The Norton Anthology
of Literature by Women

SECOND EDITION

The Norton Anthology of Literature by Women
The Traditions in English

SECOND EDITION

SANDRA M. GILBERT
UNIVERSITY OF CALIFORNIA, DAVIS

SUSAN GUBAR
INDIANA UNIVERSITY

W · W · NORTON & COMPANY · New York · London

The text of this book is composed in Electra with the display set in
Bernhard Modern. Composition by New England Typographic Service, Inc.
Manufacturing by R. R. Donnelly. Book design by Antonina Krass.

Cover illustration: *Bacchante* by Mary Cassatt. Reproduced courtesy of the
Pennsylvania Academy of Fine Arts, Philadelphia. Gift of John Frederick Lewis.

Since this page cannot legibly accommodate all the copyright notices,
pages 2431–2440 constitute an extension of the copyright page.

Library of Congress Cataloging-in-Publication Data

The Norton anthology of literature by women: the traditions in
English / [compiled by] Sandra M. Gilbert, Susan Gubar. — 2nd ed.
 p. cm.
 Includes bibliographical references (p.) and index.
 ISBN 0-393-96825-1 (pbk.)
 1. American literature—Women authors. 2. English literature-
-Women authors. 3. Women—Literary collections. I. Gilbert,
Sandra M. II. Gubar, Susan, 1944–
PS508.W7N67 1996
820.8'09287—dc20 96-5751
 CIP

W. W. Norton & Company, Inc., 500 Fifth Avenue, New York, New York 10110
 http://web.wwnorton.com
W. W. Norton & Company Ltd., 10 Coptic Street, London WC1A 1PU

4 5 6 7 8 9 0

Contents

Literature of the Seventeenth and Eighteenth Centuries 63

Literature of the Nineteenth Century 283

Turn-of-the-Century Literature

Early-Twentieth-Century Literature

Later-Twentieth-Century Literature

Preface

I think I was enchanted
When first a sombre Girl—
I read that Foreign Lady—
The Dark—felt beautiful . . .

So wrote the brilliant American poet Emily Dickinson in the mid-nine-teenth century, as she contemplated the literary achievements of "that Foreign Lady," the great British poet Elizabeth Barrett Browning, then living in exile in Italy. We begin our Preface to the Second Edition of *The Norton Anthology of Literature by Women* with this tribute from one woman of letters to another because it emphasizes the international intellectual bonds that link readers and writers across time and space. In 1985, we began our Preface to the First Edition with Virginia Woolf's remark in *A Room of One's Own* that "books continue each other." Woolf, we noted, was urging her audience to contemplate the connections between the Restoration iconoclast Aphra Behn, the eighteenth-century lyricist Anne Finch, and the four great novelists of the nineteenth century—Jane Austen, Charlotte Brontë, Emily Brontë, and George Eliot—but by implication she was also arguing for the places occupied in her "fairly long series" by such American writers as Harriet Beecher Stowe and Dickinson. It was the tradition constituted by this series that the First Edition brought to a new audience of students and general readers.

Today, however, we can see more clearly just how complex and multi-faceted Woolf's set of women writers really is. For during the eleven years that have intervened between editions, the interlocked fields of Women's Studies and Feminist Criticism have evolved in ways we might not have anticipated during the early eighties. Numerous scholars have continued the excavation and assessment that provisionally defined women's literary history in the sev-enties and eighties, and we are grateful to them for the newly recovered works of literature, better edited texts, and new contextual writings. In particular, however, we owe to them contributions that enrich the original pages of this volume so radically as to make possible a crucial emendation in our subtitle, pointing to the most significant change within the anthology: whereas the book was originally subtitled "The Tradition in English," we now subtitle it "The Traditions in English." That simple revision underlines the evolution of feminist criticism from its early preoccupation with women's shared experi-ences to its more recent absorption in the diversity of women's experiences, diversity of cultural heritage, racial identification, geographical background, sexual preference, religious practice, and class privilege.

To be sure, despite (or perhaps because of) its enlarged parameters, this re-vised edition of *The Norton Anthology of Literature by Women* continues to re-

mind readers of Woolf's affirmation that "books continue each other." To this day, this collection remains the only book that documents her point by representing the exuberant variety of literature that English-speaking women have produced between the fourteenth century and the present. Like all historically oriented Norton anthologies, our volume still provides a broad chronological overview of its subject—an overview that allows readers to appreciate fully the female literary tradition which, for several centuries, has coexisted with, revised, and influenced male literary models. *The Norton Anthology of Literature by Women* chronicles both the evolution in and the revolutions of women's literature (and women's images of women) in England, the United States, Canada, Australia, India, Africa, and other English-speaking regions.

In addition, as what is essentially a course-in-a-book, the anthology maintains a commitment to offering complete, major works in every genre. As we did in the First Edition, we include in their entirety Charlotte Brontë's *Jane Eyre* and Kate Chopin's *The Awakening*, along with a full-length novel by the Nobel prizewinner Toni Morrison, in this case *Sula*. As before, these works are supplemented by Jane Austen's *Love and Freindship*, George Eliot's *The Lifted Veil*, Rebecca Harding Davis's *Life in the Iron Mills*, and Willa Cather's *Coming, Aphrodite!* To this list we add four long prose fictions: Aphra Behn's pioneering *Oroonoko*, Eliza Haywood's racy *Fantomina*, Maria Edgeworth's poignant *The Grateful Negro*, and Carson McCullers's bitter *Ballad of the Sad Café*. In addition, the Second Edition offers not two but four full-length plays—Augusta Gregory's *Spreading the News*, Susan Glaspell's *Trifles*, Edna St. Vincent Millay's *Aria da Capo*, and Caryl Churchill's *Top Girls*—as well as a number of complete long poems or poem cycles, most notably Christina Rossetti's *Goblin Market*, H. D.'s *The Master*, Millay's *Sonnets from an Ungrafted Tree*, Muriel Rukeyser's *Käthe Kollwitz*, Gwendolyn Brooks's *The Sundays of Satin-Legs Smith*, Adrienne Rich's *An Atlas of the Difficult World*, Sylvia Plath's *Bee* sequence, Marilyn Hacker's *Ballad of Ladies Lost and Found*, and Jorie Graham's *Concerning the Right to Life*.

As these summaries make clear, the new edition has been strengthened by many texts. For these additions, we are indebted not just to new scholarship but also to the suggestions of countless teachers and students who have used the book in many different educational settings. To be more specific about our revisions: through consultations and questionnaires completed by a broad range of colleagues, we ascertained which texts, because infrequently assigned, could be replaced by others in greater demand. In fact, because of the notably larger, handsomer, and easier-to-use format of this new volume, we were able to add works by no fewer than forty-five new authors besides supplementing the selections of authors already anthologized in the First Edition.

In this last respect, we have made many changes which strengthened our representation of "classic" or "standard" women writers. In some cases, we have replaced earlier selections with even more resonant texts; we now offer, for example, self-contained excerpts from Harriet Beecher Stowe's *Uncle Tom's Cabin* and Louisa May Alcott's *Little Women*, along with new stories by such widely read authors as Sarah Orne Jewett, Katherine Mansfield, Dorothy Parker, May Sinclair, and Doris Lessing. In other instances, we have added works by a number of major figures—for example, Anne Finch, Emily Dickinson, Amy Lowell, Virginia Woolf, Marianne Moore, Judith Wright,

Gwendolyn Brooks, Sylvia Plath, Adrienne Rich, Audre Lorde, and Margaret Atwood—that will deepen students' appreciation of their oeuvres.

But perhaps the most striking feature of the new edition is the generic, geographic, ethnic and historical diversity of the writers whose texts are to be found on our table of contents. Perhaps indeed, the word "diversity" best encapsulates the principles that guided our revisions of *The Norton Anthology of Literature by Women*, just as the word "diversity" reflects the range of scholarly and critical viewpoints now enlivening feminist studies.

—*Diversity in genre.* From Juliana Berners's fifteenth-century handbook for young hunters, and Helen Maria Williams's letters home about the French revolution, to Djuna Barnes's early-twentieth-century political journalism and Gloria Anzaldúa's contemporary Chicana literary manifesto, the Second Edition now supplements its core novels stories, poems, and plays with lesser-studied forms of writing.

—*Diversity in ethnic and geographical traditions.* Not only have we included a host of writers who extend our coverage of English, Scottish, Welsh, Irish, Canadian, Australian, Indian, African, Euro-American, Native American, African American, Jewish American, and Asian American authors, but also the anthology now contains new writers from India, Nigeria, Ghana, Botswana, Ireland and the Caribbean as well as newly emerging voices in Chicana Literature.

—*Diversity in the representation of individual authors.* Such writers as Margaret Cavendish, Aphra Behn, Mary Astell, Mary Shelley, Dorothy Richardson, Alice Dunbar-Nelson, Edna St. Vincent Millay, Djuna Barnes, Elizabeth Bishop, Audre Lorde, and Margaret Atwood are now portrayed in more than one genre—that is, by critical as well as creative prose, by drama as well as lyric, or by fiction as well as poetry.

We have continued to organize these diverse writings chronologically, for we still believe that, though conventional literary periodization does not suit women's aesthetic past, the history of women's literary traditions does have significant phases of its own. Thus, here as in the First Edition, we have for the most part omitted references to the usual literary "ages" (i.e., Augustan, Romantic, Victorian) and instead organized our authors by birthdate into six eras, which our period introductions discuss in a way that will reveal the historical and thematic coherence of the material within each section: (1) Literature of the Middle Ages and the Renaissance; (2) Literature of the Seventeenth and Eighteenth Centuries; (3) Literature of the Nineteenth Century; (4) Turn-of-the-Century Literature; (5) Early-Twentieth-Century Literature; and (6) Later-Twentieth Century Literature. Since all of these periods are so dramatically affected by the manifold literary "traditions in English" that we represent, it will be useful to summarize the additions to each section.

Literature of the Middle Ages and the Renaissance. Juliana Berners's versified hunting manual, Isabella Whitney's poetic "Will and Testament," and selections from Elizabeth Cary's verse-play *The Tragedy of Mariam* are included here for the first time. In addition, a sample of Mary Sidney Herbert's translations from the Psalms as well as Aemilia Lanyer's courtly meditation on "Cooke-ham" complement these writers' earlier work. Finally, portions of Mary Wroth's elegant and eloquent sonnet sequence, *Pamphilia to Amphilanthus*, only recently recovered from long critical neglect, will allow students

to examine the rhetorical complexity of a form that was of particular impor-
tance in the Renaissance.

Literature of the Seventeenth and Eighteenth Centuries. Two major prose
narratives now underscore women's contributions to the history of fiction in
this period: Aphra Behn's innovative and influential proto-novel about slavery,
Oroonoko, along with the less-well-known but exceptionally lively romantic
tale *Fantomina* by the prolific, popular Eliza Haywood. In addition, two ex-
cerpts from Delarivier Manley's *The New Atalantis* comment wittily on love
and marriage. We have greatly strengthened verse offerings with poems by
Margaret Cavendish and Mary Astell along with more verses by Anne
Bradstreet, Katherine Philips, Anne Killigrew, Anne Finch, Lady Mary
Wortley Montagu, and Phillis Wheatley. At the turn of the eighteenth cen-
tury into the nineteenth, the addition of poems by Anna Letitia Barbauld and
Mary Robinson, along with texts by Charlotte Smith, enables students to
study women's contributions to the Romantic period. Also useful for ex-
tended analysis of the late eighteenth century are the vivid letters and politi-
cal commentaries of Abigail Adams and Helen Maria Williams.

Literature of the Nineteenth Century. Generally viewed as the strongest
pages of the original edition, this section now supplements Mary Shelley's fic-
tion with her critical introduction to *Frankenstein.* Along with more verse by
Frances E. W. Harper, two new prose works—Maria Edgeworth's *The Grateful
Negro* and the "Slave Warehouse" chapter from Harriet Beecher Stowe's
Uncle Tom's Cabin—facilitate further studies of race relations and literary
representation. At the same time, new selections from Fanny Fern and Louisa
May Alcott add humor writing and children's literature to pedagogical pic-
tures of the Victorian period. Finally, a number of new poems continue to dra-
matize the range of Emily Dickinson's poetic art.

Turn-of-the-Century Literature. Four new inclusions in this section of the
book are brilliant short stories—Constance Fenimore Woolson's *Miss Grief,*
Sarah Orne Jewett's *A White Heron,* May Sinclair's *Where Their Fire Is Not
Quenched,* and Mary Austin's *The Walking Woman*—that both tell of women's
achievements in regionalist fiction and provide vivid explorations of aesthetic
and erotic desire. To her classic *The Yellow Wallpaper,* we have added three
poems by the versatile and prolific Charlotte Perkins Gilman.

Early-Twentieth-Century Literature. Most of the major modernist authors
from the First Edition—Dorothy Richardson, Amy Lowell, Gertrude Stein,
Virginia Woolf, Anzia Yezierska, H. D., Marianne Moore, Katherine
Mansfield, Edna St. Vincent Millay, Djuna Barnes, Dorothy Parker, and Jean
Rhys—have more capacious entries or are represented by stronger, more
teachable selections. So, for example, Millay's verse drama *Aria da Capo* sup-
plements a broad selection of her verse. At the same time, the section newly
includes texts that speak to major intellectual and historical issues: essays by
Dorothy Richardson and Djuna Barnes on the women's movement in the
early part of this century; H. D.'s poem *The Master,* about Sigmund Freud;
Katherine Mansfield's *The Fly,* about the First World War; and Jean Rhys's
The Insect World, about the Second. In addition, we have added four new
modern writers, including the Native American Gertrude Bonnin (Zitkala
Ša), the avant-garde expatriate Mina Loy, and the Harlem Renaissance writers
Anne Spencer and Marita Bonner.

Later-Twentieth-Century Literature. This section introduces a range of new figures—Dilys Laing, M. F. K. Fisher, Mary Lavin, Gwen Harwood, Patricia Beer, and Hisaye Yamamoto—as well as revised and expanded selections for Anaïs Nin, Muriel Rukeyser, and Ruth Stone. Prose fiction is highlighted here with the "Southern Gothic" work of Carson McCullers (*Ballad of the Sad Café*), the brilliantly ironic stories of Muriel Spark and Doris Lessing, and Toni Morrison's superbly artful *Sula*, among many other works.

As the table of contents, organized by birthdate, moves toward the present moment, new and diverse writers proliferate: Cynthia Ozick, Ursula Fanthorpe, Paule Marshall, Bessie Head, Bharati Mukherjee, Gloria Anzaldúa, Marilyn Hacker, Sharon Olds, Eavan Boland, Buchi Emecheta, Annie Dillard, Linda Hogan, Jamaica Kincaid, Jorie Graham, Rita Dove, Luci Tapahonso, Lorna Dee Cervantes, Louise Erdrich, Cathy Song, and Rebecca Brown, all included for the first time. Just as important, most of the authors retained from the First Edition—Fleur Adcock, Margaret Atwood, and Louise Glück, for instance—now appear with extended entries: more poems or more recent prose. In this way, we have attempted to foreground some recent achievements by contemporary literary women.

Of course no anthology can pretend to completeness. Editors inevitably find themselves unable to trace the ongoing evolution of every literary movement and tradition. In addition, permissions problems sometimes lead to the exclusion of important texts, and space restrictions often require similar exclusions. Thus we regret that permissions problems or financial constraints have made it impossible to reprint works by the modernist poet/critic Laura (Riding) Jackson, the British poet Kathleen Raine, and the Chicana fiction writer Sandra Cisneros. Finally, moreover, we regret that we have not had room to include texts by countless women writers whose achievements we much admire. We are convinced, however, that the texts we have chosen will expand the contours of the canon. In addition, we continue to believe that whatever the subject, form, or provenance of our anthology's texts, we here reprint works whose historical, intellectual, or aesthetic significance clearly merits inclusion.

Adopting editorial procedures that have proved helpful in other Norton anthologies, we have in every case used what seemed to us the most accurate texts. In some instances, in order to make a work more easily accessible to the reader, we have modernized spelling and Americanized punctuation; otherwise, the spelling and punctuation of our texts is that of their authors or—as in the case of, say, Emily Brontë or Emily Dickinson—their editors. After every selection, we have indicated the date of first periodical or book publication (and, when appropriate, the date of a revised reprinting) on the right; whenever the facts are available, we have also indicated the date of composition on the left. Difficult allusions, foreign phrases, unfamiliar idioms, and arcane words have been glossed in annotations, many newly revised and expanded in this edition, at the bottom of the page. Whenever we found it necessary to present a text only in part, we have indicated internal cuts by three asterisks and prefaced the title of the work by the word "from." If we have supplied our own title for an excerpt, that title is enclosed in square brackets. A much-updated bibliography in standard Norton format has been provided at the end of the volume in order to encourage and expedite further reading and research by students.

In addition, we have tried to compose (and revise) headnotes and period introductions that are as lucid and informative as possible, providing necessary historical and biographical background without interposing our own critical interpretations between the reader and the text. Following our usual collaborative procedures, each of the two editors drafted approximately half the headnotes, then exchanged and helped revise the drafts of the other editor. Two period introductions—those on Literature of the Middle Ages and the Renaissance and on Later-Twentieth-Century Literature—were written entirely in collaboration, while the other four were composed individually, then exchanged and revised: Susan Gubar drafted the introductions to Literature of the Seventeenth and Eighteenth Centuries and Turn-of-the-Century Literature; Sandra Gilbert drafted the introductions to Literature of the Nineteenth Century and Early-Twentieth-Century Literature.

We began these prefatory remarks with references to Emily Dickinson's tribute to Elizabeth Barrett Browning and Virginia Woolf's pioneering essay on women and fiction; we want to now acknowledge our deep intellectual indebtedness to the hundreds of teachers all over the world who have for the last several decades responded to Woolf's impassioned explanation that "we think back through our mothers if we are women" by laboring to recover the female literary inheritance that we have attempted to reconstitute here. We have included a separate list of acknowledgments in which we thank the many teachers, critics, and scholars who prepared detailed critiques of our material or offered special textual suggestions, but their ideas—like our own—seem to us to be a part of a larger and ongoing collective enterprise on the part of countless researchers to whom we must all be profoundly grateful.

We want also to express our gratitude to a number of research and secretarial assistants, institutions, colleagues, friends, and relatives whose aid facilitated our work on this edition. Specifically, we thank John Beckman, Lisa Harper, Ashley Tidey, and Dan Wenger for helpful library work, but in particular we thank Katharine Ings and Chris Sindt for invaluable all-round research assistance. At W. W. Norton, Susan Brekka, Virginia Creeden, Candace Levy, Diane O'Connor, and Tara Parmiter were consistently patient and helpful. As always, moreover, we are grateful to our home institutions—the University of California, Davis, and Indiana University—for financial and secretarial support. In addition, we wish to thank a number of colleagues and friends— Joanne Feit Diehl, Florence Elon, Mary Favret, Dorothy Gilbert, Robert J. Griffin, Kenneth Gros Louis, Mary Moore, Mary Jo Weaver, Robin Wiegman—for advice and assistance with many matters. As well, Sandra Gilbert wishes to thank the University of California, Davis, Humanities Institute and the Rockefeller Foundation Study Center, Bellagio, for research and secretarial support; Susan Gubar would like to thank the Indiana University Distinguished Professors' fund for similar support. And we are as usual grateful to members of our innermost circles: our children—Roger, Katherine, and Suanna Gilbert as well as Marah and Simone Gubar—and our life companions—David Gale and Donald Gray.

Finally, though, our greatest debt is to five co-workers who in some sense helped author this book. Alice Falk's meticulous and scrupulous scholarship facilitated wise and detailed revisions of our annotations. Marian Johnson's extraordinary efficiency and organizational skill as well as her never-faltering

tact helped us confront what seemed at times like mountains of "tegras," galleys, and page proofs. Julia Reidhead's unflagging enthusiasm, support, and guidance buoyed us up even at our rockiest moments and made much of our work a great pleasure. The perpetually sagacious example of M. H. Abrams, Class of 1916 Professor Emeritus of English at Cornell and general editor of Norton anthologies, offered us a continual model of pedagogical and critical good sense. And perhaps most important of all, the late John Benedict, our first editor at Norton. continued to function (the way he always did) as a kind of muse whose spirit hovered over and sustained this project. His editorial expertise and personal brilliance inspired whatever was best in the First Edition, and it is to his memory that we dedicate the Second Edition of *The Norton Anthology of Literature by Women*

Acknowledgments

Among our many advisors and friends, the following were of special help in providing critiques of particular periods or of the anthology as a whole, or assisting in preparing texts and editorial matter: Elizabeth Abel (University of California, Berkeley); Ruth A. Banes (University of South Florida); Nina Baym (University of Illinois); Elizabeth Beaulieu (Providence College); Betty Louise Bell (University of Michigan); Frank Bidart (Wellesley College); Elyse M. Blankley (California State University, Long Beach); Christine Blouch (Bradley University); Bonnie Braendlin (Florida State University); Julia Briggs (Hertford College, Oxford University); Pamela S. Bromberg (Simmons College); Lawrence Buell (Harvard University); Gina Campbell; Miriam Cavanaugh (American International College); Barbara Christian (University of California, Berkeley); Beverly Clark (Wheaton College); Suzanne Clark (Oregon State University); Stuart Curran (University of Pennsylvania); Elizabeth R. Curry (Slippery Rock University of Pennsylvania); Ruth Dawson (University of Hawaii); Elin Diamond (Rutgers University); Joanne Feit Diehl (University of California, Davis); Angela Elliott (Centenary College); Florence Elon (University of California, Berkeley); Mary Favret (Indiana University); Paula R. Feldman (University of South Carolina); Margaret Ferguson (University of Colorado at Boulder); Leora Fisher (Georgetown University); Penelope Laurans Fitzgerald (Yale University); Stuart Friebert (Oberlin College); Susan Stanford Friedman (University of Wisconsin, Madison); J. Ellen Gainor (Cornell University); Judith Kegan Gardiner (University of Illinois, Chicago Circle); Blanche Gelfant (Dartmouth College); Albert Gelpi (Stanford University); Barbara Gelpi (Stanford University); Dorothy Gilbert; Roger Gilbert (Cornell University); Diane Gillespie (Washington State University); Katherine Clowes (Sierra College); Catherine Golden (Skidmore College); Myrna Goldenberg (Montgomery College); Marah Gubar; Jeane Harris (Arkansas State University); Tamar Heller (Williams College); Barbara Johnson (Harvard University); Sandra Kempe; Jean Klene (Saint Mary's College); Diane LeBow (Cañada College); Andrea Lebowitz (Simon Fraser University); Rebecca Lee (University of Hawaii); Susan Levin (Stevens Institute of Technology); Barbara Lewalski (Harvard University); Joanna Lipking (Northwestern University); Lawrence Lipking (Northwestern University); Dusky Loebel (Tulane University); Marlene Longenecker (The Ohio State University); Janet Thormann Mackintosh (College of Marin); Caitriona Maloney (Holy Names College); Jane Marcus (City University of New York); Wendy Martin (Claremont Graduate School); Charlotte S. McClure (Georgia State University); Marcia P. McGowan (Eastern Connecticut State University); Jeslyn Medoff (Rutgers University, New Brunswick); Anne Mellor (University of California—Los

Angeles); Diane Wood Middlebrook (Stanford University); Mary Moore (Marshall University); Timothy Morris (University of Texas at Arlington); Mary L. Morton (Nicholl State University); Mary L. Navarro (Sinclair Community College); Felicity Nussbaum (Syracuse University); Karen Carlson Ogden (University of Manitoba); Tillie Olsen; Alicia Ostriker (Rutgers University); Ruth Perry (Massachusetts Institute of Technology); Marjorie Pryse (SUNY, Albany); Susan Schibanoff (University of New Hampshire); Natalie Schroeder (University of Mississippi); Elaine Showalter (Princeton University); Sylvia Bailey Shurbutt (Shepherd College); Kenith Simmons (University of Hawaii, Hilo); Catherine Smith (Bucknell University); Susan B. Smith (Allegheny College); Valerie Smith (University of California, Los Angeles); Patricia Meyer Spacks (University of Virginia); Judith Stanton (Clemson University); Catharine Stimpson (Rutgers University); Sherry Sullivan (University of Alabama at Birmingham); Carolyn R. Swift (Rhode Island College); Carole Tabor (Louisiana Tech University); Elaine C. Thiesmeyer (Rochester Institute of Technology); Trudelle Thomas (Xavier University); Alison Townsend (Linn-Benton Community College); Marie Olesen Urbanski (University of Maine); Susan Van Dyne (Smith College); Martha Vicinus (University of Michigan); Mary Katherine Wainwright (Manatee Community College); Jean West (Rollins College); Margaret Whitt (University of Denver); Shelagh Wilkinson (York University); Alan Williamson (University of California, Davis); James Winn (University of Michigan); Susanne Woods (Franklin and Marshall College); Dorothy Zaborszky (Laurentian University); Sandra Zagarell (Oberlin College); Melody Zajdel (Montana State University).

The Norton Anthology
of Literature by Women

SECOND EDITION

Literature of the Middle Ages and the Renaissance

MEDIEVAL AND RENAISSANCE HISTORY

The years that historians define as the Old English period, the Middle Ages, and the Renaissance constitute a time of important literary activity. From the first half of the eighth century, when scholars speculate that the great Anglo-Saxon epic called *Beowulf* was composed, to the years between 1386 and 1400, when Geoffrey Chaucer wrote his *Canterbury Tales*, to 1603, when Shakespeare's *Hamlet* was first printed in London, these ages produced a number of classics. Besides *Beowulf*, the Old English era saw the composition of major poems like *The Dream of the Rood* and *The Wanderer*. In the Middle Ages, besides the *Canterbury Tales*, artists created courtly romances such as *Sir Gawain and the Green Knight* (1374–1400), dream visions such as *Piers Plowman* (c. 1372–89), and religious dramas, including *The Second Shepherd's Play* (c. 1425) and *Everyman* (after 1485). Finally, the Renaissance years that fostered Shakespeare's astounding creativity also developed the talents of such poets as Edmund Spenser (*The Faerie Queene*, 1590, 1596, 1609), Christopher Marlowe (*Doctor Faustus*, 1604, 1616), Sir Philip Sidney (*Arcadia*, 1590, 1593), Thomas Wyatt, and Ben Jonson. It is significant, however, that most of the writers who flourished in these periods were men. When we turn to the literary history of women in these nine hundred years, we find no texts in the Old English period that have been definitively identified as composed by women, hardly any works by medieval women, and comparatively few by Renaissance women.

The female writers whose works we include here suggest the kinds of women whose words have been preserved. Women's literature in Middle English is represented by just three somewhat shadowy figures: a religious recluse (Julian of Norwich); an eccentric preacher (Margery Kempe); and an enigmatic figure, possibly a prioress (Juliana Berners, whose authorship has been intermittently disputed over the centuries). More prolific and better known, Renaissance women of letters are exemplified by five innovative and influential figures: an extraordinarily charismatic queen (Elizabeth I), the aristocratic sister of a famous poet (Mary Sidney Herbert), the middle-class sister of a lawyer-poet (Isabella Whitney), the bohemian wife of a court musician (Aemilia Lanyer), and the defiantly Catholic wife of a high-ranking nobleman (Elizabeth Cary). Significantly, with the exception of Isabella Whitney, all these women were associated in one way or another with the Church or the court, institutions that would have provided unusual access to education while fostering at least tentative convictions of spiritual or secular authority that contemporary society suppressed in most women.

What were the female contemporaries of these writers doing? We know of at least two other medieval Englishwomen—each in one way or another also connected with court and Church—who made notable literary contributions. Dame Eleanor Hull (c. 1394–1460) and Lady Margaret Beaufort (1443–1509) both produced translations of devotional texts. Dame Eleanor, whose father and husband

1

served the royal family, translated a thirteenth-century French commentary on the Psalms as well as a French collection of prayers and meditations. Lady Margaret, the mother of Henry VII and grandmother of Henry VIII, rendered into English Book IV of the famous *Imitation of Christ*, a spiritual guide attributed to the medieval philosopher Thomas À Kempis (1380–1471), along with a pious work titled *The Mirror of Gold.*

In addition, we know that a number of other well-born medieval women were sufficiently literate to read and write letters, some of which are included in the cache of fifteenth-century documents, originally belonging to a family of Norfolk gentry, now known as the Paston Letters. It has been speculated, moreover, that many anonymous medieval texts were authored by women who chose not to sign their works. "Anon. was a woman," proclaimed Virginia Woolf in 1929, as she mused on the rich horde of ballads and tales whose creators have never been identified. But even some spiritual meditations—such as the early fifteenth-century vision of the afterlife known as *A Revelation Showed to a Holy Woman*—appear to have had female authors whose names have not been preserved.

When the Renaissance brought a newly secular interest in art and learning to England, increasing numbers of literary women took up their pens to write either for private circulation in aristocratic circles or, less often, for publication. The contemporaries of such learned ladies as Mary Sidney and Mary Wroth included poets like Rachel Speght (fl. 1617–1621) and polemicists like Jane Anger (fl. 1589) as well as moralists like Elizabeth Grymeston (c. 1563–1603) and Elizabeth Jocelin (1595–1622). Yet even in this more liberal period, the situation of most women was not conducive to creativity. In the words of the scholar Elaine Beilin, the "legal, theological and familial subjugation" of Renaissance women had "an inhibiting effect on women writers." As in the Middle Ages, most lived severely private lives in which, confined to the home—whether farm, castle, or convent—and constrained by cultural definitions of femininity, they had neither the experience of public life nor the expectation of an audience that would foster composition. As in the Middle Ages too, it is likely that a number of the works women did produce were not thought worth saving, while others have been handed down to us anonymously, or in some cases, if saved, have not yet been discovered in the attics, abbeys, and libraries where they may still be stored.

No wonder, then, that the medieval and Renaissance authors whose works are included here were all in one way or another spiritually or socially exceptional. Julian of Norwich, for instance, was a solitary visionary. Margery Kempe was impelled by inner voices to rebel against social conventions. Elizabeth I was England's most powerful and learned queen. Mary Sidney Herbert was the extraordinarily well-educated and wealthy patroness of many Elizabethan intellectuals, as was her niece, Mary Wroth. Isabella Whitney and Elizabeth Cary were among the very first Englishwomen to attempt composition in the genres of lyric poetry and verse tragedy, which had long been exclusively masculine preserves, and some scholars speculate that Aemilia Lanyer may actually have been the flirtatiously independent "Dark Lady" of Shakespeare's sonnets. Atypical in both education and intellectual authority, these women responded to spiritual movements and historical events about which most of their female counterparts were, at least publicly, silent.

Those events included a series of major political upheavals, a set of drastic social changes, and a dramatic succession of cultural transformations. In the years before Julian and Margery were born in the fourteenth century, English history had been shaped through the fifth-century invasion of the country by the Germanic tribes of the Angles, the Saxons, and the Jutes as well as the eleventh-century conquest of the island by French (Norman) invaders. The Anglo-Saxon language in which the heroic saga *Beowulf* is written had metamorphosed, because of the Norman

conquest, into a range of French-influenced dialects called Middle English, dialects in which such major works as *Sir Gawain and the Green Knight*, *Piers Plowman*, and *The Canterbury Tales* were composed. As English evolved, moreover, it became an ever more viable alternative to the Latin that had long been used by chroniclers, theologians, and poets to signify the seriousness of their work. In particular, it became a language in which women like Julian and Margery, who would probably never have studied Latin, could record their visions and lives.

But the lives that these women recorded must also have been determined by the shift from an essentially tribal Anglo-Saxon culture to a hierarchical society organized around a so-called feudal system in which serfs (peasants) swore loyalty to vassals (knights and landowners), who, in turn, pledged their allegiance to great lords, as well as by the slow disintegration of that system with the rise to power of a literate, mercantile, town-dwelling middle class. In addition, the lives of Julian and Margery (as well as the career of the woman known as Juliana Berners) must have been marked by the cultural centrality of the Roman Catholic Church, which increasingly dominated English life and letters after the seventh-century conversion of the Anglo-Saxons to Christianity. Julian's mystical revelations were part of a long medieval tradition of spiritual meditations, while Margery's individualistic preachings reflect a tumultuous moment in Church history, a moment when a number of revolutionary monastic orders arose throughout Europe, demanding spiritual reform.

Even more than Julian and Margery, however, the Renaissance authors included here were involved in crucial political, social, and cultural events. Indeed, Elizabeth I not only was shaped by such events but shaped them herself. By the time Elizabeth came to the throne, the Middle English of Julian and Margery had developed into something much closer to modern English, and as England was unified by Elizabeth's rule, the divergent dialects of the Middle Ages began to be consolidated into a single national language, laying the groundwork for the emergence of a national literature. Before Elizabeth's accession, moreover, the country, earlier divided by the fifteenth-century War of the Roses (which set the great houses of York and Lancaster against each other in a battle for the throne), had begun to be unified by two Tudor monarchs, Henry VII and Henry VIII. The most charismatic of the Tudor rulers, Elizabeth completed the transformation of what had been a comparatively fragmented feudal society into a centralized nation-state dominated by a single royal court. It was this court that facilitated literary production throughout the English Renaissance, and not insignificantly therefore, Mary Sidney Herbert, Aemilia Lanyer, and Mary Wroth were members of courtly circles: their respective places are made clear by the fact that Wroth was Herbert's niece and Lanyer dedicated her poems to Herbert while Herbert dedicated hers to Elizabeth.

But these women were not just associated with the centralized authority of the court. Like Cary they were also learned ladies who had the rare good fortune to be educated in the fashion recommended by the new movement called humanism— that is, they had studied the classics and had been trained in the intricacies of Renaissance rhetoric and logic. Elaborately paradoxical, stylistically ornate, and ingeniously allusive, their verse embodies the humanist passion for polemical skill and classical knowledge that was imported to England from Italy during the sixteenth century by such thinkers as Sir Thomas More, the English author of *Utopia* (1516), and Desiderius Erasmus, the Dutch-born author of *In Praise of Folly* (1510). The lives of these women also coincided with the secularization of culture brought about by humanism's renewal of interest in the pre-Christian classics of Greece and Rome, by the increasing substitution of the vernacular for churchly Latin, by the growing literacy of the non-Latin-speaking middle class, by the new nationalism of the aristocracy, and by the Reformation's questioning of papal

power. As the English Church separated itself from, on the one hand, the Rome-dominated international hierarchy of Roman Catholicism and from, on the other hand, the German and Swiss Protestantism established by Luther and Calvin, it developed a distinctive national identity, with the English monarch replacing the pope as a central earthly symbol of sacred authority. This phenomenon, along with the rise of modern English and the dramatic strength of the queen, contributed to an extraordinary cultural vitality that expressed itself in the exuberant energy of Elizabethan literature, an energy that manifests itself in the words and works of Herbert, Whitney, Lanyer, Cary, and Wroth.

Nevertheless, although their writings are infused with the energy of the age, these exceptional women rarely aspired to rival their ambitious male contemporaries. To be sure, Wroth gained notoriety when she produced both a prose romance and a sonnet sequence in the mode of works for which her uncle, Sir Philip Sidney, had become famous, while Cary daringly inscribed a verse tragedy based on a tale told by the Roman historian Josephus. But even such Renaissance aristocrats found themselves alienated and embattled in a culture that discouraged women from composing the kinds of epics, romances, lyrics, comedies, tragedies, and allegories that male poets, dramatists, and prose stylists circulated in manuscripts, staged in the theater, and published to critical acclaim throughout this dauntingly great age of English literature. And although some of the authors included here—notably Mary Herbert and Mary Wroth—moved in strikingly intellectual circles, few can be said to have belonged to literary communities comparable with the loosely organized groups of male writers who supported and encouraged the works of artists like Marlowe, Shakespeare, and Jonson. That, to represent the earliest writings of English women, we have had to conflate the Old English era, the Middle Ages, and the Renaissance into a single "early" period is simply the most dramatic sign of women's literary marginality in the years from 700 to 1600. Perhaps further evidence of their aesthetic dilemma is manifested in the themes and dreams recorded by those women who did manage to write. For while the works of these artists mirror the varying spirits of their ages, they are also—no matter when they were written—distinctively and consistently concerned with the problems creativity posed for women, and they may, therefore, seem idiosyncratic when set against the texts of male contemporaries. Haunted by the images of women that men had constructed for them, these writers created a tradition that seeks either to redefine or to resign itself to male preconceptions about femininity. Specifically, in the years from the 1370s, when Julian began to describe her revelation of divine love in the *Book of Showings*, to the 1590s, when Mary Sidney Herbert undertook to translate the Psalms into English, women had to confront the misogyny of male theologians who sought to censure and silence them as well as an ideal of courtly love that glamorized and glorified them in ways that were sometimes problematic.

MEDIEVAL AND RENAISSANCE IMAGES OF WOMEN

"By God," exclaimed Chaucer's Wife of Bath in a famous passage from *The Canterbury Tales*, "If wommen hadden writen stories / As clerkes han within hir oratories, / They wolde han writen of men more wikkednesse / Than al the merk of Adam may redresse." Afflicted by the book of "wikked wives" from which her fifth husband persistently read to her every evening, this lively female character was responding to the tradition of misogyny that extended from early Church fathers like Saints Paul and Jerome to later theologians like Augustine and Tertullian; it was, indeed, a tradition that would reach beyond her author's lifetime into the antifemale diatribes of the *Malleus Maleficarum* ("Hammer of Witches," 1486), a

fifteenth-century German handbook for witch hunters, into the portrait of the dissembling seductress Duessa in Edmund Spenser's *The Faerie Queene*, and into the punitive subjugation of Kate in William Shakespeare's *The Taming of the Shrew* (1594). While it is clear that no book of "wikked wives" will ever stifle Chaucer's exuberant Wife, such texts may well have inhibited her real-life contemporaries. Though, as we have seen, the two periods were in many ways very different, in the Middle Ages and the Renaissance alike even the most talented literary women were constrained by cultural strictures which implied that any intellectual ambition might mean they were evil. Worse still, such would-be writers had to struggle against gender definitions suggesting that femaleness itself was an intrinsically debased and secondary condition.

Defining woman's essential nature, Tertullian, the third-century philosopher of asceticism, proclaimed that she is a "temple built over a sewer." About women's history and particularly the culpability of Eve, the first woman, whose rebellious eating of forbidden fruit led to the fall of all humanity, the thirteenth-century writer Jacques de Vitry declared: "Between Adam and God in Paradise there was but one woman and she had no rest until she had succeeded in banishing her husband from the garden of delights and in condemning Christ to the torment of the cross." About woman's biological character, the views of the first-century Roman philosopher Pliny persisted: "Contact with [menstrual fluid] turns new wine sour, crops touched by it become barren . . . the edge of steel and the gleam of ivory are dulled, hives of bees die, even bronze and iron are at once seized by rust, and a horrible smell fills the air." Nor were such views unique to the particular traditions out of which these three thinkers wrote. Anglo-Saxon culture, which predated Christianity in England, was oblivious of or hostile to women. Indeed, one of the few lyrics from this period that scholars have tentatively attributed to a woman—a piece called *The Wife's Lament* (c. 900)—begins with an impassioned complaint: "I make this song sadly about myself, / about my life. I a woman say / I've been unhappy since I grew up" (translation by Willis Barnstone and Elene Kolb). In *Beowulf*, the age's major epic, moreover, women are objects of exchange, servants to men, monsters, or mothers of monsters. Similarly, the Greek philosopher Aristotle had argued in the fourth century B.C. that woman is a "deformity of nature." That pre-Christian definition, combining with the Bible's excoriation of Eve, informed the work of such major medieval thinkers as St. Augustine and St. Thomas Aquinas, both of whom believed that women were physically and spiritually inferior to men.

But if Eve, the primordial female, was both secondary (created from Adam's rib) and destructive (a temptress who condemned humanity to death and degradation), she did have a positive counterpart the mother of Christ, the Virgin Mary, who redeemed the world with the fruit of her womb. It might seem, then, that even though ambitious women were oppressed by what we now call "negative role models," they could gain strength from the sacred example of Mary. From the twelfth century to about the fifteenth, Mariolatry—the cult of the Virgin—swept Europe. As one historian has observed, "her miracles were on every lip" and "provided the stock themes for miracle plays," the festival dramas in which modern English theater had its origins. Indeed, in England, worship of the Blessed Mother seems often to have taken precedence over devotion to the Father and the Son, so much so that some scholars have seen the adoration of Mary as a lingering remnant of earlier religions that worshiped the Great Goddess. Whatever its origins, Mariolatry gave rise in sermons, songs, plays, and poems to celebrations of the female body and soul that directly controverted contemporary monastic misogyny, works in which even the sin of Eve was justified because it resulted in the sanctity of Mary, mother of the Redeemer of that sin.

A popular Middle English lyric summarized this potentially feminist theory of

what has been called the *Fortunate Fall*, the idea that the calamity brought about
by Eve's rebellion led to the redemption promised by Mary's sacred maternity:

> Ne hadde the appil take ben
> The appil taken ben,
> Ne hadde never our lady
> A ben hevene's quene
> Blessed be the time
> That appil take was
> Therefore we moun singen
> "Deo Gracias!" *

Other poems, moreover, celebrated the paradox of Mary's maidenly motherhood.
The lyric that begins "I sing of a maiden / That is makelees" (matchless), for in-
stance, affirms that "moder and maiden / Was nevere noon but she: / Wel may
swich a lady / Godes moder be" (mother and maiden—i.e., virgin—was never none
but she: well may such a lady God's mother be). Such texts implied that, far from
being man's inferior, woman, made in Mary's image, might be his superior. As one
medieval theologian argued,

> Woman is to be preferred to man, to wit in material: Adam made from clay
> and Eve from side of Adam; in place: Adam made outside paradise and Eve
> w'in; in conception: a woman conceived God which a man did not do; in ap-
> parition: Christ appeared to a woman after the Resurrection, to wit the
> Magdalene; in exaltation: a woman is exalted above the choirs of angels, to
> wit the Blessed Mary. St. Bernadine even declares thus: "It is a great grace to
> be a woman: more women are saved than men."

What is most noteworthy here is that Mary's grace sanctifies all women, even an
ostensibly fallen one such as Christ's disciple the reformed prostitute Mary
Magdalene. Thus, though Mary herself may have been unique—"alone of all her
sex," as the title of Marina Warner's useful study of Mariolatry has it—even ordi-
nary women are not to be excluded from the queendom of heaven that she rules.

The implications of such a vindication of the female were far-reaching. First,
they put in question the presuppositions of antifemale clerics and instigated a di-
alogue between misogynists like the author of the sardonic French *Quinze joies de
mariage* ("The fifteen joys of marriage") and defenders of women like the Chaucer
of *The Legend of Good Women*, a long poem praising female virtue. Second, they
even transformed some of the philosophical foundations of Western literature.
From Plato on, the European worldview had been based on what A. O. Lovejoy
called "The Great Chain of Being," a hierarchy of the created world that extended
from God down through man to woman and then to animals, plants, and stones.
With the ascendancy of Mary, however, came a seemingly subversive revision of
this system of stratification. For some late medieval writers, it was a mortal
woman, a blessed beloved such as Dante's Beatrice or Petrarch's Laura, who medi-
ated between God and the writer in just the way that the immortal Mary mediated
between God and man. Influenced by Mariolatry, these artists were also working
out of a tradition of courtly love, which functioned as a secular counterpoint to the
cult of our Lady. As early as the twelfth century, lyricists called troubadours in
France and Minnesingers in Germany had begun to praise the elegance and excel-
lence of aristocratic ladies, to whom they swore fealty and dedicated their
art. Their poems set a fashion that spread rapidly from the courts of France,

* If the apple had never been "taken"—i.e., plucked by Eve—our lady, Mary, would never have been heaven's
queen. Blessed be the time the apple was taken; therefore, we must sing "Thanks to God."

Germany, and Italy to the English court and thence to the great castles of aristocrats in all these nations. Gottfried von Strassbourg's *Tristan*, Guillaume de Loris's *Roman de la Rose* ("The Romance of the Rose"), Part I, Petrarch's sonnets to Laura, and Dante's *La Vita Nuova* ("The New Life") marked the culmination of this tradition, which for the first time identified secular desire with spiritual love, the creation of poetry with the consecration of prayer. In *Tristan*, the Cave of Love is a sacred place; in *La Vita Nuova*, Beatrice is an earthly angel; in the *Roman de la Rose*, the rose, representative of the beloved lady, is an emblem of heavenly perfection. For all these poets, and for the knights who followed the fashion they set, love was—in the phrase of the noted medieval historian Eileen Power—"feudalized," for "the lover served his lady as humbly as the vassal served his lord."

Even during the Renaissance, when medieval feudalism had begun to disintegrate, the conventions of courtly love persisted in literature, if not in life. Sir Philip Sidney's prose narrative *Arcadia*, for instance, recounts the romances of knights and ladies in a pastoral realm where the art of love represents an aesthetic ideal, while his sonnet sequence *Astrophil and Stella* (1582) explores the poet-lover's feelings for his mistress on the assumption that such passionate emotions toward a beloved woman were the most appropriate subject for lyric poetry. Influenced by the highly stylized modes and elaborately romantic themes of "Petrarchanism," a literary movement that began in Italy with Petrarch and was brought to England by Sir Thomas Wyatt, Sidney was only one of the many major Renaissance poets who produced such sonnet cycles meditating on the rapture and torment of man's love for woman. Others included Edmund Spenser (*Amoretti*, 1595), Samuel Daniel (*Delia*, 1592), and Shakespeare (*Sonnets*, 1609). In the same years when these writers were composing their celebratory sonnets, moreover, Spenser's *The Faerie Queene* offered images of pure and powerful heroines such as Una, Gloriana, and Britomart. Throughout this period, moreover, poets regularly proclaimed their aesthetic indebtedness to the female divinities known as "muses," first celebrated as sources of inspiration by the Greek and Roman bards whom many Renaissance poets strove to emulate.

Ennobling and empowering as the rhetoric of Mariolatry, the rhymes of courtly love, the sonnets of Petrarchanism, the allegorical figures of Spenser, and the concept of female muses might seem to have been for women, however, they still retained traces of the very misogyny they would appear to have replaced. About Mary, after all, one lyric declared "moder and maiden / Was nevere noon but she": no earthly woman could achieve such paradoxical grandeur. As for courtly love, it too posed problems. Highly stylized and abstract, the poet's or knight's service to the lady was often merely lip-service, even in literary works that praised her powers. Functioning as muse or mistress, the blessed damsel was usually no more than an object, albeit an object of worship. For the most part, she herself was granted no subjectivity, nor was she often portrayed as engaging in the kinds of heroic deeds that redeemed her lover.

Worse still, embedded in even the most chivalric texts are images of women as monsters and witches: any beautiful lady, these romances hint, may be a sorceress. In the medieval tale of *Sir Gawain and the Green Knight*, for instance, the hero is tested by a temptress whose wiles threaten his destruction and whose charms force him to confront his own mortality. Similarly, the medieval *Tristan* documents Tristan's death at the hands of a false Isolde even while it dramatizes the joys of the Cave of Love, and Sir Thomas Malory's fifteenth-century Arthurian cycle preserves the gestures of chivalry but also traces the way the disintegration of the Round Table is brought about by Queen Guinevere's faithlessness. Witches and bad ladies abound in medieval literature, and they are almost always associated with female sexuality, assertion, and creativity. No wonder, then, that Chaucer has his sexy, assertive, and creative Wife of Bath revise and reverse this association by telling the story of a knight who is tricked into wedding and bedding an aged crone

and rewarded for relinquishing his authority to her when she transforms herself into a beautiful lady.

If Chaucer's *Wife of Bath's Tale* parodies the courtly romance to reveal its underlying misogyny, the Wife of Bath herself is a character out of another genre, which dwelled more frankly on the defects of women: the *fabliau*. In fact, this genre makes explicit the misogyny implicit in the courtly romance. Realistic and comic, *fabliaux* were folk tales addressed to a bourgeois audience. Their plots generally turned on the machinations of cuckolding wives and cunning maids, while the resolutions they recommended for men who wanted to tame such shrews ranged from public humiliation to wife beating. At the same time, as Chaucer himself suggests in his *envoi* to *The Clerk's Tale*, about a famously submissive heroine called Patient Griselda, some writers implied, perhaps ironically and perhaps not, that woman could avoid Griselda's hardships only by taking "the high / And overpowering hand against the male." Enormously popular throughout the Middle Ages, *fabliaux* formed the basis of a number of Chaucer's narratives, including *The Miller's Tale* and *The Nun's Priest's Tale*, the first a story of a faithless young wife and the second a tale of a henpecked rooster. Good-humored though they are—in each case the storyteller clearly feels as much sympathy for the wife as for the husband—these tales deflate romantic ideals of love by depicting the female as fleshly, shrewd, earthbound.

In the same way that medieval genres which seemed to praise women covertly implied critiques of femininity and were accompanied by franker treatments of the battle of the sexes in the *fabliau*, Renaissance epics, lyrics, and dramas castigated as well as celebrated key female figures. These writings suggest that below the surface of even the most honorific language there may frequently be a secret hostility to women. Such heroines of *The Faerie Queene* as Una and Gloriana are shadowed, after all, by the sinister witch appropriately named Duessa, whose lovely facade cracks open to reveal the horror of "her neather parts, the shame of all her kind" as well as, "at her rompe," a "foxes taile, with dong all fowly dight" (decked). To be sure, *The Faerie Queene's* heroes are often balanced by sinister or villainous male figures, but the evil of those characters is never so specifically associated with sexuality. Similarly, while Shakespeare used idealizing rhetoric to praise both Mr. W. H., who was the "onlie begetter" of his famous sonnet cycle, and the "Dark Lady" to whom he also pledged erotic devotion in the cycle, he subverted that rhetoric only when he turned his attention to his mistress's femaleness. In particular, Sonnet 130 ("My mistress's eyes are nothing like the sun") ostensibly praises his beloved, but concedes that her breasts are "dun," her hair is "black wires," and her breath "reeks," while implying that such realistic descriptions should also be applied to many other women who are "belied with false compare"—that is, falsely and foolishly flattered by the metaphoric excesses of poetry.

Finally, for every Shakespeare heroine who is as ingenious and imaginative as Viola in *Twelfth Night* (1601) or as vigorously dutiful as Cordelia in *King Lear* (1606), there is a ferocious figure like Lady Macbeth in *Macbeth* (1606) and Goneril and Regan in *King Lear*. Of course, Shakespeare's dramas also offer countless examples of villainous male characters like Iago in *Othello* (1603) and Edmund in *King Lear*. But, again, the evil of such men is not usually identified with warped or excessive sexuality. By contrast, women such as Lady Macbeth, Goneril, and Regan are marked by monstrous female ambition or grotesque erotic energy. Lady Macbeth's perversity is manifested at one point by her plea "Come, unsex me here" and at another by her admission that, if she had sworn to do so, she would have "plucked" her nipple from her child's "boneless gums / And dashed [its] brains out." Similarly, the voracious lust for power and the sexual insatiability of Goneril and Regan are dramatized not only through their treatment of their aged father but also in their erotic intrigues with the bastard Edmund. Indeed, when in his madness the dispossessed King Lear proclaims that "Down from the waist" even dainty ladies are "Centaurs / Though women all above: / But to the gir-

dle do the Gods inherit, / Beneath is all the fiend's," his apparently insane misogy-
yny seems ultimately sane in light of his two older daughters' viciousness. What
clarifies the assumptions about the proper relations between the sexes that these
plays dramatized, moreover, is the fact that even attractively autonomous charac-
ters like Viola in *Twelfth Night* and Rosalind in *As You Like It* (1600) must ulti-
mately be stripped of their independence and brought to acquiesce in a husband's
power. All's well that ends well, Shakespeare declared, but to "end well" a woman
must, like Viola, become her lord's "mistress and his fancy's queen."

MEDIEVAL AND RENAISSANCE WOMEN'S LIVES

Did Shakespeare's plays reflect the reality of Renaissance women's lives? Did
courtly romances mirror the lives of aristocratic medieval ladies, and did *fabliaux*
tell the truth about ordinary women in the Middle Ages? By all accounts, both
Renaissance and medieval texts did and did not record real facts about female ex-
perience.

Women's Lives in the Middle Ages

Because feudal society was organized for war, it was essentially a masculine world
in which great landlords preserved the integrity of their estates through the rule of
primogeniture (the right of the eldest son to inherit property). As the historian
Doris Stenton has explained, women generally passed from father to husband,
with the age of marital consent for girls usually defined as twelve. Canon law (i.e.,
Church law) permitted and sometimes even encouraged wife beating, while secu-
lar as well as religious legal tradition forbade divorce and, except under special cir-
cumstances, female ownership of property. Still, although women could not serve
as judges, on juries, or in government councils, a widow could obtain some degree
of power, for she usually received a third part of her husband's estate, and in 1215
King John promised such widows a measure of freedom from royal authority: they
were no longer forced to remarry (as they had been before that year) according to
the king's wishes. Yet their daughters continued to be wed at early ages in order to
ensure the integrity of important estates, and even grown women could be sum-
marily married off, against their own wishes, unless they could purchase from their
feudal lords the right to choose their own husbands.

A number of great ladies did, however, have the power of patronage, a power to
elevate poets and knights through financial as well as personal encouragement.
From the eleventh century on, aristocratic women commissioned illuminated
manuscripts for their own uses. Because they were usually untutored in Latin
themselves and because they were often the primary tutors of the next generation,
such women had by the end of the Middle Ages been influential in promoting ver-
nacular translations of Latin religious works. As daughters, wives, and mothers,
medieval ladies also helped guard their lords' manors, regularly organizing alms-
giving, household budgets, clothing, and food for large families and retinues of ser-
vants and even, when their men were away, supervising farm affairs, lawsuits, and
other estate business.

When a family like the Pastons in Norfolk rose by acquiring large land holdings,
their sons were sent to Eton and Oxford and sometimes educated to enter the Inns
of Court, while their daughters remained at home. Yet, as the late medieval family
documents called the Paston Letters reveal, these fifteenth-century wives and
daughters actively concerned themselves with the legal, educational, and moral
welfare of their husbands and brothers. Similarly, the wives of middle-class English
farmers were responsible for looking after their husbands' stock, making butter
and cheese, helping in the fields, and producing cloth for the family from the wool
of their own sheep. From the evidence of manorial court records, it is also clear
that many widows independently farmed the holdings of their deceased husbands

and engaged in litigation on their own behalf. Moreover, country women brewed and sold ale at a profit, while bourgeois and working-class women in towns and cities earned considerable sums of money from two other major home industries—textiles (spinning and weaving) and food production (brewing and baking); wives and so-called *femes soles* (widows and unmarried women) also sometimes worked as leather sellers, wool merchants, shopkeepers, chandlers, shoemakers, bookbinders, and goldsmiths. Significantly, in 1469 the Crown awarded an annual salary of £10 to the first known English midwife, Margaret Cobbe, and in 1470 she attended the labor of Queen Elizabeth (1437–1483), wife of Edward IV (1442–1483). In addition, documents before 1200 listing needle artists refer almost exclusively to women: men's names appeared only after 1200, and men began to dominate the lists only after production came to be centered in London. In the early Middle Ages, women were often active members of craft guilds (the counterpart of modern trade unions), but as the era progressed, female workers were less frequently admitted as full members of these organizations.

To be sure, whether the working-class girl was apprenticed at an early age as a child laborer or the aristocratic daughter was given by her father in a marriage that was essentially a business contract, the lives of both women were shaped by a male-controlled socioeconomic system. In addition, their lives were shadowed by the perils of childbearing that began early and ended late, by a high infant mortality rate, and by the never-ending cares of a household that had to be sustained and maintained at great physical cost to the woman. Worse still, the peace of both was frequently threatened by the virulent phenomenon of witch hunting, an activity that became increasingly ferocious between the fourteenth and the seventeenth centuries. The ratio of women to men accused of witchcraft ranged from twenty to one in some parts of Europe to one hundred to one in other areas. Like the Jew, the witch was blamed for social ills that, in the fourteenth century, included the Black Death (the plague) and the Hundred Years' War between England and France. Like the heretic, she was believed to worship strange gods, whose ways would undermine the authority of the established Church. In this era, the *Malleus Maleficarum*, mentioned earlier, functioned with great efficiency as a handbook for witch hunters: the scholars Barbara Ehrenreich and Deirdre English have estimated that the total number of women tortured and executed during the period may have climbed into the millions.

It is hardly surprising, therefore, that a significant group of young women took refuge in the Church. Some simply turned to prayer or meditation, but others entered convents, where they could educate themselves and tutor the daughters of wealthy families, where they were safe from harassment, and where their administrative as well as intellectual abilities were given scope. Medieval nunneries were usually poorer as well as smaller in number and in population than monasteries. Their official business, especially record keeping, was frequently carried on by male chaplains who were better educated than their female counterparts. Yet these institutions did serve as sanctuaries for the unmarried daughters of the nobility and even of the middle class. A Benedictine nun like the German writer Hroswitha could pursue a serious literary career within the convent, producing hymns, Latin plays, and saints' lives. Moreover, although by the fifteenth century the nunneries of England were being faulted for worldly frivolity, and although most had never in any case been as powerful as the monasteries, a few had long been bastions of wealth. "If the Abbot of Glastonbury would marry the Abbess of Shaftesbury," observed one wit, "their heir would have more land than the King of England." While to most convents such a statement would not apply, even the poorest medieval nunneries clearly functioned as communities of women, providing their inhabitants with an autonomy unmatched in the secular world.

Like most medieval women's lives, the lives of nuns are only partially reflected in the images of women that can be drawn from most medieval texts. The ladies to whom troubadours and other courtly poets swore fealty, for instance, did have the

power of patronage, but that power was translated in works like *La Vita Nuova*, the *Roman de la Rose*, and *Gawain and the Green Knight* into images of the beloved woman not as a financial investor but as a muse. Similarly, as we have seen, many bourgeois women were as enterprising and inventive as Chaucer's Wife of Bath, but their creative industry was reflected in *The Canterbury Tales'* characterization of a Wife whose business is not, say, brewing but matrimony. Finally, a number of nuns did, like Chaucer's Prioress, achieve significant independence in the convent, but few were either as elegant or as frivolous as Chaucer's portrait of that figure might suggest; indeed, far from possessing such emblems of conspicuous consumption as the Prioress's well-fed lapdog and her expensive jewelry, most were obliged to support themselves as "educators" who functioned more as high-class baby-sitters than as real teachers. Thus, even though literary works did summarize some key contemporary visions of women, social historians must inevitably draw more information from guild records and legal documents than they do from courtly romances and *fabliaux*. As we shall suggest, Renaissance scholars must depend on similar sources to supplement the images they find in plays, prose romances, and sonnet cycles.

Women's Lives in the Renaissance

During the Renaissance, women in England continued to be defined as either *femes sole* (unmarried or widowed women) or *femes covert* ("covered" or married women). Some of those who belonged to the first of these groups might have—as they had had in the Middle Ages—considerable freedom. Aristocratic widows could manage their own property; choose second, third, or fourth husbands; and handle marriage settlements for themselves. Middle-class widows could establish businesses, join guilds, enter into foreign trade and even, in some cases, sue or be sued. Similarly, some of those who belonged to the second group were also surprisingly independent. Although as *femes covert* they had practically no legal rights, they were often entrusted by their husbands with major responsibilities. As in the Middle Ages, aristocratic wives supervised great estates, including large landholdings, and frequently functioned almost as the business partners of the men to whom they were married. Similarly, middle-class wives—like medieval bourgeoises—often shared in their husbands' mercantile enterprises or oversaw home industries (spinning, weaving, silkmaking, bookbinding, brewing) that could be quite remunerative.

In fact, the only Renaissance women who may be said to have been entirely without legal, economic, or social power of any kind were young unmarried women, especially girls from wealthy families, who might bring large financial settlements to their future husbands. These girls were frequently pressured or forced by their parents to enter into marriages of convenience to consolidate important estates. Worse still, if they had any property of their own, they were sometimes subject to abduction by unscrupulous adventurers who would hold them as prisoners until they agreed to marry (and surrender their property). That this problem was no small matter is suggested by the fact that statutes to protect "ladies, gentlewomen, and other women sole" from such treatment were passed in 1453, 1557, and 1597; in that last year, as one historian reports, "maids . . . and widows with property were still being abducted and defiled or forced into marriage."

Of course, as in the Middle Ages, *all* women were enjoined to be submissive and modest in their relations to men. The Renaissance scholar Pearl Hogrefe observes that "Tudor women would have been models of chaste, passive obedience if they had only followed the advice given them in much didactic literature of the sixteenth century." But then, as the same writer also remarks, in this era as in so many others, there was a notable difference between the "ideal" woman and the real woman. Indeed, visiting England in 1592, Frederick, duke of Wirtemberg, wittily declared that "England is a paradise for women, a prison for servants, and a hell or

purgatory for horses—for the females have great liberty and are almost like mas-
ters." Though ultimately his remark must be considered hyperbolical, he and a few
other contemporaries—most notably the Protestant reformer John Knox, author
of *The First Blast of the Trumpet against the Monstrous Regiment [Government] of
Women* (1558)—thought the British Isles had "unnaturally" succumbed to the
rule of women because England and Scotland were governed by queens like Mary
Tudor, Mary Stuart, and Elizabeth I, and because a few great ladies had consider-
able power in courtly circles.

Nevertheless, the average woman very likely did not feel that she lived in a "par-
adise." It is true that after 1500 a surprising number of aristocratic women began,
for the first time, to receive the same kind of education in the classics that their
brothers did; the unprecedented training in Greek and Latin that marked the up-
bringing of women like Elizabeth I, Mary Sidney Herbert, and Elizabeth Cary was
a strong positive consequence of the humanist Sir Thomas More's idea that both
sexes were "equally suited for the knowledge of learning by which reason is culti-
vated." But most girls, even the very well born, received little education. In addi-
tion, although many middle-class women did undertake to carry on their own
businesses, historians have demonstrated that in the years between 1485 and 1500
the numbers of such women declined drastically. Evidently, the rise of an increas-
ingly ambitious group of male entrepreneurs institutionalized and professional-
ized work that had previously gone on somewhat informally, so that Renaissance
men tended to take over guilds and industries where medieval women had earlier
dominated or at least participated on an equal basis.

It should finally be noted that the power wielded by *femes covert* who joined
with their husbands in the supervision of estates or businesses depended on the
good will of the husbands. If a husband was brutal, oppressive, or merely indiffer-
ent, his wife had no legal recourse because she had no rights of her own. Thus,
though plays like Shakespeare's *The Taming of the Shrew* or his *Twelfth Night* may
subtly misrepresent the reality of most women's lives—the first exaggerating the
Renaissance ideology of male dominance and the second glamorizing a portrait of
female independence followed by an even more romantic vision of female surren-
der—both contain at least a modicum of truth. Because marriage was a woman's
principal goal and the role of wife her primary role, she must always—unless she
was a unique exception like Elizabeth, the "virgin" queen—define herself in rela-
tion to men. Given such a self-definition, however, it would be hard indeed for her
to gain the intellectual authority required for writing serious works. Not surpris-
ingly, then, even the most learned ladies often assumed secondary positions in re-
lation to literary tradition: talented though they might have been, many became
translators (of male texts) and patronesses (of male artists). As we shall see, more-
over, much female-authored writing adopted at least a surface stance of piety and
decorum, in part, perhaps, because any female artist who flouted convention was
sharply censured: when Lady Mary Wroth's long but unfinished prose romance
The Countess of Montgomery's Urania appeared in 1621, it was greeted by a chorus
of protest because, as the critic Barbara Lewalski has pointed out, it included
disguised references to "scandals and personages of the Jacobean court."
Understandably distressed, Lady Mary withdrew the work from circulation. Her
decision dramatizes at least one of the more obvious ways in which a female liter-
ary career could be discouraged or deformed.

MEDIEVAL AND RENAISSANCE WOMEN WRITERS

Despite the sense of secondariness that had been instilled in so many medieval
and Renaissance women, a yearning for a female community, together with a
corollary vision of female power, informed much of the literature by women in this
period. Such a yearning, for instance, characterized the work of perhaps the most
prominent early European feminist, the fifteenth-century writer Christine de

Pisan, whose *La Cité des Dames* ("The City of Ladies") offered an unprecedented dream vision of a female utopia in which what Renaissance thinkers called "Women Worthies"—great women from all ages and nations—were gathered to prove the worthiness of women.

Participating in an early version of the French debate over femininity that was termed the "*Querelle des Femmes*" ("quarrel about women"), Christine assumed equality with male thinkers to contest Jean de Meun's misogynistic continuation of Guillaume de Loris's *Roman de la Rose*, a satire on women's wiles in which Jean scathingly repudiated the courtly humility toward the female Rose that was cultivated by his predecessor, Guillaume. Besides producing her fervent affirmation not just of the rights but also of the achievements of women, the widowed Christine wrote a number of other books and became, as a French scholar has noted, the first female "man of letters" to support herself (along with three children) by her pen. Yet like the writing of so many medieval and Renaissance women, her major feminist treatise was out of print from the sixteenth century to the twentieth. Nevertheless, despite its long neglect, *The City of Ladies* summarized a vision of female power that would also be recorded in various ways by mystics like Julian of Norwich and Margery Kempe and by secular gentlewomen like Mary Sidney Herbert and Aemilia Lanyer.

None of the Englishwomen represented here can be said to have had professional literary careers comparable to Christine's. Whether they were cloistered like Julian of Norwich, well off like Margery Kempe, richly married like Mary Sidney Herbert, or precariously attached to the court like Aemilia Lanyer, these women were not in any modern sense "men of letters." On the contrary, several of them—notably Queen Elizabeth and Mary Sidney Herbert, countess of Pembroke—were themselves important literary patronesses. Others, among them Elizabeth Cary and Lady Mary Wroth, also contributed to the production of poetry by financing such male artists as Thomas Nashe, Ben Jonson, and John Donne. Although they wielded some power as patronesses, these English women of letters were almost always economically dependent on Church or state. (An exception was Isabella Whitney, a daughter of the minor gentry whose sisters actually may have been in service in London.) Unlike the independent bourgeoise Christine de Pisan, then, most English women writers of the Middle Ages and the Renaissance frequently articulate conventionally submissive attitudes toward woman's "place" in the cultural scheme. As Elaine Beilin observes, "At a time when writing could be considered an inappropriate activity for women, the woman writer early on created a little island for herself in the literary stream by writing pious works." In fact, she argues, "many women took pains . . . to emphasize that they themselves were virtuous—specifically chaste, modest, and obedient—and that women, far from inheriting Eve's penchant for rebellion, were determined to redeem her through virtuous words and deeds." Such conservatism, she continues, "almost guaranteed that most women would not participate in the literary experimentation or secularization carried on by men of the period." Yet a passion not unlike Christine's frequently disrupted the careful decorum so many of these Englishwomen cultivated. Julian redefined Christ as a mother; Kempe revised the rules of marriage to liberate herself from her husband; Herbert compared Queen Elizabeth to God; Lanyer justified the ways of Eve to man. Cary and Wroth dared to work in genres traditionally associated with the male imagination, while with imperious panache Whitney wittily "bequeathed" the entire city of London to her descendants. As for Queen Elizabeth herself, she provided a paradigm of female regality for all her contemporaries, and in her own verse, sparse though it was, she vaunted and flaunted her power, threatening to "poll" the "tops" (cut off the heads) of those who vexed her.

To be sure, however, all these women were extraordinary and extraordinarily fortunate—a point they themselves generally understood, for most of their female contemporaries had neither a medieval flowering nor a Renaissance. If

Shakespeare was the common man transformed into Western culture's most un-common genius, he had no woman counterpart drawn, as he was, from the intel-lectually ambitious, aspiring middle class. In 1928, Virginia Woolf told us why. Had Shakespeare had a "wonderfully gifted sister," she explained in *A Room of One's Own*, the girl would have been given no education; her parents would have forced her to do dull domestic chores and tried to make her marry young; she would have run away to London, only to be seduced and abandoned by a predatory theatrical entrepreneur; finally, she would have died a suicide, though "the birds that sang in the hedge were not more musical than she was [and] she had the quickest fancy, a gift like her brother's for the tune of words." But for the first six-teen hundred years after Christ was born to Mary, Queen of Heaven, the tune of words was not fostered in women. Given the fact that for the female imagination the so-called Dark Ages persisted well beyond the male-defined Renaissance, it is impressive enough that a small but talented set of writers implicitly chose to de-clare, with Aemilia Lanyer, that "Our Mother Eve, who tasted of the tree . . . was simply good" and therefore to dream, as Lanyer did, that women might "have our liberty again."

JULIAN OF NORWICH

1342–C. 1416

"Because I am a woman should I therefore believe that I ought not to tell you about the goodness of God since I saw at the time that it is his will that it be known?" Specifically, what Julian of Norwich saw were sixteen "showings" or direct experiences of God's goodness, which she described in a powerful spiritual medi-tation. While she considered herself "a woman, unlettered, feeble and frail," this first English woman of letters drew her authority from "the showing of Him who is Sovereign Teacher" and was thereby empowered to record her mystical visions in a prose remarkable for its brilliant transformations of images drawn from everyday experiences.

Julian's revelations occurred in two days of her thirtieth year, during a near-fatal illness when she experienced pity for Christ's suffering. After receiving last rites, she perceived a "sudden change" that was accompanied by the series of visions of Christ, which comprise the substance of her book. A recluse or anchoress in St. Julian's Church, Norwich, Julian most likely underwent a rite of enclosure, which resembled a burial service for the soul that sought to die to the world in order to live more fully with Christ. In a cell attached to the church, probably with a maidservant, an anchoress like Julian could dedicate herself to solitary medita-tion and silent prayer. Little else is known about her, although she clearly had some renown as a pious woman, for she was visited by Margery Kempe, another vision-ary, who sought spiritual advice and counsel. Modesty, ignorance of Latin, or literal illiteracy may have caused Julian to consider herself "unlettered"; however, she drew on biblical imagery and on a range of books that included the works of Richard Rolle, *The Cloud of Unknowing*, and the *Ancren Riwle*, all popular reli-gious texts in her time.

Two records of her revelations exist, either written by her or dictated to an amanuensis: a shorter account, which is thought to have been written first and which vividly presents the sixteen revelations, and a longer version, in which she records the growth in her understanding of the revelations over a period of some twenty years. The survival of a number of manuscripts may indicate the popularity of Julian's work, although after the Reformation it ceased to attract readers. The text modernized here by Edmund Colledge and James Walsh is from the longer version. In the context of Thomas Aquinas's assertion of the inferiority of women

in his *Summa Theologica* (1265–77), Julian's description of the maternity of God may seem startling. Yet, as Caroline Walker Bynum has shown in *Jesus as Mother*, the image of "mother Jesus" flowered in twelfth-century works by Anselm of Canterbury and Bernard of Clairvaux. Throughout *A Book of Showings* (sometimes called *A Revelation of Divine Love*), Julian associated her "bodily" and "ghostly" visions of Christ with the "words [which] formed in my understanding." In the excerpt printed here, she implies that the incarnation has a unique meaning for women, who can affirm their spirituality and creativity through imagery of conception, birth, and nurturance.

From A Book of Showings
[*God the Mother*]
FROM THE FIFTY-NINTH CHAPTER

* * *

As truly as God is our Father, so truly is God our Mother, and he revealed that in everything, and especially in these sweet words where he says: I am he;[1] that is to say: I am he, the power and goodness of fatherhood; I am he, the wisdom and the lovingness of motherhood; I am he, the light and the grace which is all blessed love; I am he, the Trinity;[2] I am he, the unity; I am he, the great supreme goodness of every kind of thing; I am he who makes you to love; I am he who makes you to long; I am he, the endless fulfilling of all true desires. For where the soul is highest, noblest, most honourable, still it is lowest, meekest and mildest.

And from this foundation in substance we have all the powers of our sensuality by the gift of nature, and by the help and the furthering of mercy and grace, without which we cannot profit. Our great Father, a mighty God, who is being, knows us and loved us before time began. Out of this knowledge, in his most wonderful deep love, by the prescient eternal counsel of all the blessed Trinity he wanted the second person to become our Mother, our brother and our saviour. From this it follows that as truly as God is our Father, so truly is God our Mother. Our Father wills, our Mother works, our good Lord the Holy Spirit confirms. And therefore it is our part to love our God in whom we have our being, reverently thanking and praising him for our creation, mightily praying to our Mother for mercy and pity, and to our Lord the Holy Spirit for help and grace. For in these three is all our life: nature, mercy and grace, of which we have mildness, patience and pity, and hatred of sin and wickedness; for the virtues must of themselves hate sin and wickedness.

And so Jesus is our true Mother in nature by our first creation, and he is our true Mother in grace by his taking our created nature. All the lovely works and all the sweet loving offices of beloved motherhood are appropriated to the second person, for in him we have this godly will, whole and safe forever, both in nature and in grace, from his own goodness proper to him.

I understand three ways of contemplating motherhood in God. The first is the foundation of our nature's creation; the second is his taking of our nature, where the motherhood of grace begins; the third is the motherhood at work.

1. In a series of visions in the previous chapters, Christ showed himself to Julian and spoke words that she then interprets in the later chapters.

2. The first person of the Trinity is God, the second person is Jesus Christ, and the third is the Holy Spirit; all three, however, may bear the name God.

And in that, by the same grace, everything is penetrated, in length and in breadth, in height and in depth without end; and it is all one love.

THE SIXTIETH CHAPTER

But now I should say a little more about this penetration, as I understood our Lord to mean: How we are brought back by the motherhood of mercy and grace into our natural place, in which we were created by the motherhood of love, a mother's love which never leaves us.

Our Mother in nature, our Mother in grace, because he wanted altogether to become our Mother in all things, made the foundation of his work most humbly and most mildly in the maiden's womb. And he revealed that in the first revelation, when he brought that meek maiden before the eye of my understanding in the simple stature which she had when she conceived; that is to say that our great God, the supreme wisdom of all things, arrayed and prepared himself in this humble place, all ready in our poor flesh, himself to do the service and the office of motherhood in everything. The mother's service is nearest, readiest and surest: nearest because it is most natural, readiest because it is most loving, and surest because it is truest. No one ever might or could perform this office fully, except only him. We know that all our mothers bear us for pain and for death. O, what is that? But our true Mother Jesus, he alone bears us for joy and for endless life, blessed may he be. So he carries us within him in love and travail, until the full time when he wanted to suffer the sharpest thorns and cruel pains that ever were or will be, and at the last he died. And when he had finished, and had borne us so for bliss, still all this could not satisfy his wonderful love. And he revealed this in these great surpassing words of love. If I could suffer more, I would suffer more.[3] He could not die any more, but he did not want to cease working; therefore he must needs nourish us, for the precious love of motherhood has made him our debtor.

The mother can give her child to suck of her milk, but our precious Mother Jesus can feed us with himself, and does, most courteously and most tenderly, with the blessed sacrament,[4] which is the precious food of true life; and with all the sweet sacraments he sustains us most mercifully and graciously, and so he meant in these blessed words, where he said: I am he whom Holy Church preaches and teaches to you.[5] That is to say: All the health and the life of the sacraments, all the power and the grace of my word, all the goodness which is ordained in Holy Church for you, I am he.

The mother can lay her child tenderly to her breast, but our tender Mother Jesus can lead us easily into his blessed breast through his sweet open side, and show us there a part of the godhead and of the joys of heaven, with inner certainty of endless bliss. And that he revealed in the tenth revelation,[6] giving us the same understanding in these sweet words which he says: See, how I love you, looking into his blessed side, rejoicing.

This fair lovely word "mother" is so sweet and so kind in itself that it cannot truly be said of anyone or to anyone except of him and to him who is the true Mother of life and of all things. To the property of motherhood belong nature, love, wisdom and knowledge, and this is God. For though it may be so that our

3. In the ninth revelation, Christ spoke these words to Julian.
4. The bread and wine consumed during the Catholic mass, which represent the body and blood of Christ.

5. In the twelfth revelation.
6. In the tenth revelation Christ showed Julian a wound in his side, through which she saw "his blessed heart riven in two."

bodily bringing to birth is only little, humble and simple in comparison with our spiritual bringing to birth, still it is he who does it in the creatures by whom it is done. The kind, loving mother who knows and sees the need of her child guards it very tenderly, as the nature and condition of motherhood will have. And always as the child grows in age and in stature, she acts differently, but she does not change her love. And when it is even older, she allows it to be chastised to destroy its faults, so as to make the child receive virtues and grace. This work, with everything which is lovely and good, our Lord performs in those by whom it is done.[7] So he is our Mother in nature by the operation of grace in the lower part, for love of the higher part. And he wants us to know it, for he wants to have all our love attached to him; and in this I saw that every debt which we owe by God's command to fatherhood and motherhood is fulfilled in truly loving God, which blessed love Christ works in us. And this was revealed in everything, and especially in the great bounteous words when he says: I am he whom you love.[8]

THE SIXTY-FIRST CHAPTER

And in our spiritual bringing to birth he uses more tenderness, without any comparison, in protecting us. By so much as our soul is more precious in his sight, he kindles our understanding, he prepares our ways, he eases our conscience, he comforts our soul, he illumines our heart and gives us partial knowledge and love of his blessed divinity, with gracious memory of his sweet humanity and his blessed Passion,[9] with courteous wonder over his great surpassing goodness, and makes us to love everything which he loves for love of him, and to be well satisfied with him and with all his works. And when we fall, quickly he raises us up with his loving embrace and his gracious touch. And when we are strengthened by his sweet working, then we willingly choose him by his grace, that we shall be his servants and his lovers, constantly and forever.

And yet after this he allows some of us to fall more heavily and more grievously than ever we did before, as it seems to us. And then we who are not all wise think that everything which we have undertaken was all nothing. But it is not so, for we need to fall, and we need to see it; for if we did not fall, we should not know how feeble and how wretched we are in ourselves, nor, too, should we know so completely the wonderful love of our Creator.

For we shall truly see in heaven without end that we have sinned grievously in this life; and notwithstanding this, we shall truly see that we were never hurt in his love, nor were we ever of less value in his sight. And by the experience of this falling we shall have a great and marvellous knowledge of love in God without end; for enduring and marvellous is that love which cannot and will not be broken because of offences.

And this was one profitable understanding; another is the humility and meekness which we shall obtain by the sight of our fall, for by that we shall be raised high in heaven, to which raising we might never have come without that meekness. And therefore we need to see it; and if we do not see it, though we fell, that would not profit us. And commonly we first fall and then see it; and both are from the mercy of God.

The mother may sometimes suffer[1] the child to fall and to be distressed in various ways, for its own benefit, but she can never suffer any kind of peril to

7. I.e., in disciplining her child the mother acts as an agent of God's will.
8. In the twelfth revelation.

9. The crucifixion, in which Christ sacrificed his own life as payment for humanity's sins.
1. Allow.

come to her child, because of her love. And though our earthly mother may suffer her child to perish, our heavenly Mother Jesus may never suffer us who are his children to perish, for he is almighty, all wisdom and all love, and so is none but he, blessed may he be.

But often when our falling and our wretchedness are shown to us, we are so much afraid and so greatly ashamed of ourselves that we scarcely know where we can put ourselves. But then our courteous Mother does not wish us to flee away, for nothing would be less pleasing to him; but he then wants us to behave like a child. For when it is distressed and frightened, it runs quickly to its mother; and if it can do no more, it calls to the mother for help with all its might. So he wants us to act as a meek child, saying: My kind Mother, my gracious Mother, my beloved Mother, have mercy on me. I have made myself filthy and unlike you, and I may not and cannot make it right except with your help and grace.

And if we do not then feel ourselves eased, let us at once be sure that he is behaving as a wise Mother. For if he sees that it is profitable to us to mourn and to weep, with compassion and pity he suffers that until the right time has come, out of his love. And then he wants us to show a child's characteristics, which always naturally trusts in its mother's love in well-being and in woe. And he wants us to commit ourselves fervently to the faith of Holy Church, and find there our beloved Mother in consolation and true understanding, with all the company of the blessed. For one single person may often be broken, as it seems to him, but the entire body of Holy Church was never broken, nor ever will be without end. And therefore it is a certain thing, and good and gracious to will, meekly and fervently, to be fastened and united to our mother Holy Church, who is Christ Jesus. For the flood of mercy which is his dear blood and precious water is plentiful to make us fair and clean. The blessed wounds of our saviour are open and rejoice to heal us. The sweet gracious hands of our Mother are ready and diligent about us; for he in all this work exercises the true office of a kind nurse, who has nothing else to do but attend to the safety of her child.

It is his office to save us, it is his glory to do it, and it is his will that we know it; for he wants us to love him sweetly and trust in him meekly and greatly. And he revealed this in these gracious words: I protect you very safely.[2]

<div align="right">1390</div>

2. In Chapter Thirty-seven after the thirteenth revelation.

MARGERY KEMPE
c. 1373–1438

When Margery Kempe visited Julian of Norwich, the aging anchoress and author of *A Book of Showings*, she sought "good counsel" about her own divine revelations. The forty-year-old Margery had decided, after almost twenty years of marriage and fourteen children, that she was meant to be married not to her husband but to Christ. While Julian confirmed Margery's grace, the anchoress also warned her visitor about "the language of the world, for the more despite, shame and reproof that ye have in the world," Julian explained, "the more is your merit in the sight of God." What Julian seemed to understand in

her "holy dalliance" with Margery was the vulnerability of a "sister" whose spirituality took a quite different form from her own, for Margery dramatically enacted her religious enthusiasm in the world. Indeed, dressed all in white, wearing a ring (engraved "Jesus Christ is my love"), frequently called to fast or weep, Margery traveled throughout England and went on pilgrimages to Jerusalem, Rome, Germany, and in the Baltic. Not dedicated to the vow of silence, she reproved even the highest church officials for what she considered their moral lapses and preached to people wherever she found them. Whether her audience threatened to burn her at the stake as a heretic or promised to follow what they deemed her saintly tales and exhortations, Margery exhibited notable courage, inventiveness, and zeal, or so it seems in the major source we have of her life, *The Book of Margery Kempe*.

The same feisty energy that characterized Margery's life must have impelled her to write the first extant autobiography in the vernacular. *The Book of Margery Kempe* was narrated to several scribes, who recorded what Kempe remembered about her adventures as a spiritual teacher. Margery did not focus on her youth in Lynn, where she was raised by a prosperous mayor named John Brunham, or her marriage in 1393 to John Kempe, a tax collector, brewer, and miller by turns. Instead, she began when she was twenty-one, pregnant, and in the midst of a disabling spiritual struggle, which she placed in the context of her visions of Christ on the one hand and her marital responsibilities on the other. Margery's eventual marriage to Christ, which she attained by bargaining with her husband for freedom from sexual relations, evidently involved a sexualized relation with God not uncommon in the mystical tradition. While some scholars have diagnosed Kempe as hysterical, others have compared her brash vitality to the irreverence of Chaucer's candid Wife of Bath or her spiritual ecstasy to the intensity of St. Bridget of Sweden, who also claimed to have visions of being present at Christ's birth.

As the self-defined "creature" of her Creator, Margery recorded both mystical revelations and homely anecdotes. Invariably, she defended herself against the injunction, based on the teachings of St Paul, that "no woman should preach," by explaining "I preach not sin; I come into no pulpit. I use but communication and good words, and that I will do while I live." Unlike Julian who meditated exclusively on the growth of her spiritual understanding, Margery produced a lively, realistic narrative as well as an illuminating document of fifteenth-century society.

A modernization of *The Book of Margery Kempe* was not printed until 1936, when it was produced by W. Butler-Bowden, and we are indebted to him in the selections printed here. A critical edition of the original manuscript was published in 1940 by S. B. Meech and H. E. Allen.

From The Book of Margery Kempe[1]

[On Female Celibacy]

CHAPTER 3. HER VISION OF PARADISE. SHE DESIRES TO LIVE APART FROM HER HUSBAND. DOES PENANCE AND WEARS A HAIR-CLOTH.[2]

On a night, as this creature[3] lay in her bed with her husband, she heard a sound of melody so sweet and delectable, that she thought she had been in Paradise, and therewith she started out of her bed and said:—

1. The first two chapters of this third-person spiritual autobiography recount Margery's worldly desires and ambitions, before her Christian renunciation of the world.
2. A garment made from an extremely rough and un-

comfortable fabric containing horsehair, worn by penitents as punishment for their sins.
3. I.e., Margery, who refers to herself in the third person.

"Alas, that ever I did sin! It is full merry in Heaven."

This melody was so sweet that it surpassed all melody that ever might be heard in this world, without any comparison, and caused her, when she heard any mirth or melody afterwards, to have full plenteous and abundant tears of high devotion, with great sobbings and sighings after the bliss of Heaven, not dreading the shames and the spites of this wretched world. Ever after this inspiration, she had in her mind the mirth and the melody that was in Heaven, so much, that she could not well restrain herself from speaking thereof, for wherever she was in any company she would say oftentimes:—"It is full merry in Heaven."

And they that knew her behavior beforetime, and now heard her speaking so much of the bliss of Heaven, said to her:—

"Why speak ye so of the mirth that is in Heaven? Ye know it not, and ye have not been there, any more than we." And were wroth with her, for she would not hear nor speak of worldly things as they did, and as she did beforetime.

And after this time she had never desired to commune fleshly with her husband, for the debt of matrimony was so abominable to her that she would rather, she thought, have eaten or drunk the ooze and the muck in the gutter than consent to any fleshly communing, save only for obedience.

So she said to her husband:—"I may not deny you my body, but the love of my heart and my affections are withdrawn from all earthly creatures, and set only in God."

He would have his will and she obeyed, with great weeping and sorrowing that she might not live chaste. And oftentimes this creature counselled her husband to live chaste, and said that they often, she knew well, had displeased God by their inordinate love, and the great delectation they each had in using the other, and now it was good that they should, by the common will and consent of them both, punish and chastise themselves wilfully by abstaining from the lust of their bodies. Her husband said it was good to do so, but he might not yet. He would when God willed. And so he used her as he had done before. He would not spare her. And ever she prayed to God that she might live chaste; and three or four years after, when it pleased Our Lord, he made a vow of chastity, as shall be written afterwards, by leave of Jesus.

And also, after this creature heard this heavenly melody, she did great bodily penance. She was shriven sometimes twice or thrice on a day, and specially of that sin she so long had (hid), concealed and covered, as is written in the beginning of the book.[4]

She gave herself up to great fasting and great watching; she rose at two or three of the clock, and went to church, and was there at her prayers unto the time of noon and also all the afternoon. Then she was slandered and reproved by many people, because she kept so strict a life. She got a hair-cloth from a kiln, such as men dry malt on, and laid it in her kirtle[5] as secretly and privily as she might, so that her husband should not espy it. Nor did he, and she lay by him every night in his bed and wore the hair-cloth every day, and bore children in the time.

Then she had three years of great labor with temptations which she bore as meekly as she could, thanking Our Lord for all His gifts, and was as merry

4. In Chapter 1 we learned that Margery had not made a practice of going to confession (i.e., being shriven).

5. Skirt.

when she was reproved, scorned and japed[6] for Our Lord's love, and much more merry than she was beforetime in the worship of the world. For she knew right well she had sinned greatly against God and was worthy of more shame and sorrow than any man could cause her, and despite[7] of the world was the right way Heavenwards, since Christ Himself had chosen that way. All His apostles, martyrs, confessors and virgins, and all that ever came to Heaven, passed by the way of tribulation, and she, desiring nothing so much as Heaven, then was glad in her conscience when she believed that she was entering the way that would lead her to the place she most desired.

And this creature had contrition and great compunction with plenteous tears and many boisterous sobbings for her sins and for her unkindness against her Maker. She repented from her childhood for unkindness, as Our Lord would put it in her mind, full many a time. Then, beholding her own wickedness, she could but sorrow and weep and ever pray for mercy and forgiveness. Her weeping was so plenteous and continuing, that many people thought she could weep and leave off, as she liked. And therefore many men said she was a false hypocrite, and wept before the world for succor and worldly goods. Then full many forsook her that loved her before while she was in the world, and would not know her. And ever, she thanked God for all, desiring nothing but mercy and forgiveness of sin.

CHAPTER 4. HER TEMPTATION TO ADULTERY WITH A MAN, WHO, WHEN SHE CONSENTS, REJECTS HER.

The first two years when this creature was thus drawn to Our Lord, she had great quiet in spirit from any temptations. She could well endure to fast, and it did not trouble her. She hated the joys of the world. She felt no rebellion in her flesh. She was so strong, as she thought, that she dreaded no devil in Hell, as she did such great bodily penance. She thought that she loved God more than He did her. She was smitten with the deadly wound of vainglory, and felt it not, for she many times desired that the crucifix should loosen His hands from the Cross, and embrace her in token of love. Our Merciful Lord Jesus Christ, seeing this creature's presumption, sent her, as is written before, three years of great temptations, one of the hardest of which I purpose to write as an example to those who come after, so that they should not trust in themselves, or have joy in themselves, as she had. For, no dread, our ghostly enemy sleepeth not, but he full busily searcheth our complexions and dispositions and where he findeth us most frail, there, by Our Lord's sufferance, he layeth his snare, which no man may escape by his own power.

So he laid before this woman the snare of lechery, when she believed that all fleshly lust had wholly been quenched in her. And so for a long time she was tempted with the sin of lechery, for aught that she could do. Yet she was often shriven, she wore her hair-cloth, and did great bodily penance and wept many a bitter tear, and prayed full often to Our Lord that He should preserve her and keep her, so that she should not fall into temptation, for she thought she would rather be dead than consent thereto. All this time she had no lust to commune with her husband; but it was very painful and horrible unto her.

In the second year of her temptation, it so fell that a man whom she loved well, said unto her on St. Margaret's Eve[8] before evensong that, for anything,

6. Mocked.
7. Contempt or defiance.
8. I.e., the evening before St. Margaret's feast day

(July 20). St. Margaret was a 3rd-century virgin martyr who was very popular in late medieval England.

he would lie by her and have his lust of his body, and she should not withstand him, for if he did not have his will that time, he said he would anyhow have it another time; she should not choose. And he did it to see what she would do, but she thought that he had meant it in full earnest at that time, and said but little thereto. So they parted then and both went to hear evensong, for her church was that of Saint Margaret. This woman was so labored with the man's words that she could not hear her evensong, nor say her Paternoster,[9] or think any other good thought, but was more troubled than ever she was before.

The devil put into her mind that God had forsaken her, or else she would not be so tempted. She believed the devil's persuasion, and began to consent because she could think no good thought. Therefore thought she that God had forsaken her, and when evensong was done, she went to the man aforesaid, so that he could have his lust, as she thought he had desired, but he made such simulation[1] that she could not know his intent, and so they parted asunder for that night. This creature was so labored and vexed all that night, that she never knew what she might do. She lay by her husband, and to commune with him was so abominable to her that she could not endure it, and yet it was lawful unto her, in lawful time, if she would. But ever she was labored with the other man, to sin with him inasmuch as he had spoken to her. At last, through the importunity of temptation, and lack of discretion, she was overcome and consented in her mind, and went to the man to know if he would then consent to her, and he said he never would, for all the gold in this world; he would rather be hewn as small as flesh for the pot.

She went away all shamed and confused in herself at seeing his stability and her own instability. Then thought she of the grace that God had given her before; how she had had two years of great quiet in her soul, repenting of her sin with many bitter tears of compunction, and a perfect will never again to turn to her sin, but rather to die. Now she saw how she had consented in her will to do sin, and then fell she half into despair. She thought she must have been in Hell for the sorrow she felt. She thought she was worthy of no mercy, for her consent was so wilfully done, nor ever worthy to do Him service, because she was so false to Him. Nevertheless she was shriven many times and often, and did whatever penance her confessor would enjoin her to do, and was governed by the rules of the Church. That grace, God gave his creature, blessed may He be, but He withdrew not her temptation, but rather increased it, as she thought.

Therefore she thought He had forsaken her, and dared not trust to His mercy, but was afflicted with horrible temptations to lechery and despair all the next year following. But Our Lord, of His mercy, as she said herself, gave her each day for the most part two hours of sorrow for her sins, with many bitter tears. Afterwards, she was labored with temptation to despair as she was before, and was as far from feelings of grace, as they that never felt any, and that she could not bear, and so she gave way to despair. But for the time that she felt grace, her labors were so wonderful that she could evil fare[2] with them, but ever mourned and sorrowed as though God had forsaken her.

* * *

9. Latin version of the Lord's Prayer. 2. I.e., travel through.
1. Unclear; he feigned indifference, or gave her conflicting signs of his desire.

CHAPTER 11. ON THE WAY BACK FROM YORK, SHE AND HER HUSBAND
ARGUE AS TO THEIR CARNAL RELATIONSHIP TO EACH OTHER.

It befell on a Friday on Midsummer Eve in right hot weather, as this crea-
ture was coming from York-ward carrying a bottle with beer in her hand, and
her husband a cake in his bosom, that he asked his wife this question:—

"Margery, if there came a man with a sword, who would strike off my head,
unless I should commune naturally with you as I have done before, tell me on
your conscience—for ye say ye will not lie—whether ye would suffer my head
to be smitten off, or whether ye would suffer me to meddle with you again, as
I did at one time?"

"Alas, sir," said she, "why raise this matter, when we have been chaste these
eight weeks?"

"For I will know the truth of your heart."

And then she said with great sorrow:—"Forsooth, I would rather see you
being slain, than that we should turn again to our uncleanness."

And he replied:—"Ye are no good wife."

She then asked her husband what was the cause that he had not meddled
with her for eight weeks, since she lay with him every night in his bed. He said
he was made so afraid when he would have touched her, that he dare do no
more.

"Now, good sir, amend your ways, and ask God's mercy, for I told you nearly
three years ago that ye[3] should be slain suddenly, and now is this the third year,
and so I hope I shall have my desire. Good sir, I pray you grant me what I ask,
and I will pray for you that ye shall be saved through the mercy of Our Lord
Jesus Christ, and ye shall have more reward in Heaven than if ye wore a hair-
cloth or a habergeon.[4] I pray you, suffer me to make a vow of chastity at what
bishop's hand God wills."

"Nay," he said, "that I will not grant you, for now may I use you without
deadly sin, and then might I not do so."

Then she said to him:—"If it be the will of the Holy Ghost to fulfil what I
have said, I pray God that ye may consent thereto; and if it be not the will of
the Holy Ghost, I pray God ye never consent to it."

Then they went forth towards Bridlington in right hot weather, the creature
having great sorrow and dread for her chastity. As they came by a cross, her
husband sat down under the cross, calling his wife to him and saying these
words unto her:—"Margery, grant me my desire, and I shall grant you your de-
sire. My first desire is that we shall lie together in bed as we have done before;
the second, that ye shall pay my debts, ere ye go to Jerusalem; and the third,
that ye shall eat and drink with me on the Friday[5] as ye were wont to do."

"Nay, sir," said she, "to break the Friday, I will never grant you whilst I live."

"Well," said he, "then I shall meddle with you again."

She prayed him that he would give her leave to say her prayers, and he
granted it kindly. Then she knelt down beside a cross in the field and prayed in
this manner, with a great abundance of tears:—

"Lord God, Thou knowest all things. Thou knowest what sorrow I have had
to be chaste in my body to Thee all these three years, and now might I have my
will, and dare not for love of Thee. For if I should break that manner of fasting

3. According to one editor, ye should be read as "your
lust"; but her emphasis on his salvation suggests it is a
literal death as well. Christ gave her this prophecy
(told in Chapter 9) while she was praying.

4. A coat of armor sometimes worn for penance.
5. Friday is a traditional day of fasting in the Catholic
Church.

which Thou commandest me to keep on the Friday, without meat or drink, I should now have my desire. But, Blessed Lord, Thou knowest that I will not contravene Thy will, and much now is my sorrow unless I find comfort in Thee. Now, Blessed Jesus, make Thy will known to me unworthy, that I may follow it thereafter and fulfil it with all my might."

Then Our Lord Jesus Christ with great sweetness, spoke to her, commanding her to go again to her husband, and pray him to grant her what she desired, "And he shall have what he desireth. For, my dearworthy daughter, this was the cause that I bade thee fast, so that thou shouldst the sooner obtain and get thy desire, and now it is granted to thee. I will no longer that thou fast. Therefore I bid thee in the Name of Jesus, eat and drink as thy husband doth."

Then this creature thanked Our Lord Jesus Christ for His grace and goodness, and rose up and went to her husband, saying to him:—

"Sir, if it please you, ye shall grant me my desire, and ye shall have your desire. Grant me that ye will not come into my bed, and I grant you to requite your debts ere I go to Jerusalem. Make my body free to God so that ye never make challenge to me, by asking any debt of matrimony. After this day, whilst ye live, I will eat and drink on the Friday at your bidding."

Then said her husband:—"As free may your body be to God, as it hath been to me."

This creature thanked God, greatly rejoicing that she had her desire, praying her husband that they should say three Paternosters in worship of the Trinity for the great grace that He had granted them. And so they did, kneeling under a cross, and afterwards they ate and drank together in great gladness of spirit. This was on a Friday on Midsummer's Eve. Then went they forth Bridlingtonward and also to many other countries and spoke with God's servants, both anchorites[6] and recluses, and many others of Our Lord's lovers, with many worthy clerks, doctors of divinity and bachelors also, in divers places. And this creature, to many of them, shewed her feelings and her contemplations, as she was commanded to do, to find out if any deceit were in her feelings.

6. Religiously motivated recluses. 1436–38

JULIANA BERNERS
c. 1388–?

Little is known of Juliana Berners, who evidently authored a guide to hunting as well as several essays on beasts of the field that were included in an early treatise on these matters titled *The Book of St. Albans* (1486). Some scholars have identified her as the daughter of Sir James Berners, a favorite of Richard II, while others speculate that she dwelled at the manor of Julians Barnes. Still others claim that she was the prioress of Sopwell Abbey, near St. Albans, where she translated and versified two prose treatises on hunting as educational texts for upper-class children. If, as is likely, she did in fact compose the portion of *The Book of St. Albans* from which our selection is drawn, she was one of the first Englishwomen to work in what was to become a rich tradition of female-authored advice literature.

The excerpts printed here have been rendered into modern English by the scholar and translator Dorothy Gilbert, but their verse style preserves the terse vitality of the original. Frank and practical, these passages focus with remarkable

clarity on the anatomy and physiology of game animals (the deer, the hare) as they were viewed by medieval thinkers. Like the other portions of *The Book of St. Albans* probably composed by Juliana Berners, they reveal that women in this period were rarely squeamish about the physical details of field and kitchen, hunt and home.

FROM THE BOOK OF ST. ALBANS[1]

Hunting Terminology

Beasts of Venery[2]

Wherever you fare by forest or fell[3]
My dear child, take heed how Tristram[4] doth you tell,
The kinds of animals for hunting that he knew,
Listen to your mother; she will teach them to you.
Four kinds of hunted animals there are: 5
The first of them is the hart;[5] the second is the hare;
 One of them is the boar;
 The wolf, too; and no more.

Beasts of the Chase

Wherever you go, on what plain, in what place,
I will tell you which are the beasts of the chase.
One of them is the buck, the other is the doe,
The fox and the marten and the wild roe,[6]
And you shall, my dear child, with the other beasts all, 5
Wherever you find them, "rascal"[7] them call,
 In woodland or fell,
 Or forest; this I tell.

Note Here the Age of a Hart

Now to speak of the hart, if you will learn it here,
You shall call him a calf, when his age is a year.
"Brocket" is what you call him when he is two,
"Spayad" when he is three; thus you learn what to do.
 Call him a stag, when he is four, 5
At five, call him a great stag; mind your mother's lore.
 Call him a hart, when he is six;
 Do so, my child, while you have your wits.

1. Translated and annotated by Dorothy Gilbert.
2. Hunting Game animals were classified either as "beasts of venery" or as "beasts of chase." The distinction appears to have been one of etiquette and tradition, not law, though it may be that a higher prestige was associated with the hunting of beasts of venery, since they were also listed as "beasts of the forest," i.e., beasts that were protected by the law that governed the royal forests, while they lived on land that formed part of the forest domain. Beasts of the chase, on the other hand, were protected only by the common law, while they lived in a "chase" or enclosure.
3. A hill or ridge; here, probably a wild, elevated, or precipitous stretch of moorland or open pasture, as contrasted with a wooded area. The original has "by fryth or by feil," a conventional phrase meaning "by woods or by (open, high) hill."
4. Sir Tristram (or Tristan), in Arthurian tradition the lover of Isolde and nephew of King Mark, was famed for his consummate skill as a hunter and his knowledge of all the lore and etiquette of the subject.
5. Male red deer.
6. Deer; a small, delicately formed Eurasian species, known in England from Anglo-Saxon times. "Marten": a thick-furred animal resembling a weasel.
7. Animals not hunted as game, e.g., skunks and badgers.

The Hare

Now to speak of the hare, my son, certainly
This beast shall be called king of all venery.
For all hunting's fine terms and brave blasts,[1] be aware,
Grow out of the tracking and finding of the hare.
For, my dear child, I can take it on hand[2] 5
He is the most wonderful beast in any land.
For he casts droppings, and pellets, he has suet and fat,[3]
Chews his cud constantly, and has front teeth that stick out.
And sometimes he is male, and like a male creature,
And sometimes he is female, and bears young by nature.[4] 10
And when he is female, and his young are formed within,
They grow in three stages, before he parts with them:
First rough, and then smooth, the two babies will be,
And then unformed lumps, during his pregnancy,[5]
When his phase is female. 15
 So I tell my tale.

The Reward for the Hounds

When your hounds by main force have the hare, and she's dead,
The hunter shall reward them then with the head,
The shoulders, flanks, bowels of the animal,
And all things in the belly save only the gall,
And the viscera; that 5
They do not get.
This reward for the dogs that is dealt out on the ground
Good hunters call the "hallow," the hare's parts for the hound.
Then the loins of the hare, look you do not forget,
But bring them to the kitchen, for the lord's meat.[6] 10
 And of this same hare
 Speak we no more.

More about the Hare: Why the Hare Voids Its Dung Standing Up, and Makes Pellets of It

"Yet, master, I would know, if you'll lend me your wit,
Why the hare voids dung standing, and makes pellets of it,
When all other hunted beasts, game generally,
Void standing or squatting, as we can see."
"That I can surely tell thee," the master answered then, 5
"Why the hare stands and makes pellets, as is known to men.

1. Of the horn.
2. I guarantee, I undertake; I assure you.
3. Aristotle (*Hist. Anim.* II.17) describes suet and fat as occurring in different animals: "those with teeth in both jaws have fat, those without have suet." Thus the hare may be unusual.
4. The medieval belief in the hare's hermaphroditism and other sexual peculiarities, found in Terence (a school text), Latin encyclopedias, and biblical com-

mentary, seems to have been widespread.
5. Both Aristotle (*Hist. Anim.* VI.33) and the Roman Pliny (*Nat. Hist.* VIII.81.217) state that a hare can conceive young while already pregnant and/or nursing. This belief probably gave rise to comments like Berners'.
6. "Meete" in the original means "food, nourishment."

He stands because his body is so full of suet,
And he makes pellets, men say, because of all his fat.
And he crouches on his hocks when he lets it go—
No other game does that, as far as men know." 10
"How many beasts voic standing, I would fain find out,
And also I would learn, how many of them squat?"
"To tell you that," said the master, "is a job done easily.
All beasts that bear suet, and stand upright, you must see,
Let their scat fall when they stand, you may be sure of that, 15
And other beasts—the squatting kind—get rid of it when they squat."

1486

QUEEN ELIZABETH I

1533–1603

By 1558, when Elizabeth Tudor ascended the throne at the age of twenty-five, she was proficient in Greek and Latin as well as French, Italian, Spanish, and German. Her translations, speeches, and poems illustrate her political genius and her rhetorical ingenuity. She needed both of these assets, for she faced personal, political, and religious opposition to her rule. As the daughter of Henry VIII and Anne Boleyn, she had been declared illegitimate by Pope Clement VII, who refused to sanction her father's remarriage, and even after her supremacy had been established, she confronted public reservations about her unmarried state. As monarch, she was caught in the middle: she had to deal with a Protestant Parliament; papal objection to her legitimacy; and constant threat of war from the Catholic powers, Spain and France. As the head of the Church established by her father, Elizabeth presided over an institution that, in its structure, doctrines, and rituals, was effectively Roman Catholic; Henry had simply replaced the pope as the supreme ruler of the Church in England. Elizabeth was opposed on the one hand by Catholics, who resented Henry's rejection of papal supremacy, and on the other hand by Puritan Protestants, who believed that the Church had not been sufficiently "purified" of its Roman Catholic elements. Neither Protestant nor Catholic, Elizabeth, to ensure peace in England, followed a *via media* (a middle course), which eventually prevailed and became Anglicanism.

Most historians agree that, paradoxically enough, Queen Elizabeth achieved complete sovereignty only after a papal condemnation of 1570 excommunicated her and released her subjects from their allegiance to her rule. Public opinion consolidated against her Catholic rival, Mary Queen of Scots, and in favor of Elizabeth, who quickly became the symbol of English nationalism. When, in 1588, she commanded land forces and supervised naval raids against a papal-financed Spanish fleet (the famous Armada) that was planning to invade Britain, she defeated the last pretender to the throne, Philip II of Spain. Her resulting popularity was enhanced by the diplomatic course she maintained in strengthening the Anglican Church to resist the influence of both the Catholics and the Puritans. During the prolific literary age that was named for her forty-five-year-long reign, she was celebrated in many poems and plays as a uniquely English embodiment of the female power associated with such biblical and mythological heroines as Judith, Esther, Diana, and Minerva. In her own writing, moreover, she revealed the same witty intelligence that distinguishes so much Elizabethan literature.

The Doubt of Future Foes[1]

The doubt of future foes exiles my present joy,
And wit[2] me warns to shun such snares as threaten mine annoy;
For falsehood now doth flow, and subjects' faith doth ebb,
Which should not be if reason ruled or wisdom weaved the web.
But clouds of joys untried do cloak aspiring minds, 5
Which turn to rain of late repent by changéd course of winds.
The top of hope supposed the root upreared shall be,[3]
And fruitless all their grafted[4] guile, as shortly ye shall see.
The dazzled eyes with pride, which great ambition blinds,
Shall be unsealed by worthy wights whose foresight falsehood[5]
 finds. 10
The daughter of debate that discord aye[6] doth sow
Shall reap no gain where former rule still peace hath taught to
 know.
No foreign banished wight shall anchor in this port;
Our realm brooks not seditious sects, let them elsewhere resort.
My rusty sword through rest shall first his edge employ 15
To poll their tops[7] that seek such change or gape for future joy.

1570 1589

On Monsieur's Departure[1]

I grieve and dare not show my discontent,
I love and yet am forced to seem to hate,
I do, yet dare not say I ever meant,[2]
I seem stark mute but inwardly do prate.[3]
 I am and not, I freeze and yet am burned, 5
 Since from myself another self I turned.

My care is like my shadow in the sun,
Follows me flying, flies when I pursue it,
Stands and lies by me, doth what I have done.
His too familiar care doth make me rue it. 10
 No means I find to rid him from my breast,
 Till by the end of things[4] it be suppressed.

Some gentler passion slide into my mind,
For I am soft and made of melting snow;
Or be more cruel, love, and so be kind. 15
Let me or float or sink, be high or low.
 Or let me live with some more sweet content,
 Or die and so forget what love ere meant.

1600 1823

1. "The poem concerns Elizabeth's Roman Catholic
cousin, Mary Stuart, Queen of Scotland, who in 1568
sought refuge in England from her rebellious subjects.
Mary was the focus of several Roman Catholic conspir-
acies to place her on the English throne in place of
Elizabeth. 'Doubt': fear" [Barbara Lewalski's note].
2. Intelligence.
3. I.e., her enemies' unfounded hopes concentrate on
the "top," or outcome of their schemes, while
Elizabeth defeats them by pulling up their "roots."
4. Continues the botanical metaphor: her enemies
have unsuccessfully tried to "graft" their plans onto
roots that will not support them.
5. "Wights": men.
6. Always. "Discord" is the object of "sow."
7. To prune or crop the tops of trees, with an obvious
suggestion of beheading.
1. "Monsieur" has been identified as either the
French duke of Anjou, with whom Elizabeth had nego-
tiated marriage, or the earl of Essex, one of her favorite
courtiers.
2. I.e., meant to do.
3. Chatter.
4. The Day of Judgment.

Speech to the Troops at Tilbury[1]

My loving people,

We have been persuaded by some that are careful of [2] our safety, to take heed how we commit our selves to armed multitudes, for fear of treachery; but I assure you I do not desire to live to distrust my faithful and loving people. Let tyrants fear. I have always so behaved myself that, under God, I have placed my chiefest strength and safeguard in the loyal hearts and good-will of my subjects; and therefore I am come amongst you, as you see, at this time, not for my recreation and disport,[3] but being resolved, in the midst and heat of the battle, to live or die amongst you all; to lay down for my God, and for my kingdom, and my people, my honor and my blood, even in the dust. I know I have the body but of a weak and feeble woman; but I have the heart and stomach of a king, and of a king of England too, and think foul scorn that Parma or Spain, or any prince of Europe, should dare to invade the borders of my realm; to which rather than any dishonor shall grow by me, I myself will take up arms, I myself will be your general, judge, and rewarder of every one of your virtues in the field. I know already, for your forwardness you have deserved rewards and crowns;[4] and We do assure you in the word of a prince, they shall be duly paid you. In the mean time, my lieutenant general[5] shall be in my stead, than whom never prince commanded a more noble or worthy subject; not doubting but by your obedience to my general, by your concord in the camp, and your valour in the field, we shall shortly have a famous victory over those enemies of my God, of my kingdom, and of my people.

1588 1752

1 Delivered by Elizabeth to land forces that had assembled at Tilbury in anticipation of the landing of the Spanish Armada, a fleet of warships sent by Philip II to invade England. In fact the Armada was defeated at sea, and so never reached England, but Elizabeth's courage in personally leading her troops was not diminished.

2. Anxious for.
3. Entertainment.
4. An English monetary unit; also possibly honorary titles.
5. Robert Dudley, earl of Leicester (1532–1588).

MARY SIDNEY HERBERT, COUNTESS OF PEMBROKE
1562–1621

Mary Sidney Herbert is probably best known today as the sister of the poet Sir Philip Sidney and one of the sixteenth century's great patronesses of learning. But besides facilitating the work of others, she was herself a translator and poet of considerable skill. Aemilia Lanyer, dedicating her verse narrative of "the passion of Christ" to Herbert, self-deprecatingly admitted "many books she writes that are more rare," while other literary figures such as Edmund Spenser, John Donne, and Ben Jonson praised what Spenser called the "heavenly gifts and graces of her mind."

The third of seven children, Herbert was born at Tickenhill Palace in Worcestershire, into an aristocratic family. Her father was the godson of Henry VIII and a close friend of Edward VI. Her mother was a lady in waiting to Queen Elizabeth, a post Mary herself was to fill between 1575 and 1577. Exceptionally well educated for her time—she knew Latin as well as French and Italian—she was always partic-

ularly close to her older brother Philip, with whom she shared a passion for litera-
ture. Married in 1577 to Henry Herbert, the earl of Pembroke, she settled with him
at Wilton House, near Salisbury, one of the most majestic of England's stately
homes, and in 1580, when Philip Sidney was temporarily exiled from Elizabeth's
court, the poet made a number of long visits to her there. "In her time," remem-
bered the seventeenth-century diarist John Aubrey, "Wilton House was like a col-
lege, there were so many learned and ingenious persons." It is likely that Philip
wrote portions of his *Arcadia* and wrote or revised his *Apology for Poetry* when he
was in residence. In addition—to name only a few other members of the Wilton
House circle—the poet Samuel Daniel was employed as a tutor for the countess's
sons, and the chemist Adrian Gilbert, half-brother of Sir Walter Raleigh, had a lab-
oratory in the house.

 After Philip was killed fighting in the Netherlands in 1586, his sister devoted
herself to editing and publishing his poems. During the 1590s, she also began
working on translations of her own. Her most enduring accomplishment, however,
was a continuation of the English version of the Psalms that her brother had begun
before his death. Fascinating in its metrical variety and stanzaic inventiveness, the
150-psalm sequence—first published in its entirety in 1823—is a virtual com-
pendium of Elizabethan verse strategies. Herbert's renderings start with Psalm 44,
and her style is brilliantly complex, as both *To the Thrice-Sacred Queen Elizabeth*
(her dedication of the psalms to the queen) and her version of Psalm 58 suggest.
Whether she wrote other original poems is not known; many manuscripts may
have been lost in a fire that destroyed the Wilton House library in 1647, twenty-six
years after the countess's death. But even as it stands, Herbert's achievement in
translation and versification justifies Lanyer's description of her as "a Lady whom
Minerva [the goddess of wisdom] chose / To live with her in height of all respect."

To the Thrice-Sacred Queen Elizabeth[1]

1

Even now that care[2] which on thy crown attends
And with thy happy[3] greatness daily grows
Tells me, thrice-sacred Queen, my muse offends,
And of respect to thee the line out goes.[4]
One instant will or willing can she lose[5] 5
I say not reading, but receiving rhymes,
On whom in chief dependeth to dispose[6]
What Europe acts in these most active times?

2

Yet dare I so, as humbleness may dare,
Cherish some hope they shall acceptance find; 10
Now weighing less thy state, lighter thy care,
But knowing more thy grace, abler thy mind.
What heavenly powers thee highest throne assigned,
Assigned thee goodness suiting that degree,[7]
And by thy strength thy burthen so designed,[8] 15
To others toil is exercise to thee.

1. This poem was written to accompany a translation of the Psalms of David, begun by Herbert's brother Sir Philip Sidney and completed by Herbert after his death. Sidney was exiled from Elizabeth's court when he incurred her disfavor by counseling against a marriage with the duke of Anjou.
2. Burden.
3. Fortunate.
4. I.e., the meter is broken.
5. I.e., will she, or can she willingly, lose one instant?
6. Arrange, settle.
7. I.e., the throne.
8. I.e., those powers designated your responsibilities according to your strength.

3

Cares though still great, cannot be greatest still,
Business must ebb, though leisure never flow;
Then these the posts[9] of duty and goodwill
Shall press to offer what their senders[1] owe, 20
Which once in two, now in one subject go,
The poorer left, the richer rest[2] away,
Who better might (O might, ah word of woe)
Have given for me what I for him defray.[3]

4

How can I name whom sighing signs extend,[4] 25
And not unstop my tears' eternal spring?
But he did warp, I weaved this web to end;[5]
The stuff[6] not ours, our work no curious thing,
Wherein yet well we thought the Psalmist King
How English denizened,[7] though Hebrew born, 30
Would to thy music undispleaséd sing,
Oft having worse, without repining worn;

5

And I the cloth in both our names present,
A livery robe to be bestowed[8] by thee;
Small parcel of the undischargéd rent, 35
From which no pains nor payments can us free.
And yet enough to cause our neighbors see
We will our best, though scanted[9] in our will;
And those nigh fields where sown they favors be
Unwealthy do, not else unworthy till. 40

6

For in our work what bring we but thine own?
What English is, by many names is thine,
There humble laurels[2] in thy shadows grown
To garland others would themselves repine.[3]
Thy breast the cabinet, thy seat[4] the shrine, 45
Where muses hang their vowéd memories,
Where wit, where art, where all that is divine
Conceivéd[5] best, and best defended lies.

9. The poems as sent to Elizabeth.
1. I.e., Herbert and the late Sidney. "Press": eagerly advance.
2. Perhaps a variation of "wrested," seized and pulled (by death). "The richer": Sidney.
3. Pay metaphorically, present a tribute.
4. I.e., how can I name him (Sidney) to whom sighs, the signs of grief, are extended?
5. In clothmaking, to lay down the first set of threads (the warp), which is then intersected by another set (the woof). Herbert is referring to the fact that Sidney only began the Psalms, which she completed.
6. Accomplished, ingenious. "Stuff": raw material (i.e., the Bible).
7. Naturalized as an English subject. I.e., if David ("the Psalmist King") were an English subject, he

would willingly serve you, since he had served under a worse ruler (the tyrant Saul) without complaining.
5. Employed or stored. "Robe": courtly dress.
3. Limited, or possibly presumed to be inadequate perhaps a reference to Elizabeth's anger at Sidney). "Will": desire to do.
1. I.e., we till the fields of your favor without shows of wealth (as in costly gifts), but otherwise worthily.
2. Leaves associated with great poets.
3 I e., the laurels themselves would complain at being worn by others, since all English art ultimately stems from Elizabeth.
4. Place of abode and of rulership. "Cabinet": small room.
5. Understood. "Wit": intelligence.

7

Which if men did not (as they do) confess,[6]
And wronging worlds would otherwise consent,[7] 50
Yet here who minds so meet a patroness[8]
For authors' state or writings' argument?[9]
A King should only to a Queen be sent;
God's lovéd choice unto his chosen love;
Devotion to devotion's president;[1] 55
What all applaud, to her whom none reprove.

8

And who sees ought, but sees[2] how justly square[3]
His haughty ditties to thy glorious days?
How well beseeming thee his triumphs[4] are?
His hope, his zeal, his prayer, plaint, and praise, 60
Needless thy person[5] to their height to raise;
Less need to bend them down to thy degree;
These holy garments each good soul assays,[6]
Some sorting all, all sort[7] to none but thee.

9

For even thy rule is painted[8] in his reign; 65
Both clear in right; both nigh by wrong oppressed;[9]
And each at length (man crossing God in vain)
Possessed of place, and each in peace possessed.
Proud Philistines did interrupt his rest,
The foes of heaven no less have been thy foes; 70
He with great conquest, thou with greater blessed;
Thou sure to win, and he secure to lose.[1]

10

Thus hand in hand with him thy glories walk;
But who can trace them where alone they go?
Of thee who hemispheres on honor talk,[2] 75
And lands and seas thy trophies[3] jointly show.
The very winds did on thy party blow,
And rocks in arms thy foemen eft[4] defy.
But soft, my muse, thy pitch[5] is earthly love;
Forbear this heaven where only eagles fly. 80

6. I.e., if men did not agree that Elizabeth is the author of all English works.
7. Agree in opinion. "Wronging": doing a great wrong.
8. I.e., who in England can remember so fitting a supporter?
9. Plot or meaning. "State": financial condition.
1. One who presides, leads (as queen, Elizabeth was the head of the Church of England). "Devotion . . . devotion": worship or prayer; the second use is closer to piety, devoutness.
2. I.e., who sees anything, who does not see?
3. A verb meaning "correspond," "fit."
4. Both victories and triumphal songs. "Beseeming": matching, resembling.
5. Self.
6. Tries on. "Holy garments": i.e., the Psalms.
7. A play on *sort*: (1) going through, (2) are appropriate.

8. Represented, figured.
9. Probably closer to "defeated" than in its modern meaning. Both Elizabeth and David reigned during times of war; their enemies, the Spanish and the Philistines, were perceived as enemies of the true religion. "Nigh": almost.
1. I.e., facing overwhelming odds against winning.
2. I.e., talk of your honor.
3. Victories. In 1588 England defeated the Spanish Armada, with the aid of the weather.
4. Probably a misprint for "oft." "Rocks": an allusion to David's killing of the Philistine Goliath with a single stone; here they represent cannonballs. The rocks defy or challenge the foemen.
5. In music, a tone or level of dynamics. Here, the subject of the muse's song. Herbert feels she is not qualified to write of war, traditionally a male subject.

11

Kings on a Queen enforced their states to lay;[6]
Mainlands for emp're waiting on[7] an isle;
Men drawn by worth a woman to obey;
One moving all, herself unmoved the while;
Truth's restitution, vanity exile, 85
Wealth sprung of want, war held without annoy,[8]
Let subject be of some inspired style,
Till then the object of her subjects' joy.

12

Thy utmost[9] can but offer to her sight
Her handmaids' task, which most her will endears;[1] 90
And pray unto thy pains life from that light
Which lively light some, court and kingdom cheers,[2]
What[3] wish she may (far past her living peers
And rival still to Judah's faithful king)[4]
In more than he and more triumphant years,[5] 90 95
Sing what God doth, and do what men may sing.

1599 1962

Psalm 58 *Si Vere Utique*[1]

And call ye this to utter what is just
 You that of justice hold the sovereign throne?
And call ye this, to yield, O sons of dust,
 To wrongéd brethren every man his own?
O no! It is your long malicious will 5
 Now to the world to make by practice known
With whose oppression you the balance fill:
 Just to yourselves, indifferent else[2] to none.

But what could they, who even in birth declined
 From truth and right to lies and injuries? 10
To show the venom of their cankered[3] mind
 The adder's image scarcely can suffice;
Nay, scarce the aspic[4] may with them contend,
 On whom the charmer all in vain applies
His skilfull'st spells, aye missing of his end, 15
 While she, self-deaf and unaffected, lies.

6. I.e., kings forced to place their states under
Elizabeth's rule; Herbert is somewhat exaggerating
Elizabeth's gains in power.
7. Obeying; also courting. "Empire": government.
8. Vexation
9. I.e., Herbert's muse's greatest effort.
1. I.e., simple tokens of loyalty are more endearing to
the queen than great works.
2. I.e., that lively light (Elizabeth) that is cheered by
court and kingdom. The meaning of "some" here is

not clear; it may be a misprint.
3. Who (i.e., court and kingdom).
4. David. "Judah" is another name for Israel.
5. I.e., in a longer and more triumphant reign.
1. If indeed holy (Latin). The first line of this psalm,
in the King James version, reads, "Do ye indeed speak
righteousness, O congregation?"
2. Otherwise impartial.
3. Infected with evil.
4. Asp: a poisonous snake.

Lord, crack their teeth! Lord, crush these lions' jaws!
　　So let them sink as water in the sand.
When deadly bow their aiming fury draws,
　　Shiver the shaft ere past the shooter's hand.　　　　　　20
So make them melt as the dishouséd snail,
　　Or as the embryo whose vital band
Breaks ere it holds, and formless eyes do fail
　　To see the sun, though brought to lightful land.

O let their brood, a brood of springing thorns,　　　　　　25
　　Be by untimely rooting overthrown;
Ere bushes waxed, they push with pricking horns,[5]
　　As fruits yet green are oft by tempest blown.
The good with gladness this revenge shall see
　　And bathe his feet in blood of wicked one　　　　　　30
While all shall say, "The just rewarded be;
　　There is a God that carves to each his own."

1599　　　　　　　　　　　　　　　　　　　　　　　　1820

5. Thorns. "Waxed": grew.

ISABELLA WHITNEY

fl. 1567–1573

"Till some household cares me tie, / My books and pen I will apply," declared the young Isabella Whitney in a verse letter to a married sister. The first English-woman to publish a book of poems, Whitney abbreviated her name to "Is. W." when she signed both her broadside *Copy of a Letter Lately Written in Meter, by a Young Gentlewoman: to her Unconstant Lover. With an Admonition to All Young Gentlewomen, and to all Other Maids in General to Beware of Men's Flattery* (1567) and her major collection, *A Sweet Nosegay or Pleasant Posy, Containing a Hundred and Ten Philosophical Flowers* (1573). Yet even so modest a signature was a daring gesture.

　　Born into a middle-class, Reformist family, Whitney appears to have had two brothers, including one who authored a collection of poems titled *A Choice of Emblems* (1586), along with several sisters who served in genteel London house-holds. Little else is known of her life except that by 1600 she may have acquired a husband and two children. Her most ambitious work, *The Author . . . Maketh Her Will and Testament*, is a mock will in which she bequeaths to the city of London all its most salient characteristics. Often sardonic in its portrayal of contemporary so-cial institutions (shops, prisons, markets, Inns of Court), the poem records vivid details of daily life in urban sixteenth-century England, from the lucrative activi-ties of tailors ("such as make the sweeping cloaks") to the unlucky lot of the mad (those in Bedlam who "out of tune do talk"). But despite Whitney's wit and vital-ity, some four centuries later *A Sweet Nosegay*, in which her *Will and Testament* ap-pears, has not yet been republished in its entirety. Our excerpt was rendered in modern English by the scholar and poet Mary Moore.

The Author . . . Maketh Her Will and Testament[1]

The Author, though loath to leave the City, upon her friend's procurement is constrained to depart, wherefore she feigneth as she would die and maketh her Will and Testament as followeth, with large legacies of such goods and riches which she most abundantly hath left behind her, and thereof maketh London sole executor . . .

A Communication Which the Author Had to London
Before She Made Her Will

The time is come I must depart
 from thee, ah, famous city:
I never yet to rue my smart[2]
 did find that thou hadst pity.
Wherefore, small cause there is that I 5
 would grieve from thee [to] go,
But many women foolishly,
 like me and other more,
Do such a fixed fancy set
 on those which least deserve 10
That long it is ere wit[3] we get
 away from them to swerve;
But Time with pity oft will tell,
 to those that will her try,
Whether it best be more to mell[4] 15
 or utterly defy;
And now hath time me put in mind
 Of thy great cruelness,
That never once a help would find
 To ease me in distress. 20
Thou never yet wouldst credit give
 to board me for a year
Nor with apparel me relieve
 except thou paid were.[5]
No, no, thou never didst me good 25
 nor ever will, I know;
Yet am I in no angry mood
 but will, or ere[6] I go,
In perfect love and charity
 my Testament here write 30
And leave to thee such Treasury
 as I in it recite.
Now stand aside and give me leave
 to write my latest will,
And see that none you do deceive 35
 of[7] that I leave them till.

1. We are also grateful for the editing and anno-
tations by Mary Moore.
2. Regret my pain.
3. Intelligence.

4. Interfere, concern oneself.
5. I.e., to board and clothe her on credit.
6. Before.
7. Cheat out of.

The Manner of Her Will and What She Left to London and to All Those in It at Her Departing

I, whole in body and in mind
 but very weak in purse,
Do make and write my testament
 for fear it will be worse;[8]
And first I wholly do commend 5
 my soul and body eke[9]
To God, the Father, and the Son,
 So long as I can speak;
And after speech, my soul to him
 And body to the grave, 10
Till time that all shall rise again
 their Judgement for to have;
And then I hope they both[1] shall meet
 to dwell for aye in joy,
Whereas I trust to see my friends 15
 released from all annoy.[2]
Thus have you heard touching my soul
 and body what I mean:
I trust you all will witness bear
 I have a steadfast brain; 20
And now let me dispose such things
 as I shall leave behind,
That those which will receive the same
 may know my willing mind.
I first of all to London leave, 25
 because I there was bred,
Brave buildings rare, of churches store,
 and Paul's to the head.[3]
Between the same, fair streets there be
 and people goodly store; 30
Because their keeping craveth cost,[4]
 I yet will leave [them] more.
First, for their food, I butchers leave
 That every day shall kill;
By Thames you shall have brewers store 35
 and bakers at your will,
And such as orders[5] do observe
 and eat fish thrice a week;
I leave two streets full fraught[6] therewith;
 they need not far to seek. 40
Watling Street and Canwick Street
 I full of woolen leave,

8. I.e., she will not be whole in body and mind.
9. Also.
1. I.e., body and soul.
2. Trouble, hardship.
3. I.e., I leave to London fine buildings, many "store" churches, and before them all St. Paul's.

4. Requires expenditure.
5. Those who are ministers or clergymen.
6. Supplied, filled.

And linen store in Friday Street
 If they me not deceive;
And those which are of calling such
 that costlier they require, 45
I mercers[7] leave with silk so rich
 as any would desire.

<center>* * *</center>

For women shall you tailors have;
 by Bow the chiefest dwell;
In every lane you some shall find
 can do indifferent well;[8] 80
And for the men few streets or lanes,
 but bodymakers be,
And such as make the sweeping cloaks,
 with gards[9] beneath the knee.

<center>* * *</center>

Now when thy folk are fed and clad
 with such as I have named,
For dainty mouths and stomachs weak,
 some junkets must be framed, 90
Wherefore, I pothecaries leave
 and banquets[1] in their shop,
Physicians also for the sick 95
 diseases for to stop.
Some royst'rers still must bide in thee
 and such as cut it out[2]
That with the guiltless quarrel will
 to let their blood about. 100
For them I cunning surgeons leave
 some plasters[3] to apply,
That ruffians may not still be hanged
 nor quiet persons die.
For salt, oatmeal, candles, soap, 105
 or what you else do want,
In many places shops are full:
 I left you nothing scant.[4]
If they that keep what you leave
 Ask money when they sell it, 110
At Mint there is such store, it is
 impossible to tell[5] it.
At Stiliard store of wines there be
 your dulled wits to glad
And handsome men that must not wed 115
 except they leave their trade.

7. Those who deal in textile fabrics, especially in costly materials.
8. Fairly well.
9. Stripes. "Bodymakers": clothes for the body.
1. Sweetmeats. "Junkets": confections or delicacies. "Pothecaries": apothecaries originally sold spices, preserves, and other commodities besides drugs.

2. Flaunt, make a show. "Roysters": riotous or swaggering fellows.
3. Medicated dressings.
4. I.e. plenty.
5. Count.

They oft shall seek for proper girls,
 and some perhaps shall find,
That need compels or lucre lures
 to satisfy their mind. 120

* * *

Now for the people in thee left,
 I have done as I may,
And that the poor when I am gone 135
 Have cause for me to pray,
I will to prisons portions leave,
 what though but very small,
Yet that they may remember me
 occasion be it shall.[6] 140

* * *

To all the bookbinders by Paul's,
 because I like their art,
They ery[7] week shall money have 195
 when they from books depart.
Amongst them all, my printer must
 have somewhat to his share:
I will my friends these books to buy
 of him with other ware.[8] 200
To maidens poor, I widowers rich
 do leave, that oft shall dote,
And by that means shall marry them
 To set the girls afloat;
And wealthy widows will I leave 205
 to help young gentlemen,
Which when you have, in any case,
 be courteous to them then,
And see their plate[9] and jewels eke
 may not be marred with rust, 210
Nor let their bags[1] too long be full
 for fear that they do burst.

* * *

And Bedlam[2] must not be forgot 225
 for that was oft my walk;
I people there too many leave
 that out of tune do talk.

* * *

For such as cannot quiet be
 and strive for house or land,

6. I.e., perhaps the charity will cause those in prison to
remember her in their prayers.
7. Every.
8. I.e., her friends will use other goods to buy books
from her printer.

9. Goods made out of precious metal.
1. Money bags, purses.
2. The oldest insane asylum in England.

At the Inns of Court, I lawyers leave 235
　　to take their cause in hand;
And also leave I, at each Inn
　　of Court or Chancery,
Of gentlemen a youthful rout[3]
　　full of activity, 240
For whom I store of books have left
　　at each bookbinder's stall
And part of all that London hath
　　to furnish them withall;
And when they are with study cloyed,[4] 245
　　to recreate their mind,
Of tennis courts, of dancing schools,
　　And fence,[5] they store shall find,
And every Sunday at the least
　　I leave, to make them sport,[6] 250
In divers places players[7] that
　　of wonders shall report.
Now, London, have I for thy sake,
　　within thee and without,
As comes into my memory, 255
　　dispersed round about
Such needful things as they should have,
　　here left now unto thee.
When I am gone, with conscience
　　let them dispersed be; 260
And though I nothing named have
　　to bury me withall,
Consider that above the ground,
　　annoyance be I shall;[8]
And let me have a shrouding sheet 265
　　to cover me from shame;
And in oblivion bury me,
　　And never more me name.
Ringings[9] nor other ceremonies
　　[use] you not for cost, 270
Nor at my burial, make no feast;
　　your money were but lost.
Rejoice in God that I am gone
　　out of this vale so vile,
And that, of each thing, left such store 275
　　as may your wants exile.
I make thee sole executor because
　　I loved thee best,
And thee I put in trust to give
　　the goods unto the rest. 280

<p style="text-align:center">*　　*　　*</p>

3. A company; also, a disorderly crowd.
4. Disgusted or wearied with excess.
5. Fencing.
6. Amuse themselves.
7. Actors.
8. I shall be troublesome.
9. I.e., bell ringing

And, though I am persuaded that I
 shall never more thee see, 310
Yet to the last I shall not cease
 to wish much good to thee.
this XX of October, I,
 in Anno Domini
A thousand five hundred seventy three, 315
 as almanacs descry,[1]
Did write this will with mine own hand
 and it to London gave,
In witness of the standers by
 Whose names, if you will have, 320
Paper, Pen and Standish[2] were
 at that same present by,
With Time, who promised to reveal
 so fast as she could hie
The same, lest of my nearer kin, 325
 for any thing should vary,[3]
So finally I make an end;
 no longer can I tary.
Finis.[4] by Is. W.

 1573

1. Make known.
2. Ink stand.
3. I.e., so my relatives won't try to change anything in

the will. "Hie": speed, hasten.
4. The end (Latin).

AEMILIA LANYER
1569–1645

Known in her own day as a woman "of distinguished . . . learning," Aemilia Lanyer spent much of her career at court during the reigns of Elizabeth I, James I, and Charles I. The daughter of Baptist Bassano, an Italian musician at the English court, and his common-law wife, Margaret Johnson, she bore the son of Henry Cary, Lord Hunsden, soon after an arranged marriage to Alphonso Lanyer, a royal musician. After her husband's death in 1613, she appears to have been involved with his relatives in various legal squabbles over his estate. Otherwise her history is shadowy, although the historian A. L. Rowse has argued that she may well have been the "Dark Lady" of Shakespeare's sonnets, the independent and impetuous mistress to whom the great playwright claimed he was hopelessly enthralled.

 Whatever the truth about this poet's life, her verse is striking and accomplished, so much so that Rowse uses its radicalism as a basis for his assertion about her role in Shakespeare's poetry. In particular, her retelling of the biblical story of the Fall functions as a kind of pioneering vindication of the rights of "Our Mother Eve," who, declares Lanyer, gave Adam "What she held most dear"—the apple of knowledge—because she was "simply good." In fact, insists Lanyer, Eve's primordial female act of "betrayal" was performed in unconscious innocence, while men are more culpable because they consciously betrayed Jesus Christ to his crucifixion: "If one weak woman simply did offend, / This sin of yours hath no excuse, nor end." Significantly, in sketching out such a feminist version of two of Western culture's major legends, Lanyer outlined a pattern of revisionary mythmaking that was to be followed by many female descendants who may never even have read her work.

The selections printed here include both prose and verse examples of Lanyer's skill at theological argument. In addition, her elegant celebration of Cooke-ham—the country seat of her patroness Margaret, countess of Cumberland—offers a vision of a kind of female paradise ost.

From Salve Deus Rex Judaeorum[1]

[To the Virtuous Reader]

Often have I heard, that it is the property of some women, not only to emulate the virtues and perfections of the rest, but also by all their powers of ill speaking, to eclipse the brightness of their deserved fame: now contrary to their custom, which men I hope unjustly lay to their charge, I have written this small volume, or little book, for the general use of all virtuous ladies and gentlewomen of this kingdom; and in commendation of some particular persons of our own sex, such as for the most part, are so well known to myself, and others, that I dare undertake Fame dares not to call any better. And this have I done, to make known to the world, that all women deserve not to be blamed though some forgetting they are women themselves, and in danger to be condemned by the words of their own mouths, fall into so great an error, as to speak unadvisedly against the rest of their sex; which if it be true, I am persuaded they can show their own imperfection in nothing more: and therefore could wish (for their own case, modesties, and credit) they would refer such points of folly, to be practiced by evil disposed men, who forgetting they were born of women, nourished of women, and that if it were not by the means of women, they would be quite extinguished out of the world, and a final end of them all, do like vipers deface the wombs wherein they were bred, only to give way and utterance to their want of discretion and goodness. Such as these, were they that dishonored Christ his Apostles and Prophets, putting them to shameful deaths. Therefore we are not to regard any imputations, that they undeservedly lay upon us, not otherwise than to make use of them to our own benefits, as spur to virtue, making us fly all occasions that may color their unjust speeches to pass current. Especially considering that they have tempted even the patience of God himself, who gave power to wise and virtuous women, to bring down their pride and arrogancy. As was cruel Cesarus by the discreet counsel of noble Deborah, judge and prophetess of Israel: and resolution of Jael wife of Heber the Kenite:[2] wicked Haman, by the divine prayers and prudent proceedings of beautiful Hester:[3] blasphemous Holofernes, by the invincible courage, rare wisdom, and confident carriage of Judeth: and the unjust Judges, by the innocency of chaste Susanna:[4] with infinite others, which for brevity sake I will omit. As also in respect it pleased our Lord and Savior Jesus Christ, without the assistance of man, being free from original and all other sins,[5] from the time of his conception, till the hour of his death,

1. Hail God, King of the Jews (Latin).
2 Deborah delivered Sisera, a Canaanite captain (i.e. a leader or "Caesar") and his army into the hand of Barak. Sisera fled to the tent of Jael, whose husband's house was at peace with the Canaanite king; she feigned friendship but then drove a tent spike through his temples into the ground while he slept (Judges 4).
3. The Book of Esther relates the story of how Esther, the Jewish wife of Ahasuerus (Xerxes I), foiled the plot of the king's minister, Haman, to kill all the Jews in the kingdom.

4. Both stories are found in the Apocrypha. In the Book of Judith, the beautiful widow saved Judea by encouraging the attentions of the Assyrian general Holfernes and decapitating him while he was drunk. In the Book of Susannah, the beautiful and righteous widow, falsely accused of adultery by the two elders (the judges) whose sexual advances she had refused, is exonerated by the wise intervention of Daniel.
5. State of sin of all humanity that resulted from the Fall of Adam and Eve.

to be begotten of a woman, born of a woman, nourished of a woman, obedient
to a woman; and that he healed women, pardoned women, comforted women:
yea, even when he was in his greatest agony and bloody sweat, going to be cru-
cified, and also in the last hour of his death, took care to dispose of a woman:[6]
after his resurrection, appeared first to a woman, sent a woman[7] to declare his
most glorious resurrection to the rest of his Disciples. Many other examples I
could allege of divers faithful and virtuous women, who have in all ages, not
only been confessors, but also endured most cruel martyrdom for their faith in
Jesus Christ. All which is sufficient to enforce all good Christians and honor-
able-minded men to speak reverently of our sex, and especially of all virtuous
and good women. To the modest censures of both which, I refer these my im-
perfect endeavors, knowing that according to their own excellent dispositions,
they will rather, cherish, nourish, and increase the least spark of virtue where
they find it; by their favorable and best interpretations, than quench it by
wrong constructions. To whom I wish all increase of virtue, and desire their
best opinions.

[Eve's Apology in Defense of Women]

Now Pontius Pilate is to judge the cause[8]
Of faultless Jesus, who before him stands,
Who neither hath offended prince, nor laws,
Although he now be brought in woeful bands.
"O noble governor, make thou yet a pause, 5
Do not in innocent blood imbrue[9] thy hands;
 But hear the words of thy most worthy wife,[1]
 Who sends to thee, to beg her Savior's life.

"Let barbarous cruelty far depart from thee,
And in true justice take affliction's part; 10
Open thine eyes, that thou the truth mayest see.
Do not the thing that goes against thy heart,
Condemn not him that must thy Savior be;
But view his holy life, his good desert.
 Let not us women glory in men's fall.[2] 15
 Who had power given to overrule us all.

"Till now your indiscretion sets us free,
And makes our former fault[3] much less appear;
Our mother Eve, who tasted of the tree,
Giving to Adam what she held most dear, 20
Was simply good, and had no power to see;[4]
The after-coming harm did not appear:

6. Jesus asked his apostle John to care for his mother,
Mary (John 19:26–27).
7. Mary Magdalene (John 20:11–18).
8. Case. Pontius Pilate was the Roman official who au-
thorized Christ's execution.
9. Stain.
1. According to Matthew, Pilate's wife wrote a letter to
her husband telling him of a dream she had, which
warned against harming Jesus.

2. Of both Adam and Christ (perhaps also Pilate).
3. Eve traditionally is blamed for the tempting of
Adam in Eden.
4. According to the Book of Genesis, Eve, the first
woman, was persuaded by the serpent to eat fruit from
the forbidden Tree of Knowledge, which she gave to
her husband, Adam. As punishment God banished
Adam and Eve from the Garden of Eden and brought
death into the world.

The subtle serpent that our sex betrayed
Before our fall so sure a plot had laid

"That undiscerning ignorance perceived 25
No guile or craft that was by him intended;
For had she known of what we were bereaved,[5]
To his request she had not condescended.
But she, poor soul, by cunning was deceived;
No hurt therein her harmless heart intended: 30
 For she alleged God's word, which he[6] denies,
 That they should die, but even as gods be wise.

"But surely Adam cannot be excused;
Her fault though great, yet he was most to blame.
What weakness offered, strength might have refused; 35
Being lord of all, the greater was his shame;
Although the serpent's craft had her abused,
God's holy word ought all his actions frame.[7]
 For he was lord and king of all the earth,
 Before poor Eve had either life or breath, 40

"Who being framed[8] by God's eternal hand
The perfectest man that ever breathed on earth,
And from God's mouth received that strait[9] command,
The breach whereof he knew was present death;
Yea, having power to rule both sea and land, 45
Yet with one apple won to lose that breath[1]
 Which God had breathéd in his beauteous face,
 Bringing us all in danger and disgrace;

"And then to lay the fault on patience's back,
That we (poor women) must endure it all; 50
We know right well he did discretion lack,
Being not persuaded thereunto at all.[2]
If Eve did err, it was for knowledge sake;
The fruit being fair persuaded him to fall.
 No subtle serpent's falsehood did betray him; 55
 If he would eat it, who had power to stay[3] him?

"Not Eve, whose fault was only too much love,
Which made her give this present to her dear,
That what she tasted he likewise might prove,[4]
Whereby his knowledge might become more clear; 60
He never sought her weakness to reprove
With those sharp words which he of God did hear;
 Yet met will boast of knowledge, which he took
 From Eve's fair hand, as from a learned book.

5. Deprived, specifically of immortal life.
6. The referent is unclear; it may be either the serpent or Adam. In any case, Eve seems aware that the consequences of her act are mortality, but prefers godlike wisdom to immortal ignorance. "Alleged": cited repeated.
7. Enclose, determine.
8. Here, made or fashioned.
9. Strict.
1. I.e., the breath of immortal life.
2. Because Adam took the fruit without Eve's saying anything.
3. Prevent.
4. Experience.

"If any evil did in her remain, 65
Being made of him,[5] he was the ground of all.
If one of many worlds[6] could lay a stain
Upon our sex, and work so great a fall
To wretched man by Satan's subtle train,[7]
What will so foul a fault amongst you all?[8] 70
 Her weakness did the serpent's words obey,
 But you in malice God's dear son betray,

"Whom, if unjustly you condemn to die,
Her sin was small to what you do commit.
All mortal sins[9] that do for vengeance cry 75
Are not to be compared unto it;
If many worlds would altogether try
By all their sins the wrath of God to get,
 This sin of yours surmounts them all as far
 As doth the sun another little star[1] 80

"Then let us have our liberty again,
And challenge[2] to yourselves no sovereignty.
You came not in the world without our pain,
Make that a bar[3] against your cruelty;
Your fault being greater, why should you disdain 85
Our being your equals, free from tyranny?
 If one weak woman simply did offend,
 This sin of yours hath no excuse nor end,[4]

"To which, poor souls, we never gave consent
Witness, thy wife, O Pilate, speaks for all, 90
Who did but dream, and yet a message sent
That thou shouldest have nothing to do at all
With that just man;[5] which, if thy heart relent,
Why wilt thou be a reprobate with Saul[6]
 To seek the death of him that is so good, 95
 For thy soul's health to shed his dearest blood?"

 1611

The Description of *Cooke-ham*

Farewell (sweet *Cooke-ham*) where I first obtained
Grace from the grace where perfect grace remained:[1]
And where the Muses gave their full consent,
I should have power the virtuous to content:

5. In Genesis, Eve was formed from Adam's rib.
6. Suggests great quantities. I.e., one woman out of many.
7. Satan's serpentine arguments to Eve. Later tradition identified Satan with the serpent; Genesis makes no such connection.
8. Implicitly, how great a stigma will your crime cast upon your sex?
9. Sins punishable by eternal damnation.
1. It was then assumed, on the Ptolemaic model, that the sun actually was larger than the stars.

2. Claim.
3. Check, prevention.
4. Purpose.
5. Christ.
6. King of Israel who attempted to kill David, who had been his protégé. "Reprobate": morally unprincipled person.
1. I.e., favor from the noble person in whom perfect virtue remained. That person is Margaret, countess of Cumberland (d. 1616).

Where princely palace willed me to indite,[2] 5
The sacred story of the soul's delight.
Farewell (sweet place) where virtue then did rest,
And all delights did harbor in her breast:
Never shall my sad eyes again behold
Those pleasures which my thoughts did then unfold: 10
Yet you (great Lady) Mistress of that place,
From whose desires did spring this work of grace;
Vouchsafe[3] to think upon those pleasures past,
As fleeting worldly joys that could not last:
Or, as dim shadows of celestial pleasures, 15
Which are desired above all earthly treasures.
Oh how (me thought) against[4] you thither came,
Each part did seem some new delight to frame!
The house received all ornaments to grace it,
And would endure no foulness to deface it. 20
The walks put on their summer liveries,
And all things else did hold like similes:[5]
The trees with leaves, with fruits, with flowers clad,
Embraced each other, seeming to be glad,
Turning themselves to beauteous canopies, 25
To shade the bright sun from your brighter eyes:
The crystal streams with silver spangles gracéd,
While by the glorious sun they were embracéd:
The little birds in chirping notes did sing,
To entertain both you and that sweet spring. 30
And *Philomela* with her sundry lays,[6]
Both you and that delightful place did praise.
Oh how me thought each plant, each flower, each tree
Set forth their beauties then to welcome thee:
The very hills right humbly did descend, 35
When you to tread upon them did intend.
And as you set your feet, they still did rise,
Glad that they could receive so rich a prize.
The gentle winds did take delight to be
Among those woods that were so graced by thee. 40
And in sad[7] murmur uttered pleasing sound,
That pleasure in that place might more abound:
The swelling banks delivered all their pride,
When such a *Phoenix*[8] once they had espied.
Each arbor, bank, each seat, each stately tree, 45
Thought themselves honored in supporting thee.
The pretty birds would oft come to attend thee,
Yet fly away for fear they should offend thee:
The little creatures in the burrow by
Would come abroad to sport them in your eye 50
Yet fearful of the bow in your fair hand,
Would run away when you did make a stand.

2. Write.
3. Grant.
4. Before.
5. Comparisons; i.e., different parts of nature are compared to the liveried servants of the countess of Cumberland. "Liveries": uniforms; distinctive dress.

6 Songs. "Philomela": the nightingale (from the name of the woman who, according to Greek myth, was turned into this bird).
7. Heavy.
8. A legendary bird that lives five hundred years, then burns to death and is reborn from the ashes.

Now let me come unto that stately tree,
Wherein such goodly prospects you did see;
That oak that did in height his fellows pass, 55
As much as lofty trees, low growing grass:
Much like a comely cedar straight and tall,
Whose beauteous stature far exceeded all:
How often did you visit this fair tree,
Which seeming joyful in receiving thee, 60
Would like a palm tree spread his arms abroad,
Desirous that you there should make abode:
Whose fair green leaves much like a comely veil,
Defended *Phoebus*[9] when he would assail:
Whose pleasing boughs did yield a cool fresh air, 65
Joying[1] his happiness when you were there.
Where being seated, you might plainly see,
Hills, vales, and woods, as if on bended knee
They had appeared, your honor to salute,
Or to prefer some strange unlooked for suit:[2] 70
All interlaced with brooks and crystal springs,
A prospect fit to please the eyes of kings:
And thirteen shires[3] appeared all in your sight,
Europe could not afford much more delight.
What was there then but gave you all content, 75
While you the time in meditation spent,
Of their Creator's power, which there you saw,
In all his creatures held a perfect law;
And in their beauties did you plain descry,[4]
His beauty, wisdom, grace, love, majesty. 80
In these sweet woods how often did you walk,
With Christ and his Apostles there to talk;
Placing his holy writ in some fair tree,
To meditate what you therein did see:
With *Moses* you did mount his holy hill,[5] 85
To know his pleasure, and perform his will.
With lowly *David* you did often sing,
His holy hymns[6] to heaven's Eternal King.
And in sweet music did your soul delight,
To sound his praises, morning, noon, and night. 90
With blessed *Joseph*[7] you did often feed
Your pinéd brethren, when they stood in need.
And that sweet lady sprung from *Clifford*'s race,
Of noble *Bedford*'s blood, fair stream of grace;
To honorable *Dorset* now espoused,[8] 95
In whose fair breast true virtue then was housed:

9. Protected against the sun (identified here with
Phoebus Apollo).
1. Rejoicing at.
2. Entreaty. "Prefer": present.
3. Counties.
4. Perceive, observe.
5. Mount Sinai, which Moses climbed to speak with
God and to receive the Ten Commandments (Exodus
24).
6. Tradition remembers the biblical King David as a

musician and poet, and he is credited with many of the
poems in Psalms.
7. A son of Jacob; his brothers had sold him into slav-
ery, but he became powerful in Egypt and later aided
his family during a great famine (Genesis 37–47).
8. The countess of Cumberland's daughter, Anne
(1590–1676); she was related to the Cliffords (earls of
Cumberland) and the Russells (earls of Bedford),
through her father and mother, and married Richard
Sackville, earl of Dorset.

Oh what delight did my weak spirits find
In those pure parts of her well framéd mind:
And yet it grieves me that I cannot be
Near unto her, whose virtues did agree 100
With those fair ornaments of outward beauty,
Which did enforce from all both love and duty.
Unconstant Fortune, thou art most to blame,
Who casts us down into so low a frame:
Where our great friends we cannot daily see, 105
So great a difference is there in degree.
Many are placed in those orbs of state,
Parters in honor,[9] so ordained by fate;
Nearer in show, yet farther off in love,
In which, the lowest always are above.[1] 110
But whither am I carried in conceit?
My wit too weak to conster[2] of the great.
Why not? although we are but born of earth,
We may behold the heavens, despising death;
And loving heaven that is so far above, 115
May in the end vouchsafe us entire love.
Therefore sweet Memory do thou retain
Those pleasures past, which will not turn again:
Remember beauteous *Dorset*'s former sports,[3]
So far from being touched by ill reports; 120
Wherein myself did always bear a part,
While reverend Love presented my true heart:
Those recreations let me bear in mind,
Which her sweet youth and noble thoughts did find:
Whereof deprived, I evermore must grieve, 125
Hating blind fortune, careless to relieve.[4]
And you sweet *Cooke-ham*, whom these ladies leave,
I now must tell the grief you did conceive[5]
At their departure; when they went away,
How everything retained a sad dismay: 130
Nay long before, when once an inkling came,
Methought each thing did unto sorrow frame:[6]
The trees that were so glorious in our view,
Forsook both flowers and fruit, when once they knew
Of your depart, their very leaves did wither, 135
Changing their colors as they grew together.
But when they saw this had no power to stay you,
They often wept, though speechless, could not pray[7] you;
Letting their tears in your fair bosoms fall,
As if they said, Why will ye leave us all? 140
This being vain, they cast their leaves away,
Hoping that pity would have made you stay:
Their frozen tops like age's hoary hairs,
Shows their disasters, languishing in fears:

9. Those set apart in rank.
1. I.e., the one lower in rank is "above" the higher born in loving more.
2 Construe, interpret. "Conceit": figure of language.
3 Pleasant pastimes. "Beauteous Dorset's": Anne's.
4. Having no care to rise again.
5. Take on.
6. Give shape to sorrow.
7. Beg.

A swarthy riveled rind[8] over all spread, 145
Their dying bodies half alive, half dead.
But your occasions[9] called you so away,
That nothing there had power to make you stay:
Yet did I see a noble grateful mind,
Requiting[1] each according to their kind, 150
Forgetting not to turn and take your leave
Of these sad creatures, powerless to receive
Your favor when with grief you did depart,
Placing their former pleasures in your heart;
Giving great charge to noble Memory, 155
There to preserve their love continually:
But specially the love of that fair tree,
That first and last you did vouchsafe to see:
In which it pleased you oft to take the air,
With noble *Dorset*, then a virgin fair:[2] 160
Where many a learned book was read and scanned
To this fair tree, taking me by the hand,
You did repeat the pleasures which had past,
Seeming to grieve they could no longer last.
And with a chaste, yet loving kiss took leave, 165
Of which sweet kiss I did it soon bereave:[3]
Scorning a senseless creature should possess
So rare a favor, so great happiness.
No other kiss it could receive from me
For fear to give back what it took of thee: 170
So I ungrateful creature did deceive[4] it,
Of that which you vouchsafed in love to leave it.
And though it often had given me much content,
Yet this great wrong I never could repent:
But of the happiest made it most forlorn, 175
To show that nothing's free from Fortune's scorn.
While all the rest with this most beauteous tree,
Made their sad consort[5] sorrow's harmony.
The flowers that on the banks and walks did grow,
Crept in the ground, the grass did weep for woe. 180
The winds and waters seemed to chide together,
Because you went away they know not whither:
And those sweet brooks that ran so fair and clear,
With grief and trouble wrinkled did appear.
Those pretty birds that wonted[6] were to sing, 185
Now neither sing, nor chirp, nor use their wing;
But with their tender feet on some bare spray,
Warble forth sorrow, and their own dismay.
Fair *Philomela* leaves her mournful ditty,
Drowned in dead sleep, yet can procure no pity: 190
Each arbor, bank, each seat, each stately tree,

8. Dark wrinkled bark.
9. Necessary business.
1. Rewarding.
2. Before she was married.
3. I.e., by kissing the tree after the countess, Lanyer

takes away the kiss for herself.
4. Cheat.
5. A set of musicians as well as company more generally.
6. Accustomed.

Looks bare and desolate now for want[7] of thee;
Turning green tresses into frosty gray,
While in cold grief they wither all away.
The sun grew weak, his beams no comfort gave, 195
While all green things did make the earth their grave:
Each briar, each bramble, when you went away,
Caught fast your clothes, thinking to make you stay:
Delightful Echo wonted to reply
To our last words, did now for sorrow die: 200
The house cast off each garment that might grace it,
Putting on dust and cobwebs to deface it.
All desolation then there did appear,
When you were going whom they held so dear.
This last farewell to Cooke-ham here I give. 205
When I am dead thy name in this may live,
Wherein I have performed her noble hest,[8]
Whose virtues lodge in my unworthy breast,
And ever shall, so long as life remains,
Tying my heart to her by those rich chains. 210

 1611

7. Lack. 8. The bidding of the countess of Cumberland.

ELIZABETH CARY

1585–1639

One of the most precocious and prolific Elizabethan women of letters, Elizabeth
Cary wrote her ambitious verse play, *The Tragedy of Mariam, the Faire Queene of
Jewry*, at the age of seventeen. As a child, she had taught herself a range of lan-
guages (including French, Latin, and Hebrew), completed a number of transla-
tions, and begun the wide reading in theology that resulted in her conversion to
Catholicism in 1626. Married at fifteen or sixteen to Henry Cary, later viscount
Falkland, she bore him eleven children before he separated from her; in an effort to
punish her for her conversion, he denied her financial support and custody of her
children. Although the Privy Council later ordered her estranged husband to sup-
port her and the couple eventually reconciled, Cary remained a Roman Catholic,
as did several of her children. One of her daughters produced a respectful manu-
script biography of her, *The Lady Falkland: Her Life*, which was finally published—
centuries later—in 1861.

Published in 1613, a decade after it was written, *Mariam* was the first full-length
play by an Englishwoman to appear in print. An eloquent record of a woman's am-
bivalence toward marriage and male authority, the work is based on tales of Herod,
his wife Mariam, and his sister Salome that are told in contemporary translations
of *Jewish Antiquities*, written by the Roman traveler Josephus. The plot of the
drama turns on Herod's perfidy and Mariam's resistance: appointed by Rome to
rule the Jews, Herod leaves his wife, Doris, for Mariam, granddaughter of
Hircanus, the rightful king, and then has Hircanus killed and Mariam's brother
drowned; finally, after Salome convinces him that Mariam is trying to poison him,
he condemns the heroine herself to death.

Significantly, Josephus portrays the "Queen of Jewry" as selfish and manipula-
tive, while Cary depicts her as a noble rebel whose defiance of her husband heralds

the new law of Christianity. Yet despite the piety that infused her art, this writer's rebellion against what she saw in both art and life as conjugal tyranny left her with a reputation of impropriety and unwomanliness. Two years after she died, one commentator declared that she was "a lady of a most masculine understanding, allayed with the passions and infirmities of her own sex," while as recently as 1962 another critic described her as a woman of "literary, masculine, and eccentric character."

From The Tragedy of Mariam, the Faire Queene of Jewry

From Act 3, Scene 3

[ON THE DUTIES OF A WIFE]

CHORUS. 'Tis not enough for one that is a wife 215
To keep her[1] spotless from an act of ill:
But from suspicion she should free her life,
And bare herself of[2] power as well as will.
 'Tis not so glorious for her to be free,
 As by her proper[3] self restrained to be. 220

When she hath spacious ground to walk upon,
Why on the ridge should she desire to go?
It is no glory to forbear alone[4]
Those things that may her honor overthrow.
 But 'tis thankworthy if she will not take 225
 All lawful liberties for honor's sake.

That wife her hand against her fame doth rear,
That more than to her lord alone will give
A private word to any second ear,
And though she may with reputation live, 230
 Yet though most chaste, she doth her glory blot,
 And wounds her honor, though she kills it not.

When to their husbands they themselves do bind,
Do they not wholly give themselves away?
Or give they but their body, not their mind,
Reserving that, though best, for others' prey?[5] 235
 No sure, their thoughts no more can be their own,
 And therefore should to none but one be known.

Then she usurps upon another's right,
That seeks to be by public language graced: 240
And though her thoughts reflect with purest light,
Her mind if not peculiar[6] is not chaste.
 For in a wife it is no worse to find,
 A common body than a common mind.

1. I.e., herself.
2. I.e., keep herself from.
3. I.e., her own.
4. To only do without.

5. I.e., keeping their minds from their husbands to be the prey of others.
6. Exclusively one's own.

And every mind, though free from thought of ill, 245
That out of glory seeks a worth to show,
When any's ears but one therewith they fill,
Doth in a sort her pureness overthrow.
 Now Mariam had (but that to this she bent)[7]
 Been free from fear, as well as innocent. 250

From Act 4, Scene 8

[MARIAM'S FATE]

MARIAM. Am I the Mariam that presumed so much, 525
And deemed my face must needs preserve my breath?
Ay, I it was that thought my beauty such,
As it alone could countermand my death.
Now death will teach me: he can pale as well
A cheek of roses as a cheek less bright, 530
And dim an eye whose shine doth most excel,
As soon as one that casts a meaner light.
Had not myself against myself conspired,
No plot, no adversary from without
Could Herod's love from Mariam have retired,[8] 535
Or from his heart have thrust my semblance out.
The wanton queen that never loved for love,
False Cleopatra, wholly set on gain,
With all her sleights did prove, yet vainly prove,[9]
For her the love of Herod to obtain. 540
Yet her allurements, all her courtly guile,
Her smiles, her favors, and her smooth deceit
Could not my face from Herod's mind exile,
But were with him of less than little weight.
That face and person that in Asia late 545
For beauty's goddess, Paphos' queen,[1] was ta'en:
That face that did captive great Julius' fate,
That very face that was Anthonius' bane,
That face that to be Egypt's pride was born,
That face that all the world esteemed so rare: 550
Did Herod hate, despise, neglect, and scorn,
When with the same, he Mariam's did compare.
This made that I improvidently wrought,
And on the wager even my life did pawn:
Because I thought, and yet but truly thought, 555
That Herod's love could not from me be drawn.
But now, though out of time,[2] I plainly see
It could be drawn, though never drawn from me,
Had I but with humility been graced,
As well as fair I might have proved me wise: 560
But I did think because I knew me chaste,
One virtue for a woman might suffice.

7. I.e., if only she had inclined to this course.
8. Withdrawn.
9. Try. Cleopatra (68–31 B.C.), queen of Egypt.
1. Aphrodite, the Greek goddess of love. Cleopatra

first captured the love of Julius Caesar and then Mark Anthony, who ultimately was drawn by her into an unsuccessful war against Rome.
2. I.e., in the wrong time; too late.

That mind for glory of our sex might stand,
Wherein humility and chastity
Doth march with equal paces hand in hand. 565
But one, if single seen, who setteth by?[3]
And I had singly one, but 'tis my joy,
That I was ever innocent, though sour:
And therefore can they but my life destroy,
My soul is free from adversary's power. [*Enter* DORIS[4]] 570
You princes great in power, and high in birth,
Be great and high, I envy not your hap:[5]
Your birth must be from dust, your power on earth;
In Heaven shall Mariam sit in Sara's lap.[6]
DORIS. Ay, Heaven—your beauty cannot bring you thither, 575
Your soul is black and spotted, full of sin:
You in adultery lived nine year together,
And Heaven will never let adultery in.
MARIAM. What art thou that dost poor Mariam pursue,
Some spirit sent to drive me to despair? 580
Who sees for truth that Mariam is untrue?
If fair she be, she is as chaste as fair.
DORIS. I am that Doris that was once beloved,
Beloved by Herod, Herod's lawful wife:
'Twas you that Doris from his side removed, 585
And robbed from me the glory of my life.
MARIAM. Was that adultery? Did not Moses say,
That he that being matched did deadly hate:
Might by permission put his wife away,
And take a more beloved to be his mate?[7] 590
DORIS. What did he hate me for: for simple truth?
For bringing beauteous babes, for love to him?
For riches, noble birth, or tender youth?
Or for no stain did Doris' honor dim?
Oh, tell me, Mariam, tell me if you know, 595
Which fault of these made Herod Doris' foe?
These thrice three years have I with hands held up,
And bowèd knees fast nailèd to the ground,
Besought for thee the dregs of that same cup,
That cup of wrath that is for sinners found. 600
And now thou art to drink it: Doris' curse
Upon thyself did all this wile attend,
But now it shall pursue thy children worse.
MARIAM. Oh, Doris, now to thee my knees I bend,
That heart that never bowed to thee doth bow: 605
Curse not mine infants, let it thee suffice,
That Heaven doth punishment to me allow.
Thy curse is cause that guiltless Mariam dies.
DORIS. Had I ten thousand tongues, and every tongue
Inflamed with poison's power, and steeped in gall: 610

3. Disregards.
4. Herod's first wife, whom he set aside so that he
might marry Mariam.
5. Fortune.

6. The lap of Abraham's wife; i.e., with the blessed
dead.
7. This is not quite what Moses says; see
Deuteronomy 24:1–4.

My curses would not answer for my wrong,
Though I in cursing thee employed them all.
Hear thou that didst Mount [Gerizim] command,[8]
To be a place whereon with cause to curse:
Stretch thy revenging arm, thrust forth thy hand, 615
And plague the mother much: the children worse.
Throw flaming fire upon the baseborn heads
That were begotten in unlawful beds.
But let them live till they have sense to know
What 'tis to be in miserable state: 620
Then be their nearest friends their overthrow,
Attended by they by suspicious hate.
And, Mariam, I do hope this boy of mine
Shall one day come to be the death of thine. [*Exit.*]
MARIAM. Oh! Heaven forbid. I hope the world shall see, 625
This curse of thine shall be returned on thee:
Now, earth, farewell, though I be yet but young,
Yet I, methinks, have known thee too too long. [*Exit.*]

CHORUS. The fairest action of our human life
Is scorning to revenge an injury: 630
For who forgives without a further strife,
His adversary's heart to him doth tie.
 And 'tis a firmer conquest truly said,
 To win the heart than overthrow the head.

If we a worthy enemy do find, 635
To yield to worth, it must be nobly done:
But if of baser metal[9] be his mind,
In base revenge there is no honor won.
 Who would a worthy courage overthrow,
 And who would wrestle with a worthless foe? 640

We say our hearts are great and cannot yield;
Because they cannot yield it proves them poor:
Great hearts are tasked beyond their power but seld,[1]
The weakest lion will the loudest roar.
 Truth's school for certain doth this same allow, 645
 High-heartedness doth sometimes teach to bow.

A noble heart doth teach a virtuous scorn:
To scorn to owe a duty overlong,
To scorn to be for benefits forborne,[2]
To scorn to lie, to scorn to do a wrong, 650
 To scorn to bear an injury in mind,
 To scorn a freeborn heart slavelike to bind.

8. According to Deuteronomy 27:11–26, Moses commanded his people to stand on Mount Gerizim to bless and Mount Ebal to curse.
9. I.e., mettle; quality of disposition or character.
1. Seldom.
2. I.e., not to repay an obligation.

But if for wrongs we needs revenge must have,
Then be our vengeance of the noblest kind:
Do we his body from our fury save, 655
And let our hate prevail against our mind?
 What can 'gainst him a greater vengeance be,
 Than make his foe more worthy far than he?

Had Mariam scorned to leave a due unpaid,
She would to Herod then have paid her love: 660
And not have been by sullen passion swayed.
To fix her thoughts all injury above
 Is virtuous pride. Had Mariam thus been proved,
 Long famous life to her had been allowed.

1602 1613

MARY WROTH
1587?–1651/53

Aristocratic, controversial and adventurous, Mary Wroth was a major literary heiress. Her father, Sir Robert Sidney (later earl of Leicester), was himself a reputable poet; even better known were her uncle, Sir Philip Sidney, and her aunt, Lady Mary Sidney Herbert, the countess of Pembroke. Perhaps energized by such distinguished origins, she became the first Englishwoman to produce a full-length prose romance and the first to compose a sonnet sequence.

Raised in an atmosphere of wealth and privilege, Wroth was the eldest of four girls and two boys raised by fond parents and was nurtured in particular by a mother whom the poet Ben Jonson praised for her hospitality and generosity. "My Lady," wrote Sir Robert's steward, "sees [her children] well taught, and brought up in Learning, and Qualities, fitt for theire Birth and Condicion." The young Mary Sidney's happy childhood came to an end, however, when she entered into what was evidently an unhappy marriage with Sir Robert Wroth, whom Jonson called a "Jealous husband." After Robert's untimely death in 1614, his widow was left with an infant son and a heavily indebted estate. Two years later, her son died, and her indebtedness intensified when even his share of the estate was entailed away from her. As the critic Ann Rosalind Jones has observed, moreover, her difficulties were "probably intensified" by the long affair into which she then entered with her cousin William, earl of Pembroke, who became the father of her two surviving children.

From the perspective of her contemporaries, Wroth's literary career was at least as unconventional as her personal life. Her major work—the prose romance *The Countess of Montgomery's Urania*, to which the sonnet sequence *Pamphilia to Amphilanthus* was appended—infuriated several courtiers whose thinly disguised portraits appeared in it. Most vituperative was one Lord Denny, who castigated the author for writing "lascivious tales and amorous toys." Though Wroth defended herself in a set of passionate "Railing Rimes," she gained little support from others in her circle and within six months withdrew the volume she had so boldly and hopefully published.

Paradoxically, however, the eponymous heroine of Wroth's romance is a pure and noble shepherdess based on an offstage character in Sir Philip Sidney's famous *Arcadia*, while Pamphilia, whose name means "all-loving" and who is the

speaker of her sonnet sequence, represents female constancy, chastity, and "heroic virtue" in a fallen world. Indeed, as several critics have noted, Pamphilia's merits have much in common with the glories attributed to Elizabeth I herself: "shee is upright and just," remarks one of Wroth's characters, "in her government mild, and loving to her subjects," and "she hath . . . a brave and manlike spirit, and wondrous wise shee is." At the same time, throughout the technically accomplished and melodious verses in which this fictive woman of letters speaks, Wroth reveals the aesthetic potential of the woman poet even while, as Ann Jones puts it, she "expands the possibilities of a female poetic voice to encompass passion, purgation, and vision."

Most of the texts we reprint here have been modernized by the scholar and poet Mary Moore, to whom we are also indebted for some annotations.

From Pamphilia to Amphilanthus

1

When night's black mantle could most darkness prove,[1]
　And sleep, death's Image, did my senses hire[2]
　From knowledge of myself, then thoughts did move
　Swifter than those most swiftness need require:
In sleep, a chariot drawn by winged desire　　　　　　　　　　5
　I saw, where sat bright Venus, Queen of love,
　And at her feet, her son,[3] still adding fire
　To burning hearts, which she did hold above;
But one heart flaming more than all the rest
　The goddess held and put it to my breast.　　　　　　　　　10
　"Dear son, now shut,"[4] said she, "Thus must we win";
He her obeyed and martyred my poor heart;
　I, waking, hoped as dreams it would depart,
　Yet since, O me, a lover I have been.

8

Love, leave to urge: thou know'st thou hast the hand.[5]
　T'is cowardice to strive where none resist;
　Pray thee leave off; I yield unto thy band
　Do not thus still in thine own power persist;
Behold, I yield: let forces be dismissed;　　　　　　　　　　5
　I am thy subject, conquered, bound to stand,
　Never thy foe, but did thy claim assist,
　Seeking thy due of those who did withstand;[6]
But now it seems thou wouldst I should thee love;
　I do confess: t'was thy will made me choose,　　　　　　　10
　And thy fair shows made me a lover prove,
　When I my freedom did for pain refuse.
Yet this, Sir god: your boyship I despise:
　Your charms I obey, but love not want[7] of eyes.

1. Display; also, test.
2. Bribe.
3. Cupid, Roman god of love.
4. I.e., shut the flaming heart into Pamphilia's breast; also, because Cupid is associated with the darts or ar-

rows of love, "shut" is here a pun on "shoot."
5. I.e., the upper hand. "Leave": omit, cease.
6. I.e., from those who resisted.
7. I.e., both lack and desire.

11

The weary traveler who, tired, sought
 In places distant far, yet found no end
 Of pain or labor nor his state to mend,[8]
 At last with joy is to his home back brought—
Finds not more ease, though he with joy be fraught[9] 5
 (When past is fear, content like souls ascend),[1]
 Than I, on whom new pleasures do descend,
 Which now as high as first born bliss[2] is wrought;
He tired with his pains, I, with my mind;
 He all content receives by ease of limbs; 10
 I, greatest happiness that I do find
 Belief for faith,[3] while hope in pleasure swims;
Truth says it was wrong conceit bred my despite,[4]
Which once acknowledged brings my heart's delight.

24

When last I saw thee, I did not thee see;
 It was thine image, which in my thoughts lay
 So lively figured as no time's delay
 Could suffer[5] me in heart to parted be;
And sleep so favorable is to me 5
 As not to let thy loved remembrance stray,
 Lest that I, waking, might have cause to say
 There was one minute found to forget thee;
Then, since my faith is such, so kind my sleep
 That gladly thee presents into my thought, 10
 And still true-lover-like thy face doth keep
 So[6] as some pleasure shadow-like is wrought,
Pity my loving, nay, of conscience, give
Reward to me, in whom thy self doth live.

25

Like to the Indians,[7] scorched with the sun,
 The sun, which they do as their God adore,
 So am I used by love, for ever more
 I worship him, less favors have I won;
Better are they who thus to blackness run 5
 And so can only whiteness' want deplore,
 Than, I, who, pale and white am with grief's store,[8]
 Nor can have hope but to see hopes undone;[9]
Besides, their sacrifice received is in sight
 Of their chose[1] saint; mine hid as worthless rite. 10

8. I.e., nor any way to mend his state.
9. Supplied, filled.
1. When fear is past, contentment ascends like souls.
2. The joy of giving birth to one's first child. "Which": i.e., pleasures.
3. I.e., I receive belief through faith as he receives contentment from physical ease.
4. Disdain, ill-will. "Conceit": thought, idea (or perhaps a fanciful expression).

5. Permit.
6. Refers back to the lover's face (i.e., keep as it is) and forward as a conjunction (i.e., so pity my loving).
7. Inhabitants of India, or of the East more generally.
8. With storing grief.
9. Defeated (primary meaning); but Wroth spelled the word *undunn*, which also puns on *dun*, "dull and dark."
1. Chosen.

Grant me to see where I my offerings give;
Then let me wear the mark of Cupid's might
 In heart, as they in skin of Phoebus'[2] light,
Not ceasing offerings to love while I live.

43

Night, welcome art thou to my mind distressed,
 Dark, heavy, sad, yet not more sad than I;
 Never could'st thou find fitter company
For thine own humor[3] than I, thus oppressed.
If thou be dark, my wrongs still unredressed 5
 Saw never light, nor smallest bliss can spy;[4]
 If heavy, joy from me too fast doth hie,
And care outgoes[5] my hope of quiet rest.
Then now in friendship, join with hapless me,
 Who am as sad and dark as thou canst be, 10
 Hating all pleasure or delight of life;
Silence and grief, with thee I best do love,
 And from you three, I know I cannot move;
 Then let us live, companions without strife.

64

Love like a juggler comes to play his prize[6]
 And all minds draw his wonders to admire,
 To see how cunningly he, wanting[7] eyes,
Can yet deceive the best sight of desire;
The wanton child, how he can feign his fire 5
 So prettily[8] as none sees his disguise,
 How finely do his tricks, while we fools hire
The badge and office[9] of his tyrannies,
For in the end, such juggling he doth make
 As he our hearts, instead of eyes, doth take; 10
 For men can only by their sleights abuse
The sight with nimble and delightful skill,
 But if he play, his gain is our lost will;
 Yet, childlike, we cannot his sports[1] refuse.

74

SONG

Love, a child, is ever crying;
 Please him, and he straight is flying;
 Give him, he the more is craving,
 Never satisfied with having;

2. The sun, whose mark the Indians wear on their
skin.
3. Temperament; also, in ancient and medieval physi-
ology, one of the four fluids that determine a person's
temperament (the dark and heavy one is melancholy).
4. I.e., the speaker's unredressed wrongs are more
thoroughly dark even than night.

5. Outstrips. "Hie": quickly depart.
6. Game.
7. Lacking and desiring.
8. Skillfully.
9. I.e., the signs and service.
1. Games.

His desires have no measure; 5
 Endless folly is his treasure;
 What he promiseth, he breaketh;
 Trust not one word that he speaketh;

He vows nothing but false matter
 And to cousen[2] you, he'll flatter; 10
 Let him gain the hand, he'll leave you
 And still glory to deceive you;

He will triumph in your wailing
 And yet cause be of your failing;
 These his virtues are and slighter 15
 Are his gifts, his favors lighter;

Feathers are as firm in staying;
 Wolves no fiercer in their preying.
 As a child, then, leave him crying
 Nor seek him so given to flying. 20

From A *Crown of Sonnets Dedicated to Love*[3]
77 [*First of the Corona*]

In this strange labyrinth, how shall I turn?
 Ways are on all sides, while the way, I miss;
 If to the right hand, there, in love I burn;
 Let me go forward, therein danger is;
If to the left, suspicion hinders bliss;[4] 5
 Let me turn back, shame cries I ought return,
 Nor faint, though crosses[5] with my fortunes kiss;
 Standstill is harder, although sure to mourn;[6]
Thus, let me take the right or left hand way,
 Go forward, or stand still, or back retire, 10
 I must these doubts endure without allay[7]
 Or help, but travail find for my best hire;
Yet that which most my troubled sense doth move
Is to leave all and take the thread of love.[8]

78 [*Second of the Corona*]

Is to leave all and take the thread of love,
 Which line straight leads unto the soul's content,

2. I.e., cozen, "cheat"; possibly punning on *cousin.*
Wroth's reputed lover was her cousin William
Herbert, who was the son of Mary Sidney Herbert, the
countess of Pembroke.
3. Poems 77, 78, 79, and 89 are from a "crown" or
"corona" of sonnets, a sequence in which the last line
of each sonnet becomes the first line of the following
one, until a circle, or "crown," is completed by the last
line of the final poem, which is the same as the first
line of the first one.

4. The left side was regarded as the unlucky side for
omens (the left is "sinister").
5. Obstacles.
6. I.e., the speaker would mourn, and standstill would
lead to mourning.
7. Abatement, lessening.
8. I.e., as in Greek mythology Theseus found his way
through the first labyrinth with the help of thread sup-
plied by Ariadne, so for the speaker love will provide
the way out.

Where choice delights with pleasure's wings do move,
 And idle fantasy never room had lent;
When chaste thoughts guide us, then our minds are bent 5
 To take that good which ills from us remove,
 Light of true love, brings fruit which none repent,
 But constant lovers seek and wish to prove;
Love is the shining star of blessings light,
 The fervent fire of zeal,[9] the root of peace, 10
 The lasting lamp, fed with the oil of right,
 Image of faith, and womb for joy's increase.
Love is true virtue and his ends delight;
His flames are joys; his bands[1] true lovers' might.

79 [Third of the Corona]

His flames are joys, his bands, true lovers' might;
 No stain is there but pure as purest white,
 Where no cloud can appear to dim his light,
 Nor spot defile, but shame will soon requite;[2]
Here are affections tried[3] by love's just might, 5
 As gold by fire, and black discerned by white,
 Error by truth, and darkness known by light,
 Where faith is valued for love to requite;
Please him and serve him, glory in his might,
 And firm he'll be as innocency white,[4] 10
 Clear as the air, warm as sun beams, as day, light,[5]
 Just as truth, constant as fate, joyed to requite;
Then love obey; strive to observe his might,
And be in his brave court a glorious light.

89 [Thirteenth of the Corona]

Free from all fogs but shining fair and clear,
 Wise in all good and innocent in ill,
 Where holy friendship is esteemed dear
 With truth in love and justice in our will,
In love these titles only have their fill[6] 5
 Of happy life, maintainer, and the mere
 Defense of right, the punisher of skill
 And fraud, from whence directions[7] doth appear;
To thee, then, lord commander of all hearts
 Ruler of our affections, kind and just, 10
 Great King of Love, my soul from feigned smarts
 Or thought of change, I offer to your trust,
This crown, my self, and all that I have more,
Except my heart which you bestowed before.

9. Like other imagery in this stanza, the word *zeal* has religious connotations.
1. Shackles.
2. Retaliate for.
3. Proved.
4. I.e., love will be as firm as innocence is white.

5. I.e., warm as sun beams, warm as daylight, and light as day.
6. I.e., the titles are "fulfilled" as accurate descriptions.
7. Love is a place as well as a personified being.

91

SONG

Sweet, let me enjoy thy sight,
　　More clear, more bright than morning sun,
Which in spring time gives delight[8]
　　And by which summer's pride is won;

Present sight doth pleasures move, 5
　　Which, in sad absence, we must miss,
But, when met again in love,
　　Then twice redoubled is our bliss,

Yet this comfort absence gives—
　　And only faithful loving tries— 10
That, though parted, love's force lives
　　As just[9] in heart as in our eyes,

But such comfort banish quite;
　　Far sweeter is it still to find
Favor in thy loved sight, 15
　　Which, present, smiles with joys combined

Eyes of gladness, lips of love,
　　And hearts from passion not to turn,
But in sweet affections move
　　In flames of faith, to live and burn; 20

Dearest, then, this kindness give,
　　And grant me life which is your sight,
Wherein I more blessed live
　　Than graced with sun's fair light.

96

Late in the forest I did Cupid[1] see
　　Cold, wet, and crying, he had lost his way,
　　And, being blind, was farther like to stray,
　　Which sight a kind compassion bred in me;
I kindly took and dried him while that he, 5
　　Poor child, complained he starved was with stay,[2]
　　And pined for want of his accustomed prey,
　　For none in that wild place his host would be;
I was glad of his finding, thinking sure[3]
　　This service should my freedom still procure, 10
　　And in my arms I took him then unharmed,
Carrying him safe unto a Myrtle bower,
　　But on the way he made me feel his power,
　　Burning my heart, who had him kindly warmed.

8. Because seeing was thought to involve active emis-
sions from the eyes, "sight" acts like the sun. The word
sight also has its present meanings (the act of seeing or
the thing seen).

9. I.e., just as.
1. Roman god of love, son of Venus.
2. With being stopped (i.e., from preying on lovers).
3. Surely.

103

My muse, now happy, lay thy self to rest;
 Sleep in the quiet of a faithful love;
 Write you no more but let these fantasies move
 Some other hearts; wake not to new unrest,
But, if you study, be those thoughts addressed 5
 To truth, which shall eternal goodness prove,
 Enjoying of true joy the most and best,
 The endless gain which never will remove;
Leave the discourse of Venus and her son
 To young beginners, and their brains inspire 10
 With stories of great love, and from that fire,
 Get heat to write the fortunes they have won,
And thus leave off; what's past shows you can love;
Now let your constancy your honor prove.

1621

4. Both Venus' *son* Cupid and love as the *sun* of our lives.

Literature of the Seventeenth and Eighteenth Centuries

AN AGE OF CHANGE

In her fantasy, *Orlando* (1928), Virginia Woolf told the story of a writer, representing English literary history, who was born male during the Renaissance and started life as an Elizabethan, but turned into a woman in the second half of the seventeenth century. Her protagonist's sex change dramatizes a major event in the history of English letters, namely, the entrance of women into the literary marketplace. Not insignificantly, a number of women began to write and publish just when the production of literature became commercialized, when the patron started to give way to the printer, and when the small courtly audience began to give way to a large reading public. For the first time, too, many of these women were not exceptionally privileged by virtue of their aristocratic rank or religious calling; some, indeed, were ordinary middle-class women.

What in *A Room of One's Own* Woolf considers "a change" of "greater importance than the Crusades or the Wars of the Roses"—the moment when the middle-class woman began to write—took place during an era of transition that is usually associated with the emergence of the modern world. Such vocations as law, medicine, science, journalism, and politics became professionalized in ways that would have been unimaginable before. On both sides of the Atlantic, the religious disputes of the seventeenth century gave way to the commercial growth of the eighteenth century: the Church of England was supplemented as a central cultural institution by the Bank of England, and the early Puritan settlers, pilgrims searching for an earthly paradise, were succeeded by American citizens determined to establish their economic independence. The religious, intellectual, and social movements that accompanied this transformation—Puritanism, empiricism, and urbanization—had a paradoxical and complex impact on women's lives, on the one hand, overtly excluding women or further subjecting them to male regulation and, on the other hand, implicitly providing precedents for questioning the conventional authorities who had defined women as the second sex. While, as many historians have argued, women's contribution to production decreased when the English and American economies shifted from agriculture to manufacturing and commerce, the spread of education and the expansion of middle-class professions helped make possible the emergence of productive, publishing literary women, who began to form unique traditions of their own.

Put in the starkest terms, the seventeenth century was marked by political conflicts and religious disputes, while the eighteenth century was remarkable for its moderation, tolerance, and prosperity. Even the American Revolution at the end of the period could be said to dramatize optimistic assumptions about the common sense and morality of ordinary citizens as well as the secularization of civic activity. Nor did the loss of the colonies deter England from expanding and

63

consolidating its empire elsewhere around the globe. Although the shifting of political power from the court to the city and of literary power from the patron to the printer did not conveniently occur during any single interval at the midpoint of these two hundred years, this transformation nevertheless distinguished the quite different atmospheres in which authors wrote and readers read. As both producers and consumers, many women with literary aspirations and tastes profited from the change.

POLITICAL BACKGROUND

English Revolution and Consolidation

English political history in the seventeenth century, which has been characterized as "a history of hurts," included two revolutions within fifty years, two kings deposed and one killed, and an Anglican Church that was consolidated, overthrown, and rebuilt. Civil strife was a direct result of religious disputes dating back to the Reformation, when the Church of England separated from the Catholic Church, for radical reformers continued to believe that the Church had to "purify" itself further of Catholic rites and creeds. Attacking the Church—i.e., the official Church of England—such Puritans fought for civic and religious freedom from the authority of the bishops and the authoritarianism of the Stuart kings, James I (r. 1603–25) and Charles I (r. 1625–49). They were, therefore, viewed as rebels by both moderate Protestants and Catholics. But a crisis ensued when the Stuart monarchs aligned themselves with Rome, levied high taxes, and attempted to assert, as James I did, that "kings are not only God's lieutenants on earth, but even by God himself they are called gods." Many moderate Protestants in Parliament, elected representatives of men of property, united with the reformers against the Crown. By 1642, the struggle between Parliament and king—Puritans and Royalists, country and court—culminated in armed conflict. The execution of King Charles I in 1649 and the succession of Oliver Cromwell, the leader of the parliamentary army and lord protector of England (1653–58), hastened the rise to power of the middle class, led to the persecution of such supposedly tradition-bound groups as Anglicans and Catholics, and—perhaps most important—effectively ended the divine right of kings.

Before, during, and after the English Civil War, many Parliamentarians and Royalists feared the chaos associated with a growing number of radical Protestant sects. Such anxious citizens as Samuel Pepys and John Evelyn recorded the confusion of the times in their diaries. Pepys, for example, described a Royalist uncle condemned in the Tower of London while another uncle served as a captain in the parliamentary militia, and Evelyn protested against an anarchistic mechanic preaching "feculent stuff" from a church pulpit. Nevertheless, the political upheavals of the seventeenth century had a liberating impact on the lives of many women, for the Puritan Revolution created a crisis in which women on both sides were charged with new, unforeseen responsibilities. Royalists like Margaret Cavendish, duchess of Newcastle, and Charlotte Stanley, countess of Derby, defended their homes against parliamentary armies or traveled back and forth between England and France on their husbands' behalf. Similarly, Puritans like Lucy Hutchinson and Quakers like Margaret Fell recorded their efforts to help their families survive quickly shifting political circumstances. Still, their virtual exclusion from political institutions meant that their role was confined mainly to personal influence in a time when revolutionary instability was followed first by conservative reaction and then by compromise.

Internal disputes among Parliamentarians, fear of fanaticism and the mob, desire for stability, and dislike of military rule resulted in the Restoration of the Stuart monarchy of Charles II (r. 1660–85). Whereas Catholic families and Royalist bishops had been persecuted under Cromwell, Puritans were excluded from positions of civil and religious authority during the reign of Charles II. In

stark contrast to the Puritans, who had closed the theaters and instituted fines against swearing, drinking, and dancing, aristocratic courtiers in the Restoration quickly became infamous for the sexual freedom that was reflected in the comedies now performed regularly on the reopened stage, not only by actors but, for the first time, by actresses too. In spite of the courtly decadence associated with, for instance, Charles II's actress-mistress Nell Gwyn, the king had to conform to the policies of a Parliament that worked to strengthen England's trading and agricultural industries, for the balance of power had already begun to shift from the court to the city, from the king to the two-party system: the Tories, associated with a conservative aristocracy, and the Whigs, identified with the growing commercial class. When the restored Stuart monarchs again asserted their autonomy as well as their sympathy with Roman Catholicism, popular sentiment led to the so-called Glorious Revolution of 1689. Charles II's successor, James II (r. 1685–88), was forced to relinquish the crown to his Protestant daughter and her husband, a nonviolent change in government that promised an end to a century of violent upheaval and the beginning of a stable equilibrium. John Dryden expressed the relieved optimism of the next generation when, in his Secular Masque (1700), he exclaimed, " 'Tis well an old age is out, / And time to begin a new."

As divisive as these civil and religious disorders undoubtedly were, they had, by the middle of the eighteenth century, given way to a secularized, parliamentary government. Church and state had been effectively separated, and the Act of Toleration (1689) freed Dissenters (Protestants outside the Church of England) from religious persecution. Parliament also joined Scotland with England and established the stability of royal succession. Religious toleration and governmental continuity were matched by freedom of the press and free trade. With Parliament now controlling taxation and foreign policy, England became the wealthiest world power. Throughout the eighteenth century, the authority of government continued to shift from the court to the Parliament and the ministerial cabinet, an institution that took shape during the reign of Anne (1702–14) and became dominant during Sir Robert Walpole's long ministry (1721–42), in part because the three King Georges (1712–1820) were less than charismatic leaders. By midcentury, when the last Stuart heir was defeated in his effort to restore a more orthodox monarchy, mercantile interests provided the impetus for a series of wars against France, which led to England's acquisition of an empire reaching from India to Gibraltar to Canada. Paradoxically, however, the very principles of religious toleration, civic autonomy, and vigorous mercantile development that infused eighteenth-century English growth would lead in America to a revolt against English rule.

The New World

The Puritans began to leave England before the British Civil War. From 1629 to 1640, thousands, mostly from the middle classes, emigrated to New England in the hope of finding a place free from the religious persecution and economic harassment they associated with the Old World. After an arduous, three-month voyage across the Atlantic, the emigrants embarked on what the colonist Samuel Danforth described as "an errand into the wilderness." They were strengthened to face the threats of illness, privation, wild animals, and homesickness by the conviction that, like the tribe of Moses in search of the Promised Land, they had received a divine covenant, which would enable them to build a holy "city on the hill" in the New World. Puritan leaders in the Massachusetts Bay Colony like John Winthrop and Cotton Mather saw America as an ideal location for a "new Zion," a theocracy in which God's will could be carried out without interference from Anglican bishops or English monarchs.

Whether the impetus for settlement was predominantly religious, as in Pennsylvania, where the Quakers sought refuge, or financial, as in Virginia, with its

profitable tobacco crop, many later colonists saw the New World as an inspiring, if sometimes bewildering, opportunity for development. Yet the eastern edge of the American continent was also being populated by prisoners sent by their jailors, convicts transported by their judges, indentured servants, and slaves sold to Southern planters by English, French, Portuguese, and Spanish traders. By the 1770s and 1780s, seventy thousand African slaves were landed annually, half of them carried in British ships. Chained into overcrowded and filthy quarters, thousands of Africans died of smallpox, dysentery, insanity, and suicidal mutinies throughout the eighteenth century. Meanwhile, the number of colonists grew from 111,000 in 1670 to 1,600,000 by 1760. During the second half of the century, they were joined by additional Dutch, French Protestant, and German settlers. Together, the colonists appropriated the lands of the American Indians, who were forced either to migrate or to fight.

Economic impediments, brought about by parliamentary acts, led the colonists toward the independence movement. England's policy of taxation without representation fueled American resentment, and political resistance to George III reached new heights in a skeptical generation that no longer espoused the Puritanism of the pioneers: Benjamin Franklin, for example, began his publishing career by writing the *Silence Dogood Papers* (1722), a satire on Cotton Mather's *Essays to Do Good* (1710). If America was still viewed as "the most perfect society now existing in the world," as it was by the French settler Jean de Crèvecoeur in 1782, it was precisely because it was free of the religious fervor prevalent in Europe, for "zeal in Europe is confined . . . a grain of powder enclosed; here it burns away in the open air, and consumes without effect." Essayists and philosophers based their arguments for separation from England on the national identity of America, as did poets like Philip Freneau and Hugh Henry Brackenridge when they delivered the collaborative *Poem on the Rising Glory of America* at the 1771 Princeton commencement. Attempts of king and Parliament to control the political and economic life of the American colonies finally led to the revolution of 1776. That insurrection was also justified by English-born men like Tom Paine and Joseph Priestley, who supported the inalienable rights of ordinary citizens as opposed to the tyrannies of kings, states, and churches. Their ideal had informed the English Civil War, and it would profoundly affect not only the lives but the letters of women.

INTELLECTUAL AND SOCIAL BACKGROUND

Puritanism

Puritanism, which shaped English history and American identity throughout the seventeenth century, dramatically endowed the inner life of the self and the historical development of the state with divine significance. Early English and colonial Puritans believed that, after the Fall, God had offered a covenant of grace through Christ to certain elect souls. Because God was thought to visit his grace directly on each of these individuals, the Puritans minimized the rule of Church ritual and liturgy, and instead emphasized each individual's need to study the self, the world, and the Bible so as to attain spiritual certitude and moral rectitude. Advocating what the historian Christopher Hill has called "a doctrine of spiritual equality" ("one good man was as good as another, and better than a bad peer or bishop or king"), the Puritans in England posed the challenge of individual conscience to civil and religious institutions, for the "Witness of the Indwelling Spirit" was a better spiritual authority than the Anglican Church, which had not yet "purified" itself "to recover," in the phrase of William Bradford, first governor of Plymouth, "primitive order, liberty, and beauty."

Besides raising the individual's conscience above the dictates of the Church, the doctrine of predestination meant that "though none are Sav'd that wickednesse imbrace, / Yet none are Damn'd that have Inherent Grace," or so it was in-

terpreted by the colonial poet Edward Taylor in his *God's Determinations Touching His Elect* (c. 1690). Puritans could not earn grace through good works; however, English preachers like Thomas Taylor explained that ' we teach that only doers shall be saved, and by their doing though not for their doing." In the cosmic drama of salvation that they witnessed in their private and public lives, therefore, Puritan poets and preachers were motivated by a high sense of moral purpose that paradoxically infused not only their struggle to wean the soul away from earthly desire but also their effort to serve the community through productive labor. If Puritanism thereby fostered self-education and spiritual introspection, it also contributed, as a number of sociologists have pointed out, to the rise of capitalism.

Before and after the Civil War in England, the Puritans were stereotyped as sternly self-absorbed fanatics, opposed to the frivolity and idolatry of the arts. Both English and colonial writers did, in fact, express their distrust of the imagination, in much the same strain as Cotton Mather when, in 1726, he warned ministry students to "beware of a boundless and sickly appetite for the reading of the poems which now the rickety nation swarms withal." Yet the aim of Puritanism was not to obliterate imaginative literature, but to turn it toward the search for evidences of God's grace. During the Civil War, pulpit oratory and political pamphleteering resulted in a simpler, more functional prose style. Not only the bawdy satires of Ben Jonson and the melodramatic tragedies of John Webster but also the elaborately paradoxical poems of Richard Crashaw and John Donne were succeeded by introspective, spiritual meditations on biblical themes. The publication of the King James version of the Bible in 1611 had already made that book more widely read than ever before. Second only in popularity during this period was John Bunyan's *The Pilgrim's Progress* (1678), a prose allegory written while Bunyan was in jail for his religious beliefs. Just as Bunyan in England stressed the virtues of faith and industry, American Puritans like John Winthrop and Cotton Mather traced the New World's mission in terms of God's covenant with humankind. A similar confidence that history develops according to a providential plan characterizes the highly popular captivity narrative authored by Mary Rowlandson, who witnessed her own and her children's injuries and escapes as divine signs of God's grand design.

In its emphasis on the importance of each soul, its association of atheism with illiteracy, and its concomitant commitment to the education of the laity, Puritanism allowed a number of women to explore and articulate the authority of their spiritual experiences. Although, as the historian Sheila Rowbotham has argued, Puritan culture reenforced the power of the father as the head of the family, it defined the wife as her husband's partner: her soul was equal to his in the sight of God. The emphasis on conscience, not only in Puritanism but also in other dissenting Protestant sects, meant that women were sometimes allowed to preach, as Jane Holmes, Anne Wentworth, and Margaret Fox did in the seventeenth century and as Ann Lee, Joanna Southcott, and Betty Gray did in the eighteenth century. Significantly, the Protestant mystic Jane Lead prophesied a female savior, a "woman clothed with the sun," while the Quaker Margaret Fell argued that Christ was the same in men and women, who could both speak of and for him. An early autobiographical narrative, the *Life of Elizabeth Ashbridge* (1774), typifies the ways in which spiritual introspection would empower American women to take responsibility for and control over their own lives. In addition, implicitly granting authority to the female conscience as well as to the male, the self-consciousness of Puritanism made possible Anne Bradstreet's meditative poetry.

Nevertheless, like most Puritan women, Bradstreet was forbidden to participate publicly in the interpretation of Scripture and excluded from the governing boards that ruled over civic and religious issues. Both English literary history and American social history provide evidence that, as potentially liberating as Puritanism could be for women, it was embedded in a patriarchal ideology that was hostile to women. The clash between the midwife-preacher Anne Hutchinson

and the Puritan theocracy of Boston demonstrates just how threatening a woman preacher could seem, for Hutchinson was attacked by civil and religious authorities after she had attracted as many as sixty people to her discussions of the "indwelling Christ." Found guilty of heresy, she was excommunicated by the Church and banished from the colony. Subsequent lecturers in Boston described an infant Hutchinson had miscarried in prison as a "monstrous birth" that "embodied her spiritual errors" and as "the work of the devil," an apelike being with horns and claws. Like that of Bradstreet's sister, who was also excommunicated for her preaching, the case of Hutchinson highlights the misogyny that informed the Salem witchcraft trials. Nineteen people and two dogs were hanged for witchcraft in those trials, and few people appear to have had the audacity of Sarah Good, who, when convicted during one such trial, cried out on the scaffold to the Reverend Nicholas Noye, "You are a liar. I am no more a witch than you are a wizard, and if you take away my life God will give you blood to drink."

In England, the two-edged implications of Puritan thought were probably best expressed by John Milton, who composed the age's principal hymn to matrimonial love in his epic poem *Paradise Lost* (1667). In the garden of Eden, Adam and Eve express pleasure at finding the mutuality of their desire for each other, for sexuality is the "perpetual fountain of domestic sweets," and Adam's higher reason is said to complement Eve's greater sensitivity. Drawing on Puritan arguments for freedom of choice in marriage and on the idea of the wife as a helpmate, Milton argued in a number of tracts that wives could sue for divorce from husbands and that "unchastity" was worse in men than in women. Yet in *Paradise Lost*, Milton portrayed an Eve created out of and for Adam. Following the biblical story, moreover, he allotted culpability for the Fall to a woman who disobeys not only God's commandment but Milton's description of her proper place: "He for God only, she for God in him." Eve's fascination with Satan leads to the Fall and humankind's punishment: expulsion from paradise, mortality, and labor. Just as important, Eve's alliance with Satan is prefigured in the poem by the thralldom of the allegorical figure Sin, who also serves Satan and brings death into the world. To be sure, in the moral scheme of Milton's epic, Sin signifies a great deal more than maternity. But because she is the only mother in the work, it seems crucial that she foreshadows the painful maternity that is God's punishment of Eve by embodying a nauseated sense of female generativity, for Sin breeds innumerable hellhounds, animals that emerge from and return to her womb, where they bark and howl unseen. Milton's Puritan radicalism—his defense of regicide, republicanism, and freedom of the press—did not extend to women, as Mary Astell would point out when she wondered why a man so concerned about freedom did not "cry up liberty to poor female slaves." Images of women in *Paradise Lost* would haunt women writers from Mary Wollstonecraft to Charlotte Brontë, Virginia Woolf, and Laura Riding Jackson. As the scholar Hilda L. Smith has argued, however, the Puritan protest against tyranny that Milton articulated may have contributed to the rise of feminism, because in that protest women could witness their exclusion from even the most radical movement of their time.

Science and Rationalism

Perhaps, as some historians have suggested, it was precisely the civic and religious upheavals of the seventeenth century that gave rise to the belief that no single creed could be accepted over all the others. In any case, the tolerant pluralism that characterized eighteenth-century intellectual history was in part the result of direct challenges to traditional religion, challenges associated with the rise of mathematics, physics, and anatomy. The telescope, which furnished evidence of a Copernican universe, and the microscope, which provided proof of the corpuscular composition of the blood and thereby added the final support to Harvey's theory of circulation, were both invented in the seventeenth century, as were such

instruments as the barometer and the thermometer. At the beginning of the century, Francis Bacon (1561–1626) emphasized the need to liberate knowledge from blind acceptance of Greek and medieval philosophies by testing authority against experience. Already in Bacon's time, poets and theologians like John Donne worried that the "new philosophy calls all in doubt; / The element of fire is quite put out," for the world seemed "all in pieces, all coherence gone." By the Restoration, however, science had become fashionable in court, and the Royal Society, a scientific institute, was founded with the motto *Nullius in verba*, meaning "on the word of no one."

Although advances like Robert Boyle's substitution of chemistry for medieval alchemy were viewed by many as a direct assault on religion, the scientists' investigations of physical experience were not unrelated to the Puritans' spiritual examination of personal experience. By the turn of the century, moreover, a number of empiricists sought to affirm the principles of a new faith based on the "laws" of nature that Sir Isaac Newton (1642–1727) had discovered by applying mathematics to physics. The result was Deism, a philosophy that viewed nature as a well-ordered mechanism in which God functioned only as a divine mechanic. Rejecting the need for supernatural revelation in general and for Christian doctrine in particular, the Deists assumed that logic and observation would allow them to deduce the intelligibility and coherence of the universe. Just as the philosopher John Locke (1632–1704) explained with confidence that "the works of nature in every part of them sufficiently evidence a Deity," Alexander Pope proclaimed in his *Essay on Man* (1733–34), "All are but parts of one stupendous whole: / Whose body Nature is, and God the soul."

Both the new science and Deism exerted a profound effect on eighteenth-century literature. Gone were the baroque rhetorical flourishes of "false wit," replaced by what Jonathan Swift hailed as a "clear, masculine, and smooth" style. Inspiration was derided by English satirists as "enthusiasm," which was associated with the madness of the Puritans in particular and the Whigs in general, for some of the most prominent writers of this period were conservatives whose satire attempted to right the wrongs of an age descending into crass commercialism and individualism. Modeling their work on the poetry produced by Virgil and Horace in the Rome of Augustus, these Augustan or neoclassical writers assumed that if nature had its laws then poetry probably did too. While literary critics began to enumerate the rules that regulated various genres, poets like Dryden and Pope assumed that the classics best articulated general truths about the nature of man, so that 'Homer and Nature were," in fact, "the same." They chose the heroic couplet—two rhymed lines composed in iambic pentameter—for a discursive, public poetry that was as didactic as the new science was utilitarian.

While many of the satirists were pessimistic about the depravity of humanity and society, Pope's optimism in *Essay on Man*—"Whatever IS, is RIGHT"—resembled the cheerful argument of the Whig philosopher Anthony Ashley Cooper, third earl of Shaftesbury; because human nature is as well constructed as physical nature, Shaftesbury reasoned, an innate benevolence governs the moral instincts of human beings. The cult of feeling that would develop out of this idea was associated with the sympathetic tears that heroes and heroines alike shed from the 1720s on in sentimental comedies on the English stage. Paradoxically, however, Deism also contributed to the formation of what the title of a book by Tom Paine called *The Age of Reason* (1795); not only did Paine's book begin with the assertion that all institutions of faith have tyrannized over humankind, it also went on to attack the Bible, contrasting a corrupt Solomon, with his seven hundred wives and three hundred concubines, to an enlightened Benjamin Franklin, whose "mind was ever young, [whose] temper ever serene; science, that never grows gray, was always his mistress." The new secularism doubtless molded Benjamin Franklin and Thomas Jefferson, both of whom played important roles in the American version of the Royal Society. Indeed, Franklin's experiments in electricity reflected the

sanguine practicality of his famous *Almanac* (1732–57) and *Autobiography* (1791), just as Jefferson's rejection of "superstition" in *The Life and Morals of Jesus of Nazareth* represented the same confidence in a well-regulated universe that inspired him to construct a government that would "govern least."

By the middle of the eighteenth century, the new empiricism had contributed to a general decline in traditional religion, which was only further accelerated in England by the complacency of the Church. On both sides of the Atlantic, the 1740s saw religious revivals that were clearly a reaction against the weakening of traditional faith. In England, John Wesley began to preach salvation through Christ to large middle- and working-class crowds in open air meetings. Although his followers, known as Methodists, were initially ridiculed as illiterate fanatics, the spiritual fervor of this movement had after a time a major impact within the Church, inspiring the growth of evangelicalism. In America, the first Great Awakening was led, in part, by the eminent American preacher Jonathan Edwards, and it too gave rise to a great number of what Edwards himself called "surprising conversions."

That Edwards was eventually forced to resign from his church by his own congregation, however, illustrates the changing religious temper of the times. The inductive method, respect for each individual's experience, and belief in the innate benevolence of the creator undermined the influences of Edwards's sovereign and arbitrary God. For all the severity of his sermon *Sinners in the Hands of an Angry God* (1741), moreover, Edwards himself wrote a scientific essay, *Of Insects*, early in life; read John Locke at Yale University; and ended his career by returning to the mystical pantheism of his youth. Similarly, Wesley, who preached forty thousand sermons and traveled many thousands of miles on horseback, tried to keep his followers within the Church of England and maintained a lively, observant journal that was published posthumously. In other words, even those thinkers who opposed the secularization of culture demonstrated the new fascination with documentation, which manifested itself in proliferating diaries, biographies, travelogues, histories, natural histories, and encyclopedias.

Not a few women lamented the fact that men "refuse to let us know / What sacred Science doth impart." Yet, from Margaret Cavendish's scientific investigations to Sarah Frye Egerton's poem in praise of Robert Boyle and Mary Wortley Montagu's pioneering advocacy of innoculation, literary women were involved in the scientific revolution of their time. As with Puritanism, the impact of the new science on women's history was complex. On the one hand, as the scholar Carolyn Merchant has shown, Bacon's view that nature had to be "hounded in her wanderings"—that the scientist should "torture nature's secrets from her"— paralleled the widespread torture of witches in the early seventeenth century and reduced men's sense of responsibility to an earth no longer viewed as a nurturing mother. On the other hand, the materialistic philosophers associated with this revolution called into question the divine right of patriarchal authority. In his *Leviathan* (1651), Thomas Hobbes described the state of nature as a matriarchy in which "every woman that bears children, becomes both a mother and a lord." Although Hobbes argued that the predatory precultural state is bestial and must be replaced by the consent of men to the authority of a powerful king, his theory nevertheless undermined the idea of the father's natural ownership of the child, as did John Locke's direct attack on the "absolute arbitrary dominion of the father."

Just as important, Locke's psychological model of the mind as a *tabula rasa* (blank tablet) implied that all knowledge is the result of sensuous experience. Besides opening up the discourse of rights and responsibilities, then, Locke paved a way to the realism that would allow many eighteenth-century women to record in letters and journals the private experiences that had shaped their development. Similarly, both the cult of sentimentality fostered by Deist benevolence and the

religious revivals of the 1740s quickly became associated with women, who had, since Milton's time, been identified with an emotional receptivity thought to complement male rationalism: it is hardly insignificant that John Wesley, the founder of Methodism, was said to have acquired his new doctrines from his mother's preachings and that the sensitive heroine of Samuel Richardson's *Pamela* (1740), a best-seller both in England and America, embodied the middle-class virtues of industry, moral integrity, and upward mobility. Yet the rise of the novel, which was so important to women's history, depended not only on the new empiricism and the cult of sentimentality but also on the formation of a middle-class reading public, a development that reflected the extraordinary growth of capitalism in the late eighteenth century.

Urbanization

As England moved from a predominantly rural economy of local farmers and yeomen to an industrial economy of large landholders and national markets, it became what the novelist Daniel Defoe (1659–1731) called "the most flourishing and opulent country in the world." After the founding of the Bank of England (1694) and the world's first stock exchange (1689) made possible vast investments both in England and in the colonies, inventions like Newcomen's steam pump (1712), Kemp's flying shuttle (1733), Hargreaves's spinning jenny (1764), Arkwright's water frame (1764), and Cartwright's power loom (1785–87) began to transform the woolen industry, which manufactured England's most stable export. In addition, large landowners began consolidating open fields previously cultivated by tenant farmers, and this process (called *enclosure*) permitted techniques of farming to be applied on a more productive scale, although it also turned many independent smallholders into agricultural laborers. Coal mining and ironmongering grew, sustained by Watt's new steam engine (1769), so that the midland cities began to expand. With the shift of population to industrial towns, the English working class began to face the exploitative conditions that would give rise at the end of the century to trade unionism.

London remained the center of what was now the first of the industrialized countries. After the Great Fire of 1666 destroyed many sections of the city, the capital was rebuilt on a larger scale, and the architect Sir Christopher Wren established his reputation with St. Paul's Church while the painter William Hogarth gained renown with his portrayals of London street scenes. Celia Fienne's *Journey through England on Side Saddle in the Time of William and Mary* (1702) described the hazardous road conditions outside London in the late seventeenth century, but by the middle of the eighteenth century turnpikes and macadamized roads connected the capital to the rest of Great Britain, as did canals, which gave the country the most efficient system of transport it had known. A falling death rate after 1740 and a rising birth rate caused the population to grow steadily in the last decades of the eighteenth century. A similar growth spurt in America created three cities—Boston, New York, and Philadelphia—that were larger than any English towns other than London.

The growth of these urban centers throughout the eighteenth century was reflected in the cosmopolitan wit of much writing, which focused on topical social and political issues. The first daily newspapers—for instance, *The Daily Courant* (1702) in England and the *News-Letter* (1704) in Boston—as well as periodicals like *The Spectator*, *The Gentleman's Magazine*, and *The American Magazine* published reviews, stories, social instruction, and moral essays for the literati, who populated coffeehouses on both sides of the Atlantic. In addition, by the second decade of the eighteenth century there were already more than seventy printing and publishing shops in London. Although the Augustan wits leveled much of their satire against the mediocrity they associated with commercial writing, the

literary marketplace had been transformed. "Writing," as Defoe explained in 1725, had "become a very considerable branch of the English commerce," a view corroborated by the fact that he sold eighty thousand copies of *The True-Born Englishman*.

Pope was the first major English poet to support himself through the sales of his books, and his most influential successor, Dr. Samuel Johnson, the son of a Lichfield bookseller, was the first major author to establish his reputation through scholarship (his *Dictionary*, 1755), criticism (his *Lives of the Poets*, 1779–81), and conversational genius (preserved in James Boswell's *Life*, 1791). With the proliferation of publishing houses in America, moreover, American writers were less dependent on English acceptance than they had been at the beginning of the century. But the threat to neoclassical standards posed by the commercialization of literature and the emergence of subscription sales and circulating libraries is probably best gauged by the growing popularity of a new form that was appropriately called the novel. Both Daniel Defoe, a journalist-turned-novelist who wrote about an entrepreneurial adventurer in *Robinson Crusoe* (1719), and Samuel Richardson, a printer-turned-novelist who wrote about an industrious servant girl in *Pamela*, articulated the bourgeois values of the large reading public who bought unprecedented numbers of their books.

Perhaps no other change had a greater impact on literary women than the demise of the older, more closed patronage system for the support of authors, and this change was instantaneous. After Charles II licensed two theatrical companies, women dramatists from Aphra Behn to Susannah Centlivre, Mary Pix, and Catherine Trotter began producing and publishing their own plays. Between 1695 and the death of Queen Anne in 1714, at least forty plays were written by women dramatists. Their work was probably made possible by mutual support as well as improved morality in the theater and by the increasing number of educated women who attended performances. It was important, too, that in these years women were for the first time able to appear on stage as actresses. Aphra Behn produced the first lines written by a woman for a woman to speak specifically to women in a hit play that allowed her to earn sellout box office receipts for two nights.

Behn's *Oroonoko* (1688), sometimes considered the first English novel, marks the beginning of the exceptionally popular prose fiction produced by women of letters. Although at times such writers as Behn, Delarivier Manley, and Eliza Haywood were criticized for their reliance on scandalous material, they gained unprecedented fame from their productions of epistolary novellas and romantic narratives. Novelists, in particular, began to realize that literature was one of the few lucrative professions open to women, and economic need quickly became a defense for publication. As Sarah Fielding explained in the preface to *David Simple* (1744), "Perhaps the best excuse that can be made for a woman's venturing to write at all, is that which really produced this book; distress in her circumstances: which she could not so well remove by any other means in her power." While the poets Anne Bradstreet, Katherine Philips, and Phillis Wheatley depended on male relatives and friends to publish their books, historians like Catharine Macaulay and essayists like Elizabeth Montagu increasingly negotiated with booksellers and printers themselves. Eventually, the philanthropist Hannah More and the novelists Charlotte Smith and Susanna Rowson helped support their families by publishing numerous books on manners and morals. In addition, the predominantly middle-class women who frequented the circulating libraries provided such writers with an audience interested in the private lives of wives and daughters. Women participated vigorously in almost all of the major literary movements and genres in the eighteenth century, frequently supporting themselves in the process; however, their contributions remained distinctive, no doubt because of the myths and realities that differentiated the female experience from the male in this period.

IMAGES OF WOMEN

Literary ladies, no less than other women, had to confront the misogynist images of women still prevalent in their culture, for popular writers like Joseph Swetnam continued to castigate women during the seventeenth century in phrases that harked back to medieval times: "Eagles eat not men till they are dead but women devour them alive, for a woman will pick thy pocket and empty thy purse, laugh in thy face and cut thy throat, they are ungrateful, perjured, full of fraud, flouting and deceit, unconstant, waspish, toyish, light, sullen, proud, discourteous, and cruel." (*The Arraignment of Lewd, Idle, Forward and Unconstant Women*, 1615). During the period before the English Civil War, there were many portraits of conniving, ambitious ladies like those attacked by the likes of Swetnam, but there were also patronesses and mistresses idealized in courtly poetry. Yet even in the many erotic and romantic verses of seventeenth-century lyricists, the visions of women that such works recorded were often projections of, on the one hand, male anxieties and, on the other hand, male desire. To be sure, great poems like John Donne's 1633 *The Ecstasy, A Valediction: Forbidding Mourning*, and *The Relic* acknowledged female subjectivity and even argued that in their love the poet and his mistress transcended gender: "Difference of sex no more we knew," wrote Donne in *The Relic*, "than our guardian angels do." Yet even Donne, for instance in such a work as *Elegy XIX: To His Mistress Going to Bed* (1669), tended to make an object out of woman, possessively defining his beloved as "my America! my new-found-land, / My kingdom; safeliest when with one man manned." Moreover, if Donne celebrated his conquest of his mistress in terms of the laying of the land, in such sardonic pieces as *Song: Go and Catch a Falling Star* and *Woman's Constancy*, both 1633, he argued that "nowhere / Lives a woman true and fair."

In this regard, his attitudes were typical of those held by many of his contemporaries, who not only reproached women for inconstancy but also blamed them for unnatural eroticism. Ben Jonson's scathing *To Fine Lady Would-Be* (1616), for example, savagely excoriates a court lady for loving to make love but refusing to bear children, noting that "the world reputes you barren; but I know / Your 'pothecary, and his drug says no." Accusing her of using medicinal arts either to abort babies or prevent conception, Jonson concludes, "Write, then on thy womb, / Of the not born, yet buried, here's the tomb." But if Donne and Jonson reproached women for inconstancy or wanton sexuality, such poets as Andrew Marvell, Robert Herrick, and even Jonson himself censured women for clinging to virginity. Poems urging women to yield themselves to their lovers were so ubiquitous in the period as to constitute a literary tradition of their own. Based on the so-called *carpe diem* (seize the day) theme, such verses urged the beloved to yield to the importunities of her lover before it was too late. Jonson's *Come, My Celia* (1606) argues that the lovers should "prove, / While we can, the sports of love" because "Time will not be ours forever; / He at length our good will sever"; Andrew Marvell's *To His Coy Mistress* (1681) explains that, if his mistress does not yield herself, "worms shall try that long preserved virginity"; and Robert Herrick's *To the Virgins, to Make Much of Time* notoriously advises young girls to "Gather ye rosebuds while ye may, / Old time is still a-flying."

A number of Restoration and early-eighteenth-century literary works also protested against chastity in women, but less through erotic lyricism than through the negative image of the gossiping shrew, the affected devout, or the proud prude. As satire gained literary prominence, however, more artists drew on the classical writer Juvenal's *Sixth Satire* to bemoan the demise of female fidelity, modesty, and purity, and to express their horror of female sexuality. "Let the porter, and the groom, / Things designed for dirty slaves; / Drudge in fair Aurelia's womb, / To get supplies for age and graves," John Wilmot, second earl of Rochester, exclaimed in *A Song* (1691), as if to illustrate the satirists' equation of the womb with the tomb. From John Oldham's *A Satire upon a Woman, Who by Her Falsehood and Scorn*

Was the Death of His Friend (1678) to Jonathan Swift's *Strephon and Chloe* (1731) and *A Beautiful Young Nymph Going to Bed* (1734), misogynist poems portrayed women as adulterous wantons, syphilitic prostitutes, and flirtatious coquettes: Oldham—who cursed his female subject as "Vil'st of that viler sex, who damn'd us all!"—was just as scatological in his depiction of women as Swift, who stripped away the makeup, clothing, perfume, and wigs that adorned women to reveal that "Caelia, Caelia, Caelia shits!" Frequently using mock-pastoral conventions to uncover the filthy physicality of the contaminating whore who lurks behind the idealized shepherdess, the satirists projected on the female figure their horror at materialistic acquisition, pride, and hypocrisy, a perversion of values that would eventually result in the death of culture. But if female inconstancy and physicality implied deceitfulness and death, they also meant, in Pope's famous line, that " 'Most women have no characters at all.' " It is hardly surprising, in the context established by his *Epistle to a Lady* (1735), that the only female model Pope could imagine was described as a "contradiction," "a softer man."

As the century progressed, more and more thinkers came to counsel women, in the words of Lord Lyttleton, "Seek to be good, but aim not to be great: / A woman's noblest station is retreat: / Her fairest virtues fly from public sight, / Domestic worth, that shuns too strong a light." As satire gave way to sentiment, moreover, popular pamphlets, conduct books, sermons, and essays analyzed the proper duties of wives and daughters with the more genteel condescension of Lord Chesterfield, explaining that "women are but children of a larger growth." Middle-class women, now increasingly confined to the domestic sphere, were told by essayists like Richard Steele that all they have "to do in this world, is contained within the duties of a daughter, a sister, a wife, and a mother." As the literature about domestic conduct proliferated, it applied the ideal of politeness implicit in Augustan literature to women, who were now expected to be modest and decorous: as the naturalist-poet Erasmus Darwin explained, "The Muses are young ladies; we expect to see them dressed."

Such literature also began to contribute to the sentimentality implicit in Shaftesbury's Deism, creating a middle-class cult of weeping and delicacy in women praised for their emotional sensitivity as well as their purity and passivity. Sentimental fiction, as the critic Katharine Rogers has pointed out, featured moral ideals of gentleness and refined feelings that were considered feminine. By the time Richardson published *Pamela* and *Clarissa* (1747–48), the bourgeoisie had associated its moral superiority with the image of an angelic, chaste woman who was engaged in a struggle for supremacy with a predatory, masculine nobility. To be sure, comic novelists like Henry Fielding continued to criticize Richardson's heroines as conniving upstarts, while pornographers like John Cleland continued to focus on the exotic pleasures provided by whores. But in countless popular novels imitating Richardson's astonishingly successful fiction, female characters were transformed from demonic sinners into domestic saints, much to the delight of the many middle-class women who read these works.

Clearly, both eighteenth-century satires on female vice and celebrations of feminine virtue were informed by medieval portraits of a destructive Eve and a redemptive Mary. More striking, however, was the emergence of a new image of woman, a satiric portrait of the female artist, which constituted a reaction against the growing visibility of literary women. The late-seventeenth- and eighteenth-century attacks on literary ladies are important not only because they demonstrate why many women were unable to write or publish but also because they explain why those who did write and publish frequently felt it necessary to apologize or justify their efforts. As the scholar Wendy Martin has explained, Puritan scorn for so-called scribbling women is aptly illustrated by Thomas Parker's 1650 condemnation of his sister: "Your printing of a book beyond the custom of your sex," Parker wrote in a public letter, "doth rankly smell." Similarly, as the literary historian Myra Reynolds has shown, both the plays and the poetry produced in England

after the Restoration attacked women writers, readers, and speakers, who were only represented as mangling the language they wrote, read, or regurgitated. From a learned lady named "Bisarre" in George Farquahar's *The Inconstant* (1703) to Sophronia and Lady Wrangle in Colly Cibber's *The Refusal* (1721), female erudition was satirized as affectation. But feminine addiction to romantic literature was also attacked: Biddy Tipkins in Steele's *The Tender Husband* (1705), who would rather be called "Elismonda" or "Deidania," inhabits a hodgepodge world of shepherds, knights, and groves: she is a type of the "female Quixote" Charlotte Lennox would popularize in 1752, whose descendants were George Colman's Polly Honeycomb (1760) and Richard Sheridan's Lydia Languish (1775).

Just as the American Puritan John Winthrop had bemoaned the lot of a woman who had "fallen into a sad infirmity, the loss of her understanding, and reason, which had been growing upon her diverse years, by occasion of her giving herself wholly to reading and writing, and written many books" (1645), the Augustan satirists implied that reading and writing would derange weaker female minds. In *Three Hours after Marriage* (1717), Pope, Swift, and Arbuthnot directly satirized the poet Anne Finch as Phoebe Clinket, a prototypical female dunce who proves the point Pope had made earlier in *The Rape of the Lock* (1714), that "the poetic and the hysteric fit" are near allied in the female. A loose lady novelist is the prize in a contest between hack writers in one of Pope's early versions of *The Dunciad* (1728) while a monstrous Goddess of Criticism represents the self-indulgence of modern literature in Swift's *Tale of a Tub* (1704) and a nursing Goddess of Dullness is the deity of the hacks in the last book of *The Dunciad* (1743). Toward the end of the century, when Dr. Johnson compared a woman preacher to a dancing dog, or when he condemned portrait-painting as improper in women because "public practice of any art . . . and staring in men's faces, is very indelicate in a female," he was assuming that "creativity" and "femininity" were contradictory terms.

WOMEN'S LIVES

If the literary woman suffered from being considered an anomaly, all women in this period were burdened by the judgments prescribed by judicial authorities. In 1632 the author of *The Laws' Resolution of Women's Rights* succinctly explained that women "have nothing to do in constituting laws, of consenting to them, in interpreting of laws, or in hearing them interpreted . . . and yet they stand strictly tied to men's establishments, little or nothing excused by ignorance." Within the legal system throughout the seventeenth and eighteenth centuries, women were held to different standards of behavior than men and were punished more severely for departing from those standards. For example, mothers of stillborn babies could be charged with infanticide (if they could not produce witnesses to prove the child born dead) until 1803. So-called scolding women were punished with the "brank" (an iron framework caging the head) or the "ducking stool" (a chair with straps that was let down into a river) before 1809. As late as 1770 Parliament passed a statute declaring that "all women of whatever age, rank, profession, or degree, whether virgin maid or widow, that shall from and after such Act impose upon, seduce, and betray into matrimony any of His Majesty's subjects by means of scent, paints, cosmetics, washes, artificial teeth, false hair, Spanish wool, iron stays, hoops, high-heeled shoes, or bolstered hips, shall incur the penalty of the law now in force against witchcraft and like misdemeanours, and that the marriage upon conviction shall stand null and void."

The misogyny implicit in such a statute also informed laws unrelated to criminality. Although an unmarried woman could own property and a widow was entitled to a portion of her deceased husband's estate, a married woman throughout this period could neither own property nor make a will, "for the husband is entitled to the fruits of his wife's labour." By virtue of the judicial concept of the *feme*

covert ("covered" woman), the woman's legal existence was suspended by marriage: she was theoretically incorporated into the person of her husband, under whose protection she carried on all her activities. With no right to divorce and no rights with respect to her own children, she also had no rights over her own body, for English husbands could imprison wives in their houses until 1891. While in America the concept of civil marriage resulted in a slightly more tolerant attitude toward divorce, and the patriarchal rule of primogeniture (the right of the oldest son to inherit the estate) was more erratic, legal conditions were almost as difficult for women.

Although women clearly labored under legal disadvantages, both men and women in this period gained greater freedom in choosing a marriage partner. To be sure, in wealthy families marriage was often still settled through treaties, and a number of women were forced either to marry against their wishes or to wait many years for their fathers' consent. But many women were allowed to follow the dictates of their affection in choosing husbands. Both married and single aristocrats, like the duchess of Marlborough, intimate friend of Queen Anne, and Lady Hester Stanhope, niece of the prime minister William Pitt, exercised considerable political influence and lived luxurious, even adventurous, lives. But middle- and working-class single women, wives, and widows lost many of their previously important economic roles. For the middle class, in particular, the assumption that husbands should support their wives gave rise to an ideology of female idleness, a belief that wives were symbols of their husbands' status by virtue of their leisure.

Many historians agree that working-class women lost much of their economic independence during the period when England and America moved from agricultural to industrial production. The specialization that accompanied industrialization meant that a number of home industries previously open to women (spinning, baking, preserving, sewing, farming, and brewing) steadily decreased. In the country, yeoman's wives tended to withdraw from agricultural labor, and in the city journeymen's wives were less involved in their husbands' trades. Though women continued to work as brewsters and spinsters, they were beginning to be excluded from many other industries by the separation of the workplace from the home.

In America, of course, the lady on a Southern plantation or the wife of a Massachusetts fisherman would be expected to help carry on her husband's business. When exploration and Indian wars resulted in labor shortages, moreover, women worked in craftsmaking, innkeeping, and shopkeeping. In southern England, too, women continued to specialize in dairy and poultry work. But with the enclosures of the second half of the eighteenth century, as Sir Frederick Eden remarked in 1797, "the acquisition of the necessities of life required by a labourer's family, rests entirely in the husband." Working-class women could, of course, always become servants, yet even Dr. Johnson could not give Boswell a satisfactory reason why "women servants . . . have much lower wages than men servants" although "our female house servants work much harder than the male." Toward the end of the eighteenth century, women began working in the developing mills and factories; however, they generally earned only two-thirds of a man's pay.

Perhaps there is no better example of how professionalization excluded women than the struggle between midwives and physicians. In the sixteenth century, church examiners certified midwives; in the seventeenth century, greater emphasis was placed on medical knowledge, and examiners were frequently members of the College of Physicians. Two writers defended the autonomy of midwives: Jane Sharp, in *The Midwives' Book* (1671), attempted to provide women with the anatomical information men received in universities, and Elizabeth Cellier, in *A Scheme for the Foundation of a Royal Hospital*, proposed a corporation that would establish standards for midwives. Yet, castigated as witches or incompetents, midwives were replaced throughout the eighteenth century by male physicians, both

in lying-in hospitals and in middle-class homes. Using new instruments like the forceps, placing women in beds instead of on birthing stools, doctors, who worked under covers to protect women's modesty, were reminded in textbooks that "Degorges, one of the best obstetricians of his time, was blind." Yet despite their best efforts, infant mortality rates remained quite high throughout the period. None of Queen Anne's seventeen offspring outlived her. Only about one child in four born in London survived in the early part of the eighteenth century. One baby died out of every fifteen born at the British Lying-In Hospital between 1749 and 1759.

That midwives were excluded from the medical education that would have ensured their professional survival illustrates widespread acceptance of Lord Halifax's view that "there is inequality in the sexes, and that for the better economy of the world, the men, who were to be the lawgivers, had the larger share of reason bestowed upon them." Frequently reprinted in England and advertised extensively in colonial newspapers, Halifax's *The Lady's New Year's Gift; or, Advice to a Daughter* (1688) was far more typical than, say, Defoe's advocacy of equalizing the educational opportunities of the sexes (*Essay on Projects*, 1697). Even within the increasingly popular boarding schools for middle-class girls in Defoe's time, a "liberal education" consisted mainly of embroidery, modeling in wax, painting on glass, and musical accomplishments, although some girls' schools did put on plays and teach cooking skills. Between 1698 and 1715, more than one hundred charity schools were established in London and Westminster, but most of the girls who attended were trained there for domestic service. There was, of course, no formal higher education for women of any class. Like Oxford and Cambridge, the American universities founded in this period—Harvard (1636), Yale (1701), and Princeton (1746)—were closed to women.

As the anonymous author of *An Essay in Defense of the Female Sex* (1696) explained, "We are taught only our mother tongue, or perhaps French," while "the other sex by means of a more extensive education to the knowledge of the Roman and Greek languages, have a vaster field for the imaginations to rove in, and their capacities thereby enlarged." Yet with classical imitation, allusion, and translation playing a major role in neoclassical literature, a knowledge of Greek and Latin was virtually a prerequisite for poetic authorship. When an exceptional woman like Elizabeth Elstob was encouraged by her family to become an Anglo-Saxon scholar, her publications did not save her from pecuniary difficulties after she lost that support: following her brother's death, the author of *Rudiments of Grammar for the Anglo-Saxon Tongue* (1715) was forced to become first a poorly paid teacher and then a dependent governess. Furthermore, such a learned woman was constantly cautioned, in the words of the moralist Dr. Gregory, to "keep [her learning] a profound secret, especially from the men, who generally look with a jealous and malignant eye on a woman of great parts or a cultivated understanding" (*A Father's Legacy to His Daughters*, 1774). Still, in spite of such discouragement, by the 1760s in London a small circle of aristocratic ladies, imitating the salons of French hostesses, became renowned for learning and grace. Elizabeth Montagu, Elizabeth Carter, and Frances Boscawen were called "bluestockings," a phrase associated with the informality of their conversational gatherings, where worsted stockings (as opposed to silk) could be worn. Montagu's *Essays on the Writings and Genius of Shakespeare* (1769), along with Catharine Macaulay's *History of England* (1763–83) and Hester Mulso Chapone's *Letters on the Improvements of the Mind* (1773), contributed to the growing recognition of women's intellectual abilities.

WOMEN'S NEW PROFESSION OF LETTERS

Although it subjected them to ridicule and censure, writing was one of the few professions open to middle-class women, one they could pursue in their homes

with financial success. Some women—by virtue of their leisure—were able to follow Joseph Addison's advice that they should "apply themselves to letters," for "they have more spare time on their hands, and lead a more sedentary life" than men. Yet, constantly reminded of their inadequacies, not a few shared the views of the poet Mary Oxlie, who meditated anxiously on the impediments to female creativity posed by women's lack of education and their domestic preoccupations, and by the resentment such confinement necessarily breeds:

> Perfection in a woman's work is rare;
> From an untroubled mind should verses flow;
> My discontents make mine too muddy show;
> And hoarse encumbrances of household care,
> Where these remain the Muses ne'er repair.

Because "all heroic actions, public employments, powerful governments and eloquent pleadings are denied our sex in this age," Margaret Cavendish believed that her own "restless" ambition caused her "to run upon every subject." Women who refused to submit to the distraction or the notoriety she suffered understandably wrote only in private and in forms considered "trivial," like Dorothy Osborne, whose observant, witty letters in the 1650s were meant only for her lover, William Temple. Sara Kemble Knight's *Private Journal of a Journey from Boston to New York*, which was composed during 1704 and 1705 but not published until 1825, typified many diaries and autobiographies that were written by women who kept them as private or familial forms of communication. If women agreed to publication, it was often—as with Katherine Philips—"with the same reluctancy as I would cut off a limb to save my life," and frequently they published anonymously.

A few women writers, especially if protected by anonymity or rank, directly questioned male assumptions about female inferiority. The nameless author of a poem in praise of the poet Sarah Egerton, for example, declared in 1706, "No more let haughty man with fierce disdain, / Despise the product of a female brain." Later in the century, Mary Wortley Montagu explained her conviction, after reading *Gulliver's Travels*, that "if there was a commonwealth of rational horses (as Doctor Swift has supposed), it would be an established maxim among them that a mare could not be taught to pace." Later still, in a poem published in *The Gentleman's Magazine* (1771) to which the scholar Roger Gilbert has called attention, an anonymous literary lady complained of "Mr. Pope's characters of women": "By custom doomed to folly, sloth, and ease, / No wonder Pope such female triflers sees; / But, would the satirist confess the truth, / Nothing so like as male and female youth." But more frequently women's opinions were like those of the poet Anne Finch, who contrasted the "happy . . . race of men" with the sadness of female "ciphers," to lament the fact that "since the Fall (by our seducement wrought) / Ours is the greater loss as ours the greater fault." Finally, conservative writers like Mrs. Chapone, Mrs. Trimmer, and Mrs. Barbauld accepted the view that their own literary success was an aberration: Hannah More advised girls to "aspire only to those virtues that are *peculiar to your sex*; follow your natural modesty, and think it your greatest commendation not to be talked of one way or another."

Yet even Hannah More changed her mind as the eighteenth century progressed, writing in 1799 that women's potential is unknown, for their minds have been as "stunted and cramped" as the "crippled" feet of Chinese women. In an age that equated reason with virtue, it was a protest against female miseducation that motivated and shaped a new form of writing. Proposals to reform women's morals and manners were, to be sure, based on the earlier arguments of Anna von Schurman, whose *The Learned Maid; or, Whether a Maid May Be a Scholar* was translated into English in 1659, and Bathsua Pell (Mrs. Makin), who published an essay to revive

the *Ancient Education of Gentlewomen* in 1673. From Mary Astell to Lady Mary Wortley Montagu and Catharine Macaulay, the foundation was laid for the radical vindication of women's rights that Mary Wollstonecraft published in 1792. In the crucible of revolutionary idealism associated with the French and the American revolutions, Wollstonecraft made the connection between the ideals of fraternity and those of sorority, much as Abigail Adams, wife of John Adams, did in letters that admonished her husband to "remember the ladies," for they were "determined to foment a rebellion" and refused to be "bound by any laws in which we have no voice, or representation" (1776). In addition, Adams's compatriot Judith Sargent Murray produced a polemical tract against female miseducation, while one woman of letters, Helen Maria Williams, who witnessed the French Revolution firsthand during what became an extended sojourn in France, published influential and largely sympathetic accounts in *Letters Written in France in the Summer of 1790*, a work which earned her many admirers and, later, many detractors.

Like the polemicists, female poets both participated in and diverged from the literary conventions and genres established by their male contemporaries. Aphra Behn used the sexual license of the Restoration to satirize male impotence rather than female debauchery, while Anne Finch, who composed in all the conventional Augustan forms (song, satire, fable, tragedy), frequently resisted the closure of the heroic couplet in her verse and rejected the prevailing political didacticism for a more personal observation of nature. Katherine Philips's poems on the pleasures of female friendship are no less marked by her gender than Lady Chudleigh's bitter attack on marriage in *To the Ladies*. In a quite different mode, Anne Bradstreet placed her Puritan spiritual meditations in a domestic and maternal context, and Phillis Wheatley presented her decidedly pious poems in terms of her experience as a slave. On both sides of the Atlantic, then, women poets both used and subverted the literary traditions they inherited from an overwhelmingly male-dominated literary history.

Though the classical forms and subjects of eighteenth-century verse were not always suited to an exploration of women's lives, the increasingly popular prose narratives of this period were ideal for such a project. At the end of the seventeenth and the beginning of the eighteenth century, narratives like Behn's *Oroonoko*, Manley's *The Adventures of Rivella* (1714), and Haywood's *Love in Excess* (1719–20) combined romantic intrigue with adventure plots and achieved instant success; *Love in Excess*, for example, became the most popular novel in England besides *Robinson Crusoe*. Later, nonfictional prose included moralizing tracts, conduct books, and personal essays along with collections of letters; the letters of aristocrats like Lady Russell and Mrs. Delaunay, for instance, were as popular as Hester Thrale's account of Dr. Johnson's life. The writers in this last group elevated social and literary gossip into a suitable subject of analysis, and as the critic Ian Watt has explained, it was only a small step from such minute accounts of authentic experience to the production of what purported to be such an account. In addition, the realistic mode allowed female authors to record the domestic experiences of women, who were doubtless also encouraged to write in this mode by the fact that the conventional identification of the speaking subject as a male in poetry did not hold true in eighteenth-century fiction.

In other words, the significance of the female narrators invented by Defoe (in *Moll Flanders*, 1722, or *Roxana*, 1724) and Richardson (in *Pamela* or *Clarissa*) would not have been lost on women writers. Richardson, who presented his novels as collections of letters, and Defoe, who presented his as autobiographies, were fictionalizing genres already popular with women readers and writers. Richardson, in particular, involved a circle of female friends in his subtle analyses of emotional reactions, going so far as to send a copy of *Pamela* to a friend's daughters with interleaved pages for their corrections. Empowered by the extraordinary popularity of these books, especially with women readers, women writers began to produce their

own heroines in novels of manners and Gothic romances. With the publication of commercially successful novels like Frances (Fanny) Burney's *Evelina* (1778), Susanna Rowson's *Charlotte Temple* (1791), and Ann Radcliffe's *The Mysteries of Udolpho* (1794), the female imagination had found the forms and the themes that would sustain it for another, even more productive century. Often just as popular, the verse of Radcliffe's poetic contemporaries—Anna Letitia Barbauld, Charlotte Smith, Joanna Baillie, and Mary Robinson—exhibited a new sensibility in poetry at the end of the eighteenth century, one that literary historians associate with the rise of Romanticism. Expressing personal emotion, describing the beauty of the natural world, returning to the sonnet form, and displaying a fascination with the specificity of ordinary experiences, these writers influenced and were influenced by such male contemporaries as William Wordsworth and William Hazlitt, with whom they entered into an implicit dialogue.

As Virginia Woolf understood, the seventeenth century inaugurated a new age of female creativity. Literary women like Sarah Egerton were determined to reject the strictures of male contemporaries and to keep on writing: "My daring pen will bolder sallies make," she declared, "And like myself, an unchecked freedom take." No monolithic voice emerges from the compositions of Egerton's diverse contemporaries and descendants. Tonal differences distinguish the more licentious productions of Delarivier Manley and Eliza Haywood from the more respectable, domestic writings of Frances Burney; seventeenth-century female poets may have found it more difficult to find an audience than did eighteenth-century women novelists; the apparently humble apologies of Anne Bradstreet and Anne Finch contrast with the witty satires of Lady Mary Wortley Montagu. Obviously, too, the attacks against slavery mounted by an English writer like Aphra Behn cannot be conflated with those composed by Americans reacting to institutionalized slavery close at hand. However, by the middle of the eighteenth century, the female imagination had come into its own, a fact evidenced by some notable efforts to justify and commemorate a feminine canon. In 1748, Thomas Seward, the father of the poet Anna Seward, published *The Female Right to Literature*; in 1752, George Ballard compiled *Memoirs of Several Ladies of Great Britain who have been Celebrated for their Writings*; and in 1755, George Colman and Bonnell Thornton edited *Poems by Eminent Ladies*, an anthology in two volumes meant as "standing proof that great abilities are not confined to the men, and that genius often glows with equal warmth, and perhaps with more delicacy, in the breast of a female." No wonder, then, that by Queen Anne's reign Woolf's artistic heroine, Orlando, "was apt to think of poetry when she should have been thinking of taffeta." Although "there was something in the sneer of Mr. Pope, in the condescension of Mr. Addison . . . which took away her relish for the society of wits," Orlando creates a salon and discovers the pleasures of writing as a woman.

ANNE BRADSTREET

1612–1672

When she arrived in America in 1630, Anne Bradstreet later remembered, "I found a new world and new manners, at which my heart rose. But," she added, "after I was convinced it was the way of God, I submitted to it and joined to the church at Boston." Combining a rebellious spirit with the scrupulousness of conscience fostered by the Puritan community to which she belonged, her statement reveals both the independence and the integrity that characterized this woman whose *The Tenth Muse Lately Sprung Up in America* was to become the first

collection of verse produced in the New World and, according to contemporary booksellers, one of the "most vendible"—i.e., one of the most salable—volumes in seventeenth-century London. Born in England, Bradstreet was raised in luxurious surroundings on the estates of the earl of Lincoln, where her father, Thomas Dudley, managed the nobleman's property. Both her parents were well born and well bred; she herself was educated by private tutors and was evidently quite early given access to the earl's extensive library. In 1628, at the age of sixteen, she married Simon Bradstreet, a cultivated Cambridge graduate nine years her senior, who had also worked as the earl's steward. Her life in England would seem to have been one of easy elegance so that she might well, in that year, have looked forward to a comfortable and civilized future.

Besides being humane and genteel, however, the Dudley family were devout Puritans, for whom life's trials symbolized God's intention to educate the soul. As a child of six or seven, Bradstreet recalled in a memoir, "I began to make conscience of my ways," confessing that "as I grew up to be about 14 or 15, I found my heart more carnal, and sitting loose from God." Just before her marriage, she therefore continued, "the Lord laid His hand sore upon me and smote me with the smallpox." Even before her arrival in Puritan New England, then, she felt she had experienced considerable "affliction," and she had learned to see the world as a text in which the divine will was inscribed. Still, nothing in her English girlhood could have entirely prepared this disciplined young woman for the hardships of the wilderness outpost to which the whole Dudley family, including the recently married Bradstreets, journeyed in 1630, when Anne was eighteen. Like the other Massachusetts colonists, they had come to escape the political and religious persecutions to which Puritans were subject in the old country, and though they were of higher rank than most—indeed, both Bradstreet's father and her husband were to become governors of Massachusetts—they had to confront the same rigors that troubled all the settlers: famine and fever, severe winters and scorching summers, a savage coast and a mysterious new land that stretched, it must have seemed, indefinitely off to the west.

For the Dudleys and the Bradstreets, as for the other colonists, there was only one way to survive such difficulties with sanity and with what the Puritans called "grace": one clung to God and to the Bible that was his word, one ceaselessly examined experience to interpret its theological message, and one redefined life as a passionate pilgrimage to a better life after death. Inevitably, however, in defending themselves with such religious intensity against the dangers of the New World, the settlers became fiercely doctrinaire, and their righteously reiterated dogmas had some especially problematic implications for women. By God's will, the Puritans felt, woman was created as man's helpmate and subordinate; thus a good wife must be submissive and self-abnegating, renouncing what would seem to be egotistical ambitions and desires for intellectual self-advancement or self-fulfillment. Indeed, such desires were often seen as potentially dangerous. In 1645, John Winthrop, then the governor of the colony, wrote sorrowfully about "a godly young woman," who had gone mad by "giving herself wholly to reading and writing, and written many books." Less than a decade earlier, moreover, in 1637 and 1638, Winthrop's election as governor had facilitated the trial, imprisonment, and banishment of the unorthodox Anne Hutchinson, who was accused of "traducing the ministers and their ministry" by preaching her own interpretations of Puritan theology.

Given such strictures against female ambition, it is no wonder that, so far as biographers can tell, Bradstreet never attempted to publish her poetry in her own lifetime. Rather, in 1650 her brother-in-law, John Woodbridge, arranged without her knowledge (or so he claimed) to have *The Tenth Muse* printed in London. When he did so he wrote a careful foreword, explaining that her verse was "the work of a woman, honoured and esteemed where she lives, for . . . her exact dili-

gence in her place, and discreet managing of her family occasions, and . . . these poems are but the fruit of some few hours, curtailed from her sleep and other refreshments." And in fact, at this point, Bradstreet was the diligent mother of a growing family—she eventually had eight children—as well as the devoted wife of an increasingly prosperous settler. The poems collected in *The Tenth Muse*, moreover, betray little overt rebellion against such a lot; although largely written before she was thirty, they do show considerable learning and literary ambition. Bradstreet had obviously studied the works of Sir Walter Raleigh and Sir Philip Sidney with care, and she was deeply influenced by Joshua Sylvester's translation of Guillaume du Bartas's *La Septmaine du Creation*, a compendious poem that appeared in English as *The Divine Weeks and Works* and which, in Bradstreet's own words, was marked by a mastery of "natural philosophy . . . grave divinity . . . high astronomy . . . anatomy . . . music and state policy." But, perhaps precisely because their composition had been so consciously scholarly and their author was so decorous, poems like *The Humours*, *The Ages of Man*, and *The Four Monarchies* read like studiously versified notes rather than personal utterances.

Even in the 1650 edition of *The Tenth Muse*, though, we can discern, if not a rebellion against woman's domestic "place," a rising of the heart against female intellectual subordination. *The Prologue*, for instance, claims to be the product of a "foolish, broken, blemished Muse," a talent "made . . . irreparable" by nature, for "men can do best, and women know it well." But at the same time, the poet allows herself a flash of anger. "I am obnoxious to each carping tongue / Who says my hand a needle better fits," she observes tartly, adding that "if what I do prove well, it won't advance, / They'll say it's stolen, or else it was by chance." The modesty of the poem's conclusion, in which Bradstreet renounces what would be an artist's natural desire to be crowned with the laurel or bay wreath of Apollo that traditionally announced a poet's success ("Give thyme or parsley wreath, I ask no bays"), can be seen as sardonic. Similarly, her fine elegy *In Honour of That High and Mighty Princess Queen Elizabeth of Happy Memory* may seem at first like a conventional celebration of royalty, full of rhetorical flourishes and elegant compliments. But again, a vein of feminist anger embedded in the work surfaces when the poet declares, "Nay masculines, you have thus taxed us long, / But she, though dead, will vindicate our wrong. / Let such as say our sex is void of reason, / Know 'tis a slander now but once was treason." Clearly this diligent wife and mother knew her own worth, and in the "few hours, curtailed from her sleep and other refreshment" when she ostensibly wrote her poems, she confronted her role as domestic helpmate with a sharp wit.

Ultimately, however, Bradstreet's situation as wife and mother was to prove not an obstacle to creativity but an inspiration, for the poems and prose meditations she wrote after the 1650 publication of *The Tenth Muse* depended heavily on images and metaphors drawn from her life as a woman. Her verses to her husband and children, her *Meditations Divine and Moral*, and her famous *Upon the Burning of Our House* all show the ways in which, as she matured into "Mistress Anne Bradstreet," a powerful matron and patroness of the Massachusetts Bay Colony, the domestic and the theological merged and glowed in her mind, even God himself coming to be seen (in the *Meditations*) as a nursing mother or a "prudent mother" so that the converse of such a proposition might also be true: the nursing mother or the "prudent mother" might be considered analogous to God.

Anne Bradstreet died in 1672, after decades of intermittent "affliction" that she sought, in characteristic Puritan fashion, to transform into a divine education; the second edition of *The Tenth Muse*, containing numerous corrections and additions to the 1650 volume, was not published until six years later. As time went by, her reputation declined, so that by the nineteenth century, critics of American literature were defining her achievement as "a pitiful indication of the literary poverty of the days and land in which it was popular." Still, over the years, poets from the

seventeenth-century writer Edward Taylor to the twentieth-century artists Conrad Aiken and John Berryman have rendered her respect in their various ways, with Berryman's *Homage to Mistress Anne Bradstreet* constituting a major acknowledgment of her genius. For after all, as Adrienne Rich has argued, "to have written . . . the first good poems in America, while rearing eight children, lying frequently sick, keeping house at the edge of the wilderness, was to have managed a poet's range and extension within confines as severe as any American poet has confronted."

The Prologue

1

To sing of wars, of captains, and of kings,
Of cities founded, commonwealths begun,
For my mean[1] pen are too superior things:
Or how they all or each their dates have run,[2]
Let poets and historians set these forth; 5
My obscure lines shall not so dim their worth.

2

But when my wondering eyes and envious heart
Great Bartas'[3] sugared lines do but read o'er,
Fool I do grudge the Muses did not part
'Twixt him and me that overfluent store;[4] 10
A Bartas can do what a Bartas will,
But simple I according to my skill.[5]

3

From schoolboy's tongue no rhetoric we expect,
Nor yet a sweet consort[6] from broken strings,
Nor perfect beauty where's a main defect: 15
My foolish, broken, blemished Muse so sings,
And this to mend, alas, no art is able,
'Cause nature made it so irreparable.

4

Nor can I, like that fluent sweet-tongued Greek,
Who lisped at first,[7] in future times speak plain. 20
By art he gladly found what he did seek,
A full requital of his striving pain.
Art can do much, but this maxim's most sure:
A weak or wounded brain admits no cure.

1. Humble lowly.
2. I.e., how their sequences of events fell.
3. Guillaume du Bartas (1544–1590), author of *The Divine Weeks*, an epic poem on Christian history.
4. I.e., I foolishly regret that the Muses (nine Greek goddesses of the arts, learning, and inspiration) did not equally divide their overflowing wealth between us both.
5. I.e., a simple person like me can only do what she has the ability to do. "Will": desires.
6. Harmony, as in music. "Rhetoric": eloquent language.
7. Demosthenes (c. 383–322 B.C.), a Greek orator who overcame a speech defect by placing pebbles in his mouth and addressing the sea.

5

I am obnoxious to each carping[8] tongue 25
Who says my hand a needle better fits;
A poet's pen all scorn I should thus wrong,[9]
For such despite they cast on female wits;[1]
If what I do prove well, it won't advance,[2]
They'll say it's stolen, or else it was by chance. 30

6

But sure the antique[3] Greeks were far more mild,
Else of our sex why feignéd they those nine,[4]
And poesy made Calliope's[5] own child?
So 'mongst the rest they placed the arts divine.
But this weak knot they[6] will full soon untie: 35
The Greeks did nought but play the fools and lie.[7]

7

Let Greeks be Greeks, and women what they are,
Men have precedency and still excel.
It is but vain unjustly[8] to wage war;
Men can do best, and women know it well. 40
Preeminence in all and each is yours;
Yet grant some small acknowledgement of ours.

8

And oh ye highflown quills that soar the skies,
And ever with your prey[9] still catch your praise,
If e'er you deign[1] these lowly lines your eyes, 45
Give thyme or parsley wreath, I ask no bays;[2]
This mean and unrefinéd ore of mine
Will make your glistering gold but more to shine.

 1650

In Honor of That High and Mighty Princess Queen Elizabeth[1] of Happy Memory

The Proem[2]

Although, great Queen, thou now in silence lie
Yet thy loud herald[3] Fame doth to the sky
Thy wondrous worth proclaim in every clime,
And so hath vowed while there is world or time.
So great's thy glory and thine excellence, 5

8. Complaining. "Obnoxious": vulnerable, exposed
to.
9. I.e., all scornfully say abuse.
1. Intelligence. "Despite": contempt.
2. Be recognized, praised. "Prove": turn out.
3. Ancient.
4. I.e., why did they invent the Muses?
5. The Muse of epic poetry.
6. The speaker's critics. "Knot": argument.
7. This line anticipates what the critics will say.

8. On false premises.
9. Metaphorically, the poets' works. "Quills": pens
made from birds' feathers; by association, poets.
1. Condescend to give.
2. Laurel leaves, associated with great poets.
1. Elizabeth Tudor (1533–1603, queen of England
1558–1603).
2. Brief introductory verse.
3. Royal crier or messenger.

The sound thereof rapts[4] every human sense,
That men account it no impiety
To say thou wert a fleshly deity.
Thousands bring offerings (though out of date)
Thy world of honors to accumulate; 10
'Mongst hundred hecatombs[5] of roaring verse,
Mine bleating stands before thy royal hearse.[6]
Thou never diest nor canst thou now disdain
T'accept the tribute of a loyal brain.
Thy clemency did erst[7] esteem as much 15
The acclamations of the poor as rich,
Which makes me deem my rudeness is no wrong,
Though I resound thy praises 'mongst the throng.

The Poem

No Phoenix[8] pen, nor Spenser's poetry,
No Speed's nor Camden's learned history, 20
Eliza's works, wars, praise, can e'er compact;[9]
The world's the theatre where she did act.
No memories nor volumes can contain
The 'leven Olympiads[1] of her happy reign,
Who was so good, so just, so learned, so wise, 25
From all the kings on earth she won the prize.
Nor say I more than duly is her due,
Millions will testify that this is true.
She hath wiped off th' aspersion of her sex,
That women wisdom lack to play the rex.[2] 30
Spain's monarch says not so, nor yet his host;[3]
She taught them better manners, to their cost.
The Salic law[4] in force now had not been,
If France had ever hoped for such a queen.
But can you, doctors,[5] now this point dispute, 35
She's argument enough to make you mute.
Since first the Sun did run his ne'er run race,
And earth had, once a year, a new old face,
Since time was time, and unmanly man,
Come show me such a phoenix if you can 40
Was ever people better ruled than hers?
Was ever land more happy freed from stirs?[6]
Did ever wealth in England more abound?

4. Holds the complete attention of.
5. Honorary tributes (literally, sacrificial slaughter of animals).
6. Frame placed over a coffin or tomb for holding candles and epitaphs.
7. Formerly, at one time "Clemency": leniency.
8. A mythical bird that immolates itself and is then reborn from its own ashes. Bradstreet associates the bird with the immortality of both great poetry and Elizabeth's name. "No": neither.
9. Condense, summarize. The allusions are to Edmund Spenser (1552–1599), major English poet; John Speed (1542–1629), English historian and mapmaker; and William Camden (1551–1623), English historian.

1. The four-year period between Olympic games in ancient Greece; thus Elizabeth reigned for forty-four years.
2. King (Latin).
3. Army. Philip II (1527–1598) was king of Spain, Portugal, and the Netherlands; under his rule the Spanish Armada, a fleet of warships, attempted to invade England and was defeated in 1588.
4. Forbade women to inherit land, used in France and Spain to prevent the ascension of female monarchs.
5. Scholars.
6. Conflicts, wars.

Her victories in foreign coasts resound;
Ships more invincible than Spain's, her foe, 45
She wracked, she sacked,[7] she sunk his Armado;
Her stately troops advanced to Lisbon's wall,
Don Anthony in's right there to install.
She frankly helped Frank's brave distresséd king;[8]
The states united now her fame do sing. 50
She their protectrix was; they well do know
Unto our dread virago,[9] what they owe,
Her nobles sacrificed their noble blood,
Nor men nor coin she spared to do them good.
The rude untaméd Irish she did quell; 55
Before her picture the proud Tyrone[1] fell.
Had ever prince such counsellors as she?
Herself Minerva[2] caused them so to be.
Such captains and such soldiers never seen,
As were the subjects of our Pallas[3] queen. 60
Her seamen though all straits the world did round;
Terra incognita[4] might know the sound.
Her Drake came laden home with Spanish gold;
Her Essex took Cadiz, their Herculean[5] hold.
But time would fail me, so my tongue would too, 65
To tell of half she did, or she could do.
Semiramis[6] to her is but obscure,
More infamy than fame she did procure.
She build her glory but on Babel's walls,[7]
World's wonder for a while, but yet it falls. 70
Fierce Tomris[8] (Cyrus' headsman) Scythians' queen,
Had put her harness off, had she but seen
Our Amazon in th' Camp of Tilbury,[9]
Judging all valor and all majesty
Within that princess to have residence, 75
And prostrate yielded to her excellence,
Dido,[1] first foundress of proud Carthage walls
(Who living consummates her funerals),
A great Eliza, but compared with ours,
How vanisheth her glory, wealth, and powers. 80

7. Looted. "Wracked": destroyed.
8. The references are, first to Philip II's unsuccessful rival for the throne of Portugal, supported by England and France (Lisbon is the capital city of Portugal). Then, to Henri IV, who assumed the throne of France in 1589 and was aided generously with money and arms by Elizabeth in fighting the Catholic rebels backed by Spain.
9. "Protectrix": female protector. A strong, courageous woman.
1. Nobleman who led the Irish rebellion against English rule, assisted by the Spanish; defeated at Kinsale.
2. Roman name for the Greek goddess of wisdom, Athena, protectress of the city of Athens.
3. Another name for Athena.
4. "Unknown land" (Latin).
5. Strong, mighty; from the Greek hero Hercules. Sir Francis Drake (1540–1596), English admiral and ex-
plorer. "Essex": reference to Robert Devereux, second earl of Essex, English soldier and statesman. Cádiz is a city in southern Spain.
6. Legendary Assyrian queen, noted for her wisdom and beauty.
7. According to Genesis 11, a great tower was built in the ancient city of Babylon. To punish the builders' presumption, God confused their languages and scattered them.
8. She executed Cyrus, founder of the Persian Empire.
9. Site of Elizabeth's famous speech to her troops (see above, p. 29); "Amazon": member of a mythical race of women possessed of great strength and courage.
1. Queen of Carthage, an ancient city in North Africa; her abandonment by her lover Aeneas and subsequent self-immolation on her own funeral pyre are recounted in Virgil's epic *The Aeneid*.

Profuse, proud Cleopatra,[2] whose wrong name,
Instead of glory, proved her country's shame,
Of her what worth in stories to be seen,
But that she was a rich Egyptian queen.
Zenobya,[3] potent empress of the East, 85
And of all these without compare the best,
Whom none but great Aurelius[4] could quell;
Yet for our Queen is no fit parallel.
She was a phoenix queen, so shall she be,
Her ashes not revived, more phoenix she. 90
Her personal perfections, who would tell
Must dip his pen in th' Heleconian well,[5]
Which I may not; my pride doth but aspire
To read what others write and so admire.
Now say, have women worth? or have they none? 95
Or had they some, but with our Queen is't gone?
Nay masculines, you have thus taxed[6] us long,
But she, though dead, will vindicate our wrong.
Let such as say our sex is void of reason
Know 'tis a slander now but once was treason. 100
But happy England which had such a queen;
Yea happy, happy, had those days still been.
But happiness lies in the higher sphere,
Then wonder not Eliza moves not here.
Full fraught with honor, riches and with days 105
She set, she set, like Titan in his rays.
No more shall rise or set so glorious sun
Until the heaven's great revolution.[7]
If then new things their old forms shall retain,
Eliza shall rule Albion[8] once again. 110

Her Epitaph

Here sleeps the queen, this is the royal bed
Of th' damask rose, sprung from the white and red,[9]
Whose sweet perfume fills the all-filling air.
This rose is withered, once so lovely fair.
On neither tree did grow such rose before, 115
The greater was our gain, our loss the more.

Another

Here lies the pride of queens, pattern of kings,
So blaze[1] it, Fame, here's feathers for thy wings
Here lies the envied, yet unparalleled prince,

2. Queen of Egypt and mistress of Roman statesmen Julius Caesar and Mark Antony (69–30 B.C.). Her name means "glory to the father" (or "fatherland").
3. Queen of Palmyra (A.D. 267–72), an ancient city in Syria.
4. I.e., Aurelian, emperor of Rome (A.D. 161–80), who captured Zenobia and destroyed her kingdom.
5. Well found on Helicon, mountain of poetic inspiration in Greek myth.
6. Accused.
7. The Day of Judgment.
8. Britain.
9. The colors of the two houses in the War of the Roses (1455–85) "Damask rose": a fragrant red rose symbolic of the Tudors' union of the warring houses of York and Lancaster.
1. Blazon, proclaim.

Whose living virtues speak (though dead long since). 120
If many worlds, as that fantastic framed,[2]
In every one be her great glory famed.

1650

The Author to Her Book[1]

Thou ill-formed offspring of my feeble brain,
Who after birth didst by my side remain,
Till snatched from thence by friends, less wise than true,
Who thee abroad, exposed to public view,
Made thee in rags, halting to th' press to trudge, 5
Where errors were not lessened (all may judge).
At thy return my blushing was not small,
My rambling brat (in print) should mother call,
I cast thee by as one unfit for light,
Thy visage was so irksome in my sight; 10
Yet being mine own, at length affection would
Thy blemishes amend, if so I could:
I washed thy face, but more defects I saw,
And rubbing off a spot still made a flaw.
I stretched thy joints to make thee even feet,[2] 15
Yet still thou run'st more hobbling than is meet;[3]
In better dress to trim thee was my mind,
But nought save homespun cloth i' th' house I find.
In this array 'mongst vulgars[4] may'st thou roam.
In critic's hands beware thou dost not come, 20
And take thy way where yet thou art not known
If for thy father asked, say thou hadst none;
And for thy mother, she alas is poor,
Which caused her thus to send thee out of door.

1678

To My Dear and Loving Husband

If ever two were one, then surely we.
If ever man were loved by wife, then thee;
If ever wife was happy in a man,
Compare with me ye women if you can.
I prize thy love more than whole mines of gold, 5
Or all the riches that the East doth hold.
My love is such that rivers cannot quench,

2. I.e., as that visionary or demented person theo-
rized. This may be a reference to the Polish astronomer
Nicolaus Copernicus (1473–1543), who challenged
the Ptolemaic model of the universe, which placed the
earth at the center, by asserting that the earth revolved
around the sun along with the other planets.
1. Bradstreet's volume of poems *The Tenth Muse* was

published in 1650 without her knowledge; this poem
was probably written while she was preparing a revised
second edition for publication.
2. I.e., metrical feet; thus, to smooth out the meter of
the lines.
3. Appropriate, decorous.
4. Common people.

Nor ought but love from thee, give recompense.[1]
Thy love is such I can no way repay.
The heavens reward thee manifold[2] I pray. 10
Then while we live, in love let's so persevere,
That when we live no more, we may live ever.

1678

A Letter to Her Husband, Absent upon Public Employment

My head, my heart, mine eyes, my life, nay, more,
My joy, my magazine[1] of earthly store,
If two be one, as surely thou and I,
How stayest thou there, whilst I at Ipswich[2] lie?
So many steps, head from the heart to sever, 5
If but a neck, soon should we be together.
I, like the Earth this season, mourn in black,
My Sun is gone so far in's zodiac,[3]
Whom whilst I 'joyed, nor storms, nor frost I felt,
His warmth such frigid colds did cause to melt. 10
My chilled limbs now numbed lie forlorn:
Return, return, sweet Sol, from Capricorn;[4]
In this dead time, alas, what can I more
Than view those fruits which through thy heat I bore?
Which sweet contentment yield me for a space, 15
True living pictures of their father's face.
O strange effect! now thou art southward gone,
I weary grow the tedious day so long;
But when thou northward to me shalt return,
I wish my Sun may never set, but burn 20
Within the Cancer[5] of my glowing breast,
The welcome house of him my dearest guest.
Where ever, ever stay, and go not thence,
Till nature's sad decree shall call thee hence;
Flesh of thy flesh, bone of thy bone, 25
I here, thou there, yet both but one.

1678

To Her Father with Some Verses

Most truly honored, and as truly dear,
If worth in me or ought I do appear,
Who can of right better demand the same

1. Can adequately return.
2. Many times.
1. Warehouse.
2. Town in Massachusetts, north of Boston.
3. The path of the sun and planets through the heav-
ens. "My Sun": her husband.

4. The tenth sign of the zodiac, which rises in winter.
"Sol": the sun
5. The fourth sign of the zodiac, which rises in sum-
mer.

Than may your worthy self from whom it came?
The principal[1] might yield a greater sum, 5
Yet handled ill, amounts but to this crumb;
My stock's so small I know not how to pay,
My bond remains in force unto this day:[2]
Yet for part payment take this simple mite,[3]
Where nothing's to be had, kings loose their right. 10
Such is my debt I may not say forgive,
But as I can, I'll pay it while I live;
Such is my bond, none can discharge but I,
Yet paying is not paid until I die.

 1678

For Deliverance from a Fever

When sorrows had begirt me round,
And pains within and out,
When in my flesh no part was found,[1]
Then didst Thou rid me out.[2]
My burning flesh in sweat did boil, 5
My aching head did break,
From side to side for ease I toil,
So faint I could not speak.
Beclouded was my soul with fear
Of Thy displeasure sore, 10
Nor could I read my evidence
Which oft I read before.
"Hide not Thy face from me!" I cried,
"From burnings keep my soul.
Thou know'st my heart, and hast me tried; 15
I on Thy mercies roll."
"O heal my soul," Thou know'st I said,
"Though flesh consume to nought,
What though in dust it shall be laid,
To glory 't shall be brought." 20
Thou heard'st, Thy rod Thou didst remove
And spared my body frail,
Thou show'st to me Thy tender love,
My heart no more might quail
O, praises to my mighty God, 25
Praise to my Lord, I say,
Who hath redeemed my soul from pit,
Praises to Him for aye.[3]

 1867

1. Sum of money that accrues interest. 1. I.e., no healthy part.
2. I.e., I am still indebted to you. 2. Rid me of illness. "Thou": God.
3. Small contribution that is all one can afford. 3. Always. "Pit": hell.

From Meditations Divine and Moral

6

The finest bread hath the least bran, the purest honey the least wax, and the sincerest Christian the least self-love.

8

Downy beds make drowsy persons, but hard lodging keeps the eyes open; a prosperous state makes a secure Christian, but adversity makes him consider.

9

Sweet words are like honey: a little may refresh, but too much gluts the stomach.

10

Diverse children have their different natures: some are like flesh[1] which nothing but salt will keep from putrefaction, some again like tender fruits that are best preserved with sugar. Those parents are wise that can fit their nurture according to their nature.

12

Authority without wisdom is like a heavy axe without an edge: fitter to bruise than polish.

16

That house which is not often swept makes the cleanly inhabitant soon loathe it, and that heart which is not continually purifying itself is no fit temple for the spirit of God to dwell in.

19

Corn,[2] till it have passed through the mill and been ground to powder, is not fit for bread. God so deals with his servants: he grinds them with grief and pain till they turn to dust, and then are they fit manchet[3] for his mansion.

38

Some children are hardly weaned; although the teat be rubbed with wormwood[4] or mustard, they will either wipe it off, or else suck down sweet and bitter together. So is it with some Christians: let God embitter all the sweets of this life, that so they might feed upon more substantial food, yet they are so childishly sottish[5] that they are still hugging and sucking these empty breasts that God is forced to hedge up their way with thorns or lay affliction on their loins that so they might shake hands with the world, before it bid them farewell.

39

A prudent mother will not clothe her little child with a long and cumbersome garment; she easily forsees what events it is like to produce, at the best, but falls and bruises or perhaps somewhat worse. Much more will the all-wise God proportion His dispensations according to the stature and strength of the person He bestows them on. Large endowments of honor, wealth, or a healthful

1. Meat.
2. Grain.
3. White bread made from the finest flour.

4. A bitter extract placed on a mother's breast ("teat"), to wean her child from breast-feeding.
5. Both drunken and addicted to drink.

body would quite overthrow some weak Christian; therefore God cuts their garments short to keep them in such a trim that they might run the ways of His commandment.

<div align="right">1867</div>

Here Follows Some Verses upon the Burning of Our House July 10th, 1666. Copied out of a Loose Paper

In silent night when rest I took
For sorrow near I did not look
I wakened was with thund'ring noise
And piteous shrieks of dreadful voice.
That fearful sound of "Fire!" and "Fire!" 5
Let no man know is my desire.
I, starting up, the light did spy,
And to my God my heart did cry
To strengthen me in my distress
And not to leave me succorless.[1] 10
Then, coming out, beheld a space[2]
The flame consume my dwelling place.
And when I could no longer look,
I blest His name that gave and took,
That laid my goods now in the dust. 15
Yea, so it was, and so 'twas just.
It was His own, it was not mine,
Far be it that I should repine;[3]
He might of all justly bereft[4]
But yet sufficient for us left. 20
When by the ruins oft I passed
My sorrowing eyes aside did cast,
And here and there the places spy
Where oft I sat and long did lie:
Here stood that trunk, and there that chest, 25
There lay that store I counted best.
My pleasant things in ashes lie,
And them behold no more shall I.
Under thy roof no guest shall sit,
Nor at thy table eat a bit. 30
No pleasant tale shall e'er be told,
Nor things recounted done of old.
No candle e'er shall shine in thee,
Nor bridegroom's voice e'er heard shall be.
In silence ever shall thou lie, 35
Adieu, Adieu, all's vanity.[5]
Then straight I 'gin my heart to chide,
And did thy wealth on earth abide?
Didst fix thy hope on mold'ring dust?

1. Helpless.
2. For a short period of time.
3. Complain.

4. I.e., he might have taken everything from us with good cause.
5. Empty, worthless.

The arm of flesh didst make thy trust? 40
Raise up thy thoughts above the sky
That dunghill mists away may fly.
Thou hast an house on high erect,
Framed by that mighty Architect,
With glory richly furnishéd, 45
Stands permanent though this be fled.
It's purchaséd and paid for too
By Him who hath enough to do.
A price so vast is is unknown
Yet by His gift is made thine own; 50
There's wealth enough, I need no more.
Farewell, my pelf,[6] farewell my store.
The world no longer let me love,
My hope and treasure lies above.

1867

6. Money, usually falsely gained.

MARGARET CAVENDISH, DUCHESS OF NEWCASTLE

1623–1673

"What a vision of loneliness and riot the thought of Margaret Cavendish brings to mind!" exclaimed Virginia Woolf in 1928. The author of "philosophical fancies" and scientific speculations, poems and plays, the woman who so bemused Woolf was born Margaret Lucas to an aristocratic Essex family where "all the brothers were valiant, and all the sisters virtuous," and although many at court disliked her for her shyness and eccentricity, she became a maid of honor to the queen. In 1645 she married William Cavendish, duke of Newcastle, a Royalist soldier with whom she lived on the Continent in poverty and exile during Cromwell's reign. After the Restoration, the couple returned to their English estate, where the childless duchess pursued her literary career with diligence. But although she published numerous books in her lifetime—including *Poems and Fancies* (1653), *Nature's Pictures Drawn by Fancie's Pencil* (1656), and *Plays Written by the thrice Noble, Illustrious and Excellent Princess, the Lady Marchioness of Newcastle* (1667)— most of Cavendish's contemporaries regarded her as a freak because of the oddity of her writings and the peculiarity of her dress. At a time when it was considered bold for women to produce even the tamest of compositions, "the crazy duchess" tried to combine Metaphysical poetry with scientific speculation, philosophical meditation with fanciful fantasizing. No wonder, then, that Dorothy Osborne, a seventeenth-century letter writer, believed "the poor woman is a little distracted, she could never have been so ridiculous else as to venture at writing books and in verse too."

Despite her undoubted strangeness, however, the duchess at her best produced some witty verse as well as some lively and thoughtful prose. Though her work was never as strong as the poetry of her American contemporary Anne Bradstreet, her imagery, like Bradstreet's, often drew on the realities of female life—fashion, cooking, housekeeping. In addition, her speculations on the meaning of femininity—in particular those dramatized in *Female Orations*—were unusually sophisticated in their acknowledgment of the complex problems posed by woman's cultural situa-

tion. Similarly, *The Poetess's Hasty Resolution* and *An Excuse for So Much Writ Upon My Verses* illuminate the anxieties authorship also instilled in Bradstreet. Clearly, Cavendish had scrutinized her own psychological reactions to the process of writing and used them to explore women's attitudes toward femininity and creativity.

The Poetess's Hasty Resolution

Reading my verses, I liked them so well,
Self-love did make my judgment to rebel.
Thinking them so good, I thought more to write;
Considering not how others would them like.
I writ so fast, I thought if I lived long, 5
A pyramid of fame to build thereon.
Reason observing which way I was bent,
Did stay my hand, and asked me what I meant;
Will you, said she, thus waste your time in vain,
On that which in the world small praise shall gain? 10
For shame leave off, said she, the Printer spare,
He'll lose by your ill poetry, I fear.
Besides the world hath already such a weight
Of useless books, as it is over fraught.[1]
Then pity take, do the world a good turn, 15
And all you write cast in the fire, and burn.
Angry I was, and Reason struck away,
When I did hear, what she to me did say.
Then all in haste I to the press it sent,
Fearing persuasion might my book prevent: 20
But now 'tis done, with grief repent do I,
Hang down my head with shame, blush, sigh, and cry.
Take pity, and my drooping spirits raise,
Wipe off my tears with handkerchiefs of praise.

 1653

An Excuse for So Much Writ upon My Verses

Condemn me not for making such a coil[2]
About my book, alas it is my child.
Just like a bird, when her young are in nest,
Goes in, and out, and hops, and takes no rest;
But when their young are fledged,[3] their heads out peep, 5
Lord what a chirping does the old one keep.
So I, for fear, my strengthless child should fall
Against a door, or stool, aloud I call,
Bid have a care of such a dangerous place:
Thus write I much, to hinder all disgrace. 10

 1653

1. Laden. 3. Feathered.
2. Turmoil, stir.

Female Orations

I

Ladies, gentlewomen, and other inferior women, but not less worthy I have been industrious to assemble you together, and wish I were so fortunate as to persuade you to make frequent assemblies, associations, and combinations amongst our sex, that we may unite in prudent counsels, to make ourselves as free, happy, and famous as men; whereas now we live and die as if we were produced from beasts, rather than from men; for men are happy, and we women are miserable; they possess all the ease, rest, pleasure, wealth, power, and fame; whereas women are restless with labor, easeless with pain, melancholy for want of pleasures, helpless for want of power, and die in oblivion, for want of fame. Nevertheless, men are so unconscionable and cruel against us that they endeavor to bar us of all sorts of liberty, and will not suffer us freely to associate amongst our own sex; but would fain bury us in their houses or beds, as in a grave. The truth is, we live like bats or owls, labor like beasts, and die like worms.

II

Ladies, gentlewomen, and other inferior women: The lady that spoke to you hath spoken wisely and eloquently, in expressing our unhappiness; but she hath not declared a remedy, or showed us a way to come out of our miseries; but, if she could or would be our guide, to lead us out of the labyrinth men have put us into, we should not only praise and admire her, but adore and worship her as our goddess: but alas! men, that are not only our tyrants but our devils, keep us in the hell of subjection, from whence I cannot perceive any redemption or getting out; we may complain and bewail our condition, yet that will not free us; we may murmur and rail against men, yet they regard not what we say. In short, our words to men are as empty sounds; our sighs, as puffs of winds; and our tears, as fruitless showers; and our power is so inconsiderable, that men laugh at our weakness.

III

Ladies, gentlewomen, and other inferior women: The former orations were exclamations against men, repining at their condition and mourning for our own; but we have no reason to speak against men, who are our admirers and lovers; they are our protectors, defenders, and maintainers; they admire our beauties, and love our persons; they protect us from injuries, defend us from dangers, are industrious for our subsistence, and provide for our children; they swim great voyages by sea, travel long journeys by land, to get us rarities and curiosities; they dig to the center of the earth for gold for us; they dive to the bottom of the sea for jewels for us; they build to the skies houses for us; they hunt, fowl, fish, plant, and reap for food for us. All which, we could not do ourselves; and yet we complain of men, as if they were our enemies, whenas[1] we could not possibly live without them, which shows we are as ungrateful as inconstant. But we have more reason to murmur against Nature, than against men, who hath made men more ingenious, witty,[2] and wise than women; more strong, industrious, and laborious than women; for women are witless and strengthless, and unprofitable creatures, did they not bear children.

1. While on the other hand. 2. Intelligent.

Wherefore, let us love men, praise men, and pray for men; for without men, we should be the most miserable creatures that Nature hath made or could make.

IV

Noble ladies, gentlewomen, and other inferior women: The former ora-toress says we are witless and strengthless; if so, it is that we neglect the one and make no use of the other, for strength is increased by exercise, and wit is lost for want of conversation. But to show men we are not so weak and foolish as the former oratoress doth express us to be, let us hawk, hunt, race, and do the like exercises that men have; and let us converse in camps,[3] courts, and cities; in schools, colleges, and courts of judicature; in taverns, brothels, and gaming houses; all of which will make our strength and wit known, both to men and to our own selves, for we are as ignorant of ourselves as men are of us. And how should we know ourselves, when we never made a trial of ourselves? Or how should men know us, when they never put us to the proof?[4] Wherefore my advice is, we should imitate men; so will our bodies and minds appear more masculine, and our power will increase by our actions.

V

Noble, honorable, and virtuous women: The former oration was to per-suade us to change the custom of our sex, which is a strange and unwise per-suasion, since we cannot change the nature of our sex, nor make ourselves men; and to have female bodies, and yet to act masculine parts, will be very preposterous and unnatural. In truth, we shall make ourselves like the defects of Nature, and be hermaphroditical,[5] neither perfect women, nor perfect men, but corrupt and imperfect creatures. Wherefore let me persuade you, since we cannot alter the nature of our persons, not to alter the course of our lives; but to rule so our lives and behaviors that we be acceptable and pleasing to God and men; which is, to be modest, chaste, temperate, humble, patient, and pious; also, be housewifely, cleanly, and of few words. All which will gain us praise from men and blessing from Heaven; love in this world and glory in the next.

VI

Worthy women: The former oratoress's oration endeavored to persuade us that it would not only be a reproach and disgrace, but unnatural, for women in their actions and behavior to imitate men: we may as well say it will be a re-proach, disgrace, and unnatural to imitate the gods, which imitation we are commanded both by the gods and their ministers; and shall we neglect the imitation of men, which is more easy and natural than the imitation of the gods? For how can terrestrial creatures imitate celestial deities? Yet one terres-trial may imitate another, although in different sorts of creatures. Wherefore, since all terrestrial imitations ought to ascend to the better and not to de-scend to the worse, women ought to imitate men, as being a degree in nature more perfect than they themselves; and all masculine women ought to be as much praised as effeminate men to be dispraised; for the one advances to per-fection, the other sinks to imperfection; that so, by our industry, we may come, at last, to equal men, both in perfection and power.

3. I.e., military camps.
4. Test.
5. Male and female within one body (from the name in Greek legend of the son of the gods Hermes and Aphrodite, who was joined, in one body, with a nymph).

VII

Noble ladies, honorable gentlewomen, and worthy female-commoners: The former oratoress's speech was to persuade us out of ourselves and to be that which Nature never intended us to be, to wit, masculine. But why should we desire to be masculine, since our own sex and condition is far the better? For if men have more courage, they have more danger; and if men have more strength, they have more labor than women have; if men are more eloquent in speech, women are more harmonious in voice; if men be more active, women are more graceful; if men have more liberty, women have more safety; for we never fight duels nor battles, nor do we go long travels or dangerous voyages; we labor not in building nor digging in mines, quarries, or pits, for metal, stone, or coals; neither do we waste or shorten our lives with university or scholastical studies, questions, and disputes; we burn not our faces with smiths' forges or chemists'[6] furnaces; and hundreds of other actions which men are employed in; for they would not only fade the fresh beauty, spoil the lovely features, and decay the youth of women, causing them to appear old, when they are young; but would break their small limbs, and destroy their tender lives. Wherefore women have no reason to complain against Nature or the god of Nature, for although the gifts are not the same as they have given to men, yet those gifts they have given to women are much better; for we women are much more favored by Nature than men, in giving us such beauties, features, shapes, graceful demeanor, and such insinuating and enticing attractives, that men are forced to admire us, love us, and be desirous of us; insomuch that rather than not have and enjoy us, they will deliver to our disposals their power, persons, and lives, enslaving themselves to our will and pleasures; also, we are their saints, whom they adore and worship; and what can we desire more than to be men's tyrants, destinies, and goddesses?

1662

6. Alchemists'.

JANE LEAD

1624–1704

A mystic and spiritual autobiographer, the visionary writer Jane Lead was born Jane Ward in Norfolk and educated "like other girls" until at the age of fifteen she heard a miraculous voice speaking to her amid Christmas festivities and resolved to lead a devotional life. When she was twenty-one, she married William Lead, a distant relative six years her senior, with whom she had four daughters. After his death, when she was forty-six, she renewed her commitment to mystical theology and to what she called "Spiritual Virginity." At around this time, moreover, she had the striking vision, excerpted here, of a female figure whom the critic Catherine Smith regards as "Lead's revision of Sophia, the Virgin Wisdom of God in esoteric theology and apocalyptic tradition."

Already a student of the works of the radical German theologian Jacob Boehme (1575–1624), Lead now became even more passionately mystical, and in 1674 she moved into the household of Dr. John Pordage, the leader of one of the many nonconformist congregations that were springing up in England around this time. In 1681, after Pordage's death, she began to publish her own spiritual writings, and in 1694, with the assistance of a young disciple, Dr. Francis Lee, she founded the

Philadelphia Society, a nonconformist group (like the Diggers and the Ranters) based on Boehme's teachings. Her books include *The Heavenly Cloud Now Breaking* (1681), *The Enochian Walks With God* (1694), and perhaps most important, the four-volume *A Fountain of Gardens, Watered by the Rivers of Divine Pleasure* (1697–1701). Although her works are primarily religious and she was not consciously a feminist, her writing was consistently energized by images of the magical woman within the soul who, she believed, would bring redemption to male and female spirits alike, and her metaphors of rebirth are distinctively feminine.

From A Fountain of Gardens[1]

[*The First Vision*]

The first vision that appeared to me was in the month of April, 1670, which was on this wise—

Being my lot at that time to visit a friend in a solitary country place, where I had great advantage of retirement, often frequenting lonely walks in a grove or wood, contemplating the happy state of the angelical world and how desirous I was to have my conversation there, my thoughts were much exercised upon Solomon's choice, which was to find out the noble stone of divine Wisdom;[2] for by acquainting myself with her, all desirable good in spiritual things would meet upon me. The report and fame that Solomon gave of Wisdom did much excite me to seek her favor and friendship; demurring in myself from whence she was descended, still questioning whether she was a distinct being from the Deity or no? Which while in this debate within my mind, there came upon me an overshadowing bright cloud, and in the midst of it the figure of a woman, most richly adorned with transparent gold, her hair hanging down, and her face as the terrible crystal for brightness, but her countenance was sweet and mild. At which sight I was somewhat amazed, but immediately this voice came, saying, "Behold, I am God's eternal Virgin Wisdom, whom thou hast been inquiring after; I am to unseal the treasures of God's deep wisdom unto thee, and will be as Rebecca[3] was unto Jacob, a true natural mother; for out of my womb thou shalt be brought forth after the manner of a spirit, conceived and born again; this thou shalt know by a new motion of life, stirring and giving a restlessness, till wisdom be born within the inward parts of thy soul. Now consider of my saying till I return to thee again."

This vision took great impression on me, yet I kept it for the present hid, but it operated so much upon me, as indeed I was incapable to converse with any mortals; which was taken notice of, that some extraordinary thing had happened, for the which I begged my friend's excuse and desired that she would give me the liberty to be much alone, and to walk in the silent woods, where I might contemplate what had so lately happened. Now after three days, sitting under a tree, the same figure in greater glory did appear, with a crown upon her

1. The full title is *A Fountain of Gardens, Watered by the Rivers of Divine Pleasure, and Springing Up in All the Variety of Spiritual Plants; Blown Up by the Pure Breath into a Paradise*.
2. The biblical king Solomon, noted for his wisdom, is here associated with the legendary philosopher's stone, which was reputed to change base metals into gold.
3. The mother of Jacob and his older twin Esau. She helped Jacob deceive his dying father, Isaac, into giving him the blessing that was promised to Esau (Genesis 27).

head, full of majesty, saying, "Behold me as thy mother, and know thou art to enter into covenant[4] to obey the new creation laws, that shall be revealed unto thee." Then did she hold out a golden book, with three[5] seals upon it, saying, "Herein lieth hidden the deep wonders of Jehovah's wisdom, which hath been sealed up, that none could or ever shall break up, but such as of her virgin off-spring shall appear to be, who will her laws receive and keep, as they shall spring daily in the new heart and mind." This appearance and words was wonderfully sweet and refreshing in my soul; at which I bowed and prostrated at her feet, promising to be obedient to all her laws. So the vision shut up for that time.

Pondering this in my heart with great comfort, that this daystar[6] had visited me from on high, I returned to London to my own habitation, retiring myself from all my acquaintance, saving one person that was highly illuminated,[7] who encouraged me still to wait upon this vision, for he was acquainted with somewhat of this kind. So after six days the vision appeared again, with a train of virgin spirits, and with an angelical host; and called to me to come and see the virgin queen, with her first-born children; asking me whether I was willing to be joined amongst this virgin company? At which I replied, "All willing to offer up myself most free." Then immediately I was encompassed about with this heavenly host, and made a spirit of light. Then these words from the Virgin proceeded, saying, "I shall now cease to appear in a visible figure unto thee, but I will not fail to transfigure myself in thy mind and there open the spring of Wisdom and understanding, that so thou mayst come to know the only True God, in and by the formation of Christ, the anointed prophet in thee; that shall reveal great and wonderful things unto thee, that are to be made known and public in its time and day. Therefore be watchful, and to thy mother Wisdom's counsel give good heed, and thou shalt greatly prosper, and succeed the prophets and apostles to perfect what was left behind, for completing as to Christ the fullness of God's great mystery: so go on, and nothing fear or doubt; for I thy glass[8] for divine seeing shall evermore stand before thee." Then my spirit replied, "According to thy word let all this be fulfilled." And so this glory withdrew; but an inward glory did my heart fill, for a burning love to all of those heavenly beings did kindle within my heart vehemently.

[The Second Vision]

In the Month of August

The mind of Wisdom thus opened itself in me, as I waited in my spirit upon her; she did show me what key would open the great mystery, which lay deeply hid in myself. It was wrought and carved out of such pure gold as had passed though many fires; many keys I had tried, but could not turn in this secret enclosed lock, but still it shut upon me, though I thought I had that key which was compounded of such metals as would have made its entrance, as love, faith, patience, humility,[9] which with strong supplication and prayer I presented, as the key of the work. All which was too short to reach it. Whereupon I was put to a loss altogether to seek how this gate should be opened, having compassed the Holy City,[1] and waited and tried every way, where I might find

4. Solemn agreement; here alluding to God's covenant with the Israelites (Genesis 6:18).
5. A mystic number—as in the Holy Trinity.
6. I.e., morning star.

7. Enlightened spirit ually.
8. Lens.
9. These echo some of the cardinal virtues.
1. I.e., the New Jerusalem of Revelations.

passage, circling from one path to another, from prayer to prayer, and from faith to faith; so that in good earnest I began to consider I had not found this wonderful key, for want[2] of which I might run out in waste all my days, and grope as in the dark, yet never find the door which opens into my true shepherd's fold.[3] Whereupon being cast into a deep astonishing silence and stillness, the word of Wisdom thus opened itself unto me: "Oh, thou deep searching spirit, marvel not thou hast been so long frustrated, for as to thy present state and dispensation, thou couldst never reach me to all eternity, for my birth in thee lies deeper than thy present gift of faith and prayer can open; thou hast with many others been in a great mistake. But in as much thou ownest and bewailest thy unskillfulness, I will make known to thee what key will turn this great wheel of my Wisdom, so as it may move and manifest itself in thee through all thy properties,[4] if thou canst bid up to the price of it. For understand that it is compounded of all pure gold, subsisting in a burning furnace of many fires. And although this wonderful key is of Wisdom's carving out, and her free gift, yet, O thou seeking spirit, she will cost thee very dear, if ever thou obtainest her. Yet she goeth about seeking such as are worthy of her, and will show herself within the walls of the mind, and meet them in every thought that waits for her laws and counsel, and brings a kingdom which will be well worth thy selling all for. But the great thing," saith Wisdom, "now is to discipline and make thy spirit a cunning artist, to give it knowledge of what matter in number, weight, and measure this pure key is made up of, which is all pure deity in the number THREE, which is weighty indeed, being one exceeding weighty glory, fitting in the circle of the heavens within man's heart, measuring with the line of his power, the temple and inward court, with the worshippers therein. This is Wisdom's key, which will make our hands drop with sweet-smelling myrrh[5] upon the handles of her lock." Which while I was opening her privy[6] door with this key, my soul failed within me, and I retained no strength; my sun of reason and the moon of my outward sense were folded up and withdrew. I knew nothing by myself, as to those working properties from nature and creature,[7] and the wheel of the motion standing still, another moved from a central fire;[8] so that I felt myself transmuted into one pure flame. Then came that word to me, "This is no other than the gate of my eternal deep; canst thou subsist in this fiery region, which is Wisdom's mansion where she meets with holy abstracted spirits, and gives forth a fiery law, which if thereunto thou canst give heed, so as to come up to her requirings, then no secret shall be withheld from thee." Thus far am I admitted to come into the entrance of her house, where I must stop till I hear further from her.

Now as I was attending to obtain a fresh visit, being entered into this first mansion of her house,[9] to hear and learn further, she said on this wise, that I was greatly beloved, and she would be my mother, and so should I own her and call her, who would now be to me as Rebecca was to Jacob, to contrive and put me in a way how I should obtain the birthright blessing. For if I would apply

2. Lack.
3. Pen for sheep; the shepherd is Christ.
4. I.e., personal qualities.
5. An aromatic resin, one of the gifts of the Magi to the Christ child (Matthew 2:11).
6. Private.
7. I.e., she knew nothing of her natural human functions.

8. I.e., the wheel of ordinary motion stopping, another wheel (i.e., the wheel of Wisdom) moved from a central fire.
9. See John 14:2: "In my Father's house are many mansions" (i.e., rooms).

myself to her doctrine, and draw my life's food from no other breast, I should then know the recovery of a lost kingdom; at which salutation I was dissolved and melted, the fervent heat of this love strongly impulsing me to a resolve for to obey her in all things.

When pure oil from Wisdom's vessel stopping, it opened again not till October the 20th in the morning watch; then heard I her voice thus, "Sequester and draw out of thy animal sensitive life[1] that is too gross: I cannot appear till that disappear. There must be spirit with spirit, light with light." No sooner had I this caution, but I felt power which suspended the active busy mind, which for a time was expired into silence. "Know then," said the same voice, "thou shalt supplant thy brother Esau, who according to the figure, is a cunning hunter in the out-birth[2] and field of nature. While he with his subtlety seeking it abroad in the wild properties of the external region, I will now help thee to it near at hand, even in thy own enclosed ground. There the true scapegoat[3] feeds, of which I will make savory meat, such as God thy Father loves." Hearing this salutation from my late known mother, I was deadly ravished in the spirit, in the light of the Lord, and feared to return to the dark house of my outward senses again; which opened a spring of intercession in me, that as one of the friends of the bridegroom[4] I might hear his voice still, which indeed was so pleasant and sweet as I could well have admitted of a dissolution of my elementary being, rather than this conference should not still be maintained with this renowned pearl of wisdom. But I have learned to observe her time and seasons; I witness her opening as in the twinkling of an eye, a pure bright, subtle, swift spirit, a working motion, a circling fire, a penetrating oil.

<div align="right">1697–1701</div>

1. I.e., life of the senses.
2. Progeny, something brought forth.
3. In Leviticus 16, the scapegoat is heaped with the sins of the people and sent into the wilderness while the goat of the Lord is offered as a sacrifice. Lead may

also be thinking of Christ as "the true scapegoat."
4. I.e., Jesus. In Matthew 9:15 he says, "Can the children of the bridechamber mourn, as long as the bridegroom is with them?"

KATHERINE PHILIPS
1632–1664

Known in her own day as "The Matchless Orinda," Katherine Philips was the daughter of John Fowler, a London merchant. In 1648 she married James Philips, a wealthy Puritan some years her senior, who shared many of her interests and supported her literary career with enthusiasm. At Cardigan Priory, their Welsh home, the pair saw themselves as the center of an intellectual circle called the Society of Friendship, in which each member was given a playfully neoclassical pseudonym. Katherine herself, for instance, became "Orinda" and James became "Antenor," while Katherine's friend Anne Owen, viscountess of Dungannon, was the original of the "Excellent Lucasia" to whom a number of Orinda's pieces on friendship are dedicated.

Though few of Philips's poems were published in her lifetime, she did have several translations of Corneille's plays performed to great acclaim, and her verses, circulated privately, received much praise from such contemporary poets and intellectuals as Abraham Cowley, Jeremy Taylor, and John Dryden. The mother of

two children, one of whom died in infancy, she clearly had a "room of her own" in which to write and leisure for friendship as well as literary activity. As our selections indicate, she wrote on a wide range of subjects, including courtship, marriage, and her own painfully thwarted maternity. But that her most loving poems are addressed to female friends suggests the bonds that were beginning to develop between seventeenth-century intellectual women, who felt that they had found "all the world" in each other rather than in romanticized heroes. Nevertheless, "The Matchless Orinda" was admired by male as well as female readers. When she died of smallpox at the early age of thirty-two, countless tributes appeared, eulogizing her. Though some of her work was conventionally pious or sentimental, her first collection of plays and poems, posthumously printed, was extraordinarily popular; as the poet Anne Killigrew somewhat enviously remarked, "every laurel to her laurel bowed"—i.e., every respected poet praised her artistry.

Friendship's Mysteries, to My Dearest Lucasia

Set by Mr. H. Lawes.

1

Come, my Lucasia, since we see
 That miracles men's faith do move
By wonder and by prodigy,[1]
 To the dull, angry world let's prove
There's a religion in our love. 5

2

For though we were designed[2] t'agree,
 That fate no liberty destroys,
But our election[3] is as free
 As Angels, who with greedy choice
Are yet determined to their joys. 10

3

Our hearts are doubled by their loss,[4]
 Here mixture is addition grown;
We both diffuse, and both engross,[5]
 And we, whose minds are so much one,
Never, yet ever, are alone. 15

4

We court our own captivity,
 Then thrones more[6] great and innocent:
'Twere banishment to be set free,
 Since we wear fetters whose intent
Not bondage is, but ornament. 20

5

Divided joys are tedious found,

1. Something extraordinary that acts as an omen.
2. Minded, resolved.
3. Exercise of deliberate choice. The mention of angels (line 9) suggests also the notion of "divine election," God's choice of some for eternal salvation.
4. I.e., to one another.
5. Gather together, condense. "Diffuse": spread abroad, become diffused.
6. More than thrones.

And griefs united easier grow:
We are our selves but by rebound,[7]
And all our titles shuffled so,
 Both princes, and both subjects too. 25

6
Our hearts are mutual victims laid,
 While they (such power in friendship lies)
Are altars, priests, and offerings made,
 And each heart which thus kindly dies,
 Grows deathless by the sacrifice. 30

1655

To My Excellent Lucasia, on Our Friendship

I did not live until this time
 Crowned my felicity,
When I could say without a crime,[1]
 I am not thine, but thee.

This carcass breathed, and walked, and slept, 5
 So that the world believed
There was a soul the motions kept;[2]
 But they were all deceived.

For as a watch by art[3] is wound
 To motion, such was mine: 10
But never had Orinda[4] found
 A soul till she found thine;

Which now inspires,[5] cures and supplies,
 And guides my darkened breast:
For thou art all that I can prize, 15
 My joy, my life, my rest.

No bridegroom's nor crown-conqueror's[6] mirth
 To mine compared can be:
They have but pieces of the earth,
 I've all the world in thee. 20

Then let our flames still light and shine,
 And no false fear control,
As innocent as our design,[7]
 Immortal as our soul.

1667

7. Reflection. 4. Philips herself
1. I.e., lying. 5. Fills with air.
2. I.e., that controlled the body's movements. 6. One who has become a monarch by force.
3. Artificial means, skill. 7. Intention.

On the Death of My First and Dearest Child, Hector Philips, Borne the 23ᵈ of April, and Died the 2ᵈ of May 1655

Set by Mr. Lawes.

1

Twice forty months in wedlock I did stay,
 Then had my vows crowned with a lovely boy.
And yet in forty days he dropped away;
 O! swift vicissitude of human joy!

2

I did but see him, and he disappeared, 5
 I did but touch the rosebud, and it fell;
A sorrow unforeseen and scarcely feared,
 So ill can mortals their afflictions spell.[1]

3

And now (sweet babe) what can my trembling heart
 Suggest to right my doleful fate or thee? 10
Tears are my muse, and sorrow all my art,
 So piercing groans must be thy elegy.

4

Thus whilst no eye is witness of my moan,
 I grieve thy loss (Ah, boy too dear to live!)
And let the unconcerned world alone, 15
 Who neither will, nor can refreshment give.

5

An offering too for thy sad tomb I have,
 Too just a tribute to thy early hearse;
Receive these gasping numbers[2] to thy grave,
 The last of thy unhappy mother's verse. 20

1667

To Sir Amorous La Fool

Bless us, here's a do[1] indeed!
That she must so much courtship need.
Scorn sits so handsome on this face,
With such an unaffected grace,
That I could wish my sex were changed to be 5
A lover only of your cruelty.

Women, men say, are fools they know,
But what are they that call us so,
When their sighs and amorous ware,
But more serious follies are.[2] 10

1. Understand, decipher.
2. Lines of poetry.

1. Fuss.
2. "But . . . are": are but, are only.

What time we spend to curl and dress our hair,
You spend to think us, though we are not, fair.

What pretty dotage[3] call you this,
To weep and groan and glance and kiss;
Unkindness makes your heart to break, 15
And not a word of sense to speak.
And court the careless, when with far less pain,
Some wholesome milkmaid would say yours again.

 1667

A Married State

A married state affords but little ease:
The best of husbands are so hard to please.
This in wives' careful faces you may spell,
Though they dissemble[1] their misfortunes well.
A virgin state is crowned with much content, 5
It's always happy as it's innocent.
No blustering husbands to create your fears,
No pangs of childbirth to extort your tears,
No children's cries for to offend your ears,
Few worldly crosses to distract your prayers. 10
Thus are you freed from all the cares that do
Attend on matrimony and a husband too.
Therefore, madam, be advised by me:
Turn, turn apostate to love's levity.
Suppress wild nature if she dare rebel, 15
There's no such thing as leading apes in hell.[2]

 1667

3. Foolish affection.
1. Disguise. "Spell": make out with difficulty.
2. See Shakespeare's *Taming of the Shrew* 2.1.33–34: "I

must dance barefoot on her wedding-day, / And for
your love to her lead apes in hell."

MARY ROWLANDSON
C. 1636–1711

At dawn on February 10, 1676, Mary Rowlandson, her six-year-old daughter, and her two older children were captured by a group of New England Indians. Both Rowlandson and the six-year-old were wounded, and they were separated from the older children. Though a number of people, including Rowlandson's sister, were killed in the raid, her husband—a minister—survived because he was away from home. During a three-month imprisonment that followed, Rowlandson lived with the members of the Wampanoag woman Weetamoo's household, migrating with them into southwestern New Hampshire, visiting, when possible, with her son, Joseph, and her daughter, Mary, coping with cold by reading a Bible that was given to her and with hunger by knitting or sewing in exchange for pancakes and bear meat. Her resiliency and survival skills seem to have surprised even herself: before

the Indian raid she had believed that she would "choose rather to be killed by them than taken alive." But, she explains in a narrative that has since become a classic of frontier literature, "when it came to the trial my mind changed; their glittering weapons so daunted my spirit, that I chose rather to go along with those (as I may say) ravenous beasts, than that moment to end my days."

The raid on her house had been part of a year-long series of attacks on colonial outposts led by Metacomet, or "Philip," as the white settlers called him. Rowlandson was understandably irate, if not racist, about the "merciless heathen" who taunted her and tormented her children. Yet even her account implies that the Wampanoag Indians were themselves starving and uprooted. In fact, what became known as "King Philip's War" was a futile effort on the part of the American Indians to reclaim the homeland they had lost to Puritans like the Rowlandsons. By May 2, 1676, Rowlandson was thankful that the Indian community assented to the ransom her husband offered for her, that several of its representatives provided a hood and scarf for her journey, and that during her captivity "not one of them ever offered me the least abuse of unchastity to me, in word or action."

After moving with her husband to Wethersfield, Connecticut, where he died in 1678, Rowlandson married Captain Samuel Talcott in 1679 and published her *Narrative* in 1682. It has remained a prototype of the captivity narrative, a popular American genre mined not only by early writers who experienced captivities in their lives but also by later novelists like James Fenimore Cooper and William Faulkner, who composed fictionalized versions of the form.

Documenting, as it does, her shifting attitudes toward Native American culture, her capacity for endurance, and the Puritan rhetorical tradition, Rowlandson's captivity narrative, which she wrote for her surviving children, has been exceptionally popular, going through more than thirty editions after it was published in 1682.

From A Narrative of the Captivity and Restoration of Mrs. Mary Rowlandson

The Third Remove[1]

The morning being come, they prepared to go on their way. One of the Indians got up upon a horse, and they set me up behind him, with my poor sick babe in my lap. A very wearisome and tedious day I had of it; what with my own wound, and my child's being so exceeding sick, and in a lamentable condition with her wound. It may be easily judged what a poor feeble condition we were in, there being not the least crumb of refreshing that came within either of our mouths from Wednesday night to Saturday night, except only a little cold water. This day in the afternoon, about an hour by sun, we came to the place where they intended, *viz.* an Indian town, called Wenimesset, northward of Quabaug. When we were come, Oh the number of pagans (now merciless enemies) that there came about me, that I may say as David, "I had fainted, unless I had believed, etc." (Psalm 27:13).[2] The next day was the sabbath. I then remembered how careless I had been of God's holy time; how many sabbaths I had lost and misspent, and how evilly I had walked in God's sight; which lay so close unto my spirit, that it was easy for me see how right-

1. I.e., departure. From February 12 to 27 Rowlandson and her captors stayed at an American Indian village on the Ware River, near New Braintree.

2. The verse continues "to see the goodness of the Lord in the land of the living."

eous it was with God to cut off the thread of my life and cast me out of His presence for ever. Yet the Lord still showed mercy to me, and upheld me; and as He wounded me with one hand, so he healed me with the other. This day there came to me one Robert Pepper (a man belonging to Roxbury) who was taken in Captain Beers's fight and had been now a considerable time with the Indians; and up with them almost as far as Albany, to see King Philip, as he told me, and was now very lately come into these parts.[3] Hearing, I say, that I was in this Indian town, he obtained leave to come and see me. He told me he himself was wounded in the leg at Captain Beer's fight; and was not able some time to go, but as they carried him, and as he took oaken leaves and laid to his wound, and through the blessing of God he was able to travel again. Then I took oaken leaves and laid to my side, and with the blessing of God it cured me also; yet before the cure was wrought, I may say as it is in Psalm 38:5–6, "My wounds stink and are corrupt, I am troubled, I am bowed down greatly, I go mourning all the day long." I sat much alone with a poor wounded child in my lap, which moaned night and day, having nothing to revive the body, or cheer the spirits of her, but instead of that, sometimes one Indian would come and tell me one hour that "your master will knock your child in the head," and then a second, and then a third, "your master will quickly knock your child in the head."

This was the comfort I had from them, miserable comforters are ye all, as he[4] said. Thus nine days I sat upon my knees, with my babe in my lap, till my flesh was raw again; my child being even ready to depart this sorrowful world, they bade me carry it out to another wigwam (I suppose because they would not be troubled with such spectacles) whither I went with a very heavy heart, and down I sat with the picture of death in my lap. About two hours in the night, my sweet babe like a lamb departed this life on Feb. 18, 1675.[5] It being about six years, and five months old. It was nine days from the first wounding, in this miserable condition, without any refreshing of one nature or other, except a little cold water. I cannot but take notice how at another time I could not bear to be in the room where any dead person was, but now the case is changed; I must and could lie down by my dead babe, side by side all the night after. I have thought since of the wonderful goodness of God to me in preserving me in the use of my reason and senses in that distressed time, that I did not use wicked and violent means to end my own miserable life. In the morning, when they understood that my child was dead they sent for me home to my master's wigwam (by my master in this writing, must be understood Quanopin, who was a Sagamore,[6] and married King Philip's wife's sister; not that he first took me, but I was sold to him by another Narraganset Indian, who took me when first I came out of the garrison). I went to take up my dead child in my arms to carry it with me, but they bid me let it alone; there was no resisting, but go I must and leave it. When I had been at my master's wigwam, I took the first opportunity I could get to go look after my dead child. When I came I asked them what they had done with it; then they told me it was upon the hill. Then they went and showed me where it was, where I saw the ground was newly digged, and there they told me they had buried it. There I left that

3. Captain Beers battled to rescue the garrison of Northfield, Massachusetts, September 4, 1675.
4. I.e., Job 16:2: "I have heard many such things: miserable comforters are ye all."
5. Using the present Gregorian calendar, March 1, 1676.
6. A subordinate chief among Algonquin Indians. Quanopin was Weetamoo's husband; Rowlandson became her servant.

child in the wilderness, and must commit it, and myself also in this wil-
derness-condition, to Him who is above all. God having taken away this dear
child, I went to see my daughter Mary, who was at this same Indian town, at a
wigwam not very far off, though we had little liberty or opportunity to see one
another. She was about ten years old, and taken from the door at first by a
Praying Ind. and afterward sold for a gun. When I came in sight, she would fall
aweeping; at which they were provoked, and would not let me come near her,
but bade me be gone; which was a heart-cutting word to me. I had one child
dead, another in the wilderness, I knew not where, the third they would not let
me come near to: "Me (as he said) have ye bereaved of my Children, Joseph is
not, and Simeon is not, and ye will take Benjamin also, all these things are
against me."[7] I could not sit still in this condition, but kept walking from one
place to another. And as I was going along, my heart was even overwhelmed
with the thoughts of my condition, and that I should have children, and a na-
tion which I knew not, ruled over them. Whereupon I earnestly entreated the
Lord, that He would consider my low estate, and show me a token for good,
and if it were His blessed will, some sign and hope of some relief. And indeed
quickly the Lord answered, in some measure, my poor prayers; for as I was
going up and down mourning and lamenting my condition, my son came to
me, and asked me how I did. I had not seen him before, since the destruction
of the town, and I knew not where he was, till I was informed by himself, that
he was amongst a smaller parcel of Indians, whose place was about six miles
off. With tears in his eyes, he asked me whether his sister Sarah was dead; and
told me he had seen his sister Mary; and prayed me, that I would not be trou-
bled in reference to himself. The occasion of his coming to see me at this time,
was this: there was, as I said, about six miles from us, a small plantation of
Indians, where it seems he had been during his captivity; and at this time,
there were some forces of the Ind. gathered out of our company, and some also
from them (among whom was my son's master) to go to assault and burn
Medfield.[8] In this time of the absence of his master, his dame brought him to
see me. I took this to be some gracious answer to my earnest and unfeigned
desire. The next day, viz. to this, the Indians returned from Medfield, all the
company, for those that belonged to the other small company, came through
the town that now we were at. But before they came to us, Oh! the outrageous
roaring and hooping that there was. They began their din about a mile before
they came to us. By their noise and hooping they signified how many they had
destroyed (which was at that time twenty three.) Those that were with us at
home were gathered together as soon as they heard the hooping, and every
time that the other went over their number, these at home gave a shout, that
the very earth rung again. And thus they continued till those that had been
upon the expedition were come up to the Sagamore's wigwam; then, Oh, the
hideous insulting and triumphing that there was over some Englishmen's
scalps that they had taken (as their manner is) and brought with them. I can-
not but take notice of the wonderful mercy of God to me in those afflictions,
in sending me a Bible. One of the Indians that came from Medfield fight, had
brought some plunder, came to me, and asked me, if I would have a Bible, he
had got one in his basket. I was glad of it, and asked him, whether he thought

7. The lament of Jacob (Genesis 42:36).
8. This attack on Medfield, Massachusetts, took place on February 21.

the Indians would let me read? He answered, yes. So I took the Bible, and in that melancholy time, it came into my mind to read first the 28th chapter of Deuteronomy,[9] which I did, and when I had read it, my dark heart wrought on this manner: that there was no mercy for me, that the blessings were gone, and the curses come in their room, and that I had lost my opportunity. But the Lord helped me still to go on reading till I came to Chap. 30, the seven first verses, where I found, there was mercy promised again, if we would return to Him by repentance;[1] and though we were scattered from one end of the earth to the other, yet the Lord would gather us together, and turn all those curses upon our enemies. I do not desire to live to forget this Scripture, and what comfort it was to me.

Now the Ind. began to talk of removing from this place, some one way, and some another. There were now besides myself nine English captives in this place (all of them children, except one woman) I got an opportunity to go and take my leave of them. They being to go one way, and I another, I asked them whether they were earnest with God for deliverance. They told me they did as they were able, and it was some comfort to me that the Lord stirred up children to look to Him. The woman, *viz.* goodwife[2] Joslin, told me she should never see me again, and that she could find in her heart to run away. I wished her not to run away by any means, for we were near thirty miles from any English town, and she very big with child, and had but one week to reckon, and another child in her arms, two years old, and bad rivers there were to go over, and we were feeble, with our poor and coarse entertainment.[3] I had my Bible with me, I pulled it out, and asked her whether she would read. We opened the Bible and lighted on Psalm 27, in which Psalm we especially took notice of that, *ver. ult.*,[4] "Wait on the Lord, Be of good courage, and he shall strengthen thine Heart, wait I say on the Lord."[5]

1682

9. This chapter concerns God's blessings and curses on those who obey and disobey him.
1. "That then the Lord thy God will turn thy captivity, and have compassion upon thee, and will return and gather thee from all the nations" (Deuteronomy 30:3).
2. I.e., mistress of the house.
3. Food
4. "Ver. ult.": the last verse (Latin).
5. Verse 14.

APHRA BEHN
1640–1689

Spy and playwright, traveler and wit, Aphra Behn was England's first professional woman writer. In an age when many women of letters were intellectual aristocrats like Anne Finch, countess of Winchilsea, and Margaret Cavendish, duchess of Newcastle, wealthy ladies who claimed to write only for pleasure and "fame" among their friends, Behn was a middle-class widow who frankly wrote for money and public acclaim. Of uncertain parentage, she seems to have traveled to the West Indies at the age of sixteen when her father was appointed lieutenant governor of Surinam. Her adventures are said by some biographers to have included an involvement in a slave rebellion and a visit to a group of American Indians who had never before seen Europeans (though it should be remembered that her autobiographical accounts were composed to sell books, and therefore, many of the facts of her life remain elusive). Returning to England in 1664, Behn was briefly married to a man about whom little is known except that he was a London merchant

of Dutch ancestry, who very likely died in the terrible plague of 1665.

In 1666, widowed and casting about for some means of support, Behn entered the intelligence service of King Charles II, though as she later acknowledged, such "public toils of state affairs" were "unusual with my sex, or in my years." Assigned to work as a spy in Antwerp, she carried out her mission "remarkably well," according to Angeline Goreau, the author of one biography, but the king's agents never paid her properly for her labors, so that she ended up spending some time in 1668 in a London debtors' prison. Apparently it was the trauma of this last experience that decided her on what was, for a woman, an unprecedented step: writing for money. By 1670, Aphra Behn's first play, *The Forced Marriage*, was successfully produced on the London stage.

From 1670 on, Behn's groundbreaking literary career was characterized by remarkable productivity. She had always been a literary young woman, a fluent diarist, and an enthusiastic reader of French romances. Now, as she became a professional playwright, she moved from writing somewhat derivative tragicomedies to producing farces in the style of such contemporaries as the comic dramatist William Wycherley. Altogether, during her years in the theater she wrote and published some fourteen plays, including *The Rover* (1677), *Sir Patient Fancy* (1678), *The Roundheads* (1681), and *The City Heiress* (1682). At the same time, inquiring "What has poor woman done that she must be / Debarred from sacred poetry?" and demanding freedom to assert what society defined as "my masculine part, the poet in me," Behn was composing and publishing a series of briskly witty verses, some marked by an erotic honesty that scandalized many of her readers. For although the Restoration circles in which she traveled permitted extraordinary license to male artists like Behn's libertine friend and patron the poet John Wilmot, earl of Rochester, the same circles expected women to remain decently silent about their own desires. As her poem *The Disappointment* suggests, however, Behn did not maintain such a silence, so that even a supporter like the writer Anne Finch was later to concede that "a little too loosely she writ."

In Behn's later years, the London theaters on which she had depended for her livelihood suffered a number of reverses, and her income from playwriting was severely reduced. Enterprising as ever, she turned her talents in yet another direction, writing and publishing a set of pioneering prose fictions—*Love Letters between a Nobleman and His Sister* (1684–86), *The Fair Jilt* (1688), *Agnes de Castro* (1688), and most notably, *Oroonoko* (1688). Loosely based on "real life," with the revolutionary *Oroonoko* supposedly recounting Behn's early experiences in Surinam and including a passionate protest against the institution of slavery, these literary novelties were to play a part in the development of a new form, the novel, in which, as some critics have suggested, women of letters were at last to find a genre of their own. Part-travel narrative, part-memoir, part-fantasy, part-biography, *Oroonoko* is complex in its treatment of racial difference, yet ultimately Behn's sympathy for her heroic royal slave and her outrage against the injustice of slavery give the book extraordinary resonance. Following in her footsteps, such white women of letters as Maria Edgeworth and Elizabeth Barrett Browning (in England) along with Elizabeth Cady Stanton and Harriet Beecher Stowe (in the United States) produced polemics against the savagery of supposedly civilized societies that denied full humanity to all human beings. In so doing, they echoed the protests of African-American contemporaries from Sojourner Truth to Frederick Douglass.

Behn died in pain and poverty within a year of the publication of *Oroonoko*, and her reputation was to be obscured or defaced for centuries after her death. Yet she had once again broken new ground. "All women together ought to let flowers fall upon the tomb of Aphra Behn," declared the author of *A Room of One's Own*, "for it was she who earned them the right to speak their minds." Her grave—somewhat surprisingly located in Westminster Abbey—is marked by a censorious stone that

reads "Here lies a Proof that wit can never be / Defence against mortality." But Virginia Woolf's tribute to her memory was more apt than such a motto.

The Willing Mistress[1]

Amyntas led me to a grove,
 Where all the trees did shade us;
The sun itself, though it had strove,
 It could not have betrayed us.[2]
The place secured from human eyes 5
 No other fear allows
But when the winds that gently rise
 Do kiss the yielding boughs.

Down there we sat upon the moss,
 And did begin to play 10
A thousand amorous tricks,[3] to pass
 The heat of all the day.
A many kisses did he give
 And I returned the same,
Which made me willing to receive 15
 That which I dare not name.

His charming eyes no aid required
 To tell their softening tale:
On her that was already fired [4]
 'Twas easy to prevail. 20
He did but kiss and clasp me round,
 Whilst those his thoughts expressed:
And laid me gently on the ground;
 Ah who can guess the rest?

1673

Love Armed[1]

Love in fantastic triumph[2] sat
Whilst bleeding hearts around him flowed,
For whom fresh[3] pains he did create
And strange tyrannic power he showed.

From thy bright eyes he took the fires 5
Which round about in sport he hurled,

1. This song appears in Behn's play *The Dutch Lover* where it is sung by a maidservant to her mistress.
2. I.e., revealed us to others.
3. Games, amusements.
4. I.e., made warm with desire.
1. A song in Behn's play *Abdelazer; or, The Moor's Revenge.* "Love" in this poem is Cupid, often depicted during the Renaissance as a cruel and arbitrary god (see, for example, the Maske of Cupid in Spenser's *The Faerie Queene* .7).
2. In a splendid procession.
3. New.

But 'twas from mine he took desires
Enough t'undo the amorous world.[4]

From me he took his sighs and tears,
From thee his pride and cruelty; 10
From me his languishments and fears.
And every killing dart[5] from thee.

Thus thou and I the God have armed
And set him up a deity;
But my poor heart alone is harmed, 15
Whilst thine the victor is, and free.

 1676

The Disappointment[1]

One day the amorous Lysander,
By an impatient passion swayed,[2]
Surprised fair Cloris, that lovéd maid,
Who could defend herself no longer.
All things did with his love conspire;[3] 5
The gilded planet[4] of the day,
In his gay chariot drawn by fire,
Was now descending to the sea,
And left no light to guide the world
But what from Cloris' brighter eyes was hurled. 10

In a lone thicket made for love,
Silent as yielding maid's consent,
She with a charming languishment,
Permits his force, yet gently strove;[5]
Her hands his bosom softly meet, 15
But not to put him back designed,
Rather to draw 'em on inclined:
Whilst he lay trembling at her feet,
Resistance 'tis in vain to show:
She wants[6] the power to say—*Ah! what d'ye do?* 20

Her bright eyes sweet and yet severe,
Where love and shame confusedly strive,
Fresh vigor to Lysander give;
And breathing faintly in his ear,
She cried—*Cease, cease—your vain desire,* 25
Or I'll call out—what would you do?

4. To destroy the world's lovers in the sufferings of
desire.
5. Cupid's darts.
1. Based on the first half of a French poem titled
L'Occasion perdue recouverte, i.e., a lost chance recov-
ered.

2. By desire moved.
3. I.e., the outside world seemed to encourage his
love.
4. The sun.
5. Struggled.
6. Lacks.

My dearer honor[7] even to you
I cannot, must not give—Retire,[8]
Or take this life, whose chiefest part
I gave you with the conquest of my heart. 30

But he as much unused to fear,
As he was capable of love,
The blessed minutes to improve[9]
Kisses her mouth, her neck, her hair;
Each touch her new desire alarms; 35
His burning, trembling hand he pressed
Upon her swelling snowy breast,
While she lay panting in his arms.
All her unguarded beauties lie
The spoils and trophies of the enemy. 40

And now without respect or fear
He seeks the object of his vows
(His love no modesty allows)
By swift degrees advancing—where
His daring hand that altar[1] seized, 45
Where gods of love do sacrifice:
That awful throne, that paradise
Where rage is calmed, and anger pleased;
That fountain where delight still flows,
And gives the universal world repose. 50

Her balmy lips encountering his,
Their bodies, as their souls, are joined;
Where both in transports unconfined
Extend themselves upon the moss.
Cloris half dead and breathless lay; 55
Her soft eyes cast a humid light
Such as divides the day and night;
Or falling stars, whose fires decay:
And now no signs of life she shows,
But what in short-breathed sighs returns and goes. 60

He saw how at her length she lay;
He saw her rising bosom bare;
Her loose thin robes, through which appear
A shape designed for love and play;
Abandoned by her pride and shame 65
She does her softest joys dispense,
Offering her virgin innocence
A victim to love's sacred flame;
While the o'er-ravished shepherd lies
Unable to perform the sacrifice. 70

7. Virginity.
8. Leave.

9. Make more pleasurable.
1. I.e., her genitals.

Ready to taste a thousand joys,
The too transported hapless swain[2]
Found the vast pleasure turned to pain;
Pleasure which too much love destroys:
The willing garments[3] by he laid, 75
And heaven all opened to his view.
Mad to possess, himself he threw
On the defenseless lovely maid.
But oh what envying god conspires
To snatch his power, yet leave him the desire! 80

Nature's support (without whose aid
She can no human being give)
Itself now wants the art[4] to live;
Faintness its slackened nerves invade:
In vain th'enragéd youth essayed 85
To call its fleeting vigor back;
No motion 'twill from motion take;
Excess of love his love betrayed:
In vain he toils, in vain commands:
The insensible fell weeping in his hand. 90

In this so amorous cruel strife,
Where love and fate were too severe,
The poor Lysander in despair
Renounced his reason with his life:
Now all the brisk and active fire 95
That should the nobler part[5] inflame
Served to increase his rage and shame,
And left no spark for new desire:
Not all her naked charms could move
Or calm that rage that had debauched[6] his love. 100

Cloris returning from the trance
Which love and soft desire had bred,
Her timorous hand she gently laid
(Or guided by design or chance)
Upon that fabulous Priapus,[7] 105
That potent god, as poets feign:[8]
But never did young shepherdess,
Gathering the fern upon the plain,
More nimbly draw her fingers back,
Finding beneath the verdant[9] leaves a snake, 110

Than Cloris her fair hand withdrew,
Finding that god of her desires
Disarmed of all his awful fires,

2. Unfortunate lover. 7. I.e., his erect penis (from Priapus, the always-erect
3. I.e., hers. Greek god of fertility).
4. Lacks the ability. 8. Claim, but also pretend falsely.
5. His reason, but also his impotent phallus. 9. Green. "Nimbly": quickly.
6. Corrupted.

And cold as flowers bathed in the morning dew.
Who can the nymph's confusion guess? 115
The blood forsook the hinder place,
And strewed[1] with blushes all her face,
Which both disdain and shame expressed:
And from Lysander's arms she fled,
Leaving him fainting on the gloomy bed. 120

Like lightning through the grove she hies,
Or Daphne[2] from the Delphic god;
No print upon the grassy road
She leaves, to instruct pursuing eyes.
The wind that wantoned[3] in her hair 125
And with her ruffled garments played,
Discovered[4] in the flying maid
All that the gods e'er made, if fair.
So Venus, when her love was slain,[5]
With fear and haste flew o'er the fatal plain. 130

The nymph's resentments none but I
Can well imagine or condole:
But none can guess Lysander's soul,
But those who swayed[6] his destiny.
His silent griefs swell up to storms, 135
And not one god his fury spares;
He cursed his birth, his fate, his stars.
But more the shepherdess's charms,
Whose soft bewitching influence
Had damned him to the hell of impotence. 140

1680

On Her Loving Two Equally

I

How strong does my passion flow,
Divided equally twixt[1] two?
Damon had ne'er subdued my heart
Had not Alexis took his part;
Nor could Alexis powerful prove,[2] 5
Without my Damon's aid, to gain my love.

II

When my Alexis present is,
Then I for Damon sigh and mourn;
But when Alexis I do miss,

1. Scattered, covered. "Hinder place": her genitals.
2. In Greek myth, a nymph who escapes the god
Apollo's lecherous pursuit by turning into a laurel tree.
3. Played wildly, frolicked.
4. Uncovered, displayed.
5. Venus is the Roman name for Aphrodite, the Greek
goddess of love. Her lover Adonis was slain by a boar.
6. Governed, directed; compare line 2. "Those": i.e.,
the gods.
1. Between.
2. Show himself.

 Damon gains nothing but my scorn. 10
 But if it chance they both are by,[3]
 For both alike I languish, sigh, and die.

 III
 Cure then, thou mighty wingéd god,[4]
 This restless fever in my blood;
 One golden-pointed dart[5] take back: 15
 But which, O Cupid, wilt thou take?
 If Damon's, all my hopes are crossed;[6]
 Or that of my Alexis, I am lost.

 1684

To the Fair Clarinda, Who Made Love to Me, Imagined More than Woman[1]

 Fair lovely maid, or if that title be
 Too weak, too feminine for nobler thee,
 Permit a name that more approaches truth:
 And let me call thee lovely charming youth.
 This last will justify my soft complaint,[2] 5
 While that[3] may serve to lessen my constraint;
 And without blushes I the youth pursue,
 When so much beauteous woman is in view.
 Against thy charms we struggle but in vain;
 With thy deluding form thou givest us pain, 10
 While the bright nymph betrays us to the swain.[4]
 In pity to our sex sure thou wert sent,
 That we might love, and yet be innocent:[5]
 For sure no crime[6] with thee we can commit;
 Or if we should—thy form excuses it. 15
 For who that gathers fairest flowers believes
 A snake lies hid beneath the fragrant leaves.

 Thou beauteous wonder of a different kind,
 Soft Cloris with the dear Alexis joined;
 Whene'er the manly part of thee would plead[7] 20
 Thou tempts us with the image of the maid,
 While we the noblest passions[8] do extend
 The love to Hermes, Aphrodite the friend.[9]

 1688

3. Near.
4. Cupid.
5. According to myth, Cupid shot darts of lead and of gold at the hearts of lovers, corresponding to false and true love, respectively.
6. Blocked, ruined.
1. I.e., as a hermaphrodite, a union of male and female in one body.
2. Declaration of love. "This last": the title of youth (male).
3. "That": the title of maid (female).
4. A male shepherd. "Nymph": a mythic female spirit, also more generally a young woman. That is, her feminine beauty induces us to surrender to her masculine aggressiveness.
5. I.e., virginal.
6. Sexual transgression.
7. I.e., beg for sexual favors.
8. Love and friendship, sharply distinguished in the 18th century.
9. I.e., friendship. The Greek messenger god (Hermes) and the Greek goddess of love (Aphrodite), whose son, Hermaphroditus, became an androgyne.

Oroonoko, or The Royal Slave[1]

I do not pretend, in giving you the history of this royal slave, to entertain my reader with the adventures of a feigned hero, whose life and fortunes fancy may manage at the poet's pleasure, not in relating the truth, desire to adorn it with any accidents but such as arrived in earnest to him. And it shall come simply into the world, recommended by its own proper merits and natural intrigues, there being enough of reality to support it, and to render it diverting, without the addition of invention.

I was myself an eyewitness to a great part of what you will find here set down, and what I could not be witness of, I received from the mouth of the chief actor in this history, the hero himself, who gave us the whole transactions of his youth; and though I shall omit for brevity's sake a thousand little accidents of his life, which, however pleasant to us, where history was scarce and adventures very rare, yet might prove tedious and heavy to my reader, in a world where he finds diversions for every minute, new and strange. But we who were perfectly charmed with the character of this great man were curious to gather ever circumstance of his life.

The scene of the last part of his adventures lies in a colony in America called Surinam,[2] in the West Indies.

But before I give you the story of this gallant slave, 'tis fit I tell you the manner of bringing them to these new colonies, for those they make use of there are not natives of the place; for those we live with in perfect amity, without daring to command 'em, but on the contrary caress 'em with all the brotherly and friendly affection in the world, trading with 'em for their fish, venison, buffaloes,[3] skins, and little rarities; as marmosets, a sort of monkey as big as a rat or weasel but of a marvelous and delicate shape, and has face and hands like a human creature, and cousheries,[4] a little beast in the form and fashion of a lion, as big as a kitten, but so exactly made in all parts like that noble beast, that it is it in miniature. Then for little parakeetoes, great parrots, macaws, and a thousand other birds and beasts of wonderful and surprising forms, shapes, and colors. For skins of prodigious snakes, of which there are some threescore yards in length, as is the skin of one that may be seen at his Majesty's antiquaries'; where are also some rare flies[5] of amazing forms and colors, presented to 'em by myself, some as big as my fist, some less, and all of various excellencies, such as art cannot imitate. Then we trade for feathers which they order into all shapes, make themselves little short habits of 'em, and glorious wreaths for their heads, necks, arms and legs, whose tinctures are unconceivable. I had a set of these presented to me, and I gave 'em to the King's theater, and it was the dress of the Indian Queen,[6] infinitely admired by persons of quality, and were unimitable. Besides these, a thousand little knacks and rarities in nature, and some of art, as their baskets, weapons, aprons, et cetera. We dealt with 'em with beads of all colors, knives, axes, pins and needles, which they used only as tools to drill holes with in their ears,

1. The text, prepared by Joanna Lipking, is based on the 1688 edition, the sole edition published during Behn's lifetime. The critical edition of G.C. Duchovnay (1971), which collates the four 17th-century editions, has been consulted.
2. A British sugar colony on the South American coast south of Venezuela, later Dutch Guiana.
3. Wild oxen of various species.

4 A name appearing in local descriptions, but the animal is not clearly identified; possibly the *cujara* (Portuguese), a swamp rodent known as the rice rat.
5. Butterflies.
6. The title character in the 1664 heroic play by Sir Robert Howard and John Dryden, which was noted for its lavish production. There are contemporary records of "speckled plumes" and feather headdresses.

noses, and lips, where they hang a great many little things, as long beads, bits of tin, brass, or silver beat thin, and any shining trinket. The beads they weave into aprons about a quarter of an ell long, and of the same breadth,[7] working them very prettily in flowers of several colors of beads; which apron they wear just before 'em, as Adam and Eve did the fig leaves, the men wearing a long stripe of linen which they deal with us for. They thread these beads also on long cotton threads and make girdles to tie their aprons to, which come twenty times or more about the waist, and then cross, like a shoulder belt, both ways, and round their necks, arms, and legs. This adornment, with their long black hair, and the face painted in little specks or flowers here and there, makes 'em a wonderful figure to behold.

Some of the beauties which indeed are finely shaped, as almost all are, and who have pretty features, are very charming and novel; for they have all that is called beauty, except the color, which is a reddish yellow; or after a new oiling, which they often use to themselves, they are of the color of a new brick, but smooth, soft, and sleek. They are extreme[8] modest and bashful, very shy and nice[9] of being touched. And though they are all thus naked, if one lives forever among 'em there is not to be seen an indecent action or glance; and being continually used to see one another so unadorned, so like our first parents before the Fall, it seems as if they had no wishes; there being nothing to heighten curiosity, but all you can see you see at once, and every moment see, and where there is no novelty there can be no curiosity. Not but I have seen a handsome young Indian dying for love of a very beautiful young Indian maid; but all his courtship was to fold his arms, pursue her with his eyes, and sighs were all his language; while she, as if no such lover were present, or rather, as if she desired none such, carefully guarded her eyes from beholding him, and never approached him but she looked down with all the blushing modesty I have seen in the most severe and cautious of our world. And these people represented to me an absolute idea of the first state of innocence, before man knew how to sin. And 'tis most evident and plain that simple Nature is the most harmless, inoffensive, and virtuous mistress. 'Tis she alone, if she were permitted, that better instructs the world than all the inventions of man. Religion would here but destroy that tranquillity they possess by ignorance, and laws would but teach 'em to know offense, of which now they have no notion. They once made mourning and fasting for the death of the English governor, who had given his hand to come on such a day to 'em and neither came nor sent, believing when once a man's word was passed, nothing but death could or should prevent his keeping it. And when they saw he was not dead, they asked him what name they had for a man who promised a thing he did not do. The governor told them, such a man was a liar, which was a word of infamy to a gentleman. Then one of 'em replied, "Governor, you are a liar, and guilty of that infamy." They have a native justice which knows no fraud, and they understand no vice or cunning, but when they are taught by the white men. They have plurality of wives, which, when they grow old, they serve those that succeed 'em, who are young, but with a servitude easy and respected; and unless they take slaves in war, they have no other attendants.

Those on that continent where I was had no king, but the oldest war captain

7. About a foot square. 9. Shy, reluctant.
8. Extremely.

was obeyed with great resignation. A war captain is a man who has led them on to battle with conduct[1] and success, of whom I shall have occasion to speak more hereafter, and of some other of their customs and manners, as they fall in my way.

With these people, as I said, we live in perfect tranquillity and good understanding, as it behooves us to do, they knowing all the places where to seek the best food of the country and the means of getting it, and for very small and unvaluable trifles, supply us with what 'tis impossible for us to get; for they do not only in the wood and over the savannas, in hunting, supply the parts of hounds, by swiftly scouring through those almost impassable places, and by the mere activity of their feet run down the nimblest deer and other eatable beasts; but in the water one would think they were gods of the rivers, or fellow citizens of the deep, so rare an art they have in swimming, diving, and almost living in water, by which they command the less swift inhabitants of the floods. And then for shooting, what they cannot take, or reach with their hands, they do with arrows, and so admirable an aim that they will split almost a hair; and at any distance that an arrow can reach, they will shoot down oranges and other fruit, and only touch the stalk with the dart's point, that they may not hurt the fruit. So that they being, on all occasions, very useful to us, we find it absolutely necessary to caress 'em as friends, and not to treat 'em as slaves; nor dare we do other, their numbers so far surpassing ours in that continent.

Those then whom we make use of to work in our plantations of sugar are Negroes, black slaves altogether, which are transported thither in this manner. Those who want slaves make a bargain with a master or captain of a ship and contract to pay him so much apiece, a matter of twenty pound a head for as many as he agrees for, and to pay for 'em when they shall be delivered on such a plantation. So that when there arrives a ship laden with slaves, they who have so contracted go aboard and receive their number by lot; and perhaps in one lot that may be for ten, there may happen to be three or four men, the rest women and children. Or be there more or less of either sex, you are obliged to be contented with your lot.

Coramantien,[2] a country of blacks so called, was one of those places in which they found the most advantageous trading for these slaves, and thither most of our great traders in that merchandise trafficked; for that nation is very warlike and brave, and having a continual campaign, being always in hostility with one neighboring prince or other, they had the fortune to take a great many captives; for all they took in battle were sold as slaves, at least those common men who could not ransom themselves. Of these slaves so taken, the general only has all the profit; and of these generals, our captains and masters of ships buy all their freights.

The King of Coramantien was himself a man of a hundred and odd years old, and had no son, though he had many beautiful black wives; for most certainly there are beauties that can charm of that color. In his younger years he had had many gallant men to his sons, thirteen of which died in battle, conquering when they fell; and he had only left him for his successor one grand-

1. Aptitude for leadership.

2. Until 1665 a fortified British trading station on the Gold Coast of Africa, in modern-day Ghana. Persons transported from the region were called Cormantines and impressed many European observers by their beauty and bearing; their fierceness in war, and their extreme dignity under captivity or torture.

child, son to one of these dead victors, who, as soon as he could bear a bow in his hand and a quiver at his back, was sent into the field, to be trained up by one of the oldest generals to war; where, from his natural inclination to arms and the occasions given him, with the good conduct of the old general, he became, at the age of seventeen, one of the most expert captains and bravest soldiers that ever saw the field of Mars. So that he was adored as the wonder of all that world, and the darling of the soldiers. Besides, he was adorned with a native beauty so transcending all those of his gloomy race that he struck an awe and reverence even in those that knew not his quality; as he did in me, who beheld him with surprise and wonder, when afterwards he arrived in our world.

He had scarce arrived at his seventeenth year, when fighting by his side, the general was killed with an arrow in his eye, which the Prince Oroonoko (for so was this gallant Moor[3] called) very narrowly avoided; nor had he, if the general, who saw the arrow shot, and perceiving it aimed at the Prince, had not bowed his head between, on purpose to receive it in his own body rather than it should touch that of the Prince, and so saved him.

'Twas then, afflicted as Oroonoko was, that he was proclaimed general in the old man's place; and then it was, at the finishing of that war, which had continued for two years, that the Prince came to court, where he had hardly been a month together from the time of his fifth year to that of seventeen; and 'twas amazing to imagine where it was he learned so much humanity; or to give his accomplishments a juster name, where 'twas he got that real greatness of soul, those refined notions of true honor, that absolute generosity, and that softness that was capable of the highest passions of love and gallantry, whose objects were almost continually fighting men, or those mangled or dead; who heard no sounds but those of war and groans. Some part of it we may attribute to the care of a Frenchman of wit and learning, who, finding it turn to very good account to be a sort of royal tutor to this young black, and perceiving him very ready, apt, and quick of apprehension, took a great pleasure to teach him morals, language, and science, and was for it extremely beloved and valued by him. Another reason was, he loved, when he came from war, to see all the English gentlemen that traded thither, and did not only learn their language but that of the Spaniards also, with whom he traded afterwards for slaves.

I have often seen and conversed with this great man, and been a witness to many of his mighty actions, and do assure my reader the most illustrious courts could not have produced a braver man, both for greatness of courage and mind, a judgment more solid, a wit more quick, and a conversation more sweet and diverting. He knew almost as much as if he had read much. He had heard of and admired the Romans; he had heard of the late civil wars in England, and the deplorable death of our great monarch,[4] and would discourse of it with all the sense and abhorrence of the injustice imaginable. He had an extreme good and graceful mien, and all the civility of a well-bred great man. He had nothing of barbarity in his nature, but in all points addressed himself as if his education had been in some European court.

This great and just character of Oroonoko gave me an extreme curiosity to see him, expecially when I knew he spoke French and English, and that I could talk with him. But though I had heard so much of him, I was as greatly sur-

3. Loosely used for any black-skinned person.
4. British Charles I, beheaded in 1649 during the Civil War between the Royalists and Parliamentarians. In 1688, this remark and others would have signaled Behn's ardent support of James II, the last of the Stuart kings, who would be forced into exile within the year.

prised when I saw him as if I had heard nothing of him, so beyond all report I found him. He came into the room and addressed himself to me, and some other women, with the best grace in the world. He was pretty tall, but of a shape the most exact that can be fancied. The most famous statuary[5] could not form the figure of a man more admirably turned from head to foot. His face was not of that brown, rusty black which most of that nation are, but a perfect ebony or polished jet. His eyes were the most awful that could be seen, and very piercing, the white of 'em being like snow, as were his teeth. His nose was rising and Roman, instead of African and flat; his mouth the finest shaped that could be seen, far from those great turned lips which are so natural to the rest of the Negroes. The whole proportion and air of his face was so noble and exactly formed that, bating[6] his color, there could be nothing in nature more beautiful, agreeable, and handsome. There was no one grace wanting that bears the standard of true beauty. His hair came down to his shoulders by the aids of art; which was by pulling it out with a quill and keeping it combed, of which he took particular care. Nor did the perfections of his mind come short of those of his person, for his discourse was admirable upon almost any subject; and whoever had heard him speak would have been convinced of their errors, that all fine wit is confined to the white men, especially those of Christendom, and would have confessed that Oroonoko was as capable even of reigning well, and of governing as wisely, had as great a soul, as politic maxims, and was as sensible[7] of power, as any prince civilized in the most refined schools of humanity and learning, or the most illustrious courts.

This prince, such as I have described him, whose soul and body were so admirably adorned, was (while yet he was in the court of his grandfather), as I said, as capable of love as 'twas possible for a brave and gallant man to be; and in saying that, I have named the highest degree of love, for sure, great souls are most capable of that passion.

I have already said, the old general was killed by the shot of an arrow, by the side of this prince, in battle, and that Oroonoko was made general. This old dead hero had one only daughter left of his race, a beauty that, to describe her truly, one need say only she was female to the noble male, the beautiful black Venus to our young Mars, as charming in her person as he, and of delicate virtues. I have seen a hundred white men sighing after her, and making a thousand vows at her feet, all vain and unsuccessful. And she was, indeed, too great for any but a prince of her own nation to adore.

Oroonoko coming from the wars (which were now ended), after he had made his court to his grandfather, he thought in honor he ought to make a visit to Imoinda, the daughter of his foster-father, the dead general; and to make some excuses to her, because his preservation was the occasion of her father's death; and to present her with those slaves that had been taken in this last battle, as the trophies of her father's victories. When he came, attended by all the young soldiers of any merit, he was infinitely surprised at the beauty of this fair queen of night, whose face and person was so exceeding all he had ever beheld; that lovely modesty with which she received him; that softness in

5. Sculptor.
6. Except for. The singling out of Africans with European looks or moral values is by no means unique to Behn; for example, Edward Long's 1774 *History of Jamaica* reports of the Cormantines that "their fea-
tures are very different from the rest of the African Negroes, being smaller, and more of the European turn."
7. Cognizant, conscious. "Politic" shrewd, sagacious.

her look, and sighs, upon the melancholy occasion of this honor that was done
by so great a man as Oroonoko, and a prince of whom she had heard such ad-
mirable things: the awfulness[8] wherewith she received him, and the sweetness
of her words and behavior while he stayed, gained a perfect conquest over his
fierce heart, and made him feel the victor could be subdued. So that having
made his first compliments, and presented her a hunded and fifty slaves in fet-
ters, he told her with his eyes that he was not insensible of her charms; while
Imoinda, who wished for nothing more than so glorious a conquest, was
pleased to believe she understood that silent language of newborn love, and
from that moment put on all her additions to beauty.

The prince returned to court with quite another humor than before; and
though he did not speak much of the fair Imoinda, he had the pleasure to hear
all his followers speak of nothing but the charms of that maid, insomuch that,
even in the presence of the old king, they were extolling her and heightening,
if possible, the beauties they had found in her. So that nothing else was talked
of, no other sound was heard in every corner where there were whisperers, but
"Imoinda! Imoinda!"

'Twill be imagined Oroonoko stayed not long before he made his second
visit, nor, considering his quality, not much longer before he told her he
adored her. I have often heard him say that he admired[9] by what strange inspi-
ration he came to talk things so soft and so passionate, who never knew love,
nor was used to the conversation[1] of women; but (to use his own words) he
said, most happily some new and till then unknown power instructed his heart
and tongue in the language of love, and at the same time, in favor of him, in-
spired Imoinda with a sense of his passion. She was touched with what he said,
and returned it all in such answers as went to his very heart, with a pleasure
unknown before. Nor did he use those obligations[2] ill that love had done him,
but turned all his happy moments to the best advantage; and as he knew no
vice, his flame aimed at nothing but honor, if such a distinction may be made
in love; and especially in that country, where men take to themselves as many
as they can maintain, and where the only crime and sin with woman is to turn
her off, to abandon her to want, shame, and misery. Such ill morals are only
practiced in Christian countries, where they prefer the bare name of religion,
and, without virtue or morality, think that's sufficient. But Oroonoko was
none of those professors, but as he had right notion of honor, so he made her
such propositions as were not only and barely such; but contrary to the custom
of his country, he made her vows she should be the only woman he would pos-
sess while he lived; that no age or wrinkles should incline him to change, for
her soul would be always fine and always young, and he should have an eternal
idea in his mind of the charms she now bore, and should look into his heart for
that idea when he could find it no longer in her face.

After a thousand assurances of his lasting flame, and her eternal empire over
him, she condescended to receive him for her husband, or rather, received him
as the greatest honor the gods could do her.

There is a certain ceremony in these cases to be observed, which I forgot to
ask him how performed; but 'twas concluded on both sides that, in obedience
to him, the grandfather was to be first made acquainted with the design, for

8. Reverence. 1. Company.
9. Marveled. 2. Benefits.

they pay a most absolute resignation to the monarch, especially when he is a parent also.

On the other side, the old king, who had many wives and many concubines, wanted not court flatterers to insinuate in his heart a thousand tender thoughts for this young beauty, and who represented her to his fancy as the most charming he had ever possessed in all the long race of his numerous years. At this character his old heart, like an extinguished brand, most apt to take fire, felt new sparks of love and began to kindle; and now grown to his second childhood, longed with impatience to behold this gay thing, with whom, alas! he could but innocently play. But how he should be confirmed she was this wonder, before he used his power to call her to court (where maidens never came, unless for the King's private use). he was next to consider; and while he was so doing, he had intelligence brought him that Imoinda was most certainly mistress to the Prince Oroonoko. This gave him some chagrin; however, it gave him also an opportunity, one day when the Prince was a-hunting. to wait on a man of quality as his slave and attendant, who should go and make a present to Imoinda as from the Prince; he should then, unknown, see this fair maid, and have an opportunity to hear what message she would return the Prince for his present, and from thence gather the state of her heart and degree of her inclination. This was put in execution, and the old monarch saw, and burned. He found her all he had heard, and would not delay his happiness, but found he should have some obstacle to overcome her heart; for she expressed her sense of the present the Prince had sent her in terms so sweet, so soft and pretty, with an air of love and joy that could not be dissembled, insomuch that 'twas past doubt whether she love Oroonoko entirely. This gave the old king some affliction, but he salved it with this, that the obedience the people pay their king was not at all inferior to what they paid their gods; and what love would not oblige Imoinda to do, duty would compel her to.

He was therefore no sooner got to his apartment but he sent the royal veil to Imoinda, that is, the ceremony of invitation: he sends the lady he has a mind to honor with his bed a veil, with which she is covered, and secured for the King's use; and 'tis death to disobey, besides held a most impious disobedience.

'Tis not to be imagined the surprise and grief that seized this lovely maid at this news and sight. However, as delays in these cases are dangerous and pleading worse than treason, trembling, and almost fainting, she was obliged to suffer herself to be covered and led away.

They brought her thus to court; and the King, who had caused a very rich bath to be prepared, was led into it, where he sat under a canopy, in state, to receive this longed-for virgin; whom he having commanded should be brought to him, they (after disrobing her) led her to the bath, and making fast the doors, left her to descend. The King, without more courtship, bade her throw off her mantle and come to his arms. But Imoinda, all in tears, threw herself on the marble, on the brink of the bath, and besought him to hear her. She told him. as she was a maid, how proud of the divine glory she should have been, of having it in her power to oblige her king; but as by the laws he could not, and from his royal goodness would not, take from any man his wedded wife, so she believed she should be the occasion of making him commit a great sin, if she did not reveal her state and condition, and tell him she was another's, and could not be so happy to be his.

The King, enraged at this delay, hastily demanded the name of the bold
man that had married a woman of her degree without his consent. Imoinda,
seeing his eyes fierce and his hands tremble (whether with age or anger, I know
not, but she fancied the last), almost repented she had said so much, for now
she feared the storm would fall on the Prince. She therefore said a thousand
things to appease the raging of his flame, and to prepare him to hear who it
was with calmness; but before she spoke, he imagined who she meant, but
would not seem to do so, but commanded her to lay aside her mantle and suf-
fer herself to receive his caresses; or by his gods, he swore that happy man
whom she was going to name should die, though it were even Oroonoko him-
self. "Therefore," said he, "deny this marriage, and swear thyself a maid."
"That," replied Imoinda, "by all our powers I do, for I am not yet known to my
husband." "'Tis enough," said the King; " 'tis enough to satisfy both my con-
science and my heart." And rising from his seat, he went and led her into the
bath, it being in vain for her to resist.

In this time the Prince, who was returned from hunting, went to visit his
Imoinda, but found her gone; and not only so, but heard she had received the
royal veil. This raised him to a storm, and in his madness they had much ado
to save him from laying violent hands on himself. Force first prevailed, and
then reason. They urged all to him that might oppose his rage, but nothing
weighed so greatly with him as the King's old age, uncapable of injuring him
with Imoinda. He would give way to that hope, because it pleased him most,
and flattered best his heart. Yet this served not altogether to make him cease
his different passions, which sometimes raged within him, and sometimes
softened into showers. 'Twas not enough to appease him, to tell him his grand-
father was old and could not that way injure him, while he retained that awful
duty which the young men are used there to pay to their grave relations. He
could not be convinced he had no cause to sigh and mourn for the loss of a
mistress he could not with all his strength and courage retrieve. And he would
often cry, "O my friends! Were she in walled cities or confined from me in for-
tifications of the greatest strength, did enchantments or monsters detain her
from me, I would venture through any hazard to free her. But here, in the arms
of a feeble old man, my youth, my violent love, my trade in arms, and all my
vast desire of glory avail me nothing. Imoinda is as irrecoverably lost to me as
if she were snatched by the cold arms of Death. Oh! she is never to be re-
trieved. If I would wait tedious years, till fate should bow the old king to his
grave, even that would not leave me Imoinda free; but still that custom that
makes it so vile a crime for a son to marry his father's wives or mistresses would
hinder my happiness, unless I would either ignobly set an ill precedent to my
successors, or abandon my country and fly with her to some unknown world,
who never heard our story."

But it was objected to him that his case was not the same; for Imoinda being
his lawful wife, by solemn contract, 'twas he was the injured man and might if
he so pleased take Imoinda back, the breach of the law being on his grandfa-
ther's side; and that if he could circumvent him and redeem her from the
Otan, which is the palace of the King's women, a sort of seraglio, it was both
just and lawful for him so to do.

This reasoning had some force upon him, and he should have been entirely
comforted, but for the thought that she was possessed by his grandfather.
However, he loved so well that he was resolved to believe what most favored

his hope, and to endeavor to learn from Imoinda's own mouth what only she could satisfy him in, whether she was robbed of that blessing which was only due to his faith and love. But as it was very hard to get a sight of the women (for no men ever entered into the Otan but when the King went to entertain himself with some one of his wives or mistresses, and 'twas death at any other time for any other to go in), so he knew not how to contrive to get a sight of her.

While Oroonoko felt all the agonies of love, and suffered under a torment the most painful in the world, the old king was not exempted from his share of affliction. He was troubled for having been forced by an irresistible passion to rob his son[3] of a treasure he knew could not but be extemely dear to him, since she was the most beautiful that ever had been seen, and had besides all the sweetness and innocence of youth and modesty, with a charm of wit surpassing all. He found that, however she was forced to expose her lovely person to his withered arms, she could only sigh and weep there, and think of Oroonoko; and oftentimes could not forbear speaking of him, though her life were, by custom, forfeited by owning her passion. But she spoke not of a lover only, but of a prince dear to him to whom she spoke, and of the praises of a man who, till now, filled the old man's soul with joy at every recital of his bravery, or even his name. And 'twas this dotage on our young hero that gave Imoinda a thousand privileges to speak of him without offending, and this condescension in the old king that made her take the satisfaction of speaking of him so very often.

Besides, he many times inquired how the Prince bore himself; and those of whom he asked, being entirely slaves to the merits and virtues of the Prince, still answered what they thought conduced best to his service; which was to make the old king fancy that the Prince had no more interest in Imoinda, and had resigned her willingly to the pleasure of the King, that he diverted himself with his mathematicians, his fortifications, his officers, and his hunting.

This pleased the old lover, who failed not to report these things again to Imoinda, that she might, by the example of her young lover, withdraw her heart, and rest better contented in his arms. But however she was forced to receive this unwelcome news, in all appearance with unconcern and content, her heart was bursting within, and she was only happy when she could get alone, to vent her griefs and moans with sighs and tears.

What reports of the Prince's conduct were made to the King, he thought good to justify as far as possibly he could by his actions, and when he appeared in the presence of the King, he showed a face not at all betraying his heart. So that in a little time, the old man being entirely convinced that he was no longer a lover of Imoinda, he carried him with him in his train to the Otan, often to banquet with his mistress. But as soon as he entered, one day, into the apartment of Imoinda with the King, at the first glance from her eyes, notwithstanding all his determined resolution, he was ready to sink in the place where he stood, and had certainly done so but for the support of Aboan, a young man who was next to him; which, with his change of countenance, had betrayed him, had the King chanced to look that way. And I have observed, 'tis a very great error, in those who laugh when one says a Negro can change color, for I have seen 'em as frequently blush, and look pale, and that as visibly as ever I saw in the most beautiful white. And 'tis certain that both

3. I.e., grandson.

these changes were evident, this day, in both these lovers. And Imoinda, who saw with some joy the change in the Prince's face, and found it in her own, strove to divert the King from beholding either by a forced caress, with which she met him, which was a new wound in the heart of the poor dying Prince. But as soon as the King was busied in looking on some fine thing of Imoinda's making, she had time to tell the Prince with her angry but love-darting eyes that she resented his coldness, and bemoaned her own miserable captivity. Nor were his eyes silent, but answered hers again, as much as eyes could do, instructed by the most tender and most passionate heart that ever loved. And they spoke so well and so effectually, as Imoinda no longer doubted but she was the only delight and the darling of that soul she found pleading in 'em its right of love, which none was more willing to resign than she. And 'twas this powerful language alone that in an instant conveyed all the thoughts of their souls to each other, that[4] they both found there wanted but opportunity to make them both entirely happy. But when he saw another door opened by Onahal, a former old wife of the King's who now had charge of Imoinda, and saw the prospect of a bed of state made ready with sweets and flowers for the dalliance of the King, who immediately led the trembling victim from his sight into that prepared repose, what rage, what wild frenzies seized his heart! which forcing to keep within bounds, and to suffer without noise, it became the more insupportable, and rent his soul with ten thousand pains. He was forced to retire to vent his groans, where he fell down on a carpet and lay struggling a long time, and only breathing now and then, "—O Imoinda!"

When Onahal had finished her necessary affair within, shutting the door, she came forth to wait till the King called; and hearing someone sighing in the other room, she passed on, and found the Prince in that deplorable condition, which she thought needed her aid. She gave him cordials, but all in vain, till finding the nature of his disease by his sighs and naming Imoinda. She told him, he had not so much cause as he imagined to afflict himself, for if he knew the King so well as she did, he would not lose a moment in jealousy, and that she was confident that Imoinda bore, at this minute, part in his affliction. Aboan was of the same opinion, and both together persuaded him to reassume his courage; and all sitting down on the carpet, the Prince said so many obliging things to Onahal that he half persuaded her to be of his party. And she promised him she would thus far comply with his just desires, that she would let Imoinda know how faithful he was, what he suffered, and what he said.

This discourse lasted till the King called, which gave Oroonoko a certain satisfaction, and with the hope Onahal had made him conceive, he assumed a look as gay as 'twas possible a man in his circumstances could do; and presently after, he was called in with the rest who waited without. The King commanded music to be brought, and several of his young wives and mistresses came all together by his command to dance before him; where Imoinda performed her part with an air and grace so passing all the rest as her beauty was above 'em, and received the present ordained as a prize. The Prince was every moment more charmed with the new beauties and graces he beheld in this fair one. And while he gazed, and she danced, Onahal was retired to a window with Aboan.

4. So that.

This Onahal, as I said, was one of the cast[5] mistresses of the old king; and 'twas these (now past their beauty) that were made guardians or governants[6] to the new and the young ones, and whose business it was to teach them all those wanton arts of love with which they prevailed and charmed heretofore in their turn; and who now treated the triumphing happy ones with all the severity, as to liberty and freedom that was possible, in revenge of those honors they rob them of; envying them those satisfactions, those gallantries and presents, that were once made to themselves, while youth and beauty lasted, and which they now saw pass regardless by, and were paid only to the bloomings. And certainly nothing is more afflicting to a decayed beauty than to behold in itself declining charms that were once adored, and to find those caresses paid to new beauties to which once she laid a claim; to hear 'em whisper as she passes by, "That once was a delicate woman." These abandoned ladies therefore endeavor to revenge all the despites[7] and decays of time on these flourishing happy ones. And 'twas this severity that gave Oroonoko a thousand fears he should never prevail with Onahal to see Imoinda. But, as I said, she was now retired to a window with Aboan.

This young man was not only one of the best quality,[8] but a man extremely well made and beautiful; and coming often to attend the King to the Otan, he had subdued the heart of the antiquated Onahal, which had not forgot how pleasant it was to be in love. And though she had some decays in her face, she had none in her sense and wit; she was there agreeable still, even to Aboan's youth, so that he took pleasure in entertaining her with discourses of love. He knew also that to make his court to these she-favorites was the way to be great, these being the persons that do all affairs and business at court. He had also observed that she had given him glances more tender and inviting than she had done to others of his quality. And now, when he saw that her favor could so absolutely oblige the Prince, he failed not to sigh in her ear and to look with eyes all soft upon her, and give her hope that she had made some impresssions on his heart. He found her pleased at this, and making a thousand advances to him; but the ceremony ending and the King departing broke up the company for that day, and his conversation.

Aboan failed not that night to tell the Prince of his success, and how advantageous the service of Onahal might be to his amour with Imoinda. The Prince was overjoyed with this good news and besought him, if it were possible, to caress her so as to engage her entirely, which he could not fail to do, if he complied with her desires. "For then," said the Prince, "her life lying at your mercy, she must grant you the request you make in my behalf." Aboan understood him, and assured him he would make love so effectually that he would defy the most expert mistress of the art to find out whether he dissembled it or had it really. And 'twas with impatience they waited the next opportunity of going to the Otan.

The wars came on, the time of taking the field approached, and 'twas impossible for the Prince to delay his going at the head of his army to encounter the enemy. So that every day seemed a tedious year till he saw his Imoinda, for he believed he could not live if he were forced away without being so happy. 'Twas with impatience, therefore, that he expected the next visit the King would make, and according to his wish, it was not long.

5. Cast-off.
6. Female teachers or chaperones
7. Insults.
8. Rank.

The parley of the eyes of these two lovers had not passed so secretly but an old jealous lover could spy it; or rather, he wanted not flatterers who told him they observed it. So that the Prince was hastened to the camp, and this was the last visit he found he should make to the Otan; he therefore urged Aboan to make the best of this last effort, and to explain himself so to Onahal that she, deferring her enjoyment of her young lover no longer, might make way for the Prince to speak to Imoinda.

The whole affair being agreed on between the Prince and Aboan, they attended the King, as the custom was, to the Otan, where, while the whole company was taken up in beholding the dancing and antic posture the women-royal made to divert the King, Onahal singled out Aboan, whom she found most pliable to her wish. When she had him where she believed she could not be heard, she sighed to him, and softly cried, "Ah, Aboan! When will you be sensible of my passion? I confess it with my mouth, because I would not give my eyes the lie; and you have but too much already perceived they have confessed my flame. Nor would I have you believe that because I am the abandoned mistress of a king, I esteem myself altogether divested of charms. No, Aboan; I have still a rest[9] of beauty enough engaging, and have learned to please too well not to be desirable. I can have lovers still, but will have none but Aboan." "Madam," replied the half-feigning youth, "you have already, by my eyes, found you can still conquer, and I believe 'tis in pity of me you condescend to this kind confession. But, Madam, words are used to be so small a part of our country courtship, that 'tis rare one can get so happy an opportunity as to tell one's heart, and those few minutes we have are forced to be snatched for more certain proofs of love than speaking and sighing: and such I languish for."

He spoke this with such a tone that she hoped it true, and could not forbear believing it; and being wholly transported with joy, for having subdued the finest of all the King's subjects to her desires, she took from her ears two large pearls and commanded him to wear 'em in his. He would have refused 'em, crying, "Madam, these are not the proofs of your love that I expect; 'tis opportunity, 'tis a lone hour only, that can make me happy." But forcing the pearls into his hand, she whispered softly to him, "Oh! Do not fear a woman's invention, when love sets her a-thinking." And pressing his hand, she cried, "This night you shall be happy. Come to the gate of the orange groves behind the Otan, and I will be ready, about midnight, to receive you." 'Twas thus agreed, and she left him, that no notice might be taken of their speaking together.

The ladies were still dancing, and the King, laid on a carpet, with a great deal of pleasure was beholding them, especially Imoinda, who that day appeared more lovely than ever, being enlivened with the good tidings Onahal had brought her of the constant passion the Prince had for her. The Prince was laid on another carpet at the other end of the room, with his eyes fixed on the object of his soul; and as she turned or moved, so did they, and she alone gave his eyes and soul their motions. Nor did Imoinda employ her eyes to any other use than in beholding with infinite pleasure the joy she produced in those of the Prince. But while she was more regarding him than the steps she took, she chanced to fall, and so near him as that, leaping with extreme force from the carpet, he caught her in his arms as she fell; and 'twas visible to the whole pres-

9. Remnant.

ence[1] the joy wherewith he received her. He clasped her close to his bosom, and quite forgot that reverence that was due to the mistress of a king, and that punishment that is the reward of a boldness of this nature; and had not the presence of mind of Imoinda (fonder of his safety than her own) befriended him, in making her spring from his arms and fall into her dance again, he had at that instant met his death; for the old king, jealous to the last degree, rose up in rage, broke all the diversion, and led Imoinda to her apartment, and sent out word to the Prince to go immediately to the camp, and that if he were found another night in court he should suffer the death ordained for disobedient offenders.

You may imagine how welcome this news was to Oroonoko, whose unseasonable transport and caress of Imoinda was blamed by all men that loved him; and now he perceived his fault, yet cried that for such another moment, he would be content to die.

All the Otan was in disorder about this accident; and Onahal was particularly concerned, because on the Prince's stay depended her happiness, for she could no longer expect that of Aboan. So that ere they departed, they contrived it so that the Prince and he should come both that night to the grove of the Otan which was all of oranges and citrons, and that there they should wait her orders.

They parted thus, with grief enough, till night, leaving the King in possession of the lovely maid. But nothing could appease the jealousy of the old lover. He would not be imposed on, but would have it that Imoinda made a false step on purpose to fall into Oroonoko's bosom, and that all things looked like a design on both sides; and 'twas in vain she protested her innocence. He was old and obstinate, and left her more than half assured that his fear was true.

The King going to his apartment sent to know where the Prince was, and if he intended to obey his command. The messenger returned and told him, he found the Prince pensive and altogether unpreparing for the campaign, that he lay negligently on the ground, and answered very little. This confirmed the jealousy of the King, and he commanded that they should very narrowly and privately watch his motions, and that he should not stir from his apartment but one spy or other should be employed to watch him. So that the hour approaching wherein he was to go to the citron grove, and taking only Aboan along with him, he leaves his apartment, and was watched to the very gate of the Otan where he was seen to enter, and where they left him, to carry back the tidings to the King.

Oroonoko and Aboan were no sooner entered but Onahal led the Prince to the apartment of Imoinda, who, not knowing anything of her happiness, was laid in bed. But Onahal only left him in her chamber, to make the best of his opportunity, and took her dear Aboan to her own, where he showed the heighth of complaisance for his prince, when, to give him an opportunity, he suffered himself to be caressed in bed by Onahal.

The Prince softly wakened Imoinda, who was not a little surprised with joy to find him there; and yet she trembled with a thousand fears. I believe he omitted saying nothing to this young maid that might persuade her to suffer him to seize his own, and take the rights of love; and I believe she was not long

1. Company.

resisting those arms where she so longed to be; and having opportunity, night and silence, youth, love and desire, he soon prevailed, and ravished in a moment what his old grandfather had been endeavoring for so many months.

'Tis not to be imagined the satisfaction of these two young lovers; not the vows she made him that she remained a spotless maid till that night, and that what she did with his grandfather had robbed him of no part of her virgin honor, the gods in mercy and justice having reserved that for her plighted lord, to whom of right it belonged. And 'tis impossible to express the transports he suffered, while he listened to a discourse so charming from her loved lips, and clasped that body in his arms for whom he had so long languished; and nothing now afflicted him but his sudden departure from her; for he told her the necessity and his commands, but should depart satisfied in this, that since the old king had hitherto not been able to deprive him of those enjoyments which only belonged to him, he believed for the future he would be less able to injure him; so that abating the scandal of the veil, which was no otherwise so than that she was wife to another, he believed her safe, even in the arms of the King, and innocent; yet would he have ventured at the conquest of the world, and have given it all, to have had her avoided that honor of receiving the royal veil. 'Twas thus, between a thousand caresses, that both bemoaned the hard fate of youth and beauty, so liable to that cruel promotion. 'Twas a glory that could well have been spared here, though desired and aimed at by all the young females of that kingdom.

But while they were thus fondly employed, forgetting how time ran on, and that the dawn must conduct him far away from his only happiness, they heard a great noise in the Otan, and unusual voices of men; at which the Prince, starting from the arms of the frighted Imoinda, ran to a little battle-ax he used to wear by his side, and having not so much leisure as to put on his habit, he opposed himself against some who were already opening the door; which they did with so much violence that Oroonoko was not able to defend it, but was forced to cry out with a commanding voice, "Whoever ye are that have the boldness to attempt to approach this apartment thus rudely, know that I, the Prince Oroonoko, will revenge it with the certain death of him that first enters. Therefore stand back, and know, this place is sacred to love and me this night; tomorrow 'tis the King's."

This he spoke with a voice so resolved and assured that they soon retired from the door, but cried, "'Tis by the King's command we are come; and being satisfied by thy voice, O Prince, as much as if we had entered, we can report to the King the truth of all his fears, and leave thee to provide for thy own safety, as thou art advised by thy friends."

At these words they departed, and left the Prince to take a short and sad leave of his Imoinda, who, trusting in the strength of her charms, believed she should appease the fury of a jealous king by saying she was surprised, and that it was by force of arms he got into her apartment. All her concern now was for his life, and therefore she hastened him to the camp, and with much ado prevailed on him to go. Nor was it she alone that prevailed; Aboan and Onahal both pleaded, and both assured him of a lie that should be well enough contrived to secure Imoinda. So that at last, with a heart sad as death, dying eyes, and sighing soul, Oroonoko departed and took his way to the camp.

It was not long after the King in person came to the Otan, where, beholding Imoinda with rage in his eyes, he upbraided her wickedness and perfidy, and

threatening her royal lover, she fell on her face at his feet, bedewing the floor
with her tears and imploring his pardon for a fault which she had not with her
will committed, as Onahal, who was also prostrate with her, could testify; that
unknown to her, he had broke into her apartment, and ravished her. She spoke
this much against her conscience, but to save her own life 'twas absolutely
necessary she should feign this falsity. She knew it could not injure the Prince,
he being fled to an army that would stand by him against any injuries that
should assault him. However, this last thought of Imoinda's being ravished
changed the measures of his revenge; and whereas before he designed to be
himself her executioner, he now resolved she should not die. But as it is the
greatest crime in nature amongst 'em to touch a woman after having been
possessed by a son, a father, or a brother, so now he looked on Imoinda as a pol-
luted thing, wholly unfit for his embrace; nor would he resign her to his grand-
son, because she had received the royal veil. He therefore removes her from
the Otan, with Onahal; whom he put into safe hands, with order they should
be both sold off as slaves to another country, either Christian or heathen; 'twas
no matter where.

 This cruel sentence, worse than death, they implored might be reversed;
but their prayers were vain, and it was put in execution accordingly, and that
with so much secrecy that none, either without or within the Otan, knew any-
thing of their absence or their destiny.

 The old king, nevertheless, executed this with a great deal of reluctancy; but
he believed he had made a very great conquest over himself, when he had once
resolved, and had performed what he resolved. He believed now that his love
had been unjust, and that he could not expect the gods, or Captain of the
Clouds (as they call the unknown power), should suffer a better consequence
from so ill a cause. He now begins to hold Oroonoko excused, and to say he
had reason for what he did. And now everybody could assure the King how
passionately Imoinda was beloved by the Prince; even those confessed it now,
who said the contrary before his flame was abated. So that the King being old,
and not able to defend himself in war, and having no sons of all his race re-
maining alive but only this, to maintain him on his throne; and looking on this
as a man disobliged, first by the rape of his mistress, or rather wife; and now by
depriving of him wholly of her, he feared, might make him desperate and do
some cruel thing, either to himself or his old grandfather, the offender: he
began to repent him extremely of the contempt he had, in his rage, put on
Imoinda. Besides, he considered he ought in honor to have killed her for this
offense, if it had been one. He ought to have had so much value and consider-
ation for a maid of her quality as to have nobly put her to death, and not to
have sold her like a common slave, the greatest revenge and the most dis-
graceful of any; and to which they a thousand times prefer death, and implore
it, as Imoinda did, but could not obtain that honor. Seeing therefore it was
certain that Oroonoko would highly resent this affront, he thought good to
make some excuse for his rashness to him; and to that end he sent a messen-
ger to the camp, with orders to treat with him about the matter, to gain his
pardon, and to endeavor to mitigate his grief; but that by no means he should
tell him she was sold, but secretly put to death, for he knew he should never
obtain his pardon for the other.

 When the messenger came, he found the Prince upon the point of engaging
with the enemy; but as soon as he heard of the arrival of the messenger, he

commanded him to his tent, where he embraced him and received him with joy; which was soon abated by the downcast looks of the messenger, who was instantly demanded the cause by Oroonoko, who, impatient of delay, asked a thousand questions in a breath, and all concerning Imoinda. But there needed little return, for he could almost answer himself of all he demanded, from his sighs and eyes. At last, the messenger casting himself at the Prince's feet, and kissing them with all the submission of a man that had something to implore which he dreaded to utter, he besought him to hear with calmness what he had to deliver to him, and to call up all his noble and heroic courage to encounter with his words, and defend himself against the ungrateful[2] things he must relate. Oroonoko replied, with a deep sigh and a languishing voice, "I am armed against their worst efforts—; for I know they will tell me, Imoinda is no more—and after that, you may spare the rest." Then, commanding him to rise, he laid himself on a carpet, under a rich pavilion, and remained a good while silent, and was hardly heard to sigh. When he was come a little to himself, the messenger asked him leave to deliver that part of his embassy which the Prince had not yet divined. And the Prince cried, "I permit thee—." Then he told him the affliction the old king was in, for the rashness he had committed in his cruelty to Imoinda; and how he deigned to ask pardon for his offense, and to implore the Prince would not suffer that loss to touch his heart too sensibly, which now all the gods could not restore him, but might recompense him in glory, which he begged he would pursue; and that Death, that common revenger of all injuries, would soon even the account between him and a feeble old man.

Oroonoko bade him return his duty to his lord and master, and to assure him, there was no account of revenge to be adjusted between them; if there were, 'twas he was the aggressor, and that Death would be just and, maugre[3] his age, would see him righted; and he was contented to leave his share of glory to youths more fortunate and worthy of that favor from the gods. That henceforth he would never lift a weapon or draw a bow, but abandon the small remains of his life to sighs and tears, and the continual thoughts of what his lord and grandfather had thought good to send out of the world, with all that youth, that innocence, and beauty.

After having spoken this, whatever his greatest officers and men of the best rank could do, they could not raise him from the carpet, or persuade him to action and resolutions of life; but commanding all to retire, he shut himself into his pavilion all that day, while the enemy was ready to engage; and wondering at the delay, the whole body of the chief of the army then addressed themselves to him, and to whom they had much ado to get admittance. They fell on their faces at the foot of his carpet, where they lay and besought him with earnest prayers and tears to lead 'em forth to battle, and not let the enemy take advantages of them; and implored him to have regard to his glory, and to the world, that depended on his courage and conduct. But he made no other reply to all their supplications but this, that he had now no more business for glory; and for the world, it was a trifle not worth his care. "Go," continued he, sighing, "and divide it amongst you; and reap with joy what you so vainly prize, and leave me to my more welcome destiny."

They then demanded what they should do, and whom he would constitute

2. Offensive. 3. In spite of. Oroonoko is saying that he will die first.

in his room, that the confusion of ambitious youth and power might not ruin their order and make them a prey to the enemy. He replied, he would not give himself the trouble—; but wished 'em to choose the bravest man amongst 'em, let his quality or birth be what it would. "For, O my friends!" said he, "it is not titles make men brave or good, or birth that bestows courage and generosity, or makes the owner happy. Believe this, when you behold Oroonoko, the most wretched and abandoned by fortune of all the creation of the gods." So turning himself about, he would make no more reply to all they could urge or implore.

The army, beholding their officers return unsuccessful, with sad faces and ominous looks that presaged no good luck, suffered a thousand fears to take possession of their hearts, and the enemy to come even upon 'em, before they would provide for their safety by any defense; and though they were assured by some, who had a mind to animate 'em, that they should be immediately headed by the Prince, and that in the meantime Aboan had orders to command as general, yet they were so dismayed for want of that great example of bravery that they could make but a very feeble resistance; and at last downright fled before the enemy, who pursued 'em to the very tents, killing 'em. Nor could all Aboan's courage, which that day gained him immortal glory, shame 'em into a manly defense of themselves. The guards that were left behind about the Prince's tent, seeing the soldiers flee before the enemy and scatter themselves all over the plain, in great disorder, made such outcries as roused the Prince from his amorous slumber, in which he had remained buried for two days without permitting any sustenance to approach him. But in spite of all his resolutions, he had not the constancy of grief to that degree, as to make him insensible of the danger of his army; and in that instant he leaped from his couch and cried, "—Come, if we must die, let us meet Death the noblest way; and 'twill be more like Oroonoko to encounter him at an army's head, opposing the torrent of a conquering foe, than lazily on a couch to wait his lingering pleasure, and die every moment by a thousand wrecking[4] thoughts; or be tamely taken by an enemy, and led a whining, lovesick slave to adorn the triumphs of Jamoan, that young victor, who already is entered beyond the limits I had prescribed him."

While he was speaking, he suffered his people to dress him for the field, and sallying out of his pavilion, with more life and vigor in his countenance than ever he showed, he appeared like some divine power descended to save his country from destruction; and his people had purposely put on him all things that might make him shine with most splendor, to strike a reverend awe into the beholders. He flew into the thickest of those that were pursuing his men, and being animated with despair, he fought as if he came on purpose to die, and did such things as will not be believed that human strength could perform, and such as soon inspired all the rest with new courage and new order. And now it was that they began to fight indeed, and so as if they would not be outdone even by their adored hero; who, turning the tide of the victory, changing absolutely the fate of the day, gained an entire conquest; and Oroonoko having the good fortune to single out Jamoan, he took him prisoner with his own hand, having wounded him almost to death.

This Jamoan afterwards became very dear to him, being a man very gallant

4. Racking.

and of excellent graces and fine parts; so that he never put him amongst the rank of captives, as they used to do, without distinction, for the common sale or market; but kept him in his own court, where he retained nothing of the prisoner but the name, and returned no more into his own country, so great an affection he took for Oroonoko; and by a thousand tales and adventures of love and gallantry flattered[5] his disease of melancholy and languishment, which I have often heard him say had certainly killed him, but for the conversation of this prince and Aboan, and the French governor he had from his childhood, of whom I have spoken before, and who was a man of admirable wit, great ingenuity and learning, all which he had infused into his young pupil. This Frenchman was banished out of his own country for some heretical notions he held, and though he was a man of very little religion, he had admirable morals and a brave soul.

After the total defeat of Jamoan's army, which all fled, or were left dead upon the place, they spent some time in the camp, Oroonoko choosing rather to remain a while there in his tents than enter into a palace or live in a court where he had so lately suffered so great a loss. The officers, therefore, who saw and knew his cause of discontent, invented all sorts of diversions and sports to entertain their prince; so that what with those amusements abroad and others at home, that is, within their tents, with the persuasions, arguments, and care of his friends and servants that he more peculiarly prized, he wore off in time a great part of that chagrin and torture of despair which the first efforts of Imoinda's death had given him. Insomuch as having received a thousand kind embassies from the King, and invitations to return to court, he obeyed, though with no little reluctancy; and when he did so, there was a visible change in him, and for a long time he was much more melancholy than before. But time lessens all extremes, and reduces 'em to mediums and unconcern; but no motives or beauties, though all endeavored it, could engage him in any sort of amour, though he had all the invitations to it, both from his own youth and others' ambitions and designs.

Oroonoko was no sooner returned from this last conquest, and received at court with all the joy and magnificence that could be expressed to a young victor, who was not only returned triumphant but beloved like a deity, when there arrived in the port an English ship.

This person[6] had often before been in these countries and was very well known to Oroonoko, with whom he had trafficked for slaves, and had used to do the same with his predecessors.

This commander was a man of a finer sort of address and conversation, better bred and more engaging than most of that sort of men are, so that he seemed rather never to have been bred out of a court than almost all his life at sea. This captain therefore was always better received at court than most of the traders to those countries were; and especially by Oroonoko, who was more civilized, according to the European mode, than any other had been, and took more delight in the white nations, and above all men of parts and wit. To this captain he sold abundance of his slaves, and for the favor and esteem he had for him, made him many presents, and obliged him to stay at court as long as possibly he could. Which the captain seemed to take as a very great honor done him, entertaining the Prince every day with globes and maps, and math-

5. Soothed. 6. The ship's captain.

ematical discourses and instruments; eating, drinking, hunting, and living with him with so much familiarity that it was not to be doubted but he had gained very greatly upon the heart of this gallant young man. And the captain, in return of all these mighty favors, besought the Prince to honor his vessel with his presence, some day or other, to dinner before he should set sail; which he condescended to accept, and appointed his day. The captain, on his part, failed not to have all things in a readiness, in the most magnificent order he could possibly. And the day being come, the captain in his boat, richly adorned with carpets and velvet cushions, rowed to the shore to receive the Prince, with another longboat where was placed all his music and trumpets, with which Oroonoko was extremely delighted; who met him on the shore attended by his French governor, Jamoan, Aboan, and about a hundred of the noblest of the youths of the court. And after they had first carried the Prince on board, the boats fetched the rest off; where they found a very splendid treat, with all sorts of fine wines, and were as well entertained as 'twas possible in such a place to be.

The Prince, having drunk hard of punch and several sorts of wine, as did all the rest (for great care was taken they should want nothing of that part of the entertainment), was very merry, and in great admiration of the ship, for he had never been in one before; so that he was curious of beholding every place where he decently might descend. The rest, no less curious, who were not quite overcome with drinking, rambled at their pleasure fore and aft, as their fancies guided 'em. So that the captain, who had well laid his design before, gave the word, and seized on all his guests; they clapping great irons suddenly on the Prince, when he was leaped down in the hold to view that part of the vessel, and locking him fast down, secured him. The same treachery was used to all the rest; and all in one instant, in several places of the ship, were lashed fast in irons, and betrayed to slavery. That great design over, they set all hands to work to hoise[7] sail; and with as treacherous and fair a wind, they made from the shore with this innocent and glorious prize, who thought of nothing less than such an entertainment.

Some have commended this act as brave in the captain; but I will spare my sense of it, and leave it to my reader to judge as he pleases.

It may be easily guessed in what manner the Prince resented this indignity, who may be best resembled to a lion taken in a toil; so he raged, so he struggled for liberty, but all in vain; and they had so wisely managed his fetters that he could not use a hand in his defense, to quit himself of a life that would by no means endure slavery, nor could he move from the place where he was tied to any solid part of the ship, against which he might have beat his head, and have finished his disgrace that way. So that being deprived of all other means, he resolved to perish for want of food. And pleased at last with that thought, and toiled and tired by rage and indignation, he laid himself down, and sullenly resolved upon dying, and refused all things that were brought him.

This did not a little vex the captain, and the more so because he found almost all of 'em of the same humor; so that the loss of so many brave slaves, so tall and goodly to behold, would have been very considerable. He therefore ordered one to go from him (for he would not be seen himself) to Oroonoko, and to assure him he was afflicted for having rashly done so unhospitable a deed,

7. Hoist.

and which could not be now remedied, since they were far from shore; but since he resented it in so high a nature, he assured him he would revoke his resolution, and set both him and his friends ashore on the next land they should touch at; and of this the messenger gave him his oath, provided he would resolve to live. And Oroonoko, whose honor was such as he never had violated a word in his life himself, much less a solemn asseveration, believed in an instant what this man said, but replied, he expected for a confirmation of this to have his shameful fetters dismissed. This demand was carried to the captain, who returned him answer that the offense had been so great which he had put upon the Prince that he durst not trust him with liberty while he remained in the ship, for fear lest by a valor natural to him, and a revenge that would animate that valor, he might commit some outrage fatal to himself and the King his master, to whom his vessel did belong. To this Oroonoko replied, he would engage his honor to behave himself in all friendly order and manner, and obey the command of the captain, as he was lord of the King's vessel and general of those men under his command.

This was delivered to the still doubting captain, who could not resolve to trust a heathen, he said, upon his parole,[8] a man that had no sense or notion of the God that he worshipped. Oroonoko then replied, he was very sorry to hear that the captain pretended to the knowledge and worship of any gods who had taught him no better principles than not to credit as he would be credited; but they told him the difference of their faith occasioned that distrust. For the captain had protested to him upon the word of a Christian, and sworn in the name of a great god, which if he should violate, he would expect eternal torment in the world to come. "Is that all the obligation he has to be just to his oath?" replied Oroonoko. "Let him know I swear by my honor; which to violate, would not only render me contemptible and despised by all brave and honest men, and so give myself perpetual pain, but it would be eternally offending and diseasing all mankind, harming, betraying, circumventing and outraging all men; but punishments hereafter are suffered by one's self, and the world takes no cognizances whether this god have revenged 'em or not, 'tis done so secretly and deferred so long. While the man of no honor suffers every moment the scorn and contempt of the honester world, and dies every day ignominiously in his fame, which is more valuable than life. I speak not this to move belief, but to show you how you mistake, when you imagine that he who will violate his honor will keep his word with his gods." So turning from him with a disdainful smile, he refused to answer him, when he urged him to know what answer he should carry back to his captain; so that he departed without saying any more.

The captain pondering and consulting what to do, it was concluded that nothing but Oroonoko's liberty would encourage any of the rest to eat, except the Frenchman, whom the captain could not pretend to keep prisoner, but only told him he was secured because he might act something in favor of the Prince, but that he should be freed as soon as they came to land. So that they concluded it wholly necessary to free the Prince from his irons, that he might show himself to the rest; that they might have an eye upon him, and that they could not fear a single man.

This being resolved, to make the obligation the greater, the captain himself

8. Word of honor.

went to Oroonoko; where after many compliments, and assurances of what he had already promised, he receiving from the Prince his parole and his hand for his good behavior, dismissed his irons and brought him to his own cabin; where after having treated and reposed him a while, for he had neither eat[9] nor slept in four days before, he besought him to visit those obstinate people in chains, who refused all manner of sustenance, and entreated him to oblige 'em to eat, and assure 'em of their liberty the first opportunity.

Oroonoko, who was too generous not to give credit to his words, showed himself to his people, who were transported with excess of joy at the sight of their darling prince, falling at his feet and kissing and embracing 'em, believing, as some divine oracle, all he assured 'em. But he besought 'em to bear their chains with that bravery that became those whom he had seen act so nobly in arms; and that they could not give him greater proofs of their love and friendship, since 'twas all the security the captain (his friend) could have, against the revenge, he said, they might possibly justly take for the injuries sustained by him. And they all with one accord assured him, they could not suffer enough, when it was for his repose and safety.

After this they no longer refused to eat, but took what was brought 'em, and were pleased with their captivity, since by it they hoped to redeem the Prince, who, all the rest of the voyage, was treated with all the respect due to his birth, though nothing could divert his melancholy; and he would often sigh for Imoinda, and think this a punishment due to his misfortune, in having left that noble maid behind him that fatal night, in the Otan, when he fled to the camp.

Possessed with a thousand thoughts of past joys with this fair young person, and a thousand griefs for her eternal loss, he endured a tedious voyage, and at last arrived at the mouth of the river of Surinam, a colony belonging to the King of England, and where they were to deliver some part of their slaves. There the merchants and gentlemen of the country going on board to demand those lots of slaves they had already agreed on, and, amongst those, the overseers of those plantations where I then chanced to be, the captain, who had given the word, ordered his men to bring up those noble slaves in fetters whom I have spoken of; and havin' put 'em some in one and some in other lots, with women and children (which they call pickaninnies), they sold 'em off as slaves to several merchants and gentlemen; not putting any two in one lot, because they would separate 'em far from each other, not daring to trust 'em together, lest rage and courage should put 'em upon contriving some great action, to the ruin of the colony.

Oroonoko was first seized on, and sold to our overseer, who had the first lot, with seventeen more of all sorts and sizes, but not one of quality with him. When he saw this, he found what they meant, for, as I said, he understood English pretty well; and being wholly unarmed and defenseless, so as it was in vain to make any resistance, he only beheld the captain with a look all fierce and disdainful, upbraiding him with eyes that forced blushes on his guilty cheeks; he only cried, in passing over the side of the ship, "Farewell, sir. 'Tis worth my suffering, to gain so true a knowledge both of you and of your gods by whom you swear." And desiring those that held him to forbear their pains, and telling 'em he would make no resistance, he cried, "Come, my fellow

9. The past form of *eat*.

slaves; let us descend, and see if we can meet with more honor and honesty in the next world we shall touch upon." So he nimbly leaped into the boat, and showing no more concern, suffered himself to be rowed up the river with his seventeen companions.

The gentleman that bought him was a young Cornish gentleman whose name was Trefry, a man of great wit and fine learning, and was carried into those parts by the Lord——, Governor,[1] to manage all his affairs. He reflecting on the last words of Oroonoko to the captain, and beholding the richness of his vest,[2] no sooner came into the boat but he fixed his eyes on him; and finding something so extraordinary in his face, his shape and mien, a greatness of look and haughtiness in his air, and finding he spoke English, had a great mind to be inquiring into his quality and fortune; which, though Oroonoko endeavored to hide, by only confessing he was above the rank of common slaves, Trefry soon found he was yet something greater than he confessed, and from that moment began to conceive so vast an esteem for him that he ever after loved him as his dearest brother, and showed him all the civilities due to so great a man.

Trefry was a very good mathematician and a linguist, could speak French and Spanish; and in the three days they remained in the boat (for so long were they going from the ship to the plantation) he entertained Oroonoko so agreeably with his art and discourse, that he was no less pleased with Trefry than he was with the Prince; and he thought himself at least fortunate in this, that since he was a slave, as long as he would suffer himself to remain so, he had a man of so excellent wit and parts for a master. So that before they had finished their voyage up the river, he made no scruple of declaring to Trefry all his fortunes, and most part of what I have here related, and put himself wholly into the hands of his new friend, whom he found resenting all the injuries were done him, and was charmed with all the greatness of his actions; which were recited with that modesty and delicate sense as wholly vanquished him, and subdued him to his interest. And he promised him on his word and honor, he would find the means to reconduct him to his own country again, assuring him, he had a perfect abhorrence of so dishonorable an action, and that he would sooner have died than have been the author of such a perfidy. He found the Prince was very much concerned to know what became of his friends, and how they took their slavery; and Trefry promised to take care about the inquiring after their condition, and that he should have an account of 'em.

Though, as Oroonoko afterwards said, he had little reason to credit the words of a *backearary*,[3] yet he knew not why, but he saw a kind of sincerity and awful truth in the face of Trefry; he saw an honesty in his eyes, and he found him wise and witty enough to understand honor; for it was one of his maxims, a man of wit could not be a knave or villain.

In their passage up the river they put in at several houses for refreshment, and ever when they landed, numbers of people would flock to behold this man; not but their eyes were daily entertained with the sight of slaves, but the fame of Oroonoko was gone before him, and all people were in admiration of his beauty. Besides, he had a rich habit on, in which he was taken, so different

1. Lord Willoughby of Parham, coproprietor of Surinam by royal grant. John Trefry was his plantation overseer.
2. An outer garment or robe.
3. White person or master; a variant of *backra*, from an Ibo word transported with the slaves to Surinam and the Caribbean.

from the rest, and which the captain could not strip him of, because he was forced to surprise his person in the minute he sold him. When he found his habit made him liable, as he thought, to be gazed at the more, he begged Trefry to give him something more befitting a slave, which he did, and took off his robes. Nevertheless, he shone through all; and his osenbrigs (a sort of brown holland[4] suit he had on) could not conceal the graces of his locks and mien, and he had no less admirers than when he had his dazzling habit on. The royal youth appeared in spite of the slave, and people could not help treating him after a different manner, without designing it. As soon as they approached him they venerated and esteemed him; his eyes insensibly commanded respect, and his behavior insinuated it into every soul. So that there was nothing talked of but this young and gallant slave, even by those who yet knew not that he was a prince.

I ought to tell you that the Christians never buy any slaves but they give 'em some name of their own, their native ones being likely very barbarous and hard to pronounce; so that Mr. Trefry gave Oroonoko that of Caesar, which name will live in that country as long as that (scarce more) glorious one of the great Roman; for 'tis most evident, he wanted[5] no part of the personal courage of that Caesar, and acted things as memorable, had they been done in some part of the world replenished with people and historians that might have given him his due. But his misfortune was to fall in an obscure world, that afforded only a female pen to celebrate his fame; though I doubt not but it had lived from others' endeavors, if the Dutch, who immediately after his time took that country,[6] had not killed, banished, and dispersed all those that were capable of giving the world this great man's life, much better than I have done. And Mr. Trefry, who designed it, died before he began it, and bemoaned himself for not having undertook it in time.

For the future, therefore, I must call Oroonoko Caesar, since by that name only he was known in our western world, and by that name he was received on shore at Parham House, where he was destined a slave. But if the King himself (God bless him) had come ashore, there could not have been greater expectations by all the whole plantation, and those neighboring ones, than was on ours at that time; and he was received more like a governor than a slave. Notwithstanding, as the custom was, they assigned him his portion of land, his house, and his business, up in the plantation. But as it was more for form than any design to put him to his task, he endured no more of the slave but the name, and remained some days in the house, receiving all visits that were made him, without stirring towards that part of the plantation where the Negroes were.

At last he would needs go view his land, his house, and the business assigned him. But he no sooner came to the houses of the slaves, which are like a little town by itself, the Negroes all having left work, but they all came forth to behold him, and found he was that prince who had, at several times, sold most of 'em to these parts; and from a veneration they pay to great men, especially if they know 'em, and from the surprise and awe they had at the sight of him, they all cast themselves at his feet, crying out in their language, "Live, O King! Long live, O King!" and kissing his feet, paid him even divine homage.

4. Coarse cotton or linen, sometimes called osnaburg, after a German cloth-manufacturing town.
5. Lacked.

6 In 1667 the Dutch attacked and conquered Surinam, and England ceded it by treaty in exchange for New York.

Several English gentlemen were with him; and what Mr. Trefry had told 'em was here confirmed, of which he himself before had no other witness than Caesar himself. But he was infinitely glad to find his grandeur confirmed by the adoration of all the slaves.

Caesar, troubled with their over-joy and over-ceremony, besought 'em to rise and to receive him as their fellow slave, assuring them he was no better. At which they set up with one accord a most terrible and hideous mourning and condoling, which he and the English had much ado to appease; but at last they prevailed with 'em, and they prepared all their barbarous music, and everyone killed and dressed something of his own stock (for every family has their land apart, on which, at their leisure times, they breed all eatable things), and clubbing it together,[7] made a most magnificent supper, inviting their *Grandee Captain*, their prince, to honor it with his presence; which he did, and several English with him; where they all waited on him, some playing, others dancing before him all the time, according to the manners of their several nations, and with unwearied industry endeavoring to please and delight him.

While they sat at meat Mr. Trefry told Caesar that most of these young slaves were undone in love with a fine she-slave, whom they had had about six months on their land. The Prince, who never heard the name of love without a sigh, nor any mention of it without the curiosity of examining further into that tale, which of all discourses was most agreeable to him, asked how they came to be so unhappy as to be all undone for one fair slave. Trefry, who was naturally amorous and loved to talk of love as well as anybody, proceeded to tell him, they had the most charming black that ever was beheld on their plantation, about fifteen or sixteen years old, as he guessed; that for his part, he had done nothing but sigh for her ever since she came, and that all the white beauties he had seen never charmed him so absolutely as this fine creature had done; and that no man, of any nation, ever beheld her that did not fall in love with her; and that she had all the slaves perpetually at her feet, and the whole country resounded with the fame of Clemene, "for so," said he, "we have christened her. But she denies us all with such a noble disdain, that 'tis a miracle to see that she, who can give such eternal desires, should herself be all ice and all unconcern. She is adorned with the most graceful modesty that ever beautified youth; the softest sigher—that, if she were capable of love, one would swear she languished for some absent happy man; and so retired, as if she feared a rape even from the god of day,[8] or that the breezes would steal kisses from her delicate mouth. Her task of work some sighing lover every day makes it his petition to perform for her, which she accepts blushing and with reluctancy, for fear he will ask her a look for a recompense, which he dares not presume to hope, so great an awe she strikes into the hearts of her admirers." "I do not wonder," replied the Prince, "that Clemene should refuse slaves, being as you say so beautiful, but wonder how she escapes those who can entertain her as you can do; or why, being your slave, you do not oblige her to yield." "I confess," said Trefry, "when I have, against her will, entertained her with love so long as to be transported with my passion, even above decency, I have been ready to make use of those advantages of strength and force nature has given me. But oh! she disarms me with that modesty and weeping, so ten-

7. Contributing jointly. 8. The sun.

der and so moving that I retire, and thank my stars she overcame me." The company laughed at his civility to a slave, and Caesar only applauded the nobleness of his passion and nature, since that slave might be noble or, what was better, have true notions of honor and virtue in her. Thus passed they this night, after having received from the slaves all imaginable respect and obedience.

The next day, Trefry asked Caesar to walk, when the heat was allayed, and designedly carried him by the cottage of the fair slave, and told him she whom he spoke of last night lived there retired. "But," says he, "I would not wish you to approach, for I am sure you will be in love as soon as you behold her." Caesar assured him he was proof against all the charms of that sex, and that if he imagined his heart could be so perfidious to love again, after Imoinda, he believed he should tear it from his bosom. They had no sooner spoke, but a little shock dog[9] that Clemene had presented her, which she took great delight in, ran out; and she, not knowing anybody was there, ran to get it in again, and bolted out on those who were just speaking of her. When seeing them, she would have run in again, but Trefry caught her by the hand and cried, "Clemene, however you fly a lover, you ought to pay some respect to this stranger" (pointing to Caesar). But she, as if she had resolved never to raise her eyes to the face of a man again, bent 'em the more to the earth when he spoke, and gave the Prince the leisure to look the more at her. There needed no long gazing or consideration to examine who this fair creature was; he soon saw Imoinda all over her; in a minute he saw her face, her shape, her air, her modesty, and all that called forth his soul with joy at his eyes, and left his body destitute of almost life: it stood without motion, and for a minute knew not that it had a being; and I believe he had never come to himself, so oppressed he was with over-joy, if he had not met with this allay, that he perceived Imoinda fall dead in the hands of Trefry. This awakened him, and he ran to her aid and caught her in his arms, where by degrees she came to herself; and 'tis needless to tell with what transports, what ecstasies of joy, they both a while beheld each other, without speaking; then snatched each other to their arms; then gaze again, as if they still doubted whether they possessed the blessing they grasped; but when they recovered their speech, 'tis not to be imagined what tender things they expressed to each other, wondering what strange fate had brought 'em together again. They soon informed each other of their fortunes, and equally bewailed their fate; but at the same time they mutually protested that even fetters and slavery were soft and easy, and would be supported with joy and pleasure, while they could be so happy to possess each other and to be able to make good their vows. Caesar swore he disdained the empire of the world while he could behold his Imoinda; and she despised grandeur and pomp, those vanities of her sex, when she could gaze on Oroonoko. He adored the very cottage where she resided, and said that little inch of the world would give him more happiness than all the universe could do; and she vowed it was a palace, while adorned with the presence of Oroonoko.

Trefry was infinitely pleased with this novel,[1] and found this Clemene was the fair mistress of whom Caesar had before spoke; and was not a little satis-

9. A long-haired dog or poodle, especially associated with women of fashion. 1. Novel event or piece of news.

fied that heaven was so kind to the Prince as to sweeten his misfortunes by so lucky an accident; and leaving the lovers to themselves, was impatient to come down to Parham House (which was on the same plantation) to give me an account of what had happened. I was as impatient to make these lovers a visit, having already made a friendship with Caesar, and from his own mouth learned what I have related; which was confirmed by his Frenchman, who was set on shore to seek his fortunes, and of whom they could not make a slave, because a Christian, and he came daily to Parham Hill to see and pay his respects to his pupil prince. So that concerning and interesting myself in all that related to Caesar, whom I had assured of liberty as soon as the Governor arrived, I hasted presently to the place where the lovers were, and was infinitely glad to find this beautiful young slave (who had already gained all our esteems, for her modesty and her extraordinary prettiness) to be the same I had heard Caesar speak so much of. One may imagine then we paid her a treble respect; and though, from her being carved in fine flowers and birds all over her body, we took her to be of quality before, yet when we knew Clemene was Imoinda, we could not enough admire her.

I had forgot to tell you that those who are nobly born of that country are so delicately cut and rased[2] all over the forepart of the trunk of their bodies, that it looks as if it were japanned, the works being raised light high point round the edges of the flowers. Some are only carved with a little flower or bird at the sides of the temples, as was Caesar; and those who are so carved over the body resemble our ancient Picts,[3] that are figured in the chronicles, but these carvings are more delicate.

From that happy day Caesar took Clemene for his wife, to the general joy of all people; and there was as much magnificence as the country would afford at the celebration of this wedding: and in a very short time after she conceived with child, which made Caesar ever adore her, knowing he was the last of his great race. This new accident made him more impatient of liberty, and he was every day treating with Trefry for his and Clemene's liberty, and offered either gold or a vast quantity of slaves, which should be paid before they let him go, provided he could have any security that he should go when his ransom was paid. They fed him from day to day with promises, and delayed him till the Lord Governor should come; so that he began to suspect them of falsehood, and that they would delay him till the time of his wife's delivery and make a slave of that too, for all the breed is theirs to whom the parents belong. This thought made him very uneasy, and his sullenness gave them some jealousies[4] of him; so that I was obliged, by some persons who feared a mutiny (which is very fatal sometimes in those colonies, that abound so with slaves that they exceed the whites in vast numbers), to discourse with Caesar, and to give him all the satisfaction I possibly could; they knew he and Clemene were scarce an hour in a day from my lodgings, that they eat with me, and that I obliged 'em in all things I was capable of. I entertained him with the lives of the Romans, and great men, which charmed him to my company, and her with teaching her all the pretty works[5] that I was mistress of, and telling her stories of nuns, and endeavoring to bring her to the knowledge of the true God. But of all dis-

2. Incised. The carving is likened to figured lacquerwork in the Japanese style and to elaborate "high point" lace.
3. A North British people appearing in histories of England and Scotland.
4. Suspicions.
5. Decorative needlework or other handiwork.

courses Caesar liked that the worst, and would never be reconciled to our no-
tions of the Trinity, of which he ever made a jest; it was a riddle, he said, would
turn his brain to conceive, and one could not make him understand what faith
was. However, these conversations failed not altogether so well to divert him
that he liked the company of us women much above the men, for he could not
drink, and he is but an ill companion in that country that cannot. So that
obliging him to love us very well, we had all the liberty of speech with him, es-
pecially myself, whom he called his Great Mistress; and indeed my word
would go a great way with him. For these reasons, I had opportunity to take no-
tice to him that he was not well pleased of late as he used to be, was more re-
tired and thoughtful; and told him I took it ill he should suspect we would
break our words with him, and not permit both him and Clemene to return to
his own kingdom, which was not so long a way but when he was once on his
voyage he would quickly arrive there. He made me some answers that showed
a doubt in him, which made me ask him what advantage it would be to doubt.
It would but give us a fear of him, and possibly compel us to treat him so as I
should be very loath to behold; that is, it might occasion his confinement.
Perhaps this was not so luckily spoke of me, for I perceived he resented that
word, which I strove to soften again in vain. However, he assured me that
whatsoever resolutions he should take, he would act nothing upon the white
people; and as for myself and those upon that plantation where he was, he
would sooner forfiet his eternal liberty, and life itself, that lift his hand against
his greatest enemy on that place. He besought me to suffer no fears upon his
account, for he could do nothing that honor should not dictate; but he ac-
cused himself for having suffered slavery so long; yet he charged that weakness
on Love alone, who was capable of making him neglect even glory itself, and
for which now he reproaches himself every moment of the day. Much more to
this effect he spoke, with an air impatient enough to make me know he would
not be long in bondage; and though he suffered only the name of a slave, and
had nothing of the toil and labor of one, yet that was sufficient to render him
uneasy; and he had been too long idle, who used to always in action and in
arms. He had a spirit all rough and fierce, and that could not be tamed to lazy
rest; and though all endeavors were used to exercise himself in such actions
and sports as this world afforded, as running, wrestling, pitching the bar,[6]
hunting and fishing, chasing and killing tigers[7] of a monstrous size, which this
continent affords in abundance, and wonderful snakes, such as Alexander is
reported to have encountered at the river of Amazons,[8] and which Caesar took
great delight to overcome, yet these were not actions great enough for his large
soul, which was still panting after more renowned action.

Before I parted that day with him, I got, with much ado, a promise from him
to rest yet a little longer with patience, and wait the coming of the Lord
Governor, who was every day expected on our shore; he assured me he would,
and this promise he desired me to know was given perfectly in complaisance
to me, in whom he had an entire confidence.

After this, I neither thought it convenient to trust him much out of our
view, nor did the country, who feared him; but with one accord it was advised

6. A game in which players compete in throwing a
heavy bar or rod.
7. Wild cats, including the South American jaguar
and cougar.

8. Alexander the Great is supposed to have encoun-
tered both snakes and Amazons (warrior women) in a
campaign against India.

to treat him fairly, and oblige him to remain within such a compass, and that he should be permitted as seldom as could be to go up to the plantations of the Negroes or, if he did, to be accompanied by some that should be rather in appearance attendants than spies. This care was for some time taken, and Caesar looked upon it as a mark of extraordinary respect, and was glad his discontent had obliged 'em to be more observant to him. He received new assurance from the overseer, which was confirmed to him by the opinion of all the gentlemen of the country, who made their court to him. During this time that we had his company more frequently than hitherto we had had, it may not be unpleasant to relate to you the diversions we entertained him with, or rather he us.

My stay was to be short in the country, because my father died at sea, and never arrived to possess the honor was designed him (which was lieutenant general of six and thirty islands, besides the continent[9] of Surinam) nor the advantages he hoped to reap by them; so that though we were obliged to continue on our voyage, we did not intend to stay upon the place. Though, in a word, I must say thus much of it, that certainly had his late Majesty, of sacred memory, but seen and known what a vast and charming world he had been master of in that continent, he would never have parted so easily with it to the Dutch. 'Tis a continent whose vast extent was never yet known, and may contain more noble earth than all the universe besides, for, they say, it reaches from east to west, one way as far as China and another to Peru. It affords all things both for beauty and use; 'tis there eternal spring, always the very months of April, May, and June; the shades are perpetual, the trees bearing at once all degrees of leaves and fruit, from blooming buds to ripe autumn: groves of oranges, lemons, citrons, figs, nutmegs, and noble aromatics, continually bearing their fragrancies. The trees appearing all like nosegays adorned with flowers of different kinds; some are all white, some purple, some scarlet, some blue, some yellow; bearing, at the same time, ripe fruit and blooming young, or producing every day new. The very wood of all these trees has an intrinsic value above common timber, for they are, when cut, of different colors, glorious to behold, and bear a price considerable, to inlay withal. Besides this they yield rich balm and gums, so that we make our candles of such an aromatic substance as does not only give a sufficient light, but, as they burn, they cast their perfumes all about. Cedar is the common firing, and all the houses are built with it. The very meat we eat, when set on the table, if it be native, I mean of the country, perfumes the whole room; especially a little beast called an armadilly, a thing which I can liken to nothing so well as a rhinoceros; 'tis all in white armor, so jointed that it moves as well in it as if it had nothing on; this beast is about the bigness of a pig of six weeks old. But it were endless to give an account of all the diverse wonderful and strange things that country affords, and which we took a very great delight to go in search of, though those adventures are oftentimes fatal and at least dangerous. But while we had Caesar in our company on these designs we feared no harm, nor suffered any.

As soon as I came into the country, the best house in it was presented me, called St. John's Hill. It stood on a vast rock of white marble, at the foot of which the river ran a vast depth down, and not to be descended on that side;

9. "Land not disjoined by the sea from other lands" (Johnson's *Dictionary*), i.e., the mainland portion.

the little waves still dashing and washing the foot of this rock made the softest murmurs and purlings in the world; and the opposite bank was adorned with such vast quantities of different flowers eternally blowing,[1] and every day and hour new, fenced behind 'em with lofty trees of a thousand rare forms and colors, that the prospect was the most ravishing that fancy can create. On the edge of this white rock, towards the river, was a walk or grove of orange and lemon trees, about half the length of the Mall[2] here, whose flowery and fruitbearing branches met at the top and hindered the sun, whose rays are very fierce there, from entering a beam into the grove; and the cool air that came from the river made it not only fit to entertain people in, at all the hottest hours of the day, but refreshed the sweet blossoms and made it always sweet and charming; and sure the whole globe of the world cannot show so delightful a place as this grove was. Not all the gardens of boasted Italy can produce a shade to outvie this, which nature had joined with art to render so exceeding fine; and 'tis a marvel to see how such vast trees, as big as English oaks, could take footing on so solid a rock and in so little earth as covered that rock; but all things by nature there are rare, delightful, and wonderful. But to our sports.

Sometimes we would go surprising,[3] and in search of young tigers in their dens, watching when the old ones went forth to forage for prey; and oftentimes we have been in great danger and have fled apace for our lives when surprised by the dams. But once, above all other times, we went on this design, and Caesar was with us, who had no sooner stolen a young tiger from her nest but, going off, we encountered the dam, bearing a buttock of a cow which he[4] had torn off with his mighty paw, and going with it towards his den. We had only four women, Caesar, and an English gentleman, brother to Harry Martin, the great Oliverian;[5] we found there was no escaping this enraged and ravenous beast. However, we women fled as fast as we could from it; but our heels had not saved our lives if Caesar had not laid down his cub, when he found the tiger quit her prey to make the more speed towards him, and taking Mr. Martin's sword, desired him to stand aside, or follow the ladies. He obeyed him, and Caesar met this monstrous beast of might, size, and vast limbs, who came with open jaws upon him; and fixing his awful stern eyes full upon those of the beast, and putting himself into a very steady and good aiming posture of defense, ran his word quite through his breast down to his very heart, home to the hilt of the sword. The dying beast stretched forth her paw, and going to grasp his thigh, surprised with death in that very moment, did him no other harm than fixing her long nails in his flesh very deep, feebly wounded him, but could not grasp the flesh to tear off any. When he had done this, he hallooed to us to return, which, after some assurance of his victory, we did, and found him lugging out the sword from the bosom of the tiger, who was laid in her blood on the ground; he took up the cub, and with an unconcern that had nothing of the joy or gladness of a victory, he came and laid the whelp at my feet. We all extremely wondered at his daring, and at the bigness of the beast, which was about the heighth of a heifer but of mighty, great, and strong limbs.

Another times, being in the woods, he killed a tiger which had long infested

1. Blooming.
2. Fashionable walk in St. James's Park in London.
3. A military term for making sudden raids.
4. The very jarring mixture of pronouns in the two accounts of the tigers may perhaps suggest a reluctance to use a feminine pronoun in moments of extreme violence. The first account was left uncorrected in all four 17th-century editions.
5 Supporter of Oliver Cromwell.

that part, and borne away abundance of sheep and oxen, and other things that
were for the support of those to whom they belonged; abundance of people as-
sailed this beast, some affirming they had shot her with several bullets quite
through the body at several times, and some swearing they shot her through
the very heart, and they believed she was a devil rather than a mortal thing.
Caesar had often said he had a mind to encounter this monster, and spoke
with several gentlemen who had attempted her, one crying, "I shot her with so
many poisoned arrows," another with his gun in this part of her, and another
in that; so that he, remarking all these places where she was shot, fancied still
he should overcome her by giving her another sort of a wound than any had
yet done; and one day said (at the table), "What trophies and garlands, ladies,
will you make me, if I bring you home the heart of this ravenous beast that eats
up all your lambs and pigs?" We all promised he should be rewarded at all our
hands. So taking a bow, which he choosed out of a great many, he went up in
the wood, with two gentlemen, where he imagined this devourer to be; they
had not passed very far in it but they heard her voice, growling and grumbling,
as if she were pleased with something she was doing. When they came in view,
they found her muzzling in the belly of a new ravished sheep, which she had
torn open; and seeing herself approached, she took fast hold of her prey with
her forepaws and and set a very fierce raging look on Caesar, without offering
to approach him, for fear at the same time of losing what she had in posses-
sion. So that Caesar remained as good while, only taking aim, and getting an
opportunity to shoot her where he designed; 'twas some time before he could
accomplish it, and to wound her and not kill her would but have enraged her
more, and endangered him. He had a quiver of arrows at his side, so that if one
failed he could be supplied; at last, retiring a little, he gave her opportunity to
eat, for he found she was ravenous, and fell to as soon as she saw him retire,
being more eager of her prey than of doing new mischiefs. When he going
softly to one side of her, and hiding his person behind certain herbage that
grew high and thick, he took so good aim that, as he intended, he shot her just
into the eye, and the arrow was sent with so good a will and so sure a hand that
it stuck in her brain, and made her caper and become mad for a moment or
two; but being seconded by another arrow, he fell dead upon the prey. Caesar
cut him open with a knife, to see where those wounds were that had been re-
ported to him, and why he did not die of 'em. But I shall now relate a thing
that possibly will find no credit among men, because 'tis a notion commonly
received with us, that nothing can receive a wound in the heart and live; but
when the heart of this courageous animal was taken out, there were seven bul-
lets of lead in it, and the wounds seamed up with great scars, and she lived
with the bullets a great while, for it was long since they were shot. This heart
the conqueror brought up to us, and 'twas a very great curiosity, which all the
country came to see, and which gave Caesar occasion of many fine discourses,
of accidents in war and strange escapes.

At other times he would go a-fishing; and discoursing on that diversion, he
found we had in that country a very strange fish, called a numb eel[6] (an eel of
which I have eaten), that while it is alive, it has a quality so cold, that those
who are angling, though with a line of never so great a length with a rod at the
end of it, it shall, in the same minute the bait is touched by this eel, seize him

6. Electric eel.

or her that holds the rod with benumbedness, that shall deprive 'em of sense
for a while; and some have fallen into the water, and others dropped as dead on
the banks of the rivers where they stood, as soon as this fish touches the bait.
Caesar used to laugh at this, and believed it impossible a man could lose his
force at the touch of a fish, and could not understand that philosophy,[7] that a
cold quality should be of that nature. However, he had a great curiosity to try
whether it would have the same effect on him it had on others, and often
tried, but in vain. At last the sought for fish came to the bait, as he stood an-
gling on the bank; and instead of throwing away the rod or giving it a sudden
twitch out of the water, whereby he might have caught both the eel and have
dismissed the rod, before it could have too much power over him, for experi-
ment sake he grasped it but the harder, and fainting fell into the river; and
being still possessed of the rod, the tide carried him, senseless as he was, a
great way, till an Indian boat took him up, and perceived when they touched
him a numbness seize them. and by that knew the rod was in his hand; which
with a paddle (that is, a short oar) they struck away, and snatched it into the
boat, eel and all. If Caesar were almost dead with the effect of this fish, he was
more so with that of the water, where he had remained the space of going a
league, and they found they had much ado to bring him back to life. But at
last they did, and brought him home, where he was in a few hours well recov-
ered and refreshed, and not a little ashamed to find he should be overcome by
an eel, and that all the people who heard his defiance would laugh at him. But
we cheered him up; and he being convinced, we had the eel at supper, which
was a quarter of an ell about and most delicate meat, and was of the more
value, since it cost so dear as almost the life of so gallant a man.

About this time we were in many mortal fears about some disputes the
English had with the Indians, so that we could scarce trust ourselves, without
great numbers, to go to any Indian towns or place where they abode, for fear
they should fall upon us, as they did immediately after my coming away; and
that it was in the possession of the Dutch, who used 'em not so civilly as the
English, so that they cut in pieces all they could take, getting into houses and
hanging up the mother and all her children about her, and cut a footman I left
behind me all in joints, and nailed him to trees.

This feud began while I was there, so that I lost half the satisfaction I pro-
posed, in not seeing and visiting the Indian towns. But one day, bemoaning of
our misfortunes upon this account, Caesar told us we need not fear, for if we
had a mind to go, he would undertake to be our guard. Some would, but most
would not venture; about eighteen of us resolved and took barge, and after
eight days arrived near an Indian town. But approaching it, the hearts of some
of our company failed, and they would not venture on shore; so we polled who
would and who would not. For my part, I said if Caesar would, I would go; he
resolved; so did my brother and my woman, a maid of good courage. Now
none of us speaking the language of the people, and imagining we should have
a half diversion in gazing only and not knowing what they said, we took a fish-
erman that lived at the mouth of the river, who had been a long inhabitant
there, and obliged him to go with us. But because he was known to the
Indians, as trading among 'em, and being by long living there become a per-
fect Indian in color, we, who resolved to surprise 'em by making 'em see some-

7. "Hypothesis or system upon which natural effects are explained" (Johnson's *Dictionary*).

thing they never had seen (that is, white people), resolved only myself, my brother and woman should go; so Caesar, the fisherman, and the rest, hiding behind some thick reeds and flowers that grew on the banks, let us pass on towards the town, which was on the bank of the river all along. A little distant from the houses, or huts, we saw some dancing, others busied in fetching and carrying of water from the river. They had no sooner spied us but they set up a loud cry, that frighted us at first; we thought it had been for those that should kill us, but it seems it was of wonder and amazement. They were all naked, and we were dressed so as is most commode[8] for the hot countries, very glittering and rich, so that we appeared extremely fine; my own hair was cut short, and I had a taffety cap with black feathers on my head; my brother was in a stuff[9] suit, with silver loops and buttons and abundance of green ribbon. This was all infinitely surprising to them, and because we saw them stand still till we approached 'em, we took heart and advanced, came up to 'em, and offered 'em our hands; which they took, and looked on us round about, calling still for more company; who came swarming out, all wondering and crying out *"Tepeeme,"* taking their hair up in their hands and spreading it wide to those they called out to, as if they would say (as indeed it signified) "Numberless wonders," or not to be recounted, no more than to number the hair of their heads. By degrees they grew more bold, and from gazing upon us round, they touched us, laying their hands upon all the features of our faces, feeling our breasts and arms, taking up one petticoat, then wondering to see another; admiring our shoes and stockings, but more our garters, which we gave 'em, and they tied about their legs, being laced with silver lace at the ends, for they much esteem any shining things. In fine, we suffered 'em to survey us as they pleased, and we thought they would never have done admiring us. When Caesar and the rest saw we were received with such wonder, they came up to us; and finding the Indian trader whom they knew (for 'tis by these fishermen, called Indian traders, we hold a commerce with 'em, for they love not to go far from home, and we never go to them), when they saw him therefore they set up a new joy, and cried, in their language, "Oh! here's our *tiguamy,* and we shall now know whether those things can speak." So advancing to him some of 'em gave him their hands and cried, *"Amora tiguamy,"* which is as much as, "How do you?" or "Welcome, friend," and all with one din began to gabble to him and asked if we had sense and wit; if we could talk of affairs of life and war, as they could do; if we could hunt, swim, and do a thousand things they use. He answered 'em, we could. Then they invited us into their houses, and dressed venison and buffalo for us; and going out, gathered a leaf of a tree called a *sarumbo* leaf, of six yards long, and spread it on the ground for a tablecloth; and cutting another in pieces instead of plates, setting us on little bow Indian stools, which they cut out of one entire piece of wood and paint in a sort of japan work. They serve everyone their mess on these pieces of leaves, and it was very good, but too high seasoned with pepper. When we had eat, my brother and I took out our flutes and played to 'em, which gave 'em new wonder; and I soon perceived, by an admiration that is natural to these people, and by the extreme ignorance and simplicity of 'em, it were not difficult to establish any unknown or extravagant religion among them, and to impose any notions or fictions upon 'em. For seeing a kinsman of mine set some paper afire

8. Suitable. 9. Woven fabric, worsted.

with a burning glass, a trick they had never before seen, they were like to have
adored him for a god, and begged he would give them the characters or figures
of his name, that they might oppose it against winds and storms; which he did,
and they held it up in those seasons, and fancied it had a charm to conquer
them, and kept it like a holy relic. They are very superstitious, and called him
the great *Peeie*, that is, prophet. They showed us their Indian *Peeie*, a youth of
about sixteen years old, as handsome as nature could make a man. They con-
secrate a beautiful youth from his infancy, and all arts are used to complete
him in the finest manner, both in beauty and shape. He is bred to all the little
arts and cunning they are capable of, to all the legerdemain tricks and sleight
of hand, whereby he imposes upon the rabble, and is both a doctor in physic
and divinity; and by these tricks makes the sick believe he sometimes eases
their pains, by drawing from the afflicted part little serpents, to odd flies, or
worms, or any strange thing; and though they have besides undoubted good
remedies for almost all their diseases, they cure the patient more by fancy than
by medicines, and make themselves feared, loved, and reverenced. This young
Peeie had a very young wife, who seeing my brother kiss her, came running and
kissed me; after this they kissed one another, and made it a very great jest, it
being so novel; and new admiration and laughing went round the multitude,
that they never will forget that ceremony, never before used or known. Caesar
had a mind to see and talk with their war captains, and we were conducted to
one of their houses, where we beheld several of the great captains, who had
been at council. But so frightful a vision it was to see 'em no fancy can create;
no such dreams can represent so dreadful a spectacle. For my part I took 'em
got hobgoblins or fiends rather than men; but however their shapes appeared,
their souls were very humane and noble; but some wanted their noses, some
their lips, some both noses and lips, some their ears, and others cut through
each check with long slashes, through which their teeth appeared; they had
other several formidable wounds and scars, or rather dismemberings. They
had *comitas* or little aprons before 'em, and girdles of cotton, with their knives
naked, stuck in it; a bow at their backs and a quiver of arrows on their thighs;
and most had feathers on their heads of diverse colors. They cried "*Amora
tiguamy*" to us at our entrance, and were pleased we said as much to 'em; they
seated us, and gave us drink of the best sort and wondered, as much as the oth-
ers had done before, to see us. Caesar was marveling as much at their faces,
wondering how they should all be so wounded in war; he was impatient to
know how they all came by those frightful marks of rage or malice, rather than
wounds got in noble battle. They told us, by our interpreter, that when any war
was waging, two men chosen out by some old captain whose fighting was past,
and who could only teach the theory of war, these two men were to stand in
competition for the generalship, or great war captain; and being brought be-
fore the old judges, now past labor, they are asked what they dare do to show
they are worthy to lead an army. When he who is first asked, making no reply,
cuts off his nose, and throws it contemptibly[1] on the ground; and the other
does something to himself that he thinks surpasses him, and perhaps deprives
himself of lips and an eye; so they slash on till one gives out, and many have
died in this debate. And 'tis by a passive valor they show and prove their activ-

1. With contempt.

ity, a sort of courage too brutal to be applauded by our black hero; nevertheless he expresses his esteem of 'em.

In this voyage Caesar begot so good an understanding between the Indians and the English that there were no more fears or heart-burnings during our stay, but we had a perfect, open, and free trade with 'em. Many things remarkable and worthy reciting we met with in this short voyage, because Caesar made it his business to search out and provide for our entertainment, especially to please his dearly adored Imoinda, who was a sharer in all our adventures; we being resolved to make her chains easy as we could, and to compliment the Prince in that manner that most obliged him.

As we were coming up again, we met with some Indians of strange aspects; that is, of a larger size and other sort of features than those of our country. Our Indian slaves that rowed us asked 'em some questions, but they could not understand us; but showed us a long cotton string with several knots on it, and told us, they had been coming from the mountains so many moons as there were knots. They were habited in skins of a strange beast, and brought along with 'em bags of gold dust, which, as well as they could give us to understand, came streaming in little small channels down the high mountains when the rains fell; and offered to be the convoy to any body or persons that would go to the mountains. We carried these men up to Parham, where they were kept till the Lord Governor came. And because all the country was mad to be going on this golden adventure, the Governor by his letters commanded (for they sent some of the gold to him) that a guard should be set at the mouth of the river of Amazons[2] (a river so called, almost as broad as the river of Thames) and prohibited all people from going up that river, it conducting to those mountains of gold. But we going off for England before the project was further prosecuted, and the Governor being drowned in a hurricane, either the design died, or the Dutch have the advantage of it. And 'tis to be bemoaned what his Majesty lost by losing that part of America.

Though this digression is a little from my story, however since it contains some proofs of the curiosity and daring of this great man, I was content to omit nothing of his character.

It was thus for some time we diverted him; but now Imoinda began to show she was with child, and did nothing but sigh and weep for the captivity of her lord, herself, and the infant yet unborn, and believed if it were so hard to gain the liberty of two, 'twould be more difficult to get that for three. Her griefs were so many darts in the great heart of Caesar; and taking his opportunity one Sunday when all the whites were overtaken in drink, as there were abundance of several trades and slaves for four years[3] that inhabited among the Negro houses, and Sunday was their day of debauch (otherwise they were a sort of spies upon Caesar), he went pretending out of goodness to 'em to feast amongst 'em; and sent all his music, and ordered a great treat for the whole gang, about three hundred Negroes; and about a hundred and fifty were able to bear arms, such as they had, which were sufficient to do execution[4] with spirits accordingly. For the English had none but rusty swords that no strength could draw from a scabbard, except the people of particular quality, who took care to oil 'em and keep 'em in good order. The guns also, unless here and there

2. The mouth of the Amazon, in Brazil, is far distant from Surinam.
3. Tradesmen, and whites who for crimes or debt were indentured for a fixed period.
4. Harm, slaughter.

one, or those newly carried from England, would do no good or harm; for 'tis the nature of that country to rust and eat up iron, or any metals but gold and silver. And they are very unexpert at the bow, which the Negroes and Indians are perfect masters of.

Caesar, having singled out these men from the women and children, made an harangue to 'em of the miseries and ignominies of slavery, counting up all their toils and sufferings, under such loads, burdens, and drudgeries as were fitter for beasts than men, senseless brutes than human souls. He told 'em, it was not for days, months, or years, but for eternity; there was no end to be of their misfortunes. They suffered not like men, who might find a glory and fortitude in oppression, but like dogs that loved the whip and bell,[5] and fawned the more they were beaten. That they had lost the divine quality of men and were become insensible asses, fit only to bear; nay, worse: an ass, or dog, or horse, having done his duty, could lie down in retreat and rise to work again, and while he did his duty endured no stripes; but men, villainous, senseless men such as they, toiled on all the tedious week till Black Friday;[6] and then, whether they worked or not, whether they were faulty or meriting, they promiscuously, the innocent with the guilty, suffered the infamous whip, the sordid stripes, from their fellow slaves, till their blood trickled from all parts of their body, blood whose every drop ought to be revenged with a life of some of those tyrants that impose it. "And why," said he, "my dear friends and fellow sufferers, should we be slaves to an unknown people? Have they vanquished us nobly in fight? Have they won us in honorable battle? And are we by the chance of war become their slaves? This would not anger a noble heart, this would not animate a soldier's soul; no, but we are bought and sold like apes or monkeys, to be the sport of women, fools, and cowards, and the support of rogues, runagades,[7] that have abandoned their own countries for rapine, murders, thefts, and villainies. Do you not hear every day how they upbraid each other with infamy of life, below the wildest savages; and shall we render obedience to such a degenerate race, who have no one human virtue left to distinguish 'em from the vilest creatures? Will you, I say, suffer the lash from such hands?" They all replied, with one accord, "No, no, no; Caesar has spoke like a great captain, like a great king."

After this he would have proceeded, but was interrupted by a tall Negro of some more quality than the rest; his name was Tuscan; who bowing at the feet of Caesar, cried, "My lord, we have listened with joy and attention to what you have said, and, were we only men, would follow so great a leader through the world. But oh! consider, we are husbands and parents too, and have things more dear to us than life, our wives and children, unfit for travel in these unpassable woods, mountains, and bogs; we have not only difficult lands to overcome, but rivers to wade, and monsters to encounter, ravenous beasts of prey—." To this, Caesar replied that honor was the first principle in nature that was to be obeyed; but as no man would pretend to that, without all the acts of virtue, compassion, charity, love, justice, and reason, he found it not inconsistent with that to take an equal care of their wives and children as they would of themselves; and that he did not design, when he led them to free

5. Proverbial for something that distracts from comfort or pleasure, from the protective charm on chariots of triumphing generals in ancient Rome.
6. Here, a day of customary beating; more widely, a

Friday bringing some notable disaster, from students' slang for examination day.
7. Renegades or fugitives.

dom and glorious liberty, that they should leave that better part of themselves to perish by the hand of the tyrant's whip. But if there were a woman among them so degenerate from love and virtue to choose slavery before the pursuit of her husband, and with the hazard of her life to share with him in his fortunes, that such a one ought to be abandoned, and left as a prey to the common enemy.

To which they all agreed—and bowed. After this, he spoke of the impassable woods and rivers, and convinced 'em, the more danger, the more glory. He told them that he had heard of one Hannibal, a great captain, had cut his way through mountains of solid rocks;[8] and should a few shrubs oppose them, which they could fire before 'em? No, 'twas a trifling excuse to men resolved to die or overcome. As for bogs, they are with a little labor filled and hardened; and the rivers could be no obstacle, since they swam by nature, at least by custom, from their first hour of birth. That when the children were weary they must carry them by turns, and the woods and their own industry would afford them food. To this they all assented with joy.

Tuscan then demanded what he would do. He said, they would travel towards the sea, plant a new colony, and defend it by their valor; and when they could find a ship, either driven by stress of weather or guided by Providence that way, they would seize it and make it a prize, till it had transported them to their own countries; at least, they should be made free in his kingdom, and be esteemed as his fellow sufferers, and men that had the courage and the bravery to attempt, at least, for liberty; and if they died in the attempt it would be more brave than to live in perpetual slavery.

They bowed and kissed his feet at this resolution, and with one accord vowed to follow him to death. And that night was appointed to begin their march; they made it known to their wives, and directed them to tie their hamaca[9] about their shoulder and under their arm like a scarf, and to lead their children that could go, and carry those that could not. The wives, who pay an entire obedience to their husbands, obeyed, and stayed for 'em where they were appointed. The men stayed but to furnish themselves with what defensive arms they could get; and all met at the rendezvous, where Caesar made a new encouraging speech to 'em, and led 'em out.

But as they could not march far that night, on Monday early, when the overseers went to call 'em all together to go to work, they were extremely surprised to find not one upon the place, but all fled with what baggage they had. You may imagine this news was not only suddenly spread all over the plantation, but soon reached the neighboring ones; and we had by noon about six hundred men they call the militia of the county, that came to assist us in the pursuit of the fugitives. But never did one see so comical an army march forth to war. The men of any fashion would not concern themselves, though it were almost the common cause, for such revoltings are very ill examples, and have very fatal consequences oftentimes in many colonies. But they had a respect for Caesar, and all hands were against the Parhamites, as they called those of Parham plantation, because they did not, in the first place, love the Lord Governor, and secondly they would have it that Caesar was ill used, and baffled with;[1] and 'tis not impossible but some of the best in the country was of

8. The Carthaginian general and his troops literally 9. Hammock.
hacked their way down the Alps into Italy to attack 1. Cheated.
Rome.

his counsel in this flight, and depriving us of all the slaves; so that they of the better sort would not meddle in the matter. The deputy governor,[2] of whom I have had no great occasion to speak, and who was the most fawning fair-tongued fellow in the world and one that pretended the most friendship to Caesar, was now the only violent man against him; and though he had nothing, and so need fear nothing, yet talked and looked bigger than any man. He was a fellow whose character s not fit to be mentioned with the worst of the slaves. This fellow would lead his army forth to meet Caesar, or rather to pursue him; most of their arms were of those sort of cruel whips they call cat with nine tails; some had rusty useless guns for show, others old basket hilts[3] whose blades had never seen the light in this age, and others had long staffs and clubs. Mr. Trefry went along, rather to be a mediator than a conqueror in such a battle; for he foresaw and knew, if by fighting they put the Negroes into despair, they were a sort of sullen fellows that would drown or kill themselves before they would yield; and he advised that fair means was best. But Byam was one that abounded in his own wit[4] and would take his own measures.

It was not hard to find these fugitives; for as they fled they were forced to fire and cut the woods before 'em, so that night or day they pursued 'em by the light they made and by the path they had cleared. But as soon as Caesar found he was pursued, he put himself in posture of defense, placing all the women and children in the rear, and himself with Tuscan by his side, or next to him, all promising to die or conquer. Encouraged thus they never stood to parley, but fell on pell-mell upon the English, and killed some and wounded a good many, they having recourse to their whips as the best of their weapons. And as they observed no order, they perplexed the enemy so sorely with lashing 'em in the eyes; and the women and children seeing their husbands so treated, being of fearful cowardly dispositions, and hearing the English cry out, "Yield and live, yield and be pardoned," they all run in amongst their husbands and fathers, and hung about 'em, crying out, "Yield, yield; and leave Caesar to their revenge"; that by degrees the slaves abandoned Caesar, and left him only Tuscan and his heroic Imoinda; who, grown big as she was, did nevertheless press near her lord, having a bow and a quiver full of poisoned arrows, which she managed with such dexterity that she wounded several, and shot the governor into the shoulder; of which wound he had like to have died, but that an Indian woman, his mistress, sucked the wound and cleansed it from the venom. But however, he stirred not from the place till he had parleyed with Caesar, who he found was resolved to die fighting, and would not be taken; no more would Tuscan, or Imoinda. But he, more thirsting after revenge of another sort than that of depriving him of life, now made use of all his art of talking and dissembling, and besought Caesar to yield himself upon terms which he himself should propose, and should be sacredly assented to and kept by him. He told him, it was not that he any longer feared him, or could believe the force of two men, and a young heroine, could overcome all them, with all the slaves now on their side also; but it was the vast esteem he had for his person, the desire he had to serve so gallant a man, and to hinder himself from the reproach hereafter of having been the occasion of the death of a prince whose valor and

2. William Byam. There are recorded complaints against him for high-handedness and from him about insubordination by settlers and slaves.
3. Swords with protective hilt guards. "Cat with nine

tails": a whip with nine knotted lashes, used for punishment in the British navy and army until 1881.
4. Intelligence.

magnanimity deserved the empire of the world. He protested to him, he looked upon this action as gallant and brave, however tending to the prejudice of his lord and master, who would by it have lost so considerable a number of slaves; that this flight of his should be looked on as a heat of youth, and rashness of a too forward courage, and an unconsidered impatience of liberty, and no more; and that he labored in vain to accomplish that which they would effectually perform as soon as any ship arrived that would touch on his coast. "So that if you will be pleased," continued he, "to surrender yourself, all imaginable respect shall be paid you; and yourself, your wife, and child, if it be here born, shall depart free out of our land."

But Caesar would hear of no compsition;[5] though Byam urged, if he pursued and went on in his design, he would inevitably perish, either by great snakes, wild beasts, or hunger; and he ought to have regard to his wife, whose condition required ease, and not the fatigues of tedious travel, where she could not be secured from being devoured. But Caesar told him, there was no faith in the white men or the gods they adored, who instructed 'em in principles so false that honest men could not live amongst 'em; though no people professed so much, none performed so little; that he knew what he had to do when he dealt with men of honor, but with them a man ought to be eternally on his guard, and never to eat and drink with Christians without his weapon of defense in his hand; and for his own security, never to credit one word they spoke. As for the rashness and inconsiderateness of his action, he would confess the governor is in the right; and that he was ashamed of what he had done, in endeavoring to make those free who were by nature slaves, poor wretched rogues, fit to be used as Christian's tools; dogs, treacherous and cowardly, fit for such masters; and they wanted only but to be whipped into the knowledge of the Christian gods to be the vilest of all creeping things, to learn to worship such deities as had not power to make 'em just, brave, or honest. In fine, after a thousand things of this nature, not fit here to be recited, he told Byam he had rather die than live upon the same earth with such dogs. But Trefry and Byam pleaded and protested together so much that Trefry, believing the governor to mean what he said, and speaking very cordially himself, generously put himself into Caesar's hands, and took him aside and persuaded him, even with tears, to live, by surrendering himself, and to name his conditions. Caesar was overcome by his wit and reasons, and in consideration of Imoinda; and demanding what he desired, and that it should be ratified by their hands in writing, because he had perceived that was the common way of contract between man and man, amongst the whites. All this was performed, and Tuscan's pardon was put in, and they surrender to the governor, who walked peaceably down into the plantation with 'em, after giving order to bury their dead. Casear was very much toiled with the bustle of the day, for he had fought like a fury; and what mischief was done he and Tuscan performed alone, and gave their enemies a fatal proof that they durst do anything and feared no mortal force.

But they were no sooner arrived at the place where all the slaves receive their punishments of whipping, but they laid hands on Caesar and Tuscan, faint with heat and toil; and surprising them, bound them to two several stakes, and whipped them in a most deplorable and inhuman manner, rending the very

5. Settlement.

flesh from their bones; especially Caesar, who was not perceived to make any moan or to alter his face, only to roll his eyes on the faithless governor, and those he believed guilty, with fierceness and indignation; and to complete his rage, he saw every one of those slaves, who but a few days before adored him as something more than mortal, now had a whip to give him some lashes, when he strove not to break his fetters; though if he had, it were impossible. But he pronounced a woe and revenge from his eyes, that darted fire that 'twas at once both awful and terrible to behold.

When they thought they were sufficiently revenged on him, they untied him, almost fainting with loss of blood from a thousand wounds all over his body, from which they had rent his clothes, and led him bleeding and naked as he was, and loaded him all over with irons; and then rubbed his wounds, to complete their cruelty, with Indian pepper, which had like to have made him raving mad; and in this condition made him so fast to the ground that he could not stir, if his pains and wounds would have given him leave. They spared Imoinda, and did not let her see this barbarity committed towards her lord, but carried her down to Parham and shut her up; which was not in kindness to her, but for fear she should die with the sight, or miscarry, and then they should lose a young slave and perhaps the mother.

You must know, that when the news was brought on Monday morning that Caesar had betaken himself to the woods and carried with him all the Negroes, we were possessed with extreme fear, which no persuasions could dissipate, that he would secure himself till night, and then that he would come down and cut all our throats. This apprehension made all the females of us fly down the river, to be secured; and while we were away they acted this cruelty. For I suppose I had authority and interest enough there, had I suspected any such thing, to have prevented it; but we had not gone many leagues but the news overtook us that Caesar was taken and whipped like a common slave. We met on the river with Colonel Martin, a man of great gallantry, wit, and goodness, and whom I have celebrated in a character of my new comedy[6] by his own name, in memory of so brave a man. He was wise and eloquent and, from the fineness of his parts, bore a great sway over the hearts of all the colony. He was a friend to Caesar, and resented this false dealing with him very much. We carried him back to Parham, thinking to have made an accommodation; when we came, the first news we heard was that the governor was dead of a wound Imoinda had given him; but it was not so well. But it seems he would have the pleasure of beholding the revenge he took on Caesar and before the cruel ceremony was finished, he dropped down; and then they perceived the wound he had on his shoulder was by a venomed arrow, which, as I said, his Indian mistress healed by sucking the wound.

We were no sooner arrived but we went up to the plantation to see Caesar, whom we found in a very miserable and unexpressible condition; and I have a thousand times admired how he lived, in so much tormenting pain. We said all things to him that trouble, pity, and good nature could suggest, protesting our innocency of the fact and our abhorrence of such cruelties; making a thousand professions of services to him and begging as many pardons for the offenders, till we said so much that he believed we had no hand in his ill treatment; but told us he could never pardon Byam; as for Trefry, he confessed

6. *The Younger Brother, or The Amorous Jilt*, not produced until 1696 despite this piece of promotion.

he saw his grief and sorrow for his suffering, which he could not hinder, but was like to have been beaten down by the very slaves for speaking in his defense. But for Byam, who was their leader, their head—and should, by his justice and honor, have been an example to 'em—for him, he wished to live, to take a dire revenge of him, and said, "It had been well for him if he had sacrificed me, instead of giving me the contemptible[7] whip." He refused to talk much, but begging us to give him our hands, he took 'em, and protested never to lift up his to do us any harm. He had a great respect for Colonel Martin, and always took his counsel like that of a parent, and assured him he would obey him in anything but his revenge on Byam. "Therefore," said he, "for his own safety, let him speedily dispatch me; for if I could dispatch myself I would not, till that justice were done to my injured person, and the contempt of a soldier. No, I would not kill myself, even after a whipping, but will be content to live with that infamy, and be pointed at by every grinning slave, till I have completed my revenge; and then you shall see that Oroonoko scorns to live with the indignity that was put on Caesar." All we could do could get no more words from him; and we took care to have him put immediately into a healing bath to rid him of his pepper, and ordered a chirurgeon[8] to anoint him with healing balm, which he suffered; and in some time he began to be able to walk and eat. We failed not to visit him every day, and to that end had him brought to an apartment at Parham.

The governor was no sooner recovered, and had heard of the menaces of Caesar, but he called his council; who (not to disgrace them, or burlesque the government there) consisted of such notorious villains as Newgate[9] never transported; and possibly originally were such who understood neither the laws of God or man, and had no sort of principles to make 'em worthy the name of men; but at the very council table would contradict and fight with one another, and swear so bloodily that 'twas terrible to hear and see 'em. (Some of 'em were afterwards hanged when the Dutch took possession of the place, others sent off in chains.) But calling these special rulers of the nation together, and requiring their counsel in this weighty affair, they all concluded that (Damn 'em) it might be their own cases; and that Caesar ought to be made an example to all the Negroes, to fright 'em from daring to threaten their betters, their lords and masters; and at this rate no man was safe from his own slaves; and concluded, *nemine contradicente*,[1] that Caesar should be hanged.

Trefry then thought it time to use his authority, and told Byam his command did not extend to his lord's plantation, and that Parham was as much exempt from the law as Whitehall;[2] and that they ought no more to touch the servants of the Lord—(who there represented the King's person) than they could those about the King himself; and that Parham was a sanctuary; and though his lord were absent in person, his power was still in being there, which he had entrusted with him as far as the dominions of his particular plantations reached, and all that belonged to it; the rest of the country, as Byam was lieutenant to his lord, he might exercise his tyranny upon. Trefry had others as powerful, or more, that interested themselves in Caesar's life, and absolutely

7. Showing contempt.
8. Surgeon.
9. The major London prison, from which criminals were transported to the colonies.

1. No one disagreeing (Latin).
2. The king's palace in London. Treffry stands as Lord Willoughby's deputy on his private land. Byam in the colony at large.

said he should be defended. So turning the governor and his wise council out of the doors (for they sat at Parham House), they set a guard upon our landing place, and would admit none but those we called friends to us and Caesar.

The governor having remained wounded at Parham till his recovery was completed, Caesar did not know but he was still there; and indeed, for the most part his time was spent there for he was one that loved to live at other people's expense; and if he were a day absent, he was ten present there, and used to play and walk and hunt and fish with Caesar. So that Caesar did not at all doubt, if he once recovered strength, but he should find an opportunity of being revenged on him. Though after such a revenge, he could not hope to live, for if he escaped the fury of the English mobile,[3] who perhaps would have been glad of the occasion to have killed him, he was resolved not to survive his whipping; yet he had, some tender hours, a repenting softness, which he called his fits of coward, wherein he struggled with Love for the victory of his heart, which took part with his charming Imoinda there; but for the most part his time was passed in melancholy thought and black designs. He considered, if he should do this deed and die, either in the attempt or after it, he left his lovely Imoinda a prey, or at best a slave, to the enraged multitude; his great heart could not endure that thought. 'Perhaps,' said he, "she may be first ravished by every brute, exposed first to their nasty lusts and then a shameful death." No; he could not live a moment under that apprehension, too insupportable to be borne. These were his thoughts and his silent arguments with his heart, as he told us afterwards; so that now resolving not only to kill Byam but all those he thought had enraged him, pleasing his great heart with the fancied slaughter he should make over the whole face of the plantation, he first resolved on a deed, that (however horrid it at first appeared to us all), when we had heard his reasons, we thought it brave and just. Being able to walk and, as he believed, fit for the execution of his great design, he begged Trefry to trust him into the air, believing a walk would do him good, which was granted him; and taking Imoinda with him, as he used to do in his more happy and calmer days, he led her up into a wood, where, after (with a thousand sighs, and long gazing silently on her face, while tears gushed, in spite of him, from his eyes) he told her his design first of killing her, and then his enemies, and next himself, and the impossibility of escaping, and therefore he told her the necessity of dying, he found the heroic wife faster pleading for death than he was to propose it, when she found his fixed resolution, and on her knees besought him not to leave her a prey to his enemies. He (grieved to death) yet pleased at her noble resolution, took her up, and embracing her with all the passion and languishment of a dying lover, drew his knife to kill this treasure of his soul, this pleasure of his eyes; while tears trickled down his cheeks, hers were smiling with joy she should die by so noble a hand, and be sent in her own country (for that's their notion of the next world) by him she so tenderly loved and so truly adored in this; for wives have a respect for their husbands equal to what any other people pay a deity, and when a man finds any occasion to quit his wife, if he love her, she dies by his hand; if not, he sells her, or suffers some other to kill her. It being thus, you may believe the deed was soon resolved on; and 'tis not to be doubted but the parting, the eternal leave-taking of two such lovers, so greatly born, so sensible,[4] so beautiful, so young, and so fond, must

3. Common people or mob. 4. Sensitive.

be very moving, as the relation of it was to me afterwards.

All that love could say in such cases being ended, and all the intermitting ir-resolutions being adjusted, the lovely, young, and adored victim lays herself down before the sacrificer; while he, with a hand resolved and a heart breaking within, gave the fatal stroke; first cutting her throat, and then severing her yet smiling face from that delicate body, pregnant as it was with fruits of tenderest love. As soon as he had done, he laid the body decently on leaves and flowers, of which he made a bed, and concealed it under the same coverlid of nature; only her face he left yet bare to look on. But when he found she was dead and past all retrieve, never more to bless him with her eyes and soft language, his grief swelled up to rage; he tore, he raved, he roared, like some monster of the wood, calling on the loved name of Imoinda. A thousand times he turned the fatal knife that did the deed toward his own heart, with a resolution to go im-mediately after her; but dire revenge, which now was a thousand times more fierce in his soul than before, prevents him; and he would cry out, "No; since I have sacrificed Imoinda to my revenge, shall I lose that glory which I have pur-chased so dear as at the price of the fairest, dearest, softest creature that ever nature made? No, no!" Then, at her name, grief would get the ascendant of rage, and he would lie down by her side and water her face with showers of tears, which never were wont to fall from those eyes. And however bent he was on his intended slaughter, he had not power to stir from the sight of this dear object, now more beloved and more adored than ever.

He remained in this deploring condition for two days, and never rose from the ground where he had made his sad sacrifice. At last, rousing from her side, and accusing himself with living too long now Imoinda was dead, and that the deaths of those barbarous enemies were deferred too long, he resolved now to finish the great work; but offering to rise, he found his strength so decayed that he reeled to and fro, like boughs assailed by contrary winds; so that he was forced to lie down again, and try to summons all his courage to his aid. He found his brains turned round, and his eyes were dizzy, and objects appeared not the same to him they were wont to do; his breath was short, and all his limbs surprised with a faintness he had never felt before. He had not eat in two days, which was one occasion of this feebleness, but excess of grief was the greatest; yet still he hoped he should recover vigor to act his design, and lay ex-pecting it yet six days longer, still mourning over the dead idol of his heart, and striving every day to rise, but could not.

In all this time you may believe we were in no little affliction for Caesar and his wife; some were of opinion he was escaped never to return; others thought some accident had happened to him. But however, we failed not to send out an hundred people several ways to search for him; a party of about forty went that way he took, among whom was Tuscan, who was perfectly reconciled to Byam. They had not gone very far into the wood but they smelt an unusual smell, as of a dead body; for stinks must be very noisome that can be distin-guished among such a quantity of natural sweets as every inch of that land produces. So that they concluded they should find him dead, or somebody that was so. They passed on towards it, as loathsome as it was, and made such a rustling among the leaves that lie thick on the ground, by continual falling, that Caesar heard he was approached; and though he had during the space of these eight days endeavored to rise, but found he wanted strength, yet looking up and seeing his pursuers, he rose and reeled to a neighboring tree, against

which he fixed his back; and being within a dozen yards of those that advanced and saw him, he called out to them and bid them approach no nearer, if they would be safe. So that they stood still, and hardly believing their eyes, that would persuade them that it was Caesar that spoke to 'em, so much was he altered, they asked him what he had done with his wife, for they smelt a stink that almost struck them dead. He, pointing to the dead body, sighing, cried, "Behold her there." They put off the flowers that covered her with their sticks, and found she was killed, and cried out, "Oh, monster! that hast murdered thy wife." Then asking him why he did so cruel a deed, he replied, he had no leisure to answer impertinent questions. "You may go back," continued he, "and tell the faithless governor he may thank fortune that I am breathing my last, and that my arm is too feeble to obey my heart in what it had designed him." But his tongue faltering, and trembling, he could scarce end what he was saying. The English, taking advantage by his weakness, cried, "Let us take him alive by all means." He heard 'em; and as if he had revived from a fainting, or a dream, he cried out, "No, gentlemen, you are deceived; you will find no more Caesars to be whipped, no more find a faith in me. Feeble as you think me, I have strength yet left to secure me from a second indignity." They swore all anew, and he only shook his head and beheld them with scorn. Then they cried out, "Who will venture on this single man? Will nobody?" They stood all silent while Caesar replied, "Fatal will be the attempt to the first adventurer, let him assure himself," and at that word, held up his knife in a menacing posture. "Look ye, ye faithless crew," said he, "'tis not life I seek, nor am I afraid of dying," and at that word cut a piece of flesh from his own throat, and threw it at 'em; "yet still I would live if I could, till I had perfected my revenge. But oh! it cannot be; I feel life gliding from my eyes and heart, and if I make not haste, I shall yet fall a victim to the shameful whip." At that, he ripped up his own belly, and took his bowels and pulled 'em out, with what strength he could; while some, on their knees imploring, besought him to hold his hand. But when they saw him tottering, they cried out, "Will none venture on him?" A bold English cried, "Yes, if he were the devil" (taking courage when he saw him almost dead); and swearing a horrid oath for his farewell to the world, he rushed on him; Caesar, with his armed hand, met him so fairly as stuck him to the heart, and he fell dead at his feet. Tuscan, seeing that, cried out, "I love thee, O Caesar, and therefore will not let thee die, if possible." And running to him, took him in his arms; but at the same time warding a blow that Caesar made at his bosom, he received it quite through his arm; and Caesar having not the strength to pluck the knife forth, though he attempted it, Tuscan neither pulled it out himself nor suffered it to be pulled out, but came down with it sticking in his arm; and the reason he gave for it was, because the air should not get into the wound. They put their hands across, and carried Caesar between six of 'em, fainted as he was, and they thought dead, or just dying; and they brought him to Parham, and laid him on a couch, and had the chirurgeon immediately to him, who dressed his wounds and sewed up his belly, and used means to bring him to life, which they effected. We ran all to see him, and if before we thought him so beautiful a sight, he was now so altered that his face was like a death's head blacked over, nothing but teeth and eyeholes. For some days we suffered nobody to speak to him, but caused cordials to be poured down his throat, which sustained his life; and in six or seven days he recovered his senses. For you must know that

wounds are almost to a miracle cured in the Indies, unless wounds in the legs, which rarely ever cure.

When he was well enough to speak, we talked to him, and asked him some questions about his wife, and the reasons why he killed her; and he then told us what I have related of that resolution, and of his parting; and he besought us we would let him die, and was extremely afflicted to think it was possible he might live; he assured us if we did not dispatch him, he would prove very fatal to a great many. We said all we could to make him live, and gave him new assurances; but he begged we would not think so poorly of him, or of his love to Imoinda, to imagine we could flatter him to life again; but the chirurgeon assured him he could not live, and therefore he need not fear. We were all (but Caesar) afflicted at this news; and the sight was gashly;[5] his discourse was sad, and the earthly smell about him so strong that I was persuaded to leave the place for some time (being myself but sickly, and very apt to fall into fits of dangerous illness upon any extraordinary melancholy). The servants and Trefry and the chirurgeons promised all to take what possible care they could of the life of Caesar, and I, taking boat, went with other company to Colonel Martin's, about three days' journey down the river; but I was no sooner gone, but the governor taking Trefry about some pretended earnest business a day's journey up the river, having communicated his design to one Banister, a wild Irishman and one of the council, a fellow of absolute barbarity, and fit to execute any villainy, but was rich: he came up to Parham, and forcibly took Caesar, and had him carried to the same post where he was whipped; and causing him to be tied to it, and a great fire made before him, he told him he should die like a dog, as he was. Caesar replied, this was the first piece of bravery that ever Banister did, and he never spoke sense till he pronounced that word; and if he would keep it, he would declare, in the other world, that he was the only man of all the whites that ever he heard speak truth. And turning to the men that bound him, he said, "My friends, am I to die, or to be whipped?" And they cried, "Whipped! No, you shall not escape so well." And then he replied, smiling, "A blessing on thee," and assured them they need not tie him, for he would stand fixed like a rock, and endure death so as should encourage them to die. "But if you whip me," said he, "be sure you tie me fast."

He had learned to take tobacco; and when he was assured he should die, he desired they would give him a pipe in his mouth, ready lighted, which they did; and the executioner came, and first cut off his members,[6] and threw them into the fire; after that, with an ill-favored knife, they cut his ears, and his nose, and burned them; he still smoked on, as if nothing had touched him. Then they hacked off one of his arms, and still he bore up, and held his pipe; but at the cutting off the other arm, his head sunk, and his pipe dropped, and he gave up the ghost, without a groan or a reproach. My mother and sister were by him all the while, but not suffered to save him, so rude and wild were the rabble, and so inhuman were the justices, who stood by to see the execution, who after paid dearly enough for their insolence. They cut Caesar in quarters, and sent them to several of the chief plantations. One quarter was sent to Colonel Martin, who refused it, and swore he had rather see the quarters of Banister and the governor himself than those of Caesar on his planta-

5. Ghastly.　　　　　　　　　　　　　　6. Genitals.

tions, and that he could govern his Negroes without terrifying and grieving them with frightful spectacles of a mangled king.

Thus died this great man, worthy of a better fate, and a more sublime wit than mine to write his praise; yet, I hope, the reputation of my pen is considerable enough to make his glorious name to survive to all ages, with that of the brave, the beautiful, and the constant Imoinda.

1688

LADY MARY CHUDLEIGH

1656–1710

In the preface to her *Poems on Several Occasions* (1703), Lady Mary Chudleigh explained that readers would discover in her verse "a picture of my mind, my sentiments all laid open to their view." *To the Ladies* suggests that she was unhappily married to Sir George Chudleigh, of Ashton, Devon. But as the critic Joanna Lipking has argued, the poem's technical expertise also places it in a highly stylized genre, whose poetic conventions Chudleigh may be expertly following. Little is known about her personal life except that she suffered over her daughter dying young. Yet Lady Mary also reveals her strikingly feminist sentiments in *The Ladies' Defense* (1701) and *Essays upon Several Subjects* (1710). These books—the former in verse and the latter in prose—respond to a minister, John Sprint, whose wedding sermon *The Bride-Woman's Counselor* (1700) argued that a wife's whole duty was to love, honor, and obey her husband. Indignant that women are "debarred from knowledge, banished from the schools, / And with the utmost industry bred fools," Lady Mary scorns the "mean low trivial cares of life," asserting that women must "read and think, and think and read again, / And on our minds bestow the utmost pain." Although she attained some renown in her day—her *Poems* and her book of essays went through several editions—at her death Chudleigh left a number of works unpublished. A new collection of her writing has recently been edited by Margaret J. M. Ezell.

From The Ladies' Defense:
Or, a Dialogue Between
Sir John Brute, Sir William Loveall, Melissa, and a Parson

Melissa's Answer

* * *

'Tis hard we should be by the men despised,
Yet kept from knowing what would make us prized:
Debarred from knowledge, banished from the schools,
And with the utmost industry bred fools. 515
Laughed out of reason, jested out of sense,
And nothing left but native innocence:
Then told we are incapable of wit,[1]

1. Intelligence. "Native": innate.

And only for the meanest drudgeries fit:
Made slaves to serve their luxury and pride, 520
And with innumerable hardships tried,
Till pitying heaven release us from our pain,
Kind heaven to whom alone we dare complain.
Th' ill-natured world will no compassion show;
Such as are wretched, it would still have so: 525
It gratifies its envy and its spite;
The most in others' miseries take delight.
While we are present they some pity spare,
And feast us on a thin repast of air:
Look grave and sigh, when we our wrongs relate, 530
And in a complement accuse[2] our fate:
Blame those to whom we our misfortunes owe,
And all the signs of real friendship show.
But when we're absent, we their sport are made,
They fan the flame, and our oppressors aid; 535
Join with the stronger, the victorious side,
And all our sufferings, all our griefs deride.
Those generous few, whom kinder thoughts inspire,
And who the happiness of all desire;
Who wish we were from barbarous usage free, 540
Exempt from toils, and shameful slavery,
Yet let us unreproved, misspend our hours,
And to mean purposes employ our nobler powers.
They think if we our thoughts can but express,
And know but how to work, to dance and dress, 545
It is enough, as much as we should mind,
As if we were for nothing else designed,
But made, like puppets, to divert mankind.
O that my sex would all such toys despise;
And only study to be good, and wise: 550
Inspect themselves, and every blemish find,
Search all the close recesses of the mind,
And leave no vice, no ruling passion there,
Nothing to raise a blush, or cause a fear:
Their memories with solid notions fill, 555
And let their reason dictate to their will.
Instead of novels, histories peruse,
And for their guides the wiser ancients choose,
Through all the labyrinths of learning go,
And grow more humble, as they more do know. 560
By doing this, they will respect procure,
Silence the men, and lasting fame secure;
And to themselves the best companions prove,
And neither fear their malice, nor desire their love.

1701

2. Reveal, disclose. "Complement": compliment.

To the Ladies

Wife and servant are the same,
But only differ in the name:
For when that fatal knot is tied,
Which nothing, nothing can divide:
When she the word *obey* has said, 5
And man by law supreme has made,
Then all that's kind is laid aside,
And nothing left but state[1] and pride:
Fierce as an Eastern prince he grows,
And all his innate rigor shows: 10
Then but to look, to laugh, or speak,
Will the nuptial contract break.
Like mutes she signs alone must make,
And never any freedom take:
But still be governed by a nod, 15
And fear her husband as her God:
Him still must serve, him still obey,
And nothing act, and nothing say,
But what her haughty lord thinks fit,
Who with the power, has all the wit.[2] 20
Then shun, oh! shun that wretched state,
And all the fawning flatt'rers hate:
Value your selves, and men despise,
You must be proud, if you'll be wise.

1703

1. Pomp. 2. Intelligence.

ANNE KILLIGREW
1660–1685

The author of a small but skilful body of verse, Anne Killigrew is best known today as the subject of John Dryden's famous elegy *To the Pious Memory of the Accomplished Young Lady Mrs. Anne Killigrew* (1686). Born in London shortly before the Restoration, she was the daughter of Dr. Henry Killigrew, chaplain to the duke of York and himself a dramatist whose genius, Dryden declared, had been "transfused into [her] blood." Because of her father's position, she was raised in an atmosphere where female talent was encouraged; she frequented court circles; and she became maid of honor to Mary Modena, duchess of York. But though, when Killigrew died of smallpox at the age of twenty-five, Dryden defined her as a modern equivalent of the famous Greek woman poet Sappho, her literary career cannot have been quite as successful as his ceremonial eulogy suggested. Certainly her plaintive *Upon the Saying That My Verses Were Made by Another* implies a literary anxiety comparable with the fear expressed by Anne Bradstreet when she wrote in her *Prologue*, "If what I do prove well, it won't advance, / They'll say it's stolen, or else it was by chance." At the same time, the almost excessively elaborate modesty of *To My Lord Colrane* suggests that her nervousness about attacks from others inevitably inspired considerable self-doubt. The hazards of female authorship were not insignificant, even in an age when women intellectuals were beginning to gain some strength.

Upon the Saying That My Verses Were Made by Another

Next heaven,[1] my vows to thee, O sacred Muse!
I offered up, nor didst thou them refuse.

 O queen of verse, said I, if thou'lt inspire,
And warm my soul with thy poetic fire,
No love of gold shall share with thee my heart,
Or yet ambition in my breast have part,
More rich, more noble I will ever hold 5
The Muse's laurel,[2] than a crown of gold.
An undivided sacrifice I'll lay
Upon thine altar, soul and body pay;
Thou shalt my pleasure, my employment be,
My all I'll make a holocaust[3] to thee. 10

 The deity that ever does attend
Prayers so sincere, to mine did condescend.[4]
I writ, and the judicious praised my pen:
Could any doubt ensuing glory then?
What pleasing raptures filled my ravished sense, 15
How strong, how sweet, fame, was thy influence!
And thine, false hope, that to my flattered sight
Did'st glories represent so near and bright!
By thee deceived, methought each verdant[5] tree
Apollo's transformed Daphne[6] seemed to be; 20
And every fresher branch, and every bough,
Appeared as garlands to empale[7] my brow.
The learn'd in love say, thus the winged boy[8]
Does first approach, dressed up in welcome joy;
At first he to the cheated[9] lover's sight 25
Nought represents but rapture and delight,
Alluring hopes, soft fears, which stronger bind
Their hearts, than when they more assurance find.

 Emboldened thus, to fame I did commit
(By some few hands,) my most unlucky wit.[1] 30
But ah, the sad effects that from it came!
What ought t'have brought me honor, brought me shame!
Like Aesop's painted jay,[2] I seemed to all,
Adorned in plumes, I not my own could call:
Rifled like her, each one my feathers tore, 35
And, as they thought, unto the owner bore.
My laurels thus another's brow adorned,

1. I.e., next to heaven.
2. Leaves of a tree traditionally associated with famous poets.
3. Burnt offering.
4. Assent. "Attend": hear.
5. Green.
6. Nymph who was transformed into a laurel tree to escape the lecherous pursuit of Apollo, god of the sun and of poetry in Greek myth.
7. Surround.
8. Cupid, the Greek god of love.
9. Deceived.
1. Imagination. "Some few hands": i.e., those who helped to circulate her work.
2. In one of Aesop's fables, a jay adorns himself in a peacock's feathers and is angrily attacked by the other birds.

My numbers[3] they admired, but me they scorned:
Another's brow, that had so rich a store
Of sacred wreaths that circled it before; 40
While mine quite lost (like a small stream that ran
Into a vast and boundless ocean,)
Was swallowed up with what it joined, and drowned.
And that abyss yet no accession[4] found.

 Orinda (Albion's[5] and her sex's grace) 45
Owed not her glory to a beauteous face;
It was her radiant soul that shone within,
Which struck a luster through her outward skin;
That did her lips and cheeks with roses dye,
Advanced[6] her height, and sparked in her eye. 50
Nor did her sex at all obstruct her fame,
But higher 'mong the stars it fixed her name;
What she did write, not only all allowed,[7]
But every laurel to her laurel bowed!

 The envious age, only to me alone, 55
Will not allow what I do write, my own;
But let them rage, and 'gainst a maid conspire,
So deathless numbers from my tuneful lyre[8]
Do ever flow; so, Phoebus,[9] I by thee
Divinely inspired and possessed may be, 60
I willingly accept Cassandra's[1] fate,
To speak the truth, although believed too late.

1686

To My Lord Colrane,[1] In Answer to His Complemental Verses Sent Me under the Name of Cleanor

Long my dull muse in heavy slumbers lay,
Indulging sloth, and to soft ease gave way,
Her fill of rest resolving to enjoy,
Or fancying little worthy her employ.
When noble Cleanor's obliging strains 5
Her, the neglected lyre to tune, constrains.
Confused at first, she raised her drowsy head,
Pondered a while, then pleased, forsook her bed.
Surveyed each line with fancy richly fraught,
Re-read, and then revolved them in her thought. 10

 And can it be? she said, and can it be?
That 'mong the Great Ones I a poet see?

3. Meter; more generally, poetry.
4. Addition.
5. I.e., England. "Orinda": i.e., Katherine Philips (see p. 101).
6. Increased.
7. Acknowledged.

8. A Greek musical instrument like a small harp.
9. Apollo.
1. A Trojan princess gifted by Apollo with prophecy; in anger at being spurned by her, he brought it to pass that no one believed her predictions.
1. Henry Hare, second baron Colraine (1636–1708).

The Great Ones? who their ill-spent time divide,
'Twixt dangerous politics, and formal pride,
Destructive vice, expensive vanity, 15
In worse ways yet, if worse there any be:
Leave to inferiors the despised arts,
Let their retainers be the Men of Parts.[2]
But here with wonder and with joy I find,
I'th' noble born, a no less noble mind; 20
One, who on ancestors, does not rely
For fame, in merit, as in title, high!

 The Severe Goddess thus approved the lays:[3]
Yet too much pleased, alas, with her own praise.
But to vain pride, my muse, cease to give place, 25
Virgil's immortal numbers once did grace
A *Smothered Gnat*:[4] by high applause is shown,
If undeserved, the praisers' worth alone:
Nor that you should believ't, is't always meant,[5]
'Tis often for instruction only sent, 30
To praise men to amendment, and display,
By its perfection, where their weakness lay.
This use of these applauding numbers make
Them for example, not encomium, take.

 1686

2. I.e., of ability or talent.
3. Poems.
4. A mock-heroic poem once thought to be by Virgil

and paraphrased by Edmund Spenser as *Virgil's Gnat.*
"Numbers": verses.
5. I.e., you should not always believe it is meant.

ANNE FINCH, COUNTESS OF WINCHILSEA
1661–1720

The very first poem in Anne Finch's 1713 collection of verse—the only volume she published in her lifetime—outlines her gloomy vision of the literary woman's situation. Accomplished artist though she was, Finch had every reason to feel bitterness, for she had long been, in the words of the critic Cora Kaplan, "a prime butt for anti-'bluestocking' jokes on the stage and in verse." Even her sometime friend Alexander Pope, for instance, had caricatured her in a play called *Three Hours after Marriage* (coauthored with John Gay and John Arbuthnot) as a mad poetess named "Phoebe Clinket," and as late as 1954 Sylvia Plath, herself destined to become one of the twentieth century's major literary women, was amused by that character's "high flown and very funny ambitions to write poetry." Nor is there any evidence that Plath, who played the part of Phoebe Clinket in a Cambridge University production of Pope's comedy, ever read the verse written by Anne Finch herself.

 Yet this woman who feared she would be thought "a presumptuous creature" was a perceptive and productive poet. Her work was admired by many in her own day, and after her death discriminating readers from William Wordsworth to Virginia Woolf continued to celebrate her talent. The daughter of Sir William Kingsmill and Anne Hazlewood, both members of wealthy upper-class families, she was raised in aristocratic circles. Carefully nurtured and well educated, she went to court in 1683 as a maid of honor—an attendant—to Mary Modena,

duchess of York, a position in which she may well have known Anne Killigrew, who was also one of the duchess's ladies in waiting. Apparently, the young Anne Kingsmill was charming and beautiful; when Heneage Finch, also a royal attendant—a "gentleman of the bedchamber"—met her in those years, he courted her vigorously. The couple wed in 1684, and their marriage was a happy one, as many of Finch's poems—for instance, her *Letter to Daphnis*—testify.

When the former duke of York, now King James II, was exiled in the late 1680s and replaced as king by William of Orange, the Finches remained stubbornly loyal to their former patron and his wife. Swept out of court, they lived in comparative poverty among their relatives, in a kind of political exile of their own. In 1690, however, Heneage Finch's distant cousin, the earl of Winchilsea, died unexpectedly, and the former gentleman of the bedchamber inherited both his title and his luxurious estate at Eastwell; here the couple settled into a life of comfortable retirement, with Anne, now countess of Winchilsea, writing many poems in praise of rural pleasures. A work like her *Nocturnal Reverie*, for instance, with its accurate and detailed descriptions of night-time meadows and groves, reveals how attentively she observed the pastoral world she loved so much and explains why William Wordsworth, the great Romantic poet of nature, was to remark in 1815 that this poem contained almost the only "new image[s] of external nature" produced between Milton's *Paradise Lost* and Thomson's *The Seasons*.

For Anne Finch, however, the serenity of the countryside around Eastwell was more than an emblem of nature's beauty; it symbolized escape from a society where "all's confused"—and where the role of a literary woman was particularly confusing. Even during her days in the service of Mary Modena, this imaginative woman had written poetry. But, perhaps mindful of Anne Killgrew's fate, she had refused to publish it, explaining later that "I was not so far abandoned by my prudence as, out of mistaken vanity, to let any attempts of mine in poetry show themselves while I lived in such a public place as the court, where every one would have made their remarks upon a versifying maid of honor, and far the greater number with prejudice, if not contempt." Living and writing at Eastwell, though, she became the center of a circle of intellectual friends not unlike the group that had gathered around Katherine Philips a few decades earlier, and her poems were read in manuscript by many of these people. But while the reputation she thus achieved brought a good deal of admiration, it also brought from some quarters exactly the "prejudice, if not contempt," that she had earlier feared. No wonder, then, that in many of her verses she meditated with some bitterness on woman's lot. "How are we fallen, fallen by mistaken rules?" she asked in *The Introduction*, wondering, as Mary Wollstonecraft was also to wonder, if women are "education's more than nature's fools." Moreover, just as Anne Bradstreet had mused nostalgically on the reign of Queen Elizabeth, when it was "treason" to consider the female sex "void of reason," Finch dreamed of an age when women were not "fallen" and wished to be told "fables of women that excelled of old"—stories of exemplary biblical heroines like Miriam and Deborah, for instance.

Perhaps because her sense of woman's "fall" was so keen, Finch was often a prey to melancholy as well as bitterness. Some of her most famous works brood on the state of depression and anxiety that her contemporaries called "the spleen," and others, like *Ardelia to Melancholy*, try to combat such feelings. To Woolf, meditating in *A Room of One's Own* on this poet's career, it seemed "a thousand pities that [her mind] should have been forced to [such] anger and bitterness," yet sympathetic readers can see now that even "spleen" became an important source of inspiration for Finch. In addition, we can see that her "spleen" was at least partly justified. Even today, more than two hundred and seventy-five years after her death, there is no complete edition of her poetic works; the most recent collection, edited in 1903 by Myra Reynolds, omits an important group of manuscripts that Reynolds did not know about.

A Letter to Daphnis,[1] April 2, 1685

This to the crown and blessing of my life,
The much loved husband of a happy wife,
To him whose constant passion found the art[2]
To win a stubborn and ungrateful heart;
And to the world by tenderest proof discovers[3] 5
They err, who say that husbands can't be lovers.
With such return of passion, as is due,
Daphnis I love, Daphnis my thoughts pursue,
Daphnis, my hopes, my joys, are bounded all in you:
Even I, for Daphnis, and my promise[4] sake, 10
What I in women censure,[5] undertake.
But this from love, not vanity, proceeds;
You know who writes; and I who 'tis that reads.
Judge not my passion by my want of skill,
Many love well, though they express it ill; 15
And I your censure could with pleasure bear,
Would you but soon return, and speak it here.

1685 1713

The Introduction

Did I my lines intend for public view,
How many censures[1] would their faults pursue,
Some would, because such words they do affect,
Cry they're insipid, empty, uncorrect.
And many have attained, dull and untaught, 5
The name of wit[2] only by finding fault.
True judges might condemn their want[3] of wit,
And all might say they're by a woman writ.
Alas! a woman that attempts the pen
Such an intruder on the rights of men, 10
Such a presumptuous creature is esteemed,
The fault can by no virtue be redeemed.
They tell us we mistake our sex and way;
Good breeding, fashion, dancing, dressing, play
Are the accomplishments we should desire; 15
To write, or read, or think, or to enquire
Would cloud our beauty, and exhaust our time,
And interrupt the conquests of our prime;[4]
Whilst the dull manage of a servile house[5]
Is held by some our utmost art, and use. 20
 Sure 'twas not ever thus, nor are we told
Fables,[6] of women that excelled of old;
To whom, by the diffusive[7] hand of Heaven

1. Finch's neoclassical name for her husband, 2. Intelligence, learning.
Heneage Finch. 3. Lack.
2. Skill. 4. Maturity. "Conquests": i.e., amorous ones.
3. Reveals. 5. A house full of servants.
4. I.e., her wedding vows. 6. Falsehoods.
5. Criticize, namely servility, devotion. 7. Scattering.
1. Severe criticisms.

Some share of wit and poetry was given.
On that glad day on which the Ark⁵ returned, 25
The holy pledge for which the land had mourned,
The joyful tribes attend it on the way,
The Levites do the sacred charge⁹ convey,
Whilst various instruments before it play;
Here holy virgins in the concert join, 30
The louder notes to soften and refine,
And with alternate verse complete the hymn divine.¹
Lo! the young poet, after God's own heart,
By Him inspired, and taught the Muses' art,²
Returned from conquest, a bright chorus meets, 35
That sing his slain ten thousand in the streets.
In such loud numbers they his acts declare,
Proclaim the wonders of his early war,
That Saul upon the vast applause does frown,
And feels its mighty thunder shake the crown. 40
What, can the threatened judgment now prolong?³
Half of the kingdom⁴ is already gone;
The fairest half, whose influence guides the rest,
Have David's empire o'er their hearts confessed.
 A woman here leads fainting Israel on, 45
She fights, she wins, she triumphs with a song,⁵
Devout, majestic, for the subject fit,
And far above her arms exalts her wit,
Then to the peaceful, shady palm withdraws,
And rules the rescued nation with her laws. 50
How are we fallen, fallen by mistaken rules?
And education's, more than nature's fools,
Debarred from all improvements of the mind,
And to be dull, expected and designed;⁶
And if some one would soar above the rest, 55
With warmer fancy⁷ and ambition pressed,
So strong th'opposing faction still appears.
The hopes to thrive can ne'er outweigh the fears.
Be cautioned then my Muse, and still retired;⁸
Nor be despised, aiming to be admired; 60
Conscious of wants, still with contracted wing,
To some few friends and to thy sorrows sing;
For groves of laurel⁹ thou wert never meant;
Be dark enough thy shades, and be thou there content.

1689? 1713

8. The Ark of the Covenant, a chest containing the Ten Commandments engraved on stone tablets, was carried by the Israelites during their desert wanderings; the Ark was carried into Jerusalem by the priests of the Levites amid great celebration (1 Chronicles 15).

9. i.e., the Ark

1. i.e., the virgins' voices alternate with the men's in song.

2. Greek goddesses of art, learning, and inspiration; according to a later convention, all artists have their own personal muse. "Young poet": David, a young Israelite musician and warrior, who slew the giant Goliath and defeated the Philistine army, earning the love of his people and the jealousy of Saul, king of Israel (1 Samuel 17–18).

3. Be prolonged; Saul's doom had been foreshadowed.

4. I.e., the women.

5. Deborah, an Israelite judge, led her people in battle and wrote a song celebrating their victory (Judges 4–5).

6. Destined, formed.

7. More intense imagination.

8. Withdrawn, restrained.

9. Tree whose leaves are associated with poetic achievement.

The Spleen[1]

A *Pindaric Poem*[2]

What art thou, Spleen, which ev'ry thing dost ape.[3]
 Thou Proteus[4] to abused mankind;
 Who never yet thy real cause could find,
Or fix thee to remain in one continued[5] shape
 Still varying thy perplexing form, 5
 Now a Dead Sea[6] thou'lt represent,
 A calm of stupid discontent,
Then, dashing on the rocks, wilt rage into a storm.
 Trembling sometimes thou dost appear,
 Dissolved into a panic fear; 10
 On sleep intruding dost thy shadows spread,
 Thy gloomy terrors round the silent bed,
And crowd with boding[7] dreams the melancholy head;
 Or, when the midnight hour is told,[8]
 And drooping lids thou still dost waking hold, 15
 Thy fond delusions cheat[9] the eyes:
 Before them antic[1] spectres dance,
Unusual fires their pointed heads advance,
 And airy phantoms rise.
 Such was the monstrous vision seen, 20
When Brutus (now beneath his cares oppressed,
And all Rome's fortunes rolling on his breast,
 Before Philippi's latest field,
Before his fate did to Octavius lead)
 Was vanquished by the spleen.[2] 25

 Falsely the mortal part[3] we blame
 Of our depressed and pond'rous frame,[4]
 Which, till the first degrading sin[5]
 Let thee, its dull attendant, in,
 Still with the other did comply, 30
Nor clogged the active soul, disposed to fly,
And range[6] the mansions of its native sky.
 Nor, whilst in his own heaven he dwelt,
 Whilst man his Paradise possessed,
His fertile garden in the fragrant east, 35
 And all united odors smelt,
 No arméd sweets,[7] until thy reign,

1. One of the four humors, a bodily fluid thought to cause depression or melancholy.
2. A poetic form derived from the Greek poet Pindar, consisting of several units called strophes, generally addressed to some spiritual or material object; also called an ode.
3. Imitate.
4. In Greek mythology, a divinity of the sea who was capable of changing shape at will.
5. Constant, unchanging.
6. A salt lake in the Middle East, lacking tidal movement.
7. Foreboding, menacing.
8. Tolled, as by a bell.

9. Deceive.
1. Fantastic, clownlike.
2. In Shakespeare's *Julius Caesar*, the Roman leader Brutus is visited by the ghost of Caesar, whom he has assassinated, on the eve of his battle on the plains of Philippi with Octavius, the rival claimant to Roman rule.
3. The body. "Part": the flesh.
4. Eve and Adam's eating of the forbidden fruit in Eden (Genesis 3).
5. I.e., the soul. "Attendant": accompaniment.
6. Travel through. "Disposed": accustomed, desiring.
7. Painfully sweet fragrances.

Could shock the sense, or in the face
A flushed unhandsome color place.
Now the jonquil[8] o'ercomes the feeble brain; 40
We faint beneath the aromatic pain,
Till some offensive scent thy pow'rs appease,
And pleasure we resign[9] for short, and nauseous ease.

In ev'ry one thou dost possess
New are thy motions,[1] and thy dress: 45
Now in some grove a list'ning friend
Thy false suggestions must attend,
Thy whispered griefs, thy fancied[2] sorrows hear,
Breathed in a sigh, and witnessed by a tear;
Whilst in the light and vulgar[3] crowd, 50
Thy slaves, more clamorous and loud,
By laughters unprovoked, thy influence too confess.
In the imperious wife thou vapors[4] art,
Which from o'er-heated passions rise
In clouds to the attractive brain,[5] 55
Until descending thence again,
Through the o'er-cast, and show'ring eyes,
Upon her husband's softened heart,
He the disputed point must yield,
Something resign of the contested field:[6] 60
Till lordly man, born to imperial sway,
Compounds for peace, to make that[7] right away,
And woman, armed with Spleen, does servilely obey.

The fool, to imitate the wits,
Complains of thy pretended fits,[8] 65
And dullness, born with him, would lay
Upon thy accidental[9] sway;
Because, sometimes, thou dost presume
Into the ablest heads to come:
That, often, men of thoughts refined, 70
Impatient of unequal sense,
Such slow returns, where they so much dispense,
Retiring from the crowd, are to thy shades inclined.
O'er me alas! thou dost too much prevail:
I feel thy force, whilst I against thee rail;[2] 75
I feel my verse decay, and my cramped numbers[3] fail.
Through thy black jaundice,[4] I all objects see,

8. A fragrant yellow and white flower.
9. Give up.
1. Effects.
2. Imagined. "Attend": listen to.
3. Frivolous and common. "Witnessed": confirmed, validated.
4. Brief attacks of faintness and dizziness to which 18th-century women were thought extremely susceptible. "Unprovoked": without cause.
5. I.e., the brain attracts vapors from the more bodily "passions" or emotions
6. The passage describes a wife's hypocritical use of tears to win an argument with her husband.

7. I.e., "imperial sway" (power). "Compounds": makes a concession.
8. I.e., falsely complains of fits of spleen. "Wits": intelligent, educated people.
9. Not innate, but circumstantial. "Dullness": stupidity. "Lay": blame.
1. I.e., impatient at receiving so little intellectual stimulation when they provide so much.
2. Complain bitterly.
3. Bad verse.
4. I.e., discoloration of the tissues caused by accumulation of bile; usually yellow, but spleen is black bile.

As dark, and terrible as thee,
My lines decried, and my employment[5] thought
An useless folly, or presumptuous fault: 80
 Whilst in the Muses' paths I stray,
Whilst in their groves, and by their secret springs
My hand delights to trace unusual things,
And deviates from the known, and common way;
 Nor will in fading silks compose[6] 85
 Faintly th' inimitable rose,
Fill up an ill-drawn bird, or paint on glass
The sov'reign's blurred and undistinguished face,
The threat'ning angel, and the speaking ass.[7]

Patron thou art to ev'ry gross abuse,[8] 90
 The sullen husband's feigned excuse,
When the ill humor with his wife he spends,
And bears recruited[9] wit and spirits to his friends.
 The son of Bacchus[1] pleads thy pow'r,
As to the glass he still repairs,[2] 95
 Pretends but to remove thy cares,
Snatch from thy shades one gay and smiling hour,
And drown thy kingdom in a purple show'r.
When the coquette,[3] whom ev'ry fool admires,
 Would in variety be fair, 100
And, changing hastily the scene
From light, impertinent, and vain,
Assumes a soft, a melancholy air,
And of her eyes rebates[4] the wand'ring fires,
The careless posture, and the head reclined, 105
 The thoughtful, and composéd[5] face,
Proclaiming the withdrawn, the absent mind,
Allows the fop[6] more liberty to gaze,
Who gently for the tender cause enquires:
The cause, indeed, is a defect in sense, 110
Yet is the Spleen alleged[7] and still the dull pretense.
 But these are thy fantastic[8] harms,
 The tricks of thy pernicious stage,
 Which do the weaker sort engage;
Worse are the dire effects of thy more pow'rful charms. 115
 By thee religion, all we know,
 That should enlighten here below,
 Is veiled in darkness, and perplexed
 With anxious doubts, with endless scruples[9] vexed,
And some restraint implied from each perverted text[1] 120

5. I.e., as a poet.
6. Embroider, thought to be a woman's pastime.
7. Women's "artistic" activities: coloring or painting biblical scenes on glass (the speaking ass appears in Numbers 22).
8. Blatant wrongdoing.
9. Replenished. "Ill humour": spleen. "Spends": exhausts.
1. I.e., the drunkard Bacchus was the Roman god of wine and revelry, whose son is one who follows his example.

2. Turns, resorts.
3. Flirtatious woman.
4. Removes.
5. Calm.
6. Vain, fashionable young man.
7. Blamed. "Sense": intelligence.
8. Outward, theatrical.
9. Hesitations of conscience.
1. I.e., prohibitions inferred from distorted readings of the Bible.

Whilst touch not, taste not, what is freely giv'n,
Is but thy niggard[2] voice, disgracing bounteous heav'n.
 From speech restrained, by thy deceits abused,
 To deserts banished, or in cells reclused
 Mistaken vot'ries[3] to the Powers Divine, 125
 Whilst they a purer sacrifice design,[4]
Do but the Spleen obey, and worship at thy shrine.
 In vain to chase thee ev'ry art we try,
 In vain all remedies apply,
 In vain the Indian leaf infuse, 130
 Or the parched eastern berry[5] bruise;
Some pass, in vain, those bounds, and nobler liquors use.
 Now harmony, in vain, we bring,
 Inspire the flute and touch the string.
 From harmony no help is had; 135
Music but soothes thee, if too sweet y sad,
And if too light, but turns thee gaily mad.
 Though the physician's greatest gains,
 Although his growing wealth he sees
 Daily increased by ladies' fees, 140
 Yet dost thou baffle all his studious pains.
 Not skilful Lower[5] thy source could find,
 Or, through the well-dissected body trace
 The secret, the mysterious ways,
By which thou dost surprise, and prey upon the mind. 145
 Though in the search, too deep for human thought,
 With unsuccessful toil he wrought,[7]
 Till thinking thee to've catched, himself by thee caught,
 Retained thy pris'ner, thy acknowledged slave,
 And sank beneath thy chain to a lamented grave. 150

1701 1713

To the Nightingale

Exert thy voice, sweet harbinger[1] of spring!
 This moment is thy time to sing,
 This moment I attend to praise,
And set my numbers to thy lays.[2]
 Free as thine shall be my song, 5
 As thy music, short, or long.
Poets, wild as thee, were born,
 Pleasing best when unconfined,
 When to please is least designed,
Soothing but their cares to rest;[3] 10
 Cares do still their thoughts molest,

2. Miserly.
3. Persons bound by religious vows.
4. Intend.
5. Coffee. "Indian leaf": tea.
6. Richard Lower (1631–1691), famous British physiologist who studied the human nervous system.

7. Worked.
1. Forerunner.
2. Songs "Attend": devote. "Numbers": verses.
3. I.e., they intend only to soothe their own cares, not to please others.

And still th'unhappy poet's breast,
Like thine, when best he sings, is placed against a thorn.
She begins. Let all be still!
 Muse, thy promise now fulfill! 15
Sweet, oh! sweet, still sweeter yet
Can thy words such accents fit,[4]
Canst thou syllables refine,
Melt a sense that shall retain
Still some spirit of the brain,[5] 20
Till with sounds like these it join.
 'Twill not be! then change thy note;
 Let division[6] shake thy throat.
Hark! Division now she tries;
Yet as far the muse outflies. 25
 Cease then, prithee, cease thy tune;
 Trifler[7] wilt thou sing till June?
Till thy business all lies waste,
And the time of building's past!
 Thus we poets that have speech, 30
Unlike what thy forests teach,
 If a fluent vein[8] be shown
 That's transcendent[9] to our own,
Criticize, reform, or preach,
Or censure what we cannot reach. 35

1702? 1713

The Circuit of Apollo[1]

Apollo as lately a circuit he made
Through the lands of the muses when Kent[2] he surveyed
And saw there that poets were not very common,
But most that pretended to verse[3] were the women,
Resolved to encourage the few that he found, 5
And she that writ best with a wreath[4] should be crowned.
A summons sent out was obeyed but by four,
When Phoebus, afflicted[5] to meet with no more,
And standing where sadly he now might descry
From the banks of the Stoure the desolate Wye,[6] 10
He lamented for Behn[7] o'er that place of her birth,
And said amongst femens[8] was not on the earth
Her superior in fancy,[9] in language, or wit,
Yet owned that a little too loosely[1] she writ,

4. I.e., can the muse's poetry match the bird's music?
5. The speaker asks her muse for a more musical strain of poetry that will still have an intellectual content, i.e., will not be mere sound. The metaphor is of refining or melting base ore into purer metals.
6. A musical term, defining a series of rapid decorative runs or variations on a melody.
7. Frivolous person.
8. Stream, metaphorically of song or poetry.
9. Superior.
1. I.e., the circular journey or tour of the Greek god of the sun and of poetry.

2. The county in England where Finch lived. "Muses": Greek goddesses of art, learning, and inspiration.
3. Claimed to be poets.
4. Of laurel.
5. Pained, saddened. "Phoebus": i.e., Apollo.
6. Two rivers that flow through Kent.
7. Aphra Behn, English poet (see p. 109).
8. Women.
9. Imagination.
1. With too much sexual explicitness.

Since the art of the muse is to stir up soft thoughts, 15
Yet to make all hearts beat without blushes or faults.

But now to proceed, and their merits to know
Before he on any the bays[2] would bestow,
He ordered them each in their several[3] way
To show him their papers, to sing or to say 20
Whate'er they thought best, their pretensions might prove,
When Alinda began, with a song upon love.
So easy the verse, yet composed with such art,
That not one expression fell short of the heart.
Apollo himself did their influence obey; 25
He catched up his lyre, and a part[4] he would play,
Declaring no harmony else could be found
Fit to wait upon[5] words of so moving a sound.
The wreath he reached out, to have placed on her head,
If Laura not quickly a paper had read, 30
Wherein she Orinda[6] has praiséd so high,
He owned it had reached him while yet in the sky,
That he thought with himself when it first struck his ear,
Whoe'er could write that ought the laurel to wear.
Betwixt them he stood in a musing suspense, 35
Till Valeria withdrew him a little from thence,
And told him as soon as she'd got him aside
Her works by no other but him should be tried;[7]
Which so often he read, and with still new delight,
That judgment 'twas thought would not pass till 'twas night; 40
Yet at length he restored them, but told her withal[8]
If she kept it still close, he'd the talent recall.
Ardelia[9] came last as expecting least praise,
Who writ for her pleasure and not for the bays,
But yet, as occasion or fancy should sway, 45
Would sometimes endeavor to pass a dull day
In composing a song, or a scene of a play
Not seeking for fame, which so little does last
That ere we can taste it the pleasure is past.
But Apollo replied, though so careless[1] she seemed, 50
Yet the bays, if her share, would be highly esteemed.

And now he was going to make an oration,
Had thrown by one lock with a delicate fashion,
Upon the left foot most genteelly did stand,
Had drawn back the other and waved his white hand, 55
When calling to mind how the prize, although given
By Paris[2] to her who was fairest in heaven,

2. Leaves of the laurel.
3. Individual, distinct.
4. Piece. "Lyre": a Greek instrument like a small harp.
5. Accompany.
6. I.e., Katherine Philips (see p. 101).
7. Judged.
8. Nevertheless.
9. Finch's neoclassical penname. The other names in the poem may refer to women Finch knew (see also n. 6, p. 177).

1. Indifferent.
2. The son of King Priam of Troy, he was asked to decide which of the three goddesses Hera, Aphrodite, and Athena was the most beautiful, by awarding one of them a golden apple. Paris chose Aphrodite in return for the most beautiful woman in the world. His abduction of Helen, wife of the Greek Menelaus, instigated the Trojan War and ultimately brought about the fall of his city and dynasty ("house").

Had pulled on the rash, inconsiderate boy
The fall of his house, with the ruin of Troy;
Since in wit or in beauty it never was heard 60
One female could yield to have another preferred,
He changed his design, and divided his praise,
And said that they all had a right to the bays,
And that 'twere injustice one brow to adorn
With a wreath which so fitly by each might be worn; 65
Then smiled to himself, and applauded his art,[3]
Who thus nicely[4] has acted so subtle a part
Four women to wheedle, but found 'em too many,
For who would please all can never please any.
In vain then he thought it, there longer to stay, 70
But told them he now must go drive on the day,[5]
Yet the case to Parnassus[6] should soon be referred,
And there in a council of muses be heard,
Who of their own sex best the title might try,
Since no man upon earth, nor Himself in the sky 75
Would be so imprudent, so dull, or so blind,
To lose three parts in four amongst womankind.

 1702

Adam Posed[1]

Could our first father, at his toilsome plough,
Thorns in his path, and labor on his brow,
Clothed only in a rude, unpolished skin,
Could he a vain fantastic nymph[2] have seen,
In all her airs, in all her antic graces, 5
Her various fashions, and more various faces;
How had it posed that skill, which late assigned
Just appellations to each several kind,[3]
A right idea of the sight to frame;
T'have guessed from what new element she came; 10
T'have hit[4] the wavering form, or given this thing a name!

 1709

Friendship between Ephelia and Ardelia[1]

Eph. What friendship is, Ardelia, show.
Ard. 'Tis to love, as I love you.
Eph. This account, so short (though kind)
 Suits not my inquiring mind.
 Therefore farther now repeat: 5
 What is friendship when complete?[2]

3. Skill.
4. Cleverly, prudently.
5. In Greek mythology, Apollo drove the chariot that
pulled the sun across the sky.
6. The mountain where the Muses lived.
1. Puzzled.

2. Fanciful woman of fashion.
3. Adam was given the task of naming all living crea-
tures (Genesis 2:19–20).
4. Exactly suited.
1. Finch's neoclassical penname.
2. Perfect.

Ard. 'Tis to share all joy and grief;
 'Tis to lend all due relief
 From the tongue, the heart the hand;
 'Tis to mortgage house and land; 10
 For a friend be sold a slave;
 'Tis to die upon a grave,
 If a friend therein do lie.
Eph. This indeed, though carried high,
 This, though more than e'er was done 15
 Underneath the rolling sun.
 This has all been said before.
 Can Ardelia say no more?
Ard. Words indeed no more can show:
 But 'tis to love, as I love you. 20

 1713

A Nocturnal Reverie

In such a night, when every louder wind
Is to its distant cavern safe confined;
And only gentle Zephyr[1] fans his wings,
And lonely Philomel,[2] still waking, sings;
Or from some tree, famed for the owl's delight, 5
She, hollowing clear, directs the wanderer right:
In such a night, when passing clouds give place,[3]
Or thinly veil the heavens' mysterious face;
When in some river, overhung with green,
The waving moon and trembling leaves are seen; 10
When freshened grass now bears itself upright,
And makes cool banks to pleasing rest invite,
Whence springs the woodbind, and the bramble-rose,
And where the sleepy cowslip sheltered grows;
Whilst now a paler hue the foxglove takes, 15
Yet checkers still with red the dusky brakes;[4]
When scattered glow-worms, but in twilight fine,[5]
Show trivial beauties watch their hour to shine;
Whilst Salisbury[6] stands the test of every light,
In perfect charm and perfect virtue bright: 20
When odors, which declined repelling day,
Through temperate air uninterrupted stray;
When darkened groves their softest shadows wear,
And falling waters we distinctly hear;
When through the gloom more venerable shows 25
Some ancient fabric, awful[7] in repose,
While sunburnt hills their swarthy looks conceal,

1. The west wind.
2. A Greek woman who was changed into a nightingale, according to the Roman poets.
3. Disappear. "Hollowing": sounding.
4. Thickets.

5. Handsome, i.e., the glowworms demonstrate that small beauties must choose their moment to be seen.
6. An allusion to Finch's friend Anne Tafton, countess of Salisbury.
7. Awesome. "Ancient fabric": building, structure.

And swelling haycocks[8] thicken up the vale:
When the loosed horse now, as his pasture leads,
Comes slowly grazing through th'adjoining meads.[9] 30
Whose stealing pace and lengthened shade we fear,
Till torn up forage[1] in his teeth we hear:
When nibbling sheep at large pursue their food,
And unmolested kine[2] rechew the cud;
When curlews cry beneath the village-walls, 35
And to her straggling brood the partridge calls;
Their shortlived jubilee the creatures keep,
Which but endures, whilst tyrant-man does sleep;
When a sedate content the spirit feels,
And no fierce light disturbs, whilst it reveals; 40
But silent musings urge the mind to seek
Something, too high for syllables to speak;
Till the free soul to a composedness charmed,
Finding the elements of rage disarmed,
O'er all below a solemn quiet grown, 45
Joys in th'inferior world,[3] and thinks it like her own:
In such a night let me abroad remain,
Till morning breaks, and all's confused again;
Our cares, our toils, our clamors are renewed,
Or pleasures, seldom reached, again pursued. 50

 1713

The Apology

'Tis true I write and tell me by what rule
I am alone forbid to play the fool:
To follow through the groves a wandering muse
And feigned[1] ideas for my pleasures choose.
Why should it in my pen be held a fault 5
Whilst Mira paints her face, to paint a thought;
Whilst Lamia to the manly bumper[2] flies
And borrowed spirits sparkle in her eyes;
Why should it be in me a thing so vain
To heat with poetry my colder brain? 10
But I write ill and therefore should forbear.
Does Flavia cease now at her fortieth year
In every place to let that face be seen
Which all the town rejected at fifteen?
Each woman has her weakness; mine indeed 15
Is still to write though hopeless to succeed.

8. Conical mounds of hay. "Swarthy": dark, especially 3. The material world, thought to be lower than the
of skin. spiritual world.
9. Meadows. 1. Invented, imagined.
1. Food of grazing animals. 2. Large glass of wine.
2. Cattle.

Nor to the men is this so easy found
Even in most works with which the wits abound.
(So weak are all since our first breach[3] with Heaven)
There's less to be applauded than forgiven. 20

1713

The Answer

[to Pope's Impromptu][1]

Disarmed with so genteel an air,
 The contest I give o'er;
Yet, Alexander, have a care,
 And shock the sex[2] no more.
We rule the world our life's whole race,[3] 5
 Men but assume[4] that right;
First slaves to every tempting face,
 Then martyrs to our spite.
You of one Orpheus[5] sure have read,
 Who would like you have writ 10
Had he in London town been bred,
 And polished too his wit;
But he poor soul thought all was well,
 And great should be his fame,
When he had left his wife in hell, 15
 And birds and beasts could tame.
Yet venturing then with scoffing rhymes
 The women to incense,
Resenting heroines[6] of those times
 Soon punished his offense. 20
And as the Hebrus[7] rolled his skull
 And harp besmeared with blood,
They clashing as the waves grew full
 Still harmonized the flood.

3. The disobedience of Adam and Eve in eating the forbidden fruit form the Tree of Knowledge (Genesis 3) "Wits": intelligent people.
1. A short poem by Alexander Pope addressed to Finch, with the subtitle "Occasioned by four satirical verses on women wits in *The Rape of the Lock*." The lines from Pope's great mock-epic say suggest that some women "scribble plays" as a manifestation of the same disorder that causes others to "take physic" (medicine) and that female discontent expresses itself alternately in "the hysteric or poetic fit." Finch, a friend of Pope's, evidently took issue with this, as might be expected, and seems to have argued with him in person on the issue of female poetic talent. Pope responded with his brief *Impromptu* (improvisation), in which he flattered Finch by claiming that all the exam-

ples of female poets she cites pale beside her own accomplishments. *The Answer* is Finch's correspondingly deferential reply.
2. I.e., the female sex.
3. Length.
4. Claim without truly possessing.
5. Mythical Greek poet whose wife, Eurydice, was forced to remain behind in the underworld when he looked back at her as they were leaving, against the instruction of Hades, god of the dead. Orpheus' singing had the power to charm wild animals.
6. A band of frenzied women, who tore Orpheus to pieces.
7. River into which Orpheus' head and lyre were cast after he was dismembered (see Ovid's *Metamorphoses* 11.50–51).

But you our follies gently[8] treat, 25
 And spin so fine the thread,
You need not fear his awkward fate,
 The lock won't cost the head.[9]
Our admiration you command
 For all that's gone before; 30
What next we look for at your hand
 Can only raise it more.
Yet sooth[1] the ladies I advise
 (As me too pride has wrought[2]),
We're born to wit, but to be wise 35
 By admonitions taught.

 1717

8. Genteelly, wittily. 1. Truly.
9. A reference to *The Rape of the Lock*, in which a lock 2. Shaped, influenced.
of hair is stolen from Belinda, the heroine.

DELARIVIER MANLEY

c. 1663–1724

The daughter of a historian father and the granddaughter of a Dutch diplomat, Delarivier Manley was educated for the most part at home in the British Channel Island of Jersey. After she married a cousin (into whose care she and her two sisters had been consigned after the death of their father) and bore a son, she discovered that her husband's first wife was alive and the marriage bigamous. Despite her lost reputation and near destitution, her subsequent travels around southwest England resulted in her first publications: *Letters by Mrs. Manley* (1696) appeared the same year her first play, *The Lost Lover*, was produced at Drury Lane. But it was the commercial success of *The Secret History, of Queen Zarah, and the Zarazians* (1705), a thinly veiled attack on Sarah, duchess of Marlborough and favorite of Queen Anne, that brought Manley fame as the author of scurrilous, political narratives.

Describing herself as "the only person of her sex [who] knows how to love," Manley became a powerful satirist, the author of six plays as well as the autobiographical fiction *Rivella* (1714), and the editor of and contributor to such periodicals as the *Female Tatler* and the *Examiner*. So sensational a best-seller was her *Secret Memoirs and Manners of Several Persons of Quality, of Both Sexes from the New Atalantis* (1709–10) that it went through seven editions by 1736. Its instant popularity led Alexander Pope's hero in *The Rape of the Lock* (1714) to boast that his fame would endure "As long as *Atalantis* shall be read." Yet Manley soon suffered a number of economic and physical hardships, and she died in obscurity.

Based on rumors and details about thinly disguised notable people, the *New Atalantis* employs the mythical character of Astrea, goddess of justice, who has come down to earth from the moon to witness the vices of human beings. Our first selection includes Manley's ironic portrait of another woman artist, the poet Sarah Fyge Egerton, composed primarily from the point of view of Egerton's tormented husband. At least in part based on Egerton's acrimonious divorce suit, it presents a farcical battle between the sexes. Our second selection hints at precisely the shocking sexual escapades with which Manley's own name was repeatedly linked.

From The New Atalantis[1]

[*A Fury of a Wife: On Sarah Egerton*]

Intelligence, who neither bore him nor the countrywoman any great good will for usurping upon her province and forcing her to a long and painful silence, drew away the ladies to attend the shrieks and cries that came from a little house, at the end of a neighboring village. The door was open, and a vast crowd about it. The sight was pleasant enough—an old, thin, rawboned priest in his sacerdotal habit, combatting his wife, who buffeted him again, and seemed to be the aggressor. He had not only lost his hat and peruke[2] in the scuffle, but his face looked all over besmeared with something, nobody could tell what, but at last it was known to be piping-hot apple pie out of the oven, which she had scalded him with in a very handsome manner, but was so kind to throw a pound of butter immediately after, to cool him again. His righteous spirit, raised by the smart of the burning, catched hold of her top-knot[3] to demolish that fabric. It was fastened so close to her head that he pulled and pulled in vain. She shrieked out as he pulled, and well she might, for he had tore a piece of ear from her head, which made the blood run down, and was easier to come off than the headgear, which was so interwove with pins, top-knots, false and true curls, that it stood impenetrable, like a rock buffeted by the waves. Astrea assumed a visibility to part the combatants, which none but herself and her companions endeavored at among the great crowd of people. They knew her too well and were delighted to see the scuffle. As soon as they were parted, the priestess flounced out of the house, called for her coachman and bid him put in his horses for away would she go (in that very condition) to sue for justice, if there were any justice in the nation. The poor fellow durst not but obey her, though he loved his master ten times better.

Intelligence was very forward to inform herself about the combat. The good old gentleman had water brought him to wash off the baked mask from his face. The gazers dismissed from the gate and then, after recovering a little vital air, he begged Astrea and her companions to repose themselves and have pity upon a poor man who, for his sins, was matched to the she-devil incarnate. "You see what she is for person, my good friends and new acquaintance," said the priest. "Nothing was ever so homely. Her face is made in part like a blackamoor, flat-nosed, blobber-lipped.[4] There's no sign of life in her complexion. It savors all of mortality. She looks as if she had been buried a twelve-month. Neither her cheeks nor lips can claim any distinction; they are all of an earthy hue, her teeth rotten and sweet as the grave, or charnel-house.[5] And yet, the devil was in me, I married her for love. Lord bless us! Love of what? Not her good conditions, I'm sure. But I am an old man, as you see, and she's a wit. That took me, though I understood never a word of what she writes or says. Deliver me from a poetical wife, and all honest men for my sake! She rumbles in verses of atoms, artic and artartic,[6] of gods and strange things, foreign to all fashionable understanding. Because she was ingenious, I thought

1. This is a *roman à clef*; however, identifications of the historical persons will be supplied only when they are essential to understanding the text or of interest to the contemporary reader.
2. Wig.
3. A bow of ribbon worn on top of the head.
4. With thick or protruding lips. Though "black-

amoor" need not itself have depreciatory force here, the casual racism of identifying ugliness with stereotypically negroid features would have been unremarkable to Manley's contemporaries.
5. Vault in which the bones of the dead are piled.
6. She wrote of the Arctic and Antarctic in a poem.

she'd have been a helpmeet to my memory, being something decayed, but she hates her duties to me, and to the gods, and never goes to the temple above twice a year, and then she falls into counterfeit fits. The bottle of hartshorn's[7] sent for, and herself carried in a languishing posture home. Her tongue is at perpetual war, her discourse one continued reproach, derogating from[8] mine and my children's honor. If there be anybody present, then she's sure to be the most virulent. If I happen to hear it with heroic patience, she is defeated and undone, falls into fits, beats herself to be revenged on me. She has often kicked all the bedclothes off, and her own linen, till she has been stark naked, when the under-priest, the coachman and boy, have been holding of her down. Yet I've good reason to think all this but a sham. I mean her fits, for if you'll let her alone, she'll quickly come to herself. But anybody that compassionates her (as people are apt to do till they know her), she'll hold 'em tack[9] from one frolic to another for four long hours and then to complete all, as if nothing had ailed her, she'll start up of an sudden, and fall a-boxing of me courageously, or her chambermaid, or both. When she has had her revenge, she is at ease. But if by chance she finds my mind unguarded (against the bitter assaults of her tongue), and that I do fall into a passion, as it is not possible always for me to forbear, then she's pleased, then she's delighted, and finds her joy in my torments. Is this anything but the temper of the devil? The day before I'm to sacrifice,[1] she's sure to perplex me all night long, on purpose to discompose and put my mind out of frame. I've often attempted, upon such occasions, to lie in another bed, but that won't do, I should be too much at my ease and that would be her hell. Up she comes roaring, and stamps her foot impetuously and incessantly upon the door, till 'tis broke open. She's as strong in her freaks as a grenadier.[2] Then she falls a-howling and sobbing, tells me she can't sleep without me, and either forces me to rise to her bed, or comes to bed to me, and is sure to keep me awake all night long with her scolding. As that's all her end and design, there's no intervals, no truce to be had with her. She has frightened away all my children, won't suffer one of 'em in my house, had once like to have choked my daughter, that's a woman grown, by flying upon her with her two hands about her throat. She had stopped her windpipe, till the poor girl's tongue hung out of her mouth and her face was grown black, and had certainly killed her in a few minutes more, if I had not come and prevented her. What safety (think you) can my life be in with such a fury? And yet I know not what's the remedy. She won't go from me, if I were to give her all that I have (though she's sordidly covetous), because she dares not torment anybody else as she does me, and yet I keep her a coach and four servants, have a plentiful income and an estate of my own, and she had little or no fortune. I was bewitched to marry her. Then she's in love with all the handsome fellows she sees, but her face protects her chastity, for none sure was ever yet so courageous as to assault it. She vents her passion in love-verses and dialogues of Clarinda and Daphnis. A pitiful lawyer's clerk was a long time her Alexis,[3] and there was love-letters and verses printed with rattling epithets, bombast descriptions, romantic flights, and, in short, nothing of nature in 'em. Yet these must be printed with an epistle to her adored Meneses, who, I've understood

7. Smelling salts.
8. Taking away.
9. Be a match for them.
1. Hold a service.

2. Originally, a grenade thrower; the grenadiers were the tallest and finest men in the regiment.
3. These are conventional names in pastoral poetry given to lovers.

since, was a foolish apothecary that used to recover her from her fits without the help of Galen, or Hippocrates.[4] Then, for her morals, a lady whom she had invited to stay at our house that summer, assumed the reasonable freedom to advise her against passion and anger. She took it so ill at their hands that, to be revenged, she made herself a voluntary evidence in a lawsuit against her, of all the discourse they had together in freedom and, by adding a great deal of false to the true, made her lose her cause. I had been abroad today about my business and had missed my dinner. Coming home, I asked for something to eat. She had took care (after dining plentifully herself) that there should be nothing left for me. One of the maids whispered me, that there was a large apple pie in the oven to be kept hot for the gentlewoman's supper, but I was to know nothing of it. Being pretty sharp-set,[5] I went to the oven; as by instinct, out I drew the pie, got a plate of butter and fell to buttering of it in happy security, as I thought, because she had retired to her closet, pleased with putting the victuals out of the way that I should have nothing to eat. The devil would not let her rest long without tormenting of poor me. Down she comes and, before I was aware, snatches the pie and, by a dexterous whirl of her hand, sends it full in my face and eyes. The plate of butter followed, then the tankard full of drink and, in short, whatever came to hand. Enraged at the pain I felt, my usual moderation forsook me. I leaped briskly at her top-knots, she squalled, which alarmed the neighbors and your selves to behold this comical combat. 'Twas nuts[6] to those rogues, my neighbors, who would not have parted us, though we had killed ourselves upon the spot. But for you, my good friends, I am much obliged to your endeavors, but I see small hopes of redressing these grievances that lie heavy upon me. Were I of another profession than I am, by a just indignation, I would assert the authority of a husband; but our talent is expected to be meek under persecution, long-suffering. Particular scandal often rests upon the general. My brethren may be aspersed[7] for my sake, so that I content myself to sit down under this chastisement, coming from the hand of heaven as a punishment for my sins in marrying a wife not above half so young as myself, when I had children grown up to keep my house and administer comfortably to my necessities."

Here, the two divinities, by stroking with their hands and applying a proper antidote, expelled the fire that had swelled the poor priest's face and eyes in a terrible manner. He returned them a thousand thanks for their civility. They took their leaves very courteously, often regretting the miseries he seemed to suffer with such a fury of a wife.

[The New Cabal: [8] New-Formed Amities against the Hymeneal Union]

But to satisfy your Excellency, these ladies are of the new Cabal, a sect (however innocent in itself) that does not fail from meeting its share of censure from the world. Alas! what can they do? How unfortunate are women? If they seek their diversion out of themselves and include the other sex, they must be criminal? If in themselves (as those of the new Cabal), still they are criminal? Though censurers must carry their imaginations a much greater length than I am able to do mine, to explain this hypothesis with success.

4. Galen (2nd century A.D.) and Hippocrates (5th century B.C.), Greek physicians and writers of medical books.
5. Very hungry

6. A source of pleasure or delight.
7. Slandered, vilified.
8. Small body of persons engaged in secret intrigue.

They pretend to find in these the vices[9] of old Rome revived and quote you certain detestable authors who (to amuse posterity) have introduced you lasting monuments of vice, which could only subsist in imagination and can, in reality, have no other foundation than what are to be found in the dreams of poets and the ill nature of those censurers, who will have no diversions innocent, but what themselves advance!

Oh how laudable! how extraordinary! how wonderful! is the uncommon happiness of the Cabal? They have wisely excluded that rapacious sex who, making a prey of the honor of ladies, find their greatest satisfaction (some few excepted) in boasting of their good fortune, the very chocolate-house[1] being witnesses of their self-love where, promiscuously among the known and unknown, they expose the letters of the fair, explain the mysterious and refine upon the happy part, in their redundancy of vanity consulting nothing but what may feed the insatiable hydra![2]

The Cabal run no such dangers, they have all the happiness in themselves! Two beautiful ladies joined in an excess of amity (no word is tender enough to express their new delight) innocently embrace! For how can they be guilty? They vow eternal tenderness, they exclude the men, and condition that they will always do so. What irregularity can there be in this? 'Tis true, some things may be strained a little too far, and that causes reflections to be cast upon the rest. One of the fair could not defend herself from receiving an importunate visit from a person of the troublesome sex. The lady who was her favorite came unexpectedly at the same time upon another. Armida heard her chair set down in the hall and presently knew her voice, inquiring with precipitation who was above? Having observed a common coach at the gate without a livery, the lover became surprised to the last degree to see Armida's. She trembled! she turned pale! she conjured him to pass into her closet and consent to be concealed till the lady was gone! His curiosity made him as obliging as she could desire; he was no sooner withdrawn, but his fair rival entered the chamber enraged, her voice shrill, her tone inquisitive and menacing, the extremes of jealousy in her eyes and air. "Where is this inconstant—where is this ungrateful girl—? What happy wretch is it upon whom you bestow my rites? To whom do you deliver the possession of my kisses and embraces? Upon whom bestow that heart so invaluable and for which I have paid the equivalent?— Come let us see this monster to whom my happiness is sacrificed—Are you not sufficiently warned by the ruin of so many? Are you also eager to be exposed, to be undone, to be food for vanity, to fill the detestable creatures with vain glory! What recompense—ah, what satisfaction!—Can there be in any heart of theirs, more than in mine—Have they more tenderness—more endearments—their truth cannot come in comparison! Besides, they find their account in treachery and boasting, their pride is gratified, whilst our interest is in mutual secrecy, in natural justice and in mutual constancy."

Such excursions as these have given occasion to the enemies of the Cabal to refine, as much as they please, upon the mysteries of it. There are, who will not allow of innocency in any intimacies, detestable censurers who, after the manner of the Athenians, will not believe so great a man as Socrates (him whom

9. So-called decadent behavior, especially homosexuality.
1. Chocolate, which was first sold in London in the 16th century, became a fashionable drink, and many shops opened, some of which became men's clubs.
2. A many-headed snake, killed by Heracles, that grew back its heads when they were cut off. Here, scandal.

the oracle delivered to be the wisest of all men) could see every hour the beauty of an Alcibiades without taxing his sensibility.[3] How did they recriminate for his affection, for his cares, his tenderness to the lovely youth? How have they delivered him down to posterity as blameable for too guilty a passion for his beautiful pupil?—Since then it is not in the fate of even so wise a man to avoid the censure of the busy and the bold, care ought to be taken by others (less fortified against occasion of detraction, in declining such unaccountable intimacies) to prevent the ill-natured world's refining upon their mysterious innocence.

The persons who passed us in those three coaches were returning from one of their private, I was going to say silent, meetings, but far be it from me to detract from any of the attributes of the sex. The Lady L——and her daughters make four of the cabal. They have taken a little lodging about twelve furlongs from Angela in a place obscure and pleasant with a magazine[4] of good wine and necessary conveniences as to chambers of repose, a tolerable garden and the country in prospect. They wear away the indulgent happy hours according to their own taste. Their coaches and people (of whom they always take as few with them as possible) are left to wait at the convenient distance of a field in length, an easy walk to their bower of bliss. The day and hour of their *rendezvous* is appointed beforehand; they meet, they caress, they swear inviolable secrecy and amity. The glass corroborates their endearments. They momently exclude the men: fortify themselves in the precepts of virtue and chastity against all their detestable undermining arts: arraign without pity or compassion those who have been so unfortunate as to fall into their snare: propagate their principles of exposing them without mercy: give rules to such of the Cabal who are not married how to behave themselves to such who they think fit they should marry, no such weighty affair being to be accomplished without the mutual consent of the society, at the same time lamenting the custom of the world, that has made it convenient (nay, almost indispensable) for all ladies once to marry. To those that have husbands, they have other instructions, in which this is sure to be one: to reserve their heart their tender amity for their fair friend, an article in this well-bred, wilfully undistinguishing age which the husband seems to be rarely solicitous of.

Those who are in their opinion so happy as to be released from the imposing matrimonial fetters are thought the ornament of the Cabal and by all most happy. They claim an ascendant, a right of governing, of admitting or extending; in both they are extremely nice, with particular reserve to the constitution of the novice, they strictly examine her genius,[5] whether it have fitted her for the mysteries of the Cabal, as if she may be rendered insensible on the side of Nature. Nature, who has the trick of making them dote on the opposite improving[6] sex, for if her foible be found directed to what Nature inspires, she is unanimously excluded, and particular injunctions bestowed upon all members of this distinguishing society from admitting her to their bosom, or initiating her in the mysteries of their endearments.

Secrecy is also a material article. This they inviolably promise, nor is it the

3. Socrates (4th century B.C.), Greek philosopher, who according to Plato's *Symposium*, was executed on the grounds that he had corrupted Athenian youth and introduced new gods; he resisted the solicitations of the politician and general Alcibiades, an admirer some twenty years his younger.
4. Storehouse.
5. Natural ability or capacity. "Nice": fastidious, particular.
6. Disapproving, censuring.

least part of the instruction given to a new bride, lest she let her husband into a mystery (however innocent) that may expose and ridicule the community as it happened in the case of the beautiful virgin Euphelia. No sooner did she appear as attendant to the Queen, but all the eyes of all the circle were directed to her. The men adored, the ladies would have discovered something to destroy that adoration if it had been possible, except the Marchioness de Lerma who, bold and masculine, loudly taxed these invidious spectators of ill nature and malice. She took the fair maid into especial consideration, sheltered her under her distinguished protections and, in short, introduced her into the Cabal of which, they say, the Marchioness was one of the first founders in Atalantis, having something so robust in her air and mien that the other sex would have certainly claimed her for one of theirs, if she had not thought fit to declare herself by her habit (alone) to be of the other, insomuch that I have often heard it lamented by the curious, who have taxed themselves of negligence, and were intimate with her lord, when living, that they did not desire him to explain upon that query.

Euphelia flourished under the shine of so great a favorite. The Marquis de los Minos fell in love with her. There was nothing to obstruct his happiness but the Marchioness de Lerma's jealousy. Enraged to lose her beautiful pupil, she traversed her advancement all that lay in her power, but the honor of such a marriage being conspicuous on the young virgin's side, she was forced to give up the secrets of the Cabal and sacrifice the marchioness's honor to preserve the opinion of her own.

Some few such discoveries have happened to cast a taint upon the innocency of the Cabal. How malicious is the world? Who would not avoid their censure if it were possible? We must do justice to the endeavors of the witty Marchioness of Sandomire when she used to mask her diversions in the habit of the other sex and, with her female favorite, Ianthe, wander through the gallant quarter of Atalantis in search of adventures. But what adventures? Good heaven! none that could in reality wound her chastity! Her virtue sacred to her lord and the marriage bed was preserved inviolable! For what could reflect back upon it with any prejudice in the little liberties she took with her own sex whom she used to cajole with the affected seeming gallantry of the other, engage and carry them to the public gardens, and houses of entertainment with music and all diversions?[7] These creatures of hire failed not to find their account in obliging the Marchioness's and Ianthe's peculiar taste, by all the liberties that belonged to women of their loose character and indigence. Though I should look upon it as an excess of mortification were I the marchioness to see the corruption of the sex and to what extremes vice may step by step lead those who were born and probably educated in the road of innocence. It may be surely counted an inhumane curiosity and shows a height of courage, more blameable than otherwise, not to be dejected at the brutality, the degeneracy, of those of our own specie.[8]

* * *

ASTREA: It is something so new and uncommon, so laudable and blameable, that we don't know how to determine, especially wanting light even to guess at what you call the mysteries of the Cabal. If only tender friendship, invio-

7. Not infrequently of a bawdy nature. 8. I.e., species, kind.

able and sincere, be the regard, what can be more meritorious or a truer em-
blem of their happiness above? 'Tis by imitation, the nearest approach they
can make, a feint, a distant landscape of immortal joys. But if they carry it a
length beyond what nature designed and fortify themselves by these new-
formed amities against the hymenial union, or give their husbands but a sec-
ond place in their affections and cares, 'tis wrong and to be blamed. Thus far
as to the merit of the thing itself, but when we look with true regard to the
world, if it permit a shadow of suspicion, a bare imagination, that the myster-
ies they pretend have anything in 'em contrary to kind, and that strict mod-
esty and virtue do not adorn and support their conversation, 'tis to be avoided
and condemned, lest they give occasion for obscene laughter, new invented
satire, fanciful jealousies and impure distrusts in that nice, unforgiving sex,
who arbitrarily decide that woman was only created (with all her beauty, soft-
ness, passions and complete tenderness) to adorn the husband's reign, perfect
his happiness, and propagate the kind.

<p style="text-align:center">* * *</p>

She that was in the coach with her is one of the widows of the new Cabal.
What an irregularity of taste is theirs? They do not in reality love men, but
dote of the representation of men in women. Hence it is that those ladies are
so fond of the dress en cavaliere,[9] though it is extremely against my liking, I
would have the sex distinguished as well by their garb as by their manner. That
bewitching modesty which is so becoming to the opening veil is against kind
in the confirmed, bold and agreeable air of the hat, feather and peruke. If in
this dress you retain the shamefacedness of the other, you lose the native
charm that recommends it. If you dismiss it, you dismiss the highest beauty of
the sex, for, without regard to that much-in-fashion virtue assurance, next to
real innate modesty in ladies (which indeed never fails of giving the appear-
ance), I think the outward blush and seeming habitude of it one of the great-
est ornaments they can wear.

But to return to my widow of the new Cabal. She fell in love with one of the
fair female comedians when she was acting the part of a young lover and a lib-
ertine. The widow sent for the girl and made her very considerable presents,
ordered her picture in that dress to be taken at length by one of the best hands,
and carried her to remain with her during the season at her villa. The come-
dian was dazzled at those endearments and advances from a lady of fortune
and did not know how to behave herself in a manner regular enough (for her
conversation[1] had been pretty much at large); however, she added her whole
endeavors and by that means became tolerably uneasy to herself, not abun-
dantly used to decorum and constraint. The widow redoubled her kindness
and caresses, assured her of her tenderness and amity; she even proceeded to
gentle squeezes and embraces. Nothing could be more innocently endearing
than her transports! The comedian was at a loss to know not only how to merit
so many favors, but of the meaning of 'em. She was also weary of the solitude
and splendor of the widow's family and wanted to return to the amorous hurry
and theatrical littleness she had been used to and therefore received those
honors with no new Cabal air, but, as if rather disgusted at such amiable
proofs of amity, told the lady she did not like those hugs and endearments

9. I.e., as a man.
1. Society, acquaintance; also a term for sexual intercourse.

from her own sex, they seemed unnatural: did they come from a man, she should be able to guess at his design, but here she was at a loss—. The widow found her companion not of a taste virtuous enough for the mysteries of their union; her mind ran all upon what she had been too much used to, the other sex. The comedian had been vitiated by amour! by abominable intrigue with the filthy, odious men! and was not therefore worthy the honor of being admitted into their community. She withdrew those airs of fondness from a tasteless undeserving wretch, assumed more coldness in her behavior to her whilst in the country and, at her coming back, by little and little, dropped her very acquaintance. When she returned to her house in town, to show the lurkings of her malice, or rather her detestation to vice, though but in effigy, she caused the comedian's picture to be let down and with her own hand cut out the face, so stamped upon and abused sent it back to her whom it represented, at the same time causing her to be told she had by her loose libertine life made it a scandal to her house to have such a picture seen in it. The poor comedian fell a crying and said she might have let her alone: she did not for her part seek nor covet the acquaintance: she was no worse now than when 'twas first drawn, neither could her manner of life be a secret to the virtuous widow: she should have objected it to her then, before she gave her the trouble of sitting not to affront her picture so, but she guessed the reason, and would leave her Ladyship to be punished by the reflection of it.

1709–10

MARY ASTELL
1666–1731

In her preface to a collection of Lady Mary Wortley Montagu's Turkish Embassy letters (1724), Mary Astell compared them favorably with the travel literature composed by men and encouraged women readers to "be pleased that a *woman* triumphs." The mutual esteem of these two learned friends, evidenced not only by Astell's pride in Lady Mary's epistolary triumphs but also by Lady Mary's financial support of Astell's writing career, epitomizes the ideal that had earlier impelled Astell to write *A Serious Proposal to the Ladies* (1694), her project to establish a retreat in which women could educate themselves even as they pursued the "blessings" of friendship. Clearly Astell's description of this intellectual community of women was a response to the frequent attacks on the vanity of female wishes in Restoration literature: while a number of satiric poems and plays criticized flirtatiousness and dilettantism as inherently female, Astell believed that religious and philosophic training could correct such feminine failings.

Astell's proposal, therefore, begins by arguing that women have been debarred from advantages, which they are later reproached for not having, and inculcated with vices, for which they are then upbraided. Uncompromising as she was in this claim, Astell accepted the legal, vocational, and economic subordination of women. Although she was quite conservative in subsequent essays on the inalterable subjugation of wives to husbands, in her proposal she could insist, by emphasizing the moral benefits of what amounts to a Protestant convent, on women's natural equality with men. Thus, as Katharine M. Rogers has argued in *Feminism in Eighteenth-Century England*, "Astell was able to combine acceptance of the ex-

ternal status quo with radical questioning of the alleged natural superiority on which men based their prerogatives," and she was able to do so, in part, because she limited her claims to single women.

Significantly, Astell herself remained single, and in *A Serious Proposal to the Ladies*, which went through several editions, she attempted to provide a feasible alternative to marriage for other women. Although this daughter of a Newcastle merchant must have counted herself lucky to be given an education by an uncle who was a clergyman, she dedicated her quiet life in Chelsea to championing other women's right to learn. Eighteen years old when she composed the poem *Ambition*, she consistently sought to debate those "Who falsely say that women have no soul," publishing under the pseudonym "a Lover of her Sex." Anthologized in *The Ladies Library* (1714) by Richard Steele and satirized in *The Tatler* by Jonathan Swift, she established a considerable reputation within her own lifetime.

Ambition

Mar 30. 1684

I

What's this that with such vigor fills my breast?
　　Like the first mover[1] finds no rest,
　　And with its force does all things draw,
Makes all submit to its imperial law!
Sure 'tis a spark 'bove what Prometheus[2] stole, 5
　　Kindled by a heavenly coal,
　　Their sophistry[3] I can control,
Who falsely say that women have no soul.

II

Vile greatness! I disdain to bow to thee,
　　Thou art below even lowly me, 10
　　I would no fame, no titles have,
And no more land than what will make a grave.
I scorn to weep for worlds, may I but reign
　　And empire o'er my self obtain,
　　In Caesar's throne I'd not sit down, 15
Nor would I stoop for Alexander's[4] crown.

III

Let me obscured be, and never known.
　　Or pointed at about the town,
　　Short-winded fame shall not transmit
My name, that the next age may censure it: 20
If I write sense no matter what they say,

1. In the medieval astronomical system that pictured the heavens as concentric spheres, the *primum mobile* was the outermost moving sphere, which communicates its motion to all the others.
2. According to Greek legend, he stole fire from the gods for humanity (whom he had created).
3. Clever but deceptive argumentation.
4. Alexander the Great (356–323 B.C.), king of Macedon and conqueror of Greece and Persia. "Caesar's throne": Caesar was the name taken by Roman emperors from the first, Augustus (ruled 29 B.C.–A.D 14), to Domitian (ruled 81–96).

Whether they call it dull, or pay
 A reverence such as Virgil claims,
Their breath's infectious,[5] I have higher aims.

IV

Mean-spirited men! that bait at honor, praise, 25
 A wreath of laurel or of bays,[6]
How short's their immortality!
But oh a crown of glory ne'er will die!
This I'm ambitious of, no pains will spare
 To have a higher mansion[7] there, 30
 There all are kings, here let me be,
Great O my God, great in humility.

1689 1988

From A Serious Proposal to the Ladies

[A *Religious Retirement*]

Now as to the proposal, it is to erect a monastery, or if you will (to avoid giving offence to the scrupulous and injudicious, by names which though innocent in themselves, have been abused by superstitious practices),[1] we will call it a religious retirement, and such as shall have a double aspect, being not only a retreat from the world for those who desire that advantage, but likewise, an institution and previous discipline, to fit us to do the greatest good in it; such an institution as this (if I do not mightily deceive my self) would be the most probable method to amend the present, and improve the future age. * * *

You are therefore ladies, invited into a place, where you shall suffer no other confinement, but to be kept out of the road of sin: * * * Happy retreat! which will be the introducing you into such a paradise as your mother Eve forfeited,[2] where you shall feast on pleasures, that do not, like those of the world, disappoint your expectations, pall your appetites, and by the disgust they give you put you on the fruitless search after new delights, which when obtained are as empty as the former; but such as will make you truly happy now, and prepare you to be perfectly so hereafter. Here are no serpents to deceive you, whilst you entertain your selves in these delicious gardens. No provocations will be given in this amicable society, but to love and to good works, which will afford such an entertaining employment, that you'll have as little inclination as leisure to pursue those follies, which in the time of your ignorance passed with you under the name of love, although there is not in nature two more different things, than true love and that brutish passion, which pretends to ape it. Here will be no rivalling but for the love of God, no ambition but to procure his favour, to which nothing will more effectually recommend you, than a great and dear affection to each other. * * *

5. Morally contaminating. Virgil (70–19 B.C.), whose poetry includes the epic *The Aeneid*, is the dominant poet in Latin literature and was particularly highly regarded through the Middle Ages.
6. In classical Greece, victors were crowned with a wreath of laurel; bay is a kind of laurel. "Bait": stop.
7. I.e., a room in heaven, see John 14:2: "In my

Father's house are many mansions."
1. Monks had acquired a reputation among English anti-Papists for dabbling in the supernatural.
2. Eve was cast out of the Garden of Eden with Adam when she ate the fruit from the tree of knowledge (Genesis 3:6).

One great end of this institution shall be, to expel that cloud of ignorance which custom has involved us in, to furnish our minds with a stock of solid and useful knowledge, that the souls of women may no longer be the only unadorned and neglected things. It is not intended that our religious should waste their time, and trouble their heads about such unconcerning matters, as the vogue of the world has turned up for learning, the impertinency of which has been excellently exposed by an ingenious pen,[3] but busy themselves in a serious inquiry after necessary and perfective truths, something which it concerns them to know, and which tends to their real interest and perfection, and what that is the excellent author just now mentioned will sufficiently inform them. Such a course of study will neither be too troublesome nor out of the reach of a female virtuoso;[4] for it is not intended she should spend her hours in learning words but things, and therefore no more languages than are necessary to acquaint her with useful authors. Nor need she trouble her self in turning over a great number of books, but take care to understand and digest a few well chosen and good ones. Let her but obtain right ideas, and be truly acquainted with the nature of those objects that present themselves to her mind, and then no matter whether or no she be able to tell what fanciful people have said about them: And thoroughly to understand Christianity as professed by the Church of England,[5] will be sufficient to confirm her in the truth, though she have not a catalogue of those particular errors which oppose it. Indeed a learned education of the women will appear so unfashionable, that I began to startle at the singularity of the proposition, but was extremely pleased when I found a late ingenious author (whose book I met with since the writing of this) agree with me in my opinion.[6] For speaking of the repute that learning was in about 150 years ago, "It was so very modish," says he "that the fair sex seemed to believe that Greek and Latin added to their charms: and Plato and Aristotle untranslated. were frequent ornaments of their closets. One would think by the effects, that it was a proper way of educating them, since there are no accounts in history of so many great women in any one age, as are to be found between the years 15 and 1500."

For since God has given women as well as men intelligent souls, why should they be forbidden to improve them? Since he has not denied us the faculty of thinking, why should we not (at least in gratitude to him) employ our thoughts on himself their noblest object, and not unworthily bestow them on trifles and gaieties and secular affairs? Being[7] the soul was created for the contemplation of truth as well as for the fruition of good, is it not as cruel and unjust to exclude women from the knowledge of the one as from the enjoyment of the other? Especially since the will is blind, and cannot choose but by the direction of the understanding; or to speak more properly, since the soul always wills according as she understands, so that if she understands amiss, she wills amiss. And as exercise enlarges and exalts any faculty, so through want of using it becomes cramp and lessened; if therefore we make little or no use of our understandings, we shall shortly have none to use; and the more contracted and unemployed the deliberating and directive power is, the more liable is the elective to unworthy and mischievous choices. What is it but the

3. Mr. Nor. *Conduct of Hum. Life* [Astell's note].
4. I.e., one interested in the pursuit of knowledge.
5. The Church of England set itself against the doctrines and ceremonies of the Catholic Church.

6. Astell's note cites William Wotton's *Reflections upon Ancient and Modern Learning* (1691).
7. I.e., given that.

want[8] of an ingenious education, that renders the generality of feminine conversations so insipid and foolish and their solitude so insupportable? Learning is therefore necessary to render them more agreeable and useful in company, and to furnish them with becoming entertainments when alone, that so they may not be driven to those miserable shifts,[9] which too many make use of to put off their time, that precious talent that never lies on the hands of a judicious person. And since our happiness in the next world, depends so far on those dispositions which we carry along with us out of this, that without a right habitude and temper of mind we are not capable of felicity; and seeing our beatitude consists in the contemplation of the divine truth and beauty, as well as in the fruition of his goodness, can ignorance be a fit preparative for Heaven? Is't likely that she whose understanding has been busied about nothing but froth and trifles, should be capable of delighting her self in noble and sublime truths? Let such therefore as deny us the improvement of our intellectuals, either take up his[1] Paradox, who said that women have no souls, which at a time when the most contend to have them allowed to brutes, would be as unphilosophical as it is unmannerly, or else let them permit us to cultivate and improve them. There is a sort of learning indeed which is worse than the greatest ignorance: A woman may study plays and romances all her days, and be a great deal more knowing but never a jot the wiser. Such a knowledge as this serves only to instruct and put her forward in the practice of the greatest follies, yet how can they justly blame her who forbid, or at least won't afford opportunity of better? A rational mind will be employed, it will never be satisfied in doing nothing, and if you neglect to furnish it with good materials, 'tis like to take up with such as come to hand.

We pretend not that women should teach in the church, or usurp authority where it is not allowed them; permit us only to understand our own duty, and not be forced to take it upon trust from others; to be at least so far learned, as to be able to form in our minds a true idea of Christianity, it being so very necessary to fence us against the danger of these last and perilous days, in which deceivers a part of whose character is to lead captive silly women, need not creep into houses since they have authority to proclaim their errors on the housetop. And let us also acquire a true practical knowledge, such as will convince us of the absolute necessity of holy living as well as of right believing, and that no heresy is more dangerous than that of an ungodly and wicked life. And since the French tongue is understood by most ladies, methinks they may much better improve it by the study of philosophy (as I hear the French ladies do) Descartes, Malebranche[2] and others, than by reading idle novels and romances. 'Tis strange we shou'd be so forward to imitate their fashions and fopperies, and have no regard to what really deserves our imitation. And why shall it not be thought as genteel to understand French philosophy, as to be accoutred in a French mode? Let therefore the famous Madam D'acier, Scudery, &c, and our own incomparable Orinda,[3] excite the emulation of the English ladies.

8. Lack.
9. Expedients, here evidently referring to women's traditional leisure activities, such as music, embroidery, etc.
1. Perhaps Mohammed, who was commonly thought to have claimed in the Koran that women lacked souls.
2. René Descartes (1596–1650) and Nicholas de

Malebranche (1638–1715), well-known 17th-century philosophers.
3. Katherine Philips (1631–1664), English poet known as "the Matchless Orinda" (see p. 101). Anne Lefebvre D'Acier (1654–1720), French classical scholar who translated the *Iliad* and *Odyssey*. Magdeleine de Scudéry (1607–1701), French poet and novelist.

The ladies, I'm sure, have no reason to dislike this proposal, but I know not how the men will resent it to have their enclosure broke down, and women invited to taste of that tree of knowledge they have so long unjustly monopolized. But they must excuse me, if I be as partial to my own sex as they are to theirs, and think women as capable of learning as men are, and that it becomes them as well. For I cannot imagine wherein the hurt lies, if instead of doing mischief to one another, by an uncharitable and vain conversation, women be enabled to inform and instruct those of their own sex at least; the holy ghost having left it on record, that Priscilla as well as her husband, catechized the eloquent Apollos[4] and the great Apostle found no fault with her. It will therefore be very proper for our ladies to spend part of their time in this retirement, in adorning their minds with useful knowledge.

1694

4. In Acts 18 26, an eloquent preacher named Apollos, who knows only the teachings of John the Baptist, is educated in Christianity by Priscilla and her husband Aquila, two followers of the Apostle Paul.

LADY MARY WORTLEY MONTAGU
1689–1762

At twenty-one years of age, Lady Mary Pierrepont sent her translation of the *Enchiridion of Epictetus* to her mentor, Bishop Burnet, with a letter in which she explained, "My sex is usually forbid studies of this nature, and folly reckoned so much our proper sphere, that we are sooner pardoned any excesses of that, than the least pretensions to reading or good sense." Although she knew that "there is hardly a character in the world more despicable, or more liable to universal ridicule than that of a learned woman," through her witty conversation and the candid letters and sardonic poems she circulated to friends, the woman who became Lady Mary Wortley Montagu went on to attain a reputation for learning that gained her staunch friends and merciless foes. Writing in the age of great epistolary productions, Lady Mary fashioned her letters into a fascinating record of women's customs and conduct both in England and abroad. The explicit sexual themes she addressed in her poems made her vulnerable to scandalous rumors, but she was also hailed by contemporaries as a "she meteor" or "the female traveler."

Almost every major event in Lady Mary's life was recorded in letters to her sister, her husband, and her daughter. It was a life of privilege and publicity. Her father was a wealthy Whig peer, Evelyn Pierrepont, who became fifth earl of Kingston in 1690 and first duke of Kingston in 1713; her mother, Mary Fielding, died when Lady Mary was five years old. The education she pursued in her father's library was stimulated by her uncle and Bishop Burnet, and by two close friends, Mary Astell and Anne Montagu. After Montagu's death in 1709, her brother continued this correspondence. When it turned into a courtship, which Lady Mary's father opposed, Edward Wortley Montagu and Lady Mary eloped in 1712. Montagu was made ambassador to Constantinople in 1716, and for two years Lady Mary sent letters home describing her journeys and adventures in Turkey, where she explored Constantinople in disguise and even visited a harem. On her return to England, she helped to popularize smallpox inoculation by having her own two children inoculated: a 1724 article in *The Plaindealer* viewed her education of an antagonistic medical profession as proof "that England has owed to women the greatest blessings she has been distinguished by."

Throughout her adult life, Lady Mary was active at the center of London's cultural coteries: she helped advance the career of her cousin, the dramatist and novelist Henry Fielding; she maintained friendships with Joseph Addison and Richard Steele, the author-editors of the influential periodical *The Spectator*; in 1717 she received Alexander Pope's *Eloisa to Abelard*, which was addressed to her as to a close friend, and in 1735 she withstood Pope's furious attack on her as a slovenly "Sappho" in *Epistle II: To a Lady*. After a bitter political feud with Pope and the marriage of her daughter in 1739, she fell in love with Francesco Algarotti, a young writer she followed to Italy. She never established a lasting relationship with him, but she remained separated from her husband, returning to England only after his death in 1761 for the remaining year of her own life. A year after her death, the Turkish Embassy letters consolidated her literary reputation; she had prepared them for publication herself, keeping copies of those she mailed and deleting the more personal passages. Forty years later, her other correspondences began to appear in print, and today they total almost nine hundred letters. A number of her poems—*Town Eclogues* and *Court Poems*—appeared in a pirated volume in 1716, a portion of which was reprinted in 1747. In 1837, Lord Wharncliffe produced an edition of her *Letters and Works*. But her poems have only recently begun to receive the attention they deserve. Satires on feminine narcissism and on masculine arrogance, urbane assessments of urban life, and savvy evaluations of literary fashions, the poems of Lady Mary Wortley Montagu deploy traditional neoclassical forms with exceptional vigor and notable skill.

Saturday—The Small-Pox[1]

Flavia

The wretched Flavia, on her couch reclined;
Thus breathed the anguish of a wounded mind,
A glass reversed in her right hand she bore,
For now she shunned the face she sought before.
 "How am I changed! alas! how am I grown 5
A frightful spectre to myself unknown!
Where's my complexion? where my radiant bloom,
That promised happiness for years to come?
Then with what pleasure I this face surveyed!
To look once more, my visits oft delayed! 10
Charmed with the view, a fresher red would rise,
And a new life shot sparkling from my eyes!
 "Ah! faithless glass, my wonted bloom restore;
Alas! I rave, that bloom is now no more!
The greatest good the gods on men bestow, 15
Even youth itself, to me is useless now.
There was a time (oh! that I could forget!)
When opera-tickets poured before my feet;
And at the ring, where brightest beauties shine,
The earliest cherries of the spring were mine. 20
Witness, O Lilly; and thou, Motteux, tell,

1. Lady Mary herself contracted smallpox (1715), though she was not badly marked. Later she worked to introduce into England the practice of inoculation against smallpox, which she had observed in Turkey.

How much japan² these eyes have made ye sell.
With what contempt ye saw me oft despise
The humble offer of the raffled prize;
For at each raffle stil. each prize I bore, 25
With scorn rejected, or with triumph wore!
Now beauty's fled, and presents are no more!
 "For me the patriot has the House³ forsook,
And left debates to catch a passing look.
For me the soldier has soft verses writ: 30
For me the beau has aimed to be a wit.
For me the wit to nonsense was betrayed;
The gamester has for me his dun delayed,
And overseen⁴ the card he would have played.
The bold and haughty, by success made vain, 35
Awed by my eyes have trembled to complain:
The bashful 'squire, touched by a wish unknown,
Has dared to speak with spirit not his own:
Fired by one wish, all did alike adore;
Now beauty's fled, and lovers are no more! 40
 "As round the room I turn my weeping eyes,
New unaffected scenes of sorrow rise.
Far from my sight that killing picture⁵ bear,
The face disfigure, and the canvas tear:
That picture which with pride I used to show, 45
The lose resemblance that upbraids me now.
And thou, my toilette!⁶ where I oft have sat,
While hours unheeded passed in deep debate
How curls should fall or where a patch to place;
If blue or scarlet best became my face: 50
Now on some happier nymph your aid bestow;
On fairer heads, ye useless jewels, glow!
No borrowed lustre can my charms restore;
Beauty is fled, and dress is now no more!
 "Ye meaner beauties, I permit ye shine; 55
Go, triumph in the hearts that once were mine:
But 'midst your triumphs with confusion know,
'Tis to my ruin all your charms ye owe.
Would pitying heaven restore my wonted mien,
Ye still might move unthought of and unseen: 60
But oh, how vain, how wretched is the boast
Of beauty faded, and of empire lost!
What now is left but, weeping, to deplore
My beauty fled, and empire now no more!
 "Ye cruel chemists, what withheld your aid? 65
Could no pomatum⁷ save a trembling maid?

2. I.e., Japanese goods. Charles Lillie, associated with the publication of *The Tatler* (a journal published 1607–1711) and a perfumer and apparently sold Japanese goods. Peter Motteux (1660–1718), translator and dramatist, who also dealt in tea and Chinese and Indian wares.
3. I.e., the House of Commons, the lower house of Parliament.
4. Overlooked. "Dun": debt collector.
5. I.e., a painting that "kills" her with its "unaffected scenes" because it shows her face unscarred by small-pox.
6. Dressing table.
7. Scented ointment. "Chemists": druggists.

How false and trifling is that art ye boast!
No art can give me back my beauty lost.
In tears, surrounded by my friends, I lay
Masked o'er, and trembled at the sight of day; 70
Mirmillio came my fortune to deplore
(A golden-headed cane well carved he bore),
Cordials, he cried, my spirits must restore!
Beauty is fled, and spirit is no more!
 "Galen, the grave officious Squirt was there, 75
With fruitless grief and unavailing care;
Machaon[8] too, the great Machaon, known
By his red cloak and his superior frown;
And why, he cried, this grief and this despair?
You shall again be well, again be fair; 80
Believe my oath (with that an oath he swore);
False was his oath; my beauty was no more!
 "Cease, hapless maid, no more thy tale pursue,
Forsake mankind, and bid the world adieu!
Monarchs and beauties rule with equal sway: 85
All strive to serve, and glory to obey:
Alike unpitied when deposed they grow,
Men mock the idol of their former vow.
 "Adieu! ye parks—in some obscure recess,
Where gentle streams will weep at my distress, 90
Where no false friend will in my grief take part,
And mourn my ruin with a joyful heart;
There let me live in some deserted place,
There hide in shades this lost inglorious face.
Plays, operas, circles,[9] I no more must view! 95
My toilette, patches, all the world adieu!"

1715 1716

Epitaph[1]

Here lies John Hughs and Sarah Drew.
Perhaps you'll say, what's that to you?
Believe me, friend, much may be said
On this poor couple that are dead.
On Sunday next they should have married; 5
But see how oddly things are carried.
On Thursday last it rained and lightened,
These tender lovers sadly frightened
Sheltered beneath the cocking hay[2]
In hopes to pass the storm away. 10

8. The son of Asclepius (the Greek god of healing) and one of the Greek heroes in the Trojan War; he healed many fellow soldiers. Galen (2nd century A.D.), great Greek physician and medical writer. "Squirt": doctor (slang).
9. Tiers of seats in a theater.
1. On 1 Sept. 1718 Pope sent Lady Mary his two sentimental epitaphs on the lovers killed by lightning at Stanton Harcourt (*Corr.* 1. 493–6). She was roused by his suggestions that the pair would otherwise have lived in pastoral bliss, that their death was a reward for virtue, and that it in turn would be rewarded by "a tear from the finest eyes in the world." Her poem addresses itself less to the lovers' death than to Pope's celebration.
2. I.e., hay cocks (conical heaps).

But the bold thunder found them out
(Commissioned for that end no doubt)
And seizing on their trembling breath
Consigned them to the shades of death.
Who knows if 'twas not kindly done? 15
For had they seen the next year's sun
A beaten wife and cuckold swain[3]
Had jointly cursed the marriage chain.
Now they are happy in their doom
For P. has wrote upon their tomb.[4] 20

1718 1763

An Answer to a Love Letter in Verse[1]

Is it to me, this sad-lamenting strain?
Are heaven's choicest gifts bestowed in vain?
A plenteous fortune, and a beauteous bride,
Your love rewarded, and content your pride!
Yet leaving her—'tis me that you pursue, 5
Without one single charm, but being new.
 How vile is man! How I detest the ways
Of artful falsehood, and designing praise!
Tasteless, an easy Happiness you slight.
Ruin your joy, and mischief your delight. 10
Why should poor Pug[2] (the mimic of your kind)
Wear a rough chain, and be to box confined?
Some cup perhaps he breaks, or tears a fan,
While moves unpunished the destroyer, man.
Not bound by vows, and unrestrained by shame, 15
In sport you break the heart, and rend the fame.[3]
Not that your art can be successful here,
Th'already plundered need no robber fear,
Nor sighs, nor charms, nor flattery can move,
Too well secured against a second love, 20
Once, and but once, that devil charmed my mind,
To reason deaf, to observation blind,
I idly hoped (what cannot love persuade?)
My fondness equaled, and my truth repaid,
Slow to distrust, and willing to believe, 25
Long hushed my doubts, and would my self deceive;
But oh too soon—this tale would ever last,
Sleep, sleep my wrongs and let me think 'em past.
 For you who mourn with counterfeited grief
And ask so boldly like a begging thief; 30
May soon some other nymph inflict the pain
You know so well, with cruel art to feign,

3. A rustic, especially a lover in pastoral poetry.
4. In 1713, Alexander Pope (1688–1744), English
poet, wrote three epitaphs on John Hewet and Sarah
Drew, two of which were highly sentimental in empha-
sizing the pair's purity and faithfulness; it is to these
that Lady Mary is responding.

1. Lady Mary was replying to a letter from a "Mr. T." or
"Mr. T——n." One "sad-lamenting" suitor sent her a
verse epistle dated 31 May 1725; there were no doubt
others.
2. Monkey.
3. Reputation.

Though long you've sported with Don Cupid's[4] dart,
You may see eyes, and you may feel a heart.
 So the brisk wits[5] who stop the evening coach 35
Laugh at the fear that follows their approach,
With idle mirth, and haughty scorn despise
The passenger's pale cheek, and staring eyes;
But seized by justice, find a fright no jest
And all the terror doubled in their breast. 40

1720 1750

Epistle from Mrs. Yonge to Her Husband[1]

Think not this paper comes with vain pretense
To move your pity, or to mourn th' offense.
Too well I know that hard obdurate heart;
No softening mercy there will take my part,
Nor can a woman's arguments prevail. 5
When even your patron's[2] wise example fails.
But this last privilege I still retain;
Th' oppressed and injured always may complain.
 Too, too severely laws of honor bind
The weak submissive sex of womankind. 10
If sighs have gained or force compelled our hand,
Deceived by art,[3] or urged by stern command,
Whatever motive binds the fatal tie,
The judging world expects our constancy.
 Just heaven! (for sure in heaven does justice reign, 15
Though tricks below that sacred name profane)
To you appealing I submit my cause,
Nor fear a judgment from impartial laws.
All bargains but conditional[4] are made;
The purchase void, the creditor unpaid, 20
Defrauded servants are from service free;
A wounded slave regains his liberty.
For wives ill used[5] no remedy remains,
To daily racks condemned, and to eternal chains.
 From whence is this unjust distinction grown? 25
Are we not formed with passions like your own?
Nature with equal fire our souls endued,[6]
Our minds as haughty, and as warm our blood;
O'er the wide world your pleasures you pursue,
The change is justified by something new; 30

4. Roman god of love, who shoots his victims with arrows. "Don": master (archaic).
5. I.e., highway robbers.
1. The editors gratefully acknowledge the permission of Lawrence Lipking to use information contained in his notes to this poem in *The Norton Anthology of English Literature*. In this epistle, or verse-letter, Lady Mary assumes the role of Mary Yonge, a woman who, having separated from her adulterous husband, William, herself took a lover and was then publicly disgraced by the divorce proceedings that her husband instigated. Intimate details of her relationship with her lover were revealed during the trial, and the court awarded Mr. Yonge his wife's dowry and the greater part of her fortune.
2. Sir Robert Walpole, a powerful friend of Yonge's at court, who was said to tolerate his own wife's infidelity.
3. Artifice.
4. Only conditionally.
5. Poorly treated.
6. Endowed.

But we must sigh in silence—and be true.
Our sex's weakness you expose and blame
(Of every prattling fop the common theme),
Yet from this weakness you suppose is due
Sublimer virtue than your Cato[7] knew. 35
Had heaven designed us trials so severe,
It would have formed our tempers then to bear.[8]
 And I have borne (oh what have I not borne!)
The pang of jealousy, the insults of scorn.
Wearied at length, I from your sight remove, 40
And place my future hopes in secret love.
In the gay bloom of glowing youth retired,
I quit[9] the woman's joy to be admired,
With that small pension your hard heart allows,
Renounce your fortune, and release your vows. 45
To custom (though unjust) so much is due;
I hide my frailty from the public view.
My conscience clear, yet sensible of shame,
My life I hazard, to preserve my fame.
And I prefer this low inglorious state 50
To vile dependence on the thing I hate—
But you pursue me to this last retreat.
Dragged into light, my tender crime is shown
And every circumstance of fondness known.
Beneath the shelter of the law you stand, 55
And urge my ruin with a cruel hand,
While to my fault thus rigidly severe,
Tamely submissive to the man you fear.[1]
 This wretched outcast, this abandoned wife,
Has yet this joy to sweeten shameful life: 60
By your mean conduct, infamously loose,[2]
You are at once my accuser and excuse.
Let me be damned by the censorious prude
(Stupidly dull, or spiritually lewd),
My hapless case will surely pity find 65
From every just and reasonable mind.
When to the final sentence I submit,
The lips condemn me, but their souls acquit.
 No more my husband, to your pleasures go,
The sweets of your recovered freedom know. 70
Go: court the brittle friendship of the great,
Smile at his board or at his levee[3] wait;
And when dismissed, to madam's toilet fly,[4]
More than her chambermaids, or glasses,[5] lie,
Tell her how young she looks, how heavenly fair, 75
Admire the lilies and the roses there.
Your high ambition may be gratified,

7. A Roman statesman known for his self-discipline.
8. I.e., capable of bearing such trials. "Tempers":
characters.
9. Gave up.
1. I.e., Walpole.
2. Immoral (i.e., adulterous). "Mean": low.

3. Morning reception of visitors. "Board": dining
table.
4. It was fashionable for upper-class women to re-
ceive visitors during the last stages of dressing (their
"toilet").
5. Mirrors.

Some cousin of her own be made your bride,
And you the father of a glorious race
Endowed with Ch——l's strength and Low——r's face.[6] 80

1724 1977

Verses[1]

Addressed to the imitator of the first satire of the second book of Horace.

In two large columns on thy motley page,
Where Roman wit is striped with English rage;
Where ribaldry to satire makes pretense,
And modern scandal rolls with ancient sense:
Whilst on one side we see how Horace thought, 5
And on the other how he never wrote;
Who can believe, who view the bad, the good,
That the dull copyist better understood
That spirit he pretends to imitate,
Than heretofore that Greek he did translate?[2] 10
 Thine is just such an image of *his* pen,
As thou thyself art of the sons of men,
Where our own species in burlesque we trace,
A sign-post likeness of the human race,
That is at once resemblance and disgrace.[3] 15
 Horace can laugh, is delicate, is clear,
You only coarsely rail, or darkly sneer;
His style is elegant, his diction pure,
Whilst none thy crabbed numbers can endure;
Hard as thy heart, and as thy birth obscure.[4] 20
 If *he* has thorns, they all on roses grow;
Thine like thistles, and mean brambles show;
With this exception, that, though rank the soil,
Weeds as they are, they seem produced by toil.
 Satire should, like a polished razor, keen, 25
Wound with a touch, that's scarcely felt or seen:
Thine is an oyster-knife, that hacks and hews;
The rage, but not the talent to abuse;
And is in *hate*, what *love* is in the stews.[5]
 'Tis the gross *lust* of hate, that still annoys, 30
Without distinction, as gross love enjoys:
Neither to folly, not to vice confined,
The object of thy spleen[6] is humankind:

6. Antony Lowther, a notorious lady's man. General Churchill, rumored to have had an affair with Lady Walpole. Lady Mary insinuates that Yonge's next wife may be as untrue as his first.
1. Lady Mary's vitriolic attack on Alexander Pope (1688–1744) was occasioned by a couplet in his Horatian imitation (*Satire* 2.1)(1733) that she took as applying to her: "From furious *Sappho* scarce a milder Fate, / P——x'd [poxed] by her Love, or libell'd by her Hate" (lines 83–84).
2. Pope translated Homer's *Iliad* and most of the *Odyssey* with considerable financial success; but from its inception, the project came under attack from some who questioned Pope's knowledge of Greek and found the results un-Homeric. See the famous verdict of the classicist Richard Bentley (1662–1742) on Pope's *Iliad*: "It is a pretty poem, Mr. Pope, but you must not call it Homer."
3. Pope was hunchbacked and only about four and a half feet tall.
4. The rank and station of Pope's parents was unclear, though not as low as Lady Mary implies; his father was in trade. "Crabbed numbers": ill-natured and inelegant verse.
5. Brothels.
6. Violent ill-humor.

It preys on all who yield, or who resist:
To thee 'tis provocation to exist. 35
 But if thou seest a great and generous heart,
Thy bow is doubly bent to force a dart.
Nor dignity nor innocence is spared,
Nor age, nor sex, nor thrones, nor graves, revered.
Nor only justice vainly we demand, 40
But even benefits can't rein thy hand;
To this or that alike in vain we trust,
Nor find thee less ungrateful than unjust.
 Not even youth and beauty can control
The universal rancor of thy soul; 45
Charms that might soften superstition's rage,
Might humble pride, or thaw the ice of age.
But how should'st thou by beauty's force be moved,
No more for loving made than to be loved?
It was the equity of righteous Heaven, 50
That such a soul to such a form was given;
And shows the uniformity of fate,
That one so odious should be born to hate.
 When God created thee, one would believe
He said the same as to the snake of Eve; 55
To human race antipathy declare,
"Twixt them and thee be everlasting war.'
But oh! the sequel of the sentence dread,
And whilst you *bruise their heel,* beware your head.
Nor think thy weakness shall be thy defense, 60
The female scold's protection in offense.
Sure 'tis as fair to beat who cannot fight,
As 'tis to libel those who cannot write.
And if thou draw'st thy pen to aid the law,
Others a cudgel, or a rod, may draw. 65
If none with vengeance yet thy crimes pursue,
Or give thy manifold affronts their due;
If limbs unbroken, skin without a stain,
Unwhipped, unblanketed, unkicked, unslain,
That wretched little carcass you retain, 70
The reason is, not that the world wants eyes,
But thou'rt so mean,[8] they see, and they despise:
When fretful *porcupine,* with rancorous will,
From mounted back shoots forth a harmless quill,
Cool the spectators stand; and all the while 75
Upon the angry little monster smile.
Thus 'tis with thee:—while impotently safe,
You strike unwounding, we unhurt can laugh.
Who but must laugh, this bully when he sees,
A puny insect shivering at a breeze?' 80
One over-matched by every blast of wind,
Insulting and provoking all mankind.

7. God cursed the snake for its part in convincing
Adam and Eve to eat the forbidden fruit, promising it
that woman's seed "shall bruise thy head, and thou
shalt bruise his heel" (Genesis 3:15).

8. Low, gnoble.
9. See Pope's *Epistle to Burlington* (1731): "'Who but
must laugh, the Master when he sees, / A puny insect
shiv'ring at a breeze!'" (lines 107–8).

Is this the *thing* to keep mankind in awe,
To make those trouble who escape the law?[1]
Is this *the ridicule* to live so long, 85
The deathless satire and *immortal song?*[2]
No: like the self-blown praise, thy scandal flies;
And, as we're told of wasps, it stings and dies.
 If none do yet return th' intended blow,
You all your safety to your dullness owe: 90
But whilst that armor thy poor corse[3] defends,
'Twill make thy readers few, as are thy friends:
Those, who thy nature loathed, yet loved thy art,
Who liked thy head, and yet abhorred thy heart:
Chose thee to read, but never to converse, 95
And scorned in prose him whom they prized in verse
Even they shall now their partial error see,
Shall shun thy writings like thy company;
And to thy books shall ope their eyes no more
Than to thy person they would do their door. 100
 Nor thou the justice of the world disown,
That leaves thee thus an outcast and alone;
For though in law to murder be to kill,
In equity the murder's in the will:
Then whilst with coward-hand you stab a name, 105
And try at least t' assassinate our fame,
Like the first bold assassin's be thy lot,
Ne'er be thy guilt forgiven, or forgot;
But, as thou hat'st, be hated my mankind,
And with the emblem of thy crooked mind 110
Marked on thy back, like Cain by God's own hand,[4]
Wander, like him, accursed through the land.

 1747

To the Countess of Bute, Lady Montagu's Daughter

[On Her Granddaughter]

Jan 28, N.S.[1] (1753)

 Dear Child,—You have given me a great deal of satisfaction by your account of your eldest daughter. I am particularly pleased to hear she is a good arithmetician; it is the best proof of understanding: the knowledge of numbers is one of the chief distinctions between us and the brutes.[2] If there is anything in blood, you may reasonably expect your children should be endowed with an uncommon share of good sense. Mr. Wortley's family and mine have both produced some of the greatest men that have been born in England: I mean Admiral Sandwich, and my grandfather, who was distinguished by the

1. Compare Pope's imitation of Horace's *Satire* 2.1.118: "Hear this, and tremble! you, who 'scape the Laws."
2. In his *Epilogue to the Satires: Dialogue 2* (1738), Pope suggests that truth makes his satire immortal (line 247).
3. Body.

4. God set a mark on Cain, who had killed his brother Abel, so that no one would kill him as he wandered in his punishment (Genesis 4:8–15).
1. "New style" date (i.e., of the Gregorian reformed calendar, which was not accepted in England until 1752).
2. Beasts.

name of Wise William. I have heard Lord Bute's father mentioned as an extraordinary genius, though he had not many opportunities of showing it; and his uncle, the present Duke of Argyll, has one of the best heads I ever knew.

I will therefore speak to you as supposing Lady Mary[3] not only capable, but desirous of learning: in that case by all means let her be indulged in it. You will tell me I did not make it a part of your education: your prospect was very different from hers. As you had no defect either in mind or person to hinder, and much in your circumstances to attract, the highest offers it seemed your business to learn how to live in the world, as it is hers to know how to be easy[4] but of it. It is the common error of builders and parents to follow some plan they think beautiful (and perhaps is so), without considering that nothing is beautiful that is misplaced. Hence we see so many edifices raised that the raisers can never inhabit, being too large for their fortunes. Vistas[5] are laid open over barren heaths, and apartments contrived for a coolness very agreeable in Italy, but killing in the north of Britain: thus every woman endeavors to breed her daughter a fine lady, qualifying her for a station in which she will never appear, and at the same time incapacitating her for that retirement[6] to which she is destined. Learning, if she has a real taste for it, will not only make her contented, but happy in it. No entertainment is so cheap as reading, nor any pleasure so lasting. She will not want new fashions, nor regret the loss of expensive diversions, or variety of company, if she can be amused with an author in her closet.[7] To render this amusement extensive, she should be permitted to learn the languages. I have heard it lamented that boys lose so many years in mere learning of words: this is no objection to a girl, whose time is not so precious: she cannot advance herself in any profession, and has therefore more hours to spare: and as you say her memory is good, she will be very agreeably employed this way.

There are two cautions to be given on this subject—first, not to think herself learned when she can read Latin, or even Greek. Languages are more properly to be called vehicles of learning than learning itself, as may be observed in many schoolmasters, who, though perhaps critics in grammar are the most ignorant fellows upon earth. True knowledge consists in knowing things, not words. I would wish her no further a linguist than to enable her to read books in their originals that are often corrupted, and always injured by translations. Two hours' application every morning will bring this about much sooner than you can imagine and she will have leisure enough besides to run over the English poetry, which is a more important part of a woman's education than it is generally supposed. Many a young damsel has been ruined by a fine copy of verses, which she would have laughed at if she had known it had been stolen from Mr. Waller.[8] I remember when I was a girl, I saved one of my companions from destruction who communicated to me an epistle she was quite charmed with. As she had a natural good taste, she observed the lines were not so smooth as Prior's or Pope's[9] but had more thought and spirit than any of theirs. She was wonderfully delighted with such a demonstration of her lover's sense and passion, and not a little pleased with her own charms, that had force enough to inspire such elegancies. In the midst of this triumph I showed her

3. Lady Mary's granddaughter.
4. At ease, contented. "The world": high society. Apparently Montagu did not consider her granddaughter to be "marriageable."
5. A passage between trees or buildings opening onto a distant prospect.

6. I.e., like of solitude.
7. Small, private room attached to a bedroom.
8. Edmund Waller (1606–1687), English poet.
9. Alexander Pope (1688–1744), English poet. Matthew Prior (1664–1721), English diplomat and poet.

that they were taken from Randolph's[1] poems and the unfortunate transcriber was dismissed with the scorn he deserved. To say truth, the poor plagiary[2] was very unlucky to fall into my hands; that author being no longer in fashion, would have escaped any one of less universal reading than myself. You should encourage your daughter to talk over with you what she reads; and, as you are very capable of distinguishing, take care she does not mistake pert folly for wit[3] and humor, or rhyme for poetry, which are the common errors of young people, and have a train of ill consequences.

The second caution to be given her (and which is most absolutely necessary) is to conceal whatever learning she attains, with as much solicitude as she would hide crookedness or lameness; the parade[4] of it can only serve to draw on her the envy, and consequently the most inveterate hatred, of all he and she fools, which will certainly be at least three parts in four of all her acquaintance. The use of knowledge in our sex, besides the amusement of solitude, is to moderate the passions, and learn to be contented with a small expense which are the certain effects of a studious life; and it may be preferable even to that fame which men have engrossed[5] to themselves, and will not suffer us to share. You will tell me I have not observed this rule myself: but you are mistaken: it is only inevitable accident that has given me any reputation that way. I have always carefully avoided it and ever thought it a misfortune.

The explanation of this paragraph would occasion a long digression, which I will not trouble you with it being my present design only to say what I think useful for the instruction of my granddaughter, which I have much at heart. If she has the same inclination (I should say passion) for learning that I was born with history, geography, and philosophy will furnish her with materials to pass away cheerfully a longer life than is allotted to mortals. I believe there are few heads capable of making Sir I. Newton's[6] calculations, but the result of them is not difficult to be understood by a moderate capacity. Do not fear this should make her affect the character of Lady ——— or Lady ———, or Mrs.———. Those women are ridiculous, not because they have learning but because they have it not. One thinks herself a complete historian after reading Echard's *Roman History*; another a profound philosopher, having got by heart some of Pope's unintelligible essays; and a third an able divine, on the strength of Whitefield's[7] sermons: thus you hear them screaming politics and controversy. It is a saying of Thucydides,[8] ignorance is bold, and knowledge reserved. Indeed, it is impossible to be far advanced in it without being more humbled by a conviction of human ignorance, than elated by learning. At the same time I recommend books, I neither exclude work[9] nor drawing. I think it as scandalous for a woman not to know how to use a needle, as for a man not to know how to use a sword. I was once extreme fond of my pencil,[1] and it was a great mortification to me when my father turned off my master, having made a considerable progress for a short time I learnt. My overeagerness in the pursuit of it had brought a weakness on my eyes, that made it necessary to leave it off;

1. Thomas Randolph (1605–1635); his *Poems* was published in 1638.
2. Plagiarist.
3. Intelligence.
4. Proud display.
5. Appropriated.
6. English scientist, founder of modern physics (1642–1727).
7. George Whitefield (1714–1770), famous

Methodist preacher who published many of his sermons. Lawrence Echard (1670–1730) wrote *Roman History* (1695–98). Pope wrote several essays in verse. "Divine": theologian.
8. Greek historian of the 5th century B.C.; Lady Mary is paraphrasing a line from his *Peloponnesian War*.
9. Embroidery.
1. A fine brush for artwork.

and all the advantage I got was the improvement of my hand.[2] I see, by hers, that practice will make her a ready writer: she may attain it by serving you for a secretary, when your health or affairs make it troublesome to you to write yourself: and custom will make it an agreeable amusement to her. She cannot have too many for that station of life which will probably be her fate. The ultimate end of your education was to make you a good wife (and I have the comfort to hear that you are one): hers ought to be, to make her happy in a virgin state. I will not say it is happier; but it is undoubtedly safer than any marriage. In a lottery, where there are (at the lowest computation) ten thousand blanks to a prize it is the most prudent choice not to venture.

I have always been so thoroughly persuaded of this truth, that, notwithstanding the flattering views I had for you (as I never intended you a sacrifice to my vanity), I thought I owed you the justice to lay before you all the hazards attending matrimony: you may recollect I did so in the strongest manner. Perhaps you may have more success in the instructing your daughter: she has so much company at home, she will not need seeking it abroad, and will more readily take the notions you think fit to give her. As you were alone in my family, it would have been thought a great cruelty to suffer[3] you no companions of your own age, especially having so many near relations, and I do not wonder their opinions influenced yours. I was not sorry to see you not determined on a single life, knowing it was not your father's intention, and contented myself with endeavoring to make your home so easy that you might not be in haste to leave it.

I am afraid you will think this a very long and insignificant letter. I hope the kindness of the design will excuse it, being willing to give you every proof in my power that I am

Your most affectionate mother.

1753 1763

2. Handwriting. 3. Allow.

ELIZA HAYWOOD
1693?–1756

Prolific even by eighteenth-century standards, Eliza Haywood authored more than sixty titles—including short fiction, novels, plays, periodicals, political works, and poetry—in a career that spanned nearly forty years. Yet her early life remains shrouded in obscurity. Apparently abandoned by her husband before she was twenty-one, Haywood pursued a theater career, first at Dublin's Smock Alley theater and later in London. There she turned to fiction, and from the date of her first publication—the best-selling *Love in Excess: Or, The Fatal Inquiry* (1719–20)— she was quickly established in literary London as the figure whom Henry Fielding dubbed "Mrs. Novel." In part, Haywood acquired a significant readership in the 1720s with a series of often racy popular novels; perhaps as a result, too, she also acquired critics such as Alexander Pope, who lampooned her for immorality and commercial sensationalism in the *Dunciad* (1728).

Haywood's later career was more circumspect, but even more versatile. Within a year of the publication of Samuel Richardson's best-selling novel *Pamela* (1740), she had produced both a satire and an imitation in *Anti-Pamela: Or, Feign'd Innocence Detected* (1741) and *The Virtuous Villager: Or, Virgin's Victory* (1742).

Her later works included periodicals (*The Female Spectator*, 1744–46), allegorical prose (*Life's Progress through the Passions: Or, The Adventures of Natura*, 1748), a political pamphlet for which she was briefly jailed (*A Letter from H— G—, Esq.*, 1750), and advice manuals (*The Wife* and *The Husband*, 1756). At her death in 1756, Haywood was working on her last periodical, *The Young Lady*.

Fantomina: Or, Love in a Maze (1724) was written at the height of Haywood's early career. As the scholar Christine Blouch explains, "An unnamed protagonist uses the occasion of attending the theater to create her own drama, which is a swiftly and intricately staged series of progressive identities that transgress social and sexual boundaries. *Fantomina* is about a young woman who decides to become mistress of her own identity." Of particular interest to contemporary readers is Haywood's depiction of a desirous female character whose brilliant masquerades easily dupe a gullible man. Yet just as fascinating as her analysis of the rhythms of dawning and dwindling desire is Haywood's gloomy conviction that at the story's end her impudent heroine must be severely punished for such erotic transgressions and impersonations.

Fantomina: Or, Love in a Maze[1]

Being a Secret History of an Amour Between Two Persons of Condition

> In love the victors from vanquished fly.
> They fly that wound, and they pursue that die.
>
> Waller

A young lady of distinguished birth, beauty, wit, and spirit, happened to be in a box one night at the playhouse; where, though there were a great number of celebrated toasts, she perceived several gentlemen extremely pleased themselves with entertaining a woman who sat in a corner of the pit, and, by her air and manner of receiving them, might easily be known to be one of those who come there for no other purpose, than to create acquaintance with as many as seem desirous of it. She could not help testifying her contempt of men, who, regardless either of the play, or circle,[2] threw away their time in such a manner, to some ladies that sat by her: but they, either less surprised by being more accustomed to such sights than she who had been bred for the most part in the country, or not of a disposition to consider anything very deeply, took but little notice of it. She still thought of it, however; and the longer she reflected on it, the greater was her wonder, that men, some of whom she knew were accounted to have wit, should have tastes so very depraved.—This excited a curiosity in her to know in what manner these creatures were addressed:—she was young, a stranger to the world, and consequently to the dangers of it; and having nobody in town, at that time, to whom she was obliged to be accountable for her actions, did in everything as her inclinations or humors rendered most agreeable to her: therefore thought it not in the least a fault to put in practice a little whim which came immediately into her head, to dress herself as near as she could in the fashion of those women who make sale of their favors, and set herself in the way of being accosted as such a one, having at that time no other aim, than the gratification of an innocent curiosity.—She no sooner designed this frolic, than she put it in execution; and muffling her

1. We are indebted to Marah Gubar for bringing this text to our attention. "Toasts" (line 3): the bells of the season.
2. Tier of seats in the theater. "Testifying": asserting.

hoods over her face, went the next night into the gallery-box, and practicing as
much as she had observed at that distance, the behavior of that woman, was
not long before she found her disguise had answered the ends she wore it
for:—a crowd of purchasers of all degrees and capacities were in a moment
gathered about her, each endeavoring to outbid the other, in offering her a
price for her embraces.—She listened to 'em all, and was not a little diverted
in her mind at the disappointment she should give to so many, each of which
thought himself secure of gaining her.—She was told by 'em all, that she was
the most lovely woman in the world; and some cried, *Gad, she is mighty like my
fine Lady Such-a-one,*—naming her own name. She was naturally vain, and re-
ceived no small pleasure in hearing herself praised, though in the person of an-
other, and a supposed prostitute; but she dispatched as soon as she could all
that had hitherto attacked her, when she saw the accomplished *Beauplaisir*[3]
was making his way through the crowd as fast as he was able, to reach the
bench she sat on. She had often seen him in the drawing-room, had talked
with him; but then her quality and reputed virtue kept him from using her
with that freedom she now expected he would do, and had discovered some-
thing in him, which had made her often think she should not be displeased, if
he would abate some part of his reserve.—Now was the time to have her
wishes answered:—he looked in her face, and fancied, as many others had
done, that she very much resembled that lady whom she really was; but the
vast disparity there appeared between their characters prevented him from
entertaining even the most distant thought that they could be the same.—He
addressed her at first with the usual salutations of her pretended profession,
as, *Are you engaged, Madam?—Will you permit me to wait on you home after the
play?—By Heaven, you are a fine girl!—How long have you used this house?*—
and such like questions; but perceiving she had a turn of wit, and a genteel
manner in her raillery, beyond what is frequently to be found among those
wretches, who are for the most part gentlewomen but by necessity, few of 'em
having had an education suitable to what they affect to appear, he changed
the form of his conversation, and showed her it was not because he under-
stood no better that he had made use of expressions so little polite.—In fine,
they were infinitely charmed with each other: he was transported to find so
much beauty and wit in a woman, who he doubted not but on very easy terms
he might enjoy; and she found a vast deal of pleasure in conversing with him
in this free and unrestrained manner. They passed their time all the play with
an equal satisfaction; but when it was over, she found herself involved in a dif-
ficulty, which before never entered into her head, but which she knew not well
how to get over.—The passion he professed for her, was not of that humble na-
ture which can be content with distant adorations:—he resolved not to part
from her without the gratifications of those desires she had inspired; and pre-
suming on the liberties which her supposed function allowed of, told her she
must either go with him to some convenient house of his procuring, or permit
him to wait on her to her own lodgings.—Never had she been in such a
dilemma: three or four times did she open her mouth to confess her real qual-
ity; but the influence of her ill stars prevented it, by putting an excuse into her
head, which did the business as well, and at the same time did not take from
her the power of seeing and entertaining him a second time with the same

3. "Good pleasure" (French).

freedom she had done this.—She told him, she was under obligations to a man who maintained her, and whom she durst not disappoint, having promised to meet him that night at a house hard by.—This story so like what those ladies sometimes tell was not at all suspected by *Beauplaisir*; and assuring her he would be far from doing her a prejudice,[4] desired that in return for the pain he should suffer in being deprived of her company that night, that she would order her affairs, so as not to render him unhappy the next. She gave a solemn promise to be in the same box on the morrow evening; and they took leave of each other; he to the tavern to drown the remembrance of his disappointment; she in a hackney-chair[5] hurried home to indulge contemplation on the frolic she had taken, designing nothing less on her first reflections than to keep the promise she had made him, and hugging herself with joy, that she had the good luck to come off undiscovered.

But these cogitations were but of a short continuance; they vanished with the hurry of her spirits, and were succeeded by others vastly different and ruinous:—all the charms of *Beauplaisir* came fresh into her mind; she languished, she almost died for another opportunity of conversing with him; and not all the admonitions of her discretion were effectual to oblige her to deny laying hold of that which offered itself the next night.—She depended on the strength of her virtue, to bear her fate through trials more dangerous than she apprehended this to be, and never having been addressed by him as Lady— was resolved to receive his devoirs as a town-mistress,[6] imagining a world of satisfaction to herself in engaging him in the character of such a one, observing the surprise he would be in to find himself refused by a woman, who he supposed granted her favors without exception.—Strange and unaccountable were the whimsies she was possessed of—wild and incoherent her desires— unfixed and undetermined her resolutions, but in that of seeing *Beauplaisir* in the manner she had lately done. As for her proceedings with him, or how a second time to escape him, without discovering who she was, she could neither assure herself, nor whether or not in the last extremity she would do so.— Bent, however, on meeting him, whatever should be the consequence, she went out some hours before the time of going to the playhouse, and took lodgings in a house not very far from it, intending, that if he should insist on passing some part of the night with her, to carry him there, thinking she might with more security to her honor entertain him at a place where she was mistress, than at any of his own choosing.

The appointed hour being arrived, she had the satisfaction to find his love in his assiduity: he was there before her; and nothing could be more tender than the manner in which he accosted her: but from the first moment she came in, to that of the play being done, he continued to assure her no consideration should prevail with him to part from her again, as she had done the night before; and she rejoiced to think she had taken that precaution of providing herself with a lodging, to which she thought she might invite him, without running any risk, either of her virtue or reputation.—Having told him she would admit of his accompanying her home, he seemed perfectly satisfied; and leading her to the place, which was not above twenty houses distant, would have ordered a collation[7] to be brought after them. But she would not

4. An injury from misjudgment.
5. A hired closed vehicle for one person, carried on two poles by two bearers.

6. Prostitute.
7. Light meal.

permit it, telling him she was not one of those who suffered themselves to be treated at their own lodgings; and as soon she was come in, sent a servant, belonging to the house, to provide a very handsome supper, and wine, and everything was served to table in a manner which showed the director neither wanted money, nor was ignorant how it should be laid out.

This proceeding, though it did not take from him the opinion that she was what she appeared to be, yet it gave him thoughts of her, which he had not before.—He believed her a *mistress*, but believed her to be one of a superior rank, and began to imagine the possession of her would be much more expensive than at first he had expected: but not being of a humor to grudge anything for his pleasures, he gave himself no farther trouble than what were occasioned by fears of not having money enough to reach her price, about him.

Supper being over, which was intermixed with a vast deal of amorous conversation, he began to explain himself more than he had done; and both by his words and behavior let her know he would not be denied that happiness the freedoms she allowed had made him hope.— t was in vain; she would have retracted the encouragement she had given:—in vain she endeavored to delay, till the next meeting, the fulfilling of his wishes:—she had now gone too far to retreat:—*he* was bold;—he was resolute: *she* fearful—confused, altogether unprepared to resist in such encounters, and rendered more so, by the extreme liking she had to him.—Shocked, however, at the apprehension of really losing her honor, she struggled all she could, and was just going to reveal the whole secret of her name and quality, when the thoughts of the liberty he had taken with her, and those he still continued to prosecute,[8] prevented her, with representing the danger of being exposed, and the whole affair made a theme for public ridicule.—Thus much, indeed, she told him, that she was a virgin, and had assumed this manner of behavior only to engage him. But that he little regarded, or if he had, would have been far from obliging him to desist;—nay, in the present burning eagerness of desire, 'tis probable, that had he been acquainted both with who and what she really was, the knowledge of her birth would not have influenced him with respect sufficient to have curbed the wild exuberance of his luxurious wishes, or made him in that longing—that impatient moment, change the form of his addresses. In fine, she was undone; and he gained a victory, so highly rapturous, that had he known over whom, scarce could he have triumphed more. Her tears, however, and the distraction she appeared in, after the ruinous ecstasy was past, as it heightened his wonder, so it abated his satisfaction:—he could not imagine for what reason a woman, who, if she intended not to be a *mistress*, had counterfeited the part of one, and taken so much pains to engage him, should lament a consequence which she could not but expect, and till the last test, seemed inclinable to grant; and was both surprised and troubled at the mystery.—He omitted nothing that he thought might make her easy; and still retaining an opinion that the hope of interest had been the chief motive which had led her to act in the manner she had done, and believing that she might know so little of him, as to suppose, now she had nothing left to give, he might not make that recompense she expected for her favors: to put her out of that pain, he pulled out of his pocket a purse of gold, entreating her to accept of that as an earnest of what he intended to do for her; assuring her, with ten thousand protestations, that he

8. Persist in, carry on.

would spare nothing, which his whole estate could purchase, to procure her content and happiness. This treatment made her quite forget the part she had assumed, and throwing it from her with an air of disdain, Is this a reward (*said she*) for condescensions,[9] such as I have yielded to?—Can all the wealth you are possessed of make a reparation for my loss of honor?—Oh! no, I am undone beyond the power of heaven itself to help me!—She uttered many more such exclamations; which the amazed *Beauplaisir* heard without being able to reply to, till by degrees sinking from that rage of temper, her eyes resumed their softening glances, and guessing at the consternation he was in, No, my dear *Beauplaisir*, (*added she*) your love alone can compensate for the shame you have involved me in; be you sincere and constant, and I hereafter shall, perhaps, be satisfied with my fate, and forgive myself the folly that betrayed me to you.

Beauplaisir thought he could not have a better opportunity than these words gave him of inquiring who she was, and wherefore she had feigned herself to be of a profession which he was now convinced she was not; and after he had made her a thousand vows of an affection, as inviolable and ardent as she could wish to find in him, entreated she would inform him by what means his happiness had been brought about, and also to whom he was indebted for the bliss he had enjoyed.—Some remains of yet unextinguished modesty, and sense of shame, made her blush exceedingly at this demand; but recollecting herself in a little time, she told him so much of the truth, as to what related to the frolic she had taken of satisfying her curiosity in what manner *mistresses*, of the sort she appeared to be were treated by those who addressed them; but forbore discovering her true name and quality, for the reasons she had done before, resolving, if he boasted of this affair, he should not have it in his power to touch her character: she therefore said she was the daughter of a country gentleman, who was come to town to buy clothes, and that she was called *Fantomina*. He had no reason to distrust the truth of this story, and was therefore satisfied with it; but did not doubt by the beginning of her conduct, but that[1] in the end she would be in reality, the thing she so artfully had counterfeited; and had good nature enough to pity the misfortunes he imagined would be her lot: but to tell her so, or offer his advice in that point, was not his business, at least, as yet.

They parted not till towards morning; and she obliged him to a willing vow of visiting her the next day at three in the afternoon. It was too late for her to go home that night, therefore contented herself with lying there. In the morning she sent for the woman of the house to come up to her; and easily perceiving, by her manner, that she was a woman who might be influenced by gifts, made her a present of a couple of broad pieces, and desired her, that if the gentleman, who had been there the night before, should ask any questions concerning her, that he should be told, she was lately come out of the country, had lodged there about a fortnight, and that her name was *Fantomina*. I shall (*also added she*) lie but seldom here; nor, indeed, ever come but in those times when I expect to meet him: I would, therefore, have you order it so, that he may think I am but just gone out, if he should happen by any accident to call when I am not here; for I would not, for the world, have him imagine I do not

9. Acts of consent. 1. I.e., her conduct never made him doubt that.

constantly lodge here. The landlady assured her she would do everything as she desired, and gave her to understand she wanted not the gift of secrecy.

Everything being ordered at this home for the security of her reputation, she repaired to the other, where she easily excused to an unsuspecting aunt, with whom she boarded, her having been abroad all night, saying, she went with a gentleman and his lady in a barge, to a little country seat of theirs up the river, all of them designing to return the same evening; but that one of the bargemen happening to be taken ill on the sudden, and no other waterman to be got that night, they were obliged to tarry till morning. Thus did this lady's wit and vivacity assist her in all, but where it was most needed.—She had discernment to foresee, and avoid all those ills which might attend the loss of her *reputation*, but was wholly blind to those of the ruin of her *virtue*; and having managed her affairs so as to secure the *one*, grew perfectly easy with the remembrance she had forfeited the *other*.—The more she reflected on the merits of *Beauplaisir*, the more she excused herself for what she had done; and the prospect of that continued bliss she expected to share with him took from her all remorse for having engaged in an affair which promised her so much satisfaction, and in which she found not the least danger of misfortune.—If he is really (*said she, to herself*) the faithful, the constant lover he has sworn to be, how charming will be our amor?—And if he should be false, grow satiated, like other men, I shall but, at the worst, have the private vexation of knowing I have lost him;—the intrigue being a secret, my disgrace will be so too:—I shall hear no whispers as I pass—She is forsaken:—the odious word *forsaken* will never wound my ears; nor will my wrongs excite either the mirth or pity of the talking world:—it would not be even in the power of my undoer himself to triumph over me; and while he laughs at, and perhaps despises the fond, the yielding *Fantomina*, he will revere and esteem the virtuous, the reserved lady.—In this manner did she applaud her own conduct, and exult with the imagination that she had more prudence than all her sex beside. And it must be confessed, indeed, that she preserved an economy in the management of this intrigue beyond what almost any woman but herself ever did: in the first place, by making no person in the world a confident in it; and in the next, in concealing from *Beauplaisir* himself the knowledge who she was; for though she met him three or four days in a week, at that lodging she had taken for that purpose, yet as much as he employed her time and thoughts, she was never missed from any assembly she had been accustomed to frequent.—The business of her love has engrossed her till six in the evening, and before seven she has been dressed in a different habit, and in another place.—Slippers, and a night-gown loosely flowing, has been the garb in which he has left the languishing *Fantomina*;—laced and adorned with all the blaze of jewels has he, in less than an hour after, beheld at the royal chapel, the palace gardens, drawing-room, opera, or play, the haughty awe-inspiring lady—a thousand times has he stood amazed at the prodigious likeness between his little mistress and this court beauty; but was still as far from imagining they were the same as he was the first hour he had accosted her in the playhouse, though it is not impossible but that her resemblance to this celebrated lady might keep his inclination alive something longer than otherwise they would have been; and that it was to the thoughts of this (as he supposed) unenjoyed charmer she owed in great measure the vigor of his latter caresses.

But he varied not so much from his sex as to be able to prolong desire to any

great length after possession: the rifled charms of *Fantomina* soon lost their potency, and grew tasteless and insipid; and when the season of the year inviting the company to the *Bath*,[2] she offered to accompany him, he made an excuse to go without her. She easily perceived his coldness, and the reason why he pretended her going would be inconvenient, and endured as much from the discovery as any of her sex could do: she dissembled it, however, before him, and took her leave of him with the show of no other concern than his absence occasioned: but this she did to take from him all suspicion of her following him, as she intended, and had already laid a scheme for.—From her first finding out that he designed to leave her behind, she plainly saw it was for no other reason, than that being tired of her conversation, he was willing to be at liberty to pursue new conquests; and wisely considering that complaints, tears, swoonings, and all the extravagancies which women make use of in such cases, have little prevalence over a heart inclined to rove, and only serve to render those who practice them more contemptible, by robbing them of that beauty which alone can bring back the fugitive lover, she resolved to take another course; and remembering the height of transport she enjoyed when the agreeable *Beauplaisir* kneeled at her feet, imploring her first favors, she longed to prove the same again. Not but a woman of her beauty and accomplishments might have beheld a thousand in that condition *Beauplaisir* had been; but with her sex's modesty, she had not also thrown off another virtue equally valuable, though generally unfortunate, *constancy*: she loved *Beauplaisir*; it was only he whose solicitations could give her pleasure; and had she seen the whole species[3] despairing, dying for her sake, it might, perhaps, have been a satisfaction to her pride, but none to her more tender inclination.—Her design was once more to engage him, to hear him sigh, to see him languish, to feel the strenuous pressures of his eager arms, to be compelled, to be sweetly forced to what she wished with equal ardor, was what she wanted, and what she had formed a stratagem to obtain, in which she promised herself success.

She no sooner heard he had left the town, than making a pretense to her aunt, that she was going to visit a relation in the country, went towards *Bath*, attended but by two servants, who she found reasons to quarrel with on the road and discharged: clothing herself in a habit she had brought with her, she forsook the coach, and went into a wagon, in which equipage she arrived at *Bath*. The dress she was in was a round-eared cap, a short red petticoat, and a little jacket of gray stuff; all the rest of her accoutrements were answerable to[4] these, and joined with a broad country dialect, a rude unpolished air, which she, having been bred in these parts, knew very well how to imitate, with her hair and eye-brows blacked, made it impossible for her to be known, or taken for any other than what she seemed. Thus disguised did she offer herself to service in the house where *Beauplaisir* lodged, having made it her business to find out immediately where he was. Notwithstanding this metamorphosis she was still extremely pretty; and the mistress of the house happening at that time to want a maid was very glad of the opportunity of taking her. She was presently received into the family; and had a post in it (such as she would have chose, had she been left at her liberty), that of making the gentlemen's beds, getting them their breakfasts, and waiting on them in their chambers. Fortune

2. A city with hot mineral waters that was a fashionable gathering place. "Rifled": stolen.

3. I.e., of men. "Solicitations": sexual entreaties.

4. In agreement with.

in this exploit was extremely on her side; there were no others of the male-sex
in the house than an old gentleman, who had lost the use of his limbs with the
rheumatism, and had come thither for the benefit of the waters, and her
beloved *Beauplaisir*; so that she was in no apprehensions of any amorous vio-
lence, but where she wished to find it. Nor were her designs disappointed: He
was fired with the first sight of her; and though he did not presently take any
farther notice of her, than giving her two or three hearty kisses, yet she, who
now understood that language but too well, easily saw they were the prelude
to more substantial joys.—Coming the next morning to bring his chocolate,
as he had ordered, he catched her by the pretty leg, which the shortness of her
petticoat did not in the least oppose; then pulling her gently to him, asked her,
how long she had been at service?—How many sweethearts she had? If she
had ever been in love? and many other such questions, befitting one of the de-
gree she appeared to be: all which she answered with such seeming innocence,
as more enflamed the amorous heart of him who talked to her. He compelled
her to sit in his lap; and gazing on her blushing beauties, which, if possible, re-
ceived addition from her plain and rural dress, he soon lost the power of con-
taining himself.—His wild desires burst out in all his words and actions: he
called her little angel, cherubim, swore he must enjoy her, though death were
to be the conseqence, devoured her lips, her breasts with greedy kisses, held to
his burning bosom her half-yielding, half-reluctant body, nor suffered her to
get loose, till he had ravaged all, and glutted each rapacious sense with the
sweet beauties of the pretty *Celia*, for that was the name she bore in this sec-
ond expedition.—Generous as liberality itself to all who gave him joy this way,
he gave her a handsome sum of gold, which she durst not now refuse, for fear
of creating some mistrust, and losing the heart she so lately had regained;
therefore taking it with an humble courtesy, and a well counterfeited show of
surprise and joy, cried, O law, Sir! what must I do for all this? He laughed at her
simplicity, and kissing her again, though less fervently than he had done be-
fore, bad her not be out of the way when he came home at night. She
promised she would not, and very obediently kept her word.

His stay at *Bath* exceeded not a month; but in that time his supposed coun-
try lass had persecuted him so much with her fondness, that in spite of the ea-
gerness with which he first enjoyed her, he was at last grown more weary of her,
than he had been of *Fantomina*; which she perceiving, would not be trouble-
some, but quitting her service, remained privately in the town till she heard he
was on his return; and in that time provided herself of another disguise to
carry on a third plot, which her inventing brain had furnished her with, once
more to renew his twice-decayed ardors. The dress she had ordered to be
made, was such as widows wear in their first mourning, which, together with
the most afflicted and penitential countenance that ever was seen, was no
small alteration to her who used to seem all gaiety.—To add to this, her hair,
which she was accustomed to wear very loose, both when *Fantomina* and
Celia, was now tied back so straight, and her pinners[5] coming so very forward,
that there was none of it to be seen. In fine, her habit and her air were so much
changed, that she was not more difficult to be known in the rude country *girl*,
than she was now in the sorrowful *widow*.

She knew that *Beauplaisir* came alone in his chariot to the *Bath*, and in the

5. Long flaps on a headdress.

time of her being servant in the house where he lodged, heard nothing of any
body that was to accompany him to *London*, and hoped he would return in the
same manner he had gone: She therefore hired horses and a man to attend her
to an inn about ten miles on this side of *Bath*, where having discharged them,
she waited till the chariot should come by; which when it did, and she saw that
he was alone in it, she called to him that drove it to stop a moment, and going
to the door saluted the master with these words:

The distressed and wretched, Sir (*said she*), never fail to excite compassion
in a generous mind; and I hope I am not deceived in my opinion that yours is
such:—You have the appearance of a gentleman, and cannot, when you hear
my story, refuse that assistance which is in your power to give to an unhappy
woman, who without it, may be rendered the most miserable of all created be-
ings.

It would not be very easy to represent the surprise, so odd an address created
in the mind of him to whom it was made.—She had not the appearance of one
who wanted charity; and what other favor she required he could not conceive:
but telling her she might command any thing in his power gave her encour-
agement to declare herself in this manner: You may judge (*resumed she*), by
the melancholy garb I am in, that I have lately lost all that ought to be valuable
to womankind; but it is impossible for you to guess the greatness of my
misfortune, unless you had known my husband, who was master of every per-
fection to endear him to a wife's affections.—But, notwithstanding, I look on
myself as the most unhappy of my sex in out-living him, I must so far obey the
dictates of my discretion, as to take care of the little fortune he left behind
him, which being in the hands of a brother of his in *London*, will be all carried
off to *Holland*, where he is going to settle; if I reach not the town before he
leaves it, I am undone for ever.—To which end I left *Bristol*, the place where
we lived, hoping to get a place in the stage at *Bath*, but they were all taken up
before I came; and being, by a hurt I got in a fall, rendered incapable of travel-
ing any long journey on horseback, I have no way to go to *London*, and must be
inevitably ruined in the loss of all I have on earth, without you have good na-
ture enough to admit me to take part of your chariot.

Here the feigned widow ended her sorrowful tale, which had been several
times interrupted by a parenthesis of sighs and groans; and *Beauplaisir*, with a
complaisant and tender air, assured her of his readiness to serve her in things
of much greater consequence than what she desired of him; and told her it
would be an impossibility of denying a place in his chariot to a lady who he
could not behold without yielding one in his heart. She answered the compli-
ments he made her but with tears, which seemed to stream in such abundance
from her eyes, that she could not keep her handkerchief from her face one mo-
ment. Being come into the chariot, *Beauplaisir* said a thousand handsome
things to persuade her from giving way to so violent a grief; which, he told her,
would not only be destructive to her beauty, but likewise her health. But all his
endeavors for consolement appeared ineffectual, and he began to think he
should have but a dull journey, in the company of one who seemed so obsti-
nately devoted to the memory of her dead husband, that there was no getting
a word from her on any other theme:—but bethinking himself of the cele-
brated story of the *Ephesian* matron,[6] it came into his head to make trial, she

6. In the *Satyricon* by the Roman author Petronius, a soldier persuaded a widow from Ephesus who was keeping
watch in her husband's tomb to eat and then to make love.

who seemed equally susceptible of *sorrow*, might not also be so too of *love*: and
having began a discourse on almost every other topic, and finding her still in-
capable of answering, resolved to put it to the proof, if this would have no
more effect to rouse her sleeping spirits:—with a gay air, therefore, though
accompanied with the greatest modesty and respect, he turned the con-
versation, as though without design, on that joy-giving passion, and soon dis-
covered that was indeed the subject she was best pleased to be entertained
with; for on his giving her a hint to begin upon, never any tongue run more
voluble than hers, on the prodigious power it had to influence the souls of
those possessed of it, to actions even the most distant from their intentions,
principles, or humors.—From that she passed to a description of the happi-
ness of mutual affection;—the unspeakable ecstasy of those who meet with
equal ardency; and represented it in colors so lively, and disclosed by the ges-
tures with which her words were accompanied, and the accent of her voice so
true a feeling of what she said, that *Beauplaisir*, without being as stupid, as he
was really the contrary, could not avoid perceiving there were seeds of fire, not
yet extinguished, in this fair widow's soul, which wanted but the kindling
breath of tender sighs to light into a blaze.—He now thought himself as for-
tunate, as some moments before he had the reverse; and doubted not, but,
that before they parted, he should find a way to dry the tears of this lovely
mourner, to the satisfaction of them both. He did not, however, offer, as he
had done to *Fantomina* and *Celia*, to urge his passion directly to her, but by a
thousand little softening artifices, which he well knew how to use, gave her
leave to guess he was enamored. When they came to the inn where they were
to lie, he declared himself somewhat more freely, and perceiving she did not
resent it past forgiveness, grew more encroaching still:—he now took the lib-
erty of kissing away her tears, and catching the sighs as they issued from her
lips; telling her if grief was infectious, he was resolved to have his share;
protesting he would gladly exchange passions with her, and be content to bear
her load of *sorrow*, if she would as willingly ease the burden of his *love*.—She
said little in answer to the strenuous pressures with which at last he ventured
to enfold her, but not thinking it decent, for the character she had assumed, to
yield so suddenly, and unable to deny both his and her own inclinations, she
counterfeited a fainting, and fell motionless upon his breast.—He had no
great notion that she was in a real fit, and the room they supped in happening
to have a bed in it, he took her in his arms and laid her on it, believing, that
whatever her distemper was, that was the most proper place to convey her
to—He laid himself down by her, and endeavored to bring her to herself; and
she was too grateful to her kind physician at her returning sense, to remove
from the posture he had put her in, without his leave.

It may, perhaps, seem strange that *Beauplaisir* should in such near in-
timacies continue still deceived: I know there are men who will swear it is an
impossibility, and that no disguise could hinder them from knowing a woman
they had once enjoyed. In answer to these scruples, I can only say, that besides
the alteration which the change of dress made in her, she was so admirably
skilled in the art of feigning, that she had the power of putting on almost what
face she pleased, and knew so exactly how to form her behavior to the charac-
ter she represented, that all the comedians at both playhouses are infinitely
short of her performances: she could vary her very glances, tune her voice to
accents the most different imaginable from those in which she spoke when
she appeared herself.—These aids from nature, joined to the wiles of art, and

the distance between the places where the imagined *Fantomina* and *Celia* were, might very well prevent his having any thought that they were the same, or that the fair *widow* was either of them: it never so much as entered his head, and though he did fancy he observed in the face of the latter, features which were not altogether unknown to him, yet he could not recollect when or where he had known them;—and being told by her, that from her birth, she had never removed from *Bristol*, a place where he never was, he rejected the belief of having seen her, and supposed his mind had been deluded by an idea of some other, whom she might have a resemblance of.

They passed the time of their journey in as much happiness as the most luxurious gratification of wild desires could make them; and when they came to the end of it, parted not without a mutual promise of seeing each other often.—He told her to what place she should direct a letter to him; and she assured him she would send to let him know where to come to her, as soon as she was fixed in lodgings.

She kept her promise; and charmed with the continuance of his eager fondness, went not home, but into private lodgings, whence she wrote to him to visit her the first opportunity, and inquire for the Widow *Bloomer*.—She had no sooner dispatched this billet, than she repaired to the house where she had lodged as *Fantomina*, charging the people if *Beauplaisir* should come there, not to let him know she had been out of town. From thence she wrote to him, in a different hand, a long letter of complaint, that he had been so cruel in not sending one letter to her all the time he had been absent, entreated to see him, and concluded with subscribing herself his unalterably affectionate *Fantomina*. She received in one day answers to both these. The first contained these lines:

To the Charming Mrs. Bloomer,

It would be impossible, my Angel! for me to express the thousandth part of that infinity of transport, the sight of your dear letter gave me.—Never was woman formed to charm like you: never did any look like you,—write like you,— bless like you;—nor did ever man adore as I do.—Since yesterday we parted, I have seemed a body without a soul; and had you not by this inspiring billet, gave me new life, I know not what by tomorrow I should have been.—I will be with you this evening about five:—O, 'tis an age till then!—But the cursed formalities of duty oblige me to dine with my lord—who never rises from table till that hour;— therefore adieu till then sweet lovely mistress of the soul and all the faculties of

Your most faithful,
Beauplaisir.

The other was in this manner:

To the Lovely Fantomina,

If you were half so sensible as you ought of your own power of charming, you would be assured, that to be unfaithful or unkind to you, would be among the things that are in their very natures impossibilities.—It was my misfortune, not my fault, that you were not persecuted every post with a declaration of my unchanging passion; but I had unluckily forgot the name of the woman at whose

house you are, and knew not how to form a direction that it might come safe to
your hands.—And, indeed, the reflection how you might misconstrue my silence,
brought me to town some weeks sooner than I intended—If you knew how I have
languished to renew those blessings I am permitted to enjoy in your society, you
would rather pity than condemn

<div align="right">

Your ever faithful,
Beauplaisir.

</div>

P.S. *I fear I cannot see you till tomorrow; some business has unluckily fallen out*
that will engross my hours till then.—Once more, my dear, Adieu.

Traitor! (*cried she*) as soon as she had read them, 'tis thus our silly, fond,
believing sex are served when they put faith in man: so had I been deceived
and cheated, had I like the rest believed, and sat down mourning in absence,
and vainly waiting recovered tendernesses.—How do some women (*continued
she*) make their life a hell, burning in fruitless expectations, and dreaming out
their days in hopes and fears, then wake at last to all the horror of despair?—
But I have outwitted even the most subtle of the deceiving kind, and while he
thinks to fool me, is himself the only beguiled person.

She made herself, most certainly, extremely happy in the reflection on the
success of her stratagems; and while the knowledge of his inconstancy and lev-
ity of nature kept her from having that real tenderness for him she would else
have had, she found the means of gratifying the inclination she had for his
agreeable person, in as full a manner as she could wish. She had all the sweets
of love, but as yet had tasted none of the gall, and was in a state of content-
ment, which might be envied by the more delicate.

When the expected hour arrived, she found that her lover had lost no part
of the fervency with which he had parted from her; but when the next day she
received him as *Fantomina*, she perceived a prodigious difference; which led
her again into reflections on the unaccountableness of men's fancies, who still
prefer the last conquest, only because it is the last.—Here was an evident
proof of it; for there could not be a difference in merit, because they were the
same person; but the Widow *Bloomer* was a more new acquaintance than
Fantomina, and therefore esteemed more valuable. This, indeed, must be said
of *Beauplaisir*, that he had a greater share of good nature than most of his sex,
who, for the most part, when they are weary of an intrigue, break it entirely off,
without any regard to the despair of the abandoned nymph. Though he
retained no more than a bare pity and complaisance[7] for *Fantomina*, yet be-
lieving she loved him to an excess, would not entirely forsake her, though the
continuance of his visits was now become rather a penance than a pleasure.

The Widow *Bloomer* triumphed some time longer over the heart of this in-
constant, but at length her sway was at an end, and she sunk in this character,
to the same degree of tastelessness, as she had done before in that of
Fantomina and *Celia*.—She presently perceived it, but bore it as she had al-
ways done; it being but what she expected, she had prepared herself for it, and
had another project in *embrio*,[8] which she soon ripened into action. She did
not, indeed, complete it altogether so suddenly as she had done the others, by
reason there must be persons employed in it; and the aversion she had to any

7. Politeness. 8. In embryo (Latin), i.e., in the beginning stage.

confidents in her affairs, and the caution with which she had hitherto acted, and which she was still determined to continue, made it very difficult for her to find a way without breaking through that resolution to compass what she wished.—She got over the difficulty at last, however, by proceeding in a manner, if possible, more extraordinary than all her former behavior:—muffling herself up in her hood one day, she went into the park about the hour when there are a great many necessitous gentlemen, who think themselves above doing what they call little things for a maintenance, walking in the *Mall*, to take a *Camelion* Treat,[9] and fill their stomachs with air instead of meat. Two of those, who by their physiognomy she thought most proper for her purpose, she beckoned to come to her; and taking them into a walk more remote from company, began to communicate the business she had with them in these words: I am sensible, gentlemen (*said she*), that, through the blindness of fortune, and partiality of the world, merit frequently goes unrewarded, and that those of the best pretentions meet with the least encouragement:—I ask your pardon (*continued she*), perceiving they seemed surprised, if I am mistaken in the notion, that you two may, perhaps, be of the number of those who have reason to complain of the injustice of fate; but if you are such as I take you for, I have a proposal to make you, which may be of some little advantage to you. Neither of them made any immediate answer, but appeared buried in consideration for some moments. At length, We should, doubtless, madam (*said one of them*), willingly come into any measures to oblige you, provided they are such as may bring us into no danger, either as to our persons or reputations. That which I require of you (*resumed she*), has nothing in it criminal: All that I desire is *secrecy* in what you are entrusted, and to disguise yourselves in such a manner as you cannot be known, if hereafter seen by the person on whom you are to impose.—In fine, the business is only an innocent frolic, but if blazed abroad, might be taken for too great a freedom in me:—Therefore, if you resolve to assist me, here are five pieces[1] to drink my health, and assure you, that I have not discoursed you on an affair, I design not to proceed in; and when it is accomplished fifty more lie ready for your acceptance. These words, and, above all, the money, which was a sum which, 'tis probable, they had not seen of a long time, made them immediately assent to all she desired, and press for the beginning of their employment: but things were not yet ripe for execution; and she told them, that the next day they should be let into the secret, charging them to meet her in the same place at an hour she appointed. 'Tis hard to say, which of these parties went away best pleased; *they*, that fortune had sent them so unexpected a windfall; or *she*, that she had found persons, who appeared so well qualified to serve her.

Indefatigable in the pursuit of whatsoever her humor was bent upon, she had no sooner left her new-engaged emissaries, than she went in search of a house for the completing of her project.—She pitched on one very large, and magnificently furnished, which she hired by the week, giving them the money beforehand, to prevent any inquiries. The next day she repaired to the park, where she met the punctual 'squires of low degree; and ordering them to follow her to the house she had taken, told them they must condescend to

9. Chameleons were thought to live on air. "Necessitous": poor, needy. "The Mall": a walk in London's St. James Park, which was a fashionable promenade.
1. Gold coins.

appear like servants, and gave each of them a very rich livery. Then writing a
letter to *Beauplaisir*, in a character vastly different from either of those she
had made use of, as *Fantomina*, or the fair Widow *Bloomer*, ordered one of
them to deliver it into his own hands, to bring back an answer, and to be care-
ful that he sifted out nothing of the truth.—I do not fear (*said she*), that you
should discover to him who I am, because that is a secret, of which you your-
selves are ignorant; but I would have you be so careful in your replies, that he
may not think the concealment springs from any other reasons than your great
integrity to your trust.—Seem therefore to know my whole affairs; and let
your refusing to make him partaker in the secret, appear to be only the effect
of your zeal for my interest and reputation. Promises of entire fidelity on the
one side, and reward on the other, being past, the messenger made what haste
he could to the house of *Beauplaisir*; and being there told where he might find
him, performed exactly the injunction that had been given him. But never as-
tonishment exceeding that which *Beauplaisir* felt at the reading this billet, in
which he found these lines:

To the All-conquering Beauplaisir.

*I imagine not that 'tis a new thing to you, to be told, you are the greatest charm
in nature to our sex: I shall therefore, not to fill up my letter with any impertinent
praises on your wit or person, only tell you, that I am infinite in love with both,
and if you have a heart not too deeply engaged, should think myself the happiest
of my sex in being capable of inspiring it with some tenderness.—There is but
one thing in my power to refuse you, which is the knowledge of my name, which
believing the sight of my face will render no secret, you must not take it ill that I
conceal from you.—The bearer of this is a person I can trust; send by him your
answer; but endeavor not to dive into the meaning of this mystery, which will be
impossible for you to unravel, and at the same time very much disoblige me:—
But that you may be in no apprehensions of being imposed on by a woman un-
worthy of your regard, I will venture to assure you, the first and greatest men in
the kingdom would think themselves blessed to have that influence over me you
have, though unknown to yourself acquired.—But I need not go about to raise
your curiosity, by giving you any idea of what my person is; if you think fit to be
satisfied, resolve to visit me tomorrow about three in the afternoon; and though
my face is hid, you shall not want sufficient demonstration, that she who takes
these unusual measures to commence a friendship with you, is neither old, nor
deformed. Till then I am,*

<div align="right">

Yours,
Incognita.

</div>

He had scarce come to the conclusion, before he asked the person who
brought it, from what place he came;—the name of the lady he served;—if she
were a wife, or widow, and several other questions directly opposite to the di-
rections of the letter; but silence would have availed him as much as did all
these testimonies of curiosity: no *Italian Bravo*,[2] employed in a business of the
like nature, performed his office with more artifice; and the impatient inquirer

2. Hired soldier.

was convinced, that nothing but doing as he was desired, could give him any light into the character of the woman who declared so violent a passion for him; and little fearing any consequence which could ensue from such an encounter, resolved to rest satisfied till[3] he was informed of everything from herself, not imagining this *Incognita* varied so much from the generality of her sex, as to be able to refuse the knowledge of anything to the man she loved with that transcendency of passion she professed, and which his many successes with the ladies gave him encouragement enough to believe. He therefore took pen and paper, and answered her letter in terms tender enough for a man who had never seen the person to whom he wrote. The words were as follows:

To the Obliging and Witty[4] Incognita.

Though to tell me I am happy enough to be liked by a woman, such, as by your manner of writing, I imagine you to be, is an honor which I can never sufficiently acknowledge, yet I know not how I am able to content myself with admiring the wonders of your wit alone: I am certain, a soul like yours must shine in your eyes with a vivacity, which must bless all they look on.—I shall, however, endeavor to restrain myself in those bounds you are pleased to set me, till by the knowledge of my inviolable fidelity, I may be thought worthy of gazing on that heaven I am now but to enjoy in contemplation.—You need not doubt my glad compliance with your obliging summons: there is a charm in your lines, which gives too sweet an idea of their lovely author to be resisted.—I am all impatient for the blissful moment, which is to throw me at your feet, and give me an opportunity of convincing you that I am,

> Your everlasting slave,
> Beauplaisir.

Nothing could be more pleased than she, to whom it was directed, at the receipt of this letter; but when she was told how inquisitive he had been concerning her character and circumstances, she could not forbear laughing heartily to think of the tricks she had played him, and applauding her own strength of genius, and force of resolution, which by such unthought-of ways could triumph over her lover's inconstancy, and render that very temper, which to other women is the greatest curse, a means to make herself more blessed.—Had he been faithful to me (*said she, to herself*), either as *Fantomina*, or *Celia*, or the Widow *Bloomer*, the most violent passion, if it does not change its object, in time will wither: possession naturally abates the vigor of desire, and I should have had, at best, but a cold, insipid, husband-like lover in my arms; but by these arts of passing on him as a new mistress whenever the ardor, which alone makes love a blessing, begins to diminish, for the former one, I have him always raving, wild, impatient, longing, dying.—O that all neglected wives, and fond abandoned nymphs would take this method!— Men would be caught in their own snare, and have no cause to scorn our easy, weeping, wailing sex! Thus did she pride herself as if secure she never should have any reason to repent the present gaiety of her humor. The hour drawing near in which he was to come, she dressed herself in as magnificent a manner,

3. Not to rest satisfied until. 4. Intelligent.

as if she were to be that night at a ball at court, endeavoring to repair the want
of those beauties which the vizard⁵ should conceal, by setting forth the others
with the greatest care and exactness. Her fine shape, and air, and neck ap-
peared to great advantage; and by that which was to be seen of her, one might
believe the rest to be perfectly agreeable. *Beauplaisir* was prodigiously
charmed, as well with her appearance, as with the manner she entertained
him: but though he was wild with impatience for the sight of a face which be-
longed to so exquisite a body, yet he would not immediately press for it, be-
lieving before he left her he should easily obtain that satisfaction.—A noble
collation being over, he began to sue for the performance of her promise of
granting everything he could ask, excepting the sight of her face, and knowl-
edge of her name. It would have been a ridiculous piece of affection⁶ in her to
have seemed coy in complying with what she herself had been the first in de-
siring: she yielded without even a show of reluctance: and if there be any true
felicity in an amour such as theirs, both here enjoyed it to the full. But not in
the height of all their mutual raptures, could he prevail on her to satisfy his cu-
riosity with the sight of her face: she told him that she hoped he knew so much
of her, as might serve to convince him she was not unworthy of his tenderest
regard; and if he could not content himself with that which she was willing to
reveal, and which was the conditions of their meeting, dear as he was to her,
she would rather part with him for ever, than consent to gratify an inquisitive-
ness, which, in her opinion, had no business with his love. It was in vain that
he endeavored to make her sensible of her mistake: and that this restraint was
the greatest enemy imaginable to the happiness of them both: she was not to
be persuaded, and he was obliged to desist his solicitations, though deter-
mined in his mind to compass what he so ardently desired, before he left the
house. He then turned the discourse wholly on the violence of the passion he
had for her; and expressed the greatest discontent in the world at the appre-
hensions of being separated;—swore he could dwell for ever in her arms, and
with such an undeniable earnestness pressed to be permitted to tarry with her
the whole night, that had she been less charmed with his renewed eagerness of
desire, she scarce would have had the power of resisting him; but in granting
this request, she was not without a thought that he had another reason for
making it besides the extremity of his passion, and had it immediately in her
head how to disappoint him.

 The hours of repose being arrived, he begged she would retire to her cham-
ber; to which she consented, but obliged him to go to bed first; which he did
not much oppose, because he supposed she would not lie in her mask, and
doubted not but the morning's dawn would bring the wished discovery.—The
two imagined servants ushered him to his new lodging; where he lay some mo-
ments in all the perplexity imaginable at the oddness of this adventure. But
she suffered not these cogitations to be of any long continuance: she came,
but came in the dark; which being no more than he expected by the former
part of her proceedings, he said nothing of; but as much satisfaction as he
found in her embraces, nothing ever longed for the approach of day with more
impatience than he did. At last it came; but how great was his disappoint-
ment, when by the noises he heard in the street, the hurry of the coaches, and
the cries of penny-merchants, he was convinced it was night nowhere but with

5. Mask. 6. Affectation.

him? He was still in the same darkness as before; for she had taken care to blind the windows in such a manner, that not the least chink was left to let in day.—He complained of her behavior in terms that she would not have been able to resist yielding to, if she had not been certain it would have been the ruin of her passion:—she, therefore, answered him only as she had done before; and getting out of the bed from him, flew out of the room with too much swiftness for him to have overtaken her, if he had attempted it. The moment she left him, the two attendants entered the chamber, and plucking down the implements which had screened him from the knowledge of that which he so much desired to find out, restored his eyes once more to day:—they attended to assist him in dressing, brought him tea, and by their obsequiousness, let him see there was but one thing which the mistress of them would not gladly oblige him in.—He was so much out of humor, however, at the disappointment of his curiosity, that he resolved never to make a second visit.—Finding her in an outer room, he made no scruple of expressing the sense he had of the little trust she reposed in him, and at last plainly told her, he could not submit to receive obligations from a lady, who thought him uncapable of keeping a secret, which she made no difficulty of letting her servants into.—He resented—he once more entreated—he said all that man could do, to prevail on her to unfold the mystery; but all his adjurations were fruitless; and he went out of the house determined never to re-enter it, till she should pay the price of his company with the discovery of her face and circumstances.—She suffered[7] him to go with this resolution, and doubted not but he would recede from it, when he reflected on the happy moments they had passed together; but if he did not, she comforted herself with the design of forming some other stratagem, with which to impose on him a fourth time.

She kept the house, and her gentlemen-equipage for about a fortnight, in which time she continued to write to him as *Fantomina* and the Widow *Bloomer*, and received the visits he sometimes made to each; but his behavior to both was grown so cold, that she began to grow as weary of receiving his now insipid caresses as he was of offering them: she was beginning to think in what manner she should drop these two characters, when the sudden arrival of her mother, who had been some time in a foreign country, obliged her to put an immediate stop to the course of her whimsical adventures.—That lady, who was severely virtuous, did not approve of many things she had been told of the conduct of her daughter; and though it was not in the power of any person in the world to inform her of the truth of what she had been guilty of, yet she heard enough to make her keep her afterwards in a restraint, little agreeable to her humor, and the liberties to which she had been accustomed.

But this confinement was not the greatest part of the trouble of this now afflicted lady: she found the consequences of her amorous follies would be, without almost a miracle, impossible to be concealed:—she was with child; and though she would easily have found means to have screened even this from the knowledge of the world, had she been at liberty to have acted with the same unquestionable authority over herself, as she did before the coming of her mother, yet now all her invention was at a loss for a stratagem to impose on a woman of her penetration:—by eating little, lacing prodigious straight, and the advantage of a great hoop-petticoat, however, her bigness was not

7. Allowed.

taken notice of, and, perhaps, she would not have been suspected till the time
of her going into the country, where her mother designed to send her, and
from whence she intended to make her escape to some place where she might
be delivered with secrecy, if the time of it had not happened much sooner than
she expected.—A ball being at court, the good old lady was willing she should
partake of the diversion of it as a farewell to the town.—It was there she was
seized with those pangs, which none in her condition are exempt from:—she
could not conceal the sudden rack which all at once invaded her; or had her
tongue been mute, her wildly rolling eyes, the distortion of her features, and
the convulsions which shook her whole frame, in spite of her, would have
revealed she labored under some terrible shock of nature.—Everybody was
surprised, everybody was concerned, but few guessed at the occasion.—Her
mother grieved beyond expression, doubted not but she was struck with the
hand of death; and ordered her to be carried home in a chair, while herself fol-
lowed in another.—A physician was immediately sent for: but he presently
perceiving what was her distemper, called the old lady aside, and told her, it
was not a doctor of his sex, but one of her own, her daughter stood in need
of.—Never was astonishment and horror greater than that which seized the
soul of this afflicted parent at these words: she could not for a time believe the
truth of what she heard; but he insisting on it, and conjuring her to send for a
midwife, she was at length convinced of it.—All the pity and tenderness she
had been for some moment before possessed of now vanished, and were suc-
ceeded by an adequate shame and indignation:—she flew to the bed where
her daughter was lying, and telling her what she had been informed of, and
which she was now far from doubting commanded her to reveal the name of
the person whose insinuations had drawn her to this dishonor.—It was a great
while before she could be brought to confess anything, and much longer be-
fore she could be prevailed on to name the man whom she so fatally had loved;
but the rack of nature growing more fierce, and the enraged old lady protest-
ing no help should be afforded her while she persisted in her obstinacy, she,
with great difficulty and hesitation in her speech, at last pronounced the
name of *Beauplaisir*. She had no sooner satisfied her weeping mother, than
that sorrowful lady sent messengers at the same time, for a midwife, and
for that gentleman who had occasioned the other's being wanted.—He
happened by accident to be at home, and immediately obeyed the summons,
though prodigiously surprised what business a lady so much a stranger to him
could have to impart.—But how much greater was his amazement, when
taking him into her closet, she there acquainted him with her daughter's
misfortune, of the discovery she had made, and how far he was concerned in
it?—All the idea one can form of wild astonishment, was mean to what he
felt:—he assured her, that the young lady her daughter was a person whom he
had never, more than at a distance, admired:—that he had indeed, spoke to
her in public company, but that he never had a thought which tended to her
dishonor.—His denials, if possible, added to the indignation she was before
enflamed with:—she had no longer patience; and carrying him into the cham-
ber where she was just delivered of a fine girl, cried out, I will not be imposed
on the truth by one of you shall be revealed.—*Beauplaisir* being brought to
the bedside, was beginning to address himself to the lady in it, to beg she
would clear the mistake her mother was involved in; when she, covering her-
self with the cloths, and ready to die a second time with the inward agitations

of her soul, shrieked out, Oh, I am undone!—I cannot live, and bear this shame!—But the old lady believing that now or never was the time to dive into the bottom of this mystery, forcing her to rear her head, told her, she should not hope to escape the scrutiny of a parent she had dishonored in such a manner, and pointing to *Beauplaisir*, Is this the gentleman (*said she*), to whom you owe your ruin? or have you deceived me by a fictitious tale? Oh! no (*resumed the trembling creature*), he is, indeed, the innocent cause of my un-doing:—Promise me your pardon (*continued she*), and I will relate the means. Here she ceased, expecting what she would reply, which, on hearing *Beauplaisir* cry out, What mean you, madam? I your undoing, who never har-bored the least design on you in my life, she did in these words, Though the injury you have done your family (*said sh*e), is of a nature which cannot justly hope forgiveness, yet be assured, I shall much sooner excuse you when satis-fied of the truth, than while I am kept in a suspense, if possible, as vexatious as the crime itself is to me. Encouraged by this she related the whole truth. And 'tis difficult to determine, if *Beauplaisir*, or the lady, were most surprised at what they heard; he, that he should have been blinded so often by her arti-fices; or she, that so young a creature should have the skill to make use of them. Both sat for some time in a profound reverie; till at length she broke it first in these words: Pardon, sir (*said she*), the trouble I have given you: I must confess it was with a design to oblige you to repair the supposed injury you had done this unfortunate girl, by marrying her, but now I know not what to say:— The blame is wholly hers, and I have nothing to request further of you, than that you will not divulge the distracted folly she has been guilty of.—He an-swered her in terms perfectly polite; but made no offer of that which, perhaps, she expected, though could not, now informed of her daughter's proceedings, demand. He assured her, however, that if she would commit the newborn lady to his care, he would discharge it faithfully. But neither of them would consent to that; and he took his leave, full of cogitations, more confused than ever he had known in his whole life. He continued to visit there, to inquire after her health every day; but the old lady perceiving there was nothing likely to ensue from these civilities, but, perhaps, a renewing of the crime, she entreated him to refrain; and as soon as her daughter was in a condition, sent her to a monastery in *France*, the abbess of which had been her particular friend. And thus ended an intrigue, which, considering the time it lasted, was as full of va-riety as any, perhaps, that many ages has produced.

1724

ANNA LETITIA BARBAULD
1743–1825

An indefatigable essayist, editor, pamphleteer, and poet, Anna Letitia Barbauld was brought up in a family of Dissenters—religious nonconformists who encour-aged her to read, write, and learn French, Italian, Latin, and Greek. With her cler-gyman husband, whom she married in 1774, she ran a boys' school in Suffolk while publishing poems, essays, and works for children, some in collaboration with her brother John. After the school was sold in 1785, the pace of her literary activity

quickened: she wrote political pamphlets, a poem combating the slave trade (*Epistle to William Wilberforce*, 1791), and a controversial antiwar poem (*Eighteen Hundred and Eleven*, 1811), while editing the poetry of Akenside (1794) and Collins (1797) as well as the letters of Samuel Richardson, a fifty-volume edition of *The British Novelists* (1810), and *The Female Speaker* (1811), a collection of prose and poetry intended for young women readers.

In 1808, Barbauld's husband became insane and killed himself, yet though she was deeply grieved, she valiantly continued her literary work. Never a feminist, she declined to run a girls' school because she thought women should be "good wives or agreeable companions" rather than bluestockings. Yet she herself belonged to a circle of learned ladies that included such notable intellectuals as the playwright Joanna Baillie, the novelist Maria Edgeworth, and the essayist Hannah More.

The Rights of Woman

Yes, injured Woman! rise, assert thy right!
Woman! too long degraded, scorned, oppressed;
O born to rule in partial Law's despite,[1]
Resume thy native empire[2] o'er the breast!

Go forth arrayed in panoply divine, 5
That angel pureness which admits no stain;
Go, bid proud Man his boasted rule resign
And kiss the golden sceptre of thy reign.

Go, gird thyself with grace, collect thy store
Of bright artillery glancing from afar; 10
Soft melting tones thy thundering cannon's roar,
Blushes and tears thy magazine of war.

Thy rights are empire; urge no meaner claim,—
Felt, not defined, and if debated, lost;
Like sacred mysteries, which withheld from fame, 15
Shunning discussion, are revered the most.

Try all that wit and art suggest to bend
Of thy imperial foe the stubborn knee;
Make treacherous Man thy subject, not thy friend;
Thou mayest command, but never canst be free. 20

Awe the licentious and restrain the rude;
Soften the sullen, clear the cloudy brow:
Be, more than princes' gifts, thy favors sued;—
She hazards all, who will the least allow.

But hope not, courted idol of mankind, 25
On this proud eminence secure to stay;
Subduing and subdued, thou soon shalt find
Thy coldness soften, and thy pride give way.

1. In defiance of unfair law. 2. Innate rule.

Then, then, abandon each ambitious thought;
Conquest or rule thy heart shall feebly move, 30
In Nature's school, by her soft maxims taught
That separate rights are lost in mutual love.

1795 1825

Washing-Day

The Muses are turned gossips; they have lost
The buskined[1] step, and clear high-sounding phrase,
Language of gods. Come then, domestic Muse,
In slipshod measure[2] loosely prattling on
Of farm or orchard, pleasant curds and cream, 5
Or drowning flies, or shoe lost in the mire
By little whimpering boy, with rueful face;
Come, Muse, and sing the dreaded Washing-Day.
Ye who beneath the yoke of wedlock bend,
With bowed soul, full well ye ken[3] the day 10
Which week, smooth sliding after week, brings on
Too soon;—for to that day nor peace belongs
Nor comfort; ere the first gray streak of dawn,
The red-armed washers come and chase[4] repose.
Nor pleasant smile, nor quaint device of mirth, 15
E'er visited that day: the very cat,
From the wet kitchen scared, and reeking hearth,
Visits the parlor,—an unwonted guest.
The silent breakfast-meal is soon dispatched;
Uninterrupted, save by anxious looks 20
Cast at the lowering[5] sky, if sky should lower.
From that last evil, O preserve us, heavens!
For should the skies pour down, adieu to all
Remains of quiet: then expect to hear
Of sad disasters—dirt and gravel stains 25
Hard to efface, and loaded lines at once
Snapped short—and linen-horse[6] by dog thrown down,
And all the petty miseries of life.
Saints have been calm while stretched upon the rack,
And Guatimozin[7] smiled on burning coals; 30
But never yet did housewife notable
Greet with a smile a rainy washing-day.
—But grant the welkin[8] fair, require not thou
Who call'st thyself perchance the master there,
Or[9] study swept, or nicely dusted coat, 35
Or usual 'tendance[1]—ask not, indiscreet,

1. Buskins were the high boots worn by actors of an-
cient Greek tragedies. "Muses": goddesses not just of
tragedy but of the arts and learning more generally.
2. Meter.
3. Know.
4. I.e., chase away.
5. Gloomy, threatening.

6. A wooden frame for drying linen on.
7. Cuauhtémoc (c. 1495–1522), the last Aztec em-
peror, was tortured by his Spanish captors; his stoicism
and refusal to speak became proverbial.
8. Sky.
9. Either.
1. Attendance, service.

Thy stockings mended, though the yawning rents
Gape wide as Erebus;[2] nor hope to find
Some snug recess impervious: shouldst thou try
The 'customed garden walks, thine eye shall rue 40
The budding fragrance of thy tender shrubs,
Myrtle or rose, all crushed beneath the weight
Of coarse-checked apron—with impatient hand
Twitched off when showers impend: or crossing lines
Shall mar thy musings, as the wet cold sheet 45
Flaps in thy face abrupt. Woe to the friend
Whose evil stars have urged him forth to claim
On such a day the hospitable rites![3]
Looks, blank at best, and stinted courtesy,
Shall he receive. Vainly he feeds his hopes 50
With dinner of roast chicken, savory pie,
Or tart or pudding:—pudding he nor tart
That day shall eat: nor, though the husband try,
Mending what can't be helped, to kindle mirth
From cheer deficient, shall his consort's brow 55
Clear up propitious:—the unlucky guest
In silence dines, and early slinks away
I well remember, when a child, the awe
This day struck into me; for then the maids,
I scarce knew why, looked cross, and drove me from them: 60
Nor soft caress could I obtain, no hope
Usual indulgencies; jelly or creams,
Relic[4] of costly suppers, and set by
For me their petted one; or buttered toast,
When butter was forbid: or thrilling tale 65
Of ghost, or witch, or murder—so I went
And sheltered me beside the parlor fire:
There my dear grandmother, eldest of forms,
Tended the little ones, and watched from harm,
Anxiously fond, though oft her spectacles 70
With elfin cunning hid, and oft the pins
Drawn from her ravelled stocking, might have soured
One less indulgent.—
At intervals my mother's voice was heard,
Urging dispatch: briskly the work went on, 75
All hands employed to wash, to rinse, to wring,
To fold, and starch, and clap, and iron, and plait.
Then would I sit me down, and ponder much
Why washings were. Sometimes through hollow bowl
Of pipe amused we blew, and sent aloft 80
The floating bubbles; little dreaming then
To see, Montgolfier,[5] thy silken ball
Ride buoyant through the clouds—so near approach

2. In Greek mythology, the place of darkness between the earth and the underworld.
3. Hospitality (a mock-epic expression).
4. Leftover food. "Jelly": a gelatinous dessert made from fruit juice and boiling water.
5. Joseph Michel Montgolfier (1740–1810) and his brother, Jacques Étienne (1745–1799), together invented the first practical hot-air balloon.

The sports of children and the toils of men.
Earth, air, and sky, and ocean, hath its bubbles, 85
And verse is one of them—this most of all.

 1797

ABIGAIL ADAMS

1744–1818

Born in Weymouth, Massachusetts, to a wealthy Congregational minister and his
wife, Abigail Adams was kept out of school because of her poor health and there-
fore always felt herself to be uneducated. Yet she had access to her father's library,
and she received an informal education from her grandmother. After marriage in
1764 to John Adams, then a lawyer, she raised their four children and helped run
the family farm. In 1774, her husband became a delegate to the first Continental
Congress and their voluminous correspondence began, eventually totaling more
than three hundred letters. A lively, active correspondent whose letters have been
in print since her grandson published a selection in 1840, she chronicled the tur-
bulent years of the Revolutionary War and early republican era. Yet this eight-
eenth-century New Englander frequently asked the recipients of her "rough
unpolished" messages to burn them. Perhaps they were originally preserved be-
cause her husband became the second president of the United States and her son,
John Quincy Adams, the sixth. In any case, her comments on patriotism and
citizenship, on education and religion, on household and national economies con-
tribute to a portrait of an independent yet dedicated wife, one who learned to
undertake the family's business enterprises when her husband's attention was
consumed by public service. According to the historian Linda K. Kerber, in the
many letters Adams wrote she remained "a shrewd commentator on the political
scene, assuming as active an obligation to judge good and evil as if she were called
upon annually to vote."

LETTERS TO JOHN ADAMS
[Man Is a Dangerous Creature][1]

 November 27 1775

Tis a fortnight to Night since I wrote you a line during which, I have been
confined with the Jaundice, Rhumatism and a most violent cold; I yesterday
took a puke which has relieved me, and I feel much better to day. Many, very
many people who have had the dysentery, are now afflicted both with the
Jaundice and Rhumatism, some it has left in Hecticks, some in dropsies.[2]

The great and incessant rains we have had this fall (the like cannot be recol-
lected) may have occasiond some of the present disorders. The Jaundice is
very prevelant in the Camp. We have lately had a week of very cold weather, as

1. Adams's spelling has been preserved.
2. Edemas, accumulation of fluid. "Heckticks": wasting fevers.

cold as January, and a flight of snow, which I hope will purify the air of some of the noxious vapours. It has spoild many hundreds of Bushels of Apples, which were designd for cider, and which the great rains had prevented people from making up. Suppose[3] we have lost 5 Barrels by it.

Col. Warren returnd last week to Plymouth, so that I shall not hear any thing from you till he goes back again which will not be till the last of this month.

He Damp'd my Spirits greatly by telling me that the Court had prolonged your Stay an other month.[4] I was pleasing myself with the thoughts that you would soon be upon your return. Tis in vain to repine. I hope the publick will reap what I sacrifice.

I wish I knew what mighty things were fabricating. If a form of Goverment is to be established here what one will be assumed? Will it be left to our assemblies to chuse one? and will not many men have many minds? and shall we not run into Dissentions among ourselves?

I am more and more convinced that Man is a dangerous creature, and that power whether vested in many or a few is ever grasping, and like the grave cries give, give. The great fish swallow up the small, and he who is most strenuous for the Rights of the people, when vested with power, is as eager after the perogatives[5] of Goverment. You tell me of degrees of perfection to which Humane Nature is capable of arriving, and I believe it, but at the same time lament that our admiration should arise from the scarcity of the instances.

The Building up a Great Empire, which was only hinted at by my correspondent may now I suppose be realized even by the unbelievers. Yet will not ten thousand Difficulties arise in the formation of it? The Reigns of Goverment have been so long slakned, that I fear the people will not quietly submit to those restraints which are necessary for the peace, and security, of the community; if we separate from Brittain, what Code of Laws will be established. How shall we be governd so as to retain our Liberties? Can any goverment be free which is not administred by general stated Laws? Who shall frame these Laws? Who will give them force and energy? Tis true your Resolution[s] as a Body have heithertoo had the force of Laws. But will they continue to have?

When I consider these things and the prejudices of people in favour of Ancient customs and Regulations, I feel anxious for the fate of our Monarchy or Democracy or what ever is to take place. I soon get lost in a Labyrinth of perplexities, but whatever occurs, may justice and righteousness be the Stability of our times, and order arise out of confusion. Great difficulties may be surmounted, by patience and perseverance.

I believe I have tired you with politicks. As to news we have not any at all. I shudder at the approach of winter when I think I am to remain desolate. Suppose your weather is warm yet. Mr. Mason and Thaxter live with me, and render some part of my time less disconsolate. Mr. Mason is a youth who will please you, he has Spirit, taste and Sense. His application to his Studies is constant and I am much mistaken if he does not make a very good figure in his profession.

I have with me now, the only Daughter[6] of your Brother; I feel a tenderer af-

3. I.e., I suppose.
4. I.e., the Congress then meeting in Philadelphia.
5. I.e., prerogatives; special powers or rights.
6. Susanna (1766–1826), daughter of Elihu Adams.

fection for her as she has lost a kind parent. Though too young to be sensible of her own loss, I can pitty her. She appears to be a child of a very good Disposition—only wants to be a little used to company.

Our Little ones send Duty to pappa and want much to see him. Tom says he[7] wont come home till the Battle is over—some strange notion he has got into his head. He has got a political cread to say to him when he returns.

I must bid you good night. Tis late for one who am much of an invalide. I was dissapointed last week in receiving a packet by the post, and upon unsealing it found only four news papers. I think you are more cautious than you need be. All Letters I believe have come safe to hand. I have Sixteen from you, and wish I had as many more. Adieu. Yours.

[Remember the Ladies]

Braintree March 31 1776

I wish you would ever write me a Letter half as long as I write you; and tell me if you may where your Fleet are gone? What sort of Defence Virginia can make against our common Enemy? Whether it is so situated as to make an able Defence? Are not the Gentery Lords and the common people vassals, are they not like the uncivilized Natives Brittain represents us to be? I hope their Riffel Men[1] who have shewen themselves very savage and even Blood thirsty; are not a specimen of the Generality of the people.

I am willing to allow the Colony great merrit for having produced a Washington but they have been shamefully duped by a Dunmore.[2]

I have sometimes been ready to think that the passion for Liberty cannot be Eaquelly Strong in the Breasts of those who have been accustomed to deprive their fellow Creatures of theirs. Of this I am certain that it is not founded upon that generous and christian principal of doing to others as we would that others should do unto us.

Do not you want to see Boston;[3] I am fearfull of the small pox, or I should have been in before this time. I got Mr. Crane to go to our House and see what state it was in. I find it has been occupied by one of the Doctors of a Regiment, very dirty, but no other damage has been done to it. The few things which were left in it are all gone. Cranch has the key which he never deliverd up. I have wrote to him for it and am determined to get it cleand as soon as possible and shut it up. I look upon it a new acquisition of property, a property which one month ago I did not value at a single Shilling, and could with pleasure have seen it in flames.

The Town in General is left in a better state than we expected, more oweing to a percipitate flight than any Regard to the inhabitants, tho some individuals discoverd a sense of honour and justice and have left the rent of the Houses in which they were, for the owners and the furniture unhurt, or if damaged sufficient to make it good.

7. I.e., John Adams.
1. Virginians played an important part in the 18th-century French and Indian Wars.
2. John Morris, earl of Dunmore (1732–1809), colonial governor of Virginia (1771–76), attempted to disarm the colonists and declared martial law after the Massachusetts battle of Lexington and Concord in 1775. George Washington was born in Virginia.
3. In response to the Boston Tea Party of December 1773, British troops occupied the city from May 1774 until they were driven out in March 1776.

Others have committed abominable Ravages. The Mansion House of your President is safe and the furniture unhurt whilst both the House and Furniture of the Solisiter General[4] have fallen a prey to their own merciless party. Surely the very Fiends feel a Reverential awe for Virtue and patriotism, whilst they Detest the paricide and traitor.

I feel very differently at the approach of spring to what I did a month ago. We knew not then whether we could plant or sow with safety, whether when we had toild we could reap the fruits of our own industery, whether we could rest in our own Cottages, or whether we should not be driven from the sea coasts to seek shelter in the wilderness, but now we feel as if we might sit under our own vine and eat the good of the land.

I feel a gaieti de Coar[5] to which before I was a stranger. I think the Sun looks brighter, the Birds sing more melodiously and Nature puts on a more chearfull countanance. We feel a temporary peace, and the poor fugitives are returning to their deserted habitations.

Tho we felicitate ourselves, we sympathize with those who are trembling least the Lot of Boston should be theirs. But they cannot be in similar circumstances unless pusilanimity and cowardise should take possession of them. They have time and warning given them to see the Evil and shun it.—I long to hear that you have declared an independancy—and by the way in the new Code of Laws which I suppose it will be necessary for you to make I desire you would Remember the Ladies, and be more generous and favourable to them than your ancestors. Do not put such unlimited power into the hands of the Husbands. Remember all Men would be tyrants if they could. If perticuliar care and attention is not paid to the Laidies we are determined to foment a Rebelion, and will not hold ourselves bound by any Laws in which we have no voice, or Representation.

That your Sex are Naturally Tyrannical is a Truth so thoroughly established as to admit of no dispute, but such of you as wish to be happy willingly give up the harsh title of Master for the more tender and endearing one of Friend. Why then, not put it out of the power of the vicious and the Lawless to use us with cruelty and indignity with impunity. Men of Sense in all Ages abhor those customs which treat us only as the vassals of your Sex. Regard us then as Beings placed by providence under your protection and in immitation of the Supreem Being make use of that power only for our happiness.

April 5

Not having an opportunity of sending this I shall add a few lines more; tho not with a heart so gay. I have been attending the sick chamber of our Neighbour Trot whose affliction I most sensibly feel but cannot discribe, striped of two lovely children in one week. Gorge the Eldest died on wedensday and Billy the youngest on fryday, with the Canker fever,[6] a terible disorder so much like the thr[o]at distemper, that it differs but little from it. Betsy Cranch has been very bad, but upon the recovery. Becky Peck they do not expect will live out the day. Many grown person[s] are now sick with it, in this

4. Samuel Quincy (1735–1789), soliciter general of the province of Massachusetts, who was himself a loyalist. "President": John Hancock (1737–1793), who presided over the First and Second Congresses of Massachusetts.
5. I.e., *gaieté de coeur* cheerfulness (French).
6. An ulcerated throat.

[street?] 5. It rages much in other Towns. The Mumps too are very frequent. Isaac is now confined with it. Our own little flock are yet well. My Heart trembles with anxiety for them. God preserve them.

I want to hear much oftener from you than I do. March 8 was the last date of any that I have yet had.—You inquire of whether I am making Salt peter.[7] I have not yet attempted it, but after Soap making believe I shall make the experiment. I find as much as I can do to manufacture cloathing for my family which would else be Naked. I know of but one person in this part of the Town who has made any, that is Mr. Tertias Bass as he is calld who has got very near an hundred weight which has been found to be very good. I have heard of some others in the other parishes. Mr. Reed of Weymouth has been applied to, to go to Andover to the mills which are now at work, and has gone. I have lately seen a small Manuscrip de[s]cribing the proportions for the various sorts of powder, fit for cannon, small arms and pistols. If it would be of any Service your way I will get it transcribed and send it to you.—Every one of your Friend[s] send their Regards, and all the little ones. Your Brothers youngest child lies bad with convulsion fitts.[8] Adieu. I need not say how much I am Your ever faithfull Friend.

[Absolute Power over Wives]

B[raintre]e May 7 1776

How many are the solitary hours I spend, ruminating upon the past, and anticipating the future, whilst you overwhelmd with the cares of State, have but few moments you can devote to any individual. All domestick pleasures and injoyments are absorbed in the great and important duty you owe your Country "for our Country is as it were a secondary God, and the First and greatest parent. It is to be preferred to Parents, Wives, Children, Friends and all things the Gods only excepted. For if our Country perishes it is as imposible to save an Individual, as to preserve one of the fingers of a Mortified Hand." Thus do I supress every wish, and silence every Murmer, acquiesceing in a painfull Seperation from the companion of my youth, and the Friend of my Heart.

I believe tis near ten days since I wrote you a line. I have not felt in a humour to entertain you. If I had taken up my pen perhaps some unbecomeing invective might have fallen from it; the Eyes of our Rulers have been closed and a Lethargy has seazd almost every Member. I fear a fatal Security has taken possession of them. Whilst the Building is on flame they tremble at the expence of water to quench it, in short two months has elapsed since the evacuation of Boston, and very little has been done in that time to secure it, or the Harbour from future invasion till the people are all in a flame; and no one among us that I have heard of even mentions expence, they think universally that there has been an amaizing neglect some where. Many have turnd out as volunteers to work upon Nodles Island, and many more would go upon Nantaskit if it was once set on foot.[1] "Tis a Maxim of state That power and Liberty are like Heat

7. A substance used in medicine and preserving food (as well as in gunpowder).
8. Susanna, daughter of Peter Boylston Adams, died within the month at less than a year of age.
1. I.e., put into action.

and moisture; where they are well mixt every thing prospers, where they are single, they are destructive."

A Goverment of more Stability is much wanted in this colony, and they are ready to receive it from the Hands of the Congress, and since I have begun with Maxims of State I will add another viz. that a people may let a king fall, yet still remain a people, but if a king et his people slip from him, he is no longer a king. And as this is most certainly our case, why not proclaim to the World in decisive terms your own importance?

Shall we not be dispiced by foreign powers for hesitateing so long at a word?

I can not say that I think you very generous to the Ladies, for whilst you are proclaiming peace and good will to Men, Emancipating all Nations, you insist upon retaining an absolute power over Wives. But you must remember that Arbitrary power is like most other things which are very hard, very liable to be broken—and notwithstanding all your wise Laws and Maxims we have it in our power not only to free ourselves but to subdue our Masters, and without voilence throw both your natural and legal authority at our feet—

> "Charm by accepting, by submitting sway
> Yet have our Humour most when we obey."[2]

I thank you for several Letters which I have received since I wrote Last. They alleviate a tedious absence, and I long earnestly for a Saturday Evening, and experience a similar pleasure to that which I used to find in the return of my Friend upon that day after a weeks absence. The Idea of a year dissolves all my Phylosophy.

Our Little ones whom you so often recommend to my care and instruction shall not be deficient in virtue or probity if the precepts of a Mother have their desired Effect, but they would be doubly inforced could they be indulged with the example of a Father constantly before them; I often point them to their Sire

> "engaged in a corrupted State
> Wrestling with vice and faction."

May 9

I designd to have finished the sheet, but an opportunity offering I close only just inform you that May the 7 our privateers took two prises in the Bay in fair sight of the Man of war, one a Brig from Irland the other from fyall [Fayal] loaded with wine Brandy and the other Beef &c. The wind was East and a flood tice, so that the tenders could not get out tho they tried several times, the Light house fired Signal guns, but all would not do, they took them in triumph and carried them into Lyn.

Johnny and Charls have the Mumps, a bad disorder, but they are not very bad. Pray be kind enough to remember me at all times and write as often as you possibly can to your

Portia[3]

2. Slightly misquoted from Alexander Pope's *Epistle 2: To a Lady* (1735), lines 263–64.

3. Adams used this signature fairly often after May 1775.

CHARLOTTE SMITH
1749–1806

Describing herself in *Beachy Head* (1807) as "an early worshipper at Nature's shrine," the poet-novelist Charlotte Smith was an important precursor of such Romantic poets as William Wordsworth and Samuel Taylor Coleridge as well as a significant ancestor of the Victorian poet Elizabeth Barrett Browning. Though she has been largely forgotten until quite recently, Smith's productivity was extraordinary: even while bearing and rearing ten children, she wrote and published more than twenty novels and books of verse, many of which were both popular and influential; her *Elegiac Sonnets, and Other Essays* (1784) had gone through eleven editions by 1851.

At sixteen, after a comfortable childhood at Bignor Park in Sussex, Charlotte Turner married Benjamin Smith, the extravagant son of a London merchant. From the start, the marriage was an unhappy one, although even when Benjamin was at one point sent to debtors' prison, his wife stayed with him during his incarceration. Finally, separated from her husband and burdened with the responsibility of raising (and supporting) eight growing children, Smith undertook to write and publish both poetry and prose fiction in the hope of solving the family's financial problems. Her many novels included the Gothic works *Emmeline, the Orphan of the Castle* (1788) and *The Old Manor House* (1793) as well as the more doctrinaire, political works *Desmond* (1792) and *The Young Philosopher* (1798), both of which show the influence of the philosopher Jean Jacques Rousseau and an enthusiastic sympathy with the ideals that motivated the French Revolution of 1789.

Smith's sonnet *Pressed by the Moon, Mute Arbitress of Tides* reveals a Romantic tendency toward self-analysis, even self-dramatization, that is quite consistent with the spirit of many of her novels. Her witty and genial *Thirty-eight* is more surprising, however, coming as it does from an artist whose lifelong struggle for financial survival must often have seemed to be "doomed" by intransigent circumstances. Perhaps most characteristic are such ambitious, long, blank-verse poems as *The Emigrants* (1793) and *Beachy Head*, both of which shaped and were shaped by what the critic Stuart Curran calls "an alternate Romanticism that seeks not to transcend or to absorb nature but to contemplate and honor" it. If Smith's life was a hard one and her literary reputation obscured for many years, she did survive, at least through the effect her proto-Romantic modes had on disparate but unquestionably major descendants, from Wordsworth and Coleridge to Barrett Browning.

[Pressed by the moon, mute arbitress of tides]

Written in the churchyard at Middleton in Sussex

Pressed by the moon, mute arbitress of tides,
 While the loud equinox[1] its power combines,
 The sea no more its swelling surge confines,
But o'er the shrinking land sublimely rides.
The wild blast, rising from the western cave, 5

1. I.e., equinoctial (powerful) wind.

Drives the huge billows from their heaving bed,
Tears from their grassy tombs the village dead,
And breaks the silent sabbath[2] of the grave!
With shells and seaweed mingled, on the shore
 Lo! their bones whiten in the frequent wave; 10
 But vain to them the winds and waters rave;
They hear the warring elements no more!
While I am doomed—by life's long storm oppressed,
To gaze with envy on their gloomy rest.

 1786

Thirty-Eight

Addressed to Mrs. H—y

In early youth's unclouded scene,
The brilliant morning of eighteen,
With health and sprightly joy elate
 We gazed on life's enchanting spring,
 Nor thought how quickly time would bring 5
The mournful period[1]—Thirty-eight.

Then the starch maid or matron sage,
Already of that sober age,
We viewed with mingled scorn and hate,
 In whose sharp words or sharper face 10
 With thoughtless mirth we loved to trace
The sad effects of—Thirty-eight.

Till saddening, sickening at the view,
We learned to dread what time might do;
And then preferred[2] a prayer to fate 15
 To end our days ere that arrived,
 When (power and pleasure long survived)
We met neglect and—Thirty-eight.

But time, in spite of wishes, flies,
And fate our simple prayer denies, 20
And bids us death's own hour await:
 The auburn locks are mixed with gray,
 The transient roses fade away,
But reason comes at—Thirty-eight.

Her voice the anguish contradicts 25
That dying vanity inflicts;
Her hand new pleasures can create.
 For us she opens to the view
 Prospects less bright—but far more true,
And bids us smile at—Thirty-eight. 30

2. I.e., rest.
1. I.e., occasion. 2. Offered.

No more shall scandal's breath destroy
The social converse we enjoy
With bard or critic tête à tête;[3]
 O'er youth's bright blooms her blights shall pour,
 But spare the improving friendly hour 35
That science[4] gives to—Thirty-eight.

Stripped of their gaudy hues by truth,
We view the glitt'ring toys of youth,
And blush to think how poor the bait
 For which to public scenes we ran 40
 And scorned of sober sense the plan
Which gives content at—Thirty-eight.

Though time's inexorable sway
Has torn the myrtle bands away,
For other wreaths 'tis not too late; 45
 The amaranth's purple glow survives,
 And still Minerva's olive[5] lives
On the calm brow of—Thirty-eight.

With eye more steady we engage
To contemplate approaching age, 50
And life more justly estimate.
 With firmer souls and stronger powers,
 With reason, faith, and friendship ours,
 We'll not regret the stealing hours
That lead from Thirty—even to Forty-eight. 55

1786

From Beachy Head[1]

[Imperial lord of the high southern coast]

On thy stupendous summit, rock sublime!
That o'er the channel reared, halfway at sea
The mariner at early morning hails,
I would recline; while Fancy should go forth,
And represent the strange and awful hour 5
Of vast concussion; when the Omnipotent
Stretched forth his arm, and rent the solid hills,
Bidding the impetuous main flood rush between
The rifted shores, and from the continent
Eternally divided this green isle. 10
Imperial lord of the high southern coast!
From thy projecting headland I would mark
Far in the east the shades of night disperse,

3. In privacy (French).
4. I.e., knowledge.
5. Sacred to Minerva, Roman goddess of wisdom. "Myrtle": sacred to Venus, goddess of love. "Amaranth": legendary flower that never faded.

1. "In crossing the Channel from the coast of France, Beachy-Head is the first land made" [Smith's note]. These high chalk cliffs are on the south coast of Sussex.

Melting and thinned, as from the dark blue wave
Emerging, brilliant rays of arrowy light 15
Dart from the horizon; when the glorious sun
Just lifts above it his resplendent orb.
Advances now, with feathery silver touched,
The rippling tide of flood; glisten the sands,
While, inmates of the chalky clefts that scar 20
Thy sides precipitous, with shrill harsh cry,
Their white wings glancing in the level beam,
The terns, and gulls, and tarrocks,[2] seek their food,
And thy rough hollows echo to the voice
Of the gray choughs, and ever restless daws,[3] 25
With clamor, not unlike the chiding hounds,
While the lone shepherd, and his baying dog,
Drive to thy turfy crest his bleating flock.

The high meridian of the day is past,
And Ocean now, reflecting the calm Heaven, 30
Is of cerulean hue; and murmers low
The tide of ebb, upon the level sands.
The sloop, her angular canvas shifting still,
Catches the light and variable airs
That but a little crisp the summer sea, 35
Dimpling its tranquil surface.

* * *

[An early worshipper at Nature's shrine]

Ah! who *is* happy? Happiness! a word— 255
That like false fire,[4] from marsh effluvia born,
Misleads the wanderer, destined to contend
In the world's wilderness, with want or woe—
Yet *they* are happy, who have never asked
What good or evil means. The boy 260
That on the river's margin gaily plays,
Has heard that Death is there[.]—He knows not Death,
And therefore fears it not; and venturing in
He gains a bullrush, or a minnow—then,
At certain peril, for a worthless prize, 265
A crow's, or raven's nest, he climbs the boll[5]
Of some tall pine; and of his prowess proud,
Is for a moment happy. Are *your* cares,
Ye who despise him, never worse applied?
The village girl is happy, who sets forth 270
To distant fair, gay in her Sunday suit,
With cherry colored knots, and flourished shawl,
And bonnet newly purchased. So is he
Her little brother, who his mimic drum
Beats, till he drowns her rural lovers' oaths 275
Of constant faith, and still increasing love;

2. Sea birds.
3. "Choughs" and "daws" are crows.
4. I.e., *ignis fatuus.*
5. Tree trunk.

Ah! yet a while, and half those oaths believed,
Her happiness is vanished; and the boy
While yet a stripling, finds the sound he loved
Has led him on,[6] till he has given up 280
His freedom, and his happiness together.
I once was happy, when while yet a child,
I learned to love these upland solitudes,
And, when elastic as the mountain air,
To my light spirit, care was yet unknown 285
And evil unforeseen:—Early it came,
And childhood scarcely passed, I was condemned,
A guiltless exile, silently to sigh,
While Memory, with faithful pencil, drew
The contrast; and regretting, I compared 290
With the polluted smoky atmosphere
And dark and stifling streets, the southern hills
That to the setting Sun, their graceful heads
Rearing, o'erlook the frith, where Vecta[7] breaks
With her white rocks, the strong impetuous tide, 295
When western winds the vast Atlantic urge
To thunder on the coast[.]—Haunts of my youth!
Scenes of fond daydreams, I behold ye yet!
Where 'twas so pleasant by thy northern slopes
To climb the winding sheep-path, aided oft 300
By scattered thorns: whose spiny branches bore
Small woolly tufts, spoils of the vagrant lamb
There seeking shelter from the noonday sun;
And pleasant, seated on the short soft turf,
To look beneath upon the hollow way 305
While heavily upward moved the laboring wain,[8]
And stalking slowly by, the sturdy hind
To ease his panting team, stopped with a stone
The grating wheel.

 Advancing higher still
The prospect widens, and the village church 310
But little, o'er the lowly roofs around
Rears its gray belfry, and its simple vane;
Those lowly roofs of thatch are half concealed
By the rude arms of trees,[9] lovely in spring,
When on each bough, the rosy-tinctured bloom 315
Sits thick, and promises autumnal plenty.
For even those orchards round the Norman Farms,
Which, as their owners mark the promised fruit,
Console them for the vineyards of the south,
Surpass not these.

 Where woods of ash, and beech, 320
And partial copses, fringe the green hill foot,

6. I.e., to becoming a soldier. 8. Cart.
7. The Isle of Wight. "Frith": or firth, an arm of the 9. Apple trees, which blossom in the spring and are
sea. harvested in the autumn.

The upland shepherd rears his modest home,
There wanders by, a little nameless stream
That from the hill wells forth, bright now and clear,
Or after rain with chalky mixture gray, 325
But still refreshing in its shallow course
The cottage garden; most for use designed,
Yet not of beauty destitute. The vine
Mantles the little casement; yet the briar
Drops fragrant dew among the July flowers; 330
And pansies rayed, and freaked and mottled pinks
Grow among balm, and rosemary and rue
There honeysuckles flaunt, and roses blow[1]
Almost uncultured: Some with dark green leaves
Contrast their flowers of pure unsullied white; 335
Others, like velvet robes of regal state
Of richest crimson, while in thorny moss
Enshrined and cradled, the most lovely, wear
The hues of youthful beauty's glowing cheek.—
With fond regret I recollect e'en now 340
In Spring and Summer, what delight I felt
Among these cottage gardens, and how much
Such artless nosegays, knotted with a rush
By village housewife or her ruddy maid,
Were welcome to me; soon and simple pleased. 345

An early worshipper at Nature's shrine,
I loved her rudest scenes—warrens, and heaths,[2]
And yellow commons, and birch-shaded hollows,
And hedge rows, bordering unfrequented lanes
Bowered with wild roses, and the clasping woodbine 350
Where purple tassels of the tangling vetch
With bittersweet, and bryony inweave,
And the dew fills the silver bindweed's cups—
I loved to trace the brooks whose humid banks
Nourish the harebell, and the freckled pagil;[3] 355
And stroll among o'ershadowing woods of beech,
Lending in Summer, from the heats of noon
A whispering shade; while haply there reclines
Some pensive lover of uncultured flowers,
Who, from the tumps[4] with bright green mosses clad, 360
Plucks the wood sorrel, with its light thin leaves,
Heart-shaped, and triply folded; and its root
Creeping like beaded coral; or who there
Gathers, the copse's pride, anemones,
With rays like golden studs on ivory laid 365
Most delicate: but touched with purple clouds,
Fit crown for April's fair but changeful brow.

Ah! hills so early loved! in fancy still
I breathe your pure keen air; and still behold

1. Blossom
2. Open, uncultivated ground. "Warrens" uncultivated ground where rabbits breed.
3. These are all particular plants and wildflowers.
4. Dry mounds in a bog. "Uncultur'd": uncultivated.

Those widely spreading views, mocking alike 370
The Poet and the Painter's utmost art.
And still, observing objects more minute,
Wondering remark the strange and foreign forms
Of seashells; with the pale calcareous[5] soil
Mingled, and seeming of resembling substance. 375
Though surely the blue Ocean (from the heights
Where the downs westward trend, but dimly seen)
Here never rolled its surge. Does Nature then
Mimic, in wanton mood, fantastic shapes
Of bivalves, and inwreathed volutes,[6] that cling 380
To the dark sea-rock of the wat'ry world?
Or did this range of chalky mountains, once
Form a vast bason,[7] where the Ocean waves
Swelled fathomless? What time these fossil shells,
Buoyed on their native element, were thrown 385
Among the imbedding calx:[8] when the huge hill
Its giant bulk heaved, and in strange ferment
Grew up a guardian barrier, 'twixt the sea
And the green level of the sylvan weald.[9]

Ah! very vain is Science' proudest boast, 390
And but a little light its flame yet lends
To its most ardent votaries; since from whence
These fossil forms are seen, is but conjecture,
Food for vague theories, or vain dispute,
While to his daily task the peasant goes, 395
Unheeding such inquiry; with no care
But that the kindly change of sun and shower,
Fit for his toil the earth he cultivates.
As little recks the herdsman of the hill,
Who on some turfy knoll, idly reclined, 400
Watches his wether[1] flock, that deep beneath
Rest the remains of men, of whom is left
No traces in the records of mankind,
Save what these half obliterated mounds
And half filled trenches doubtfully impart 405
To some lone antiquary; who on times remote,
Since which two thousand years have rolled away,
Loves to contemplate. He perhaps may trace,
Or fancy he can trace, the oblong square
Where the mailed legions, under Claudius,[2] reared 410
The rampire, or excavated fossé[3] delved;
What time the huge unwieldy Elephant[4]
Auxiliary reluctant, hither led,
From Afric's forest glooms and tawny sands,

5. Chalky (compare line 20, "chalky clefts").
6. Shellfish with spiral shells.
7. I.e., basin.
8. Lime.
9. Forest.
1. Castrated sheep. "Recks": takes heed.
2. Roman emperor (A.D. 41–54), who in 43 landed in

Britain, which he made a province.
3. Ditch, trench. "Rampire": rampart.
4. In the year 1740, some workmen digging in the part at Burton in Sussex, discovered, nine feet below the surface, the teeth and bones of an elephant. . . . The Romans under the Emperor Claudius probably brought elephants into Britain [Smith's note].

First felt the Northern blast, and his vast frame 415
Sunk useless; whence in after ages found,
The wondering hinds, on those enormous bones
Gazed; and in giants dwelling on the hills
Believed and marvelled—

 Hither, Ambition come!
Come and behold the nothingness of all 420
For which you carry through the oppressed Earth,
War, and its train of horrors—see where tread
The innumerous hoofs of flocks above the works
By which the warrior sought to register
His glory, and immortalize his name[.]— 425
The pirate Dane,[5] who from his circular camp
Bore in destructive robbery, fire and sword
Down through the vale, sleeps unremembered here;
And here, beneath the green sward, rests alike
The savage native, who his acorn meal 430
Shared with the herds, that ranged the pathless woods;
And the centurion, who on these wide hills
Encamping, planted the Imperial Eagle.[6]
All, with the lapse of Time, have passed away,
Even as the clouds, with dark and dragon shapes, 435
Or like vast promontories crowned with towers,
Cast their broad shadows on the downs: then sail
Far to the northward, and their transient gloom
Is soon forgotten.
 * * *

 1807

5 The incursions of the Danes were for many ages the
scourge of this island [Smith's note].

6 The standard of a subdivision of a Roman legion,
which was led by a "centurion."

FRANCES BURNEY

1752–1840

At fifteen years of age, with her twelve-year-old sister Susan sobbing by her side, Frances Burney burned all of her early writing because her stepmother felt that a reputation for scribbling would harm the girl's marriage prospects and because she herself was early impressed "with ideas that fastened degradation to this class of composition" then, as now, called the novel. Soon after, however, Burney began to keep a secret journal addressed to "A Certain Miss Nobody," because "to Nobody can I be wholly unreserved." While she would eventually write her diary for the members of her family, her early determination to counterpoint decorous public submission with private literary assertion was to play a crucial role in her life.

The third of six children, Burney was eight years old when the family moved from King's Lynn to London, and ten years old when she lost her mother, Esther (Seepe) Burney. She became greatly attached to her father, the historian of music Dr. Charles Burney, and to his friend Samuel ("Daddy") Crisp, the recipient of many of her early confidences. Although she was said to be shy and had only re-ceived a few months of formal schooling, through her gregarious father she met a

number of artists and intellectuals. Her first and most important nove', *Evelina* (1778), explored the social development of a heroine who proves herself worthy of her well-born suitor. Published anonymously when Burney was twenty-six, this epistolary fiction was an instant success. After its author's identity became known, first to her family and then to the public, it won Burney such prominent friends as the essayist and lexicographer Samuel Johnson, his companion Mrs. Hester Thrale, the painter Sir Joshua Reynolds, the playwright Richard Sheridan, and the philosopher Edmund Burke, all of whom appear in the *Diary*. With the encouragement of these supporters, her father, and "Daddy" Crisp, Burney next published *Cecilia; or, Memoirs of an Heiress* (1782). While not as popular as *Evelina*, it also analyzed the social and economic problems of women. In both of these novels, Burney self-consciously tried to raise the status of the novel by combining verisimilitude with instruction. In the process, she helped establish a new genre, the novel of manners. Indeed, she conveyed the manners and morals of polite society with a relish for the ridiculous and a respect for the conventional that explain why Jane Austen found both the theme and the title of *Pride and Prejudice* in the concluding chapter of *Cecilia*.

In spite of enthusiastic reviews, Burney felt she had exhausted her subject with *Cecilia* and, again with the encouragement of her father, she accepted a place at court in 1786. Although the position of second keeper of the robes to Queen Charlotte secured her a salary of two hundred pounds a year, it involved such official duties as mixing the queen's snuff and attending to her dressing, even as it placed Burney under the grating supervision of the first keeper of the robes, a Mrs. Schwellenberg. In 1791 Burney was allowed to retire with a pension of one hundred pounds, and two years later, at the age of forty-one, she married a penniless French exile, General Alexandre D'Arblay. She continued to publish, first *Brief Revelations Relative to the Emigrant French Clergy* (1793), and later *Camilla; or, Female Difficulties* (1796) and *The Wanderer* (1814). From 1802 to 1812, she lived with her husband and their son in France, where she received the title of countess from Louis XVIII. After fleeing to Brussels during Napoleon's Hundred Days, she returned with her family to London. She remained in retirement after her husband's death in 1818, editing her father's memoirs (1832). Three years after her death, her niece, Charlotte Frances Barrett, began issuing the *Diary and Letters*, but the *Early Diary* was not published until 1889. The selection printed here from the *Diary and Letters of Madame d'Arblay* (7 volumes) demonstrates Burney's ear for dialogue and her eye for social detail.

From The Diary and Letters of Madame D'Arblay

Letter from Miss F. Burney to Mrs. Phillips[1] *[Authoress of "Evelina"]*

I thank you most heartily for your two sweet letters, my ever dearest Susy, and equally for the kindness they contain and the kindness they accept. And, as I have a frank[2] and a subject, I will leave my *brothers*, and write you and my dear brother Molesworth a little account of a *rout* I have just been at, at the house of Mr. Paradise.[3]

You will wonder, perhaps, in this time of hurry, why I went thither: but when I tell you Pacchierotti[4] was there, you will not think it surprising.

There was a crowd of company; Charlotte[5] and I went together; my father

1. Susan Burney Phillips, the author's sister.
2. An envelope marked or signed by an official so that it can be mailed without postage.
3. An acquaintance in polite society. "Rout": fashion-
able gathering.
4. A well-known operatic singer.
5. Burney's youngest sister.

came afterwards. Mrs. Paradise received us very graciously, and led me imme-
diately up to Miss Thrale, who was sitting by the Pac.[6] The Miss Kirwans, you
may be sure, were not far off, and so I did pretty well. There was nobody else I
knew but Dr. Solander, Mr. Coxe, the traveller, Sir Sampson and Lady Gideon
(Streatham acquaintances), Mr. Sastres, and Count Zenobia, a noble
Venetian, whom I have often met lately at Mrs. Thrale's.

We were very late, for we had waited cruelly for the coach, and Pac. had
sung a song out of *Artaxerxes*, composed for a tenor, which we lost, to my infi-
nite regret.[7] Afterwards he sang "Dolce speme," set by Bertoni, less elegantly
than by Sacchini, but more expressively for the words. He sang it delightfully.
It was but the second time I have heard him in a room since his return to
England.

After this he went into another room, to try if it would be cooler; and Mrs.
Paradise, leaning over the Kirwans and Charlotte, who hardly got a seat all
night for the crowd, said she begged to speak to me. I squeezed my great per-
son out, and she then said,

"Miss Burney, Lady Say and Sele[8] desires the honor of being introduced to
you."

Her ladyship stood by her side. She seems pretty near fifty—at least turned
forty; her head was full of feathers, flowers, jewels, and gee-gaws, and as high
as Lady Archer's; her dress was trimmed with beads, silver, persian sashes, and
all sort of fine fancies; her face is thin and fiery, and her whole manner spoke a
lady all alive.

"Miss Burney," cried she, with great quickness, and a look all curiosity, "I am
very happy to see you; I have longed to see you a great while; I have read your
performance,[9] and I am quite delighted with it. I think it's the most elegant
novel I ever read in my life. Such a style! I am quite surprised at it. I can't think
where you got so much invention!"

You may believe this was a reception not to make me very loquacious. I did
not know which way to turn my head.

'I must introduce you," continued her ladyship, "to my sister; she'll be
quite delighted to see you. She has written a novel herself; so you are sister au-
thoresses. A most elegant thing it is, I assure you; almost as pretty as yours,
only not quite so elegant. She has written two novels, only one is not so pretty
as the other. But I shall insist upon your seeing them. One is in letters, like
yours, only yours is prettiest: it's called the *Mausoleum of Julia!*"

What unfeeling things, thought I, are *my* sisters! I'm sure I never heard
them go about thus praising *me*!

Mrs. Paradise then again came forward, and taking my hand, led me up to
her ladyship's sister, Lady Hawke, saying aloud, and with a courteous smirk,
"Miss Burney, ma'am, authoress of *Evelina*."

'Yes," cried my friend, Lady Say and Sele, who followed me close, "it's the
authoress of *Evelina*; so you are sister authoresses!"

Lady Hawke arose and curtsied. She is much younger than her sister, and
rather pretty; extremely languishing, delicate, and pathetic;[1] apparently ac-
customed to be reckoned the genius of her family, and well contented to be
looked upon as a creature dropped from the clouds.

6. I.e., Pacchierotti.
7. I.e., they arrived too late to hear it.
8. A title, not a name; her husband is the Baron Say
and Sele.
9. Burney's first published novel, Evelina.
1. I.e., arousing sympathy, tenderness.

I was then seated between their ladyships, and Lady S. and S., drawing as near to me as possible, said,

"Well, and so you wrote this pretty book!—and pray did your papa know of it?"

"No, ma'am; not till some months after the publication."

"So I've heard; it's surprising! I can't think how you invented it!—there's a vast deal of invention in it! And you've got so much humor, too! Now my sister has no humor—hers is all sentiment. You can't think how I was entertained with that old grandmother and her son!"

I suppose she meant Tom Branghton for the son.

"How much pleasure you must have had in writing it; had not you?"

"Y—e—s, ma'am."

"So has my sister; she's never without a pen in her hand; she can't help writing for her life. When Lord Hawke is travelling about with her, she keeps writing all the way."

"Yes," said Lady Hawke; "I really can't help writing. One has great pleasure in writing the things; has not one, Miss Burney?"

"Y—e—s, ma'am."

"But your novel," cried Lady Say and Sele, "is in such a style!—so elegant! I am vastly glad you made it end happily. I hate a novel that don't end happy."

"Yes," said Lady Hawke, with a languid smile, "I was vastly glad when she married Lord Orville. I was sadly afraid it would not have been."

"My sister intends," said Lady Say and Sele, "to print her *Mausoleum*, just for her own friends and acquaintances."

"Yes," said Lady Hawke, "I have never printed yet."

"I saw Lady Hawke's name," quoth I to my first friend, "ascribed to the play of *Variety*."[2]

"Did you indeed?" cried Lady Say, in an ecstasy. "Sister! do you know Miss Burney saw your name in the newspapers, about the play!"

"Did she?" said Lady Hawke, smiling complacently. "But I really did not write it; I never wrote a play in my life."

"Well," cried Lady Say, "but do repeat that sweet part that I am so fond of— you know what I mean; Miss Burney *must* hear it,—out of your novel, you know!"

Lady H.—No, I can't; I have forgot it.

Lady S.—Oh no! I am sure you have not; I insist upon it.

Lady H.—But I know you can repeat it yourself; you have so fine a memory; I am sure you can repeat it.

Lady S.—Oh, but I should not do it justice! that's all,—I should not do it justice!

Lady Hawke then bent forward, and repeated—" 'If, when he made the declaration of his love, the sensibility[3] that beamed in his eyes was felt in his heart, what pleasing sensations and soft alarms might not that tender avowal awaken!' "

"And from what, ma'am," cried I, astonished, and imagining I had mistaken them, "is this taken?"

"From my sister's novel!" answered the delighted Lady Say and Sele, expecting my raptures to be equal to her own; "it's in the *Mausoleum*,—did not

2. I.e., a play by the name of *Variety*, anonymously produced at Drury Lane. The author was actually Richard Griffith.
3. Sensitivity, emotion.

you know that? Well, I can't think how you can write these sweet novels! And it's all just like that part. Lord Hawke himself says it's all poetry. For my part, I'm sure I never could write so. I suppose, Miss Burney, you are producing another,—a'n't you?"

"No, ma'am."

"Oh, I daresay you are. I daresay you are writing one at this very minute!"

Mrs. Paradise now came up to me again, followed by a square man, middle-aged, and humdrum, who, I found, was Lord Say and Sele, afterwards from the Kirwans; for though they introduced him to me, I was so confounded by their vehemence and their manners, that I did not hear his name.

"Miss Burney," said Mrs. P., presenting me to him, "authoress of *Evelina*."

"Yes," cried Lady Say and Sele, starting up, "'tis the authoress of *Evelina*!"

"Of what?" cried he.

"Of *Evelina*. You'd never think it,—she looks so young, to have so much invention, and such an elegant style! Well, I could write a play, I think, but I'm sure I could never write a novel."

"Oh yes, you could, if you would try," said Lady Hawke.

"Oh no, I could not," answered she; "I could not get a style—that's the thing—I could not tell how to get a style! and a novel's nothing without a style, you know!"

"Why no," said Lady Hawke; "that's true. But then you write such charming letters, you know!"

"Letters!" repeated Lady S. and S., simpering; "do you think so? Do you know I wrote a long letter to Mrs. Ray just before I came here, this very afternoon,—quite a long letter! I did, I assure you!"

Here Mrs. Paradise came forward with another gentleman, younger, slimmer, and smarter, and saying to me, "Sir Gregory Page Turner," said to him, "Miss Burney, authoress of *Evelina*."

At which Lady Say and Sele, in fresh transport, again arose, and rapturously again repeated—"Yes, she's authoress of *Evelina*! Have you read it?"

"No; is it to be had?"[4]

"Oh dear, yes! it's been printed these two years! You'd never think it! But it's the most elegant novel I ever read in my life. Writ in such a style!"

"Certainly," said he, very civilly; "I have every inducement to get it. Pray where is it to be had? everywhere, I suppose?"

"Oh, nowhere, I hope!" cried I, wishing at that moment it had been never in human ken.[5]

My *square* friend, Lord Say and Sele, then putting his head forward, said, very solemnly, "I'll purchase it."

His lady then mentioned to me a hundred novels that I had never heard of, asking my opinion of them, and whether I knew the authors; Lady Hawke only occasionally and languidly joining in the discourse: and then Lady S. and S., suddenly arising, begged me not to move, for she should be back again in a minute, and flew to the next room.

I took, however, the first opportunity of Lady Hawke's casting down her eyes, and reclining her delicate head, to make away from this terrible set; and, just as I was got by the piano-forte, where I hoped Pacchierotti would soon present himself, Mrs. Paradise again came to me, and said,

4. For sale. 5. Range of vision or knowledge.

"Miss Burney, Lady Say and Sele wishes vastly to cultivate your acquaintance, and begs to know if she may have the honor of your company to an assembly at her house next Friday?—and I will do myself the pleasure to call for you, if you will give me leave."

"Her ladyship does me much honor, but I am unfortunately engaged," was my answer, with as much promptness as I could command. F.B.

1782

PHILLIS WHEATLEY
c. 1753–1784

Just enough is known about Phillis Wheatley's life to suggest the extent of her poetic talent, for she developed it against great odds. The time and place of Wheatley's birth are as unknown as her African name, but she probably came from what is now called Senegal or Gambia. Purchased directly off a slave ship in Boston by a wealthy tailor, John Wheatley, in 1761, she was losing her first teeth, and so she was believed to be about seven years of age. Because of her precocity, the girl, who became Mrs. Susannah Wheatley's personal servant, was treated beneficently by the standards of the time. She learned English in sixteen months, and soon studied Latin, as well as the Bible and English poetry by Alexander Pope and Thomas Gray. She began writing religious verse when she was thirteen, and she could not have been more than seventeen years old when she published one of her first poems, an elegy on the death of the English evangelical preacher George Whitefield. In 1773, in poor health, she was sent to England with the Wheatleys' son, and there her only book, *Poems on Various Subjects, Religious and Moral*, was published. After she returned to Boston to witness first Mrs. and then Mr. Wheatley's death, she was freed and married John Peters, a freedman who seems later to have been imprisoned for debt. Two of her three children died, and eventually Wheatley worked in a dilapidated lodging house to support herself and the third child, who died soon after she did.

Even the scanty information we have about Wheatley's career implies that she lived the life of a prodigy. Whether praised as an exemplary figure or scrutinized as a strange aberration, she was famous for her wit in conversation, her modesty, and her social poise. Certainly, her poems are decorous and pious in their stylistic use of conventional neoclassical couplets and in their thematic focus on spiritual salvation achieved through Christ. She was the guest of the countess of Huntingdon in London and met General George Washington after publishing a poem about him in the April 1776 issue of the *Philadelphia Magazine*. The volume of verse the countess of Huntingdon helped publish contains a foreword attesting to Wheatley's talents and is signed by eighteen prominent Massachusetts men, including John Hancock. Yet none of these testimonials saved her from the obscurity and destitution of her life after slavery. *Poems on Various Subjects* was published in America in 1786. But Wheatley's fame as the first black American woman poet was not established until Margaretta M. Odell published a *Memoir* in her 1834 edition of the *Poems*. Only recently has Wheatley received the scholarly attention her unprecedented achievement deserves. As the critic Henry Louis Gates Jr. has pointed out, her poetry marks the simultaneous literary origin of two aesthetic lineages: the black American literary tradition and the black female literary tradition. At the same time, her work is marked by a confident eloquence suggesting that she felt herself to be very much part of an intellectual mainstream in her addresses to such diverse figures as "S. M., a young African painter" and "His Excellency General Washington."

On Being Brought from Africa to America

'Twas mercy brought me from my pagan land,
Taught my benighted[1] soul to understand
That there's a God, that there's a Savior too:
Once I redemption neither sought nor knew.
Some view that sable[2] race with scornful eye: 5
"Their color is a diabolic dye."
Remember, Christians, Negroes black as Cain[3]
May be refined and join the angelic strain.[4]

1773

To the Right Honorable William, Earl of Dartmouth,[1] His Majesty's Principal Secretary of State for North America, Etc.

Hail, happy day, when, smiling like the morn,
Fair Freedom rose New England to adorn:
The northern clime[2] beneath her genial ray,
Dartmouth, congratulates thy blissful sway:[3]
Elate with hope her race no longer mourns, 5
Each soul expands, each grateful bosom burns,
While in thine hand with pleasure we behold
The silken reins, and Freedom's charms unfold.
Long lost to realms beneath the northern skies
She shines supreme, while hated Faction dies: 10
Soon as appeared the goddess[4] long desired,
Sick at the view, she[5] languished and expired;
Thus from the splendors of the morning light
The owl in sadness seeks the caves of night.

No more, America, in mournful strain[6] 15
Of wrongs, and grievance unredressed complain,
No longer shalt thou dread the iron chain
Which wanton Tyranny with lawless hand
Had made, and with it meant to enslave the land.

Should you, my lord, while you peruse my song, 20
Wonder from whence my love of Freedom sprung,
Whence flow these wishes for the common good,
By feeling hearts alone best understood,
I, young in life, by seeming cruel fate,

1. Unenlightened.
2. Black.
3. After Cain murdered his brother Abel, God
"marked" him so that no one would kill him (Genesis
4:15) This has sometimes been interpreted as the
story of the origin of blacks.
4. Race. "Refined": purified (possibly punning on
cane sugar).
1. He was appointed secretary in charge of the

American colonies in August 1772, replacing the stern
Lord Hillsborough. American sympathizers in Eng-
land were hopeful that Dartmouth would prove to be
more amenable to the colonies' grievances.
2. Region.
3. Reign, leadership.
4. I.e., Freedom.
5. I.e., Faction (internal conflict).
6. Eloquent burst of language or melody.

Was snatched from Afric's fancied happy seat:[7] 25
What pangs excruciating must molest,
What sorrows labor in my parents' breast?
Steeled was that soul and by no misery moved
That from a father seized his babe beloved:
Such, such my case. And can I then but pray 30
Others may never feel tyrannic sway?

 For favors past, great Sir, our thanks are due,
And thee we ask thy favors to renew,
Since[8] in thy power, as in thy will before,
To soothe the griefs which thou didst once deplore. 35
May heavenly grace the sacred sanction give
To all thy works, and thou forever live
Not only on the wings of fleeting Fame,
Though praise immortal crowns the patriot's[9] name,
But to conduct to heaven's refulgent fane,[1] 40
May fiery coursers sweep the ethereal plain,[2]
And bear thee upwards to that blessed abode,
Where, like the prophet,[3] thou shalt find thy God.

 1773

To S. M.,[1] A Young *African* Painter, on Seeing His Works

To show the laboring bosom's deep intent,
And thought in living characters to paint,
When first thy pencil did those beauties give,
And breathing figures learnt from thee to live,
How did those prospects give my soul delight, 5
A new creation rushing on my sight?
Still, wond'rous youth! each noble path pursue,
On deathless glories fix thine ardent view:
Still may the painter's and the poet's fire
To aid thy pencil, and thy verse conspire! 10
And may the charms of each seraphic theme
Conduct thy footsteps to immortal fame!
High to the blissful wonders of the skies
Elate thy soul, and raise thy wishful eyes.
Thrice happy, when exalted to survey 15
That splendid city, crowned with endless day,
Whose twice six gates on radiant hinges ring:
Celestial Salem[2] blooms in endless spring.

 Calm and serene thy moments glide along,
And may the muse inspire each future song! 20

7. Place of abode. "Fancied": imagined.
8. I.e., since it is in thy power. The line draws a distinction between Dartmouth's powerless state of sympathy for the colonies before his appointment, and his newfound ability to help them.
9. I.e., Dartmouth's.

1. Shining temple.
2. Heaven. "Coursers": swift horses.
3. Elijah, who was borne up into heaven on a chariot of fire (2 Kings 2:11).
1. Scipio Moorhead, a servant in Boston.
2. I.e., Jerusalem (in heaven).

Still, with the sweets of contemplation blessed,
May peace with balmy wings your soul invest!
But when these shades of time are chased away,
And darkness ends in everlasting day,
On what seraphic pinions[3] shall we move, 25
And view the landscapes in the realms above?
There shall thy tongue in heavenly murmurs flow,
And there my muse with heavenly transport glow:
No more to tell of Damon's tender sighs,
Or rising radiance of Aurora's[4] eyes, 30
For nobler themes demand a nobler strain,
And purer language on the ethereal plain.
Cease, gentle muse! the solemn gloom of night
Now seals the fair creation from my sight.

 1773

To His Excellency, General Washington

The following letter and verses, were written by the famous Phillis Wheatley,
the African Poetess, and presented to his Excellency Gen. Washington.

Sir,

I have taken the freedom to address your Excellency in the enclosed poem,
and entreat your acceptance, though I am not insensible of its inaccuracies.
Your being appointed by the Grand Continental Congress to be Generalis-
simo of the armies of North America, together with the fame of your virtues,
excite sensations not easy to suppress. Your generosity, therefore, I presume,
will pardon the attempt. Wishing your Excellency all possible success in the
great cause you are so generously engaged in I am,

 Your Excellency's most obedient humble servant,

 Phillis Wheatley

Providence, Oct. 26, 1775
His Excellency Gen. Washington

 Celestial choir! enthroned in realms of light,
 Columbia's[1] scenes of glorious toils I write.
 While freedom's cause her anxious breast alarms,
 She flashes dreadful in refulgent arms.
 See mother earth her offspring's fate bemoan, 5
 And nations gaze at scenes before unknown!
 See the bright beams of heaven's revolving light
 Involved in sorrows and the veil of night!
 The goddess[2] comes, she moves divinely fair,
 Olive and laurel binds her golden hair: 10
 Wherever shines this native of the skies,

3. Angels' wings.
4. Damon and Aurora are the subjects of a conven-
tional love poem, unsuited to heaven.

1. America's.
2. Probably Liberty personified, here associated (in
line 10) with Athena ("olive") and victory ("laurel").

Unnumbered charms and recent graces rise.
 Muse! bow propitious while my pen relates
How pour her armies through a thousand gates:
As when Eolus[3] heaven's fair face deforms, 15
Enwrapped in tempest and a night of storms;
Astonished ocean feels the wild uproar,
The refluent surges beat the sounding shore;
Or thick as leaves in Autumn's golden reign,
Such, and so many, moves the warrior's train. 20
In bright array they seek the work of war,
Where high unfurled the ensign[4] waves in air.
Shall I to Washington their praise recite?
Enough thou knowest them in the fields of fight.
Thee, first in place and honors,—we demand 25
The grace and glory of thy martial band.
Famed for thy valor, for thy virtues more,
Hear every tongue thy guardian aid implore!
 One century scarce performed its destined round,
When Gallic[5] powers Columbia's fury found; 30
And so may you, whoever dares disgrace
The land of freedom's heaven-defended race!
Fixed are the eyes of nations on the scales,
For in their hopes Columbia's arm prevails.
Anon Britannia droops the pensive head, 35
While round increase the rising hills of dead.
Ah! cruel blindness to Columbia's state!
Lament thy thirst of boundless power too late.
 Proceed, great chief, with virtue on thy side,
Thy every action let the goddess guide. 40
A crown, a mansion, and a throne that shine,
With gold unfading, WASHINGTON! be thine.

1775–76 1776, 1834

3. God of winds. "Muse": goddess of art and learning, 4. Banner, flag.
conventionally invoked for inspiration and informa- 5. French.
tion.

MARY ROBINSON

1758–1800

A famous beauty somewhat sardonically labeled "pretty, charming 'Perdita'" by
Oscar Wilde, Mary Robinson led an adventurous life as wife, mother, actress, mis-
tress, and prolific woman of letters. Born in Bristol and raised in London, she mar-
ried Thomas Robinson in 1774, when she was still a teenager, gave birth to a
daughter, and when her husband was imprisoned for debt spent ten months in
prison with him and her baby. There she wrote a collection of poems that appeared
in 1775, earning the patronage of the duchess of Devonshire. On leaving prison,
she began a successful career as an actress.
 Robinson's glamorous performance as Perdita in Shakespeare's *The Winter's
Tale* earned her a permanent pseudonym and charmed the seventeen-year-old
prince of Wales, who made her royal mistress for a year, but then abandoned her

with no compensation and an unsavory reputation. Unwilling to return to the stage, she began writing in earnest after several other romantic relationships failed and a miscarriage left her partially paralyzed. Wide-ranging, lively and lucrative, her literary output includes several collections of poetry, among them an erotic sonnet sequence (*Sappho and Phaon*, 1796), a satiric comedy (*Nobody*, 1794), a verse tragedy (*The Sicilian Lover*, 1795), eight novels, including the best-selling gothic romance *Vicenza, or the Dangers of Credulity*, 1796), and a feminist polemic (*A Letter to the Woman of England on the Injustice of Mental Subordination*, 1799).

Moving in intellectual circles that included Wordsworth, Coleridge, Mary Wollstonecraft, and William Godwin, Robinson was painted by such major contemporary artists as Romney, Gainsborough, and Reynolds. Yet despite her many triumphs, she died relatively young, at the age of forty-two, after years of ill health and of the disillusionment she expressed in *January, 1795*, where she deplored a world of "Authors who can't earn a dinner;/Many a subtle rogue a winner" and "Taste and talents quite deserted;/All the laws of truth perverted."

London's Summer Morning

Who has not waked to list the busy sounds
Of summer's morning, in the sultry smoke
Of noisy London? On the pavement hot
The sooty chimney-boy, with dingy face
And tattered covering, shrilly bawls his trade, 5
Rousing the sleepy housemaid. At the door
The milk-pail rattles, and the tinkling bell
Proclaims the dustman's office;[1] while the street
Is lost in clouds impervious. Now begins
The din of hackney-coaches,[2] wagons, carts; 10
While tinmen's shops, and noisy trunk-makers,
Knife-grinders, coopers,[3] squeaking cork-cutters,
Fruit-barrows, and the hunger-giving cries
Of vegetable venders, fill the air.
Now every shop displays its varied trade, 15
And the fresh-sprinkled pavement cools the feet
Of early walkers. At the private door
The ruddy housemaid twirls the busy mop,
Annoying the smart 'prentice, or neat girl,
Tripping with band-box[4] lightly. Now the sun 20
Darts burning splendor on the glittering pane,
Save where the canvas awning throws a shade
On the gay merchandise. Now, spruce and trim,
In shops (where beauty smiles with industry)
Sits the smart damsel; while the passenger 25
Peeps through the window, watching every charm.
Now pastry dainties catch the eye minute
Of humming insects, while the limy snare[5]
Waits to enthrall them. Now the lamp-lighter
Mounts the tall ladder, nimbly venturous, 30

1. I.e., carting away garbage.
2. Hired carriages.
3. Those who make barrels and buckets.
4. Hat box.
5. Bird lime is a sticky substance.

To trim the half-filled lamp; while at his feet
The pot-boy[6] yells discordant! All along
The sultry pavement, the old-clothes-man cries
In tone monotonous, and side-long views
The area for his traffic: now the bag 35
Is slyly opened, and the half-worn suit
(Sometimes the pilfered treasure of the base
Domestic spoiler[7]), for one half its worth,
Sinks in the green abyss. The porter now
Bears his huge load along the burning way; 40
And the poor poet wakes from busy dreams,
To paint the summer morning.

1794 1806

January, 1795

Pavement slippery, people sneezing,
Lords in ermine, beggars freezing;
Titled gluttons dainties carving,
Genius in a garret starving.

Lofty mansions, warm and spacious; 5
Courtiers cringing and voracious;[1]
Misers scarce the wretched heeding;
Gallant soldiers fighting, bleeding.

Wives who laugh at passive spouses;
Theatres, and meeting-houses; 10
Balls, where simpering misses languish;
Hospitals, and groans of anguish.

Arts and sciences bewailing;
Commerce drooping, credit failing;
Placemen[2] mocking subjects loyal; 15
Separations, weddings royal.

Authors who can't earn a dinner;
Many a subtle rogue a winner;
Fugitives for shelter seeking;
Misers hoarding, tradesmen breaking.[3] 20

Taste and talents quite deserted;
All the laws of truth perverted;
Arrogance o'er merit soaring;
Merit silently deploring.

Ladies gambling night and morning; 25
Fools the works of genius scorning;

6. A boy who carries beer to outside customers.
7. I.e., a thieving servant.
1. Greedy.

2. A disparaging term for those with appointed positions in
government.
3. I.e., "breaking" them financially by not paying them.

Ancient dames for girls mistaken,
Youthful damsels quite forsaken.

Some in luxury delighting;
More in talking than in fighting; 30
Lovers old, and beaux decrepit;
Lordlings empty and insipid.

Poets, painters, and musicians;
Lawyers, doctors, politicians;
Pamphlets, newspapers, and odes, 35
Seeking fame by different roads.

Gallant souls with empty purses,
Generals only fit for nurses;
School-boys, smit with martial spirit,
Taking place of veteran merit. 40

Honest men who can't get places,
Knaves who show unblushing faces;
Ruin hastened, peace retarded;
Candor spurned, and art[4] rewarded.

1795 1806

To the Poet Coleridge[1]

RAPT in the visionary theme!
 SPIRIT DIVINE! with THEE I'll wander,
Where the blue, wavy, lucid stream,
 'Mid forest glooms, shall slow meander!
With THEE I'll trace the circling bounds 5
 Of thy NEW PARADISE[2] extended;
And listen to the varying sounds
 Of winds, and foamy torrents blended.

Now by the source which laboring heaves
 The mystic fountain, bubbling, panting, 10
While gossamer its network weaves,
 Adown the blue lawn slanting
I'll mark thy *sunny dome*,[3] and view
Thy *Caves of Ice*, thy fields of dew!
Thy ever-blooming mead, whose flower 15
Waves to the cold breath of the moonlight hour![4]

4. I.e., craftiness, cunning.
1. Samuel Taylor Coleridge (1772–1834), poet and
critic, who, along with his friend William Wordsworth,
is most often linked with the beginnings of Romantic
poetry in England. Coleridge was strongly influenced
by German philosophy in his ideas of aesthetics and
the imaginative process.
2. Perhaps a reference to the last line of Coleridge's

Kubla Khan (written c. 1797–98; published 1816) as
well as to a construction of the poets' imaginations.
3. The speaker in *Kubla Khan* wishes he could build
with music "That sunny dome! those caves of ice!"
4. Two of Coleridge's best-known poems, *Frost at Midnight*
(1798) and *Dejection: A Ode* (1802), are set in moonlight.
"Mead": meadow.

Or when the day-star, peering bright
On the gray wing of parting night;
While more than vegetating power[5]
Throbs grateful to the burning hour, 20
As summer's whispered sighs unfold
Her million, million buds of gold;
Then will I climb the breezy bounds,
 Of thy NEW PARADISE extended,
And listen to the distant sounds 25
 Of winds, and foamy torrents blended!

SPIRIT DIVINE! with THEE I'll trace
Imagination's boundless space!
With thee, beneath thy *sunny dome,*
 I'll listen to the minstrel's lay, 30
 Hymning the gradual close of day;
In *Caves of Ice* enchanted roam,
Where on the glittering entrance plays
The moon's-beam with its silvery rays;
 Or, when glassy stream, 35
 That through the deep dell flows,
 Flashes the noon's hot beam;
 The noon's hot beam, that midway shows
Thy flaming Temple, studded o'er
With all PERUVIA's[6] lustrous store! 40
There will I trace the circling bounds
 Of thy NEW PARADISE extended!
And listen to the awful sounds,
 Of winds, and foamy torrents blended!

And now I'll pause to catch the moan 45
 Of distant breezes, cavern-pent;
Now, ere the twilight tints are flown,
Purpling the landscape, far and wide,
On the dark promontory's side
 I'll gather wild flowers, dew besprent, 50
And weave a crown for THEE,
GENIUS OF HEAVEN-TAUGHT POESY!
While, opening to my wondering eyes,
Thou bidst a new creation rise,
I'll raptured trace the circling bounds 55
 Of thy RICH PARADISE extended,
And listen to the varying sounds
 Of winds, and foaming torrents blended.

And now, with lofty tones inviting,
Thy nymph,[7] her dulcimer swift smiting, 60
Shall wake me in ecstatic measures!
Far, far removed from mortal pleasures!

5. Growing power, also with the sense of "the power that causes vegetation."
6. I.e., of Peru, whose chief mineral, copper, would make a building "flame."
7. The "damsel with a dulcimer" in the last stanza of *Kubla Khan.*

In cadence rich, in cadence strong,
Proving the wondrous witcheries of song!
 I hear her voice! thy *sunny dome*, 65
Thy *caves of ice*, loud repeat,
Vibrations, maddening sweet,
 Calling the visionary wanderer home.
She sings of THEE, O favored child
Of *Minstrelsy*, SUBLIMELY WILD![8] 70
Of thee, whose soul can feel the tone
Which gives to airy dreams *a magic* ALL THY OWN!

1797

8. Coleridge's description in *Kubla Khan* of a "deep roman-
tic chasm" provides a fine example of the late-18th-century
notion of the sublime: the grand and lofty—in nature associ-
ated with the fearful, wild, and violent—to which we re-
spond emotionally.

MARY WOLLSTONECRAFT
1759–1797

"It is time to effect a revolution in female manners—time to restore to them their lost dignity—and make them, as part of the human species, labor by reforming themselves, to reform the world": Mary Wollstonecraft's fervent radicalism extended from a critique of private property and political oppression to a protest against the subjection of women. Her most famous book, *A Vindication of the Rights of Woman* (1792), is a justification of women's rights and an attack against the wrongs inflicted on women, in which this author claims that women's manners have been corrupted by a culture that exalts feminine inferiority. Vanity, triviality, duplicity, and selfishness are the secondary characteristics of a creature, called female, who has been constructed to suit society. It is in this context that *A Vindication of the Rights of Woman* presents the first fully elaborated feminist criticism of misogynist images of women in literature as well as the first sustained argument for female political, economic, and legal equality. To be sure, a number of polemical tracts on the injustice of women's situation preceded Wollstonecraft's, with Catharine Macaulay's *Letters on Education*, which Wollstonecraft reviewed, published only two years earlier. But Wollstonecraft's impassioned plea against the miseducation of women constituted a groundbreaking demonstration of how the very protection offered women confines them to the vices and virtues of an inferior class and thereby inhibits both women and men from establishing their common humanity.

Wollstonecraft's own education seems to have been acquired in spite of the impoverishment and instability of her family, but the energy of her revolt against injustice was very much shaped by her struggle for independence from that family. The woman who would dedicate her philosophical inquiries to a protest against arbitrary tyranny found political impetus in the personal injustices she both witnessed and experienced. The second of five children, Wollstonecraft suffered from the brutality of her father and the submissiveness of her mother. Although Edward John Wollstonecraft inherited a fortune from his father, a weaver, he lost it in a succession of farming failures that led to drunken physical abuse of his wife. Wollstonecraft tried to protect her mother, sleeping on the landing outside her mother's room on more than one occasion; however, she was regarded or regarded herself as second to her older brother in her mother's affections. As the family

moved from London to Yorkshire to Wales, and back to London, Wollstonecraft suffered from the financial constraints that eventually led her father to use up most of the money settled on his daughters. To relieve him from debt and to extricate herself from his intolerable rule, she left home in 1778, at the age of nineteen, earning her living as a companion to a widow in Bath. Later, she would strive for her independence by opening a school and by becoming a governess. The school failed and the mother of her charges discharged her, but Wollstonecraft pursued her education, teaching herself both French and German, even as she sustained and was sustained by a succession of friendships.

In contrast to the violence she identified with her parents' marriage, friendships provided the bonds of affection in Wollstonecraft's life. At the age of eleven, in Beverley, for example, she wrote vivid letters to her best friend, Jane Arden, whom she would see again in Bath. She met her most cherished friend, Fanny Blood, in 1774, and their relationship flourished when, two years later, Wollstonecraft's father brought the family to Walworth. Two years older than Wollstonecraft, Fanny Blood lived in almost as difficult a home, with an improvident father and a patient mother who took in sewing to eke out a living for the family. When, in 1782, her mother died, Wollstonecraft, then twenty-three, joined the Blood family, where she sewed with Mrs. Blood and Fanny from sunrise to sunset.

During this same period, the two friends joined forces to rescue one of Wollstonecraft's younger sisters from a marriage she found intolerable: after giving birth to a child, Eliza Wollstonecraft Bishop suffered a severe emotional breakdown; Fanny Blood moved Eliza's belongings, while Mary Wollstonecraft removed Eliza from her husband and child. Whether the friends' audacious plan was heartless and foolhardy (the child died later that year) or redemptive and courageous (divorce was difficult for women to obtain), it illustrates Wollstonecraft's rebellious independence and her identification with women's suffering. Both traits are evident in her continued commitment to Fanny Blood. When, in 1785, Fanny Blood was pregnant in a foreign country, Wollstonecraft undertook the arduous voyage to Lisbon to be with her friend for the delivery. The despondency she experienced after the subsequent death of Fanny would haunt her for the rest of her life, although she continued to give financial support to her friend's relatives as well as to her own.

It was not until Wollstonecraft arrived in London in 1787 that she identified her ambitions with the profession of writing. Earlier, at her girls' school in Newington Green, she had benefited from the intellectual companionship of Richard Price, a famous liberal author of the period, and she had written *Thoughts on the Education of Daughters* on her return from Portugal. But under the auspices of Joseph Johnson, the mainstay of publishing associated with the revolutionary movements in France and America, she earned her living by writing essays for his *Analytic Review* and by translating Jacques Necker's *Of the Importance of Religious Opinions* (1788) and Christian Salzmann's *Elements of Morality* (1790). The appearances of her first novel, *Mary, a Fiction*; her children's book, *Original Stories*; and her no longer extant anthology, *The Female Reader*, in 1788 and 1789 were followed in 1790 by the instantaneous success of her *Vindication of the Rights of Men*. Wollstonecraft had clearly profited from the intellectual stimulation of Johnson's circle of acquaintances, men like the mystic poet William Blake, who illustrated the second edition of *Original Stories*; the physician Dr. George Fordyce, a fellow of the Royal Society; the revolutionary theorist Tom Paine; and the Romantic painter Henry Fuseli.

Although later readers of *A Vindication of the Rights of Men* have faulted the book as disorganized, and although it was obscured by the subsequent popularity of Tom Paine's *The Rights of Man* (1791–92), it was the first rebuttal of Edmund Burke's *Reflections on the Revolution in France* (1790). Wollstonecraft responded to Burke's eloquent attack on the French Revolution and his conservative idealiza-

tion of England by defending the radical principles of her friend Price and by analyzing the exploitation of the working class and the disproportionate privileges of the propertied class in England. Her next work, *A Vindication of the Rights of Woman*, can be read as a sequel to *A Vindication of the Rights of Men*, an extension of her enthusiastic response to the French Revolution. Written in six weeks, it was dedicated to the revolutionary French statesman Talleyrand to argue that the goals of liberty, equality, and fraternity would be undermined by the exclusion of women and their rights from programs for social reform. By the time she published her second *Vindication*, Wollstonecraft had joined the ranks of such professional literary women as Frances Burney and Hannah More. Indeed, she had exceeded them, for the philosophic breadth of her writing established links between radicalism, Romanticism, and feminism that would be of lasting importance.

Throughout her career, Wollstonecraft confronted the discrepancy between her revolutionary theories and the material realities they sought to address and redress. Nowhere is this more evident than in the tension between the ideal of male-female friendship in her polemical writing and the torment of romantic thralldom she suffered in her life. In spite of her growing reputation, after she had analyzed the destructiveness of romance in her second *Vindication*, Wollstonecraft left England when it became clear that she could not join the household of Fuseli, the married man she had begun to love. Escaping to France to witness the Revolution firsthand, she fell in love with an American, Gilbert Imlay, and was registered as his wife, to gain the protection of American citizenship. Yet she refused the legal claim of marriage. Imlay had been an officer in the American revolutionary army and had published a book about the Kentucky wilderness, but he was engaged in shady political and financial intrigues about which Wollstonecraft knew little or nothing. When he abandoned her in Paris under dangerous circumstances—with her baby daughter, Fanny, during the Reign of Terror—she wrote numerous letters lamenting his lack of feeling. When she returned to London from a trip through the Scandinavian countries, which he had arranged for her, she discovered his infidelity and tried to kill herself by throwing herself off Putney Bridge into the Thames. Astonishingly, however, she never stopped writing during this period, publishing *A Historical and Moral View of the Origins and Progress of the French Revolution* in 1794, the same year she gave birth to her daughter, and *Letters Written during a Short Residence in Sweden, Norway, and Denmark* in 1796, less than a year after her suicide attempt. Indeed, this book was constructed out of letters to Imlay, which were returned at her request.

The next year Wollstonecraft went to visit William Godwin. The already established philosopher and novelist had met her earlier at Johnson's, but now Godwin was looking for a lifelong companion. Their ideas and careers meshed, and in spite of their principles, they decided to legalize the relationship when Wollstonecraft became pregnant for the second time. Tragically however, their marriage lasted less than a year: Wollstonecraft died at thirty-six of puerperal fever, eleven days after she gave birth to Mary Wollstonecraft Godwin. The physicians, who may have caused blood poisoning in their efforts to remove the placenta, were hampered by the primitive state of medicine in this period. They could counteract the painful effects of Wollstonecraft's infection only with wine, of her lactation only with puppies brought in to draw the milk from her breasts. She had been unable to complete her last project, a novel titled *Maria; or, The Wrongs of Women*.

The gruesome irony of Wollstonecraft's personal tragedies when viewed from the perspective of her pioneering principles is also apparent in the use made of Godwin's laudatory *Memoirs of the Author of "A Vindication of the Rights of Woman"* (1798) and his edition of her *Posthumous Works* (1798), in which he reprinted her love letters to Imlay. The scandal that resulted caused Wollstonecraft to be castigated as a "hyena in petticoats" and a "philosophical wanton." It also effectively erased her philosophic achievement for more than a

century. Yet women from George Eliot to Ruth Benedict continued to be fasci-
nated by Wollstonecraft's life. The personal suffering that she dramatized in her
novels and the visionary reforms for which she called in her political writing are
twin aspects of what she saw as the injustice of a social system that defined women
as male property. While in A *Vindication of the Rights of Woman* she condemned
Milton, Pope, Chesterfield, and Rousseau for promulgating pernicious images of
women, she was equally contemptuous of the reading habits of women, whose ad-
diction to romance seemed to her to propagate only ignorance and further depen-
dency. In all these respects, Wollstonecraft became a foremother, not only for her
biological daughter Mary Wollstonecraft Godwin Shelley, who read her parents'
books while sitting by her mother's grave, but also for literary women from
Margaret Fuller and Florence Nightingale to Charlotte Perkins Gilman, Olive
Schreiner, Virginia Woolf, and Adrienne Rich, all of whom have extended the tra-
dition of feminist polemic she established.

From A Vindication of the Rights of Woman[1]

Introduction

After considering the historic page, and viewing the living world with anx-
ious solicitude, the most melancholy emotions of sorrowful indignation have
depressed my spirits, and I have sighed when obliged to confess, that either
nature has made a great difference between man and man, or that the civiliza-
tion which has hitherto taken place in the world has been very partial. I have
turned over various books written on the subject of education, and patiently
observed the conduct of parents and the management of schools; but what
has been the result?—a profound conviction that the neglected education of
my fellow-creatures is the grand source of the misery I deplore; and that
women, in particular, are rendered weak and wretched by a variety of concur-
ring causes, originating from one hasty conclusion. The conduct and manners
of women, in fact, evidently prove that their minds are not in a healthy state;
for, like the flowers which are planted in too rich a soil, strength and usefulness
are sacrificed to beauty; and the flaunting leaves, after having pleased a fastid-
ious eye, fade, disregarded on the stalk, long before the season when they
ought to have arrived at maturity.—One cause of this barren blooming I at-
tribute to a false system of education, gathered from the books written on this
subject by men who, considering females rather as women than human crea-
tures, have been more anxious to make them alluring mistresses than affec-
tionate wives and rational mothers; and the understanding of the sex has been
so bubbled[2] by this specious homage, that the civilized women of the present
century, with a few exceptions, are only anxious to inspire love, when they
ought to cherish a nobler ambition, and by their abilities and virtues exact
respect.

In a treatise, therefore, on female rights and manners, the works which have
been particularly written for their improvement must not be overlooked; es-
pecially when it is asserted, in direct terms, that the minds of women are en-
feebled by false refinement; that the books of instruction, written by men of
genius, have had the same tendency as more frivolous productions; and that,

1. The text is from the second revised edition of 1792, as edited by Carol H. Poston from the Norton Critical Edition of A *Vindication* (1975). The editors gratefully acknowledge Poston's permission to make use of the information in her annotations.
2. Deceived by "bubbles," i.e., insubstantial fictions.

in true style of Mahometanism, they are treated as a kind of subordinate beings, and not as a part of the human species, when improveable reason is allowed to be the dignified distinction which raises men above the brute creation, and puts a natural sceptre in a feeble hand.

Yet because I am a woman, I would not lead my readers to suppose that I mean violently to agitate the contested question respecting the equality or inferiority of the sex; but as the subject lies in my way, and I cannot pass it over without subjecting the main tendency of my reasoning to misconstruction, I shall stop a moment to deliver, in a few words, my opinion.—In the government of the physical world it is observable that the female in point of strength is, in general, inferior to the male. This is the law of nature; and it does not appear to be suspended or abrogated in favor of women. A degree of physical superiority cannot, therefore, be denied—and it is a noble prerogative! But not content with this natural pre-eminence, men endeavor to sink us still lower, merely to render us alluring objects for a moment; and women, intoxicated by the adoration which men, under the influence of their senses, pay them, do not seek to obtain a durable interest in their hearts, or to become the friends of the low creatures who find amusement in their society.

I am aware of an obvious inference:—from every quarter have I heard exclamations against masculine women; but where are they to be found? If by this appellation men mean to inveigh against their ardor in hunting, shooting, and gaming, I shall most cordially join in the cry; but if it be against the imitation of manly virtues, or, more properly speaking, the attainment of those talents and virtues, the exercise of which ennobles the human character, and which raise females in the scale of animal being, when they are comprehensively termed mankind;—all those who view them with a philosophic eye must, I should think, wish with me, that they may every day grow more and more masculine.

This discussion naturally divides the subject. I shall first consider women in the grand light of human creatures, who, in common with men, are placed on this earth to unfold their faculties; and afterwards I shall more particularly point out their peculiar designation.

I wish also to steer clear of an error which many respectable writers have fallen into; for the instruction which has hitherto been addressed to women, has rather been applicable to *ladies*, if the little indirect advice, that is scattered through Sandford and Merton,[4] be excepted; but, addressing my sex in a firmer tone, I pay particular attention to those in the middle class, because they appear to be in the most natural state.[5] Perhaps the seeds of false-refinement, immorality, and vanity, have ever been shed by the great. Weak, artificial being, raised above the common wants and affections of their race, in a premature unnatural manner, undermine the very foundation of virtue, and spread corruption through the whole mass of society! As a class of mankind they have the strongest claim to pity; the education of the rich tends to render them vain and helpless, and the unfolding mind is not strengthened by the practice of those duties which dignify the human character.—They only live

3. Europeans commonly though mistakenly assumed that the Koran, the sacred text of Muslims, teaches that women have no souls.
4. The popular children's story *The History of Sandford and Merton*, by Thomas Day, was published in three volumes (1786–89). The tutor in it frequently cites the moral superiority of Harry Sandford, son of a poor farmer, over Tommy Merton, the son of a rich family.
5. The middle class is here considered more "natural" than the rich because uncorrupted by titles, property, and wealth.

to amuse themselves, and by the same law which in nature invariably produces certain effects, they soon only afford barren amusement.

But as I purpose taking a separate view of the different ranks of society and of the moral character of women, in each, this hint is, for the present, sufficient; and I have only alluded to the subject, because it appears to me to be the very essence of an introduction to give a cursory account of the contents of the work it introduces.

My own sex, I hope, will excuse me, if I treat them like rational creatures instead of flattering their *fascinating* graces, and viewing them as if they were in a state of perpetual childhood, unable to stand alone. I earnestly wish to point out in what true dignity and human happiness consists—I wish to persuade women to endeavor to acquire strength, both of mind and body, and convince them that the soft phrases, susceptibility of heart, delicacy of sentiment, and refinement of taste, are almost synonymous with epithets of weakness, and that those beings who are only the objects of pity and that kind of love, which has been termed its sister, will soon become objects of contempt.

Dismissing then those pretty feminine phrases, which the men condescendingly use to soften our slavish dependence, and despising that weak elegancy of mind, exquisite sensibility, and sweet docility of manners, supposed to be the sexual characteristics of the weaker vessel, I wish to shew that elegance is inferior to virtue, that the first object of laudable ambition is to obtain a character as a human being, regardless of the distinction of sex; and that secondary views should be brought to this simple touchstone.

This is a rough sketch of my plan; and should I express my conviction with the energetic emotions that I feel whenever I think of the subject, the dictates of experience and reflection will be felt by some of my readers. Animated by this important object, I shall disdain to cull[6] my phrases or polish my style;—I aim at being useful, and sincerity will render me unaffected; for wishing rather to persuade by the force of my arguments, than dazzle by the elegance of my language, I shall not waste my time in rounding periods,[7] or in fabricating the turgid bombast of artificial feelings, which, coming from the head, never reach the heart.—I shall be employed about things, not words!—and, anxious to render my sex more respectable members of society, I shall try to avoid that flowery diction which has slided from essays into novels, and from novels into familiar letters and conversation.

These pretty superlatives, dropping glibly from the tongue, vitiate the taste, and create a kind of sickly delicacy that turns away from simple unadorned truth, and a deluge of false sentiments and overstretched feelings, stifling the natural emotions of the heart, render the domestic pleasures insipid, that ought to sweeten the exercise of those severe duties, which educate a rational and immortal being for a nobler field of action.

The education of women has, of late, been more attended to than formerly; yet they are still reckoned a frivolous sex, and ridiculed or pitied by the writers who endeavor by satire or instruction to improve them. It is acknowledged that they spend many of the first years of their lives in acquiring a smattering of accomplishments; meanwhile strength of body and mind are sacrificed to

6. Be selective in.
7. A formal sentence made up of balanced clauses; i.e., in rounding out elaborate sentences.

From *Chapter II*

THE PREVAILING OPINION OF A SEXUAL CHARACTER DISCUSSED

To account for, and excuse the tyranny of man, many ingenious arguments have been brought forward to prove, that the two sexes, in the acquirement of virtue, ought to aim at attaining a very different character: or, to speak explic-itly, to establish notions of beauty, to the desire of establishing themselves—the only way women can rise in the world—by marriage. And this desire making mere animals of them, when they marry they act as such children may be expected to act:—they dress; they paint, and nickname God's creatures.[8]—Surely these weak beings are only fit for a seraglio![9]—Can they be expected to govern a family with judgment, or take care of the poor babes whom they bring into the world?

If then it can be fairly deduced from the present conduct of the sex, from the prevalent fondness for pleasure which takes place of ambition and those nobler passions that open and enlarge the soul; that the instruction which women have hitherto received has only tended, with the constitution of civil society, to render them insignificant objects of desire—mere propagators of fools!—if it can be proved that in aiming to accomplish them, without culti-vating their understandings, they are taken out of their sphere of duties, and made ridiculous and useless when the short-lived bloom of beauty is over,[1] I presume that *rational* men will excuse me for endeavouring to persuade them to become more masculine and respectable.

Indeed the word masculine is only a bugbear:[2] there is little reason to fear that women will acquire too much courage or fortitude; for their apparent in-feriority with respect to bodily strength, must render them, in some degree, dependent on men in the various relations of life; but why should it be in-creased by prejudices that give a sex to virtue, and confound simple truths with sensual reveries?

Women are, in fact, so much degraded by mistaken notions of female ex-cellence, that I do not mean to add a paradox when I assert, that this artificial weakness produces a propensity to tyrannize, and gives birth to cunning, the natural opponent of strength, which leads them to play off those con-temptible infantine airs that undermine esteem even whilst they excite desire. Let men become more chaste and modest, and if women do not grow wiser in the same ratio, it will be clear that they have weaker understandings. It seems scarcely necessary to say, that I now speak of the sex in general. Many individ-uals have more sense than their male relatives; and, as nothing preponderates where there is a constant struggle for an equilibrium, without it has naturally more gravity, some women govern their husbands without degrading them-selves, because intellect will always govern.

1. "A lively writer, I cannot recollect his name, asks what business women turned of forty have to do in the world?" [Wollstonecraft's note]. In her edition of the *Vindication*, Poston suggests that the passage may be from Frances Burney's *Evelina* (1778), a novel in which a licentious rake exclaims, "I don't know what the devil a woman lives for after thirty: she is only in other folks' way."
2. An object of dread.
3. Useless.
8. Hamlet accuses Ophelia of "female" faults: "You jig, you amble, and you lisp; you nickname God's crea-tures and make your wantonness your ignorance" (*Hamlet* 3.1.150).
9. Harem, the women's quarters in a Muslim palace.

itly, women are not allowed to have sufficient strength of mind to acquire what really deserves the name of virtue. Yet it should seem, allowing them to have souls, that there is but one way appointed by Providence to lead *mankind* to either virtue or happiness.

If then women are not a swarm of ephemeron[4] triflers, why should they be kept in ignorance under the specious name of innocence? Men complain, and with reason, of the follies and caprices of our sex, when they do not keenly satirize our headstrong passions and groveling vices.—Behold, I should answer, the natural effect of ignorance! The mind will ever be unstable that has only prejudices to rest on, and the current will run with destructive fury when there are no barriers to break its force. Women are told from their infancy, and taught by the example of their mothers, that a little knowledge of human weakness, justly termed cunning, softness of temper, *outward* obedience, and a scrupulous attention to a puerile kind of propriety, will obtain for them the protection of man; and should they be beautiful, everything else is needless, for, at least, twenty years of their lives.

Thus Milton describes our first frail mother; though when he tells us that women are formed for softness and sweet attractive grace,[5] I cannot comprehend his meaning, unless, in the true Mahometan strain, he meant to deprive us of souls and insinuate that we were beings only designed by sweet attractive grace, and docile blind obedience, to gratify the senses of man when he can no longer soar on the wing of contemplation.

How grossly do they insult us who thus advise us only to render ourselves gentle, domestic brutes![6] For instance, the winning softness so warmly, and frequently, recommended, that governs by obeying. What childish expressions, and how insignificant is the being—can it be an immortal one! who will condescend to govern by such sinister methods! "Certainly," says Lord Bacon, "man is of kin to the beasts by his body; and if he be not of kin to God by his spirit, he is a base and ignoble creature!"[7] Men, indeed, appear to me to act in a very unphilosophical manner when they try to secure the good conduct of women by attempting to keep them always in a state of childhood. Rousseau[8] was more consistent when he wished to stop the progress of reason in both sexes, for if men eat of the tree of knowledge, women will come in for a taste but, from the imperfect cultivation which their understandings now receive, they only attain a knowledge of evil.

Children, I grant, should be innocent; but when the epithet is applied to men, or women, it is but a civil[9] term for weakness. For if it be allowed that women were destined by Providence to acquire human virtues, and by the exercise of their understandings, that stability of character which is the firmest ground to rest our future hopes upon, they must be permitted to turn to the fountain of light, and not forced to shape their course by the twinkling of a mere satellite.[1] Milton, I grant, was of a very different opinion; for he only bends to the indefeasible right of beauty, though it would be difficult to ren-

4. A flying insect that lives only one day.

5. Milton's, *Paradise Lost* 4.297–99. "For contemplation he and valor form'd, / For softness she and sweet attractive grace; / He for God only, she for God in him."

6. Purely physical beings, lacking reason and intelligence.

7. Francis Bacon's *Of Atheism* (1597).

8. Jean-Jacques Rousseau (1712–1778), who advocated intuition and instinct over rationality. His views on the education of women, alluded to throughout Wollstonecraft's treatise, are set forth in *Émile* (1762), especially in Book 5: *Sophy; or, Woman.*

9. Polite; euphemistic.

1. Any body that orbits a larger body.

der two passages which I now mean to contrast, consistent. But into similar in-consistencies are great men often led by their senses.

> To whom thus Eve with *perfect beauty* adorned.
> My Author and Disposer, what thou bidst
> *Unargued* I obey; So God ordains;
> God is thy *law*, thou *mine*:—to know no more
> Is Woman's *happiest* knowledge and her *praise*.[2]

These are exactly the arguments that I have used to children; but I have added, your reason is now gaining strength, and, till it arrives at some degree of maturity, you must look up to me for advice—then you ought to *think*, and only rely on God.

Yet in the following lines Milton seems to coincide with me; when he makes Adam thus expostulate with his Maker.

> Hast thou not made me here thy substitute,
> And these inferior far beneath me set?
> Among *unequals* what society
> Can sort, what harmony or true delight?
> Which must be mutual, in proportion due
> Giv'n and *received*; but in *disparity*
> The one intense, the other still remiss
> Cannot well suit with either, but soon prove
> Tedious alike: of *fellowship* I speak
> Such as I seek, fit to participate
> All rational delight—[3]

In treating, therefore, of the manners of women, let us, disregarding sensual arguments, trace what we should endeavor to make them in order to co-oper-ate, if the expression be not too bold, with the supreme Being.

By individual education, I mean, for the sense of the word is not precisely defined, such an attention to a child as will slowly sharpen the senses, form the temper,[4] regulate the passions as they begin to ferment, and set the understanding to work before the body arrives at maturity; so that the man may only have to proceed, not to begin, the important task of learning to think and reason.

To prevent any misconstruction, I must add, that I do not believe that a private education can work the wonders which some sanguine writers have attributed to it. Men and women must be educated, in a great degree, by the opinions and manners of the society they live in. In every age there has been a stream of popular opinion that has carried all before it, and given a family character, as it were, to the century. It may then fairly be inferred, that, till society be differently constituted, much cannot be expected from education It is, however, sufficient for my present purpose to assert, that, whatever effect circumstances have on the abilities, every being may become virtuous by the exercise of its own reason; for if but one being was created with vicious incli-nations, that is positively bad, what can save us from atheism? or if we worship a god, is not that god a devil?

2. *Paradise Lost* 4.634–38 (Wollstonecraft's italics). 4. Temperament, character.
3. *Paradise Lost* 7.331–92 (Wollstonecraft's italics).

Consequently, the most perfect education, in my opinion, is such an exercise of the understanding as is best calculated to strengthen the body and form the heart. Or, in other words, to enable the individual to attain such habits of virtue as will render it independent. In fact, it is a farce to call any being virtuous whose virtues do not result from the exercise of its own reason. This was Rousseau's opinion respecting men: I extend it to women, and confidently assert that they have been drawn out of their sphere by false refinement, and not by an endeavor to acquire masculine qualities. Still the regal homage which they receive is so intoxicating, that till the manners of the times are changed, and formed on more reasonable principles, it may be impossible to convince them that the illegitimate power, which they obtain, by degrading themselves, is a curse, and that they must return to nature and equality, if they wish to secure the placid satisfaction that unsophisticated affections impart. But for this epoch we must wait—wait, perhaps, till kings and nobles, enlightened by reason, and, preferring the real dignity of man to childish state[5] throw off their gaudy hereditary trappings: and if then women do not resign the arbitrary power of beauty—they will prove that they have *less* mind than man.

I may be accused of arrogance; still I must declare what I firmly believe, that all the writers who have written on the subject of female education and manners from Rousseau to Dr. Gregory,[6] have contributed to render women more artificial, weak characters, than they would otherwise have been, and, consequently, more useless members of society. I might have expressed this conviction in a lower key; but I am afraid it would have been the whine of affectation, and not the faithful expression of my feelings, of the clear result, which experience and reflection have led me to draw. When I come to that division of the subject, I shall advert to the passages that I more particularly disapprove of, in the works of the authors I have just alluded to; but it is first necessary to observe, that my objection extends to the whole purport of those books, which tend, in my opinion, to degrade one half of the human species, and render women pleasing at the expense of every solid virtue.

Though, to reason on Rousseau's ground, if man did attain a degree of perfection of mind when his body arrived at maturity, it might be proper, in order to make a man and his wife *one*, that she should rely entirely on his understanding: and the graceful ivy, clasping the oak that supported it, would form a whole in which strength and beauty would be equally conspicuous. But, alas! husbands, as well as their helpmates, are often only overgrown children: nay, thanks to early debauchery, scarcely men in their outward form—and if the blind lead the blind, one need not come from heaven to tell us the consequence.

Many are the causes that, in the present corrupt state of society, contribute to enslave women by cramping their understandings and sharpening their senses. One, perhaps, that silently does more mischief than all the rest, is their disregard of order.

To do everything in an orderly manner, is a most important precept, which women, who, generally speaking, receive only a disorderly kind of education, seldom attend to with that degree of exactness that men, who from their in-

5. Pomp, rich display.
6. John Gregory (1724–1773), author of a popular

book on the education of women, *A Father's Legacy to His Daughters* (1774).

fancy are broken into method, observe. This negligent kind of guess-work, for what other epithet can be used to point out the random exertions of a sort of instinctive common sense, never brought to the test of reason* prevents their generalizing matters of fact—so they do today, what they did yesterday, merely because they did it yesterday.

This contempt of the understanding in early life has more baneful consequences than is commonly supposed; for the little knowledge which women of strong minds attain, is, from various circumstances, of a more desultory kind than the knowledge of men, and it is acquired more by sheer observations on real life, than from comparing what has been individually observed with the results of experience generalized by speculation. Led by their dependent situation and domestic employments more into society, what they learn is rather by snatches; and as learning is with them, in general, only a secondary thing, they do not pursue any one branch with that persevering ardor necessary to give vigor to the faculties, and clearness to the judgment. In the present state of society, a little learning is required to support the character of a gentleman; and boys are obliged to submit to a few years of discipline. But in the education of women, the cultivation of the understanding is always subordinate to the acquirement of some corporeal accomplishment: even while enervated by confinement and false notions of modesty, the body is prevented from attaining that grace and beauty which relaxed half-formed limbs never exhibit. Besides, in youth their faculties are not brought forward by emulation; and having no serious scientific study, if they have natural sagacity it is turned too soon on life and manners. They dwell on effects, and modifications, without tracing them back to causes; and complicated rules to adjust behavior are a weak substitute for simple principles.

As a proof that education gives this appearance of weakness to females, we may instance the example of military men, who are, like them, sent into the world before their minds have been stored with knowledge or fortified by principles. The consequences are similar; soldiers acquire a little superficial knowledge, snatched from the muddy current of conversation, and, from continually mixing with society, they gain, what is termed a knowledge of the world; and this acquaintance with manners and customs has frequently been confounded with a knowledge of the human heart. But can the crude fruit of casual observation, never brought to the test of judgment, formed by comparing speculation and experience, deserve such a distinction? Soldiers, as well as women, practice the minor virtues with punctilious politeness. Where is then the sexual difference, when the education has been the same? All the difference that I can discern, arises from the superior advantage of liberty, which enables the former to see more of life.

* * *

Probably the prevailing opinion, that woman was created for man, may have taken its rise from Moses's poetical story;[7] yet, as very few, it is presumed, who have bestowed any serious thought on the subject, ever supposed that Eve was, literally speaking, one of Adam's ribs, the deduction must be allowed to fall to the ground; or, only be so far admitted as it proves that man, from the

7. Until the 19th century, Moses was believed to have written the first five books of the Bible. The reference is to the story of Eve's creation from one of the ribs of Adam (Genesis 2:21–22).

remotest antiquity, found it convenient to exert his strength to subjugate his companion, and his invention to shew that she ought to have her neck bent under the yoke, because the whole creation was only created for his convenience or pleasure.

Let it not be concluded that I wish to invert the order of things; I have already granted, that, from the constitution of their bodies, men seem to be designed by Providence to attain a greater degree of virtue.[8] I speak collectively of the whole sex; but I see not the shadow of a reason to conclude that their virtues should differ in respect to their nature. In fact, how can they, if virtue has only one eternal standard? I must therefore, if I reason consequentially, as strenuously maintain that they have the same simple direction, as that there is a God.

It follows then that cunning should not be opposed to wisdom, little cares to great exertions, or insipid softness, varnished over with the name of gentleness, to that fortitude which grand views alone can inspire.

I shall be told that woman would then lose many of her peculiar graces, and the opinion of a well known poet might be quoted to refute my unqualified assertion. For Pope has said, in the name of the whole male sex,

> Yet ne'er so sure our passion to create,
> As when she touched the brink of all we hate.[9]

In what light this sally places men and women, I shall leave to the judicious to determine: meanwhile I shall content myself with observing, that I cannot discover why, unless[1] they are mortal, females should always be degraded by being made subservient to love or lust.

To speak disrespectfully of love is, I know, high treason against sentiment and fine feelings; but I wish to speak the simple language of truth, and rather to address the head than the heart. To endeavor to reason love out of the world, would be to out Quixote Cervantes,[2] and equally offend against common sense; but an endeavor to restrain this tumultuous passion, and to prove that it should not be allowed to dethrone superior powers, or to usurp the sceptre which the understanding should ever coolly wield, appears less wild.

Youth is the season for love in both sexes; but in those days of thoughtless enjoyment provision should be made for the more important years of life, when reflection takes place of sensation. But Rousseau, and most of the male writers who have followed his steps, have warmly inculcated that the whole tendency of female education ought to be directed to one point:—to render them pleasing.

Let me reason with the supporters of this opinion who have any knowledge of human nature, do they imagine that marriage can eradicate the habitude of life? The woman who has only been taught to please will soon find that her charms are oblique sun-beams, and that they cannot have much effect on her husband's heart when they are seen every day, when the summer is passed and gone. Will she then have sufficient native energy to look into herself for comfort, and cultivate her dormant faculties? or, is it not more rational to expect

8. I.e., men have more passions and greater physical strength than women and must, therefore, exercise greater restraint.
9. Alexander Pope's *Moral Essays II, Of the Characters of Women*, (1735), lines 51–52.

1. Except.
2. I.e., to outdo the hero of Cervantes's *Don Quixote* (1605) in attempting the impossible.

that she will try to please other men; and, in the emotions raised by the expectation of new conquests, endeavor to forget the mortification her love or pride has received? When the husband ceases to be a lover—and the time will inevitably come, her desire of pleasing will then grow languid, or become a spring of bitterness; and love, perhaps, the most evanescent of all passions, gives place to jealousy or vanity.

I now speak of women who are restrained by principle or prejudice; such women, though they would shrink from an intrigue[3] with real abhorrence, yet, nevertheless, wish to be convinced by the homage of gallantry that they are cruelly neglected by their husbands; or, days and weeks are spent in dreaming of the happiness enjoyed by congenial souls till their health is undermined and their spirits broken by discontent. How then can the great art of pleasing be such a necessary study? It is only useful to a mistress; the chaste wife, and serious mother, should only consider her power to please as the polish of her virtues, and the affection of her husband as one of the comforts that render her task less difficult and her life happier.—But, whether she be loved or neglected, her first wish should be to make herself respectable[4] and not to rely for all her happiness on a being subject to like infirmities with herself.

The worthy Dr. Gregory fell into a similar error. I respect his heart; but entirely disapprove of his celebrated *Legacy to His Daughters.*

He advises them to cultivate a fondness for dress, because a fondness for dress, he asserts, is natural to them. I am unable to comprehend what either he or Rousseau mean, when they frequently use this indefinite term.[5] If they told us that in a pre-existent state the soul was fond of dress, and brought this inclination with it into a new body, I should listen to them with a half smile, as I often do when I hear a rant about innate elegance.—But if he only meant to say that the exercise of the faculties will produce this fondness—I deny it—It is not natural, but arises, like false ambition in men, from a love of power.

Dr. Gregory goes much further; he actually recommends dissimulation, and advises an innocent girl to give the lie to her feelings, and not dance with spirit, when gaiety of heart would make her feet eloquent without making her gestures immodest. In the name of truth and common sense, why should not one woman acknowledge that she can take more exercise than another? or, in other words, that she has a sound constitution; and why to damp innocent vivacity, is she darkly to be told that men will draw conclusions which she little thinks of?[6]—Let the libertine draw what inference he pleases; but, I hope, that no sensible mother will restrain the natural frankness of youth by instilling such indecent cautions. Out of the abundance of the heart the mouth speaketh;[7] and a wiser than Solomon hath said, that the heart should be made clean,[8] and not trivial ceremonies observed, which it is not very difficult to fulfill with scrupulous exactness when vice reigns in the heart.

Women ought to endeavor to purify their heart; but can they do so when their uncultivated understandings make them entirely dependent on their

3. An extramarital affair.
4. I.e., morally worthy of respect.
5. I.e., natural.
6. Gregory, in *A Father's Legacy to His Daughters,* writes: "I would have you to dance with spirit; but never allow yourselves to be so far transported with mirth, as to forget the delicacy of your sex.—Many a girl dancing in the gaiety and innocence of her heart, is thought to discover [reveal] a spirit she little dreams of."
7. Matthew 12:34.
8. Psalm 24:3–4: 'Who shall ascend into the hill of the Lord? or who shall stand in his holy place? He that hath clean hands, and a pure heart." The psalm is attributed to David, the "wiser than Solomon."

senses for employment and amusement, when no noble pursuit sets them above the little vanities of the day, or enables them to curb the wild emotions that agitate a reed over which every passing breeze has power? To gain the affections of a virtuous man is affectation necessary? Nature has given woman a weaker frame[9] than man; but, to ensure her husband's affections, must a wife, who by the exercise of her mind and body whilst she was discharging the duties of a daughter, wife, and mother, has allowed her constitution to retain its natural strength, and her nerves a healthy tone, is she, I say, to condescend to use art[1] and feign a sickly delicacy in order to secure her husband's affection? Weakness may excite tenderness, and gratify the arrogant pride of man; but the lordly caresses of a protector will not gratify a noble mind that pants for, and deserves to be respected. Fondness is a poor substitute for friendship!

In a seraglio, I grant, that all these arts are necessary; the epicure[2] must have his palate tickled, or he will sink into apathy, but have women so little ambition as to be satisfied with such a condition? Can they supinely dream life away in the lap of pleasure, or the languor of weariness, rather than assert their claim to pursue reasonable pleasures and render themselves conspicuous by practising the virtues which dignify mankind? Surely she has not an immortal soul who can loiter life away merely employed to adorn her person, that she may amuse the languid hours, and soften the cares of a fellow-creature who is willing to be enlivened by her smiles and tricks, when the serious business of life is over.

Besides, the woman who strengthens her body and exercises her mind will, by managing her family and practicing various virtues, become the friend, and not the humble dependent of her husband; and if she, by possessing such substantial qualities, merit his regard, she will not find it necessary to conceal her affection, nor to pretend to an unnatural coldness of constitution to excite her husband's passions. In fact, if we revert to history, we shall find that the women who have distinguished themselves have neither been the most beautiful nor the most gentle[3] of their sex.

Nature, or, to speak with strict propriety, God, has made all things right; but man has sought him out many inventions to mar the work. I now allude to that part of Dr. Gregory's treatise, where he advises a wife never to let her husband know the extent of her sensibility or affection. Voluptuous precaution, and as ineffectual as absurd.—Love, from its very nature, must be transitory. To seek for a secret that would render it constant, would be as wild a search as for the philosopher's stone, or the grand panacea[4] and the discovery would be equally useless, or rather pernicious to mankind. The most holy band of society is friendship. It has been well said, by a shrewd satirist, "that rare as true love is, true friendship is still rarer."[5]

This is an obvious truth, and the cause not lying deep, will not elude a slight glance of inquiry.

Love, the common passion,[6] in which chance and sensation take place of choice and reason, is, in some degree, felt by the mass of mankind; for it is not

9. Body.
1. Artifice, deceit.
2. In this sense, a person devoted to sensual pleasure; here, the sultan catered to sexually by his harem ("seraglio").
3. Genteel, refined.

4. A medicine reputed to cure all illness. "Philosopher's stone": substance that alchemists believed could transform base matter into gold.
5. Maxim 473 of de La Rochefoucauld (1613–1680), great French epigrammist.
6. Emotion.

necessary to speak, at present, of the emotions that rise above or sink below love. This passion, naturally increased by suspense and difficulties, draws the mind out of its accustomed state, and exalts the affections; but the security of marriage. allowing the fever of love to subside, a healthy temperature is thought insipid, only by those who have not sufficient intellect to substitute the calm tenderness of friendship, the confidence of respect instead of blind admiration, and the sensual emotions of fondness.

This is, must be, the course of nature.—Friendship or indifference inevitably succeeds love.—And this constitution seems perfectly to harmonize with the system of government which prevails in the moral world. Passions are spurs to action, and open the mind; but they sink into mere appetites, become a personal and momentary gratification, when the object is gained, and the satisfied mind rests in enjoyment. The man who had some virtue whilst he was struggling for a crown, often becomes a voluptuous tyrant when it graces his brow; and, when the lover is not lost in the husband, the dotard, a prey to childish caprices, and fond jealousies, neglects the serious duties of life, and the caresses which should excite confidence in his children are lavished on the overgrown child, his wife.

In order to fulfill the duties of life, and to be able to pursue with vigor the various employments which form the moral character, a master and mistress of a family ought not to continue to love each other with passion. I mean to say, that they ought not to indulge those emotions which disturb the order of society, and engross the thoughts that should be otherwise employed. The mind that has never been engrossed by one object wants[7] vigor—if it can long be so, it is weak.

A mistaken education, a narrow, uncultivated mind, and many sexual prejudices, tend to make women more constant than men; but, for the present, I shall not touch on this branch of the subject. I will go still further, and advance, without dreaming of a paradox, that an unhappy marriage is often very advantageous to a family, and that the neglected wife is, in general, the best mother.[8] And this would almost always be the consequence if the female mind were more enlarged: for, it seems to be the common dispensation of Providence, that what we gain in present enjoyment should be deducted from the treasure of life, experience; and that when we are gathering the flowers of the day and revelling in pleasure, the solid fruit of toil and wisdom should not be caught at the same time. The way lies before us, we must turn to the right or left; and he who will pass life away in bounding from one pleasure to another, must not complain if he acquire neither wisdom nor respectability of character.

Supposing, for a moment, that the soul is not immortal, and that man was only created for the present scene,—I think we should have reason to complain that love, infantine fondness, ever grew insipid and palled upon the sense. Let us eat, drink, and love, for tomorrow we die, would be, in fact, the language of reason, the morality of life; and who but a fool would part with a reality for a fleeting shadow? But, if awed by observing the improbable[9] powers of the mind, we disdain to confine our wishes or thoughts to such a compara-

7. Lacks.

8. Wollstonecraft sounds somewhat more cynical about married love here than she really is; she simply means that a woman not completely preoccupied with her husband has more time and energy for her children.

9. Poston suggests that this is a misprint in the second edition for "improbable," i.e., unknowable.

tively mean field of action; that only appears grand and important, as it is connected with a boundless prospect and sublime hopes, what necessity is there for falsehood in conduct, and why must the sacred majesty of truth be violated to detain a deceitful good that saps the very foundation of virtue? Why must the female mind be tainted by coquetish arts to gratify the sensualist, and prevent love from subsiding into friendship, or compassionate tenderness, when there are not qualities on which friendship can be built? Let the honest heart shew itself, and *reason* teach passion to submit to necessity; or, let the dignified, pursuit of virtue and knowledge raise the mind above those emotions which rather embitter than sweeten the cup of life, when they are not restrained within due bounds.

I do not mean to allude to the romantic passion,[1] which is the concomitant of genius.—Who can clip its wing? But that grand passion not proportioned to the puny enjoyments of life, is only true to the sentiment, and feeds on itself. The passions which have been celebrated for their durability have always been unfortunate. They have acquired strength by absence and constitutional melancholy.—The fancy[2] has hovered round a form of beauty dimly seen— but familiarity might have turned admiration into disgust; or, at least, into indifference, and allowed the imagination leisure to start fresh game. With perfect propriety, according to this view of things, does Rousseau make the mistress of his soul, Eloisa, love St. Preux when life was fading before her;[3] but this is no proof of the immortality of the passion.

Of the same complexion is Dr. Gregory's advice respecting delicacy of sentiment, which he advises a woman not to acquire, if she have determined to marry. This determination, however, perfectly consistent with his former advice, he calls *indelicate*, and earnestly persuades his daughters to conceal it, though it may govern their conduct;—as if it were indelicate to have the common appetites of human nature.

Noble morality! and consistent with the cautious prudence of a little soul that cannot extend its views beyond the present minute division of existence. If all the faculties of woman's mind are only to be cultivated as they respect her dependence on man; if, when a husband be obtained, she have arrived at her goal, and meanly proud rests satisfied with such a paltry crown, let her grovel contentedly, scarcely raised by her employments above the animal kingdom; but, if, struggling for the prize of her high calling, she look beyond the present scene, let her cultivate her understanding without stopping to consider what character the husband may have whom she is destined to marry. Let her only determine, without being too anxious about present happiness, to acquire the qualities that ennoble a rational being, and a rough inelegant husband may shock her taste without destroying her peace of mind. She will not model her soul to suit the frailties of her companion, but to bear with them: his character may be a trial, but not an impediment to virtue.

If Dr. Gregory confined his remark to romantic expectations of constant love and congenial feelings, he should have recollected that experience will banish what advice can never make us cease to wish for, when the imagination is kept alive at the expense of reason.

1. I.e., the creative imagination.
2. The imagination.
3. In Rousseau's novel *Julie; ou, La Nouvelle Héloise* (1761), Julie reveals on her deathbed to her husband, Wolmar, that her real, passionate love is for her former lover St. Preux. Julie or "Eloisa" was thought to represent a woman with whom Rousseau was in love at the time.

I own it frequently happens that women who have fostered a romantic un-natural delicacy of feeling, waste their[4] lives in *imagining* how happy they should have been with a husband who could love them with a fervid increasing affection every day, and all day. But they might as well pine married as single—and would not be a jot more unhappy with a bad husband than longing for a good one. That a proper education; or, to speak with more precision, a well stored mind, would enable a woman to support a single life with dignity, I grant; but that she should avoid cultivating her taste, lest her husband should occasionally shock it, is quitting a substance for a shadow. To say the truth, I do not know of what use is an improved taste, if the individual be not rendered more independent of the casualties of life; if new sources of enjoyment, only dependent on the solitary operations of the mind, are not opened. People of taste, married or single, without distinction, will ever be disgusted by various things that touch not less observing minds. On this conclusion the argument must not be allowed to hinge; but in the whole sum of enjoyment is taste to be denominated a blessing?

The question is, whether it procures most pain or pleasure? The answer will decide the propriety of Dr. Gregory's advice, and shew how absurd and tyrannic it is thus to lay down a system of slavery; or to attempt to educate moral beings by any other rules than those deduced from pure reason, which apply to the whole species.

Gentleness of manners, forbearance and long-suffering, are such amiable Godlike qualities, that in sublime poetic strains the Deity has been invested with them; and perhaps, no representation of his goodness so strongly fastens on the human affections as those that represent him abundant in mercy and willing to pardon. Gentleness, considered in this point of view, bears on its front all the characteristics of grandeur, combined with the winning graces of condescension;[5] but what a different aspect it assumes when it is the submissive demeanor of dependence, the support of weakness that loves, because it wants protection, and is forbearing, because it must silently endure injuries; smiling under the lash at which it dare not snarl. Abject as this picture appears, it is the portrait of an accomplished woman, according to the received opinion of female excellence, separated by specious reasoners from human excellence. Or, they[6] kindly restore the rib, and make one moral being a man and woman; not forgetting to give her all the "submissive charms."[7]

How women are to exist in that state where there is to be neither marrying nor giving in marriage,[8] we are not told. For though moralists have agreed that the tenor of life seems to prove that man is prepared by various circumstances for a future state, they constantly concur in advising *woman* only to provide for the present. Gentleness, docility, and a spaniel-like affection are, on this ground, consistently recommended as the cardinal virtues of the sex; and, disregarding the arbitrary economy of nature, one writer has declared that it is

4. "For example, the herd of Novelists" [Wollstonecraft's note]. Wollstonecraft is referring both to women who base their expectations in love on the distortions of sentimental novels, and to women who indulge their fantasies by writing such novels.
5. Gracious difference.
6. "Vide [see] Rousseau and Swedenborg" [Wollstonecraft's note]. Rousseau asserted that a married couple formed a single unit. Emmanuel

Swedenborg (1688–1772), Swedish theologian, believed that in heaven, husband and wife are united in a single body.
7. *Paradise Lost* 4.497–99: "he in delight / Both of her Beauty and submissive charms / Smiled with superior love."
8. "For in the resurrection they neither marry, nor are given in marriage, but are as the angels of God in heaven" (Matthew 22:30).

masculine for a woman to be melancholy.[9] She was created to be the toy of man, his rattle, and it must jingle in his ears whenever, dismissing reason, he chooses to be amused.

To recommend gentleness, indeed, on a broad basis is strictly philosophical. A frail being should labor to be gentle. But when forbearance confounds right and wrong, it ceases to be a virtue; and, however convenient it may be found in a companion—that companion will ever be considered as an inferior, and only inspire a vapid tenderness, which easily degenerates into contempt. Still, if advice could really make a being gentle, whose natural disposition admitted not of such a fine polish, something towards the advancement of order would be attained; but if, as might quickly be demonstrated, only affectation be produced by this indiscriminate counsel, which throws a stumbling-block in the way of gradual improvement, and true melioration of temper, the sex is not much benefited by sacrificing solid virtues to the attainment of superficial graces, though for a few years they may procure the individuals regal sway.

As a philosopher, I read with indignation the plausible epithets which men use to soften their insults, and, as a moralist, I ask what is meant by such heterogeneous associations, as fair defects, amiable weaknesses, &c.?[1] If there be but one criterion of morals, but one archetype for man, women appear to be suspended by destiny, according to the vulgar tale of Mahomet's coffin,[2] they have neither the unerring instinct of brutes, nor are allowed to fix the eye of reason on a perfect model. They were made to be loved, and must not aim at respect, lest they should be hunted out of society as masculine.

But to view the subject in another point of view. Do passive indolent women make the best wives? Confining our discussion to the present moment of existence, let us see how such weak creatures perform their part? Do the women who, by the attainment of a few superficial accomplishments, have strengthened the prevailing prejudice, merely contribute to the happiness of their husbands? Do they display their charms merely to amuse them? And have women, who have early imbibed notions of passive obedience, sufficient character to manage a family or educate children? So far from it, that, after surveying the history of woman, I cannot help, agreeing with the severest satirist, considering the sex as the weakest as well as the most oppressed half of the species. What does history disclose but marks of inferiority, and how few women have emancipated themselves from the galling yoke of sovereign man?—So few, that the exceptions remind me of an ingenious conjecture respecting Newton: that he was probably a being of a superior order, accidentally caged in a human body.[3] Following the same train of thinking, I have been led to imagine that the few extraordinary women who have rushed in eccentrical directions out of the orbit prescribed to their sex, were *male* spirits, confined by mistake in female frames. But if it be not philosophical to think of sex when the soul is mentioned, the inferiority must depend on the organs; or the heavenly fire, which is to ferment the clay, is not given in equal portions.

But avoiding, as I have hitherto done, any direct comparison of the two

9. Perhaps a reference to Edmund Burke's *Inquiry* into the sublime, where he associates melancholy with the nonfeminine.

1. *Paradise Lost* 10.891–92: "This fair defect / Of nature," and Pope's *Moral Essays* 2.44: "Fine by defect, and delicately weak."

2. According to popular ("vulgar") legend, Mo-

hammed's coffin hovers magically inside his tomb.

3. Wollstonecraft may be recalling Pope's *Essay on Man* 2:31–34: "Superior beings . . . / Admired such wisdom in an earthly shape, / And showed a Newton as we show an ape." Isaac Newton (1642–1727), great English scientist who founded modern physics.

sexes collectively, or frankly acknowledging the inferiority of woman, accord-
ing to the present appearance of things, I shall only insist that men have in-
creased that inferiority till women are almost sunk below the standard of
rational creatures. Let their faculties have room to unfold, and their virtues to
gain strength, and then determine where the whole sex must stand in the in-
tellectual scale. Yet let it be remembered, that for a small number of distin-
guished women I do not ask a place.

* * *

From *Chapter XII!*

SOME INSTANCES OF THE FOLLY WHICH THE IGNORANCE OF WOMEN GENERATES; WITH CONCLUDING REFLECTIONS ON THE MORAL IMPROVEMENT THAT A REVOLUTION IN FEMALE MANNERS MIGHT NATURALLY BE EXPECTED TO PRODUCE

Another instance of that feminine weakness of character, often produced
by a confined education, is a romantic twist of the mind, which has been very
properly termed *sentimental*.

Women subjected by ignorance to their sensations, and only taught to look
for happiness in love, refine[4] on sensual feelings, and adopt metaphysical no-
tions respecting that passion, which lead them shamefully to neglect the du-
ties of life, and frequently in the midst of these sublime refinements they
plump into actual vice.

These are the women who are amused by the reveries of the stupid novel-
ists, who, knowing little of human nature, work up stale tales, and describe
meretricious scenes, all retailed[5] in a sentimental jargon, which equally tend
to corrupt the taste, and draw the heart aside from its daily duties. I do not
mention the understanding, because never having been exercised, its slum-
bering energies rest inactive, like the lurking particles of fire which are sup-
posed universally to pervade matter.[6]

Females, in fact, denied all political privileges, and not allowed, as married
women, excepting in criminal cases, a civil existence, have their attention nat-
urally drawn from the interest of the whole community to that of the minute
parts, though the private duty of any member of society must be very imper-
fectly performed when not connected with the general good. The mighty
business of female life is to please, and restrained from entering into more im-
portant concerns by political and civil oppression, sentiments become events,
and reflection deepens what it should, and would have effaced, if the under-
standing had been allowed to take a wider range.

But, confined to trifling employments, they naturally imbibe opinions
which the only kind of reading calculated to interest an innocent frivolous
mind, inspires. Unable to grasp any thing great, is it surprising that they find
the reading of history a very dry task, and disquisitions addressed to the un-
derstanding intolerably tedious, and almost unintelligible? Thus are they nec-
essarily dependent on the novelist for amusement. Yet, when I exclaim against
novels, I mean when contrasted with those works which exercise the under-

4. Intensify, heighten.
5. Recounted.
6. Popular belief held that all matter was made up of four elements in varying proportions: air, earth, fire, and water.

standing and regulate the imagination.—For any kind of reading I think better than leaving a blank still a blank, because the mind must receive a degree of enlargement and obtain a little strength by a slight exertion of its thinking powers; besides, even the productions that are only addressed to the imagination, raise the reader a little above the gross gratification of appetites, to which the mind has not given a shade of delicacy.

This observation is the result of experience; for I have known several notable women, and one in particular, who was a very good woman—as good as such a narrow mind would allow her to be, who took care that her daughters (three in number) should never see a novel. As she was a woman of fortune and fashion, they had various masters to attend them, and a sort of menial governess to watch their footsteps. From their masters they learned how tables, chairs. &c. were called in French and Italian; but as the few books thrown in their way were far above their capacities, or devotional, they neither acquired ideas nor sentiments, and passed their time, when not compelled to repeat *words*, in dressing, quarrelling with each other, or conversing with their maids by stealth, till they were brought into company as marriageable.

Their mother, a widow, was busy in the meantime in keeping up her connections, as she termed a numerous acquaintance, lest her girls should want a proper introduction into the great world. And these young ladies, with minds vulgar in every sense of the word, and spoiled tempers, entered life puffed up with notions of their own consequence, and looking down with contempt on those who could not vie with them in dress and parade.

With respect to love, nature, or their nurses, had taken care to teach them the physical meaning of the word; and, as they had few topics of conversation, and fewer refinements of sentiment, they expressed their gross[7] wishes not in very delicate phrases, when they spoke freely, talking of matrimony.

Could these girls have been injured by the perusal of novels? I almost forgot a shade[8] in the character of one of them; she affected a simplicity bordering on folly, and with a simper would utter the most immodest remarks and questions, the full meaning of which she had learned whilst secluded from the world, and afraid to speak in her mother's presence, who governed with a high hand: they were all educated, as she prided herself, in a most exemplary manner; and read their chapters and psalms before breakfast, never touching a silly novel.

This is only one instance; but I recollect many other women who, not led by degrees to proper studies, and not permitted to choose for themselves, have indeed been overgrown children; or have obtained, by mixing in the world, a little of what is termed common sense: that is, a distinct manner of seeing common occurrences, as they stand detached: but what deserves the name of intellect, the power of gaining general or abstract ideas, or even intermediate ones, was out of the question. Their minds were quiescent, and when they were not roused by sensible objects and employments of that kind, they were low-spirited, would cry, or go to sleep.

When, therefore, I advise my sex not to read such flimsy works, it is to induce them to read something superior; for I coincide in opinion with a sagacious man, who, having a daughter and niece under his care, pursued a very different plan with each.

The niece, who had considerable abilities, had, before she was left to his

7. Unrefined, blatant. 8. Mark, flaw.

guardianship, been indulged in desultory reading. Her he endeavored to lead, and did lead to history and moral essays; but his daughter, whom a fond weak mother had indulged, and who consequently was averse to every thing like application, he allowed to read novels: and used to justify his conduct by saying, that if she ever attained a relish for reading them he should have some foundation to work upon; and that erroneous opinions were better than none at all.

In fact the female mind has been so totally neglected, that knowledge was only to be acquired from this muddy source, till from reading novels some women of superior talents learned to despise them.

The best method, I believe, that can be adopted to correct a fondness for novels is to ridicule them: not indiscriminately, for then it would have little effect; but, if a judicious person, with some turn for humor, would read several to a young girl, and point out both by tones, and apt comparisons with pathetic[9] incidents and heroic characters in history how foolishly and ridiculously they caricatured human nature, just opinions might be substituted instead of romantic sentiments.

In one respect, however, the majority of both sexes resemble, and equally show a want of taste and modesty. Ignorant women, forced to be chaste to preserve their reputation, allow their imagination to revel in the unnatural and meretricious scenes sketched by the novel writers of the day, slighting as insipid the sober dignity and matron graces of history[1] whilst men carry the same vitiated taste into life, and fly for amusement to the wanton, from the unsophisticated charms of virtue, and the grave respectability of sense.

Besides, the reading of novels makes women, and particularly ladies of fashion, very fond of using strong expressions and superlatives in conversation; and, though the dissipated artificial life which they lead prevents their cherishing any strong legitimate passion, the language of passion in affected tones slips forever from their glib tongues, and every trifle produces those phosphoric bursts which only mimic in the dark the flame of passion.

1792

9. Stirring.
1. "I am not now alluding to that superiority of mind which leads to the creation of ideal beauty, when he, surveyed with a penetrating eye, appears a tragicomedy, in which little can be seen to satisfy the heart without the help of fancy" [Wollstonecraft's note]. "He" refers to the superior person, presumably an artist or poet.

HELEN MARIA WILLIAMS

1762?–1827

After the death of her father, a Welsh army officer, Helen Maria Williams was educated with her two sisters at home in Berwick-on-Tweed by her Scots mother. At the age of nineteen, Williams set out for London with her first long poem completed, and in her twenties she began publishing sonnets (admired by the young William Wordsworth), political poems against slavery, and sentimental fiction. An invitation from a French acquaintance led to a visit to France, which resulted in the first of her influential accounts of events across the Channel—*Letters Written*

from France in the Summer of 1790—and eventually resulted in her decision to live out most of the rest of her life in France.

In thirteen volumes describing thirty years of French history, Helen Maria Williams retained her sympathy for the principles of the Revolution. Her letters attracted attention because of their emotional immediacy and because of her personal engagement in political events. In 1793, during the general arrest of British subjects, Williams was herself briefly imprisoned; in 1794, she moved to Switzerland out of fear of reprisals for her writings against the Jacobin Terror; after the fall of Robespierre, she returned to Paris, maintaining her libertarian ideals despite the atrocities she had witnessed and recorded. Her view that "liberty is innocent of the outrages committed under its borrowed sanction" meant that her reputation with the British reading public suffered as her English contemporaries reacted with alarm to the violence of the Reign of Terror and the rise of Napoleon.

Williams's prestige continued to decline during the writing of the later volumes of *Letters from France*, when she entertained extensively in Paris, gaining notoriety not only for the large parties she generously sprinkled with social and artistic celebrities but also because of her decision to live with a divorced man, John Hurford Stone, whom she may have secretly married in 1794. Although she continued to publish books about French history as well as a number of English translations of French works, she had clearly alienated many of her readers. Yet when the first and most successful volume of *Letters from France* appeared in 1790, Williams's sympathetic description of the fall of the Bastille was widely admired and taken by some as an answer to Edmund Burke's criticism of the uprising in his *Reflections on the Revolution in France* (1790). About Williams's accounts, the critic Mary Favret has claimed that "despite their initial dependence on sentimental and romantic fictions," they "eventually serve as registers for political rather than emotional turbulence. They become the instruments probing the inner workings of power structures." An incisive observer, an astute commentator, and a sophisticated expatriate, Williams was a pioneering woman journalist who mediated between two cultures with subtlety and verve.

From Letters Written from France

Volume 1, Letter 1

I arrived at Paris, by a very rapid journey, the day before the Federation;[1] and when I am disposed to murmur at the evils of my destiny, I shall henceforth put this piece of good fortune into the opposite scale, and reflect how many disappointments it ought to counterbalance. Had the packet[2] which conveyed me from Brighton to Dieppe sailed a few hours later; had the wind been contrary; in short, had I not reached Paris at the moment I did reach it, I should have missed the most sublime spectacle, which, perhaps, was ever represented on the theater of this earth.

I shall send you once a week the details which I promised when we parted, though I am well aware how very imperfectly I shall be able to describe the images which press upon my mind. It is much easier to feel what is sublime, than to paint it; and all I shall be able to give you will be a faint sketch, to which your own imagination must add coloring and spirit. The night before the

1. The revolutionary "Festival of the Federation" on July 14, 1790, at which the national guards from all over France met in Paris to renew their oaths before King Louis XVI.
2. Mail boat.

Federation, by way of prelude to the solemnities of that memorable day, the Te Deum[3] was performed at the church of Notre Dame by a greater number of musicians than have ever been assembled together, excepting at Westminster Abbey.[4] The Overture which preceded the Te Deum was simple and majestic; the music, highly expressive, had the power of electrifying the hearers: and near the conclusion of the piece, the composer, by artful discords, produced a melancholy emotion; and then, by exciting ideas of trouble and inquietude, prepared the mind for a recitative which affected the audience in a very powerful manner, by recalling the images of that consternation and horror which prevailed in Paris on the 13th of July, 1789, the day before that on which the Bastile[5] was taken. The words were, as well as I can recollect, what follows:—"People, your enemies advance, with hostile sentiments, with menacing looks! They come to bathe their hands in your blood! Already they encompass the walls of your city! Rise, rise from the inaction in which you are plunged, seize your arms, and fly to the combat! God will combat with you!" These words were succeeded by a chorus of instruments and voices, deep and solemn, which seemed to chill the soul. But what completed the effect was, when the sound of a loud and heavy bell mixed itself with this awful concert, in imitation of the alarm-bell, which, the day before the taking of the Bastille, was rung in every church and convent in Paris; and which, it is said, produced a confusion of sounds inexpressibly horrible. At this moment the audience appeared to breathe with difficulty; every heart seemed frozen with terror: till at length the bell ceased, the music changed its tone, and another recitative announced the entire defeat of the enemy; and the whole terminated, after a flourish of drums and trumpets, with an hymn of thanksgiving to the Supreme Being.

Volume 2, Letter 1

I again take up the pen to write to you at the Chateau of Mons. du F——,[6] from which place I last year sent you the history of his misfortunes; those misfortunes which have led me to love, as well as admire, the revolution. For you know we are so framed that, while we contemplate the deliverance of millions with a sublime emotion of wonder and exultation, the tears of tenderness, the throbbings of sympathy, are reserved for the moment when we select one happy family from the great national group, and when, amidst the loud acclamations of an innumerable multitude, we can distinguish the soothing sounds of domestic felicity. I have beheld with awful astonishment the sun of liberty spreading its broad blaze over the French hemisphere; but I have traced with inexpressible delight that benignant beam which has chased every cloud of calamity from the dwelling of Mons. du F——.

It seems the recompense of my French patriotism that I have on several occasions had the good fortune to witness those scenes of general felicity, in which it requires but common sensibility to partake. I went to Rouen the very

3. A liturgical Christian hymn of praise to God.
4. Gothic church in London in which British monarchs are coronated and buried. "Notre Dame": a Gothic church that is the cathedral of Paris.
5. The state prison in Paris, stormed by a mob on July 14, 1789.

6. I.e., du Fossé, whose story Williams tells elsewhere in her Letters: imprisoned and disinherited by a royal lettre de cachet because of his father's anger at his marrying out of the aristocracy, he was freed by the Revolution and reclaimed his patrimony.

day before the King accepted the constitution.[7] When the courier arrived with this intelligence, the cannons were immediately fired, the bells of all the churches rung, and the people displayed their joy by crowding the streets with bonfires, at the distance of every eight or ten yards. I observed some of the people, who were too poor to contribute a portion of wood, bring for their offering, a part of an old bedstead, a leg of a broken chair, etc. to feed the flame.

Strangers stopped, and congratulated one another in the streets, which resounded with cries of exultation, among which the sounds of "Vive le Roi des François," were almost lost amidst those of "Vive la nation." "C'est la nation qui triomphe. C'est la constitution qui triomphe."[8]

In the afternoon Te Deum was sung in the cathedral. The eight hundred electors of the department, who were at that time assembled at Rouen, walked in procession, attended by all the officers of the administration, and several battalions of the national guard. An immense multitude filled every part of the cathedral; the sounds of the organ and the drums, the voices of the choir, and the acclamations of the people, were mingled together, and rolled through the long aisles of the building. It was impossible to witness this religious solemnity, and reflect on the greatness of the occasion which had called so immense a multitude together, that of having completed the glorious work of a free government, without catching the enthusiasm which beat high in every bosom.

Indeed living in France at present, appears to me somewhat like living in a region of romance. Events the most astonishing and marvelous are here the occurrences of the day, and every newspaper is filled with articles of intelligence that will form a new era in the history of mankind. The sentiments of the people also are elevated far above the pitch of common life. All the motives which most powerfully stimulate the mind in its ordinary state, seem repressed in consideration of the public good, and every selfish interest is sacrificed with fond alacrity at the altar of the country. For my part, while I contemplate these things, I sometimes think that the age of chivalry, instead of being past forever, is just returned; not indeed in its erroneous notions of loyalty, honor, and gallantry, which are as little "à l'ordre du jour,"[9] as its dwarfs, giants, and imprisoned damsels; but in its noble contempt of sordid cares, its spirit of unsullied generosity, and its heroic zeal for the happiness of others.

The completion of the new government has been celebrated by general demonstrations of joy throughout the whole kingdom; and thus begins, under the auspices of liberty, the constitutional reign of Lewis the Sixteenth.

It is said that the Abbé Maury, who left France as soon as the constitution was accepted, is going to Rome, and that the pope intends to give him a cardinal's hat, in recompense for the obstinate battle he has so long fought against reason and philosophy. The patriots declare that the pope by so doing will prove that he has more power than the whole National Assembly, "car il fera rougir l'Abbé Maury."[1]

7. On September 27, 1791, Louis XVI signed the constitution, written by the National Assembly, that created a limited monarchy and an elected unicameral legislature.
8. Long live the King of the French; Long live the nation. It is the nation that triumphs. It is the constitution that triumphs [Williams's translation].

9. The order of the day [Williams's translation].
1. "For he will make the Abbé Maury redden" [Williams's translation]. The distinguishing insignia of a cardinal is the red hat he is given by the pope; Pope Pius VI opposed the nationalization of church lands and state-imposed clerical reforms that attended the French Revolution.

Volume 3, Letter 1

Paris, January 25, 1793

Dear Sir,

The event which has this week taken place[2] in Paris, will no doubt furnish you with ample matter for speculation. Imagination contemplates with an overwhelming emotion that extraordinary vicissitude of fortune which conducted Louis the Sixteenth from the radiant palace of Versailles, to the gloomy tower of the Temple[3]—from the first throne of Europe, to the scaffold and the block—while the feelings of the heart, which run a faster pace than the reasonings of the head, reject for a while all calculations of general good or evil, and melt in mournful sympathy over "greatness fallen from its high estate." But, when we consider the importance which this event may have in its consequences, not only to this country, but to all Europe, we lose sight of the individual sufferer, to meditate upon the destiny of mankind

While you observe from a distance the great drama which is acting in France, I am a spectator of the representation.—I am placed near enough the scene to discern every look and every gesture of the actors, and every passion excited in the minds of the audience. I shall therefore endeavor to fill up the outline of that picture which France has presented to your contemplation since the memorable epoch of the tenth of August.[4]

That conflict which after the King's acceptance of the new constitution existed in this country between the executive and legislative powers, between the court and the people, has since the tenth of August been succeeded by a conflict far more terrible; a conflict between freedom and anarchy, knowledge and ignorance, virtue and vice. While the real patriots of France, in their different conflicts with the ancient despotism, risked their lives, and shed their blood, and by their desperate valor confirmed the liberty of their country, a set of men, who exposed not their persons to the smallest danger in the enterprise, contrived, without peril or exertion, to seize upon a considerable portion of power; and never surely in the annals of tyranny have we heard of power more shamefully abused. Those demagogues, known by the appellation of the "Commune provisoire de Paris,"[5] have, during the short period of their usurpation, committed more crimes than despotism itself would have achieved in ages. The crimes of tyrants, by exciting our abhorrence, serve to promote the cause of freedom. It was reserved for the Commune of Paris to check the generous glow of sympathy with a great and magnanimous nation, which had nobly emancipated itself from slavery, and to lead all the feelings of humanity to take part with its oppressors. Surrounding nations, who might perhaps have been animated by the example of a country which has long served as a model to the rest of Europe, have heard of the second of September,[6] and have shrunk back into the torpor of slavery. They have beheld, in the room of the pure and sublime worship of liberty, the grim idol of anarchy set up, and have seen her altar smeared with sanguinary rites. They have beheld the inhuman judges of that night wearing the municipal scarf[7]

2. Louis XVI was executed on January 21, 1793.
3. A 13th-century monastery in Paris; one of its towers was used as a prison for Louis XVI and his family after their arrest and until their execution. Versailles was the residence of French kings, built for Louis XIV and located in the city of the same name.
4. On August 10, 1792, the Tuileries Palace in Paris was stormed, the royal family arrested, and the republic proclaimed.

5. The provisional Paris commune; the municipal authorities of the revolution set up on August 10.
6. Mass arrests of royalist sympathizers followed the arrest of the royal family. On September 2–3, mobs massacred hundreds in their prisons.
7. A sash signifying office.

which their polluting touch profaned, surrounded by men armed with pikes and sabers dropping with blood—while a number of blazing torches threw their glaring light on the ferocious visages of those execrable judges, who, mixing their voices with the shrieks of the dying, passed sentence with a savage mockery of justice, on victims devoted to their rage. They have beheld the infernal executioners of that night, with their arms bared for the purposes of murder, dragging forth those victims to modes of death at which nature shudders.—Ah! ye slaughtered heroes of the immortal 14th of July, was it for this ye overthrew the towers of the Bastille, and burst open its gloomy dungeons?—was it for this, ye generous patriots, that with heroic contempt of life ye shed your blood to give liberty and happiness to your enslaved country?—Ah! had ye foreseen that the fanatics of liberty, fierce as the fanatics of superstition, would have their day of St. Bartholomew,[8] would not your victorious arms have been unnerved? Would not the sacred glow of freedom have been frozen in your veins? Ah! what is become of the delightful visions which elevated the enthusiastic heart?—What is become of the transport which beat high in every bosom, when an assembled million of the human race vowed on the altar of their country, in the name of the represented nation, inviolable fraternity and union—an eternal federation![9] This was indeed the golden age of the revolution.—But it is past!—the enchanting spell is broken, and the fair scenes of beauty and of order, through which imagination wandered, are transformed into the desolation of the wilderness, and clouded by the darkness of the tempest. If the genius of Liberty—profaned Liberty! does not arise in his might, and crush those violators of freedom, whose crimes have almost broken the heart of humanity, the inhabitants of Paris may indeed "wish for the wings of the dove, that they may fly away and be at rest—for there is violence and strife in the city."[1]

At the head of this band of conspirators is Robespierre[2]—gloomy and saturnine in his disposition, with a countenance of such dark aspect as seems the index of no ordinary guilt—fanatical and exaggerated in his avowed principles of liberty, possessing that species of eloquence which gives him power over the passions, and that cool determined temper which regulates the most ferocious designs with the most calm and temperate prudence. His crimes do not appear to be the result of passion, but of some deep and extraordinary malignity, and he seems formed to subvert and to destroy. "One, next to him in power, and next in crime," is Danton,[3] who, though not inferior to his associate in vice, and superior in ability, having less self-command, is consequently less dangerous.—This man, at the period of the massacres, was Minister of Justice, and, being conjured to exert his authority in putting a stop to those horrors, coolly answered, "Quand le peuple ont exercé *leurs* droits, je reprendrai les *miennes*."[4]

<hr/>

8. A reference to the Massacre of St. Bartholomew's Day, the massacre of French Protestant leaders that began in Paris on August 24, 1572.
9. A reference to the Festival of the Federation (see n.1, p. 276).
1. See Psalm 55:6, 9: "And I said, Oh that I had wings like a dove! for then I would fly away, and be at rest. . . . for I have seen violence and strife in the city."
2. Maximilien Robespierre (1758–1794), leader of the left wing in the National Assembly and a key opponent

of the more moderate Girondists in the subsequent National Convention.
3. George-Jacques Danton (1759–1794), leader in Paris who helped plan the overthrow of the monarchy on August 10, 1792, and later named minister of justice. The quote is from Milton's *Paradise Lost* (1667), 1.79; Beelzebub is being compared with Satan.
4. "When the people have exerted *their* rights, I will resume [mine]" [Williams's translation].

Marat,[5] though sometimes spoken of as one of the leaders of this faction, is in reality only one of its instruments—

> A fellow by the hand of nature marked,
> Quoted, and signed to do a deed of shame;
> And taking note of his abhorred aspect,
> Finding him fit for bloody villainy,[6]

he is employed to execute the purposes of more able heads.

This triumvirate, resembling the celebrated triumvirate of Rome[7] in everything that bears the marks of baseness and of crimes, had associated in their guilt a number of lesser chiefs, who in their turn had enlisted others as instruments of the same horrid purpose. The organization of this executive assembly was formed with so much address,[8] that the less confidential members of it were ignorant how they came together, while those who were the primary movers were careful to leave no positive traces of their guilt. Hence arises the extreme difficulty of punishing these murderers; for though the complicated chain of evidence may be pursued to a certain length, yet it always breaks off in the link that leads to conviction.

<p style="text-align:center">* * *</p>

5. Jean-Paul Marat (1743–1793), one of the strongest popular leaders of the revolution and a proponent of violence and revolt.
6. *King John* 4.2.221–22 and a slight paraphrase of 224–25.
7. Both the unofficial alliance of the First Triumvirate (Pompey, Licinius Crassus, and Julius Caesar; 60 B.C.) and the Second Triumvirate, formally established to protect the republic (Mark Antony, Lepidus, and Octavian—who would become Augustus Caesar; 43 B.C.) ended in civil war and a single dictator.
8. Readiness, skill.

Literature of the
Nineteenth Century

THE WORLD OF THE NINETEENTH CENTURY

"There can be no question that the present epoch is initiating an empire of the higher reason, of arts, affections, aspirations; and for that epoch the genius of woman has been reserved," declared Thomas Wentworth Higginson in 1859. The editor of the *Atlantic Monthly* and the sometime mentor of the American poet Emily Dickinson, Higginson was neither alone nor eccentric in holding such a belief. For both in England and America the nineteenth century saw unprecedented changes in the conditions of women's lives as well as the consolidation of a powerful female literary tradition. Battling for the vote, demanding the right to own property and retain custody of their children after divorce; entering institutions of higher education; studying to be physicians and nurses, lawyers and journalists; forming trade unions; establishing businesses and writing best-sellers, women both at home and abroad had become so dramatically visible that by the end of the century the so-called Woman Question—the issue of just what woman's "place" ought to be in a proper society—had begun to obsess a startling range of thinkers. That for three-quarters of a century, one woman—Queen Victoria—had occupied a place of extraordinary international significance may have added to the intensity with which such matters were discussed, for, though she was no feminist, the increasingly bulky figure of the queen loomed ever larger as the age progressed.

The nineteenth century was in any case an era of remarkable, even shocking cultural transformation. In London for Victoria's 1897 Diamond Jubilee, sixty years after she had ascended the throne in 1837, the American writer Mark Twain mused that though "British history is two thousand years old . . . in a good many ways the world has moved farther ahead since the Queen was born than it moved in all the rest of the two thousand put together." His observation applied with special force to the "moves ahead" experienced or imagined for the first time by women. Yet those particular changes were inextricably related to more general changes. As the feminist historian Ray Strachey wrote in *The Cause* (1928), her account of the British struggle for female emancipation, "The true history of the Woman's Movement is the whole history of the nineteenth century; nothing which occurred in those years could be irrelevant to the great social change which was going on and nothing was without its share of influence upon it." No doubt she was referring to exactly the kinds of sociocultural shifts Twain himself was contemplating: revolutionary upheaval, industrialization, imperialist expansion, political reform, and the so-called disappearance of God.

Revolutionary Ideologies

The eighteenth century had ended with two revolutions that radically redefined Western politics. The American Revolution (1776) revised the relationship between the Old World and the New. The French Revolution (1789), at least partly influenced by recent events in North America, brought the threat of such changes

dramatically, and in the end bloodily, home to Europe. Together, the two revolutions reminded both the ruling class and the intellectual class whom the French called the "third estate" that old hierarchies were inexorably disintegrating. Both the middle class (rising merchants and professionals) and the proletariat (the peasant and working classes) were no longer willing to acquiesce in a system that taxed or oppressed them while denying them the power to make significant decisions about their own futures. Though the American Revolution has been seen by some commentators as upper middle class or even aristocratic in its origins while the French Revolution seems to many historians to represent a more genuine rising of "the people," both events have in common an ideology based for the first time on a passionately articulated vision of what Enlightenment thinkers from the French Jean Jacques Rousseau to the American Thomas Paine called "the Rights of Man."

To men of letters, such a vision was profoundly inspiring, so that they greeted, in William Blake's phrases, the "stiff shudderings" that "shook the heavenly thrones" of European tradition with outbursts of enthusiasm. Blake himself acclaimed the passing of the old order and the coming of the new, while William Wordsworth, describing the hopes for social metamorphosis that had been aroused in the early days of the uprising in France, recalled that "bliss was it in that dawn to be alive/But to be young was very heaven." Similarly, to such literary women as Mary Wollstonecraft and Helen Maria Williams, this revolutionary "dawn" seemed at first to promise major cultural transformations. And though these and other writers were later to be in various degrees disillusioned by the failures of both revolutions to live up to the great expectations they had elicited, the common ideology that both events dramatized was, as we shall see, to be profoundly influential throughout the nineteenth century and up to our own day, not only on middle-of-the-road political movements like the one that led to the first Reform Act of 1832 but on more radical movements like chartism, abolitionism, and women's suffrage.

Industrialization and Its Implications

What equally, and just as urgently, impelled these movements, however, was a very different kind of revolution: the so-called Industrial Revolution. As early as the mid-eighteenth century, methods of manufacturing had begun to become more technologically sophisticated, especially in England and particularly in the production of textiles, one of the country's major industries. By the 1760s, the invention of the steam engine and the spinning jenny had pointed the way to an age when the work of spinning and weaving would go on in large, centralized factories rather than individual cottages and when such work would require ever larger amounts of coal to fire the engines that drove increasingly complex machines. At the same time, the English Enclosure Acts of the mid-eighteenth century had transformed communally worked lands into private agricultural businesses, forcing many small farmers to migrate to urban centers, where they joined the new class of industrial laborers required by the burgeoning factory system, while the opening of textile mills, paper factories, and other industries had begun to create a similar working class in America.

The striking metamorphoses of both England and America (but, again, especially England) from essentially agrarian nations to modern states commanding all the resources of power looms, printing presses, railroads, steamships, and telegraphs fostered a virtual religion of progress, which was exhilarating to many, not least to a number of writers. In 1833, for instance, William Wordsworth, the sometime celebrant of pastoral nature, wrote a sonnet praising the wonders of *Steamboats, Viaducts, and Railways*, while in *Locksley Hall* (1842) Alfred, Lord Tennyson created a speaker who glorified the achievements of "men the workers, ever reaping something new." Similarly, some decades later, Walt Whitman in

America wrote his paean *To a Locomotive in Winter* (1876), in which he exulted in the great engine as a "type of the modern—emblem of motion and power," and his reclusive contemporary Emily Dickinson admitted to similar feelings about what was then called "the iron horse," confiding that "I like to see it lap the Miles" (c. 1862). In articulating such sentiments, moreover, these writers were simply expressing a prevailing cultural attitude.

Soon enough, however, the industrial "progress" such poems celebrated began to reveal its darker side. Quite early in the nineteenth century, sensitive observers had become aware of the dreadful conditions under which many of their contemporaries lived and worked. In the first decade of the new age, William Blake had prophetically inveighed against "dark Satanic Mills," the products of an unbridled rationalism that he saw threatening to disfigure "England's green and pleasant Land." The meaning of such mills, however, was more forcefully brought home to those who labored in them for what were practically starvation wages as well as to those whose traditional employments as handloom weavers, spinners, dyers, and other craftsworkers were annihilated by their technology. In the teens, a number of workers, both those who were exploited by the new system and those who were dispossessed by it, tried sporadically to unite, in some cases actually attempting to destroy the machines that were oppressing them, in others holding mass meetings to demand reform. But their efforts were unsuccessful. The policy known as "laissez-faire" (let it be), advocated by many contemporary thinkers, held that socio-economic factors should and would adjust themselves without governmental intervention so that all would turn out for the best in the end, and conservative governments in both England and America were committed to that policy. In 1812, England's House of Lords passed a bill requiring the death penalty for anyone who destroyed the apparatus used in the stocking industry, and in 1819 British troops charged a huge but peaceful crowd that had gathered at St. Peter's Fields, Manchester, to press for reform, killing nine and injuring hundreds of others.

By the 1840s, the situation in England, particularly in the industrial north, was appalling: in the slums of Manchester and Liverpool, hungry families were packed into filthy hovels; five-year-old children and pregnant women worked like mules for fifteen-hour days, dragging loads of coal in the mines outside Nottingham; London seamstresses toiled for eighteen hours at a time during the height of the four-month social "season" and starved for the rest of the year; for workers who inhaled the polluted air of badly ventilated mills and factories the death rate from tuberculosis was double the national average; and protective tariffs known as the "Corn Laws" kept foreign grain from entering the country so that the price of the bread made from English wheat could be inflated to exorbitant levels.

Friedrich Engels's radical *Condition of the Working Class in England* (1845) meticulously documented many of these problems, but even an "establishment" politician like Benjamin Disraeli raised his voice in dismay, arguing in the subtitle of his 1845 novel, *Sybil*, that there were really "two nations" in England—the rich and the poor. For of course what made the situation of the workers even more poignant was the fact that their labor had contributed to the steady rise of a newly rich group of capitalist entrepreneurs—tradesmen and factory owners, stockbrokers and professional managers—who were anything but hungry. Prosperous and often piously smug, it was this comfortable middle class that set the tone of nineteenth-century society in both England and America, decorously imitating what they believed to be the manners of the aristocracy, furnishing their parlors with ornate bric-a-brac, dressing their women in expensively complicated costumes— and, more often than not, ignoring or scorning the sufferings of the poor.

If conditions for the workers in the United States were not quite so extreme as they were in England, that was because the possibility of westward migration often acted as a kind of escape valve. Nevertheless, even as it created a newly wealthy middle class in centers like Boston and New York, industrialization took its toll in Britain's former colony, particularly in the factory towns of New England, where

workers in the textile and paper industries, among others—frequently young girls from poor rural families or recent refugees from the great Irish potato famine—labored from sunup to sundown for meager wages. Not surprisingly, then, many writers on both sides of the Atlantic indited passionate protests against the abuses fostered by the new technology and by the capitalist system that sponsored it, decrying the powerlessness and pain of the poor as well as the insensitivity and materialism of the rich. As early as 1819, Percy Bysshe Shelley had responded to the massacre at St. Peter's Fields with his hortatory *Song to the Men of England*, in which he demanded, "Wherefore plough / For the lords who lay ye low?" As time passed and conditions deteriorated further, other writers took up the theme, if not quite so radically. Novels like Charles Dickens's *Bleak House* (1853), along with Elizabeth Gaskell's *Mary Barton* (1848) and Charlotte Brontë's *Shirley* (1849), incisively portrayed both the wretchedness and the rebellion of the laboring classes, and tales like Herman Melville's *The Paradise of Bachelors and the Tartarus of Maids* (1855) set the comfortably "heavenly" lives of the wealthy—in this case a group of bachelors dwelling in London's Inns of Court—against the metaphorically infernal existence of New England factory girls.

Imperialism and Reform

If both a religion of progress and a reaction against technology's discontents were contradictory consequences of the Industrial Revolution, a third was equally problematic. Creating a need for fresh markets as well as a demand for raw materials that could not be supplied at home, the new age of the machine inevitably led to the definitive expansion of the British Empire into "underdeveloped" parts of the globe that was called imperialism. Africa, Egypt, India—all previously colonized, to be sure—now became crucially interdependent segments of a new international organism, administered in London, Cairo, Calcutta, and elsewhere by a class of bureaucrats who felt it was, in the words of the late-nineteenth-century writer Rudyard Kipling, "the white man's burden" to bring civilization to supposedly barbaric natives. Even those who had expressed doubts about the efficacy of nineteenth-century progress often pledged allegiance to this enterprise; as the speaker of Tennyson's *Locksley Hall* declared, "Better fifty years of Europe / Than a cycle of Cathay."

At the same time, the only recently "United" States, themselves former colonies, were engaging in similar efforts of expansion and colonization. Following the eighteenth-century English philosopher George Berkeley's dictum that "Westward the course of Empire takes its way," Americans of European descent set out to conquer the wild frontiers of the New World they saw as their own, in the process exterminating or subordinating countless Native American peoples. Furthermore, to acquire laborers to work the vast cotton and tobacco plantations they had established in the South, American settlers purchased black slaves from traders who ruthlessly raided the coast of West Africa to steal human "raw materials" in a grim apotheosis of the imperialist impulse. By 1800, such activity had, of course, been going on for more than a century, and though in 1808 slave trading had been officially discontinued by both England and the United States, the practice continued unabated: traders often "dumped" their manacled cargo (sometimes as many as five hundred to seven hundred and fifty men and women) overboard if a patrol ship were sighted. By 1830, scholars estimate that there were approximately two million "assimilated" slaves—Africans who had learned to speak English and to do plantation work—in the United States; by 1860, when the Civil War began, there were almost four million, and in a number of Southern states, such as Virginia and North Carolina, the "major cash crop," as the historian Eleanor Flexner has remarked, "was not cotton, or tobacco—but slaves," for black laborers were bred like cattle to reproduce more laborers, and young women in particular were prized for their "generating qualities."

Given the predatory impulses on which the imperialist imperatives of expansion and exploitation were based, it was probably inevitable that they should have triggered wars and uprisings in Europe, North America, and elsewhere. These ranged from struggles between competing imperial powers (like the Crimean War of 1850–53, in which England and France attempted to wrest control of portions of the disintegrating Ottoman Empire from Russia) to wars of colonial conquest (like the so-called Indian wars in the American West) and native insurrections (like the sporadic mutinies in nineteenth-century British India and the continuing battle for home rule in colonial Ireland). But perhaps the most dramatic of these conflicts was the American Civil War (1861–65), which combined elements of several different kinds of struggles, representing at the same time a war of liberation for the enslaved blacks and a conflict of economic interests between two quasi-imperial powers, the industrial North and the agrarian South.

Not surprisingly, the Civil War was preceded and accompanied by a reiteration of the ideology of human rights that was earlier associated with the American and French Revolutions, an ideology that was rapidly to become crucial to leaders of liberation movements in colonized countries around the world and to the founders of the British and American women's suffrage movements. Expressing their horror at what Melville called "man's foulest crime"—black slavery—white writers of both sexes on both sides of the Atlantic, from Henry David Thoreau and John Stuart Mill to Walt Whitman, from Harriet Beecher Stowe and Louisa May Alcott to Elizabeth Barrett Browning, argued for human dignity, freedom, and self-determination, while a new generation of black writers and speakers, including Frederick Douglass, Sojourner Truth, Harriet Jacobs (writing as "Linda Brent"), Harriet E. Wilson, and Frances E. W. Harper, arose in the United States to testify from personal experience about the iniquity of slavery. Their commitment to justice was finally rewarded when, after a tragic and bloody five-year struggle, the Union defeated the Confederacy, and the Congress of the newly reunited country enacted the Thirteenth Amendment to the Constitution, which permanently outlawed slavery, thereby freeing all slaves and, within a few years, leading to the Fifteenth Amendment, which enfranchised all black men.

Dramatic as it was, however, the widespread protest of intellectuals against slavery and the major constitutional amendments to which it led were symptomatic of quieter protests that were also based on the ideology of human rights and that fostered important, if less sweeping, political reforms throughout the nineteenth century. Chief among these were the moves in England to extend the vote to middle- and working-class men and to repeal the Corn Laws. In 1832, the first Reform Bill was passed, enfranchising all men owning property worth £10 or more in annual rent; in 1867, after much agitation from a working-class party known as the Chartists (because they proposed a "People's Charter" allowing for universal suffrage), the second Reform Bill was enacted, which in effect extended the right to vote to all English men; and in 1846 the Corn Laws were repealed, reducing tariffs on imported grain and alleviating the inflationary conditions that had made the lives of the poor not only harsh but hungry.

The Disappearance of God

The agitations and anxieties that surrounded such vast social changes soon took their toll on the spiritual serenity of those bred in an old order that was rapidly giving way to a new one. As factories darkened the landscape of England and battles of "brother against brother" raged in the valleys of America, it no longer seemed possible to share the philosophical confidence in the destined progress of humanity that had marked the thinking of the eighteenth century. Indeed, despite the proclamations of some nineteenth-century optimists that, as one of Robert Browning's characters observes, "the best is yet to be" and the insistence of others that social and industrial advances sped humanity ever closer to what Tennyson

called the "one far-off divine event, / To which the whole creation moves," to many thinkers it no longer seemed possible to believe in God or in the divine at all. Writing in *The Scholar Gypsy* (1853) about "this strange disease of modern life," Matthew Arnold warned of "the infection of our mental strife," and in *Dover Beach* (1867) he described the "melancholy, long, withdrawing roar" of "the Sea of Faith." He was responding to what the critic J. Hillis Miller has called the "disappearance of God" from the intellectual horizon of many contemporary thinkers.

There were, it is true, a number of figures who tried desperately to revive and revise old creeds, including American Transcendentalists like Emerson and Thoreau, who substituted a belief in the luminous beneficence of Nature for more orthodox faiths, and British conservatives like John Henry, Cardinal Newman, who argued for the redemptive powers of a return to Roman Catholic traditions. But many poets were haunted by a nightmarish refrain like that of Arthur Hugh Clough's *Dipsychus* (1865)—"Ting, ting, there is no God; ting, ting— / Dong, there is no God; dong"—and they were convinced that the supposed piety of their more conventional middle-class countrymen was merely hypocritical, even mercenary in its motives. What intensified the skepticism of such thinkers was precisely the industrial "progress" of which so many nineteenth-century citizens were proud. For more often than not such advances issued in social and scientific research that subverted the very foundations of traditional faith. The "condition of the working class" as described by Engels, after all, had inexorably led to the *Communist Manifesto* (1847), coauthored by Engels and Karl Marx, a document that severely questioned what had once seemed to be the almost divine rights of rulers and property owners. Similarly, the empirical impulses that fostered the invention of steamships and railways led just as inexorably to the discoveries of Charles Darwin, whose *Origin of Species* (1859) definitively supplanted the old idea of a seven-day divine creation of Adam and Eve with the new and unnerving concept of human evolution from lower organisms. Looking at a world in which a man seemed no "higher" than an animal, and men treated each other (as well as women and children) like animals, it is no wonder that Tennyson had an anxious vision of "Nature red in tooth and claw." Though the Victorian poet laureate (official national poet) himself recovered from his moment of doubt, many of his contemporaries could not free themselves from such pessimism and skepticism. Thus the changes that Mark Twain observed—the "move[s] ahead" the world had made in Queen Victoria's lifetime—were both radical and radically unsettling.

WOMAN'S SPHERE

For women, though the nineteenth century's startling changes often triggered considerable unease, such shifts were always significant and frequently beneficial. In 1800, however, eight years after the publication of Mary Wollstonecraft's *A Vindication of the Rights of Woman* (1792), nothing could have seemed more unlikely than the possibility that for this "epoch the genius of woman has been reserved." Indeed, despite the new conceptions of human rights dramatized by the American and French revolutions and the arguments for women's rights eloquently advanced by Wollstonecraft and earlier by writers such as Hannah More and Anne Finch, almost all women were still confined by law and custom in a secondary, private "sphere." Worse still, even some of the most liberal thinkers of the age helped formulate a concept of a "woman's sphere" that was in its way no less oppressive than the misogyny of medieval monks and the antifeminism of Augustan wits.

The Ideology of Femininity

Ironically enough, in the middle of the eighteenth century the French philosopher Jean Jacques Rousseau, whose demands for human liberty had been influential on

a number of movements for political reform, forcefully articulated some of the most restrictive tenets of what can be called the nineteenth century's ideology of femininity, declaring in *Émile* (1762) that "the whole education of women ought to be relative to men. To please them, to be useful to them, to make themselves loved and honored by them, to educate them when young, to care for them when grown, to counsel them, to console them, and to make life sweet and agreeable to them—these are the duties of women at all times, and what should be taught them from their infancy." The ideal women he thus envisioned—a pure, submissive, decorous, and even angelic creature—was only one particularly notable representative of a standard against which every middle- and upper-class woman's conduct was measured, and other writers, female as well as male, elaborated on the virtues of such an ideal.

In 1844, for instance, the selflessness of the model woman was discussed by the English writer Mrs. Sarah Ellis, who admonished readers of her conduct books (volumes of advice on manners and morals) that " 'what shall I do to gratify myself—to be admired—or to vary the tenor of my existence?' are not the questions which a woman of right feelings asks on first waking to the avocations of the day. Much more congenial to the highest attributes of woman's character are inquiries such as these: 'How shall I endeavor through this day to turn the time, the health and the means permitted me to enjoy to the best account?' " In 1854, in a long and very popular poem about femininity with the telling title *The Angel in the House*, Coventry Patmore described such selflessness more extravagantly, casting it in terms that suggest self-sacrifice, even self-immolation:

> Man must be pleased; but him to please
> Is woman's pleasure; down the gulf
> Of his condoled necessities
> She casts her best, she flings herself.

In fact, for many writers, such a self-sacrificing and angelic woman became the paradigm of renunciatory Christian love. Working out of a tradition that went back at least as far as the German poet-novelist Goethe, whose Faust (in *Faust*, 1808/1832) is redeemed by the "Eternal Feminine" (*das Ewige Weibliche*) that draws man's mind to "higher" things, such thinkers employed a rhetoric drawn from religion to characterize the good mother as a kind of Madonna and the dutiful maiden as a virginal angel. Significantly, as the critic Nina Auerbach has observed, it was only in the nineteenth century that painters began regularly portraying angels as female; perhaps even more significantly, as Auerbach has also noted, the Victorian cult of the "angel in the house" can be associated with the "disappearance of God" we discussed earlier, with its theological imagery arising in part from a displacement of traditional metaphors for the sacred onto the secular figure of the woman.

Where some writers characterized the feminine ideal through a vocabulary drawn from religion, others used a rhetoric of chivalry. If for such thinkers the model woman was not an "angel," she was at least a "queen." John Ruskin's *Of Queens' Gardens* (1865), with its assertion that woman's "great function is Praise; she enters into no contest but infallibly judges the crown of contest," implicitly alludes to medieval jousts and tournaments to characterize the regal lady whose "intellect is not for invention or creation" but who "rules" man's home so that it is "the place of Peace." Just a few years later the American writer Louisa May Alcott would argue in similar terms in *Little Women* (1869) that "a woman's happiest kingdom is home."

Whether a selfless angel or a serene queen, the model woman was often seen by both British and American ideologists of femininity as delicate, frail, ethereal. To certify her spirituality and refinement, she must look and act like a fragile creature.

Instructions as to how a young girl, or even an older woman, was to manage such a task often ranged from the ridiculous to the bizarre. Marriageable maidens on both sides of the Atlantic drank vinegar to cultivate an "interesting" pallor, tight-laced themselves into narrow corsets so as to achieve an uncannily slender waist (eighteen inches was the ideal), and practiced the "art" of fainting to remind beaux of their delicacy. More problematic still, many medical men and laymen believed that a "good"—that is, a well-bred middle- or upper-class—woman was essentially passionless: if men were beasts ruled by sexual desire, their pure wives and daughters knew nothing of such matters. To be sure, as the historian Peter Gay has documented, a number of nineteenth-century women both experienced and expressed erotic pleasure. Nevertheless, in public it was generally agreed that on her wedding night, the angelic virgin should in one way or another behave as Queen Victoria was said to have: close her eyes "and think of England." As for childbirth, the details of confinement and delivery constituted a darkly secret knowledge that was to be confined only to those who had already delivered, and even for such initiates they were "functions" not to be "dwelt upon" at any length, certainly not in public.

At its most extreme, this nineteenth-century ideal of the frail, even sickly female ultimately led to a glorification of the dead or dying woman. The most fruitful subject for literature, announced the American romancer Edgar Allan Poe in 1846, is "the death . . . of a beautiful woman," and four years later, in *The Blessed Damozel* (1850), the English poet Dante Gabriel Rossetti offered a postmortem vision of a seductive angel-lady leaning over the golden walls of heaven and yearning toward her earthly lover. But if dead women were fascinating, dying girl-children were even more enthralling: the extravagantly sentimental death scenes of Charles Dickens's "Little Nell" (in *The Old Curiosity Shop*, 1840) and Harriet Beecher Stowe's "Little Eva" (in *Uncle Tom's Cabin*, 1851–52) are only two examples of brilliantly morbid melodramas that center on such figures. What these episodes seem to do, however, is to bring to the surface an extraordinary imperative that underlay much of the nineteenth-century ideology of femininity: in one way or another, woman must be "killed" into passivity for her to acquiesce in what Rousseau and others considered her duty of self-abnegation "relative to men."

But what of women who refused to be passive or, just as problematic, were forced by circumstance into "unwomanly" activity? For nineteenth-century ideologists of femininity, these fell into two categories: subordinate working-class women and insubordinate middle- or upper-class ladies. About the first category, most ideologists had comparatively little to say: although the working-class woman could never be a lady—and indeed the verbal distinction between "woman" and "lady" was a crucial one—at her best she could reflect the lady's virtues. If she was neither angelically delicate nor gracefully regal, she could still mimic the characteristics of such figures by making herself into a kind of proletarian Madonna who submerged her own interests in those of husband and children, as Rousseau had advised the more educated woman to do. Were she single, however, her situation was far more perilous, for whether she worked on a farm or in a factory, as a kitchen helper or a parlormaid, moralists feared that she was constantly in danger of becoming a "fallen woman," a prostitute. Dante Gabriel Rossetti's 1870 poem *Jenny* brilliantly articulated the horror felt by a representative middle-class speaker at the "poor flower" of "lazy laughing, languid Jenny, / Fond of a kiss and fond of a guinea," a golden-haired whore whose favors he himself has just enjoyed. If the idealized lady was in some sense "sick"—fragile, pale, ethereal—her fallen contemporary was figuratively sickening: her "beauty goads / A man tonight to think of toads!" Indeed, even the virtue of the lady is finally put in question by Jenny's troublesome vice. Though the young prostitute is "like a rose shut in a book / In which pure women may not look," the speaker confesses his secret belief that she and her respectable counterpart are really sisters under the

skin: "Of the same lump (it has been said) / For honor and dishonor made, / Two sister vessels."

The anxious notion that the angel and the whore might be counterparts was a crucial one. Rossetti implicitly conceded that Jenny and others of her class may have been forced to "fall" by poverty or ignorance, but what of those who "fell" by their own free will? More particularly, what of those who fell not merely by demanding the sexual liberty that the Victorian double standard gave to men and forbade to women but by asserting just those emotional and intellectual needs that Rousseau thought should be sacrificed to the claims of husbands, fathers, and sons? As if to warn against such female insubordination, nineteenth-century novelists and poets, in both England and America, frequently counterpointed glowing portraits of angelic ladies with fearful depictions of demonic madwomen and murderesses or, less extravagantly but just as censoriously, biting portrayals of scheming sorceresses, social climbers, and female intellectuals.

Thackeray's delineation of the ambitious Becky Sharp in *Vanity Fair* (1848) was a fairly typical example of the way in which a number of nineteenth-century writers perceived a sharp-witted woman's refusal to be selfless as ultimately pernicious. Paralleling the figure of Amelia Sedley, an almost maddeningly angelic heroine (at whom Thackeray also pokes fun), Becky is an apparently realistic character, embedded in the scrupulously observed minutiae of Victorian society. Yet her shrewd charm cracks open when Thackeray sardonically reminds his readers that he hasn't "showed the monster's [i.e., Becky's] hideous tail above water." More explicitly fantastic portraits of unladylike ladies counterpointed pictures of ethereal maidens to make similar points in other novels. The passionate self-will of Zenobia, for instance, the dark heroine of Hawthorne's *Blithedale Romance* (1852), is unfavorably compared to the spiritual self-abnegation of her half-sister Priscilla, and the first of these women is punished with a hideous death by drowning when she fails to accept her sometime lover's dictum that "woman is a monster . . . without man as her acknowledged principal." Similarly, Charles Dickens's fallen aristocrat, Lady Dedlock, is contrasted to her illegitimate but virtuous daughter, Esther Summerson, and horribly murdered in *Bleak House* (1853); the reader is clearly meant to understand that her punishment appropriately fits her early crime of sexual indulgence. Fictions by women were also haunted by such double images of female self-assertion and self-abnegation: Charlotte Brontë's Bertha Mason Rochester, the madwoman in *Jane Eyre* (1847), is the counterpart of the novel's decorous heroine, Jane, and Elizabeth Barrett Browning's Lady Waldemar, the villainness of *Aurora Leigh* (1857), is set against the poem's noble protagonist, Aurora. For both sexes, these sometimes stereotypical figures originated in an ideology of femininity that stipulated the moral possibilities of "woman's sphere" by defining conflicting extremes: angel and monster, virgin and whore.

The Reality of Female Life

Were Victorian wives and daughters in fact angels and queens, monsters and madwoman? A reading of the literature of the period would at first suggest that such sentimental or melodramatic figures were to be found in every other British and American drawing room. Yet although a few women no doubt tried to replicate some of these fictional prototypes in their own lives, it is unlikely that many succeeded, given the intransigent facts of their social, economic, and cultural status. Qualified, to be sure, by class and (in the United States and the British colonies) race, the female situation in England and America continued to be as problematic as ever for most of the century.

Despite her ostensible power to rule, even the most queenly or angelic married lady had in fact few legal rights. On her marriage, as her ancestresses had from the

Middle Ages on, she still became what the eighteenth-century English jurist Sir William Blackstone, echoing earlier legal commentators, described as a *feme covert* (a "covered" woman). "By marriage," Blackstone declared in a magisterial passage that was repeatedly cited throughout the nineteenth century, "the very being or legal existence of a woman is suspended, or at least it is incorporated or consolidated into that of the husband, under whose wing, protection, and cover she performs everything, and she is therefore called in our law a feme covert." Such an obliteration of legal reality, or "civil death," as it was sometimes termed, was also the lot of American married women, for the traditions of English common law were long the foundations of colonial jurisprudence.

Practically speaking, the consequences of such a definition of the wife's status were drastic indeed. In the year 1800 and long into the century that followed, a married woman could not own property, even what she herself might have brought to the marriage or inherited after she was wed. Furthermore, her husband could, and sometimes did, will his estate—including what had been her own inheritance—away from her. Finally, if he died intestate (without having made a will), her rights in the property they might have jointly accumulated were minimal; the historian Eleanor Flexner has reported that in New York State, for instance, a widow was allowed nothing but the family Bible and a few other books, some cattle and household goods, and no matter how many children she had, "one table, six chairs, six knives and forks, six tea-cups and saucers, one sugar dish, one milk-pot, one tea-pot, and six spoons." In addition, a husband's power over his wife's property extended to power over her earnings, such as they were.

As for a woman's children, her husband had sole rights in their guardianship if the couple were separated for any reason, including his moral turpitude. Nor was it easy for wives to escape even the worst husbands: until past the middle of the nineteenth century, divorce was virtually unobtainable in both England and America, except by extraordinary legislative or parliamentary decrees (almost all of which were enacted at the behest of husbands), and a woman did not even have an inalienable entitlement to her own physical liberty; as the British suffragist Ray Strachey pointed out, in England "the right of a man to imprison his wife in his own house was not questioned till 1891." Finally, the married woman's moral as well as legal obliteration was signaled by the fact that until fairly late in the nineteenth century she could neither sue nor be sued: her husband was held responsible for all her acts and debts as if she were minor, defective, or mentally ill.

In addition to legal denials and constraints, severe restrictions were imposed on women by education and social custom. On the face of it, Rousseau's prescription that a girl be taught to subordinate her interests to men's should not necessarily entail the relegation of young women to virtual ignorance. To converse intelligently with gentlemen, after all, it might seem that a girl would have to be taught history, mathematics, classics—all subjects her brothers had studied and of which presumably they might like to speak. In practice, though, middle- and upper-class female education meant a minimal training in modern languages, a study of drawing or watercoloring, embroidery, and music together with a strict training in "propriety," which, wrote the influential educator Hannah More in 1799, "is to a woman what the great Roman critic says action is to an orator: it is the first, the second, the third requisite."

As for more serious subjects, such fields as classics or mathematics were considered absolutely improper for women, though a few, like Elizabeth Barrett Browning and George Eliot, were privileged to study them on their own. Rather, to complete the lady's training and render her figure "elegant," she was often strapped to a "backboard"—an iron collar fastened to a board and fixed over the shoulders—for many hours every day, while her less aristocratic but almost equally genteel middle-class sister might be obliged to spend many tedious hours embroidering homiletic samplers and reading aloud from the Bible. How a spirited upper-

class girl responded to such an education is made clear in Barrett Browning's *Aurora Leigh*, where the poet-heroine describes the "cage-bird life" for which her aristocratic English aunt educated her. Similarly, the reaction of a lively middle-class girl to the lugubrious education in "propriety" offered by a charitable board-ing school is dramatized in the great Lowood episode of Charlotte Brontë's *Jane Eyre*, in which pedagogical humiliations that the Brontë sisters themselves had to endure are vividly and movingly recounted.

Where law and education restricted many possibilities of intellectual develop-ment for nineteenth-century ladies, custom closed off almost all the rest. The very doctrine of woman's "sphere," for instance, implied that there was an almost un-bridgeable gulf between the public world of politics and business, ruled by men, and the domestic world of the household, ostensibly "ruled" but, more accurately, inhabited by women. "Man for the field and woman for the hearth,/Man for the sword and for the needle she,/Man with the head and woman with the heart,/Man to command and woman to obey," intones a solidly old-fashioned king in Tennyson's *The Princess* (1847), and his precepts aptly summarize the guidelines by which middle- and upper-class married women lived: a lady could not go out alone, especially not in the city and certainly not at night; her days were to be spent supervising her servants, doing needlework, and making or receiving visits; her mind was to be occupied largely with fashion and society and perhaps to some small extent with charitable projects.

To be sure, she did have to bear children, and she often bore a great many. Despite efforts by a few radical physicians on both sides of the Atlantic to educate the public about birth control, contraceptive methods were still primitive as well as obscure in the nineteenth century, so that, if in theory a lady was an angel, she was often in practice transformed by multiple pregnancies into a "poor animal," as Jane Austen pityingly described one young female relative. Once her children were born, however, and if they survived—for infant mortality rates remained high throughout the century—they were handed over to nurses and governesses who did the major work of raising them, depriving the lady of at least one meaningful function she might have had. As the Industrial Revolution progressed and more newly wealthy entrepreneurial families rose into the middle and upper classes, moreover, the division of woman's sphere from man's became increasingly sharp. With more money to pay more servants, the lady's household duties virtually dis-appeared, and with man's work—once done in or near the home and shared by wives on farms or in family trades—now located in offices and factories, the two spheres were geographically as well as socially separated.

No wonder, then, that Florence Nightingale complained in 1852 that "women's life is spent in pastime, men's in business," adding bitterly:

> A married woman's life consists in superintending what she does not know how to do.... [She] is to direct the servants, who are to provide conve-niences and luxuries not thought of formerly She has never learnt, and does not know how, but she must take care to provide them. She must su-perintend the nurse, and the governess of her children, though she knows nothing and has learnt nothing of the nurse's work. And the governess ... what is she to do? She must direct the characters of her pupils. How is she fit for it? ... Over her, so little prepared, the mother so little prepared is to preside.

Nightingale's mention of the "little prepared" governess reminds us that it was not only married upper- and middle-class women who suffered from the constraints of law, education, and custom: the situation of the unmarried woman of "gentle" birth was equally difficult, if not more so. She could only comparatively rarely, and in unusual circumstances, inherit property. Most fortunes in England (and

America as well) devolved on eldest sons, and in England great estates were frequently "entailed" on the male line, so that in the absence of sons some distant male relative would inherit a man's property—precisely the situation that triggers the comic action of Jane Austen's *Pride and Prejudice* (1813). Under the circumstances, it is not surprising that most women would prefer the subjugation of matrimony to the uncertainties of spinsterhood, not surprising that mothers struggled, often desperately, to further their daughters' chances on the "marriage market." No matter how gentle her birth, a portionless young woman who did not wed was frequently obliged to live as a maiden aunt on the good will of male relations or married sisters, or she survived on a meager income as what Jane Austen sardonically called a "ridiculous old maid, the proper sport of boys and girls."

Worse still, if she had neither charitable relations nor a modest income of her own, such a woman was generally obliged to turn to the only genteel careers open to her: in England, governessing, and in England and America, schoolteaching. Ill-paid, badly trained, and overworked, both governesses and schoolteachers often lived lives of quiet desperation, dreaming of matrimonial rescue. The governess's lot was especially difficult because, while the schoolteacher at least had some authority in her classroom, the governess, living with a single family, was continually subject to the whims of her employers, who often insisted that in addition to her instructional tasks, she care for infants, do much of the family sewing, and perform countless other miscellaneous chores. What made the governess's situation even more problematic was the fact that she frequently suffered from an anxiety that one social historian has termed "status incongruence": since she was herself of "good birth," she felt equal and akin to the family in which she lived, yet she was, after all, as much a servant as any kitchen maid. A contemporary observer commented that though "the Governess is a class rapidly on the increase" because such employment is "the only recourse left to young girls in the highest ranks of society who are forced to earn their living," the sorrowful practitioner of that profession "may be known at a glance from her plain and quiet style of dress" and because "on her face [there] is a fixed sad look of despair."

One reason why the governess represented a class "on the increase" was the phenomenon of so-called redundant women in Victorian England. Historians speculate that the emigration of large numbers of single men to America and to the Commonwealth colonies had left nineteenth-century England with a disproportionate mass of single women: according to the Victorian social critic H. R. Greg, 30 out of every 100 British women were unmarried in 1851, and 12 were widows; altogether, he estimated that 1,148,000 women in England and Wales were, as he put it, "unnaturally" single. The problem of such female "redundancy" was endlessly discussed in newspapers and magazines, but according to contemporary statistics at least 25,000 of these hapless "old maids" mournfully resolved their difficulties by becoming governesses.

Much as they may have deviated from the nineteenth-century ideology of femininity, however, the real lives of nineteenth-century upper- and middle-class women did not swerve quite so radically from literary stereotypes as did the lives of their working-class sisters. Whether married or single, working-class women were usually expected, indeed obliged, to labor in both the private and the public spheres. Before the Industrial Revolution, such women had lived hard enough lives—spinning, sewing, cooking, and sharing farm work with their husbands, fathers, or brothers—but after 1800 their situation became even more difficult, in both England and America. Because women were often willing to work for lower wages and longer hours than men, factories in both countries depended heavily on female labor, a fact that aroused considerable male resentment. As the historian Sheila Rowbotham observes, "One of the frequent complaints in the early stages of the Industrial Revolution was that although women and children could find work, the men could not." Whether a husband was employed or unemployed, however, the working-class wife was still his property—and his servant. After long

hours of factory work, she still had her domestic duties to do; in addition, if her children were not old enough to go into factories themselves, she had to arrange for their care. Nursing mothers often rushed home during factory breaks to breast-feed their infants, but many, inevitably, weaned their babies as early as they could, feeding them what Rowbotham describes as "watered-down, often infected cow's milk," a formula that accounts, at least in part, for the high infant mortality rate among the working classes.

Women who labored in dressmaking or in the mines struggled with equally harsh conditions. Young seamstresses often worked virtually around the clock during the London season, crowded into dark, ill-ventilated rooms that one contemporary witness described as "worse than in the worst-conducted factories," adding that "the dressmakers themselves state their belief that 'no man could sustain the labor which is imposed on these young and delicate women.'" As for women in the mines, their situation, according to a Mines Commission report (1842), was if anything, more extreme: even in the advanced stages of pregnancy, they "always did the lifting or heavy part of the work, and neither they nor the children [who labored alongside them] were treated like human beings." Testified one woman worker: "I have a belt round my waist and a chain passing between my legs and go on my hands and feet [pulling loads of coal]. . . . I have drawn till I have had the skin off me; the belt and chain is worse when we are in the family way."

Though the working conditions of female domestic servants (of whom there were 750,000 in England alone in 1851) were not so extreme, such conditions too were arduous, marked by low pay, long hours, and little leisure time—usually only one half-day per week. Worse still, of course, were the living and working conditions of black slaves in America. Bred like cattle to produce crops of new workers, subject to sexual exploitation and harrassment by their white masters, frequently separated from husbands and children, forced to perform endless hours of unpaid labor in cotton fields and plantation houses, these women were no doubt the most oppressed of all nineteenth-century female workers. Paradoxically, however, such diverse writers as the black memoirist Harriet Jacobs ("Linda Brent") and the white novelist Harriet Beecher Stowe frequently see these women—forced to be single and to sustain families against overwhelming odds—as repositories of strength, even as heroic figures. And indeed, the career of the legendary Harriet Tubman, a former slave who became a "conductor" on the Underground Railroad, which funneled Southern blacks to freedom in the North, more than supported such a view. Called "Moses" by her contemporaries, Tubman undertook some nineteen journeys into slave territory and liberated at least three hundred people.

Along with black heroines like Harriet Tubman, the only women workers who might seem to have achieved a rough equality with men and some control over their own lives were the pioneer women who labored to settle the American West. These women did work together with their husbands, as agricultural women traditionally had in England, and while they were frequently exhausted by the hardships they encountered, they could at least in some sense reap the rewards of their labor. The French writer Alexis de Tocqueville described one such woman with admiration, praising her energetic offspring as "true children of the wilderness" and noting that "she does not regret what [their upbringing has] cost her." But the American suffrage leader Anna Howard Shaw was less celebratory in her recollection of her own mother's first encounter with the primitive cabin in the backwoods of Michigan where her father (who remained in Massachusetts to work in a textile mill) sent his family: "Something within her seemed to give way and she sank upon the floor. She could not realize . . . that this was really the place father had prepared for us, that here he expected us to live."

If the married lady had no rights, the working-class woman had none either. The wages she earned were, of course, her husband's money, and she had no reciprocal claim on his earnings, nor did she have the right to leave or divorce him. On the contrary; as Ray Strachey reminds us, "If a man was displeased with the way his

wife worked for him—or with any other aspect of her conduct—he had a perfect right to beat her with a stick, provided it was not thicker than his own thumb." Moreover, if the lady's education was a training in submissive "propriety," the working-class woman's education—if she had any at all—was a training in industrious submission. In England, parish or "ragged" schools, charitable institutions for poor children, taught girls sewing, knitting, and other household skills, along with just enough reading to enable them to study the Bible; at one such institution, children over five worked from 5:00 A.M. to 6:00 P.M. at a "manufactory" and then attended school. Similarly, in America poor girls were expected to sew and knit while their brothers studied arithmetic and other subjects. Moreover, for many girls in both countries—but especially in England—a job as a domestic "apprentice" took the place of formal schooling altogether. Theoretically, such children were being trained to be good servants, but in fact most were simply exploited as household "slaveys," expected at the ages of seven or eight to do a full day's work in the kitchen or the laundry. As for the young black girls who were slaves in America, they generally received no education at all but worked alongside their parents in the cottonfields and cookhouses of the South.

Considering how few attractive vocational or personal alternatives working-class women had in the nineteenth century, it is surprising that more did not "fall," like Rossetti's "languid Jenny," into a life of prostitution. As it was, however, a number did, on both sides of the Atlantic. In the middle of the century, some contemporary observers estimated that there were approximately fifty thousand "streetwalkers" in London alone, and proportionally similar numbers may have been concentrated in other urban centers like Edinburgh, New York, Chicago, and New Orleans. The "unskilled daughters of the unskilled classes," as one historian has defined them, these were mostly young women who turned to what was called "the life" when they could not support themselves as seamstresses and domestics, or in the hope—futile, as they usually discovered—of earning extra luxuries and mimicking the glittering fashions of upper-class ladies. Many rapidly contracted syphilis and other venereal diseases; some married and retired or established businesses, including brothels, of their own; few achieved even the small comforts Rossetti characterizes his Jenny as possessing, and fewer still looked as stylish as the heroine of Thomas Hardy's sardonic *The Ruined Maid* (1866), who boasts to a roughly clad country cousin with chapped hands and a sunburnt face that she is elegantly dressed and fair-complexioned because she is "ruined."

In fact, tattered and ill, most prostitutes were seen not only as diseased but as a source of disease, and worse still, every working-class woman was defined as potentially a prostitute. In England in 1864, 1866, and 1869 Parliament passed what were known as the "Contagious Diseases Acts," legislation that empowered the police in certain districts to arrest any working-class woman on suspicion of prostitution and subject her to enforced gynecological examinations. If a woman refused such an examination, it was generally assumed she was guilty in any case; if she acquiesced in the examination, that too proved her culpability. (Men who might have been the customers of such women were not subject to similar treatment, though they too, of course, might be considered responsible for the spread of venereal disease.) Enforcing a double standard of morality that humiliated women while encouraging male sexual exploitation, the Contagious Diseases Acts may finally summarize the problematic reality that shadowed the nineteenth century's ideology of femininity. In particular, an anxiety about the female body led, on the one hand, to fantasies about the upper-class woman's rare spirituality and, on the other hand, to imaginings of the working-class woman's corrosive sexuality.

WOMAN'S REVOLUTION

Throughout the history of Western culture there had always, of course, been a notable dissonance between what we have here been calling the ideology of feminin-

ity and what we have just defined as the reality of women's lives. During the nineteenth century, however, this discrepancy between fiction and fact became so striking that it created precisely the revolution to which Higginson was alluding when he claimed in 1859 that "now Cinderella [is thinking] of putting on her royal robes." Historians have speculated that the egalitarian ideologies with which the era began, along with the impulses toward political reform that accompanied such ideologies, were essential to the battle for women's rights and votes that marked this century. Similarly, the demands of women for higher education and their eagerness to enter trades and professions were fostered by those radical ideas about the world, while the large-scale social changes impelled by the Industrial Revolution forced many working-class women out of the home and into the factory, at the same time making a number of middle- and upper-class women unpleasantly aware of just how unproductive a "lady's" leisure was. Finally, the rebelliousness of even the most religious women was implicitly encouraged by the newly antihierarchical thinking associated with the so-called disappearance of God.

Rights and Votes

It is not surprising that women, and some men as well, should early have understood the feminist implications of the intellectual assumptions that underlay the French Revolution and also, to some extent, the American War for Independence. As early as 1819, the Chartists who assembled at the disastrous St Peter's Fields meeting near Manchester to demand government attention to their plight included not only a number of working-class women but also some men who supported their right to join in political protests. By the early 1830s, French socialist and utopian thinkers had begun to proselytize in England for causes that included "the emancipation of women." Among the middle classes, too, similar ideas were stirring: in 1831, the *Westminster Review* published an anonymous article advocating female suffrage, and in 1832 a Member of Parliament presented a petition to the House of Commons, asking that "every unmarried female possessing the necessary pecuniary qualification . . . be allowed to vote."

At the same time, even the most apparently privileged aristocratic women had begun to become aware of the disadvantages of their sex, and as Ray Strachey observes, one of them brought about "the first legislative attempt to improve the position of women in England": Lady Caroline Norton, a dashing and witty London hostess, was divorced by her husband and denied custody of her children in 1836; in despair, she wrote a series of fierce pamphlets, including *The Natural Right of a Mother to the Custody of Her Child* (1837), which finally resulted in Parliament's passage of the Infants' Custody Act of 1839. This bill was, as Strachey remarks, "a timid and hesitating measure," but nevertheless it represented a legal landmark because it actually conceded some rights to women, who had hitherto had none.

In the United States, however, it was the antislavery movement that most dramatically inaugurated a feminist groundswell. Beginning in the 1830s, countless American women were active in the struggle to emancipate the blacks in the South. Their participation ranged from work in the Underground Railroad, which helped escaping slaves to find their way to freedom, to membership in the first National Female Anti-Slavery Society, founded in 1837. Among the most prominent speakers for the abolitionist cause were the Grimké sisters, Sarah and Angelina, who early saw a connection between their own political powerlessness and the subjugation of slaves. If women were not allowed to speak in the public sphere, they argued, how could they bear witness to what they knew was just? "I surrender not our claim to equality," declared Sarah Grimké in 1838, emphasizing her belief that "*whatsoever it is morally right for a man to do, it is morally right for a woman to do.*" In a sardonic poem titled *The Times That Try Men's Souls*, her con-

temporary and co-worker Maria Weston Chapman surfaced the protofeminist beliefs that informed such a statement: women, she exclaimed with mock horror, have

> . . . taken a notion to speak for themselves,
> And are wielding the tongue and the pen;
> They've mounted the rostrum; the termagent elves,
> And—oh horrid!—are talking to men!

Some few years after Chapman wrote these lines, the dilemma of both American and English women who wanted to speak for the rights of slaves was powerfully dramatized by an event that occurred in London. A group of American women were denied the right to be seated as delegates to an 1840 World Anti-Slavery Convention. Nothing could have more effectively clarified the disparity between the male abolitionists' transatlantic rhetoric of liberation and the reality of their misogyny, a misogyny that seemed to their female colleagues a shocking shadow of more general social feelings about women. Eight years later, in 1848, two of the would-be delegates to the London Anti-Slavery Convention—Lucretia Mott and Elizabeth Cady Stanton—were among five women who called a meeting of their own at Seneca Falls, in New York State. The resulting Woman's Rights Convention revised the American Declaration of Independence to support the proposition that sometimes "in the course of human events it becomes necessary for one portion of the family of man to assume among the people of the earth a position different from that they have hitherto occupied."

Many other English and American figures were among the nineteenth-century women who contributed to the feminist effort. In the United States, for instance, Margaret Fuller published her impassioned and influential *Woman in the Nineteenth Century* in 1845, while Lucy Stone began a brilliant career as what Eleanor Flexner calls a lecturer "on behalf of the oppressed," declaring: "I expect to plead not for the slave only, but for suffering humanity everywhere. ESPECIALLY DO I MEAN TO LABOR FOR THE ELEVATION OF MY SEX." By 1851, Susan B. Anthony had joined Stone, Mott, and Stanton as one of the leaders of the suffrage movement; Sojourner Truth had risen in Akron, Ohio, to speak for the rights of black women; Frances E. W. Harper had begun to write eloquent poetry demanding the liberation of slaves and women; and countless other American women, black and white, of all ages and classes, had become converts to "the cause." Their work was slow and arduous. They wrote pamphlets, made speeches, carried petitions from house to house in villages, towns, and cities throughout the nation, testified before legislative bodies that were frequently amused or hostile, and marched in demonstrations. Their struggle—the longest single political battle in American history—did not gain them the vote nationally for more than three-quarters of a century. Yet they did make progress in achieving some rights for women. By 1860, Married Women's Property Acts had been passed in fourteen states, including Massachusetts, New York, and Illinois, while a few states and territories (for instance, Wyoming and Utah in 1870, Colorado in 1893, and Idaho in 1896) gradually extended voting rights to women.

The U.S. movement had a specific transatlantic impact through a story about the first Worcester (Massachusetts) Women's Rights convention written in 1851 for the *Westminster Review* by Harriet Taylor, a young Englishwoman, who described the proceedings and stated the case for women's rights. In the same year, Taylor married the philosopher John Stuart Mill, a figure whose intensely feminist *The Subjection of Women*, written in 1861 and published in 1869, was to formulate arguments for female equality that would become central to the British women's movement. The book's ideas, insisted Mill, were "acquired mainly through [his wife's] teaching," and though some critics have disputed this claim, it is at least

clear that the couple had an egalitarian relationship, which was essential in shaping Mill's thought, and that Taylor had lucidly summarized some important American feminist concepts.

Even before Mill had started to draft his feminist treatise, however, a number of Englishwomen had begun to organize committees for women's rights roughly comparable to the groups working in America. Foremost among these early pioneers was Barbara Leigh Smith, later Barbara Bodichon: in 1855 she undertook to circulate petitions in support of a Married Women's Property Act; in 1857 she was instrumental in founding a feminist paper called *The Englishwoman's Journal*; and in 1865, at a meeting of a Kensington Ladies' Discussion Society, she adopted a strong position in favor of women's suffrage, a position that led to the formation of England's first Women's Suffrage Committee. In 1866, a year after John Stuart Mill had been elected to Parliament, this group presented him with several petitions, containing thousands of signatures in support of votes for women, which allowed him to bring about the first parliamentary debate on women's suffrage, an action he himself defined as "by far the most important public service" he performed during his membership in the House of Commons.

Still, despite the energy and enthusiasm of Bodichon, Mill, and others, the progress of the woman's "revolution" was as slow in England as in America. The first Married Women's Property Act was defeated in 1856, and Parliament passed a far more conservative Marriage and Divorce Law in 1857, an act that served to defuse demands for the much-needed property bill. Similarly, the Contagious Diseases Acts of the 1860s, legislation that, as we noted, allowed the harrassment of countless working-class women, were stubbornly defended by the government for several decades. Finally, despite a brilliant speech by Mill, the 1866 bill for women's suffrage received comparatively few votes. It was not until 1882 that a serious and effective Married Women's Property Act was passed in England, and not until 1886 that the Contagious Diseases Acts were formally repealed, after a long and vigorous campaign led by Josephine Butler. As for suffrage, by the 1870s and 1880s the battle in England had barely been joined, and like their American sisters, Englishwomen would have to wait for the vote until after World War I.

Education, Trades, and Professions

Though feminist political and legal advances came only gradually and sporadically, nineteenth-century women did make extraordinary progress in other ways. The philosophy of human rights that shaped so many of the suffrage and abolition movements' assumptions proved an equally crucial influence on theories about women's education. In the United States, such thinkers as Emma Willard, Frances Wright, and Catherine Beecher, each in her own way, insisted on demanding serious training for girls, and in 1833 what is now Oberlin College became the first institution to admit young women "coeds." Perhaps an even more important milestone in the history of women's fight for learning was the founding of Mount Holyoke in 1837. Mary Lyon, the school's principal, was determined to teach her students such varied (and heretofore masculine) subjects as rhetoric and logic, human physiology and "intellectual philosophy," astronomy and chemistry. A number of interested observers in New England and elsewhere were impressed, for the establishment of Mount Holyoke was followed by the opening of Vassar in 1865, of Smith and Wellesley in 1875, of the "Harvard Annex" (Radcliffe) in 1879, and of Bryn Mawr in 1885.

During these years, similar struggles for educational opportunities were being waged by women in England. In the 1840s, Christian Socialists concerned about the condition of governesses founded a Governesses' Benevolent Institution designed to provide annuities for "ladies in temporary distress," but they discovered they could hardly meet the needs of all those who applied for assistance.

Reasoning that if such women "could teach better they could command higher salaries," the founders of the Benevolent Institution initiated a series of "Lectures to Ladies," which by 1848 had evolved into Queens College for Women in London, a kind of adult education school that offered basic courses in literature, science, and philosophy.

In addition, just as American feminists fought for admission to Harvard and managed to establish Radcliffe as the "Harvard Annex," so British feminists laid siege to the great universities of Cambridge and Oxford. Their leader in this struggle was Emily Davies, who worked for years to arrange the admission of women, first to London University, and then to Cambridge. Though she did not achieve her goal in London, she triumphed when in 1870 Girton College for Women, now part of Cambridge University, was established. A year later, Anne Jemima Clough, another pioneering educator, was instrumental in founding what is now Newnham College, Cambridge. Finally, in the 1870s and 1880s, two more women's colleges—Somerville and Lady Margaret Hall—were established at Oxford. By 1884, women were allowed to study at both major British universities—although, they were still, for many years, denied the right to earn formal degrees.

A natural consequence of women's entrance into higher education was an intensification of female interest in joining the professions. Perhaps the most dramatic struggle here was the fight of a few courageous young women to enter medical schools and become practicing physicians. Again, it was an American who led this battle: despite much opposition, Elizabeth Blackwell gained admission to Geneva College as a medical student and graduated at the head of her class in 1849. Journeying to Europe for further training, she met and was influenced by the young Florence Nightingale, and later she returned to England, where she supported the long but successful struggles of two English women, Elizabeth Garrett and Sophia Jex-Blake, to gain medical degrees of their own.

Of course, such accomplishments as medical degrees and university study were largely the prerogative of upper- and middle-class women. But working-class women, too, began to fight for their rights and to unite in newly vital ways during the nineteenth century, for the philosophy of human rights preached by Chartists in England and similar reformers in America influenced all classes. In Lowell, Massachusetts, textile workers edited and published a widely known magazine, *The Lowell Offering*, and, even more important, organized the Female Labor Reform Association, which served as a model for a number of comparable groups that sprang up in other New England mill towns. Although working-class women were not quite so active in England, similar organizations were also established there throughout the century. In the 1830s, as Sheila Rowbotham notes, Female Reform Societies and Female Political Unions supported the protests of male workers, while in 1874 Emma Paterson formed the Women's Protective and Provident League and the National Union of Working Women to encourage female trade unionism. The passion for justice of these activist women on both sides of the Atlantic, like the feminist principles of their middle- and upper-class sisters, was aptly expressed by what Eleanor Flexner explains was "a parody on an old song, *I Can't Be a Nun*," which striking factory girls in Lowell, Massachusetts, sang as they marched through the town in 1836:

> Oh, I cannot be a slave,
> I will not be a slave,
> For I'm so fond of liberty
> That I cannot be a slave.

A GOLDEN AGE OF WOMEN'S LITERATURE

It is no coincidence that this century of feminist revolution was a kind of golden age of women's literature. In the nineteenth century, after a female—and, more

particularly, a feminist—tradition had earlier begun to establish itself in the words and works of, say, Bradstreet, Finch, and Wollstonecraft. the female imagination flourished. Significantly, the women Woolf defined as "the four great novelists"— Jane Austen, Charlotte and Emily Brontë, and George Eliot—were all nineteenth-century artists and artists very much of their time. Similarly, the era produced such major poets as Emily Dickinson. Elizabeth Barrett Browning, and Christina Rossetti. In addition, the century fostered the work of a range of political or quasi-political figures—Margaret Fuller, Harriet Beecher Stowe, Frances E. W. Harper, and Florence Nightingale—as well as the art of novelists like Maria Edgeworth and Elizabeth Gaskell, whose achievements appear "minor" only when they are set against the extraordinary accomplishments of the Brontës. Austen, and Eliot. Clearly, the spirit of the age that motivated such activists as Mott and Stanton, Bodichon and Blackwell also inspired the imaginings of their literary sisters. Indeed, as their texts suggest, nineteenth-century women writers were as haunted as were American and English suffragists by the discrepancy between ideology and reality, a discrepancy that frequently forced these artists to tell tales of pain even while it fueled their fantasies of freedom. Still, though the writings of nineteenth-century women in England and America often drew, implicitly or explicitly, on precisely the impulses that energized the contemporary women's movement, the nature of those writings cannot be completely understood in isolation from the literary achievements of nineteenth-century men.

Male and Female Traditions

As in earlier eras, women writers in the nineteenth century worked both with and against the grain of male aesthetic assumptions and practices. There were no toweringly great women Romantic poets contemporary with Wordsworth and Coleridge, Shelley, Byron, and Keats, for instance, yet some women artists did write poetry that can clearly be identified as Romantic in its praise of the unspoiled beauty of wild landscapes, its commitment to the power of the imagination, and its philosophy of what the critic M. H. Abrams, following Thomas Carlyle, has called "Natural Supernaturalism." The poet-novelist Charlotte Smith, for instance, produced Beachy Head (1807), a long meditation on nature, as well as a series of Elegiac Sonnets (1784), which pioneered in the formation of the Romantic aesthetic, while the poet Mary Tighe (1772–1810) produced a Spenserian narrative titled Cupid and Psyche (1805), which influenced John Keats's famous Ode to Psyche (1820).

At the same time, a number of the ideas formulated by the male Romantics (and earlier by Smith and Tighe). as well as some recurrent Romantic themes and images, had considerable impact on the nineteenth-century female contemporaries and descendants of writers like Wordsworth and Byron. Obviously, the writings of such relatives of poets as Dorothy Wordsworth (William Wordsworth's sister) and Mary Shelley (Percy Shelley's wife) would reveal these influences: Dorothy Wordsworth's journals are marked by (and themselves influenced) exactly the steady, detailed, and reverent observations of nature that characterize her brother's Lyrical Ballads (1798) and The Prelude (1850), while Mary Shelley's tales and novels, especially Frankenstein (1818), exhibit just the concern with issues of liberty and authority, will and imagination, that works of her husband's like Prometheus Unbound (1820) and The Triumph of Life (1824) dramatize. Yet even a fiction writer like Jane Austen, notable for preferring "sense" to "sensibility" (as her novel titled Sense and Sensibility, 1811, demonstrates). had to confront questions about the world that were raised by the Romantics: in her early, parodic Northanger Abbey (composed before 1803), for instance, she comically yet seriously considered the implications for women of the Gothic romance that obsessed many of her contemporaries as well as the cult of the picturesque that so influenced the Romantics, while in her late Persuasion (1818) she meditated on just

the relationships between individual desire and social authority that also interested her male contemporaries.

Paradoxically, however, it is in the work of midcentury novelists like Charlotte and Emily Brontë that we can find the most vivid traces of Romanticism as it was defined by male poets like Byron, Shelley, and their precursor William Blake. Jane Eyre's impassioned plea for social and spiritual liberty is, after all, both a Byronic assertion of the claims of the self and a Shelleyan demand for social transformation, while the characterization of Jane's darkly brooding lover, Edward Rochester, clearly draws on the traits of such haunting Byronic heroes as Manfred and Childe Harold. In fact, the Byronic hero—a dashing yet Satanic rebel who seized the imagination of readers throughout Europe in the first decades of the nineteenth century—provided a model of simultaneously tempting and terrifying masculinity for many women writers, including, besides Charlotte Brontë, Charlotte's sister Emily. Heathcliff, the mysteriously demonic foundling whose vengeful passions trigger the plot of *Wuthering Heights* (1847), clearly derives much of his power from that Romantic paradigm even while his hellish energies recall the subversive intensity of earlier, quasi-mythic figures like William Blake's Orc and Los.

At the same time, however, the Byronic hero also provided a pattern for a new kind of character: a Byronic *heroine.* Charlotte Brontë's rebellious Jane Eyre and Emily Brontë's fierce Catherine Earnshaw are each in her own way revisions of this brooding outcast who rejects any cultural commandments that fail to meet the needs of his or her own soul. Similarly, Elizabeth Barrett Browning's Aurora Leigh, at least at the moment when she refuses to acquiesce in Romney's demand that she abnegate her own ambition to become his helpmate, argues with defiant passion for the authority of her own desire, while Emily Dickinson, in a number of her most intensely rebellious poems, assumes a posture of Byronic alienation from God and man alike. Considering that most of these women artists were confronting exactly the dissonance between ideology and reality that their feminist-activist contemporaries were, it is not surprising that they should have adopted such a revolutionary stance. What is impressive, however, is the inventiveness with which they transformed a male figure into a female (and implicitly feminist) model.

But of course Byronic Romanticism was only a single strain in the literary chorus nineteenth-century women writers heard on both sides of the Atlantic. In the United States, that strain, modified by the writings of the Victorian sage Thomas Carlyle and by the ideas of German Romantic philosophers, modulated into the concept of "self-reliance," which was central to such Transcendentalists as Emerson and Thoreau, a concept that Margaret Fuller turned to feminist purposes in the brilliant polemics of *The Great Lawsuit,* later published as *Woman in the Nineteenth Century.* In England, the questioning of authority that had marked the texts of all the British Romantics evolved into a Victorian skepticism about received theology and a commitment to the common life, a commitment to serious public service in the complex world of the "here and now" that often virtually replaced traditional religious faith not only in the writings of Tennyson, Browning, and Carlyle himself but also in the works of George Eliot and Elizabeth Barrett Browning. In other words, throughout the century the male and female literary traditions in England and America continued to be both intertwined and interdependent.

Yet those traditions could not be identical, despite the connections that we can trace between them. For one thing, although a number of literary women did manage to achieve not only greatness but fame in the course of the age, most continued to experience precisely the anxieties about literary authority that had been expressed by such precursors as Anne Bradstreet and Anne Finch. That artists like Charlotte and Emily Brontë and Marian Evans had to publish their works under male pseudonyms (respectively, Currer and Ellis Bell and George Eliot) is one in-

dication that such anxieties persisted. That poets like Elizabeth Barrett Browning, Emily Dickinson, and Christina Rossetti had, in various degrees, to withdraw from the public world is another indication that the old anxieties lingered: Barrett Browning confined herself to a sickroom for more than a decade; Dickinson not only imprisoned herself in her "Father's house" (as she put it) but refused to publish; and Rossetti, at least metaphorically, immured herself in the convent of her own soul.

Finally, that a number of these writers, both novelists and poets, frequently had to follow Byronic assertions of ambition with qualifying avowals of renunciation—a phenomenon we can see in the works of women from Jane Austen to Emily Dickinson, from Charlotte Brontë to Christina Rossetti—is yet another sign of continuing anxiety. If a "lady" was supposed to be an angel in the house, after all, how could she allow herself to make the kinds of self-confident claims for her own creativity that empowered her male contemporaries? "I think I shall be among the English Poets after my death," John Keats had written in 1818, but his American descendant, Emily Dickinson—who may have felt equal certainty—had to be more careful in her self-definitions: calling herself "the slightest in the House," she remarked ironically that "they shut me up in Prose. . . . Because they liked me 'still.'" Similarly, Christina Rossetti reminded herself in *The Lowest Room* that it was best to be "last," and George Eliot defined Dorothea Brooke, the protagonist of *Middlemarch* (1872) and perhaps this novelist's favorite heroine, as "the foundress of nothing."

Nevertheless, even while expressing and enacting such striking conflicts, these women did continue to write, and as we have already observed, they created what was in some sense a golden age of the female imagination. How did they do it? Clearly, they were energized by the unprecedented fact that they *did* have female precursors as well as a growing number of highly visible female contemporaries.

For novelists from Austen and the Brontës to Stowe, Eliot, and Alcott, there was a newly viable—and popular—genre in which they could work, a genre that had been developed by such eighteenth-century precursors as Frances (Fanny) Burney and Anne Radcliffe, and that was in their own century to be exploited with great commercial success by best-selling writers including (in England) the sensational novelists Mary Elizabeth Braddon (1837–1915) and Rhoda Broughton (1849–1920), and (in America) the sentimental novelists Susan Warner (1819–1885) and Maria Cummins (1827–1866). That a sensational work like Braddon's *Lady Audley's Secret* (1862) was often scorned by elite male critics as merely a "thriller" and that a sentimental work like Cummins's *The Wide, Wide World* (1851) was frequently dismissed as little more than a tearjerker could not disguise from readers of both sexes the fact that women like the authors of these novels had finally become key presences in a literary marketplace that had hitherto been primarily dominated by male writers and editors. Nathaniel Hawthorne's complaint in 1855 that his art was being threatened by a "damned mob of scribbling women" represents the reaction of many men of letters to this new female commercial power, but—despite George Eliot's diatribe *Silly Novels by Lady Novelists*—many women of letters must have been encouraged rather than disturbed by such power.

Similarly, poets including Barrett Browning, Rossetti, and Dickinson must have been heartened by the examples of such well-known women poets as Felicia Hemans (1793–1835), L.E.L. (Letitia Elizabeth Landon, 1802–1838), and many more. That some of these artists, like such popular novelists as Braddon and Warner, were scorned as effusive and sentimental (the American Lydia Sigourney, for instance, was labeled "The Sweet Singer of Hartford") does not mean that their presence was not in some sense a strengthening one for, say, Barrett Browning and Rossetti (both of whom wrote elegies on the death of L.E.L.) and even for Dickinson (who frequently attempted to "rewrite" in her own style the hearts-and-

flowers verses of women poets whose works she read in the *Springfield Gazette*). In addition, of course, ambitious writers like Dickinson and Rossetti were profoundly inspired by the powerful example of Barrett Browning, a poet whose work, unlike that of Sigourney and L.E.L., was so widely admired in the nineteenth century that she was very seriously considered for the position of English poet laureate after William Wordsworth died in 1850.

Besides the existence of significant precursors and contemporaries, however, the revolutionary social changes to which Mark Twain was referring when he remarked that the world had been transformed in the seventy-five years of Queen Victoria's reign affected women writers at least as strongly as they affected male artists. Some of these women—for instance the legendary speaker Sojourner Truth, the escaped slave Harriet Jacobs ("Linda Brent"), and the feminist orator Elizabeth Cady Stanton—were of course integrally involved in the various public movements that brought about these changes. But even those women who lived less overtly political lives saw that the tumult of the age required a record, and Elizabeth Barrett Browning provided one in her verse-novel *Aurora Leigh* just as George Eliot offered one in *Middlemarch*, Rebecca Cox Jackson in her journal, Harriet Beecher Stowe in *Uncle Tom's Cabin*, Harriet Wilson in *Our Nig*, Florence Nightingale in *Cassandra*, and Rebecca Harding Davis in *Life in the Iron-Mills*. Working in all the forms in which their aesthetic brothers worked—the novel, the essay, the long poem, the sonnet, the lyric—these diverse artists wrote their way out of the female "sphere" to which they had been confined.

As their texts show, such nineteenth-century women writers were often only covertly subversive, producing decorous surfaces that erupted to reveal indecorous, even Byronic, passions for liberty, as if many had decided to follow Emily Dickinson's dictum to "tell all the truth / But tell it slant." Yet their power was irrepressible. With Elizabeth Barrett Browning's poet-heroine Aurora Leigh, each would have asserted that "every creature, female as the male, / Stands single in responsible act and thought," and, also with Aurora, each would have insisted that "I too have my vocation,—work to do. . . . Most serious work, most necessary work / As any of the economists." Significantly, it was Barrett Browning herself who once lamented that she looked "everywhere for [poetic] grandmothers, and found none." But after she and the other female artists of her century had made their enduring contributions to our culture, no aspiring young woman writer would ever have to level such a complaint again. At least in literature, what Thomas Wentworth Higginson called an "epoch" reserved for "the genius of woman" had finally begun—an era that certainly did not exclude the contributions of men but at last also, definitively, included women's achievements.

MARIA EDGEWORTH
1768–1849

Maria Edgeworth was born at Black Bourton, Oxfordshire, the second of the twenty-one children of Richard Lovell Edgeworth, a brilliant, if eccentric, inventor and educator of Anglo-Irish descent. Her mother, Anna Maria Elers, was apparently the least loved of his several wives, and after her death in 1773, Maria Edgeworth grew up under the care of three successive stepmothers. After attending one school at Derby and another in London, she accompanied her father and her current stepmother to Ireland in 1782. On the family estate, Edgeworthstown, Richard Edgeworth completed her education first by instructing her himself, then by involving her in local politics, and finally by collaborating with her on *Practical Education* (1798), a book that demonstrates his interest in the pedagogic theories

of the French philosopher Jean Jacques Rousseau. Maria Edgeworth had already begun to teach her younger siblings and, at her father's request, to translate works of the conservative moralist Madame de Genlis.

When the publication of Genlis's *Adelaide and Théodore* was canceled because of the subsequent appearance of another English version, her father's friend Thomas Day wrote a congratulatory letter, for, as Maria Edgeworth explained later, he was basically of the opinion "that the extent of a woman's erudition should consist in her knowing her simple letters, without their mischievous combinations." Her first signed work, *Letters for Literary Ladies* (1795), appropriately begins with an exchange of letters between a liberal father and his conservative friend on the subject of female authorship. Although these figures, modeled on Richard Edgeworth and Day, contend over the propriety of women writing, they agree that women are meant to be wives and mothers, two roles Edgeworth would extol in her fiction and avoid in her life. Just as her early efforts repeat her father's opinions in fictional forms, her later work would gloss his social theories. Under the supervision of her father, she produced financially successful moral tales and children's stories that contemporary reviewers praised for their instructiveness. Although many critics have viewed her father's influence as a form of control, Marilyn Butler has recently argued that such a perspective derives from a hostile Victorian reading of his character and that he played a "subordinate position of supplier of detail, or the less exalted role of proof-reader.'

During the same period in which she was writing *Letters for Literary Ladies*, Edgeworth entertained her family with specimens of the speech of their Irish steward. An early dramatic monologue grew into her most famous novel, *Castle Rackrent* (1800), a humorous but telling critique of exploitative Irish landlords recounted by a shrewdly observant family retainer. Her realism in portraying Irish customs and speech was unprecedented. It also shaped the later novel *The Absentee* (1812), which criticized absentee Irish gentry ashamed of their origins. By the end of her life, when she helped relieve sufferers during the Irish potato famine of 1847, Edgeworth had become an honorary member of the Irish Royal Academy. Her contribution to Irish literature led Sir Walter Scott to explain that he hoped to attain for his country—Scotland—"the rich humor, pathetic tenderness, and admirable taste" she had "so fortunately achieved for Ireland."

Edgeworth had begun writing, she explained, "to please my father," and "to please him I continued." Although she traveled several times to London, France, and Switzerland, where, on one occasion, she rejected a marriage proposal, she focused in her novels on the conventions of the domestic life she led. With the publication of *Belinda* (1801) and *Ormond* (1817), Edgeworth extended the tradition first established in Frances Burney's novel of manners and later perfected in Jane Austen's comic fiction. Like Austen, Edgeworth wrote in the common sitting room; in fact, she sat at a desk on which her father later inscribed his view that, "in these works which were chiefly written to please me," his daughter had "improved and amused her own mind, and gratified her heart, which I do believe is better than her head." After his death, she completed only one novel and his *Memoirs of Richard Lovell Edgeworth, Esq.* (1820); without his presence she seemed to lack a motive for writing. But for the youthful Austen, Maria Edgeworth, like Burney, had succeeded in securing the status of the novel by producing works "in which the greatest powers of the mind are displayed, in which the most thorough knowledge of human nature, the happiest delineation of its varieties, the liveliest effusions of wit and humor, are conveyed to the world in the best-chosen language."

In its topical subject and subtle rhetorical maneuvers, *The Grateful Negro* demonstrates how Edgeworth became one of the most incisive as well as one of the most commercially successful novelists of her time. The work's analysis of moral issues pertaining to family ties, domestic responsibilities, and social duties extends this artist's characteristic concerns to the more exotic locale of Jamaica

and the more atypical subject of a slave rebellion. Like many later literary women, Edgeworth uses her own high valuation of the family to critique a slave economy that abrogates family ties. Just as interesting is Edgeworth's analysis of the complex ethical effects of gratitude, affection, sympathy, and sentiment on master-slave relationships. Since Edgeworth's character Caesar achieves through his high moral sense the status of a royal slave, he bears comparison with Aphra Behn's hero in *Oroonoko*.

The Grateful Negro

In the island of Jamaica there lived two planters, whose methods of managing their slaves were as different as possible. Mr. Jefferies considered the Negroes as an inferior species, incapable of gratitude, disposed to treachery, and to be roused from their natural indolence only by force; he treated his slaves, or rather suffered his overseer to treat them, with the greatest severity.

Jefferies was not a man of a cruel, but of a thoughtless and extravagant temper. He was of such a sanguine disposition, that he always calculated upon having a fine season, and fine crops on his plantation; and never had the prudence to make allowance for unfortunate accidents: he required, as he said, from his overseer produce and not excuses.

Durant, the overseer, did not scruple to use the most[1] cruel and barbarous methods of forcing the slaves to exertions beyond their strength. Complaints of his brutality, from time to time, reached his master's ears; but though Mr. Jefferies was moved to momentary compassion, he shut his heart against conviction: he hurried away to the jovial banquet, and drowned all painful reflections in wine.

He was this year much in debt; and, therefore, being more than usually anxious about his crop, he pressed his overseer to exert himself to the utmost.

The wretched slaves upon his plantation thought themselves still more unfortunate when they compared their condition with that of the Negroes on the estate of Mr. Edwards. This gentleman treated his slaves with all possible humanity and kindness. He wished that there was no such thing as slavery in the world; but he was convinced, by the arguments of those who have the best means of obtaining information, that the sudden emancipation of the Negroes would rather increase than diminish their miseries. His benevolence, therefore, confined itself within the bounds of reason. He adopted those plans for the amelioration of the state of the slaves which appeared to him the most likely to succeed without producing any violent agitation or revolution.[2] For instance, his Negroes had reasonable and fixed daily tasks; and when these were finished, they were permitted to employ their time for their own advantage or amusement. If they chose to employ themselves longer for their master, they were paid regular wages for their extra work. This reward, for as such it was considered, operated most powerfully upon the slaves. Those who are animated by hope can perform what would seem impossibilities to those who are under the depressing influence of fear. The wages which Mr. Edwards promised, he took care to see punctually paid.

1. *The Negro Slaves* (1796)—a fine drama, by (August von) Kotzebue. It is to be hoped that such horrible instances of cruelty are not now to be found in nature. Bryan Edwards, in his *History of Jamaica* (1793), says that most of the planters are humane; but he allows that some facts can be cited in contradiction of this assertion [Edgeworth's note].

2. (Edward's) *History of the West Indies* (1793), from which these ideas are adopted—not stolen [Edgeworth's note].

He had an excellent overseer, of the name of Abraham Bayley, a man of a mild but steady temper, who was attached not only to his master's interests but to his virtues; and who, therefore, was more intent upon seconding his humane views than upon squeezing from the labor of the Negroes the utmost produce. Each Negro had, near his cottage, a portion of land, called his provision-ground; and one day in the week was allowed for its cultivation.

It is common in Jamaica for the slaves to have provision-grounds, which they cultivate for their own advantage; but it too often happens, that, when a good Negro has successfully improved his little spot of ground, when he has built himself a house, and begins to enjoy the fruits of his industry, his acquired property is seized upon by the sheriff's officer for the payment of his master's debts; he is forcibly separated from his wife and children, dragged to public auction, purchased by a stranger, and perhaps sent to terminate his miserable existence in the mines of Mexico; excluded forever from the light of heaven; and all this without any crime or imprudence on his part, real or pretended. He is punished because his master is unfortunate!

To this barbarous injustice the Negroes on Mr. Edwards' plantation were never exposed. He never exceeded his income; he engaged in no wild speculations; he contracted no debts; and his slaves, therefore, were in no danger of being seized by a sheriff's officer: their property was secured to them by the prudence as well as by the generosity of their master.

One morning, as Mr. Edwards was walking in that part of his plantation which joined to Mr. Jefferies' estate, he thought he heard the voice of distress at some distance. The lamentations grew louder and louder as he approached the cottage, which stood upon the borders of Jeffries' plantation.

This cottage belonged to a slave of the name of Caesar, the best Negro in Mr. Jefferies' possession. Such had been his industry and exertion, that, notwithstanding the severe tasks imposed by Durant, the overseer, Caesar found means to cultivate his provision-ground to a degree of perfection no where else to be seen on this estate. Mr. Edwards had often admired this poor fellow's industry, and now hastened to inquire what misfortune had befallen him.

When he came to the cottage, he found Caesar standing with his arms folded, and his eyes fixed upon the ground. A young and beautiful female Negro was weeping bitterly, as she knelt at the feet of Durant, the overseer, who regarding her with a sullen aspect, repeated. "He must go. I tell you, woman, he must go. What signifies all this nonsense?"

At the sight of Mr. Edwards, the overseer's countenance suddenly changed, and assumed an air of obsequious civility. The poor woman retired to the farther corner of the cottage, and continued to weep. Caesar never moved. "Nothing is the matter, sir," said Durant, "but that Caesar is going to be sold. That is what the woman is crying for. They were to be married; but we'll find Clara another husband, I tell her; and she'll get the better of her grief, you know, sir, as I tell her, in time."

"Never! never!" said Clara.

"To whom is Caesar going to be sold? and for what sum?"

"For what can be got for him," replied Durant, laughing; "and to whoever will buy him. The sheriff's officer is here. who has seized him for debt, and must make the most of him at market."

"Poor fellow!" said Mr. Edwards; "and must he leave this cottage which he has built, and these bananas which he has planted?"

Caesar now for the first time looked up, and fixing his eyes upon Mr. Edwards for a moment, advanced with an intrepid rather than an imploring countenance, and said, "Will you be my master? Will you be her master? Buy both of us. You shall not repent of it. Caesar will serve you faithfully."

On hearing these words Clara sprang forward, and clasping her hands together, repeated, "Caesar will serve you faithfully."

Mr. Edwards was moved by their entreaties, but he left them without declaring his intentions. He went immediately to Mr. Jefferies, whom he found stretched on a sofa, drinking coffee. As soon as Mr. Edwards mentioned the occasion of his visit, and expressed his sorrow for Caesar, Jefferies exclaimed, "Yes, poor devil! I pity him from the bottom of my soul. But what can I do? I leave all those things to Durant. He says the sheriff's officer has seized him; and there's an end of the matter. You know, money must be had. Besides, Caesar is not worse off than any other slave sold for debt. What signifies talking about the matter, as if it were something that never happened before! Is not it a case that occurs every day in Jamaica?"

"So much the worse," replied Mr. Edwards.

"The worse for them, to be sure," said Jefferies. "But, after all, they are slaves, and are used to be treated as such; and they tell me the Negroes are a thousand times happier here, with us, than they ever were in their own country."

"Did the Negroes tell you so themselves?"

"No; but people better informed than Negroes have told me so; and, after all, slaves there must be; for indigo,[3] and rum, and sugar, we must have."

"Granting it to be physically impossible that the world should exist without rum, sugar, and indigo, why could they not be produced by freemen as well as by slaves? If we hired Negroes for laborers, instead of purchasing them for slaves, do you think they would not work as well as they do now? Does any Negro, under the fear of the overseer, work harder than a Birmingham journeyman, or a Newcastle collier,[4] who toil for themselves and their families?"

"Of that I don't pretend to judge. All I know is, that the West India planters would be ruined if they had no slaves; and I am a West India planter."

"So am I; yet I do not think they are the only people whose interests ought to be considered in this business."

"Their interests, luckily, are protected by the laws of the land; and though they are rich men, and white men, and freemen, they have as good a claim to their rights as the poorest black slave on any of our plantations."

"The law, in our case, seems to make the right; and the very reverse ought to be done—the right should make the law."

"Fortunately for us planters, we need not enter into such nice distinctions. You could not, if you would, abolish the trade. Slaves would be smuggled into the islands."

"What! if nobody would buy them? You know that you cannot smuggle slaves into England. The instant a slave touches English ground he becomes free. Glorious privilege! Why should it not be extended to all her dominions? If the future importation of slaves into these islands were forbidden by law, the trade must cease. No man can either sell or possess slaves without its being known: they cannot be smuggled like lace or brandy."

3. A blue dye made from plants.
4. Coal miner. "Journeyman": one who works for another for day wages (Birmingham, England, experienced great industrial development and population growth in the 17th century).

"Well, well!" retorted Jefferies, a little impatiently, "as yet the law is on our side. I can do nothing in this business, nor can you."

"Yes, we can do something; we can endeavor to make our Negroes as happy as possible."

"I leave the management of these people to Durant."

"That is the very thing of which they complain; forgive me for speaking to you with the frankness of an old acquaintance."

"Oh! you can't oblige me more: I love frankness of all things! To tell you the truth, I have heard complaints of Durant's severity; but I make it a principle to turn a deaf ear to them, for I know nothing can be done with these fellows without it. You are partial to Negroes; but even you must allow they are a race of beings naturally inferior to us. You may in vain think of managing a black as you would a white. Do what you please for a Negro, he will cheat you the first opportunity he finds. You know what their maxim is: 'God gives black men what white men forget.'"

To these common-place desultory observations Mr. Edwards made no reply; but recurred to poor Caesar, and offered to purchase both him and Clara, at the highest price the sheriff's officer could obtain for them at market. Mr. Jefferies, with the utmost politeness to his neighbor, but with the most perfect indifference to the happiness of those whom he considered of a different species from himself, acceded to this proposal. Nothing could be more reasonable, he said; and he was happy to have it in his power to oblige a gentleman for whom he had such a high esteem.

The bargain was quickly concluded with the sheriff's officer; for Mr. Edwards willingly paid several dollars more than the market price for the two slaves. When Caesar and Clara heard that they were not to be separated, their joy and gratitude were expressed with all the ardor and tenderness peculiar to their different characters. Clara was an Eboe, Caesar a Koromantyn[5] Negro: the Eboes are soft, languishing, and timid; the Koromantyns are frank, fearless, martial, and heroic.

Mr. Edwards took his new slaves home with him, desired Bayley, his overseer, to mark out a provision-ground for Caesar, and to give him a cottage, which happened at this time to be vacant.

"Now, my good friend," said he to Caesar, "you may work for yourself, without fear that what you earn may be taken from you; or that you should ever be sold, to pay your master's debts. If he does not understand what I am saying," continued Mr. Edwards, turning to his overseer, "you will explain it to him."

Caesar perfectly understood all that Mr. Edwards said; but his feelings were at this instant so strong that he could not find expression for his gratitude: he stood like one stupefied! Kindness was new to him; it overpowered his manly heart; and at hearing the words "my good friend," the tears gushed from his eyes: tears which no torture could have extorted! Gratitude swelled in his bosom; and he longed to be alone, that he might freely yield to his emotions.

He was glad when the conch-shell sounded to call the Negroes to their daily labor, that he might relieve the sensations of his soul by bodily exertion. He performed his task in silence; and an inattentive observer might have thought him sullen.

In fact, he was impatient for the day to be over, that he might get rid of a heavy load which weighed upon his mind.

5. I.e., from Africa's Gold Coast. "Eboe": from Benin, a former kingdom of West Africa.

The cruelties practiced by Durant, the overseer of Jefferies' plantation, had exasperated the slaves under his dominion.

They were all leagued together in a conspiracy, which was kept profoundly secret. Their object was to extirpate every white man, woman, and child, in the island. Their plans were laid with consummate art; and the Negroes were urged to execute them by all the courage of despair.

The confederacy extended to all the Negroes in the island of Jamaica, excepting those on the plantation of Mr. Edwards. To them no hint of the dreadful secret had yet been given; their countrymen, knowing the attachment they felt to their master, dared not trust them with these projects of vengeance. Hector, the Negro who was at the head of the conspirators, was the particular friend of Caesar, and had imparted to him all his designs. These friends were bound to each other by the strongest ties. Their slavery and their sufferings began in the same hour; they were both brought from their own country in the same ship. This circumstance alone forms, among the Negroes, a bond of connection not easily to be dissolved. But the friendship of Caesar and Hector commenced even before they were united by the sympathy of misfortune; they were both of the same nation, both Koromantyns. In Africa they had both been accustomed to command; for they had signalized themselves by superior fortitude and courage. They respected each other for excelling in all which they had been taught to consider as virtuous; and with them revenge was a virtue!

Revenge was the ruling passion of Hector: in Caesar's mind it was rather a principle instilled by education. The one considered it as a duty, the other felt it as a pleasure. Hector's sense of injury was acute in the extreme; he knew not how to forgive. Caesar's sensibility was yet more alive to kindness than to insult. Hector would sacrifice his life to extirpate an enemy. Caesar would devote himself for the defense of a friend; and Caesar now considered a white man as his friend.

He was now placed in a painful situation. All his former friendships, all the solemn promises by which he was bound to his companions in misfortune, forbade him to indulge that delightful feeling of gratitude and affection, which, for the first time, he experienced for one of that race of beings whom he had hitherto considered as detestable tyrants—objects of implacable and just revenge!

Caesar was most impatient to have an interview with Hector, that he might communicate his new sentiments, and dissuade him from those schemes of destruction which he meditated. At midnight, when all the slaves except himself were asleep, he left his cottage, and went to Jefferies' plantation, to the hut in which Hector slept. Even in his dreams Hector breathed vengeance. "Spare none! Sons of Africa, spare none!" were the words he uttered in his sleep, as Caesar approached the mat on which he lay. The moon shone full upon him. Caesar contemplated the countenance of his friend, fierce even in sleep. "Spare none! Oh, yes! There is one that must be spared. There is one for whose sake all must be spared."

He wakened Hector by this exclamation. "Of what were you dreaming?" said Caesar.

"Of that which, sleeping or waking, fills my soul—revenge! Why did you waken me from my dream? It was delightful. The whites were weltering in their blood! But silence! we may be overheard."

"No; everyone sleeps but ourselves," replied Caesar. "I could not sleep without speaking to you on—a subject that weighs upon my mind. You have seen Mr. Edwards?"

"Yes. He that is now your master."

"He that is now my benefactor—my friend!"

"Friend! Can you call a white man friend?" cried Hector, starting up with a look of astonishment and indignation.

"Yes," replied Caesar, with firmness. "And you would speak, ay, and would feel, as I do, Hector, if you knew this white man. Oh, how unlike he is to all of his race, that we have ever seen! Do not turn from me with so much disdain. Hear me with patience, my friend."

"I cannot," replied Hector, "listen with patience to one who between the rising and the setting sun can forget all his resolutions, all his promises; who by a few soft words can be so wrought upon as to forget all the insults, all the injuries he has received from this accursed race; and can even call a white man friend!"

Caesar, unmoved by Hector's anger, continued to speak of Mr. Edwards with the warmest expressions of gratitude; and finished by declaring he would sooner forfeit his life than rebel against such a master. He conjured Hector to desist from executing his designs; but all was in vain. Hector sat with his elbows fixed upon his knees, leaning his head upon his hands, in gloomy silence.

Caesar's mind was divided between love for his friend and gratitude to his master: the conflict was violent and painful. Gratitude at last prevailed: he repeated his declaration, that he would rather die than continue in a conspiracy against his benefactor!

Hector refused to except him from the general doom. "Betray us if you will!" cried he. "Betray our secrets to him whom you call your benefactor! to him whom a few hours have made your friend! To him sacrifice the friend of your youth, the companion of your better days, of your better self! Yes, Caesar, deliver me over to the tormentors: I can endure more than they can inflict. I shall expire without a sigh, without a groan. Why do you linger here, Caesar? Why do you hesitate? Hasten this moment to your master; claim your reward for delivering into his power hundreds of your countrymen! Why do you hesitate? Away! The coward's friendship can be of use to none. Who can value his gratitude? Who can fear his revenge?"

Hector raised his voice so high, as he pronounced these words, that he wakened Durant, the overseer, who slept in the next house. They heard him call out suddenly, to inquire who was there: and Caesar had but just time to make his escape, before Durant appeared. He searched Hector's cottage; but finding no one, again retired to rest. This man's tyranny made him constantly suspicious; he dreaded that the slaves should combine against him; and he endeavored to prevent them, by every threat and every stratagem he could devise, from conversing with each other.

They had, however, taken their measures, hitherto, so secretly, that he had not the slightest idea of the conspiracy which was forming in the island. Their schemes were not yet ripe for execution; but the appointed time approached. Hector, when he coolly reflected on what had passed between him and Caesar, could not help admiring the frankness and courage with which he had avowed his change of sentiments. By this avowal, Caesar had in fact exposed his own life to the most imminent danger, from the vengeance of the conspirators,

who might be tempted to assassinate him who had their lives in his power. Notwithstanding the contempt with which, in the first moment of passion, he had treated his friend, he was extremely anxious that he should not break off all connection with the conspirators. He knew that Caesar possessed both intrepidity and eloquence, and that his opposition to their schemes would perhaps entirely frustrate their whole design. He therefore determined to use every possible means to bend him to their purposes.

He resolved to have recourse to one of those persons who, among the Negroes, are considered as sorceresses.[6] Esther, an old Koromantyn Negress, had obtained by her skill in poisonous herbs, and her knowledge of venomous reptiles, a high reputation among her countrymen. She soon taught them to believe her to be possessed of supernatural powers; and she then worked their imagination to what pitch and purpose she pleased.

She was the chief instigator of this intended rebellion. It was she who had stimulated the revengeful temper of Hector almost to frenzy. She now promised him that her arts should be exerted over his friend; and it was not long before he felt their influence. Caesar soon perceived an extraordinary change in the countenance and manner of his beloved Clara. A melancholy hung over her, and she refused to impart to him the cause of her dejection. Caesar was indefatigable in his exertions to cultivate and embellish the ground near his cottage, in hopes of making it an agreeable habitation for her; but she seemed to take no interest in any thing. She would stand beside him immovable, in a deep reverie; but when he inquired whether she was ill, she would answer no, and endeavor to assume an air of gaiety: but this cheerfulness was transient; she soon relapsed into despondency. At length, she endeavored to avoid her lover, as if she feared his farther inquiries.

Unable to endure this state of suspense, he one evening resolved to bring her to an explanation. "Clara," said he, "you once loved me: I have done nothing, have I, to forfeit your confidence?"

"I once loved you!" said she, raising her languid eyes, and looking at him with reproachful tenderness; "and can you doubt my constancy? Oh, Caesar, you little know what is passing in my heart! You are the cause of my melancholy!"

She paused and hesitated, as if afraid that she had said too much; but Caesar urged her with so much vehemence, and so much tenderness, to open to him her whole soul, that, at last, she could not resist his eloquence. She reluctantly revealed to him that secret of which she could not think without horror. She informed him, that unless he complied with what was required of him by the sorceress Esther, he was devoted to die. What it was that Esther required of him, Clara knew not: she knew nothing of the conspiracy. The timidity of her character was ill-suited to such a project; and everything relating to it had been concealed from her with the utmost care.

When she explained to Caesar the cause of her dejection, his natural courage resisted these superstitious fears; and he endeavored to raise Clara's spirits. He endeavored in vain: she fell at his feet; and with tears, and the most tender supplications, conjured him to avert the wrath of the sorceress, by obeying her commands, whatever they might be!

"Clara," replied he, "you know not what you ask!"

6. Those knowledgeable in *obeah* practices of sorcery and magic ritual.

"I ask you to save your life " said she. "I ask you, for my sake, to save your life, while yet it is in your power!"

"But would you, to save my life, Clara, make me the worst of criminals? Would you make me the murderer of my benefactor?"

Clara started with horror.

"Do you recollect the day, the moment, when we were on the point of being separated forever, Clara? Do you remember the white man's coming to my cottage? Do you remember his look of benevolence—his voice of compassion? Do you remember his generosity? Oh! Clara, would you make me the murderer of this man?"

"Heaven forbid!" said Clara. "This cannot be the will of the sorceress!"

"It is," said Caesar. "But she shall not succeed, even though she speaks with the voice of Clara. Urge me no further; my resolution is fixed. I should be unworthy of your love if I were capable of treachery and ingratitude."

"But is there no means of averting the wrath of Esther?" said Clara. "Your life—"

"Think, first, of my honor," interrupted Caesar. "Your fears deprive you of reason. Return to this sorceress, and tell her that I dread not her wrath. My hands shall never be imbrued in the blood of my benefactor. Clara! can you forget his look when he told us that we should never more be separated?"

"It went to my heart," said Clara, bursting into tears. "Cruel, cruel Esther!" Why do you command us to destroy such a generous master?"

The conch sounded to summon the Negroes to their morning's work. It happened this day, that Mr. Edwards, who was continually intent upon increasing the comforts and happiness of his slaves, sent his carpenter, while Caesar was absent, to fit up the inside of his cottage; and when Caesar returned from work, he found his master pruning the branches of a tamarind tree that over-hung the thatch. "How comes it, Caesar," said he, "that you have not pruned these branches?"

Caesar had no knife. "Here is mine for you," said Mr. Edwards. "It is very sharp," added he, smiling; "but I am not one of those master who are afraid to trust their Negroes with sharp knives."

These words were spoken with perfect simplicity: Mr. Edwards had no suspicion, at this time, of what was passing in the Negro's mind. Caesar received the knife without uttering a syllable; but no sooner was Mr. Edwards out of sight than he knelt down, and, in a transport of gratitude, swore that, with this knife, he would stab himself to the heart sooner than betray his master!

The principle of gratitude conquered every other sensation. The mind of Caesar was not insensible to the charms of freedom: he knew the Negro conspirators had so taken their measures that there was the greatest probability of their success. His heart beat high at the idea of recovering his liberty: but he was not to be seduced from his duty, not even by this delightful hope; nor was he to be intimidated by the dreadful certainty that his former friends and countrymen, considering him as a deserter from their cause, would become his bitterest enemies. The loss of Hector's esteem and affection was deeply felt by Caesar. Since the night that the decisive conversation relative to Mr. Edwards passed, Hector and he had never exchanged a syllable.

This visit proved the cause of much suffering to Hector, and to several of the slaves on Jefferies' plantation. We mentioned that Durant had been awakened by the raised voice of Hector. Though he could not find anyone in the

cottage, yet his suspicions were not dissipated; and an accident nearly brought the whole conspiracy to light. Durant had ordered one of the Negroes to watch a boiler of sugar: the slave was overcome by the heat, and fainted. He had scarcely recovered his senses when the overseer came up, and found that the sugar had fermented, by having remained a few minutes too long in the boiler. He flew into a violent passion, and ordered that the Negro should receive fifty lashes. His victim bore them without uttering a groan; but, when his punishment was over, and when he thought the overseer was gone, he exclaimed, "It will soon be our turn!"

Durant was not out of hearing. He turned suddenly, and observed that the Negro looked at Hector when he pronounced these words, and this confirmed the suspicion that Hector was carrying on some conspiracy. He immediately had recourse to that brutality which he considered as the only means of governing black men: Hector and three other Negroes were lashed unmercifully; but no confessions could be extorted.

Mr. Jefferies might perhaps have forbidden such violence to be used, if he had not been at the time carousing with a party of jovial West Indians, who thought of nothing but indulging their appetites in all the luxuries that art and nature could supply. The sufferings which had been endured by many of the wretched Negroes to furnish out this magnificent entertainment were never once thought of by these selfish epicures. Yet so false are the general estimates of character, that all these gentlemen passed for men of great feeling and generosity! The human mind, in certain situations, becomes so accustomed to ideas of tyranny and cruelty, that they no longer appear extraordinary or detestable: they rather seem part of the necessary and immutable order of things.

Mr. Jefferies was stopped, as he passed from his dining-room into his drawing-room, by a little Negro child, of about five years old, who was crying bitterly. He was the son of one of the slaves who were at this moment under the torturer's hand. "Poor little devil!" said Mr. Jeffries, who was more than half intoxicated. "Take him away; and tell Durant, some of ye, to pardon his father—if he can."

The child ran, eagerly, to announce his father's pardon; but he soon returned, crying more violently than before. Durant would not hear the boy; and it was now no longer possible to appeal to Mr. Jefferies, for he was in the midst of an assembly of fair ladies, and no servant belonging to the house dared to interrupt the festivities of the evening. The three men, who were so severely flogged to extort from them confessions, were perfectly innocent: they knew nothing of the confederacy; but the rebels seized the moment when their minds were exasperated by this cruelty and injustice, and they easily persuaded them to join the league. The hope of revenging themselves upon the overseer was a motive sufficient to make them brave death in any shape.

Another incident, which happened a few days before the time destined for the revolt of the slaves, determined numbers who had been undecided. Mrs. Jefferies was a languid beauty, or rather a languid fine lady who had been a beauty, and who spent all that part of the day which was not devoted to the pleasures of the table, or to reclining on a couch, in dress. She was one day extended on a sofa, fanned by four slaves, two at her head and two at her feet, when news was brought that a large chest, directed to her, was just arrived from London.

This chest contained various articles of dress of the newest fashions. The Jamaica ladies carry their ideas of magnificence to a high pitch: they willingly give a hundred guineas for a gown, which they perhaps wear but once or twice. In the elegance and variety of her ornaments, Mrs. Jefferies was not exceeded by any lady in the island, except by one who had lately received a cargo from England. She now expected to outshine her competitor, and desired that the chest should be unpacked in her presence.

In taking out one of the gowns, it caught on a nail in the lid, and was torn. The lady, roused from her natural indolence by this disappointment to her vanity, instantly ordered that the unfortunate female slave should be severely chastised. The woman was the wife of Hector; and this fresh injury worked up his temper, naturally vindictive, to the highest point. He ardently longed for the moment when he might satiate his vengeance.

The plan the Negroes had laid was to set fire to the canes, at one and the same time, on every plantation; and when the white inhabitants of the island should run to put out the fire, the blacks were to seize this moment of confusion and consternation to fall upon them, and make a general massacre. The time when this scheme was to be carried into execution was not known to Caesar; for the conspirators had changed their day, as soon as Hector told them that his friend was no longer one of the confederacy. They dreaded he should betray them; and it was determined that he and Clara should both be destroyed, unless they could be prevailed upon to join the conspiracy.

Hector wished to save his friend, but the desire of vengeance overcame every other feeling. He resolved, however, to make an attempt, for the last time, to change Caesar's resolution.

For this purpose, Esther was the person he employed: she was to work upon his mind by means of Clara. On returning to her cottage one night, she found suspended from the thatch one of those strange fantastic charms with which the Indian sorceresses terrify those whom they have prescribed. Clara, unable to conquer her terror, repaired again to Esther, who received her first in mysterious silence; but, after she had implored her forgiveness for the past, and with all possible humility conjured her to grant her future protection, the sorceress deigned to speak. Her commands were that Clara should prevail upon her lover to meet her, on this awful spot, the ensuing night.

Little suspecting what was going forward on the plantation of Jefferies, Mr. Edwards that evening gave his slaves a holiday. He and his family came out at sunset, when the fresh breeze had sprung up, and seated themselves under a spreading palm-tree, to enjoy the pleasing spectacle of this Negro festival. His Negroes were all well clad, and in the gayest colors, and their merry countenances suited the gaiety of their dress. While some were dancing, and some playing on the tambourine, others appeared among the distant trees, bringing baskets of avocado pears, grapes, and pineapples, the produce of their own provision-grounds; and others were employed in spreading their clean trenchers, or the calabashes,[7] which served for plates and dishes. The Negroes continued to dance and divert themselves till late in the evening. When they separated and retired to rest, Caesar, recollecting his promise to Clara, repaired secretly to the habitation of this sorceress. It was situated in the recess

7. Hollowed gourds. "Trenchers": plates.

of a thick wood. When he arrived there, he found the door fastened; and he was obliged to wait some time before it was opened by Esther.

The first object he beheld was his beloved Clara, stretched on the ground, apparently a corpse! The sorceress had thrown her into a trance by a preparation of deadly nightshade. The hag burst into an infernal laugh, when she beheld the despair that was painted in Caesar's countenance. "Wretch!" cried she, "you have defied my power; behold its victim!"

Caesar, in a transport of rage, seized her by the throat: but his fury was soon checked.

"Destroy me," said the fiend, "and you destroy your Clara. She is not dead: but she lies in the sleep of death, into which she has been thrown by magic art, and from which no power but mine can restore her to the light of life. Yes! look at her, pale and motionless! Never will she rise from the earth, unless, within one hour, you obey my commands. I have administered to Hector and his companions the solemn fetish oath, at the sound of which every Negro in Africa trembles? You know my object."

"Fiend, I do!" replied Caesar, eyeing her sternly; "but, while I have life, it shall never be accomplished."

"Look yonder!" cried she, pointing to the moon; "in a few minutes that moon will set: at that hour Hector and his friends will appear. They come armed—armed with weapons which I shall steep in poison for their enemies. Themselves I will render invulnerable. Look again!" continued she; "if my dim eyes mistake not, yonder they come. Rash man, you die if they cross my threshold."

"I wish for death," said Caesar. "Clara is dead!"

"But you can restore her to life by a single word."

Caesar, at this moment, seemed to hesitate.

"Consider! Your heroism is vain," continued Esther. "You will have the knives of fifty of the conspirators in your bosom, if you do not join them; and, after you have fallen, the death of your master is inevitable. Here is the bowl of poison, in which the Negro knives are to be steeped. Your friends, your former friends, your countrymen, will be in arms in a few minutes; and they will bear down everything before them—Victory, Wealth, Freedom, and Revenge, will be theirs."

Caesar appeared to be more and more agitated. His eyes were fixed upon Clara. The conflict in his mind was violent: but his sense of gratitude and duty could not be shaken by hope, fear, or ambition; nor could it be vanquished by love. He determined, however, to appear to yield. As if struck with panic, at the approach of the confederate Negroes, he suddenly turned to the sorceress, and said, in a tone of feigned submission, "It is in vain to struggle with fate. Let my knife, too, be dipped in your magic poison."

The sorceress clapped her hands with infernal joy in her countenance. She bade him instantly give her his knife, that she might plunge it to the hilt in the bowl of poison, to which she turned with savage impatience. His knife was left in his cottage, and, under pretence of going in search of it, he escaped. Esther promised to prepare Hector and all his companions to receive him with their ancient cordiality on his return. Caesar ran with the utmost speed along a bye-path out of the wood, met none of the rebels, reached his master's house, scaled the wall of his bed-chamber, got in at the window, and wakened him, exclaiming, "Arm—arm yourself, my dear master! Arm all your slaves! They

will fight for you, and die for you; as I will the first. The Koromantyn yell of war will be heard in Jefferies plantation this night! Arm—arm yourself, my dear master, and let us surround the rebel leaders while it is yet time. I will lead you to the place where they are all assembled, on condition that their chief, who is my friend, shall be pardoned."

Mr. Edwards armed himself and the Negroes on his plantation, as well as the whites; they were all equally attached to him. He followed Caesar into the recesses of the wood

They proceeded with all possible rapicity, but in perfect silence, till they reached Esther s habitation: which they surrounded completely, before they were perceived by the conspirators.

Mr. Edwards looked through a hole in the wall; and, by the blue flame of a cauldron, over which the sorceress was stretching her shriveled hands, he saw Hector and five stout Negroes standing, intent upon her incantations. These Negroes held their knives in their hands, ready to dip them into the bowl of poison. It was proposed, by one of the whites, to set fire immediately to the hut, and thus to force the rebels to surrender. The advice was followed; but Mr. Edwards charged his people to spare their prisoners. The moment the rebels saw that the thatch of the hut was in flames they set up the Koromantyn yell of war, and rushed out with frantic desperation.

"Yield! You are pardoned, Hector," cried Mr. Edwards, in a loud voice.

"You are pardoned, my friend!" repeated Caesar.

Hector, incapable at this instant of listening to anything but revenge, sprang forwards, and plunged his knife into the bosom of Caesar. The faithful servant staggered back a few paces: his master caught him in his arms. "I die content," said he. "Bury me with Clara."

He swooned from loss of blood as they were carrying him home; but when his wound was examined, it was found not to be mortal. As he recovered from his swoon, he stared wildly round him, trying to recollect where he was, and what had happened. He thought that he was still in a dream, when he saw his beloved Clara standing beside him. The opiate, which the pretended sorceress had administered to her, had ceased to operate; she wakened from her trance just at the time the Koromantyr yell commenced. Caesar's joy!—we must leave that to the imagination

In the meantime, what became of the rebel Negroes, and Mr. Edwards?

The taking the chief conspirators prisoners did not prevent the Negroes upon Jefferies' plantation from insurrection. The moment they heard the war-whoop, the signal agreed upon, they rose in a body; and, before they could be prevented, either by the whites on the estate, or by Mr. Edwards' adherents, they had set fire to the overseer's house, and to the canes. The overseer was the principal object of their vengeance—he died in tortures, inflicted by the hands of those who had suffered most by his cruelties. Mr. Edwards, however, quelled the insurgents before rebellion spread to any other estates in the island. The influence of his character, and the effect of his eloquence upon the minds of the people, were astonishing: nothing but his interference could have prevented the total destruction of Mr. Jefferies and his family, who, as it was computed, lost this night upwards of fifty thousand pounds. He was never afterwards able to recover his losses, or to shake off his constant fear of a fresh insurrection among his slaves. At length, he and his lady returned to England, where they were obliged to live in obscurity and indigence. They had no con-

solation in their misfortunes but that of railing at the treachery of the whole race of slaves. Our readers, we hope, will think that at least one exception may be made, in favor of THE GRATEFUL NEGRO.

March 1802 1804

DOROTHY WORDSWORTH

1771–1855

Through times of personal crisis, she "preserved me still a Poet," wrote William Wordsworth about his younger sister, Dorothy, in Book XI of *The Prelude*. Earlier, in *Tintern Abbey*(1798), his great meditation on the redemptive powers of nature, he was more explicit. Addressing Dorothy as his "dearest Friend," he told her that "in thy voice I catch / The language of my former heart, and read / My former pleasures in the shooting lights / Of thy wild eyes." Though she was hardly as childlike as that last quotation implies, the woman who elicited such praise was in fact her brother's "dearest Friend" for most of his life. Born in 1771, the only girl among five Wordsworth children, Dorothy Wordsworth was twenty-one months William's junior. After their mother's death when Dorothy was quite young, the girl was raised by various relatives and saw her brothers only occasionally. But in 1795, when she was twenty-four, William came into a legacy that enabled the two to settle together permanently, first in a cottage in Dorsetshire, then at Grasmere, in the English Lake District Wordsworth was to celebrate throughout his poetic career.

At Alfoxden, in Dorsetshire, Dorothy began the journals which she later continued at Grasmere and which constitute the achievement on which her own reputation chiefly rests today: she began them because, as she noted, "I shall give William Pleasure" by undertaking such a task. For many readers, then—as for Dorothy herself—the principal virtue of these works inheres in the source material they provided for the writer's brother, along with the William Wordsworth biography they record. As the critic Helen Darbishire once observed, they are important documents that show us "the life of a great poet." At the same time, however, Dorothy's diaries are extraordinarily compelling in and of themselves.

Vividly observed, often passionately frank, these journals are written with a hasty energy that perfectly captures the kaleidoscope of the Wordsworths' rural yet literary world. Though outwardly serene, that world was full of variety and vitality, as Dorothy continually demonstrates. Daily life alternated domesticity with adventure: Dorothy baked pies, broiled beefsteaks, and climbed craggy hillsides in rainy weather. William brooded on new poems, and Dorothy soothed his headaches, then wandered along country roads where she met a host of beggars, tinkers, and other itinerants who would provide him with subjects for more poems and her with further observations. Throughout the *Journals*, her narration of such matters is unfailingly brisk yet extraordinarily meticulous. On parting with her brother, for instance, she noted that "after a flood of tears my heart was easier," then demonstrated her recovery with keen observations of wildflowers and of "a blind man, driving a very large beautiful Bull and a cow." Nor did she ever yield to excessive sentimentality, even about her adored William: she could not, for example, resist recording an episode in a meadow when the poet "took a sheep for me, and then me for a sheep."

On the day William Wordsworth married Mary Hutchinson in October 1802, his sister was so distraught—as her journal entry, included here, reveals—that she

could not attend the wedding. Yet after the couple returned to Grasmere, Dorothy went on living with them, and there is every indication that the family was harmonious. Not only did Dorothy continue to "preserve" her brother as a poet but she became a fond nurse to his children, for whom she wrote some accomplished verses. As these works suggest, and as the piece titled *Peaceful Our Valley* also indicates, she may well have had considerable poetic ability of her own. Why she did not produce more poetry than she did is thus a troublesome question, for, as her journals reveal, she was never merely her brother's literary handmaiden, though critics have often defined her that way. Perhaps, as Virginia Woolf was to speculate in *A Room of One's Own*, she turned her talents to prose because "the poetry" is most often "denied outlet" in women. In any case, she continued writing her lively and scrupulously detailed journals until 1828. In 1829, she suffered a serious illness that would lead to the onset of arteriosclerosis, and she lingered on in what M. H. Abrams has called a kind of "half-life" for another twenty years; for most of that time she was devotedly nursed by the brother to whom her own devotion had once been so important.

From The Grasmere Journals

1800

May 14 [Wednesday]. Wm. and John set off into Yorkshire after dinner at $\frac{1}{2}$ past 2 o'clock, cold pork in their pockets.[1] I left them at the turning of the Low-wood bay under the trees. My heart was so full that I could hardly speak to W. when I gave him a farewell kiss. I sate a long time upon a stone at the margin of the lake, and after a flood of tears my heart was easier. The lake looked to me I knew not why dull and melancholy, and the weltering on the shores seemed a heavy sound. I walked as long as I could amongst the stones of the shore. The wood rich in flowers. A beautiful yellow, palish yellow flower, that looked thick round and double, and smelt very sweet—I supposed it was a ranunculus—Crowfoot, the grassy-leaved Rabbit-toothed white flower, strawberries, geranium—scentless violet, anemones two kinds, orchises, primroses. The heckberry very beautiful, the crab coming out as a low shrub. Met a blind man, driving a very large beautiful Bull and a cow—he walked with two sticks. Came home by Clappersgate. The valley very green, many sweet views up to Rydale head when I could juggle away the fine houses,[2] but they disturbed me even more than when I have been happier. One beautiful view of the Bridge, without Sir Michael's.[3] Sat down very often, though it was cold. I resolved to write a journal of the time till W. and J. return, and I set about keeping my resolve because I will not quarrel with myself, and because I shall give Wm Pleasure by it when he comes home again. At Rydale a woman of the village, stout and well dressed, begged a halfpenny—she had never she said done it before, but these hard times——Arrived at home with a bad headache, set some slips of privett.[4] The evening cold, had a fire—my face now flame-coloured. It is nine o'clock. I shall soon go to bed. A young woman begged at the door—she had come from Manchester on Sunday morn with two shillings and a slip of paper which she supposed a Bank note—it was a

1. The poet William Wordsworth and his younger brother, John, were on the way to visit Mary Hutchinson, whom William would marry two years later.

2. I.e., keep them out of view.
3. Sir Michael le Fleming's estate, Rydal Hall.
4. I.e., arranged cuttings from a privet, a kind of shrub.

cheat. She had buried her husband and three children within a year and a half—all in one grave—burying very dear—paupers all put in one place—20 shillings paid for as much ground as will bury a man—a stone to be put over it or the right will be lost—each time the ground is opened. Oh! that I had a letter from William!

* * *

1801

November 27 [Friday]. Snow upon the ground thinly scattered. It snowed after we got up and then the sun shone and it was very warm though frosty— now the sun shines sweetly. A woman came who was travelling with her husband—he had been wounded and was going with her to live at Whitehaven. She had been at Ambleside the night before, offered 4d[5] at the Cock for a bed—they sent her to one Harrison's where she and her husband had slept upon the hearth and bought a pennyworth of chips for a fire. Her husband was gone before very lame—"Aye" says she "I was once an officer's wife I, as you see me now. My first husband married me at Appleby. I had 18£ a year for teaching a school and because I had no fortune his father turned him out of doors. I have been in the West Indies. I lost the use of this finger just before he died he came to me and said he must bid farewell to his dear children and me. I had a muslin gown on like yours—I seized hold of his coat as he went from me and slipped the joint of my finger. He was shot directly. I came to London and married this man. He was clerk to Judge Chambray, *that man*, that man that's going on the Road now. If he, Judge Chambray, had been at Kendal he would [have] given us a guinea or two and made nought of it, for he is very generous." Before dinner we set forward to walk intending to return to dinner. But as we had got as far as Rydale Wm thought he would go on to Mr Luff's. We accompanied him under Loughrigg, and parted near the stepping stones.

* * *

December 22 [Tuesday]. Still thaw. I washed my head. Wm and I went to Rydale for letters. The road was covered with dirty snow, rough and rather slippery. We had a melancholy letter from C.,[6] for he had been very ill, though he was better when he wrote. We walked home almost without speaking. Wm composed a few lines of the Pedlar. We talked about Lamb's Tragedy[7] as we went down the White Moss. We stopped a long time in going to watch a little bird with a salmon coloured breast—a white cross or T upon its wings, and a brownish back with faint stripes. It was pecking the scattered Dung upon the road. It began to peck at the distance of 4 yards from us and advanced nearer and nearer till it came within the length of Wm's stick without any apparent fear of us. As we came up the White Moss we met an old man, who I saw was a beggar by his two bags hanging over his shoulder, but from a half laziness, half indifference and a wanting to try him if he would speak I let him pass. He said nothing, and my heart smote me. I turned back and said You are begging? "Ay," says he. I gave him a halfpenny. William, judging from his appearance joined in, I suppose you were a sailor? "Ay," he replied, "I have been 57 years at sea, 12 of them on board a man-of-war under Sir Hugh Palmer." Why have you not a pension? "I have no pension, but I could have got into Greenwich hospi-

5. Fourpence.
6. Samuel Taylor Coleridge (1772–1834), poet and

friend of the Wordsworths.
7. *John Woodvil* (1802), by Charles Lamb.

tal[8] but all my officers are dead." He was 75 years of age, had a freshish colour in his cheeks, grey hair, a decent hat with a binding round the edge, the hat worn brown and glossy, his shoes were small thin shoes low in the quarters, pretty good. They had belonged to a gentleman. His coat was blue, frock shaped coming over his thighs it had been joined up at the seams behind with paler blue to let it out, and there were three Bell-shaped patches of darker blue behind where the buttons had been. His breeches were either of fustian or grey cloth, with strings hanging down, whole and tight; he had a checked shirt on, and a small coloured handkerchief tied round his neck. His bags were hung over each shoulder and lay on each side of him, below his breast. One was brownish and of coarse stuff, the other was white with meal[9] on the outside, and his blue waist-coat was whitened with meal. In the coarse bag I guessed he put his scraps of meat etc. He walked with a slender stick decently stout, but his legs bowed outwards. We overtook old Fleming[1] at Rydale, leading his little Dutchmanlike grandchild along the slippery road. The same pace seemed to be natural to them both, the old man and the little child, and they went hand in hand, the grandfather cautious, yet looking proud of his charge.

* * *

December 29 [Tuesday]. A fine morning. A thin fog upon the hills which soon disappeared. The sun shone. Wilkinson went with us to the top of the hill. We turned out of the road at the 2nd mile stone and passed a pretty cluster of houses at the foot of St. John's Vale. The houses were among tall trees partly of Scotch fir, and some naked forest trees. We crossed a Bridge just below these houses and the river winded sweetly along the meadows. Our road soon led us along the sides of dreary bare hills. but we had a glorious prospect to the left of Saddleback, half way covered with snow and underneath the comfortable white houses and the village of Threlkeld. These houses and the village want trees about them. Skiddaw was behind us and dear Coleridge's desert[2] home——As we ascended the hills it grew very cold and slippery. Luckily the wind was at our backs and helped us on. A sharp hail shower gathered at the head of Matterdale and the view upwards was very grand—the wild cottages seen through the hurrying hail shower. The wind drove and eddied about and about and the hills looked large and swelling through the storm. We thought of Coleridge. O the bonny nooks and windings and curlings of the Beck down at the bottom of the steep green mossy Banks.

* * *

1802

January 31 [Sunday]. William had slept very ill—he was tired and had a bad headache. We walked round the two lakes. Grasmere was very soft and Rydale was extremely beautiful from the pasture side. Nab Scar was just topped by a cloud which cutting it off as high as it could be cut off made the mountain look uncommonly lofty. We sate down a long time in different places. I always love to walk that way because it is the way I first came to Rydale and Grasmere, and because our dear Coleridge did also. When I came with Wm $6\frac{1}{2}$ years ago it was just at sunset. There was a rich yellow light on the

8. The royal hospital for seamen. "Man-o'-war" (p. 320): a warship.
9. Flour.

1. Thomas Fleming, an innkeeper at Rydale.
2. Deserted.

waters and the Islands were reflected there. Today it was grave and soft but not perfectly calm. William says it was much such a day as when Coleridge came with him. The sun shone out before we reached Grasmere. We sate by the roadside at the foot of the Lake close to Mary's dear name which she had cut herself upon the stone. William cut at it with his knife to make it plainer. We amused ourselves for a long time in watching the Breezes some as if they came from the bottom of the lake spread in a circle, brushing along the surface of the water, and growing more delicate, as it were thinner and of a *paler* colour till they died away. Others spread out like a peacock's tail, and some went right forward this way and that in all directions. The lake was still where these breezes were not, but they made it all alive. I found a strawberry blossom in a rock. The little slender flower had more courage than the green leaves, for *they* were but half expanded and half grown, but the blossom was spread full out. I uprooted it rashly, and I felt as if I had been committing an outrage, so I planted it again. It will have but a stormy life of it, but let it live if it can. * * * Mr Simpson drank tea with us. We payed our rent to Benson. William's head bad after Mr S. was gone. I petted him on the carpet and began a letter to Sara.

* * *

February 14 [Sunday]. * * * After dinner a little before sunset I walked out. About 20 yards above glowworm Rock I met a Carman, a Highlander I suppose, with 4 carts, the first 3 belonging to himself, the last evidently to a man and his family who had joined company with him and who I guessed to be Potters. The carman was cheering his horses and talking to a little lass about 10 years of age who seemed to make him her companion. She ran to the Wall and took up a large stone to support the wheel of one of his carts and ran on before with it in her arms to be ready for him. She was a beautiful creature and there was something uncommonly impressive in the lightness and joyousness of her manner. Her business seemed to be all pleasure—pleasure in her own motions—and the man looked at her as if he too was pleased and spoke to her in the same tone in which he spoke to his horses. There was a wildness in her whole figure, not the wildness of a Mountain lass but a *Road* lass, a traveller from her Birth, who had wanted neither food nor clothes. Her Mother followed the last cart with a lovely child, perhaps about a year old, at her Back and a good-looking girl about 15 years old walked beside her. All the children were like the mother. She had a very fresh complexion, but she was blown with fagging up the hill with the steepness of the hill and the Bairn[3] that she carried. Her husband was helping the horse to drag the cart up by pushing it with his Shoulder. I got tea when I reached home and read German till about 9 o'clock. Then Molly went away and I wrote to Coleridge. Went to bed at about 12 o'clock. I slept in Wm's bed, and I slept badly, for my thoughts were full of William.

* * *

March 4 [Thursday]. Before we had quite finished Breakfast Calvert's man brought the horses for Wm.[4] We had a deal to do to shave—pens to make— poems to put in order for writing, to settle the dress pack up etc. The man came before the pens were made and he was obliged to leave me with only

3. Baby. "Blown with fagging": i.e., tired with struggling.

4. In preparation for an expedition to Keswick, to meet Coleridge.

two. Since he has left me (at $\frac{1}{2}$ past 11) it is now 2 I have been putting the Drawers into order, laid by his clothes which we had thrown here and there and everywhere, filed two months' newspapers and got my dinner 2 boiled eggs and 2 apple tarts. I have set Molly on to clear the garden a little, and I myself have helped. I transplanted some snowdrops—The Bees are busy—Wm has a nice bright day. It was hard frost in the night. The Robins are singing sweetly. Now for my walk. I *will* be busy, I *will* look well and be well when he comes back to me. O the Darling! Here is one of his bitten apples! I can hardly find in my heart to throw it into the fire. I must wash myself, then off—I walked round the two Lakes crossed the stepping stones at Rydale Foot. Sate down where we always sit. I was full of thoughts about my darling. Blessings on him. I came home at the foot of our own hill under Loughrigg. They are making sad ravages in the woods. Benson's Wood is going and the wood above the River. The wind has blown down a [?small] fir tree on the Rock that terminates John's path—I suppose the wind of Wednesday night. I read German after my return till tea time. After tea I worked and read the LB, enchanted with the Idiot Boy.[5] Wrote to Wm then went to Bed. It snowed when I went to Bed.

* * *

March 18 [Thursday]. A very fine morning. The sun shone but it was far colder than yesterday. I felt myself weak, and William charged me not to go to Mrs Lloyd's I seemed indeed, to myself unfit for it but when he was gone[6] I thought I would get the visit over if I could—So I ate a Beef-steak thinking it would strengthen me so it did, and I went off. I had a very pleasant walk. Rydale vale was full of life and motion. The wind blew briskly and the lake was covered all over with Bright silver waves that were there each the twinkling of an eye, then others rose up and took their place as fast as they went away. The Rocks glittered in the sunshine, the crows and the ravens were busy, and the thrushes and little Birds sang. I went through the fields, and sate $\frac{1}{2}$ an hour afraid to pass a Cow. The Cow looked at me and I looked at the Cow and whenever I stirred the Cow gave over eating. I was not very much tired when I reached Lloyds, I walked in the garden. Charles is all for agriculture. Mrs L. in her kindest way. A parcel came in from Birmingham, with Lamb's play for us and for C. They came with me as far as Rydale. As we came along Ambleside vale in the twilight—it was a grave evening—there was something in the air that compelled me to serious thought. The hills were large, closed in by the sky. It was nearly dark when I parted from the Lloyds that is, night was come on and the moon came out from behind a mountain mass of Black clouds—O the unutterable darkness of the sky and the earth below the moon! and the glorious brightness of the moon itself! There was a vivid sparkling streak of light at this end of Rydale water but the rest was very dark and Loughrigg fell and Silver How were white and bright as if they were covered with hoar frost. The moon retired again and appeared and disappeared several times before I reached home. Once there was no moonlight to be seen but upon the Island house and the promontory of the Island where it stands, "That needs must be a holy place"[7] etc. etc. I had many very exquisite feelings and when I saw this

5. "LB": *Lyrical Ballads*, the book of poems which Wordsworth and Coleridge published together in 1798. *The Idiot Boy* was one of William's contributions.

6. To Keswick.

7. Source unknown; possibly from an early version of Coleridge's *Kubla Khan*.

lowly Building in the waters among the Dark and lofty hills, with that bright soft light upon it, it made me more than half a poet. I was tired when I reached home. I could not sit down to reading and tried to write verses but alas! I gave up expecting William and went soon to bed. Fletcher's carts came home late.

* * *

April 15 [Thursday]. It was a threatening misty morning—but mild. We set off after dinner from Eusemere. * * * When we were in the woods beyond Gowbarrow park we saw a few daffodils close to the water side. We fancied that the lake had floated the seeds ashore and that the little colony had so sprung up. But as we went along there were more and yet more and at last under the boughs of the trees, we saw that there was a long belt of them along the shore, about the breadth of a country turnpike road. I never saw daffodils so beautiful they grew among the mossy stones about and about them, some rested their heads upon these stones as on a pillow for weariness and the rest tossed and reeled and danced and seemed as if they verily laughed with the wind that blew upon them over the lake, they looked so gay ever glancing ever changing. This wind blew directly over the lake to them. There was here and there a little knot and a few stragglers a few yards higher up but they were so few as not to disturb the simplicity and unity and life of that one busy high-way.[8] We rested again and again. The Bays were stormy, and we heard the waves at different distances and in the middle of the water like the sea.

* * *

April 29 [Thursday]. A beautiful morning. The sun shone and all was pleas-ant. * * * We * * * went to John's Grove, sate a while at first. Afterwards William lay, and I lay in the trench under the fence—he with his eyes shut and listening to the waterfalls and the Birds. There was no one waterfall above an-other—it was a sound of waters in the air—the voice of the air. William heard me breathing and rustling now and then but we both lay still, and unseen by one another. He thought that it would be as sweet thus to lie so in the grave, to hear the *peaceful* sounds of the earth and just to know that our dear friends were near. The Lake was still. There was a Boat out. Silver How reflected with delicate purple and yellowish hues as I have seen Spar. Lambs on the island and running races together by the half dozen in the round field near us. The copses greenish, hawthorn green.—Came home to dinner then went to Mr. Simpson. We rested a long time under a wall. Sheep and lambs were in the field—cottages smoking. As I lay down on the grass, I observed the glittering silver line on the ridges of the Backs of the sheep, owing to their situation re-specting the Sun—which made them look beautiful but with something of strangeness, like animals of another kind—as if belonging to a more splendid world.

* * *

September 24. Mary first met us in the avenue. She looked so fat and well that we were made very happy by the sight of her. Then came Sara, and last of all Joanna.[9] Tom was forking corn standing upon the corn cart. We dressed

8. Two years later William wrote a poem about the daffodils, *I Wandered Lonely as a Cloud*, which appears to rely heavily on Dorothy's prose description.
9. The occasion is the marriage of William and Mary.

All of Mary's sisters and brothers were present, but only three attended the wedding, apparently because Dorothy was overwrought.

ourselves immediately and got tea—the garden looked gay with asters and sweet peas. I looked at everything with tranquility and happiness—was ill on Saturday and on Sunday and continued to be during most of the time of our stay. Jack and George came on Friday Evening 1st October. On Saturday 2nd we rode to Hackness, William Jack George and Sara single, I behind Tom. On Sunday 3rd Mary and Sara were busy packing. On Monday 4th October 1802, my Brother William was married to Mary Hutchinson. I slept a good deal of the night and rose fresh and well in the morning. At a little after 8 o'clock I saw them go down the avenue towards the Church. William had parted from me upstairs. I gave him the wedding ring—with how deep a blessing! I took it from my forefinger where I had worn it the whole of the night before—he slipped it again onto my finger and blessed me fervently. When they were absent my dear little Sara prepared the breakfast. I kept myself as quiet as I could, but when I saw the two men running up the walk, coming to tell us it was over, I could stand it no longer and threw myself on the bed where I lay in stillness, neither hearing or seeing anything, till Sara came upstairs to me and said "They are coming" This forced me from the bed where I lay and I moved I knew not how straight forward, faster than my strength could carry me till I met my beloved William and fell upon his bosom. He and John Hutchinson led me to the house and there I stayed to welcome my dear Mary. As soon as we had breakfasted we departed.[1] It rained when we set off. Poor Mary was much agitated when she parted from her Brothers and Sisters and her home. Nothing particular occurred till we reached Kirby We had sunshine and showers, pleasant talk, love and cheerfulness. * * * It rained very hard when we reached Windermere. We sate in the rain at Wilcock's to change horses, and arrived at Grasmere at about 6 o'clock on Wednesday Evening, the 6th of October 1802. Molly was overjoyed to see us, for my part I cannot describe what I felt, and our dear Mary's feelings would I dare say not be easy to speak of. We went by candle light into the garden and were astonished at the growth of the Brooms, Portugal Laurels, etc. etc. etc. The next day, Thursday, we unpacked the Boxes. On Friday 8th we baked Bread, and Mary and I walked, first upon the Hill side, and then in John's Grove, then in view of Rydale, the first walk that I had taken with my Sister.

1800–03 1971

Peaceful Our Valley, Fair and Green

Peaceful our valley, fair and green;
 And beautiful the cottages
Each in its nook, its sheltered hold,
 Or underneath its tuft of trees.

Many and beautiful they are; 5
 But there is one that I love best,
A lowly roof in truth it is,
 A brother of the rest.

1. Dorothy traveled back to Grasmere Cottage with William and Mary.

Yet when I sit on rock or hill
 Down-looking on the valley fair, 10
That cottage with its grove of trees
 Summons my heart; it settles there.

Others there are whose small domain
 Of fertile fields with hedgerows green
Might more seduce the traveler's mind 15
 To wish that there his home had been.

Such wish be his! I blame him not,
 My fancies they, perchance, are wild;
I love that house because it is
 The very mountain's child. 20

Fields hath it of its own, green fields;
 But they are craggy, steep, and bare;
Their fence is of the mountain stone,
 And moss and lichen flourish there.

And when the storm comes from the North 25
 It lingers near that pastoral spot,
And piping through the mossy walls,
 It seems delighted with its lot.

And let it take its own delight,
 And let it range the pastures bare 30
Until it reach that grove of trees
 —It may not enter there!

A green unfading grove it is,
 Skirted with many a lesser tree,
Hazel and holly, beech and oak, 35
 A fair and flourishing company!

Precious the shelter of those trees!
 They screen the cottage that I love;
The sunshine pierces to the roof
 And the tall pine trees tower above. 40

When first I saw that dear abode
 It was a lovely winter's day:
After a night of perilous storm
 The West wind ruled with gentle sway;

A day so mild, it might have been 45
 The first day of the gladsome spring;
The robins warbled; and I heard
 One solitary throstle sing:

A stranger in the neighborhood,
 All faces then to me unknown, 50

I left my sole companion-friend
 To wander out alone.

Lured by a little winding path,
 I quitted soon the public road,
A smooth and tempting path it was 55
 By sheep and shepherds trod.

Eastward, toward the mighty hills
 This pathway led me on,
Until I reached a lofty Rock
 With velvet moss o'ergrown. 60

With russet Oak and tufts of Fern
 Its top was richly garlanded;
Its sides adorned with Eglantine
 Bedropped with hips of glossy red.

There too in many a sheltered chink 65
 The foxglove's broad leaves flourished fair,
And silver birch whose purple twigs
 Bend to the softest breathing air.

Beneath that rock my course I stayed
 And, looking to its summit high, 70
"Thou wear'st," said I, "a splendid garb,
 Here winter keeps his revelry.

"I've been a dweller on the plains,
 Have sighed when summer days were gone;
No more I'll sigh; for winter here 75
 Hath gladsome gardens of his own.

"What need of flowers? The splendid moss
 Is gayer than an April mead;
More rich its hues of various green,
 Orange and gold and glowing red." 80

—Beside that gay and lovely rock
 There came with merry voice
A foaming streamlet glancing by
 It seemed to say "Rejoice!"

My youthful wishes all fulfilled 85
 Wishes matured by thoughtful choice,
I stood an Inmate[1] of this vale,
 How could I but rejoice?

 1892

1. Inhabitant.

JANE AUSTEN
1775–1817

In 1816, writing to her nephew about his fiction and her own, Jane Austen asked, "What should I do with your strong, manly spirited sketches, full of variety and glow?—How could I possibly join them on to the little bit (two inches wide) of ivory on which I work with so fine a brush, as produces little effect after much labor?" This modest deprecation of her miniature art recalls the discreet figure Virginia Woolf evokes in A Room of One's Own, an Austen who sits writing in the common sitting room, readying herself for inevitable interruptions by providing herself with a blotter under which she can hide her manuscript. Yet by the time Austen was corresponding with J. Edward Austen at her desk in the common sitting room, she had already published four of the six novels that would gain her immediate and lasting acclaim. Northanger Abbey (1818), Sense and Sensibility (1811), Pride and Prejudice (1813), Mansfield Park (1814), Emma (1816), and Persuasion (1818) are unprecedented achievements inaugurating the great novelistic tradition that continues in the work of Mary Shelley, the Brontës, George Eliot, and Virginia Woolf herself.

Although Austen did not publish until she was thirty-six years old, she had two periods of literary productivity, first in her father's rectory when she was in her teens and early twenties, and second at Chawton, during the last decade of her life. Though shrouded in obscurity, the biographical background of her achievement has always been considered singularly uneventful. The daughter of George Austen, a rector and schoolteacher, and Cassandra (Leigh) Austen, the niece of the master of Balliol College, Oxford, Jane Austen was the seventh of eight children. Five of her six brothers married, and their children participated in the lively correspondence Austen maintained throughout her life. But her most intimate companion and correspondent was her older sister, Cassandra, a painter who was also, according to Austen, "the finest comic writer of the present age." Although Jane, beginning at six, and Cassandra, at nine, were sent away briefly to three different schools, they received most of their education at home from their father. When Mr. Austen discontinued his school, the two sisters shared a sitting room, which included Jane's piano and notebooks and Cassandra's drawing implements. From this period, 1787–93, date such precocious juvenilia as Love and Freindship (Austen's youthful spelling) and The Beautiful Cassandra. Four years later, Austen also drafted First Impressions (1797), which was the original version of Pride and Prejudice, Elinor and Marianne (begun in 1795), the original of Sense and Sensibility, and Northanger Abbey (begun in 1788 and sold in 1803 but not published in her lifetime). Whether performing in home theatricals or circulating her manuscripts, Austen found in her immediate family her first and most enthusiastic audience. And Austen's characters would be drawn almost entirely from her family's class, the country gentry that distinguished itself from both the growing commercial class and the wealthier aristocracy.

In 1801, Mr. Austen gave his Steventon living (his Church office and the revenue attached to it) over to his eldest son, and moved with his wife and daughters to Bath. Either before or directly after leaving Steventon—the evidence is contradictory and unclear—Austen may have been in love with a young man who died, exactly the experience Cassandra had apparently endured in 1797. In any case, the subsequent death of her father in 1805 left her mother with an inadequate income of £210 a year, which was subsequently raised by her brothers to the barely adequate sum of £450. After a short stay in Southampton, Mrs. Austen and her daughters settled down in a cottage on Edward Austen's estate. In what must have been confining circumstances at Chawton—living with her mother, Cassandra, an

unmarried friend, and occasionally, her brother James's daughter—Austen began revising and publishing her novels in rapid succession. Although she published anonymously, the immediate success of her fiction led to the identification of its author. Yet Austen managed to maintain a life of obscurity that Cassandra abetted after her sister's death by burning many of her letters. A year of an undetermined illness ended Austen's life when she was forty-two years of age. She was mourned by many relatives, but by none more grievously than her sister, who wrote, "She was the sun of my life, the gilder of every pleasure, the soother of every sorrow, I had not a thought concealed from her, and it is as if I had lost a part of myself."

Modesty and a desire for anonymity characterize Austen's most famous pronouncements, whether she is describing her subject ("three or four families in a country village") or defining herself ("the most unlearned and uninformed female who ever dared to be an authoress"). Yet she was well read in the eighteenth-century and Romantic classics of Richardson, Fielding, Pope, Goldsmith, Hume, Johnson, Scott, Cowper, and Byron. She was also an avid reader of books by her female contemporaries, especially Frances Burney, Mary Brunton, Ann Radcliffe, and Maria Edgeworth. Indeed in works like *Love and Freindship*, *Volume the First*, and *Northanger Abbey*, she began to define herself as a writer by self-consciously satirizing not only the female tradition in literature but also its effects on the growth and development of the female imagination: focusing either on the sentimental romance and the epistolary form or the Gothic novel, Austen comically criticized the overvaluation of love, the miseducation of women, the subterfuges of the marriage market, the rivalry among women for male approval, the female cult of weakness and dependency, the discrepancy between women's private sphere and public (male) history. Precisely these themes, moreover, would inform her major novels.

From *Sense and Sensibility* to *Persuasion*, Austen delineated the lot of upper-middle-class girls who can escape the constraints of family life only by marrying. Just as the Dashwood sisters of *Sense and Sensibility* watch the family's fortune going to their half-brother, the Bennet daughters realize that their father's property has been entailed to a male cousin in *Pride and Prejudice*, Fanny Price in *Mansfield Park* is a poor dependent, and Anne Elliot of *Persuasion* is resigned to an impoverished spinsterhood. Even Austen's peremptory Emma, the heroine "whom no one but myself will much like," must learn to respect the ethical and economic authority of the well-named Mr. Knightley. Given the financial, social, and political power of men, Austen implies, female survival depends on gaining male approval and protection. As each heroine learns to distinguish among several apparently eligible suitors, Austen satirizes the bombastic self-importance of some clergymen, the autocratic pride of many aristocrats, the crudity of the nouveau riche, and always, the flightiness of girls who delude themselves into thinking they are the masters of their own or anyone else's fate. Beneath the bright, sparkling tone of the narrator's voice, then, Austen's "two inches of ivory" become, in Dorothy Van Ghent's phrase, "a lady's fan," which is "in substance an elephant's tusk; it is a savagely probing instrument as well as a masterpiece of refinement." And Austen seems supremely confident about the scope and subject of her comedy. When, after the publication of *Emma*, the prince regent transmitted a message to her that she could "dedicate any future book to H.R.H." and his librarian suggested that it be "an historical romance illustrative of the august House of Cobourg," Austen explained, "I could not sit down seriously to write a serious romance under any motive than to save my life; and if it were indispensable for me to keep it up and never relax into laughing at myself or at any other, I am sure I should be hung before I finished the first chapter. I must keep to my own style and go on in my own way."

The limits Austen set for her art are exactly the limits she perceived as imposed on female experience. By analyzing the manners and morals of women whose lives were confined to the common sitting room, with exuberant hilarity in the juvenilia

and a more ironic wit in the mature fiction, Austen provides a subtle portrayal of female values, a precise examination of female grief and joy. While a few readers, most famously Mark Twain and Ralph Waldo Emerson, took her own assessment at face value and faulted her fiction for its limitations, most have followed the example of such dissimilar artists as Scott, Macaulay, Tennyson, Trollope, Kipling, and Woolf in placing Austen's accomplishment next to Shakespeare's. For Woolf, Austen is ultimately "a mistress of much deeper emotion than appears upon the surface. She stimulates us to provide what is not there. What she offers is, apparently, a trifle, yet is composed of something that expands in the reader's mind and endows with the enduring form of life scenes which are outwardly trivial." Austen is, therefore, "the most perfect artist among women."

Love and Freindship

A Novel in a Series of Letters[1]

"Deceived in Freindship & Betrayed in Love"

Letter the First. From Isabel to Laura

How often, in answer to my repeated intreaties that you would give my Daughter a regular detail of the Misfortunes and Adventures of your Life, have you said "No, my freind never will I comply with your request till I may be no longer in Danger of again experiencing such dreadful ones." Surely that time is now at hand. You are this Day 55. If a woman may ever be said to be in safety from the determined Perseverance of disagreable Lovers and the cruel Persecutions of obstinate Fathers, surely it must be at such a time of Life.

Isabel

Letter 2d. Laura to Isabel

Altho' I cannot agree with you in supposing that I shall never again be exposed to Misfortunes as unmerited as those I have already experienced, yet to avoid the imputation of Obstinacy or ill-nature, I will gratify the curiosity of your daughter; and may the fortitude with which I have suffered the many Afflictions of my past Life, prove to her a useful Lesson for the support of those which may befall her in her own.

Laura

Letter 3d. Laura to Marianne

As the Daughter of my most intimate friend I think you entitled to that knowledge of my unhappy Story, which your Mother has so often solicited me to give you.

My Father was a native of Ireland & an inhabitant of Wales; My Mother was the natural Daughter of a Scotch Peer by an italian Opera-girl[2]—I was born in Spain & received my Education at a Convent in France.

1. The epistolary novel (i.e., a novel cast as a series of letters) was a popular form in the 18th century, the most famous example being Richardson's *Clarissa*; Austen is satirizing this extremely sentimental genre. Following R. W. Chapman, we have retained Austen's idiosyncratic spelling and capitalization throughout this text.
2. Dancer in the ballet, which was then a regular part of all operas; thought to be of loose morals. "Natural": illegitimate.

When I had reached my eighteenth Year I was recalled by my Parents to my paternal roof in Wales. Our mansion was situated in one of the most romantic parts of the Vale of Uske. Tho' my Charms are now considerably softened and somewhat impaired by the Misfortunes I have undergone, I was once beautiful. But lovely as I was the Graces of my Person were the least of my Perfections. Of every accomplishment accustomary to my sex, I was Mistress. When in the Convent, my progress had always exceeded my instructions, my Acquirements had been wonderfull for my Age, and I had shortly surpassed my Masters.

In my Mind, every Virtue that could adorn it was centered; it was the Rendezvous of every good Quality & of every noble sentiment.

A sensibility[3] too tremblingly alive to every affliction of my Freinds, my Acquaintance and particularly to every affliction of my own, was my only fault, if a fault it could be called. Alas! how altered now! Tho' indeed my own misfortunes do not make less impression on me than they ever did, yet now I never feel for those of an other. My accomplishments too, begin to fade—I can neither sing so well nor Dance so gracefully as I once did and I have entirely forgot the Minuet Dela Cour[4]

Adeiu

Laura

Letter 4th. Laura to Marianne

Our neighbourhood was small, for it consisted only of your mother. She may probably have already told you that being left by her Parents in indigent Circumstances she had retired into Wales on eoconomical motives. There it was, our freindship first commenced. Isabel was then one and twenty—Tho' pleasing both in her Person and Manners (between ourselves) she never possessed the hundredth part of my Beauty or Accomplishments. Isabel had seen the World. She had passed 2 Years at one of the first Boarding schools in London; had spent a fortnight in Bath & had supped one night in Southampton.[5]

"Beware my Laura (she would often say) Beware of the insipid Vanities and idle Dissipations of the Metropolis of England; Beware of the unmeaning Luxuries of Bath & of the Stinking fish of Southampton."

"Alas! (exclaimed I) how am I to avoid those evils I shall never be exposed to? What probability is there of my ever tasting the Dissipations of London, the Luxuries of Bath or the stinking Fish of Southampton? I who am doomed to waste my Days of Youth & Beauty in an humble Cottage in the Vale of Uske."

Ah! little did I then think I was ordained so soon to quit that humble Cottage for the Deceitfull Pleasures of the World.

adeiu

Laura

Letter 5th. Laura to Marianne

One Evening in December as my Father my Mother and myself, were

3. A strong capacity for emotional response, highly valued especially by upper-class women.
4. "Minuet of the court," an elegant French dance

popular at the time.
5. An English port city. Bath is an English resort famous for its mineral springs.

arranged in social converse round our Fireside, we were on a sudden, greatly astonished, by hearing a violent knocking on the outward Door of our rustic Cot.[6]

My Father started—"What noise is that," (said he.) "It sounds like a loud rapping at the Door"—(replied my Mother.) "it does indeed." (cried I.) "I am of your opinion; (said my Father) it certainly does appear to proceed from some uncommon violence exerted against our unoffending Door." "Yes (exclaimed I) I cannot help thinking it must be somebody who knocks for Admittance."

"That is another point (replied he;) We must not pretend to determine on what motive the person may knock—tho' that someone *does* rap at the Door, I am partly convinced."

Here, a 2d tremendous rap interrupted my Father in his speech and somewhat alarmed my Mother and me.

"Had we not better go and see who it is,? (said she) the Servants are out." "I think we had." (replied I.) "Certainly, (added my Father) by all means." "Shall we go now?" (said my Mother.) "The sooner the better." (answered he). "Oh! let no time be lost." (cried I.)

A third more violent Rap than ever again assaulted our ears. "I am certain there is somebody knocking at the Door." (said my Mother.) "I think there must," (replied my Father) "I fancy the Servants are returned; (said I) I think I hear Mary going to the Door." "I'm glad of it (cried my Father) for I long to know who it is."

I was right in my Conjecture; for Mary instantly entering the Room, informed us that a young Gentleman & his Servant were at the Door, who had lossed their way, were very cold and begged leave to warm themselves by our fire.

"Wont you admit them?" (said I) "You have no objection, my Dear?" (said my Father.) "None in the World." (replied my Mother.)

Mary, without waiting for any further commands immediately left the room and quickly returned introducing the most beauteous and amiable Youth, I had ever beheld. The servant, She kept to herself.

My natural Sensibility had already been greatly affected by the sufferings of the unfortunate Stranger and no sooner did I first behold him, than I felt that on him the happiness or Misery of my future Life must depend.

<div style="text-align: right">adeiu
Laura</div>

Letter 6th. Laura to Marianne

The noble Youth informed us that his name was Lindsay—for particular reasons howewer I shall conceal it under that of Talbot. He told us that he was the son of an English Baronet,[7] that his Mother had been many years no more and that he had a Sister of the middle size. "My Father (he continued) is a mean and mercenary wretch—it is only to such particular freinds as this Dear Party that I would thus betray his failings. Your Virtues my amiable Polydore (addressing himself to my father) yours Dear Claudia and yours my Charming Laura call on me to repose in you, my Confidence." We bowed. "My Father, seduced by the false glare of Fortune and the Deluding Pomp of Title, insisted

6. Cottage. 7. One of the less prestigious British titles.

on my giving my hand to Lady Dorothea. No never exclaimed I. Lady Dorothea is lovely and Engaging; I prefer no woman to her; but know Sir, that I scorn to marry her in compliance with your wishes. No! Never shall it be said that I obliged my Father."

We all admired the noble Manliness of his reply. He continued.

"Sir Edward was surprized; he had perhaps little expected to meet with so spirited an opposition to his will.

Where Edward in the name of wonder (sa d he) did you pick up this unmeaning Gibberish? You have been studying Novels I suspect.

I scorned to answer: it would have been beneath my Dignity. I mounted my Horse and followed by my faithful William set forwards for my Aunts."

"My Father's house is situated in Bedfordshire my Aunt's in Middlesex, and tho' I flatter myself with being a tolerable proficienz in Geography, I know not how it happened, but I found myself entering this beautiful Vale which I find is in South Wales, when I had expected to have reached my Aunts.[8]

"After having wandered some time on the Banks of the Uske without knowing which way to go, I began to lament my cruel Destiny in the bitterest and most pathetic Manner. It was now perfectly dark, not a single Star was there to direct my steps, and I know not what might have befallen me had I not at length discerned thro' the solemn Gloom that surrounded me a distant Light, which as I approached it, I discovered to be the chearfull Blaze of your fire. Impelled by the combination of Misfortunes under which I laboured, namely Fear, Cold and Hunger I hesitated not to ask admittance which at length I have gained; and now my Adorable Laura (continued he taking my Hand) when may I hope to receive that reward of all the painfull sufferings I have undergone during the course of my Attachment to you, to which I have ever aspired? Oh! when will you reward me with Yourself?"

"This instant, Dear and Amiable Edward" (replied I.). We were immediately united by my Father, who tho' he had never taken orders had been bred to the Church.

<div align="right">adeiu
Laura</div>

Letter 7th. Laura to Marianne

We remained but a few Days after our Marriage, in the Vale of Uske. After taking an affecting Farewell of my father, my Mother and my Isabel, I accompanied Edward to his Aunt's in Middlesex. Philippa received us both with every expression of affectionate Love. My arrival was indeed a most agreable surprize to her as she had not only been totally ignorant of my Marriage with her Nephew, but had never even had the slightest idea of there being such a person in the World.

Augusta, the sister of Edward was on a visit to her when we arrived. I found her exactly what her Brother had described her to be—of the middle size. She received me with equal surprize though not with equal Cordiality, as Philippa. There was a Disagreable Coldness and Forbidding Reserve in her reception of me which was equally Distressing and Unexpected. None of that interesting Sensibility or amiable Simpathy in her Manners and Address to me which

8. Instead of traveling south less than forty miles, he went almost one hundred miles west.

should have Distinguished our introduction to each other. Her Language was neither warm, nor affectionate, her expressions of regard were neither animated nor cordial; her arms were not opened to receive me to her Heart, tho' my own were extended to press her to mine.

A short Conversation between Augusta and her Brother, which I accidentally overheard encreased my Dislike to her, and convinced me that her Heart was no more formed for the soft ties of Love than for the endearing intercourse of Freindship.

"But do you think that my Father will ever be reconciled to this imprudent connection?" (said Augusta.)

"Augusta (replied the noble Youth) I thought you had a better opinion of me, than to imagine I would so abjectly degrade myself as to consider my Father's Concurrence in any of my Affairs, either of Consequence or concern to me. Tell me Augusta tell me with sincerity; did you ever know me consult his inclinations or follow his Advice in the least trifling Particular since the age of fifteen?"

"Edward (replied she) you are surely too diffident in your own praise. Since you were fifteen only!—My Dear Brother since you were five years old, I entirely acquit you of ever having willingly contributed to the Satisfaction of your Father. But still I am not without apprehensions of your being shortly obliged to degrade yourself in your own eyes by seeking a Support for your Wife in the Generosity of Sir Edward."

"Never, never Augusta will I so demean myself. (said Edward). Support! What Support will Laura want which she can receive from him?"

"Only those very insignificant ones of Victuals and Drink." (answered she.)

"Victuals and Drink! (replied my Husband in a most nobly contemtuous Manner) and dost thou then imagine that there is no other support for an exalted Mind (such as is my Laura's) than the mean and indelicate employment of Eating and Drinking?"

"None that I know of, so efficacious." (returned Augusta).

"And did you then never feel the pleasing Pangs of Love, Augusta? (replied my Edward). Does it appear impossible to your vile and corrupted Palate, to exist on Love? Can you not conceive the Luxury of living in every Distress that Poverty can inflict, with the object of your tenderest Affection?"

"You are too ridiculous (said Augusta) to argue with; perhaps however you may in time be convinced that. . . ."

Here I was prevented from hearing the remainder of her Speech, by the Appearance of a very Handsome Young Woman, who was ushered into the Room at the Door of which I had been listening. On hearing her announced by the Name of "Lady Dorothea", I instantly quitted my Post and followed her into the Parlour, for I well remembered that she was the Lady, proposed as a Wife for my Edward by the Cruel and Unrelenting Baronet.

Altho' Lady Dorothea's visit was nominally to Philippa and Augusta, yet I have some reason to imagine that (acquainted with the Marriage and arrival of Edward) to see me was a principal motive to it.

I soon perceived that though lovely and Elegant in her Person and tho' Easy and Polite in her Address, she was of that inferior order of Beings with regard to Delicate feeling, tender Sentiments, and refined Sensibility, of which Augusta was one.

She staid but half an hour and neither in the Course of her Visit, confided

to me any of her Secret thoughts, nor requested me to confide in her, any of mine. You will easily imagine therefore my Dear Marianne that I could not feel any ardent Affection or very sincere Attachment for Lady Dorothea.

<div align="right">Adeiu

Laura</div>

Letter 8th. Laura to Marianne, in continuation

Lady Dorothea had not left us long before another visitor as unexpected a one as her Ladyship, was announced. It was Sir Edward, who informed by Augusta of her Brother's marriage, came doubtless to reproach him for having dared to unite himself to me without his Knowledge. But Edward foreseeing his Design, approached him with heroic fortitude as soon as he entered the Room, and addressed him in the following Manner.

"Sir Edward, I know the motive of your Journey here—You come with the base Design of reproaching me for having entered into an indissoluble engagement with my Laura without your Consent—But Sir, I glory in the Act—. It is my greatest boast that I have incurred the Displeasure of my Father!"

So saying, he took my hand and whilst Sir Edward, Philippa, and Augusta were doubtless reflecting with Admiration on his undaunted Bravery, led me from the Parlor to his Father's Carriage, which yet remained at the Door and in which we were instantly conveyed from the pursuit of Sir Edward.

The Postilions[9] had at first received orders only to take the London road; as soon as we had sufficiently reflected However, we ordered them to Drive to M——, the seat of Edward's most particular freind, which was but a few miles distant.

At M——. we arrived in a few hours; and on sending in our names were immediately admitted to Sophia, the Wife of Edward's freind. After having been deprived during the course of 3 weeks of a real freind (for such I term your Mother) imagine my transports[1] at beholding one, most truly worthy of the Name. Sophia was rather above the middle size; most elegantly formed. A soft Languor spread over her lovely features, but increased their Beauty.—It was the Charectaristic of her Mind—. She was all Sensibility and Feeling. We flew into each others arms & after having exchanged vows of mutual Freindship for the rest of our Lives, instantly unfolded to each other the most inward Secrets of our Hearts—. We were interrupted in this Delightfull Employment by the entrance of Augustus, (Edward's freind) who was just returned from a solitary ramble.

Never did I see such an affecting Scene as was the meeting of Edward and Augustus.

"My Life! my Soul!" (exclaimed the former) "My Adorable Angel!" (replied the latter) as they flew into each other's arms. It was too pathetic for the feelings of Sophia and myself—We fainted Alternately on a Sofa.

<div align="right">Adeiu

Laura</div>

Letter the 9th. From the Same to the Same

Towards the close of the Day we received the following Letter from Philippa.

9. Riders who guide the horses drawing a coach. 1. Joy

"Sir Edward is greatly incensed by your abrupt departure; he has taken back Augusta with him to Bedfordshire. Much as I wish to enjoy again your charming society, I cannot determine to snatch you from that, of such dear & deserving Freinds—When your Visit to them is terminated, I trust you will return to the arms of your"

<div align="right">"Philippa."</div>

We returned a suitable answer to this affectionate Note & after thanking her for her kind invitation assured her that we would certainly avail ourselves of it, whenever we might have no other place to go to. Tho' certainly nothing could to any reasonable Being, have appeared more satisfactory, than so gratefull a reply to her invitation, yet I know not how it was, but she was certainly capricious enough to be displeased with our behaviour and in a few weeks after, either to revenge our Conduct, or releive her own solitude, married a young and illiterate Fortune-hunter. This imprudent Step (tho' we were sensible that it would probably deprive us of that fortune which Philippa had ever taught us to expect) could not on our own accounts, excite from our exalted Minds a single sigh; yet fearfull lest it might prove a source of endless misery to the deluded Bride, our trembling Sensibility was greatly affected when we were first informed of the Event. The affectionate Entreaties of Augustus and Sophia that we would for ever consider their House as our Home, easily prevailed on us to determine never more to leave them—. In the Society of my Edward & this Amiable Pair, I passed the happiest moments of my Life: Our time was most delightfully spent, in mutual Protestations of Freindship, and in vows of unalterable Love, in which we were secure from being interrupted, by intruding & disagreable Visitors, as Augustus & Sophia had on their first Entrance in the Neighbourhood, taken due care to inform the surrounding Families, that as their Happiness centered wholly in themselves, they wished for no other society. But alas! my Dear Marianne such Happiness as I then enjoyed was too perfect to be lasting. A most severe & unexpected Blow at once destroyed every Sensation of Pleasure. Convinced as you must be from what I have already told you concerning Augustus & Sophia, that there never were a happier Couple, I need not I imagine inform you that their union had been contrary to the inclinations of their Cruel & Mercenary Parents; who had vainly endeavoured with obstinate Perseverance to force them into a Marriage with those whom they had ever abhorred, but with an Heroic Fortitude worthy to be related & Admired, they had both, constantly refused to submit to such despotic Power.

After having so nobly disentangled themselves from the Shackles of Parental Authority, by a Clandestine Marriage, they were determined never to forfeit the good opinion they had gained in the World, in so doing, by accepting any proposals of reconciliation that might be offered them by their Fathers—to this farther tryal of their noble independance however they never were exposed.

They had been married but a few months when our visit to them commenced during which time they had been amply supported by a considerable sum of Money which Augustus had gracefully purloined from his Unworthy father's Escritoire,[2] a few days before his union with Sophia.

2. A writing desk.

By our arrival their Expences were considerably encreased tho' their means for supplying them were then nearly exhausted. But they, Exalted Creatures! scorned to reflect a moment on their pecuniary Distresses & would have blushed at the idea of paying their Debts.—Alas! what was their Reward for such disinterested Eehaviour The beautifull Augustus was arrested and we were all undone. Such perfidious Treachery in the merciless perpetrators of the Deed will shock your gentle nature Dearest Marianne as much as it then affected the Delicate Sensibility of Edward, Sophia, your Laura, & of Augustus himself. To compleat such unparaleled Barbarity we were informed that an Execution[3] in the House would shortly take place. Ah! what could we do but what we did! We sighed & fainted on the Sofa.

<div style="text-align:right">

Adeiu

Laura

</div>

Letter 10th. Laura in continuation

When we were somewhat recovered from the overpowering Effusions of our Grief, Edward desired that we would consider what was the most prudent step to be taken in our unhappy situation while he repaired to his imprisoned freind to lament over his misfortunes. We promised that we would, & he set forwards on his Journey to Town. During his Absence we faithfully complied with his Desire & after the most mature Deliberation, at length agreed that the best thing we could do was to leave the House; of which we every moment expected the Officers of Justice to take possession. We waited therefore with the greatest impatience, for the return of Edward in order to impart to him the result of our Deliberations—. But no Edward appeared—. In vain did we count the tedious Moments of his Absence—in vain did we weep—in vain even did we sigh—no Edward returned—. This was too cruel, too unexpected a Blow to our Gentle Sensibility—. we could not support it—we could only faint—. At length collecting all the Resolution I was Mistress of, I arose & after packing up some necessary Apparel for Sophia & myself, I dragged her to a Carriage I had ordered & instantly we set out for London. As the Habitation of Augustus was within twelve miles of Town, it was not long e'er we arrived there, & no sooner had we entered Holbourn than letting down one of the Front Glasses I enquired of every decent-looking Person that we passed "If they had seen my Edward"?

But as we drove too rapidly to allow them to answer my repeated Enquiries, I gained little, or indeed, no information concerning him. "Where am I to Drive?" said the Fostilion. "To Newgate[4] Gentle Youth (replied I), to see Augustus." "Oh! no, no, (exclaimed Sophia) I cannot go to Newgate; I shall not be able to support the sight of my Augustus in so cruel a confinement— my feelings are sufficiently shocked by the *recital*, of his Distress, but to behold it will overpower my Sensibility." As I perfectly agreed with her in the Justice of her Sentiments the Postilion was instantly directed to return into the Country. You may perhaps have been somewhat surprised my Dearest Marianne, that in the Distress I then endured, destitute of any Support, & unprovided with any Habitation, I should never once have remembered my Father & Mother or my paternal Cottage in the Vale of Uske. To account for this seeming forgetfullness I must inform you of a trifling Circumstance con-

3. Legal seizure of property to pay bad debts. 4. A well-known British prison.

cerning them which I have as yet never mentioned—. The death of my Parents a few weeks after my Departure, is the circumstance I allude to. By their decease I became the lawfull Inheritress of their House & Fortune. But alas! the House had never been their own & their Fortune had only been an Annuity[5] on their own Lives. Such is the Depravity of the World! To your Mother I should have returned with Pleasure, should have been happy to have introduced to her, my Charming Sophia & should have with Chearfullness have passed the remainder of my Life in their dear Society in the Vale of Uske, had not one obstacle to the execution of so agreable a Scheme, intervened; which was the Marriage & Removal of your Mother to a Distant part of Ireland.

<div align="right">

Adeiu

Laura

</div>

Letter 11th. Laura in continuation

"I have a Relation in Scotland (said Sophia to me as we left London) who I am certain would not hesitate in receiving me." "Shall I order the Boy to drive there?" said I—but instantly recollecting myself, exclaimed "Alas I fear it will be too long a Journey for the Horses." Unwilling however to act only from my own inadequate Knowledge of the Strength & Abilities of Horses, I consulted the Postilion, who was entirely of my Opinion concerning the Affair. We therefore determined to change Horses at the next Town & to travel Post[6] the remainder of the Journey.—. When we arrived at the last Inn we were to stop at, which was but a few miles from the House of Sophia's Relation, unwilling to intrude our Society on him unexpected & unthought of, we wrote a very elegant & well-penned Note to him containing an Account of our Destitute & melancholy Situation, and of our intention to spend some months with him in Scotland. As soon as we had dispatched this letter, we immediately prepared to follow it in person & were stepping into the Carriage for that Purpose when our Attention was attracted by the Entrance of a coroneted Coach & 4[7] into the Inn-yard. A Gentleman considerably advanced in years, descended from it—. At his first Appearance my Sensibility was wonderfully affected & e'er I had gazed at him a 2d time, an instinctive Sympathy whispered to my Heart, that he was my Grandfather.

Convinced that I could not be mistaken in my conjecture I instantly sprang from the Carriage I had just entered, & following the Venerable Stranger into the Room he had been shewn to, I threw myself on my knees before him & besought him to acknowledge me as his Grand Child.—He started, & after having attentively examined my features, raised me from the Ground & throwing his Grand-fatherly arms around my neck, exclaimed, "Acknowledge thee! Yes dear resemblance of my Laurina & my Laurina's Daughter, sweet image of my Claudia & my Claudia's Mother, I do acknowledge thee as the Daughter of the one & the Grandaughter of the other." While he was thus tenderly embracing me, Sophia astonished at my precipitate Departure, entered the Room in search of me—. No sooner had she caught the eye of the venerable Peer, than he exclaimed with every mark of Astonishment—"Another Grandaughter! Yes, yes, I see you are the Daughter of my Laurina's eldest Girl;

5. A sum of money paid annually for life.
6. In relays, changing horses at intervals.

7. A fancy coach drawn by four horses. "Coroneted": marked with a crown denoting nobility.

Your resemblance to the beauteous Matilda sufficiently proclaims it." "Oh.!"
replied Sophia, "when I first beheld you the instinct of Nature whispered me
that we were in some degree related—But whether Grandfathers, or
Grandmothers, I could not pretend to determine." He folded her in his arms,
and whilst they were tenderly embracing, the Door of the Apartment opened
and a most beautifull Young Man appeared. On perceiving him Lord St. Clair
started and retreating back a few paces, with uplifted Hands, said, "Another
Grandchild! What an unexpected Happiness is this! to discover in the space
of 3 minutes, as many of my Descendants! This, I am certain is Philander[8] the
son of my Laurina's 3d Girl the amiable Bertha; there wants now but the pres-
ence of Gustavus to compleat the Union of my Laurina's Grand-Children."

"And here he is; (said a Gracefull Youth who that instant entered the room)
here is the Gustavus you desire to see. I am the son of Agatha your Laurina's
4th & Youngest Daughter." "I see you are indeed; replied Lord St. Clair—But
tell me (continued he looking fearfully towards the Door) tell me, have I any
other Grand-Children in the House." "None my Lord." "Then I will provide
for you all without further delay—Here are 4 Banknotes of 50£ each—Take
them & remember I have done the Duty of a Grandfather—." He instantly
left the Room & immediately afterwards the House.

<div align="right">Adeiu

Laura</div>

Letter the 12th. Laura in continuation

You may imagine how greatly we were surprised by the sudden depar-
ture of Lord St. Clair. "Ignoble Grand-sire!" exclaimed Sophia. "Unworthy
Grandfather!" said I, & instantly fainted in each other's arms. How long we re-
mained in this situation I know not; but when we recovered we found our-
selves alone, without either Gustavus, Philander or the Bank-notes. As we
were deploring our unhappy fate, the Door of the Apartment opened &
"Macdonald" was announced. He was Sophia's cousin. The haste with which
he came to our relief so soon after the receipt of our Note, spoke so greatly in
his favour that I hesitated not to pronounce him at first sight, a tender &
Simpathetic Freind. Alas! he little deserved the name—for though he told us
that he was much concerned at our Misfortunes, yet by his own account it ap-
peared that the perusal of them, had neither drawn from him a single sigh, nor
induced him to bestow one curse on our vindictive Stars.—. He told Sophia
that his Daughter depended on her returning with him to Macdonald-Hall, &
that as his Cousin's freind he should be happy to see me there also. To
Macdonald-Hall, therefore, we went, and were received with great kindness by
Janetta the daughter of Macdonald, & the Mistress of the Mansion. Janetta
was then only fifteen; naturally well disposed, endowed with a susceptible
Heart, and a simpathetic Disposition, she might, had these amiable Qualities
been properly encouraged, have been an ornament to human Nature; but un-
fortunately her Father possessed not a sou sufficiently exalted to admire so
promising a Disposition, and had endeavoured by every means in his power to
prevent its encreasing with her Years. He had actually so far extinguished the
natural noble Sensibility of her Heart, as to prevail on her to accept an offer

8. Traditional name for a lover or flirt.

from a young man of his Recommendation. They were to be married in a few months, and Graham, was in the House when we arrived. We soon saw through his Character.—. He was just such a Man as one might have expected to be the choice of Macdonald. They said he was Sensible, well-informed, and Agreable; we did not pretend to Judge of such trifles, but as we were convinced he had no soul, that he had never read the *Sorrows of Werter*,[9] & that his Hair bore not the slightest resemblance to Auburn, we were certain that Janetta could feel no affection for him, or at least that she ought to feel none. The very circumstance of his being her father's choice too, was so much in his disfavour, that had he been deserving her, in every other respect yet *that* of itself ought to have been a sufficient reason in the Eyes of Janetta for rejecting him. These considerations we were determined to represent to her in their proper light & doubted not of meeting with the desired success from one naturally so well disposed, whose errors in the Affair had only arisen from a want of proper confidence in her own opinion, & a suitable contempt of her father's. We found her indeed all that our warmest wishes could have hoped for; we had no difficulty to convince her that it was impossible she could love Graham, or that it was her duty to disobey her Father; the only thing at which she rather seemed to hesitate was our assertion that she must be attached to some other Person. For some time, she persevered in declaring that she knew no other young Man for whom she had the smallest Affection; but upon explaining the impossibility of such a thing she said that she believed she *did like* Captain M'Kenzie better than any one she knew besides. This confession satisfied us and after having enumerated the good Qualities of M'Kenzie & assured her that she was violently in love with him, we desired to know whether he had ever in any wise declared his Affection to her.

"So far from having ever declared it, I have no reason to imagine that he has ever felt any for me." said Janetta. "That he certainly adores you (replied Sophia) there can be no doubt—. The Attachment must be reciprocal—. Did he never gaze on you with Admiration—tenderly press your hand—drop an involuntary tear—& leave the room abruptly?" "Never (replied She) that I remember—he has always left the room indeed when his visit has been ended, but has never gone away particularly abruptly or without making a bow". "Indeed my Love (said I) you must be mistaken—: for it is absolutely impossible that he should ever have left you but with Confusion, Despair, & Precipitation[1]—. Consider but for a moment Janetta, & you must be convinced how absurd it is to suppose that he could ever make a Bow, or behave like any other Person." Having settled this Point to our satisfaction, the next we took into consideration was, to determine in what manner we should inform M'Kenzie of the favourable Opinion Janetta entertained of him.—. We at length agreed to acquaint him with it by an anonymous Letter which Sophia drew up in the following Manner.

"Oh! happy Lover of the beautifull Janetta, oh! enviable Possessor of her Heart whose hand is destined to another, why do you thus delay a confession of your Attachment to the amiable Object of it? Oh! consider that a few weeks will at once put an end to every flattering Hope that you may now entertain,

9. *The Sorrows of Young Werther* was an extremely influential sentimental novel by Johann Wolfgang von Goethe (1749–1832), which records the brief and stormy life of a passionate young man.
1. I.e., tears.

by uniting the unfortunate Victim of her father's Cruelty to the execrable &
detested Graham."

"Alas! why do you thus so cruelly connive at the projected Misery of her & of
yourself by delaying to communicate that scheme which had doubtless long
possessed your imagination? A secret Union will at once secure the felicity of
both."

The amiable M'Kenzie, whose modesty as he afterwards assured us had
been the only reason of his having so long concealed the violence of his affec-
tion for Janetta, on receiving this Billet[2] flew on the wings of Love to
Macdonald-Hall, and so powerfully pleaded his Attachment to her who in-
spired it, that after a few more private interviews, Sophia & I experienced the
Satisfaction of seeing them depart for Gretna-Green, which they chose for the
celebration of their Nuptials, in preference to any other place although it was
at a considerable distance from Macdonald-Hall.

<div align="right">Adeiu
Laura</div>

Letter the 13th. Laura in Continuation

They had been gone nearly a couple of Hours, before either Macdonald or
Graham had entertained any suspicion of the affair—. And they might not
even then have suspected it, but for the following little Accident. Sophia hap-
pening one Day to open a private Drawer in Macdonald's Library with one of
her own keys, discovered that it was the Place where he kept his Papers of con-
sequence & amongst them some bank notes of considerable amount. This
discovery she imparted to me; and having agreed together that it would be a
proper treatment of so vile a Wretch as Macdonald to deprive him of money,
perhaps dishonestly gained, it was determined that the next time we should
either of us happen to go that way, we would take one or more of the Bank
notes from the drawer. This well-meant Plan we had often successfully put in
Execution; but alas! on the very day of Janetta's Escape, as Sophia was majes-
tically removing the 5th Bank-note from the Drawer to her own purse, she was
suddenly most impertinently interrupted in her employment by the entrance
of Macdonald himself, in a most abrupt & precipitate Manner. Sophia (who
though naturally all winning sweetness could when occasions demanded it
call forth the Dignity of her Sex) instantly put on a most forbidding look, &
darting an angry frown on the undaunted Culprit, demanded in a haughty
tone of voice "Wherefore her retirement[3] was thus insolently broken in on?"
The unblushing Macdonald, without even endeavouring to exculpate himself
from the crime he was charged with, meanly endeavoured to reproach Sophia
with ignobly defrauding him of his Money. The dignity of Sophia was
wounded; "Wretch (exclaimed she, hastily replacing the Bank-note in the
Drawer) how darest thou to accuse me of an Act, of which the bare idea makes
me blush?" The base wretch was still unconvinced & continued to upbraid the
justly-offended Sophia in such opprobrious Language, that at length he so
greatly provoked the gentle sweetness of her Nature, as to induce her to re-
venge herself on him by informing him of Janetta's Elopement, and of the ac-
tive Part we had both taken in the Affair. At this period of their Quarrel I

2. Note. 3. Privacy, solitude.

entered the Library and was as you may imagine equally offended as Sophia at the ill-grounded Accusations of the malevolent and contemptible Macdonald. "Base Miscreant (cried I) how canst thou thus undauntedly endeavour to sully the spotless reputation of such bright Excellence? Why dost thou not suspect my innocence as soon?" "Be satisfied Madam (replied he) I do suspect it, & therefore must desire that you will both leave this House in less than half an hour."

"We shall go willingly; (answered Sophia) our hearts have long detested thee, & nothing but our freindship for thy Daughter could have induced us to remain so long beneath thy roof."

"Your Freindship for my Daughter has indeed been most powerfully exerted by throwing her into the arms of an unprincipled Fortune-hunter." (replied he)

"Yes, (exclaimed I) amidst every misfortune, it will afford us some consolation to reflect that by this one act of Freindship to Janetta, we have amply discharged every obligation that we have received from her father."

"It must indeed be a most gratefull reflection, to your exalted minds." (said he.)

As soon as we had packed up our wardrobe & valuables, we left Macdonald Hall, & after having walked about a mile & a half we sate down by the side of a clear limpid stream to refresh our exhausted limbs. The place was suited to meditation.—.A Grove of full-grown Elms sheltered us from the East—. A Bed of full-grown Nettles from the West—. Before us ran the murmuring brook & behind us ran the turn-pike road. We were in a mood for contemplation & in a Disposition to enjoy so beautifull a spot. A mutual Silence which had for some time reigned between us, was at length broke by my exclaiming—"What a lovely Scene! Alas why are not Edward & Augustus here to enjoy its Beauties with us?"

"Ah! my beloved Laura (cried Sophia) for pity's sake forbear recalling to my remembrance the unhappy situation of my imprisoned Husband. Alas, what would I not give to learn the fate of my Augustus! to know if he is still in Newgate, or if he is yet hung. But never shall I be able so far to conquer my tender sensibility as to enquire after him. Oh! do not I beseech you ever let me again hear you repeat his beloved name—. It affects me too deeply—. I cannot bear to hear him mentioned, it wounds my feelings."

"Excuse me my Sophia for having thus unwillingly offended you—" replied I—and then changing the conversation, desired her to admire the Noble Grandeur of the Elms which Sheltered us from the Eastern Zephyr.[4] "Alas! my Laura (returned she) avoid so melancholy a subject, I intreat you.—Do not again wound my Sensibility by Observations on those elms. They remind me of Augustus—. He was like them, tall, magestic—he possessed that noble grandeur which you admire in them."

I was silent, fearfull lest I might any more unwillingly distress her by fixing on any other subject of conversation which might again remind her of Augustus.

"Why do you not speak my Laura?" (said she after a short pause) "I cannot support this silence—you must not leave me to my own reflections; they ever recur to Augustus."

4. Gentle breeze.

"What a beautifull Sky! (said I) How charmingly is the azure varied by those delicate streaks of white!"

"Oh! my Laura (replied she hastily withdrawing her Eyes from a momentary glance at the sky) do not thus distress me by calling my Attention to an object which so cruelly reminds me of my Augustus's blue sattin Waist-coat striped with white! In pity to your unhappy freind avoid a subject so distressing." What could I do? The feelings of Sophia were at that time so exquisite, & the tenderness she felt for Augustus so poignant that I had not the power to start any other topic, justly fearing that it might in some unforseen manner again awaken all her sensibility by directing her thoughts to her Husband.— Yet to be silent would be cruel; She had intreated me to talk.

From this Dilemma I was most fortunately relieved by an accident truly apropos; it was the lucky overturning of a Gentleman's Phaeton,[5] on the road which ran murmuring behind us. It was a most fortunate Accident as it diverted the Attention of Sophia from the melancholy reflections which she had been before indulging. We instantly quitted our seats & ran to the rescue of those who but a few moments before had been in so elevated a situation as a fashionably high Phaeton, but who were now laid low and sprawling in the Dust—. "What an ample subject for reflection on the uncertain Enjoyments of this World, would not that Phaeton & the Life of Cardinal Wolsey[6] afford a thinking Mind!" said I to Sophia as we were hastening to the field of Action.

She had not time to answer me for every thought was now engaged by the horrid Spectacle before us. Two Gentlemen most elegantly attired but weltering in their blood was what first struck our Eyes—we approached—they were Edward & Augustus—Yes dearest Marianne they were our Husbands. Sophia shreiked & fainted on the Ground—I screamed and instantly ran mad—. We remained thus mutually deprived of our Senses some minutes, & on regaining them were deprived of them again—. For an Hour & a Quarter did we continue in this unfortunate Situation—Sophia fainting every moment & I running Mad as often. At length a Groan from the hapless Edward (who alone retained any share of Life) restored us to ourselves—. Had we indeed before imagined that either of them lived, we should have been more sparing of our Greif—but as we had supposed when we first beheld them that they were no more, we knew that nothing could remain to be done but what we were about—. No sooner therefore did we hear my Edward's groan than postponing our Lamentations for the present, we hastily ran to the Dear Youth and kneeling on each side of him implored him not to die—. "Laura (said He fixing his now languid Eyes on me) I fear I have been overturned."

I was overjoyed to find him yet sensible—.

"Oh! tell me Edward (said I) tell me I beseech you before you die, what has befallen you since that unhappy Day in which Augustus was arrested & we were separated—"

"I will" (said he) and instantly fetching a Deep sigh, expired—. Sophia immediately sunk again into a swoon—. My Greif was more audible, My voice faltered, My Eyes assumed a vacant Stare, My face became as pale as Death, and my Senses were considerably impaired—.

"Talk not to me of Phaetons (said I, raving in a frantic, incoherent man-

5. A light, open carriage.
6. Thomas Wolsey (c. 1475–1530), British cardinal who fell from power as a result of a quarrel with Henry VIII.

ner)—Give me a violin—. I'll play to him & sooth him in his melancholy
Hours—Beware ye gentle Nymphs of Cupid's Thunderbolts, avoid the pierc-
ing Shafts of Jupiter[7]—Look at that Grove of Firs—I see a Leg of Mutton—
They told me Edward was not Dead; but they deceived me—they took him for
a Cucumber—" Thus I continued wildly exclaiming on my Edward's death—.
For two Hours did I rave thus madly and should not then have left off, as I was
not in the least fatigued, had not Sophia who was just recovered from her
swoon, intreated me to consider that Night was now approaching and that the
Damps began to fall. "And whither shall we go (said I) to shelter us from ei-
ther"? "To that white Cottage." (replied she pointing to a neat building which
rose up amidst the Grove of Elms & which I had not before observed—) I
agreed & we instantly walked to it—we knocked at the door—it was opened by
an old Woman; on being requested to afford us a Night's Lodging, she in-
formed us that her House was but small, that she had only two Bed-rooms, but
that However we should be wellcome to one of them. We were satisfied & fol-
lowed the good Woman into the House where we were greatly cheered by the
sight of a comfortable fire—. She was a Widow & had only one Daughter, who
was then just Seventeen—One of the best of ages; but alas! she was very plain
& her name was Bridget. Nothing therefore could be expected from
her—she could not be supposed to posses either exalted Ideas, Delicate
Feelings or refined Sensibilities—She was nothing more than a mere good-
tempered, civil & obliging Young Woman; as such we could scarcely dislike
her—she was only an Object of Contempt—.

<div align="right">

Adeiu

Laura

</div>

Letter the 14th. Laura in continuation

Arm yourself my amiable Young Freind with all the philosophy you are
Mistress of; summon up all the fortitude you possess, for Alas! in the perusal
of the following Pages your sensibility will be most severely tried. Ah! what
were the Misfortunes I had before experienced & which I have already related
to you, to the one I am now going to inform you of. The Death of my Father,
my Mother, and my Husband though almost more than my gentle Nature
could support, were trifles in comparison to the misfortune I am now pro-
ceeding to relate. The morning after our arrival at the Cottage, Sophia com-
plained of a violent pain in her delicate limbs, accompanied with a disagreable
Head-ake. She attributed it to a cold caught by her continued faintings in the
open Air as the Dew was falling the Evening before. This I feared was but too
probably the case; since how could it be otherwise accounted for that I should
have escaped the same indisposition, but by supposing that the bodily
Exertions I had undergone in my repeated fits of frenzy, had so effectually cir-
culated & warmed my Blood as to make me proof against the chilling Damps
of Night, whereas, Sophia lying totally inactive on the Ground must have been
exposed to all their Severity. I was most seriously alarmed by her illness which
trifling as it may appear to you, a certain instinctive Sensibility whispered me,
would in the End be fatal to her.

7. Cupid is the god of love in Roman mythology, tradi-
tionally armed with arrows, while Jupiter is the sover-
eign god who brandishes thunderbolts; Laura has
confused the two. "Nymphs": mythical female spirits,
but the word may also refer to young girls in general.

Alas! my fears were but too fully justified; she grew gradually worse & I daily became more alarmed for her.—At length she was obliged to confine herself solely to the Bed allotted us by our worthy Land lady— Her disorder turned to a galloping Consumption[8] & in a few Days carried her off. Amidst all my Lamentations for her (& violent you may suppose they were) I yet received some consolation in the reflection of my having paid every Attention to her, that could be offered, in her illness I had wept over her every Day—had bathed her sweet face with my tears & had pressed her fair Hands continually in mine—. "My beloved Laura (said she to me a few Hours before she died) take warning from my unhappy End & avoid the imprudent conduct which has occasioned it . . beware of fainting-fits . . Though at the time they may be refreshing & Agreable yet beleive me they will in the end, if too often repeated & at improper seasons, prove destructive to your Constitution My fate will teach you this . . I die a Martyr to my greif for the loss of Augustus One fatal swoon has cost me my Life Beware of swoons Dear Laura . . . A frenzy fit is not one quarter so pernicious; it is an exercise to the Body & if not too violent, is I dare say conducive to Health in its consequences—Run mad as often as you chuse; but do not faint—".

These were the last words she ever adressed to me . . . It was her dieing Advice to her afflicted Laura, who has ever most faithfully adhered to it.

After having attended my lamented freind to her Early Grave, I immediately (tho' late at night) left the detested Village in which she died, & near which had expired my Husband & Augustus. I had not walked many yards from it before I was overtaken by a Stage-Coach, in which I instantly took a place, determined to proceed in it to Edinburgh, where I hoped to find some kind pitying Freind who would receive and comfort me in my Afflictions.

It was so dark when I entered the Coach that I could not distinguish the Number of my Fellow-travellers; I could only perceive that they were Many. Regardless however of any thing concerning them, I gave myself up to my own sad Reflections. A general Silence prevailed—A Silence, which was by nothing interrupted but by the loud & repeated snores of one of the Party.

"What an illiterate villain must that Man be! (thought I to myself) What a total Want of delicate refinement must he have who can thus shock our senses by such a brutal Noise! He must I am certain be capable of every bad Action! There is no crime too black for such a Character!" Thus reasoned I within myself, & doubtless such were the reflections of my fellow travellers.

At length, returning Day enabled me to behold the unprincipled Scoundrel who had so violently disturbed my feelings. It was Sir Edward the father of my Deceased Husband. By his side, sate Augusta, & on the same seat with me were your Mother & Lady Dorothea. Imagine my Surprise at finding myself thus seated amongst my old Acquaintance. Great as was my astonishment, it was yet increased, when on look out of Windows, I beheld the Husband of Philippa, with Philippa by his side, on the Coach-box, & when on looking behind, I beheld, Philander & Gustavus in the Basket.[9] "Oh! Heavens, (exclaimed I) is it possible that I should so unexpectedly be surrounded by my nearest Relations and Connections"? These words roused the rest of the Party, and every eye was directed to the corner in which I sat. "Oh! my Isabel (continued I throwing myself across Lady Dorothea into her arms) receive once

8. Tuberculosis. 9. The rear compartment of a coach.

more to your Bosom the unfortunate Laura. Alas! when we last parted in the
Vale of Usk, I was happy in being united to the best of Edwards; I had then a
Father and a Mother, & had never known misfortunes—But now deprived of
every freind but you—".

"What! (interrupted Augusta) is my Brother dead then? Tell us I intreat
you what is become of him?" "Yes, cold & insensible Nymph, (replied I) that
luckless Swain[1] your Brother, is no more, & you may now glory in being the
Heiress of Sir Edward's fortune."

Although I had always despised her from the Day I had overheard her con-
versation with my Edward, yet in civility I complied with hers & Sir Edward's
intreaties that I would inform them of the whole melancholy Affair. They were
greatly shocked—Even the obdurate Heart of Sir Edward & the insensible one
of Augusta, were touched with Sorrow, by the unhappy tale. At the request of
your Mother I related to them every other misfortune which had befallen me
since we parted. Of the imprisonment of Augustus & the absence of
Edward—of our arrival in Scotland—of our unexpected Meeting with our
Grandfather and our cousins—of our visit to Macdonald-Hall—of the singu-
lar Service we there performed towards Janetta—of her Fathers ingratitude for
it of his inhuman Behaviour, unaccountable suspicions, & barbarous
treatment of us, in obliging us to leave the House of our Lamentations
on the loss of Edward & Augustus & finally of the melancholy Death of my
beloved Companion.

Pity & Surprise were strongly depictured in your Mother's Countenance,
during the whole of my narration, but I am sorry to say, that to the eternal re-
proach of her Sensibility, the latter infinitely predominated. Nay, faultless
as my Conduct had certainly been during the whole Course of my late
Misfortunes & Adventures, she pretended to find fault with my Behaviour in
many of the situations in which I had been placed. As I was sensible myself,
that I had always behaved in a manner which reflected Honour on my Feelings
& Refinement, I paid little attention to what she said, & desired her to satisfy
my Curiosity by informing me how she came there, instead of wounding my
spotless reputation with unjustifiable Reproaches. As soon as she had com-
plyed with my wishes in this particular & had given me an accurate detail of
every thing that had befallen her since our separation (the particulars of which
if you are not already acquainted with, your Mother will give you) I applied to
Augusta for the same information respecting herself, Sir Edward & Lady
Dorothea.

She told me that having a considerable taste for the Beauties of Nature, her
curiosity to behold the delightful scenes it exhibited in that part of the World
had been so much raised by Gilpin's Tour to the Highlands,[2] that she had pre-
vailed on her Father to undertake a Tour of Scotland & had persuaded Lady
Dorothea to accompany them. That they had arrived at Edinburgh a few days
before & from thence had made daily Excursions into the Country around in
the Stage Coach they were then in, from one of which Excursions they were at
that time returning. My next enquiries were concerning Philippa & her
Husband, the latter of whom I learned having spent all her fortune, had re-

1. "Nymph" and "swain" are terms derived from pas-
toral poetry designating young women and men (often
lovers).
2. William Gilpin (1724–1804) was a British clergy-

man who wrote a number of works on landscapes and
helped to begin the 18th-century cult of the "pic-
turesque."

course for subsistance to the talent in which, he had always most excelled, namely, Driving, & that having sold every thing which belonged to them except their Coach, had converted it into a Stage,[3] & in order to be removed from any of his former Acquaintance, had driven it to Edinburgh from whence he went to Sterling every other Day. That Philippa still retaining her affection for her ungratefull Husband, had followed him to Scotland & generally accompanied him in his little Excursions to Sterling. "It has only been to throw a little money into their Pockets (continued Augusta) that my Father has always travelled in their Coach to veiw the beauties of the Country since our arrival in Scotland—for it would certainly have been much more agreable to us, to visit the Highlands in a Postchaise" than merely to travel from Edinburgh to Sterling & from Sterling to Edinburgh every other Day in a crouded & uncomfortable Stage." I perfectly agreed with her in her sentiments on the Affair, & secretly blamed Sir Edward for thus sacrificing his Daughter's pleasure for the sake of a ridiculous old Woman whose folly in marrying so young a Man ought to be punished. His Behaviour however was entirely of a piece with his general Character; for what could be expected from a Man who possessed not the smallest atom of Sensibility, who scarcely knew the meaning of Simpathy, & who actually snored—.

<div align="right">Adeiu
Laura</div>

Letter the 15th. Laura in continuation

When we arrived at the town where we were to Breakfast, I was determined to speak with Philander & Gustavus, & to that purpose as soon as I left the Carriage, I went to the Basket & tenderly enquired after their Health, expressing my fears of the uneasiness of their Situation. At first they seemed rather confused at my Appearance dreading no doubt that I might call them to account for the money which our Grandfather had left me & which they had unjustly deprived me of, but finding that I mentioned nothing of the Matter, they desired me to step into the Basket as we might there converse with greater ease. Accordingly I entered & whilst the rest of the party were devouring Green tea & buttered toast, we feasted ourselves in a more refined & Sentimental Manner by a confidential Conversation. I informed them of every thing which had befallen me during the course of my Life, and at my request they related to me every incident of theirs.

"We are the sons as you already know, of the two youngest Daughters which Lord St. Clair had by Laurina an italian opera girl. Our mothers could neither of them exactly ascertain who were our fathers; though it is generally believed that Philander, is the son of one Philip Jones a Bricklayer and that my father was Gregory Staves a Staymaker of Edinburgh. This is however of little consequence, for as our Mothers were certainly never married to either of them, it reflects no Dishonour on our Blood which is of a most ancient & unpolluted kind. Bertha (the Mother of Philander) & Agatha (my own Mother) always lived together. They were neither of them very rich; their united fortunes had originally amounted to nine thousand Pounds, but as they had always lived upon the principal of it, when we were fifteen it was diminished to nine

3. A coach that carries passengers for money. 4. A closed carriage that transports mail and passengers.

Hundred. This nine Hundred, they always kept in a Drawer in one of the Tables which stood in our common sitting Parlour, for the Convenience of having it always at Hand. Whether it was from this circumstance, of its being easily taken, or from a wish of being independant, or from an excess of Sensibility (for which we were always remarkable) I cannot now determine, but certain it is that when we had reached our 15th year, we took the Nine Hundred Pounds & ran away. Having obtained this prize we were determined to manage it with eoconomy & not to spend it either with folly or Extravagance. To this purpose we therefore divided it into nine parcels, one of which we devoted to Victuals, the 2d to Drink, the 3d to Housekeeping, the 4th to Carriages, the 5th to Horses, the 6th to Servants, the 7th to Amusements, the 8th to Cloathes & the 9th to Silver Buckles. Having thus arranged our Expences for two Months (for we expected to make the nine Hundred Pounds last as long) we hastened to London & had the good luck to spend it in 7 weeks & a Day which was 6 Days sooner than we had intended. As soon as we had thus happily disencumbered ourselves from the weight of so much Money, we began to think of returning to our Mothers, but accidentally hearing that they were both starved to death, we gave over the design & determined to engage ourselves to some strolling Company of Players, as we had always a turn for the Stage. Accordingly we offered our services to one & were accepted; our Company was indeed rather small, as it consisted only of the Manager his wife & ourselves, but there were fewer to pay and the only inconvenience attending it was the Scarcity of Plays which for want of People to fill the Characters, we could perform.—. We did not mind trifles however—. One of our most admired Performances was *Macbeth*, in which we were truly great. The Manager always played *Banquo* himself, his Wife my *Lady Macbeth*. I did the *Three Witches* & Philander acted *all the rest*. To say the truth this tragedy was not only the Best, but the only Play we ever performed; & after having acted it all over England, and Wales, we came to Scotland to exhibit it over the remainder of Great Britain. We happened to be quartered in that very Town, where you came and met your Grandfather—. We were in the Inn-yard when his Carriage entered & perceiving by the Arms to whom it belonged, & knowing that Lord St. Clair was our Grandfather, we agreed to endeavour to get something from him by discovering the Relationship—. You know how well it succeeded—. Having obtained the two Hundred Pounds, we instantly left the Town, leaving our Manager & his wife to act *Macbeth* by themselves, & took the road to Sterling, where we spent our little fortune with great *eclat*. We are now returning to Edinburgh to get some preferment[5] in the Acting way; & such my Dear Cousin is our History."

I thanked the amiable Youth for his entertaining Narration, & after expressing my Wishes for their Welfare & Happiness, left them in their little Habitation & returned to my other Freinds who impatiently expected me.

My Adventures are now drawing to a close my dearest Marianne; at least for the present.

When we arrived at Edinburgh Sir Edward told me that as the Widow of his Son, he desired I would accept from his Hands of four Hundred a year. I graciously promised that I would, but could not help observing that the unsim-

5. Employment. "Eclat": flamboyance, conspicuousness.

pathetic Baronet offered it more on account of my being the Widow of Edward than in being the refined & Amiable Laura

I took up my Residence in a romantic Village in the Highlands of Scotland, where I have ever since continued, & where I can uninterrupted by unmeaning Visits, indulge in a melancholy soltude, my unceasing Lamentations for the Death of my Father, my Mother, my Husband & my Freind.

Augusta has been for several Years united to Graham the Man of all others most suited to her; she became acquainted with him during her stay in Scotland.

Sir Edward in hopes of gaining an Heir to his Title & Estate, at the same time married Lady Dorothea—. His wishes have been answered.

Philander & Gustavus, after having raised their reputation by their Performances in the Theatrical Line at Edinburgh, removed to Covent Garden,[6] where they still Exhibit under the assumed names of *Lewis & Quick*.

Philippa has long paid the Debt of Nature, Her Husband however still continues to drive the Stage-Coach from Edinburgh to Sterling:—

<div align="right">Adeiu my Dearest Marianne
Laura</div>

June 13th 1790 1922

6. A theater in London.

REBECCA COX JACKSON
1795–1871

In a moving account of her self-education, the Shaker visionary and preacher Rebecca Jackson remembered a moment when her shame at her own illiteracy "pierced my soul like a sword" so that she "could not keep from crying." But then, she explained, "these words were spoken in my heart, 'Be faithful, and the time shall come when you can write.'" Not long after that, she added, an inner voice reminded her that God, "who learned the first man to read . . . can learn you," and in fact, apparently quite miraculously, she started that very day to read the Bible. Some years later, moreover, she began to write the striking spiritual autobiography excerpted here, and she continued composing this memoir on and off throughout her religious career.

Jackson was a free black woman. She was born just outside Philadelphia and for many years worked as a seamstress, a job that brought her some financial independence. Her husband, Samuel J. Jackson, lived with her, her older brother, Joseph Cox, and her brother's children in a comfortable house in Philadelphia. Jackson renounced the security of this life, however, after being profoundly transformed by a powerful experience of religious "awakening" that seized her during a thunderstorm in July 1830. Suddenly feeling herself to be an instrument of divine authority, she chose—like such earlier women as the fourteenth-century visionary Margery Kempe or the seventeenth-century mystic Jane Lead—to leave her husband, her home, and her family for a career of spiritual commitment. After having achieved considerable success as an itinerant preacher whose "gift," according to a contemporary witness, "was to travel some and speak to the people," she joined the radical sect known as the Shakers, a group of Protestant believers who advocated the Motherhood as well as the Fatherhood of God and who seemed to her,

with their austere dress and communal ways, to be "living to live forever." Throughout these years, she lived and journeyed through the countryside with a younger woman disciple named Rebecca Perot; known as "the two Rebeccas," the women were evidently both inseparable and inspiring.

Around 1843, Jackson undertook to write her memoirs, including a series of dreams and visions. Although these remained unpublished until the historian Jean McMahon Humez edited them in 1981, Shaker scholars transcribed and preserved them during the nineteenth century. In their dramatizations of violence as well as in their magical meditations on domesticity, such passages as *The Dream of Slaughter*, *The Dream of the Cakes*, and *The Dream of Washing Quilts* suggest the intensity with which an apparently unschooled woman could enrich her inner life with imagery drawn from "ordinary" reality. Moreover, in the simultaneous sense of peril and resistance that these dreams convey as well as in their sometimes haunted consciousness of racial difference, Jackson's memoirs imply that even for a supposedly "free" black woman nineteenth-century America was hardly an un-threatening place. As another nineteenth-century black woman preacher, Amanda Smith, remarked, "Some people would understand the quintessence of sanctify-ing grace if they could be black about twenty-four hours."

From Gifts of Power

A Dream of Slaughter

In a night or two after I had this dream,[1] I also dreamed I was in a house, en-tered in at the south door. I heard a footstep quick behind me and looked at the east window and saw a man coming. I run upstairs, told the child's nurse a robber was in the house. She fled. I went to the east window, then to the west, to jump out. I found in so doing I should kill myself, so I sat down on a chair by the west window with my face to the north. He came up and came right to me. He took a lance and laid my nose open and then he cut my head on the right side, from the back to the front above my nose, and pulled the skin down over that side. Then he cut the left, did the same way, and pulled the skin down. The skin and blood covered me like a veil from my head to my lap. All my body was covered with blood. Then he took a long knife and cut my chest open in the form of the cross and took all my bowels out and laid them on the floor by my right side, and then went in search of all the rest of the family. This was a family that I sewed in. When the lance was going through my nose it felt like a feather was going over my nose. I sat in silent prayer all the time saying these words in my mind, "Lord Jesus, receive my spirit."

After I found he was gone I thought I would make my escape before he re-turned. I was afraid if he found me alive he would want to treat me more cruel. But a voice above my head told me to sit still, as though I was dead, for that was the only thing that would save me. And this was the way I sat all the time he was amangling my body—as though I was dead. So in a moment after those words were spoken to me, he came in and came to me as if he was agoing to do something else to me, and I was afraid. I thought I would implore his mercy to save my life, but the same voice spoke to me and said, "He can show no mercy." And in the same moment, the same voice from above spoke to him and asked, "What is your occupation?" (and also the man that was with him).

1. She has just recounted a dream in which, by her own interpretation, she has learned to resist carnal pleasures and to follow God.

He said the man rid[2] the entrails but he opened the heart. And He commanded him not to touch me again. And they both fled from before me by the power of that voice. And then I found what it was that keep me alive. He had not as yet taken out my heart, but my entrails were laying all this time by my right side on the floor.

And then I awoke and my dream troubled me. I was so faint when I woke I could not get up for sometime. And when I did I cried, "I shall die! I shall die!" Samuel said, "What is the matter?" "Oh my dream! My dream!" And I was all in a tremble. And these words were spoken to me, "Thy life is hid in Christ. Thy life is hid in Christ. Thy life is hid in Christ." Three times these words were spoken to me. And I was strengthened and my soul filled with the love of God. And I began to walk the floor back and forth apraising the Lord as though nothing had been.

* * *

The Dream of the Cakes

A dream. I thought I was going to bake some cakes. A sister come in that belonged to the Covenant. I said, "I am glad you have come!" "Why?" "Because I am going to bake some cakes." I sat down on a low stool before the griddle. It laid on two bricks, the fire under it. It stood in the northeast corner of the room on the floor. The fireplace was on the west side of the room. However, I greased the griddle, put on a little batter, about a tablespoonful. It run all over the griddle, a beautiful brown on both sides, though I did not turn it. And in a moment the people ate it all up—they were all white.[3] I did not see them before I saw them eating my cake. I knowed not where they came from—I looked at the sister. "Did you see that? Well, I will try it again."

I poured on another. It run all over, under, and into the fire. They ate it out of the fire and off of the griddle. And the people increased as the cake enlarged. I put on the third. It run all over the griddle, on the fire, under it, on the ashes, under it, and spread about one yard around. The people ate it off the griddle, off the fire, from under it, off the ashes, under the ashes. They ate it all, except a little piece about one inch in length, a half inch in width. This little piece lay before my right foot in the ashes. It was all I seen. I picked it up and said, "Let us taste it. They ate it so good." I broke it and put the piece in my mouth. It was the sweetest I ever tasted. I gave her the other, said, "Here, taste. No wonder they ate it up!"

So the people increased at the baking of the third cake to a large multitude.[4] I don't think I put on more than a spoonful each time—it is my manner in baking any kind of batter cakes to try the griddle with batter enough to make a cake the size of a half a dollar, so that if it sticks, then there is not much batter wasted.

And I woke in the morning. I told my dream. My dreams became a burden to my family. I shall only mention a few of them in this writing in order to show how it pleased God in His wisdom to lead a poor unlearned ignorant woman, without the aid of mortal.

2. Removed.
3. According to one editor, this dream reflects the fact that Jackson's early congregations were largely white.

4. Compare Jesus' feeding of thousands with a few loaves and fishes (e.g., Mark 6:37–44).

The Dream of Washing Quilts

A dream. I was washing. I was squatting down, washing three bed quilts and singing as I was awashing. And this same sister[5] came to the south door and said, "What are you adoing here?" "I am awashing." "Ain't you afraid to be here?" "No." "Why, you are in great danger."

I then looked and saw I was in a place walled all around with stone. The place was four square. I was in the center of it. There was no window in it, only one door. That was in the southwest corner, opened in. The south door she stood in, which brought her behind me, rather to my left. My face was east. Under me was a pool of water. This walled place was full of water like a bowl. Nobody could get to me. There were three pieces of boards about one yard in length. They were all one size. On one of them I sat. On the one at my right side sat a tub. In it was two quilts, which I had washed in this pool, though I knowed not I was in such a dangerous place till she spoke. Yet I did not feel to move till I had done my washing. So I sat still singing until I was done.

Then I picked up my tub with my three clean quilts in, put the tub on my head, came out with great ease and went eastward, came into a street ran north and south. I then stopped, turned around to see where I had come from, found I was standing by a gate as though I had come through it, saw a bridge alongside the gate. This bridge was over a stream of water. I could not tell whether I had come through this gate or over the bridge.

While I stood here awonder, I looked up, saw the gate post on the south side had a steeple on it, and on the top of the steeple was a gold ball. As I looked from the top to where I stood, I found a little white cord hanging right by my right hand. I caught hold of it, made a squat, then leaped into the air, placed my right foot on the ball, with my left foot swinging in the air. I was above all earthly things. I saw three cities, one in the east, one in the south, one in the west. These cities were clean and beautiful. Then I leaped down with as great ease as I ascended.

Then I heard this same sister speak behind me. "What are you doing here?" "Why, I have been on that pinnacle." She doubted. I caught hold of the cord and leaped upon it again. This I done three times—I had done it twice before she came. I then went through the gate and along this stream of water until I headed it. This was the same way I had come with my clean quilts in the tub upon my head, but I did not see this water nor this gate nor this bridge until I got into the street that ran north and south. This street which I came in from the washing ran east and west. Now as I returned the same way, it brought me westward, and when I headed this stream, I went south—but when I found myself at that gate, I had no tub nor quilts.

So now I went south. After I got far in the south, I looked up to the heavens, saw three pictures all of one size and of one appearance, very majestic, long, and beautiful, of the male order. They were some distance apart. They faced the north. Each one was on a black cloud. And there was three heavy claps of thunder. Each clap came out of each cloud. I found I had traveled a long distance—no house nor shelter near, as far as my eyes could see, and I saw a heavy thunderstorm rising. I wondered what I should do. It was said, "Turn back." I turned, and when I turned in the same road that I came—for I never turned

5. Jackson reveals later that this "sister" (the same who appeared in the previous dream) is jealous of her influence over the Covenant Meeting.

out of the road in all my journey—being turned on my right (that is, on my right hand side off the road, east), I saw a beautiful white cottage into which I was told to enter, which I did. And when I found myself in so beautiful a house, sheltered from the storm, I was filled with joy and rejoicing. And it was said to me, "This is yours."

Then I heard this sister holler behind the cottage, "What are you adoing here?" "Why, I live here." "You live here?" "Yes, I live here." "Why, how can you live here? Nobody lives here." "Why, this is my cottage, and I am as happy as a lord." "Why, the sun never rises here." "The sun never rises here?" As I made this reply I advanced to the door which I came in at, which was in the south side of the cottage. (She was on the north side which made her behind the cottage—I only heard her voice.) And when I went out and looked in the west, I saw the fourth picture, like the three I saw in the south—same size, same height in the heavens—and it faced the east and it was on a black cloud. And as I kept repeating, "The sun never rises here? No? Why, yonder she is arising—arising now!" "Well, she has only rose to you."

The sun, while I looked in the faces of the pictures, rose from behind the picture as though it came out of the cloud. And it rose out on the south side of this fourth picture, bearing her course toward these three pictures in the south, out of which came three claps of heavy thunder. The thunder out of the three black clouds behind the three pictures in the south, the sun out of the black cloud behind the fourth picture in the west. Then I waked.

1843–45 1981

MARY SHELLEY
1797–1851

Mary Wollstonecraft Godwin Shelley, wrote her friend Leigh Hunt in his *Blue Stocking Revels* (1837), was "four-famed—for her parents, her lord, / And the poor lone impossible monster abhorred." Amiably sardonic though it is, this couplet tersely summarizes some of the major facts of this author's remarkable career. The daughter of the feminist theoretician Mary Wollstonecraft (famous for her *Vindication of the Rights of Woman*, 1792) and the rationalist philosopher William Godwin (equally well known for his *Enquiry Concerning Political Justice*, 1793), she eloped with the Romantic poet Percy Bysshe Shelley when she was only seventeen, and when she was merely nineteen she wrote *Frankenstein*, perhaps the most memorable and influential science fiction fantasy ever published in English.

Putting aside the intellectual achievements of her mother and father, Mary Shelley's existence was marked from the first by emotional extremes. Though her parents were radically opposed to marriage (Godwin had called it "the worst of all laws" and Wollstonecraft had defined it as "legalized prostitution"), they had somewhat embarrassedly wed not only to legitimize the birth of their child but also with every expectation of a peaceful life together. But Wollstonecraft died of puerperal fever just after giving birth to her daughter Mary, and Godwin, left in charge of his motherless infant as well as Wollstonecraft's illegitimate daughter, Fanny Imlay, was plunged into gloom. Nor did conditions substantially improve after Mary's father remarried, when she was four. His new wife, the widowed Mary Jane Clairmont, had two children of her own, Charles and Jane, to whom she was

clearly partial, so that Mary soon began to feel like a rebellious Cinderella. Idolizing her scholarly but distant father, she grew up headstrong and literary, educating herself through voracious reading, scorning her stepmother, and making long brooding pilgrimages to her mother's grave.

Sent to live with family friends in Scotland when she was fifteen, Mary spent a good deal of time "scribbling." On her return to London in 1814, when she was nearly seventeen, she was immediately drawn to a young friend of her father's, the poet Percy Bysshe Shelley, who appears to have been equally drawn to her. Injudiciously married at the age of nineteen to the sixteen-year-old Harriet Westbrook, Shelley was now twenty-two, the scion of an aristocratic family, who had glamorously repudiated his heritage to devote himself to art and ideas. In a few years, however, he had wearied of the comparatively ordinary wife who had already borne him one child and was about to give birth to another; evidently he was ready for amorous redemption. A disciple of Godwin's, Shelley had also long venerated the by now mythical Mary Wollstonecraft, and no doubt Mary Godwin's physical charm—she was evidently a coolly attractive girl—together with her imaginative power and her fascinating heritage enthralled him as rapidly as his poetic charisma enchanted her. Within a month, the pair had confessed their feelings to each other, appropriately enough at Wollstonecraft's grave, and fled to the Continent together, bringing Mary's stepsister Jane—who had now renamed herself "Claire"—Clairmont with them; Mary was already pregnant with their first child.

It is an understatement to say that Mary's years with Shelley were hectic ones. Almost from the beginning, they were tragic. At the age of seventeen, she gave birth to her first child, a premature daughter who died in two weeks. Her journal entries from this period are hauntingly evocative. Indeed, as the feminist critic Ellen Moers has pointed out, their preoccupation with death and resurrection prefigures some of the central concerns of *Frankenstein*. "Dream that my little baby came to life again," she wrote on Sunday, March 19, 1815; "that it had been only cold, and that we rubbed it before the fire, and it lived." An imaginative, theatrical girl, Mary Shelley was being gradually transformed into a woman subject to genuine terrors. In 1816, both Fanny Imlay and Harriet Shelley committed suicide. Now Shelley was able to wed Mary, but to his distress he was never considered respectable enough to be given custody of his two children by Harriet. Married at last, the young couple wandered between England, Switzerland, and Italy, often impoverished and always beset by importunate friends and relatives. At the same time, many of their relationships were richly rewarding: Keats, Byron, Leigh Hunt, Thomas Love Peacock, James Hogg, Edward Trelawney, and many other notable Romantics enlivened their social circle, and their growing intellectual as well as emotional dependence on each other seems also to have helped them endure many difficulties.

Though such difficulties must often have appeared unremitting, then, the Shelleys did have respites of relative calm. It was during one of these periods that Mary began the composition of *Frankenstein*. Summering in Geneva in 1816, she, Shelley, their six-month-old son William, and Claire occupied a small house near Lord Byron's grander Villa Diodati; Claire was embroiled in a fitful affair with Byron, and Shelley, too, had become close to the aristocratic poet, who was already celebrated, even notorious, for both his work and his womanizing. Years later, in her wonderfully vivid introduction to the 1831 edition of the book, reprinted here, Mary was to respond to a question that, she explained, she was often asked: "How I, then a young girl, came to think of . . . so very hideous an idea?" One night, she recalled, the group—which also included Byron's eccentric young Italian physician, William Polidori—were regaling each other with tales of the supernatural in the villa's candlelit salon when Byron suddenly declared, "We will each write a ghost story." Mary was at first frustratingly empty of inspiration, but after brooding for a few days, she had a terrifying nightmare about a "pale student of unhallowed

arts" who employed a "powerful engine" to awaken "the hideous phantasm of a man." Almost at once she understood that this horrifying dream might be the basis of "my ghost story—my tiresome, unlucky ghost story!" for she longed to "contrive [a tale] which would frighten my reader as I myself had been frightened that night!"

Frightening *Frankenstein* certainly is, but as readers from 1818 to the present have generally realized, it is considerably more than that. Subtitled *The Modern Prometheus* and prefaced with an epigraph from Milton's *Paradise Lost* in which the fallen Adam reproaches God for having abandoned him, the novel openly meditates on large issues of responsibility and desire, science and sinfulness. Far more covertly, it reimagines Aeschylus's overreachingly ambitious Prometheus (whom Shelley himself was later to vindicate in his great verse drama *Prometheus Unbound*) and Milton's arrogantly vengeful Satan to consider questions about woman's anatomy and destiny that had always concerned Mary's own mother. For in "giving life" to a monster assembled from parts of corpses dug up in a nearby graveyard, the novel's protagonist, Victor Frankenstein, not only usurps the creative function of God, he enacts the maternal role of a woman, while, in experiencing himself as a lonely outcast, barred from education and inheritance, the book's nameless monster represents in exaggerated form some of the feelings a nineteenth-century daughter might well have had about her own place in a society where she had only the most minimal rights. Although such interpretations did not occur to the tale's earliest critics, most knew at once that they were encountering a work that was almost inexplicably resonant, and Mary Shelley herself was driven to contemplate the mysterious origins of her "hideous" idea. The explanation of these origins, as a number of recent writers have suggested, lay at least partly in the way early traumas of loss and sexuality, maternity and death had become intertwined in her life.

After the popular success of *Frankenstein* such traumas unfortunately continued unabated. In the fall of 1817, six months before the publication of her novel, Mary had given birth to a daughter, Clara Everina: in the fall of 1818, six months after the book's appearance, the child died of dysentery in Venice. A year and a half later, in June 1819, the Shelleys' three-year-old son William succumbed to a similar malady in Rome. Mary, in particular, was devastated, and to distract herself she began a novel, *Mathilda*, which was unpublished in her lifetime but which served "to quell my wretchedness temporarily." Even more therapeutic was the birth of her son Percy Florence in November of the same year. He was the only one among her children to survive, and though he grew up to be a comparatively ordinary man—unworthy, as some thought, of the Godwin-Wollstonecraft-Shelley heritage—he soon became his mother's only consolation. For, two and a half years later, in the summer of 1822, Shelley himself, along with his friend Edward Williams, drowned in the bay of Lerici when the poet's boat, the *Ariel*, was overturned.

Shortly before the catastrophe, Mary herself had suffered a miscarriage; overwrought and exhausted, she had parted with her husband coldly before he embarked on his fateful voyage—a failing for which she was never to forgive herself. But in any case this last blow was almost overwhelmingly heavy. A journal entry she wrote shortly after Shelley's death hardly seems to overstate the intensity of the dramas through which she had lived in the eight years since her elopement:

> I am now on the eve of completing my five & twentieth year—how drearily young for one so lost as I! How young in years for one lives ages each day in sorrow—think you that these moments are counted in my life as in other people's?—oh no! . . . what I have suffered . . . will write years on my brow & intrench them in my heart.

Despite such a sense of enduring pain, Mary was to live some thirty more years after Shelley's death, and in those years she remained consistently productive,

publishing a number of tales, five more novels—*Valperga* (1823), *The Last Man* (1826), *Perkin Warbeck* (1830), *Lodore* (1835), and *Falkner* (1837)—essays, travel sketches, and a series of biographies, as well as a set of useful and perceptive notes to her husband's poems. Vigorously inventive, her prose continued to enthrall many readers, though only *The Last Man* begins to compare with *Frankenstein* in force and originality. Significantly, that novel, like her brief tale *The Mortal Immortal*, expressed her anguished sense of having survived what seemed to be the deaths of almost everyone around her. And indeed she had, for not only were her husband and three of her children gone but so were Shelley's friend Keats, who had died in Rome not long before Shelley himself drowned, and the couple's friend Byron, who died at Missolonghi in 1824, where he had gone to fight for the cause of Greek independence, as well as her father, who died in 1836, and her half-sister Fanny Imlay, who had committed suicide in 1816.

Yet Mary herself stubbornly survived, writing, raising her son Percy, recovering from smallpox, and refusing to remarry, with the proud explanation that she wanted the name "Mary Shelley" to be engraved on her tombstone. Always conscious of her maternal inheritance, she once declared: "If I have never written to vindicate the rights of women, I have ever befriended women when oppressed. At every risk I have befriended and supported victims to the social system." But she need not have struggled to justify herself, for with her imaginative energy she had accomplished at least as much as her mother had.

Introduction to *Frankenstein*

The Publishers of the Standard Novels, in selecting "Frankenstein" for one of their series, expressed a wish that I should furnish them with some account of the origin of the story. I am the more willing to comply, because I shall thus give a general answer to the question, so very frequently asked me—"How I, then a young girl, came to think of, and to dilate upon,[1] so very hideous an idea?" It is true that I am very averse to bringing myself forward in print; but as my account will only appear as an appendage to a former production, and as it will be confined to such topics as have connection with my authorship alone, I can scarcely accuse myself of a personal intrusion.

It is not singular that, as the daughter of two persons of distinguished literary celebrity,[2] I should very early in life have thought of writing. As a child I scribbled; and my favorite pastime, during the hours given me for recreation, was to "write stories." Still I had a dearer pleasure than this, which was the formation of castles in the air—the indulging in waking dreams—the following up trains of thought, which had for their subject the formation of a succession of imaginary incidents. My dreams were at once more fantastic and agreeable than my writings. In the latter I was a close imitator—rather doing as others had done, than putting down the suggestions of my own mind. What I wrote was intended at least for one other eye—my childhood's companion and friend; but my dreams were all my own; I accounted for them to nobody; they were my refuge when annoyed—my dearest pleasure when free.

I lived principally in the country as a girl, and passed a considerable time in Scotland. I made occasional visits to the more picturesque parts; but my habitual residence was on the blank and dreary northern shores of the Tay, near

1. Describe at length.
2. Mary Wollstonecraft (1759–1797) and William Godwin (1756–1836), both well-known authors.

Dundee. Blank and dreary on retrospection I call them; they were not so to me then. They were the aerie[3] of freedom, and the pleasant region where unheeded I could commune with the creatures of my fancy. I wrote then—but in a most commonplace style. It was beneath the trees of the grounds belonging to our house, or on the bleak sides of the woodless mountains near, that my true compositions, the airy flights of my imagination, were born and fostered. I did not make myself the heroine of my tales Life appeared to me too commonplace an affair as regarded myself. I could not figure to myself that romantic woes or wonderful events would ever be my lot; but I was not confined to my own identity, and I could people the hours with creations far more interesting to me at that age, than my own sensations.

After this my life became busier, and reality stood in place of fiction. My husband, however, was from the first, very anxious that I should prove myself worthy of my parentage, and enroll myself on the page of fame. He was forever inciting me to obtain literary reputation, which even on my own part I cared for then, though since I have become infinitely indifferent to it. At this time he desired that I should write, not so much with the idea that I could produce anything worthy of notice, but that he might himself judge how far I possessed the promise of better things hereafter Still I did nothing. Traveling, and the cares of a family, occupied my time; and study, in the way of reading, or improving my ideas in communication with his far more cultivated mind, was all of literary employment that engaged my attention.

In the summer of 1816, we visited Switzerland, and became the neighbors of Lord Byron. At first we spent our pleasant hours on the lake, or wandering on its shores; and Lord Byron, who was writing the third canto of *Childe Harold*,[4] was the only one among us who put his thoughts upon paper. These, as he brought them successively to us, clothed in all the light and harmony of poetry, seemed to stamp as divine the glories of heaven and earth, whose influences we partook with him.

But it proved a wet, ungenial summer, and incessant rain often confined us for days to the house. Some volumes of ghost stories, translated from the German into French, fell into our hands. There was *The History of the Inconstant Lover*, who, when he thought to clasp the bride to whom he had pledged his vows, found himself in the arms of the pale ghost of her whom he had deserted. There was the tale of the sinful founder of his race, whose miserable doom it was to bestow the kiss of death on all the younger sons of his fated house, just when they reached the age of promise. His gigantic, shadowy form, clothed like the ghost in *Hamlet*, in complete armor, but with the beaver[5] up, was seen at midnight, by the moon's fitful beams, to advance slowly along the gloomy avenue. The shape was lost beneath the shadow of the castle walls, but soon a gate swung back, a step was heard, the door of the chamber opened, and he advanced to the couch of the blooming youths, cradled in healthy sleep. Eternal sorrow sat upon his face as he bent down and kissed the forehead of the boys, who from that hour withered like flowers snapped upon the stalk. I have not seen these stories since then; but their incidents are as fresh in my mind as if I had read them yesterday.

3. The nest of a bird on a cliff or mountaintop, or any isolated or secluded dwelling.
4. The first two cantos of Byron's long poem *Childe Harold* were published to enormous popular acclaim in 1812.
5. The piece of armor/helmet that protects the lower part of the face.

"We will each write a ghost story," said Lord Byron; and his proposition was acceded to. There were four of us. The noble author began a tale, a fragment of which he printed at the end of his poem of *Mazeppa*.[6] Shelley, more apt to embody ideas and sentiments in the radiance of brilliant imagery, and in the music of the most melodious verse that adorns our language, than to invent the machinery of a story, commenced one founded on the experiences of his early life. Poor Polidori[7] had some terrible idea about a skull-headed lady, who was so punished for peeping through a key-hole—what to see I forget—something very shocking and wrong of course; but when she was reduced to a worse condition than the renowned Tom of Coventry, he did not know what to do with her, and was obliged to despatch her to the tomb of the Capulets,[8] the only place for which she was fitted. The illustrious poets also, annoyed by the platitude of prose, speedily relinquished their uncongenial task.

I busied myself *to think of a story*,—a story to rival those which had excited us to this task. One which would speak to the mysterious fears of our nature, and awaken thrilling horror—one to make the reader dread to look round, to curdle the blood, and quicken the beatings of the heart. If I did not accomplish these things, my ghost story would be unworthy of its name. I thought and pondered—vainly. I felt that blank incapability of invention which is the greatest misery of authorship, when dull Nothing replies to our anxious invocations. *Have you thought of a story?* I was asked each morning, and each morning I was forced to reply with a mortifying negative.

Everything must have a beginning, to speak in Sanchean phrase;[9] and that beginning must be linked to something that went before. The Hindus give the world an elephant to support it, but they make the elephant stand upon a tortoise. Invention, it must be humbly admitted, does not consist in creating out of void, but out of chaos; the materials must, in the first place, be afforded: it can give form to dark, shapeless substances, but cannot bring into being the substance itself. In all matters of discovery and invention, even of those that appertain to the imagination, we are continually reminded of the story of Columbus and his egg.[1] Invention consists in the capacity of seizing on the capabilities of a subject, and in the power of molding and fashioning ideas suggested to it.

Many and long were the conversations between Lord Byron and Shelley, to which I was a devout but nearly silent listener. During one of these, various philosophical doctrines were discussed, and among others the nature of the principle of life, and whether there was any probability of its ever being discovered and communicated. They talked of the experiments of Dr. Darwin[2] (I speak not of what the Doctor really did, or said that he did, but, as more to my purpose, of what was then spoken of as having been done by him), who preserved a piece of vermicelli in a glass case, till by some extraordinary means it

6. *Mazeppa, a Poem* (1819).
7. John William Polidori (1795–1821), Byron's doctor and friend, whose other attempts to write also met with little success.
8. Shakespeare's *Romeo and Juliet* ends with the unhappy pair dead in the tomb of Juliet's family. Tom of Coventry was the "peeping Tom," who alone looked at Lady Godiva when, according to legend, she rode naked through Coventry (so that her husband would lift a tax); his eyes shriveled in his head.
9. I.e., befitting the down-to-earth and practical

squire in Cervantes's *Don Quixote* (1615); perhaps a direct allusion to Sancho Panza's statement about the importance of beginnings in Part 2, Chapter 33.
1. The story that Columbus, when told that others could find the Indies, challenged the listeners to stand an egg on its end. When none could, he struck the egg on the table and left it standing on its broken end, to prove that the way would be easy to follow once he had shown it.
2. Erasmus Darwin (1731–1802), physician, poet, and scientist.

began to move with voluntary motion. Not thus, after all, would life be given. Perhaps a corpse would be reanimated; galvanism[3] had given token of such things: perhaps the component parts of a creature might be manufactured, brought together, and endued with vital warmth.

Night waned upon this talk, and even the witching hour had gone by, before we retired to rest. When I placed my head on my pillow, I did not sleep, nor could I be said to think. My imagination, unbidden, possessed and guided me, gifting the successive images that arose in my mind with a vividness far beyond the usual bounds of reverie. I saw—with shut eyes, but acute mental vision,—I saw the pale student of unhallowed arts kneeling beside the thing he had put together. I saw the hideous phantasm of a man stretched out, and then, on the working of some powerful engine, show signs of life, and stir with an uneasy, half vital motion. Frightful must it be; for supremely frightful would be the effect of any human endeavor to mock the stupendous mechanism of the Creator of the world. His success would terrify the artist; he would rush away from his odious handiwork, horror-stricken. He would hope that, left to itself, the slight spark of life which he had communicated would fade; that this thing, which had received such imperfect animation, would subside into dead matter; and he might sleep in the belief that the silence of the grave would quench for ever the transient existence of the hideous corpse which he had looked upon as the cradle of life. He sleeps; but he is awakened; he opens his eyes; behold the horrid thing stands at his bedside, opening his curtains, and looking on him with yellow, watery, but speculative eyes.

I opened mine in terror. The idea so possessed my mind, that a thrill of fear ran through me, and I wished to exchange the ghastly image of my fancy for the realities around. I see them still; the very room, the dark *parquet*,[4] the closed shutters, with the moonlight struggling through, and the sense I had that the glassy lake and white high Alps were beyond. I could not so easily get rid of my hideous phantom; still it haunted me. I must try to think of something else. I recurred to my ghost story,—my tiresome unlucky ghost story! O! if I could only contrive one which would frighten my reader as I myself had been frightened that night!

Swift as light and as cheering was the idea that broke in upon me. "I have found it! What terrified me will terrify others; and I need only describe the specter which had haunted my midnight pillow." On the morrow I announced that I had *thought of a story.* I began that day with the words, *It was on a dreary night of November*, making only a transcript of the grim terrors of my waking dream.

At first I thought but of a few pages—of a short tale; but Shelley urged me to develop the idea at greater length. I certainly did not owe the suggestion of one incident, nor scarcely of one train of feeling, to my husband, and yet but for his incitement, it would never have taken the form in which it was presented to the world. From this declaration I must except the preface. As far as I can recollect, it was entirely written by him.

And now, once again, I bid my hideous progeny go forth and prosper. I have an affection for it, for it was the offspring of happy days, when death and grief were but words, which found no true echo in my heart. Its several pages speak

3. Application of electricity developed by chemical action, especially to stimulate plants or muscles. 4. Patterned wooden floor.

of many a walk, many a drive, and many a conversation, when I was not alone; and my companion was one who, in this world, I shall never see more. But this is for myself; my readers have nothing to do with these associations.

I will add but one word as to the alterations I have made. They are principally those of style. I have changed no portion of the story, nor introduced any new ideas of circumstances. I have mended the language where it was so bald as to interfere with the interest of the narrative; and these changes occur almost exclusively in the beginning of the first volume. Throughout they are entirely confined to such parts as are mere adjuncts to the story, leaving the core and substance of it untouched.

1831

The Mortal Immortal

A Tale

July 16, 1833.—This is a memorable anniversary for me; on it I complete my three hundred and twenty-third year!

The Wandering Jew?[1]—certainly not. More than eighteen centuries have passed over his head. In comparison with him, I am a very young immortal.

Am I, then, immortal? This is a question which I have asked myself, by day and night, for now three hundred and three years, and yet cannot answer it. I detected a gray hair amidst my brown locks this very day—that surely signifies decay. Yet it may have remained concealed there for three hundred years—for some persons have become entirely white-headed before twenty years of age.

I will tell my story, and my reader shall judge for me. I will tell my story, and so contrive to pass some few hours of a long eternity, become so wearisome to me. Forever! Can it be? to live forever! I have heard of enchantments, in which the victims were plunged into a deep sleep, to wake, after a hundred years, as fresh as ever: I have heard of the Seven Sleepers[2]—thus to be immortal would not be so burthensome: but, oh! the weight of never-ending time—the tedious passage of the still-succeeding hours! How happy was the fabled Nourjahad![3]—But to my task.

All the world has heard of Cornelius Agrippa.[4] His memory is as immortal as his arts have made me. All the world has also heard of his scholar, who, unawares, raised the foul fiend during his master's absence, and was destroyed by him. The report, true or false, of this accident, was attended with many inconveniences to the renowned philosopher. All his scholars at once deserted him—his servants disappeared. He had no one near him to put coals on his ever-burning fires while he slept, or to attend to the changeful colors of his medicines while he studied. Experiment after experiment failed, because one pair of hands was insufficient to complete them: the dark spirits laughed at him for not being able to retain a single mortal in his service.

I was then very young—very poor—and very much in love. I had been for

1. According to medieval legend, a Jew who mocked Jesus on his way to the Cross was condemned by Christ to wander through the world until Judgment Day.
2. A legend about seven youths of Ephesus who slept in a cave for 187 years to escape persecution.

3. The hero of Frances Sherwood's *History of Nourjahad* (1767) was happy because he safely learned how undesirable immortality is.
4. Heinrich Cornelius Agrippa von Nettesheim (1486–1535), German occult philosopher and alchemist.

about a year the pupil of Cornelius, though I was absent when this accident took place. On my return, my friends implored me not to return to the alchemist's abode. I trembled as I listened to the dire tale they told; I required no second warning; and when Cornelius came and offered me a purse of gold if I would remain under his roof, I felt as if Satan himself tempted me. My teeth chattered—my hair stood on end:—I ran off as fast as my trembling knees would permit.

My failing steps were directed whither for two years they had every evening been attracted,—a gently bubbling spring of pure living waters, beside which lingered a dark-haired girl, whose beaming eyes were fixed on the path I was accustomed each night to tread. I cannot remember the hour when I did not love Bertha; we had been neighbors and playmates from infancy—her parents, like mine, were of humble life, yet respectable—our attachment had been a source of pleasure to them. In an evil hour, a malignant fever carried off both her father and mother, and Bertha became an orphan. She would have found a home beneath my paternal roof, but, unfortunately, the old lady of the near castle, rich, childless, and solitary, declared her intention to adopt her. Henceforth Bertha was clad in silk—inhabited a marble palace—and was looked on as being highly favored by fortune. But in her new situation among her new associates, Bertha remained true to the friend of her humbler days; she often visited the cottage of my father, and when forbidden to go thither, she would stray towards the neighboring wood, and meet me beside its shady fountain.

She often declared that she owed no duty to her new protectress equal in sanctity to that which bound us. Yet still I was too poor to marry, and she grew weary of being tormented on my account. She had a haughty but an impatient spirit, and grew angry at the obstacles that prevented our union. We met now after an absence, and she had been sorely beset while I was away; she complained bitterly, and almost reproached me for being poor. I replied hastily,—

"I am honest, if I am poor!—were I not, I might soon become rich!"

This exclamation produced a thousand questions. I feared to shock her by owning[5] the truth, but she drew it from me; and then, casting a look of disdain on me, she said—

"You pretend to love, and you fear to face the Devil for my sake!"

I protested that I had only dreaded to offend her;—while she dwelt on the magnitude of the reward that I should receive. Thus encouraged—shamed by her—led on by love and hope, laughing at my late fears, with quick steps and a light heart, I returned to accept the offers of the alchemist, and was instantly installed in my office.

A year passed away. I became possessed of no insignificant sum of money. Custom had banished my fears. In spite of the most painful vigilance, I had never detected the trace of a cloven foot;[6] nor was the studious silence of our abode ever disturbed by demoniac howls. I still continued my stolen interviews with Bertha, and Hope dawned on me—Hope—but not perfect joy; for Bertha fancied that love and security were enemies, and her pleasure was to divide them in my bosom. Though true of heart, she was somewhat of a coquette in manner; and I was jealous as a Turk. She slighted me in a thousand

5. Admitting.
6. A feature thought to be possessed by the devil and his servants.

ways, yet would never acknowledge herself to be in the wrong. She would drive me mad with anger, and then force me to beg her pardon. Sometimes she fancied that I was not sufficiently submissive, and then she had some story of a rival, favored by her protectress. She was surrounded by silk-clad youths—the rich and gay—What chance had the sad-robed scholar of Cornelius compared with these?

On one occasion, the philosopher made such large demands upon my time, that I was unable to meet her as I was wont. He was engaged in some mighty work, and I was forced to remain, day and night, feeding his furnaces and watching his chemical preparations. Bertha waited for me in vain at the fountain. Her haughty spirit fired at this neglect; and when at last I stole out during the few short minutes allotted to me for slumber, and hoped to be consoled by her, she received me with disdain, dismissed me in scorn, and vowed that any man should possess her hand rather than he who could not be in two places at once for her sake. She would be revenged!—And truly she was. In my dingy retreat I heard that she had been hunting, attended by Albert Hoffer. Albert Hoffer was favored by her protectress, and the three passed in cavalcade before my smoky window. Methought that they mentioned my name—it was followed by a laugh of derision, as her dark eyes glanced contemptuously towards my abode.

Jealousy, with all its venom, and all its misery, entered my breast. Now I shed a torrent of tears, to think that I should never call her mine; and, anon,[7] I imprecated a thousand curses on her inconstancy. Yet, still I must stir the fires of the alchemist, still attend on the changes of his unintelligible medicines.

Cornelius had watched for three days and nights, nor closed his eyes. The progress of his alembics[8] was slower than he expected: in spite of his anxiety, sleep weighed upon his eyelids. Again and again he threw off drowsiness with more than human energy; again and again it stole away his senses. He eyed his crucibles wistfully. "Not ready yet," he murmured; "will another night pass before the work is accomplished? Winzy,[9] you are vigilant—you are faithful—you have slept, my boy—you slept last night. Look at that glass vessel. The liquid it contains is of a soft rose-color: the moment it begins to change its hue, awaken me—till then I may close my eyes. First, it will turn white, and then emit golden flashes; but wait not till then; when the rose-color fades, rouse me." I scarcely heard the last words, muttered, as they were, in sleep. Even then he did not quite yield to nature. "Winzy, my boy," he again said, "do not touch the vessel—do not put it to your lips; it is a philter—a philter to cure love; you would not[1] cease to love your Bertha—beware to drink!"

And he slept. His venerable head sunk on his breast, and I scarce heard his regular breathing. For a few minutes I watched the vessel—the rosy hue of the liquid remained unchanged. Then my thoughts wandered—they visited the fountain, and dwelt on a thousand charming scenes never to be renewed—never! Serpents and adders were in my heart as the word "Never!" half formed itself on my lips. False girl!—false and cruel! Never more would she smile on me as that evening she smiled on Albert. Worthless, detested woman! I would not remain unrevenged—she should see Albert expire at her feet—she should die beneath my vengeance. She had smiled in disdain and triumph—she

7. Shortly afterward.
8. Apparatus used for distilling fluids.

9. The name of the narrator.
1. Do not wish to. "Philter": a potion or charm.

knew my wretchedness and her power. Yet what power had she?—the power of exciting my hate—my utter scorn—my—oh, all but indifference! Could I attain that—could I regard her with careless eyes, transferring my rejected love to one fairer and more true, that were indeed a victory!

A bright flash darted before my eyes. I had forgotten the medicine of the adept;[2] I gazed on it with wonder: flashes of admirable beauty, more bright than those which the diamond emits when the sun's rays are on it, glanced from the surface of the liquid; an odor the most fragrant and grateful stole over my sense; the vessel seemed one globe of living radiance, lovely to the eye, and most inviting to the taste. The first thought, instinctively inspired by the grosser sense, was, I will—I must drink. I raised the vessel to my lips. "It will cure me of love—of torture!" Already I had quaffed half of the most delicious liquor ever tasted by the palate of man, when the philosopher stirred. I started—I dropped the glass—the fluid flamed and glanced along the floor, while I felt Cornelius's grip at my throat, as he shrieked aloud, "Wretch! you have destroyed the labor of my life!"

The philosopher was totally unaware that I had drunk any portion of his drug. His idea was, and I gave a tacit assent to it, that I had raised the vessel from curiosity, and that, frighted at its brightness, and the flashes of intense light it gave forth, I had let it fall. I never undeceived him. The fire of the medicine was quenched—the fragrance died away—he grew calm, as a philosopher should under the heaviest trials, and dismissed me to rest.

I will not attempt to describe the sleep of glory and bliss which bathed my soul in paradise during the remaining hours of that memorable night. Words would be faint and shallow types[3] of my enjoyment, or of the gladness that possessed my bosom when I woke. I trod air—my thoughts were in heaven. Earth appeared heaven, and my inheritance upon it was to be one trance of delight. "This it is to be cured of love," I thought; "I will see Bertha this day, and she will find her lover cold and regardless; too happy to be disdainful, yet how utterly indifferent to her!"

The hours danced away. The philosopher, secure that he had once succeeded, and believing that he might again, began to concoct the same medicine once more. He was shut up with his books and drugs, and I had a holiday. I dressed myself with care; I looked in an old but polished shield, which served me for a mirror; methought my good looks had wonderfully improved. I hurried beyond the precincts of the town, joy in my soul, the beauty of heaven and earth around me. I turned my steps towards the castle—I could look on its lofty turrets with lightness of heart, for I was cured of love. My Bertha saw me afar off, as I came up the avenue. I know not what sudden impulse animated her bosom, but at the sight, she sprung with a light fawn-like bound down the marble steps, and was hastening towards me. But I had been perceived by another person. The old high-born hag, who called herself her protectress, and was her tyrant, had seen me, also; she hobbled, panting, up the terrace; a page, as ugly as herself, held up her train, and fanned her as she hurried along, and stopped my fair girl with a "How, now, my bold mistress? whither so fast? Back to your cage—hawks are abroad!"

Bertha clasped her hands—her eyes were still bent on my approaching figure. I saw the contest. How I abhorred the old crone who checked the kind im-

2. Alchemist who has learned the secrets of his art. 3. Signs, specimens.

pulses of my Bertha's softening heart. Hitherto, respect for her rank had caused me to avoid the lady of the castle; now I disdained such trivial considerations. I was cured of love, and lifted above all human fears; I hastened forwards, and soon reached the terrace. How lovely Bertha looked! her eyes flashing fire, her cheeks glowing with impatience and anger, she was a thousand times more graceful and charming than ever—I no longer loved—Oh! no, I adored—worshiped—idolized her!

She had that morning been persecuted, with more than usual vehemence, to consent to an immediate marriage with my rival. She was reproached with the encouragement that she had shown him—she was threatened with being turned out of doors with disgrace and shame. Her proud spirit rose in arms at the threat; but when she remembered the scorn that she had heaped upon me, and how, perhaps, she had thus lost one whom she now regarded as her only friend, she wept with remorse and rage. At that moment I appeared. "O, Winzy!" she exclaimed, "take me to your mother's cot;[4] swiftly let me leave the detested luxuries and wretchedness of this noble dwelling—take me to poverty and happiness."

I clasped her in my arms with transport. The old lady was speechless with fury, and broke forth into invective only when we were far on our road to my natal cottage. My mother received the fair fugitive, escaped from a gilt cage to nature and liberty, with tenderness and joy; my father, who loved her, welcomed her heartily; it was a day of rejoicing, which did not need the addition of the celestial potion of the alchemist to steep me in delight.

Soon after this eventful day, I became the husband of Bertha. I ceased to be the scholar of Cornelius, but I continued his friend. I always felt grateful to him for having, unawares, procured me that delicious draught of a divine elixir, which, instead of curing me of love (sad cure! solitary and joyless remedy for evils which seem blessings to the memory), had inspired me with courage and resolution, thus winning for me an inestimable treasure in my Bertha.

I often called to mind that period of trance-like inebriation with wonder. The drink of Cornelius had not fulfilled the task for which he affirmed that it had been prepared, but its effects were more potent and blissful than words can express. They had faded by degrees, yet they lingered long—and painted life in hues of splendor. Bertha often wondered at my lightness of heart and unaccustomed gaiety; for, before, I had been rather serious, or even sad, in my disposition. She loved me the better for my cheerful temper, and our days were winged by joy.

Five years afterwards I was suddenly summoned to the bedside of the dying Cornelius. He had sent for me in haste, conjuring my instant presence. I found him stretched on his pallet,[5] enfeebled even to death; all of life that yet remained animated his piercing eyes, and they were fixed on a glass vessel, full of a roseate liquid.

"Behold," he said, in a broken and inward voice, "the vanity of human wishes! a second time my hopes are about to be crowned, a second time they are destroyed. Look at that liquor—you remember five years ago I had prepared the same, with the same success;—then, as now, my thirsting lips expected to taste the immortal elixir—you dashed it from me! and at present it is too late."

4. Cottage. 5. Thin mattress.

He spoke with difficulty, and fell back on his pillow. I could not help saying,—

"How, revered master, can a cure for love restore you to life?"

A faint smile gleamed across his face as I listened earnestly to his scarcely intelligible answer.

"A cure for love and for all things—the Elixir of Immortality. Ah! if now I might drink, I should live for ever!"

As he spoke, a golden flash gleamed from the fluid; a well-remembered fragrance stole over the air; he raised himself, all weak as he was—strength seemed miraculously to reenter his frame—he stretched forth his hand—a loud explosion startled me—a ray of fire shot up from the elixir, and the glass vessel which contained it was shivered to atoms! I turned my eyes towards the philosopher; he had fallen back—his eyes were glassy—his features rigid—he was dead!

But I lived, and was to live forever! So said the unfortunate alchemist, and for a few days I believed his words. I remembered the glorious drunkenness that had followed my stolen draught. I reflected on the change I had felt in my frame—in my soul. The bounding elasticity of the one—the buoyant lightness of the other. I surveyed myself in a mirror, and could perceive no change in my features during the space of the five years which had elapsed. I remembered the radiant hues and grateful scent of that delicious beverage—worthy the gift it was capable of bestowing—I was, then, IMMORTAL!

A few days after I laughed at my credulity. The old proverb, that "a prophet is least regarded in his own country," was true with respect to me and my defunct master. I loved him as a man—I respected him as a sage—but I derided the notion that he could command the powers of darkness, and laughed at the superstitious fears with which he was regarded by the vulgar.[6] He was a wise philosopher, but had no acquaintance with any spirits but those clad in flesh and blood. His science was simply human; and human science, I soon persuaded myself, could never conquer nature's laws so far as to imprison the soul for ever within its carnal habitation. Cornelius had brewed a soul-refreshing drink—more inebriating than wine—sweeter and more fragrant than any fruit: it possessed probably strong medicinal powers, imparting gladness to the heart and vigor to the limbs; but its effects would wear out; already were they diminished in my frame. I was a lucky fellow to have quaffed health and joyous spirits, and perhaps long life, at my master's hands; but my good fortune ended there: longevity was far different from immortality.

I continued to entertain this belief for many years. Sometimes a thought stole across me—Was the alchemist indeed deceived? But my habitual credence was, that I should meet the fate of all the children of Adam[7] at my appointed time—a little late, but still at a natural age. Yet it was certain that I retained a wonderfully youthful look. I was laughed at for my vanity in consulting the mirror so often, but I consulted it in vain—my brow was untrenched[8]—my cheeks—my eyes—my whole person continued as untarnished as in my twentieth year.

I was troubled. I looked at the faded beauty of Bertha—I seemed more like her son. By degrees our neighbors began to make similar observations, and I found at last that I went by the name of the Scholar bewitched. Bertha herself

6. Common, uneducated people.
7. According to Genesis 3, the first man, who brought death into the world when he and Eve ate the forbid-
den fruit in Eden.
8. Unwrinkled.

grew uneasy. She became jealous and peevish, and at length she began to question me. We had no children; we were all in all to each other; and though, as she grew older, her vivacious spirit became a little allied to ill-temper, and her beauty sadly diminished, I cherished her in my heart as the mistress I had idolized, the wife I had sought and won with such perfect love.

At last our situation became intolerable: Bertha was fifty—I twenty years of age. I had, in very shame, in some measure adopted the habits of a more advanced age; I no longer mingled in the dance among the young and gay, but my heart bounded along with them while I restrained my feet; and a sorry figure I cut among the Nestors[9] of our village. But before the time I mention, things were altered—we were universally shunned; we were—at least, I was—reported to have kept up an iniquitous acquaintance with some of my former master's supposed friends. Poor Bertha was pitied, but deserted. I was regarded with horror and detestation.

What was to be done? we sat by our winter fire—poverty had made itself felt, for none would buy the produce of my farm; and often I had been forced to journey twenty miles, to some place where I was not known, to dispose of our property. It is true we had saved something for an evil day—that day was come.

We sat by our lone fireside—the old-hearted youth and his antiquated wife. Again Bertha insisted on knowing the truth; she recapitulated all she had ever heard said about me, and added her own observations. She conjured me to cast off the spell; she described how much more comely gray hairs were than my chestnut locks; she descanted[1] on the reverence and respect due to age—how preferable to the slight regard paid to mere children: could I imagine that the despicable gifts of youth and good looks outweighed disgrace, hatred, and scorn? Nay, in the end I should be burned as a dealer in the black art, while she, to whom I had not deigned to communicate any portion of my good fortune, might be stoned as my accomplice. At length she insinuated that I must share my secret with her, and bestow on her like benefits to those I myself enjoyed, or she would denounce me—and then she burst into tears.

Thus beset, methought it was the best way to tell the truth. I revealed it as tenderly as I could, and spoke only of *a very long life*, not of immortality—which representation, indeed, coincided best with my own ideas. When I ended, I rose and said,

"And now, my Bertha, will you denounce the lover of your youth?—You will not, I know. But it is too hard, my poor wife, that you should suffer from my ill-luck and the accursed arts of Cornelius. I will leave you—you have wealth enough, and friends will return in my absence. I will go; young as I seem, and strong as I am, I can work and gain my bread among strangers, unsuspected and unknown. I loved you in youth; God is my witness that I would not desert you in age, but that your safety and happiness require it."

I took my cap and moved towards the door; in a moment Bertha's arms were round my neck, and her lips were pressed to mine. "No, my husband, my Winzy," she said, "you shall not go alone—take me with you; we will remove from this place, and, as you say, among strangers we shall be unsuspected and safe. I am not so very old as quite to shame you, my Winzy; and I dare say the

9. Old men; Nestor was an aged counselor in Homer's 1. Discoursed.
Iliad.

charm will soon wear off, and, with the blessing of God, you will become more elderly-looking, as is fitting; you shall not leave me."

I returned the good soul's embrace heartily. "I will not, my Bertha; but for your sake I had not thought of such a thing.[2] I will be your true, faithful husband while you are spared to me, and do my duty by you to the last."

The next day we prepared secretly for our emigration. We were obliged to make great pecuniary sacrifices—it could not be helped. We realized a sum sufficient, at least, to maintain us while Bertha lived; and, without saying adieu to any one, quitted our native country to take refuge in a remote part of western France.

It was a cruel thing to transport poor Bertha from her native village, and the friends of her youth, to a new country, new language, new customs. The strange secret of my destiny rendered this removal immaterial to me; but I compassionated her deeply, and was glad to perceive that she found compensation for her misfortunes in a variety of little ridiculous circumstances. Away from all tell-tale chroniclers, she sought to decrease the apparent disparity of our ages by a thousand feminine arts—rouge, youthful dress, and assumed juvenility of manner. I could not be angry—Did not I myself wear a mask? Why quarrel with hers, because it was less successful? I grieved deeply when I remembered that this was my Bertha, whom I had loved so fondly, and won with such transport—the dark-eyed, dark-haired girl, with smiles of enchanting archness and a step like a fawn—this mincing, simpering, jealous old woman. I should have revered her gray locks and withered cheeks; but thus!—It was my work, I knew; but I did not the less deplore this type of human weakness.

Her jealousy never slept. Her chief occupation was to discover that, in spite of outward appearances, I was myself growing old. I verily believe that the poor soul loved me truly in her heart, but never had woman so tormenting a mode of displaying fondness. She would discern wrinkles in my face and decrepitude in my walk, while I bounded along in youthful vigor, the youngest looking of twenty youths. I never dared address another woman: on one occasion, fancying that the belle of the village regarded me with favoring eyes, she bought me a gray wig. Her constant discourse among her acquaintances was, that though I looked so young, there was ruin at work within my frame; and she affirmed that the worst symptom about me was my apparent health. My youth was a disease, she said, and I ought at all times to prepare, if not for a sudden and awful death, at least to awake some morning white-headed, and bowed down with all the marks of advanced years. I let her talk—I often joined in her conjectures. Her warnings chimed in with my never-ceasing speculations concerning my state, and I took an earnest, though painful, interest in listening to all that her quick wit and excited imagination could say on the subject.

Why dwell on these minute circumstances? We lived on for many long years. Bertha became bed-rid and paralytic: I nursed her as a mother might a child. She grew peevish, and still harped upon one string—of how long I should survive her. It has ever been a source of consolation to me, that I performed my duty scrupulously towards her. She had been mine in youth, she was mine in age, and at last, when I heaped the sod over her corpse, I wept to feel that I had lost all that really bound me to humanity.

Since then how many have been my cares and woes, how few and empty my

2. I.e., I thought of it only for your sake.

enjoyments! I pause here in my history—I will pursue it no further. A sailor without rudder or compass, tossed on a stormy sea—a traveller lost on a widespread heath, without landmark or star to guide him—such have I been: more lost, more hopeless than either. A nearing ship, a gleam from some far cot, may save them; but I have no beacon except the hope of death.

Death! mysterious, ill-visaged friend of weak humanity! Why alone of all mortals have you cast me from your sheltering fold?[3] O, for the peace of the grave! the deep silence of the iron-bound tomb! that thought would cease to work in my brain, and my heart beat no more with emotions varied only by new forms of sadness!

Am I immortal? I return to my first question. In the first place, is it not more probable that the beverage of the alchemist was fraught rather with longevity than eternal life? Such is my hope. And then be it remembered, that I only drank *half* of the potion prepared by him. Was not the whole necessary to complete the charm? To have drained half the Elixir of Immortality is but to be half immortal—my Forever is thus truncated and null.

But again, who shall number the years of the half of eternity? I often try to imagine by what rule the infinite may be divided. Sometimes I fancy age advancing upon me. One gray hair I have found. Fool! do I lament? Yes, the fear of age and death often creeps coldly into my heart; and the more I live, the more I dread death, even while I abhor life. Such an enigma is man—born to perish—when he wars, as I do, against the established laws of his nature.

But for this anomaly of feeling surely I might die: the medicine of the alchemist would not be proof against[4] fire—sword—and the strangling waters. I have gazed upon the blue depths of many a placid lake, and the tumultuous rushing of many a mighty river, and have said, peace inhabits those waters; yet I turned my steps away, to live yet another day. I have asked myself, whether suicide would be a crime in one to whom thus only the portals of the other world could be opened. I have done all, except presenting myself as a soldier or duelist, an object of destruction to my—no, *not* my fellow-mortals, and therefore I have shrunk away. They are not my fellows. The inextinguishable power of life in my frame, and their ephemeral existence, place us wide as the poles asunder. I could not raise a hand against the meanest[5] or the most powerful among them.

Thus I have lived on for many a year—alone, and weary of myself—desirous of death, yet never dying—a mortal immortal. Neither ambition nor avarice can enter my mind, and the ardent love that gnaws at my heart, never to be returned—never to find an equal on which to expend itself—lives there only to torment me.

This very day I conceived a design by which I may end all—without self-slaughter, without making another man a Cain[6]—an expedition, which mortal frame can never survive, even endued[7] with the youth and strength that inhabits mine. Thus I shall put my immortality to the test, and rest for ever— or return, the wonder and benefactor of the human species.

Before I go, a miserable vanity has caused me to pen these pages. I would not die, and leave no name behind. Three centuries have passed since I

3. An enclosure for sheep. Christ is traditionally represented as a shepherd; here Shelley places Death in that protective role.
4. Able to resist or repel.
5. Lowest.

6. I.e., a murderer. In Genesis 4, Cain, the son of Adam and Eve, murders his brother Abel and is cast out into the world.
7. Endowed.

quaffed the fatal beverage: another year shall not elapse before, encountering gigantic dangers—warring with the powers of frost in their home—beset by famine, toil, and tempest—I yield this body, too tenacious a cage for a soul which thirsts for freedom, to the destructive elements of air and water—or, if I survive, my name shall be recorded as one of the most famous among the sons of men; and, my task achieved, I shall adopt more resolute means, and, by scattering and annihilating the atoms that compose my frame, set at liberty the life imprisoned within, and so cruelly prevented from soaring from this dim earth to a sphere more congenial to its immortal essence.

1833 1834

SOJOURNER TRUTH
c. 1797–1883

Our understanding of both the life and the art of Sojourner Truth is limited, for this woman, who by all accounts became a brilliant speechmaker, exemplifies an oral tradition only partially preserved. As Erlene Stetson and Linda David have demonstrated in their book about this orator, "illiteracy did not exclude Truth from political discourse," because she relied on access to the written word, especially the Bible and newspapers, which she heard read aloud and which she refashioned in her remarkable speeches. Born into slavery in Hurley, Ulster County, New York, she was called Isabella, and after she fled to freedom in 1827, she took the last name of the family that protected her. Isabella Van Wagenen had already witnessed the sale of two of her four surviving children when she settled as a domestic servant with her son in New York City in or around 1829. There she worked with the evangelical preacher Elijah Pierson, who encouraged her efforts to convert prostitutes, and Robert Matthew, whose communal household, "Zion Hill," in Sing Sing, New York, was her home for two years. In 1843, mystical visions and voices gave her the new name "Sojourner Truth." So christened, she sojourned alone to speak the truth on tours that would make her famous throughout the United States.

Her religious zeal was linked to abolitionist goals when, at a communal farm in Northampton, Massachusetts, in that first winter of her travels, she came into contact with George W. Benson, brother-in-law of the newspaper editor William Lloyd Garrison. Subsequently hailed by abolitionist leaders, she toured Ohio, Indiana, Missouri, and Kansas throughout the 1850s, singing gospel songs, engaging large crowds with her speeches, and selling the *Narrative of Sojourner Truth* (1850), an autobiographical account transcribed and edited by Olive Gilbert. Illiterate all of her life, speaking an English accented with her original language, Dutch, Sojourner Truth was effective even with hostile audiences. In an essay in the April 1863 issue of the *Atlantic Monthly*, Harriet Beecher Stowe described the subtle power of this "sibyl" who had found enough charity to declare, "Lord, Lord, I can love *even de white folk!*" During the postwar period, encouraged by Elizabeth Cady Stanton, Sojourner Truth began speaking for the cause of women's suffrage, but she never relinquished her spiritual and racial themes. Her later call for a "Negro State" met with no success; however, she continued to lecture and sing in many eastern and midwestern states until, in her mid-eighties, she retired to Battle Creek, Michigan, where she died.

As one of the most effective female orators of her time, Sojourner Truth spoke for oppressed people with humor and courage that are evident, too, in the story of her response to allegations that she was a man: she was said to have bared her

breast at a women's rights convention. Although we must depend on the records of her white friends, in her speeches Sojourner Truth emerges, as the scholar Sterling Stuckey has observed, with the vitality of a great blues singer who sustains the most essential values of her people.

We are indebted to Miriam Schneir for her modernization of Truth's speeches in *Feminism: The Essential Historical Writings* (1972); the speeches were originally recorded in Elizabeth Cady Stanton et al., *The History of Woman Suffrage* (1881–87).

Ain't I a Woman?

Well, children, where there is so much racket there must be something out of kilter. I think that 'twixt the negroes of the South and the women at the North, all talking about rights, the white men will be in a fix pretty soon. But what's all this here talking about?

That man over there says that women need to be helped into carriages, and lifted over ditches, and to have the best place everywhere. Nobody ever helps me into carriages, or over mud-puddles, or gives me any best place! And ain't I a woman? Look at me! Look at my arm! I have ploughed and planted, and gathered into barns, and no man could head[1] me! And ain't I a woman? I could work as much and eat as much as a man—when I could get it—and bear the lash as well! And ain't I a woman? I have borne thirteen children, and seen them most all sold off to slavery, and when I cried out with my mother's grief, none but Jesus heard me! And ain't I a woman?

Then they talk about this thing in the head; what's this they call it? [Intellect, someone whispers.] That's it, honey. What's that got to do with women's rights or negro's rights? If my cup won't hold but a pint, and yours holds a quart, wouldn't you be mean not to let me have my little half-measure full?

Then that little man in black there, he says women can't have as much rights as men, 'cause Christ wasn't a woman! Where did your Christ come from? Where did your Christ come from? From God and a woman! Man had nothing to do with Him.

If the first woman God ever made was strong enough to turn the world upside down all alone, these women together ought to be able to turn it back, and get it right side up again! And now they is asking to do it, the men better let them.

Obliged to you for hearing me, and now old Sojourner ain't got nothing more to say.

1851 1881–86

What Time of Night It Is

Is it not good for me to come and draw forth a spirit,[2] to see what kind of spirit people are of? I see that some of you have got the spirit of a goose, and some have got the spirit of a snake. I feel at home here. I come to you, citizens of New York, as I suppose you ought to be. I am a citizen of the state of New

1. Get in front of, surpass. 2. An energetic response.

York; I was born in it, and I was a slave in the state of New York; and now I am a good citizen of this state. I was born here, and I can tell you I feel at home here. I've been lookin' round and watchin' things, and I know a little mite[3] 'bout Woman's Rights, too. I come forth to speak 'bout Woman's Rights, and want to throw in my little mite, to keep the scales a-movin'. I know that it feels a kind o' hissin' and ticklin' like to see a colored woman get up and tell you about things, and Woman's Rights. We have all been thrown down so low that nobody thought we'd ever get up again; but we have been long enough trodden now; we will come up again, and now I am here.

I was a-thinkin', when I see women contendin' for their rights, I was a-thinkin' what a difference there is now, and what there was in old times. I have only a few minutes to speak; but in the old times the kings of the earth would[n't] hear a woman. There was a king in the Scriptures;[4] and then it was the kings of the earth would kill a woman if she come into their presence; but Queen Esther come forth, for she was oppressed, and felt there was a great wrong, and she said I will die or I will bring my complaint before the king. Should the king of the United States be greater, or more crueler, or more harder? But the king, he raised up his sceptre and said: "Thy request shall be granted unto thee—to the half of my kingdom will I grant it to thee!" Then he said he would hang Haman on the gallows he had made up high. But that is not what women come forward to contend. The women want their rights as Esther. She only wanted to explain her rights. And he was so liberal that he said, "the half of my kingdom shall be granted to thee," and he did not wait for her to ask, he was so liberal with her.

Now, women do not ask half of a kingdom, but their rights, and they don't get 'em. When she comes to demand 'em, don't you hear how sons hiss their mothers like snakes because they ask for their rights; and can they ask for anything less? The king ordered Haman to be hung on the gallows which he prepared to hang others; but I do not want any man to be killed, but I am sorry to see them so short-minded. But we'll have our rights; see if we don't; and you can't stop us from them; see if you can. You may hiss as much as you like, but it is comin'. Women don't get half as much rights as they ought to; we want more, and we will have it. Jesus says: "What I say to one, I say to all—watch!"[5] I'm a-watchin'. God says: "Honor your father and your mother."[6] Sons and daughters ought to behave themselves before their mothers, but they do not. I can see them a-laughin', and pointin' at their mothers up here on the stage. They hiss when an aged woman comes forth. If they'd been brought up proper they'd have known better than hissin' like snakes and geese. I'm 'round watchin' these things, and I wanted to come up and say these few things to you, and I'm glad of the hearin' you give me. I wanted to tell you a mite about Woman's Rights, and so I came out and said so. I am sittin' among you to watch; and every once and awhile I will come out and tell you what time of night it is.

1853 1881–86

3. Bit.
4. Men and women who came before King Ahasuerus uncalled were put to death unless he held out his golden scepter, as he did to Esther, his Jewish queen, who saved her people from a massacre planned by Haman (see the Book of Esther, which this paragraph echoes).
5. Compare Mark 13:37: "And what I say unto you I say unto all, Watch."
6. One of the Ten Commandments issued by God to Moses.

Keeping the Thing Going while Things Are Stirring

My friends, I am rejoiced that you are glad, but I don't know how you will feel when I get through. I come from another field—the country of the slave. They have got their liberty—so much good luck to have slavery partly destroyed; not entirely. I want it root and branch destroyed. Then we will all be free indeed. I feel that if I have to answer for the deeds done in my body just as much as a man, I have a right to have just as much as a man. There is a great stir about colored men getting their rights,[1] but not a word about the colored women; and if colored men get their rights, and not colored women theirs, you see the colored men will be masters over the women, and it will be just as bad as it was before. So I am for keeping the thing going while things are stirring; because if we wait till it is still, it will take a great while to get it going again. White women are a great deal smarter, and know more than colored women, while colored women do not know scarcely anything. They go out washing, which is about as high as a colored woman gets, and their men go about idle, strutting up and down; and when the women come home, they[2] ask for their money and take it all, and then scold because there is no food. I want you to consider on that, chil'n. I call you chil'n; you are somebody's chil'n, and I am old enough to be mother of all that is here. I want women to have their rights. In the courts women have no right, no voice; nobody speaks for them. I wish woman to have her voice there among the pettifoggers.[3] If it is not a fit place for women, it is unfit for men to be there.

I am above eighty years old; it is about time for me to be going. I have been forty years a slave and forty years free, and would be here forty years more to have equal rights for all. I suppose I am kept here because something remains for me to do; I suppose I am yet to help to break the chain. I have done a great deal of work; as much as a man, but did not get so much pay. I used to work in the field and bind grain, keeping up with the cradler;[4] but men doing no more, got twice as much pay; so with the German women. They work in the field and do as much work, but do not get the pay. We do as much, we eat as much, we want as much. I suppose I am about the only colored woman that goes about to speak for the rights of the colored women. I want to keep the thing stirring, now that the ice is cracked. What we want is a little money. You men know that you get as much again as women when you write, or for what you do. When we get our rights we shall not have to come to you for money, for then we shall have money enough in our own pockets; and may be you will ask us for money. But help us now until we get it. It is a good consolation to know that when we have got this battle once fought we shall not be coming to you any more. You have been having our rights so long, that you think, like a slaveholder, that you own us. I know that it is hard for one who has held the reins for so long to give up; it cuts like a knife. It will feel all the better when it closes up again. I have been in Washington about three years, seeing about these colored people. Now colored men have the right to vote. There ought to be equal rights now more than ever, since colored people have got their freedom. I am

1. The Fourteenth and Fifteenth Amendments to the Constitution, proposed in 1866 and adopted in 1868, gave blacks the vote but omitted any reference to women.
2. I.e., the men.
3. Unscrupulous lawyers.
4. A worker who reaps grain and lays it flat.

going to talk several times while I am here; so now I will do a little singing. I have not heard any singing since I came here.

1867 1881–86

ELIZABETH BARRETT BROWNING
1806–1861

Elizabeth Barrett Browning is probably best known today for her romance with Robert Browning. Her *Sonnets from the Portuguese*, a series of love poems dedicated to him, are still popular, while the dramatic elopement of the two writers has been the subject of many books and at least one play, *The Barretts of Wimpole Street* (1930) by Rudolf Besier. Yet in her own era this prolific, scholarly, and highly political poet was considered a major author rather than a romance heroine. Older and more famous than the husband whose reputation has since eclipsed hers, she was seriously mentioned for the post of poet laureate when Wordsworth died in 1850. Admired by such diverse figures as William Makepeace Thackeray and Harriet Martineau, Edgar Allan Poe and Harriet Beecher Stowe, Alfred, Lord Tennyson and Margaret Fuller, she was an accomplished student and translator of Greek, the center of a lively circle of English expatriates in mid-nineteenth-century Florence, a passionate abolitionist, a powerful supporter of the movement for Italian unification, and a strong feminist. Indeed nothing could be more misleading than the twentieth-century image of "Mrs. Browning" as a swooning Victorian invalid, languishing on a sofa, smelling salts in one hand and sentimental verses in the other.

Born on a pleasant estate at Durham in Herefordshire, Elizabeth Barrett was the oldest of eleven children. Her father, Edward Moulton Barrett, owned extensive plantations in Jamaica, from which the family fortune derived, though Elizabeth herself was later to be troubled by the link with slavery such holdings represented. Strong-willed and autocratic, he dominated the household, and Elizabeth's submissive mother, Mary Barrett, was evidently an appropriate wife for him: she was "one of those women," the poet later wrote, who "in . . . bowing themselves make a mark, a plait, within—a sign of suffering." Yet Elizabeth clearly loved and admired her; after Mrs. Barrett's death in 1828, she indicated in letters and journals that, like her heroine Aurora Leigh, she "felt a mother-want about the world."

A precocious child, Barrett Browning started to write poetry early. According to some reports, she composed verses at the age of four, and when she was fourteen her father—whose patriarchal sternness did not prevent him from taking pride in his oldest child's accomplishments—had her "epic," *The Battle of Marathon*, privately printed. At the age of sixteen, she wrote a long philosophical poem, *An Essay on Mind*, and around this time she began studying Greek, with special attention to the Greek Christian poets. Her life was not entirely carefree, however. In 1821 she suffered what was defined as a "nervous collapse"; her general health had, in any case, always been precarious. Quite early, therefore, like so many other nineteenth-century invalids, she began using what she called "muriate of morphine . . . in a combination with ether" to ease both physical pain and mental distress. For much of her adult life, especially her years of confinement in the famous house at 50 Wimpole Street from which Browning rescued her, she seems to have been virtually dependent on such drugs.

Despite these problems, Barrett Browning's earliest years at Wimpole Street were by no means bleak. After some financial losses, the family had moved there in

1838, just as Elizabeth was beginning to establish a considerable literary reputation with her first books, a translation of Aeschylus's *Prometheus Bound* (1833) and a collection of her own verse, *The Seraphim and Other Poems* (1838). After her mother's death, she and her father had become particularly close—she was evidently always a special favorite of his—and she was also devoted to her brothers and sisters, especially her brother Edward ("Bro"), the sibling closest to her in age. In addition, she had formed friendships with a number of notable literary figures, including the essayist Mary Russell Mitford, the dramatist Richard Horne, and the man of letters John Kenyon. Her health continued to be poor, however, and in 1838 she was advised by doctors to vacation in Cornwall, where the climate was supposed to be good for invalids. She persuaded her father that Bro should accompany her there, and in what may well have been the major catastrophe of her life, the young man was drowned that year in a sailing accident off Torquay. Earlier in the year, her brother Samuel had also died, and the loss of Bro, coming so soon after another fatality, dealt her a terrible blow. Plunged into "hopeless grief," feeling herself to be "dead before death," and "living on the outside of my life," she retired into the notorious sickroom at Wimpole Street, from which she was not to emerge for another five years.

Still, although she was ill and in mourning, Barrett Browning continued her indefatigable correspondence and her vigorous composition. In 1844 she published a two-volume collection of her poems, with an American edition that had an introduction by Edgar Allan Poe. Friends visited her, she maintained a lively interest in London's literary world, and she continued her study of Greek; her *Account of the Greek Christian Poets* appeared serially in the *Athenaeum*, a major British periodical, in 1842. Finally, in 1845, she received a surprising letter from an admirer, Robert Browning, a little-known but increasingly well-regarded poet whose veneration of her work was to change her life. "I do . . . love these books with all my heart—and I love you too," he wrote, imploring her for the privilege of a meeting. At their first encounter, and thereafter, the two poets discovered many mutual affinities; within a year and a half of Browning's first letter to Elizabeth Barrett, they eloped to the Continent together.

Six years younger than his wife-to-be, Browning was a struggling experimental writer when the pair met. Because he was extraordinarily intellectual, his work was often considered "obscure," but in an effort to surmount such judgments he had been trying to write popular dramas, a labor that no doubt influenced his later mastery of the dramatic monologue and that must also have left its mark on his wife's work, perhaps enhancing her interest in capturing the theatrical intensity of immediate events. Because Elizabeth Barrett was far more established than Robert Browning at the time of their first meeting, however, it is just as likely that her stylistic inventiveness influenced his writing. Certainly, even in his first letter to her, he expressed his respect for her work, defining himself "as a loyal fellow-craftsman." Their flight from the dark house at Wimpole Street to the sunnier streets of France and Italy was obviously romantic: Edward Moulton Barrett had long refused to allow any of his children to marry, so the couple had to wed furtively in a London church, with only Elizabeth's maid and a cousin of Robert's as witnesses. But what was ultimately more crucial than the crisis of their love was the seriousness of their aesthetic as well as emotional engagement with each other and the psychological support that the poet formerly known as Elizabeth Barrett was to derive from that many-leveled relationship.

That she did derive such support from Browning is made clear by the intensity of the verse she wrote in the fifteen years of her marriage, years when the couple lived primarily in Florence at the house called Casa Guidi, which she memorialized in *Casa Guidi Windows*, her brilliant meditation on the successes and setbacks of the Italian nationalist movement. Traveling through France, where Elizabeth insisted on meeting and doing homage to the novelist George Sand—

about whom she had already written several sonnets—the Brownings came to Italy, the land that was to become a significant second home for both. Here the two began to write what were obviously ambitious and major works. Elizabeth, for instance, produced her *Poems* of 1850, which included such fierce political statements as *The Runaway Slave at Pilgrim's Point*. Shortly thereafter, she published *Sonnets from the Portuguese*, a sequence that adapted the usually male-oriented genre of the sonnet cycle to female requirements, telling the story of a love affair from a woman's, instead of a man's, point of view. Then, in 1851, she produced *Casa Guidi Windows*, and in 1857 her "epic-novel" *Aurora Leigh* appeared. Finally, in 1860, she published *Poems before Congress*, a collection of frankly political manifestos dedicated to the cause of Italian unification; and in 1862, the year after her death from complications of bronchitis, her *Last Poems* were assembled by her husband. To the end, she had been vital and productive.

Aesthetically energized, Barrett Browning had also been socially and intellectually refreshed by her new life. In Florence she made many friends, including the American writers Harriet Beecher Stowe and Margaret Fuller as well as the increasingly eccentric English poet Walter Savage Landor, and she developed new interests, including—along with the Italian "cause"—the popular spiritualist movement. Most important, in Florence in 1849, after several miscarriages, she gave birth to a son, Robert Wiedeman Barrett-Browning, called "Pennini" (or "Pen" for short). Like marriage, maternity seemed only to enhance her creative imagination. Her "own young Florentine" with "brave blue English eyes" appears as a redemptive figure at the conclusion of *Casa Guidi Windows*, and again, thinly disguised, as a sacramental child in *Aurora Leigh*. Gracing poems and romping in parlors, he seems to have been a muse rather than an encumbrance for his forty-three-year-old mother.

If her own real child functioned as a herald of art as well as reality for Barrett Browning, however, that is because, especially during her Italian years, she had evolved a passionate aesthetic of reality. In *Aurora Leigh*, her heroine, a poet like herself, articulates this creed, and following such beliefs, Barrett Browning wrote with commitment about the problem of slavery in the United States, an issue she dramatized in *The Runaway Slave at Pilgrim's Point*, and about the pain of impoverished children in England, a matter she had already begun to treat in the early polemics of *The Cry of the Children* and that she later took up in *A Song for the Ragged Schools of London*. More elaborately, she recorded not only her aesthetic of reality but also her protofeminist philosophy in the book-length verse-novel *Aurora Leigh*, where she attacked the degrading education most nineteenth-century women received and defended their right to intellectual self-determination. Attempting a range of forms and meters—the sonnet and the verse drama, the ballad and the blank verse epic—she constantly tested herself against the highest standards of male-defined poetic genres, as if to declare, with her Aurora, "I too have my vocation—work to do . . . most serious work."

A True Dream

(Dreamed at Sidmouth[1] 1833)

I had not an evil end in view,
 Though I trod the evil way;
And why I practiced the magic art,
 My dream it did not say.

1. An English seaside town

I unsealed the vial mystical,
 I outpoured the liquid thing,
And while the smoke came wreathing out,
 I stood unshuddering.

The smoke came wreathing, wreathing out,
 All mute, and dark, and slow,
Till its cloud was stained with a fleshly hue,
 And a fleshly form 'gan show.

Then paused the smoke—the fleshly form
 Looked steadfast in mine ee,[2]
His beard was black as a thundercloud,
 But I trembled not to see.[3]

I unsealed the vial mystical,
 I outpoured the liquid thing,
And while the smoke came wreathing out,
 I stood unshuddering.

The smoke came wreathing, wreathing out,
 All mute, and dark, and slow,
Till its cloud was stained with a fleshly hue,
 And a fleshly form 'gan show.

Then paused the smoke—but the mortal form
 A garment swart[4] did veil,
I looked on it with fixéd heart,
 Yea—not a pulse did fail!

I unsealed the vial mystical,
 I outpoured the liquid thing,
And while the smoke came wreathing out,
 I stood unshuddering.

The smoke came wreathing, wreathing out,
 And now it was faster and lighter,
And it bore on its folds the rainbow's hues,
 Heaven could not show them brighter.

Then paused the smoke, the rainbow's hues
 Did a childish face express—
The rose in the cheek, the blue in the eyne,
 The yellow in the tress.

The fair young child shook back her hair,
 And round me her arms did wreathe,
Her lips were hard and cold as stone,
 They sucked away my breath.

5

10

15

20

25

30

35

40

2. Archaic form of "eye"; Barrett Browning is evoking both the language and form of old English ballads like "Sir Patrick Spens" here.

3. I.e., did not tremble to see him.

4. Black or dark colored.

I cast her off as she clung to me, 45
 With hate and shuddering;
I brake the vials, and foresware
 The curséd, curséd thing.

Anon[5] outspake a brother of mine—
 "Upon the pavement, see, 50
Besprent with noisome[6] poison slime,
 Those twining serpents three."

Anon outspake my wildered[7] heart
 As I saw the serpent train—
"I have called up three existences 55
 I cannot quench again."

"Alas! with unholy company,
 My lifetime they will scathe;
They will hiss in the storm, and on sunny days
 Will gleam and thwart my path." 60

Outspake that pitying brother of mine—
 "Now nay, my sister, nay,
I will pour on them oil of vitriol,[8]
 And burn their lives away."

"Now nay, my brother, torture not, 65
 Now hold thine hand, and spare."
He poured on them oil of vitriol,
 And did not heed my prayer.

I saw the drops of torture fall;
 I heard the shriekings rise, 70
While the serpents writhed in agony
 Beneath my dreaming eyes.

And while they shrieked, and while they writhed,
 And inward and outward wound,
They waxéd larger, and their wail 75
 Assumed a human sound.

And glared their eyes, and their slimy scales
 Were roundly and redly bright,
Most like the lidless sun, what time[9]
 Through the mist he meets your sight. 80

And larger and larger they waxéd still,
 And longer still and longer;
And they shrieked in their pain, "Come, come to us,
 We are stronger, we are stronger."

5. Then, shortly after.
6. Repulsive. "Besprent": sprinkled.
7. Bewildered.

8. A caustic chemical substance.
9. When. "Lidless sun": the sun is compared to an eye with no lid.

Upon the ground I laid mine head, 85
 And heard the wailing sound;
I did not wail, I did not writhe—
 I laid me on the ground.

And larger and larger they waxéd still
 And longer still and longer; 90
And they shrieked in their pangs, "Come, come to us,
 We are stronger, we are stronger."

Then up I raised my burning brow,
 My quiv'ring arms on high;
I spake in prayer, and I named aloud 95
 The name of sanctity.

And as in my anguish I prayed and named
 Aloud the holy name,
The impious mocking serpent voice
 Did echo back the same. 100

And larger and larger they waxéd still,
 And stronger still and longer!
And they shrieked in their pangs, "Come, come to us,
 We are stronger, we are stronger."

Then out from among them arose a form 105
 In shroud of death indued[1]—
I fled from him with wings of wind,
 With whirlwinds he pursued.

 . . .

I stood by a chamber door, and thought
 Within its gloom to hide; 110
I locked the door, and the while forgot
 That I stood on the outer side.

And the knell of mine heart was wildly tolled
 While I graspéd still the key;
For I felt beside me the icy breath, 115
 And knew that *that* was *he*.

I heard these words, "Who'er doth *taste*,
 Will *drink* the magic bowl;
So her body may do my mission here
 Companioned by her soul." 120

Mine hand was cold as the key it held,
 Mine heart had an iron weight;
I saw a gleam, I heard a sound—
 The clock was striking eight.

1833 1913

1. I.e., wrapped or covered.

Grief

I tell you, hopeless grief is passionless;
That only men incredulous of despair,
Half-taught in anguish, through the midnight air
Beat upward to God's throne in loud access
Of shrieking and reproach. Full desertness, 5
In souls as countries, lieth silent-bare
Under the blanching, vertical eye-glare
Of the absolute heavens. Deep-hearted man, express
Grief for thy dead in silence like to death—
Most like a monumental statue set 10
In everlasting watch and moveless woe
Till itself crumble to the dust beneath.
Touch it; the marble eyelids are not wet:
If it could weep, it could arise and go.

 1844

To George Sand[1]

A Desire

Thou large-brained woman and large-hearted man,
Self-called George Sand! whose soul, amid the lions[2]
Of thy tumultuous senses, moans defiance
And answers roar for roar, as spirits can:
I would some mild miraculous thunder ran 5
Above the applauded circus, in appliance
Of thine own nobler nature's strength and science,
Drawing two pinions,[3] white as wings of swan,
From thy strong shoulders, to amaze the place
With holier light! that thou to woman's claim 10
And man's, mightst join beside the angel's grace
Of a pure genius sanctified from blame,
Till child and maiden pressed to thine embrace
To kiss upon thy lips a stainless fame.[4]

 1844

To George Sand[1]

A Recognition

True genius, but true woman! dost deny
The woman's nature with a manly scorn,
And break away the gauds[2] and armlets worn

1. Outburst.
1. French female novelist (1804–1876) whose novels and style of life were considered immoral by some.
2. In the ancient Roman "circus" or arena slaves were pitted against lions for the amusement of spectators.
3. Wings.

4. I.e., a fame unstained by immorality.
1. See second n. 1, this page.
2. Ornaments, here representing womanly things Sand has rejected, such as a woman's name and the role of a wife.

By weaker women in captivity?
Ah, vain denial! that revolted cry 5
Is sobbed in by a woman's voice forlorn,—
Thy woman's hair, my sister, all unshorn
Floats back disheveled strength in agony,
Disproving thy man's name: and while before
The world thou burnest in a poet-fire, 10
We[3] see thy woman-heart beat evermore
Through the large flame. Beat purer, heart, and higher,
Till God unsex thee on the heavenly shore
Where unincarnate spirits purely aspire!

 1844

The Cry of the Children[1]

Φεῦ, φεῦ, τί προδδέρκεδσέ μ' ὄμμαδιυ, τέκυα;[2]
 —Medea.

I

Do ye hear the children weeping, O my brothers,
 Ere the sorrow comes with years?
They are leaning their young heads against their mothers,
 And *that* cannot stop their tears.
The young lambs are bleating in the meadows, 5
 The young birds are chirping in the nest,
The young fawns are playing with the shadows,
 The young flowers are blowing[3] toward the west—
But the young, young children, O my brothers,
 They are weeping bitterly! 10
They are weeping in the playtime of the others,
 In the country of the free.

II

Do you question the young children in the sorrow
 Why their tears are falling so?
The old man may weep for his tomorrow 15
 Which is lost in long ago;
The old tree is leafless in the forest,
 The old year is ending in the frost,
The old wound, if stricken, is the sorest,
 The old hope is hardest to be lost: 20
But the young, young children, O my brothers,
 Do you ask them why they stand
Weeping sore before the bosoms of their mothers,
 In our happy fatherland?

3. I.e., chiefly Barrett Browning herself, perhaps along
with a select few who see Sand's true nature.
1. This poem was inspired by a contemporary govern-
ment report on the employment of children in mines
and factories, one of the major social issues in England
at the time.
2. Alas, alas, why do you look at me with your eyes,
children? (Greek). Spoken by Medea (Euripides'
Medea 1040); the title quotes the chorus (line 1271).
3. Blooming.

III

They look up with their pale and sunken faces, 25
 And their looks are sad to see.
For the man's hoary[4] anguish draws and presses
 Down the cheeks of infancy;
"Your old earth," they say, "is very dreary,
 Our young feet," they say, "are very weak; 30
Few paces have we taken, yet are weary—
 Our grave-rest is very far to seek
Ask the aged why they weep, and not the children,
 For the outside earth is cold,
And we young ones stand without, in our bewildering, 35
 And the graves are for the old.

IV

"True," say the children, "it may happen
 That we die before our time:
Little Alice died last year, her grave is shapen
 Like a snowball, in the rime.[5] 40
We looked into the pit prepared to take her:
 Was no room for any work in the close clay!
From the sleep wherein she lieth none will wake her,
 Crying, 'Get up, little Alice! it is day.'
If you listen by that grave, in sun and shower, 45
 With your ear down, little Alice never cries;
Could we see her face, be sure we should not know her,
 For the smile has time for growing in her eyes:
And merry go her moments, lulled and stilled in
 The shroud by the kirk-chime.[6] 50
It is good when it happens," say the children,
 "That we die before our time."

V

Alas, alas, the children! they are seeking
 Death in life, as best to have:
They are binding up their hearts away from breaking, 55
 With a cerement[7] from the grave.
Go out, children, from the mine and from the city,
 Sing out, children, as the little thrushes do;
Pluck your handfuls of the meadow-cowslips pretty.
 Laugh aloud, to feel your fingers let them through! 60
But they answer, "Are your cowslips of the meadows
 Like our weeds anear the mine?
Leave us quiet in the dark of the coal-shadows,
 From your pleasures fair and fine!

VI

"For oh," say the children, "we are weary, 65
 And we cannot run or leap;
If we cared for any meadows, it were merely

4. White-haired, extremely old.
5. Frost.
6. Church bell.

7. Shroud for the dead. "Binding up": wrapping to strengthen, reinforce.

To drop down in them and sleep.
Our knees tremble sorely in the stooping,
 We fall upon our faces, trying to go; 70
And, underneath our heavy eyelids drooping
 The reddest flower would look as pale as snow.
For, all day, we drag our burden tiring
 Through the coal-dark, underground;
Or, all day, we drive the wheels of iron 75
 In the factories, round and round.

VII

"For all day the wheels are droning, turning;
 Their wind comes in our faces,
Till our hearts turn, our heads with pulses burning,
 And the walls turn in their places: 80
Turns the sky in the high window, blank and reeling,
 Turns the long light that drops adown the wall,
Turn the black flies that crawl along the ceiling:
 All are turning, all the day, and we with all.
And all day the iron wheels are droning, 85
 And sometimes we could pray,
'O ye wheels' (breaking out in a mad moaning),
 'Stop! be silent for today!' "

VIII

Ay, be silent! Let them hear each other breathing
 For a moment, mouth to mouth! 90
Let them touch each other's hands, in a fresh wreathing
 Of their tender human youth!
Let them feel that this cold metallic motion
 Is not all the life God fashions or reveals:
Let them prove[8] their living souls against the notion 95
 That they live in you, or under you, O wheels!
Still, all day, the iron wheels go onward,
 Grinding life down from its mark;
And the children's souls, which God is calling sunward,
 Spin on blindly in the dark. 100

IX

Now tell the poor young children, O my brothers,
 To look up to Him and pray;
So the blessèd One who blesseth all the others,
 Will bless them another day.
They answer, "Who is God that He should hear us, 105
 While the rushing of the iron wheels is stirred?
When we sob aloud, the human creatures near us
 Pass by, hearing not, or answer not a word.
And we hear not (for the wheels in their resounding)
 Strangers speaking at the door: 110
Is it likely God, with angels singing round Him,
 Hears our weeping anymore?

8. Test.

X

"Two words, indeed, of praying we remember,
 And at midnight's hour of harm.
'Our Father,'[9] looking upward in the chamber,
 We say softly for a charm.
We know no other words except 'Our Father,'
 And we think that, in some pause of angels' song,
God may pluck them with the silence sweet to gather,
 And hold both within his right hand which is strong.
'Our Father!' If He heard us, He would surely
 (For they call Him good and mild)
Answer, smiling down the steep world very purely,
 'Come and rest with me, my child.'

115

120

XI

"But, no!" say the children, weeping faster,
 "He is speechless as a stone;
And they tell us, of His image is the master[1]
 Who commands us to work on.
Go to!" say the children,—"up in Heaven,
 Dark, wheel-like, turning clouds are all we find.
Do not mock us; grief has made us unbelieving:
 We look up for God, but tears have made us blind."
Do you hear the children weeping and disproving,
 O my brothers, what ye preach?
For God's possible is taught by his world s loving,
 And the children doubt of each.

125

130

135

XII

And well may the children weep before you!
 They are weary ere they run;
They have never seen the sunshine, nor the glory
 Which is brighter than the sun.
They know the grief of man, without its wisdom;
 They sink in man's despair, without its calm;
Are slaves, without the liberty in Christdom,
 Are martyrs, by the pang without the palm:[2]
Are worn as if with age, yet unretrievingly
 The harvest of its memories cannot reap,—
Are orphans of the earthly love and heavenly.
 Let them weep! let them weep!

140

145

XIII

They look up with their pale and sunken faces,
 And their look is dread to see,
For they mind[3] you of their angels in high places,
 With eyes turned on Deity.
"How long," they say, "how long, O cruel nation,
 Will you stand, to move the world, on a child's heart,—
Stifle down with a mailéd heel its palpitation,

150

155

9. The first words of the Lord's Prayer.
1. Even the cruel taskmaster of the children was made
in God's image.

2. Symbol of triumph; thus martyrs by their suffering
only, not by their redemption.
3. Remind.

And tread onward to your throne amid the mart?[4]
Our blood splashes upward, O goldheaper,
 And your purple[5] shows your path!
But the child's sob in the silence curses deeper
 Than the strong man in his wrath."

1844

The Runaway Slave at Pilgrim's Point[1]

I

I stand on the mark beside the shore
 Of the first white pilgrim's bended knee,
Where exile turned to ancestor,[2]
 And God was thanked for liberty.
I have run through the night, my skin is as dark, 5
I bend my knee down on this mark:
 I look on the sky and the sea.

II

O pilgrim-souls, I speak to you!
 I see you come proud and slow
From the land of the spirits pale as dew 10
 And round me and round me ye go.
O pilgrims, I have gasped and run
All night long from the whips of one
 Who in your names works sin and woe!

III

And thus I thought that I would come 15
 And kneel here where ye knelt before,
And feel your souls around me hum
 In undertone to the ocean's roar;
And lift my black face, my black hand,
Here, in your names, to curse this land 20
 Ye blessed in freedom's, evermore.

IV

I am black, I am black,
 And yet God made me, they say:
But if He did so, smiling back
 He must have cast his work away 25
Under the feet of his white creatures,
 With a look of scorn, that the dusky features
 Might be trodden again to clay.

V

And yet He has made dark things
 To be glad and merry as light: 30
There's a little dark bird sits and sings,

4. Market.
5. I.e., the blood left in their trail after trampling the children.
1. The point at Plymouth Rock, Massachussetts, where the Puritans, fleeing persecution in England, first landed their ships in the 17th century.
2. I.e., where the pilgrims, exiled from one nation, became ancestors to a new one.

There's a dark stream ripples out of sight,
And the dark frogs chant in the safe morass,[3]
And the sweetest stars are made to pass
 O'er the face of the darkest night. 35

VI

But we who are dark, we are dark!
 Ah God, we have no stars!
About our souls in care and cark[4]
 Our blackness shuts like prison-bars:
The poor souls crouch so far behind 40
That never a comfort can they find
 By reaching through the prison-bars.

VII

Indeed we live beneath the sky,
 That great smooth Hand of God stretched out
On all his children fatherly, 45
 To save them from the dread and doubt
Which would be if, from this low place,
All opened straight up to his face
 Into the grand eternity.

VIII

And still God's sunshine and his frost, 50
 They make us hot, they make us cold,
As if we were not black and lost;
 And the beasts and birds, in wood and fold,
Do fear and take us for very men:
Could the whippoorwill or the cat of the glen 55
 Look into my eyes and be bold?

IX

I am black, I am black!
 But, once, I laughed in girlish glee,
For one of my color stood in the track
 Where the drivers drove, and looked at me, 60
And tender and full was the look he gave—
Could a slave look so at another slave?—
 I look at the sky and the sea.

X

And from that hour our spirits grew
 As free as if unsold, unbought: 65
Oh, strong enough, since we were two,
 To conquer the world, we thought.
The drivers drove us day by day;
We did not mind, we went one way,
 And no better a freedom sought. 70

XI

In the sunny ground between the canes,[5]
 He said "I love you" as he passed;

3. Swamp.
4. Distress.

5. Sugar canes; the two worked on a sugar plantation.

When the shingle-roof rang sharp with the rains,
 I heard how he vowed it fast:
While others shook he smiled in the hut, 75
As he carved me a bowl of the coconut
 Through the roar of the hurricanes.

XII

I sang his name instead of a song,
 Over and over I sang his name,
Upward and downward I drew it along 80
 My various notes,—the same, the same!
I sang it low, that the slave-girls near
Might never guess, from aught they could hear,
 It was only a name—a name.

XIII

I look on the sky and the sea. 85
 We were two to love and two to pray:
Yes, two, O God, who cried to Thee,
 Though nothing didst Thou say!
Coldly Thou sat'st behind the sun:
And now I cry who am but one, 90
 Thou wilt not speak today.

XIV

We were black, we were black,
 We had no claim to love and bliss,
What marvel if each went to wrack?[6]
 They wrung my cold hands out of his, 95
They dragged him—where? I crawled to touch
His blood's mark in the dust . . . not much,
 Ye pilgrim-souls, though plain as *this*![7]

XV

Wrong, followed by a deeper wrong!
 Mere grief's too good for such as I: 100
So the white men brought the shame ere long
 To strangle the sob of my agony.
They would not leave me for my dull
Wet eyes!—it was too merciful
 To let me weep pure tears and die. 105

XVI

I am black, I am black!
 I wore a child upon my breast,
An amulet that hung too slack,
 And, in my unrest, could not rest:
Thus we went moaning, child and mother, 110
One to another, one to another,
 Until all ended for the best.

XVII

For hark! I will tell you low, low,
 I am black, you see,—

6. Destruction.
7. The "mark beside the shore" where the speaker stands.

And the babe who lay on my bosom so, 115
 Was far too white, too white for me;
As white as the ladies who scorned to pray
Beside me at church but yesterday,
 Though my tears had washed a place for my knee.

<div align="center">XVIII</div>

My own, own child! I could not bear 120
 To look in his face, it was so white;
I covered him up with a kerchief there,
 I covered his face in close and tight:
And he moaned and struggled, as well might be,
For the white child wanted his liberty— 125
 Ha, ha! he wanted the master-right.

<div align="center">XIX</div>

He moaned and beat with his head and feet,
 His little feet that never grew;
He struck them out, as it was meet,
 Against my heart to break it through: 130
I might have sung and made him mild,
But I dared not sing to the white-faced child
 The only song I knew.

<div align="center">XX</div>

I pulled the kerchief very close:
 He could not see the sun, I swear, 135
More, then, alive, than now he does
 From between the roots of the mango . . . where?
I know where. Close! A child and mother
Do wrong to look at one another
 When one is black and one is fair. 140

<div align="center">XXI</div>

Why, in that single glance I had
 Of my child's face, . . . I tell you all,
I saw a look that made me mad!
 The *master's* look, that used to fall
On my soul like his lash . . . or worse! 145
And so, to save it from my curse,
 I twisted it round in my shawl.

<div align="center">XXII</div>

And he moaned and trembled from foot to head,
 He shivered from head to foot;
Till after a time, he lay instead 150
 Too suddenly still and mute.
I felt, beside, a stiffening cold:
I dared to lift up just a fold,
 As in lifting a leaf of the mango-fruit.

<div align="center">XXIII</div>

But *my* fruit . . . Ha, ha!—there, had been 155
 (I laugh to think on't at this hour!)
Your fine white angels (who have seen
 Nearest the secret of God's power)
And plucked my fruit to make them wine,

And sucked the soul of that child of mine 160
 As the hummingbird sucks the soul of the flower.

XXIV

Ha, ha, the trick of the angels white!
 They freed the white child's spirit so.
I said not a word, but day and night
 I carried the body to and fro, 165
And it lay on my heart like a stone, as chill.
—The sun may shine out as much as he will:
 I am cold, though it happened a month ago.

XXV

From the white man's house, and the black man's hut,
 I carried the little body on: 170
The forest's arms did round us shut,
 And silence through the trees did run:
They asked no question as I went,
They stood too high for astonishment,
 They could see God sit on his throne. 175

XXVI

My little body, kerchiefed fast,
 I bore it on through the forest, on;
And when I felt it was tired at last,
 I scooped a hole beneath the moon:
Through the forest-tops the angels far, 180
With a white sharp finger from every star,
 Did point and mock at what was done.

XXVII

Yet when it was all done aright,—
 Earth,'twixt me and my baby, strewed,—
All, changed to black earth,—nothing white,— 185
 A dark child in the dark!—ensued
Some comfort, and my heart grew young;
I sate down smiling there and sung
 The song I learnt in my maidenhood.

XXVIII

And thus we two were reconciled, 190
 The white child and black mother, thus;
For as I sang it soft and wild,
 The same song, more melodious,
Rose from the grave whereon I sate:
It was the dead child singing that, 195
 To join the souls of both of us.

XXIX

I look on the sea and the sky.
 Where the pilgrims' ships first anchored lay
The free sun rideth gloriously,
 But the pilgrim ghosts have slid away 200
Through the earliest streaks of the morn:
My face is black, but it glares with a scorn
 Which they dare not meet by day.

XXX

Ha!—in their stead, their hunter sons!
 Ha, ha! they are on me—they hunt in a ring! 205
Keep off! I brave you all at once,
 I throw off your eyes like snakes that sting!
You have killed the black eagle at nest, I think:
Did you ever stand still in your triumph, and shrink
 From the stroke of her wounded wing? 210

XXXI

(Man, drop that stone you dared to lift!—)
 I wish you who stand there five abreast,
Each, for his own wife's joy and gift,
 A little corpse as safely at rest
As mine in the mangoes! Yes, but *she* 215
May keep live babies on her knee,
 And sing the song she likes the best.

XXXII

I am not mad: I am black.
 I see you staring in my face—
I know you staring, shrinking back,
 Ye are born of the Washington-race,[8] 220
And this land is the free America,
And this mark on my wrist—(I prove[9] what I say)
 Ropes tied me up here to the flogging-place.

XXXIII

You think I shrieked then? Not a sound. 225
 I hung, as a gourd hangs in the sun;
I only cursed them all around
 As softly as I might have done
My very own child: from these sands
Up to the mountains, lift your hands, 230
 O slaves, and end what I begun!

XXXIV

Whips, curses; these must answer those!
 For in this union you have set
Two kinds of men in adverse rows,
 Each loathing each; and all forget 235
The seven wounds in Christ's body fair,
While He sees gaping everywhere
 Our countless wounds that pay no debt.[1]

XXXV

Our wounds are different. Your white men
 Are, after all, not gods indeed, 240
Nor able to make Christs again
 Do good with bleeding. We who bleed
(Stand off!) we help not in our loss!
We are too heavy for our cross,
 And fall and crush you and your seed. 245

8. I.e., the race of George Washington.
9. Demonstrate.

1. According to the Bible, Jesus Christ died on the cross in payment for the sins of humanity.

XXXVI

I fall, I swoon![2] I look at the sky.
 The clouds are breaking on my brain;
I am floated along, as if I should die
 Of liberty's exquisite pain.
In the name of the white child waiting for me 250
In the death-dark where we may kiss and agree,
White men, I leave you all curse-free
 In my broken heart's disdain!

1850

Hiram Powers' "Greek Slave"[1]

They say ideal beauty cannot enter
The house of anguish. On the threshold stands
An alien image with enshackled hands,
Called the Greek Slave! as if the artist meant her
(That passionless perfection which he lent her, 5
Shadowed not darkened where the sill expands)[2]
To so confront man's crimes in different lands
With man's ideal sense. Pierce to the center,
Art's fiery finger, and break up ere long
The serfdom of this world. Appeal, fair stone, 10
From God's pure heights of beauty against man's wrong!
Catch up in thy divine face, not alone
East griefs but west,[3] and strike and shame the strong,
By thunders of white silence, overthrown.

1850

From Sonnets from the Portuguese[1]

V

I lift my heavy heart up solemnly,
As once Electra[2] her sepulchral urn,
And, looking in thine eyes, I overturn
The ashes at thy feet. Behold and see
What a great heap of grief lay hid in me, 5
And how the red wild sparkles dimly burn
Through the ashen grayness. If thy foot in scorn
Could tread them out to darkness utterly,
It might be well perhaps. But if instead

2. Possibly an echo of Shelley's *Ode to the West Wind:* "I fall upon the thorns of life! I bleed!"
1. The work of an American sculptor who became a close friend of the Brownings while they were living in Florence.
2. I.e., where the threshold to the house of anguish begins; her beauty is not lessened by that threshold, only given a more somber cast.
3. Greek slavery was a grief of the East; Barrett Browning may be thinking here of American slavery as a grief of the West.
1. All the sonnets in the sequence are addressed to Elizabeth's husband, Robert, himself a famous poet.
2. In Sophocles' play *Electra*, the heroine's brother Orestes disguises himself and presents his sister with a funeral urn that he claims contains her brother's ashes.

Thou wait beside me for the wind to blow 10
The gray dust up, . . . those laurels[3] on thine head,
O my Belovéd, will not shield thee so,
That none of all the fires shall scorch and shred
The hair beneath. Stand farther off then! go.

XXII

When our two souls stand up erect and strong,
Face to face, silent, drawing nigh[4] and nigher,
Until the lengthening wings break into fire
At either curvéd point,—what bitter wrong
Can the earth do to us, that we should not long 5
Be here contented? Think. In mounting higher,
The angels would press on us and aspire
To drop some golden orb[5] of perfect song
Into our deep, dear silence. Let us stay
Rather on earth, Belovéd,—where the unfit 10
Contrarious moods of men recoil away
And isolate pure spirits, and permit
A place to stand and love in for a day,
With darkness and the death-hour rounding it.

XLIII

How do I love thee? Let me count the ways.
I love thee to the depth and breadth and height
My soul can reach, when feeling out of sight
For the ends of Being and ideal Grace.
I love thee to the level of everyday's 5
Most quiet need, by sun and candle light.
I love thee freely, as men strive for Right;
I love thee purely, as they turn from Praise.
I love thee with the passion put to use[6]
In my old griefs, and with my childhood's faith. 10
I love thee with a love I seemed to lose
With my lost saints,—I love thee with the breath,
Smiles, tears, and all my life!—and, if God choose,
I shall but love thee better after death.

1850

From Aurora Leigh

Book I [Aurora's Parents][1]

* * * My mother was a Florentine,[2]
Whose rare blue eyes were shut from seeing me 30

3. Leaves associated with poetic achievement.
4. Near.
5. Ball or sphere. The image may recall the old notion of the "music of the spheres," created by the motions of stars and planets.
6. I.e., a natural reserve of passion that had formerly been directed to grief, now transformed to love.
1. In Book I, the poet-to-be Aurora, born in Italy of an

Italian mother and an English father, is orphaned early and brought to England, where she is raised and educated by her father's sister, an austere British lady. The first selection from Book I covers her memories of her mother, and the second records some of her reactions to her Victorian training in decorum.
2. Florence was a center of Renaissance art and culture.

When scarcely I was four years old, my life
A poor spark snatched up from a failing lamp
Which went out therefore. She was weak and frail;
She could not bear the joy of giving life,
The mother's rapture slew her. If her kiss 35
Had left a longer weight upon my lips
It might have steadied the uneasy breath,
And reconciled and fraternized my soul
With the new order.[3] As it was, indeed,
I felt a mother-want about the world, 40
And still went seeking, like a bleating lamb
Left out at night in shutting up the fold,[4]—
As restless as a nest-deserted bird
Grown chill through something being away, though what
It knows not. * * * 45

My father was an austere Englishman, 65
Who, after a dry lifetime spent at home
In college-learning, law, and parish talk,
Was flooded with a passion unaware,
His whole provisioned and complacent past
Drowned out from him that moment. As he stood 70
In Florence, where he had come to spend a month
And note the secret of Da Vinci's drains,[5]
He musing somewhat absently perhaps
Some English question . . . whether men should pay
The unpopular but necessary tax 75
With left or right hand—in the alien sun
In that great square of the Santissima[6]
There drifted past him (scarcely marked enough
To move his comfortable island scorn)
A train of priestly banners, cross and psalm, 80
The white-veiled rose-crowned maidens holding up
Tall tapers, weighty for such wrists, aslant
To the blue luminous tremor of the air,
And letting drop the white wax as they went
To eat the bishop's wafer at the church;[7] 85
From which long trail of chanting priests and girls,
A face flashed like a cymbal on his face
And shook with silent clangor brain and heart,
Transfiguring him to music. Thus, even thus,
He too received his sacramental gift 90
With eucharistic[8] meanings; for he loved.

And thus beloved, she died. * * * 92

 * * *Father, then, and child, 120
We lived among the mountains many years,
God's silence on the outside of the house,

3. I.e., her motherless state.
4. An enclosure for sheep.
5. Leonardo da Vinci (1452–1519), artist, scientist, and engineer, devised a system of irrigation for the plains of Lombardy.
6. The *piazza* or square before the 13th-century Church of Santissima Annunziata.
7. I.e., to receive Holy Communion—in which a wafer and wine, thought to reincarnate the body and blood of Christ, are consumed—from the bishop.
8. Relating to Holy Communion.

And we who did not speak too loud within,
And old Assunta to make up the fire,
Crossing herself whene'er a sudden flame 125
Which lightened from the firewood, made alive
That picture of my mother on the wall.

The painter drew it after she was dead,
And when the face was finished, throat and hands,
Her cameriera[9] carried him, in hate 130
Of the English-fashioned shroud, the last brocade
She dressed in at the Pitti;[1] "he should paint
No sadder thing than that," she swore, "to wrong
Her poor signora." Therefore very strange
The effect was. I, a little child, would crouch 135
For hours upon the floor with knees drawn up,
And gaze across them, half in terror, half
In adoration, at the picture there,—
That swan-like supernatural white life
Just sailing upward from the red stiff silk 140
Which seemed to have no part in it nor power
To keep it from quite breaking out of bounds.
For hours I sat and stared. Assunta's awe
And my poor father's melancholy eyes
Still pointed that way. That way went my thoughts 145
When wandering beyond sight. And as I grew
In years, I mixed, confused, unconsciously,
Whatever I last read or heard or dreamed,
Abhorrent, admirable, beautiful,
Pathetical, or ghastly, or grotesque, 150
With still that face . . . which did not therefore change,
But kept the mystic level of all forms,
Hates, fears, and admirations, was by turns
Ghost, fiend, and angel, fairy, witch, and sprite,
A dauntless Muse who eyes a dreadful Fate, 155
A loving Psyche who loses sight of Love,
A still Medusa[2] with mild milky brows
All curdled and all clothed upon with snakes
Whose slime falls fast as sweat will; or anon
Our Lady of the Passion, stabbed with swords[3] 160
Where the Babe sucked, or Lamia[4] in her first
Moonlighted pallor, ere she shrunk and blinked
And shuddering wriggled down to the unclean;
Or my own mother, leaving her last smile
In her last kiss upon the baby-mouth 165
My father pushed down on the bed for that,—
Or my dead mother, without smile or kiss,
Buried at Florence. * * *

9. Lady's maid.
1. The Pitti Palace in Florence, once occupied by no-
bility.
2. A mythological female with snakes for hair. A Muse
is a Greek goddess of the arts and learning. The Fates
are three sisters who decide the destiny of each human
being. Psyche, according to Greek myth, was a beauti-
ful maiden who was wooed by Cupid (Love), by night,
until she attempted to catch sight of him, and he fled.
3. The virgin Mary, "stabbed" with grief by her son
Jesus' Crucifixion and suffering (the Passion).
4. In Keats's poem Lamia, a young man falls in love
with a beautiful woman who is then revealed to be a
serpent.

Book I [Aurora's Journey to England and Education There by Her Father's Sister]

I think I see my father's sister stand 270
Upon the hall-step of her country-house
To give me welcome. She stood straight and calm,
Her somewhat narrow forehead braided tight
As if for taming accidental thoughts
From possible pulses,[5] brown hair pricked with gray 275
By frigid use of life (she was not old,
Although my father's elder by a year),
A nose drawn sharply, yet in delicate lines;
A close mild mouth, a little soured about
The ends, through speaking unrequited loves 280
Or peradventure[6] niggardly half-truths;
Eyes of no color,—once they might have smiled,
But never, never have forgot themselves
In smiling; cheeks, in which was yet a rose
Of perished summers, like a rose in a book, 285
Kept more for ruth[7] than pleasure,—if past bloom,
Past fading also.
 She had lived, we'll say,
A harmless life, she called a virtuous life,
A quiet life, which was not life at all
(But that, she had not lived enough to know), 290
Between the vicar and the country squires,
The lord-lieutenant looking down sometimes
From the empyrean[8] to assure their souls
Against chance vulgarisms, and, in the abyss,
The apothecary, looked on once a year 295
To prove their soundness of humility.
The poor-club[9] exercised her Christian gifts
Of knitting stockings, stitching petticoats,
Because we are of one flesh, after all,
And need one flannel (with a proper sense 300
Or difference in the quality)—and still
The book-club, guarded from your modern trick
Of shaking dangerous questions from the crease,[1]
Preserved her intellectual. She had lived
A sort of cage-bird life, born in a cage, 305
Accounting that to leap from perch to perch
Was act and joy enough for any bird.
Dear heaven, how silly are the things that live
In thickets, and eat berries!
 I, alas,
A wild bird scarcely fledged, was brought to her cage, 310
And she was there to meet me. Very kind.
Bring the clean water, give out the fresh seed.

* * *

5. Excitements. 8. The highest reaches of heaven.
6. Perhaps. 9. Charitable organization.
7. Pity, remorse. 1. I.e., of finding subversive ideas hidden in books.

I broke the copious curls upon my head 385
In braids, because she liked smooth-ordered hair.
I left off saying my sweet Tuscan words[2]
Which still at any stirring of the heart
Came up to float across the English phrase
As lilies (*Bene* or *Che che*[3]), because 390
She liked my father's child to speak his tongue
I learnt the collects and the catechism,
The creeds, from Athanasius back to Nice,
The Articles, the Tracts[4] *against* the times
(By no means Buonaventure's "Prick of Love"), 395
And various popular synopses of
Inhuman doctrines never taught by John,[5]
Because she liked instructed piety.
I learnt my complement of classic French
(Kept pure of Balzac and neologism[6]) 400
And German also, since she liked a range
Of liberal education,—tongues, not books,
I learnt a little algebra, a little
Of the mathematics,—brushed with extreme flounce[7]
The circle of the sciences, because 405
She misliked women who are frivolous.
I learnt the royal genealogies
Of Oviedo, the internal laws
Of the Burmese empire,[8]—by how many feet
Mount Chimborazo outsoars Teneriffe, 410
What navigable river joins itself
To Lara, and what census of the year five
Was taken at Klagenfurt,—because she liked
A general insight into useful facts.
I learnt much music,—such as would have been 415
As quite impossible in Johnson's day[9]
As still it might be wished—fine sleights of hand
And unimagined fingering, shuffling off
The hearer's soul through hurricanes of notes
To a noisy Tophet; and I drew . . . costumes 420
From French engravings, nereids[1] neatly draped
(With smirks of simmering godship): I washed in
Landscapes from nature (rather say, washed out).
I danced the polka and Cellarius,[2]

2. The dialect of Tuscany, the region of Italy where Florence is located.

3. What's the matter? "*Bene*": good.

4. The Thirty-Nine Articles are the creed of the Church of England. "Collects": opening prayers in the Anglican Church. The collect varies with the day. "Creeds": articles of Christian faith; one early creed was proclaimed at Nicaea (Nice), a Church council attended by Athanasius.

5. All the works in this list are strict religious primers and treatises. "Tracts against the times" is a humorous reference to *Tracts for the Times* by Newman, Pusey, and Keble, which condemned Anglican Church reform. Buonaventure's *Prick of Love* is a religious work that prefers love to reason. John, author of one of the Gospels, did not concern himself with fine technical points of theology.

6. New words. Honoré de Balzac (1799–1850) wrote many popular novels dealing with the corruption of Parisian society. "Neologism": new doctrines.

7. Abruptness, impatience.

8. Burma is an Asian country. Oviedo is a city in Spain. All the facts mentioned in this passage are noteworthy only for being esoteric, unrelated to Aurora's real concerns.

9. Samuel Johnson (1709–1784) was a famous critic and writer. When told how difficult was a piece of music that a young lady was playing, he is said to have answered "I would it had been impossible."

1. Sea nymphs. "Tophet": hell.

2. A kind of waltz. "Washed in": painted watercolors.

Spun glass, stuffed birds, and modelled flowers in wax, 425
Because she liked accomplishments in girls.
I read a score of books on womanhood
To prove, if women do not think at all,
They may teach thinking (to a maiden aunt
Or else the author),—books that boldly assert 430
Their right of comprehending husband's talk
When not too deep, and even of answering
With pretty "may it please you," or "so it is,"—
Their rapid insight and fine aptitude,
Particular worth and general missionariness,[3] 435
As long as they keep quiet by the fire
And never say "no" when the world says "ay,"
For that is fatal,—their angelic reach[4]
Of virtue, chiefly used to sit and darn,
And fatten household sinners,—their, in brief, 440
Potential faculty in everything
Of abdicating power in it: she owned
She liked a woman to be womanly,
And English women, she thanked God and sighed
(Some people always sigh in thanking God), 445
Were models to the universe. And last
I learnt cross-stitch, because she did not like
To see me wear the night with empty hands
A-doing nothing. So, my shepherdess
Was something after all (the pastoral[5] saints 450
Be praised for't), leaning lovelorn with pink eyes
To match her shoes, when I mistook the silks;
Her head uncrushed by that round weight of hat
So strangely similar to the tortoise shell
Which slew the tragic poet.[6]
 By the way, 455
The works of women are symbolical.
We sew, sew, prick our fingers, dull our sight,
Producing what? A pair of slippers, sir,
To put on when you're weary—or a stool
To stumble over and vex you . . . "curse that stool!" 460
Or else at best, a cushion, where you lean
And sleep, and dream of something we are not
But would be for your sake. Alas, alas!
This hurts most, this—that, after all, we are paid
The worth of our work, perhaps
 In looking down 465
Those years of education (to return)
I wonder if Brinvilliers[7] suffered more
In the water-torture . . . flood succeeding flood
To drench the incapable throat and split the veins . . .
 Than I did. Certain of your feebler souls 470

3. I.e., desire to convert others to virtue.
4. Coventry Patmore's popular book-length poem *The Angel in the House* (1854) celebrated the ideals of domestic virtue.
5. Pertaining to shepherdry.
6. The Greek tragedian Aeschylus was reputedly killed when an eagle dropped a tortoise on his head.
7. The Marquise de Brinvilliers was tortured by having water forced down her throat, because she allegedly murdered her husband's relatives to win his fortune for herself and her lover.

Go out[8] in such a process; many pine
To a sick, inodorous light; my own endured:
I had relations in the Unseen, and drew
The elemental nutriment and heat
From nature, as earth feels the sun at nights, 475
Or as a babe sucks surely in the dark.
I kept the life thrust on me, on the outside
Of the inner life with all its ample room
For heart and lungs, for will and intellect,
Inviolable by conventions. God, 480
I thank thee for that grace of thine!

 * * *

Book II [Romney's Proposal of Marriage to Aurora and Her Refusal][9]

 "Then, must it be
Indeed farewell? And was I so far wrong
In hope and in illusion, when I took 420
The woman to be nobler than the man,
Yourself the noblest woman, in the use[1]
And comprehension of what love is,—love,
That generates the likeness of itself
Through all heroic duties? so far wrong, 425
In saying bluntly, venturing truth on love,
'Come, human creature, love and work with me,'—
Instead of 'Lady, thou art wondrous fair,
And, where the Graces[2] walk before, the Muse
Will follow at the lightning of their eyes, 430
And where the Muse walks, lovers need to creep:
Turn round and love me, or I die of love.' "
With quiet indignation I broke in.
"You misconceive the question like a man,
Who sees the woman as the complement 435
Of his sex merely. You forget too much
That every creature, female as the male,
Stands single in responsible act and thought
As also in birth and death. Whoever says
To a loyal woman, 'Love and work with me,' 440
Will get fair answers if she work and love,
Being good themselves, are good for her—the best
She was born for. Women of a softer mood,
Surprised by men when scarcely awake to life,
Will sometimes only hear the first word, love, 445
And catch up with it any kind of work,
Indifferent, so that dear love go with it.
I do not blame such women, though, for love,

8. I.e., die.
9. In this selection Aurora's cousin Romney Leigh, now the head of the family, has proposed to her, arguing that it would be better for her to join him in working for social welfare than to continue with her plan to become a poet, since he believes that women cannot

write effective verse. In lines 418–32, Romney is speaking. In the next paragraph, Aurora reiterates her refusal, insisting on her commitment to her chosen vocation.
1. Practice.
2. Greek goddesses of charm and beauty.

They pick much oakum;[3] earth's fanatics make
Too frequently heaven's saints. But *me* your work 450
Is not the best for,—nor your love the best,
Nor able to commend the kind of work
For love's sake merely. Ah, you force me, sir,
To be overbold in speaking of myself:
I too have my vocation,—work to do, 455
The heavens and earth have set me since I changed
My father's face for theirs, and, though your world
Were twice as wretched as you represent,
Most serious work, most necessary work
As any of the economists'.[4] Reform, 460
Make trade a Christian possibility,
And individual right no general wrong;
Wipe out earth's furrows of the Thine and Mine,
And leave one green for men to play at bowls,[5]
With innings for them all! . . . What then, indeed, 465
If mortals are not greater by the head
Than any of their prosperities? what then,
Unless the artist keep up open roads
Betwixt the seen and unseen,—bursting through
The best of your conventions with his best, 470
The speakable, imaginable best
God bids him speak, to prove what lies beyond
Both speech and imagination? A starved man
Exceeds a fat beast: we'll not barter, sir,
The beautiful for barley.—And, even so, 475
I hold you will not compass your poor ends
Of barley-feeding and material ease,
Without a poet's individualism
To work your universal. It takes a soul,
To move a body: it takes a high-souled man, 480
To move the masses, even to a cleaner stye:[6]
It takes the ideal, to blow a hair's-breadth off
The dust of the actual.—Ah, your Fouriers[7] failed,
Because not poets enough to understand
That life develops from within.—For me, 485
Perhaps I am not worthy, as you say,
Of work like this: perhaps a woman's soul
Aspires, and not creates: yet we aspire,
And yet I'll try out your perhapses, sir,
And if I fail . . . why, burn me up my straw 490
Like other false works—I'll not ask for grace;
Your scorn is better, cousin Romney. I
Who love my art, would never wish it lower
To suit my stature. I may love my art.
You'll grant that even a woman may love art, 495

3. Loose hemp or fiber derived from untwisting old
rope; i.e., they are condemned to hard labor.
4. The economists wished to reform British trade;
Aurora hopes to reform the British soul.
5. A form of outdoor bowling.

6. Enclosure for pigs.
7. François Fourier (1772–1837), French social theo-
rist who advocated communal property as a basis for
social harmony.

Seeing that to waste true love on anything
Is womanly, past question."

*　*　*

Book V [Aurora's Theories of Poetry][8]

The critics say that epics have died out
With Agamemnon and the goat-nursed[9] gods; 140
I'll not believe it. I could never deem
As Payne Knight did (the mythic mountaineer
Who traveled higher than he was born to live,
And showed sometimes the goiter[1] in his throat
Discoursing of an image seen through fog), 145
That Homer's heroes measured twelve feet high.
They were but men:—his Helen's[2] hair turned gray
Like any plain Miss Smith's who wears a front;[3]
And Hector's infant[4] whimpered at a plume
As yours last Friday at a turkey-cock. 150
All actual heroes are essential men,
And all men possible heroes: every age,
Heroic in proportions, double-faced,
Looks backward and before, expects a morn
And claims an epos.[5]
 Ay, but every age 155
Appears to souls who live in't (ask Carlyle[6])
Most unheroic. Ours, for instance, ours:
The thinkers scout it, and the poets abound
Who scorn to touch it with a fingertip:
A pewter age[7]—mixed metal, silver-washed; 160
An age of scum, spooned off the richer past,
An age of patches for old gaberdines,
An age of mere transition,[8] meaning nought
Except that what succeeds must shame it quite
If God please. That's wrong thinking, to my mind, 165
And wrong thoughts make poor poems.
 Every age,
Through being beheld too close, is ill-discerned
By those who have not lived past it. We'll suppose
Mount Athos[9] carved, as Alexander schemed,
To some colossal statue of a man. 170

8. In this selection, Aurora, now a struggling poet liv-
ing in London, formulates her artistic beliefs and
goals, distinguishing her ideas about poetry from those
of her contemporaries. In a sense, this aesthetic mani-
festo will prove to be the foundation of the success she
achieves later in Barrett Browning's verse-novel.
9. The god Zeus was nursed by a goat. Agamemnon
was a famous Greek king who led the war against Troy.
1. A disease often found in mountainous areas,
when the diet lacks iodine. Richard Payne Knight
(1750–1824), a classical scholar.
2. Helen of Troy, a renowned beauty whose abduction
caused the Trojan War.
3. False hair.
4. In Homer's *Iliad*, the son of Hector (the greatest
Trojan warrior) was terrified of his father's armor and

the crest of his helmet.
5. Epic poem.
6. Thomas Carlyle (1795–1881) Scottish historian
and essayist who celebrated the heroic ideal in such
works as *Heroes and Hero-Worship* and *Past and
Present.*
7. An allusion to the classical idea of civilization's de-
cline from a Golden Age through silver, bronze, and so
on. Pewter is a metal alloy.
8. In *The Spirit of the Age* (1831) J. S. Mill called the
present age "an age of transition." "Gaberdines": coats
made of gabardine, a twilled fabric.
9. A mountain in northern Greece that an architect-
builder proposed to carve into a likeness of Alexander
the Great.

The peasants, gathering brushwood in his ear,
Had guessed as little as the browsing goats
Of form or feature of humanity
Up there,—in fact, had traveled five miles off
Or ere the giant image broke on them, 175
Full human profile, nose and chin distinct,
Mouth, muttering rhythms of silence up the sky
And fed at evening with the blood of suns;
Grand torso,—hand, that flung perpetually
The largesse of a silver river down 180
To all the country pastures. 'Tis even thus
With times we live in,—evermore too great
To be apprehended near.
 But poets should
Exert a double vision; should have eyes
To see near things as comprehensively 185
As if afar they took their point of sight,
And distant things as intimately deep
As if they touched them. Let us strive for this.
I do distrust the poet who discerns
No character or glory in his times, 190
And trundles back his soul five hundred years,
Past moat and drawbridge, into a castle-court,
To sing—oh, not of lizard or of toad
Alive i' the ditch there,—'t were excusable,
But of some black chief, half knight, half sheep-lifter, 195
Some beauteous dame, half chattel[1] and half queen,
As dead as must be, for the greater part,
The poems made on their chivalric bones;
And that's no wonder: death inherits death.

Nay, if there's room for poets in this world 200
A little overgrown (I think there is),
Their sole work is to represent the age,
Their age, not Charlemagne's,[2]—this live, throbbing age,
That brawls, cheats, maddens, calculates, aspires,
And spends more passion, more heroic heat, 205
Betwixt the mirrors of its drawing-rooms,
Than Roland[3] with his knights at Roncesvalles.
To flinch from modern varnish, coat or flounce,
Cry out for togas and the picturesque,
Is fatal,—foolish too. King Arthur's self 210
Was commonplace to Lady Guenever;
And Camelot to minstrels seemed as flat
As Fleet Street[4] to our poets. Never flinch,
But still, unscrupulously epic, catch
Upon the burning lava of a song 215
The full-veined, heaving, double-breasted Age:

1. Property. "Sheep-lifter": thief of livestock.
2. King of the Franks (A.D. 724–818) who created an empire and became a hero of legend and poetry.
3. A knight and nephew of Charlemagne, killed in battle at Roncesvalles and immortalized in the 11th-
century poem *Chanson de Roland*.
4. A London street, headquarters for the press. "Camelot": legendary British seat of King Arthur and his knights.

That, when the next shall come, the men of that
May touch the impress[5] with reverent hand, and say
"Behold,—behold the paps[6] we all have sucked!
This bosom seems to beat still, or at least 220
It sets ours beating: this is living art,
Which thus presents and thus records true life."

<div align="center">* * *</div>

<div align="right">1857</div>

A Curse for a Nation[1]

Prologue

I heard an angel speak last night,
 And he said "Write!
Write a Nation's curse for me,
And send it over the Western Sea."

I faltered, taking up the word: 5
 "Not so, my lord!
If curses must be, choose another
To send thy curse against my brother.

"For I am bound by gratitude,
 By love and blood, 10
To brothers of mine across the sea,
Who stretch out kindly hands to me."

"Therefore," the voice said, "shalt thou write
 My curse tonight.
From the summits of love a curse is driven, 15
As lightning is from the tops of heaven."

"Not so," I answered. "Evermore
 My heart is sore
For my own land's sins: for little feet
Of children bleeding along the street: 20

"For parked-up[2] honors that gainsay
 The right of way:
For almsgiving through a door that is
Not open enough for two friends to kiss:

"For love of freedom which abates 25
 Beyond the Straits:[3]
For patriot virtue starved to vice on
Self-praise, self-interest, and suspicion:

5. The image is of a molten substance being molded by the present age, which leaves its "impress" in the metal.
6. Breasts.
1. The nation is the United States, then practicing slavery.
2. Gathered in one place.
3. The Strait of Gibraltar, which divides Europe from Africa, where England had extensive colonies and imperial interests.

"For an oligarchic parliament,[4]
 And bribes well-meant.
What curse to another land assign,
When heavy-souled for the sins of mine?" 30

"Therefore," the voice said, "shalt thou write
 My curse tonight.
Because thou hast strength to see and hate 35
A foul thing done *within* thy gate."

"Not so," I answered once again.
 "To curse, choose men.
For I, a woman, have only known
How the heart melts and the tears run down." 40

"Therefore," the voice said, "shalt thou write
 My curse tonight.
Some women weep and curse, I say
(And no one marvels), night and day.

"And thou shalt take their part tonight, 45
 Weep and write.
A curse from the depths of womanhood
Is very salt, and bitter, and good."

So thus I wrote, and mourned indeed,
 What all may read. 50
And thus, as was enjoined on me,
I send it over the Western Sea.

The Curse

I

Because ye have broken your own chain
 With the strain
Of brave men climbing a Nation's height, 55
Yet thence bear down with brand and thong
On souls of others,—for this wrong
 This is the curse. Write.

Because yourselves are standing straight
 In the state 60
Of Freedom's foremost acolyte,
Yet keep calm footing all the time
On writhing bond-slaves,—for this crime
 This is the curse. Write.

Because ye prosper in God's name, 65
 With a claim

4. I.e., a parliament controlled by an aristocratic elite.

To honor in the old world's sight,
Yet do the fiend's work perfectly
In strangling martyrs,—for this lie
 This is the curse. Write. 70

II

Ye shall watch while kings conspire
Round the people's smouldering fire
 And, warm for your part,
Shall never dare—O shame!
To utter the thought into flame 75
 Which burns at your heart.
 This is the curse. Write.

Ye shall watch while nations strive
With the bloodhounds, die or survive,
 Drop faint from their jaws, 80
Or throttle them backward to death;
And only under your breath
 Shall favor the cause.
 This is the curse. Write.

Ye shall watch while strong men draw 85
The nets of feudal law
 To strangle the weak;
And, counting the sin for a sin,
Your soul shall be sadder within
 Than the word ye shall speak. 90
 This is the curse. Write.

When good men are praying erect
That Christ may avenge his elect
 And deliver the earth,
The prayer in your ears, said low, 95
Shall sound like the tramp of a foe
 That's driving you forth.
 This is the curse. Write.

When wise men give you their praise,
They shall pause in the heat of the phrase, 100
 As if carried too far.
When ye boast your own charters kept true,
Ye shall blush; for the thing which ye do
 Derides what ye are.
 This is the curse. Write. 105

When fools cast taunts at your gate,
Your scorn ye shall somewhat abate
 As ye look o'er the wall;
For your conscience, tradition, and name
Explode with a deadlier blame 110
 Than the worst of them all.
 This is the curse. Write.

Go, wherever ill deeds shall be done,
Go, plant your flag in the sun
　　Beside the ill-doers! 115
And recoil from clenching the curse
Of God's witnessing Universe
　　With a curse of yours.
　　THIS is the curse.　　Write.

　　　　　　　　　　　　　　　　　　　　　　　　　　　1860

Mother and Poet

Turin, after News from Gaeta, 1861[1]

1

Dead! One of them shot by the sea in the east,
　　And one of them shot in the west by the sea.
Dead! both my boys! When you sit at the feast
　　And are wanting a great song for Italy free,
　　　　Let none look at *me*! 5

2

Yet I was a poetess only last year,
　　And good at my art, for a woman, men said;
But *this* woman, *this*, who is agonized here,
　　—The east sea and west sea rhyme on in her head
　　　　For ever instead. 10

3

What art can a woman be good at? Oh, vain!
　　What art *is* she good at, but hurting her breast
With the milk-teeth of babes, and a smile at the pain?
　　Ah boys, how you hurt! you were strong as you pressed,
　　　　And I proud, by that test. 15

4

What art's for a woman? To hold on her knees
　　Both darlings! to feel all their arms round her throat,
Cling, strangle a little! to sew by degrees
　　And 'broider the long-clothes and neat little coat;
　　　　To dream and to doat. 20

5

To teach them . . . It stings there! I made them indeed
　　Speak plain the word *country*. I taught them, no doubt,
That a country's a thing men should die for at need.
　　I prated of liberty, rights, and about
　　　　The tyrant cast out. 25

6

And when their eyes flashed . . . O my beautiful eyes! . . .
　　I exulted: nay, let them go forth at the wheels

1. "The mother was Laura Savio of Turin, poet and patriot, whose two sons were killed at Ancona and Gaeta" [Browning's note]. At this time Italy was struggling to free itself from foreign rule and become a unified state.

Of the guns, and denied not. But then the surprise
 When one sits quite alone! Then one weeps, then one kneels!
 God, how the house feels! 30

7

At first, happy news came, in gay letters moiled[2]
 With my kisses,—of camp-life and glory, and how
They both loved me; and, soon coming home to be spoiled
 In return would fan off every fly from my brow
 With their green laurel-bough. 35

8

Then was triumph at Turin: "Ancona was free!"
 And someone came out of the cheers in the street,
With a face pale as stone, to say something to me.
 My Guido was dead! I fell down at his feet,
 While they cheered in the street. 40

9

I bore it; friends soothed me; my grief looked sublime
 As the ransom of Italy. One boy remained
To be leant on and walked with, recalling the time
 When the first grew immortal, while both of us strained
 To the height he had gained. 45

10

And letters still came, shorter, sadder, more strong,
 Writ now but in one hand, "I was not to faint,—
One loved me for two—would be with me ere long:
 And Viva l'Italia![3]—he died for, our saint,
 Who forbids our complaint." 50

11

My Nanni would add, "he was safe, and aware
 Of a presence that turned off the balls,[4]—was imprest
It was Guido himself, who knew what I could bear,
 And how 'twas impossible, quite dispossessed
 To live on for the rest." 55

12

On which, without pause, up the telegraph line
 Swept smoothly the next news from Gaeta:—Shot.
Tell his mother. Ah, ah, "his," "their" mother—not "mine,"
 No voice says "My mother" again to me. What!
 You think Guido forgot? 60

13

Are souls straight so happy that, dizzy with Heaven,
 They drop earth's affections, conceive not of woe?
I think not. Themselves were too lately forgiven
 Through THAT Love and Sorrow which reconciled so
 The Above and Below.[5] 65

2. Smeared.
3. Long live Italy!

4. Bullets
5. I.e., the love and sorrow of Jesus Christ.

14

O Christ of the five wounds, who look'dst through the dark
 To the face of thy mother! consider, I pray,
How we common mothers stand desolate, mark,
 Whose sons, not being Christs, die with eyes turned away,
 And no last word to say! 70

15

Both boys dead? but that's out of nature. We all
 Have been patriots, yet each house must always keep one.
'Twere imbecile, hewing out roads to a wall;
 And, when Italy's made, for what end is it done
 If we have not a son? 75

16

Ah, ah, ah! when Gaeta's taken, what then?
 When the fair wicked queen sits no more at her sport
Of the fire-balls of death crashing souls out of men?
 When the guns of Cavalli[6] with final retort
 Have cut the game short? 80

17

When Venice and Rome keep their new jubilee,
 When your flag takes all heaven for its white, green, and red,[7]
When *you* have your country from mountain to sea,
 When King Victor has Italy's crown on his head,
 (And I have my dead)— 85

18

What then? Do not mock me. Ah, ring your bells low,
 And burn your lights faintly! *My* country is *there*,
Above the star pricked by the last peak of snow:
 My Italy's there, with my brave civic pair,
 To disfranchise despair! 90

19

Forgive me. Some women bear children in strength,
 And bite back the cry of their pain in self-scorn;
But the birth-pangs of nations will wring us at length
 Into wail such as this—and we sit on forlorn
 When the man-child is born. 95

20

Dead! One of them shot by the sea in the east,
 And one of them shot in the west by the sea.
Both! both my boys! If in keeping the feast
 You want a great song for your Italy free,[8]
 Let none look at *me*! 100

1862

6. Cavalli was the general in command at Gaeta. "The fair wicked queen" was Maria, wife of Francis II, the last ruler of the Neapolitan government, who had retreated to Gaeta.

7. The colors of the new Italian flag, symbolizing national unity.
8. I.e., the holiday celebrating the unification of Italy in 1861.

MARGARET FULLER

1810–1850

After Margaret Fuller's untimely death at forty years of age, Elizabeth Barrett Browning honored her "truth and courage," Ralph Waldo Emerson mourned that he had "lost in her my audience," Nathaniel Hawthorne censured her as "a great humbug" in his journal and as Zenobia in *The Blithedale Romance* (1852), Henry James brooded over the "haunting Margaret-ghost," and Henry David Thoreau spent five days on Fire Island, New York, searching for the remains of her body and her last book. Whether they castigated or praised her, however, all agreed that, in Barrett Browning's words, her "writings [were] curiously inferior to . . . her conversation." Indeed, their mixed response of awe at her personal power and uncertainty about the written evidence of that power typifies the problem Fuller poses for contemporary readers as well. But her prose nevertheless struggles to effect a cultural transformation that would reflect her own search for fulfillment, a search of epic proportions: "Such a predetermination to eat this big Universe as her oyster or egg," the English essayist and historian Thomas Carlyle wrote, "I have not before seen in any human soul."

Fuller's mother, Margaret (Crane) Fuller, was notable for her patient submissiveness as she bore nine children and raised the seven who survived past infancy. Her father, Timothy Fuller, was an energetic and independent graduate of Harvard, the speaker of the Massachusetts House of Representatives, a Unitarian in religion and a Jeffersonian in politics. He taught his precocious first child Latin and English grammar at an early age, even as he encouraged direct discourse and discouraged stereotypically "feminine" hesitation, apology, or euphemism. This strenuous education produced a child prodigy who read Virgil, Ovid, and Horace at the age of seven, and who suffered terrifying nightmares and recurrent headaches for most of her life. Torn between her training as her father's "son" and her knowledge of her female self, Fuller felt that womanhood was "too straitly bounded" to give her scope, but she suffered feelings of inauthenticity when she "played" the part of the great man.

After a short stay at the Misses Prescott's School in Groton, Massachusetts, presumably designed to address this dilemma, Fuller continued her education at home in Cambridgeport until, after a move to Groton, her father died. To support the family, she taught at Bronson Alcott's experimental school in Boston and then at the Greene Street School in Providence. At both establishments she began to cultivate the friendships that would play a prominent role throughout her life. After more than one adolescent infatuation with female friends, she began her "conversations," meetings or classes usually composed of an elite group of Bostonians who discussed such topics as ethics and Greek mythology. From 1839 to 1840, New England's version of the salon took place in Elizabeth Peabody's bookstore, where Fuller could draw on the connections she had already established in Cambridge intellectual society, which was composed of Transcendentalists like Frederic Henry Hedge, W. E. Channing, and James Freeman Clarke. From 1840 to 1842, with the encouragement of Emerson, she edited the Transcendentalists' magazine, *The Dial*. In 1844, Horace Greeley, editor of the *New York Daily Tribune*, hired her to write literary criticism and moved her to New York.

As the first self-supporting American woman journalist, the translator of Johann Peter Eckermann's *Conversations with Goethe* (1839), and the author of *Summer on the Lakes* (1844), Fuller undertook to mediate between American society and European culture, represented by such figures as the German poet-dramatist Goethe, the Romantic poet Lord Byron, and the French novelist George Sand. While her *Papers on Literature and Art*, published in 1846, consolidated her repu-

tation, her fame today depends largely on *Woman in the Nineteenth Century* (1845). Originally a *Dial* essay titled *The Great Lawsuit* (1843), this feminist polemic applied to women Transcendentalist tenets regarding the sacred duty of self-development, but it also solved the problem of Fuller's own sense of self-division: "there is no wholly masculine man," she proclaimed, "no purely feminine woman." Hortatory in tone, *Woman in the Nineteenth Century* resembles a sermon, insisting, as it does, that men and women alike must fulfill their potential for the greater spiritual good of both sexes. Although her prose is sometimes marred by strained rhetoric, the broadly based humanism Fuller stressed here was to inform the rest of her life as she widened her concerns from feminism to the politics of liberation.

Already, in New York, she had helped establish a "halfway house" for convicts and translated one of the earliest discussions of Karl Marx and Friedrich Engels to be offered in the United States. After she sailed for Europe as a foreign correspondent, she met Giuseppe Mazzini, the Italian patriot in exile as well as two artists associated with sexual liberation, the French novelist George Sand and the exiled Polish writer Adam Mickiewicz. Eventually, she settled in Italy, where she took Giovanni Angelo, marchese d'Ossoli, as her lover. Ten years her junior, he was instrumental in consolidating her commitment to the cause of Italian independence. Her son, Angelo Eugene, was born on September 5, 1848, and in November Fuller left him to rejoin Ossoli in Rome. There she witnessed and reported on the arrival of the Italian nationalist Giuseppe Garibaldi, the proclamation of the Roman Republic, and the intervention of the French on behalf of the pope. During the French siege, she took over an emergency hospital, but when the Republic was overthrown in July, she fled with Ossoli and her child, first to Florence and then to America. It is unclear whether the two married before leaving Italy, although it is known that Fuller was working on a history of the Roman revolution at this time.

Just outside of New York's harbor, the ship bearing Fuller, Ossoli, and their child drove into a sandbar during a storm. The baby's body was washed ashore, but neither Margaret Fuller nor Ossoli was ever found. In spite of the fame Fuller had attained during her relatively short lifetime, the contemporary scholars Bell Gale Chevigny and Marie Olesen Urbanski have demonstrated how subsequent editors and biographers trivialized this woman of letters's image. Yet, as Chevigny and Urbanski also show, Fuller continued to exert a profound influence on the growing American women's movement. In the words of the nineteenth-century suffragist Ednah Cheney, "Whatever she spoke of revealed a hidden meaning, and everything seemed to be put into true relation. . . . I was no longer the limitation of myself, but I felt that the whole wealth of the universe was open to me." Cheney understood, as did many of her contemporaries, that Fuller's famous presumption—her saying, for example, "I accept the universe"—could be misinterpreted as conceit, but what it truly signified was "consciousness of the illimitable ego, the divinity in the soul."

From Woman in the Nineteenth Century

[*Prejudice against Women*]

* * * Knowing that there exists in the minds of men a tone of feeling toward women as toward slaves, such as is expressed in the common phrase, "Tell that to women and children"; that the infinite soul[1] can only work through them in already ascertained limits; that the gift of reason, Man's highest prerogative, is

1. A Transcendentalist concept probably derived from Emerson's *Over-Soul*.

allotted to them in much lower degree; that they must be kept from mischief and melancholy by being constantly engaged in active labor, which is to be furnished and directed by those better able to think, etc., etc.,—we need not multiply instances, for who can review the experience of last week without recalling words which imply, whether in jest or earnest, these views, or views like these,—knowing this, can we wonder that many reformers think that measures are not likely to be taken in behalf of women, unless their wishes could be publicly represented by women?

"That can never be necessary," cry the other side. "All men are privately influenced by women; each has his wife, sister, or female friends, and is too much biased by these relations to fail of representing their interests; and, if this is not enough, let them propose and enforce their wishes with the pen. The beauty of home would be destroyed, the delicacy of the sex be violated, the dignity of halls of legislation degraded, by an attempt to introduce them there. Such duties are inconsistent with those of a mother;" and then we have ludicrous pictures of ladies in hysterics at the polls, and senate-chambers filled with cradles.

But if, in reply, we admit as truth that Woman seems destined by nature rather for the inner circle, we must add that the arrangements of civilized life have not been, as yet, such as to secure it to her Her circle, if the duller, is not the quieter. If kept from "excitement," she is not from drudgery. Not only the Indian squaw carries the burdens of the camp, but the favorites of Louis XIV[2] accompany him in his journeys, and the washerwoman stands at her tub, and carries home her work at all seasons, and in all states of health. Those who think the physical circumstances of Woman would make a part in the affairs of national government unsuitable, are by no means those who think it impossible for negresses to endure fieldwork, even during pregnancy, or for sempstresses to go through their killing labors.

As to the use of the pen, there was quite as much opposition to Woman's possessing herself of that help to free agency as there is now to her seizing on the rostrum or the desk; and she is likely to draw, from a permission to plead her cause that way, opposite inferences to what might be wished by those who now grant it.

As to the possibility of her filling with grace and dignity any such position, we should think those who had seen the great actresses, and heard the Quaker preachers of modern times, would not doubt that Woman can express publicly the fulness of thought and creation, without losing any of the peculiar beauty of her sex. What can pollute and tarnish is to act thus from any motive except that something needs to be said or done. Woman could take part in the processions, the songs, the dances of old religion; no one fancied her delicacy was impaired by appearing in public for such a cause.

As to her home, she is not likely to leave it more than she now does for balls, theatres, meetings for promoting missions, revival meetings, and others to which she flies, in hope of an animation for her existence commensurate with what she sees enjoyed by men. Governors of ladies'-fairs are no less engrossed by such a charge, than the governor of a state by his; presidents of Washingtonian societies[3] no less away from home than presidents of conven-

2. Women in favor at the court of the French king
3. Temperance groups. "Ladies'-fairs": bazaars organized by women.

tions. If men look straitly to it, they will find that, unless their lives are domestic, those of the women will not be. A house is no home unless it contain food and fire for the mind as well as for the body. The female Greek, of our day, is as much in the street as the male to cry, "What news?"[4] We doubt not it was the same in Athens of old. The women, shut out from the marketplace, made up for it at the religious festivals. For human beings are not so constituted that they can live without expansion. If they do not get it in one way, they must in another, or perish.

As to men's representing women fairly at present, while we hear from men who owe to their wives not only all that is comfortable or graceful, but all that is wise, in the arrangement of their lives, the frequent remark, "You cannot reason with a woman,"—when from those of delicacy, nobleness, and poetic culture, falls the contemptuous phrase "women and children," and that in no light sally of the hour, but in works intended to give a permanent statement of the best experiences,—when not one man, in the million, shall I say? no, not in the hundred million, can rise above the belief that Woman was made *for Man*,—when such traits as these are daily forced upon the attention, can we feel that Man will always do justice to the interests of Woman? Can we think that he takes a sufficiently discerning and religious view of her office and destiny ever to do her justice, except when prompted by sentiment,—accidentally or transiently, that is, for the sentiment will vary according to the relations in which he is placed? The lover, the poet, the artist, are likely to view her nobly. The father and the philosopher have some chance of liberality; the man of the world, the legislator for expediency, none.

Under these circumstances, without attaching importance, in themselves, to the changes demanded by the champions of Woman, we hail them as signs of the times. We would have every arbitrary barrier thrown down. We would have every path laid open to Woman as freely as to Man. Were this done, and a slight temporary fermentation allowed to subside, we should see crystallizations more pure and of more various beauty. We believe the divine energy would pervade nature to a degree unknown in the history of former ages, and that no discordant collision, but a ravishing harmony of the spheres,[5] would ensue.

Yet, then and only then will mankind be ripe for this, when inward and outward freedom for Woman as much as for Man shall be acknowledged as a *right*, not yielded as a concession. As the friend of the Negro assumes that one man cannot by right hold another in bondage, so should the friend of Woman assume that Man cannot by right lay even well-meant restrictions on Woman. If the Negro be a soul, if the woman be a soul, apparelled in flesh, to one Master only are they accountable. There is but one law for souls, and, if there is to be an interpreter of it, he must come not as man, or son of man, but as son of God.

Were thought and feeling once so far elevated that Man should esteem himself the brother and friend, but nowise the lord and tutor, of Woman,— were he really bound with her in equal worship,—arrangements as to function and employment would be of no consequence. What Woman needs is not as a woman to act or rule, but as a nature to grow, as an intellect to discern, as a

4. Greek men were satirized for newsmongering, just as the Latin *quid nunc* became a term for male busybodies.

5. According to ancient astronomical belief, the motions of the stars and planets created a music of order and perfection.

soul to live freely and unimpeded, to unfold such powers as were given her when we left our common home. If fewer talents were given her, yet if allowed the free and full employment of these, so that she may render back to the giver his own with usury,[6] she will not complain; nay. I dare to say she will bless and rejoice in her earthly birth-place, her earthly lot. Let us consider what obstructions impede this good era, and what signs give reason to hope that it draws near.

I was talking on this subject with Miranda[7] a woman, who, if any in the world could, might speak without heat and bitterness of the position of her sex. Her father was a man who cherished no sentimental reverence for Woman, but a firm belief in the equality of the sexes. She was his eldest child, and came to him at an age when he needed a companion. From the time she could speak and go alone, he addressed her not as a plaything, but as a living mind. Among the few verses he ever wrote was a copy addressed to this child, when the first locks were cut from her head; and the reverence expressed on this occasion for that cherished head, he never belied. It was to him the temple of immortal intellect. He respected his child, however, too much to be an indulgent parent. He called on her for clear judgment, for courage, for honor and fidelity; in short, for such virtues as he knew. In so far as he possessed the keys to the wonders of this universe, he allowed free use of them to her, and, by the incentive of a high expectation, he forbade, so far as possible, that she should let the privilege lie idle.

Thus this child was early led to feel herself a child of the spirit. She took her place easily, not only in the world of organized being, but in the world of mind. A dignified sense of self-dependence was given as all her portion, and she found it a sure anchor. Herself securely anchored, her relations with others were established with equal security. She was fortunate in a total absence of those charms which might have drawn to her bewildering flatteries, and in a strong electric[8] nature, which repelled those who did not belong to her, and attracted those who did. With men and women her relations were noble,—affectionate without passion, intellectual without coldness. The world was free to her, and she lived freely in it. Outward adversity came, and inward conflict; but that faith and self-respect had early been awakened which must always lead, at last, to an outward serenity and an inward peace.

Of Miranda I had always thought as an example, that the restraints upon the sex were insuperable only to those who think them so, or who noisily strive to break them. She had taken a course of her own, and no man stood in her way. Many of her acts had been unusual, but excited no uproar. Few helped, but none checked her; and the many men who knew her mind and her life, showed to her confidence as to a brother, gentleness as to a sister. And not only refined, but very coarse men approved and aided one in whom they saw resolution and clearness of design. Her mind was often the leading one, always effective.

When I talked with her upon these matters, and had said very much what I have written, she smilingly replied "And yet we must admit that I have been fortunate, and this should not be.[9] My good father's early trust gave the first bias, and the rest followed, of course. It is true that I have had less outward aid,

6. Interest.
7. Reflects an idealized version of Fuller's own experiences and opinions.
8 Quick exciting.
9 I.e., I would not be as I am without my good fortune.

in after years, than most women; but that is of little consequence. Religion was early awakened in my soul,—a sense that what the soul is capable to ask it must attain, and that, though I might be aided and instructed by others, I must depend on myself as the only constant friend. This self-dependence, which was honored in me, is deprecated as a fault in most women. They are taught to learn their rule from without, not to unfold it from within.

"This is the fault of Man, who is still vain, and wishes to be more important to Woman than, by right, he should be."

"Men have not shown this disposition toward you," I said.

"No; because the position I early was enabled to take was one of self-reliance.[1] And were all women as sure of their wants as I was, the result would be the same. But they are so overloaded with precepts by guardians, who think that nothing is so much to be dreaded for a woman as originality of thought or character, that their minds are impeded by doubts till they lose their chance of fair, free proportions. The difficulty is to get them to the point from which they shall naturally develop self-respect, and learn self-help.

"Once I thought that men would help to forward this state of things more than I do now. I saw so many of them wretched in the connections[2] they had formed in weakness and vanity. They seemed so glad to esteem women whenever they could.

" 'The soft arms of affection,' said one of the most discerning spirits, 'will not suffice for me, unless on them I see the steel bracelets of strength.'

"But early I perceived that men never, in any extreme of despair, wished to be women. On the contrary, they were ever ready to taunt one another, at any sign of weakness, with,

> Art thou not like the women, who,—

The passage ends various ways, according to the occasion and rhetoric of the speaker. When they admired any woman, they were inclined to speak of her as 'above her sex.' Silently I observed this, and feared it argued a rooted scepticism, which for ages had been fastening on the heart, and which only an age of miracles could eradicate. Ever I have been treated with great sincerity; and I look upon it as a signal instance of this, that an intimate friend of the other sex said, in a fervent moment, that I 'deserved in some star to be a man.' He was much surprised when I disclosed my view of my position and hopes, when I declared my faith that the feminine side, the side of love, of beauty, of holiness, was now to have its full chance, and that, if either were better, it was better now to be a woman; for even the slightest achievement of good was furthering an especial work of our time. He smiled incredulously. 'She makes the best she can of it,' thought he. 'Let Jews believe the pride of Jewry, but I am of the better sort, and know better.'

"Another used as highest praise, in speaking of a character in literature, the words 'a manly woman.'

"So in the noble passage of Ben Jonson:[3]

1. Another Emersonian concept, expressing a faith in individualism.
2. Marriages, relationships.
3. English poet (1572–1637). The passage is slightly misquoted from Epigrams 76: *To Lucy, Countess of Bedford*.

> I meant the day-star should not brighter ride,
> Nor shed like influence from its lucent seat;
> I meant she should be courteous, facile, sweet,
> Free from that solemn vice of greatness, pride;
> I meant each softest virtue there should meet,
> Fit in that softer bosom to abide,
> Only a learned and a manly soul
> I purposed her, that should with even powers
> The rock, the spindle, and the shears control
> Of destiny,[4] and spin her own free hours."

"Methinks," said I, "you are too fasticious in objecting to this. Jonson, in using the word 'manly,' only meant to heighten the picture of this, the true, the intelligent fate, with one of the deeper colors."

"And yet," said she, "so invariable is the use of this word where a heroic quality is to be described, and I feel so sure that persistence and courage are the most womanly no less than the most manly qualities, that I would exchange these words for others of a larger sense, at the risk of marring the fine tissue of the verse.[5] Read, 'A heavenward and instructed soul,' and I should be satisfied. Let it not be said, wherever there is energy or creative genius, 'She has a masculine mind.'"

[Muse and Minerva]

There are two aspects of Woman's nature, represented by the ancients as Muse and Minerva.[6] It is the former to which the writer in the Pathfinder[7] looks. It is the latter which Wordsworth has in mind, when he says,

> With a placid brow,
> Which woman ne'er should forfeit, keep thy vow.[8]

The especial genius of Woman I believe to be electrical in movement, intuitive in function, spiritual in tendency. She excels not so easily in classification, or recreation,[9] as in an instinctive seizure of causes, and a simple breathing out of what she receives, that has the singleness of life, rather than the selecting and energizing of art.

More native is it to her to be the living model of the artist than to set apart from herself any one form in objective reality; more native to inspire and receive the poem, than to create it. In so far as soul is in her completely developed, all soul is the same; but in so far as it is modified in her as Woman, it flows, it breathes, it sings, rather than deposits soil, or finishes work; and that which is especially feminine flushes, in blossom, the face of earth, and pervades, like air and water, all this seeming solid globe, daily renewing and purifying its life. Such may be the especially feminine element spoken of as Femality. But it is no more the order of nature that it should be incarnated pure in any form, than that the masculine energy should exist unmingled with it in any form

Male and female represent the two sides of the great radical dualism. But, in

4. The Fates spin out the thread of each person's destiny, cutting it when the time of death arrives.
5. I.e., its prosody.
6. The ancient goddess of wisdom, known as Athena in Greek myth. "Muse": any of nine sister goddesses in Greek mythology, presides over learning and creative arts.
7. The New York Pathfinder, a periodical in existence at the time.
8. William Wordsworth's Liberty: Sequel to the Preceding (1835).
9. Careful analysis.

fact, they are perpetually passing into one another. Fluid hardens to solid, solid rushes to fluid. There is no wholly masculine man, no purely feminine woman.

History jeers at the attempts of physiologists to bind great original laws by the forms which flow from them. They make a rule; they say from observation what can and cannot be. In vain! Nature provides exceptions to every rule. She sends women to battle, and sets Hercules spinning;[1] she enables women to bear immense burdens, cold, and frost; she enables the man, who feels maternal love, to nourish his infant like a mother. Of late she plays still gayer pranks. Not only she deprives organizations, but organs, of a necessary end. She enables people to read with the top of the head, and see with the pit of the stomach. Presently she will make a female Newton, and a male Siren.

Man partakes of the feminine in the Apollo,[2] Woman of the masculine as Minerva.

What I mean by the Muse is that unimpeded clearness of the intuitive powers, which a perfectly truthful adherence to every admonition of the higher instincts would bring to a finely organized human being. It may appear as prophecy or as poesy. It enabled Cassandra to foresee the results of actions passing round her; the Seeress[3] to behold the true character of the person through the mask of his customary life. (Sometimes she saw a feminine form behind the man, sometimes the reverse.) It enabled the daughter of Linnaeus to see the soul of the flower exhaling from the flower.[4] It gave a man, but a poet-man, the power of which he thus speaks: "Often in my contemplation of nature, radiant intimations, and as it were sheaves of light, appear before me as to the facts of cosmogony, in which my mind has, perhaps, taken especial part." He wisely adds, "but it is necessary with earnestness to verify the knowledge we gain by these flashes of light." And none should forget this. Sight must be verified by light before it can deserve the honors of piety and genius. Yet sight comes first, and of this sight of the world of causes, this approximation to the region of primitive motions, women I hold to be especially capable. Even without equal freedom with the other sex, they have already shown themselves so; and should these faculties have free play, I believe they will open new, deeper and purer sources of joyous inspiration than have as yet refreshed the earth.

Let us be wise, and not impede the soul. Let her work as she will. Let us have one creative energy, one incessant revelation. Let it take what form it will, and let us not bind it by the past to man or woman, black or white. Jove sprang from Rhea, Pallas from Jove.[5] So let it be.

If it has been the tendency of these remarks to call Woman rather to the Minerva side,—if I, unlike the more generous writer, have spoken from society no less than the soul,—let it be pardoned! It is love that has caused this,—love for many incarcerated souls, that might be freed, could the idea of religious

1. A Greek hero; he was forced to wear women's clothes and spin yarn.
2. The Greek god of the sun and of poetry. Sir Isaac Newton (1642–1727), major English scientist. "Siren": mythical female who lures sailors onto rocks through the enchanting power of her song.
3. Female seer or clairvoyant. Cassandra, daughter of the king of Troy, was a prophetess.
4. The daughter of Linnaeus [18th-century botanist]

states, that, while looking steadfastly at the red lily, she saw its spirit hovering above it, as a red flame. It is true, this, like many fair spirit-stories, may be explained away as an optical illusion, but its poetic beauty and meaning would, even then, make it valuable, as an illustration of the spiritual fact [Fuller's note].
5. Zeus, the king of the Greek gods, whose mother was Rhea. Pallas is Minerva, goddess of wisdom, said to have been born from the head of Jove.

self-dependence be established in them, could the weakening habit of depen-
dence on others be broken up?

Proclus[6] teaches that every life has, in its sphere, a totality or wholeness of
the animating powers of the other spheres; having only, as its own characteris-
tic, a predominance of some one power. Thus Jupiter comprises, within him-
self, the other twelve powers,[7] which stand thus: The first triad is *demiurgic* or
fabricative, that is, Jupiter, Neptune, Vulcan; the second, *defensive*, Vesta,
Minerva, Mars; the third, *vivific*, Ceres, Juno, Diana; and the fourth, Mercury,
Venus, Apollo, *elevating and harmonic*. In the sphere of Jupiter, energy is pre-
dominant—with Venus, beauty; but each comprehends and apprehends all
the others.

When the same community of life and consciousness of mind begin among
men, humanity will have, positively and finally, subjugated its brute elements
and Titanic[8] childhood; criticism will have perished; arbitrary limits and igno-
rant censure be impossible; all will have entered upon the liberty of law,[9] and
the harmony of common growth.

Then Apollo will sing to his lyre what Vulcan forges on the anvil, and the
Muse weave anew the tapestries of Minerva.

It is, therefore, only in the present crisis that the preference is given to
Minerva. The power of continence must establish the legitimacy of freedom,
the power of self-poise the perfection of motion.

Every relation, every gradation of nature is incalculably precious, but only
to the soul which is poised upon itself, and to whom no loss, no change, can
bring dull discord, for it is in harmony with the central soul.[1]

* * *

Women must leave off asking [men] and being influenced by them, but re-
tire within themselves, and explore the ground-work of life till they find their
peculiar secret. Then, when they come forth again, renovated and baptized,
they will know how to turn all dross[2] to gold, and will be rich and free though
they live in a hut, tranquil if in a crowd. Then their sweet singing shall not be
from passionate impulse, but the lyrical overflow of a divine rapture, and a
new music shall be evolved from this many-chorded world.

Grant her, then, for a while, the armor and the javelin. Let her put from her
the press of other minds, and meditate in virgin loneliness. The same idea
shall reappear in due time as Muse, or Ceres,[3] the all-kindly, patient Earth-
Spirit.

[The Future of Women]

And now I have designated in outline, if not in fulness, the stream which is
ever flowing from the heights of my thought.

In the earlier tract[4] I was told I did not make my meaning sufficiently clear.
In this I have consequently tried to illustrate it in various ways, and may have
been guilty of much repetition. Yet, as I am anxious to leave no room for

6. Greek philosopher and mystic (A.D. 412–485).
7. Each is a god or goddess.
8. The Titans were a race of giants who were suc-
ceeded by the gods in Greek myth.
9. Natural law or necessity.
1. Another reference to the Emersonian doctrine of

the *Over-Soul*.
2. Waste materials found in metals
3. Roman goddess of agriculture.
4. Her first version of this work, *The Great Lawsuit*,
was criticized when it appeared in the *Dial* (1843).

doubt, I shall venture to retrace, once more, the scope of my design in points, as was done in old-fashioned sermons.

Man is a being of two-fold relations, to nature beneath, and intelligences above him. The earth is his school, if not his birth-place; God his object; life and thought his means of interpreting nature, and aspiring to God.

Only a fraction of this purpose is accomplished in the life of any one man. Its entire accomplishment is to be hoped only from the sum of the lives of men, or Man considered as a whole.

As this whole has one soul and one body, any injury or obstruction to a part, or to the meanest member, affects the whole. Man can never be perfectly happy or virtuous, till all men are so.

To address[5] Man wisely, you must not forget that his life is partly animal, subject to the same laws with Nature.

But you cannot address him wisely unless you consider him still more as soul, and appreciate the conditions and destiny of soul.

The growth of Man is twofold, masculine and feminine.

So far as these two methods can be distinguished, they are so as

Energy and Harmony;

Power and Beauty;

Intellect and Love;

or by some such rude classification; for we have not language primitive and pure enough to express such ideas with precision.

These two sides are supposed to be expressed in Man and Woman, that is, as the more and the less, for the faculties have not been given pure to either, but only in preponderance. There are also exceptions in great number, such as men of far more beauty than power, and the reverse. But, as a general rule, it seems to have been the intention to give a preponderance on the one side, that is called masculine, and on the other, one that is called feminine.

There cannot be a doubt that, if these two developments were in perfect harmony, they would correspond to and fulfill one another, like hemispheres, or the tenor and bass in music.

But there is no perfect harmony in human nature; and the two parts answer one another only now and then; or, if there be a persistent consonance, it can only be traced at long intervals, instead of discoursing an obvious melody.

What is the cause of this?

Man, in the order of time, was developed first; as energy comes before harmony; power before beauty.

Woman was therefore under his care as an elder. He might have been her guardian and teacher.

But, as human nature goes not straightforward, but by excessive action and then reaction in an undulated course, he misunderstood and abused his advantages, and became her temporal master instead of her spiritual sire.

On himself came the punishment. He educated Woman more as a servant than a daughter, and found himself a king without a queen.

The children of this unequal union showed unequal natures, and, more and more, men seemed sons of the handmaid, rather than princess.

At last, there were so many Ishmaelites that the rest grew frightened and in-

5. Consider.

dignant. They laid the blame on Hagar,[6] and drove her forth into the wilderness.

But there were none the fewer Ishmaelites for that.

At last men became a little wiser, and saw that the infant Moses was, in every case, saved by the pure instincts of Woman's breast.[7] For, as too much adversity is better for the moral nature than too much prosperity, Woman, in this respect, dwindled less than Man, though in other respects still a child in leading-strings.[8]

So Man did her more and more justice, and grew more and more kind.

But yet—his habits and his will corrupted by the past—he did not clearly see that Woman was half himself; that her interests were identical with his; and that, by the law of their common being, he could never reach his true proportions while she remained in any wise shorn[9] of hers.

And so it has gone on to our day; both ideas developing, but more slowly than they would under a clearer recognition of truth and justice, which would have permitted the sexes their due influence on one another, and mutual improvement from more dignified relations.

Wherever there was pure love, the natural influences were, for the time, restored.

Wherever the poet or artist gave free course to his genius, he saw the truth, and expressed it in worthy forms, for these men especially share and need the feminine principle. The divine birds need to be brooded[1] into life and song by mothers.

Wherever religion (I mean the thirst for truth and good, not the love of sect and dogma) had its course, the original design was apprehended in its simplicity, and the dove presaged sweetly from Dodona's oak.[2]

I have aimed to show that no age was left entirely without a witness of the equality of the sexes in function, duty, and hope.

Also that, when there was unwillingness or ignorance, which prevented this being acted upon, women had not the less power for their want of light and noble freedom. But it was power which hurt alike them and those against whom they made use of the arms of the servile,—cunning, blandishment, and unreasonable emotion.

That now the time has come when a clearer vision and better action are possible—when Man and Woman may regard one another as brother and sister, the pillars of one porch, the priests of one worship.

I have believed and intimated that this hope would receive an ampler fruition, than ever before, in our own land.

And it will do so if this land carry out the principles from which sprang our national life.

I believe that, at present, women are the best helpers of one another.

Let them think; let them act; till they know what they need.

We only ask of men to remove arbitrary barriers. Some would like to do

6. Egyptian servant who bore an illegitimate son, Ishmael, to Abraham, and was driven into the desert because of her contempt for his childless wife Sarah. "Ishmaelites": i.e., outcasts from society.

7. Moses was found floating on the river Nile in a basket by the pharoah's daughter, who rescued him.

8. Strings used to support a child who is learning to walk.

9. In any way deprived.

1. Hatched.

2. An ancient Greek oracle; the rustling oak leaves revealed Zeus's message. The tree's sanctity had been made known by a dove that spoke.

more. But I believe it needs that Woman show herself in her native dignity, to teach them how to aid her; their minds are so encumbered by tradition.

When Lord Edward Fitzgerald travelled with the Indians, his manly heart obliged him at once to take the packs from the squaws and carry them. But we do not read that the red men followed his example, though they are ready enough to carry the pack of the white woman, because she seems to them a superior being.

Let Woman appear in the mild majesty of Ceres, and rudest churls[3] will be willing to learn from her.

You ask, what use will she make of liberty, when she has so long been sustained and restrained?

I answer; in the first place, this will not be suddenly given. I read yesterday a debate of this year on the subject of enlarging women's rights over property. It was a leaf from the class-book that is preparing for the needed instruction. The men learned visibly as they spoke. The champions of Woman saw the fallacy of arguments on the opposite side, and were startled by their own convictions. With their wives at home, and the readers of the paper, it was the same. And so the stream flows on; thought urging action, and action leading to the evolution of still better thought.

But, were this freedom to come suddenly, I have no fear of the consequences. Individuals might commit excesses, but there is not only in the sex a reverence for decorums and limits inherited and enhanced from generation to generation, which many years of other life could not efface, but a native love, in Woman as Woman, of proportion, of "the simple art of not too much,"—a Greek moderation, which would create immediately a restraining party, the natural legislators and instructors of the rest, and would gradually establish such rules as are needed to guard, without impeding, life.

The Graces[4] would lead the choral dance, and teach the rest to regulate their steps to the measure of beauty.

But if you ask me what offices they may fill, I reply—any. I do not care what case you put; let them be sea-captains, if you will. I do not doubt there are women well fitted for such an office, and, if so, I should be as glad to see them in it, as to welcome the maid of Saragossa, or the maid of Missolonghi, or the Suliote heroine, or Emily Plater.[5]

I think women need, especially at this juncture, a much greater range of occupation than they have, to rouse their latent powers. A party of travelers lately visited a lonely hut on a mountain. There they found an old woman, who told them she and her husband had lived there forty years. "Why," they said, "did you choose so barren a spot?" She "did not know; *it was the man's notion.*"

And, during forty years, she had been content to act, without knowing why, upon "the man's notion." I would not have it so.

In families that I know, some little girls like to saw wood, others to use carpenters' tools. Where these tastes are indulged, cheerfulness and good-humor

3. Uneducated men.
4. Three Greek goddesses of beauty and charm.
5. Commanded a company in the Polish army fighting against Russia (1831). The Maid of Saragossa was Maria Austin, who fought against the French in Spain

(1808). The Maid of Missolonghi, an unidentified Greek, fought during the Turkish sieges of 1822 or 1826. The Suliote heroine was probably Moscha, who led a band of women during the siege of Souli in Albania (1803).

are promoted. Where they are forbidden, because "such things are not proper for girls," they grow sullen and mischievous.

Fourier[6] had observed these wants of women, as no one can fail to do who watches the desires of little girls, or knows the ennui that haunts grown women, except where they make to themselves a serene little world by art of some kind. He, therefore, in proposing a great variety of employments, in manufactures or the care of plants and animals, allows for one third of women as likely to have a taste for masculine pursuits, one third of men for feminine.

Who does not observe the immediate glow and serenity that is diffused over the life of women, before restless or fretful, by engaging in gardening, building, or the lowest department of art? Here is something that is not routine, something that draws forth life towards the infinite.

I have no doubt, however, that a large proportion of women would give themselves to the same employments as now, because there are circumstances that must lead them. Mothers will delight to make the nest soft and warm. Nature would take care of that; no need to clip the wings of any bird that wants to soar and sing, or finds in itself the strength of pinion[7] for a migratory flight unusual to its kind. The difference would be that *all* need not be constrained to employments for which *some* are unfit.

I have urged upon the sex self-subsistence in its two forms of self-reliance and self-impulse, because I believe them to be the needed means of the present juncture.

I have urged on Woman independence of Man, not that I do not think the sexes mutually needed by one another, but because in Woman this fact has led to an excessive devotion, which has cooled love, degraded marriage, and prevented either sex from being what it should be to itself or the other.

I wish Woman to live, *first* for God's sake. Then she will not make an imperfect man her god, and thus sink to idolatry. Then she will not take what is not fit for her from a sense of weakness and poverty. Then, if she finds what she needs in Man embodied, she will know how to love, and be worthy of being loved.

By being more a soul, she will not be less Woman, for nature is perfected through spirit.

Now there is no woman, only an overgrown child.

That her hand may be given with dignity, she must be able to stand alone. I wish to see men and women capable of such relations as are depicted by Landor[8] in his Pericles and Aspasia, where grace is the natural garb of strength, and the affections are calm, because deep. The softness is that of a firm tissue, as when

> The gods approve
> The depth, but not the tumult of the soul,
> A fervent, not ungovernable love.

A profound thinker has said, "No married woman can represent the female world, for she belongs to her husband. The idea of Woman must be represented by a virgin."

6. François Fourier (1772–1837), French social theorist.

7. Wing.

8. Walter Savage Landor (1775–1864), English poet.

But that is the very fault of marriage, and of the present relation between the sexes, that the woman *does* belong to the man, instead of forming a whole with him. Were it otherwise, there would be no such limitation to the thought.

Woman, self-centered, would never be absorbed by any relation; it would be only an experience to her as to man. It is a vulgar error that love, a love, to Woman is her whole existence;[9] she also is born for Truth and Love in their universal energy. Would she but assume her inheritance, Mary would not be the only virgin mother. Not Manzoni[1] alone would celebrate in his wife the virgin mind with the maternal wisdom and conjugal affections. The soul is ever young, ever virgin.

And will not she soon appear?—the woman who shall vindicate their birthright for all women; who shall teach them what to claim, and how to use what they obtain? Shall not her name be for her era Victoria, for her country and life Virginia?[2] Yet predictions are rash; she herself must teach us to give her the fitting name.

1845

9. See, e.g., Byron's *Don Juan* (1819): "Man's love of man's life a thing apart, / 'Tis a woman's whole existence" (Canto 1, Stanza 194).
1. Alessandro Manzoni (1785–1873), Italian novelist and poet.

2. Victoria was then queen of England; Virginia is a reference both to America, where Fuller sees woman's future lying, and to the virginity of soul she celebrates here.

ELIZABETH CLEGHORN GASKELL
1810–1865

Although she was born in London, the woman who gained fame as "Mrs. Gaskell" was destined to become one of the nineteenth century's foremost recorders of life in England's provinces during the height of the Industrial Revolution. Her father, William Stevenson, a sometime Unitarian minister, had come to the capital to take up a position as keeper of the records to the treasury, but soon after his wife's death, when Elizabeth—the last of eight children—was still very young, he sent this youngest daughter to live with an aunt at Knutsford, the small rural town that inspired her later depictions of isolated, pastoral "Cranford." There, at the age of twenty-one, she married the Reverend William Gaskell, also a Unitarian minister, with whom she was to live happily for the rest of her life.

After their marriage, the Gaskells settled in the industrial city of Manchester, where the Reverend Gaskell had his church, and within a decade or so the couple were the parents of four children, whose upbringing constituted a full-time job for Mrs. Gaskell until 1845. In that year, her son William died, and although she had another child within a year, she may have begun writing what was to be her first novel, *Mary Barton* (1848), to "divert her mind," as one biographer puts it, from the pain of her loss. Even before she started to take herself seriously as a potential novelist, however, Elizabeth Gaskell had clearly developed the observational skills that give her works such force. Manchester in the 1840s was a city in turmoil, with fiercely expanding factories dominating both the town and the lives of its enormous, increasingly impoverished population. In 1843, the historian-philosopher Thomas Carlyle published his *Past and Present*, a work that addressed itself in part to the crises afflicting such cities; in 1845, the German thinker Friedrich Engels, who was later to coauthor with Karl Marx *The Communist Manifesto* (1848), pro-

duced *The Condition of the Working Class in England*, which offered an extended analysis of the plight of Manchester's industrial laborers. Like these men—or perhaps even more—Mrs. Gaskell had countless opportunities to observe the misery that lay all around her. She had collaborated with her husband on the beginning of a series titled *Sketches among the Poor* in 1837; in addition, as the wife of a minister, she was frequently obliged to visit and console sufferers; as a nascent novelist, too, she had a keen sense of the drama that marked what Virginia Woolf was to call the "lives of the obscure."

Not surprisingly, then, *Mary Barton* constituted a memorable portrait of a series of those lives at the same time that it offered a detailed examination of the tensions between industrial leaders and industrial laborers that shadowed and sometimes shattered the public world of Manchester. In later novels, moreover—particularly *Ruth* (1853), the story of an unwed working-class mother, and *North and South* (1855), a tale that explicitly compared the industrialized north of England to the more agrarian south—Mrs. Gaskell continued to undertake fictional studies of what nineteenth-century writers called the "condition of England" question.

Set against Gaskell's other works, *Cranford* (1853) may at first appear to be little more than a nostalgic idyll of village life in the early Victorian period. Yet this writer's loving descriptions of the "elegant economy" practiced by her heroines of gentle birth but slender means are as incisive in their way as her more obviously analytical evocations of class conflict in Manchester. Begun as a series of sketches commissioned by Charles Dickens for *Household Words*, a weekly journal he founded in 1850, *Cranford* quickly evolved from a quietly comic memoir to a more searching but still humorous consideration of the relationship between old and new ways of life in a society that was rapidly changing. For though Miss Jenkyns and her friends appear to inhabit a timeless world of decorous customs and delicate china, their old-fashioned sphere seems increasingly like some fragile object that has been artificially preserved, and its tenuous elegance is continually threatened by forces from the "modern" industrial towns that come ever nearer. Disturbed by critics who argued that in *Mary Barton* she had been guilty of class prejudice, preferring the workers to their employers, Gaskell clearly set out in *Cranford* to show the trials of a vanishing genteel class even while she both celebrated and satirized the foibles of that class.

As she honed the novelistic skills she displayed in books as diverse as *Mary Barton* and *Cranford*, Mrs. Gaskell quickly became one of England's most successful writers and the friend of such notables as Charles Dickens, Harriet Beecher Stowe, John Ruskin, and Florence Nightingale. But her most important literary relationship was with Charlotte Brontë, whom she met in 1850, when the author of *Jane Eyre* was at the height of her fame. Although the two women saw each other only a few times, they corresponded regularly, and Gaskell was increasingly moved by both Brontë's sufferings and her fortitude. "Such a life as Miss B's I never heard of before [it was] described . . . to me," she wrote in awe to one of her friends, shortly after learning about the hardships of the novelist's history from a mutual acquaintance. After Brontë's death in 1855, Gaskell explored the conditions of that existence more fully when the Reverend Patrick Brontë asked her to write a life of his daughter, and the work she produced, despite inaccuracies and omissions designed to spare the feelings of the family, is a classic of English biography.

Mrs. Gaskell's special ability to enter with sensitivity and sympathy into circumstances so different from her own constitutes yet another indication of the range of her literary talents. Some critics have considered those talents as distinctively "womanly" because of their delineation of "women's oddities" in a work like *Cranford*, but Gaskell's skills might just as easily be defined as distinctively humane in their combination of scrupulous observation and com-

passionate imagination. Given her novelistic energy, she must certainly have been planning more works when she died quite suddenly at The Lawn, a country house she had just purchased as a retirement gift for her husband. She was buried in the town she had memorialized as "Cranford," an appropriate gesture because, as she once wrote to the critic John Ruskin, "Whenever I am ailing or ill, I take *Cranford* and—I was going to say, *enjoy* it! (but that would not be pretty!) laugh over it afresh!"

From Cranford[1]

Chapter I. Our Society

In the first place, Cranford is in possession of the Amazons;[2] all the holders of houses above a certain rent are women. If a married couple come to settle in the town, somehow the gentleman disappears; he is either fairly frightened to death by being the only man in the Cranford evening parties, or he is accounted for by being with his regiment, his ship, or closely engaged in business all the week in the great neighboring commercial town of Drumble, distant only twenty miles on a railroad. In short, whatever does become of the gentlemen, they are not at Cranford. What could they do if they were there? The surgeon has his round of thirty miles, and sleeps at Cranford; but every man cannot be a surgeon. For keeping the trim gardens full of choice flowers without a weed to speck them; for frightening away little boys who look wistfully at the said flowers through the railings; for rushing out at the geese that occasionally venture in to the gardens if the gates are left open; for deciding all questions of literature and politics without troubling themselves with unnecessary reasons or arguments; for obtaining clear and correct knowledge of everybody's affairs in the parish; for keeping their neat maid-servants in admirable order; for kindness (somewhat dictatorial) to the poor, and real tender good offices to each other whenever they are in distress, the ladies of Cranford are quite sufficient. "A man," as one of them observed to me once, "is so in the way in the house." Although the ladies of Cranford know all each other's proceedings, they are exceedingly indifferent to each other's opinions. Indeed, as each has her own individuality, not to say eccentricity, pretty strongly developed, nothing is so easy as verbal retaliation; but, somehow, goodwill reigns among them to a considerable degree.

The Cranford ladies have only an occasional little quarrel, spirted out in a few peppery words and angry jerks of the head; just enough to prevent the even tenor of their lives from becoming too flat. Their dress is very independent of fashion; as they observe, "What does it signify how we dress here at Cranford, where everybody knows us?" And if they go from home, their reason is equally cogent, "What does it signify how we dress here, where nobody knows us?" The materials of their clothes are, in general, good and plain, and most of them are nearly as scrupulous as Miss Tyler, of cleanly memory; but I will answer for it, the last gigot,[3] the last tight and scanty petticoat in wear in England, was seen at Cranford—and seen without a smile.

1. The two opening chapters of *Cranford*, printed here, were originally published in 1851 as a single self-contained episode titled *Our Society at Cranford* in Charles Dickens's journal *Household Words*.

2. A mythical race of women warriors who live independently of men.

3. A ballooning sleeve tightly gathered at the wrist.

I can testify to a magnificent family red silk umbrella, under which a gentle little spinster, left alone of many brothers and sisters, used to patter to church on rainy days. Have you any red silk umbrellas in London? We had a tradition of the first that had ever been seen in Cranford; and the little boys mobbed it, and called it "a stick in petticoats." It might have been the very red silk one I have described, held up by a strong father over a troop of little ones; the poor little lady—the survivor of all—could scarcely carry it.

Then there were rules and regulations for visiting and calls; and they were announced to any young people who might be staying in the town, with all the solemnity with which the old Manx laws were read once a year on the Tinwald Mount.[4]

"Our friends have sent to inquire how you are after your journey tonight, my dear" (fifteen miles in a gentleman's carriage); "they will give you some rest tomorrow, but the next day, I have no doubt, they will call; so be at liberty after twelve—from twelve to three are our calling hours."

Then, after they had called:

"It is the third day; I dare say your mamma has told you, my dear, never to let more than three days elapse between receiving a call and returning it; and also, that you are never to stay longer than a quarter of an hour."

"But am I to look at my watch? How am I to find out when a quarter of an hour has passed?"

"You must keep thinking about the time, my dear, and not allow yourself to forget it in conversation."

As everybody had this rule in their minds, whether they received or paid a call, of course no absorbing subject was ever spoken about. We kept ourselves to short sentences of small talk, and were punctual to our time.

I imagine that a few of the gentlefolks of Cranford were poor, and had some difficulty in making both ends meet; but they were like the Spartans,[5] and concealed their smart under a smiling face. We none of us spoke of money, because that subject savoured of commerce and trade, and though some might be poor, we were all aristocratic. The Cranfordians had that kindly *esprit de corps*[6] which made them overlook all deficiencies in success when some among them tried to conceal their poverty. When Mrs. Forrester, for instance, gave a party in her baby-house of a dwelling, and the little maiden disturbed the ladies on the sofa by a request that she might get the tea-tray out from underneath, every one took this novel proceeding as the most natural thing in the world, and talked on about household forms and ceremonies as if we all believed that our hostess had a regular servants' hall, second table, with housekeeper and steward, instead of the one little charity-school maiden,[7] whose short ruddy arms could never have been strong enough to carry the tray upstairs, if she had not been assisted in private by her mistress, who now sat in state,[8] pretending not to know what cakes were sent up, though she knew, and we knew, and she knew that we knew, and we knew that she knew that we knew, she had been busy all the morning making tea-bread and sponge-cakes.

There were one or two consequences arising from this general but unacknowledged poverty, and this very much acknowledged gentility, which were

4. "Manx laws": those of the Isle of Man, off Great Britain in the Irish Sea. The island's traditional legislature, known as the Tynwald, met for centuries in an open-air assembly once a year.

5. Citizens of a Greek city known for their austerity.
6. Group feeling (French).
7. A poor girl hired out by a public institution.
8. Regal pomp.

not amiss, and which might be introduced into many circles of society to their great improvement. For instance, the inhabitants of Cranford kept early hours, and clattered home in their pattens,[9] under the guidance of a lantern-bearer, about nine o'clock at night; and the whole town was abed and asleep by half-past ten. Moreover, it was considered "vulgar" (a tremendous word in Cranford) to give anything expensive, in the way of eatable or drinkable, at the evening entertainments. Wafer bread-and-butter and sponge-biscuits were all that the Honorable Mrs. Jamieson gave; and she was sister-in-law to the late Earl of Glenmire, although she did practice such "elegant economy."

"Elegant economy!" How naturally one falls back into the phraseology of Cranford! There, economy was always "elegant," and moneyspending always "vulgar and ostentatious"; a sort of sour-grapeism which made us very peaceful and satisfied. I never shall forget the dismay felt when a certain Captain Brown came to live at Cranford, and openly spoke about his being poor—not in a whisper to an intimate friend, the doors and windows being previously closed, but in the public street! in a loud military voice! alleging his poverty as a reason for not taking a particular house. The ladies of Cranford were already rather moaning over the invasion of their territories by a man and a gentleman. He was a half-pay captain, and had obtained some situation on a neighboring railroad, which had been vehemently petitioned against by the little town; and if, in addition to his masculine gender, and his connection with the obnoxious railroad, he was so brazen as to talk of being poor—why, then, indeed, he must be sent to Coventry.[1] Death was as true and as common as poverty; yet people never spoke about that, loud out in the streets. It was a word not to be mentioned to ears polite. We had tacitly agreed to ignore that any with whom we associated on terms of visiting equality could ever be prevented by poverty from doing anything that they wished. If we walked to or from a party, it was because the night was so fine, or the air so refreshing, not because sedan-chairs[2] were expensive. If we wore prints, instead of summer silks, it was because we preferred a washing material; and so on, till we blinded ourselves to the vulgar fact that we were, all of us, people of very moderate means. Of course, then, we did not know what to make of a man who could speak of poverty as if it was not a disgrace. Yet, somehow, Captain Brown made himself respected in Cranford, and was called upon, in spite of all resolutions to the contrary. I was surprised to hear his opinions quoted as authority at a visit which I paid to Cranford about a year after he had settled in the town. My own friends had been among the bitterest opponents of any proposal to visit the Captain and his daughters, only twelve months before; and now he was even admitted in the tabooed hours before twelve. True, it was to discover the cause of a smoking chimney, before the fire was lighted; but still Captain Brown walked upstairs, nothing daunted, spoke in a voice too large for the room, and joked quite in the way of a tame man about the house. He had been blind to all the small slights, and omissions of trivial ceremonies, with which he had been received. He had been friendly, though the Cranford ladies had been cool; he had answered small sarcastic compliments in good faith; and with his manly frankness had overpowered all the shrinking which met him as a man who was not ashamed to be poor. And, at last, his excellent masculine

9. Wooden sandals. 2. A portable enclosed chair carried by two men.
1. Idiomatic for socially ostracized.

common sense, and his facility in devising expedients to overcome domestic dilemmas, had gained him an extraordinary place as an authority among the Cranford ladies. He himself went on in his course, as unaware of his popularity as he had been of the reverse; and I am sure he was startled one day when he found his advice so highly esteemed as to make some counsel which he had given in jest to be taken in sober, serious earnest.

It was on this subject: An old lady had an Alderney cow, which she looked upon as a daughter. You could not pay the short quarter of an hour call without being told of the wonderful milk or wonderful intelligence of this animal. The whole town knew and kindly regarded Miss Betsy Barker's Alderney; therefore great was the sympathy and regret when, in an unguarded moment, the poor cow tumbled into a lime-pit.[3] She moaned so loudly that she was soon heard and rescued; but meanwhile the poor beast had lost most of her hair, and came out looking naked, cold, and miserable, in a bare skin. Everybody pitied the animal, though a few could not restrain their smiles at her droll appearance. Miss Betsy Barker absolutely cried with sorrow and dismay; and it was said she thought of trying a bath of oil. This remedy, perhaps, was recommended by some one of the number whose advice she asked; but the proposal, if ever it was made, was knocked on the head by Captain Brown's decided "Get her a flannel waistcoat and flannel drawers, ma'am, if you wish to keep her alive. But my advice is, kill the poor creature at once."

Miss Betsy Barker dried her eyes, and thanked the Captain heartily; she set to work, and by and by all the town turned out to see the Alderney meekly going to her pasture, clad in dark gray flannel. I have watched her myself many a time. Do you ever see cows dressed in gray flannel in London?

Captain Brown had taken a small house on the outskirts of the town, where he lived with his two daughters. He must have been upwards of sixty at the time of the first visit I paid to Cranford after I had left it as a residence. But he had a wiry, well-trained, elastic figure, a stiff military throw-back of his head, and a springing step, which made him appear much younger than he was. His eldest daughter looked almost as old as himself, and betrayed the fact that his real was more than his apparent age. Miss Brown must have been forty; she had a sickly, pained, careworn expression on her face, and looked as if the gaiety of youth had long faded out of sight. Even when young she must have been plain and hard-featured. Miss Jessie Brown was ten years younger than her sister, and twenty shades prettier. Her face was round and dimpled. Miss Jenkyns once said, in a passion against Captain Brown (the cause of which I will tell you presently), "that she thought it was time for Miss Jessie to leave off her dimples, and not always to be trying to look like a child." It was true there was something childlike in her face; and there will be, I think, till she dies, though she should live to a hundred. Her eyes were large blue wondering eyes, looking straight at you; her nose was unformed and snub, and her lips were red and dewy; she wore her hair, too, in little rows of curls, which heightened this appearance. I do not know whether she was pretty or not; but I liked her face, and so did everybody, and I do not think she could help her dimples. She had something of her father's jauntiness of gait and manner; and any female observer might detect a slight difference in the attire of the two sisters—that of Miss Jessie being about two pounds per annum more expensive than Miss

3. A pit filled with lime, for disposing of waste.

Brown's. Two pounds was a large sum in Captain Brown's annual disbursements.

Such was the impression made upon me by the Brown family when I first saw them all together in Cranford Church. The Captain I had met before—on the occasion of the smoky chimney, which he had cured by some simple alteration in the flue. In church, he held his double eye-glass[4] to his eyes during the Morning Hymn, and then lifted up his head erect and sang out loud and joyfully. He made the responses louder than the clerk—an old man with a piping feeble voice, who, I think, felt aggrieved at the Captain's sonorous bass, and quavered higher and higher in consequence.

On coming out of church, the brisk Captain paid the most gallant attention to his two daughters. He nodded and smiled to his acquaintances, but he shook hands with none until he had helped Miss Brown to unfurl her umbrella, had relieved her of her prayer-book, and had waited patiently till she, with trembling nervous hands, had taken up her gown to walk through the wet roads.

I wondered what the Cranford ladies did with Captain Brown at their parties. We had often rejoiced, in former days, that there was no gentleman to be attended to, and to find conversation for, at the card-parties. We had congratulated ourselves upon the snugness of the evenings; and, in our love for gentility, and distaste of mankind, we had almost persuaded ourselves that to be a man was to be "vulgar"; so that when I found my friend and hostess, Miss Jenkyns, was going to have a party in my honor, and that Captain and the Miss Browns were invited, I wondered much what would be the course of the evening. Card-tables, with green baize tops, were set out by daylight, just as usual; it was the third week in November, so the evenings closed in about four. Candles, and clean packs of cards, were arranged on each table. The fire was made up; the neat maid-servant had received her last directions; and there we stood, dressed in our best, each with a candle-lighter in our hands, ready to dart at the candles as soon as the first knock came. Parties in Cranford were solemn festivities, making the ladies feel gravely elated as they sat together in their best dresses. As soon as three had arrived, we sat down to "Preference,"[5] I being the unlucky fourth. The next four comers were put down immediately to another table; and presently the tea-trays, which I had seen set out in the store-room as I passed in the morning, were placed each on the middle of a card-table. The china was delicate eggshell; the old-fashioned silver glittered with polishing; but the eatables were of the slightest description. While the trays were yet on the tables, Captain and the Miss Browns came in: and I could see that, somehow or other, the Captain was a favorite with all the ladies present. Ruffled brows were smoothed, sharp voices lowered at his approach. Miss Brown looked ill, and depressed almost to gloom. Miss Jessie smiled as usual, and seemed nearly as popular as her father. He immediately and quietly assumed the man's place in the room; attended to every one's wants, lessened the pretty maid-servant's labor by waiting on empty cups and bread-and-butterless ladies; and yet did it all in so easy and dignified a manner, and so much as if it were a matter of course for the strong to attend to the weak, that he was a true man throughout. He played for threepenny points with as grave an interest as if they had been pounds; and yet, in all his attention to strangers,

4. An early form of spectacles. 5. A card game.

he had an eye on his suffering daughter—for suffering I was sure she was, though to many eyes she might only appear to be irritable. Miss Jessie could not play cards: but she talked to the sitters-out, who, before her coming, had been rather inclined to be cross. She sang, too, to an old cracked piano, which I think had been a spinet in its youth. Miss Jessie sang *Jock of Hazeldean* a little out of tune; but we were none of us musical, though Miss Jenkyns beat time, out of time, by way of appearing to be so.

It was very good of Miss Jenkyns to do this; for I had seen that, a little before, she had been a good deal annoyed by Miss Jessie Brown's unguarded admission (apropos of Shetland wool) that she had an uncle, her mother's brother, who was a shopkeeper in Edinburgh. Miss Jenkyns tried to drown this confession by a terrible cough—for the Honorable Mrs. Jamieson was sitting at the card-table nearest Miss Jessie, and what would she say or think if she found out she was in the same room with a shopkeeper's niece! But Miss Jessie Brown (who had no tact, as we all agreed the next morning) *would* repeat the information, and assure Miss Pole she could easily get her the identical Shetland wool required, "through my uncle, who has the best assortment of Shetland goods of any one in Edinbro'." It was to take the taste of this out of our mouths, and the sound of this out of our ears, that Miss Jenkyns proposed music; so I say again, it was very good of her to beat time to the song.

When the trays reappeared with biscuits and wine, punctually at a quarter to nine, there was conversation, comparing of cards, and talking over tricks; but by and by Captain Brown sported a bit of literature.

"Have you seen any numbers of *The Pickwick Papers*?"[6] said he. (They were then publishing in parts.) "Capital thing!"

Now Miss Jenkyns was daughter of a deceased rector of Cranford; and, on the strength of a number of manuscript sermons, and a pretty good library of divinity, considered herself literary, and looked upon any conversation about books as a challenge to her. So she answered and said, "Yes, she had seen them; indeed, she might say she had read them."

"And what do you think of them?" exclaimed Captain Brown. "Aren't they famously good?"

So urged Miss Jenkyns could not but speak.

"I must say, I don't think they are by any means equal to Dr. Johnson.[7] Still, perhaps, the author is young. Let him persevere, and who knows what he may become if he will take the great Doctor for his model?" This was evidently too much for Captain Brown to take placidly; and I saw the words on the tip of his tongue before Miss Jenkyns had finished her sentence.

"It is quite a different sort of thing, my dear madam," he began.

"I am quite aware of that," returned she. "And I make allowances, Captain Brown."

"Just allow me to read you a scene out of this month's number," pleaded he. "I had it only this morning, and I don't think the company can have read it yet."

"As you please," said she, settling herself with an air of resignation. He read the account of the "swarry" which Sam Weller gave at Bath.[8] Some of us

6. *The Posthumous Papers of the Pickwick Club*, a comic novel by Charles Dickens, originally published in serial form in 1835–37.
7. Samuel Johnson (1709–1784), British poet, critic, and essayist, upholder of high moral standards in literature.
8. A popular British resort. "Swarry": anglicization of the French *scirée*, an elegant evening party. Sam Weller is a comic manservant in *The Pickwick Papers*.

laughed heartily. I did not dare, because I was staying in the house. Miss Jenkyns sat in patient gravity. When it was ended, she turned to me, and said with mild dignity:

"Fetch me *Rasselas*,[9] my dear, out of the book-room."

When I had brought it to her, she turned to Captain Brown.

"Now allow *me* to read you a scene, and then the present company can judge between your favorite, Mr. Boz,[1] and Dr. Johnson."

She read one of the conversations between Rasselas and Imlac, in a high-pitched, majestic voice: and when she had ended, she said: "I imagine I am now justified in my preference of Dr. Johnson as a writer of fiction." The Captain screwed his lips up, and drummed on the table, but he did not speak. She thought she would give him a finishing blow or two.

"I consider it vulgar, and below the dignity of literature, to publish in numbers."

"How was the *Rambler*[2] published, ma'am?" asked Captain Brown in a low voice, which I think Miss Jenkyns could not have heard.

"Dr. Johnson's style is a model for young beginners. My father recommended it to me when I began to write letters—I have formed my own style upon it; I recommend it to your favorite."

"I should be very sorry for him to exchange his style for any such pompous writing," said Captain Brown.

Miss Jenkyns felt this as a personal affront, in a way of which the Captain had not dreamed. Epistolary writing she and her friends considered as her *forte*. Many a copy of many a letter have I seen written and corrected on the slate, before she "seized the half-hour just previous to post-time to assure" her friends of this or of that; and Dr. Johnson was, as she said, her model in these compositions. She drew herself up with dignity, and only replied to Captain Brown's last remark by saying, with marked emphasis on every syllable: "I prefer Dr. Johnson to Mr. Boz."

It is said—I won't vouch for the fact—that Captain Brown was heard to say, *sotto voce*,[3] "D——n Dr. Johnson!" If he did, he was penitent afterwards, as he showed by going to stand near Miss Jenkyns's arm-chair, and endeavoring to beguile her into conversation on some more pleasing subject. But she was inexorable. The next day she made the remark I have mentioned about Miss Jessie's dimples.

Chapter II. The Captain

It was impossible to live a month at Cranford and not know the daily habits of each resident; and long before my visit was ended I knew much concerning the whole Brown trio. There was nothing new to be discovered respecting their poverty; for they had spoken simply and openly about that from the very first. They made no mystery of the necessity for their being economical. All that remained to be discovered was the Captain's infinite kindness of heart, and the various modes in which, unconsciously to himself, he manifested it. Some little anecdotes were talked about for some time after they occurred. As we did not read much, and as all the ladies were pretty well suited with servants, there

9. Johnson's didactic romance *The History of Rasselas, Prince of Abissinia* (1759), in which characters engage in protracted moral debates.
1. Dickens's pseudonym in his early work.

2. A weekly paper put out by Johnson, consisting chiefly of his essays.
3. Under his breath (Italian).

was a dearth of subjects for conversation. We therefore discussed the circumstance of the Captain taking a poor old woman's dinner out of her hands one very slippery Sunday. He had met her returning from the bakehouse as he came from church, and noticed her precarious footing; and, with the grave dignity with which he did everything, he relieved her of her burden, and steered along the street by her side, carrying her baked mutton and potatoes safely home. This was thought very eccentric; and it was rather expected that he would pay a round of calls on the Monday morning, to explain and apologize to the Cranford sense of propriety: but he did no such thing: and then it was decided that he was ashamed, and was keeping out of sight. In a kindly pity for him, we began to say: "After all, the Sunday morning's occurrence showed great goodness of heart," and it was resolved that he should be comforted on his next appearance amongst us; but, lo! he came down upon us, untouched by any sense of shame, speaking loud and bass as ever, his head thrown back, his wig as jaunty and well-curled as usual, and we were obliged to conclude he had forgotten all about Sunday.

Miss Pole and Miss Jessie Brown had set up a kind of intimacy on the strength of the Shetland wool and the new knitting stitches; so it happened that when I went to visit Miss Pole I saw more of the Browns than I had done while staying with Miss Jenkyns, who had never got over what she called Captain Brown's disparaging remarks upon Dr. Johnson as a writer of light and agreeable fiction. I found that Miss Brown was seriously ill of some lingering, incurable complaint, the pain occasioned by which gave the uneasy expression to her face that I had taken for unmitigated crossness. Cross, too, she was at times, when the nervous irritability occasioned by her disease became past endurance. Miss Jessie bore with her at these times, even more patiently than she did with the bitter self-upbraidings by which they were invariably succeeded. Miss Brown used to accuse herself, not merely of hasty and irritable temper, but also of being the cause why her father and sister were obliged to pinch, in order to allow her the small luxuries which were necessaries in her condition. She would so fain have made sacrifices for them, and have lightened their cares, that the original generosity of her disposition added acerbity to her temper. All this was borne by Miss Jessie and her father with more than placidity—with absolute tenderness. I forgave Miss Jessie her singing out of tune, and her juvenility of dress, when I saw her at home. I came to perceive that Captain Brown's dark Brutus wig[4] and padded coat (alas! too often threadbare) were remnants of the military smartness of his youth, which he now wore unconsciously. He was a man of infinite resources, gained in his barrack experience. As he confessed, no one could black his boots to please him except himself; but, indeed, he was not above saving the little maid-servant's labors in every way—knowing, most likely, that his daughter's illness made the place a hard one.

He endeavored to make peace with Miss Jenkyns soon after the memorable dispute I have named, by a present of a wooden fire-shovel (his own making), having heard her say how much the grating of an iron one annoyed her. She received the present with cool gratitude, and thanked him formally. When he was gone, she bade me put it away in the lumber-room; feeling, probably, that

4. A wig arranged in the pseudo-Roman style and favored during the Regency period. Marcus Jurius Brutus (85?–42 B.C.) was a Roman general.

no present from a man who preferred Mr. Boz to Dr. Johnson could be less jar-
ring than an iron fire-shovel.

Such was the state of things when I left Cranford and went to Drumble. I
had, however, several correspondents, who kept me *au fait*[5] as to the proceed-
ings of the dear little town. There was Miss Pole, who was becoming as much
absorbed in crochet as she had been once in knitting, and the burden of whose
letter was something like: "But don't you forget the white worsted at Flint's"
of the old song; for at the end of every sentence of news came a fresh direction
as to some crochet commission which I was to execute for her. Miss Matilda
Jenkyns (who did not mind being called Miss Matty, when Miss Jenkyns was
not by) wrote nice, kind, rambling letters, now and then venturing into an
opinion of her own; but suddenly pulling herself up, and either begging me
not to name what she had said, as Deborah thought differently, and *she* knew,
or else putting in a postscript to the effect that, since writing the above, she
had been talking over the subject with Deborah, and was quite convinced
that, etc.—(here probably followed a recantation of every opinion she had
given in the letter). Then came Miss Jenkyns—*Deborah* as she liked Miss
Matty to call her, her father having once said that the Hebrew name ought to
be so pronounced. I secretly think she took the Hebrew prophetess for a model
in character; and, indeed, she was not unlike the stern prophetess in some
ways, making allowance, of course, for modern customs and difference in
dress. Miss Jenkyns wore a cravat, and a little bonnet like a jockey-cap, and al-
together had the appearance of a strong-minded woman; although she would
have despised the modern idea of women being equal to men. Equal, indeed!
she knew they were superior. But to return to her letters. Everything in them
was stately and grand like herself. I have been looking them over (dear Miss
Jenkyns, how I honoured her!) and I will give an extract, more especially be-
cause it relates to our friend Captain Brown:

"The honorable Mrs. Jamieson has only just quitted me; and, in the course
of conversation, she communicated to me the intelligence that she had yes-
terday received a call from her revered husband's quondam[6] friend, Lord
Mauleverer. You will not easily conjecture what brought his lordship within
the precincts of our little town. It was to see Captain Brown, with whom, it
appears, his lordship was acquainted in the plumed wars,[7] and who had the
privilege of averting destruction from his lordship's head when some great
peril was impending over it, off the misnomered Cape of Good Hope. You
know our friend the Honorable Mrs. Jamieson's deficiency in the spirit of in-
nocent curiosity, and you will therefore not be so much surprised when I tell
you she was quite unable to disclose to me the exact nature of the peril in
question. I was anxious, I confess, to ascertain in what manner Captain
Brown, with his limited establishment, could receive so distinguished a guest;
and I discovered that his lordship retired to rest, and, let us hope, to refreshing
slumbers, at the Angel Hotel; but shared the Brunonian[8] meals during the two
days that he honored Cranford with his august presence. Mrs. Johnson, our
civil butcher's wife, informs me that Miss Jessie purchased a leg of lamb; but,
besides this, I can hear of no preparation whatever to give a suitable reception
to so distinguished a visitor. Perhaps they entertained him with the feast of

5. At the fact (French, literal trans.); informed. 7. Wars against France under Napoleon.
6. Former. 8. Latinate adjectival form of "Brown."

reason and the flow of soul, and to us, who are acquainted with Captain Brown's sad want[9] of relish for the pure wells of English undefiled, it may be matter for congratulation that he has had the opportunity of improving his taste by holding converse with an elegant and refined member of the British aristocracy. But from some mundane failings who is altogether free?"

Miss Pole and Miss Matty wrote to me by the same post. Such a piece of news as Lord Mauleverer's visit was not to be lost on the Cranford letter-writers: they made the most of it. Miss Matty humbly apologized for writing at the same time as her sister, who was so much more capable than she to describe the honor done to Cranford, but in spite of a little bad spelling, Miss Matty's account gave me the best idea of the commotion occasioned by his lordship's visit, after it had occurred; for, except the people at the "Angel," the Browns, Mrs. Jamieson, and a little lad his lordship had sworn at for driving a dirty hoop against the aristocratic legs, I could not hear of any one with whom his lordship had held conversation.

My next visit to Cranford was in the summer. There had been neither births, deaths, nor marriages since I was there last. Everybody lived in the same house, and wore pretty nearly the same well-preserved, old-fashioned clothes. The greatest event was, that Miss Jenkyns had purchased a new carpet for the drawing-room. Oh, the busy work Miss Matty and I had in chasing the sunbeams, as they fell in an afternoon right down on this carpet through the blindless window! We spread newspapers over the places and sat down to our book or our work; and, lo! in a quarter of an hour the sun had moved, and was blazing away on a fresh spot; and down again we went on our knees to alter the position of the newspapers. We were very busy, too, one whole morning, before Miss Jenkyns gave her party, in following her directions, and in cutting out and stitching together pieces of newspaper so as to form little paths to every chair set for the expected visitors, lest their shoes might dirty or defile the purity of the carpet. Do you make paper paths for every guest to walk upon in London?

Captain Brown and Miss Jenkyns were not very cordial to each other. The literary dispute, of which I had seen the beginning, was a "raw,"[1] the slightest touch on which made them wince. It was the only difference of opinion they had ever had; but that difference was enough. Miss Jenkyns could not refrain from talking at Captain Brown; and, though he did not reply, he drummed with his fingers, which action she felt and resented as very disparaging to Dr. Johnson. He was rather ostentatious in his preference of the writings of Mr. Boz; would walk through the streets so absorbed in them that he all but ran against Miss Jenkyns; and though his apologies were earnest and sincere, and though he did not, in fact, do more than startle her and himself, she owned to me she had rather he had knocked her down, if he had only been reading a higher style of literature. The poor, brave Captain! he looked older, and more worn, and his clothes were very threadbare. But he seemed as bright and cheerful as ever, unless he was asked about his daughter's health.

"She suffers a great deal, and she must suffer more: we do what we can to alleviate her pain—God's will be done!" He took off his hat at these last words. I found, from Miss Matty, that everything had been done, in fact. A medical man, of high repute in that country neighborhood, had been sent for, and

9. Lack. 1. Sore spot.

every injunction he had given was attended to, regardless of expense. Miss Matty was sure they denied themselves many things in order to make the invalid comfortable; but they never spoke about it; and as for Miss Jessie!—"I really think she's an angel," said poor Miss Matty, quite overcome. "To see her way of bearing with Miss Brown's crossness, and the bright face she puts on after she's been sitting up a whole night and scolded above half of it, is quite beautiful. Yet she looks as neat and as ready to welcome the Captain at breakfast-time as if she had been asleep in the Queen's bed all night. My dear! you could never laugh at her prim little curls or her pink bows again if you saw her as I have done." I could only feel very penitent, and greet Miss Jessie with double respect when I met her next. She looked faded and pinched; and her lips began to quiver, as if she was very weak, when she spoke of her sister. But she brightened, and sent back the tears that were glittering in her pretty eyes, as she said:

"But, to be sure, what a town Cranford is for kindness! I don't suppose any one has a better dinner than usual cooked but the best part of all comes in a little covered basin for my sister. The poor people will leave their earliest vegetables at our door for her. They speak short and gruff, as if they were ashamed of it: but I am sure it often goes to my heart to see their thoughtfulness." The tears now came back and overflowed; but after a minute or two she began to scold herself, and ended by going away the same cheerful Miss Jessie as ever.

"But why does not this Lord Mauleverer do something for the man who saved his life?" said I.

"Why, you see, unless Captain Brown has some reason for it, he never speaks about being poor; and he walked along by his lordship looking as happy and cheerful as a prince; and as they never called attention to their dinners by apologies, and as Miss Brown was better that day, and all seemed bright, I dare say his lordship never knew how much care there was in the background. He did send game in the winter pretty often, but now he is gone abroad."

I had often occasion to notice the use that was made of fragments and small opportunities in Cranford; the rose-leaves that were gathered ere they fell to make into a pot-pourri for someone who had no garden; the little bundles of lavender flowers sent to strew the drawers of some town-dweller, or to burn in the chamber of some invalid. Things that many would despise, and actions which it seemed scarcely worth while to perform, were all attended to in Cranford. Miss Jenkyns stuck an apple full of cloves, to be heated and smell pleasantly in Miss Brown's room; and as she put in each clove she uttered a Johnsonian sentence. Indeed, she never could think of the Browns without talking Johnson; and, as they were seldom absent from her thoughts just then, I heard many a rolling, three-piled sentence.[2]

Captain Brown called one day to thank Miss Jenkyns for many little kindnesses, which I did not know until then that she had rendered. He had suddenly become like an old man; his deep bass voice had a quavering in it, his eyes looked dim, and the lines on his face were deep. He did not—could not—speak cheerfully of his daughter's state, but he talked with manly, pious resignation, and not much. Twice over he said: "What Jessie has been to us, God only knows!" and after the second time, he got up hastily, shook hands all round without speaking, and left the room.

2. Johnson was famous for his long, periodic sentences. "Three-piled" refers to the number of clauses.

That afternoon we perceived little groups in the street, all listening with faces aghast to some tale or other. Miss Jenkyns wondered what could be the matter for some time before she took the undignified step of sending Jenny out to inquire.

Jenny came back with a white face of terror. "Oh, ma'am! Oh, Miss Jenkyns, ma'am! Captain Brown is killed by them nasty cruel railroads!" and she burst into tears. She, along with many others, had experienced the poor Captain's kindness.

"How?—where—where? Good God! Jenny, don't waste time in crying, but tell us something." Miss Matty rushed out into the street at once, and collared the man who was telling the tale.

"Come in—come to my sister at once. Miss Jenkyns, the rector's daughter. Oh, man, man! say it is not true." she cried, as she brought the affrighted carter, sleeking down his hair, into the drawing-room, where he stood with his wet boots on the new carpet, and no one regarded it.

"Please, mum, it is true. I seed it myself," and he shuddered at the recollection. "The Captain was a-reading some new book as he was deep in, a-waiting for the down train; and there was a little lass as wanted to come to its mammy, and gave its sister the slip, and came toddling across the line. And he looked up sudden, at the sound of the train coming, and seed the child, and he darted on the line and cotched it up, and his foot slipped, and the train came over him in no time. O Lord, Lord! Mum, it's quite true, and they've come over to tell his daughters. The child's safe, though, with only a bang on its shoulder as he threw it to its mammy. Poor Captain would be glad of that, mum, wouldn't he? God bless him." The great rough carter puckered up his manly face, and turned away to hide his tears. I turned to Miss Jenkyns. She looked very ill, as if she were going to faint, and signed to me to open the window.

"Matilda, bring me my bonnet. I must go to those girls. God pardon me, if ever I have spoken contemptuously to the Captain!"

Miss Jenkyns arrayed herself to go out, telling Miss Matilda to give the man a glass of wine. While she was away, Miss Matty and I huddled over the fire, talking in a low and awestruck voice. I know we cried quietly all the time.

Miss Jenkyns came home in a silent mood, and we durst not ask her many questions. She told us that Miss Jessie had fainted, and that she and Miss Pole had had some difficulty in bringing her round; but that, as soon as she recovered, she begged one of them to go and sit with her sister.

"Mr. Hoggins says she cannot live many days, and she shall be spared this shock," said Miss Jessie, shivering with feelings to which she dared not give way.

"But how can you manage, my dear?" asked Miss Jenkyns; "you cannot bear up, she must see your tears."

"God will help me—I will not give way—she was asleep when the news came; she may be asleep yet. She would be so utterly miserable, not merely at my father's death, but to think of what would become of me; she is so good to me." She looked up earnestly in their faces with her soft true eyes, and Miss Pole told Miss Jenkyns afterwards she could hardly bear it, knowing, as she did, how Miss Brown treated her sister.

However, it was settled according to Miss Jessie's wish. Miss Brown was to be told her father had been summoned to take a short journey on railway business. They had managed it in some way—Miss Jenkyns could not exactly say

how. Miss Pole was to stop with Miss Jessie. Mrs. Jamieson had sent to inquire. And this was all we heard that night; and a sorrowful night it was. The next day a full account of the fatal accident was in the county paper which Miss Jenkyns took in. Her eyes were very weak, she said, and she asked me to read it. When I came to the "gallant gentleman was deeply engaged in the perusal of a number of *Pickwick*, which he had just received," Miss Jenkyns shook her head long and solemnly, and then sighed out: "Poor, dear, infatuated man!"

The corpse was to be taken from the station to the parish church, there to be interred. Miss Jessie had set her heart on following it to the grave; and no dissuasives could alter her resolve. Her restraint upon herself made her almost obstinate; she resisted all Miss Pole's entreaties and Miss Jenkyns's advice. At last Miss Jenkyns gave up the point; and after a silence, which I feared portended some deep displeasure against Miss Jessie, Miss Jenkyns said she should accompany the latter to the funeral.

"It is not fit for you to go alone. It would be against both propriety and humanity were I to allow it."

Miss Jessie seemed as if she did not half like this arrangement; but her obstinacy, if she had any, had been exhausted in her determination to go to the interment. She longed, poor thing, I have no doubt, to cry alone over the grave of the dear father to whom she had been all in all, and to give way, for one little half-hour, uninterrupted by sympathy and unobserved by friendship. But it was not to be. That afternoon Miss Jenkyns sent out for a yard of black crape, and employed herself busily in trimming the little black silk bonnet I have spoken about. When it was finished she put it on, and looked at us for approbation—admiration she despised. I was full of sorrow, but, by one of those whimsical thoughts which come unbidden into our heads, in times of deepest grief, I no sooner saw the bonnet than I was reminded of a helmet; and in that hybrid bonnet, half helmet, half jockey-cap, did Miss Jenkyns attend Captain Brown's funeral, and, I believe, supported Miss Jessie with a tender, indulgent firmness which was invaluable, allowing her to weep her passionate fill before they left.

Miss Pole, Miss Matty, and I, meanwhile attended to Miss Brown: and hard work we found it to relieve her querulous and never-ending complaints. But if we were so weary and dispirited, what must Miss Jessie have been! Yet she came back almost calm, as if she had gained a new strength. She put off her mourning dress, and came in, looking pale and gentle, thanking us each with a soft long pressure of the hand. She could even smile—a faint, sweet, wintry smile—as if to reassure us of her power to endure; but her look made our eyes fill suddenly with tears, more than if she had cried outright.

It was settled that Miss Pole was to remain with her all the watching live-long night; and that Miss Matty and I were to return in the morning to relieve them, and give Miss Jessie the opportunity for a few hours of sleep. But when the morning came, Miss Jenkyns appeared at the breakfast-table, equipped in her helmet-bonnet, and ordered Miss Matty to stay at home, as she meant to go and help to nurse. She was evidently in a state of great friendly excitement, which she showed by eating her breakfast standing, and scolding the household all round.

No nursing—no energetic strong-minded woman could help Miss Brown now. There was that in the room as we entered which was stronger than us all, and made us shrink into solemn awestruck helplessness. Miss Brown was

dying. We hardly knew her voice, it was so devoid of the complaining tone we had always associated with it. Miss Jessie told me afterwards that it, and her face too, were just what they had been formerly, when her mother's death left her the young anxious head of the family, of whom only Miss Jessie survived.

She was conscious of her sister's presence, though not, I think, of ours. We stood a little behind the curtain: Miss Jessie knelt with her face near her sister's, in order to catch the last soft awful whispers.

"Oh, Jessie! Jessie! How selfish I have been! God forgive me for letting you sacrifice yourself for me as you did! I have so loved you—and yet, I have thought only of myself. God forgive me!"

"Hush, love! hush!" said Miss Jessie, sobbing.

"And my father, my dear, dear father! I will not complain now, if God will give me strength to be patient. But, oh, Jessie! tell my father how I longed and yearned to see him at last, and to ask his forgiveness. He can never know now how I loved him—oh! if I might but tell him, before I die. What a life of sorrow his has been, and I have done so little to cheer him!"

A light came into Miss Jessie's face. "Would it comfort you, dearest, to think that he does know?—would it comfort you, love, to know that his cares, his sorrows"—Her voice quivered, but she steadied it into calmness—"Mary! he has gone before you to the place where the weary are at rest. He knows now how you loved him."

A strange look, which was not distress, came over Miss Brown's face. She did not speak for some time, but then we saw her lips form the words, rather than heard the sound—"Father, mother. Harry, Archy'—then, as if it were a new idea throwing a filmy shadow over her darkened mind—"But you will be alone, Jessie!"

Miss Jessie had been feeling this all during the silence, I think; for the tears rolled down her cheeks like rain, at these words, and she could not answer at first. Then she put her hands together tight, and lifted them up, and said—but not to us—"Though He slay me, yet will I trust in Him."[3]

In a few moments more Miss Brown lay calm and still—never to sorrow or murmur more.

After this second funeral, Miss Jenkyns insisted that Miss Jessie should come to stay with her rather than go back to the desolate house, which, in fact, we learned from Miss Jessie, must now be given up, as she had not wherewithal to maintain it. She had something above twenty pounds a year, besides the interest of the money for which the furniture would sell; but she could not live upon that: and so we talked over her qualifications for earning money.

"I can sew neatly," said she, "and I like nursing. I think, too, I could manage a house, if any one would try me as housekeeper; or I would go into a shop as saleswoman, if they would have patience with me at first."

Miss Jenkyns declared, in an angry voice, that she should do no such thing; and talked to herself about "some people having no idea of their rank as a captain's daughter," nearly an hour afterwards, when she brought Miss Jessie up a basin of delicately-made arrowroot, and stood over her like a dragoon[4] until the last spoonful was finished: then she disappeared. Miss Jessie began to tell me some more of the plans which had suggested themselves to her, and insen-

3. Job 13:15.
4. A mounted infantryman. "Arrowroot": a kind of starchy pudding.

sibly fell into talking of the days that were past and gone, and interested me so much I neither knew nor heeded how time passed. We were both startled when Miss Jenkyns reappeared, and caught us crying. I was afraid lest she would be displeased, as she often said that crying hindered digestion, and I knew she wanted Miss Jessie to get strong; but, instead, she looked queer and excited, and fidgeted round us without saying anything. At last she spoke.

"I have been so much startled—no, I've not been at all startled—don't mind me, my dear Miss Jessie—I've been very much surprised —in fact, I've had a caller, whom you knew once, my dear Miss Jessie"—

Miss Jessie went very white, then flushed scarlet, and looked eagerly at Miss Jenkyns.

"A gentleman, my dear, who wants to know if you would see him."

"Is it?—it is not"—stammered out Miss Jessie—and got no farther.

"This is his card," said Miss Jenkyns, giving it to Miss Jessie; and while her head was bent over it, Miss Jenkyns went through a series of winks and odd faces to me, and formed her lips into a long sentence, of which, of course, I could not understand a word.

"May he come up?" asked Miss Jenkyns at last.

"Oh, yes! certainly!" said Miss Jessie, as much as to say, this is your house, you may show any visitor where you like. She took up some knitting of Miss Matty's and began to be very busy, though I could see how she trembled all over.

Miss Jenkyns rang the bell, and told the servant who answered it to show Major Gordon upstairs; and, presently, in walked a tall, fine, frank-looking man of forty or upwards. He shook hands with Miss Jessie; but he could not see her eyes, she kept them so fixed on the ground. Miss Jenkyns asked me if I would come and help her to tie up the preserves in the store-room; and though Miss Jessie plucked at my gown, and even looked up at me with begging eye, I durst not refuse to go where Miss Jenkyns asked. Instead of tying up preserves in the store-room, however, we went to talk in the dining-room; and there Miss Jenkyns told me what Major Gordon had told her; how he had served in the same regiment with Captain Brown, and had become acquainted with Miss Jessie, then a sweet-looking, blooming girl of eighteen; how the acquaintance had grown into love on his part, though it had been some years before he had spoken; how, on becoming possessed, through the will of an uncle, of a good estate in Scotland, he had offered and been refused, though with so much agitation and evident distress that he was sure she was not indifferent to him; and how he had discovered that the obstacle was the fell disease which was, even then, too surely threatening her sister. She had mentioned that the surgeons foretold intense suffering; and there was no one but herself to nurse her poor Mary, or cheer and comfort her father during the time of illness. They had had long discussions; and on her refusal to pledge herself to him as his wife when all should be over, he had grown angry, and broken off entirely, and gone abroad, believing that she was a cold-hearted person whom he would do well to forget. He had been traveling in the East, and was on his return home when, at Rome, he saw the account of Captain Brown's death in *Galignani*.[5]

Just then Miss Matty, who had been out all the morning, and had only lately returned to the house, burst in with a face of dismay and outraged propriety.

5. A Roman newspaper.

"Oh, goodness me!" she said. "Deborah, there's a gentleman sitting in the drawing-room with his arm round Miss Jessie's waist!" Miss Matty's eyes looked large with terror.

Miss Jenkyns snubbed her down in an instant.

"The most proper place in the world for his arm to be in. Go away, Matilda, and mind your own business." This from her sister, who had hitherto been a model of feminine decorum, was a blow for poor Miss Matty, and with a double shock she left the room.

The last time I ever saw poor Miss Jenkyns was many years after this. Mrs. Gordon had kept up a warm and affectionate intercourse with all at Cranford. Miss Jenkyns, Miss Matty, and Miss Pole had all been to visit her, and returned with wonderful accounts of her house, her husband, her dress, and her looks. For, with happiness, something of her early bloom returned; she had been a year or two younger than we had taken her for. Her eyes were always lovely, and, as Mrs. Gordon, her dimples were not out of place. At the time to which I have referred, when I last saw Miss Jenkyns, that lady was old and feeble, and had lost something of her strong mind. Little Flora Gordon was staying with the Misses Jenkyns, and when I came in she was reading aloud to Miss Jenkyns, who lay feeble and changed on the sofa. Flora put down the *Rambler* when I came in

"Ah!" said Miss Jenkyns, "you find me changed, my dear. I can't see as I used to do. If Flora were not here to read to me, I hardly know how I should get through the day. Did you ever read the *Rambler*? It's a wonderful book—wonderful! and the most improving reading for Flora" (which I dare say it would have been, if she could have read half the words without spelling, and could have understood the meaning of a third), "better than that strange old book, with the queer name, poor Captain Brown was killed for reading—that book by Mr. Boz, you know—Old Poz; when I was a girl—but that's a long time ago—I acted Lucy in Old Poz " She babbled on long enough for Flora to get a good long spell at the *Christmas Carol*,[6] which Miss Matty had left on the table.

<div style="text-align:right">1851, 1853</div>

6. Charles Dickens's *A Christmas Carol* (1843).

FANNY FERN (SARA WILLIS PARTON)

1811–1872

A leading columnist, journalist, novelist, and activist, Sara Willis Parton was born in Maine, married twice, widowed, divorced, and was the mother of three by the time she published her first collection of essays. Originally written for Boston newspapers under the pseudonym "Fanny Fern," *Fern Leaves from Fanny's Portfolio* (1853) became an instant best-seller and was followed by several other equally successful books, whose popularity earned their author a prominent position as a regular weekly columnist for the New York *Ledger.* Married for a third time—to James Parton, himself a well-known literary man—Fanny Fern settled in New York City, where she wielded considerable influence as a commentator on current affairs, with a special interest in social inequities and women's issues.

Besides her celebrated columns, most of which were collected in such other volumes as *Fresh Leaves* (1857), *Ginger Snaps* (1870), and *Caper Sauce* (1872), Fern produced two novels, *Ruth Hall* (1855) and *Rose Clark* (1856). Her work was admired by Hawthorne (who praised *Ruth Hall*) and Whitman (who imitated the cover design of *Fern Leaves* in the first edition of his *Leaves of Grass*, 1855). Sometimes sentimental and melodramatic, as in *Hour-Glass Thoughts*, and sometimes satiric, as in *Mr. Pipkin's Ideas of Family Retrenchment*, she was always first and foremost an incisive observer of her culture's foibles and frailties. Moreover, although her "Fern Leaves" may occasionally appear misogynistic (as in *Lady Doctors*), she had an intense commitment to women's rights and even in so brief a sketch as *Mrs. Adolphus Smith Sporting the "Blue Stocking"* dramatized the obstacles confronting female intellectual ambition with comic verve.

Mrs. Adolphus Smith Sporting the "Blue Stocking"[1]

Well, I think I'll finish that story for the editor of the "Dutchman." Let me see; where did I leave off? The setting sun was just gilding with his last ray—"Ma, I want some bread and molasses"—(yes, dear,) gilding with his last ray the church spire—"Wife, where's my Sunday pants?" (*Under the bed, dear,*) the church spire of Inverness, when a—"There's nothing under the bed, dear, but your lace cap"—(Perhaps they are in the coal hod[2] in the closet,) when a horseman was seen approaching—"Ma'am, the *pertators* is out;[3] not one for dinner"—(Take some turnips,) approaching, covered with dust, and—"Wife! the baby has swallowed a button"—(*Reverse him*, dear—take him by the heels,) and waving in his hand a banner, on which was written—"Ma! I've torn my pantaloons"—liberty or death! The inhabitants rushed *en masse*—"Wife! *will* you leave off scribbling?" (Don't be disagreeable, Smith, I'm just getting inspired,) to the public square, where De Begnis, who had been secretly—"Butcher wants to see you, ma'am"—secretly informed of the traitors'—"Forgot *which* you said, ma'am, sausages or mutton chop"—movements, gave orders to fire; not less than twenty—"My gracious! Smith, you haven't been *reversing* that child all this time; he's as black as your coat; and that boy of *yours* has torn up the first sheet of my manuscript. There! it's no use for a married woman to cultivate her intellect.—Smith, hand me those twins."

1853

Hour-Glass Thoughts

The bride stands waiting at the altar; the corpse lies waiting for burial.

Love vainly implores of Death a reprieve; Despair vainly invokes his coming.

The starving wretch, who purloins a crust, trembles in the hall of Justice; liveried sin,[1] unpunished, riots in high places.

Brothers, clad "in purple and fine linen, fare sumptuously every day"; Sisters, in linsey-woolsey, toil in garrets and shrink, trembling, from insults[2] that no fraternal arm avenges.

1. Derisive term for an intellectual or literary woman (from an 18th-century literary society).
2. Coal scuttle (pail).
3. I.e., they are out of potatoes.

1. I.e., sin by those of rank, who have servants in the distinctive clothing of livery.
2. Sexual affronts. "Linsey-woolsey": coarse fabric of wool and flax, often woven at home.

The Village Squire sows, reaps and garners golden harvests; the Parish Clergyman sighs, as his[3] casting vote cuts down his already meager salary.

The unpaid sempstress be-gems with tears the fairy festal robe; proud beauty floats in it through the ballroom, like a thing of air.

Church spires point, with tapering fingers to the rich man's heaven; Penitence, in rags, tearful and altarless, meekly stays its timid foot at the threshold.

Sneaking Vice, wrapped in the labeled cloak of Piety, finds "open sesame"; shrinking Conscientiousness, jostled rudely aside, weeps in secret its fancied unworthiness.

The Editor grows plethoric[4] on the applause of the public and mammoth subscription lists; the unrecognized journalist, who, behind the scenes, mixes so deftly the newspaperial salad, lives on the smallest possible stipend, and looks like an undertaker's walking advertisement.

The Wife, pure, patient, loving, trustful, sits singing, by the evening fire, re-pairing, with the busy fingers of economy, the time-worn garment; the Husband, favored by darkness, seeks, with stealthy steps and costly gifts, the syren[5] of the hour, squandering hundreds to win a smile which is ever in the market for the highest bidder.

The polluted libertine, with foul lips, hackneyed heart, but polished man-ners, finds smiling welcome at the beauteous lips of Virtue; while, from the brow on which that libertine has ineffaceably written "Magdalen,"[6] "beau-teous Virtue" turns scornfully away.

Wives rant of their "Woman's Rights" in public; Husbands eat bad dinners and tend crying babies at home.

Mothers toil in kitchens; Daughters lounge in parlors.

Fathers drive the plow; Sons drive tandem.[7]

1853

Mr. Pipkin's Ideas of Family Retrenchment

Mrs. Pipkin, I am under the disagreeable necessity of informing you, that our family expenses are getting to be enormous. I see that carpet woman charged you a dollar for one day's work. Why, that is positively a man's wages;—such presumption is intolerable. Pity you did not make it yourself, Mrs. Pipkin; wives ought to lift their end of the yoke; that's my creed.

Little Tom Pipkin.—Papa, may I have this bit of paper on the floor? it is your tailor's bill—says, "$400 for your last year's clothes."

Mr. Pipkin.—Tom, go to bed, and learn never to interrupt your father when he is talking. Yes, as I was saying, Mrs. Pipkin, wives should hold up their end of the yoke; and it is high time there was a little retrenchment here; super-fluities must be dispensed with.

Bridget.—Please, sir, there are three baskets of champagne just come for you, and four boxes of cigars.

Mr. Pipkin.—Will you please lock that door, Mrs. Pipkin, till I can get a chance to say what I have to say to you on this subject. I was thinking today, that you might dispense with your nursery maid, and take care of baby your-

3. The squire's.
4. Swollen.
5. I.e., siren: a temptress.

6. "Fallen" woman.
7. I.e., drive a tandem—a two-seated carriage drawn by two horses.

self. He don't cry much, except nights; and since I've slept alone upstairs, I don't hear the little tempest at all. It is really quite a relief—that child's voice is a perfect ear-splitter.

I think I shall get you, too, to take charge of the marketing and providing, (on a stipulated allowance from me, of course,) it will give me so much more time to—attend to *business*, Mrs. Pipkin. I shall take my own dinners down town at the —— House. I hear Stevens is an excellent "caterer"; (though that's nothing to me, of course, as my only object in going is to meet business acquaintances from different parts of the Union, to drive a bargain, etc., etc.)

Well—it will cost you and the children little or nothing for your dinners. There's nothing so disgusting to a man of refinement, like myself, as to see a *woman* fond of eating; and as to children, any fool knows they ought not to be allowed to stuff their skins, like little anacondas.[1] Yes, our family expenses are enormous. My partner sighed like a pair of bellows at that last baby you had, Mrs. Pipkin; oh, it's quite ruinous—but I can't stop to talk now, I'm going to try a splendid horse which is offered me at a bargain—(too frisky for you to ride, my dear, but just the thing for me.)

You had better dismiss your nursery girl this afternoon; that will begin to look like retrenchment. Good-by; if I am not home till late, don't sit up for me, as I have ordered a supper at —— House for my old friend, Tom Hillar, of New Orleans. We'll drink this toast, my dear: "Here's hoping the last little Pipkin may never have his nose put out of joint."

 1853

Lady Doctors

And so the female doctors are prospering and getting practice. I am sure I am heartily glad of it, for several reasons; one of which is, that it is an honest and honorable deliverance from the everlasting, nonremunerating, consumptive-provoking,[1] monotonous needle. Another is, that it is a more excellent way of support, than by the mercenary and unretraceable road, through the church-door to the altar, into which so many nonreliant women are driven. Having said this, I feel at liberty to remark that we all have our little fancies, and one of mine is, that a hat is a pleasanter object of contemplation in a sick room than a bonnet. I think, too, that my wrist reposes more comfortably in a big hand than a little one, and if my mouth is to be inspected, I prefer submitting it to a beard than to a flounce. Still, this may be a narrow prejudice—I dare say it is—but like most of my prejudices, I am afraid no amount of fire will burn it out of me.

A female doctor! Great Esculapius![2] Before swallowing her pills (of which she would be the first), I should want to make sure that I had never come between her and a lover, or a new bonnet, or been the innocent recipient of a gracious smile from her husband. If I desired her undivided attention to my case, I should first remove the looking-glass, and if a consultation seemed advisable, I should wish to arm myself with a gridiron,[3] or a darning-needle, or some other appropriate weapon, before expressing such a wish. If my female doctor

1. Constrictors, snakes that swallow their prey whole. 2. Greco-Roman god of medicine.
1. Causing consumption (tuberculosis). 3. Grate for broiling food.

recommended a blister on my head, I should strongly doubt its necessity if my hair happened to be handsome, also the expediency of a scar-defacing plaster for my neck, if it happened to be plump and white. Still, these may be little prejudices; very like they are but this I will say before the breath is taken out of me by any female doctor, that while I am in my senses I will never exchange my gentlemanly, soft-voiced, soft-stepping, experienced, intelligent, handsome doctor, for all the female M. D.'s who ever carved up dead bodies or live characters—or tore each other's caps.

1853

Moral Molasses; or, Too Sweet by Half

The most thorough emetic[1] I know of, is in the shape of "Guide to Young Wives," and kindred books; as if one rule could. by any possibility, apply to all persons; as if every man living did not require different management (bless me, I did not intend to use that torpedo word,[2] but it is out now); as if, when things go wrong, a wife had only to fly upstairs. read a chapter in the "Young Wife's Guide," supposed to be suited to her complaint, and then go downstairs and apply the worthless plaster to the matrimonial sore. Pshaw! as well might a doctor send a peck of pills into a hospital, to be distributed by the hands of the nurse, to any and every male patient brought there, without regard to complaints or constitutional tendencies. I have no patience with such matrimonial nostrums.

"Always meet your husband with a smile." That is one of them. Suppose we put the boot on the other foot, and require the men to come grinning home? no matter how many of their notes may have been protested; no matter how, like Beelzebub,[3] their business partner may have tormented them; no matter how badly elections go—when they do it, may I be there to see! Nor should they. Passing over the everlasting monotony of that everlasting "Guide Book" smile, let us consider, brethren (sisters not admitted), what matrimony was intended for. As I look at it, as much to share each other's sorrows as to share each other's joys; neither of the twain to shoulder wholly the one or the other. Those of you, brethren, who agree with me in this lucid view of the subject, please to signify it by rising.

'Tis a vote.

Well then, do people in moments of perplexity generally grin? Is it not asking too much of female, and too much of male nature, to do it when a man's store burns down, and there is no insurance? or when a misguided and infatuated baby stuffs beans up its nose, while its mamma is putting new cuffs on her husband's coat, hearing Katy say her lesson, and telling the cook about dinner? And when this sorely afflicted couple meet, would it not be best to make a clean breast of their troubles, sympathize together over them, have a nice matrimonial cry on each other's shoulders, and wind up with a first-class kiss?

'Tis a vote.

Well then—to the mischief with your grinning over a volcano;—erupt, and

1. A substance that induces vomiting. 3. The fallen angel ranking next to Satan.
2. I.e., an explosive word.

have done with it! so shall you love each other more for your very sorrows; so shall you avoid hypocrisy and kindred bedevilments, and pull evenly in the matrimonial harness. I speak as unto *wise* men.

Lastly, brethren, what I particularly admire, is the indirect compliment to your sex, which this absurd rule I have quoted implies; the devotion, magnanimity, fortitude, and courage, it gives *you* fair-weather sailors credit for! But what is the use of talking about it? These guide books are mainly written by sentimental old maids; who, had they ever been within kissing distance of a beard, would not so abominably have wasted pen, ink, and paper; or, by some old bachelor, tip-toeing on the outskirts of the promised land, without a single clear idea of its resources and requirements, or courage enough to settle there if he had.

1853

The Boston Woman

The Boston woman draweth down her mouth, rolleth up her eyes, foldeth her hands, and walketh on a crack.[1] She rejoiceth in anatomical and chemical lectures. She prateth of Macaulay and Carlyle;[2] belongeth to many and divers reading-classes, and smileth in a chaste, moonlight kind of way on literary men. She dresseth (to her praise be it spoken) plainly in the street, and considereth India-rubbers, a straw bonnet, and a thick shawl, the fittest costume for damp and cloudy weather. She dresseth her children more for comfort than show, and bringeth them up also to walk on a crack. She maketh the tour of the Common twice or three times a day, without regard to the barometer. She goeth to church twice or three times on Sunday, sandwiched with Bible-classes and Sabbath-schools. She thinketh London, Vienna, or Paris—fools to Boston; and the "Boulevards" and "Tuileries" not to be mentioned with the Frog Pond and the Common.[3] She is well posted up as to politics—"thinketh as Pa does," and sticketh to it through thunder and lightning. When asked to take a gentleman's arm, she hooketh the tip of her little finger circumspectly on to his male coat sleeve. She is as prim as a bolster,[4] as stiff as a ram-rod, as frigid as an icicle, and not even matrimony with a New Yorker could thaw her.

1853

1. I.e., does not deviate from her course.
2. The historians and essayists Thomas Macaulay (1800–1859) and Thomas Carlyle (1795–1881) are very serious reading.

3. I.e., the pond and park in Boston surpass the streets and famous gardens of Paris.
4. Long, firm pillow.

HARRIET BEECHER STOWE

1811–1896

Harriet Beecher Stowe is still one of the most popular of the women novelists who published best-sellers in America during the mid-nineteenth century. Approximately 350,000 copies of *Uncle Tom's Cabin; or, Life among the Lowly* (1851–52) were purchased during the first year of its printing, bringing its author $10,000 in

just the first three months. While the book, which sold more than a million pirated copies in England, earned Stowe friends like George Eliot and Charles Dickens, within three years it had given rise to some thirty anti–Uncle Tom novels by Southern sympathizers. As a protest against the Fugitive Slave Act, which denied runaway slaves sanctuary and made it criminal to assist them, Stowe's novel preached the evils of slavery to a nation shown to be in need of Christian humility. By now Uncle Tom's Cabin has transcended both the partisanship of Northern abolitionists, who used it for propaganda purposes during the Civil War, and the more recent critical reaction of African-American scholars, who have objected to the docility of "Uncle Tomism." Yet its controversial reception may have been responsible for obscuring the fact that Stowe published more than twenty-five other novels, essays, and stories.

To what familial influences can Stowe's prolific career be attributed? First, most biographers agree, Stowe's father, the eminent Congregational minister Lyman Beecher, was instrumental in instilling a sense of mission in his children: all nine of them were educated, according to his Calvinist values, for a life of public service as ministers or mothers, depending on their gender. Stowe received a theological education from her father, and all her life she struggled with despair over her inability to meet his spiritual standards, even as she sought to emulate the conversion work she saw him effecting in his church in her childhood hometown of Litchfield, Connecticut, and in the Lane Theological Seminary in Cincinnati, Ohio, where the family moved in 1832 when he became president of Lane. Stowe's mother, Roxana (Foote) Beecher, exerted her influence more as an absence than a presence: dead by the time her seventh child reached the age of four, she was remembered and cherished as a pious, devoted mother. Stowe was also imbued with a sense of the moral power of women by her older sister, Catharine Beecher, who took over their mother's household duties in 1815. After Harriet graduated from Miss Sarah Pierce's school in Litchfield, she attended the female seminary established by Catharine in Hartford. There she learned the lesson Catharine Beecher taught throughout her prominent career, the doctrine that women in their traditional roles could transform and redeem American culture through their exemplary Christian benevolence.

If the Beecher inheritance sustained and shaped the ethical impulse informing Stowe's subsequent fiction, her marriage to Calvin Ellis Stowe in 1836 provided her with a financial impetus for writing. This professor of biblical literature at Lane shared her New England background, as well as her propensity for nervous depression and religious compunction. Never well paid, by 1844 he handed over the management of the family's finances to his wife, who discovered, to her relief, that she could lighten the load of what she considered "domestic slavery" by hiring a helper with the money she gained from publishing stories. In 1850, after six pregnancies and the death in infancy of her sixth baby, and with a seventh child on the way, Stowe moved with her husband to Maine, where he taught at Bowdoin College and where she experienced what she later called her "vision" of the death scene of Uncle Tom.

Her reading of abolitionist literature; the letters of her brother Charles, which recorded the voice of a sadistic Louisiana overseer he knew; the sermons of her other two brothers, Edward and Henry Ward, who denounced the Fugitive Slave Act from their pulpits; as well as the threat to one of her servants, who was claimed as a slave and managed to escape through the help of the family—all of these contributed to Stowe's growing reaction against slavery, as had the death of her six-month-old baby, which taught her, she later explained, "what a poor slave mother may feel when her child is torn from her." If Stowe's pattern of imagery in Uncle Tom's Cabin is any index, she was haunted by a feeling of maternal loss—the loss of her infant and the earlier death of her mother—that she brilliantly described as the byproduct of slavery. The faith in Christian humility she preached was associated with the spiritual agency of women, for her portraits of the submissive Tom,

the angelic little Eva, and the maternal Quaker Rachel dramatized her attack on a slave system that divided mother and child. When *Uncle Tom's Cabin* was met by a storm of protests, she answered with *A Key to Uncle Tom's Cabin* (1853), documenting the horror of slavery she had fictionalized so effectively. After a triumphal European tour, recorded in *Sunny Memories of Foreign Lands* (1854), she wrote *Dred* (1856), a novel that depicts the disabling ethical effects of slavery on the white race.

Throughout her life, Stowe continued to support her family with writings that contributed to the formation of a national American literature. Turning to her native New England, she fashioned a regionalist perspective marked by respect for women's domestic sphere, a perspective that would later characterize the stories of Sarah Orne Jewett and Mary Wilkins Freeman. *The Minister's Wooing* (1859), *The Pearl of Orr's Island* (1862), *Oldtown Folks* (1869), and *Poganuc People* (1878) contain her finest portraits of New Englanders, dramatized through dialect, set in a somber physical landscape, and infused with a sometimes severe Calvinist spiritual atmosphere. *The Minister's Housekeeper*, which is reprinted here from *Sam Lawson's Oldtown Fireside Stories* (1872), is narrated by a lazy but lively village storyteller Stowe had created in *Oldtown Folks* for comic relief. In the Oldtown tales, as in her children's stories, housekeeping manuals, and journalism, she achieved remarkable popularity and diversity.

Stowe had purchased an orange plantation in Mandarin, Florida, to escape Hartford winters after Calvin Stowe retired and to provide a rehabilitating occupation for her alcoholic son, Frederick William. She continued to support this son, her husband, and two unmarried daughters until her husband died in 1886. Suffering from senility and depression, she spent the last ten years of her life in Hartford. Seven years after her death, the Stowe cabinet in the library of the Woman's Building at the World's Columbian Exposition in Chicago contained a complete set of her works in twenty volumes, forty-two translations of *Uncle Tom's Cabin*, and a bust of the author done by the successful Boston sculptor Anne Whitney. The display was a fitting tribute to Stowe's achievement.

From Uncle Tom's Cabin

Chapter XXX. *The Slave Warehouse*

A slave warehouse! Perhaps some of my readers conjure up horrible visions of such a place. They fancy some foul, obscure den, some horrible *Tartarus* "*informis, ingens, ad lumen ademptum.*"[1] But no, innocent friend; in these days men have learned the art of sinning expertly and genteelly, so as not to shock the eyes and senses of respectable society. Human property is high in the market; and is, therefore, well fed, well cleaned, tended, and looked after, that it may come to sale sleek, and strong, and shining. A slave-warehouse in New Orleans is a house externally not much unlike many others, kept with neatness; and where every day you may see arranged, under a sort of shed along the outside, rows of men and women, who stand there as a sign of the property sold within.

Then you shall be courteously entreated to call and examine, and shall find an abundance of husbands, wives, brothers, sisters, fathers, mothers, and young children, to be "sold separately, or in lots to suit the convenience of the purchaser;" and that soul immortal, once bought with blood and anguish by

1. Tartarus "hideous, huge, without light" (Latin); in Virgil's *Aeneid* 3.658 a similar phrase is applied to the blinded Cyclops Polyphemus. Tartarus is the place of punishment in the underworld.

the Son of God, when the earth shook, and the rocks rent, and the graves were opened,[2] can be sold, leased, mortgaged, exchanged for groceries or dry goods, to suit the phases of trade, or the fancy of the purchaser.

It was a day or two after the conversation between Marie and Miss Ophelia, that Tom, Adolph, and about half a dozen others of the St Clare estate, were turned over to the loving kindness of Mr. Skeggs, the keeper of a depot on ———— street, to await the auction, next day.

Tom had with him quite a sizable trunk full of clothing, as had most others of them. They were ushered, for the night, into a long room, where many other men, of all ages, sizes, and shades of complexion, were assembled, and from which roars of laughter and unthinking merriment were proceeding.

"Ah, ha! that's right. Go it, boys,—go it!" said Mr. Skeggs, the keeper. "My people are always so merry! Sambo, I see!" he said, speaking approvingly to a burly negro who was performing tricks of low buffoonery, which occasioned the shouts which Tom had heard.

As might be imagined, Tom was in no humor to join these proceedings; and, therefore, setting his trunk as far as possible from the noisy group, he sat down on it, and leaned his face against the wall.

The dealers in the human article make scrupulous and systematic efforts to promote noisy mirth among them, as a means of drowning reflection, and rendering them insensible to their condition. The whole object of the training to which the negro is put, from the time he is sold in the northern market till he arrives south, is systematically directed towards making him callous, unthinking, and brutal. The slave-dealer collects his gang in Virginia or Kentucky, and drives them to some convenient, healthy place,—often a watering place,—to be fattened. Here they are fed full daily; and, because some incline to pine, a fiddle is kept commonly going among them, and they are made to dance daily; and he who refuses to be merry—in whose soul thoughts of wife, or child, or home, are too strong for him to be gay—is marked as sullen and dangerous, and subjected to all the evils which the ill will of an utterly irresponsible and hardened man can inflict upon him. Briskness, alertness, and cheerfulness of appearance, especially before observers, are constantly enforced upon them, both by the hope of thereby getting a good master, and the fear of all that the driver may bring upon them, if they prove unsalable.

"What dat ar nigger doin here?" said Sambo, coming up to Tom, after Mr. Skeggs had left the room. Sambo was a full black, of great size, very lively, voluble, and full of trick and grimace.

"What you doin here?" said Sambo, coming up to Tom, and poking him facetiously in the side. "Meditatin', eh?"

"I am to be sold at the auction, to-morrow!" said Tom, quietly.

"Sold at auction,—haw! haw! boys, an't this yer fun? I wish't I was gwine that ar way!—tell ye, would n't I make em laugh? But how is it,—dis yer whole lot gwine tomorrow?" said Sambo, laying his hand freely on Adolph's shoulder.

"Please to let me alone!" said Adolph, fiercely, straightening himself up, with extreme disgust.

"Law, now, boys! dis yer's one o' yer white niggers,—kind o' cream color, ye know, scented!" said he, coming up to Adolph and snuffing. "O, Lor! he'd do

2. A reference to the Harrowing of Hell, the story that Christ descended into Hell after his death to release the souls held there.

for a tobaccer-shop; they could keep him to scent snuff! Lor, he'd keep a whole shop agwine,—he would!"

"I say, keep off, can't you?" said Adolph, enraged.

"Lor, now, how touchy we is,—we white niggers! Look at us, now!" and Sambo gave a ludicrous imitation of Adolph's manner; "here's de airs and graces. We's been in a good family, I specs."

"Yes," said Adolph; "I had a master that could have bought you all for old truck!"[3]

"Laws, now, only think," said Sambo, "the gentlemens that we is!"

"I belonged to the St. Clare family," said Adolph, proudly.

"Lor, you did! Be hanged if they ar' n't lucky to get shet of ye. Spects they 's gwine to trade ye off with a lot o' cracked tea-pots and sich like!" said Sambo, with a provoking grin.

Adolph, enraged at this taunt, flew furiously at his adversary, swearing and striking on every side of him. The rest laughed and shouted, and the uproar brought the keeper to the door.

"What now, boys? Order,—order!" he said, coming in and flourishing a large whip.

All fled in different directions, except Sambo, who, presuming on the favor which the keeper had to him as a licensed wag, stood his ground, ducking his head with a facetious grin, whenever the master made a dive at him.

"Lor, Mas'r, 'tan't us,—we's reglar stiddy,—it's these yer new hands; they's real aggravatin',—kinder pickin' at us, all time!"

The keeper, at this, turned upon Tom and Adolph, and distributing a few kicks and cuffs without much inquiry, and leaving general orders for all to be good boys and go to sleep, left the apartment.

While this scene was going on in the men's sleeping-room, the reader may be curious to take a peep at the corresponding apartment allotted to the women. Stretched out in various attitudes over the floor, he may see number-less sleeping forms of every shade of complexion, from the purest ebony to white, and of all years, from childhood to old age, lying now asleep. Here is a fine bright girl, of ten years, whose mother was sold out yesterday, and who to-night cried herself to sleep when nobody was looking at her. Here, a worn old negress, whose thin arms and callous fingers tell of hard toil, waiting to be sold to-morrow, as a cast-off article, for what can be got for her; and some forty or fifty others, with heads variously enveloped in blankets or articles of clothing, lie stretched around them. But, in a corner, sitting apart from the rest, are two females of a more interesting appearance than common. One of these is a respectably-dressed mulatto woman between forty and fifty, with soft eyes and a gentle and pleasing physiognomy. She has on her head a high-raised turban, made of a gay red Madras handkerchief, of the first quality, and her dress is neatly fitted, and of good material, showing that she has been provided for with a careful hand. By her side, and nestling closely to her, is a young girl of fifteen,—her daughter. She is a quadroon,[4] as may be seen from her fairer complexion, though her likeness to her mother is quite discernible. She has the same soft, dark eye, with longer lashes, and her curling hair is of a luxuri-ant brown. She also is dressed with great neatness, and her white, delicate hands betray very little acquaintance with servile toil. These two are to be sold

3. Odds and end, trash. 4. One-quarter black.

tomorrow, in the same lot with the St. Clare servants; and the gentleman to whom they belong, and to whom the money for their sale is to be transmitted, is a member of a Christian church in New York, who will receive the money, and go thereafter to the sacrament of his Lord and theirs, and think no more of it.

These two, whom we shall call Susan and Emmeline, had been the personal attendants of an amiable and pious lady of New Orleans, by whom they had been carefully and piously instructed and trained. They had been taught to read and write, diligently instructed in the truths of religion, and their lot had been as happy an one as in their condition it was possible to be. But the only son of their protectress had the management of her property; and, by carelessness and extravagance involved it to a large amount, and at last failed. One of the largest creditors was the respectable firm of B. & Co., in New York. B & Co. wrote to their lawyer in New Orleans, who attached the real estate (these two articles and a lot of plantation hands formed the most valuable part of it), and wrote word to that effect to New York. Brother B., being, as we have said, a Christian man, and a resident in a free State, felt some uneasiness on the subject. He didn't like trading in slaves and souls of men,—of course, he didn't; but, then, there were thirty thousand dollars in the case, and that was rather too much money to be lost for a principle; and so, after much considering, and asking advice from those that he knew would advise to suit him, Brother B. wrote to his lawyer to dispose of the business in the way that seemed to him the most suitable, and remit the proceeds.

The day after the letter arrived in New Orleans, Susan and Emmeline were attached, and sent to the depot to await a general auction on the following morning; and as they glimmer faintly upon us in the moonlight which steals through the grated window, we may listen to their conversation. Both are weeping, but each quietly, that the other may not hear.

"Mother, just lay your head on my lap, and see if you can't sleep a little," says the girl, trying to appear calm.

"I haven't any heart to sleep, Em; I can't; it's the last night we may be together!"

"O, mother, don't say so! perhaps we shall get sold together,—who knows?"

"If 't was anybody's else case, I should say so, too, Em," said the woman; "but I'm so feard of losin' you that I don't see anything but the danger."

"Why, mother, the man said we were both likely, and would sell well."

Susan remembered the man's looks and words. With a deadly sickness at her heart, she remembered how he had looked at Emmeline's hands, and lifted up her curly hair, and pronounced her a first-rate article. Susan had been trained as a Christian, brought up in the daily reading of the Bible, and had the same horror of her child's being sold to a life of shame that any other Christian mother might have; but she had no hope,—no protection.

"Mother, I think we might do first rate, if you could get a place as cook, and I as chamber-maid or seamstress, in some family. I dare say we shall. Let's both look as bright and lively as we can, and tell all we can do, and perhaps we shall," said Emmeline.

"I want you to brush your hair all back straight, tomorrow," said Susan.

"What for, mother? I don't look near so well, that way."

"Yes, but you'll sell better so."

"I don't see why!" said the child.

"Respectable families would be more apt to buy you, if they saw you looked plain and decent, as if you wasn't trying to look handsome. I know their ways better 'n you do," said Susan.

"Well, mother, then I will."

"And, Emmeline, if we shouldn't ever see each other again, after tomorrow,—if I'm sold way up on a plantation somewhere, and you somewhere else,—always remember how you've been brought up, and all Missis has told you; take your Bible with you, and your hymn-book; and if you're faithful to the Lord, he 'll be faithful to you."

So speaks the poor soul, in sore discouragement; for she knows that tomorrow any man, however vile and brutal, however godless and merciless, if he only has money to pay for her, may become owner of her daughter, body and soul; and then, how is the child to be faithful? She thinks of all this, as she holds her daughter in her arms, and wishes that she were not handsome and attractive. It seems almost an aggravation to her to remember how purely and piously, how much above the ordinary lot, she has been brought up. But she has no resort but to *pray*; and many such prayers to God have gone up from those same trim, neatly-arranged, respectable slave-prisons,—prayers which God has not forgotten, as a coming day shall show; for it is written, "Who causeth one of these little ones to offend, it were better for him that a millstone were hanged about his neck, and that he were drowned in the depths of the sea."[5]

The soft, earnest, quiet moonbeam looks in fixedly, marking the bars of the grated windows on the prostrate, sleeping forms. The mother and daughter are singing together a wild and melancholy dirge, common as a funeral hymn among the slaves:

"O, where is weeping Mary?
O, where is weeping Mary?
'Rived in the goodly land.
She is dead and gone to Heaven;
She is dead and gone to Heaven;
'Rived in the goodly land."

These words, sung by voices of a peculiar and melancholy sweetness, in an air which seemed like the sighing of earthly despair after heavenly hope, floated through the dark prison rooms with a pathetic cadence, as verse after verse was breathed out:

"O, where are Paul and Silas?
O, where are Paul and Silas?
Gone to the the goodly land.
They are dead and gone to Heaven;
They are dead and gone to Heaven;
'Rived in the goodly land."

Sing on, poor souls! The night is short, and the morning will part you forever!

5. Compare Luke 17:2: "It were better for him that a millstone were hanged about his neck, and he cast into the sea."

But now it is morning, and everybody is astir; and the worthy Mr. Skeggs is busy and bright, for a lot of goods is to be fitted out for auction. There is a brisk look-out on the toilet; injunctions passed around to every one to put on their best face and be spry; and now all are arranged in a circle for a last review, before they are marched up to the Bourse.[6]

Mr. Skeggs, with his palmetto on and his cigar in his mouth, walks around to put farewell touches on his wares.

"How's this?" he said, stepping in front of Susan and Emmeline. "Where's your curls, gal?"

The girl looked timidly at her mother, who, with the smooth adroitness common among her class, answers,

"I was telling her, last night, to put up her hair smooth and neat, and not havin' it flying about in curls; looks more respectable so."

"Bother!" said the man, peremptorily, turning to the girl; "you go right along, and curl yourself real smart!" He added, giving a crack to a rattan he held in his hand, "And be back in quick time, too!"

"You go and help her," he added, to the mother. "Them curls may make a hundred dollars difference in the sale of her."

Beneath a splendid dome were men of all nations, moving to and fro, over the marble pave. On every side of the circular area were little tribunes, or stations, for the use of speakers and auctioneers. Two of these, on opposite sides of the area, were now occupied by brilliant and talented gentlemen, enthusiastically forcing up, in English and French commingled, the bids of connoisseurs in their various wares. A third one, on the other side, still unoccupied, was surrounded by a group, waiting the moment of sale to begin. And here we may recognize the St. Clare servants,—Tom, Adolph, and others; and there, too, Susan and Emmeline, awaiting their turn with anxious and dejected faces. Various spectators, intending to purchase, or not intending, as the case might be, gathered around the group, handling, examining, and commenting on their various points and faces with the same freedom that a set of jockeys discuss the merits of a horse.

"Hulloa, Alf! what brings you here?" said a young exquisite, slapping the shoulder of a sprucely-dressed young man, who was examining Adolph through an eye-glass.

'Well, I was wanting a valet, and I heard that St. Clare's lot was going. I thought I'd just look at his—"

'Catch me ever buying any of St. Clare's people! Spoilt niggers, every one. Impudent as the devil!" said the other.

"Never fear that!" said the first. "If I get 'em, I'll soon have their airs out of them; they'll soon find that they've another kind of master to deal with than Monsieur St. Clare. 'Pon my word, I'll buy that fellow. I like the shape of him."

"You'll find it'll take all you've got to keep him. He's deucedly extravagant!"

"Yes, but my lord will find that he can't be extravagant with me. Just let him be sent to the calaboose[7] a few times, and thoroughly dressed down! I'll tell you if it don't bring him to a sense of his ways! O, I'll reform him, up hill and down,—you'll see. I buy him, that's flat!"

Tom had been standing wistfully examining the multitude of faces throng-

6. Exchange, market. 7. Jail.

ing around him, for one whom he would wish to call master. And if you should ever be under the necessity, sir, of selecting, out of two hundred men, one who was to become your absolute owner and disposer, you would, perhaps, realize, just as Tom did, how few there were that you would feel at all comfortable in being made over to. Tom saw abundance of men,—great, burly, gruff men; little, chirping, dried men; long-favored, lank, hard men; and every variety of stubbed-looking, commonplace men, who pick up their fellow-men as one picks up chips, putting them into the fire or a basket with equal unconcern, according to their convenience; but he saw no St. Clare.

A little before the sale commenced, a short, broad, muscular man, in a checked shirt considerably open at the bosom, and pantaloons much the worse for dirt and wear, elbowed his way through the crowd, like one who is going actively into a business; and, coming up to the group, began to examine them systematically. From the moment that Tom saw him approaching, he felt an immediate and revolting horror at him, that increased as he came near. He was evidently, though short, of gigantic strength. His round, bullet head, large, light-gray eyes, with their shaggy, sandy eye-brows, and stiff, wiry, sun-burned hair, were rather unprepossessing items, it is to be confessed; his large, coarse mouth was distended with tobacco, the juice of which, from time to time, he ejected from him with great decision and explosive force; his hands were immensely large, hairy, sun-burned, freckled, and very dirty, and garnished with long nails, in a very foul condition. This man proceeded to a very free personal examination of the lot. He seized Tom by the jaw, and pulled open his mouth to inspect his teeth; made him strip up his sleeve, to show his muscle; turned him round, made him jump and spring, to show his paces.

"Where was you raised?" he added, briefly, to these investigations.

"In Kintuck, Mas'r," said Tom, looking about, as if for deliverance.

"What have you done?"

"Had care of Mas'r's farm," said Tom.

"Likely story!" said the other, shortly, as he passed on. He paused a moment before Dolph; then spitting a discharge of tobacco-juice on his well-blacked boots, and giving a contemptuous umph, he walked on. Again he stopped before Susan and Emmeline. He put out his heavy, dirty hand, and drew the girl towards him; passed it over her neck and bust, felt her arms, looked at her teeth, and then pushed her back against her mother, whose patient face showed the suffering she had been going through at every motion of the hideous stranger.

The girl was frightened, and began to cry.

"Stop that, you minx!" said the salesman; "no whimpering here,—the sale is going to begin." And accordingly the sale begun.

Adolph was knocked off, at a good sum, to the young gentleman who had previously stated his intention of buying him; and the other servants of the St. Clare lot went to various bidders.

"Now, up with you, boy! d'ye hear?" said the auctioneer to Tom.

Tom stepped upon the block, gave a few anxious looks round; all seemed mingled in a common, indistinct noise,—the clatter of the salesman crying off his qualifications in French and English, the quick fire of French and English bids; and almost in a moment came the final thump of the hammer, and the clear ring on the last syllable of the word "*dollars*," as the auctioneer announced his price, and Tom was made over.—He had a master!

He was pushed from the block;—the short, bullet-headed man seizing him roughly by the shoulder, pushed him to one side, saying, in a harsh voice, "Stand there, *you!*"

Tom hardly realized anything; but still the bidding went on,—rattling, clattering, now French, now English. Down goes the hammer again,—Susan is sold! She goes down from the block, stops, looks wistfully back,—her daughter stretches her hands towards her. She looks with agony in the face of the man who has bought her,—a respectable middle-aged man, of benevolent countenance.

"O, Mas'r, please do buy my daughter!"

"I'd like to, but I'm afraid I can't afford it." said the gentleman, looking, with painful interest, as the young girl mounted the block, and looked around her with a frightened and timid glance.

The blood flushes painfully in her otherwise colorless cheek, her eye has a feverish fire, and her mother groans to see that she looks more beautiful than she ever saw her before. The auctioneer sees his advantage, and expatiates volubly in mingled French and English, and bids rise in rapid succession.

"I'll do anything in reason," said the benevolent-looking gentleman, pressing in and joining with the bids. In a few moments they have run beyond his purse. He is silent; the auctioneer grows warmer; but bids gradually drop off. It lies now between an aristocratic old citizen and our bullet-headed acquaintance. The citizen bids for a few turns, contemptuously measuring his opponent; but the bullet-head has the advantage over him, both in obstinacy and concealed length of purse, and the controversy lasts but a moment; the hammer falls,—he has got the girl, body and soul, unless God help her!

Her master is Mr. Legree, who owns a cotton plantation on the Red river. She is pushed along into the same lot with Tom and two other men, and goes off, weeping as she goes.

The benevolent gentleman is sorry; but, then, the thing happens every day! One sees girls and mothers crying, at these sales, *always!* it can't be helped, etc.; and he walks off, with his acquisition, in another direction.

Two days after, the lawyer of the Christian firm of B & Co., New York, sent on their money to them. On the reverse of that draft, so obtained, let them write these words of the great Paymaster, to whom they shall make up their account in a future day: "When he maketh inquisition for blood, he forgetteth not the cry of the humble!"[8]

1852

The Minister's Housekeeper[1]

SCENE.—*The shady side of a blueberry-pasture.—Sam Lawson with the boys, picking blueberries.—Sam, loq.*[2]

"Wal, you see, boys, 't was just here,—Parson Carryl's wife she died along in the forepart o' March: my cousin Huldy she undertook to keep house for him. The way on't was, that Huldy she went to take care o' Mis' Carryl in the fust

8. Psalm 9:12.
1. This is part of a series of stories narrated by Sam
Lawson, the village loafer in a New England town
2. *Loquitur*; i.e., Sam speaks.

on't, when she fust took sick. Huldy was a tailoress by trade; but then she was one o' these 'ere facultized[3] persons that has a gift for most anything, and that was how Mis' Carryl come to set sech store by her, that, when she was sick, nothin' would do for her but she must have Huldy round all the time: and the minister he said he'd make it good to her all the same, and she shouldn't lose nothin' by it. And so Huldy she stayed with Mis' Carryl full three months afore she died, and got to seein' to everything pretty much round the place.

"Wal, arter Mis' Carryl died, Parson Carryl he'd got so kind o' used to hevin' on her round, takin' care o' things, that he wanted her to stay along a spell; and so Huldy she stayed along a spell, and poured out his tea, and mended his close, and made pies and cakes, and cooked and washed and ironed, and kep' everything as neat as a pin. Huldy was a dreful chipper sort o' gal; and work sort o' rolled off from her like water off a duck's back. There wa'n't no gal in Sherburne that could put sich a sight o' work through as Huldy; and yet, Sunday mornin', she always come out in the singers' seat[4] like one o' these 'ere June roses, lookin' so fresh and smilin', and her voice was jest as clear and sweet as a meadow lark's—Lordy massy! I 'member how she used to sing some o' them 'ere places where the treble and counter[5] used to go together: her voice kind o' trembled a little, and it sort o' went through and through a feller! tuck him right where he lived!"

Here Sam leaned contemplatively back with his head in a clump of sweet-fern, and refreshed himself with a chew of young wintergreen. "This 'ere young wintergreen, boys, is jest like a feller's thoughts o' things that happened when he was young: it comes up jest so fresh and tender every year, the longest time you hev to live; and you can't help chawin' on't though't is sort o' stingin'. I don't never get over likin' young wintergreen."

"But about Huldah, Sam?"

"Oh yes! about Huldy. Lordy massy! when a feller is Indianin' round,[6] these 'ere pleasant summer days, a feller's thoughts gits like a flock o' young partridges: they's up and down and everywhere; 'cause one place is jest about as good as another, when they's all so kind o' comfortable and nice. Wal, about Huldy,—as I was a-sayin'. She was jest as handsome a gal to look at as a feller could have; and I think a nice, well-behaved young gal in the singers' seat of a Sunday is a means o' grace: it's sort o' drawin' to the unregenerate, you know. Why, boys, in them days, I've walked ten miles over to Sherburne of a Sunday mornin', jest to play the bass-viol in the same singers' seat with Huldy. She was very much respected, Huldy was; and, when she went out to tailorin', she was allers bespoke[7] six months ahead, and sent for in waggins up and down for ten miles round; for the young fellers was allers 'mazin' anxious to be sent after Huldy, and was quite free to offer to go for her. Wal, after Mis' Carryl died, Huldy got to be sort o' housekeeper at the minister's, and saw to everything, and did everything: so that there wa'n't a pin out o' the way.

"But you know how 'tis in parishes: there allers is women that thinks the minister's affairs belongs to them, and they ought to have the rulin' and guidin' of 'em; and, if a minister's wife dies, there's folks that allers has their eyes open on providences,[8]—lookin' out who's to be the next one.

3. A hybrid word, apparently of Sam's invention, meaning multitalented.
4. The pew in a church where the choir sits.
5. High and low female parts in a choral work.
6. Loafing.

7. Hired or engaged beforehand. "Went out to tailorin' ": hired herself out as a seamstress.
8. Opportunities, presumed to be "provided" by God.

"Now, there was Mis' Amaziah Pipperidge, a widder with snappin' black eyes, and a hook nose,—kind o' like a hawk; and she was one o' them up-and-down commandin' sort o' women, that feel that they have a call to be seein' to everything that goes on in the parish, and 'specially to the minister.

"Folks did say that Mis' Pipperidge sort o' set her eye on the Parson for herself: wal, now that 'ere might 'a' been, or it might not. Some folks thought it was a very suitable connection. You see, she hed a good property of her own, right nigh to the minister's lot, and was allers kind o' active and busy; so, takin' one thing with another, I shouldn't wonder if Mis' Pipperidge should a thought that Providence p'inted that way. At any rate, she went up to Deakin[9] Blodgett's wife, and they two sort o' put their heads together a-mournin' and condolin' about the way things was likely to go on at the minister's now Mis' Carryl was dead. Ye see, the parson's wife, she was one of them women who hed their eyes everywhere and on everything. She was a little thin woman, but tough as Inger rubber,[1] and smart as a steel trap; and there wa'n't a hen laid an egg, or cackled, but Mis' Carryl was right there to see about it; and she hed the garden made in the spring, and the medders mowed in summer, and the cider made, and the corn husked, and the apples got in the fall; and the doctor, he hedn't nothin' to do but jes' sit stock-still a-meditatin' on Jerusalem and Jericho and them things that ministers think about. But Lordy massy! he didn't know nothin' about where anything he eat or drunk or wore come from or went to: his wife jest led him round in temporal things[2] and took care on him like a baby.

"Wal, to be sure, Mis' Carryl looked up to him in spirituals, and thought all the world on him; for there wa'n't a smarter minister nowhere round. Why, when he preached on decrees and election,[3] they used to come clear over from South Parish, and West Sherburne, and Oldtown to hear him; and there was sich a row o' waggins tied along by the meetin-house that the stables was all full, and all the hitchin'-posts was full clean up to the tavern, so that folks said the doctor made the town look like a gineral trainin' day[4] a Sunday.

"He was gret on texts, the doctor was. When he hed a p'int to prove, he'd jest go through the Bible, and drive all the texts ahead o' him like a flock o' sheep; and then, if there was a text that seemed agin him, why, he'd come out with his Greek and Hebrew, and kind o' chase it round a spell, jest as ye see a feller chase a contrary bell-wether,[5] and make him jump the fence arter the rest. I tell you, there wa'n't no text in the Bible that could stand agin the doctor when his blood was up. The year arter the doctor was app'inted to preach the 'lection sermon in Boston he made such a figger that the Brattle Street Church sent a committee right down to see if they couldn't get him to Boston; and then the Sherburne folks, they up and raised his salary; ye see, there ain't nothin' wakes folks up like somebody else's wantin' what you've got. Wal, that fall they made him a Doctor o' Divinity at Cambridge College,[6] and so they sot more by him than ever. Wal, you see, the doctor, of course he felt kind o' lonesome and afflicted when Mis' Carryl was gone; but railly and truly, Huldy was so up to everything about 'ouse, that the doctor didn't miss nothin' in a

9. Deacon, a church administrator.
1. India rubber.
2. Worldly matters, as opposed to the eternal.
3. Divine choice in Puritan theology, the belief in predestination.

4. Day for training or parade by a volunteer military company.
5. Leading sheep of a flock.
6. Harvard University in Cambridge, Massachusetts.

temporal way. His shirt-bosoms was pleated finer than they ever was, and them ruffles round his wrists was kep' like the driven snow; and there wa'n't a brack[7] in his silk stockin's, and his shoe-buckles was kep' polished up, and his coats brushed, and then there wa'n't no bread and biscuit like Huldy's; and her butter was like solid lumps o' gold; and there weren't no pies to equal hers; and so the doctor never felt the loss o' Mis' Carryl at table. Then there was Huldy allers oppisite to him, with her blue eyes and her cheeks like two fresh peaches. She was kind o' pleasant to look at; and the more the doctor looked at her the better he liked her; and so things seemed to be goin' on quite quiet and comfortable ef it hadn't been that Mis' Pipperidge and Mis' Deakin Blodgett and Mis' Sawin got their heads together a-talkin' about things.

" 'Poor man,' says Mis' Pipperidge, 'what can that child that he's got there do towards takin' the care of all that place? It takes a mature woman,' she says, 'to tread in Mis' Carryl's shoes.'

" 'That it does,' said Mis' Blodgett; 'and, when things once get to runnin' downhill, there ain't no stoppin' on 'em,' says she.

"Then Mis' Sawin she took it up. (Ye see, Mis' Sawin used to go out to dressmakin', and was sort o' jealous, 'cause folks sot more by Huldy than they did by her.) 'Well,' says she, 'Huldy Peters is well enough at her trade. I never denied that, though I do say I never did believe in her way o' makin' button-holes; and I must say, if 't was the dearest friend I hed, that I thought Huldy tryin' to fit Mis' Kittridge's plum-colored silk was a clear piece o' presumption; the silk was jist sp'iled, so 't wa'n't fit to come into the meetin'-house. I must say, Huldy's a gal that's always too ventersome about takin 'sponsibilities she don't know nothin' about.'

" 'Of course she don't,' said Mis' Deakin Blodgett. 'What does she know about all the lookin' and seein' to that there ought to be in guidin' the minister's house. Huldy's well meanin', and she's good at her work, and good in the singers' seat; but Lordy massy! she hain't got no experience. Parson Carryl ought to have an experienced woman to keep house for him. There's the spring house-cleanin' and the fall house-cleanin' to be seen to, and the things to be put away from the moths; and then the gettin' ready for the Association[8] and all the ministers' meetin's; and the makin' the soap and the candles, and settin' the hens and turkeys, watchin' the calves, and seein' after the hired men and the garden; and there that 'ere blessed man jist sets there at home as serene, and has nobody round but that 'ere gal, and don't even know how things must be a-runnin' to waste!'

"Wal, the upshot on't was, they fussed and fuzzled and wuzzled[9] till they'd drinked up all the tea in the teapot; and then they went down and called on the parson, and wuzzled him all up talkin' about this, that, and t'other that wanted lookin' to, and that it was no way to leave everything to a young chit[1] like Huldy, and that he ought to be lookin' about for an experienced woman. The parson he thanked 'em kindly, and said he believed their motives was good, but he didn't go no further. He didn't ask Mis' Pipperidge to come and stay there and help him, nor nothin' o' that kind; but he said he'd attend to matters himself. The fact was, the parson had got such a likin' for havin' Huldy round, that he couldn't think o' such a thing as swappin' her off for the Widder Pipperidge.

7. Flaw.
8. Regional association of churches.

9. I.e., gossipped and worried.
1. Pert young woman.

"But he thought to himself, 'Huldy is a good girl; but I oughtn't to be a-leavin' everything to her,—it's too hard on her. I ought to be instructin' and guidin' and helpin' of her; 'cause't ain't everybody could be expected to know and do what Mis' Carryl did;' and so at it he went; and Lordy massy! didn't Huldy hev a time on't when the minister began to come out of his study, and want to tew round and see to things? Huldy, you see, thought all the world of the minister, and she was 'most afraid to laugh; but she told me she couldn't, for the life of her, help it when his back was turned, for he wuzzled things up in the most singular way. But Huldy she'd jest say, 'Yes, sir,' and get him off into his study, and go on her own way.

" 'Huldy,' says the minister one day, 'you ain't experienced outdoors; and, when you want to know anything, you must come to me.'

" 'Yes, sir,' says Huldy.

" 'Now, Huldy,' says the parson, 'you must be sure to save the turkey-eggs, so that we can have a lot of turkeys for Thanksgiving.'

" 'Yes, sir,' says Huldy; and she opened the pantry-door, and showed him a nice dishful she'd been a-savin' up. Wal, the very next day the parson's hen-turkey was found killed up to old Jim Scrogg's barn. Folks said Scroggs killed it; though Scroggs he stood to it he didn't: at any rate, the Scroggses they made a meal on't; and Huldy she felt bad about it, 'cause she'd set her heart on raisin' the turkeys; and says she, 'Oh, dear! I don't know what I shall do. I was just ready to set her.' "[2]

" 'Do, Huldy?' says the parson. 'Why, there's the other turkey, out there by the door; and a fine bird, too, he is.'

"Sure enough, there was the old tom-turkey a-struttin' and a-sidlin' and a-quitterin', and a-floutin' his tail-feathers in the sun, like a lively young widower, all ready to begin life over ag'in.

" 'But,' says Huldy, 'you know *he* can't set on eggs.'

" 'He can't? I'd like to know why,' says the parson. 'He shall set on eggs, and hatch 'em too.'

" 'O doctor!' says Huldy, all in a tremble; 'cause, you know, she didn't want to contradict the minister, and she was afraid she should laugh,—'I never heard that a tom-turkey would set on eggs.'

" 'Why, they ought to,' said the parson, getting quite 'arnest; 'what else be they good for? you just bring out the eggs, now, and put 'em in the nest, and I'll make him set on 'em.'

"So Huldy she thought there weren't no way to convince him but to let him try: so she took the eggs out, and fixed 'em all nice in the nest; and then she come back and found old Tom a-skirmishin' with the parson pretty lively, I tell ye. Ye see, old Tom he didn't take the idee at all; and he flopped and gobbled, and fit the parson; and the parson's wig got round so that his cue[3] stuck straight out over his ear, but he'd got his blood up. Ye see, the old doctor was used to carryin' his p'ints o' doctrine; and he hadn't fit the Arminians and Socinians[4] to be beat by a tom-turkey; so finally he made a dive, and ketched him by the neck in spite o' his floppin', and stroked him down, and put Huldy's apron round him.

" 'There, Huldy,' he says, quite red in the face, 'we've got him now;' and he *traveled* off to the barn with him as lively as a cricket.

2. I.e., allow her to hatch her eggs by sitting on them.
3. I.e., queue—the braid of his wig.

4. Two religious sects that opposed parts of the Calvinist doctrine of religious faith.

"Huldy came behind jist chokin' with laugh, and afraid the minister would look round and see her.

" 'Now, Huldy, we'll crook his legs, and set him down,' says the parson, when they got him to the nest; 'you see he is getting quiet, and he'll set there all right.'

"And the parson he sot him down; and old Tom he sot there solemn enough, and held his head down all droopin', lookin' like a rail pious old cock, as long as the parson sot by him.

" 'There! you see how still he sets,' says the parson to Huldy.

"Huldy was 'most dyin' for fear she should laugh. 'I'm afraid he'll get up,' says she, 'when you do.'

" 'Oh no, he won't!' says the parson, quite confident. 'There, there,' says he, layin' his hands on him, as if pronouncin' a blessin'. But when the parson riz up, old Tom he riz up too, and began to march over the eggs.

" 'Stop, now!' says the parson. 'I'll make him get down ag'in: hand me that corn-basket; we'll put that over him.'

"So he crooked old Tom's legs, and got him down ag'in; and they put the corn-basket over him, and then they both stood and waited.

" 'That'll do the thing, Huldy,' said the Parson.

" 'I don't know about it,' says Huldy.

" 'Oh yes, it will, child! I understand,' says he.

"Just as he spoke, the basket rïz right up and stood, and they could see old Tom's long legs.

" 'I'll make him stay down, confound him,' says the parson; for, ye see, par-sons is men, like the rest on us, and the doctor had got his spunk up.

" 'You just hold him a minute, and I'll get something that'll make him stay, I guess;' and out he went to the fence, and brought in a long, thin, flat stone, and laid it on old Tom's back.

"Old Tom he wilted down considerable under this, and looked railly as if he was goin' to give in. He stayed still there a good long spell, and the minister and Huldy left him there and come up to the house; but they hadn't more than got in the door before they see Tom a-hippin' along, as high-steppin' as ever, sayin', 'Talk! talk! and quitter! quitter!' and struttin' and gobblin' as if he'd come through the Red Sea, and got the victory.[5]

" 'Oh, my eggs!' says Huldy. 'I'm afraid he's smashed 'em!'

"And sure enough, there they was, smashed flat enough under the stone.

" 'I'll have him killed,' said the parson: 'we won't have such a critter round.'

"But the parson he slep' on't, and then didn't do it; he only come out next Sunday with a tiptop sermon on the 'Riginal Cuss' that was pronounced on things in gineral, when Adam fell,[6] and showed how everything was allowed to go contrary ever since. There was pigweed, and pusley, and Canady thistles, cut-worms, and bag-worms, and canker-worms, to say nothin' of rattlesnakes. The doctor made it very impressive and sort o' improvin'; but Huldy she told me, goin' home, that she hardly could keep from laughin' two or three times in the sermon when she thought of old Tom a-standin' up with the corn-basket on his back.

5. Moses led the Israelites across the Red Sea and de-feated the Egyptians, who pursued them (Exodus 14:19–31).

6. In Genesis Adam falls from grace by eating a fruit from the Tree of Knowledge, thus bringing the curse of death and labor on himself and his descendants (Genesis 3). " 'Riginal Cuss": Original Curse or Sin.

"Wal, next week Huldy she jist borrowed the minister's horse and side-saddle, and rode over to South Parish to her Aunt Bascome's,—Widder Bascome's, you know, that lives there by the trout-brook,—and got a lot o' turkey-eggs o' her, and come back and set a hen on 'em, and said nothin'; and in good time there was as nice a lot o' turkey-chicks as ever ye see.

"Huldy never said a word to the minister about his experiment, and he never said a word to her; but he sort o' kep' more to his books, and didn't take it on him to advise so much.

"But not long arter he took it into his head that Huldy ought to have a pig to be a-fattin' with the buttermilk. Mis' Pipperidge set him up to it; and jist then old Tim Bigelow, out to Juniper Hill, told him if he'd call over he'd give him a little pig.

"So he sent for a man, and told him to build a pig-pen right out by the well, and have it all ready when he came home with his pig.

"Huldy she said she wished he might put a curb round the well out there, because in the dark, sometimes, a body might stumble into it; and the parson he told him he might do that.

"Wal, old Aikin, the carpenter, he didn't come till most the middle of the arternoon; and then he sort o' idled, so that he didn't get up the well-curb till sundown; and then he went off and said he'd come and do the pig-pen next day.

"Wal, arter dark, Parson Carryl he driv into the yard, full chizel,[7] with his pig. He'd tied up his mouth to keep him from squealin'; and he see what he thought was the pig-pen,—he was rather near-sighted,—and so he ran and threw piggy over; and down he dropped into the water, and the minister put out his horse and pranced off into the house quite delighted.

" 'There, Huldy, I've got you a nice little pig.'

" 'Dear me!' says Huldy: 'where have you put him?'

" 'Why, out there in the pig-pen, to be sure.'

" 'Oh dear me!' says Huldy: 'that's the well-curb. There ain't no pig-pen built,' says she.

" 'Lordy massy!' says the parson: 'then I've thrown the pig in the well!'

"Wal, Huldy she worked and worked, and finally she fished piggy out in the bucket, but he was dead as a door-nail; and she got him out o' the way quietly, and didn't say much; and the parson he took to a great Hebrew book in his study; and says he, 'Huldy, I ain't much in temporals,' says he. Huldy says she kind o' felt her heart go out to him, he was so sort o' meek and helpless and larned; and says she, 'Wal, Parson Carryl, don't trouble your head no more about it; I'll see to things;' and sure enough, a week arter there was a nice pen, all ship-shape, and two little white pigs that Huldy bought with the money for the butter she sold at the store.

" 'Wal, Huldy,' said the parson, 'you are a most amazin' child: you don't say nothin,' but you do more than most folks.'

"Arter that the parson set sich store by Huldy that he come to her and asked her about everything, and it was amazin' how everything she put her hand to prospered. Huldy planted marigolds and larkspurs, pinks and carnations, all up and down the path to the front door, and trained up mornin'-glories and scarlet-runners round the windows. And she was always a-gettin' a root here,

7. Full speed.

and a sprig there, and a seed from somebody else,—for Huldy was one o' them that has the gift, so that ef you jist give 'em the leastest sprig of anything they make a great bush out of it right away; so that in six months Huldy had roses and geraniums and lilies, sich as it would a took a gardener to raise. The parson he took no notice at fust; but when the yard was all ablaze with flowers he used to come and stand in a kind o' maze[8] at the front door, and say, 'Beautiful, beautiful! Why, Huldy, I never see anything like it.' And then when her work was done arternoons, Huldy would sit with her sewin' in the porch, and sing and trill away till she'd draw the meadow larks and the bobolinks and the ori- oles to answer her, and the great big elm-tree overhead would get perfectly rackety with the birds; and the parson, settin' there in his study, would git to kind o' dreamin' about the angels, and golden harps, and the New Jerusalem;[9] but he wouldn't speak a word, 'cause Huldy she was jist like them wood- thrushes, she never could sing so well when she thought folks was hearin'. Folks noticed, about this time, that the parson's sermons got to be like Aaron's rod, that budded and blossomed;[1] there was things in 'em about flowers and birds, and more 'special about the music o' heaven. And Huldy she noticed, that ef there was a hymn run in her head while she was round a-workin' the minister was sure to give it out next Sunday. You see, Huldy was jist like a bee: she always sung when she was workin', and you could hear her trillin', now down in the corn-patch, while she was pickin' the corn; and now in the but- tery, while she was workin' the butter; and now she'd go singin' down cellar, and then she'd be singin' up overhead, so that she seemed to fill a house chock full o' music.

"Huldy was so sort o' chipper and fair-spoken that she got the hired men all under her thumb: they come to her and took her orders jist as meek as so many calves; and she traded at the store, and kep' the accounts, and she hed her eyes everywhere, and tied up all the ends so tight that there wa'n't no gettin' round her. She wouldn't let nobody put nothin' off[2] on Parson Carryl, 'cause he was a minister. Huldy was allers up to anybody that wanted to make a hard bargain; and, afore he knew jist what he was about, she'd got the best end of it, and everybody said that Huldy was the most capable gal that they'd ever traded with.

"Wal, come to the meetin' of the Association, Mis' Deakin Blodgett and Mis' Pipperidge come callin' up to the Parson's, all in a stew, and offerin' their services to get the house ready; but the doctor he jist thanked 'em quite quiet, and turned 'em over to Huldy; and Huldy she told 'em that she'd got every- thing ready, and showed 'em her pantries, and her cakes and her pies and her puddin's, and took 'em all over the house; and they went peekin' and pokin', openin' cupboard doors, and lookin' into drawers; and they couldn't find so much as a thread out o' the way, from garret to cellar, and so they went off quite discontented. Arter that the women set a new trouble a-brewin'. Then they begun to talk that it was a year now since Mis' Carryl died; and it railly wasn't proper such a young gal to be stayin' there, who everybody could see was a-settin' her cap for the minister.

"Mis' Pipperidge said that, so long as she looked on Huldy as the hired gal,

8. State of amazement.
9. Holy city where redeemed souls abide.
1. In Numbers 17:1–10 the high priest Aaron's rod is caused to blossom by Moses as a sign of God's favor to Aaron and the priests.
 2. Cheat.

she hadn't thought much about it; but Huldy was railly takin' on airs as an equal, and appearin' as mistress o' the house in a way that would make talk if it went on. And Mis' Pipperidge she driv round up to Deakin Abner Snow's, and down to Mis' Lijah Perry's, and asked them if they wasn't afraid that the way the parson and Huldy was a-goin' on might make talk. And they said they hadn't thought on't before, but now, come to think on't, they was sure it would; and they all went and talked with somebody else, and asked them if they didn't think it would make talk. So come Sunday, between meetin's there wa'n't nothin' else talked about; and Huldy saw folks a-noddin' and a-winkin', and a-look-in' arter her, and she begun to feel dreful sort o' disagreeable. Finally Mis' Sawin she says to her. 'My dear, didn't you never think folks would talk about you and the minister?'

" 'No: why should they?' says Huldy, quite innocent.

" 'Wal, dear,' says she, 'I think it's a shame; but they say you're tryin' to catch him, and that it's so bold and improper for you to be courtin' of him right in his own house,—you know folks will talk,—I thought I'd tell you 'cause I think so much of you,' says she.

"Huldy was a gal of spirit, and she despised the talk, but it made her dreful uncomfortable; and when she got home at night she sat down in the mornin'-glory porch, quite quiet, and didn't sing a word.

"The minister he had heard the same thing from one of his deakins that day; and when he saw Huldy so kind o' silent he says to her, 'Why don't you sing, my child?'

"He hed a pleasant sort o' way with him, the minister had, and Huldy had got a likin' to be with him, and it all come over her that perhaps she ought to go away; and her throat kind o' filled up so she couldn't hardly speak; and, says she, 'I can't sing tonight.'

"Says he, 'You don't know how much good your singin' has done me, nor how much good you have done me in all ways, Huldy. I wish I knew how to show my gratitude.'

" 'O sir!' says Huldy, 'is it improper for me to be here?'

" 'No dear,' says the minister, 'but ill-natured folks will talk; but there is one way we can stop it, Huldy—if you will marry me. You'll make me very happy, and I'll do all I can to make you happy. Will you?'

"Wal, Huldy never told me jist what she said to the minister,—gals never does give you the particulars of them 'ere things jist as you'd like 'em,—only I know the upshot and the hull on't was, that Huldy she did a consid'able lot o' clear starchin' and ironin' the next two days; and the Friday o' next week the minister and she rode over together to Dr. Lothrop's in Oldtown; and the doctor, he jist made 'em man and wife, 'spite of envy of the Jews,' as the hymn says. Wal, you'd better believe there was a-starin' and a-wonderin' next Sunday mornin' when the second bell was a-tollin', and the minister walked up the broad aisle with Huldy, all in white, arm in arm with him, and he opened the minister's pew, and handed her in as if she was a princess; for, you see, Parson Carryl come of a good family, and was a born gentleman, and ad a sort o' grand way o' bein' polite to womenfolks. Wal, I guess there was a-rus'lin' among the bunnets. Mis' Pipperidge gin a great bounce, like corn pop-pin' on a shovel, and her eyes glared through her glasses at Huldy as if they'd a' sot her afire; and everybody in the meetin'-house was a-starin', I tell yew. But they couldn't none of 'em say nothin' agin Huldy's looks; for there wa'n't a

crimp nor a frill about her that wa'n't jis' so; and her frock was white as the driven snow, and she had her bunnet all trimmed up with white ribbins; and all the fellows said the old doctor had stole a march, and got the handsomest gal in the parish.

"Wal, arter meetin' they all come round the parson and Huldy at the door, shakin' hands and laughin'; for by that time they was about agreed that they'd got to let putty well alone.

" 'Why, Parson Carryl,' says Mis' Deakin Blodgett, 'how you've come it over us.'[3]

" 'Yes,' says the parson, with a kind o' twinkle in his eye. 'I thought,' says he, 'as folks wanted to talk about Huldy and me, I'd give 'em somethin' wuth talkin' about.' "

1872

3. I.e., fooled or surprised us.

HARRIET JACOBS

c. 1813–1897

"Slavery is terrible for men; but it is far more terrible for women. Superadded to the burden common to all, *they* have wrongs, and sufferings, and mortifications peculiarly their own": Harriet Jacobs, under the pseudonym "Linda Brent," dramatically documented this claim in her 1861 autobiography, *Incidents in the Life of a Slave Girl*. From her description of her sexual harassment by her owner, Dr. Flint, to her account of how she was prevented from marrying, Jacobs used her narrator and fictionalized surrogate, Brent, to analyze the wrongs inflicted on slave women. In spite of Victorian taboos against so-called indelicate subjects, moreover, she also explained why women like her were drawn into sexual relationships with white men other than their masters ("It seems less degrading to give one's self, than to submit to compulsion"), and the difficulty these women had in obtaining freedom for their children. Although both the names and the locations in her narrative are fictitious (to protect the safety of those who helped her), she deals directly with the racial impact of slave revolts like the Nat Turner uprising of 1831 and legislation like the Fugitive Slave Act of 1850, which subjected runaways in the North to deportation back to the South.

As the scholarship of Jean Fagan Yellin has demonstrated, Harriet Jacobs fashioned her life story into Linda Brent's first-person account of a heroic mother and a fallen woman who endured twenty-seven years of slavery. After the death of her parents, Brent was nurtured by her maternal grandmother, a freed slave of extraordinary industry and piety. At fifteen years of age, Brent began resisting her owner's efforts at sexual exploitation. Much to Dr. Flint's outrage, she gave birth to a son and a daughter, both fathered by a white man she calls Mr. Sands, who promised to buy them for her. Much of her narrative is taken up with her efforts to secure freedom from both Dr. Flint and Mr. Sands for herself and her children. More than ten years after her escape, Brent's author met the white historical novelist and abolitionist Lydia Maria Child, who introduced and edited Jacobs account. "With trifling exceptions, both the ideas and the language are her own," Child explained, adding that Brent's first mistress taught her how to read and write. For both Child and Jacobs, the publication of *Incidents in the Life of a Slave Girl* was a political effort to help other "sisters in bondage." The selection printed here has been taken from the point in the narrative when Linda Brent has convinced her owner that

she has fled to New York. Actually, after running away to a swamp, where she encountered "large, venomous snakes [that] were less dreadful to my imagination than the white men in that community called civilization," she has hidden out in the same Southern town in which Dr. Flint and Mr. Sands live, at her grandmother's house. Determined to shield herself and her children from harm, she has not revealed to her son or daughter her presence in the house where they, too, are living.

From Incidents in the Life of a Slave Girl

Chapter XXI. The Loophole of Retreat

A small shed had been added to my grandmother's house years ago. Some boards were laid across the joists at the top, and between these boards and the roof was a very small garret, never occupied by anything but rats and mice. It was a pent[1] roof, covered with nothing but shingles, according to the southern custom for such buildings. The garret was only nine feet long and seven wide. The highest part was three feet high, and sloped down abruptly to the loose board floor. There was no admission for either light or air. My uncle Phillip, who was a carpenter, had very skilfully made a concealed trap-door, which communicated with the storeroom. He had been doing this while I was waiting in the swamp. The storeroom opened upon a piazza. To this hole I was conveyed as soon as I entered the house. The air was stifling; the darkness total. A bed had been spread on the floor. I could sleep quite comfortably on one side; but the slope was so sudden that I could not turn on the other without hitting the roof. The rats and mice ran over my bed; but I was weary, and I slept such sleep as the wretched may, when a tempest has passed over them. Morning came. I knew it only by the noises I heard; for in my small den day and night were all the same. I suffered for air even more than for light. But I was not comfortless. I heard the voices of my children. There was joy and there was sadness in the sound. It made my tears flow. How I longed to speak to them! I was eager to look on their faces; but there was no hole, no crack, through which I could peep. This continued darkness was oppressive. It seemed horrible to sit or lie in a cramped position day after day, without one gleam of light. Yet I would have chosen this, rather than my lot as a slave, though white people considered it an easy one; and it was so compared with the fate of others. I was never cruelly overworked; I was never lacerated with the whip from head to foot; I was never so beaten and bruised that I could not turn from one side to the other; I never had my heel-strings cut to prevent my running away; I was never chained to a log and forced to drag it about, while I toiled in the fields from morning till night; I was never branded with hot iron, or torn by bloodhounds. On the contrary, I had always been kindly treated, and tenderly cared for, until I came into the hands of Dr. Flint.[2] I had never wished for freedom till then. But though my life in slavery was comparatively devoid of hardships, God pity the woman who is compelled to lead such a life!

My food was passed up to me through the trap-door my uncle had contrived; and my grandmother, my uncle Phillip, and aunt Nancy would seize such opportunities as they could, to mount up there and chat with me at the

1. Sloping. 2. Brent's owner.

HARRIET JACOBS

opening. But of course this was not safe in the daytime. It must all be done in darkness. It was impossible for me to move in an erect position, but I crawled about my den for exercise. One day I hit my head against something, and found it was a gimlet. My uncle had left it sticking there when he made the trap-door. I was as rejoiced as Robinson Crusoe[3] could have been at finding such a treasure. It put a lucky thought into my head. I said to myself, "Now I will have some light. Now I will see my children." I did not dare to begin my work during the daytime, for fear of attracting attention. But I groped round; and having found the side next the street, where I could frequently see my children, I stuck the gimlet in and waited for evening. I bored three rows of holes, one above another; then I bored out the interstices between. I thus succeeded in making one hole about an inch long and an inch broad. I sat by it till late into the night, to enjoy the little whiff of air that floated in. In the morning I watched for my children. The first person I saw in the street was Dr. Flint. I had a shuddering, superstitious feeling that it was a bad omen. Several familiar faces passed by. At last I heard the merry laugh of children, and presently two sweet little faces were looking up at me, as though they knew I was there, and were conscious of the joy they imparted. How I longed to tell them I was there!

My condition was now a little improved. But for weeks I was tormented by hundreds of little red insects, fine as a needle's point, that pierced through my skin, and produced an intolerable burning. The good grandmother gave me herb teas and cooling medicines, and finally I got rid of them. The heat of my den was intense, for nothing but thin shingles protected me from the scorching summer's sun. But I had my consolations. Through my peeping-hole I could watch the children, and when they were near enough, I could hear their talk. Aunt Nancy brought me all the news she could hear at Dr. Flint's. From her I learned that the doctor had written to New York to a colored woman, who had been born and raised in our neighborhood, and had breathed his contaminating atmosphere. He offered her a reward if she could find out any thing about me. I know not what was the nature of her reply; but he soon after started for New York in haste, saying to his family that he had business of importance to transact. I peeped at him as he passed on his way to the steamboat. It was a satisfaction to have miles of land and water between us, even for a little while; and it was a still greater satisfaction to know that he believed me to be in the Free States. My little den seemed less dreary than it had done. He returned, as he did from his former journey to New York, without obtaining any satisfactory information. When he passed our house next morning, Benny[4] was standing at the gate. He had heard them say that he had gone to find me, and he called out, "Dr. Flint, did you bring my mother home? I want to see her." The doctor stamped his foot at him in a rage, and exclaimed, "Get out of the way, you little damned rascal! If you don't, I'll cut off your head."

Benny ran terrified into the house, saying, "You can't put me in jail again. I don't belong to you now." It was well that the wind carried the words away from the doctor's ear. I told my grandmother of it, when we had our next conference at the trap-door; and begged of her not to allow the children to be impertinent to the irascible old man.

3. Shipwrecked hero of the novel (1719) by Daniel Defoe. "Gimlet": a small tool used for boring holes. 4. Her son. Her daughter's name is Ellen.

Autumn came, with a pleasant abatement of heat. My eyes had become accustomed to the dim light, and by holding my book or work in a certain position near the aperture I contrived to read and sew. That was a great relief to the tedious monotony of my life. But when winter came, the cold penetrated through the thin shingle roof, and I was dreadfully chilled. The winters there are not so long, or so severe, as in northern latitudes; but the houses are not built to shelter from cold, and my little den was peculiarly comfortless. The kind grandmother brought me bed-clothes and warm drinks. Often I was obliged to lie in bed all day to keep comfortable; but with all my precautions, my shoulders and feet were frostbitten. O, those long, gloomy days, with no object for my eye to rest upon, and no thoughts to occupy my mind, except the dreary past and the uncertain future! I was thankful when there came a day sufficiently mild for me to wrap myself up and sit at the loophole to watch the passers by. Southerners have the habit of stopping and talking in the streets, and I heard many conversations not intended to meet my ears. I heard slave-hunters planning how to catch some poor fugitive. Several times I heard allusions to Dr. Flint, myself, and the history of my children, who, perhaps, were playing near the gate. One would say, "I wouldn't move my little finger to catch her, as old Flint's property," Another would say, "I'll catch any nigger for the reward. A man ought to have what belongs to him, if he is a damned brute." The opinion was often expressed that I was in the Free States. Very rarely did any one suggest that I might be in the vicinity. Had the least suspicion rested on my grandmother's house, it would have been burned to the ground. But it was the last place they thought of. Yet there was no place, where slavery existed, that could have afforded me so good a place of concealment.

Dr. Flint and his family repeatedly tried to coax and bribe my children to tell something they had heard said about me. One day the doctor took them into a shop, and offered them some bright little silver pieces and gay handkerchiefs if they would tell where their mother was. Ellen shrank away from him, and would not speak; but Benny spoke up, and said, "Dr. Flint, I don't know where my mother is. I guess she's in New York; and when you go there again, I wish you'd ask her to come home, for I want to see her; but if you put her in jail, or tell her you'll cut her head off, I'll tell her to go right back."

From Chapter XXIX. Preparations for Escape[5]

I hardly expect that the reader will credit me, when I affirm that I lived in that little dismal hole, almost deprived of light and air, and with no space to move my limbs, for nearly seven years. But it is a fact. and to me a sad one, even now; for my body still suffers from the effects of that long imprisonment, to say nothing of my soul. Members of my family, now living in New York and Boston, can testify to the truth of what I say.

Countless were the nights that I sat late at the little loophole scarcely large enough to give me a glimpse of one twinkling star. There, I heard the patrols and slave-hunters conferring together about the capture of runaways, well knowing how rejoiced they would be to catch me.

Season after season, year after year, I peeped at my children's faces, and heard their sweet voices, with a heart yearning all the while to say, "Your

5. In the omitted chapters, Brent reveals herself to her daughter, Ellen, who subsequently escapes to the North.

mother is here." Sometimes it appeared to me as if ages had rolled away since I entered upon that gloomy, monotonous existence. At times, I was stupefied and listless; at other times I became very impatient to know when these dark years would end, and I should again be allowed to feel the sunshine, and breathe the pure air. * * *

* * * My restlessness increased. I had lived too long in bodily pain and anguish of spirit. Always I was in dread that by some accident, or some contrivance, slavery would succeed in snatching my children from me. This thought drove me nearly frantic, and I determined to steer for the North Star[6] at all hazards. At this crisis, Providence opened an unexpected way for me to escape. My friend Peter came one evening, and asked to speak with me. "Your day has come, Linda," said he. "I have found a chance for you to go to the Free States. You have a fortnight to decide." The news seemed too good to be true; but Peter explained his arrangements, and told me all that was necessary was for me to say I would go.[7] * * *

The anticipation of being a free woman proved almost too much for my weak frame. The excitement stimulated me, and at the same time bewildered me. I made busy preparations for my journey, and for my son to follow me. I resolved to have an interview with him before I went, that I might give him cautions and advice, and tell him how anxiously I should be waiting for him at the north. Grandmother stole up to me as often as possible to whisper words of counsel. She insisted upon my writing to Dr. Flint, as soon as I arrived in the Free States, and asking him to sell me to her. She said she would sacrifice her house, and all she had in the world, for the sake of having me safe with my children in any part of the world. If she could only live to know *that* she could die in peace. I promised the dear old faithful friend that I would write to her as soon as I arrived, and put the letter in a safe way to reach her; but in my own mind I resolved that not another cent of her hard earnings should be spent to pay rapacious slave-holders for what they called their property. And even if I had not been unwilling to buy what I had already a right to possess, common humanity would have prevented me from accepting the generous offer, at the expense of turning my aged relative out of house and home, when she was trembling on the brink of the grave.

I was to escape in a vessel; but I forbear to mention any further particulars.[8] * * *

I made all my arrangements to go on board as soon as it was dusk. The intervening time I resolved to spend with my son. I had not spoken to him for seven years, though I had been under the same roof, and seen him every day, when I was well enough to sit at the loophole. I did not dare to venture beyond the storeroom; so they brought him there, and locked us up together, in a place concealed from the piazza door. It was an agitating interview for both of us. After we had talked and wept together for a little while, he said, "Mother, I'm glad you're going away. I wish I could go with you. I knew you was here; and I have been so afraid they would come and catch you!"

6. "This was the only guide of many a fleeing slave, hiding by day and running by night" [note by Walter Teller, editor of our text].

7. In the omitted passage, Brent at first hesitates to escape because of her son but is persuaded by her uncle Phillip to "seize the chance so unexpectedly offered"; Phillip also tells her grandmother.

8. In the omitted passage, Brent's grandmother is frightened by the murder of another fugitive slave. Brent, therefore, at first decides to remain with her grandmother and sends her friend Fanny to the ship in her place; Brent is, however, discovered by a neighbor when talking to her grandmother, who now tells her that she must go, too.

I was greatly surprised, and asked him how he had found it out.

He replied, "I was standing under the eaves, one day, before Ellen went away, and I heard somebody cough up over the wood shed. I don't know what made me think it was you, but I did think so. I missed Ellen, the night before she went away; and grandmother brought her back into the room in the night;[9] and I thought maybe she'd been to see *you*, before she went, for I heard grandmother whisper to her, 'Now go to sleep; and remember never to tell.' "

I asked him if he ever mentioned his suspicions to his sister. He said he never did; but after he heard the cough, if he saw her playing with other children on that side of the house, he always tried to coax her round to the other side, for fear they would hear me cough, too. He said he had kept a close lookout for Dr. Flint, and if he saw him speak to a constable, or a patrol, he always told grandmother. I now recollected that I had seen him manifest uneasiness, when people were on that side of the house, and I had at the time been puzzled to conjecture a motive for his actions. Such prudence may seem extraordinary in a boy of twelve years, but slaves, being surrounded by mysteries, deceptions, and dangers, early learn to be suspicious and watchful, and prematurely cautious and cunning. He had never asked a question of grandmother, or uncle Phillip, and I had often heard him chime in with other children, when they spoke of my being at the north.

I told him I was now really going to the Free States, and if he was a good, honest boy, and a loving child to his dear old grandmother, the Lord would bless him, and bring him to me, and we and Ellen would live together.

<div align="right">1861</div>

9. Ellen had spent her last night with her mother.

ELIZABETH CADY STANTON
1815–1902

"In thought and sympathy we were one," Elizabeth Cady Stanton wrote about herself and Susan B. Anthony, "and in the division of labor we exactly complemented each other. I am the better writer, she the better critic. She supplied the facts and statistics, I the philosophy and rhetoric, and, together, we have made arguments that stood unshaken through the storms of long years; arguments that no one has answered. Our speeches may be considered the united product of our two brains." Through Anthony's efficiency and Stanton's eloquence, these two reformers managed to dislodge feminist demands from the margins of other liberal movements. As different as they were temperamentally, together they formed the National Woman Suffrage Association (NWSA), which shaped the women's movement in America.

The woman who took literary responsibility for this effective collaboration was the fourth child of Daniel and Margaret (Livingston) Cady. After studying at home in Johnstown, New York, at the Johnstown Academy, and later at Emma Willard's Troy Female Seminary Elizabeth Cady married Henry Brewster Stanton, a journalist and reformer, in 1840, and they attended the World Anti-Slavery Convention in London on their honeymoon. There, with Lucretia Mott, Stanton became involved in a protest against the exclusion of women delegates, and planned a women's rights convention that was to take place on July 19, 1848, at Seneca Falls, New York. Stanton's draft of the *Declaration of Sentiments* for the

Seneca Falls Convention initiated a writing career that included the articles she published under the pseudonym "Sun Flower" in Amelia Bloomer's paper, the *Lily*, and the numerous speeches she delivered first in New York and later during several trips to the western states, tours that were undertaken, in part, to finance the education of her seven children. Stanton had met Anthony in 1851, when they began working together in the temperance and abolitionist movements. Before, during, and after the Civil War, they devoted themselves to the cause of women, organizing women's rights conventions and editing the weekly paper *Revolution*. As the president of NWSA for twenty-one years, Stanton became the major spokesperson for the women's movement. After the death of her husband in 1887, she extended her interest beyond suffrage, especially in her controversial feminist critique of the masculine bias in Judeo-Christian tradition, *The Woman's Bible* (1895, 1898). At this time, too, she published her lively autobiography, *Eighty Years and More* (1898). She continued lecturing on divorce, religion, and women's rights until she died in her sleep at the age of eighty-six, just after writing a letter to President Theodore Roosevelt in which she urged him to support women's suffrage.

From Address to the New York State Legislature, 1860[1]

You who have read the history of nations, from Moses[2] down to our last election, where have you ever seen one class looking after the interests of another? Any of you can readily see the defects in other governments, and pronounce sentence against those who have sacrificed the masses to themselves; but when we come to our own case, we are blinded by custom and self-interest. Some of you who have no capital can see the injustice which the laborer suffers; some of you who have no slaves, can see the cruelty of his oppression; but who of you appreciate the galling humiliation, the refinements of degradation, to which women (the mothers, wives, sisters, and daughters of freemen) are subject, in this the last half of the nineteenth century? How many of you have ever read even the laws concerning them that now disgrace your statute-books? In cruelty and tyranny, they are not surpassed by any slaveholding code in the Southern states; in fact they are worse, by just so far as woman, from her social position, refinement, and education, is on a more equal ground with the oppressor.

Allow me just here to call the attention of that party now so much interested in the slave of the Carolinas, to the similarity in his condition and that of the mothers, wives, and daughters of the Empire State.[3] The Negro has no name. He is Cuffy Douglas or Cuffy Brooks, just whose Cuffy he may chance to be. The woman has no name. She is Mrs. Richard Roe or Mrs. John Doe, just whose Mrs. she may chance to be. Cuffy has no right to his earnings; he can not buy or sell, or lay up anything that he can call his own. Mrs. Roe has no right to her earnings; she can neither buy nor sell, make contracts, nor lay up anything that she can call her own. Cuffy has no right to his children; they can be sold from him at any time. Mrs. Roe has no right to her children; they may be bound out to cancel a father's debts of honor. The unborn child, even, by

1. This speech, delivered by Stanton, was, like all the work of Stanton and Anthony (1881–86), the product of intensive collaboration. Anthony declared that it was up to Stanton to "move the hearts of our lawmakers at this time"; moreover, she came to live with Stanton to write the speech with her and to help in the household.
2. In the Old Testament, leader of the Israelites out of Egypt to the Promised Land.
3. New York State.

the last will of the father, may be placed under the guardianship of a stranger and a foreigner. Cuffy has no legal existence; he is subject to restraint and moderate chastisement. Mrs. Roe has no legal existence; she has not the best right to her own person. The husband has the power to restrain, and administer moderate chastisement.

Blackstone[4] declares that the husband and wife are one, and learned commentators have decided that that one is the husband. In all civil codes, you will find them classified as one. Certain rights and immunities, such and such privileges are to be secured to white male citizens. What have women and Negroes to do with rights? What know they of government, war, or glory?

The prejudice against color, of which we hear so much, is no stronger than that against sex. It is produced by the same cause, and manifested very much in the same way. The Negro's skin and the woman's sex are both *prima facie*[5] evidence that they were intended to be in subjection to the white Saxon man. The few social privileges which the man gives the woman, he makes up to the Negro in civil rights. The woman may sit at the same table and eat with the white man; the free Negro may hold property and vote. The woman may sit in the same pew with the white man in church; the free Negro may enter the pulpit and preach. Now, with the black man's right to suffrage, the right unquestioned, even by Paul, to minister at the altar,[6] it is evident that the prejudice against sex is more deeply rooted and more unreasonably maintained than that against color. * * *

Just imagine an inhabitant of another planet entertaining himself some pleasant evening in searching over our great national compact, our Declaration of Independence, our Constitutions, or some of our statute-books; what would he think of those "women and Negroes" that must be so fenced in, so guarded against? Why, he would certainly suppose we were monsters, like those fabulous giants or Brobdingnagians[7] of olden times, so dangerous to civilized man, from our size, ferocity, and power. Then let him take up our poets, from Pope down to Dana;[8] let him listen to our Fourth of July toasts, and some of the sentimental adulations of social life, and no logic could convince him that this creature of the law, and this angel of the family altar, could be one and the same being. Man is in such a labyrinth of contradictions with his marital and property rights; he is so befogged on the whole question of maidens, wives, and mothers, that from pure benevolence we should relieve him from this troublesome branch of legislation. We should vote, and make laws for ourselves. Do not be alarmed, dear ladies! You need spend no time reading Grotius, Coke, Puffendorf, Blackstone, Bentham, Kent, and Story[9] to find out what you need. We may safely trust the shrewd selfishness of the white man, and consent to live under the same broad code where he has so comfortably ensconced himself. Any legislation that will do for man, we may abide by most cheerfully. * * *

Now do not think, gentlemen, we wish you to do a great many troublesome things for us. We do not ask our legislators to spend a whole session in fixing

4. Sir William Blackstone, author of the influential *Commentaries on the Laws of England* (1765–69), had articulated the principle that "by marriage the very being or legal existence of a woman is suspended."
5. On first view (Latin).
6. In 1 Timothy 2:12, St. Paul refuses to allow "a woman to teach"; she must "be in silence."

7. The race of giants in Jonathan Swift's *Gulliver's Travels* (1735).
8. Alexander Pope (1688–1744) and Richard Henry Dana Sr. (1787–1879), male authors who wrote about women either satirically or romantically.
9. All, like Blackstone, writers on the law.

up a code of laws to satisfy a class of most unreasonable women. We ask no more than the poor devils in the Scripture asked, "Let us alone." In mercy, let us take care of ourselves, our property, our children, and our homes. True, we are not so strong, so wise, so crafty as you are, but if any kind friend leaves us a little money, or we can by great industry earn fifty cents a day, we would rather buy bread and clothes for our children than cigars and champagne for our legal protectors. There has been a great deal written and said about protection. We, as a class, are tired of one kind of protection, that which leaves us everything to do, to dare, and to suffer, and strips us of all means for its accomplishment. We would not tax man to take care of us. No, the Great Father has endowed all his creatures with the necessary powers for self-support, self-defense, and protection. We do not ask man to represent us; it is hard enough in times like these for man to carry backbone enough to represent himself. So long as the mass of men spend most of their time on the fence, not knowing which way to jump, they are surely in no condition to tell us where we had better stand. In pity for man, we would no longer hang like a mill-stone round his neck. Undo what man did for us in the Dark Ages, and strike out all special legislation for us; strike the words "white male" from all your constitutions, and then, with fair sailing, let us sink or swim, live or die, survive or perish together.

1860 1881–86

CHARLOTTE BRONTË

1816–1855

"Ten years ago we professed an orthodox system of novel-making. Our lovers were humble and devoted," remembered the Victorian journalist Margaret Oliphant in 1855, "when suddenly, without warning, *Jane Eyre* stole upon the scene, and the most alarming revolution of modern times has followed the invasion of *Jane Eyre*." When she spoke of "orthodox . . . novel-making," Oliphant no doubt meant to refer to the sentimental novels of manners that had been so popular in the earlier decades of the century. Certainly nothing could have been more different from such books than *Jane Eyre*. Indeed, although in our own century this revolutionary work has usually been thought of as a romance, the model for hundreds of best-selling love stories about darkly mysterious heroes and frail but feisty heroines, it is considerably more than that, as its first readers quickly understood. "*Jane Eyre* is throughout the personification of an unregenerate and undisciplined spirit," declared the reviewer Elizabeth Rigney in 1848, four years after the novel was published, and in 1853, another reviewer, Anne Mozley, recalled that the book seemed to many to have been written by "an alien . . . from society [who was] amenable to none of its laws."

 The author of this electrifying best-seller was born on April 21, 1816, the third child of Patrick Brontë, a clergyman of Irish descent, and his wife, Maria Branwell. In 1820, the family settled in the small Yorkshire town of Haworth, where the Reverend Brontë was curate of the local church. Both parents were evidently literary—Reverend Brontë produced several books of poetry, a novel, and a collection of sermons, and his wife wrote essays—but what might, despite modest means, have been a pleasant home became sorrowful when Mrs. Brontë died of cancer after giving birth to six children in rapid succession. Her husband tried in vain to remarry and finally invited his wife's sister, Elizabeth Branwell, to help care for his

orphaned family. A strict and forbidding woman, "Aunt Branwell" lived with the Brontës until her death in 1842, but she seems never to have provided the warmth that they lost with their mother's death. Another catastrophe added further gloom to the household: in 1824, seeking to enrich his children's lives, Reverend Brontë sent his four oldest girls to Clergy Daughters' School at Cowan Bridge, a charitable institution for the daughters of impoverished clergymen that Charlotte Brontë was later to memorialize as *Jane Eyre's* grim Lowood. By all accounts, her description in the novel was unfailingly accurate. Not only were the students subject to a tyrannical disciplinary system, they were so badly fed and housed that many became ill. Among the sickest were the Brontës. Maria and Elizabeth, the two oldest girls, succumbed to a combination of typhoid fever and consumption before their anxious relatives realized how dangerous conditions were; Charlotte and Emily were withdrawn from the school just in time to save their lives.

Isolated in their north England village on the edge of the Yorkshire moors, the four surviving children—Charlotte, Branwell, Emily, and Anne—drew together for comfort and eventually transformed Reverend Brontë's lonely parsonage into their own literary community. When their father brought Branwell a set of wooden soldiers, each child chose one, named it, and invented a history for it. Soon the tales they wove around these visionary beings evolved into a series of continuing fantasies about two imaginary kingdoms, "Angria" and "Gondal." Eventually, Branwell and Charlotte began to collaborate in recording the chronicles of Angria, while Emily and Anne transcribed the history of Gondal. Voracious readers, they reproduced the styles and themes of writers, most notably the popular Scottish novelist Sir Walter Scott and the Romantic poet Lord Byron, as well as the formats of journals like *Blackwood's*, in tiny volumes "printed" in a microscopic hand so as to look like miniaturized versions of real books.

What is more striking still, the Brontës continued creating and transcribing these romantic tales even after Charlotte had once again been sent away to school—this time, in 1831–32, to Roe Head, a far more comfortable and convenient establishment than Cowan Bridge had been—and even after she had returned to Roe Head in 1835 as a member of the teaching staff. In fact, in some ways Brontë's fantasizings about Angria intensified as she entered the workaday world of the schoolroom, where, as she noted, she had to toil in "irritation and weariness" to teach recalcitrant pupils "the distinction between an article and a substantive." Feeling herself trapped in "wretched bondage" to a career for which she had no natural vocation, she confided to her journal, "I should be agonised if I had not the dream [of Angria] to repose on," and in moments of "divine leisure" she transcribed the "fascinating spell" that the "infernal world" of her daydreams cast on her, writing in a kind of trance, with her eyes closed and her mind full of visions.

Despite Charlotte Brontë's sense that as a teacher or governess she was in "bondage," she knew that such jobs offered the only source of income to genteel but impoverished young women. As the unmarried daughter of a country clergyman with small means, Brontë had to find a way of supporting herself. Marriage was always, of course, a solution to a spinster's financial problems, but this independent young woman was determined to marry only a man she could respect, and though she had several proposals, none came from such a person. Inevitably, then, she was consigned to the schoolroom or the nursery. After teaching at Roe Head, she went on to several "situations" as private governess, and it is no doubt from these that she learned a truth that stands behind so many of the pained exclamations of her governess-heroine, Jane Eyre: "a private governess has no existence, is not considered as a living and rational being except as connected with the wearisome duties she has to fulfill."

In the summer of 1842, however, Charlotte Brontë and her younger sister Emily were suddenly given a chance for escape from such "wearisome duties." Troubled by her nieces' dilemma, the Brontës' severe Aunt Branwell quite unexpectedly of-

fered them a small sum of money so that they could open a school of their own. But if they were to attempt such an enterprise, they would have to be better educated than they were, and so a second plan was set in motion: Charlotte and Emily were to be sent to Brussels, to a finishing school for young ladies called the Pensionnat Héger, where they would acquire the facility in foreign languages and the continental polish that would fit them to be self-employed headmistresses.

Run by Constantin Héger, an impetuous but brilliant teacher, and his wife, Zoe, the daughter of a cultivated French emigré family, the Pensionnat was a small but exceptionally enlightened educational institution. It was here, however, that Charlotte Brontë found herself involved in real life in the kind of romantic struggle that she had up till now only encountered in her Angrian daydreams. For, perhaps within a few months of her arrival in Brussels, she began to fall in love with Mr. Héger, although, as a married man and a devout Catholic, he gave no sign of returning her feelings. At the end of a year, Aunt Branwell died and the sisters returned to Haworth, where Emily decided to stay and keep house for her father. But Charlotte could not repress her feelings; in the words of her fine biographer Winifred Gerin, she was drawn as by a "somnambulist's compulsion" to return to Brussels, where she spent a year as a teacher at the Pensionnat and where both the charisma and the increasing coolness of the "master" she loved gave her what was to become essential material for all four of her novels.

Those novels were not begun until two years after Charlotte had retreated to England in an effort to cure her unrequited passion. Still hoping to begin their school, the Brontë sisters drew up circulars and mailed them to prospective pupils, while in the meantime Charlotte wrote a series of pathetic letters to Héger, declaring that her correspondence with him was now her "only joy on earth." But there was little or no response to either the school circulars or the love letters. Not a single pupil expressed interest in "The Misses Brontë's Establishment," and Héger replied to Charlotte's pleas for understanding at first with perfunctory friendliness and then with prolonged silence. By 1845, it was clear that this rebellious governess would not find redemption either in romance or in private enterprise. Her salvation lay in the writing that had always been her vocation, and in the community of imagination that she shared with her sisters, Anne and Emily.

It was Emily who provided the first impulse toward the creative resurrection that marked the years 1845 to 1848 for Charlotte Brontë. Accidentally discovering some of the verses the author-to-be of *Wuthering Heights* had been composing for years about the inhabitants of *her* fantasy kingdom, Gondal, Charlotte was struck by their distinctive intensity. Always decisive when she thought she saw a way out of the poverty in which the sisters were ensnared, she resolved at once to send the poems to a publisher, adding some works of her own and Anne's for good measure. Before doing so, she rechristened the three newly professional writers with *noms de plume* that were deliberately ambiguous in gender: Charlotte, Emily, and Anne Brontë became Currer, Ellis, and Acton Bell, ostensibly because, as Charlotte was somewhat disingenuously to explain later, "What author would be without the advantage of being able to walk invisible?" but more likely because women's works were not usually received with sufficient seriousness by reviewers.

The volume called *Poems by Currer, Ellis, and Acton Bell* was hardly received at all, in any case, for it sold only two copies in the year after its publication. Undaunted by this failure, however, the three Brontës turned to fiction, and here Charlotte's painful love for Héger, together with her years of transforming her daydreams about Angria into vivid romances, stood her in good stead. Her first novel, *The Professor* (published posthumously), drew directly on her experiences in Brussels, although it was told by a male narrator, as if its author were trying to disguise her own pain from herself. Her third novel, *Shirley* (1849), featured a hero who was a French tutor. Her fourth, *Villette* (1853), was set again in Brussels, and it was in good part devoted to an extraordinarily accurate portrait of the "master" she loved. Despite a surface realism, however, all three works were infused by

Romantic and Gothic elements—dreams, visions, dramatic encounters—as well as by an energy of imagination that transformed biographical materials into compelling art.

But it was in Charlotte Brontë's second novel, *Jane Eyre* (1847), that all the elements of her life were most effectively transmuted into a powerful work of fiction. Her early trauma at Cowan Bridge, her hardships as a governess, and her love for Héger—all these experiences helped shape the fictional autobiography of a heroine who, like Brontë herself, seemed small, plain, and decorous even while her apparently "unregenerate spirit" brought about "the most alarming revolution of modern times." At the same time, this book in which a determined female narrator spoke with what was in 1847 surprising authority about a woman's desire for liberty—"for liberty I gasped; for liberty I uttered a prayer"—was also shaped and strengthened by a fantastic subplot for which there was no real-life precedent: the story of Bertha Mason Rochester. As if commenting on Jane's apparent decorum, Bertha's fierce mutterings and secret midnight wanderings suggest more sinister and subversive strategies to which women might be driven in their search for "liberty."

When *Jane Eyre* appeared, this unprecedented romance—combining an account of an independent woman's dreams and desires with a fantasy about explosive madness—took the reading public by storm. Shy by nature and profoundly unused to the sophistication of London circles, "Currer Bell" found herself almost overnight a literary "lion." Years later Anne Ritchie the daughter of the novelist William Makepeace Thackeray, still remembered her father's first meeting with the acclaimed author, and Elizabeth Gaskell reverently recorded her first impressions of Charlotte Brontë in a letter she later reprinted in her 1857 *Life of Charlotte Brontë*. Despite the fact that she continued to live quietly in Haworth, the governess who had seemed to have "no existence" had now a dramatic public life.

For Brontë herself, however, such success was bittersweet. Soon after the publication of *Jane Eyre*, her brother Branwell died in painful circumstances. Ostensibly an art student and painter, he had for years been both an alcoholic and a drug addict, and like his sister Charlotte but without her resilience, he had endured the pains of unrequited love. Within months, his death was followed by the deaths from tuberculosis of Emily and Anne. Bereft of the siblings who had constituted the only literary society she really wanted to join Charlotte could not be consoled by her newly won fame. A determined survivor, she went on writing and keeping house for her father, but the Brontë parsonage was now lonelier and more sorrowful than ever, so that when Mrs. Gaskell visited in 1853 she was as struck by the silence as by the "exquisite" cleanliness of the household.

Perhaps in an attempt to cheer her solitude and her father's, Charlotte Brontë married Arthur Bell Nicholls, the Reverend Brontë's curate, in 1854. The marriage seems to have been reasonably content, although the new Mrs. Nicholls did complain to a friend that "the married woman can call but a very small portion of each day her own." Toward the end of the year, however, she became pregnant and suffered so severe a case of what it is almost an understatement to call "morning sickness" that by March of 1855 she was bedridden and emaciated. Some biographers have speculated that her illness was complicated by the same tuberculosis that killed her sisters; others have suggested that she could no longer continue the life that had consumed so many of those she loved. Whatever the medical causes, she died on March 31, 1855, and was buried near her sisters and brother in Haworth churchyard

If Brontë's body had not been equal to the task of survival, however, her imagination had been more than equal to that job. "Imagination is a strong, restless faculty which claims to be heard and exercised: are we to be quite deaf to her cry and insensate to her struggles?" she once wrote to the man of letters George Henry Lewes. For her, such a question had only one answer. Through all the hardships of

an exceptionally difficult life, Brontë herself had attended with special intensity to the claims of imagination, so that, as Virginia Woolf declared seventy years after this writer's death, even now when we read *Jane Eyre* "we are steeped through and through with the genius, the vehemence, the indignation of Charlotte Brontë."

Jane Eyre[1]

Chapter I

There was no possibility of taking a walk that day. We had been wandering, indeed, in the leafless shrubbery an hour in the morning; but since dinner (Mrs. Reed, when there was no company, dined early) the cold winter wind had brought with it clouds so somber, and a rain so penetrating, that further outdoor exercise was now out of the question.

I was glad of it: I never liked long walks, especially on chilly afternoons: dreadful to me was the coming home in the raw twilight, with nipped fingers and toes, and a heart saddened by the chidings of Bessie, the nurse, and humbled by the consciousness of my physical inferiority to Eliza, John, and Georgiana Reed.

The said Eliza, John, and Georgiana were now clustered round their mamma in the drawing-room: she lay reclined on the sofa by the fireside, and with her darlings about her (for the time neither quarreling nor crying) looked perfectly happy. Me, she had dispensed from joining the group; saying, "She regretted to be under the necessity of keeping me at a distance; but that until she heard from Bessie and could discover by her own observation that I was endeavoring in good earnest to acquire a more sociable and childlike disposition, a more attractive and sprightly manner—something lighter, franker, more natural, as it were—she really must exclude me from privileges intended only for contented, happy, little children."

"What does Bessie say I have done?" I asked.

"Jane, I don't like cavilers or questioners: besides, there is something truly forbidding in a child taking up her elders in that manner. Be seated somewhere; and until you can speak pleasantly, remain silent."

A small breakfast-room adjoined the drawing-room. I slipped in there. It contained a bookcase: I soon possessed myself of a volume, taking care that it should be one stored with pictures. I mounted into the window-seat: gathering up my feet, I sat cross-legged like a Turk; and, having drawn the red moreen curtain nearly close, I was shrined in double retirement.

Folds of scarlet drapery shut in my view to the right hand; to the left were the clear panes of glass, protecting, but not separating me from the drear November day. At intervals, while turning over the leaves of my book, I studied the aspect of that winter afternoon. Afar, it offered a pale blank of mist and cloud; near, a scene of wet lawn and storm-beat shrub, with ceaseless rain sweeping away wildly before a long and lamentable blast.

I returned to my book—Bewick's *History of British Birds:*[2] the letterpress thereof I cared little for, generally speaking; and yet there were certain intro-

1. We are indebted to Richard J. Dunn for information contained in his notes to the Norton Critical Edition of *Jane Eyre*.

2. I.e., the text. Thomas Bewick, *History of British Birds* (1804).

ductory pages that, child as I was, I could not pass quite as a blank. They were those which treat of the haunts of sea-fowl; of "the solitary rocks and promontories" by them only inhabited; of the coast of Norway, studded with isles from its southern extremity, the Lindeness, or Naze, to the North Cape————

> Where the Northern Ocean, in vast whirls,
> Boils round the naked, melancholy isles
> Of farthest Thule; and the Atlantic surge
> Pours in among the stormy Hebrides.[3]

Nor could I pass unnoticed the suggestion of the bleak shores of Lapland, Siberia, Spitzbergen, Nova Zembla, Iceland, Greenland, with the "vast sweep of the Arctic Zone, and those forlorn regions of dreary space—that reservoir of frost and snow, where firm fields of ice, the accumulation of centuries of winters, glazed in Alpine heights above heights, surround the pole, and concentre the multiplied rigors of extreme cold." Of these death-white realms I formed an idea of my own: shadowy, like all the half-comprehended notions that float dim through children's brains, but strangely impressive. The words in these introductory pages connected themselves with the succeeding vignettes, and gave significance to the rock standing up alone in a sea of billow and spray; to the broken boat stranded on a desolate coast; to the cold and ghastly moon glancing through bars of cloud at a wreck just sinking.

I cannot tell what sentiment haunted the quite solitary churchyard, with its inscribed headstone; its gate, its two trees, its low horizon, girdled by a broken wall, and its newly-risen crescent, attesting the hour of eventide.

The two ships becalmed on a torpid sea I believed to be marine phantoms.

The fiend pinning down the thief's pack behind him I passed over quickly: it was an object of terror.

So was the black, horned thing seated aloof on a rock, surveying a distant crowd surrounding a gallows.

Each picture told a story; mysterious often to my undeveloped understanding and imperfect feelings, yet ever profoundly interesting: as interesting as the tales Bessie sometimes narrated on winter evenings, when she chanced to be in good humor; and when, having brought her ironing-table to the nursery-hearth, she allowed us to sit about it, and while she got up Mrs. Reed's lace frills, and crimped her night-cap borders, fed our eager attention with passages of love and adventure taken from old fairy tales and older ballads; or (as at a later period I discovered) from the pages of "Pamela," and "Henry, Earl of Moreland."[4]

With Bewick on my knee, I was then happy: happy at least in my way. I feared nothing but interruption and that came too soon. The breakfast-room door opened.

"Bah! Madame Mope." cried the voice of John Reed; then he paused: he found the room apparently empty.

"Where the dickens is she?" he continued. "Lizzy! Georgy! (calling to his sisters) Joan[5] is not here: tell mamma she is run out into the rain—bad animal!"

3. From James Thomson's *Seasons*, *Autumn*, lines 862–65.
4. The popular 18th-century novel by Samuel

Richardson and an abridgement of the novel by Henry Brooke.
5. "Jane" is a variant of "Joan."

"It is well I drew the curtain," thought I; and I wished fervently he might not discover my hiding-place: nor would John Reed have found it out himself; he was not quick either of vision or conception; but Eliza just put her head in at the door, and said at once:—"She is in the window-seat, to be sure, Jack."

And I came out immediately, for I trembled at the idea of being dragged forth by the said Jack.

"What do you want?" I asked, with awkward diffidence.

"Say, 'what do you want, Master Reed?' " was the answer. "I want you to come here"; and sitting himself in an arm-chair, he intimated by a gesture that I was to approach and stand before him.

John Reed was a schoolboy of fourteen years old; four years older than I, for I was but ten; large and stout for his age, with a dingy and unwholesome skin; thick lineaments in a spacious visage, heavy limbs and large extremities. He gorged himself habitually at table, which made him bilious, and gave him a dim and bleared eye and flabby cheeks. He ought now to have been at school; but his mamma had taken him home for a month or two, "on account of his delicate health." Mr. Miles, the master, affirmed that he would do very well if he had fewer cakes and sweetmeats sent him from home; but the mother's heart turned from an opinion so harsh, and inclined rather to the more refined idea that John's sallowness was owing to over-application and, perhaps, to pining after home.

John had not much affection for his mother and sisters, and an antipathy to me. He bullied and punished me; not two or three times in the week, nor once or twice in the day, but continually: every nerve I had feared him, and every morsel of flesh on my bones shrank when he came near. There were moments when I was bewildered by the terror he inspired, because I had no appeal whatever against either his menaces or his inflictions; the servants did not like to offend their young master by taking my part against him, and Mrs. Reed was blind and deaf on the subject: she never saw him strike or heard him abuse me, though he did both now and then in her very presence; more frequently, however, behind her back.

Habitually obedient to John, I came up to his chair: he spent some three minutes in thrusting out his tongue at me as far as he could without damaging the roots: I knew he would soon strike, and while dreading the blow, I mused on the disgusting and ugly appearance of him who would presently deal it. I wonder if he read that notion in my face; for, all at once, without speaking, he struck suddenly and strongly. I tottered, and regaining my equilibrium retired back a step or two from his chair.

"That is for your impudence in answering mamma a while since," said he, "and for your sneaking way of getting behind curtains, and for the look you had in your eyes two minutes since, you rat!"

Accustomed to John Reed's abuse, I never had an idea of replying to it; my care was how to endure the blow which would certainly follow the insult.

"What were you doing behind the curtain?" he asked.

"I was reading."

"Show the book."

I returned to the window and fetched it thence.

"You have no business to take our books; you are a dependent, mamma says; you have no money; your father left you none; you ought to beg, and not live here with gentlemen's children like us, and eat the same meals we do, and

wear clothes at our mamma's expense. Now, I'll teach you to rummage my book-shelves: for they *are* mine; all the house belongs to me, or will do in a few years. Go and stand by the door, out of the way of the mirror and the windows."

I did so, not at first aware what was his intention; but when I saw him lift and poise the book and stand in act to hurl it, I instinctively started aside with a cry of alarm: not soon enough, however; the volume was flung, it hit me, and I fell, striking my head against the door and cutting it. The cut bled, the pain was sharp: my terror had passed its climax; other feelings succeeded.

"Wicked and cruel boy!" I said. "You are like a murderer—you are like a slave-driver—you are like the Roman emperors!"

I had read Goldsmith's *History of Rome*,[6] and had formed my opinion of Nero, Caligula, etc. Also I had drawn parallels in silence, which I never thought thus to have declared aloud.

"What! what!" he cried. "Did she say that to me? Did you hear her, Eliza and Georgiana? Won't I tell mamma? but first———"

He ran headlong at me: I felt him grasp my hair and my shoulder: he had closed with a desperate thing. I really saw in him a tyrant: a murderer. I felt a drop or two of blood from my head trickle down my neck, and was sensible of somewhat pungent suffering: these sensations for the time predominated over fear, and I received him in frantic sort. I don't very well know what I did with my hands, but he called me "Rat! rat!" and bellowed out aloud. Aid was near him: Eliza and Georgiana had run for Mrs. Reed, who was gone upstairs; she now came upon the scene, followed by Bessie and her maid Abbot. We were parted: I heard the words:—"Dear! dear! What a fury to fly at Master John!"

"Did ever anybody see such a picture of passion!"

Then Mrs. Reed subjoined:—"Take her away to the red-room, and lock her in there." Four hands were immediately laid upon me, and I was borne upstairs.

Chapter II

I resisted all the way: a new thing for me, and a circumstance which greatly strengthened the bad opinion Bessie and Miss Abbot were disposed to entertain of me. The fact is, I was a trifle beside myself; or rather *out* of myself, as the French would say: I was conscious that a moment's mutiny had already rendered me liable to strange penalties, and, like any other rebel slave, I felt resolved, in my desperation, to go all lengths.

"Hold her arms, Miss Abbot: she's like a mad cat."

"For shame! for shame!" cried the lady's-maid. "What shocking conduct, Miss Eyre, to strike a young gentleman, your benefactress's son! Your young master."

"Master! How is he my master? Am I a servant?"

"No; you are less than a servant, for you do nothing for your keep. There, sit down, and think over your wickedness."

They had got me by this time into the apartment indicated by Mrs. Reed, and had thrust me upon a stool: my impulse was to rise from it like a spring; their two pairs of hands arrested me instantly.

6. Oliver Goldsmith's *The Roman History* (1769).

"If you don't sit still, you must be tied down," said Bessie. "Miss Abbot, lend me your garters; she would break mine directly."

Miss Abbot turned to divest a stout leg of the necessary ligature. This preparation for bonds, and the additional ignominy it inferred, took a little of the excitement out of me.

"Don't take them off," I cried; "I will not stir."

In guarantee whereof I attached myself to my seat by my hands.

"Mind you don't," said Bessie; and when she had ascertained that I was really subsiding, she loosened her hold of me; then she and Miss Abbot stood with folded arms, looking darkly and doubtfully on my face, as incredulous of my sanity.

"She never did so before," at last said Bessie, turning to the Abigail.[7]

"But it was always in her," was the reply. "I've told Missis often my opinion about the child, and Missis agreed with me. She's an underhand little thing: I never saw a girl of her age with so much cover."[8]

Bessie answered not; but ere long, addressing me, she said:

"You ought to be aware, Miss, that you are under obligations to Mrs. Reed: she keeps you: if she were to turn you off,[9] you would have to go to the poorhouse."

I had nothing to say to these words: they were not new to me: my very first recollections of existence included hints of the same kind. This reproach of my dependence had become a vague singsong in my ear; very painful and crushing, but only half intelligible. Miss Abbot joined in:—"And you ought not to think yourself on an equality with the Misses Reed and Master Reed, because Missis kindly allows you to be brought up with them. They will have a great deal of money, and you will have none: it is your place to be humble, and to try to make yourself agreeable to them."

"What we tell you is for your good," added Bessie, in no harsh voice: "you should try to be useful and pleasant, then, perhaps, you would have a home here; but if you become passionate and rude, Missis will send you away, I am sure."

"Besides," said Miss Abbot, "God will punish her: He might strike her dead in the midst of her tantrums, and then where would she go? Come, Bessie, we will leave her: I wouldn't have her heart for anything. Say your prayers, Miss Eyre, when you are by yourself; for if you don't repent, something bad might be permitted to come down the chimney, and fetch you away."

They went, shutting the door, and locking it behind them.

The red-room was a spare chamber, very seldom slept in; I might say never, indeed, unless when a chance influx of visitors at Gateshead Hall rendered it necessary to turn to account all the accommodation it contained: yet it was one of the largest and stateliest chambers in the mansion. A bed supported on massive pillars of mahogany, hung with curtains of deep red damask, stood out like a tabernacle in the center; the two large windows, with their blinds always drawn down, were half shrouded in festoons and falls of similar drapery; the carpet was red; the table at the foot of the bed was covered with a crimson cloth; the walls were a soft fawn color, with a blush of pink in it; the wardrobe, the toilet-table, the chairs were of darkly-polished old mahogany. Out of these

7. A lady's personal servant (after a character in a play by Beaumont and Fletcher).
8. Deception.
9. Turn you out.

deep surrounding shades rose high, and glared white, the piled-up mattresses and pillows of the bed, spread with a snowy Marseilles counterpane. Scarcely less prominent was an ample, cushioned easy-chair near the head of the bed, also white, with a footstool before it; and looking, as I thought, like a pale throne.

This room was chill, because it seldom had a fire; it was silent, because remote from the nursery and kitchens; solemn, because it was known to be so seldom entered. The housemaid alone came here on Saturdays, to wipe from the mirrors and the furniture a week's quiet dust: and Mrs. Reed herself, at far intervals, visited it to review the contents of a certain secret drawer in the wardrobe, where were stored divers parchments, her jewel-casket, and a miniature of her deceased husband; and in those last words lies the secret of the red-room—the spell which kept it so lonely in spite of its grandeur.

Mr. Reed had been dead nine years: it was in this chamber he breathed his last; here he lay in state; hence his coffin was borne by the undertaker's men; and, since that day, a sense of dreary consecration had guarded it from frequent intrusion.

My seat, to which Bessie and the bitter Miss Abbot had left me riveted, was a low ottoman near the marble chimney-piece; the bed rose before me; to my right hand there was the high, dark wardrobe, with subdued, broken reflections varying the gloss of its panels. to my left were the muffled windows; a great looking-glass between them repeated the vacant majesty of the bed and room. I was not quite sure whether they had locked the door; and, when I dared move, I got up, and went to see. Alas! yes: no jail was ever more secure. Returning, I had to cross before the looking-glass; my fascinated glance involuntarily explored the depth it revealed. All looked colder and darker in that visionary hollow than in reality: and the strange little figure there gazing at me, with a white face and arms specking the gloom, and glittering eyes of fear moving where all else was still, had the effect of a real spirit: I thought it like one of the tiny phantoms, half fairy, half imp, Bessie's evening stories represented as coming out of lone, ferny dells in moors, and appearing before the eyes of belated travelers. I returned to my stool.

Superstition was with me at that moment; but it was not yet her hour for complete victory: my blood was still warm; the mood of the revolted slave was still bracing me with its bitter vigor; I had to stem a rapid rush of retrospective thought before I quailed to the dismal present.

All John Reed's violent tyrannies, all his sisters' proud indifference, all his mother's aversion, all the servant's partiality, turned up in my disturbed mind like a dark deposit in a turbid well. Why was I always suffering, always browbeaten, always accused, forever condemned? Why could I never please? Why was it useless to try to win any one's favor? Eliza, who was headstrong and selfish, was respected. Georgiana, who had a spoiled temper, a very acrid spite, a captious and insolent carriage, was universally indulged. Her beauty, her pink cheeks and golden curls, seemed to give delight to all who looked at her, and to purchase indemnity for every fault. John, no one thwarted, much less punished; though he twisted the necks of the pigeons, killed the little pea-chicks,[1] set the dogs at the sheep, stripped the hothouse vines of their fruit, and broke the buds off the choicest plants in the conservatory: he called his mother "old

1. Peacock chicks.

girl," too; sometimes reviled her for her dark skin, similar to his own; bluntly disregarded her wishes; not unfrequently tore and spoiled her silk attire; and he was still "her own darling." I dared commit no fault; I strove to fulfill every duty; and I was termed naughty and tiresome, sullen and sneaking, from morning to noon, and from noon to night.

My head still ached and bled with the blow and fall I had received: no one had reproved John for wantonly striking me; and because I had turned against him to avert farther irrational violence, I was loaded with general opprobrium.

"Unjust!—unjust!" said my reason, forced by the agonizing stimulus into precocious though transitory power; and Resolve, equally wrought up, insti-gated some strange expedient to achieve escape from insupportable oppres-sion—as running away, or, if that could not be effected, never eating or drinking more, and letting myself die.

What a consternation of soul was mine that dreary afternoon! How all my brain was in tumult, and all my heart in insurrection! Yet in what darkness, what dense ignorance, was the mental battle fought! I could not answer the ceaseless inward question—*why* I thus suffered; now, at the distance of—I will not say how many years, I see it clearly.

I was a discord in Gateshead Hall; I was like nobody there; I had nothing in harmony with Mrs. Reed or her children, or her chosen vassalage. If they did not love me, in fact, as little did I love them. They were not bound to regard with affection a thing that could not sympathize with one amongst them; a heterogeneous thing, opposed to them in temperament, in capacity, in propensities; a useless thing, incapable of serving their interest, or adding to their pleasure; a noxious thing, cherishing the germs of indignation at their treatment, of contempt of their judgment. I know that had I been a sanguine, brilliant, careless, exacting, handsome, romping child—though equally de-pendent and friendless—Mrs. Reed would have endured my presence more complacently; her children would have entertained for me more of the cor-diality of fellow-feeling; the servants would have been less prone to make me the scapegoat of the nursery.

Daylight began to forsake the red-room; it was past four o'clock, and the be-clouded afternoon was tending to drear twilight. I heard the rain still beating continuously on the staircase window, and the wind howling in the grove be-hind the hall; I grew by degrees cold as a stone, and then my courage sank. My habitual mood of humiliation, self-doubt, forlorn depression, fell damp on the embers of my decaying ire. All said I was wicked, and perhaps I might be so: what thought had I been but just conceiving of starving myself to death? That certainly was a crime: and was I fit to die? Or was the vault under the chancel of Gateshead Church an inviting bourne? In such vault I had been told did Mr. Reed lie buried; and led by this thought to recall his idea, I dwelt on it with gathering dread. I could not remember him; but I knew that he was my own uncle—my mother's brother—that he had taken me when a parentless infant to his house; and that in his last moments he had required a promise of Mrs. Reed that she would rear and maintain me as one of her own children. Mrs. Reed probably considered she had kept this promise; and so she had, I dare say, as well as her nature would permit her; but how could she really like an inter-loper not of her race,[2] and unconnected with her, after her husband's death, by

2. I.e., family.

any tie? It must have been most irksome to find herself bound by a hard-wrung pledge to stand in the stead of a parent to a strange child she could not love, and to see an uncongenial alien permanently intruded on her own family group.

A singular notion dawned upon me. I doubted not—never doubted—that if Mr. Reed had been alive he would have treated me kindly; and now, as I sat looking at the white bed and overshadowed walls—occasionally also turning a fascinated eye towards the dimly gleaming mirror—I began to recall what I had heard of dead men, troubled in their graves by the violation of their last wishes, revisiting the earth to punish the perjured and avenge the oppressed; and I thought Mr. Reed's spirit, harassed by the wrongs of his sister's child, might quit its abode—whether in the church vault, or in the unknown world of the departed—and rise before me in this chamber. I wiped my tears and hushed my sobs, fearful lest any sign of violent grief might waken a preternatural voice to comfort me, or elicit from the gloom some haloed face, bending over me with strange pity. This idea, consolatory in theory, I felt would be terrible if realized: with all my might I endeavored to stifle it—I endeavored to be firm. Shaking my hair from my eyes, I lifted my head and tried to look boldly round the dark room. At this moment a light gleamed on the wall. Was it, I asked myself, a ray from the moon penetrating some aperture in the blind? No; moonlight was still, and this stirred; while I gazed, it glided up to the ceiling and quivered over my head. I can now conjecture readily that this streak of light was, in all likelihood, a gleam from a lantern carried by some one across the lawn: but then, prepared as my mind was for horror, shaken as my nerves were by agitation, I thought the swift-darting beam was a herald of some coming vision from another world. My heart beat thick, my head grew hot; a sound filled my ears, which I deemed the rushing of wings: something seemed near me; I was oppressed, suffocated: endurance broke down; I rushed to the door and shook the lock in desperate effort. Steps came running along the outer passage; the key turned, Bessie and Abbot entered.

"Miss Eyre, are you ill?" said Bessie.

"What a dreadful noise! it went quite through me!" exclaimed Abbot.

"Take me out! let me go into the nursery!" was my cry.

"What for? Are you hurt? Have you seen something?" again demanded Bessie.

"Oh! I saw a light, and I thought a ghost would come." I had now got hold of Bessie's hand, and she did not snatch it from me.

"She has screamed out on purpose," declared Abbot, in some disgust. "And what a scream! If she had been in great pain one would have excused it, but she only wanted to bring us all here: I know her naughty tricks."

"What is all this?" demanded another voice, peremptorily; and Mrs. Reed came along the corridor, her cap flying wide, her gown rustling stormily. "Abbot and Bessie, I believe I gave orders that Jane Eyre should be left in the red-room till I came to her myself."

"Miss Jane screamed so loud, ma'am," pleaded Bessie.

"Let her go," was the only answer. "Loose Bessie's hand, child: you cannot succeed in getting out by these means, be assured. I abhor artifice, particularly in children; it is my duty to show you that tricks will not answer: you will now stay here an hour longer, and it is only on condition of perfect submission and stillness that I shall liberate you then."

"Oh aunt, have pity! Forgive me! I cannot endure it—let me be punished some other way! I shall be killed if——"

"Silence! This violence is all most repulsive": and so, no doubt, she felt it. I was a precocious actress in her eyes: she sincerely looked on me as a compound of virulent passions, mean spirit, and dangerous duplicity.

Bessie and Abbot having retreated, Mrs. Reed, impatient of my now frantic anguish and wild sobs, abruptly thrust me back and locked me in, without far-ther parley. I heard her sweeping away; and soon after she was gone I suppose I had a species of fit: unconsciousness closed the scene.

Chapter III

The next thing I remember is, waking up with a feeling as if I had had a frightful nightmare, and seeing before me a terrible red glare, crossed with thick black bars. I heard voices, too, speaking with a hollow sound, as if muf-fled by a rush of wind or water: agitation, uncertainty, and an all-predominat-ing sense of terror confused my faculties. Ere long I became aware that some one was handling me; lifting me up and supporting me in a sitting posture, and that more tenderly than I had ever been raised or upheld before. I rested my head against a pillow or an arm, and felt easy.

In five minutes more the cloud of bewilderment dissolved: I knew quite well that I was in my own bed, and that the red glare was the nursery fire. It was night: a candle burned on the table; Bessie stood at the bed-foot with a basin in her hand, and a gentleman sat in a chair near my pillow, leaning over me.

I felt an inexpressible relief, a soothing conviction of protection and secu-rity, when I knew that there was a stranger in the room, an individual not be-longing to Gateshead, and not related to Mrs. Reed. Turning from Bessie (though her presence was far less obnoxious to me than that of Abbot, for in-stance, would have been), I scrutinized the face of the gentleman: I knew him; it was Mr. Lloyd, an apothecary, sometimes called in by Mrs. Reed when the servants were ailing: for herself and the children she employed a physician.

"Well, who am I?" he asked.

I pronounced his name, offering him at the same time my hand: he took it, smiling and saying, "We shall do very well by-and-by." Then he laid me down, and addressing Bessie, charged her to be very careful that I was not disturbed during the night. Having given some further directions, and intimated that he should call again the next day, he departed—to my grief: I felt so sheltered and befriended while he sat in the chair near my pillow; and as he closed the door after him all the room darkened and my heart again sank: inexpressible sad-ness weighed it down.

"Do you feel as if you should sleep, Miss?" asked Bessie, rather softly.

Scarcely dared I answer her; for I feared the next sentence might be rough. "I will try."

"Would you like to drink, or could you eat anything?"

"No, thank you, Bessie."

"Then I think I shall go to bed, for it is past twelve o'clock; but you may call me if you want anything in the night."

Wonderful civility this! It emboldened me to ask a question.

"Bessie, what is the matter with me? Am I ill?"

"You fell sick, I suppose, in the red-room with crying; you'll be better soon, no doubt."

Bessie went into the housemaid's apartment, which was near. I heard her say—"Sarah, come and sleep with me in the nursery; I daren't for my life be alone with that poor child tonight; she might die; it's such a strange thing she should have that fit: I wonder if she saw anything. Missis was rather too hard."

Sarah came back with her; they both went to bed; they were whispering together for half an hour before they fell asleep. I caught scraps of their conversation, from which I was able only too distinctly to infer the main subject discussed.

"Something passed her, all dressed in white, and vanished"—"A great black dog behind him"—"Three loud raps on the chamber door"—"A light in the churchyard just over his grave"—etc. etc.

At last both slept: the fire and the candle went out. For me, the watches of that long night passed in ghastly wakefulness; ear, eye, and mind were alike strained by dread: such dread as children only can feel.

No severe or prolonged bodily illness followed this incident of the red-room: it only gave my nerves a shock, of which I feel the reverberation to this day. Yes, Mrs. Reed, to you I owe some fearful pangs of mental suffering. But I ought to forgive you, for you knew not what you did:[3] while rending my heart-strings, you thought you were only uprooting my bad propensities.

Next day, by noon, I was up and dressed, and sat wrapped in a shawl by the nursery hearth. I felt physically weak and broken down; but my worst ailment was an unutterable wretchedness of mind: a wretchedness which kept drawing from me silent tears; no sooner had I wiped one salt drop from my cheek than another followed. Yet I thought I ought to have been happy, for none of the Reeds were there, they were all gone out in the carriage with their mamma: Abbot, too, was sewing in another room, and Bessie, as she moved hither and thither, putting away toys and arranging drawers, addressed to me every now and then a word of unwonted kindness. This state of things should have been to me a paradise of peace, accustomed as I was to a life of ceaseless reprimand and thankless fagging;[4] but, in fact, my racked nerves were now in such a state that no calm could soothe, and no pleasure excite them agreeably.

Bessie had been down into the kitchen, and she brought up with her a tart on a certain brightly painted china plate, whose bird of paradise, nestling in a wreath of convolvuli and rosebuds, had been wont to stir in me a most enthusiastic sense of admiration; and which plate I had often petitioned to be allowed to take in my hand in order to examine it more closely, but had always hitherto been deemed unworthy of such a privilege. This precious vessel was now placed on my knee, and I was cordially invited to eat the circlet of delicate pastry upon it. Vain favor! coming, like most other favors long deferred and often wished for, too late! I could not eat the tart: and the plumage of the bird, the tints of the flowers, seemed strangely faded: I put both plate and tart away. Bessie asked if I would have a book: the word *book* acted as a transient stimulus, and I begged her to fetch *Gulliver's Travels*[5] from the library. This book I had again and again perused with delight. I considered it a narrative of facts and discovered in it a vein of interest deeper than what I found in fairy tales: for as to the elves, having sought them in vain among foxglove leaves and bells, under mushrooms and beneath the ground-ivy mantling old wall-nooks, I had at length made up my mind to the sad truth, that they were all gone out

3. An echo of Christ's words on the cross: "Father, for- 4. Hard work.
give them; for they know not what they do" (Luke 5. Jonathan Swift's *Gulliver's Travels* (1726).
23:34).

of England to some savage country where the woods were wilder and thicker, and the population more scant; whereas, Lilliput and Brobdingnag being, in my creed, solid parts of the earth's surface, I doubted not that I might one day, by taking a long voyage, see with my own eyes the little fields, houses, and trees, the diminutive people, the tiny cows, sheep, and birds of the one realm; and the corn-fields forest-high, the mighty mastiffs, the monster cats, the tower-like men and women, of the other. Yet when this cherished volume was now placed in my hand—when I turned over its leaves, and sought in its marvelous pictures the charm I had, till now, never failed to find—all was eerie and dreary; the giants were gaunt goblins, the pigmies malevolent and fearful imps, Gulliver a most desolate wanderer in most dread and dangerous regions. I closed the book, which I dared no longer peruse, and put it on the table, beside the untasted tart.

Bessie had now finished dusting and tidying the room, and having washed her hands, she opened a certain little drawer, full of splendid shreds of silk and satin, and began making a new bonnet for Georgiana's doll. Meantime she sang: her song was—

> In the days when we went gipsying,
> A long time ago.[6]

I had often heard the song before, and always with lively delight; for Bessie had a sweet voice—at least I thought so. But now, though her voice was still sweet, I found in its melody an indescribable sadness. Sometimes, preoccupied with her work, she sang the refrain very low, very lingeringly; "A long time ago" came out like the saddest cadence of a funeral hymn. She passed into another ballad, this time a really doleful one.

> My feet they are sore, and my limbs they are weary;
> Long is the way, and the mountains are wild;
> Soon will the twilight close moonless and dreary
> Over the path of the poor orphan child.
>
> Why did they send me so far and so lonely,
> Up where the moors spread and gray rocks are piled?
> Men are hard-hearted, and kind angels only
> Watch o'er the steps of a poor orphan child.
>
> Yet distant and soft the night-breeze is blowing,
> Clouds there are none, and clear stars beam mild;
> God, in His mercy, protection is showing,
> Comfort and hope to the poor orphan child.
>
> Ev'n should I fall o'er the broken bridge passing,
> Or stray in the marshes, by false lights beguiled,
> Still will my Father, with promise and blessing,
> Take to His bosom the poor orphan child.
>
> There is a thought that for strength should avail me,
> Though both of shelter and kindred despoiled;

6. A popular song of the period.

Heaven is a home, and a rest will not fail me;
God is a friend to the poor orphan child.

"Come, Miss Jane, don't cry," said Bessie, as she finished. She might as well have said to the fire, "don't burn!" but how could she divine the morbid suffering to which I was a prey? In the course of the morning Mr. Lloyd came again.

"What, already up!" said he, as he entered the nursery. "Well, nurse, how is she?"

Bessie answered that I was doing very well.

"Then she ought to look more cheerful. Come here, Miss Jane; your name is Jane, is it not?"

"Yes, sir, Jane Eyre."

"Well, you have been crying, Miss Jane Eyre; can you tell me what about? Have you any pain?"

"No, sir."

"Oh! I daresay she is crying because she could not go out with Missis in the carriage," interposed Bessie.

"Surely not! why, she is too old for such pettishness."

I thought so too; and my self-esteem being wounded by the false charge, I answered promptly, "I never cried for such a thing in my life: I hate going out in the carriage. I cry because I am miserable."

"Oh fie, Miss!" said Bessie.

The good apothecary appeared a little puzzled. I was standing before him; he fixed his eyes on me very steadily: his eyes were small and gray: not very bright, but I daresay I should think them shrewd now: he had a hard-featured yet good-natured looking face. Having considered me at leisure, he said: "What made you ill yesterday?"

"She had a fall," said Bessie, again putting in her word.

"Fall! why that is like a baby again! Can't she manage to walk at her age? She must be eight or nine years old."

"I was knocked down," was the blunt explanation jerked out of me by another pang of mortified pride: "but that did not make me ill," I added; while Mr. Lloyd helped himself to a pinch of snuff.

As he was returning the box to his waistcoat pocket, a loud bell rang for the servants' dinner; he knew what it was. "That's for you, nurse," said he; "you can go down; I'll give Miss Jane a lecture till you come back."

Bessie would rather have stayed, but she was obliged to go, because punctuality at meals was rigidly enforced at Gateshead Hall.

"The fall did not make you ill; what did, then?" pursued Mr. Lloyd, when Bessie was gone.

"I was shut up in a room where there is a ghost till after dark."

I saw Mr. Lloyd smile and frown at the same time: "Ghost! What, you are a baby after all! You are afraid of ghosts?"

"Of Mr. Reed's ghost I am: he died in that room, and was laid out there. Neither Bessie nor any one else will go into it at night, if they can help it; and it was cruel to shut me up alone without a candle,—so cruel that I think I shall never forget it."

"Nonsense! And is it that makes you so miserable? Are you afraid now in daylight?"

"No: but night will come again before long: and besides,—I am unhappy,—very unhappy, for other things."

"What other things? Can you tell me some of them?"

How much I wished to reply fully to this question! How difficult it was to frame any answer. Children can feel, but they cannot analyze their feelings; and if the analysis is partially effected in thought, they know not how to express the result of the process in words. Fearful, however, of losing this first and only opportunity of relieving my grief by imparting it, I, after a disturbed pause, contrived to frame a meager, though, as far as it went, true response.

"For one thing, I have no father or mother, brothers or sisters."

"You have a kind aunt and cousins."

Again I paused; then bunglingly enounced: "But John Reed knocked me down, and my aunt shut me up in the red-room."

Mr. Lloyd a second time produced his snuff-box.

"Don't you think Gateshead Hall a very beautiful house?" asked he. "Are you not very thankful to have such a fine place to live at?"

"It is not my house, sir; and Abbot says I have less right to be here than a servant."

"Pooh! you can't be silly enough to wish to leave such a splendid place?"

"If I had anywhere else to go, I should be glad to leave it; but I can never get away from Gateshead till I am a woman."

"Perhaps you may—who knows? Have you any relations besides Mrs. Reed?"

"I think not, sir."

"None belonging to your father?"

"I don't know: I asked aunt Reed once, and she said possibly I might have some poor, low relations called Eyre, but she knew nothing about them."

"If you had such, would you like to go to them?"

I reflected. Poverty looks grim to grown people; still more so to children: they have not much idea of industrious, working, respectable poverty; they think of the word only as connected with ragged clothes, scanty food, fireless grates, rude manners, and debasing vices: poverty for me was synonymous with degradation.

"No; I should not like to belong to poor people," was my reply.

"Not even if they were kind to you?"

I shook my head: I could not see how poor people had the means of being kind; and then to learn to speak like them, to adopt their manners, to be uneducated, to grow up like one of the poor women I saw sometimes nursing their children or washing their clothes at the cottage doors of the village of Gateshead: no, I was not heroic enough to purchase liberty at the price of caste.

"But are your relatives so very poor? Are they working people?"

"I cannot tell; aunt Reed says, if I have any, they must be a beggarly set: I should not like to go a begging."

"Would you like to go to school?"

Again I reflected: I scarcely knew what school was; Bessie sometimes spoke of it as a place where young ladies sat in the stocks, wore backboards,[7] and were expected to be exceedingly genteel and precise: John Reed hated his school, and abused his master; but John Reed's tastes were no rule for mine, and if

7. Boards to which 19th-century young women were strapped to improve their posture. "Stocks": a wooden frame that restrained a culprit's feet and hands.

Bessie's accounts of school discipline (gathered from the young ladies of a family where she had lived before coming to Gateshead) were somewhat appalling, her details of certain accomplishments attained by these same young ladies were, I thought, equally attractive. She boasted of beautiful paintings of landscapes and flowers by them executed; of songs they could sing and pieces they could play, of purses they could net, of French books they could translate; till my spirit was moved to emulation as I listened. Besides, school would be a complete change: it implied a long journey, an entire separation from Gateshead, an entrance into a new life.

"I should indeed like to go to school," was the audible conclusion of my musings."

"Well, well; who knows what may happen?" said Mr. Lloyd, as he got up: "The child ought to have change of air and scene,' he added, speaking to himself; "nerves not in a good state."

Bessie now returned; at the same moment the carriage was heard rolling up the gravel-walk.

"Is that your mistress, nurse?" asked Mr. Lloyd. "I should like to speak to her before I go."

Bessie invited him to walk into the breakfast-room, and led the way out. In the interview which followed between him and Mrs. Reed, I presume, from after-occurrences, that the apothecary ventured to recommend my being sent to school; and the recommendation was no doubt readily enough adopted; for as Abbot said, in discussing the subject with Bessie when both sat sewing in the nursery one night, after I was in bed, and, as they thought, asleep, "Missis was, she dared say, glad enough to get rid of such a tiresome, ill-conditioned child, who always looked as if she were watching everybody, and scheming plots underhand." Abbot, I think, gave me credit for being a sort of infantine Guy Fawkes.[8]

On that same occasion I learned, for the first time, from Miss Abbot's communications to Bessie, that my father had been a poor clergyman; that my mother had married him against the wishes of her friends, who considered the match beneath her; that my grandfather Reed was so irritated at her disobedience, he cut her off without a shilling; that after my mother and father had been married a year, the latter caught the typhus fever while visiting among the poor of a large manufacturing town where his curacy was situated, and where that disease was then prevalent; that my mother took the infection from him, and both died within a month of each other.

Bessie, when she heard this narrative, sighed and said, "Poor Miss Jane is to be pitied, too, Abbot."

"Yes," responded Abbot, "if she were a nice, pretty child, one might compassionate her forlornness; but one really cannot care for such a little toad as that."

"Not a great deal, to be sure," agreed Bessie "at any rate, a beauty like Miss Georgiana would be more moving in the same condition."

"Yes, I doat on Miss Georgiana!" cried the fervent Abbot. "Little darling!— with her long curls and her blue eyes, and such a sweet color as she has; just as if she were painted!—Bessie, I could fancy a Welsh rabbit for supper."

"So could I—with a roast onion. Come, we'll go down." They went.

8. Famous 16th-century English traitor who conspired to blow up the houses of Parliament.

Chapter IV

From my discourse with Mr. Lloyd, and from the above-reported confer-ence between Bessie and Abbot, I gathered enough of hope to suffice as a mo-tive for wishing to get well: a change seemed near,—I desired and waited it in silence. It tarried, however: days and weeks passed: I had regained my normal state of health, but no new allusion was made to the subject over which I brooded. Mrs. Reed surveyed me at times with a severe eye, but seldom ad-dressed me: since my illness she had drawn a more marked line of separation than ever between me and her own children; appointing me a small closet to sleep in by myself, condemning me to take my meals alone, and pass all my time in the nursery, while my cousins were constantly in the drawing-room. Not a hint, however, did she drop about sending me to school: still I felt an in-stinctive certainty that she would not long endure me under the same roof with her; for her glance, now more than ever, when turned on me, expressed an insuperable and rooted aversion.

Eliza and Georgiana, evidently acting according to orders, spoke to me as little as possible: John thrust his tongue in his cheek whenever he saw me, and once attempted chastisement; but as I instantly turned against him, roused by the same sentiment of deep ire and desperate revolt which had stirred my cor-ruption before, he thought it better to desist, and ran from me, uttering exe-crations, and vowing I had burst his nose. I had indeed leveled at that prominent feature as hard a blow as my knuckles could inflict; and when I saw that either that or my look daunted him, I had the greatest inclination to fol-low up my advantage to purpose; but he was already with his mamma. I heard him in a blubbering tone commence the tale of how "that nasty Jane Eyre" had flown at him like a mad cat: he was stopped rather harshly—"Don't talk to me about her, John: I told you not to go near her; she is not worthy of notice; I do not choose that either you or your sisters should associate with her."

Here, leaning over the banister, I cried out suddenly, and without at all de-liberating on my words,—"They are not fit to associate with me."

Mrs. Reed was rather a stout woman; but on hearing this strange and auda-cious declaration, she ran nimbly up the stair, swept me like a whirlwind into the nursery, and crushing me down on the edge of my crib, dared me in an em-phatic voice to rise from that place, or utter one syllable, during the remainder of the day.

"What would uncle Reed say to you, if he were alive?" was my scarcely vol-untary demand. I say scarcely voluntary, for it seemed as if my tongue pro-nounced words without my will consenting to their utterance: something spoke out of me over which I had no control.

"What?" said Mrs. Reed under her breath: her usually cold composed gray eye became troubled with a look like fear; she took her hand from my arm, and gazed at me as if she really did not know whether I were child or fiend. I was now in for it.

"My uncle Reed is in heaven, and can see all you do and think; and so can papa and mamma: they know how you shut me up all day long, and how you wish me dead."

Mrs. Reed soon rallied her spirits: she shook me most soundly, she boxed both my ears, and then left me without a word. Bessie supplied the hiatus by a homily of an hour's length, in which she proved beyond a doubt that I was the

most wicked and abandoned child ever reared under a roof. I half believed her; for I felt indeed only bad feelings surging in my breast.

November, December, and half of January passed away. Christmas and the New Year had been celebrated at Gateshead with the usual festive cheer; presents had been interchanged, dinners and evening parties given. From every enjoyment I was, of course, excluded: my share of the gaiety consisted in witnessing the daily apparelling of Eliza and Georgiana, and seeing them descend to the drawing-room, dressed out in thin muslin frocks and scarlet sashes, with hair elaborately ringletted; and afterwards, in listening to the sound of the piano or the harp played below to the passing to and fro of the butler and footman, to the jingling of glass and china as refreshments were handed, to the broken hum of conversation as the drawing-room doors opened and closed. When tired of this occupation, I would retire from the stairhead to the solitary and silent nursery: there, though somewhat sad, I was not miserable. To speak truth, I had not the least wish to go into company, for in company I was very rarely noticed; and if Bessie had but been kind and companionable, I should have deemed it a treat to spend the evenings quietly with her, instead of passing them under the formidable eye of Mrs. Reed, in a room full of ladies and gentlemen. But Bessie, as soon as she had dressed her young ladies, used to take herself off to the lively regions of the kitchen and the house-keeper's room, generally bearing the candle along with her. I then sat with my doll on my knee, till the fire got low, glancing round occasionally to make sure that nothing worse than myself haunted the shadowy room; and when the embers sank to a dull red, I undressed hastily, tugging at knots and strings as I best might, and sought shelter from cold and darkness in my crib. To this crib I always took my doll; human beings must love something, and in the dearth of worthier objects of affection, I contrived to find a pleasure in loving and cherishing a faded graven image, shabby as a miniature scarecrow. It puzzles me now to remember with what absurd sincerity I doated on this little toy, half fancying it alive and capable of sensation. I could not sleep unless it was folded in my night-gown; and when it lay there safe and warm, I was comparatively happy, believing it to be happy likewise.

Long did the hours seem while I waited the departure of the company, and listened for the sound of Bessie's step on the stairs: sometimes she would come up in the interval to seek her thimble or her scissors, or perhaps to bring me something by way of supper—a bun or a cheese-cake—then she would sit on the bed while I ate it, and when I had finished, she would tuck the clothes round me, and twice she kissed me and said, "Good night, Miss Jane." When thus gentle, Bessie seemed to me the best, prettiest, kindest being in the world; and I wished most intensely that she would always be so pleasant and amiable, and never push me about, or scold, or task me unreasonably, as she was too often wont to do. Bessie Lee must, I think, have been a girl of good natural capacity, for she was smart in all she did, and had a remarkable knack of narrative; so, at least, I judge from the impression made on me by her nursery tales. She was pretty, too, if my recollections of her face and person are correct. I remember her as a slim young woman, with black hair, dark eyes, very nice features, and good, clear complexion; but she had a capricious and hasty temper, and indifferent ideas of principle or justice: still, such as she was, I preferred her to any one else at Gateshead Hall.

It was the fifteenth of January, about nine o'clock in the morning: Bessie

was gone down to breakfast; my cousins had not yet been summoned to their mamma; Eliza was putting on her bonnet and warm garden-coat to go and feed her poultry, an occupation of which she was fond: and not less so of selling the eggs to the housekeeper and hoarding up the money she thus obtained. She had a turn for traffic,[9] and a marked propensity for saving; shown not only in the vending of eggs and chickens, but also in driving hard bargains with the gardener about flower-roots, seeds, and slips of plants; that functionary having orders from Mrs. Reed to buy of his young lady all the products of her parterre[1] she wished to sell: and Eliza would have sold the hair off her head if she could have made a handsome profit thereby. As to her money, she first secreted it in odd corners, wrapped in a rag or an old curl-paper; but some of these hoards having been discovered by the housemaid, Eliza, fearful of one day losing her valued treasure, consented to entrust it to her mother, at a usurious rate of interest—fifty or sixty per cent.; which interest she exacted every quarter, keeping her accounts in a little book with anxious accuracy.

Georgiana sat on a high stool, dressing her hair at the glass, and interweaving her curls with artificial flowers and faded feathers, of which she had found a store in a drawer in the attic. I was making my bed, having received strict orders from Bessie to get it arranged before she returned (for Bessie now frequently employed me as a sort of under-nurserymaid, to tidy the room, dust the chairs, etc.). Having spread the quilt, and folded my night-dress, I went to the window-seat to put in order some picture-books and doll's house furniture scattered there; an abrupt command from Georgiana to let her playthings alone (for the tiny chairs and mirrors, the fairy plates and cups were her property) stopped my proceedings; and then, for lack of other occupation, I fell to breathing on the frost-flowers with which the window was fretted, and thus clearing a space in the glass through which I might look out on the grounds, where all was still and petrified under the influence of a hard frost.

From this window were visible the porter's lodge and the carriage-road, and just as I had dissolved so much of the silver-white foliage veiling the panes as left room to look out, I saw the gates thrown open and a carriage roll through. I watched it ascending the drive with indifference: carriages often came to Gateshead, but none ever brought visitors in whom I was interested; it stopped in front of the house, the door-bell rang loudly, the new-comer was admitted. All this being nothing to me, my vacant attention soon found livelier attraction in the spectacle of a little hungry robin, which came and chirruped on the twigs of the leafless cherry-tree nailed against the wall near the casement. The remains of my breakfast of bread and milk stood on the table, and having crumbled a morsel of roll, I was tugging at the sash to put out the crumbs on the window-sill, when Bessie came running upstairs into the nursery.

"Miss Jane, take off your pinafore: what are you doing there? Have you washed your hands and face this morning?" I gave another tug before I answered, for I wanted the bird to be secure of its bread: the sash yielded; I scattered the crumbs, some on the stone sill, some on the cherry-tree bough, then, closing the window, I replied:—"No, Bessie; I have only just finished dusting."

"Troublesome, careless child! and what are you doing now? You look quite red, as if you had been about some mischief: what were you opening the window for?"

9. Bartering. 1. Ornamental garden.

I was spared the trouble of answering, for Bessie seemed in too great a hurry to listen to explanations: she hauled me to the wash-stand, inflicted a merciless, but happily brief scrub on my face and hands with soap, water, and a coarse towel; disciplined my head with a bristly brush, denuded me of my pinafore, and then, hurrying me to the top of the stairs, bid me go down directly, as I was wanted in the breakfast-room.

I would have asked who wanted me: I would have demanded if Mrs. Reed was there; but Bessie was already gone, and had closed the nursery-door upon me: I slowly descended. For nearly three months I had never been called to Mrs. Reed's presence: restricted so long to the nursery, the breakfast, dining, and drawing-rooms were become for me awful regions, on which it dismayed me to intrude.

I now stood in the empty hall; before me was the breakfast-room door, and I stopped, intimidated and trembling. What a miserable little poltroon had fear, engendered of unjust punishment, made of me in those days! I feared to return to the nursery, and feared to go forward to the parlor; ten minutes I stood in agitated hesitation: the vehement ringing of the breakfast-room bell decided me; I *must* enter.

"Who could want me?" I asked inwardly, as with both hands I turned the stiff door-handle, which, for a second or two, resisted my efforts. "What should I see besides aunt Reed in the apartment?—a man or a woman?" The handle turned, the door unclosed, and passing through and curtseying low I looked up at—a black pillar! such, at least, appeared to me, at first sight, the straight, narrow, sable-clad shape standing erect on the rug: the grim face at the top was like a carved mask, placed above the shaft by way of capital.

Mrs. Reed occupied her usual seat by the fireside: she made a signal to me to approach; I did so, and she introduced me to the stony stranger with the words: "This is the little girl respecting whom I applied to you."

He, for it was a man, turned his head slowly towards where I stood, and having examined me with the two inquisitive-looking gray eyes which twinkled under a pair of bushy brows, said solemnly, and in a bass voice: "Her size is small: what is her age?"

"Ten years."

"So much?" was the doubtful answer; and he prolonged his scrutiny for some minutes. Presently he addressed me:

"Your name, little girl?"

"Jane Eyre, sir."

In uttering these words I looked up: he seemed to me a tall gentleman; but then I was very little: his features were large, and they and all the lines of his frame were equally harsh and prim.

"Well, Jane Eyre, and are you a good child?"

Impossible to reply to this in the affirmative: my little world held a contrary opinion: I was silent. Mrs. Reed answered for me by an expressive shake of the head, adding soon, "Perhaps the less said on that subject the better, Mr. Brocklehurst."

"Sorry indeed to hear it! she and I must have some talk;" and bending from the perpendicular, he installed his person in the arm-chair, opposite Mrs. Reed's. "Come here," he said.

I stepped across the rug; he placed me square and straight before him. What a face he had, now that it was almost on a level with mine! what a great nose! and what a mouth! and what large prominent teeth!

"No sight so sad as that of a naughty child," he began, "especially a naughty little girl. Do you know where the wicked go after death?"

"They go to hell," was my ready and orthodox answer.

"And what is hell? Can you tell me that?"

"A pit full of fire."

"And should you like to fall into that pit, and to be burning there forever?"

"No, sir."

"What must you do to avoid it?"

I deliberated a moment; my answer, when it did come, was objectionable: "I must keep in good health and not die."

"How can you keep in good health? Children younger than you die daily. I buried a little child of five years old only a day or two since,—a good little child, whose soul is now in heaven. It is to be feared the same could not be said of you, were you to be called hence."

Not being in a condition to remove his doubt, I only cast my eyes down on the two large feet planted on the rug, and sighed, wishing myself far enough away.

"I hope that sigh is from the heart, and that you repent of ever having been the occasion of discomfort to your excellent benefactress."

"Benefactress! benefactress!" said I, inwardly: "they all call Mrs. Reed my benefactress; if so, a benefactress is a disagreeable thing."

"Do you say your prayers night and morning?" continued my interrogator.

"Yes, sir."

"Do you read your Bible?"

"Sometimes."

"With pleasure? Are you fond of it?"

"I like Revelations, and the book of Daniel, and Genesis and Samuel, and a little bit of Exodus, and some parts of Kings and Chronicles, and Job and Jonah."

"And the Psalms? I hope you like them?"

"No, sir."

"No? Oh, shocking! I have a little boy, younger than you, who knows six Psalms by heart: and when you ask him which he would rather have, a ginger-bread-nut to eat, or a verse of a Psalm to learn he says: 'Oh! the verse of a Psalm! angels sing Psalms,' says he; 'I wish to be a little angel here below'; he then gets two nuts in recompense for his infant piety."

"Psalms are not interesting," I remarked.

"That proves you have a wicked heart; and you must pray to God to change it: to give you a new and clean one: to take away your heart of stone and give you a heart of flesh."

I was about to propound a question, touching the manner in which that operation of changing my heart was to be performed, when Mrs. Reed interposed, telling me to sit down; she then proceeded to carry on the conversation herself.

"Mr. Brocklehurst, I believe I intimated in the letter which I wrote to you three weeks ago, that this little girl has not quite the character and disposition I could wish: should you admit her into Lowood school, I should be glad if the superintendent and teachers were requested to keep a strict eye on her, and above all, to guard against her worst fault, a tendency to deceit. I mention this in your hearing, Jane, that you may not attempt to impose on Mr. Brocklehurst."

Well might I dread, well might I dislike Mrs. Reed; for it was her nature to wound me cruelly: never was I happy in her presence: however carefully I obeyed, however strenuously I strove to please her, my efforts were still repulsed and repaid by such sentences as the above. Now, uttered before a stranger, the accusation cut me to the heart: I dimly perceived that she was already obliterating hope from the new phase of existence which she destined me to enter; I felt, though I could not have expressed the feeling, that she was sowing aversion and unkindness along my future path: I saw myself transformed under Mr. Brocklehurst's eye into an artful noxious child, and what could I do to remedy the injury?

"Nothing, indeed," thought I, as I struggled to repress a sob, and hastily wiped away some tears, the impotent evidences of my anguish.

"Deceit is, indeed, a sad fault in a child," said Mr. Brocklehurst "it is akin to falsehood, and all liars will have their portion in the lake burning with fire and brimstone: she shall, however, be watched, Mrs. Reed; I will speak to Miss Temple and the teachers."

"I should wish her to be brought up in a manner suiting her prospects," continued my benefactress; "to be made useful, to be kept humble: as for the vacations, she will, with your permission, spend them always at Lowood."

"Your decisions are perfectly judicious, madam," returned Mr. Brocklehurst. "Humility is a Christian grace, and one peculiarly appropriate to the pupils of Lowood: I, therefore, direct that especial care shall be bestowed on its cultivation among them. I have studied how best to mortify in them the worldly sentiment of pride; and, only the other day, I had a pleasing proof of my success. My second daughter, Augusta, went with her mamma to visit the school, and on her return she exclaimed: 'Oh, dear papa, how quiet and plain all the girls at Lowood look; with their hair combed behind their ears, and their long pinafores, and those little holland² pockets outside their frocks— they are almost like poor people's children! and,' said she, 'they looked at my dress and mamma's, as if they had never seen a silk gown before.'"

"This is the state of things I quite approve," returned Mrs. Reed; "had I sought all England over, I could scarcely have found a system more exactly fitting a child like Jane Eyre. Consistency, my dear Mr. Brocklehurst; I advocate consistency in all things."

"Consistency, madam, is the first of Christian duties; and it has been observed in every arrangement connected with the establishment of Lowood: plain fare, simple attire, unsophisticated accommodations, hardy and active habits; such is the order of the day in the house and its inhabitants."

"Quite right, sir. I may then depend upon this child being received as a pupil at Lowood, and there being trained in conformity to her position and prospects?"

"Madam, you may: she shall be placed in that nursery of chosen plants— and I trust she will show herself grateful for the inestimable privilege of her election."

"I will send her, then, as soon as possible, Mr. Brocklehurst; for, I assure you, I feel anxious to be relieved of a responsibility that was becoming too irksome."

"No doubt, no doubt, madam, and now I wish you good morning. I shall re-

2. Plain-weave heavy fabric

turn to Brocklehurst Hall in the course of a week or two: my good friend, the Archdeacon, will not permit me to leave him sooner. I shall send Miss Temple notice that she is to expect a new girl, so that there will be no difficulty about receiving her. Good-bye."

"Good-bye, Mr. Brocklehurst; remember me to Mrs. and Miss Brocklehurst, and to Augusta and Theodore, and Master Broughton Brocklehurst."

"I will, madam. Little girl, here is a book entitled the 'Child's Guide';[3] read it with prayer, especially that part containing 'an account of the awfully sudden death of Martha G——, a naughty child addicted to falsehood and deceit.'"

With these words Mr. Brocklehurst put into my hand a thin pamphlet sewn in a cover, and having rung for his carriage he departed.

Mrs. Reed and I were left alone: some minutes passed in silence: she was sewing, I was watching her. Mrs. Reed might be at that time some six or seven and thirty; she was a woman of robust frame, square-shouldered and strong-limbed, not tall, and, though stout, not obese: she had a somewhat large face, the under-jaw being much developed and very solid; her brow was low, her chin large and prominent, mouth and nose sufficiently regular; under her light eyebrows glimmered an eye devoid of ruth; her skin was dark and opaque, her hair nearly flaxen; her constitution was sound as a bell—illness never came near her; she was an exact, clever manager, her household and tenantry were thoroughly under her control; her children, only, at times defied her authority, and laughed it to scorn; she dressed well, and had a presence and port[4] calculated to set off handsome attire.

Sitting on a low stool, a few yards from her arm-chair, I examined her figure; I perused her features. In my hand I held the tract containing the sudden death of the Liar: to which narrative my attention had been pointed as to an appropriate warning. What had just passed; what Mrs. Reed had said concerning me to Mr. Brocklehurst; the whole tenor of their conversation, was recent, raw, and stinging in my mind; I had felt every word as acutely as I had heard it plainly, and a passion of resentment fomented now within me.

Mrs. Reed looked up from her work; her eye settled on mine, her fingers at the same time suspended their nimble movements.

"Go out of the room; return to the nursery," was her mandate. My look or something else must have struck her as offensive, for she spoke with extreme, though suppressed irritation. I got up, I went to the door; I came back again; I walked to the window, across the room, then close up to her.

Speak I must; I had been trodden on severely, and *must* turn: but how? What strength had I to dart retaliation at my antagonist? I gathered my energies and launched them in this blunt sentence:—"I am not deceitful: if I were, I should say I loved *you*; but I declare I do not love you: I dislike you the worst of anybody in the world except John Reed; and this book about the liar, you may give to your girl, Georgiana, for it is she who tells lies, and not I."

Mrs. Reed's hands still lay on her work inactive: her eye of ice continued to dwell freezingly on mine.

"What more have you to say?" she asked, rather in the tone in which a person might address an opponent of adult age than such as is ordinarily used to a child.

3. One of the heavily didactic and religious children's 4. Manner.
magazines of the period, such as *The Children's Friend*.

That eye of hers, that voice stirred every antipathy I had. Shaking from head to foot, thrilled with ungovernable excitement, I continued:—"I am glad you are no relation of mine: I will never call you aunt again as long as I live. I will never come to see you when I am grown up; and if any one asks me how I liked you, and how you treated me, I will say the very thought of you makes me sick, and that you treated me with miserable cruelty."

"How dare you affirm that, Jane Eyre?"

"How dare I, Mrs. Reed? How dare I? Because it is the *truth*. You think I have no feelings, and that I can do without one bit of love or kindness; but I cannot live so: and you have no pity. I shall remember how you thrust me back—roughly and violently thrust me back—into the red-room, and locked me up there, to my dying day; though I was in agony; though I cried out, while suffocating with distress, 'Have mercy! Have mercy, aunt Reed!' And that punishment you made me suffer because your wicked boy struck me—knocked me down for nothing. I will tell anybody who asks me questions this exact tale. People think you a good woman, but you are bad; hard-hearted. *You* are deceitful!"

Ere I had finished this reply my soul began to expand, to exult, with the strangest sense of freedom, of triumph, I ever felt. It seemed as if an invisible bond had burst, and that I had struggled out into unhoped-for liberty. Not without cause was this sentiment: Mrs. Reed looked frightened; her work had slipped from her knee; she was lifting up her hands, rocking herself to and fro, and even twisting her face as if she would cry.

"Jane, you are under a mistake: what is the matter with you? Why do you tremble so violently? Would you like to drink some water?"

"No, Mrs. Reed."

"Is there anything else you wish for, Jane? I assure you, I desire to be your friend."

"Not you. You told Mr. Brocklehurst I had a bad character, a deceitful disposition; and I'll let everybody at Lowood know what you are, and what you have done."

"Jane, you don't understand these things: children must be corrected for their faults."

"Deceit is not my fault!" I cried out in a savage, high voice.

"But you are passionate, Jane, that you must allow: and now return to the nursery—there's a dear—and lie down a little."

"I am not your dear; I cannot lie down: send me to school soon, Mrs. Reed, for I hate to live here."

"I will indeed send her to school soon," murmured Mrs. Reed, *sotto voce;*[5] and gathering up her work, she abruptly quitted the apartment.

I was left there alone—winner of the field. It was the hardest battle I had fought, and the first victory I had gained: I stood awhile on the rug, where Mr. Brocklehurst had stood, and I enjoyed my conqueror's solitude. First, I smiled to myself and felt elate; but this fierce pleasure subsided in me as fast as did the accelerated throb of my pulses. A child cannot quarrel with its elders, as I had done; cannot give its furious feelings uncontrolled play, as I had given mine, without experiencing afterwards the pang of remorse and the chill of reaction. A ridge of lighted heath, alive, glancing, devouring, would have been a

5. Under her breath (Italian).

meet[6] emblem of my mind when I accused and menaced Mrs. Reed: the same ridge, black and blasted after the flames are dead, would have represented as meetly my subsequent condition, when half an hour's silence and reflection had shown me the madness of my conduct, and the dreariness of my hated and hating position.

Something of vengeance I had tasted for the first time; as aromatic wine it seemed, on swallowing, warm and racy: its afterflavor, metallic and corroding, gave me a sensation as if I had been poisoned. Willingly would I now have gone and asked Mrs. Reed's pardon; but I knew, partly from experience and partly from instinct, that was the way to make her repulse me with double scorn, thereby re-exciting every turbulent impulse of my nature.

I would fain exercise some better faculty than that of fierce speaking; fain find nourishment for some less fiendish feeling than that of sombre indignation. I took a book—some Arabian tales; I sat down and endeavored to read. I could make no sense of the subject; my own thoughts swam always between me and the page I had usually found fascinating. I opened the glass-door in the breakfast-room: the shrubbery was quite still: the black frost reigned, unbroken by sun or breeze, through the grounds. I covered my head and arms with the skirt of my frock, and went out to walk in a part of the plantation which was quite sequestered: but I found no pleasure in the silent trees, the falling fir-cones, the congealed relics of autumn, russet leaves, swept by past winds in heaps, and now stiffened together. I leaned against a gate, and looked into an empty field where no sheep were feeding, where the short grass was nipped and blanched. It was a very gray day; a most opaque sky, "onding on snaw,"[7] canopied all; thence flakes fell at intervals, which settled on the hard path and on the hoary lea without melting. I stood, a wretched child enough, whispering to myself over and over again, "What shall I do?—what shall I do?"

All at once I heard a clear voice call, "Miss Jane! where are you? Come to lunch!"

It was Bessie, I knew well enough; but I did not stir; her light step came tripping down the path.

"You naughty little thing!" she said. "Why don't you come when you are called?"

Bessie's presence, compared with the thoughts over which I had been brooding, seemed cheerful; even though, as usual, she was somewhat cross. The fact is, after my conflict with and victory over Mrs. Reed, I was not disposed to care much for the nursemaid's transitory anger; and I was disposed to bask in her youthful lightness of heart. I just put my two arms round her, and said, "Come, Bessie! don't scold."

The action was more frank and fearless than any I was habituated to indulge in: somehow it pleased her.

"You are a strange child, Miss Jane," she said, as she looked down at me: "a little, roving, solitary thing: and you are going to school, I suppose?"

I nodded.

"And won't you be sorry to leave poor Bessie?"

"What does Bessie care for me? She is always scolding me."

"Because you're such a queer, frightened, shy, little thing. You should be bolder."

6. Proper. 7. Appearing ready to snow (Northern dialect).

"What! to get more knocks?"

"Nonsense! But you are rather put upon, that's certain. My mother said, when she came to see me last week, that she would not like a little one of her own to be in your place. Now, come in, and I've some good news for you."

"I don't think you have, Bessie."

"Child! what do you mean? What sorrowful eyes you fix on me! Well! but Missis and the young ladies and Master John are going out to tea this afternoon, and you shall have tea with me. I'll ask cook to bake you a little cake, and then you shall help me to look over your drawers for I am soon to pack your trunk. Missis intends you to leave Gateshead in a day or two, and you shall choose what toys you like to take with you."

"Bessie, you must promise not to scold me any more till I go."

"Well, I will: but mind you are a very good girl, and don't be afraid of me. Don't start when I chance to speak rather sharply: it's so provoking."

"I don't think I shall ever be afraid of you again, Bessie, because I have got used to you; and I shall soon have another set of people to dread."

"If you dread them, they'll dislike you."

"As you do, Bessie?"

"I don't dislike you, Miss; I believe I am fonder of you than of all the others."

"You don't show it."

"You little sharp thing! you've got quite a new way of talking. What makes you so venturesome and hardy?"

"Why, I shall soon be away from you, and besides—" I was going to say something about what had passed between me and Mrs. Reed; but on second thoughts I considered it better to remain silent on that head.

"And so you're glad to leave me?"

"Not at all, Bessie; indeed, just now I am rather sorry."

"Just now! and rather! How coolly my little lady says it! I daresay now if I were to ask you for a kiss you wouldn't give it me: you'd say you'd *rather* not."

"I'll kiss you and welcome: bend your head down." Bessie stooped; we mutually embraced, and I followed her into the house quite comforted. That afternoon lapsed in peace and harmony; and in the evening Bessie told me some of her most enchanting stories, and sang me some of her sweetest songs. Even for me life had its gleams of sunshine.

Chapter V

Five o'clock had hardly struck on the morning of the 19th of January, when Bessie brought a candle into my closet, and found me already up and nearly dressed. I had risen half an hour before her entrance, and had washed my face, and put on my clothes by the light of a half-moon just setting, whose rays streamed through the narrow window near my crib. I was to leave Gateshead that day by a coach which passed the lodge gates at six A.M. Bessie was the only person yet risen; she had lit a fire in the nursery, where she now proceeded to make my breakfast. Few children can eat when excited with the thoughts of a journey; nor could I. Bessie, having pressed me in vain to take a few spoonfuls of the boiled milk and bread she had prepared for me, wrapped up some biscuits in a paper and put them into my bag; then she helped me on with my pelisse[8] and bonnet, and wrapping herself in a shawl, she and I left the nursery.

8. Long coat or cloak.

As we passed Mrs. Reed's bedroom, she said, "Will you go in and bid Missis good-bye?"

"No, Bessie: she came to my crib last night when you were gone down to supper, and said I need not disturb her in the morning, or my cousins either; and she told me to remember that she had always been my best friend, and to speak of her and be grateful to her accordingly."

"What did you say, Miss?"

"Nothing: I covered my face with the bed-clothes, and turned from her to the wall."

"That was wrong, Miss Jane."

"It was quite right, Bessie: your Missis has not been my friend: she has been my foe."

"Oh, Miss Jane! don't say so!"

"Good-bye to Gateshead!" cried I, as we passed through the hall and went out at the front door.

The moon was set, and it was very dark; Bessie carried a lantern, whose light glanced on wet steps and gravel road sodden by a recent thaw. Raw and chill was the winter morning: my teeth chattered as I hastened down the drive. There was a light in the porter's lodge: when we reached it, we found the porter's wife just kindling her fire: my trunk, which had been carried down the evening before, stood corded at the door. It wanted but a few minutes of six, and shortly after that hour had struck the distant roll of wheels announced the coming coach; I went to the door, and watched its lamps approach rapidly through the gloom.

"Is she going by herself?" asked the porter's wife.

"Yes."

"And how far is it?"

"Fifty miles."

"What a long way! I wonder Mrs. Reed is not afraid to trust her so far alone."

The coach drew up; there it was at the gates with its four horses and its top laden with passengers: the guard and coachman loudly urged haste; my trunk was hoisted up; I was taken from Bessie's neck, to which I clung with kisses.

"Be sure and take good care of her," cried she to the guard, as he lifted me into the inside.

"Ay, ay!" was the answer: the door was slapped to, a voice exclaimed, "All right," and on we drove. Thus was I severed from Bessie and Gateshead: thus whirled away to unknown, and, as I then deemed, remote and mysterious regions.

I remember but little of the journey: I only know that the day seemed to me of a preternatural length, and that we appeared to travel over hundreds of miles of road. We passed through several towns, and in one, a very large one, the coach stopped; the horses were taken out, and the passengers alighted to dine. I was carried into an inn, where the guard wanted me to have some dinner; but, as I had no appetite, he left me in an immense room with a fire-place at each end, a chandelier pendent from the ceiling, and a little red gallery high up against the wall filled with musical instruments. Here I walked about for a long time, feeling very strange, and mortally apprehensive of some one coming in and kidnapping me; for I believed in kidnappers, their exploits having frequently figured in Bessie's fireside chronicles. At last the guard returned:

once more I was stowed away in the coach, my protector mounted his own seat, sounded his hollow horn, and away we rattled over the "stony street" of L——.

The afternoon came on wet and somewhat misty: as it waned into dusk I began to feel that we were getting very far indeed from Gateshead: we ceased to pass through towns; the country changed; great gray hills heaved up round the horizon: as twilight deepened we descended a valley, dark with wood, and long after night had overclouded the prospect I heard a wild wind rushing amongst trees.

Lulled by the sound, I at last dropped asleep: I had not long slumbered when the sudden cessation of motion awoke me; the coach-door was open, and a person like a servant was standing at it: I saw her face and dress by the light of the lamps.

"Is there a little girl called Jane Eyre here?" she asked. I answered "Yes," and was then lifted out; my trunk was handed down, and the coach instantly drove away.

I was stiff with long sitting, and bewildered with the noise and motion of the coach: gathering my faculties, I looked about me. Rain, wind, and darkness filled the air; nevertheless, I dimly discerned a wall before me and a door open in it; through this door I passed with my new guide: she shut and locked it behind her. There was now visible a house or houses—for the building spread far—with many windows, and lights burning in some; we went up a broad pebbly path, splashing wet, and were admitted at a door; then the servant led me through a passage into a room with a fire, where she left me alone.

I stood and warmed my numbed fingers over the blaze, then I looked round; there was no candle, but the uncertain light from the hearth showed, by intervals, papered walls, carpet, curtains shining mahogany furniture: it was a parlour, not so spacious or splendid as the drawing-room at Gateshead, but comfortable enough. I was puzzling to make out the subject of a picture on the wall, when the door opened, and an individual carrying a light entered; another followed close behind.

The first was a tall lady with dark hair, dark eyes, and a pale and large forehead; her figure was partly enveloped in a shawl, her countenance was grave, her bearing erect.

"The child is very young to be sent alone," said she, putting her candle down on the table. She considered me attentively for a minute or two, then further added:

"She had better be put to bed soon; she looks tired: are you tired?" she asked, placing her hand on my shoulder.

"A little, ma'am."

"And hungry too, no doubt: let her have some supper before she goes to bed, Miss Miller. Is this the first time you have left your parents to come to school, my little girl?"

I explained to her that I had no parents. She inquired how long they had been dead; then how old I was, what was my name, whether I could read, write, and sew a little: then she touched my cheek gently with her forefinger, and saying, "She hoped I should be a good child," dismissed me along with Miss Miller.

The lady I had left might be about twenty-nine; the one who went with me appeared some years younger: the first impressed me by her voice, look, and

air. Miss Miller was more ordinary; ruddy in complexion, though of a careworn countenance; hurried in gait and action, like one who had always a multiplicity of tasks on hand: she looked, indeed, what I afterwards found she really was, an under-teacher. Led by her, I passed from compartment to compartment, from passage to passage, of a large and irregular building; till, emerging from the total and somewhat dreary silence pervading that portion of the house we had traversed, we came upon the hum of many voices, and presently entered a wide, long room, with great deal tables, two at each end, on each of which burnt a pair of candles, and seated all round on benches a congregation of girls of every age, from nine or ten to twenty. Seen by the dim light of the dips, their number to me appeared countless, though not in reality exceeding eighty; they were uniformly dressed in brown stuff frocks of quaint fashion, and long holland pinafores. It was the hour of study; they were engaged in conning over their tomorrow's task, and the hum I had heard was the combined result of their whispered repetitions.

Miss Miller signed to me to sit on a bench near the door, then walking up to the top of the long room, she cried out:

"Monitors, collect the lesson-books and put them away!"

Four tall girls arose from different tables, and going round, gathered the books and removed them. Miss Miller again gave the word of command:

"Monitors, fetch the supper-trays!"

The tall girls went out, and returned presently, each bearing a tray, with portions of something, I knew not what, arranged thereon, and a pitcher of water and mug in the middle of each tray. The portions were handed round; those who liked took a draught of the water, the mug being common to all. When it came to my turn, I drank, for I was thirsty, but did not touch the food, excitement and fatigue rendering me incapable of eating: I now saw, however, that it was a thin oaten cake, shared into fragments.

The meal over, prayers were read by Miss Miller, and the classes filed off, two and two, upstairs. Overpowered by this time with weariness, I scarcely noticed what sort of a place the bedroom was; except that, like the schoolroom, I saw it was very long. Tonight I was to be Miss Miller's bedfellow; she helped me to undress: when laid down I glanced at the long rows of beds, each of which was quickly filled with two occupants; in ten minutes the single light was extinguished; amidst silence and complete darkness, I fell asleep.

The night passed rapidly: I was too tired even to dream; I only once awoke to hear the wind rave in furious gusts, and the rain fall in torrents, and to be sensible that Miss Miller had taken her place by my side. When I again unclosed my eyes, a loud bell was ringing: the girls were up and dressing; day had not yet begun to dawn, and a rush-light or two burned in the room. I too rose reluctantly; it was bitter cold, and I dressed as well as I could for shivering, and washed when there was a basin at liberty, which did not occur soon, as there was but one basin to six girls on the stands down the middle of the room. Again the bell rang: all formed in file, two and two, and in that order descended the stairs and entered the cold and dimly-lit schoolroom: here prayers were read by Miss Miller; afterwards she called out:—"Form classes!"

A great tumult succeeded for some minutes, during which Miss Miller repeatedly exclaimed, "Silence!" and "Order!" When it subsided, I saw them all drawn up in four semicircles, before four chairs, placed at the four tables; all held books in their hands, and a great book, like a Bible, lay on each table, before the vacant seat. A pause of some seconds succeeded, filled up by the low,

vague hum of numbers; Miss Miller walked from class to class, hushing this indefinite sound.

A distant bell tinkled: immediately three ladies entered the room, each walked to a table and took her seat; Miss Miller assumed the fourth vacant chair, which was that nearest the door, and around which the smallest of the children were assembled: to this inferior class I was called, and placed at the bottom of it.

Business now began: the day's Collect[9] was repeated, then certain texts of Scripture were said, and to these succeeded a protracted reading of chapters in the Bible, which lasted an hour. By the time that exercise was terminated day had fully dawned. The indefatigable bell now sounded for the fourth time: the classes were marshalled and marched into another room to breakfast: how glad I was to behold a prospect of getting something to eat! I was now nearly sick from inanition, having taken so little the day before.

The refectory was a great, low-ceiled, gloomy room; on two long tables smoked basins of something hot, which, however, to my dismay, sent forth an odor far from inviting. I saw a universal manifestation of discontent when the fumes of the repast met the nostrils of those destined to swallow it: from the van of the procession, the tall girls of the first class, rose the whispered words:—"Disgusting! The porridge is burned again!"

"Silence!" ejaculated a voice; not that of Miss Miller, but one of the upper teachers, a little and dark personage, smartly dressed, but of somewhat morose aspect, who installed herself at the top of one table, while a more buxom lady presided at the other. I looked in vain for her I had first seen the night before; she was not visible: Miss Miller occupied the foot of the table where I sat, and a strange, foreign looking, elderly lady, the French teacher, as I afterwards found, took the corresponding seat at the other board. A long grace was said and a hymn sung; then a servant brought in some tea for the teachers, and the meal began.

Ravenous, and now very faint, I devoured a spoonful or two of my portion without thinking of its taste; but the first edge of hunger blunted, I perceived I had got in hand a nauseous mess: burned porridge is almost as bad as rotten potatoes; famine itself soon sickens over it. The spoons were moved slowly: I saw each girl taste her food and try to swallow it; but in most cases the effort was soon relinquished. Breakfast was over, and none had breakfasted. Thanks being returned for what we had not got, and a second hymn chanted, the refectory was evacuated for the schoolroom. I was one of the last to go out, and in passing the tables, I saw one teacher take a basin of the porridge and taste it; she looked at the others; all their countenances expressed displeasure, and one of them, the stout one, whispered:—"Abominable stuff! How shameful!"

A quarter of an hour passed before lessons again began, during which the schoolroom was in a glorious tumult; for that space of time, it seemed to be permitted to talk loud and more freely, and they used their privilege. The whole conversation ran on the breakfast, which one and all abused roundly. Poor things! it was the sole consolation they had. Miss Miller was now the only teacher in the room: a group of great girls standing about her, spoke with serious and sullen gestures. I heard the name of Mr. Brocklehurst pronounced by some lips; at which Miss Miller shook her head disapprovingly; but she made no great effort to check the general wrath: doubtless she shared in it.

9. A short prayer, which varies with the days.

A clock in the schoolroom struck nine; Miss Miller left her circle, and standing in the middle of the room, cried:—"Silence! To your seats!"

Discipline prevailed: in five minutes the confused throng was resolved into order, and comparative silence quelled the Babel clamor of tongues. The upper teachers now punctually resumed their posts: but still, all seemed to wait. Ranged on benches down the sides of the room, the eighty girls sat motionless and erect: a quaint assemblage they appeared, all with plain locks combed from their faces, not a curl visible; in brown dresses, made high and surrounded by a narrow tucker about the throat, with little pockets of holland (shaped something like a Highlander's purse) tied in front of their frocks, and destined to serve the purpose of a work-bag: all too wearing woolen stockings and country-made shoes, fastened with brass buckles. Above twenty of those clad in this costume were full-grown girls, or rather young women; it suited them ill, and gave an air of oddity even to the prettiest.

I was still looking at them, and also at intervals examining the teachers—none of whom precisely pleased me; for the stout one was a little coarse, the dark one not a little fierce, the foreigner harsh and grotesque, and Miss Miller, poor thing! looked purple, weatherbeaten, and overworked—when, as my eye wandered from face to face, the whole school rose simultaneously, as if moved by a common spring.

What was the matter? I had heard no order given: I was puzzled. Ere I had gathered my wits, the classes were again seated: but as all eyes were now turned to one point, mine followed the general direction, and encountered the personage who had received me last night. She stood at the bottom of the long room, on the hearth; for there was a fire at each end: she surveyed the two rows of girls silently and gravely. Miss Miller approaching, seemed to ask her a question, and having received her answer, went back to her place, and said aloud,—"Monitor of the first class, fetch the globes!"

While the direction was being executed, the lady consulted moved slowly up the room. I suppose I have a considerable organ of Veneration,[1] for I retain yet the sense of admiring awe with which my eyes traced her steps. Seen now, in broad daylight, she looked tall, fair, and shapely; brown eyes, with a benignant light in their irids,[2] and a fine penciling of long lashes round, relieved the whiteness of her large front; on each of her temples her hair, of a very dark brown, was clustered in round curls, according to the fashion of those times, when neither smooth bands nor long ringlets were in vogue; her dress, also in the mode of the day, was of purple cloth, relieved by a sort of Spanish trimming of black velvet; a gold watch (watches were not so common then as now) shone at her girdle. Let the reader add, to complete the picture, refined features; a complexion, if pale, clear; and a stately air and carriage, and he will have, at least, as clearly as words can give it, a correct idea of the exterior of Miss Temple—Maria Temple, as I afterwards saw the name written in a prayer-book entrusted to me to carry to church.

The superintendent of Lowood (for such was this lady) having taken her seat before a pair of globes placed on one of the tables, summoned the first class round her, and commenced giving a lesson in geography; the lower classes were called by the teachers: repetitions in history, grammar, etc., went

1. A reference to the "science" of phrenology, much in vogue in the 19th century, according to which a person's mental and moral character could be determined by the shape of the skull.
2. Plural of *iris*.

on for an hour; writing and arithmetic succeeded, and music lessons were given by Miss Temple to some of the elder girls. The duration of each lesson was measured by the clock, which at last struck twelve. The superintendent rose:—"I have a word to address to the pupils," said she.

The tumult of cessation from lessons was already breaking forth, but it sank at her voice. She went on:—"You had this morning a breakfast which you could not eat; you must be hungry. I have ordered that a lunch of bread and cheese shall be served to all."

The teachers looked at her with a sort of surprise.

"It is to be done on my responsibility," she added, in an explanatory tone to them, and immediately afterwards left the room.

The bread and cheese was presently brought in and distributed, to the high delight and refreshment of the whole school. The order was now given, "To the garden!" Each put on a coarse straw bonnet, with strings of colored calico, and a cloak of gray frieze. I was similarly equipped, and, following the stream, I made my way into the open air.

The garden was a wide enclosure, surrounded with walls so high as to exclude every glimpse of prospect; a covered verandah ran down one side, and broad walks bordered a middle space divided into scores of little beds: these beds were assigned as gardens for the pupils to cultivate, and each bed had an owner. When full of flowers they would doubtless look pretty; but now, at the latter end of January, all was wintry blight and brown decay. I shuddered as I stood and looked around me: it was an inclement day for outdoor exercise; not positively rainy, but darkened by a drizzling yellow fog; all underfoot was still soaking wet with the floods of yesterday. The stronger among the girls ran about and engaged in active games, but sundry pale and thin ones herded together for shelter and warmth in the veranda; and among these, as the dense mist penetrated to their shivering frames, I heard frequently the sound of a hollow cough.

As yet I had spoken to no one, nor did anybody seem to take notice of me; I stood lonely enough: but to that feeling of isolation I was accustomed; it did not oppress me much. I leant against a pillar of the veranda, drew my gray mantle close about me, and trying to forget the cold which nipped me without, and the unsatisfied hunger which gnawed me within, delivered myself up to the employment of watching and thinking. My reflections were too undefined and fragmentary to merit record: I hardly yet knew where I was; Gateshead and my past life seemed floated away to an immeasurable distance; the present was vague and strange, and of the future I could form no conjecture. I looked round the convent-like garden, and then up at the house; a large building, half of which seemed gray and old, the other half quite new. The new part, containing the schoolroom and dormitory, was lit by mullioned and latticed windows, which gave it a church-like aspect; a stone tablet over the door, bore this inscription:—

LOWOOD INSTITUTION.

THIS PORTION WAS REBUILT A.D. —, BY NAOMI BROCKLEHURST, OF BROCKLEHURST HALL, IN THIS COUNTY.

"Let your light so shine before men that they may see your good works, and glorify your Father which is in heaven."—St. Matt. V. 16.

I read these words over and over again: I felt that an explanation belonged to them, and was unable fully to penetrate their import. I was still pondering the signification of "Institution," and endeavoring to make out a connection between the first words and the verse of Scripture, when the sound of a cough close behind me, made me turn my head. I saw a girl sitting on a stone bench near; she was bent over a book, on the perusal of which she seemed intent: from where I stood I could see the title—it was *Rasselas*[3]; a name that struck me as strange, and consequently attractive. In turning a leaf she happened to look up, and I said to her directly:—"Is your book interesting?" I had already formed the intention of asking her to lend it to me some day.

"I like it," she answered, after a pause of a second or two, during which she examined me.

"What is it about?" I continued. I hardly know where I found the hardihood thus to open a conversation with a stranger; the step was contrary to my nature and habits: but I think her occupation touched a chord of sympathy somewhere; for I too liked reading, though of a frivolous and childish kind; I could not digest or comprehend the serious or substantial.

"You may look at it," replied the girl, offering me the book.

I did so; a brief examination convinced me that the contents were less taking than the title: *Rasselas* looked dull to my trifling taste; I saw nothing about fairies, nothing about genii; no bright variety seemed spread over the closely printed pages. I returned it to her; she received it quietly, and without saying anything she was about to relapse into her former studious mood: again I ventured to disturb her:—"Can you tell me what the writing on that stone over the door means? What is Lowood Institution?"

"This house where you are come to live."

"And why do they call it Institution? Is it in any way different from other schools?"

"It is partly a charity-school: you and I, and all the rest of us, are charity children. I suppose you are an orphan: are not either your father or your mother dead?"

"Both died before I can remember."

"Well, all the girls here have lost either one or both parents, and this is called an institution for educating orphans."

"Do we pay no money? Do they keep us for nothing?"

"We pay, or our friends pay, fifteen pounds a year for each."

"Then why do they call us charity children?"

"Because fifteen pounds is not enough for board and teaching, and the deficiency is supplied by subscription."

"Who subscribes?"

"Different benevolent-minded ladies and gentlemen in this neighborhood and in London."

"Who was Naomi Brocklehurst?"

"The lady who built the new part of this house as that tablet records, and whose son overlooks and directs everything here."

"Why?"

"Because he is treasurer and manager of the establishment."

3. *The History of Rasselas, Prince of Abyssinia* was a popular didactic romance by Samuel Johnson (1759).

"Then this house does not belong to that tall lady who wears a watch, and who said we were to have some bread and cheese."

"To Miss Temple? Oh, no! I wish it did: she has to answer to Mr. Brocklehurst for all she does. Mr. Brocklehurst buys all our food and all our clothes."

"Does he live here?"

"No—two miles off, at a large hall."

"Is he a good man?"

"He is a clergyman, and is said to do a great deal of good."

"Did you say that tall lady was called Miss Temple?"

"Yes."

"And what are the other teachers called?"

"The one with red cheeks is called Miss Smith; she attends to the work, and cuts out—for we make our own clothes, our frocks, and pelisses, and everything; the little one with black hair is Miss Scatcherd; she teaches history and grammar, and hears the second class repetitions; and the one who wears a shawl, and has a pocket-handkerchief tied to her side with a yellow riband, is Madame Pierrot: she comes from Lisle, in France, and teaches French."

"Do you like the teachers?"

"Well enough."

"Do you like the little black one and the Madame————?—I cannot pronounce her name as you do."

"Miss Scatcherd is hasty—you must take care not to offend her; Madame Perrot is not a bad sort of person."

"But Miss Temple is the best—isn't she?"

"Miss Temple is very good, and very clever: she is above the rest, because she knows far more than they do."

"Have you been long here?"

"Two years."

"Are you an orphan?"

"My mother is dead."

"Are you happy here?"

"You ask rather too many questions. I have given you answers enough for the present: now I want to read."

But at the moment the summons sounded for dinner: all reentered the house. The odor which now filled the refectory was scarcely more appetizing than that which had regaled our nostrils at breakfast: the dinner was served in two huge tin-plated vessels, whence rose a strong steam redolent of rancid fat. I found the mess to consist of indifferent potatoes and strange shreds of rusty meat, mixed and cooked together. Of this preparation a tolerably abundant plateful was opportioned to each pupil. I ate what I could, and wondered within myself whether every day's fare would be like this.

After dinner, we immediately adjourned to the schoolroom: lessons recommenced, and were continued till five o'clock.

The only marked event of the afternoon was, that I saw the girl with whom I had conversed in the veranda, dismissed in disgrace, by Miss Scatcherd, from a history class, and sent to stand in the middle of the large schoolroom. The punishment seemed to me in a high degree ignominious, especially for so great a girl—she looked thirteen or upwards. I expected she would show signs of great distress and shame; but to my surprise she neither wept nor blushed:

composed, though grave, she stood, the central mark of all eyes. "How can she bear it so quietly—so firmly?" I asked of myself. "Were I in her place, it seems to me I should wish the earth to open and swallow me up. She looks as if she were thinking of something beyond her punishment—beyond her situation: of something not round her nor before her. I have heard of daydreams—is she in a daydream now? Her eyes are fixed on the floor, but I am sure they do not see it—her sight seems turned in, gone down into her heart: she is looking at what she can remember, I believe; not at what is really present. I wonder what sort of a girl she is—whether good or naughty?"

Soon after five P.M. we had another meal, consisting of a small mug of cof-fee, and half a slice of brown bread. I devoured my bread and drank my coffee with relish; but I should have been glad of as much more—I was still hungry. Half an hour's recreation succeeded, then study: then the glass of water and the piece of oat-cake, prayers and bed. Such was my first day at Lowood.

Chapter VI

The next day commenced as before, getting up and dressing by rush-light; but this morning we were obliged to dispense with the ceremony of washing: the water in the pitchers was frozen. A change had taken place in the weather the preceding evening, and a keen north-east wind, whistling through the crevices of our bed-room windows all night long, had made us shiver in our beds, and turned the contents of the ewers to ice.

Before the long hour and a half of prayers and Bible reading was over, I felt ready to perish with cold. Breakfast-time came at last, and this morning the porridge was not burned; the quality was eatable, the quantity small; how small my portion seemed! I wished it had been doubled.

In the course of the day I was enrolled a member of the fourth class, and reg-ular tasks and occupations were assigned me: hitherto, I had only been a spec-tator of the proceedings at Lowood, I was now to become an actor therein. At first, being little accustomed to learn by heart, the lessons appeared to me both long and difficult: the frequent change from task to task, too, bewildered me; and I was glad, when, about three o'clock in the afternoon, Miss Smith put into my hands a border of muslin two yards long, together with needle, thimble, etc., and sent me to sit in a quiet corner of the schoolroom, with di-rections to hem the same. At that hour most of the others were sewing like-wise; but one class still stood round Miss Scatcherd's chair reading, and as all was quiet, the subject of their lessons could be heard, together with the man-ner in which each girl acquitted herself, and the animadversions[4] or commen-dations of Miss Scatcherd on the performance. It was English history: among the readers, I observed my acquaintance of the veranda: at the commence-ment of the lesson, her place had been at the top of the class, but for some error of pronunciation or some inattention to stops, she was suddenly sent to the very bottom. Even in that obscure position, Miss Scatcherd continued to make her an object of constant notice: she was continually addressing to her such phrases as the following:—

"Burns" (such it seems was her name: the girls here were all called by their surnames, as boys are elsewhere), "Burns, you are standing on the side of your

4. Critical remarks.

shoe, turn your toes out immediately." "Burns, you poke your chin out most unpleasantly, draw it in." "Burns, I insist on your holding your head up: I will not have you before me in that attitude," etc., etc.

A chapter having been read through twice, the books were closed and the girls examined. The lesson had comprised part of the reign of Charles I, and there were sundry questions about tonnage and poundage, and ship-money, which most of them appeared unable to answer; still, every little difficulty was solved instantly when it reached Burns: her memory seemed to have retained the substance of the whole lesson, and she was ready with answers on every point. I kept expecting that Miss Scatcherd would praise her attention; but, instead of that, she suddenly cried out:—

"You dirty, disagreeable girl! you have never cleaned your nails this morning!"

Burns made no answer: I wondered at her silence.

"Why," thought I, "does she not explain that she could neither clean her nails nor wash her face, as the water was frozen?"

My attention was now called off by Miss Smith desiring me to hold a skein of thread: while she was winding it, she talked to me from time to time, asking whether I had ever been at school before, whether I could mark, stitch, knit, etc.; till she dismissed me, I could not pursue my observations on Miss Scatcherd's movements. When I returned to my seat, that lady was just delivering an order, of which I did not catch the import; but Burns immediately left the class, and, going into the small inner room where the books were kept, returned in half a minute, carrying in her hand a bundle of twigs tied together at one end. This ominous tool she presented to Miss Scatcherd with a respectful curtsy; then she quietly, and without being told, unloosed her pinafore, and the teacher instantly and sharply inflicted on her neck a dozen strokes with the bunch of twigs. Not a tear rose to Burns' eye; and, while I paused from my sewing, because my fingers quivered at this spectacle with a sentiment of unavailing and impotent anger, not a feature of her pensive face altered its ordinary expression.

"Hardened girl!" exclaimed Miss Scatcherd; "nothing can correct you of your slatternly habits: carry the rod away."

Burns obeyed: I looked at her narrowly as she emerged from the book-closet; she was just putting back her handkerchief into her pocket, and the trace of a tear glistened on her thin cheek.

The play-hour in the evening I thought the pleasantest fraction of the day at Lowood: the bit of bread, the draught of coffee swallowed at five o'clock had revived vitality, if it had not satisfied hunger; the long restraint of the day was slackened; the schoolroom felt warmer than in the morning—its fires being allowed to burn a little more brightly to supply, in some measure, the place of candles, not yet introduced; the ruddy gloaming, the licensed uproar, the confusion of many voices, gave one a welcome sense of liberty.

On the evening of the day on which I had seen Miss Scatcherd flog her pupil, Burns, I wandered as usual among the forms and tables and laughing groups without a companion, yet not feeling lonely; when I passed the windows, I now and then lifted a blind and looked out; it snowed fast, a drift was already forming against the lower panes; putting my ear close to the window, I could distinguish from the gleeful tumult within, the disconsolate moan of the wind outside.

Probably, if I had lately left a good home and kind parents, this would have been the hour when I should most keenly have regretted the separation: that wind would then have saddened my heart; this obscure chaos would have disturbed my peace: as it was, I derived from both a strange excitement, and reckless and feverish, I wished the wind to howl more wildly, the gloom to deepen to darkness, and the confusion to rise to clamor.

Jumping over forms, and creeping under tables, I made my way to one of the fire-places: there, kneeling by the high wire fender, I found Burns, absorbed, silent, abstracted from all round her by the companionship of a book, which she read by the dim glare of the embers.

"Is it still *Rasselas?*" I asked, coming behind her.

"Yes," she said, "and I have just finished it."

And in five minutes more she shut it up. I was glad of this.

"Now," thought I, "I can perhaps get her to talk." I sat down by her on the floor.

"What is your name besides Burns?"

"Helen."

"Do you come a long way from here?"

"I come from a place further north; quite on the borders of Scotland."

"Will you ever go back?"

"I hope so; but nobody can be sure of the future."

"You must wish to leave Lowood?"

"No: why should I? I was sent to Lowood to get an education; and it would be of no use going away until I have attained that object."

"But that teacher, Miss Scatcherd, is so cruel to you?"

"Cruel? Not at all! She is severe: she dislikes my faults."

"And if I were in your place I should dislike her; I should resist her; if she struck me with that rod, I should get it from her hand; I should break it under her nose."

"Probably you would do nothing of the sort: but if you did, Mr. Brocklehurst would expel you from the school; that would be a great grief to your relations. It is far better to endure patiently a smart which nobody feels but yourself, than to commit a hasty action whose evil consequences will extend to all connected with you; and, besides, the Bible bids us return good for evil."

"But then it seems disgraceful to be flogged, and to be sent to stand in the middle of a room full of people; and you are such a great girl: I am far younger than you, and I could not bear it."

"Yet it would be your duty to bear it, if you could not avoid it: it is weak and silly to say you *cannot bear* what it is your fate to be required to bear."

I heard her with wonder: I could not comprehend this doctrine of endurance; and still less could I understand or sympathize with the forbearance she expressed for her chastiser. Still I felt that Helen Burns considered things by a light invisible to my eyes. I suspected she might be right and I wrong; but I would not ponder the matter deeply: like Felix, I put it off to a more convenient season.[5]

"You say you have faults, Helen: what are they? To me you seem very good."

"Then learn from me, not to judge by appearances: I am, as Miss Scatcherd said, slatternly; I seldom put, and never keep, things in order; I am careless; I

5. Felix, the Roman governor of Judea, was impressed by the eloquence of the apostle Paul, and so put off his trial for two years (Acts 24:24–27).

forget rules; I read when I should learn my lessons; I have no method; and sometimes I say, like you, I cannot bear to be subjected to systematic arrangements. This is all very provoking to Miss Scatcherd, who is naturally neat, punctual, and particular."

"And cross and cruel," I added; but Helen Burns would not admit my addition: she kept silence.

"Is Miss Temple as severe to you as Miss Scatcherd?"

At the utterance of Miss Temple's name, a soft smile flitted over her grave face.

"Miss Temple is full of goodness; it pains her to be severe to anyone, even the worst in the school; she sees my errors, and tells me of them gently; and, if I do anything worthy of praise, she gives me my meed liberally. One strong proof of my wretchedly defective nature is, that even her expostulations, so mild, so rational, have not influence to cure me of my faults; and even her praise, though I value it most highly, cannot stimulate me to continued care and foresight."

"That is curious," said I: "it is so easy to be careful."

"For you I have no doubt it is. I observed you in your class this morning, and saw you were closely attentive: your thoughts never seemed to wander while Miss Miller explained the lesson and questioned you. Now, mine continually rove away: when I should be listening to Miss Scatcherd, and collecting all she says with assiduity, often I lose the very sound of her voice; I fall into a sort of dream. Sometimes I think I am in Northumberland, and that the noises I hear round me are the bubbling of a little brook which runs through Deepden near our house;—then, when it comes to my turn to reply, I have to be wakened; and, having heard nothing of what was read for listening to the visionary brook, I have no answer ready."

"Yet how well you replied this afternoon."

"It was mere chance: the subject on which we had been reading had interested me. This afternoon, instead of dreaming of Deepden, I was wondering how a man who wished to do right could act so unjustly and unwisely as Charles the First sometimes did; and I thought what a pity it was that, with his integrity and conscientiousness, he could see no farther than the prerogatives of the crown. If he had but been able to look to a distance, and see to what they call the spirit of the age was tending! Still, I like Charles—I respect him—I pity him, poor murdered king! Yes, his enemies were the worst: they shed blood they had no right to shed. How dared they kill him!"

Helen was talking to herself now: she had forgotten I could not very well understand her—that I was ignorant, or nearly so, of the subject she discussed. I recalled her to my level.

"And when Miss Temple teaches you, do your thoughts wander then?"

"No, certainly, not often; because Miss Temple has generally something to say which is newer than my own reflections: her language is singularly agreeable to me, and the information she communicates is often just what I wished to gain."

"Well, then, with Miss Temple you are good?"

"Yes, in a passive way: I make no effort; I follow as inclination guides me. There is no merit in such goodness."

"A great deal: you are good to those who are good to you. It is all I ever desire to be. If people were always kind and obedient to those who are cruel and un-

just, the wicked people would have it all their own way; they would never feel afraid, and so they would never alter, but would grow worse and worse. When we are struck at without a reason, we should strike back again very hard; I am sure we should—so hard as to teach the person who struck us never to do it again."

"You will change your mind, I hope, when you grow older: as yet you are but a little untaught girl."

"But I feel this, Helen: I must dislike those who, whatever I do to please them, persist in disliking me; I must resist those who punish me unjustly. It is as natural as that I should love those who show me affection, or submit to punishment when I feel it is deserved."

"Heathens and savage tribes hold that doctrine; but Christians and civilized nations disown it."

"How? I don't understand."

"It is not violence that best overcomes hate—nor vengeance that most certainly heals injury."

"What then?"

"Read the New Testament, and observe what Christ says, and how he acts; make his word your rule, and his conduct your example."

"What does he say?"

"Love your enemies; bless them that curse you; do good to them that hate you and despitefully use you."[6]

"Then I should love Mrs. Reed, which I cannot do; I should bless her son John, which is impossible."

In her turn, Helen Burns asked me to explain, and I proceeded forthwith to pour out, in my own way, the tale of my sufferings and resentments. Bitter and truculent when excited, I spoke as I felt, without reserve or softening.

Helen heard me patiently to the end: I expected she would then make a remark, but she said nothing.

"Well," I asked impatiently, "is not Mrs. Reed a hard-hearted, bad woman?"

"She has been unkind to you, no doubt; because, you see, she dislikes your cast of character, as Miss Scatcherd does mine: but how minutely you remember all she has done and said to you! What a singularly deep impression her injustice seems to have made on your heart! No ill-usage so brands its record on my feelings. Would you not be happier if you tried to forget her severity, together with the passionate emotions it excited? Life appears to me too short to be spent in nursing animosity, or registering wrongs. We are, and must be, one and all, burdened with faults in this world: but the time will soon come when, I trust, we shall put them off in putting off our corruptible bodies; when debasement and sin will fall from us with this cumbrous frame of flesh, and only the spark of the spirit will remain,—the impalpable principle of life and thought, pure as when it left the Creator to inspire the creature: whence it came it will return; perhaps again to be communicated to some being higher than man—perhaps to pass through gradations of glory, from the pale human soul to brighten to the seraph! Surely it will never, on the contrary, be suffered to degenerate from man to fiend? No; I cannot believe that: I hold another creed; which no one ever taught me, and which I seldom mention; but in which I delight, and to which I cling: for it extends hope to all: it makes

6. Matthew 5:44.

Eternity a rest—a mighty home, not a terror and an abyss. Besides, with this creed, I can so clearly distinguish between the criminal and his crime; I can so sincerely forgive the first while I abhor the last: with this creed revenge never worries my heart, degradation never too deeply disgusts me, injustice never crushes me too low: I live in calm, looking to the end."

Helen's head, always drooping, sank a little lower as she finished this sentence. I saw by her look she wished no longer to talk to me, but rather to converse with her own thoughts. She was not allowed much time for meditation; a monitor, a great rough girl, presently came up, exclaiming in a strong Cumberland accent,—

"Helen Burns, if you don't go and put your drawer in order, and fold up your work this minute, I'll tell Miss Scatcherd to come and look at it!"

Helen sighed as her reverie fled, and getting up, obeyed the monitor without reply as without delay.

Chapter VII

My first quarter at Lowood seemed an age; and not the golden age either: it comprised an irksome struggle with difficulties in habituating myself to new rules and unwonted tasks. The fear of failure in these points harassed me worse than the physical hardships of my lot; though these were no trifles.

During January, February, and part of March, the deep snows, and, after their melting, the almost impassable roads, prevented our stirring beyond the garden walls, except to go to church; but within these limits we had to pass an hour every day in the open air. Our clothing was insufficient to protect us from the severe cold: we had no boots, the snow got into our shoes and melted there; our ungloved hands became numbed and covered with chilblains, as were our feet: I remember well the distracting irritation I endured from this cause every evening, when my feet inflamed; and the torture of thrusting the swelled, raw, and stiff toes into my shoes in the morning. Then the scanty supply of food was distressing: with the keen appetites of growing children, we had scarcely sufficient to keep alive a delicate invalid. From this deficiency of nourishment resulted an abuse, which pressed hardly on the younger pupils: whenever the famished great girls had an opportunity, they would coax or menace the little ones out of their portion. Many a time I have shared between two claimants the precious morsel of brown bread distributed at teatime; and after relinquishing to a third, half the contents of my mug of coffee, I have swallowed the remainder with an accompaniment of secret tears, forced from me by the exigency of hunger.

Sundays were dreary days in that wintry season. We had to walk two miles to Brocklebridge Church, where our patron officiated. We set out cold, we arrived at church colder: during the morning service we became almost paralyzed. It was too far to return to dinner, and an allowance of cold meat and bread, in the same penurious proportion observed in our ordinary meals, was served round between the services.

At the close of the afternoon service we returned by an exposed and hilly road, where the bitter winter wind, blowing over a range of snowy summits to the north, almost flayed the skin from our faces.

I can remember Miss Temple walking lightly and rapidly along our drooping line, her plaid cloak, which the frosty wind fluttered, gathered close about her, and encouraging us, by precept and example, to keep up our spirits, and

march forward, as she said, "like stalwart soldiers." The other teachers, poor things, were generally themselves too much dejected to attempt the task of cheering others.

How we longed for the light and heat of a blazing fire when we got back! But, to the little ones at least, this was denied: each hearth in the schoolroom was immediately surrounded by a double row of great girls, and behind them the younger children crouched in groups, wrapping their starved[7] arms in their pinafores.

A little solace came at tea-time, in the shape of a double ration of bread—a whole, instead of a half, slice—with the delicious addition of a thin scrape of butter: it was the hebdomadal treat to which we all looked forward from Sabbath to Sabbath. I generally contrived to reserve a moiety[8] of this boun-teous repast for myself; but the remainder I was invariably obliged to part with.

The Sunday evening was spent in repeating, by heart, the Church Catechism, and the fifth, sixth, and seventh chapters of St. Matthew; and in listening to a long sermon, read by Miss Miller, whose irrepressible yawns at-tested her weariness. A frequent interlude of these performances was the en-actment of the part of Eutychus by some half dozen of little girls; who, overpowered with sleep, would fall down, if not out of the third loft, yet off the fourth form, and be taken up half dead.[9] The remedy was, to thrust them for-ward into the center of the schoolroom, and oblige them to stand there till the sermon was finished. Sometimes their feet failed them, and they sank to-gether in a heap; they were then propped up with the monitors' high stools.

I have not yet alluded to the visits of Mr. Brocklehurst; and indeed that gen-tleman was from home during the greater part of the first month after my ar-rival; perhaps prolonging his stay with his friend the archdeacon: his absence was a relief to me. I need not say that I had my own reasons for dreading his coming: but come he did at last.

One afternoon (I had then been three weeks at Lowood), as I was sitting with a slate in my hand, puzzling over a sum in long division, my eyes, raised in abstraction to the window, caught sight of a figure just passing: I recognized almost instinctively that gaunt outline; and when two minutes after, all the school, teachers included, rose *en masse*, it was not necessary for me to look up in order to ascertain whose entrance they thus greeted. A long stride measured the schoolroom, and presently beside Miss Temple, who herself had risen, stood the same black column which had frowned on me so ominously from the hearth-rug of Gateshead. I now glanced sideways at this piece of architec-ture. Yes, I was right: it was Mr. Brocklehurst, buttoned up in a surtout,[1] and looking longer, narrower, and more rigid than ever.

I had my own reasons for being dismayed at this apparition: too well I re-membered the perfidious hints given by Mrs. Reed about my disposition, etc.; the promise pledged by Mr. Brocklehurst to apprise Miss Temple and the teachers of my vicious nature. All along I had been dreading the fulfillment of this promise,—I had been looking out daily for the "Coming Man," whose in-formation respecting my past life and conversation was to brand me as a bad

7. Frozen: literally, starved for warmth.
8. Half. "Hebdomadal": weekly.
9. Eutychus fell asleep while listening to the apostle

Paul and consequently fell from a third-story window ("third loft") (Acts 20:7–12).
1. Long, close-fitting overcoat.

child forever: now there he was. He stood at Miss Temple's side; he was speaking low in her ear: I did not doubt he was making disclosures of my villainy; and I watched her eye with painful anxiety, expecting every moment to see its dark orb turn on me a glance of repugnance and contempt. I listened too; and as I happened to be seated quite at the top of the room, I caught most of what he said: its import relieved me from immediate apprehension.

"I suppose, Miss Temple, the thread I bought at Lowton will do; it struck me that it would be just of the quality for the calico chemises, and I sorted the needles to match. You may tell Miss Smith that I forgot to make a memorandum of the darning needles, but she shall have some papers sent in next week; and she is not, on any account, to give out more than one at a time to each pupil: if they have more, they are apt to be careless and lose them. And, oh ma'am! I wish the woolen stockings were better looked to!—when I was here last, I went into the kitchen-garden and examined the clothes drying on the line; there was a quantity of black hose in a very bad state of repair: from the size of the holes in them I was sure they had not been well mended from time to time."

He paused.

"Your directions shall be attended to, sir," said Miss Temple.

"And, ma'am," he continued, "the laundress tells me some of the girls have two clean tuckers[2] in the week: it is too much; the rules limit them to one."

"I think I can explain that circumstance, sir. Agnes and Catherine Johnstone were invited to take tea with some friends at Lowton last Thursday, and I gave them leave to put on clean tuckers for the occasion."

Mr. Brocklehurst nodded.

"Well, for once it may pass; but please not to let the circumstance occur too often. And there is another thing which surprised me: I find, in settling accounts with the housekeeper, that a lunch, consisting of bread and cheese, has twice been served out to the girls during the past fortnight. How is this? I look over the regulations, and I find no such meal as lunch mentioned. Who introduced this innovation? and by what authority?"

"I must be responsible for the circumstance, sir," replied Miss Temple: "the breakfast was so ill-prepared that the pupils could not possibly eat it; and I dared not allow them to remain fasting till dinnertime."

"Madam, allow me an instant. You are aware that my plan in bringing up these girls is, not to accustom them to habits of luxury and indulgence, but to render them hardy, patient, self-denying. Should any little accidental disappointment of the appetite occur, such as the spoiling of a meal, the under or the over dressing of a dish, the incident ought not to be neutralized by replacing with something more delicate the comfort lost, thus pampering the body and obviating the aim of this institution; it ought to be improved to the spiritual edification of the pupils, by encouraging them to evince fortitude under the temporary privation. A brief address on those occasions would not be mistimed, wherein a judicious instructor would take the opportunity of referring to the sufferings of the primitive Christians; to the torments of martyrs; to the exhortations of our blessed Lord himself, calling upon his disciples to take up their cross and follow him; to his warnings that man shall not live by bread alone, but by every word that proceedeth out of the mouth of God; to

2. Pieces of cloth in the neckline of a dress.

his divine consolations, 'if ye suffer hunger or thirst for my sake, happy are ye.'[3] Oh, madam, when you put bread and cheese, instead of burned porridge, into these children's mouths, you may indeed feed their vile bodies, but you little think how you starve their immortal souls!"

Mr. Brocklehurst again paused—perhaps overcome by his feelings. Miss Temple had looked down when he first began to speak to her; but she now gazed straight before her, and her face, naturally pale as marble, appeared to be assuming also the coldness and fixity of that material; especially her mouth, closed as if it would have required a sculptor's chisel to open it, and her brow settled gradually into petrified severity.

Meantime, Mr. Brocklehurst, standing on the hearth with his hands behind his back, majestically surveyed the whole school. Suddenly his eye gave a blink, as if it had met something that either dazzled or shocked its pupil; turning, he said in more rapid accents than he had hitherto used:—"Miss Temple, Miss Temple, what—*what* is that girl with curled hair? Red hair, ma'am, curled—curled all over?" And extending his cane he pointed to the awful object, his hand shaking as he did so.

"It is Julia Severn," replied Miss Temple, very quietly.

"Julia Severn, ma'am! And why has she, or any other, curled hair? Why, in defiance of every precept and principle of this house, does she conform to the world so openly—here in an evangelical, charitable establishment—as to wear her hair one mass of curls?"

"Julia's hair curls naturally," returned Miss Temple, still more quietly.

"Naturally! Yes, but we are not to conform to nature: I wish these girls to be the children of Grace: and why that abundance? I have again and again intimated that I desire the hair to be arranged closely, modestly, plainly. Miss Temple, that girl's hair must be cut off entirely; I will send a barber tomorrow: and I see others who have far too much of the excrescence—that tall girl, tell her to turn round. Tell all the first form to rise up and direct their faces to the wall."

Miss Temple passed her handkerchief over her lips, as if to smooth away the involuntary smile that curled them; she gave the order, however, and when the first class could take in what was required of them, they obeyed. Leaning a little back on my bench, I could see the looks and grimaces with which they commented on this maneuver: it was a pity Mr. Brocklehurst could not see them too; he would perhaps have felt that, whatever he might do with the outside of the cup and platter, the inside was further beyond his interference than he imagined.[4]

He scrutinized the reverse of these living medals some five minutes, then pronounced sentence. These words fell like the knell of doom:—"All those top-knots must be cut off."

Miss Temple seemed to remonstrate.

"Madam," he pursued, "I have a master to serve whose kingdom is not of this world: my mission is to mortify in these girls the lusts of the flesh; to teach them to clothe themselves with shamefacedness and sobriety, not with braided hair and costly apparel; and each of the young persons before us has a

3. Brocklehurst misquotes Matthew 5:6: "Blessed are they which do hunger and thirst after righteousness: for they shall be filled."
4. "Woe to you, scribes and Pharisees, hypocrites! for ye make clean the outside of the cup and of the platter, but within they are full of extortion and excess" (Matthew 23:25).

string of hair twisted in plaits which vanity itself might have woven: these, I repeat, must be cut off; think of the time wasted, of——"

Mr. Brocklehurst was here interrupted: three other visitors, ladies, now entered the room. They ought to have come a little sooner to have heard his lecture on dress, for they were splendidly attired in velvet, silk, and furs. The two younger of the trio (fine girls of sixteen and seventeen) had gray beaver hats, then in fashion, shaded with ostrich plumes, and from under the brim of this graceful head-dress fell a profusion of light tresses, elaborately curled; the elder lady was enveloped in a costly velvet shawl, trimmed with ermine, and she wore a false front of French curls.

These ladies were deferentially received by Miss Temple, as Mrs. and the Misses Brocklehurst, and conducted to seats of honor at the top of the room. It seems they had come in the carriage with their reverend relative, and had been conducting a rummaging scrutiny of the rooms upstairs, while he transacted business with the housekeeper, questioned the laundress, and lectured the superintendent. They now proceeded to address divers remarks and reproofs to Miss Smith, who was charged with the care of the linen and the inspection of the dormitories: but I had no time to listen to what they said; other matters called off and enchained my attention.

Hitherto, while gathering up the discourse of Mr. Brocklehurst and Miss Temple, I had not, at the same time, neglected precautions to secure my personal safety; which I thought would be effected, if I could only elude observation. To this end, I had sat well back on the form, and while seeming to be busy with my sum, had held my slate in such a manner as to conceal my face: I might have escaped notice, had not my treacherous slate somehow happened to slip from my hand and falling with an obtrusive crash, directly drawn every eye upon me; I knew it was all over now, and, as I stooped to pick up the two fragments of slate, I rallied my forces for the worst. It came.

"A careless girl!" said Mr. Brocklehurst, and immediately after—"It is the new pupil, I perceive." And before I could draw breath, "I must not forget I have a word to say respecting her." Then aloud: how loud it seemed to me! "Let the child who broke her slate, come forward."

Of my own accord, I could not have stirred: I was paralyzed: but the two great girls who sat on each side of me, set me on my legs and pushed me towards the dread judge, and then Miss Temple gently assisted me to his very feet, and I caught her whispered counsel,—"Don't be afraid, Jane, I saw it was an accident; you shall not be punished."

The kind whisper went to my heart like a dagger.

"Another minute, and she will despise me for a hypocrite," thought I; and an impulse of fury against Reed, Brocklehurst, and Co. bounded in my pulses at the conviction. I was no Helen Burns. "Fetch that stool," said Mr. Brocklehurst, pointing to a very high one from which a monitor had just risen: it was brought.

"Place the child upon it."

And I was placed there, by whom I don't know: I was in no condition to note particulars: I was only aware that they had hoisted me up to the height of Mr. Brocklehurst's nose, that he was within a yard of me, and that a spread of shot orange and purple silk pelisses, and a cloud of silvery plumage extended and waved below me.

Mr. Brocklehurst hemmed.

"Ladies," said he, turning to his family; "Miss Temple, teachers, and children, you all see this girl?"

Of course they did; for I felt their eyes directed like burning-glasses against my scorched skin.

"You see she is yet young; you observe she possesses the ordinary form of childhood; God has graciously given her the shape that he has given to all of us; no signal deformity points her out as a marked character. Who would think that the Evil One had already found a servant and agent in her? Yet such, I grieve to say, is the case."

A pause—in which I began to steady the palsy of my nerves, and to feel that the Rubicon was passed;[5] and that the trial, no longer to be shirked, must be firmly sustained.

"My dear children," pursued the black marble clergyman, with pathos, "this is a sad, a melancholy occasion; for it becomes my duty to warn you, that this girl, who might be one of God's own lambs, is a little castaway: not a member of the true flock, but evidently an interloper and an alien. You must be on your guard against her; you must shun her example: if necessary, avoid her company, exclude her from your sports, and shut her out from your converse. Teachers, you must watch her: keep your eyes on her movements, weigh well her words, scrutinize her actions, punish her body to save her soul: if, indeed, such salvation be possible, for (my tongue falters while I tell it) this girl, this child, the native of a Christian land, worse than many a little heathen who says its prayers to Brahma and kneels before Juggernaut[6]—this girl is—a liar!"

Now came a pause of ten minutes; during which I, by this time in perfect possession of my wits, observed all the female Brocklehursts produce their pocket-handkerchiefs and apply them to their optics, while the elderly lady swayed herself to and fro, and the two younger ones whispered, "How shocking!"

Mr. Brocklehurst resumed.

"This I learned from her benefactress; from the pious and charitable lady who adopted her in her orphan state, reared her as her own daughter, and whose kindness, whose generosity the unhappy girl repaid by an ingratitude so bad, so dreadful, that at last her excellent patroness was obliged to separate her from her own young ones, fearful lest her vicious example should contaminate their purity: she has sent her here to be healed, even as the Jews of old sent their diseased to the troubled pool of Bethesda;[7] and, teachers, superintendent, I beg of you not to allow the waters to stagnate round her."

With this sublime conclusion, Mr. Brocklehurst adjusted the top button of his surtout, muttered something to his family, who rose, bowed to Miss Temple, and then all the great people sailed in state from the room. Turning at the door, my judge said:—"Let her stand half an hour longer on that stool, and let no one speak to her during the remainder of the day."

There was I, then, mounted aloft: I, who had said I could not bear the shame of standing on my natural feet in the middle of the room, was now exposed to general view on a pedestal of infamy. What my sensations were, no language can describe: but just as they all rose, stifling my breath and constricting my throat, a girl came up and passed me: in passing, she lifted her

5. I.e., the point of no return was crossed.
6. Hindu gods.

7. Bethesda, literally, "house of grace," was the place where Jesus healed an invalid (John 5:2–9).

eyes. What a strange light inspired them! What an extraordinary sensation that ray sent through me! How the new feeling bore me up! It was as if a martyr, a hero, had passed a slave or victim, and imparted strength in the transit. I mastered the rising hysteria, lifted up my head, and took a firm stand on the stool. Helen Burns asked some slight question about her work of Miss Smith, was chidden for the triviality of the inquiry, returned to her place, and smiled at me as she again went by. What a smile! I remember it now, and I know that it was the effluence of fine intellect, of true courage; it lit up her marked lineaments, her thin face, her sunken gray eye, like a reflection from the aspect of an angel. Yet at that moment Helen Burns wore on her arm the "untidy badge"; scarcely an hour ago I had heard her condemned by Miss Scatcherd to a dinner of bread and water on the morrow, because she had blotted an exercise in copying it out. Such is the imperfect nature of man! such spots are there on the disc of the clearest planet; and eyes like Miss Scatcherd's can only see those minute defects, and are blind to the full brightness of the orb.

Chapter VIII

Ere the half-hour ended, five o'clock struck; school was dismissed and all were gone into the refectory to tea. I now ventured to descend: it was deep dusk; I retired into a corner and sat down on the floor. The spell by which I had been so far supported began to dissolve; reaction took place, and soon, so overwhelming was the grief that seized me, I sank prostrate with my face to the ground. Now I wept: Helen Burns was not here; nothing sustained me; left to myself I abandoned myself, and my tears watered the boards. I had meant to be so good, and to do so much at Lowood: to make so many friends, to earn respect, and win affection. Already I had made visible progress: that very morning I had reached the head of my class; Miss Miller had praised me warmly; Miss Temple had smiled approbation; she had promised to teach me drawing, and to let me learn French, if I continued to make similar improvement two months longer: and then I was well-received by my fellow-pupils; treated as an equal by those of my own age, and not molested by any; now, here I lay again crushed and trodden on; and could I ever rise more?

"Never," I thought; and ardently I wished to die. While sobbing out this wish in broken accents, someone approached: I started up—again Helen Burns was near me; the fading fires just showed her coming up the long, vacant room; she brought my coffee and bread.

"Come, eat something," she said; but I put both away from me, feeling as if a drop or a crumb would have choked me in my present condition. Helen regarded me, probably with surprise: I could not now abate my agitation, though I tried hard; I continued to weep aloud. She sat down on the ground near me, embraced her knees with her arms, and rested her head upon them; in that attitude she remained silent as an Indian. I was the first who spoke:—

"Helen, why do you stay with a girl whom everybody believes to be a liar?"

"Everybody, Jane? Why, there are only eighty people who have heard you called so, and the world contains hundreds of millions."

"But what have I to do with millions? The eighty I know despise me."

"Jane, you are mistaken: probably not one in the school either despises or dislikes you: many, I am sure, pity you much."

"How can they pity me after what Mr. Brocklehurst said?"

"Mr. Brocklehurst is not a god: nor is he even a great and admired man: he is

little liked here; he never took steps to make himself liked. Had he treated you as an especial favorite, you would have found enemies, declared or covert, all around you: as it is, the greater number would offer you sympathy if they dared. Teachers and pupils may look coldly on you for a day or two, but friendly feelings are concealed in their hearts; and if you persevere in doing well, these feelings will ere long appear so much the more evident for their temporary suppression. Besides, Jane,"—she paused.

"Well, Helen?" said I, putting my hand into hers: she chafed my fingers gently to warm them, and went on:—

"If all the world hated you, and believed you wicked, while your own conscience approved you, and absolved you from guilt, you would not be without friends."

"No; I know I should think well of myself; but that is not enough: if others don't love me, I would rather die than live—I cannot bear to be solitary and hated, Helen. Look here; to gain some real affection from you, or Miss Temple, or any other whom I truly love, I would willingly submit to have the bone of my arm broken, or to let a bull toss me, or to stand behind a kicking horse, and let it dash its hoof at my chest,"—

"Hush, Jane! you think too much of the love of human beings, you are too impulsive, too vehement: the sovereign hand that created your frame, and put life into it, has provided you with other resources than your feeble self, or than creatures feeble as you. Besides this earth, and besides the race of men, there is an invisible world and a kingdom of spirits: that world is round us, for it is everywhere; and those spirits watch us, for they are commissioned to guard us; and if we were dying in pain and shame, if scorn smote us on all sides, and hatred crushed us, angels see our tortures, recognize our innocence (if innocent we be: as I know you are of this charge which Mr. Brocklehurst has weakly and pompously repeated at second-hand from Mrs. Reed; for I read a sincere nature in your ardent eyes and on your clear front), and God waits only the separation of spirit from flesh to crown us with a full reward. Why, then, should we ever sink overwhelmed with distress, when life is so soon over, and death is so certain an entrance to happiness—to glory?"

I was silent: Helen had calmed me; but in the tranquility she imparted there was an alloy of inexpressible sadness. I felt the impression of woe as she spoke, but I could not tell whence it came; and when, having done speaking, she breathed a little fast and coughed a short cough, I momentarily forgot my own sorrows to yield to a vague concern for her.

Resting my head on Helen's shoulder, I put my arms round her waist; she drew me to her, and we reposed in silence. We had not sat long thus, when another person came in. Some heavy clouds, swept from the sky by a rising wind, had left the moon bare; and her light, streaming in through a window near, shone full both on us and on the approaching figure, which we at once recognized as Miss Temple.

"I came on purpose to find you, Jane Eyre," said she; "I want you in my room; and as Helen Burns is with you, she may come too."

We went; following the superintendent's guidance, we had to thread some intricate passages, and mount a staircase before we reached her apartment; it contained a good fire, and looked cheerful. Miss Temple told Helen Burns to be seated in a low arm-chair on one side of the hearth, and herself taking another, she called me to her side.

"Is it all over?" she asked, looking down at my face. "Have you cried your grief away?"

"I am afraid I never shall do that."

"Why?"

"Because I have been wrongly accused; and you, ma'am, and everybody else will now think me wicked."

"We shall think you what you prove yourself to be, my child. Continue to act as a good girl, and you will satisfy me."

"Shall I, Miss Temple?"

"You will," said she, passing her arm round me "And now tell me who is the lady whom Mr. Brocklehurst called your benefactress?"

"Mrs. Reed, my uncle's wife. My uncle is dead, and left me to her care."

"Did she not, then, adopt you of her own accord?"

"No, ma'am; she was sorry to have to do it: but my uncle, as I have often heard the servants say, got her to promise before he died, that she would always keep me."

"Well, now, Jane, you know, or at least I will tell you, that when a criminal is accused, he is always allowed to speak in his own defence. You have been charged with falsehood; defend yourself to me as well as you can. Say whatever your memory suggests as true; but add nothing and exaggerate nothing."

I resolved, in the depth of my heart, that I would be most moderate—most correct; and, having reflected a few minutes in order to arrange coherently what I had to say, I told her all the story of my sad childhood. Exhausted by emotion, my language was more subdued than it generally was when it developed that sad theme; and mindful of Helen's warnings against the indulgence of resentment, I infused into the narrative far less of gall and wormwood than ordinary. Thus restrained and simplified, it sounded more credible: I felt as I went on that Miss Temple fully believed me.

In the course of the tale I had mentioned Mr. Lloyd as having come to see me after the fit: for I never forgot the, to me, frightful episode of the red-room; in detailing which, my excitement was sure, in some degree, to break bounds; for nothing could soften in my recollection the spasm of agony which clutched my heart when Mrs. Reed spurned my wild supplication for pardon, and locked me a second time in the dark and haunted chamber.

I had finished: Miss Temple regarded me a few minutes in silence; she then said:—"I know something of Mr. Lloyd; I shall write to him; if his reply agrees with your statement, you shall be publicly cleared from every imputation: to me, Jane, you are clear now."

She kissed me, and still keeping me at her side (where I was well contented to stand, for I derived a child's pleasure from the contemplation of her face, her dress, her one or two ornaments, her white forehead, her clustered and shining curls, and beaming dark eyes), she proceeded to address Helen Burns.

"How are you tonight, Helen? Have you coughed much today?"

"Not quite so much, I think, ma'am."

"And the pain in your chest?"

"It is a little better."

Miss Temple got up, took her hand and examined her pulse; then she returned to her own seat: as she resumed it, I heard her sigh low. She was pensive a few minutes, then rousing herself, she said cheerfully:—"But you two are my visitors tonight; I must treat you as such." She rang her bell.

"Barbara," she said to the servant who answered it, "I have not yet had tea; bring the tray, and place cups for these two young ladies."

And a tray was soon brought. How pretty, to my eyes, did the china cups and bright teapot look, placed on the little round table near the fire! How fragrant was the steam of the beverage, and the scent of the toast! of which, however, I, to my dismay (for I was beginning to be hungry), discerned only a very small portion: Miss Temple discerned it too:—"Barbara," said she, "can you not bring a little more bread and butter? There is not enough for three."

Barbara went out: she returned soon:—"Madam, Mrs. Harden says she has sent up the usual quantity."

Mrs. Harden, be it observed, was the housekeeper: a woman after Mr. Brocklehurst's own heart, made up of equal parts of whalebone and iron.

"Oh, very well!" returned Miss Temple; "we must make it do, Barbara, I suppose." And as the girl withdrew, she added, smiling, "Fortunately, I have it in my power to supply deficiencies for this once."

Having invited Helen and me to approach the table, and placed before each of us a cup of tea with one delicious but thin morsel of toast, she got up, unlocked a drawer, and taking from it a parcel wrapped in paper, disclosed presently to our eyes a good-sized seed-cake.

"I meant to give each of you some of this to take with you," said she; "but as there is so little toast, you must have it now," and she proceeded to cut slices with a generous hand.

We feasted that evening as on nectar and ambrosia; and not the least delight of the entertainment was the smile of gratification with which our hostess regarded us, as we satisfied our famished appetites on the delicate fare she liberally supplied. Tea over and the tray removed, she again summoned us to the fire; we sat one on each side of her, and now a conversation followed between her and Helen, which it was indeed a privilege to be admitted to hear.

Miss Temple had always something of serenity in her air, of state in her mien, of refined propriety in her language, which precluded deviation into the ardent, the excited, the eager: something which chastened the pleasure of those who looked on her and listened to her, by a controlling sense of awe; and such was my feeling now; but as to Helen Burns, I was struck with wonder.

The refreshing meal, the brilliant fire, the presence and kindness of her beloved instructress, or, perhaps, more than all these, something in her own unique mind, had roused her powers within her. They woke, they kindled: first, they glowed in the bright tint of her cheek, which till this hour I had never seen but pale and bloodless; then they shone in the liquid luster of her eyes, which had suddenly acquired a beauty more singular than that of Miss Temple's—a beauty neither of fine color nor long eyelash, nor penciled brow, but of meaning, of movement, of radiance. Then her soul sat on her lips, and language flowed, from what source I cannot tell: has a girl of fourteen a heart large enough, vigorous enough, to hold the swelling spring of pure full, fervid eloquence? Such was the characteristic of Helen's discourse on that, to me, memorable evening; her spirit seemed hastening to live within a very brief span as much as many live during a protracted existence.

They conversed of things I had never heard of: of nations and times past; of countries far away: of secrets of nature discovered or guessed at: they spoke of books: how many they had read! What stores of knowledge they possessed! Then they seemed so familiar with French names and French authors: but my

amazement reached its climax when Miss Temple asked Helen if she some-
times snatched a moment to recall the Latin her father had taught her, and
taking a book from a shelf, bade her read and construe a page of "Virgil"; and
Helen obeyed, my organ of Veneration expanding at every sounding line. She
had scarcely finished ere the bell announced bedtime: no delay could be ad-
mitted; Miss Temple embraced us both, saying, as she drew us to her heart:—
"God bless you, my children!"

Helen she held a little longer than me: she let her go more reluctantly; it was
Helen her eye followed to the door; it was for her she a second time breathed a
sad sigh; for her she wiped a tear from her cheek.

On reaching the bedroom, we heard the voice of Miss Scatcherd: she was
examining drawers; she had just pulled out Helen Burns' and when we entered
Helen was greeted with a sharp reprimand, and told that tomorrow she should
have half a dozen of untidily-folded articles pinned to her shoulder.

"My things were indeed in shameful disorder," murmured Helen to me, in a
low voice: "I intended to have arranged them, but I forgot."

Next morning, Miss Scatcherd wrote in conspicuous characters on a piece
of pasteboard the word "Slattern," and bound it like a phylactery[8] round
Helen's large, mild, intelligent, and benign-looking forehead. She wore it till
evening, patient, unresentful, regarding it as a deserved punishment. The mo-
ment Miss Scatcherd withdrew after afternoon-school, I ran to Helen, tore it
off, and thrust it into the fire: the fury of which she was incapable had been
burning in my soul all day, and tears, hot and large, had continually been
scalding my cheek; for the spectacle of her sad resignation gave me an intoler-
able pain at the heart.

About a week subsequently to the incidents above narrated, Miss Temple,
who had written to Mr. Lloyd, received his answer: it appeared that what he
said went to corroborate my account. Miss Temple, having assembled the
whole school, announced that inquiry had been made into the charges alleged
against Jane Eyre, and that she was most happy to be able to pronounce her
completely cleared from every imputation. The teachers then shook hands
with me and kissed me, and a murmur of pleasure ran through the ranks of my
companions.

Thus relieved of a grievous load, I from that hour set to work afresh, re-
solved to pioneer my way through every difficulty: I toiled hard, and my suc-
cess was proportionate to my efforts; my memory, not naturally tenacious,
improved with practice: exercise sharpened my wits; in a few weeks I was pro-
moted to a higher class; in less than two months I was allowed to commence
French and drawing. I learned the first two tenses of the verb Etre,[9] and
sketched my first cottage (whose walls, by-the-by, outrivaled in slope those of
the leaning tower of Pisa), on the same day. That night, on going to bed, I for-
got to prepare in imagination the Barmecide[1] supper of hot roast potatoes, or
white bread and new milk, with which I was wont to amuse my inward crav-
ings: I feasted instead on the spectacle of ideal drawings, which I saw in the
dark; all the work of my own hands: freely pencilled houses and trees, pic-
turesque rocks and ruins, Cuyplike groups of cattle,[2] sweet paintings of but-

8. Box containing scriptural passages, worn by
Orthodox Jewish men during prayers.
9. To be (French).
1. A wealthy man in The Arabian Nights who invites a

beggar to an imaginary banquet.
2. Unblossomed. Albert Cuyp (1620–1691), Dutch
landscape painter.

terflies hovering over unblown roses, of birds picking at ripe cherries, of wrens' nests enclosing pearl-like eggs, wreathed about with young ivy sprays. I examined, too, in thought, the possibility of my ever being able to translate currently[3] a certain little French story-book which Madame Pierrot had that day shown me; nor was the problem solved to my satisfaction ere I fell sweetly asleep.

Well has Solomon said—"Better is a dinner of herbs where love is, than a stalled ox and hatred therewith."[4]

I would not now have exchanged Lowood with all its privations, for Gateshead and its daily luxuries.

Chapter IX

But the privations, or rather the hardships, of Lowood lessened. Spring drew on: she was indeed already come; the frosts of winter had ceased; its snows were melted, its cutting winds ameliorated. My wretched feet, flayed and swollen to lameness by the sharp air of January, began to heal and subside under the gentler breathings of April; the nights and mornings no longer by their Canadian temperature froze the very blood in our veins; we could now endure the play-hour passed in the garden: sometimes on a sunny day it began even to be pleasant and genial, and a greenness grew over those brown beds, which, freshening daily, suggested the thought that Hope traversed them at night, and left each morning brighter traces of her steps. Flowers peeped out amongst the leaves; snowdrops, crocuses, purple auriculas, and golden-eyed pansies. On Thursday afternoons (half-holidays) we now took walks, and found still sweeter flowers opening by the wayside, under the hedges.

I discovered, too, that a great pleasure, an enjoyment which the horizon only bounded, lay all outside the high and spike-guarded walls of our garden: this pleasure consisted in prospect of noble summits girdling a great hill-hollow, rich in verdure and shadow; in a bright beck, full of dark stones and sparkling eddies. How different had this scene looked when I viewed it laid out beneath the iron sky of winter, stiffened in frost, shrouded with snow!—when mists as chill as death wandered to the impulse of east winds along those purple peaks, and rolled down "ing" and holm till they blended with the frozen fog of the beck.[5] That beck itself was then a torrent, turbid and curbless: it tore asunder the wood, and sent a raving sound through the air, often thickened with wild rain or whirling sleet; and for the forest on its banks, *that* showed only ranks of skeletons.

April advanced to May: a bright, serene May it was; days of blue sky, placid sunshine, and soft western or southern gales filled up its duration. And now vegetation matured with vigor; Lowood shook loose its tresses; it became all green, all flowery; its great elm, ash, and oak skeletons were restored to majestic life; woodland plants sprang up profusely in its recesses; unnumbered varieties of moss filled its hollows, and it made a strange ground-sunshine out of the wealth of its wild primrose plants: I have seen their pale gold gleam in overshadowed spots like scatterings of the sweetest luster. All this I enjoyed

3. Jane transliterates the French word *couramment*, "fluently."
4. Proverbs 15:17.

5. Brook. "Ing": meadow. "Holm": low ground beside a brook.

often and fully, free, unwatched, and almost alone: for this unwonted liberty and pleasure there was a cause, to which it now becomes my task to advert.

Have I not described a pleasant site for a dwelling, when I speak of it as bosomed in hill and wood, and rising from the verge of a stream? Assuredly, pleasant enough: but whether healthy or not is another question.

That forest-dell, where Lowood lay, was the cradle of fog and fog-bred pestilence; which, quickening with the quickening spring, crept into the Orphan Asylum, breathed typhus through its crowded school-room and dormitory, and, ere May arrived, transformed the seminary into a hospital.

Semistarvation and neglected colds had predisposed most of the pupils to receive infection: forty-five out of the eighty girls lay ill at one time. Classes were broken up, rules relaxed. The few who continued well were allowed almost unlimited license; because the medical attendant insisted on the necessity of frequent exercise to keep them in health: and had it been otherwise, no one had leisure to watch or restrain them. Miss Temple's whole attention was absorbed by the patients: she lived in the sick-room, never quitting it except to snatch a few hours' rest at night. The teachers were fully occupied with packing up and making other necessary preparations for the departure of those girls who were fortunate enough to have friends and relations able and willing to remove them from the seat of contagion. Many, already smitten, went home only to die: some died at the school, and were buried quietly and quickly, the nature of the malady forbidding delay.

While disease had thus become an inhabitant of Lowood, and death its frequent visitor; while there was gloom and fear within its walls; while its rooms and passages steamed with hospital smells, the drug and the pastille striving vainly to overcome the effluvia[6] of mortality, that bright May shone unclouded over the bold hills and beautiful woodland out of doors. Its garden, too, glowed with flowers: hollyhocks had sprung up tall as trees, lilies had opened, tulips and roses were in bloom; the borders of the little beds were gay with pink thrift and crimson double-daisies; the sweetbriers gave out, morning and evening, their scent of spice and apples; and these fragrant treasures were all useless for most of the inmates of Lowood, except to furnish now and then a handful of herbs and blossoms to put in a coffin.

But I, and the rest who continued well, enjoyed fully the beauties of the scene and season: they let us ramble in the wood, like gipsies, from morning till night; we did what we liked, went where we liked: we lived better too. Mr. Brocklehurst and his family never came near Lowood now: household matters were not scrutinized into; the cross housekeeper was gone, driven away by the fear of infection; her successor, who had been matron at the Lowton Dispensary, unused to the ways of her new abode, provided with comparative liberality. Besides, there were fewer to feed: the sick could eat little; our breakfast-basins were better filled: when there was no time to prepare a regular dinner, which often happened, she would give us a large piece of cold pie, or a thick slice of bread and cheese, and this we carried away with us to the wood, where we each chose the spot we liked best, and dined sumptuously.

My favorite seat was a smooth and broad stone, rising white and dry from the very middle of the beck, and only to be got at by wading through the water; a feat I accomplished barefoot. The stone was just broad enough to accom-

6. Offensive smells. "Pastille" an aromatic paste for fumigating a room's air.

modate, comfortably, another girl and me, at that time my chosen comrade—
one Mary Ann Wilson; a shrewd, observant personage, whose society I took
pleasure in, partly because she was witty and original, and partly because she
had a manner which set me at my ease. Some years older than I, she knew
more of the world, and could tell me many things I liked to hear: with her my
curiosity found gratification: to my faults also she gave ample indulgence,
never imposing curb or rein on anything I said. She had a turn for narrative, I
for analysis; she liked to inform, I to question; so we got on swimmingly to-
gether, deriving much entertainment, if not much improvement, from our
mutual intercourse.

And where, meantime, was Helen Burns? Why did I not spend these sweet
days of liberty with her? Had I forgotten her? or was I so worthless as to have
grown tired of her pure society? Surely the Mary Ann Wilson I have men-
tioned was inferior to my first acquaintance: she could only tell me amusing
stories, and reciprocate any racy and pungent gossip I chose to indulge in;
while, if I have spoken truth of Helen, she was qualified to give those who en-
joyed the privilege of her converse, a taste of far higher things.

True, reader; and I knew and felt this: and though I am a defective being,
with many faults and few redeeming points, yet I never tired of Helen Burns;
nor ever ceased to cherish for her a sentiment of attachment, as strong, tender,
and respectful as any that ever animated my heart. How could it be otherwise,
when Helen, at all times and under all circumstances, evinced for me a quiet
and faithful friendship, which ill-humor never soured, nor irritation ever trou-
bled? But Helen was ill at present: for some weeks she had been removed from
my sight to I knew not what room upstairs. She was not, I was told, in the hos-
pital portion of the house with the fever patients; for her complaint was con-
sumption,[7] not typhus: and by consumption I, in my ignorance, understood
something mild, which time and care would be sure to alleviate.

I was confirmed in this idea by the fact of her once or twice coming down-
stairs on very warm sunny afternoons, and being taken by Miss Temple into
the garden: but, on these occasions, I was not allowed to go and speak to her; I
only saw her from the schoolroom window, and then not distinctly; for she was
much wrapped up, and sat at a distance under the veranda.

One evening, in the beginning of June, I had stayed out very late with Mary
Ann in the wood; we had, as usual, separated ourselves from the others and
had wandered far: so far that we lost our way, and had to ask it at a lonely cot-
tage, where a man and woman lived, who looked after a herd of half-wild swine
that fed on the mast in the wood. When we got back it was after moon-rise: a
pony, which we knew to be the surgeon's, was standing at the garden door.
Mary Ann remarked that she supposed some one must be very ill, as Mr. Bates
had been sent for at that time of the evening. She went into the house; I
stayed behind a few minutes to plant in my garden a handful of roots I had
dug up in the forest, and which I feared would wither if I left them till the
morning. This done, I lingered yet a little longer: the flowers smelt so sweet as
the dew fell; it was such a pleasant evening, so serene, so warm; the still glow-
ing west promised so fairly another fine day on the morrow; the moon rose
with such majesty in the grave east. I was noting these things and enjoying
them as a child might, when it entered my mind as it had never done before:—

7. Tuberculosis.

"How sad to be lying now on a sick bed, and to be in danger of dying! This world is pleasant—it would be dreary to be called from it, and to have to go who knows where?"

And then my mind made its first earnest effort to comprehend what had been infused into it concerning heaven and hell: and for the first time it recoiled, baffled; and for the first time glancing behind, on each side, and before it, it saw all round an unfathomed gulf: it felt the one point where it stood—the present; all the rest was formless cloud and vacant depth: and it shuddered at the thought of tottering, and plunging amid that chaos. While pondering this new idea, I heard the front door open; Mr. Bates came out, and with him was a nurse. After she had seen him mount his horse and depart, she was about to close the door, but I ran up to her.

"How is Helen Burns?"

"Very poorly," was the answer.

"Is it her Mr. Bates has been to see?"

"Yes."

"And what does he say about her?"

"He says she'll not be here long."

This phrase, uttered in my hearing yesterday, would have only conveyed the notion that she was about to be removed to Northumberland, to her own home. I should not have suspected that it meant she was dying; but I knew instantly now: it opened clear on my comprehension that Helen Burns was numbering her last days in this world, and that she was going to be taken to the region of spirits, if such region there were. I experienced a shock of horror, then a strong thrill of grief, then a desire—a necessity to see her. and I asked in what room she lay.

"She is in Miss Temple's room," said the nurse.

"May I go up and speak to her?"

"Oh, no, child! It is not likely; and now it is time for you to come in; you'll catch the fever if you stop out when the dew is falling."

The nurse closed the front door; I went in by the side entrance which led to the schoolroom: I was just in time; it was nine o'clock, and Miss Miller was calling the pupils to go to bed.

It might be two hours later, probably near eleven, when I—not having been able to fall asleep, and deeming, from the perfect silence of the dormitory, that my companions were all wrapt in profound repose—rose softly, put on my frock over my night-dress, and, without shoes, crept from the apartment, and set off in quest of Miss Temple's room. It was quite at the other end of the house; but I knew my way; and the light of the unclouded summer moon, entering here and there at passage windows, enabled me to find it without difficulty. An odor of camphor and burned vinegar warned me when I came near the fever room: and I passed its door quickly, fearful lest the nurse who sat up all night should hear me. I dreaded being discovered and sent back; for I *must* see Helen,—I must embrace her before she died.—I must give her one last kiss, exchange with her one last word.

Having descended a staircase, traversed a portion of the house below, and succeeded in opening and shutting, without noise, two doors, I reached another flight of steps; these I mounted, and then just opposite to me was Miss Temple's room. A light shone through the key-hole, and from under the door; a profound stillness pervaded the vicinity. Coming near, I found the door

slightly ajar; probably to admit some fresh air into the close abode of sickness. Indisposed to hesitate, and full of impatient impulses—soul and senses quivering with keen throes—I put it back and looked in. My eye sought Helen, and feared to find death.

Close by Miss Temple's bed, and half covered with its white curtains, there stood a little crib. I saw the outline of a form under the clothes, but the face was hid by the hangings: the nurse I had spoken to in the garden sat in an easy-chair, asleep; an unsnuffed candle burned dimly on the table. Miss Temple was not to be seen; I knew afterwards that she had been called to a delirious patient in the fever-room. I advanced; then paused by the crib side: my hand was on the curtain, but I preferred speaking before I withdrew it. I still recoiled at the dread of seeing a corpse.

"Helen!" I whispered softly, "are you awake?"

She stirred herself, put back the curtain, and I saw her face, pale, wasted, but quite composed: she looked so little changed that my fear was instantly dissipated.

"Can it be you, Jane?" she asked in her own gentle voice.

"Oh!" I thought, "she is not going to die: they are mistaken: she could not speak and look so calmly if she were."

I got on to her crib and kissed her: her forehead was cold, and her cheek both cold and thin, and so were her hand and wrist; but she smiled as of old.

"Why are you come here, Jane? It is past eleven o'clock: I heard it strike some minutes since."

"I came to see you, Helen: I heard you were very ill, and I could not sleep till I had spoken to you."

"You came to bid me good-bye, then: you are just in time probably."

"Are you going somewhere, Helen? Are you going home?"

"Yes; to my long home—my last home."

"No, no, Helen!" I stopped distressed. While I tried to devour my tears, a fit of coughing seized Helen; it did not, however, wake the nurse; when it was over, she lay some minutes exhausted; then she whispered:—"Jane, your little feet are bare; lie down and cover yourself with my quilt."

I did so: she put her arm over me, and I nestled close to her. After a long silence, she resumed; still whispering,—

"I am very happy, Jane; and when you hear that I am dead, you must be sure and not grieve: there is nothing to grieve about. We all must die one day, and the illness which is removing me is not painful; it is gentle and gradual: my mind is at rest. I leave no one to regret me much: I have only a father; and he is lately married, and will not miss me. By dying young, I shall escape great sufferings. I had not qualities or talents to make my way very well in the world; I should have been continually at fault."

"But where are you going to, Helen? Can you see? Do you know?"

"I believe: I have faith: I am going to God."

"Where is God? What is God?"

"My Maker and yours, who will never destroy what he created. I rely implicitly on his power, and confide wholly in his goodness: I count the hours till that eventful one arrives which shall restore me to him, reveal him to me."

"You are sure, then, Helen, that there is such a place as heaven; and that our souls can get to it when we die?"

"I am sure there is a future state; I believe God is good; I can resign my im-

mortal part to him without any misgiving. God is my father; God is my friend: I love him; I believe he loves me."

"And shall I see you again, Helen, when I die?"

"You will come to the same region of happiness: be received by the same mighty, universal Parent, no doubt, dear Jane."

Again I questioned; but this time only in thought. "Where is that region? Does it exist?" And I clasped my arms closer round Helen; she seemed dearer to me than ever; I felt as if I could not let her go; I lay with my face hidden on her neck. Presently she said in the sweetest tone,—"How comfortable I am! That last fit of coughing has tired me a little; I feel as if I could sleep: but don't leave me, Jane; I like to have you near me."

"I'll stay with you, *dear* Helen: no one shall take me away."

"Are you warm, darling?"

"Yes."

"Goodnight, Jane."

"Good-night, Helen."

She kissed me, and I her; and we both soon slumbered.

When I awoke it was day: an unusual movement roused me, I looked up; I was in somebody's arms; the nurse held me; she was carrying me through the passage back to the dormitory. I was not reprimanded for leaving my bed; people had something else to think about: no explanation was afforded then to my many questions; but a day or two afterwards I learned that Miss Temple, on returning to her own room at dawn, had found me laid in a little crib; my face against Helen Burns' shoulder, my arms around her neck. I was asleep, and Helen was—dead.

Her grave is in Brocklebridge churchyard: for fifteen years after her death it was only covered by a grassy mound; but now a gray marble tablet marks the spot, inscribed with her name, and the word "Resurgam."[8]

Chapter X

Hitherto I have recorded in detail the events of my insignificant existence: to the first ten years of my life, I have given almost as many chapters. But this is not to be a regular autobiography: I am only bound to invoke memory where I know her responses will possess some degree of interest; therefore I now pass a space of eight years almost in silence: a few lines only are necessary to keep up the links of connection.

When the typhus fever had fulfilled its mission of devastation at Lowood, it gradually disappeared from thence; but not till its virulence and the number of its victims had drawn public attention on the school. Inquiry was made into the origin of the scourge, and by degrees various facts came out which excited public indignation in a high degree. The unhealthy nature of the site; the quantity and quality of the children's food; the brackish, fetid water used in its preparation; the pupils' wretched clothing and accommodation: all these things were discovered; and the discovery produced a result mortifying to Mr. Brocklehurst, but beneficial to the institution.

Several wealthy and benevolent individuals in the county subscribed largely for the erection of a more convenient building in a better situation; new regu-

8. I shall rise again (Latin).

lations were made; improvements in diet and clothing introduced; the funds of the school were entrusted to the management of a committee. Mr. Brocklehurst, who, from his wealth and family connections, could not be over-looked, still retained the post of treasurer; but he was aided in the discharge of his duties by gentlemen of rather more enlarged and sympathizing minds: his office of inspector, too, was shared by those who knew how to combine reason with strictness, comfort with economy, compassion with uprightness. The school, thus improved, became in time a truly useful and noble institution. I remained an inmate of its walls, after its regeneration, for eight years: six as pupil, and two as teacher; and in both capacities I bear my testimony to its value and importance.

During these eight years my life was uniform: but not unhappy, because it was not inactive. I had the means of an excellent education placed within my reach. A fondness for some of my studies, and a desire to excel in all, together with a great delight in pleasing my teachers, especially such as I loved, urged me on: I availed myself fully of the advantages offered me. In time I rose to be the first girl of the first class; then I was invested with the office of teacher; which I discharged with zeal for two years; but at the end of that time I altered.

Miss Temple, through all changes, had thus far continued superintendent of the seminary: to her instruction I owed the best part of my acquirements; her friendship and society had been my continual solace: she had stood me in the stead of mother, governess, and, latterly, companion. At this period she married, removed with her husband (a clergyman, an excellent man, almost worthy of such a wife) to a distant county, and consequently was lost to me.

From the day she left I was no longer the same: with her was gone every set-tled feeling, every association that had made Lowood in some degree a home to me. I had imbibed from her something of her nature and much of her habits: more harmonious thoughts: what seemed better-regulated feelings had become the inmates of my mind. I had given in allegiance to duty and order; I was quiet; I believed I was content: to the eyes of others, usually even to my own, I appeared a disciplined and subdued character.

But destiny, in the shape of the Rev. Mr. Nasmyth, came between me and Miss Temple: I saw her in her traveling dress step into a post-chaise, shortly after the marriage ceremony; I watched the chaise mount the hill and disap-pear beyond its brow; and then retired to my own room, and there spent in solitude the greatest part of the half-holiday granted in honour of the occa-sion.

I walked about the chamber most of the time. I imagined myself only to be regretting my loss, and thinking how to repair it; but when my reflections were concluded, and I looked up and found that the afternoon was gone, and evening far advanced, another discovery dawned on me, namely, that in the interval I had undergone a transforming process; that my mind had put off all it had borrowed of Miss Temple—or rather that she had taken with her the serene atmosphere I had been breathing in her vicinity—and that now I was left in my natural element, and beginning to feel the stirring of old emotions. It did not seem as if a prop were withdrawn, but rather as if a motive were gone; it was not the power to be tranquil which had failed me, but the reason for tranquility was no more. My world had for some years been in Lowood: my experience had been of its rules and systems; now I remembered that the real

world was wide, and that a varied field of hopes and fears, of sensations and excitements, awaited those who had courage to go forth into its expanse, to seek real knowledge of life amid its perils.

I went to my window, opened it, and looked out. There were the two wings of the building; there was the garden; there were the skirts of Lowood; there was the hilly horizon. My eye passed all other objects to rest on those most remote, the blue peaks: it was those I longed to surmount; all within their boundary of rock and heath seemed prison-ground, exile limits. I traced the white road winding round the base of one mountain, and vanishing in a gorge between two: how I longed to follow it further! I recalled the time when I had traveled that very road in a coach; I remembered descending that hill at twilight: an age seemed to have elapsed since the day which brought me first to Lowood, and I had never quitted it since. My vacations had all been spent at school: Mrs. Reed had never sent for me to Gateshead; neither she nor any of her family had ever been to visit me. I had had no communication by letter or message with the outer world: school-rules, school-duties, school-habits and notions, and voices, and faces, and phrases, and costumes, and preferences, and antipathies: such was what I knew of existence. And now I felt that it was not enough: I tired of the routine of eight years in one afternoon. I desired liberty; for liberty I gasped; for liberty I uttered a prayer; it seemed scattered on the wind then faintly blowing. I abandoned it and framed a humbler supplication; for change, stimulus: that petition, too, seemed swept off into vague space: "Then," I cried, half desperate, "grant me at least a new servitude!"

Here a bell, ringing the hour of supper, called me downstairs.

I was not free to resume the interrupted chain of my reflections till bedtime: even then a teacher who occupied the same room with me kept me from the subject to which I longed to recur, by a prolonged effusion of small talk. How I wished sleep would silence her! It seemed as if, could I but go back to the idea which had last entered my mind as I stood at the window, some inventive suggestion would rise for my relief.

Miss Gryce snored at last; she was a heavy Welshwoman, and till now her habitual nasal strains had never been regarded by me in any other light than as a nuisance; tonight I hailed the first deep notes with satisfaction; I was debarrassed[9] of interruption; my half-effaced thought instantly revived.

"A new servitude! There is something in that," I soliloquized (mentally, be it understood; I did not talk aloud). "I know there is, because it does not sound too sweet; it is not like such words as Liberty, Excitement, Enjoyment: delightful sounds truly; but no more than sounds for me; and so hollow and fleeting that it is mere waste of time to listen to them. But Servitude! That must be matter of fact. Any one may serve: I have served here eight years; now all I want is to serve elsewhere. Can I not get so much of my own will? Is not the thing feasible? Yes—yes—the end is not so difficult; if I had only a brain active enough to ferret out the means of attaining it."

I sat up in bed by way of arousing this said brain: it was a chilly night; I covered my shoulders with a shawl, and then I proceeded to *think* again with all my might.

"What do I want? A new place, in a new house, amongst new faces, under new circumstances: I want this because it is of no use wanting anything better.

9. Jane transliterates the French *debarassée*, literally, "freed of."

How do people do to get a new place? They apply to friends, I suppose: I have no friends. There are many others who have no friends, who must look about for themselves and be their own helpers; and what is their resource?"

I could not tell: nothing answered me; I then ordered my brain to find a response, and quickly. It worked and worked faster: I felt the pulses throb in my head and temples; but for nearly an hour it worked in chaos, and no result came of its efforts. Feverish with vain labor, I got up and took a turn in the room; undrew the curtain, noted a star or two, shivered with cold, and again crept to bed.

A kind fairy, in my absence, had surely dropped the required suggestion on my pillow; for as I lay down it came quietly and naturally to my mind:—"Those who want situations advertise; you must advertise in the——*shire Herald.*"

"How? I know nothing about advertising."

Replies rose smooth and prompt now:—"You must inclose the advertisement and the money to pay for it under a cover directed to the Editor of the *Herald*; you must put it, the first opportunity you have, into the post at Lowton; answers must be addressed to J. E. at the post-office there: you can go and inquire in about a week after you send your letter, if any are come, and act accordingly."

This scheme I went over twice, thrice; it was then digested in my mind: I had it in a clear practical form; I felt satisfied, and fell asleep.

With earliest day I was up: I had my advertisement written, inclosed, and directed before the bell rang to rouse the school: it ran thus:—

"A young lady accustomed to tuition" (had I not been a teacher two years?) "is desirous of meeting with a situation in a private family where the children are under fourteen" (I thought that as I was barely eighteen, it would not do to undertake the guidance of pupils nearer my own age). "She is qualified to teach the usual branches of a good English education, together with French, Drawing, and Music" (in those days, reader, this now narrow catalog of accomplishments would have been held tolerably comprehensive). "Address, J. E., Post-office, Lowton, ——shire."

This document remained locked in my drawer all day: after tea, I asked leave of the new superintendent to go to Lowton, in order to perform some small commissions for myself and one or two of my fellow-teachers; permission was readily granted: I went. It was a walk of two miles, and the evening was wet, but the days were still long; I visited a shop or two, slipped the letter into the post-office, and came back through heavy rain, with streaming garments, but with a relieved heart.

The succeeding week seemed long: it came to an end at last, however, like all sublunary things, and once more, towards the close of a pleasant autumn day, I found myself afoot on the road to Lowton. A picturesque track it was, by the way, lying along the side of the beck and through the sweetest curves of the dale: but that day I thought more of the letters, that might or might not be awaiting me at the little burgh whither I was bound, than of the charms of lea and water.

My ostensible errand on this occasion was to get measured for a pair of shoes; so I discharged that business first, and when it was done, I stepped across the clean and quiet little street from the shoemaker's to the post-office; it was kept by an old dame, who wore horn spectacles on her nose and black mittens on her hands.

"Are there any letters for J. E.?" I asked.

She peered at me over her spectacles, and then she opened a drawer, and fumbled among its contents for a long time—so long that my hopes began to falter. At last, having held a document before her glasses for nearly five minutes, she presented it across the counter, accompanying the act by another inquisitive and mistrustful glance—it was for J. E.

"Is there only one?" I demanded

"There are no more," said she; and I put it in my pocket and turned my face homeward: I could not open it then; rules obliged me to be back by eight, and it was already half-past seven.

Various duties awaited me on my arrival: I had to sit with the girls during their hour of study; then it was my turn to read prayers; to see them to bed: afterwards I supped with the other teachers. Even when we finally retired for the night, the inevitable Miss Gryce was still my companion: we had only a short end of candle in our candlestick, and I dreaded lest she should talk till it was all burnt out: fortunately, however, the heavy supper she had eaten produced a soporific effect: she was already snoring before I had finished undressing. There still remained an inch of candle: I now took out my letter; the seal was an initial F.; I broke it: the contents were brief

"If J. E., who advertised in the——shire *Herald* of last Thursday, possesses the acquirements mentioned, and if she is in a position to give satisfactory references as to character and competency; a situation can be offered her where there is but one pupil—a little girl, under ten years of age—and where the salary is thirty pounds per annum. J. E. is requested to send references, name, address, and all particulars to the direction, 'Mrs. Fairfax, Thornfield, near Millcote,——shire.' "

I examined the document long: the writing was old-fashioned and rather uncertain, like that of an elderly lady. This circumstance was satisfactory: a private fear had haunted me that, in thus acting for myself, and by my own guidance, I ran the risk of getting into some scrape and, above all things, I wished the result of my endeavors to be respectable, proper, *en règle*.[1] I now felt that an elderly lady was no bad ingredient in the business I had on hand. Mrs. Fairfax! I saw her in a black gown and widow's cap,—frigid, perhaps, but not uncivil: a model of elderly English respectability. Thornfield! that, doubtless, was the name of her house—a neat, orderly spot, I was sure, though I failed in my efforts to conceive a correct plan of the premises. Millcote, ——shire. I brushed up my recollections of the map of England; yes, I saw it, both the shire and the town. ——shire was seventy miles nearer London than the remote county where I now resided; that was a recommendation to me. I longed to go where there was life and movement. Millcote was a large manufacturing town on the banks of the A——: a busy place, enough, doubtless: so much the better; it would be a complete change at least Not that my fancy was much captivated by the idea of long chimneys and clouds of smoke—"but," I argued, "Thornfield will, probably, be a good way from the town."

Here the socket of the candle dropped, and the wick went out.

Next day new steps were to be taken; my plans could no longer be confined to my own breast: I must impart them in order to achieve their success. Having sought and obtained an audience of the superintendent during the noontide recreation, I told her I had a prospect of getting a new situation

1. By the rule. (French).

where the salary would be double what I now receive (for at Lowood I only got fifteen pounds per annum), and requested she would break the matter for me to Mr. Brocklehurst, or some of the committee, and ascertain whether they would permit me to mention them as references. She obligingly consented to act as mediatrix in the matter. The next day she laid the affair before Mr. Brocklehurst, who said that Mrs. Reed must be written to, as she was my natural guardian. A note was accordingly addressed to that lady, who returned for answer, that "I might do as I pleased: she had long relinquished all interference in my affairs." This note went the round of the committee, and, at last, after what appeared to me most tedious delay, formal leave was given me to better my condition if I could; and an assurance added that, as I had always conducted myself well, both as teacher and pupil, at Lowood, a testimonial of character and capacity, signed by the inspectors of that institution, should forthwith be furnished me.

This testimonial I accordingly received in about a month, forwarded a copy of it to Mrs. Fairfax, and got that lady's reply, stating that she was satisfied, and fixing that day fortnight as the period for my assuming the post of governess in her house.

I now busied myself in preparations: the fortnight passed rapidly. I had not a very large wardrobe, though it was adequate to my wants; and the last day sufficed to pack my trunk,—the same I had brought with me eight years ago from Gateshead.

The box was corded, the card nailed on. In half an hour the carrier was to call for it to take it to Lowton, whither I myself was to repair at an early hour the next morning to meet the coach. I had brushed my black stuff traveling dress, prepared my bonnet, gloves, and muff; sought in all my drawers to see that no article was left behind; and now, having nothing more to do, I sat down and tried to rest. I could not, though I had been on foot all day—I could not now repose an instant—I was too much excited. A phase of my life was closing tonight, a new one opening tomorrow: impossible to slumber in the interval; I must watch feverishly while the change was being accomplished.

"Miss," said a servant who met me in the lobby, where I was wandering like a troubled spirit, "a person below wishes to see you."

"The carrier, no doubt," I thought, and ran downstairs without inquiry. I was passing the back parlour, or teachers' sitting-room, the door of which was half-open, to go to the kitchen, when someone ran out.

"It's her, I am sure!—I could have told her anywhere!" cried the individual who stopped my progress and took my hand.

I looked. I saw a woman attired like a well-dressed servant, matronly, yet still young; very good-looking, with black hair and eyes, and lively complexion.

"Well, who is it?" she asked, in a voice and with a smile I half recognized! "You've not quite forgotten me, I think, Miss Jane?"

In another second I was embracing and kissing her rapturously. "Bessie! Bessie! Bessie!" that was all I said; whereat she half laughed, half cried, and we both went into the parlor. By the fire stood a little fellow of three years old, in plaid frock and trousers.

"That is my little boy," said Bessie, directly.

"Then you are married, Bessie?"

"Yes: nearly five years since, to Robert Leaven, the coachman, and I've a little girl besides Bobby there that I've christened Jane."

"And you don't live at Gateshead?"

"I live at the lodge: the old porter has left."

"Well, and how do they all get on? Tell me everything about them, Bessie: but sit down first; and, Bobby, come and sit on my knee, will you?" But Bobby preferred sidling over to his mother.

"You're not grown so very tall, Miss Jane, nor so very stout," continued Mrs. Leaven. "I dare say they've not kept you too well at school: Miss Reed is the head and shoulders taller than you are; and Miss Georgiana would make two of you in breadth."

"Georgiana is handsome, I suppose, Bessie?"

"Very. She went up to London last winter with her mamma, and there everybody admired her, and a young lord fell in love with her: but his relations were against the match; and—what do you think?—he and Miss Georgiana made it up to run away: but they were found out and stopped. It was Miss Reed that found them out: I believe she was envious; and now she and her sister lead a cat and dog life together; they are always quarrelling."

"Well, and what of John Reed?"

"Oh, he is not doing so well as his mamma could wish. He went to college, and he got—plucked,[2] I think they call it: and then his uncles wanted him to be a barrister, and study the law: but he is such a dissipated young man, they will never make much of him, I think."

"What does he look like?"

"He is very tall: some people call him a fine-looking young man; but he has such thick lips."

"And Mrs. Reed?"

"Missis looks stout and well enough in the face, but I think she's not quite easy in her mind: Mr. John's conduct does not please her—he spends a deal of money."

"Did she send you here, Bessie?"

"No, indeed: but I have long wanted to see you, and when I heard that there had been a letter from you, and that you were going to another part of the country, I thought I'd just set off, and get a look at you before you were quite out of my reach."

"I am afraid you are disappointed in me, Bessie." I said this laughing: I perceived that Bessie's glance, though it expressed regard, did in no shape denote admiration.

"No, Miss Jane, not exactly: you are genteel enough; you look like a lady, and it is as much as ever I expected of you: you were no beauty as a child."

I smiled at Bessie's frank answer: I felt that it was correct, but I confess I was not quite indifferent to its import: at eighteen most people wish to please, and the conviction that they have not an exterior likely to second that desire brings anything but gratification.

"I dare say you are clever, though." continued Bessie, by way of solace. "What can you do? Can you play on the piano?"

"A little."

There was one in the room; Bessie went and opened it, and then asked me to sit down and give her a tune: I played a waltz or two, and she was charmed.

2. Expelled for failing examinations.

"The Miss Reeds could not play as well!" said she exultingly. "I always said you would surpass them in learning: and can you draw?"

"That is one of my paintings over the chimney-piece." It was a landscape in watercolors, of which I had made a present to the superintendent, in acknowledgment of her obliging mediation with the committee on my behalf, and which she had framed and glazed.

"Well, that is beautiful, Miss Jane! It is as fine a picture as any Miss Reed's drawing-master could paint, let alone the young ladies themselves, who could not come near it: and have you learnt French?"

"Yes, Bessie, I can both read it and speak it."

"And you can work on muslin and canvas?"

"I can."

"Oh, you are quite a lady, Miss Jane! I knew you would be: you will get on whether your relations notice you or not. There was something I wanted to ask you. Have you ever heard anything from your father's kinsfolk, the Eyres?"

"Never in my life."

"Well, you know Missis always said they were poor and quite despicable: and they may be poor; but I believe they are as much gentry as the Reeds are; for one day, nearly seven years ago, a Mr. Eyre came to Gateshead and wanted to see you. Missis said you were at school fifty miles off. He seemed so much disappointed, for he could not stay: he was going on a voyage to a foreign country, and the ship was to sail from London in a day or two. He looked quite a gentleman, and I believe he was your father's brother."

"What foreign country was he going to, Bessie?"

"An island thousands of miles off, where they make wine—the butler did tell me"—

"Madeira?" I suggested.

"Yes, that is it—that is the very word."

"So he went?"

"Yes; he did not stay many minutes in the house: Missis was very high with him; she called him afterwards a 'sneaking tradesman.' My Robert believes he was a wine-merchant."

"Very likely," I returned; "or perhaps clerk or agent to a wine-merchant."

Bessie and I conversed about old times an hour longer, and then she was obliged to leave me. I saw her again for a few minutes the next morning at Lowton, while I was waiting for the coach. We parted finally at the door of the "Brocklehurst Arms" there. Each went our separate way: she set off for the brow of Lowood Fell to meet the conveyance which was to take her back to Gateshead; I mounted the vehicle which was to bear me to new duties and a new life in the unknown environs of Millcote.

Chapter XI

A new chapter in a novel is something like a new scene in a play: and when I draw up the curtain this time, reader, you must fancy you see a room in the "George Inn" at Millcote, with such large figured papering on the walls as inn rooms have; such a carpet, such furniture, such ornaments on the mantelpiece, such prints; including a portrait of George the Third, and another of the Prince of Wales, and a representation of the death of Wolfe. All this is visible to you by the light of an oil lamp hanging from the ceiling, and by that of an excellent fire, near which I sit in my cloak and bonnet; my muff and umbrella

lie on the table, and I am warming away the numbness and chill contracted by
sixteen hours' exposure to the rawness of an October day: I left Lowton at four
o'clock A.M., and the Millcote town clock is now just striking eight.

Reader, though I look comfortably accommodated, I am not very tranquil
in my mind. I thought when the coach stopped here there would be someone
to meet me; I looked anxiously round as I descended the wooden steps the
"boots" placed for my convenience, expecting to hear my name pronounced,
and to see some description of carriage waiting to convey me to Thornfield.
Nothing of the sort was visible; and when I asked a waiter if any one had been
to inquire after a Miss Eyre, I was answered in the negative: so I had no re-
source but to request to be shown into a private room: and here I am waiting,
while all sorts of doubts and fears are troubling my thoughts.

It is a very strange sensation to inexperienced youth to feel itself quite alone
in the world, cut adrift from every connection, uncertain whether the port to
which it is bound can be reached, and prevented by many impediments from
returning to that it has quitted. The charm of adventure sweetens that sensa-
tion, the glow of pride warms it; but then the throb of fear disturbs it; and fear
with me became predominant, when half an hour elapsed and still I was alone.
I bethought myself to ring the bell.

"Is there a place in this neighborhood called Thornfield?" I asked of the
waiter who answered the summons.

"Thornfield? I don't know, ma'am; I'll inquire at the bar." He vanished, but
reappeared instantly:—"Is your name Eyre, Miss?"

"Yes."

"Person here waiting for you."

I jumped up, took my muff and umbrella, and hastened into the inn-pas-
sage: a man was standing by the open door, and in the lamp-lit street I dimly
saw a one-horse conveyance.

"This will be your luggage, I suppose?" said the man rather abruptly when
he saw me, pointing to my trunk in the passage.

"Yes." He hoisted it on to the vehicle, which was a sort of car, and then I got
in: before he shut me up I asked him how far it was to Thornfield.

"A matter of six miles."

"How long shall we be before we get there?"

"Happen an hour and a half."

He fastened the car door, climbed to his own seat outside, and we set off.
Our progress was leisurely, and gave me ample time to reflect; I was content to
be at length so near the end of my journey; and as I leaned back in the com-
fortable though not elegant conveyance, I meditated much at my ease.

"I suppose," thought I, "judging from the plainness of the servant and car-
riage, Mrs. Fairfax is not a very dashing person: so much the better; I never
lived among fine people but once, and I was very miserable with them. I won-
der if she lives alone except this little girl; if so, and if she is in any degree ami-
able, I shall surely be able to get on with her! I will do my best: it is a pity that
doing one's best does not always answer. At Lowood, indeed, I took that reso-
lution, kept it, and succeeded in pleasing; but with Mrs. Reed, I remember, my
best was always spurned with scorn. I pray God Mrs. Fairfax may not turn out
a second Mrs. Reed; but if she does, I am not bound to stay with her: let the
worst come to the worst, I can advertise again. How far are we on our road now,
I wonder?"

I let down the window and looked out: Millcote was behind us; judging by

the number of its lights, it seemed a place of considerable magnitude, much larger than Lowton. We were now, as far as I could see, on a sort of common; but there were houses scattered all over the district; I felt we were in a different region to Lowood, more populous, less picturesque; more stirring, less romantic.

The roads were heavy, the night misty; my conductor let his horse walk all the way, and the hour and a half extended, I verily believe, to two hours; at last he turned in his seat and said: "You're noan so far fro' Thornfield now."

Again I looked out: we were passing a church: I saw its low broad tower against the sky, and its bell was tolling a quarter; I saw a narrow galaxy of lights too, on a hillside, marking a village or hamlet. About ten minutes after the driver got down and opened a pair of gates; we passed through, and they clashed to behind us. We now slowly ascended a drive, and came upon the long front of a house: candle-light gleamed from one curtained bow-window; all the rest were dark. The car stopped at the front door; it was opened by a maidservant; I alighted and went in.

"Will you walk this way, ma'am," said the girl; and I followed her across a square hall with high doors all round: she ushered me into a room whose double illumination of fire and candle at first dazzled me, contrasting as it did with the darkness to which my eyes had been for two hours inured; when I could see, however, a cozy and agreeable picture presented itself to my view.

A snug, small room; a round table by a cheerful fire; an arm-chair high-backed and old-fashioned, wherein sat the neatest imaginable little elderly lady, in widow's cap, black silk gown, and snowy muslin apron: exactly like what I had fancied Mrs. Fairfax, only less stately and milder-looking. She was occupied in knitting; a large cat sat demurely at her feet; nothing in short was wanting to complete the beau ideal[3] of domestic comfort. A more reassuring introduction for a new governess could scarcely be conceived: there was no grandeur to overwhelm, no stateliness to embarrass; and then, as I entered, the old lady got up, and promptly and kindly came forward to meet me.

"How do you do, my dear? I am afraid you have had a tedious ride; John drives so slowly: you must be cold; come to the fire."

"Mrs. Fairfax, I suppose?" said I.

"Yes, you are right: do sit down."

She conducted me to her own chair, and then began to remove my shawl and untie my bonnet-strings. I begged she would not give herself so much trouble.

"Oh, it is no trouble; I dare say your own hands are almost numbed with cold. Leah, make a little hot negus[4] and cut a sandwich or two: here are the keys of the storeroom."

And she produced from her pocket a most housewifely bunch of keys, and delivered them to the servant.

"Now, then, draw nearer to the fire," she continued. "You've brought your luggage with you, haven't you, my dear?"

"Yes, ma'am."

"I'll see it carried into your room," she said, and bustled out.

"She treats me like a visitor," thought I. "I little expected such a reception;

3. The perfect type or model (French). 4. A wine punch.

I anticipated only coldness and stiffness: this is not like what I have heard of the treatment of governesses but I must not exult too soon."

She returned, with her own hands cleared her knitting apparatus and a book or two from the table, to make room for the tray which Leah now brought, and then herself handed me the refreshments. I felt rather confused at being the object of more attention than I had ever before received, and that too, shown by my employer and superior; but as she did not herself seem to consider she was doing anything out of her place, I thought it better to take her civilities quietly.

"Shall I have the pleasure of seeing Miss Fairfax tonight?" I asked, when I had partaken of what she offered me.

"What did you say, my dear? I am a little deaf," returned the good lady, approaching her ear to my mouth.

I repeated the question more distinctly.

"Miss Fairfax? Oh, you mean Miss Varens! Varens is the name of your future pupil."

"Indeed! Then she is not your daughter?"

"No,—I have no family."

I should have followed up my first inquiry by asking in what way Miss Varens was connected with her; but I recollected it was not polite to ask too many questions: besides, I was sure to hear in time.

"I am so glad," she continued, as she sat down opposite to me, and took the cat on her knee; "I am so glad you are come; it will be quite pleasant living here now with a companion. To be sure it is pleasant at any time; for Thornfield is a fine old hall, rather neglected of late years perhaps, but still it is a respectable place; yet you know in winter time one feels dreary quite alone, in the best quarters. I say alone—Leah is a nice girl to be sure, and John and his wife are very decent people; but then you see they are only servants, and one can't converse with them on terms of equality: one must keep them at due distance, for fear of losing one's authority. I'm sure last winter (it was a very severe one, if you recollect, and when it did not snow, it rained and blew) not a creature but the butcher and postman came to the house from November til February; and I really got quite melancholy with sitting night after night alone. I had Leah in to read to me sometimes; but I don't think the poor girl liked the task much: she felt it confining. In spring and summer one got on better: sunshine and long days make such a difference; and then, just at the commencement of this autumn, little Adela Varens came and her nurse: a child makes a house alive all at once; and now you are here I shall be quite gay."

My heart really warmed to the worthy lady as I heard her talk: and I drew my chair a little nearer to her, and expressed my sincere wish that she might find my company as agreeable as she anticipated.

"But I'll not keep you sitting up late tonight," said she; "it is on the stroke of twelve now, and you have been traveling all day: you must feel tired. If you have got your feet well warmed I'll show you your bedroom. I've had the room next to mine prepared for you; it is only a small apartment, but I thought you would like it better than one of the large front chambers: to be sure they have finer furniture, but they are so dreary and solitary, I never sleep in them myself."

I thanked her for her considerate choice, and as I really felt fatigued with my long journey, expressed my readiness to retire. She took her candle, and I fol-

lowed her from the room. First she went to see if the hall-door was fastened; having taken the key from the lock, she led the way upstairs. The steps and banisters were of oak; the staircase window was high and latticed; both it and the long gallery into which the bedroom doors opened looked as if they belonged to a church rather than a house. A very chill and vaultlike air pervaded the stairs and gallery, suggesting cheerless ideas of space and solitude; and I was glad when finally ushered into my chamber to find it of small dimensions, and furnished in ordinary modern style.

When Mrs. Fairfax had bidden me a kind good-night, and I had fastened my door, gazed leisurely round, and in some measure effaced the eerie impression made by that wide hall, that dark and spacious staircase, and that long, cold gallery, by the livelier aspect of my little room, I remembered that after a day of bodily fatigue and mental anxiety I was now at last in safe haven. The impulse of gratitude swelled my heart, and I knelt down at the bedside, and offered up thanks where thanks were due; not forgetting, ere I rose, to implore aid on my further path, and the power of meriting the kindness which seemed so frankly offered me before it was earned. My couch had no thorns in it that night; my solitary room no fears. At once weary and content, I slept soon and soundly: when I awoke it was broad day.

The chamber looked such a bright little place to me as the sun shone in between the gay blue chintz window curtains, showing papered walls and a carpeted floor, so unlike the bare planks and stained plaster of Lowood that my spirits rose at the view. Externals have a great effect on the young: I thought that a fairer era of life was beginning for me, one that was to have its flowers and pleasures, as well as its thorns and toils. My faculties, roused by the change of scene, the new field offered to hope, seemed all astir. I cannot precisely define what they expected, but it was something pleasant: not perhaps that day or that month, but at an indefinite future period.

I rose; I dressed myself with care: obliged to be plain—for I had no article of attire that was not made with extreme simplicity—I was still by nature solicitous to be neat. It was not my habit to be disregardful of appearance, or careless of the impression I made: on the contrary, I ever wished to look as well as I could, and to please as much as my want of beauty would permit. I sometimes regretted that I was not handsomer: I sometimes wished to have rosy cheeks, a straight nose, and small cherry mouth; I desired to be tall, stately, and finely developed in figure; I felt it a misfortune that I was so little, so pale, and had features so irregular and so marked. And why had I these aspirations and these regrets? It would be difficult to say: I could not then distinctly say it to myself; yet I had a reason, and a logical, natural reason too. However, when I had brushed my hair very smooth, and put on my black frock—which, Quaker-like as it was, at least had the merit of fitting to a nicety—and adjusted my clean white tucker, I thought I should do respectably enough to appear before Mrs. Fairfax; and that my new pupil would not at least recoil from me with antipathy. Having opened my chamber window, and seen that I left all things straight and neat on the toilet table, I ventured forth.

Traversing the long and matted gallery, I descended the slippery steps of oak; then I gained the hall: I halted there a minute: I looked at some pictures on the walls (one I remember represented a grim man in a cuirass, and one a lady with powdered hair and a pearl necklace), at a bronze lamp pendent from the ceiling, at a great clock whose case was of oak curiously carved, and ebon

black with time and rubbing. Everything appeared very stately and imposing to me: but then I was so little accustomed to grandeur. The hall-door, which was half of glass, stood open; I stepped over the threshold. It was a fine autumn morning; the early sun shone serenely on embrowned groves and still green fields: advancing on to the lawn, I looked up and surveyed the front of the mansion. It was three stories high, of proportions not vast, though considerable: a gentleman's manor-house, not a nobleman's seat: battlements round the top gave it a picturesque look. Its gray front stood out well from the background of a rookery, whose cawing tenants were now on the wing: they flew over the lawn and grounds to alight in a great meadow, from which these were separated by a sunk fence, and where an array of mighty old thorn trees, strong, knotty, and broad as oaks, at once explained the etymology of the mansion's designation. Farther off were hills: not so lofty as those round Lowood, nor so craggy, nor so like barriers of separation from the living world; but yet quiet and lonely hills enough, and seeming to embrace Thornfield with a seclusion I had not expected to find existent so near the stirring locality of Millcote. A little hamlet whose roofs were blent with trees straggled up the side of one of these hills; the church of the district stood nearer Thornfield: its old tower-top looked over a knoll between the house and gates.

I was yet enjoying the calm prospect and pleasant fresh air, yet listening with delight to the cawing of the rooks, yet surveying the wide, hoary front of the hall, and thinking what a great place it was for one lonely little dame like Mrs. Fairfax to inhabit, when that lady appeared at the door.

"What! out already?" said she. "I see you are an early riser." I went up to her, and was received with an affable kiss and shake of the hand.

"How do you like Thornfield?" she asked. I told her I liked it very much.

"Yes," she said, "it is a pretty place: but I fear it will be getting out of order, unless Mr. Rochester should take it into his head to come and reside here permanently; or, at least, visit it rather oftener: great houses and fine grounds require the presence of the proprietor."

"Mr. Rochester!" I exclaimed. "Who is he?"

"The owner of Thornfield," she responded quietly. "Did you not know he was called Rochester?"

Of course I did not—I had never heard of him before; but the old lady seemed to regard his existence as a universally understood fact, with which everybody must be acquainted by instinct.

"I thought," I continued, "Thornfield belonged to you."

"To me? Bless you, child; what an idea! To me? I am only the housekeeper— the manager. To be sure I am distantly related to the Rochesters by the mother's side; or, at least, my husband was: he was a clergyman, incumbent of Hay—that little village yonder on the hill—and that church near the gates was his. The present Mr. Rochester's mother was a Fairfax, and second cousin to my husband; but I never presume on the connection—in fact it is nothing to me; I consider myself quite in the light of an ordinary house-keeper: my employer is always civil, and I expect nothing more."

"And the little girl—my pupil?"

"She is Mr. Rochester's ward; he commissioned me to find a governess for her. He intends to have her brought up in ——shire, I believe. Here she comes with her 'bonne,' as she calls her nurse." The enigma then was explained: this affable and kind little widow was no great dame, but a dependent like myself.

I did not like her the worse for that; on the contrary, I felt better pleased than ever. The equality between her and me was real; not the mere result of condescension on her part: so much the better—my position was all the freer.

As I was meditating on this discovery, a little girl, followed by her attendant, came running up the lawn. I looked at my pupil, who did not at first appear to notice me: she was quite a child, perhaps seven or eight years old, slightly built, with a pale, small-featured face, and a redundancy of hair falling in curls to her waist.

"Good-morning, Miss Adela," said Mrs. Fairfax. "Come and speak to the lady who is to teach you, and to make you a clever woman some day." She approached.

"C'est là ma gouvernante?" said she, pointing to me, and addressing her nurse; who answered: "Mais oui, certainement."[5]

"Are they foreigners?" I inquired, amazed at hearing the French language.

"The nurse is a foreigner, and Adela was born on the Continent, and, I believe, never left it till within six months ago. When she first came here she could speak no English; now she can make shift to talk it a little: I don't understand her, she mixes it so with French; but you will make out her meaning very well, I daresay."

Fortunately I had had the advantage of being taught French by a French lady; and as I had always made a point of conversing with Madame Pierrot as often as I could, and had, besides, during the last seven years, learnt a portion of French by heart daily—applying myself to take pains with my accent, and imitating as closely as possible the pronunciation of my teacher—I had acquired a certain degree of readiness and correctness in the language, and was not likely to be much at a loss with Mademoiselle Adela. She came and shook hands with me when she heard that I was her governess; and as I led her into breakfast I addressed some phrases to her in her own tongue: she replied briefly at first, but after we were seated at the table, and she had examined me some ten minutes with her large hazel eyes, she suddenly commenced chattering fluently.

"Ah!" cried she, in French, "you speak my language as well as Mr. Rochester does: I can talk to you as I can to him, and so can Sophie. She will be glad: nobody here understands her: Madame Fairfax is all English. Sophie is my nurse; she came with me over the sea in a great ship with a chimney that smoked—how it did smoke!—and I was sick, and so was Sophie, and so was Mr. Rochester. Mr. Rochester lay down on a sofa in a pretty room called the salon, and Sophie and I had little beds in another place. I nearly fell out of mine; it was like a shelf. And Mademoiselle—what is your name?"

"Eyre—Jane Eyre."

"Aire?[6] Bah! I cannot say it. Well: our ship stopped in the morning, before it was quite daylight, at a great city—a huge city, with very dark houses and all smoky; not at all like the pretty clean town I came from; and Mr. Rochester carried me in his arms over a plank to the land, and Sophie came after, and we all got into a coach, which took us to a beautiful large house, larger than this and finer, called an hotel. We stayed there nearly a week. I and Sophie used to walk every day in a great green place full of trees, called the Park; and there

were many children there besides me, and a pond with beautiful birds in it, that I fed with crumbs."

"Can you understand her when she runs on so fast?" asked Mrs. Fairfax.

I understood her very well, for I had been accustomed to the fluent tongue of Madame Pierrot.

"I wish," continued the good lady, "you would ask her a question or two about her parents: I wonder if she remembers them?"

"Adèle," I inquired, "with whom did you live when you were in that pretty clean town you spoke of?"

"I lived long ago with mamma; but she is gone to the Holy Virgin. Mamma used to teach me to dance and sing, and to say verses. A great many gentlemen and ladies came to see mamma, and I used to dance before them, or to sit on their knees and sing to them: I liked it. Shall I let you hear me sing now?"

She had finished her breakfast, so I permitted her to give a specimen of her accomplishments. Descending from her chair, she came and placed herself on my knee; then, folding her little hands demurely before her, shaking back her curls and lifting her eyes to the ceiling, she commenced singing a song from some opera. It was the strain of a forsaken lady, who, after bewailing the perfidy of her lover, calls pride to her aid; desires her attendant to deck her in her brightest jewels and richest robes, and resolves to meet the false one that night at a ball, and prove to him, by the gaiety of her demeanor, how little his desertion has affected her.

The subject seemed strangely chosen for an infant singer; but I suppose the point of the exhibition lay in hearing the notes of love and jealousy warbled with the lisp of childhood; and in very bad taste that point was: at least I thought so.

Adèle sang the canzonette tunefully enough, and with the naïveté of her age. This achieved, she jumped from my knee and said, "Now, Mademoiselle, I will repeat you some poetry."

Assuming an attitude, she began "La Ligue des Rats: fable de la Fontaine."[7] She then declaimed the little piece with an attention to punctuation and emphasis, a flexibility of voice and an appropriateness of gesture, very unusual indeed at her age, and which proved she had been carefully trained.

"Was it your mamma who taught you that piece?" I asked.

"Yes; and she just used to say it in this way: 'Qu'avez vous donc? lui dit un de ces rats; parlez!'[8] She made me lift my hand—so—to remind me to raise my voice at the question. Now shall I dance for you?"

"No, that will do: but after your mamma went to the Holy Virgin, as you say, with whom did you live then?"

"With Madame Frédéric and her husband: she took care of me, but she is nothing related to me. I think she is poor, for she had not so fine a house as mamma. I was not long there. Mr. Rochester asked me if I would like to go and live with him in England, and I said yes; for I knew Mr. Rochester before I knew Madame Frédéric, and he was always kind to me and gave me pretty dresses and toys. But you see he has not kept his word, for he has brought me to England, and now he is gone back again himself, and I never see him."

7. *The League of Rats*, a fable by La Fontaine. In this fable a mouse is eaten by a cat when the rescue attempts of other rodents fail. "Canzonette": short song.

8. What's the matter? says one of the rats to her; speak! (French).

After breakfast Adèle and I withdrew to the library; which room, it appears, Mr. Rochester had directed should be used as the schoolroom. Most of the books were locked up behind glass doors; but there was one bookcase left open, containing everything that could be needed in the way of elementary works, and several volumes of light literature, poetry, biography, travels, a few romances, etc. I suppose he had considered that these were all the governess would require for her private perusal; and, indeed, they contented me amply for the present; compared with the scanty pickings I had now and then been able to glean at Lowood, they seemed to offer an abundant harvest of entertainment and information. In this room, too, there was a cabinet piano,[9] quite new and of superior tone; also an easel for painting, and a pair of globes.

I found my pupil sufficiently docile, though disinclined to apply: she had not been used to regular occupation of any kind. I felt it would be injudicious to confine her too much at first; so, when I had talked to her a great deal, and got her to learn a little, and when the morning had advanced to noon, I allowed her to return to her nurse. I then proposed to occupy myself till dinner-time in drawing some little sketches for her use.

As I was going upstairs to fetch my portfolio and pencils, Mrs. Fairfax called to me: "Your morning school-hours are over now, I suppose," said she. She was in a room the folding-doors of which stood open: I went in when she addressed me. It was a large, stately apartment, with purple chairs and curtains, a Turkey carpet, walnut-paneled walls, one vast window rich in stained glass, and a lofty ceiling, nobly molded. Mrs. Fairfax was dusting some vases of fine purple spar, which stood on a sideboard.

"What a beautiful room!" I exclaimed, as I looked round; for I had never before seen any half so imposing.

"Yes; this is the dining-room. I have just opened the window, to let in a little air and sunshine; for everything gets so damp in apartments that are seldom inhabited: the drawing-room yonder feels like a vault."

She pointed to a wide arch corresponding to the window, and hung like it with a Tyrian-dyed[1] curtain, now looped up. Mounting to it by two broad steps and looking through, I thought I caught a glimpse of a fairy place, so bright to my novice eyes appeared the view beyond. Yet it was merely a very pretty drawing-room, and within it a boudoir, both spread with white carpets, on which seemed laid brilliant garlands of flowers; both ceiled with snowy moldings of white grapes and vine-leaves, beneath which glowed in rich contrast crimson couches and ottomans; while the ornaments on the pale Parian mantelpiece were of sparkling Bohemian glass, ruby red; and between the windows large mirrors repeated the general blending of snow and fire.

"In what order you keep these rooms, Mrs. Fairfax!" said I. "No dust, no canvas coverings: except that the air feels chilly, one would think they were inhabited daily."

"Why, Miss Eyre, though Mr. Rochester's visits here are rare, they are always sudden and unexpected; and as I observed that it put him out to find everything swathed up, and to have a bustle of arrangement on his arrival, I thought it best to keep the rooms in readiness."

"Is Mr. Rochester an exacting, fastidious sort of man?"

9. Small upright piano. 1. Purple or crimson.

"Not particularly so; but he has a gentleman's tastes and habits, and he expects to have things managed in conformity to them."

"Do you like him? Is he generally liked?"

"Oh, yes; the family have always been respected here. Almost all the land in this neighborhood, as far as you can see, has belonged to the Rochesters time out of mind."

"Well, but, leaving his land out of the question, do you like him? Is he liked for himself?"

"I have no cause to do otherwise than like him; and I believe he is considered a just and liberal landlord by his tenants: but he has never lived much amongst them."

"But has he no peculiarities? What, in short, is his character?"

"Oh! his character is unimpeachable, I suppose. He is rather peculiar, perhaps: he has traveled a great deal, and seen a great deal of the world, I should think. I daresay he is clever: but I never had much conversation with him."

"In what way is he peculiar?"

"I don't know—it is not easy to describe—nothing striking, but you feel it when he speaks to you: you cannot be always sure whether he is in jest or earnest, whether he is pleased or the contrary; you don't thoroughly understand him, in short—at least, I don't: but it is of no consequence, he is a very good master."

This was all the account I got from Mrs. Fairfax of her employer and mine. There are people who seem to have no notion of sketching a character, or observing and describing salient points, either in persons or things: the good lady evidently belonged to this class; my queries puzzled, but did not draw her out. Mr. Rochester was Mr. Rochester in her eyes; a gentleman, a landed proprietor—nothing more: she inquired and searched no further, and evidently wondered at my wish to gain a more definite notion of his identity.

When we left the dining-room, she proposed to show me over the rest of the house; and I followed her upstairs and downstairs, admiring as I went; for all was well arranged and handsome. The large front chambers I thought especially grand; and some of the third-story rooms, though dark and low, were interesting from their air of antiquity. The furniture once appropriated to the lower apartments had from time to time been removed here, as fashions changed; and the imperfect light entering by their narrow casements showed bedsteads of a hundred years old; chests in oak or walnut, looking with their strange carvings of palm branches and cherubs' heads, like types of the Hebrew ark;[2] rows of venerable chairs, high-backed and narrow; stools still more antiquated, on whose cushioned tops were yet apparent traces of half-effaced embroideries, wrought by fingers that for two generations had been coffin-dust. All these relics gave to the third story of Thornfield Hall the aspect of a home of the past: a shrine of memory. I liked the hush, the gloom, the quaintness of these retreats in the day; but I by no means coveted a night's repose on one of those wide and heavy beds: shut in, some of them, with doors of oak; shaded, others, with wrought old-English hangings crusted with thick work, portraying effigies of strange flowers, and stranger birds, and strangest human beings,—all which would have looked strange, indeed, by the pallid gleam of moonlight.

2. The sacred chest containing the Ten Commandments, described in Exodus 25:10–22.

"Do the servants sleep in these rooms?" I asked.

"No; they occupy a range of smaller apartments to the back; no one ever sleeps here: one would almost say that, if there were a ghost at Thornfield Hall, this would be its haunt."

"So I think: you have no ghost, then?"

"None that I ever heard of," returned Mrs. Fairfax, smiling.

"Nor any traditions of one? no legends or ghost stories?"

"I believe not. And yet it is said the Rochesters have been rather a violent than a quiet race in their time: perhaps, though, that is the reason they rest tranquilly in their graves now."

"Yes—'after life's fitful fever they sleep well,'"[3] I muttered. "Where are you going now, Mrs. Fairfax?" for she was moving away.

"On to the leads;[4] will you come and see the view from thence?" I followed still, up a very narrow staircase to the attics, and thence by a ladder and through a trap-door to the roof of the hall. I was now on a level with the crow colony, and could see into their nests. Leaning over the battlements and looking far down, I surveyed the grounds laid out like a map: the bright and velvet lawn closely girdling the gray base of the mansion; the field, wide as a park, dotted with its ancient timber; the wood, dun and sere, divided by a path visibly overgrown, greener with moss than the trees were with foliage; the church at the gates, the road, the tranquil hills, all reposing in the autumn day's sun: the horizon bounded by a propitious sky, azure, marbled with pearly white. No feature in the scene was extraordinary, but all was pleasing. When I turned from it and repassed the trap-door, I could scarcely see my way down the ladder: the attic seemed black as a vault compared with that arch of blue air to which I had been looking up, and to that sunlit scene of grove, pasture, and green hill of which the hall was the center, and over which I had been gazing with delight.

Mrs. Fairfax stayed behind a moment to fasten the trap-door; I, by dint of groping, found the outlet from the attic, and proceeded to descend the narrow garret staircase. I lingered in the long passage to which this led, separating the front and back rooms of the third story: narrow, low, and dim, with only one little window at the far end, and looking, with its two rows of small black doors all shut, like a corridor in some Bluebeard's castle.[5]

While I paced softly on the last sound I expected to hear in so still a region, a laugh, struck my ear. It was a curious laugh; distinct, formal, mirthless. I stopped: the sound ceased, only for an instant; it began again louder: for at first, though distinct, it was very low. It passed off in a clamorous peal that seemed to wake an echo in every lonely chamber; though it originated but in one, and I could have pointed out the door whence the accents issued.

"Mrs. Fairfax!" I called out: for I now heard her descending the great stairs. "Did you hear that loud laugh? Who is it?"

"Some of the servants, very likely," she answered: "perhaps Grace Poole."

"Did you hear it?" I again inquired.

"Yes, plainly: I often hear her; she sews in one of these rooms. Sometimes Leah is with her: they are frequently noisy together."

3. Shakespeare's *Macbeth* 3.2.23.
4. Roof.
5. In the fairy tale *Bluebeard*, by Charles Perrault (1628–1703), the young wife is allowed to enter all the rooms in her husband's castle but one, where the bodies of his former wives are kept.

The laugh was repeated in its low, syllabic tone, and terminated in an odd murmur.

"Grace!" exclaimed Mrs. Fairfax.

I really did not expect any Grace to answer; for the laugh was as tragic, as preternatural a laugh as any I ever heard; and, but that it was high noon, and that no circumstance of ghostliness accompanied the curious cachinnation, but that neither scene nor season favored fear, I should have been superstitiously afraid. However, the event showed me I was a fool for entertaining a sense even of surprise.

The door nearest me opened, and a servant came out,—a woman of between thirty and forty; a set, square-made figure, red-haired, and with a hard, plain face: any apparition less romantic or less ghostly could scarcely be conceived.

"Too much noise, Grace," said Mrs. Fairfax. "Remember directions!" Grace curtseyed silently and went in.

"She is a person we have to sew and assist Leah in her house-maid's work," continued the widow; "not altogether unobjectionable in some points, but she does well enough. By-the-by, how have you got on with your new pupil this morning?"

The conversation, thus turned on Adèle, continued till we reached the light and cheerful region below. Adèle came running to meet us in the hall, exclaiming,—"Mesdames. vous etes servies!" adding, "J'ai bien faim, moi!"[6]

We found dinner ready and waiting for us in Mrs. Fairfax's room.

Chapter XII

The promise of a smooth career, which my first calm introduction to Thornfield Hall seemed to pledge, was not belied on a longer acquaintance with the place and its inmates. Mrs. Fairfax turned out to be what she appeared, a placid-tempered, kind-natured woman, of competent education and average intelligence. My pupil was a lively child, who had been spoiled and indulged, and therefore was sometimes wayward; but as she was committed entirely to my care, and no injudicious interference from any quarter ever thwarted my plans for her improvement, she soon forgot her little freaks, and became obedient and teachable. She had no great talents, no marked traits of character, no peculiar development of feeling or taste which raised her one inch above the ordinary level of childhood; but neither had she any deficiency or vice which sunk her below it. She made reasonable progress, entertained for me a vivacious, though perhaps not very profound, affection; and by her simplicity, gay prattle, and efforts to please, inspired me, in return, with a degree of attachment sufficient to make us both content in each other's society.

This, *par parenthèse*,[7] will be thought cool language by persons who entertain solemn doctrines about the angelic nature of children, and the duty of those charged with their education to conceive for them an idolatrous devotion: but I am not writing to flatter parental egotism, to echo cant, or prop up humbug; I am merely telling the truth. I felt a conscientious solicitude for Adèle's welfare and progress, and a quiet liking to her little self; just as I cher-

6. My ladies, dinner is served! . . . I am very hungry! 7. Parenthetically.

ished towards Mrs. Fairfax a thankfulness for her kindness, and a pleasure in her society proportionate to the tranquil regard she had for me, and the moderation of her mind and character.

Anybody may blame me who likes when I add further that now and then, when I took a walk by myself in the grounds, when I went down to the gates and looked through them along the road, or when, while Adèle played with her nurse, and Mrs. Fairfax made jellies in the store-room, I climbed the three staircases, raised the trap-door of the attic, and having reached the leads, looked out afar over sequestered field and hill, and along dim sky-line—that then I longed for a power of vision which might overpass that limit; which might reach the busy world, towns, regions full of life I had heard of but never seen: that then I desired more of practical experience than I possessed; more of intercourse with my kind, of acquaintance with variety of character, than was here within my reach. I valued what was good in Mrs. Fairfax, and what was good in Adèle; but I believed in the existence of other and more vivid kinds of goodness, and what I believed in I wished to behold.

Who blames me? Many, no doubt; and I shall be called discontented. I could not help it: the restlessness was in my nature; it agitated me to pain sometimes. Then my sole relief was to walk along the corridor of the third story, backwards and forwards, safe in the silence and solitude of the spot and allow my mind's eye to dwell on whatever bright visions rose before it—and, certainly, they were many and glowing; to let my heart be heaved by the exultant movement, which, while it swelled it in trouble, expanded it with life; and, best of all, to open my inward ear to a tale that was never ended—a tale my imagination created, and narrated continuously; quickened with all of incident, life, fire, feeling, that I desired and had not in my actual existence.

It is in vain to say human beings ought to be satisfied with tranquillity: they must have action; and they will make it if they cannot find it. Millions are condemned to a stiller doom than mine, and millions are in silent revolt against their lot. Nobody knows how many rebellions besides political rebellions ferment in the masses of life which people earth. Women are supposed to be very calm generally: but women feel just as men feel; they need exercise for their faculties and a field for their efforts as much as their brothers do; they suffer from too rigid a restraint, too absolute a stagnation, precisely as men would suffer; and it is narrow-minded in their more privileged fellow-creatures to say that they ought to confine themselves to making puddings and knitting stockings, to playing on the piano and embroidering bags. It is thoughtless to condemn them, or laugh at them, if they seek to do more or learn more than custom has pronounced necessary for their sex.

When thus alone I not unfrequently heard Grace Poole's laugh: the same peal, the same low, slow ha! ha! which, when first heard, had thrilled me: I heard, too, her eccentric murmurs; stranger than her laugh. There were days when she was quite silent; but there were others when I could not account for the sounds she made. Sometimes I saw her; she would come out of her room with a basin, or a plate, or a tray in her hand, go down to the kitchen, and shortly return, generally (oh, romantic reader, forgive me for telling the plain truth:) bearing a pot of porter.[8] Her appearance always acted as a damper to the curiosity raised by her oral oddities: hard-featured and staid, she had no

8. Weak stout.

point to which interest could attach. I made some attempts to draw her into conversation, but she seemed a person of few words: a monosyllabic reply usually cut short every effort of that sort.

The other members of the household, viz. John and his wife, Leah the housemaid, and Sophie the French nurse, were decent people: but in no respect remarkable. With Sophie I used to talk French, and sometimes I asked her questions about her native country; but she was not of a descriptive or narrative turn, and generally gave such vapid and confused answers as were calculated rather to check than encourage inquiry.

October, November, December passed away. One afternoon in January Mrs. Fairfax had begged a holiday for Adèle because she had a cold; and, as Adèle seconded the request with an ardor that reminded me how precious occasional holidays had been to me in my own childhood, I accorded it, deeming that I did well in showing pliability on the point. It was a fine, calm day, though very cold; I was tired of sitting still in the library through a whole long morning: Mrs. Fairfax had just written a letter which was waiting to be posted, so I put on my bonnet and cloak and volunteered to carry it to Hay; the distance, two miles, would be a pleasant winter afternoon walk. Having seen Adèle comfortably seated in her little chair by Mrs. Fairfax's parlor fireside, and given her her best wax doll (which I usually kept enveloped in silver paper in a drawer) to play with, and a story-book for change of amusement; and having replied to her "Revenez bientôt, ma bonne amie, ma chère Mdlle. Jeannette,"[9] with a kiss, I set out.

The ground was hard, the air was still, my road was lonely; I walked fast till I got warm, and then I walked slowly to enjoy and analyze the species of pleasure brooding for me in the hour and situation. It was three o'clock; the church bell tolled as I passed under the belfry: the charm of the hour lay in its approaching dimness, in the low-gliding and pale-beaming sun. I was a mile from Thornfield, in a lane noted for wild roses in summer, for nuts and blackberries in autumn, and even now possessing a few coral treasures in hips and haws, but whose best winter delight lay in its utter solitude and leafless repose. If a breath of air stirred, it made no sound here; for there was not a holly, not an evergreen to rustle, and the stripped hawthorn and hazel bushes were as still as the white, worn stones which causewayed the middle of the path. Far and wide, on each side, there were only fields, where no cattle now browsed; and the little brown birds, which stirred occasionally in the hedge, looked like single russet leaves that had forgotten to drop.

This lane inclined uphill all the way to Hay: having reached the middle I sat down on a stile which led thence into a field. Gathering my mantle about me, and sheltering my hands in my muff, I did not feel the cold, though it froze keenly; as was attested by a sheet of ice covering the causeway, where a little brooklet, now congealed, had overflowed after a rapid thaw some days since. From my seat I could look down on Thornfield: the gray and battlemented hall was the principal object in the vale below me; its woods and dark rookery rose against the west. I lingered till the sun went down among the trees, and sank crimson and clear behind them. I then turned eastward.

On the hilltop above me sat the rising moon; pale yet as a cloud, but brightening momently: she looked over Hay, which, half lost in trees, sent up a blue

9. Come back soon, my good friend, my dear Miss Jane.

smoke from its few chimneys; it was yet a mile distant, but in the absolute hush I could hear plainly its thin murmurs of life. My ear too felt the flow of currents; in what dales and depths I could not tell: but there were many hills beyond Hay, and doubtless many becks threading their passes. That evening calm betrayed alike the tinkle of the nearest streams, the sough of the most remote.

A rude noise broke on these fine ripplings and whisperings, at once so far away and so clear: a positive tramp, tramp; a metallic clatter, which effaced the soft wave-wanderings; as, in a picture, the solid mass of a crag, or the rough boles of a great oak, drawn in dark and strong on the foreground, efface the aërial distance of azure hill, sunny horizon, and blended clouds, where tint melts into tint.

The din was on the causeway; a horse was coming; the windings of the lane yet hid it, but it approached. I was just leaving the stile; yet, as the path was narrow, I sat still to let it go by. In those days I was young, and all sorts of fancies bright and dark tenanted my mind: the memories of nursery stories were there amongst other rubbish; and when they recurred, maturing youth added to them a vigor and vividness beyond what childhood could give. As this horse approached, and as I watched for it to appear through the dusk, I remembered certain of Bessie's tales, wherein figured a North-of-England spirit, called a "Gytrash," which, in the form of horse, mule, or large dog, haunted solitary ways, and sometimes came upon belated travelers, as this horse was now coming upon me.

It was very near, but not yet in sight, when, in addition to the tramp, tramp, I heard a rush under the hedge, and close down by the hazel stems glided a great dog, whose black and white color made him a distinct object against the trees. It was exactly one mask of Bessie's Gytrash,—a lion-like creature with long hair and a huge head: it passed me, however, quietly enough; not staying to look up, with strange pretercanine eyes, in my face, as I half expected it would. The horse followed,—a tall steed, and on its back a rider. The man, the human being, broke the spell at once. Nothing ever rode the Gytrash: it was always alone; and goblins, to my notions, though they might tenant the dumb carcasses of beasts, could scarce covet shelter in the common-place human form. No Gytrash was this,—only a traveler taking the short cut to Millcote. He passed, and I went on: a few steps, and I turned: a sliding sound and an exclamation of "What the deuce is to do now?" and a clattering tumble, arrested my attention. Man and horse were down; they had slipped on the sheet of ice which glazed the causeway. The dog came bounding back, and seeing his master in a predicament, and hearing the horse groan, barked till the evening hills echoed the sound, which was deep in proportion to his magnitude. He snuffed round the prostrate group, and then he ran up to me; it was all he could do,—there was no other help at hand to summon. I obeyed him, and walked down to the traveler, by this time struggling himself free of his steed. His efforts were so vigorous I thought he could not be much hurt; but I asked him the question:—"Are you injured, sir?"

I think he was swearing, but am not certain; however, he was pronouncing some formula which prevented him from replying to me directly.

"Can I do anything?" I asked again.

"You must just stand on one side," he answered as he rose, first to his knees, and then to his feet. I did; whereupon began a heaving, stamping, clattering

process, accompanied by a barking and baying which removed me effectually
some yards' distance; but I would not be driven quite away till I saw the event.
This was finally fortunate; the horse was re-established, and the dog was si-
lenced with a "Down, Pilot!" The traveler now, stooping, felt his foot and leg,
as if trying whether they were sound; apparently something ailed them, for he
halted to the stile whence I had just risen, and sat down.

I was in the mood for being useful, or at least officious, I think, for I now
drew near him again.

"If you are hurt, and want help, sir, I can fetch some one either from
Thornfield Hall or from Hay."

"Thank you; I shall do: I have no broken bones—only a sprain"; and again
he stood up and tried his foot, but the result extorted an involuntary "Ugh!"

Something of daylight still lingered, and the moon was waxing bright: I
could see him plainly. His figure was enveloped in a riding cloak, fur collared,
and steel clasped; its details were not apparent, but I traced the general points
of middle height, and considerable breadth of chest. He had a dark face, with
stern features and a heavy brow; his eyes and gathered eyebrows looked ireful
and thwarted just now; he was past youth, but had not reached middle age;
perhaps he might be thirty-five. I felt no fear of him, and but little shyness.
Had he been a handsome, heroic-looking young gentleman, I should not have
dared to stand thus questioning him against his will, and offering my services
unasked. I had hardly ever seen a handsome youth; never in my life spoken to
one. I had a theoretical reverence and homage for beauty, elegance, gallantry,
fascination; but had I met those qualities incarnate in masculine shape, I
should have known instinctively that they neither had nor could have sympa-
thy with anything in me, and should have shunned them as one would fire,
lightning, or anything else that is bright but antipathetic.

If even this stranger had smiled and been good-humored to me when I ad-
dressed him; if he had put off my offer of assistance gaily and with thanks, I
should have gone on my way and not felt any vocation to renew inquiries: but
the frown, the roughness of the traveler, set me at my ease: I retained my sta-
tion when he waved to me to go, and announced:—"I cannot think of leaving
you, sir, at so late an hour, in this solitary lane, till I see you are fit to mount
your horse."

He looked at me when I said this: he had hardly turned his eyes in my direc-
tion before.

"I should think you ought to be at home yourself," said he, "if you have a
home in this neighborhood: where do you come from?"

"From just below; and I am not at all afraid of being out late when it is
moonlight: I will run over to Hay for you with pleasure, if you wish it; indeed,
I am going there to post a letter."

"You live just below—do you mean at that house with the battlements?"
pointing to Thornfield Hall, on which the moon cast a hoary gleam, bringing
it out distinct and pale from the woods, that, by contrast with the western sky,
now seemed one mass of shadow.

"Yes, sir."

"Whose house is it?"

"Mr. Rochester's."

"Do you know Mr. Rochester?"

"No, I have never seen him."

"He is not resident, then?"

"No."

"Can you tell me where he is?"

"I cannot."

"You are not a servant at the hall, of course. You are—" He stopped, ran his eye over my dress, which, as usual, was quite simple: a black merino cloak, a black beaver bonnet: neither of them half fine enough for a lady's maid. He seemed puzzled to decide what I was: I helped him.

"I am the governess."

"Ah, the governess!" he repeated; "deuce take me, if I had not forgotten! The governess!" and again my raiment underwent scrutiny. In two minutes he rose from the stile: his face expressed pain when he tried to move.

"I cannot commission you to fetch help," he said; "but you may help me a little yourself, if you will be so kind."

"Yes, sir."

"You have not an umbrella that I can use as a stick?"

"No."

"Try to get hold of my horse's bridle and lead him to me: you are not afraid!"

I should have been afraid to touch a horse when alone, but when told to do it I was disposed to obey. I put down my muff on the stile, and went up to the tall steed; I endeavored to catch the bridle, but it was a spirited thing, and would not let me come near its head; I made effort on effort, though in vain: meantime, I was mortally afraid of its trampling fore-feet. The traveler waited and watched for some time, and at last he laughed.

"I see," he said, "the mountain will never be brought to Mahomet, so all you can do is to aid Mahomet to go to the mountain; I must beg of you to come here."[1]

I came. "Excuse me," he continued: "necessity compels me to make you useful." He laid a heavy hand on my shoulder, and leaning on me with some stress, limped to his horse. Having once caught the bridle, he mastered it directly, and sprang to his saddle; grimacing grimly as he made the effort, for it wrenched his sprain.

"Now," said he, releasing his under lip from a hard bite, "just hand me my whip; it lies there under the hedge."

I sought it and found it.

"Thank you: now make haste with the letter to Hay, and return as fast as you can."

A touch of a spurred heel made his horse first start and rear, and then bound away; the dog rushed in his traces: all three vanished,

> Like heath that, in the wilderness,
> The wild wind whirls away.[2]

I took up my muff and walked on. The incident had occurred and was gone for me: it *was* an incident of no moment, no romance, no interest in a sense; yet it marked with change one single hour of a monotonous life. My help had been needed and claimed; I had given it: I was pleased to have done something; trivial, transitory though the deed was, it was yet an active thing, and I

1. According to legend, the Muslim prophet Muhammad summoned Mount Safa to come to him, in order to display his powers. When the mountain did not come, he told the spectators he would go to it.
2. From Thomas Moore's *Fallen Is Thy Throne, Sacred Songs* (1816).

was weary of an existence all passive. The new face, too, was like a new picture introduced to the gallery of memory, and it was dissimilar to all the others hanging there: firstly, because it was masculine; and, secondly, because it was dark, strong, and stern. I had it still before me when I entered Hay, and slipped the letter into the post-office; I saw it as I walked fast down hill all the way home. When I came to the stile, I stopped a minute, looked round and listened, with an idea that a horse's hoof might ring on the causeway again, and that a rider in a cloak, and a Gytrash-like Newfoundland dog, might be again apparent: I saw only the hedge and a pollard willow before me, rising up still and straight to meet the moonbeams; I heard only the faintest waft of wind roaming fitful among the trees round Thornfield, a mile distant; and when I glanced down in the direction of the murmur, my eye, traversing the hall-front, caught a light kindling in a window: it reminded me that I was late, and I hurried on.

I did not like reentering Thornfield. To pass its threshold was to return to stagnation; to cross the silent hall, to ascend the darksome staircase, to seek my own lonely little room, and then to meet tranquil Mrs. Fairfax, and spend the long winter evening with her, and her only, was to quell wholly the faint excitement wakened by my walk,—to slip again over my faculties the viewless fetters of an uniform and too still existence; of an existence whose very privileges of security and ease I was becoming incapable of appreciating. What good it would have done me at that time to have been tossed in the storms of an uncertain struggling life, and to have been taught by rough and bitter experience to long for the calm amid which I now repined! Yes, just as much good as it would do a man tired of sitting still in a "too easy chair"[3] to take a long walk; and just as natural was the wish to stir, under my circumstances, as it would be under his.

I lingered at the gates; I lingered on the lawn; I paced backwards and forwards on the pavement: the shutters of the glass door were closed; I could not see into the interior; and both my eyes and spirit seemed drawn from the gloomy house—from the gray hollow filled with rayless cells, as it appeared to me—to that sky expanded before me,—a blue sea absolved from taint of cloud; the moon ascending it in solemn march; her orb seeming to look up as she left the hilltops, from behind which she had come, far and farther below her, and aspired to the zenith, midnight-dark in its fathomless depth and measureless distance: and for those trembling stars that followed her course; they made my heart tremble, my veins glow when I viewed them. Little things recall us to earth: the clock struck in the hall; that sufficed; I turned from moon and stars, opened a side door, and went in.

The hall was not dark, nor yet was it lit, only by the high-hung bronze lamp: a warm glow suffused both it and the lower steps of the oak staircase. This ruddy shine issued from the great dining-room, whose two-leaved door stood open, and showed a genial fire in the grate, glancing on marble hearth and brass fire-irons, and revealing purple draperies and polished furniture, in the most pleasant radiance. It revealed, too, a group near the mantelpiece: I had scarcely caught it, and scarcely become aware of a cheerful mingling of voices, amongst which I seemed to distinguish the tones of Adèle, when the door closed.

3. Alexander Pope's *The Dunciad* (1743) 4.342.

I hastened to Mrs. Fairfax's room: there was a fire there too, but no candle, and no Mrs. Fairfax. Instead, all alone, sitting upright on the rug, and gazing with gravity at the blaze, I beheld a great black and white long-haired dog, just like the Gytrash of the lane. It was so like it that I went forward and said—"Pilot," and the thing got up and came to me and snuffed me. I caressed him, and he wagged his great tail: but he looked an eerie creature to be alone with, and I could not tell whence he had come. I rang the bell, for I wanted a candle; and I wanted, too, to get an account of this visitant. Leah entered.

"What dog is this?"

"He came with master."

"With whom?"

"With master—Mr. Rochester—he is just arrived."

"Indeed! and is Mrs. Fairfax with him?"

"Yes, and Miss Adgela; they are in the dining-room, and John is gone for a surgeon: for master has had an accident; his horse fell and his ankle is sprained."

"Did the horse fall in Hay Lane?"

"Yes, coming down hill; it slipped on some ice."

"Ah! Bring me a candle, will you, Leah?"

Leah brought it; she entered, followed by Mrs. Fairfax, who repeated the news; adding that Mr. Carter the surgeon was come, and was now with Mr. Rochester: then she hurried out to give orders about tea, and I went upstairs to take off my things.

Chapter XIII

Mr. Rochester, it seems, by the surgeon's orders, went to bed early that night; nor did he rise soon next morning. When he did come down, it was to attend to business: his agent and some of his tenants were arrived, and waiting to speak with him.

Adèle and I had now to vacate the library: it would be in daily requisition as a reception-room for callers. A fire was lit in an apartment upstairs, and there I carried our books, and arranged it for the future schoolroom. I discerned in the course of the morning that Thornfield Hall was a changed place: no longer silent as a church, it echoed every hour or two to a knock at the door, or a clang of the bell; steps, too, often traversed the hall, and new voices spoke in different keys below; a rill from the outer world was flowing through it; it had a master: for my part I liked it better.

Adèle was not easy to teach that day; she could not apply: she kept running to the door and looking over the banisters to see if she could get a glimpse of Mr. Rochester; then she coined pretexts to go downstairs, in order, as I shrewdly suspected, to visit the library, where I knew she was not wanted; then, when I got a little angry, and made her sit still, she continued to talk incessantly of her "ami, Monsieur Edouard Fairfax *de* Rochester,"[4] as she dubbed him (I had not before heard his prenomens), and to conjecture what presents he had brought her: for it appears he had intimated the night before, that when his luggage came from Millcote there would be found among it a little box in whose contents she had an interest.

"Et cela doit signifier," said she, "qu'il y aura là dedans un cadeau pour moi,

4. She adds the "de" as a sign of nobility. "Ami": friend.

et peut-être pour vous aussi, mademoiselle Monsieur a parlé de vous: il m'a demandé le nom de ma gouvernante, et si elle n'était pas une petite personne, assez mince et un peu pâle. J'ai dit qu'oui: car c'est vrai, n'est-ce pas, mademoiselle?"[5]

I and my pupil dined as usual in Mrs. Fairfax's parlor; the afternoon was wild and snowy, and we passed it in the schoolroom. At dark I allowed Adèle to put away books and work, and to run downstairs; for, from the comparative silence below, and from the cessation of appeals to the doorbell, I conjectured that Mr. Rochester was now at liberty. Left alone, I walked to the window; but nothing was to be seen thence: twilight and snowflakes together thickened the air, and hid the very shrubs on the lawn. I let down the curtain and went back to the fireside.

In the clear embers I was tracing a view, not unlike a picture I remembered to have seen of the castle of Heidelberg, on the Rhine, when Mrs. Fairfax came in, breaking up by her entrance the fiery mosaic I had been piecing together, and scattering too some heavy unwelcome thoughts that were beginning to throng on my solitude.

"Mr. Rochester would be glad if you and your pupil would take tea with him in the drawing-room this evening," said she: "he has been so much engaged all day that he could not ask to see you before."

"When is his tea-time?" I inquired.

"Oh, at six o'clock: he keeps early hours in the country. You had better change your frock now; I will go with you and fasten it. Here is a candle."

"Is it necessary to change my frock?"

"Yes, you had better: I always dress for the evening when Mr. Rochester is here."

This additional ceremony seemed somewhat stately; however, I repaired to my room, and, with Mrs. Fairfax's aid, replaced my black stuff dress by one of black silk: the best and the only additional one I had, except one of light gray, which, in my Lowood notions of the toilette, I thought too fine to be worn, except on first-rate occasions.

"You want a brooch," said Mrs. Fairfax. I had a single little pearl ornament which Miss Temple gave me as a parting keepsake: I put it on, and then we went downstairs. Unused as I was to strangers, it was rather a trial to appear thus formally summoned in Mr. Rochester's presence. I let Mrs. Fairfax precede me into the dining-room, and kept in her shade as we crossed that apartment; and, passing the arch, whose curtain was now dropped, entered the elegant recess beyond.

Two wax candles stood lighted on the table, and two on the mantelpiece; basking in the light and heat of a superb fire lay Pilot—Adèle knelt near him. Half reclined on a couch appeared Mr. Rochester, his foot supported by the cushion; he was looking at Adèle and the dog: the fire shone full on his face. I knew my traveler with his broad and jetty eyebrows; his square forehead, made squarer by the horizontal sweep of his black hair I recognized his decisive nose, more remarkable for character than beauty; his full nostrils, denoting, I thought, choler;[6] his grim mouth, chin, and jaw—yes, all three were very grim,

5. "And that must mean," said she, "that there will be a present inside for me, and perhaps for you, too, Miss Eyre. Mr. Rochester talked about you; he asked me my governess's name, and if she wasn't a small person, rather thin and a little pale. I said yes: because it's true, isn't it, Miss Eyre?"

6. Anger originally, one of the four humors thought to dominate a person's makeup).

and no mistake. His shape, now divested of cloak, I perceived harmonized in squareness with his physiognomy: I suppose it was a good figure in the athletic sense of the term—broad-chested and thin-flanked, though neither tall nor graceful.

Mr. Rochester must have been aware of the entrance of Mrs. Fairfax and myself; but it appeared he was not in the mood to notice us, for he never lifted his head as we approached.

"Here is Miss Eyre, sir," said Mrs. Fairfax, in her quiet way. He bowed, still not taking his eyes from the group of the dog and child.

"Let Miss Eyre be seated," said he: and there was something in the forced stiff bow, in the impatient yet formal tone, which seemed further to express, "What the deuce is it to me whether Miss Eyre be there or not? At this moment I am not disposed to accost her."

I sat down quite disembarrassed. A reception of finished politeness would probably have confused me: I could not have returned or repaid it by answering grace and elegance on my part; but harsh caprice laid me under no obligation; on the contrary, a decent quiescence, under the freak of manner, gave me advantage. Besides, the eccentricity of the proceeding was piquant: I felt interested to see how he would go on.

He went on as a statue would, that is, he neither spoke nor moved. Mrs. Fairfax seemed to think it necessary that some one should be amiable, and she began to talk. Kindly, as usual—and, as usual, rather trite—she condoled with him on the pressure of business he had had all day; on the annoyance it must have been to him with that painful sprain: then she commended his patience and perseverance in going through with it.

"Madam, I should like some tea," was the sole rejoinder she got. She hastened to ring the bell; and, when the tray came, she proceeded to arrange the cups, spoons, etc., with assiduous celerity. I and Adèle went to the table; but the master did not leave his couch.

"Will you hand Mr. Rochester's cup?" said Mrs. Fairfax to me; "Adèle might perhaps spill it."

I did as requested. As he took the cup from my hand, Adèle, thinking the moment propitious for making a request in my favor, cried out:—"N'est-ce pas, monsieur, qu'il y a un cadeau pour Mademoiselle Eyre, dans votre petit coffre?"[7]

"Who talks of cadeaux?" said he gruffly: "did you expect a present, Miss Eyre? Are you fond of presents?" and he searched my face with eyes that I saw were dark, irate, and piercing.

"I hardly know, sir; I have little experience of them: they are generally thought pleasant things."

"Generally thought? But what do you think?"

"I should be obliged to take time, sir, before I could give you an answer worthy of your acceptance: a present has many faces to it, has it not? and one should consider all before pronouncing an opinion as to its nature."

"Miss Eyre, you are not so unsophisticated as Adèle: she demands a 'cadeau,' clamorously, the moment she sees me: you beat about the bush."

"Because I have less confidence in my deserts than Adèle has: she can prefer the claim of old acquaintance, and the right too of custom; for she says you

7. Isn't it so, sir, that there is a present for Miss Eyre, in your little chest?

have always been in the habit of giving her playthings; but if I had to make a case I should be puzzled, since I am a stranger, and have done nothing to entitle me to an acknowledgment."

"Oh, don't fall back on over-modesty! I have examined Adèle, and find you have taken great pains with her; she is not bright, she has no talents; yet in a short time she has made much improvement."

"Sir, you have now given me my 'cadeau'; I am obliged to you: it is the meed teachers most covet; praise of their pupil's progress."

"Humph!" said Mr. Rochester, and he took his tea in silence.

"Come to the fire," said the master, when the tray was taken away, and Mrs. Fairfax had settled into a corner with her knitting; while Adèle was leading me by the hand round the room, showing me the beautiful books and ornaments on the consoles and chiffonnières. We obeyed, as in duty bound; Adèle wanted to take a seat on my knee, but she was ordered to amuse herself with Pilot.

"You have been resident in my house three months?"

"Yes, sir."

"And you come from——?"

"From Lowood school, in ——shire."

"Ah! a charitable concern.—How long were you there?"

"Eight years."

"Eight years! you must be tenacious of life. I thought half the time in such a place would have done up any constitution! No wonder you have rather the look of another world. I marveled where you had got that sort of face. When you came on me in Hay Lane last night, I thought unaccountably of fairy tales, and had half a mind to demand whether you had bewitched my horse: I am not sure yet. Who are your parents?"

"I have none."

"Nor ever had, I suppose: do you remember them?"

"No."

"I thought not. And so you were waiting for your people when you sat on the stile?"

"For whom, sir?"

"For the men in green: it was a proper moonlight evening for them. Did I break through one of your rings,[8] that you spread that damned ice on the causeway?"

I shook my head. "The men in green all forsook England a hundred years ago," said I, speaking as seriously as he had done. "And not even in Hay Lane, or the fields about it, could you find a trace of them. I don't think either summer or harvest, or winter moon, will ever shine on their revels more."

Mrs. Fairfax had dropped her knitting, and, with raised eyebrows, seemed wondering what sort of talk this was.

"Well," resumed Mr. Rochester, "if you disown parents you must have some sort of kinsfolk: uncles and aunts?"

"No; none that I ever saw."

"And your home?"

"I have none."

"Where do your brothers and sisters live?"

8. Enchanted circles where fairies dance.

"I have no brothers and sisters."

"Who recommended you to come here?"

"I advertised, and Mrs. Fairfax answered my advertisement."

"Yes," said the good lady, who now knew what ground we were upon, "and I am daily thankful for the choice Providence led me to make. Miss Eyre has been an invaluable companion to me, and a kind and careful teacher to Adèle."

"Don't trouble yourself to give her a character," returned Mr. Rochester: "eulogiums will not bias me; I shall judge for myself. She began by felling my horse."

"Sir?" said Mrs. Fairfax.

"I have to thank her for this sprain."

The widow looked bewildered.

"Miss Eyre, have you ever lived in a town?"

"No, sir."

"Have you seen much society?"

"None but the pupils and teachers of Lowood; and now the inmates of Thornfield."

"Have you read much?"

"Only such books as came in my way; and they have not been numerous or very learned."

"You have lived the life of a nun: no doubt you are well drilled in religious forms;—Brocklehurst, who I understand directs Lowood, is a parson, is he not?"

"Yes, sir."

"And you girls probably worshipped him, as a convent full of religieuses[9] would worship their director?"

"Oh, no."

"You are very cool! No! What! A novice not worship her priest! That sounds blasphemous."

"I disliked Mr. Brocklehurst; and I was not alone in the feeling. He is a harsh man; at once pompous and meddling: he cut off our hair; and for economy's sake bought us bad needles and thread, with which we could hardly sew."

"That was very false economy," remarked Mrs. Fairfax, who now again caught the drift of the dialogue.

"And was that the head and front of his offending?"[1] demanded Mr. Rochester.

"He starved us when he had the sole superintendence of the provision department, before the committee was appointed; and he bored us with long lectures once a week, and with evening readings from books of his own inditing,[2] about sudden deaths and judgments, which made us afraid to go to bed."

"What age were you when you went to Lowood?"

"About ten."

"And you stayed there eight years: you are now, then, eighteen?"

I assented.

"Arithmetic, you see, is useful; without its aid I should hardly have been able to guess your age. It is a point difficult to fix where the features and coun-

9. Nuns.
1. From *Othello* 1.3.80.
2. Written by him.

tenance are so much at variance as in your case. And now, what did you learn at Lowood? Can you play?"

"A little."

"Of course: that is the established answer. Go into the library—I mean, if you please. (Excuse my tone of command; I am used to say 'Do this,' and it is done: I cannot alter my customary habits for one new inmate.) Go then, into the library; take a candle with you; leave the door open; sit down to the piano, and play a tune."

I departed, obeying his directions.

"Enough!" he called out in a few minutes. "You play a *little*, I see, like any other English schoolgirl: perhaps rather better than some, but not well."

I closed the piano and returned. Mr. Rochester continued:

"Adèle showed me some sketches this morning which she said were yours. I don't know whether they were entirely of your doing: probably a master aided you?"

"No, indeed!" I interjected.

"Ah! that pricks pride. Well, fetch me your portfolio, if you can vouch for its contents being original; but don't pass your word unless you are certain: I can recognize patchwork."

"Then I will say nothing, and you shall judge for yourself, sir."

I brought the portfolio from the library.

"Approach the table," said he; and I wheeled it to his couch. Adèle and Mrs. Fairfax drew near to see the pictures.

"No crowding," said Mr. Rochester: "take the drawings from my hand as I finish with them; but don't push your faces up to mine."

He deliberately scrutinized each sketch and painting. Three he laid aside; the others, when he had examined them, he swept from him.

"Take them off to the other table, Mrs. Fairfax," said he, "and look at them with Adèle;—you" (glancing at me) "resume your seat, and answer my questions. I perceive these pictures were done by one hand: was that hand yours?"

"Yes."

"And when did you find time to do them? They have taken much time, and some thought."

"I did them in the last two vacations I spent at Lowood, when I had no other occupation."

"Where did you get your copies?"

"Out of my head."

"That head I see now on your shoulders?"

"Yes, sir."

"Has it other furniture of the same kind within?"

"I should think it may have: I should hope—better."

He spread the pictures before him, and again surveyed them alternately.

While he is so occupied I will tell you, reader, what they are: and first, I must premise that they are nothing wonderful. The subjects had, indeed, risen vividly on my mind. As I saw them with the spiritual eye, before I attempted to embody them, they were striking; but my hand would not second my fancy, and in each case it had wrought out but a pale portrait of the thing I had conceived.

These pictures were in watercolors. The first represented clouds low and livid, rolling over a swollen sea all the distance was in eclipse; so, too, was the

foreground; or, rather, the nearest billows, for there was no land. One gleam of light lifted into relief a half-submerged mast, on which sat a cormorant, dark and large, with wings flecked with foam: its beak held a gold bracelet, set with gems, that I had touched with as brilliant tints as my palette could yield, and as glittering distinctness as my pencil could impart. Sinking below the bird and mast, a drowned corpse glanced through the green water; a fair arm was the only limb clearly visible, whence the bracelet had been washed or torn.

The second picture contained for foreground only the dim peak of a hill, with grass and some leaves slanting as if by a breeze. Beyond and above spread an expanse of sky, dark blue as at twilight: rising into the sky was a woman's shape to the bust, portrayed in tints as dusk and soft as I could combine. The dim forehead was crowned with a star; the lineaments below were seen as through the suffusion of vapor; the eyes shone dark and wild; the hair streamed shadowy, like a beamless cloud torn by storm or by electric travail. On the neck lay a pale reflection like moonlight; the same faint luster touched the train of thin clouds from which rose and bowed this vision of the Evening Star.

The third showed the pinnacle of an iceberg piercing a polar winter sky: a muster of northern lights reared their dim lances, close serried, along the horizon. Throwing these into distance, rose, in the foreground, a head,—a colossal head, inclined towards the iceberg, and resting against it. Two thin hands, joined under the forehead, and supporting it, drew up before the lower features a sable veil; a brow quite bloodless, white as bone, and an eye hollow and fixed, blank of meaning but for the glassiness of despair, alone were visible. Above the temples, amidst wreathed turban folds of black drapery, vague in its character and consistency as cloud, gleamed a ring of white flame, gemmed with sparkles of a more lurid tinge. This pale crescent was "The likeness of a Kingly Crown"; what it diademed was "the shape which shape had none."[3]

"Were you happy when you painted these pictures?" asked Mr. Rochester, presently.

"I was absorbed, sir: yes, and I was happy. To paint them, in short, was to enjoy one of the keenest pleasures I have ever known."

"That is not saying much. Your pleasures, by your own account, have been few; but I daresay you did exist in a kind of artist's dreamland while you blent and arranged these strange tints. Did you sit at them long each day?"

"I had nothing else to do, because it was the vacation, and I sat at them from morning till noon, and from noon till night: the length of the midsummer days favored my inclination to apply."

"And you felt self-satisfied with the result of your ardent labors?"

"Far from it. I was tormented by the contrast between my idea and my handiwork: in each case I had imagined something which I was quite powerless to realize."

"Not quite: you have secured the shadow of your thought: but no more, probably. You had not enough of the artist's skill and science to give it full being: yet the drawings are, for a schoolgirl, peculiar. As to the thoughts, they are elfish. These eyes in the Evening Star you must have seen in a dream. How could you make them look so clear, and yet not at all brilliant? for the planet

3. From Milton's *Paradise Lost* (1674) 2.666–73. These lines are a description of Death, the son of Satan.

above quells their rays. And what meaning is that in their solemn depth? And who taught you to paint wind? There is a high gale in that sky, and on this hill-top. Where did you see Latmos?[4] For that is Latmos. There,—put the drawings away!"

I had scarce tied the strings of the portfolio when, looking at his watch, he said abruptly,—"It is nine o'clock: what are you about, Miss Eyre, to let Adèle sit up so long? Take her to bed."

Adèle went to kiss him before quitting the room: he endured the caress, but scarcely seemed to relish it more than Pilot would have done, nor so much.

"I wish you all good-night, now." said he, making a movement of the hand towards the door, in token that he was tired of our company, and wished to dismiss us. Mrs. Fairfax folded up her knitting. I took my portfolio: we curtseyed to him, received a frigid bow in return, and so withdrew.

"You said Mr. Rochester was not strikingly peculiar, Mrs. Fairfax," I observed, when I rejoined her in her room, after putting Adèle to bed.

"Well, is he?"

"I think so: he is very changeful and abrupt."

"True: no doubt he may appear so to a stranger, but I am so accustomed to his manner I never think of it; and then, if he has peculiarities of temper, allowance should be made."

"Why?"

"Partly because it is his nature—and we can none of us help our nature; and, partly, he has painful thoughts, no doubt, to harass him, and make his spirits unequal."

"What about?"

"Family troubles, for one thing."

"But he has no family."

"Not now, but he has had—or, at least, relatives. He lost his elder brother a few years since."

"His *elder* brother?"

"Yes. The present Mr. Rochester has not been very long in possession of the property; only about nine years."

"Nine years is a tolerable time. Was he so very fond of his brother as to be still inconsolable for his loss?"

"Why, no—perhaps not. I believe there were some misunderstandings between them. Mr. Rowland Rochester was not quite just to Mr. Edward; and, perhaps, he prejudiced his father against him. The old gentleman was fond of money, and anxious to keep the family estate together. He did not like to diminish the property by division, and yet he was anxious that Mr. Edward should have wealth too, to keep up the consequence of the name; and, soon after he was of age, some steps were taken that were not quite fair, and made a great deal of mischief. Old Mr. Rochester and Mr. Rowland combined to bring Mr. Edward into what he considered a painful position, for the sake of making his fortune: what the precise nature of that position was I never clearly knew, but his spirit could not brook what he had to suffer in it. He is not very forgiving: he broke with his family, and now for many years he has led an unsettled kind of life. I don't think he has ever been resident at Thornfield for a fort-

4. A mountain in Caria, mythic scene of the story of Selene and Encymion.

night together since the death of his brother without a will left him master of the estate; and, indeed, no wonder he shuns the old place."

"Why should he shun it?"

"Perhaps he thinks it gloomy."

The answer was evasive—I should have liked something clearer; but Mrs. Fairfax either could not, or would not, give me more explicit information of the origin and nature of Mr. Rochester's trials. She averred they were a mystery to herself, and that what she knew was chiefly from conjecture. It was evident, indeed, that she wished me to drop the subject, which I did accordingly.

Chapter XIV

For several subsequent days I saw little of Mr. Rochester. In the mornings he seemed much engaged with business, and in the afternoon gentlemen from Millcote or the neighborhood called, and sometimes stayed to dine with him. When his sprain was well enough to admit of horse exercise, he rode out a good deal; probably to return these visits, as he generally did not come back till late at night.

During this interval even Adèle was seldom sent for to his presence, and all my acquaintance with him was confined to an occasional rencontre in the hall, on the stairs, or in the gallery, when he would sometimes pass me haughtily and coldly, just acknowledging my presence by a distant nod or a cool glance, and sometimes bow and smile with gentlemanlike affability. His changes of mood did not offend me, because I saw that I had nothing to do with their alternation; the ebb and flow depended on causes quite disconnected with me.

One day he had had company to dinner, and had sent for my portfolio; in order, doubtless, to exhibit its contents. The gentlemen went away early, to attend a public meeting at Millcote, as Mrs. Fairfax informed me; but the night being wet and inclement, Mr. Rochester did not accompany them. Soon after they were gone, he rang the bell: a message came that I and Adèle were to go downstairs. I brushed Adèle's hair and made her neat, and having ascertained that I was myself in my usual Quaker trim, where there was nothing to retouch—all being too close and plain, braided locks included, to admit of disarrangement—we descended, Adèle wondering whether the *petit coffre* was at length come; for, owing to some mistake, its arrival had hitherto been delayed. She was gratified: there it stood, a little carton, on the table when we entered the dining-room. She appeared to know it by instinct.

"Ma boîte! ma boîte!"[5] exclaimed she, running towards it.

"Yes—there is your 'boîte' at last: take it into a corner, you genuine daughter of Paris, and amuse yourself with disemboweling it," said the deep and rather sarcastic voice of Mr. Rochester, proceeding from the depths of an immense easy-chair at the fireside. "And mind," he continued, "don't bother me with any details of the anatomical process, or any notice of the condition of the entrails: let your operation be conducted in silence: tiens-toi tranquille, enfant; comprends-tu?"[6]

Adèle seemed scarcely to need the warning; she had already retired to a sofa with her treasure, and was busy untying the cord which secured the lid. Having

5. Box. 6. Keep still, child; do you understand?

removed this impediment, and lifted certain silvery envelopes of tissue-paper, she merely exclaimed:—"Oh ciel! Que c'est beau!"[7] and then remained absorbed in ecstatic contemplation.

"Is Miss Eyre there?" now demanded the master, half rising from his seat to look round to the door, near which I still stood.

"Ah! well; come forward: be seated here." He drew a chair near his own. "I am not fond of the prattle of children," he continued; "for, old bachelor as I am, I have no pleasant associations connected with their lisp. It would be intolerable to me to pass a whole evening *tête-à-tête* with a brat. Don't draw that chair further off, Miss Eyre; sit down exactly where I placed it—if you please, that is. Confound these civilities! I continually forget them. Nor do I particularly affect simple-minded old ladies. By-the-bye, I must have mine in mind; it won't do to neglect her. she is a Fairfax, or wed to one; and blood is said to be thicker than water."

He rang and dispatched an invitation to Mrs. Fairfax, who soon arrived, knitting-basket in hand.

"Good-evening, madam; I sent to you for a charitable purpose: I have forbidden Adèle to talk to me about her presents, and she is bursting with repletion; have the goodness to serve her as auditress and interlocutrice:[8] it will be one of the most benevolent acts you ever performed."

Adèle, indeed, no sooner saw Mrs. Fairfax than she summoned her to the sofa, and there quickly filled her lap with the porcelain, the ivory, the waxen contents of her "boîte"; pouring out, meantime, explanations and raptures in such broken English as she was mistress of.

"Now I have performed the part of a good host," pursued Mr. Rochester, "put my guests into the way of amusing each other, I ought to be at liberty to attend to my own pleasure. Miss Eyre, draw your chair still a little further forward: you are yet too far back; I cannot see you without disturbing my position in this comfortable chair, which I have no mind to do."

I did as I was bid, though I would much rather have remained somewhat in the shade: but Mr. Rochester had such a direct way of giving orders, it seemed a matter of course to obey him promptly.

We were, as I have said, in the dining-room: the luster,[9] which had been lit for dinner, filled the room with a festal breadth of light; the large fire was all red and clear; the purple curtains hung rich and ample before the lofty windows and loftier arch; everything was still, save the subdued chat of Adèle (she dared not speak loud), and, filling up each pause, the beating of winter rain against the panes.

Mr. Rochester, as he sat in his damask-covered chair, looked different to what I had seen him look before; not quite so stern—much less gloomy. There was a smile on his lips, and his eyes sparkled, whether with wine or not I am not sure; but I think it very probable. He was, in short, in his after-dinner mood; more expanded and genial, and also more self-indulgent than the frigid and rigid temper of the morning: still he looked preciously grim, cushioning his massive head against the swelling back of his chair, and receiving the light of the fire on his granite-hewn features, and in his great, dark eyes; for he had great, dark eyes, and very fine eyes too—not without a certain change in their

7. Oh heavens! How beautiful!
8. Female interlocutor or fellow speaker.
9. Chandelier.

depths sometimes, which, if it was not softness, reminded you, at least, of that feeling.

He had been looking two minutes at the fire, and I had been looking the same length of time at him, when turning suddenly, he caught my gaze fastened on his physiognomy.

"You examine me, Miss Eyre," said he: "do you think me handsome?"

I should, if I had deliberated, have replied to this question by something conventionally vague and polite; but the answer somehow slipped from my tongue before I was aware:—"No, sir."

"Ah! By my word! there is something singular about you," said he: "you have the air of a little nonnette,[1] quaint, quiet, grave, and simple, as you sit with your hands before you, and your eyes generally bent on the carpet (except, by-the-bye, when they are directed piercingly to my face; as just now, for instance); and when one asks you a question, or makes a remark to which you are obliged to reply, you rap out a round rejoinder, which, if not blunt, is at least brusque. What do you mean by it?"

"Sir, I was too plain: I beg your pardon. I ought to have replied that it was not easy to give an impromptu answer to a question about appearances; that tastes differ; that beauty is of little consequence, or something of that sort."

"You ought to have replied no such thing. Beauty of little consequence, indeed! And so, under pretence of softening the previous outrage, of stroking and soothing me into placidity, you stick a sly penknife under my ear! Go on: what fault do you find with me, pray? I suppose I have all my limbs and all my features like any other man?"

"Mr. Rochester, allow me to disown my first answer. I intended no pointed repartee: it was only a blunder."

"Just so: I think so: and you shall be answerable for it. Criticize me: does my forehead not please you?"

He lifted up the sable waves of hair which lay horizontally over his brow, and showed a solid enough mass of intellectual organs, but an abrupt deficiency where the suave sign of benevolence should have risen.

"Now, ma'am, am I a fool?"

"Far from it, sir. You would, perhaps, think me rude if I inquired in return whether you are a philanthropist?"

"There again! Another stick of the penknife, when she pretended to pat my head: and that is because I said I did not like the society of children and old women (low be it spoken!). No, young lady, I am not a general philanthropist; but I bear a conscience"; and he pointed to the prominences which are said to indicate that faculty, and which, fortunately for him, were sufficiently conspicuous; giving, indeed, a marked breadth to the upper part of his head: "and, besides, I once had a kind of rude tenderness of heart. When I was as old as you I was a feeling fellow enough; partial to the unfledged, unfostered, and unlucky; but fortune has knocked me about since: she has even kneaded me with her knuckles, and now I flatter myself I am hard and tough as an India-rubber ball; pervious, though, through a chink or two still, and with one sentient point in the middle of the lump. Yes: does that leave hope for me?"

"Hope of what, sir?"

"Of my final retransformation from India-rubber back to flesh?"

1. A young nun.

"Decidedly he has had too much wine," I thought; and I did not know what answer to make to his queer question: how could I tell whether he was capable of being re-transformed?

"You look very much puzzled, Miss Eyre; and though you are not pretty any more than I am handsome, yet a puzzled air becomes you; besides, it is convenient, for it keeps those searching eyes of yours away from my physiognomy, and busies them with the worsted flowers of the rug; so puzzle on. Young lady, I am disposed to be gregarious and communicative tonight."

With this announcement he rose from his chair, and stood, leaning his arm on the marble mantelpiece: in that attitude his shape was seen plainly as well as his face; his unusual breadth of chest, disproportionate almost to his length of limb. I am sure most people would have thought him an ugly man; yet there was so much unconscious pride in his port so much ease in his demeanor; such a look of complete indifference to his own external appearance; so haughty a reliance on the power of other qualities, intrinsic or adventitious, to atone for the lack of mere personal attractiveness, that, in looking at him, one inevitably shared the indifference, and, even in a blind, imperfect sense, put faith in the confidence.

"I am disposed to be gregarious and communicative tonight," he repeated; "and that is why I sent for you: the fire and the chandelier were not sufficient company for me; nor would Pilot have been, for none of these can talk. Adèle is a degree better, but still far below the mark; Mrs. Fairfax ditto; you, I am persuaded, can suit me if you will: you puzzled me the first evening I invited you down here. I have almost forgotten you since: other ideas have driven yours from my head; but tonight I am resolved to be at ease; to dismiss what importunes, and recall what pleases. It would please me now to draw you out—to learn more of you—therefore speak."

Instead of speaking, I smiled; and not a very complacent or submissive smile either.

"Speak," he urged.

"What about, sir?"

"Whatever you like. I leave both the choice of subject and the manner of treating it entirely to yourself."

Accordingly I sat and said nothing: "If he expects me to talk for the mere sake of talking and showing off, he will find he has addressed himself to the wrong person," I thought.

"You are dumb, Miss Eyre."

I was dumb still. He bent his head a little towards me, and with a single hasty glance seemed to dive into my eyes.

"Stubborn?" he said, "and annoyed. Ah, it is consistent. I put my request in an absurd, almost insolent form. Miss Eyre, I beg your pardon. The fact is, once for all, I don't wish to treat you like an inferior: that is (correcting himself), I claim only such superiority as must result from twenty years' difference in age and a century's advance in experience. This is legitimate, et j'y tiens,[2] as Adèle would say; and it is by virtue of this superiority and this alone that I desire you to have the goodness to talk to me a little now, and divert my thoughts, which are galled with dwelling on one point—cankering as a rusty nail."

2. And I accept it

He had deigned an explanation; almost an apology: I did not feel insensible to his condescension, and would not seem so.

"I am willing to amuse you if I can, sir: quite willing; but I cannot introduce a topic, because how do I know what will interest you? Ask me questions, and I will do my best to answer them."

"Then, in the first place, do you agree with me that I have a right to be a little masterful, abrupt; perhaps exacting, sometimes, on the grounds I stated; namely, that I am old enough to be your father, and that I have battled through a varied experience with many men of many nations, and roamed over half the globe, while you have lived quietly with one set of people in one house?"

"Do as you please, sir."

"That is no answer; or rather it is a very irritating, because a very evasive one; reply clearly."

"I don't think, sir, you have a right to command me merely because you are older than I, or because you have seen more of the world than I have; your claim to superiority depends on the use you have made of your time and experience."

"Humph! Promptly spoken. But I won't allow that, seeing that it would never suit my case; as I have made an indifferent, not to say a bad, use of both advantages. Leaving superiority out of the question, then, you must still agree to receive my orders now and then, without being piqued or hurt by the tone of command—will you?"

I smiled: I thought to myself Mr. Rochester is peculiar—he seems to forget that he pays me £30 per annum for receiving his orders.

"The smile is very well," said he, catching instantly the passing expression; "but speak too."

"I was thinking, sir, that very few masters would trouble themselves to inquire whether or not their paid subordinates were piqued and hurt by their orders."

"Paid subordinates! What, you are my paid subordinate, are you? Oh, yes, I had forgotten the salary! Well, then, on that mercenary ground, will you agree to let me hector a little?"

"No, sir, not on that ground: but, on the ground that you did forget it, and that you care whether or not a dependent is comfortable in his dependency, I agree heartily."

"And will you consent to dispense with a great many conventional forms and phrases, without thinking that the omission arises from insolence?"

"I am sure, sir, I should never mistake informality for insolence: one I rather like, the other nothing free-born would submit to, even for a salary."

"Humbug! Most things free-born will submit to anything for a salary; therefore, keep to yourself, and don't venture on generalities of which you are intensely ignorant. However, I mentally shake hands with you for your answer, despite its inaccuracy; and as much for the manner in which it was said as for the substance of the speech: the manner was frank and sincere; one does not often see such a manner: no, on the contrary, affectation, or coldness, or stupid, coarse-minded misapprehension of one's meaning are the usual rewards of candor. Not three in three thousand raw school-girl governesses would have answered me as you have just done. But I don't mean to flatter you: if you are cast in a different mold to the majority, it is no merit of yours: Nature did it.

And then, after all, I go too fast in my conclusions: for what I yet know, you may be no better than the rest; you may have intolerable defects to counterbalance your few good points."

"And so may you," I thought. My eye met his as the idea crossed my mind: he seemed to read the glance, answering as if its import had been spoken as well as imagined:—

"Yes, yes, you are right," said he; "I have plenty of faults of my own: I know it, and I don't wish to palliate them, I assure you. God wot I need not be too severe about others; I have a past existence, a series of deeds, a color of life to contemplate within my own breast, which might well call my sneers and censures from my neighbors to myself. I started, or rather (for, like other defaulters, I like to lay half the blame on ill fortune and adverse circumstances) was thrust on to a wrong tack at the age of one-and-twenty, and have never recovered the right course since: but I might have been very different; I might have been as good as you—wiser, almost as stainless. I envy you your peace of mind, your clean conscience, your unpolluted memory. Little girl, a memory without blot or contamination must be an exquisite treasure—an inexhaustible source of pure refreshment: is it not?"

"How was your memory when you were eighteen, sir?"

"All right then; limpid, salubrious: no gush of bilge water had turned it to fetid puddle. I was your equal at eighteen—quite your equal. Nature meant me to be, on the whole, a good man, Miss Eyre one of the better kind; and you see I am not so. You would say you don't see it: at least I flatter myself I read as much in your eye (beware, by-the-bye, what you express with that organ, I am quick at interpreting its language). Then take my word for it,—I am not a villain: you are not to suppose that—not to attribute to me any such bad eminence; but, owing, I verily believe, rather to circumstances than to my natural bent, I am a trite commonplace sinner, hackneyed in all the poor petty dissipations with which the rich and worthless try to put on life. Do you wonder that I avow this to you? Know, that in the course of your future life you will often find yourself elected the involuntary confidant of your acquaintances' secrets: people will instinctively find out, as I have done, that it is not your forte to tell of yourself, but to listen while others talk of themselves; they will feel, too, that you listen with no malevolent scorn of their indiscretion, but with a kind of innate sympathy; not the less comforting and encouraging because it is very unobstrusive in its manifestations."

"How do you know?—how can you guess all this, sir?"

"I know it well; therefore I proceed almost as freely as if I were writing my thoughts in a diary. You would say, I should have been superior to circumstances; so I should—so I should; but you see I was not. When fate wronged me, I had not the wisdom to remain cool: I turned desperate; then I degenerated. Now, when any vicious simpleton excites my disgust by his paltry ribaldry, I cannot flatter myself that I am better than he: I am forced to confess that he and I are on a level. I wish I had stood firm—God knows I do! Dread remorse when you are tempted to err, Miss Eyre: remorse is the poison of life."

"Repentance is said to be its cure, sir."

"It is not its cure. Reformation may be its cure; and I could reform—I have strength yet for that—if—but where is the use of thinking of it, hampered, burdened, cursed as I am? Besides, since happiness is irrevocably denied me, I have a right to get pleasure out of life: and I will get it, cost what it may."

"Then you will degenerate still more, sir."

"Possibly: yet why should I, if I can get sweet, fresh pleasure? And I may get it as sweet and fresh as the wild honey the bee gatherers on the moor."

"It will sting—it will taste bitter, sir."

"How do you know?—you never tried it. How very serious—how very solemn you look: and you are as ignorant of the matter as this cameo head" (taking one from the mantelpiece). "You have no right to preach to me, you neophyte, that have not passed the porch of life, and are absolutely unacquainted with its mysteries."

"I only remind you of your own words, sir: you said error brought remorse, and you pronounced remorse the poison of existence."

"And who talks of error now? I scarcely think the notion that flitted across my brain was an error. I believe it was an inspiration rather than a temptation: it was very genial, very soothing,—I know that. Here it comes again! It is no devil, I assure you; or if it be, it has put on the robes of an angel of light. I think I must admit so fair a guest when it asks entrance to my heart."

"Distrust it, sir, it is not a true angel."

"Once more, how do you know? By what instinct do you pretend to distinguish between a fallen seraph of the abyss and a messenger from the eternal throne—between a guide and a seducer?"

"I judged by your countenance, sir; which was troubled: when you said the suggestion had returned upon you. I feel sure it will work you more misery if you listen to it."

"Not at all—it bears the most gracious message in the world: for the rest, you are not my conscience-keeper, so don't make yourself uneasy. Here, come in, bonny wanderer!"

He said this as if he spoke to a vision, viewless to any eye but his own; then, folding his arms, which he had half extended, on his chest, he seemed to enclose in their embrace the invisible being.

"Now," he continued, again addressing me, "I have received the pilgrim—a disguised deity, as I verily believe. Already it has done me good: my heart was a sort of charnel; it will now be a shrine."

"To speak truth, sir, I don't understand you at all: I cannot keep up the conversation, because it has got out of my depth. Only one thing I know: you said you were not as good as you should like to be, and that you regretted your own imperfection;—one thing I can comprehend: you intimated that to have a sullied memory was a perpetual bane. It seems to me, that if you tried hard, you would in time find it possible to become what you yourself would approve; and that if from this day you began with resolution to correct your thoughts and actions, you would in a few years have laid up a new and stainless store of recollections, to which you might revert with pleasure."

"Justly thought; rightly said, Miss Eyre; and, at this moment, I am paving hell with energy."

"Sir?"

"I am laying down good intentions, which I believe durable as flint. Certainly, my associates and pursuits shall be other than they have been."

"And better?"

"And better—so much better as pure ore is than foul dross. You seem to doubt me; I don't doubt myself: I know what my aim is, what my motives are;

and at this moment I pass a law, unalterable as that of the Medes and Persians,[3] that both are right."

"They cannot be, sir, if they require a new statute to legalize them."

"They are, Miss Eyre, though they absolutely require a new statute; unheard-of combinations of circumstances demand unheard-of-rules."

"That sounds a dangerous maxim, sir; because one can see at once that it is liable to abuse."

"Sententious sage! so it is: but I swear by my household gods not to abuse it."

"You are human and fallible."

"I am: so are you—what then?"

"The human and fallible should not arrogate a power with which the divine and perfect alone can be safely entrusted."

"What power?"

"That of saying of any strange, unsanctioned line of action,—'Let it be right.'"

" 'Let it be right'—the very words: you have pronounced them."

"*May* it be right then." I said, as I rose, deeming it useless to continue a discourse which was all darkness to me; and, besides, sensible that the character of my interlocutor was beyond my penetration; at least, beyond its present reach; and feeling the uncertainty, the vague sense of insecurity, which accompanies a conviction of ignorance.

"Where are you going?"

"To put Adèle to bed: it is past her bedtime."

"You are afraid of me, because I talk like a Sphinx."[4]

"Your language is enigmatical, sir: but though I am bewildered, I am certainly not afraid."

"You *are* afraid—your self-love dreads a blunder."

"In that sense I do feel apprehensive—I have no wish to talk nonsense."

"If you did, it would be in such a grave, quiet manner, I should mistake it for sense. Do you never laugh, Miss Eyre? Don't trouble yourself to answer—I see, you laugh rarely; but you can laugh very merrily: believe me, you are not naturally austere, any more than I am naturally vicious. The Lowood constraint still clings to you somewhat; controlling your features, muffling your voice, and restricting your limbs; and you fear in the presence of a man and a brother—or father, or master, or what you will—to smile too gaily, speak too freely, or move too quickly: but, in time, I think you will learn to be natural with me, as I find it impossible to be conventional with you; and then your looks and movements will have more vivacity and variety than they dare offer now. I see at intervals the glance of a curious sort of bird through the close-set bars of a cage; a vivid, restless, resolute captive is there; were it but free, it would soar cloud-high. You are still bent on going?"

"It has struck nine, sir."

"Never mind,—wait a minute: Adèle is not ready to go to bed yet. My position, Miss Eyre, with my back to the fire, and my face to the room, favors observation. While talking to you, I have also occasionally watched Adèle; (I

3. Two peoples noted for the strictness of their nations' legislative procedures.

4. I.e., one who speaks in riddles, like the mythical Greek monster.

have my own reasons for thinking her a curious study,—reasons that I may, nay that I shall, impart to you some day;) she pulled out of her box, about ten minutes ago, a little pink silk frock; rapture lit her face as she unfolded it; coquetry runs in her blood, blends with her brains, and seasons the marrow of her bones. 'Il faut que je l'essaie,' cried she; 'et à l'instant même!'[5] and she rushed out of the room. She is now with Sophie, undergoing a robing process: in a few minutes she will reenter; and I know what I shall see,—a miniature of Céline Varens, as she used to appear on the boards at the rising of——: but never mind that. However, my tenderest feelings are about to receive a shock: such is my presentiment; stay now, to see whether it will be realized."

Ere long Adèle's little foot was heard tripping across the hall. She entered, transformed as her guardian had predicted. A dress of rose-colored satin, very short, and as full in the skirt as it could be gathered, replaced the brown frock she had previously worn; a wreath of rosebuds circled her forehead; her feet were dressed in silk stockings and small white satin sandals.

"Est-ce que ma robe va bien?" cried she, bounding forwards; "et mes souliers? et mes bas? Tenez, je croix que je vais danser."[6]

And spreading out her dress, she chasséed across the room; till, having reached Mr. Rochester, she wheeled lightly round before him on tiptoe, then dropped on one knee at his feet, exclaiming:—

"Monsieur, je vous remercie mille fois de votre bonté"; then rising, she added, "C'est comme cela que maman faisait, n'est-ce pas, monsieur?"[7]

"Pre-cise-ly!" was the answer; "and, 'comme cela,'[8] she charmed my English gold out of my British breeches pocket. I have been green, too, Miss Eyre,—ay, grass green: not a more vernal tint freshens you now than once freshened me. My Spring is gone, however: but it has left me that French floweret on my hands; which, in some moods, I would fain be rid of. Not valuing now the root whence it sprang; having found that it was of a sort which nothing but gold dust could manure, I have but half a liking to the blossom: especially when it looks so artificial as just now. I keep it and rear it rather on the Roman Catholic principle of expiating numerous sins, great or small, by one good work. I'll explain all this some day. Good-night."

Chapter XV

Mr. Rochester did, on a future occasion, explain it.

It was one afternoon, when he chanced to meet me and Adèle in the grounds; and while she played with Pilot and her shuttlecock, he asked me to walk up and down a long beech avenue within sight of her.

He then said that she was the daughter of a French opera-dancer, Céline Varens, towards whom he had once cherished what he called a "grande passion."[9] This passion Céline had professed to return with even superior ardor. He thought himself her idol; ugly as he was: he believed, as he said, that she preferred his "taille d'athlète" to the elegance of the Apollo Belvidere.[1]

"And, Miss Eyre, so much was I flattered by this preference of the Gallic sylph for her British gnome, that I installed her in an hotel; gave her a com-

5. I must try it, . . . and this very instant!
6. Is my dress all right? . . . and my shoes? and my stockings? Wait, I think I'm going to dance.
7. Sir, I thank you a thousand times for your goodness; . . . It's just as Mamma used to do it, isn't it, sir?
8. Like that.
9. Great passion.
1. A famous statue of Apollo is housed in the Belvedere wing of the Vatican. "Taille d'athlète": athletic figure.

plete establishment of servants, a carriage, cashmeres, diamonds, dentelles, etc. In short, I began the process of ruining myself in the received style, like any other spoony.[2] I had not it seems, the originality to chalk out a new road to shame and destruction, but trod the old track with stupid exactness not to deviate an inch from the beaten center. I had—as I deserved to have—the fate of all other spoonies. Happening to call one evening when Céline did not expect me, I found her out; but it was a warm night, and I was tired with strolling through Paris, so I sat down in her boudoir; happy to breathe the air consecrated so lately by her presence. No,—I exaggerate; I never thought there was any consecrating virtue about her: it was rather a sort of pastille perfume she had left, a scent of musk and amber, than an odor of sanctity. I was just beginning to stifle with the fumes of conservatory flowers and sprinkled essences, when I bethought myself to open the window and step out on to the balcony. It was moonlight and gas-light besides, and very still and serene. The balcony was furnished with a chair or two; I sat down, took out a cigar,—I will take one now, if you will excuse me."

Here ensued a pause, filled up by the producing and lighting of a cigar; having placed it to his lips and breathed a trail of Havannah incense on the freezing and sunless air, he went on:—

"I liked bonbons too, in those days, Miss Eyre, and I was *croquant*—overlook the barbarism—*croquant t*[3] chocolate comfits, and smoking alternately, watching meantime the equipages that rolled along the fashionable streets towards the neighboring opera-house, when in an elegant close carriage drawn by a beautiful pair of English horses, and distinctly seen in the brilliant city-night, I recognized the 'voiture'[4] I had given Céline. She was returning: of course my heart thumped with impatience against the iron rails I leaned upon. The carriage stopped, as I had expected, at the hotel door; my flame (that is the very word for an opera inamorata[5] alighted: though muffled in a cloak—an unnecessary encumbrance, by-the-bye, on so warm a June evening—I knew her instantly by her little foot, seen peeping from the skirt of her dress, as she skipped from the carriage-step. Bending over the balcony, I was about to murmur, 'Mon ange'[6]—in a tone, of course, which should be audible to the ear of love alone—when a figure jumped from the carriage after her; cloaked also; but that was a spurred heel which had rung on the pavement, and that was a hatted head which now passed under the arched *porte-cochère* of the hotel.

"You never felt jealousy, did you, Miss Eyre? Of course not: I need not ask you: because you never felt love. You have both sentiments yet to experience: your soul sleeps; the shock is yet to be given which shall waken it. You think all existence lapses in as quiet a flow as that in which your youth has hitherto slid away. Floating on with closed eyes and muffled ears, you neither see the rocks bristling not far off in the bed of the flood, nor hear the breakers boil at their base. But I tell you—and you may mark my words—you will come some day to a craggy pass of the channel, where the whole of life's stream will be broken up into whirl and tumult, foam and noise: either you will be dashed to atoms on

2. Fool. "Dentelles": laces.
3. Crunching. Rochester's "barbarism" may be his use of an English grammatical construction with a French verb.
4. Carriage
5. Beloved woman.
6. My angel.

crag points, or lifted up and borne on by some master wave into a calmer cur-
rent—as I am now.

"I like this day: I like that sky of steel; I like the sternness and stillness of the
world under this frost. I like Thornfield: its antiquity; its retirement; its old
crow-trees and thorn-trees; its gray façade, and lines of dark windows reflect-
ing that metal welkin: and yet how long have I abhorred the very thought of it;
shunned it like a great plague-house! How I do still abhor——"

He ground his teeth and was silent: he arrested his step and struck his boot
against the hard ground. Some hated thought seemed to have him in its grip,
and to hold him so tightly that he could not advance.

We were ascending the avenue when he thus paused; the hall was before us.
Lifting his eye to its battlements, he cast over them a glare such as I never saw
before or since. Pain, shame, ire—impatience, disgust, detestation—seemed
momentarily to hold a quivering conflict in the large pupil dilating under his
ebon eyebrow. Wild was the wrestle which should be paramount; but another
feeling rose and triumphed: something hard and cynical; self-willed and res-
olute: it settled his passion and petrified his countenance: he went on:—
"During the moment I was silent, Miss Eyre, I was arranging a point with my
destiny. She stood there, by that beech-trunk—a hag like one of those who ap-
peared to 'Macbeth' on the heath of Forres. 'You like Thornfield?' she said, lift-
ing her finger; and then she wrote in the air a memento, which ran in lurid
hieroglyphics all along the house-front, between the upper and lower row of
windows. 'Like it if you can! Like it if you dare!'

"'I will like it,' said I. 'I dare like it'; and (he subjoined moodily) I will keep
my word: I will break obstacles to happiness, to goodness—yes, goodness; I
wish to be a better man than I have been; than I am—as Job's leviathan broke
the spear, the dart and the habergeon, hindrances which others count as iron
and brass I will esteem but straw and rotten wood."[7]

Adèle here ran before him with her shuttlecock. "Away!" he cried harshly;
"keep at a distance, child; or go in to Sophie!" Continuing then to pursue his
walk in silence, I ventured to recall him to the point whence he had abruptly
diverged:—"Did you leave the balcony, sir," I asked, "when Mdlle. Varens en-
tered?"

I almost expected a rebuff for this hardly well-timed question: but, on the
contrary, waking out of his scowling abstraction, he turned his eyes towards
me, and the shade seemed to clear off his brow. "Oh, I had forgotten Céline!
Well, to resume. When I saw my charmer thus come in accompanied by a
cavalier, I seemed to hear a hiss, and the green snake of jealousy, rising on un-
dulating coils from the moonlit balcony, glided within my waistcoat, and ate
its way in two minutes to my heart's core. Strange!" he exclaimed, suddenly
starting again from the point. "Strange that I should choose you for the confi-
dant of all this, young lady: passing strange that you should listen to me qui-
etly, as if it were the most usual thing in the world for a man like me to tell
stories of his opera-mistresses to a quaint, inexperienced girl like you! But the
last singularity explains the first, as I intimated once before: you, with your
gravity, considerateness, and caution, were made to be the recipient of secrets.
Besides, I know what sort of a mind I have placed in communication with my
own: I know it is one not liable to take infection: it is a peculiar mind; it is an

7. Job 41:26–27.

unique one. Happily I do not mean to harm it: but, if I did, it would not take harm from me. The more you and I converse, the better; for while I cannot blight you, you may refresh me." After this digression, he proceeded:—"I remained in the balcony. 'They will come to her boudoir, no doubt,' thought I: 'let me prepare an ambush.' So putting my hand in through the open window, I drew the curtain over it, leaving only an opening through which I could take observations; then I closed the casement, all but a chink just wide enough to furnish an outlet to lovers' whispered vows: then I stole back to my chair; and as I resumed it the pair came in. My eye was quickly at the aperture. Céline's chambermaid entered, lit a lamp, left it on the table, and withdrew. The couple were thus revealed to me clearly: both removed their cloaks, and there was 'the Varens'[8] shining in satin and jewels,—my gifts of course,—and there was her companion in an officer's uniform; and I knew him for a young roué of a vicomte[9]—a brainless and vicious youth whom I had sometimes met in society, and had never thought of hating because I despised him so absolutely. On recognizing him, the fang of the snake, jealousy, was instantly broken; because at the same moment my love for Céline sank under an extinguisher. A woman who could betray me for such a rival was not worth contending for: she deserved only scorn; less, however, than I, who had been her dupe.

"They began to talk; their conversation eased me completely: frivolous, mercenary, heartless, and senseless, it was rather calculated to weary than enrage a listener. A card of mine lay on the table; this being perceived, brought my name under discussion. Neither of them possessed energy or wit to belabor me soundly; but they insulted me as coarsely as they could in their little way: especially Céline; who even waxed rather brilliant on my personal defects—deformities she termed them. Now it had been her custom to launch out into fervent admiration of what she called my 'beauté mâle':[1] wherein she differed diametrically from you, who told me point-blank, at the second interview, that you did not think me handsome. The contrast struck me at the time, and—"

Adèle here came running up again.

"Monsieur, John has just been to say that your agent has called and wishes to see you."

"Ah! in that case I must abridge. Opening the window, I walked in upon them; liberated Céline from my protection; gave her notice to vacate her hotel; offered her a purse for immediate exigencies; disregarded screams, hysterics, prayers, protestations, convulsions; made an appointment with the vicomte for a meeting at the Bois de Boulogne. Next morning I had the pleasure of encountering him; left a bullet in one of his poor etiolated arms, feeble as the wing of a chicken in the pip, and then thought I had done with the whole crew. But unluckily the Varens, six months before, had given me this filette[2] Adèle; who she affirmed was my daughter; and perhaps she may be, though I see no proofs of such grim paternity written in her countenance. Pilot is more like me than she. Some years after I had broken with the mother she abandoned her child and ran away to Italy with a musician or singer. I acknowledged no natural claim on Adèle's part to be supported by me; nor do I now

8. Literal translation of the French 'la Varens": a common Gallic idiom for identifying a well-known female stage performer was to use her last name, preceded by "la."

9. Viscount: a nobleman.
1. Masculine beauty.
2. Little girl.

acknowledge any, for I am not her father; but hearing that she was quite destitute, I e'en took the poor thing out of the slime and mud of Paris, and transplanted it here, to grow up clean in the wholesome soil of an English country garden. Mrs. Fairfax found you to train it; but now you know that it is the illegitimate offspring of a French opera-girl, you will perhaps think differently of your post and protégée. You will be coming to me some day with notice that you have found another place—that you beg me to look out for a new governess, etc.—eh?"

"No. Adèle is not answerable for either her mother's faults or yours. I have a regard for her, and now that I know she is, in a sense, parentless—forsaken by her mother and disowned by you, sir—I shall cling closer to her than before. How could I possibly prefer the spoilt pet of a wealthy family, who would hate her governess as a nuisance, to a lonely little orphan, who leans towards her as a friend?"

"Oh, that is the light in which you view it! Well, I must go in now; and you too: it darkens."

But I stayed out a few minutes longer with Adgele and Pilot—ran a race with her, and played a game of battledore and shuttlecock.[3] When we went in, and I had removed her bonnet and coat, I took her on my knee; kept her there an hour, allowing her to prattle as she liked, not rebuking even some little freedoms and trivialities into which she was apt to stray when much noticed; and which betrayed in her a superficiality of character, inherited probably from her mother, hardly congenial to an English mind. Still she had her merits; and I was disposed to appreciate all that was good in her to the utmost. I sought in her countenance and features a likeness to Mr. Rochester, but found none—no trait, no turn of expression announced relationship. It was a pity: if she could but have been proved to resemble him, he would have thought more of her.

It was not till after I had withdrawn to my own chamber for the night that I steadily reviewed the tale Mr. Rochester had told me. As he had said, there was probably nothing at all extraordinary in the substance of the narrative itself—a wealthy Englishman's passion for a French dancer, and her treachery to him, were everyday matters enough, no doubt, in society—but there was something decidedly strange in the paroxysm of emotion which had suddenly seized him, when he was in the act of expressing the present contentment of his mood, and his newly-revived pleasure in the old hall and its environs. I meditated wonderingly on this incident: but gradually quitting it, as I found it for the present inexplicable, I turned to the consideration of my master's manner to myself. The confidence he had thought fit to repose in me seemed a tribute to my discretion. I regarded and accepted it as such. His deportment had now for some weeks been more uniform towards me than at the first. I never seemed in his way; he did not take fits of chilling hauteur; when he met me unexpectedly, the encounter seemed welcome—he had always a word and sometimes a smile for me; when summoned by formal invitation to his presence, I was honored by a cordiality of reception that made me feel I really possessed the power to amuse him, and that these evening conferences were sought as much for his pleasure as for my benefit.

I, indeed, talked comparatively little; but I heard him talk with relish. It was

3. Badminton.

his nature to be communicative—he liked to open to a mind unacquainted with the world glimpses of its scenes and ways (I do not mean its corrupt scenes and wicked ways, but such as derived their interest from the great scale on which they were acted, the strange novelty by which they were characterised); and I had a keen delight in receiving the new ideas he offered, in imagining the new pictures he portrayed, and following him in thought through the new regions he disclosed, never startled or troubled by one noxious allusion.

The ease of his manner freed me from painful restraint; the friendly frankness, as correct as cordial, with which he treated me, drew me to him. I felt at times as if he were my relation, rather than my master: yet he was imperious sometimes still; but I did not mind that; I saw it was his way. So happy, so gratified did I become with this new interest added to life, that I ceased to pine after kindred. My thin crescent-destiny seemed to enlarge; the blanks of existence were filled up; my bodily health improved; I gathered flesh and strength.

And was Mr. Rochester now ugly in my eyes? No, reader. Gratitude, and many associations, all pleasurable and genial, made his face the object I best liked to see; his presence in a room was more cheering than the brightest fire. Yet I had not forgotten his faults—indeed, I could not, for he brought them frequently before me. He was proud, sardonic, harsh to inferiority of every description. In my secret soul I knew that his great kindness to me was balanced by unjust severity to many others. He was moody, too—unaccountably so. I more than once, when sent for to read to him, found him sitting in his library alone, with his head bent on his folded arms; and, when he looked up, a morose, almost a malignant scowl, blackened his features. But I believed that his moodiness, his harshness, and his former faults of morality (I say *former*, for now he seemed corrected of them) had their source in some cruel cross of fate. I believed he was naturally a man of better tendencies, higher principles, and purer tastes than such as circumstances had developed, education instilled, or destiny encouraged. I thought there were excellent materials in him; though for the present they hung together somewhat spoiled and tangled. I cannot deny that I grieved for his grief, whatever that was, and would have given much to assuage it.

Though I had now extinguished my candle and was laid down in bed, I could not sleep for thinking of his look when he paused in the avenue, and told how his destiny had risen up before him, and dared him to be happy at Thornfield.

"Why not?" I asked myself. "What alienates him from the house? Will he leave it again soon? Mrs. Fairfax said he seldom stayed here longer than a fortnight at a time, and he has now been resident eight weeks. If he does go, the change will be doleful. Suppose he should be absent spring, summer, and autumn: how joyless sunshine and fine days will seem."

I hardly know whether I had slept or not after this musing; at any rate, I started wide awake on hearing a vague murmur, peculiar and lugubrious, which sounded, I thought, just above me. I wished I had kept my candle burning: the night was drearily dark; my spirits were depressed. I rose and sat up in bed, listening. The sound was hushed.

I tried again to sleep; but my heart beat anxiously: my inward tranquillity was broken. The clock, far down in the hall, struck two. Just then it seemed my chamber-door was touched; as if fingers had swept the panels in groping a way

along the dark gallery outside. I said, "Who is there?" Nothing answered. I was chilled with fear.

All at once I remembered that it might be Pilot: who, when the kitchen-door chanced to be left open, not unfrequently found his way up to the threshold of Mr. Rochester's chamber: I had seen him lying there myself, in the mornings. The idea calmed me somewhat: I lay down. Silence composes the nerves; and as an unbroken hush now reigned again through the whole house, I began to feel the return of slumber. But it was not fated that I should sleep that night. A dream had scarcely approached my ear, when it fled affrighted, scared by a marrow-freezing incident enough.

This was a demoniac laugh—low, suppressed, and deep—uttered, as it seemed, at the very key-hole of my chamber-door. The head of my bed was near the door, and I thought at first the goblin-laughter stood at my bedside—or rather, crouched by my pillow: but I rose, looked round, and could see nothing; while, as I still gazed, the unnatural sound was reiterated: and I knew it came from behind the panels. My first impulse was to rise and fasten the bolt; my next again, to cry out, "Who is there?"

Something gurgled and moaned. Ere long, steps retreated up the gallery towards the third story staircase: a door had lately been made to shut in that staircase; I heard it open and close, and all was still.

"Was that Grace Poole? and is she possessed with a devil?" thought I. Impossible now to remain longer by myself: I must go to Mrs. Fairfax. I hurried on my frock and a shawl; I withdrew the bolt, and opened the door with a trembling hand. There was a candle burning just outside, left on the matting in the gallery. I was surprised at this circumstance: but still more was I amazed to perceive the air quite dim, as if filled with smoke; and, while looking to the right hand and left, to find whence these blue wreaths issued, I became further aware of a strong smell of burning.

Something creaked: it was a door ajar; and that door was Mr. Rochester's, and the smoke rushed in a cloud from thence. I thought no more of Mrs. Fairfax; I thought no more of Grace Poole or the laugh: in an instant, I was within the chamber. Tongues of flame darted round the bed: the curtains were on fire. In the midst of blaze and vapor, Mr. Rochester lay stretched motionless, in deep sleep.

"Wake! wake!" I cried—I shook him, but he only murmured and turned: the smoke had stupefied him. Not a moment could be lost: the very sheets were kindling. I rushed to his basin and ewer; fortunately, one was wide and the other deep, and both were filled with water. I heaved them up, deluged the bed and its occupant, flew back to my own room, brought my own water-jug, baptized the couch afresh, and, by God's aid, succeeded in extinguishing the flames which were devouring it.

The hiss of the quenched element, the breakage of a pitcher which I flung from my hand when I had emptied it, and, above all, the splash of the shower-bath I had liberally bestowed, roused Mr. Rochester at last. Though it was now dark, I knew he was awake; because I heard him fulminating strange anathemas[4] at finding himself lying in a pool of water.

"Is there a flood?" he cried.

"No, sir," I answered; "but there has been a fire: get up, do, you are quenched now; I will fetch you a candle."

4. Curses.

"In the name of all the elves in Christendom, is that Jane Eyre?" he demanded. "What have you done with me, witch, sorceress? Who is in the room beside you? Have you plotted to drown me?"

"I will fetch you a candle, sir; and, in Heaven's name, get up. Somebody has plotted something: you cannot too soon find out who and what it is."

"There—I am up now; but at your peril you fetch a candle yet: wait two minutes till I get into some dry garments, if any dry there be—yes, here is my dressing-gown. Now run!"

I did run; I brought the candle which still remained in the gallery. He took it from my hand, held it up, and surveyed the bed, all blackened and scorched, the sheets drenched, the carpet round swimming in water.

"What is it? and who did it?" he asked.

I briefly related to him what had transpired: the strange laugh I had heard in the gallery: the step ascending to the third story; the smoke,—the smell of fire which had conducted me to his room; in what state I had found matters there, and how I had deluged him with all the water I could lay hands on.

He listened very gravely; his face, as I went on, expressed more concern than astonishment; he did not immediately speak when I had concluded.

"Shall I call Mrs. Fairfax?" I asked.

"Mrs. Fairfax? No: what the deuce would you call her for? What can she do? Let her sleep unmolested."

"Then I will fetch Leah, and wake John and his wife."

"Not at all: just be still. You have a shawl on? If you are not warm enough, you may take my cloak yonder; wrap it about you, and sit down in the arm-chair: there,—I will put it on. Now place your feet on the stool, to keep them out of the wet. I am going to leave you a few minutes. I shall take the candle. Remain where you are till I return: be as still as a mouse. I must pay a visit to the third story. Don't move, remember, or call any one."

He went: I watched the light withdraw. He passed up the gallery very softly, unclosed the staircase door with as little noise as possible, shut it after him, and the last ray vanished. I was left in total darkness. I listened for some noise, but heard nothing. A very long time elapsed. I grew weary: it was cold, in spite of the cloak; and then I did not see the use of staying, as I was not to rouse the house. I was on the point of risking Mr. Rochester's displeasure, by disobeying his orders, when the light once more gleamed dimly on the gallery-wall, and I heard his unshod feet tread the matting. "I hope it is he," thought I, "and not something worse."

He reentered, pale and very gloomy. 'I have found it all out,' said he, setting his candle down on the wash-stand; "it is as I thought."

"How, sir?"

He made no reply, but stood with his arms folded, looking on the ground. At the end of a few minutes, he inquired in rather a peculiar tone:—"I forget whether you said you saw anything when you opened your chamber door."

"No, sir, only the candlestick on the ground."

"But you heard an odd laugh? You have heard that laugh before, I should think, or something like it?"

"Yes, sir: there is a woman who sews here, called Grace Poole—she laughs in that way. She is a singular person."

"Just so. Grace Poole—you have guessed it. She is, as you say, singular,—very. Well, I shall reflect on the subject. Meantime, I am glad that you are the only person, besides myself, acquainted with the precise details of tonight's

incident. You are no talking fool: say nothing about it. I will account for this state of affairs (pointing to the bed): and now return to your own room. I shall do very well on the sofa in the library for the rest of the night. It is near four:— in two hours the servants will be up."

"Good-night, then, sir," said I, departing.

He seemed surprised—very inconsistently so, as he had just told me to go.

"What!" he exclaimed, "are you quitting me already: and in that way?"

"You said I might go, sir."

"But not without taking leave; not without a word or two of acknowledgment and good will: not, in short, in that brief, dry fashion. Why, you have saved my life!—snatched me from a horrible and excruciating death!—and you walk past me as if we were mutual strangers! At least shake hands."

He held out his hand; I gave him mine: he took it first in one, then in both his own.

"You have saved my life: I have a pleasure in owing you so immense a debt. I cannot say more. Nothing else that has being would have been tolerable to me in the character of creditor for such an obligation: but you: it is different;—I feel your benefits no burden, Jane."

He paused; gazed at me: words almost visible trembled on his lips,—but his voice was checked.

"Good night again, sir. There is no debt, benefit, burden, obligation, in the case."

"I knew," he continued, "you would do me good in some way, at some time;—I saw it in your eyes when I first beheld you: their expression and smile did not—(again he stopped)—did not (he proceeded hastily) strike delight to my very inmost heart so for nothing. People talk of natural sympathies; I have heard of good genii—there are grains of truth in the wildest fable. My cherished preserver, good night!"

Strange energy was in his voice, strange fire in his look.

"I am glad I happened to be awake," I said; and then I was going.

"What! you *will* go?"

"I am cold, sir."

"Cold? Yes,—and standing in a pool! Go, then, Jane; go!" But he still retained my hand, and I could not free it. I bethought myself of an expedient.

"I think I hear Mrs. Fairfax move, sir," said I.

"Well, leave me." He relaxed his fingers, and I was gone.

I regained my couch, but never thought of sleep. Till morning dawned I was tossed on a buoyant but unquiet sea, where billows of trouble rolled under surges of joy. I thought sometimes I saw beyond its wild waters a shore, sweet as the hills of Beulah;[5] and now and then a freshening gale wakened by hope, bore my spirit triumphantly towards the bourne; but I could not reach it, even in fancy,—a counteracting breeze blew off land, and continually drove me back. Sense would resist delirium, judgment would warn passion. Too feverish to rest, I rose as soon as day dawned.

Chapter XVI

I both wished and feared to see Mr. Rochester on the day which followed this sleepless night. I wanted to hear his voice again, yet feared to meet his eye.

5. Name (meaning "married") given to the Jews' land restored after their exile in Babylon (Isaiah 62:4).

During the early part of the morning, I momentarily expected his coming. He was not in the frequent habit of entering the schoolroom; but he did step in for a few minutes sometimes, and I had the impression that he was sure to visit it that day.

But the morning passed just as usual. Nothing happened to interrupt the quiet course of Adèle's studies; only, soon after breakfast, I heard some bustle in the neighborhood of Mr. Rochester's chamber, Mrs. Fairfax's voice, and Leah's, and the cook's—that is, John's wife—and even John's own gruff tones. There were exclamations of, "What a mercy master was not burned in his bed!" "It is always dangerous to keep a candle lit at night." "How providential that he had presence of mind to think of the water-jug!" "I wonder he waked nobody!" "It is to be hoped he will not take cold with sleeping on the library sofa," etc.

To much confabulation succeeded a sound of scrubbing and setting to rights; and when I passed the room, in going downstairs to dinner, I saw through the open door that all was again restored to complete order—only the bed was stripped of its hangings. Leah stood up in the window-seat, rubbing the panes of glass dimmed with smoke. I was about to address her, for I wished to know what account had been given of the affair; but, on advancing, I saw a second person in the chamber—a woman sitting on a chair by the bedside, and sewing rings to new curtains. That woman was no other than Grace Poole.

There she sat, staid and taciturn-looking, as usual, in her brown stuff gown, her check apron, white handkerchief, and cap. She was intent on her work, in which her whole thoughts seemed absorbed. On her hard forehead, and in her commonplace features, was nothing either of the paleness or desperation one would have expected to see marking the countenance of a woman who had attempted murder, and whose intended victim had followed her last night to her lair, and (as I believed) charged her with the crime she wished to perpetrate. I was amazed—confounded. She looked up, while I still gazed at her: no start, no increase or failure of color betrayed emotion, consciousness of guilt, or fear of detection. She said, "Good morning, Miss," in her usual phlegmatic and brief manner; and taking up another ring and more tape, went on with her sewing.

"I will put her to some test," thought I. "Such absolute impenetrability is past comprehension."

"Good morning, Grace," I said. "Has anything happened here? I thought I heard the servants all talking together a while ago."

"Only master had been reading in his bed last night. He fell asleep with his candle lit, and the curtains got on fire; but, fortunately, he awoke before the bed-clothes or the wood-work caught, and contrived to quench the flame with the water in the ewer."

"A strange affair!" I said, in a low voice; then, looking at her fixedly, "Did Mr. Rochester wake nobody? Did no one hear him move?"

She again raised her eyes to me; and this time there was something of consciousness in their expression. She seemed to examine me warily; then she answered, "The servants sleep so far off, you know, Miss, they would not be likely to hear. Mrs. Fairfax's room and yours are the nearest to master's; but Mrs. Fairfax said she heard nothing: when people get elderly, they often sleep heavy." She paused, and then added, with a sort of assumed indifference, but still in a marked and significant tone, "But you are young, Miss, and I should say a light sleeper. Perhaps you may have heard a noise?"

"I did," said I, dropping my voice, so that Leah, who was still polishing the panes, could not hear me, "and at first I thought it was Pilot; but Pilot cannot laugh, and I am certain I heard a laugh, and a strange one."

She took a new needleful of thread, waxed it carefully, threaded her needle with a steady hand, and then observed, with perfect composure,—"It is hardly likely master would laugh, I should think, Miss, when he was in such danger: you must have been dreaming."

"I was not dreaming," I said, with some warmth, for her brazen coolness provoked me. Again she looked at me, and with the same scrutinizing and conscious eye.

"Have you told master that you heard a laugh?" she inquired.

"I have not had the opportunity of speaking to him this morning."

"You did not think of opening your door and looking out into the gallery?" she further asked.

She appeared to be cross-questioning me—attempting to draw from me information unawares. The idea struck me that if she discovered I knew or suspected her guilt, she would be playing off some of her malignant pranks on me. I thought it advisable to be on my guard.

"On the contrary," said I, "I bolted my door."

"Then you are not in the habit of bolting your door every night before you get into bed?"

"Fiend! she wants to know my habits, that she may lay her plans accordingly!" Indignation again prevailed over prudence; I replied sharply, "Hitherto I have often omitted to fasten the bolt: I did not think it necessary. I was not aware any danger or annoyance was to be dreaded at Thornfield Hall; but in future" (and I laid marked stress on the words) "I shall take good care to make all secure before I venture to lie down."

"It will be wise so to do," was her answer. "This neighborhood is as quiet as any I know, and I never heard of the hall being attempted by robbers since it was a house though there are hundreds of pounds' worth of plate in the plate-closet, as is well known. And you see, for such a large house, there are very few servants, because master has never lived here much, and when he does come, being a bachelor, he needs little waiting on; but I always think it best to err on the safe side: a door is soon fastened, and it is as well to have a drawn bolt between one and any mischief that may be about. A deal of people, Miss, are for trusting all to Providence; but I say Providence will not dispense with the means, though He often blesses them when they are used discreetly." And here she closed her harangue: a long one for her, and uttered with the demureness of a Quakeress.

I still stood absolutely dumfounded at what appeared to me her miraculous self-possession and most inscrutable hypocrisy, when the cook entered.

"Mrs. Poole," said she, addressing Grace, "the servants' dinner will soon be ready. Will you come down?"

"No. Just put my pint of porter and bit of pudding on a tray, and I'll carry it upstairs."

"You'll have some meat?"

"Just a morsel, and a taste of cheese, that's all."

"And the sago?"[6]

6. A cereal, eaten in the West Indies, made from palm tree trunks.

"Never mind it at present. I shall be coming down before tea-time. I'll make it myself."

The cook here turned to me, saying that Mrs. Fairfax was waiting for me: so I departed.

I hardly heard Mrs. Fairfax's account of the curtain conflagration during dinner, so much was I occupied in puzzling my brains over the enigmatical character of Grace Poole, and still more in pondering the problem of her position at Thornfield; in questioning why she had not been given into custody that morning, or, at the very least, dismissed from her master's service. He had almost as much as declared his conviction of her criminality last night: what mysterious cause withheld him from accusing her? Why had he enjoined me, too, to secrecy? It was strange—a bold, vindictive, and haughty gentleman seemed somehow in the power of one of the meanest of his dependants; so much in her power, that even when she lifted her hand against his life, he dared not openly charge her with the attempt, much less punish her for it.

Had Grace been young and handsome, I should have been tempted to think that tenderer feelings than prudence or fear influenced Mr. Rochester in her behalf; but, hard-favored and matronly as she was, the idea could not be admitted. "Yet," I reflected, "she has been young once; her youth would be contemporary with her master's. Mrs. Fairfax told me once she had lived here many years. I don't think she can ever have been pretty; but, for aught I know, she may possess originality and strength of character to compensate for the want of personal advantages. Mr. Rochester is an amateur of the decided and eccentric—Grace is eccentric at least. What if a former caprice (a freak very possible to a nature so sudden and headstrong as his) has delivered him into her power, and she now exercises over his actions a secret influence, the result of his own indiscretion, which he cannot shake off, and dare not disregard?" But, having reached this point of conjecture, Mrs. Poole's square, flat figure, and uncomely, dry, even coarse face, recurred so distinctly to my mind's eye, that I thought, "No; impossible! my supposition cannot be correct. Yet," suggested the secret voice which talks to us in our own hearts, "you are not beautiful either, and perhaps Mr. Rochester approves you—at any rate, you have often felt as if he did; and last night—remember his words; remember his look; remember his voice!"

I well remembered all—language, glance, and tone seemed at the moment vividly renewed. I was now in the schoolroom. Adèle was drawing. I bent over her and directed her pencil. She looked up with a sort of start.

"Qu'avez-vous, mademoiselle?" said she; "Vos doigts tremblent comme la feuille, et vos joues sont rouges: mais, rouges comme des cerises!"[7]

"I am hot, Adèle, with stooping " She went on sketching, I went on thinking.

I hastened to drive from my mind the hateful notion I had been conceiving respecting Grace Poole: it disgusted me. I compared myself with her, and found we were different. Bessie Leaven had said I was quite a lady; and she spoke truth: I was a lady. And now I looked much better than I did when Bessie saw me: I had more color and more flesh; more life, more vivacity; because I had brighter hopes and keener enjoyments.

"Evening approaches," said I, as I looked towards the window. "I have never

7. What's wrong, miss? . . . Your fingers are trembling like a leaf, and your cheeks are red: red as cherries!

heard Mr. Rochester's voice or step in the house today; but surely I shall see him before night: I feared the meeting in the morning: now I desire it, because expectation has been so long baffled that it is grown impatient."

When dusk actually closed, and when Adèle left me to go and play in the nursery with Sophie, I did most keenly desire it. I listened for the bell to ring below; I listened for Leah coming up with a message; I fancied sometimes I heard Mr. Rochester's own tread, and I turned to the door, expecting it to open and admit him. The door remained shut: darkness only came in through the window. Still it was not late: he often sent for me at seven and eight o'clock, and it was yet but six. Surely I should not be wholly disappointed tonight, when I had so many things to say to him! I wanted again to introduce the subject of Grace Poole, and to hear what he would answer; I wanted to ask him plainly if he really believed it was she who had made last night's hideous attempt; and if so, why he kept her wickedness a secret. It little mattered whether my curiosity irritated him; I knew the pleasure of vexing and soothing him by turns; it was one I chiefly delighted in, and a sure instinct always prevented me from going too far: beyond the verge of provocation I never ventured; on the extreme brink I liked well to try my skill. Retaining every minute form of respect, every propriety of my station, I could still meet him in argument without fear or uneasy restraint: this suited both him and me.

A tread creaked on the stairs at last; Leah made her appearance, but it was only to intimate that tea was ready in Mrs. Fairfax's room. Thither I repaired, glad at least to go downstairs, for that brought me, I imagined, nearer to Mr. Rochester's presence.

"You must want your tea," said the good lady, as I joined her, "you ate so little at dinner. I am afraid," she continued, "you are not well to-day, you looked flushed and feverish."

"Oh, quite well! I never felt better."

"Then you must prove it by evincing a good appetite; will you fill the teapot while I knit off this needle?" Having completed her task, she rose to draw down the blind which she had hitherto kept up, by way, I suppose, of making the most of daylight: though dusk was now fast deepening into total obscurity.

"It is fair tonight," said she, as she looked through the panes, "though not starlight; Mr. Rochester has, on the whole, had a favorable day for his journey."

"Journey!—Is Mr. Rochester gone anywhere? I did not know he was out."

"Oh, he set off the moment he had breakfasted! He is gone to the Leas, Mr. Eshton's place, ten miles on the other side Millcote; I believe there is quite a party assembled there—Lord Ingram, Sir George Lynn, Colonel Dent, and others."

"Do you expect him back tonight?"

"No—nor tomorrow either; I should think he is very likely to stay a week or more. When these fine, fashionable people get together, they are so surrounded by elegance and gaiety, so well provided with all that can please and entertain, they are in no hurry to separate. Gentlemen, especially, are often in request on such occasions; and Mr. Rochester is so talented and so lively in society, that I believe he is a general favorite—the ladies are very fond of him—though you would not think his appearance calculated to recommend him particularly in their eyes; but I suppose his acquirements and abilities, perhaps his wealth and good blood, make amends for any little fault of looks."

"Are there ladies at the Leas?"

"There are Mrs. Eshton and her three daughters—very elegant young

ladies, indeed; and there are the Honorable Blanche and Mary Ingram—most beautiful women, I suppose: indeed, I have seen Blanche, six or seven years since, when she was a girl of eighteen. She came here to a Christmas ball and party Mr. Rochester gave. You should have seen the dining-room that day— how richly it was decorated, how brilliantly lit up! I should think there were fifty ladies and gentlemen present—all of the first county families; and Miss Ingram was considered the belle of the evening."

"You saw her, you say, Mrs. Fairfax: what was she like?"

"Yes, I saw her. The dining-room doors were thrown open, and, as it was Christmas-time, the servants were allowed to assemble in the hall, to hear some of the ladies sing and play. Mr. Rochester would have me to come in, and I sat down in a quiet corner and watched them. I never saw a more splendid scene: the ladies were magnificently dressed: most of them—at least most of the younger ones—looked handsome, but Miss Ingram was certainly the queen."

"And what was she like?"

"Tall, fine bust, sloping shoulders, long, graceful neck; olive complexion, dark and clear; noble features; eyes rather like Mr. Rochester's, large and black, and as brilliant as her jewels. And then she had such a fine head of hair, raven-black, and so becomingly arranged; a crown of thick plaits behind, and in front the longest, the glossiest curls I ever saw. She was dressed in pure white, an amber-colored scarf was passed over her shoulder and across her breast, tied at the side, and descending in long, fringed ends below her knee. She wore an amber-colored flower, too, in her hair: it contrasted well with the jetty mass of her curls."

"She was greatly admired, of course?"

"Yes, indeed, and not only for her beauty, but for her accomplishments. She was one of the ladies who sang; a gentleman accompanied her on the piano. She and Mr. Rochester sang a duet."

"Mr. Rochester? I was not aware he could sing."

"Oh! he has a fine bass voice, and an excellent taste for music."

"And Miss Ingram, what sort of a voice had she?"

"A very rich and powerful one—she sang delightfully—it was a treat to listen to her; and she played afterwards. I am no judge of music, but Mr. Rochester is, and I heard him say her execution was remarkably good."

"And this beautiful and accomplished lady is not yet married?"

"It appears not: I fancy neither she nor her sister have very large fortunes. Old Lord Ingram's estates were chiefly entailed, and the eldest son came in for everything almost."

"But I wonder no wealthy nobleman or gentleman has taken a fancy to her: Mr. Rochester, for instance. He is rich, is he not?"

"Oh! yes. But you see there is a considerable difference in age: Mr. Rochester is near forty; she is but twenty-five."

"What of that? More unequal matches are made every day."

"True: yet I should scarcely fancy Mr. Rochester would entertain an idea of the sort. But you eat nothing: you have scarcely tasted since you began tea."

"No: I am too thirsty to eat. Will you let me have another cup?"

I was about again to revert to the probability of a union between Mr. Rochester and the beautiful Blanche; but Adèle came in, and the conversation was turned into another channel.

When once more alone, I reviewed the information I had got; looked into

my heart, examined its thoughts and feelings, and endeavored to bring back with a strict hand such as had been straying through imagination's boundless and trackless waste, into the safe fold of common sense.

Arraigned at my own bar, Memory having given her evidence of the hopes, wishes, sentiments I had been cherishing since last night—of the general state of mind in which I had indulged for nearly a fortnight past; Reason having come forward and told in her own quiet way, a plain, unvarnished tale, showing how I had rejected the real, and rabidly devoured the ideal;—I pronounced judgment to this effect:—That a greater fool than Jane Eyre had never breathed the breath of life: that a more fantastic idiot had never surfeited herself on sweet lies, and swallowed poison as if it were nectar.

"You," I said, "a favorite with Mr. Rochester? You gifted with the power of pleasing him? You of importance to him in any way? Go! your folly sickens me. And you have derived pleasure from occasional tokens of preference—equivocal tokens, shown by a gentleman of family, and a man of the world, to a dependant and a novice. How dared you? Poor stupid dupe!—Could not even self-interest make you wiser? You repeated to yourself this morning the brief scene of last night?—Cover your face and be ashamed! He said something in praise of your eyes, did he? Blind puppy! Open their bleared lids and look on your own accursed senselessness! It does good to no woman to be flattered by her superior, who cannot possibly intend to marry her; and it is madness in all women to let a secret love kindle within them, which, if unreturned and unknown, must devour the life that feeds it; and, if discovered and responded to, must lead, *ignis-fatuus*-like,[8] into miry wilds, whence there is no extrication.

"Listen, then, Jane Eyre, to your sentence: tomorrow, place the glass before you, and draw in chalk your own picture, faithfully; without softening one defect: omit no harsh line, smooth away no displeasing irregularity; write under it, 'Portrait of a Governess, disconnected, poor, and plain.'

"Afterwards, take a piece of smooth ivory—you have one prepared in your drawing-box: take your palette, mix your freshest, finest, clearest tints; choose your most delicate camel-hair pencils; delineate carefully the loveliest face you can imagine; paint it in your softest shades and sweetest hues, according to the description given by Mrs. Fairfax of Blanche Ingram: remember the raven ringlets, the Oriental eye;—what! you revert to Mr. Rochester as a model! Order! No snivel!—no sentiment!—no regret! I will endure only sense and resolution. Recall the august yet harmonious lineaments, the Grecian neck and bust: let the round and dazzling arm be visible, and the delicate hand; omit neither diamond ring nor gold bracelet; portray faithfully the attire, aërial lace and glistening satin, graceful scarf and golden rose: call it 'Blanche, an accomplished lady of rank.'

"Whenever, in future, you should chance to fancy Mr. Rochester thinks well of you, take out these two pictures and compare them: say, 'Mr. Rochester might probably win that noble lady's love, if he chose to strive for it; is it likely he would waste a serious thought on this indigent and insignificant plebian?'"

"I'll do it," I resolved: and having framed this determination, I grew calm, and fell asleep.

I kept my word. An hour or two sufficed to sketch my own portrait in crayons; and in less than a fortnight I had completed an ivory miniature of an

8. Like a will-o'-the-wisp.

imaginary Blanche Ingram. It looked a lovely face enough, and when compared with the real head in chalk, the contrast was as great as self-control could desire. I derived benefit from the task: it had kept my head and hands employed, and had given force and fixedness to the new impressions I wished to stamp indelibly on my heart.

Ere long, I had reason to congratulate myself on the course of wholesome discipline to which I had thus forced my feelings to submit: thanks to it, I was able to meet subsequent occurrences with a decent calm; which, had they found me unprepared, I should probably have been unequal to maintain, even externally.

Chapter XVII

A week passed, and no news arrived of Mr. Rochester: ten days, and still he did not come. Mrs. Fairfax said she should not be surprised if he were to go straight from the Leas to London, and thence to the Continent and not show his face again at Thornfield for a year to come: he had not unfrequently quitted it in a manner quite as abrupt and unexpected. When I heard this I was beginning to feel a strange chill and failing at the heart. I was actually permitting myself to experience a sickening sense of disappointment: but rallying my wits, and recollecting my principles, I at once called my sensations to order; and it was wonderful how I got over the temporary blunder—how I cleared up the mistake of supposing Mr. Rochester's movements a matter in which I had any cause to take a vital interest. Not that I humbled myself by a slavish notion of inferiority: on the contrary, I just said—"You have nothing to do with the master of Thornfield, further than to receive the salary he gives you for teaching his protégée, and to be grateful for such respectful and kind treatment as, if you do your duty, you have a right to expect at his hands. Be sure that is the only tie he seriously acknowledges between you and him: so don't make him the object of your fine feelings, your raptures, agonies, and so forth. He is not of your order: keep to your caste, and be too self-respecting to lavish the love of the whole heart, soul, and strength, where such a gift is not wanted and would be despised."

I went on with my day's business tranquilly: but ever and anon vague suggestions kept wandering across my brain of reasons why I should quit Thornfield; and I kept involuntarily framing advertisements and pondering conjectures about new situations; these thoughts I did not think it necessary to check; they might germinate and bear fruit if they could.

Mr. Rochester had been absent upwards of a fortnight, when the post brought Mrs. Fairfax a letter.

"It is from the master," said she as she looked at the direction. "Now I suppose we shall know whether we are to expect his return or not."

And while she broke the seal and perused the document, I went on taking my coffee (we were at breakfast); it was hot, and I attributed to that circumstance a fiery glow which suddenly rose to my face. Why my hand shook, and why I involuntarily spilt half the contents of my cup into my saucer, I did not choose to consider.

"Well—I sometimes think we are too quiet: but we run a chance of being busy enough now: for a little while at least," said Mrs. Fairfax, still holding the note before her spectacles.

Ere I permitted myself to request an explanation, I tied the string of Adèle's pinafore, which happened to be loose: having helped her also to another bun, and refilled her mug with milk, I said, nonchalantly:—"Mr. Rochester is not likely to return soon, I suppose?"

"Indeed, he is—in three days, he says; that will be next Thursday; and not alone either. I don't know how many of the fine people at the Leas are coming with him. He sends directions for all the best bedrooms to be prepared; and the library and drawing-rooms are to be cleaned out; and I am to get more kitchen hands from the George Inn, at Millcote, and from wherever else I can; and the ladies will bring their maids and the gentlemen their valets: so we shall have a full house of it." And Mrs. Fairfax swallowed her breakfast and hastened away to commence operations.

The three days were, as she had foretold, busy enough. I had thought all the rooms at Thornfield beautifully clean and well-arranged, but it appears I was mistaken. Three women were got to help; and such scrubbing, such brushing, such washing of paint and beating of carpets, such taking down and putting up of pictures, such polishing of mirrors and lusters, such lighting of fires in bedrooms, such airing of sheets and feather-beds on hearths, I never beheld either before or since. Adèle ran quite wild in the midst of it: the preparations for company, and the prospect of their arrival, seemed to throw her into ec- stasies. She would have Sophie to look over all her "toilettes," as she called frocks; to furbish up any that were "passées,"[9] and to air and arrange the new. For herself, she did nothing but caper about in the front chambers, jump on and off the bedsteads, and lie on the mattresses and piled-up bolsters and pil- lows before the enormous fires roaring in the chimneys. From school duties she was exonerated: Mrs. Fairfax had pressed me into her service, and I was all day in the storeroom, helping (or hindering) her and the cook; learning to make custards and cheesecakes and French pastry, to truss game and garnish dessert dishes.

The party were expected to arrive on Thursday afternoon, in time for dinner at six. During the intervening period I had no time to nurse chimeras; and I believe I was as active and gay as anybody—Adèle excepted. Still, now and then, I received a damping check to my cheerfulness; and was, in spite of my- self, thrown back on the region of doubts and portents, and dark conjectures. This was when I chanced to see the third story staircase door (which of late had always been kept locked) open slowly, and give passage to the form of Grace Poole, in prim cap, white apron, and handerchief; when I watched her glide along the gallery, her quiet tread muffled in a list slipper; when I saw her look into the bustling, topsy-turvy bedrooms,—just say a word, perhaps, to the charwoman about the proper way to polish a grate, or clean a marble mantle- piece, or take stains from papered walls, and then pass on. She would thus de- scend to the kitchen once a day, eat her dinner, smoke a moderate pipe on the hearth, and go back, carrying her pot of porter with her, for her private solace, in her own gloomy, upper haunt. Only one hour in the twenty-four did she pass with her fellow-servants below; all the rest of her time was spent in some low-ceiled, oaken chamber of the third story: there she sat and sewed—and probably laughed drearily to herself—as companionless as a prisoner in his dungeon.

9. Out of style.

The strangest thing of all was, that not a soul in the house, except me, noticed her habits, or seemed to marvel at them; no one discussed her position or employment; no one pitied her solitude or isolation. I once, indeed, overheard part of a dialogue between Leah and one of the charwomen, of which Grace formed the subject. Leah had been saying something I had not caught, and the charwoman remarked—"She gets good wages, I guess?"

"Yes," said Leah; "I wish I had as good; not that mine are to complain of,—there's no stinginess at Thornfield; but they're not one-fifth of the sum Mrs. Poole receives. And she is laying by: she goes every quarter to the bank at Millcote. I should not wonder but she has saved enough to keep her independent if she liked to leave; but I suppose she's got used to the place; and then she's not forty yet, and strong and able for anything. It is too soon for her to give up business."

"She is a good hand, I daresay," said the charwoman.

"Ah! she understands what she has to do,—nobody better,"—rejoined Leah, significantly; "and it is not every one could fill her shoes; not for all the money she gets."

"That it is not!" was the reply. "I wonder whether master——"

The charwoman was going on; but here Leah turned and perceived me, and she instantly gave her companion a nudge.

"Doesn't she know?" I heard the woman whisper.

Leah shook her head, and the conversation was of course dropped. All I had gathered from it amounted to this,—that there was a mystery at Thornfield; and that from participation in that mystery I was purposely excluded.

Thursday came: all work had been completed the previous evening; carpets were laid down, bed-hangings festooned, radiant white counterpanes spread, toilet-tables arranged, furniture rubbed, flowers piled in vases: both chambers and saloons looked as fresh and bright as hands could make them. The hall, too, was scoured; and the great carved clock, as well as the steps and banisters of the staircase, were polished to the brightness of glass: in the dining-room, the sideboard flashed resplendent with plate; in the drawing-room and boudoir, vases of exotics bloomed on all sides.

Afternoon arrived: Mrs. Fairfax assumed her best black satin gown, her gloves, and her gold watch; for it was her part to receive the company—to conduct the ladies to their rooms, etc. Adèle, too, would be dressed: though I thought that she had little chance of being introduced to the party that day, at least. However, to please her, I allowed Sophie to apparel her in one of her short, full muslin frocks. For myself, I had no need to make any change; I should not be called upon to quit my sanctum of the schoolroom; for a sanctum it was now become to me—"a very pleasant refuge in time of trouble."[1]

It had been a mild, serene spring day; one of those days which, towards the end of March or the beginning of April, rise shining over the earth as heralds of summer. It was drawing to an end now; but the evening was even warm, and I sat at work in the schoolroom with the window open.

"It gets late," said Mrs. Fairfax, entering in rustling state. "I am glad I ordered dinner an hour after the time Mr. Rochester mentioned; for it is past six now. I have sent John down to the gates to see if there is anything on the road:

1. Psalm 46:1.

one can see a long way from thence in the direction of Millcote." She went to the window. "Here he is!" said she. "Well, John" (leaning out), "any news?"

"They're coming, ma'am," was the answer. "They'll be here in ten minutes."

Adèle flew to the window. I followed; taking care to stand on one side, so that, screened by the curtain, I could see without being seen.

The ten minutes John had given seemed very long, but at last wheels were heard; four equestrians galloped up the drive, and after them came two open carriages. Fluttering veils and waving plumes filled the vehicles; two of the cavaliers were young, dashing-looking gentlemen; the third was Mr. Rochester, on his black horse, Mesrour;[2] Pilot bounding before him: at his side rode a lady, and he and she were the first of the party. Her purple riding-habit almost swept the ground, her veil streamed long on the breeze; mingling with its transparent folds, and gleaming through them, shone rich raven ringlets.

"Miss Ingram!" exclaimed Mrs. Fairfax, and away she hurried to her post below.

The cavalcade, following the sweep of the drive, quickly turned the angle of the house, and I lost sight of it. Adèle now petitioned to go down; but I took her on my knee and gave her to understand that she must not on any account think of venturing in sight of the ladies, either now or at any other time, unless expressly sent for; that Mr. Rochester would be very angry, etc. "Some natural tears she shed"[3] on being told this; but as I began to look very grave, she consented at last to wipe them.

A joyous stir was now audible in the hall; gentlemen's deep tones and ladies' silvery accents blent harmoniously together, and distinguishable above all, though not loud, was the sonorous voice of the master of Thornfield Hall, welcoming his fair and gallant guests under its roof. Then light steps ascended the stairs; and there was a tripping through the gallery, and soft cheerful laughs, and opening and closing doors, and for a time, a hush.

"Elles changent de toilettes,"[4] said Adèle; who, listening attentively, had followed every movement; and she sighed.

"Chez maman," said she, "quand il y avait du monde, je le suivais partout, au salon et à leurs chambres; souvent je regardais les femmes de chambre coiffer et habiller les dames, et c'était si amusant: comme cela on apprend."[5]

"Don't you feel hungry, Adèle?"

"Mais oui, mademoiselle: voilà cinq ou six heures que nous n'avons pas mangé."[6]

"Well now, while the ladies are in their rooms, I will venture down and get you something to eat."

And issuing from my asylum with precaution, I sought a backstairs which conducted directly to the kitchen. All in that region was fire and commotion; the soup and fish were in the last stage of projection, and the cook hung over her crucibles in a frame of mind and body threatening spontaneous combustion.[7] In the servants' hall two coachmen and three gentlemen's gentlemen

2. The name of a royal executioner in *The Arabian Nights*.
3. *Paradise Lost* 12.645.
4. They are changing clothes.
5. At mama's, . . . when there were a lot of people, I would follow them everywhere, in the drawing room and to their rooms; I often watched the maids dress and groom the ladies, and it was so amusing: that is how one learns.
6. Yes, of course, miss: it's been five or six hours since we've eaten.
7. A playful reference to alchemy, in which metals and powders are placed in crucibles in an attempt to make gold.

stood or sat round the fire; the Abigails, I suppose, were upstairs with their
mistresses: the new servants that had been hired from Millcote were bustling
about everywhere. Threading this chaos, I at last reached the larder; there I
took possession of a cold chicken, a roll of bread, some tarts, a plate or two, and
a knife and fork: with this booty I made a hasty retreat. I had regained the
gallery, and was just shutting the back-door behind me, when an accelerated
hum warned me that the ladies were about to issue from their chambers. I
could not proceed to the schoolroom without passing some of their doors, and
running the risk of being surprised with my cargo of victualage; so I stood still
at this end, which, being windowless, was dark quite dark now, for the sun was
set and twilight gathering.

Presently the chambers gave up their fair tenants one after another; each
came out gaily and airily, with dress that gleamed lustrous through the dusk.
For a moment they stood grouped together at the other extremity of the
gallery, conversing in a key of sweet subdued vivacity; they then descended the
staircase almost as noiselessly as a bright mist rolls down a hill. Their collec-
tive appearance had left on me an impression of high-born elegance, such as I
had never before received.

I found Adèle peeping through the schoolroom door, which she held ajar.
"What beautiful ladies!" cried she in English. "Oh, I wish I might go to them!
Do you think Mr. Rochester will send for us by-and-by, after dinner?"

"No, indeed, I don't; Mr. Rochester has something else to think about.
Never mind the ladies tonight; perhaps you will see them tomorrow; here is
your dinner."

She was really hungry, so the chicken and tarts served to divert her attention
for a time. It was well I secured this forage; or both she, I and Sophie, to whom
I conveyed a share of our repast, would have run a chance of getting no dinner
at all: every one downstairs was too much engaged to think of us. The dessert
was not carried out till after nine; and at ten footmen were still running to and
fro with trays and coffee-cups. I allowed Adèle to sit up much later than usual;
for she declared she could not possibly go to sleep while the doors kept open-
ing and shutting below, and people bustling about. Besides, she added, a mes-
sage might possibly come from Mr. Rochester when she was undressed; "et
alors quel dommage!"[8]

I told her stories as long as she would listen to them; and then for a change
I took her out into the gallery. The hall lamp was now lit, and it amused her to
look over the balustrade and watch the servants passing backwards and for-
wards. When the evening was far advanced, a sound of music issued from the
drawing-room, whither the piano had been removed. Adèle and I sat down on
the top step of the stairs to listen. Presently a voice blent with the rich tones of
the instrument; it was a lady who sang, and very sweet her notes were. The solo
over, a duet followed, and then a glee: a joyous conversational murmur filled
up the intervals. I listened long: suddenly I discovered that my ear was wholly
intent on analysing the mingled sounds, and trying to discriminate amidst the
confusion of accents those of Mr. Rochester; and when it caught them, which
it soon did, it found a further task in framing the tones, rendered by distance
inarticulate, into words.

The clock struck eleven. I looked at Adèle whose head leant against my

8. And then what a shame!

shoulder; her eyes were waxing heavy, so I took her up in my arms and carried her off to bed. It was near one before the gentlemen and ladies sought their chambers.

The next day was as fine as its predecessor; it was devoted by the party to an excursion to some sight in the neighborhood. They set out early in the forenoon, some on horseback, the rest in carriages; I witnessed both the departure and the return. Miss Ingram, as before, was the only lady equestrian; and, as before, Mr. Rochester galloped at her side; the two rode a little apart from the rest. I pointed out this circumstance to Mrs. Fairfax, who was standing at the window with me:—"You said it was not likely they should think of being married," said I, "but you see Mr. Rochester evidently prefers her to any of the other ladies."

"Yes; I daresay: no doubt he admires her."

"And she him," I added; "look how she leans her head towards him as if she were conversing confidentially; I wish I could see her face; I have never had a glimpse of it yet."

"You will see her this evening," answered Mrs. Fairfax. "I happened to remark to Mr. Rochester how much Adèle wished to be introduced to the ladies, and he said: 'Oh! let her come into the drawing-room after dinner; and request Miss Eyre to accompany her.'"

"Yes—he said that from mere politeness: I need not go, I am sure," I answered.

"Well, I observed to him that as you were unused to company, I did not think you would like appearing before so gay a party—all strangers—and he replied, in his quick way: 'Nonsense! If she objects, tell her it is my particular wish; and if she resists, say I shall come and fetch her in case of contumacy.'"[9]

"I will not give him that trouble," I answered. "I will go, if no better may be: but I don't like it. Shall you be there, Mrs. Fairfax?"

"No; I pleaded off, and he admitted my plea. I'll tell you how to manage so as to avoid the embarrassment of making a formal entrance, which is the most disagreeable part of the business. You must go into the drawing-room while it is empty, before the ladies leave the dinner-table; choose your seat in any quiet nook you like; you need not stay long after the gentlemen come in, unless you please: just let Mr. Rochester see you are there and then slip away—nobody will notice you."

"Will these people remain long, do you think?"

"Perhaps two or three weeks; certainly not more. After the Easter recess, Sir George Lynn, who was lately elected member for Millcote, will have to go up to town and take his seat; I daresay Mr. Rochester will accompany him: it surprises me that he has already made so protracted a stay at Thornfield."

It was with some trepidation that I perceived the hour approach when I was to repair with my charge to the drawing-room. Adèle had been in a state of ecstasy all day, after hearing she was to be presented to the ladies in the evening; and it was not till Sophie commenced the operation of dressing her that she sobered down. Then the importance of the process quickly steadied her; and by the time she had her curls arranged in well-smoothed, drooping clusters, her pink satin frock put on, her long sash tied, and her lace mittens adjusted, she looked as grave as any judge. No need to warn her not to disarrange her attire: when she was dressed, she sat demurely down in her little chair, taking

9. Stubborn resistance to authority.

care previously to lift up the satin skirt for fear she should crease it, and assured me she would not stir thence till I was ready. This I quickly was; my best dress (the silver-gray one, purchased for Miss Temple's wedding, and never worn since) was soon put on; my hair was soon smoothed; my sole ornament, the pearl brooch, soon assumed. We descended.

Fortunately there was another entrance to the drawing-room than that through the saloon where they were all seated at dinner. We found the apartment vacant, a large fire burning silently on the marble hearth, and wax candles shining in bright solitude, amid the exquisite flowers with which the tables were adorned. The crimson curtain hung before the arch: slight as was the separation this drapery formed from the party in the adjoining saloon, they spoke in so low a key that nothing of their conversation could be distinguished beyond a soothing murmur.

Adèle, who appeared to be still under the influence of a most solemnizing impression, sat down, without a word, on the footstool I pointed out to her. I retired to a window-seat, and, taking a book from a table near, endeavored to read. Adèle brought her stool to my feet; ere long she touched my knee.

"What is it, Adèle?"

"Est-ce que je ne puis pas prendre une seule de ces fleurs magnifiques, mademoiselle? Seulement pour compléter ma toilette."[1]

"You think too much of your 'toilette,' Adèle, but you may have a flower." And I took a rose from a vase and fastened it in her sash. She sighed a sigh of ineffable satisfaction, as if her cup of happiness were now full. I turned my face away to conceal a smile I could not suppress: there was something ludicrous as well as painful in the little Parisienne's earnest and innate devotion to matters of dress.

A soft sound of rising now became audible; the curtain was swept back from the arch; through it appeared the dining-room with its lit luster pouring down light on the silver and glass of a magnificent dessert-service covering a long table; a band of ladies stood in the opening; they entered, and the curtain fell behind them.

There were but eight, yet somehow as they flocked in, they gave the impression of a much larger number. Some of them were very tall, many were dressed in white, and all had a sweeping amplitude of array that seemed to magnify their persons as a mist magnifies the moon. I rose and curtseyed to them; one or two bent their heads in return, the others only stared at me.

They dispersed about the room, reminding me, by the lightness and buoyancy of their movements, of a flock of white plumy birds. Some of them threw themselves in half-reclining positions on the sofas and ottomans, some bent over the tables and examined the flowers and books, the rest gathered in a group round the fire—all talked in a low but clear tone which seemed habitual to them. I knew their names afterwards, and may as well mention them now.

First there was Mrs. Eshton and two of her daughters. She had evidently been a handsome woman, and was well preserved still. Of her daughters, the eldest, Amy, was rather little; naïve, and childlike in face and manner, and piquant in form: her white muslin dress and blue sash became her well. The second, Louisa, was taller and more elegant in figure, with a very pretty face, of that order the French term "minois chiffonné";[2] both sisters were fair as lilies.

1. Couldn't I take just one of these magnificent flowers, miss? Just to complete my costume. 2. A sweet, slightly petulant face.

Lady Lynn was a large and stout personage of about forty, very erect, very haughty-looking, richly dressed in a satin robe of changeful sheen: her dark hair shone glossily under the shade of an azure plume, and within the circlet of a band of gems.

Mrs. Colonel Dent was less showy, but, I thought, more ladylike. She had a slight figure, a pale, gentle face, and fair hair. Her black satin dress, her scarf of rich foreign lace, and her pearl ornaments, pleased me better than the rainbow radiance of the titled dame.

But the three most distinguished—partly, perhaps, because the tallest figures of the band—were the Dowager Lady Ingram and her daughters, Blanche and Mary. They were all three of the loftiest stature of woman. The dowager might be between forty and fifty; her shape was still fine; her hair (by candle-light at least) still black; her teeth, too, were still apparently perfect. Most people would have termed her a splendid woman of her age: and so she was, no doubt, physically speaking; but then there was an expression of almost insupportable haughtiness in her bearing and countenance. She had Roman features and a double chin, disappearing into a throat like a pillar: these features appeared to me not only inflated and darkened, but even furrowed with pride; and the chin was sustained by the same principle, in a position of almost preternatural erectness. She had, likewise, a fierce and a hard eye: it reminded me of Mrs. Reed's; she mouthed her words in speaking; her voice was deep, its inflections very pompous, very dogmatical—very intolerable, in short. A crimson velvet robe, and a shawl turban of some gold-wrought Indian fabric, invested her (I suppose she thought) with a truly imperial dignity.

Blanche and Mary were of equal stature—straight and tall as poplars. Mary was too slim for her height; but Blanche was molded like a Dian.[3] I regarded her, of course, with special interest. First, I wished to see whether her appearance accorded with Mrs. Fairfax's description; secondly, whether it at all resembled the fancy miniature I had painted of her; and thirdly—it will out!—whether it were such as I should fancy likely to suit Mr. Rochester's taste.

As far as person went, she answered point for point, both to my picture and Mrs. Fairfax's description. The noble bust, the sloping shoulders, the graceful neck, the dark eyes and black ringlets were all there—but her face? Her face was like her mother's; a youthful unfurrowed likeness: the same low brow, the same high features, the same pride. It was not, however, so saturnine a pride: she laughed continually; her laugh was satirical, and so was the habitual expression of her arched and haughty lip.

Genius is said to be self-conscious: I cannot tell whether Miss Ingram was a genius, but she was self-conscious—remarkably self-conscious indeed. She entered into a discourse on botany with the gentle Mrs. Dent. It seems Mrs. Dent had not studied that science: though, as she said, she liked flowers, "especially wild ones"; Miss Ingram had, and she ran over its vocabulary with an air. I presently perceived she was (what is vernacularly termed) *trailing* Mrs. Dent; that is playing on her ignorance; her *trail* might be clever, but it was decidedly not good-natured. She played; her execution was brilliant; she sang; her voice was fine; she talked French apart to her mamma; and she talked it well, with fluency and with a good accent.

3. I.e., Diana, beautiful Roman virgin goddess of hunting.

Mary had a milder and more open countenance than Blanche; softer features too, and a skin some shades fairer (Miss Ingram was dark as a Spaniard)—but Mary was deficient in life; her face lacked expression, her eye lustre; she had nothing to say, and having once taken her seat, remained fixed like a statue in its niche. The sisters were both attired in spotless white.

And did I now think Miss Ingram such a choice as Mr. Rochester would be likely to make? I could not tell—I did not know his taste in female beauty. If he liked the majestic, she was the very type of majesty: then she was accomplished, sprightly. Most gentlemen would admire her, I thought; and that he *did* admire her, I already seemed to have obtained proof: to remove the last shade of doubt, it remained but to see them together.

You are not to suppose, reader, that Adèle has all this time been sitting, motionless, on the stool at my feet: no; when the ladies entered, she rose, advanced to meet them, made a stately reverence, and said, with gravity,—"Bon jour, mesdames."[4]

And Miss Ingram had looked down at her with a mocking air, and exclaimed, "Oh, what a little puppet!"

Lady Lynn had remarked, "It is Mr. Rochester's ward, I suppose—the little French girl he was speaking of."

Mrs. Dent had kindly taken her hand, and given her a kiss. Amy and Louisa Eshton had cried out simultaneously—

"What a love of a child!"

And then they had called her to a sofa, where she now sat, ensconced between them, chattering alternately in French and broken English: absorbing not only the young ladies' attention, but that of Mrs Eshton and Lady Lynn, and getting spoiled to her heart's content.

At last coffee is brought in, and the gentlemen are summoned. I sit in the shade—if any shade there be in this brilliantly-lit apartment; the window curtain half hides me. Again the arch yawns: they come. The collective appearance of the gentlemen, like that of the ladies, is very imposing: they are all costumed in black; most of them are tall, some young. Henry and Frederick Lynn are very dashing sparks, indeed; and Colonel Dent is a fine soldierly man. Mr. Eshton, the magistrate of the district, is gentleman-like: his hair is quite white, his eyebrows and whiskers still dark, which gives him something of the appearance of a "père noble de théâtre."[5] Lord Ingram, like his sisters, is very tall; like them, also, he is handsome; but he shares Mary's apathetic and listless look: he seems to have more length of limb than vivacity of blood or vigour of brain.

And where is Mr. Rochester?

He comes in last: I am not looking at the arch, yet I see him enter. I try to concentrate my attention on those netting-needles, on the meshes of the purse I am forming—I wish to think only of the work I have in my hands, to see only the silver beads and silk threads that lie in my lap; whereas, I distinctly behold his figure, and I inevitably recall the moment when I last saw it: just after I had rendered him, what he deemed an essential service—and he, holding my hand, and looking down on my face, surveyed me with eyes that revealed a heart full and eager to overflow; in whose emotions I had a part. How

4. Hello, ladies.
5. Distinguished old gentleman, as portrayed in the theater.

near had I approached him at that moment! What had occurred since, calculated to change his and my relative positions? Yet now, how distant, how far estranged we were! So far estranged, that I did not expect him to come and speak to me. I did not wonder, when, without looking at me, he took a seat at the other side of the room, and began conversing with some of the ladies.

No sooner did I see that his attention was riveted on them, and that I might gaze without being observed, than my eyes were drawn involuntarily to his face: I could not keep their lids under control: they would rise, and the irids would fix on him. I looked, and had an acute pleasure in looking,—a precious, yet poignant pleasure; pure gold, with a steely point of agony: a pleasure like what the thirst-perishing man might feel who knows the well to which he has crept is poisoned, yet stoops and drinks divine draughts nevertheless.

Most true is it that "beauty is in the eye of the gazer." My master's colorless, olive face, square, massive brow, broad and jetty eyebrows, deep eyes, strong features, firm, grim mouth,—all energy, decision, will,—were not beautiful, according to rule; but they were more than beautiful to me: they were full of an interest, an influence that quite mastered me,—that took my feelings from my own power and fettered them in his. I had not intended to love him: the reader knows I had wrought hard to extirpate from my soul the germs of love there detected; and now, at the first renewed view of him, they spontaneously revived, green and strong! He made me love him without looking at me.

I compared him with his guests. What was the gallant grace of the Lynns, the languid elegance of Lord Ingram,—even the military distinction of Colonel Dent, contrasted with his look of native pith and genuine power? I had no sympathy with their appearance, their expression; yet I could imagine that most observers would call them attractive, handsome, imposing; while they would pronounce Mr. Rochester at once harsh-featured and melancholy-looking. I saw them smile, laugh—it was nothing; the light of the candles had as much soul in it as their smile; the tinkle of the bell as much significance as their laugh. I saw Mr. Rochester smile—his stern features softened; his eye grew both brilliant and gentle, its ray both searching and sweet. He was talking, at the moment, to Louisa and Amy Eshton. I wondered to see them receive with calm that look which seemed to me so penetrating; I expected their eyes to fall, their color to rise under it; yet I was glad when I found they were in no sense moved. "He is not to them what he is to me," I thought: "he is not of their kind. I believe he is of mine;—I am sure he is,—I feel akin to him,—I understand the language of his countenance and movements; though rank and wealth sever us widely, I have something in my brain and heart, in my blood and nerves, that assimilates me mentally to him. Did I say, a few days since, that I had nothing to do with him but to receive my salary at his hands? Did I forbid myself to think of him in any other light than as a paymaster? Blasphemy against nature! Every good, true, vigorous feeling I have, gathers impulsively round him. I know I must conceal my sentiments; I must smother hope; I must remember that he cannot care much for me. For when I say that I am of his kind, I do not mean that I have his force to influence, and his spell to attract; I mean only that I have certain tastes and feelings in common with him. I must then repeat continually that we are for ever sundered;—and yet, while I breathe and think I must love him."

Coffee is handed. The ladies, since the gentlemen entered, have become lively as larks; conversation waxes brisk and merry. Colonel Dent and Mr.

Eshton argue on politics; their wives listen. The two proud dowagers, Lady Lynn and Lady Ingram, confabulate together. Sir George—whom, by-the-by, I have forgotten to describe—a very big and very fresh-looking country gentleman, stands before their sofa, coffee-cup in hand, and occasionally puts in a word. Mr. Frederick Lynn has taken a seat beside Mary Ingram, and is showing her the engravings of a splendid volume; she looks, smiles now and then, but apparently says little. The tall and phlegmatic[6] Lord Ingram leans with folded arms on the chair-back of the little and lively Amy Eshton; she glances up at him, and chatters like a wren: she likes him better than she does Mr. Rochester. Henry Lynn has taken possession of an ottoman at the feet of Louisa; Adèle shares it with him: he is trying to talk French with her, and Louisa laughs at his blunders. With whom will Blanche Ingram pair? She is standing alone at the table, bending gracefully over an album. She seems waiting to be sought; but she will not wait too long: she herself selects a mate.

Mr. Rochester, having quitted the Eshtons, stands on the hearth as solitary as she stands by the table; she confronts him, taking her station on the opposite side of the mantlepiece.

"Mr. Rochester, I thought you were not fond of children?"

"Nor am I."

"Then, what induced you to take charge of such a little doll as that?" (pointing to Adèle). "Where did you pick her up?"

"I did not pick her up, she was left on my hands."

"You should have sent her to school."

"I could not afford it; schools are so dear."

"Why, I suppose you have a governess for her; I saw a person with her just now—is she gone? Oh, no, there she is still behind the window-curtain. You pay her, of course. I should think it quite as expensive—more so, for you have them both to keep in addition."

I feared—or should I say, hoped—the allusion to me would make Mr. Rochester glance my way; and I involuntarily shrank further into the shade; but he never turned his eyes.

"I have not considered the subject," said he indifferently, looking straight before him.

"No—you men never do consider economy and common sense. You should hear mamma on the chapter of governess. Mary and I have had, I should think, a dozen at least in our day; half of them detestable and the rest ridiculous, and all incubi[7]—were they not, mamma?"

"Did you speak, my own?"

The young lady thus claimed as the dowager's special property reiterated her question with an explanation.

"My dearest, don't mention governesses; the word makes me nervous. I have suffered a martyrdom from their incompetency and caprice; I thank Heaven I have now done with them!"

Mrs. Dent here bent over to the pious lady, and whispered something in her ear; I suppose, from the answer elicited, it was a reminder that one of the anathematised race was present.

"Tant pis!"[8] said her ladyship, "I hope it may do her good." Then, in a lower

6. Slow and unemotional; phlegm was one of the four humors (see n. 6, p. 551).

7. Evil spirits.

8. Too bad!

tone, but still loud enough for me to hear, "I noticed her; I am a judge of physiognomy, and in hers I see all the faults of her class."

"What are they, madam?" inquired Mr. Rochester aloud.

"I will tell you in your private ear," replied she, wagging her turban three times with portentous significancy.

"But my curiosity will be past its appetite; it craves food now."

"Ask Blanche; she is nearer you than I."

"Oh, don't refer him to me, mamma! I have just one word to say of the whole tribe; they are a nuisance. Not that I ever suffered much from them; I took care to turn the tables. What tricks Theodore and I used to play on our Miss Wilsons, and Mrs. Greys, and Madame Jouberts! Mary was always too sleepy to join in a plot with spirit. The best fun was with Madame Joubert. Miss Wilson was a poor sickly thing, lachrymose and low-spirited: not worth the trouble of vanquishing, in short; and Mrs. Grey was coarse and insensible: no blow took effect on her. But poor Madame Joubert! I see her yet in her raging passions, when we had driven her to extremities—spilled our tea, crumbled our bread and butter, tossed our books up to the ceiling, and played a charivari[9] with the ruler and desk, the fender and fire-irons. Theodore, do you remember those merry days?"

"Yaas, to be sure I do," drawled Lord Ingram; "and the poor old stick used to cry out, 'Oh, you villains[1] childs!' and then we sermonized her on the presumption of attempting to teach such clever blades as we were, when she was herself so ignorant."

"We did; and Tedo, you know I helped you in prosecuting (or persecuting) your tutor, whey-faced Mr. Vining—the parson in the pip,[2] as we used to call him. He and Miss Wilson took the liberty of falling in love with each other— at least Tedo and I thought so; we surprised sundry tender glances and sighs which we interpreted as tokens of 'la belle passion,'[3] and I promise you the public soon had the benefit of our discovery; we employed it as a sort of lever to hoist our dead-weights from the house. Dear mamma, there, as soon as she got an inkling of the business, found out that it was of an immoral tendency. Did you not, my lady-mother?"

"Certainly, my best. And I was quite right, depend on that: there are a thousand reasons why liaisons between governesses and tutors should never be tolerated a moment in any well-regulated house; firstly,——."

"Oh, gracious, mamma! Spare us the enumeration! Au reste,[4] we all know them: danger of bad example to innocence of childhood—distractions and consequent neglect of duty on the part of the attached—mutual alliance and reliance; confidence thence resulting—insolence accompanying—mutiny and general blow-up. Am I right, Baroness Ingram, of Ingram Park?"

"My lily-flower, you are right now, as always."

"Then no more need be said; change the subject."

Amy Eshton, not hearing or not heeding this dictum, joined in with her soft infantine tone: "Louisa and I used to quiz[5] our governess too; but she was such a good creature, she would bear anything; nothing put her out. She was never cross with us; was she, Louisa?"

9. A noisy serenade to newlyweds.
1. Naughty.
2. Like a chick in its shell.

3. The beautiful passion.
4. At any rate.
5. Mock. A "quiz" is an eccentric person.

"No, never; we might do what we pleased—ransack her desk and her work-box, and turn her drawers inside out; and she was so good-natured, she would give us anything we asked for."

"I suppose now," said Miss Ingram, curling her lips sarcastically, "we shall have an abstract of the memoirs of all the governesses extant; in order to avert such a visitation, I again move the introduction of a new topic. Mr. Rochester, do you second my motion?"

"Madam, I support you on this point as on every other."

"Then on me be the onus of bringing it forward. Signor Eduardo, are you in voice tonight?"

"Donna Bianca,[6] if you command it, I will be."

"Then, signor, I lay on you my sovereign behest to furbish up your lungs and other vocal organs, as they will be wanted on my royal service."

"Who would not be the Rizzio of so divine a Mary?"

"A fig for Rizzio!" cried she, tossing her head with all its curls, as she moved to the piano. "It is my opinion the fiddler David must have been an insipid sort of fellow; I like black Bothwell better. To my mind a man is nothing with-out a spice of the devil in him; and history may say what it will of James Hepburn,[7] but I have a notion he was just the sort of wild, fierce, bandit hero whom I could have consented to gift with my hand."

"Gentlemen, you hear! Now which of you most resembles Bothwell?" cried Mr. Rochester.

"I should say the preference lies with you," responded Colonel Dent.

"On my honor, I am much obliged to you," was the reply.

Miss Ingram, who had now seated herself with proud grace at the piano, spreading out her snowy robes in queenly amplitude, commenced a brilliant prelude; talking meantime. She appeared to be on her high-horse tonight; both her words and her air seemed intended to excite not only the admiration, but the amazement of her auditors; she was evidently bent on striking them as something very dashing and daring indeed.

"Oh, I am so sick of the young men of the present day!" exclaimed she, rat-tling away at the instrument. "Poor puny things not fit to stir a step beyond papa's park-gates: nor to go even so far without mamma's permission and guardianship! Creatures so absorbed in care about their pretty faces and their white hands, and their small feet; as if a man had anything to do with beauty! As if loveliness were not the special prerogative of woman—her legitimate ap-panage[8] and heritage! I grant an ugly *woman* is a blot on the fair face of cre-ation; but as to the *gentlemen*, let them be solicitous to possess only strength and valour: let their motto be—Hunt, shoot, and fight; the rest is not worth a fillip. Such should be my device, were I a man."

"Whenever I marry," she continued after a pause which none interrupted, "I am resolved my husband shall not be a rival, but a foil to me. I will suffer no competitor near the throne; I shall exact an undivided homage; his devotions shall not be shared between me and the shape he sees in his mirror. Mr. Rochester, now sing, and I will play for you."

"I am all obedience," was the response.

6. Mr. Edward . . . Miss Blanche (Italian).
7. David Rizzio was an Italian who joined the house-hold of Mary, queen of Scots, as a singer, then became the queen's confidant and lover. Her second husband, Lord Darnley, had Rizzio killed. James Hepburn, fourth earl of Bothwell, in turn had Darnley murdered and married the queen, becoming her third husband.
8. I.e., endowment.

"Here then is a Corsair-song. Know that I doat on Corsairs; and for that reason, sing it 'con spirito.'"[9]

"Commands from Miss Ingram's lips would put spirit into a mug of milk and water."

"Take care, then: if you don't please me, I will shame you by showing how such things *should* be done."

"That is offering a premium on incapacity; I shall now endeavor to fail."

"Gardez-vous en bien![1] If you err wilfully, I shall devise a proportionate punishment."

"Miss Ingram ought to be clement, for she has it in her power to inflict a chastisement beyond mortal endurance."

"Ha! explain!" commanded the lady.

"Pardon me, madam; no need of explanation; your own fine sense must inform you that one of your frowns would be a sufficient substitute for capital punishment."

"Sing!" said she, and again touching the piano, she commenced an accompaniment in spirited style.

"Now is my time to slip away," thought I; but the tones that then severed the air arrested me. Mrs. Fairfax had said Mr. Rochester possessed a fine voice; he did—a mellow powerful bass, into which he threw his own feeling, his own force; finding a way through the ear to the heart, and there waking sensation strangely. I waited till the last deep and full vibration had expired—till the tide of talk, checked an instant, had resumed its flow; I then quitted my sheltered corner and made my exit by the side-door, which was fortunately near. Thence a narrow passage led into the hall; in crossing it, I perceived my sandal was loose; I stopped to tie it, kneeling down for that purpose on the mat at the foot of the staircase. I heard the dining-room door unclose; a gentleman came out; rising hastily, I stood face to face with him; it was Mr. Rochester.

"How do you do?" he asked.

"I am very well, sir."

"Why did you not come and speak to me in the room?"

I thought I might have retorted the question on him who put it; but I would not take that freedom. I answered:—"I did not wish to disturb you, as you seemed engaged, sir."

"What have you been doing during my absence?"

"Nothing particular; teaching Adèle as usual."

"And getting a good deal paler than you were—as I saw at first sight. What is the matter?"

"Nothing at all, sir."

"Did you take any cold that night you half drowned me?"

"Not the least."

"Return to the drawing-room; you are deserting too early."

"I am tired, sir."

He looked at me for a minute.

"And a little depressed," he said. "What about? Tell me."

"Nothing—nothing, sir. I am not depressed."

"But I affirm that you are: so much depressed that a few more words would bring tears to your eyes—indeed, they are there now, shining and swimming;

9. With spirit. 1. Be very careful.

and a bead has slipped from the lash and fallen on to the flag. If I had time, and was not in mortal dread of some prating prig of a servant passing, I would know what all this means. Well, tonight I excuse you; but understand that so long as my visitors stay, I expect you to appear in the drawing-room every evening; it is my wish; don't neglect it. Now go, and send Sophie for Adèle. Good-night, my——" He stopped, bit his lip, and abruptly left me.

Chapter XVIII

Merry days were these at Thornfield Hall; and busy days too: how different from the first three months of stillness, monotony, and solitude I had passed beneath its roof! All sad feelings seemed now driven from the house, all gloomy associations forgotten: there was life everywhere, movement all day long. You could not now traverse the gallery, once so hushed, nor enter the front chambers, once so tenantless, without encountering a smart lady's maid, or a dandy valet.

The kitchen, the butler's pantry, the servants' hall, the entrance hall, were equally alive; and the saloons were only left void and still when the blue sky and halcyon sunshine of the genial spring weather called their occupants out into the grounds. Even when that weather was broken, and continuous rain set in for some days, no damp seemed cast over enjoyment; indoor amusements only became more lively and varied, in consequence of the stop put to outdoor gaiety.

I wondered what they were going to do the first evening a change of entertainment was proposed; they spoke of "playing charades," but in my ignorance I did not understand the term. The servants were called in, the dining-room tables wheeled away, the lights otherwise disposed, the chairs placed in a semicircle opposite the arch. While Mr. Rochester and the other gentlemen directed these alterations, the ladies were running up and down stairs ringing for their maids. Mrs. Fairfax was summoned to give information respecting the resources of the house in shawls, dresses, draperies of any kind; and certain wardrobes of the third story were ransacked, and their contents, in the shape of brocaded and hooped petticoats, satin sacques, black modes, lace lappets,[2] etc., were brought down in armfuls by the Abigails; then a selection was made, and such things as were chosen were carried to the boudoir within the drawing-room.

Meantime, Mr. Rochester had again summoned the ladies round him, and was selecting certain of their number to be of his party. "Miss Ingram is mine, of course," said he; afterwards he named the two Misses Eshton, and Mrs. Dent. He looked at me; I happened to be near him, as I had been fastening the clasp of Mrs. Dent's bracelet, which had got loose.

"Will you play?" he asked. I shook my head. He did not insist, which I rather feared he would have done; he allowed me to return quietly to my usual seat.

He and his aids now withdrew behind the curtain; the other party, which was headed by Colonel Dent, sat down on the crescent of chairs. One of the gentlemen, Mr. Eshton, observing me, seemed to propose that I should be asked to join them; but Lady Ingram instantly negatived the notion.

"No," I heard her say: "she looks too stupid for any game of the sort."

Ere long, a bell tinkled, and the curtain drew up. Within the arch the bulky

2. Streamers attached to headgear. "Sacques": loose gowns. "Modes": clothing made of thin, light silk.

figure of Sir George Lynn, whom Mr. Rochester had likewise chosen, was seen enveloped in a white sheet; before him, on a table, lay open a large book; and at his side stood Amy Eshton, draped in Mr. Rochester's cloak, and holding a book in her hand. Somebody, unseen, rang the bell merrily; then Adèle (who had insisted on being one of her guardian's party), bounded forward, scattering round her the contents of a basket of flowers she carried on her arm. Then appeared the magnificent figure of Miss Ingram, clad in white, a long veil on her head, and a wreath of roses round her brow; by her side walked Mr. Rochester, and together they drew near the table. They knelt, while Mrs. Dent and Louisa Eshton, dressed also in white, took up their stations behind them. A ceremony followed, in dumb show, in which it was easy to recognize the pantomime of a marriage. At its termination Colonel Dent and his party consulted in whispers for two minutes, then the Colonel called out,—"Bride!" Mr. Rochester bowed, and the curtain fell.

A considerable interval elapsed before it again rose. Its second rising displayed a more elaborately prepared scene than the last. The drawing-room, as I have before observed, was raised two steps above the dining-room, and on the top of the upper step, placed a yard or two back within the room, appeared a large marble basin, which I recognized as an ornament of the conservatory— where it usually stood, surrounded by exotics, and tenanted by gold fish—and whence it must have been transported with some trouble, on account of its size and weight.

Seated on the carpet, by the side of this basin, was seen Mr. Rochester, costumed in shawls, with a turban on his head. His dark eyes and swarth skin and Paynim features suited the costume exactly: he looked the very model of an Eastern emir; an agent or a victim of the bowstring. Presently advanced into view Miss Ingram. She, too, was attired in Oriental fashion: a crimsom scarf tied sashlike round the waist; an embroidered handkerchief knotted about her temples; her beautifully-molded arms bare, one of them up-raised in the act of supporting a pitcher, poised gracefully on her head. Both her cast of form and feature, her complexion and her general air, suggested the idea of some Israelitish princess of the patriarchal days; and such was doubtless the character she intended to represent.

She approached the basin, and bent over it as if to fill her pitcher; she again lifted it to her head. The personage on the well-brink now seemed to accost her; to make some request,—"She hasted, let down her pitcher on her hand and gave him to drink." From the bosom of his robe he then produced a casket, opened it and showed magnificent bracelets and earrings; she acted astonishment and admiration; kneeling, he laid the treasure at her feet; incredulity and delight were expressed by her looks and gestures; the stranger fastened the bracelets on her arms, and the rings in her ears. It was Eliezer and Rebecca; the camels only were wanting.[3]

The divining party again laid their heads together; apparently they could not agree about the word or syllable this scene illustrated. Colonel Dent, their spokesman, demanded "the tableau of the Whole";[4] whereupon the curtain again descended.

3. A servant of Abraham was instructed to find a wife for Abraham's son Isaac; the servant resolved to approach the first woman who was willing to serve water to him and his camels. In this way he met and wooed Rebecca, who became Isaac's wife (Genesis 24:14–67). 4. A depiction of a scene representing the entire word, rather than a single syllable.

On its third rising only a portion of the drawing-room was disclosed; the rest being concealed by a screen, hung with some sort of dark and coarse drapery. The marble basin was removed; in its place stood a deal table and a kitchen chair: these objects were visible by a very dim light proceeding from a horn lantern, the wax candles being all extinguished.

Amidst this sordid scene sat a man with his clenched hands resting on his knees, and his eyes bent on the ground. I knew Mr. Rochester; though the begrimed face, the disordered dress (his coat hanging loose from one arm, as if it had been almost torn from his back in a scuffle), the desperate and scowling countenance, the rough, bristling hair might well have disguised him. As he moved a chain clanked; to his wrists were attached fetters.

"Bridewell!"[5] exclaimed Colonel Dent, and the charade was solved.

A sufficient interval having elapsed for the performers to resume their ordinary costume, they reentered the dining-room. Mr. Rochester led in Miss Ingram; she was complimenting him on his acting.

"Do you know," said she, "that, of the three characters, I liked you in the last best? Oh, had you but lived a few years earlier, what a gallant gentleman-high-wayman you would have made!"

"Is all the soot washed from my face?" he asked, turning it towards her.

"Alas, yes; the more's the pity! Nothing could be more becoming to your complexion than that ruffian's rouge.'

"You would like a hero of the road then?"

"An English hero of the road would be the next best thing to an Italian bandit; and that could only be surpassed by a Levantine pirate."

"Well, whatever I am, remember you are my wife; we were married an hour since, in the presence of all these witnesses." She giggled, and her color rose.

"Now, Dent," continued Mr. Rochester, "it is your turn." And as the other party withdrew, he and his band took the vacated seats. Miss Ingram placed herself at her leader's right hand; the other diviners filled the chairs on each side of him and her. I did not now watch the actors; I no longer waited with interest for the curtain to rise; my attention was absorbed by the spectators; my eyes, erewhile fixed on the arch, were now irresistibly attracted to the semicircle of chairs. What charade Colonel Dent and his party played, what word they chose, how they acquitted themselves, I no longer remember; but I still see the consultation which followed each scene: I see Mr. Rochester turn to Miss Ingram, and Miss Ingram to him; I see her incline her head towards him till the jetty curls almost touch his shoulder and wave against his cheek; I hear their mutual whisperings; I recall their interchanged glances; and something even of the feeling roused by the spectacle returns in memory at this moment.

I have told you, reader, that I had learned to love Mr. Rochester; I could not unlove him now, merely because I found that he had ceased to notice me—because I might pass hours in his presence and he would never once, turn his eyes in my direction—because I saw all his attentions appropriated by a great lady, who scorned to touch me with the hem of her robes as she passed; who, if ever her dark and imperious eye fell on me by chance, would withdraw it instantly as from an object too mean to merit observation. I could not unlove him, because I felt sure he would soon marry this very lady—because I read daily in her a proud security in his intentions respecting her—because I wit-

5. A prison.

nessed hourly in him a style of courtship which, if careless and choosing rather to be sought than to seek, was yet, in its very carelessness, captivating, and in its very pride, irresistible.

There was nothing to cool or banish love in these circumstances; though much to create despair. Much too, you will think, reader, to engender jealousy; if a woman, in my position, could presume to be jealous of a woman in Miss Ingram's. But I was not jealous; or very rarely;—the nature of the pain I suffered could not be explained by that word. Miss Ingram was a mark beneath jeaousy: she was too inferior to excite the feeling. Pardon the seeming paradox; I mean what I say. She was very showy, but she was not genuine: she had a fine person, many brilliant attainments; but her mind was poor, her heart barren by nature; nothing bloomed spontaneously on that soil; no unforced natural fruit delighted by its freshness. She was not good; she was not original: she used to repeat sounding phrases from books: she never offered, nor had, an opinion of her own. She advocated a high tone of sentiment; but she did not know the sensations of sympathy and pity; tenderness and truth were not in her. Too often she betrayed this, by the undue vent she gave to a spiteful antipathy she had conceived against little Adèle: pushing her away with some contumelious[6] epithet if she happened to approach her; sometimes ordering her from the room, and always treating her with coldness and acrimony. Other eyes besides mine watched these manifestations of character—watched them closely, keenly, shrewdly. Yes: the future bridegroom, Mr. Rochester himself, exercised over his intended a ceaseless surveillance: and it was from this sagacity—this guardedness of his—this perfect, clear consciousness of his fair one's defects—this obvious absence of passion in his sentiments towards her, that my ever-torturing pain arose.

I saw he was going to marry her, for family, perhaps political reasons; because her rank and connections suited him; I felt he had not given her his love, and that her qualifications were ill adapted to win from him that treasure. This was the point—this was where the nerve was touched and teased—this was where the fever was sustained and fed: *she could not charm him.*

If she had managed the victory at once, and he had yielded and sincerely laid his heart at her feet, I should have covered my face, turned to the wall, and (figuratively) have died to them. If Miss Ingram had been a good and noble woman, endowed with force, fervor, kindness, sense, I should have had one vital struggle with two tigers—jealousy and despair: then, my heart torn out and devoured, I should have admired her—acknowledged her excellence, and been quiet for the rest of my days: and the more absolute her superiority, the deeper would have been my admiration—the more truly tranquil my quiescence. But as matters really stood, to watch Miss Ingram's efforts at fascinating Mr. Rochester; to witness their repeated failure—herself unconscious that they did fail; vainly fancying that each shaft launched hit the mark, and infatuatedly pluming herself on success, when her pride and self-complacency repelled further and further what she wished to allure—to witness *this,* was to be at once under ceaseless excitation and ruthless restraint.

Because, when she failed, I saw how she might have succeeded. Arrows that continually glanced off from Mr. Rochester's breast and fell harmless at his feet, might, I knew, if shot by a surer hand, have quivered keen in his proud

6. Humiliating.

heart—have called love into his stern eye and softness into his sardonic face; or, better still, without weapons a silent conquest might have been won.

"Why can she not influence him more, when she is privileged to draw so near to him?" I asked myself. "Surely she cannot truly like him, or not like him with true affection. If she did, she need not coin her smiles so lavishly, flash her glances so unremittingly, manufacture airs so elaborate, graces so multitudinous. It seems to me that she might, by merely sitting quietly at his side, saying little and looking less, get nigher his heart. I have seen in his face a far different expression from that which hardens it now while she is so vivaciously accosting him; but then it came of itself, it was not elicited by meretricious arts and calculated manuevers; and one had but to accept it—to answer what he asked without pretension, to address him when needful without grimace— and it increased and grew kinder and more genial, and warmed one like a fostering sunbeam. How will she manage to please him when they are married? I do not think she will manage it; and yet it might be managed and his wife might, I verily believe, be the very happiest woman the sun shines on."

I have not yet said anything condemnatory of Mr. Rochester's project of marrying for interest and connections. It surprised me when I first discovered that such was his intention; I had thought him a man unlikely to be influenced by motives so commonplace in his choice of a wife; but the longer I considered the position, education, etc., of the parties, the less I felt justified in judging and blaming either him or Miss Ingram, for acting in conformity to ideas and principles instilled into them, doubtless, from their childhood. All their class held these principles; I supposed, then, they had reasons for holding them such as I could not fathom. It seemed to me that, were I a gentleman like him, I would take to my bosom only such a wife as I could love; but the very obviousness of the advantages to the husband's own happiness, offered by this plan, convinced me that there must be arguments against its general adoption of which I was quite ignorant; otherwise I felt sure all the world would act as I wished to act.

But in other points, as well as this, I was growing very lenient to my master: I was forgetting all his faults, for which I had once kept a sharp look-out. It had formerly been my endeavor to study all sides of his character; to take the bad with the good; and from the just weighing of both to form an equitable judgment. Now I saw no bad. The sarcasm that had repelled, the harshness that had startled me once, were only like keen condiments in a choice dish: their presence was pungent, but their absence would be felt as comparatively insipid. And as for the vague something—was it a sinister or a sorrowful, a designing or a desponding expression?—that opened upon a careful observer, now and then, in his eye and closed again before one could fathom the strange depth partially disclosed; that something which used to make me fear and shrink, as if I had been wandering amongst volcanic-looking hills, and had suddenly felt the ground quiver, and seen it gape; that something I at intervals beheld still, and with throbbing heart, but not with palsied nerves. Instead of wishing to shun, I longed only to dare—to divine it; and I thought Miss Ingram happy, because one day she might look into the abyss at her leisure, explore its secrets, and analyse their nature.

Meantime, while I thought only of my master and his future bride—saw only them, heard only their discourse, and considered only their movements of importance—the rest of the party were occupied with their own separate

interests and pleasures. The ladies Lynn and Ingram continued to consort in solemn conferences, when they nodded their two turbans at each other, and held up their four hands in confronting gestures of surprise, or mystery, or horror, according to the theme on which their gossip ran, like a pair of magnified puppets. Mild Mrs. Dent talked with good-natured Mrs. Eshton; and the two sometimes bestowed a courteous word or smile on me. Sir George Lynn, Colonel Dent, and Mr. Eshton discussed politics, or county affairs, or justice business. Lord Ingram flirted with Amy Eshton; Louisa played and sang to and with one of the Messrs. Lynn; and Mary Ingram listened languidly to the gallant speeches of the other. Sometimes all, as with one consent, suspended their by-play to observe and listen to the principal actors; for, after all, Mr. Rochester, and—because closely connected with him—Miss Ingram, were the life and soul of the party. If he was absent from the room an hour, a perceptible dulness seemed to steal over the spirits of his guests, and his re-entrance was sure to give a fresh impulse to the vivacity of conversation.

The want of his animating influence appeared to be peculiarly felt one day that he had been summoned to Millcote on business, and was not likely to return till late. The afternoon was wet: a walk the party had proposed to take to see a gipsy camp, lately pitched on a common beyond Hay, was consequently deferred. Some of the gentlemen were gone to the stables; the younger ones, together with the younger ladies, were playing billiards in the billiard-room. The dowagers Ingram and Lynn sought solace in a quiet game at cards. Blanche Ingram, after having repelled, by supercilious taciturnity, some efforts of Mrs. Dent and Mrs. Eshton to draw her into conversation, had first murmured over some sentimental tunes and airs on the piano, and then, having fetched a novel from the library, had flung herself in haughty listlessness on a sofa, and prepared to beguile, by the spell of fiction, the tedious hours of absence. The room and the house were silent; only now and then the merriment of the billiard players was heard from above.

It was verging on dusk, and the clock had already given warning of the hour to dress for dinner, when little Adèle, who knelt by me in the drawing-room window-seat, exclaimed,—"Voilà Monsieur Rochester, qui revient!"[7]

I turned, and Miss Ingram darted forwards from her sofa; the others, too, looked up from their several occupations; for at the same time a crunching of wheels, and a splashing tramp of horse-hoofs became audible on the wet gravel. A post-chaise was aproaching.

"What can possess him to come home in that style?" said Miss Ingram. "He rode Mesrour (the black horse), did he not, when he went out? and Pilot was with him,—what has he done with the animals?"

As she said this, she approached her tall person and ample garments so near the window, that I was obliged to bend back almost to the breaking of my spine; in her eagerness she did not observe me at first, but when she did, she curled her lip and moved to another casement. The post-chaise stopped, the driver rang the door bell, and a gentleman alighted, attired in traveling garb; but it was not Mr. Rochester; it was a tall, fashionable-looking man, a stranger.

"Provoking!" exclaimed Miss Ingram: "you tiresome monkey!" (apostrophizing Adèle) "who perched you up in the window to give false intelligence?" and she cast on me an angry glance, as if I were in fault.

7. Here is Mr. Rochester, he's returned!

Some parleying was audible in the hall, and soon the new-comer entered. He bowed to Lady Ingram, as deeming her the eldest lady present.

"It appears I come at an inopportune time madam," said he; "when my friend, Mr. Rochester, is from home; but I arrive from a very long journey, and I think I may presume so far on old and intimate acquaintance as to instal myself here till he returns."

His manner was polite; his accent, in speaking, struck me as being somewhat unusual,—not precisely foreign, but still not altogether English; his age might be about Mr. Rochester's,—between thirty and forty; his complexion was singularly sallow; otherwise he was a fine-looking man, at first sight especially. On closer examination you detected something in his face that displeased; or rather, that failed to please. His features were regular, but too relaxed; his eye was large and well cut, but the life looking out of it was a tame, vacant life—at least so I thought.

The sound of the dressing-bell dispersed the party. It was not till after dinner that I saw him again; he then seemed quite at his ease. But I liked his physiognomy even less than before; it struck me as being, at the same time, unsettled and inanimate. His eye wandered, and had no meaning in its wandering; this gave him an odd look, such as I never remembered to have seen. For a handsome and not an unamiable-looking man, he repelled me exceedingly; there was no power in that smooth-skinned face of a full oval shape; no firmness in that aquiline nose. and small cherry mouth. there was no thought on the low, even forehead; no command in that blank, brown eye.

As I sat in my usual nook, and looked at him with the light of the girandoles on the mantelpiece beaming full over him—for he occupied an arm-chair, drawn close to the fire, and kept shrinking still nearer as if he were cold—I compared him with Mr. Rochester. I think (with deference be it spoken) the contrast could not be much greater between a sleek gander and a fierce falcon: between a meek sheep and the rough-coated keen-eyed dog, its guardian.

He had spoken of Mr. Rochester as an old friend. A curious friendship theirs must have been: a pointed illustration, indeed, of the old adage that "extremes meet."

Two or three of the gentlemen sat near him, and I caught at times scraps of their conversation across the room. At first I could not make much sense of what I heard. for the discourse of Louisa Eshton and Mary Ingram, who sat nearer to me. confused the fragmentary sentences that reached me at intervals. These last were discussing the stranger: they both called him a "beautiful man." Louisa said he was "a love of a creature," and she "adored him": and Mary instanced his "pretty little mouth. and nice nose," as her ideal of the charming.

"And what a sweet-tempered forehead he has!" cried Louisa,—"so smooth—none of those frowning irregularities I dislike so much: and such a placid eye and smile!"

And then, to my great relief, Mr. Henry Lynn summoned them to the other side of the room, to settle some point about the deferred excursion to Hay Common.

I was now able to concentrate my attention on the group by the fire, and I presently gathered that the new-comer was called Mr. Mason: then I learned that he was but just arrived in England, and that he came from some hot country: which was the reason, doubtless, his face was so sallow, and that he

sat so near the hearth, and wore a surtout in the house. Presently the words, Jamaica, Kingston, Spanish Town, indicated the West Indies as his residence; and it was with no little surprise I gathered, ere long, that he had there first seen and become acquainted with Mr. Rochester. He spoke of his friend's dislike of the burning heats, the hurricanes, and rainy seasons of that region. I knew Mr. Rochester had been a traveler: Mrs. Fairfax had said so; but I thought the continent of Europe had bounded his wanderings: till now I had never heard a hint given of visits to more distant shores.

I was pondering these things, when an incident, and a somewhat unexpected one, broke the thread of my musing. Mr. Mason, shivering as some one chanced to open the door, asked for more coal to be put on the fire, which had burned out its flame, though its mass of cinder still shone hot and red. The footman who brought in the coal, in going out, stopped near Mr. Eshton's chair, and said something to him in a low voice, of which I heard only the words, "old woman,"—"quite troublesome."

"Tell her she shall be put in the stocks if she does not take herself off," replied the magistrate.

"No—stop!" interrupted Colonel Dent. "Don't send her away, Eshton; we might turn the thing to account; better consult the ladies." And speaking aloud, he continued, "Ladies, you talked of going to Hay Common to visit the gipsy camp; Sam, here, says that one of the old Mother Bunches[8] is in the servants' hall at this moment, and insists upon being brought in before 'the quality,' to tell them their fortunes. Would you like to see her?"

"Surely, colonel," cried Lady Ingram, "you would not encourage such a low impostor. Dismiss her, by all means, at once!"

"But I cannot persuade her to go away, my lady," said the footman; "nor can any of the servants: Mrs. Fairfax is with her just now, entreating her to be gone; but she has taken a chair in the chimney-corner, and says nothing shall stir her from it till she gets leave to come in here."

"What does she want?" asked Mrs. Eshton.

"'To tell the gentry their fortunes,' she says, ma'am; and she swears she must and will do it."

"What is she like?" inquired the Misses Eshton in a breath.

"A shockingly ugly old creature, miss; almost as black as a crock."

"Why, she's a real sorceress!" cried Frederick Lynn. "Let us have her in, of course."

"To be sure," rejoined his brother; "it would be a thousand pities to throw away such a chance of fun."

"My dear boys, what are you thinking about?" exclaimed Mrs. Lynn.

"I cannot possibly countenance any such inconsistent proceeding," chimed in the Dowager Ingram.

"Indeed, mamma, but you can—and will," pronounced the haughty voice of Blanche, as she turned round on the piano-stool; where till now she had sat silent, apparently examining sundry sheets of music. "I have a curiosity to hear my fortune told: therefore, Sam, order the beldame[9] forwards."

"My darling Blanche! recollect——"

"I do—I recollect all you can suggest; and I must have my will—quick, Sam!"

8. A 16th-century London keeper of an alehouse 9. Old woman.
whose name was used in many 17th-century jestbooks.

"Yes—yes—yes!" cried all the juveniles, both ladies and gentlemen. "Let her come—it will be excellent sport!"

The footman still lingered. "She looks such a rough one," said he.

"Go!" ejaculated Miss Ingram, and the man went.

Excitement instantly seized the whole party: a running fire of raillery and jests was proceeding when Sam returned.

"She won't come now," said he. "She says it's not her mission to appear before the 'vulgar herd' (them's her words). I must show her into a room by herself, and then those who wish to consult her must go to her one by one."

"You see now, my queenly Blanche," began Lady Ingram, "she encroaches. Be advised, my angel girl—and——"

"Show her into the library, of course," cut in the "angel girl." "It is not my mission to listen to her before the vulgar herd either: I mean to have her all to myself. Is there a fire in the library?"

"Yes, ma'am—but she looks such a tinker."[1]

"Cease that chatter, blockhead! and do my bidding."

Again Sam vanished; and mystery, animation, expectation rose to full flow once more.

"She's ready now," said the footman, as he reappeared. 'She wishes to know who will be her first visitor.'

"I think I had better just look in upon her before any of the ladies go," said Colonel Dent.

"Tell her, Sam, a gentleman is coming."

Sam went and returned.

"She says, sir, that she'll have no gentlemen; they need not trouble themselves to come near her: nor," he added, with difficulty suppressing a titter, "any ladies either, except the young and single."

"By Jove, she has taste!" exclaimed Henry Lynn.

Miss Ingram rose solemnly: "I go first," she said, in a tone which might have befitted the leader of a forlorn hope, mounting a breach in the van of his men.

"Oh, my best! oh, my dearest! pause—reflect!" was her mamma's cry; but she swept past her in stately silence, passed through the door which Colonel Dent held open, and we heard her enter the library.

A comparative silence ensued. Lady Ingram thought it "le cas"[2] to wring her hands: which she did accordingly. Miss Mary declared she felt, for her part, she never dared venture. Amy and Louisa Eshton tittered under their breath, and looked a little frightened.

The minutes passed very slowly: fifteen were counted before the library-door again opened. Miss Ingram returned to us through the arch.

Would she laugh? Would she take it as a joke? All eyes met her with a glance of curiosity, and she met all eyes with one of rebuff and coldness: she looked neither flurried nor merry; she walked stiffly to her seat, and took it in silence.

"Well, Blanche?" said Lord Ingram.

"What did she say, sister?" asked Mary.

"What did you think? How do you feel? Is she a real fortune-teller?" demanded the Misses Eshton.

"Now, now, good people," returned Miss Ingram, "don't press upon me. Really your organs of wonder and credulity are easily excited: you seem by the

1. Itinerant metal-worker, often a gypsy. 2. The right moment.

importance you all—my good mamma included—ascribe to this matter—absolutely to believe we have a genuine witch in the house, who is in close alliance with the old gentleman.[3] I have seen a gipsy-vagabond; she has practiced in hackneyed fashion the science of palmistry, and told me what such people usually tell. My whim is gratified; and now I think Mr. Eshton will do well to put the hag in the stocks tomorrow morning, as he threatened."

Miss Ingram took a book, leant back in her chair, and so declined further conversation. I watched her for nearly half an hour: during all that time she never turned a page, and her face grew momently darker, more dissatisfied, and more sourly expressive of disappointment. She had obviously not heard anything to her advantage: and it seemed to me, from her prolonged fit of gloom and taciturnity, that she herself, notwithstanding her professed indifference, attached undue importance to whatever revelations had been made her.

Meantime, Mary Ingram, Amy and Louisa Eshton, declared they dared not go alone; and yet they all wished to go. A negotiation was opened through the medium of the ambassador, Sam; and after much pacing to and fro, till, I think, the said Sam's calves must have ached with the exercise, permission was at last, with great difficulty extorted from the rigorous Sibyl,[4] for the three to wait upon her in a body.

Their visit was not so still as Miss Ingram's had been: we heard hysterical giggling and little shrieks proceeding from the library; and at the end of about twenty minutes they burst the door open, and came running across the hall, as if they were half-scared out of their wits.

"I'm sure she is something not right!" they cried one and all. "She told us such things! She knows all about us!" and they sank breathless into the various seats the gentlemen hastened to bring them.

Pressed for further explanation they declared she had told them of things they had said and done when they were mere children; described books and ornaments they had in their boudoirs at home; keepsakes that different relations had presented to them. They affirmed that she had even divined their thoughts, and had whispered in the ear of each the name of the person she liked best in the world, and informed them of what they most wished for.

Here the gentlemen interposed with earnest petitions to be further enlightened on these two last-named points; but they got only blushes, ejaculations, tremors, and titters, in return for their importunity. The matrons, meantime, offered vinaigrettes[5] and wielded fans; and again and again reiterated the expression of their concern that their warning had not been taken in time; and the elder gentlemen laughed, and the younger urged their services on the agitated fair ones.

In the midst of the tumult, and while my eyes and ears were fully engaged in the scene before me, I heard a hem close at my elbow: I turned and saw Sam.

"If you please, miss, the gipsy declares that there is another young single lady in the room who has not been to her yet, and she swears she will not go till she has seen all. I thought it must be you: there is no one else for it. What shall I tell her?"

"Oh, I will go by all means," I answered; and I was glad of the unexpected

3. I.e., the devil.
4. Prophetess.

5. Small ornamental bottles, often containing smelling salts.

opportunity to gratify my much-excited curiosity. I slipped out of the room, unobserved by any eye—for the company were gathered in one mass about the trembling trio just returned—and I closed the door quietly behind me.

"If you like, miss," said Sam. "I'll wait in the hall for you; and if she frightens you, just call and I'll come in."

"No, Sam, return to the kitchen: I am not in the least afraid." Nor was I; but I was a good deal interested and excited.

Chapter XIX

The library looked tranquil enough as I entered it. and the Sibyl—if Sibyl she were—was seated snugly enough in an easy chair at the chimney-corner. She had on a red cloak and a black bonnet: or rather, a broad-brimmed gipsy hat, tied down with a striped handkerchief under her chin. An extinguished candle stood on the table: she was bending over the fire, and seemed reading in a little black book, like a prayer-book, by the light of the blaze: she muttered the words to herself, as most old women do, while she read; she did not desist immediately on my entrance: it appeared she wished to finish a paragraph.

I stood on the rug and warmed my hands, which were rather cold with sitting at a distance from the drawing-room fire. I felt now as composed as ever I did in my life: there was nothing indeed in the gipsy's appearance to trouble one's calm. She shut her book and slowly looked up; her hat-brim partially shaded her face, yet I could see as she raised it, that it was a strange one. It looked all brown and black: elf-locks bristled out from beneath a white band which passed under her chin, and came half over her cheeks or rather jaws; her eye confronted me at once, with a bold and direct gaze.

"Well, and you want your fortune told?" she said in a voice as decided as her glance, as harsh as her features.

"I don't care about it, mother; you may please yourself; but I ought to warn you, I have no faith."

"It's like your impudence to say so: I expected it of you; I heard it in your step as you crossed the threshold."

"Did you? You've a quick ear."

"I have; and a quick eye, and a quick brain."

"You need them all in your trade."

"I do; especially when I've customers like you to deal with. Why don't you tremble?"

"I'm not cold."

"Why don't you turn pale?"

"I am not sick."

"Why don't you consult my art?"

"I'm not silly."

The old crone "nichered" a laugh under her bonnet and bandage: she then drew out a short, black pipe, and lighting it began to smoke. Having indulged a while in this sedative, she raised her bent body, took the pipe from her lips, and while gazing steadily at the fire, said very deliberately:—"You are cold; you are sick; and you are silly."

"Prove it," I rejoined.

"I will; in few words. You are cold, because you are alone: no contact strikes the fire from you that is in you. You are sick: because the best of feelings, the

highest and the sweetest given to man, keeps far away from you. You are silly, because, suffer as you may, you will not beckon it to approach; nor will you stir one step to meet it where it waits you."

She again put her short, black pipe to her lips, and renewed her smoking with vigor.

"You might say all that to almost any one who, you knew, lived as a solitary dependant in a great house."

"I might say it to almost any one; but would it be true of almost any one?"

"In my circumstances."

"Yes; just so, in *your* circumstances: but find me another precisely placed as you are."

'It would be easy to find you thousands."

"You could scarcely find me one. If you knew it, you are peculiarly situated: very near happiness; yes; within reach of it. The materials are all prepared; there only wants a movement to combine them. Chance laid them somewhat apart; let them be once approached and bliss results."

"I don't understand enigmas. I never could guess a riddle in my life."

"If you wish me to speak more plainly, show me your palm."

"And I must cross it with silver, I suppose?"

"To be sure."

I gave her a shilling: she put it into an old stocking-foot which she took out of her pocket, and having tied it round and returned it, she told me to hold out my hand. I did. She approached her face to the palm, and pored over it without touching it.

"It is too fine," said she. "I can make nothing of such a hand as that; almost without lines: besides, what is in a palm? Destiny is not written there."

"I believe you," said I.

"No," she continued, "it is in the face: on the forehead, about the eyes, in the eyes themselves, in the lines of the mouth. Kneel, and lift up your head."

"Ah! now you are coming to reality," I said as I obeyed her. "I shall begin to put some faith in you presently."

I knelt within half a yard of her. She stirred the fire, so that a ripple of light broke from the disturbed coal: the glare, however, as she sat, only threw her face into deeper shadow: mine, it illumined.

"I wonder with what feelings you came to me tonight," she said, when she had examined me a while. "I wonder what thoughts are busy in your heart during all the hours you sit in yonder room with the fine people flitting before you like shapes in a magic lantern: just as little sympathetic communion passing between you and them, as if they were really mere shadows of human forms and not the actual substance."

"I feel tired often, sleepy sometimes; but seldom sad."

"Then you have some secret hope to buoy you up and please you with whispers of the future?"

"Not I. The utmost I hope is, to save money enough out of my earnings to set up a school some day in a little house rented by myself."

"A mean nutriment for the spirit to exist on: and sitting in that window-seat (you see I know your habits)——"

"You have learned them from the servants."

"Ah! you think yourself sharp. Well—perhaps I have: to speak truth, I have an acquaintance with one of them—Mrs. Poole——"

I started to my feet when I heard the name.

"You have—have you?" thought I; "there is diablerie[6] in the business after all, then!"

"Don't be alarmed," continued the strange being; "she's a safe hand, is Mrs. Poole: close and quiet: any one may repose confidence in her. But, as I was saying: sitting in that window-seat, do you think of nothing but your future school? Have you no present interest in any of the company who occupy the sofas and chairs before you? Is there not one face you study? One figure whose movements you follow with, at least, curiosity?"

"I like to observe all the faces, and all the figures."

"But do you never single one from the rest—or it may be, two?"

"I do frequently; when the gestures or looks of a pair seem telling a tale: it amuses me to watch them."

"What tale do you like best to hear?"

"Oh, I have not much choice! They generally run on the same theme—courtship; and promise to end in the same catastrophe—marriage."

"And do you like that monotonous theme?"

"Positively, I don't care about it: it is nothing to me."

"Nothing to you? When a lady, young and full of life and health, charming with beauty and endowed with the gifts of rank and fortune, sits and smiles in the eyes of a gentleman you——"

"I what?"

"You know—and, perhaps, think well of?"

"I don't know the gentlemen here. I have scarcely interchanged a syllable with one of them; and as to thinking well of them, I consider some respectable and stately, and middle-aged, and others young, dashing, handsome and lively: but certainly they are all at liberty to be the recipients of whose smiles they please, without my feeling disposed to consider the transaction of any moment to me."

"You don't know the gentlemen here? You have not exchanged a syllable with one of them? Will you say that of the master of the house?"

"He is not at home."

"A profound remark! A most ingenious quibble! He went to Millcote this morning, and will be back here tonight, or tomorrow: does that circumstance exclude him from the list of your acquaintance—blot him, as it were, out of existence?"

"No: but I can scarcely see what Mr. Rochester has to do with the theme you had introduced."

"I was talking of ladies smiling in the eyes of gentlemen; and of late so many smiles have been shed into Mr. Rochester's eyes that they overflow like two cups filled above the brim: have you never remarked that?"

"Mr. Rochester has a right to enjoy the society of his guests."

"No question about his right: but have you never observed that, of all the tales told here about matrimony, Mr. Rochester has been favored with the most lively and the most continuous?"

"The eagerness of a listener quickens the tongue of a narrator." I said this rather to myself than to the gipsy; whose strange talk, voice, manner, had by this time wrapped me in a kind of dream. One unexpected sentence came

6. Devilry.

from her lips after another, till I got involved in a web of mystification; and wondered what unseen spirit had been sitting for weeks by my heart watching its workings and taking record of every pulse.

"Eagerness of a listener!" repeated she: "yes; Mr. Rochester has sat by the hour, his ear inclined to the fascinating lips that took such delight in their task of communicating; and Mr. Rochester was so willing to receive and looked so grateful for the pastime given him: you have noticed this?"

"Grateful! I cannot remember detecting gratitude in his face."

"Detecting! You have analyzed, then. And what did you detect, if not gratitude?"

I said nothing.

"You have seen love: have you not?—and, looking forward, you have seen him married and beheld his bride happy?"

"Humph! Not exactly. Your witch's skill is rather at fault sometimes."

"What the devil have you seen, then?"

"Never mind: I came here to inquire, not to confess. Is it known that Mr. Rochester is to be married?"

"Yes; and to the beautiful Miss Ingram."

"Shortly?"

"Appearances would warrant that conclusion; and, no doubt (though, with an audacity that wants chastising out of you, you seem to question it), they will be a superlatively happy pair. He must love such a handsome, noble, witty, accomplished lady; and probably she loves him: or, if not his person, at least his purse. I know she considers the Rochester estate eligible to the last degree; though (God pardon me!) I told her something on that point about an hour ago, which made her look wondrous grave: the corners of her mouth fell half an inch. I would advise her blackaviced[7] suitor to look out: if another comes with a longer, or clearer rent-roll,—he's dished——"

"But, mother, I did not come to hear Mr. Rochester's fortune: I came to hear my own; and you have told me nothing of it."

"Your fortune is yet doubtful: when I examined your face, one trait contradicted another. Chance has meted you a measure of happiness: that I know. I knew it before I came here this evening. She has laid it carefully on one side for you. I saw her do it. It depends on yourself to stretch out your hand, and take it up; but whether you will do so, is the problem I study. Kneel again on the rug."

"Don't keep me long; the fire scorches me."

I knelt. She did not stoop towards me, but only gazed leaning back in her chair. She began muttering,—"The flame flickers in the eye, the eye shines like dew: it looks soft and full of feeling; it smiles at my jargon: it is susceptible; impression follows impression through its clear sphere; where it ceases to smile, it is sad; an unconscious lassitude weighs on the lid: that signifies melancholy resulting from loneliness. It turns from me; it will not suffer farther scrutiny; it seems to deny, by a mocking glance, the truth of the discoveries I have already made,—to disown the charge both of sensibility and chagrin: its pride and reserve only confirm me in my opinion. The eye is favorable.

"As to the mouth, it delights at times in laughter; it is disposed to impart all that the brain conceives; though I daresay it would be silent on much the

7. I.e., blackavised, i.e., of a dark complexion.

heart experiences. Mobile and flexible, it was never intended to be compressed in the eternal silence of solitude: it is a mouth which should speak much and smile often and have human affection for its interlocutor. That feature too is propitious.

"I see no enemy to a fortunate issue but in the brow; and that brow professes to say—'I can live alone if self-respect and circumstances require me so to do. I need not sell my soul to buy bliss. I have an inward treasure, born with me, which can keep me alive if all extraneous delights should be withheld; or offered only at a price I cannot afford to give.' The forehead declares, 'Reason sits firm and holds the reins, and she will not let the feelings burst away and hurry her to wild chasms. The passions may rage furiously, like true heathens, as they are; and the desires may imagine all sorts of vain things: but judgment shall still have the last word in every argument, and the casting vote in every decision. Strong wind, earthquake-shock, and fire may pass by: but I shall follow the guiding of that still small voice which interprets the dictates of conscience.'

"Well said, forehead; your declaration shall be respected. I have formed my plans—right plans I deem them—and in them I have attended to the claims of conscience, the counsels of reason. I know how soon youth would fade and bloom perish, if, in the cup of bliss offered, but one dreg of shame, or one flavor of remorse were detected; and I do not want sacrifice, sorrow, dissolution—such is not my taste. I wish to foster, not to blight—to earn gratitude, not to wring tears of blood—no, nor of brine: my harvest must be in smiles, in endearments, in sweet—That will do. I think I rave in a kind of exquisite delirium. I should wish now to protract this moment *ad infinitum*; but I dare not. So far I have governed myself thoroughly. I have acted as I inwardly swore I would act; but farther might try me beyond my strength. Rise, Miss Eyre: leave me; 'the play is played out.' "[8]

Where was I? Did I wake or sleep? Had I been dreaming? Did I dream still? The old woman's voice had changed: her accent, her gesture, and all were familiar to me as my own face in a glass—as the speech of my own tongue. I got up, but did not go. I looked; I stirred the fire, and I looked again: but she drew her bonnet and her bandage closer about her face, and again beckoned me to depart. The flame illuminated her hand stretched out: roused now, and on the alert for discoveries, I at once noticed that hand. It was no more the withered limb of eld than my own; it was a rounded supple member, with smooth fingers, symmetrically turned; a broad ring flashed on the little finger, and stooping forward I looked at it, and saw a gem I had seen a hundred times before. Again I looked at the face; which was no longer turned from me—on the contrary, the bonnet was doffed, the bandage displaced, the head advanced.

"Well, Jane, do you know me?" asked the familiar voice.

"Only take off the red cloak, sir, and then——"

"But the string is in a knot—help me."

"Break it, sir."

"There, then—'Off, ye lendings' "[9]

And Mr. Rochester stepped out of his disguise.

"Now, sir, what a strange idea!"

8. The next to last line of Shakespeare's *Twelfth Night* IV 2.4.53, "Play out the play."
is "But that's all one, our play is done"; see also I *Henry* 9 *King Lear* 3.4.114.

"But well carried out, eh? Don't you think so?"

"With the ladies you must have managed well."

"But not with you?"

"You did not act the character of a gipsy with me."

"What character did I act? My own?"

"No; some unaccountable one. In short, I believe you have been trying to draw me out—or in; you have been talking nonsense to make me talk nonsense. It is scarcely fair, sir."

"Do you forgive me, Jane?"

"I cannot tell till I have thought it all over. If, on reflection, I find I have fallen into no great absurdity, I shall try to forgive you; but it was not right."

"Oh! you have been very correct—very careful, very sensible."

I reflected, and thought, on the whole, I had. It was a comfort; but, indeed, I had been on my guard almost from the beginning of the interview. Something of masquerade I suspected. I knew gipsies and fortune-tellers did not express themselves as this seeming old woman had expressed herself; besides, I had noted her feigned voice, her anxiety to conceal her features. But my mind had been running on Grace Poole—that living enigma, that mystery of mysteries, as I considered her. I had never thought of Mr. Rochester.

"Well," said he, "what are you musing about? What does that grave smile signify?"

"Wonder and self-congratulation, sir. I have your permission to retire now, I suppose?"

"No; stay a moment; and tell me what the people in the drawing-room yonder are doing."

"Discussing the gipsy, I daresay."

"Sit down!—Let me hear what they said about me."

"I had better not stay long, sir; it must be near eleven o'clock. Oh! are you aware, Mr. Rochester, that a stranger has arrived here since you left this morning?"

"A stranger!—no; who can it be? I expected no one; is he gone?"

"No; he said he had known you long, and that he could take the liberty of installing himself here till you returned."

"The devil he did! Did he give his name?"

"His name is Mason, sir; and he comes from the West Indies; from Spanish Town, in Jamaica, I think."

Mr. Rochester was standing near me; he had taken my hand, as if to lead me to a chair. As I spoke, he gave my wrist a convulsive grip; the smile on his lips froze: apparently a spasm caught his breath.

"Mason!—the West Indies!" he said, in the tone one might fancy a speaking automaton to enounce its single words; "Mason!—the West Indies!" he reiterated; and he went over the syllables three times, growing, in the intervals of speaking, whiter than ashes: he hardly seemed to know what he was doing.

"Do you feel ill, sir?" I inquired.

"Jane, I've got a blow;—I've got a blow, Jane!" he staggered.

"Oh!—lean on me, sir."

"Jane, you offered me your shoulder once before; let me have it now."

"Yes, sir, yes; and my arm."

He sat down, and made me sit beside him. Holding my hand in both his own, he chafed it; gazing on me, at the same time, with the most troubled and dreary look.

"My little friend!" said he, "I wish I were in a quiet island with only you; and trouble, and danger, and hideous recollections removed from me."

"Can I help you, sir?—I'd give my life to serve you."

"Jane, if aid is wanted, I'll seek it at your hands; I promise you that."

"Thank you, sir; tell me what to do,—I'll try, at least, to do it."

"Fetch me now, Jane, a glass of wine from the dining-room; they will be at supper there; and tell me if Mason is with them, and what he is doing."

I went. I found all the party in the dining-room at supper, as Mr. Rochester had said; they were not seated at table,—the supper was arranged on the sideboard; each had taken what he chose, and they stood about here and there in groups, their plates and glasses in their hands. Every one seemed in high glee; laughter and conversation were general and animated. Mr. Mason stood near the fire, talking to Colonel and Mrs. Dent, and appeared as merry as any of them. I filled a wine-glass (I saw Miss Ingram watch me frowningly as I did so: she thought I was taking a liberty, I daresay), and I returned to the library.

Mr. Rochester's extreme pallor had disappeared, and he looked once more firm and stern. He took the glass from my hand.

"Here is to your health, ministrant spirit!" he said: he swallowed the contents and returned it to me. "What are they doing, Jane?"

"Laughing and talking, sir."

"They don't look grave and mysterious, as if they had heard something strange?"

"Not at all—they are full of jests and gaiety."

"And Mason?"

"He was laughing too."

"If all these people came in a body and spat at me, what would you do, Jane?"

"Turn them out of the room, sir, if I could."

He half smiled. "But if I were to go to them, and they only looked at me coldly, and whispered sneeringly among each other, and then drop off and left me one by one, what then? Would you go with them?"

"I rather think not, sir: I should have more pleasure in staying with you."

"To comfort me?"

"Yes, sir, to comfort you, as well as I could."

"And if they laid you under a ban for adhering to me?"

"I, probably, should know nothing about their ban; and if I did, I should care nothing about it."

"Then, you could dare censure for my sake?"

"I could dare it for the sake of any friend who deserved my adherence; as you, I am sure, do."

"Go back now into the room; step quietly up to Mason, and whisper in his ear that Mr. Rochester is come and wishes to see him: show him in here and then leave me."

"Yes, sir."

I did his behest. The company all stared at me as I passed straight among them. I sought Mr. Mason, delivered the message, and preceded him from the room: I ushered him into the library, and then I went upstairs.

At a late hour, after I had been in bed some time, I heard the visitors repair to their chambers: I distinguished Mr. Rochester's voice, and heard him say, "This way, Mason; this is your room."

He spoke cheerfully: the gay tones set my heart at ease. I was soon asleep.

Chapter XX

I had forgotten to draw my curtain,[1] which I usually did; and also to let down my window-blind. The consequence was, that when the moon, which was full and bright (for the night was fine), came in her course to that space in the sky opposite my casement, and looked in at me through the unveiled panes, her glorious gaze roused me. Awaking in the dead of night, I opened my eyes on her disk—silver-white and crystal-clear. It was beautiful, but too solemn: I half rose, and stretched my arm to draw the curtain.

Good God! What a cry!

The night—its silence—its rest, was rent in twain, by a savage, a sharp, a shrilly sound that ran from end to end of Thornfield Hall.

My pulse stopped: my heart stood still; my stretched arm was paralyzed. The cry died, and was not renewed. Indeed, whatever being uttered that fearful shriek could not soon repeat it: not the widest-winged condor on the Andes could, twice in succession, send out such a yell from the cloud shrouding his eyrie. The thing delivering such utterance must rest ere it could repeat the effort.

It came out of the third story; for it passed overhead. And overhead—yes, in the room just above my chamber ceiling—I now heard a struggle: a deadly one it seemed from the noise; and a half-smothered voice shouted—"Help! help! help!" three times rapidly.

"Will no one come?" it cried; and then, while the staggering and stamping went on wildly, I distinguished through plank and plaster:—"Rochester! Rochester! for God's sake, come!"

A chamber door opened: some one ran, or rushed, along the gallery. Another step stamped on the flooring above, and something fell; and there was silence.

I had put on some clothes, though horror shook all my limbs: I issued from my apartment. The sleepers were all aroused: ejaculations, terrified murmurs, sounded in every room; door after door unclosed: one looked out and another looked out; the gallery filled. Gentlemen and ladies alike had quitted their beds; and "Oh! what is it?"—"Who is hurt?"—"What has happened?"—"Fetch a light!"—"Is it fire?"—"Are there robbers?"—"Where shall we run?" was demanded confusedly on all hands. But for the moonlight they would have been in complete darkness. They ran to and fro; they crowded together; some sobbed, some stumbled: the confusion was inextricable.

"Where the devil is Rochester?" cried Colonel Dent. "I cannot find him in his bed."

"Here! here!" was shouted in return. "Be composed, all of you: I'm coming."

And the door at the end of the gallery opened, and Mr. Rochester advanced with a candle: he had just descended from the upper story. One of the ladies ran to him directly; she seized his arm: it was Miss Ingram.

"What awful event has taken place?" said she. "Speak! let us know the worst at once!"

"But don't pull me down or strangle me," he replied: for the Misses Eshton were clinging about him now; and the two dowagers, in vast white wrappers, were bearing down on him like ships in full sail.

1. I.e., the curtain on her poster bed.

"All's right!—all's right!" he cried. "It's a mere rehearsal of Much Ado About Nothing. Ladies, keep off; or I shall wax dangerous."

And dangerous he looked: his black eyes darted sparks. Calming himself by an effort, he added:—"A servant has had the nightmare; that is all. She's an excitable, nervous person she construed her dream into an apparition, or something of that sort, no doubt; and has taken a fit with fright. Now, then, I must see you all back into your rooms; for, till the house is settled she cannot be looked after. Gentlemen, have the goodness to set the ladies the example. Miss Ingram, I am sure you will not fail in evincing superiority to idle terrors. Amy and Louisa, return to your nests like a pair of doves, as you are. Mesdames" (to the dowagers), "you will take cold to a dead certainty, if you stay in this chill gallery any longer."

And so, by dint of alternate coaxing and commanding, he contrived to get them all once more enclosed in their separate dormitories. I did not wait to be ordered back to mine; but retreated unnoticed: as unnoticed I had left it.

Not, however, to go to bed: on the contrary, I began and dressed myself carefully. The sounds I had heard after the scream, and the words that had been uttered, had probably been heard only by me; for they had proceeded from the room above mine: but they assured me that it was not a servant's dream which had thus struck horror through the house; and that the explanation Mr. Rochester had given was merely an invention framed to pacify his guests. I dressed, then, to be ready for emergencies. When dressed, I sat a long time by the window, looking out over the silent grounds and silvered fields, and waiting for I knew not what. It seemed to me that some event must follow the strange cry, struggle, and call.

No: stillness returned: each murmur and movement ceased gradually, and in about an hour Thornfield Hall was again as hushed as a desert. It seemed that sleep and night had resumed their empire. Meantime the moon declined: she was about to set. Not liking to sit in the cold and darkness, I thought I would lie down on my bed, dressed as I was. I left the window, and moved with little noise across the carpet; as I stooped to take off my shoes, a cautious hand tapped low at the door.

"Am I wanted?" I asked.

"Are you up?" asked the voice I expected to hear, viz. my master's.

"Yes, sir."

"And dressed?"

"Yes."

"Come out, then, quietly."

I obeyed. Mr. Rochester stood in the gallery, holding a light.

"I want you," he said: "come this way: take your time and make no noise."

My slippers were thin: I could walk the matted floor as softly as a cat. He glided up the gallery and up the stairs, and stopped in the dark, low corridor of the fateful third story: I had followed and stood at his side.

"Have you a sponge in your room?" he asked in a whisper.

"Yes, sir."

"Have you any salts—volatile salts?"

"Yes."

"Go back and fetch both."

I returned, sought the sponge on the wash-stand, the salts in my drawer, and once more retraced my steps. He still waited; he held a key in his hand: ap-

proaching one of the small, black doors, he put it in the lock; he paused and addressed me again.

"You don't turn sick at the sight of blood?"

"I think I shall not: I have never been tried yet."

I felt a thrill while I answered him; but no coldness, and no faintness.

"Just give me your hand," he said; "it will not do to risk a fainting fit."

I put my fingers into his. "Warm and steady," was his remark: he turned the key and opened the door.

I saw a room I remembered to have seen before; the day Mrs. Fairfax showed me over the house: it was hung with tapestry; but the tapestry was now looped up in one part, and there was a door apparent, which had then been concealed. This door was open; a light shone out of the room within: I heard thence a snarling, snatching sound, almost like a dog quarreling. Mr. Rochester, putting down his candle, said to me, "Wait a minute," and he went forward to the inner apartment. A shout of laughter greeted his entrance; noisy at first, and terminating in Grace Poole's own goblin ha! ha! She then was there. He made some sort of arrangement, without speaking; though I heard a low voice address him: he came out and closed the door behind him.

"Here, Jane!" he said; and I walked round to the other side of a large bed, which with its drawn curtains concealed a considerable portion of the chamber. An easy-chair was near the bed-head: a man sat in it, dressed with the exception of his coat; he was still; his head leaned back; his eyes were closed. Mr. Rochester held the candle over him; I recognised in his pale and seemingly lifeless face—the stranger, Mason: I saw too that his linen on one side, and one arm, was almost soaked in blood.

"Hold the candle," said Mr. Rochester, and I took it; he fetched a basin of water from the wash-stand: "Hold that," said he. I obeyed. He took the sponge, dipped it in and moistened the corpse-like face: he asked for my smelling-bottle, and applied it to the nostrils. Mr. Mason shortly unclosed his eyes; he groaned. Mr. Rochester opened the shirt of the wounded man, whose arm and shoulder were bandaged: he sponged away blood, trickling fast down.

"Is there immediate danger?" murmured Mr. Mason.

"Pooh! No—a mere scratch. Don't be so overcome, man: bear up! I'll fetch a surgeon for you now, myself: you'll be able to be removed by morning, I hope. Jane," he continued.

"Sir?"

"I shall have to leave you in this room with this gentleman, for an hour, or perhaps two hours; you will sponge the blood as I do when it returns: if he feels faint, you will put the glass of water on that stand to his lips, and your salts to his nose. You will not speak to him on any pretext—and—Richard—it will be at the peril of your life if you speak to her: open your lips—agitate yourself—and I'll not answer for the consequences."

Again the poor man groaned: he looked as if he dared not move: fear, either of death or of something else, appeared almost to paralyze him. Mr. Rochester put the now bloody sponge into my hand, and I proceeded to use it as he had done. He watched me a second, then saying, "Remember!—No conversation," he left the room. I experienced a strange feeling as the key grated in the lock, and the sound of his retreating step ceased to be heard.

Here then I was in the third story, fastened into one of its mystic cells; night around me; a pale and bloody spectacle under my eyes and hands; a murderess

hardly separated from me by a single door: yes—that was appalling—the rest I could bear; but I shuddered at the thought of Grace Poole bursting out upon me.

I must keep to my post, however. I must watch this ghastly countenance—these blue, still lips forbidden to unclose—these eyes now shut, now opening, now wandering through the room, now fixing on me, and ever glazed with the dulness of horror. I must dip my hand again and again in the basin of blood and water, and wipe away the trickling gore. I must see the light of the un-snuffed candle wane on my employment; the shadows darken on the wrought-antique tapestry round me, and grow black under the hangings of the vast old bed, and quiver strangely over the doors of a great cabinet opposite—whose front, divided into twelve panels, bore in grim design the heads of the twelve apostles, each inclosed in its separate panel as in a frame; while above them at the top rose an ebon crucifix and a dying Christ.

According as the shifting obscurity and flickering gleam hovered here or glanced there, it was now the bearded physician, Luke, that bent his brow; now St. John's long hair that waved; and anon the devilish face of Judas, that grew out of the panel, and seemed gathering life and threatening a revelation of the arch-traitor—of Satan himself—in his subordinate's form.

Amidst all this, I had to listen as well as watch: to listen for the movements of the wild beast or the fiend in yonder side den. But since Mr. Rochester's visit it seemed spell-bound: all the night I heard but three sounds at three long intervals,—a step creak, a momentary renewal of the snarling, canine noise, and a deep human groan.

Then my own thoughts worried me. What crime was this, that lived incarnate in this sequestered mansion, and could neither be expelled nor subdued by the owner?—What mystery, that broke out, now in fire and now in blood, at the deadest hours of night? What creature was it, that, masked in an ordinary woman's face and shape, uttered the voice, now of a mocking demon, and anon of a carrion-seeking bird of prey?

And this man I bent over—this commonplace, quiet stranger—how had he become involved in the web of horror? and why had the Fury[2] flown at him? What made him seek this quarter of the house at an untimely season, when he should have been asleep in bed? I had heard Mr. Rochester assign him an apartment below—what brought him here? And why, now, was he so tame under the violence or treachery done him? Why did he so quietly submit to the concealment Mr. Rochester enforced? Why did Mr. Rochester enforce this concealment? His guest had been outraged, his own life on a former occasion had been hideously plotted against; and both attempts he smothered in secrecy and sank in oblivion! Lastly, I saw Mr. Mason was submissive to Mr. Rochester; that the impetuous will of the latter held complete sway over the inertness of the former: the few words which had passed between them assured me of this. It was evident that in their former intercourse, the passive disposition of the one had been habitually influenced by the active energy of the other: whence then had arisen Mr. Rochester's dismay when he heard of Mr. Mason's arrival? Why had the mere name of this unresisting individual—whom his word now sufficed to control like a child—fallen on him, a few hours since, as a thunderbolt might fall on an oak?

2. Greek female spirit of vengeance.

Oh! I could not forget his look and his paleness when he whispered: "Jane, I have got a blow—I have got a blow, Jane." I could not forget how the arm had trembled which he had rested on my shoulder: and it was no light matter which could thus bow the resolute spirit and thrill the vigorous frame of Fairfax Rochester.

"When will he come? When will he come?" I cried inwardly, as the night lingered and lingered—as my bleeding patient drooped, moaned, sickened: and neither day nor aid arrived. I had, again and again, held the water to Mason's white lips; again and again offered him the stimulating salts: my efforts seemed ineffectual: either bodily or mental suffering, or loss of blood, or all three combined, were fast prostrating his strength. He moaned so, and looked so weak, wild, and lost, I feared he was dying; and I might not even speak to him.

The candle, wasted at last, went out; as it expired, I perceived streaks of gray light edging the window curtains: dawn was then approaching. Presently I heard Pilot bark far below, out of his distant kennel in the courtyard: hope revived. Nor was it unwarranted: in five minutes more the grating key, the yielding lock, warned me my watch was relieved. It could not have lasted more than two hours: many a week has seemed shorter.

Mr. Rochester entered, and with him the surgeon he had been to fetch.

"Now, Carter, be on the alert," he said to this last: "I give you but half an hour for dressing the wound, fastening the bandages, getting the patient downstairs and all."

"But is he fit to move, sir?"

"No doubt of it; it is nothing serious: he is nervous, his spirits must be kept up. Come, set to work."

Mr. Rochester drew back the thick curtain, drew up the holland blind, let in all the daylight he could; and I was surprised and cheered to see how far dawn was advanced: what rosy streaks were beginning to brighten the east. Then he approached Mason, whom the surgeon was already handling.

"Now, my good fellow, how are you?" he asked.

"She's done for me, I fear," was the faint reply.

"Not a whit!—courage! This day fortnight you'll hardly be a pin the worse of it: you've lost a little blood; that's all. Carter, assure him there's no danger."

"I can do that conscientiously," said Carter, who had now undone the bandages; "only I wish I could have got here sooner: he would not have bled so much—but how is this? The flesh on the shoulder is torn as well as cut. This wound was not done with a knife: there have been teeth here!"

"She bit me," he murmured. "She worried me like a tigress, when Rochester got the knife from her."

"You should not have yielded: you should have grappled with her at once," said Mr. Rochester.

"But under such circumstances, what could one do?" returned Mason. "Oh, it was frightful!" he added, shuddering. "And I did not expect it: she looked so quiet at first."

"I warned you," was his friend's answer; "I said—be on your guard when you go near her. Besides, you might have waited till tomorrow, and had me with you: it was mere folly to attempt the interview tonight and alone."

"I thought I could have done some good."

"You thought! you thought! Yes; it makes me impatient to hear you: but, however, you have suffered, and are likely to suffer enough for not taking my

advice; so I'll say no more. Carter—hurry!—hurry! The sun will soon rise, and I must have him off."

"Directly, sir; the shoulder is just bandaged. I must look to this other wound in the arm: she has had her teeth here too, I think."

"She sucked the blood: she said she'd drain my heart," said Mason.

I saw Mr. Rochester shudder: a singularly marked expression of disgust, horror, hatred, warped his countenance almost to distortion; but he only said:— "Come, be silent, Richard, and never mind her gibberish: don't repeat it."

"I wish I could forget it," was the answer.

"You will when you are out of the country: when you get back to Spanish Town, you may think of her as dead and buried—or rather, you need not think of her at all."

"Impossible to forget this night!"

"It is not impossible: have some energy, man. You thought you were as dead as a herring two hours since, and you are all alive and talking now. There!— Carter has done with you or nearly so: I'll make you decent in a trice. Jane" (he turned to me for the first time since his reentrance), "take this key: go down into my bedroom, and walk straight forward into my dressing-room; open the top drawer of the wardrobe and take out a clean shirt and neck-handkerchief: bring them here, and be nimble."

I went; sought the repository he had mentioned, found the articles named and returned with them.

"Now," said he, "go to the other side of the bed while I order his toilet; but don't leave the room: you may be wanted again."

I retired as directed.

"Was anybody stirring below when you went down, Jane?" inquired Mr. Rochester, presently.

"No, sir; all was very still."

"We shall get you off cannily, Dick: and it will be better, both for your sake, and for that of the poor creature in yonder. I have striven long to avoid exposure, and I should not like it to come at last. Here, Carter, help him on with his waistcoat. Where did you leave your furred cloak? You can't travel a mile without that, I know, in this damned cold climate. In your room?—Jane, run down to Mr. Mason's room,—the one next mine,—and fetch a cloak you will see there."

Again I ran, and again returned, bearing an immense mantle lined and edged with fur.

"Now I've another errand for you," said my untiring master; "you must away to my room again. What a mercy you are shod with velvet, Jane!—a clod-hopping messenger would never do at this juncture. You must open the middle drawer of my toilet-table and take out a little phial and a little glass you will find there,—quick!"

I flew thither and back, bringing the desired vessels.

"That's well! Now, doctor, I shall take the liberty of administering a dose myself; on my own responsibility. I got this cordial at Rome of an Italian charlatan—a fellow you would have kicked, Carter. It is not a thing to be used indiscriminately, but it is good upon occasion: as now, for instance. Jane, a little water."

He held out the tiny glass, and I half filled it from the water bottle on the wash-stand.

"That will do—now wet the lip of the phial."

I did so: he measured twelve drops of a crimson liquid, and presented it to Mason.

"Drink, Richard: it will give you the heart you lack, for an hour or so."

"But will it hurt me?—is it inflammatory?"

"Drink! drink! drink!"

Mr. Mason obeyed, because it was evidently useless to resist. He was dressed now: he still looked pale, but he was no longer gory and sullied. Mr. Rochester let him sit three minutes after he had swallowed the liquid; he then took his arm.

"Now I am sure you can get on your feet," he said—"try."

The patient rose.

"Carter, take him under the other shoulder. Be of good cheer, Richard; step out—that's it!"

"I do feel better," remarked Mr. Mason.

"I am sure you do. Now, Jane, trip on before us away to the back-stairs; unbolt the side-passage door, and tell the driver of the post-chaise you will see in the yard—or just outside, for I told him not to drive his rattling wheels over the pavement—to be ready; we are coming: and, Jane, if any one is about, come to the foot of the stairs and hem."[3]

It was by this time half-past five, and the sun was on the point of rising; but I found the kitchen still dark and silent. The side-passage door was fastened; I opened it with as little noise as possible: all the yard was quiet; but the gates stood wide open, and there was a post-chaise, with horses ready harnessed, and driver seated on the box, stationed outside. I approached him, and said the gentlemen were coming; he nodded: then I looked carefully round and listened. The stillness of early morning slumbered everywhere; the curtains were yet drawn over the servants' chamber windows; little birds were just twittering in the blossom-blanched orchard trees, whose boughs drooped like white garlands over the wall enclosing one side of the yard; the carriage horses stamped from time to time in their closed stables: all else was still.

The gentlemen now appeared. Mason, supported by Mr. Rochester and the surgeon, seemed to walk with tolerable ease: they assisted him into the chaise; Carter followed.

"Take care of him," said Mr. Rochester to the latter, "and keep him at your house till he is quite well: I shall ride over in a day or two to see how he gets on. Richard, how is it with you?"

"The fresh air revives me, Fairfax."

"Leave the window open on his side, Carter; there is no wind—good-bye, Dick."

"Fairfax——"

"Well, what is it?"

"Let her be taken care of; let her be treated as tenderly as may be: let her ——" he stopped and burst into tears.

"I do my best; and have done it, and will do it," was the answer: he shut up the chaise door, and the vehicle drove away.

"Yet would to God there was an end of all this!" added Mr. Rochester, as he closed and barred the heavy yard-gates. This done, he moved with slow step and abstracted air towards a door in the wall bordering the orchard. I, suppos-

3. Cough.

ing he had done with me, prepared to return to the house; again, however, I
heard him call "Jane!" He had opened the portal and stood at it, waiting for
me.

"Come where there is some freshness, for a few moments," he said; "that
house is a mere dungeon: don't you feel it so?"

"It seems to me a splendid mansion, sir."

"The glamor of inexperience is over your eyes," he answered; "and you see it
through a charmed medium: you cannot discern that the gilding is slime and
the silk draperies cobwebs; that the marble is sordid slate, and the polished
woods mere refuse chips and scaly bark. Now *here*" (he pointed to the leafy en-
closure we had entered) "all is real, sweet, and pure."

He strayed down a walk edged with box; with apple trees, pear trees, and
cherry trees on one side, and a border on the other, full of all sorts of old-fash-
ioned flowers, stocks sweet-williams, primroses, pansies, mingled with south-
ern-wood, sweet-briar, and various fragrant herbs. They were fresh now as a
succession of April showers and gleams, followed by a lovely spring morning,
could make them: the sun was just entering the dappled east, and his light il-
lumined the wreathed and dewy orchard trees and shone down the quiet walks
under them.

"Jane, will you have a flower?"

He gathered a half-blown rose, the first on the bush, and offered it to me.

"Thank you, sir."

"Do you like this sunrise, Jane? That sky with its high and light clouds
which are sure to melt away as the day waxes warm—this placid and balmy at-
mosphere?"

"I do, very much."

"You have passed a strange night, Jane."

"Yes, sir."

"And it has made you look pale—were you afraid when I left you alone with
Mason?"

"I was afraid of some one coming out of the inner room."

"But I had fastened the door—I had the key in my pocket: I should have
been a careless shepherd if I had left a lamb—my pet lamb—so near a wolf's
den, unguarded: you were safe."

"Will Grace Poole live here still, sir?"

"Oh, yes! don't trouble your head about her—put the thing out of your
thoughts."

"Yet it seems to me your life is hardly secure while she stays."

"Never fear—I will take care of myself."

"Is the danger you apprehended last night gone by now sir?"

"I cannot vouch for that till Mason is out of England: nor even then. To live,
for me, Jane, is to stand on a crater-crust which may crack and spue fire any
day."

"But Mr. Mason seems a man easily led. Your influence, sir, is evidently po-
tent with him: he will never set you at defiance, or wilfully injure you."

"Oh, no! Mason will not defy me; nor, knowing it, will he hurt me—but, un-
intentionally, he might in a moment, by one careless word, deprive me, if not
of life, yet for ever of happiness."

"Tell him to be cautious, sir: let him know what you fear, and show him how
to avert the danger."

He laughed sardonically, hastily took my hand, and as hastily threw it from him.

"If I could do that, simpleton, where would the danger be? Annihilated in a moment. Ever since I have known Mason I have only had to say to him 'Do that,' and the thing has been done. But I cannot give him orders in this case: I cannot say 'Beware of harming me, Richard'; for it is imperative that I should keep him ignorant that harm to me is possible. Now you look puzzled; and I will puzzle you farther. You are my little friend, are you not?"

"I like to serve you, sir, and to obey you in all that is right."

"Precisely: I see you do. I see genuine contentment in your gait and mien, your eye and face, when you are helping me and pleasing me—working for me, and with me, in, as you characteristically say, *'all that is right'*: for if I bid you do what you thought wrong, there would be no light-footed running, no neat-handed alacrity, no lively glance and animated complexion. My friend would then turn to me, quiet and pale, and would say, 'No, sir; that is impossible: I cannot do it, because it is wrong'; and would become immutable as a fixed star. Well, you too have power over me, and may injure me: yet I dare not show you where I am vulnerable, lest, faithful and friendly as you are, you should transfix me at once."

"If you have no more to fear from Mr. Mason than you have from me, sir, you are very safe."

"God grant it may be so! Here, Jane, is an arbour; sit down."

The arbor was an arch in the wall, lined with ivy; it contained a rustic seat. Mr. Rochester took it, leaving room, however, for me: but I stood before him.

"Sit," he said; "the bench is long enough for two. You don't hesitate to take a place at my side, do you? Is that wrong, Jane?"

I answered him by assuming it: to refuse would, I felt, have been unwise.

"Now, my little friend, while the sun drinks the dew—while all the flowers in this old garden awake and expand, and the birds fetch their young ones' breakfast out of the cornfield, and the early bees do their first spell of work—I'll put a case to you; which you must endeavor to suppose your own: but first, look at me, and tell me you are at ease, and not fearing that I err in detaining you, or that you err in staying."

"No, sir; I am content."

"Well then, Jane, call to aid your fancy—suppose you were no longer a girl well reared and disciplined, but a wild boy indulged from childhood upwards; imagine yourself in a remote foreign land; conceive that you there commit a capital error, no matter of what nature or from what motives, but one whose consequences must follow you through life and taint all your existence. Mind, I don't say a *crime*; I am not speaking of shedding of blood or any other guilty act, which might make the perpetrator amenable to the law: my word is *error*. The results of what you have done become in time to you utterly insupport-able; you take measures to obtain relief: unusual measures, but neither unlaw-ful nor culpable. Still you are miserable; for hope has quitted you on the very confines of life: your sun at noon darkens in an eclipse, which you feel will not leave it till the time of setting. Bitter and base associations have become the sole food of your memory: you wander here and there, seeking rest in exile: happiness in pleasure—I mean in heartless, sensual pleasure—such as dulls intellect and blights feeling. Heart-weary and soul-withered, you come home after years of voluntary banishment; you make a new acquaintance—how or

where no matter: you find in this stranger much of the good and bright quali-
ties which you have sought for twenty years, and never before encountered;
and they are all fresh, healthy, without soil and without taint. Such society re-
vives, regenerates: you feel better days come back—higher wishes, purer feel-
ings; you desire to recommence your life, and to spend what remains to you of
days in a way more worthy of an immortal being. To attain this end, are you
justified in overleaping an obstacle of custom—a mere conventional impedi-
ment, which neither your conscience sanctifies nor your judgment approves?"

He paused for an answer: and what was I to say? Oh, for some good spirit to
suggest a judicious and satisfactory response! Vain aspiration! The west wind
whispered in the ivy round me; but no gentle Ariel[4] borrowed its breath as a
medium of speech: the birds sang in the tree-tops; but their song, however
sweet, was inarticulate.

Again Mr. Rochester propounded his query.

"Is the wandering and sinful, but now rest-seeking and repentant, man jus-
tified in daring the world's opinion, in order to attach to him for ever this gen-
tle, gracious, genial stranger, thereby securing his own peace of mind and
regeneration of life?"

"Sir," I answered, "a wanderer's repose or a sinner's reformation should
never depend on a fellow-creature. Men and women die; philosophers falter in
wisdom, and Christians in goodness: if any one you know has suffered and
erred, let him look higher than his equals for strength to amend, and solace to
heal."

"But the instrument—the instrument! God, who does the work, ordains
the instrument. I have myself—I tell it you without parable—been a worldly,
dissipated, restless man; and I believe I have found the instrument for my
cure, in——"

He paused: the birds went on caroling, the leaves lightly rustling. I almost
wondered they did not check their songs and whispers to catch the suspended
revelation: but they would have had to wait many minutes—so long was the
silence protracted. At last I looked up at the tardy speaker: he was looking ea-
gerly at me.

"Little friend," said he, in quite a changed tone—while his face changed
too; losing all its softness and gravity, and becoming harsh and sarcastic—"you
have noticed my tender penchant for Miss Ingram: don't you think if I mar-
ried her she would regenerate me with a vengeance?"

He got up instantly, went quite to the other end of the walk, and when he
came back he was humming a tune.

"Jane, Jane," said he, stopping before me, "you are quite pale with your vig-
ils: don't you curse me for disturbing your rest?"

"Curse you? No sir."

"Shake hands in confirmation of the word. What cold fingers! They were
warmer last night when I touched them at the door of the mysterious cham-
ber. Jane, when will you watch with me again?"

"Whenever I can be useful, sir."

"For instance, the night before I am married! I am sure I shall not be able to
sleep. Will you promise to sit up with me to bear me company? To you I can
talk of my lovely one: for now you have seen her and know her."

4. Spirit (in Shakespeare's *Tempest*).

"Yes, sir."

"She's a rare one, is she not, Jane?"

"Yes, sir."

"A strapper—a real strapper, Jane: big, brown, and buxom; with hair just such as the ladies of Carthage must have had. Bless me! there's Dent and Lynn in the stables! Go in by the shrubbery, through that wicket."

As I went one way, he went another, and I heard him in the yard, saying cheeringly:—"Mason got the start of you all this morning; he was gone before sunrise: I rose at four to see him off."

Chapter XXI

Presentiments are strange things! and so are sympathies; and so are signs: and the three combined make one mystery to which humanity has not yet found the key. I never laughed at presentiments in my life; because I have had strange ones of my own. Sympathies, I believe, exist: (for instance, between far-distant, long-absent, wholly estranged relatives; asserting, notwithstanding their alienation, the unity of the source to which each traces his origin) whose workings baffle mortal comprehension. And signs, for aught we know, may be but the sympathies of Nature with man.

When I was a little girl, only six years old, I, one night, heard Bessie Leaven say to Martha Abbot that she had been dreaming about a little child; and that to dream of children was a sure sign of trouble, either to one's self or one's kin. The saying might have worn out of my memory, had not a circumstance immediately followed which served indelibly to fix it there. The next day Bessie was sent for home to the deathbed of her little sister.

Of late I had often recalled this saying and this incident; for during the past week scarcely a night had gone over my couch that had not brought with it a dream of an infant: which I sometimes hushed in my arms, sometimes dandled on my knee, sometimes watched playing with daisies on a lawn; or again, dabbling its hands in running water. It was a wailing child this night, and a laughing one the next: now it nestled close to me, and now it ran from me; but whatever mood the apparition evinced, whatever aspect it wore, it failed not for seven successive nights to meet me the moment I entered the land of slumber.

I did not like this iteration of one idea—this strange recurrence of one image; and I grew nervous as bedtime approached, and the hour of the vision drew near. It was from companionship with this baby-phantom I had been roused on that moonlight night when I heard the cry; and it was on the afternoon of the day following I was summoned downstairs by a message that some one wanted me in Mrs. Fairfax's room. On repairing thither, I found a man waiting for me, having the appearance of a gentleman's servant: he was dressed in deep mourning, and the hat he held in his hand was surrounded with a crape band.

"I daresay you hardly remember me, miss," he said, rising as I entered; "but my name is Leaven: I lived coachman with Mrs. Reed when you were at Gateshead eight or nine years since, and I live there still."

"Oh, Robert! how do you do? I remember you very well: you used to give me a ride sometimes on Miss Georgiana's bay pony. And how is Bessie? You are married to Bessie?"

"Yes, miss: my wife is very hearty, thank you; she brought me another little one about two months since—we have three now—and both mother and child are thriving."

"And are the family well at the house, Robert?"

"I am sorry I can't give better news of them, miss: they are very badly at present—in great trouble."

"I hope no one is dead," I said glancing at his black dress. He too looked down at the crape round his hat and replied,—"Mr. John died yesterday was a week, at his chambers in London."

"Mr. John?"

"Yes."

"And how does his mother bear it?"

"Why you see, Miss Eyre, it is not a common mishap: his life has been very wild: these last three years he gave himself up to strange ways; and his death was shocking."

"I heard from Bessie he was not doing well."

"Doing well! He could not do worse: he ruined his health and his estate amongst the worst men and the worst women. He got into debt and into jail: his mother helped him out twice, but as soon as he was free he returned to his old companions and habits. His head was not strong: the knaves he lived amongst fooled him beyond anything I ever heard. He came down to Gateshead about three weeks ago and wanted Missis to give up all to him. Missis refused: her means have long been much reduced by his extravagance; so he went back again, and the next news was that he was dead. How he died, God knows!—they say he killed himself."

I was silent: the tidings were frightful. Robert Leaven resumed:—"Missis had been out of health herself for some time: she had got very stout, but was not strong with it; and the loss of money and fear of poverty were quite break-ing her down. The information about Mr. John's death and the manner of it came too suddenly: it brought on a stroke. She was three days without speak-ing; but last Tuesday she seemed rather better: she appeared as if she wanted to say something, and kept making signs to my wife and mumbling. It was only yesterday morning, however, that Bessie understood she was pronouncing your name; and at last she made out the words, 'Bring Jane—fetch Jane Eyre: I want to speak to her.' Bessie is not sure whether she is in her right mind, or means anything by the words; but she told Miss Reed and Miss Georgiana, and advised them to send for you. The young ladies put it off at first: but their mother grew so restless, and said, 'Jane, Jane,' so many times, that at last they consented. I left Gateshead yesterday; and if you can get ready, miss, I should like to take you back with me early tomorrow morning."

"Yes, Robert, I shall be ready: it seems to me that I ought to go."

"I think so too, miss. Bessie said she was sure you would not refuse: but I suppose you will have to ask leave before you can get off?"

"Yes; and I will do it now"; and having directed him to the servants' hall, and recommended him to the care of John's wife, and the attentions of John himself, I went in search of Mr. Rochester.

He was not in any of the lower rooms; he was not in the yard, the stables, or the grounds. I asked Mrs. Fairfax if she had seen him;—yes: she believed he was playing billiards with Miss Ingram. To the billiard-room I hastened: the click of balls and the hum of voices resounded thence: Mr. Rochester, Miss

Ingram, the two Misses Eshton, and their admirers, were all busied in the game. It required some courage to disturb so interesting a party; my errand, however, was one I could not defer, so I approached the master where he stood at Miss Ingram's side. She turned as I drew near and looked at me haughtily: her eyes seemed to demand, "What can the creeping creature want now?" and when I said, in a low voice, "Mr. Rochester," she made a movement as if tempted to order me away. I remember her appearance at the moment,—it was very graceful and very striking: she wore a morning robe of sky-blue crape; a gauzy azure scarf was twisted in her hair. She had been all animation with the game, and irritated pride did not lower the expression of her haughty lineaments.

"Does that person want you?" she inquired of Mr. Rochester; and Mr. Rochester turned to see who the "person" was. He made a curious grimace,— one of his strange and equivocal demonstrations—threw down his cue and followed me from the room.

"Well, Jane?" he said, as he rested his back against the schoolroom door, which he had shut.

"If you please, sir, I want leave of absence for a week or two."

"What to do?—Where to go?"

"To see a sick lady who has sent for me."

"What sick lady?—Where does she live?"

"At Gateshead, in ——shire."

"——shire? That is a hundred miles off! Who may she be that sends for people to see her that distance?"

"Her name is Reed, sir,—Mrs. Reed."

"Reed of Gateshead? There was a Reed of Gateshead, a magistrate."

"It is his widow, sir."

"And what have you to do with her? How do you know her?"

"Mr. Reed was my uncle,—my mother's brother."

"The deuce he was! You never told me that before: you always said you had no relations."

"None that would own me, sir. Mr. Reed is dead, and his wife cast me off."

"Why?"

"Because I was poor, and burdensome, and she disliked me."

"But Reed left children?—you must have cousins? Sir George Lynn was talking of a Reed of Gateshead, yesterday—who, he said, was one of the veriest rascals in town; and Ingram was mentioning a Georgiana Reed of the same place, who was much admired for her beauty, a season or two ago, in London."

"John Reed is dead, too, sir: he ruined himself and half-ruined his family, and is supposed to have committed suicide. The news so shocked his mother that it brought on an apoplectic attack."

"And what good can you do her? Nonsense, Jane! I would never think of running a hundred miles to see an old lady who will, perhaps, be dead before you reach her: besides, you say she cast you off."

"Yes, sir, but that is long ago; and when her circumstances were very different: I could not be easy to neglect her wishes now."

"How long will you stay?"

"As short a time as possible, sir."

"Promise me only to stay a week——"

"I had better not pass my word: I might be obliged to break it."

"At all events you *will* come back: you will not be induced under any pretext to take up a permanent residence with her."

"Oh, no! I shall certainly return if all be well."

"And who goes with you? You don't travel a hundred miles alone."

"No, sir, she has sent her coachman."

"A person to be trusted?"

"Yes, sir, he has lived ten years in the family."

Mr. Rochester meditated. "When do you wish to go?"

"Early tomorrow morning, sir."

"Well, you must have some money; you can't travel without money, and I daresay you have not much: I have given you no salary yet. How much have you in the world, Jane?" he asked, smiling.

I drew out my purse; a meager thing it was. "Five shillings, sir." He took the purse, poured the hoard into his palm and chuckled over it as if its scantiness pleased him. Soon he produced his pocket-book: "Here," said he, offering me a note: it was fifty pounds, and he owed me but fifteen. I told him I had no change.

"I don't want change: you know that. Take your wages."

I declined accepting more than was my due. He scowled at first; then, as if recollecting something, he said:—"Right, right! Better not give you all now: you would perhaps, stay away three months if you had fifty pounds. There are ten: is it not plenty?"

"Yes, sir, but now you owe me five."

"Come back for it then: I am your banker for forty pounds."

"Mr. Rochester, I may as well mention another matter of business to you while I have the opportunity."

"Matter of business? I'm curious to hear it."

"You have as good as informed me, sir, that you are going shortly to be married?"

"Yes: what then?"

"In that case, sir, Adèle ought to go to school: I am sure you will perceive the necessity of it."

"To get her out of my bride's way; who might otherwise walk over her rather too emphatically. There's sense in the suggestion; not a doubt of it: Adèle, as you say, must go to school; and you, of course, must march straight to—the devil?"

"I hope not, sir: but I must seek another situation somewhere."

"In course!" he exclaimed, with a twang of voice and a distortion of features equally fantastic and ludicrous. He looked at me some minutes.

"And old Madam Reed, or the Misses, her daughters, will be solicited by you to seek a place, I suppose?"

"No, sir; I am not on such terms with my relatives as would justify me in asking favors of them—but I shall advertise."

"You shall walk up the pyramids of Egypt!" he growled. "At your peril you advertise! I wish I had only offered you a sovereign instead of ten pounds. Give me back nine pounds, Jane; I've a use for it."

"And so have I, sir," I returned, putting my hands and my purse behind me. "I could not spare the money on any account."

"Little niggard!" said he, "refusing me a pecuniary request! Give me five pounds, Jane."

"Not five shillings, sir; nor five pence."

"Just let me look at the cash."

"No, sir; you are not to be trusted."

"Jane!"

"Sir?"

"Promise me one thing."

"I'll promise you anything, sir, that I think I am likely to perform."

"Not to advertise: and to trust this quest of a situation to me. I'll find you one in time."

"I shall be glad so to do, sir, if you, in your turn, will promise that I and Adèle shall be both safe out of the house before your bride enters it"

"Very well! very well! I'll pledge my word on it. You go tomorrow, then?"

"Yes, sir; early."

"Shall you come down to the drawing-room after dinner?"

"No, sir, I must prepare for the journey."

"Then you and I must bid good-bye for a little while?"

"I suppose so, sir."

"And how do people perform that ceremony of parting, Jane? Teach me; I'm not quite up to it."

"They say, Farewell; or any other form they prefer."

"Then say it."

"Farewell, Mr. Rochester, for the present."

"What must I say?"

"The same, if you like, sir."

"Farewell, Miss Eyre, for the present: is that all?"

"Yes."

"It seems stingy, to my notions, and dry and unfriendly. I should like something else: a little addition to the rite. If one shook hands, for instance; but no—that would not content me either. So you'll do no more than say Farewell, Jane?"

"It is enough, sir: as much good will may be conveyed in one hearty word as in many."

"Very likely; but it is blank and cool—'farewell.'"

"How long is he going to stand with his back against the door?" I asked myself; "I want to commence my packing." The dinner-bell rang, and suddenly away he bolted, without another syllable: I saw him no more during the day, and was off before he had risen in the morning.

I reached the lodge at Gateshead about five o'clock in the afternoon of the first of May: I stepped in there before going up to the hall. It was very clean and neat: the ornamental windows were hung with little white curtains; the floor was spotless; the grate and fire-irons were burnished bright, and the fire burned clear. Bessie sat on the hearth nursing her last-born, and Robert and his sister played quietly in a corner.

"Bless you!—I knew you would come!" exclaimed Mrs. Leaven, as I entered.

"Yes, Bessie," said I, after I had kissed her; "and I trust I am not too late. How is Mrs. Reed?—Alive still, I hope."

"Yes, she is alive; and more sensible and collected than she was. The doctor says she may linger a week or two yet; but he hardly thinks she will finally recover."

"Has she mentioned me lately?"

"She was talking of you only this morning, and wishing you would come: but she is sleeping now; or was ten minutes ago, when I was up at the house. She generally lies in a kind of lethargy all the afternoon, and wakes up about six or seven. Will you rest yourself here an hour, miss, and then I will go up with you?"

Robert here entered, and Bessie laid her sleeping child in the cradle and went to welcome him: afterwards she insisted on my taking off my bonnet and having some tea; for she said I looked pale and tired. I was glad to accept her hospitality; and I submitted to be relieved of my travelling garb just as passively as I used to let her undress me when a child.

Old times crowded fast back on me as I watched her bustling about—setting out the tea-tray with her best china, cutting bread-and-butter, toasting a tea-cake, and, between whiles, giving little Robert or Jane an occasional tap or push, just as she used to give me in former days. Bessie had retained her quick temper as well as her light foot and good looks.

Tea ready, I was going to approach the table; but she desired me to sit still, quite in her old, peremptory tones. I must be served at the fireside, she said; and she placed before me a little round stand with my cup and a plate of toast, absolutely as she used to accommodate me with some privately purloined dainty on a nursery chair: and I smiled and obeyed her as in bygone days.

She wanted to know if I was happy at Thornfield Hall, and what sort of a person the mistress was; and when I told her there was only a master, whether he was a nice gentleman, and if I liked him. I told her he was rather an ugly man, but quite a gentleman; and that he treated me kindly, and I was content. Then I went on to describe to her the gay company that had lately been staying at the house: and to these details Bessie listened with interest: they were precisely of the kind she relished.

In such conversation an hour was soon gone: Bessie restored to me my bonnet, etc., and, accompanied by her, I quitted the lodge for the hall. It was also accompanied by her that I had, nearly nine years ago, walked down the path I was now ascending. On a dark, misty, raw morning in January, I had left a hostile roof with a desperate and embittered heart—a sense of outlawry and almost of reprobation—to seek the chilly harborage of Lowood: that bourne[5] so far away and unexplored. The same hostile roof now again rose before me: my prospects were doubtful yet; and I had yet an aching heart. I still felt as a wanderer on the face of the earth; but I experienced firmer trust in myself and my own powers, and less withering dread of oppression. The gaping wound of my wrongs, too, was now quite healed; and the flame of resentment extinguished.

"You shall go into the breakfast-room first,' said Bessie, as she preceded me through the hall; "the young ladies will be there."

In another moment I was within that apartment. There was every article of furniture looking just as it did on the morning I was first introduced to Mr. Brocklehurst: the very rug he had stood upon still covered the hearth. Glancing at the book-cases, I thought I could distinguish the two volumes of *Bewick's British Birds* occupying their old place on the third shelf, and *Gulliver's Travels* and the *Arabian Nights* ranged just above. The inanimate objects were not changed: but the living things had altered past recognition.

5. Destination.

Two young ladies appeared before me; one very tall, almost as tall as Miss Ingram,—very thin too, with a sallow face and severe mien. There was something ascetic in her look, which was augmented by the extreme plainness of a straight-skirted, black, stuff dress, a starched linen collar, hair combed away from the temples, and the nun-like ornament of a string of ebony beads and a crucifix. This I felt sure was Eliza, though I could trace little resemblance to her former self in that elongated and colorless visage.

The other was as certainly Georgiana: but not the Georgiana I remembered—the slim and fairy-like girl of eleven. This was a full-blown, very plump damsel, fair as wax-work; with handsome and regular features, languishing blue eyes, and ringleted yellow hair. The hue of her dress was black too; but its fashion was so different from her sister's—so much more flowing and becoming—it looked as stylish as the other's looked puritanical.

In each of the sisters there was one trait of the mother—and only one: the thin and pallid elder daughter had her parent's Cairngorm eye: the blooming and luxuriant younger girl had her contour of jaw and chin,—perhaps a little softened, but still imparting an indescribable hardness to the countenance, otherwise so voluptuous and buxom.

Both ladies, as I advanced, rose to welcome me, and both addressed me by the name of "Miss Eyre." Eliza's greeting was delivered in a short, abrupt voice, without a smile; and then she sat down again, fixed her eyes on the fire, and seemed to forget me. Georgiana added to her "How d'ye do?" several common-places about my journey, the weather and so on, uttered in rather a drawling tone: and accompanied by sundry side-glances that measured me from head to foot—now traversing the folds of my drab merino pelisse, and now lingering on the plain trimming of my cottage bonnet. Young ladies have a remarkable way of letting you know that they think you a "quiz" without actually saying the words. A certain superciliousness of look, coolness of manner, nonchalance of tone, express fully their sentiments on the point, without committing them by any positive rudeness in word or deed.

A sneer, however, whether covert or open, had now no longer that power over me it once possessed: as I sat between my cousins, I was surprised to find how easy I felt under the total neglect of the one and the semi-sarcastic attentions of the other—Eliza did not mortify, nor Georgiana ruffle me. The fact was, I had other things to think about; within the last few months feelings had been stirred in me so much more potent than any they could raise—pains and pleasures so much more acute and exquisite had been excited, than any it was in their power to inflict or bestow—that their airs gave me no concern either for good or bad.

"How is Mrs. Reed?" I asked soon, looking calmly at Georgiana; who thought fit to bridle at the direct address, as if it were an unexpected liberty.

"Mrs. Reed? Ah! mama you mean; she is extremely poorly: I doubt if you can see her tonight."

"If," said I, "you would just step upstairs and tell her I am come, I should be much obliged to you."

Georgiana almost started, and she opened her blue eyes wild and wide. "I know she had a particular wish to see me," I added, "and I would not defer attending to her desire longer than is absolutely necessary."

"Mama dislikes being disturbed in an evening," remarked Eliza. I soon rose, quietly took off my bonnet and gloves, uninvited, and said I would just step

out to Bessie—who was, I dared say, in the kitchen—and ask her to ascertain whether Mrs. Reed was disposed to receive me or not tonight. I went, and having found Bessie and despatched her on my errand, I proceeded to take further measures. It had heretofore been my habit always to shrink from arrogance: received as I had been today, I should, a year ago, have resolved to quit Gateshead the very next morning; now, it was disclosed to me all at once, that that would be a foolish plan. I had taken a journey of a hundred miles to see my aunt, and I must stay with her till she was better—or dead: as to her daughters' pride or folly, I must put it on one side; make myself independent of it. So I addressed the house-keeper; asked her to show me a room, told her I should probably be a visitor here for a week or two, had my trunk conveyed to my chamber, and followed it thither myself. I met Bessie on the landing.

"Missis is awake," said she; "I have told her you are here: come and let us see if she will know you."

I did not need to be guided to the well-known room to which I had so often been summoned for chastizement or reprimand in former days. I hastened before Bessie, I softly opened the door: a shaded light stood on the table, for it was now getting dark. There was the great four-post bed with amber hangings as of old: there the toilet-table, the arm-chair, and the foot-stool: at which I had a hundred times been sentenced to kneel, to ask pardon for offences, by me uncommitted. I looked into a certain corner near, half-expecting to see the slim outline of a once-dreaded switch; which used to lurk there, waiting to leap out imp-like and lace my quivering palm or shrinking neck. I approached the bed; I opened the curtains and leaned over the high-piled pillows.

Well did I remember Mrs. Reed's face, and I eagerly sought the familiar image. It is a happy thing that time quells the longings of vengeance, and hushes the promptings of rage and aversion: I had left this woman in bitterness and hate, and I came back to her now with no other emotion than a sort of ruth for her great sufferings, and a strong yearning to forget and forgive all injuries—to be reconciled and clasp hands in amity.

The well-known face was there: stern, relentless as ever—there was that peculiar eye which nothing could melt; and the somewhat raised, imperious, despotic eyebrow. How often had it lowered on me menace and hate! and how the recollection of childhood's terrors and sorrows revived as I traced its harsh line now! And yet I stooped down and kissed her: she looked at me.

"Is this Jane Eyre?" she said.

"Yes, aunt Reed. How are you, dear aunt?"

I had once vowed that I would never call her aunt again: I thought it no sin to forget and break that vow now. My fingers had fastened on her hand which lay outside the sheet: had she pressed mine kindly, I should at that moment have experienced true pleasure. But unimpressionable natures are not so soon softened, nor are natural antipathies so readily eradicated: Mrs. Reed took her hand away, and, turning her face rather from me, she remarked that the night was warm. Again she regarded me, so icily, I felt at once that her opinion of me—her feeling towards me—was unchanged, and unchangeable. I knew by her stony eye—opaque to tenderness, indissoluble to tears—that she was resolved to consider me bad to the last: because to believe me good, would give her no generous pleasure: only a sense of mortification.

I felt pain, and then I felt ire; and then I felt a determination to subdue her—to be her mistress in spite both of her nature and her will. My tears had

risen, just as in childhood: I ordered them back to their source. I brought a chair to the bed-head: I sat down and leaned over the pillow.

"You sent for me," I said, "and I am here; and it is my intention to stay till I see how you get on."

"Oh, of course! You have seen my daughters?"

"Yes."

"Well, you may tell them I wish you to stay till I can talk some things over with you I have on my mind: tonight it is too late, and I have a difficulty in re-calling them. But there was something I wished to say—let me see——"

The wandering look and changed utterance told what wreck had taken place in her once-vigorous frame. Turning restlessly, she drew the bed-clothes round her; my elbow, resting on a corner of the quilt, fixed it down: she was at once irritated.

"Sit up!" said she; "don't annoy me with holding the clothes fast—are you Jane Eyre?"

"I am Jane Eyre."

"I have had more trouble with that child than anyone would believe. Such a burden to be left on my hands—and so much annoyance as she caused me, daily and hourly, with her incomprehensible disposition, and her sudden starts of temper, and her continual, unnatural watchings of one's movements! I de-clare she talked to me once like something mad, or like a fiend—no child ever spoke or looked as she did; I was glad to get her away from the house. What did they do with her at Lowood? The fever broke out there, and many of the pupils died. She, however, did not die: but I said she did—I wish she had died!"

"A strange wish, Mrs. Reed: why do you hate her so?"

"I had a dislike to her mother always; for she was my husband's only sister, and a great favorite with him: he opposed the family's disowning her when she made her low marriage; and when news came of her death, he wept like a sim-pleton. He would send for the baby; though I entreated him rather to put it out to nurse and pay for its maintenance. I hated it the first time I set my eyes on it—a sickly, whining, pining thing! It would wail in its cradle all night long—not screaming heartily like any other child, but whimpering and moan-ing. Reed pitied it; and he used to nurse it and notice it as if it had been his own: more, indeed, than he ever noticed his own at that age. He would try to make my children friendly to the little beggar: the darlings could not bear it, and he was angry with them when they showed their dislike. In his last illness, he had it brought continually to his bedside; and but an hour before he died, he bound me by vow to keep the creature. I would as soon have been charged with a pauper brat out of a workhouse: but he was weak, naturally weak. John does not at all resemble his father, and I am glad of it: John is like me and like my brothers—he is quite a Gibson. Oh, I wish he would cease tormenting me with letters for money! I have no more money to give him: we are getting poor. I must send away half the servants and shut up part of the house; or let it off. I can never submit to do that—yet how are we to get on? Two-thirds of my in-come goes in paying the interest of mortgages. John gambles dreadfully, and always loses—poor boy! He is beset by sharpers: John is sunk and degraded—his look is frightful—I feel ashamed for him when I see him."

She was getting much excited. "I think I had better leave her now," said I to Bessie, who stood on the other side of the bed.

"Perhaps you had, miss: but she often talks in this way towards night—in the morning she is calmer."

I rose. "Stop!" exclaimed Mrs. Reed. "There is another thing I wished to say. He threatens me—he continually threatens me with his own death, or mine: and I dream sometimes that I see him laid out with a great wound in his throat, or with a swollen and blackened face. I am come to a strange pass: I have heavy troubles. What is to be done? How is the money to be had?"

Bessie now endeavored to persuade her to take a sedative draught: she succeeded with difficulty. Soon after, Mrs. Reed grew more composed, and sank into a dozing state. I then left her.

More than ten days elapsed before I had again any conversation with her. She continued either delirious or lethargic; and the doctor forbade every thing which could painfully excite her. Meantime, I got on as well as I could with Georgiana and Eliza. They were very cold, indeed, at first. Eliza would sit half the day sewing, reading, or writing, and scarcely utter a word either to me or her sister. Georgiana would chatter nonsense to her canary bird by the hour, and take no notice of me. But I was determined not to seem at a loss for occupation or amusement: I had brought my drawing materials with me, and they served me for both.

Provided with a case of pencils, and some sheets of paper, I used to take a seat apart from them, near the window, and busy myself in sketching fancy vignettes, representing any scene that happened momentarily to shape itself in the ever-shifting kaleidoscope of imagination: a glimpse of sea between two rocks; the rising moon, and a ship crossing its disk; a group of reeds and water-flags, and a naiad's head crowned with lotus-flowers, rising out of them; an elf sitting in a hedge-sparrow's nest, under a wreath of hawthorn-bloom.

One morning I fell to sketching a face: what sort of a face it was to be, I did not care or know. I took a soft black pencil, gave it a broad point, and worked away. Soon I had traced on the paper a broad and prominent forehead, and a square lower outline of visage: that contour gave me pleasure; my fingers proceeded actively to fill it with features. Strongly-marked horizontal eyebrows must be traced under that brow; then followed, naturally, a well-defined nose, with a straight ridge and full nostrils; then a flexible-looking mouth, by no means narrow; then a firm chin with a decided cleft down the middle of it: of course, some black whiskers were wanted, and some jetty hair, tufted on the temples, and waved above the forehead. Now for the eyes: I had left them to the last, because they required the most careful working. I drew them large; I shaped them well: the eyelashes I traced long and sombre; the irids lustrous and large. "Good! but not quite the thing," I thought, as I surveyed the effect: "They want more force and spirit," and I wrought the shades blacker, that the lights might flash more brilliantly—a happy touch or two secured success. There, I had a friend's face under my gaze; and what did it signify that those young ladies turned their backs on me? I looked at it; I smiled at the speaking likeness: I was absorbed and content.

"Is that a portrait of some one you know?" asked Eliza, who had approached me unnoticed. I responded that it was merely a fancy head, and hurried it beneath the other sheets. Of course, I lied: it was, in fact, a very faithful representation of Mr. Rochester. But what was that to her, or to any one but myself? Georgiana also advanced to look. The other drawings pleased her much, but she called that "an ugly man." They both seemed surprised at my skill. I of-

fered to sketch their portraits; and each, in turn, sat for a pencil outline. Then Georgiana produced her album. I promised to contribute a water-color drawing: this put her at once into good humor. She proposed a walk in the grounds. Before we had been out two hours, we were deep in a confidential conversation: she had favored me with a description of the brilliant winter she had spent in London two seasons ago—of the admiration she had there excited—the attention she had received: and I even got hints of the titled conquest she had made. In the course of the afternoon and evening these hints were enlarged on: various soft conversations were reported, and sentimental scenes represented; and, in short, a volume of a novel of fashionable life was that day improvised by her for my benefit. The communications were renewed from day to day: they always ran on the same theme—herself, her loves, and woes. It was strange she never once adverted either to her mother's illness, or her brother's death, or the present gloomy state of the family prospects. Her mind seemed wholly taken up with reminiscences of past gaiety, and aspirations after dissipations to come. She passed about five minutes each day in her mother's sick-room and no more.

Eliza still spoke little: she had evidently no time to talk. I never saw a busier person than she seemed to be: yet it was difficult to say what she did: or rather, to discover any result of her diligence. She had an alarum to call her up early. I know not how she occupied herself before breakfast, but after that meal she divided her time into regular portions; and each hour had its allotted task. Three times a day she studied a little book, which I found, on inspection, was a Common Prayer-book. I asked her once what was the great attraction of that volume, and she said "the Rubric."[6] Three hours she gave to stitching, with gold thread, the border of a square crimson cloth, almost large enough for a carpet. In answer to my inquiries after the use of this article, she informed me it was a covering for the altar of a new church lately erected near Gateshead. Two hours she devoted to her diary; two to working by herself in the kitchen-garden; and one to the regulation of her accounts. She seemed to want no company; no conversation. I believe she was happy in her way: this routine sufficed to her; and nothing annoyed her so much as the occurrence of any incident which forced her to vary its clock-work regularity.

She told me one evening, when more disposed to be communicative than usual, that John's conduct, and the threatened ruin of the family, had been a source of profound affliction to her: but she had now, she said, settled her mind, and formed her resolution. Her own fortune she had taken care to secure; and when her mother died,—and it was wholly improbable, she tranquilly remarked, that she should either recover or linger long,—she would execute a long-cherished project: seek a retirement where punctual habits would be permanently secured from disturbance, and place safe barriers between herself and a frivolous world. I asked if Georgiana would accompany her.

"Of course not. Georgiana and she had nothing in common: they never had had. She would not be burdened with her society for any consideration. Georgiana should take her own course; and she, Eliza, would take hers."

Georgiana, when not unburdening her heart to me, spent most of her time in lying on the sofa, fretting about the dulness of the house, and wishing over

6. The section stating the rules for services.

and over again that her aunt Gibson would send her an invitation up to town. "It would be so much better," she said, "if she could only get out of the way for a month or two, till all was over." I did not ask what she meant by "all being over," but I suppose she referred to the expected decease of her mother and the gloomy sequel of funeral rites. Eliza generally took no more notice of her sister's indolence and complaints than if no such murmuring, lounging object had been before her. One day however, as she put away her account book, and unfolded her embroidery, she suddenly took her up thus:—"Georgiana, a more vain and absurd animal than you, was certainly never allowed to cumber the earth. You had no right to be born: for you make no use of life. Instead of living for, in, and with yourself, as a reasonable being ought, you seek only to fasten your feebleness on some other person's strength: if no one can be found willing to burden her or himself with such a fat, weak, puffy, useless thing, you cry out that you are ill-treated, neglected, miserable. Then, too, existence for you must be a scene of continual change and excitement, or else the world is a dungeon: you must be admired, you must be courted, you must be flattered— you must have music, dancing, and society—or you languish, you die away. Have you no sense to devise a system which will make you independent of all efforts, and all wills, but your own? Take one day; share it into sections; to each section apportion its task: leave no stray unemployed quarters of an hour, ten minutes, five minutes, include all; do each piece of business in its turn with method, with rigid regularity. The day will close almost before you are aware it has begun; and you are indebted to no one for helping you to get rid of one vacant moment; you have had to seek no one's company, conversation, sympathy, forbearance: you have lived, in short, as an independent being ought to do. Take this advice: the first and last I shall offer you; then you will not want me or anyone else, happen what may. Neglect it—go on as heretofore, craving, whining, and idling—and suffer the results of your idiocy, however bad and insufferable they may be. I tell you this plainly; and listen: for though I shall no more repeat what I am now about to say, I shall steadily act on it. After my mother's death, I wash my hands of you: from the day her coffin is carried to the vault in Gateshead Church, you and I will be as separate as if we had never known each other. You need not think that because we chanced to be born of the same parents, I shall suffer you to fasten me down by even the feeblest claim; I can tell you this—if the whole human race, ourselves excepted, were swept away, and we two stood alone on the earth, I would leave you in the old world, and betake myself to the new."

She closed her lips.

"You might have spared yourself the trouble of delivering that tirade," answered Georgiana. "Everybody knows you are the most selfish, heartless creature in existence: and I know your spiteful hatred towards me; I have had a specimen of it before in the trick you played me about Lord Edwin Vere: you could not bear me to be raised above you, to have a title, to be received into circles where you dare not show your face, and so you acted the spy and informer, and ruined my prospects for ever." Georgiana took out her handkerchief and blew her nose for an hour afterwards. Eliza sat cold, impassible, and assiduously industrious.

True, generous feeling is made small account of by some: but here were two natures rendered, the one intolerably acrid, the other despicably savourless for the want of it. Feeling without judgment is a washy draught indeed; but judg-

ment untempered by feeling is too bitter and husky a morsel for human deglutition.[7]

It was a wet and windy afternoon: Georgiana had fallen asleep on the sofa over the perusal of a novel; Eliza was gone to attend a saint's-day service at the new church—for in matters of religion she was a rigid formalist: no weather ever prevented the punctual discharge of what she considered her devotional duties: fair or foul, she went to church thrice every Sunday, and as often on week-days as there were prayers.

I bethought myself to go upstairs and see how the dying woman sped, who lay there almost unheeded: the very servants paid her but a remittent attention: the hired nurse, being little looked after, would slip out of the room whenever she could. Bessie was faithful; but she had her own family to mind, and could only come occasionally to the hall. I found the sick-room unwatched, as I had expected: no nurse was there; the patient lay still, and seemingly lethargic; her livid face sunk in the pillows: the fire was dying in the grate. I renewed the fuel, re-arranged the bed-clothes, gazed awhile on her who could not now gaze on me, and then I moved away to the window.

The rain beat strongly against the panes, the wind blew tempestuously: "One lies there," I thought, "who will soon be beyond the war of earthly elements. Whither will that spirit—now struggling to quit its material tenement—flit when at length released?"

In pondering the great mystery, I thought of Helen Burns, recalled her dying words—her faith—her doctrine of equality of disembodied souls. I was still listening in thought to her well-remembered tones—still picturing her pale and spiritual aspect, her wasted face and sublime gaze, as she lay on her placid deathbed, and whispered her longing to be restored to her divine Father's bosom—when a feeble voice murmured from the couch behind: "Who is that?"

I knew Mrs. Reed had not spoken for days: was she reviving? I went up to her.

"It is I, aunt Reed."

"Who—I?" was her answer. "Who are you?" looking at me with surprise and a sort of alarm, but still not wildly. "You are quite a stranger to me—where is Bessie?"

"She is at the lodge, aunt."

"Aunt!" she repeated. "Who calls me aunt? You are not one of the Gibsons; and yet I know you—that face, and the eyes and forehead are quite familiar to me: you are like—why you are like Jane Eyre!"

I said nothing: I was afraid of occasioning some shock by declaring my identity.

"Yet," said she, "I am afraid it is a mistake: my thoughts deceive me. I wished to see Jane Eyre, and I fancy a likeness where none exists: besides, in eight years she must be so changed."

I now gently assured her that I was the person she supposed and desired me to be: and seeing that I was understood, and that her senses were quite collected, I explained how Bessie had sent her husband to fetch me from Thornfield.

"I am very ill, I know," she said ere long. "I was trying to turn myself a few

<hr>

7. Swallowing.

minutes since, and find I cannot move a limb. It is as well I should ease my mind before I die: what we think little of in health, burdens us at such an hour as the present is to me. Is the nurse here? or is there no one in the room but you?"

I assured her we were alone.

"Well, I have twice done you a wrong which I regret now. One was in breaking the promise which I gave my husband to bring you up as my own child; the other—" she stopped. "After all it is of no great importance, perhaps," she murmured to herself: "and then I may get better; and to humble myself so to her is painful."

She made an effort to alter her position, but failed: her face changed; she seemed to experience some inward sensation—the precursor, perhaps, of the last pang.

"Well: I must get it over. Eternity is before me: I had better tell her.—Go to my dressing-case, open it, and take out a letter you will see there."

I obeyed her directions.

"Read the letter," she said.

It was short and thus conceived:

"Madam,—

"Will you have the goodness to send me the address of my niece, Jane Eyre, and to tell me how she is: it is my intention to write shortly and desire her to come to me at Madeira. Providence has blessed my endeavors to secure a competency; and as I am unmarried and childless, I wish to adopt her during my life, and bequeath her at my death whatever I may have to leave.

I am, Madam, etc. etc.
John Eyre, Madeira."

It was dated three years back.

"Why did I never hear of this?" I asked.

"Because I disliked you too fixedly and thoroughly ever to lend a hand in lifting you to prosperity. I could not forget your conduct to me, Jane—the fury with which you once turned on me; the tone in which you declared you abhorred me the worst of anybody in the world; the unchildlike look and voice with which you affirmed that the very thought of me made you sick, and asserted that I had treated you with miserable cruelty. I could not forget my own sensations when you thus started up and poured out the venom of your mind: I felt fear, as if an animal that I had struck or pushed had looked up at me with human eyes and cursed me in a man's voice.—Bring me some water! Oh, make haste!"

"Dear Mrs. Reed," said I, as I offered her the draught she required, "think no more of all this, let it pass away from your mind. Forgive me for my passionate language: I was a child then; eight, nine years have passed since that day."

She heeded nothing of what I said; but when she had tasted the water and drawn breath, she went on thus:—"I tell you I could not forget it; and I took my revenge: for you to be adopted by your uncle, and placed in a state of ease and comfort, was what I could not endure. I wrote to him; I said I was sorry for his disappointment, but Jane Eyre was dead: she had died of typhus fever at Lowood. Now act as you please: write and contradict my assertion—expose

my falsehood as soon as you like. You were born, I think, to be my torment: my last hour is racked by the recollection of a deed which, but for you, I should never have been tempted to commit."

"If you could but be persuaded to think no more of it, aunt, and to regard me with kindness and forgiveness"——

"You have a very bad disposition," said she, "and one to this day I feel it impossible to understand: how for nine years you could be patient and quiescent under any treatment, and in the tenth break out all fire and violence, I can never comprehend."

"My disposition is not so bad as you think: I am passionate, but not vindictive. Many a time, as a little child, I should have been glad to love you if you would have let me; and I long earnestly to be reconciled to you now: kiss me, aunt."

I approached my cheek to her lips: she would not touch it. She said I oppressed her by leaning over the bed; and again demanded water. As I laid her down—for I raised her and supported her on my arm while she drank—I covered her ice-cold and clammy hand with mine: the feeble fingers shrank from my touch—the glazing eyes shunned my gaze.

"Love me, then, or hate me, as you will," I said at last; "you have my full and free forgiveness: ask now for God's; and be at peace."

Poor, suffering woman! it was too late for her to make now the effort to change her habitual frame of mind: living, she had ever hated me—dying, she must hate me still.

The nurse now entered, and Bessie followed. I yet lingered half an hour longer, hoping to see some sign of amity: but she gave none. She was fast relapsing into stupor; nor did her mind again rally: at twelve o'clock that night she died. I was not present to close her eyes; nor were either of her daughters. They came to tell us the next morning that all was over. She was by that time laid out. Eliza and I went to look at her: Georgiana, who had burst out into loud weeping, said she dared not go. There was stretched Sarah Reed's once robust and active frame, rigid and still: her eye of flint was covered with its cold lid; her brow and strong traits wore yet the impress of her inexorable soul. A strange and solemn object was that corpse to me. I gazed on it with gloom and pain: nothing soft, nothing sweet, nothing pitying, or hopeful, or subduing, did it inspire; only a grating anguish for *her* woes—not my loss—and a somber tearless dismay at the fearfulness of death in such a form.

Eliza surveyed her parent calmly. After a silence of some minutes she observed, "With her constitution she should have lived to a good old age: her life was shortened by trouble." And then a spasm constricted her mouth for an instant: as it passed away she turned and left the room, and so did I. Neither of us had dropped a tear.

Chapter XXII

Mr. Rochester had given me but one week's leave of absence: yet a month elapsed before I quitted Gateshead. I wished to leave immediately after the funeral; but Georgiana entreated me to stay till she could get off to London: whither she was now at last invited by her uncle, Mr. Gibson; who had come down to direct his sister's interment and settle the family affairs. Georgiana said she dreaded being left alone with Eliza; from her she got neither sympa-

thy in her dejection, support in her fears, nor aid in her preparations; so I bore with her feeble-minded quailings, and selfish lamentations, as well as I could, and did my best in sewing for her, and packing her dresses. It is true that while I worked she would idle; and I thought to myself, "If you and I were destined to live always together, cousin, we would commence matters on a different footing. I should not settle tamely down into being the forbearing party; I should assign you your share of labor, and compel you to accomplish it, or else it should be left undone: I should insist, also, on your keeping some of those drawling, half-insincere complaints hushed in your own breast. It is only because our connection happens to be very transitory, and comes at a peculiarly mournful season, that I consent thus to render it so patient and compliant on my part."

At last I saw Georgiana off; but now it was Eliza's turn to request me to stay another week. Her plans required all her time and attention, she said: she was about to depart for some unknown bourne; and all day long she stayed in her own room, her door bolted within, filling trunks, emptying drawers, burning papers, and holding no communication with anyone. She wished me to look after the house, to see callers, and answer notes of condolence.

One morning she told me I was at liberty. "And," she added, "I am obliged to you for your valuable services and discreet conduct! There is some difference between living with such a one as you, and with Georgiana: you perform you own part in life, and burden no one. Tomorrow," she continued, "I set out for the Continent. I shall take up my abode in a religious house near Lisle—a nunnery you would call it: there I shall be quiet and unmolested. I shall devote myself for a time to the examination of the Roman Catholic dogmas, and to a careful study of the workings of their system; if I find it to be, as I half suspect it is, the one best calculated to ensure the doing of all things decently and in order, I shall embrace the tenets of Rome and probably take the veil."

I neither expressed surprise at this resolution nor attempted to dissuade her from it. "The vocation will fit you to a hair," I thought: "much good may it do you!"

When we parted, she said: "Good-bye, cousin Jane Eyre; I wish you well: you have some sense."

I then returned: "You are not without sense, cousin Eliza; but what you have I suppose in another year will be walled up alive in a French convent. However, it is not my business, and so it suits you—I don't much care."

"You are in the right," said she: and with these words we each went our separate way. As I shall not have occasion to refer either to her or her sister again, I may as well mention here that Georgiana made an advantageous match with a wealthy worn-out man of fashion; and that Eliza actually took the veil, and is at this day superior of the convent where she passed the period of her noviatiate: and which she endowed with her fortune.

How people feel when they are returning home from an absence, long or short, I did not know: I had never experienced the sensation. I had known what it was to come back to Gateshead when a child, after a long walk—to be scolded for looking cold or gloomy; and later, what it was to come back from church to Lowood—to long for a plenteous meal and a good fire, and to be unable to get either. Neither of these returnings were very pleasant or desirable: no magnet drew me to a given point, increasing in its strength of attraction the nearer I came. The return to Thornfield was yet to be tried.

My journey seemed tedious—very tedious: fifty miles one day, a night spent at an inn; fifty miles the next day. During the first twelve hours I thought of Mrs. Reed in her last moments: I saw her disfigured and discolored face, and heard her strangely altered voice. I mused on the funeral day, the coffin, the hearse, the black train of tenants and servants—few was the number of relatives—the gaping vault, the silent church, the solemn service. Then I thought of Eliza and Georgiana: I beheld one the cynosure[8] of a ball-room, the other the inmate of a convent cell; and I dwelt on and analyzed their separate peculiarities of person and character. The evening arrival at the great town of ———— scattered these thoughts; night gave them quite another turn: laid down on my traveller's bed, I left reminiscence for anticipation.

I was going back to Thornfield: but how long was I to stay there? Not long; of that I was sure. I had heard from Mrs. Fairfax in the interim of my absence: the party at the hall was dispersed; Mr. Rochester had left for London three weeks ago, but he was then expected to return in a fortnight. Mrs. Fairfax surmized that he was gone to make arrangements for his wedding, as he had talked of purchasing a new carriage: she said the idea of his marrying Miss Ingram still seemed strange to her; but from what everybody said, and from what she had herself seen, she could no longer doubt that the event would shortly take place. "You would be strangely incredulous if you did doubt it," was my mental comment. "I don't doubt it."

The question followed, "Where was I to go?" I dreamt of Miss Ingram all the night: in a vivid morning dream I saw her closing the gates of Thornfield against me and pointing me out another road; and Mr. Rochester looked on with his arms folded—smiling sardonically, as it seemed, at both her and me.

I had not notified to Mrs. Fairfax the exact day of my return; for I did not wish either car or carriage to meet me at Millcote. I proposed to walk the distance quietly by myself; and very quietly, after leaving my box in the ostler's care, did I slip away from the George Inn, about six o'clock of a June evening, and take the old road to Thornfield: a road which lay chiefly through fields, and was now little frequented.

It was not a bright or splendid summer evening, though fair and soft: the haymakers were at work all along the road; and the sky, though far from cloudless, was such as promised well for the future: its blue—where blue was visible—was mild and settled, and its cloud strata high and thin. The west, too, was warm: no watery gleam chilled it—it seemed as if there was a fire lit, an altar burning behind its screen of marbled vapor, and out of apertures shone a golden redness.

I felt glad as the road shortened before me: so glad that I stopped once to ask myself what that joy meant: and to remind reason that it was not to my home I was going, or to a permanent resting-place, or to a place where fond friends looked out for me and waited my arrival. "Mrs. Fairfax will smile you a calm welcome, to be sure," said I; "and little Adèle will clap her hands and jump to see you; but you know very well you are thinking of another than they; and that he is not thinking of you."

But what is so headstrong as youth? What so blind as inexperience? These affirmed that it was pleasure enough to have the privilege of again looking on Mr. Rochester, whether he looked on me or not; and they added—"Hasten! hasten! be with him while you may: but a few more days or weeks, at most, and

8. Center of attention.

you are parted with him for ever!" And then I strangled a new-born agony—a deformed thing which I could not persuade myself to own and rear—and ran on.

They are making hay, too, in Thornfield meadows: or, rather, the laborers are just quitting their work, and returning home with their rakes on their shoulders: now, at the hour I arrive. I have but a field or two to traverse, and then I shall cross the road and reach the gates. How full the hedges are of roses! But I have no time to gather any; I want to be at the house. I passed a tall briar, shooting leafy and flowery branches across the path; I see the narrow stile with stone steps; and I see—Mr. Rochester sitting there, a book and a pencil in his hand: he is writing.

Well, he is not a ghost; yet every nerve I have is unstrung: for a moment I am beyond my own mastery. What does it mean? I did not think I should tremble in this way when I saw him—or lose my voice or the power of motion in his presence. I will go back as soon as I can stir: I need not make an absolute fool of myself. I know another way to the house. It does not signify if I knew twenty ways; for he has seen me.

"Hallo!" he cries; and he puts up his book and his pencil. "There you are! Come on, if you please."

I suppose I do come on; though in what fashion I know not: being scarcely cognizant of my movements, and solicitous only to appear calm; and, above all, to control the working muscles of my face—which I feel rebel insolently against my will, and struggle to express what I had resolved to conceal. But I have a veil—it is down: I may make shift yet to behave with decent composure.

"And this is Jane Eyre? Are you coming from Millcote, and on foot? Yes— just one of your tricks: not to send for a carriage, and come clattering over the street and road like a common mortal, but to steal into the vicinage of your home along with twilight, just as if you were a dream or a shade. What the deuce have you done with yourself this last month?"

"I have been with my aunt, sir, who is dead."

"A true Janian reply! Good angels be my guard! She comes from the other world—from the abode of people who are dead; and tells me so when she meets me alone here in the gloaming! If I dared, I'd touch you, to see if you are substance or shadow, you elf!—but I'd as soon offer to take hold of a blue *ignis fatuus*[9] light in a marsh. Truant! truant!" he added, when he had paused an instant. "Absent from me a whole month: and forgetting me quite, I'll be sworn!"

I knew there would be pleasure in meeting my master again; even though broken by the fear that he was so soon to cease to be my master, and by the knowledge that I was nothing to him: but there was ever in Mr. Rochester (so at least I thought) such a wealth of the power of communicating happiness, that to taste but of the crumbs he scattered to stray and stranger birds like me was to feast genially. His last words were balm: they seemed to imply that it imported something to him whether I forgot him or not. And he had spoken of Thornfield as my home—would that it were my home!

He did not leave the stile, and I hardly liked to ask to go by. I inquired soon if he had not been to London.

"Yes: I suppose you found that out by second-sight."

9. Light from marsh gas.

for such an event. Almost every day I asked Mrs. Fairfax if she had yet heard anything decided: her answer was always in the negative. Once, she said, she had actually put the question to Mr. Rochester as to when he was going to bring his bride home; but he had answered her only by a joke, and one of his queer looks, and she could not tell what to make of him.

One thing specially surprised me, and that was, there were no journeyings backward and forward, no visits to Ingram Park: to be sure it was twenty miles off, on the borders of another county; but what was that distance to an ardent lover? To so practiced and indefatigable a horseman as Mr. Rochester it would be but a morning's ride. I began to cherish hopes I had no right to conceive: that the match was broken off; that rumor had been mistaken; that one or both parties had changed their minds. I used to look at my master's face to see if it were sad or fierce; but I could not remember the time when it had been so uniformly clear of clouds or evil feelings. If, in the moments I and my pupil spent with him, I lacked spirits and sank into inevitable dejection, he became even gay. Never had he called me more frequently to his presence; never been kinder to me when there—and, alas! never had I loved him so well.

Chapter XXII

A splendid Midsummer shone over England: skies so pure, suns so radiant as were then seen in long succession, seldom favor, even singly, our wave-girt land. It was as if a band of Italian days had come from the South, like a flock of glorious passenger birds, and lighted to rest them on the cliffs of Albion.[5] The hay was all got in; the fields round Thornfield were green and shorn; the roads white and baked; the trees were in their dark prime; hedge and wood, full-leaved and deeply tinted, contrasted well with the sunny hue of the cleared meadows between.

On Midsummer-eve, Adèle, weary with gathering wild strawberries in Hay Lane half the day, had gone to bed with the sun. I watched her drop asleep, and when I left her I sought the garden.

It was now the sweetest hour of the twenty-four:—"Day its fervid fires had wasted,"[6] and dew fell cool on panting plain and scorched summit. Where the sun had gone down in simple state—pure of the pomp of clouds—spread a solemn purple, burning with the light of red jewel and furnace flame at one point, on one hill-peak, and extending high and wide, soft and still softer, over half heaven. The east had its own charm of fine, deep blue, and its own modest gem, a rising and solitary star: soon it would boast the moon; but she was yet beneath the horizon.

I walked a while on the pavement; but a subtle, well-known scent—that of a cigar—stole from some window; I saw the library casement open a hand-breath; I knew I might be watched thence; so I went apart into the orchard. No nook in the grounds more sheltered and more Eden-like; it was full of trees, it bloomed with flowers: a very high wall shut it out from the court, on one side; on the other, a beech avenue screened it from the lawn. At the bottom was a sunk fence; its sole separation from lonely fields; a winding walk, bordered with laurels and terminating in a giant horse-chestnut, circled at the base by a seat, led down to the fence. Here one could wander unseen. While such

5. England. 6. From Thomas Campbell's *The Turkish Lady*.

honey-dew fell, such silence reigned, such gloaming[7] gathered, I felt as if I could haunt such shade for ever: but in threading the flower and fruit parterres at the upper part of the enclosure, enticed there by the light the now-rising moon casts on this more open quarter, my step is stayed—not by sound, not by sight, but once more by a warning fragrance.

Sweet briar and southernwood, jasmine, pink, and rose, have long been yielding their evening sacrifice of incense: this new scent is neither of shrub nor flower; it is—I know it well—it is Mr. Rochester's cigar. I look round, and I listen. I see trees laden with ripening fruit. I hear a nightingale warbling in a wood half a mile off; no moving form is visible, no coming step audible; but that perfume increases: I must flee. I make for the wicket leading to the shrub-bery, and I see Mr. Rochester entering. I step aside into the ivy recess; he will not stay long: he will soon return whence he came, and if I sit still he will never see me.

But no—eventide is as pleasant to him as to me, and this antique garden as attractive; and he strolls on, now lifting the gooseberry tree branches to look at the fruit, large as plums, with which they are laden; now taking a ripe cherry from the wall; now stooping towards a knot of flowers, either to inhale their fragrance or to admire the dew-beads on their petals. A great moth goes hum-ming by me; it alights on a plant at Mr. Rochester's foot: he sees it, and bends to examine it.

"Now he has his back towards me," thought I, "and he is occupied too; per-haps, if I walk softly, I can slip away unnoticed."

I trod on an edging of turf that the crackle of the pebbly gravel might not betray me: he was standing among the beds at a yard or two distant from where I had to pass; the moth apparently engaged him. "I shall get by very well," I meditated. As I crossed his shadow, thrown long over the garden by the moon, not yet risen high, he said quietly without turning:—"Jane, come and look at this fellow."

I had made no noise: he had not eyes behind—could his shadow feel? I started at first, and then I approached him.

"Look at his wings," said he; "he reminds me rather of a West Indian insect; one does not often see so large and gay a night-rover in England: there! he is flown."

The moth roamed away. I was sheepishly retreating also; but Mr. Rochester followed me, and when we reached the wicket, he said:—"Turn back: on so lovely a night it is a shame to sit in the house; and surely no one can wish to go to bed while sunset is thus at meeting with moonrise."

It is one of my faults that, though my tongue is sometimes prompt enough at an answer, there are times when it sadly fails me in framing an excuse; and always the lapse occurs at some crisis, when a facile word or plausible pretext is specially wanted to get me out of painful embarrassment. I did not like to walk at this hour alone with Mr. Rochester in the shadowy orchard; but I could not find a reason to allege for leaving him. I followed with lagging step, and thoughts busily bent on discovering a means of extrication; but he himself looked so composed, and so grave also, I became ashamed of feeling any con-fusion: the evil—if evil existent or prospective there was—seemed to lie with me only; his mind was unconscious and quiet.

7. Twilight.

"Jane," he recommenced, as we entered the laurel walk, and slowly strayed down in the direction of the sunk fence and the horse-chestnut, "Thornfield is a pleasant place in summer, is it not?"

"Yes, sir."

"You must have become in some degree attached to the house,—you, who have an eye for natural beauties, and a good deal of the organ of Adhesiveness?"

"I am attached to it, indeed."

"And though I don't comprehend how it is, I perceive you have acquired a degree of regard for that foolish little child, Adèle, too; and even for simple dame Fairfax?"

"Yes, sir; in different ways, I have an affection for both."

"And would be sorry to part with them?"

"Yes."

"Pity!" he said, and sighed and paused. "It is always the way of events in this life," he continued presently: "no sooner have you got settled in a pleasant resting-place, than a voice calls out to you to rise and move on, for the hour of repose is expired."

"Must I move on, sir?" I asked. "Must I leave Thornfield?"

"I believe you must, Jane. I am sorry, Janet, but I believe indeed you must."

This was a blow: but I did not let it prostrate me.

"Well, sir, I shall be ready when the order to march comes."

"It is come now—I must give it tonight."

"Then you are going to be married, sir?"

"Ex-act-ly—pre-cise-ly: with your usual acuteness, you have hit the nail straight on the head."

"Soon, sir?"

"Very soon, my——that is, Miss Eyre: and you'll remember, Jane, the first time I, or Rumor, plainly intimated to you that it was my intention to put my old bachelor's neck into the sacred noose, to enter into the holy estate of matrimony—to take Miss Ingram to my bosom, in short (she's an extensive armful: but that's not to the point—one can't have too much of such a very excellent thing as my beautiful Blanche): well, as I was saying—listen to me, Jane! You're not turning your head to look after more moths, are you? That was only a lady-clock,[8] child, 'flying away home.' I wish to remind you that it was you who first said to me, with that discretion I respect in you—with that foresight, prudence, and humility which befit your responsible and dependent position—that in case I married Miss Ingram—both you and little Adèle had better trot forthwith. I pass over the sort of slur conveyed in this suggestion on the character of my beloved; indeed, when you are far away, Janet, I'll try to forget it: I shall notice only its wisdom; which is such that I have made it my law of action. Adèle must go to school; and you, Miss Eyre, must get a new situation.'

"Yes, sir, I will advertise immediately: and meantime, I suppose"——I was going to say, "I suppose I may stay here till I find another shelter to betake myself to:" but I stopped, feeling it would not do to risk a long sentence, for my voice was not quite under command.

"In about a month I hope to be a bridegroom," continued Mr. Rochester;

8. Ladybug.

"and in the interim I shall myself look out for employment and an asylum for you."

"Thank you, sir; I am sorry to give——"

"Oh, no need to apologize! I consider that when a dependent does her duty as well as you have done yours, she has a sort of claim upon her employer for any little assistance he can conveniently render her; indeed I have already, through my future mother-in-law, heard of a place that I think will suit: it is to undertake the education of the five daughters of Mrs. Dionysius O'Gall, of Bitternutt Lodge, Connaught, Ireland. You'll like Ireland, I think: they're such warm-hearted people there, they say."

"It is a long way off, sir."

"No matter—a girl of your sense will not object to the voyage or the distance."

"Not the voyage, but the distance: and then the sea is a barrier——"

"From what, Jane?"

"From England and from Thornfield: and——"

"Well?"

"From *you*, sir."

I said this almost involuntarily; and, with as little sanction of free will, my tears gushed out. I did not cry so as to be heard, however; I avoided sobbing. The thought of Mrs. O'Gall and Bitternutt Lodge struck cold to my heart; and colder the thought of all the brine and foam, destined, as it seemed, to rush between me and the master at whose side I now walked! and coldest the re-membrance of the wider ocean—wealth, caste, custom intervened between me and what I naturally and inevitably loved.

"It is a long way," I again said.

"It is to be sure; and when you get to Bitternutt Lodge, Connaught, Ireland, I shall never see you again, Jane: that's morally certain. I never go over to Ireland, not having myself much of a fancy for the country. We have been good friends, Jane; have we not?"

"Yes, sir."

"And when friends are on the eve of separation, they like to spend the little time that remains to them close to each other. Come—we'll talk over the voy-age and the parting quietly, half an hour or so, while the stars enter into their shining life up in heaven yonder: here is the chestnut tree: here is the bench at its old roots. Come, we will sit there in peace tonight, though we should never more be destined to sit there together." He seated me and himself.

"It is a long way to Ireland, Janet, and I am sorry to send my little friend on such weary travels; but if I can't do better, how is it to be helped? Are you any-thing akin to me, do you think, Jane?"

I could risk no sort of answer by this time: my heart was full.

"Because," he said, "I sometimes have a queer feeling with regard to you—especially when you are near me, as now: it is as if I had a string somewhere under my left ribs, tightly and inextricably knotted to a similar string situated in the corresponding quarter of your little frame. And if that boisterous chan-nel, and two hundred miles or so of land come broad between us, I am afraid that cord of communion will be snapped; and then I've a nervous notion I should take to bleeding inwardly. As for you—you'd forget me."

"That I *never* should, sir: you know"——impossible to proceed.

"Jane, do you hear that nightingale singing in the wood? Listen!"

In listening, I sobbed convulsively; for I could repress what I endured no longer; I was obliged to yield, and I was shaken from head to foot with acute distress. When I did speak, it was only to express an impetuous wish that I had never been born, or never come to Thornfield.

"Because you are sorry to leave it?"

The vehemence of emotion, stirred by grief and love within me, was claiming mastery, and struggling for full sway; and asserting a right to predominate: to overcome, to live, rise, and reign at last; yes,—and to speak.

"I grieve to leave Thornfield: I love Thornfield—I love it, because I have lived in it a full and delightful life,—momentarily at least. I have not been trampled on. I have not been petrified. I have not been buried with inferior minds, and excluded from every glimpse of communion with what is bright and energetic, and high. I have talked, face to face, with what I reverence; with what I delight in,—with an original, a vigorous, an expanded mind. I have known you, Mr. Rochester; and it strikes me with terror and anguish to feel I absolutely must be torn from you for ever. I see the necessity of departure; and it is like looking on the necessity of death."

"Where do you see the necessity?" he asked, suddenly.

"Where? You, sir, have placed it before me."

"In what shape?"

"In the shape of Miss Ingram; a noble and beautiful woman,—your bride."

"My bride! What bride? I have no bride!"

"But you will have."

"Yes;—I will!—I will!" He set his teeth.

"Then I must go—you have said it yourself."

"No: you must stay! I swear it—and the oath shall be kept."

"I tell you I must go!" I retorted, roused to something like passion. "Do you think I can stay to become nothing to you? Do you think I am an automaton?—a machine without feelings? and can bear to have my morsel of bread snatched from my lips, and my drop of living water dashed from my cup? Do you think, because I am poor, obscure, plain, and little, I am soulless and heartless? You think wrong!—I have as much soul as you,—and full as much heart! And if God had gifted me with some beauty and much wealth, I should have made it as hard for you to leave me, as it is now for me to leave you. I am not talking to you now through the medium of custom, conventionalities, nor even of mortal flesh—it is my spirit that addresses your spirit; just as if both had passed through the grave, and we stood at God's feet, equal,—as we are!"

"As we are!" repeated Mr. Rochester—"so," he added, enclosing me in his arms, gathering me to his breast, pressing his lips on my lips: "So, Jane!"

"Yes, so, sir," I rejoined: "and yet not so; for you are a married man—or as good as a married man, and wed to one inferior to you—to one with whom you have no sympathy—whom I do not believe you truly love; for I have seen and heard you sneer at her. I would scorn such a union: therefore I am better than you—let me go!"

"Where, Jane? To Ireland?"

"Yes—to Ireland. I have spoken my mind, and can go anywhere now."

"Jane, be still; don't struggle so, like a wild, frantic bird that is rending its own plumage in its desperation."

"I am no bird; and no net ensnares me: I am a free human being with an independent will; which I now exert to leave you."

Another effort set me at liberty, and I stood erect before him.

"And your will shall decide your destiny," he said: "I offer you my hand, my heart, and a share of all my possessions."

"You play a farce, which I merely laugh at."

"I ask you to pass through life at my side—to be my second self, and best earthly companion."

"For that fate you have already made your choice, and must abide by it."

"Jane, be still a few moments; you are over-excited: I will be still too."

A waft of wind came sweeping down the laurel walk, and trembled through the boughs of the chestnut: it wandered away—away—to an indefinite distance—it died. The nightingale's song was then the only voice of the hour: in listening to it, I again wept. Mr. Rochester sat quiet, looking at me gently and seriously. Some time passed before he spoke; he at last said:—"Come to my side, Jane, and let us explain and understand one another."

"I will never again come to your side: I am torn away now, and cannot return."

"But, Jane, I summon you as my wife: it is you only I intend to marry."

I was silent: I thought he mocked me.

"Come, Jane—come hither."

"Your bride stands between us."

He rose, and with a stride reached me.

"My bride is here," he said, again drawing me to him, "because my equal is here, and my likeness. Jane, will you marry me?"

Still I did not answer, and still I writhed myself from his grasp: for I was still incredulous.

"Do you doubt me, Jane?"

"Entirely."

"You have no faith in me?"

"Not a whit."

"Am I a liar in your eyes?" he asked passionately. "Little sceptic, you *shall* be convinced. What love have I for Miss Ingram? None: and that you know. What love has she for me? None: as I have taken pains to prove; I caused a rumor to reach her that my fortune was not a third of what was supposed, and after that I presented myself to see the result; it was coldness both from her and her mother. I would not—I could not—marry Miss Ingram. You—you strange—you almost unearthly thing!—I love as my own flesh. You—poor and obscure, and small and plain as you are—I entreat to accept me as a husband."

"What, me!" I ejaculated: beginning in his earnestness—and especially in his incivility—to credit his sincerity: "me who have not a friend in the world but you—if you are my friend: not a shilling but what you have given me?"

"You, Jane. I must have you for my own—entirely my own. Will you be mine? Say yes, quickly."

"Mr. Rochester, let me look at your face: turn to the moonlight."

"Why?"

"Because I want to read your countenance; turn!"

"There: you will find it scarcely more legible than a crumpled, scratched page. Read on: only make haste, for I suffer."

His face was very much agitated and very much flushed, and there were strong workings in the features, and strange gleams in the eyes.

"Oh, Jane, you torture me!" he exclaimed. "With that searching and yet faithful and generous look, you torture me!"

"How can I do that? If you are true, and your offer real, my only feelings to you must be gratitude and devotion—they cannot torture."

"Gratitude!" he ejaculated; and added wildly—"Jane, accept me quickly. Say, Edward—give me my name—Edward—I will marry you."

"Are you in earnest?—Do you truly love me? Do you sincerely wish me to be your wife?"

"I do; and if an oath is necessary to satisfy you, I swear it."

"Then sir, I will marry you."

"Edward—my little wife!"

"Dear Edward!"

"Come to me—come to me entirely now," said he: and added, in his deepest tone, speaking in my ear as his cheek was laid on mine, "Make my happiness—I will make yours."

"God pardon me!" he subjoined ere long: "and man meddle not with me: I have her, and will hold her."

"There is no one to meddle, sir I have no kindred to interfere."

"No—that is the best of it," he said.

And if I loved him less I should have thought his accent and look of exultation savage; but, sitting by him, roused from the nightmare of parting—called to the paradise of union—I thought only of the bliss given me to drink in so abundant a flow. Again and again he said,"Are you happy, Jane?" and again and again I answered, "Yes." After which he murmured, "It will atone—it will atone. Have I not found her friendless, and cold, and comfortless? Will I not guard, and cherish, and solace her? Is there not love in my heart, and constancy in my resolves? It will expiate at God's tribunal. I know my Maker sanctions what I do. For the world's judgment—I wash my hands thereof. For man's opinion—I defy it."

But what had befallen the night? The moon was not yet set, and we were all in shadow: I could scarcely see my master's face, near as I was. And what ailed the chestnut tree? it writhed and groaned; while wind roared in the laurel walk, and came sweeping over us.

"We must go in," said Mr. Rochester: "the weather changes. I could have sat with thee till morning, Jane."

"And so," thought I, "could I with you." I should have said so, perhaps, but a livid, vivid spark leapt out of a cloud at which I was looking, and there was a crack, a crash, and a close rattling peal; and I thought only of hiding my dazzled eyes against Mr. Rochester's shoulder.

The rain rushed down. He hurried me up the walk, through the grounds, and into the house; but we were quite wet before we could pass the threshold. He was taking off my shawl in the hall, and shaking the water out of my loosened hair, when Mrs. Fairfax emerged from her room. I did not observe her at first, nor did Mr. Rochester. The lamp was lit. The clock was on the stroke of twelve.

"Hasten to take off your wet things," said he; "and before you go, good-night—good-night, my darling!"

He kissed me repeatedly. When I looked up, on leaving his arms, there stood the widow, pale, grave, and amazed. I only smiled at her, and ran upstairs. "Explanation will do for another time," thought I. Still, when I reached my chamber, I felt a pang at the idea that she should even temporarily misconstrue what she had seen. But joy soon effaced every other feeling; and loud as the wind blew, near and deep as the thunder crashed, fierce and frequent as

the lightning gleamed, cataract-like as the rain fell during a storm of two hour's duration, I experienced no fear, and little awe. Mr. Rochester came thrice to my door in the course of it, to ask if I was safe and tranquil: and that was comfort, that was strength for anything.

Before I left my bed in the morning, little Adèle came running in to tell me that the great horse-chestnut at the bottom of the orchard had been struck by lightning in the night, and half of it split away.

Chapter XXIV

As I rose and dressed, I thought over what had happened, and wondered if it were a dream. I could not be certain of the reality till I had seen Mr. Rochester again, and heard him renew his words of love and promise.

While arranging my hair, I looked at my face in the glass, and felt it was no longer plain: there was hope in its aspect, and life in its color; and my eyes seemed as if they had beheld the fount of fruition, and borrowed beams from the lustrous ripple. I had often been unwilling to look at my master, because I feared he could not be pleased at my look; but I was sure I might lift my face to his now, and not cool his affection by its expression. I took a plain but clean and light summer dress from my drawer and put it on: it seemed no attire had ever so well become me; because none had I ever worn in so blissful a mood.

I was not surprised, when I ran down into the hall, to see that a brilliant June morning had succeeded to the tempest of the night; and to feel, through the open glass door, the breathing of a fresh and fragrant breeze. Nature must be gladsome when I was so happy. A beggar-woman and her little boy—pale, ragged objects both—were coming up the walk, and I ran down and gave them all the money I happened to have in my purse—some three or four shillings: good or bad, they must partake of my jubilee. The rooks cawed, and blither birds sang; but nothing was so merry or so musical as my own rejoicing heart.

Mrs. Fairfax surprised me by looking out of the window with a sad countenance, and saying gravely:—"Miss Eyre, will you come to breakfast?" During the meal she was quiet and cool: but I could not undeceive her then. I must wait for my master to give explanations; and so must she. I ate what I could, and then I hastened upstairs. I met Adèle leaving the school-room.

"Where are you going? It is time for lessons."

"Mr. Rochester has sent me away to the nursery."

"Where is he?"

"In there," pointing to the apartment she had left; and I went in, and there he stood.

"Come and bid me good-morning," said he. I gladly advanced; and it was not merely a cold word now, or even a shake of the hand that I received, but an embrace and a kiss. It seemed natural; it seemed genial to be so well-loved, so caressed by him.

"Jane, you look blooming, and smiling, and pretty," said he: "truly pretty this morning. Is this my pale, little elf? Is this my mustard-seed?[9] This little sunny-faced girl with the dimpled cheek and rosy lips; the satin-smooth hazel hair, and the radiant hazel eyes?" (I had green eyes, reader; but you must excuse the mistake: for him they were new-dyed, I suppose.)

"It is Jane Eyre, sir."

9. Name of one of the fairies in Shakespeare's A *Midsummer Night's Dream.*

"Soon to be Jane Rochester," he added: "in four weeks, Janet, not a day more. Do you hear that?"

I did, and I could not quite comprehend it: it made me giddy. The feeling, the announcement sent through me, was something stronger than was consistent with joy—something that smote and stunned: it was, I think, almost fear.

"You blushed, and now you are white, Jane: what is that for?"

"Because you gave me a new name—Jane Rochester; and it seems so strange."

"Yes, Mrs. Rochester," said he; "young Mrs. Rochester—Fairfax Rochester's girl-bride."

"It can never be, sir; it does not sound likely. Human beings never enjoy complete happiness in this world. I was not born for a different destiny to the rest of my species: to imagine such a lot befalling me is a fairy tale—a day-dream."

"Which I can and will realize. I shall begin today. This morning I wrote to my banker in London to send me certain jewels he has in his keeping,—heirlooms for the ladies of Thornfield. In a day or two I hope to pour them into your lap: for every privilege, every attention shall be yours, that I would accord a peer's daughter, if about to marry her."

"Oh, sir!—never mind jewels! I don't like to hear them spoken of. Jewels for Jane Eyre sounds unnatural and strange: I would rather not have them."

"I will myself put the diamond chain round your neck, and the circlet on your forehead,—which it will become: for nature, at least, has stamped her patent of nobility on this brow, Jane; and I will clasp the bracelets on these fine wrists, and load these fairy-like fingers with rings."

"No, no, sir! think of other subjects, and speak of other things, and in another strain. Don't address me as if I were a beauty; I am your plain, Quakerish governess."

"You are a beauty, in my eyes; and a beauty just after the desire of my heart,—delicate and aërial."

"Puny and insignificant, you mean. You are dreaming, sir,—or you are sneering. For God's sake, don't be ironical!"

"I will make the world acknowledge you a beauty too," he went on, while I really became uneasy at the strain he had adopted; because I felt he was either deluding himself, or trying to delude me. "I will attire my Jane in satin and lace, and she shall have roses in her hair and I will cover the head I love best with a priceless veil."

"And then you won't know me, sir; and I shall not be your Jane Eyre any longer, but an ape in a harlequin's[1] jacket,—a jay in borrowed plumes. I would as soon see you, Mr. Rochester, tricked out in stage-trappings, as myself clad in a court-lady's robe; and I don't call you handsome, sir, though I love you most dearly: far too dearly to flatter you. Don't flatter me."

He pursued his theme, however, without noticing my deprecation. "This very day I shall take you in the carriage to Millcote, and you must choose some dresses for yourself. I told you we shall be married in four weeks. The wedding is to take place quietly, in the church down below yonder; and then I shall waft you away at once to town. After a brief stay there, I shall bear my treasure to regions nearer the sun: to French vineyards and Italian plains; and she shall see

1. I.e., clown's.

whatever is famous in old story and in modern record: she shall taste, too, of the life of cities; and she shall learn to value herself by just comparison with others."

"Shall I travel?—and with you, sir?"

"You shall sojourn at Paris, Rome, and Naples: at Florence, Venice, and Vienna: all the ground I have wandered over shall be retrodden by you: wherever I stamped my hoof, your sylph's[2] foot shall step also. Ten years since, I flew through Europe half mad; with disgust, hate, and rage, as my companions; now I shall revisit it healed and cleansed, with a very angel as my comforter."

I laughed at him as he said this. "I am not an angel," I asserted; "and I will not be one till I die: I will be myself. Mr. Rochester, you must neither expect nor exact anything celestial of me—for you will not get it, any more than I shall get it of you: which I do not at all anticipate."

"What do you anticipate of me?"

"For a little while you will perhaps be as you are now,—a very little while; and then you will turn cool; and then you will be capricious; and then you will be stern, and I shall have much ado to please you: but when you get well used to me, you will perhaps like me again—*like* me, I say, not *love* me. I suppose your love will effervesce in six months, or less. I have observed in books written by men, that period assigned as the farthest to which a husband's ardor extends. Yet, after all, as a friend and companion, I hope never to become quite distasteful to my dear master."

"Distasteful! and like you again! I think I shall like you again and yet again: and I will make you confess I do not only *like*, but *love* you—with truth, fervor, constancy."

"Yet are you not capricious, sir?"

"To women who please me only by their faces, I am the very devil when I find out they have neither souls nor hearts—when they open to me a perspective of flatness, triviality, and perhaps imbecility, coarseness, and ill-temper: but to the clear eye and eloquent tongue, to the soul made of fire, and the character that bends but does not break—at once supple and stable, tractable and consistent—I am ever tender and true."

"Had you ever experience of such a character, sir? Did you ever love such an one?"

"I love it now."

"But before me: if I, indeed, in any respect come up to that difficult standard?"

"I never met your likeness. Jane: you please me, and you master me—you seem to submit, and I like the sense of pliancy you impart: and while I am twining the soft, silken skein round my finger, it sends a thrill up my arm to my heart. I am influenced—conquered; and the influence is sweeter than I can express; and the conquest I undergo has a witchery beyond any triumph *I* can win. Why do you smile, Jane? What does that inexplicable, that uncanny turn of countenance mean?"

"I was thinking, sir (you will excuse the idea; it was involuntary), I was thinking of Hercules and Samson[3] with their charmers——"

2. A being who inhabits air.

3. He was charmed by Delilah, who betrayed him to his enemies. Hercules was "charmed" by various women, especially by his wife, Deianira, who was responsible for his death.

"You were, you little elfish——"

"Hush, sir! You don't talk very wisely just now; any more than those gentlemen acted very wisely. However, had they been married, they would no doubt by their severity as husbands have made up for their softness as suitors; and so will you, I fear. I wonder how you will answer me a year hence, should I ask a favor it does not suit your convenience or pleasure to grant."

"Ask me something now, Janet—the least thing: I desire to be entreated——"

"Indeed, I will, sir; I have my petition all ready."

"Speak! But if you look up and smile with that countenance, I shall swear concession before I know to what, and that will make a fool of me."

"Not at all, sir; I ask only this don't send for the jewels, and don't crown me with roses: you might as well put a border of gold lace round that plain pocket handkerchief you have there."

"I might as well 'gild refined gold.'[4] I know it: your request is granted then—for the time. I will remand the order I despatched to my banker. But you have not yet asked for anything; you have prayed a gift to be withdrawn: try again."

"Well, then, sir; have the goodness to gratify my curiosity, which is much piqued on one point."

He looked disturbed. "What? what?" he said hastily. "Curiosity is a dangerous petition: it is well I have not taken a vow to accord every request——"

"But there can be no danger in complying with this, sir."

"Utter it, Jane: but I wish that instead of a mere inquiry into perhaps, a secret, it was a wish for half my estate."

"Now, king Ahasuerus![5] What do I want with half your estate? Do you think I am a Jew-usurer, seeking good investment in land? I would much rather have all your confidence. You will not exclude me from your confidence, if you admit me to your heart?"

"You are welcome to all my confidence that is worth having, Jane: but for God's sake don't desire a useless burden! Don't long for poison—don't turn out a downright Eve[6] on my hands!"

"Why not, sir? You have just been telling me how much you like to be conquered, and how pleasant over-persuasion is to you. Don't you think I had better take advantage of the confession, and begin and coax, and entreat—even cry and be sulky if necessary for the sake of a mere essay of my power?"

"I dare you to any such experiment. Encroach, presume, and the game is up."

"Is it, sir? You soon give in. How stern you look now! Your eyebrows have become as thick as my finger, and your forehead resembles, what, in some very astonishing poetry, I once saw styled 'a blue-piled thunderloft.'[7] That will be your married look, sir, I suppose?"

"If that will be your married look, I, as a Christian, will soon give up the notion of consorting with a mere sprite or salamander.[8] But what had you to ask, thing?—out with it!"

"There, you are less than civil now; and I like rudeness a great deal better than flattery. I had rather be a *thing* than an angel. This is what I have to ask:— Why did you take such pains to make me believe you wished to marry Miss Ingram?"

4. Shakespeare's *King John* 4.2.11.
5. Fabulously rich Persian king in the Book of Esther.
6. I.e., one desiring forbidden and harmful knowl-
edge.
7. Perhaps from the Brontë's own poetry.
8. A mythical being that can inhabit fire.

"Is that all? Thank God, it is no worse!"

And now he unknit his black brows; looked down, smiling at me, and stroked my hair, as if well pleased at seeing a danger averted.

"I think I may confess," he continued, "even although I should make you a little indignant, Jane—and I have seen what a fire-spirit you can be when you are indignant. You glowed in the cool moonlight last night, when you mutinied against fate, and claimed your rank as my equal. Janet, by-the-by, it was you who made me the offer."

"Of course, I did. But to the point if you please, sir—Miss Ingram?"

"Well, I feigned courtship of Miss Ingram, because I wished to render you as madly in love with me as I was with you; and I knew jealousy would be the best ally I could call in for the furtherance of that end."

"Excellent!—now you are small—not one whit bigger than the end of my little finger. It was a burning shame, and a scandalous disgrace to act in that way. Did you think nothing of Miss Ingram's feelings, sir?"

"Her feelings are concentrated in one—pride; and that needs humbling. Were you jealous, Jane?"

"Never mind, Mr. Rochester: it is in no way interesting to you to know that. Answer me truly once more. Do you think Miss Ingram will not suffer from your dishonest coquetry? Won't she feel forsaken and deserted?"

"Impossible!—when I told you how she, on the contrary, deserted me: the idea of my insolvency cooled, or rather extinguished, her flame in a moment."

"You have a curious designing mind, Mr. Rochester. I am afraid your principles on some points are eccentric."

"My principles were never trained, Jane: they may have grown a little awry for want of attention."

"Once again, seriously; may I enjoy the great good that has been vouchsafed to me, without fearing that any one else is suffering the bitter pain I myself felt a while ago?"

"That you may, my good little girl: there is not another being in the world has the same pure love for me as yourself—for I lay that pleasant unction to my soul, Jane, a belief in your affection."

I turned my lips to the hand that lay on my shoulder. I loved him very much—more than I could trust myself to say—more than words had power to express.

"Ask something more," he said presently; "it is my delight to be entreated, and to yield."

I was again ready with my request.

"Communicate your intentions to Mrs. Fairfax, sir: she saw me with you last night in the hall, and she was shocked. Give her some explanation before I see her again. It pains me to be misjudged by so good a woman."

"Go to your room, and put on your bonnet," he replied. "I mean you to accompany me to Millcote this morning; and while you prepare for the drive, I will enlighten the old lady's understanding. Did she think, Janet, you had given the world for love, and considered it well lost?"[9]

"I believe she thought I had forgotten my station, and yours, sir."

"Station! station!—your station is in my heart, and on the necks of those who would insult you, now or hereafter—Go."

9. *All for Love; or, The World Well Lost* (1678), is the title of a heroic tragedy by John Dryden.

I was soon dressed; and when I heard Mr. Rochester quit Mrs. Fairfax's parlor, I hurried down to it. The old lady had been reading her morning portion of Scripture—the lesson for the day; her Bible lay open before her, and her spectacles were upon it. Her occupation, suspended by Mr. Rochester's announcement, seemed now forgotten: her eyes, fixed on the blank wall opposite, expressed the surprise of a quiet mind, stirred by unwonted tidings. Seeing me, she roused herself: she made a sort of effort to smile, and framed a few words of congratulation; but the smile expired, and the sentence was abandoned unfinished. She put up her spectacles, shut the Bible, and pushed her chair back from the table.

"I feel so astonished," she began, "I hardly know what to say to you, Miss Eyre. I have surely not been dreaming, have I? Sometimes I half fall asleep when I am sitting alone, and fancy things that have never happened. It has seemed to me more than once when I have been in a doze, that my dear husband, who died fifteen years since, has come in and sat down beside me; and that I have even heard him call me by my name, Alice, as he used to do. Now, can you tell me whether it is actually true that Mr. Rochester has asked you to marry him? Don't laugh at me. But I really thought he came in here five minutes ago, and said, that in a month you would be his wife."

"He has said the same thing to me," I replied.

"He has! Do you believe him? Have you accepted him?"

"Yes."

She looked at me bewildered.

"I could never have thought it. He is a proud man: all the Rochesters were proud: and his father, at least, liked money. He, too, has always been called careful. He means to marry you?"

"He tells me so."

She surveyed my whole person: in her eyes I read that they had there found no charm powerful enough to solve the enigma.

"It passes me!" she continued: "but no doubt it is true since you say so. How it will answer, I cannot tell: I really don't know. Equality of position and fortune is often advisable in such cases; and there are twenty years of difference in your ages. He might almost be your father."

"No, indeed, Mrs. Fairfax!" exclaimed I, nettled: "he is nothing like my father! No one, who saw us together, would suppose it for an instant. Mr. Rochester looks as young, and is as young, as some men at five-and-twenty."

"Is it really for love he is going to marry you?" she asked.

I was so hurt by her coldness and scepticism that the tears rose to my eyes.

"I am sorry to grieve you," pursued the widow; "but you are so young, and so little acquainted with men, I wished to put you on your guard. It is an old saying that 'all is not gold that glitters'; and in this case I do fear there will be something found to be different to what either you or I expect."

"Why?—am I a monster?" I said: "is it impossible that Mr. Rochester should have a sincere affection for me?"

"No: you are very well; and much improved of late: and Mr. Rochester, I daresay, is fond of you. I have always noticed that you were a sort of pet of his. There are times when, for your sake, I have been a little uneasy at his marked preference, and have wished to put you on your guard: but I did not like to suggest even the possibility of wrong. I knew such an idea would shock, perhaps offend you; and you were so discreet, and so thoroughly modest and sensible,

I hoped you might be trusted to protect yourself. Last night I cannot tell you what I suffered when I sought all over the house, and could find you nowhere, nor the master either; and then, at twelve o'clock, saw you come in with him."

"Well, never mind that now," I interrupted impatiently: "it is enough that all was right."

"I hope all will be right in the end," she said: "but believe me, you cannot be too careful. Try and keep Mr. Rochester at a distance: distrust yourself as well as him. Gentlemen in his station are not accustomed to marry their governesses."

I was growing truly irritated: happily, Adèle ran in.

"Let me go,—let me go to Millcote too!" she cried. "Mr. Rochester won't: though there is so much room in the new carriage. Beg him to let me go, mademoiselle."

"That I will, Adèle," and I hastened away with her, glad to quit my gloomy monitress. The carriage was ready: they were bringing it round to the front, and my master was pacing the pavement, Pilot following him backwards and forwards.

"Adèle may accompany us, may she not, sir?"

"I told her no. I'll have no brats!—I'll have only you."

"Do let her go, Mr. Rochester, if you please: it would be better."

"Not it: she will be a restraint."

He was quite peremptory, both in look and voice. The chill of Mrs. Fairfax's warnings, and the damp of her doubts were upon me: something of unsubstantiality and uncertainty had beset my hopes. I half lost the sense of power over him. I was about mechanically to obey him, without further remonstrance; but as he helped me into the carriage, he looked at my face.

"What is the matter?" he asked; "all the sunshine is gone. Do you really wish the bairn to go? Will it annoy you if she is left behind?"

"I would far rather she went, sir."

"Then off for your bonnet, and back, like a flash of lightning!" cried he to Adèle.

She obeyed him with what speed she might.

"After all, a single morning's interruption will not matter much," said he, "when I mean shortly to claim you—your thoughts, conversation, and company—for life."

Adèle, when lifted in, commenced kissing me, by way of expressing her gratitude for my intercession: she was instantly stowed away into a corner on the other side of him. She then peeped round to where I sat; so stern a neighbor was too restrictive: to him, in his present fractious mood she dared whisper no observations, nor ask of him any information.

"Let her come to me," I entreated: "she will, perhaps, trouble you, sir: there is plenty of room on this side."

He handed her over as if she had been a lap-dog; "I'll send her to school yet," he said, but now he was smiling.

Adèle heard him, and asked if she was to go school "sans[1] mademoiselle."

"Yes," he replied,"absolutely sans mademoiselle; for I am to take mademoiselle to the moon, and there I shall seek a cave in one of the white valleys among the volcano-tops, and mademoiselle shall live with me there, and only me."

1. Without.

"She will have nothing to eat: you will starve her," observed Adèle.

"I shall gather manna for her morning and night: the plains and hillsides in the moon are bleached with manna, Adèle."

"She will want to warm herself: what will she do for a fire?"

"Fire rises out of the lunar mountains: when she is cold, I'll carry her up to a peak and lay her down on the edge of a crater."

"Oh, qu'elle y sera mal—peu confortable![2] And her clothes, they will wear out: how can she get new ones?"

Mr. Rochester professed to be puzzled. "Hem?" said he. "What would you do, Adèle? Cudgel your brains for an expedient. How would a white or a pink cloud answer for a gown, do you think? And one could cut a pretty enough scarf out of a rainbow."

"She is far better as she is," concluded Adèle, after musing some time: "besides, she would get tired of living with only you in the moon. If I were mademoiselle, I would never consent to go with you."

"She has consented: she has pledged her word."

"But you can't get her there: there is no road to the moon: it is all air; and neither you nor she can fly."

"Adèle, look at that field." We were now outside Thornfield gates, and bowling lightly along the smooth road to Millcote, where the dust was well-laid by the thunder-storm, and where the low hedges and lofty timber trees on each side glistened green and rain-refreshed.

"In that field, Adèle, I was walking late one evening about a fortnight since—the evening of the day you helped me to make hay in the orchard meadows; and as I was tired with raking swaths, I sat down to rest me on a stile; and there I took out a little book and a pencil, and began to write about a misfortune that befell me long ago and a wish I had for happy days to come: I was writing away very fast, though daylight was fading from the leaf, when something came up the path and stopped two yards off me. I looked at it. It was a little thing with a veil of gossamer on its head. I beckoned it to come near me; it stood soon at my knee. I never spoke to it, and it never spoke to me, in words: but I read its eyes, and it read mine; and our speechless colloquy was to this effect:—It was a fairy, and come from Elf-land, it said; and its errand was to make me happy: I must go with it out of the common world to a lonely place—such as the moon, for instance—and it nodded its head towards her horn, rising over Hay-hill: it told me of the alabaster cave and silver vale where we might live. I said I should like to go; but reminded it, as you did me, that I had no wings to fly.

" 'Oh,' returned the fairy, 'that does not signify! Here is a talisman will remove all difficulties;' and she held out a pretty gold ring. 'Put it,' she said, 'on the fourth finger of my left hand, and I am yours, and you are mine; and we shall leave earth, and make our own heaven yonder.' She nodded again at the moon. The ring, Adèle, is in my breeches-pocket, under the disguise of a sovereign: but I mean soon to change it to a ring again."

"But what has mademoiselle to do with it? I don't care for the fairy: you said it was mademoiselle you would take to the moon?"——

"Mademoiselle is a fairy," he said, whispering mysteriously. Whereupon I told her not to mind his badinage; and she, on her part, evinced a fund of genuine French scepticism: denominating Mr. Rochester "un vrai menteur,"[3] and

2 Oh, she'll be uncomfortable there! 3. A real liar.

assuring him that she had made no account whatever of his "Contes de fée," and that "du reste, il n'y avait pas de fées, et quand même il y en avait,"[4] she was sure they would never appear to him, nor ever give him rings, or offer to live with him in the moon. The hour spent at Millcote was a somewhat harassing one to me. Mr. Rochester obliged me to go to a certain silk warehouse: there I was ordered to choose half a dozen dresses. I hated the business, I begged leave to defer it: no—it should be gone through with now. By dint of entreaties expressed in energetic whispers I reduced the half-dozen to two: these, however, he vowed he would select himself. With anxiety I watched his eye rove over the gay stores: he fixed on a rich silk of the most brilliant amethyst dye, and a superb pink satin. I told him in a new series of whispers, that he might as well buy me a gold gown and a silver bonnet at once: I should certainly never venture to wear his choice. With infinite difficulty, for he was stubborn as a stone, I persuaded him to make an exchange in favor of a sober black satin and pearl-gray silk. "It might pass for the present," he said; "but he would yet see me glittering like a parterre."

Glad was I to get him out of the silk warehouse, and then out of a jeweller's shop: the more he bought me, the more my cheek burned with a sense of annoyance and degradation. As we reentered the carriage, and I sat back feverish and fagged, I remembered what in the hurry of events, dark and bright, I had wholly forgotten—the letter of my uncle, John Eyre, to Mrs. Reed: his intention to adopt me and make me his legatee. "It would, indeed, be a relief," I thought, "if I had ever so small an independency; I never can bear being dressed like a doll by Mr. Rochester, or sitting like a second Danae with the golden shower falling daily round me.[5] I will write to Madeira the moment I get home, and tell my uncle John I am going to be married, and to whom: if I had but a prospect of one day bringing Mr. Rochester an accession of fortune, I could better endure to be kept by him now." And somewhat relieved by this idea (which I failed not to execute that day), I ventured once more to meet my master's and lover's eye; which most pertinaciously sought mine, though I averted both face and gaze. He smiled; and I thought his smile was such as a sultan might, in a blissful and fond moment, bestow on a slave his gold and gems had enriched: I crushed his hand, which was ever hunting mine, vigorously, and thrust it back to him red with the passionate pressure—

"You need not look in that way," I said: "if you do I'll wear nothing but my old Lowood frocks to the end of the chapter. I'll be married in this lilac gingham—you may make a dressing-gown for yourself out of the pearl-gray silk, and an infinite series of waist-coats out of the black satin."

He chuckled; he rubbed his hands: "Oh, it is rich to see and hear her!" he exclaimed. "Is she original? Is she piquant? I would not exchange this one little English girl for the grand Turk's whole seraglio;[6] gazelle-eyes, houri forms, and all!"

The Eastern allusion bit me again: "I'll not stand you an inch in the stead of a seraglio," I said; "so don't consider me an equivalent for one; if you have a fancy for anything in that line, away with you, sir, to the bazaars of Stamboul

4. Fairy tales, and that furthermore, there were no fairies, and even so there were some (*quand même* may be Brontë's error for *même se*, "even if").

5. Zeus, as a shower of gold, made love to Danae.
6. I.e., harem.

without delay; and lay out in extensive slave-purchases some of that spare cash you seem at a loss to spend satisfactorily here."

"And what will you do, Janet, while I am bargaining for so many tons of flesh and such an assortment of black eyes?"

"I'll be preparing myself to go out as a missionary to preach liberty to them that are enslaved—your harem inmates amongst the rest. I'll get admitted there, and I'll stir up mutiny; and you, three-tailed bashaw[7] as you are, sir, shall in a trice find yourself fettered amongst our hands: nor will I, for one, consent to cut your bonds till you have signed a charter, the most liberal that despot ever yet conferred."

"I would consent to be at your mercy, Jane."

"I would have no mercy, Mr. Rochester, if you supplicated for it with an eye like that. While you looked so, I should be certain that whatever charter you might grant under coercion, your first act, when released, would be to violate its conditions."

"Why, Jane, what would you have? I fear you will compel me to go through a private marriage ceremony, besides that performed at the altar. You will stipulate, I see, for peculiar terms—what will they be?"

"I only want an easy mind, sir; not crushed by crowded obligations. Do you remember what you said of Céline Varens?—of the diamonds, the cashmeres you gave her? I will not be your English Céline Varens. I shall continue to act as Adèle's governess; by that I shall earn my board and lodging, and thirty pounds a year besides. I'll furnish my own wardrobe out of that money, and you shall give me nothing but"——

"Well, but what?"

"Your regard; and if I give you mine in return, that debt will be quit."

"Well, for cool native impudence, and pure innate pride, you haven't your equal," said he. We were now approaching Thornfield. "Will it please you to dine with me today?" he asked, as we re-entered the gates.

"No, thank you, sir."

"And what for, 'no, thank you,' if one may inquire?"

"I never have dined with you, sir: and I see no reason why I should now: till"——

"Till what? You delight in half-phrases."

"Till I can't help it."

"Do you suppose I eat like an ogre, or a ghoul, that you dread being the companion of my repast?"

"I have formed no supposition on the subject, sir; but I want to go on as usual for another month."

"You will give up your governessing slavery at once."

"Indeed! begging your pardon, sir, I shall not. I shall just go on with it as usual. I shall keep out of your way all day, as I have been accustomed to do: you may send for me in the evening, when you feel disposed to see me, and I'll come then; but at no other time."

"I want a smoke, Jane, or a pinch of snuff, to comfort me under all this, 'pour me donner une contenance,'[8] as Adèle would say: and unfortunately I have neither my cigar-case, nor my snuff-box. But listen—whisper—it is your

7. Pasha (a grand Turk). 8. To steady me.

time now, little tyrant, but it will be mine presently: and when once I have fairly seized you, to have and to hold, I'll just—figuratively speaking—attach you to a chain like this" (touching his watch-guard).

"Yes, bonny wee thing, I'll wear you in my bosom, lest my jewel I should tyne."[9]

He said this as he helped me to alight from the carriage; and while he afterwards lifted out Adèle, I entered the house, and made good my retreat upstairs.

He duly summoned me to his presence in the evening. I had prepared an occupation for him; for I was determined not to spend the whole time in a *tête-à-tête* conversation. I remembered his fine voice; I knew he liked to sing—good singers generally do. I was no vocalist myself, and, in his fastidious judgment, no musician either; but I delighted in listening when the performance was good. No sooner had twilight, that hour of romance, begun to lower her blue and starry banner over the lattice, than I rose, opened the piano, and entreated him, for the love of heaven, to give me a song. He said I was a capricious witch, and that he would rather sing another time; but I averred that no time was like the present.

"Did I like his voice?" he asked.

"Very much." I was not fond of pampering that susceptible vanity of his; but for once, and from motives of expediency, I would e'en soothe and stimulate it.

"Then, Jane, you must play the accompaniment."

"Very well, sir; I will try."

I did try, but was presently swept off the stool and denominated "a little bungler." Being pushed unceremoniously to one side—which was precisely what I wished—he unsurped my place, and proceeded to accompany himself: for he could play as well as sing. I hied me to the window-recess; and while I sat there and looked out on the still trees and dim lawn, to a sweet air was sung in mellow tones the following strain:—

> The truest love that ever heart
> Felt at its kindled core
> Did through each vein, in quickened start,
> The tide of being pour.
>
> Her coming was my hope each day,
> Her parting was my pain;
> The chance that did her steps delay
> Was ice in every vein.
>
> I dreamed it would be nameless bliss,
> As I loved, loved to be;
> And to this object did I press
> As blind as eagerly.
>
> But wide as pathless was the space
> That lay, our lives, between,
> And dangerous as the foamy race
> Of ocean-surges green.

9. Lose.

And haunted as a robber-path
 Through wilderness or wood;
For Might and Right, and Woe and Wrath,
 Between our spirits stood.

I dangers dared; I hind'rance scorned;
 I omens did defy:
Whatever menaced, harassed, warned,
 I passed impetuous by.

On sped my rainbow, fast as light;
 I flew as in a dream;
For glorious rose upon my sight
 That child of Shower and Gleam.

Still bright on clouds of suffering dim
 Shines that soft, solemn joy.
Nor care I now, how dense and grim
 Disasters gather nigh.

I care not in this moment sweet,
 Though all I have rushed o'er
Should come on pinion, strong and fleet,
 Proclaiming vengeance sore

Though haughty Hate should strike me down,
 Right, bar approach to me.
And grinding Might, with furious frown,
 Swear endless enmity.

My love has placed her little hand
 With noble faith in mine,
And vowed that wedlock's sacred band
 Our nature shall entwine.

My love has sworn, with sealing kiss,
 With me to live—to die;
I have at last my nameless bliss:
 As I love—loved am I!

He rose and came towards me, and I saw his face all kindled, and his full fal-
con-eye flashing, and tenderness and passion in every lineament. I quailed
momentarily—then I rallied. Soft scene, daring demonstration, I would not
have; and I stood in peril of both: a weapon of defence must be prepared—I
whetted my tongue: as he reached me, I asked with asperity, "whom he was
going to marry now?"

"That was a strange question to be put by his darling Jane."

"Indeed! I considered it a very natural and necessary one: he had talked of
his future wife dying with him. What did he mean by such a pagan idea? I had
no intention of dying with him—he might depend on that."

"Oh, all he longed, all he prayed for, was that I might live with him! Death
was not for such as I."

"Indeed it was: I had as good a right to die when my time came as he had: but I should bide that time, and not be hurried away in a suttee."[1]

"Would I forgive him for the selfish idea, and prove my pardon by a reconciling kiss?"

"No: I would rather be excused."

Here I heard myself apostrophized as a "hard little thing;" and it was added, "any other woman would have been melted to marrow at hearing such stanzas crooned in her praise."

I assured him I was naturally hard—very flinty, and that he would often find me so; and that, moreover, I was determined to show him divers rugged points in my character before the ensuing four weeks elapsed: he should know fully what sort of a bargain he had made, while there was yet time to rescind it.

"Would I be quiet, and talk rationally?"

"I would be quiet if he liked; and as to talking rationally, I flattered myself I was doing that now."

He fretted, pished and pshawed. "Very good," I thought; "you may fume and fidget as you please: but this is the best plan to pursue with you, I am certain. I like you more than I can say; but I'll not sink into a bathos of sentiment: and with this needle of repartee I'll keep you from the edge of the gulf too; and, moreover, maintain by its pungent aid that distance between you and myself most conducive to our real mutual advantage."

From less to more, I worked him up to considerable irritation; then, after he had retired, in dudgeon, quite to the other end of the room, I got up, and saying, "I wish you good-night, sir," in my natural and wonted respectful manner, I slipped out by the side-door and got away.

The system thus entered on I pursued during the whole season of probation; and with the best success. He was kept, to be sure, rather cross and crusty: but on the whole I could see he was excellently entertained; and that a lamb-like submission and turtle-dove sensibility, while fostering his despotism more, would have pleased his judgment, satisfied his common-sense, and even suited his taste, less.

In other people's presence I was, as formerly, deferential and quiet; any other line of conduct being uncalled for: it was only in the evening conferences I thus thwarted and afflicted him. He continued to send for me punctually the moment the clock struck seven; though when I appeared before him now, he had no such honeyed terms as "love" and "darling" on his lips: the best words at my service were "provoking puppet," "malicious elf," "sprite," "changeling," etc. For caresses, too, I now got grimaces; for a pressure of the hand, a pinch on the arm; for a kiss on the cheek, a severe tweak of the ear. It was all right: at present I decidely preferred these fierce favors to anything more tender. Mrs. Fairfax, I saw, approved me: her anxiety on my account vanished; therefore I was certain I did well. Meantime, Mr. Rochester affirmed I was wearing him to skin and bone, and threatened awful vengeance for my present conduct at some period fast coming. I laughed in my sleeve at his menaces: "I can keep you in reasonable check now," I reflected; "and I don't doubt to be able to do it hereafter: if one expedient loses its virtue, another must be devised."

Yet after all my task was not an easy one; often I would rather have pleased

1. Custom according to which a Hindu widow was cremated on her husband's funeral pyre.

than teased him. My future husband was becoming to me my whole world; and more than the world: almost my hope of heaven. He stood between me and every thought of religion, as an eclipse intervenes between man and the broad sun. I could not, in those days, see God for his creature: of whom I had made an idol.

Chapter XXV

The month of courtship had wasted: its very last hours were being numbered. There was no putting off the day that advanced—the bridal day; and all preparations for its arrival were complete. I, at least, had nothing more to do: there were my trunks, packed locked, corded, ranged in a row along the wall of my little chamber: to-morrow, at this time, they would be far on their road to London: and so should I (D.V.),[2]—or rather, not I, but one Jane Rochester, a person whom as yet I knew not. The cards of address alone remained to nail on: they lay, four little squares, on the drawer. Mr. Rochester had himself written the direction, "Mrs. Rochester, ———— Hotel, London," on each: I could not persuade myself to affix them, or to have them affixed. Mrs. Rochester! She did not exist: she would not be born till tomorrow, some time after eight o'clock A.M.; and I would wait to be assured she had come into the world alive before I assigned to her all that property. It was enough that in yonder closet, opposite my dressing-table, garments said to be hers had already displaced my black stuff Lowood frock and straw bonnet: for not to me appertained that suit of wedding raiment, the pearl-colored robe, the vapory veil, pendent from the usurped portmanteau. I shut the closet, to conceal the strange, wraith-like apparel it contained; which, at this evening hour—nine o'clock—gave out certainly a most ghostly shimmer through the shadow of my apartment.

"I will leave you by yourself, white dream," I said. "I am feverish: I hear the wind blowing: I will go out of doors and feel it."

It was not only the hurry of preparation that made me feverish; not only the anticipation of the great change—the new life which was to commence tomorrow: both these circumstances had their share, doubtless, in producing that restless, excited mood which hurried me forth at this late hour into the darkening grounds; but a third cause influenced my mind more than they.

I had at heart a strange and anxious thought. Something had happened which I could not comprehend; no one knew of or had seen the event but myself: it had taken place the preceding night. Mr. Rochester that night was absent from home; nor was he yet returned: business had called him to a small estate of two or three farms he possessed thirty miles off—business it was requisite he should settle in person, previously to his meditated departure from England. I waited now his return; eager to disburthen my mind, and to seek of him the solution of the enigma that perplexed me. Stay till he comes, reader; and, when I disclose my secret to him, you shall share the confidence.

I sought the orchard: driven to its shelter by the wind, which all day had blown strong and full from the south; without, however, bringing a speck of rain. Instead of subsiding as night drew on, it seemed to augment its rush and deepen its roar: the trees blew steadfastly one way, never writhing round, and scarcely tossing back their boughs once in an hour; so continuous was the

2. *Deo volente* (God willing; Latin).

strain bending their branchy heads northward—the clouds drifted from pole to pole, fast following, mass on mass: no glimpse of blue sky had been visible that July day.

It was not without a certain wild pleasure I ran before the wind delivering my trouble of mind to the measureless air-torrent thundering through space. Descending the laurel-walk, I faced the wreck of the chestnut-tree; it stood up, black and riven: the trunk, split down the center, gasped ghastly. The cloven halves were not broken from each other, for the firm base and strong roots kept them unsundered below; though community of vitality was destroyed—the sap could flow no more: their great boughs on each side were dead, and next winter's tempests would be sure to fell one or both to earth: as yet, however, they might be said to form one tree—a ruin, but an entire ruin.

"You did right to hold fast to each other," I said: as if the monster splinters were living things, and could hear me. "I think, scathed as you look, and charred and scorched, there must be a little sense of life in you yet; rising out of that adhesion at the faithful, honest roots: you will never have green leaves more—never more see birds making nests and singing idyls in your boughs; the time of pleasure and love is over with you; but you are not desolate: each of you has a comrade to sympathize with him in his decay." As I looked up at them, the moon appeared momentarily in that part of the sky which filled their fissure; her disk was blood-red and half overcast; she seemed to throw on me one bewildered, dreary glance, and buried herself again instantly in the deep drift of cloud. The wind fell, for a second, round Thornfield; but far away over wood and water, poured a wild, melancholy wail: it was sad to listen to, and I ran off again.

Here and there I strayed through the orchard, gathered up the apples with which the grass round the tree roots was thickly strewn: then I employed myself in dividing the ripe from the unripe; I carried them into the house and put them away in the store-room. Then I repaired to the library to ascertain whether the fire was lit; for, though summer, I knew on such a gloomy evening Mr. Rochester would like to see a cheerful hearth when he came in: yes, the fire had been kindled some time, and burnt well. I placed his arm-chair by the chimney-corner: I wheeled the table near it: I let down the curtain, and had the candles brought in ready for lighting. More restless than ever, when I had completed these arrangements I could not sit still, nor even remain in the house: a little timepiece in the room and the old clock in the hall simultaneously struck ten.

"How late it grows!" I said: "I will run down to the gates: it is moonlight at intervals; I can see a good way on the road. He may be coming now, and to meet him will save some minutes of suspense."

The wind roared high in the great trees which enbowered the gates; but the road as far as I could see, to the right hand and the left, was all still and solitary: save for the shadows of clouds crossing it at intervals, as the moon looked out, it was but a long pale line, unvaried by one moving speck.

A puerile tear dimmed my eye while I looked—a tear of disappointment and impatience: ashamed of it, I wiped it away. I lingered; the moon shut herself wholly within her chamber, and drew close her curtain of dense cloud; the night grew dark; rain came driving fast on the gale.

"I wish he would come! I wish he would come!" I exclaimed, seized with hypochondriac foreboding. I had expected his arrival before tea; now it was

dark: what could keep him? Had an accident happened? The event of last night again recurred to me. I interpreted it as a warning of disaster. I feared my hopes were too bright to be realized; and I had enjoyed so much bliss lately that I imagined my fortune had passed its meridian, and must now decline.

"Well, I cannot return to the house," I thought; "I cannot sit by the fireside while he is abroad in inclement weather: better tire my limbs than strain my heart; I will go forward and meet him."

I set out; I walked fast, but not far: ere I had measured a quarter of a mile I heard the tramp of hoofs; a horseman came on, full gallop; a dog ran by his side. Away with evil presentiment! It was he: here he was, mounted on Mesrour, followed by Pilot. He saw me; for the moon had opened a blue field in the sky, and rode in it watery bright: he took his hat off, and waved it round his head. I now ran to meet him.

"There!" he exclaimed, as he stretched out his hand and bent from the saddle: "You can't do without me, that is evident. Step on my boot-toe; give me both hands: mount!"

I obeyed: joy made me agile: I sprang up before him. A hearty kissing I got for a welcome; and some boastful triumph; which I swallowed as well as I could. He checked himself in his exultation to demand, "But is there anything the matter, Janet, that you come to meet me at such an hour? Is there anything wrong?"

"No; but I thought you would never come. I could not bear to wait in the house for you, especially with this rain and wind."

"Rain and wind, indeed! Yes, you are dripping like a mermaid; pull my cloak round you: but I think you are feverish, Jane: both your cheek and hand are burning hot. I ask again, is there anything the matter?"

"Nothing, now: I am neither afraid nor unhappy."

"Then you have been both?"

"Rather: but I'll tell you all about it by-and-by, sir; and I daresay you will only laugh at me for my pains."

"I'll laugh at you heartily when tomorrow's past; till then I dare not: my prize is not certain. This is you; who have been as slippery as an eel this last month, and as thorny as a briar-rose. I could not lay a finger anywhere but I was pricked; and now I seem to have gathered up a stray lamb in my arms: you wandered out of the fold to seek your shepherd, did you, Jane?"

"I wanted you: but don't boast. Here we are at Thornfield: now let me get down."

He landed me on the pavement. As John took his horse, and he followed me into the hall, he told me to make haste and put something dry on, and then return to him in the library; and he stopped me, as I made for the staircase, to extort a promise that I would not be long: nor was I long: in five minutes I rejoined him. I found him at supper.

"Take a seat and bear me company, Jane: please God, it is the last meal but one you will eat at Thornfield Hall for a long time."

I sat down near him; but told him I could not eat.

"Is it because you have the prospect of a journey before you, Jane? Is it the thoughts of going to London that takes away your appetite?"

"I cannot see my prospects clearly tonight, sir; and I hardly know what thoughts I have in my head. Everything in life seems unreal."

"Except me: I am substantial enough:—touch me."

"You, sir, are the most phantom-like of all: you are a mere dream."

He held out his hand, laughing: "Is that a dream?" said he, placing it close to my eyes. He had a rounded, muscular, and vigorous hand, as well as a long, strong arm.

"Yes; though I touch it, it is a dream," said I, as I put it down from before my face. "Sir, have you finished supper?"

"Yes, Jane."

I rang the bell, and ordered away the tray. When we were again alone, I stirred the fire, and then took a low seat at my master's knee.

"It is near midnight," I said.

"Yes: but remember, Jane, you promised to wake with me the night before my wedding."

"I did; and I will keep my promise, for an hour or two at least: I have no wish to go to bed."

"Are all your arrangements complete?"

"All, sir."

"And on my part, likewise," he returned.

"I have settled everything; and we shall leave Thornfield tomorrow, within half an hour after our return from church."

"Very well, sir."

"With what an extraordinary smile you uttered that word—'very well,' Jane! What a bright spot of color you have on each cheek! and how strangely your eyes glitter! Are you well?"

"I believe I am."

"Believe! What is the matter?—Tell me what you feel."

"I could not, sir: no words could tell you what I feel. I wish this present hour would never end: who knows with what fate the next may come charged?"

"This is hypochondria, Jane. You have been over-excited, or over-fatigued."

"Do you, sir, feel calm and happy?"

"Calm?—no: but happy—to the heart's core."

I looked up at him to read the signs of bliss in his face: it was ardent and flushed.

"Give me your confidence, Jane," he said: "relieve your mind of any weight that oppresses it by imparting it to me. What do you fear?—that I shall not prove a good husband?"

"It is the idea farthest from my thoughts."

"Are you apprehensive of the new sphere you are about to enter?—of the new life into which you are passing?"

"No."

"You puzzle me, Jane: your look and tone of sorrowful audacity perplex and pain me. I want an explanation."

"Then, sir—listen. You were from home last night?"

"I was: I know that; and you hinted a while ago at something which had happened in my absence:—nothing, probably, of consequence; but, in short, it has disturbed you. Let me hear it. Mrs. Fairfax has said something, perhaps? or you have overheard the servants talk?—your sensitive self-respect has been wounded?"

"No, sir." It struck twelve—I waited till the timepiece had concluded its silver chime, and the clock its hoarse, vibrating stroke, and then I proceeded.

"All day yesterday I was very busy, and very happy in my ceaseless bustle; for

I am not, as you seem to think, troubled by any haunting fears about the new sphere, et cetera: I think it a glorious thing to have the hope of living with you, because I love you. No, sir, don't caress me now—let me talk undisturbed. Yesterday I trusted well in Providence, and believed that events were working together for your good and mine: it was a fine day, if you recollect—the calmness of the air and sky forbade apprehensions respecting your safety or comfort on your journey. I walked a little while on the pavement after tea, thinking of you; and I beheld you in imagination so near me I scarcely missed your actual presence. I thought of the life that lay before me—*your* life, sir—an existence more expansive and stirring than my own: as much more so as the depths of the sea to which the brook runs are than the shallows of its own strait channel. I wondered why moralists call this world a dreary wilderness; for me it blossomed like a rose. Just at sunset the air turned cold and the sky cloudy: I went in. Sophie called me upstairs to look at my wedding-dress, which they had just brought; and under it in the box I found your present— the veil which, in your princely extravagance, you sent for from London: resolved, I suppose, since I would not have jewels, to cheat me into accepting something as costly. I smiled as I unfolded it, and devised how I would tease you about your aristocratic tastes, and your efforts to masque your plebeian bride in the attributes of a peeress. I thought how I would carry down to you the square of unembroidered blond[3] I had myself prepared as a covering for my low-born head, and ask if that was not good enough for a woman who could bring her husband neither fortune, beauty, nor connections. I saw plainly how you would look; and heard your impetuous republican answers, and your haughty disavowal of any necessity on your part to augment your wealth, or elevate your standing, by marrying either a purse or a coronet."

"How well you read me, you witch!" interposed Mr. Rochester; "but what did you find in the veil besides its embroidery? Did you find poison, or a dagger, that you look so mournful now?"

"No, no, sir; besides the delicacy and richness of the fabric, I found nothing save Fairfax Rochester's pride; and that did not scare me, because I am used to the sight of the demon. But, sir, as it grew dark the wind rose: it blew yesterday evening, not as it blows now—wild and high—but 'with a sullen, moaning sound'[4] far more eerie. I wished you were at home. I came into this room, and the sight of the empty chair and fireless hearth chilled me. For some time after I went to bed I could not sleep—a sense of anxious excitement distressed me. The gale still rising seemed to my ear to muffle a mournful under-sound; whether in the house or abroad I could not at first tell, but it recurred, doubtful, yet doleful at every lull: at last I made out it must be some dog howling at a distance. I was glad when it ceased. On sleeping, I continued in dreams the idea of a dark and gusty night. I continued also the wish to be with you, and experienced a strange, regretful consciousness of some barrier dividing us. During all my first sleep I was following the windings of an unknown road; total obscurity environed me; rain pelted me; I was burdened with the charge of a little child: a very small creature, too young and feeble to walk, and which shivered in my cold arms and wailed piteously in my ear. I thought, sir, that you were on the road a long way before me; and I strained every nerve to over

3. A kind of silk lace.
4. Sir Walter Scott's *The Lay of the Last Minstrel* (1805) 1.13.1.

take you, and made effort on effort to utter your name and entreat you to stop—but my movements were fettered; and my voice still died away inarticulate; while you, I felt, withdrew farther and farther every moment."

"And these dreams weigh on your spirits now, Jane, when I am close to you? Little nervous subject! Forget visionary woe, and think only of real happiness! You say you love me, Janet: yes—I will not forget that; and you cannot deny it. *Those* words did not die inarticulate on your lips. I heard them clear and soft: a thought too solemn perhaps, but sweet as music—'I think it is a glorious thing to have the hope of living with you, Edward, because I love you.'—Do you love me, Jane? Repeat it."

"I do, sir.—I do with my whole heart."

"Well," he said, after some minutes' silence, "it is strange; but that sentence has penetrated my breast painfully. Why? I think because you said it with such an earnest, religious energy: and because your upward gaze at me now is the very sublime of faith, truth, and devotion: it is too much as if some spirit were near me. Look wicked, Jane; as you know well how to look; coin one of your wild, shy, provoking smiles; tell me you hate me—tease me, vex me; do anything but move me: I would rather be incensed than saddened."

"I will tease you and vex you to your heart's content when I have finished my tale: but hear me to the end."

"I thought, Jane, you had told me all. I thought I had found the source of your melancholy in a dream!"

I shook my head. "What! is there more? But I will not believe it to be anything important. I warn you of incredulity beforehand. Go on."

The disquietude of his air, the somewhat apprehensive impatience of his manner, surprised me: but I proceeded.

"I dreamt another dream, sir: that Thornfield Hall was a dreary ruin, the retreat of bats and owls. I thought that of all the stately front nothing remained but a shell-like wall, very high, and very fragile-looking. I wandered, on a moonlight night, through the grass-grown enclosure within: here I stumbled over a marble hearth, and there over a fallen fragment of cornice. Wrapped up in a shawl, I still carried the unknown little child: I might not lay it down anywhere, however tired were my arms—however much its weight impeded my progress, I must retain it. I heard the gallop of a horse at a distance on the road: I was sure it was you; and you were departing for many years, and for a distant country. I climbed the thin wall with frantic, perilous haste, eager to catch one glimpse of you from the top: the stones rolled from under my feet, the ivy branches I grasped gave way, the child clung round my neck in terror, and almost strangled me: at last I gained the summit. I saw you like a speck on a white track, lessening every moment. The blast blew so strong I could not stand. I sat down on the narrow ledge; I hushed the scared infant in my lap: you turned an angle of the road; I bent forward to take a last look; the wall crumbled; I was shaken; the child rolled from my knee, I lost my balance, fell, and woke."

"Now, Jane, that is all."

"All the preface, sir; the tale is yet to come. On waking, a gleam dazzled my eyes: I thought—oh, it is daylight! But I was mistaken: it was only candlelight. Sophie, I supposed, had come in. There was a light on the dressing-table, and the door of the closet, where, before going to bed, I had hung my wedding-dress and veil, stood open: I heard a rustling there. I asked, 'Sophie, what are

you doing?' No one answered; but a form emerged from the closet: it took the light, held it aloft, and surveyed the garments pendent from the portmanteau. 'Sophie! Sophie!' I again cried: and still it was silent I had risen up in bed; I bent forward: first, surprise, then bewilderment, came over me; and then my blood crept cold through my veins. Mr. Rochester, this was not Sophie, it was not Leah, it was not Mrs. Fairfax: It was not—no, I was sure of it, and am still—it was not even that strange woman, Grace Poole."

"It must have been one of them," interrupted my master.

"No, sir, I solemnly assure you to the contrary. The shape standing before me had never crossed my eyes within the precincts of Thornfield Hall before; the height, the contour, were new to me."

"Describe it, Jane."

"It seemed, sir, a woman, tall and large, with thick and dark hair hanging long down her back. I know not what dress she had on: it was white and straight; but whether gown, sheet, or shroud, I cannot tell."

"Did you see her face?"

"Not at first. But presently she took my veil from its place; she held it up, gazed at it long, and then she threw it over her own head, and turned to the mirror. At that moment I saw the reflection of the visage and features quite distinctly in the dark oblong glass."

"And how were they?"

"Fearful and ghastly to me—oh, sir, I never saw a face like it! It was a discolored face—it was a savage face. I wish I could forget the roll of the red eyes and the fearful blackened inflation of the lineaments."

"Ghosts are usually pale, Jane."

"This, sir, was purple: the lips were swelled and dark; the brow furrowed; the black eyebrows widely raised over the bloodshot eyes. Shall I tell you of what it reminded me?"

"You may."

"Of the foul German specter—the Vampire."

"Ah?—What did it do?"

"Sir, it removed my veil from its gaunt head, rent it in two parts, and flinging both on the floor, trampled on them."

"Afterwards?"

"It drew aside the window-curtain and looked out: perhaps it saw dawn approaching, for, taking the candle, it retreated to the door. Just at my bedside the figure stopped: the fiery eye glared upon me—she thrust up her candle close to my face, and extinguished it under my eyes. I was aware her lurid visage flamed over mine, and I lost consciousness: for the second time in my life—only the second time—I became insensible from terror."

"Who was with you when you revived?"

"No one, sir; but the broad day. I rose, bathed my head and face in water, drank a long draught; felt that though enfeebled I was not ill, and determined that to none but you would I impart this vision. Now, sir, tell me who and what that woman was?"

"The creature of an over-stimulated brain; that is certain. I must be careful of you, my treasure: nerves like yours were not made for rough handling."

"Sir, depend on it, my nerves were not in fault; the thing was real: the transaction actually took place."

"And your previous dreams: were they real too? Is Thornfield Hall a ruin?

Am I severed from you by insuperable obstacles? Am I leaving you without a tear—without a kiss—without a word?"

"Not yet."

"Am I about to do it?—Why, the day is already commenced which is to bind us indissolubly; and when we are once united, there shall be no recurrence of these mental terrors: I guarantee that."

"Mental terrors, sir! I wish I could believe them to be only such: I wish it more now than ever; since even you cannot explain to me the mystery of that awful visitant."

"And since I cannot do it, Jane, it must have been unreal."

"But, sir, when I said so to myself on rising this morning, and when I looked round the room to gather courage and comfort from the cheerful aspect of each familiar object in full daylight, there—on the carpet—I saw what gave the distinct lie to my hypothesis,—the veil, torn from top to bottom, in two halves!"

I felt Mr. Rochester start and shudder; he hastily flung his arms round me.

"Thank God!" he exclaimed, "that if anything malignant did come near you last night, it was only the veil that was harmed.—Oh, to think what might have happened!"

He drew his breath short, and strained me so close to him I could scarcely pant. After some minutes' silence, he continued, cheerily:— "Now, Janet, I'll explain to you all about it. It was half dream, half reality: a woman did, I doubt not, enter your room: and that woman was—must have been—Grace Poole. You call her a strange being yourself: from all you know you have reason so to call her—what did she do to me? what to Mason? In a state between sleeping and waking you noticed her entrance and her actions; but feverish, almost delirious as you were, you ascribed to her goblin appearance different from her own: the long dishevelled hair, the swelled black face, the exaggerated stature, were figments of imagination; results of nightmare: the spiteful tearing of the veil was real: and it is like her. I see you would ask why I keep such a woman in my house: when we have been married a year and a day, I will tell you; but not now. Are you satisfied, Jane? Do you accept my solution of the mystery?"

I reflected, and in truth it appeared to me the only possible one: satisfied I was not, but to please him I endeavored to appear so—relieved, I certainly did feel; so I answered him with a contented smile. And now, as it was long past one, I prepared to leave him.

"Does not Sophie sleep with Adèle in the nursery?" he asked, as I lit my candle.

"Yes, sir."

"And there is room enough in Adèle's little bed for you. You must share it with her tonight, Jane: it is no wonder that the incident you have related should make you nervous, and I would rather you did not sleep alone: promise me to go to the nursery."

"I shall be very glad to do so, sir."

"And fasten the door securely on the inside. Wake Sophie when you go upstairs, under pretence of requesting her to rouse you in good time tomorrow; for you must be dressed and have finished breakfast before eight. And now, no more somber thoughts: chase dull care away, Janet. Don't you hear to what soft whispers the wind has fallen? and there is no more beating of rain against the window-panes: look here" (he lifted up the curtain)— "it is a lovely night!"

It was. Half heaven was pure and stainless: the clouds, now trooping before the wind, which had shifted to the west, were filing off eastward in long, silvered columns. The moon shone peacefully.

"Well," said Mr. Rochester, gazing inquiringly into my eyes, "how is my Janet now?"

"The night is serene, sir; and so am I."

"And you will not dream of separation and sorrow tonight; but of happy love and blissful union."

This prediction was but half fulfilled: I did not indeed dream of sorrow, but as little did I dream of joy; for I never slept at all. With little Adèle in my arms, I watched the slumber of childhood—so tranquil, so passionless, so innocent—and waited for the coming day: all my life was awake and astir in my frame; and as soon as the sun rose I rose too. I remember Adèle clung to me as I left her; I remember I kissed her as I loosened her little hands from my neck; and I cried over her with strange emotion, and quitted her because I feared my sobs would break her still sound repose. She seemed the emblem of my past life; and he, I was now to array myself to meet the dread, but adored, type of my unknown future day.

Chapter XXVI

Sophie came at seven to dress me; she was very long indeed in accomplishing her task—so long that Mr. Rochester, grown, I suppose, impatient of my delay, sent up to ask why I did not come. She was just fastening my veil (the plain square of blond after all) to my hair with a brooch; I hurried from under her hands as soon as I could.

"Stop!" she cried in French

"Look at yourself in the mirror: you have not taken one peep."

So I turned at the door: I saw a robed and veiled figure, so unlike my usual self that it seemed almost the image of a stranger. "Jane!" called a voice, and I hastened down. I was received at the foot of the stairs by Mr. Rochester.

"Lingerer," he said, "my brain is on fire with impatience; and you tarry so long!"

He took me into the dining-room, surveyed me keenly all over, pronounced me "fair as a lily, and not only the pride of his life, but the desire of his eyes," and then, telling me he would give me but ten minutes to eat some breakfast, he rang the bell. One of his lately hired servants, a footman, answered it.

"Is John getting the carriage ready?"

"Yes, sir."

"Is the luggage brought down?"

"They are bringing it down, sir."

"Go you to the church: see if Mr. Wood (the clergyman) and the clerk are there: return and tell me."

The church, as the reader knows, was but just beyond the gates; the footman soon returned.

"Mr. Wood is in the vestry, sir, putting on his surplice."

"And the carriage?"

"The horses are harnessing."

"We shall not want it to go to church; but it must be ready the moment we return, all the boxes and luggage arranged and strapped on, and the coachman in his seat."

"Yes, sir."

"Jane, are you ready?"

I rose. There were no groomsmen, no bridesmaids, no relatives to wait for or marshal: none but Mr. Rochester and I. Mrs. Fairfax stood in the hall as we passed. I would fain have spoken to her, but my hand was held by a grasp of iron: I was hurried along by a stride I could hardly follow; and to look at Mr. Rochester's face was to feel that not a second of delay would be tolerated for any purpose. I wonder what other bridegroom ever looked as he did—so bent up to a purpose, so grimly resolute: or who, under such steadfast brows, ever revealed such flaming and flashing eyes.

I know not whether the day was fair or foul; in descending the drive, I gazed neither on sky nor earth; my heart was with my eyes; and both seemed migrated into Mr. Rochester's frame. I wanted to see the invisible thing on which, as we went along, he appeared to fasten a glance fierce and fell.[5] I wanted to feel the thoughts whose force he seemed breasting and resisting.

At the churchyard wicket he stopped: he discovered I was quite out of breath.

"Am I cruel in my love?" he said. "Delay an instant: lean on me, Jane."

And now I can recall the picture of the gray old house of God rising calm before me, of a rook wheeling round the steeple, of a ruddy morning sky beyond. I remember something, too, of the green grave-mounds; and I have not forgotten, either, two figures of strangers, straying among the low hillocks, and reading the mementoes graven on the few mossy head-stones. I noticed them, because, as they saw us, they passed round to the back of the church; and I doubted not they were going to enter by the side-aisle door, and witness the ceremony. By Mr. Rochester they were not observed; he was earnestly looking at my face, from which the blood had, I daresay, momentarily fled: for I felt my forehead dewy, and my cheeks and lips cold. When I rallied, which I soon did, he walked gently with me up the path to the porch.

We entered the quiet and humble temple; the priest waited in his white surplice at the lowly altar, the clerk beside him. All was still: two shadows only moved in a remote corner. My conjecture had been correct: the strangers had slipped in before us, and they now stood by the vault of the Rochesters, their backs towards us, viewing through the rails the old time-stained marble tomb, where a kneeling angel guarded the remains of Damer de Rochester, slain at Marston Moor[6] in the time of the civil wars; and of Elizabeth, his wife.

Our place was taken at the communion rails. Hearing a cautious step behind me, I glanced over my shoulder: one of the strangers—a gentleman, evidently—was advancing up the chancel. The service began. The explanation of the intent of matrimony was gone through; and then the clergyman came a step further forward, and, bending slightly towards Mr. Rochester, went on.

"I require and charge you both (as ye will answer at the dreadful day of judgment, when the secrets of all hearts shall be disclosed), that if either of you know any impediment why ye may not lawfully be joined in matrimony, ye do now confess it; for be ye well assured that so many as are coupled together otherwise than God's word doth allow, are not joined together by God, neither is their matrimony lawful."

5. Piercing, terrible.
6. Parliamentarian victory over the Royalists (July 2, 1644) during the English Civil War.

He paused, as the custom is. When is the pause after that sentence ever broken by reply? Not, perhaps, once in a hundred years. And the clergyman, who had not lifted his eyes from his book, and had held his breath but for a moment, was proceeding: his hand was already stretched towards Mr. Rochester, as his lips unclosed to ask, "Wilt thou have this woman for thy wedded wife?"—when a distinct and near voice said:— "The marriage cannot go on: I declare the existence of an impediment."

The clergyman looked up at the speaker, and stood mute; the clerk did the same; Mr. Rochester moved slightly, as if an earthquake had rolled under his feet: taking a firmer footing, and not turning his head or eyes; he said, "Proceed."

Profound silence fell when he had uttered that word, with deep but low intonation. Presently Mr. Wood said:— "I cannot proceed without some investigation into what has been asserted, and evidence of its truth or falsehood."

"The ceremony is quite broken off," subjoined the voice behind us. "I am in a condition to prove my allegation: an insuperable impediment to this marriage exists."

Mr. Rochester heard, but heeded not: he stood stubborn and rigid: making no movement, but to possess himself of my hand. What a hot and strong grasp he had!—and how like quarried marble was his pale, firm, massive front at this moment! How his eye shone, still, watchful, and yet wild beneath!

Mr. Wood seemed at a loss.

"What is the nature of the impediment?" he asked. "Perhaps it may be got over—explained away?"

"Hardly," was the answer: "I have called it insuperable, and I speak advisedly."

The speaker came forwards and leaned on the rails. He continued, uttering each word distinctly, calmly, steadily, but not loudly.

"It simply consists in the existence of a previous marriage. Mr. Rochester has a wife now living."

My nerves vibrated to those low-spoken words as they had never vibrated to thunder—my blood felt their subtle violence as it had never felt frost or fire: but I was collected, and in no danger of swooning. I looked at Mr. Rochester: I made him look at me. His whole face was colorless rock: his eye was both spark and flint. He disavowed nothing: he seemed as if he would defy all things. Without speaking, without smiling, without seeming to recognize in me a human being, he only twined my waist with his arm, and riveted me to his side.

"Who are you?" he asked of the intruder.

"My name is Briggs—a solicitor of —— Street, London."

"And you would thrust on me a wife?"

"I would remind you of your lady's existence, sir; which the law recognizes, if you do not."

"Favor me with an account of her—with her name, her parentage, her place of abode."

"Certainly." Mr. Briggs calmly took a paper from his pocket, and read out in a sort of official, nasal voice:—

" 'I affirm and can prove that on the 20th of October, A.D.——(a date of fifteen years back), Edward Fairfax Rochester, of Thornfield Hall, in the county of ——, and of Ferndean Manor, in—— shire, England, was married to my sister, Bertha Antoinetta Mason, daughter of Jonas Mason, merchant,

and of Antoinetta his wife, a Creole—at —— church, Spanish Town, Jamaica. The record of the marriage will be found in the register of that church—a copy of it is now in my possession. Signed, Richard Mason.' "

"That—if a genuine document—may prove I have been married, but it does not prove that the woman mentioned therein as my wife is still living."

"She was living three months ago," returned the lawyer.

"How do you know?"

"I have a witness to the fact, whose testimony even you, sir, will scarcely controvert."

"Produce him—or go to hell."

"I will produce him first—he is on the spot: Mr. Mason, have the goodness to step forward."

Mr. Rochester, on hearing the name, set his teeth; he experienced, too, a sort of strong convulsive quiver; near to him as I was, I felt the spasmodic movement of fury or despair run through his frame. The second stranger, who had hitherto lingered in the background, now drew near; a pale face looked over the solicitor's shoulder—yes, it was Mason himself. Mr. Rochester turned and glared at him. His eye, as I have often said, was a black eye: it had now a tawny, nay a bloody light in its gloom; and his face flushed—olive cheek and hueless forehead received a glow, as from spreading, ascending heart-fire: and he stirred, lifted his strong arm—he could have struck Mason—dashed him on the church-floor—shocked by ruthless blow the breath from his body—but Mason shrank away, and cried faintly, "Good God!" Contempt fell cool on Mr. Rochester—his passion died as if a blight had shrivelled it up: he only asked, "What have *you* to say?"

An inaudible reply escaped Mason's white lips.

"The devil is in it if you cannot answer distinctly. I again demand, what have *you* to say?"

"Sir—sir"—interrupted the clergyman, "do not forget you are in a sacred place." Then, addressing Mason, he inquired gently, "Are you aware, sir, whether or not this gentleman's wife is still living?"

"Courage," urged the lawyer,— "speak out."

"She is now living at Thornfield Hall," said Mason, in more articulate tones: "I saw her there last April. I am her brother."

"At Thornfield Hall!" ejaculated the clergyman. "Impossible! I am an old resident in this neighbourhood, sir, and I never heard of a Mrs. Rochester at Thornfield Hall."

I saw a grim smile contort Mr. Rochester's lip, and he muttered:— "No—by God! I took care that none should hear of it—or of her under that name." He mused—for ten minutes he held counsel with himself: he formed his resolve, and announced it:— "Enough—all shall bolt out at once, like a bullet from the barrel.—Wood, close your book, and take off your surplice; John Green (to the clerk) leave the church: there will be no wedding today." the man obeyed.

Mr. Rochester continued, hardily and recklessly: "Bigamy is an ugly word!— I meant, however, to be a bigamist; but fate has outmaneuvered me; or Providence has checked me,—perhaps the last. I am little better than a devil at this moment; and, as my pastor there would tell me, deserve no doubt the sternest judgments of God,—even to the quenchless fire and deathless worm. Gentlemen, my plan is broken up!—what this lawyer and his client say is true: I have been married; and the woman to whom I was married lives! You say you

never heard of a Mrs Rochester at the house up yonder, Wood: but I dare say you have many a time inclined your ear to gossip about the mysterious lunatic kept there under watch and ward. Some have whispered to you that she is my bastard half-sister: some, my cast-off mistress; I now inform you that she is my wife, whom I married fifteen years ago,—Bertha Mason by name; sister of this resolute personage, who is now, with his quivering limbs and white cheeks, showing you what a stout heart men may bear. Cheer up, Dick!—never fear me!—I'd almost as soon strike a woman as you. Bertha Mason is mad; and she came of a mad family;—idiots and maniacs through three generations! Her mother, the Creole[7], was both a mad-woman and a drunkard!—as I found out after I had wed the daughter: for they were silent on family secrets before. Bertha, like a dutiful child, copied her parent in both points. I had a charming partner—pure, wise, modest: you can fancy I was a happy man.—I went through rich scenes! Oh! my experience has been heavenly, if you only knew it! But I owe you no further explanation. Briggs, Wood, Mason,—I invite you all to come up to the house and visit Mrs. Poole's patient, and *my wife!* You shall see what sort of a being I was cheated into espousing, and judge whether or not I had a right to break the compact, and seek sympathy with something at least human. This girl," he continued, looking at me, "knew no more than you, Wood, of the disgusting secret: she thought all was fair and legal; and never dreamt she was going to be entrapped into a feigned union with a de-frauded wretch, already bound to a bad, mad, and embruted partner! Come, all of you, follow."

Still holding me fast, he left the church: the three gentlemen came after. At the front door of the hall we found the carriage.

"Take it back to the coach-house, John," said Mr. Rochester, coolly; "it will not be wanted today."

At our entrance Mrs. Fairfax, Adèle, Sophie, Leah, advanced to meet and greet us.

"To the right about—every soul!" cried the master: "away with your con-gratulations! Who wants them?—Not I!—they are fifteen years too late!"

He passed on and ascended the stairs, still holding my hand, and still beck-oning the gentlemen to follow him; which they did. We mounted the first staircase, passed up the gallery, proceeded to the third storey: the low, black door, opened by Mr. Rochester's master key, admitted us to the tapestried room, with its great bed and its pictorial cabinet.

"You know this place, Mason," said our guide; "she bit and stabbed you here."

He lifted the hangings from the wall, uncovering the second door: this, too, he opened In a room without a window there burned a fire, guarded by a high and strong fender, and a lamp suspended from the ceiling by a chain. Grace Poole bent over the fire, apparently cooking something in a saucepan. In the deep shade, at the further end of the room, a figure ran backwards and for-wards. What it was, whether beast or human being, one could not, at first sight, tell: it grovelled, seemingly, on all fours; it snatched and growled like some strange wild animal: but it was covered with clothing; and a quantity of dark, grizzled hair, wild as a mane, hid its head and face.

7. In the West Indies, a person of European descent.

"Good-morrow, Mrs. Poole!" said Mr. Rochester. "How are you? and how is your charge today?"

"We're tolerable, sir, I thank you," replied Grace, lifting the boiling mess carefully on to the hob: "rather snappish, but not 'rageous."

A fierce cry seemed to give the lie to her favorable report: the clothed hyena rose up, and stood tall on its hind feet.

"Ah, sir, she sees you!" exclaimed Grace: "you'd better not stay."

"Only a few moments, Grace: you must allow me a few moments."

"Take care then, sir!—for God's sake, take care!"

The maniac bellowed: she parted her shaggy locks from her visage, and gazed wildly at her visitors. I recognized well that purple face—those bloated features. Mrs. Poole advanced.

"Keep out of the way," said Mr. Rochester, thrusting her aside: "she has no knife now, I suppose? and I'm on my guard."

"One never knows what she has, sir: she is so cunning: it is not in mortal discretion to fathom her craft."

"We had better leave her," whispered Mason.

"Go to the devil!" was his brother-in-law's recommendation.

" 'Ware!" cried Grace. The three gentlemen retreated simultaneously. Mr. Rochester flung me behind him: the lunatic sprang and grappled his throat viciously, and laid her teeth to his cheek: they struggled. She was a big woman, in stature almost equaling her husband, and corpulent besides: she showed virile force in the contest—more than once she almost throttled him, athletic as he was. He could have settled her with a well-planted blow; but he would not strike: he would only wrestle. At last he mastered her arms; Grace Poole gave him a cord, and he pinioned them behind her: with more rope, which was at hand, he bound her to a chair. The operation was performed amidst the fiercest yells and the most convulsive plunges. Mr. Rochester then turned to the spectators: he looked at them with a smile both acrid and desolate.

"That is *my wife*," said he. "Such is the sole conjugal embrace I am ever to know—such are the endearments which are to solace my leisure hours! And *this* is what I wished to have" (laying his hand on my shoulder): "this young girl, who stands so grave and quiet at the mouth of hell, looking collectedly at the gambols of a demon. I wanted her just as a change after that fierce ragout. Wood and Briggs, look at the difference! Compare these clear eyes with the red balls yonder—this face with that mask—this form with that bulk; then judge me, priest of the gospel and man of the law, and remember, with what judgment ye judge ye shall be judged![8] Off with you now. I must shut up my prize."

We all withdrew. Mr. Rochester stayed a moment behind us to give some further order to Grace Poole. The solicitor addressed me as he descended the stair.

"You, madam," said he, "are cleared from all blame: your uncle will be glad to hear it—if, indeed, he should be still living—when Mr. Mason returns to Madeira."

"My uncle! What of him? Do you know him?"

"Mr. Mason does: Mr. Eyre has been the Funchal correspondent of his house for some years. When your uncle received your letter intimating the contemplated union between yourself and Mr. Rochester, Mr. Mason, who

8. Matthew 7:1–2.

was staying at Madeira to recruit his health, on his way back to Jamaica, happened to be with him. Mr. Eyre mentioned the intelligence; for he knew that my client here was acquainted with a gentleman of the name of Rochester. Mr. Mason, astonished and distressed as you may suppose, revealed the real state of matters. Your uncle, I am sorry to say, is now on a sick bed; from which, considering the nature of his disease—decline—and the stage it has reached, it is unlikely he will ever rise. He could not then hasten to England himself, to extricate you from the snare into which you had fallen, but he implored Mr. Mason to lose no time in taking steps to prevent the false marriage. He referred him to me for assistance. I used all despatch, and am thankful I was not too late: as you, doubtless, must be also. Were I not morally certain that your uncle will be dead ere you reach Madeira, I would advise you to accompany Mr. Mason back: but as it is, I think you had better remain in England till you can hear further, either from or of Mr. Eyre. Have we anything else to stay for?" he inquired of Mr. Mason.

"No, no—let us be gone," was the anxious reply; and without waiting to take leave of Mr. Rochester, they made their exit at the hall door. The clergyman stayed to exchange a few sentences, either of admonition or reproof, with his haughty parishioner: this duty done, he too departed.

I heard him go as I stood at the half-open door of my own room, to which I had now withdrawn. The house cleared, I shut myself in, fastened the bolt that none might intrude, and proceeded—not to weep, not to mourn, I was yet too calm for that, but—mechanically to take off the wedding-dress, and replace it by the stuff gown I had worn yesterday, as I thought, for the last time. I then sat down: I felt weak and tired. I leaned my arms on a table, and my head dropped on them. And now I thought: till now I had only heard, seen, moved—followed up and down where I was led or dragged—watched event rush on event, disclosure open beyond disclosure: but *now, I thought*.

The morning had been a quiet morning enough—all except the brief scene with the lunatic: the transaction in the church had not been noisy; there was no explosion of passion, no loud altercation, no dispute, no defiance or challenge, no tears, no sobs: a few words had been spoken, a calmly pronounced objection to the marriage made: some stern, short questions put by Mr. Rochester; answers, explanations given, evidence adduced; an open admission of the truth had been uttered by my master; then the living proof had been seen: the intruders were gone and all was over.

I was in my own room as usual—just myself, without obvious change: nothing had smitten me, or scathed me, or maimed me. And yet, where was the Jane Eyre of yesterday?—where was her life?—where were her prospects?

Jane Eyre, who had been an ardent, expectant woman—almost a bride—was a cold, solitary girl again: her life was pale; her prospects were desolate. A Christmas frost had come at midsummer; a white December storm had whirled over June; ice glazed the ripe apples, drifts crushed the blowing roses; on hay-field and corn-field lay a frozen shroud: lanes which last night blushed full of flowers, today were pathless with untrodden snow; and the woods, which twelve hours since waved leafy and fragrant as groves between the tropics, now spread, waste, wild, and white as pine-forests in wintry Norway. My hopes were all dead—struck with a subtle doom, such as in one night, fell on all the first-born in the land of Egypt.[9] I looked on my cherished wishes, yes-

9. Exodus 12.

terday so blooming and glowing: they lay stark, chill, livid corpses that could never revive. I looked at my love: that feeling which was my master's—which he had created; it shivered in my heart, like a suffering child in a cold cradle; sickness and anguish had seized it; it could not seek Mr. Rochester's arms—it could not derive warmth from his breast. Oh, never more could it turn to him; for faith was blighted—confidence destroyed! Mr. Rochester was not to me what he had been; for he was not what I had thought him. I would not ascribe vice to him; I would not say he had betrayed me: but the attribute of stainless truth was gone from his idea; and from his presence I must go; *that* I perceived well. When—how—whither, I could not yet discern; but he himself, I doubted not, would hurry me from Thornfield. Real affection, it seemed, he could not have for me; it had been only fitful passion: that was balked; he would want me no more. I should fear even to cross his path now: my view must be hateful to him. Oh, how blind had been my eyes! How weak my conduct!

My eyes were covered and closed: eddying darkness seemed to swim round me, and reflection came in as black and confused a flow. Self-abandoned, relaxed, and effortless, I seemed to have laid me down in the dried-up bed of a great river; I heard a flood loosened in remote mountains, and felt the torrent come: to rise I had no will, to flee I had no strength. I lay faint; longing to be dead. One idea only still throbbed life-like within me—a remembrance of God: it begot an unuttered prayer: these words went wandering up and down in my rayless mind, as something that should be whispered; but no energy was found to express them:— "Be not far from me, for trouble is near: there is none to help."[1]

It was near: and as I had lifted no petition to Heaven to avert it—as I had neither joined my hands, nor bent my knees, nor moved my lips—it came: in full, heavy swing the torrent poured over me. The whole consciousness of my life lorn, my love lost, my hope quenched, my faith death-struck, swayed full and mighty above me in one sullen mass. That bitter hour cannot be described: in truth, "the waters came into my soul; I sank in deep mire: I felt no standing; I came into deep waters; the floods overflowed me."[2]

Chapter XXVII

Some time in the afternoon I raised my head, and looking round and seeing the western sun gilding the sign of its decline on the wall, I asked, "What am I to do?"

But the answer my mind gave—"Leave Thornfield at once"—was so prompt, so dread, that I stopped my ears: I said, I could not bear such words now. "That I am not Edward Rochester's bride is the least part of my woe," I alleged: "that I have wakened out of most glorious dreams, and found them all void and vain, is a horror I could bear and master; but that I must leave him decidedly, instantly, entirely, is intolerable. I cannot do it."

But, then, a voice within me averred that I could do it; and foretold that I should do it. I wrestled with my own resolution: I wanted to be weak that I might avoid the awful passage of further suffering I saw laid out for me; and conscience, turned tyrant, held passion by the throat, told her tauntingly she

1. Psalm 22:11. 2. Psalm 69:1–2.

had yet but dipped her dainty foot in the slough, and swore that with that arm of iron he would thrust her down to unsounded depths of agony.

"Let me be torn away, then!" I cried. "Let another help me!"

"No; you shall tear yourself away, none shall help you: you shall, yourself, pluck out your right eye: yourself cut off your right hand: your heart shall be the victim; and you, the priest, to transfix it "[3]

I rose up suddenly, terror-struck at the solitude which so ruthless a judge haunted,—at the silence which so awful a voice filled. My head swam as I stood erect: I perceived that I was sickening from excitement and inanition; neither meat nor drink had passed my lips that day, for I had taken no break-fast. And, with a strange pang, I now reflected that, long as I had been shut up here, no message had been sent to ask how I was, or to invite me to come down: not even little Adèle had tapped at the door; not even Mrs. Fairfax had sought me. "Friends always forget those whom fortune forsakes," I murmured, as I undrew the bolt and passed out. I stumbled over an obstacle: my head was still dizzy, my sight was dim, and my limbs were feeble. I could not soon re-cover myself. I fell, but not on to the ground; an out-stretched arm caught me; I looked up—I was supported by Mr. Rochester, who sat in a chair across my chamber threshold.

"You come out at last," he said. "Well, I have been waiting for you long, and listening: yet not one movement have I heard, nor one sob: five minutes more of that death-like hush, and I should have forced the lock like a burglar. So, you shun me?—you shut yourself up and grieve alone! I would rather you had come and upbraided me with vehemence. You are passionate: I expected a scene of some kind. I was prepared for the hot rain of tears; only I wanted them to be shed on my breast: now a senseless floor has received them, or your drenched handkerchief. But I err: you have not wept at all! I see a white cheek and a faded eye, but no trace of tears. I suppose, then, your heart has been weeping blood?

"Well, Jane; not a word of reproach? Nothing bitter—nothing poignant? Nothing to cut a feeling or sting a passion? You sit quietly where I have placed you, and regard me with a weary, passive look.

"Jane, I never meant to wound you thus. If the man who had but one little ewe lamb that was dear to him as a daughter, that ate of his bread and drank of his cup, and lay in his bosom, had by some mistake slaughtered it at the sham-bles, he would not have rued his bloody blunder more than I now rue mine.[4] Will you ever forgive me?"

Reader!—I forgave him at the moment, and on the spot. There was such deep remorse in his eye, such true pity in his tone, such manly energy in his manner; and, besides, there was such unchanged love in his whole look and mien—I forgave him all: yet not in words, not outwardly; only at my heart's core.

"You know I am a scoundrel, Jane?" ere long he inquired wistfully—wonder-ing, I suppose, at my continued silence and tameness: the result rather of weakness than of will.

"Yes, sir."

3. In Matthew 5.27–30 Jesus redefines the Old Testament concept of adultery to include one's thoughts and uses this language to describe the neces-sary response.

4. 2 Samuel 12:1–4 tells of the rich man's deliberate slaughter of the poor man's lamb. "Shambles": slaugh-terhouse.

"Then tell me so roundly and sharply—don't spare me."

"I cannot: I am tired and sick. I want some water." He heaved a sort of shuddering sigh, and taking me in his arms, carried me downstairs. At first I did not know to what room he had borne me; all was cloudy to my glazed sight: presently I felt the reviving warmth of a fire; for, summer as it was, I had become icy cold in my chamber. He put wine to my lips; I tasted it and revived; then I ate something he offered me, and was soon myself. I was in the library—sitting in his chair—he was quite near. "If I could go out of life now, without too sharp a pang, it would be well for me," I thought; "then I should not have to make the effort of cracking my heart-strings in rending them from among Mr. Rochester's. I must leave him, it appears. I do not want to leave him—I cannot leave him."

"How are you now, Jane?"

"Much better, sir: I shall be well soon."

"Taste the wine again, Jane."

I obeyed him; then he put the glass on the table, stood before me, and looked at me attentively. Suddenly he turned away, with an inarticulate exclamation, full of passionate emotion of some kind; he walked fast through the room and came back: he stooped towards me as if to kiss me; but I remembered caresses were now forbidden. I turned my face away, and put his aside.

"What!—How is this?" he exclaimed hastily. "Oh, I know! you won't kiss the husband of Bertha Mason? You consider my arms filled and my embraces appropriated?"

"At any rate, there is neither room nor claim for me, sir."

"Why, Jane? I will spare you the trouble of much talking: I will answer for you—because I have a wife already, you would reply.—I guess rightly?"

"Yes."

"If you think so, you must have a strange opinion of me: you must regard me as a plotting profligate—a base and low rake who has been simulating disinterested love in order to draw you into a snare deliberately laid, and strip you of honor, and rob you of self-respect. What do you say to that? I see you can say nothing: in the first place, you are faint still, and have enough to do to draw your breath; in the second place, you cannot yet accustom yourself to accuse and revile me; and, besides, the flood-gates of tears are opened, and they would rush out if you spoke much; and you have no desire to expostulate, to upbraid, to make a scene: you are thinking how to *act*, —*talking*, you consider, is of no use. I know you—I am on my guard."

"Sir, I do not wish to act against you," I said; and my unsteady voice warned me to curtail my sentence.

"Not in *your* sense of the word, but in *mine*, you are scheming to destroy me. You have as good as said that I am a married man—as a married man you will shun me, keep out of my way: just now you have refused to kiss me. You intend to make yourself a complete stranger to me; to live under this roof only as Adèle's governess: if ever I say a friendly word to you, if ever a friendly feeling inclines you again to me, you will say,— 'That man had nearly made me his mistress: I must be ice and rock to him'; and ice and rock you will accordingly become."

I cleared and steadied my voice to reply: "All is changed about me, sir; I must change too—there is no doubt of that; and to avoid fluctuations of feeling, and continual combats with recollections and associations, there is only one way—Adèle must have a new governess, sir."

"Oh, Adèle will go to school—I have settled that already; nor do I mean to torment you with the hideous associations and recollections of Thornfield Hall—this accursed place—this tent of Achan[5]—this insolent vault, offering the ghastliness of living death to the light of the open sky—this narrow stone hell, with its one real fiend, worse than a legion of such as we imagine.—Jane, you shall not stay here, nor will I. I was wrong ever to bring you to Thornfield Hall, knowing as I did how it was haunted I charged them to conceal from you, before I ever saw you, al knowledge of the curse of the place; merely because I feared Adèle never would have a governess to stay if she knew with what inmate she was housed, and my plans would not permit me to remove the maniac elsewhere—though I possess an old house, Ferndean Manor, even more retired and hidden than this, where I could have lodged her safely enough, had not a scruple about the unhealthiness of the situation, in the heart of a wood, made my conscience recoil from the arrangement. Probably those damp walls would soon have eased me of her charge: but to each villain his own vice; and mine is not a tendency to indirect assassination, even of what I most hate.

"Concealing the mad-woman's neighborhood from you, however, was something like covering a child with a cloak, and laying it down near a upas-tree:[6] that demon's vicinage is poisoned, and always was. But I'll shut up Thornfield Hall: I'll nail up the front door, and board the lower windows: I'll give Mrs. Poole two hundred a year to live here with *my wife*, as you term that fearful hag: Grace will do much for money and she shall have her son, the keeper at Grimsby Retreat, to bear her company and be at hand to give her aid in the paroxysms when *my wife* is prompted by her familiar to burn people in their beds at night, to stab them, to bite their flesh from their bones, and so on "—

"Sir," I interrupted him, "you are inexorable for that unfortunate lady: you speak of her with hate—with vindictive antipathy. It is cruel—she cannot help being mad."

"Jane, my little darling (so I will call you for so you are), you don't know what you are talking about; you misjudge me again: it is not because she is mad I hate her. If you were mad, do you think I should hate you?"

"I do indeed, sir."

"Then you are mistaken, and you know nothing about me, and nothing about the sort of love of which I am capable. Every atom of your flesh is as dear to me as my own: in pain and sickness it would still be dear. Your mind is my treasure, and if it were broken, it would be my treasure still: if you raved, my arms should confine you, and not a strait wais-coat—your grasp, even in fury, would have a charm for me: if you flew at me as wildly as that woman did this morning, I should receive you in an embrace at least as fond as it would be re-strictive. I should not shrink from you with disgust as I did from her: in your quiet moments you should have no watcher and no nurse but me; and I could hang over you with untiring tenderness, though you gave me no smile in re-turn; and never weary of gazing into your eyes, though they had no longer a ray of recognition for me.—But why do I follow that train of ideas? I was talking of removing you from Thornfield. All, you know, is prepared for prompt depar-ture: tomorrow you shall go. I only ask you to endure one more night under

5. Achan concealed stolen treasure in his tent (Joshua 7).

6. A legendary poisonous tree that killed all the life around it

this roof, Jane: and then, farewell to its miseries and terrors for ever! I have a place to repair to which will be a secure sanctuary from hateful reminiscences, from unwelcome intrusion—even from falsehood and slander."

"And take Adèle with you, sir," I interrupted; "she will be a companion for you."

"What do you mean, Jane? I told you I would send Adèle to school: and what do I want with a child for a companion? and not my own child,—a French dancer's bastard. Why do you importune me about her? I say, why do you assign Adèle to me for a companion?"

"You spoke of a retirement, sir; and retirement and solitude are dull: too dull for you."

"Solitude! solitude!" he reiterated, with irritation. "I see I must come to an explanation. I don't know what sphinx-like expression is forming in your countenance. *You* are to share my solitude. Do you understand?"

I shook my head: it required a degree of courage, excited as he was becoming, even to risk that mute sign of dissent. He had been walking fast about the room, and he stopped, as if suddenly rooted to one spot. He looked at me long and hard: I turned my eyes from him, fixed them on the fire, and tried to assume and maintain a quiet, collected aspect.

"Now for the hitch in Jane's character," he said at last, speaking more calmly than from his look I had expected him to speak. "The reel of silk has run smoothly enough so far; but I always knew there would come a knot and a puzzle: here it is. Now for vexation, and exasperation, and endless trouble! By God! I long to exert a fraction of Samson's strength, and break the entanglement like tow!"

He recommenced his walk: but soon again stopped, and this time just before me.

"Jane! will you hear reason?" (he stooped and approached his lips to my ear) "because, if you won't, I'll try violence." His voice was hoarse; his look that of a man who is just about to burst an insufferable bond and plunge headlong into wild license. I saw that in another moment, and with one impetus of frenzy more, I should be able to do nothing with him. The present—the passing second of time—was all I had in which to control and restrain him: a movement of repulsion, flight, fear, would have sealed my doom,—and his. But I was not afraid: not in the least. I felt an inward power; a sense of influence, which supported me. The crisis was perilous; but not without its charm: such as the Indian, perhaps, feels when he slips over the rapid in his canoe. I took hold of his clenched hand; loosened the contorted fingers, and said to him, soothingly,— "Sit down; I'll talk to you as long as you like, and hear all you have to say, whether reasonable or unreasonable."

He sat down: but he did not get leave to speak directly. I had been struggling with tears for some time; I had taken great pains to repress them, because I knew he would not like to see me weep. Now, however, I considered it well to let them flow as freely and as long as they liked. If the flood annoyed him, so much the better. So I gave way and cried heartily.

Soon I heard him earnestly entreating me to be composed. I said I could not while he was in such a passion.

"But I am not angry, Jane: I only love you too well; and you had steeled your little pale face with such a resolute, frozen look, I could not endure it. Hush, now, and wipe your eyes."

His softened voice announced that he was subdued; so I, in my turn, became calm. Now he made an effort to rest his head on my shoulder; but I would not permit it. Then he would draw me to him: no.

"Jane! Jane!" he said, in such an accent of bitter sadness it thrilled along every nerve I had, "you don't love me, then? It was only my station, and the rank of my wife, that you valued? Now that you think me disqualified to become your husband you recoil from my touch as if I were some toad or ape."

These words cut me: yet what could I do or say? I ought probably to have done or said nothing: but I was so tortured by a sense of remorse at thus hurting his feelings I could not control the wish to drop balm where I had wounded.

"I *do* love you," I said, "more than ever: but I must not show or indulge the feeling: and this is the last time I must express it."

"The last time, Jane! What! do you think you can live with me, and see me daily, and yet, if you still love me, be always cold and distant?"

"No, sir, that I am certain I could not; and therefore I see there is but one way: but you will be furious if I mention it."

"Oh, mention it! If I storm, you have the art of weeping."

"Mr. Rochester, I must leave you."

"For how long, Jane? For a few minutes, while you smooth your hair—which is somewhat dishevelled; and bathe your face—which looks feverish?"

"I must leave Adèle and Thornfield. I must part with you for my whole life: I must begin a new existence amongst strange faces and strange scenes."

"Of course: I told you you should. I pass over the madness about parting from me. You mean you must become a part of me. As to the new existence, it is all right: you shall yet be my wife: I am not married. You shall be Mrs. Rochester—both virtually and nominally. I shall keep only to you so long as you and I live. You shall go to a place I have in the south of France: a whitewashed villa on the shores of the Mediterranean. There you shall live a happy, and guarded, and most innocent life. Never fear that I wish to lure you into error—to make you my mistress. Why do you shake your head? Jane, you must be reasonable; or in truth I shall again become frantic."

His voice and hand quivered; his large nostrils dilated; his eye blazed; still I dared to speak:— "Sir, your wife is living: that is a fact acknowledged this morning by yourself. If I lived with you as you desire, I should then be your mistress: to say otherwise is sophistical—is false."

"Jane, I am not a gentle-tempered man—you forget that: I am not long-enduring; I am not cool and dispassionate. Out of pity to me and yourself, put your finger on my pulse, feel how it throbs, and—beware!"

He bared his wrist and offered it to me: the blood was forsaking his cheek and lips; they were growing livid; I was distressed on all hands. To agitate him thus deeply, by a resistance he so abhorred, was cruel: to yield was out of the question. I did what human beings do instinctively when they are driven to utter extremity—looked for aid to one higher than man: the words "God help me!" burst involuntarily from my lips.

"I am a fool!" cried Mr. Rochester suddenly. "I keep telling her I am not married, and do not explain to her why. I forget she knows nothing of the character of that woman, or of the circumstances attending my infernal union with her. Oh, I am certain Jane will agree with me in opinion when she knows all that I know! Just put your hand in mine, Janet, that I may have the evi-

dence of touch as well as sight to prove you are near me—and I will in a few words show you the real state of the case. Can you listen to me?"

"Yes, sir; for hours if you will."

"I ask only minutes. Jane, did you ever hear or know that I was not the eldest son of my house; that I had once a brother older than I?"

"I remember Mrs. Fairfax told me so once."

"And did you ever hear that my father was an avaricious grasping man?"

"I have understood something to that effect."

"Well, Jane, being so, it was his resolution to keep the property together; he could not bear the idea of dividing his estate and leaving me a fair portion: all, he resolved, should go to my brother Rowland. Yet as little could he endure that a son of his should be a poor man. I must be provided for by a wealthy marriage. He sought me a partner betimes. Mr. Mason, a West India planter and merchant, was his old acquaintance. He was certain his possessions were real and vast: he made inquiries. Mr. Mason, he found, had a son and daughter; and he learned from him that he could and would give the latter a fortune of thirty thousand pounds: that sufficed. When I left college I was sent out to Jamaica, to espouse a bride already courted for me. My father said nothing about her money: but he told me Miss Mason was the boast of Spanish Town for her beauty: and this was no lie. I found her a fine woman, in the style of Blanche Ingram; tall, dark, and majestic. Her family wished to secure me, because I was of a good race; and so did she. They showed her to me in parties, splendidly dressed. I seldom saw her alone, and had very little private conversation with her. She flattered me, and lavishly displayed for my pleasure her charms and accomplishments. All the men in her circle seemed to admire her and envy me. I was dazzled, stimulated: my senses were excited; and being ignorant, raw, and inexperienced, I thought I loved her. There is no folly so besotted that the idiotic rivalries of society, the prurience, the rashness, the blindness of youth, will not hurry a man to its commission. Her relatives encouraged me; competitors piqued me; she allured me: a marriage was achieved almost before I knew where I was. Oh, I have no respect for myself when I think of that act!—an agony of inward contempt masters me. I never loved, I never esteemed, I did not even know her. I was not sure of the existence of one virtue in her nature: I had marked neither modesty, nor benevolence, nor candor, nor refinement in her mind or manners—and, I married her:—gross, groveling, mole-eyed blockhead that I was! With less sin I might have—but let me remember to whom I am speaking.

"My bride's mother I had never seen: I understood she was dead. The honeymoon over, I learned my mistake; she was only mad, and shut up in a lunatic asylum. There was a younger brother, too, a complete dumb idiot. The elder one, whom you have seen (and whom I cannot hate, whilst I abhor all his kindred, because he has some grains of affection in his feeble mind; shown in the continued interest he takes in his wretched sister, and also in a dog-like attachment he once bore me), will probably be in the same state one day. My father, and my brother Rowland, knew all this; but they thought only of the thirty thousand pounds, and joined in the plot against me.

"These were vile discoveries; but, except for the treachery of concealment, I should have made them no subject of reproach to my wife: even when I found her nature wholly alien to mine; her tastes obnoxious to me; her cast of mind common, low, narrow, and singularly incapable of being led to anything

higher, expanded to anything larger—when I found that I could not pass a single evening, nor even a single hour of the day, with her in comfort: that kindly conversation could not be sustained between us, because whatever topic I started immediately received from her a turn at once coarse and trite, perverse and imbecile—when I perceived that I should never have a quiet or settled household, because no servant would bear the continued outbreaks of her violent and unreasonable temper, or the vexations of her absurd, contradictory, exacting orders—even then I restrained myself: I eschewed upbraiding, I curtailed remonstrance; I tried to devour my repentance and disgust in secret; I repressed the deep antipathy I felt.

"Jane, I will not trouble you with abominable details: some strong words shall express what I have to say. I lived with that woman upstairs four years, and before that time she had tried me indeed: her character ripened and developed with frightful rapidity; her vices sprang up fast and rank: they were so strong, only cruelty could check them; and I would not use cruelty. What a pigmy intellect she had—and what giant propensities! How fearful were the curses those propensities entailed on me! Bertha Mason,—the true daughter of an infamous mother,—dragged me through all the hideous and degrading agonies which must attend a man bound to a wife at once intemperate and unchaste.

"My brother in the interval was dead; and at the end of the four years my father died too. I was rich enough now—yet poor to hideous indigence: a nature the most gross, impure, depraved, I ever saw, was associated with mine, and called by the law and by society a part of me. And I could not rid myself of it by any legal proceedings: for the doctors now discovered that *my wife* was mad—her excesses had prematurely developed the germs of insanity:—Jane, you don't like my narrative; you look almost sick—shall I defer the rest to another day?"

"No, sir, finish it now: I pity you—I do earnestly pity you."

"Pity, Jane, from some people is a noxious and insulting sort of tribute, which one is justified in hurling back in the teeth of those who offer it; but that is the sort of pity native to callous, selfish hearts: it is a hybrid, egotistical pain at hearing of woes, crossed with ignorant contempt for those who have endured them. But that is not your pity, Jane: it is not the feeling of which your whole face is full at this moment—with which your eyes are now almost overflowing—with which your heart is heaving—with which your hand is trembling in mine. Your pity, my darling, is the suffering mother of love: its anguish is the very natal pang of the divine passion. I accept it, Jane; let the daughter have free advent—my arms wait to receive her."

"Now, sir, proceed: what did you do when you found she was mad?"

"Jane—I approached the verge of despair: a remnant of self-respect was all that intervened between me and the gulf. In the eyes of the world I was doubtless covered with grimy dishonor: but I resolved to be clean in my own sight—and to the last I repudiated the contamination of her crimes, and wrenched myself from connection with her mental defects. Still, society associated my name and person with hers! I yet saw her and heard her daily: something of her breath (faugh!) mixed with the air I breathed; and, besides, I remembered I had once been her husband—that recollection was then, and is now, inexpressibly odious to me: moreover, I knew that while she lived I could never be the husband of another and better wife; and though five years my senior (her

family and her father had lied to me even in the particular of her age), she was likely to live as long as I, being as robust in frame as she was infirm in mind. Thus, at the age of twenty-six, I was hopeless.

"One night I had been awakened by her yells—(since the medical men had pronounced her mad she had of course been shut up)—it was a fiery West Indian night; one of the description that frequently precede the hurricanes of those climates; being unable to sleep in bed, I got up and opened the window. The air was like sulfur-steams—I could find no refreshment anywhere. Mosquitoes came buzzing in and hummed sullenly round the room; the sea, which I could hear from thence, rumbled dull like an earthquake—black clouds were casting up over it; the moon was setting in the waves, broad and red, like a hot cannon-ball—she threw her last bloody glance over a world quivering with the ferment of tempest. I was physically influenced by the atmosphere and scene, and my ears were filled with the curses the maniac still shrieked out; wherein she momentarily mingled my name with such a tone of demon-hate, with such language!—no professed harlot ever had a fouler vocabulary than she: though two rooms off, I heard every word—the thin partitions of the West India house opposing but slight obstruction to her wolfish cries.

"'This life,' said I at last, 'is hell! this is the air—those are the sounds of the bottomless pit! I have a right to deliver myself from it if I can. The sufferings of this mortal state will leave me with the heavy flesh that now cumbers my soul. Of the fanatic's burning eternity I have no fear; there is not a future state worse than this present one—let me break away, and go home to God!'

"I said this whilst I knelt down at and unlocked a trunk which contained a brace of loaded pistols: I meant to shoot myself. I only entertained the intention for a moment; for not being insane, the crisis of exquisite and unalloyed despair which had originated the wish and design of self-destruction was past in a second.

"A wind fresh from Europe blew over the ocean and rushed through the open casement: the storm broke, streamed, thundered, blazed, and the air grew pure. I then framed and fixed a resolution. While I walked under the dripping orange-trees of my wet garden, and among its drenched pomegranates and pineapples, and while the refulgent dawn of the tropics kindled round me—I reasoned thus, Jane:—and now listen; for it was true Wisdom that consoled me in that hour, and showed me the right path to follow.

"The sweet wind from Europe was still whispering in the refreshed leaves, and the Atlantic was thundering in glorious liberty; my heart, dried up and scorched for a long time, swelled to the tone, and filled with living blood—my being longed for renewal—my soul thirsted for a pure draught. I saw Hope revive—and felt Regeneration possible. From a flowery arch at the bottom of my garden I gazed over the sea—bluer than the sky: the old world was beyond; clear prospects opened thus:—

"'Go,' said Hope, 'and live again in Europe: there it is not known what a sullied name you bear, nor what a filthy burden is bound to you. You may take the maniac with you to England; confine her with due attendance and precautions at Thornfield: then travel yourself to what clime you will, and form what new tie you like. That woman, who has so abused your long-suffering—so sullied your name; so outraged your honor; so blighted your youth—is not your wife; nor are you her husband. See that she is cared for as her condition de-

mands, and you have done all that God and Humanity require of you. Let her identity, her connection with yourself, be buried in oblivion: you are bound to impart them to no living being. Place her in safety and comfort: shelter her degradation with secrecy, and leave her.'

"I acted precisely on this suggestion. My father and brother had not made my marriage known to their acquaintance; because, in the very first letter I wrote to apprise them of the union—having already begun to experience extreme disgust of its consequences; and from the family character and constitution seeing a hideous future opening to me—I added an urgent charge to keep it secret; and very soon the infamous conduct of the wife my father had selected for me was such as to make him blush to own her as his daughter-in-law. Far from desiring to publish the connection, he became as anxious to conceal it as myself.

"To England, then, I conveyed her; a fearful voyage I had with such a monster in the vessel. Glad was I when I at last got her to Thornfield, and saw her safely lodged in that third-story room, of whose secret inner cabinet she has now for ten years made a wild beast's den—a goblin's cell. I had some trouble in finding an attendant for her: as it was necessary to select one on whose fidelity dependence could be placed; for her ravings would inevitably betray my secret: besides, she had lucid intervals of days—sometimes weeks—which she filled up with abuse of me. At last I hired Grace Poole, from the Grimsby Retreat. She and the surgeon, Carter (who dressed Mason's wounds that night he was stabbed and worried), are the only two I have ever admitted to my confidence. Mrs. Fairfax may indeed have suspected something; but she could have gained no precise knowledge as to facts. Grace has, on the whole, proved a good keeper; though, owing partly to a fault of her own, of which it appears nothing can cure her, and which is incident to her harassing profession, her vigilance has been more than once lulled and baffled. The lunatic is both cunning and malignant; she has never failed to take advantage of her guardian's temporary lapses; once to secrete the knife with which she stabbed her brother, and twice to possess herself of the key of her cell, and issue therefrom in the night-time. On the first of these occasions she perpetrated the attempt to burn me in my bed; on the second she paid that ghastly visit to you. I thank Providence, who watched over you, that she then spent her fury on your wedding apparel; which perhaps brought back vague reminiscences of her own bridal days; but on what might have happened I cannot endure to reflect. When I think of the thing which flew at my throat this morning hanging its black and scarlet visage over the nest of my dove my blood curdles"——

"And what, sir," I asked, while he paused, "did you do when you had settled her here? Where did you go?"

"What did I do, Jane? I transformed myself into a Will-o'-the-wisp. Where did I go? I pursued wanderings as wild as those of the March-spirit. I sought the Continent, and went devious through all its lands. My fixed desire was to seek and find a good and intelligent woman whom I could love: a contrast to the fury I left at Thornfield"——

"But you could not marry, sir."

"I had determined, and was convinced that I could and ought. It was not my original intention to deceive, as I have deceived you. I meant to tell my tale plainly, and make my proposals openly: and it appeared to me so absolutely rational that I should be considered free to love and be loved, I never doubted

some woman might be found willing and able to understand my case and accept me, in spite of the curse with which I was burdened."

"Well, sir?"

"When you are inquisitive, Jane, you always make me smile. You open your eyes like an eager bird, and make every now and then a restless movement; as if answers in speech did not flow fast enough for you, and you wanted to read the tablet of one's heart. But before I go on tell me what you mean by your 'Well, sir?' It is a small phrase very frequent with you; and which many a time has drawn me on and on through interminable talk: I don't very well know why."

"I mean—What next? How did you proceed? What came of such an event?"

"Precisely: and what do you wish to know now?"

"Whether you found any one you liked: whether you asked her to marry you; and what she said."

"I can tell you whether I found any one I liked, and whether I asked her to marry me: but what she said is yet to be recorded in the book of Fate. For ten long years I roved about, living first in one capital, then another: sometimes in St. Petersburg; oftener in Paris; occasionally in Rome, Naples, and Florence. Provided with plenty of money and the passport of an old name, I could choose my own society: no circles were closed against me. I sought my ideal of a woman among English ladies, French countesses, Italian signoras, and German gräfinnen.[7] I could not find her. Sometimes, for a fleeting moment, I thought I caught a glance, heard a tone, beheld a form, which announced the realization of my dream: but I was presently undeceived. You are not to suppose that I desired perfection either of mind or person. I longed only for what suited me—for the antipodes of the Creole: and I longed vainly. Amongst them all I found not one whom, had I been ever so free, I—warned as I was of the risks, the horrors, the loathings of incongruous unions—would have asked to marry me. Disappointment made me reckless. I tried dissipation—never debauchery: that I hated, and hate. That was my Indian Messalina's[8] attribute: rooted disgust at it and her restrained me much, even in pleasure. Any enjoyment that bordered on riot seemed to approach me to her and her vices, and I eschewed it.

"Yet I could not live alone; so I tried the companionship of mistresses. The first I chose was Céline Varens—another of those steps which make a man spurn himself when he recalls them. You already know what she was, and how my liaison with her terminated. She had two successors: an Italian, Giacinta, and a German, Clara; both considered singularly handsome. What was their beauty to me in a few weeks? Giacinta was unprincipled and violent: I tired of her in three months. Clara was honest and quiet; but heavy, mindless, unimpressible: not one whit to my taste. I was glad to give her a sufficient sum to set her up in a good line of business, and so get decently rid of her. But, Jane, I see by your face you are not forming a very favorable opinion of me just now. You think me an unfeeling, loose-principled rake: don't you?"

"I don't like you so well as I have done sometimes, indeed, sir. Did it not seem to you in the least wrong to live in that way: first with one mistress and then another? You talk of it as a mere matter of course."

7. Countesses.
8. Dissipated wife of the Roman emperor Claudius. "Antipodes": exact opposites.

"It was with me: and I did not like it. It was a groveling fashion of existence: I should never like to return to it. Hiring a mistress is the next worst thing to buying a slave: both are often by nature, and always by position, inferior: and to live familiarly with inferiors is degrading. I now hate the recollection of the time I passed with Céline, Giacinta, and Clara."

I felt the truth of these words; and I drew from them the certain inference, that if I were so far to forget myself and all the teaching that had ever been instilled into me as—under any pretext—with any justification—through any temptation—to become the successor of these poor girls, he would one day regard me with the same feeling which now in his mind desecrated their memory. I did not give utterance to this conviction: it was enough to feel it. I impressed it on my heart, that it might remain there to serve me as aid in the time of trial.

"Now, Jane, why don't you say 'Well, sir?' I have not done. You are looking grave. You disapprove of me still, I see. But let me come to the point. Last January, rid of all mistresses—in a harsh, bitter frame of mind, the result of a useless, roving, lonely life—corroded with disappointment, sourly disposed against all men, and especially against all *womankind* (for I began to regard the notion of an intellectual, faithful, loving woman as a mere dream), recalled by business, I came back to England.

"On a frosty winter afternoon I rode in sight of Thornfield Hall. Abhorred spot! I expected no peace—no pleasure there. On a stile in Hay Lane I saw a quiet little figure sitting by itself. I passed it as negligently as I did the pollard willow opposite to it; I had no presentiment of what it would be to me; no inward warning that the arbitress of my life—my genius for good or evil—waited there in humble guise. I did not know it even when, on the occasion of Mesrour's accident, it came up and gravely offered me help. Childish and slender creature! It seemed as if a linnet had hopped on my foot and proposed to bear me on its tiny wing. I was surly; but the thing would not go: it stood by me with strange perseverance, and looked and spoke with a sort of authority. I must be aided, and by that hand: and aided I was.

"When once I had pressed the frail shoulder, something new—a fresh sap and sense—stole into my frame. It was well I had learnt that this elf must return to me—that it belonged to my house down below—or I could not have felt it pass away from under my hand, and seen it vanish behind the dim hedge, without singular regret. I heard you come home that night, Jane: though probably you were not aware that I thought of you, or watched for you. The next day I observed you—myself unseen—for half an hour, while you played with Adèle in the gallery. It was a snowy day, I recollect, and you could not go out of doors. I was in my room; the door was ajar: I could both listen and watch. Adèle claimed your outward attention for a while; yet I fancied your thoughts were elsewhere: but you were very patient with her, my little Jane; you talked to her and amused her a long time. When at last she left you, you lapsed at once into deep reverie: you betook yourself slowly to pace the gallery. Now and then, in passing a casement you glanced out at the thick-falling snow; you listened to the sobbing wind, and again you paced gently on and dreamed. I think those day visions were not dark; there was a pleasurable illumination in your eye occasionally, a soft excitement in your aspect, which told of no bitter, bilious, hypochondriac brooding: your look revealed rather the sweet musings, of youth, when its spirit follows on willing wings the flight of Hope, up and on to an ideal heaven. The voice of Mrs. Fairfax, speaking to a

servant in the hall, wakened you: and how curiously you smiled to and at yourself, Janet! There was much sense in your smile: it was very shrewd, and seemed to make light of your own abstraction. It seemed to say—'My fine visions are all very well, but I must not forget they are absolutely unreal. I have a rosy sky, and a green flowery Eden in my brain; but without, I am perfectly aware, lies at my feet a rough tract to travel, and around me gather black tempests to encounter.' You ran downstairs and demanded of Mrs. Fairfax some occupation: the weekly house accounts to make up, or something of that sort, I think it was. I was vexed with you for getting out of my sight.

"Impatiently I waited for evening, when I might summon you to my presence. An unusual—to me—a perfectly new character I suspected was yours: I desired to search it deeper, and know it better. You entered the room with a look and air at once shy and independent: you were quaintly dressed—much as you are now. I made you talk—ere long I found you full of strange contrasts. Your garb and manner were restricted by rule; your air was often diffident, and altogether that of one refined by nature, but absolutely unused to society, and a good deal afraid of making herself disadvantageously conspicuous by some solecism or blunder; yet when addressed you lifted a keen, a daring, and a glowing eye to your interlocutor's face: there was penetration and power in each glance you gave; when plied by close questions, you found ready and round answers. Very soon you seemed to get used to me; I believe you felt the existence of sympathy between you and your grim and cross master, Jane; for it was astonishing to see how quickly a certain pleasant ease tranquilized your manner: snarl as I would, you showed no surprise, fear, annoyance, or displeasure at my moroseness; you watched me, and now and then smiled at me with a simple yet sagacious grace I cannot describe. I was at once content and stimulated with what I saw: I liked what I had seen, and wished to see more. Yet, for a long time, I treated you distantly, and sought your company rarely. I was an intellectual epicure, and wished to prolong the gratification of making this novel and piquant acquaintance: besides, I was for a while troubled with a haunting fear that if I handled the flower freely its bloom would fade—the sweet charm of freshness would leave it. I did not then know that it was no transitory blossom; but rather the radiant resemblance of one, cut in an indestructible gem. Moreover, I wished to see whether you would seek me if I shunned you—but you did not: you kept in the school-room as still as your own desk and easel; if by chance I met you, you passed me as soon, and with as little token of recognition, as was consistent with respect. Your habitual expression in those days, Jane, was a thoughtful look; not despondent, for you were not sickly; but not buoyant, for you had little hope, and no actual pleasure. I wondered what you thought of me—or if you ever thought of me; to find this out I resumed my notice of you. There was something glad in your glance and genial in your manner when you conversed: I saw you had a social heart; it was the silent schoolroom—it was the tedium of your life—that made you mournful. I permitted myself the delight of being kind to you; kindness stirred emotion soon: your face became soft in expression, your tones gentle; I liked my name pronounced by your lips in a grateful, happy accent. I used to enjoy a chance meeting with you, Jane, at this time: there was a curious hesitation in your manner: you glanced at me with a slight trouble—a hovering doubt: you did not know what my caprice might be—whether I was going to play the master and be stern, or the friend and be benignant. I was now too

fond of you often to stimulate the first whim; and, when I stretched my hand out cordially, such bloom and light and bliss rose to your young, wistful features, I had much ado often to avoid straining you then and there to my heart."

"Don't talk any more of those days, sir," I interrupted, furtively dashing away some tears from my eyes; his language was torture to me; for I knew what I must do—and do soon—and all these reminiscences and these revelations of his feelings only made my work more difficult.

"No, Jane," he returned: "what necessity is there to dwell on the Past, when the Present is so much surer—the Future so much brighter?"

I shuddered to hear the infatuated assertion.

"You see now how the case stands—do you not?" he continued. "After a youth and manhood passed half in unutterable misery and half in dreary solitude, I have for the first time found what I can truly love—I have found *you*. You are my sympathy—my better self—my good angel—I am bound to you with a strong attachment. I think you good, gifted, lovely: a fervent, a solemn passion is conceived in my heart; it leans to you, draws you to my center and spring of life, wraps my existence about you—and, kindling in pure, powerful flame, fuses you and me in one.

"It was because I felt and knew this that I resolved to marry you. To tell me that I had already a wife is empty mockery: you know now that I had but a hideous demon. I was wrong to attempt to deceive you; but I feared a stubbornness that exists in your character. I feared early instilled prejudice: I wanted to have you safe before hazarding confidences. This was cowardly: I should have appealed to your nobleness and magnanimity at first, as I do now—opened to you plainly my life of agony—described to you my hunger and thirst after a higher and worthier existence—shown to you, not my *resolution* (that word is weak), but my resistless *bent* to love faithfully and well where I am faithfully and well loved in return. Then I should have asked you to accept my pledge of fidelity, and to give me yours: Jane—give it me now."

A pause.

"Why are you silent, Jane?"

I was experiencing an ordeal: a hand of fiery iron grasped my vitals. Terrible moment: full of struggle, blackness, burning! Not a human being that ever lived could wish to be loved better than I was loved; and him who thus loved me I absolutely worshiped: and I must renounce love and idol. One drear word comprised my intolerable duty—"Depart!"

"Jane, you understand what I want of you? Just this promise—'I will be yours, Mr. Rochester.' "

"Mr. Rochester, I will *not* be yours."

Another long silence.

"Jane!" recommenced he, with a gentleness that broke me down with grief, and turned me stone-cold with ominous terror—for this still voice was the pant of a lion rising—"Jane, do you mean to go one way in the world, and to let me go another?"

"I do."

"Jane" (bending towards and embracing me), "do you mean it now?"

"I do."

"And now?" softly kissing my forehead and cheek.

"I do"—extricating myself from restraint rapidly and completely.

"Oh, Jane, this is bitter! This—this is wicked. It would not be wicked to love me."

"It would to obey you."

A wild look raised his brows—crossed his features: he rose; but he forbore yet. I laid my hand on the back of the chair for support: I shook, I feared—but I resolved.

"One instant, Jane. Give one glance to my horrible life when you are gone. All happiness will be torn away with you. What then is left? For a wife I have but the maniac upstairs: as well might you refer me to some corpse in yonder churchyard. What shall I do, Jane? Where turn for a companion, and for some hope?"

"Do as I do: trust in God and yourself. Believe in heaven. Hope to meet again there."

"Then you will not yield?"

"No."

"Then you condemn me to live wretched, and to die accursed?" His voice rose.

"I advise you to live sinless; and I wish you to die tranquil."

"Then you snatch love and innocence from me? You fling me back on lust for a passion—vice for an occupation?"

"Mr. Rochester, I no more assign this fate to you than I grasp at it for myself. We were born to strive and endure—you as well as I: do so. You will forget me before I forget you."

"You make me a liar by such language: you sully my honor. I declared I could not change: you tell me to my face I shall change soon. And what a distortion in your judgment, what a perversity in your ideas, is proved by your conduct! Is it better to drive a fellow-creature to despair than to transgress a mere human law—no man being injured by the breach? For you have neither relatives nor acquaintances whom you need fear to offend by living with me."

This was true: and while he spoke my very conscience and reason turned traitors against me, and charged me with crime in resisting him. They spoke almost as loud as Feeling: and that clamored wildly. "Oh, comply!" it said. "Think of his misery; think of his danger—look at his state when left alone; remember his headlong nature; consider the recklessness following on despair—soothe him; save him; love him; tell him you love him and will be his. Who in the world cares for *you*? or who will be injured by what you do?"

Still indomitable was the reply—"*I* care for myself. The more solitary, the more friendless, the more unsustained I am, the more I will respect myself. I will keep the law given by God; sanctioned by man. I will hold to the principles received by me when I was sane, and not mad—as I am now. Laws and principles are not for the times when there is no temptation: they are for such moments as this, when body and soul rise in mutiny against their rigor; stringent are they; inviolate they shall be. If at my individual convenience I might break them, what would be their worth? They have a worth—so I have always believed; and if I cannot believe it now, it is because I am insane—quite insane: with my veins running fire, and my heart beating faster than I can count its throbs. Preconceived opinions, foregone determinations, are all I have at this hour to stand by: there I plant my foot."

I did. Mr. Rochester, reading my countenance, saw I had done so. His fury was wrought to the highest: he must yield to it for a moment, whatever fol-

lowed; he crossed the floor and seized my arm, and grasped my waist. He seemed to devour me with his flaming glance: physically, I felt, at the moment, powerless as stubble exposed to the draught and glow of a furnace— mentally, I still possessed my soul, and with it the certainty of ultimate safety. The soul, fortunately, has an interpreter—often an unconscious, but still a truthful interpreter—in the eye. My eye rose to his; and while I looked in his fierce face, I gave an involuntary sigh: his grip was painful, and my overtasked strength almost exhausted.

"Never," said he, as he ground his teeth, "never was anything at once so frail and so indomitable. A mere reed she feels in my hand!" (And he shook me with the force of his hold.) "I could bend her with my finger and thumb: and what good would it do if I bent, if I uptore, if I crushed her? Consider that eye: consider the resolute, wild, free thing looking out of it, defying me, with more than courage—with a stern triumph. Whatever I do with its cage, I cannot get at it—the savage, beautiful creature! If I tear, if I rend the slight prison, my outrage will only let the captive loose. Conqueror I might be of the house; but the inmate would escape to heaven before I could call myself possessor of its clay dwelling-place. And it is you, spirit—with will and energy, and virtue and purity—that I want: not alone your brittle frame. Of yourself, you could come with soft flight and nestle against my heart, if you would: seized against your will you will elude the grasp like an essence—you will vanish ere I inhale your fragrance. Oh! come, Jane, come!"

As he said this he released me from his clutch, and only looked at me. The look was far worse to resist than the frantic strain: only an idiot, however, would have succumbed now. I had dared and baffled his fury; I must elude his sorrow: I retired to the door.

"You are going, Jane?"

"I am going, sir."

"You are leaving me?"

"Yes."

"You will not come?—You will not be my comforter, my rescuer?—My deep love, my wild woe, my frantic prayer, are all nothing to you?"

What unutterable pathos was in his voice! How hard it was to reiterate firmly, "I am going."

"Jane!"

"Mr. Rochester!"

"Withdraw, then,—I consent—but remember, you leave me here in anguish. Go up to your own room; think over all I have said, and, Jane, cast a glance on my sufferings—think of me."

He turned away; he threw himself on his face on the sofa. "Oh, Jane! my hope—my love—my life!" broke in anguish from his lips. Then came a deep, strong sob.

I had already gained the door: but, reader, I walked back—walked back as determinedly as I had retreated. I knelt down by him; I turned his face from the cushion to me; I kissed his cheek; I smoothed his hair with my hand.

"God bless you, my dear master!" I said. 'God keep you from harm and wrong—direct you, solace you—reward you well for your past kindness to me."

"Little Jane's love would have been my best reward," he answered: "without it, my heart is broken. But Jane will give me her love: yes—nobly, generously."

Up the blood rushed to his face; forth flashed the fire from his eyes; erect he sprang; he held his arms out; but I evaded the embrace, and at once quitted the room.

"Farewell!" was the cry of my heart as I left him. Despair added, "Farewell, for ever!"

That night I never thought to sleep; but a slumber fell on me as soon as I lay down in bed. I was transported in thought to the scenes of childhood; I dreamed I lay in the red-room at Gateshead; that the night was dark, and my mind impressed with strange fears. The light that long ago had struck me into syncope,[9] recalled in this vision, seemed glidingly to mount the wall, and tremblingly to pause in the center of the obscured ceiling. I lifted up my head to look: the roof resolved to clouds, high and dim; the gleam was such as the moon imparts to vapors she is about to sever. I watched her come—watched with the strangest anticipation; as though some word of doom were to be written on her disk. She broke forth as never moon yet burst from cloud: a hand first penetrated the sable folds and waved them away; then, not a moon, but a white human form shone in the azure, inclining a glorious brow earthward. It gazed and gazed and gazed on me. It spoke to my spirit: immeasurably distant was the tone, yet so near, it whispered in my heart—"My daughter, flee temptation!"

"Mother, I will."

So I answered after I had waked from the trance-like dream. It was yet night, but July nights are short: soon after midnight dawn comes. "It cannot be too early to commence the task I have to fulfill," thought I. I rose: I was dressed; for I had taken off nothing but my shoes. I knew where to find in my drawers some linen, a locket, a ring. In seeking these articles I encountered the beads of a pearl necklace Mr. Rochester had forced me to accept a few days ago. I left that; it was not mine: it was the visionary bride's, who had melted in air. The other articles I made up in a parcel; my purse, containing twenty shillings (it was all I had), I put in my pocket: I tied on my straw bonnet, pinned my shawl, took the parcel and my slippers, which I would not put on yet, and stole from my room.

"Farewell, kind Mrs. Fairfax!" I whispered, as I glided past her door. "Farewell, my darling Adèle!" I said, as I glanced towards the nursery. No thought could be admitted of entering to embrace her. I had to deceive a fine ear: for aught I knew, it might now be listening.

I would have got past Mr. Rochester's chamber without a pause; but my heart momentarily stopping its beat at that threshold, my foot was forced to stop also. No sleep was there: the inmate was walking restlessly from wall to wall; and again and again he sighed while I listened. There was a heaven—a temporary heaven—in this room for me, if I chose: I had but to go in and to say—"Mr. Rochester, I will love you and live with you through life till death," and a fount of rapture would spring to my lips. I thought of this.

That kind master, who could not sleep now, was waiting with impatience for day. He would send for me in the morning; I should be gone. He would have me sought for: vainly. He would feel himself forsaken; his love rejected: he would suffer; perhaps grow desperate. I thought of this too. My hand moved towards the lock; I caught it back, and glided on.

9. A faint.

Drearily I wound my way downstairs: I knew what I had to do, and I did it mechanically. I sought the key of the side-door in the kitchen; I sought, too, a phial of oil and a feather; I oiled the key and the lock. I got some water, I got some bread for perhaps I would have to walk far; and my strength, sorely shaken of late, must not break down. All this I did without one sound. I opened the door, passed out, shut it softly. Dim dawn glimmered in the yard. The great gates were closed and locked; but a wicket in one of them was only latched. Through that I departed: it, too, I shut. and now I was out of Thornfield.

A mile off, beyond the fields, lay a road which stretched in the contrary direction to Millcote; a road I had never traveled, but often noticed, and wondered where it led: thither I bent my steps. No reflection was to be allowed now: not one glance was to be cast back; not even one forward. Not one thought was to be given either to the past or the future. The first was a page so heavenly sweet—so deadly sad—that to read one line of it would dissolve my courage and break down my energy. That last was an awful blank: something like the world when the deluge was gone by.

I skirted fields, and hedges, and lanes, till after sunrise. I believe it was a lovely summer morning: I know my shoes, which I had put on when I left the house, were soon wet with dew. But I looked neither to rising sun, nor smiling sky, nor wakening nature. He who is taken out to pass through a fair scene to the scaffold thinks not of the flowers that smile on his road, but of the block and axe-edge; of the disseverment of bone and vein; of the grave gaping at the end: and I thought of drear flight and homeless wandering—and, oh! with agony I thought of what I left. I could not help it. I thought of him now—in his room—watching the sunrise; hoping I should soon come to say I would stay with him, and be his. I longed to be his; I panted to return: it was not too late; I could yet spare him the bitter pang of bereavement. As yet my flight, I was sure, was undiscovered. I could go back and be his comforter—his pride; his redeemer from misery; perhaps from ruin. Oh, that fear of his self-abandonment—far worse than my abandonment—how it goaded me! It was a barbed arrow-head in my breast; it tore me when I tried to extract it; it sickened me when remembrance thrust it further in. Birds began singing in brake and copse: birds were faithful to their mates; birds were emblems of love. What was I? In the midst of my pain of heart, and frantic effort of principle, I abhorred myself. I had no solace from self-approbation: none even from self-respect. I had injured—wounded—left my master. I was hateful in my own eyes. Still I could not turn, nor retrace one step. God must have led me on. As to my own will or conscience, impassioned grief had trampled one and stifled the other. I was weeping wildly as I walked along my solitary way: fast, fast I went, like one delirious. A weakness, beginning inwardly, extending to the limbs, seized me, and I fell: I lay on the ground some minutes, pressing my face to the wet turf. I had some fear—or hope—that here I should die: but I was soon up; crawling forwards on my hands and knees, and then again raised to my feet—as eager and as determined as ever to reach the road.

When I got there I was forced to sit to rest me under the hedge; and while I sat, I heard wheels, and saw a coach come on. I stood up and lifted my hand; it stopped. I asked where it was going: the driver named a place a long way off, and where I was sure Mr. Rochester had no connections. I asked for what sum he would take me there: he said thirty shillings; I answered I had but twenty;

well, he would try to make it do. He further gave me leave to get into the inside, as the vehicle was empty: I entered, was shut in, and it rolled on its way.

Gentle reader, may you never feel what I then felt! May your eyes never shed such stormy, scalding, heart-wrung tears as poured from mine. May you never appeal to Heaven in prayers so hopeless and so agonised as in that hour left my lips: for never may you, like me, dread to be the instrument of evil to what you wholly love.

Chapter XXVIII

Two days are passed. It is a summer evening; the coachman has set me down at a place called Whitcross; he could take me no farther for the sum I had given, and I was not possessed of another shilling in the world. The coach is a mile off by this time; I am alone. At this moment I discover that I forgot to take my parcel out of the pocket of the coach, where I had placed it for safety; there it remains, there it must remain; and now, I am absolutely destitute.

Whitcross is no town, nor even a hamlet; it is but a stone pillar set up where four roads meet: white-washed, I suppose, to be more obvious at a distance and in darkness. Four arms spring from its summit: the nearest town to which these point is, according to the inscription, distant ten miles; the farthest, above twenty. From the well-known names of these towns I learn in what county I have lighted; a north-midland shire, dusk with moorland, ridged with mountain: this I see. There are great moors behind and on each hand of me; there are waves of mountains far beyond that deep valley at my feet. The population here must be thin, and I see no passengers on these roads: they stretch out east, west, north, and south—white, broad, lonely; they are all cut in the moor, and the heather grows deep and wild to their very verge. Yet a chance traveler might pass by; and I wish no eye to see me now: strangers would wonder what I am doing, lingering here at the sign-post, evidently objectless and lost. I might be questioned: I could give no answer but what would sound incredible and excite suspicion. Not a tie holds me to human society at this moment—not a charm or hope calls me where my fellow-creatures are—none that saw me would have a kind thought or a good wish for me. I have no relative but the universal mother, Nature: I will seek her breast and ask repose.

I struck straight into the heath; I held on to a hollow I saw deeply furrowing the brown moorside; I waded knee-deep in its dark growth; I turned with its turnings, and finding a moss-blackened granite crag in a hidden angle, I sat down under it. High banks of moor were about me; the crag protected my head: the sky was over that.

Some time passed before I felt tranquil even here: I had a vague dread that wild cattle might be near, or that some sportsman or poacher might discover me. If a gust of wind swept the waste. I looked up, fearing it was the rush of a bull; if a plover whistled, I imagined it a man. Finding my apprehensions unfounded, however, and calmed by the deep silence that reigned as evening declined at nightfall, I took confidence. As yet I had not thought; I had only listened, watched, dreaded; now I regained the faculty of reflection.

What was I to do? Where to go? Oh, intolerable questions, when I could do nothing and go nowhere!—when a long way must yet be measured by my weary, trembling limbs, before I could reach human habitation—when cold charity must be entreated before I could get a lodging: reluctant sympathy

importuned: almost certain repulse incurred: before my tale could be listened
to, or one of my wants relieved!

I touched the heath: it was dry, and yet warm with the heat of the summer-
day. I looked at the sky; it was pure: a kindly star twinkled just above the chasm
ridge. The dew fell, but with propitious softness; no breeze whispered. Nature
seemed to me benign and good; I thought she loved me, outcast as I was; and
I, who from man could anticipate only mistrust, rejection, insult, clung to her
with filial fondness. Tonight, at least, I would be her guest—as I was her child:
my mother would lodge me without money and without price. I had one
morsel of bread yet: the remnant of a roll I had bought in a town we passed
through at noon with a stray penny—my last coin. I saw ripe bilberries gleam-
ing here and there, like jet beads in the heath: I gathered a handful and ate
them with the bread. My hunger, sharp before, was, if not satisfied, appeased
by this hermit's meal. I said my evening prayers at its conclusion, and then
chose my couch.

Beside the crag the heath was very deep: when I lay down my feet were
buried in it; rising high on each side, it left only a narrow space for the night-
air to invade. I folded my shawl double, and spread it over me for a coverlet; a
low, mossy swell was my pillow. Thus lodged I was not, at least at the com-
mencement of the night, cold.

My rest might have been blissful enough, only a sad heart broke it. It
plained of its gaping wounds, its inward bleeding, its riven chords, It trembled
for Mr. Rochester and his doom: it bemoaned him with bitter pity; it de-
manded him with ceaseless longing: and, impotent as a bird with both wings
broken, it still quivered its shattered pinions in vain attempts to seek him.

Worn out with this torture of thought, I rose to my knees. Night was come,
and her planets were risen: a safe, still night; too serene for the companionship
of fear. We know that God is everywhere; but certainly we feel His presence
most when His works are on the grandest scale spread before us: and it is in the
unclouded night-sky, where His worlds wheel their silent course, that we read
clearest His infinitude, His omnipotence, His omnipresence. I had risen to my
knees to pray for Mr Rochester. Looking up, I, with tear-dimmed eyes, saw the
mighty Milky Way. Remembering what it was—what countless systems there
swept space like a soft trace of light—I felt the might and strength of God.
Sure was I of His efficiency to save what He had made: convinced I grew that
neither earth should perish nor one of the souls it treasured. I turned my
prayer to thanksgiving: the Source of Life was also the Savior of spirits. Mr.
Rochester was safe: he was God's, and by God would he be guarded. I again
nestled to the breast of the hill; and ere long in sleep, forgot sorrow.

But next day Want came to me, pale and bare. Long after the little birds had
left their nests; long after bees had come in the sweet prime of day to gather
the heath honey before the dew was dried—when the long morning shadows
were curtailed, and the sun filled earth and sky—I got up, and I looked round
me.

What a still, hot, perfect day! What a golden desert this spreading moor!
Everywhere sunshine. I wished I could live in it and on it. I saw a lizard run
over the crag; I saw a bee busy among the sweet bilberries. I would fain at the
moment have become bee or lizard, that I might have found fitting nutri-
ment, permanent shelter here. But I was a human being, and had a human
being's wants: I must not linger where there was nothing to supply them. I

rose; I looked back at the bed I had left. Hopeless of the future, I wished but this—that my Maker had that night thought good to require my soul of me while I slept; and that this weary frame, absolved by death from further conflict with fate, had now but to decay quietly, and mingle in peace with the soil of this wilderness. Life, however, was yet in my possession; with all its requirements, and pains, and responsibilities. The burden must be carried; the want provided for; the suffering endured; the responsibility fulfilled. I set out.

Whitcross regained, I followed a road which led from the sun, now fervent and high. By no other circumstance had I will to decide my choice. I walked a long time, and when I thought I had nearly done enough, and might conscientiously yield to the fatigue that almost overpowered me—might relax this forced action, and, sitting down on a stone I saw near, submit resistlessly to the apathy that clogged heart and limb—I heard a bell chime—a church bell.

I turned in the direction of the sound, and there, amongst the romantic hills, whose changes and aspect I had ceased to note an hour ago, I saw a hamlet and a spire. All the valley at my right hand was full of pasture-fields, and corn-fields, and wood; and a glittering stream ran zig-zag through the varied shades of green, the mellowing grain, the sombre wood-land, the clear and sunny lea. Recalled by the rumbling of wheels to the road before me, I saw a heavily-laden waggon laboring up the hill; and not far beyond were two cows and their drover. Human life and human labor were near. I must struggle on: strive to live and bend to toil like the rest.

About two o'clock P.M. I entered the village. At the bottom of its one street there was a little shop with some cakes of bread in the window. I coveted a cake of bread. With that refreshment I could perhaps regain a degree of energy; without it, it would be difficult to proceed. The wish to have some strength and some vigour returned to me as soon as I was amongst my fellow-beings. I felt it would be degrading to faint with hunger on the causeway of a hamlet. Had I nothing about me I could offer in exchange for one of these rolls? I considered. I had a small silk handkerchief tied round my throat; I had my gloves. I could hardly tell how men and women in extremities of destitution proceeded. I did not know whether either of these articles would be accepted: probably they would not; but I must try.

I entered the shop: a woman was there. Seeing a respectably-dressed person, a lady as she supposed, she came forward with civility. How could she serve me? I was seized with shame: my tongue would not utter the request I had prepared. I dared not offer her the half-worn gloves, the creased handkerchief: besides, I felt it would be absurd. I only begged permission to sit down a moment, as I was tired. Disappointed in the expectation of a customer, she coolly acceded to my request. She pointed to a seat; I sank into it. I felt sorely urged to weep; but conscious how unseasonable such a manifestation would be, I restrained it. Soon I asked her, "if there were any dressmaker or plain-work-woman in the village?"

"Yes; two or three. Quite as many as there was employment for."

I reflected. I was driven to the point now. I was brought face to face with Necessity. I stood in the position of one without a resource: without a friend; without a coin. I must do something. What? I must apply somewhere. Where?

"Did she know of any place in the neighborhood where a servant was wanted?"

"Nay; she couldn't say."

"What was the chief trade in this place? What did most of the people do?"

"Some were farm laborers; a good deal worked at Mr. Oliver's needle-factory, and at the foundry."

"Did Mr. Oliver employ women?"

"Nay; it was men's work."

"And what do the women do?"

"I knawn't," was the answer. "Some does one thing, and some another. Poor folk mun get on as they can."

She seemed to be tired of my questions: and, indeed, what claim had I to importune her? A neighbor or two came in; my chair was evidently wanted. I took leave.

I passed up the street, looking as I went at all the houses to the right hand and to the left: but I could discover no pretext, nor see an inducement, to enter any. I rambled round the hamlet, going sometimes to a little distance and returning again, for an hour or more. Much exhausted, and suffering greatly now for want of food, I turned aside into a lane and sat down under the hedge. Ere many minutes had elapsed I was again on my feet, however, and again searching for something—a resource, or at least an informant. A pretty little house stood at the top of the lane, with a garden before it; exquisitely neat, and brilliantly blooming. I stopped at it. What business had I to approach the white door or touch the glittering knocker? In what way could it possibly be the interest of the inhabitants of that dwelling to serve me? Yet I drew near and knocked. A mild-looking, cleanly-attired young woman opened the door. In such a voice as might be expected from a hopeless heart and fainting frame—a voice wretchedly low and faltering—I asked if a servant was wanted here?

"No," said she; "we do not keep a servant."

"Can you tell me where I could get employment of any kind?" I continued. "I am a stranger, without acquaintance, in this place. I want some work: no matter what."

But it was not her business to think for me, or to seek a place for me: besides, in her eyes, how doubtful must have appeared my character, position, tale. She shook her head; she "was sorry she could give me no information," and the white door closed, quite gently and civilly: but it shut me out. If she had held it open a little longer, I believe I should have begged a piece of bread; for I was now brought low.

I could not bear to return to the sordid village; where, besides, no prospect of aid was visible. I should have longed rather to deviate to a wood I saw not far off, which appeared in its thick shade to offer inviting shelter; but I was so sick, so weak, so gnawed with nature's cravings, instinct kept me roaming round abodes where there was a chance of food. Solitude would be no solitude—rest no rest—while the vulture, hunger, thus sank beak and talons in my side.

I drew near houses; I left them, and came back again, and again I wandered away: always repelled by the consciousness of having no claim to ask—no right to expect interest in my isolated lot. Meantime the afternoon advanced, while I thus wandered about like a lost and starving dog. In crossing a field I saw the church spire before me: I hastened towards it. Near the churchyard, and in the middle of a garden, stood a well-built though small house, which I had no doubt was the parsonage. I remembered that strangers who arrive at a place

where they have no friends, and who want employment, sometimes apply to the clergyman for introduction and aid. It is the clergyman's function to help—at least with advice—those who wished to help themselves. I seemed to have something like a right to seek counsel here. Renewing, then, my courage, and gathering my feeble remains of strength, I pushed on. I reached the house, and knocked at the kitchen-door. An old woman opened: I asked was this the parsonage?

"Yes."

"Was the clergyman in?"

"No."

"Would he be in soon?"

"No, he was gone from home."

"To a distance?"

Not so far—happen three mile. He had been called away by the sudden death of his father: he was at Marsh End now, and would very likely stay there a fortnight longer.

"Was there any lady of the house?"

"Nay, there was naught but her, and she was housekeeper;" and of her, reader, I could not bear to ask the relief for want of which I was sinking; I could not yet beg; and again I crawled away.

Once more I took off my handkerchief—once more I thought of the cakes of bread in the little shop. Oh, for but a crust! for but one mouthful to allay the pang of famine! Instinctively I turned my face again to the village; I found the shop again, and I went in; and though others were there besides the woman, I ventured the request: "Would she give me a roll for this handker-chief?"

She looked at me with evident suspicion: "Nay, she never sold stuff i' that way."

Almost desperate, I asked for half a cake; she again refused. "How could she tell where I had got the handkerchief?" she said.

"Would she take my gloves?"

"No! what could she do with them?"

Reader, it is not pleasant to dwell on these details. Some say there is enjoy-ment in looking back to painful experience past; but at this day I can scarcely bear to review the times to which I allude: the moral degradation, blent with the physical suffering, form too distressing a recollection ever to be willingly dwelt on. I blamed none of those who repulsed me. I felt it was what was to be expected, and what could not be helped: an ordinary beggar is frequently an object of suspicion; a well-dressed beggar inevitably so. To be sure what I begged was employment: but whose business was it to provide me with em-ployment? Not, certainly, that of persons who saw me then for the first time, and who knew nothing about my character. And as to the woman who would not take my handkerchief in exchange for her bread, why, she was right; if the offer appeared to her sinister, or the exchange unprofitable. Let me condense now. I am sick of the subject.

A little before dark I passed a farm-house, at the open door of which the farmer was sitting, eating his supper of bread and cheese; I stopped, and said:—"Will you give me a piece of bread? for I am very hungry." He cast on me a glance of surprise; but without answering he cut a thick slice from his loaf, and gave it to me. I imagine he did not think I was a beggar, but only an

eccentric sort of lady, who had taken a fancy to his brown loaf. As soon as I was out of sight of his house, I sat down and ate it.

I could not hope to get a lodging under a roof, and sought it in the wood I have before alluded to. But my night was wretched, my rest broken: the ground was damp, the air cold: besides intruders passed near me more than once, and I had again and again to change my quarters: no sense of safety or tranquillity befriended me. Towards morning it rained; the whole of the following day was wet. Do not ask me, reader, to give a minute account of that day; as before, I sought work; as before, I was repulsed; as before, I starved: but once did food pass my lips. At the door of a cottage I saw a little girl about to throw a mess of cold porridge into a pig trough. "Will you give me that?" I asked.

She stared at me. "Mother!" she exclaimed, "there is a woman wants me to give her this porridge."

"Well, lass," replied a voice within, "give it her if she's a beggar. T' pig doesn't want it."

The girl emptied the stiffened mold into my hand, and I devoured it ravenously.

As the wet twilight deepened, I stopped in a solitary bridle-path, which I had been pursuing an hour or more.

"My strength is quite failing me," I said, in soliloquy. "I feel I cannot go much further. Shall I be an outcast again this night? While the rain descends so, must I lay my head on the cold, drenched ground? I fear I cannot do otherwise: for who will receive me? But it will be very dreadful, with this feeling of hunger, faintness, chill, and this sense of desolation—this total prostration of hope. In all likelihood, though, I should die before morning. And why cannot I reconcile myself to the prospect of death? Why do I struggle to retain a valueless life? Because I know, or believe, Mr. Rochester is still living: and then, to die of want and cold, is a fate to which nature cannot submit passively. Oh, Providence! sustain me a little longer! Aid—direct me!"

My glazed eye wandered over the dim and misty landscape. I saw I had strayed far from the village: it was quite out of sight. The very cultivation surrounding it had disappeared. I had, by cross-ways and by-paths, once more drawn near the tract of moorland; and now, only a few fields, almost as wild and unproductive as the heath from which they were scarcely reclaimed, lay between me and the dusky hill.

"Well, I would rather die yonder than in a street, or on a frequented road," I reflected. "And far better that crows and ravens—if any ravens there be in these regions—should pick my flesh from my bones, than that they should be prisoned in a workhouse coffin and moulder in a pauper's grave."

To the hill, then, I turned. I reached it. It remained now only to find a hollow where I could lie down, and feel at least hidden, if not secure: but all the surface of the waste looked level. It showed no variation but of tint; green, where rush and moss overgrew the marshes; black, where the dry soil bore only heath. Dark as it was getting, I could still see these changes; though but as mere alternations of light and shade: for color had faded with the day-light.

My eye still roved over the sullen swell, and along the moor-edge, vanishing amidst the wildest scenery; when at one dim point, far in among the marshes and the ridges, a light sprang up. "That is an *ignis fatuus*," was my first thought; and I expected it would soon vanish. It burned on, however, quite steadily; neither receding nor advancing. "Is it then, a bonfire just kindled?" I

questioned. I watched to see whether it would spread: but no; as it did not diminish, so it did not enlarge. "It may be a candle in a house," I then conjectured: "but if so, I can never reach it. It is much too far away: and were it within a yard of me, what would it avail? I should but knock at the door to have it shut in my face."

And I sank down where I stood, and hid my face against the ground. I lay still a while: the night-wind swept over the hill and over me, and died moaning in the distance; the rain fell fast, wetting me afresh to the skin. Could I but have stiffened to the still frost—the friendly numbness of death—it might have pelted on: I should not have felt it; but my yet living flesh shuddered to its chilling influence. I rose ere long.

The light was yet there: shining dim, but constant, through the rain. I tried to walk again: I dragged my exhausted limbs slowly towards it. It led me aslant over the hill, through a wide bog; which would have been impassable in winter, and was splashy and shaking even now, in the height of summer. Here I fell twice; but as often I rose and rallied my faculties. This light was my forlorn hope: I must gain it.

Having crossed the marsh, I saw a trace of white over the moor. I approached it; it was a road or a track: it led straight up to the light, which now beamed from a sort of knoll, amid a clump of trees—firs, apparently, from what I could distinguish of the character of their forms and foliage through the gloom. My star vanished as I drew near: some obstacle had intervened between me and it. I put out my hand to feel the dark mass before me; I discriminated the rough stones of a low wall—above it, something like palisades, and within, a high and prickly hedge. I groped on. Again a whitish object gleamed before me: it was a gate—a wicket; it moved on its hinges as I touched it. On each side stood a sable bush—holly or yew.

Entering the gate and passing the shrubs, the silhouette of a house rose to view; black, low, and rather long; but the guiding light shone nowhere. All was obscurity. Were the inmates retired to rest? I feared it must be so. In seeking the door, I turned an angle: there shot out the friendly gleam again, from the lozenged panes of a very small latticed window, within a foot of the ground; made still smaller by the growth of ivy or some other creeping plant, whose leaves clustered thick over the portion of the house wall in which it was set. The aperture was so screened and narrow that curtain or shutter had been deemed unnecessary; and when I stooped down and put aside the spray of foliage shooting over it, I could see all within. I could see clearly a room with a sanded floor, clean scoured; a dresser of walnut, with pewter plates ranged in rows, reflecting the redness and radiance of a glowing peat-fire. I could see a clock, a white deal table, some chairs. The candle, whose ray had been my beacon, burnt on the table; and by its light an elderly woman, somewhat rough-looking, but scrupulously clean, like all about her, was knitting a stocking.

I noticed these objects cursorily only—in them there was nothing extraordinary. A group of more interest appeared near the hearth, sitting still amidst the rosy peace and warmth suffusing it. Two young, graceful women—ladies in every point—sat, one in a low rocking-chair, the other on a lower stool; both wore deep mourning of crape and bombazeen, which sombre garb singularly set off very fair necks and faces: a large old pointer dog rested its massive head on the knee of one girl—in the lap of the other was cushioned a black cat.

A strange place was this humble kitchen for such occupants! Who were they? They could not be the daughters of the elderly person at the table; for

she looked like a rustic, and they were all delicacy and cultivation. I had nowhere seen such faces as theirs: and yet, as I gazed on them, I seemed intimate with every lineament. I cannot call them handsome—they were too pale and grave for the word: as they each bent over a book, they looked thoughtful almost to severity. A stand between them supported a second candle and two great volumes, to which they frequently referred; comparing them seemingly with the smaller books they held in their hands, like people consulting a dictionary to aid them in the task of translation. This scene was as silent as if all the figures had been shadows, and the fire-lit apartment a picture: so hushed was it, I could hear the cinders fall from the grate, the clock tick in its obscure corner; and I even fancied I could distinguish the click-click of the woman's knitting-needles. When, therefore, a voice broke the strange stillness at last, it was audible enough to me.

"Listen, Diana," said one of the absorbed students; "Franz and old Daniel are together in the night-time, and Franz is telling a dream from which he has awakened in terror—listen!" And in a low voice she read something, of which not one word was intelligible to me; for it was in an unknown tongue—neither French nor Latin. Whether it were Greek or German I could not tell.

"That is strong," she said, when she had finished: "I relish it." The other girl, who had lifted her head to listen to her sister, repeated, while she gazed at the fire, a line of what had been read. At a later day, I knew the language and the book; therefore I will here quote the line: though when I first heard it it was only like a stroke on sounding brass to me—conveying no meaning:— "'Da trat hervor Einer, anzusehen wie die Sternen Nacht.' Good! good!" she exclaimed, while her dark and deep eye sparkled. "There you have a dim and mighty archangel fitly set before you! The line is worth a hundred pages of fustian. 'Ich wäge die Gedanken in der Schale meines Zornes und die Werke mit dem Gewichte meines Grimms.'[1] I like it!"

Both were again silent.

"Is there ony country where they talk i' that way?" asked the old woman, looking up from her knitting.

"Yes, Hannah—a far larger country than England; where they talk in no other way."

"Well, for sure case, I knawn't how they can understand t' one t' other: and if either o' ye went there, ye could tell what they said, I guess?"

"We could probably tell something of what they said, but not all—for we are not as clever as you think us, Hannah. We don't speak German, and we cannot read it without a dictionary to help us."

"And what good does it do you?"

"We mean to teach it some time—or at least the elements, as they say; and then we shall get more money than we do now."

"Varry like: but give ower studying: ye've done enough for tonight."

"I think we have: at least I'm tired. Mary, are you?"

"Mortally: after all, it's tough work fagging away at a language with no master but a lexicon."

"It is: especially such a language as this crabbed but glorious Deutsch. I wonder when St. John will come home."

1. Then there stepped forth one, in appearance like the starry sky. . . . I weigh thoughts in the scale of my anger, and deeds with the weight of my wrath! From Johann von Schiller's *The Robbers* (1781) 5.1. "Fustian": pretentious writing.

"Surely he will not be long now: it is just ten" (looking at a little gold watch she drew from her girdle). "It rains fast. Hannah, will you have the goodness to look at the fire in the parlor?"

The woman rose: she opened a door, through which I dimly saw a passage: soon I heard her stir a fire in an inner room; she presently came back.

"Ah, childer!" said she, "it fair troubles me to go into yond' room now: it looks so lonesome wi' the chair empty and set back in a corner."

She wiped her eyes with her apron: the two girls, grave before, looked sad now.

"But he is in a better place," continued Hannah: "we shouldn't wish him here again. And then, nobody need to have a quieter death nor he had."

"You say he never mentioned us?" inquired one of the ladies.

"He hadn't time, bairn: he was gone in a minute—was your father. He had been a bit ailing like the day before, but naught to signify; and when Mr. St. John asked if he would like either o' ye to be sent for, he fair laughed at him. He began again with a bit of a heaviness in his head the next day—that is, a fortnight sin"—and he went to sleep and niver wakened: he wor' a'most stark when your brother went into t' chamber and fand him. Ah, childer! that's t' last o' t' old stock—for ye and Mr. St. John is like of a different soart to them 'at's gone; for all your mother wor mich i' your way; and a'most as book-learned. She wor the pictur' o' ye, Mary: Diana is more like your father."

I thought them so similar I could not tell where the old servant (for such I now concluded her to be) saw the difference. Both were fair complexioned and slenderly made; both possessed faces full of distinction and intelligence. One, to be sure, had hair a shade darker than the other, and there was a difference in their style of wearing it: Mary's pale brown locks were parted and braided smooth; Diana's duskier tresses covered her neck with thick curls. The clock struck ten.

"Ye'll want your supper, I am sure," observed Hannah; "and so will Mr. St. John when he comes in."

And she proceeded to prepare the meal. The ladies rose; they seemed about to withdraw to the parlor. Till this moment I had been so intent on watching them, their appearance and conversation had excited in me so keen an interest, I had half-forgotten my own wretched position: now it recurred to me. More desolate, more desperate than ever, it seemed from contrast. And how impossible did it appear to touch the inmates of this house with concern on my behalf; to make them believe in the truth of my wants and woes—to induce them to vouchsafe a rest for my wanderings! As I groped out the door, and knocked at it hesitatingly, I felt that last idea to be a mere chimera. Hannah opened.

"What do you want?" she inquired, in a voice of surprise, as she surveyed me by the light of the candle she held.

"May I speak to your mistresses?" I said.

"You had better tell me what you have to say to them. Where do you come from?"

"I am a stranger."

"What is your business here at this hour?"

"I want a night's shelter in an outhouse or anywhere, and a morsel of bread to eat."

Distrust, the very feeling I dreaded, appeared in Hannah's face. "I'll give

you a piece of bread,' she said, after a pause: "but we can't take in a vagrant to
lodge. It isn't likely."

"Do let me speak to your mistresses."

"No; not I. What can they do for you? You should not be roving about now;
it looks very ill."

"But where shall I go if you drive me away? What shall I do?"

"Oh, I'll warrant you know where to go, and what to do. Mind you don't do
wrong, that's all. Here is a penny; now go" ——

"A penny cannot feed me, and I have no strength to go farther. Don't shut
the door:—oh, don't, for God's sake!"

"I must; the rain is driving in" ——

"Tell the young ladies.—Let me see them" ——

"Indeed, I will not. You are not what you ought to be or you wouldn't make
such a noise. Move off."

"But I must die if I am turned away."

"Not you. I'm fear'd you have some ill plans agate,[2] that bring you about
folk's houses at this time o' night. If you've any followers—housebreakers or
such like—anywhere near, you may tell them we are not by ourselves in the
house; we have a gentleman, and dogs, and guns." Here the honest but inflex-
ible servant clapped the door to and bolted it within.

This was the climax. A pang of exquisite suffering—a throe of true de-
spair—rent and heaved my heart. Worn out, indeed, I was; not another step
could I stir. I sank on the wet door-step: I groaned—I wrung my hands—I wept
in utter anguish. Oh, this specter of death! Oh, this last hour, approaching in
such horror! Alas, this isolation—this banishment from my kind! Not only the
anchor of home, but the footing of fortitude was gone—at least for a moment:
but the last I soon endeavored to regain.

"I can but die," I said, "and I believe in God. Let me try to wait His will in
silence."

These words I not only thought, but uttered; and thrusting back all my mis-
ery into my heart, I made an effort to compel it to remain there—dumb and
still.

"All men must die," said a voice quite close at hand; "but all are not con-
demned to meet a lingering and premature doom, such as yours would be if
you perished here of want."

"Who or what speaks?" I asked, terrified at the unexpected sound, and in-
capable now of deriving from any occurrence a hope of aid. A form was near—
what form the pitch-dark night and my enfeebled vision prevented me from
distinguishing. With a loud long knock the new comer appealed to the door.

"Is it you, Mr. St. John?" cried Hannah.

"Yes—yes; open quickly."

"Well, how wet and cold you must be, such a wild night as it is! Come in—
your sisters are quite uneasy about you, and I believe there are bad folks about.
There has been a beggar-woman—I declare she is not gone yet!—laid down
there. Get up! for shame! Move off, I say!"

"Hush, Hannah! I have a word to say to the woman. You have done your
duty in excluding, now let me do mine in admitting her. I was near, and lis-

2. Under way (literally "on gate").

tened to both you and her. I think this is a peculiar case—I must at least examine into it. Young woman, rise, and pass before me into the house."

With difficulty I obeyed him. Presently I stood within that clean, bright kitchen—on the very hearth—trembling, sickening; conscious of an aspect in the last degree ghastly, wild and weatherbeaten. The two ladies, their brother, Mr. St. John, the old servant, were all gazing at me.

"St. John, who is it?" I heard one ask.

"I cannot tell: I found her at the door," was the reply.

"She does look white," said Hannah.

"As white as clay or death," was responded. "She will fall: let her sit."

And indeed my head swam: I dropped; but a chair received me. I still possessed my senses; though just now I could not speak.

"Perhaps a little water would restore her. Hannah, fetch some. But she is worn to nothing. How very thin, and how very bloodless!"

"A mere specter!"

"Is she ill, or only famished?"

"Famished, I think. Hannah, is that milk? Give it me, and a piece of bread."

Diana (I knew her by the long curls which I saw drooping between me and the fire as she bent over me) broke some bread, dipped it in milk, and put it to my lips. Her face was near mine: I saw there was pity in it, and I felt sympathy in her hurried breathing. In her simple words, too, the same balm-like emotion spoke: "Try to eat."

"Yes—try," repeated Mary gently; and Mary's hand removed my sodden bonnet and lifted my head. I tasted what they offered me: feebly at first, eagerly soon.

"Not too much at first—restrain her," said the brother; "she has had enough." And he withdrew the cup of milk and the plate of bread.

"A little more, St. John—look at the avidity in her eyes."

"No more at present, sister. Try if she can speak now—ask her her name."

I felt I could speak, and I answered—"My name is Jane Elliott." Anxious as ever to avoid discovery, I had before resolved to assume an *alias*.

"And where do you live? Where are your friends?"

I was silent.

"Can we send for any one you know?"

I shook my head.

"What account can you give of yourself?"

Somehow, now that I had once crossed the threshold of this house, and once was brought face to face with its owners, I felt no longer outcast, vagrant, and disowned by the wide world. I dared to put off the mendicant—to resume my natural manner and character. I began once more to know myself; and when Mr. St. John demanded an account—which at present I was far too weak to render—I said after a brief pause,—"Sir, I can give you no details tonight."

"But what, then," said he, "do you expect me to do for you?"

"Nothing," I replied. My strength sufficed for but short answers. Diana took the word:—

"Do you mean," she asked, "that we have now given you what aid you require? and that we may dismiss you to the moor and the rainy night?"

I looked at her. She had, I thought, a remarkable countenance; instinct both with power and goodness. I took sudden courage. Answering her compassionate gaze with a smile, I said: "I will trust you. If I were a masterless and stray dog, I know that you would not turn me from your hearth tonight: as it is, I

really have no fear. Do with me and for me as you like; but excuse me from much discourse—my breath is short—I feel a spasm when I speak." All three surveyed me, and all three were silent.

"Hannah," said Mr. St. John at last, "let her sit there at present, and ask her no questions; in ten minutes more, give her the remainder of that milk and bread. Mary and Diana, let us go into the parlor and talk the matter over."

They withdrew. Very soon one of the ladies returned—I could not tell which. A kind of pleasant stupor was stealing over me as I sat by the genial fire. In an undertone she gave some directions to Hannah. Ere long, with the servant's aid, I contrived to mount a staircase; my dripping clothes were removed; soon a warm, dry bed received me. I thanked God—experienced amid unutterable exhaustion a glow of grateful joy—and slept.

Chapter XXIX

The recollection of about three days and nights succeeding this is very dim in my mind. I can recall some sensations felt in that interval; but few thoughts framed, and no actions performed. I knew I was in a small room, and in a narrow bed. To that bed I seemed to have grown; I lay on it motionless as a stone; and to have torn me from it would have been almost to kill me. I took no note of the lapse of time—of the change from morning to noon, from noon to evening. I observed when any one entered or left the apartment; I could even tell who they were; I could understand what was said when the speaker stood near to me; but I could not answer; to open my lips or move my limbs was equally impossible. Hannah, the servant, was my most frequent visitor. Her coming disturbed me. I had a feeling that she wished me away: that she did not understand me or my circumstances: that she was prejudiced against me. Diana and Mary appeared in the chamber once or twice a day. They would whisper sentences of this sort at my bedside:—

"It is very well we took her in."

"Yes; she would certainly have been found dead at the door in the morning, had she been left out all night. I wonder what she has gone through?"

"Strange hardships, I imagine—poor, emaciated, pallid wanderer!"

"She is not an uneducated person, I should think, by her manner of speaking; her accent was quite pure; and the clothes she took off, though splashed and wet, were little worn and fine."

"She has a peculiar face; fleshless and haggard as it is, I rather like it; and when in good health and animated, I can fancy her physiognomy would be agreeable."

Never once in their dialogues did I hear a syllable of regret at the hospitality they had extended to me; or of suspicion of, or aversion to, myself. I was comforted.

Mr. St. John came but once: he looked at me, and said my state of lethargy was the result of reaction from excessive and protracted fatigue. He pronounced it needless to send for a doctor: nature, he was sure, would manage best left to herself. He said every nerve had been overstrained in some way, and the whole system must sleep torpid awhile. There was no disease. He imagined my recovery would be rapid enough when once commenced. These opinions he delivered in a few words, in a quiet, low voice; and added, after a pause, in the tone of a man little accustomed to expansive comment, "rather an unusual physiognomy; certainly not indicative of vulgarity or degradation."

"Far otherwise," responded Diana."To speak truth, St. John, my heart rather warms to the poor little soul. I wish we may be able to benefit her permanently."

"That is hardly likely," was the reply. "You will find she is some young lady who has had a misunderstanding with her friends and has probably injudiciously left them. We may, perhaps, succeed in restoring her to them, if she is not obstinate: but I trace lines of force in her face which make me sceptical of her tractability." He stood considering me some minutes; then added, "She looks sensible, but not at all handsome."

"She is so ill, St. John."

"Ill or well, she would always be plain. The grace and harmony of beauty are quite wanting in those features."

On the third day I was better; on the fourth, I could speak, move, rise in bed, and turn. Hannah had brought me some gruel and dry toast, about, as I supposed, the dinner hour. I had eaten with relish: the food was good—void of the feverish flavor which had hitherto poisoned what I had swallowed. When she left me, I felt comparatively strong and revived; ere long satiety of repose and desire for action stirred me. I wished to rise; but what could I put on? Only my damp and bemired apparel, in which I had slept on the ground and fallen in the marsh. I felt ashamed to appear before my benefactors so clad. I was spared the humiliation.

On a chair by the bedside were all my own things, clean and dry. My black silk frock hung against the wall. The traces of the bog were removed from it; the creases left by the wet smoothed out: it was quite decent. My very shoes and stockings were purified and rendered presentable. There were the means of washing in the room, and a comb and brush to smooth my hair. After a weary process, and resting every five minutes, I succeeded in dressing myself. My clothes hung loose on me, for I was much wasted; but I covered deficiencies with a shawl, and once more, clean and respectable-looking—no speck of the dirt, no trace of the disorder I so hated, and which seemed so to degrade me, left—I crept down a stone staircase with the aid of the banisters to a narrow low passage, and found my way presently to the kitchen.

It was full of the fragrance of new bread and the warmth of a generous fire. Hannah was baking. Prejudices, it is well known, are most difficult to eradicate from the heart whose soil has never been loosened or fertilized by education: they grow there, firm as weeds among stones. Hannah had been cold and stiff, indeed, at the first: latterly she had begun to relent a little; and when she saw me come in tidy and well-dressed, she even smiled.

"What, you have got up?" she said. "You are better, then. You may sit you down in my chair on the hearthstone, if you will."

She pointed to the rocking-chair: I took it. She bustled about, examining me every now and then with the corner of her eye. Turning to me, as she took some loaves from the oven, she asked, bluntly—"Did you ever go a-begging afore you came here?"

I was indignant for a moment; but remembering that anger was out of the question, and that I had indeed appeared as a beggar to her, I answered quietly, but still not without a certain marked firmness—"You are mistaken in supposing me a beggar. I am no beggar: any more than yourself or your young ladies."

After a pause, she said, "I dunnut understand that: you've like no house, nor no brass, I guess?"

"The want of house or brass (by which I suppose you mean money) does not make a beggar in your sense of the word."

"Are you book-learned?" she inquired, presently.

"Yes, very."

"But you've never been to a boarding-school!"

"I was at a boarding-school eight years."

She opened her eyes wide.

"Whatever cannot ye keep yourself for, then?"

"I have kept myself; and, I trust, shall keep myself again. What are you going to do with these gooseberries?" I inquired, as she brought out a basket of the fruit.

"Mak'em into pies."

"Give them to me and I'll pick them."

"Nay; I dunnut want ye to do nought."

"But I must do something. Let me have them."

She consented; and she even brought me a clean towel to spread over my dress, "lest," as she said, "I should mucky it."

"Ye've not been used to a sarvant's wark, I see by your hands," she remarked. "Happen ye've been a cressmaker."

"No, you are wrong. And, now, never mind what I have been: don't trouble your head further about me; but tell me the name of the house where we are."

"Some calls it Marsh End, and some calls it Moor House."

"And the gentleman who lives here is called Mr. St. John?"

"Nay; he doesn't live here: he is only staying a while. When he is at home, he in his own parish at Morton."

"That village a few miles off?"

"Aye."

"And what is he?"

"He is a parson."

I remembered the answer of the old housekeeper at the parsonage, when I had asked to see the clergyman. "This, then, was his father's residence?"

"Aye; old Mr. Rivers lived here, and his father, and grandfather, and gurt (great) grandfather afore him."

"The name, then, of that gentleman is Mr. St. John Rivers?"

"Aye; St. John is like his kirstened name."

"And his sisters are called Diana and Mary Rivers?"

"Yes."

"Their father is dead?"

"Dead three weeks sin' of a stroke."

"They have no mother?"

"The mistress has been dead this mony a year."

"Have you lived with the family long?"

"I've lived here thirty year. I nursed them all three."

"That proves you must have been an honest and faithful servant. I will say so much for you, though you have had the incivility to call me a beggar."

She again regarded me with a surprised stare. "I believe," she said, "I was quite mista'en in my thoughts of you: but there is so mony cheats goes about, you mun forgie me."

"And though," I continued, rather severely "you wished to turn me from the door, on a night when you should not have shut out a dog."

"Well, it was hard: but what can a body do? I thought more o' th' childer nor of mysel': poor things! They've like nobody to tak' care on 'em but me. I'm like to look sharpish."

I maintained a grave silence for some minutes.

"You munnut think too hardly of me," she again remarked.

"But I do think hardly of you," I said; "and I'll tell you why—not so much because you refused to give me shelter, or regarded me as an impostor, as because you just now made it a species of reproach that I had no 'brass,' and no house. Some of the best people that ever lived have been as destitute as I am; and if you are a Christian, you ought not to consider poverty a crime."

"No more I ought," said she: "Mr. St. John tells me so too; and I see I wor wrang—but I've clear a different notion on you now to what I had. You look a raight down dacent little crater."

"That will do—I forgive you now. Shake hands."

She put her floury and horny hand into mine: another and heartier smile illumined her rough face: and from that moment we were friends.

Hannah was evidently fond of talking. While I picked the fruit and she made the paste for the pies, she proceeded to give me sundry details about her deceased master and mistress, and "the childer," as she called the young people.

Old Mr. Rivers, she said, was a plain man enough; but a gentleman, and of as ancient a family as could be found. Marsh End had belonged to the Rivers' ever since it was a house: and it was, she affirmed, "aboon two hundred year old—for all it looked but a small, humble place, naught to compare wi' Mr. Oliver's grand hall down i' Morton Vale. But she could remember Bill Oliver's father a journeyman needle-maker; and th' Rivers' wor gentry i' thi' owd days o' th' Henrys, as onybody might see by looking into th' registers i' Morton Church vestry." Still, she allowed, "the owd maister was like other folk—naught mich out o' t' common way: stark mad o' shooting, and farming, and sich like." The mistress was different. She was a great reader, and studied a deal; and the "bairns" had taken after her. There was nothing like them in these parts, nor ever had been; they had liked learning, all three, almost from the time they could speak; and they had always been "of a mak' of their own." Mr. St. John, when he grew up, would go to college and be a parson; and the girls, as soon as they left school, would seek places as governesses: for they had told her their father had some years ago lost a great deal of money by a man he had trusted turning bankrupt; and as he was now not rich enough to give them fortunes, they must provide for themselves. They had lived very little at home for a long while, and were only come now to stay a few weeks on account of their father's death: but they did so like Marsh End and Morton, and all these moors and hills about. They had been in London, and many other grand towns; but they always said there was no place like home; and then they were so agreeable with each other—never fell out nor "threaped."[3] She did not know where there was such a family for being united.

Having finished my task of gooseberry picking, I asked where the two ladies and their brother were now.

"Gone over to Morton for a walk; but they would be back in half an hour to tea."

They returned within the time Hannah had allotted them: they entered by

3. Quarreled.

the kitchen door. Mr. St. John, when he saw me, merely bowed and passed through; the two ladies stopped: Mary, in a few words, kindly and calmly expressed the pleasure she felt in seeing me well enough to be able to come down; Diana took my hand: she shook her head at me.

"You should have waited for my leave to descend," she said. "You still look very pale—and so thin! Poor child!—poor girl."

Diana had a voice toned, to my ear, like the cooing of a dove. She possessed eyes whose gaze I delighted to encounter. Her whole face seemed to me full of charm. Mary's countenance was equally intelligent—her features equally pretty: but her expression was more reserved; and her manners, though gentle, more distant. Diana looked and spoke with a certain authority: she had a will, evidently. It was my nature to feel pleasure in yielding to an authority supported like hers: and to bend, where my conscience and self-respect permitted, to an active will.

"And what business have you here?" she continued. "It is not your place. Mary and I sit in the kitchen sometimes, because at home we like to be free, even to licence—but you are a visitor, and must go into the parlor."

"I am very well here."

"Not at all—with Hannah bustling about and covering you with flour."

"Besides, the fire is too hot for you," interposed Mary.

"To be sure," added her sister. "Come, you must be obedient." And still holding my hand, she made me rise, and led me into the inner room.

"Sit there," she said, placing me on the sofa, "while we take our things off and get the tea ready; it is another privilege we exercise in our little moorland home—to prepare our own meals when we are so inclined; or when Hannah is baking, brewing, washing, or ironing."

She closed the door, leaving me solus with Mr. St. John, who sat opposite, a book or newspaper in his hand. I examined, first, the parlor, and then its occupant.

The parlor was rather a small room, very plainly furnished; yet comfortable, because clean and neat. The old-fashioned chairs were very bright, and the walnut-wood table was like a looking-glass. A few strange antique portraits of the men and women of other days decorated the stained walls; a cupboard with glass doors contained some books and an ancient set of china. There was no superfluous ornament in the room—not one modern piece of furniture, save a brace of work-boxes and a lady's desk in rosewood, which stood on a side-table: everything—including the carpet and curtains—looked at once well worn and well saved.

Mr. St. John—sitting as still as one of the dusky pictures on the walls, keeping his eyes fixed on the page he perused and his lips mutely sealed, was easy enough to examine. Had he been a statue instead of a man, he could not have been easier. He was young—perhaps from twenty-eight to thirty—tall, slender; his face riveted the eye; it was like a Greek face, very pure in outline: quite a straight, classic nose; quite an Athenian mouth and chin. It is seldom, indeed, an English face comes so near the antique models as did his. He might well be a little shocked at the irregularity of my lineaments, his own being so harmonious. His eyes were large and blue, with brown lashes; his high forehead, colorless as ivory, was partially streaked over by careless locks of fair hair.

This is a gentle delineation, is it not, reader? Yet he whom it describes scarcely impressed one with the idea of a gentle, a yielding, an impressible, or even of a placid nature. Quiescent as he now sat, there was something about

his nostril, his mouth, his brow, which, to my perceptions, indicated elements within either restless, or hard, or eager. He did not speak to me one word, nor even direct to me one glance, till his sisters returned. Diana, as she passed in and out in the course of preparing tea, brought me a little cake, baked on the top of the oven.

"Eat that now," she said: "you must be hungry. Hannah says you have had nothing but some gruel since breakfast."

I did not refuse it, for my appetite was awakened and keen. Mr. Rivers now closed his book, approached the table, and, as he took a seat, fixed his blue pictorial-looking eyes full on me. There was an unceremonious directness, a searching, decided steadfastness in his gaze now, which told that intention, and not diffidence, had hitherto kept it averted from the stranger.

"You are very hungry," he said.

"I am, sir." It is my way—it always was my way, by instinct—ever to meet the brief with brevity, the direct with plainness.

"It is well for you that a low fever has forced you to abstain for the last three days: there would have been danger in yielding to the cravings of your appetite at first. Now you may eat; though still not immoderately."

"I trust I shall not eat long at your expense, sir," was my very clumsily-contrived, unpolished answer.

"No," he said coolly: "when you have indicated to us the residence of your friends, we can write to them, and you may be restored to home."

"That, I must plainly tell you, is out of my power to do; being absolutely without home and friends."

The three looked at me, but not distrustfully; I felt there was no suspicion in their glances: there was more of curiosity. I speak particularly of the young ladies. St. John's eyes, though clear enough in a literal sense, in a figurative one were difficult to fathom. He seemed to use them rather as instruments to search other people's thoughts, than as agents to reveal his own: the which combination of keenness and reserve was considerably more calculated to embarrass than to encourage.

"Do you mean to say," he asked, "that you are completely isolated from every connection?"

"I do. Not a tie links me to any living thing: not a claim do I possess to admittance under any roof in England."

"A most singular position at your age!"

Here I saw his glance directed to my hands, which were folded on the table before me. I wondered what he sought there: his words soon explained the quest.

"You have never been married? You are a spinster?"

Diana laughed.

"Why, she can't be above seventeen or eighteen years old, St. John," said she.

"I am near nineteen: but I am not married. No."

I felt a burning glow mount to my face; for bitter and agitating recollections were awakened by the allusion to marriage. They all saw the embarrassment and the emotion. Diana and Mary relieved me by turning their eyes elsewhere than to my crimsoned visage; but the colder and sterner brother continued to gaze, till the trouble he had excited forced out tears as well as color.

"Where did you last reside?" he now asked.

"You are too inquisitive, St. John," murmured Mary, in a low voice; but he

leaned over the table and required an answer by a second firm and piercing look.

"The name of the place where, and of the person with whom I lived, is my secret," I replied, concisely.

"Which, if you like, you have, in my opinion, a right to keep both from St. John and every other questioner," remarked Diana.

"Yet if I know nothing about you or your history, I cannot help you," he said. "And you need help: do you not?"

"I need it, and I seek it; so far, sir, that some true philanthropist will put me in the way of getting work which I can do, and the remuneration for which will keep me: if but in the barest necessaries of life."

"I know not whether I am a true philanthropist; yet I am willing to aid you to the utmost of my power, in a purpose so honest. First, then, tell me what you have been accustomed to do, and what you *can* do."

I had now swallowed my tea. I was mightily refreshed by the beverage; as much so as a giant with wine: it gave new tone to my unstrung nerves, and enabled me to address this penetrating young judge steadily.

"Mr. Rivers," I said, turning to him, and looking at him, as he looked at me, openly and without diffidence, "you and your sisters have done me a great service—the greatest man can do his fellow-being; you have rescued me, by your noble hospitality, from death. This benefit conferred gives you an unlimited claim on my gratitude; and a claim, to a certain extent, on my confidence. I will tell you as much of the history of the wanderer you have harbored as I can tell without compromising my own peace of mind—my own security, moral and physical, and that of others.

"I am an orphan; the daughter of a clergyman. My parents died before I could know them. I was brought up a dependent; educated in a charitable institution. I will even tell you the name of the establishment where I passed six years as a pupil and two as a teacher—Lowood Orphan Asylum,——shire: you will have heard of it, Mr. Rivers?—the Rev. Robert Brocklehurst is the treasurer."

"I have heard of Mr. Brocklehurst, and I have seen the school."

"I left Lowood nearly a year since to become a private governess. I obtained a good situation, and was happy. This place I was obliged to leave four days before I came here. The reason of my departure I cannot and ought not to explain: it would be useless—dangerous; and would sound incredible. No blame attached to me; I am as free from culpability as any one of you three. Miserable I am, and must be for a time; for the catastrophe which drove me from a house I had found a paradise was of a strange and direful nature. I observed but two points in planning my departure—speed, secrecy: to secure these I had to leave behind me everything I possessed except a small parcel; which, in my hurry and trouble of mind, I forgot to take out of the coach that brought me to Whitcross. To this neighborhood, then, I came, quite destitute. I slept two nights in the open air, and wandered about two days without crossing a threshold: but twice in that space of time did I taste food; and it was when brought by hunger, exhaustion and despair almost to the last gasp that you, Mr. Rivers, forbade me to perish of want at your door, and took me under the shelter of your roof. I know all your sisters have done for me since—for I have not been insensible during my seeming torpor—and I owe to their spontaneous, genuine, genial compassion, as large a debt as to your evangelical charity."

"Don't make her talk any more now, St. John," said Diana, as I paused; "she is evidently not yet fit for excitement. Come to the sofa, and sit down now, Miss Elliott."

I gave an involuntary half-start at hearing the alias; I had forgotten my new name. Mr. Rivers, whom nothing seemed to escape, noticed it at once.

"You said your name was Jane Elliott?" he observed.

"I did say so; and it is the name by which I think it expedient to be called at present: but it is not my real name, and when I hear it, it sounds strange to me."

"Your real name you will not give?"

"No: I fear discovery above all things; and whatever disclosure would lead to it, I avoid."

"You are quite right, I am sure," said Diana. "Now do, brother, let her be at peace a while."

But when St. John had mused a few moments, he recommenced, as imperturbably, and with as much acumen as ever.

"You would not like to be long dependent on our hospitality—you would wish, I see, to dispense as soon as may be with my sisters' compassion; and, above all, with my *charity* (I am quite sensible of the distinction drawn, nor do I resent it—it is just): you desire to be independent of us?"

"I do: I have already said so. Show me how to work, or how to seek work: that is all I now ask; then let me go, if it be but to the meanest cottage—but *till then* allow me to stay here: I dread another essay of the horrors of homeless destitution."

"Indeed, you *shall* stay here," said Diana, putting her white hand on my head.

"You *shall*," repeated Mary, in the tone of undemonstrative sincerity which seemed natural to her.

"My sisters, you see, have a pleasure in keeping you," said Mr. St. John, "as they would have a pleasure in keeping and cherishing a half-frozen bird some wintry wind might have driven through their casement. I feel more inclination to put you in the way of keeping yourself: and shall endeavor to do so: but observe, my sphere is narrow. I am but the incumbent of a poor country parish: my aid must be of the humblest sort. And if you are inclined to despise the day of small things, seek some more efficient succour than such as I can offer."

"She has already said that she is willing to do anything honest she *can* do," answered Diana for me; "and you know, St. John, she has no choice of helpers: she is forced to put up with such crusty people as you."

"I will be a dressmaker: I will be a plain-work-woman; I will be a servant, a nurse-girl, if I can be no better," I answered.

"Right," said Mr. St. John, quite coolly. "If such is your spirit, I promise to aid you; in my own time and way."

He now resumed the book with which he had been occupied before tea. I soon withdrew; for I had talked as much, and sat up as long, as my present strength would permit.

Chapter XXX

The more I knew of the inmates of Moor House, the better I liked them. In a few days I had so far recovered my health that I could sit up all day, and walk

out sometimes. I could join with Diana and Mary in all their occupations; con-
verse with them as much as they wished, and aid them when and where they
would allow me. There was a reviving pleasure in this intercourse, of a kind
now tasted by me for the first time—the pleasure arising from perfect conge-
niality of tastes, sentiments, and principles.

I liked to read what they liked to read: what they enjoyed, delighted me;
what they approved, I reverenced. They loved their sequestered home. I, too,
in the gray, small, antique structure, with its low roof, its latticed casements,
its moldering walls, its avenue of aged firs—all grown aslant under the stress of
mountain winds; its garden, dark with yew and holly—and where no flowers
but of the hardiest species would bloom—found a charm both potent and
permanent. They clung to the purple moors behind and around their
dwelling—to the hollow vale into which the pebbly bridle-path leading from
their gate descended; and which wound between fern-banks first, and then
amongst a few of the wildest little pasture-fields that ever bordered a wilder-
ness of heath, or gave sustenance to a flock of gray moorland sheep, with their
little mossy-faced lambs:—they clung to this scene, I say, with a perfect en-
thusiasm of attachment. I could comprehend the feeling, and share both its
strength and truth. I saw the fascination of the locality. I felt the consecration
of its loneliness: my eye feasted on the outline of swell and sweep—on the
wild coloring communicated to ridge and dell by moss, by heath-bell, by
flower-sprinkled turf, by brilliant bracken and mellow granite crag. These de-
tails were just to me what they were to them—so many pure and sweet sources
of pleasure. The strong blast and the soft breeze; the rough and the halcyon
day; the hours of sunrise and sunset; the moonlight and the clouded night, de-
veloped for me, in these regions, the same attraction as for them—wound
round my faculties the same spell that entranced theirs.

Indoors we agreed equally well. They were both more accomplished and
better read than I was: but with eagerness I followed in the path of knowledge
they had trodden before me. I devoured the books they lent me: then it was
full satisfaction to discuss with them in the evening what I had perused during
the day. Thought fitted thought; opinion met opinion: we coincided, in short,
perfectly.

If in our trio there was a superior and a leader, it was Diana. Physically, she
far excelled me: she was handsome; she was vigorous. In her animal spirits
there was an affluence of life and certainty of flow, such as excited my wonder,
while it baffled my comprehension. I could talk a while when the evening
commenced: but the first gush of vivacity and fluency gone, I was fain to sit on
a stool at Diana's feet, to rest my head on her knee, and listen alternately to
her and Mary; while they sounded thoroughly the topic on which I had but
touched. Diana offered to teach me German. I liked to learn of her: I saw the
part of instructress pleased and suited her; that of scholar pleased and suited
me no less. Our natures dovetailed: mutual affection—of the strongest
kind—was the result. They discovered I could draw: their pencils and color-
boxes were immediately at my service. My skill, greater in this one point than
theirs, surprised and charmed them. Mary would sit and watch me by the hour
together: then she would take lessons; and a docile, intelligent, assiduous
pupil she made. Thus occupied, and mutually entertained, days passed like
hours and weeks like days.

As to Mr. St. John, the intimacy which had arisen so naturally and rapidly

between me and his sisters did not extend to him. One reason of the distance yet observed between us was that he was comparatively seldom at home: a large proportion of his time appeared devoted to visiting the sick and poor among the scattered population of his parish.

No weather seemed to hinder him in these pastoral excursions: rain or fair, he would, when his hours of morning study were over, take his hat, and, followed by his father's old pointer Carlo, go out on his mission of love or duty— I scarcely know in which light he regarded it. Sometimes, when the day was very unfavourable, his sisters would expostulate. He would then say, with a peculiar smile, more solemn than cheerful,—"And if I let a gust of wind or a sprinkling of rain turn me aside from these easy tasks, what preparation would such sloth be for the future I propose to myself?"

Diana and Mary's general answer to this question was a sigh, and some minutes of apparently mournful meditation.

But besides his frequent absences, there was another barrier to friendship with him: he seemed of a reserved, an abstracted, and even of a brooding nature. Zealous in his ministerial labors, blameless in his life and habits, he yet did not appear to enjoy that mental serenity, that inward content, which should be the reward of every sincere Christian and practical philanthropist. Often, of an evening, when he sat at the window, his desk and papers before him, he would cease reading or writing, rest his chin on his hand, and deliver himself up to I know not what course of thought; but that it was perturbed and exciting might be seen in the frequent flash and changeful dilation of his eye.

I think, moreover, that Nature was not to him that treasury of delight it was to his sisters. He expressed once, and but once in my hearing, a strong sense of the rugged charm of the hills, and an inborn affection for the dark roof and hoary walls he called his home; but there was more of gloom than pleasure in the tone and words in which the sentiment was manifested; and never did he seem to roam the moors for the sake of their soothing silence—never seek out or dwell upon the thousand peaceful delights they could yield.

Incommunicative as he was, some time elapsed before I had an opportunity of gauging his mind. I first got an idea of its caliber when I heard him preach in his own church at Morton. I wish I could describe that sermon; but it is past my power. I cannot even render faithfully the effect it produced on me.

It began calm—and indeed, as far as delivery and pitch of voice went, it was calm to the end: an earnestly felt, yet strictly restrained zeal breathed soon in the distinct accents, and prompted the nervous language. This grew to force—compressed, condensed, controlled. The heart was thrilled, the mind astonished, by the power of the preacher: neither was softened. Throughout there was a strange bitterness; an absence of consolatory gentleness; stern allusions to Calvinistic doctrines—election, predestination, reprobation—were frequent; and each reference to these points sounded like a sentence pronounced for doom. When he had done, instead of feeling better, calmer, more enlightened by his discourse, I experienced an inexpressible sadness; for it seemed to me—I know not whether equally so to others—that the eloquence to which I had been listening had sprung from a depth where lay turbid dregs of disappointment—where moved troubling impulses of insatiate yearnings and disquieting aspirations. I was sure St. John Rivers—pure-lived, conscientious, zealous as he was—had not yet found that peace of God which passeth

all understanding;[4] he had no more found it, I thought, then had I; with my concealed and racking regrets for my broken idol and lost elysium[5]—regrets to which I have latterly avoided referring; but which possessed me and tyrannized over me ruthlessly.

Meantime a month was gone. Diana and Mary were soon to leave Moor House, and return to the far different life and scene which awaited them, as governesses in a large, fashionable, south-of-England city, where each held a situation in families, by whose wealthy and haughty members they were regarded only as humble dependents, and who neither knew nor sought one of their innate excellences, and appreciated only their acquired accomplishments as they appreciated the skill of their cook or the taste of their waiting-woman. Mr. St. John had said nothing to me yet about the employment he had promised to obtain for me; yet it became urgent that I should have a vocation of some kind. One morning, being left alone with him a few minutes in the parlor, I ventured to approach the window-recess—which his table, chair, and desk consecrated as a kind of study—and I was going to speak; though not very well knowing in what words to frame my inquiry—for it is at all times difficult to break the ice of reserve glassing over such natures as his—when he saved me the trouble by being the first to commence a dialogue.

Looking up as I drew near— "You have a question to ask of me?" he said.

"Yes; I wish to know whether you have heard of any service I can offer myself to undertake."

"I found or devised something for you three weeks ago; but as you seemed both useful and happy here—as my sisters had evidently become attached to you, and your society gave them unusual pleasure—I deemed it inexpedient to break in on your mutual comfort till their approaching departure from Marsh End should render yours necessary."

"And they will go in three days now?" I said.

"Yes; and when they go I shall return to the parsonage at Morton: Hannah will accompany me; and this old house will be shut up."

I waited for a few moments, expecting he would go on with the subject first broached; but he seemed to have entered another train of reflection; his look denoted abstraction from me and my business. I was obliged to recall him to a theme which was of necessity one of close and anxious interest to me.

"What is the employment you had in view, Mr. Rivers? I hope this delay will not have increased the difficulty of securing it."

"Oh, no; since it is an employment which depends only on me to give, and you to accept."

He again paused: there seemed a reluctance to continue. I grew impatient: a restless movement or two, and an eager and exacting glance fastened on his face, conveyed the feeling to him as effectually as words could have done, and with less trouble.

"You need be in no hurry to hear," he said; "let me frankly tell you, I have nothing eligible or profitable to suggest. Before I explain, recall, if you please, my notice, clearly given, that if I helped you, it must be as the blind man would help the lame. I am poor; for I find that, when I have paid my father's debts, all the patrimony remaining to me will be this crumbling grange, the row of scathed firs behind, and the patch of moorish soil, with the yew-trees

4. Philippians 4:7. 5. I.e., paradise.

and holly-bushes in front. I am obscure: Rivers is an old name; but of the three sole descendants of the race, two earn the dependent's crust among strangers, and the third considers himself an alien from his native country—not only for life, but in death. Yes, and deems, and is bound to deem, himself honored by the lot, and aspires but after the day when the cross of separation from fleshly ties shall be laid on his shoulders, and when the Head of that church-militant, of whose humblest members he is one, shall give the word, 'Rise, follow Me!' "

St. John said these words as he pronounced his sermons, with a quiet, deep voice; with an unflushed cheek, and a coruscating radiance of glance. He resumed:— "And since I am myself poor and obscure, I can offer you but a service of poverty and obscurity. You may even think it degrading—for I see now your habits have been what the world calls refined: your tastes lean to the ideal; and your society has at least been amongst the educated—but I consider that no service degrades which can better our race. I hold that the more arid and unreclaimed the soil where the Christian laborer's task of tillage is appointed him—the scantier the meed his toil brings—the higher the honor. His, under such circumstances, is the destiny of the pioneer; and the first pioneers of the Gospel were the Apostles—their captain was Jesus, the Redeemer, Himself."

"Well?" I said, as he again paused—"proceed."

He looked at me before he proceeded: indeed, he seemed leisurely to read my face, as if its features and lines were characters on a page. The conclusions drawn from this scrutiny he partially expressed in his succeeding observations.

"I believe you will accept the post I offer you," said he; "and hold it for a while: not permanently, though: any more than I could permanently keep the narrow and narrowing—the tranquil, hidden office of English country incumbent: for in your nature is an alloy as detrimental to repose as that in mine; though of a different kind."

"Do explain," I urged, when he halted once more.

"I will; and you shall hear how poor the proposal is,—how trivial—how cramping. I shall not stay long at Morton, now that my father is dead, and that I am my own master. I shall leave the place probably in the course of a twelve-month: but while I do stay I will exert myself to the utmost for its improvement. Morton, when I came to it two years ago, had no school: the children of the poor were excluded from every hope of progress. I established one for boys: I mean now to open a second school for girls. I have hired a building for the purpose, with a cottage of two rooms attached to it for the mistress's house. Her salary will be thirty pounds a year; her house is already furnished, very simply, but sufficiently, by the kindness of a lady, Miss Oliver; the only daughter of the sole rich man in my parish—Mr. Oliver, the proprietor of a needle-factory and iron-foundry in the valley. The same lady pays for the education and clothing of an orphan from the workhouse; on condition that she shall aid the mistress in such menial offices connected with her own house and the school as her occupation of teaching will prevent her having time to discharge in person. Will you be this mistress?"

He put the question rather hurriedly; he seemed half to expect an indignant, or at least a disdainful, rejection of the offer: not knowing all my thoughts and feelings, though guessing some, he could not tell in what light the lot would appear to me. In truth it was humble—but then it was sheltered, and I wanted a safe asylum: it was plodding—but then, compared with that of

a governess in a rich house, it was independent; and the fear of servitude with strangers entered my soul like iron: it was not ignoble—not unworthy—not mentally degrading. I made my decision.

"I thank you for the proposal, Mr. Rivers; and I accept it with all my heart."

"But you comprehend me?" he said. "It is a village school: your scholars will be only poor girls—cottagers' children—at the best, farmers' daughters. Knitting, sewing, reading, writing, cyphering, will be all you will have to teach. What will you do with your accomplishments? What with the largest portion of your mind—sentiments—tastes?"

"Save them till they are wanted. They will keep."

"You know what you undertake; then?"

"I do."

He now smiled: and not a bitter or a sad smile, but one well pleased and deeply gratified.

"And when will you commence the exercise of your function?"

"I will go to my house tomorrow; and open the school, if you like, next week."

"Very well: so be it."

He rose and walked through the room. Standing still, he again looked at me. He shook his head.

"What do you disapprove of, Mr. Rivers?" I asked.

"You will not stay at Morton long: no, no!"

"Why! What is your reason for saying so?"

"I read it in your eye; it is not of that description which promises the maintenance of an even tenor in life."

"I am not ambitious."

He started at the word "ambitious." He repeated, "No. What made you think of ambition? Who is ambitious? I know I am: but how did you find it out?"

"I was speaking of myself."

"Well, if you are not ambitious, you are"——He paused.

"What?"

"I was going to say, impassioned: but perhaps you would have misunderstood the word, and been displeased. I mean, that human affections and sympathies have a most powerful hold on you. I am sure you cannot long be content to pass your leisure in solitude, and to devote your working hours to a monotonous labor wholly void of stimulus; any more than I can be content," he added, with emphasis, "to live here buried in morass, pent in with mountain—my nature, that God gave me, contravened; my faculties, heaven-bestowed, paralyzed—made useless. You hear now how I contradict myself. I, who preached contentment with a humble lot, and justified the vocation even of hewers of wood, and drawers of water, in God's service—I, His ordained minister, almost rave in my restlessness. Well, propensities and principles must be reconciled by some means."

He left the room. In this brief hour I had learnt more of him than in the whole previous month: yet still he puzzled me.

Diana and Mary Rivers became more sad and silent as the day approached for leaving their brother and their home. They both tried to appear as usual; but the sorrow they had to struggle against was one that could not be entirely conquered or concealed. Diana intimated that this would be a different part-

ing from any they had ever yet known. It would probably, as far as St. John was concerned, be a parting for years: it might be a parting for life.

"He will sacrifice all to his long-framed resolves," she said: "natural affection and feelings more potent still. St. John looks quiet, Jane; but he hides a fever in his vitals. You would think him gentle, yet in some things he is inexorable as death; and the worst of it is, my conscience will hardly permit me to dissuade him from his severe decision: certainly, I cannot for a moment blame him for it. It is right, noble, Christian: yet it breaks my heart." And the tears gushed to her fine eyes. Mary bent her head low over her work.

"We are now without father: we shall soon be without home and brother," she murmured.

At that moment a little accident supervened which seemed decreed by fate purposely to prove the truth of the adage that "misfortunes never come singly": and to add to their distresses the vexing one of the slip between the cup and the lip. St. John passed the window reading a letter. He entered.

"Our uncle John is dead," said he.

Both the sisters seemed struck: not shocked or appalled; the tidings appeared in their eyes rather momentous than afflicting.

"Dead?" repeated Diana.

"Yes."

She riveted a searching gaze on her brother's face. "And what then?" she demanded, in a low voice.

"What then, Di?" he replied, maintaining a marble immobility of feature. "When then? Why—nothing. Read."

He threw the letter into her lap. She glanced over it, and handed it to Mary. Mary perused it in silence, and returned it to her brother. All three looked at each other, and all three smiled—a dreary, pensive smile enough.

"Amen! We can yet live," said Diana at last.

"At any rate, it makes us no worse off than we were before," remarked Mary.

"Only it forces rather strongly on the mind the picture of what *might have been*," said Mr. Rivers; "and contrasts it somewhat too vividly with what *is*."

He folded the letter, locked it in his desk, and again went out.

For some minutes no one spoke. Diana then turned to me.

"Jane, you will wonder at us and our mysteries," she said, "and think us hard-hearted beings not to be more moved at the death of so near a relation as an uncle; but we have never seen him or known him. He was my mother's brother. My father and he quarreled long ago. It was by his advice that my father risked most of his property in the speculation that ruined him. Mutual recrimination passed between them: they parted in anger, and were never reconciled. My uncle engaged afterwards in more prosperous undertakings: it appears he realized a fortune of twenty thousand pounds. He was never married, and had no near kindred but ourselves, and one other person, not more closely related than we. My father always cherished the idea that he would atone for his error by leaving his possessions to us: that letter informs us that he has bequeathed every penny to the other relation; with the exception of thirty guineas, to be divided between St. John, Diana, and Mary Rivers, for the purchase of three mourning rings. He had a right, of course, to do as he pleased: and yet a momentary damp is cast on the spirits by the receipt of such news. Mary and I would have esteemed ourselves rich with a thousand pounds each; and to St. John such a sum would have been valuable, for the good it would have enabled him to do."

This explanation given, the subject was dropped, and no further reference made to it, by either Mr. Rivers or his sisters. The next day I left Marsh End for Morton. The day after, Diana and Mary quitted it for distant B——. In a week, Mr. Rivers and Hannah repaired to the parsonage: and so the old grange was abandoned.

Chapter XXXI

My home, then,—when I at last find a home,—is a cottage: a little room with white-washed walls and a sanded floor; containing four painted chairs and a table, a clock, a cupboard, with two or three plates and dishes, and a set of tea-things in delf.[6] Above, a chamber of the same dimensions as the kitchen, with a deal bedstead and chest of drawers; small, yet too large to be filled with my scanty wardrobe: though the kindness of my gentle and generous friends has increased that by a modest stock of such things as are necessary.

It is evening. I have dismissed, with the fee of an orange, the little orphan who serves me as a handmaid. I am sitting alone on the hearth. This morning the village school opened. I had twenty scholars. But three of the number can read: none write or cypher. Several knit, and a few sew a little. They speak with the broadest accent of the district. At present they and I have a difficulty in understanding each other's language. Some of them are unmannered, rough, intractable, as well as ignorant; but others are docile, have a wish to learn, and evince a disposition that pleases me. I must not forget that these coarsely-clad little peasants are of flesh and blood as good as the scions of gentlest genealogy; and that the germs of native excellence, refinement, intelligence, kind feeling, are as likely to exist in their hearts as in those of the best-born. My duty will be to develop these germs: surely I shall find some happiness in discharging that office. Much enjoyment I do not expect in the life opening before me: yet it will, doubtless, if I regulate my mind, and exert my powers as I ought, yield me enough to live on from day to day.

Was I very gleeful, settled, content, during the hours I passed in yonder bare, humble schoolroom this morning and afternoon? Not to deceive myself, I must reply—No: I felt desolate to a degree. I felt—yes, idiot that I am—I felt degraded. I doubted I had taken a step which sank instead of raising me in the scale of social existence. I was weakly dismayed at the ignorance, the poverty, the coarseness of all I heard and saw round me. But let me not hate and despise myself too much for these feelings: I know them to be wrong—that is a great step gained; I shall strive to overcome them. Tomorrow, I trust, I shall get the better of them partially; and in a few weeks, perhaps, they will be quite subdued. In a few months, it is possible, the happiness of seeing progress, and a change for the better in my scholars, may substitute gratification for disgust.

Meantime, let me ask myself one question—Which is better?—To have surrendered to temptation; listened to passion; made no painful effort—no struggle;—but to have sunk down in the silken snare; fallen asleep on the flowers covering it; wakened in a southern clime, among the luxuries of a pleasure villa: to have been now living in France, Mr. Rochester's mistress; delirious with his love half my time—for he would—oh, yes, he would have loved me well for a while. He *did* love me—no one will ever love me so again. I shall never more know the sweet homage given to beauty, youth, and grace—for

6. I.e., delft, Dutch pottery.

never to anyone else shall I seem to possess these charms. He was fond and proud of me—it is what no man besides will ever be.—But where am I wondering, and what am I saying; and, above all, feeling? Whether is it better, I ask, to be a slave in a fool's paradise at Marseilles—fevered with delusive bliss one hour—suffocating with the bitterest tears of remorse and shame the next—or to be a village schoolmistress, free and honest, in a breezy mountain nook in the healthy heart of England?

Yes; I feel now that I was right when I adhered to principle and law, and scorned and crushed the insane promptings of a frenzied moment. God directed me to a correct choice: I thank His providence for the guidance.

Having brought my eventide musings to this point, I rose, went to my door, and looked at the sunset of the harvest-day, and at the quiet fields before my cottage; which, with the school, was distant half a mile from the village. The birds were singing their last strains—

"The air was mild; the dew was balm."[7]

While I looked, I thought myself happy, and was surprised to find myself ere long weeping—and why? For the doom which had reft me from adhesion to my master: for him I was no more to see; for the desperate grief and fatal fury—consequences of my departure—which might now, perhaps, be dragging him from the path of right, too far to leave hope of ultimate restoration thither. At this thought, I turned my face aside from the lovely sky of eve and lonely vale of Morton—I say *lonely*, for in that bend of it visible to me there was no building apparent save the church and the parsonage, half-hid in trees; and, quite at the extremity, the roof of Vale Hall, where the rich Mr. Oliver and his daughter lived. I hid my eyes, and leant my head against the stone frame of my door; but soon a slight noise near the wicket which shut in my tiny garden from the meadow beyond it made me look up. A dog—old Carlo, Mr. Rivers' pointer, as I saw in a moment—was pushing the gate with his nose, and St. John himself leaned upon it with folded arms; his brow knit, his gaze, grave almost to displeasure, fixed on me. I asked him to come in.

"No, I cannot stay; I have only brought you a little parcel my sisters left for you. I think it contains a color-box, pencils, and paper."

I approached to take it: a welcome gift it was. He examined my face, I thought, with austerity, as I came near: the traces of tears were doubtless very visible upon it.

"Have you found your first day's work harder than you expected?" he asked.

"Oh, no! On the contrary, I think in time I shall get on with my scholars very well."

"But perhaps your accommodations—your cottage—your furniture—have disappointed your expectations? They are, in truth, scanty enough; but——"

I interrupted:— "My cottage is clean and weather-proof; my furniture sufficient and commodious. All I see has made me thankful, not despondent. I am not absolutely such a fool and sensualist as to regret the absence of a carpet, a sofa, and silver plate: besides, five weeks ago I had nothing—I was an outcast, a beggar, a vagrant; now I have acquaintance, a home, a business. I wonder at the goodness of God; the generosity of my friends; the bounty of my lot. I do not repine."

7. From Sir Walter Scott's *The Lay of the Last Minstrel* 3.24.3–4.

"But you feel solitude an oppression? The little house there behind you is dark and empty."

"I have hardly had time yet to enjoy a sense of tranquillity, much less to grow impatient under one of loneliness."

"Very well; I hope you feel the content you express: at any rate, your good sense will tell you that it is too soon yet to yield to the vacillating fears of Lot's wife.[8] What you had left before I saw you, of course I do not know; but I counsel you to resist, firmly, every temptation which would incline you to look back: pursue your present career steadily, for some months at least."

"It is what I mean to do," I answered.

St. John continued:— "It is hard work to control the workings of inclination, and turn the bent of nature; but that it may be done I know from experience. God has given us, in a measure, the power to make our own fate; and when our energies seem to demand a sustenance they cannot get—when our will strains after a path we may not follow—we need neither starve from inanition, nor stand still in despair: we have but to seek another nourishment for the mind, as strong as the forbidden fruit it longed to taste—and perhaps purer; and to hew out for the adventurous foot a road as direct and broad as the one Fortune has blocked up against us, if rougher than it.

"A year ago I was myself intensely miserable, because I thought I had made a mistake in entering the ministry: its uniform duties wearied me to death. I burnt for the more active life of the world—for the more exciting toils of a literary career—for the destiny of an artist, author, orator; anything rather than that of a priest: yes, the heart of a politician, of a soldier, of a votary of glory, a lover of renown, a luster after power, beat under my curate's surplice. I considered; my life was so wretched, it must be changed, or I must die. After a season of darkness and struggling, light broke and relief fell: my cramped existence all at once spread out to a plain without bounds—my powers heard a call from heaven to rise, gather their full strength, spread their wings, and mount beyond ken. God had an errand for me; to bear which afar, to deliver it well, skill and strength, courage and eloquence, the best qualifications of soldier, statesman, and orator, were all needed: for these all center in the good missionary.

"A missionary I resolved to be. From that moment my state of mind changed; the fetters dissolved and dropped from every faculty, leaving nothing of bondage but its galling soreness—which time only can heal. My father, indeed, opposed the determination, but since his death I have not a legitimate obstacle to contend with; some affairs settled, a successor for Morton provided, an entanglement or two of the feelings broken through or cut asunder—a last conflict with human weakness, in which I know I shall overcome, because I have vowed that I *will* overcome—and I leave Europe for the East."

He said this in his peculiar, subdued, yet emphatic voice; looking, when he had ceased speaking, not at me, but at the setting sun, at which I looked too. Both he and I had our backs towards the path leading up the field to the wicket. We had heard no step on that grass-grown track; the water running in the vale was the one lulling sound of the hour and scene; we might well then start when a gay voice, sweet as a silver bell, exclaimed:— "Good evening, Mr. Rivers. And good evening, old Carlo. Your dog is quicker to recognize his

8. Fleeing the destruction of Sodom, Lot's wife looked backward and was turned into a pillar of salt (Genesis 19:24–26).

friends than you are, sir; he pricked his ears and wagged his tail when I was at the bottom of the field, and you have your back towards me now."

It was true. Though Mr. Rivers had started at the first of those musical accents, as if a thunderbolt had split a cloud over his head, he stood yet, at the close of the sentence, in the same attitude in which the speaker had surprised him—his arm resting on the gate, his face directed towards the west. He turned at last, with measured deliberation. A vision, as it seemed to me, had risen at his side. There appeared, within three feet of him, a form clad in pure white—a youthful, graceful form: full, yet fine in contour; and when, after bending to caress Carlo, it lifted up its head, and threw back a long veil, there bloomed under his glance a face of perfect beauty. Perfect beauty is a strong expression; but I do not retrace or qualify it: as sweet features as ever the temperate clime of Albion molded; as pure hues of rose and lily as ever her humid gales and vapory skies generated and screened justified, in this instance, the term. No charm was wanting, no defect was perceptible; the young girl had regular and delicate lineaments; eyes shaped and colored as we see them in lovely pictures, large, and dark, and full; the long and shadowy eyelash which encircles a fine eye with so soft a fascination; the penciled brow which gives such clearness; the white, smooth forehead which adds such repose to the livelier beauties of tint and ray; the cheek, oval, fresh, and smooth; the lips, fresh too, ruddy, healthy, sweetly formed; the even and gleaming teeth without flaw; the small dimpled chin; the ornament of rich, plenteous tresses—all advantages, in short, which, combined, realize the ideal of beauty were fully hers. I wondered, as I looked at this fair creature: I admired her with my whole heart. Nature had surely formed her in a partial mood; and, forgetting her usual stinted stepmother dole of gifts, had endowed this, her darling, with a granddame's bounty.

What did St. John Rivers think of this earthly angel? I naturally asked myself that question as I saw him turn to her and look at her; and, as naturally, I sought the answer to the inquiry in his countenance. He had already withdrawn his eye from the Peri,[9] and was looking at a humble tuft of daisies which grew by the wicket.

"A lovely evening, but late for you to be out alone," he said, as he crushed the snowy heads of the closed flowers with his foot.

"Oh, I only came home from S——" (she mentioned the name of a large town some twenty miles distant) "this afternoon. Papa told me you had opened your school, and that the new mistress was come; and so I put on my bonnet after tea, and ran up the valley to see her: this is she?" pointing to me.

"It is," said St. John.

"Do you think you shall like Morton?" she asked of me, with a direct and naïve simplicity of tone and manner, pleasing, if childlike.

"I hope I shall. I have many inducements to do so."

"Did you find your scholars as attentive as you expected?"

"Quite."

"Do you like your house?"

"Very much."

"Have I furnished it nicely?"

"Very nicely indeed."

9. Fairy, beautiful girl.

"And made a good choice of an attendant for you in Alice Wood?"

"You have, indeed. She is teachable and handy." (This, then, I thought, is Miss Oliver, the heiress, favored, it seems, in the gifts of fortune, as well as in those of nature! What happy combination of the planets presided over her birth, I wonder?)

"I shall come up and help you to teach sometimes," she added. "It will be a change for me to visit you now and then; and I like a change. Mr. Rivers, I have been so gay during my stay at S——. Last night, or rather this morning, I was dancing till two o'clock. The ——th regiment are stationed there since the riots; and the officers are the most agreeable men in the world: they put all our young knife-grinders and scissor merchants to shame."

It seemed to me that Mr. St. John's under lip protruded, and his upper lip curled a moment. His mouth certainly looked a good deal compressed, and the lower part of his face unusually stern and square, as the laughing girl gave him this information. He lifted his gaze, too, from the daisies, and turned it on her. An unsmiling, a searching, a meaning gaze it was. She answered it with a second laugh, and laughter well became her youth, her roses, her dimples, her bright eyes.

As he stood, mute and grave, she again fell to caressing Carlo. "Poor Carlo loves me," said she. "He is not stern and distant to his friends; and if he could speak, he would not be silent."

As she patted the dog's head, bending with native grace before his young and austere master, I saw a glow rise to that master's face. I saw his solemn eye melt with sudden fire, and flicker with resistless emotion. Flushed and kindled thus, he looked nearly as beautiful for a man as she for a woman. His chest heaved once, as if his large heart, weary of despotic constriction, had expanded, despite the will, and made a vigorous bound for the attainment of liberty. But he curbed it, I think, as a resolute rider would curb a rearing steed. He responded neither by word nor movement to the gentle advances made him.

"Papa says you never come to see us now," continued Miss Oliver, looking up. "You are quite a stranger at Vale Hall. He is alone this evening, and not very well: will you return with me and visit him?"

"It is not a seasonable hour to intrude on Mr. Oliver," answered St. John.

"Not a seasonable hour! But I declare it is. It is just the hour when papa most wants company: when the works are closed, and he has no business to occupy him. Now, Mr. Rivers, do come. Why are you so very shy, and so very somber?"

She filled up the hiatus his silence left by a reply of her own.

"I forgot!" she exclaimed, shaking her beautiful curled head, as if shocked at herself. "I am so giddy and thoughtless! Do excuse me. It had slipped my memory that you have good reasons to be indisposed for joining in my chatter. Diana and Mary have left you, and Moor House is shut up, and you are so lonely. I am sure I pity you. Do come and see papa."

"Not tonight, Miss Rosamond, not tonight."

Mr. St. John spoke almost like an automaton: himself only knew the effort it cost him thus to refuse.

"Well, if you are so obstinate, I will leave you; for I dare not stay any longer: the dew begins to fall. Good-evening!"

She held out her hand. He just touched it. "Good-evening!" he repeated, in a voice low and hollow as an echo. She turned; but in a moment returned.

"Are you well?" she asked. Well might she put the question: his face was blanched as her gown.

"Quite well," he enunciated; and, with a bow, he left the gate. She went one way; he another. She turned twice to gaze after him, as she tripped fairy-like down the field; he, as he strode firmly across, never turned at all.

This spectacle of another's suffering and sacrifice rapt my thoughts from exclusive meditation on my own. Diana Rivers had designated her brother "inexorable as death." She had not exaggerated.

Chapter XXXII

I continued the labors of the village-school as actively and faithfully as I could. It was truly hard work at first. Some time elapsed before, with all my efforts, I could comprehend my scholars and their nature. Wholly untaught, with faculties quite torpid, they seemed to me hopelessly dull; and, at first sight, all dull alike: but I soon found I was mistaken. There was a difference among them as among the educated; and when I got to know them, and they me, this difference rapidly developed itself. Their amazement at me, my language, my rules, and ways, once subsided, I found some of these heavy-looking, gaping rustics wake up into sharp-witted girls enough. Many showed themselves obliging, and amiable too; and I discovered among them not a few examples of natural politeness and innate self-respect, as well as of excellent capacity, that won both my goodwill and my admiration. These soon took a pleasure in doing their work well; in keeping their persons neat; in learning their tasks regularly; in acquiring quiet and orderly manners. The rapidity of their progress, in some instances, was even surprising; and an honest and happy pride I took in it: besides, I began personally to like some of the best girls; and they liked me. I had among my scholars several farmers' daughters: young women grown, almost. These could already read, write, and sew; and to them I taught the elements of grammar, geography, history, and the finer kinds of needlework. I found estimable characters among them—characters desirous of information, and disposed for improvement—with whom I passed many a pleasant evening hour in their own homes. Their parents then (the farmer and his wife) loaded me with attentions. There was an enjoyment in accepting their simple kindness, and in repaying it by a consideration—a scrupulous regard to their feelings—to which they were not, perhaps, at all times accustomed, and which both charmed and benefited them; because, while it elevated them in their own eyes, it made them emulous to merit the deferential treatment they received.

I felt I became a favorite in the neighborhood. Whenever I went out, I heard on all sides cordial salutations, and was welcomed with friendly smiles. To live amid general regard, though it be but the regard of working-people, is like "sitting in sunshine, calm and sweet:"[1] serene inward feelings bud and bloom under the ray. At this period of my life my heart far oftener swelled with thankfulness than sank with dejection: and yet, reader, to tell you all, in the midst of this calm, this useful existence—after a day passed in honorable exertion among my scholars, an evening spent in drawing or reading contentedly alone—I used to rush into strange dreams at night: dreams many-colored, agitated, full of the ideal, the stirring, the stormy—dreams where, amid unusual

1. From Thomas Moore's *Lalla Rookh* (1817), *Third Day*, 346.

scenes, charged with adventure, with agitating risk and romantic chance, I still
again and again met Mr. Rochester, always at some exciting crisis; and then
the sense of being in his arms, hearing his voice, meeting his eye, touching his
hand and cheek, loving him, being loved by him—the hope of passing a life-
time at his side, would be renewed, with all its first force and fire. Then I
awoke. Then I recalled where I was, and how situated. Then I rose up on my
curtainless bed, trembling and quivering; and then the still, dark night wit-
nessed the convulsion of despair and heard the burst of passion. By nine
o'clock the next morning I was punctually opening the school; tranquil, set-
tled, prepared for the steady duties of the day.

Rosamond Oliver kept her word in coming to visit me. Her call at the school
was generally made in the course of her morning ride. She would canter up to
the door on her pony, followed by a mounted livery servant. Anything more ex-
quisite than her appearance, in her purple habit, with her Amazon's cap of
black velvet placed gracefully above the long curls that kissed her cheek and
floated to her shoulders, can scarcely be imagined: and it was thus she would
enter the rustic building, and glide through the dazzled ranks of the village
children. She generally came at the hour when Mr. Rivers was engaged in giv-
ing his daily catechising lesson. Keenly, I fear, did the eye of the visitress pierce
the young pastor's heart. A sort of instinct seemed to warn him of her en-
trance, even when he did not see it; and when he was looking quite away from
the door, if she appeared at it his cheek would glow and his marble-seeming
features, though they refused to relax, changed indescribably: and in their very
quiescence became expressive of a repressed fervor, stronger than working
muscle or darting glance could indicate.

Of course she knew her power: indeed, he did not, because he could not,
conceal it from her. In spite of his Christian stoicism, when she went up and
addressed him, and smiled gaily, encouragingly, even fondly in his face, his
hand would tremble and his eye burn. He seemed to say, with his sad and res-
olute look, if he did not say it with his lips, "I love you, and I know you prefer
me. It is not despair of success that keeps me dumb. If I offered my heart, I be-
lieve you would accept it. But that heart is already laid on a sacred altar: the
fire is arranged round it. It will soon be no more than a sacrifice consumed."

And then she would pout like a disappointed child; a pensive cloud would
soften her radiant vivacity; she would withdraw her hand hastily from his, and
turn in transient petulance from his aspect, at once so heroic and so martyr-
like. St. John, no doubt, would have given the world to follow, recall, retain her,
when she thus left him: but he would not give one chance of Heaven; nor re-
linquish, for the elysium of her love, one hope of the true, eternal Paradise.
Besides, he could not bound all that he had in his nature—the rover, the aspi-
rant, the poet, the priest—in the limits of a single passion. He could not—he
would not—renounce his wide field of mission warfare for the parlors and the
peace of Vale Hall. I learnt so much from himself, in an inroad I once, despite
his reserve, had the daring to make on his confidence.

Miss Oliver already honored me with frequent visits to my cottage. I had
learnt her whole character; which was without mystery or disguise: she was co-
quettish, but not heartless; exacting, but not worthlessly selfish. She had been
indulged from her birth, but was not absolutely spoiled. She was hasty, but
good-humored; vain (she could not help it, when every glance in the glass
showed her such a flush of loveliness), but not affected; liberal-handed; inno-

cent of the pride of wealth; ingenuous; sufficiently intelligent; gay, lively, and unthinking: she was very charming, in short, even to a cool observer of her own sex like me; but she was not profoundly interesting or thoroughly impressive. A very different sort of mind was hers from that, for instance, of the sisters of St. John. Still, I liked her almost as I liked my pupil Adèle: except that for a child whom we have watched over and taught a closer affection is engendered than we can give an equally attractive adult acquaintance.

She had taken an amiable caprice to me. She said I was like Mr. Rivers (only, certainly, she allowed, "not one-tenth so handsome: though I was a nice neat little soul enough, but he was an angel"). I was, however, good, clever, composed, and firm, like him. I was a *lusus naturae*,[2] she affirmed, as a village schoolmistress: she was sure my previous history, if known, would make a delightful romance.

One evening, while, with her usual childlike activity, and thoughtless yet not offensive inquisitiveness, she was rummaging the cupboard and the table-drawer of my little kitchen, she discovered first two French books, a volume of Schiller, a German grammar and dictionary; and then my drawing-materials and some sketches, including a pencil-head of a pretty little cherub-like girl, one of my scholars, and sundry views from nature, taken in the Vale of Morton and on the surrounding moors. She was first transfixed with surprise, and then electrified with delight.

"Had I done these pictures? Did I know French and German? What a love—what a miracle I was! I drew better than her master in the first school in S——. Would I sketch a portrait of her, to show to papa?"

"With pleasure," I replied; and I felt a thrill of artist-delight at the idea of copying from so perfect and radiant a model. She had then on a dark-blue silk dress; her arms and her neck were bare; her only ornament was her chestnut tresses, which waved over her shoulders with all the wild grace of natural curls. I took a sheet of fine cardboard, and drew a careful outline. I promised myself the pleasure of coloring it; and, as it was getting late then, I told her she must come and sit another day.

She made such a report of me to her father that Mr. Oliver himself accompanied her next evening—a tall, massive-featured, middle-aged, and gray-headed man, at whose side his lovely daughter looked like a bright flower near a hoary turret. He appeared a taciturn, and perhaps a proud personage; but he was very kind to me. The sketch of Rosamond's portrait pleased him highly: he said I must make a finished picture of it. He insisted, too, on my coming the next day to spend the evening at Vale Hall.

I went. I found it a large, handsome residence, showing abundant evidences of wealth in the proprietor. Rosamond was full of glee and pleasure all the time I stayed. Her father was affable; and when he entered into conversation with me after tea, he expressed in strong terms his approbation of what I had done in Morton school; and said he only feared, from what he saw and heard, I was too good for the place, and would soon quit it for one more suitable.

"Indeed!" cried Rosamond, "she is clever enough to be a governess in a high family, papa."

I thought—I would far rather be where I am than in any high family in the land. Mr. Oliver spoke of Mr. Rivers—of the Rivers family—with great respect. He said it was a very old name in that neighborhood; that the ancestors of the

2. Sport of nature (Latin).

house were wealthy; that all Morton had once belonged to them, that even now he considered the representative of that house might, if he liked, make an alliance with the best. He accounted it a pity that so fine and talented a young man should have formed the design of going out as a missionary; it was quite throwing a valuable life away. It appeared, then, that her father would throw no obstacle in the way of Rosamond's union with St. John. Mr. Oliver evidently regarded the young clergyman's good birth, old name, and sacred profession as sufficient compensation for the want of fortune.

It was the 5th of November, and a holiday.[3] My little servant, after helping me to clean my house, was gone, well satisfied with the fee of a penny for her aid. All about me was spotless and bright—scoured floor, polished grate, and well-rubbed chairs. I had also made myself neat, and had now the afternoon before me to spend as I would.

The translation of a few pages of German occupied an hour; then I got my palette and pencils, and fell to the more soothing, because easier occupation, of completing Rosamond Oliver's miniature. The head was finished already: there was but the background to tint and the drapery to shade off; a touch of carmine, too, to add to the ripe lips—a soft curl here and there to the tresses—a deeper tinge to the shadow of the lash under the azured eyelid. I was absorbed in the execution of these nice details when, after one rapid tap, my door unclosed, admitting St. John Rivers.

"I am come to see how you are spending your holiday," he said. "Not, I hope, in thought? No, that is well: while you draw you will not feel lonely. You see, I mistrust you still: though you have borne up wonderfully so far. I have brought you a book for evening solace," and he laid on the table a new publication—a poem: one of those genuine productions so often vouchsafed to the fortunate public of those days—the golden age of modern literature. Alas! the readers of our era are less favored. But, courage! I will not pause either to accuse or repine. I know poetry is not dead, nor genius lost; nor has Mammon[4] gained power over either, to bind or slay: they will both assert their existence, their presence, their liberty and strength again one day. Powerful angels, safe in heaven! they smile when sordid souls triumph, and feeble ones weep over their destruction. Poetry destroyed? Genius banished? No! Mediocrity, no: do not let envy prompt you to the thought. No; they not only live, but reign, and redeem: and without their divine influence spread everywhere you would be in hell—the hell of your own meanness."

While I was eagerly glancing at the bright pages of Marmion[5] (for Marmion it was) St. John stooped to examine my drawing. His tall figure sprang erect again with a start: he said nothing. I looked up at him: he shunned my eye. I knew his thoughts well, and could read his heart plainly; at the moment I felt calmer and cooler than he: I had then temporarily the advantage of him, and I conceived an inclination to do him some good, if I could.

"With all his firmness and self-control," thought I, "he tasks himself too far: locks every feeling and pang within—expresses, confesses, imparts nothing. I am sure it would benefit him to talk a little about this sweet Rosamond, whom he thinks he ought not to marry: I will make him talk."

I said first: "Take a chair, Mr. Rivers." But he answered, as he always did, that he could not stay. "Very well," I responded, mentally, "stand if you like; but you

3. I.e., Guy Fawkes Day, anniversary of the ill-fated Gunpowder Plot (to blow up the houses of Parliament) of 1605.

4. I.e., money.

5. Sir Walter Scott's *Marmion* (1808).

shall not go just yet, I am determined: solitude is at least as bad for you as it is
for me. I'll try if I cannot discover the secret spring of your confidence, and
find an aperture in that marble breast through which I can shed one drop of
the balm of sympathy."

"Is this portrait like?" I asked bluntly.

"Like! Like whom? I did not observe it closely."

"You did, Mr. Rivers."

He almost started at my sudden and strange abruptness: he looked at me as-
tonished. "Oh, that is nothing yet," I muttered within. "I don't mean to be
baffled by a little stiffness on your part; I'm prepared to go to considerable
lengths." I continued, "You observed it closely and distinctly: but I have no ob-
jection to your looking at it again," and I rose and placed it in his hand.

"A well-executed picture," he said; "very soft, clear colouring; very graceful
and correct drawing."

"Yes, yes; I know all that. But what of the resemblance? Who is it like?"

Mastering some hesitation, he answered, "Miss Oliver, I presume."

"Of course. And now, sir, to reward you for the accurate guess I will promise
to paint you a careful and faithful duplicate of this very picture, provided you
admit that the gift would be acceptable to you. I don't wish to throw away my
time and trouble on an offering you would deem worthless."

He continued to gaze at the picture: the longer he looked, the firmer he
held it, the more he seemed to covet it. "It is like!" he murmured; "the eye is
well managed: the colour, light, expression, are perfect. It smiles!"

"Would it comfort or would it wound you to have a similar painting? Tell
me that. When you are at Madagascar, or at the Cape, or in India, would it be
a consolation to have that memento in your possession? or would the sight of
it bring recollections calculated to enervate and distress?"

He now furtively raised his eyes: he glanced at me, irresolute, disturbed; he
again surveyed the picture.

"That I should like to have it is certain: whether it would be judicious or
wise is another question."

Since I had ascertained that Rosamond really preferred him, and that her
father was not likely to oppose the match, I—less exalted in my views than St.
John—had been strongly disposed in my own heart to advocate their union. It
seemed to me that, should he become the possessor of Mr. Oliver's large for-
tune, he might do as much good with it as if he went and laid his genius out to
wither and his strength to waste under a tropical sun. With this persuasion I
now answered:— "As far as I can see, it would be wiser and more judicious if
you were to take to yourself the original at once."

By this time he had sat down: he had laid the picture on the table before
him, and with his brow supported on both hands hung fondly over it. I dis-
cerned he was now neither angry nor shocked at my audacity. I saw even that
to be thus frankly addressed on a subject he had deemed unapproachable—to
hear it thus freely handled—was beginning to be felt by him as a new plea-
sure—an unhoped-for relief. Reserved people often really need the frank dis-
cussion of their sentiments and griefs more than the expansive. The
sternest-seeming stoic is human after all; and to "burst" with boldness and
goodwill into "the silent sea"[6] of their souls is often to confer on them the first
of obligations.

6. Samuel Taylor Coleridge's *The Rime of the Ancient Mariner* (1798), lines 105–6.

"She likes you, I am sure," said I, as I stood behind his chair, "and her father respects you. Moreover, she is a sweet girl—rather thoughtless; but you would have sufficient thought for both yourself and her. You ought to marry her."

"*Does* she like me?" he asked.

"Certainly; better than she likes any one else. She talks of you continually: there is no subject she enjoys so much or touches upon so often."

"It is very pleasant to hear this," he said—"very: go on for another quarter of an hour." And he actually took out his watch and laid it upon the table to measure the time.

"But where is the use of going on," I asked, "when you are probably preparing some iron blow of contradiction, or forging a fresh chain to fetter your heart?"

"Don't imagine such hard things. Fancy me yielding and melting, as I am doing: human love rising like a freshly opened fountain in my mind and overflowing with sweet inundation all the field I have so carefully, and with such labour prepared—so assiduously sown with the seeds of good intentions, of self-denying plans. And now it is deluged with a nectarous flood—the young germs swamped—delicious poison cankering them: now I see myself stretched on an ottoman in the drawing-room at Vale Hall, at my bride Rosamond Oliver's feet: she is talking to me with her sweet voice—gazing down on me with those eyes your skilful hand has copied so well—smiling at me with these coral lips. She is mine—I am hers—this present life and passing world suffice to me. Hush! say nothing—my heart is full of delight—my senses are entranced—let the time I marked pass in peace."

I humored him: the watch ticked on: he breathed fast and low: I stood silent. Amidst this hush the quarter sped; he replaced the watch, laid the picture down, rose, and stood on the hearth.

"Now," said he, "that little space was given to delirium and delusion. I rested my temples on the breast of temptation, and put my neck voluntarily under her yoke of flowers; I tasted her cup. The pillow was burning; there is an asp in the garland; the wine has a bitter taste; her promises are hollow—her offers false; I see and know all this."

I gazed at him in wonder.

"It is strange," pursued he, "that while I love Rosamond Oliver so wildly—with all the intensity, indeed, of a first passion, the object of which is exquisitely beautiful, graceful, and fascinating—I experience at the same time a calm, unwarped consciousness that she would not make me a good wife; that she is not the partner suited to me; that I should discover this within a year after marriage; and that to twelve months' rapture would succeed a lifetime of regret. This I know."

"Strange, indeed!" I could not help ejaculating.

"While something in me," he went on, "is acutely sensible to her charms, something else is as deeply impressed with her defects; they are such that she could sympathize in nothing I aspired to—cooperate in nothing I undertook. Rosamond a sufferer, a laborer, a female apostle? Rosamond a missionary's wife? No!"

"But you need not be a missionary. You might relinquish that scheme."

"Relinquish! What! my vocation? My great work? My foundation laid on earth for a mansion in heaven? My hopes of being numbered in the band who have merged all ambition in the glorious one of bettering their race—of carrying knowledge into the realms of ignorance—of substituting peace for war—

freedom for bondage—religion for superstition—the hope of heaven for the fear of hell? Must I relinquish that? It is dearer than the blood in my veins. It is what I have to look forward to and to live for."

After a considerable pause, I said, —"And Miss Oliver? Are her disappointment and sorrow of no interest to you?"

"Miss Oliver is ever surrounded by suitors and flatterers; in less than a month my image will be effaced from her heart. She will forget me; and will marry, probably some one who will make her far happier than I should do."

"You speak coolly enough; but you suffer in the conflict. You are wasting away."

"No. If I get a little thin, it is with anxiety about my prospects, yet unsettled—my departure, continually procrastinated. Only this morning I received intelligence that the successor, whose arrival I have been so long expecting, cannot be ready to replace me for three months to come yet; and perhaps the three months may extend to six."

"You tremble and become flushed whenever Miss Oliver enters the schoolroom."

Again the surprised expression crossed his face. He had not imagined that a woman would dare to speak so to a man. For me, I felt at home in this sort of discourse. I could never rest in communication with strong, discreet, and refined minds, whether male or female, till I had passed the outworks of conventional reserve, and crossed the threshold of confidence, and won a place by their heart's very hearthstone.

"You *are* original," said he, "and not timid. There is something brave in your spirit, as well as penetrating in your eye; but allow me to assure you that you partially misinterpret my emotions. You think them more profound and potent than they are. You give me a larger allowance of sympathy than I have a just claim to. When I colour, and when I shake before Miss Oliver, I do not pity myself. I scorn the weakness. I know it is ignoble; a mere fever of the flesh: not, I declare, a convulsion of the soul. *That* is just as fixed as a rock firm set in the depths of a restless sea. Know me to be what I am—a cold, hard man."

I smiled incredulously.

"You have taken my confidence by storm," he continued: "and now it is much at your service. I am simply, in my original state—stripped of that blood-bleached robe with which Christianity covers human deformity—a cold, hard, ambitious man. Natural affection only, of all the sentiments, has permanent power over me. Reason, and not Feeling, is my guide: my ambition is unlimited; my desire to rise higher, to do more than others, insatiable. I honor endurance, perseverance, industry, talent; because these are the means by which men achieve great ends and mount to lofty eminence. I watch your career with interest, because I consider you a speciment of a diligent, orderly, energetic woman; not because I deeply compassionate what you have gone through, or what you still suffer."

"You would describe yourself as a mere pagan philosopher," I said.

"No. There is this difference between me and deistic philosophers: I believe; and I believe the Gospel. You missed your epithet. I am not a pagan, but a Christian philosopher—a follower of the sect of Jesus. As His disciple I adopt His pure, His merciful, His benignant doctrines. I advocate them: I am sworn to spread them. Won in youth to religion, she has cultivated my original qualities thus:—From the minute germ, natural affection, she has developed the overshadowing tree, philanthropy. From the wild, stringy root of human

uprightness, she has reared a due sense of the Divine justice. Of the ambition to win power and renown for my wretched self, she has formed the ambition to spread my Master's kingdom; to achieve victories for the standard of the cross. So much has religion done for me; turning the original materials to the best account; pruning and training nature. But she could not eradicate nature: nor will it be eradicated 'till this mortal shall put on immortality.' "[7]

Having said this, he took his hat, which lay on the table beside my palette. Once more he looked at the portrait.

"She *is* lovely," he murmured. "She is well named the Rose of the World, indeed!"

"And may I not paint one like it for you?"

"*Cui bono?*[8] No."

He drew over the picture the sheet of thin paper on which I was accustomed to rest my hand in painting to prevent the cardboard from being sullied. What he suddenly saw on this blank paper it was impossible for me to tell: but something had caught his eye. He took it up with a snatch; he looked at the edge; then shot a glance at me, inexpressibly peculiar and quite incomprehensible: a glance that seemed to take and make note of every point in my shape, face, and dress; for it traversed all, quick, keen as lightning. His lips parted, as if to speak: but he checked the coming sentence, whatever it was.

"What is the matter?" I asked.

"Nothing in the world," was the reply; and, replacing the paper, I saw him dexterously tear a narrow slip from the margin. It disappeared in his glove; and, with one hasty nod and "good-afternoon," he vanished.

"Well!" I exclaimed, using an expression of the district, "that caps the globe,[9] however!"

I, in my turn, scrutinized the paper, but saw nothing on it save a few dingy stains of paint where I had tried the tint in my pencil. I pondered the mystery a minute or two; but finding it insolvable, and being certain it could not be of much moment, I dismissed and soon forgot it

Chapter XXXII

When Mr. St. John went it was beginning to snow; the whirling storm continued all night. The next day a keen wind brought fresh and blinding falls; by twilight the valley was drifted up and almost impassable. I had closed my shutter, laid a mat to the door to prevent the snow from blowing in under it, trimmed my fire, and after sitting nearly an hour on the hearth listening to the muffled fury of the tempest, I lit a candle, took down Marmion, and beginning—

> Day set on Norham's castled steep,
> And Tweed's fair river broad and deep,
> And Cheviot's mountains lone;
> The massive towers, the donjon keep,
> The flanking walls that round them sweep,
> In yellow luster shone.

I soon forgot storm in music.

I heard a noise: the wind, I thought, shook the door. No; it was St. John

7. I Corinthians 15:53–54. 9. Tops everything.
8. Who stands to benefit? (Latin).

Rivers, who, lifting the latch, came in out of the frozen hurricane—the howl-ing darkness—and stood before me: the cloak that covered his tall figure all white as a glacier. I was almost in consternation; so little had I expected any guest from the blocked-up vale that night.

"Any ill news?" I demanded. "Has anything happened?"

"No. How very easily alarmed you are!" he answered, removing his cloak and hanging it up against the door, towards which he again coolly pushed the mat which his entrance had deranged. He stamped the snow from his boots.

"I shall sully the purity of your floor," said he, "but you must excuse me for once." Then he approached the fire: "I have had hard work to get here, I assure you," he observed, as he warmed his hands over the flame. "One drift took me up to the waist; happily the snow is quite soft yet."

"But why are you come?" I could not forbear saying.

"Rather an inhospitable question to put to a visitor; but since you ask it, I answer simply to have a little talk with you; I got tired of my mute books and empty rooms. Besides, since yesterday I have experienced the excitement of a person to whom a tale has been half-told, and who is impatient to hear the sequel."

He sat down. I recalled his singular conduct of yesterday, and really I began to fear his wits were touched. If he were insane, however, his was a very cool and collected insanity: I had never seen that handsome-featured face of his look more like chiseled marble than it did just now, as he put aside his snow-wet hair from his forehead and let the firelight shine free on his pale brow and cheek as pale, where it grieved me to discover the hollow trace of care or sor-row now so plainly graved. I waited, expecting he would say something I could at least comprehend; but his hand was now at his chin, his finger on his lip: he was thinking. It struck me that his hand looked wasted like his face. A perhaps uncalled-for gush of pity came over my heart: I was moved to say:—"I wish Diana or Mary would come and live with you: it is too bad that you should be quite alone; and you are recklessly rash about your own health."

"Not at all," said he: "I care for myself when necessary; I am well now. What do you see amiss in me?"

This was said with a careless, abstracted indifference, which showed that my solicitude was, at least in his opinion, wholly superfluous. I was silenced.

He still slowly moved his finger over his upper lip, and still his eye dwelt dreamily on the glowing grate. Thinking it urgent to say something, I asked him presently if he felt any cold draught from the door, which was behind him.

"No, no," he responded, shortly and somewhat testily.

"Well," I reflected, "if you won't talk, you may be still; I'll let you alone now, and return to my book."

So I snuffed the candle, and resumed the perusal of Marmion. He soon stirred; my eye was instantly drawn to his movements; he only took out a mo-rocco pocket-book, thence produced a letter, which he read in silence, folded it, put it back, relapsed into meditation. It was vain to try to read with such an inscrutable fixture before me; nor could I, in my impatience, consent to be dumb; he might rebuff me if he liked, but talk I would.

"Have you heard from Diana and Mary lately?"

"Not since the letter I showed you a week ago."

"There has not been any change made about your own arrangements? You will not be summoned to leave England sooner than you expected?"

"I fear not, indeed: such chance is too good to befall me." Baffled so far I changed my ground—I bethought myself to talk about the school and my scholars.

"Mary Garrett's mother is better, and Mary came back to the school this morning, and I shall have four new girls next week from the Foundry Close—they would have come today but for the snow."

"Indeed!"

"Mr. Oliver pays for two."

"Does he?"

"He means to give the whole school a treat at Christmas."

"I know."

"Was it your suggestion?"

"No."

"Whose, then?"

"His daughter's, I think."

"It is like her: she is so good-natured."

"Yes."

Again came the blank of a pause: the clock struck eight strokes. It aroused him; he uncrossed his legs, sat erect, turned to me.

"Leave your book a moment, and come a little nearer the fire," he said.

Wondering, and of my wonder finding no end, I complied.

"Half an hour ago," he pursued, "I spoke of my impatience to hear the sequel of a tale: on reflection, I find the matter will be better managed by my assuming the narrator's part, and converting you into a listener. Before commencing it is but fair to warn you that the story will sound somewhat hackneyed in your ears: but stale details often regain a degree of freshness when they pass through new lips. For the rest, whether trite or novel, it is short.

"Twenty years ago a poor curate—never mind his name at this moment—fell in love with a rich man's daughter; she fell in love with him, and married him, against the advice of all her friends; who consequently disowned her immediately after the wedding. Before two years passed the rash pair were both dead, and laid quietly side by side under one slab. (I have seen their grave; it formed part of the pavement of a huge churchyard surrounding the grim, soot-black old cathedral of an overgrown manufacturing town in ——shire.) They left a daughter, which, at its very birth, Charity received in her lap—cold as that of the snow-drift I almost stuck fast in to-night. Charity carried the friendless thing to the house of its rich maternal relations; it was reared by an aunt-in-law called (I come to names now) Mrs. Reed, of Gateshead—you start—did you hear a noise? I daresay it is only a rat scrambling along the rafters of the adjoining schoolroom: it was a barn before I had it repaired and altered, and barns are generally haunted by rats.—To proceed. Mrs. Reed kept the orphan ten years: whether it was happy or not with her I cannot say, never having been told; but at the end of that time she transferred it to a place you know—being no other than Lowood School, where you so long resided yourself. It seems her career there was very honorable: from a pupil she became a teacher, like yourself—really it strikes me there are parallel points in her history and yours—she left it to be a governess: there, again, your fates were analogous; she undertook the education of the ward of a certain Mr. Rochester."

"Mr. Rivers!" I interrupted.

"I can guess your feelings," he said, "but restrain them for a while: I have

nearly finished; hear me to the end. Of Mr. Rochester's character I know noth-
ing, but the one fact that he professed to offer honorable marriage to this
young girl, and that at the very altar she discovered he had a wife yet alive,
though a lunatic. What his subsequent conduct and proposals were is a mat-
ter of pure conjecture; but when an event transpired which rendered inquiry
after the governess necessary, it was discovered she was gone—no one could
tell when, where, or how. She had left Thornfield Hall in the night; every re-
search after her course had been vain: the country had been scoured far and
wide; no vestige of information could be gathered respecting her. Yet that she
should be found is become a matter of serious urgency: advertisements have
been put in all the papers; I myself have received a letter from one Mr. Briggs,
a solicitor, communicating the details I have just imparted. Is it not an odd
tale?"

"Just tell me this," said I, "and since you know so much you surely *can* tell it
me—what of Mr. Rochester? How and where is he? What is he doing? Is he
well?"

"I am ignorant of all concerning Mr. Rochester: the letter never mentions
him but to narrate the fraudulent and illegal attempt I have adverted to. You
should rather ask the name of the governess—the nature of the event which
requires her appearance."

"Did no one go to Thornfield Hall then? Did no one see Mr. Rochester?"

"I suppose not."

"But they wrote to him?"

"Of course."

"And what did he say? Who has his letters?"

"Mr. Briggs intimates that the answer to his application was not from Mr.
Rochester, but from a lady: it is signed 'Alice Fairfax.' "

I felt cold and dismayed: my worst fears then were probably true: he had in
all probability left England, and rushed in reckless desperation to some former
haunt on the Continent. And what opiate for his severe sufferings—what ob-
ject for his strong passions—had he sought there? I dared not answer the ques-
tion. Oh, my poor master—once almost my husband—whom I had often
called "my dear Edward!"

"He must have been a bad man," observed Mr. Rivers.

"You don't know him—don't pronounce an opinion upon him," I said, with
warmth.

"Very well," he answered, quietly: "and indeed my head is otherwise occu-
pied than with him: I have my tale to finish. Since you won't ask the gov-
erness's name, I must tell it of my own accord—stay—I have it here—it is
always more satisfactory to see important points written down, fairly commit-
ted to black and white."

And the pocket-book was again deliberately produced, opened, sought
through; from one of its compartments was extracted a shabby slip of paper,
hastily torn off: I recognized in its texture and its stains of ultramarine and
lake and vermilion the ravished margin of the portrait-cover. He got up, held it
close to my eyes: and I read, traced in Indian ink, in my own handwriting, the
words "Jane Eyre"—the work doubtless of some moment of abstraction.

"Briggs wrote to me of a Jane Eyre," he said; "the advertisements demanded
a Jane Eyre: I knew a Jane Elliott.—I confess I had my suspicions, but it was
only yesterday afternoon they were at once resolved into certainty. You own
the name and renounce the *alias?*"

"Yes—yes—but where is Mr. Briggs? He perhaps knows more of Mr. Rochester than you do."

"Briggs is in London; I should doubt his knowing anything at all about Mr. Rochester; it is not in Mr. Rochester he is interested. Meantime you forget essential points in pursuing trifles: you do not inquire why Mr. Briggs sought after you—what he wanted with you."

"Well, what did he want?"

"Merely to tell you that your uncle, Mr. Eyre of Madeira, is dead; that he has left you all his property, and that you are now rich—merely that—nothing more."

"I rich?"

"Yes, you, rich—quite an heiress."

Silence succeeded.

"You must prove your identity, of course," resumed St. John, presently: "a step which will offer no difficulties: you can then enter on immediate possession. Your fortune is vested in the English funds; Briggs has the will and the necessary documents."

Here was a new card turned up! It is a fine thing, reader, to be lifted in a moment from indigence to wealth—a very fine thing: but not a matter one can comprehend, or consequently enjoy, all at once. And then there are other chances in life far more thrilling and rapture-giving; *this* is solid, an affair of the actual world, nothing idea about it: all its associations are solid and sober, and its manifestations are the same. One does not jump, and spring, and shout hurrah! at hearing one has got a fortune; one begins to consider responsibilities and to ponder business; on a base of steady satisfaction rise certain grave cares—and we contain ourselves, and brood over our bliss with a solemn brow.

Besides, the words Legacy, Bequest, go side by side with the words Death, Funeral. My uncle I had heard was dead—my only relative; ever since being made aware of his existence I had cherished the hope of one day seeing him: now, I never should. And then this money came only to me: not to me and a rejoicing family, but to my isolated self. It was a grand boon doubtless; and independence would be glorious—yes, I felt that—*that* thought swelled my heart.

"You unbend your forehead at last," said Mr. Rivers: "I thought Medusa[1] had looked at you, and that you were turning to stone—perhaps now you will ask how much you are worth?"

"How much am I worth?"

"Oh, a trifle! Nothing of course to speak of—twenty thousand pounds, I think they say—but what is that?"

"Twenty thousand pounds?"

Here was a new stunner—I had been calculating on four or five thousand. This news actually took my breath for a moment: Mr. St. John, whom I had never heard laugh before, laughed now.

"Well," said he, "if you had committed a murder, and I had told you your crime was discovered, you could scarcely look more aghast."

"It is a large sum—don't you think there is a mistake?"

"No mistake at all."

"Perhaps you have read the figures wrong—it may be 2,000!"

1. Mythological Gorgon; turned to stone all who looked at her.

"It is written in letters, not figures,—twenty thousand."

I again felt rather like an individual of but average gastronomical powers sitting down to feast alone at a table spread with provisions for a hundred. Mr. Rivers rose now and put his cloak on.

"If it were not such a very wild night," he said, "I would send Hannah down to keep you company: you look too desperately miserable to be left alone. But Hannah, poor woman! could not stride the drifts so well as I: her legs are not quite so long: so I must e'en leave you to your sorrows. Good-night."

He was lifting the latch: a sudden thought occurred to me.

"Stop one minute!" I cried.

"Well?"

"It puzzles me to know why Mr. Briggs wrote to you about me; or how he knew you, or could fancy that you, living in such an out-of-the-way place, had the power to aid in my discovery."

"Oh! I am a clergyman," he said; "and the clergy are often appealed to about odd matters."

Again the latch rattled.

"No: that does not satisfy me!" I exclaimed: and, indeed, there was something in the hasty and unexplanatory reply which, instead of allaying, piqued my curiosity more than ever.

"It is a very strange piece of business," I added. "I must know more about it."

"Another time."

"No: tonight!—tonight!" and as he turned from the door I placed myself between it and him. He looked rather embarrassed.

"You certainly shall not go till you have told me all!" I said.

"I would rather not, just now."

"You shall!—you must!"

"I would rather Diana or Mary informed you."

Of course these objections wrought my eagerness to a climax: gratified it must be, and that without delay; and I told him so.

"But I apprised you that I was a hard man," said he; "difficult to persuade."

"And I am a hard woman,—impossible to put off."

"And then," he pursued, "I am cold: no fervor infects me."

"Whereas I am hot, and fire dissolves ice. The blaze there has thawed all the snow from your cloak; by the same token it has streamed on to my floor, and made it like a trampled street. As you hope ever to be forgiven, Mr. Rivers, the high crime and misdemeanor of spoiling a sanded kitchen, tell me what I wish to know."

"Well, then," he said, "I yield; if not to your earnestness, to your perseverance: as stone is worn by continual dropping. Besides, you must know some day,—as well now as later. Your name is Jane Eyre?"

"Of course: that was all settled before."

"You are not, perhaps, aware that I am your namesake?—that I was christened St. John Eyre Rivers?"

"No, indeed! I remember now seeing the letter E comprised in your initials written in books you have at different times lent me; but I never asked for what name it stood. But what then? Surely"——

I stopped: I could not trust myself to entertain, much less to express, the thought that rushed upon me—that embodied itself,—that, in a second,

stood out a strong, solid probability. Circumstances knit themselves, fitted themselves, shot into order: the chain that had been lying hitherto a formless lump of links was drawn out straight,—every ring was perfect, the connection complete. I knew, by instinct, how the matter stood before St. John had said another word: but I cannot expect the reader to have the same intuitive perception, so I must repeat his explanation.

"My mother's name was Eyre; she had two brothers; one a clergyman, who married Miss Jane Reed, of Gateshead; the other, John Eyre, Esq., merchant, late of Funchal, Madeira. Mr. Briggs, being Mr. Eyre's solicitor, wrote to us last August to inform us of our uncle's death; and to say that he had left his property to his brother the clergyman's orphan daughter; overlooking us, in consequence of a quarrel, never forgiven, between him and my father. He wrote again a few weeks since, to intimate that the heiress was lost; and asking if we knew anything of her. A name casually written on a slip of paper has enabled me to find her out. You know the rest." Again he was going. but I set my back against the door.

"Do let me speak," I said; "let me have one moment to draw breath and reflect." I paused—he stood before me, hat in hand, looking composed enough. I resumed: "Your mother was my father's sister?"

"Yes."

"My aunt, consequently?"

He bowed.

"My uncle John was your uncle John? You, Diana and Mary, are his sister's children; as I am his brother's child?"

"Undeniably."

"You three, then, are my cousins; half our blood on each side flows from the same source?"

"We are cousins; yes."

I surveyed him. It seemed I had found a brother: one I could be proud of,— one I could love; and two sisters whose qualities were such that, when I knew them but as mere strangers, they had inspired me with genuine affection and admiration. The two girls on whom, kneeling down on the wet ground, and looking through the low, latticed window of Moor House kitchen, I had gazed with so bitter a mixture of interest and despair were my near kinswomen; and the young and stately gentleman who had found me almost dying at his threshold was my blood relation. Glorious discovery to a lonely wretch! This was wealth indeed!—wealth to the heart!—a mine of pure, genial affections. This was a blessing, bright, vivid, and exhilarating;—not like the ponderous gift of gold: rich and welcome enough in its way, but sobering from its weight. I now clapped my hands in sudden joy—my pulse bounded, my veins thrilled.

"Oh, I am glad!—I am glad " I exclaimed.

St. John smiled. "Did I not say you neglected essential points to pursue trifles?" he asked. "You were serious when I told you you had got a fortune; and now, for a matter of no moment, you are excited."

"What can you mean? It may be of no moment to you; you have sisters, and don't care for a cousin; but I had nobody; and now three relations,—or two, if you don't choose to be counted,—are born into my world full grown. I say again, I am glad!"

I walked fast through the room: I stopped, half suffocated with the thoughts that rose faster than I could receive, comprehend, settle them:—

thoughts of what might, could, would, and should be, and that ere long. I
looked at the blank wall: it seemed a sky, thick with ascending stars,—every
one lit me to a purpose or delight. Those who had saved my life, whom till this
hour I had loved barrenly, I could now benefit. They were under a yoke: I could
free them: they were scattered,—I could reunite them—the independence,
the affluence which was mine might be theirs too. Were we not four? Twenty
thousand pounds shared equally would be five thousand each, enough and to
spare: justice would be done,—mutual happiness secured. Now the wealth did
not weigh on me: now it was not a mere bequest of coin,—it was a legacy of
life, hope, enjoyment.

How I looked while these ideas were taking my spirit by storm I cannot tell;
but I perceived soon that Mr. Rivers had placed a chair behind me, and was
gently attempting to make me sit down on it. He also advised me to be com-
posed: I scorned the insinuation of helplessness and distraction, shook off his
hand, and began to walk about again.

"Write to Diana and Mary tomorrow," I said, "and tell them to come home
directly; Diana said they would both consider themselves rich with a thousand
pounds, so with five thousand they will do very well."

"Tell me where I can get you a glass of water," said St. John; "you must really
make an effort to tranquilize your feelings."

"Nonsense! and what sort of an effect will the bequest have on you? Will it
keep you in England, induce you to marry Miss Oliver, and settle down like an
ordinary mortal?"

"You wander: your head becomes confused. I have been too abrupt in com-
municating the news; it has excited you beyond your strength."

"Mr. Rivers! you quite put me out of patience; I am rational enough; it is
you who misunderstand; or rather who affect to misunderstand."

"Perhaps if you explained yourself a little more fully I should comprehend
better."

"Explain! What is there to explain? You cannot fail to see that twenty thou-
sand pounds, the sum in question, divided equally between the nephew and
three nieces of our uncle will give five thousand to each? What I want is, that
you should write to your sisters and tell them of the fortune that has accrued
to them."

"To you, you mean."

"I have intimated my view of the case: I am incapable of taking any other. I
am not brutally selfish, blindly unjust, or fiendishly ungrateful. Besides, I am
resolved I will have a home and connections. I like Moor House, and I will live
at Moor House; I like Diana and Mary, and I will attach myself for life to Diana
and Mary. It would please and benefit me to have five thousand pounds; it
would torment and oppress me to have twenty thousand; which, moreover,
could never be mine in justice, though it might in law. I abandon to you, then,
what is absolutely superfluous to me. Let there be no opposition, and no dis-
cussion about it; let us agree among each other, and decide the point at once."

"This is acting on first impulses; you must take days to consider such a mat-
ter, ere your word can be regarded as valid."

"Oh! if all you doubt is my sincerity, I am easy: you see the justice of the
case?"

"I *do* see a certain justice; but it is contrary to all custom. Besides, the entire
fortune is your right: my uncle gained it by his own efforts; he was free to leave

it to whom he would: he left it to you. After all, justice permits you to keep it: you may, with a clear conscience, consider it absolutely your own."

"With me," said I, "it is fully as much a matter of feeling as of conscience: I must indulge my feelings; I so seldom have had an opportunity of doing so. Were you to argue, object, and annoy me for a year, I could not forego the delicious pleasure of which I have caught a glimpse—that of repaying, in part, a mighty obligation, and winning to myself life-long friends."

"You think so now," rejoined St. John; "because you do not know what it is to possess, nor consequently to enjoy wealth: you cannot form a notion of the importance twenty thousand pounds would give you; of the place it would enable you to take in society; of the prospects it would open to you: you cannot——"

"And you," I interrupted, "cannot at all imagine the craving I have for fraternal and sisterly love. I never had a home, I never had brothers and sisters; I must and will have them now: you are not reluctant to admit me and own me, are you?"

"Jane: I will be your brother—my sisters will be your sisters—without stipulating for this sacrifice of your just rights."

"Brother? Yes; at the distance of a thousand leagues! Sisters? Yes; slaving amongst strangers! I, wealthy—gorged with gold I never earned and do not merit! You, penniless! Famous equality and fraternization! Close union! Intimate attachment!"

"But, Jane, your aspirations after family ties and domestic happiness may be realised otherwise than by the means you contemplate: you may marry."

"Nonsense again! Marry! I don't want to marry, and never shall marry."

"That is saying too much: such hazardous affirmations are a proof of the excitement under which you labor."

"It is not saying too much: I know what I feel, and how averse are my inclinations to the bare thought of marriage. No one would take me for love; and I will not be regarded in the light of a mere money-speculation. And I do not want a stranger—unsympathizing alien, different from me; I want my kindred: those with whom I have full fellow-feeling. Say again you will be my brother: when you uttered the words I was satisfied, happy; repeat them, if you can repeat them sincerely."

"I think I can. I know I have always loved my own sisters; and I know on what my affection for them is grounded,—respect for their worth and admiration of their talents. You too have principle and mind: your tastes and habits resemble Diana's and Mary's; your presence is always agreeable to me; in your conversation I have already for some time found a salutary solace. I feel I can easily and naturally make room in my heart for you, as my third and youngest sister."

"Thank you: that contents me for tonight. Now you had better go; for if you stay longer you will perhaps irritate me afresh by some mistrustful scruple."

"And the school, Miss Eyre? It must now be shut up, I suppose?"

"No. I will retain my post of mistress till you get a substitute."

He smiled approbation: we shook hands, and he took leave.

I need not narrate in detail the further struggles I had and arguments I used to get matters regarding the legacy settled as I wished. My task was a very hard one: but, as I was absolutely resolved—as my cousins saw at length that my mind was really and immutably fixed on making a just division of the property—as they would have done precisely what I wished to do—they yielded at

length so far as to consent to put the affair to arbitration. The judges chosen were Mr. Oliver and an able lawyer: both coincided in my opinion: I carried my point. The instruments of transfer were drawn out: St. John, Diana, Mary, and I, each became possessed of a competency.[2]

Chapter XXXIV

It was near Christmas by the time all was settled: the season of general holiday approached. I now closed Morton school, taking care that the parting should not be barren on my side. Good fortune opens the hand as well as the heart wonderfully; and to give somewhat when we have largely received, is but to afford a vent to the unusual ebullition of the sensations. I had long felt with pleasure that many of my rustic scholars liked me, and when we parted that consciousness was confirmed: they manifested their affection plainly and strongly. Deep was my gratification to find I had really a place in their unsophisticated hearts: I promised them that never a week should pass in future that I did not visit them, and give them an hour's teaching in their school.

Mr. Rivers came up, as—having seen the classes, now numbering sixty girls, file out before me, and locked the door—I stood with the key in my hand, exchanging a few words of special farewell with some half-dozen of my best scholars: as decent, respectable, modest, and well-informed young women as could be found in the ranks of the British peasantry. And that is saying a great deal; for after all the British peasantry are the best taught, best mannered, most self-respecting of any in Europe: since those days I have seen paysannes and Bäuerinnen:[3] and the best of them seemed to me ignorant, coarse, and besotted, compared with my Morton girls.

"Do you consider you have got your reward for a season of exertion?" asked Mr. Rivers when they were gone. "Does not the consciousness of having done some real good in your day and generation give pleasure?"

"Doubtless."

"And you have only toiled a few months! Would not a life devoted to the task of regenerating your race be well spent?"

"Yes," I said; "but I could not go on for ever so: I want to enjoy my own faculties as well as to cultivate those of other people. I must enjoy them now; don't recall either my mind or body to the school: I am out of it, and disposed for full holiday."

He looked grave. "What now? What sudden eagerness is this you evince? What are you going to do?"

"To be active: as active as I can. And first I must beg you to set Hannah at liberty, and get somebody else to wait on you."

"Do you want her?"

"Yes, to go with me to Moor House. Diana and Mary will be at home in a week, and I want to have everything in order against their arrival."

"I understand: I thought you were for flying off on some excursion. It is better so: Hannah shall go with you."

"Tell her to be ready by tomorrow then; and here is the schoolroom key: I will give you the key of my cottage in the morning."

He took it. "You give it up very gleefully," said he: "I don't quite understand

2. I.e., sufficient money. 3. Peasant women (French and German).

your light-heartedness; because I cannot tell what employment you propose to yourself as a substitute for the one you are relinquishing. What aim, what purpose, what ambition in life have you now?"

"My first aim will be to *clean down* (do you comprehend the full force of the expression?) to *clean down* Moor House from chamber to cellar; my next to rub it up with beeswax, oil, and an indefinite number of cloths, till it glitters again; my third, to arrange every chair, table, bed, carpet, with mathematical precision; afterwards I shall go near to ruin you in coals and peat to keep up good fires in every room; and lastly, the two days preceding that on which your sisters are expected will be devoted by Hannah and me to such a beating of eggs, sorting of currants, grating of spices, compounding of Christmas cakes, chopping up of materials for mince-pies, and solemnizing of other culinary rites, as words can convey but an inadequate notion of to the uninitiated like you. My purpose, in short, is to have all things in an absolutely perfect state of readiness for Diana and Mary before next Thursday; and my ambition is to give them a beau-ideal of a welcome when they come."

St. John smiled slightly: still he was dissatisfied.

"It is all very well for the present," said he: "but seriously, I trust that when the first flush of vivacity is over you will look a little higher than domestic endearments and household joys."

"The best things the world has!" I interrupted.

"No, Jane, no: this world is not the scene of fruition; do not attempt to make it so: nor of rest; do not turn slothful."

"I mean, on the contrary, to be busy."

"Jane, I excuse you for the present: two months' grace I allow you for the full enjoyment of your new position, and for pleasing yourself with this late-found charm of relationship; but *then* I hope you will begin to look beyond Moor House and Morton, and sisterly society, and the selfish calm and sensual comfort of civilised affluence. I hope your energies will then once more trouble you with their strength."

I looked at him with surprise.

"St. John," I said, "I think you are almost wicked to talk so. I am disposed to be as content as a queen, and you try to stir me up to restlessness! To what end?"

"To the end of turning to profit the talents which God has committed to your keeping; and of which He will surely one day demand a strict account. Jane, I shall watch you closely and anxiously—I warn you of that. And try to restrain the disproportionate fervor with which you throw yourself into common-place home pleasures. Don't cling so tenaciously to ties of the flesh; save your constancy and ardor for an adequate cause; forbear to waste them on trite transient objects. Do you hear, Jane?"

"Yes; just as if you were speaking Greek. I feel I have adequate cause to be happy, and I *will* be happy. Good-bye!"

Happy at Moor House I was, and hard I worked; and so did Hannah: she was charmed to see how jovial I could be amidst the bustle of a house turned topsy-turvy—how I could brush, and dust, and clean, and cook. And really after a day or two of confusion worse confounded it was delightful, by degrees, to invoke order from the chaos ourselves had made. I had previously taken a journey to S—— to purchase some new furniture: my cousins having given me carte blanche to effect what alterations I pleased, and a sum having been

set aside for that purpose. The ordinary sitting-room and bedrooms I left much as they were: for I knew Diana and Mary would derive more pleasure from seeing again the old homely tables and chairs and beds than from the spectacle of the smartest innovations. Still some novelty was necessary, to give to their return the piquancy with which I wished it to be invested. Dark handsome new carpets and curtains, an arrangement of some carefully selected antique ornaments in porcelain and bronze, new coverings, and mirrors, and dressing-cases for the toilet-tables, answered the end: they looked fresh without being glaring. A spare parlor and bedroom I refurnished entirely with old mahogany and crimson upholstery: I laid canvas on the passage and carpets on the stairs. When all was finished, I thought Moor House as complete a model of bright modest snugness within as it was, at this season, a specimen of wintry waste and desert dreariness without.

The eventful Thursday at length came. They were expected about dark, and ere dusk fires were lit upstairs and below; the kitchen was in perfect trim; Hannah and I were dressed, and all was in readiness.

St. John arrived first. I had entreated him to keep quite clear of the house till everything was arranged: and, indeed, the bare idea of the commotion, at once sordid and trivial, going on within its walls sufficed to scare him to estrangement. He found me in the kitchen, watching the progress of certain cakes for tea, then baking. Approaching the hearth, he asked, "If I was at last satisfied with housemaid's work?" I answered by inviting him to accompany me on a general inspection of the result of my labours. With some difficulty I got him to make the tour of the house. He just looked in at the doors I opened; and when he had wandered upstairs and downstairs, he said I must have gone through a great deal of fatigue and trouble to have effected such considerable changes in so short a time: but not a syllable did he utter indicating pleasure in the improved aspect of his abode.

This silence damped me. I thought perhaps the alterations had disturbed some old associations he valued. I inquired whether this was the case: no doubt in a somewhat crestfallen tone.

"Not at all; he had, on the contrary, remarked that I had scrupulously respected every association: he feared, indeed, I must have bestowed more thought on the matter than it was worth. How many minutes, for instance, had I devoted to studying the arrangement of this very room?—By-the-bye, could I tell him where such a book was?"

I showed him the volume on the shelf: he took it down, and withdrawing to his accustomed window recess, he began to read it.

Now, I did not like this, reader. St. John was a good man; but I began to feel he had spoken truth of himself when he said he was hard and cold. The humanities and amenities of life had no attraction for him—its peaceful enjoyments no charm. Literally, he lived only to aspire—after what was good and great, certainly; but still he would never rest; nor approve of others resting round him. As I looked at his lofty forehead, still and pale as a white stone—at his fine lineaments fixed in study—I comprehended all at once that he would hardly make a good husband: that it would be a trying thing to be his wife. I understood, as by inspiration, the nature of his love for Miss Oliver; I agreed with him that it was but a love of the senses. I comprehended how he should despise himself for the feverish influence it exercised over him; how he should wish to stifle and destroy it; how he should mistrust its ever conducing permanently to his happiness, or hers. I saw he was of the material from which na-

ture hews her heroes—Christian and Pagan—her lawgivers, her statesmen, her conquerors; a steadfast bulwark for great interests to rest upon; but, at the fireside, too often a cold cumbrous column, gloomy and out of place.

"This parlor is not his sphere," I reflected; "the Himalayan ridge, or Caffre[4] bush, even the plague-cursed Guinea Coast swamp, would suit him better. Well may he eschew the calm of domestic life; it is not his element: there his faculties stagnate—they cannot develop or appear to advantage. It is in scenes of strife and danger—where courage is proved, and energy exercised, and fortitude tasked—that he will speak and move, the leader and superior. A merry child would have the advantage of him on this hearth. He is right to choose a missionary's career—I see it now."

"They are coming! they are coming!" cried Hannah, throwing open the parlour door. At the same moment old Carlo barked joyfully. Out I ran. It was now dark: but a rumbling of wheels was audible. Hannah soon had a lantern lit. The vehicle had stopped at the wicket; the driver opened the door: first one well-known form, then another, stepped out. In a minute I had my face under their bonnets, in contact first with Mary's soft cheek, then with Diana's flowing curls. They laughed—kissed me—then Hannah: patted Carlo, who was half wild with delight, asked eagerly if all was well; and being assured in the affirmative, hastened into the house.

They were stiff with their long and jolting drive from Whitcross, and chilled with the frosty night-air; but their pleasant countenances expanded to the cheerful fire-light. While the driver and Hannah brought in the boxes, they demanded St. John. At this moment he advanced from the parlor. They both threw their arms round his neck at once. He gave each one quiet kiss, said in a low tone a few words of welcome, stood a while to be talked to, and then, intimating that he supposed they would soon rejoin him in the parlor, withdrew there as to a place of refuge.

I had lit their candles to go upstairs, but Diana had first to give hospitable orders respecting the driver; this done, both followed me. They were delighted with the renovation and decoration of their rooms; with the new drapery, and fresh carpets, and rich tinted china vases: they expressed their gratification ungrudgingly. I had the pleasure of feeling that my arrangements met their wishes exactly; and that what I had done added a vivid charm to their joyous return home.

Sweet was that evening. My cousins, full of exhilaration, were so eloquent in narrative and comment, that their fluency covered St. John's taciturnity: he was sincerely glad to see his sisters; but in their glow of fervour and flow of joy he could not sympathize. The event of the day—that is, the return of Diana and Mary—pleased him; but the accompaniments of that event, the glad tumult, the garrulous glee of reception, irked him: I saw he wished the calmer morrow was come. In the very meridian of the night's enjoyment, about an hour after tea, a rap was heard at the door. Hannah entered with the intimation that "a poor lad was come, at that unlikely time, to fetch Mr. Rivers to see his mother, who was drawing away."

"Where does she live, Hannah?"

"Clear up at Whitcross Brow, almost four miles off; and moor and moss all the way."

"Tell him I will go."

4. Kaffir, African.

"I'm sure, sir, you had better not. It's the worst road to travel after dark that can be: there's no track at all over the bog. And then it is such a bitter night— the keenest wind you ever felt. You had better send word, sir, that you will be there in the morning."

But he was already in the passage, putting on his cloak; and without one objection, one murmur, he departed. It was then nine o'clock: he did not return till midnight. Starved and tired enough he was: but he looked happier than when he set out. He had performed an act of duty; made an exertion; felt his own strength to do and deny, and was on better terms with himself.

I am afraid the whole of the ensuing week tried his patience. It was Christmas week: we took to no settled employment, but spent it in a sort of merry domestic dissipation. The air of the moors, the freedom of home, the dawn of prosperity, acted on Diana and Mary's spirits like some life-giving elixir: they were gay from morning till noon, and from noon till night. They could always talk; and their discourse, witty, pithy, original, had such charms for me, that I preferred listening to, and sharing in it, to doing anything else. St. John did not rebuke our vivacity; but he escaped from it: he was seldom in the house; his parish was large, the population scattered, and he found daily business in visiting the sick and poor in its different districts.

One morning, at breakfast, Diana, after looking a little pensive for some minutes, asked him, "If his plans were yet unchanged?"

"Unchanged and unchangeable," was the reply. And he proceeded to inform us that his departure from England was now definitively fixed for the ensuing year.

"And Rosamond Oliver?" suggested Mary: the words seeming to escape her lips involuntarily: for no sooner had she uttered them, than she made a gesture as if wishing to recall them. St. John had a book in his hand—it was his unsocial custom to read at meals—he closed it, and looked up.

"Rosamond Oliver," said he, "is about to be married to Mr. Granby; one of the best connected and most estimable residents in S——, grandson and heir to Sir Frederic Granby: I had the intelligence from her father yesterday."

His sisters looked at each other, and at me; we all three looked at him: he was serene as glass.

"The match must have been got up hastily," said Diana: "they cannot have known each other long."

"But two months: they met in October at the county ball at S——. But where there are no obstacles to a union, as in the present case, where the connection is in every point desirable, delays are unnecessary: they will be married as soon as S—— Place, which Sir Frederic gives up to them, can be refitted for their reception."

The first time I found St. John alone after this communication, I felt tempted to inquire if the event distressed him: but he seemed so little to need sympathy, that, so far from venturing to offer him more, I experienced some shame at the recollection of what I had already hazarded. Besides, I was out of practice in talking to him: his reserve was again frozen over, and my frankness was congealed beneath it. He had not kept his promise of treating me like his sisters; he continually made little chilling differences between us, which did not at all tend to the development of cordiality: in short, now that I was acknowledged his kinswoman, and lived under the same roof with him, I felt the distance between us to be far greater than when he had known me only as the

village schoolmistress. When I remembered how far I had once been admitted to his confidence, I could hardly comprehend his present frigidity.

Such being the case, I felt not a little surprised when he raised his head suddenly from the desk over which he was stooping, and said:— "You see, Jane, the battle is fought and the victory won."

Startled at being thus addressed, I did not immediately reply: after a moment's hesitation I answered:— "But are you sure you are not in the position of those conquerors whose triumphs have cost them too dear? Would not such another ruin you?"

"I think not; and if I were, it does not much signify; I shall never be called upon to contend for such another. The event of the conflict is decisive: my way is now clear; I thank God for it!" So saying, he returned to his papers and his silence.

As our mutual happiness (i.e. Diana's, Mary's, and mine) settled into a quieter character, and we resumed our usual habits and regular studies, St. John stayed more at home: he sat with us in the same room, sometimes for hours together. While Mary drew, Diana pursued a course of encyclopaedic reading she had (to my awe and amazement) undertaken, and I fagged away at German, he pondered a mystic lore of his own: that of some Eastern tongue, the acquisition of which he thought necessary to his plans.

Thus engaged, he appeared, sitting in his own recess, quiet and absorbed enough; but that blue eye of his had a habit of leaving the outlandish-looking grammar, and wandering over, and sometimes fixing upon us, his fellow students, with a curious intensity of observation: if caught, it would be instantly withdrawn; yet ever and anon it returned searchingly to our table. I wondered what it meant: I wondered, too, at the punctual satisfaction he never failed to exhibit on an occasion that seemed to me of small moment, namely,—my weekly visit to Morton school; and still more was I puzzled when, if the day was unfavorable, if there was snow, or rain, or high wind, and his sisters urged me not to go, he would invariably make light of their solicitude, and encourage me to accomplish the task without regard to the elements.

"Jane is not such a weakling as you would make her," he would say: "she can bear a mountain blast, or a shower, or a few flakes of snow, as well as any of us. Her constitution is both sound and elastic;—better calculated to endure variations of climate than many more robust."

And when I returned, sometimes a good deal tired and not a little weather-beaten, I never dared complain, because I saw that to murmur would be to vex him: on all occasions fortitude pleased him; the reverse was a special annoyance.

One afternoon, however, I got leave to stay at home, because I really had a cold. His sisters were gone to Morton in my stead: I sat reading Schiller; he, deciphering his crabbed Oriental scrolls. As I exchanged a translation for an exercise, I happened to look his way: there I found myself under the influence of the ever-watchful blue eye. How long it had been searching me through and through, and over and over, I cannot tell: so keen was it, and yet so cold, I felt for the moment superstitious—as if I were sitting in the room with something uncanny.

"Jane, what are you doing?"

"Learning German."

"I want you to give up German, and learn Hindostanee."

"You are not in earnest?"

"In such earnest that I must have it so: and I will tell you why."

He then went on to explain that Hindostanee was the language he was himself at present studying: that, as he advanced, he was apt to forget the commencement; that it would assist him greatly to have a pupil with whom he might again and again go over the elements, and so fix them thoroughly in his mind; that his choice had hovered for some time between me and his sisters; but that he had fixed on me, because he saw I could sit at a task the longest of the three. Would I do him this favor? I should not, perhaps, have to make the sacrifice long; as it wanted now barely three months to his departure.

St. John was not a man to be lightly refused: you felt that every impression made on him, either for pain or pleasure, was deep-graved and permanent. I consented. When Diana and Mary returned, the former found her scholar transferred from her to her brother: she laughed; and both she and Mary agreed that St. John should never have persuaded them to such a step. He answered, quietly: "I know it."

I found him a very patient, very forbearing, and yet an exacting master: he expected me to do a great deal; and when I fulfilled his expectations, he, in his own way, fully testified his approbation. By degrees, he acquired a certain influence over me that took away my liberty of mind: his praise and notice were more restraining than his indifference. I could no longer talk or laugh freely when he was by, because a tiresomely importunate instinct reminded me that vivacity (at least in me) was distasteful to him. I was so fully aware that only serious moods and occupations were acceptable, that in his presence every effort to sustain or follow any other became vain: I fell under a freezing spell. When he said "go," I went; "come," I came; "do this," I did it. But I did not love my servitude: I wished, many a time, he had continued to neglect me.

One evening when, at bedtime, his sisters and I stood round him, bidding him good-night, he kissed each of them, as was his custom; and, as was equally his custom, he gave me his hand. Diana, who chanced to be in a frolicsome humor (*she* was not painfully controlled by his will; for hers, in another way, was as strong), exclaimed:—"St. John! you used to call Jane your third sister, but you don't treat her as such: you should kiss her too."

She pushed me towards him. I thought Diana very provoking, and felt uncomfortably confused; and while I was thus thinking and feeling, St. John bent his head; his Greek face was brought to a level with mine, his eyes questioned my eyes piercingly—he kissed me. There are no such things as marble kisses, or ice kisses, or I should say my ecclesiastical cousin's salute belonged to one of these classes; but there may be experiment kisses, and his was an experiment kiss. When given, he viewed me to learn the result; it was not striking: I am sure I did not blush; perhaps I might have turned a little pale, for I felt as if this kiss were a seal affixed to my fetters. He never omitted the ceremony afterwards, and the gravity and quiescence with which I underwent it seemed to invest it for him with a certain charm.

As for me, I daily wished more to please him: but to do so, I felt daily more and more that I must disown half my nature, stifle half my faculties, wrest my tastes from their original bent, force myself to the adoption of pursuits for which I had no natural vocation. He wanted to train me to an elevation I could never reach; it racked me hourly to aspire to the standard he uplifted. The thing was as impossible as to mold my irregular features to his correct and clas-

sic pattern, to give to my changeable green eyes the sea-blue tint and solemn lustre of his own.

Not his ascendancy alone, however, held me in thrall at present. Of late it had been easy enough for me to look sad: a cankering evil sat at my heart and drained my happiness at its source—the evil of suspense.

Perhaps you think I had forgotten Mr. Rochester, reader, amid these changes of place and fortune. Not for a moment. His idea was still with me; because it was not a vapor sunshine could disperse; nor a sand-traced effigy storms could wash away: it was a name graven on a tablet, fated to last as long as the marble it inscribed. The craving to know what had become of him followed me everywhere; when I was at Morton, I reentered my cottage every evening to think of that: and now at Moor House, I sought my bedroom each night to brood over it.

In the course of my necessary correspondence with Mr. Briggs about the will, I had inquired if he knew anything of Mr. Rochester's present residence and state of health; but, as St. John had conjectured, he was quite ignorant of all concerning him. I then wrote to Mrs. Fairfax, entreating information on the subject. I had calculated with certainty on this step answering my end: I felt sure it would elicit an early answer. I was astonished when a fortnight passed without reply; but when two months wore away, and day after day the post arrived and brought nothing for me, I fell a prey to the keenest anxiety.

I wrote again: there was a chance of my first letter having missed. Renewed hope followed renewed effort: it shone like the former for some weeks, then, like it, it faded, flickered: not a line, not a word reached me. When half a year wasted in vain expectancy my hope died out: and then I felt dark indeed.

A fine spring shone round me, which I could not enjoy. Summer approached; Diana tried to cheer me: she said I looked ill, and wished to accompany me to the sea-side. This St. John opposed; he said I did not want dissipation, I wanted employment; my present life was too purposeless, I required an aim; and, I suppose, by way of supplying deficiencies, he prolonged still further my lessons in Hindostanee, and grew more urgent in requiring their accomplishment: and I, like a fool, never thought of resisting him—I could not resist him.

One day I had come to my studies in lower spirits than usual; the ebb was occasioned by a poignantly felt disappointment: Hannah had told me in the morning there was a letter for me, and when I went down to take it, almost certain that the long looked-for tidings were vouchsafed me at last, I found only an unimportant note from Mr. Briggs on business. The bitter check had wrung from me some tears; and now as I sat poring over the crabbed characters and flourishing tropes of an Indian scribe, my eyes filled again.

St. John called me to his side to read; in attempting to do this my voice failed me: words were lost in sobs. He and I were the only occupants of the parlour: Diana was practicing her music in the drawing-room, Mary was gardening—it was a very fine May-day, clear, sunny, and breezy. My companion expressed no surprise at this emotion, nor did he question me as to its cause; he only said:—"We will wait a few minutes, Jane, till you are more composed." And while I smothered the paroxysm with all haste, he sat calm and patient, leaning on his desk and looking like a physician watching with the eye of science an expected and fully understood crisis in a patient's malady. Having stifled my sobs, wiped my eyes, and muttered something about not being very

well that morning, I resumed my task, and succeeded in completing it. St. John put away my books and his, locked his desk, and said:—"Now, Jane, you shall take a walk; and with me."

"I will call Diana and Mary."

"No. I want only one companion this morning, and that must be you: put on your things; go out by the kitchen door; take the road towards the head of Marsh Glen: I will join you in a moment."

I know no medium: I never in my life have known any medium in my dealings with positive, hard characters, antagonistic to my own, between absolute submission and determined revolt. I have always faithfully observed the one, up to the very moment of bursting, sometimes with volcanic vehemence, into the other; and as neither present circumstances warranted, nor my present mood inclined me to mutiny, I observed careful obedience to St. John's directions; and in ten minutes I was treading the wild track of the glen, side by side with him.

The breeze was from the west: it came over the hill, sweet with scents of heath and rush; the sky was of stainless blue; the stream descending the ravine, swelled with past spring rains, poured along plentiful and clear, catching golden gleams from the sun, and sapphire tints from the firmament. As we advanced and left the track, we trod a soft turf, mossy fine and emerald green, minutely enamelled with a tiny white flower and spangled with a star-like yellow blossom: the hills, meantime, shut us quite in; for the glen, towards its head, wound to the very core.

"Let us rest here," said St. John, as we reached the first stragglers of a battalion of rocks, guarding a sort of pass, beyond which the beck rushed down a waterfall; and where, still a little further, the mountain shook off turf and flower, had only heath for raiment, and crag for gem—where it exaggerated the wild to the savage, and exchanged the fresh for the frowning—where it guarded the forlorn hope of solitude, and a last refuge for silence.

I took a seat: St. John stood near me. He looked up the pass and down the hollow; his glance wandered away with the stream, and returned to traverse the unclouded heaven which colored it; he removed his hat, let the breeze stir his hair and kiss his brow. He seemed in communion with the genius of the haunt: with his eye he bade farewell to something.

"And I shall see it again," he said aloud, "in dreams, when I sleep by the Ganges: and again, in a more remote hour—when another slumber overcomes me—on the shore of a darker stream."

Strange words of a strange love! An austere patriot's passion for his fatherland! He sat down; for half an hour we never spoke; neither he to me nor I to him: that interval past, he recommenced:—"Jane, I go in six weeks; I have taken my berth in an East Indiaman which sails on the twentieth of June."

"God will protect you; for you have undertaken His work," I answered.

"Yes," said he, "there is my glory and joy. I am the servant of an infallible master. I am not going out under human guidance, subject to the defective laws and erring control of my feeble fellow-worms: my king, my lawgiver, my captain, is the All-perfect. It seems strange to me that all round me do not burn to enlist under the same banner,—to join in the same enterprise."

"All have not your powers: and it would be folly for the feeble to wish to march with the strong."

"I do not speak to the feeble, or think of them: I address only such as are worthy of the work, and competent to accomplish it."

"Those are few in number, and difficult to discover."

"You say truly: but when found, it is right to stir them up—to urge and ex-hort them to the effort—to show them what their gifts are, and why they were given—to speak Heaven's message in their ear,—to offer them, direct from God, a place in the ranks of His chosen."

"If they are really qualified for the task, will not their own hearts be the first to inform them of it?"

I felt as if an awful charm was framing round and gathering over me: I trem-bled to hear some fatal word spoken which would at once declare and rivet the spell.

"And what does *your* heart say?" demanded St. John.

"My heart is mute,—my heart is mute," I answered, struck and thrilled.

"Then I must speak for it," continued the deep, relentless voice. "Jane, come with me to India: come as my help-meet and fellow laborer."

The glen and sky spun round: the hills heaved! It was as if I had heard a summons from Heaven—as f a visionary messenger, like him of Macedonia, had enounced, "Come over and help us!"[5] But I was no apostle,—I could not behold the herald,—I could not receive his call.

"Oh, St. John!" I cried, "have some mercy!"

I appealed to one who, in the discharge of what he believed his duty, knew neither mercy nor remorse. He continued:—"God and nature intended you for a missionary's wife. It is rot personal, but mental endowments they have given you: you are formed for labor, not for love. A missionary's wife you must—shall be. You shall be mine: I claim you—not for my pleasure, but for my Sovereign's service."

"I am not fit for it: I have no vocation," I said.

He had calculated on these first objections: he was not irritated by them. Indeed, as he leaned back against the crag behind him, folded his arms on his chest, and fixed his countenance, I saw he was prepared for a long and trying opposition, and had taken in a stock of patience to last him to its close—re-solved, however, that that close should be conquest for him.

"Humility, Jane," said he, "is the groundwork of Christian virtues: you say right that you are not fit for the work. Who is fit for it? Or who, that ever was truly called, believed himself worthy of the summons? I, for instance, am but dust and ashes. With St. Paul, I acknowledge myself the chiefest of sinners: but I do not suffer this sense of my personal vileness to daunt me. I know my Leader: that He is just as well as mighty; and while He has chosen a feeble in-strument to perform a great task, He will, from the boundless stores of His providence, supply the inadequacy of the means to the end. Think like me, Jane—trust like me. It is the Rock of Ages I ask you to lean on: do not doubt but it will bear the weight of your human weakness."

"I do not understand a missionary life: I have never studied missionary labors."

"There, I, humble as I am, can give you the aid you want: I can set you your task from hour to hour; stand by you always; help you from moment to mo-ment. This I could do in the beginning: soon (for I know your powers) you would be as strong and apt as myself, and would not require my help."

"But my powers—where are they for this undertaking? I do not feel them. Nothing speaks or stirs in me while you talk I am sensible of no light kin-

5. A Macedonian appeared in a vision to Paul, asking him to come and help the Macedonians (Acts 16:9).

dling—no life quickening—no voice counseling or cheering. Oh, I wish I could make you see how much my mind is at this moment like a rayless dungeon, with one shrinking fear fettered in its depths—the fear of being persuaded by you to attempt what I cannot accomplish!"

"I have an answer for you—hear it. I have watched you ever since we first met: I have made you my study for ten months. I have proved you in that time by sundry tests: and what have I seen and elicited? In the village school I found you could perform well, punctually, uprightly, labor uncongenial to your habits and inclinations; I saw you could perform it with capacity and tact: you could win while you controlled. In the calm with which you learnt you had become suddenly rich, I read a mind clear of the vice of Demas:—lucre had no undue power over you.[6] In the resolute readiness with which you cut your wealth into four shares, keeping but one to yourself, and relinquishing the three others to the claim of abstract justice, I recognized a soul that reveled in the flame and excitement of sacrifice. In the tractability with which, at my wish, you forsook a study in which you were interested, and adopted another because it interested me; in the untiring assiduity with which you have since persevered in it—in the unflagging energy and unshaken temper with which you have met its difficulties—I acknowledge the complement of the qualities I seek. Jane, you are docile, diligent, disinterested, faithful, constant, and courageous; very gentle, and very heroic: cease to mistrust yourself—I can trust you unreservedly. As a conductress of Indian schools, and a helper amongst Indian women, your assistance will be to me invaluable."

My iron shroud contracted round me; persuasion advanced with slow sure step. Shut my eyes as I would, these last words of his succeeded in making the way, which had seemed blocked up, comparatively clear. My work, which had appeared so vague, so hopelessly diffuse, condensed itself as he proceeded, and assumed a definite form under his shaping hand. He waited for an answer. I demanded a quarter of an hour to think, before I again hazarded a reply.

"Very willingly," he rejoined: and rising, he strode a little distance up the pass, threw himself down on a swell of heath, and there lay still.

"I *can* do what he wants me to do: I am forced to see and acknowledge that," I meditated—"That is, if life be spared me. But I feel mine is not the existence to be long protracted under an Indian sun.—What then? He does not care for that: when my time came to die he would resign me, in all serenity and sanctity, to the God who gave me. The case is very plain before me. In leaving England, I should leave a loved but empty land—Mr. Rochester is not there: and if he were, what is, what can that ever be to me? My business is to live without him now: nothing so absurd, so weak as to drag on from day to day, as if I were waiting some impossible change in circumstances, which might reunite me to him. Of course (as St. John once said) I must seek another interest in life to replace the one lost: is not the occupation he now offers me truly the most glorious man can adopt or God assign? Is it not, by its noble cares and sublime results, the one best calculated to fill the void left by uptorn affections and demolished hopes? I believe I must say, Yes—and yet I shudder. Alas! If I join St. John, I abandon half myself: if I go to India, I go to premature death. And how will the interval between leaving England for India, and India for the grave, be filled? Oh, I know well! That, too, is very clear to my vision. By straining to satisfy St. John till my sinews ache, I *shall* satisfy him—to the

6. Demas's love of the world made him desert Paul (2 Timothy 4:10).

finest central point and farthest outward circle of his expectations. If I do go with him—if I do make the sacrifice he urges, I will make it absolutely: I will throw all on the altar—heart, vitals, the entire victim. He will never love me; but he shall approve me; I will show him energies he has not yet seen, resources he was never suspected. Yes: I can work as hard as he can; and with as little grudging.

"Consent, then, to his demand is possible: but for one item—one dreadful item. It is—that he asks me to be his wife, and has no more of a husband's heart for me than that frowning giant of a rock, down which the stream is foaming in yonder gorge. He prizes me as a soldier would a good weapon; and that is all. Unmarried to him, this would never grieve me; but can I let him complete his calculations—coolly put into practice his plans—go through the wedding ceremony? Can I receive from him the bridal ring, endure all the forms of love (which I doubt not he would scrupulously observe) and know that the spirit was quite absent? Can I bear the consciousness that every endearment he bestows is a sacrifice made on principle? No: such a martyrdom would be monstrous. I will never undergo it. As his sister, I might accompany him—not as his wife: I will tell him so."

I looked toward the knoll: there he lay, still as a prostrate column; his face turned to me: his eye beaming, watchful, and keen. He started to his feet, and approached me.

"I am ready to go to India, if I may go free."

"Your answer requires a commentary," he said; "it is not clear."

"You have hitherto been my adopted brother: I, your adopted sister; let us continue as such: you and I had better not marry."

He shook his head. "Adopted fraternity will not do in this case. If you were my real sister it would be different: I should take you and seek no wife. But as it is, either our union must be consecrated and sealed by marriage, or it cannot exist: practical obstacles oppose themselves to any other plan. Do you not see it, Jane? Consider a moment—your strong sense will guide you."

I did consider: and still my sense, such as it was, directed me only to the fact that we did not love each other as man and wife should; and therefore it inferred we ought not to marry. I said so. "St. John," I returned, "I regard you as a brother—you, me as a sister: so let us continue."

"We cannot—we cannot," he answered, with short, sharp determination: "it would not do. You have said you will go with me to India: remember—you have said that."

"Conditionally."

"Well—well. To the main point—the departure with me from England, the cooperation with me in my future labors—you do not object. You have already as good as put your hand to the plow: you are too consistent to withdraw it. You have but one end to keep in view—how the work you have undertaken can best be done. Simplify your complicated interests, feelings, thoughts, wishes, aims; merge all considerations in one purpose: that of fulfilling with effect—with power—the mission of your great Master. To do so, you must have a coadjutor—not a brother: that is a loose tie: but a husband. I, too, do not want a sister; a sister might any day be taken from me. I want a wife: the sole helpmeet I can influence efficiently in life and retain absolutely till death."

I shuddered as he spoke: I felt his influence in my marrow—his hold on my limbs.

"Seek one elsewhere than in me, St. John: seek one fitted to you."

"One fitted to my purpose, you mean—fitted to my vocation. Again I tell you it is not the insignificant private individual—the mere man, with the man's selfish senses—I wish to mate: it is the missionary."

"And I will give the missionary my energies—it is all he wants—but not myself: that would be only adding the husk and shell to the kernel. For them he has no use: I retain them."

"You cannot—you ought not. Do you think God will be satisfied with half an oblation?[7] Will He accept a mutilated sacrifice? It is the cause of God I advocate: it is under His standard I enlist you. I cannot accept on His behalf a divided allegiance: it must be entire."

"Oh! I will give my heart to God," I said. "*You* do not want it."

I will not swear, reader, that there was not something of repressed sarcasm both in the tone in which I uttered this sentence, and in the feeling that accompanied it. I had silently feared St. John till now, because I had not understood him. He had held me in awe, because he had held me in doubt. How much of him was saint, how much mortal, I could not heretofore tell: but revelations were being made in this conference: the analysis of his nature was proceeding before my eyes. I saw his fallibilities: I comprehended them. I understood that, sitting there where I did, on the bank of heath, and with that handsome form before me, I sat at the feet of a man, erring as I. The veil fell from his hardness and despotism. Having felt in him the presence of these qualities, I felt his imperfection, and took courage. I was with an equal—one with whom I might argue—one whom, if I saw good, I might resist.

He was silent after I had uttered the last sentence, and I presently risked an upward glance at his countenance. His eye, bent on me, expressed at once stern surprise and keen inquiry. "Is she sarcastic, and sarcastic to *me*!" it seemed to say. "What does this signify?"

"Do not let us forget that this is a solemn matter," he said ere long: "one of which we may neither think nor talk lightly without sin. I trust, Jane, you are in earnest when you say you will give your heart to God: it is all I want. Once wrench your heart from man, and fix it on your Maker, the advancement of that Maker's spiritual kingdom on earth will be your chief delight and endeavor; you will be ready to do at once whatever furthers that end. You will see what impetus would be given to your efforts and mine by our physical and mental union in marriage: the only union that gives a character of permanent conformity to the destinies and designs of human beings: and, passing over all minor caprices—all trivial difficulties and delicacies of feeling—all scruple about the degree, kind, strength or tenderness of mere personal inclination— you will hasten to enter into that union at once."

"Shall I?" I said briefly; and I looked at his features, beautiful in their harmony, but strangely formidable in their still severity; at his brow, commanding but not open; at his eyes, bright and deep, and searching, but never soft; at his tall, imposing figure; and fancied myself in idea *his wife*. Oh! it would never do! As his curate, his comrade, all would be right: I would cross oceans with him in that capacity; toil under eastern suns, in Asia deserts with him in that office; admire and emulate his courage and devotion, and vigor; accommodate quietly to his masterhood; smile undisturbed at his ineradicable ambition; discriminate the Christian from the man: profoundly esteem the one, and freely forgive the other. I should suffer often, no doubt, attached to him

7. Offering.

only in this capacity: my body would be under rather a stringent yoke, but my heart and mind would be free. I should still have my unblighted self to turn to: my natural unenslaved feelings with which to communicate in moments of loneliness. There would be recesses in my mind which would be only mine, to which he never came; and sentiments growing there fresh and sheltered, which his austerity could never blight, nor his measured warrior-march trample down: but as his wife—at his side always, and always restrained, and always checked—forced to keep the fire of my nature continually low, to compel it to burn inwardly and never utter a cry, though the imprisoned flame consumed vital after vital—*this* would be unendurable.

"St. John!" I exclaimed, when I had got so far in my meditation.

"Well?" he answered icily.

"I repeat: I freely consent to go with you as your fellow-missionary; but not as your wife; I cannot marry you and become part of you."

"A part of me you must become," he answered steadily; "otherwise the whole bargain is void. How can I, a man not yet thirty, take out with me to India a girl of nineteen, unless she be married to me? How can we be for ever together—sometimes in solitudes, sometimes amid savage tribes—and unwed?"

"Very well," I said shortly; "under the circumstances, quite as well as if I were either your real sister, or a man and a clergyman like yourself."

"It is known that you are not my sister; I cannot introduce you as such: to attempt it would be to fasten injurious suspicions on us both. And for the rest, though you have a man's vigorous brain, you have a woman's heart, and—it would not do."

"It would do," I affirmed with some disdain, "perfectly well. I have a woman's heart; but not where you are concerned; for you I have only a comrade's constancy; a fellow-soldier's frankness, fidelity, fraternity, if you like; a neophyte's respect and submission to his hierophant:[8] nothing more—don't fear."

"It is what I want," he said, speaking to himself; "it is just what I want. And there are obstacles in the way: they must be hewn down. Jane, you would not repent marrying me; be certain of that; we *must* be married. I repeat it: there is no other way; and undoubtedly enough of love would follow upon marriage to render the union right even in your eyes."

"I scorn your idea of love," I could not help saying, as I rose up and stood before him, leaning my back against the rock. "I scorn the counterfeit sentiment you offer: yes, St. John, and I scorn you when you offer it."

He looked at me fixedly: compressing his well-cut lips while he did so. Whether he was incensed or surprised, or what, it was not easy to tell: he could command his countenance thoroughly.

"I scarcely expected to hear that expression from you," he said: "I think I have done and uttered nothing to deserve scorn."

I was touched by his gentle tone, and overawed by his high, calm mien.

"Forgive me the words, St. John: but it is your own fault that I have been roused to speak so unguardedly. You have introduced a topic on which our natures are at variance—a topic we should never discuss: the very name of love is an apple of discord[9] between us—if the reality were required what should we

<hr>

8. Priest (in ancient Greece). "Neophyte" new convert.

9. Mythical apple thrown among the Greek goddesses by Eris, goddess of strife.

do? How should we feel? My dear cousin, abandon your scheme of marriage—forget it."

"No," said he; "it is a long-cherished scheme, and the only one which can secure my great end: but I shall urge you no further at present. Tomorrow I leave home for Cambridge: I have many friends there to whom I should wish to say farewell. I shall be absent a fortnight—take that space of time to consider my offer: and do not forget that if you reject it, it is not me you deny, but God. Through my means, He opens to you a noble career; as my wife only can you enter upon it. Refuse to be my wife, and you limit yourself for ever to a track of selfish ease and barren obscurity. Tremble lest in that case you should be numbered with those who have denied the faith, and are worse than infidels!"

He had done. Turning from me, he once more

Looked to river, looked to hill:[1]

But this time his feelings were all pent in his heart: I was not worthy to hear them uttered. As I walked by his side homeward, I read well in his iron silence all he felt towards me: the disappointment of an austere and despotic nature, which has met resistance where it expected submission—the disapprobation of a cool, inflexible judgment, which has detected in another feelings and views in which it has no power to sympathize: in short, as a man, he would have wished to coerce me into obedience: it was only as a sincere Christian he bore so patiently with my perversity, and allowed so long a space for reflection and repentance.

That night, after he had kissed his sisters, he thought proper to forget even to shake hands with me; but left the room in silence. I—who, though I had no love, had much friendship for him—was hurt by the marked omission: so much hurt that tears started to my eyes.

"I see you and St. John have been quarreling, Jane," said Diana, "during your walk on the moor. But go after him; he is now lingering in the passage, expecting you—he will make it up."

I have not much pride under such circumstances: I would always rather be happy than dignified; and I ran after him—he stood at the foot of the stairs.

"Good-night, St. John," said I.

"Good-night, Jane," he replied calmly.

"Then shake hands," I added.

What a cold, loose touch he impressed on my fingers! He was deeply displeased by what had occurred that day: cordiality would not warm, nor tears move him. No happy reconciliation was to be had with him—no cheering smile or generous word: but still the Christian was patient and placid; and when I asked him if he forgave me, he answered that he was not in the habit of cherishing the remembrance of vexation; that he had nothing to forgive: not having been offended.

And with that answer he left me. I would much rather he had knocked me down.

Chapter XXXV

He did not leave for Cambridge the next day, as he had said he would. He deferred his departure a whole week; and during that time he made me feel

1. Sir Walter Scott's *The Lay of the Last Minstrel* 5.26.1

what severe punishment a good yet stern, a conscientious yet implacable man can inflict on one who has offended him. Without one overt act of hostility, one upbraiding word, he contrived to impress me momently with the conviction that I was put beyond the pale of his favor.

Not that St. John harbored a spirit of unchristian vindictiveness—not that he would have injured a hair of my head, if it had been fully in his power to do so. Both by nature and principle he was superior to the mean gratification of vengeance: he had forgiven me for saying I scorned him and his love, but he had not forgotten the words; and as long as he and I lived he never would forget them. I saw by his look, when he turned to me, that they were always written on the air between me and him; whenever I spoke, they sounded in my voice to his ear; and their echo toned every answer he gave me.

He did not abstain from conversing with me: he even called me as usual each morning to join him at his desk; and I fear the corrupt man within him had a pleasure unimparted to, and unshared by, the pure Christian, in evincing with what skill he could, while acting and speaking apparently just as usual, extract from every deed and every phrase the spirit of interest and approval which had formerly communicated a certain austere charm to his language and manner. To me, he was in reality become no longer flesh, but marble; his eye was a cold, bright, blue gem; his tongue, a speaking instrument—nothing more.

All this was torture to me—refined, lingering torture. It kept up a slow fire of indignation, and a trembling trouble of grief, which harassed and crushed me altogether. I felt how, if I were his wife, this good man, pure as the deep sunless source, could soon kill me: without drawing from my veins a single drop of blood, or receiving on his own crystal conscience the faintest stain of crime. Especially I felt this when I made any attempt to propitiate him. No ruth[2] met my ruth. He experienced no suffering from estrangement—no yearning after reconciliation; and though, more than once, my fast falling tears blistered the page over which we both bent, they produced no more effect on him than if his heart had been really a matter of stone or metal. To his sisters, meantime, he was somewhat kinder than usual: as if afraid that mere coldness would not sufficiently convince me how completely I was banished and banned, he added the force of contrast: and this I am sure he did, not by malice, but on principle.

The night before he left home, happening to see him walking in the garden about sunset, and remembering, as I looked at him, that this man, alienated as he now was, had once saved my life, and that we were near relations, I was moved to make a last attempt to regain his friendship. I went out and approached him, as he stood leaning over the little gate: I spoke to the point at once.

"St. John, I am unhappy, because you are still angry with me. Let us be friends."

"I hope we are friends," was the unmoved reply; while he still watched the rising of the moon, which he had been contemplating as I approached.

"No, St. John, we are not friends as we were. You know that."

"Are we not? That is wrong. For my part, I wish you no ill and all good."

"I believe you, St. John; for I am sure you are incapable of wishing anyone

2. Compassion, pity.

ill: but, as I am your kinswoman, I should desire somewhat more of affection than that sort of general philanthropy you extend to mere strangers."

"Of course," he said.

"Your wish is reasonable; and I am far from regarding you as a stranger."

This, spoken in a cool, tranquil tone, was mortifying and baffling enough. Had I attended to the suggestions of pride and ire, I should immediately have left him: but something worked within me more strongly than those feelings could. I deeply venerated my cousin's talent and principle. His friendship was of value to me: to lose it tried me severely. I would not so soon relinquish the attempt to reconquer it.

"Must we part in this way, St. John? And when you go to India, will you leave me so, without a kinder word than you have yet spoken?"

He now turned quite from the moon, and faced me.

"When I go to India, Jane, will I leave you? What! do you not go to India?"

"You said I could not, unless I married you."

"And you will not marry me? You adhere to that resolution?"

Reader, do you know, as I do, what terror those cold people can put into the ice of their questions? How much of the fall of the avalanche is in their anger? of the breaking up of the frozen sea in their displeasure?

"No, St. John, I will not marry you. I adhere to my resolution."

The avalanche had shaken and slid a little forward; but it did not yet crash down.

"Once more, why this refusal?" he asked.

"Formerly," I answered, "because you did not love me; now, I reply, because you almost hate me. If I were to marry you, you would kill me. You are killing me now."

His lips and cheeks turned white—quite white.

"*I should kill you—I am killing you?* Your words are such as ought not to be used: violent, unfeminine, and untrue. They betray an unfortunate state of mind: they merit severe reproof: they would seem inexcusable; but that it is the duty of man to forgive his fellow, even until seventy-and-seven times."[3]

I had finished the business now. While earnestly wishing to erase from his mind the trace of my former offence, I had stamped on that tenacious surface another and far deeper impression: I had burned it in."

"Now, you will indeed hate me," I said. "It is useless to attempt to conciliate you: I see I have made an eternal enemy of you."

A fresh wrong did these words inflict: the worse because they touched on the truth. That bloodless lip quivered to a temporary spasm. I knew the steely ire I had whetted. I was heart-wrung.

"You utterly misinterpret my words," I said, at once seizing his hand:

"I have no intention to grieve or pain you—indeed, I have not."

Most bitterly he smiled—most decidedly he withdrew his hand from mine. "And now you recall your promise, and will not go to India at all, I presume?" said he, after a considerable pause.

"Yes I will, as your assistant," I answered.

A very long silence succeeded. What struggle there was in him between Nature and Grace in this interval I cannot tell; only singular gleams scintillated in his eyes, and strange shadows passed over his face. He spoke at last.

3. Matthew 18:21–22.

"I before proved to you the absurdity of a single woman of your age propos-
ing to accompany abroad a single man of mine. I proved it to you in such
terms as, I should have thought, would have prevented your ever again allud-
ing to the plan. That you have done so, I regret—for your sake."

I interrupted him. Anything like a tangible reproach gave me courage at
once.

"Keep to common sense, St. John: you are verging on nonsense. You pretend
to be shocked by what I have said. You are not really shocked; for, with your su-
perior mind, you cannot be either so dull or so conceited as to misunderstand
my meaning. I say again, I will be your curate, if you like, but never your wife."

Again he turned lividly pale; but, as before, controlled his passion perfectly.
He answered emphatically, but calmly: "A female curate, who is not my wife,
would never suit me. With me, then, it seems, you cannot go: but if you are
sincere in your offer, I will, while in town, speak to a married missionary, whose
wife needs a coadjutor. Your own fortune will make you independent of the
Society's aid; and thus you may still be spared the dishonor of breaking your
promise, and deserting the band you engaged to join."

Now I never had, as the reader knows, either given any formal promise, or
entered into any engagement; and this language was all much too hard, and
much too despotic for the occasion. I replied: "There is no dishonor; no
breach of promise; no desertion in the case. I am not under the slightest oblig-
ation to go to India especially with strangers. With you I would have ventured
much; because I admire, confide in, and, as a sister, I love you: but I am con-
vinced that, go when and with whom I would, I should not live long in that
climate."

"Ah! you are afraid of yourself," he said, curling his lip.

"I am. God did not give me my life to throw away; and to do as you wish me
would, I begin to think, be almost equivalent to committing suicide.
Moreover, before I definitively resolve in quitting England, I will know for cer-
tain whether I cannot be of greater use by remaining in it than by leaving it."

"What do you mean?"

"It would be fruitless to attempt to explain: but there is a point on which I
have long endured painful doubt; and I can go nowhere till by some means
that doubt is removed."

"I know where your heart turns and to what it clings. The interest you cher-
ish is lawless and unconsecrated. Long since you ought to have crushed it: now
you should blush to allude to it. You think of Mr. Rochester?"

It was true. I confessed it by silence.

"Are you going to seek Mr. Rochester?"

"I must find out what is become of him."

"It remains for me, then," he said, "to remember you in my prayers; and to
entreat God for you, in all earnestness, that you may not indeed become a
castaway. I had thought I recognized in you one of the chosen. But God sees
not as man sees: His will be done."

He opened the gate, passed through it, and strayed away down the glen. He
was soon out of sight.

On reentering the parlor, I found Diana standing at the window, looking
very thoughtful. Diana was a great deal taller than I: she put her hand on my
shoulder, and, stooping, examined my face.

"Jane," she said, "you are always agitated and pale now. I am sure there is

something the matter. Tell me what business St. John and you have on hand. I have watched you this half-hour from the window: you must forgive my being such a spy, but for a long time I have fancied I hardly know what. St. John is a strange being——"

She paused—I did not speak: soon she resumed:—"That brother of mine cherishes peculiar views of some sort respecting you, I am sure: he has long distinguished you by a notice and interest he never showed to any one else—to what end? I wish he loved you—does he Jane?"

I put her cool hand to my hot forehead: "No, Di, not one whit."

"Then why does he follow you so with his eyes—and get you so frequently alone with him, and keep you so continually at his side? Mary and I had both concluded he wished you to marry him."

"He does—he has asked me to be his wife."

Diana clapped her hands. "That is just what we hoped and thought! And you will marry him, Jane, won't you? And then he will stay in England."

"Far from that, Diana; his sole idea in proposing to me is to procure a fitting fellow-laborer in his Indian toils."

"What! He wishes you to go to India?"

"Yes."

"Madness!" she exclaimed. "You would not live three months there, I am certain. You never shall go: you have not consented—have you, Jane?"

"I have refused to marry him——"

"And have consequently displeased him?" she suggested.

"Deeply: he will never forgive me, I fear: yet I offered to accompany him as his sister."

"It was frantic folly to do so, Jane. Think of the task you undertook—one of incessant fatigue: where fatigue kills even the strong; and you are weak. St. John—you know him—would urge you to impossibilities: with him there would be no permission to rest during the hot hours; and unfortunately, I have noticed, whatever he exacts, you force yourself to perform. I am astonished you found courage to refuse his hand. You do not love him then, Jane?"

"Not as a husband."

"Yet he is a handsome fellow."

"And I am so plain, you see, Di. We should never suit."

"Plain! You? Not at all. You are much too pretty, as well as too good, to be grilled alive in Calcutta." And again she earnestly conjured me to give up all thoughts of going out with her brother.

"I must, indeed," I said; "for when just now I repeated the offer of serving him for a deacon, he expressed himself shocked at my want of decency. He seemed to think I had committed an impropriety in proposing to accompany him unmarried: as if I had not from the first hoped to find in him a brother; and habitually regarded him as such."

"What makes you say he does not love you, Jane?"

"You should hear himself on the subject. He has again and again explained that it is not himself, but his office he wishes to mate. He has told me I am formed for labor—not for love: which is true, no doubt. But, in my opinion, if I am not formed for love, it follows that I am not formed for marriage. Would it not be strange, Di, to be chained for life to a man who regarded one but as a useful tool?"

"Insupportable—unnatural—out of the question!"

"And then," I continued, "though I have only sisterly affection for him now, yet, if forced to be his wife, I can imagine the possibility of conceiving an inevitable, strange, torturing kind of love for him: because he is so talented; and there is often a certain heroic grandeur in his look, manner, and conversation. In that case, my lot would become unspeakably wretched. He would not want me to love him; and if I showed the feeling, he would make me sensible that it was a superfluity, unrequired by him, unbecoming in me. I know he would."

"And yet St. John is a good man," said Diana.

"He is a good and a great man: but he forgets, pitilessly, the feelings and claims of little people, in pursuing his own large views. It is better, therefore, for the insignificant to keep out of his way; lest, in his progress, he should trample them down. Here he comes! I will leave you, Diana." And I hastened upstairs, as I saw him entering the garden.

But I was forced to meet him again at supper. During that meal he appeared just as composed as usual. I had thought he would hardly speak to me, and I was certain he had given up the pursuit of his matrimonial scheme: the sequel showed I was mistaken on both points. He addressed me precisely in his ordinary manner, or what had, of late, been his ordinary manner; one scrupulously polite. No doubt he had invoked the help of the Holy Spirit to subdue the anger I had roused in him, and now believed he had forgiven me once more.

For the evening reading before prayers, he selected the twenty-first chapter of Revelation. It was at all times pleasant to listen while from his lips fell the words of the Bible: never did his fine voice sound at once so sweet and full—never did his manner become so impressive in its noble simplicity, as when he delivered the oracles of God: and tonight that voice took a more solemn tone—that manner a more thrilling meaning—as he sat in the midst of his household circle (the May moon shining in through the uncurtained window, and rendering almost unnecessary the light of the candle on the table): as he sat there, bending over the great old Bible, and described from its page the vision of the new heaven and the new earth—told how God would come to dwell with men, how He would wipe away all tears from their eyes, and promised that there should be no more death, neither sorrow nor crying, nor any more pain, because the former things were passed away.

The succeeding words thrilled me strangely as he spoke them: especially as I felt, by the slight, indescribable alteration in sound, that in uttering them, his eye had turned on me.

"He that overcometh shall inherit all things; and I will be his God, and he shall be my son. But," was slowly, distinctly read, "the fearful, the unbelieving, etc. shall have their part in the lake which burneth with fire and brimstone, which is the second death."

Henceforth I knew what fate St. John feared for me.

A calm, subdued triumph, blent with a longing earnestness, marked his enunciation of the last glorious verses of that chapter. The reader believed his name was already written in the Lamb's book of life, and he yearned after the hour which should admit him to the city to which the kings of the earth bring their glory and honor; which has no need of sun or moon to shine in it, because the glory of God lightens it, and the Lamb is the light thereof.

In the prayer following the chapter, all his energy gathered—all his stern

zeal woke: he was in deep earnest, wrestling with God, and resolved on a conquest. He supplicated strength for the weak-hearted; guidance for wanderers from the fold: a return, even at the eleventh hour, for those whom the temptations of the world and the flesh were luring from the narrow path. He asked, he urged, he claimed the boon of a brand snatched from the burning. Earnestness is ever deeply solemn: first, as I listened to that prayer, I wondered at his; then, when it continued and rose, I was touched by it, and at last awed. He felt the greatness and goodness of his purpose so sincerely: others who heard him plead for it, could not but feel it too.

The prayer over, we took leave of him: he was to go at a very early hour in the morning. Diana and Mary having kissed him, left the room—in compliance, I think, with a whispered hint from him: I tendered my hand, and wished him a pleasant journey.

"Thank you, Jane. As I said, I shall return from Cambridge in a fortnight: that space, then, is yet left you for reflection. If I listened to human pride, I should say no more to you of marriage with me; but I listen to my duty, and keep steadily in view my first aim—to do all things to the glory of God. My Master was long-suffering: so will I be. I cannot give you up to perdition as a vessel of wrath: repent—resolve; while there is yet time. Remember, we are bid to work while it is day—warned that 'the night cometh when no man shall work.'[4] Remember the fate of Dives,[5] who had his good things in this life. God give you strength to choose that better part which shall not be taken from you!"

He laid his hand on my head as he uttered the last words. He had spoken earnestly, mildly: his look was not, indeed, that of a lover beholding his mistress; but it was that of a pastor recalling his wandering sheep—or better, of a guardian angel watching the soul for which he is responsible. All men of talent, whether they be men of feeling or not; whether they be zealots, or aspirants, or despots—provided only they be sincere—have their sublime moments: when they subdue and rule. I felt veneration for St. John—veneration so strong that its impetus thrust me at once to the point I had so long shunned. I was tempted to cease struggling with him—to rush down the torrent of his will into the gulf of his existence, and there lose my own. I was almost as hard beset by him now as I had been once before, in a different way, by another. I was a fool both times. To have yielded then would have been an error of principle; to have yielded now would have been an error of judgment. So I think at this hour, when I look back to the crisis through the quiet medium of time: I was unconscious of folly at the instant.

I stood motionless under my hierophant's touch. My refusals were forgotten—my fears overcome—my wrestlings paralyzed. The impossible—*i.e.* my marriage with St. John—was fast becoming the Possible. All was changing utterly, with a sudden sweep. Religion called—Angels beckoned—God commanded—life rolled together like a scroll—death's gates opening, showed eternity beyond: it seemed, that for safety and bliss there, all here might be sacrificed in a second. The dim room was full of visions.

"Could you decide now?" asked the missionary. The inquiry was put in gentle tones: he drew me to him as gently. Oh, that gentleness! how far more potent is it than force! I could resist St. John's wrath: I grew pliant as a reed under

4. John 9:4. 5. In Luke 16:19–31, Dives, the rich man, goes to hell.

his kindness. Yet I knew all the time, if I yielded now, I should not the less be made to repent, some day, of my former rebellion. His nature was not changed by one hour of solemn prayer: it was only elevated.

"I could decide if I were but certain," I answered: "were I but convinced that it is God's will I should marry you, I could vow to marry you here and now—come afterwards what would!"

"My prayers are heard!" ejaculated St. John. He pressed his hand firmer on my head, as if he claimed me: he surrounded me with his arm, *almost* as if he loved me (I say *almost*—I knew the difference—for I had felt what it was to be loved; but, like him, I had now put love out of the question, and thought only of duty): I contended with my inward dimness of vision, before which clouds yet rolled. I sincerely, deeply, fervently longed to do what was right; and only that. "Show me, show me the path!" I entreated of Heaven. I was excited more than I had ever been; and whether what followed was the effect of excitement, the reader shall judge.

All the house was still; for I believe all, except St. John and myself, were now retired to rest. The one candle was dying out: the room was full of moonlight. My heart beat fast and thick: I heard its throb. Suddenly it stood still to an inexpressible feeling that thrilled it through, and passed at once to my head and extremities. The feeling was not like an electric shock; but it was quite as sharp, as strange, as startling: it acted on my senses as if their utmost activity hitherto had been but torpor; from which they were now summoned, and forced to wake. They rose expectant: eye and ear waited, while the flesh quivered on my bones.

"What have you heard? What do you see?" asked St. John. I saw nothing: but I heard a voice somewhere cry—"Jane! Jane! Jane!" nothing more.

"Oh God! what is it?" I gasped.

I might have said, "Where is it?" for it did not seem in the room—nor in the house—nor in the garden: it did not come out of the air—nor from under the earth—nor from overhead. I had heard it—where, or whence, for ever impossible to know! And it was the voice of a human being—a known, loved, well-remembered voice—that of Edward Fairfax Rochester; and it spoke in pain and woe wildly, eerily, urgently.

"I am coming!" I cried. "Wait for me! Oh, I will come!" I flew to the door, and looked into the passage: it was dark. I ran out into the garden: it was void.

"Where are you?" I exclaimed.

The hills beyond Marsh Glen sent the answer faintly back—"Where are you?" I listened. The wind sighed low in the firs: all was moorland loneliness and midnight hush.

"Down superstition!" I commented, as that specter rose up black by the black yew at the gate. "This is not thy deception, nor thy witchcraft: it is the work of nature. She was roused, and did—no miracle—but her best."

I broke from St. John, who had followed, and would have detained me. It was *my* time to assume ascendancy. *My* powers were in play and in force. I told him to forbear question or remark; I desired him to leave me: I must, and would be alone. He obeyed at once. Where there is energy to command well enough, obedience never fails. I mounted to my chamber; locked myself in; fell on my knees; and prayed in my way—a different way to St. John's, but effective in its own fashion. I seemed to penetrate very near a Mighty Spirit; and my soul rushed out in gratitude at His feet. I rose from the thanksgiving—

took a resolve—and lay down, unscared, enlightened—eager but for the daylight.

Chapter XXXVI

The daylight came. I rose at dawn. I busied myself for an hour or two with arranging my things in my chamber, drawers, and wardrobe, in the order wherein I should wish to leave them during a brief absence. Meantime, I heard St. John quit his room. He stopped at my door: I feared he would knock—no, but a slip of paper was passed under the door. I took it up. It bore these words—

"You left me too suddenly last night. Had you stayed but a little longer, you would have laid your hand on the Christian's cross and the angel's crown. I shall expect your clear decision when I return this day fortnight. Meantime, watch and pray that you enter not into temptation: the spirit, I trust, is willing, but the flesh, I see, is weak.[6] I shall pray for you hourly,—Yours, St. John."

"My Spirit," I answered mentally, "is willing to do what is right; and my flesh, I hope, is strong enough to accomplish the will of Heaven, when once that will is distinctly known to me. At any rate, it shall be strong enough to search—inquire—to grope an outlet from this cloud of doubt, and find the open day of certainty."

It was the first of June; yet the morning was overcast and chilly: rain beat fast on my casement. I heard the front-door open, and St. John pass out. Looking through the window, I saw him traverse the garden. He took the way over the misty moors in the direction of Whitcross—there he would meet the coach.

"In a few more hours I shall succeed you in that track, cousin," thought I: "I too have a coach to meet at Whitcross. I too have some to see and ask after in England, before I depart for ever."

It wanted yet two hours of breakfast-time. I filled the interval in walking softly about my room, and pondering the visitation which had given my plans their present bent. I recalled that inward sensation I had experienced: for I could recall it, with all its unspeakable strangeness. I recalled the voice I had heard; again I questioned whence it came, as vainly as before: it seemed in *me* —not in the external world. I asked, was it a mere nervous impression—a delusion? I could not conceive or believe: it was more like an inspiration. The wondrous shock of feeling had come like the earthquake which shook the foundations of Paul and Silas's prison:[7] it had opened the doors of the soul's cell, and loosed its bands—it had wakened it out of its sleep, whence it sprang trembling, listening, aghast; then vibrated thrice a cry on my startled ear, and in my quaking heart, and through my spirit; which neither feared nor shook, but exulted as if in joy over the success of one effort it had been privileged to make, independent of the cumbrous body.

"Ere many days," I said, as I terminated my musings, "I will know something of him whose voice seemed last night to summon me. Letters have proved of no avail—personal inquiry shall replace them."

At breakfast I announced to Diana and Mary that I was going a journey, and should be absent at least four days.

6. Matthew 26:41. 7. Acts 16:25–26.

"Alone, Jane?" they asked.

"Yes; it was to see, or hear news of, a friend about whom I had for some time been uneasy."

They might have said, as I have no doubt they thought, that they had believed me to be without any friends save them; for, indeed, I had often said so; but with their true natural delicacy, they abstained from comment; except that Diana asked me if I was sure I was well enough to travel. I looked very pale, she observed. I replied, that nothing ailed me save anxiety of mind, which I hoped soon to alleviate.

It was easy to make my further arrangements; for I was troubled with no inquiries—no surmises. Having once explained to them that I could not now be explicit about my plans, they kindly and wisely acquiesced in the silence with which I pursued them; according to me the privilege of free action I should, under similar circumstances, have accorded them.

I left Moor House at three o'clock P.M., and soon after four I stood at the foot of the sign-post of Whitcross, waiting the arrival of the coach which was to take me to distant Thornfield. Amid the silence of those solitary roads and desert hills, I heard it approach from a great distance. It was the same vehicle whence, a year ago, I had alighted one summer evening on this very spot—how desolate, and hopeless, and objectless! It stopped as I beckoned. I entered—not now obliged to part with my whole fortune as the price of its accommodation. Once more on the road to Thornfield, I felt like the messenger-pigeon flying home.

It was a journey of six-and-thirty hours. I had set out from Whitcross on a Tuesday afternoon, and early on the succeeding Thursday morning the coach stopped to water the horses at a wayside inn, situated in the midst of scenery whose green hedges and large fields and low pastoral hills (how mild of feature and verdant of hue compared with the stern north-midland moors of Morton!) met my eye like the lineaments of a once familiar face. Yes, I knew the character of this landscape: I was sure we were near my bourne.

"How far is Thornfield Hall from here?" I asked of the ostler.

"Just two miles, ma'am, across the fields."

"My journey is closed," I thought to myself. I got out of the coach, gave a box I had into the ostler's charge, to be kept till I called for it; paid my fare; satisfied the coachman, and was going: the brightening day gleamed on the sign of the inn, and I read in gilt letters, "The Rochester Arms." My heart leaped up: I was already on my master's very lands. It fell again: the thought struck it:—

"Your master himself may be beyond the British Channel, for aught you know: and then, if he is at Thornfield Hall, towards which you hasten, who besides him is there? His lunatic wife: and you have nothing to do with him: you dare not speak to him or seek his presence. You have lost your labor—you had better go no farther," urged the monitor. "Ask information of the people at the inn; they can give you all you seek: they can solve your doubts at once. Go up to that man, and inquire if Mr. Rochester be at home."

The suggestion was sensible; and yet I could not force myself to act on it. I so dreaded a reply that would crush me with despair. To prolong doubt was to prolong hope. I might yet once more see the Hall under the ray of her star. There was the stile before me—the very fields through which I had hurried, blind, deaf, distracted, with a revengeful fury tracking and scourging me, on

the morning I fled from Thornfield: ere I well knew what course I had resolved to take, I was in the midst of them. How fast I walked! How I ran sometimes! How I looked forward to catch the first view of the well-known woods! With what feelings I welcomed single trees I knew, and familiar glimpses of meadow and hill between them!

At last the woods rose; the rookery clustered dark; a loud cawing broke the morning stillness. Strange delight inspired me: on I hastened. Another field crossed—a lane threaded—and there were the courtyard walls—the back of-fices: the house itself, the rookery still hid. "My first view of it shall be in front," I determined, "where its bold battlements will strike the eye nobly at once, and where I can single out my master's very window: perhaps he will be standing at it—he rises early: perhaps he is now walking in the orchard, or on the pavement in front. Could I but see him!—but a moment! Surely, in that case, I should not be so mad as to run to him? I cannot tell—I am not certain. And if I did—what then? God bless him! What then? Who would be hurt by my once more tasting the life his glance can give me?—I rave: perhaps at this moment he is watching the sun rise over the Pyrenees, or on the tideless sea of the south."

I had coasted along the lower wall of the orchard—turned its angle: there was a gate just there, opening into the meadow, between two stone pillars, crowned by stone balls. From behind one pillar I could peep round quietly at the full front of the mansion. I advanced my head with precaution, desirous to ascertain if any bedroom window-blinds were yet drawn up: battlements, win-dows, long front—all from this sheltered station were at my command.

The crows sailing overhead perhaps watched me while I took this survey. I wonder what they thought: they must have considered I was very careful and timid at first, and that gradually I grew very bold and reckless. A peep, and then a long stare; and then a departure from my niche and a straying out into the meadow; and a sudden stop full in front of the great mansion, and a pro-tracted, hardy gaze towards it. "What affectation of diffidence was this at first?" they might have demanded. "What stupid regardlessness now?"

Hear an illustration, reader.

A lover finds his mistress asleep on a mossy bank; he wishes to catch a glimpse of her fair face without waking her. He steals softly over the grass, careful to make no sound; he pauses—fancying she has stirred: he withdraws; not for worlds would be be seen. All is still: he again advances: he bends above her; a light veil rests on her features: he lifts it, bends lower; now his eyes an-ticipate the vision of beauty—warm, and blooming, and lovely, in rest. How hurried was their first glance! But how they fix! How he starts! How he sud-denly and vehemently clasps in both arms the form he dared not, a moment since, touch with his finger! How he calls aloud a name, and drops his burden, and gazes on it wildly! He thus grasps and cries, and gazes, because he no longer fears to waken by any sound he can utter—by any movement he can make. He thought his love slept sweetly: he finds she is stone-dead.

I looked with timorous joy towards a stately house: I saw a blackened ruin.

No need to cower behind a gate-post, indeed!—to peep up at chamber lat-tices, fearing life was astir behind them! No need to listen for doors opening—to fancy steps on the pavement or the gravel-walk! The lawn, the grounds were trodden and waste: the portal yawned void. The front was, as I had once seen it in a dream, but a shell-like wall, very high and very fragile looking, perfo-

rated with paneless windows: no roof, no battlements, no chimneys—all had crashed in.

And there was the silence of death about it: the solitude of a lonesome wild. No wonder that letters addressed to people here had never received an answer: as well despatch epistles to a vault in a church aisle. The grim blackness of the stones told by what fate the Hall had fallen—by conflagration: but how kindled? What story belonged to this disaster? What loss, besides mortar and marble and wood-work, had followed upon it? Had life been wrecked, as well as property? If so, whose? Dreadful question: there was no one here to answer it—not even dumb sign, mute token.

In wandering round the shattered walls and through the devastated interior, I gathered evidence that the calamity was not of late occurrence. Winter snows, I thought, had drifted through that void arch, winter rains beaten in at those hollow casements; for, amid the drenched piles of rubbish, spring had cherished vegetation: grass and weed grew here and there between the stones and fallen rafters. And oh! where, meantime, was the hapless owner of this wreck? In what land? Under what auspices? My eye involuntarily wandered to the gray church tower near the gates, and I asked, "Is he with Damer de Rochester, sharing the shelter of his narrow marble house?"

Some answer must be had to these questions. I could find it nowhere but at the inn, and thither, ere long, I returned. The host himself brought my breakfast into the parlor. I requested him to shut the door and sit down: I had some questions to ask him. But when he complied, I scarcely knew how to begin; such horror had I of the possible answers. And yet the spectacle of desolation I had just left prepared me in a measure for a tale of misery. The host was a respectable-looking, middle-aged man.

"You know Thornfield Hall, of course?" I managed to say at last.

"Yes, ma'am; I lived there once."

"Did you?" Not in my time, I thought: you are a stranger to me.

"I was the late Mr. Rochester's butler," he added.

The late! I seemed to have received with full force the blow I had been trying to evade.

"The late!" I gasped. "Is he dead?"

"I mean the present gentleman Mr. Edward's father," he explained.

I breathed again: my blood resumed its flow. Fully assured by these words that Mr. Edward—my Mr. Rochester (God bless him, wherever he was!)—was at least alive: was, in short, 'the present gentleman.' Gladdening words! It seemed I could hear all that was to come—whatever the disclosures might be—with comparative tranquillity. Since he was not in the grave, I could bear, I thought, to learn that he was at the Antipodes.

"Is Mr. Rochester living at Thornfield Hall now?" I asked, knowing, of course, what the answer would be, but yet desirous of deferring the direct question as to where he really was.

"No, ma'am—oh, no! No one is living there. I suppose you are a stranger in these parts, or you would have heard what happened last autumn,— Thornfield Hall is quite a ruin: it was burnt down just about harvest time. A dreadful calamity! such an immense quantity of valuable property destroyed: hardly any of the furniture could be saved. The fire broke out at dead of night, and before the engines arrived from Millcote, the building was one mass of flame. It was a terrible spectacle: I witnessed it myself."

"At dead of night!" I muttered. Yes, that was ever the hour of fatality at Thornfield. "Was it known how it originated?" I demanded.

"They guessed, ma'am: they guessed. Indeed, I should say it was ascertained beyond a doubt. You are not perhaps aware," he continued, edging his chair a little nearer the table, and speaking low, "that there was a lady,—a—a lunatic, kept in the house?"

"I have heard something of it."

"She was kept in very close confinement, ma'am; people even for some years was not absolutely certain of her existence. No one saw her: they only knew by rumor that such a person was at the Hall; and who or what she was it was difficult to conjecture. They said Mr. Edward had brought her from abroad; and some believed she had been his mistress. But a queer thing happened a year since—a very queer thing."

I feared now to hear my own story. I endeavored to recall him to the main fact.

"And this lady?"

"This lady, ma'am," he answered, "turned out to be Mr. Rochester's wife! The discovery was brought about in the strangest way. There was a young lady, a governess at the Hall, that Mr. Rochester fell in——"

"But the fire," I suggested.

"I'm coming to that, ma'am—that Mr. Edward fell in love with. The servants say they never saw anybody so much in love as he was: he was after her continually. They used to watch him—servants will, you know, ma'am—and he set store on her past everything: for all, nobody but him thought her so very handsome. She was a little small thing, they say, almost like a child. I never saw her myself; but I've heard Leah, the housemaid, tell of her. Leah liked her well enough. Mr. Rochester was about forty, and this governess not twenty; and you see, when gentlemen of his age fall in love with girls, they are often like as if they were bewitched: well, he would marry her."

"You shall tell me this part of the story another time," I said; "but now I have a particular reason for wishing to hear all about the fire. Was it suspected that this lunatic, Mrs. Rochester, had any hand in it?"

"You've hit it, ma'am: it's quite certain that it was her and nobody but her, that set it going. She had a woman to take care of her called Mrs. Poole—an able woman in her line, and very trustworthy, but for one fault—a fault common to a deal of them nurses and matrons—*she kept a private bottle of gin by her*, and now and then took a drop over much. It is excusable, for she had a hard life of it: but still it was dangerous; for when Mrs. Poole was fast asleep, after the gin-and-water, the mad lady, who was as cunning as a witch, would take the keys out of her pocket, let herself out of her chamber, and go roaming about the house, doing any wild mischief that came into her head. They say she had nearly burned her husband in his bed once: but I don't know about that. However, on this night, she set fire first to the hangings of the room next her own; and then she got down to a lower story, and made her way to the chamber that had been the governess's—(she was like as if she knew somehow how matters had gone on, and had a spite at her)—and she kindled the bed there; but there was nobody sleeping in it fortunately. The governess had run away two months before; and for all Mr. Rochester sought her as if she had been the most precious thing he had in the world, he never could hear a word of her; and he grew savage—quite savage in his disappointment: he never was a wild man, but he got dangerous after he lost her. He would be alone, too. He sent Mrs. Fairfax, the housekeeper, away to her friends at a distance; but he

did it handsomely, for he settled an annuity on her for life: and she deserved it—she was a very good woman. Miss Adèle, a ward he had, was put to school. He broke off acquaintance with all the gentry, and shut himself up, like a hermit, at the Hall."

"What! did he not leave England?"

"Leave England? Bless you, no! He would not cross the door-stones of the house; except at night, when he walked just like a ghost about the grounds and in the orchard as if he had lost his senses—which it is my opinion he had; for a more spirited, bolder, keener gentleman than he was before that midge of a governess crossed him, you never saw, ma'am. He was not a man given to wine, or cards, or racing, as some are, and he was not so very handsome; but he had a courage and a will of his own, if ever man had. I knew him from a boy, you see: and for my part I have often wished that Miss Eyre had been sunk in the sea before she came to Thornfield Hall."

"Then Mr. Rochester was at home when the fire broke out?"

"Yes, indeed was he; and he went up to the attics when all was burning above and below, and got the servants out of their beds and helped them down himself—and went back to get his mad wife out of her cell. And then they called out to him that she was on the roof; where she was standing, waving her arms, above the battlements, and shouting out till they could hear her a mile off; I saw her and heard her with my own eyes. She was a big woman, and had long black hair: we could see it streaming against the flames as she stood. I witnessed, and several more witnessed Mr. Rochester ascend through the skylight on to the roof: we heard him call 'Bertha!' We saw him approach her; and then, ma'am, she yelled, and gave a spring, and the next minute she lay smashed on the pavement."

"Dead?"

"Dead? Ay, dead as the stones on which her brains and blood were scattered."

"Good God!"

"You may well say so, ma'am: it was frightful!"

He shuddered.

"And afterwards?" I urged.

"Well, ma'am, afterwards the house was burned to the ground: there are only some bits of walls standing now."

"Were any other lives lost?"

"No—perhaps it would have been better if there had."

"What do you mean?"

"Poor Mr. Edward!" he ejaculated, "I little thought ever to have seen it! Some say it was a just judgment on him for keeping his first marriage secret, and wanting to take another wife while he had one living: but I pity him, for my part."

"You said he was alive?" I exclaimed.

"Yes, yes: he is alive; but many think he had better be dead."

"Why? How?" My blood was again running cold. "Where is he?" I demanded. "Is he in England?"

"Ay—ay—he's in England: he can't get out of England, I fancy—he's a fixture now."

What agony was this! And the man seemed resolved to protract it.

"He is stone-blind," he said at last. "Yes—he is stone-blind—is Mr. Edward."

I had dreaded worse. I had dreaded he was mad. I summoned strength to ask what had caused this calamity.

"It was all his own courage, and a body may say, his kindness, in a way, ma'am: he wouldn't leave the house till every one else was out before him. As he came down the great staircase at last, after Mrs. Rochester had flung herself from the battlements, there was a great crash—all fell. He was taken out from under the ruins, alive, but sadly hurt: a beam had fallen in such a way as to protect him partly; but one eye was knocked out, and one hand so crushed that Mr. Carter, the surgeon, had to amputate it directly. The other eye inflamed: he lost the sight of that also. He is now helpless, indeed—blind and a cripple."

"Where is he? Where does he now live?"

"At Ferndean, a manor-house on a farm he has, about thirty miles off: quite a desolate spot."

"Who is with him?"

"Old John and his wife: he would have none else. He is quite broken down, they say."

"Have you any sort of conveyance?"

"We have a chaise, ma'am, a very handsome chaise."

"Let it be got ready instantly; and if your post-boy can drive me to Ferndean before dark this day, I'll pay both you and him twice the hire you usually demand."

Chapter XXXVII

The manor-house of Ferndean was a building of considerable antiquity, moderate size, and no architectural pretensions, deep buried in a wood. I had heard of it before. Mr. Rochester often spoke of it, and sometimes went there. His father had purchased the estate for the sake of the game covers. He would have let the house; but could find no tenant, in consequence of its ineligible and insalubrious site. Ferndean then remained uninhabited and unfurnished; with the exception of some two or three rooms fitted up for the accommodation of the squire when he went there in the season to shoot.

To this house I came, just ere dark, on an evening marked by the characteristics of sad sky, cold gale, and continued small, penetrating rain. The last mile I performed on foot, having dismissed the chaise and driver with the double remuneration I had promised. Even when within a very short distance of the manor-house you could see nothing of it; so thick and dark grew the timber of the gloomy wood about it. Iron gates between granite pillars showed me where to enter, and passing through them, I found myself at once in the twilight of close-ranked trees. There was a grass-grown track descending the forest aisle, between hoar and knotty shafts and under branched arches. I followed it, expecting soon to reach the dwelling; but it stretched on and on, it wound far and farther: no sign of habitation or grounds was visible.

I thought I had taken a wrong direction and lost my way. The darkness of natural as well as of sylvan dusk gathered over me. I looked round in search of another road. There was none: all was interwoven stem, columnar trunk, dense, summer foliage—no opening anywhere.

I proceeded: at last my way opened, the trees thinned a little: presently I beheld a railing, then the house—scarce, by this dim light, distinguishable from the trees; so dank and green were its decaying walls. Entering a portal, fastened only by a latch, I stood amidst a space of enclosed ground, from which

the wood swept away in a semicircle. There were no flowers, no garden-beds; only a broad gravel-walk girdling a grass-plat, and this set in the heavy frame of the forest. The house presented two pointed gables in its front; the windows were latticed and narrow; the front door was narrow too, one step led up to it. The whole looked, as the host of the Rochester Arms had said, "quite a desolate spot." It was as still as a church on a week-day: the pattering rain on the forest leaves was the only sound audible in its vicinage.

"Can there be life here?" I asked.

Yes: life of some kind there was: for I heard a movement—that narrow front door was unclosing, and some shape was about to issue from the grange.

It opened slowly: a figure came out into the twilight and stood on the step; a man without a hat: he stretched forth his hand as if to feel whether it rained. Dusk as it was, I had recognized him—it was my master, Edward Fairfax Rochester and no other.

I stayed my step, almost my breath, and stood to watch him—to examine him, myself unseen, and alas! to him invisible. It was a sudden meeting, and one in which rapture was kept well in check by pain. I had no difficulty in restraining my voice from exclamation, my step from hasty advance.

His form was of the same strong and stalwart contour as ever: his port was still erect, his hair was still raven-black; nor were his features altered or sunk: not in one year's space, by any sorrow, could his athletic strength be quelled, or his vigorous prime blighted. But in his countenance I saw a change: that looked desperate and brooding—that reminded me of some wronged and fettered wild beast or bird, dangerous to approach in his sullen woe. The caged eagle, whose gold-ringed eyes cruelty has extinguished, might look as looked that sightless Samson.

And, reader, do you think I feared him in his blind ferocity?—if you do, you little know me. A soft hope blent with my sorrow that soon I should dare to drop a kiss on that brow of rock, and on those lips so sternly sealed beneath it: but not yet. I would not accost him yet.

He descended the one step, and advanced slowly and gropingly towards the grass-plat. Where was his daring stride now? Then he paused, as if he knew not which way to turn. He lifted his hand and opened his eyelids; gazed blank, and with a straining effort, on the sky, and towards the amphitheatre of trees: one saw that all to him was void darkness. He stretched his right hand (the left arm, the mutilated one, he kept hidden in his bosom); he seemed to wish by touch to gain an idea of what lay around him: he met but vacancy still; for the trees were some yards off where he stood. He relinquished the endeavor, folded his arms, and stood quiet and mute in the rain, now falling fast on his uncovered head. At this moment John approached him from some quarter.

"Will you take my arm, sir?" he said; "there is a heavy shower coming on: had you not better go in?"

"Let me alone," was the answer.

John withdrew, without having observed me. Mr. Rochester now tried to walk about: vainly,—all was too uncertain. He groped his way back to the house, and, reentering it, closed the door.

I now drew near and knocked: John's wife opened for me. "Mary," I said, "how are you?"

She started as if she had seen a ghost: I calmed her. To her hurried "Is it really you, miss, come at this late hour to this lonely place?" I answered by taking her hand; and then I followed her into the kitchen, where John now sat by a

good fire. I explained to them, in few words, that I had heard all which had happened since I left Thornfield, and that I was come to see Mr. Rochester. I asked John to go down to the turnpike-house, where I had dismissed the chaise, and bring my trunk, which I had left there: and then, while I removed my bonnet and shawl, I questioned Mary as to whether I could be accommodated at the Manor House for the night; and finding that arrangements to that effect, though difficult, would not be impossible, I informed her I should stay. Just at this moment the parlor-bell rang.

"When you go in," said I, "tell your master that a person wishes to speak to him, but do not give my name."

"I don't think he will see you," she answered; "he refuses everybody."

When she returned I inquired what he had said.

"You are to send in your name and your business," she replied. She then proceeded to fill a glass with water, and place it on a tray, together with candles.

"Is that what he rang for?" I asked.

"Yes: he always has candles brought in at dark, though he is blind."

"Give the tray to me, I will carry it in."

I took it from her hand: she pointed me out the parlor door. The tray shook as I held it; the water spilled from the glass; my heart struck my ribs loud and fast. Mary opened the door for me, and shut it behind me.

This parlor looked gloomy: a neglected handful of fire burned low in the grate; and, leaning over it, with his head supported against the high, old-fashioned mantelpiece, appeared the blind tenant of the room. His old dog, Pilot, lay on one side, removed out of the way, and coiled up as if afraid of being inadvertently trodden upon. Pilot pricked up his ears when I came in: then he jumped up with a yelp and a whine, and bounded towards me: he almost knocked the tray from my hands. I set it on the table; then patted him, and said softly, "Lie down!" Mr. Rochester turned mechanically to *see* what the commotion was: but as he *saw* nothing, he returned and sighed.

"Give me the water, Mary," he said.

I approached him with the now only half-filled glass. Pilot followed me, still excited.

"What is the matter?" he inquired.

"Down, Pilot!" I again said. He checked the water on its way to his lips, and seemed to listen: he drank, and put the glass down. "This is you, Mary, is it not?"

"Mary is in the kitchen," I answered.

He put out his hand with a quick gesture, but not seeing where I stood, he did not touch me. "Who is this? Who is this?" he demanded, trying, as it seemed, to *see* with those sightless eyes—unavailing and distressing attempt! "Answer me—speak again!" he ordered, imperiously and aloud.

"Will you have a little more water, sir? I spilled half of what was in the glass," I said.

"*Who* is it? *What* is it? Who speaks?"

"Pilot knows me, and John and Mary know I am here. I came only this evening," I answered.

"Great God!—what delusion has come over me? What sweet madness has seized me?"

"No delusion—no madness: your mind, sir, is too strong for delusion, your health too sound for frenzy."

"And where is the speaker? Is it only a voice? Oh! I cannot see, but I must feel, or my heart will stop and my brain burst. Whatever—whoever you are—be perceptible to the touch or I cannot live!"

He groped; I arrested his wandering hand, and prisoned it in both mine.

"Her very fingers!" he cried; "her small, slight fingers! If so, there must be more of her."

The muscular hand broke from my custody; my arm was seized, my shoulder—neck—waist—I was entwined and gathered to him.

"Is it Jane? *What* is it? This is her shape—this is her size——"

"And this her voice," I added. "She is all here: her heart, too. God bless you, sir! I am glad to be so near you again."

"Jane Eyre!—Jane Eyre!" was all he said.

"My dear master," I answered, "I am Jane Eyre: I have found you out—I am come back to you."

"In truth?—in the flesh? My living Jane?"

"You touch me, sir,—you hold me, and fast enough; I am not cold like a corpse, nor vacant like air, am I?"

"My living darling! These are certainly her limbs, and these her features; but I cannot be so blest, after all my misery. It is a dream; such dreams as I have had at night when I have clasped her once more to my heart, as I do now; and kissed her, as thus—and felt that she loved me, and trusted that she would not leave me."

"Which I never will, sir, from this day."

"Never will, says the vision? But I always woke and found it an empty mockery; and I was desolate and abandoned—my life dark, lonely, hopeless—my soul athirst and forbidden to drink—my heart famished and never to be fed. Gentle, soft dream, nestling in my arms now, you will fly, too, as your sisters have all fled before you: but kiss me before you go—embrace me, Jane."

"There, sir—and there!"

I pressed my lips to his once brilliant and now rayless eyes—I swept his hair from his brow, and kissed that too. He suddenly seemed to arouse himself: the conviction of the reality of all this seized him.

"It is you—is it Jane? You are come back to me then?"

"I am."

"And you do not lie dead in some ditch under some stream? And you are not a pining outcast amongst strangers?"

"No, sir; I am an independent woman now."

"Independent! What do you mean, Jane?"

"My uncle in Madeira is dead, and he left me five thousand pounds."

"Ah, this is practical—this is real!" he cried: "I should never dream that. Besides, there is that peculiar voice of hers, so animating and piquant, as well as soft: it cheers my withered heart; it puts life into it.—What, Janet! Are you an independent woman? A rich woman?"

"Quite rich, sir. If you won't let me live with you, I can build a house of my own close up to your door, and you may come and sit in my parlor when you want company of an evening."

"But as you are rich, Jane, you have now, no doubt, friends who will look after you, and not suffer you to devote yourself to a blind lameter[8] like me?"

"I told you I am independent, sir, as well as rich: I am my own mistress."

8. Cripple.

"And you will stay with me?"

"Certainly—unless you object. I will be your neighbor, your nurse, your housekeeper. I find you lonely: I will be your companion—to read to you, to walk with you, to sit with you, to wait on you, to be eyes and hands to you. Cease to look so melancholy, my dear master; you shall not be left desolate, so long as I live."

He replied not: he seemed serious—abstracted; he sighed; he half-opened his lips as if to speak: he closed them again. I felt a little embarrassed. Perhaps I had too rashly overleaped conventionalities; and he, like St. John, saw impropriety in my inconsiderateness. I had indeed made my proposal from the idea that he wished and would ask me to be his wife: an expectation, not the less certain because unexpressed, had buoyed me up, that he would claim me at once as his own. But no hint to that effect escaping him, and his countenance becoming more overcast, I suddenly remembered that I might have been all wrong and was perhaps playing the fool unwittingly; and I began gently to withdraw myself from his arms—but he eagerly snatched me closer.

"No—no—Jane: you must not go. No—I have touched you, heard you, felt the comfort of your presence—the sweetness of your consolation: I cannot give up these joys. I have little left in myself—I must have you. The world may laugh—may call me absurd, selfish—but it does not signify. My very soul demands you: it will be satisfied: or it will take deadly vengeance on its frame."

"Well, sir, I will stay with you: I have said so."

"Yes—but you understand one thing by staying with me; and I understand another. You, perhaps, could make up your mind to be about my hand and chair—to wait on me as a kind little nurse (for you have an affectionate heart and a generous spirit, which prompt you to make sacrifices for those you pity), and that ought to suffice for me no doubt. I suppose I should now entertain none but fatherly feelings for you: do you think so? Come—tell me."

"I will think what you like, sir: I am content to be only your nurse, if you think it better."

"But you cannot always be my nurse, Janet: you are young—you must marry one day."

"I don't care about being married."

"You should care, Janet: if I were what I once was, I would try to make you care—but—a sightless block!"

He relapsed again into gloom. I, on the contrary, became more cheerful, and took fresh courage: these last words gave me an insight as to where the difficulty lay; and as it was no difficulty with me, I felt quite relieved from my previous embarrassment. I resumed a livelier vein of conversation.

"It is time some one undertook to rehumanize you," said I, parting his thick and long uncut locks; "for I see you are being metamorphosed into a lion, or something of that sort. You have 'a faux air' of Nebuchadnezzar in the fields[9] about you, that is certain: your hair reminds me of eagle's feathers; whether your nails are grown like bird's claws or not, I have not yet noticed."

"On this arm I have neither hand nor nails," he said, drawing the multilated limb from his breast, and showing it to me. "It is a mere stump—a ghastly sight! Don't you think so, Jane?"

"It is a pity to see it; and a pity to see your eyes—and the scar of fire on your

9. In Daniel 4:32–37 Nebuchadnezzar is driven into the fields to repent. "Faux air": semblance.

forehead: and the worst of it is, one is in danger of loving you too well for all this; and making too much of you."

"I thought you would be revolted, Jane, when you saw my arm and cicatrised visage."[1]

"Did you? Don't tell me so—lest I should say something disparaging to your judgment. Now, let me leave you an instant, to make a better fire, and have the hearth swept up. Can you tell when there is a good fire?"

"Yes, with the right eye I see a glow—a ruddy haze."

"And you see the candles?"

"Very dimly—each is a luminous cloud."

"Can you see me?"

"No, my fairy: but I am only too thankful to hear and feel you."

"When do you take supper?"

"I never take supper."

"But you shall have some tonight. I am hungry: so are you, I daresay, only you forget."

Summoning Mary, I soon had the room in more cheerful order: I prepared him, likewise, a comfortable repast. My spirits were excited, and with pleasure and ease I talked to him during supper, and for a long time after. There was no harassing restraint, no repressing of glee and vivacity with him; for with him I was at perfect ease, because I knew I suited him: all I said or did seemed either to console or revive him. Delightful consciousness! It brought to life and light my whole nature: in his presence I thoroughly lived; and he lived in mine. Blind as he was, smiles played over his face, joy dawned on his forehead; his lineaments softened and warmed.

After supper he began to ask me many questions, of where I had been, what I had been doing, how I had found him out but I gave him only very partial replies: it was too late to enter into particulars that night. Besides, I wished to touch no deep-thrilling chord—to open no fresh well of emotion in his heart: my sole present aim was to cheer him. Cheered, as I have said, he was: and yet but by fits. If a moment's silence broke the conversation, he would turn restless, touch me, then say, "Jane."

"You are altogether a human being, Jane? You are certain of that?"

"I conscientiously believe so, Mr. Rochester."

"Yet how, on this dark and doleful evening, could you so suddenly rise on my lone hearth? I stretched my hand to take a glass of water from a hireling, and it was given me by you: I asked a question, expecting John's wife to answer me, and your voice spoke at my ear."

"Because I had come in, in Mary's stead, with the tray."

"And there is enchantment in the very hour I am now spending with you. Who can tell what a dark, dreary, hopeless life I have dragged on for months past? Doing nothing, expecting nothing; merging night in day; feeling but the sensation of cold when I let the fire go out, of hunger when I forgot to eat: and then a ceaseless sorrow, and, at times, a very delirium of desire to behold my Jane again. Yes: for her restoration I longed, far more than for that of my lost sight. How can it be that Jane is with me, and says she loves me? Will she not depart as suddenly as she came? Tomorrow, I fear, I shall find her no more."

A common-place, practical reply, out of the train of his own disturbed ideas,

1. Scarred.

was, I was sure, the best and most reassuring for him in this frame of mind. I passed my finger over his eyebrows, and remarked that they were scorched, and that I would apply something which should make them grow as broad and black as ever.

"Where is the use of doing me good in any way, beneficent spirit, when, at some fatal moment, you will again desert me—passing like a shadow, whither and how to me unknown; and for me remaining afterwards undiscoverable?"

"Have you a pocket comb about you, sir?"

"What for, Jane?"

"Just to comb out this shaggy black mane. I find you rather alarming when I examine you close at hand: you talk of my being a fairy; but I am sure you are more like a brownie."[2]

"Am I hideous, Jane?"

"Very, sir: you always were, you know."

"Humph! The wickedness has not been taken out of you, wherever you have sojourned."

"Yet I have been with good people; far better than you: a hundred times better people; possessed of ideas and views you never entertained in your life: quite more refined and exalted."

"Who the deuce have you been with?"

"If you twist in that way you will make me pull the hair out of your head; and then I think you will cease to entertain doubts of my substantiality."

"Who have you been with, Jane?"

"You shall not get it out of me tonight, sir; you must wait till tomorrow; to leave my tale half told will, you know, be a sort of security that I shall appear at your breakfast table to finish it. By-the-bye, I must mind not to rise on your hearth with only a glass of water, then: I must bring an egg at the least, to say nothing of fried ham."

"You mocking changeling—fairy-born and human-bred! You make me feel as I have not felt these twelve months. If Saul could have had you for his David, the evil spirit would have been exorcised without the aid of the harp."[3]

"There, sir, you are redd up[4] and made decent. Now I'll leave you: I have been traveling these last three days, and I believe I am tired. Good-night."

"Just one word, Jane: were there only ladies in the house where you have been?"

I laughed and made my escape, still laughing as I ran upstairs. "A good idea!" I thought, with glee. "I see I have the means of fretting him out of his melancholy for some time to come."

Very early the next morning I heard him up and astir, wandering from one room to another. As soon as Mary came down I heard the question: "Is Miss Eyre here?" Then: "Which room did you put her into? Was it dry? Is she up? Go and ask if she wants anything; and when she will come down."

I came down as soon as I thought there was a prospect of breakfast. Entering the room very softly, I had a view of him before he discovered my presence. It was mournful indeed to witness the subjugation of that vigorous spirit to a corporeal infirmity. He sat in his chair,—still, but not at rest: expectant evidently; the lines of now habitual sadness marking his strong features.

2. A benevolent spirit, of shaggy appearance. 4. Tidied.
3. 1 Samuel 16:23.

His countenance reminded one of a lamp quenched, waiting to be relit—
and alas! it was not himself that could now kindle the luster of animated ex-
pression: he was dependent on another for that office! I had meant to be gay
and careless, but the powerlessness of the strong man touched my heart to the
quick: still I accosted him with what vivacity I could: "It is a bright, sunny
morning, sir," I said. "The rain is over and gone, and there is a tender shining
after it: you shall have a walk soon."

I had wakened the glow: his features beamed.

"Oh, you are indeed there my sky-lark! Come to me. You are not gone: not
vanished? I heard one of your kind an hour ago, singing high over the wood:
but its song had no music for me, any more than the rising sun had rays. All
the melody on earth is concentrated in my Jane's tongue to my ear (I am glad
it is not naturally a silent one): all the sunshine I can feel is in her presence."

The water stood in my eyes to hear this avowal of his dependence: just as if
a royal eagle, chained to a perch, should be forced to entreat a sparrow to be-
come its purveyor. But I would not be lachrymose: I dashed off the salt drops,
and busied myself with preparing breakfast.

Most of the morning was spent in the open air. I led him out of the wet and
wild wood into some cheerful fields: I described to him how brilliantly green
they were; how the flowers and hedges looked refreshed; how sparkingly blue
was the sky. I sought a seat for him in a hidden and lovely spot: a dry stump of
a tree: nor did I refuse to let him, when seated, place me on his knee: why
should I, when both he and I were happier near than apart? Pilot lay beside us:
all was quiet. He broke out suddenly while clasping me in his arms: "Cruel,
cruel deserter! Oh, Jane, what did I feel when I discovered you had fled from
Thornfield, and when I could nowhere find you; and, after examining your
apartment, ascertained that you had taken no money, nor anything which
could serve as an equivalent A pearl necklace I had given you lay untouched
in its little casket; your trunks were left corded and locked as they had been
prepared for the bridal tour. What could my darling do, I asked, left destitute
and penniless? And what did she do? Let me hear now."

Thus urged, I began the narrative of my experience for the last year. I soft-
ened considerably what related to the three days of wandering and starvation,
because to have told him all would have been to inflict unnecessary pain: the
little I did say lacerated his faithful heart deeper than I wished.

I should not have left him thus, he said, without any means of making my
way: I should have told him my intention. I should have confided in him: he
would never have forced me to be his mistress. Violent as he had seemed in his
despair, he, in truth, loved me far too well and too tenderly to constitute him-
self my tyrant: he would have given me half his fortune, without demanding
so much as a kiss in return, rather than I should have flung myself friendless on
the wide world. I had endured, he was certain, more than I had confessed to
him.

"Well, whatever my sufferings had been, they were very short," I answered:
and then I proceeded to tell him how I had been received at Moor House; how
I had obtained the office of schoolmistress, etc. The accession of fortune, the
discovery of my relations, followed in due order. Of course St. John Rivers'
name came in frequently in the progress of my tale. When I had done that
name was immediately taken up.

"This St. John, then, is your cousin?"

"Yes."

"You have spoken of him often: do you like him?"

"He was a very good man, sir; I could not help liking him."

"A good man? Does that mean a respectable, well-conducted man of fifty? Or what does it mean?"

"St. John was only twenty-nine, sir."

"'*Jeune encore*,'[5] as the French say. Is he a person of low stature, phlegmatic, and plain? A person whose goodness consists rather in his guiltlessness of vice than in his prowess in virtue?"

"He is untiringly active. Great and exalted deeds are what he lives to perform."

"But his brain? That is probably rather soft? He means well: but you shrug your shoulders to hear him talk?"

"He talks little, sir: what he does say is ever to the point. His brain is first-rate, I should think not impressible, but vigorous."

"Is he an able man, then?"

"Truly able."

"A thoroughly educated man?"

"St. John is an accomplished and profound scholar."

"His manners, I think, you said are not to your taste?—priggish and parsonic?"

"I never mentioned his manners; but, unless I had a very bad taste, they must suit it; they are polished, calm, and gentlemanlike."

"His appearance,—I forget what description you gave of his appearance;—a sort of raw curate, half-strangled with his white neckcloth, and stilted up on his thick-soled high-lows,[6] eh?"

"St. John dresses well. He is a handsome man: tall, fair, with blue eyes and a Grecian profile."

(*Aside*.) "Damn him!" —(*To me*.) "Did you like him, Jane?"

"Yes, Mr. Rochester, I liked him: but you asked me that before."

I perceived, of course, the drift of my interlocutor. Jealousy had got hold of him: she stung him; but the sting was salutary: it gave him respite from the gnawing fang of melancholy. I would not, therefore, immediately charm the snake.

"Perhaps you would rather not sit any longer on my knee, Miss Eyre?" was the next somewhat unexpected observation.

"Why not, Mr. Rochester?"

"The picture you have just drawn is suggestive of a rather too overwhelming contrast. Your words have delineated very prettily a graceful Apollo: he is present to your imagination,—tall, fair, blue-eyed, and with a Grecian profile. Your eyes dwell on a Vulcan,[7]—a real blacksmith, brown, broad-shouldered; and blind and lame into the bargain."

"I never thought of it before; but you certainly are rather like Vulcan, sir."

"Well,—you can leave me, ma'am: but before you go" (and he retained me by a firmer grasp than ever), "you will be pleased just to answer me a question or two." He paused.

"What questions, Mr. Rochester?"

5. Still young.
6. High-fastening shoes.

7. The lame god of fire who worked at a forge. Apollo was the handsome sun god of Greek mythology.

Then followed this cross-examination.

"St. John made you schoolmistress of Morton before he knew you were his cousin?"

"Yes."

"You would often see him? He would visit the school sometimes?"

"Daily."

"He would approve of your plans, Jane? I know they would be clever, for you are a talented creature."

"He approved of them—yes."

"He would discover many things in you he could not have expected to find? Some of your accomplishments are not ordinary."

"I don't know about that."

"You had a little cottage near the school, you say: did he ever come there to see you?"

"Now and then."

"Of an evening?"

"Once or twice."

A pause.

"How long did you reside with him and his sisters after the cousinship was discovered?"

"Five months."

"Did Rivers spend much time with the ladies of his family?"

"Yes; the back parlor was both his study and ours: he sat near the window, and we by the table."

"Did he study much?"

"A good deal."

"What?"

"Hindostanee."

"And what did you do meantime?"

"I learned German, at first."

"Did he teach you?"

"He did not understand German."

"Did he teach you nothing?"

"A little Hindostanee."

"Rivers taught you Hindostanee?"

"Yes, sir."

"And his sisters also?"

"No."

"Only you?"

"Only me."

"Did you ask to learn?"

"No."

"He wished to teach you?"

"Yes."

A second pause.

"Why did he wish it? Of what use could Hindostanee be to you?"

"He intended me to go with him to India."

"Ah! here I reach the root of the matter. He wanted you to marry him?"

"He asked me to marry him."

"That is a fiction—an impudent invention to vex me."

"I beg your pardon, it is the literal truth: he asked me more than once, and was as stiff about urging his point as ever you could be."

"Miss Eyre, I repeat, you can leave me. How often am I to say the same thing? Why do you remain pertinaciously perched on my knee, when I have given you notice to quit?"

"Because I am comfortable there."

"No, Jane, you are not comfortable there, because your heart is not with me: it is with this cousin—this St. John. Oh, till this moment I thought my little Jane was all mine! I had a belief she loved me even when she left me: that was an atom of sweet in much bitter. Long as we have been parted, hot tears as I have wept over our separation, I never thought that while I was mourning her she was loving another! But it is useless grieving. Jane, leave me: go and marry Rivers."

"Shake me off, then, sir—push me away, for I'll not leave you of my own accord."

"Jane, I ever like your tone of voice: it still renews hope, it sounds so truthful. When I hear it, it carries me back a year. I forget that you have formed a new tie. But I am not a fool—go——"

"Where must I go, sir?"

"Your own way—with the husband you have chosen."

"Who is that?"

"You know—this St. John Rivers."

"He is not my husband, nor ever will be. He does not love me: I do not love him. He loves (as he *can* love, and that is not as you love) a beautiful young lady called Rosamond. He wanted to marry me only because he thought I should make a suitable missionary's wife, which she would not have done. He is good and great, but severe; and, for me, cold as an iceberg. He is not like you, sir: I am not happy at his side, nor near him, nor with him. He has no indulgence for me—no fondness. He sees nothing attractive in me; not even youth—only a few useful mental points.—Then I must leave you, sir, to go to him?"

I shuddered involuntarily, and clung instinctively closer to my blind but beloved master. He smiled.

"What, Jane! Is this true? Is such really the state of matters between you and Rivers?"

"Absolutely, sir. Oh, you need not be jealous! I wanted to tease you a little to make you less sad: I thought anger would be better than grief. But if you wish me to love you, could you but see how much I *do* love you, you would be proud and content. All my heart is yours, sir: it belongs to you; and with you it would remain were fate to exile the rest of me from your presence for ever."

Again, as he kissed me, painful thoughts darkened his aspect.

"My seared vision! my crippled strength!" he murmured regretfully.

I caressed, in order to soothe him. I knew of what he was thinking, and wanted to speak for him; but dared not. As he turned aside his face a minute I saw a tear slide from under the sealed eyelid, and trickle down the manly cheek. My heart swelled.

"I am no better than the old lightning-struck chestnut-tree in Thornfield orchard," he remarked ere long. " And what right would that ruin have to bid a budding woodbine cover its decay with freshness?"

"You are no ruin, sir—no lightning-struck tree: you are green and vigorous.

Plants will grow about your roots, whether you ask them or not, because they take delight in your bountiful shadow; and as they grow they will lean towards you, and wind round you, because your strength offers them so safe a prop."

Again he smiled: I gave him comfort.

"You speak of friends, Jane?" he asked.

"Yes: of friends." I answered rather hesitatingly: for I knew I meant more than friends, but could not tell what other word to employ. He helped me.

"Ah! Jane. But I want a wife."

"Do you, sir?"

"Yes: is it news to you?"

"Of course: you said nothing about it before."

"Is it unwelcome news?"

"That depends on circumstances, sir—on your choice."

"Which you shall make for me, Jane. I will abide by your decision."

"Choose then, sir—*her who loves you best*."

"I will at least choose—*her I love best*. Jane, will you marry me?"

"Yes, sir."

"A poor blind man, whom you will have to lead about by the hand?"

"Yes, sir."

"A crippled man, twenty years older than you, whom you will have to wait on?"

"Yes, sir."

"Truly, Jane?"

"Most truly, sir."

"Oh! my darling! God bless you and reward you!"

"Mr. Rochester, if ever I did a good deed in my life—if ever I thought a good thought—if ever I prayed a sincere and blameless prayer—if ever I wished a righteous wish,—I am rewarded now. To be your wife is, for me, to be as happy as I can be on earth."

"Because you delight in sacrifice."

"Sacrifice! What do I sacrifice? Famine for food, expectation for content. To be privileged to put my arms round what I value—to press my lips to what I love—to repose on what I trust: is that to make a sacrifice? If so, then certainly I delight in sacrifice."

"And to bear with my infirmities, Jane: to overlook my deficiencies."

"Which are none, sir, to me. I love you better now, when I can really be useful to you, than I did in your state of proud independence, when you disdained every part but that of the giver and protector."

"Hitherto I have hated to be helped—to be led henceforth, I feel, I shall hate it no more. I did not like to put my hand into a hireling's, but it is pleasant to feel it circled by Jane's little fingers. I preferred utter loneliness to the constant attendance of servants; but Jane's soft ministry will be a perpetual joy. Jane suits me: do I suit her?"

"To the finest fiber of my nature, sir."

"The case being so, we have nothing in the world to wait for: we must be married instantly."

He looked and spoke with eagerness: his old impetuosity was rising.

"We must become one flesh without any delay, Jane: there is but the license to get—then we marry."

"Mr. Rochester, I have just discovered the sun is far declined from its meridian, and Pilot is actually gone home to his dinner. Let me look at your watch."

"Fasten it into your girdle, Janet, and keep it hence-forward: I have no use for it."

"It is nearly four o'clock in the afternoon, sir. Don't you feel hungry?"

"The third day from this must be our wedding-day, Jane. Never mind fine clothes and jewels now: all that is not worth a fillip."

"The sun has dried up all the rain-drops, sir. The breeze is still: it is quite hot."

"Do you know, Jane, I have your little pearl necklace at this moment fastened round my bronze scrag under my cravat? I have worn it since the day I lost my only treasure: as a memento of her."

"We will go home through the wood: that will be the shadiest way."

He pursued his own thoughts without heeding me.

"Jane! you think me, I daresay, an irreligious dog: but my heart swells with gratitude to the beneficent God of this earth just now. He sees not as man sees, but far clearer: judges not as man judges, but far more wisely. I did wrong: I would have sullied my innocent flower—breathed guilt on its purity: the Omnipotent snatched it from me. I, in my stiff-necked rebellion, almost cursed the dispensation: instead of bending to the decree, I defied it. Divine justice pursued its course; disasters came thick on me: I was forced to pass through the valley of the shadow of death. *His* chastisements are mighty; and one smote me which has humbled me for ever. You know I was proud of my strength; but what is it now, when I must give it over to foreign guidance, as a child does its weakness? Of late, Jane—only—only of late—I began to see and acknowledge the hand of God in my doom. I began to experience remorse, repentance; the wish for reconcilement to my Maker. I began sometimes to pray: very brief prayers they were, but very sincere.

"Some days since: nay, I can number them—four; it was last Monday night, a singular mood came over me: one in which grief replaced frenzy—sorrow, sullenness. I had long had the impression that since I could nowhere find you, you must be dead. Late that night—perhaps it might be between eleven and twelve o'clock—ere I retired to my dreary rest, I supplicated God that, if it seemed good to Him, I might soon be taken from this life, and admitted to that world to come, where there was still hope of rejoining Jane.

"I was in my own room, and sitting by the window, which was open: it soothed me to feel the balmy night-air: though I could see no stars and only by a vague, luminous haze, knew the presence of a moon. I longed for thee, Janet! Oh, I longed for thee both with soul and flesh! I asked of God, at once in anguish and humility, if I had not been long enough desolate, afflicted, tormented; and might not soon taste bliss and peace once more. That I merited all I endured I acknowledged—that I could scarcely endure more I pleaded; and the Alpha and Omega of my heart's wishes broke involuntarily from my lips in the words— 'Jane! Jane! Jane!' "

"Did you speak these words aloud?"

"I did, Jane. If any listener had heard me, he would have thought me mad: I pronounced them with such frantic energy."

"And it was last Monday night: somewhere near midnight?"

"Yes; but the time is of no consequence: what followed is the strange point. You will think me superstitious,—some superstition I have in my blood, and always had: nevertheless, this is true—true at least it is that I heard what I now relate.

"As I exclaimed 'Jane! Jane! Jane!' a voice—I cannot tell whence the voice came, but I know whose voice it was—replied, 'I am coming: wait for me;' and a moment after went whispering on the wind the words—'Where are you?'"

"I'll tell you, if I can, the idea, the picture these words opened to my mind: yet it is difficult to express what I want to express. Ferndean is buried, as you see, in a heavy wood, where sound falls dull, and dies unreverberating. 'Where are you?' seemed spoken among mountains; for I heard a hill-sent echo repeat the words. Cooler and fresher at the moment the gale seemed to visit my brow: I could have deemed that in some wild, lone scene, I and Jane were meeting. In spirit, I believe, we must have met. You no doubt were, at that hour, in unconscious sleep, Jane: perhaps your soul wandered from its cell to comfort mine; for those were your accents—as certain as I live—they were yours!"

Reader, it was on Monday night—near midnight—that I too had received the mysterious summons: those were the very words by which I replied to it. I listened to Mr. Rochester's narrative; but made no disclosure in return. The coincidence struck me as too awful and inexplicable to be communicated or discussed. If I told anything, my tale would be such as must necessarily make a profound impression on the mind of my hearer: and that mind, yet from its sufferings too prone to gloom, needed not the deeper shade of the supernatural. I kept these things then, and pondered them in my heart.[8]

"You cannot now wonder," continued my master, "that when you rose upon me so unexpectedly last night I had difficulty in believing you any other than a mere voice and vision: something that would melt to silence and annihilation, as the midnight whisper and mountain echo had melted before. Now, I thank God! I know it to be otherwise. Yes, I thank God!"

He put me off his knee, rose, and reverently lifting his hat from his brow, and bending his sightless eyes to the earth, he stood in mute devotion. Only the last words of the worship were audible.

"I thank my Maker that in the midst of judgment He has remembered mercy. I humbly entreat my Redeemer to give me strength to lead henceforth a purer life than I have done hitherto!"

Then he stretched his hand out to be led. I took that dear hand, held it a moment to my lips, then let it pass round my shoulder: being so much lower of stature than he, I served both for his prop and guide. We entered the wood, and wended homeward.

Chapter XXXVIII

CONCLUSION

Reader, I married him. A quiet wedding we had: he and I, the parson and clerk, were alone present. When we got back from church, I went into the kitchen of the manor-house, where Mary was cooking the dinner, and John cleaning the knives, and I said: "Mary, I have been married to Mr. Rochester this morning." The housekeeper and her husband were both of that decent phlegmatic order of people to whom one may at any time safely communicate a remarkable piece of news without incurring the danger of having one's ears pierced by some shrill ejaculation, and subsequently stunned by a torrent of

8. Luke 2:19.

wordy wonderment. Mary did look up, and she did stare at me: the ladle with which she was basting a pair of chickens roasting at the fire did for some three minutes hang suspended in air; and for the same space of time John's knives also had rest from the polishing process: but Mary, bending again over the roast, said only: "Have you, Miss? Well, for sure!"

A short time after she pursued: "I seed you go out with the master, but I didn't know you were gone to church to be wed;" and she basted away. John, when I turned to him, was grinning from ear to ear.

"I told Mary how it would be," he said: "I knew what Mr. Edward" (John was an old servant, and had known his master when he was the cadet[9] of the house, therefore he often gave him his Christian name)—"I knew what Mr. Edward would do; and I was certain he would not wait long neither: and he's done right, for aught I know. I wish you joy, Miss!" and he politely pulled his forelock.

"Thank you, John. Mr. Rochester told me to give you and Mary this." I put into his hand a five-pound note. Without waiting to hear more, I left the kitchen. In passing the door of that sanctum some time after I caught the words: "She'll happen do better for him nor ony o' t' grand ladies." And again, "If she ben't one o' th' handsomest, she's noan faâl and varry good-natured; and i' his een[1] she's fair beautiful, onybody may see that."

I wrote to Moor House and to Cambridge immediately to say what I had done: fully explaining also why I had thus acted. Diana and Mary approved the step unreservedly. Diana announced that she would just give me time to get over the honeymoon, and then she would come and see me.

"She had better not wait till then, Jane," said Mr. Rochester, when I read her letter to him; "if she does, she will be too late, for our honeymoon will shine our life-long: its beams will only fade over your grave or mine."

How St. John received the news I don't know; he never answered the letter in which I communicated it: yet six months after he wrote to me; without, however, mentioning Mr. Rochester's name, or alluding to my marriage. His letter was then calm: and though very serious, kind. He has maintained a regular, though not frequent correspondence ever since: he hopes I am happy, and trusts I am not of those who live without God in the world, and only mind earthly things.

You have not quite forgotten little Adèle, have you, reader? I had not; I soon asked and obtained leave of Mr. Rochester to go and see her at the school where he had placed her. Her frantic joy at beholding me again moved me much. She looked pale and thin: she said she was not happy. I found the rules of the establishment were too strict, its course of study too severe, for a child of her age: I took her home with me. I meant to become her governess once more; but I soon found this impracticable; my time and cares were now required by another—my husband needed them all. So I sought out a school conducted on a more indulgent system; and near enough to permit of my visiting her often, and bringing her home sometimes. I took care she should never want for anything that could contribute to her comfort: she soon settled in her new abode, became very happy there, and made fair progress in her studies. As she grew up a sound English education corrected in a great measure her French defects; and when she left school I found in her a pleasing and

9. Younger son. 1. Eyes. "Noan faâl": no fool.

obliging companion: docile, good-tempered, and well-principled. By her grateful attention to me and mine she has long since well repaid any little kindness I ever had in my power to offer her.

My tale draws to its close: one word respecting my experience of married life, and one brief glance at the fortunes of those whose names have most frequently recurred in this narrative, and I have done.

I have now been married ten years. I know what it is to live entirely for and with what I love best on earth. I hold myself supremely blest—blest beyond what language can express; because I am my husband's life as fully as he is mine. No woman was ever nearer to her mate than I am; ever more absolutely bone of his bone and flesh of his flesh.[2]

I know no weariness of my Edward's society: he knows none of mine, any more than we each do of the pulsation of the heart that beats in our separate bosoms; consequently, we are ever together. To be together is for us to be at once as free as in solitude, as gay as in company. We talk, I believe, all day long: to talk to each other is but a more animated and an audible thinking. All my confidence is bestowed on him, all his confidence is devoted to me; we are precisely suited in character—perfect concord is the result.

Mr. Rochester continued blind the first two years of our union: perhaps it was that circumstance that drew us so very near—that knit us so very close! for I was then his vision, as I am still his right hand. Literally, I was (what he often called me) the apple of his eye. He saw nature—he saw books through me; and never did I weary of gazing for his behalf, and of putting into words the effect of field, tree, town, river, cloud, sunbeam—of the landscape before us; of the weather round us—and impressing by sound on his ear what light could no longer stamp on his eye. Never did I weary of reading to him: never did I weary of conducting him where he wished to go: of doing for him what he wished to be done. And there was a pleasure in my services, most full, most exquisite, even though sad—because he claimed these services without painful shame or damping humiliation. He loved me so truly that he knew no reluctance in profiting by my attendance: he felt I loved him so fondly that to yield that attendance was to indulge my sweetest wishes.

One morning at the end of the two years, as I was writing a letter to his dictation, he came and bent over me, and said—"Jane, have you a glittering ornament round your neck?"

I had a gold watch-chain: I answered, "Yes."

"And have you a pale blue dress on?"

I had. He informed me then that for some time he had fancied the obscurity clouding one eye was becoming less dense; and that now he was sure of it.

He and I went up to London. He had the advice of an eminent oculist; and he eventually recovered the sight of that one eye. He cannot now see very distinctly: he cannot read or write much; but he can find his way without being led by the hand: the sky is no longer a blank to him—the earth no longer a void. When his firstborn was put into his arms, he could see that the boy had inherited his own eyes, as they once were—large, brilliant, and black. On that occasion he again, with a full heart, acknowledged that God had tempered judgment with mercy.

My Edward and I, then, are happy: and the more so because those we most

2. Genesis 2:23.

love are happy likewise. Diana and Mary Rivers are both married: alternately, once every year, they come to see us, and we go to see them. Diana's husband is a captain in the navy; a gallant officer and a good man. Mary's is a clergyman: a college friend of her brother's; and, from his attainments and principles, worthy of the connection. Both Captain Fitzjames and Mr. Wharton love their wives, and are loved by them.

As to St. John Rivers, he left England: he went to India. He entered on the path he had marked for himself; he pursues it still. A more resolute, indefatigable pioneer never wrought amidst rocks and dangers. Firm, faithful, and devoted; full of energy, and zeal, and truth, he labors for his race: he clears their painful way to improvement: he hews down like a giant the prejudices of creed and caste that encumber it. He may be stern; he may be exacting: he may be ambitious yet; but his is the sternness of the warrior Greatheart, who guards his pilgrim convoy from the onslaught of Apollyon.[3] His is the exaction of the apostle, who speaks but for Christ when he says—"Whosoever will come after Me, let him deny himself, and take up his cross and follow Me."[4] His is the ambition of the high master-spirit, which aims to fill a place in the first rank of those who are redeemed from the earth—who stand without fault before the throne of God; who share the last mighty victories of the Lamb; who are called, and chosen, and faithful.

St. John is unmarried: he never will marry now. Himself has hitherto sufficed to the toil; and the toil draws near its close: his glorious sun hastens to its setting. The last letter I received from him drew from my eyes human tears, and yet filled my heart with Divine joy: he anticipated his sure reward, his incorruptible crown. I know that a stranger's hand will write to me next, to say that the good and faithful servant has been called at length into the joy of his Lord. And why weep for this? No fear of death will darken St. John's last hour: his mind will be unclouded; his heart will be undaunted; his hope will be sure; his faith steadfast. His own words are a pledge of this:—"My Master," he says, "has forewarned me. Daily he announces more distinctly,—'Surely I come quickly!'[5] and hourly I more eagerly respond,— 'Amen; even so come, Lord Jesus!'"

1847

3. In Bunyan's *The Pilgrim's Progress* (1678), Apollyon is the angel of the bottomless pit. Greatheart is the Christian warrior.

4. Mark 8:34.

5. Revelation 22:20; the next to last verse of the Old Testament of the Bible.

EMILY BRONTË
1818–1848

"Stronger than a man, simpler than a child, her nature stood alone," wrote Charlotte Brontë of her sister Emily in a *Biographical Notice of Ellis and Acton Bell* that she published after the deaths of the authors of *Wuthering Heights* and *Agnes Grey*. A few years later, Constantin Héger, Emily's schoolmaster for a year in Brussels, added an equally striking tribute: "She should have been a man—a great navigator . . . her strong, imperious will would never have been daunted by opposition or difficulty." Paradoxically, however, the woman who inspired such dramatic statements appeared to many as a shy yet practical housekeeper who baked bread

that was "always light and excellent" while studying German and scribbling poems on odd scraps of paper. Perhaps, indeed, it is because of such contradictions that the life story of Emily Brontë has long haunted biographers as well as more casual readers of her work.

Born in 1818, Emily Brontë was the fifth child of Patrick Brontë, a literarily inclined clergyman, and his wife, Maria Branwell Brontë, a lively but fragile woman who died not long after the birth of her last child, Anne. Like her equally famous sister Charlotte, Emily was raised at Haworth Parsonage in Yorkshire by her mother's pious sister, Elizabeth Branwell, who moved from Cornwall to her brother-in-law's home in order to care for his motherless children when he failed to remarry after his wife's death. Like Charlotte, too, Emily was briefly enrolled in the Clergy Daughters' School at Cowan Bridge, where she was one of the youngest pupils and was summarily brought home after her older sisters, Maria and Elizabeth, fell ill and died of a combination of typhoid fever and tuberculosis. Unlike Charlotte, however, Emily appeared—at least on the surface—to have transcended that traumatic experience unscathed, or so the biographer Winifred Gérin, has argued.

After the deaths of Maria and Elizabeth, Emily received a haphazard education at home, along with her older brother, Branwell, and her remaining sisters, Charlotte and Anne. Because their father was an intellectual of sorts, the children had access to a literary collection that included not only the works of writers like Milton, Byron, and Scott but also the latest issues of contemporary periodicals like *Blackwood's* magazine. Equally obsessed with politics and poetry, history and fiction, they began early to incorporate such matters into what Charlotte called their "Bed Plays"—elaborate fantasies, which were eventually to become more real to Emily than her daily life. Most notably, when their father brought Branwell a set of wooden soldiers, each child chose a figure with which to identify. Emily's was "Parry," named (as if in anticipation of Héger's later description of her) after her childhood hero Edward Parry the Arctic explorer, and at first this dashing character figured in "plays" primarily of Charlotte and Branwell's invention. Eventually, however, Emily, together with her sister Anne, incorporated his adventures into a series of sagas that were uniquely their own. These were the chronicles of "Gondal," an imaginary country in the North Pacific that was ruled by a tempestuous queen known, variously, as Augusta Geraldine Almeda, A. G. A., Rosina of Alcona, A. S., Sidonia's deity, and Gondal's queen. Astonishingly, these two young women sustained their involvement in the "history" of this imaginary country long past their teens: much of Emily Brontë's poetry, the critic Fannie Ratchford has shown, was conceived as part of a Gondal "cycle" whose prose portions have been lost.

What is perhaps even more impressive about Emily Brontë's commitment to Gondal is the way she was able both to extend and to elaborate her fantasy in the midst of an apparently prosaic reality. The "Diary Papers" she and her sister Anne wrote on their birthdays indicate the ease with which Emily moved from her existence as a housekeeping daughter to her imaginative experience as Gondal's queen. In 1834, for instance, when she was just sixteen, she juxtaposed domestic detail and mysterious drama in a statement that began by noting "I fed Rainbow, Diamond Snowflake Jasper" (pet birds), went on to observe that "Taby" (the family servant) "said just now Come Anne pilloputate" (peel a potato) and then declared that "the Gondals are discovering the interior of Gaaldine" (their exotic continent). Rarely have English writers combined such minutely accurate transcriptions of ordinary life—kitchens and potato peels—with such imaginings of high adventure. Yet it is precisely this configuration of the prosaic and the poetic that gives Emily Brontë's one novel, *Wuthering Heights*, its distinctive power.

As her Diary Papers suggest, Emily's housekeeping life at Haworth Parsonage was by no means an imprisonment. Rather, she felt constrained and confined on

the few occasions when she had to leave home. In 1835, she briefly attended Roe Head, a girls' boarding school where Charlotte was employed as a teacher, and in 1837 she herself spent some six months teaching at Law Hill, a similar institution. Both experiences were unpleasant, indeed almost disastrous, for her. "I felt in my heart she would die, if she did not go home," Charlotte remembered about her sister's time at Roe Head, explaining that "liberty was the breath of Emily's nostrils; without it, she perished." Nevertheless, despite her attachment to such "liberty"—which she evidently found only on the moors near Haworth—Emily accompanied Charlotte to Brussels in 1842, where the two studied at a Belgian school, the Pensionnat Héger, in the hope that they might prepare themselves to found an educational establishment of their own. In November 1842, however, receiving word that their "Aunt Branwell" had died, the sisters returned to Haworth, and although Charlotte went back to Brussels for another term, Emily was never really to leave home again.

Despite its apparent quietness, Emily's life in Yorkshire from 1842 to 1848 was eventful. In the autumn of 1845, Charlotte "accidentally alighted," as she later put it, "on a MS volume of verses in my sister Emily's handwriting," and finding that these works had "a peculiar music—wild, melancholy, and elevating," she conceived a plan to publish them, along with poems by herself and Anne; thus in 1846 a volume titled *Poems by Currer, Ellis, and Acton Bell* appeared in London. The pseudonyms had been chosen because they concealed the femininity of the three authors at the same time that they were "not positively masculine." Yet Ellis Bell's gender was an important factor in her sister's appreciation of her work: "I know no woman that ever lived who wrote such poetry before," she exclaimed in a letter to her publisher. No doubt she was referring to the visionary sternness that set Emily's poems apart from the sentimental effusions that "ladies" were supposed to produce. But although a few reviewers received the verse of the Bells with approbation, and at least one singled out Ellis's "power of wing" for special praise, the reading public did not share either his admiration or Charlotte's. In the year after the Bells' *Poems* appeared, only two copies were sold.

Undaunted, the sisters set out to try their fortunes as fiction writers. The books they produced were Charlotte's *Jane Eyre*; Anne's *Agnes Grey*; and Emily's *Wuthering Heights*, a novel that was not greeted with anything like the wave of popular enthusiasm that met *Jane Eyre*. Some reviewers, generally the most sympathetic, thought it an early, immature work by "Currer Bell" himself. Others, shocked at the book's frank portrayals of passion and dissolution, commented that it was "a disagreeable story" and speculated that, like the novel, its author must be "dogged, brutal, and morose." In fact, *Wuthering Heights* is none of these: brilliantly organized by an interlocking series of first-person narratives, it is a tale of love, revenge, and redemption that comments on the tensions of nineteenth-century society even while it offers a vision of a spiritual region beyond ordinary "reality." Like Wordsworth and Carlyle, Brontë invested the world with a kind of "natural supernaturalism" that gave mystical radiance to the earthly realm of moors and cliffs, and even to the emotional relationships of men and women, parents and children. Like Blake and Byron, she defined her visionary system as one that was beyond good and evil. Indeed, in *Wuthering Heights*'s satanic hero, Heathcliff, she created a figure who "stalked apart" from ordinary mortals and conventional morality as so many of Byron's heroes did, a figure whose fierce passions, like those of his beloved Catherine Earnshaw Linton, often seem to represent the author's own desire for the subversive *Marriage of Heaven and Hell* that William Blake had imagined some fifty years earlier.

That Emily Brontë quite consciously shaped *Wuthering Heights* not just as a Gothic romance but also as a radically visionary work becomes quite clear when one studies her poems. Here, in verses spoken in her "own" voice as well as in dramatic monologues written for Gondalian characters like A. G. A. and her band of troubled lovers, the poet expressed her own alienation from social conventions

and her own yearning for the "dazzling sea" of infinity, her own defiance of time and mortality, and her own commitment to the inspiring "night wind" of imagination. *No Coward Soul Is Mine*, perhaps her most famous poem, articulated the severe yet ecstatic creed by which she lived and that informs her other verses, along with her one novel. "No trembler in the world's storm-troubled sphere," she relied in true Romantic fashion on the "God within my breast" to redeem her from pain, and, in true mystical fashion, she saw that inner "God" as one with an outer spirit of "Undying Life." At the same time, however, in a poem that her sister Charlotte published after her death, Emily Brontë insisted that she would not renounce the reality of nature, for "The earth that wakes *one* human heart to feeling / Can centre both the worlds of Heaven and Hell."

If she had experienced a kind of terrestrial heaven on the moors, however, Brontë was destined to live through a domestic hell in her own household. Never a man of strong character, her brother, Branwell, had dramatically deteriorated over the years, and when he was rejected by a married woman with whom he had been in love, he declined into alcoholism and opium addiction. By all accounts, it was Emily who watched over him in his last days, waiting up night after night to lead him to bed when he came home drunk or drugged. In September 1848, "his constitution shattered," as Charlotte put it, he died; and October 1, the day of his funeral, was the last day on which Emily went out of her house. Apparently she caught a cold at the funeral service, but what might have been a minor ailment quickly turned into consumption, possibly hastened by the trauma through which she had just lived. Characteristically, she refused to see a doctor and forced herself to go about her usual business during the entire two-month period of her fatal sickness. Even on the day of her death, she stubbornly rose and dressed. Yet the extent of her illness can be judged from the report of the carpenter who made her coffin in December 1848: he claimed he had never made so narrow a coffin for an adult; it was, he said, five feet six inches in length, sixteen inches in width.

Always stoic, Emily Brontë had sworn to the end that "I'll walk where my own nature would be leading: / It vexes me to choose another guide." After her death, such independence was to be recognized as one of the qualities that gave her writing extraordinary power. But even in her lifetime, those closest to her had recognized her special genius: her poems "stirred my heart like the sound of a trumpet when I read them alone and in secret," Charlotte once confided to a friend, "for Ellis Bell is of no . . . ordinary materials."

[Tell me, tell me, smiling child]

Tell me, tell me, smiling child,
What the past is like to thee?
"An Autumn evening soft and mild
With a wind that sighs mournfully."

Tell me, what is the present hour? 5
"A green and flowery spray
Where a young bird sits gathering its power
To mount and fly away."

And what is the future, happy one?
"A sea beneath a cloudless sun; 10
A mighty, glorious, dazzling sea
Stretching into infinity."

[I am the only being whose doom]

I am the only being whose doom[1]
No tongue would ask, no eye would mourn;
I never caused a thought of gloom,
A smile of joy, since I was born.

In secret pleasure, secret tears, 5
This changeful life has slipped away,
As friendless after eighteen years,
As lone as on my natal day.

There have been times I cannot hide,
There have been times when this was drear, 10
When my sad soul forgot its pride
And longed for one to love me here.

But those were in the early glow
Of feelings since subdued by care;
And they have died so long ago, 15
I hardly now believe they were.[2]

First melted off the hope of youth,
Then fancy's[3] rainbow fast withdrew;
And then experience told me truth
In mortal bosoms never grew. 20

'Twas grief enough to think mankind
All hollow, servile, insincere;
But worse to trust to my own mind
And find the same corruption there.

May 17, 1837 1910

[Alone I sat; the summer day]

Alone I sat; the summer day
Had died in smiling light away;
I saw it die, I watched it fade
From misty hill and breezeless glade:

And thoughts in my soul were gushing, 5
And my heart bowed beneath their power;
And tears within my eyes were rushing
Because I could not speak the feeling,
The solemn joy around me stealing
In that divine, untroubled hour. 10

I asked myself, "O why has heaven
Denied the precious gift to me,

1. Death or fate. 3. Imagination's.
2. I.e., existed.

The glorious gift to many given
To speak their thoughts in poetry?

"Dreams have encircled me " I said, 15
"From careless childhood's sunny time;
Visions by ardent fancy fed
Since life was in its morning prime."[1]

But now, when I had hoped to sing,
My fingers strike a tuneless string; 20
And still the burden of the strain[2]
Is "Strive no more; 'tis all in vain."

August 1837 1941

F. de Samara to A. G. A.[1]

Light up thy halls! 'Tis closing day.
I'm drear and lone and far away—
Cold blows on my breast the northwind's bitter sigh,
And oh, my couch is bleak beneath the rainy sky!

Light up thy halls—and think not of me; 5
That face is absent now, thou hast hated so to see—
Bright be thine eyes, undimmed their dazzling shine,
For never, never more shall they encounter mine!

The desert[2] moor is dark; there is tempest in the air;
I have breathed my only wish in one last, one burning prayer— 10
A prayer that would come forth, although it lingered long;
That set on fire my heart, but froze upon my tongue.

And now, it shall be done before the morning rise:
I will not watch the sun ascend in yonder skies.
One task alone remains—thy pictured face to view; 15
And then I go to prove[3] if God, at least, be true!

Do I not see thee now? Thy black resplendent hair;
Thy glory-beaming brow, and smile, how heavenly fair!
Thine eyes are turned away—those eyes I would not see;
Their dark, their deadly ray, would more than madden me. 20

There, go, Deceiver, go! My hand is streaming wet;
My heart's blood flows to buy the blessing—To forget!
Oh could that lost heart give back, back again to thine,
One tenth part of the pain that clouds my dark decline[4]

1. First hour, beginning.
2. Tune. "Burden": bass or accompanying part.
1. A. G. A. is Augusta Geraldine Almeda, the heroine of an intricate dynastic story set in the mythological kingdom of Gondal. Both Anne and Emily Brontë participated in creating the story. The speaker of the poem is one of A. G. A.'s betrayed lovers. C. W. Hatfield argues that Emily Brontë made a mistake in copying the poem and that the speaker is really Lord Alfred of Aspin Castle, A. G. A.'s deserted husband, and not the youth Fernando de Samara (see Hatfield's *The Complete Poems of EB*, p. 16).
2. Deserted.
3. Test.
4. End, death.

Oh could I see thy lids weighed down in cheerless woe; 25
Too full to hide their tears, too stern to overflow;
Oh could I know thy soul with equal grief was torn,
This fate might be endured—this anguish might be borne!

How gloomy grows the night! 'Tis Gondal's wind that blows;
I shall not tread again the deep glens where it rose— 30
I feel it on my face—"Where, wild blast, dost thou roam?
What do we, wanderer,[5] here, so far away from home?

"I do not need thy breath to cool my death-cold brow;
But go to that far land, where she is shining now;
Tell Her my latest wish, tell Her my dreary doom;[6] 35
Say that *my* pangs are past, but *Hers* are yet to come."

Vain words—vain, frenzied thoughts! No ear can hear me call—
Lost in the vacant air my frantic curses fall—
And could she see me now, perchance her lip would smile,
Would smile in careless pride and utter scorn the while! 40

And yet for all her hate, each parting glance would tell
A stronger passion breathed, burned, in this last farewell.
Unconquered in my soul the Tyrant[7] rules me still;
Life bows to my control, but *Love* I cannot kill!

November 1, 1838 1941

The Night-Wind

In summer's mellow midnight,
A cloudless moon shone through
Our open parlor window
And rosetrees wet with dew.

I sat in silent musing, 5
The soft wind waved my hair:
It told me Heaven was glorious,
And sleeping Earth was fair.

I needed not its breathing
To bring such thoughts to me, 10
But still it whispered lowly,
"How dark the woods will be!

"The thick leaves in my murmur
Are rustling like a dream,
And all their myriad voices 15
Instinct[1] with spirit seem."

I said, "Go, gentle singer,
Thy wooing voice is kind,

5. The speaker addresses the wind. 7. I.e., love.
6. The speaker's death or fate; also his curse. 1. Infused.

But do not think its music
Has power to reach my mind. 20

"Play with the scented flower,
The young tree's supple bough,
And leave my human feelings
In their own course to flow."

The wanderer would not leave[2] me. 25
Its kiss grew warmer still—
"O come," it sighed so sweetly,
"I'll win thee 'gainst thy will.

"Have we not been from childhood friends?
Have I not loved thee long? 30
As long as thou hast loved the night
Whose silence wakes my song.

"And when thy heart is laid at rest
Beneath the church-yard stone
I shall have time enough to mourn 35
And thou to be alone."

September 11, 1840 1850

[Riches I hold in light esteem]

Riches I hold in light esteem
And Love I laugh to scorn
And lust of Fame was but a dream
That vanished with the morn—

And if I pray, the only prayer 5
That moves my lips for me
Is—"Leave the heart that now I bear
And give me liberty."

Yes, as my swift days near their goal
'Tis all that I implore— 10
Through life and death, a chainless soul
With courage to endure!

March 1, 1841 1846

[Aye, there it is! It wakes to-night][1]

Aye, there it[2] is! It wakes to-night
Sweet thoughts that will not die

2. An alternative reading of the manuscript is "heed."
1. Possibly addressed to one of Emily Brontë's sib-
lings. Charlotte Brontë supplied the following note:
"In these stanzas a louder gale has roused the sleeper
on her pillow the wakened soul struggles to blend with
the storm by which it is swayed."
2. I.e., the gale wind.

And feeling's fires flash all as bright
As in the years gone by!

And I can tell by thine altered cheek 5
And by thy kindled gaze
And by the words thou scarce dost speak,
How wildly fancy[3] plays.

Yes, I could swear that glorious wind
Has swept the world aside, 10
Has dashed its memory from thy mind
Like foam-bells[4] from the tide—

And thou art now a spirit pouring
Thy presence into all—
The essence of the Tempest's roaring 15
And of the Tempest's fall—

A universal influence
From thine own influence free;
A principle of life, intense,
Lost to mortality. 20

Thus truly when that breast is cold
Thy prisoned soul shall rise,
The dungeon mingle with the mold[5]—
The captive with the skies.

July 6, 1841 1850

A Day Dream

On a sunny brae[1] alone I lay
One summer afternoon;
It was the marriage-time of May
With her young lover, June.[2]

From her Mother's[3] heart seemed loath to part 5
That queen of bridal charms,
But her Father[4] smiled on the fairest child
He ever held in his arms.

The trees did wave their plumy crests,
The glad birds caroled clear; 10
And I, of all the wedding guests,
Was only sullen there.

There was not one but wished to shun
My aspect void of cheer;

3. Imagination.
4. Bubbles.
5. Earth or decaying flesh in the earth.
1. Hillside along a river.

2. I.e., it was the end of May.
3. The earth's.
4. The sun.

The very gray rocks, looking on, 15
Asked, "What do you do here?"

And I could utter no reply:
In sooth I did not know
Why I had brought a clouded eye
To greet the general glow. 20

So, resting on a heathy bank,
I took my heart to me;
And we together sadly sank
Into a reverie.

We thought, "When winter comes again, 25
Where will these bright things be?
All vanished, like a vision vain,
An unreal mockery!

"The birds that now so blithely sing,
Through deserts frozen dry, 30
Poor spectres of the perished Spring
In famished troops will fly.

"And why should we be glad at all?
The leaf is hardly green,
Before a token of the fall⁵ 35
Is on its surface seen."

Now whether it were really so
I never could be sure;
But as, in fit of peevish woe,
I stretched me on the moor, 40

A thousand thousand glancing fires
Seemed kindling in the air;
A thousand thousand silvery lyres
Resounded far and near:

Methought the very breath I breathed 45
Was full of sparks divine,
And all my heather-couch was wreathed
By that celestial shine.

And while the wide Earth echoing rang
To their strange minstrelsy, 50
The little glittering spirits sang,
Or seemed to sing, to me:

"O mortal, mortal, let them die;
Let Time and Tears destroy,

5. Both autumn and the Fall of Adam and Eve.

That we may overflow the sky 55
With universal joy.

"Let Grief distract the sufferer's breast,
And Night obscure his way;
They hasten him to endless rest,
And everlasting day. 60

"To Thee the world is like a tomb,
A desert's naked shore;
To us, in unimagined bloom,
It brightens more and more.

"And could we lift the veil and give 65
One brief glimpse to thine eye
Thou would'st rejoice for those that live,
Because they live to die."

The music ceased—the noonday Dream
Like dream of night withdrew 70
But Fancy still will sometimes deem
Her fond[6] creation true.

March 5, 1844 1846

R. Alcona to J. Brenzaida[1]

Cold in the earth, and the deep snow piled above thee!
Far, far removed, cold in the dreary grave!
Have I forgot, my Only Love, to love thee,
Severed at last by Time's all-wearing wave?

Now, when alone, do my thoughts no longer hover 5
Over the mountains on Angora's shore;
Resting their wings where heath and fern-leaves cover
That noble heart for ever, ever more?

Cold in the earth, and fifteen wild Decembers
From those brown hills have melted into spring— 10
Faithful indeed is the spirit that remembers
After such years of change and suffering!

Sweet Love of youth, forgive if I forget thee
While the World's tide is bearing me along:
Sterner desires and darker hopes beset me, 15
Hopes which obscure but cannot do thee wrong.

No other Sun has lightened up my heaven;
No other Star has ever shone for me:

6. Foolish. "Fancy": imagination.
1. Rosina Alcona is another name for A. G. A., the
heroine of the Gondal stories. C. W. Hatfield suggests
that Brenzaida may be A. G. A.'s first love as well as her
last husband. Here he is deceased.

All my life's bliss from thy dear life was given—
All my life's bliss is in the grave with thee. 20

But when the days of golden dreams had perished
And even Despair was powerless to destroy,
Then did I learn how existence could be cherished,
Strengthened and fed without the aid of joy;

Then did I check the tears of useless passion, 25
Weaned my young soul from yearning after thine;
Sternly denied its burning wish to hasten
Down to that tomb already more than mine!

And even yet, I dare not let it languish,
Dare not indulge in Memory's rapturous pain; 30
Once drinking deep of that divinest anguish,
How could I seek the empty world again?

March 3, 1845 1846

[Ah! why, because the dazzling sun]

Ah! why, because the dazzling sun
Restored my earth to joy
Have you[1] departed, every one,
And left a desert sky?

All through the night, your glorious eyes 5
Were gazing down in mine.
And with a full heart's thankful sighs
I blessed that watch divine.

I was at peace, and drank your beams
As they were life to me 10
And revelled in my changeful dreams
Like petrel[2] on the sea.

Thought followed thought—star followed star
Through boundless regions on,
While one sweet influence, near and far, 15
Thrilled through and proved us one.

Why did the morning rise to break
So great, so pure a spell,
And scorch with fire the tranquil cheek
Where your cool radiance fell? 20

Blood-red he rose,[3] and arrow-straight
His fierce beams struck my brow:

1. The speaker addresses the stars. 3 The sun.
2. Sea birds.

The soul of Nature sprang elate,
But mine sank sad and low!

My lids closed down—yet through their veil 25
I saw him blazing still;
And bathe in gold the misty dale,
And flash upon the hill.

I turned me to the pillow then
To call back Night, and see 30
Your worlds of solemn light, again
Throb with my heart and me!

It would not do—the pillow glowed
And glowed both roof and floor,
And birds sang loudly in the wood, 35
And fresh winds shook the door.

The curtains waved, the wakened flies
Were murmuring round my room,
Imprisoned there, till I should rise
And give them leave to roam. 40

O Stars and Dreams and Gentle Night;
O Night and Stars return!
And hide me from the hostile light
That does not warm, but burn—

That drains the blood of suffering men; 45
Drinks tears, instead of dew:
Let me sleep through his blinding reign,
And only wake with you!

April 14, 1845 1846

The Prisoner

A *Fragment*

In the dungeon crypts[1] idly did I stray,
Reckless of the lives wasting there away;
"Draw the ponderous bars! open, Warder stern!"
He dared not say me nay—the hinges harshly turn.

"Our guests are darkly lodged," I whispered, gazing through 5
The vault, whose grated eye showed heaven more gray than blue
(This was when glad Spring laughed in awaking pride);
"Aye, darkly lodged enough!" returned my sullen guide.

Then, God forgive my youth! forgive my careless tongue!
I scoffed, as the chill chains on the damp flagstones rung: 10

1. Underground vaults. The speaker, a man, is wandering through the dungeon in the castle of his father.

"Confined in triple walls, art thou so much to fear,
That we must bind thee down and clench thy fetters here?"

The captive raised her face; it was as soft and mild
As sculptured marble saint; or slumbering unweaned child;
It was so soft and mild, it was so sweet and fair, 15
Pain could not trace a line, or grief a shadow there!

The captive raised her hand and pressed it to her brow;
"I have been struck," she said, "and I am suffering now;
Yet these are little worth, your bolts and irons strong:
And, were they forged in steel, they could not hold me long." 20

Hoarse laughed the jailor grim: "Shall I be won to hear;
Dost think, fond,[2] dreaming wretch, that _I_ shall grant thy prayer?
Or, better still, wilt melt my master's heart with groans?
Ah! sooner might the sun thaw down these granite stones.

"My master's voice is low, his aspect bland and kind, 25
But hard as hardest flint the soul that lurks behind;
And I am rough and rude, yet not more rough to see
Than is the hidden ghost that has its home in me."

About her lips there played a smile of a most scorn.
"My friend," she gently said, "you have not heard me mourn; 30
When you my kindred's lives, _my_ lost life can restore,
Then may I weep and sue—but never, friend, before!

"Still, let my tyrants know, I am not doomed to wear
Year after year in gloom, and desolate despair;
A messenger of Hope comes every night to me, 35
And offers for short life, eternal liberty.

"He comes with western winds, with evening's wandering airs,
With that clear dusk of heaven that brings the thickest stars,
Winds take a pensive tone, and stars a tender fire,
And visions rise, and change, that kill me with desire. 40

"Desire for nothing known in my maturer years,
When Joy grew mad with awe, at counting future tears.
When, if my spirit's sky was full of flashes warm,
I knew not whence they came, from sun or thunderstorm.

"But, first, a hush of peace—a soundless calm descends; 45
The struggle of distress and fierce impatience ends;
Mute music soothes my breast—unuttered harmony,
That I could never dream, till Earth was lost to me.

"Then dawns the Invisible; the Unseen its truth reveals;
My outward sense is gone, my inward essence feels 50
Its wings are almost free—its home, its harbor found,
Measuring the gulf, it stoops—and dares the final bound.

2. Foolish.

"Oh! dreadful is the check—intense the agony—
When the ear begins to hear, and the eye begins to see;
When the pulse begins to throb, the brain to think again; 55
The soul to feel the flesh, and the flesh to feel the chain.

"Yet I would lose no sting, would wish no torture less;
The more that anguish racks, the earlier it will bless;
And robed in fires of hell, or bright with heavenly shine,
If it but herald death, the vision is divine!" 60

She ceased to speak, and we, unanswering, turned to go—
We had no further power to work the captive woe:
Her cheek, her gleaming eye, declared that man had given
A sentence, unapproved, and overruled by Heaven.

October 9, 1845 1846

[No coward soul is mine][1]

No coward soul is mine
No trembler in the world's storm-troubled sphere
I see Heaven's glories shine
And Faith shines equal arming me from Fear

O God within my breast 5
Almighty ever-present Deity
Life, that in me hast rest
As I Undying Life, have power in Thee

Vain are the thousand creeds
That move men's hearts, unutterably vain, 10
Worthless as withered weeds
Or idlest froth amid the boundless main

To waken doubt in one
Holding so fast by thy infinity
So surely anchored on 15
The steadfast rock of Immortality

With wide-embracing love
Thy spirit animates eternal years
Pervades and broods above,
Changes, sustains, dissolves, creates and rears 20

Though Earth and moon were gone
And suns and universes ceased to be
And thou wert left alone
Every Existence would exist in thee

There is not room for Death 25

1. The following are the last lines my sister Emily ever wrote [Charlotte Brontë's note].

Nor atom that his might could render void
 Since thou art Being and Breath
 And what thou art may never be destroyed.

January 2, 1846 1850

Stanzas[1]

Often rebuked, yet always back returning
 To those first feelings that were born with me,
And leaving busy chase of wealth and learning
 For idle dreams of things which cannot be:

To-day, I will seek not the shadowy region;[2] 5
 Its unsustaining vastness waxes drear;
And visions rising, legion after legion,
 Bring the unreal world too strangely near.

I'll walk, but not in old heroic traces,[3]
 And not in paths of high morality, 10
And not among the half-distinguished faces,
 The clouded forms of long-past history.

I'll walk where my own nature would be leading:
 It vexes[4] me to choose another guide:
Where the gray flocks in ferny glens are feeding; 15
 Where the wild wind blows on the mountain side.

What have those lonely mountains worth revealing?
 More glory and more grief than I can tell:
The earth that wakes *one* human heart to feeling
 Can center both the worlds of Heaven and Hell. 20

 1850

1. As no manuscript exists for this poem, there is some speculation that Charlotte may have written it instead of Emily; however, the poem seems to summarize much of Emily's characteristic vision.

2. The shadowy world of the imagination, specifically the private myth of Gondal.
3. Paths or, alternatively, straps that form a harness.
4. Provokes.

GEORGE ELIOT
1819–1880

Known as Mary Anne, Mary Ann, and Marian Evans to her family, "Clematis" (meaning mental beauty) to a youthful friend, "Deutera" (which "*means* second and *sounds* a little like daughter") to her first scholarly mentor, Mrs. Lewes to her correspondents, "Our Lady" to the women she considered her spiritual daughters, "Mutter" to her adopted sons, and Mrs. John W. Cross to her eulogists, one of the most celebrated sages of Victorian England was best known to the reading public as "George Eliot." By adopting this name, she paid tribute to the man who nurtured her literary efforts, George Henry Lewes, but she also placed herself in a tra-

dition that goes back to George Sand (Aurore Dupin Dudevant) and the Bells (the Brontës). It was the name George Eliot that her readers associated with the blend of compassion, wisdom, and humor that characterizes the omniscient voice of her novels. However, as Ruby Redinger has demonstrated in her biography, the very proliferation of feminine names by which Eliot was known dramatizes the problem she had to solve when she began to publish fiction under a male pseudonym at the age of thirty-eight. Although she would eventually attain the appropriate distinction of being represented in the *English Men of Letters* series, Eliot was aware that her identification with masculine achievement threatened to undermine her consciousness of herself as a woman: a talented but embittered female artist in Eliot's last novel exclaims, "You may try, but you cannot imagine what it is to have a man's force of genius in you, yet to suffer the slavery of being a girl." Nevertheless, Eliot's greatest accomplishment may have been her dramatization of just this contradiction.

In Eliot's most autobiographical novel, *The Mill on the Floss* (1860), Maggie Tulliver's acute sense of her own female "slavery" reflects some of the early frustration that resulted in the headaches, depressions, and sensitivity toward cold that Eliot suffered all of her adult life. Maggie's imaginative curiosity earns, from an otherwise affectionate father, the sardonic comment that "an over-'cute [over-acute] woman's no better nor a long-tailed sheep—she'll fetch none the bigger price for that." While Eliot's father was more prosperous as a farmer and agent for a neighboring estate than the miller who is Maggie's father, Robert Evans was just as traditional in his support of the Church of England, the Tory Party, and their implicitly conservative assumptions about the appropriate sphere of women. Maggie's mother, Mrs. Tulliver, seems more attached to her son, and even to her monographed linen, than to her daughter, just as Eliot always believed her own mother favored her older brother, Isaac. Similarly, in *The Mill on the Floss*, the sister who is destined never to receive the affection she craves from her brother associates her emotional deprivation with Lucy Dean, the conventionally pretty cousin who is as neat as Maggie is messy, as obedient as Maggie is rebellious; in Eliot's childhood this role was played by her older sister Chrissey. From her depiction of Maggie's angry torturing of her doll to her portrayal of the girl's voracious reading and her running away to become queen of the Gypsies, Eliot dramatizes the "hunger of the heart" for sympathy it never receives. Maggie's warring impulses—her desire for intellectual stimulation as opposed to her dutiful efforts at renunciation—reflect Eliot's own self-division as well as her awareness of the constraints of provincial life.

Yet looking backward on provincial life remained the motivating impulse and subject of most of Eliot's fiction. Her nostalgia for the everyday scenes of the preindustrial past turned them into "the mother tongue of our imagination," but what she herself humorously portrayed as the shrewd narrow-mindedness of rural characters was precisely what hindered her own development. From the age of five, Eliot attended three different schools, making friends with at least one headmistress, Maria Lewis. From the time she left school at fifteen, when her mother died, until she was thirty, when her father died, however, she was hampered by the household and nursing duties she assiduously performed. At home, she continued to study Italian, German, and music, corresponding frequently with Miss Lewis, who developed an evangelical strain of puritanism in the young girl. Only when Isaac married and she moved with her father from Griff to a house in Coventry did Eliot begin to find acquaintances who would pose challenging philosophic questions to her.

People like Charles Bray, the author of *The Philosophy of Necessity*, and his wife, Caroline (Hennell) Bray, whose brother wrote *An Inquiry Concerning the Origins of Christianity*, encouraged Eliot's intellectual development, which issued in a typically Victorian crisis of faith. After a painful struggle, she renounced tradi-

tional Christianity, but she could make peace with her father only by promising to accompany him to church on Sundays. During this time, she completed her first major translation, David Friedrich Strauss's *Das Leben Jesu* ("The Life of Jesus," 1846). Published anonymously it contributed, as did her other translations, to the belief that animated her subsequent fiction, "that the idea of God, so far as it has been a highly spiritual influence, is the ideal of a goodness entirely human." The struggle with her spiritual Father was an index of her struggle with her own father, whose death evoked contradictory responses: 'What shall I be without my father?" Eliot mused during his dying. "It will seem as if part of my moral nature were gone. I had a vision of myself last night becoming earthly sensual and devilish for want of that purifying restraining influence." Retrospectively, however, her comment that his dying days were "the happiest" of her life indicates some intimation that his death meant her release.

After a recuperative trip to Switzerland, Eliot was introduced by the Brays to John Chapman, editor of the *Westminster Review*, and she moved to London, where she worked hard to become a member of the literary establishment. As assistant editor of the *Westminster*, she corresponded and negotiated with authors, read proofs, and wrote reviews of philosophic and religious books. She met such eminent Victorians as Charles Dickens, James Froude, Harriet Martineau, John Stuart Mill, and most important, the philosopher Herbert Spencer. As the biographer Gordon Haight has demonstrated, her earlier propensity to glorify a father figure to whom she could dedicate her labor now meant that she did not receive the credit she deserved for turning the *Westminster* into one of England's leading reviews. Ensconced in Chapman's household, she found herself contending with his jealous wife and mistress. In the presence of Chapman and Spencer, moreover, she became even more acutely self-conscious about what Hallam Tennyson would call her "strong masculine face."

This painful but stimulating period was ended when Spencer introduced Eliot to the writer and editor George Henry Lewes, a married man who had separated from his wife. After they began seeing each other, they made the highly unconventional decision to live together despite the fact that Lewes could not obtain a divorce. Although she faced the censure not only of her brother, Isaac, but also of polite London society, Eliot went off to the Continent in 1854 to begin life with Lewes as an unmarried wife. No wonder, then, that she objected to the plot of *Jane Eyre*, specifically to Jane's refusal to live with the married Rochester: "All self-sacrifice is good," she character stically conceded, "but one would like it to be in a somewhat nobler cause than a diabolical law which chains a man body and soul to a putrifying carcass." The number of those who refused to visit the woman who returned to London calling herself "Marian Lewes" should not be minimized: even so tolerant a writer as Mrs. Gaskell wrote to her, "I wish you *were* Mrs. Lewes."

By 1856 Eliot was clearly assessing the current state of fiction, specifically condemning "silly novels" by "lady novelists." In the *Westminster Review*, she asked, "Why can we not have pictures of religious life among the industrial classes in England, as interesting as Mrs. Stowe's pictures of religious life among the Negroes?" Not to be discounted in considering Eliot's late productivity is the intellectual stimulation that Lewes's own work supplied: a versatile physiologist, biographer, novelist, essayist, and editor, he was the author of a *Biographical History of Philosophy* (1854–56) and an article on *The Lady Novelists* (1852). It was he who encouraged her to compose and publish her first stories in *Blackwood's* "Maga," which were collected in *Scenes of Clerical Life* (1858). Here, as so often, her title was deceptive, for these three stories actually focus on three female characters, a patient but dying wife-mother, a foreign girl goaded into murderous rage by a faithless lover, and a woman who, having been physically abused by her husband, takes refuge in alcohol.

Lewes had believed that "people would have sniffed" at Eliot's first novel, *Adam*

Bede (1859), "if they had known the writer to be a woman," and its instant success did place George Eliot in the ranks of major novelists such as Dickens and Thackeray. Even after her true identity became known, Lewes continued to protect her career, writing letters for her to publishers, keeping back unfavorable reviews that would have troubled her, and suggesting certain scenes for novels in progress. Because Lewes and Eliot had to support themselves and his three sons through their writing, they welcomed the £12,000 *Adam Bede* brought. *Silas Marner* (1861) was so popular that her publisher, Blackwood, had to double the original edition of four thousand copies within a month after publication. By this time Eliot had become a careful businesswoman who negotiated herself for the £7,000 she received for *Romola* (1863).

How are the private lives of men and women related to the public issues of culture and society? This question was the recurrent subject of Eliot's mature novels: *Felix Holt* (1866), *Middlemarch* (1871–72), and *Daniel Deronda* (1874–76). Perhaps *Middlemarch*, with its subtitle, *A Study of Provincial Life*, best exemplifies Eliot's panoramic range. Set in the 1830s, with its aristocratic landlords and clergymen, its middle-class bankers and doctors, and its working-class grocers and horse dealers, the novel insists on the complex interrelationships between the sexes and the classes by developing a metaphor of a web or labyrinth and even by elaborating an image of the multitudinous scratches on the surface of a pier glass (a mirror): "place now against it a lighted candle as a centre of illumination, and lo! the scratches will seem to arrange themselves in a fine series of concentric circles round that little sun." Eliot explained that this "parable" signifies the egoism produced by any single perspective, the "flattering illusion" of a concentric arrangement of events that both delights and deludes. For her narrator, who studies this "exclusive optical selection" with patient omniscience, the novel becomes a philosophic study of domestic incompatibility and religious hypocrisy, political discord and legal intrigue. As a composite of the novel's chorus of characters, the narrator maintains a tolerant tone and sympathetic stance that assume that even the most common lives illustrate how "the growing good of the world is partly dependent on unhistoric acts."

Of course the unhistoric acts of Eliot's heroine, Dorothea Brooke, play a central role in *Middlemarch*. As the critic Barbara Hardy has observed, the heroines of all of Eliot's novels share "the *ex-officio* disability of being a woman." For Dorothea, as for the others, this disability is associated with ignorance, the absence of a vocation, and the desire for knowledge "such as great men know." Married to an aging scholar because she wishes to become wise herself in order to do good works, Dorothea discovers not only that she cannot learn from her husband, the author of the projected *Key to All Mythologies*, but that he is hardly wise himself. Thus she becomes a "foundress of nothing," for Eliot consistently denied her heroines the worldly success she herself achieved. Yet, through her suffering, Dorothea attains the growth in sympathy that is always an index of ethical maturity in Eliot's world. For a contemporary like Emily Dickinson, Eliot's achievement was monumental: "What do I think of *Middlemarch*? What do I think of glory?" she wrote, adding that "the mysteries of human nature surpass the 'mysteries of redemption.'"

When Lewes died in 1878, Eliot went into mourning. Previously, in times of stress she had relied on a succession of close female friends: Maria Lewis, Sara Hennell, Barbara Smith Bodichon, and Edith Simcox. But if Eliot felt that her pseudonym encoded her special dependency on Lewes ("To L —— I owe it"), then she must have known that no one could take his place and that her writing career was over. Yet, on May 6, 1880, much to her friends' surprise and dismay, Eliot announced her marriage to John Walter Cross. More than twenty years her junior, he had met her in 1867 when he was traveling on the Continent with his mother. The marriage ended seven months after the wedding, when Eliot died. Cross used her letters to write the first and most laudatory of her biographies, but in spite of

his efforts, the next generation of readers considered Eliot's fiction too moralistic, earnest, and diffuse. Women writers from Eliza Linton and Mrs. Oliphant to Katherine Mansfield envied the protection Eliot had received from Lewes, but they distrusted her assumption of masculine superiority. Nevertheless, by integrating philosophy and fiction, Eliot exerted a profound influence on the shape of the novel as it was developed by writers as diverse as Henry James, D. H. Lawrence, and Margaret Drabble.

The selections printed here represent two different aspects of Eliot's career. *The Lifted Veil* (1859), which appeared anonymously in *Blackwood's*, reflects her reaction to the lifting of her own veil of anonymity when the public was discovering her identity. Eccentric though it is in her oeuvre, the tale questions the ideal of sympathetic identification Eliot usually espoused, for, as a surrogate of the author, Latimer experiences nothing but pain from the telepathy that reveals to him the subjectivity of others. *The Lifted Veil* also extends the tradition of female Gothic established in Shelley's *The Mortal Immortal* and Brontë's *Jane Eyre*. *Brother and Sister* represents Eliot as a poet. Written in the period when she composed *The Spanish Gypsy* (1868) and *Armgart* (1871), it explores the same sibling relationship she had placed at the center of her semiautobiographical *The Mill on the Floss*.

The Lifted Veil

Give me no light, great Heaven, but such as turns
To energy of human fellowship;
No powers beyond the growing heritage
That makes completer manhood.[1]

Chapter I

The time of my end approaches. I have lately been subject to attacks of *angina pectoris*,[2] and in the ordinary course of things, my physician tells me, I may fairly hope that my life will not be protracted many months. Unless, then, I am cursed with an exceptional physical constitution, as I am cursed with an exceptional mental character, I shall not much longer groan under the wearisome burden of this earthly existence. If it were to be otherwise,—if I were to live on to the age most men desire and provide for,—I should for once have known whether the miseries of delusive expectation can outweigh the miseries of true prevision. For I foresee when I shall die, and everything that will happen in my last moments.

Just a month from this day, on the 20th of September, 1850, I shall be sitting in this chair, in this study, at ten o'clock at night, longing to die, weary of incessant insight and foresight, without delusions and without hope. Just as I am watching a tongue of blue flame rising in the fire, and my lamp is burning low, the horrible contraction will begin at my chest. I shall only have time to reach the bell, and pull it violently, before the sense of suffocation will come. No one will answer my bell. I know why. My two servants are lovers, and will have quarreled. My housekeeper will have rushed out of the house in a fury, two hours before, hoping that Perry will believe she has gone to drown herself. Perry is alarmed at last, and is gone out after her. The little scullery-maid is asleep on a bench: she never answers the bell; it does not wake her. The sense

1. The epigraph is by Eliot. 2. A painful heart disease.

of suffocation increases: my lamp goes out with a horrible stench: I make a great effort, and snatch at the bell again. I long for life, and there is no help. I thirsted for the unknown: the thirst is gone. O God, let me stay with the known, and be weary of it: I am content. Agony of pain and suffocation,—and all the while the earth, the fields, the pebbly brook at the bottom of the rookery,[3] the fresh scent after the rain, the light of the morning through my chamber-window, the warmth of the hearth after the frosty air,—will darkness close over them forever?

Darkness,—darkness,—no pain,—nothing but darkness: but I am passing on and on through the darkness: my thought stays in the darkness, but always with a sense of moving onward. . . .

Before that time comes, I wish to use my last hours of ease and strength in telling the strange story of my experience. I have never fully unbosomed myself to any human being; I have never been encouraged to trust much in the sympathy of my fellow-men. But we have all a chance of meeting with some pity, some tenderness, some charity, when we are dead: it is the living only who cannot be forgiven,—the living only from whom men's indulgence and reverence are held off, like the rain by the hard east wind. While the heart beats, bruise it,—it is your only opportunity; while the eye can still turn towards you with moist timid entreaty, freeze it with an icy unanswering gaze; while the ear, that delicate messenger to the inmost sanctuary of the soul, can still take in the tones of kindness, put it off with hard civility, or sneering compliment, or envious affectation of indifference; while the creative brain can still throb with the sense of injustice, with the yearning for brotherly recognition,— make haste,—oppress it with your ill-considered judgments, your trivial comparisons, your careless misrepresentations. The heart will by and by be still,—*ubi sæva indignatio ulterius cor lacerare nequit;*[4] the eye will cease to entreat; the ear will be deaf; the brain will have ceased from all wants as well as from all work. Then your charitable speeches may find vent; then you may remember and pity the toil and the struggle and the failure; then you may give due honor to the work achieved; then you may find extenuation for errors, and may consent to bury them.

That is a trivial schoolboy text; why do I dwell on it? It has little reference to me, for I shall leave no works behind me for men to honor. I have no near relatives who will make up, by weeping over my grave, for the wounds they inflicted on me when I was among them. It is only the story of my life that will perhaps win a little more sympathy from strangers when I am dead, than I ever believed it would obtain from my friends while I was living.

My childhood perhaps seems happier to me than it really was, by contrast with all the after-years. For then the curtain of the future was as impenetrable to me as to other children: I had all their delight in the present hour, their sweet indefinite hopes for the morrow; and I had a tender mother: even now, after the dreary lapse of long years, a slight trace of sensation accompanies the remembrance of her caress as she held me on her knee,—her arms round my little body, her cheek pressed on mine. I had a complaint of the eyes that made me blind for a little while, and she kept me on her knee from morning till night. That unequaled love soon vanished out of my life, and even to my childish consciousness it was as if that life had become more chill. I rode my

3. A nesting place of rooks or ravens.
4. "Inscription on Swift's tombstone" [Eliot's note].
Where fierce indignation can no longer tear his heart (Latin).

little white pony with the groom by my side as before, but there were no loving
eyes looking at me as I mounted, no glad arms opened to me when I came
back. Perhaps I missed my mother's love more than most children of seven or
eight would have done, to whom the other pleasures of life remained as be-
fore; for I was certainly a very sensitive child. I remember still the mingled
trepidation and delicious excitement with which I was affected by the tramp-
ing of the horses on the pavement in the echoing stables, by the loud reso-
nance of the grooms' voices, by the booming bark of the dogs as my father's
carriage thundered under the archway of the courtyard, by the din of the gong
as it gave notice of luncheon and dinner. The measured tramp of soldiery
which I sometimes heard—for my father's house lay near a country town
where there were large barracks—made me sob and tremble; and yet when
they were gone past, I longed for them to come back again.

I fancy my father thought me an odd child, and had little fondness for me;
though he was very careful in fulfilling what he regarded as a parent's duties.
But he was already past the middle of life, and I was not his only son. My
mother had been his second wife, and he was five-and-forty when he married
her. He was a firm, unbending, intensely orderly man, in root and stem a
banker, but with a flourishing graft[5] of the active landholder, aspiring to
county influence: one of those people who are always like themselves from day
to day, who are uninfluenced by the weather, and neither know melancholy
nor high spirits. I held him in great awe, and appeared more timid and sensi-
tive in his presence than at other times; a circumstance which, perhaps,
helped to confirm him in the intention to educate me on a different plan from
the prescriptive one with which he had complied in the case of my elder
brother, already a tall youth at Eton.[6] My brother was to be his representative
and successor; he must go to Eton and Oxford, for the sake of making connec-
tions, of course: my father was not a man to underrate the bearing of Latin
satirists or Greek dramatists on the attainment of an aristocratic position.
But, intrinsically, he had slight esteem for "those dead but sceptred spirits;"
having qualified himself for forming an independent opinion by reading
Potter's "Æschylus," and dipping into Francis's "Horace."[7] To this negative
view he added a positive one, derived from a recent connection with mining
speculations; namely, that a scientific education was the really useful training
for a younger son. Moreover, it was clear that a shy, sensitive boy like me was
not fit to encounter the rough experience of a public school. Mr. Letherall had
said so very decidedly. Mr. Letherall was a large man in spectacles, who one day
took my small head between his large hands, and pressed it here and there in
an exploratory, suspicious manner,—then placed each of his great thumbs on
my temples, and pushed me a little way from him, and stared at me with glit-
tering spectacles. The contemplation appeared to displease him, for he
frowned sternly, and said to my father, drawing his thumbs across my eye-
brows,—

"The deficiency is there, sir,—there, and here," he added, touching the
upper sides of my head,—"here is the excess. That must be brought out, sir,
and this must be laid to sleep."[8]

5. Part of a plant that has been attached to another
plant of a different species.
6. Famous English private school (in Britain, called a
"public school"), with a classical curriculum.
7. English translations of the Greek tragedian and

Latin poet.
8. Letherall is practicing the "science" of phrenology,
much in vogue in the later 19th-century, according to
which a person's mental character could be deter-
mined by the shape of his or her skull.

I was in a state of tremor, partly at the vague idea that I was the object of reprobation, partly in the agitation of my first hatred,—hatred of this big, spectacled man, who pulled my head about as if he wanted to buy and cheapen it.

I am not aware how much Mr. Letherall had to do with the system afterwards adopted towards me, but it was presently clear that private tutors, natural history, science, and the modern languages were the appliances by which the defects of my organization were to be remedied. I was very stupid about machines, so I was to be greatly occupied with them; I had no memory for classification, so it was particularly necessary that I should study systematic zoölogy and botany; I was hungry for human deeds and human emotions, so I was to be plentifully crammed with the mechanical powers, the elementary bodies, and the phenomena of electricity and magnetism. A better-constituted boy would certainly have profited under my intelligent tutors, with their scientific apparatus; and would, doubtless, have found the phenomena of electricity and magnetism as fascinating as I was, every Thursday, assured they were. As it was, I could have paired off, for ignorance of whatever was taught me, with the worst Latin scholar that was ever turned out of a classical academy. I read Plutarch, and Shakespeare, and Don Quixote[9] by the sly, and supplied myself in that way with wandering thoughts, while my tutor was assuring me that "an improved man, as distinguished from an ignorant one, was a man who knew the reason why water ran down-hill." I had no desire to be this improved man; I was glad of the running water; I could watch it and listen to it gurgling among the pebbles, and bathing the bright green water-plants, by the hour together. I did not want to know *why* it ran; I had perfect confidence that there were good reasons for what was so very beautiful.

There is no need to dwell on this part of my life. I have said enough to indicate that my nature was of the sensitive, unpractical order, and that it grew up in an uncongenial medium, which could never foster it into happy, healthy development. When I was sixteen I was sent to Geneva[1] to complete my course of education; and the change was a very happy one to me, for the first sight of the Alps, with the setting sun on them, as we descended the Jura,[2] seemed to me like an entrance into heaven; and the three years of my life there were spent in a perpetual sense of exaltation, as if from a draught of delicious wine, at the presence of Nature in all her awful loveliness. You will think, perhaps, that I must have been a poet, from this early sensibility[3] to Nature. But my lot was not so happy as that. A poet pours forth his song and *believes* in the listening ear and answering soul, to which his song will be floated sooner or later. But the poet's sensibility without his voice,—the poet's sensibility that finds no vent but in silent tears on the sunny bank, when the noonday light sparkles on the water or in an inward shudder at the sound of harsh human tones, the sight of a cold human eye,—this dumb passion brings with it a fatal solitude of soul in the society of one's fellow-men. My least solitary moments were those in which I pushed off in my boat, at evening, towards the center of the lake; it seemed to me that the sky, and the glowing mountain-tops, and the wide blue water surrounded me with a cherishing love such as no human face

9. *Don Quixote* is the comic novel by Cervantes. Plutarch was a Greek historian and biographer.
1. A city in Switzerland known for its fine schools.

2. A mountain range in Germany.
3. I.e., sensitivity. "Awful": awe-inspiring.

had shed on me since my mother's love had vanished out of my life. I used to do as Jean Jacques[4] did,—lie down in my boat and let it glide where it would, while I looked up at the departing glow leaving one mountain-top after the other, as if the prophet's chariot of fire[5] were passing over them on its way to the home of light. Then, when the white summits were all sad and corpse-like, I had to push homeward, for I was under careful surveillance, and was allowed no late wanderings. This disposition of mine was not favorable to the formation of intimate friendships among the numerous youths of my own age who are always to be found studying at Geneva. Yet I made *one* such friendship; and, singularly enough, it was with a youth whose intellectual tendencies were the very reverse of my own. I shall call him Charles Meunier; his real surname—an English one, for he was of English extraction—having since become celebrated. He was an orphan, who lived on a miserable pittance while he pursued the medical studies for which he had a special genius. Strange! that with my vague mind, susceptible and unobservant, hating inquiry and given up to contemplation, I should have been drawn towards a youth whose strongest passion was science. But the bond was not an intellectual one; it came from a source that can happily blend the stupid with the brilliant, the dreamy with the practical: it came from community of feeling. Charles was poor and ugly, derided by Genevese *gamins*,[6] and not acceptable in drawing-rooms. I saw that he was isolated, as I was, though from a different cause, and, stimulated by a sympathetic resentment, I made timid advances towards him. It is enough to say that there sprang up as much comradeship between us as our different habits would allow; and in Charles's rare holidays we went up the Salève together, or took the boat to Vevey, while I listened dreamily to the monologues in which he unfolded his bold conceptions of future experiment and discovery. I mingled them confusedly in my thought with glimpses of blue water and delicate floating cloud, with the notes of birds and the distant glitter of the glacier. He knew quite well that my mind was half absent, yet he liked to talk to me in this way; for don't we talk of our hopes and our projects even to dogs and birds, when they love us? I have mentioned this one friendship because of its connection with a strange and terrible scene which I shall have to narrate in my subsequent life.

This happier life at Geneva was put an end to by a severe illness, which is partly a blank to me, partly a time of dimly remembered suffering, with the presence of my father by my bed from time to time. Then came the languid monotony of convalescence, the days gradually breaking into variety and distinctness as my strength enabled me to take longer and longer drives. On one of these more vividly remembered days, my father said to me, as he sat beside my sofa,—

"When you are quite well enough to travel, Latimer, I shall take you home with me. The journey will amuse you and do you good, for I shall go through the Tyrol and Austria, and you will see many new places. Our neighbors, the Filmores, are come; Alfred will join us at Basle, and we shall all go together to Vienna, and back by Prague—"

My father was called away before he had finished his sentence, and he left

4. Jean Jacques Rousseau (1712–1778). French philosopher who believed in the goodness of nature. This description of the power of nature also recalls Wordsworth's *Prelude* (1850) 1.351–400.

5. The prophet Elijah was carried into heaven on a flaming chariot (2 Kings 2).

6. Street urchins.

my mind resting on the word *Prague*, with a strange sense that a new and won-
drous scene was breaking upon me: a city under the broad sunshine, that
seemed to me as if it were the summer sunshine of a long-past century ar-
rested in its course,—unrefreshed for ages by the dews of night or the rushing
rain-cloud; scorching the dusty, weary, time-eaten grandeur of a people
doomed to live on in the stale repetition of memories, like deposed and super-
annuated kings in their regal gold-inwoven tatters. The city looked so thirsty
that the broad river seemed to me a sheet of metal; and the blackened statues,
as I passed under their blank gaze, along the unending bridge, with their an-
cient garments and their saintly crowns, seemed to me the real inhabitants
and owners of this place, while the busy, trivial men and women, hurrying to
and fro, were a swarm of ephemeral visitants infesting it for a day. It is such
grim, stony beings as these, I thought, who are the fathers of ancient faded
children, in those tanned time-fretted dwellings that crowd the steep before
me; who pay their court in the worn and crumbling pomp of the palace which
stretches its monotonous length on the height; who worship wearily in the sti-
fling air of the churches, urged by no fear or hope, but compelled by their
doom to be ever old and undying, to live on in the rigidity of habit, as they live
on in perpetual mid-day, without the repose of night or the new birth of morn-
ing.

A stunning clang of metal suddenly thrilled through me, and I became con-
scious of the objects in my room again: one of the fire-irons had fallen as Pierre
opened the door to bring me my draught.[7] My heart was palpitating violently,
and I begged Pierre to leave my draught beside me; I would take it presently.

As soon as I was alone again, I began to ask myself whether I had been sleep-
ing. Was this a dream,—this wonderfully distinct vision,—minute in its dis-
tinctness down to a patch of rainbow light on the pavement, transmitted
through a colored lamp in the shape of a star,—of a strange city, quite unfa-
miliar to my imagination? I had seen no picture of Prague: it lay in my mind as
a mere name, with vaguely remembered historical associations,—ill-defined
memories of imperial grandeur and religious wars.

Nothing of this sort had ever occurred in my dreaming experience before,
for I had often been humiliated because my dreams were only saved from
being utterly disjointed and commonplace by the frequent terrors of night-
mare. But I could not believe that I had been asleep, for I remembered dis-
tinctly the gradual breaking-in of the vision upon me, like the new images in a
dissolving view, or the growing distinctness of the landscape as the sun lifts up
the veil of the morning mist. And while I was conscious of this incipient vi-
sion, I was also conscious that Pierre came to tell my father Mr. Filmore was
waiting for him, and that my father hurried out of the room. No, it was not a
dream; was it,—the thought was full of tremulous exultation,—was it the
poet's nature in me, hitherto only a troubled yearning sensibility, now mani-
festing itself suddenly as spontaneous creation? Surely it was in this way that
Homer saw the plain of Troy, that Dante saw the abodes of the departed, that
Milton saw the earthward flight of the Tempter.[8] Was it that my illness had
wrought some happy change in my organization,—given a firmer tension to
my nerves,—carried off some dull obstruction? I had often read of such ef-

7. Drink.
8. In the *Iliad*, the *Divine Comedy*, and *Paradise Lost*, respectively.

fects,—in works of fiction at least. Nay; in genuine biographies I had read of the subtilizing or exalting influence of some diseases on the mental powers. Did not Novalis feel his inspiration intensified under the progress of consumption?[9]

When my mind had dwelt for some time on this blissful idea, it seemed to me that I might perhaps test it by an exertion of my will. The vision had begun when my father was speaking of our going to Prague. I did not for a moment believe it was really a representation of that city; I believed—I hoped it was a picture that my newly liberated genius had painted in fiery haste, with the colours snatched from lazy memory. Suppose I were to fix my mind on some other place,—Venice, for example, which was far more familiar to my imagination than Prague: perhaps the same sort of result would follow. I concentrated my thoughts on Venice; I stimulated my imagination with poetic memories, and strove to feel myself present in Venice, as I had felt myself present in Prague. But in vain. I was only coloring the Canaletto[1] engravings that hung in my old bedroom at home; the picture was a shifting one, my mind wandering uncertainly in search of more vivid images; I could see no accident of form or shadow without conscious labor after the necessary conditions. It was all prosaic effort, not rapt passivity, such as I had experienced half an hour before. I was discouraged; but I remembered that inspiration was fitful.

For several days I was in a state of excited expectation, watching for a recurrence of my new gift. I sent my thoughts ranging over my world of knowledge, in the hope that they would find some object which would send a reawakening vibration through my slumbering genius. But no; my world remained as dim as ever, and that flash of strange light refused to come again, though I watched for it with palpitating eagerness.

My father accompanied me every day in a drive, and a gradually lengthening walk as my powers of walking increased: and one evening he had agreed to come and fetch me at twelve the next day, that we might go together to select a musical box, and other purchases rigorously demanded of a rich Englishman visiting Geneva. He was one of the most punctual of men and bankers, and I was always nervously anxious to be quite ready for him at the appointed time. But, to my surprise, at a quarter past twelve he had not appeared. I felt all the impatience of a convalescent who has nothing particular to do, and who has just taken a tonic[2] in the prospect of immediate exercise that would carry off the stimulus.

Unable to sit still and reserve my strength, I walked up and down the room, looking out on the current of the Rhone, just where it leaves the dark-blue lake; but thinking all the while of the possible causes that could detain my father.

Suddenly I was conscious that my father was in the room, but not alone: there were two persons with him. Strange! I had heard no footstep, I had not seen the door open; but I saw my father, and at his right hand our neighbor Mrs. Filmore, whom I remembered very well, though I had not seen her for five years. She was a commonplace middle-aged woman, in silk and cashmere; but the lady on the left of my father was not more than twenty, a tall, slim, wil-

9. Tuberculosis. Novalis (1772–1801), German Romantic poet.

1. Venetian painter (1697–1768).
2. An invigorating drug.

lowy figure, with luxuriant blond hair, arranged in cunning braids and folds that looked almost too massive for the slight figure and the small-featured, thin-lipped face they crowned. But the face had not a girlish expression: the features were sharp, the pale gray eyes at once acute, restless, and sarcastic. They were fixed on me in half-smiling curiosity, and I felt a painful sensation as if a sharp wind were cutting me. The pale-green dress, and the green leaves that seemed to form a border about her pale blond hair, made me think of a Water-Nixie[3]—for my mind was full of German lyrics, and this pale, fatal-eyed woman, with the green weeds, looked like a birth from some cold sedgy stream, the daughter of an aged river.

"Well, Latimer, you thought me long," my father said. . . .

But while the last word was in my ears, the whole group vanished, and there was nothing between me and the Chinese painted folding-screen that stood before the door. I was cold and trembling; I could only totter forward and throw myself on the sofa. This strange new power had manifested itself again. . . . But *was* it a power? Might it not rather be a disease,—a sort of intermittent delirium, concentrating my energy of brain into moments of unhealthy activity, and leaving my saner hours all the more barren? I felt a dizzy sense of unreality in what my eye rested on; I grasped the bell convulsively, like one trying to free himself from nightmare, and rang it twice. Pierre came with a look of alarm in his face.

"Monsieur ne se trouve pas bien?"[4] he said anxiously.

"I'm tired of waiting, Pierre," I said, as distinctly and emphatically as I could, like a man determined to be sober in spite of wine; "I'm afraid something has happened to my father,—he's usually so punctual. Run to the Hôtel des Bergues and see if he is there."

Pierre left the room at once, with a soothing "Bien, Monsieur;" and I felt the better for this scene of simple, waking prose. Seeking to calm myself still further, I went into my bedroom, adjoining the *salon*, and opened a case of eau-de-Cologne; took out a bottle; went through the process of taking out the cork very neatly, and then rubbed the reviving spirit over my hands and forehead, and under my nostrils, drawing a new delight from the scent because I had procured it by slow details of labor, and by no strange sudden madness. Already I had begun to taste something of the horror that belongs to the lot of a human being whose nature is not adjusted to simple human conditions.

Still enjoying the scent, I returned to the *salon*, but it was not unoccupied, as it had been before I left it. In front of the Chinese folding-screen there was my father, with Mrs. Filmore on his right hand, and on his left, the slim blond-haired girl, with the keen face and the keen eyes fixed on me in half-smiling curiosity.

"Well, Latimer, you thought me long," my father said. . . .

I heard no more, felt no more, till I became conscious that I was lying with my head low on the sofa, Pierre and my father by my side. As soon as I was thoroughly revived, my father left the room, and presently returned, saying,—

"I've been to tell the ladies how you are, Latimer. They were waiting in the next room. We shall put off our shopping expedition to-day."

Presently he said, "That young lady is Bertha Grant, Mrs. Filmore's orphan niece. Filmore has adopted her, and she lives with them, so you will have her

3. In Germanic folklore, a water sprite. 4. Monsieur is not well?

for a neighbor when we go home,—perhaps for a near relation; for there is a tenderness between her and Alfred, I suspect, and I should be gratified by the match, since Filmore means to provide for her in every way as if she were his daughter. It had not occurred to me that you knew nothing about her living with the Filmores."

He made no further allusion to the fact of my having fainted at the moment of seeing her, and I would not for the world have told him the reason: I shrank from the idea of disclosing to anyone what might be regarded as a pitiable peculiarity, most of all from betraying it to my father, who would have suspected my sanity ever after.

I do not mean to dwell with particularity on the details of my experience. I have described these two cases at length, because they had definite, clearly traceable results in my after-lot.

Shortly after this last occurrence—I think the very next day—I began to be aware of a phase in my abnormal sensibility, to which, from the languid and slight nature of my intercourse with others since my illness, I had not been alive before. This was the obtrusion on my mind of the mental process going forward in first one person, and then another, with whom I happened to be in contact: the vagrant, frivolous ideas and emotions of some uninteresting acquaintance—Mrs. Filmore, for example—would force themselves on my consciousness like an importunate, ill-played musical instrument, or the loud activity of an imprisoned insect. But this unpleasant sensibility was fitful, and left me moments of rest, when the souls of my companions were once more shut out from me, and I felt a relief such as silence brings to wearied nerves. I might have believed this importunate insight to be merely a diseased activity of the imagination, but that my prevision of incalculable words and actions proved it to have a fixed relation to the mental process in other minds. But this superadded consciousness, wearying and annoying enough when it urged on me the trivial experience of indifferent people, became an intense pain and grief when it seemed to be opening to me the souls of those who were in a close relation to me,—when the rational talk, the graceful attentions, the wittily turned phrases, and the kindly deeds, which used to make the web of their characters, were seen as if thrust asunder by a microscopic vision, that showed all the intermediate frivolities, all the suppressed egoism, all the struggling chaos of puerilities, meanness, vague capricious memories, and indolent make-shift thoughts, from which human words and deeds emerge like leaflets[5] covering a fermenting heap.

At Basle we were joined by my brother Alfred, now a handsome self-confident man of six-and-twenty,—a thorough contrast to my fragile, nervous, ineffectual self. I believe I was held to have a sort of half-womanish, half-ghostly beauty; for the portrait-painters, who are thick as weeds at Geneva, had often asked me to sit to them, and I had been the model of a dying minstrel in a fancy picture. But I thoroughly disliked my own *physique*, and nothing but the belief that it was a condition of poetic genius would have reconciled me to it. That brief hope was quite fled, and I saw in my face now nothing but the stamp of a morbid organization, framed for passive suffering,—too feeble for the sublime resistance of poetic production. Alfred, from whom I had been almost constantly separated, and who, in his present stage of character and ap-

5. Small leaves.

pearance, came before me as a perfect stranger, was bent on being extremely friendly and brother-like to me. He had the superficial kindness of a good-humored, self-satisfied nature, that fears no rivalry, and has encountered no contrarieties. I am not sure that my disposition was good enough for me to have been quite free from envy towards him, even if our desires had not clashed, and if I had been in the healthy human condition which admits of generous confidence and charitable construction.[6] There must always have been an antipathy between our natures. As it was, he became in a few weeks an object of intense hatred to me; and when he entered the room, still more when he spoke, it was as if a sensation of grating metal had set my teeth on edge. My diseased consciousness was more intensely and continually occupied with his thoughts and emotions than with those of any other person who came in my way. I was perpetually exasperated with the petty promptings of his conceit and his love of patronage, with his self-complacent belief in Bertha Grant's passion for him, with his half-pitying contempt for me—seen not in the ordinary indications of intonation and phrase and slight action, which an acute and suspicious mind is on the watch for, but in all their naked skinless complication.

For we were rivals, and our desires clashed, though he was not aware of it. I have said nothing yet of the effect Bertha Grant produced in me on a nearer acquaintance. That effect was chiefly determined by the fact that she made the only exception, among all the human beings about me, to my unhappy gift of insight. About Bertha I was always in a state of uncertainty: I could watch the expression of her face, and speculate on its meaning; I could ask for her opinion with the real interest of ignorance; I could listen for her words and watch for her smile with hope and fear: she had for me the fascination of an unraveled destiny. I say it was this fact that chiefly determined the strong effect she produced on me: for, in the abstract, no womanly character could seem to have less affinity for that of a shrinking, romantic, passionate youth than Bertha's. She was keen, sarcastic, unimaginative, prematurely cynical, remaining critical and unmoved in the most impressive scenes, inclined to dissect all my favorite poems, and especially contemptuous towards the German lyrics which were my pet literature at that time. To this moment I am unable to define my feeling towards her: it was not ordinary boyish admiration, for she was the very opposite, even to the color of her hair, of the ideal woman who still remained to me the type[7] of loveliness; and she was without that enthusiasm for the great and good, which, even at the moment of her strongest dominion over me, I should have declared to be the highest element of character. But there is no tyranny more complete than that which a self-centered negative nature exercises over a morbidly sensitive nature perpetually craving sympathy and support. The most independent people feel the effect of a man's silence in heightening their value for his opinion,—feel an additional triumph in conquering the reverence of a critic habitually captious and satirical: no wonder, then, that an enthusiastic self-distrusting youth should watch and wait before the closed secret of a sarcastic woman's face, as if it were the shrine of the doubtfully benignant deity who ruled his destiny. For a young enthusiast is unable to imagine the total negation in another mind of the emotions which are stirring his own: they may be feeble, latent, inactive, he thinks, but

6. Interpretation. 7. Standard, ideal.

they are there,—they may be called forth; sometimes, in moments of happy hallucination, he believes they may be there in all the greater strength because he sees no outward sign of them. And this effect, as I have intimated, was heightened to its utmost intensity in me, because Bertha was the only being who remained for me in the mysterious seclusion of soul that renders such youthful delusion possible. Doubtless there was another sort of fascination at work,—that subtle physical attraction which delights in cheating our psychological predictions, and in compelling the men who paint sylphs to fall in love with some *bonne et brave femme*,[8] heavy-heeled and freckled.

Bertha's behavior towards me was such as to encourage all my illusions, to heighten my boyish passion, and make me more and more dependent on her smiles. Looking back with my present wretched knowledge, I conclude that her vanity and love of power were intensely gratified by the belief that I had fainted on first seeing her purely from the strong impression her person had produced on me. The most prosaic woman likes to believe herself the object of a violent, a poetic passion; and without a grain of romance in her, Bertha had that spirit of intrigue which gave piquancy to the idea that the brother of the man she meant to marry was dying with love and jealousy for her sake. That she meant to marry my brother was what at that time I did not believe; for though he was assiduous in his attentions to her, and I knew well enough that both he and my father had made up their minds to this result, there was not yet an understood engagement,—there had been no explicit declaration; and Bertha habitually, while she flirted with my brother, and accepted his homage in a way that implied to him a thorough recognition of its intention, made me believe, by the subtlest looks and phrases,—feminine nothings which could never be quoted against her,—that he was really the object of her secret ridicule; that she thought him, as I did, a coxcomb,[9] whom she would have pleasure in disappointing. Me she openly petted in my brother's presence, as if I were too young and sickly ever to be thought of as a lover; and that was the view he took of me. But I believe she must inwardly have delighted in the tremors into which she threw me by the coaxing way in which she patted my curls, while she laughed at my quotations. Such caresses were always given in the presence of our friends; for when we were alone together, she affected a much greater distance towards me, and now and then took the opportunity, by words or slight actions, to stimulate my foolish timid hope that she really preferred me. And why should she not follow her inclination? I was not in so advantageous a position as my brother, but I had fortune, I was not a year younger than she was, and she was an heiress, who would soon be of age to decide for herself.

The fluctuations of hope and fear, confined to this one channel, made each day in her presence a delicious torment. There was one deliberate act of hers which especially helped to intoxicate me. When we were at Vienna her twentieth birthday occurred, and as she was very fond of ornaments, we all took the opportunity of the splendid jewelers' shops in that Teutonic Paris to purchase her a birthday present of jewelry. Mine, naturally, was the least expensive; it was an opal ring,—the opal was my favorite stone, because it seems to blush and turn pale as if it had a soul. I told Bertha so when I gave it her, and said

8. Good and hearty woman. "Sylph-": elemental be- 9. A conceited young man.
ings that inhabit the air.

that it was an emblem of the poetic nature, changing with the changing light of heaven and of woman's eyes. In the evening she appeared elegantly dressed, and wearing conspicuously all the birthday presents except mine. I looked eagerly at her fingers, but saw no opal. I had no opportunity of noticing this to her during the evening; but the next day, when I found her seated near the window alone, after breakfast, I said: "You scorn to wear my poor opal. I should have remembered that you despised poetic natures, and should have given you coral, or turquoise, or some other opaque unresponsive stone." "Do I despise it?" she answered, taking hold of a delicate gold chain which she always wore round her neck and drawing out the end from her bosom with my ring hanging to it; "it hurts me a little, I can tell you," she said, with her usual dubious smile, "to wear it in that secret place; and since your poetical nature is so stupid as to prefer a more public position, I shall not endure the pain any longer."

She took off the ring from the chain and put it on her finger, smiling still, while the blood rushed to my cheeks, and I could not trust myself to say a word of entreaty that she would keep the ring where it was before.

I was completely fooled by this, and for two days shut myself up in my own room whenever Bertha was absent, that I might intoxicate myself afresh with the thought of this scene and all it implied.

I should mention that during these two months,—which seemed a long life to me from the novelty and intensity of the pleasures and pains I underwent,—my diseased participation in other people's consciousness continued to torment me; now it was my father, and now my brother, now Mrs. Filmore or her husband, and now our German courier, whose stream of thought rushed upon me like a ringing in the ears not to be got rid of, though it allowed my own impulses and ideas to continue their uninterrupted course. It was like a preternaturally heightened sense of hearing, making audible to one a roar of sound where others find perfect stillness.[1] The weariness and disgust of this involuntary intrusion into other souls was counteracted only by my ignorance of Bertha, and my growing passion for her,—a passion enormously stimulated, if not produced, by that ignorance. She was my oasis of mystery in the dreary desert of knowledge. I had never allowed my diseased condition to betray itself, or to drive me into any unusual speech or action, except once, when, in a moment of peculiar bitterness against my brother, I had forestalled some words which I knew he was going to utter,—a clever observation, which he had prepared beforehand. He had occasionally a slightly affected hesitation in his speech, and when he paused an instant after the second word, my impatience and jealousy impelled me to continue the speech for him, as if it were something we had both learned by rote. He colored and looked astonished, as well as annoyed; and the words had no sooner escaped my lips than I felt a shock of alarm lest such an anticipation of words—very far from being words of course, easy to divine—should have betrayed me as an exceptional being, a sort of quiet energumen,[2] whom everyone, Bertha above all, would shudder at and avoid. But I magnified, as usual, the impression any word or deed of mine could produce on others; for no one gave any sign of having noticed my inter-

1. Eliot uses this simile again in a famous passage in *Middlemarch* (Chapter 28): "If we had a keen vision and feeling of all ordinary human life, it would be like hearing the grass grow and the squirrel's heart beat, and we should die of that roar which lies on the other side of silence."

2. One who is possessed by a devil.

ruption as more than a rudeness, to be forgiven me on the score of my feeble nervous condition.

While this superadded consciousness of the actual was almost constant with me, I had never had a recurrence of that distinct prevision which I have described in relation to my first interview with Bertha; and I was waiting with eager curiosity to know whether or not my vision of Prague would prove to have been an instance of the same kind. A few days after the incident of the opal ring, we were paying one of our frequent visits to the Lichtenberg Palace. I could never look at many pictures in succession; for pictures, when they are at all powerful, affect me so strongly that one or two exhaust all my capability of contemplation. This morning I had been looking at Giorgione's picture of the cruel-eyed woman, said to be a likeness of Lucrezia Borgia.[3] I had stood long alone before it, fascinated by the terrible reality of that cunning, relentless face, till I felt a strange poisoned sensation, as if I had long been inhaling a fatal odor, and was just beginning to be conscious of its effects. Perhaps even then I should not have moved away, if the rest of the party had not returned to this room, and announced that they were going to the Belvedere Gallery to settle a bet which had arisen between my brother and Mr. Filmore about a portrait. I followed them dreamily, and was hardly alive to what occurred till they had all gone up to the gallery, leaving me below; for I refused to come within sight of another picture that day. I made my way to the Grand Terrace, since it was agreed that we should saunter in the gardens when the dispute had been decided. I had been sitting here a short space, vaguely conscious of trim gardens, with a city and green hills in the distance, when, wishing to avoid the proximity of the sentinel, I rose and walked down the broad stone steps, intending to seat myself farther on in the gardens. Just as I reached the gravel-walk, I felt an arm slipped within mine, and a light hand gently pressing my wrist. In the same instant a strange intoxicating numbness passed over me, like the continuance or climax of the sensation I was still feeling from the gaze of Lucrezia Borgia. The gardens, the summer sky, the consciousness of Bertha's arm being within mine, all vanished, and I seemed to be suddenly in darkness, out of which there gradually broke a dim firelight, and I felt myself sitting in my father's leather chair in the library at home. I knew the fireplace,—the dogs for the wood-fire,—the black marble chimney-piece with the white marble medallion of the dying Cleopatra[4] in the centre. Intense and hopeless misery was pressing on my soul; the light became stronger, for Bertha was entering with a candle in her hand,—Bertha, my wife,—with cruel eyes, with green jewels and green leaves on her white ball-dress; every hateful thought within her present to me. . . . "Madman, idiot! why don't you kill yourself, then?" It was a moment of hell. I saw into her pitiless soul,—saw its barren worldliness, its scorching hate,—and felt it clothe me round like an air I was obliged to breathe. She came with her candle and stood over me with a bitter smile of contempt; I saw the great emerald brooch on her bosom, a studded serpent with diamond eyes. I shuddered,—I despised this woman with the barren soul and mean thoughts; but I felt helpless before her, as if she clutched my bleeding heart, and would clutch it till the last drop of life-blood ebbed away. She was my wife, and we hated each other. Gradually the hearth,

3. Borgia (1480–1519), member of a powerful Italian family famous for licentiousness, intrigue, and violence, whose second husband was murdered.

Giorgione (c 1478–1511), Italian painter.
4. Egyptian queen who killed herself by letting a poisonous asp bite her.

the dim library, the candle-light disappeared,—seemed to melt away into a background of light, the green serpent with the diamond eyes remaining a dark image on the retina. Then I had a sense of my eyelids quivering, and the living daylight broke in upon me; I saw gardens, and heard voices; I was seated on the steps of the Belvedere Terrace, and my friends were round me.

The tumult of mind into which I was thrown by this hideous vision made me ill for several days, and prolonged our stay at Vienna. I shuddered with horror as the scene recurred to me; and it recurred constantly, with all its minutiæ, as if they had been burnt into my memory; and yet, such is the madness of the human heart under the influence of its immediate desires, I felt a wild hell-braving joy that Bertha was to be mine; for the fulfilment of my former prevision concerning her first appearance before me, left me little hope that this last hideous glimpse of the future was the mere diseased play of my own mind, and had no relation to external realities. One thing alone I looked towards as a possible means of casting doubt on my terrible conviction,—the discovery that my vision of Prague had been false,—and Prague was the next city on our route.

Meanwhile I was no sooner in Bertha's society again, than I was as completely under her sway as before. What if I saw into the heart of Bertha, the matured woman,—Bertha, my wife? Bertha, the *girl*, was a fascinating secret to me still: I trembled under her touch; I felt the witchery of her presence; I yearned to be assured of her love. The fear of poison is feeble against the sense of thirst. Nay, I was just as jealous of my brother as before,—just as much irritated by his small patronizing ways; for my pride, my diseased sensibility, were there as they had always been, and winced as inevitably under every offence as my eye winced from an intruding mote. The future, even when brought within the compass of feeling by a vision that made me shudder, had still no more than the force of an idea, compared with the force of present emotion,—of my love for Bertha, of my dislike and jealousy towards my brother.

It is an old story, that men sell themselves to the tempter, and sign a bond with their blood, because it is only to take effect at a distant day; then rush on to snatch the cup their souls thirst after with an impulse not the less savage because there is a dark shadow beside them forevermore. There is no short cut, no patent tram-road[5] to wisdom: after all the centuries of invention, the soul's path lies through the thorny wilderness which must be still trodden in solitude, with bleeding feet, with sobs for help, as it was trodden by them of old time.

My mind speculated eagerly on the means by which I should become my brother's successful rival, for I was still too timid, in my ignorance of Bertha's actual feeling, to venture on any step that would urge from her an avowal of it. I thought I should gain confidence even for this, if my vision of Prague proved to have been veracious; and yet, the horror of that certitude! Behind the slim girl Bertha, whose words and looks I watched for, whose touch was bliss, there stood continually that Bertha with the fuller form, the harder eyes, the more rigid mouth,—with the barren selfish soul laid bare; no longer a fascinating secret, but a measured fact, urging itself perpetually on my unwilling sight. Are you unable to give me your sympathy,—you who read this? Are you unable to imagine this double consciousness at work within me, flowing on like two par-

5. A road made of metal rails for streetcars.

allel streams which never mingle their waters and blend into a common hue? Yet you must have known something of the presentiments that spring from an insight at war with passion; and my visions were only like presentiments intensified to horror. You have known the powerlessness of ideas before the might of impulse; and my visions, when once they had passed into memory, were mere ideas,—pale shadows that beckoned in vain, while my hand was grasped by the living and the loved.

In after days I thought with bitter regret that if I had foreseen something more or something different,—if instead of that hideous vision which poisoned the passion it could not destroy, or if even along with it I could have had a foreshadowing of that moment when I looked on my brother's face for the last time, some softening influence would have been shed over my feeling towards him: pride and hatred would surely have been subdued into pity, and the record of those hidden sins would have been shortened. But this is one of the vain thoughts with which we men flatter ourselves. We try to believe that the egoism within us would have easily been melted, and that it was only the narrowness of our knowledge which hemmed in our generosity, our awe, our human piety, and hindered them from submerging our hard indifference to the sensations and emotions of our fellow. Our tenderness and self-renunciation seem strong when our egoism has had its day,—when, after our mean striving for a triumph that is to be another's loss, the triumph comes suddenly, and we shudder at it, because it is held out by the chill hand of death.

Our arrival in Prague happened at night, and I was glad of this, for it seemed like a deferring of a terribly decisive moment to be in the city for hours without seeing it. As we were not to remain long in Prague, but to go on speedily to Dresden, it was proposed that we should drive out the next morning and take a general view of the place, as well as visit some of its specially interesting spots, before the heat became oppressive,—for we were in August, and the season was hot and dry. But it happened that the ladies were rather late at their morning toilet,[6] and to my father's politely repressed but perceptible annoyance, we were not in the carriage till the morning was far advanced. I thought with a sense of relief, as we entered the Jews' quarter, where we were to visit the old synagogue, that we should be kept in this flat, shut-up part of the city, until we should all be too tired and too warm to go farther, and so we should return without seeing more than the streets through which we had already passed. That would give me another day's suspense,—suspense, the only form in which a fearful spirit knows the solace of hope. But as I stood under the blackened, groined arches of that old synagogue, made dimly visible by the seven thin candles in the sacred lamp, while our Jewish cicerone reached down the Book of the Law,[7] and read to us in its ancient tongue,—I felt a shuddering impression that this strange building, with its shrunken lights, this surviving withered remnant of mediæval Judaism, was of a piece with my vision. Those darkened dusty Christian saints, with their loftier arches and their larger candles, needed the consolatory scorn with which they might point to a more shrivelled death-in-life than their own.

As I expected, when we left the Jews' quarter the elders of our party wished to return to the hotel. But now, instead of rejoicing in this, as I had done be-

6. Bathing and dressing.
7. The Torah (the first five books of the Bible). "Cicerone": guide.

forehand, I felt a sudden overpowering impulse to go on at once to the bridge, and put an end to the suspense I had been wishing to protract. I declared, with unusual decision, that I would get out of the carriage and walk on alone; they might return without me. My father, thinking this merely a sample of my usual "poetic nonsense," objected that I should only do myself harm by walking in the heat; but when I persisted, he said angrily that I might follow my own absurd devices, but that Schmidt (our courier) must go with me. I assented to this, and set off with Schmidt towards the bridge. I had no sooner passed from under the archway of the grand old gate leading on to the bridge, than a trembling seized me, and I turned cold under the mid-day sun; yet I went on: I was in search of something,—a small detail which I remembered with special intensity as part of my vision. There it was,—the patch of rainbow light on the pavement transmitted through a lamp in the shape of a star.

Chapter II

Before the autumn was at an end, and while the brown leaves still stood thick on the beeches in our park, my brother and Bertha were engaged to each other, and it was understood that their marriage was to take place early in the next spring. In spite of the certainty I had felt from that moment on the bridge at Prague, that Bertha would one day be my wife, my constitutional timidity and distrust had continued to benumb me, and the words in which I had sometimes premeditated a confession of my love had died away unuttered. The same conflict had gone on within me as before,—the longing for an assurance of love from Bertha's lips, the dread lest a word of contempt and denial should fall upon me like a corrosive acid. What was the conviction of a distant necessity to me? I trembled under a present glance, I hungered after a present joy, I was clogged and chilled by a present fear. And so the days passed on: I witnessed Bertha's engagement and heard her marriage discussed as if I were under a conscious nightmare,—knowing it was a dream that would vanish, but feeling stifled under the grasp of hard-clutching fingers.

When I was not in Bertha's presence,—and I was with her very often, for she continued to treat me with a playful patronage that wakened no jealousy in my brother,—I spent my time chiefly in wandering, in strolling, or taking long rides while the daylight lasted, and then shutting myself up with my unread books; for books had lost the power of chaining my attention. My self-consciousness was heightened to that pitch of intensity in which our own emotions take the form of a drama which urges itself imperatively on our contemplation, and we begin to weep, less under the sense of our suffering than at the thought of it. I felt a sort of pitying anguish over the pathos of my own lot: the lot of a being finely organized for pain, but with hardly any fibers that responded to pleasure,—to whom the idea of future evil robbed the present of its joy, and for whom the idea of future good did not still the uneasiness of a present yearning or a present dread. I went dumbly through that stage of the poet's suffering, in which he feels the delicious pang of utterance, and makes an image of his sorrows.

I was left entirely without remonstrance concerning this dreamy wayward life: I knew my father's thought about me: "That lad will never be good for anything in life: he may waste his years in an insignificant way on the income that falls to him: I shall not trouble myself about a career for him."

One mild morning in the beginning of November, it happened that I was

standing outside the portico patting lazy old Cæsar, a Newfoundland almost blind with age, the only dog that ever took any notice of me,—for the very dogs shunned me, and fawned on the happier people about me,—when the groom brought up my brother's horse which was to carry him to the hunt, and my brother himself appeared at the door, florid, broad-chested, and self-complacent, feeling what a good-natured fellow he was not to behave insolently to us all on the strength of his great advantages.

"Latimer, old boy," he said to me in a tone of compassionate cordiality, "what a pity it is you don't have a run with the hounds now and then! The finest thing in the world for low spirits!"

"Low spirits!" I thought bitterly, as he rode away; "that is the sort of phrase with which coarse, narrow natures like yours think to describe experience of which you can know no more than your horse knows. It is to such as you that the good of this world falls: ready dulness, healthy selfishness, good-tempered conceit,—these are the keys to happiness."

The quick thought came, that my selfishness was even stronger than his,—it was only a suffering selfishness instead of an enjoying one. But then, again, my exasperating insight into Alfred's self-complacent soul, his freedom from all the doubts and fears, the unsatisfied yearnings, the exquisite tortures of sensitiveness, that had made the web of my life, seemed to absolve me from all bonds towards him. This man needed no pity, no love; those fine influences would have been as little felt by him as the delicate white mist is felt by the rock it caresses. There was no evil in store for him: if he was not to marry Bertha, it would be because he had found a lot pleasanter to himself.

Mr. Filmore's house lay not more than half a mile beyond our own gates, and whenever I knew my brother was gone in another direction, I went there for the chance of finding Bertha at home. Later on in the day I walked thither. By a rare accident she was alone, and we walked out in the grounds together, for she seldom went on foot beyond the trimly swept gravel-walks. I remember what a beautiful sylph she looked to me as the low November sun shone on her blond hair, and she tripped along teasing me with her usual light banter, to which I listened half fondly, half moodily; it was all the sign Bertha's mysterious inner self ever made to me. Today perhaps the moodiness predominated, for I had not yet shaken off the access[8] of jealous hate which my brother had raised in me by his parting patronage. Suddenly I interrupted and startled her by saying, almost fiercely, "Bertha, how can you love Alfred?"

She looked at me with surprise for a moment, but soon her light smile came again, and she answered sarcastically, "Why do you suppose I love him?"

"How can you ask that, Bertha?"

"What! your wisdom thinks I must love the man I'm going to marry? The most unpleasant thing in the world. I should quarrel with him; I should be jealous of him; our ménage[9] would be conducted in a very ill-bred manner. A little quiet contempt contributes greatly to the elegance of life."

"Bertha, that is not your real feeling. Why do you delight in trying to deceive me by inventing such cynical speeches?"

"I need never take the trouble of invention in order to deceive you, my small Tasso"[1] (that was the mocking name she usually gave me). "The easiest way to deceive a poet is to tell him the truth."

8. Outburst.
9. Household.
1. Torcuato Tasso (1544–1595), Italian poet, author

of the epic Gerusalemme Liberata; he was twice confined as insane.

She was testing the validity of her epigram in a daring way, and for a moment the shadow of my vision—the Bertha whose soul was no secret to me—passed between me and the radiant girl, the playful sylph whose feelings were a fascinating mystery. I suppose I must have shuddered, or betrayed in some other way my momentary chill of horror.

"Tasso!" she said, seizing my wrist and peeping round into my face, "are you really beginning to discern what a heartless girl I am? Why, you are not half the poet I thought you were; you are actually capable of believing the truth about me."

The shadow passed from between us, and was no longer the object nearest to me. The girl whose light fingers grasped me, whose elfish charming face looked into mine,—who, I thought, was betraying an interest in my feelings that she would not have directly avowed,—this warm-breathing presence again possessed my senses and imagination like a returning siren[2] melody which had been overpowered for an instant by the roar of threatening waves. It was a moment as delicious to me as the waking up to a consciousness of youth after a dream of middle age. I forgot everything but my passion, and said with swimming eyes,—

"Bertha, shall you love me when we are first married? I wouldn't mind if you really loved me only for a little while."

Her look of astonishment, as she loosed my hand and started away from me, recalled me to a sense of my strange, my criminal indiscretion.

"Forgive me," I said hurriedly, as soon as I could speak again; "I did not know what I was saying."

"Ah, Tasso's mad fit has come on, I see," she answered quietly, for she had recovered herself sooner than I had. "Let him go home and keep his head cool. I must go in, for the sun is setting."

I left her,—full of indignation against myself. I had let slip words which, if she reflected on them, might rouse in her a suspicion of my abnormal mental condition,—a suspicion which of all things I dreaded. And besides that, I was ashamed of the apparent baseness I had committed in uttering them to my brother's betrothed wife. I wandered home slowly, entering our park through a private gate instead of by the lodges.[3] As I approached the house, I saw a man dashing off at full speed from the stable-yard across the park. Had any accident happened at home? No; perhaps it was only one of my father's peremptory business errands that required this headlong haste. Nevertheless I quickened my pace without any distinct motive, and was soon at the house. I will not dwell on the scene I found there. My brother was dead,—had been pitched from his horse, and killed on the spot by a concussion of the brain.

I went up to the room where he lay, and where my father was seated beside him with a look of rigid despair. I had shunned my father more than any one since our return home, for the radical antipathy between our natures made my insight into his inner self a constant affliction to me. But now, as I went up to him, and stood beside him in sad silence, I felt the presence of a new element that blended us as we had never been blent before. My father had been one of the most successful men in the money-getting world: he had had no sentimental sufferings, no illness. The heaviest trouble that had befallen him was

2. The sirens are mythological maidens who lure sailors toward rocks by the power of their song.

3. Small houses on large private estates used by caretakers, gamekeepers, and other servants.

the death of his first wife. But he married my mother soon after; and I remember he seemed exactly the same, to my keen childish observation, the week after her death as before. But now, at last, a sorrow had come,—the sorrow of old age, which suffers the more from the crushing of its pride and its hopes, in proportion as the pride and hope are narrow and prosaic. His son was to have been married soon,—would probably have stood for the borough[4] at the next election. That son's existence was the best motive that could be alleged for making new purchases of land every year to round off the estate. It is a dreary thing to live on doing the same things year after year, without knowing why we do them. Perhaps the tragedy of disappointed youth and passion is less piteous than the tragedy of disappointed age and worldliness.

As I saw into the desolation of my father's heart, I felt a movement of deep pity towards him, which was the beginning of a new affection,—an affection that grew and strengthened in spite of the strange bitterness with which he regarded me in the first month or two after my brother's death. If it had not been for the softening influence of my compassion for him,—the first deep compassion I had ever felt,—I should have been stung by the perception that my father transferred the inheritance of an eldest son to me with a mortified sense that fate had compelled him to the unwelcome course of caring for me as an important being. It was only in spite of himself that he began to think of me with anxious regard. There is hardly any neglected child for whom death has made vacant a more favored place, who will not understand what I mean.

Gradually, however, my new deference to his wishes, the effect of that patience which was born of my pity for him, won upon his affection, and he began to please himself with the endeavor to make me fill my brother's place as fully as my feebler personality would admit. I saw that the prospect which by and by presented itself of my becoming Bertha's husband was welcome to him, and he even contemplated in my case what he had not intended in my brother's,—that his son and daughter-in-law should make one household with him. My softened feeling towards my father made this the happiest time I had known since childhood;—these last months in which I retained the delicious illusion of loving Bertha, of longing and doubting and hoping that she might love me. She behaved with a certain new consciousness and distance towards me after my brother's death; and I too was under a double constraint,—that of delicacy towards my brother's memory and of anxiety as to the impression my abrupt words had left on her mind. But the additional screen this mutual reserve erected between us only brought me more completely under her power: no matter how empty the adytum,[5] so that the veil be thick enough. So absolute is our soul's need of something hidden and uncertain for the maintenance of that doubt and hope and effort which are the breath of its life, that if the whole future were laid bare to us beyond today, the interest of all mankind would be bent on the hours that lie between; we should pant after the uncertainties of our one morning and our one afternoon; we should rush fiercely to the Exchange for our last possibility of speculation, of success, of disappointment; we should have a glut of political prophets foretelling a crisis or a no-crisis within the only twenty-four hours left open to prophecy. Conceive the condition of the human mind if all propositions what-

4. I.e., have run as a parliamentary representative for 5. Innermost sanctuary of a temple.
his district.

soever were self-evident except one, which was to become self-evident at the close of a summer's day, but in the mean time might be the subject of question, of hypothesis, of debate. Art and philosophy, literature and science, would fasten like bees on that one proposition which had the honey of probability in it, and be the more eager because their enjoyment would end with sunset. Our impulses, our spiritual activities, no more adjust themselves to the idea of their future nullity, than the beating of our heart, or the irritability of our muscles.

Bertha, the slim, fair-haired girl, whose present thoughts and emotions were an enigma to me amid the fatiguing obviousness of the other minds around me, was as absorbing to me as a single unknown today,—as a single hypothetic proposition to remain problematic till sunset; and all the cramped, hemmed-in belief and disbelief, trust and distrust, of my nature welled out in this one narrow channel.

And she made me believe that she loved me. Without ever quitting her tone of *badinage*[6] and playful superiority, she intoxicated me with the sense that I was necessary to her, that she was never at ease unless I was near her, submitting to her playful tyranny. It costs a woman so little effort to besot us in this way! A half-repressed word, a moment's unexpected silence, even an easy fit of petulance on our account, will serve us as *hashish* for a long while. Out of the subtlest web of scarcely perceptible signs, she set me weaving the fancy that she had always unconsciously loved me better than Alfred, but that, with the ignorant fluttered sensibility of a young girl, she had been imposed on by the charm that lay for her in the distinction of being admired and chosen by a man who made so brilliant a figure in the world as my brother. She satirized herself in a very graceful way for her vanity and ambition. What was it to me that I had the light of my wretched prevision on the fact that now it was I who possessed at least all but the personal part of my brother's advantages? Our sweet illusions are half of them conscious illusions, like effects of color that we know to be made up of tinsel, broken glass, and rags.

We were married eighteen months after Alfred's death, one cold, clear morning in April, when there came hail and sunshine both together; and Bertha, in her white silk and pale-green leaves, and the pale hues of her hair and face, looked like the spirit of the morning. My father was happier than he had thought of being again: my marriage, he felt sure, would complete the desirable modification of my character, and make me practical and worldly enough to take my place in society among sane men. For he delighted in Bertha's tact and acuteness, and felt sure she would be mistress of me, and make me what she chose: I was only twenty-one, and madly in love with her. Poor father! He kept that hope a little while after our first year of marriage, and it was not quite extinct when paralysis came and saved him from utter disappointment.

I shall hurry through the rest of my story, not dwelling so much as I have hitherto done on my inward experience. When people are well known to each other, they talk rather of what befalls them externally, leaving their feelings and sentiments to be inferred.

We lived in a round of visits for some time after our return home, giving splendid dinner-parties, and making a sensation in our neighborhood by the

6. Joking, trifling.

new luster of our equipage, for my father had reserved this display of his increased wealth for the period of his son's marriage; and we gave our acquaintances liberal opportunity for remarking that it was a pity I made so poor a figure as an heir and a bridegroom. The nervous fatigue of this existence, the insincerities and platitudes which I had to live through twice over,—through my inner and outward sense,—would have been maddening to me, if I had not had that sort of intoxicated callousness which came from the delights of a first passion. A bride and bride-groom, surrounded by all the appliances of wealth, hurried through the day by the whirl of society, filling their solitary moments with hastily snatched caresses, are prepared for their future life together as the *novice* is prepared for the cloister,—by experiencing its utmost contrast.

Through all these crowded excited months, Bertha's inward self remained shrouded from me, and I still read her thoughts only through the language of her lips and demeanor: I had still the human interest of wondering whether what I did and said pleased her, of longing to hear a word of affection, of giving a delicious exaggeration of meaning to her smile But I was conscious of a growing difference in her manner towards me; sometimes strong enough to be called haughty coldness, cutting and chilling me as the hail had done that came across the sunshine on our marriage morning; sometimes only perceptible in the dexterous avoidance of a *tête-à-tête* walk or dinner to which I had been looking forward. I had been deeply pained by this,—had even felt a sort of crushing of the heart, from the sense that my brief day of happiness was near its setting; but still I remained dependent on Bertha, eager for the last rays of a bliss that would soon be gone forever, hoping and watching for some after-glow more beautiful from the impending night.

I remember—how should I not remember?—the time when that dependence and hope utterly left me, when the sadness I had felt in Bertha's growing estrangement became a joy that I looked back upon with longing, as a man might look back on the last pains in a paralyzed limb. It was just after the close of my father's last illness which had necessarily withdrawn us from society and thrown us more upon each other. It was the evening of my father's death. On that evening the veil which had shrouded Bertha's soul from me—had made me find in her alone among my fellow-beings the blessed possibility of mystery and doubt and expectation—was first withdrawn. Perhaps it was the first day since the beginning of my passion for her, in which that passion was completely neutralized by the presence of an absorbing feeling of another kind. I had been watching by my father's death-bed: I had been witnessing the last fitful yearning glance his soul had cast back on the spent inheritance of life,—the last faint consciousness of love he had gathered from the pressure of my hand. What are all our personal loves when we have been sharing in that supreme agony? In the first moments when we come away from the presence of death, every other relation to the living is merged, to our feeling, in the great relation of a common nature and a common destiny.

In that state of mind I joined Bertha in her private sitting-room. She was seated in a leaning posture on a settee, with her back towards the door, the great rich coils of her pale blond hair surmounting her small neck, visible above the back of the settee. I remember, as I closed the door behind me, a cold tremulousness seizing me, and a vague sense of being hated and lonely,— vague and strong, like a presentiment. I know how I looked at that moment, for I saw myself in Bertha's thought as she lifted her cutting gray eyes, and

looked at me: a miserable ghost-seer, surrounded by phantoms in the noonday, trembling under a breeze when the leaves were still, without appetite for the common objects of human desire, but pining after the moonbeams. We were front to front with each other, and judged each other. The terrible moment of complete illumination had come to me, and I saw that the darkness had hidden no landscape from me, but only a blank prosaic wall: from that evening forth, through the sickening years which followed, I saw all round the narrow room of this woman's soul,—saw petty artifice and mere negation where I had delighted to believe in coy sensibilities and in wit at war with latent feeling,— saw the light floating vanities of the girl defining themselves into the systematic coquetry, the scheming selfishness, of the woman,—saw repulsion and antipathy harden into cruel hatred, giving pain only for the sake of wreaking itself.

For Bertha too; after her kind, felt the bitterness of disillusion. She had believed that my wild poet's passion for her would make me her slave; and that, being her slave, I should execute her will in all things. With the essential shallowness of a negative, unimaginative nature, she was unable to conceive the fact that sensibilities were anything else than weaknesses. She had thought my weaknesses would put me in her power, and she found them unmanageable forces. Our positions were reversed. Before marriage she had completely mastered my imagination, for she was a secret to me; and I created the unknown thought before which I trembled as if it were hers. But now that her soul was laid open to me, now that I was compelled to share the privacy of her motives, to follow all the petty devices that preceded her words and acts, she found herself powerless with me, except to produce in me the chill shudder of repulsion,—powerless, because I could be acted on by no lever within her reach. I was dead to worldly ambitions, to social vanities, to all the incentives within the compass of her narrow imagination, and I lived under influences utterly invisible to her.

She was really pitiable to have such a husband, and so all the world thought. A graceful, brilliant woman, like Bertha, who smiled on morning callers, made a figure in ball-rooms, and was capable of that light repartee which, from such a woman, is accepted as wit, was secure of carrying off all sympathy from a husband who was sickly, abstracted, and, as some suspected, crack-brained. Even the servants in our house gave her the balance of their regard and pity. For there were no audible quarrels between us; our alienation, our repulsion from each other, lay within the silence of our own hearts; and if the mistress went out a great deal, and seemed to dislike the master's society, was it not natural, poor thing? The master was odd. I was kind and just to my dependants, but I excited in them a shrinking, half-contemptuous pity; for this class of men and women are but slightly determined in their estimate of others by general considerations, or even experience, of character. They judge of persons as they judge of coins, and value those who pass current at a high rate.

After a time I interfered so little with Bertha's habits, that it might seem wonderful how her hatred towards me could grow so intense and active as it did. But she had begun to suspect, by some involuntary betrayals of mine, that there was an abnormal power of penetration in me,—that fitfully, at least, I was strangely cognizant of her thoughts and intentions, and she began to be haunted by a terror of me, which alternated every now and then with defiance. She meditated continually how the incubus[7] could be shaken off her life,—

7. Evil spirit thought in medieval times to have sexual intercourse with women while they are asleep.

how she could be freed from this hateful bond to a being whom she at once despised as an imbecile, and dreaded as an inquisitor. For a long while she lived in the hope that my evident wretchedness would drive me to the commission of suicide; but suicide was not in my nature. I was too completely swayed by the sense that I was in the grasp of unknown forces, to believe in my power of self-release. Towards my own destiny I had become entirely passive; for my one ardent desire had spent itself, and impulse no longer predominated over knowledge. For this reason I never thought of taking any steps towards a complete separation, which would have made our alienation evident to the world. Why should I rush for help to a new course, when I was only suffering from the consequences of a deed which had been the act of my intensest will? That would have been the logic of one who had desires to gratify, and I had no desires. But Bertha and I lived more and more aloof from each other. The rich find it easy to live married and apart.

That course of our life which I have indicated in a few sentences filled the space of years. So much misery, so slow and hideous a growth of hatred and sin, may be compressed into a sentence! And men judge of each other's lives through this summary medium. They epitomize[8] the experience of their fellow-mortal, and pronounce judgment on him in neat syntax, and feel themselves wise and virtuous,—conquerors over the temptations they define in well-selected predicates. Seven years of wretchedness glide glibly over the lips of the man who has never counted them out in moments of chill disappointment, of head and heart throbbings, of dread and vain wrestling, of remorse and despair. We learn words by rote, but not their meaning; *that* must be paid for with our life-blood, and printed in the subtle fibers of our nerves.

But I will hasten to finish my story. Brevity is justified at once to those who readily understand, and to those who will never understand.

Some years after my father's death, I was sitting by the dim firelight in my library one January evening,—sitting in the leather chair that used to be my father's,—when Bertha appeared at the door, with a candle in her hand, and advanced towards me. I knew the ball-dress she had on,—the white ball-dress with the green jewels, shone upon by the light of the wax candle which lit up the medallion of the dying Cleopatra on the mantelpiece. Why did she come to me before going out? I had not seen her in the library, which was my habitual place, for months. Why did she stand before me with the candle in her hand, with her cruel contemptuous eyes fixed on me, and the glittering serpent, like a familiar demon, on her breast? For a moment I thought this fulfillment of my vision at Vienna marked some dreadful crisis in my fate, but I saw nothing in Bertha's mind, as she stood before me, except scorn for the look of overwhelming misery with which I sat before her. . . . "Fool, idiot, why don't you kill yourself, then?"—that was her thought. But at length her thoughts reverted to her errand, and she spoke aloud. The apparently indifferent nature of the errand seemed to make a ridiculous anticlimax to my prevision and my agitation.

"I have had to hire a new maid. Fletcher is going to be married, and she wants me to ask you to let her husband have the public-house and farm at Molton. I wish him to have it. You must give the promise now, because Fletcher is going tomorrow morning,—and quickly, because I'm in a hurry."

8. Summarize.

"Very well; you may promise her," I said indifferently; and Bertha swept out of the library again.

I always shrank from the sight of a new person, and all the more when it was a person whose mental life was likely to weary my reluctant insight with worldly ignorant trivialities. But I shrank especially from the sight of this new maid, because her advent had been announced to me at a moment to which I could not cease to attach some fatality: I had a vague dread that I should find her mixed up with the dreary drama of my life,—that some new sickening vision would reveal her to me as an evil genius.[9] When at last I did unavoidably meet her, the vague dread was changed into definite disgust. She was a tall, wiry, dark-eyed woman, this Mrs. Archer, with a face handsome enough to give her coarse hard nature the odious finish of bold, self-confident coquetry. That was enough to make me avoid her, quite apart from the contemptuous feeling with which she contemplated me. I seldom saw her; but I perceived that she rapidly became a favorite with her mistress, and, after the lapse of eight or nine months, I began to be aware that there had arisen in Bertha's mind towards this woman a mingled feeling of fear and dependence, and that this feeling was associated with ill-defined images of candle-light scenes in her dressing-room, and the locking up of something in Bertha's cabinet. My interviews with my wife had become so brief and so rarely solitary that I had no opportunity of perceiving these images in her mind with more definiteness. The recollections of the past become contracted in the rapidity of thought till they sometimes bear hardly a more distinct resemblance to the external reality than the forms of an oriental alphabet to the objects that suggested them.

Besides, for the last year or more a modification had been going forward in my mental condition, and was growing more and more marked. My insight into the minds of those around me was becoming dimmer and more fitful, and the ideas that crowded my double consciousness became less and less dependent on any personal contact. All that was personal in me seemed to be suffering a gradual death, so that I was losing the organ through which the personal agitations and projects of others could affect me. But along with this relief from wearisome insight, there was a new development of what I concluded—as I have since found rightly,—to be a prevision of external scenes. It was as if the relation between me and my fellow-men was more and more deadened, and my relation to what we call the inanimate was quickened into new life. The more I lived apart from society, and in proportion as my wretchedness subsided from the violent throb of agonized passion into the dulness of habitual pain, the more frequent and vivid became such visions as that I had had of Prague,—of strange cities, of sandy plains, of gigantic ruins, of midnight skies with strange bright constellations, of mountain-passes, of grassy nooks flecked with the afternoon sunshine through the boughs: I was in the midst of such scenes, and in all of them one presence seemed to weigh on me in all these mighty shapes,—the presence of something unknown and pitiless. For continual suffering had annihilated religious faith within me: to the utterly miserable—the unloving and the unloved—there is no religion possible, no worship but a worship of devils. And beyond all these, and continually recurring, was the vision of my death,—the pangs, the suffocation, the last struggle, when life would be grasped at in vain.

9. Spirit or influence.

Things were in this state near the end of the seventh year. I had become entirely free from insight, from my abnormal cognizance of any other consciousness than my own, and, instead of intruding involuntarily into the world of other minds, was living continually in my own solitary future. Bertha was aware that I was greatly changed. To my surprise she had of late seemed to seek opportunities of remaining in my society, and had cultivated that kind of distant yet familiar talk which is customary between a husband and wife who live in polite and irrevocable alienation. I bore this with languid submission, and without feeling enough interest in her motives to be roused into keen observation; yet I could not help perceiving something triumphant and excited in her carriage and the expression of her face,—something too subtle to express itself in words or tones, but giving one the idea that she lived in a state of expectation or hopeful suspense. My chief feeling was satisfaction that her inner self was once more shut out from me; and I almost revelled for the moment in the absent melancholy that made me answer her at cross purposes, and betray utter ignorance of what she had been saying. I remember well the look and the smile with which she one day said, after a mistake of this kind on my part: "I used to think you were a clairvoyant, and that was the reason why you were so bitter against other clairvoyants, wanting to keep your monopoly; but I see now you have become rather duller than the rest of the world."

I said nothing in reply. It occurred to me that her recent obtrusion of herself upon me might have been prompted by the wish to test my power of detecting some of her secrets; but I let the thought drop again at once: her motives and her deeds had no interest for me, and whatever pleasures she might be seeking, I had no wish to balk her. There was still pity in my soul for every living thing, and Bertha was living,—was surrounded with possibilities of misery.

Just at this time there occurred an event which roused me somewhat from my inertia, and gave me an interest in the passing moment that I had thought impossible for me. It was a visit from Charles Meunier, who had written me word that he was coming to England for relaxation from too strenuous labor, and would like to see me. Meunier had now a European reputation; but his letter to me expressed that keen remembrance of an early regard, an early debt of sympathy, which is inseparable from nobility of character: and I too felt as if his presence would be to me like a transient resurrection into a happier preexistence.

He came, and as far as possible, I renewed our old pleasure of making *tête-à-tête* excursions, though, instead of mountains and glaciers and the wide blue lake, we had to content ourselves with mere slopes and ponds and artificial plantations. The years had changed us both, but with what different result! Meunier was now a brilliant figure in society, to whom elegant women pretended to listen, and whose acquaintance was boasted of by noblemen ambitious of brains. He repressed with the utmost delicacy all betrayal of the shock which I am sure he must have received from our meeting, or of a desire to penetrate into my condition and circumstances, and sought by the utmost exertion of his charming social powers to make our reunion agreeable. Bertha was much struck by the unexpected fascinations of a visitor whom she had expected to find presentable only on the score of his celebrity, and put forth all her coquetries and accomplishments. Apparently she succeeded in attracting his admiration, for his manner towards her was attentive and flattering. The effect of his presence on me was so benignant, especially in those renewals of

our old *tête-à-tête* wanderings, when he poured forth to me wonderful narratives of his professional experience, that more than once, when his talk turned on the psychological relations of disease, the thought crossed my mind that, if his stay with me were long enough, I might possibly bring myself to tell this man the secrets of my lot. Might there not lie some remedy for *me*, too, in his science? Might there not at least lie some comprehension and sympathy ready for me in his large and susceptible mind? But the thought only flickered feebly now and then, and died out before it could become a wish. The horror I had of again breaking in on the privacy of another soul made me, by an irrational instinct, draw the shroud of concealment more closely around my own, as we automatically perform the gesture we feel to be wanting in another.

When Meunier's visit was approaching its conclusion, there happened an event which caused some excitement in our household, owing to the surprisingly strong effect it appeared to produce on Bertha,—on Bertha, the self-possessed, who usually seemed inaccessible to feminine agitations, and did even her hate in a self-restrained hygienic manner. This event was the sudden severe illness of her maid, Mrs. Archer. I have reserved to this moment the mention of a circumstance which had forced itself on my notice shortly before Meunier's arrival, namely, that there had been some quarrel between Bertha and this maid, apparently during a visit to a distant family, in which she had accompanied her mistress. I had overheard Archer speaking in a tone of bitter insolence, which I should have thought an adequate reason for immediate dismissal. No dismissal followed; on the contrary, Bertha seemed to be silently putting up with personal inconveniences from the exhibitions of this woman's temper. I was the more astonished to observe that her illness seemed a cause of strong solicitude to Bertha; that she was at the bedside night and day, and would allow no one else to officiate as head-nurse. It happened that our family doctor was out on a holiday, an accident which made Meunier's presence in the house doubly welcome, and he apparently entered into the case with an interest which seemed so much stronger than the ordinary professional feeling, that one day when he had fallen into a long fit of silence after visiting her, I said to him,—

"Is this a very peculiar case of disease, Meunier?"

"No," he answered, "it is an attack of peritonitis, which will be fatal, but which does not differ physically from many other cases that have come under my observation. But I'll tell you what I have on my mind. I want to make an experiment on this woman, if you will give me permission. It can do her no harm,—will give her no pain,—for I shall not make it until life is extinct to all purposes of sensation. I want to try the effect of transfusing blood into her arteries after the heart has ceased to beat for some minutes. I have tried the experiment again and again with animals that have died of this disease, with astounding results, and I want to try it on a human subject. I have the small tubes necessary, in a case I have with me, and the rest of the apparatus could be prepared readily. I should use my own blood,—take it from my own arm. This woman won't live through the night, I'm convinced, and I want you to promise me your assistance in making the experiment. I can't do without another hand, but it would perhaps not be well to call in a medical assistant from among your provincial doctors. A disagreeable foolish version of the thing might get abroad."

"Have you spoken to my wife on the subject?" I said, "because she appears to be peculiarly sensitive about this woman: she has been a favorite maid."

"To tell you the truth," said Meunier, "I don't want her to know about it. There are always insuperable difficulties with women in these matters, and the effect on the supposed dead body may be startling. You and I will sit up together, and be in readiness. When certain symptoms appear I shall take you in, and at the right moment we must manage to get every one else out of the room."

I need not give our farther conversation on the subject. He entered very fully into the details, and overcame my repulsion from them, by exciting in me a mingled awe and curiosity concerning the possible results of his experiment.

We prepared everything, and he instructed me in my part as assistant. He had not told Bertha of his absolute conviction that Archer would not survive through the night, and endeavored to persuade her to leave the patient and take a night's rest. But she was obstinate, suspecting the fact that death was at hand, and supposing that he wished merely to save her nerves. She refused to leave the sick-room. Meunier and I sat up together in the library, he making frequent visits to the sick-room, and returning with the information that the case was taking precisely the course he expected. Once he said to me, "Can you imagine any cause of ill feeling this woman has against her mistress, who is so devoted to her?"

"I think there was some misunderstanding between them before her illness. Why do you ask?"

"Because I have observed for the last five or six hours,—since, I fancy, she has lost all hope of recovery,—there seems a strange prompting in her to say something which pain and failing strength forbid her to utter; and there is a look of hideous meaning in her eyes, which she turns continually towards her mistress. In this disease the mind often remains singularly clear to the last."

"I am not surprised at an indication of malevolent feeling in her," I said. "She is a woman who has always inspired me with distrust and dislike, but she managed to insinuate herself into her mistress's favor." He was silent after this, looking at the fire with an air of absorption, till he went upstairs again. He stayed away longer than usual, and on returning, said to me quietly, "Come now."

I followed him to the chamber where death was hovering. The dark hangings of the large bed made a background that gave a strong relief to Bertha's pale face as I entered. She started forward as she saw me enter, and then looked at Meunier with an expression of angry inquiry; but he lifted up his hand as if to impose silence, while he fixed his glance on the dying woman and felt her pulse. The face was pinched and ghastly, a cold perspiration was on the forehead and the eyelids were lowered so as almost to conceal the large dark eyes. After a minute or two, Meunier walked round to the other side of the bed where Bertha stood, and with his usual air of gentle politeness towards her begged her to leave the patient under our care,—everything should be done for her,—she was no longer in a state to be conscious of an affectionate presence. Bertha was hesitating, apparently almost willing to believe his assurance and to comply. She looked round at the ghastly dying face, as if to read the confirmation of that assurance, when for a moment the lowered eyelids were raised again, and it seemed as if the eyes were looking towards Bertha, but blankly. A shudder passed through Bertha's frame, and she returned to her station near the pillow, tacitly implying that she would not leave the room.

The eyelids were lifted no more. Once I looked at Bertha as she watched the face of the dying one. She wore a rich *peignoir*, and her blond hair was half cov-

ered by a lace cap: in her attire she was, as always, an elegant woman, fit to fig-
ure in a picture of modern aristocratic life: but I asked myself how that face of
hers could ever have seemed to me the face of a woman born of woman, with
memories of childhood, capable of pain, needing to be fondled? The features
at that moment seemed so preternaturally sharp, the eyes were so hard and
eager,—she looked like a cruel immortal, finding her spiritual feast in the ago-
nies of a dying race. For across those hard features there came something like
a flash when the last hour had been breathed out, and we all felt that the dark
veil had completely fallen. What secret was there between Bertha and this
woman? I turned my eyes from her with a horrible dread lest my insight should
return, and I should be obliged to see what had been breeding about two
unloving women's hearts. I felt that Bertha had been watching for the mo-
ment of death as the sealing of her secret: I thanked Heaven it could remain
sealed for me.

Meunier said quietly, "She is gone." He then gave his arm to Bertha, and she
submitted to be led out of the room.

I suppose it was at her order that two female attendants came into the
room, and dismissed the younger one who had been present before. When
they entered, Meunier had already opened the artery in the long thin neck
that lay rigid on the pillow, and I dismissed them, ordering them to remain at
a distance till we rang: the doctor, I said, had an operation to perform,—he
was not sure about the death. For the next twenty minutes I forgot everything
but Meunier and the experiment in which he was so absorbed that I think his
senses would have been closed against all sounds or sights which had no rela-
tion to it. It was my task at first to keep up the artificial respiration in the body
after the transfusion had been effected, but presently Meunier relieved me,
and I could see the wondrous slow return of life; the breast began to heave, the
inspirations became stronger, the eyelids quivered, and the soul seemed to
have returned beneath them. The artificial respiration was withdrawn: still
the breathing continued, and there was a movement of the lips.

Just then I heard the handle of the door moving: I suppose Bertha had heard
from the women that they had been dismissed: probably a vague fear had
arisen in her mind, for she entered with a look of alarm. She came to the foot
of the bed and gave a stifled cry.

The dead woman's eyes were wide open, and met hers in full recognition,—
the recognition of hate. With a sudden strong effort, the hand that Bertha had
thought forever still was pointed towards her, and the haggard face moved.
The gasping eager voice said,—

"You mean to poison your husband . . . the poison is in the black cabinet . . .
I got it for you . . . you laughed at me, and told lies about me behind my back,
to make me disgusting . . . because you were jealous . . . are you sorry . . . now?"

The lips continued to murmur, but the sounds were no longer distinct.
Soon there was no sound,—only a slight movement: the flame had leaped out,
and was being extinguished the faster. The wretched woman's heart-strings
had been set to hatred and vengeance; the spirit of life had swept the chords
for an instant, and was gone again forever. Great God! Is this what it is to live
again . . . to wake up with our unstilled thirst upon us, with our unuttered
curses rising to our lips, with our muscles ready to act out their half-commit-
ted sins?

Bertha stood pale at the foot of the bed, quivering and helpless, despairing

of devices,[1] like a cunning animal whose hiding-places are surrounded by swift-advancing flame. Even Meunier looked paralyzed; life for that moment ceased to be a scientific problem to him. As for me, this scene seemed of one texture with the rest of my existence: horror was my familiar,[2] and this new revelation was only like an old pain recurring with new circumstances.

Since then Bertha and I have lived apart,—she in her own neighborhood, the mistress of half our wealth; I as a wanderer in foreign countries, until I came to this Devonshire nest to die. Bertha lives pitied and admired; for what had I against that charming woman, whom every one but myself could have been happy with? There had been no witness of the scene in the dying room except Meunier, and while Meunier lived his lips were sealed by a promise to me.

Once or twice, weary of wandering, I rested in a favorite spot, and my heart went out towards the men and women and children whose faces were becoming familiar to me; but I was driven away again in terror at the approach of my old insight,—driven away to live continually with the one Unknown Presence revealed and yet hidden by the moving curtain of the earth and sky. Till at last disease took hold of me and forced me to rest here,—forced me to live in dependence on my servants. And then the curse of insight, of my double consciousness, came again, and has never left me. I knew all their narrow thoughts their feeble regard, their half-wearied pity.

It is the 20th of September, 1850. I know these figures I have just written, as if they were a long familiar inscription. I have seen them on this page in my desk unnumbered times, when the scene of my dying struggle has opened upon me. . . .

1859

Brother and Sister[1]

I

I cannot choose but think upon the time
When our two lives grew like two buds that kiss
At lightest thrill from the bee's swinging chime,
Because the one so near the other is.

He was the elder and a little man 5
Of forty inches, bound to show no dread,
And I the girl that puppy-like now ran,
Now lagged behind my brother's larger tread.

I held him wise, and when he talked to me
Of snakes and birds, and which God loved the best, 10
I thought his knowledge marked the boundary
Where men grew blind, though angels knew the rest.

1. I.e., losing hope in her plans.
2. Familiar spirit or demon.

1. George Eliot is remembering her childhood affection for her brother, Isaac Evans.

If he said "Hush!" I tried to hold my breath;
Wherever he said "Come!" I stepped in faith.

II

Long years have left their writing on my brow, 15
But yet the freshness and the dew-fed beam
Of those young mornings are about me now,
When we two wandered toward the far-off stream

With rod and line. Our basket held a store
Baked for us only, and I thought with joy 20
That I should have my share, though he had more,
Because he was the elder and a boy.

The firmaments of daisies since to me
Have had those mornings in their opening eyes,
The bunchèd cowslip's pale transparency 25
Carries that sunshine of sweet memories,

And wild-rose branches take their finest scent
From those blest hours of infantine content.

III

Our mother bade us keep the trodden ways,
Stroked down my tippet,[2] set my brother's frill, 30
Then with the benediction of her gaze
Clung to us lessening, and pursued us still

Across the homestead to the rookery[3] elms,
Whose tall old trunks had each a grassy mound,
So rich for us, we counted them as realms 35
With varied products: here were earth-nuts found,

And here the Lady-fingers in deep shade;
Here sloping toward the Moat the rushes grew,
The large to split for pith,[4] the small to braid:
While over all the dark rooks cawing flew, 40

And made a happy strange solemnity,
A deep-toned chant from life unknown to me.

IV

Our meadow-path had memorable spots:
One where it bridged a tiny rivulet,
Deep hid by tangled blue Forget-me-nots; 45
And all along the waving grasses met

2. A shoulder cape of fur or cloth. 4. Spongy interior of plant stalks.
3. Nesting place of rooks or ravens.

My little palm, or nodded to my cheek,
When flowers with upturned faces gazing grew
My wonder downward, seeming all to speak
With eyes of souls that dumbly heard and knew. 50

Then came the copse,[5] where wild things rushed unseen,
And black-scathed grass betrayed the past abode
Of mystic gypsies, who still lurked between
Me and each hidden distance of the road.

 A gypsy once had startled me at play, 55
 Blotting with her dark smile my sunny day.

V

Thus rambling we were schooled in deepest lore,
And learned the meanings that give words a soul,
The fear, the love, the primal passionate store,
Whose shaping impulses make manhood whole. 60

Those hours were seed to all my after good;
My infant gladness, through eye, ear, and touch,
Took easily as warmth a various food
To nourish the sweet skill of loving much.

For who in age shall roam the earth and find 65
Reasons for loving that will strike out love
With sudden rod from the hard year-pressed mind?
Were reasons sown as thick as stars above,

 'Tis love must see them, as the eye sees light:
 Day is but Number[6] to the darkened sight. 70

VI

Our brown canal was endless to my thought;
And on its banks I sat in dreamy peace,
Unknowing how the good I loved was wrought,
Untroubled by the fear that it would cease.

Slowly the barges floated into view 75
Rounding a grassy hill to me sublime
With some Unknown beyond it whither flew
The parting cuckoo toward a fresh spring time.

The wide-arched bridge, the scented elder-flowers,
The wondrous watery rings that died too soon, 80
The echoes of the quarry, the still hours
With white robe sweeping on the shadeless noon,

5. Small thicket or grove 6. I.e., an abstraction unrelated to experience.

Were but my growing self, are part of me,
My present Past, my root of piety.

VII

Those long days measured by my little feet 85
Had chronicles which yield me many a text;
Where irony still finds an image meet[7]
Of full-grown judgments in this world perplext.

One day my brother left me in high charge,
To mind the rod, while he went seeking bait, 90
And bade me, when I saw a nearing barge,
Snatch out the line, lest he should come too late.

Proud of the task, I watched with all my might
For one whole minute, till my eyes grew wide,
Till sky and earth took on a strange new light 95
And seemed a dream-world floating on some tide—

A fair pavilioned boat for me alone
Bearing me onward through the vast unknown.

VIII

But sudden came the barge's pitch-black prow,
Nearer and angrier came my brother's cry, 100
And all my soul was quivering fear, when lo!
Upon the imperilled line, suspended high,

A silver perch! My guilt that won the prey,
Now turned to merit, had a guerdon[8] rich
Of hugs and praises, and made merry play, 105
Until my triumph reached its highest pitch

When all at home were told the wondrous feat,
And how the little sister had fished well.
In secret, though my fortune tasted sweet,
I wondered why this happiness befell. 110

"The little lass had luck," the gardener said:
And so I learned, luck was with glory wed.

IX

We had the self-same world enlarged for each
By loving difference of girl and boy:
The fruit that hung on high beyond my reach 115
He plucked for me, and oft he must employ

A measuring glance to guide my tiny shoe
Where lay firm stepping-stones, or call to mind

7. Suitable. 8. Reward.

"This thing I like my sister may not do
For she is little, and I must be kind " 120

Thus boyish Will the nobler mastery learned
Where inward vision over impulse reigns,
Widening its life with separate life discerned,
A Like unlike, a Self that self restrains.

His years with others must the sweeter be 125
For those brief days he spent in loving me.

X

His sorrow was my sorrow, and his joy
Sent little leaps and laughs through all my frame;
My doll seemed lifeless and no girlish toy
Had any reason when my brother came. 130

I knelt with him at marbles, marked his fling
Cut the ringed stem and make the apple drop,
Or watched him winding close the spiral string
That looped the orbits of the humming top.

Grasped by such fellowship my vagrant thought 135
Ceased with dream-fruit dream-wishes to fulfil;
My aëry-picturing fantasy was taught
Subjection to the harder, truer skill

That seeks with deeds to grave[9] a thought-tracked line,
And by "What is," "What will be" to define. 140

XI

School parted us; we never found again
That childish world where our two spirits mingled
Like scents from varying roses that remain
One sweetness, nor can evermore be singled.

Yet the twin habit of that early time 145
Lingered for long about the heart and tongue:
We had been natives of one happy clime,
And its dear accents to our utterance clung.

Till the dire years whose awful name is Change
Had grasped our souls still yearning in divorce,[1] 150
And pitiless shaped them in two forms that range
Two elements which sever their life's course.[2]

But were another childhood-world my share,
I would be born a little sister there.

1869 1874

9. I.e., engrave, trace
1. Separation.

2. I.e., their souls have now become separate elements

FLORENCE NIGHTINGALE

1820–1910

Florence Nightingale was famous in her lifetime as a nurse, hospital administrator, sanitation reformer, and founder of the Nightingale School for Nursing as well as the Training School for Midwives. She was also the author of a polemical tract titled *Cassandra*. The title of this protest against the feminization of women dramatizes Nightingale's anxious awareness that her own complaint might be just as ineffectual as that of Cassandra, the virgin-priestess of Apollo whose divinely inspired prophecy is destined to go unheeded.

Nightingale's protest was part of a personal rebellion against her family's traditionally Victorian expectations for her. The family was extremely well-to-do, with residences in Derbyshire, the New Forest, and London's fashionable Mayfair district. It was her mother, Fanny, and her older sister, Parthenope, who represented a feminine ideal that Nightingale found stultifying. Although William Edward Nightingale educated his two children in Greek and Latin, history and philosophy, both girls were clearly intended to grace a fairly typical upper-class household and to marry well. Florence Nightingale reacted to such values by falling into trances, depressions, and daydreams: "The whole occupation of Parthe and Mama," Nightingale later wrote, "was to lie on two sofas and tell one another not to get tired by putting flowers into water." In 1837 the first of what she described as four calls from God enjoined her to a life of active service. Strengthened in her resolve to defy the family's prescriptions, she rejected a marriage proposal from Richard Monckton Milnes, a prosperous social reformer. Between her seventeenth and thirty-second years she struggled to free herself from her mother's acceptance of Parthenope's extreme emotional dependency. In her guilt over this conflict, Nightingale resembled the speaker whose suicidal speeches frame *Cassandra*: "My present life is suicide," she wrote in her diary. "In my 31st year I see nothing desirable but death; What am I that their life is not good enough for me? Oh God what am I?"

Cassandra, which was originally part of a work titled *Suggestions for Thought to Searchers after Religious Truth*, dates from this period in 1851 and 1852 when Nightingale was struggling with the issue of her own self-definition. This three-volume book has never been publicly printed, and *Cassandra* was not available until 1928, when Ray Strachey included it in *The Cause*, her history of the women's movement. The writing of *Suggestions for Thought*, however, cleared a way for Nightingale herself: at thirty-two years of age, she left home to train as a nurse at the Institute for Deaconesses at Kaiserwerth on the Rhine. In spite of her family's disapprobation, in 1853 she returned to England to become the Superintendent of the Institute for the Care of Sick Gentlewomen in Distressed Circumstances, when her father agreed to settle an annual £500 on her to ensure her independence. The next year she began her famous work at Scutari in the Crimea.

With ten Roman Catholic nuns, fourteen Anglican sisters, and fourteen hospital nurses, Nightingale confronted the cholera, typhus, gangrene, dysentery, and scurvy that were destroying the British army. In spite of the initial hostility of army officials, Nightingale was determined to help the thousands of men who were dying because of lack of sanitation, lack of equipment, and lack of space in the barracks hospital. She dispensed food and clothing, organized a laundry, built a new wing, and equipped it with everything from towels to arrowroot in huge milk pails. On her return, a national heroine at the age of thirty-six, the "Lady of the Lamp" suffered an illness that at least one scholar, George Pickering, concludes was "a weapon to protect herself from her family."

An invalid's life guaranteed Nightingale's privacy so she could devote herself to

the two hundred–odd books and reports she wrote on world hunger, education, taxation, hospital construction, reform of the Poor Law, and the administration of the army in India. Significantly, too, after her mother's death in 1880 and Parthenope's in 1890, her health began to improve; however, she never relinquished her horror of what her mother and sister had represented. During her years of invalidism, she had worked through the agency of a succession of prominent men, including Sidney Herbert, Arthur Clough, and Sir John Sutherland. Friendly with each "exactly like two men," she had declared earlier to Harriet Martineau that "I am brutally indifferent to the wrongs or rights of my sex." Paradoxically, however, in *Cassandra*, the work that liberated her to reject the idleness of her mother and sister, Nightingale produced what the critic Elaine Showalter has aptly termed "a major text of English feminism, a link between Wollstonecraft and Woolf."

From Cassandra

[Women's Time][1]

"Yet I would spare no pang,
 Would wish no torture less,
 The more that anguish racks,
 The earlier it will bless."

Give us back our suffering, we cry to Heaven in our hearts—suffering rather than indifferentism; for out of nothing comes nothing.[2] But out of suffering may come the cure. Better have pain than paralysis! A hundred struggle and drown in the breakers. One discovers the new world. But rather, ten times rather, die in the surf, heralding the way to that new world, than stand idly on the shore!

Passion, intellect, moral activity—these three have never been satisfied in a woman. In this cold and oppressive conventional atmosphere, they cannot be satisfied. To say more on this subject would be to enter into the whole history of society, of the present state of civilization.

Look at that lizard—"It is not hot," he says, "I like it. The atmosphere which enervates you is life to me." The state of society which some complain of makes others happy. Why should these complain to those? *They* do not suffer. *They* would not understand it, any more than that lizard would comprehend the sufferings of a Shetland sheep.

The progressive[3] world is necessarily divided into two classes—those who take the best of what there is and enjoy it—those who wish for something better and try to create it. Without these two classes the world would be badly off. They are the very conditions of progress, both the one and the other. Were there none who were discontented with what they have, the world would never reach anything better. And, through the other class, which is constantly taking the best of what the first is creating for them, a balance is secured, and that which is conquered is held fast. But with neither class must we quarrel for not possessing the privileges of the other. The laws of the nature of each make it impossible.

Is discontent a privilege?

1. Part II of *Cassandra*.
2. An echo of *King Lear* 1.1.90: "Nothing will come of

nothing."
3. I.e., progressing or developing.

Yes, it is a privilege for you to suffer for your race—a privilege not reserved to the Redeemer,[4] and the martyrs alone, but one enjoyed by numbers in every age.

The common-place life of thousands; and in that is its only interest—its only merit as a history; viz. that it is the type of common sufferings—the story of one who has not the courage to resist nor to submit to the civilization of her time—is this.

Poetry and imagination begin life. A child will fall on its knees on the gravel walk at the sight of a pink hawthorn in full flower, when it is by itself, to praise God for it.

Then comes intellect. It wishes to satisfy the wants which intellect creates for it. But there is a physical, not moral, impossibility of supplying the wants of the intellect in the state of civilization at which we have arrived. The stimulus, the training, the time, are all three wanting to us; or, in other words, the means and inducements are not there.

Look at the poor lives we lead. It is a wonder that we are so good as we are, not that we are so bad. In looking round we are struck with the power of the organizations we see, not with their want[5] of power. Now and then, it is true, we are conscious that *there* is an inferior organization, but, in general, just the contrary. Mrs. A. has the imagination, the poetry of a Murillo,[6] and has sufficient power of execution to show that she might have had a great deal more. Why is she not a Murillo? From a material difficulty, not a mental one. If she has a knife and fork in her hands for three hours of the day, she cannot have a pencil or brush. Dinner is the great sacred ceremony of this day, the great sacrament. To be absent from dinner is equivalent to being ill. Nothing else will excuse us from it. Bodily incapacity is the only apology valid. If she has a pen and ink in her hands during other three hours, writing answers for the penny post, again, she cannot have her pencil,[7] and *so ad infinitum* through life. People have no type[8] before them in their lives, neither fathers nor mothers, nor the children themselves. They look at things in detail. They say, "It is very desirable that A., my daughter, should go to such a party, should know such a lady, should sit by such a person." It is true. But what standard have they before them of the nature and destination of man? The very words are rejected as pedantic. But might they not, at least, have a type in their minds that such an one might be a discoverer through her intellect, such another through her art, a third through her moral power?

Women often try one branch of intellect after another in their youth, *e.g.* mathematics. But that, least of all is compatible with the life of "society." It is impossible to follow up anything systematically. Women often long to enter some man's profession where they would find direction, competition (or rather opportunity of measuring the intellect with others) and, above all, time.

In those wise institutions, mixed as they are with many follies, which will last as long as the human race lasts, because they are adapted to the wants of the human race; those institutions which we call monasteries, and which, embracing much that is contrary to the laws of nature, are yet better adapted to the union of the life of action and that of thought than any other mode of life

4. Christ.
5. Lack.
6. Bartolomé Murillo (1618–1682), Spanish painter of
religious and peasant subjects.
7. Artist's pencil or brush.
8. Model.

with which we are acquainted; in many such, four and a half hours, at least, are daily set aside for thought, rules are given for thought, training and opportunity afforded. Among us there is *no* time appointed for this purpose, and the difficulty is that, in our social life, we must be always doubtful whether we ought not to be with somebody else or be doing something else.

Are men better off than women in this?

If one calls upon a friend in London and sees her son in the drawing-room, it strikes one as odd to find a young man sitting idle in his mother's drawing-room in the morning. For men, who are seen much in those haunts, there is no end of the epithets we have: "knights of the carpet," "drawing-room heroes," "ladies' men." But suppose we were to see a number of men in the morning sitting round a table in the drawing-room, looking at prints, doing worsted work,[9] and reading little books, how we should laugh! A member of the House of Commons was once known to do worsted work. Of another man was said, "His only fault is that he is too good; he drives out with his mother every day in the carriage, and if he is asked anywhere he answers that he must dine with his mother, but, if she can spare him, he will come in to tea, and he does not come."

Now, why is it more ridiculous for a man than for a woman to do worsted work and drive out every day in the carriage? Why should we laugh if we were to see a parcel of men sitting round a drawing-room table in the morning, and think it all right if they were women?

Is man's time more valuable than woman's? or is the difference between man and woman this, that woman has confessedly nothing to do?

Women are never supposed to have any occupation of sufficient importance *not* to be interrupted, except "suckling their fools";[1] and women themselves have accepted this, have written books to support it, and have trained themselves so as to consider whatever they do as *not* of such value to the world or to others, but that they can throw it up at the first "claim of social life." They have accustomed themselves to consider intellectual occupation as a merely selfish amusement, which it is their "duty" to give up for every trifler more selfish than themselves.

A young man (who was afterwards useful and known in his day and generation) when busy reading and sent for by his proud mother to shine in some morning visit, came; but, after it was over, he said, "Now, remember, this is not to happen again. I came that you might not think me sulky, but I shall not come again." But for a young woman to send such a message to her mother and sisters, how impertinent it would be! A woman of great administrative powers said that she never undertook anything which she "could not throw by at once, if necessary."

How do we explain then the many cases of women who have distinguished themselves in classics, mathematics, even in politics?

Widowhood, ill-health, or want of bread, these three explanations or excuses are supposed to justify a woman taking up an occupation. In some cases, no doubt, an indomitable force of character will suffice without any of these three, but such are rare.

But see how society fritters away the intellects of those comitted to her

9. Knitting.
1. Iago on women's role: "To suckle fools and chronicle small beer" (*Othello* 2.1.159).

charge! It is said that society is necessary to sharpen the intellect. But what do we seek society for? It does sharpen the intellect, because it is a kind of *tour-de-force* to say something at a pinch,—unprepared and uninterested with any subject, to improvise something under difficulties. But what "go we out for to seek"? To take the chance of some one having something to say which we want to hear? or of finding something to say which *they* want to hear? You have a little to say, but not much. You often make a stipulation with someone else, "Come in ten minutes, for I shall not be able to find enough to spin out longer than that." You are not to talk of anything very interesting, for the essence of society is to prevent any long conversations and all tête-à-têtes. *Glissez, n'appuyez pas* is its very motto. The praise of a good *maîtresse demaison*[2] consists in this, that she allows no one person to be too much absorbed in, or too long about, a conversation. She always recalls them to their "duty." People do not go into the company of their fellow-creatures for what would seem a very sufficient reason, namely, that they have something to say to them, or something that they want to hear from them; but in the vague hope that they may find something to say.

Then as to solitary opportunities. Women never have an half-hour in all their lives (excepting before or after anybody is up in the house) that they can call their own, without fear of offending or of hurting someone. Why do people sit up so late, or, more rarely, get up so early? Not because the day is not long enough, but because they have "no time in the day to themselves."

If we do attempt to do anything in company, what is the system of literary exercise which we pursue? Everybody reads aloud out of their own book or newspaper—or, every five minutes, something is said. And what is it to be "read aloud to"? The most miserable exercise of the human intellect. Or rather, is it any exercise at all? It is like lying on one's back, with one's hands tied and having liquid poured down one's throat. Worse than that, because suffocation would immediately ensue and put a stop to this operation. But no suffocation would stop the other.

So much for the satisfaction of the intellect. Yet for a married woman in society, it is even worse. A married woman was heard to wish that she could break a limb that she might have a little time to herself. Many take advantage of the fear of "infection" to do the same.

It is a thing *so* accepted among women that they have nothing to do, that one woman has not the least scruple in saying to another, "I will come and spend the morning with you." And you would be thought quite surly and absurd, if you were to refuse it on the plea of occupation. Nay, it is thought a mark of amiability and affection, if you are "on such terms" that you can "come in" "any morning you please."

In a country house, if there is a large party of young people, "You will spend the morning with us," they say to the neighbors, "we will drive together in the afternoon," "tomorrow we will make an expedition, and we will spend the evening together." And this is thought friendly and spending time in a pleasant manner. So women play through life. Yet time is the most valuable of all things. If they had come every morning and afternoon and robbed us of half-a-crown we should have had redress from the police. But it is laid down, that our time is of no value. If you offer a morning visit to a professional man, and

2. Mistress of the house (French). "*Glissez, n'appuyez pas*": slide, don't lean (French).

say, "I will just stay an hour with you, if you will allow me, till so and so comes back to fetch me"; it costs him the earnings of an hour, and therefore he has a right to complain. But women have no right, because it is "only their time."

Women have no means given them, whereby they *can* resist the "claims of social life." They are taught from their infancy upwards that it is a wrong, ill-tempered, and a misunderstanding of "woman's mission" (with a great M) if they do not allow themselves *willingly* to be interrupted at all hours. If a woman has once put in a claim to be treated as a man by some work of science or art or literature, which she can *show* as the "fruit of her leisure," then she will be considered justified in *having* leisure (hardly, perhaps, even then). But if not, not. If she has nothing to show, she must resign herself to her fate.

[*The Savior of Her Race*]

V

"L'enthousiasme est la faiblesse d'un temps où l'intelligence monte très haut, entrainée par l'imagination, et tombe très bas, écrasée par une réalité, sans poésie et sans grandeur."[3]

Women dream till they have no longer the strength to dream; those dreams against which they so struggle, so honestly, vigorously, and conscientiously, and so in vain, yet which are their life, without which they could not have lived; those dreams go at last. All their plans and visions seem vanished, and they know not where; gone, and they cannot recall them. They do not even remember them. And they are left without the food of reality or of hope.

Later in life, they neither desire nor dream, neither of activity, nor of love, nor of intellect. The last often survives the longest. They wish, if their experiences would benefit anybody, to give them to someone. But they never find an hour free in which to collect their thoughts, and so discouragement becomes ever deeper and deeper, and they less and less capable of undertaking anything.

It seems as if the female spirit of the world were mourning everlastingly over blessings, not *lost*, but which she has never had, and which, in her discouragement she feels that she never will have, they are so far off.

The more complete a woman's organization, the more she will feel it, till at last there shall arise a woman, who will resume,[4] in her own soul all the sufferings of her race, and that woman will be the Savior of her race.

Jesus Christ raised women above the condition of mere slaves, mere ministers to the passions of the man, raised them by His sympathy, to be Ministers of God. He gave them moral activity. But the Age, the World, Humanity, must give them the means to exercise this moral activity, must give them intellectual cultivation, spheres of action.

There is perhaps no century where the woman shows so meanly as in this.[5] Because her education seems entirely to have parted company with her voca-

3. Enthusiasm is the weakness of a time when intelligence mounts very high, dragged by the imagination, and falls very low, crushed by a reality without poetry and without grandeur.
4. Encompass, go through in summary form.
5. At almost every period of social life, we find, as it were, two undercurrents running different ways. There is the noble woman who dreams the following out her useful vocation; but there is also the selfish dreamer now, who is ever turning to something new, regardless of the expectations she has voluntarily excited, who is ever talking about "making a life for herself," heedless that she is spoiling another life, undertaken, perhaps, at her own bidding. This is the ugly reverse of the medal [Nightingale's note].

tion; there is no longer unity between the woman as inwardly developed, and as outwardly manifested.

In the last century it was not so. In the succeeding one let us hope that it will no longer be so.

But now she is like the Archangel Michael as he stands upon Saint Angelo at Rome. She has an immense provision of wings, which seem as if they would bear her over earth and heaven; but when she tries to use them, she is petrified into stone, her feet are grown into the earth, chained to the bronze pedestal.

Nothing can well be imagined more painful than the present position of woman, unless, on the one hand, she renounces all outward activity and keeps herself within the magic sphere, the bubble of her dreams; or, on the other, surrendering all aspiration, she gives herself to her real life, soul and body. For those to whom it is possible, the latter is best; for out of activity may come thought, out of mere aspiration can come nothing.

But now—when the young imagination is so high and so developed, and reality is so narrow and conventional—there is no more parallelism between life in the thought and life in the actual than between the corpse, which lies motionless in its narrow bed, and the spirit, which, in our imagination, is at large among the stars.

The ideal life is passed in noble schemes of good consecutively followed up, of devotion to a great object, of sympathy given and received for high ideas and generous feelings. The actual life is passed in sympathy given and received for a dinner, a party, a piece of furniture, a house built or a garden laid out well, in devotion to your guests—(a too real devotion, for it implies that of all your time)—in schemes of schooling for the poor, which you follow up perhaps in an odd quarter of an hour, between luncheon and driving out in the carriage—broth and dripping are included in the plan[6]—and the rest of your time goes in ordering the dinner, hunting for a governess for your children, and sending pheasants and apples to your poorer relations. Is there anything in *this* life which can be called an Incarnation of the ideal life within? Is it a wonder that the unhappy woman should prefer to keep them entirely separate? not to take the bloom off her Ideal by mixing it up with her Actual; not to make her Actual still more unpalatable by trying to *inform* it with her Ideal? And then she is blamed, and her own sex unites against her, for not being content with the "day of small things." She is told that "trifles make the sum of human things"; they do indeed. She is contemptuously asked, "Would she abolish domestic life?" Men are afraid that their houses will not be so comfortable, that their wives will make themselves "remarkable" women that they will make themselves distasteful to men; they write books (and very wisely) to teach themselves to dramatize "little things," to persuade themselves that "domestic life is their sphere" and to idealize the "sacred hearth." Sacred it is indeed. Sacred from the touch of their sons almost as soon as they are out of childhood—from its dulness and its tyrannous trifling *these* recoil. Sacred from the grasp of their daughters' affections upon which it has so light a hold that they seize the first opportunity of marriage, *their* only chance of emancipation. The "sacred hearth"; sacred to their husband's sleep, their sons' absence in the body and their daughters' in mind.

Oh! mothers, who talk about this hearth, how much do you know of your

6. I.e., little bits of time are intermingled like broth and dripping.

son's real life, how much of your daughter's imaginary one? Awake, ye women, all ye that sleep, awake! If this domestic life were so very good, would your young men wander away from it, your maidens think of something else?

The time is come when women must do something more than the "domestic hearth," which means nursing the infants, keeping a pretty house, having a good dinner and an entertaining party.

You say, "It is true, our young men see visions, and our maidens dream dreams," but what of? Does not the woman intend to marry, and have over again what she has at home? and the man ultimately too? Yes, but not the same; she *will* have the same, that is, if circumstances are not altered to prevent it; but her *ideal* is very different, though that ideal and the reality will never come together to mould each other. And it is not only the unmarried woman who dreams. The married woman also holds long imaginary conversations but too often.

VI

We live in the world, it is said, and must walk in its ways.

Was Christ called a complainer against the world? Yet all these great teachers and preachers must have had a most deep and ingrained sense, a continual feeling of the miseries and wrongs of the world. Otherwise they would not have been impelled to devote life and death to redress them. Christ, Socrates, Howard,[7] they must have had no ear for the joys, compared to that which they had for the sorrows of the world.

They acted, however, and we complain. The great reformers of the world turn into the great misanthropists, if circumstances or organization do not permit them to act. Christ, if He had been a woman, might have been nothing but a great complainer. Peace be with the misanthropists! They have made a step in progress; the next will make them great philanthropists; they are divided but by a line.

The next Christ will perhaps be a female Christ. But do we see one woman who looks like a female Christ? or even like "the messenger before" her "face," to go before her and prepare the hearts and minds for her?

To this will be answered that half the inmates of Bedlam begin in this way, by fancying that they are "the Christ."[8]

People talk about imitating Christ, and imitate Him in the little trifling formal things, such as washing the feet, saying His prayer, and so on; but if anyone attempts the real imitation of Him, there are no bounds to the outcry with which the presumption of that person is condemned.

For instance, Christ was saying something to the people one day, which in-

7. Probably a reference to John Howard (1726–1790), an English prison reformer.

8. "It is quite true that insanity, sensuality, and monstrous fraud have constantly assumed to be 'the Christ,' *vide* the *Agapemone* and the Mormons. 'Believing' a man of the name of Prince 'to be the tabernacle of God on earth,' poor deluced women transfer to him all their stock in the Three per Cents. We hear of the Mormons, etc., being the 'recipients and mouthpieces of God's Spirit.' They profess to be 'incarnations of the Deity,' 'witnesses of the Almighty,' 'solely knowing God's will, and being the medium of communicating it to man,' and so forth. It does not appear to us that this blasphemy is very dangerous to the cause of true religion in general, any more than forgery is very dangerous to commerce in general. It is the universal dishonesty in religion, as in trade, which is really dangerous" [Nightingale's note]. The Agapemone was a group in England, founded in 1849 by Henry James Prince, made up of both sexes and based on community of goods. The religion of the Mormons was founded in New York State in 1830 by Joseph Smith.

terested Him very much, and interested them very much; and Mary and His brothers came in the middle of it, and wanted to interrupt Him, and take Him home to dinner, very likely—(how natural that story is! does it not speak more home than any historic evidences of the Gospel's reality?), and He, instead of being angry with their interruption of Him in such an important work for some trifling thing, answers, "Who is my mother? and who are my brethren? Whosoever shall do the will of my Father which is in heaven, the same is my brother and sister and mother."[9] But if *we* were to say that, we should be accused of "destroying the family tie, of diminishing the obligation of the home duties."

He might well say, "Heaven and earth shall pass away, but my words shall not pass away."[1] His words will never pass away. If He had said, "Tell them that I am engaged at this moment in something very important; that the instruction of the multitude ought to go before any personal ties; that I will remember to come when I have done," no one would have been impressed by His words; but how striking is that, "Behold my mother and my brethren!"

VII

The dying woman to her mourners:—"Oh! if you knew how gladly I leave this life, how much more courage I feel to take the chance of another, than of anything I see before me in this, you would put on your wedding-clothes instead of mourning for me!"

"But," they say, "so much talent! so many gifts! such good which you might have done!"

"The world will be put back some little time by my death," she says; "you see I estimate my powers at least as highly as you can; but it is by the death which has taken place some years ago in me, not by the death which is about to take place now." And so is the world put back by the death of every one who has to sacrifice the development of his or her peculiar gifts (which were meant, not for selfish gratification, but for the improvement of that world) to conventionality.

"My people were like children playing on the shore of the eighteenth century. I was their hobby-horse, their plaything; and they drove me to and fro, dear souls! never weary of the play themselves, till I, who had grown to woman's estate and to the ideas of the nineteenth century, lay down exhausted, my mind closed to hope, my heart to strength.

"Free—free—oh! divine freedom, art thou come at last? Welcome, beautiful death!"

Let neither name nor date be placed on her grave, still less the expression of regret or of admiration; but simply the words, "I believe in God."

1852–59 1928

9. Mark 3:33–35.　　　　　　　　　　1. Matthew 24:35.

FRANCES E. W. HARPER

1825–1911

Of the black women writers who contributed to the abolition movement, the one with the most successful publishing career was Frances Ellen Watkins Harper. Although her first collection of poetry and prose, *Forest Leaves* (c. 1845), is no longer available, her volume of antislavery verse, *Poems on Miscellaneous Subjects* (1854), sold twelve thousand copies by 1858 and went through some twenty editions by 1874. Her narrative poems, which dramatized her protest against white injustice to blacks, were exceptionally popular with lecture audiences. Just as the *The Two Offers* (Anglo-African Magazine, 1859) was described as "the first short story published by an American Negro," *Iola Leroy; or, Shadows Uplifted* (1892) was recognized as the first novel by a black author to describe Reconstruction. According to the African-American scholar Hazel V. Carby, the novel—"rooted in the authority of Harper's experience as abolitionist, lecturer, poet, teacher, feminist, and black woman"—should be understood as an attempt to "re-arm the black intellectual and to contest the terrain of racist retrenchment." Throughout her life, Harper integrated her literary career with public service dedicated to the moral education of whites and blacks.

Born in Baltimore, Maryland, the only child of free black parents, Frances Watkins was orphaned at the age of three and raised by her uncle, the Reverend William Watkins. At fourteen, after attending his school for free blacks, she supported herself as a nursemaid and later as a seamstress and teacher. Through contacts with abolitionists involved in the Underground Railroad in the early 1850s, she lectured widely for antislavery societies in Massachusetts, Pennsylvania, Maine, New Jersey, New York, and Ohio, sometimes using the lecture podium for readings of her poetry. On November 22, 1860, she married Fenton Harper, a widower who died four years later. When she resumed her lecturing, she toured the South, addressing both black and mixed audiences. From 1871, when she settled in Philadelphia with her daughter, until her death at eighty-five, Harper worked actively in social and civic organizations, as a participant in two conventions of the American Woman Suffrage Association, as the director of the American Association of Education of Colored Youth, and as the vice president of the National Association of Colored Women.

Her verse, written to dramatize her political commitments, was sometimes as sentimental as the poetry of her contemporary, Felicia Hemans. Yet, at her best, Harper used biblical characters and black dialect to define the terrible experience of slavery from the point of view of black women, and to record the subversive survival skills such women contributed to slave culture.

The Slave Mother

Heard you that shriek? It rose
 So wildly on the air,
It seemed as if a burdened heart
 Was breaking in despair.

Saw you those hands so sadly clasped— 5
 The bowed and feeble head—
The shuddering of that fragile form—
 That look of grief and dread?

Saw you the sad, imploring eye?
 Its every glance was pain, 10
As if a storm of agony
 Were sweeping through the brain.

She is a mother, pale with fear,
 Her boy clings to her side,
And in her kirtle[1] vainly tries 15
 His trembling form to hide.

He is not hers, although she bore
 For him a mother's pains;
He is not hers, although her blood
 Is coursing through his veins! 20

He is not hers, for cruel hands
 May rudely tear apart
The only wreath of household love
 That binds her breaking heart.

His love has been a joyous light 25
 That o'er her pathway smiled,
A fountain gushing ever new,
 Amid life's desert wild.

His lightest word has been a tone
 Of music round her heart, 30
Their lives a streamlet blent in one—
 Oh, Father! must they part?

They tear him from her circling arms,
 Her last and fond embrace.
Oh! never more may her sad eyes 35
 Gaze on his mournful face.

No marvel, then, these bitter shrieks
 Disturb the listening air:
She is a mother, and her heart
 Is breaking in despair. 40

 1854

The Tennessee Hero

"He had heard his comrades plotting to obtain their liberty, and rather than
betray them he received 750 lashes and died."

He stood before the savage throng,
 The base and coward crew;
A tameless light flashed from his eye,
 His heart beat firm and true.

1. Outer skirt.

He was the hero of his band,
 The noblest of them all;
Though fetters galled his weary limbs,
 His spirit spurned their thrall.[1]

And towered in its manly might,
 Above the murderous crew.
Oh! liberty had nerved his heart,
 And every pulse beat true.

"Now tell us," said the savage troop,
 "And life thy gain shall be!
Who are the men that plotting, say—
 'They must and will be free!' "

Oh, could you have seen the hero then,
 As his lofty soul arose,
And his dauntless eyes defiance flashed
 On his mean and craven foes!

"I know the men who would be free;
 They are the heroes of your land;
But death and torture I defy,
 Ere I betray that band.

And what! oh, what is life to me,
 Beneath your base control?
Nay! do your worst. Ye have no chains
 To bind my free-born soul."

They brought the hateful lash and scourge,
 With murder in each eye.
But a solemn vow was on his lips—
 He had resolved to die.

Yes, rather than betray his trust,
 He'd meet a death of pain;
'T was sweeter far to meet it thus
 Than wear a treason stain!

Like storms of wrath, of hate and pain,
 The blows rained thick and fast;
But the monarch soul kept true
 Till the gates of life were past.

And the martyr spirit fled
 To the throne of God on high,
And showed his gaping wounds
 Before the unslumbering eye.

1854

1. Bondage.

Vashti[1]

She leaned her head upon her hand
 And heard the king's decree—
"My lords are feasting in my halls,
 Bid Vashti come to me.

"I've shown the treasures of my house, 5
 My costly jewels rare,
But with the glory of her eyes
 No rubies can compare.

"Adorned and crowned I'd have her come,
 With all her queenly grace, 10
And, 'mid my lords and mighty men,
 Unveil her lovely face.

"Each gem that sparkles in my crown,
 Or glitters on my throne,
Grows poor and pale when she appears, 15
 My beautiful, my own!"

All waiting stood the chamberlains
 To hear the Queen's reply,
They saw her cheek grow deathly pale,
 But light flash'd to her eye: 20

"Go, tell the King," she proudly said,
 "That I am Persia's Queen,
And by his crowds of merry men
 I never will be seen.

"I'll take the crown from off my head 25
 And tread it 'neath my feet
Before their rude and careless gaze
 My shrinking eyes shall meet.

"A queen unveiled before the crowd!—
 Upon each lip my name!— 30
Why, Persia's women all would blush
 And weep for Vashti's shame!

"Go back!" she cried, and waved her hand,
 And grief was in her eye:
"Go, tell the King," she sadly said, 35
 "That I would rather die."

They brought her message to the King,
 Dark flashed his angry eye;
'Twas as the lightning ere the storm
 Hath swept in fury by. 40

1. The queen of Ahasuerus refused to dance before him and was banished from his sight (Esther 1: 9–19).

Then bitterly outspoke the King,
 Through purple lips of wrath—
"What shall be done to her who dares
 To cross your monarch's path?"

Then spake his wily counsellors— 45
 "O King of this fair land!
From distant Ind to Ethiop
 All bow to thy command

"But if, before thy servants' eyes,
 This thing they plainly see,
That Vashti doth not heed thy will 50
 Nor yield herself to thee,

"The women, restive 'neath our rule,
 Would learn to scorn our name,
And from her deed to us would come 55
 Reproach and burning shame.

"Then, gracious King, sign with thy hand
 This stern but just decree,
That Vashti lay aside her crown,
 Thy Queen no more to be." 60

She heard again the King's command,
 And left her high estate,
Strong in her earnest womanhood,
 She calmly met her fate,

And left the palace of the King, 65
 Proud of her spotless name—
A woman who could bend to grief,
 But would not bow to shame.

1871

Aunt Chloe's Politics

Of course, I don't know very much
 About these politics,
But I think that some who run 'em,
 Do mighty ugly tricks.

I've seen 'em honey-fugle[1] round, 5
 And talk so awful sweet,
That you'd think them full of kindness,
 As an egg is full of meat.[2]

2. Rank or standing in society.
1. Sweet-talk, deceive through empty rhetoric

2. I.e., yolk and albumen.

Now I don't believe in looking
 Honest people in the face, 10
And saying when you're doing wrong,
 That "I haven't sold my race."[3]

When we want to school our children,
 If the money isn't there,
Whether black or white have took it, 15
 The love we all must share.

And this buying up each other
 Is something worse than mean,
Though I thinks a heap of voting,
 I go for voting clean.[4] 20

1872

Learning to Read

Very soon the Yankee teachers
 Came down and set up school;
But, oh! how the Rebs[1] did hate it,—
 It was agin' their rule.

Our masters always tried to hide 5
 Book learning from our eyes;
Knowledge didn't agree with slavery—
 'Twould make us all too wise.

But some of us would try to steal
 A little from the book, 10
And put the words together,
 And learn by hook or crook.

I remember Uncle Caldwell,
 Who took pot liquor fat[2]
And greased the pages of his book, 15
 And hid it in his hat.

And had his master ever seen
 The leaves upon his head,
He'd have thought them greasy papers,
 But nothing to be read. 20

And there was Mr. Turner's Ben,
 Who heard the children spell,
And picked the words right up by heart,
 And learned to read 'em well.

3. I.e., wronged my people.
4. During the post–Civil War period white politicians tried to buy black votes.
1. The southern "rebels." The poem takes place after the Civil War, during the period of Reconstruction when Northern teachers came to the South to educate the newly freed slaves. It had been illegal to teach slaves to read.
2. The fat that floats to the top of the pot.

Well, the Northern folks kept sending 25
 The Yankee teachers down;
And they stood right up and helped us,
 Though Rebs did sneer and frown.

And, I longed to read my Bible,
 For precious words it said; 30
But when I begun to learn it,
 Folks just shook their heads,

And said there is no use trying,
 Oh! Chloe, you're too late;
But as I was rising sixty,[3] 35
 I had no time to wait.

So I got a pair of glasses,
 And straight to work I went,
And never stopped till I could read
 The hymns and Testament. 40

Then I got a little cabin
 A place to call my own—
And I felt as independent
 As the queen upon her throne.

1872

3. Nearing sixty.

HARRIET E. ADAMS WILSON
1828?–1870?

Harriet E. Wilson was the first black woman to publish a novel in English and the first African-American to publish a novel in the United States. Her sardonically entitled *Our Nig* was printed (apparently at her own expense) by the Massachusetts firm of George C. Rand and Avery in September 1859. Even more than the phrase "our nig"—a phrase that would have been as shocking in the nineteenth century as it is today—the book's full title emphasized the author's political motivation, as well as her irony, for it read

OUR NIG.
or,
Sketches from the
Life of a Free Black,
In a Two-Story White House, North.
SHOWING THAT SLAVERY'S SHADOWS
FALL EVEN THERE.

by "OUR NIG."

Our Nig received no reviews, evidently had hardly any sales, and was almost completely forgotten until the scholar Henry Louis Gates Jr. reissued it in a facsimile edition in 1983.

As Gates observed, Wilson's use of the controversial, emotionally charged word *nig* in her title may in fact have been partly responsible for the obscurity into which the novel fell; in addition, he argues that the opening of the tale, which portrays a comparatively happy marriage between a black man and a white woman, may have made the work unacceptable to black and white readers alike. In any case, the book's failure undoubtedly accounts for the paucity of information about Wilson herself. She was born in New Hampshire, she may have been trained as a hat maker, she married and was evidently deserted by a sailor named Thomas Wilson, and she subsequently gave birth in a "county house" (a poor house) to a child named George Mason Wilson, who died in 1860 at the age of seven: these are among the few facts known about her. Nevertheless, *Our Nig* itself offers a vivid picture of the kind of life she must have lived as a free black in New England, for the novel appears to be based on personal experiences.

The selection included here, for instance, recounts the circumstances of the childhood of "our nig," a mulatto girl named Alfrado, or "Frado" for short. When this passage begins, the child is seven, her father has died, and her mother has deserted her, leaving her with a wealthy white family, the Bellmonts, who have decided to keep her in the household as a servant.

From Our Nig

[*Frado's Childhood*]

Frado was called early in the morning by her new mistress. Her first work was to feed the hens. She was shown how it was *always* to be done, and in no other way; any departure from this rule to be punished by a whipping. She was then accompanied by Jack[1] to drive the cows to pasture, so she might learn the way. Upon her return she was allowed to eat her breakfast, consisting of a bowl of skimmed milk, with brown bread crusts, which she was told to eat, standing, by the kitchen table, and must not be over ten minutes about it. Meanwhile the family were taking their morning meal in the dining-room. This over, she was placed on a cricket[2] to wash the common dishes; she was to be in waiting always to bring wood and chips, to run hither and thither from room to room.

A large amount of dish-washing for small hands followed dinner. Then the same after tea and going after the cows finished her first day's work. It was a new discipline to the child. She found some attractions about the place, and she retired to rest at night more willing to remain. The same routine followed day after day, with slight variation; adding a little more work, and spicing the toil with "words that burn," and frequent blows on her head. These were great annoyances to Frado, and had she known where her mother was, she would have gone at once to her. She was often greatly wearied, and silently wept over her sad fate. At first she wept aloud, which Mrs. Bellmont noticed by applying a rawhide,[3] always at hand in the kitchen. It was a symptom of discontent and complaining which must be "nipped in the bud," she said.

Thus passed a year. No intelligence of Mag.[4] It was now certain Frado was to become a permanent member of the family. Her labors were multiplied; she was quite indispensable, although but seven years old. She had never learned to read, never heard of a school until her residence in the family.

1. The son of the Bellmont family.
2. A footstool.
3. I.e., a whip.
4. Frado's mother.

Mrs. Bellmont was in doubt about the utility of attempting to educate people of color, who were incapable of elevation. This subject occasioned a lengthy discussion in the family, Mr. Bellmont, Jane and Jack arguing for Frado's education; Mary and her mother objecting. At last Mr. Bellmont declared decisively that she *should* go to school. He was a man who seldom decided controversies at home. The word once spoken admitted of no appeal; so, notwithstanding Mary's objection that she would have to attend the same school she did, the word became law.

It was to be a new scene to Frado, and Jack had many queries and conjectures to answer. He was himself too far advanced to attend the summer school, which Frado regretted, having had too many opportunities of witnessing Miss Mary's temper to feel safe in her company alone.

The opening day of school came. Frado sauntered on far in the rear of Mary, who was ashamed to be seen "walking with a nigger." As soon as she appeared, with scanty clothing and bared feet, the children assembled, noisily published her approach: "See that nigger," shouted one. "Look! look!" cried another. "I won't play with her," said one little girl. "Nor I neither," replied another.

Mary evidently relished these sharp attacks, and saw a fair prospect of lowering Nig where, according to her views, she belonged. Poor Frado, chagrined and grieved, felt that her anticipations of pleasure at such a place were far from being realized. She was just deciding to return home, and never come there again, when the teacher appeared, and observing the downcast looks of the child, took her by the hand, and led her into the school-room. All followed, and, after the bustle of securing seats was over, Miss Marsh inquired if the children knew "any cause for the sorrow of that little girl?" pointing to Frado. It was soon all told. She then reminded them of their duties to the poor and friendless; their cowardice in attacking a young innocent child; referred them to one who looks not on outward appearances, but on the heart. "She looks like a good girl; I think *I* shall love her, so lay aside all prejudice, and vie with each other in shewing kindness and good-will to one who seems different from you," were the closing remarks of the kind lady. These kind words! The most agreeable sound which ever meets the ear of sorrowing, grieving childhood.

Example rendered her words efficacious. Day by day there was a manifest change of deportment towards "Nig." Her speeches often drew merriment from the children; no one could do more to enliven their favorite pastimes than Frado. Mary could not endure to see her thus noticed, yet knew not how to prevent it. She could not influence her schoolmates as she wished. She had not gained their effections by winning ways and yielding points of controversy. On the contrary, she was self-willed, domineering; every day reported "mad" by some of her companions. She availed herself of the only alternative, abuse and taunts, as they returned from school. This was not satisfactory; she wanted to use physical force "to subdue her," to "keep her down."

There was, on their way home, a field intersected by a stream over which a single plank was placed for a crossing. It occurred to Mary that it would be a punishment to Nig to compel her to cross over; so she dragged her to the edge, and told her authoritatively to go over. Nig hesitated, resisted. Mary placed herself behind the child, and, in the struggle to force her over, lost her footing and plunged into the stream. Some of the larger scholars being in sight, ran, and thus prevented Mary from drowning and Frado from falling. Nig scampered home fast as possible, and Mary went to the nearest house, dripping, to

procure a change of garments. She came loitering home, half crying, exclaiming, "Nig pushed me into the stream!" She then related the particulars. Nig was called from the kitchen. Mary stood with anger flashing in her eyes. Mr. Bellmont sat quietly reading his paper. He had witnessed too many of Miss Mary's outbreaks to be startled. Mrs. Bellmont interrogated Nig.

"I did n't do it! I did n't do it!" answered Nig, passionately, and then related the occurrence truthfully.

The discrepancy greatly enraged Mrs. Bellmont. With loud accusations and angry gestures she approached the child. Turning to her husband, she asked.

"Will you sit still, there, and hear that black nigger call Mary a liar?"

"How do we know but she has told the truth? I shall not punish her," he replied, and left the house, as he usually did when a tempest threatened to envelop him. No sooner was he out of sight than Mrs. B. and Mary commenced beating her inhumanly; then propping her mouth open with a piece of wood, shut her up in a dark room, without any supper. For employment, while the tempest raged within, Mr. Bellmont went for the cows, a task belonging to Frado, and thus unintentionally prolonged her pain. At dark Jack came in, and seeing Mary, accosted her with, "So you thought you'd vent your spite on Nig, did you? Why can't you let her alone? It was good enough for you to get a ducking, only you did not stay in half long enough."

"Stop!" said his mother. "You shall never talk so before me. You would have that little nigger trample on Mary, would you? She came home with a lie; it made Mary's story false."

"What was Mary's story?" asked Jack.

It was related.

"Now," said Jack, sallying into a chair, "the school-children happened to see it all, and they tell the same story Nig does. Which is most likely to be true, what a dozen agree they saw, or the contrary?"

"It is very strange you will believe what others say against your sister," retorted his mother, with flashing eye. "I think it is time your father subdued you."

"Father is a sensible man," argued Jack. "He would not wrong a dog. Where *is* Frado?" he continued.

"Mother gave her a good whipping and shut her up," replied Mary.

Just then Mr. Bellmont entered, and asked if Frado was "shut up yet."

The knowledge of her innocence, the perfidy of his sister, worked fearfully on Jack. He bounded from his chair, searched every room till he found the child; her mouth wedged apart, her face swollen, and full of pain.

How Jack pitied her! He relieved her jaws, brought her some supper, took her to her room, comforted her as well as he knew how, sat by her till she fell asleep, and then left for the sitting room. As he passed his mother, he remarked, "If that was the way Frado was to be treated, he hoped she would never wake again!" He then imparted her situation to his father, who seemed untouched, till a glance at Jack exposed a tearful eye. Jack went early to her next morning. She awoke sad, but refreshed. After breakfast Jack took her with him to the field, and kept her through the day. But it could not be so generally. She must return to school, to her household duties. He resolved to do what he could to protect her from Mary and his mother. He bought her a dog, which became a great favorite with both. The invalid, Jane, would gladly befriend her; but she had not the strength to brave the iron will of her mother. Kind words and affectionate glances were the only expressions of sympathy she

could safely indulge in. The men employed on the farm were always glad to hear her prattle; she was a great favorite with them. Mrs. Bellmont allowed them the privilege of talking with her in the kitchen. She did not fear but she should have ample opportunity of subduing her when they were away. Three months of schooling, summer and winter, she enjoyed for three years. Her winter over-dress was a cast-off overcoat, once worn by Jack, and a sun-bonnet. It was a source of great merriment to the scholars, but Nig's retorts were so mirthful, and their satisfaction so evident in attributing the selection to "Old Granny Bellmont," that it was not painful to Nig or pleasurable to Mary. Her jollity was not to be quenched by whipping or scolding. In Mrs. Bellmont's presence she was under restraint; but in the kitchen, and among her schoolmates, the pent up fires burst forth. She was ever at some sly prank when unseen by her teacher, in school hours; not unfrequently some outburst of merriment, of which she was the original, was charged upon some innocent mate, and punishment inflicted which she merited. They enjoyed her antics so fully that any of them would suffer wrongfully to keep open the avenues of mirth. She would venture far beyond propriety, thus shielded and countenanced.

The teacher's desk was supplied with drawers, in which were stored his books and other *et ceteras* of the profession. The children observed Nig very busy there one morning before school, as they flitted in occasionally from their play outside. The master came; called the children to order; opened a drawer to take the book the occasion required; when out poured a volume of smoke. "Fire! fire!" screamed he, at the top of his voice. By this time he had become sufficiently acquainted with the peculiar odor, to know he was imposed upon. The scholars shouted with laughter to see the terror of the dupe, who, feeling abashed at the needless fright, made no very strict investigation, and Nig once more escaped punishment. She had provided herself with cigars, and puffing, puffing away at the crack of the drawer, had filled it with smoke, and then closed it tightly to deceive the teacher, and amuse the scholars. The interim of terms was filled up with a variety of duties new and peculiar. At home, no matter how powerful the heat when sent to rake hay or guard the grazing herd, she was never permitted to shield her skin from the sun. She was not many shades darker than Mary now; what a calamity it would be ever to hear the contrast spoken of. Mrs. Bellmont was determined the sun should have full power to darken the shade which nature had first bestowed upon her as best befitting.

1859

EMILY DICKINSON
1830–1886

In 1881 a young woman named Mabel Loomis Todd wrote her parents about "the *character* of Amherst . . . a lady whom the people call the '*Myth*': She has not been outside of her own house in fifteen years. . . . She dresses wholly in white, and her mind is said to be perfectly wonderful." So began the legend of Emily Dickinson, one of the greatest poets of the nineteenth century, who was for years portrayed by biographers and critics as an eccentric recluse, a "little home-keeping person," a

mad spinster who had been disappointed in love. For, four years after this New England woman in white died in 1886, the same Mabel Loomis Todd brought out a volume containing selections from 1,776 strange and passionate poems, which had been found, neatly sewed into booklets, in her bureau drawers, and the imagination of the public was immediately seized by the mysterious discrepancy between what seemed to be the isolation of Dickinson's life and the intensity of her art. To many, indeed, the "case" of Emily Dickinson—only eight of whose poems had been published in her lifetime—seemed to offer a crucial model for the situation of the woman poet. Eccentricity, reclusiveness, and most of all, thwarted romance—these appeared to be the conditions that might drive a woman to what was, for women, the perversity of writing verse.

Despite the equivocal glamour of the legend Todd helped create, however, the "Myth of Amherst" had a conventional enough childhood, and even in its apparent isolation, her adult life was marked not so much by longing for lost love as by aesthetic and intellectual commitment to her art, in whose cause she continually demanded "severer service" of herself. The second child of Edward Dickinson, an austere but ambitious lawyer, and his retiring wife, Emily, she was born on December 10, 1830 into one of Amherst's leading families. With her older brother, Austin, and her younger sister, Lavinia, she seems to have had a cheerful home and, by the standards of her time and place, a good education at Amherst Academy. When she was seventeen, moreover, she even went for a year to what was to become one of the first women's colleges—Mount Holyoke Female Seminary, a few miles outside Amherst.

It was at Mount Holyoke that Dickinson's independence and imagination began to manifest themselves. Two episodes, in particular, tell us something about the kind of resourceful and rebellious girl she was. The first, about which Todd heard from the poet's sister, has to do with geometry: "When the [geometry] examination came and [Emily] had never studied it, she went to the blackboard and gave such a glib exposition of imaginary figures that the dazed teacher passed her with the highest mark." The second, which was reported by a classmate, has to do with religion: when Mary Lyon, the school principal, was proselytizing for an evangelical revival, she "asked all those who wanted to be Christians to rise," but because Emily could not "honestly accede to" the request, she, and only she, "remained seated."

Geometry may have been a subject that the young Dickinson was able to "imagine," but orthodox religious conversion evidently was not, and, as many biographers have speculated, it was quite possibly Lyon's evangelical revival that decided the poet on leaving Mount Holyoke, though her father's desire to have his older daughter back at home also played a part in the move. In any case, after only a year she left school, never to return, and from then on her life became increasingly withdrawn, as she slowly developed the fear of public places (known as agoraphobia) that marked her later years. Her trips out of town were few. As a girl, she traveled to Boston, Cambridge, and Worcester several times to vacation with relatives. In 1855, she and her sister "Vinnie" accompanied their congressman father to Washington and Philadelphia for a visit of almost two months. Finally, in 1864, she spent some weeks in Cambridge because she was being treated by a Boston specialist for what recent scholars have theorized was a bad case of an eye disorder called exotropia. Except for these excursions, she remained in Amherst—a kind of Yankee princess deliberately training herself to see, as she put it, "New Englandly"—until her death in 1886 of Bright's disease.

To be sure, throughout her career, Dickinson maintained a voluminous, lively, and often brilliant correspondence with personal and family friends as well as literary acquaintances. Within her circle of intimates, moreover, she was evidently quite warmly nurtured both as a woman and as an artist by her sister-in-law Susan Gilbert Dickinson, the especially beloved companion about whom she once wrote that "when my hand is cut, hers will be found inside."

But even in Amherst, what Dickinson called the "circumference" of her daily life gradually narrowed. At first a high-spirited girl, helping to hostess her father's parties, paying visits to neighbors, and composing whimsical valentines for undergraduates at Amherst College, she eventually took to dressing "wholly in white," assured the editor Thomas Wentworth Higginson—one of her major correspondents—that "I do not cross my Father's ground to any house in town," refused for the most part to appear before callers, and even in her last illness allowed a doctor to "examine" her only as she walked past a partially opened door in the next room. Becoming a "Myth," she "manifested" her presence, like a priestess of some mysterious religion, only through tokens of flowers, cakes, and wine, transmitted by her sister or the family servant, or as one famous story has it, through playful gifts of sweets to children, arranged in a basket let down from her bedroom window.

What could have accounted for such behavior in a woman who had been a witty and energetic girl? For years, biographers of Dickinson assumed that sometime in the early 1860s she had fallen hopelessly in love with a man whose identity has never been established, though the leading candidate for the position was long supposed to be the Reverend Charles Wadsworth, a glamorous but married clergyman, whom she was thought to have met during her 1855 stay in Philadelphia. A series of tormented, often frankly erotic letters to a man enigmatically addressed as "Master," in which Dickinson variously defines herself as a wounded bird, a childlike "Daisy," a "culprit," a "smaller life," reinforced the sense of such biographers that both this writer's withdrawal from the world and her impassioned art were inspired by a tragic romance. More recently, however, critics have begun to question the sentimental assumptions on which such interpretations of her life and work were based.

To be sure, as these scholars concede, there may well have been an emotional event that inspired both Dickinson's poetry and her self-protectiveness. Yet her "Master" letters, with their deliberate effacement of the addressee's identity, are just as clearly explorations of the general relationship between male power and female powerlessness, male authority and female dependency, as they are pleas for romantic reassurance from a particular man. Moreover, in these letters as in so many of her most impassioned verses, the poet is obviously both disguising and dramatizing herself, as if to document a crucial confession that she made to Thomas Wentworth Higginson, the *Atlantic Monthly* editor who became her literary mentor: "When I state myself, as the Representative of the Verse—it does not mean—me—but a supposed person."

Anticipating modern theories of the poet's "persona," Dickinson's definition of herself as a "supposed person" reveals just how self-consciously literary she was, even while its suggestion of a commitment to fantasy recalls the imaginary geometry she sketched on a Mount Holyoke blackboard. In many other ways, moreover, her correspondence with Higginson reinforces these points, as contemporary critics have begun to notice. Struck by an essay titled *A Letter to a Young Contributor*, which the *Atlantic* editor published in 1862, Dickinson began to write to Higginson in that year, inquiring if her verses were "alive" and asking if she might be his "scholar." Though his responses were sometimes equivocal—he often objected to her eccentric language or to the meters that she called "the Bells whose jingling cooled my tramp"—his basic reaction was encouraging, and in 1870 he even journeyed to Amherst to meet her, becoming one of the few visitors to whom she appeared in person in her later life. For all his faults of perception, he seems to have understood, as many Dickinson biographers after him did not, the extent and intensity of her aesthetic vocation.

A further indication of Dickinson's literary intensity—her professionalism, even—can be found in records of her reading. According to family members, the walls of this poet's bedroom were hung with pictures of favorite writers—George Eliot, Thomas Carlyle, Elizabeth Barrett Browning, a selection that reveals how she ranged from the male to the female literary traditions and from prose to poetry

in her search for intellectual models. Most persistently, however, she defined herself as a woman writer, reading the works of female precursors with special care, attending to the implications of novels like Charlotte Brontë's *Jane Eyre*, Emily Brontë's *Wuthering Heights*, and George Eliot's *Middlemarch* with the same absorbed delight that characterized her devotion to Elizabeth Barrett Browning's *Aurora Leigh*. Finally, then, the key to her enigmatic identity as a "supposed person" who was called the "Myth of Amherst" may rest not in investigations of her questionable romance, but in studies of her unquestionably serious reading as well as in analyses of her disquietingly powerful writing. Elliptically phrased, intensely compressed, her poems are more linguistically innovative than any other nineteenth-century verses, with the possible exception of some works by Walt Whitman and Gerard Manley Hopkins, her two most radical male contemporaries. Throughout her largely secret but always brilliant career, moreover, she confronted precisely the questions about the individual and society, time and death, flesh and spirit, that major precursors from Milton to Keats had faced. Dreaming of "Amplitude and Awe," she recorded sometimes vengeful, sometimes mystical visions of social and personal transformation in poems as inventively phrased and imaginatively constructed as any in the English language.

Clearly such accomplishments required not only extraordinary talent but also some measure of freedom. Yet because she was the unmarried daughter of conservative New Englanders, Dickinson was obliged to take on many household tasks; as a nineteenth-century New England wife, she would have had the same number of obligations, if not more. Some of these she performed with pleasure; in 1856, for instance, she was judge of a bread-baking contest, and in 1857 she won a prize in that contest. But as Higginson's "scholar," as a voracious reader and an ambitious writer, Dickinson had to win herself time for "Amplitude and Awe," and it is increasingly clear that she did so through a strategic withdrawal from her ordinary world. A story related by her niece Martha Dickinson Bianchi reveals that the poet herself knew from the first what both the price and the prize might be: on one occasion, said Bianchi, Dickinson took her up to the room in which she regularly sequestered herself and, mimicking locking herself in, "thumb and forefinger closed on an imaginary key," said "with a quick turn of her wrist, 'It's just a turn—and freedom, Matty!'"

In the freedom of her solitary, but not lonely, room, Dickinson may have become what her Amherst neighbors saw as a bewildering "myth." Yet there, too, she created myths of her own. Reading the Brontës and Barrett Browning, studying Transcendentalism and the Bible, she contrived a theology that is powerfully expressed in many of her poems. That it was at its most hopeful a female-centered theology is revealed in verses like those she wrote about the women artists she admired, as well as in more general works like her gravely pantheistic address to the "Sweet Mountains" who "tell me no lie," with its definition of the hills around Amherst as "strong Madonnas" and its description of the writer herself as "The Wayward Nun—beneath the Hill—/ Whose service is to You—." As Dickinson's admirer and descendant Adrienne Rich has accurately observed, this passionate poet consistently chose to confront her society—to "have it out"—"on her own premises."

24

There is a morn by men unseen—
Whose maids upon remoter green
Keep their Seraphic[1] May—

1. Angelic.

And all day long, with dance and game,
And gambol I may never name— 5
Employ their holiday.

Here to light measure, move the feet
Which walk no more the village street—
Nor by the wood are found—
Here are the birds that sought the sun 10
When last year's distaff² idle hung
And summer's brows were bound.

Ne'er saw I such a wondrous scene—
Ne'er such a ring on such a green—
Nor so serene array— 15
As if the stars some summer night
Should swing their cups of Chrysolite³—
And revel till the day—

Like thee to dance—like thee to sing—
People upon the mystic green— 20
I ask, each new May Morn.
I wait thy far, fantastic⁴ bells—
Announcing me in other dells—
Unto the different dawn!

c. 1858 1945

103

I have a King, who does not speak—
So—wondering—thro' the hours meek
I trudge the day away—
Half glad when it is night, and sleep,
If, haply thro' a dream, to peep 5
In parlors, shut by day.

And if I do—when morning comes—
It is as if a hundred drums
Did round my pillow roll,
and shouts fill all my Childish sky, 10
And Bells keep saying "Victory"
From steeples in my soul!

And if I don't—the little Bird
Within the Orchard, is not heard,
And I omit to pray 15
"Father, thy will be done"⁵ today
For my will goes the other way,
And it were perjury!

c. 1859 1896

2. Staff that holds unspun wool.
3. A goldlike mineral.
4. Imaginary.

5. From the Lord's Prayer (see Matthew 6:10 and
Luke 11:2).

209

With thee, in the Desert—
With thee in the thirst—
With thee in the Tamarind wood—
Leopard breathes—at last!

c. 1860 1945

211

Come slowly—Eden!
Lips unused to Thee—
Bashful—sip thy Jessamines[6]—
As the fainting Bee—

Reaching late his flower, 5
Round her chamber hums—
Counts his nectars—
Enters—and is lost in Balms.[7]

c. 1860 1890

249

Wild Nights—Wild Nights!
Were I with thee
Wild Nights should be
Our luxury!

Futile—the Winds— 5
To a Heart in port—
Done with the Compass—
Done with the Chart!

Rowing in Eden—
Ah, the Sea!
Might I but moor—Tonight— 10
In Thee!

c. 1861 1891

258

There's a certain Slant of light,
Winter Afternoons—
That oppresses, like the Heft[8]
Of Cathedral Tunes—

6. Jasmines. 8. Weight.
7. Perfumes.

Heavenly Hurt, it gives us— 5
We can find no scar,
But internal difference,
Where the Meanings, are—

None may teach it—Any—
'Tis the Seal Despair— 10
An imperial affliction
Sent us of the Air—

When it comes, the Landscape listens—
Shadows—hold their breath—
When it goes, 'tis like the Distance 15
On the look of Death—

c. 1861 1890

271

A solemn thing—it was—I said—
A woman—white—to be—
And wear—if God should count me fit—
Her blameless mystery—

A hallowed thing—to drop a life 5
Into the purple well—
Too plummetless[9]— that it return—
Eternity—until—

I pondered how the bliss would lock—
And would it feel as big— 10
When I could take it in my hand—
As hovering—seen—through fog—

And then—the size of this "small" life—
The Sages—call it small—
Swelled—like Horizons—in my vest[1]— 15
And I sneered—softly—"small"!

c. 1861 1896

280

I felt a Funeral, in my Brain,
And Mourners to and fro
Kept treading—treading—till it seemed
That Sense was breaking through[2]—

9. Bottomless. 2. I.e., sense or reason was collapsing.
1. Clothing.

And when they all were seated, 5
A Service, like a Drum—
Kept beating—beating—till I thought
My Mind was going numb—

And then I heard them lift a Box
And creak across my Soul 10
With those same Boots of Lead, again,
Then Space—began to toll,

As all the Heavens were a Bell,
And Being, but an Ear,
And I, and Silence, some strange Race 15
Wrecked, solitary, here—

And then a Plank in Reason, broke,
And I dropped down, and down—
And hit a World, at every plunge,
And Finished knowing—then— 20

c. 1861 1896

288

I'm Nobody! Who are you?
Are you—Nobody—Too?
Then there's a pair of us?
Don't tell! they'd advertise[3]—you know!

How dreary—to be—Somebody! 5
How public—like a Frog—
To tell one's name—the livelong June—
To an admiring Bog!

c. 1861 1891

303

The Soul selects her own Society—
Then—shuts the Door—
To her divine Majority—
Present no more—

Unmoved—she notes the Chariots—pausing— 5
At her low Gate—
Unmoved—an Emperor be kneeling
Upon her Mat—

I've known her—from an ample nation—
Choose One— 10

3. Announce, publicize.

Then—close the Valves of her attention—
Like Stone—

c. 1862 1890

312

Her—"last Poems"[4]—
Poets—ended—
Silver—perished—with her Tongue—
Not on Record—bubbled o'her,
Flute—or Woman— 5
So divine—
Not unto its Summer—Morning
Robin—uttered Half the Tune—
Gushed too free for the Adoring—
From the Anglo-Florentine[5]— 10
Late—the Praise—
'Tis dull—conferring
On the Head too High to Crown—
Diadem—or Ducal Showing[6]—
Be its Grave—sufficient sign— 15
Nought—that We—No Poet's Kinsman—
Suffocate—with easy woe—
What, and if, Ourself a Bridegroom—
Put Her down—in Italy?[7]

c. 1862 1914

322

There came a Day at Summer's full,
Entirely for me—
I thought that such were for the Saints,
Where Resurrections—be—

The Sun, as common, went abroad, 5
The flowers, accustomed blew,[8]
As if no soul the solstice passed
That maketh all things new—

The time was scarce profaned, by speech—
The symbol of a word 10
Was needless, as at Sacrament,[9]
The Wardrobe—of our Lord—

4. This poem is an homage to Elizabeth Barrett Browning (1806–1861), whose *Last Poems* were posthumously published in 1862.
5. Barrett Browning lived with her husband, Robert Browning, in Florence during the last years of her life.
6. I.e., ducal crown.

7. I.e., how much would I grieve for her were I her husband and had buried her in Italy?
8. Bloomed.
9. One of the Christian rites instituted by Jesus Christ.

Each was to each The Sealed Church,
Permitted to commune this—time—
Lest we too awkward show 15
At Supper of the Lamb.[1]

The Hours slid fast—as Hours will,
Clutched tight, by greedy hands—
So faces on two Decks, look back,
Bound to opposing lands— 20

And so when all the time had leaked,
Without external sound
Each bound the Other's Crucifix—
We gave no other Bond—

Sufficient troth, that we shall rise— 25
Deposed—at length, the Grave—
To that new Marriage,
Justified—through Calvaries[2] of Love—

c. 1861 1890

327

Before I got my eye put out
I liked as well to see—
As other Creatures, that have Eyes
And know no other way—

But were it told to me—Today— 5
That I might have the sky
For mine—I tell you that my Heart
Would split, for size of me—

The Meadows—mine—
The Mountains—mine— 10
All Forests—Stintless Stars—
As much of Noon as I could take
Between my finite eyes—

The Motions of the Dipping Birds—
The Morning's Amber Road— 15
For mine—to look at when I liked—
The News would strike me dead—

So safer—guess—with just my soul
Upon the Window pane—
Where other Creatures put their eyes— 20
Incautious—of the Sun—

c. 1862 1891

1. I.e., Jesus. "Sealed": authenticated.
2. Intense sufferings (Calvary was the site of Jesus' Crucifixion). "Justified": judged worthy of salvation.

341

After great pain, a formal feeling comes—
The Nerves sit ceremonious, like Tombs—
The stiff Heart questions was it He, that bore,
And Yesterday, or Centuries before?

The Feet, mechanical, go round— 5
Of Ground, or Air, or Ought—
A Wooden way
Regardless grown,
A Quartz contentment, like a stone—

This is the Hour of Lead— 10
Remembered, if outlived,
As Freezing persons, recollect the Snow—
First—Chill—then Stupor—then the letting go—

c. 1862 1929

365

Dare you see a Soul *at the White Heat*?
Then crouch within the door—
Red—is the Fire's common tint—
But when the vivid Ore
Has vanquished Flame's conditions, 5
It quivers from the Forge
Without a color, but the light
Of unanointed Blaze.
Least[3] Village has its Blacksmith
Whose Anvil's even ring 10
Stands symbol for the finer Forge
That soundless tugs—within—
Refining these impatient Ores
With Hammer, and with Blaze
Until the Designated Light 15
Repudiate the Forge[4]—

c. 1862 1891

384

No Rack[5] can torture me—
My Soul—at Liberty—
Behind this mortal Bone
There knits a bolder One[6]—

3. I.e., the smallest. 5. A device used to torture prisoners.
4. Metaphorically, the world in which her soul has 6. I.e., bone.
been refined.

You cannot prick with saw— 5
Nor pierce with Scimitar—
Two Bodies—therefore be—
Bind One—The Other fly—

The Eagle of his Nest
No easier divest[7]— 10
And gain the Sky
Than mayest Thou—

Except[8] Thyself may be
Thine Enemy—
Captivity is Consciousness— 15
So's Liberty.

c. 1862 1890

392

Through the Dark Sod—as Education—
The Lily passes sure[9]—
Feels her white foot—no trepidation—
Her faith—no fear—

Afterward—in the Meadow— 5
Swinging her Beryl[1] Bell—
The Mold-life[2]—all forgotten—now—
In Ecstasy—and Dell—

c. 1862 1929

401

What Soft—Cherubic Creatures—
These Gentlewomen are—
One would as soon assault a Plush[3]—
Or violate a Star—

Such Dimity[4] Convictions— 5
A Horror so refined
Of freckled Human Nature—
Of Deity—ashamed—

It's such a common—Glory—
A Fisherman's[5]—Degree— 10

7. I.e., it is no easier for the eagle to leave his nest. 2. Its life in the soil.
8. Unless. 3. A thick, rich fabric.
9. Both the sod and the lily's passage through it are 4. A sheer cotton fabric.
comparable to education. 5. An allusion to Christ.
1. Blue.

Redemption—Brittle Lady—
Be so—ashamed of Thee—

c. 1862 1896

425

Good Morning—Midnight—
I'm coming Home—
Day—got tired of Me—
How could I—of Him?

Sunshine was a sweet place— 5
I liked to stay—
But Morn—didn't want me—now—
So—Goodnight—Day!

I can look—can't I—
When the East is Red? 10
The Hills—have a way—then—
That puts the Heart—abroad—

You—are not so fair—Midnight—
I chose—Day—
But—please take a little Girl— 15
He turned away!

c. 1862 1929

435

Much Madness is divinest Sense—
To a discerning Eye—
Much Sense—the starkest Madness—
'Tis the Majority
In this, as All, prevail— 5
Assent—and you are sane—
Demur—you're straightway dangerous—
And handled with a Chain—

c. 1862 1890

441

This is my letter to the World
That never wrote to Me—
The simple News that Nature told—
With tender Majesty

Her[6] Message is committed 5
To Hands I cannot see—
For love of Her—Sweet—countrymen—
Judge tenderly—of Me

c. 1862 1890

454

It was given to me by the Gods—
When I was a little Girl—
They give us Presents most—you know—
When we are new—and small.
I kept it in my Hand— 5
I never put it down—
I did not dare to eat—or sleep—
For fear it would be gone—
I heard such words as "Rich"—
When hurrying to school— 10
From lips at Corners of the Streets—
And wrestled with a smile.
Rich! 'Twas Myself—was rich—
To take the name of Gold—
And Gold to own—in solid Bars— 15
The Difference—made me bold—

c. 1862 1945

462

Why make it[7] doubt—it hurts it so—
So sick—to guess—
So strong—to know—
So brave—upon its little Bed
To tell the very last They said 5
Unto Itself—and smile—And shake—
For that dear—distant—dangerous—Sake—
But—the Instead—the Pinching fear
That Something—it did do—or dare—
Offend the Vision—and it flee— 10
And They no more remember me—
Nor ever turn to tell me why—
Oh, Master, This is Misery—

c. 1862 1929

6. I.e., Nature's. her reference to her *Master,* see letters 233 (p. 886) and
7. For Dickinson's use of *it* to describe herself and for 248 (p. 888).

465

I heard a Fly buzz—when I died—
The Stillness in the Room
Was like the Stillness in the Air—
Between the Heaves of Storm—

The Eyes around—had wrung them dry— 5
And Breaths were gathering firm
For that last Onset—when the King
Be witnessed—in the Room—

I willed my Keepsakes—Signed away
What portion of me be 10
Assignable—and then it was
There interposed a Fly—

With Blue—uncertain stumbling Buzz—
Between the light—and me—
And then the Windows failed—and then 15
I could not see to see—

c. 1862 1896

479

She dealt her pretty words like Blades—
How glittering they shone—
And every One unbared a Nerve
Or wantoned[8] with a Bone—

She never deemed—she hurt— 5
That—is not Steel's Affair—
A vulgar grimace in the Flesh—
How ill the Creatures bear—

To Ache is human—not polite—
The Film upon the eye 10
Mortality's old Custom—
Just locking up—to Die

c. 1862 1929

508

I'm ceded—I've stopped being Theirs—
The name They dropped upon my face
With water, in the country church
Is finished using, now,

8. Toyed.

And They can put it with my Dolls, 5
My childhood, and the string of spools,
I've finished threading—too—

Baptized, before, without the choice,
But this time, consciously, of Grace—
Unto supremest name— 10
Called to my Full—The Crescent[9] dropped—
Existence's whole Arc, filled up,
With one small Diadem.

My second Rank—too small the first—
Crowned—Crowing—on my Father's breast— 15
A half unconscious Queen—
But this time—Adequate—Erect,
With Will to choose, or to reject,
And I choose, just a Crown—

c. 1862 1890

512

The Soul has Bandaged moments—
When too appalled to stir—
She feels some ghastly Fright come up
And stop to look at her—

Salute her—with long fingers— 5
Caress her freezing hair—
Sip, Goblin, from the very lips
The Lover—hovered—o'er—
Unworthy, that a thought so mean
Accost a Theme—so—fair— 10

The soul has moments of Escape—
When bursting all the doors—
She dances like a Bomb, abroad,
And swings upon the Hours,

As do the Bee—delirious borne— 15
Long Dungeoned from his Rose—
Touch Liberty—then know no more,
But Noon, and Paradise—

The Soul's retaken moments—
When, Felon led along, 20
With shackles on the plumed feet,[1]
And staples, in the Song,

9. I.e., the crescent moon, symbolizing the immature rity.
self, compared with the full moon, representing matu- 1. I.e., winged feet.

The Horror welcomes her, again,
These, are not brayed of Tongue—

c. 1862 1945

520

I started Early—Took my Dog—
And visited the Sea—
The Mermaids in the Basement
Came out to look at me—

And Frigates—in the Upper Floor 5
Extended Hempen[2] Hands—
Presuming Me to be a Mouse—
Aground—upon the Sands—

But no Man moved Me—till the Tide
Went past my simple Shoe— 10
And past my Apron—and my Belt
And past my Bodice—too—

And made as He would eat me up—
As wholly as a Dew
Upon a Dandelion's Sleeve— 15
And then—I started—too—

And He—He followed—close behind—
I felt His Silver Heel
Upon my Ankle—Then my Shoes
Would overflow with Pearl— 20

Until We met the Solid Town—
No One He seemed to know—
And bowing—with a Mighty look—
At me—The Sea withdrew—

c. 1862 1891

528

Mine—by the Right of the White Election!
Mine—by the Royal Seal!
Mine—by the Sign in the Scarlet prison—
Bars—cannot conceal!

Mine—here—in Vision—and in Veto! 5
Mine—by the Grave's Repeal—

2. I.e., of rope and sail.

Titled—Confirmed—
Delirious Charter!
Mine—long as Ages steal!

c. 1862 1890

569

I reckon[3]—when I count at all—
First—Poets—Then the Sun—
Then Summer—Then the Heaven of God—
And then—the List is done—

But, looking back—the First so seems 5
To Comprehend the Whole—
The Others look a needless Show—
So I write—Poets—All—

Their Summer—lasts a Solid Year—
They can afford a Sun 10
The East—would deem extravagant—
And if the Further Heaven—

Be Beautiful as they prepare[4]
For Those who worship Them—
It is too difficult a Grace— 15
To justify the Dream—

c. 1862 1929

579

I had been hungry, all the Years—
My Noon had Come—to dine—
I trembling drew the Table near—
And touched the Curious Wine—

'Twas this on Tables I had seen— 5
When turning, hungry, Home
I looked in Windows, for the Wealth
I could not hope—for Mine—

I did not know the ample Bread—
'Twas so unlike the Crumb 10
The Birds and I, had often shared
In Nature's—Dining Room—

The Plenty hurt me—'twas so new—
Myself felt ill—and odd—

3. Take into account, add up. 4. I.e., as the one which they prepare.

As Berry—of a Mountain Bush— 15
Transplanted—to the Road—

Nor was I hungry—so I found
That Hunger—was a way
Of Persons outside Windows—
The Entering—takes away— 20

c. 1862 1891

593

I think I was enchanted
When first a sombre Girl—
I read that Foreign Lady[5]—
The Dark—felt beautiful—

And whether it was noon at night— 5
Or only Heaven—at Noon—
For very Lunacy of Light
I had not power to tell—

The Bees—became as Butterflies—
The Butterflies—as Swans— 10
Approached—and spurned the narrow Grass—
And just the meanest Tunes

That Nature murmured to herself
To keep herself in Cheer—
I took for Giants—practising 15
Titanic Opera—

The Days—to Mighty Metres stept—
The Homeliest—adorned
As if unto a Jubilee
'Twere suddenly confirmed— 20

I could not have defined the change—
Conversion of the Mind
Like Sanctifying in the Soul—
Is witnessed—not explained—

'Twas a Divine Insanity— 25
The Danger to be Sane
Should I again experience—
'Tis Antidote to turn—

To Tomes of solid Witchcraft—
Magicians be asleep— 30

5. A reference to Elizabeth Barrett Browning.

But Magic—hath an Element
Like Deity—to keep—

c. 1862 1935

601

A still—Volcano—Life—
That flickered in the night—
When it was dark enough to do
Without erasing sight—

A quiet—Earthquake Style— 5
Too subtle to suspect
By natures this side Naples[6]—
The North cannot detect

The Solemn—Torrid—Symbol—
The lips that never lie— 10
Whose hissing Corals part—and shut—
And Cities—ooze away—

c. 1862 1929

613

They shut me up in Prose—
As when a little Girl
They put me in the Closet—
Because they liked me "still"—

Still! Could themself have peeped— 5
And seen my Brain—go round—
They might as wise have lodged a Bird
For Treason—in the Pound[7]—

Himself has but to will
And easy as a Star 10
Abolish his Captivity—
And laugh—No more have I[8]—

c. 1862 1935

642

Me from Myself—to banish—
Had I Art[9]—

6. The Italian city closest to the famous volcano 8. I.e., I have to do no more than the bird to be free.
Vesuvius. 9. Skill.
7. An enclosure for animals, here roofless.

Impregnable my Fortress
Unto All Heart—

But since Myself—assault Me— 5
How have I peace
Except by subjugating
Consciousness?

And since We're mutual Monarch
How this be 10
Except by Abdication—
Me—of Me?

c. 1862 1929

657

I dwell in Possibility—
A fairer House than Prose—
More numerous of Windows—
Superior—for Doors—

Of Chambers as the Cedars— 5
Impregnable of Eye—
And for an Everlasting Roof
The Gambrels[1] of the Sky—

Of Visitors—the fairest—
For Occupation[2]—This— 10
The spreading wide my narrow Hands
To gather Paradise—

c. 1862 1929

669

No Romance sold unto[3]
Could so enthrall a Man
As the perusal of
His individual One—
'Tis Fiction's—to dilute to Plausibility 5
Our Novel—When 'tis small enough
To Credit[4]—'Tisn't true!

c. 1862 1914

1. Slanted roofs. 3. I.e., no fantastic tale sold to [a man].
2. Principal business. 4. Believe.

670

One need not be a Chamber—to be Haunted—
One need not be a House—
The Brain has Corridors—surpassing
Material Place—

Far safer, of a Midnight Meeting 5
External Ghost
Than its interior Confronting—
That Cooler Host.

Far safer, through an Abbey gallop,
The Stones a'chase— 10
Than Unarmed, one's a' self encounter—
In lonesome Place—

Ourself behind ourself, concealed—
Should startle most—
Assassin hid in our Apartment 15
Be Horror's least.

The Body—borrows a Revolver—
He bolts the Door—
O'erlooking a superior spectre—
Or More— 20

c. 1863 1891

709

Publication—is the Auction
Of the Mind of Man—
Poverty—be justifying
For so foul a thing

Possibly—but We—would rather 5
From Our Garret go
White—Unto the White Creator—
Than invest—Our Snow—

Thought belong to Him who gave it—
Then—to Him Who bear 10
Its Corporeal illustration—Sell
The Royal Air—

In the Parcel—Be the Merchant
Of the Heavenly Grace—
But reduce no Human Spirit 15
To Disgrace of Price—

c. 1863 1929

712

Because I could not stop for Death—
He kindly stopped for me—
The Carriage held but just Ourselves—
And Immortality.

We slowly drove—He knew no haste 5
And I had put away
My labor and my leisure too,
For His Civility—

We passed the School, where Children strove
At Recess—in the Ring— 10
We passed the Fields of Gazing Grain—
We passed the Setting Sun—

Or rather—He passed Us—
The Dews drew quivering and chill—
For only Gossamer, my Gown— 15
My Tippet—only Tulle[5]—

We paused before a House that seemed
A Swelling of the Ground[6]—
The Roof was scarcely visible—
The Cornice—in the Ground— 20

Since then—'tis Centuries—and yet
Feels shorter than the Day
I first surmised the Horses' Heads
Were toward Eternity—

c. 1863 1890

722

Sweet Mountains—Ye tell Me no lie—
Never deny Me—Never fly—
Those same unvarying Eyes
Turn on Me—when I fail—or feign,
Or take the Royal names in vain— 5
Their far—slow—Violet Gaze—

My Strong Madonnas[7]—Cherish still—
The Wayward Nun—beneath the Hill—
Whose service—is to You—
Her latest[8] Worship—When the Day 10

5. A fine silk net. "Tippet": a feminine garment that
covers the shoulders.
6. I.e., a grave.
7. Italian name for the Virgin Mary; not normally
plural.
8. Last.

Fades from the Firmament away—
To lift Her Brows on You[9]—

c. 1863 1945

732

She rose to His Requirement—dropt
The Playthings of Her life
To take the honorable Work
Of Woman, and of Wife—

If ought She missed in Her new Day, 5
Of Amplitude, or Awe—
Or first Prospective—Or the Gold
In using, wear away,

It lay unmentioned—as the Sea
Develop Pearl, and Weed, 10
But only to Himself—be known
The Fathoms they abide—

c. 1863 1890

754

My Life had stood—a Loaded Gun—
In Corners—till a Day
The Owner passed—identified—
And carried Me away—

And now We roam in Sovereign Woods— 5
And now We hunt the Doe—
And every time I speak for Him—
The Mountains straight reply—

And do I smile, such cordial light
Upon the Valley glow— 10
It is as a Vesuvian[1] face
Had let its pleasure through—

And when at Night—Our good Day done—
I guard My Master's Head—
'Tis better than the Eider Duck's[2] 15
Deep Pillow—to have shared—

To foe of His—I'm deadly foe—
None stir the second time—

9. I.e., to look at you. 2. From which eiderdown is taken.
1. Volcanic, after Mount Vesuvius.

On whom I lay a Yellow Eye—
Or an emphatic Thumb— 20

Though I than He—may longer live
He longer must—than I—
For I have but the power to kill,
Without—the power to die—

c. 1863 1929

858

This Chasm, Sweet, upon my life
I mention it to you,
When Sunrise through a fissure drop
The Day must follow too.

If we demur, its gaping sides 5
Disclose as 'twere a Tomb
Ourself am lying straight wherein
The Favorite of Doom.

When it has just contained a Life
Then, Darling, it will close 10
And yet so bolder every Day
So turbulent it grows

I'm tempted half to stitch it up
With a remaining Breath
I should not miss in yielding, though 15
To Him, t would be Death—

And so I bear it big about
My Burial—before
A Life quite ready to depart
Can harass me no more— 20

c. 1864 1945

959

A loss of something ever felt I—
The first that I could recollect
Bereft I was—of what I knew not
Too young that any should suspect

A Mourner walked among the children 5
I notwithstanding went about
As one bemoaning a Dominion
Itself[3] the only Prince cast out—

3. I.e., the or e bemoaning.

Elder, Today, a session wiser
And fainter, too, as Wiseness is— 10
I find myself still softly searching
For my Delinquent[4] Palaces—

And a Suspicion, like a Finger
Touches my Forehead now and then
That I am looking oppositely 15
For the site of the Kingdom of Heaven—

c. 1864 1945

986

A narrow Fellow in the Grass
Occasionally rides—
You may have met Him—did you not
His notice sudden is—

The Grass divides as with a Comb— 5
A spotted shaft is seen—
And then it closes at your feet
And opens further on—

He likes a Boggy Acre
A Floor too cool for Corn— 10
Yet when a Boy, and Barefoot—
I more than once at Noon
Have passed, I thought, a Whip lash
Unbraiding in the Sun
When stooping to secure it[5] 15
It wrinkled, and was gone—

Several of Nature's People
I know, and they know me—
I feel for them a transport
Of cordiality— 20

But never met this Fellow
Attended,[6] or alone
Without a tighter breathing
And Zero at the Bone—

c. 1865 1866

—— 1072

Title divine—is mine!
The Wife—without the Sign!

4. Lost.
5. I.e., take it. 6. I.e., with others.

Acute Degree—conferred on me—
Empress of Calvary![7]
Royal—all but the Crown! 5
Betrothed—without the swoon
God sends us Women—
When you—hold—Garnet[8] to Garnet—
Gold—to Gold—
Born—Bridalled—Shrouded— 10
In a Day—
Tri Victory
"My Husband"—women say—
Stroking the Melody—
Is *this*—the way? 15

c. 1862 1924

1129

Tell all the Truth but tell it slant—
Success in Circuit[9] lies
Too bright for our infirm Delight
The Truth's superb surprise

As Lightning to the Children eased 5
With explanation kind
The Truth must dazzle gradually
Or every man be blind—

c. 1868 1945

1138

A Spider sewed at Night
Without a Light
Upon an Arc of White.

If Ruff it was of Dame
Or Shroud of Gnome 5
Himself himself inform.[1]

Of Immortality
His Strategy
Was Physiognomy.

c. 1869 1891

7. The hill on which Christ was crucified. 9. I.e., circuitousness.
8. A dark red gemstone. 1. I.e., only he could tell himself.

1282

Art thou the thing I wanted?
Begone—my Tooth has grown[2]—
Supply the minor Palate
That has not starved so long—
I tell thee while I waited 5
The mystery of Food
Increased till I abjured it
And dine without Like God—

First draft

Art thou the thing I wanted?
Begone—my Tooth has grown— 10
Affront a minor palate
Thou could'st not goad so long—

I tell thee while I waited—
The mystery of Food
Increased till I abjured it 15
Subsisting now like God—

Second draft, c. 1873 1945

1317

Abraham to kill him
Was distinctly told[3]—
Isaac was an Urchin—
Abraham was old—

Not a hesitation— 5
Abraham complied—
Flattered by Obeisance
Tyranny demurred—

Isaac—to his children
Lived to tell the tale— 10
Moral—with a Mastiff
Manners may prevail.

c. 1874 1945

1445

Death is the supple Suitor
That wins at last—
It is a stealthy Wooing

2. Both "my taste has matured" and "I am longer in
the tooth" (i.e., older).

3. For the story of Abraham's offering Isaac for sacri-
fice, see Genesis 22.

 Conducted first
 By pallid innuendoes 5
 And dim approach
 But brave at last with Bugles
 And a bisected Coach
 It bears away in triumph
 To Troth unknown 10
 And Kindred as responsive
 As Porcelain.

c. 1878 1945

1562

Her[4] Losses make our Gains ashamed—
She bore Life's empty Pack
As gallantly as if the East
Were swinging at her Back.
Life's empty Pack is heaviest, 5
As every Porter knows—
In vain to punish Honey—
It only sweeter grows.

c. 1883 1894

1651 — ?

 A Word made Flesh[5] is seldom
 And tremblingly partook
 Nor then perhaps reported
 But have I not mistook
 Each one of us has tasted 5
 With ecstasies of stealth
 The very food debated
 To our specific strength—

 A Word that breathes distinctly
 Has not the power to die 10
 Cohesive as the Spirit
 It may expire if He—
 "Made Flesh and dwelt among us"
 Could condescension be
 Like this consent of Language 15
 This loved Philology.[6]

? 1955

4. George Eliot's. Dickinson wrote this poem imme-
diately after reading John Cross s biography of the late
novelist and enclosed it in a letter to the publisher
Thomas Niles, in which she wrote, "The Life of
Marian Evans had much I never knew. A Doom of
Fruit without the Bloom, like the Niger Fig."
5. A biblical description of Christ: "And the Word was
made flesh" (John 1:14).
6. The study of language.

1657

Eden is that old-fashioned House
We dwell in every day
Without suspecting our abode
Until we drive away.

How fair on looking back, the Day 5
We sauntered from the Door—
Unconscious our returning,
But discover it no more.

? 1914

1670

In Winter in my Room
I came upon a Worm—
Pink, lank and warm—
But as he was a worm
And worms presume 5
Not quite with him at home—
Secured him by a string
To something neighboring
And went along.

A Trifle[7] afterward 10
A thing occurred
I'd not believe it if I heard
But state with creeping blood—
A snake with mottles rare
Surveyed my chamber floor 15
In feature as the worm before
But ringed with power—
The very string with which
I tied him—too
When he was mean[8] and new 20
That string was there—

I shrank—"How fair you are"!
Propitiation's claw—
"Afraid," he hissed
"Of me"? 25
"No cordiality"—
He fathomed me—
Then to a Rhythm *Slim*
Secreted in his Form
As Patterns swim 30
Projected him.[9]

7. Shortly.
8. Low, small.

9. I.e., he advanced.

That time I flew
Both eyes his way
Lest he pursue
Nor ever ceased to run 35
Till in a distant Town
Towns on from mine
I set me down
This was a dream.

? 1914

1705

Volcanoes be in Sicily
And South America
I judge from my Geography
Volcanoes nearer here
A Lava step at any time 5
Am I inclined to climb
A Crater I may contemplate
Vesuvius[1] at Home.

? 1914

1732

My life closed twice before its close—
It yet remains to see
If Immortality unveil
A third event to me

So huge, so hopeless to conceive 5
As these that twice befell.
Parting is all we know of heaven,
And all we need of hell.

? 1896

1737

Rearrange a "Wife's" affection!
When they dislocate my Brain!
Amputate my freckled Bosom!
Make me bearded like a man!

Blush, my spirit, in thy Fastness[2]— 5
Blush, my unacknowledged clay[3]—

1. A volcano near Naples, Italy. 3. Flesh.
2. Firm, secure, or constrained position.

Seven years of troth[4] have taught thee
More than Wifehood ever may!

Love that never leaped its socket—
Trust entrenched in narrow pain— 10
Constancy thro' fire—awarded—
Anguish—bare of anodyne![5]

Burden—borne so far triumphant—
None suspect me of the crown,
For I wear the "Thorns"[6] till *Sunset*— 15
Then—my Diadem put on.

Big my Secret but it's *bandaged*—
It will never get away
Till the Day its Weary Keeper
Leads it through the Grave to thee. 20

? 1945

Letters

233 [*Daisy and Her Master*]

TO RECIPIENT UNKNOWN
C. 1861
Master.

If you saw a bullet hit a Bird—and he told you he was'nt shot—you might weep at his courtesy, but you would certainly doubt his word.

One drop more from the gash that stains your Daisy's[1] bosom—then would you *believe*? Thomas' faith in Anatomy, was stronger than his faith in faith.[2] God made me—[Sir][3] Master—I did'nt be—myself. I dont know how it was done. He built the heart in me—Bye and bye it outgrew me—and like the little mother—with the big child—I got tired holding him. I heard of a thing called "Redemption"—which rested men and women. You remember I asked you for it—you gave me something else. I forgot the Redemption [in the Redeemed—I did'nt tell you for a long time, but I knew you had altered me— I] and was tired—no more—[so dear did this stranger become that were it, or my breath—the Alternative—I had tossed the fellow away with a smile.] I am older—tonight, Master—but the love is the same—so are the moon and the crescent. If it had been God's will that I might breathe where you breathed— and find the place—myself—at night—if I (can) never forget that I am not with you—and that sorrow and frost are nearer than I—if I wish with a might I cannot repress—that mine were the Queen's place—the love of the

4. Fidelity, betrothal.
5. Medicine that relieves pain.
6. Christ was made to wear a crown of thorns at his crucifixion.
1. Dickinson's name for herself when writing to her "Master," whose identity is unknown.
2. In John 20:25, "doubting Thomas" refuses to be-

lieve in Christ's Resurrection until "I shall see in his hands the print of the nails, and put my finger into the print of the nails, and thrust my hand into his side."
3. Words which ED crossed out are here enclosed in brackets; alternative readings are in parentheses [Thomas H. Johnson's, Dickinson's editor, note.].

Plantagenet[4] is my only apology—To come nearer than presbyteries[5]—and nearer than the new Coat—that the Tailor made—the prank of the Heart at play on the Heart—in holy Holiday—is forbidden me—You make me say it over—I fear you laugh—when I do not see—[but] "Chillon"[6] is not funny. Have you the Heart in your breast—Sir—is it set like mine—a little to the left—has it the misgiving—if it wake in the night—perchance—itself to it—a timbrel[7] is it—itself to it a tune?

These things are [reverent] holy, Sir, I touch them [reverently] hallowed, but persons who pray—dare remark [our] "Father" You say I do not tell you all—Daisy confessed—and denied not.

Vesuvius dont talk—Etna dont—[Thy] one of them—said a syllable—a thousand years ago, and Pompeii[8] heard it, and hid forever—She could'nt look the world in the face, afterward—I suppose—Bashfull Pompeii! "Tell you of the want"—you know what a leech is, dont you—and [remember that] Daisy's arm is small—and you have felt the horizon hav'nt you—and did the sea—never come so close as to make you dance?

I dont know what you can do for it—thank you—Master—but if I had the Beard on my cheek—like you—and you—had Daisy's petals—and you cared so for me—what would become of you? Could you forget me in fight, or flight—or the foreign land? Could'nt Carlo,[9] and you and I walk in the meadows an hour—and nobody care but the Bobolink—and his—a silver scruple? I used to think when I died—I could see you—so I died as fast as I could—but the "Corporation"[1] are going Heaven too so Eternity] wont be sequestered—now [at all]—Say I may wait for you—say I need go with no stranger to the to me—untried [country] fold—I waited a long time—Master—but I can wait more—wait till my hazel hair is dappled—and you carry the cane—then I can look at my watch—and if the Day is too far declined—we can take the chances [of] for Heaven—What would you do with me if I came "in white?" Have you the little chest to put the Alive—in?

I want to see you more—Sir—than all I wish for in this world—and the wish—altered a little—will be my only one—for the skies.

Could you come to New England—[this summer—could] would you come to Amherst—Would you like to come—Master?

[Would it do harm—yet we both fear God—] Would Daisy disappoint you—no—she would'nt—Sir—it were comfort forever—just to look in your face, while you looked in mine—then I could play in the woods till Dark—till you take me where Sundown cannot find us—and the true keep coming—till the town is full. [Will you tell me if you will?]

I did'nt think to tell you, you did'nt come to me "in white," nor ever told me why,

No Rose, yet felt myself a'bloom,
No Bird—yet rode in Ether.

4. I.e., the love of royalty for royalty (the Plantagenets were an English royal family).
5. The parts of churches reserved for officiating clergy. There has been some speculation that the "Master" was one Reverend Charles Wadsworth.
6. A reference, probably, to Byron's poem *The Prisoner*
of *Chillon* (1816).
7. Small drum or tambourine.
8. A Roman town, buried by an eruption of Mount Vesuvius in A.D. 79. Etna is also a volcano in Italy.
9. Dickinson's dog.
1. The ruling elders of a church.

248 [Daisy Kneels a Culprit]

TO RECIPIENT UNKNOWN
EARLY 1862?

Oh, did I offend it—[Did'nt it want me to tell it the truth] Daisy—Daisy—offend it—who bends her smaller life to his (it's) meeker (lower) every day—who only asks—a task—[who] something to do for love of it—some little way she cannot guess to make that master glad—

A love so big it scares her, rushing among her small heart—pushing aside the blood and leaving her faint (all) and white in the gust's arm—

Daisy—who never flinched thro' that awful parting, but held her life so tight he should not see the wound—who would have sheltered him in her childish bosom (Heart)—only it was'nt big eno' for a Guest so large—*this* Daisy—grieve her Lord—and yet it (she) often blundered—Perhaps she grieved (grazed) his taste—perhaps her odd—Backwoodsman [life] ways [troubled] teased his finer nature (sense). Daisy [fea] knows all that—but must she go unpardoned—teach her, preceptor grace—teach her majesty—Slow (Dull) at patrician things—Even the wren upon her nest learns (knows) more than Daisy dares—

Low at the knee that bore her once unto [royal] wordless rest [now] Daisy [stoops a] kneels a culprit—tell her her [offence] fault—Master—if it is [not so] small eno' to cancel with her life, [Daisy] she is satisfied—but punish [do not] dont banish her—shut her in prison, Sir—only pledge that you will forgive— sometime—before the grave, and Daisy will not mind—She will awake in [his] your likeness.

Wonder stings me more than the Bee—who did never sting me—but made gay music with his might wherever I [may] [should] did go—Wonder wastes my pound, you said I had no size to spare—

You send the water over the Dam in my brown eyes—

I've got a cough as big as a thimble—but I dont care for that—I've got a Tomahawk in my side but that dont hurt me much. [If you] Her master stabs her more—

Wont he come to her—or will he let her seek him, never minding [whatever] so long wandering [out] if to him at last.

Oh how the sailor strains, when his boat is filling—Oh how the dying tug, till the angel comes. Master—open your life wide, and take me in forever, I will never be tired—I will never be noisy when you want to be still. I will be [glad] [as the] your best little girl—nobody else will see me, but you—but that is enough—I shall not want any more—and all that Heaven only will disappoint me—will be because it's not so dear

260 [Say If My Verse Is Alive?]

TO T. W. HIGGINSON[2]
15 APRIL 1862
Mr Higginson,

Are you too deeply occupied to say if my Verse is alive?

The Mind is so near itself—it cannot see, distinctly—and I have none to ask—

2. Thomas Wentworth Higginson (1823–1911), a clergyman and then an essayist and lecturer, had published a *Letter to a Young Contributor* in the *Atlantic Monthly*. Dickinson wrote this letter in response, beginning a correspondence that lasted the rest of Dickinson's life.

Should you think it breathed—and had you the leisure to tell me, I should feel quick gratitude—

If I make the mistake—that you dared to tell me—would give me sincerer honor—toward you—

I enclose my name—asking you, if you please—Sir—to tell me what is true?

That you will not betray me—it is needless to ask—since Honor is its own pawn—

261 [My "Companions"]

To T. W. HIGGINSON
25 APRIL 1862
Mr Higginson,

Your kindness claimed earlier gratitude—but I was ill—and write today, from my pillow.

Thank you for the surgery—it was not so painful as I supposed. I bring you others—as you ask—though they might not differ—

While my thought is undressed—I can make the distinction, but when I put them in the Gown—they look alike, and numb.

You asked how old I was? I made no verse—but one or two—until this winter—Sir—

I had a terror—since September—I could tell to none—and so I sing, as the Boy does by the Burying Ground—because I am afraid—You inquire my Books—For Poets—I have Keats—and Mr and Mrs Browning. For Prose—Mr Ruskin—Sir Thomas Browne—and the Revelations.[3] I went to school—but in your manner of the phrase—had no education. When a little Girl, I had a friend, who taught me Immortality—but venturing too near, himself—he never returned—Soon after, my Tutor, died—and for several years, my Lexicon—was my only companion—Then I found one more—but he was not contented I be his scholar—so he left the Land.

You ask of my Companions Hills—Sir—and the Sundown—and a Dog—large as myself, that my Father bought me—They are better than Beings—because they know—but do not tell—and the noise in the Pool, at Noon—excels my Piano. I have a Brother and Sister—My Mother does not care for thought—and Father, too busy with his Briefs—to notice what we do—He buys me many Books—but begs me not to read them—because he fears they joggle the Mind. They are religious—except me—and address an Eclipse, every morning—whom they call their "Father." But I fear my story fatigues you—I would like to learn—Could you tell me how to grow—or is it unconveyed—like Melody—or Witchcraft?

You speak of Mr Whitman[4]—I never read his Book—but was told that he was disgraceful—

I read Miss Prescott's[5] "Circumstance," but it followed me, in the Dark—so I avoided her—

Two Editors of Journals came to my Father's House, this winter—and asked

3. The visionary last book of the Bible. John Keats (1795–1821), English Romantic poet. Robert Browning, (1812–1889) and Elizabeth Barrett Browning, (1806–1861) English poets. John Ruskin (1819–1900), English art critic and essayist Sir Thomas Browne (1605–1682), English prose writer noted for his ornate style. Higginson's Letter to a Young Contributor had mentioned Ruskin and Browne. 4. A number of contemporary reviewers had attacked the sexually frank Leaves of Grass, by the American poet Walt Whitman (1819–1892), which included poems described as "coarse," "vulgar," and "indecent." 5. Harriet Prescott (1835–1921), popular short-story writer.

me for my Mind—and when I asked them "Why," they said I was penurious—
and they, would use it for the World—

I could not weigh myself—Myself—

My size felt small—to me—I read your Chapters in the Atlantic—and ex-
perienced honor for you—I was sure you would not reject a confiding ques-
tion—

Is this—Sir—what you asked me to tell you?

<div style="text-align: right">Your friend,
E—Dickinson.</div>

<div style="text-align: center">265 [Fame]</div>

To T. W. Higginson
7 June 1862
Dear friend.

Your letter gave no Drunkenness, because I tasted Rum before—Domingo[6]
comes but once—yet I have had few pleasures so deep as your opinion, and if
I tried to thank you, my tears would block my tongue—

My dying Tutor told me that he would like to live till I had been a poet, but
Death was much of Mob as I could master[7]—then—And when far after-
ward—a sudden light on Orchards, or a new fashion in the wind troubled my
attention—I felt a palsy, here—the Verses just relieve—

Your second letter surprised me, and for a moment, swung—I had not sup-
posed it. Your first—gave no dishonor, because the True—are not ashamed—
I thanked you for your justice—but could not drop the Bells whose jingling
cooled my Tramp—Perhaps the Balm, seemed better, because you bled me,
first.

I smile when you suggest that I delay "to publish"—that being foreign to
my thought, as Firmament to Fin—

If fame belonged to me, I could not escape her—if she did not, the longest
day would pass me on the chase—and the approbation of my Dog, would for-
sake me—then—My Barefoot-Rank is better—

You think my gait "spasmodic"[8]—I am in danger—Sir—

You think me "uncontrolled"—I have no Tribunal.

Would you have time to be the "friend" you should think I need? I have a
little shape—it would not crowd your Desk—nor make much Racket as the
Mouse, that dents your Galleries—

If I might bring you what I do—not so frequent to trouble you—and ask
you if I told it clear—'twould be control, to me—

The Sailor cannot see the North—but knows the Needle[9] can—

The "hand you stretch me in the Dark," I put mine in, and turn away—I
have no Saxon,[1] now—

6. Santo Domingo, capital of the Dominican
Republic in the West Indies. Dickinson used the name
in several poems; here it is invoked as a source of rum.
7. I.e., I was unable to write for a "mob"—a popular
audience.
8. I.e., does not scan in proper measures.
9. Compass needle.
1. Language fails me [Johnson's note].

As if I asked a common Alms,
And in my wondering hand
A Stranger pressed a Kingdom,
And I, bewildered, stand—
As if I asked the Orient
Had it for me a Morn—
And it should lift it's purple Dikes,
And shatter me with Dawn!

But, will you be my Preceptor, Mr Higginson?

Your friend
E Dickinson—

268 [My Business Is Circumference]

TO T. W. HIGGINSON
JULY 1862

Could you believe me—without? I had no portrait, now, but am small, like
the Wren, and my Hair is bold, like the Chestnut Bur—and my eyes, like the
Sherry in the Glass, that the Guest leaves—Would this do just as well?

It often alarms Father—He says Death might occur, and he has Molds[2] of
all the rest—but has no Mold of me, but I noticed the Quick wore off those
things, in a few days, and forestall the dishonor—You will think no caprice of
me—

You said "Dark." I know the Butterfly—and the Lizard—and the Orchis[3]—
Are not those *your* Countrymen?

I am happy to be your scholar, and will deserve the kindness, I cannot repay.
If you truly consent, I recite, now—

Will you tell me my fault, frankly as to yourself, for I had rather wince, than
die. Men do not call the surgeon, to commend—the Bone, but to set it, Sir,
and fracture within, is more critical. And for this, Preceptor, I shall bring you—
Obedience—the Blossom from my Garden, and every gratitude I know.
Perhaps you smile at me. I could not stop for that—My Business is
Circumference[4]—An ignorance, not of Customs, but if caught with the
Dawn—or the Sunset see me—Myself the only Kangaroo among the Beauty,
Sir, if you please, it afflicts me, and I thought that instruction would take it
away.

Because you have much business, beside the growth of me—you will ap-
point, yourself, how often I shall come—without your inconvenience. And if
at any time—you regret you received me, or I prove a different fabric to that
you supposed—you must banish me—

When I state myself, as the Representative of the Verse—it does not
mean—me—but a supposed person. You are true, about the "perfection."

Today, makes Yesterday mean.

2. I.e., photographs or pictures.
3. Small orchid; Higginson had written a number of
nature essays.

4. This important Dickinsonian word has been de-
fined by Johnson as "a projection of her imagination
into all relationships of man, nature, and spirit."

You spoke of Pippa Passes[5]—I never heard anybody speak of Pippa Passes—
before.

You see my posture is benighted.

To thank you, baffles me. Are you perfectly powerful? Had I a pleasure you
had not, I could delight to bring it.

Your Scholar

5. Dramatic poem (1841) by Robert Browning.

CHRISTINA ROSSETTI
1830–1894

Admired by such varied contemporaries and descendants as Algernon Charles
Swinburne and Gerard Manley Hopkins, Virginia Woolf and Edith Sitwell,
Christina Rossetti has often been considered a sort of nun of art, a reclusive poet
who lived an uneventful life of austere piety. Yet this apparently retiring woman of
letters began her days as a rebelliously willful child, and what her brother referred
to as her "hushed life-drama" informed a long literary career marked by struggle
and success. Born in 1830, Rossetti was the youngest of four children in an exuber-
ant Anglo-Italian family. Her father, Gabriele Rossetti, had been a famous poet
and politician in Naples. Forced to emigrate because he was a member of the
Carbonari, a revolutionary group seeking to establish a Neapolitan republic, he
settled in London. There he taught Italian, wrote long scholarly treatises on
Dante, and married Frances Polidori, a lively sometime governess who was the
daughter of Gaetano Polidori, another distinguished Italian emigré, and an
Englishwoman named Anna Louisa Pierce. Not surprisingly, all the children of the
Rossetti marriage were energetic and ambitious. Maria, the oldest, wrote her own
study of Dante and eventually joined an Anglican sisterhood devoted to social
work; Dante Gabriel, the second child (known in the family as Gabriel), became a
poet and painter, one of the members of the so-called Pre-Raphaelite Brother-
hood, a group of young men whose radical ideas about aesthetic style were to
influence English art for several generations; and William Michael, the third,
became a well-known man of letters.

Like the four Brontë children, the four young Rossettis read voraciously and
produced several family journals for which both Gabriel and Christina supplied
poems from an early age. Unlike the Brontës, however, the Rossetti children grew
up in a cosmopolitan setting. William later recalled that, bilingual from their
youth, they listened, fascinated, as numerous Italian expatriates "engaged in ani-
mated talk on the affairs of Europe . . . with frequent and fervent recitations of po-
etry." In addition, they spent many summers at the country cottage of their
grandfather Polidori, who introduced them to the pleasures of rural life and who,
in 1847, when Christina was seventeen, published her first volume of verses on his
private printing press. Then, in the summer of 1848, when Gabriel and six friends
formed the Pre-Raphaelite Brotherhood, Christina became romantically involved
with James Collinson, a poet-painter who was one of the "brothers," and the pair
were engaged that autumn. Though their relationship did not finally end in mar-
riage, it is likely that through Collinson, as well as through Gabriel, the young poet
was exposed to some of the most advanced cultural and aesthetic ideas then cur-
rent in London, including a neo-Romantic revival of medievalism that marked
some of her early poems and ballads. Certainly, her work appeared in several issues
of *The Germ*, a short-lived journal that was published by the Brotherhood, and she
sometimes posed as a model for various artists in the group.

Educated at home, Christina Rossetti was raised a strict Anglican, so strict that one of her reasons for breaking her engagement to Collinson was said to be his conversion in 1850 to Roman Catholicism. But she began early to read secular as well as religious poetry from both the Italian and English traditions. Like her sister, Maria, she was meant to follow in her mother's footsteps and become a governess, but such employment seemed hopelessly dreary to her. Perhaps it was no coincidence, then, that in her adolescence she developed a number of mysterious ailments which made it difficult for her to work outside her home. As early as 1855, when she was temporarily employed as a governess, she confessed in a note to William that "I am rejoiced to feel that my health does really unfit me for miscellaneous governessing *en permanence.*"

From the 1850s on, therefore, Christina Rossetti lived mostly at home with her parents, helping to nurse her father, who had become seriously ill in 1843, and after his death in 1854 helping her mother to run the household. Still, she was by no means a recluse. From 1860 to 1870, she did social work at the St. Mary Magdalen Home for Fallen Women on Highgate Hill, and in 1854 she volunteered for service with Florence Nightingale's expedition of nurses to Scutari; evidently, it was only because of her youth that she was not accepted. Besides her involvement in welfare organizations, she led an active social life. In 1862, her brother Gabriel, who had been rootless and depressed after the 1861 suicide of his wife (and one-time mistress), the former Elizabeth Siddal, leased a luxurious residence called Tudor House. There he became the center of a glittering circle that included Meredith, Swinburne, Browning, and Lewis Carroll. Much admired by members of this set, Christina spent a good deal of time at Tudor House.

It was in the 1850s and 1860s, too, that Christina Rossetti had what seem to have been several love affairs whose vicissitudes she may have recorded in the stream of intensely erotic and sometimes painfully renunciatory poems that she produced in this period, including a sequence of love poems in Italian—*Il Rossegiao dell'oriente* (The reddening dawn)—that was discovered after her death. Her brother William consistently claimed that some of her most sorrowful poems were written about her failed relationship with James Collinson, and that others were responses to an amorous entanglement with Charles Bagot Cayley, who proposed to her (and was refused) in 1866. More recently, Lona Mosk Packer, the author of a 1963 biography, has argued that for much of her life Christina was hopelessly in love with William Bell Scott, a friend of the family and a married man, who only briefly returned her affection. Whatever the facts—and it is always possible that Christina's tragic "affair" was more imaginary than real—her poems suggest that at this time she was both scrupulous and sensual, both rigorously moral and richly romantic.

Most important, however, Rossetti's poems of this period reveal that she was already an accomplished artist. Her first collection, *Goblin Market, and Other Poems,* appeared in 1862, with a second edition in 1865. Her second book, *The Prince's Progress, and Other Poems,* was published in 1866. Both volumes included illustrations by her brother Gabriel, and both met with critical acclaim. Thus, by the 1870s Christina had become a seasoned writer with a considerable reputation. In 1870 she published a collection of short stories, in 1872 a book of inventive and charming nursery rhymes, and in 1874 a Lewis Carroll–like tale for children titled *Speaking Likenesses.* In addition, she produced four more books of poems in the course of her career as well as several essays on Dante and six volumes of religious essays. The subject of many critical tributes and the object of a few literary pilgrimages, she developed a briskly professional attitude toward her own work. At a time when there were not yet any international copyright laws to protect the interests of authors, she entered vigorously into royalty negotiations, pressed publishers to see that her books were issued promptly and printed properly, and energetically insisted on retaining what she called "my dear Copyright."

Such professional keenness may at first seem rather at odds with the character

of the voice that emerges from Rossetti's poems. For the most part, her verses are marked by a delicate austerity of style that appears incompatible with some of her businesslike correspondence. Yet it is important to remember that Rossetti was always a highly conscious craftswoman and that she came from a family of aesthetically sophisticated intellectuals, with her brothers, in particular, frequently helping her to revise her work and always helping to guard her professional interests. At the same time, it is important to consider the possibility that Rossetti was quite aware of the distinction between her own position in the world and that occupied by the very brothers for whose assistance she had often to be grateful. Though she had been glad to be liberated from the prison of "governessing *en permanence*," she was then obliged to live decorously at home, a chaste Victorian "spinster," while Gabriel, along with his Pre-Raphaelite Brothers, sowed wild oats and took London by storm, and William pursued a more sedate but equally unconstrained career as a critic and editor.

Even though her letters to publishers hint that she knew her own literary worth, Rossetti's poems suggest that she often had to struggle to renounce or at least moderate worldly ambition as well as to reconcile herself to losses in love. In their various ways, for instance, *Goblin Market* and *The World* meditate on the dangers of desire, especially the dangers of female desire, while *Shut Out, Symbols*, and *The Convent Threshold* explore the arduous difficulties of renunciation. More specifically, *A Triad, A Soul, In an Artist's Studio, Eve*, and *Enrica, 1865* contemplate the limited and sometimes limiting (but sometimes enlivening) range of alternatives available to women, and such so-called mortuary verses as *After Death* and *Dead before Death*—verses written about or from the vantage point of the dead—mourn those limitations. Finally, however, an exuberant fantasy like *Venus's Looking Glass* hints at the possibility of a transfigured world in which female power would be liberated and celebrated.

That Rossetti did allow herself to record hopeful visions is significant in view of the increasingly intense religiosity as well as the undeniable somberness that characterized her later life. In 1871 she suffered a severe attack of Graves' disease, a thyroid disorder that seriously disfigured and debilitated her, and around this time she began to write the devotional essays collected in six volumes published by the Society for the Propagation of Christian Knowledge. When she recovered, her brother William, with whom she, her mother, and two elderly aunts had been living, married Lucy Brown, the daughter of Ford Madox Brown, another one of the Pre-Raphaelite Brotherhood. Tensions arose between Christina and Lucy; though the poet tried hard to assuage these strains, within two years she, her mother, and her aunts established a separate household of their own.

After the three older women died, Christina was left alone, and in 1894 she succumbed to cancer. During the last weeks of her life, a neighbor complained that she could be heard screaming for several hours every evening, and one wonders if such outbursts—which her physician attributed to "hysteria" rather than pain—might represent some portion of the cost exacted by her long renunciation of desire. Despite that cost, however, and though she herself often dreamed of dying into another, more spiritually loving world, the works of this woman whom an admirer once described as a "playful saint" won through to many significant artistic triumphs.

Song

When I am dead, my dearest,
 Sing no sad songs for me;
Plant thou no roses at my head,
 Nor shady cypress tree:

Be the green grass above me 5
 With showers and dewdrops wet;
And if thou wilt, remember,
 And if thou wilt, forget.

I shall not see the shadows,
 I shall not feel the rain;
I shall not hear the nightingale 10
 Sing on, as if in pain
And dreaming through the twilight
 That doth not rise nor set,
Haply[1] I may remember, 15
 And haply may forget.

1848 1862

Symbols

I watched a rosebud very long
 Brought on by dew and sun and shower,
 Waiting to see the perfect[2] flower:
Then, when I thought it should be strong,
 It opened at the matin[3] hour 5
 And fell at evensong.

I watched a nest from day to day,
 A green nest full of pleasant shade,
 Wherein three speckled eggs were laid:
But when they should have hatched in May, 10
 The two old birds had grown afraid
 Or tired, and flew away.

Then in my wrath I broke the bough
 That I had tended so with care,
 Hoping its scent should fill the air; 15
I crushed the eggs, not heeding how
 Their ancient promise had been fair:
 I would have vengeance now.

But the dead branch spoke from the sod,[4]
 And the eggs answered me again: 20
 Because we failed dost thou complain?
Is thy wrath just? And what if God,
 Who waiteth for thy fruits in vain,
 Should also take the rod?[5]

1849 1862

1. Perhaps; by chance.
2. Finished, full-grown.
3. Morning.
4. In Genesis 4.10, God says to Cain, who has mur-

dered his brother Abel, "the voice of thy brother's
blood crieth unto me from the ground."
5. I.e., punish.

After Death

The curtains were half drawn, the floor was swept
 And strewn with rushes, rosemary and may[6]
 Lay thick upon the bed on which I lay,
Where thro' the lattice ivy-shadows crept.
He leaned above me, thinking that I slept 5
 And could not hear him; but I heard him say:
 "Poor child, poor child": and as he turned away
Came a deep silence, and I knew he wept.
He did not touch the shroud, or raise the fold
 That hid my face, or take my hand in his, 10
 Or ruffle the smooth pillows for my head:
 He did not love me living; but once dead
 He pitied me; and very sweet it is
To know he still is warm tho' I am cold.

1849 1862

A Soul

She stands as pale as Parian statues[7] stand;
Like Cleopatra when she turned at bay,
 And felt her strength above the Roman sway,[8]
And felt the aspic[9] writhing in her hand.
Her face is steadfast toward the shadowy land, 5
 For dim beyond it looms the land of day:
 Her feet are steadfast, all the arduous way
That foot-track doth not waver on the sand.
She stands there like a beacon through the night,
 A pale clear beacon where the storm-drift is— 10
She stands alone, a wonder deathly-white:
She stands there patient nerved with inner might,
 Indomitable in her feebleness,
Her face and will athirst against the light.

1854 1896

The World

By day she[1] wooes me, soft, exceeding fair:
 But all night as the moon so changeth she;
 Loathsome and foul with hideous leprosy
And subtle serpents gliding in her hair.
By day she wooes me to the outer air, 5
 Ripe fruits, sweet flowers, and full satiety:

6. Green, flowering branches associated with spring.
7. Ancient statues made with the beautiful white marble from the Greek island of Paros.
8. Sovereign power. Cleopatra (69–30 B.C.), queen of Egypt, was captured by the Romans, who planned to parade her before the populace. Rather than become a public spectacle, she killed herself by letting a poisonous snake bite her; she feels her strength to be greater because she has taken control of her destiny.
9. Variation of "asp," a venomous Egyptian snake.
1. I.e., the world.

But thro' the night, a beast she grins at me,
A very monster void of love and prayer.
By day she stands a lie: by night she stands
 In all the naked horror of the truth 10
With pushing horns and clawed and clutching hands.
Is this a friend indeed; that I should sell
 My soul to her, give her my life and youth,
Till my feet, cloven[2] too, take hold on hell?

1854 1862

Dead before Death

Ah! changed and cold, how changed and very cold!
 With stiffened smiling lips and cold calm eyes:
 Changed, yet the same; much knowing, little wise;
This was the promise of the days of old!
Grown hard and stubborn in the ancient mold,[3] 5
 Grown rigid in the sham of lifelong lies:
 We hoped for better things as years would rise,
But it is ever as a tale once told.
All fallen the blossom that no fruitage bore,
 All lost the present and the future time, 10
All lost, all lost, the lapse[4] that went before:
So lost till death shut-to the opened door,
 So lost from chime to everlasting chime,
So cold and lost for ever evermore.

1854 1862

Cobwebs

It is a land with neither night nor day,
 Nor heat nor cold, nor any wind nor rain,
 Nor hills nor valleys: but one even plain
Stretches through long unbroken miles away,
While through the sluggish air a twilight gray 5
 Broodeth: no moons or seasons wax and wane,
 No ebb and flow are there along the main,[5]
No bud-time, no leaf-falling, there for aye:[6]—
No ripple on the sea, no shifting sand,
 No beat of wings to stir the stagnant space: 10
 No pulse of life through all the loveless land
And loveless sea; no trace of days before,
 No guarded home, no toil-won resting-place,
No future hope, no fear for evermore.

1855 1896

2. The devil is traditionally thought to have cloven hooves.
3. Both a hollow form in which something is given shape, and soil rich in decaying organic matter.

4. Fall (perhaps a reference to the Fall of Adam and Eve in Genesis).
5. Sea.
6. Always.

Shut Out

The door was shut. I looked between
 Its iron bars; and saw it lie,
 My garden, mine, beneath the sky,
Pied⁷ with all flowers bedewed and green:

From bough to bough the song-birds crossed, 5
 From flower to flower the moths and bees;
 With all its nests and stately trees
It had been mine, and it was lost.

A shadowless spirit kept the gate,
 Blank and unchanging like the grave. 10
 I peering thro' said: "Let me have
Some buds to cheer my outcast state."

He answered not. "Or give me, then,
 But one small twig from shrub or tree;
 And bid my home remember me 15
Until I come to it again."

The spirit was silent; but he took
 Mortar and stone to build a wall;
 He left no loophole great or small
Thro' which my straining eyes might look: 20

So now I sit here quite alone
 Blinded with tears; nor grieve for that,
 For nought is left worth looking at
Since my delightful land is gone.

A violet bed is budding near, 25
 Wherein a lark has made her nest:
 And good they are, but not the best;
And dear they are, but not so dear.

1856 1862

A Triad⁸

Three sang of love together: one with lips
 Crimson, with cheeks and bosom in a glow,
Flushed to the yellow hair and finger tips;
 And one there sang who soft and smooth as snow
 Bloomed like a tinted hyacinth at a show; 5
And one was blue with famine after love,
 Who like a harpstring snapped rang harsh and low
The burden⁹ of what those were singing of.

7. Covered with multicolored patches.
8. A musical chord formed of three notes; also simply, a group of three.
9. In music, a bass part.

One shamed herself in love; one temperately
 Grew gross[1] in soulless love, a sluggish wife; 10
One famished died for love. Thus two of three
 Took death for love and won him after strife;
One droned in sweetness like a fattened bee:
 All on the threshold, yet all short of life.

1856 1862

A Birthday

My heart is like a singing bird
 Whose nest is in a watered shoot;
My heart is like an apple tree
 Whose boughs are bent with thickset fruit;
My heart is like a rainbow shell 5
 That paddles in a halcyon sea;
My heart is gladder than all these
 Because my love is come to me.

Raise me a dais[2] of silk and down;
 Hang it with vair[3] and purple dyes; 10
Carve it in doves and pomegranates,
 And peacocks with a hundred eyes;
Work it in gold and silver grapes,
 In leaves and silver fleurs-de-lys,[4]
Because the birthday of my life 15
 Is come, my love is come to me.

1857 1861

Up-hill

Does the road wind up-hill all the way?
 Yes, to the very end.
Will the day's journey take the whole long day?
 From morn to night, my friend.

But is there for the night a resting-place? 5
 A roof for when the slow dark hours begin.
May not the darkness hide it from my face?
 You cannot miss that inn.[5]

Shall I meet other wayfarers at night?
 Those who have gone before. 10
Then must I knock, or call when just in sight?
 They will not keep you standing at that door.

1. Fat.
2. A platform, often hung with cloth and ornately dec-
orated.
3. Gray and white squirrel fur.

4. Conventionalized emblem of an iris, used in her-
aldry.
5. I.e., death.

> Shall I find comfort, travel-sore and weak?
> Of labor you shall find the sum.
> Will there be beds for me and all who seek? 15
> Yea, beds for all who come.

1858 1861

The Convent Threshold

There's blood between us, love, my love,
There's father's blood, there's brother's blood;
And blood's a bar I cannot pass:
I choose the stairs that mount above,
Stair after golden skyward stair, 5
To city and to sea of glass.
My lily feet are soiled with mud,
With scarlet mud which tells a tale
Of hope that was, of guilt that was,
Of love that shall not yet avail; 10
Alas, my heart, if I could bare
My heart, this selfsame stain is there:
I seek the sea of glass and fire[1]
To wash the spot, to burn the snare;[2]
Lo, stairs are meant to lift us higher: 15
Mount with me, mount the kindled stair.

Your eyes look earthward, mine look up.
I see the far-off city grand,
Beyond the hills a watered land,
Beyond the gulf a gleaming strand 20
Of mansions where the righteous sup;
Who sleep at ease among their trees,
Or wake to sing a cadenced hymn
With Cherubim and Seraphim;[3]
They bore the Cross, they drained the cup,[4] 25
Racked, roasted, crushed, wrenched limb from limb,
They the offscouring[5] of the world:
The heaven of starry heavens unfurled,
The sun before their face is dim.

You looking earthward, what see you? 30
Milk-white, wine-flushed among the vines,
Up and down leaping, to and fro,
Most glad, most full, made strong with wines,
Blooming as peaches pearled with dew,
Their golden windy hair afloat, 35
Love-music warbling in their throat,
Young men and women come and go.

1. An image taken from St. John's vision of the Day of Judgment in Revelation 15:2.
2. The spot and the snare are emblems of worldly sin and temptation.
3. Two orders of angels in heaven.
4. Jesus's Crucifixion is spoken of in the New Testament as a bitter cup.
5. Garbage, filth.

You linger, yet the time is short:
Flee for your life, gird up your strength
To flee: the shadows stretched at length
Show that day wanes, that night draws nigh; 40
Flee to the mountain, tarry not
Is this a time for smile and sigh
For songs among the secret trees
Where sudden blue birds nest and sport? 45
The time is short and yet you stay:
Today while it is called today
Kneel, wrestle, knock, do violence, pray:
Today is short, tomorrow nigh:
Why will[6] you die? why will you die? 50

You sinned with me a pleasant sin:
Repent with me, for I repent.
Woe's me the lore I must unlearn!
Woe's me that easy way we went
So rugged when I would return! 55
How long until my sleep begin.
How long shall stretch these nights and days?
Surely, clean Angels cry, she prays;
She laves[7] her soul with tedious tears:
How long must stretch these years and years? 60

I turn from you my cheeks and eyes,
My hair which you shall see no more—
Alas for joy that went before,
For joy that dies, for love that dies.
Only my lips still turn to you, 65
My livid lips that cry, Repent.
Oh weary life, Oh weary Lent,[8]
Oh weary time whose stars are few.

How should I rest in Paradise,
Or sit on steps of heaven alone? 70
If Saints and Angels spoke of love
Should I not answer from my throne:
Have pity upon me, ye my friends,
For I have heard the sound thereof:
Should I not turn with yearning eyes, 75
Turn earthwards with a pitiful pang?
Oh save me from a pang in heaven.
By all the gifts we took and gave,
Repent, repent, and be forgiven:
This life is long, but yet it ends; 80
Repent and purge your soul and save:
No gladder song the morning stars

6. I.e., do you wish?
7. Washes.
8. In the Christian church, the period of forty days be-

fore Easter observed with penitance and fasting to re-
call Christ's fasting in the wilderness. More generally, a
time of pious self-deprivation.

Upon their birthday morning sang
Than Angels sing when one repents.

I tell you what I dreamed last night: 85
A spirit with transfigured face
Fire-footed clomb an infinite space.
I heard his hundred pinions[9] clang,
Heaven-bells rejoicing rang and rang,
Heaven-air was thrilled with subtle scents, 90
Worlds spun upon their rushing cars:[1]
He mounted shrieking: "Give me light."
Still light was poured on him, more light;
Angels, Archangels[2] he outstripped

Exultant in exceeding might, 95
And trod the skirts of Cherubim.
Still "Give me light," he shrieked; and dipped
His thirsty face, and drank a sea,
Athirst with thirst it could not slake.
I saw him, drunk with knowledge, take 100
From aching brows the aureole[3] crown—
His locks writhed like a cloven snake—
He left his throne to grovel down
And lick the dust of Seraphs' feet:
For what is knowledge duly weighed? 105
Knowledge is strong, but love is sweet;
Yea all the progress he had made
Was but to learn that all is small
Save love, for love is all in all.

I tell you what I dreamed last night: 110
It was not dark, it was not light,
Cold dews had drenched my plenteous hair
Thro' clay;[4] you came to seek me there.
And "Do you dream of me?" you said.
My heart was dust that used to leap 115
To you; I answered half asleep:
"My pillow is damp, my sheets are red,
There's a leaden tester[5] to my bed:
Find you a warmer playfellow,
A warmer pillow for your head, 120
A kinder love to love than mine."
You wrung your hands; while I like lead
Crushed downwards thro' the sodden earth:
You smote your hands but not in mirth,
And reeled but were not drunk with wine. 125

For all night long I dreamed of you:
I woke and prayed against my will,

9. Wings. "Clomb": climbed. 3. Halo.
1. Chariots. 4. The clay of the grave.
2. The highest order of angels. 5. Canopy; here the coffin's lid.

Then slept to dream of you again.
At length I rose and knelt and prayed:
I cannot write the words I said, 130
My words were slow, my tears were few;
But thro' the dark my silence spoke
Like thunder. When this morning broke,
My face was pinched, my hair was gray,
And frozen blood was on the sill 135
Where stifling in my struggle I lay.

If now you saw me you would say:
Where is the face I used to love?
And I would answer: Gone before;
It tarries veiled in paradise. 140
When once the morning star shall rise,
When earth with shadow flees away
And we stand safe within the door,
Then you shall lift the veil thereof.
Look up, rise up: for far above 145
Our palms[6] are grown, our place is set;
There we shall meet as once we met
And love with old familiar love.

1858 1862

Goblin Market

Morning and evening
Maids heard the goblins cry:
"Come buy our orchard fruits,
Come buy, come buy:
Apples and quinces, 5
Lemons and oranges,
Plump unpecked cherries,
Melons and raspberries,
Bloom-down-cheeked peaches,
Swart-headed[1] mulberries, 10
Wild free-born cranberries,
Crabapples, dewberries,
Pineapples, blackberries,
Apricots, strawberries;—
All ripe together 15
In summer weather,—
Morns that pass by,
Fair eyes that fly;
Come buy, come buy:
Our grapes fresh from the vine, 20
Pomegranates full and fine,
Dates and sharp bullaces,

6. Trees whose leaves are associated with victory, tri- 1. Black-headed.
umph.

Rare pears and greengages,
Damsons[2] and bilberries,
Taste them and try: 25
Currants and gooseberries,
Bright-fire-like barberries,
Figs to fill your mouth,
Citrons from the South,
Sweet to tongue and sound to eye; 30
Come buy, come buy."

Evening by evening
Among the brookside rushes,
Laura bowed her head to hear,
Lizzie veiled her blushes: 35
Crouching close together
In the cooling weather,
With clasping arms and cautioning lips,
With tingling cheeks and finger tips.
"Lie close," Laura said, 40
Pricking up her golden head:
"We must not look at goblin men,
We must not buy their fruits:
Who knows upon what soil they fed
Their hungry thirsty roots?" 45
"Come buy," call the goblins
Hobbling down the glen.
"Oh," cried Lizzie, "Laura, Laura,
You should not peep at goblin men."
Lizzie covered up her eyes, 50
Covered close lest they should look;
Laura reared her glossy head,
And whispered like the restless brook:
"Look, Lizzie, look, Lizzie,
Down the glen tramp little men. 55
One hauls a basket,
One bears a plate,
One lugs a golden dish
Of many pounds' weight.
How fair the vine must grow 60
Whose grapes are so luscious;
How warm the wind must blow
Through those fruit bushes."
"No," said Lizzie: "No, no, no;
Their offers should not charm us, 65
Their evil gifts would harm us."
She thrust a dimpled finger
In each ear, shut eyes and ran:
Curious Laura chose to linger
Wondering at each merchant man. 70
One had a cat's face,
One whisked a tail,

2. Bullaces, greengages, and damsons are plums.

One tramped at a rat's pace,
One crawled like a snail,
One like a wombat prowled obtuse and furry, 75
One like a ratel tumbled hurry skurry.
She heard a voice like voice of doves
Cooing all together:
They sounded kind and full of loves
In the pleasant weather. 80

Laura stretched her gleaming neck
Like a rush-imbedded swan,
Like a lily from the beck,[4]
Like a moonlit poplar branch,
Like a vessel at the launch 85
When its last restraint is gone

Backwards up the mossy glen
Turned and trooped the goblin men,
With their shrill repeated cry,
"Come buy, come buy." 90
When they reached where Laura was
They stood stock still upon the moss,
Leering at each other,
Brother with queer brother;
Signaling each other, 95
Brother with sly brother.
One set his basket down,
One reared his plate;
One began to weave a crown
Of tendrils, leaves, and rough nuts brown 100
(Men sell not such in any town);
One heaved the golden weight
Of dish and fruit to offer her:
"Come buy, come buy," was still their cry.
Laura stared but did not stir, 105
Longed but had no money.
The whisk-tailed merchant bade her taste
In tones as smooth as honey,
The cat-faced purred,
The rat-paced spoke a word 110
Of welcome, and the snail-paced even was heard;
One parrot-voiced and jolly
Cried "Pretty Goblin" still for "Pretty Polly";
One whistled like a bird.

But sweet-tooth Laura spoke in haste 115
"Good Folk, I have no coin;
To take were to purloin:
I have no copper in my purse,
I have no silver either,
And all my gold is on the furze[5] 120

3. A South African badgerlike creature. 5. A spiny shrub.
4. Small brook.

That shakes in windy weather
Above the rusty heather."
"You have much gold upon your head."
They answered all together:
"Buy from us with a golden curl." 125
She clipped a precious golden lock,
She dropped a tear more rare than pearl,
Then sucked their fruit globes fair or red.
Sweeter than honey from the rock,
Stronger than man-rejoicing wine, 130
Clearer than water flowed that juice;
She never tasted such before,
How should it cloy with length of use?
She sucked and sucked and sucked the more
Fruits which that unknown orchard bore, 135
She sucked until her lips were sore;
Then flung the emptied rinds away
But gathered up one kernel stone,
And knew not was it night or day
As she turned home alone. 140

Lizzie met her at the gate
Full of wise upbraidings:
"Dear, you should not stay so late,
Twilight is not good for maidens;
Should not loiter in the glen 145
In the haunts of goblin men.
Do you not remember Jeanie,
How she met them in the moonlight,
Took their gifts both choice and many,
Ate their fruits and wore their flowers 150
Plucked from bowers
Where summer ripens at all hours?
But ever in the noonlight
She pined and pined away;
Sought them by night and day, 155
Found them no more, but dwindled and grew gray;
Then fell with the first snow,
While to this day no grass will grow
Where she lies low:
I planted daisies there a year ago 160
That never blow.
You should not loiter so."
"Nay, hush," said Laura:
"Nay, hush, my sister:
I ate and ate my fill, 165
Yet my mouth waters still:
Tomorrow night I will
Buy more"; and kissed her.
"Have done with sorrow;
I'll bring you plums tomorrow 170
Fresh on their mother twigs,
Cherries worth getting;

You cannot think what figs
My teeth have met in,
What melons icy-cold 175
Piled on a dish of gold
Too huge for me to hold,
What peaches with a velvet nap,
Pellucid grapes without one seed:
Odorous indeed must be the mead 180
Whereon they grow, and pure the wave they drink
With lilies at the brink,
And sugar-sweet their sap."

Golden head by golden head,
Like two pigeons in one nest 185
Folded in each other's wings,
They lay down in their curtained bed:
Like two blossoms on one stem,
Like two flakes of new-fallen snow,
Like two wands of ivory 190
Tipped with gold for awful[6] kings.
Moon and stars gazed in at them,
Wind sang to them lullaby,
Lumbering owls forebore to fly,
Not a bat flapped to and fro 195
Round their nest:
Cheek to cheek and breast to breast
Locked together in one nest.

Early in the morning
When the first cock crowed his warning, 200
Neat like bees, as sweet and busy,
Laura rose with Lizzie:
Fetched in honey, milked the cows,
Aired and set to rights the house,
Kneaded cakes of whitest wheat, 205
Cakes for dainty mouths to eat,
Next churned butter, whipped up cream,
Fed their poultry, sat and sewed;
Talked as modest maidens should:
Lizzie with an open heart, 210
Laura in an absent dream,
One content, one sick in part;
One warbling for the mere bright day's delight,
One longing for the night.

At length slow evening came: 215
They went with pitchers to the reedy brook;
Lizzie most placid in her look,
Laura most like a leaping flame,
They drew the gurgling water from its deep.

6. Awe-inspiring.

Lizzie plucked purple and rich golden flags, 220
Then turning homeward said: "The sunset flushes
Those furthest loftiest crags;
Come, Laura, not another maiden lags.
No willful squirrel wags,
The beasts and birds are fast asleep." 225
But Laura loitered still among the rushes.
And said the bank was steep.

And said the hour was early still,
The dew not fallen, the wind not chill;
Listening ever, but not catching 230
The customary cry,
"Come buy, come buy,"
With its iterated jingle
Of sugar-baited words:
Not for all her watching 235
Once discerning even one goblin
Racing, whisking, tumbling, hobbling—
Let alone the herds
That used to tramp along the glen,
In groups or single, 240
Of brisk fruit-merchant men.
Till Lizzie urged, "O Laura, come;
I hear the fruit-call, but I dare not look:
You should not loiter longer at this brook:
Come with me home. 245
The stars rise, the moon bends her arc,
Each glow-worm winks her spark,
Let us get home before the night grows dark:
For clouds may gather
Though this is summer weather, 250
Put out the lights and drench us through;
Then if we lost our way what should we do?"

Laura turned cold as stone
To find her sister heard that cry alone,
That goblin cry, 255
"Come buy our fruits, come buy."
Must she then buy no more such dainty fruit?
Must she no more such succous pasture find,
Gone deaf and blind?
Her tree of life dropped from the root: 260
She said not one word in her heart's sore ache:
But peering through the dimness, nought discerning,
Trudged home, her pitcher dripping all the way;
So crept to bed, and lay
Silent till Lizzie slept; 265
Then sat up in a passionate yearning.
And gnashed her teeth for balked desire, and wept
As if her heart would break.

Day after day, night after night,

Laura kept watch in vain
In sullen silence of exceeding pain.
She never caught again the goblin cry,
"Come buy, come buy";—
She never spied the goblin men
Hawking their fruits along the glen: 275
But when the noon waxed bright
Her hair grew thin and gray;
She dwindled, as the fair full moon doth turn
To swift decay and burn
Her fire away. 280

One day remembering her kernelstone
She set it by a wall that faced the south:
Dewed it with tears, hoped for a root,
Watched for a waxing shoot,
But there came none. 285
It never saw the sun,
It never felt the trickling moisture run:
While with sunk eyes and faded mouth
She dreamed of melons, as a traveler sees
False waves in desert drouth 290
With shade of leaf-crowned trees,
And burns the thirstier in the sandful breeze.

She no more swept the house,
Tended the fowls or cows,
Fetched honey, kneaded cakes of wheat, 295
Brought water from the brook:
But sat down listless in the chimneynook
And would not eat.

Tender Lizzie could not bear
To watch her sister's cankerous care,[7] 300
Yet not to share.
She night and morning
Caught the goblins' cry:
"Come buy our orchard fruits,
Come buy, come buy";— 305
Beside the brook, along the glen,
She heard the tramp of goblin men,
The voice and stir
Poor Laura could not hear;
Longed to buy fruit to comfort her, 310
But feared to pay too dear.
She thought of Jeanie in her grave,
Who should have been a bride;
But who for joys brides hope to have
Fell sick and died 315
In her gay prime,

7. I.e., the core eating away at her.

In earliest winter time,
With the first glazing rime,
With the first snow-fall of crisp winter time.

Till Laura dwindling 320
Seemed knocking at Death's door.
Then Lizzie weighed no more
Better and worse;
But put a silver penny in her purse,
Kissed Laura, crossed the heath with clumps of furze 325
At twilight, halted by the brook:
And for the first time in her life
Began to listen and look.

Laughed every goblin
When they spied her peeping: 330
Came towards her hobbling,
Flying, running, leaping,
Puffing and blowing,
Chuckling, clapping, crowing,
Cluckling and gobbling, 335
Mopping and mowing,
Full of airs and graces,
Pulling wry faces,
Demure grimaces,
Cat-like and rat-like, 340
Ratel- and wombat-like,
Snail-paced in a hurry,
Parrot-voiced and whistler,
Helter skelter, hurry skurry,
Chattering like magpies, 345
Fluttering like pigeons,
Gliding like fishes,—
Hugged her and kissed her:
Squeezed and caressed her:
Stretched up their dishes, 350
Panniers, and plates:
"Look at our apples
Russet and dun,
Bob at our cherries,
Bite at our peaches, 355
Citrons and dates,
Grapes for the asking,
Pears red with basking
Out in the sun,
Plums on their twigs; 360
Pluck them and suck them,
Pomegranates, figs."—

"Good folk," said Lizzie,
Mindful of Jeanie:
"Give me much and many":— 365
Held out her apron,

Tossed them her penny
"Nay, take a seat with us,
Honor and eat with us,"
They answered grinning:
"Our feast is but beginning. 370
Night yet is early,
Warm and dew-pearly,
Wakeful and starry:
Such fruits as these
No man can carry; 375
Half their bloom would fly,
Half their dew would dry,
Half their flavor would pass by
Sit down and feast with us,
Be welcome guest with us, 380
Cheer you and rest with us."—
"Thank you," said Lizzie: "But one waits
At home alone for me:
So without further parleying,
If you will not sell me any 385
Of your fruits though much and many,
Give me back my silver penny
I tossed you for a fee."—
They began to scratch their pates,
No longer wagging, purring, 390
But visibly demurring,
Grunting and snarling.
One called her proud,
Cross-grained, uncivil; 395
Their tones waxed loud,
Their looks were evil.
Lashing their tails
They trod and hustled her,
Elbowed and jostled her, 400
Clawed with their nails,
Barking, mewing, hissing, mocking,
Tore her gown and soiled her stocking,
Twitched her hair out by the roots,
Stamped upon her tender feet, 405
Held her hands and squeezed their fruits
Against her mouth to make her eat.

White and golden Lizzie stood,
Like a lily in a flood,—
Like a rock of blue-veined stone 410
Lashed by tides obstreperously,—
Like a beacon left alone
In a hoary roaring sea,
Sending up a golden fire,—
Like a fruit-crowned orange-tree 415
White with blossoms honey-sweet
Sore beset by wasp and bee,—
Like a royal virgin town

Topped with gilded dome and spire
Close beleaguered by a fleet 420
Mad to tug her standard down.

One may lead a horse to water,
Twenty cannot make him drink.
Though the goblins cuffed and caught her,
Coaxed and fought her, 425
Bullied and besought her,
Scratched her, pinched her black as ink,
Kicked and knocked her,
Mauled and mocked her,
Lizzie uttered not a word; 430
Would not open lip from lip
Lest they should cram a mouthful in:
But laughed in heart to feel the drip
Of juice that syruped all her face,
And lodged in dimples of her chin, 435
And streaked her neck which quaked like curd.
At last the evil people,
Worn out by her resistance,
Flung back her penny, kicked their fruit
Along whichever road they took, 440
Not leaving root or stone or shoot;
Some writhed into the ground,
Some dived into the brook
With ring and ripple,
Some scudded on the gale without a sound, 445
Some vanished in the distance.

In a smart, ache, tingle,
Lizzie went her way;
Knew not was it night or day;
Sprang up the bank, tore through the furze, 450
Threaded copse and dingle,
And heard her penny jingle
Bouncing in her purse,—
Its bounce was music to her ear.
She ran and ran 455
As if she feared some goblin man
Dogged her with gibe or curse
Or something worse:
But not one goblin skurried after,
Nor was she pricked by fear; 460
The kind heart made her windy-paced
That urged her home quite out of breath with haste
And inward laughter.

She cried, "Laura," up the garden,
"Did you miss me? 465
Come and kiss me.
Never mind my bruises,
Hug me, kiss me, suck my juices

Squeezed from goblin fruits for you,
Goblin pulp and goblin dew. 470
Eat me, drink me, love me;
Laura, make much of me;
For your sake I have braved the glen
And had to do with goblin merchant men."

Laura started from her chair, 475
Flung her arms up in the air,
Clutched her hair:
"Lizzie, Lizzie, have you tasted
For my sake the fruit forbidden?
Must your light like mine be hidden, 480
Your young life like mine be wasted,
Undone in mine undoing,
And ruined in my ruin,
Thirsty, cankered, goblin-ridden?"—
She clung about her sister, 485
Kissed and kissed and kissed her:
Tears once again
Refreshed her shrunken eyes,
Dropping like rain
After long sultry drouth; 490
Shaking with anguish, fear, and pain,
She kissed and kissed her with a hungry mouth.

Her lips began to scorch,
That juice was wormwood to her tongue,
She loathed the feast: 495
Writhing as one possessed she leaped and sung,
Rent all her robe, and wrung
Her hands in lamentable haste,
And beat her breast.
Her locks streamed like the torch 500
Borne by a racer at full speed,
Or like the mane of horses in their flight,
Or like an eagle when she stems[3] the light
Straight toward the sun,
Or like a caged thing freed, 505
Or like a flying flag when armies run.

Swift fire spread through her veins, knocked at her heart,
Met the fire smoldering there
And overbore its lesser flame;
She gorged on bitterness without a name: 510
Ah fool, to choose such part
Of soul-consuming care!
Sense failed in the mortal strife:
Like the watch-tower of a town
Which an earthquake shatters down, 515

8. Makes headway against.

Like a lightning-stricken mast,
Like a wind-uprooted tree
Spun about,
Like a foam-topped waterspout
Cast down headlong in the sea, 520
She fell at last;
Pleasure past and anguish past,
Is it death or is it life?

Life out of death.
That night long Lizzie watched by her, 525
Counted her pulse's flagging stir,
Felt for her breath,
Held water to her lips, and cooled her face
With tears and fanning leaves.
But when the first birds chirped about their eaves, 530
And early reapers plodded to the place
Of golden sheaves,
And dew-wet grass
Bowed in the morning winds so brisk to pass,
And new buds with new day 535
Opened of cup-like lilies on the stream,
Laura awoke as from a dream,
Laughed in the innocent old way,
Hugged Lizzie but not twice or thrice;
Her gleaming locks showed not one thread of gray, 540
Her breath was sweet as May,
And light danced in her eyes.

Days, weeks, months, years
Afterwards, when both were wives
With children of their own; 545
Their mother-hearts beset with fears,
Their lives bound up in tender lives:
Laura would call the little ones
And tell them of her early prime,
Those pleasant days long gone 550
Of not-returning time:
Would talk about the haunted glen,
The wicked quaint fruit-merchant men,
Their fruits like honey to the throat
But poison in the blood 555
(Men sell not such in any town):
Would tell them how her sister stood
In deadly peril to do her good,
And win the fiery antidote:
Then joining hands to little hands 560
Would bid them cling together,—
"For there is no friend like a sister
In calm or stormy weather;
To cheer one on the tedious way,
To fetch one if one goes astray, 565

To lift one if one totters down,
To strengthen whilst one stands."

1859 1862

In an Artist's Studio

One face looks out from all his[1] canvases,
 One selfsame figure sits or walks or leans:
 We found her hidden just behind those screens,
That mirror[2] gave back all her loveliness.
A queen in opal or in ruby dress, 5
 A nameless girl in freshest summer-greens,
 A saint, an angel—every canvas means
The same one meaning, neither more nor less.
He feeds upon her face by day and night,
 And she with true kind eyes looks back on him, 10
Fair as the moon and joyful as the light
 Not wan with waiting, not with sorrow dim;
Not as she is, but was when hope shone bright;
 Not as she is, but as she fills his dream.

1861 1896

Eve[3]

"While I sit at the door
Sick to gaze within
Mine eye weepeth sore
For sorrow and sin:
As a tree my sin stands 5
To darken all lands;
Death is the fruit it bore.

"How have Eden bowers grown
Without Adam to bend them!
How have Eden flowers blown[4] 10
Squandering their sweet breath
Without me to tend them!
The Tree of Life was ours,
Tree twelvefold-fruited,
Most lofty tree that flowers, 15
Most deeply rooted:
I chose the tree of death.

"Hadst thou but said me nay,
Adam, my brother,
I might have pined away; 20

1. Dante Gabriel Rossetti, Christina Rossetti's brother. The "face" is that of Elizabeth Siddall, whom Dante Gabriel later married. Christina herself also posed for many of his paintings.
2. The artist's eye and/or his painting. "Screens": the paintings; however, nude models were protected from the eyes of visitors to the artist's studio by screens, so the word creates an ambiguity throughout the poem.

3. The first woman and wife of Adam, who, in Genesis 3, is cajoled by the serpent into eating fruit from the forbidden Tree of Knowledge and who then gives the fruit to Adam to eat, thus bringing about the expulsion from Eden and the emergence of death into the world.
4. Blossomed

I, but none other:
God might have let thee stay
Safe in our garden,
By putting me away
Beyond all pardon. 25

"I, Eve, sad mother
Of all who must live,
I, not another,
Plucked bitterest fruit to give
My friend, husband, lover;— 30
O wanton eyes, run over;
Who but I should grieve?—
Cain hath slain his brother:[5]
Of all who must die mother,
Miserable Eve!" 35

Thus she sat weeping,
Thus Eve our mother,
Where one lay sleeping
Slain by his brother.
Greatest and least 40
Each piteous beast
To hear her voice
Forgot his joys
And set aside his feast.

The mouse paused in his walk 45
And dropped his wheaten stalk;
Grave cattle wagged their heads
In rumination;[6]
The eagle gave a cry
From his cloud station; 50
Larks on thyme beds
Forbore to mount or sing;
Bees drooped upon the wing;
The raven perched on high
Forgot his ration; 55
The conies[7] in their rock,
A feeble nation,
Quaked sympathetical;
The mocking-bird left off to mock;
Huge camels knelt as if 60
In deprecation;
The kind hart's tears were falling;
Chattered the wistful stork;
Dove-voices with a dying fall[8]
Cooed desolation 65
Answering grief by grief.

5. In Genesis 4, Adam and Eve's son Cain kills his
brother Abel.
6. Both cud chewing and, usually in human applica-
tion, deep thought.
7. Rabbits.
8. Dying away, trailing off, but also with a suggestion
of the Fall of Adam and Eve.

Only the serpent in the dust
 Wriggling and crawling,
Grinned an evil grin and thrust
 His tongue out with its fork. 70

1865 1866

Enrica, 1865[9]

She came among us from the South
 And made the North her home awhile:
 Our dimness brightened in her smile,
Our tongue[1] grew sweeter in her mouth.

We chilled beside her liberal[2] glow, 5
 She dwarfed us by her ampler scale,
 Her full-blown blossom made us pale,
She summer-like and we like snow.

We Englishwomen, trim, correct,
 All minted[3] in the selfsame mold, 10
 Warm-hearted but of semblance cold,
All-courteous out of self-respect.

She woman in her natural grace,
 Less trammelled[4] she by lore of school,
 Courteous by nature not by rule, 15
Warm-hearted and of cordial face.

So for awhile she made her home
 Among us in the rigid North,
 She who from Italy came forth
And scaled the Alps and crossed the foam. 20

But if she found us like our sea,
 Of aspect colorless and chill,
 Rock-girt; like it she found us still
Deep at our deepest, strong and free.

1865 1875

Venus's Looking-Glass

I marked where lovely Venus[5] and her court
 With song and dance and merry laugh went by;

9. The poem is about a woman of Rossetti's acquaintance named Enrica Barile, who had been abandoned by her husband (a rather eccentric man who changed his name to Filopanti, "all-loving"), and subsequently moved to London.
1. Language.

2. Generous, abundant.
3. Stamped, like coins.
4. Confined, restrained.
5. The Roman name for Aphrodite, the Greek goddess of love; dolphins and doves were sacred to her. "Marked": saw.

Weightless, their wingless feet seemed made to fly,
Bound from the ground and in mid air to sport.
Left far behind I heard the dolphins snort,　　　　　　　　　　5
　　Tracking their goddess with a wistful eye,
　　Around whose head white doves rose, wheeling high
Or low, and cooed after their tender sort.
All this I saw in Spring. Thro' Summer heat
　　I saw the lovely Queen of Love no more.　　　　　　　　　10
　　　　But when flushed Autumn thro' the woodlands went
I spied sweet Venus walk amid the wheat:
　　Whom seeing, every harvester gave o'er
　　His toil, and laughed and hoped and was content.

1872　　　　　　　　　　　　　　　　　　　　　　　　　1875

REBECCA HARDING DAVIS

1831–1910

For Tillie Olsen, the twentieth-century working-class writer who recovered *Life in the Iron-Mills* from a century of critical neglect, Rebecca Harding Davis's novella represents the triumph of a "house-bound, class-bound, sex-bound" author who was somehow able to envision the grim realities of mid-nineteenth-century industrialization in America: labor's alienated relations with managers and owners, the degradation of ignored and unjust poverty, the pollution caused by industrial waste. *Life in the Iron-Mills*, which appeared anonymously in an 1861 issue of the *Atlantic Monthly*, was immediately acknowledged as a literary landmark by Nathaniel Hawthorne and Louisa May Alcott, Henry Ward Beecher, and Ralph Waldo Emerson. Some six years before the French novelist Émile Zola began publishing what were called "naturalistic" novels, a thirty-year-old Virginian had brilliantly dramatized the socioeconomic implications of environmental determinism. Yet, by the end of her life, this innovative writer was mainly remembered as the mother of the distinguished reporter Richard Harding Davis.

Little is known about the circumstances that turned Harding Davis into a sometimes inspired, always prolific author. The eldest of five children, she was born in Washington County, Pennsylvania, but moved with her family in 1836 to the city of Wheeling (then in Virginia and now in West Virginia). Wheeling not only was a center of the booming steel industry in the late 1850s but, inside a border state, was also increasingly involved in the turbulent antagonisms preceding the Civil War. The Harding family was middle class. Richard W. Harding, an Englishman from Ireland, was successful in business, conservative in his political views, and autocratic in his demands on the family. Rachel Leet (Wilson) Harding first educated her daughter at home and then sent her to the Washington Female Seminary in Pennsylvania. After graduating in 1848 with the highest honors in her class, Rebecca Harding lived her life inside the family, educating the younger children, studying the books brought home by her brother, William, when he attended Washington College, and, perhaps most important, walking through the mills and factories of the town.

During this period, Harding sent *Life in the Iron-Mills* to the prestigious magazine that was run by James T. Fields. His acceptance letter, accompanied by $50, must have seemed like the beginning of an exciting new life, and in fact, it did lead to a longer work serialized in the *Atlantic* and later published in book form as

Margaret Howth (1862), as well as to several dramatic stories about the devastating costs of the Civil War. It also resulted in a visit to Fields, which initiated a long-lasting friendship with his wife, Annie Fields, and shorter exchanges with Hawthorne and Emerson, among others. And it precipitated a correspondence with a reader-admirer whom Harding met in 1852 and married in 1863: three years her junior, Lemuel Clarke Davis was studying for the bar and writing journalism when he decided to settle with his wife in Philadelphia.

Although Harding Davis continued to pursue an ever more professional career in journalism and fiction, the rest of her life hardly met the expectations of these exciting years. First, nursing her father through a long illness, she found little refuge back at her new home, which was shared initially with her husband's sister and her children. Next, Harding Davis fell ill with what might have been nervous exhaustion. Then, to supplement the family's income, she began writing for magazines that could pay her more than the *Atlantic*. Subsequent novels suffered from the time pressures imposed by serialization. The late *Pro Aris et Focis—A Plea for Our Altars and Hearths* (1870) proclaimed the joys of domesticity; however, the author's own domestic life seems to have been arduous. With her husband increasingly occupied by abolitionist activities and as editor of the *Philadelphia Public Ledger*, she must have found it difficult to combine her position as contributing editor of the *New York Tribune* with the raising of their two sons and daughter. Yet, in her forties, she retained her earlier determination to extend the subject of fiction to wider social and economic issues: *Put Out of the Way* (1871), for example, focuses on the laws relating to lunacy; *Earthen Pitchers* (1873–74) on two young professional women; *John Andross* (1874) on monetary corruption in government. A number of short stories collected in *Silhouettes of American Life* (1892) further developed her self-defined literary project, "to dig into this commonplace, this vulgar American life, and see what is in it."

By the time she died at seventy-nine years old, Harding Davis had witnessed a decline of interest in her work. Yet she must have known that, by writing *Life in the Iron-Mills*, she had herself confronted just the inhibitions to creativity that she had analyzed with such clarity in her portrait of a working-class sculptor's efforts to construct the form of his desire out of the refuse (the korl) of the iron-mill. Tellingly, when her editor objected to the title she had chosen to give this tale, Harding Davis's alternative was "The Korl Woman" or "Beyond," for this huge figure of a woman imbued with longing signifies not only the thwarted work of the korl cutter but also Harding Davis's own protest against a world in which she saw that class, race, and gender could condemn human beings to frustration and pain.

Life in the Iron-Mills

> "Is this the end?
> O Life, as futile, then, as frail!
> What hope of answer or redress?"[1]

A cloudy day: do you know what that is in a town of iron-works? The sky sank down before dawn, muddy, flat, immovable. The air is thick, clammy with the breath of crowded human beings. It stifles me. I open the window, and, looking out, can scarcely see through the rain the grocer's shop opposite, where a crowd of drunken Irishmen are puffing Lynchburg tobacco[2] in their pipes. I can detect the scent through all the foul smells ranging loose in the air.

1. The first line is Davis's. the next two are from 56.25–27.
Alfred, Lord Tennyson's *In Memoriam* (1850), 2. An inferior tobacco grown in Virginia.

The idiosyncrasy of this town is smoke. It rolls sullenly in slow folds from the great chimneys of the iron-foundries, and settles down in black, slimy pools on the muddy streets. Smoke on the wharves, smoke on the dingy boats, on the yellow river,—clinging in a coating of greasy soot to the house-front, the two faded poplars, the faces of the passers-by. The long train of mules, dragging masses of pig-iron[3] through the narrow street, have a foul vapor hanging to their reeking sides. Here, inside, is a little broken figure of an angel pointing upward from the mantel-shelf; but even its wings are covered with smoke, clotted and black. Smoke everywhere! A dirty canary chirps desolately in a cage beside me. Its dream of green fields and sunshine is a very old dream,—almost worn out, I think.

From the back-window I can see a narrow brick-yard sloping down to the river-side, strewed with rain-butts[4] and tubs. The river, dull and tawny-colored, (*la belle rivière!*)[5] drags itself sluggishly along, tired of the heavy weight of boats and coal-barges. What wonder? When I was a child, I used to fancy a look of weary, dumb appeal upon the face of the Negro-like river slavishly bearing its burden day after day. Something of the same idle notion comes to me to-day, when from the street-window I look on the slow stream of human life creeping past, night and morning, to the great mills. Masses of men, with dull, besotted[6] faces bent to the ground, sharpened here and there by pain or cunning; skin and muscle and flesh begrimed with smoke and ashes; stooping all night over boiling caldrons of metal, laired by day in dens of drunkenness and infamy; breathing from infancy to death an air saturated with fog and grease and soot, vileness for soul and body. What do you make of a case like that, amateur psychologist? You call it an altogether serious thing to be alive: to these men it is a drunken jest, a joke,—horrible to angels perhaps, to them commonplace enough. My fancy about the river was an idle one: it is no type of such a life. What if it be stagnant and slimy here? It knows that beyond there waits for it odorous sunlight,—quaint old gardens, dusky with soft, green foliage of apple-trees, and flushing crimson with roses,—air, and fields, and mountains. The future of the Welsh puddler[7] passing just now is not so pleasant. To be stowed away, after his grimy work is done, in a hole in the muddy graveyard, and after that,—*not* air, nor green fields, nor curious roses.

Can you see how foggy the day is? As I stand here, idly tapping the window-pane, and looking out through the rain at the dirty back-yard and the coal-boats below, fragments of an old story float up before me,—a story of this old house into which I happened to come today. You may think it a tiresome story enough, as foggy as the day, sharpened by no sudden flashes of pain or pleasure.—I know: only the outline of a dull life, that long since, with thousands of dull lives like its own, was vainly lived and lost: thousands of them,—massed, vile, slimy lives, like those of the torpid lizards in yonder stagnant water-butt.—Lost? There is a curious point for you to settle, my friend, who study psychology in a lazy, *dilettante* way. Stop a moment. I am going to be honest. This is what I want you to do. I want you to hide your disgust, take no heed to your clean clothes, and come right down with me,—here, into the thickest of the fog and mud and foul effluvia.[8] I want you to hear this story. There is a se-

3. Crude iron formed in blocks.
4. Large casks for catching rainwater.
5. The beautiful river!—an ironic recollection of the Ohio's former purity.
6. Stupid, especially with drunkenness.
7. One who "puddles," or refines metal by stirring molten vats.
8. Offensive smells or waste by-products.

cret down here, in this nightmare fog, that has lain dumb for centuries: I want to make it a real thing to you. You, Egoist, or Pantheist, or Arminian,[9] busy in making straight paths for your feet on the hills, do not see it clearly,—this terrible question which men here have gone mad and died trying to answer. I dare not put this secret into words. I told you it was dumb. These men, going by with drunken faces and brains full of unawakened power, do not ask it of Society or of God. Their lives ask it; their deaths ask it. There is no reply. I will tell you plainly that I have a great hope; and I bring it to you to be tested. It is this: that this terrible dumb question is its own reply; that it is not the sentence of death we think it, but, from the very extremity of its darkness, the most solemn prophecy which the world has known of the Hope to come. I dare make my meaning no clearer, but will only tell my story. It will, perhaps, seem to you as foul and dark as this thick vapor about us, and as pregnant with death; but if your eyes are free as mine are to look deeper, no perfume-tinted dawn will be so fair with promise of the day that shall surely come.

My story is very simple,—only what I remember of the life of one of these men,—a furnace-tender in one of Kirby & John's rolling-mills,[1]—Hugh Wolfe. You know the mills? They took the great order for the Lower Virginia railroads there last winter; run usually with about a thousand men. I cannot tell why I choose the half-forgotten story of this Wolfe more than that of myriads of these furnace-hands. Perhaps because there is a secret underlying sympathy between that story and this day with its impure fog and thwarted sunshine,—or perhaps simply for the reason that this house is the one where the Wolfes lived. There were the father and son,—both hands, as I said, in one of Kirby & John's mills for making railroad-iron,—and Deborah, their cousin, a picker[2] in some of the cotton-mills. The house was rented then to half a dozen families. The Wolfes had two of the cellar-rooms. The old man, like many of the puddlers and feeders[3] of the mills, was Welsh,—had spent half of his life in the Cornish tin-mines.[4] You may pick the Welsh emigrants, Cornish miners, out of the throng passing the windows, any day. They are a trifle more filthy; their muscles are not so brawny; they stoop more. When they are drunk, they neither yell, nor shout, nor stagger, but skulk along like beaten hounds. A pure, unmixed blood, I fancy: shows itself in the slight angular bodies and sharply-cut facial lines. It is nearly thirty years since the Wolfes lived here. Their lives were like those of their class: incessant labor, sleeping in kennel-like rooms, eating rank pork and molasses, drinking—God and the distillers only know what; with an occasional night in jail, to atone for some drunken excess. Is that all of their lives?—of the portion given to them and these their duplicates swarming the streets to-day?—nothing beneath?—all? So many a political reformer will tell you,—and many a private reformer, too, who has gone among them with a heart tender with Christ's charity and come out outraged, hardened.

One rainy night, about eleven o'clock, a crowd of half-clothed women stopped outside of the cellar-door. They were going home from the cotton-mill.

9. Respectively, one who believes in self-interest, one who believes that God is present in all things, and one who believes in free will.
1. Mills where metal is rolled into sheets, bars, and other forms.

2. Operator of a machine that separates cotton fibers.
3. Workers who feed more molten metal into the casting forms.
4. Cornwall is in southwest England, where much mining is done.

"Good-night, Deb," said one, a mulatto,[5] steadying herself against the gas-post. She needed the post to steady her. So did more than one of them.

"Dah's a ball to Miss Potts' to-night. Ye'd best come."

"Inteet, Deb, if hur'll come, hur'll hef fun,"[6] said a shrill Welsh voice in the crowd.

Two or three dirty hands were thrust out to catch the gown of the woman, who was groping for the latch of the door.

"No."

"No? Where's Kit Small, then?"

"Begorra! on the spools.[7] Alleys behint, though we helped her, we dud. An wid ye! Let Deb alone! It's ondacent frettin' a quite body. Be the powers, an' we'll have a night of it! there'll be lashin's o' drink,—the Vargent[8] be blessed and praised for 't!"

They went on, the mulatto inclining for a moment to show fight, and drag the woman Wolfe off with them; but, being pacified, she staggered away.

Deborah groped her way into the cellar, and, after considerable stumbling, kindled a match, and lighted a tallow dip[9] that sent a yellow glimmer over the room. It was low, damp,—the earthen floor covered with a green, slimy moss,—a fetid air smothering the breath. Old Wolfe lay asleep on a heap of straw, wrapped in a torn horse-blanket. He was a pale, meek little man, with a white face and red rabbit-eyes. The woman Deborah was like him; only her face was even more ghastly, her lips bluer, her eyes more watery. She wore a faded cotton gown and a slouching bonnet. When she walked, one could see that she was deformed, almost a hunchback. She trod softly, so as not to waken him, and went through into the room beyond. There she found by the half-extinguished fire an iron saucepan filled with cold boiled potatoes, which she put upon a broken chair with a pint-cup of ale. Placing the old candlestick beside this dainty repast, she untied her bonnet, which hung limp and wet over her face, and prepared to eat her supper. It was the first food that had touched her lips since morning. There was enough of it, however: there is not always. She was hungry,—one could see that easily enough,—and not drunk, as most of her companions would have been found at this hour. She did not drink, this woman,—her face told that, too,—nothing stronger than ale. Perhaps the weak, flaccid wretch had some stimulant in her pale life to keep her up,— some love or hope, it might be, or urgent need. When that stimulant was gone, she would take to whiskey. Man cannot live by work alone. While she was skinning the potatoes, and munching them, a noise behind her made her stop.

"Janey!" she called, lifting the candle and peering into the darkness. "Janey, are you there?"

A heap of ragged coats was heaved up, and the face of a young girl emerged, staring sleepily at the woman.

"Deborah," she said, at last, "I'm here the night."

"Yes, child. Hur's welcome," she said, quietly eating on.

The girl's face was haggard and sickly; her eyes were heavy with sleep and hunger: real Milesian[1] eyes they were, dark, delicate blue, glooming out from black shadows with a pitiful fright.

5. A person who is half black in ancestry.
6. Indeed, Deb, if you'll come, you'll have fun (Welsh dialect).
7. I.e., working on the spools where cotton is wound.

"Begorra": by God (Irish euphemism).
8. The Virgin Mary. "Lashin's": plenty.
9. The least expensive kind of candle.
1. Irish.

"I was alone," she said, timidly.

"Where's the father?" asked Deborah, holding out a potato, which the girl greedily seized.

"He's beyant,—wid Haley,—in the stone house." (Did you ever hear the word *jail* from an Irish mouth?) "I came here. Hugh told me never to stay me-lone."

"Hugh?"

"Yes."

A vexed frown crossed her face. The girl saw it, and added quickly,—

"I have net seen Hugh the day, Deb. The old man says his watch[2] lasts till the mornin'."

The woman sprang up, and hastily began to arrange some bread and flitch[3] in a tin pail, and to pour her own measure of ale into a bottle. Tying on her bonnet, she blew out the candle.

"Lay ye down, Janey dear," she said, gently, covering her with the old rags. "Hur can eat the potatoes, if hur's hungry."

"Where are ye goin', Deb? The rain's sharp."

"To the mill, with Hugh's supper."

"Let him bide till th' morn. Sit ye down."

"No, no,"—sharply pushing her off. "The boy'll starve."

She hurried from the cellar, while the child wearily coiled herself up for sleep. The rain was falling heavily, as the woman, pail in hand, emerged from the mouth of the alley, and turned down the narrow street, that stretched out, long and black, miles before her. Here and there a flicker of gas lighted an uncertain space of muddy footwalk and gutter; the long rows of houses, except an occasional lager-bier shop, were closed; now and then she met a band of mill-hands skulking to or from their work.

Not many even of the inhabitants of a manufacturing town know the vast machinery of system by which the bodies of workmen are governed, that goes on unceasingly from year to year. The hands of each mill are divided into watches that relieve each other as regularly as the sentinels of an army. By night and day the work goes on, the unsleeping engines groan and shriek, the fiery pools of metal boil and surge. Only for a day in the week, in half-courtesy to public censure, the fires are partially veiled; but as soon as the clock strikes midnight, the great furnaces break forth with renewed fury, the clamor begins with fresh, breathless vigor, the engines sob and shriek like "gods in pain."

As Deborah hurried down through the heavy rain, the noise of these thousand engines sounded through the sleep and shadow of the city like far-off thunder. The mill to which she was going lay on the river, a mile below the city-limits. It was far, and she was weak, aching from standing twelve hours at the spools. Yet it was her almost nightly walk to take this man his supper, though at every square she sat down to rest, and she knew she should receive small word of thanks.

Perhaps, if she had possessed an artist's eye, the picturesque oddity of the scene might have made her step stagger less, and the path seem shorter; but to her the mills were only "summat deilish[4] to look at by night."

The road leading to the mills had been quarried from the solid rock, which rose abrupt and bare on one side of the cinder-covered road, while the river,

2. Workshift.
3. Rank salt pork.
4. Somewhat devilish.

sluggish and black, crept past on the other. The mills for rolling iron are simply immense tent-like roofs, covering acres of ground, open on every side. Beneath these roofs Deborah looked in on a city of fires, that burned hot and fiercely in the night. Fire in every horrible form: pits of flame waving in the wind; liquid metal-flames writhing in tortuous streams through the sand; wide caldrons filled with boiling fire, over which bent ghastly wretches stirring the strange brewing; and through all, crowds of half-clad men, looking like revengeful ghosts in the red light, hurried, throwing masses of glittering fire. It was like a street in Hell. Even Deborah muttered, as she crept through, " 'T looks like t' Devil's place!" It did,—in more ways than one.

She found the man she was looking for, at last, heaping coal on a furnace. He had not time to eat his supper; so she went behind the furnace, and waited. Only a few men were with him, and they noticed her only by a "Hyur comes t' hunchback, Wolfe."

Deborah was stupid with sleep; her back pained her sharply; and her teeth chattered with cold, with the rain that soaked her clothes and dripped from her at every step. She stood, however, patiently holding the pail, and waiting.

"Hout, woman! ye look like a drowned cat. Come near to the fire,"—said one of the men, approaching to scrape away the ashes.

She shook her head. Wolfe had forgotten her. He turned, hearing the man, and came closer.

"I did no' think; gi' me my supper, woman."

She watched him eat with a painful eagerness. With a woman's quick instinct, she saw that he was not hungry,—was eating to please her. Her pale, watery eyes began to gather a strange light.

"Is't good, Hugh? T'ale was a bit sour, I feared."

"No, good enough." He hesitated a moment. "Ye're tired, poor lass! Bide here till I go. Lay down there on that heap of ash, and go to sleep."

He threw her an old coat for a pillow, and turned to his work. The heap was the refuse of the burnt iron, and was not a hard bed; the half-smothered warmth, too, penetrated her limbs, dulling their pain and cold shiver.

Miserable enough she looked, lying there on the ashes like a limp, dirty rag,—yet not an unfitting figure to crown the scene of hopeless discomfort and veiled crime: more fitting, if one looked deeper into the heart of things,— at her thwarted woman's form, her colorless life, her waking stupor that smothered pain and hunger,—even more fit to be a type of her class. Deeper yet if one could look, was there nothing worth reading in this wet, faded thing, half-covered with ashes? no story of a soul filled with groping passionate love, heroic unselfishness, fierce jealousy? of years of weary trying to please the one human being whom she loved, to gain one look of real heart-kindness from him? If anything like this were hidden beneath the pale, bleared eyes, and dull, washed-out-looking face, no one had ever taken the trouble to read its faint signs: not the half-clothed furnace-tender, Wolfe, certainly. Yet he was kind to her: it was his nature to be kind, even to the very rats that swarmed in the cellar; kind to her in just the same way. She knew that. And it might be that very knowledge had given to her face its apathy and vacancy more than her low, torpid life. One sees that dead, vacant look steal sometimes over the rarest, finest of women's faces,—in the very midst, it may be, of their warmest summer's day; and then one can guess at the secret of intolerable solitude that lies hid beneath the delicate laces and brilliant smile. There was no warmth, no bril-

liancy, no summer for this woman; so the stupor and vacancy had time to gnaw into her face perpetually. She was young, too, though no one guessed it; so the gnawing was the fiercer.

She lay quiet in the dark corner, listening, through the monotonous din and uncertain glare of the works, to the dull plash of the rain in the far distance,—shrinking back whenever the man Wolfe happened to look towards her. She knew, in spite of all his kindness, that there was that in her face and form which made him loathe the sight of her. She felt by instinct, although she could not comprehend it, the finer nature of the man, which made him among his fellow-workmen something unique, set apart. She knew, that, down under all the vileness and coarseness of his life, there was a groping passion for whatever was beautiful and pure,—that his soul sickened with disgust at her deformity, even when his words were kindest. Through this dull consciousness, which never left her, came, like a sting, the recollection of the dark blue eyes and lithe figure of the little Irish girl she had left in the cellar. The recollection struck through even her stupid intellect with a vivid glow of beauty and of grace. Little Janey, timid, helpless, clinging to Hugh as her only friend: that was the sharp thought, the bitter thought, that drove into the glazed eyes a fierce light of pain. You laugh at it? Are pain and jealousy less savage realities down here in this place I am taking you to than in your own house or your own heart,—your heart, which they clutch at sometimes? The note is the same, I fancy, be the octave high or low.

If you could go into this mill where Deborah lay, and drag out from the hearts of these men the terrible tragedy of their lives, taking it as a symptom of the disease of their class, no ghost Horror would terrify you more. A reality of soul-starvation, of living death, that meets you every day under the besotted faces on the street,—I can paint nothing of this, only give you the outside outlines of a night, a crisis in the life of one man: whatever muddy depth of soul-history lies beneath you can read according to the eyes God has given you.

Wolfe, while Deborah watched him as a spaniel its master, bent over the furnace with his iron pole, unconscious of her scrutiny, only stopping to receive orders. Physically, Nature had promised the man but little. He had already lost the strength and instinct vigor of a man, his muscles were thin, his nerves weak, his face (a meek, woman's face) haggard, yellow with consumption. In the mill he was known as one of the girl-men: "Molly Wolfe" was his *sobriquet*.[5] He was never seen in the cockpit, did not own a terrier,[6] drank but seldom; when he did, desperately. He fought sometimes, but was always thrashed, pommelled to a jelly. The man was game enough, when his blood was up: but he was no favorite in the mill; he had the taint of school-learning on him,—not to a dangerous extent, only a quarter or so in the free-school in fact,[7] but enough to ruin him as a good hand in a fight.

For other reasons, too, he was not popular. Not one of themselves, they felt that, though outwardly as filthy and ash-covered; silent, with foreign thoughts and longings breaking out through his quietness in innumerable curious ways: this one, for instance. In the neighboring furnace-buildings lay great heaps of the refuse from the ore after the pig-metal is run. *Korl* we call it here: a light,

5. Nickname. "Consumption": tuberculosis.
6. Terriers were bred as hunters. "Cockpit": place where cockfights are held, a violent game in which roosters are made to kill each other.
7. Most workers in the mills were illiterate, public schools almost nonexistent [Tillie Olsen's note].

porous substance, of a delicate, waxen, flesh-colored tinge. Out of the blocks of this korl, Wolfe, in his off-hours from the furnace, had a habit of chipping and moulding figures,—hideous, fantastic enough, but sometimes strangely beautiful: even the mill-men saw that, while they jeered at him. It was a curious fancy in the man, almost a passion. The few hours for rest he spent hewing and hacking with his blunt knife, never speaking, until his watch came again,—working at one figure for months, and, when it was finished, breaking it to pieces perhaps, in a fit of disappointment. A morbid, gloomy man, untaught, unled, left to feed his soul in grossness and crime, and hard, grinding labor.

I want you to come down and look at this Wolfe, standing there among the lowest of his kind, and see him just as he is, that you may judge him justly when you hear the story of this night. I want you to look back, as he does every day, at his birth in vice, his starved infancy; to remember the heavy years he has groped through as boy and man,—the slow, heavy years of constant, hot work. So long ago he began, that he thinks sometimes he has worked there for ages. There is no hope that it will ever end. Think that God put into this man's soul a fierce thirst for beauty,—to know it, to create it; to *be*—something, he knows not what,—other than he is. There are moments when a passing cloud, the sun glinting on the purple thistles, a kindly smile, a child's face, will rouse him to a passion of pain,—when his nature starts up with a mad cry of rage against God, man, whoever it is that has forced this vile, slimy life upon him. With all this groping, this mad desire, a great blind intellect stumbling through wrong, a loving poet's heart, the man was by habit only a coarse, vulgar laborer, familiar with sights and words you would blush to name. Be just: when I tell you about this night, see him as he is. Be just,—not like man's law, which seizes on one isolated fact, but like God's judging angel, whose clear, sad eye saw all the countless cankering days of this man's life, all the countless nights, when, sick with starving, his soul fainted in him, before it judged him for this night, the saddest of all.

I called this night the crisis of his life. If it was, it stole on him unawares. These great turning-days of life cast no shadow before, slip by unconsciously. Only a trifle, a little turn of the rudder, and the ship goes to heaven or hell.

Wolfe, while Deborah watched him, dug into the furnace of melting iron with his pole, dully thinking only how many rails the lump would yield. It was late,—nearly Sunday morning; another hour, and the heavy work would be done,—only the furnaces to replenish and cover for the next day. The workmen were growing more noisy, shouting, as they had to do, to be heard over the deep clamor of the mills. Suddenly they grew less boisterous,—at the far end, entirely silent. Something unusual had happened. After a moment, the silence came nearer; the men stopped their jeers and drunken choruses. Deborah, stupidly lifting up her head, saw the cause of the quiet. A group of five or six men were slowly approaching, stopping to examine each furnace as they came. Visitors often came to see the mills after night: except by growing less noisy, the men took no notice of them. The furnace where Wolfe worked was near the bounds of the works; they halted there hot and tired: a walk over one of these great foundries is no trifling task. The woman, drawing out of sight, turned over to sleep. Wolfe, seeing them stop, suddenly roused from his indifferent stupor, and watched them keenly. He knew some of them: the overseer, Clarke,—a son of Kirby, one of the mill-owners,—and a Doctor May,

one of the town-physicians. The other two were strangers. Wolfe came closer. He seized eagerly every chance that brought him into contact with this mysterious class that shone down on him perpetually with the glamour of another order of being. What made the difference between them? That was the mystery of his life. He had a vague notion that perhaps to-night he could find it out. One of the strangers sat down on a pile of bricks, and beckoned young Kirby to his side.

"This *is* hot, with a vengeance. A match, please?"—lighting his cigar. "But the walk is worth the trouble. If it were not that you must have heard it so often, Kirby, I would tell you that your works look like Dante's Inferno."[8]

Kirby laughed.

"Yes. Yonder is Farinata himself in the burning tomb,"[9]—pointing to some figure in the shimmering shadows.

"Judging from some of the faces of your men," said the other, "they bid fair to try the reality of Dante's vision, some day."

Young Kirby looked curiously around, as if seeing the faces of his hands for the first time.

"They're bad enough, that's true. A desperate set, I fancy. Eh, Clarke?"

The overseer did not hear him. He was talking of net profits just then,—giving, in fact, a schedule of the annual business of the firm to a sharp peering little Yankee, who jotted down notes on a paper laid on the crown of his hat: a reporter for one of the city-papers, getting up a series of reviews of the leading manufactories. The other gentlemen had accompanied them merely for amusement. They were silent until the notes were finished, drying their feet at the furnaces, and sheltering their faces from the intolerable heat. At last the overseer concluded with—"I believe that is a pretty fair estimate, Captain."

"Here, some of you men!" said Kirby, "bring up those boards. We may as well sit down, gentlemen, until the rain is over. It cannot last much longer at this rate."

"Pig-metal,"—mumbled the reporter,—"um!—coal facilities,—um!—hands employed, twelve hundred,—bitumen,—um!—all right, I believe, Mr. Clarke;—sinking-fund,—what did you say was your sinking-fund?"[1]

"Twelve hundred hands?" said the stranger the young man who had first spoken. "Do you control their votes, Kirby?"

"Control? No." The young man smiled complacently. "But my father brought seven hundred votes to the polls for his candidate last November. No force-work, you understand,—only a speech or two, a hint to form themselves into a society, and a bit of red and blue bunting to make them a flag. The Invincible Roughs,—I believe that is their name. I forget the motto: 'Our country's hope,' I think."

There was a laugh. The young man talking to Kirby sat with an amused light in his cool gray eye, surveying critically the half-clothed figures of the puddlers, and the slow swing of their brawny muscles. He was a stranger in the city,—spending a couple of months in the borders of a Slave State, to study the institutions of the South,[2]—a brother-in-law of Kirby's,—Mitchell. He was an amateur gymnast,—hence his anatomical eye; a patron, in a *blasé* way,

8. I.e., of Dante's vision of hell in the *Inferno*.
9. Farinata degli Uberti, one of the heretics in Canto
10 of the *Inferno*.

1. Accumulated to pay off a corporate debt.
2. I.e., slavery.

of the prize-ring; a man who sucked the essence out of a science or philosophy in an indifferent, gentlemanly way; who took Kant, Novalis, Humboldt,[3] for what they were worth in his own scales; accepting all, despising nothing, in heaven, earth, or hell, but one-idead men; with a temper yielding and brilliant as summer water, until his Self was touched, when it was ice, though brilliant still. Such men are not rare in the States.

As he knocked the ashes from his cigar, Wolfe caught with a quick pleasure the contour of the white hand, the blood-glow of a red ring he wore. His voice, too, and that of Kirby's, touched him like music,—low, even, with chording cadences. About this man Mitchell hung the impalpable atmosphere belonging to the thoroughbred gentleman. Wolfe, scraping away the ashes beside him, was conscious of it, did obeisance to it with his artist sense, unconscious that he did so.

The rain did not cease. Clark and the reporter left the mills; the others, comfortably seated near the furnace, lingered, smoking and talking in a desultory way. Greek would not have been more unintelligible to the furnace-tenders, whose presence they soon forgot entirely. Kirby drew out a newspaper from his pocket and read aloud some article, which they discussed eagerly. At every sentence, Wolfe listened more and more like a dumb, hopeless animal, with a duller, more stolid look creeping over his face, glancing now and then at Mitchell, marking acutely every smallest sign of refinement, then back to himself, seeing as in a mirror his filthy body, his more stained soul.

Never! He had no words for such a thought, but he knew now, in all the sharpness of the bitter certainty, that between them there was a great gulf never to be passed.[4] Never!

The bells of the mills rang for midnight. Sunday morning had dawned. Whatever hidden message lay in the tolling bells floated past these men unknown. Yet it was there. Veiled in the solemn music ushering the risen saviour was a key-note to solve the darkest secrets of a world gone wrong,—even this social riddle which the brain of the grimy puddler grappled with madly tonight.

The men began to withdraw the metal from the caldrons. The mills were deserted on Sundays, except by the hands who fed the fires, and those who had no lodgings and slept usually on the ash-heaps. The three strangers sat still during the next hour, watching the men cover the furnaces, laughing now and then at some jest of Kirby's.

"Do you know," said Mitchell, "I like this view of the works better than when the glare was fiercest? These heavy shadows and the amphitheatre of smothered fires are ghostly, unreal. One could fancy these red smouldering lights to be the half-shut eyes of wild beasts, and the spectral figures their victims in the den."

Kirby laughed. "You are fanciful. Come, let us get out of the den. The spectral figures, as you call them, are a little too real for me to fancy a close proximity in the darkness,—unarmed, too."

The others rose, buttoning their over-coats, and lighting cigars.

"Raining, still," said Doctor May, "and hard. Where did we leave the coach, Mitchell?"

3. Three very different 18th- and 19th-century German thinkers.
4. In Luke 16:26, Christ speaks of the "great gulf fixed" between Dives, the rich man, in hell, and Lazarus, the beggar, in heaven.

"At the other side of the works.—Kirby, what's that?"

Mitchell started back, half-frightened, as, suddenly turning a corner, the white figure of a woman faced him in the darkness,—a woman, white, of giant proportions, crouching on the ground, her arms flung out in some wild gesture of warning.

"Stop! Make that fire burn there!" cried Kirby, stopping short.

The flame burst out, flashing the gaunt figure into bold relief.

Mitchell drew a long breath.

"I thought it was alive," he said, going up curiously.

The others followed.

"Not marble, eh?" asked Kirby, touching it.

One of the lower overseers stopped.

"Korl, Sir."

"Who did it?"

"Can't say. Some of the hands; chipped it out in off-hours."

"Chipped to some purpose. I should say. What a flesh-tint the stuff has! Do you see, Mitchell?"

"I see."

He had stepped aside where the light fell boldest on the figure, looking at it in silence. There was not one line of beauty or grace in it: a nude woman's form, muscular, grown coarse with labor, the powerful limbs instinct with some one poignant longing. One idea: there it was in the tense, rigid muscles, the clutching hands, the wild, eager face, like that of a starving wolf's. Kirby and Doctor May walked around it, critical, curious. Mitchell stood aloof, silent. The figure touched him strangely.

"Not badly done," said Doctor May. "Where did the fellow learn that sweep of the muscles in the arm and hand? Look at them! They are groping,—do you see?—clutching: the peculiar action of a man dying of thirst."

"They have ample facilities for studying anatomy," sneered Kirby, glancing at the half-naked figures.

"Look," continued the Doctor, "at this bony wrist, and the strained sinews of the instep! A working-woman,—the very type[5] of her class."

"God forbid!" muttered Mitchell.

"Why?" demanded May. "What does the fellow intend by the figure? I cannot catch the meaning."

"Ask him," said the other. dryly. "There he stands,"—pointing to Wolfe, who stood with a group of men, leaning on his ash-rake.

The Doctor beckoned him with the affable smile which kind-hearted men put on, when talking with these people.

"Mr. Mitchell has picked you out as the man who did this,—I'm sure I don't know why. But what did you mean by it?"

"She be hungry."

Wolfe's eyes answered Mitchell, not the Doctor.

"Oh-h! But what a mistake you have made, my fine fellow! You have given no sign of starvation to the body. It is strong,—terribly strong. It has the mad, half-despairing gesture of drowning."

Wolfe stammered, glanced appealingly at Mitchell, who saw the soul of the thing, he knew. But the cool, probing eyes were turned on himself now,—mocking, cruel, relentless.

5. Mold, representative.

"Not hungry for meat," the furnace-tender said at last.

"What then? Whiskey?" jeered Kirby, with a coarse laugh.

Wolfe was silent a moment, thinking.

"I dunno," he said, with a bewildered look. "It mebbe. Summat to make her live, I think,—like you. Whiskey ull do it, in a way."

The young man laughed again. Mitchell flashed a look of disgust some-where,—not at Wolfe.

"May," he broke out impatiently, "are you blind? Look at that woman's face! It asks questions of God, and says, 'I have a right to know.' Good God, how hungry it is!"

They looked a moment; then May turned to the mill-owner:—

"Have you many such hands as this? What are you going to do with them? Keep them at puddling iron?"

Kirby shrugged his shoulders. Mitchell's look had irritated him.

"*Ce n'est pas mon affaire.*[6] I have no fancy for nursing infant geniuses. I sup-pose there are some stray gleams of mind and soul among these wretches. The Lord will take care of his own; or else they can work out their own salvation. I have heard you call our American system a ladder which any man can scale. Do you doubt it? Or perhaps you want to banish all social ladders, and put us all on a flat table-land,—eh, May?"

The Doctor looked vexed, puzzled. Some terrible problem lay hid in this woman's face, and troubled these men. Kirby waited for an answer, and, re-ceiving none, went on, warming with his subject.

"I tell you, there's something wrong that no talk of '*Liberté*' or '*Égalité*'[7] will do away. If I had the making of men, these men who do the lowest part of the world's work should be machines,—nothing more,—hands. It would be kind-ness. God help them! What are taste, reason, to creatures who must live such lives as that?" He pointed to Deborah, sleeping on the ash-heap. "So many nerves to sting them to pain. What if God had put your brain, with all its agony of touch, into your fingers, and bid you work and strike with that?"

"You think you could govern the world better?" laughed the Doctor.

"I do not think at all."

"That is true philosophy. Drift with the stream, because you cannot dive deep enough to find bottom, eh?"

"Exactly," rejoined Kirby. "I do not think. I wash my hands of all social prob-lems,—slavery, caste, white or black. My duty to my operatives[8] has a narrow limit,—the pay-hour on Saturday night. Outside of that, if they cut korl, or cut each other's throats, (the more popular amusement of the two,) I am not responsible."

The Doctor sighed,—a good honest sigh, from the depths of his stomach.

"God help us! Who is responsible?"

"Not I, I tell you," said Kirby, testily. "What has the man who pays them money to do with their souls' concerns, more than the grocer or butcher who takes it?"

"And yet," said Mitchell's cynical voice, "look at her! How hungry she is!"

Kirby tapped his boot with his cane. No one spoke. Only the dumb face of the rough image looking into their faces with the awful question, "What shall

6. That's not my business (French).
7. The slogan of the French Revolution was *Liberté*,

Égalité, Fraternité (Liberty, Equality, Brotherhood).
8. Workers.

we do to be saved?"[9] Only Wolfe's face, with its heavy weight of brain, its weak, uncertain mouth, its desperate eyes, out of which looked the soul of his class,—only Wolfe's face turned towards Kirby's. Mitchell laughed,—a cool, musical laugh.

"Money has spoken!" he said, seating himself lightly on a stone with the air of an amused spectator at a play. "Are you answered?"—turning to Wolfe his clear, magnetic face.

Bright and deep and cold as Arctic air, the soul of the man lay tranquil beneath. He looked at the furnace-tender as he had looked at a rare mosaic in the morning; only the man was the more amusing study of the two.

"Are you answered? Why, May, look at him! '*De profundis clamavi.*'[1] Or, to quote in English, 'Hungry and thirsty, his soul faints in him.' And so Money sends back its answer into the depths through you, Kirby! Very clear the answer, too!—I think I remember reading the same words somewhere:—washing your hands in Eau de Cologne, and saying, 'I am innocent of the blood of this man. See ye to it!' "[2]

Kirby flushed angrily.

"You quote Scripture freely."

"Do I not quote correctly? I think I remember another line, which may amend my meaning: 'Inasmuch as ye did it unto one of the least of these, ye did it unto me.' Deist?[3] Bless you, man, I was raised on the milk of the Word. Now, Doctor, the pocket of the world having uttered its voice, what has the heart to say? You are a philanthropist, in a small way,—n'est ce pas?[4] Here, boy, this gentleman can show you how to cut korl better,—or your destiny. Go on, May!"

"I think a mocking devil possesses you to-night," rejoined the Doctor, seriously.

He went to Wolfe and put his hand kindly on his arm. Something of a vague idea possessed the Doctor's brain that much good was to be done here by a friendly word or two: a latent genius to be warmed into life by a waited-for sun-beam. Here it was: he had brought it. So he went on complacently:—

"Do you know, boy, you have it in you to be a great sculptor, a great man?—do you understand?" (talking down to the capacity of his hearer: it is a way people have with children, and men like Wolfe,)—"to live a better, stronger life than I, or Mr. Kirby here? A man may make himself anything he chooses. God has given you stronger powers than many men,—me, for instance."

May stopped, heated, glowing with his own magnanimity. And it was magnanimous. The puddler had drunk in every word, looking through the Doctor's flurry, and generous heat, and self-approval, into his will, with those slow, absorbing eyes of his.

"Make yourself what you will. It is your right."

"I know," quietly. "Will you help me?"

Mitchell laughed again. The Doctor turned now, in a passion,—

"You know, Mitchell, I have not the means. You know, if I had, it is in my heart to take this boy and educate him for"——

9. The words of the keeper of the prison in Philippi after an earthquake opens the doors of his prison (Acts 16:30).

1. I have cried out of the deep [unto thee, O Lord] (Latin version of Psalm 130:1).

2. The words of Pontius Pilate, the Roman judge who permitted Christ to be crucified but refused to take responsibility (Matthew 27:24).

3. Believer in a God who created the universe and its laws but who thereafter refrains from interfering with those laws. The quote is from Matthew 25:40

4. Isn't that right?

"The glory of God, and the glory of John May."

May did not speak for a moment; then, controlled, he said,—

"Why should one be raised, when myriads are left?—I have not the money, boy," to Wolfe, shortly.

"Money?" He said it over slowly, as one repeats the guessed answer to a riddle, doubtfully. "That is it? Money?"

"Yes, money,—that is it," said Mitchell, rising, and drawing his furred coat about him. "You've found the cure for all the world's diseases.—Come, May, find your good-humor, and come home. This damp wind chills my very bones. Come and preach your Saint-Simonian[5] doctrines to-morrow to Kirby's hands. Let them have a clear idea of the rights of the soul, and I'll venture next week they'll strike for higher wages. That will be the end of it."

"Will you send the coach-driver to this side of the mills?" asked Kirby, turning to Wolfe.

He spoke kindly: it was his habit to do so. Deborah, seeing the puddler go, crept after him. The three men waited outside. Doctor May walked up and down, chafed. Suddenly he stopped.

"Go back, Mitchell! You say the pocket and the heart of the world speak without meaning to these people. What has its head to say? Taste, culture, refinement? Go!"

Mitchell was leaning against a brick wall. He turned his head indolently, and looked into the mills. There hung about the place a thick, unclean odor. The slightest motion of his hand marked that he perceived it, and his insufferable disgust. That was all. May said nothing, only quickened his angry tramp.

"Besides," added Mitchell, giving a corollary to his answer, "it would be of no use. I am not one of them."

"You do not mean"—said May, facing him.

"Yes, I mean just that. Reform is born of need, not pity. No vital movement of the people's has worked down, for good or evil; fermented, instead, carried up the heaving, cloggy mass. Think back through history, and you will know it. What will this lowest deep—thieves, Magdalens,[6] negroes—do with the light filtered through ponderous Church creeds, Baconian theories, Goethe schemes? Some day, out of their bitter need will be thrown up their own light-bringer,—their Jean Paul, their Cromwell,[7] their Messiah."

"Bah!" was the Doctor's inward criticism. However, in practice, he adopted the theory; for, when, night and morning, afterwards, he prayed that power might be given these degraded souls to rise, he glowed at heart, recognizing an accomplished duty.

Wolfe and the woman had stood in the shadow of the works as the coach drove off. The Doctor had held out his hand in a frank, generous way, telling him to "take care of himself, and to remember it was his right to rise." Mitchell had simply touched his hat, as to an equal, with a quiet look of thorough recognition. Kirby had thrown Deborah some money, which she found, and clutched eagerly enough. They were gone now, all of them. The man sat down on the cinder-road, looking up into the murky sky.

5. Socialist; after Claude Henri de Rouvroy, Comte de Saint-Simon (1760–1825), French social theorist.
6. Prostitutes (from Mary Magdalen, anciently identified with the repentant prostitute who anointed Jesus' feet [Luke 7:37–50]).
7. Oliver Cromwell (1599–1658) led the revolt against the British monarchy. Francis Bacon (1561–1626), a philosopher, and Johann Wolfgang von Goethe (1749–1832), a poet, developed complicated abstract theories. Jean Paul Richter (1763–1825) was a German novelist.

" 'T be late, Hugh. Wunnot hur come?"

He shook his head doggedly, and the woman crouched out of his sight against the wall. Do you remember rare moments when a sudden light flashed over yourself, your world, God? when you stood on a mountain-peak, seeing your life as it might have been, as it is? one quick instant, when custom lost its force and every-day usage? when your friend, wife, brother, stood in a new light? your soul was bared, and the grave,—a foretaste of the nakedness of the Judgment-Day? So it came before him, his life, that night. The slow tides of pain he had borne gathered themselves up and surged against his soul. His squalid daily life, the brutal coarseness eating into his brain, as the ashes into his skin: before, these things had been a dull aching into his consciousness; to-night, they were reality. He gripped the filthy red shirt that clung, stiff with soot, about him, and tore it savagely from his arm. The flesh beneath was muddy with grease and ashes,—and the heart beneath that! And the soul? God knows.

Then flashed before his vivid poetic sense the man who had left him,—the pure face, the delicate, sinewy limbs, in harmony with all he knew of beauty or truth. In his cloudy fancy he had pictured a Something like this. He had found it in this Mitchell, even when he idly scoffed at his pain: a Man all-knowing, all-seeing, crowned by Nature, reigning,—the keen glance of his eye falling like a sceptre on other men. And yet his instinct taught him that he too—He! He looked at himself with sudden loathing, sick, wrung his hands with a cry, and then was silent. With all the phantoms of his heated, ignorant fancy, Wolfe had not been vague in his ambitions. They were practical, slowly built up before him out of his knowledge of what he could do. Through years he had day by day made this hope a real thing to himself,—a clear, projected figure of himself, as he might become.

Able to speak, to know what was best, to raise these men and women working at his side up with him: sometimes he forgot this defined hope in the frantic anguish to escape,—only to escape,—out of the wet, the pain, the ashes, somewhere, anywhere,—only for one moment of free air on a hill-side, to lie down and let his sick soul throb itself out in the sunshine. But to-night he panted for life. The savage strength of his nature was roused; his cry was fierce to God for justice.

"Look at me!" he said to Deborah, with a low, bitter laugh, striking his puny chest savagely. "What am I worth, Deb? Is it my fault that I am no better? My fault? My fault?"

He stopped, stung with a sudden remorse, seeing her hunchback shape writhing with sobs. For Deborah was crying thankless tears, according to the fashion of women.

"God forgi' me, woman! Things go harder wi' you nor me. It's a worse share."

He got up and helped her to rise; and they went doggedly down the muddy street, side by side.

"It's all wrong," he muttered, slowly,—"all wrong! I dunnot understan'. But it'll end some day."

"Come home, Hugh!" she said, coaxingly; for he had stopped, looking around bewildered.

"Home,—and back to the mill!" He went on saying this over to himself, as if he would mutter down every pain in this dull despair.

She followed him through the fog, her blue lips chattering with cold. They reached the cellar at last. Old Wolfe had been drinking since she went out, and had crept nearer the door. The girl Janey slept heavily in the corner. He went up to her, touching softly the worn white arm with his fingers. Some bitterer thought stung him, as he stood there. He wiped the drops from his forehead, and went into the room beyond, livid, trembling. A hope, trifling, perhaps, but very dear, had died just then out of the poor puddler's life, as he looked at the sleeping, innocent girl,—some plan for the future, in which she had borne a part. He gave it up that moment, then and forever. Only a trifle, perhaps, to us: his face grew a shade paler,—that was all. But, somehow, the man's soul, as God and the angels looked down on it, never was the same afterwards.

Deborah followed him into the inner room. She carried a candle, which she placed on the floor, closing the door after her. She had seen the look on his face, as he turned away: her own grew deadly. Yet, as she came up to him her eyes glowed. He was seated on an old chest, quiet, holding his face in his hands.

"Hugh!" she said, softly.

He did not speak.

"Hugh, did hur hear what the man said,—him with the clear voice? Did hur hear? Money, money,—that it wud do all?"

He pushed her away,—gently, but he was worn out; her rasping tone fretted him.

"Hugh!"

The candle flared a pale yellow light over the cobwebbed brick walls, and the woman standing there. He looked at her. She was young, in deadly earnest; her faded eyes, and wet, ragged figure caught from their frantic eagerness a power akin to beauty.

"Hugh, it is true! Money ull do it! Oh, Hugh, boy, listen till me! He said it true! It is money!"

"I know. Go back! I do not want you here."

"Hugh, it is t' last time. I'll never worrit hur again."[8]

There were tears in her voice now, but she choked them back.

"Hear till me only to-night! If one of t'witch people wud come, them we heard of t' home, and gif hur all hur wants, what then? Say, Hugh!"

"What do you mean?"

"I mean money."

Her whisper shrilled through his brain.

"If one of t' witch dwarfs wud come from t' lane moors to-night, and gif hur money, to go out,—*out*, I say,—out, lad, where t' sun shines, and t' heath grows, and t' ladies walk in silken gownds, and God stays all t' time,—where t' man lives that talked to us to-night,—Hugh knows,—Hugh could walk there like a king!"

He thought the woman mad, tried to check her, but she went on, fierce in her eager haste.

"If I were t' witch dwarf, if I had t' money, wud hur thank me? Wud hur take

8. I'll never bother you again (Welsh dialect).

me out o' this place wid hur and Janey? I wud not come into the gran' house hur wud build, to vex hur wid t' hunch,—only at night, when t' shadows were dark, stand far off to see hur."

Mad? Yes! Are many of us mad in this way?

"Poor Deb! poor Deb!" he said, soothingly.

"It is here," she said, suddenly jerking into his hand a small roll. "I took it! I did it! Me, me!—not hur! I shall be hanged, I shall be burnt in hell, if anybody knows I took it! Out of his pocket, as he leaned against t' bricks. Hur knows?"

She thrust it into his hand, and then, her errand done, began to gather chips together to make a fire, choking down hysteric sobs.

"Has it come to this?"

That was all he said. The Welsh Wolfe blood was honest. The roll was a small green pocket-book containing one or two gold pieces, and a check for an incredible amount, as it seemed to the poor puddler. He laid it down, hiding his face again in his hands.

"Hugh, don't be angry wud me! It's only poor Deb,—hur knows?"

He took the long skinny fingers kindly in his.

"Angry? God help me, no! Let me sleep. I am tired."

He threw himself heavily down on the wooden bench, stunned with pain and weariness. She brought some old rags to cover him.

It was late on Sunday evening before he awoke. I tell God's truth, when I say he had then no thought of keeping this money. Deborah had hid it in his pocket. He found it there. She watched him eagerly, as he took it out.

"I must gif it to him," he said, reading her face.

"Hur knows," she said with a bitter sigh of disappointment. "But it is hur right to keep it."

His right! The word struck him. Doctor May had used the same. He washed himself, and went out to find this man Mitchell. His right! Why did this chance word cling to him so obstinately? Do you hear the fierce devils whisper in his ear, as he went slowly down the darkening street?

The evening came on, slow and calm. He seated himself at the end of an alley leading into one of the larger streets. His brain was clear to-night, keen, intent, mastering. It would not start back, cowardly, from any hellish temptation, but meet it face to face. Therefore the great temptation of his life came to him veiled by no sophistry, but bold, defiant, owning its own vile name, trusting to one bold blow for victory.

He did not deceive himself. Theft! That was it. At first the word sickened him; then he grappled with it. Sitting there on a broken cart-wheel, the fading day, the noisy groups, the church-bells' tolling passed before him like a panorama,[9] while the sharp struggle went on within. This money! He took it out, and looked at it. If he gave it back, what then? He was going to be cool about it.

People going by to church saw only a sickly mill-boy watching them quietly at the alley's mouth. They did not know that he was mad, or they would not have gone by so quietly: mad with hunger; stretching out his hands to the world, that had given so much to them, for leave to live the life God meant him to live. His soul within him was smothering to death; he wanted so much, thought so much, and knew—nothing. There was nothing of which he was

9. I.e., like the continuous scenes painted on rolls of canvas that were unrolled before an audience; a popular 19th-century theatrical pastime.

certain, except the mill and things there. Of God and heaven he had heard so little, that they were to him what fairy-land is to a child: something real, but not here; very far off. His brain, greedy, dwarfed, full of thwarted energy and unused powers, questioned these men and women going by, coldly, bitterly, that night. Was it not his right to live as they,—a pure life, a good, true-hearted life, full of beauty and kind words? He only wanted to know how to use the strength within him. His heart warmed, as he thought of it. He suffered[1] himself to think of it longer. If he took the money?

Then he saw himself as he might be, strong, helpful, kindly. The night crept on, as this one image slowly evolved itself from the crowd of other thoughts and stood triumphant. He looked at it. As he might be! What wonder, if it blinded him to delirium,—the madness that underlies all revolution, all progress, and all fall?

You laugh at the shallow temptation? You see the error underlying its argument so clearly,—that to him a true life was one of full development rather than self-restraint? that he was deaf to the higher tone in a cry of voluntary suffering for truth's sake than in the fullest flow of spontaneous harmony? I do not plead his cause. I only want to show you the mote in my brother's eye: then you can see clearly to take it out.[2]

The money,—there it lay on his knee, a little blotted slip of paper, nothing in itself; used to raise him out of the pit; something straight from God's hand. A thief! Well, what was it to be a thief? He met the question at last, face to face, wiping the clammy drops of sweat from his forehead. God made this money—the fresh air, too—for his children's use. He never made the difference between poor and rich. The Something who looked down on him that moment through the cool gray sky had a kindly face, he knew,—loved his children alike. Oh, he knew that!

There were times when the soft floods of color in the crimson and purple flames, or the clear depth of amber in the water below the bridge, had somehow given him a glimpse of another world than this,—of an infinite depth of beauty and of quiet somewhere,—somewhere,—a depth of quiet and rest and love. Looking up now, it became strangely real. The sun had sunk quite below the hills, but his last rays struck upward, touching the zenith. The fog had risen, and the town and river were steeped in its thick, gray damp; but over-head, the sun-touched smoke-clouds opened like a cleft ocean,—shifting, rolling seas of crimson mist, waves of billowy silver veined with blood-scarlet, inner depths unfathomable of glancing light. Wolfe's artist-eye grew drunk with color. The gates of that other world! Fading, flashing before him now! What, in that world of Beauty, Content, and Right, were the pretty laws, the mine and thine, of mill-owners and mill-hands?

A consciousness of power stirred within him. He stood up. A man,—he thought, stretching out his hands,—free to work, to live, to love! Free! His right! He folded the scrap of paper in his hand. As his nervous fingers took it in, limp and blotted, so his soul took in the mean temptation, lapped it in fancied rights, in dreams of improved existences, drifting and endless as the cloud-seas of color. Clutching it, as if the tightness of his hold would

1. Allowed.
2. In the Sermon on the Mount Christ asks, "And why beholdest thou the mote that is in thy brother's eye, but considerest not the beam that is in thine own eye? Or how wilt thou say to thy brother, Let me pull out the mote out of thine eye; and, behold, a beam is in thine own eye?" (Matthew 7:3–4). The contrast is between a speck of dust and a large timber.

strengthen his sense of possession, he went aimlessly down the street. It was his watch at the mill. He need not go, need never go again, thank God!—shaking off the thought with unspeakable loathing.

Shall I go over the history of the hours of that night? how the man wandered from one to another of his old haunts, with a half-consciousness of bidding them farewell,—lanes and alleys and back-yards where the mill-hands lodged,—noting, with a new eagerness, the filth and drunkenness, the pig-pens, the ash-heaps covered with potato-skins, the bloated, pimpled women at the doors,—with a new disgust, a new sense of sudden triumph, and, under all, a new, vague dread, unknown before, smothered down, kept under, but still there? It left him but once during the night, when, for the second time in his life, he entered a church. It was a sombre Gothic pile,[3] where the stained light lost itself in far-retreating arches; built to meet the requirements and sympathies of a far other class than Wolfe's. Yet it touched, moved him uncontrollably. The distances, the shadows, the still, marble figures, the mass of silent kneeling worshippers, the mysterious music, thrilled, lifted his soul with a wonderful pain. Wolfe forgot himself, forgot the new life he was going to live, the mean terror gnawing underneath. The voice of the speaker strengthened the charm; it was clear, feeling, full, strong. An old man, who had lived much, suffered much; whose brain was keenly alive, dominant; whose heart was summer-warm with charity. He taught it to-night. He held up Humanity in its grand total; showed the great world-cancer to his people. Who could show it better? He was a Christian reformer; he had studied the age thoroughly; his outlook at man had been free, world-wide, over all time. His faith stood sublime upon the Rock of Ages;[4] his fiery zeal guided vast schemes by which the gospel was to be preached to all nations. How did he preach it to-night? In burning, light-laden words he painted the incarnate Life, Love, the universal Man: words that became reality in the lives of these people,—that lived again in beautiful words and actions, trifling, but heroic. Sin, as he defined it, was a real foe to them; their trials, temptations, were his. His words passed far over the furnace-tender's grasp, toned to suit another class of culture; they sounded in his ears a very pleasant song in an unknown tongue. He meant to cure this world-cancer with a steady eye that had never glared with hunger, and a hand that neither poverty nor strychnine-whiskey[5] had taught to shake. In this morbid, distorted heart of the Welsh puddler he had failed.

Wolfe rose at last, and turned from the church down the street. He looked up; the night had come on foggy, damp; the golden mists had vanished, and the sky lay dull and ash-colored. He wandered again aimlessly down the street, idly wondering what had become of the cloud-sea of crimson and scarlet. The trial-day of this man's life was over, and he had lost the victory. What followed was mere drifting circumstance,—a quicker walking over the path,—that was all. Do you want to hear the end of it? You wish me to make a tragic story out of it? Why, in the police-reports of the morning paper you can find a dozen such tragedies: hints of shipwrecks unlike any that ever befell on the high seas; hints that here a power was lost to heaven,—that there a soul went down where no tide can ebb or flow. Commonplace enough the hints are,—jocose sometimes, done up in rhyme.

3. Large building.
4. I.e., strong Christian faith.

5. A kind of cheap whisky (strychnine, which is highly poisonous, acts as a stimulant in small amounts).

Doctor May, a month after the night I have told you of, was reading to his wife at breakfast from this fourth column of the morning-paper: an unusual thing,—these police-reports not being, in general, choice reading for ladies; but it was only one item he read.

"Oh, my dear! You remember that man I told you of, that we saw at Kirby's mill?—that was arrested for robbing Mitchell? Here he is; just listen:—'Circuit Court. Judge Day. Hugh Wolfe, operative in Kirby & John's Loudon Mills. Charge, grand larceny. Sentence, nineteen years hard labor in penitentiary.'—Scoundrel! Serves him right! After all our kindness that night! Picking Mitchell's pocket at the very time!"

His wife said something about the ingratitude of that kind of people, and then they began to talk of something else.

Nineteen years! How easy that was to read! What a simple word for Judge Day to utter! Nineteen years! Half a lifetime![6]

Hugh Wolfe sat on the window-ledge of his cell, looking out. His ankles were ironed. Not usual in such cases; but he had made two desperate efforts to escape. "Well," as Haley, the jailer, said, "small blame to him! Nineteen years' imprisonment was not a pleasant thing to look forward to." Haley was very good-natured about it, though Wolfe had fought him savagely.

"When he was first caught," the jailer said afterwards, in telling the story, "before the trial, the fellow was cut down at once,—laid there on that pallet like a dead man, with his hands over his eyes. Never saw a man so cut down in my life. Time of the trial, too, came the queerest dodge of any customer I ever had. Would choose no lawyer. Judge gave him one, of course. Gibson it was. He tried to prove the fellow crazy; but it wouldn't go. Thing was plain as daylight: money found on him. 'Twas a hard sentence,—all the law allows; but it was for 'xample's sake. These mill-hands are gettin' onbearable. When the sentence was read, he just looked up, and said the money was his by rights, and that all the world had gone wrong. That night, after the trial, a gentleman came to see him here, name of Mitchell,—him as he stole from. Talked to him for an hour. Thought he came for curiosity, like. After he was gone, thought Wolfe was remarkable quiet, and went into his cell. Found him very low; bed all bloody. Doctor said he had been bleeding at the lungs. He was as weak as a cat; yet, if ye'll b'lieve me, he tried to get a-past me and get out. I just carried him like a baby, and threw him on the pallet. Three days after, he tried it again: that time reached the wall. Lord help you! he fought like a tiger,—giv' some terrible blows. Fightin' for life, you see; for he can't live long, shut up in the stone crib down yonder. Got a death-cough now. 'T took two of us to bring him down that day; so I just put the irons on his feet. There he sits, in there. Goin' to-morrow, with a batch more of 'em. That woman, hunchback, tried with him,—you remember?—she's only got three years. 'Complice. But *she's* a woman, you know. He's been quiet ever since I put on irons: giv' up, I suppose. Looks white, sick-lookin'. It acts different on 'em, bein' sentenced. Most of 'em gets reckless, devilish-like. Some prays awful, and sings them vile songs of the mills, all in a breath. That woman, now, she's desper't'. Been beggin' to

6. Nineteen years was literally half a lifetime. Life expectancy for a male in the 1850's was thirty-seven years. Hugh Wolfe is nineteen years old, for all his "lifetime" in the mills, the "slow heavy years of con- stant hot work." As was common at the time, he had probably been in the mills since he was nine or ten [Olsen's note].

see Hugh, as she calls him, for three days. I'm a-goin' to let her in. She don't go
with him. Here she is in this next cell. I'm a-goin' now to let her in."

He let her in. Wolfe did not see her. She crept into a corner of the cell, and
stood watching him. He was scratching the iron bars of the window with a
piece of tin which he had picked up, with an idle, uncertain, vacant stare, just
as a child or idiot would do.

"Tryin' to get out, old boy?" laughed Haley. "Them irons will need a crow-
bar beside your tin, before you can open 'em."

Wolfe laughed, too, in a senseless way.

"I think I'll get out," he said.

"I believe his brain's touched," said Haley, when he came out.

The puddler scraped away with the tin for half an hour. Still Deborah did
not speak. At last she ventured nearer, and touched his arm.

"Blood?" she said, looking at some spots on his coat with a shudder.

He looked up at her. "Why, Deb!" he said, smiling,—such a bright, boyish
smile, that it went to poor Deborah's heart directly, and she sobbed and cried
out loud.

"Oh, Hugh, lad! Hugh! du not look at me, when it wur my fault! To think I
brought hur to it! And I loved hur so! Oh, lad, I dud!"

The confession, even in this wretch, came with the woman's blush through
the sharp cry.

He did not seem to hear her,—scraping away diligently at the bars with the
bit of tin.

Was he going mad? She peered closely into his face. Something she saw
there made her draw suddenly back,—something which Haley had not seen,
that lay beneath the pinched vacant look it had caught since the trial, or the
curious gray shadow that rested on it. That gray shadow,—yes, she knew what
that meant. She had often seen it creeping over women's faces for months,
who died at last of slow hunger or consumption. That meant death, distant,
lingering: but this—Whatever it was the woman saw, or thought she saw, used
as she was to crime and misery, seemed to make her sick with a new horror.
Forgetting her fear of him, she caught his shoulders, and looked keenly,
steadily, into his eyes.

"Hugh!" she cried, in a desperate whisper,—"oh, boy, not that! for God's
sake, not *that*!"

The vacant laugh went off his face, and he answered her in a muttered word
or two that drove her away. Yet the words were kindly enough. Sitting there on
his pallet, she cried silently a hopeless sort of tears, but did not speak again.
The man looked up furtively at her now and then. Whatever his own trouble
was, her distress vexed him with a momentary sting.

It was market-day. The narrow window of the jail looked down directly on
the carts and wagons drawn up in a long line, where they had unloaded. He
could see, too, and hear distinctly the clink of money as it changed hands, the
busy crowd of whites and blacks shoving, pushing one another, and the chaf-
fering[7] and swearing at the stalls. Somehow, the sound, more than anything
else had done, wakened him up,—made the whole real to him. He was done
with the world and the business of it. He let the tin fall, and locked out, press-
ing his face close to the rusty bars. How they crowded and pushed! And he,—

7. Bargaining.

he should never walk that pavement again! There came Neff Sanders, one of the feeders at the mill, with a basket on his arm. Sure enough, Neff was married the other week. He whistled, hoping he would look up; but he did not. He wondered if Neff remembered he was there,—if any of the boys thought of him up there, and thought that he never was to go down that old cinder-road again. Never again! He had not quite understood it before; but now he did. Not for days or years, but never!—that was it.

How clear the light fell on that stall in front of the market! and how like a picture it was, the dark-green heaps of corn, and the crimson beets, and golden melons! There was another with game: how the light flickered on that pheasant's breast, with the purplish blood dripping over the brown feathers! He could see the red shining of the drops, it was so near. In one minute he could be down there. It was just a step. So easy, as it seemed, so natural to go! Yet it could never be—not in all the thousands of years to come—that he should put his foot on that street again! He thought of himself with a sorrowful pity, as of some one else. There was a dog down in the market, walking after his master with such a stately, grave look!—only a dog, yet he could go backwards and forwards just as he pleased: he had good luck! Why, the very vilest cur, yelping there in the gutter, had not lived his life, had been free to act out whatever thought God had put into his brain; while he—No, he would not think of that! He tried to put the thought away, and to listen to a dispute between a countryman and a woman about some meat; but it would come back. He, what had he done to bear this?

Then came the sudden picture of what might have been, and now. He knew what it was to be in the penitentiary,—how it went with men there. He knew how in these long years he should slowly die, but not until soul and body had become corrupt and rotten,—how, when he came out, if he lived to come, even the lowest of the mill-hands would jeer him,—how his hands would be weak, and his brain senseless and stupid. He believed he was almost that now. He put his hand to his head, with a puzzled, weary look. It ached, his head, with thinking. He tried to quiet himself. It was only right, perhaps; he had done wrong. But was there right or wrong for such as he? What was right? And who had ever taught him? He thrust the whole matter away. A dark, cold quiet crept through his brain. It was all wrong; but let it be! It was nothing to him more than the others. Let it be!

The door grated, as Haley opened it.

"Come, my woman! Must lock up for t' night. Come, stir yerself!"

She went up and took Hugh's hand.

"Good-night, Deb," he said, carelessly.

She had not hoped he would say more; but the tired pain on her mouth just then was bitterer than death. She took his passive hand and kissed it.

"Hur'll never see Deb again!" she ventured, her lips growing colder and more bloodless.

What did she say that for? Did he not know it? Yet he would not be impatient with poor old Deb. She had trouble of her own, as well as he.

"No, never again," he said, trying to be cheerful.

She stood just a moment, looking at him. Do you laugh at her, standing there, with her hunchback, her rags, her bleared, withered face, and the great despised love tugging at her heart?

"Come, you!" called Haley, impatiently.

She did not move.

"Hugh!" she whispered.

It was to be her last word. What was it?

"Hugh, boy, not THAT!"

He did not answer. She wrung her hands, trying to be silent, looking in his face in an agony of entreaty. He smiled again, kindly.

"It is best, Deb. I cannot bear to be hurted any more."

"Hur knows," she said, humbly.

"Tell my father good-bye; and—and kiss little Janey."

She nodded, saying nothing, looked in his face again, and went out of the door. As she went, she staggered.

"Drinkin' to-day?" broke out Haley, pushing her before him. "Where the Devil did you get it? Here, in with ye!" and he shoved her into her cell, next to Wolfe's, and shut the door.

Along the wall of her cell there was a crack low down by the floor, through which she could see the light from Wolfe's. She had discovered it days before. She hurried in now, and, kneeling down by it, listened, hoping to hear some sound. Nothing buy the rasping of the tin on the bars. He was at his old amusement again. Something in the noise jarred on her ear, for she shivered as she heard it. Hugh rasped away at the bars. A dull old bit of tin, not fit to cut korl with.

He looked out of the window again. People were leaving the market now. A tall mulatto girl, following her mistress, her basket on her head, crossed the street just below, and looked up. She was laughing; but, when she caught sight of the haggard face peering out through the bars, suddenly grew grave, and hurried by. A free, firm, step, a clear-cut olive face, with a scarlet turban tied on one side, dark, shining eyes, and on the head the basket poised, filled with fruit and flowers, under which the scarlet turban and bright eyes looked out half-shadowed. The picture caught his eye. It was good to see a face like that. He would try to-morrow, and cut one like it. To-morrow! He threw down the tin, trembling, and covered his face with his hands. When he looked up again, the daylight was gone.

Deborah, crouching near by on the other side of the wall, heard no noise. He sat on the side of the low pallet, thinking. Whatever was the mystery which the woman had seen on his face, it came out now slowly, in the dark there, and became fixed,—a something never seen on his face before. The evening was darkening fast. The market had been over for an hour; the rumbling of the carts over the pavement grew more infrequent: he listened to each, as it passed, because he thought it was to be for the last time. For the same reason, it was, I suppose, that he strained his eyes to catch a glimpse of each passer-by, wondering who they were, what kind of homes they were going to, if they had children,—listening eagerly to every chance word in the street, as if—(God be merciful to the man! what strange fancy was this?)—as if he never should hear human voices again.

It was quite dark at last. The street was a lonely one. The last passenger, he thought, was gone. No,—there was a quick step: Joe Hill, lighting the lamps. Joe was a good old chap; never passed a fellow without some joke or other. He remembered once seeing the place where he lived with his wife. "Granny Hill" the boys called her. Bedridden she was; but so kind as Joe was to her! kept the room so clean!—and the old woman, when he was there, was laughing at

"some of t' lad's foolishness." The step was far down the street; but he could
see him place the ladder, run up, and light the gas. A longing seized him to be
spoken to once more.

"Joe!" he called, out of the grating. "Good-bye, Joe!"

The old man stopped a moment, listening uncertainly; then hurried on.
The prisoner thrust his hand out of the window, and called again, louder; but
Joe was too far down the street. It was a little thing; but it hurt him,—this dis-
appointment.

"Good-bye, Joe!" he called, sorrowfully enough.

"Be quiet!" said one of the jailers, passing the door, striking on it with his
club.

Oh, that was the last, was it?

There was an inexpressible bitterness on his face, as he lay down on the bed,
taking the bit of tin, which he had rasped to a tolerable degree of sharpness, in
his hand,—to play with, it may be. He bared his arms, looking intently at their
corded veins and sinews. Deborah, listening in the next cell, heard a slight
clicking sound, often repeated. She shut her lips tightly, that she might not
scream, the cold drops of sweat broke over her, in her dumb agony.

"Hur knows best," she muttered at last, fiercely clutching the boards where
she lay.

If she could have seen Wolfe, there was nothing about him to frighten her.
He lay quite still, his arms outstretched, looking at the pearly stream of moon-
light coming into the window. I think in that one hour that came then he lived
back over all the years that had gone before. I think that all the low, vile life, all
his wrongs, all his starved hopes, came then, and stung him with a farewell
poison that made him sick unto death. He made neither moan nor cry, only
turned his worn face now and then to the pure light, that seemed so far off, as
one that said, "How long, O Lord? how long?"[8]

The hour was over at last. The moon, passing over her nightly path, slowly
came nearer, and threw the light across his bed on his feet. He watched it
steadily, as it crept up, inch by inch, slowly. It seemed to him to carry with it a
great silence. He had been so hot and tired there always in the mills! The years
had been so fierce and cruel! There was coming now quiet and coolness and
sleep. His tense limbs relaxed, and settled in a calm languor. The blood ran
fainter and slow from his heart. He did not think now with a savage anger of
what might be and was not; he was conscious only of deep stillness creeping
over him. At first he saw a sea of faces: the mill-men,—women he had known,
drunken and bloated,—Janeys timid and pitiful,—poor old Debs: then they
floated together like a mist, and faded away, leaving only the clear, pearly
moonlight.

Whether, as the pure light crept up the stretched-out figure, it brought with
it calm and peace, who shall say? His dumb soul was alone with God in judg-
ment. A Voice may have spoken for it from far-off Calvary, "Father, forgive
them, for they know not what they do!"[9] Who dare say? Fainter and fainter
the heart rose and fell, slower and slower the moon floated from behind a
cloud, until, when at last its full tide of white splendor swept over the cell, it
seemed to wrap and fold into a deeper stillness the dead figure that never

8. From Thomas Babington Macaulay (1800–1859), 6:3 and Revelation 6:10.
Marriage of Tirzah and Ahirad. This also echoes Psalm 9. Christ's words on the cross (Luke 23:34).

should move again. Silence deeper than the Night! Nothing that moved, save the black nauseous stream of blood dripping slowly from the pallet to the floor!

There was outcry and crowd enough in the cell the next day. The coroner and his jury, the local editors, Kirby himself and boys with their hands thrust knowingly into their pockets and heads on one side, jammed into the corners. Coming and going all day. Only one woman. She came late, and outstayed them all. A Quaker, or Friend,[1] as they call themselves. I think this woman was known by that name in heaven. A homely body, coarsely dressed in gray and white. Deborah (for Haley had let her in) took notice of her. She watched them all—sitting on the end of the pallet, holding his head in her arms—with the ferocity of a watch-dog, if any of them touched the body. There was no meekness, or sorrow, in her face; the stuff out of which murderers are made, instead. All the time Haley and the woman were laying straight the limbs and cleaning the cell, Deborah sat still, keenly watching the Quaker s face. Of all the crowd there that day, this woman alone had not spoken to her,—only once or twice had put some cordial to her lips. After they all were gone, the woman, in the same still, gentle way, brought a vase of wood-leaves and berries, and placed it by the pallet, then opened the narrow window. The fresh air blew in, and swept the woody fragrance over the dead face. Deborah looked up with a quick wonder.

"Did hur know my boy wud like it? Did hur know Hugh?"

"I know Hugh now."

The white fingers passed in a slow, pitiful way over the dead, worn face. There was a heavy shadow in the quiet eyes.

"Did hur know where they'll bury Hugh?" said Deborah in a shrill tone, catching her arm.

This had been the question hanging on her lips all day.

"In t' town-yard? Under t' mud and ash? T' lad'll smother, woman! He wur born on t' lane moor, where t' air is frick[2] and strong. Take hur out, for God's sake, take hur out where t' air blows!"

The Quaker hesitated, but only for a moment. She put her strong arm around Deborah and led her to the window.

"Thee sees the hills, friend, over the river? Thee sees how the light lies warm there, and the winds of God blow all the day? I live there,—where the blue smoke is, by the trees. Look at me." She turned Deborah s face to her own, clear and earnest. "Thee will believe me? I will take Hugh and bury him there to-morrow."

Deborah did not doubt her. As the evening wore on, she leaned against the iron bars, looking at the hills that rose far off, through the thick sodden clouds, like a bright, unattainable calm. As she looked, a shadow of their solemn repose fell on her face: its fierce discontent faded into a pitiful, humble quiet. Slow, solemn tears gathered in her eyes: the poor weak eyes turned so hopelessly to the place where Hugh was to rest, the grave heights looking higher and brighter and more solemn than ever before. The Quaker watched her keenly. She came to her at last, and touched her arm.

"When thee comes back," she said, in a low, sorrowful tone, like one who

1. The Society of Friends, a religious sect that began in 17th-century England. 2. Fresh.

speaks from a strong heart deeply moved with remorse or pity, "thee shall begin thy life again,—there on the hills. I came too late; but not for thee,—by God's help, it may be."

Not too late. Three years after, the Quaker began her work. I end my story here. At evening-time it was light. There is no need to tire you with the long years of sunshine, and fresh air, and slow, patient Christ-love, needed to make healthy and hopeful this impure body and soul. There is a homely pine house, on one of these hills, whose windows overlook broad, wooded slopes and clover-crimsoned meadows,—niched into the very place where the light is warmest, the air freest. It is the Friends' meeting-house. Once a week they sit there, in their grave, earnest way, waiting for the Spirit of Love to speak, open-ing their simple hearts to receive His words. There is a woman, old, deformed, who takes a humble place among them: waiting like them: in her gray dress, her worn face, pure and meek, turned now and then to the sky. A woman much loved by these silent, restful people; more silent than they, more humble, more loving. Waiting: with her eyes turned to hills higher and purer than these on which she lives,—dim and far off now, but to be reached some day. There may be in her heart some latent hope to meet there the love denied her here,—that she shall find him whom she lost, and that then she will not be all-unworthy. Who blames her? Something is lost in the passage of every soul from one eternity to the other,—something pure and beautiful, which might have been and was not: a hope, a talent, a love, over which the soul mourns, like Esau[3] deprived of his birthright. What blame to the meek Quaker, if she took her lost hope to make the hills of heaven more fair?

Nothing remains to tell that the poor Welsh puddler once lived, but this fig-ure of the mill-woman cut in korl. I have it here in a corner of my library. I keep it hid behind a curtain,—it is such a rough, ungainly thing. Yet there are about it touches, grand sweeps of outline, that show a master's hand. Sometimes,—to-night, for instance,—the curtain is accidentally drawn back, and I see a bare arm stretched out imploringly in the darkness, and an eager, wolfish face watching mine: a wan, woeful face, through which the spirit of the dead korl-cutter looks out, with its thwarted life, its mighty hunger, its unfinished work. Its pale, vague lips seem to tremble with a terrible question. "Is this the End?" they say,—"nothing beyond?—no more?" Why, you tell me you have seen that look in the eyes of dumb brutes,—horses dying under the lash. I know.

The deep of the night is passing while I write. The gas-light wakens from the shadows here and there the objects which lie scattered through the room: only faintly, though; for they belong to the open sunlight. As I glance at them, they each recall some task or pleasure of the coming day. A half-moulded child's head; Aphrodite;[4] a bough of forest-leaves; music; work; homely frag-ments, in which lie the secrets of all eternal truth and beauty. Prophetic all! Only this dumb, woeful face seems to belong to and end with the night. I turn to look at it. Has the power of its desperate need commanded the darkness away? While the room is yet steeped in heavy shadow, a cool, gray light sud-denly touches its head like a blessing hand, and its groping arm points through the broken cloud to the far East, where, in the flickering, nebulous crimson, God has set the promise of the Dawn.

1861

3. The son of Isaac and Rebecca, who sold his birthright to his brother Jacob (Genesis 25:31). 4. The Greek goddess of love.

LOUISA MAY ALCOTT

1832–1888

If American girls between 1870 and the present were to vote for their favorite fictional heroine, Louisa May Alcott's Jo March would be among the election's finalists. The central character of Alcott's *Little Women* (1869), high-spirited Jo is a literarily inclined tomboy, the second oldest of four sisters whose domestic adventures have had an enduring appeal for generations of young readers. Though the novel in which they appear is frequently didactic, drawing for both its narrative structure and its moral strictures on John Bunyan's allegorical *Pilgrim's Progress* (1678), it is continually enlivened by realistic details of New England home life during the Civil War period as well as by incisive depictions of the pressures associated with growing up female in nineteenth-century America. More specifically, the tale is made dramatic by its sympathetic examination of rambunctious Jo's initial rebellion against, and ultimate reconciliation to, what the historian Nancy Cott has called "the bonds of womanhood."

No doubt one factor that gave this portrait of the artist as a "little woman" special force was that in many ways the tale of Jo's pilgrim's progress toward maturity was Alcott's own story. Born in 1832, Louisa May Alcott was, like Jo, the second of four sisters; her older sister, Anna, inspired the character of Jo's sister Meg; her younger sisters, Elizabeth and Abbie, were depicted in barely disguised forms as Jo's sisters Beth and Amy. Like gentle philosophical Mr. March, who is away fighting in the Civil War for much of the book, "Lu" Alcott's father was an unworldly philosopher who was often absent from home on lecture and walking tours. The friend of such notable New England intellectuals as Emerson and Thoreau, Bronson Alcott was an experimental educator, a Transcendentalist, and a social reformer whose commitment to idealistic causes—for instance, the short-lived utopian community called "Fruitlands" —frequently left his family on the edge of poverty. Like *Little Women*'s patient and diligent "Marmee," his wife, Abba, was a strong, supportive woman who kept the household going, both emotionally and financially, through all kinds of vicissitudes. Most likely it was from her example that the young Louisa gained the determination to shoulder what *Little Women*, following *Pilgrim's Progress*, calls the "burdens" of life. Certainly it was to assist her overworked mother that she resolved, at the age of eighteen, to become self-supporting, and, more, to make enough money so that Abba Alcott could "have a lovely, quiet home . . . with no debts or troubles."

Although, as she herself observed, the range of careers available to nineteenth-century girls was severely limited, Alcott held positions as a seamstress, a domestic servant, a governess, a teacher, a lady's "companion," and an army nurse—all jobs whose oppressions and rewards she was later to describe in her novel *Work* (1873) and in several other volumes. Even while she labored at these often menial occupations, however, she was steadily writing fiction, poetry, and journalistic sketches. Like Jo March, she had always been an imaginative girl, and like Jo, she composed Gothic thrillers (which she published under the pseudonym A. M. Barnard) when she was still a teenager. Again like Jo—who learns to renounce her desire for romantic "blood and thunder" in a chapter of *Little Women* called "Literary Lessons"—Alcott moved during her career from romance to realism, from melodramatizing to moralizing. In 1863 she published a well-received collection of *Hospital Sketches*, describing her experiences as a Civil War army nurse with poignant accuracy, and in 1864 she published a promising first novel, *Moods*. Then, early in 1868, she became the editor of *Merry's Museum*, a magazine for girls, and, when a Boston publisher suggested that she herself might write a novel for young people, she composed *Little Women* in two six-week periods. The book

was an instant success, establishing her as one of America's best-selling writers. For the next twenty years, until her death in 1888, she was to maintain and enhance her reputation, producing, on the average, a book a year, including seven more novels for girls and two for adults, as well as sixteen collections of stories and sketches for children and adolescents.

From *Little Women* onward, Alcott's fiction reveals her continuing concern with social reform, especially her sense of the ways in which young women were exploited by a society that obliged them to support themselves but offered them few opportunities for self-improvement. Similarly, her early thrillers, recently collected in two volumes—*Behind a Mask* and *Plots and Counterplots*—frequently suggest a secret rage at female powerlessness, a rage that is briefly expressed by even the ever-patient Marmee in *Little Women*, when she confesses that "I have been angry every day of my life." Not surprisingly, then, Louisa May Alcott was active in the nineteenth-century feminist movement. She was the first woman to register in Concord when Massachusetts gave women limited suffrage in 1879, for instance, and she helped facilitate the 1881 publication of Harriet Hanson Robinson's *Massachusetts in the Woman Suffrage Movement*, claiming that she took "more pride" in such gestures toward political reform "than in all the books I ever wrote." But as even the opening chapters of *Little Women* (reprinted here) reveal, this rebellious feminist also inherited from her mother a more general sense of socal responsibility for the welfare of those less fortunate than herself.

Perhaps, indeed, it was because her private as well as public responsibilities had been so heavy and of such long standing that Alcott's success as a writer brought her comparatively little satisfaction. Despite the fact that she was lionized on literary tours and treated as a celebrity in her home town of Concord, she disliked the attentions of her many admirers, complaining that "I asked for bread, and got a stone,—in the shape of a pedestal." Sadly, her last years were shadowed by a range of ailments, many very likely psychosomatic in nature, while her family, particularly her aging father and her widowed sister Anna, continued to be burdens to her. It may be no coincidence that she died, of what was diagnosed as either meningitis or apoplexy, on the very day of her father's funeral: the moral responsibilities of her pilgrim's progress ended only with the end of her life.

From Little Women

Chapter 1. Playing Pilgrims

"Christmas won't be Christmas without any presents," grumbled Jo, lying on the rug.

"It's so dreadful to be poor!" sighed Meg, looking down at her old dress.

"I don't think it's fair for some girls to have plenty of pretty things, and other girls nothing at all," added little Amy, with an injured sniff.

"We've got father and mother and each other," said Beth, contentedly, from her corner.

The four young faces on which the firelight shone brightened at the cheerful words, but darkened again as Jo said sadly:

"We haven't got father, and shall not have him for a long time." She didn't say "perhaps never," but each silently added it, thinking of father far away, where the fighting was.

Nobody spoke for a minute; then Meg said in an altered tone:

"You know the reason mother proposed not having any presents this Christmas was because it is going to be a hard winter for everyone; and she

thinks we ought not to spend money for pleasure when our men are suffering so in the army.[1] We can't do much, but we can make our little sacrifices, and ought to do it gladly. But I am afraid I don't"; and Meg shook her head, and she thought regretfully of all the pretty things she wanted.

"But I don't think the little we should spend would do any good. We've each got a dollar, and the army wouldn't be much helped by our giving that. I agree not to expect anything from mother or you, but I do want to buy *Undine and Sintram*[2] for myself; I've wanted it so long," said Jo, who was a bookworm.

"I planned to spend mine on new music,' said Beth, with a little sigh, which no one heard but the hearth-brush and kettle-holder.

"I shall get a nice box of Faber's drawing pencils; I really need them," said Amy, decidedly.

"Mother didn't say anything about our money, and she won't wish us to give up everything. Let's each buy what we want, and have a little fun; I'm sure we work hard enough to earn it," cried Jo, examining the heels of her shoes in a gentlemanly manner.

"I know I do—teaching those tiresome children nearly all day when I am longing to enjoy myself at home," began Meg, in the complaining tone again.

"You don't have half such a hard time as I do," said Jo. "How would you like to be shut up for hours with a nervous, fussy old lady, who keeps you trotting, is never satisfied, and worries you till you're ready to fly out of the window or cry?"

"It's naughty to fret; but I do think washing dishes and keeping things tidy is the worst work in the world. It makes me cross; and my hands get so stiff, I can't practice[3] well at all"; and Beth looked at her rough hands with a sigh that anyone could hear that time.

"I don't believe any of you suffer as I do," cried Amy; "for you don't have to go to school with impertinent girls, who plague you if you don't know your lessons, and laugh at your dresses, and label your father if he isn't rich, and insult you when your nose isn't nice."

"If you mean *libel*, I'd say so, and not talk about *labels*, as if papa was a pickle-bottle," advised Jo, laughing.

"I know what I mean, and you needn't be *statirical* about it. It's proper to use good words, and improve your *vocabulary*," returned Amy, with dignity.

"Don't peck at one another, children. Don't you wish we had the money papa lost when we were little, Jo? Dear me! how happy and good we'd be, if we had no worries!" said Meg, who could remember better times.

"You said, the other day, you thought we were a deal happier than the King children, for they were fighting and fretting all the time, in spite of their money."

"So I did, Beth. Well, I think we are; for, though we do have to work, we make fun for ourselves, and are a pretty jolly set, as Jo would say."

"Jo does use such slang words!" observed Amy, with a reproving look at the long figure stretched on the rug. Jo immediately sat up, put her hands in her pockets, and began to whistle.

"Don't, Jo; it's so boyish!"

"That's why I do it."

"I detest rude, unladylike girls!"

1. I.e., in the Union forces fighting in the Civil War.
2. Tales by the German Romantic author Friedrich von Fouqué (1777–1843).
3. I.e., the piano.

"I hate affected, niminy-piminy chits!"

"'Birds in their little nests agree,'"[4] sang Beth, the peacemaker, with such a funny face that both sharp voices softened to a laugh, and the "pecking" ended for that time.

"Really, girls, you are both to be blamed," said Meg, beginning to lecture in her elder-sisterly fashion. "You are old enough to leave off boyish tricks, and to behave better, Josephine. It didn't matter so much when you were a little girl; but now you are so tall, and turn up your hair, you should remember that you are a young lady."

"I'm not! and if turning up my hair makes me one, I'll wear it in two tails till I'm twenty," cried Jo, pulling off her net, and shaking down her chestnut mane. "I hate to think I've got to grow up, and be Miss March, and wear long gowns, and look as prim as a China-aster![5] It's bad enough to be a girl, anyway, when I like boys' games and work and manners! I can't get over my disappointment in not being a boy; and it's worse than ever now, for I'm dying to go and fight with papa, and I can only stay at home and knit, like a poky old woman!" And Jo shook the blue army sock till the needles rattled like castanets, and her ball bounded across the room.

"Poor Jo! It's too bad, but it can't be helped; so you must try to be contented with making your name boyish, and playing brother to us girls," said Beth, stroking the rough head at her knee with a hand that all the dish-washing and dusting in the world could not make ungentle in its touch.

"As for you, Amy," continued Meg, "you are altogether too particular and prim. Your airs are funny now; but you'll grow up an affected little goose, if you don't take care. I like your nice manners and refined ways of speaking when you don't try to be elegant; but your absurd words are as bad as Jo's slang."

"If Jo is a tomboy and Amy a goose, what am I, please?" asked Beth, ready to share the lecture.

"You're a dear, and nothing else," answered Meg, warmly; and no one contradicted her, for the "Mouse" was the pet of the family.

As young readers like to know "how people look," we will take this moment to give them a little sketch of the four sisters, who sat knitting away in the twilight, while the December snow fell quietly without, and the fire crackled cheerfully within. It was a comfortable old room, though the carpet was faded and the furniture very plain; for a good picture or two hung on the walls, books filled the recesses, chrysanthemums and Christmas roses bloomed in the windows, and a pleasant atmosphere of home-peace pervaded it.

Margaret, the eldest of the four, was sixteen, and very pretty, being plump and fair, with large eyes, plenty of soft, brown hair, a sweet mouth, and white hands, of which she was rather vain. Fifteen-year-old Jo was very tall, thin, and brown, and reminded one of a colt; for she never seemed to know what to do with her long limbs, which were very much in her way. She had a decided mouth, a comical nose, and sharp, gray eyes, which appeared to see everything, and were by turns fierce, funny, or thoughtful. Her long, thick hair was her one beauty; but it was usually bundled in a net, to be out of her way. Round shoulders had Jo, big hands and feet, a fly-away look to her clothes, and the uncomfortable appearance of a girl who was rapidly shooting up into a

4. From Isaac Watt's "Love between Brothers and 5. Flower.
Sisters" (1715). "Chits": pert girls.

woman, and didn't like it. Elizabeth—or Beth, as everyone called her—was a
rosy, smooth-haired, bright-eyed girl of thirteen, with a shy manner, a timid
voice, and a peaceful expression, which was seldom disturbed. Her father
called her "Little Tranquillity," and the name suited her excellently; for she
seemed to live in a happy world of her own, only venturing out to meet the few
whom she trusted and loved. Amy, though the youngest, was a most impor-
tant person—in her own opinion at least. A regular snow-maiden, with blue
eyes, and yellow hair, curling on her shoulders, pale and slender, and always
carrying herself like a young lady mindful of her manners. What the charac-
ters of the four sisters were we will leave to be found out.

The clock struck six; and, having swept up the hearth, Beth put a pair of
slippers down to warm. Somehow the sight of the old shoes had a good effect
upon the girls; for mother was coming, and everyone brightened to welcome
her. Meg stopped lecturing, and lighted the lamp, Amy got out of the easy-
chair without being asked, and Jo forgot how tired she was as she sat up to hold
the slippers nearer to the blaze.

"They are quite worn out; Marmee must have a new pair."

"I thought I'd get her some with my dollar," said Beth.

"No, I shall!" cried Amy.

"I'm the oldest," began Meg, but Jo cut in with a decided:

"I'm the man of the family now papa is away, and I shall provide the slip-
pers, for he told me to take special care of mother while he was gone."

"I'll tell you what we'll do," said Beth; "let's each get her something for
Christmas, and not get anything for ourselves."

"That's like you, dear! What will we get?" exclaimed Jo.

Every one thought soberly for a minute; then Meg announced as if the idea
was suggested by the sight of her own pretty hands, "I shall give her a nice pair
of gloves."

"Army shoes, best to be had," cried Jo.

"Some handkerchiefs, all hemmed," said Beth.

"I'll get a little bottle of cologne; she likes it, and it won't cost much, so I'll
have some left to buy my pencils," added Amy.

"How will we give the things?" asked Meg.

"Put them on the table, and bring her in and see her open the bundles.
Don't you remember how we used to do on our birthdays?" answered Jo.

"I used to be so frightened when it was my turn to sit in the big chair with
the crown on, and see you all come marching round to give the presents, with
a kiss. I liked the things and the kisses, but it was dreadful to have you sit look-
ing at me while I opened the bundles," said Beth, who was toasting her face
and the bread for tea, at the same time.

"Let Marmee think we are getting things for ourselves, and then surprise
her. We must go shopping tomorrow afternoon, Meg; there is so much to do
about the play for Christmas night," said Jo, marching up and down, with her
hands behind her back and her nose in the air.

"I don't mean to act any more after this time; I'm getting too old for such
things," observed Meg, who was as much a child as ever about "dressing-up"
frolics.

"You won't stop, I know, as long as you can trail round in a white gown with
your hair down, and wear gold-paper jewellery. You are the best actress we've
got, and there'll be an end of everything if you quit the boards," said Jo. "We

ought to rehearse tonight. Come here, Amy, and do the fainting scene, for you are as stiff as a poker in that."

"I can't help it; I never saw anyone faint, and I don't choose to make myself all black and blue, tumbling flat as you do. If I can go down easily, I'll drop; if I can't, I shall fall into a chair and be graceful; I don't care if Hugo does come at me with a pistol," returned Amy, who was not gifted with dramatic power, but was chosen because she was small enough to be borne out shrieking by the villain of the piece.

"Do it this way; clasp your hands so, and stagger across the room, crying frantically, 'Roderigo! save me! save me!'" and away went Jo, with a melodramatic scream which was truly thrilling.

Amy followed, but she poked her hands out stiffly before her, and jerked herself along as if she went by machinery; and her "Ow!" was more suggestive of pins being run into her than of fear and anguish. Jo gave a despairing groan, and Meg laughed outright, while Beth let her bread burn as she watched the fun with interest.

"It's no use! Do the best you can when the time comes, and if the audience laugh, don't blame me. Come on, Meg."

Then things went smoothly, for Don Pedro defied the world in a speech of two pages without a single break; Hagar, the witch, chanted an awful incantation over her kettleful of simmering toads, with weird effect; Roderigo rent his chains asunder manfully, and Hugo died in agonies of remorse and arsenic with a wild "Ha! ha!"

"It's the best we've had yet," said Meg, as the dead villain sat up and rubbed his elbows.

"I don't see how you can write and act such splendid things, Jo. You're a regular Shakespeare!" exclaimed Beth, who firmly believed that her sisters were gifted with wonderful genius in all things.

"Not quite," replied Jo modestly. "I do think 'The Witch's Curse, An Operatic Tragedy,' is rather a nice thing; but I'd like to try *Macbeth*, if we only had a trap-door for Banquo. I always wanted to do the killing part. 'Is that a dagger I see before me?'" muttered Jo, rolling her eyes and clutching at the air, as she had seen a famous tragedian do.

"No, it's the toasting fork, with mother's shoe on it instead of the bread. Beth's stage-struck!" cried Meg, and the rehearsal ended in a general burst of laughter.

"Glad to find you so merry, my girls," said a cheery voice at the door, and actors and audience turned to welcome a tall, motherly lady, with a "can-I-help-you" look about her which was truly delightful. She was not elegantly dressed, but a noble-looking woman, and the girls thought the gray cloak and unfashionable bonnet covered the most splendid mother in the world.

"Well, dearies, how have you got on today? There was so much to do, getting the boxes ready to go tomorrow, that I didn't come home to dinner. Has anyone called, Beth? How is your cold, Meg? Jo, you look tired to death. Come and kiss me, baby."

While making these maternal inquiries, Mrs. March got her wet things off, her warm slippers on, and sitting down in the easy-chair, drew Amy to her lap, preparing to enjoy the happiest hour of her busy day. The girls flew about, trying to make things comfortable, each in her own way. Meg arranged the tea-table; Jo brought wood and set chairs, dropping, overturning, and clattering

everything she touched; Beth trotted to and fro between parlor and kitchen, quiet and busy; while Amy gave directions to everyone, as she sat with her hands folded.

As they gathered about the table, Mrs. March said, with a particularly happy face, "I've got a treat for you after supper."

A quick, bright smile went round like a streak of sunshine. Beth clapped her hands, regardless of the biscuit she held, and Jo tossed up her napkin, crying, "A letter! a letter! Three cheers for father!"

"Yes, a nice long letter. He is well, and thinks he shall get through the cold season better than we feared. He sends all sorts of loving wishes for Christmas, and an especial message to you girls," said Mrs. March, patting her pocket as if she had got a treasure there.

"Hurry and get done! Don't stop to quirk your little finger, and simper over your plate, Amy," cried Jo, choking in her tea, and dropping her bread, butter side down, on the carpet in her haste to get at the treat.

Beth ate no more, but crept away, to sit in her shadowy corner and brood over the delight to come, till the others were ready.

"I think it was so splendid of father to go as chaplain when he was too old to be drafted, and not strong enough for a soldier," said Meg, warmly.

"Don't I wish I could go as a drummer, a vivan⁶—what's its name? or a nurse, so I could be near him and help him," exclaimed Jo, with a groan.

"It must be very disagreeable to sleep in a tent, and eat all sorts of bad-tasting things, and drink out of a tin mug," sighed Amy.

"When will he come home, Marmee?" asked Beth, with a little quiver in her voice.

"Not for many months, dear, unless he is sick. He will stay and do his work faithfully as long as he can, and we won't ask for him back a minute sooner than he can be spared. Now come and hear the letter."

They all drew to the fire, mother in the big chair, with Beth at her feet, Meg and Amy perched on either arm of the chair, and Jo leaning on the back, where no one would see any sign of emotion if the letter should happen to be touching. Very few letters were written in those hard times that were not touching, especially those which fathers sent home. In this one little was said of the hardships endured, the dangers faced, or the home-sickness conquered; it was a cheerful, hopeful letter, full of lively descriptions of camp life, marches, and military news; and only at the end did the writer's heart overflow with fatherly love and longing for the little girls at home.

"Give them all my dear love and a kiss. Tell them I think of them by day, pray for them by night, and find my best comfort in their affection at all times. A year seems very long to wait before I see them, but remind them that while we wait we may all work, so that these hard days need not be wasted. I know they will remember all I said to them, that they will be loving children to you, will do their duty faithfully, fight their bosom enemies bravely, and conquer themselves so beautifully, that when I come back to them I may be fonder and prouder than ever of my little women."

Everybody sniffed when they came to that part; Jo wasn't ashamed of the great tear that dropped off the end of her nose, and Amy never minded the rumpling of her curls as she hid her face on her mother's shoulder and sobbed

6. I.e., a vivandière: a woman who helps provision an army.

out, "I *am* a selfish girl! but I'll truly try to be better, so he mayn't be disappointed in me by and by."

"We all will!" cried Meg. "I think too much of my looks, and hate to work, but won't any more, if I can help it."

"I'll try and be what he loves to call me, 'a little woman,' and not be rough and wild; but do my duty here instead of wanting to be somewhere else," said Jo, thinking that keeping her temper at home was a much harder task than facing a rebel or two down South.

Beth said nothing, but wiped away her tears with the blue army sock, and began to knit with all her might, losing no time in doing the duty that lay nearest her, while she resolved in her quiet little soul to be all that father hoped to find her when the year brought round the happy coming home.

Mrs. March broke the silence that followed Jo's words, by saying in her cheery voice, "Do you remember how you used to play *Pilgrim's Progress*[7] when you were little things? Nothing delighted you more than to have me tie my piece-bags[8] on your backs for burdens, give you hats and sticks and rolls of paper, and let you travel through the house from the cellar, which was the City of Destruction, up, up, to the housetop, where you had all the lovely things you could collect to make a Celestial City."

"What fun it was, especially going by the lions, fighting Apollyon, and passing through the Valley where the hobgoblins were!" said Jo.

"I liked the place where the bundles fell off and tumbled downstairs," said Meg.

"My favorite part was when we came out on the flat roof where our flowers and arbors and pretty things were, and all stood and sang for joy up there in the sunshine," said Beth, smiling, as if that pleasant moment had come back to her.

"I don't remember much about it, except that I was afraid of the cellar and the dark entry, and always liked the cake and milk we had up at the top. If I wasn't too old for such things, I'd rather like to play it over again," said Amy, who began to talk of renouncing childish things at the mature age of twelve.

"We never are too old for this, my dear, because it is a play we are playing all the time in one way or another. Our burdens are here, our road is before us, and the longing for goodness and happiness is the guide that leads us through many troubles and mistakes to the peace which is a true Celestial City. Now, my little pilgrims, suppose you begin again, not in play, but in earnest, and see how far on you can get before Father comes home."

"Really, Mother? Where are our bundles?" asked Amy, who was a very literal young lady.

"Each of you told what your burden was just now, except Beth; I rather think she hasn't got any," said her mother.

"Yes, I have; mine is dishes and dusters, and envying girls with nice pianos, and being afraid of people."

Beth's bundle was such a funny one that everybody wanted to laugh; but nobody did, for it would have hurt her feelings very much.

"Let us do it," said Meg, thoughtfully. "It is only another name for trying to

7. John Bunyan's allegorical book (1678) tells the story of successfully journeying from this world to the next.

8. Bags for holding pieces of cloth.

be good, and the story may help us; for though we do want to be good, it's hard work, and we forget, and don't do our best."

"We were in the Slough of Despond tonight, and Mother came and pulled us out as Help did in the book. We ought to have our roll of directions, like Christian. What shall we do about that?" asked Jo, delighted with the fancy which lent a little romance to the very dull task of doing her duty.

"Look under your pillows Christmas morning, and you will find your guide-book," replied Mrs. March.

They talked over the new plan while old Hannah cleared the table; then out came the four little work-baskets, and the needles flew as the girls made sheets for Aunt March. It was uninteresting sewing, but tonight no one grumbled. They adopted Jo's plan of dividing the long seams into four parts, and calling the quarters Europe, Asia, Africa, and America, and in that way got on capitally, especially when they talked about the different counties, as they stitched their way through them

At nine they stopped work, and sang, as usual, before they went to bed. No one but Beth could get much music out of the old piano; but she had a way of softly touching the yellow keys, and making a pleasant accompaniment to the simple songs they sang Meg had a voice like a flute, and she and her mother led the little choir. Amy chirped like a cricket, and Jo wandered through the airs at her own sweet will, always coming out at the wrong place with a croak or a quaver that spoilt the most pensive tune. They had always done this from the time they could lisp

"Crinkle, crinkle, 'ittle 'tar."

and it had become a household custom, for the mother was a born singer. The first sound in the morning was her voice, and she went about the house singing like a lark; and the last sound at night was the same cheery sound, for the girls never grew too old for that familiar lullaby.

Chapter 2. A Merry Christmas

Jo was the first to wake in the gray dawn of Christmas morning. No stockings hung at the fireplace, and for a moment she felt as much disappointed as she did long ago, when her little sock fell down because it was so crammed with goodies. Then she remembered her mother's promise, and, slipping her hand under her pillow, drew out a little crimson-covered book. She knew it very well, for it was that beautiful old story of the best life ever lived, and Jo felt that it was a true guide-book for any pilgrim going the long journey. She woke Meg with a "Merry Christmas," and bade her see what was under her pillow. A green-covered book appeared, with the same picture inside, and a few words written by their mother, which made their one present very precious in their eyes. Presently Beth and Amy woke, to rummage and find their little books also—one, dove-colored, the other blue; and all sat looking at and talking about them, while the east grew rosy with the coming day.

In spite of her small vanities, Margaret had a sweet and pious nature, which unconsciously influenced her sisters, especially Jo, who loved her very tenderly, and obeyed her because her advice was so gently given.

"Girls," said Meg seriously, looking from the tumbled head beside her to the two little night-capped ones in the room beyond, "Mother wants us to read

and love and mind these books, and we must begin at once. We used to be faithful about it; but since Father went away, and all this war trouble unsettled us, we have neglected many things. You can do as you please; but *I* shall keep my book on the table here, and read a little every morning as soon as I wake, for I know it will do me good, and help me through the day."

Then she opened her new book and began to read. Jo put her arm round her, and, leaning cheek to cheek, read also, with the quiet expression so seldom seen on her restless face.

"How good Meg is! Come, Amy, let's do as they do. I'll help you with the hard words, and they'll explain things if we don't understand," whispered Beth, very much impressed by the pretty books and her sisters' example.

"I'm glad mine is blue," said Amy; and then the rooms were very still while the pages were softly turned, and the winter sunshine crept in to touch the bright heads and serious faces with a Christmas greeting.

"Where is Mother?" asked Meg, as she and Jo ran down to thank her for their gifts, half an hour later.

"Goodness only knows. Some poor creeter come a-beggin', and your ma went straight off to see what was needed. There never *was* such a woman for givin' away vittles and drink, clothes, and firin'," replied Hannah, who had lived with the family since Meg was born, and was considered by them all more as a friend than a servant.

"She will be back soon, I think; so fry your cake, and have everything ready," said Meg, looking over the presents which were collected in a basket and kept under the sofa, ready to be produced at the proper time. "Why, where is Amy's bottle of cologne?" she added, as the little flask did not appear.

"She took it out a minute ago, and went off with it to put a ribbon on it, or some such notion," replied Jo, dancing about the room to take the first stiffness off the new army-slippers.

"How nice my handkerchiefs look, don't they! Hannah washed and ironed them for me, and I marked them all myself," said Beth, looking proudly at the somewhat uneven letters which had cost her such labor.

"Bless the child! she's gone and put 'Mother' on them instead of 'M. March.' How funny!" cried Jo, taking up one.

"Isn't it right? I thought it was better to do it so, because Meg's initials are 'M. M.,' and I don't want anyone to use these but Marmee," said Beth, looking troubled.

"It's all right, dear, and a very pretty idea—quite sensible, too, for no one can ever mistake now. It will please her very much, I know," said Meg, with a frown for Jo and a smile for Beth.

"There's Mother. Hide the basket, quick!" cried Jo, as a door slammed, and steps sounded in the hall.

Amy came in hastily, and looked rather abashed when she saw her sisters all waiting for her.

"Where have you been, and what are you hiding behind you?" asked Meg, surprised to see, by her hood and cloak, that lazy Amy had been out so early.

"Don't laugh at me, Jo! I didn't mean anyone should know till the time came. I only meant to change the little bottle for a big one, and I gave *all* my money to get it, and I'm truly trying not to be selfish any more."

As she spoke, Amy showed the handsome flask which replaced the cheap one; and looked so earnest and humble in her little effort to forget herself that

Meg hugged her on the spot, and Jo pronounced her "a trump," while Beth ran to the window and picked her finest rose to ornament the stately bottle.

"You see, I felt ashamed of my present, after reading and talking about being good this morning, so I ran round the corner and changed it the minute I was up; and I'm so glad, for mine is the handsomest now."

Another bang of the street door sent the basket under the sofa, and the girls to the table, eager for breakfast.

"Merry Christmas, Marmee! Many of them! Thank you for our books; we read some, and mean to, every day," they cried, in chorus.

"Merry Christmas, little daughters! I'm glad you began at once, and hope you will keep on. But I want to say one word before we sit down. Not far away from here lies a poor woman with a little new-born baby. Six children are huddled into one bed to keep from freezing, for they have no fire. There is nothing to eat over there; and the oldest boy came to tell me they were suffering hunger and cold. My girls, will you give them your breakfast as a Christmas present?"

They were all unusually hungry, having waited nearly an hour, and for a minute no one spoke; only a minute, for Jo exclaimed impetuously:

"I'm so glad you came before we began!"

"May I go and help carry the things to the poor little children?" said Beth, eagerly.

"I shall take the cream and the muffins," added Amy, heroically, giving up the articles she most liked.

Meg was already covering the buckwheats, and piling the bread into one big plate.

"I thought you'd do it," said Mrs. March, smiling as if satisfied. "You shall all go and help me, and when we come back we will have bread and milk for breakfast, and make it up at dinner-time."

They were soon ready, and the procession set out. Fortunately it was early, and they went through back streets, so few people saw them, and no one laughed at the queer party.

A poor, bare, miserable room it was, with broken windows, no fire, ragged bed-clothes, a sick mother, wailing baby, and a group of pale, hungry children cuddled under one old quilt, trying to keep warm.

How the big eyes stared and blue lips smiled as the girls went in!

"Ach, mein Gott![9] it is good angels come to us!" said the poor woman, crying for joy.

"Funny angels in hoods and mittens," said Jo, and set them laughing.

In a few minutes it really did seem as if kind spirits had been at work there. Hannah, who had carried wood, made a fire, and stopped up the broken panes with old hats and her own cloak. Mrs. March gave the mother tea and gruel, and comforted her with promises of help, while she dressed the little baby as tenderly as if it had been her own. The girls, meantime, spread the table, set the children round the fire, and fed them like so many hungry birds—laughing, talking, and trying to understand the funny broken English.

"Das ist gut!" "Die Engelkinder!"[1] cried the poor things, as they ate, and warmed their purple hands at the comfortable blaze.

The girls had never been called angel children before, and thought it very

9. Ah, my God! (German). 1. This is good! The angel children

agreeable, especially Jo, who had been considered a "Sancho"[2] ever since she was born. That was a very happy breakfast, though they didn't get any of it; and when they went away, leaving comfort behind, I think there were not in all the city four merrier people than the hungry little girls who gave away their breakfasts and contented themselves with bread and milk on Christmas morning.

"That's loving our neighbor better than ourselves, and I like it," said Meg, as they set out their presents, while their mother was upstairs collecting clothes for the poor Hummels.

Not a very splendid show, but there was a great deal of love done up in the few little bundles; and the tall vase of red roses, white chrysanthemums, and trailing vines, which stood in the middle, gave quite an elegant air to the table.

"She's coming! Strike up, Beth! Open the door, Amy! Three cheers for Marmee!" cried Jo, prancing about, while Meg went to conduct Mother to the seat of honor.

Beth played her gayest march, Amy threw open the door, and Meg enacted escort with great dignity. Mrs. March was both surprised and touched; and smiled with her eyes full as she examined her presents, and read the little notes which accompanied them. The slippers went on at once, a new handkerchief was slipped into her pocket, well scented with Amy's cologne, the rose was fastened in her bosom, and the nice gloves were pronounced a "perfect fit."

There was a good deal of laughing and kissing and explaining, in the simple, loving fashion which makes these home festivals so pleasant at the time, so sweet to remember long afterwards, and then all fell to work.

The morning charities and ceremonies took so much time that the rest of the day was devoted to preparations for the evening festivities.

Not rich enough to afford any great outlay for private performances, the girls put their wits to work, and—necessity being the mother of invention—made whatever they needed. Very clever were some of their productions—pasteboard guitars, antique lamps made of old-fashioned butter-boats[3] covered with silver paper, gorgeous robes of old cotton glittering with tin spangle from a pickle factory, and armor covered with the same useful diamond-shaped bits, left in the sheets when the lids of tin preserve-pots were cut out. The furniture was used to being turned topsy-turvy, and the big chamber was the scene of many innocent revels.

No gentlemen were admitted; so Jo played male parts to her heart's content, and took immense satisfaction in a pair of russet-leather boots given her by a friend. These boots, an old foil, and a slashed doublet once used by an artist for some picture, were Jo's chief treasures, and appeared on all occasions. The smallness of the company made it necessary for the two principal actors to take several parts apiece; and they certainly deserved some credit for the hard work they did in learning three or four different parts, whisking in and out of various costumes, and managing the stage besides. It was excellent drill for their memories, a harmless amusement, and employed many hours which otherwise would have been idle, lonely, or spent in less profitable society.

On Christmas night, a dozen girls piled on to the bed, which was the dress-

2. I.e., like Sancho Panza, the simple and common-sensical peasant who acts as a squire in Cervantes's *Don Quixote* (1615).
3. Vessels for serving melted butter in.

circle, and sat before the blue and yellow chintz curtains in a most flattering state of expectancy. There was a good deal of rustling and whispering behind the curtain, a trifle of lamp-smoke, and an occasional giggle from Amy, who was apt to get hysterical in the excitement of the moment. Presently a bell sounded, the curtains flew apart, and the Operatic Tragedy began.

"A gloomy wood," according to the one play-bill, was represented by a few shrubs in pots, green baize[4] on the floor, and a cave in the distance. This cave was made with a clothes-horse for a roof, bureaus for walls; and in it was a small furnace in full blast, with a black spot on it, and an old witch bending over it. The stage was dark, and the glow of the furnace had a fine effect, especially as real steam issued from the kettle when the witch took off the cover. A moment was allowed for the first thrill to subside; then Hugo, the villain, stalked in with a clanking sword at his side, a slouched hat, black beard, mysterious cloak, and the boots. After pacing to and fro in much agitation, he struck his forehead, and burst out in a wild strain, singing of his hatred to Roderigo, his love for Zara, and his pleasing resolution to kill the one and win the other. The gruff tones of Hugo's voice, with an occasional shout when his feelings overcame him, were very impressive, and the audience applauded the moment he paused for breath. Bowing with the air of one accustomed to public praise, he stole to the cavern, and ordered Hagar to come forth with a commanding "What ho, minion! I need thee!"

Out came Meg, with gray horse-hair hanging about her face, a red and black robe, a staff, and cabbalistic[5] signs upon her cloak. Hugo demanded a potion to make Zara adore him, and one to destroy Roderigo. Hagar, in a fine dramatic melody, promised both, and proceeded to call up the spirit who would bring the love philtre:

> "Hither, hither, from my home,
> Airy sprite, I bid thee come!
> Born of roses, fed on dew,
> Charms and potions canst thou brew?

> "Bring me here, with elfin speed,
> The fragrant philtre which I need;
> Make it sweet and swift and strong,
> Spirit, answer now my song!"

A soft strain of music sounded, and then at the back of the cave appeared a little figure in cloudy white, with glittering wings, golden hair, and a garland of roses on its head. Waving a wand, it sang:

> "Hither I come,
> From my airy home,
> Afar in the silver moon.
> Take this magic spell,
> And use it well,
> Or its power will vanish soon!'

And, dropping a small, gilded bottle at the witch's feet, the spirit vanished. Another chant from Hagar produced another apparition—not a lovely one;

4. A coarse fabric made to imitate felt. 5. I.e., associated with the occult.

for, with a bang, an ugly black imp appeared, and, having croaked a reply, tossed a dark bottle at Hugo, and disappeared with a mocking laugh. Having warbled his thanks and put the potions in his boots, Hugo departed; and Hagar informed the audience that, as he had killed a few of her friends in times past, she has cursed him, and intends to thwart his plans, and be revenged on him. Then the curtain fell, and the audience reposed and ate candy while discussing the merits of the play.

A good deal of hammering went on before the curtain rose again; but when it became evident what a masterpiece of stage-carpentering had been got up, no one murmured at the delay. It was truly superb! A tower rose to the ceiling; half-way up appeared a window, with a lamp burning at it, and behind the white curtain appeared Zara in a lovely blue and silver dress, waiting for Roderigo. He came in gorgeous array, with plumed cap, red cloak, chestnut love-locks, a guitar, and the boots, of course. Kneeling at the foot of the tower, he sang a serenade in melting tones. Zara replied, and, after a musical dialogue, consented to fly. Then came the grand effect of the play. Roderigo produced a rope ladder, with five steps to it, threw up one end, and invited Zara to descend. Timidly she crept from her lattice, put her hand on Roderigo's shoulder, and was about to leap gracefully down, when, "Alas! alas for Zara!" she forgot her train—it caught in the window, the tower tottered, leant forward, fell with a crash, and buried the unhappy lovers in the ruins!

A universal shriek arose as the russet boots waved wildly from the wreck, and a golden head emerged, exclaiming, "I told you so! I told you so!" With wonderful presence of mind, Don Pedro, the cruel sire, rushed in, dragged out his daughter, with a hasty aside:

"Don't laugh! Act as if it was all right!"—and, ordering Roderigo up, banished him from the kingdom with wrath and scorn. Though decidedly shaken by the fall of the tower upon him, Roderigo defied the old gentleman, and refused to stir. This dauntless example fired Zara: she also defied her sire, and he ordered them both to the deepest dungeons of the castle. A stout little retainer came in with chains, and led them away, looking very much frightened, and evidently forgetting the speech he ought to have made.

Act third was the castle hall; and here Hagar appeared, having come to free the lovers and finish Hugo. She hears him coming, and hides; sees him put the potions into two cups of wine, and bid the timid little servant "Bear them to the captives in their cells, and tell them I shall come anon." The servant takes Hugo aside to tell him something, and Hagar changes the cups for two others which are harmless. Ferdinando, the "minion," carries them away, and Hagar puts back the cup which holds the poison meant for Roderigo. Hugo, getting thirsty after a long warble, drinks it, loses his wits, and, after a good deal of clutching and stamping, falls flat and dies; while Hagar informs him what she has done in a song of exquisite power and melody.

This was a truly thrilling scene, though some persons might have thought that the sudden tumbling down of a quantity of long hair rather marred the effect of the villain's death. He was called before the curtain, and with great propriety appeared, leading Hagar, whose singing was considered more wonderful than all the rest of the performance put together.

Act fourth displayed the despairing Roderigo on the point of stabbing himself, because he has been told that Zara has deserted him. Just as the dagger is at his heart, a lovely song is sung under his window, informing him that Zara is

true, but in danger, and he can save her, if he will. A key is thrown in, which unlocks the door, and in a spasm of rapture he tears off his chains, and rushes away to find and rescue his lady-love.

Act fifth opened with a stormy scene between Zara and Don Pedro. He wishes her to go into a convent, but she won't hear of it; and, after a touching appeal, is about to faint, when Roderigo dashes in and demands her hand. Don Pedro refuses, because he is not rich. They shout and gesticulate tremendously, but cannot agree, and Roderigo is about to bear away the exhausted Zara, when the timid servant enters with a letter and a bag from Hagar, who has mysteriously disappeared. The latter informs the party that she bequeaths untold wealth to the young pair, and an awful doom to Don Pedro, if he doesn't make them happy. The bag is opened, and several quarts of tin money shower down upon the stage, till it is quite glorified with the glitter. This entirely softens the "stern sire": he consents without a murmur, all join in a joyful chorus, and the curtain falls upon the lovers kneeling to receive Don Pedro's blessing in attitudes of the most romantic grace.

Tumultuous applause followed, but received an unexpected check; for the cot-bed, on which the "dress-circle"[6] was built, suddenly shut up, and extinguished the enthusiastic audience. Roderigo and Don Pedro flew to the rescue, and all were taken out unhurt, though many were speechless with laughter. The excitement had hardly subsided, when Hannah appeared, with "Mrs. March's compliments, and would the ladies walk down to supper."

This was a surprise, even to the actors; and, when they saw the table, they looked at one another in rapturous amazement. It was like Marmee to get up a little treat for them; but anything so fine as this was unheard of since the departed days of plenty. There was ice-cream—actually two dishes of it, pink and white—and cake and fruit and distracting French bonbons, and, in the middle of the table, four great bouquets of hothouse flowers.

It quite took their breath away, and they stared first at the table and then at their mother, who looked as if she enjoyed it immensely.

"Is it fairies?" asked Amy.

"It's Santa Claus," said Beth.

"Mother did it"; and Meg smiled her sweetest, in spite of her gray beard and white eyebrows.

"Aunt March had a good fit, and sent the supper," cried Jo, with a sudden inspiration.

"All wrong. Old Mr. Laurence sent it," replied Mrs. March.

"The Laurence boy's grandfather! What in the world put such a thing into his head? We don't know him!" exclaimed Meg.

"Hannah told one of his servants about your breakfast party. He is an odd old gentleman, but that pleased him. He knew my father, years ago; and he sent me a polite note this afternoon, saying he hoped I would allow him to express his friendly feeling towards my children by sending them a few trifles in honor of the day. I could not refuse; and so you have a little feast at night to make up for the bread-and-milk breakfast."

"That boy put it into his head, I know he did! He's a capital fellow, and I wish we could get acquainted. He looks as if he'd like to know us; but he's bashful, and Meg is so prim she won't let me speak to him when we pass," said

6. In a theater, the first tier of seats above the main floor.

Jo, as the plates went round, and the ice began to melt out of sight, with "Ohs!" and "Ahs!" of satisfaction.

"You mean the people who live in the big house next door, don't you?" asked one of the girls. "My mother knows old Mr. Laurence; but says he's very proud, and doesn't like to mix with his neighbors. He keeps his grandson shut up, when he isn't riding or walking with his tutor, and makes him study very hard. We invited him to our party, but he didn't come. Mother says he's very nice, though he never speaks to us girls."

"Our cat ran away once, and he brought her back, and we talked over the fence, and were getting on capitally— all about cricket, and so on—when he saw Meg coming, and walked off. I mean to know him some day; for he needs fun, I'm sure he does," said Jo decidedly.

"I like his manners, and he looks like a little gentleman; so I've no objection to your knowing him, if a proper opportunity comes. He brought the flowers himself; and I should have asked him in, if I had been sure what was going on upstairs. He looked so wistful as he went away, hearing the frolic, and evidently having none of his own."

"It's a mercy you didn't, Mother!" laughed Jo, looking at her boots. "But we'll have another play, some time, that he *can* see. Perhaps he'll help act; wouldn't that be jolly?"

"I never had such a fine bouquet before! How pretty it is!" And Meg examined her flowers with great interest.

"They *are* lovely. But Beth's roses are sweeter to me," said Mrs. March, smelling the half-dead posy in her belt.

Beth nestled up to her, and whispered softly, "I wish I could send my bunch to Father. I'm afraid he isn't having such a merry Christmas as we are."

1869

Turn-of-the-Century
Literature

A MAJOR SHIFT IN GENDER RELATIONS

Speaking about women's labor, the rebellious heroine of Olive Schreiner's *The Story of an African Farm* (1883) exclaims, "*we* bear the world, and *we* make it." Her brash affirmation of female creative primacy would be symbolized ten years later in America by the Woman's Building at the World's Columbian Exposition in Chicago. This building—the first that was funded, managed, and designed entirely by women—included Mary Cassatt's mural depicting "woman apart from her relations to man" and exhibits dedicated to British nurses, African-American and American inventors, Continental artisans, and Eastern explorers as well as the first international collection of women's books gathered by women. Opening in the same year that New Zealand granted women the vote and the English Parliament passed the last of the Married Woman's Property Acts, the Woman's Building expressed the confidence that women felt in looking back on more than a century of unusual accomplishments.

By 1900, women had become, in the words of the feminist historian Ray Strachey, "free both in their persons and their properties, their money and their consciences, their bodies and their souls." For this reason, as another cultural historian, Theodore Roszak, has demonstrated, "the 'woman problem' had become one of the most earthshattering debates in the Western world" and "by the final decades of the century, it permeated everything." Between the 1880s and the outbreak of World War I in 1914, female lives and letters on both sides of the Atlantic were transformed by the entrance of large numbers of women into the labor force, by increased educational opportunities, and by the emergence of militant suffragism. It is hardly surprising, then, that many literary figures in this period felt that they were living between two worlds, one dead and the other struggling to be born. Nor is it surprising that both sexes frequently associated accelerating historical changes with the rapidly shifting situation of women. For, as the Victorian age turned into the modern period, women's revolt was a dramatic component in a series of violent challenges to the social order that were posed by artists, workers, colonized peoples, social reformers, and free thinkers.

A TRANSITIONAL AGE

While it may be convenient to mark the end of the Victorian period as the year 1901, when Queen Victoria died after a sixty-four-year-long reign and Theodore Roosevelt began to make the White House his "bully pulpit," there was a growing realization throughout the last three decades of the nineteenth century and the first decade of the twentieth century that a major historical revolution was in the making. Already in 1873, Mark Twain and Charles Dudley Warner had called the age "gilded," rather than golden, for they were appalled by the crass materialism that was turning America into a world power, a rival to England in industrial lead-

ership. Many intellectuals agreed that Victorianism was dead, though they disagreed about the exact date of its demise: the English libertarian Edward Carpenter and the American historian Henry Adams associated this transition with the 1880s and 1890s, respectively, while the poet William Butler Yeats triumphantly announced that "Victorianism had been defeated in the year 1900," and the novelist Virginia Woolf dated that defeat in 1910, the year when Victoria's successor, King Edward VII, died. At the same time, some of Woolf's friends took the publication of Lytton Strachey's *Eminent Victorians* (1918) as the symbolic end of the nineteenth century, for Strachey's book attacked head on the respectability, earnestness, industriousness, piety, and propriety of his parents' generation.

Strachey's scathing rejection of the bourgeois values he associated with Victorian complacency had, however, been anticipated in the 1870s, when the novelist Samuel Butler criticized the patriarchal family, the Church, the law, scientific theories based on evolution, and faith in progress through technology. But throughout the late nineteenth century there were other symptoms of a breakdown of certainty and a growing alienation of intellectuals from society. Late Victorians and early modernists alike confronted nineteenth-century economic prosperity from a disillusioned perspective, born in part of their dissatisfaction with the literary marketplace, because the rapid commercialization of literature—accelerated when compulsory elementary school education in the 1890s resulted in a higher literacy rate—had led to the formation of a mass reading audience. Not a few writers echoed the protests of the novelist George Gissing, who deplored the mediocrity encouraged by the economics of the literary marketplace. At the same time, however, a number of artists felt constrained by the moralistic standards still maintained by publishers. Outrage over the sexual explicitness of Thomas Hardy's *Jude the Obscure* (1896) so angered Hardy himself that he decided to devote himself exclusively to writing poetry. Thus both England and America began to witness a schism between a financially successful popular culture and what was considered genuine, "high" art.

The writers who most flamboyantly thumbed their noses at respectable Victorian virtues, even as they sought to elevate the status of art by eliminating its utilitarian function, were the so-called aesthetes. In England, the aesthetic movement espoused the slogan "art for art's sake," the doctrine that the true artistic spirit eschews conventional morality to maintain the integrity of individual vision. As the phrase *fin de siècle* ("end of the century") itself suggests, the aesthetes' stylization of the self and of art was profoundly affected by French ideas, especially the ideas of poets like Charles Baudelaire and Arthur Rimbaud, both of whom were represented in Arthur Symons's *The Symbolist Movement in Literature* (1899). According to these thinkers, the artist was not to preach societal reformation but, in the words of Walter Pater in *Studies in the History of the Renaissance* (1873), "to burn always with [a] hard gem-like flame," for "art comes to you proposing frankly to give nothing but the highest quality to your moments as they pass, and simply for those moments' sake."

The erotic poetry of Algernon Charles Swinburne, the baroque and sometimes pornographic drawings of Aubrey Beardsley, and the figure of the dandy began to epitomize what was considered the "decadence" of this movement, while Oscar Wilde's homosexuality became a notorious emblem of bohemian defiance that was castigated in America from countless pulpits. Wilde's hero in *The Portrait of Dorian Gray* (1891) perfectly captured the era's mood of exhausted satiety when he responded to the *fin de siècle* by sighing, "I wish it were *fin du globe.*" Throughout "the mauve decade" or "the gay nineties," such periodicals as *The Yellow Book* and *The Chap-Book* flaunted the quest for a deliberately abnormal, exotic, and titillating style. Frank Harris's eleven-volume history of his sexual escapades, *My Secret Life* (c. 1890), and the dances of the American Isadora

Duncan, performed in free-flowing robes and bare feet, flouted puritanical codes as assiduously as did the art of the aesthetes.

Of course, many writers rejected the sensationalism and world-weariness of the aesthetes; however, even the eminent late Victorians George Meredith and Rudyard Kipling developed highly innovative styles: Meredith used an elaborately elliptical prose in novels that ridicule the presumption of masculine superiority, while Kipling wrote stories and poems in dialects that capture the unique perspectives of everyday soldiers and citizens. A major transformation in literary history was reflected, too, in the lyrical and novelistic experimentation of many other artists in this period. Throughout the 1870s and 1880s, Walt Whitman issued revised editions of *Leaves of Grass*, to the acclaim of such English men of letters as William Michael Rossetti and Swinburne. Several years later, Emily Dickinson's unconventional lyrics began to appear in America, while in England the Jesuit poet Gerard Manley Hopkins revived archaic words, coined compound phrases, and invented a new theory of rhythm in startlingly alliterative poetry that would not be published until 1918. In addition, Henry James and Joseph Conrad exploited in their work and explained in their critical prefaces their own complex uses of multiple narrators and points of view, thus helping to transform the novel into a more self-consciously literary form than it had ever been before.

Like the modernists Ezra Pound, Gertrude Stein, and James Joyce, Henry James was an expatriate in an art world that defined itself as an international elite. International experimentation also characterized the age's music and painting. The art critic Roger Fry selected for exhibition in London canvases by impressionists such as Manet, Cézanne, and Van Gogh, together with paintings by the post-impressionists Matisse and Picasso. Through such different events in music history as the dramatist George Bernard Shaw's defense of Richard Wagner's mythically structured operas in *The Perfect Wagnerite* (1898) and Anton von Webern's creation of atonal scores (*Passacaglia*, 1908), conventional ideas of representation and reality were being broken down, as they were also in the literature that began to appear in newly created "little" magazines. With the emergence of modernism in the years directly before the outbreak of World War I, many artists had begun to engage in an open rebellion against society at large, for they were demonstrating how all established forms of intellectual and moral certainty had lost their legitimacy.

Industrialization

What intensified such artists' feelings that they were living in a transitional time were the rise of the industrial city and the rapid advances in national wealth and population that were associated with the development of capitalism in this period. Both American and English societies were transformed by mass-production techniques employed in large factories powered by ever more complicated machines. Exciting new technological prospects also opened up with the production of radio shortwaves (1887), the invention of wireless telegraphy (1895), the discovery of radiation by the Curies (1897–1901), and the first flight by the Wright brothers (1903). In 1895, newly invented automobiles were entered in their first race (only six were able to start and their speed averaged 5.25 miles per hour) and the Underwood Typewriter Company began to market machines that enabled the typist to see what was being typed: both the car and the typewriter would quickly become enormously popular. Louis Sullivan's soaring office buildings, the construction of the Brooklyn Bridge (1883), and the first motion picture, *The Great Train Robbery* (1903), were only the most dramatic signs of how the new technology would shape modern architecture and art. Exhilarated by unfolding possibilities for personal success, popular novelists like Horatio Alger continued to publish best-selling books promulgating an ethic of individual enterprise.

But many social critics felt that, when the mid-nineteenth-century Civil "War for freedom" had been replaced by the "war for the dollar," all the inequities of industrialization were dramatized. In America, a number of "robber barons" or captains of industry had amassed huge fortunes, which they displayed in the ornate mansions of New York and Chicago. Such ostentation led the American economist Thorstein Veblen to write his *Theory of the Leisure Class* (1899). For the American novelist Edith Wharton, the conspicuous consumption of New York high society—its lavish garden parties, silver-backed hair brushes, visiting cards, and ostentatious boxes at the opera—illustrated the immorality of a class that considered only bankruptcy a sin. While industrial development proceeded more slowly in England than in the United States, both countries witnessed the growth of joint stock companies, syndicates, trusts, mergers, holding companies, and interlocking boards of directors. With the introduction of electrical energy for domestic lighting and industrial power, diesel engines, subways, plastics, refrigeration, and canning, the Industrial Revolution began to bring comparative comfort to many people for the first time. But the extension of manhood suffrage, the institution of minimum wage laws, and the passage of child labor laws could not alleviate the economic suffering that resulted from recurrent unemployment, overproduction, and wage cutbacks.

Thus, although a number of religious leaders claimed that "God has intended the great to be great and the little to be little," and so-called social Darwinists argued that the poor had proven themselves to be "evolutionary misfits" who deserved to be destroyed by the economic system, the working class began in this period to organize for collective bargaining to attain job security, shorter hours, better conditions, and higher wages. Labor unions in England developed comparatively peacefully until 1906, when their effort to get working-class spokesmen into Parliament resulted in the creation of the Labour Party; but in America the rise of unions was dramatic and bloody. After more than 110,000 miles of railroad track were built across the American continent in the 1860s and 1870s, for example, the railroad strikes of 1877, 1886, and 1894 provoked judicial and governmental opposition. The Homestead steel strike (1892) was matched in England by the 1888 strike of Bryant and May's match girls, many of whom suffered from a cancer called "phossy-jaw," caused by the phosphorus into which they dipped matches. Both skilled and unskilled workers in England and America used meetings, leaflets, lockouts, boycotts, picketing, strikes, syndicalism (general strikes), and legislative lobbying to cope with the exploitation and oppression that Karl Marx had outlined in *Das Kapital* (1867–95) and that the socialists Beatrice and Sidney Webb had described in their massive work *Poverty* (1911).

Besides leading to such public activity and political theory, utopian socialism was at least in part responsible for the growth of fantastic fiction at the turn of the century. On the one hand, H. G. Wells believed that the split between rich and poor had produced two distinct races, and in *The Time Machine* (1895), a pioneering science fiction novel, he implied that the working-class tenders of machines would cannibalize the effete and idle rich. Edward Bellamy, on the other hand, wrote a popular "fairy tale of social felicity" titled *Looking Backward* (1888), in which future collectivity eradicates all the evils of private enterprise. In addition, the poet William Morris developed utopian ideas about the aesthetic manufacturing of furniture and home decorations, ideas that contributed to the formation of the Arts and Crafts movement.

Growing social militancy also resulted in an interest in literary "realism" and "naturalism." In France, the realistic presentation of average people in middleclass society by the novelist Honoré de Balzac (1799–1850) had been succeeded by naturalism, the movement in fiction that approached working-class characters in terms of biological inheritance and economic determinism. The Goncourt brothers and Émile Zola attempted to present their readers "with a living model, or rather life itself with its entrails warm and active, its guts palpitating." As early as

1900, the Philadelphia painter Thomas Eakins discouraged his students from studying classical busts and took them instead to a bone-boiling establishment to dissect horses. George Moore, Arnold Bennett, and John Galsworthy carried on the realistic tradition in English novels about the manners of the genteel and the morals of the poor, while Frank Norris, Upton Sinclair, and Theodore Dreiser developed naturalism in America.

Given their quasi-scientific interest in cultural subsections of the population, a number of these writers appeared to agree with the novelist William Dean Howells that "our life is too large for our art to be broad." Both in ethnic and in regional literature, turn-of-the-century artists charted the rapid changes in society, which had affected different portions of the population in various ways. Ethnic voices began to articulate the special perspective of the some thirteen million immigrants who arrived in New York City between 1890 and 1919 from eastern Europe and southern Italy. Among Jewish writers, for example, Emma Lazarus wrote *The New Colossus*, for the "huddled masses yearning to breathe free." The Danish-American reformer Jacob Riis portrayed slum life in *How the Other Half Lives* (1890). Similarly, whether addressing the problems of rural villages in England or New England, such turn-of-the-century regionalists as Thomas Hardy and Mary E. Wilkins Freeman attempted to capture the uniqueness of the local customs and landscapes that frame their characters' lives. In poetry, too, A. E. Housman and Edwin Arlington Robinson described the obscure destinies of Shropshire lads and Maine butchers. Whether, like Housman and Robinson, they were resigned or, like Wells and Bellamy, they were rebellious, writers had turned their attention to much distinctively new subject matter.

The Rise and Fall of Empire

Just as nineteenth-century monopoly capitalism had developed huge corporations, nineteenth-century imperialism had portioned the entire globe into spheres of influence. Strong national pride and economic expediency caused both the English and the American governments to consolidate their colonial holdings throughout this period. The rise of imperialist fervor was perhaps most striking in America, for the expanding United States strengthened its hold on the American West, even as it began to exert its influence over foreign states. On the domestic front, large firms controlled the many transcontinental railroad lines that, for the first time, connected the eastern states to what had been the western wilderness. A vast section of northern Oklahoma Territory was leased to settler-farmers in 1893, the year that Frederick Jackson Turner attended the World's Columbian Exposition to present his famous thesis about the closing of the frontier. In 1912, the last states of the original forty-eight—New Mexico and Arizona—were admitted to the union.

The subjugation of Native Americans—a process that concluded in this period—was accompanied by opportunities for foreign conquest offered by a new policy of international imperialism. The Spanish-American War (1898) led to America's first acquisition of noncontiguous colonies with substantial populations: Hawaii, Puerto Rico, the Philippines, and Cuba were colonized in a course of action that President McKinley described as America's "manifest destiny." His successor, Theodore Roosevelt, believed that "the nation that has trained itself to a cancer of unwarlike and isolated ease is bound, in the end, to go down before other nations which have not lost the manly and adventurous virtues." Countless legislators lauded what the British writer Rudyard Kipling called the "white man's burden." Although the Monroe Doctrine (1823) was supposed to prevent European intervention in the Western Hemisphere, the construction of the Panama Canal (1907–14) demonstrated how this doctrine could be used to justify the intervention of the United States in Latin America.

The glamorization of militaristic nationalism in America reflected widespread

jlhgolshm ?

European jingoism. An ideology of aggression, which some historians associate with the international events that led to World War I, was implicit in the imperialist expansion of England. Disraeli's "Big England" policy had resulted in the purchase of Suez Canal shares in 1875 and his proclamation of Queen Victoria as "Empress of India" in 1876. By 1894, England was signing the Congo Treaty with King Leopold II of Belgium, gaining both countries' leases in Africa. In 1900 the British Empire covered nearly twenty million square miles and contained three hundred million people, and the newly created Girl Guides were themselves guided by a handbook that was subtitled *How Girls Can Help Build the Empire.*

Even in the heyday of empire building, however, there were strong voices of dissent. The Boer War in South Africa (1899–1902) not only showed that a small number of Dutch settlers could challenge English right and might but was also the first war protested by many British intellectuals. In 1905 the pamphlet *The Decline and Fall of the British Empire* sold thousands of copies in several months, reflecting widespread belief that the Empire might have passed its peak. Moreover, just when it seemed literally that the sun could not set on the British Empire, Joseph Conrad provided one of the more scathing critiques of the European invasion of Africa in *Heart of Darkness* (1902): the "white man's burden," Conrad implied, was less an ennobling mission to civilize the native African populations than a mercenary effort to wrest wealth from them.

While Cecil Rhodes, prime minister of the Cape Colony (South Africa), and the South African writer Olive Schreiner were disagreeing about the moral influence of the English presence in Africa, a number of black intellectuals in America were redefining their situation through an effort to reimagine their relationship to their ancestors' native continent. To some extent, the dialogues between men like Booker T. Washington, W. E. B. Du Bois, and Marcus Garvey presented what in our time remain the parameters of African-American identity, for each proposed a different course of liberation to blacks, disillusioned by the racism rampant in America after the abolition of slavery. The legalization of public segregation in 1896 and the growth of the Ku Klux Klan meant that blacks were in some sense colonized people who had to decide between two goals: integration with the dominant culture or an ideology of separatism. While in *Up from Slavery* (1901) Washington counseled self-improvement, which he gauged by white standards, Du Bois espoused "Pan-Africanism" during his editorship of the magazine *Crisis*, and Garvey headed the Universal Negro Improvement Association in an effort to raise racial pride and liberate Africa from colonial rule.

Both Du Bois and Garvey understood the need for cultural identity that was informing the growth of jazz in black urban communities. By 1904 Ma Rainey was touring America in a song-and-dance team with her husband, and by 1907 Bessie Smith was singing the blues at the Ivory Theatre in Chattanooga, Tennessee. Similarly, on numerous reservations throughout the southwest, American Indian communities attempted to preserve their traditional rituals and languages after the genocide perpetrated by the government's "pacification" programs. In 1879 Susette La Flesche (or Inshta Theumba, which means "Bright Eyes") began the lecture tours on behalf of Native American rights that would inspire Helen Hunt Jackson to write her pro-Indian works *A Century of Dishonor* (1881) and *Ramona* (1884).

While white supremacy came under attack in America, England experienced the growing dissent expressed by colonial rebellions that gained momentum throughout this period. Perhaps in response to such agitation, independence movements (which often excluded native populations) helped convert Canada into a federation in 1867, Australia into a commonwealth in 1900, and New Zealand into a separate dominion in 1907 as well as establishing the Union of South Africa in 1909. But, most dramatic, in Ireland Charles Stewart Parnell led the Home Rule Party in its demands for a separate Irish legislature. Parnell suffered political disaster in 1890, after he was named as a co-respondent in a divorce suit;

however, rising Irish protests against British rule continued up to the beginning of the century, when the radical Sinn Fein movement became more violent, and through World War I, when Irish patriots sought help from England's enemy, Germany. The Irish Literary Revival, or the Irish Renaissance, as it is sometimes called, was the literary expression of Irish nationalism.

Standish James O'Grady's histories of Ireland (1878, 1880) and Douglas Hyde's translations of Gaelic poetry shaped William Butler Yeats's poems on Irish heroic legends. Indeed, whether Yeats expressed disillusionment with public response to the nationalist movement ("romantic Ireland's dead and gone") or sympathy with the suffering of the militants ("a terrible beauty is born"), his poetry was as grounded in Celtic mythology and Irish politics as were the plays of Lady Augusta Gregory, the aristocrat who directed Dublin's Abbey Theatre with him. From the middle of the nineteenth century, when Oscar Wilde's mother wrote for *The Nation*, to 1914, when James Joyce's short stories, *Dubliners*, appeared in print, Ireland witnessed an extraordinary literary revival.

The Death of God

In the face of widespread discontent with the distribution of wealth and intense debates about the imperialist mission, organized religion also came under attack. If God was thought to have disappeared earlier in the century, he was now declared dead by the German philosopher Friedrich Nietzsche (1844–1900). After several decades of Darwinian speculation on the origins of the universe and a quarter century of scholarship investigating the historical backgrounds of the Bible, even so conservative a writer as the British novelist Mrs. Humphrey Ward questioned the literal truth of revelation. Like Thomas Hardy, moreover, a number of artists felt "God-Forsaken" by a deity indifferent to human suffering or, again like Hardy, they believed the world to be determined by mere chance or "Crass Casualty." In England, but more especially in America, many intellectuals and artists were disaffected by the crusading fervor of the evangelicalism that fueled the temperance and worldwide mission movements, for the rhetoric of some Protestant crusaders seemed dangerously antiforeigner, antiblack, anti-Catholic, and anti-Semitic. In the place of orthodox faith, what the American philosopher William James called "varieties of religious experience" began to proliferate.

An explosion of interest in alternative religions was fostered by and in turn fostered the development of anthropology. Sir James Frazer's study of primitive rituals in *The Golden Bough* (1890–1915) and Andrew Lang's *Myth, Ritual, and Religion* (1887, 1899) contributed to the dethronement of religious orthodoxy through their analyses of pagan mythology and folklore. In addition, Madame Blavatsky, the founder of the Theosophic Society (1875), conflated Christianity and other religions when she argued in *The Secret Doctrine* (1888) that Jesus was an incarnation of Buddha. The Tarot, astrology, and the Cabala were studied in occult groups like the Golden Dawn, which supplied the poet Yeats—an inveterate attender of seances—with much of his esoteric imagery. At the same time, psychologists, and in particular the psychologists of religion, emphasized the human origins of all faiths: not only did William James analyze how all religions seek to heal humanity's sense of unease but the philosopher George Santayana claimed that "religion and poetry are identical in essence," elevating the human imagination to a redemptive force.

But the so-called death of God also resulted in an ideology of sexual liberation. The birth-control advocate Annie Besant, for example, was drawn to Eastern forms of mysticism that she viewed as less puritanical than Christianity. With the publication of Edward Carpenter's *Love's Coming of Age* (1896, 1906) and Havelock Ellis's *Studies in the Psychology of Sex* (1897–1910), the subject of human sexuality began to emerge as a field of scientific inquiry, one that was soon to be more closely studied by the Viennese psychoanalyst Sigmund Freud, whose

dream interpretations and studies of hysteria began to be translated into English in the first two decades of the twentieth century. Arguing for toleration of homosexuality and for an acceptance of sexuality as part of human behavior, both Carpenter and Ellis saw themselves as liberating modern humanity from Victorian prudery. Although Carpenter, Ellis, and Freud were criticized or censured for their explicit treatment of desire, subjectivity and sexuality would quickly become major topics for poets and novelists.

IMAGES OF WOMEN

Not only did women participate in all the movements that challenged the balance of power among classes and nations but they were also in the process of fomenting a social revolution that would radically change the relationship between the sexes. As the cultural historian Samuel Hynes has explained, this "revolution had many implications besides the sexual," for it "involved legal, political, and economic issues, and touched on property ownership, the franchise, higher education, the birth rate, laws of marriage and divorce, the protocol of the court, and the future of the empire—in short, on nearly every aspect of . . . society." In this context, it is hardly surprising that by 1920, when Arnold Bennett published *Our Women*, he was arguing that "sex-discord" had "noticeably developed since Coventry Patmore wrote *The Angel in the House*" (1885), a poem that celebrated the virtues of the ideal bride. Patmore's ideology of feminine renunciation and domesticity continued to be influential at the turn of the century, but artists and intellectuals tended to confront what the scholar Martha Vicinus has called women's "widening sphere" more directly and overtly, whether as opponents or advocates, as the period progressed. While moralists, educators, and physicians continued to explain to women why they should lead decorous, selfless private lives as wives and mothers, a number of artists responded angrily or triumphantly to the fact that many women no longer did so.

Patmore's exemplary woman, for example, continued to haunt Henry Adams, who argued in *The Education of Henry Adams* (1907) that modern scientific energy, typified by the dynamo, had to be countered by the eternal beauty and potency he identified with the medieval figure of the Virgin. While Adams viewed the demise of the Virgin and the rise of the dynamo with trepidation, countless writers argued that women could counter the evils of industrial life if they remained within the home. But domesticity was also assumed to constitute women's primary source of satisfaction. John Cordy Jeaffreson's popular novel *A Woman in Spite of Herself* (1872) dramatized the pleasure with which its heroine relinquishes the male costume circumstances had required of her; she is relieved to admit her femininity and accept a marriage proposal that will allow her to demonstrate "the never-ceasing, ever-active delight that a true woman feels" in being the "watchful ministrant, enthusiastic slave of the man to whom she has given her heart."

Even while works like Jeaffreson's and Patmore's celebrated this angelic ministrant and slave, much late-Victorian and early-twentieth-century literature anxiously meditated on her disappearance. Henry A. Jones's play *The Case of Rebellious Susan* (1894), for example, included a scene in which an older man lectures a henpecking, selfish wife who refuses to serve dinner "while the present inequalities between the sexes remain unredressed": "Nature's darling woman," he explains to her, "is a stay-at-home woman, a woman who wants to be a good wife and a good mother, and cares very little for anything else." "Go home!" he concludes, as if anticipating the defensive stridency of the hero in Harley Granville-Barker's play *The Madras House* (1910), who argues that "women haven't morals or intellect in our sense of the words. . . . Shut them away from public life and public exhibition."

At the same time, imperiled as the Victorian cult of feminine purity was felt to

be, the ideology of separate sexual spheres was used to argue that women had feminized a previously virile culture. In countless adventure tales where boys like Mark Twain's Huck (in *Huckleberry Finn*, 1884) and Robert Louis Stevenson's Jim Hawkins (in *Treasure Island*, 1883) hear and respond to the call of the wild, they are fleeing from a society associated not only with moralistic women but with women whose refinement symbolizes the confinement of civilization. Turn-of-the-century literature abounded with images of Mrs. Grundy, a priggish puritan whose excessive zeal for gentility makes life unendurable for real men. At the same time, however, women's supposed purity was used by advocates and critics of women's increasingly active role in public life: legislators on both sides of the Atlantic argued, on the one hand, that women would purify politics if they were allowed to participate and, on the other hand, that women would be defiled by such participation. Moreover, even as women's angelic status was being characterized as repressive or endangered, the Victorian cult of feminine selflessness and fragility was also used to prove that, in the words of the antisuffragist James McGrigor Allan, "every woman is . . . always more or less an invalid."

Among the rapidly growing ranks of male gynecologists, obstetricians, and psychologists, hysteria, which was associated with women etymologically through the Greek root *hyster* ("womb"), was considered a female disease in which "the patient loses more and more of her energy and self-control, becoming capriciously fanciful about her health, imagining or feigning strange diseases." Indeed, late-nineteenth- and early-twentieth-century physicians like Henry Maudsley and S. Weir Mitchell sought to demonstrate not only that menstruation, pregnancy, and lactation turned women into helpless invalids but also that higher education and physical or even mental labor would damage women's health. Mitchell prescribed what became popular as "the rest cure": only complete immobilization—bedrest, constant feeding, and enforced idleness—would center the woman on her primary function, reproduction, and heal her neurasthenic symptoms. When the Victorian angel threatened to turn into an invalid, however, she came perilously close to functioning like her Victorian counterpart, the madwoman, for through illness she had exempted herself from her socially prescribed duties of childbearing, child-rearing, and home management. By the turn of the century, however, the angel, the madwoman, and the invalid had all been upstaged by two distinct but related images of rebelliously assertive women: the *femme fatale* and the New Woman.

From the Pre-Raphaelite paintings of Edward Burne-Jones to the art nouveau illustrations of Aubrey Beardsley, from Swinburne's sadistic Faustine to Yeats's destructive "daughters of Herodias," the sinister but sensuous figure of the *femme fatale* evoked the same fascination that Walter Pater expressed about Leonardo da Vinci's *La Gioconda* (the *Mona Lisa*). In a famous passage of *Studies in the History of the Renaissance*, Pater portrayed an alluring woman who is "older than the rocks among which she sits; like the vampire, she has been dead many times, and learned the secrets of the grave." Imbued with the sins of the Borgias, the secrets of Leda (mother of Helen of Troy), and the sanctity of St. Anne (mother of the Virgin Mary), Pater's world-weary beauty is both a lustful vampire and a potent mother, and she therefore epitomizes the contradictory qualities of the fatal female. By the turn of the century, such a figure appeared in so much poetry and fiction that the cultural historian Mario Praz has argued that "in no other literary period . . . has sex been so obviously the mainspring of works of imagination."

As a seductive rebel, for instance, the *femme fatale* emerged in such exceptionally popular late-Victorian fantasies as H. Rider Haggard's best-selling *She* (1887) and George MacDonald's *Lilith* (1895). Endowed with amazing grace, Haggard's She-Who-Must-Be-Obeyed and MacDonald's Lilith are tormented, divided creatures, burning with insatiable, destructive desire and with a power that implies mounting male anxiety about female energy, specifically those energies associated with the mother transformed into a monster. As if to illustrate this point, the hero of George Bernard Shaw's *Man and Superman* (1903) explains that "of all human

struggles there is none so treacherous and remorseless as the struggle between the artist man and the mother woman. Which shall use up the other? That is the issue between them." More generally, however, the realistic novel in this period also dramatized growing male anxiety that men were losing the battle between the sexes. In *Sister Carrie* (1900), Theodore Dreiser described the rise of an actress who triumphs on the stage while her abandoned lover commits suicide. Even in comic or farcical literature, the female seemed indomitable. Max Beerbohm's *Zuleika Dobson* (1911) portrayed the havoc that ensues in Oxford after the entrance of one *femme fatale*: all the undergraduates kill themselves because of their adoration of a flirtatious coquette.

To be sure, a number of American and English writers responded quite differently to women's rising power, for they identified with what they perceived as the growing rebelliousness of women. Following the feminist concerns of the Victorian philosopher John Stuart Mill, George Gissing, George Moore, and John Galsworthy composed novels that implicitly criticized divorce laws, custody provisions, punitive attitudes toward illegitimacy, and the impoverishment of single women. A host of books resembled Stephen Crane's *Maggie: A Girl of the Streets* (1893) in offering sympathetic treatments of the fallen woman. At the same time, moreover, the middle-class American girl emerged in much fiction as a lively representative of the independence of her culture. Praised by Rudyard Kipling, fictionalized by William Dean Howells, and caricatured as "the Gibson girl," she was to acquire spunky innocence, spontaneity, and intelligence in some of the novels of Henry James; in *The Portrait of a Lady* (1881), for example, where he located "the center of the subject in the young woman's own consciousness," James traced the fastidiousness with which his heroine moved from naive idealism to moral maturity.

Although Howells's and James's audacious innocents often ended up either dead or married, they contributed to the construction of a new character, the New Woman. In portraying this figure, who prefigures the modernist "flapper," many English and American writers used the novel and the theater to try to make the feminist cause their own. Much of their writing was influenced by the plays of Henrik Ibsen. With its concluding scene in which Nora slams the door as she leaves her husband and children, *A Doll's House* (1879) was only the most famous of the Norwegian dramatist's treatments of women's demands for release from the childish dependency and boredom of domesticity. Following Ibsen in England, Shaw brought imperious heroines on stage, represented by actresses like Elizabeth Robins and Ellen Terry. Similarly, the novels of George Meredith (*Diana of the Crossways*, 1885) and Grant Allen (*The Woman Who Did*, 1895) focused on female characters who actively and articulately expressed their dissatisfaction with conventional feminine roles. Frequently as seductive and divided as the *femme fatale*, the New Woman was a rebel who regarded marriage as incompatible with her emancipation but who just as frequently suffered a tragic penalty for her views, because even while she was often a locus for the male novelist's own discontent with sex roles, she was also often used to dramatize what many men of letters saw as the self-destructiveness of feminism.

For all the irony and ambiguity of Henry James's narrative tone, the suffrage movement is presented in *The Bostonians* (1886) in terms of a manipulative bonding between two women living in what James's hero calls "a feminine, a nervous, hysterical, chattering, canting age." Such a diagnosis of feminism reflected the views of men like Sir Almroth Wright, an eminent bacteriologist and author of *The Unexpurgated Case against Woman's Suffrage* (1913). In a 1912 letter to the *Times* Wright argued that "there is mixed up with the woman's movement much mental disorder"; with a half million "excess women" in Britain, Wright believed that "physiological emergencies" motivated the behavior of the militant suffragist. The idea that the independent woman was sick informed even Havelock Ellis's de-

fense of female homosexuality, for Ellis claimed that the "invert," as he called her, suffered the biological tragedy of being born into the wrong body. Similarly, despite Thomas Hardy's indisputable sympathies for the sufferings of his New Woman, Sue Bridehead in *Jude the Obscure* (1896), the plot of the novel implies that men will be destroyed by women, whether by a 'mere female animal' like Arabella Donn or by the conflicted spirituality of a neurasthenic Sue.

If the New Woman was a source of much imaginative energy at the turn of the century, it may have been because writers like James believed that, in the words of the critic Larzer Ziff, "women, with their free use of leisure, were the chief consumers of novels and therefore were increasingly becoming producers of them. The feminine attitude, now disengaging itself from that of men, was in point of fact coming to be all that the novel was." At least some men responded to the prominence of women writers with attacks whose defensiveness ranged from the sardonic wit that marked Oscar Wilde's discussion of "English Poetesses" in London's *Queen* magazine (1888) to the satiric ferocity that characterized Mark Twain's portrait of the adolescent poet Emmeline Grangerford in *Huckleberry Finn*. Finally, then, the turn-of-the-century obsession with figures like the *femme fatale* and the New Woman reflected not only the importance of women's issues in the public and private lives of Americans and Britons but also the growth of the female reading public and the visibility and success of women writers.

WOMEN'S LIVES

In an age when men stopped sporting beards and women started riding bicycles, one sign of the dramatic transformation of women's lives was the change in fashion that began to liberate women from the weight and confinement of crinolines and hoops, replacing them first with bustles and then with simpler, lighter skirts. By the beginning of World War I, many of the necessary conditions for female emancipation were present. As identified by the historian Gerda Lerner, these included a technology that permitted society to remove food preparation and care of the sick from the home, the mechanization of heating and laundry, the spread of health care and birth control, and the availability of education to all children. Yet, while women were, as the suffragist Ray Strachey claimed in *The Cause* (1928), "in the main, free" by 1900, Strachey herself went on to point out that they were still "politically outcast and economically oppressed; under-educated and overflattered; too much despised and too much admired."

Unlike her mother and her grandmother, the married woman in this period did have some control over her property and her children. By 1883 married women in England were as free as American women to own acquired or inherited property, and after 1886, the Guardianship of Infants' Act provided that, on a father's death, the mother would become either the sole or joint guardian of her offspring. Divorce laws, however, continued to treat the two sexes differently. In England the husband could sue solely by reason of his wife's adultery, but the wife had to prove cruelty or desertion as well as adultery, and in the United States, too, the laws were inequitable: in the state of Minnesota, for instance, a woman who was divorced by reason of her adultery had to forfeit real estate that had been her own property, while a man so divorced did not. Still, changes in property, divorce, and custody laws did imply that wives were no longer assumed to be the possessions of their husbands.

Just as legal constraints confining women were being debated and sometimes even loosened, educational restrictions were being questioned, circumvented, and overturned. To be sure, from educators like Dr. Edward H. Clarke, a Harvard professor, women continued to hear that higher education would atrophy women's uteruses. But such claims were countered by M. Carey Thomas, president of Bryn Mawr College, who argued in 1913 that "we know that college women are not only

not invalids, but that they are better physically than other women in their own class of life." At the same time, as the historians Barbara Ehrenreich and Deirdre English have demonstrated, the new subject of domestic science, or home economics, became a way of justifying higher education for women, who were now held to need scientific training to make housekeeping an efficient profession. As in America, where the daughters of the wealthy could attend Bryn Mawr, Oberlin, Vassar, or the new Harvard annex, Radcliffe, in England women could pursue their higher education not only at Girton, Newnham, and Somerville Colleges but also within London University; Oxford and Cambridge, however, still did not grant women degrees. A few African-American women were given the opportunity of higher education at schools like Bethune-Cookman College: established by Mary McLeod Bethune from sums she raised selling ice cream and sweet-potato pies to workmen on construction jobs, this college was dedicated to Bethune's commitment that all black youngsters should be given a chance to prove their worth. In 1890 the African-American reformer Anna Julia Cooper presented an important essay titled "The Higher Education of Women," which included a plea for the higher education "of colored women."

After 1870, when both boys and girls were for the first time guaranteed an elementary school education by the passage of the Education Act, educational opportunities for the working class were enhanced in England. But such opportunities were limited by the custom of training working-class daughters for domestic service. Public schools and churches in America, moreover, often channeled immigrant women into home economics programs in which they could acquire the laundering, cooking, housecleaning, and sewing skills that would prepare them for low-status, low-paying jobs. But a number of social workers tried to improve the quality of life for urban immigrant women. In 1889 Jane Addams established her famous pioneering settlement house in Chicago's slums. With a kindergarten, courses in arts and crafts, and lectures from the educator John Dewey and the architect Frank Lloyd Wright, the women who ran Hull House provided social and intellectual opportunities for their community even as they helped establish social work as a profession.

Addams's co-workers also agitated along with labor unions for the first meaningful factory laws in Illinois. The number of women workers in America had increased dramatically from approximately 4 million in 1890 to 5.33 million in 1900 and 7.5 million in 1910. Many were in domestic occupations, but thousands of others were farm laborers, teachers, sales clerks, factory workers, and textile or garment workers as well as holders of white-collar jobs—cashiers, bookkeepers, accountants, typists, and stenographers. Between 1870 and 1914 in England, the number of women clerks in the Civil Service multiplied twenty times, and thousands of women entered textile factories. In spite of this drastic rise in the number of women workers, trade union leaders were often dubious about organizing women, not infrequently because they believed with the English trade unionist Henry Broadhurst that "wives should be in their proper place at home." Male fears of job competition also perpetuated the exclusion of women and thereby fostered low pay and limited job options for women.

Although women were not unionized at the rate that men were, many women on both sides of the Atlantic did participate in the trade union movement. One of the most important early strikes in the history of American unions took place in 1909–10 among shirtwaist makers in New York and Philadelphia. Early locals of what is now called the International Ladies' Garment Workers' Union organized in the Triangle Shirt-Waist Company, which two years later was the site of a fire that killed 146 operatives. The terrible conditions created by the "sweating system"—overcrowded tenement buildings, low pay, job insecurity, dangerous and uninspected machinery, employment of very young children—were denounced by the labor organizer Ida M. Van Etten at the national convention of the American

Federation of Labor in 1890 and by the English socialist Beatrice Potter (Webb), who wrote *Pages from a Work Girl's Diary* (1888) about London East End tailoring. While the populist orator Mary Elizabeth Lease urged farmers "to raise less corn and more hell" and the organizer Mary ("Mother") Jones agitated among urban laborers, the activist Emma Goldman was repeatedly arrested and eventually deported for anarchist agitation.

That Goldman was eventually to include birth control and free love in her program for human liberation indicates how women were beginning to attempt to gain power over their own bodies. However, Goldman's emphasis in the second decade of the twentieth century on women's right to sexual pleasure was far removed from the grounds of earlier pleas for control over reproduction. As the historian Linda Gordon has shown, throughout the last quarter of the nineteenth century women based their arguments for what they called "voluntary motherhood" on their hostility toward men and toward sex. The "fearful strain" of repeated pregnancies and childbirths led nineteenth-century suffragists to attack "the lustful domination of man," just as the threat of "social diseases" (syphilis, gonorrhea) later led to the suffrage slogan *Votes for Women and Purity for Men*. Social purity campaigns, which emphasized the superior chastity of women, were also efforts to elevate the values of maternal tenderness, patience, and supportiveness. Of course, as in the Victorian era, most middle-class girls at the turn of the century were denied all information about reproduction on the grounds that it would be an affront to their purity. Long after 1901, Vera Brittain, a schoolgirl who would grow up to become a feminist writer, was given newspapers from which all paragraphs about sex had been carefully excised.

When the increasing demand for contraceptive information became evident in this period, it immediately met legal opposition. In the 1870s in England, Annie Besant was arrested for publishing George Knowlton's *Fruits of Philosophy*, a book that contained descriptions of contraceptive methods, and in America the Comstock Law (1873) prohibited the sale and the mailing "of obscene literature and articles of immoral use," including birth control information. Many moralists opposed the use of existing methods of contraception such as coitus interruptus, the vaginal sponge, the sheath, and the pessary (an intravaginal device). Just as adamantly, many medical men argued that "continence" (abstinence) was the only suitable form of birth control. Not only did ignorant physicians advise women as late as the 1880s and 1890s that the "safe" time was midway between the periods of menstruation, but the medical attack on birth control also often warned that contraception led to such disasters as hardening of the uterus or moral degeneracy. Yet the use of lamb ceca (intestines) and rubber revolutionized the manufacturing of condoms and resulted in the invention of the Mensinga diaphragm, and the developing birth control movement probably affected the rapidly falling birth rate, which in the United Kingdom dropped by nearly 30 percent between the mid-1880s and 1910.

The shift from social purity and continence to birth control in the struggle over reproductive rights paralleled a similar ideological shift in the struggle for political rights. Both in England and in America, the activist organizations of women in the 1870s and 1880s argued for reforms on the grounds of women's ethical superiority. In England, the protest led by Josephine Butler against the Contagious Diseases Acts, which forced accused prostitutes to submit to physical examinations, attacked laws that condoned (male) sexual immorality. Butler's reports of women who had been forced to submit to examinations dwelt on the indignities of "monstrous instruments" used coercively: "They seem to tear the passage open first with their hands," one victim testified, "and then they thrust in instruments, and they pull them out and push them in, and they turn and twist them about; and if you cry out they stifle you." The repeal of the Contagious Diseases Acts in 1886 was based on an ideology of feminine purity that paradoxically involved many

middle-class women in public discussions of prostitution and social diseases. Because of its emphasis on deviant or simply excessive male sexual demands, this campaign, like the social purity movement, may have also contributed to what the scholar Lillian Faderman has described as the marked development of quasi-homosexual bonds (so-called Boston marriages) between women living at the beginning of the twentieth century.

Just as committed to a standard of female-defined virtue, the Woman's Christian Temperance Union (WCTU), which grew to eight hundred thousand members between 1880 and 1920 in America, promoted the slogan "For God and Home and Native Land" to symbolize its effort to bring the purity associated with the home into the national arena. Focusing on temperance (abstinence and legal prohibition of liquor), WCTU organizers argued that women suffered physically, psychologically, and economically from men's consumption of alcohol. Although Frances Willard, the union's president, eventually placed the temperance cause within a socialist and suffragist context, she never managed to convince all her followers to look forward to "that day when the mothers, and daughters of America shall have a voice [i.e., vote] in the decision by which . . . the rum-shop is opened or shut beside their homes." Throughout the final decades of the nineteenth century, however, women attempted through reform groups, volunteer organizations, and clubs to extend their role as nurturers and moral teachers from the domestic to the public sphere. In this context, the sanctification of motherhood even became part of the argument for the vote, for women justified their entrance into public life not only in terms of their domestic responsibilities and their superior morality but also in terms of their importance as bearers of the race: in spite of its implicitly racist overtones, eugenics—the science of improving humanity through genetic control of heredity—supplied a rhetoric that lent the mother a crucial role in the development of the species.

When women on both sides of the Atlantic began organizing with increased militancy to gain female enfranchisement, their opponents included the novelist Mary Ward, the poet Christina Rossetti, and even the socialist Beatrice Webb, all of whom signed in 1889 a protest against "an emancipating process [that] has now reached the limits fixed by the physical constitution of women." Turn-of-the-century suffragists were, however, building on the work of early feminists like Elizabeth Cady Stanton and Mary Wollstonecraft and on their own experiences, not only in social purity and temperance organizations but also in the socialist and labor movements.

While none of the existing political parties in England chose to advocate women's enfranchisement, the ideological underpinnings of the struggle for the vote were established by the South African writer Olive Schreiner, whose novels and tracts identified women's secondary status with "the subjugation of large bodies of other human creatures, either as slaves, subject races, or classes." The granting of women's suffrage in New Zealand in 1893 and in South Australia in 1894 provided new impetus to the cause. After repeated efforts by the moderate National Union, led by Dame Millicent Garrett Fawcett, had failed to get a suffrage bill through Parliament, Emmeline Pankhurst in 1903 formed a new suffrage society, the Women's Social and Political Union (WSPU). Annie Kenney, a mill hand from Oldham, and Christabel Pankhurst, one of Mrs. Emmeline Pankhurst's daughters, were among the first to use the tactics—heckling, illegal speaking, seeking arrest, and enduring imprisonment—that would continue to characterize the growing militancy of the WSPU. Meetings and marches multiplied as the militants began pouring acid into letter boxes, throwing bricks and stones through shop windows, cutting telegraph wires, and slashing paintings.

Convinced that they would receive newspaper attention only through dramatic action, those militants sentenced to prison terms refused to eat, and jailors resorted to what was called the "forcible feeding" of hunger strikers. Wardens

pinned the protester to a bed and physicians pushed twenty inches of tubing down her nostrils or throat; milk and eggs were poured through a funnel into the tube. Painful and dangerous, such treatments were publicly condemned when an aristocrat, Lady Constance Lytton, disguised as a working-class woman named "Jane Wharton," was paralyzed by the practice. Nevertheless, the government responded only with what became known as the Cat and Mouse Act (1913), an act that released sick hunger strikers and allowed them to be rearrested without a fresh warrant, to continue serving their sentences when they were well. In spite of growing public support for women's suffrage during the renewed campaigns of 1913 and 1914, many moderates and socialists had been alienated by the Pankhursts' methods or by their exclusive focus on the vote. With the outbreak of war in August 1914, the movement was further split between those women who followed Mrs. Pankhurst in dedicating their energies to the war effort and others, like Olive Schreiner, who worked for world peace.

The splitting of the woman's movement into moderates and militants also occurred in America. In spite of the new leadership of Carrie Chapman Catt and Anna Howard Shaw, between 1896 and 1910 the National American Woman Suffrage Association experienced what the historian Eleanor Flexner has called "the doldrums," for many suffragists were beginning to question their state-by-state strategy, which was both arduous and frequently unsuccessful. When the national movement lost several state campaigns, two splinter groups arose, led by women deeply influenced by their experience with the militant Pankhursts. Harriot Stanton Blatch, Elizabeth Cady Stanton's daughter, traveled back to the United States from England in 1902, dismayed by the comparative inertia of American suffrage organizations. While Blatch's Equality League of Self-Supporting Women began to hold open-air meetings and parades, Alice Paul, who had been jailed in England, undertaken a hunger strike, and undergone forcible feeding, returned to America in 1910 and began describing the British movement to American suffrage groups. With the pacifist Crystal Eastman and the historian Mary Beard, Alice Paul began to campaign for a federal suffrage amendment. As different as Alice Paul's and Harriet Stanton Blatch's tactics were from those of Carrie Chapman Catt and Anna Howard Shaw, both militants and moderates depended for their intellectual framework on the analyses of female subordination provided by Charlotte Perkins Gilman, whose *Women and Economics* (1898) hailed "the woman's movement . . . as the best birth of our century." Even as the suffrage movement shaped the writing of women in this period, then, literary women also helped to clarify (and sometimes to contest) the aims of turn-of-the-century feminism.

THE WOMAN QUESTION AND WOMEN'S ARTISTIC QUEST

In Gilbert and Sullivan's comic opera *The Mikado* (1885), one singer places "that singular anomaly, the lady novelist" on a list of characters who "never would be missed"; in fact, however, women novelists and, for that matter, female poets were hardly anomalies by the turn of the century. Yet for many years their contributions were missing from the standard literary histories of this period; they had been relegated to the footnotes of literary history or placed in a predominantly male context. Not only the prominent role women of letters played but also the uniqueness of their achievement become clearer, however, when we take into account the centrality of the woman question in their lives and works.

Inevitably, the impact of the suffrage movement was greatest on the production of polemical prose. In such books as *Woman and Labor* (1911) and *Women and Economics*, Olive Schreiner and Charlotte Perkins Gilman were contributing to the mass of expository writing that was being published by feminist and antifeminist women alike. In addition, a generation of what we would now call

women's studies scholars began exploring women's cultural situation. Matilda Joslyn Gage's *Woman, Church and State* (1893) provided a female view of religious history, and Cicely Hamilton's *Marriage as a Trade* (1909) supplied a sociological analysis of the institutions that shaped women's lives. In 1910 Emma Goldman produced *The Traffic in Women*, an essay that connects the exploitation of prostitutes with the subjugation of all women, and Emily James Putnam published *The Lady*, a book about that outmoded and "somewhat dangerous" social type. By 1912, when Harriet Shaw Weaver and Dora Marsden were editing the magazine *The Freewoman*, Anna Garlin Spencer had documented the contributions of women from primitive to modern times in *Woman's Share in Social Culture*. By this time, too, Alice Meynell, Mary Elizabeth Coleridge, Mathilda Blind, and Mrs. Oliphant had produced essays and biographies about literary women.

The effort to document women's cultural situation also led the anthropologist Ruth Underhill to take down the stories of the American Indian Maria Chona (published as *The Autobiography of a Papago Woman*, 1936), just as it impelled the folkorist Mary Austin to transcribe American Indian legends in *The Basket Woman* (1914). The author of two autobiographies, Austin was one of the many women in this period who published confessional accounts of their development. A number of Victorian women's diaries and journals were issued at the turn of the century: Elizabeth Cady Stanton's *Eighty Years and More*, which analyzed her role in the feminist movement, appeared in 1898, and Mary Boykin Chestnut's *Diary*, which described life on a Southern plantation during the Civil War, was published in an abbreviated form in 1905, while the diaries of Marie Bashkirtseff (translated in 1890) and Mary MacLane (1902) were widely read. In many of these publications, women openly discussed their feelings about the female body, birth control, housework, female friendships, and aging. Alice James's *Diary*, which was privately printed several years after her death in 1892, describes not only her complex attitudes toward her famous brothers, Henry and William James, but also her resentment at a medical establishment that could not save her from an invalid's life. Just as personal and just as focused on the relationship between women and the medical establishment, Charlotte Perkins Gilman's story *The Yellow Wallpaper* (1892) analyzed female madness in terms of women's ambivalent attitudes toward men and maternity.

Besides bringing to the surface the psychological problems that women writers confronted, the feminist movement also provided a utopian vision of a world in which women might experience complete freedom. In verse, drama, fiction, and expository prose, women began to translate the visionary rhetoric of suffragism into utopian works of art. As the literary critic Elaine Showalter has reminded readers, in *Gloriana; or, The Revolution of 1900* (1890), Lady Florence Dixie envisioned a girl who disguises herself as a boy in order to enter Oxford and Parliament, while "Ellis Ethelmer," in *Woman Free* (1893), imagined what would happen if the menstrual cycle were to end. Similarly, Cicely Hamilton's and Christopher St. John's play *How the Vote Was Won* (1910) dramatized the conversion of patriarchal relatives to a triumphant suffrage cause. Elizabeth Robins, who also produced a play about the suffrage question, published *The Convert* (1907), a novel that presented suffragists who seem to be "speaking in an unknown tongue," for they desire "a world where beauty exists for beauty's sake—which is love's sake—and not for tricking money or power out of men," a future world that may be "beyond the imagining of many." Gilman herself was to focus on precisely such a world in her utopia, *Herland* (1915), which describes an all-female community of women capable of reproducing themselves without the help of men.

Even when artistic works by women participated in the literary movements dominated or defined by their male contemporaries—for instance, symbolism, naturalism, and regionalism—the contributions of women were characterized by their focus on the issues associated with the turn-of-the-century woman question.

Among poets, the women artists who were involved in a revolt against bourgeois conventionality wrote almost exclusively about their defiance of taboos placed on women. The American poet Renée Vivien, for example, lived most of her adult life in Paris, where she wrote French verse influenced by Baudelaire and Swinburne: Vivien, who flaunted her alienation from society through her identification with "decadence," undertook to mythologize the lesbian relationships she sustained with, among others, the expatriate writer Natalie Barney. In addition, the British poet Charlotte Mew used sensuous imagery in dramatic monologues frequently narrated by female characters who aspire to a spiritual grace they are destined never to receive, while her contemporary Mary Elizabeth Coleridge portrayed the tormenting self-division of a woman who sees the "hideous wound" of "a woman, wild" in *The Other Side of the Mirror*. Similar symbolist techniques were used by Olive Schreiner in allegorical meditations that explored the spiritual and aesthetic quests that shape women's dreams and dreads.

While prose writers like Vernon Lee and Marie Corelli viewed the seductive *femme fatale* as an image of powerful female beauty, Schreiner analyzed in close detail the effects of narcissism and idleness on women robbed of all functions except the aesthetic. Indeed, her discussion in *Woman and Labor* of what she called "sex-parasitism" was partially an analysis of how the role of the *femme fatale* is fatal for women. Just as concerned with the pain experienced by the woman who is perceived as fatally attractive, George Egerton (the pseudonym of Mary Chavelita Dunne) stunned London with what then seemed an erotically explicit volume of stories, *Keynotes* (1894), some of which deal with the frustration of female characters who are hampered by their distrust or ignorance of male sexuality. Like Kate Chopin, whose controversial novel *The Awakening* (1899) shocked American readers, Egerton wrote with unprecedented candor about female sexuality.

In one of her more successful stories, Egerton described the fantasy of a woman who imagines herself performing in front of a male audience that succumbs to her exotic charms. Significantly, the women who were most influenced by the idea of the *femme fatale* were female performers. The Italian actress Eleanora Duse (about whom Amy Lowell was to write a number of poems) and the English-speaking actresses Ellen Terry and Elizabeth Robins, both of whom starred in the plays of Ibsen and Shaw, led visibly eccentric lives, but they were less flamboyant than the very popular entertainer Sarah Bernhardt, who played the role of the *femme fatale* both on and off stage. Attended by a menagerie of wild beasts, engaged in a series of notorious love affairs, sleeping in a satin-lined coffin, Bernhardt reputedly wore a necklace of petrified human eyes. Equally melodramatic, one of the theater's most notorious fallen women was created by Elizabeth Robins and Florence Bell: their play *Alan's Wife* (1893) features a murderous mother who goes off to her death defending her suffocation of her sickly son as an act of mercy. At the same time, among dancers, Loie Fuller became famous in art nouveau circles for her swirling veil dances and Isadora Duncan became internationally infamous not only for what she herself called the "fantastic sensuality and ecstasy" of her dances but also for her bohemian lifestyle.

Just as aestheticism had a distinctive impact on women's art at the turn of the century, the realistic and naturalistic traditions influenced women in a special way. The early writer of naturalistic fiction Rebecca Harding Davis continued publishing throughout this period. Similarly, Mary Ward wrote novels about the degrading conditions of the London poor. But many female writers analyzed social determinism less in terms of governmental or industrial corruption than in terms of the private lives of women. Two African-American novelists, Frances Harper and Pauline Hopkins, produced pioneering works of "racial uplift" to improve the public image of black women; Harper's *Iola Leroy* (1892) and Hopkins's *Contending Forces* (1900) protested against racial discrimination as well as sexual exploitation. At the same time, the educational and social liabilities of middle-

class white women served as the mainspring of some of May Sinclair's and Edith Wharton's most successful fiction. Unlike those male contemporaries who portrayed the new freedom of the New Woman, female realists focused for the most part on the continuing confinement women confronted in an increasingly acquisitive society. Wharton, in particular, analyzed the bondage of heroines who are trapped by materialistic societal conventions that turn them into valuable objects.

Like H. H. Richardson, who located a number of her stories and novels in her native Australia, and Wharton, who became famous for her delineations of wealthy New York society, many turn-of-the-century women writers analyzed the unique mores of the local communities that had shaped their own family histories, much as Lady Gregory did in her volumes of Irish legends and in the plays she wrote for the Abbey Theatre. Studying the origins of their own identities and their cultural roots, such authors help explain the importance of regionalism in turn-of-the-century literature by women. Unlike Bret Harte, whose stories about California are dominated by romantic gamblers and sentimental miners, the short-story writers Sarah Orne Jewett and Mary E. Wilkins Freeman described the visiting, gossiping, cooking, and gardening that supplied a network of support for their communities of women. Like such Southern regionalists as Kate Chopin and Grace King, Jewett and Freeman implicitly provided a social history that might otherwise have gone unrecorded by traditional historians. Jewett's *The Country of the Pointed Firs* (1896), no less than Chopin's *Bayou Folk* (1894), set the private problems of daughters, single women, mothers, and widows into the context of economic and social issues at the turn of the century. At the same time, however, such regionalists sometimes also eulogized a pastoral, timeless realm in which women had established a harmonious, almost mythic, relationship with the physical landscape.

Reflecting the ways in which polemical, autobiographical, utopian, realistic, and regional writing by women concentrated on the situation of woman in nature and society, Chopin's important novel *The Awakening* focused on a twenty-eight-year-old, married mother of two children who is awakened socially and sexually to "her position in the universe as a human being." Indeed, this work functions not only polemically, as a plea for women's autonomy, and autobiographically, as a study of the competition between motherhood and artistry, but also as a fantasy of female sensuality, solitude, and self-discovery. Chopin had profited from her reading of Sarah Orne Jewett's stories, just as Jewett and Freeman had developed a tradition pioneered by Harriet Beecher Stowe. For although such American prose writers as Elizabeth Stuart Phelps Ward and Constance Fenimore Woolson published novels and short stories about the impossibility of being both a woman and an artist, many other turn-of-the-century women writers could begin to look back on a tradition of successful women authors.

During the span of years that witnessed the deaths of Victorian sibyls like George Eliot and Harriet Beecher Stowe, women writers felt themselves to be living through a period of transition similar to, yet somewhat different from, the transition period experienced by their male counterparts, for they were writing in an age when thousands of women were crossing the threshold from the private to the public sphere. Unlike many of their Victorian precursors, literary women no longer felt constrained to write covertly about their rebellion against socially prescribed roles. Rather, many of these artists were empowered to record both their protests and their pleas by the idea, articulated in *Woman and Labor*, that "it is the woman who is the final standard of the race." Although two classics of this period—*The Awakening* and *The Yellow Wallpaper*—are overtly pessimistic about women's fates, as are some of the stories of Woolson and Wharton, their pessimism is born of raised expectations for a fully integrated life. Whether the female contemporaries of Chopin and Gilman wrote about the possibility of industrialization ending the necessity of women's domestic service, about the similarity between ethnic discrimination and female subjugation, or about the sig-

nificance for women of the death of a patriarchal God, they would have agreed with Henry Adams that "the proper study of mankind is woman."

CONSTANCE FENIMORE WOOLSON
1840–1894

Relatively little is known about the creative development of Constance Fenimore Woolson, who spent her school years in Cleveland, Ohio, and her summers at the family cottage on Mackinac Island, Michigan, the setting of her earliest stories, *Castle Nowhere: Lake Country Sketches* (1878), and of her first novel, *Anne* (1880). The great-niece of the novelist James Fenimore Cooper, Woolson traveled along the eastern seaboard with her mother after her father's death in 1869. Ten years later, when her mother died, she moved to Europe, where she lived for the remainder of her life, primarily in Italy and Switzerland. In Florence, she met Henry James in 1880 and either or both may have conceived what Leon Edel called a "virtuous attachment," though Edel's attribution of Woolson's later unhappiness to unrequited love for James has recently been questioned. For despite her productivity—Woolson published four novels between 1883 and 1894—this writer had long felt herself to have inherited "a sort of depression that comes unexpectedly, and makes everything black."

The circumstances surrounding Woolson's death are controversial, but a number of scholars believe that she committed suicide by throwing herself from her bedroom window in Venice. Imbued with the melancholy from which its author suffered, her subtly nuanced Miss Grief provides uncanny insight into the relationships between literary men and women. Composed before Woolson's own meeting with James, it has nevertheless been read as a comment on masterful men of letters like James and even as an influence on the famous author of such studies of artists' lives and problems as *The Aspern Papers* and *The Lesson of the Master*. Not only a fascinating portrait of two quite different and competitive writers, Woolson's story also raises important questions about the basis of aesthetic judgments. How do we—why do we—term a work inspired or perverse, brilliant or flawed? On what bases are books accepted and printed by publishers? How are literary reputations established?

Miss Grief

"A conceited fool" is a not uncommon expression. Now, I know that I am not a fool, but I also know that I am conceited. But, candidly, can it be helped if one happens to be young, well and strong, passably good looking, with some money that one has inherited and more that one has earned—in all, enough to make life comfortable—and if upon this foundation rests also the pleasant superstructure of a literary success? The success is deserved, I think: certainly it was not lightly gained. Yet even with this I fully appreciate its rarity. Thus, I find myself very well entertained in life: I have all I wish in the way of society, and a deep, though of course carefully concealed, satisfaction in my own little fame; which fame I foster by a gentle system of non-interference. I know that I am spoken of as "that quiet young fellow who writes those delightful little studies of society, you know"; and I live up to that definition.

A year ago I was in Rome, and enjoying life particularly I had a large num-

ber of my acquaintances there, both American and English, and no day passed without its invitation. Of course I understood it: it is seldom that you find a literary man who is good tempered, well dressed, sufficiently provided with money, and amiably obedient to all the rules and requirements of "society." "When found, make a note of it";[1] and the note was generally an invitation.

One evening, upon returning to my lodgings, my man Simpson informed me that a person had called in the afternoon, and upon learning that I was absent had left not a card, but her name—"Miss Grief." The title lingered— Miss Grief! "Grief has not so far visited me here," I said to myself, dismissing Simpson and seeking my little balcony for a final smoke, "and she shall not now. I shall take care to be 'not at home' to her if she continues to call." And then I fell to thinking of Isabel Abercrombie, in whose society I had spent that and many evenings: they were golden thoughts.

The next day there was an excursion; it was late when I reached my rooms, and again Simpson informed me that Miss Grief had called.

"Is she coming continuously?" I said, half to myself.

"Yes, sir: she mentioned that she should call again."

"How does she look?"

"Well, sir, a lady, but not so prosperous as she was, I should say," answered Simpson, discreetly.

"Young?"

"No, sir."

"Alone?"

"A maid with her, sir."

But once outside in my little high-up balcony with my cigar, I again forgot Miss Grief and whatever she might represent. Who would not forget in that moonlight, with Isabel Abercrombie's face to remember?

The stranger came a third time, and I was absent; then she let two days pass, and began again. It grew to be a regular dialogue between Simpson and myself when I came in at night: "Grief today?"

"Yes, sir."

"What time?"

"Four, sir."

"Happy the man," I thought, "who can keep her confined to a particular hour!"

But I should not have treated my visitor so cavalierly if I had not felt sure that she was eccentric and unconventional—qualities extremely tiresome in a woman no longer young or attractive. If she were not eccentric, she would not have persisted in coming to my door day after day in this silent way, without stating her errand, leaving a note, or presenting her credentials in any shape. I made up my mind that she had something to sell—a bit of carving or some intaglio supposed to be antique. It was known that I had a fancy for oddities. I said to myself, "She has read or heard of my 'Old Gold' story, or else 'The Buried God,' and she thinks me an idealizing ignoramus upon whom she can impose. Her sepulchral name is at least not Italian; probably she is a sharp countrywoman of mine, turning, by means of the present aesthetic craze, an honest penny when she can."

She had called seven times during a period of two weeks without seeing me,

1. An allusion to a remark in Charles Dickens's (1812–1870) *Dombey and Son* (1848): "When found, make a note of" (Chapter 15).

when one day I happened to be at home in the afternoon, owing to a pouring rain and a fit of doubt concerning Miss Abercrombie. For I had constructed a careful theory of that young lady's characteristics in my own mind, and she had lived up to it delightfully until the previous evening, when with one word she had blown it to atoms and taken flight, leaving me standing, as it were, on a desolate shore, with nothing but a handful of mistaken inductions where-with to console myself. I do not know a more exasperating frame of mind, at least for a constructor of theories. I could not write, and so I took up a French novel (I model myself a little on Balzac[2]). I had been turning over its pages but a few moments when Simpson knocked, and, entering softly, said, with just a shadow of a smile on his well-trained face, "Miss Grief." I briefly consigned Miss Grief to all the Furies,[3] and then, as he still lingered—perhaps not know-ing where they resided—I asked where the visitor was.

"Outside, sir—in the hall. I told her I would see if you were at home."

"She must be unpleasantly wet if she had no carriage."

"No carriage, sir: they always come on foot. I think she *is* a little damp, sir."

"Well, let her in; but I don't want the maid. I may as well see her now, I sup-pose, and end the affair."

"Yes, sir."

I did not put down my book. My visitor should have a hearing, but not much more: she had sacrificed her womanly claims by her persistent attacks upon my door. Presently Simpson ushered her in. "Miss Grief," he said, and then went out, closing the curtain behind him.

A woman—yes, a lady—but shabby, unattractive, and more than middle-aged.

I rose, bowed slightly, and then dropped into my chair again, still keeping the book in my hand. "Miss Grief?" I said interrogatively as I indicated a seat with my eyebrows.

"Not Grief," she answered—"Crief: my name is Crief."

She sat down, and I saw that she held a small flat box.

"Not carving, then," I thought—"probably old lace, something that be-longed to Tullia or Lucrezia Borgia."[4] But, as she did not speak, I found myself obliged to begin: "You have been here, I think, once or twice before?"

"Seven times; this is the eighth."

A silence.

"I am often out; indeed, I may say that I am never in," I remarked carelessly.

"Yes; you have many friends."

"—Who will perhaps buy old lace," I mentally added. But this time I too re-mained silent; why should I trouble myself to draw her out? She had sought me; let her advance her idea, whatever it was, now that entrance was gained.

But Miss Grief (I preferred to call her so) did not look as though she could advance anything: her black gown, damp with rain, seemed to retreat fearfully to her thin self, while her thin self retreated as far as possible from me, from the chair, from everything. Her eyes were cast down; an old-fashioned lace veil

2. Honoré de Balzac (1799–1850), whose novels and stories in *The Human Comedy* were early examples of social realism in fiction.
3. Greek female spirits of vengeance.
4. Lucrezia Borgia (1480–1519), a member of a pow-erful Italian family famous for licentiousness, intrigue, and violence, whose second husband was murdered.

According to the Roman historian Livy, Tullia (c. 530 B.C.) conspired with Tarquinius Superbus to murder her husband and his wife (her sister), married Superbus, and then hounded him into deposing her father the king, over whose murdered body she drove her chariot.

with a heavy border shaded her face. She looked at the floor, and I looked at her.

I grew a little impatient, but I made up my mind that I would continue silent and see how long a time she would consider necessary to give due effect to her little pantomime. Comedy? Or was it tragedy? I suppose full five minutes passed thus in our double silence; and that is a long time when two persons are sitting opposite each other alone in a small still room.

At last my visitor, without raising her eyes, said slowly, "You are very happy, are you not, with youth, health, friends, riches, fame?"

It was a singular beginning. Her voice was clear, low, and very sweet as she thus enumerated my advantages one by one in a list. I was attracted by it, but repelled by her words, which seemed to me flattery both dull and bold.

"Thanks," I said, "for your kindness, but I fear it is undeserved. I seldom discuss myself even when with my friends."

"I am your friend," replied Miss Grief. Then, after a moment, she added slowly, "I have read every word you have written."

I curled the edges of my book indifferently; I am not a fop,[5] I hope, but—others have said the same.

"What is more, I know much of it by heart," continued my visitor. "Wait: I will show you"; and then, without pause, she began to repeat something of mine word for word, just as I had written it. On she went, and I—listened. I intended interrupting her after a moment, but I did not, because she was reciting so well, and also because I felt a desire gaining upon me to see what she would make of a certain conversation which I knew was coming—a conversation between two of my characters which was, to say the least, sphinx-like,[6] and somewhat incandescent as well. What won me a little, too, was the fact that the scene she was reciting (it was hardly more than that, though called a story) was secretly my favorite among all the sketches from my pen which a gracious public has received with favor. I never said so, but it was; and I had always felt a wondering annoyance that the aforesaid public, while kindly praising beyond their worth other attempts of mine, had never noticed the higher purpose of this little shaft, aimed not at the balconies and lighted windows of society, but straight up toward the distant stars. So she went on, and presently reached the conversation: my two people began to talk. She had raised her eyes now, and was looking at me soberly as she gave the words of the woman, quiet, gentle, cold, and the replies of the man, bitter, hot, and scathing. Her very voice changed, and took, though always sweetly, the different tones required, while no point of meaning, however small, no breath of delicate emphasis which I had meant, but which the dull types could not give, escaped an appreciative and full, almost overfull, recognition which startled me. For she had understood me—understood me almost better than I had understood myself. It seemed to me that while I had labored to interpret, partially, a psychological riddle, she, coming after, had comprehended its bearings better than I had, though confining herself strictly to my own words and emphasis. The scene ended (and it ended rather suddenly), she dropped her eyes, and moved her hand nervously to and fro over the box she held; her gloves were old and shabby, her hands small.

I was secretly much surprised by what I had heard, but my ill humor was

5. A conceited person. 6. Enigmatic, mysterious.

deep-seated that day, and I still felt sure, besides, that the box contained something which I was expected to buy.

"You recite remarkably well," I said carelessly, "and I am much flattered also by your appreciation of my attempt. But it is not, I presume, to that alone that I owe the pleasure of this visit?"

"Yes," she answered, still looking down, "it is, for if you had not written that scene I should not have sought you. Your other sketches are interiors—exquisitely painted and delicately finished, but of small scope. This is a sketch in a few bold, masterly lines—work of entirely different spirit and purpose."

I was nettled by her insight. "You have bestowed so much of your kind attention upon me that I feel your debtor," I said, conventionally. "It may be that there is something I can do for you—connected, possibly, with that little box?"

It was impertinent, but it was true; for she answered, "Yes."

I smiled, but her eyes were cast down and she did not see the smile.

"What I have to show you is a manuscript," she said after a pause which I did not break, "it is a drama. I thought that perhaps you would read it."

"An authoress! This is worse than old lace," I said to myself in dismay.— Then, aloud, "My opinion would be worth nothing, Miss Crief."

"Not in a business way, I know. But it might be—an assistance personally." Her voice had sunk to a whisper; outside, the rain was pouring steadily down. She was a very depressing object to me as she sat there with her box.

"I hardly think I have the time at present—" I began.

She had raised her eyes and was looking at me; then, when I paused, she rose and came suddenly toward my chair. "Yes, you will read it," she said with her hand on my arm—"you will read it. Look at this room; look at yourself; look at all you have. Then look at me, and have pity."

I had risen, for she held my arm, and her damp skirt was brushing my knees. Her large dark eyes looked intently into mine as she went on: "I have no shame in asking. Why should I have? It is my last endeavor; but a calm and well-considered one If you refuse I shall go away, knowing that Fate has willed it so. And I shall be content."

"She is mad," I thought. But she did not look so, and she had spoken quietly, even gently. "Sit down," I said, moving away from her. I felt as if I had been magnetized; but it was only the nearness of her eyes to mine, and their intensity. I drew forward a chair, but she remained standing.

"I cannot," she said in the same sweet, gentle tone, "unless you promise."

"Very well, I promise; only sit down."

As I took her arm to lead her to the chair, I perceived that she was trembling, but her face continued unmoved.

"You do not, of course, wish me to look at your manuscript now?" I said, temporizing; "it would be much better to leave it. Give me your address, and I will return it to you with my written opinion; though, I repeat, the latter will be of no use to you. It is the opinion of an editor or publisher that you want."

"It shall be as you please. And I will go in a moment," said Miss Grief, pressing her palms together, as if trying to control the tremor that had seized her slight frame.

She looked so pallid that I thought of offering her a glass of wine; then I remembered that if I did it might be a bait to bring her here again, and this I was desirous to prevent. She rose while the thought was passing through my mind.

Her pasteboard box lay on the chair she had first occupied; she took it, wrote an address on the cover, laid it down, and then, bowing with a little air of formality, drew her black shawl round her shoulders and turned toward the door.

I followed, after touching the bell. "You will hear from me by letter," I said.

Simpson opened the door, and I caught a glimpse of the maid, who was waiting in the anteroom. She was an old woman, shorter than her mistress, equally thin, and dressed like her in rusty black. As the door opened she turned toward it a pair of small, dim, blue eyes with a look of furtive suspense. Simpson dropped the curtain, shutting me into the inner room; he had no intention of allowing me to accompany my visitor further. But I had the curiosity to go to a bay window in an angle from whence I could command the street door, and presently I saw them issue forth in the rain and walk away side by side, the mistress, being the taller, holding the umbrella: probably there was not much difference in rank between persons so poor and forlorn as these.

It grew dark. I was invited out for the evening, and I knew that if I should go I should meet Miss Abercrombie. I said to myself that I would not go. I got out my paper for writing, I made my preparations for a quiet evening at home with myself; but it was of no use. It all ended slavishly in my going. At the last allowable moment I presented myself, and—as a punishment for my vacillation, I suppose—I never passed a more disagreeable evening. I drove homeward in a murky temper; it was foggy without, and very foggy within. What Isabel really was, now that she had broken through my elaborately built theories, I was not able to decide. There was, to tell the truth, a certain young Englishman—But that is apart from this story.

I reached home, went up to my rooms, and had a supper. It was to console myself; I am obliged to console myself scientifically once in a while. I was walking up and down afterward, smoking and feeling somewhat better, when my eye fell upon the pasteboard box. I took it up; on the cover was written an address which showed that my visitor must have walked a long distance in order to see me: "A. Crief."—"A Grief," I thought; "and so she is. I positively believe she has brought all this trouble upon me: she has the evil eye." I took out the manuscript and looked at it. It was in the form of a little volume, and clearly written; on the cover was the word "Armor" in German text,[7] and, underneath, a pen-and-ink sketch of a helmet, breastplate, and shield.

"Grief certainly needs armor," I said to myself, sitting down by the table and turning over the pages. "I may as well look over the thing now; I could not be in a worse mood." And then I began to read.

Early the next morning Simpson took a note from me to the given address, returning with the following reply: "No; I prefer to come to you; at four; A. CRIEF." These words, with their three semicolons, were written in pencil upon a piece of coarse printing paper, but the handwriting was as clear and delicate as that of the manuscript in ink.

"What sort of a place was it, Simpson?"

"Very poor, sir, but I did not go all the way up. The elder person came down, sir, took the note, and requested me to wait where I was."

"You had no chance, then, to make inquiries?" I said, knowing full well that he had emptied the entire neighborhood of any information it might possess concerning these two lodgers.

7. I.e., in black letter (or Gothic) type.

"Well, sir, you know how these foreigners will talk, whether one wants to hear or not. But it seems that these two persons have been there but a few weeks; they live alone, and are uncommonly silent and reserved. The people round there call them something that signifies 'the Madames American, thin and dumb.'"

At four the "Madames American" arrived; it was raining again, and they came on foot under their old umbrella. The maid waited in the anteroom, and Miss Grief was ushered into my bachelor's parlor. I had thought that I should meet her with great deference; but she looked so forlorn that my deference changed to pity. It was the woman that impressed me then, more than the writer—the fragile, nerveless body more than the inspired mind. For it was inspired; I had sat up half the night over her drama, and had felt thrilled through and through more than once by its earnestness, passion, and power.

No one could have been more surprised than I was to find myself thus enthusiastic. I thought I had outgrown that sort of thing. And one would have supposed, too (I myself should have supposed so the day before), that the faults of the drama, which were many and prominent, would have chilled any liking I might have felt, I being a writer myself, and therefore critical; for writers are as apt to make much of the "how," rather than the "what," as painters, who, it is well known, prefer an exquisitely rendered representation of a commonplace theme to an imperfectly executed picture of even the most striking subject. But in this case, on the contrary, the scattered rays of splendor in Miss Grief's drama had made me forget the dark spots, which were numerous and disfiguring; or, rather, the splendor had made me anxious to have the spots removed. And this also was a philanthropic state very unusual with me. Regarding unsuccessful writers, my motto had been "Væ victis!"[3]

My visitor took a seat and folded her hands; I could see, in spite of her quiet manner, that she was in breathless suspense. It seemed so pitiful that she should be trembling there before me—a woman so much older than I was, a woman who possessed the divine spark of genius, which I was by no means sure (in spite of my success) had been granted to me—that I felt as if I ought to go down on my knees before her, and entreat her to take her proper place of supremacy at once. But there! one does not go down on one's knees, combustively,[9] as it were, before a woman over fifty, plain in feature, thin, dejected, and ill dressed. I contented myself with taking her hands (in their miserable old gloves) in mine, while I said cordially, "Miss Grief, your drama seems to me full of original power. It has roused my enthusiasm: I sat up half the night reading it."

The hands I held shook, but something (perhaps a shame for having evaded the knees business) made me tighten my hold and bestow upon her also a reassuring smile. She looked at me for a moment, and then, suddenly and noiselessly, tears rose and rolled down her cheeks. I dropped her hands and retreated. I had not thought her tearful: on the contrary, her voice and face had seemed rigidly controlled. But now here she was bending herself over the side of the chair with her head resting on her arms, not sobbing aloud, but her whole frame shaken by the strength of her emotion. I rushed for a glass of wine; I pressed her to take it. I did not quite know what to do, but, putting myself in her place, I decided to praise the drama; and praise it I did. I do not

8. Woe to the defeated! (Latin). 9. I.e., in a manner to cause combustion.

know when I have used so many adjectives. She raised her head and began to wipe her eyes.

"Do take the wine," I said, interrupting myself in my cataract of language.

"I dare not," she answered; then added humbly, "that is, unless you have a biscuit here or a bit of bread."

I found some biscuit; she ate two, and then slowly drank the wine, while I resumed my verbal Niagara. Under its influence—and that of the wine too, perhaps—she began to show new life. It was not that she looked radiant—she could not—but simply that she looked warm. I now perceived what had been the principal discomfort of her appearance heretofore: it was that she had looked all the time as if suffering from cold.

At last I could think of nothing more to say, and stopped. I really admired the drama, but I thought I had exerted myself sufficiently as an anti-hysteric, and that adjectives enough, for the present at least, had been administered. She had put down her empty wineglass, and was resting her hands on the broad cushioned arms of her chair with, for a thin person, a sort of expanded content.

"You must pardon my tears," she said, smiling; "it was the revulsion of feeling. My life was at a low ebb: if your sentence had been against me, it would have been my end."

"Your end?"

"Yes, the end of my life; I should have destroyed myself."

"Then you would have been a weak as well as wicked woman," I said in a tone of disgust. I do hate sensationalism.

"Oh no, you know nothing about it. I should have destroyed only this poor worn tenement of clay. But I can well understand how *you* would look upon it. Regarding the desirableness of life, the prince and the beggar may have different opinions. We will say no more of it, but talk of the drama instead." As she spoke the word "drama" a triumphant brightness came into her eyes.

I took the manuscript from a drawer and sat down beside her. "I suppose you know that there are faults," I said, expecting ready acquiescence.

"I was not aware that there were any," was her gentle reply.

Here was a beginning! After all my interest in her—and, I may say under the circumstances, my kindness—she received me in this way! However, my belief in her genius was too sincere to be altered by her whimsies; so I persevered. "Let us go over it together," I said. "Shall I read it to you, or will you read it to me?"

"I will not read it, but recite it."

"That will never do; you will recite it so well that we shall see only the good points, and what we have to concern ourselves with now is the bad ones."

"I will recite it," she repeated.

"Now, Miss Crief," I said bluntly, "for what purpose did you come to me? Certainly not merely to recite: I am no stage manager. In plain English, was it not your idea that I might help you in obtaining a publisher?"

"Yes, yes," she answered, looking at me apprehensively, all her old manner returning.

I followed up my advantage, opened the little paper volume and began. I first took the drama line by line, and spoke of the faults of expression and structure; then I turned back and touched upon two or three glaring impossibilities in the plot. "Your absorbed interest in the motive of the whole no doubt made you forget these blemishes," I said apologetically.

But, to my surprise, I found that she did not see the blemishes—that she appreciated nothing I had said, comprehended nothing. Such unaccountable obtuseness puzzled me. I began again, going over the whole with even greater minuteness and care. I worked hard: the perspiration stood in beads upon my forehead as I struggled with her—what shall I call it—obstinacy? But it was not exactly obstinancy. She simply could not see the faults of her own work, any more than a blind man can see the smoke that dims a patch of blue sky. When I had finished my task the second time, she still remained as gently impassive as before. I leaned back in my chair exhausted, and looked at her.

Even then she did not seem to comprehend whether she agreed with it or not) what I must be thinking. "It is such a heaven to me that you like it," she murmured dreamily, breaking the silence. Then, with more animation, "And now you will let me recite it?"

I was too weary to oppose her; she threw aside her shawl and bonnet, and standing in the center of the room, began.

And she carried me along with her; all the strong passages were doubly strong when spoken, and the faults, which seemed nothing to her, were made by her earnestness to seem nothing to me, at least for that moment. When it was ended, she stood looking at me with a triumphant smile.

"Yes," I said, "I like it, and you see that I do. But I like it because my taste is peculiar. To me originality and force are everything—perhaps because I have them not to any marked degree myself—but the world at large will not overlook as I do your absolutely barbarous shortcomings on account of them. Will you trust me to go over the drama and correct it at my pleasure?" This was a vast deal for me to offer; I was surprised at myself.

"No," she answered softly, still smiling. "There shall not be so much as a comma altered." Then she sat down and fell into a reverie as though she were alone.

"Have you written anything else?" I said after a while, when I had become tired of the silence.

"Yes."

"Can I see it? Or is it them?"

"It is them. Yes, you can see all."

"I will call upon you for the purpose."

"No, you must not," she said, coming back to the present nervously. "I prefer to come to you."

At this moment Simpson entered to light the room, and busied himself rather longer than was necessary over the task. When he finally went out, I saw that my visitor's manner had sunk into its former depression: the presence of the servant seemed to have chilled her.

"When did you say I might come?" I repeated, ignoring her refusal.

"I did not say it. It would be impossible."

"Well, then, when will you come here?" There was, I fear a trace of fatigue in my tone.

"At your good pleasure, sir," she answered humbly.

My chivalry was touched by this: after all, she was a woman. "Come tomorrow," I said. "By the way, come and dine with me then; why not?" I was curious to see what she would reply.

"Why not, indeed? Yes, I will come. I am forty-three: I might have been your mother."

This was not quite true, as I am over thirty: but I look young, while she—

Well, I had thought her over fifty. "I can hardly call you 'mother,' but we might compromise upon 'aunt,'" I said, laughing. "Aunt what?"

"My name is Aaronna," she gravely answered. "My father was much disappointed that I was not a boy, and gave me as nearly as possible the name he had prepared—Aaron."

"Then come and dine with me tomorrow, and bring with you the other manuscripts, Aaronna," I said, amused at the quaint sound of the name. On the whole, I did not like "aunt."

"I will come," she answered.

It was twilight and still raining, but she refused all offers of escort or carriage, departing with her maid, as she had come, under the brown umbrella. The next day we had the dinner. Simpson was astonished—and more than astonished, grieved—when I told him that he was to dine with the maid; but he could not complain in words, since my own guest, the mistress, was hardly more attractive. When our preparations were complete, I could not help laughing: the two prim little tables, one in the parlor and one in the anteroom, and Simpson disapprovingly going back and forth between them, were irresistible.

I greeted my guest hilariously[1] when she arrived, and, fortunately, her manner was not quite so depressed as usual: I could never have accorded myself with a tearful mood. I had thought that perhaps she would make, for the occasion, some change in her attire; I have never known a woman who had not some scrap of finery, however small, in reserve for that unexpected occasion of which she is ever dreaming. But no: Miss Grief wore the same black gown, unadorned and unaltered. I was glad that there was no rain that day, so that the skirt did not at least look so damp and rheumatic.

She ate quietly, almost furtively, yet with a good appetite, and she did not refuse the wine. Then, when the meal was over and Simpson had removed the dishes, I asked for the new manuscripts. She gave me an old green copybook filled with short poems, and a prose sketch by itself; I lit a cigar and sat down at my desk to look them over.

"Perhaps you will try a cigarette?" I suggested, more for amusement than anything else, for there was not a shade of Bohemianism about her; her whole appearance was puritanical.

"I have not yet succeeded in learning to smoke."

"You have tried?" I said, turning round.

"Yes: Serena and I tried, but we did not succeed."

"Serena is your maid?"

"She lives with me."

I was seized with inward laughter, and began hastily to look over her manuscripts with my back toward her, so that she might not see it. A vision had risen before me of those two forlorn women, alone in their room with locked doors, patiently trying to acquire the smoker's art.

But my attention was soon absorbed by the papers before me. Such a fantastic collection of words, lines, and epithets I had never before seen, or even in dreams imagined. In truth, they were like the work of dreams: they were *Kubla Khan*,[2] only more so. Here and there was radiance like the flash of a diamond, but each poem, almost each verse and line, was marred by some fault or

1. Cheerfully.
2. Samuel Taylor Coleridge (1772–1834) subtitled his poem (published in 1816) "a vision in a dream."

lack which seemed wilful perversity, like the work of an evil sprite. It was like a case of jeweller's wares set before you, with each ring unfinished, each bracelet too large or too small for its purpose, each breastpin without its fastening, each necklace purposely broken. I turned the pages, marvelling. When about half an hour had passed, and I was leaning back for a moment to light another cigar, I glanced toward my visitor. She was behind me, in an easy chair before my small fire, and she was—fast asleep. In the relaxation of her unconsciousness I was struck anew by the poverty her appearance expressed; her feet were visible, and I saw the miserable worn old shoes which hitherto she had kept concealed.

After looking at her for a moment, I returned to my task and took up the prose story; in prose she must be more reasonable. She was less fantastic perhaps, but hardly more reasonable. The story was that of a profligate and commonplace man forced by two of his friends, in order not to break the heart of a dying girl who loves him, to live up to a high imaginary ideal of himself which her pure but mistaken mind has formed. He has a handsome face and sweet voice, and repeats what they tell them. Her long, slow decline and happy death, and his own inward ennui and profound weariness of the rôle he has to play, made the vivid points of the story. So far, well enough, but here was the trouble: through the whole narrative moved another character, a physician of tender heart and exquisite mercy, who practiced murder as a fine art, and was regarded (by the author) as a second Messiah! This was monstrous. I read it through twice, and threw it down; then, fatigued, I turned round and leaned back, waiting for her to wake. I could see her profile against the dark hue of the easy chair.

Presently she seemed to feel my gaze, for she stirred, then opened her eyes. "I have been asleep," she said, rising hurriedly.

"No harm in that, Aaronna."

But she was deeply embarrassed and troubled, much more so than the occasion required; so much so, indeed, that I turned the conversation back upon the manuscripts as a diversion. "I cannot stand that doctor of yours," I said, indicating the prose story; "no one would. You must cut him out."

Her self-possession returned as if by magic. "Certainly not," she answered haughtily.

"Oh, if you do not care—I had labored under the impression that you were anxious these things should find a purchaser."

"I am, I am," she said, her manner changing to deep humility with wonderful rapidity. With such alternations of feeling as this sweeping over her like great waves, no wonder she was old before her time.

"Then you must take out that doctor."

"I am willing, but do not know how," she answered, pressing her hands together helplessly. "In my mind he belongs to the story so closely that he cannot be separated from it."

Here Simpson entered, bringing a note for me: it was a line from Mrs. Abercrombie inviting me for that evening—an unexpected gathering, and therefore likely to be all the more agreeable. My heart bounded in spite of me; I forgot Miss Grief and her manuscripts for the moment as completely as though they had never existed. But, bodily, being still in the same room with her, her speech brought me back to the present.

"You have had good news?" she said.

"Oh no, nothing especial—merely an invitation."

"But good news also," she repeated. "And now, as for me, I must go."

Not supposing that she would stay much later in any case, I had that morning ordered a carriage to come for her at about that hour. I told her this. She made no reply beyond putting on her bonnet and shawl.

"You will hear from me soon," I said; "I shall do all I can for you."

She had reached the door, but before opening it she stopped, turned and extended her hand. "You are good," she said: "I give you thanks. Do not think me ungrateful or envious. It is only that you are young, and I am so—so old." Then she opened the door and passed through the anteroom without pause, her maid accompanying her and Simpson with gladness lighting the way. They were gone. I dressed hastily and went out—to continue my studies in psychology.

Time passed; I was busy, amused and perhaps a little excited (sometimes psychology is exciting). But, though much occupied with my own affairs, I did not altogether neglect my self-imposed task regarding Miss Grief. I began by sending her prose story to a friend, the editor of a monthly magazine, with a letter making a strong plea for its admittance. It should have a chance first on its own merits. Then I forwarded the drama to a publisher, also an acquaintance, a man with a taste for phantasms and a soul above mere common popularity, as his own coffers knew to their cost. This done, I waited with conscience clear.

Four weeks passed. During this waiting period I heard nothing from Miss Grief. At last one morning came a letter from my editor. "The story has force, but I cannot stand that doctor," he wrote. "Let her cut him out, and I might print it." Just what I myself had said. The package lay there on my table, travel worn and grimed; a returned manuscript is, I think, the most melancholy object on earth. I decided to wait, before writing to Aaronna, until the second letter was received. A week later it came. "Armor" was declined. The publisher had been "impressed" by the power displayed in certain passages, but the "impossibilities of the plot" rendered it "unavailable for publication"—in fact, would "bury it in ridicule" if brought before the public, a public "lamentably" fond of amusement, "seeking it, undaunted, even in the cannon's mouth." I doubt if he knew himself what he meant. But one thing, at any rate, was clear: "Armor" was declined.

Now, I am, as I have remarked before, a little obstinate. I was determined that Miss Grief's work should be received. I would alter and improve it myself, without letting her know: the end justified the means. Surely the sieve of my own good taste, whose mesh had been pronounced so fine and delicate, would serve for two. I began; and utterly failed.

I set to work first upon "Armor." I amended, altered, left out, put in, pieced, condensed, lengthened; I did my best, and all to no avail. I could not succeed in completing anything that satisfied me, or that approached, in truth, Miss Grief's own work just as it stood. I suppose I went over that manuscript twenty times: I covered sheets of paper with my copies. But the obstinate drama refused to be corrected; as it was it must stand or fall.

Wearied and annoyed, I threw it aside and took up the prose story: that would be easier. But, to my surprise, I found that that apparently gentle "doctor" would not out: he was so closely interwoven with every part of the tale that to take him out was like taking out one especial figure in a carpet: that is, impossible, unless you unravel the whole. At last I did unravel the whole, and then the story was no longer good, or Aaronna's: it was weak, and mine. All this

took time, for of course I had much to do in connection with my own life and tasks. But, though slowly and at my leisure, I really did try my best as regarded Miss Grief, and without success. I was forced at last to make up my mind that either my own powers were not equal to the task, or else that her perversities were as essential a part of her work as her inspirations, and not to be separated from it. Once during this period I showed two of the short poems to Isabel, withholding of course the writer's name. "They were written by a woman," I explained.

"Her mind must have been disordered, poor thing!" Isabel said in her gentle way when she returned them—"at least, judging by these. They are hopelessly mixed and vague."

Now, they were not vague so much as vast. But I knew that I could not make Isabel comprehend it, and (so complex a creature is man) I do not know that I wanted her to comprehend it. These were the only ones in the whole collection that I would have shown her, and I was rather glad that she did not like even these. Not that poor Aaronna's poems were evil: they were simply unrestrained, large, vast, like the skies or the wind. Isabel was bounded on all sides, like a violet in a garden bed. And I liked her so.

One afternoon, about the time when I was beginning to see that I could not "improve" Miss Grief, I came upon the maid. I was driving, and she had stopped on the crossing to let the carriage pass. I recognized her at a glance (by her general forlornness), and called to the driver to stop. "How is Miss Grief?" I said. "I have been intending to write to her for some time."

"And your note, when it comes," answered the old woman on the crosswalk fiercely, "she shall not see."

"What?"

"I say she shall not see it. Your patronizing face shows that you have no good news, and you shall not rack and stab her any more on *this* earth, please God, while I have authority."

"Who has racked or stabbed her, Serena?"

"Serena, indeed! Rubbish! I'm no Serena: I'm her aunt. And as to who has racked and stabbed her, I say you, *you*—YOU literary men!" She had put her old head inside my carriage, and flung out these words at me in a shrill, menacing tone. "But she shall die in peace in spite of you," she continued. "Vampires! you take her ideas and fatten on them, and leave her to starve. You know you do—*you* who have had her poor manuscripts these months and months!"

"Is she ill?" I asked in real concern, gathering that much at least from the incoherent tirade.

"She is dying," answered the desolate old creature, her voice softening and her dim eyes filling with tears.

"Oh, I trust not. Perhaps something can be done. Can I help you in any way?"

"In all ways if you would," she said, breaking down and beginning to sob weakly, with her head resting on the sill of the carriage window. "Oh, what have we not been through together, we two! Piece by piece I have sold all."

I am goodhearted enough, but I do not like to have old women weeping across my carriage door. I suggested, therefore, that she should come inside and let me take her home. Her shabby old skirt was soon beside me, and, following her directions, the driver turned toward one of the most wretched quarters of the city, the abode of poverty, crowded and unclean. Here, in a large bare chamber up many flights of stairs, I found Miss Grief.

As I entered I was startled: I thought she was dead. There seemed no life present until she opened her eyes, and even then they rested upon us vaguely, as though she did not know who we were. But as I approached a light came into them: she recognized me, and this sudden revivification, this return of the soul to the almost deserted body, was the most wonderful thing I ever saw. "You have good news of the drama?" she whispered as I bent over her: "tell me. I *know* you have good news."

What was I to answer? Pray, what would you have answered, puritan?

"Yes, I have good news, Aaronna," I said. "The drama will appear." (And who knows? Perhaps it will in some other world.)

She smiled, and her now brilliant eyes did not leave my face.

"He knows I'm your aunt: I told him," said the old woman, coming to the bedside.

"Did you?" whispered Miss Grief, still gazing at me with a smile. "Then please, dear Aunt Martha, give me something to eat."

Aunt Martha hurried across the room, and I followed her. "It's the first time she's asked for food in weeks," she said in a husky tone.

She opened a cupboard door vaguely, but I could see nothing within. "What have you for her?" I asked with some impatience, though in a low voice.

"Please God, nothing!" answered the poor old woman, hiding her reply and her tears behind the broad cupboard door. "I was going out to get a little something when I met you."

"Good Heavens! is it money you need? Here, take this and send; or go yourself in the carriage waiting below."

She hurried out breathless, and I went back to the bedside, much disturbed by what I had seen and heard. But Miss Grief's eyes were full of life, and as I sat down beside her she whispered earnestly, "Tell me."

And I did tell her—a romance invented for the occasion. I venture to say that none of my published sketches could compare with it. As for the lie involved, it will stand among my few good deeds, I know, at the judgment bar.

And she was satisfied. "I have never known what it was," she whispered, "to be fully happy until now." She closed her eyes, and when the lids fell I again thought that she had passed away. But no, there was still pulsation in her small, thin wrist. As she perceived my touch she smiled. "Yes, I am happy," she said again, though without audible sound.

The old aunt returned; food was prepared, and she took some. I myself went out after wine that should be rich and pure. She rallied a little, but I did not leave her: her eyes dwelt upon me and compelled me to stay, or rather my conscience compelled me. It was a damp night, and I had a little fire made. The wine, fruit, flowers, and candles I had ordered made the bare place for the time being bright and fragrant. Aunt Martha dozed in her chair from sheer fatigue—she had watched many nights—but Miss Grief was awake, and I sat beside her.

"I make you my executor," she murmured, "as to the drama. But my other manuscripts place, when I am gone, under my head, and let them be buried with me. They are not many—those you have and these. See!"

I followed her gesture, and saw under her pillows the edges of two more copybooks like the one I had. "Do not look at them—my poor dead children!" she said tenderly. "Let them depart with me—unread, as I have been."

Later she whispered, "Did you wonder why I came to you? It was the con-

trast. You were young—strong—rich—praised—loved—successful: all that I was not. I wanted to look at you—and imagine how it would feel. You had success—but I had the greater power. Tell me, did I not have it?"

"Yes, Aaronna."

"It is all in the past now. But I am satisfied."

After another pause she said with a faint smile, "Do you remember when I fell asleep in your parlor? It was the good and rich food. It was so long since I had had food like that!"

I took her hand and held it, conscience stricken, but now she hardly seemed to perceive my touch. "And the smoking?" she whispered. "Do you remember how you laughed? I saw it. But I had heard that smoking soothed—that one was no longer tired and hungry—with a cigar."

In little whispers of this sort, separated by long rests and pauses, the night passed. Once she asked if her aunt was asleep, and when I answered in the affirmative she said, "Help her to return home—to America: the drama will pay for it. I ought never to have brought her away."

I promised, and she resumed her bright-eyed silence.

I think she did not speak again. Toward morning the change came, and soon after sunrise, with her old aunt kneeling by her side, she passed away.

All was arranged as she had wished. Her manuscripts, covered with violets, formed her pillow. No one followed her to the grave save her aunt and myself: I thought she would prefer it so. Her name was not "Grief," after all, but "Moncrief"; I saw it written out by Aunt Martha for the coffin plate, as follows: "Aaronna Moncrief, aged forty-three years, two months and eight days."

I never knew more of her history than is written here. If there was more that I might have learned, it remained unlearned, for I did not ask.

And the drama? I keep it here in this locked case. I could have had it published at my own expense; but I think that now she knows its faults herself, perhaps, and would not like it.

I keep it; and, once in a while, I read it over—not as a *memento mori*[3] exactly, but rather as a memento of my own good fortune, for which I should continually give thanks. The want of one grain made all her work void, and that one grain was given to me. She, with the greater power, failed—I, with the less, succeeded. But no praise is due to me for that. When I die "Armor" is to be destroyed unread: not ever. Isabel is to see it. For women will misunderstand each other; and, dear and precious to me as my sweet wife is. I could not bear that she or anyone should cast so much as a thought of scorn upon the memory of the writer, upon my poor dead, "unavailable," unaccepted "Miss Grief."

1880

3. Remember that you must die (Latin, literal trans.); thus a reminder of death.

ALICE MEYNELL

1847–1922

"Of all the crying evils in the depraved earth . . . the greatest, judged by all the laws of God and humanity, is the miserable selfishness of men that keeps women from work," wrote the poet Alice Thompson at the age of eighteen. The daughter of cultivated, independently wealthy parents—her mother was a pianist and artist, her

father an amateur man of letters—this surprisingly feminist young woman was already beginning to write the elegant verse that would later in her life bring her considerable fame. Raised partly in Italy, where her family lived in what the critic Cora Kaplan has called a "relaxed bohemian style," she had been educated at home and had been taught, as her remark about work suggests, to take herself seriously. In addition, like her mother and sister, she was a convert to Catholicism, organizing her life as well as her art around a strong commitment to her faith.

Alice Thompson's first book of poetry, *Preludes*, appeared in 1875, and two years later she married a young Catholic journalist, Wilfred Meynell. With her husband, she founded and edited several magazines, one of which, *Merry England*, brought her the friendship of well-known contemporary poets like Coventry Patmore, Hilaire Belloc, and Francis Thompson. Besides working on *Merry England*, she also wrote an impressive number of fine essays—many on literary subjects—for such periodicals as *The Spectator* and *The Saturday Review*, and she combined this activity with a busy domestic life: her egalitarian marriage produced eight children, seven of whom survived.

Meynell's most notable achievement, however, was a body of verse that seemed, in the words of one admirer, Vita Sackville-West, to have been written "with an etching pen." Austerely lyric, poems like *A Father of Women*, *The Sunderland Children*, and *Parentage* reveal the aesthetic craft that elicited for Meynell the praise of such a major figure as John Ruskin. At the same time, the political, and often distinctively feminist, passion that infuses these works reminds us that they were written by the same woman who had longed for significant work at the age of eighteen. Not surprisingly, Meynell became a suffragist in her later years, and she drew on her deep-seated feminism in singularly powerful poems about the horrors of World War I, a conflict that she saw as having been brought about by cynical "fathers"—for, as she had already observed in *Parentage* (1896), "Theirs are armies. Death is theirs." Perhaps impressed by such intensity, the American poet Amy Lowell remembered, after Meynell's death in 1922, that this English writer's words "rang . . . like bronze cathedral bells / Down ancient lawns."

The Sunderland Children

On the 183 Sunderland children who lost their lives in a panic at the
Victoria Hall, 16th June, 1883[1]

This was the surplus childhood, held as cheap!
 Not worth the care which shields
The lambs that are to stay, the corn to reap—
 The promise of the fields.

The nation guards her future. Fruits and grass 5
 And vegetable life
Are fostered league by league. But oh, the mass
 Of childhood over-rife!

1. At a Saturday afternoon entertainment in the English mining town of Sunderland, most of the children were sitting in the cheapest seats in the gallery—about 1,500, with very few adults. Prizes had been promised to all, and as they began to be distributed on the main floor at the end of the show, the children rushed down the stairs. Because the door to the lobby could open only eighteen inches, hundreds of children became trapped on the last steps, jammed into a mass of bodies over six feet high.

O mass, O units! Oh, the separate story
 Planned for each breather of breath! 10
This futile young mankind, and transitory,
 Is left to stray to Death.

O promise, presage, menace! Upon these
 A certain seal is laid.
Unkept, unbroken, are the auguries 15
 These little children made.

For threat is bound with promise; and the nation
 Holds festival of regret
Over these dead—dead in their isolation—
 Wisely. She feared their threat. 20

 1883

Parentage

"When Augustus Caesar legislated against the unmarried citizens of
Rome, he declared them to be, in some sort, slayers of the people."

 Ah no! not these!
These, who were childless, are not they who gave
So many dead unto the journeying wave,
The helpless nurslings of the cradling seas;
Not they who doomed by infallible decrees 5
Unnumbered man to the innumerable grave.

 But those who slay
Are fathers. Theirs are armies. Death is theirs—
The death of innocences and despairs;
The dying of the golden and the gray. 10
The sentence, when these speak it, has no Nay.
And she who slays is she who bears, who bears.

 1896

A Father of Women: Ad Sororem E. B.[1]

"Thy father was transfused into thy blood."
Dryden: *Ode to Mrs. Anne Killigrew*[2]

 Our father works in us,
The daughters of his manhood. Not undone
Is he, not wasted, though transmuted thus,
 And though he left no son.

1. To Sister E. B. (Latin) E. B. is almost certainly Meynall's sister Elizabeth Thompson Butler (1844–1933), a painter of military and battle scenes.

2. A seventeenth-century poet, whose father was a well-known literary man John Dryden (1631–1700), author of the ode.

 Therefore on him I cry 5
To arm me: "For my delicate mind a casque,[3]
A breastplate for my heart, courage to die,
 Of thee, captain, I ask.

 "Nor strengthen only; press
A finger on this violent blood and pale, 10
Over this rash will let thy tenderness
 A while pause, and prevail.

 "And shepherd-father, thou
Whose staff folded[4] my thoughts before my birth,
Control them now I am of earth, and now 15
 Thou art no more of earth.

 "O liberal, constant, dear,
Crush in my nature the ungenerous art[5]
Of the inferior; set me high, and here,
 Here garner up thy heart!" 20

 Like to him now are they,
The million living fathers of the War[6]—
Mourning the crippled world, the bitter day—
 Whose striplings are no more.

 The crippled world! Come then, 25
Fathers of women with your honor in trust,
Approve, accept, know them daughters of men,
 Now that your sons are dust.

 1917

3. Helmet. 5. Artifice.
4. I.e., guided to the fold, an enclosure for sheep. 6. World War I.

ALICE JAMES
1848–1892

The journal Alice James kept for the last three years of her life is acerbic about English customs and medical practices, witty about the gossip and books she received in her sickroom, and sensitively introspective. For the most part, it was dictated to her intimate companion, Katharine Peabody Loring. These two friends, who may have furnished the impetus for Alice's brother Henry's portrait of two emotionally involved suffragists in *The Bostonians* (1886), had traveled to England to cure Katharine's sister and to visit Alice's novelist brother after the death of Alice's parents in 1882, but Alice's poor health prolonged their stay.

As the only daughter in the illustrious James family and the youngest of five siblings, Alice James was not well equipped to handle either her volatile father, who preached Christian mysticism and intellectual ambition to his children, or her mother, who was worshiped as a self-effacing madonna within the family. After a childhood punctuated by foreign travel, she grew up in Cambridge, Massachusetts. Her first mental breakdown occurred at sixteen. While her broth-

ers William and Henry were preparing for their eminent careers in psychology and literature, she was treated for stomach pains, "heart attacks," fainting spells, and paralyzed limbs with the remedies of her time "motor-therapy," "electricity," "blistering" baths, and "sulphuric ether." At thirty years of age, she was tempted to commit suicide during a profound depression, but her father's "permission"—his acknowledgment, on learning of her feelings, of her freedom to choose to die—made even that alternative seem impossible. Before and after her parents' death, she must have compared her own private suffering with her brothers' public accomplishments. A late diary entry lists Henry's *The Tragic Muse* and *The American* along with her philosopher brother William's *Psychology*: "Not a bad show for one family!" she exulted, ominously adding, 'especially if I get myself dead, the hardest job of all."

Because, as her brother Henry explained, "in our family group girls seem scarcely to have had a chance," he believed that Alice's "tragic health was, in a manner, the only solution for her of the practical problem of life." He had not known of the journal during her lifetime; however, Alice James had valued it sufficiently to ask that it be typed, and after Alice's death from breast cancer at forty-four, Loring privately printed a copy for each of the surviving brothers and one for herself. A 1934 edition was followed by Leon Edel's 1964 edition, from which the selections printed here were taken.

From The Diary

[My First Journal]

May 31st, 1889
I think that if I get into the habit of writing a bit about what happens, or rather doesn't happen, I may lose a little of the sense of loneliness and desolation which abides with me. My circumstances allowing of nothing but the ejaculation of one-syllabled reflections, a written monologue by that most interesting being, *myself*, may have its yet to be discovered consolations. I shall at least have it all my own way and it may bring relief as an outlet to that geyser of emotions, sensations, speculations and reflections which ferments perpetually within my poor old carcass for its sins; so here goes, my first Journal!

[My Microscopic Field]

July 12th [1889]
* * * It's amusing to see how, even on my microscopic field, minute events are perpetually taking place illustrative of the broadest facts of human nature. Yesterday Nurse and I had a good laugh but I must allow that decidedly she "had" me. I was thinking of something that interested me very much and my mind was suddenly flooded by one of those luminous waves that sweep out of consciousness all but the living sense and overpower one with joy in the rich, throbbing complexity of life, when suddenly I looked up at Nurse, who was dressing me, and saw her primitive, rudimentary expression (so common here) as of no inherited quarrel with her destiny of putting petticoats over my head; the poverty and deadness of it contrasted to the tide of speculation that was coursing thro' my brain made me exclaim, 'Oh! Nurse, don't you wish you were inside of *me*!"—her look of dismay and vehement disclaimer—"Inside of you, Miss, when you have just had a sick headache for five days!"—gave a greater blow to my vanity, than that much battered article has ever received.

The headache had gone off in the night and I had clean forgotten it—when the little wretch confronted me with it, at this sublime moment when I was feeling within me the potency of a Bismarck,[1] and left me powerless before the immutable law that however great we may seem to our own consciousness no human being would exchange his for ours, and before the fact that *my* glorious role was to stand for *Sick headache* to mankind! What a grotesque I am to be sure! Lying in this room, with the resistance of a thistle-down, having illusory moments of throbbing with the pulse of the Race, the Mystery to be solved at the next breath and the fountain of all Happiness within me—the sense of vitality, in short, simply proportionate to the excess of weakness!—To sit by and watch these absurdities is amusing in its way and reminds me of how I used to *listen* to my "company manners" in the days when I had 'em, and how ridiculous they sounded.

Ah! Those strange people who have the courage to be unhappy! *Are* they unhappy, by-the-way?

[Pharasaism; Death]

February 17th [1890]

I find myself as the months pass more and more stifled by the all pervasive sense of pharasaism[2] in the British constitution of things. You don't feel it at first and you can't put your finger upon it in your friends, but as the days go by you unfold it with your *Standard*,[3] in the morn. It rises dense from the P. M.G. in the evening, it creeps thro' the cracks in the window frames like the fog and envelopes you thro' the day. I asked H.[4] once how it struck him from his wider and varied field not wanting my view to become cramped upon conclusions drawn from my centimeter of observation, he said that he didn't think it could be exaggerated. It's woven of a multiplicity of minute details and incidents which elude you in the telling but which seem to exist in the texture of things and leave a dent in the mind as they file past. A monarchy to which they bow down in its tinsel capacity only, denying to it a manly movement of any sort; a boneless Church broadening itself out, up to date; the hysterical legislation over a dog with a broken leg whilst Society is engaged making bags of 4,000 pheasants, etc. etc., or gloating over foxes torn to pieces by a pack of hounds;[5] the docility with which the classes enslave themselves to respectability or non-respectability as the "good-form"[6] of the moment may be; the "sense of their betters" in the masses; the passivity with which the working man allows himself to be patted and legislated out of all independence; thus the profound ineradicables in the bone and sinew conviction that outlying regions are their preserves, that they alone of human races massacre savages out of pure virtue. It would ill-become an American to reflect upon the treatment of aboriginal races; but I never heard it suggested that our hideous dealings with the Indians was brotherly love masquerading under the disguise of pure cussedness.

1. Otto von Bismarck (1815–1898), creator and first chancellor of the German Empire, noted for his strength and ruthlessness.
2. Strict adherence to the outward forms of moral and social strictures without regard to their spirit.
3. The *Morning Standard* and the *Pall Mall Gazette* ("P.M.G.") were two London newspapers of the period.
4. Alice's brother Henry James (1843–1916), the famous novelist.
5. I.e., so-called sporting hunting. "Bag": gamebag.
6. I.e., code of behavior.

It would have been highly immoral, when Kath.[7] was here, not to get as much work out of her as possible, so the second week she began upon Woking. I had got discouraged about cremation, having been told that it was very fussy and expensive, so she wrote for the circular[8] to be sent by the Cremation people; when, lo! it's as simple and inexpensive as possible, only six guineas and one extra for a parson. Me ashes are to be put in an urn, and sent home, not as a parlor ornament for William's new house, but to be buried beside Father and Mother in the cemetery at Cam[bridge],—so that we shall not be myths as Harry suggests we might otherwise become. 'Tis a great waste that I didn't die whilst K. was here; she could have carried home the urn in her top berth and as she lay convulsed with seasickness it would have greatly assuaged her grief to have such a palpable assurance that that portion of me hitherto so susceptible to the dread thing was reduced to ashes. It seems delightfully clean to elude in this way that early riser, the unpleasant wurrum, and I am greatly in hopes that

> "The worms crawled in
> And the worms crawled out,"[9]

will not be true of my return to dust.

Then we began upon my Will, which I wanted to make over again, leaving out, of course, those who had offended me since my last, as a cousin of Lilla Walsh's used to do, who re-made hers every few weeks. K. told me that as long as I indulged in no amateur legal terminology but confined myself strictly to my vernacular it would be all right, so she wouldn't allow me even one decorative bequeath. She wrote to the Consul at Birmingham to ask him if it had to be signed in his presence and he said yes, so hearing that Lizzie Putnam was at Banbury and was coming to spend a certain afternoon, K. telegraphed to the Consul, as it was so good to get a Boston witness. The arrival of this august personage the Consul naturally caused me to "go off" and I had to be put to bed—when the most amusing scene followed. I lay in a semi-faint, draped in as many frills as could be found for the occasion, with Nurse at my head with the thickest layer of her anxious-devoted-nurse expression on, as K. told me after, when thro' a mist I vaguely saw five black figures file into my little bower, headed by the most extraordinary little man, all gesticulation and grimace, who planted himself at the foot of the bed and stroking my knees began a long harangue to the effect that he and his wife had both "laid upon a bed of sickness" which seemed to constitute uncontrovertible reason for my immediate recovery. K. with difficulty restrained him from reading the Will aloud there and then—he has doubtless not forgiven this dam thrown across to arrest the flood of his eloquence—It was so curious for me, just like a nightmare effect and I felt as if I were assisting at the reading of my own Will, surrounded by the greedy relatives, as in novels. After they had filed in and out several times and become tangled in as much resounding red-tape as the creature could reel off for the occasion they went off downstairs to an "elegant" tea where the Consul entertained them with his whole history and the digestive processes of his domestic circle, which seem to be in a sadly disorganized condition. He asked K. whether she was related to "Our great Minister to Portugal Geo. B. Loring"—imagine the condition of a Peabody-Loring having such an insult

7. Katharine P. Loring, James's intimate companion. 9. From a macabre children's song.
8. Advertising pamphlet.

hurled at her! And he also wanted to know whether Postmaster James and I were consanguineous.[1] I, not having been *born* (ahem!) was able to take things more easily, besides Mr. James, I believe, was a man to be related to whom would have been an honor. Miss Blanche Leppington, who had been asked to be a witness, told K. after that she hadn't looked at my face but that she felt as if she "ought to keep her eye fixed upon Miss James's *hand!*"—she also said the scene—"Will remain in my thoughts as the most pathetic I ever saw and in my imagination as the most picturesque and American!"—I can't complain of not being taken seriously and I think it is the first time that *picturesque* and *American*, which are usually supposed to neutralize one another so completely, were ever conjoined. In recounting the story to H. he said, "You can't say you've done nothing for your Race since you've brought that about in your own person."

[My "Hidden Self"]

October 26th [1890]

William uses an excellent expression when he says in his paper on the "Hidden Self " that the nervous victim "abandons" certain portions of his consciousness.[2] It may be the word commonly used by his kind. It is just the right one at any rate, altho' I have never unfortunately been able to abandon my consciousness and get five minutes' rest. I have passed thro' an infinite succession of conscious abandonments and in looking back now I see how it began in my childhood, altho' I wasn't conscious of the necessity until '67 or '68 when I broke down first, acutely, and had violent turns of hysteria. As I lay prostrate after the storm with my mind luminous and active and susceptible of the clearest, strongest impressions, I saw so distinctly that it was a fight simply between my body and my will, a battle in which the former was to be triumphant to the end. Owing to some physical weakness, excess of nervous susceptibility, the moral power *pauses*, as it were for a moment, and refuses to maintain muscular sanity, worn out with the strain of its constabulary functions. As I used to sit immovable reading in the library with waves of violent inclination suddenly invading my muscles taking some one of their myriad forms such as throwing myself out of the window, or knocking off the head of the benignant pater[3] as he sat with his silver locks, writing at his table, it used to seem to me that the only difference between me and the insane was that I had not only all the horrors and suffering of insanity but the duties of doctor, nurse, and strait-jacket imposed upon me, too. Conceive of never being without the sense that if you let yourself go for a moment your mechanism will fall into pie[4] and that at some given moment you must abandon it all, let the dykes break and the flood sweep in, acknowledging yourself abjectly impotent before the immutable laws. When all one's moral and natural stock in trade is a temperament forbidding the abandonment of an inch or the relaxation of a muscle, 'tis a never-ending fight. When the fancy took me of a morning at school to *study* my lessons by way of variety instead of shirking or wiggling thro' the most impossible sensations of upheaval, violent revolt in my head

1. Related.
2. Alice's brother the psychologist and philosopher William James (1842–1910) had published a paper that year called *The Hidden Self*, in which he described "contractions in the field of consciousness" in hysterical patients.
3. Father; in this case, the eminent theologian Henry James Sr. (1811–1882).
4. Disorder (literally, printer's type that is spilled or mixed).

overtook me so that I had to "abandon" my brain, as it were. So it has always been, anything that sticks of itself is free to do so, but conscious and continuous cerebration is an impossible exercise and from just behind the eyes my head feels like a dense jungle into which no ray of light has ever penetrated. So, with the rest, you abandon the pit of your stomach, the palms of your hands, the soles of your feet, and refuse to keep them sane when you find in turn one moral impression after another producing despair in the one, terror in the other, anxiety in the third and so on until life becomes one long flight from remote suggestion and complicated eluding of the multifold traps set for your undoing.

[Going Downhill]

May 31st [1891]

To him who waits, all things come! My aspirations may have been eccentric, but I cannot complain now, that they have not been brilliantly fulfilled. Ever since I have been ill, I have longed and longed for some palpable disease, no matter how conventionally dreadful a label it might have, but I was always driven back to stagger alone under the monstrous mass of subjective sensations, which that sympathetic being "the medical man" had no higher inspiration than to assure me I was personally responsible for, washing his hands of me with a graceful complacency under my very nose. Dr. Torry was the only man who ever treated me like a rational being, who did not assume, because I was victim to many pains, that I was, of necessity, an arrested mental development too.

Nothwithstanding all the happiness and comfort here, I have been going downhill at a steady trot; so they sent for Sir Andrew Clark four days ago, and the blessed being has endowed me not only with cardiac complications, but says that a lump that I have had in one of my breasts for three months, which has given me a great deal of pain, is a tumor, that nothing can be done for me but to alleviate pain, that it is only a question of time, etc. This with a delicate embroidery of "the most distressing case of nervous hyperaesthesia"[5] added to a spinal neurosis that has taken me off my legs for seven years; with attacks of rheumatic gout in my stomach for the last twenty, ought to satisfy the most inflated pathologic vanity. It is decidedly indecent to catalog oneself in this way, but I put it down in a scientific spirit, to show that though I have no productive worth, I have a certain value as an indestructible quantity.

[This Long Slow Dying]

February 2nd [1892]

This long slow dying is no doubt instructive, but it is disappointingly free from excitements: "naturalness" being carried to its supreme expression. One sloughs off the activities one by one, and never knows that they're gone, until one suddenly finds that the months have slipped away and the sofa will never more be laid upon, the morning paper read, or the loss of the new book regretted; one revolves with equal content within the narrowing circle until the vanishing point is reached I suppose.

Vanity, however, maintains its undisputed sway, and I take satisfaction in feeling as much myself as ever, perhaps simply a more concentrated essence in

5. Abnormal sensitivity to pain.

this curtailment. If I could concern myself about the fate of my soul, it would give doubtless a savor of uncertainty to the fleeting moments, but I never felt so absolutely uninterested in the poor, shabby, old thing. The fact is, I have been dead so long and it has been simply such a grim shoving of the hours behind me as I faced a ceaseless possible horror, since that hideous summer of '78, when I went down to the deep sea, its dark waters closed over me and I knew neither hope nor peace;[6] that now it's only the shriveling of an empty pea pod that has to be completed.

A little while ago we had rather an amusing episode with the kind and usually understanding Tuckey,[7] who was led away into assuring me that I should live a good bit still—I was terribly shocked and when he saw the havoc that he wrought, he reassuringly said: "but you'll be comfortable, too," at which I exclaimed: "Oh I don't care about that, but boo-hoo, it's so *inconvenient!*" and the poor man burst into a roar of laughter. I was glad afterwards that it happened, as I was taken quite by surprise, and was able to test the sincerity of my mortuary inclinations. I have always *thought* that I wanted to die, but I felt quite uncertain as to what my muscular demonstrations might be at the moment of transition, for I occasionally have a quiver as of an expected dentistical wrench[8] when I fancy the actual moment. But my substance seemed equally outraged with my mind at Tuckey's dictum, so mayhap I shall be able to maintain a calm befitting so sublimated a spirit!—at any rate there is no humbuggy "strength of mind" about it, 'tis simply physical debility, 'twould be such a bore to be perturbed.

[Physical Pain]

March 4th [1892]

I am being ground slowly on the grim grindstone of physical pain, and on two nights I had almost asked for K.'s lethal dose, but one steps hesitantly along such unaccustomed ways and endures from second to second; and I feel sure that it can't be possible but what the bewildered little hammer[9] that keeps me going will very shortly see the decency of ending his distracted career; however this may be, physical pain however great ends in itself and falls away like dry husks from the mind, whilst moral discords and nervous horrors sear the soul. These last, Katharine has completely under the control of her rhythmic hand, so I go no longer in dread. Oh the wonderful moment when I felt myself floated for the first time into the deep sea of divine *cessation,* and saw all the dear old mysteries and miracles vanish into vapor! That first experience doesn't repeat itself, fortunately, for it might become a seduction.

Katharine can't help it, she's made that way, a simple embodiment of Health, as Baldwin[1] called her, "the New England Professor of doing things."

Final Entry by Katharine P. Loring

All through Saturday the 5th and even in the night, Alice was making sentences. One of the last things she said to me was to make a correction in the sentence of March 4th "moral discords and nervous horrors."

This dictation of March 4th was rushing about in her brain all day, and al-

6. She had suffered a serious nervous breakdown.
7. James's doctor.
8. I.e., like waiting for a tooth to be pulled.

9. I.e., her heart.
1. William Wilberforce Baldwin (1850–1910), American physician and friend of Henry James.

though she was very weak and it tired her much to dictate, she could not get her head quiet until she had had it written: then she was relieved and I finished Miss Woolson's story of "Dorothy"[2] to her.

1964

2. A story by the writer Constance Fenimore Woolson (1840–1894); see above, p. 979.

SARAH ORNE JEWETT
1849–1909

In one of several tributes to Sarah Orne Jewett, Willa Cather recounted how the more experienced writer "once laughingly told me that her head was full of dear old houses and dear old women, and that when an old house and an old woman came together in her brain with a click, she knew that a story was under way." Jewett, who later advised Cather to relinquish "the masquerade" of her male narrator and write from a female point of view, crafted an art subtle enough to catch the idiomatic language and conservative values of the old women who inhabited the old houses of her native Maine, houses that often situated them in the elegiac splendor of a fading but beautiful world. No wonder, then, that Cather rated *The Country of the Pointed Firs* (1896), along with *The Scarlet Letter* and *Huckleberry Finn*, as one of the three enduring masterpieces of American literature. For, as Cather remarked, these chapters in what amounts to a lyrical novel "are living things caught in the open, with light and freedom and air-spaces about them." Like Jewett's other publications, "they melt into the land and the life of the land until they are not stories at all, but life itself."

That Jewett herself referred to her fiction as "sketches" illustrates her conscious substitution of a meditative lyricism for the neatly sustained conflicts of traditionally plotted stories. Such a focus also reflects the serenity of a life lived for the most part with a profound sense of rootedness, specifically in the southern portion of Maine. The second of the three daughters of Theodore Herman Jewett and Caroline Frances (Perry) Jewett, Theodora Sarah Orne Jewett quickly dropped her first name, which had been bestowed on her as a tribute to her father and her father's father. But she was born, was reared, and died in the pre-Revolutionary house in South Berwick that her grandfather, a prosperous shipbuilder, had bought. Both of her parents came from distinguished, well-educated families: her father, a physician, was descended from the first Bay Colony settlers, and her mother's father was a renowned surgeon. Because she was subject to ill health as a child, Jewett's father thought she would benefit from fresh air and so he took her on his rounds. Through her observation of his country patients, she acquired a deep respect for the everyday lives of common people and an equally sensitive appreciation of the region's landscape.

In her novel *The Country Doctor* (1884), she would present the struggles of a female character seeking to adopt the role of a father, who is clearly her most important mentor. Jewett's informal education with her own father was supplemented by Miss Olive Rayne's school in South Berwick and the Berwick Academy, from which she graduated in 1865. Three years later, under the pseudonym Alice or A. C. Eliot, she began publishing her first stories in the *Riverside Magazine for Young People* and the *Atlantic Monthly*. Her father's encouraging admonition— "Don't try to write *about* things: write the things themselves just as they are"— clearly shaped her aesthetic goals. By 1877 Jewett had accepted William Dean Howells's advice to collect her sketches about "things themselves," which had appeared in his *Atlantic*, in the volume she titled *Deephaven* (1877).

The letters and diaries of Jewett from this period in her life document her close relationships with a number of female friends. After her father's death in 1878, moreover, her acquaintance with Annie Adams Fields ripened into a thirty-year liaison, which the critic Josephine Donovan has placed in the context of other so-called Boston marriages: that is, female couples living together in a union comparable to marriage. Annie Fields was the wife of James T. Fields, a prominent Boston publisher who would also become the editor of the *Atlantic*. Fields was a hostess, an author, and a social welfare worker. The earliest letters between Fields and Jewett, which were omitted from Fields's 1911 edition of Jewett's letters, are dated 1877, when Fields was forty-three and Jewett was twenty-eight. The correspondence quickly became affectionately intimate, and after the death of James Fields in 1881, the two women lived together, spending part of each year on Charles Street in Boston, part in Maine, and part traveling in western Europe.

Sustained by Fields's support and the models provided by her own wide reading in nineteenth-century fiction, Jewett produced such collections as *A White Heron, and Other Stories* (1886) and *The King of Folly Island* (1888). During her lifetime, she received public acknowledgment of her contribution to American letters from established writers including John Greenleaf Whittier and James Russell Lowell and from Bowdoin College, her father's alma mater, which made her a doctor of letters in 1901. For the last seven years of her life, she suffered the consequences of a spinal concussion caused by an accident in her carriage. By the time she died in her sixtieth year, however, she had succeeded in portraying the visionary resiliency with which women responded to the economic impoverishment and the physical splendor of rural New England. Her poignant *A White Heron*, for instance, moves beyond a pastoral appreciation of nature to explore the forces that threaten the survival of the wilderness and to probe the psychology of the tale's sylvan heroine, aptly named Sylvia.

A White Heron

I

The woods were already filled with shadows one June evening, just before eight o'clock, though a bright sunset still glimmered faintly among the trunks of the trees. A little girl was driving home her cow, a plodding, dilatory, provoking creature in her behavior, but a valued companion for all that. They were going away from whatever light there was, and striking deep into the woods, but their feet were familiar with the path, and it was no matter whether their eyes could see it or not.

There was hardly a night the summer through when the old cow could be found waiting at the pasture bars; on the contrary, it was her greatest pleasure to hide herself away among the huckleberry bushes, and though she wore a loud bell she had made the discovery that if one stood perfectly still it would not ring. So Sylvia had to hunt for her until she found her, and call Co'! Co'! with never an answering Moo, until her childish patience was quite spent. If the creature had not given good milk and plenty of it, the case would have seemed very different to her owners. Besides, Sylvia had all the time there was, and very little use to make of it. Sometimes in pleasant weather it was a consolation to look upon the cow's pranks as an intelligent attempt to play hide and seek, and as the child had no playmates she lent herself to this amusement with a good deal of zest. Though this chase had been so long that the wary animal herself had given an unusual signal of her whereabouts, Sylvia

had only laughed when she came upon Mistress Moolly at the swampside, and urged her affectionately homeward with a twig of birch leaves. The old cow was not inclined to wander farther, she even turned in the right direction for once as they left the pasture, and stepped along the road at a good pace. She was quite ready to be milked now, and seldom stopped to browse. Sylvia wondered what her grandmother would say because they were so late. It was a great while since she had left home at half-past five o'clock, but everybody knew the difficulty of making this errand a short one. Mrs. Tilley had chased the hornéd torment too many summer evenings herself to blame any one else for lingering, and was only thankful as she waited that she had Sylvia, nowadays, to give such valuable assistance. The good woman suspected that Sylvia loitered occasionally on her own account; there was never such a child for straying about out-of-doors since the world was made! Everybody said that it was a good change for a little maid who had tried to grow for eight years in a crowded manufacturing town, but, as for Sylvia herself, it seemed as if she never had been alive at all before she came to live at the farm. She thought often with wistful compassion of a wretched geranium that belonged to a town neighbor.

"'Afraid of folks,'" old Mrs. Tilley said to herself, with a smile, after she had made the unlikely choice of Sylvia from her daughter's houseful of children, and was returning to the farm. "'Afraid of folks,' they said! I guess she won't be troubled no great[1] with 'em up to the old place!" When they reached the door of the lonely house and stopped to unlock it, and the cat came to purr loudly, and rub against them, a deserted pussy, indeed, but fat with young robins, Sylvia whispered that this was a beautiful place to live in, and she never should wish to go home.

The companions followed the shady wood-road, the cow taking slow steps and the child very fast ones. The cow stopped long at the brook to drink, as if the pasture were not half a swamp, and Sylvia stood still and waited, letting her bare feet cool themselves in the shoal water, while the great twilight moths struck softly against her. She waded on through the brook as the cow moved away, and listened to the thrushes with a heart that beat fast with pleasure. There was a stirring in the great boughs overhead. They were full of little birds and beasts that seemed to be wide awake, and going about their world, or else saying good-night to each other in sleepy twitters. Sylvia herself felt sleepy as she walked along. However, it was not much farther to the house, and the air was soft and sweet. She was not often in the woods so late as this, and it made her feel as if she were a part of the gray shadows and the moving leaves. She was just thinking how long it seemed since she first came to the farm a year ago, and wondering if everything went on in the noisy town just the same as when she was there, the thought of the great red-faced boy who used to chase and frighten her made her hurry along the path to escape from the shadow of the trees.

Suddenly this little woods-girl is horror-stricken to hear a clear whistle not very far away. Not a bird's-whistle, which would have a sort of friendliness, but a boy's whistle, determined, and somewhat aggressive. Sylvia left the cow to whatever sad fate might await her, and stepped discreetly aside into the

1. I.e., she won't be greatly troubled.

bushes, but she was just too late. The enemy had discovered her, and called out in a very cheerful and persuasive tone, "Halloa, little girl, how far is it to the road?" and trembling Sylvia answered almost inaudibly, "A good ways."

She did not dare to look boldly at the tall young man, who carried a gun over his shoulder, but she came out of her bush and again followed the cow, while he walked alongside.

"I have been hunting for some birds," the stranger said kindly, "and I have lost my way, and need a friend very much. Don't be afraid," he added gallantly. "Speak up and tell me what your name is, and whether you think I can spend the night at your house, and go out gunning early in the morning."

Sylvia was more alarmed than before. Would not her grandmother consider her much to blame? But who could have foreseen such an accident as this? It did not seem to be her fault, and she hung her head as if the stem of it were broken, but managed to answer "Sylvy," with much effort when her companion again asked her name.

Mrs. Tilley was standing in the doorway when the trio came into view. The cow gave a loud moo by way of explanation.

"Yes, you'd better speak up for yourself, you old trial! Where'd she tucked herself away this time, Sylvy?" But Sylvia kept an awed silence; she knew by instinct that her grandmother did not comprehend the gravity of the situation. She must be mistaking the stranger for one of the farmer-lads of the region.

The young man stood his gun beside the door, and dropped a lumpy game-bag beside it; then he bade Mrs. Tilley good-evening, and repeated his wayfarer's story, and asked if he could have a night's lodging.

"Put me anywhere you like," he said. "I must be off early in the morning before day; but I am very hungry indeed. You can give me some milk at any rate, that's plain."

"Dear sakes, yes," responded the hostess, whose long slumbering hospitality seemed to be easily awakened. "You might fare better if you went out to the main road a mile or so, but you're welcome to what we've got. I'll milk right off, and you make yourself at home. You can sleep on husks or feathers," she proffered graciously. "I raised them all myself. There's good pasturing for geese just below here towards the ma'sh. Now step round and set a plate for the gentleman, Sylvy!" And Sylvia promptly stepped. She was glad to have something to do, and she was hungry herself.

It was a surprise to find so clean and comfortable a little dwelling in this New England wilderness. The young man had known the horrors of its most primitive housekeeping, and the dreary squalor of that level of society which does not rebel at the companionship of hens. This was the best thrift of an old-fashioned farmstead, though on such a small scale that it seemed like a hermitage.[2] He listened eagerly to the old woman's quaint talk, he watched Sylvia's pale face and shining gray eyes with ever growing enthusiasm, and insisted that this was the best supper he had eaten for a month, and afterward the new-made friends sat down in the door-way together while the moon came up.

Soon it would be berry-time, and Sylvia was a great help at picking. The cow was a good milker, though a plaguy thing to keep track of, the hostess gossiped frankly, adding presently that she had buried four children, so Sylvia's mother,

2. Habitation of a hermit.

and a son (who might be dead) in California were all the children she had left. "Dan, my boy, was a great hand to go gunning," she explained sadly. "I never wanted for pa'tridges or gray squer'ls while he was to home He's been a great wand'rer, I expect, and he's no hand to write letters. There, I don't blame him, I'd ha' seen the world myself if it had been so I could."

"Sylvy takes after him," the grandmother continued affectionately, after a minute's pause. "There ain't a foot o' ground she don't know her way over, and the wild creatures counts her one o' themselves. Squer'ls she'll tame to come an' feed right out o' her hands, and all sorts o' birds. Last winter she got the jay-birds to bangeing[3] here, and I believe she'd 'a' scanted herself of her own meals to have plenty to throw out amongst 'em, if I hadn't kep' watch. Anything but crows, I tell her, I'm willing to help support—though Dan he had a tamed one o' them that did seem to have reason same as folks. It was round here a good spell after he went away. Dan an' his father they didn't hitch,—but he never held up his head ag'in after Dan had dared[4] him an' gone off."

The guest did not notice this hint of family sorrows in his eager interest in something else.

"So Sylvy knows all about birds, does she?" he exclaimed, as he looked round at the little girl who sat, very demure but increasingly sleepy, in the moonlight. "I am making a collection of birds myself. I have been at it ever since I was a boy." (Mrs. Tilley smiled.) "There are two or three very rare ones I have been hunting for these five years. I mean to get them on my own ground if they can be found."

"Do you cage 'em up?" asked Mrs. Tilley doubtfully, in response to this enthusiastic announcement.

"Oh no, they're stuffed and preserved, dozens and dozens of them," said the ornithologist, "and I have shot or snared every one myself. I caught a glimpse of a white heron a few miles from here on Saturday, and I have followed it in this direction. They have never been found in this district at all. The little white heron, it is," and he turned again to look at Sylvia with the hope of discovering that the rare bird was one of her acquaintances.

But Sylvia was watching a hop-toad in the narrow footpath.

"You would know the heron if you saw it," the stranger continued eagerly. "A queer tall white bird with soft feathers and long thin legs. And it would have a nest perhaps in the top of a high tree, made of sticks, something like a hawk's nest."

Sylvia's heart gave a wild beat; she knew that strange white bird, and had once stolen softly near where it stood in some bright green swamp grass, away over at the other side of the woods. There was an open place where the sunshine always seemed strangely yellow and hot, where tall, nodding rushes grew, and her grandmother had warned her that she might sink in the soft black mud underneath and never be heard of more. Not far beyond were the salt marshes just this side the sea itself, which Sylvia wondered and dreamed much about, but never had seen, whose great voice could sometimes be heard above the noise of the woods on stormy nights.

"I can't think of anything I should like so much as to find that heron's nest," the handsome stranger was saying. "I would give ten dollars to anybody who

3. Idling about, visiting 4. Challenged, defied. "Hitch": get along well

could show it to me," he added desperately, "and I mean to spend my whole vacation hunting for it if need be. Perhaps it was only migrating, or had been chased out of its own region by some bird of prey."

Mrs. Tilley gave amazed attention to all this, but Sylvia still watched the toad, not divining, as she might have done at some calmer time, that the creature wished to get to its hole under the door-step, and was much hindered by the unusual spectators at that hour of the evening. No amount of thought, that night, could decide how many wished-for treasures the ten dollars, so lightly spoken of, would buy.

The next day the young sportsman hovered about the woods, and Sylvia kept him company, having lost her first fear of the friendly lad, who proved to be most kind and sympathetic. He told her many things about the birds and what they knew and where they lived and what they did with themselves. And he gave her a jack-knife, which she thought as great a treasure as if she were a desert-islander. All day long he did not once make her troubled or afraid except when he brought down some unsuspecting singing creature from its bough. Sylvia would have liked him vastly better without his gun; she could not understand why he killed the very birds he seemed to like so much. But as the day waned, Sylvia still watched the young man with loving admiration. She had never seen anybody so charming and delightful; the woman's heart, asleep in the child, was vaguely thrilled by a dream of love. Some premonition of that great power stirred and swayed these young creatures who traversed the solemn woodlands with soft-footed silent care. They stopped to listen to a bird's song; they pressed forward again eagerly, parting the branches—speaking to each other rarely and in whispers; the young man going first and Sylvia following, fascinated, a few steps behind, with her gray eyes dark with excitement.

She grieved because the longed-for white heron was elusive, but she did not lead the guest, she only followed, and there was no such thing as speaking first. The sound of her own unquestioned voice would have terrified her—it was hard enough to answer yes or no when there was need of that. At last evening began to fall, and they drove the cow home together, and Sylvia smiled with pleasure when they came to the place where she heard the whistle and was afraid only the night before.

II

Half a mile from home, at the farther edge of the woods, where the land was highest, a great pine-tree stood, the last of its generation. Whether it was left for a boundary mark, or for what reason, no one could say; the woodchoppers who had felled its mates were dead and gone long ago, and a whole new forest of sturdy trees, pines and oaks and maples, had grown again. But the stately head of this old pine towered above them all and made a landmark for sea and shore miles and miles away. Sylvia knew it well. She had always believed that whoever climbed to the top of it could see the ocean; and the little girl had often laid her hand on the great rough trunk and looked up wistfully at those dark boughs that the wind always stirred, no matter how hot and still the air might be below. Now she thought of the tree with a new excitement, for why, if one climbed it at break of day could not one see all the world, and easily discover from whence the white heron flew, and mark the place, and find the hidden nest?

What a spirit of adventure, what wild ambition! What fancied triumph and delight and glory for the later morning when she could make known the secret! It was almost too real and too great for the childish heart to bear.

All night the door of the little house stood open and the whippoorwills came and sang upon the very step. The young sportsman and his old hostess were sound asleep, but Sylvia's great design kept her broad awake and watching. She forgot to think of sleep. The short summer night seemed as long as the winter darkness, and at last when the whippoorwills ceased, and she was afraid the morning would after all come too soon, she stole out of the house and followed the pasture path through the woods, hastening toward the open ground beyond, listening with a sense of comfort and companionship to the drowsy twitter of a half-awakened bird, whose perch she had jarred in passing. Alas, if the great wave of human interest which flooded for the first time this dull little life should sweep away the satisfactions of an existence heart to heart with nature and the dumb life of the forest!

There was the huge tree asleep yet in the paling moonlight, and small and silly Sylvia began with utmost bravery to mount to the top of it, with tingling, eager blood coursing the channels of her whole frame, with her bare feet and fingers, that pinched and held like bird's claws to the monstrous ladder reaching up, up, almost to the sky itself. First she must mount the white oak tree that grew alongside, where she was almost lost among the dark branches and the green leaves heavy and wet with dew; a bird fluttered off its nest, and a red squirrel ran to and fro and scolded pettishly at the harmless housebreaker. Sylvia felt her way easily. She had often climbed there, and knew that higher still one of the oak's upper branches chafed against the pine trunk, just where its lower boughs were set close together. There, when she made the dangerous pass from one tree to the other, the great enterprise would really begin.

She crept out along the swaying oak limb at last, and took the daring step across into the old pine-tree. The way was harder than she thought; she must reach far and hold fast, the sharp dry twigs caught and held her and scratched her like angry talons, the pitch made her thin little fingers clumsy and stiff as she went round and round the tree's great stem, higher and higher upward. The sparrows and robins in the woods below were beginning to wake and twitter to the dawn, yet it seemed much lighter there aloft in the pine-tree, and the child knew she must hurry if her project were to be of any use.

The tree seemed to lengthen itself out as she went up, and to reach farther and farther upward. It was like a great main-mast to the voyaging earth; it must truly have been amazed that morning through all its ponderous frame as it felt this determined spark of human spirit wending its way from higher branch to branch. Who knows how steadily the least twigs held themselves to advantage this light, weak creature on her way! The old pine must have loved his new dependent. More than all the hawks, and bats, and moths, and even the sweet voiced thrushes, was the brave, beating heart of the solitary gray-eyed child. And the tree stood still and frowned away the winds that June morning while the dawn grew bright in the east.

Sylvia's face was like a pale star, if one had seen it from the ground, when the last thorny bough was past, and she stood trembling and tired but wholly triumphant, high in the tree-top. Yes, there was the sea with the dawning sun making a golden dazzle over it, and toward that glorious east flew two hawks with slow-moving pinions. How low they looked in the air from that height when one had only seen them before far up, and dark against the blue sky.

Their gray feathers were as soft as moths; they seemed only a little way from the tree, and Sylvia felt as if she too could go flying away among the clouds. Westward, the woodlands and farms reached miles and miles into the distance; here and there were church steeples, and white villages, truly it was a vast and awesome world!

The birds sang louder and louder. At last the sun came up bewilderingly bright. Sylvia could see the white sails of ships out at sea, and the clouds that were purple and rose-colored and yellow at first began to fade away. Where was the white heron's nest in the sea of green branches, and was this wonderful sight and pageant of the world the only reward for having climbed to such a giddy height? Now look down again, Sylvia, where the green marsh is set among the shining birches and the dark hemlocks; there where you saw the white heron once you will see him again; look, look! a white spot of him like a single floating feather comes up from the dead hemlock and grows larger, and rises, and comes close at last, and goes by the landmark pine with steady sweep of wing and outstretched slender neck and crested head. And wait! wait! do not move a foot or a finger, little girl, do not send an arrow of light and consciousness from your two eager eyes, for the heron has perched on a pine bough not far beyond yours, and cries back to his mate on the nest and plumes his feathers for the new day!

The child gives a long sigh a minute later when a company of shouting catbirds comes also to the tree, and vexed by their fluttering and lawlessness the solemn heron goes away. She knows his secret now, the wild, light, slender bird that floats and wavers, and goes back like an arrow presently to his home in the green world beneath. Then Sylvia, well satisfied, makes her perilous way down again, not daring to look far below the branch she stands on, ready to cry sometimes because her fingers ache and her lamed feet slip. Wondering over and over again what the stranger would say to her, and what he would think when she told him how to find his way straight to the heron's nest.

"Sylvy, Sylvy!" called the busy old grandmother again and again, but nobody answered, and the small husk bed was empty and Sylvia had disappeared.

The guest waked from a dream, and remembering his day's pleasure hurried to dress himself that might it sooner begin. He was sure from the way the shy little girl looked once or twice yesterday that she had at least seen the white heron, and now she must really be made to tell. Here she comes now, paler than ever, and her worn old frock is torn and tattered, and smeared with pine pitch. The grandmother and the sportsman stand in the door together and question her, and the splendid moment has come to speak of the dead hemlock-tree by the green marsh.

But Sylvia does not speak after all, though the old grandmother fretfully rebukes her, and the young man's kind, appealing eyes are looking straight into her own. He can make them rich with money; he has promised it, and they are poor now. He is so well worth making happy, and he waits to hear the story she can tell.

No, she must keep silence! What is it that suddenly forbids her and makes her dumb? Has she been nine years growing and now, when the great world for the first time puts out a hand to her, must she thrust it aside for a bird's sake? The murmur of the pine's green branches is in her ears, she remembers how the white heron came flying through the golden air and how they watched the

sea and the morning together, and Sylvia cannot speak; she cannot tell the heron's secret and give its life away.

Dear loyalty, that suffered a sharp pang as the guest went away disappointed later in the day, that could have served and followed him and loved him as a dog loves! Many a night Sylvia heard the echo of his whistle haunting the pasture path as she came home with the loitering cow. She forgot even her sorrow at the sharp report of his gun and the sight of thrushes and sparrows dropping silent to the ground, their songs hushed and their pretty feathers stained and wet with blood. Were the birds better friends than their hunter might have been,—who can tell? Whatever treasures were lost to her, woodlands and summer-time, remember! Bring your gifts and graces and tell your secrets to this lonely country child!

 1886

KATE CHOPIN
1850–1904

When *The Awakening*, Kate Chopin's frank exploration of a late-nineteenth-century woman's growth toward sexual and emotional independence, appeared in 1899, critics assailed it. The novel "leaves one sick of human nature," declared one writer; "it is not a healthy book," complained another; "the purport of the story can hardly be described in language fit for publication," stormed a third. Within months, the libraries of Chopin's native city, St. Louis, had refused to carry the book, and the author herself was rebuffed by a number of acquaintances, though she had attempted to defend herself by playfully explaining in a newspaper article that "I never dreamed of Mrs. Pontellier [the novel's heroine] making such a mess of things and working out her own damnation as she did." In fact, though *The Awakening* has by now been recognized as an American classic, Chopin was never to reap the rewards of her achievement. In the years between 1899, when the work was published, and 1904, when she died, she earned hardly any royalties from the novel; her third collection of short stories was rejected by the firm that had published *The Awakening*; and—no doubt disheartened by these failures—she was able to compose only a few tales and poems. For more than three decades after Chopin's death, moreover, her allegedly scandalous masterpiece fell into oblivion; indeed, although one critic attempted to revive the book in the 1930s, *The Awakening* was not really to be recovered for readers until the 1960s.

The well-bred daughter of a wealthy St. Louis family, Katherine O'Flaherty would not, at least on the surface, have seemed likely to produce so controversial a work. On her mother's side, she was descended from French Creole aristocrats, while her father was an Irish immigrant who had become a singularly successful merchant before his death in an 1855 railway accident. Coming from such a background, Chopin herself received, at home, a typically Victorian training in decorum as well as, at school, a strict Catholic education. In 1868, when she made her debut in society, she was said to be "one of the acknowledged belles of St. Louis," and after she married Oscar Chopin, a Creole cotton trader, in 1870, she was evidently a happy and dutiful wife whom one observer later described as the notably "conscientious mother" of six children. The young couple had first settled in New Orleans, and then, with their family, they had moved to a plantation near Cloutierville, in Natchitoches (pronounced *Nack-uh-tush*) parish, an area Chopin

was eventually to memorialize in a series of brilliant stories and sketches. When her husband died of swamp fever in 1883, Chopin was said to be "inconsolable."

Painful as it was, however, Oscar's untimely death precipitated his widow into serious literary activity. She had apparently always "scribbled"—a diary as well as some sketches and poems from her youth are still held by the St. Louis Historical Society—but when she returned to her birthplace with her children, she began to write in earnest. Though they were at first received as "delightful sketches," even her earliest stories were more radical than many readers understood, suggesting that the "acknowledged belle" and the dutiful wife had always harbored a streak of rebelliousness, which was to find its fullest expression in *The Awakening*.

Chopin's family doctor, Frederick Kolbenheyer, had become one of her closest friends in these years, and according to her biographer Per Seyersted, he was a "determined agnostic" who persuaded her to read the works of such pioneering Victorian thinkers as the scientists Charles Darwin and Thomas Henry Huxley and to renounce most of the main tenets of Catholicism. In addition, she had begun to read extensively in contemporary fiction, studying, on the one hand, the works of American women regionalists like Sarah Orne Jewett and Mary E. Wilkins Freeman, and, on the other hand, the works of French naturalists like Zola, Flaubert, and Maupassant. Maupassant, in particular, had become one of her literary idols, an artist whom she defined as "a man who had escaped from tradition and authority, who had entered into himself and looked out upon life through his own being and with his own eyes." In all her short fictions, Chopin, too, was enacting just such escapes from tradition and authority. A number of tales, for instance, examined the inequities of traditional marriage; some explored the arbitrary race distinctions that characterized southern culture; others questioned the class divisions that marked even so seemingly simple a world as that of Natchitoches parish; finally, one or two actually imagined alternative ways in which society might be structured to allow individuals, especially women, more opportunities for emotional, sexual, and intellectual freedom.

But it is in *The Awakening* that Chopin most openly and vividly dramatized her own—as well as her heroine's—desire for freedom. Setting her novel in the Louisiana resort town of Grand Isle, where she herself had spent many summers as a young married woman, and in the kind of bourgeois New Orleans neighborhood where she had also lived during her marriage, she used a distinctively turn-of-the-century myth of female sexual independence to show how her protagonist, Edna Pontellier, was defined, and ultimately destroyed, by a society that could not conceive of allowing a woman—especially a wife and mother—the kind of autonomy for which she longed. Specifically, Chopin employed not only realistic strategies, learned from such cherished precursors as Jewett and Maupassant, but also images of desire and of the body's holiness, drawn from significant literary ancestors like the English poet Algernon Charles Swinburne and the American poet Walt Whitman, to explore ideas about the relationship between female sexuality and female creativity that were, in her era, almost entirely forbidden—at least to women writers.

For Edna Pontellier, who explains to her lover, "I give myself where I please," a supposedly "proper" lady has as much right to experience desire as her gentlemanly counterpart might; similarly, for Edna a lady has as much right to feel ambition as might any male peer. Nevertheless, the structure of Chopin's novel is profoundly pessimistic about such desires and ambitions: if Aphrodite, the Greek goddess of love (to whom Edna is at one point in the book compared), were reborn as a late-Victorian woman, Chopin suggests, Edna's fate might be *her* fate. For though a number of critics from the earliest reviewers to the most recent scholars have felt, with the American novelist Willa Cather, that Edna Pontellier was no more than, in Cather's words, "a Creole Bovary"—a New World version of Gustave Flaubert's foolishly sentimental Madame Bovary—*The Awakening* seems

to elaborate a shadowy story about female erotic freedom and even about feminist emotional independence.

Whether or not Chopin's death in her early fifties was related to the failure of her book, it represented a serious loss to American literature, for when she wrote *The Awakening* she was clearly at the height of her extraordinary power. Yet, despite the pain that evidently put an end to her literary career, Chopin's passionate fantasy about her heroine's fantasizings has haunted a number of readers, at least since 1969, when the scholar Per Seyersted produced a definitive two-volume edition of her works, which reintroduced the novel to a wide audience of teachers, critics, and historians. Even Edna's final swim into the sea can be seen, after all, in terms of a metaphor Florence Nightingale had used in her visionary *Cassandra*, almost half a century before Chopin had begun to imagine this surprisingly liberated woman's ambiguously significant awakening: "rather, ten times, die in the surf, heralding the way to [a] new world, than stand idly on the shore."

The Awakening[1]

I

A green and yellow parrot, which hung in a cage outside the door, kept repeating over and over:

"*Allez vous-en! Allez vous-en! Sapristi!*[2] That's all right!"

He could speak a little Spanish, and also a language which nobody understood, unless it was the mocking-bird that hung on the other side of the door, whistling his fluty notes out upon the breeze with maddening persistence.

Mr. Pontellier, unable to read his newspaper with any degree of comfort, arose with an expression and an exclamation of disgust. He walked down the gallery and across the narrow "bridges" which connected the Lebrun cottages one with the other. He had been seated before the door of the main house. The parrot and the mocking-bird were the property of Madame Lebrun, and they had the right to make all the noise they wished. Mr. Pontellier had the privilege of quitting their society when they ceased to be entertaining.

He stopped before the door of his own cottage, which was the fourth one from the main building and next to the last. Seating himself in a wicker rocker which was there, he once more applied himself to the task of reading the newspaper. The day was Sunday; the paper was a day old. The Sunday papers had not yet reached Grand Isle.[3] He was already acquainted with the market reports, and he glanced restlessly over the editorials and bits of news which he had not had time to read before quitting New Orleans the day before.

Mr. Pontellier wore eye-glasses. He was a man of forty, of medium height and slender build; he stooped a little. His hair was brown and straight, parted on one side. His beard was neatly and closely trimmed.

Once in a while he withdrew his glance from the newspaper and looked about him. There was more noise than ever over at the house. The main building was called "the house," to distinguish it from the cottages. The chattering and whistling birds were still at it. Two young girls, the Farival twins, were playing a duet from "Zampa"[4] upon the piano. Madame Lebrun was bustling

1. Notes to *The Awakening* owe much to the Norton Critical Edition prepared by Margo Culley and to the text prepared by Ronald Gottesman in *The Norton Anthology of American Literature.*

2. Go away! Go away! For God's sake!
3. Resort island, between the Gulf of Mexico and Caminada Bay, south of New Orleans.
4. Romantic opera by Louis Hérold (1791–1833).

in and out, giving orders in a high key to a yard-boy whenever she got inside the house, and directions in an equally high voice to a dining-room servant whenever she got outside. She was a fresh, pretty woman, clad always in white with elbow sleeves. Her starched skirts crinkled as she came and went. Farther down, before one of the cottages, a lady in black was walking demurely up and down, telling her beads. A good many persons of the *pension* had gone over to the *Chênière Caminada* in Beaudelet's lugger[5] to hear mass. Some young people were out under the water-oaks playing croquet. Mr. Pontellier's two children were there—sturdy little fellows of four and five. A quadroon[6] nurse followed them about with a far-away, meditative air.

Mr. Pontellier finally lit a cigar and began to smoke, letting the paper drag idly from his hand. He fixed his gaze upon a white sunshade[7] that was advancing at snail's pace from the beach. He could see it plainly between the gaunt trunks of the water-oaks and across the stretch of yellow camomile. The gulf looked far away melting hazily into the blue of the horizon. The sunshade continued to approach slowly. Beneath its pink-lined shelter were his wife, Mrs. Pontellier, and young Robert Lebrun. When they reached the cottage, the two seated themselves with some appearance of fatigue upon the step of the porch, facing each other, each leaning against a supporting post.

"What folly! to bathe[8] at such an hour in such heat!" exclaimed Mr. Pontellier. He himself had taken a plunge at daylight. That was why the morning seemed long to him.

"You are burnt beyond recognition," he added, looking at his wife as one looks at a valuable piece of personal property which has suffered some damage. She held up her hands, strong, shapely hands, and surveyed them critically, drawing up her lawn[9] sleeves above the wrists. Looking at them reminded her of her rings, which she had given to her husband before leaving for the beach. She silently reached out to him, and he, understanding, took the rings from his vest pocket and dropped them into her open palm. She slipped them upon her fingers; then clasping her knees, she looked across at Robert and began to laugh. The rings sparkled upon her fingers. He sent back an answering smile.

"What is it?" asked Pontellier, looking lazily and amused from one to the other. It was some utter nonsense; some adventure out there in the water, and they both tried to relate it at once. It did not seem half so amusing when told. They realized this, and so did Mr. Pontellier. He yawned and stretched himself. Then he got up, saying he had half a mind to go over to Klein's hotel and play a game of billiards.

"Come go along, Lebrun," he proposed to Robert. But Robert admitted quite frankly that he preferred to stay where he was and talk to Mrs. Pontellier.

"Well, send him about his business when he bores you, Edna," instructed her husband as he prepared to leave.

"Here, take the umbrella," she exclaimed, holding it out to him. He accepted the sunshade, and lifting it over his head descended the steps and walked away.

"Coming back to dinner?" his wife called after him. He halted a moment

5. Passenger boat. *"Pension"*: a bed-and-board hotel. 7. Parasol.
Chênière Caminada is an island between Grande Isle 8. Swim.
and the Louisiana coast. 9. Fine, sheer muslin.
6. I.e., with one-quarter ("quad") black ancestry.

and shrugged his shoulders. He felt in his vest pocket; there was a ten-dollar bill there. He did not know; perhaps he would return for the early dinner and perhaps he would not. It all depended upon the company which he found over at Klein's and the size of "the game." He did not say this, but she understood it, and laughed, nodding good-by to him.

Both children wanted to follow their father when they saw him starting out. He kissed them and promised to bring them back bonbons and peanuts.

II

Mrs. Pontellier's eyes were quick and bright; they were a yellowish brown, about the color of her hair. She had a way of turning them swiftly upon an object and holding them there as if lost in some inward maze of contemplation or thought.

Her eyebrows were a shade darker than her hair. They were thick and almost horizontal, emphasizing the depth of her eyes. She was rather handsome than beautiful. Her face was captivating by reason of a certain frankness of expression and a contradictory subtle play of features. Her manner was engaging.

Robert rolled a cigarette. He smoked cigarettes because he could not afford cigars, he said. He had a cigar in his pocket which Mr. Pontellier had presented him with, and he was saving it for his after-dinner smoke.

This seemed quite proper and natural on his part. In coloring he was not unlike his companion. A clean-shaven face made the resemblance more pronounced than it would otherwise have been. There rested no shadow of care upon his open countenance. His eyes gathered in and reflected the light and languor of the summer day.

Mrs. Pontellier reached over for a palmleaf fan that lay on the porch and began to fan herself, while Robert sent between his lips light puffs from his cigarette. They chatted incessantly: about the things around them; their amusing adventure out in the water—it had again assumed its entertaining aspect; about the wind, the trees, the people who had gone to the Chênière; about the children playing croquet under the oaks, and the Farival twins, who were now performing the overture to "The Poet and Peasant."[1]

Robert talked a good deal about himself. He was very young, and did not know any better. Mrs. Pontellier talked a little about herself for the same reason. Each was interested in what the other said. Robert spoke of his intention to go to Mexico in the autumn, where fortune awaited him. He was always intending to go to Mexico, but some way never got there. Meanwhile he held on to his modest position in a mercantile house in New Orleans, where an equal familiarity with English, French and Spanish gave him no small value as a clerk and correspondent.

He was spending his summer vacation, as he always did, with his mother at Grand Isle. In former times before Robert could remember, "the house" had been a summer luxury of the Lebruns. Now flanked by its dozen or more cottages, which were always filled with exclusive visitors from the "Quartier Français,"[2] it enabled Madame Lebrun to maintain the easy and comfortable existence which appeared to be her birthright.

Mrs. Pontellier talked about her father's Mississippi plantation and her girl-

1. Operetta by Franz von Suppé (1819–1895).
2. The French Quarter of New Orleans, first settled by the French in the early 18-h century and occupied at this time by wealthy, older families.

hood home in the old Kentucky blue-grass country. She was an American woman, with a small infusion of French which seemed to have been lost in dilution. She read a letter from her sister, who was away in the East, and who had engaged herself to be married. Robert was interested, and wanted to know what manner of girls the sisters were, what the father was like, and how long the mother had been dead.

When Mrs. Pontellier folded the letter it was time for her to dress for the early dinner.

"I see Léonce isn't coming back," she said, with a glance in the direction whence her husband had disappeared. Robert supposed he was not, as there were a good many New Orleans club men over at Klein's.

When Mrs. Pontellier left him to enter her room, the young man descended the steps and strolled over toward the croquet players, where, during the half-hour before dinner, he amused himself with the little Pontellier children, who were very fond of him.

III

It was eleven o'clock that night when Mr. Pontellier returned from Klein's hotel. He was in an excellent humor, in high spirits, and very talkative. His entrance awoke his wife, who was in bed and fast asleep when he came in. He talked to her while he undressed, telling her anecdotes and bits of news and gossip that he had gathered during the day. From his trousers pockets he took a fistful of crumpled bank notes and a good deal of silver coin, which he piled on the bureau indiscriminately with keys, knife, handkerchief, and whatever else happened to be in his pockets. She was overcome with sleep, and answered him with little half utterances.

He thought it very discouraging that his wife, who was the sole object of his existence, evinced so little interest in things which concerned him and valued so little his conversation.

Mr. Pontellier had forgotten the bonbons and peanuts for the boys. Notwithstanding he loved them very much, and went into the adjoining room where they slept to take a look at them and make sure that they were resting comfortably. The result of his investigation was far from satisfactory. He turned and shifted the youngsters about in bed. One of them began to kick and talk about a basket full of crabs.

Mr. Pontellier returned to his wife with the information that Raoul had a high fever and needed looking after. Then he lit a cigar and went and sat near the open door to smoke it.

Mrs. Pontellier was quite sure Raoul had no fever. He had gone to bed perfectly well, she said, and nothing had ailed him all day. Mr. Pontellier was too well acquainted with fever symptoms to be mistaken. He assured her the child was consuming[3] at that moment in the next room.

He reproached his wife with her inattention, her habitual neglect of the children. If it was not a mother's place to look after children, whose on earth was it? He himself had his hands full with his brokerage business. He could not be in two places at once; making a living for his family on the street, and staying at home to see that no harm befell them. He talked in a monotonous, insistent way.

3. I.e., "consumptive," feverish.

Mrs. Pontellier sprang out of bed and went into the next room. She soon came back and sat on the edge of the bed, leaning her head down on the pillow. She said nothing and refused to answer her husband when he questioned her. When his cigar was smoked out he went to bed, and in half a minute he was fast asleep.

Mrs. Pontellier was by that time thoroughly awake. She began to cry a little, and wiped her eyes on the sleeve of her *peignoir*. Blowing out the candle, which her husband had left burning, she slipped her bare feet into a pair of satin *mules* at the foot of the bed and went out on the porch, where she sat down in the wicker chair and began to rock gently to and fro.

It was then past midnight. The cottages were all dark. A single faint light gleamed out from the hallway of the house. There was no sound abroad except the hooting of an old owl in the top of a water-oak, and the everlasting voice of the sea, that was not uplifted at that soft hour. It broke like a mournful lullaby upon the night.

The tears came so fast to Mrs. Pontellier's eyes that the damp sleeve of her *peignoir* no longer served to dry them. She was holding the back of her chair with one hand; her loose sleeve had slipped almost to the shoulder of her uplifted arm. Turning, she thrust her face, steaming and wet, into the bend of her arm, and she went on crying there, not caring any longer to dry her face, her eyes, her arms. She could not have told why she was crying. Such experiences as the foregoing were not uncommon in her married life. They seemed never before to have weighed much against the abundance of her husband's kindness and a uniform devotion which had come to be tacit and self-understood.

An indescribable oppression, which seemed to generate in some unfamiliar part of her consciousness, filled her whole being with a vague anguish. It was like a shadow, like a mist passing across her soul's summer day. It was strange and unfamiliar; it was a mood. She did not sit there inwardly upbraiding her husband, lamenting at Fate, which had directed her footsteps to the path which they had taken. She was just having a good cry all to herself. The mosquitoes made merry over her, biting her firm, round arms and nipping at her bare insteps.

The little stinging, buzzing imps succeeded in dispelling a mood which might have held her there in the darkness half a night longer.

The following morning Mr. Pontellier was up in good time to take the rockaway[4] which was to convey him to the steamer at the wharf. He was returning to the city to his business, and they would not see him again at the Island till the coming Saturday. He had regained his composure, which seemed to have been somewhat impaired the night before. He was eager to be gone, as he looked forward to a lively week in Carondelet Street.[5]

Mr. Pontellier gave his wife half the money which he had brought away from Klein's hotel the evening before. She liked money as well as most women, and accepted it with no little satisfaction.

"It will buy a handsome wedding present for Sister Janet!" she exclaimed, smoothing out the bills as she counted them one by one.

"Oh! we'll treat Sister Janet better than that, my dear," he laughed, as he prepared to kiss her good-by.

4. Four-wheeled carriage. 5. The financial center of New Orleans.

The boys were tumbling about, clinging to his legs, imploring that numerous things be brought back to them. Mr. Pontellier was a great favorite, and ladies, men, children, even nurses, were always on hand to say good-by to him. His wife stood smiling and waving, the boys shouting, as he disappeared in the old rockaway down the sandy road.

A few days later a box arrived for Mrs. Pontellier from New Orleans. It was from her husband. It was filled with *friandises*, with luscious and toothsome bits—the finest of fruits, *pâtés*, a rare bottle or two, delicious syrups, and bonbons in abundance.

Mrs. Pontellier was always very generous with the contents of such a box; she was quite used to receiving them when away from home. The *pâtés* and fruit were brought to the dining-room; the bonbons were passed around. And the ladies, selecting with dainty and discriminating fingers and a little greedily, all declared that Mr. Pontellier was the best husband in the world. Mrs. Pontellier was forced to admit that she knew of none better.

IV

It would have been a difficult matter for Mr. Pontellier to define to his own satisfaction or any one else's wherein his wife failed in her duty toward their children. It was something which he felt rather than perceived, and he never voiced the feeling without subsequent regret and ample atonement.

If one of the little Pontellier boys took a tumble whilst at play, he was not apt to rush crying to his mother's arms for comfort; he would more likely pick himself up, wipe the water out of his eyes and the sand out of his mouth, and go on playing. Tots as they were, they pulled together and stood their ground in childish battles with doubled fists and uplifted voices, which usually prevailed against the other mother-tots. The quadroon nurse was looked upon as a huge encumbrance, only good to button up waists and panties and to brush and part hair; since it seemed to be a law of society that hair must be parted and brushed.

In short, Mrs. Pontellier was not a mother-woman. The mother-women seemed to prevail that summer at Grand Isle. It was easy to know them, fluttering about with extended, protecting wings when any harm, real or imaginary, threatened their precious brood. They were women who idolized their children, worshipped their husbands, and esteemed it a holy privilege to efface themselves as individuals and grow wings as ministering angels.

Many of them were delicious in the rôle; one of them was the embodiment of every womanly grace and charm. If her husband did not adore her, he was a brute, deserving of death by slow torture. Her name was Adèle Ratignolle. There are no words to describe her save the old ones that have served so often to picture the bygone heroine of romance and the fair lady of our dreams. There was nothing subtle or hidden about her charms; her beauty was all there, flaming and apparent: the spun-gold hair that comb nor confining pin could restrain; the blue eyes that were like nothing but sapphires; two lips that pouted, that were so red one could only think of cherries or some other delicious crimson fruit in looking at them. She was growing a little stout, but it did not seem to detract an iota from the grace of every step, pose, gesture. One would not have wanted her white neck a mite less full or her beautiful arms more slender. Never were hands more exquisite than hers, and it was a joy to

look at them when she threaded her needle or adjusted her gold thimble to her taper[6] middle finger as she sewed away on the little night-drawers or fashioned a bodice or a bib.

Madame Ratignolle was very fond of Mrs. Pontellier, and often she took her sewing and went over to sit with her in the afternoons. She was sitting there the afternoon of the day the boy arrived from New Orleans. She had possession of the rocker, and she was busily engaged in sewing upon a diminutive pair of night drawers.

She had brought the pattern of the drawers for Mrs. Pontellier to cut out— a marvel of construction, fashioned to enclose a baby's body so effectually that only two small eyes might look out from the garment, like an Eskimo's. They were designed for winter wear, when treacherous drafts came down chimneys and insidious currents of deadly cold found their way through keyholes.

Mrs. Pontellier's mind was quite at rest concerning the present material needs of her children, and she could not see the use of anticipating and making winter night garments the subject of her summer meditations. But she did not want to appear unamiable and uninterested, so she had brought forth newspapers which she spread upon the floor of the gallery, and under Madame Ratignolle's directions she had cut a pattern of the impervious garment.

Robert was there, seated as he had been the Sunday before, and Mrs. Pontellier also occupied her former position on the upper step, leaning listlessly against the post. Beside her was a box of bonbons, which she held out at intervals to Madame Ratignolle.

That lady seemed at a loss to make a selection, but finally settled upon a stick of nugat, wondering if it were not too rich; whether it could possibly hurt her. Madame Ratignolle had been married seven years. About every two years she had a baby. At that time she had three babies, and was beginning to think of a fourth one. She was always talking about her "condition." Her "condition" was in no way apparent, and no one would have known a thing about it but for her persistence in making it the subject of conversation.

Robert started to reassure her, asserting that he had known a lady who had subsisted upon nugat during the entire—but seeing the color mount into Mrs. Pontellier's face he checked himself and changed the subject.

Mrs. Pontellier, though she had married a Creole,[7] was not thoroughly at home in the society of Creoles; never before had she been thrown so intimately among them. There were only Creoles that summer at Lebrun's. They all knew each other, and felt like one large family, among whom existed the most amicable relations. A characteristic which distinguished them and which impressed Mrs. Pontellier most forcibly was their entire absence of prudery. Their freedom of expression was at first incomprehensible to her, though she had no difficulty in reconciling it with a lofty chastity which in the Creole woman seems to be inborn and unmistakable.

Never would Edna Pontellier forget the shock with which she heard Madame Ratignolle relating to old Monsieur Farival the harrowing story of one of her *accouchements*,[8] withholding no intimate detail. She was growing accustomed to like shocks, but she could not keep the mounting color back

6. I.e., tapered.
7. Descended from the original French and Spanish settlers of New Orleans; and thus at this time, an aris-
tocrat.
8. Childbirth.

from her cheeks. Oftener than once her coming had interrupted the droll story with which Robert was entertaining some amused group of married women.

A book had gone the rounds of the *pension*. When it came her turn to read it, she did so with profound astonishment. She felt moved to read the book in secret and solitude, though none of the others had done so—to hide it from view at the sound of approaching footsteps. It was openly criticised and freely discussed at table. Mrs. Pontellier gave over being astonished, and concluded that wonders would never cease.

V

They formed a congenial group sitting there that summer afternoon—Madame Ratignolle sewing away, often stopping to relate a story or incident with much expressive gesture of her perfect hands; Robert and Mrs. Pontellier sitting idle, exchanging occasional words, glances or smiles which indicated a certain advanced stage of intimacy and *camaraderie*.

He had lived in her shadow during the past month. No one thought anything of it. Many had predicted that Robert would devote himself to Mrs. Pontellier when he arrived. Since the age of fifteen, which was eleven years before, Robert each summer at Grand Isle had constituted himself the devoted attendant of some fair dame or damsel. Sometimes it was a young girl, again a widow; but as often as not it was some interesting married woman.

For two consecutive seasons he lived in the sunlight of Mademoiselle Duvigné's presence. But she died between summers; then Robert posed as an inconsolable, prostrating himself at the feet of Madame Ratignolle for whatever crumbs of sympathy and comfort she might be pleased to vouchsafe.

Mrs. Pontellier liked to sit and gaze at her fair companion as she might look upon a faultless Madonna.

"Could any one fathom the cruelty beneath that fair exterior?" murmured Robert. "She knew that I adored her once, and she let me adore her. It was 'Robert, come; go; stand up; sit down; do this; do that; see if the baby sleeps; my thimble, please, that I left God knows where. Come and read Daudet[9] to me while I sew.' "

"*Par exemple!*"[1] I never had to ask. You were always there under my feet, like a troublesome cat."

"You mean like an adoring dog. And just as soon as Ratignolle appeared on the scene, then it *was* like a dog. '*Passez! Adieu! Allez vous-en!*' "[2]

"Perhaps I feared to make Alphonse jealous," she interjoined, with excessive naïveté. That made them all laugh. The right hand jealous of the left! The heart jealous of the soul! But for that matter, the Creole husband is never jealous; with him the gangrene passion is one which has become dwarfed by disuse.

Meanwhile Robert, addressing Mrs. Pontellier, continued to tell of his one time hopeless passion for Madame Ratignolle; of sleepless nights, of consuming flames till the very sea sizzled when he took his daily plunge. While the lady at the needle kept up a little running, contemptuous comment:

"*Blagueur—farceur—gros bête, va!*"[3]

He never assumed this serio-comic tone when alone with Mrs. Pontellier.

9. Alphonse Daudet (1840–1887), French novelist.
1. For goodness sake!
2. Go on! Good-by! Go away!
3. Liar—comedian—silly, go on with you

She never knew precisely what to make of it; at that moment it was impossible for her to guess how much of it was jest and what proportion was earnest. It was understood that he had often spoken words of love to Madame Ratignolle, without any thought of being taken seriously. Mrs. Pontellier was glad he had not assumed a similar rôle toward herself. It would have been unacceptable and annoying.

Mrs. Pontellier had brought her sketching materials, which she sometimes dabbled with in an unprofessional way. She liked the dabbling. She felt in it satisfaction of a kind which no other employment afforded her.

She had long wished to try herself on Madame Ratignolle. Never had that lady seemed a more tempting subject than at that moment, seated there like some sensuous Madonna, with the gleam of the fading day enriching her splendid color.

Robert crossed over and seated himself upon the step below Mrs. Pontellier, that he might watch her work. She handled her brushes with a certain ease and freedom which came, not from long and close acquaintance with them, but from a natural aptitude. Robert followed her work with close attention, giving forth little ejaculatory expressions of appreciation in French, which he addressed to Madame Ratignolle.

"*Mais ce n'est pas mal! Elle s'y connait, elle a de la force, oui.*"[4]

During his oblivious attention he once quietly rested his head against Mrs. Pontellier's arm. As gently she repulsed him. Once again he repeated the offense. She could not but believe it to be thoughtlessness on his part; yet that was no reason she should submit to it. She did not remonstrate, except again to repulse him quietly but firmly. He offered no apology.

The picture completed bore no resemblance to Madame Ratignolle. She was greatly disappointed to find that it did not look like her. But it was a fair enough piece of work, and in many respects satisfying.

Mrs. Pontellier evidently did not think so. After surveying the sketch critically she drew a broad smudge of paint across its surface, and crumpled the paper between her hands.

The youngsters came tumbling up the steps, the quadroon following at the respectful distance which they required her to observe. Mrs. Pontellier made them carry her paints and things into the house. She sought to detain them for a little talk and some pleasantry. But they were greatly in earnest. They had only come to investigate the contents of the bonbon box. They accepted without murmuring what she chose to give them, each holding out two chubby hands scoop-like, in the vain hope that they might be filled; and then away they went.

The sun was low in the west, and the breeze soft and languorous that came up from the south, charged with the seductive odor of the sea. Children, freshly befurbelowed,[5] were gathering for their games under the oaks. Their voices were high and penetrating.

Madame Ratignolle folded her sewing, placing thimble, scissors and thread all neatly together in the roll, which she pinned securely. She complained of faintness. Mrs. Pontellier flew for the cologne water and a fan. She bathed Madame Ratignolle's face with cologne, while Robert plied the fan with unnecessary vigor.

The spell was soon over, and Mrs. Pontellier could not help wondering if

4. Why that's not bad at all! She knows what she's 5. Dressed up.
doing; yes, she has talent.

there were not a little imagination responsible for its origin, for the rose tint had never faded from her friend's face.

She stood watching the fair woman walk down the long line of galleries with the grace and majesty which queens are sometimes supposed to possess. Her little ones ran to meet her. Two of them clung about her white skirts, the third she took from its nurse and with a thousand endearments bore it along in her own fond, encircling arms. Though, as everybody well knew, the doctor had forbidden her to lift so much as a pin!

"Are you going bathing?" asked Robert of Mrs. Pontellier. It was not so much a question as a reminder.

"Oh, no," she answered, with a tone of indecision. "I'm tired; I think not." Her glance wandered from his face away toward the Gulf, whose sonorous murmur reached her like a loving but imperative entreaty.

"Oh, come!" he insisted. "You mustn't miss your bath. Come on. The water must be delicious; it will not hurt you. Come."

He reached up for her big, rough straw hat that hung on a peg outside the door, and put it on her head. They descended the steps, and walked away together toward the beach. The sun was low in the west and the breeze was soft and warm.

VI

Edna Pontellier could not have told why, wishing to go to the beach with Robert, she should in the first place have declined, and in the second place have followed in obedience to one of the two contradictory impulses which impelled her.

A certain light was beginning to dawn dimly within her,—the light which, showing the way, forbids it.

At that early period it served but to bewilder her. It moved her to dreams, to thoughtfulness, to the shadowy anguish which had over-come her the midnight when she had abandoned herself to tears.

In short, Mrs. Pontellier was beginning to realize her position in the universe as a human being, and to recognize her relations as an individual to the world within and about her. This may seem like a ponderous weight of wisdom to descend upon the soul of a young woman of twenty-eight—perhaps more wisdom than the Holy Ghost is usually pleased to vouchsafe to any woman.

But the beginning of things, of a world especially, is necessarily vague, tangled, chaotic, and exceedingly disturbing. How few of us ever emerge from such beginning! How many souls perish in its tumult!

The voice of the sea is seductive; never ceasing, whispering, clamoring, murmuring, inviting the soul to wander for a spell in abysses of solitude; to lose itself in mazes of inward contemplation.

The voice of the sea speaks to the soul. The touch of the sea is sensuous, enfolding the body in its soft, close embrace.

VII

Mrs. Pontellier was not a woman given to confidences, a characteristic hitherto contrary to her nature. Even as a child she had lived her own small life all within herself. At a very early period she had apprehended instinctively the

dual life—that outward existence which conforms, the inward life which questions.

That summer at Grand Isle she began to loose a little the mantle of reserve that had always enveloped her. There may have been—there must have been—influences, both subtle and apparent, working in their several ways to induce her to do this; but the most obvious was the influence of Adèle Ratignolle. The excessive physical charm of the Creole had first attracted her, for Edna had a sensuous susceptibility to beauty. Then the candor of the woman's whole existence, which everyone might read, and which formed so striking a contrast to her own habitual reserve—this might have furnished a link. Who can tell what metals the gods use in forging the subtle bond which we call sympathy, which we might as well call love.

The two women went away one morning to the beach together, arm in arm, under the huge white sunshade. Edna had prevailed upon Madame Ratignolle to leave the children behind, though she could not induce her to relinquish a diminutive roll of needlework, which Adèle begged to be allowed to slip into the depths of her pocket. In some unaccountable way they had escaped from Robert.

The walk to the beach was no inconsiderable one, consisting as it did of a long, sandy path, upon which a sporadic and tangled growth that bordered it on either side made frequent and unexpected inroads. There were acres of yellow camomile reaching out on either hand. Further away still, vegetable gardens abounded, with frequent small plantations of orange or lemon trees intervening. The dark green clusters glistened from afar in the sun.

The women were both of goodly height, Madame Ratignolle possessing the more feminine and matronly figure. The charm of Edna Pontellier's physique stole insensibly upon you. The lines of her body were long, clean and symmetrical; it was a body which occasionally fell into splendid poses; there was no suggestion of the trim, stereotyped fashion-plate about it. A casual and indiscriminating observer, in passing, might not cast a second glance upon the figure. But with more feeling and discernment he would have recognized the noble beauty of its modeling, and the graceful severity of poise and movement, which made Edna Pontellier different from the crowd.

She wore a cool muslin that morning—white, with a waving vertical line of brown running through it; also a white linen collar and the big straw hat which she had taken from the peg outside the door. The hat rested any way on her yellow-brown hair, that waved a little, was heavy, and clung close to her head.

Madame Ratignolle, more careful of her complexion, had twined a gauze veil about her head. She wore dogskin gloves, white gauntlets that protected her wrists. She was dressed in pure white, with a fluffiness of ruffles that became her. The draperies and fluttering things which she wore suited her rich, luxuriant beauty as a greater severity of line could not have done.

There were a number of bath-houses along the beach, of rough but solid construction, built with small, protecting galleries facing the water. Each house consisted of two compartments, and each family at Lebrun's possessed a compartment for itself, fitted out with all the essential paraphernalia of the bath and whatever other conveniences the owners might desire. The two women had no intention of bathing; they had just strolled down to the beach for a walk and to be alone and near the water. The Pontellier and Ratignolle compartments adjoined one another under the same roof.

Mrs. Pontellier had brought down her key through force of habit. Unlocking the door of her bath-room she went inside, and soon emerged, bringing a rug, which she spread upon the floor of the gallery, and two huge hair pillows covered with crash,[6] which she placed against the front of the building.

The two seated themselves there in the shade of the porch, side by side, with their backs against the pillows and their feet extended. Madame Ratignolle removed her veil, wiped her face with a rather delicate handkerchief, and fanned herself with the fan which she always carried suspended somewhere about her person by a long, narrow ribbon. Edna removed her collar and opened her dress at the throat. She took the fan from Madame Ratignolle and began to fan both herself and her companion. It was very warm, and for a while they did nothing but exchange remarks about the heat, the sun, the glare. But there was a breeze blowing, a choppy stiff wind that whipped the water into froth. It fluttered the skirts of the two women and kept them for a while engaged in adjusting, readjusting, tucking in, securing hairpins and hat-pins. A few persons were sporting some distance away in the water. The beach was very still of human sound at that hour. The lady in black was reading her morning devotions on the porch of a neighboring bath-house. Two young lovers were exchanging their hearts' yearnings beneath the children's tent, which they had found unoccupied.

Edna Pontellier, casting her eyes about, had finally kept them at rest upon the sea. The day was clear and carried the gaze out as far as the blue sky went; there were a few white clouds suspended idly over the horizon. A lateen[7] sail was visible in the direction of Cat Island, and others to the south seemed almost motionless in the far distance.

"Of whom—of what are you thinking?" asked Adèle of her companion, whose countenance she had been watching with a little amused attention, arrested by the absorbed expression which seemed to have seized and fixed every feature into a statuesque repose.

"Nothing," returned Mrs. Pontellier, with a start, adding at once: "How stupid! But it seems to me it is the reply we make instinctively to such a question. Let me see," she went on, throwing back her head and narrowing her fine eyes till they shone like two vivid points of light. "Let me see. I was really not conscious of thinking of anything; but perhaps I can retrace my thoughts."

"Oh! never mind!" laughed Madame Ratignolle. "I am not quite so exacting. I will let you off this time. It is really too hot to think, especially to think about thinking."

"But for the fun of it," persisted Edna. "First of all, the sight of the water stretching so far away, those motionless sails against the blue sky, made a delicious picture that I just wanted to sit and look at. The hot wind beating in my face made me think—without any connection that I can trace—of a summer day in Kentucky, of a meadow that seemed as big as the ocean to the very little girl walking through the grass, which was higher than her waist. She threw out her arms as if swimming when she walked, beating the tall grass as one strikes out in the water. Oh, I see the connection now!"

"Where were you going that day in Kentucky, walking through the grass?"

"I don't remember now. I was just walking diagonally across a big field. My sun-bonnet obstructed the view. I could see only the stretch of green before

6. Heavy linen fabric. "Rug": blanket. 7. Triangular.

me, and I felt as if I must walk on forever, without coming to the end of it. I don't remember whether I was frightened or pleased. I must have been entertained.

"Likely as not it was Sunday," she laughed; "and I was running away from prayers, from the Presbyterian service, read in a spirit of gloom by my father that chills me yet to think of."

"And have you been running away from prayers ever since, *ma chère?*" asked Madame Ratignolle, amused.

"No! oh, no!" Edna hastened to say. "I was a little unthinking child in those days, just following a misleading impulse without question. On the contrary, during one period of my life religion took a firm hold upon me; after I was twelve and until—until—why, I suppose until now, though I never thought much about it—just driven along by habit. But do you know," she broke off, turning her quick eyes upon Madame Ratignolle and leaning forward a little so as to bring her face quite close to that of her companion, "sometimes I feel this summer as if I were walking through the green meadow again; idly, aimlessly, unthinking and unguided."

Madame Ratignolle laid her hand over that of Mrs. Pontellier, which was near her. Seeing that the hand was not withdrawn, she clasped it firmly and warmly. She even stroked it a little, fondly, with the other hand, murmuring in an undertone, "*Pauvre chérie.*"[8]

The action was at first a little confusing to Edna, but she soon lent herself readily to the Creole's gentle caress. She was not accustomed to an outward and spoken expression of affection, either in herself or in others. She and her younger sister, Janet, had quarreled a good deal through force of unfortunate habit. Her older sister, Margaret, was matronly and dignified, probably from having assumed matronly and house-wifely responsibilities too early in life, their mother having died when they were quite young. Margaret was not effusive; she was practical. Edna had had an occasional girl friend, but whether accidentally or not, they seemed to have been all of one type—the self-contained. She never realized that the reserve of her own character had much, perhaps everything, to do with this. Her most intimate friend at school had been one of rather exceptional intellectual gifts, who wrote fine-sounding essays which Edna admired and strove to imitate; and with her she talked and glowed over the English classics, and sometimes held religious and political controversies.

Edna often wondered at one propensity which sometimes had inwardly disturbed her without causing any outward show or manifestation on her part. At a very early age—perhaps it was when she traversed the ocean of waving grass—she remembered that she had been passionately enamored of a dignified and sad-eyed cavalry officer who visited her father in Kentucky. She could not leave his presence when he was there, nor remove her eyes from his face which was something like Napoleon's, with a lock of black hair falling across the forehead. But the cavalry officer melted imperceptibly out of her existence.

At another time her affections were deeply engaged by a young gentleman who visited a lady on a neighboring plantation. It was after they went to Mississippi to live. The young man was engaged to be married to the young

8. Poor dear.

lady, and they sometimes called upon Margaret, driving over of afternoons in a buggy. Edna was a little miss, just merging into her teens; and the realization that she herself was nothing, nothing, nothing to the engaged young man was a bitter affliction to her. But he, too, went the way of dreams.

She was a grown young woman when she was overtaken by what she supposed to be the climax of her fate. It was when the face and figure of a great tragedian began to haunt her imagination and stir her senses. The persistence of the infatuation lent it an aspect of genuineness. The hopelessness of it colored it with the lofty tones of a great passion.

The picture of the tragedian stood enframed upon her desk. Any one may possess the portrait of a tragedian without exciting suspicion or comment. (This was a sinister reflection which she cherished.) In the presence of others she expressed admiration for his exalted gifts, as she handed the photograph around and dwelt upon the fidelity of the likeness. When alone she sometimes picked it up and kissed the cold glass passionately.

Her marriage to Léonce Pontellier was purely an accident, in this respect resembling many other marriages which masquerade as the decrees of Fate. It was in the midst of her secret great passion that she met him. He fell in love, as men are in the habit of doing, and pressed his suit with an earnestness and an ardor which left nothing to be desired. He pleased her; his absolute devotion flattered her. She fancied there was a sympathy of thought and taste between them, in which fancy she was mistaken. Add to this the violent opposition of her father and her sister Margaret to her marriage with a Catholic, and we need seek no further for the motives which led her to accept Monsieur Pontellier for her husband.

The acme of bliss, which would have been a marriage with the tragedian, was not for her in this world. As the devoted wife of a man who worshiped her, she felt she would take her place with a certain dignity in the world of reality, closing the portals forever behind her upon the realm of romance and dreams.

But it was not long before the tragedian had gone to join the cavalry officer and the engaged young man and a few others; and Edna found herself face to face with the realities. She grew fond of her husband, realizing with some unaccountable satisfaction that no trace of passion or excessive and fictitious warmth colored her affection, thereby threatening its dissolution.

She was fond of her children in an uneven, impulsive way. She would sometimes gather them passionately to her heart; she would sometimes forget them. The year before they had spent part of the summer with their grandmother Pontellier in Iberville.[9] Feeling secure regarding their happiness and welfare, she did not miss them except with an occasional intense longing. Their absence was a sort of relief, though she did not admit this, even to herself. It seemed to free her of a responsibility which she had blindly assumed and for which Fate had not fitted her.

Edna did not reveal so much as all this to Madame Ratignolle that summer day when they sat with faces turned to the sea. But a good part of it escaped her. She had put her head down on Madame Ratignolle's shoulder. She was flushed and felt intoxicated with the sound of her own voice and the unaccustomed taste of candor. It muddled her like wine, or like a first breath of freedom.

9. Rural parish (county) in Louisiana, west of Baton Rouge.

There was the sound of approaching voices. It was Robert, surrounded by a troop of children, searching for them. The two little Pontelliers were with him, and he carried Madame Ratignolle's little girl in his arms. There were other children beside, and two nursemaids followed, looking disagreeable and resigned.

The women at once rose and began to shake out their draperies and relax their muscles. Mrs. Pontellier threw the cushions and rug into the bath-house. The children all scampered off to the awning, and they stood there in a line, gazing upon the intruding lovers, still exchanging their vows and sighs. The lovers got up, with only a silent protest, and walked slowly away somewhere else.

The children possessed themselves of the tent, and Mrs. Pontellier went over to join them.

Madame Ratignolle begged Robert to accompany her to the house; she complained of cramp in her limbs and stiffness of the joints. She leaned draggingly upon his arm as they walked.

VIII

"Do me a favor, Robert," spoke the pretty woman at his side, almost as soon as she and Robert had started on their slow, homeward way. She looked up in his face, leaning on his arm beneath the encircling shadow of the umbrella which he had lifted.

"Granted; as many as you like," he returned, glancing down into her eyes that were full of thoughtfulness and some speculation.

"I only ask for one; let Mrs. Pontellier alone."

"*Tiens!*" he exclaimed, with a sudden, boyish laugh. "*Voilà que Madame Ratignolle est jalouse!*"[1]

"Nonsense! I'm in earnest; I mean what I say. Let Mrs. Pontellier alone."

"Why?" he asked; himself growing serious at his companion's solicitation.

"She is not one of us; she is not like us. She might make the unfortunate blunder of taking you seriously."

His face flushed with annoyance, and taking off his soft hat he began to beat it impatiently against his leg as he walked. "Why shouldn't she take me seriously?" he demanded sharply. "Am I a comedian, a clown, a jack-in-the-box? Why shouldn't she? You Creoles! I have no patience with you. Am I always to be regarded as a feature of an amusing programme? I hope Mrs. Pontellier does take me seriously. I hope she has discernment enough to find in me something besides the *blagueur*.[2] If I thought there was any doubt—"

"Oh, enough, Robert!" she broke into his heated outburst. "You are not thinking of what you are saying. You speak with about as little reflection as we might expect from one of those children down there playing in the sand. If your attentions to any married women here were ever offered with any intention of being convincing, you would not be the gentleman we all know you to be, and you would be unfit to associate with the wives and daughters of the people who trust you."

Madame Ratignolle had spoken what she believed to be the law and the gospel. The young man shrugged his shoulders impatiently.

1. So, Madame Ratignolle is jealous! 2. Joker, liar.

"Oh! well! That isn't it," slamming his hat down vehemently upon his head. "You ought to feel that such things are not flattering to say to a fellow."

"Should our whole intercourse consist of an exchange of compliments? *Ma foi!*[3]

"It isn't pleasant to have a woman tell you—" he went on, unheedingly, but breaking off suddenly: "Now if I were like Arobin—you remember Alcée Arobin and that story of the consul's wife at Biloxi?" And he related the story of Alcée Arobin and the consul's wife; and another about the tenor of the French Opera,[4] who received letters which should never have been written; and still other stories, grave and gay, till Mrs. Pontellier and her possible propensity for taking young men seriously was apparently forgotten.

Madame Ratignolle, when they had regained her cottage, went in to take the hour's rest which she considered helpful. Before leaving her. Robert begged her pardon for the impatience—he called it rudeness—with which he had received her well-meant caution.

"You made one mistake, Adèle," he said, with a light smile; "there is no earthly possibility of Mrs. Pontellier ever taking me seriously. You should have warned me against taking myself seriously. Your advice might then have carried some weight and given me subject for some reflection. *Au revoir*. But you look tired," he added, solicitously. "Would you like a cup of bouillon? Shall I stir you a toddy? Let me mix you a toddy with a drop of Angostura."[5]

She acceded to the suggestion of bouillon, which was grateful and acceptable. He went himself to the kitchen, which was a building apart from the cottages and lying to the rear of the house. And he himself brought her the golden-brown bouillon, in a dainty Sèvres[6] cup, with a flaky cracker or two on the saucer.

She thrust a bare, white arm from the curtain which shielded her open door, and received the cup from his hands. She told him he was a *bon garcon*,[7] and she meant it. Robert thanked her and turned away toward "the house."

The lovers were just entering the grounds of the *pension*. They were leaning toward each other as the water-oaks bent from the sea. There was not a particle of earth beneath their feet. Their heads might have been turned upside-down, so absolutely did they tread upon blue ether. The lady in black, creeping behind them, looked a trifle paler and more jaded than usual. There was no sign of Mrs. Pontellier and the children. Robert scanned the distance for any such apparition. They would doubtless remain away till the dinner hour. The young man ascended to his mother's room. It was situated at the top of the house, made up of odd angles and a queer, sloping ceiling. Two broad dormer windows looked out toward the Gulf, and as far across it as a man's eye might reach. The furnishings of the room were light, cool, and practical.

Madame Lebrun was busily engaged at the sewing-machine. A little black girl sat on the floor, and with her hands worked the treadle of the machine. The Creole woman does not take any chances which may be avoided of imperiling her health.

Robert went over and seated himself on the broad sill of one of the dormer windows. He took a book from his pocket and began energetically to read it, judging by the precision and frequency with which he turned the leaves. The

3. For heaven's sake!
4. In New Orleans; perhaps the most distinguished American opera company of the time. Biloxi is a coastal resort town near New Orleans.
5. Aromatic bitters.
6. Fine porcelain made in Sèvres, France.
7. Both "nice fellow" and "good waiter."

sewing-machine made a resounding clatter in the room; it was of a ponderous, by-gone make. In the lulls, Robert and his mother exchanged bits of desultory conversation.

"Where is Mrs. Pontellier?"

"Down at the beach with the children."

"I promised to lend her the Goncourt.[8] Don't forget to take it down when you go; it's there on the bookshelf over the small table." Clatter, clatter, clatter, bang! for the next five or eight minutes.

"Where is Victor going with the rockaway?"

"The rockaway? Victor?"

"Yes; down there in front. He seems to be getting ready to drive away some-where."

"Call him." Clatter, clatter!

Robert uttered a shrill, piercing whistle which might have been heard back at the wharf.

"He won't look up."

Madame Lebrun flew to the window. She called "Victor!" She waved a handkerchief and called again. The young fellow below got into the vehicle and started the horse off at a gallop.

Madame Lebrun went back to the machine, crimson with annoyance. Victor was the younger son and brother—a *tête montée*,[9] with a temper which invited violence and a will which no ax could break.

"Whenever you say the word I'm ready to thrash any amount of reason into him that he's able to hold."

"If your father had only lived!" Clatter, clatter, clatter, clatter, bang! It was a fixed belief with Madame Lebrun that the conduct of the universe and all things pertaining thereto would have been manifestly of a more intelligent and higher order had not Monsieur Lebrun been removed to other spheres during the early years of their married life.

"What do you hear from Montel?" Montel was a middle-aged gentleman whose vain ambition and desire for the past twenty years had been to fill the void which Monsieur Lebrun's taking off had left in the Lebrun household. Clatter, clatter, bang, clatter!

"I have a letter somewhere," looking in the machine drawer and finding the letter in the bottom of the work-basket. "He says to tell you he will be in Vera Cruz[1] the beginning of next month"—clatter, clatter!—"and if you still have the intention of joining him"—bang! clatter, clatter, bang!

"Why didn't you tell me so before, mother? You know I wanted—" Clatter, clatter, clatter!

"Do you see Mrs. Pontellier starting back with the children? She will be in late to luncheon again. She never starts to get ready for luncheon till the last minute." Clatter, clatter! "Where are you going?"

"Where did you say the Goncourt was?"

IX

Every light in the hall was ablaze; every lamp turned as high as it could be without smoking the chimney or threatening explosion. The lamps were fixed at intervals against the wall, encircling the whole room. Some one had gath-

ered orange and lemon branches and with these fashioned graceful festoons between. The dark green of the branches stood out and glistened against the white muslin curtains which draped the windows, and which puffed, floated, and flapped at the capricious will of a stiff breeze that swept up from the Gulf.

It was Saturday night a few weeks after the intimate conversation held between Robert and Madame Ratignolle on their way from the beach. An unusual number of husbands, fathers, and friends had come down to stay over Sunday; and they were being suitably entertained by their families, with the material help of Madame Lebrun. The dining tables had all been removed to one end of the hall, and the chairs ranged about in rows and in clusters. Each little family group had had its say and exchanged its domestic gossip earlier in the evening. There was now an apparent disposition to relax; to widen the circle of confidences and give a more general tone to the conversation.

Many of the children had been permitted to sit up beyond their usual bedtime. A small band of them were lying on their stomachs on the floor looking at the colored sheets of the comic papers which Mr. Pontellier had brought down. The little Pontellier boys were permitting them to do so, and making their authority felt.

Music, dancing, and a recitation or two were the entertainments furnished, or rather, offered. But there was nothing systematic about the programme, no appearance of prearrangement nor even premeditation.

At an early hour in the evening the Farival twins were prevailed upon to play the piano. They were girls of fourteen, always clad in the Virgin's colors, blue and white, having been dedicated to the Blessed Virgin at their baptism. They played a duet from "Zampa," and at the earnest solicitation of every one present followed it with the overture to "The Poet and the Peasant."

"*Allez vous-en! Sapristi!*" shrieked the parrot outside the door. He was the only being present who possessed sufficient candor to admit that he was not listening to these gracious performances for the first time that summer. Old Monsieur Farival, grandfather of the twins, grew indignant over the interruption, and insisted upon having the bird removed and consigned to regions of darkness. Victor Lebrun objected; and his decrees were as immutable as those of Fate. The parrot fortunately offered no further interruption to the entertainment, the whole venom of his nature apparently having been cherished up and hurled against the twins in that one impetuous outburst.

Later a young brother and sister gave recitations, which every one present had heard many times at winter evening entertainments in the city.

A little girl performed a skirt dance in the center of the floor. The mother played her accompaniments and at the same time watched her daughter with greedy admiration and nervous apprehension. She need have had no apprehension. The child was mistress of the situation. She had been properly dressed for the occasion in black tulle and black silk tights. Her little neck and arms were bare, and her hair, artificially crimped, stood out like fluffy black plumes over her head. Her poses were full of grace, and her little black-shod toes twinkled as they shot out and upward with a rapidity and a suddenness which were bewildering.

But there was no reason why every one should not dance. Madame Ratignolle could not, so it was she who gaily consented to play for the others. She played very well, keeping excellent waltz time and infusing an expression into the strains which was indeed inspiring. She was keeping up her music on

account of the children she said; because she and her husband both considered it a means of brightening the home and making it attractive.

Almost every one danced but the twins, who could not be induced to separate during the brief period when one or the other should be whirling around the room in the arms of a man. They might have danced together, but they did not think of it.

The children were sent to bed. Some went submissively; others with shrieks and protests as they were dragged away. They had been permitted to sit up till after the ice-cream, which naturally marked the limit of human indulgence.

The ice-cream was passed around with cake—gold and silver cake arranged on platters in alternate slices; it had been made and frozen during the afternoon back of the kitchen by two black women, under the supervision of Victor. It was pronounced a great success—excellent if it had only contained a little less vanilla or a little more sugar, if it had been frozen a degree harder, and if the salt might have been kept out of portions of it. Victor was proud of his achievement, and went about recommending it and urging every one to partake of it to excess.

After Mrs. Pontellier had danced twice with her husband, once with Robert, and once with Monsieur Ratignolle, who was thin and tall and swayed like a reed in the wind when he danced, she went out on the gallery and seated herself on the low window-sill, where she commanded a view of all that went on in the hall and could look out toward the Gulf. There was a soft effulgence in the east. The moon was coming up, and its mystic shimmer was casting a million lights across the distant, restless water.

"Would you like to hear Mademoiselle Reisz play?" asked Robert, coming out on the porch where she was. Of course Edna would like to hear Mademoiselle Reisz play; but she feared it would be useless to entreat her.

"I'll ask her," he said. "I'll tell her that you want to hear her. She likes you. She will come." He turned and hurried away to one of the far cottages, where Mademoiselle Reisz was shuffling away. She was dragging a chair in and out of her room, and at intervals objecting to the crying of a baby, which a nurse in the adjoining cottage was endeavoring to put to sleep. She was a disagreeable little woman, no longer young, who had quarreled with almost every one, owing to a temper which was self-assertive and a disposition to trample upon the rights of others. Robert prevailed upon her without any too great difficulty.

She entered the hall with him during a lull in the dance. She made an awkward, imperious little bow as she went in. She was a homely woman, with a small weazened face and body and eyes that glowed. She had absolutely no taste in dress, and wore a batch of rusty black lace with a bunch of artificial violets pinned to the side of her hair.

"Ask Mrs. Pontellier what she would like to hear me play," she requested of Robert. She sat perfectly still before the piano, not touching the keys, while Robert carried her message to Edna at the window. A general air of surprise and genuine satisfaction fell upon every one as they saw the pianist enter. There was a settling down, and a prevailing air of expectancy everywhere. Edna was a trifle embarrassed at being thus signaled out for the imperious little woman's favor. She would not dare to choose, and begged that Mademoiselle Reisz would please herself in selections.

Edna was what she herself called very fond of music. Musical strains, well rendered, had a way of evoking pictures in her mind. She sometimes liked to

sit in the room of mornings when Madame Ratignolle played or practiced. One piece which that lady played Edna had entitled "Solitude." It was a short, plaintive, minor strain. The name of the piece was something else, but she called it "Solitude." When she heard it there came before her imagination the figure of a man standing beside a desolate rock on the seashore. He was naked. His attitude was one of hopeless resignation as he looked toward a distant bird winging its flight away from him.

Another piece called to her mind a dainty young woman clad in an Empire gown, taking mincing dancing steps as she came down a long avenue between tall hedges. Again, another reminded her of children at play, and still another of nothing on earth but a demure lady stroking a cat.

The very first chords which Mademoiselle Reisz struck upon the piano sent a keen tremor down Mrs. Pontellier's spinal column. It was not the first time she had heard an artist at the piano. Perhaps it was the first time she was ready, perhaps the first time her being was tempered to take an impress of the abiding truth.

She waited for the material pictures which she thought would gather and blaze before her imagination. She waited in vain. She saw no pictures of solitude, of hope, of longing, or of despair. But the very passions themselves were aroused within her soul, swaying it, lashing it, as the waves daily beat upon her splendid body. She trembled, she was choking, and the tears blinded her.

Mademoiselle had finished. She arose, and bowing her stiff, lofty bow, she went away, stopping for neither thanks nor applause. As she passed along the gallery she patted Edna upon the shoulder.

"Well, how did you like my music?" she asked. The young woman was unable to answer; she pressed the hand of the pianist convulsively. Mademoiselle Reisz perceived her agitation and even her tears. She patted her again upon the shoulder as she said:

"You are the only one worth playing for. Those others? Bah!" and she went shuffling and sidling on down the gallery toward her room.

But she was mistaken about "those others." Her playing had aroused a fever of enthusiasm. "What passion!" "What an artist!" "I have always said no one could play Chopin like Mademoiselle Reisz!" "That last prelude! Bon Dieu![2] It shakes a man!"

It was growing late, and there was a general disposition to disband. But someone, perhaps it was Robert, thought of a bath at that mystic hour and under that mystic moon.

X

At all events Robert proposed it, and there was not a dissenting voice. There was not one but was ready to follow when he led the way. He did not lead the way, however, he directed the way; and he himself loitered behind with the lovers, who had betrayed a disposition to linger and hold themselves apart. He walked between them, whether with malicious or mischievous intent was not wholly clear, even to himself.

The Pontelliers and Ratignolles walked ahead; the women leaning upon the arms of their husbands. Edna could hear Robert's voice behind them, and could sometimes hear what he said. She wondered why he did not join them.

2. "Good Lord!" Frédéric Chopin (1810–1849), Polish composer and piano virtuoso.

It was unlike him not to. Of late he had sometimes held away from her for an entire day, redoubling his devotion upon the next and the next, as though to make up for hours that had been lost. She missed him the days when some pretext served to take him away from her, just as one misses the sun on a cloudy day without having thought much about the sun when it was shining.

The people walked in little groups toward the beach. They talked and laughed; some of them sang. There was a band playing down at Klein's hotel, and the strains reached them faintly, tempered by the distance. There were strange, rare odors abroad—a tangle of the sea smell and of weeds and damp, new-plowed earth, mingled with the heavy perfume of a field of white blossoms somewhere near. But the night sat light upon the sea and the land. There was no weight of darkness; there were no shadows. The white light of the moon had fallen upon the world like the mystery and the softness of sleep.

Most of them walked into the water as though into a native element. The sea was quiet now, and swelled lazily in broad billows that melted into one another and did not break except upon the beach in little foamy crests that coiled back like slow, white serpents.

Edna had attempted all summer to learn to swim. She had received instructions from both the men and women; in some instances from the children. Robert had pursued a system of lessons almost daily; and he was nearly at the point of discouragement in realizing the futility of his efforts. A certain ungovernable dread hung about her when in the water, unless there was a hand near by that might reach out and reassure her.

But that night she was like the little tottering, stumbling, clutching child, who of a sudden realizes its powers, and walks for the first time alone, boldly and with over-confidence. She could have shouted for joy. She did shout for joy, as with a sweeping stroke or two she lifted her body to the surface of the water.

A feeling of exultation overtook her, as if some power of significant import had been given her soul. She grew daring and reckless, overestimating her strength. She wanted to swim far out, where no woman had swum before.

Her unlooked-for achievement was the subject of wonder, applause, and admiration. Each one congratulated himself that his special teachings had accomplished this desired end.

"How easy it is!" she thought. "It is nothing," she said aloud: "why did I not discover before that it was nothing. Think of the time I have lost splashing about like a baby." She would not join the groups in their sports and bouts, but intoxicated with her newly conquered power, she swam out alone.

She turned her face seaward to gather in an impression of space and solitude, which the vast expanse of water, meeting and melting with moonlit sky, conveyed to her excited fancy. As she swam she seemed to be reaching out for the unlimited in which to lose herself.

Once she turned and looked toward the shore, toward the people she had left there. She had not gone any great distance—that is, what would have been great distance for an experienced swimmer. But to her unaccustomed vision the stretch of water behind her assumed the aspect of a barrier which her unaided strength would never be able to overcome.

A quick vision of death smote her soul, and for a second of time appalled and enfeebled her senses. But by an effort she rallied her staggering faculties and managed to regain the land.

She made no mention of her encounter with death and her flash of terror, except to say to her husband, "I thought I should have perished out there alone."

"You were not so very far, my dear; I was watching you," he told her.

Edna went at once to the bath-house, and she had put on her dry clothes and was ready to return home before the others had left the water. She started to walk away alone. They all called to her and shouted to her. She waved a dissenting hand, and went on paying no further heed to their renewed cries which sought to detain her.

"Sometimes I am tempted to think that Mrs. Pontellier is capricious," said Madame Lebrun, who was amusing herself immensely and feared that Edna's abrupt departure might put an end to the pleasure.

"I know she is," assented Mr. Pontellier; "sometimes, not often."

Edna had not traversed a quarter of the distance on her way home before she was overtaken by Robert.

"Did you think I was afraid?" she asked him, without a shade of annoyance.

"No; I knew you weren't afraid."

"Then why did you come? Why didn't you stay out there with the others?"

"I never thought of it."

"Thought of what?"

"Of anything. What difference does it make?"

"I'm very tired," she uttered, complainingly.

"I know you are."

"You don't know anything about it. Why should you know? I never was so exhausted in my life. But it isn't unpleasant. A thousand emotions have swept through me to-night. I don't comprehend half of them. Don't mind what I'm saying; I am just thinking aloud. I wonder if I shall ever be stirred again as Mademoiselle Reisz's playing moved me to-night. I wonder if any night on earth will ever again be like this one. It is like a night in a dream. The people about me are like some uncanny, half-human beings. There must be spirits abroad to-night."

"There are," whispered Robert. "Didn't you know this was the twenty-eighth of August?

"The twenty-eighth of August?"

"Yes. On the twenty-eighth of August, at the hour of midnight, and if the moon is shining—the moon must be shining—a spirit that has haunted these shores for ages rises up from the Gulf. With its own penetrating vision the spirit seeks some one mortal worthy to hold him company, worthy of being exalted for a few hours into realms of the semi-celestials. His search has always hitherto been fruitless, and he has sunk back, disheartened, into the sea. But tonight he found Mrs. Pontellier. Perhaps he will never wholly release her from the spell. Perhaps she will never again suffer a poor, unworthy earthling to walk in the shadow of her divine presence."

"Don't banter me," she said, wounded at what appeared to be his flippancy. He did not mind the entreaty, but the tone with its delicate note of pathos was like a reproach. He could not explain; he could not tell her that he had penetrated her mood and understood. He said nothing except to offer her his arm, for, by her own admission, she was exhausted. She had been walking alone with her arms hanging limp, letting her white skirts trail along the dewy path. She took his arm, but she did not lean upon it. She let her hand lie listlessly, as

though her thoughts were elsewhere—somewhere in advance of her body, and she was striving to overtake them.

Robert assisted her into the hammock which swung from the post before her door out to the trunk of a tree.

"Will you stay out here and wait for Mr. Pontellier?" he asked.

"I'll stay out here. Good-night."

"Shall I get you a pillow?"

"There's one here," she said, feeling about, for they were in the shadow.

"It must be so soiled; the children have been tumbling it about."

"No matter." And having discovered the pillow, she adjusted it beneath her head. She extended herself in the hammock with a deep breath of relief. She was not a supercilious or an over-dainty woman. She was not much given to reclining in the hammock, and when she did so it was with no cat-like suggestion of voluptuous ease, but with a beneficent repose which seemed to invade her whole body.

"Shall I stay with you till Mr. Pontellier comes?" asked Robert, seating himself on the outer edge of one of the steps and taking hold of the hammock rope which was fastened to the post.

"If you wish. Don't swing the hammock. Will you get my white shawl which I left on the window-sill over at the house?"

"Are you chilly?"

"No; but I shall be presently."

"Presently?" he laughed. "Do you know what time it is? How long are you going to stay out here?"

"I don't know. Will you get the shawl?"

"Of course I will," he said, rising. He went over to the house, walking along the grass. She watched his figure pass in and out of the strips of moonlight. It was past midnight. It was very quiet.

When he returned with the shawl she took it and kept it in her hand. She did not put it around her.

"Did you say I should stay till Mr. Pontellier came back?"

"I said you might if you wished to."

He seated himself again and rolled a cigarette, which he smoked in silence. Neither did Mrs. Pontellier speak. No multitude of words could have been more significant than those moments of silence, or more pregnant with the first-felt throbbings of desire.

When the voices of the bathers were heard approaching, Robert said good-night. She did not answer him. He thought she was asleep. Again she watched his figure pass in and out of the strips of moonlight as he walked away.

XI

"What are you doing out here, Edna? I thought I should find you in bed," said her husband, when he discovered her lying there. He had walked up with Madame Lebrun and left her at the house. His wife did not reply.

"Are you asleep?" he asked, bending down close to look at her.

"No." Her eyes gleamed bright and intense, with no sleepy shadows, as they looked into his.

"Do you know it is past one o'clock? Come on," and he mounted the steps and went into their room.

"Edna!" called Mr. Pontellier from within, after a few moments had gone by.

"Don't wait for me," she answered. He thrust his head through the door.

"You will take cold out there," he said, irritably. "What folly is this? Why don't you come in?"

"It isn't cold; I have my shawl."

"The mosquitoes will devour you."

"There are no mosquitoes."

She heard him moving about the room; every sound indicating impatience and irritation. Another time she would have gone in at his request. She would, through habit, have yielded to his desire; not with any sense of submission or obedience to his compelling wishes, but unthinkingly, as we walk, move, sit, stand, go through the daily treadmill of the life which has been portioned out to us.

"Edna, dear, are you not coming in soon?" he asked again, this time fondly, with a note of entreaty.

"No; I am going to stay out here."

"This is more than folly," he blurted out. "I can't permit you to stay out there all night. You must come in the house instantly."

With a writhing motion she settled herself more securely in the hammock. She perceived that her will had blazed up, stubborn and resistant. She could not at that moment have done other than denied and resisted. She wondered if her husband had ever spoken to her like that before, and if she had submitted to his command. Of course she had; she remembered that she had. But she could not realize why or how she should have yielded, feeling as she then did.

"Léonce, go to bed," she said. "I mean to stay out here. I don't wish to go in, and I don't intend to. Don't speak to me like that again; I shall not answer you."

Mr. Pontellier had prepared for bed, but he slipped on an extra garment. He opened a bottle of wine, of which he kept a small and select supply in a buffet of his own. He drank a glass of the wine and went out on the gallery and offered a glass to his wife. She did not wish any. He drew up the rocker, hoisted his slippered feet on the rail, and proceeded to smoke a cigar. He smoked two cigars; then he went inside and drank another glass of wine. Mrs. Pontellier again declined to accept a glass when it was offered to her. Mr. Pontellier once more seated himself with elevated feet, and after a reasonable interval of time smoked some more cigars.

Edna began to feel like one who awakens gradually out of a dream, a delicious, grotesque, impossible dream, to feel again the realities pressing into her soul. The physical need for sleep began to overtake her; the exuberance which had sustained and exalted her spirit left her helpless and yielding to the conditions which crowded her in.

The stillest hour of the night had come, the hour before dawn, when the world seems to hold its breath. The moon hung low, and had turned from silver to copper in the sleeping sky. The old owl no longer hooted, and the water-oaks had ceased to moan as they bent their heads.

Edna arose, cramped from lying so long and still in the hammock. She tottered up the steps, clutching feebly at the post before passing into the house.

"Are you coming in, Léonce?" she asked, turning her face toward her husband.

"Yes, dear," he answered, with a glance following a misty puff of smoke. "Just as soon as I have finished my cigar."

XII

She slept but a few hours. They were troubled and feverish hours, disturbed with dreams that were intangible, that eluded her, leaving only an impression upon her half-awakened senses of something unattainable. She was up and dressed in the cool of the early morning. The air was invigorating and steadied somewhat her faculties. However, she was not seeking refreshment or help from any source either external or from within. She was blindly following whatever impulse moved her, as if she had placed herself in alien hands for direction, and freed her soul of responsibility.

Most of the people at that early hour were still in bed and asleep. A few, who intended to go over to the *Chênière* for mass, were moving about. The lovers, who had laid their plans the night before, were already strolling toward the wharf. The lady in black with her Sunday prayer book, velvet and gold-clasped, and her Sunday silver beads, was following them at no great distance. Old Monsieur Farival was up, and was more than half inclined to do anything that suggested itself. He put on his big straw hat, and taking his umbrella from the stand in the hall, followed the lady in black, never overtaking her.

The little negro girl who worked Madame Lebrun's sewing-machine was sweeping the galleries with long, absent-minded strokes of the broom. Edna sent her up into the house to awaken Robert.

"Tell him I am going to the Chênière. The boat is ready, tell him to hurry."

He had soon joined her. She had never sent for him before. She had never asked for him. She had never seemed to want him before. She did not appear conscious that she had done anything unusual in commanding his presence. He was apparently equally unconscious of anything extraordinary in the situation. But his face was suffused with a quiet glow when he met her.

They went together back to the kitchen to drink coffee. There was no time to wait for any nicety of service. They stood outside the window and the cook passed them their coffee and a roll, which they drank and ate from the window-sill. Edna said it tasted good. She had not thought of coffee nor of anything. He told her he had often noticed that she lacked forethought.

"Wasn't it enough to think of going to the *Chênière* and waking you up?" she laughed. "Do I have to think of everything?—as Léonce says when he's in a bad humor. I don't blame him; he'd never be in a bad humor if it weren't for me."

They took a short cut across the sands. At a distance they could see the curious procession moving toward the wharf—the lovers, shoulder to shoulder, creeping; the lady in black, gaining steadily upon them; old Monsieur Farival, losing ground inch by inch, and a young barefooted Spanish girl, with a red kerchief on her head and a basket on her arm, bringing up the rear.

Robert knew the girl, and he talked to her a little in the boat. No one present understood what they said. Her name was Mariequita. She had a round, sly, piquant face and pretty black eyes. Her hands were small, and she kept them folded over the handle of her basket. Her feet were broad and coarse. She did not strive to hide them. Edna looked at her feet, and noticed the sand and slime between her brown toes.

Beaudelet grumbled because Mariequita was there, taking up so much room. In reality he was annoyed at having old Monsieur Farival, who considered himself the better sailor of the two. But he would not quarrel with so old a man as Monsieur Farival, so he quarreled with Mariequita. The girl was deprecatory at one moment, appealing to Robert. She was saucy the next, moving her head up and down, making "eyes" at Robert and making "mouths" at Beaudelet.

The lovers were all alone. They saw nothing, they heard nothing. The lady in black was counting her beads[3] for the third time. Old Monsieur Farival talked incessantly of what he knew about handling a boat, and of what Beaudelet did not know on the same subject.

Edna liked it all. She looked Mariequita up and down, from her ugly brown toes to her pretty black eyes, and back again.

"Why does she look at me like that?" inquired the girl of Robert.

"Maybe she thinks you are pretty. Shall I ask her?"

"No. Is she your sweetheart?"

"She's a married lady, and has two children."

"Oh! well! Francisco ran away with Sylvano's wife, who had four children. They took all his money and one of the children and stole his boat."

"Shut up!"

"Does she understand?"

"Oh, hush!"

"Are those two married over there—leaning on each other?"

"Of course not," laughed Robert.

"Of course not," echoed Mariequita, with a serious, confirmatory bob of the head.

The sun was high up and beginning to bite. The swift breeze seemed to Edna to bury the sting of it into the pores of her face and hands. Robert held his umbrella over her.

As they went cutting sidewise through the water, the sails bellied taut, with the wind filling and overflowing them. Old Monsieur Farival laughed sardonically at something as he looked at the sails, and Beaudelet swore at the old man under his breath.

Sailing across the bay to the *Chênière Caminada*, Edna felt as if she were being borne away from some anchorage which had held her fast, whose chains had been loosening—had snapped the night before when the mystic spirit was abroad, leaving her free to drift whithersoever she chose to set her sails. Robert spoke to her incessantly; he no longer noticed Mariequita. The girl had shrimps in her bamboo basket. They were covered with Spanish moss. She beat the moss impatiently, and muttered to herself sullenly.

"Let us go to Grande Terre[4] to-morrow?" said Robert in a low voice.

"What shall we do there?"

"Climb up the hill to the old fort and look at the little wriggling gold snakes, and watch the lizards sun themselves."

She gazed away toward Grande Terre and thought she would like to be alone there with Robert, in the sun, listening to the ocean's roar and watching the slimy lizards writhe in and out among the ruins of the old fort.

"And the next day or the next we can sail to the Bayou Brulow,"[5] he went on.

"What shall we do there?"

3. I.e., praying.
4. An island near Grande Isle.

5. A nearby village built on stilts or platforms in a marshy area (*bayou*).

"Anything—cast bait for fish."

"No; we'll go back to Grande Terre. Let the fish alone."

"We'll go wherever you like," he said. "I'll have Tonie come over and help me patch and trim my boat. We shall not need Beaudelet nor any one. Are you afraid of the pirogue?"[6]

"Oh, no."

"Then I'll take you some night in the pirogue when the moon shines. Maybe your Gulf spirit will whisper to you in which of these islands the treasures are hidden—direct you to the very spot, perhaps."

"And in a day we should be rich!" she laughed. "I'd give it all to you, the pirate gold and every bit of treasure we could dig up. I think you would know how to spend it. Pirate gold isn't a thing to be hoarded or utilized. It is something to squander and throw to the four winds, for the fun of seeing the golden specks fly."

"We'd share it, and scatter it together," he said. His face flushed.

They all went together up to the quaint little Gothic church of Our Lady of Lourdes, gleaming all brown and yellow with paint in the sun's glare.

Only Beaudelet remained behind, tinkering at his boat, and Mariequita walked away with her basket of shrimps, casting a look of childish ill-humor and reproach at Robert from the corner of her eye.

XIII

A feeling of oppression and drowsiness overcame Edna during the service. Her head began to ache, and the lights on the altar swayed before her eyes. Another time she might have made an effort to regain her composure; but her one thought was to quit the stifling atmosphere of the church and reach the open air. She arose, climbing over Robert's feet with a muttered apology. Old Monsieur Farival flurried, curious, stood up, but upon seeing that Robert had followed Mrs. Pontellier, he sank back into his seat. He whispered an anxious inquiry of the lady in black, who did not notice him or reply, but kept her eyes fastened upon the pages of her velvet prayer-book.

"I felt giddy and almost overcome," Edna said, lifting her hands instinctively to her head and pushing her straw hat up from her forehead. "I couldn't have stayed through the service." They were outside in the shadow of the church. Robert was full of solicitude.

"It was folly to have thought of going in the first place, let alone staying. Come over to Madame Antoine's; you can rest there." He took her arm and led her away, looking anxiously and continuously down into her face.

How still it was, with only the voice of the sea whispering through the reeds that grew in the salt-water pools! The long line of little gray, weather-beaten houses nestled peacefully among the orange trees. It must always have been God's day on that low, drowsy island, Edna thought. They stopped, leaning over a jagged fence made of sea-drift, to ask for water. A youth, a mild-faced Acadian,[7] was drawing water from the cistern, which was nothing more than a rusty buoy, with an opening on one side, sunk in the ground. The water which the youth handed to them in a tin pail was not cold to taste, but it was cool to her heated face, and it greatly revived and refreshed her.

Madame Antoine's cot[8] was at the far end of the village. She welcomed

6. Canoe.
7. A descendant of French-Canadians expelled from Nova Scotia in 1755.
 8 Cottage

them with all the native hospitality, as she would have opened her door to let the sunlight in. She was fat, and walked heavily and clumsily across the floor. She could speak no English, but when Robert made her understand that the lady who accompanied him was ill and desired to rest, she was all eagerness to make Edna feel at home and to dispose of her comfortably.

The whole place was immaculately clean, and the big, four-posted bed, snow-white, invited one to repose. It stood in a small side room which looked out across a narrow grass plot toward the shed, where there was a disabled boat lying keel upward.

Madame Antoine had not gone to mass. Her son Tonie had, but she supposed he would soon be back, and she invited Robert to be seated and wait for him. But he went and sat outside the door and smoked. Madame Antoine busied herself in the large front room preparing dinner. She was boiling mullets[9] over a few red coals in the huge fireplace.

Edna, left alone in the little side room, loosened her clothes, removing the greater part of them. She bathed her face, her neck and arms in the basin that stood between the windows. She took off her shoes and stockings and stretched herself in the very center of the high, white bed. How luxurious it felt to rest thus in a strange, quaint bed, with its sweet country odor of laurel lingering about the sheets and mattress! She stretched her strong limbs that ached a little. She ran her fingers through her loosened hair for a while. She looked at her round arms as she held them straight up and rubbed them one after the other, observing closely, as if it were something she saw for the first time, the fine, firm quality and texture of her flesh. She clasped her hands easily above her head, and it was thus she fell asleep.

She slept lightly at first, half awake and drowsily attentive to the things about her. She could hear Madame Antoine's heavy, scraping tread as she walked back and forth on the sanded floor. Some chickens were clucking outside the windows, scratching for bits of gravel in the grass. Later she half heard the voices of Robert and Tonie talking under the shed. She did not stir. Even her eyelids rested numb and heavily over her sleepy eyes. The voices went on—Tonie's slow, Acadian drawl, Robert's quick, soft, smooth French. She understood French imperfectly unless directly addressed, and the voices were only part of the other drowsy, muffled sounds lulling her.

When Edna awoke it was with the conviction that she had slept long and soundly. The voices were hushed under the shed. Madame Antoine's step was no longer to be heard in the adjoining room. Even the chickens had gone elsewhere to scratch and cluck. The mosquito bar[1] was drawn over her; the old woman had come in while she slept and let down the bar. Edna arose quietly from the bed, and looking between the curtains of the window, she saw by the slanting rays of the sun that the afternoon was far advanced. Robert was out there under the shed, reclining in the shade against the sloping keel of the overturned boat. He was reading from a book. Tonie was no longer with him. She wondered what had become of the rest of the party. She peeped out at him two or three times as she stood washing herself in the little basin between the windows.

Madame Antoine had laid some coarse, clean towels upon a chair, and had placed a box of *poudre de riz*[2] within easy reach. Edna dabbed the powder

9. Small fish.
1. Bar attached to the bedframe holding mosquito
netting.
2. Rice powder or talcum powder.

upon her nose and cheeks as she looked at herself closely in the little distorted mirror which hung on the wall above the basin. Her eyes were bright and wide awake and her face glowed

When she had completed her toilet she walked into the adjoining room. She was very hungry. No one was there. But there was a cloth spread upon the table that stood against the wall, and a cover was laid for one, with a crusty brown loaf and a bottle of wine beside the plate. Edna bit a piece from the brown loaf, tearing it with her strong, white teeth. She poured some of the wine into the glass and drank it down. Then she went softly out of doors, and plucking an orange from the low-hanging bough of a tree, threw it at Robert, who did not know she was awake and up.

And illumination broke over his whole face when he saw her and joined her under the orange tree.

"How many years have I slept?" she inquired. "The whole island seems changed. A new race of beings must have sprung up, leaving only you and me as past relics. How many ages ago did Madame Antoine and Tonie die? and when did our people from Grand Isle disappear from the earth?"

He familiarly adjusted a ruffle upon her shoulder.

"You have slept precisely one hundred years. I was left here to guard your slumbers; and for one hundred years I have been out under the shed reading a book. The only evil I couldn't prevent was to keep a broiled fowl from drying up."

"If it had turned to stone, still will I eat it," said Edna, moving with him into the house. "But really, what has become of Monsieur Farival and the others?"

"Gone hours ago. When they found that you were sleeping they thought it best not to awake you. Anyway, I wouldn't have let them. What was I here for?"

"I wonder if Lèonce will be uneasy!" she speculated, as she seated herself at table.

"Of course not; he knows you are with me," Robert replied, as he busied himself among sundry pans and covered dishes which had been left standing on the hearth.

"Where are Madame Antoine and her son?" asked Edna.

"Gone to Vespers,[3] and to visit some friends, I believe. I am to take you back in Tonie's boat whenever you are ready to go."

He stirred the smoldering ashes till the broiled fowl began to sizzle afresh. He served her with no mean repast, dripping the coffee anew and sharing it with her. Madame Antoine had cooked little else than the mullets, but while Edna slept Robert had foraged the island. He was childishly gratified to discover her appetite, and to see the relish with which she ate the food which he had procured for her.

"Shall we go right away?" she asked, after draining her glass and brushing together the crumbs of the crusty loaf.

"The sun isn't as low as it will be in two hours," he answered.

"The sun will be gone in two hours."

"Well, let it go; who cares!"

They waited a good while under the orange trees, till Madame Antoine came back, panting, waddling, with a thousand apologies to explain her ab-

3. Evening church service.

sence. Tonie did not dare to return. He was shy, and would not willingly face any woman except his mother.

It was very pleasant to stay there under the orange trees, while the sun dipped lower and lower, turning the western sky to flaming copper and gold. The shadows lengthened and crept out like stealthy, grotesque monsters across the grass.

Edna and Robert both sat upon the ground—that is, he lay upon the ground beside her, occasionally picking at the hem of her muslin gown.

Madame Antoine seated her fat body, broad and squat, upon a bench beside the door. She had been talking all the afternoon, and had wound herself up to the story-telling pitch.

And what stories she told them! But twice in her life she had left the *Chênière Caminada*, and then for the briefest span. All her years she had squatted and waddled there upon the island, gathering legends of the Baratarians[4] and the sea. The night came on, with the moon to lighten it. Edna could hear the whispering voices of dead men and the click of muffled gold.

When she and Robert stepped into Tonie's boat, with the red lateen sail, misty spirit forms were prowling in the shadows and among the reeds, and upon the water were phantom ships, speeding to cover.

XIV

The youngest boy, Étienne, had been very naughty, Madame Ratignolle said, as she delivered him into the hands of his mother. He had been unwilling to go to bed and had made a scene; where upon she had taken charge of him and pacified him as well as she could. Raoul had been in bed and asleep for two hours.

The youngster was in his long white nightgown, that kept tripping him up as Madame Ratignolle led him along by the hand. With the other chubby fist he rubbed his eyes, which were heavy with sleep and ill humor. Edna took him in her arms, and seating herself in the rocker, began to coddle and caress him, calling him all manner of tender names, soothing him to sleep.

It was not more than nine o'clock. No one had yet gone to bed but the children.

Léonce had been very uneasy at first, Madame Ratignolle said, and had wanted to start at once for the *Chênière*. But Monsieur Farival had assured him that his wife was only overcome with sleep and fatigue, that Tonie would bring her safely back later in the day; and he had thus been dissuaded from crossing the bay. He had gone over to Klein's, looking up some cotton broker whom he wished to see in regard to securities, exchanges, stocks, bonds, or something of the sort, Madame Ratignolle did not remember what. He said he would not remain away late. She herself was suffering from heat and oppression, she said. She carried a bottle of salts and a large fan. She would not consent to remain with Edna, for Monsieur Ratignolle was alone, and he detested above all things to be left alone.

When Étienne had fallen asleep Edna bore him into the back room, and Robert went and lifted the mosquito bar that she might lay the child comfortably in his bed. The quadroon had vanished. When they emerged from the cottage Robert bade Edna good-night. "Do you know we have been together

4. Pirates who plundered in the area of Barataria Bay.

the whole livelong day, Robert—since early this morning?" she said at parting.

"All but the hundred years when you were sleeping. Good-night."

He pressed her hard and went away in the direction of the beach. He did not join any of the others, but walked alone toward the Gulf.

Edna stayed outside, awaiting her husband's return. She had no desire to sleep or to retire nor did she feel like going over to sit with the Ratignolles, or to join Madame Lebrun and a group whose animated voices reached her as they sat in conversation before the house. She let her mind wander back over her stay at Grand Isle; and she tried to discover wherein this summer had been different from any and every other summer of her life. She could only realize that she herself—her present self—was in some way different from the other self. That she was seeing with different eyes and making the acquaintance of new conditions in herself that colored and changed her environment, she did not yet suspect.

She wondered why Robert had gone away and left her. It did not occur to her to think he might have grown tired of being with her the livelong day. She was not tired and she felt that he was not. She regretted that he had gone. It was so much more natural to have him stay, when he was not absolutely required to leave her.

As Edna waited for her husband she sang low a little song that Robert had sung as they crossed the bay. It began with "Ah! Si tu savais,"[5] and every verse ended with "si tu savais."

Robert's voice was not pretentious. It was musical and true. The voice, the notes, the whole refrain haunted her memory.

XV

When Edna entered the dining-room one evening a little late, as was her habit, an unusually animated conversation seemed to be going on. Several persons were talking at once, and Victor's voice was predominating, even over that of his mother. Edna had returned late from her bath, had dressed in some haste, and her face was flushed. Her head, set off by the dainty white gown, suggested a rich, rare blossom. She took her seat at table between old Monsieur Farival and Madame Ratignolle.

As she seated herself and was about to begin to eat her soup, which had been served when she entered the room, several persons informed her simultaneously that Robert was going to Mexico. She laid her spoon down and looked about her bewildered. He had been with her, reading to her all the morning, and had never even mentioned such a place as Mexico. She had not seen him during the afternoon; she had heard some one say he was at the house, upstairs with his mother. This she had thought nothing of, though she was surprised when he did not join her later in the afternoon, when she went down to the beach.

She looked across at him, where he sat beside Madame Lebrun, who presided. Edna's face was a blank picture of bewilderment, which she never thought of disguising. He lifted his eyebrows with the pretext of a smile as he returned her glance. He looked embarrassed and uneasy.

"When is he going?" she asked of everybody in general, as if Robert were not there to answer for himself.

"To-night!" "This very evening!" "Did you ever!" "What possesses him!"

5. "Couldst Thou but Know," a song by Michael William Balfe (1808–1870).

some of the replies she gathered, uttered simultaneously in French and English.

"Impossible!" she exclaimed. "How can a person start off from Grand Isle to Mexico at a moment's notice, as if he were going over to Klein's or to the wharf or down to the beach?"

"I said all along I was going to Mexico; I've been saying so for years!" cried Robert, in an excited and irritable tone, with the air of a man defending himself against a swarm of stinging insects.

Madame Lebrun knocked on the table with her knife handle.

"Please let Robert explain why he is going, and why he is going to-night," she called out. "Really, this table is getting to be more and more like Bedlam[6] every day, with everybody talking at once. Sometimes—I hope God will forgive me—but positively, sometimes I wish Victor would lose the power of speech."

Victor laughed sardonically as he thanked his mother for her holy wish, of which he failed to see the benefit to anybody, except that it might afford her a more ample opportunity and license to talk herself.

Monsieur Farival thought that Victor should have been taken out in mid-ocean in his earliest youth and drowned. Victor thought there would be more logic in thus disposing of old people with an established claim for making themselves universally obnoxious. Madame Lebrun grew a trifle hysterical; Robert called his brother some sharp, hard names.

"There's nothing much to explain, mother," he said; though he explained, nevertheless—looking chiefly at Edna—that he could only meet the gentleman whom he intended to join at Vera Cruz by taking such and such a steamer, which left New Orleans on such a day; that Beaudelet was going out with his lugger[7]-load of vegetables that night, which gave him an opportunity of reaching the city and making his vessel in time.

"But when did you make up your mind to all this?" demanded Monsieur Farival.

"This afternoon," returned Robert, with a shade of annoyance.

"At what time this afternoon?" persisted the old gentleman, with nagging determination, as if he were cross-questioning a criminal in a court of justice.

"At four o'clock this afternoon. Monsieur Farival," Robert replied, in a high voice and with a lofty air, which reminded Edna of some gentleman on the stage.

She had forced herself to eat most of her soup, and now she was picking the flaky bits of a *court bouillon*[8] with her fork.

The lovers were profiting by the general conversation on Mexico to speak in whispers of matters which they rightly considered were interesting to no one but themselves. The lady in black had once received a pair of prayer-beads of curious workmanship from Mexico, with very special indulgence[9] attached to them, but she had never been able to ascertain whether the indulgence extended outside the Mexican border. Father Fochel of the Cathedral had attempted to explain it; but he had not done so to her satisfaction. And she begged that Robert would interest himself, and discover, if possible, whether

6. Famous lunatic asylum in London, hence any madhouse.
7. A small boat.
8. Broth in which fish is poached.

9. According to a Roman Catholic belief, some religious articles, if specifically blessed, could remit part of the punishment for sins after death.

she was entitled to the indulgence accompanying the remarkably curious Mexican prayer-beads.

Madame Ratignolle hoped that Robert would exercise extreme caution in dealing with the Mexicans, who, she considered were a treacherous people, unscrupulous and revengeful. She trusted she did them no injustice in thus condemning them as a race. She had known personally but one Mexican, who made and sold excellent tamales, and whom she would have trusted implicitly, so soft-spoken was he. One day he was arrested for stabbing his wife. She never knew whether he had been hanged or not.

Victor had grown hilarious, and was attempting to tell an anecdote about a Mexican girl who served chocolate one winter in a restaurant in Dauphine Street. No one would listen to him but old Monsieur Farival, who went into convulsions over the droll story.

Edna wondered if they had all gone mad, to be talking and clamoring at that rate. She herself could think of nothing to say about Mexico or the Mexicans.

"At what time do you leave?" she asked Robert.

"At ten," he told her. "Beaudelet wants to wait for the moon."

"Are you all ready to go?"

"Quite ready. I shall only take a handbag, and shall pack my trunk in the city."

He turned to answer some question put to him by his mother and Edna, having finished her black coffee, left the table.

She went directly to her room. The little cottage was close and stuffy after leaving the outer air. But she did not mind; there appeared to be a hundred different things demanding her attention indoors. She began to set the toilet-stand to rights, grumbling at the negligence of the quadroon, who was in the adjoining room putting the children to bed. She gathered together stray garments that were hanging on the backs of chairs, and put each where it belonged in closet or bureau drawer. She changed her gown for a more comfortable and commodious wrapper. She rearranged her hair, combing and brushing it with unusual energy. Then she went in and assisted the quadroon in getting the boys to bed.

They were very playful and inclined to talk—to do anything but lie quiet and go to sleep. Edna sent the quadroon away to her supper and told her she need not return. Then she sat and told the children a story. Instead of soothing it excited them, and added to their wakefulness. She left them in heated argument, speculating about the conclusion of the tale which their mother promised to finish the following night.

The little black girl came in to say that Madame Lebrun would like to have Mrs. Pontellier go and sit with them over at the house till Mr. Robert went away. Edna returned answer that she had already undressed, that she did not feel quite well, but perhaps she would go over to the house later. She started to dress again, and got as far advanced as to remove her *peignoir*. But changing her mind once more she resumed the *peignoir*, and went outside and sat down before her door. She was overheated and irritable, and fanned herself energetically for a while. Madame Ratignolle came down to discover what was the matter.

"All that noise and confusion at the table must have upset me," replied Edna, "and moreover, I hate shocks and surprises. The idea of Robert starting off in such a ridiculously sudden and dramatic way! As if it were a matter of

life and death! Never saying a word about it all morning when he was with me."

"Yes," agreed Madame Ratignolle. "I think it was showing us all—you especially—very little consideration. It wouldn't have surprised me in any of the others; those Lebruns are all given to heroics. But I must say I should never have expected such a thing from Robert. Are you not coming down? Come on, dear; it doesn't look friendly."

"No," said Edna, a little sullenly. "I can't go to the trouble of dressing again; I don't feel like it."

"You needn't dress; you look all right; fasten a belt around your waist. Just look at me!"

"No," persisted Edna; "but you go on. Madame Lebrun might be offended if we both stayed away."

Madame Ratignolle kissed Edna good-night, and went away, being in truth rather desirous of joining in the general and animated conversation which was still in progress concerning Mexico and the Mexicans.

Somewhat later Robert came up, carrying his hand-bag.

"Aren't you feeling well?" he asked.

"Oh, well enough. Are you going right away?"

He lit a match and looked at his watch. "In twenty minutes," he said. The sudden and brief flare of the match emphasized the darkness for a while. He sat down upon a stool which the children had left out on the porch.

"Get a chair," said Edna.

"This will do," he replied. He put on his soft hat and nervously took it off again, and wiping his face with his handkerchief, complained of the heat.

"Take the fan," said Edna, offering it to him.

"Oh, no! Thank you. It does no good; you have to stop fanning some time, and feel all the more uncomfortable afterward."

"That's one of the ridiculous things which men always say. I have never known one to speak otherwise of fanning. How long will you be gone?"

"Forever, perhaps. I don't know. It depends upon a good many things."

"Well, in case it shouldn't be forever, how long will it be?"

"I don't know."

"This seems to me perfectly preposterous and uncalled for. I don't like it. I don't understand your motive for silence and mystery, never saying a word to me about it this morning." He remained silent, not offering to defend himself. He only said, after a moment:

"Don't part from me in an ill-humor. I never knew you to be out of patience with me before."

"I don't want to part in any ill-humor," said she. "But can't you understand? I've grown used to seeing you, to having you with me all the time, and your action seems unfriendly, even unkind. You don't even offer an excuse for it. Why, I was planning to be together, thinking of how pleasant it would be to see you in the city next winter."

"So was I," he blurted. "Perhaps that's the—" He stood up suddenly and held out his hand. "Good-by, my dear Mrs. Pontellier; good-by. You won't—I hope you won't completely forget me." She clung to his hand, striving to detain him.

"Write to me when you get there, won't you, Robert?" she entreated.

"I will, thank you. Good-by."

How unlike Robert! The merest acquaintance would have said something more emphatic than " will, thank you; good-by," to such a request.

He had evidently already taken leave of the people over at the house, for he descended the steps and went to join Beaudelet, who was out there with an oar across his shoulder waiting for Robert. They walked away in the darkness. She could only hear Beaudelet's voice; Robert had apparently not even spoken a word of greeting to his companion.

Edna bit her handkerchief convulsively, striving to hold back and to hide, even from herself as she would have hidden from another the emotion which was troubling—tearing—her. Her eyes were brimming with tears.

For the first time she recognized anew the symptoms of infatuation which she felt incipiently as a child, as a girl in her earliest teens, and later as a young woman. The recognition did not lessen the reality, the poignancy of the revelation by any suggestion or promise of instability. The past was nothing to her; offered no lesson which she was willing to heed. The future was a mystery which she never attempted to penetrate. The present alone was significant; was hers, to torture her as it was doing then with the biting conviction that she had lost that which she had held, that she had been denied that which her impassioned, newly awakened being demanded.

XVI

"Do you miss your friend greatly?" asked Mademoiselle Reisz one morning as she came creeping up behind Edna, who had just left her cottage on her way to the beach. She spent much of her time in the water since she had acquired finally the art of swimming. As their stay at Grand Isle drew near its close, she felt that she could not give too much time to a diversion which afforded her the only real pleasurable moments that she knew. When Mademoiselle Reisz came and touched her upon the shoulder and spoke to her, the woman seemed to echo the thought which was ever in Edna's mind; or, better, the feeling which constantly possessed her.

Robert's going had some way taken the brightness, the color, the meaning out of everything. The conditions of her life were in no way changed, but her whole existence was dulled, like a faded garment which seems to be no longer worth wearing. She sought him everywhere—in others whom she induced to talk about him. She went up in the mornings to Madame Lebrun's room, braving the clatter of the old sewing-machine. She sat there and chatted at intervals as Robert had done. She gazed around the room at the pictures and photographs hanging upon the wall, and discovered in some corner an old family album, which she examined with the keenest interest, appealing to Madame Lebrun for enlightenment concerning the many figures and faces which she discovered between its pages.

There was a picture of Madame Lebrun with Robert as a baby, seated in her lap, a round-faced infant with a fist in his mouth. The eyes alone in the baby suggested the man. And that was he also in kilts, at the age of five, wearing long curls and holding a whip in his hand. It made Edna laugh, and she laughed, too, at the portrait in his first long trousers; while another interested her, taken when he left for college, looking thin, long-faced, with eyes full of fire, ambition and great intentions. But there was no recent picture, none

which suggested the Robert who had gone away five days ago, leaving a void and wilderness behind him.

"Oh, Robert stopped having his pictures taken when he had to pay for them himself! He found wiser use for his money, he says," explained Madame Lebrun. She had a letter from him, written before he left New Orleans. Edna wished to see the letter, and Madame Lebrun told her to look for it either on the table or the dresser, or perhaps it was on the mantelpiece.

The letter was on the bookshelf. It possessed the greatest interest and attraction for Edna; the envelope, its size and shape, the postmark, the handwriting. She examined every detail of the outside before opening it. There were only a few lines, setting forth that he would leave the city that afternoon, that he had packed his trunk in good shape, that he was well, and sent her his love and begged to be affectionately remembered to all. There was no special message to Edna except a postscript saying that if Mrs. Pontellier desired to finish the book which he had been reading to her, his mother would find it in his room, among other books there on the table. Edna experienced a pang of jealousy because he had written to his mother rather than to her.

Every one seemed to take for granted that she missed him. Even her husband, when he came down the Saturday following Robert's departure, expressed regret that he had gone.

"How do you get on without him, Edna?" he asked.

"It's very dull without him," she admitted. Mr. Pontellier had seen Robert in the city, and Edna asked him a dozen questions or more. Where had they met? On Carondelet Street, in the morning. They had gone "in" and had a drink and a cigar together. What had they talked about? Chiefly about his prospects in Mexico, which Mr. Pontellier thought were promising. How did he look? How did he seem—grave, or gay, or how? Quite cheerful, and wholly taken up with the idea of his trip, which Mr. Pontellier found altogether natural in a young fellow about to seek fortune and adventure in a strange, queer country.

Edna tapped her foot impatiently, and wondered why the children persisted in playing in the sun when they might be under the trees. She went down and led them out of the sun, scolding the quadroon for not being more attentive.

It did not strike her as in the least grotesque that she should be making of Robert the object of conversation and leading her husband to speak of him. The sentiment which she entertained for Robert in no way resembled that which she felt for her husband, or had ever felt, or ever expected to feel. She had all her life long been accustomed to harbor thoughts and emotions which never voiced themselves. They had never taken the form of struggles. They belonged to her and were her own, and she entertained the conviction that she had a right to them and that they concerned no one but herself. Edna had once told Madame Ratignolle that she would never sacrifice herself for her children, or for any one. Then had followed a rather heated argument; the two women did not appear to understand each other or to be talking the same language. Edna tried to appease her friend, to explain.

"I would give up the unessential; I would give my money. I would give my life for my children; but I wouldn't give myself. I can't make it more clear; it's only something which I am beginning to comprehend, which is revealing itself to me."

"I don't know what you would call the essential, or what you mean by the

unessential," said Madame Ratignolle, cheerfully; 'but a woman who would give her life for her children could do no more than that—your Bible tells you so. I'm sure I couldn't do more than that."

"Oh, yes you could!" laughed Edna.

She was not surprised at Mademoiselle Reisz's question the morning that lady, following her to the beach, tapped her on the shoulder and asked if she did not greatly miss her young friend.

"Oh, good morning, Mademoiselle; it is you? Why, of course I miss Robert. Are you going down to bathe?"

"Why should I go down to bathe at the very end of the season when I haven't been in the surf all summer?" replied the woman, disagreeably.

"I beg your pardon," offered Edna, in some embarrassment, for she should have remembered that Mademoiselle Reisz's avoidance of the water had furnished a theme for much pleasantry. Some among them thought it was on account of her false hair, or the dread of getting the violets wet, while others attributed it to the natural aversion for water sometimes believed to accompany the artistic temperament. Mademoiselle offered Edna some chocolates in a paper bag, which she took from her pocket, by way of showing that she bore no ill feeling. She habitually ate chocolates for their sustaining quality; they contained much nutriment in small compass, she said. They saved her from starvation, as Madame Lebrun's table was utterly impossible; and no one save so impertinent a woman as Madame Lebrun could think of offering such food to people and requiring them to pay for it.

"She must feel very lonely without her son," said Edna, desiring to change the subject. "Her favorite son, too. It must have been quite hard to let him go."

Mademoiselle laughed maliciously.

"Her favorite son! Oh dear! Who could have been imposing such a tale upon you? Aline Lebrun lives for Victor, and for Victor alone. She has spoiled him into the worthless creature he is. She worships him and the ground he walks on. Robert is very well in a way, to give up all the money he can earn to the family, and keep the barest pittance for himself. Favorite son, indeed! I miss the poor fellow myself, my dear. I liked to see him and to hear him about the place—the only Lebrun who is worth a pinch of salt. He comes to see me often in the city. I like to play to him. That Victor! hanging would be too good for him. It's a wonder Robert hasn't beaten him to death long ago."

"I thought he had great patience with his brother," offered Edna, glad to be talking about Robert, no matter what was said.

"Oh! he thrashed him well enough a year or two ago," said Mademoiselle. "It was about a Spanish girl, whom Victor considered that he had some sort of claim upon. He met Robert one day talking to the girl, or walking with her, or bathing with her, or carrying her basket—I don't remember what;—and he became so insulting and abusive that Robert gave him a thrashing on the spot that has kept him comparatively in order for a good while. It's about time he was getting another."

"Was her name Mariequita?" asked Edna.

"Mariequita—yes, that was it. Mariequita. I had forgotten. Oh, she's a sly one, and a bad one, that Mariequita!"

Edna looked down at Mademoiselle Reisz and wondered how she could have listened to her venom so long. For some reason she felt depressed, almost

unhappy. She had not intended to go into the water; but she donned her bathing suit, and left Mademoiselle alone, seated under the shade of the children's tent. The water was growing cooler as the season advanced. Edna plunged and swam about with an abandon that thrilled and invigorated her. She remained a long time in the water, half hoping that Mademoiselle Reisz would not wait for her.

But Mademoiselle waited. She was very amiable during the walk back, and raved much over Edna's appearance in her bathing suit. She talked about music. She hoped that Edna would go to see her in the city, and wrote her address with the stub of a pencil on a piece of card which she found in her pocket.

"When do you leave?" asked Edna.

"Next Monday; and you?"

"The following week," answered Edna, adding, "It has been a pleasant summer, hasn't it, Mademoiselle?"

"Well," agreed Mademoiselle Reisz, with a shrug, "rather pleasant, if it hadn't been for the mosquitoes and the Farival twins."

XVII

The Pontelliers possessed a very charming home on Esplanade Street[1] in New Orleans. It was a large, double cottage, with a broad front veranda, whose round, fluted columns supported the sloping roof. The house was painted a dazzling white; the outside shutters, or jalousies, were green. In the yard, which was kept scrupulously neat, were flowers and plants of every description which flourishes in South Louisiana. Within doors the appointments were perfect after the conventional type. The softest carpets and rugs covered the floors; rich and tasteful draperies hung at doors and windows. There were paintings, selected with judgment and discrimination, upon the walls. The cut glass, the silver, the heavy damask which daily appeared upon the table were the envy of many women whose husbands were less generous than Mr. Pontellier.

Mr. Pontellier was very fond of walking about his house examining its various appointments and details, to see that nothing was amiss. He greatly valued his possessions, chiefly because they were his, and derived genuine pleasure from contemplating a painting, a statuette, a rare lace curtain—no matter what—after he had bought it and placed it among his household goods.

On Tuesday afternoons—Tuesday being Mrs. Pontellier's reception day[2]—there was a constant stream of callers—women who came in carriages or in the street cars, or walked when the air was soft and distance permitted. A light-colored mulatto boy, in dress coat and bearing a diminutive silver tray for the reception of cards, admitted them. A maid, in white fluted cap, offered the callers liqueur, coffee, or chocolate, as they might desire. Mrs. Pontellier, attired in a handsome reception gown, remained in the drawing-room the entire afternoon receiving her visitors. Men sometimes called in the evening with their wives.

This had been the programme which Mrs. Pontellier had religiously fol-

1. The most exclusive address of the Creole aristocracy. 2. The day when a woman was "at home" to receive visitors.

lowed since her marriage, six years before. Certain evenings during the week she and her husband attended the opera or sometimes the play.

Mr. Pontellier left his home in the mornings between nine and ten o'clock, and rarely returned before half-past six or seven in the evening—dinner being served at half-past seven.

He and his wife seated themselves at table on Tuesday evening, a few weeks after their return from Grand Isle. They were alone together. The boys were being put to bed; the patter of their bare, escaping feet could be heard occasionally, as well as the pursuing voice of the quadroon, lifted in mild protest and entreaty. Mrs Pontellier did not wear her usual Tuesday reception gown; she was in ordinary house dress. Mr. Pontellier who was observant about such things, noticed it, as he served the soup and handed it to the boy in waiting.

"Tired out, Edna? Whom did you have? Many callers?" he asked. He tasted his soup and began to season it with pepper, salt, vinegar, mustard—everything within reach.

"There were a good many," replied Edna, who was eating her soup with evident satisfaction. "I found their cards when I got home; I was out."

"Out!" exclaimed her husband, with something like genuine consternation in his voice as he laid down the vinegar cruet and looked at her through his glasses. "Why, what could have taken you out on Tuesday? What did you have to do?"

"Nothing. I simply felt like going out, and I went out."

"Well, I hope you left some suitable excuse," said her husband, somewhat appeased, as he added a dash of cayenne pepper to the soup.

"No, I left no excuse. I told Joe to say I was out, that was all."

"Why, my dear, I should think you'd understand by this time that people don't do such things; we've got to observe *les convenances*[3] if we ever expect to get on and keep up with procession. If you felt that you had to leave home this afternoon, you should have left some suitable explanation for your absence.

"This soup is really impossible; it's strange that woman hasn't learned yet to make a decent soup. Any free-lunch stand in town serves a better one. Was Mrs. Belthrop here?"

"Bring the tray with the cards, Joe. I don't remember who was here."

The boy retired and returned after a moment, bringing the tiny silver tray, which was covered with ladies' visiting cards. He handed it to Mrs. Pontellier.

"Give it to Mr. Pontellier," she said.

Joe offered the tray to Mr. Pontellier, and removed the soup.

Mr. Pontellier scanned the names of his wife's callers, reading some of them aloud, with comments as he read.

"'The Misses Delasidas.' I worked a big deal in futures[4] for their father this morning; nice girls; it's time they were getting married. 'Mrs. Belthrop.' I tell you what it is, Edna; you can't afford to snub Mrs. Belthrop. Why, Belthrop could buy and sell us ten times over. His business is worth a good, round sum to me. You'd better write her a note. 'Mrs. James Highcamp.' Hugh! the less you have to do with Mrs. Highcamp, the better. 'Madame Laforcé.' Came all the way from Carrolton,[5] too, poor old soul. 'Miss Wiggs,' 'Mrs. Eleanor Boltons.' " He pushed the cards aside.

3. The conventions.
4. A form of financial speculation.
5. Village to the west of New Orleans

"Mercy!" exclaimed Edna, who had been fuming. "Why are you taking the thing so seriously and making such a fuss over it?"

"I'm not making any fuss over it. But it's just such seeming trifles that we've got to take seriously; such things count."

The fish was scorched. Mr. Pontellier would not touch it. Edna said she did not mind a little scorched taste. The roast was in some way not to his fancy, and he did not like the manner in which the vegetables were served.

"It seems to me," he said, "we spend money enough in this house to procure at least one meal a day which a man could eat and retain his self-respect."

"You used to think the cook was a treasure," returned Edna, indifferently.

"Perhaps she was when she first came; but cooks are only human. They need looking after, like any other class of persons that you employ. Suppose I didn't look after the clerks in my office, just let them run things their own way; they'd soon make a nice mess of me and my business."

"Where are you going?" asked Edna, seeing that her husband arose from table without having eaten a morsel except a taste of the highly-seasoned soup.

"I'm going to get my dinner at the club. Good night." He went into the hall, took his hat and stick from the stand, and left the house.

She was somewhat familiar with such scenes. They had often made her very unhappy. On a few previous occasions she had been completely deprived of any desire to finish her dinner. Sometimes she had gone into the kitchen to administer a tardy rebuke to the cook. Once she went to her room and studied the cookbook during an entire evening, finally writing out a menu for the week, which left her harassed with a feeling that, after all, she had accomplished no good that was worth the name.

But that evening Edna finished her dinner alone, with forced deliberation. Her face was flushed and her eyes flamed with some inward fire that lighted them. After finishing her dinner she went to her room, having instructed the boy to tell any other callers that she was indisposed.

It was a large, beautiful room, rich and picturesque in the soft, dim light which the maid had turned low. She went and stood at an open window and looked out upon the deep tangle of the garden below. All the mystery and witchery of the night seemed to have gathered there amid the perfumes and the dusky and tortuous outlines of flowers and foliage. She was seeking herself and finding herself in just such sweet, half-darkness which met her moods. But the voices were not soothing that came to her from the darkness and the sky above and the stars. They jeered and sounded mournful notes without promise, devoid even of hope. She turned back into the room and began to walk to and fro down its whole length, without stopping, without resting. She carried in her hands a thin handkerchief, which she tore into ribbons, rolled into a ball, and flung from her. Once she stopped, and taking off her wedding ring, flung it upon the carpet. When she saw it lying there, she stamped her heel upon it, striving to crush it. But her small boot heel did not make an indenture, not a mark upon the little glittering circlet.

In a sweeping passion she seized a glass vase from the table and flung it upon the tiles of the hearth. She wanted to destroy something. The crash and clatter were what she wanted to hear.

A maid, alarmed at the din of breaking glass, entered the room to discover what was the matter.

"A vase fell upon the hearth," said Edna "Never mind; leave it till morn-
ing."

"Oh! you might get some of the glass in your feet, ma'am," insisted the
young woman, picking up bits of the broken vase that were scattered upon the
carpet. "And here's your ring, ma'am, under the chair."

Edna held out her hand, and taking the ring, slipped it upon her finger.

XVIII

The following morning Mr. Pontellier, upon leaving for his office, asked
Edna if she would not meet him in town in order to look at some new fixtures
for the library.

"I hardly think we need new fixtures, Léonce. Don't let us get anything new;
you are too extravagant. I don't believe you ever think of saving or putting by."

"The way to become rich is to make money, my dear Edna, not to save it,"
he said. He regretted that she did not feel inclined to go with him and select
new fixtures. He kissed her good-by, and told her she was not looking well and
must take care of herself. She was unusually pale and very quiet.

She stood on the front veranda as he quitted the house, and absently picked
a few sprays of jessamine that grew upon a trellis near by. She inhaled the odor
of the blossoms and thrust them into the bosom of her white morning gown.
The boys were dragging along the banquette[6] a small "express wagon," which
they had filled with block and sticks. The quadroon was following them with
little quick steps, having assumed a fictitious animation and alacrity for the
occasion. A fruit vender was crying his wares in the street.

Edna looked straight before her with a self-absorbed expression upon her
face. She felt no interest in anything about her The street, the children, the
fruit vender, the flowers growing there under her eyes, were all part and parcel
of an alien world which had suddenly become antagonistic.

She went back into the house. She had thought of speaking to the cook con-
cerning her blunders of the previous night, but Mr. Pontellier had saved her
that disagreeable mission, for which she was so poorly fitted. Mr. Pontellier's
arguments were usually convincing with those whom he employed. He left
home feeling quite sure that he and Edna would sit down that evening, and
possibly a few subsequent evenings, to a dinner deserving of the name.

Edna spent an hour or two in looking over some of her old sketches. She
could see their shortcomings and defects, which were glaring in her eyes. She
tried to work a little, but found she was not in the humor. Finally she gathered
together a few of the sketches—those which she considered the least discred-
itable; and she carried them with her when, a little later, she dressed and left
the house. She looked handsome and distinguished in her street gown. The
tan of the seashore had left her face, and her forehead was smooth, white, and
polished beneath her heavy, yellow-brown hair There were a few freckles on
her face, and a small, dark mole near the under lip and one on the temple,
half-hidden in her hair.

As Edna walked along the street she was thinking of Robert. She was still
under the spell of her infatuation. She had tried to forget him, realizing the in-
utility of remembering. But the thought of him was like an obsession, ever
pressing itself upon her. It was not that she dwelt upon details of their ac-

6. Sidewalk. "Jessamine": jasmine.

quaintance, or recalled in any special or peculiar way his personality; it was his being, his existence, which dominated her thought, fading sometimes as if it would melt into the mist of the forgotten, reviving again with an intensity which filled her with an incomprehensible longing.

Edna was on her way to Madame Ratignolle's. Their intimacy, begun at Grand Isle, had not declined, and they had seen each other with some frequency since their return to the city. The Ratignolles lived at no great distance from Edna's home, on the corner of a side street, where Monsieur Ratignolle owned and conducted a drug store which enjoyed a steady and prosperous trade. His father had been in the business before him, and Monsieur Ratignolle stood well in the community and bore an enviable reputation for integrity and clear-headedness. His family lived in commodious apartments over the store, having an entrance on the side within the *porte cochère*.[7] There was something which Edna thought very French, very foreign, about their whole manner of living. In the large and pleasant salon which extended across the width of the house, the Ratignolles entertained their friends once a fort-night with a *soirée musicale*,[8] sometimes diversified by card-playing. There was a friend who played upon the 'cello. One brought his flute and another his violin, while there were some who sang and a number who performed upon the piano with various degrees of taste and agility. The Ratignolles' *soirées musicales* were widely known, and it was considered a privilege to be invited to them.

Edna found her friend engaged in assorting the clothes which had returned that morning from the laundry. She at once abandoned her occupation upon seeing Edna, who had been ushered without ceremony into her presence.

" 'Cité can do it as well as I; it is really her business," she explained to Edna, who apologized for interrupting her. And she summoned a young black woman, whom she instructed, in French, to be very careful in checking off the list which she handed her. She told her to notice particularly if a fine linen handkerchief of Monsieur Ratignolle's, which was missing last week, had been returned; and to be sure to set to one side such pieces as required mending and darning.

Then placing an arm around Edna's waist, she led her to the front of the house, to the salon, where it was cool and sweet with the odor of great roses that stood upon the hearth in jars.

Madame Ratignolle looked more beautiful than ever there at home, in a negligé which left her arms almost wholly bare and exposed the rich, melting curves of her white throat.

"Perhaps I shall be able to paint your picture some day," said Edna with a smile when they were seated. She produced the roll of sketches and started to unfold them. "I believe I ought to work again. I feel as if I wanted to be doing something. What do you think of them? Do you think it worth while to take it up again and study some more? I might study for a while with Laidpore."

She knew that Madame Ratignolle's opinion in such a matter would be next to valueless, that she herself had not alone decided, but determined; but she sought the words and praise and encouragement that would help her to put her heart into her venture.

"Your talent is immense, dear!"

7. Porch that protects travelers alighting from or boarding a coach. 8. Musical evening.

"Nonsense!" protested Edna, well pleased

"Immense, I tell you," persisted Madame Ratignolle, surveying the sketches one by one, at close range, then holding them at arm's length, narrowing her eyes, and dropping her head on one side. "Surely, this Bavarian peasant is worthy of framing; and this basket of apples! never have I seen anything more lifelike. One might almost be tempted to reach out a hand and take one."

Edna could not control a feeling which bordered upon complacency at her friend's praise, even realizing, as she did, its true worth. She retained a few of the sketches, and gave all the rest to Madame Ratignolle, who appreciated the gift far beyond its value and proudly exhibited the pictures to her husband when he came up from the store a little later for his midday dinner.

Mr. Ratignolle was one of those men who are called the salt of the earth. His cheerfulness was unbounded, and it was matched by his goodness of heart, his broad charity, and common sense. He and his wife spoke English with an accent which was only discernible through its un-English emphasis and a certain carefulness and deliberation. Edna's husband spoke English with no accent whatever. The Ratignolles understood each other perfectly. If ever the fusion of two human beings into one has been accomplished on this sphere it was surely in their union.

As Edna seated herself at table with them she thought, "Better a dinner of herbs,"[9] though it did not take her long to discover that was no dinner of herbs, but a delicious repast, simple, choice, and in every way satisfying.

Monsieur Ratignolle was delighted to see her, though he found her looking not so well as at Grand Isle, and he advised a tonic. He talked a good deal on various topics, a little politics, some city news and neighborhood gossip. He spoke with an animation and earnestness that gave an exaggerated importance to every syllable he uttered. His wife was keenly interested in everything he said, laying down her fork the better to listen, chiming in, taking the words out of his mouth.

Edna felt depressed rather than soothed after leaving them. The little glimpse of domestic harmony which had been offered her, gave her no regret, no longing. It was not a condition of life which fitted her, and she could see in it but an appalling and hopeless ennui.[1] She was moved by a kind of commiseration for Madame Ratignolle,—a pity for that colorless existence which never uplifted its possessor beyond the region of blind contentment, in which no moment of anguish ever visited her soul, in which she would never have the taste of life's delirium. Edna vaguely wondered what she meant by "life's delirium." It had crossed her thought like some unsought, extraneous impression.

XIX

Edna could not help but think that it was very foolish, very childish, to have stamped upon her wedding ring and smashed the crystal vase upon the tiles. She was visited by no more outbursts, moving her to such futile expedients. She began to do as she liked and to feel as she liked. She completely abandoned her Tuesdays at home, and did not return the visits of those who had called upon her. She made no ineffectual efforts to conduct her household *en*

9. "Better is a dinner of herbs where love is, than a 1. Boredom
stalled ox and hatred therewith" (Proverbs 15:17)

bonne ménagère,[2] going and coming as it suited her fancy, and, so far as she was able, lending herself to any passing caprice.

Mr. Pontellier had been a rather courteous husband so long as he met a certain tacit submissiveness in his wife. But her new and unexpected line of conduct completely bewildered him. It shocked him. Then her absolute disregard for her duties as a wife angered him. When Mr. Pontellier became rude, Edna grew insolent. She had resolved never to take another step backward.

"It seems to me the utmost folly for a woman at the head of a household, and the mother of children, to spend in an atelier[3] days which would be better employed contriving for the comfort of her family."

"I feel like painting," answered Edna. "Perhaps I shan't always feel like it."

"Then in God's name paint! but don't let the family go to the devil. There's Madame Ratignolle; because she keeps up her music, she doesn't let everything go to chaos. And she's more of a musician than you are a painter."

"She isn't a musician, and I'm not a painter. It isn't on account of painting that I let things go."

"On account of what, then?"

"Oh! I don't know. Let me alone; you bother me."

It sometimes entered Mr. Pontellier's mind to wonder if his wife were not growing a little unbalanced mentally. He could see plainly that she was not herself. That is, he could not see that she was becoming herself and daily casting aside that fictitious self which we assume like a garment with which to appear before the world.

Her husband let her alone as she requested, and went away to his office. Edna went up to her atelier—a bright room in the top of the house. She was working with great energy and interest, without accomplishing anything, however, which satisfied her even in the smallest degree. For a time she had the whole household enrolled in the service of art. The boys posed for her. They thought it amusing at first, but the occupation soon lost its attractiveness when they discovered that it was not a game arranged especially for their entertainment. The quadroon sat for hours before Edna's palette, patient as a savage, while the housemaid took charge of the children, and the drawing-room went undusted. But the house-maid, too, served her term as model when Edna perceived that the young woman's back and shoulders were molded on classic lines, and that her hair, loosened from its confining cap, became an inspiration. While Edna worked she sometimes sang low the little air, "Ah! si tu savais!"

It moved her with recollections. She could hear again the ripple of the water, the flapping sail. She could see the glint of the moon upon the bay, and could feel the soft, gusty beating of the hot south wind. A subtle current of desire passed through her body, weakening her hold upon the brushes and making her eyes burn.

There were days when she was very happy without knowing why. She was happy to be alive and breathing, when her whole being seemed to be one with the sunlight, the color, the odors, the luxuriant warmth of some perfect Southern day. She liked then to wander alone into strange and unfamiliar places. She discovered many a sunny, sleepy corner, fashioned to dream in. And she found it good to dream and to be alone and unmolested.

2. As a good housewife. 3. Studio.

There were days when she' was unhappy, she did not know why,—when it did not seem worth while to be glad or sorry, to be alive or dead; when life appeared to her like a grotesque pandemonium and humanity like worms struggling blindly toward inevitable annihilation. She could not work on such a day, nor weave fancies to stir her pulses and warm her blood.

XX

It was during such a mood that Edna hunted up Mademoiselle Reisz. She had not forgotten the rather disagreeable impression left upon her by their last interview; but she nevertheless felt a desire to see her—above all, to listen while she played upon the piano. Quite early in the afternoon she started upon her quest for the pianist. Unfortunately she had mislaid or lost Mademoiselle Reisz's card, and looking up her address in the city directory, she found that the woman lived on Bienville Street, some distance away. The directory which fell into her hands was a year or more old, however, and upon reaching the number indicated, Edna discovered that the house was occupied by a respectable family of mulattoes who had *chambres garnies*[4] to let. They had been living there for six months, and knew absolutely nothing of a Mademoiselle Reisz. In fact, they knew nothing of any of their neighbors; their lodgers were all people of the highest distinction, they assured Edna. She did not linger to discuss class distinctions with Madame Pouponne, but hastened to a neighboring grocery store, feeling sure that Mademoiselle would have left her address with the proprietor.

He knew Mademoiselle Reisz a good deal better than he wanted to know her, he informed his questioner. In truth, he did not want to know her at all, anything concerning her—the most disagreeable and unpopular woman who ever lived in Bienville Street. He thanked heaven she had left the neighborhood, and was equally thankful that he did not know where she had gone.

Edna's desire to see Mademoiselle Reisz had increased tenfold since these unlooked for obstacles had arisen to thwart it. She was wondering who could give her the information she sought, when it suddenly occurred to her that Madame Lebrun would be the one most likely to do so. She knew it was useless to ask Madame Ratignolle, who was on the most distant terms with the musician, and preferred to know nothing concerning her. She had once been almost as emphatic in expressing herself upon the subject as the corner grocer.

Edna knew that Madame Lebrun had returned to the city, for it was the middle of November. And she also knew where the Lebruns lived, on Chartres Street.

Their home from the outside looked like a prison, with iron bars before the door and lower windows. The iron bars were a relic of the old *régime*,[5] and no one had ever thought of dislodging them. At the side was a high fence enclosing the garden. A gate or door opening upon the street was locked. Edna rang the bell at this side garden gate, and stood upon the banquette, waiting to be admitted.

It was Victor who opened the gate for her. A black woman, wiping her hands upon her apron, was close at his heels. Before she saw them Edna could hear them in altercation, the woman—plainly an anomaly—claiming the right to be allowed to perform her duties, one of which was to answer the bell.

4. Furnished rooms. 5. I.e., the Spanish regime (1766–1803).

Victor was surprised and delighted to see Mrs. Pontellier, and he made no attempt to conceal either his astonishment or his delight. He was a dark-browed, good-looking youngster of nineteen, greatly resembling his mother, but with ten times her impetuosity. He instructed the black woman to go at once and inform Madame Lebrun that Mrs. Pontellier desired to see her. The woman grumbled a refusal to do part of her duty when she had not been permitted to do it all, and started back to her interrupted task of weeding the garden. Whereupon Victor administered a rebuke in the form of a volley of abuse, which owing to its rapidity and incoherence, was all but incomprehensible to Edna. Whatever it was, the rebuke was convincing, for the woman dropped her hoe and went mumbling into the house.

Edna did not wish to enter. It was very pleasant there on the side porch, where there were chairs, a wicker lounge, and a small table. She seated herself, for she was tired from her long tramp; and she began to rock gently and smooth out the folds of her silk parasol. Victor drew up his chair beside her. He at once explained that the black woman's offensive conduct was all due to imperfect training, as he was not there to take her in hand. He had only come up from the island the morning before, expected to return next day. He stayed all winter at the island; he lived there, and kept the place in order and got things ready for the summer visitors.

But a man needed occasional relaxation, he informed Mrs. Pontellier, and every now and again he drummed up a pretext to bring him to the city. My! but he had had a time of it the evening before! He wouldn't want his mother to know, and he began to talk in a whisper. He was scintillant[6] with recollections. Of course, he couldn't think of telling Mrs. Pontellier all about it, she being a woman and not comprehending such things. But it all began with a girl peeping and smiling at him through the shutters as he passed by. Oh! but she was a beauty! Certainly he smiled back, and went up and talked to her. Mrs. Pontellier did not know him if she supposed he was one to let an opportunity like that escape him. Despite herself, the youngster amused her. She must have betrayed in her look some degree of interest or entertainment. The boy grew more daring, and Mrs. Pontellier might have found herself, in a little while, listening to a highly colored story but for the timely appearance of Madame Lebrun.

That lady was still clad in white, according to her custom of the summer. Her eyes beamed an effusive welcome. Would not Mrs. Pontellier go inside? Would she partake of some refreshment? Why had she not been there before? How was that dear Mr. Pontellier and how were those sweet children? Had Mrs. Pontellier ever known such a warm November?

Victor went and reclined on the wicker lounge behind his mother's chair, where he commanded a view of Edna's face. He had taken her parasol from her hands while he spoke to her, and he now lifted it and twirled it above him as he lay on his back. When Madame Lebrun complained that it was so dull coming back to the city; that she saw so few people now; that even Victor, when he came up from the island for a day or two, had so much to occupy him and engage his time, then it was that the youth went into contortions on the lounge and winked mischievously at Edna. She somehow felt like a confederate in crime, and tried to look severe and disapproving.

6. Sparkling.

There had been but two letters from Robert, with little in them they told her. Victor said it was really not worth while to go inside for the letters, when his mother entreated him to go in search of them. He remembered the contents, which in truth he rattled off very glibly when put to the test.

One letter was written from Vera Cruz and the other from the City of Mexico. He had met Montel, who was doing everything toward his advancement. So far, the financial situation was no improvement over the one he had left in New Orleans, but of course the prospects were vastly better. He wrote of the City of Mexico, the buildings, the people and their habits, the conditions of life which he found there. He sent his love to the family. He inclosed a check to his mother, and hoped she would affectionately remember him to all his friends. That was about the substance of the two letters. Edna felt that if there had been a message for her, she would have received it. The despondent frame of mind in which she had left home began again to overtake her, and she remembered that she wished to find Mademoiselle Reisz.

Madame Lebrun knew where Mademoiselle Reisz lived. She gave Edna the address, regretting that she would not consent to stay and spend the remainder of the afternoon, and pay a visit to Mademoiselle Reisz some other day. The afternoon was already well advanced.

Victor escorted her out upon the banquette, lifted her parasol, and held it over her while he walked to the car with her. He entreated her to bear in mind that the disclosures of the afternoon were strictly confidential. She laughed and bantered him a little, remembering too late that she should have been dignified and reserved.

"How handsome Mrs. Pontellier looked!" said Madame Lebrun to her son.

"Ravishing!" he admitted. "The city atmosphere has improved her. Some way she doesn't seem like the same woman."

XXI

Some people contended that the reason Mademoiselle Reisz always chose apartments up under the roof was to discourage the approach of beggars, peddlars and callers. There were plenty of windows in her little front room. They were for the most part dingy, but as they were nearly always open it did not make so much difference. They often admitted into the room a good deal of smoke and soot; but at the same time all the light and air that there was came through them. From her windows could be seen the crescent of the river, the masts of ships and the big chimneys of the Mississippi steamers. A magnificent piano crowded the apartment. In the next room she slept, and in the third and last she harbored a gasoline stove on which she cooked her meals when disinclined to descend to the neighboring restaurant. It was there also that she ate, keeping her belongings in a rare old buffet, dingy and battered from a hundred years of use.

When Edna knocked at Mademoiselle Reisz's front room door and entered, she discovered that person standing beside the window, engaged in mending or patching an old prunella gaiter.[7] The little musician laughed all over when she saw Edna. Her laugh consisted of a contortion of the face and all the muscles of the body. She seemed strikingly homely, standing there in the after-

7. A cloth button shoe.

noon light. She still wore the shabby lace and the artificial bunch of violets on the side of her head.

"So you remembered me at last," said Mademoiselle. "I had said to myself, 'Ah, bah! she will never come.' "

"Did you want me to come?" asked Edna with a smile.

"I had not thought much about it," answered Mademoiselle. The two had seated themselves on a little bumpy sofa which stood against the wall. "I am glad, however, that you came. I have the water boiling back there, and was just about to make some coffee. You will drink a cup with me. And how is *la belle dame*?[8] Always handsome! always healthy! always contented!" She took Edna's hand between her strong wiry fingers, holding it loosely without warmth, and executing a sort of double theme upon the back and palm.

"Yes," she went on; "I sometimes thought: 'She will never come. She promised as those women in society always do, without meaning it. She will not come.' For I really don't believe you like me, Mrs. Pontellier."

"I don't know whether I like you or not," replied Edna, gazing down at the little woman with a quizzical look.

The candor of Mrs. Pontellier's admission greatly pleased Mademoiselle Reisz. She expressed her gratification by repairing forthwith to the region of the gasoline stove and rewarding her guest with the promised cup of coffee. The coffee and the biscuit accompanying it proved very acceptable to Edna, who had declined refreshment at Madame Lebrun's and was now beginning to feel hungry. Mademoiselle set the tray which she brought in upon a small table near at hand, and seated herself once again on the lumpy sofa.

"I have had a letter from your friend," she remarked, as she poured a little cream into Edna's cup and handed it to her.

"My friend?"

"Yes, your friend Robert. He wrote to me from the City of Mexico."

"Wrote to *you*?" repeated Edna in amazement, stirring her coffee absently.

"Yes, to me. Why not? Don't stir all the warmth out of your coffee; drink it. Though the letter might as well have been sent to you; it was nothing but Mrs. Pontellier from beginning to end."

"Let me see it," requested the young woman, entreatingly.

"No; a letter concerns no one but the person who writes it and the one to whom it is written."

"Haven't you just said it concerned me from beginning to end?"

"It was written about you, not to you. 'Have you seen Mrs. Pontellier? How is she looking?' he asks. 'As Mrs. Pontellier says,' or 'as Mrs. Pontellier once said.' 'If Mrs. Pontellier should call upon you, play for her that Impromptu of Chopin's, my favorite. I heard it here a day or two ago, but not as you play it. I should like to know how it affects her,' and so on, as if he supposed we were constantly in each other's society."

"Let me see the letter."

"Oh, no."

"Have you answered it?"

"No."

"Let me see the letter."

8. The lovely lady.

"No, and again, no."

"Then play the Impromptu for me."

"It is growing late; what time do you have to be home?"

"Time doesn't concern me. Your question seems a little rude. Play the Impromptu."

"But you have told me nothing of yourself. What are you doing?"

"Painting!" laughed Edna. "I am becoming an artist. Think of it!"

"Ah! an artist! You have pretensions, Madame."

"Why pretensions? Do you think I could not become an artist?"

"I do not know you well enough to say. I do not know your talent or your temperament. To be an artist includes much; one must possess many gifts—absolute gifts—which have not been acquired by one's own effort. And, moreover, to succeed, the artist must possess the courageous soul."

"What do you mean by the courageous soul?"

"Courageous, ma foi![9] The brave soul. The soul that dares and defies."

"Show me the letter and play for me the Impromptu. You see that I have persistence. Does that quality count for anything in art?"

"It counts with a foolish old woman whom you have captivated," replied Mademoiselle, with her wriggling laugh.

The letter was right there at hand in the drawer of the little table upon which Edna had just placed her coffee cup. Mademoiselle opened the drawer and drew forth the letter, the topmost one. She placed it in Edna's hands, and without further comment arose and went to the piano.

Mademoiselle played a soft interlude. It was an improvisation. She sat low at the instrument, and the lines of her body settled into ungraceful curves and angles that gave it an appearance of deformity. Gradually and imperceptibly the interlude melted into the soft opening minor chords of the Chopin Impromptu.

Edna did not know when the impromptu began or ended. She sat in the sofa corner reading Robert's letter by the fading light. Mademoiselle had glided from the Chopin into the quivering love-notes of Isolde's song,[1] and back again to the Impromptu with its soulful and poignant longing.

The shadows deepened in the little room. The music grew strange and fantastic—turbulent, insistent, plaintive and soft with entreaty. The shadows grew deeper. The music filled the room. It floated out upon the night, over the housetops, the crescent of the river, losing itself in the silence of the upper air.

Edna was sobbing, just as she had wept one midnight at Grand Isle when strange, new voices awoke in her. She arose in some agitation to take her departure. "May I come again, Mademoiselle?" she asked at the threshold.

"Come whenever you feel like it. Be careful; the stairs and landings are dark; don't stumble."

Mademoiselle reëntered and lit a candle. Robert's letter was on the floor. She stooped and picked it up. It was crumpled and damp with tears. Mademoiselle smoothed the letter out, restored it to the envelope, and replaced it in the table drawer.

9. "My faith" (literal trans.); here, in fact
1. From Richard Wagner's opera Tristan und Isolde (1857–59); Isolde sings her Liebestod ("love-death") as she bids her dead lover farewell and then dies in his arms.

KATE CHOPIN

XXII

One morning on his way into town Mr. Pontellier stopped at the house of his old friend and family physican, Doctor Mandelet. The Doctor was a semi-retired physician, resting, as the saying is, upon his laurels. He bore a reputation for wisdom rather than skill—leaving the active practice of medicine to his assistants and younger contemporaries—and was much sought for in matters of consultation. A few families, united to him by bonds of friendship, he still attended when they required the services of a physician. The Pontelliers were among these.

Mr. Pontellier found the Doctor reading at the open window of his study. His house stood rather far back from the street, in the center of a delightful garden, so that it was quiet and peaceful at the old gentleman's study window. He was a great reader. He stared up disapprovingly over his eyeglasses as Mr. Pontellier entered, wondering who had the temerity to disturb him at that hour of the morning.

"Ah, Pontellier! Not sick, I hope. Come and have a seat. What news do you bring this morning?" He was quite portly, with a profusion of gray hair, and small blue eyes which age had robbed of much of their brightness but none of their penetration.

"Oh! I'm never sick, Doctor. You know that I come of tough fiber—of that old Creole race of Pontelliers that dry up and finally blow away. I come to consult—no, not precisely to consult—to talk to you about Edna. I don't know what ails her."

"Madame Pontellier not well?" marveled the Doctor. "Why I saw her—I think it was a week ago—walking along Canal Street,[2] the picture of health, it seemed to me."

"Yes, yes; she seems quite well," said Mr. Pontellier, leaning forward and whirling his stick between his two hands; "but she doesn't act well. She's odd, she's not like herself. I can't make her out, and I thought perhaps you'd help me."

"How does she act?" inquired the doctor.

"Well, it isn't easy to explain," said Mr. Pontellier, throwing himself back in his chair. "She lets the housekeeping go to the dickens."

"Well, well; women are not all alike, my dear Pontellier. We've got to consider—"

"I know that; I told you I couldn't explain. Her whole attitude—toward me and everybody and everything—has changed. You know I have a quick temper, but I don't want to quarrel or be rude to a woman, especially my wife; yet I'm driven to it, and feel like ten thousand devils after I've made a fool of myself. She's making it devilishly uncomfortable for me," he went on nervously. "She's got some sort of notion in her head concerning the eternal rights of women; and—you understand—we meet in the morning at the breakfast table."

The old gentleman lifted his shaggy eyebrows, protruded his thick nether lip, and tapped the arms of his chair with his cushioned finger-tips.

"What have you been doing to her, Pontellier?"

"Doing! *Parbleu!*"[3]

2. The main street of downtown New Orleans. 3. For heaven's sake!

"Has she," asked the Doctor, with a smile, "has she been associating of late with a circle of pseudo-intellectual women[4]—superspiritual superior beings? My wife has been telling me about them."

"That's the trouble," broke in Mr. Pontellier, "she hasn't been associating with any one. She has abandoned her Tuesdays at home, has thrown over all her acquaintances, and goes tramping about by herself, moping in the street-cars, getting in after dark. I tell you she's peculiar. I don't like it; I feel a little worried over it."

This was a new aspect for the Doctor. "Nothing hereditary?" he asked, seriously. "Nothing peculiar about her family antecedents, is there?"

"Oh, no, indeed! She comes of sound old Presbyterian Kentucky stock. The old gentleman, her father, I have heard, used to atone for his week-day sins with his Sunday devotions. I know for a fact, that his race horses literally ran away with the prettiest bit of Kentucky farming land I ever laid eyes upon. Margaret—you know Margaret—she has all the Presbyterianism undiluted. And the youngest is something of a vixen. By the way, she gets married in a couple of weeks from now."

"Send your wife up to the wedding," exclaimed the Doctor, foreseeing a happy solution. "Let her stay among her own people for a while; it will do her good."

"That's what I want her to do. She won't go to the marriage. She says a wedding is one of the most lamentable spectacles on earth. Nice thing for a woman to say to her husband!" exclaimed Mr. Pontellier, fuming anew at the recollection.

"Pontellier," said the Doctor, after a moment's reflection, "let your wife alone for a while. Don't bother her, and don't let her bother you. Woman, my dear friend, is a very peculiar and delicate organism—a sensitive and highly organized woman, such as I know Mrs. Pontellier to be, is especially peculiar. It would require an inspired psychologist to deal successfully with them. And when ordinary fellows like you and me attempt to cope with their idiosyncrasies the result is bungling. Most women are moody and whimsical. This is some passing whim of your wife, due to some cause or causes which you and I needn't try to fathom. But it will pass happily over, especially if you let her alone. Send her around to see me."

"Oh! I couldn't do that; there'd be no reason for it." objected Mr. Pontellier.

"Then I'll go around and see her," said the Doctor. "I'll drop in to dinner some evening en bon ami."[5]

"Do! by all means," urged Mr. Pontellier. "What evening will you come? Say Thursday. Will you come Thursday?" he asked, rising to take his leave.

"Very well; Thursday. My wife may possibly have some engagement for me Thursday. In case she has, I shall let you know. Otherwise, you may expect me."

Mr. Pontellier turned before leaving to say:

"I am going to New York on business very soon. I have a big scheme on hand, and want to be on the field proper to pull the ropes and handle the ribbons.[6] We'll let you in on the inside if you say so, Doctor," he laughed.

4. Women's clubs flourished during the late nineteenth century in America. They were a source of education for women as well as an arena for political organization. As the Doctor's remark indicates, the club movement was met with scorn in some quarters [Culley's note].
5. Like an old friend.
6. I.e., the reins.

"No, I thank you, my dear sir," returned the Doctor. "I leave such ventures to you younger men with the fever of life still in your blood."

"What I wanted to say," continued Mr. Pontellier, with his hand on the knob; "I may have to be absent a good while. Would you advise me to take Edna along?"

"By all means, if she wishes to go. If not, leave her here. Don't contradict her. The mood will pass, I assure you. It may take a month, two, three months—possibly longer, but it will pass; have patience."

"Well, good-by, à jeudi,"[7] said Mr. Pontellier, as he let himself out.

The Doctor would have liked during the course of conversation to ask, "Is there any man in the case?" but he knew his Creole too well to make such a blunder as that.

He did not resume his book immediately, but sat for a while meditatively looking out into the garden.

XXIII

Edna's father was in the city, and had been with them several days. She was not very warmly or deeply attached to him, but they had certain tastes in common, and when together they were companionable. His coming was in the nature of a welcome disturbance; it seemed to furnish a new direction for her emotions.

He had come to purchase a wedding gift for his daughter, Janet, and an outfit for himself in which he might make a creditable appearance at her marriage. Mr. Pontellier had selected the bridal gift, as every one immediately connected with him always deferred to this taste in such matters. And his suggestions on the question of dress—which too often assumes the nature of a problem—were of inestimable value to his father-in-law. But for the past few days the old gentleman had been upon Edna's hands, and in his society she was becoming acquainted with a new set of sensations. He had been a colonel in the Confederate army, and still maintained, with the title, the military bearing which had always accompanied it. His hair and mustache were white and silky, emphasizing the rugged bronze of his face. He was tall and thin, and wore his coats padded, which gave a fictitious breadth and depth to his shoulders and chest. Edna and her father looked very distinguished together, and excited a good deal of notice during their perambulations. Upon his arrival she began by introducing him to her atelier and making a sketch of him. He took the whole matter very seriously. If her talent had been ten-fold greater than it was, it would not have surprised him, convinced as he was that he had bequeathed to all of his daughters the germs of a masterful capability, which only depended upon their own efforts to be directed toward successful achievement.

Before her pencil he sat rigid and unflinching, as he had faced the cannon's mouth in days gone by. He resented the intrusion of the children, who gaped with wondering eyes at him, sitting so stiff up there in their mother's bright atelier. When they drew near he motioned them away with an expressive action of the foot, loath to disturb the fixed lines of his countenance, his arms, or his rigid shoulders.

Edna, anxious to entertain him, invited Mademoiselle Reisz to meet him,

having promised him a treat in her piano playing; but Mademoiselle declined the invitation. So together they attended a *soirée musicale* at the Ratignolles'. Monsieur and Madame Ratignolle made much of the Colonel, installing him as the guest of honor and engaging him at once to dine with them the following Sunday, or any day which he might select. Madame coquetted with him in the most captivating and naïve manner, with eyes, gestures, and a profusion of compliments, till the Colonel's old head felt thirty years younger on his padded shoulders. Edna marveled, not comprehending. She herself was almost devoid of coquetry.

There were one or two men whom she observed at the *soirée musicale*; but she would never have felt moved to any kittenish display to attract their notice—to any feline or feminine wiles to express herself toward them. Their personality attracted her in an agreeable way. Her fancy selected them, and she was glad when a lull in the music gave them an opportunity to meet her and talk with her. Often on the street the glance of strange eyes had lingered in her memory, and sometimes had disturbed her.

Mr. Pontellier did not attend these *soirées musicales*. He considered them *bourgeois*, and found more diversion at the club. To Madame Ratignolle he said the music dispensed at her *soirées* was "too heavy," too far beyond his untrained comprehension. His excuse flattered her. But she disapproved of Mr. Pontellier's club, and she was frank enough to tell Edna so.

"It's a pity Mr. Pontellier doesn't stay home more in the evenings. I think you would be more—well, if you don't mind my saying it—more united, if he did."

"Oh! dear no!" said Edna, with a blank look in her eyes. "What should I do if he stayed home? We wouldn't have anything to say to each other."

She had not much of anything to say to her father, for that matter; but he did not antagonize her. She discovered that he interested her, though she realized that he might not interest her long; and for the first time in her life she felt as if she were thoroughly acquainted with him. He kept her busy serving him and ministering to his wants. It amused her to do so. She would not permit a servant or one of the children to do anything for him which she might do herself. Her husband noticed, and thought it was the expression of a deep filial attachment which he had never suspected.

The Colonel drank numerous "toddies" during the course of the day, which left him, however, imperturbed. He was an expert at concocting strong drinks. He had even invented some, to which he had given fantastic names, and for whose manufacture he required diverse ingredients that it devolved upon Edna to procure for him.

When Doctor Mandelet dined with the Pontelliers on Thursday he could discern in Mrs. Pontellier no trace of that morbid condition which her husband had reported to him. She was excited and in a manner radiant. She and her father had been to the race course, and their thoughts when they seated themselves at table were still occupied with the events of the afternoon, and their talk was still of the track. The Doctor had not kept pace with turf affairs. He had certain recollections of racing in what he called "the good old times" when the Lecompte stables flourished,[8] and he drew upon this fund of memories so that he might not be left out and seem wholly devoid of the modern

8. New Orleans had been a celebrated racing center before the Civil War

spirit. But he failed to impose upon the Colonel, and was even far from impressing him with this trumped-up knowledge of bygone days. Edna had staked her father on his last venture, with the most gratifying results to both of them. Besides, they had met some very charming people, according to the Colonel's impressions. Mrs. Mortimer Merriman and Mrs. James Highcamp, who were there with Alcée Arobin, had joined them and had enlivened the hours in a fashion that warmed him to think of.

Mr. Pontellier himself had no particular leaning toward horse-racing, and was even rather inclined to discourage it as a pastime, especially when he considered the fate of that blue-grass farm in Kentucky. He endeavored, in a general way, to express a particular disapproval, and only succeeded in arousing the ire and opposition of his father-in-law. A pretty dispute followed in which Edna warmly espoused her father's cause and the Doctor remained neutral.

He observed his hostess attentively from under his shaggy brows, and noted a subtle change which had transformed her from the listless woman he had known into a being who, for the moment, seemed palpitant with the forces of life. Her speech was warm and energetic. There was no repression in her glance or gesture. She reminded him of some beautiful, sleek animal waking up in the sun.

The dinner was excellent. The claret was warm and the champagne was cold, and under their beneficent influence the threatened unpleasantness melted and vanished with the fumes of the wine.

Mr. Pontellier warmed up and grew reminiscent. He told some amusing plantation experiences, recollections of old Iberville and his youth, when he hunted 'possum in company with some friendly darky; thrashed the pecan trees, shot the grosbec,[9] and roamed the woods and fields in mischievous idleness.

The Colonel, with little sense of humor and of the fitness of things, related a somber episode of those dark and bitter days, in which he had acted a conspicuous part and always formed a central figure. Nor was the Doctor happier in his selection, when he told the old, ever new and curious story of the waning of a woman's love, seeking strange, new channels, only to return to its legitimate source after days of fierce unrest. It was one of the many little human documents which had been unfolded to him during his long career as a physician. The story did not seem especially to impress Edna. She had one of her own to tell, of a woman who paddled away with her lover one night in a pirogue and never came back. They were lost amid the Baratarian Islands, and no one ever heard of them or found trace of them from that day to this. It was a pure invention. She said that Madame Antoine had related it to her. That, also, was an invention. Perhaps it was a dream she had had. But every glowing word seemed real to those who listened. They could feel the hot breath of the Southern night; they could hear the long sweep of the pirogue through the glistening moonlit water, the beating of birds' wings, rising startled from among the reeds in the salt-water pools; they could see the faces of the lovers, pale, close together, rapt in oblivious forgetfulness, drifting into the unknown.

The champagne was cold, and its subtle fumes played fantastic tricks with Edna's memory that night.

Outside, away from the glow of the fire and the soft lamplight, the night

9. I.e., grosbeak, game birds with large (*gros*) bills.

was chill and murky. The Doctor doubled his old-fashioned cloak across his breast as he strode home through the darkness. He knew his fellow-creatures better than most men; knew that inner life which so seldom unfolds itself to unanointed eyes. He was sorry he had accepted Pontellier's invitation. He was growing old, and beginning to need rest and an imperturbed spirit. He did not want the secrets of other lives thrust upon him.

"I hope it isn't Arobin," he muttered to himself as he walked. "I hope to heaven it isn't Alcée Arobin."

XXIV

Edna and her father had a warm, and almost violent dispute upon the subject of her refusal to attend her sister's wedding. Mr. Pontellier declined to interfere, to interpose either his influence or his authority. He was following Doctor Mandelet's advice, and letting her do as she liked. The Colonel reproached his daughter for her lack of filial kindness and respect, her want of sisterly affection and womanly consideration. His arguments were labored and unconvincing. He doubted if Janet would accept any excuse—forgetting that Edna had offered none. He doubted if Janet would ever speak to her again, and he was sure Margaret would not.

Edna was glad to be rid of her father when he finally took himself off with his wedding garments and his bridal gifts, with his padded shoulders, his Bible reading, his "toddies" and ponderous oaths.

Mr. Pontellier followed him closely. He meant to stop at the wedding on his way to New York and endeavor by every means which money and love could devise to atone somewhat for Edna's incomprehensible action.

"You are too lenient, too lenient by far, Léonce," asserted the Colonel. "Authority, coercion are what is needed. Put your foot down good and hard; the only way to manage a wife. Take my word for it."

The Colonel was perhaps unaware that he had coerced his own wife into her grave. Mr. Pontellier had a vague suspicion of it which he thought it needless to mention at that late day.

Edna was not so consciously gratified at her husband's leaving home as she had been over the departure of her father. As the day approached when he was to leave her for a comparatively long stay, she grew melting and affectionate, remembering his many acts of consideration and his repeated expressions of an ardent attachment. She was solicitous about his health and his welfare. She bustled around, looking after his clothing, thinking about heavy underwear, quite as Madame Ratignolle would have done under similar circumstances. She cried when he went away, calling him her dear, good friend, and she was quite certain she would grow lonely before very long and go to join him in New York.

But after all, a radiant peace settled upon her when she at last found herself alone. Even the children were gone. Old Madame Pontellier had come herself and carried them off to Iberville with their quadroon. The old madame did not venture to say she was afraid they would be neglected during Léonce's absence; she hardly ventured to think so. She was hungry for them—even a little fierce in her attachment. She did not want them to be wholly "children of the pavement," she always said when begging to have them for a space. She wished them to know the country, with its streams, its fields, its woods, its

freedom, so delicious to the young. She wished them to taste something of the life their father had lived and known and loved when he, too, was a little child.

When Edna was at last alone, she breathed a big, genuine sigh of relief. A feeling that was unfamiliar but very delicious came over her. She walked all through the house, from one room to another, as if inspecting it for the first time. She tried the various chairs and lounges, as if she had never sat and reclined upon them before. And she perambulated around the outside of the house, investigating, looking to see if windows and shutters were secure and in order. The flowers were like new acquaintances; she approached them in a familiar spirit, and made herself at home among them. The garden walks were damp, and Edna called to the maid to bring out her rubber sandals. And there she stayed, and stooped, digging around the plants, trimming, picking dead, dry leaves. The children's little dog came out, interfering, getting in her way. She scolded him, laughing at him, played with him. The garden smelled so good and looked so pretty in the afternoon sunlight. Edna plucked all the bright flowers she could find, and went into the house with them, she and the little dog.

Even the kitchen assumed a sudden interesting character which she had never before perceived. She went in to give directions to the cook, to say that the butcher would have to bring much less meat, that they would require only half their usual quantity of bread, of milk and groceries. She told the cook that she herself would be greatly occupied during Mr. Pontellier's absence, and she begged her to take all thought and responsibility of the larder upon her own shoulders.

That night Edna dined alone. The candelabra, with a few candles in the center of the table, gave all the light she needed. Outside the circle of light in which she sat, the large dining-room looked solemn and shadowy. The cook, placed upon her mettle, served a delicious repast—a luscious tenderloin broiled à point. The wine tasted good; the marron glacé[1] seemed to be just what she wanted. It was so pleasant, too, to dine in a comfortable *peignoir*.

She thought a little sentimentally about Léonce and the children, and wondered what they were doing. As she gave a dainty scrap or two to the doggie, she talked intimately to him about Étienne and Raoul. He was beside himself with astonishment and delight over these companionable advances, and showed his appreciation by his little quick, snappy barks and a lively agitation.

Then Edna sat in the library after dinner and read Emerson[2] until she grew sleepy. She realized that she had neglected her reading, and determined to start anew upon a course of improving studies, now that her time was completely her own to do with as she liked.

After a refreshing bath, Edna went to bed. And as she snuggled comfortably beneath the eiderdown a sense of restfulness invaded her, such as she had not known before.

XXV

When the weather was dark and cloudy Edna could not work. She needed the sun to mellow and temper her mood to the sticking point. She had reached a stage when she seemed to be no longer feeling her way, working, when in the humor, with sureness and ease. And being devoid of ambition,

1. Glazed chestnuts. "À point": to a turn.
2. Ralph Waldo Emerson (1803–1882), American philosopher, essayist, and poet.

and striving not toward accomplishment, she drew satisfaction from the work in itself.

On rainy or melancholy days Edna went out and sought the society of the friends she had made at Grand Isle. Or else she stayed indoors and nursed a mood with which she was becoming too familiar for her own comfort and peace of mind. It was not despair; but it seemed to her as if life were passing by, leaving its promise broken and unfulfilled. Yet there were other days when she listened, was led on and deceived by fresh promises which her youth held out to her.

She went again to the races, and again. Alcée Arobin and Mrs. Highcamp called for her one bright afternoon in Arobin's drag.[3]

Mrs. Highcamp was a worldly but unaffected, intelligent, slim, tall blonde woman in the forties, with an indifferent manner and blue eyes that stared. She had a daughter who served her as a pretext for cultivating the society of young men of fashion. Alcée Arobin was one of them. He was a familiar figure at the race course, the opera, the fashionable clubs. There was a perpetual smile in his eyes, which seldom failed to awaken a corresponding cheerfulness in any one who looked into them and listened to his good-humored voice. His manner was quiet, and at times a little insolent. He possessed a good figure, a pleasing face, not overburdened with depth of thought or feeling; and his dress was that of the conventional man of fashion.

He admired Edna extravagantly, after meeting her at the races with her father. He had met her before on other occasions, but she had seemed to him unapproachable until that day. It was at his instigation that Mrs. Highcamp called to ask her to go with them to the Jockey Club[4] to witness the turf event of the season.

There were possibly a few track men out there who knew the race horse as well as Edna, but there was certainly none who knew it better. She sat between her two companions as one having authority to speak. She laughed at Arobin's pretensions, and deplored Mrs. Highcamp's ignorance. The race horse was a friend and intimate associate of her childhood. The atmosphere of the stables and the breath of the blue grass paddock revived in her memory and lingered in her nostrils. She did not perceive that she was talking like her father as the sleek geldings ambled in review before them. She played for very high stakes, and fortune favored her. The fever of the game flamed in her cheeks and eyes, and it got into her blood and into her brain like an intoxicant. People turned their heads to look at her, and more than one lent an attentive ear to her utterances, hoping thereby to secure the elusive but ever-desired "tip." Arobin caught the contagion of excitement which drew him to Edna like a magnet. Mrs. Highcamp remained, as usual, unmoved, with her indifferent stare and uplifted eyebrows.

Edna stayed and dined with Mrs. Highcamp upon being urged to do so. Arobin also remained and sent away his drag.

The dinner was quiet and uninteresting, save for the cheerful efforts of Arobin to enliven things. Mrs. Highcamp deplored the absence of her daughter from the races, and tried to convey to her what she had missed by going to the "Dante reading" instead of joining them.[5] The girl held a geranium leaf up to her nose and said nothing, but looked knowing and noncommittal. Mr.

3. Heavy coach.
4. The exclusive New Louisiana Jockey Club.
5. I.e., her daughter preferred intellectual activities.

Dante Alighieri (1265–1321), Italian poet, wrote *The Divine Comedy*.

Highcamp was a plain, bald-headed man, who only talked under compulsion. He was unresponsive. Mrs. Highcamp was full of delicate courtesy and consideration toward her husband. She addressed most of her conversation to him at table. They sat in the library after dinner and read the evening papers together under the drop-light;[6] while the younger people went into the drawing-room near by and talked. Miss Highcamp played some selections from Grieg[7] upon the piano. She seemed to have apprehended all of the composer's coldness and none of his poetry. While Edna listened she could not help wondering if she had lost her taste for music.

When the time came for her to go home, Mr. Highcamp grunted a lame offer to escort her, looking down at his slippered feet with tactless concern. It was Arobin who took her home. The car ride was long, and it was late when they reached Esplanade Street. Arobin asked permission to enter for a second to light his cigarette—his match safe[8] was empty. He filled his match safe, but did not light his cigarette until he left her, after she had expressed her willingness to go to the races with him again.

Edna was neither tired nor sleepy. She was hungry again, for the Highcamp dinner, though of excellent quality, had lacked abundance. She rummaged in the larder and brought forth a slice of "Gruyère"[9] and some crackers. She opened a bottle of beer which she found in the ice-box. Edna felt extremely restless and excited. She vacantly hummed a fantastic tune as she poked at the wood embers on the hearth and munched a cracker.

She wanted something to happen—something, anything; she did not know what. She regretted that she had not made Arobin stay a half hour to talk over the horses with her. She counted the money she had won. But there was nothing else to do, so she went to bed, and tossed there for hours in a sort of monotonous agitation.

In the middle of the night she remembered that she had forgotten to write her regular letter to her husband; and she decided to do so next day and tell him about her afternoon at the Jockey Club. She lay wide awake composing a letter which was nothing like the one which she wrote the next day. When the maid awoke her in the morning Edna was dreaming of Mr. Highcamp playing the piano at the entrance of a music store on Canal Street, while his wife was saying to Alcée Arobin, as they boarded an Esplanade Street car:

"What a pity that so much talent has been neglected! but I must go."

When a few days later, Alcée Arobin again called for Edna in his drag, Mrs. Highcamp was not with him. He said they would pick her up. But as the lady had not been apprised of his intention of picking her up, she was not at home. The daughter was just leaving the house to attend the meeting of a branch Folk Lore Society,[1] and regretted that she could not accompany them. Arobin appeared nonplused, and asked Edna if there were any one else she cared to ask.

She did not deem it worthwhile to go in search of any of the fashionable acquaintances from whom she had withdrawn herself. She thought of Madame Ratignolle, but knew that her fair friend did not leave the house, except to take a languid walk around the block with her husband after nightfall.

6. Gas lamp that could be lowered for reading.
7. Edvard Grieg (1843–1907), Norwegian composer.
8. I.e., matchbox.

9. Cheese originally made in Gruyère, Switzerland.
1. The New Orleans Association of the American Folklore Society.

Mademoiselle Reisz would have laughed at such a request from Edna. Madame Lebrun might have enjoyed the outing, but for some reason Edna did not want her. So they went alone, she and Arobin.

The afternoon was intensely interesting to her. The excitement came back upon her like a remittent fever. Her talk grew familiar and confidential. It was no labor to become intimate with Arobin. His manner invited easy confidence. The preliminary stage of becoming acquainted was one which he always endeavored to ignore when a pretty and engaging woman was concerned.

He stayed and dined with Edna. He stayed and sat beside the wood fire. They laughed and talked; and before it was time to go he was telling her how different life might have been if he had known her years before. With ingenuous frankness he spoke of what a wicked, ill-disciplined boy he had been, and impulsively drew up his cuff to exhibit upon his wrist the scar from a saber cut which he had received in a duel outside of Paris when he was nineteen. She touched his hand as she scanned the red cicatrice[2] on the inside of his white wrist. A quick impulse that was somewhat spasmodic impelled her fingers to close in a sort of clutch upon his hand. He felt the pressure of her pointed nails in the flesh of his palm.

She arose hastily and walked toward the mantel.

"The sight of a wound or scar always agitates and sickens me," she said. "I shouldn't have looked at it."

"I beg your pardon," he entreated, following her; "it never occurred to me that it might be repulsive."

He stood close to her, and the effrontery in his eyes repelled the old, vanishing self in her, yet drew all her awakening sensuousness. He saw enough in her face to impel him to take her hand and hold it while he said his lingering good night.

"Will you go to the races again?" he asked.

"No," she said. "I've had enough of the races. I don't want to lose all the money I've won, and I've got to work when the weather is bright, instead of—"

"Yes; work; to be sure. You promised to show me your work. What morning may I come up to your atelier? To-morrow?"

"No!"

"Day after?"

"No, no."

"Oh, please don't refuse me! I know something of such things, I might help you with a stray suggestion or two."

"No. Good night. Why don't you go after you have said good night? I don't like you," she went on in a high, excited pitch, attempting to draw away her hand. She felt that her words lacked dignity and sincerity, and she knew that he felt it.

"I'm sorry you don't like me. I'm sorry I offended you. How have I offended you? What have I done? Can't you forgive me?" And he bent and pressed his lips upon her hand as if he wished never more to withdraw them.

"Mr. Arobin," she complained, "I'm greatly upset by the excitement of the afternoon; I'm not myself. My manner must have misled you in some way. I wish you to go, please." She spoke in a monotonous, dull tone. He took his hat

2. Scar.

from the table, and stood with eyes turned from her, looking into the dying fire. For a moment or two he kept an impressive silence.

"Your manner has not misled me, Mrs. Pontellier," he said finally. "My own emotions have done that. I couldn't help it. When I'm near you, how could I help it? Don't think anything of it, don't bother, please. You see, I go when you command me. If you wish me to stay away, I shall do so. If you let me come back, I—oh! you will let me come back?"

He cast one appealing glance at her, to which she made no response. Alcée Arobin's manner was so genuine that it often deceived even himself.

Edna did not care or think whether it were genuine or not. When she was alone she looked mechanically at the back of her hand which he had kissed so warmly. Then she leaned her head down on the mantelpiece. She felt somewhat like a woman who in a moment of passion is betrayed into an act of infidelity, and realizes the significance of the act without being wholly awakened from its glamour. The thought was passing vaguely through her mind, "what would he think?"

She did not mean her husband; she was thinking of Robert Lebrun. Her husband seemed to her now like a person whom she had married without love as an excuse.

She lit a candle and went up to her room. Alcée Arobin was absolutely nothing to her. Yet his presence, his manners, the warmth of his glances, and above all the touch of his lips upon her hand had acted like a narcotic upon her.

She slept a languorous sleep, interwoven with vanishing dreams.

XXVI

Alcée Arobin wrote Edna an elaborate note of apology, palpitant with sincerity. It embarrassed her; for in a cooler, quieter moment it appeared to her absurd that she should have taken his action so seriously, so dramatically. She felt sure that the significance of the whole occurrence had lain in her own self-consciousness. If she ignored his note it would give undue importance to a trivial affair. If she replied to it in a serious spirit it would still leave in his mind the impression that she had in a susceptible moment yielded to his influence. After all, it was no great matter to have one's hand kissed. She was provoked at his having written the apology. She answered in as light and bantering a spirit as she fancied it deserved, and said she would be glad to have him look in upon her at work whenever he felt the inclination and his business gave him the opportunity.

He responded at once by presenting himself at her home with all his disarming naïveté. And then there was scarcely a day which followed that she did not see him or was not reminded of him. He was prolific in pretexts. His attitude became one of good-humored subservience and tacit adoration. He was ready at all times to submit to her moods, which were as often kind as they were cold. She grew accustomed to him. They became intimate and friendly by imperceptible degrees, and then by leaps. He sometimes talked in a way that astonished her at first and brought the crimson into her face; in a way that pleased her at last, appealing to the animalism that stirred impatiently within her.

There was nothing which so quieted the turmoil of Edna's senses as a visit to Mademoiselle Reisz. It was then, in the presence of that personality which

was offensive to her, that the woman, by her divine art, seemed to reach Edna's spirit and set it free.

It was misty, with heavy, lowering atmosphere, one afternoon, when Edna climbed the stairs to the pianist's apartments under the roof. Her clothes were dripping with moisture. She felt chilled and pinched as she entered the room. Mademoiselle was poking at a rusty stove that smoked a little and warmed the room indifferently. She was endeavoring to heat a pot of chocolate on the stove. The room looked cheerless and dingy to Edna as she entered. A bust of Beethoven, covered with a hood of dust, scowled at her from the mantelpiece.

"Ah! here comes the sunlight!" exclaimed Mademoiselle, rising from her knees before the stove. "Now it will be warm and bright enough; I can let the fire alone."

She closed the stove door with a bang, and approaching assisted in removing Edna's dripping mackintosh.

"You are cold; you look miserable. The chocolate will soon be hot. But would you rather have a taste of brandy? I have scarcely touched the bottle which you brought me for my cold." A piece of red flannel was wrapped around Mademoiselle's throat; a stiff neck compelled her to hold her head on one side.

"I will take some brandy," said Edna, shivering as she removed her gloves and overshoes. She drank the liquor from the glass as a man would have done. Then flinging herself upon the uncomfortable sofa she said, "Mademoiselle, I am going to move away from my house on Esplanade Street."

"Ah!" ejaculated the musician, neither surprised nor especially interested. Nothing ever seemed to astonish her very much. She was endeavoring to adjust the bunch of violets which had become loose from its fastening in her hair. Edna drew her down upon the sofa and taking a pin from her own hair, secured the shabby artificial flowers in their accustomed place.

"Aren't you astonished?"

"Passably. Where are you going? To New York? to Iberville? to your father in Mississippi? where?"

"Just two steps away," laughed Edna, "in a little four-room house around the corner. It looks so cozy, so inviting and restful, whenever I pass by; and it's for rent. I'm tired looking after that big house. It never seemed like mine, anyway—like home. It's too much trouble. I have to keep too many servants. I am tired bothering with them."

"That is not your true reason, *ma belle*.[3] There is no use in telling me lies. I don't know your reason, but you have not told me the truth." Edna did not protest or endeavor to justify herself.

"The house, the money that provides for it, are not mine. Isn't that enough reason?"

"They are your husband's," returned Mademoiselle, with a shrug and a malicious elevation of the eyebrows.

"Oh! I see there is no deceiving you. Then let me tell you: it is a caprice. I have a little money of my own from my mother's estate, which my father sends me by driblets. I won a large sum this winter on the races, and I am beginning to sell my sketches. Laidpore is more and more pleased with my work; he says it grows in force and individuality. I cannot judge of that myself, but I

3. My pretty

feel that I have gained in ease and confidence. However, as I said, I have sold a good many through Laidpore. I can live in the tiny house for little or nothing, with one servant. Old Celestine, who works occasionally for me, says she will come stay with me and do my work. I know I shall like it, like the feeling of freedom and independence.

"What does your husband say?"

"I have not told him yet. I only thought of it this morning. He will think I am demented, no doubt. Perhaps you think so."

Mademoiselle shook her head slowly. "Your reason is not yet clear to me," she said.

Neither was it quite clear to Edna herself; but it unfolded itself as she sat for a while in silence. Instinct had prompted her to put away her husband's bounty in casting off her allegiance. She did not know how it would be when he returned. There would have to be an understanding, an explanation. Conditions would some way adjust themselves, she felt, but whatever came, she had resolved never again to belong to another than herself.

"I shall give a grand dinner before I leave the old house!" Edna exclaimed. "You will have to come to it, Mademoiselle. I will give you everything that you like to eat and to drink. We shall sing and laugh and be merry for once." And she uttered a sigh that came from the very depth of her being.

If Mademoiselle happened to have received a letter from Robert during the interval of Edna's visits, she would give her the letter unsolicited. And she would seat herself at the piano and play as her humor prompted her while the young woman read the letter.

The little stove was roaring; it was red-hot, and the chocolate in the tin sizzled and sputtered. Edna went forward and opened the stove door, and Mademoiselle rising took a letter from under the bust of Beethoven and handed it to Edna.

"Another! so soon!" she exclaimed, her eyes filled with delight. "Tell me, Mademoiselle, does he know that I see his letters?"

"Never in the world! He would be angry and would never write to me again if he thought so. Does he write to you? Never a line. Does he send you a message? Never a word. It is because he loves you, poor fool, and is trying to forget you, since you are not free to listen to him or to belong to him."

"Why do you show me his letters, then?"

"Haven't you begged for them? Can I refuse you anything? Oh! you cannot deceive me," and Mademoiselle approached her beloved instrument and began to play. Edna did not at once read the letter. She sat holding it in her hand, while the music penetrated her whole being like an effulgence, warming and brightening the dark places of her soul. It prepared her for joy and exultation.

"Oh!" she exclaimed, letting the letter fall to the floor. "Why did you not tell me?" She went and grasped Mademoiselle's hands up from the keys. "Oh! unkind! malicious! Why did you not tell me?"

"That he was coming back? No great news, *ma foi*. I wonder he did not come long ago."

"But when, when?" cried Edna, impatiently. "He does not say when."

"He says 'very soon.' You know as much about it as I do, it is all in the letter."

"But why? Why is he coming? Oh, if I thought—" and she snatched the letters from the floor and turned the pages this way and that way, looking for the reason, which was left untold.

"If I were young and in love with a man," said Mademoiselle, turning on the stool and pressing her wiry hands between her knees as she looked down at Edna, who sat on the floor holding the letter, "it seems to me he would have to be some *grand esprit*,[4] a man with lofty aims and ability to reach them; one who stood high enough to attract the notice of his fellow-men. It seems to me if I were young and in love I should never deem a man of ordinary caliber worthy of my devotion."

"Now it is you who are telling lies and seeking to deceive me, Mademoiselle; or else you have never been in love, and know nothing about it. Why," went on Edna, clasping her knees and looking up into Mademoiselle's twisted face, "do you suppose a woman knows why she loves? Does she select? Does she say to herself: 'Go to! Here is a distinguished statesman with presidential possibilities: I shall proceed to fall in love with him.' Or, 'I shall set my heart upon this musician, whose fame is on every tongue?' Or, 'This financier, who controls the world's money markets?' "

"You are purposely misunderstanding me, *ma reine*.[5] Are you in love with Robert?"

"Yes," said Edna. It was the first time she had admitted it, and a glow overspread her face, blotching it with red spots.

"Why?" asked her companion. "Why do you love him when you ought not to?"

Edna, with a motion or two, dragged herself on her knees before Mademoiselle Reisz, who took the glowing face between her two hands.

"Why? Because his hair is brown and grows away from his temples; because he opens and shuts his eyes, and his nose is a little out of drawing; because he has two lips and a square chin, and a little finger which he can't straighten from having played baseball too energetically in his youth. Because—"

"Because you do, in short," laughed Mademoiselle. "What will you do when he comes back?" she asked.

"Do? Nothing, except feel glad and happy to be alive."

She was already glad and happy to be alive at the mere thought of his return. The murky, lowering sky, which had depressed her a few hours before, seemed bracing and invigorating as she splashed through the streets on her way home.

She stopped at a confectioner's and ordered a huge box of bonbons for the children in Iberville. She slipped a card in the box, on which she scribbled a tender message and sent an abundance of kisses.

Before dinner in the evening Edna wrote a charming letter to her husband, telling him of her intention to move for a while into the little house around the block, and to give a farewell dinner before leaving, regretting that he was not there to share it, to help her out with the menu and assist her in entertaining the guests. Her letter was brilliant and brimming with cheerfulness.

XXVII

"What is the matter with you?" asked Arobin that evening. "I never found you in such a happy mood." Edna was tired by that time, and was reclining on the lounge before the fire.

"Don't you know the weather prophet has told us we shall see the sun pretty soon?"

"Well, that ought to be reason enough," he acquiesced. "You wouldn't give

4. Grand spirit (literal trans.); here, noble soul. 5. My queen.

me another if I sat here all night imploring you." He sat close to her on a low tabouret,[6] and as he spoke his fingers lightly touched the hair that fell a little over her forehead. She liked the touch of his fingers through her hair, and closed her eyes sensitively.

"One of these days," she said, "I'm going to pull myself together for a while and think—try to determine what character of a woman I am; for, candidly, I don't know. By all the codes which I am acquainted with, I am a devilishly wicked specimen of the sex. But some way I can't convince myself that I am. I must think about it."

"Don't. What's the use? Why should you bother thinking about it when I can tell you what manner of woman you are?" His fingers strayed occasionally down to her warm, smooth cheeks and firm chin, which was growing a little full and double.

"Oh, yes! You will tell me that I am adorable; everything that is captivating. Spare yourself the effort."

"No; I shan't tell you anything of the sort, though I shouldn't be lying if I did."

"Do you know Mademoiselle Reisz?" she asked irrelevantly.

"The pianist? I know her by sight. I've heard her play."

"She says queer things sometimes in a bantering way that you don't notice at the time and you feel yourself thinking about afterward."

"For instance?"

"Well, for instance, when I left her today, she put her arms around me and felt my shoulder blades, to see if my wings were strong, she said. 'The bird that would soar above the level plain of tradition and prejudice must have strong wings. It is a sad spectacle to see the weaklings bruised, exhausted, fluttering back to earth.' "

"Whither would you soar?"

"I'm not thinking of any extraordinary flights. I only half comprehend her."

"I've heard she's partially demented," said Arobin.

"She seems to me wonderfully sane," Edna replied.

"I'm told she's extremely disagreeable and unpleasant. Why have you introduced her at a moment when I desired to talk of you?"

"Oh! talk of me if you like," cried Edna, clasping her hands beneath her head; "but let me think of something else while you do."

"I'm jealous of your thoughts to-night. They're making you a little kinder than usual; but some way I feel as if they were wandering, as if they were not here with me." She only looked at him and smiled. His eyes were very near. He leaned upon the lounge with an arm extended across her, while the other hand still rested upon her hair. They continued silently to look into each other's eyes. When he leaned forward and kissed her, she clasped his head, holding his lips to hers.

It was the first kiss of her life to which her nature had really responded. It was a flaming torch that kindled desire.

XXVIII

Edna cried a little that night after Arobin left her. It was only one phase of the multitudinous emotions which had assailed her. There was with her an overwhelming feeling of irresponsibility. There was the shock of the unex-

6. Cylindrical stool.

pected and the unaccustomed. There was her husband's reproach looking at her from external existence. There was Robert's reproach making itself felt by a quicker, fiercer, more overpowering love, which had awakened within her toward him. Above all, there was understanding. She felt as if a mist had been lifted from her eyes, enabling her to look upon and comprehend the significance of life, that monster made up of beauty and brutality. But among the conflicting sensations which assailed her, there was neither shame nor remorse. There was a dull pang of regret because it was not the kiss of love which had inflamed her, because it was not love which had held this cup of life to her lips.

XXIX

Without even waiting for an answer from her husband regarding his opinion or wishes in the matter, Edna hastened her preparations for quitting her home on Esplanade Street and moving into the little house around the block. A feverish anxiety attended her every action in that direction. There was no moment of deliberation, no interval of repose between the thought and its fulfillment. Early upon the morning following those hours passed in Arobin's society, Edna set about securing her new abode and hurrying her arrangements for occupying it. Within the precincts of her home she felt like one who has entered and lingered within the portals of some forbidden temple in which a thousand muffled voices bade her begone.

Whatever was her own in the house, everything which she had acquired aside from her husband's bounty, she caused to be transported to the other house, supplying simple and meager deficiencies from her own resources.

Arobin found her with rolled sleeves, working in company with the housemaid when he looked in during the afternoon. She was splendid and robust, and had never appeared handsomer than in the old blue gown, with a red silk handkerchief knotted at random around her head to protect her hair from the dust. She was mounted upon a high step-ladder, unhooking a picture from the wall when he entered. He had found the front door open, and had followed his ring by walking in unceremoniously.

"Come down!" he said. "Do you want to kill yourself?" She greeted him with affected carelessness, and appeared absorbed in her occupation.

If he had expected to find her languishing, reproachful, or indulging in sentimental tears, he must have been greatly surprised.

He was no doubt prepared for any emergency, ready for any one of the foregoing attitudes, just as he bent himself easily and naturally to the situation which confronted him.

"Please come down," he insisted, holding the ladder and looking up at her.

"No," she answered; "Ellen is afraid to mount the ladder. Joe is working at the 'pigeon house'—that's the name Ellen gives it, because it's so small and looks like a pigeon house—and some one has to do this."

Arobin pulled off his coat, and expressed himself ready and willing to tempt fate in her place. Ellen brought him one of her dustcaps, and went into contortions of mirth, which she found it impossible to control, which she saw him put it on before the mirror as grotesquely as he could. Edna herself could not refrain from smiling when she fastened it at his request. So it was he who in turn mounted the ladder, unhooking pictures and curtains, and dislodging ornaments as Edna directed. When he had finished he took off his dustcap and went out to wash his hands.

Edna was sitting on the tabouret, idly brushing the tips of a feather duster along the carpet when he came in again.

"Is there anything more you will let me do?" he asked.

"That is all," she answered. "Ellen can manage the rest." She kept the young woman occupied in the drawing-room, unwilling to be left alone with Arobin.

"What about the dinner?" he asked; "the grand event, the *coup d'état?*"

"It will be day after to-morrow. Why do you call it the '*coup d'état?*' Oh! it will be very fine; all my best of everything—crystal, silver and gold, Sèvres, flowers, music, and champagne to swim in. I'll let Léonce pay the bills. I won-der what he'll say when he sees the bills."

"And you ask me why I call it a *coup d'état?*" Arobin had put on his coat, and he stood before her and asked if his cravat was plumb. She told him it was, looking no higher than the tip of his collar.

"When do you go to the 'pigeon house?'—with all due acknowledgement to Ellen."

"Day after to-morrow, after the dinner. I shall sleep there."

"Ellen, will you very kindly get me a glass of water?" asked Arobin. "The dust in the curtains, if you will pardon me for hinting such a thing, has parched my throat to a crisp."

"While Ellen gets the water," said Edna, rising, "I will say good-by and let you go. I must get rid of this grime, and I have a million things to do and think of."

"When shall I see you?" asked Arobin, seeking to detain her, the maid hav-ing left the room.

"At the dinner, of course. You are invited."

"Not before?—not to-night or to-morrow morning or to-morrow noon or night? or the day after morning or noon? Can't you see yourself, without my telling you, what an eternity it is?"

He had followed her into the hall and to the foot of the stairway looking up at her as she mounted with her face half turned to him.

"Not an instant sooner," she said. But she laughed and looked at him with eyes that at once gave him courage to wait and made it torture to wait.

XXX

Though Edna had spoken of the dinner as a very grand affair, it was in truth a very small affair and very select, in so much as the invited were few and were selected with discrimination. She had counted upon an even dozen seating themselves at her round mahogany board, forgetting for the moment that Madame Ratignolle was to the last degree *souffrante*[7] and unpresentable, and not foreseeing that Madame Lebrun would send a thousand regrets at the last moment. So there were only ten, after all, which made a cozy, comfortable number.

There were Mr. and Mrs. Merriman, a pretty vivacious little woman in the thirties; her husband, a jovial fellow, something of a shallow-pate,[8] who laughed a good deal at other people's witticisms, and had thereby made him-self extremely popular. Mrs. Highcamp had accompanied them. Of course, there was Alcée Arobin; and Mademoiselle Reisz had consented to come.

7. Ill. 8. I.e., shallow-minded.

Edna had sent her a fresh bunch of violets with black lace trimmings for her hair. Monsieur Ratignolle brought himself and his wife's excuses. Victor Lebrun, who happened to be in the city, bent upon relaxation, had accepted with alacrity. There was a Miss Mayblunt, no longer in her teens, who looked at the world through lorgnettes and with the keenest interest. It was thought and said that she was intellectual; it was suspected of her that she wrote under a *nom de guerre*.[9] She had come with a gentleman by the name of Gouvernail, connected with one of the daily papers, of whom nothing special could be said, except that he was observant and seemed quiet and inoffensive. Edna herself made the tenth, and at half-past eight they seated themselves at table, Arobin and Monsieur Ratignolle on either side of their hostess.

Mrs. Highcamp sat between Arobin and Victor Lebrun. Then came Mrs. Merriman, Mr. Gouvernail, Miss Mayblunt, Mr. Merriman, and Mademoiselle Reisz next to Monsieur Ratignolle.

There was something extremely gorgeous about the appearance of the table, an effect of splendor conveyed by a cover of pale yellow satin under strips of lace-work. There were wax candles in massive brass candelabra, burning softly under yellow silk shades; full, fragrant roses, yellow and red, abounded. There were silver and gold, as she had said there would be, and crystal which glittered like the gems which the women wore.

The ordinary stiff dining chairs had been discarded for the occasion and replaced by the most commodious and luxurious which could be collected throughout the house. Mademoiselle Reisz, being exceedingly diminutive, was elevated upon cushions, as small children are sometimes hoisted at table upon bulky volumes.

"Something new, Edna?" exclaimed Miss Mayblunt, with lorgnette directed toward a magnificent cluster of diamonds that sparkled, that almost sputtered, in Edna's hair, just over the center of her forehead.

"Quite new; 'brand' new, in fact; a present from my husband. It arrived this morning from New York. I may as well admit that this is my birthday, and that I am twenty-nine. In good time I expect you to drink my health. Meanwhile, I shall ask you to begin with this cocktail, composed—would you say 'composed?' " with an appeal to Miss Mayblunt—"composed by my father in honor of Sister Janet's wedding."

Before each guest stood a tiny glass that looked and sparkled like a garnet gem.

"Then, all things considered," spoke Arobin, "it might not be amiss to start out by drinking the Colonel's health in the cocktail which he composed, on the birthday of the most charming of women—the daughter whom he invented."

Mr. Merriman's laugh at this sally was such a genuine outburst and so contagious that it started the dinner with an agreeable swing that never slackened.

Miss Mayblunt begged to be allowed to keep her cocktail untouched before her, just to look at. The color was marvelous! She could compare it to nothing she had ever seen, and the garnet lights which it emitted were unspeakably rare. She pronounced the Colonel an artist, and stuck to it.

Monsieur Ratignolle was prepared to take things seriously; the *mets*, and

9. Pseudonym.

entre-mets, the service, the decorations, even the people. He looked up from his pompono[1] and inquired of Arobin if he were related to the gentleman of that name who formed one of the firm of Laitner and Arobin, lawyers. The young man admitted that Laitner was a warm personal friend, who permitted Arobin's name to decorate the firm's letterheads and to appear upon a shingle that graced Perdido Street.

"There are so many inquisitive people and institutions abounding," said Arobin, "that one is really forced as a matter of convenience these days to assume the virtue of an occupation if he has it not."

Monsieur Ratignolle stared a little, and turned to ask Mademoiselle Reisz if she considered the symphony concerts up to the standard which had been set the previous winter. Mademoiselle Reisz answered Monseiur Ratignolle in French, which Edna thought a little rude, under the circumstances, but characteristic. Mademoiselle had only disagreeable things to say of the symphony concerts, and insulting remarks to make of all the musicians of New Orleans, singly and collectively. All her interest seemed to be centered upon the delicacies placed before her.

Mr. Merriman said that Mr. Arobin's remark about inquisitive people reminded him of a man from Waco[2] the other day at the St. Charles Hotel—but as Mr. Merriman's stories were always lame and lacking point, his wife seldom permitted him to complete them. She interrupted him to ask if he remembered the name of the author whose book she had bought the week before to send to a friend in Geneva. She was talking "books" with Mr. Gouvernail and trying to draw from him his opinion upon current literary topics. Her husband told the story of the Waco man privately to Miss Mayblunt, who pretended to be greatly amused and to think it extremely clever.

Mrs. Highcamp hung with languid but unaffected interest upon the warm and impetuous volubility of her left-hand neighbor, Victor Lebrun. Her attention was never for a moment withdrawn from him after seating herself at table; and when he turned to Mrs. Merriman, who was prettier and more vivacious than Mrs. Highcamp, she waited with easy indifference for an opportunity to reclaim his attention. There was the occasional sound of music, of mandolins, sufficiently removed to be an agreeable accompaniment rather than an interruption to the conversation. Outside the soft, monotonous splash of a fountain could be heard; the sound penetrated into the room with the heavy odor of jessamine that came through the open windows.

The golden shimmer of Edna's satin gown spread in rich folds on either side of her. There was a soft fall of lace encircling her shoulders. It was the color of her skin, without the glow, the myriad living tints that one may sometimes discover in vibrant flesh. There was something in her attitude, in her whole appearance when she leaned her head against the high-backed chair and spread her arms, which suggested the regal woman, the one who rules, who looks on, who stands alone.

But as she sat there amid her guests, she felt the old ennui overtaking her; the hopelessness which so often assailed her, which came upon her like an obsession, like something extraneous, independent of volition. It was something which announced itself; a chill breath that seemed to issue from some vast

1. Or pompano fish, a southern delicacy. "*Mets*": main course. "*Entremets*": side dishes. 2. Town in Texas.

cavern wherein discords wailed. There came over her the acute longing which always summoned into her spiritual vision the presence of the beloved one, overpowering her at once with a sense of the unattainable.

The moments glided on, while a feeling of good fellowship passed around the circle like a mystic cord, holding and binding these people together with jest and laughter. Monsieur Ratignolle was the first to break the pleasant charm. At ten o'clock he excused himself. Madame Ratignolle was waiting for him at home. She was *bien souffrante,*[3] and she was filled with vague dread, which only her husband's presence could allay.

Mademoiselle Reisz arose with Monsieur Ratignolle, who offered to escort her to the car. She had eaten well; she had tasted the good rich wines, and they must have turned her head, for she bowed pleasantly to all as she withdrew from table. She kissed Edna upon the shoulder, and whispered: "*Bonne nuit, ma reine; soyez sage.*"[4] She had been a little bewildered upon rising, or rather, descending from her cushions, and Monsieur Ratignolle gallantly took her arm and led her away.

Mrs. Highcamp was weaving a garland of roses, yellow and red. When she had finished the garland, she laid it lightly upon Victor's black curls. He was reclining far back in the luxurious chair, holding a glass of champagne to the light.

As if a magician's wand had touched him, the garland of roses transformed him into a vision of Oriental beauty. His cheeks were the color of crushed grapes, and his dusky eyes glowed with a languishing fire.

"*Sapristi!*" exclaimed Arobin.

But Mrs. Highcamp had one more touch to add to the picture. She took from the back of her chair a white silken scarf, with which she had covered her shoulders in the early part of the evening. She draped it across the boy in graceful folds, and in a way to conceal his black, conventional evening dress. He did not seem to mind what she did to him, only smiled, showing a faint gleam of white teeth, while he continued to gaze with narrowing eyes at the light through his glass of champagne.

"Oh! to be able to paint in color rather than in words!" exclaimed Miss Mayblunt, losing herself in a rhapsodic dream as she looked at him.

> "There was a graven image of Desire
> Painted with red blood on a ground of gold' "[5]

murmured Gouvernail, under his breath.

The effect of the wine upon Victor was, to change his accustomed volubility into silence. He seemed to have abandoned himself to a reverie, and to be seeing pleasing visions in the amber bead.

"Sing," entreated Mrs. Highcamp. "Won't you sing to us?"

"Let him alone," said Arobin.

"He's posing," offered Mr. Merriman; "let him have it out."

"I believe he's paralyzed," laughed Mrs. Merriman. And leaning over the youth's chair, she took the glass from his hand and held it to his lips. He sipped the wine slowly, and when he had drained the glass she laid it upon the table and wiped his lips with her little filmy handkerchief.

3. Very ill.
4. Good night, my queen, be good.

5. From A *Cameo*, by Algernon Charles Swinburne (1837–1909)

"Yes, I'll sing for you," he said, turning in his chair toward Mrs. Highcamp. He clasped his hands behind his head, and looking up at the ceiling began to hum a little, trying his voice like a musician tuning an instrument. Then, looking at Edna, he began to sing:

> "Ah! si tu savais!"

"Stop!" she cried, "don't sing that. I don't want you to sing it," and she laid her glass so impetuously and blindly upon the table as to shatter it against a caraffe. The wine spilled over Arobin's legs and some of it trickled down upon Mrs. Highcamp's black gauze gown. Victor had lost all idea of courtesy, or else he thought his hostess was not in earnest, for he laughed and went on:

> "Ah! si tu savais
> Ce que tes yeux me disent"—

"Oh! you mustn't! you mustn't," exclaimed Edna, and pushing back her chair she got up, and going behind him placed her hand over his mouth. He kissed the soft palm that pressed upon his lips.

"No, no, I won't, Mrs. Pontellier. I didn't know you meant it," looking up at her with caressing eyes. The touch of his lips was like a pleasing sting to her hand. She lifted the garland of roses from his head and flung it across the room.

"Come, Victor; you've posed long enough. Give Mrs. Highcamp her scarf."

Mrs. Highcamp undraped the scarf from about him with her own hands. Miss Mayblunt and Mr. Gouvernail suddenly conceived the notion that it was time to say good night. And Mr. and Mrs. Merriman wondered how it could be so late.

Before parting from Victor, Mrs. Highcamp invited him to call upon her daughter, who she knew would be charmed to meet him and talk French and sing French songs with him. Victor expressed his desire and intention to call upon Miss Highcamp at the first opportunity which presented itself. He asked if Arobin were going his way. Arobin was not.

The mandolin players had long since stolen away. A profound stillness had fallen upon the broad, beautiful street. The voices of Edna's disbanding guests jarred like a discordant note upon the quiet harmony of the night.

XXXI

"Well?" questioned Arobin, who had remained with Edna after the others had departed.

"Well," she reiterated, and stood up, stretching her arms, and feeling the need to relax her muscles after having been so long seated.

"What next?" he asked.

"The servants are all gone. They left when the musicians did. I have dismissed them. The house has to be closed and locked, and I shall trot around to the pigeon house, and shall send Celestine over in the morning to straighten things up."

He looked around, and began to turn out some of the lights.

"What about upstairs?" he inquired.

"I think it is all right; but there may be a window or two unlatched. We had

better look; you might take a candle and see. And bring me my wrap and hat on the foot of the bed in the middle room."

He went up with the light, and Edna began closing doors and windows. She hated to shut in the smoke and the fumes of the wine. Arobin found her cape and hat, which he brought down and helped her to put on.

When everything was secured and the lights put out, they left through the front door, Arobin locking it and taking the key, which he carried for Edna. He helped her down the steps.

"Will you have a spray of jessamine?" he asked, breaking off a few blossoms as he passed.

"No; I don't want anything."

She seemed disheartened, and had nothing to say. She took his arm, which he offered her, holding up the weight of her satin train with the other hand. She looked down, noticing the black line of his leg moving in and out so close to her against the yellow shimmer of her gown. There was the whistle of a railway train somewhere in the distance, and the midnight bells were ringing. They met no one in their short walk.

The "pigeon-house" stood behind a locked gate, and a shallow *parterre*[6] that had been somewhat neglected. There was a small front porch, upon which a long window and the front door opened. The door opened directly into the parlor; there was no side entry. Back in the yard was a room for servants, in which old Celestine had been ensconced.

Edna had left a lamp burning low upon the table. She had succeeded in making the room look habitable and homelike. There were some books on the table and a lounge near at hand. On the floor was a fresh matting, covered with a rug or two; and on the walls hung a few tasteful pictures. But the room was filled with flowers. These were a surprise to her. Arobin had sent them, and had had Celestine distribute them during Edna's absence. Her bedroom was adjoining, and across a small passage were the dining-room and kitchen.

Edna seated herself with every appearance of discomfort.

"Are you tired?" he asked.

"Yes, and chilled and miserable. I feel as if I had been wound up to a certain pitch—too tight—and something inside of me had snapped." She rested her head against the table upon her bare arm.

"You want to rest," he said, "and to be quiet. I'll go; I'll leave you and let you rest."

"Yes," she replied.

He stood up beside her and smoothed her hair with his soft magnetic hand. His touch conveyed to her a certain physical comfort. She could have fallen quietly asleep there if he had continued to pass his hand over her hair. He brushed the hair upward from the nape of her neck.

"I hope you will feel better and happier in the morning," he said. "You have tried to do too much in the past few days. The dinner was the last straw; you might have dispensed with it."

"Yes," she admitted; "it was stupid."

"No, it was delightful; but it has worn you out." His hand had strayed to her beautiful shoulders, and he could feel the response of her flesh to his touch. He seated himself beside her and kissed her lightly upon the shoulder.

6. Ornamental garden.

"I thought you were going away," she said, in an uneven voice.

"I am, after I have said good night."

"Good night," she murmured.

He did not answer, except to continue to caress her. He did not say good night until she had become supple to his gentle, seductive entreaties.

XXXII

When Mr. Pontellier learned of his wife's intention to abandon her home and take up her residence elsewhere, he immediately wrote her a letter of unqualified disapproval and remonstrance. She had given reasons which he was unwilling to acknowledge as adequate. He hoped she had not acted upon her rash impulse; and he begged her to consider first, foremost, and above all else, what people would say. He was not dreaming of scandal when he uttered this warning; that was a thing which would never have entered into his mind to consider in connection with his wife's name or his own. He was simply thinking of his financial integrity. It might get noised about that the Pontelliers had met with reverses, and were forced to conduct their *ménage*[7] on a humbler scale than heretofore. It might do incalculable mischief to his business prospects.

But remembering Edna's whimsical turn of mind of late, and foreseeing that she had immediately acted upon her impetuous determination, he grasped the situation with his usual promptness and handled it with his well-known business tact and cleverness.

The same mail which brought to Edna his letter of disapproval carried instructions—the most minute instructions—to a well-known architect concerning the remodeling of his home, changes which he had long contemplated, and which he desired carried forward during his temporary absence.

Expert and reliable packers and movers were engaged to convey the furniture, carpets, pictures—everything movable, in short—to places of security. And in an incredibly short time the Pontellier house was turned over to the artisans. There was to be an addition—a small snuggery;[8] there was to be frescoing, and hardwood flooring was to be put into such rooms as had not yet been subjected to this improvement.

Furthermore, in one of the daily papers appeared a brief notice to the effect that Mr. and Mrs. Pontellier were contemplating a summer sojourn abroad, and that their handsome residence on Esplanade Street was undergoing sumptuous alterations, and would not be ready for occupancy until their return. Mr. Pontellier had saved appearances!

Edna admired the skill of his maneuver, and avoided any occasion to balk his intentions. When the situation as set forth by Mr. Pontellier was accepted and taken for granted, she was apparently satisfied that it should be so.

The pigeon-house pleased her. It at once assumed the intimate character of a home, while she herself invested it with a charm which it reflected like a warm glow. There was with her a feeling of having descended in the social scale, with a corresponding sense of having risen in the spiritual. Every step which she took toward relieving herself from obligations added to her strength and expansion as an individual. She began to look with her own eyes; to see and to apprehend the deeper undercurrents of life. No longer was she content to "feed upon opinion" when her own soul had invited her.

7. Household. 8. Den.

After a little while, a few days, in fact, Edna went up and spent a week with her children in Iberville. They were delicious February days, with all the summer's promises hovering in the air.

How glad she was to see the children! She wept for very pleasure when she felt their little arms clasping her; their hard, ruddy cheeks pressed against her own glowing cheeks. She looked into their faces with hungry eyes that could not be satisfied with looking. And what stories they had to tell their mother! About the pigs, the cows, the mules! About riding to the mill behind Glugluq; fishing back in the lake with their Uncle Jasper; picking pecans with Lidie's little black brood, and hauling chips in their express wagon. It was a thousand times more fun to haul real chips for old lame Susie's real fire than to drag painted blocks along the banquette or Esplanade Street!

She went with them herself to see the pigs and the cows, to look at the darkies laying the cane, to thrash the pecan trees, and catch fish in the back lake. She lived with them a whole week long, giving them all of herself, and gathering and filling herself with their young existence. They listened, breathless, when she told them the house in Esplanade Street was crowded with workmen, hammering, nailing, sawing, and filling the place with clatter. They wanted to know where their bed was; what had been done with their rocking-horse; and where did Joe sleep, and where had Ellen gone, and the cook? But, above all, they were fired with a desire to see the little house around the block. Was there any place to play? Were there any boys next door? Raoul, with pessimistic foreboding, was convinced that there were only girls next door. Where would they sleep, and where would papa sleep? She told them the fairies would fix it all right.

The old Madame was charmed with Edna's visit, and showered all manner of delicate attentions upon her. She was delighted to know that the Esplanade Street house was in a dismantled condition. It gave her the promise and pretext to keep the children indefinitely.

It was with a wrench and a pang that Edna left her children. She carried away with her the sound of their voices and the touch of their cheeks. All along the journey homeward their presence lingered with her like the memory of a delicious song. But by the time she had regained the city the song no longer echoed in her soul. She was again alone.

XXXIII

It happened sometimes when Edna went to see Mademoiselle Reisz that the little musician was absent, giving a lesson or making some small necessary household purchase. The key was always left in a secret hiding-place in the entry, which Edna knew. If Mademoiselle happened to be away Edna would usually enter and wait for her return.

When she knocked at Mademoiselle Reisz's door one afternoon there was no response; so unlocking the door, as usual, she entered and found the apartment deserted, as she had expected. Her day had been quite filled up, and it was for a rest, for a refuge, and to talk about Robert, that she sought out her friend.

She had worked at her canvas—a young Italian character study—all the morning, completing the work without the model; but there had been many interruptions, some incident to her modest housekeeping, and others of a social nature.

Madame Ratignolle had dragged herself over, avoiding the too public thoroughfares, she said. She complained that Edna had neglected her much of late. Besides, she was consumed with curiosity to see the little house and the manner in which it was conducted. She wanted to hear all about the dinner party; Monsieur Ratignolle had left so early. What had happened after he left? The champagne and grapes which Edna sent over were *too* delicious. She had so little appetite; they had refreshed and toned her stomach. Where on earth was she going to put Mr. Pontellier in that little house, and the boys? And then she made Edna promise to go to her when her hour of trial overtook her.

"At any time—any time of the day or night, dear," Edna assured her.

Before leaving Madame Ratignolle said:

"In some way you seem to me like a child, Edna. You seem to act without a certain amount of reflection which is necessary in this life. That is the reason I want to say you mustn't mind if I advise you to be a little careful while you are living here alone. Why don't you have some one come and stay with you? Wouldn't Mademoiselle Reisz come?"

"No; she wouldn't wish to come, and I shouldn't want her always with me."

"Well, the reason—you know how evil-minded the world is—some one was talking of Alcée Arobin visiting you. Of course, it wouldn't matter if Mr. Arobin had not such a dreadful reputation. Monsieur Ratignolle was telling me that his attentions alone are considered enough to ruin a woman's name."

"Does he boast of his successes?" asked Edna, indifferently, squinting at her picture.

"No, I think not. I believe he is a decent fellow as far as that goes. But his character is so well known among the men. I shan't be able to come back and see you; it was very, very imprudent today."

"Mind the step!" cried Edna.

"Don't neglect me," entreated Madame Ratignolle; "and don't mind what I said about Arobin, or having some one to stay with you."

"Of course not," Edna laughed. "You may say anything you like to me." They kissed each other good-bye. Madame Ratignolle had not far to go, and Edna stood on the porch a while watching her walk down the street.

Then in the afternoon Mrs. Merriman and Mrs. Highcamp had made their "party call." Edna felt that they might have dispensed with the formality. They had also come to invite her to play *vingt-et-un*[9] one evening at Mrs. Merriman's. She was asked to go early, to dinner, and Mr. Merriman or Mr. Arobin would take her home. Edna accepted in a half-hearted way. She sometimes felt very tired of Mrs. Highcamp and Mrs. Merriman.

Late in the afternoon she sought refuge with Mademoiselle Reisz, and stayed there alone, waiting for her, feeling a kind of repose invade her with the very atmosphere of the shabby, unpretentious little room.

Edna sat at the window, which looked out over the house-tops and across the river. The window frame was filled with pots of flowers, and she sat and picked the dry leaves from a rose geranium. The day was warm, and the breeze which blew from the river was very pleasant. She removed her hat and laid it on the piano. She went on picking the leaves and digging around the plants with her hat pin. Once she thought she heard Mademoiselle Reisz approaching. But it was a young black girl, who came in, bringing a small bundle of laundry, which she deposited in the adjoining room, and went away.

9. Twenty-one, a card game.

Edna seated herself at the piano, and softly picked out with one hand the bars of a piece of music which lay open before her. A half-hour went by. There was the occasional sound of people going and coming in the lower hall. She was growing interested in her occupation of picking out the aria, when there was a second rap at the door. She vaguely wondered what these people did when they found Mademoiselle's door locked.

"Come in," she called. turning her face toward the door. And this time it was Robert Lebrun who presented himself. She attempted to rise; she could not have done so without betraying the agitation which mastered her at sight of him, so she fell back upon the stool, only exclaiming, "Why Robert!"

He came and clasped her hand, seemingly without knowing what he was saying or doing.

"Mrs. Pontellier! How do you happen—oh! how well you look! Is Mademoiselle Reisz not here? I never expected to see you."

"When did you come back?" asked Edna in an unsteady voice, wiping her face with her handkerchief. She seemed ill at ease on the piano stool, and he begged her to take the chair by the window. She did so, mechanically, while he seated himself on the stool.

"I returned day before yesterday," he answered, while he leaned his arm on the keys, bringing forth a crash of discordant sound.

"Day before yesterday!" she repeated, aloud, and went on thinking to herself, "day before yesterday," in a sort of an uncomprehending way. She had pictured him seeking her at the very first hour, and he had lived under the same sky since day before yesterday; while only by accident had he stumbled upon her. Mademoiselle must have lied when she said. "Poor fool, he loves you."

"Day before yesterday," she repeated, breaking off a spray of Mademoiselle's geranium; "then if you had not met me here to-day you wouldn't—when— that is, didn't you mean to come and see me?"

"Of course, I should have gone to see you. There have been so many things—" he turned the leaves of Mademoiselle's music nervously. "I started in at once yesterday with the old firm. After all there is as much chance for me here as there was there—that is, I might find it profitable some day. The Mexicans were not very congenial."

So he had come back because the Mexicans were not congenial; because business was as profitable here as there; because of any reason, and not because he cared to be near her. She remembered the day she sat on the floor, turning the pages of his letter, seeking the reason which was left untold.

She had not noticed how he looked—only feeling his presence; but she turned deliberately and observed him. After all, he had been absent but a few months, and was not changed. His hair—the color of hers—waved back from his temples in the same way as before. His skin was not more burned than it had been at Grand Isle. She found in his eyes, when he looked at her for one silent moment, the same tender caress, with an added warmth and entreaty which had not been there before—the same glance which had penetrated to the sleeping places of her soul and awakened them.

A hundred times Edna had pictured Robert's return, and imagined their first meeting. It was usually at her home, whither he had sought her out at once. She always fancied him expressing or betraying in some way his love for her. And here, the reality was that they sat ten feet apart. she at the window, crushing geranium leaves in her hand and smelling them, he twirling around on the piano stool, saying:

"I was very much surprised to hear of Mr. Pontellier's absence; it's a wonder Mademoiselle Reisz did not tell me; and your moving—mother told me yesterday. I should think you would have gone to New York with him, or to Iberville with the children, rather than be bothered here with housekeeping. And you are going abroad, too, I hear. We shan't have you at Grand Isle next summer; it won't seem—do you see much of Mademoiselle Reisz? She often spoke of you in the few letters she wrote."

"Do you remember that you promised to write to me when you went away?" A flush overspread his whole face.

"I couldn't believe that my letters would be of any interest to you."

"That is an excuse; it isn't the truth." Edna reached for her hat on the piano. She adjusted it, sticking the hat pin through the heavy coil of hair with some deliberation.

"Are you not going to wait for Mademoiselle Reisz?" asked Robert.

"No; I have found when she is absent this long, she is liable not to come back till late." She drew on her gloves, and Robert picked up his hat.

"Won't you wait for her?" asked Edna.

"Not if you think she will not be back till late," adding, as if suddenly aware of some discourtesy in his speech, "and I should miss the pleasure of walking home with you." Edna locked the door and put the key back in its hiding place.

They went together, picking their way across muddy streets and sidewalks encumbered with the cheap display of small tradesmen. Part of the distance they rode in the car, and after disembarking, passed the Pontellier mansion, which looked broken and half torn asunder. Robert had never known the house, and looked at it with interest.

"I never knew you in your home," he remarked.

"I am glad you did not."

"Why?" She did not answer. They went on around the corner, and it seemed as if her dreams were coming true after all, when he followed her into the little house.

"You must stay and dine with me, Robert. You see I am all alone, and it is so long since I have seen you. There is so much I want to ask you."

She took off her hat and gloves. He stood irresolute, making some excuse about his mother who expected him; he even muttered something about an engagement. She struck a match and lit the lamp on the table; it was growing dusk. When he saw her face in the lamplight, looking pained, with all the soft lines gone out of it, he threw his hat aside and seated himself.

"Oh! you know I want to stay if you will let me!" he exclaimed. All the softness came back. She laughed, and went and put her hand on his shoulder.

"This is the first moment you have seemed like the old Robert. I'll go tell Celestine." She hurried away to tell Celestine to set an extra place. She even sent her off in search of some added delicacy which she had not thought of for herself. And she recommended great care in dripping the coffee and having the omelet done to a proper turn.

When she reëntered, Robert was turning over magazines, sketches, and things that lay upon the table in great disorder. He picked up a photograph, and exclaimed:

"Alcée Arobin! What on earth is his picture doing here?"

"I tried to make a sketch of his head one day," answered Edna, "and he

thought the photograph might help me. It was at the other house. I thought it had been left there. I must have picked it up with my drawing materials."

"I should think you would give it back to him if you have finished with it."

"Oh! I have a great many such photographs. I never think of returning them. They don't amount to anything." Robert kept on looking at the picture.

"It seems to me—do you think his head worth drawing? Is he a friend of Mr. Pontellier's? You never said you knew him."

"He isn't a friend of Mr. Pontellier's; he's a friend of mine. I always knew him—that is, it is only of late that I know him pretty well. But I'd rather talk about you, and know what you have been seeing and doing and feeling out there in Mexico." Robert threw aside the picture.

"I've been seeing the waves and the white beach of Grand Isle; the quiet, grassy street of the *Chênière*; the old fort at Grande Terre. I've been working like a machine, and feeling like a lost soul. There was nothing interesting."

She leaned her head upon her hand to shade her eyes from the light.

"And what have you been seeing and doing and feeling all these days?" he asked.

"I've been seeing the waves and the white beach of Grand Isle; the quiet, grassy street of the *Chênière Caminada*: the old sunny fort at Grande Terre. I've been working with little more comprehension than a machine, and still feeling like a lost soul. There was nothing interesting."

"Mrs. Pontellier, you are cruel," he said, with feeling, closing his eyes and resting his head back in his chair. They remained in silence till old Celestine announced dinner.

XXXIV

The dining-room was very small. Edna's round mahogany would have almost filled it. As it was there was but a step or two from the little table in the kitchen, to the mantel, the small buffet, and the side door that opened out on the narrow brick-paved yard.

A certain degree of ceremony settled upon them with the announcement of dinner. There was no return to personalities. Robert related incidents of his sojourn in Mexico. and Edna talked of events likely to interest him, which had occurred during his absence The dinner was of ordinary quality, except for the few delicacies which she had sent out to purchase. Old Celestine, with a bandana *tignon* twisted about her head,[1] hobbled in and out, taking a personal interest in everything; and she lingered occasionally to talk *patois*[2] with Robert, whom she had known as a boy.

He went out to a neighboring cigar stand to purchase cigarette papers, and when he came back he found that Celestine had served the black coffee in the parlor.

"Perhaps I shouldn't have come back," he said. "When you are tired of me, tell me to go."

"You never tire me. You must have forgotten the hours and hours at Grand Isle in which we grew accustomed to each other and used to being together."

"I have forgotten nothing at Grand Isle," he said, not looking at her, but rolling a cigarette. His tobacco pouch, which he laid upon the table, was a fantastic embroidered silk affair, evidently the handiwork of a woman.

1. I.e., her hair is tied up with a scarf. 2. Dialect.

"You used to carry your tobacco in a rubber pouch," said Edna, picking up the pouch and examining the needlework.

"Yes; it was lost."

"Where did you buy this one? In Mexico?"

"It was given to me by a Vera Cruz girl; they are very generous," he replied, striking a match and lighting his cigarette.

"They are very handsome, I suppose, those Mexican women; very picturesque, with their black eyes and their lace scarfs."

"Some are; others are hideous. Just as you find women everywhere."

"What was she like—the one who gave you the pouch? You must have known her very well."

"She was very ordinary. She wasn't of the slightest importance. I knew her well enough."

"Did you visit at her house? Was it interesting? I should like to know and hear about the people you met, and the impressions they made on you."

"There are some people who leave impressions not so lasting as the imprint of an oar upon the water."

"Was she such a one?"

"It would be ungenerous for me to admit that she was of that order and kind." He thrust the pouch back in his pocket, as if to put away the subject with the trifle which had brought it up.

Arobin dropped in with a message from Mrs. Merriman, to say that the card party was postponed on account of the illness of one of her children.

"How do you do, Arobin?" said Robert, rising from the obscurity.

"Oh! Lebrun. To be sure! I heard yesterday you were back. How did they treat you down in Mexico?"

"Fairly well."

"But not well enough to keep you there. Stunning girls, though, in Mexico. I thought I should never get away from Vera Cruz when I was down there a couple of years ago."

"Did they embroider slippers and tobacco pouches and hat bands and things for you?" asked Edna.

"Oh! my! no! I didn't get so deep in their regard. I fear they made more impression on me than I made on them."

"You were less fortunate than Robert, then."

"I am always less fortunate than Robert. Has he been imparting tender confidences?"

"I've been imposing myself long enough," said Robert, rising, and shaking hands with Edna. "Please convey my regards to Mr. Pontellier when you write."

He shook hands with Arobin and went away.

"Fine fellow, that Lebrun," said Arobin when Robert had gone. "I never heard you speak of him."

"I knew him last summer at Grand Isle," she replied. "Here is that photograph of yours. Don't you want it?"

"What do I want with it? Throw it away." She threw it back on the table.

"I'm not going to Mrs. Merriman's," she said. "If you see her, tell her so. But perhaps I had better write. I think I shall write now, and say that I am sorry her child is sick, and tell her not to count on me."

"It would be a good scheme," acquiesced Arobin. "I don't blame you; stupid lot!"

Edna opened the blotter, and having procured paper and pen, began to write a note. Arobin lit a cigar and read the evening paper, which he had in his pocket.

"What is the date?" she asked. He told her.

"Will you mail this for me when you go out?"

"Certainly." He read to her little bits out of the newspaper, while she straightened things on the table.

"What do you want to do?" he asked, throwing aside the paper. "Do you want to go for a walk or a drive or anything? It would be a fine night to drive."

"No; I don't want to do anything but just be quiet. You go away and amuse yourself. Don't stay."

"I'll go away if I must; but I shan't amuse myself. You know that I only live when I am near you."

He stood up to bid her good night.

"Is that one of the things you always say to women?"

"I have said it before, but I don't think I ever came so near meaning it," he answered with a smile. There were no warm lights in her eyes; only a dreamy, absent look.

"Good night. I adore you. Sleep well." he said, and he kissed her hand and went away.

She stayed alone in a kind of reverie—a sort of stupor. Step by step she lived over every instant of the time she had been with Robert after he had entered Mademoiselle Reisz's door. She recalled his words, his looks. How few and meager they had been for her hungry heart! A vision—a transcendently seductive vision of a Mexican girl arose before her. She writhed with a jealous pang. She wondered when he would come back. He had not said he would come back. She had been with him, had heard his voice and touched his hand. But some way he had seemed nearer to her off there in Mexico.

XXXV

The morning was full of sunlight and hope. Edna could see before her no denial—only the promise of excessive joy. She lay in bed awake, with bright eyes full of speculation. "He loves you, poor fool." If she could but get that conviction firmly fixed in her mind, what mattered about the rest? She felt she had been childish and unwise the night before in giving herself over to despondency. She recapitulated the motives which no doubt explained Robert's reserve. They were not insurmountable; they would not hold if he really loved her; they could not hold against her own passion, which he must come to realize in time. She pictured him going to his business that morning. She even saw how he was dressed; how he walked down one street, and turned the corner of another; saw him bending over his desk, talking to people who entered the office, going to his lunch, and perhaps watching for her on the street. He would come to her in the afternoon or evening, sit and roll his cigarette, talk a little, and go away as he had done the night before. But how delicious it would be to have him there with her! She would have no regrets, nor seek to penetrate his reserve if he still chose to wear it.

Edna ate her breakfast only half dressed. The maid brought her a delicious printed scrawl from Raoul, expressing his love, asking her to send him some bonbons, and telling her they had found that morning ten tiny white pigs all lying in a row beside Lidie's big white pig.

A letter also came from her husband, saying he hoped to be back early in March, and then they would get ready for that journey abroad which he had promised her so long, which he felt now fully able to afford; he felt able to travel as people should, without any thought of small economies—thanks to his recent speculations in Wall Street.

Much to her surprise she received a note from Arobin, written at midnight from the club. It was to say good morning to her, to hope that she had slept well, to assure her of his devotion, which he trusted she in some faintest manner returned.

All these letters were pleasing to her. She answered the children in a cheerful frame of mind, promising them bonbons, and congratulating them upon their happy find of the little pigs.

She answered her husband with friendly evasiveness,—not with any fixed design to mislead him, only because all sense of reality had gone out of her life, she had abandoned herself to Fate, and awaited the consequences with indifference.

To Arobin's note she made no reply. She put it under Celestine's stove-lid.

Edna worked several hours with much spirit. She saw no one but a picture dealer, who asked her if it were true that she was going abroad to study in Paris.

She said possibly she might, and he negotiated with her for some Parisian studies to reach him in time for the holiday trade in December.

Robert did not come that day. She was keenly disappointed. He did not come the following day, nor the next. Each morning she awoke with hope, and each night she was a prey to despondency. She was tempted to seek him out. But far from yielding to the impulse, she avoided any occasion which might throw her in his way. She did not go to Mademoiselle Reisz's nor pass by Madame Lebrun's, as she might have done if he had still been in Mexico.

When Arobin, one night, urged her to drive with him, she went—out to the lake, on the Shell Road.[3] His horses were full of mettle, and even a little unmanageable. She liked the rapid gait at which they spun along, and the quick, sharp sound of the horses' hoofs on the hard road. They did not stop anywhere to eat or to drink. Arobin was not needlessly imprudent. But they ate and they drank when they regained Edna's little dining-room—which was comparatively early in the evening.

It was late when he left her. It was getting to be more than a passing whim with Arobin to see her and be with her. He had detected the latent sensuality, which unfolded under his delicate sense of her nature's requirements like a torpid, torrid, sensitive blossom.

There was no despondency when she fell asleep that night; nor was there hope when she awoke in the morning.

XXXVI

There was a garden out in the suburbs; a small, leafy corner, with a few green tables under the orange trees. An old cat slept all day on the stone step in the sun, and an old *mulatresse*[4] slept her idle hours away in her chair at the open window, till some one happened to knock on one of the green tables. She had

3. Road by Lake Pontchartrain.

4. A mulatto woman, of mixed black and white ancestry.

milk and cream cheese to sell, and bread and butter. There was no one who could make such excellent coffee or fry a chicken so golden brown as she.

The place was too modest to attract the attention of people of fashion, and so quiet as to have escaped the notice of those in search of pleasure and dissipation. Edna had discovered it accidentally one day when the high-board gate stood ajar. She caught sight of a little green table, blotched with the checkered sunlight that filtered through the quivering leaves overhead. Within she had found the slumbering *mulatresse*, the drowsy cat, and a glass of milk which reminded her of the milk she had tasted in Iberville.

She often stopped there during her perambulations; sometimes taking a book with her, and sitting an hour or two under the trees when she found the place deserted. Once or twice she took a quiet dinner there alone, having instructed Celestine beforehand to prepare no dinner at home. It was the last place in the city where she would have expected to meet any one she knew.

Still she was not astonished when, as she was partaking of a modest dinner late in the afternoon, looking into an open book, stroking the cat, which had made friends with her—she was not greatly astonished to see Robert come in at the tall garden gate.

"I am destined to see you only by accident," she said, shoving the cat off the chair beside her. He was surprised, ill at ease, almost embarrassed at meeting her thus so unexpectedly.

"Do you come here often?" he asked.

"I almost live here," she said.

"I used to drop in very often for a cup of Catiche's good coffee. This is the first time since I came back."

"She'll bring you a plate, and you will share my dinner. There's always enough for two—even three." Edna had intended to be indifferent and as reserved as he when she met him; she had reached the determination by a laborious train of reasoning, incident to one of her despondent moods. But her resolve melted when she saw him before her, seated there beside her in the little garden, as if a designing Providence had led him into her path.

"Why have you kept away from me, Robert?" she asked, closing the book that lay open upon the table.

"Why are you so personal, Mrs. Pontellier? Why do you force me to idiotic subterfuges?" he exclaimed with sudden warmth. "I suppose there's no use telling you I've been very busy, or that I've been sick, or that I've been to see you and not found you at home. Please let me off with any one of those excuses."

"You are the embodiment of selfishness," she said. "You save yourself something—I don't know what—but there is some selfish motive, and in sparing yourself you never consider for a moment what I think, or how I feel your neglect and indifference. I suppose this is what you would call unwomanly; but I have got into a habit of expressing myself. It doesn't matter to me, and you may think me unwomanly if you like."

"No; I only think you cruel, as I said the other day. Maybe not intentionally cruel; but you seem to be forcing me into disclosures which can result in nothing; as if you would have me bare a wound for the pleasure of looking at it, without the intention or power of healing it."

"I'm spoiling your dinner, Robert; never mind what I say. You haven't eaten a morsel."

"I only came in for a cup of coffee." His sensitive face was all disfigured with excitement.

"Isn't this a delightful place?" she remarked. "I am so glad it has never actually been discovered. It is so quiet, so sweet here. Do you notice there is scarcely a sound to be heard? It's so out of the way; and a good walk from the car. However, I don't mind walking. I always feel so sorry for women who don't like to walk; they miss so much—so many rare little glimpses of life; and we women learn so little of life on the whole.

"Catiche's coffee is always hot. I don't know how she manages it, here in the open air. Celestine's coffee gets cold bringing it from the kitchen to the dining-room. Three lumps! How can you drink it so sweet? Take some of the cress with your chop; it's so biting and crisp. Then there's the advantage of being able to smoke with your coffee out here. Now, in the city—aren't you going to smoke?"

"After a while," he said, laying a cigar on the table.

"Who gave it to you?" she laughed.

"I bought it. I suppose I'm getting reckless; I bought a whole box." She was determined not to be personal again and make him uncomfortable.

The cat made friends with him, and climbed into his lap when he smoked his cigar. He stroked her silky fur, and talked a little about her. He looked at Edna's book, which he had read; and he told her the end, to save her the trouble of wading through it, he said.

Again he accompanied her back to her home; and it was after dusk when they reached the little "pigeon-house." She did not ask him to remain, which he was grateful for, as it permitted him to stay without the discomfort of blundering through an excuse which he had no intention of considering. He helped her to light the lamp; then she went into her room to take off her hat and to bathe her face and hands.

When she came back Robert was not examining the pictures and magazines as before; he sat off in the shadow, leaning his head back on the chair as if in a reverie. Edna lingered a moment beside the table, arranging the books there. Then she went across the room to where he sat. She bent over the arm of his chair and called his name.

"Robert," she said, "are you asleep?"

"No," he answered, looking up at her.

She leaned over and kissed him—a soft, cool, delicate kiss, whose voluptuous sting penetrated his whole being—then she moved away from him. He followed, and took her in his arms, just holding her close to him. She put her hand up to his face and pressed his cheek against her own. The action was full of love and tenderness. He sought her lips again. Then he drew her down upon the sofa beside him and held her hand in both of his.

"Now you know," he said, "now you know what I have been fighting against since last summer at Grand Isle; what drove me away and drove me back again."

"Why have you been fighting against it?" she asked. Her face glowed with soft lights.

"Why? Because you were not free; you were Léonce Pontellier's wife. I couldn't help loving you if you were ten times his wife, but so long as I went away from you and kept away I could help telling you so." She put her free

hand up to his shoulder, and then against his cheek, rubbing it softly. He kissed her again. His face was warm and flushed.

"There in Mexico I was thinking of you all the time, and longing for you."

"But not writing to me," she interrupted.

"Something put into my head that you cared for me; and I lost my senses. I forgot everything but a wild dream of your some way becoming my wife."

"Your wife!"

"Religion, loyalty, everything would give way if only you cared."

"Then you must have forgotten that I was Léonce Pontellier's wife."

"Oh! I was demented, dreaming of wild, impossible things, recalling men who had set their wives free, we have heard of such things."

"Yes, we have heard of such things."

"I came back full of vague, mad intentions. And when I got here—"

"When you got here you never came near me!" She was still caressing his cheek.

"I realized what a cur I was to dream of such a thing, even if you had been willing."

She took his face between her hands and looked into it as if she would never withdraw her eyes more. She kissed him on the forehead, the eyes, the cheeks, and the lips.

"You have been a very, very foolish boy, wasting your time dreaming of impossible things when you speak of Mr. Pontellier setting me free! I am no longer one of Mr. Pontellier's possessions to dispose of or not. I give myself where I choose. If he were to say, 'Here, Robert, take her and be happy; she is yours,' I should laugh at you both."

His face grew a little white. "What do you mean?" he asked.

There was a knock at the door. Old Celestine came in to say that Madame Ratignolle's servant had come around the back way with a message that Madame had been taken sick and begged Mrs. Pontellier to go to her immediately.

"Yes, yes," said Edna, rising; "I promised. Tell her yes—to wait for me. I'll go back with her."

"Let me walk over with you," offered Robert.

"No," she said; "I will go with the servant." She went into her room to put on her hat, and when she came in again she sat once more upon the sofa beside him. He had not stirred. She put her arms about his neck.

"Good-by, my sweet Robert. Tell me good-by." He kissed her with a degree of passion which had not before entered into his caress, and strained her to him.

"I love you," she whispered, "only you; no one but you. It was you who awoke me last summer out of a life-long, stupid dream. Oh! you have made me so unhappy with your indifference. Oh! I have suffered, suffered! Now you are here we shall love each other, my Robert. We shall be everything to each other. Nothing else in the world is of any consequence. I must go to my friend; but you will wait for me? No matter how late; you will wait for me, Robert?"

"Don't go; don't go! Oh! Edna, stay with me," he pleaded. "Why should you go? Stay with me, stay with me."

"I shall come back as soon as I can; I shall find you here." She buried her face in his neck, and said good-by again. Her seductive voice, together with his

great love for her, had enthralled his senses, had deprived him of every impulse but the longing to hold her and keep her.

XXXVII

Edna looked in at the drug store. Monsieur Ratignolle was putting up a mixture himself, very carefully, dropping a red liquid into a tiny glass. He was grateful to Edna for having come; her presence would be a comfort to his wife. Madame Ratignolle's sister, who had always been with her at such trying times, had not been able to come up from the plantation, and Adèle had been inconsolable until Mrs. Pontellier so kindly promised to come to her. The nurse had been with them at night for the past week, as she lived a great distance away. And Dr. Mandelet had been coming and going all the afternoon. They were then looking for him any moment.

Edna hastened upstairs by a private stairway that led from the rear of the store to the apartments above. The children were all sleeping in a back room. Madame Ratignolle was in the salon, whither she had strayed in her suffering impatience. She sat on the sofa, clad in an ample white *peignoir*, holding a handkerchief tight in her hand with a nervous clutch. Her face was drawn and pinched, her sweet blue eyes haggard and unnatural. All her beautiful hair had been drawn back and plaited. It lay in a long braid on the sofa pillow, coiled like a golden serpent. The nurse, a comfortable looking 'Griffe'[5] woman in white apron and cap, was urging her to return to her bedroom.

"There is no use, there is no use," she said at once to Edna. "We must get rid of Mandelet; he is getting too old and careless. He said he would be here at half-past seven; now it must be eight. See what time it is, Joséphine."

The woman was possessed of a cheerful nature, and refused to take any situation too seriously, especially a situation with which she was so familiar. She urged Madame to have courage and patience. But Madame only set her teeth hard into her under lip, and Edna saw the sweat gather in beads on her white forehead. After a moment or two she uttered a profound sigh and wiped her face with the handkerchief rolled in a ball. She appeared exhausted. The nurse gave her a fresh handkerchief, sprinkled with cologne water.

"This is too much!" she cried. "Mandelet ought to be killed! Where is Alphonse? Is it possible I am to be abandoned like this—neglected by every one?"

"Neglected, indeed!" exclaimed the nurse. Wasn't she there? And here was Mrs. Pontellier leaving, no doubt, a pleasant evening at home to devote to her? And wasn't Monsieur Ratignolle coming that very instant through the hall? And Joséphine was quite sure she had heard Doctor Mandelet's coupé.[6] Yes, there it was, down at the door.

Adèle consented to go back to her room. She sat on the edge of a little low couch next to her bed.

Doctor Mandelet paid no attention to Madame Ratignolle's upbraidings. He was accustomed to them at such times, and was too well convinced of her loyalty to doubt it.

He was glad to see Edna, and wanted her to go with him into the salon and entertain him. But Madame Ratignolle would not consent that Edna should

5. I.e., the offspring of a mulatto and a black or an American Indian. 6. Closed carriage.

leave her for an instant. Between agonizing moments, she chatted a little, and said it took her mind off her sufferings.

Edna began to feel uneasy. She was seized with a vague dread. Her own like experiences seemed far away, unreal, and only half remembered. She recalled faintly an ecstasy of pain, the heavy odor of chloroform, a stupor which had deadened sensation, and an awakening to find a little new life to which she had given being, added to the great unnumbered multitude of souls that come and go.

She began to wish she had not come; her presence was not necessary. She might have invented a pretext for staying away; she might even invent a pretext now for going. But Edna did not go. With an inward agony, with a flaming, outspoken revolt against the ways of Nature, she witnessed the scene [of] torture.

She was still stunned and speechless with emotion when later she leaned over her friend to kiss her and softly say good-by. Adèle, pressing her cheek, whispered in an exhausted voice: "Think of the children, Edna. Oh think of the children! Remember them!"

XXXVIII

Edna still felt dazed when she got outside in the open air. The Doctor's coupé had returned for him and stood before the *porte cochère*. She did not wish to enter the coupé, and told Doctor Mandelet she would walk; she was not afraid, and would go alone. He directed his carriage to meet him at Mrs. Pontellier's, and he started to walk home with her.

Up—away up, over the narrow street between the tall houses, the stars were blazing. The air was mild and caressing, but cool with the breath of spring and the night. They walked slowly, the Doctor with a heavy, measured tread and his hands behind him; Edna, in an absent-minded way, as she had walked one night at Grand Isle, as if her thoughts had gone ahead of her and she was striving to overtake them.

"You shouldn't have been there, Mrs. Pontellier," he said. "That was no place for you. Adèle is full of whims at such times. There were a dozen women she might have had with her, unimpressionable women. I felt that it was cruel, cruel. You shouldn't have gone."

"Oh, well!" she answered, indifferently. "I don't know that it matters after all. One has to think of the children some time or other; the sooner the better."

"When is Léonce coming back?"

"Quite soon. Some time in March."

"And you are going abroad?"

"Perhaps—no, I am not going. I'm not going to be forced into doing things. I don't want to go abroad. I want to be let alone. Nobody has any right—except children, perhaps—and even then, it seems to me—or it did seem—" She felt that her speech was voicing the incoherency of her thoughts, and stopped abruptly.

"The trouble is," sighed the Doctor, grasping her meaning intuitively, "that youth is given up to illusions. It seems to be a provision of Nature; a decoy to secure mothers for the race. And Nature takes no account of moral consequences, of arbitrary conditions which we create, and which we feel obliged to maintain at any cost."

"Yes," she said. "The years that are gone seem like dreams—if one might go on sleeping and dreaming—but to wake up and find—oh! well! perhaps it is better to wake up after all, even to suffer, rather than to remain a dupe to illusions all one's life."

"It seems to me, my dear child," said the Doctor at parting, holding her hand, "you seem to me to be in trouble. I am not going to ask for your confidence. I will only say that if ever you feel moved to give it to me, perhaps I might help you. I know I would understand, and I tell you there are not many who would—not many, my dear."

"Some way I don't feel moved to speak of things that trouble me. Don't think I am ungrateful or that I don't appreciate your sympathy. There are periods of despondency and suffering which take possession of me. But I don't want anything but my own way. That is wanting a good deal, of course, when you have to trample upon the lives, the hearts, the prejudices of others—but no matter—still, I shouldn't want to trample upon the little lives. Oh! I don't know what I'm saying, Doctor. Good night. Don't blame me for anything."

"Yes, I will blame you if you don't come and see me soon. We will talk of things you never have dreamt of talking about before. It will do us both good. I don't want you to blame yourself, whatever comes. Good night, my child."

She let herself in at the gate, but instead of entering she sat upon the step of the porch. The night was quiet and soothing. All the tearing emotion of the last few hours seemed to fall away from her like a somber, uncomfortable garment, which she had but to loosen to be rid of. She went back to that hour before Adèle had sent for her; and her senses kindled afresh in thinking of Robert's words, the pressure of his arms, and the feeling of his lips upon her own. She could picture at that moment no greater bliss on earth than possession of the beloved one. His expression of love had already given him to her in part. When she thought that he was there at hand, waiting for her, she grew numb with the intoxication of expectancy. It was so late; he should be asleep perhaps. She would awaken him with a kiss. She hoped he would be asleep that she might arouse him with her caresses.

Still, she remembered Adèle's voice whispering, "Think of the children; think of them." She meant to think of them, that determination had driven into her soul like a death wound—but not to-night. To-morrow would be time to think of everything.

Robert was not waiting for her in the little parlor. He was nowhere at hand. The house was empty. But he had scrawled on a piece of paper that lay in the lamplight:

"I love you. Good-by—because I love you."

Edna grew faint when she read the words. She went and sat on the sofa. Then she stretched herself out there, never uttering a sound. She did not sleep. She did not go to bed. The lamp sputtered and went out. She was still awake in the morning, when Celestine unlocked the kitchen door and came in to light the fire.

XXXIX

Victor, with hammer and nails and scraps of scantling,[7] was patching a corner of one of the galleries. Mariequita sat near by, dangling her legs, watching him work, and handing him nails from the tool-box. The sun was beating

7. Small bits of wood.

down upon them. The girl had covered her head with her apron folded into a square pad. They had been talking for an hour or more. She was never tired of hearing Victor describe the dinner at Mrs. Pontellier's. He exaggerated every detail, making it appear a veritable Lucullean[8] feast. The flowers were in tubs, he said. The champagne was quaffed from huge golden goblets. Venus rising from the foam[9] could have presented no more entrancing a spectacle than Mrs. Pontellier, blazing with beauty and diamonds at the head of the board, while the other women were all of them youthful houris[1] possessed of incomparable charms.

She got it into her head that Victor was in love with Mrs. Pontellier, and he gave her evasive answers, framed so as to confirm her belief. She grew sullen and cried a little, threatening to go off and leave him to his fine ladies. There were a dozen men crazy about her at the *Chênière*; and since it was the fashion to be in love with married people, why she could run away any time she liked to New Orleans with Célina's husband.

Célina's husband was a fool, a coward, and a pig, and to prove it to her, Victor intended to hammer his head into a jelly the next time he encountered him. This assurance was very consoling to Mariequita. She dried her eyes, and grew cheerful at the prospect.

They were still talking of the dinner and the allurements of city life when Mrs. Pontellier herself slipped around the corner of the house. The two youngsters stayed dumb with amazement before what they considered to be an apparition. But it was really she in flesh and blood, looking tired and a little travel-stained.

"I walked up from the wharf," she said, "and heard the hammering. I supposed it was you, mending the porch. It's a good thing. I was always tripping over those loose planks last summer. How dreary and deserted everything looks!"

It took Victor some little time to comprehend that she had come in Beaudelet's lugger, that she had come alone, and for no purpose but to rest.

"There's nothing fixed up yet, you see. I'll give you my room; it's the only place."

"Any corner will do," she assured him.

"And if you can stand Philomel's cooking," he went on, "though I might try to get her mother while you are here. Do you think she would come?" turning to Mariequita.

Mariequita thought that perhaps Philomel's mother might come for a few days, and money enough.

Beholding Mrs. Pontellier make her appearance, the girl had at once suspected a lovers' rendezvous. But Victor's astonishment was so genuine, and Mrs. Pontellier's indifference so apparent, that the disturbing notion did not lodge long in her brain. She contemplated with the greatest interest this woman who gave the most sumptuous dinners in America, and who had all the men in New Orleans at her feet.

"What time will you have dinner?" asked Edna. "I'm very hungry; but don't get anything extra."

"I'll have it ready in little or no time," he said, bustling and packing away his

8. The first-century B.C. Roman general Lucius Licinius Lucullus was noted for his extravagant banquets.

9. The Roman goddess of love and beauty was born out of the sea foam.
1. Beautiful maidens in the Muslim paradise.

tools. "You may go to my room to brush up and rest yourself. Mariequita will show you."

"Thank you," said Edna. "But, do you know, I have a notion to go down to the beach and take a good wash and even a little swim, before dinner?"

"The water is too cold!" they both exclaimed. "Don't think of it."

"Well, I might go down and try—dip my toes in. Why, it seems to me the sun is hot enough to have warmed the very depths of the ocean. Could you get me a couple of towels? I'd better go right away, so as to be back in time. It would be a little too chilly if I waited till this afternoon."

Mariequita ran over to Victor's room, and returned with some towels, which she gave to Edna.

"I hope you have fish for dinner," said Edna, as she started to walk away; "but don't do anything extra if you haven't."

"Run and find Philomel's mother," Victor instructed the girl. "I'll go to the kitchen and see what I can do. By Gimminy! Women have no consideration! She might have sent me word."

Edna walked on down to the beach rather mechanically, not noticing anything special except that the sun was hot. She was not dwelling upon any particular train of thought. She had done all the thinking which was necessary after Robert went away, when she lay awake upon the sofa till morning.

She had said over and over to herself: "To-day it is Arobin; tomorrow it will be some one else. It makes no difference to me, it doesn't matter about Léonce Pontellier—but Raoul and Étienne!" She understood now clearly what she had meant long ago when she said to Adèle Ratignolle that she would give up the unessential, but she would never sacrifice herself for her children.

Despondency had come upon her there in the wakeful night, and had never lifted. There was no one thing in the world that she desired. There was no human being whom she wanted near her except Robert; and she even realized that the day would come when he, too, and the thought of him would melt out of her existence, leaving her alone. The children appeared before her like antagonists who had overcome her; who had overpowered her and sought to drag her into the soul's slavery for the rest of her days. But she knew a way to elude them. She was not thinking of these things when she walked down to the beach.

The water of the Gulf stretched out before her gleaming with the million lights of the sun. The voice of the sea is seductive, never ceasing, whispering, clamoring, murmuring, inviting the soul to wander in abysses of solitude. All along the white beach, up and down, there was no living thing in sight. A bird with a broken wing was beating the air above, reeling, fluttering, circling disabled down, down to the water.

Edna had found her old bathing suit still hanging, faded, upon its accustomed peg.

She put it on, leaving her clothing in the bath-house. But when she was there beside the sea, absolutely alone, she cast the unpleasant, pricking garments from her, and for the first time in her life she stood naked in the open air, at the mercy of the sun, the breeze that beat upon her, and the waves that invited her.

How strange and awful it seemed to stand naked under the sky! how delicious! She felt like some new-born creature, opening its eyes in a familiar world that it had never known.

The foamy wavelets curled up to her white feet, and coiled like serpents about her ankles. She walked out. The water was chill, but she walked on. The water was deep, but she lifted her white body and reached out with a long, sweeping stroke. The touch of the sea is sensuous, enfolding the body in its soft, close embrace.

She went on and on. She remembered the night she swam far out, and recalled the terror that seized her at the fear of being unable to regain the shore. She did not look back now, but went on and on, thinking of the blue-grass meadow that she had traversed when a little child, believing that it had no beginning and no end.

Her arms and legs were growing tired.

She thought of Léonce and the children. They were a part of her life. But they need not have thought that they could possess her, body and soul. How Mademoiselle Reisz would have laughed, perhaps sneered, if she knew! "And you call yourself an artist! What pretensions, Madame! The artist must possess the courageous soul that dares and defies."

Exhaustion was pressing upon and over-powering her.

"Good-by—because, I love you." He did not know; he did not understand. He would never understand. Perhaps Doctor Mandelet would have understood if she had seen him—but it was too late; the shore was far behind her, and her strength was gone.

She looked into the distance, and the old terror flamed up for an instant, then sank again. Edna heard her father's voice and her sister Margaret's. She heard the barking of an old dog that was chained to the sycamore tree. The spurs of the cavalry officer clanged as he walked across the porch. There was the hum of bees, and the musky odor of pinks filled the air.

1899

MARY E. WILKINS FREEMAN
1852–1930

Mary E. Wilkins Freeman's finest short stories hauntingly explore the lives of aging New England women who confront their destitution with sturdy, even ferocious, independence. Whether, like Louisa Ellis of *A New England Nun*, they refuse marriage in order to protect the seclusion and sanctity of virginity or, like Sarah Penn of *The Revolt of "Mother,"* they assert their right to control the domestic sphere in which they have been placed, Freeman's heroines recognize their isolation and defiantly struggle to preserve their integrity against the demands of the importunate suitors, husbands, and preachers who represent all that is left of a dwindling Puritan culture. Like Sarah Orne Jewett, Freeman wrote in and about a region that had experienced a striking demographic change, namely the decline of the male population after the Civil War and the depression in New England's rural village economy.

The town in which Freeman spent most of her life, Randolph, Massachusetts, was populated by farmers, cottage workers in the shoe industry, and house carpenters like her father, Warren Wilkins. Both he and his wife, Eleanor (Lothrop) Wilkins, could trace their ancestry back to seventeenth-century New England settlers. Their first surviving infant, Mary Wilkins was seven years old when her sister was born. At this age, too, in the village school, she met Mary Wales, a friend she

would cherish throughout her life. At fifteen, she moved to Brattleboro, Vermont, where her father hoped to improve the family's fortunes by becoming part-owner of a dry goods store. But the next sixteen years would be filled with disappointments. After graduating from Brattleboro High School in 1870 and spending one unhappy year at Mount Holyoke Female Seminary, Mary Wilkins apparently fell in love with one Hanson Tyler. While the biographical details of this failed relationship are obscure, it is clear that it was accompanied by a series of other difficulties: Mary Wilkins's father went out of business, her one friend left town, her younger sister died, and the family moved into the house of Hanson Tyler's father, with Eleanor Wilkins employed as the Reverend Tyler's housekeeper. When she died suddenly in 1880 and Warren Wilkins died three years later, the thirty-one-year-old Mary Wilkins found herself alone and impoverished.

What saved Freeman from destitution and depression was the literary success she had already begun to achieve. Children's poems in a local magazine, *Wide Awake,* had brought small sums, but in 1882 she had won a fifty-dollar prize offered by a leading Boston magazine for adult fiction, and that same year *Harper's Bazar* sent her twenty-five dollars with an encouraging acceptance letter. Returning to Randolph, this time to live in the Wales household, Wilkins benefited for the next twenty years from the care of her childhood friend, for Mary Wales freed her from housekeeping chores and solaced her during the nightmares that frequently disturbed her sleep and that may have been responsible for her later addiction to sedatives. A *Humble Romance and Other Stories* (1887) and *A New England Nun and Other Stories* (1891) are usually considered Wilkins's best work. After 1895, when she began traveling to Brattleboro, Boston, Chicago, and Paris, she was well established as a "local-color" realist.

In spite of her financial success and fame, one index of Wilkins's troubled state of mind was her decade-long indecision about whether or not to commit herself to marriage. She had met Dr. Charles Freeman, a nonpracticing physician, in 1892. She was forty-nine years old when, after breaking the engagement and postponing the wedding, she married him in 1902. During the first years of their marriage, he was supportive of her writing, and she published a number of stories about the local customs of her new home, Metuchen, New Jersey. But in 1909 Dr. Freeman entered a sanitarium for alcoholism, the first of a series of such confinements. Before his death, his wife had obtained a legal separation, and after it she successfully contested his will, in which he had left most of his property to someone else. Wealthy at the end of her life, she was awarded the Howells Medal for Fiction in 1926, the same year that she and Edith Wharton became the first women to be elected to membership in the National Institute of Arts and Letters. When she died at seventy-eight, Freeman had published twenty volumes of adult fiction—novels and short stories—as well as six volumes of children's stories. While those volumes have only recently received the critical attention they deserve, *Old Woman Magoun* demonstrates the impact of her best work. Used as an object of exchange or a commodity, Freeman's naive Lily Barry encounters even parental attention as a fatality that leads to her destruction.

Old Woman Magoun

The hamlet of Barry's Ford is situated in a sort of high valley among the mountains. Below it the hills lie in moveless curves like a petrified ocean; above it they rise in green-cresting waves which never break. It is *Barry's* Ford because at one time the Barry family was the most important in the place; and *Ford* because just at the beginning of the hamlet the little turbulent Barry River is fordable. There is, however, now a rude bridge across the river.

Old Woman Magoun was largely instrumental in bringing the bridge to pass. She haunted the miserable little grocery, wherein whiskey and hands of tobacco[1] were the most salient features of the stock in trade, and she talked much. She would elbow herself into the midst of a knot of idlers and talk.

"That bridge ought to be built this very summer," said Old Woman Magoun. She spread her strong arms like wings and sent the loafers, half laughing, half angry, flying in every direction. "If I were a *man*," said she, "I'd go out this very minute and lay the fust log. If I were a passel[2] of lazy men layin' round, I'd start up for once in my life, I would." The men cowered visibly—all except Nelson Barry; he swore under his breath and strode over to the counter.

Old Woman Magoun looked after him majestically. "You can cuss all you want to, Nelson Barry," said she; "I ain't afraid of you. I don't expect you to lay ary log of the bridge, but I'm goin' to have it built this very summer." She did. The weakness of the masculine element in Barry's Ford was laid low before such strenuous feminine assertion.

Old Woman Magoun and some other women planned a treat—two sucking pigs, and pies, and sweet cake—for a reward after the bridge should be finished. They even viewed leniently the increased consumption of ardent spirits.

"It seems queer to me," Old Woman Magoun said to Sally Jinks, "that men can't do nothin' without havin' to drink and chew to keep their sperits up. Lord! I've worked all my life and never done nuther."

"Men is different," said Sally Jinks.

"Yes, they be," assented Old Woman Magoun, with open contempt.

The two women sat on a bench in front of Old Woman Magoun's house, and little Lily Barry, her granddaughter, sat holding her doll on a small mossy stone near by. From where they sat they could see the men at work on the new bridge. It was the last day of the work.

Lily clasped her doll—a poor old rag thing—close to her childish bosom, like a little mother, and her face, round which curled her long yellow hair, was fixed upon the men at work. Little Lily had never been allowed to run with the other children of Barry's Ford. Her grandmother had taught her everything she knew—which was not much, but tending at least to a certain measure of spiritual growth—for she, as it were, poured the goodness of her own soul into this little receptive vase of another. Lily was firmly grounded in her knowledge that it was wrong to lie or steal or disobey her grandmother. She had also learned that one should be very industrious. It was seldom that Lily sat idly holding her doll-baby, but this was a holiday because of the bridge. She looked only a child, although she was nearly fourteen; her mother had been married at sixteen. That is, Old Woman Magoun said that her daughter, Lily's mother, had married at sixteen; there had been rumors, but no one had dared openly gainsay the old woman. She said that her daughter had married Nelson Barry, and he had deserted her. She had lived in her mother's house, and Lily had been born there, and she had died when the baby was only a week old. Lily's father, Nelson Barry, was the fairly dangerous degenerate of a good old family. Nelson's father before him had been bad. He was now the last of the family, with the exception of a sister of feeble intellect, with whom he lived in the old Barry house. He was a middle-aged man, still handsome. The shiftless popula-

1. I.e., small bunches of tobacco leaves (for chewing). 2. Group.

tion of Barry's Ford looked up to him as to an evil deity. They wondered how Old Woman Magoun dared brave him as she did. But Old Woman Magoun had within her a mighty sense of reliance upon herself as being on the right track in the midst of a maze of evil, which gave her courage. Nelson Barry had manifested no interest whatever in his daughter. Lily seldom saw her father. She did not often go to the store which was his favorite haunt. Her grandmother took care that she should not do so.

However, that afternoon she departed from her usual custom and sent Lily to the store.

She came in from the kitchen, whither she had been to baste the roasting pig. "There's no use talkin'," said she, "I've got to have some more salt. I've jest used the very last I had to dredge over that pig. I've got to go to the store."

Sally Jinks looked at Lily. "Why don't you send her?" she asked.

Old Woman Magoun gazed irresolutely at the girl. She was herself very tired. It did not seem to her that she could drag herself up the dusty hill to the store. She glanced with covert resentment at Sally Jinks. She thought that she might offer to go. But Sally Jinks said again, "Why don't you let her go?" and looked with a languid eye at Lily holding her doll on the stone.

Lily was watching the men at work on the bridge, with her childish delight in a spectacle of any kind, when her grandmother addressed her.

"Guess I'll let you go down to the store an' git some salt, Lily," said she.

The girl turned uncomprehending eyes upon her grandmother at the sound of her voice. She had been filled with one of the innocent reveries of childhood. Lily had in her the making of an artist or a poet. Her prolonged childhood went to prove it, and also her retrospective eyes, as clear and blue as blue light itself, which seemed to see past all that she looked upon. She had not come of the old Barry family for nothing. The best of the strain was in her, along with the splendid stanchness in humble lines which she had acquired from her grandmother.

"Put on your hat," said Old Woman Magoun; "the sun is hot, and you might git a headache." She called the girl to her, and put back the shower of fair curls under the rubber band which confined the hat. She gave Lily some money, and watched her knot it into a corner of her little cotton handkerchief. "Be careful you don't lose it," said she, "and don't stop to talk to anybody, for I am in a hurry for that salt. Of course, if anybody speaks to you answer them polite, and then come right along."

Lily started, her pocket-handkerchief weighted with the small silver dangling from one hand, and her rag doll carried over her shoulder like a baby. The absurd travesty of a face peeped forth from Lily's yellow curls. Sally Jinks looked after her with a sniff.

"She ain't goin' to carry that rag doll to the store?" said she.

"She likes to," replied Old Woman Magoun, in a half-shamed yet defiantly extenuating voice.

"Some girls at her age is thinkin' about beaux instead of rag dolls," said Sally Jinks.

The grandmother bristled, "Lily ain't big nor old for her age," said she. "I ain't in any hurry to have her git married. She ain't none too strong."

"She's got a good color," said Sally Jinks. She was crocheting white cotton lace, making her thick fingers fly. She really knew how to do scarcely anything except to crochet that coarse lace; somehow her heavy brain or her fingers had

mastered that.

"I know she's got a beautiful color," replied Old Woman Magoun, with an odd mixture of pride and anxiety, "but it comes an' goes."

"I've heard that was a bad sign," remarked Sally Jinks, loosening some thread from her spool.

"Yes, it is," said the grandmother. "She's nothin' but a baby, though she's quicker than most to learn."

Lily Barry went on her way to the store. She was clad in a scanty short frock of blue cotton; her hat was tipped back, forming an oval frame for her innocent face. She was very small, and walked like a child, with the clap-clap of little feet of babyhood. She might have been considered, from her looks, under ten.

Presently she heard footsteps behind her; she turned around a little timidly to see who was coming. When she saw a handsome, well-dressed man, she felt reassured. The man came alongside and glanced down carelessly at first, then his look deepened. He smiled, and Lily saw he was very handsome indeed, and that his smile was not only reassuring but wonderfully sweet and compelling.

"Well, little one," said the man, "where are you bound, you and your dolly?"

"I am going to the store to buy some salt for grandma," replied Lily, in her sweet treble. She looked up in the man's face, and he fairly started at the revelation of its innocent beauty. He regulated his pace by hers, and the two went on together. The man did not speak again at once. Lily kept glancing timidly up at him, and every time that she did so the man smiled and her confidence increased. Presently when the man's hand grasped her little childish one hanging by her side, she felt a complete trust in him. Then she smiled up at him. She felt glad that this nice man had come along, for just here the road was lonely.

After a while the man spoke. "What is your name, little one?" he asked, caressingly.

"Lily Barry."

The man started. "What is your father's name?"

"Nelson Barry," replied Lily.

The man whistled. "Is your mother dead?"

"Yes, sir."

"How old are you, my dear?"

"Fourteen," replied Lily.

The man looked at her with surprise. "As old as that?"

Lily suddenly shrank from the man. She could not have told why. She pulled her little hand from his, and he let it go with no remonstrance. She clasped both her arms around her rag doll, in order that her hand should not be free for him to grasp again.

She walked a little farther away from the man, and he looked amused.

"You still play with your doll?" he said, in a soft voice.

"Yes, sir," replied Lily. She quickened her pace and reached the store.

When Lily entered the store, Hiram Gates, the owner, was behind the counter. The only man besides in the store was Nelson Barry. He sat tipping his chair back against the wall; he was half asleep, and his handsome face was bristling with a beard of several days' growth and darkly flushed. He opened his eyes when Lily entered, the strange man following. He brought his chair down on all fours, and he looked at the man—not noticing Lily at all—with a

look compounded of defiance and uneasiness.

"Hullo, Jim!" he said.

"Hullo, old man!" returned the stranger.

Lily went over to the counter and asked for the salt, in her pretty little voice. When she had paid for it and was crossing the store, Nelson Barry was on his feet.

"Well, how are you, Lily? It is Lily, isn't it?" he said.

"Yes, sir," replied Lily, faintly.

Her father bent down and, for the first time in her life, kissed her, and the whiskey odor of his breath came into her face.

Lily involuntarily started, and shrank away from him. Then she rubbed her mouth violently with her little cotton handkerchief, which she held gathered up with the rag doll.

"Damn it all! I believe she is afraid of me," said Nelson Barry, in a thick voice.

"Looks a little like it," said the other man, laughing.

"It's that damned old woman," said Nelson Barry. Then he smiled again at Lily. "I didn't know what a pretty little daughter I was blessed with," said he, and he softly stroked Lily's pink cheek under her hat.

Now Lily did not shrink from him. Hereditary instincts and nature itself were asserting themselves in the child's innocent, receptive breast.

Nelson Barry looked curiously at Lily. "How old are you, anyway, child?" he asked.

"I'll be fourteen in September," replied Lily.

"But you still play with your doll?" said Barry, laughing kindly down at her.

Lily hugged her doll more tightly, in spite of her father's kind voice. "Yes, sir," she replied.

Nelson glanced across at some glass jars filled with sticks of candy. "See here, little Lily, do you like candy?" said he.

"Yes, sir."

"Wait a minute."

Lily waited while her father went over to the counter. Soon he returned with a package of the candy.

"I don't see how you are going to carry so much," he said, smiling. "Suppose you throw away your doll?"

Lily gazed at her father and hugged the doll tightly, and there was all at once in the child's expression something mature. It became the reproach of a woman. Nelson's face sobered.

"Oh, it's all right, Lily," he said; "keep your doll. Here, I guess you can carry this candy under your arm."

Lily could not resist the candy. She obeyed Nelson's instructions for carrying it, and left the store laden. The two men also left, and walked in the opposite direction, talking busily.

When Lily reached home, her grandmother, who was watching for her, spied at once the package of candy.

"What's that?" she asked, sharply.

"My father gave it to me," answered Lily, in a faltering voice. Sally regarded her with something like alertness.

"Your father?"

"Yes, ma'am."

"Where did you see him?"

"In the store."

"He gave you this candy?"

"Yes, ma'am."

"What did he say?"

"He asked me how old I was, and—"

"And what?"

"I don't know," replied Lily; and it really seemed to her that she did not know, she was so frightened and bewildered by it all, and, more than anything else, by her grandmother's face as she questioned her.

Old Woman Magoun's face was that of one upon whom a long-anticipated blow had fallen. Sally Jinks gazed at her with a sort of stupid alarm.

Old Woman Magoun continued to gaze at her grandchild with that look of terrible solicitude, as if she saw the girl in the clutch of a tiger. "You can't remember what else he said?" she asked, fiercely, and the child began to whimper softly.

"No, ma'am," she sobbed. "I—don't know, and—"

"And what? Answer me."

"There was another man there. A real handsome man."

"Did he speak to you?" asked Old Woman Magoun.

"Yes ma'am; he walked along with me a piece," confessed Lily, with a sob of terror and bewilderment.

"What did he say to you?" asked Old Woman Magoun, with a sort of despair.

Lily told, in her little, faltering, frightened voice, all of the conversation which she could recall. It sounded harmless enough but the look of the realization of a long-expected blow never left her grandmother's face.

The sun was getting low, and the bridge was nearing completion. Soon the workmen would be crowding into the cabin for their promised supper. There became visible in the distance, far up the road, the heavily plodding figure of another woman who had agreed to come and help. Old Woman Magoun turned again to Lily.

"You go right up-stairs to your own chamber now," said she.

"Good land! ain't you goin' to let that poor child stay up and see the fun?" said Sally Jinks.

"You jest mind your own business," said Old Woman Magoun, forcibly, and Sally Jinks shrank. "You go right up there now, Lily," said the grandmother, in a softer tone, "and grandma will bring you up a nice plate of supper."

"When be you goin' to let that girl grow up?" asked Sally Jinks, when Lily had disappeared.

"She'll grow up in the Lord's good time," replied Old Woman Magoun, and there was in her voice something both sad and threatening. Sally Jinks again shrank a little.

Soon the workmen came flocking noisily into the house. Old Woman Magoun and her two helpers served the bountiful supper. Most of the men had drunk as much as, and more than, was good for them, and Old Woman Magoun had stipulated that there was to be no drinking of anything except coffee during supper.

"I'll git you as good a meal as I know how," she said, "but if I see ary one of you drinkin' a drop, I'll run you all out. If you want anything to drink, you can go up to the store afterward. That's the place for you to to go, if you've got to make hogs of yourselves. I ain't goin' to have no hogs in my house."

Old Woman Magoun was implicitly obeyed. She had a curious authority over most people when she chose to exercise it. When the supper was in full swing, she quietly stole up-stairs and carried some food to Lily. She found the girl, with the rag doll in her arms, crouching by the window in her little rocking-chair—a relic of her infancy, which she still used.

"What a noise they are makin', grandma!" she said, in a terrified whisper, as her grandmother placed the plate before her on a chair."

"They've 'most all of 'em been drinkin'. They air a passel of hogs," replied the old woman.

"Is the man that was with—with my father down there?" asked Lily, in a timid fashion. Then she fairly cowered before the look in her grandmother's eyes.

"No, he ain't; and what's more, he never will be down there if I can help it," said Old Woman Magoun, in a fierce whisper. "I know who he is. They can't cheat me. He's one of them Willises—that family the Barrys married into. They're worse than the Barrys, ef they *have* got money. Eat your supper, and put him out of your mind, child."

It was after Lily was asleep, when Old Woman Magoun was alone, clearing away her supper dishes, that Lily's father came. The door was closed, and he knocked, and the old woman knew at once who was there. The sound of that knock meant as much to her as the whir of a bomb to the defender of a fortress. She opened the door, and Nelson Barry stood there.

"Good-evening, Mrs. Magoun," he said.

Old Woman Magoun stood before him, filling up the doorway with her firm bulk.

"Good-evening, Mrs. Magoun," said Nelson Barry again.

"I ain't got no time to waste," replied the old woman, harshly. "I've got my supper dishes to clean up after them men."

She stood there and looked at him as she might have looked at a rebellious animal which she was trying to tame. The man laughed.

"It's no use," said he. "You know me of old. No human being can turn me from my way when I am once started in it. You may as well let me come in."

Old Woman Magoun entered the house, and Barry followed her.

Barry began without any preface. "Where is the child?" asked he.

"Up-stairs. She has gone to bed."

"She goes to bed early."

"Children ought to," returned the old woman, polishing a plate.

Barry laughed. "You are keeping her a child a long while," he remarked, in a soft voice which had a sting in it.

"She *is* a child," returned the old woman, defiantly.

"Her mother was only three years older when Lily was born."

The old woman made a sudden motion toward the man which seemed fairly menacing. Then she turned again to her dish-washing.

"I want her," said Barry.

"You can't have her," replied the old woman, in a still stern voice.

"I don't see how you can help yourself. You have always acknowledged that she was my child."

The old woman continued her task, but her strong back heaved. Barry regarded her with an entirely pitiless expression.

"I am going to have the girl, that is the long and short of it," he said, "and it

is for her best good, too. You are a fool, or you would see it."

"Her best good?" muttered the old woman.

"Yes, her best good. What are you going to do with her anyway? The girl is a beauty, and almost a woman grown, although you try to make out that she is a baby. You can't live forever."

"The Lord will take care of her," replied the old woman, and again she turned and faced him, and her expression was that of a prophetess.

"Very well, let Him," said Barry, easily. "All the same I'm going to have her, and I tell you it s for her best good. Jim Willis saw her this afternoon, and—"

Old Woman Magoun looked at him. 'Jim Willis!' she fairly shrieked.

"Well, what of it?"

"One of them Willises!" repeated the old woman, and this time her voice was thick. It seemed almost as if she were stricken with paralysis. She did not enunciate clearly.

The man shrank a little. "Now what is the need of your making such a fuss?" he said. "I will take her, and Isabel will look out for her."

"Your half-witted sister?" said Old Woman Magoun.

"Yes, my half-witted sister. She knows more than you think."

"More wickedness."

"Perhaps. Well, a knowledge of evil is a useful thing. How are you going to avoid evil if you don't know what it is like? My sister and I will take care of my daughter."

The old woman continued to look at the man, but his eyes never fell. Suddenly her gaze grew inconceivably keen. It was as if she saw through all externals.

"I know what it is!" she cried. "You have been playing cards and you lost, and this is the way you will pay him."

Then the man's face reddened, and he swore under his breath.

"Oh, my God " said the old woman; and she really spoke with her eyes aloft as if addressing something outside of them both. Then she turned again to her dish-washing.

The man cast a dogged look at her back. "Well, there is no use talking. I have made up my mind," said he, "and you know me and what that means. I am going to have the girl."

"When?" said the old woman, without turning around.

"Well, I am willing to give you a week. Put her clothes in good order before she comes."

The old woman made no reply. She continued washing dishes. She even handled them so carefully that they did not rattle.

"You understand," said Barry. "Have her ready a week from to-day."

"Yes," said Old Woman Magoun, "I understand."

Nelson Barry, going up the mountain road, reflected that Old Woman Magoun had a strong character, that she understood much better than her sex in general the futility of withstanding the inevitable.

"Well," he said to Jim Willis when he reached home, "the old woman did not make such a fuss as I expected."

"Are you going to have the girl?"

"Yes; a week from to-day. Look here, Jim; you've got to stick to your promise."

"All right," said Willis. "Go you one better."

The two were playing at cards in the old parlor, once magnificent, now squalid, of the Barry house. Isabel, the half-witted sister, entered, bringing some glasses on a tray. She had learned with her feeble intellect some tricks, like a dog. One of them was the mixing of sundry drinks. She set the tray on a little stand near the two men, and watched them with her silly simper.

"Clear out now and go to bed," her brother said to her, and she obeyed.

Early the next morning Old Woman Magoun went up to Lily's little sleeping-chamber, and watched her a second as she lay asleep, with her yellow locks spread over the pillow. Then she spoke. "Lily," said she—"Lily, wake up. I am going to Greenham across the new bridge, and you can go with me."

Lily immediately sat up in bed and smiled at her grandmother. Her eyes were still misty, but the light of awakening was in them.

"Get right up," said the old woman. "You can wear your new dress if you want to."

Lily gurgled with pleasure like a baby. "And my new hat?" asked she.

"I don't care."

Old Woman Magoun and Lily started for Greenham before Barry's Ford, which kept late hours, was fairly awake. It was three miles to Greenham. The old woman said that, since the horse was a little lame, they would walk. It was a beautiful morning, with a diamond radiance of dew over everything. Her grandmother had curled Lily's hair more punctiliously than usual. The little face peeped like a rose out of two rows of golden spirals. Lily wore her new muslin dress with a pink sash, and her best hat of a fine white straw trimmed with a wreath of rosebuds; also the neatest black open-work stockings and pretty shoes. She even had white cotton gloves. When they set out, the old, heavily stepping woman, in her black gown and cape and bonnet, looked down at the little pink fluttering figure. Her face was full of the tenderest love and admiration, and yet there was something terrible about it. They crossed the new bridge—a primitive structure built of logs in a slovenly fashion. Old Woman Magoun pointed to a gap.

"Jest see that," said she. "That's the way men work."

"Men ain't very nice, be they?" said Lily, in her sweet little voice.

"No, they ain't, take them all together," replied her grandmother.

"That man that walked to the store with me was nicer than some, I guess," Lily said, in a wishful fashion. Her grandmother reached down and took the child's hand in its small cotton glove. "You hurt me, holding my hand so tight," Lily said presently, in a deprecatory little voice.

The old woman loosened her grasp. "Grandma didn't know how tight she was holding your hand," said she. "She wouldn't hurt you for nothin', except it was to save your life, or somethin' like that." She spoke with an undertone of tremendous meaning which the girl was too childish to grasp. They walked along the country road. Just before they reached Greenham they passed a stone wall overgrown with blackberry-vines, and, an unusual thing in that vicinity, a lusty spread of deadly nightshade full of berries.

"Those berries look good to eat, grandma," Lily said.

At that instant the old woman's face became something terrible to see. "You can't have any now," she said, and hurried Lily along.

"They look real nice," said Lily.

When they reached Greenham, Old Woman Magoun took her way straight to the most pretentious house there, the residence of the lawyer, whose name was Mason. Old Woman Magoun bade Lily wait in the yard for a few mo-

ments, and Lily ventured to seat herself on a bench beneath an oak-tree; then she watched with some wonder her grandmother enter the lawyer's office door at the right of the house. Presently the lawyer's wife came out and spoke to Lily under the tree. She had in her hand a little tray containing a plate of cake, a glass of milk, and an early apple She spoke very kindly to Lily; she even kissed her, and offered her the tray of refreshments, which Lily accepted gratefully. She sat eating, with Mrs. Mason watching her, when Old Woman Magoun came out of the lawyer's office with a ghastly face.

"What are you eatin'?" she asked Lily, sharply. "Is that a sour apple?"

"I thought she might be hungry," said the lawyer's wife, with loving, melancholy eyes upon the girl.

Lily had almost finished the apple. "It's real sour, but I like it; it's real nice, grandma," she said.

"You ain't been drinkin' milk with a sour apple?"

"It was real nice milk, grandma."

"You ought never to have drunk milk and eat a sour apple," said her grandmother. "Your stomach was all out of order this mornin', an' sour apples and milk is always apt to hurt anybody."

"I don't know but they are," Mrs. Mason said, apologetically, as she stood on the green lawn with her lavender muslin sweeping around her. "I am real sorry, Mrs. Magoun. I ought to have thought. Let me get some soda for her."

"Soda never agrees with her," replied the old woman, in a harsh voice. "Come," she said to Lily, "it's time we were goin' home."

After Lily and her grandmother had disappeared down the road, Lawyer Mason came out of his office and joined his wife, who had seated herself on the bench beneath the tree. She was idle, and her face wore the expression of those who review joys forever past. She had lost a little girl, her only child, years ago, and her husband always knew when she was thinking about her. Lawyer Mason looked older than his wife; he had a dry, shrewd, slightly one-sided face.

"What do you think, Maria?" he said. "That old woman came to me with the most pressing entreaty to adopt that little girl."

"She is a beautiful little girl," said Mrs. Mason, in a slightly husky voice.

"Yes, she is a pretty child," assented the lawyer, looking pityingly at his wife; "but it is out of the question, my dear. Adopting a child is a serious measure, and in this case a child who comes from Barry's Ford."

"But the grandmother seems a very good woman," said Mrs. Mason.

"I rather think she is. I never heard a word against her. But the father! No, Maria, we cannot take a child with Barry blood in her veins. The stock has run out; it is vitiated physically and morally. It won't do, my dear."

"Her grandmother had her dressed up as pretty as a little girl could be," said Mrs. Mason, and this time the tears welled into her faithful, wistful eyes.

"Well, we can't help that," said the lawyer, as he went back to his office.

Old Woman Magoun and Lily returned, going slowly along the road to Barry's Ford. When they came to the stone wall where the blackberry-vines and the deadly nightshade grew, Lily said she was tired, and asked if she could not sit down for a few minutes. The strange look on her grandmother's face had deepened. Now and then Lily glanced at her and had a feeling as if she were looking at a stranger.

"Yes, you can set down if you want to," said Old Woman Magoun, deeply and harshly.

Lily started and looked at her, as if to make sure that it was her grandmother who spoke. Then she sat down on a stone which was comparatively free of the vines.

"Ain't you goin' to set down, grandma?" Lily asked, timidly.

"No; I don't want to get into that mess," replied her grandmother. "I ain't tired. I'll stand here."

Lily sat still; her delicate little face was flushed with heat. She extended her tiny feet in her best shoes and gazed at them. "My shoes are all over dust," said she.

"It will brush off," said her grandmother, still in that strange voice.

Lily looked around. An elm-tree in the field behind her cast a spray of branches over her head; a little cool puff of wind came on her face. She gazed at the low mountains on the horizon, in the midst of which she lived, and she sighed, for no reason that she knew. She began idly picking at the blackberry-vines; there were no berries on them; then she put her little fingers on the berries of the deadly nightshade. "These look like nice berries," she said.

Old Woman Magoun, standing stiff and straight in the road, said nothing.

"They look good to eat," said Lily.

Old Woman Magoun still said nothing, but she looked up into the ineffable blue of the sky, over which spread at intervals great white clouds shaped like wings.

Lily picked some of the deadly nightshade berries and ate them. "Why, they are real sweet," said she. "They are nice." She picked some more and ate them.

Presently her grandmother spoke. "Come," she said, "it is time we were going. I guess you have set long enough."

Lily was still eating the berries when she slipped down from the wall and followed her grandmother obediently up the road.

Before they reached home, Lily complained of being very thirsty. She stopped and made a little cup of a leaf and drank long at a mountain brook. "I am dreadful dry, but it hurts me to swallow," she said to her grandmother when she stopped drinking and joined the old woman waiting for her in the road. Her grandmother's face seemed strangely dim to her. She took hold of Lily's hand as they went on. "My stomach burns," said Lily, presently. "I want some more water."

"There is another brook a little farther on," said Old Woman Magoun, in a dull voice.

When they reached that brook, Lily stopped and drank again, but she whimpered a little over her difficulty in swallowing. "My stomach burns, too," she said, walking on, "and my throat is so dry, grandma." Old Woman Magoun held Lily's hand more tightly. "You hurt me holding my hand so tight, grandma," said Lily, looking up at her grandmother, whose face she seemed to see through a mist, and the old woman loosened her grasp.

When at last they reached home, Lily was very ill. Old Woman Magoun put her on her own bed in the little bedroom out of the kitchen. Lily lay there and moaned, and Sally Jinks came in.

"Why, what ails her?" she asked. "She looks feverish."

Lily unexpectedly answered for herself. "I ate some sour apples and drank some milk," she moaned.

"Sour apples and milk are dreadful apt to hurt anybody," said Sally Jinks. She told several people on her way home that Old Woman Magoun was

dreadful careless to let Lily eat such things.

Meanwhile Lily grew worse. She suffered cruelly from the burning in her stomach, the vertigo, and the deadly nausea. "I am so sick, I am so sick, grandma," she kept moaning. She could no longer see her grandmother as she bent over her, but she could hear her talk.

Old Woman Magoun talked as Lily had never heard her talk before, as nobody had ever heard her talk before. She spoke from the depths of her soul; her voice was as tender as the coo of a dove, and it was grand and exalted. "You'll feel better very soon, little Lily," said she.

"I am so sick, grandma."

"You will feel better very soon, and then—"

"I am sick."

"You shall go to a beautiful place."

Lily moaned.

"You shall go to a beautiful place," the old woman went on.

"Where?" asked Lily, groping feebly with her cold little hands. Then she moaned again.

"A beautiful place, where the flowers grow tall."

"What color? Oh, grandma, I am so sick."

"A blue color," replied the old woman. Blue was Lily's favorite color. "A beautiful blue color, and as tall as your knees, and the flowers always stay there, and they never fade."

"Not if you pick them, grandma? Oh!"

"No, not if you pick them; they never fade, and they are so sweet you can smell them a mile off; and there are birds that sing, and all the roads have gold stones in them, and the stone walls are made of gold."

"Like the ring grandpa gave you? I am so sick, grandma."

"Yes, gold like that. And all the houses are built of silver and gold, and the people all have wings, so when they get tired walking they can fly, and—"

"I am so sick, grandma."

"And all the dolls are alive," said Old Woman Magoun. "Dolls like yours can run, and talk, and love you back again."

Lily had her poor old rag doll in bed with her, clasped close to her agonized little heart. She tried very hard with her eyes, whose pupils were so dilated that they looked black, to see her grandmother's face when she said that, but she could not. "It is dark," she moaned, feebly.

"There where you are going it is always light," said the grandmother, "and the commonest things shine like that breastpin Mrs. Lawyer Mason had on to-day."

Lily moaned pitifully, and said something incoherent. Delirium was commencing. Presently she sat straight up in bed and raved; but even then her grandmother's wonderful compelling voice had an influence over her.

"You will come to a gate with all the colors of the rainbow," said her grandmother; "and it will open, and you will go right in and walk up the gold street, and cross the field where the blue flowers come up to your knees, until you find your mother, and she will take you home where you are going to live. She has a little white room all ready for you, white curtains at the windows, and a little white looking-glass, and when you look in it you will see—"

"What will I see? I am so sick, grandma."

"You will see a face like yours, only it's an angel's; and there will be a little

white bed, and you can lay down an' rest."

"Won't I be sick, grandma?" asked Lily. Then she moaned and babbled wildly, although she seemed to understand through it all what her grandmother said.

"No, you will never be sick anymore. Talkin' about sickness won't mean anything to you."

It continued. Lily talked on wildly, and her grandmother's great voice of soothing never ceased, until the child fell into a deep sleep, or what resembled sleep; but she lay stiffly in that sleep, and a candle flashed before her eyes made no impression on them.

Then it was that Nelson Barry came. Jim Willis waited outside the door. When Nelson entered he found Old Woman Magoun on her knees beside the bed, weeping with dry eyes and a might of agony which fairly shook Nelson Barry, the degenerate of a fine old race.

"Is she sick?" he asked, in a hushed voice.

Old Woman Magoun gave another terrible sob, which sounded like the gasp of one dying.

"Sally Jinks said that Lily was sick from eating milk and sour apples," said Barry, in a tremulous voice. "I remember that her mother was very sick once from eating them."

Lily lay still, and her grandmother on her knees shook with her terrible sobs.

Suddenly Nelson Barry started. "I guess I had better go to Greenham for a doctor if she's as bad as that," he said. He went close to the bed and looked at the sick child. He gave a great start. Then he felt of her hands and reached down under the bedclothes for her little feet. "Her hands and feet are like ice," he cried out. "Good God! why didn't you send for some one—for me—before? Why, she's dying; she's almost gone!"

Barry rushed out and spoke to Jim Willis, who turned pale and came in and stood by the bedside.

"She's almost gone," he said, in a hushed whisper.

"There's no use going for the doctor, she'd be dead before he got here," said Nelson, and he stood regarding the passing child with a strange, sad face—unutterably sad, because of his incapability of the truest sadness.

"Poor little thing, she's past suffering, anyhow," said the other man, and his own face also was sad with a puzzled, mystified sadness.

Lily died that night. There was quite a commotion in Barry's Ford until after the funeral, it was all so sudden, and then everything went on as usual. Old Woman Magoun continued to live as she had done before. She supported herself by the produce of her tiny farm; she was very industrious, but people said that she was a trifle touched, since every time she went over the log bridge with her eggs or her garden vegetables to sell in Greenham, she carried with her, as one might have carried an infant, Lily's old rag doll.

1909

LADY AUGUSTA GREGORY

1852–1932

"Lady Gregory was friend and hostess," wrote the Irish poet W. B. Yeats of the woman who had been his lifelong patroness, but "neither she nor we thought her a

possible creator." Yet when she herself began to write, he added, "she became the founder of modern Irish dialect literature." Specifically, Lady Gregory produced, first, a collection of traditional tales about the ancient Gaelic hero Cuchulain (*Cuchulain of Muirthemne*, 1902); then, another important volume of Irish legends (*Gods and Fighting Men*, 1904); finally—and most important—a group of spirited, inventive, and distinctively Irish plays that made a notable mark on the theater of their time. In yet another way, moreover, this onetime "hostess" helped influence the course of twentieth-century art, for in 1893, with Yeats and the poet-playwright Edward Martyn, she founded the Irish Literary Theatre, which in 1904 moved to the famous Abbey Theatre, an institution that was as important to the history of drama as it was central in the rise of the turn-of-the-century Irish nationalist movement.

Born to a wealthy, landowning family in County Galway, in west Ireland, Isabella Augusta Persse married Sir William Gregory, a former governor of Ceylon, in 1880; after his death in 1892, she edited his memoirs and his grandfather's letters. By that time, however, she had already begun to meet, befriend, and subsidize such Irish literary men as Yeats, George Moore, Edward Martyn, John Synge, and James Joyce, all of whom—along with Lady Gregory herself—were variously concerned with reestablishing the indigenous Irish culture that had been shattered when the English conquered the country in the sixteenth century. Her volumes of Irish tales represented a significant step toward reviving lost traditions, while her work for the Abbey Theatre, with its emphasis on plays written in an accurately transcribed Irish dialect and created around plots that elaborated Irish themes and myths, was another such step. Of at least equal importance, however, were her own creations, especially witty plays like *Spreading the News*, a one-act drama that vividly evokes the world of the Irish peasantry under British imperial rule even while it reveals a keen concern with a uniquely female realm of humorous gossip and "scandal."

Lady Gregory's pieces for the Abbey Theatre had far more drawing power than Yeats's sometimes greater but usually more arcane offerings because they generally treated more popular concerns. Thus, as one observer put it, "Yeats spells empty benches . . . Lady Gregory popularity." Yet despite the solidity of her achievement, this significant woman dramatist always had a tenuous reputation. Though George Bernard Shaw defined her as "the greatest living Irishwoman," he also sardonically remarked that she was "the charwoman of the Abbey Theatre," no doubt because, as a born "hostess" and patroness, she was willing to handle so many details of what Yeats once called "theatre business, management of men." Nevertheless, at least on Yeats himself her artistic as well as her personal talent made an indelible impression: in two great late poems—*Coole Park, 1929* and *Coole Park and Ballylee, 1931*—both devoted to her deep connections with the places where she lived, he memorialized his sense of her genius, noting in *Coole Park, 1929* that this "woman's powerful character / Could keep a swallow to its first intent."

Spreading the News

PERSONS

BARTLEY FALLON	JAMES RYAN
MRS. FALLON	MRS. TARPEY
JACK SMITH	MRS. TULLY
SHAWN EARLY	A POLICEMAN, JO MULDOON
TIM CASEY	A REMOVABLE MAGISTRATE

SCENE

[*The outskirts of a Fair. An Apple Stall.* MRS. TARPEY *sitting at it.* MAGISTRATE *and* POLICEMAN *enter.*]

MAGISTRATE. So that is the Fair Green. Cattle and sheep and mud. No system. What a repulsive sight!

POLICEMAN. That is so, indeed.

MAGISTRATE. I suppose there is a good deal of disorder in this place?

POLICEMAN. There is.

MAGISTRATE. Common assault?

POLICEMAN. It's common enough.

MAGISTRATE. Agrarian crime, no doubt?

POLICEMAN. That is so.

MAGISTRATE. Boycotting? Maiming of cattle? Firing into houses?

POLICEMAN. There was one time, and there might be again.

MAGISTRATE. That is bad. Does it go any farther than that?

POLICEMAN. Far enough, indeed.

MAGISTRATE. Homicide, then! This district has been shamefully neglected! I will change all that. When I was in the Andaman Islands,[1] my system never failed. Yes, yes, I will change all that. What has that woman on her stall?

POLICEMAN. Apples mostly—and sweets.

MAGISTRATE. Just see if there are any unlicensed goods underneath—spirits or the like. We had evasions of the salt tax in the Andaman Islands.

POLICEMAN. [Sniffing cautiously and upsetting a heap of apples.] I see no spirits here—or salt.

MAGISTRATE. [To MRS. TARPEY.] Do you know this town well, my good woman?

MRS. TARPEY. [Holding out some apples.] A penny the half-dozen, your honor.

POLICEMAN. [Shouting.] The gentleman is asking do you know the town! He's the new magistrate!

MRS. TARPEY. [Rising and ducking.] Do I know the town? I do, to be sure.

MAGISTRATE. [Shouting.] What is its chief business?

MRS. TARPEY. Business, is it? What business would the people here have but to be minding one another's business?

MAGISTRATE. I mean what trade have they?

MRS. TARPEY. Not a trade. No trade at all but to be talking.

MAGISTRATE. I shall learn nothing here.

[JAMES RYAN comes in, pipe in mouth. Seeing MAGISTRATE he retreats quickly, taking pipe from mouth.]

MAGISTRATE. The smoke from that man's pipe had a greenish look; he may be growing unlicensed tobacco at home. I wish I had brought my telescope to this district. Come to the postoffice, I will telegraph for it. I found it very useful in the Andaman Islands.

[MAGISTRATE and POLICEMAN go out left.]

MRS. TARPEY. Bad luck to Jo Muldoon, knocking my apples this way and that way. [Begins arranging them.] Showing off he was to the new magistrate.

[Enter BARTLEY FALLON and MRS. FALLON.]

BARTLEY. Indeed it's a poor country and a scarce country to be living in. But I'm thinking if I went to America it's long ago the day I'd be dead!

MRS. FALLON. So you might, indeed.

[She puts her basket on a barrel and begins putting parcels in it, taking them from under her cloak.]

BARTLEY. And it's a great expense for a poor man to be buried in America.

MRS. FALLON. Never fear, Bartley Fallon, but I'll give you a good burying the day you'll die.

1. Islands governed by Great Britain, south of India.

BARTLEY. Maybe it's yourself will be buried in the graveyard of Cloonmara before me, Mary Fallon, and I myself that will be dying unbeknownst some night, and no one a-near me. And the cat itself may be gone straying through the country, and the mice squealing over the quilt.

MRS. FALLON. Leave off talking of dying. It might be twenty years you'll be living yet.

BARTLEY. [With a deep sigh.] I'm thinking if I'll be living at the end of twenty years, it's a very old man I'll be then!

MRS. TARPEY. [Turns and sees them.] Good morrow, Bartley Fallon; good morrow, Mrs. Fallon. Well, Bartley, you'll find no cause for complaining today; they are all saying it was a good fair.

BARTLEY. [Raising his voice.] It was not a good fair, Mrs. Tarpey. It was a scattered sort of a fair. If we didn't expect more, we got less. That's the way with me always; whatever I have to sell goes down and whatever I have to buy goes up. If there's ever any misfortune coming to this world, it's on myself it pitches, like a flock of crows on seed potatoes.[2]

MRS. FALLON. Leave off talking of misfortunes, and listen to Jack Smith that is coming the way, and he singing.

[Voice of JACK SMITH heard singing.]

> I thought, my first love,
> There'd be but one house between you and me,
> And I thought I would find
> Yourself coaxing my child on your knee.
> Over the tide
> I would leap with the leap of a swan,
> Till I came to the side
> Of the wife of the Red-haired man![3]

[JACK SMITH comes in; he is a red-haired man, and is carrying a hayfork.]

MRS. TARPEY. That should be a good song if I had my hearing.

MRS. FALLON. [Shouting.] It's "The Red-haired Man's Wife."

MRS. TARPEY. I know it well. That's the song that has a skin on it!

[She turns her back to them and goes on arranging her apples.]

MRS. FALLON. Where's herself, Jack Smith?

JACK SMITH. She was delayed with her washing; bleaching the clothes on the hedge she is, and she daren't leave them, with all the tinkers[4] that do be passing to the fair. It isn't to the fair I came myself, but up to the Five Acre Meadow I'm going, where I have a contract for the hay. We'll get a share of it into tramps[5] today. [He lays down hayfork and lights his pipe.]

BARTLEY. You will not get it into tramps today. The rain will be down on it by evening, and on myself too. It's seldom I ever started on a journey but the rain would come down on me before I'd find any place of shelter.

JACK SMITH. If it didn't itself, Bartley, it is my belief you would carry a leaky pail on your head in place of a hat, the way you'd not be without some cause of complaining.

[A voice heard. "Go on, now, go on out o' that. Go on I say."]

JACK SMITH. Look at that young mare of Pat Ryan's that is backing into Shaughnessy's bullocks with the dint[6] of the crowd! Don't be daunted, Pat, I'll give you a hand with her.

2. Potatoes newly planted.
3. A traditional Irish ballad.
4. Gypsies.

5. I.e., bales of hay.
6. Pressure.

[*He goes out leaving his hayfork.*]

MRS. FALLON. It's time for ourselves to be going home. I have all I bought put in the basket. Look at there, Jack Smith's hayfork he left after him! He'll be wanting it. [*Calls.*] Jack Smith! Jack Smith!—He's gone through the crowd—hurry after him, Bartley, he'll be wanting it.

BARTLEY. I'll do that. This is no safe place to be leaving it. [*He takes up fork awkwardly and upsets the basket.*] Look at that now! If there is any basket in the fair upset, it must be our own basket! [*He goes out to right.*]

MRS. FALLON. Get out of that! It is your own fault, it is. Talk of misfortunes and misfortunes will come. Glory be! Look at my new egg-cups rolling in every part—and my two pound of sugar with the paper broke—

MRS. TARPEY. [*Turning from stall.*] God help us, Mrs. Fallon, what happened your basket?

MRS. FALLON. It's himself that knocked it down, bad manners to him. [*Putting things up.*] My grand sugar that's destroyed, and he'll not drink his tea without it. I had best go back to the shop for more, much good may it do him! [*Enter* TIM CASEY]

TIM CASEY. Where is Bartley Fallon, Mrs. Fallon? I want a word with him before he'll leave the fair. I was afraid he might have gone home by this, for he's a temperate man.

MRS. FALLON. I wish he did go home! It'd be best for me if he went home straight from the fair green, or if he never came with me at all! Where is he, is it? He's gone up the road [*Jerks elbow.*] following Jack Smith with a hayfork.

[*She goes out to left.*]

TIM CASEY. Following Jack Smith with a hayfork! Did ever anyone hear the like of that. [*Shouts.*] Did you hear that news, Mrs. Tarpey?

MRS. TARPEY. I heard no news at all.

TIM CASEY. Some dispute I suppose it was that rose between Jack Smith and Bartley Fallon, and it seems Jack made off, and Bartley is following him with a hayfork!

MRS. TARPEY. Is he now? Well, that was quick work! It's not ten minutes since the two of them were here, Bartley going home and Jack going to the Five Acre Meadow; and I had my apples to settle up, that Jo Muldoon of the police had scattered, and when I looked round again Jack Smith was gone, and Bartley Fallon was gone, and Mrs. Fallon's basket upset, and all in it strewed upon the ground—the tea here—the two pound of sugar there—the eggs-cups there—Look, now, what a great hardship the deafness puts upon me, that I didn't hear the commencement of the fight! Wait till I tell James Ryan that I see below; he is a neighbor of Bartley's, it would be a pity if he wouldn't hear the news!

[*She goes out. Enter* SHAWN EARLY *and* MRS. TULLY]

TIM CASEY. Listen, Shawn Early! Listen, Mrs. Tully, to the news! Jack Smith and Bartley Fallon had a falling out, and Jack knocked Mrs. Fallon's basket into the road, and Bartley made an attack on him with a hayfork, and away with Jack, and Bartley after him. Look at the sugar here yet on the road!

SHAWN EARLY. Do you tell me so? Well, that's a queer thing, and Bartley Fallon so quiet a man!

MRS. TULLY. I wouldn't wonder at all. I would never think well of a man that would have that sort of a moldering[7] look. It's likely he has overtaken Jack by this.

7. Wasted.

[*Enter* JAMES RYAN *and* MRS. TARPEY]

JAMES RYAN. That is great news Mrs. Tarpey was telling me! I suppose that's what brought the police and the magistrate up this way. I was wondering to see them in it a while ago.

SHAWN EARLY. The police after them? Bartley Fallon must have injured Jack so. They wouldn't meddle in a fight that was only for show!

MRS. TULLY. Why wouldn't he injure him? There was many a man killed with no more of a weapon than a hayfork.

JAMES RYAN. Wait till I run north as far as Kelly's bar to spread the news! [*He goes out.*]

TIM CASEY. I'll go tell Jack Smith's first cousin that is standing there south of the church after selling his lambs. [*Goes out.*]

MRS. TULLY. I'll go telling a few of the neighbors I see beyond to the west. [*Goes out.*]

SHAWN EARLY. I'll give word of it beyond at the east of the green.

[*Is going out when* MRS. TARPEY *seizes hold of him.*]

MRS. TARPEY. Stop a minute, Shawn Early, and tell me did you see red Jack Smith's wife, Kitty Keary, in any place?

SHAWN EARLY. I did. At her own house she was, drying clothes on the hedge as I passed.

MRS. TARPEY. What did you say she was doing?

SHAWN EARLY. [*Breaking away.*] Laying out a sheet on the hedge.

[*He goes.*]

MRS. TARPEY. Laying out a sheet for the dead! The Lord have mercy on us! Jack Smith dead and his wife laying out a sheet for his burying [*Calls out.*] Why didn't you tell me that before, Shawn Early? Isn't the deafness the great hardship? Half the world might be dead without me knowing of it or getting word of it at all! [*She sits down and rocks herself.*] O my poor Jack Smith! To be going to his work so nice and so hearty, and to be left stretched on the ground in the full light of the day!

[*Enter* TIM CASEY]

TIM CASEY. What is it, Mrs. Tarpey? What happened since?

MRS. TARPEY. O my poor Jack Smith!

TIM CASEY. Did Bartley overtake him?

MRS. TARPEY. O the poor man!

TIM CASEY. Is it killed he is?

MRS. TARPEY. Stretched in the Five Acre Meadow!

TIM CASEY. The Lord have mercy on us! Is that a fact?

MRS. TARPEY. Without the rites of the Church or a ha'porth![8]

TIM CASEY. Who was telling you?

MRS. TARPEY. And the wife laying out a sheet for his corpse.

[*Sits up and wipes her eyes.*] I suppose they'll wake him the same as another?

[*Enter* MRS. TULLY, SHAWN EARLY, *and* JAMES RYAN]

MRS. TULLY. There is great talk about this work in every quarter of the fair.

MRS. TARPEY. Ochone![9] cold and dead. And myself maybe the last he was speaking to!

JAMES RYAN. The Lord save us! Is it dead he is?

TIM CASEY. Dead surely, and the wife getting provision for the wake.

SHAWN EARLY. Well, now, hadn't Bartley Fallon great venom in him?

MRS. TULLY. You may be sure he had some cause. Why would he have made an

8. Halfpenny worth.　　　　　9. Alas (Gaelic).

end of him if he had not? [*To* MRS. TARPEY, *raising her voice.*] What was it rose the dispute at all, Mrs. Tarpey?

MRS. TARPEY. Not a one of me knows. The last I saw of them, Jack Smith was standing there, and Bartley Fallon was standing there, quiet and easy, and he listening to "The Red-haired Man's Wife."

MRS. TULLY. Do you hear that, Tim Casey? Do you hear that, Shawn Early and James Ryan? Bartley Fallon was here this morning listening to red Jack Smith's wife, Kitty Keary that was! Listening to her and whispering with her! It was she started the fight so!

SHAWN EARLY. She must have followed him from her own house. It is likely some person roused him.

TIM CASEY. I never knew, before, Bartley Fallon was great[1] with Jack Smith's wife.

MRS. TULLY. How would you know it? Sure it's not in the streets they would be calling it. If Mrs. Fallon didn't know of it, and if I that have the next house to them didn't know of it, and if Jack Smith himself didn't know of it, it is not likely you would know of it, Tim Casey.

SHAWN EARLY. Let Bartley Fallon take charge of her from this out so, and let him provide for her. It is little pity she will get from any person in this parish.

TIM CASEY. How can he take charge of her? Sure he has a wife of his own. Sure you don't think he'd turn souper[2] and marry her in a Protestant church?

JAMES RYAN. It would be easy for him to marry her if he brought her to America.

SHAWN EARLY. With or without Kitty Keary, believe me it is for America he's making at this minute. I saw the new magistrate and Jo Muldoon of the police going into the postoffice as I came up—there was hurry on them—you may be sure it was to telegraph they went, the way he'll be stopped in the docks at Queenstown!

MRS. TULLY. It's likely Kitty Keary is gone with him, and not minding a sheet or a wake at all. The poor man, to be deserted by his own wife, and the breath hardly gone out yet from his body that is lying bloody in the field!

[*Enter* MRS. FALLON]

MRS. FALLON. What is it the whole of the town is talking about? And what is it you yourselves are talking about? Is it about my man Bartley Fallon you are talking? Is it lies about him you are telling, saying that he went killing Jack Smith? My grief that ever he came into this place at all!

JAMES RYAN. Be easy now, Mrs. Fallon. Sure there is no one at all in the whole fair but is sorry for you!

MRS. FALLON. Sorry for me, is it? Why would anyone be sorry for me? Let you be sorry for yourselves, and that there may be shame on you for ever and at the day of judgment, for the words you are saying and the lies you are telling to take away the character of my poor man, and to take the good name off of him, and to drive him to destruction! That is what you are doing!

SHAWN EARLY. Take comfort now, Mrs. Fallon. The police are not so smart as they think. Sure he might give them the slip yet, the same as Lynchehaun.[3]

MRS. TULLY. If they do get him, and if they do put a rope around his neck, there is no one can say he does not deserve it!

MRS. FALLON. Is that what you are saying, Bridget Tully, and is that what you

1. Intimate.
2. Roman Catholic converted to Protestantism by the attractions of free soup and other charity.

3. I.e., James Lynchehaun, a criminal who escaped to America with the help of the people of Achill Island.

think? I tell you it's too much talk you have, making yourself out to be such a great one, and to be running down every respectable person! A rope, is it? It isn't much of a rope was needed to tie up your own furniture the day you came into Martin Tully's house, and you never bringing as much as a blanket, or a penny, or a suit of clothes with you and I myself bringing seventy pounds and two feather beds. And now you are stiffer than a woman would have a hundred pounds! It is too much talk the whole of you have. A rope is it? I tell you the whole of this town is full of liars and schemers that would hang you up for half a glass of whisky. [*Turning to go.*] People they are you wouldn't believe as much as daylight from without you'd get up to have a look at it yourself. Killing Jack Smith indeed! Where are you at all, Bartley, till I bring you out of this? My nice quiet little man! My decent comrade! He that is as kind and as harmless as an innocent beast of the field! He'll be doing no harm at all if he'll shed the blood of some of you after this day's work! That much would be no harm at all. [*Calls out.*] Bartley! Bartley Fallon! Where are you? [*Going out.*] Did anyone see Bartley Fallon? [*All turn to look after her.*]

JAMES RYAN. It is hard for her to believe any such a thing, God help her!
 [*Enter* BARTLEY FALLON *from right, carrying hayfork.*]
BARTLEY. It is what I often said to myself, if there is ever any misfortune coming to this world it is on myself it is sure to come
 [*All turn round and face him.*]
BARTLEY. To be going about with this fork and to find no one to take it, and no place to leave it down, and I wanting to be gone out of this—Is that you, Shawn Early? [*Holds out fork.*] It's well I met you. You have no call to be leaving the fair for a while the way I have, and how can I go till I'm rid of this fork? Will you take it and keep it until such time as Jack Smith—
SHAWN EARLY. [*Backing.*] I will not take it, Bartley Fallon, I'm very thankful to you!
BARTLEY. [*Turning to apple stall.*] Look at it now, Mrs. Tarpey, it was here I got it; let me thrust it in under the stall. It will lie there safe enough, and no one will take notice of it until such time as Jack Smith—
MRS. TARPEY. Take your fork out of that! Is it to put trouble on me and to destroy me you want? Putting it there for the police to be rooting it out maybe. [*Thrusts him back.*]
BARTLEY. That is a very unneighborly thing for you to do, Mrs. Tarpey. Hadn't I enough care on me with that fork before this, running up and down with it like the swinging of a clock, and afeard to lay it down in any place! I wish I never touched it or meddled with it at all!
JAMES RYAN. It is a pity, indeed, you ever did.
BARTLEY. Will you yourself take it, James Ryan? You were always a neighborly man.
JAMES RYAN. [*Backing.*] There is many a thing I would do for you, Bartley Fallon, but I won't do that!
SHAWN EARLY. I tell you there is no man will give you any help or any encouragement for this day's work. If it was something agrarian now—
BARTLEY. If no one at all will take it, maybe it's best to give it up to the police.
TIM CASEY. There'd be a welcome for it with them surely!
 [*Laughter.*]
MRS. TULLY. And it is to the police Kitty Keary herself will be brought.
MRS. TARPEY. [*Rocking to and fro.*] I wonder now who will take the expense of the wake for poor Jack Smith?
BARTLEY. The wake for Jack Smith!

TIM CASEY. Why wouldn't he get a wake as well as another? Would you be-
grudge him that much?

BARTLEY. Red Jack Smith dead! Who was telling you?

SHAWN EARLY. The whole town knows of it by this.

BARTLEY. Do they say what way did he die?

JAMES RYAN. You don't know that yourself, I suppose, Bartley Fallon? You don't
know he was followed and that he was laid dead with the stab of a hayfork?

BARTLEY. The stab of a hayfork!

SHAWN EARLY. You don't know, I suppose, that the body was found in the Five
Acre Meadow?

BARTLEY. The Five Acre Meadow!

TIM CASEY. It is likely you don't know that the police are after the man that did
it?

BARTLEY. The man that did it!

MRS. TULLY. You don't know, maybe, that he was made away with for the sake
of Kitty Keary, his wife?

BARTLEY. Kitty Keary, his wife!
[Sits down bewildered.]

MRS. TULLY. And what have you to say now, Bartley Fallon?

BARTLEY. [Crossing himself.] I to bring that fork here, and to find that news be-
fore me! It is much if I can ever stir from this place at all, or reach as far as
the road!

TIM CASEY. Look, boys, at the new magistrate, and Jo Muldoon along with
him! It's best for us to quit this.

SHAWN EARLY. That is so. It is best not to be mixed in this business at all.

JAMES RYAN. Bad as he is, I wouldn't like to be an informer against any man.
[All hurry away except MRS. TARPEY, who remains behind her stall. Enter MAG-
ISTRATE and POLICEMAN]

MAGISTRATE. I knew the district was in a bad state, but I did not expect to be
confronted with a murder at the first fair I came to.

POLICEMAN. I am sure you did not, indeed.

MAGISTRATE. It was well I had not gone home. I caught a few words here and
there that roused my suspicions.

POLICEMAN. So they would, too.

MAGISTRATE. You heard the same story from everyone you asked?

POLICEMAN. The same story—or if it was not altogether the same, anyway it
was no less than the first story.

MAGISTRATE. What is that man doing? He is sitting alone with a hayfork. He
has a guilty look. The murder was done with a hayfork!

POLICEMAN. [In a whisper.] That's the very man they say did the act; Bartley
Fallon himself!

MAGISTRATE. He must have found escape difficult—he is trying to brazen it
out. A convict in the Andaman Islands tried the same game, but he could
not escape my system! Stand aside—Don't go far—have the handcuffs
ready. [He walks up to BARTLEY, folds his arms, and stands before him.] Here,
my man, do you know anything of John Smith?

BARTLEY. Of John Smith! Who is he, now?

POLICEMAN. Jack Smith, sir—Red Jack Smith!

MAGISTRATE. [Coming a step nearer and tapping him on the shoulder.] Where
is Jack Smith?

BARTLEY. [With a deep sigh, and shaking his head slowly.] Where is he, indeed?

MAGISTRATE. What have you to tell?

BARTLEY. It is where he was this morning, standing in this spot, singing his

share of songs—no, but lighting his pipe—scraping a match on the sole of
his shoe—

MAGISTRATE. I ask you, for the third time, where is he?

BARTLEY. I wouldn't like to say that. It is a great mystery, and it is hard to say of
any man, did he earn hatred or love.

MAGISTRATE. Tell me all you know.

BARTLEY. All that I know—Well, there are the three estates; there is Limbo,
and there is Purgatory, and there is[4]—

MAGISTRATE. Nonsense! This is trifling! Get to the point.

BARTLEY. Maybe you don't hold with the clergy so? That is the teaching of the
clergy. Maybe you hold with the old people. It is what they do be saying, that
the shadow goes wandering, and the soul is tired, and the body is taking a
rest—The shadow! [Starts up.] I was nearly sure I saw Jack Smith not ten
minutes ago at the corner of the forge, and I lost him again—Was it his
ghost I saw, do you think?

MAGISTRATE. [To POLICEMAN] Conscience-struck! He will confess all now!

BARTLEY. His ghost to come before me! It is likely it was on account of the
fork! I to have it and he to have no way to defend himself the time he met
with his death!

MAGISTRATE. [To POLICEMAN] I must note down his words. [Takes out note-
book. To BARTLEY] I warn you that your words are being noted.

BARTLEY. If I had ha' run faster in the beginning, this terror would not be on
me at the latter end! Maybe he will cast it up against me at the day of judg-
ment—I wouldn't wonder at all at that.

MAGISTRATE. [Writing.] At the day of judgment—

BARTLEY. It was soon for his ghost to appear to me—it is coming after me al-
ways by day it will be, and stripping the clothes off in the night time?—I
wouldn't wonder at all at that, being as I am an unfortunate man!

MAGISTRATE. [Sternly.] Tell me this truly. What was the motive of this crime?

BARTLEY. The motive, is it?

MAGISTRATE. Yes, the motive; the cause

BARTLEY. I'd sooner not say that.

MAGISTRATE. You had better tell me truly. Was it money?

BARTLEY. Not at all! What did poor Jack Smith ever have in his pockets unless
it might be his hands that would be in them?

MAGISTRATE. Any dispute about land?

BARTLEY. [Indignantly.] Not at all! He never was a grabber or grabbed from any
one!

MAGISTRATE. You will find it better for you if you tell me at once.

BARTLEY. I tell you I wouldn't for the whole world wish to say what it was—it is
a thing I would not like to be talking about.

MAGISTRATE. There is no use in hiding it. It will be discovered in the end.

BARTLEY. Well, I suppose it will, seeing that mostly everybody knows it before.
Whisper here now. I will tell no lie; where would be the use? [Puts his hand
to his mouth, and MAGISTRATE stoops.] Don't be putting the blame on the
parish, for such a thing was never done in the parish before—it was done for
the sake of Kitty Keary, Jack Smith's wife.

MAGISTRATE. [To POLICEMAN] Put on the handcuffs. We have been saved some
trouble. I knew he would confess if taken in the right way.

4. Fallon confuses the "three estates" (nobility, clergy, and common people) of medieval France with the parts of
hell.

[POLICEMAN *puts on handcuffs.*]

BARTLEY. Handcuffs now! Glory be! I always said, if there was ever any misfortune coming to this place it was on myself it would fall. I to be in handcuffs! There's no wonder at all in that. [*Enter* MRS. FALLON, *followed by the rest. She is looking back at them as she speaks.*]

MRS. FALLON. Telling lies the whole of the people of this town are; telling lies, telling lies as fast as a dog will trot! Speaking against my poor respectable man! Saying he made an end of Jack Smith! My decent comrade! There is no better man and no kinder man in the whole of the five parishes! It's little annoyance he ever gave to anyone! [*Turns and sees him.*] What in the earthly world do I see before me? Bartley Fallon in charge[5] of the police! Handcuffs on him! O Bartley, what did you do at all at all?

BARTLEY. O Mary, there has a great misfortune come upon me! It is what I always said, that if there is ever any misfortune—

MRS. FALLON. What did he do at all, or is it bewitched I am?

MAGISTRATE. This man has been arrested on a charge of murder.

MRS. FALLON. Whose charge is that? Don't believe them! They are all liars in this place! Give me back my man!

MAGISTRATE. It is natural you should take his part, but you have no cause of complaint against your neighbors. He has been arrested for the murder of John Smith, on his own confession.

MRS. FALLON. The saints of heaven protect us! And what did he want killing Jack Smith?

MAGISTRATE. It is best you should know all. He did it on account of a love affair with the murdered man's wife.

MRS. FALLON. [*Sitting down.*] With Jack Smith's wife! With Kitty Keary!— Ochone, the traitor!

THE CROWD. A great shame, indeed. He is a traitor, indeed.

MRS. TULLY. To America he was bringing her, Mrs. Fallon.

BARTLEY. What are you saying, Mary? I tell you—

MRS. FALLON. Don't say a word! I won't listen to any word you'll say! [*Stops her ears.*] O, isn't he the treacherous villain? Ohone go deo![6]

BARTLEY. Be quiet till I speak! Listen to what I say!

MRS. FALLON. Sitting beside me on the ass-car[7] coming to the town, so quiet and so respectable, and treachery like that in his heart!

BARTLEY. Is it your wits you have lost or is it I myself that have lost my wits?

MRS. FALLON. And it's hard I earned you, slaving, slaving—and you grumbling, and sighing, and coughing, and discontented, and the priest wore out anointing you, with all the times you threatened to die!

BARTLEY. Let you be quiet till I tell you!

MRS. FALLON. You to bring such a disgrace into the parish. A thing that was never heard of before!

BARTLEY. Will you shut your mouth and hear me speaking?

MRS. FALLON. And if it was for any sort of a fine handsome woman, but for a little fistful of a woman like Kitty Keary, that's not four feet high hardly, and not three teeth in her head unless she got new ones! May God reward you, Bartley Fallon, for the black treachery in your heart and the wickedness in your mind, and the red blood of poor Jack Smith that is wet upon your hand!

5. I.e., taken by.
6. Alas, my God! (Gaelic).

7. Cart drawn by a donkey.

[*Voice of* JACK SMITH *heard singing.*]

> The sea shall be dry,
> The earth under mourning and ban!
> Then loud shall he cry
> For the wife of the Red-haired man!

BARTLEY. It's Jack Smith's voice—I never knew a ghost to sing before—It is after myself and the fork he is coming! [*Goes back. Enter* JACK SMITH.] Let one of you give him the fork and I will be clear of him now and for eternity!

MRS. TARPEY. The Lord have mercy on us! Red Jack Smith! The man that was going to be waked![8]

JAMES RYAN. Is it back from the grave you are come?

SHAWN EARLY. Is it alive you are, or is it dead you are?

TIM CASEY. Is it yourself at all that's in it?

MRS. TULLY. Is it letting on you were to be dead?

MRS. FALLON. Dead or alive, let you stop Kitty Keary, your wife, from bringing my man away with her to America!

JACK SMITH. It is what I think, the wits are gone astray on the whole of you. What would my wife want bringing Bartley Fallon to America?

MRS. FALLON. To leave yourself, and to get out of you she wants, Jack Smith, and to bring him away from myself. That's what the two of them has settled together.

JACK SMITH. I'll break the head of any man that says that! Who is it says it? [*To* TIM CASEY.] Was it you said it? [*To* SHAWN EARLY.] Was it you?

ALL TOGETHER. [*Backing and shaking their heads.*] It wasn't I said it!

JACK SMITH. Tell me the name of any man that said it!

ALL TOGETHER. [*Pointing to* BARTLEY.] It was *him* that said it!

JACK SMITH. Let me at him till I break his head!

[BARTLEY *backs in terror. Neighbors hold* JACK SMITH *back.*]

JACK SMITH. [*Trying to free himself.*] Let me at him! Isn't he the pleasant sort of a scarecrow for any woman to be crossing the ocean with! It's back from the docks of New York he'd be turned [*Trying to rush at him again.*], with a lie in his mouth and treachery in his heart, and another man's wife by his side, and he passing her off as his own! Let me at him can't you.

[*Makes another rush, but is held back.*]

MAGISTRATE. [*Pointing to* JACK SMITH.] Policeman, put the handcuffs on this man. I see it all now. A case of false impersonation, a conspiracy to defeat the ends of justice. There was a case in the Andaman Islands, a murderer of the Mopsa tribe, a religious enthusiast—

POLICEMAN. So he might be, too.

MAGISTRATE. We must take both these men to the scene of the murder. We must confront them with the body of the real Jack Smith.

JACK SMITH. I'll break the head of any man that will find my dead body!

MAGISTRATE. I'll call more help from the barracks. [*Blows* POLICEMAN's *whistle.*]

BARTLEY. It is what I am thinking, if myself and Jack Smith are put together in the one cell for the night, the handcuffs will be taken off him, and his hands will be free, and murder will be done that time surely!

MAGISTRATE. Come on! [*They turn to the right.*]

1904

8. I.e., given a wake; a watch—sometimes something of a party—held over the body of the dead.

OLIVE SCHREINER

1855–1920

South African novelist, feminist, antiimperialist, socialist, and pacifist, Olive Schreiner was a celebrity in turn-of-the-century England. Her first published novel, *The Story of an African Farm* (1883), was a best-seller; her first volume of allegorical fantasies, *Dreams* (1890), was reprinted twenty-four times by 1930; her protest against the racist atrocities of white "pioneers" in Africa, *Trooper Peter Halket* (1897), was quickly translated into German, Swedish, Danish, Dutch, and French; *Woman and Labor* (1911), like its American analogue, Charlotte Perkins Gilman's *Women and Economics* (1898), was hailed by suffragists for its analysis of the historical subjection of women. Yet not only did Schreiner continue to suffer the debilitating consequences of asthma, eating disorders, headaches, and a restlessness that denied her a home, but her most ambitious projects were left unfinished at her death. "Sometimes I don't seem to be alive at all," she admitted at the height of her fame, "No one wants me. I'm [in] no relation with the life or thought in England or Africa or anywhere else." If Schreiner's work is sometimes marred by the self-indulgence that characterizes this remark, it is also frankly ambitious in its effort to align the life and thought of England and colonial Africa with the idealism that imbued her own life and thought.

Such ambition seems especially remarkable given the bleakness and destitution of Schreiner's early childhood. Born in a Wesleyan mission house, Schreiner was the ninth child of Gottlieb and Rebecca (Lyndall) Schreiner. She was six when the family began to travel over the *karroo* (the South African plains). Her father, a deeply religious missionary, was eventually expelled from the rigid London Missionary Society when he was driven by the family's dire economic need to resort to private trading. If he was sternly orthodox and naively impractical, her mother was unbending in her belief in British superiority over black African natives and Boers (Dutch settlers in Africa) and in her commitment to conventionally Victorian ideas about female decorum.

Both Schreiner's early religious doubts and her feminism reflected prevailing intellectual trends in the late Victorian period, and she read widely in the philosophical works of Herbert Spencer, John Stuart Mill, and Ralph Waldo Emerson. But she received little formal schooling: at eleven, she was sent to live with an older brother and sister; at the age of fifteen, she took the first of a series of positions as governess in Boer farming families. In these inauspicious circumstances, she composed her first two novels, *Undine* and *The Story of an African Farm*. The latter, written under the pseudonym "Ralph Iron," she brought with her to England in 1881 when seeking to train herself as a doctor. Although poor health prevented her from gaining a medical education, the successful publication of *The Story of an African Farm* won her entrance into two pioneering intellectual organizations: the Fellowship of the New Life and the Men and Women's Club. Throughout the 1880s she lived in London rooming houses, where she wrote essays on prostitution and birth control, planned an edition of Mary Wollstonecraft's *A Vindication of the Rights of Woman*, and spoke on and for the woman question.

At the age of thirty-four, Schreiner returned to South Africa, where she became involved in the antagonisms preceding the Anglo-Boer War (1899–1902). Samuel Cron Cronwright, also an anti-imperialist, was a successful cattle breeder when he and Schreiner decided to marry. Following her wishes, he took her last name and supported her efforts to write, but a series of catastrophes made writing nearly impossible. In 1895 Schreiner gave birth to a nine-pound, nine-ounce daughter, who died mysteriously after only sixteen hours of life. Subsequent miscarriages, imprisonment during the Anglo-Boer War (for her radical political stance), the loot-

ing of her Johannesburg home, and the burning of her lengthy manuscript on women and labor (presumably by British troops) only exacerbated her asthma and her writing difficulties. Still, she worked for women's suffrage and women's trade unions even after her return to London before World War I.

Perhaps it was both the pain and the courage of Schreiner's life that made her work so influential. Torn between her love for the physical beauty of Africa and her desire for the intellectual stimulation of England, she was also caught between Victorian certainties and modernist skepticism. As if to announce the advent of a new age, even before Schreiner embarked on her unconventional life she had created the most flamboyant representative of the so-called New Woman in *The Story of an African Farm*. Ironically or not, this rebellious heroine is endowed with Schreiner's mother's maiden name: Lyndall. Lyndall's rage against female socialization results in a diatribe analyzing how "the world makes men and women" out of the "little plastic beings" born into it: "To you," she explains to her male companion, "it says—*Work!* and to us it says—*Seem!*" Refusing such dissembling, Lyndall never relinquishes her faith in "a new time" that would liberate women and thereby bring about the fellowship between the sexes that Schreiner herself craved.

From Woman and Labor

[Sex-parasitism]

* * * There never has been, and as far as can be seen, there never will be, a time when the majority of the males in any society will be supported by the rest of the males in a condition of perfect mental and physical inactivity. "*Find labor or die,*" is the choice ultimately put before the human male today, as in the past; and *this* constitutes his labor problem.[1]

The labor of the man may not always be useful in the highest sense to his society, or it may even be distinctly harmful and antisocial, as in the case of the robber-barons of the Middle Ages, who lived by capturing and despoiling all who passed by their castles; or as in the case of the share speculators, stock-jobbers, ring-and-corner capitalists,[2] and monopolists of the present day, who feed upon the productive labors of society without contributing anything to its welfare. But even males so occupied are compelled to expend a vast amount of energy and even a low intelligence in their callings; and, however injurious to their societies, they run no personal risk of handing down effete and enervated constitutions to their race. Whether beneficially or unbeneficially, the human male must, generally speaking, employ his intellect, or his muscle, or die.

The position of the unemployed modern female is one wholly different. The choice before her, as her ancient fields of domestic labor slip from her, is not generally or often at the present day the choice between finding new fields

1. The nearest approach to complete parasitism on the part of a vast body of males occurred, perhaps, in ancient Rome at the time of the decay and downfall of the Empire, when the bulk of the population, male as well as female, was fed on imported corn, wine, and oil, and supplied even with entertainment, almost entirely without exertion or labor of any kind; but this condition was of short duration, and speedily contributed to the downfall of the diseased Empire itself. Among the wealthy and so-called upper classes, the males of various aristocrats have frequently tended to become completely parasitic after a lapse of time, but such a condition has always been met by a short and sharp remedy; and the class has fallen, or become extinct. The condition of the males of the upper classes in France before the Revolution affords an interesting illustration of this point [Schreiner's note].
2. I.e., capitalists who attempt to control the market by price fixing.

of labor, or death; but one far more serious in its ultimate reaction on humanity as a whole—it is the choice between finding new forms of labor or sinking slowly into a condition of more or less complete and passive *sex-parasitism!*[3]

Again and again in the history of the past, when among human creatures a certain stage of material civilization has been reached, a curious tendency has manifested itself for the human female to become more or less parasitic; social conditions tend to rob her of all forms of active conscious social labor, and to reduce her, like the field-bug, to the passive exercise of her sex functions alone. And the result of this parasitism has invariably been the decay in vitality and intelligence of the female, followed after a longer or shorter period by that of her male descendants and her entire society.

Nevertheless, in the history of the past the dangers of the sex-parasitism have never threatened more than a small section of the females of the human race, those exclusively of some dominant race or class; the mass of women beneath them being still compelled to assume many forms of strenuous activity. It is at the present day, and under the peculiar conditions of our modern civilization, that for the first time sex-parasitism has become a danger, more or less remote, to the mass of civilized women, perhaps ultimately to all.

In the very early stages of human growth, the sexual parasitism and degeneration of the female formed no possible source of social danger. Where the conditions of life rendered it inevitable that all the labor of a community should be performed by the members of that community for themselves, without the assistance of slaves or machinery, the tendency has always been rather to throw an excessive amount of social labor on the female. Under no conditions, at no time, in no place, in the history of the world have the males of any period, of any nation, or of any class, shown the slightest inclination to allow their own females to become inactive or parasitic, so long as the actual muscular labor of feeding and clothing them would in that case have devolved upon *themselves!*

The parasitism of the human female becomes a possibility only when a point in civilization is reached (such as that which was attained in the ancient civilizations of Greece, Rome, Persia, Assyria, India, and such as today exists in many of the civilizations of the East, such as those of China and Turkey), when, owing to the extensive employment of the labor of slaves, or of subject races or classes, the dominant race or class has become so liberally supplied

3. It is not without profound interest to note the varying phenomena of sex-parasitism as they present themselves in the animal world, both in the male and in the female form. Though among the greater number of species in the animal world the female form is larger and more powerful rather than the male (e.g., among birds of prey, such as eagles, falcons, vultures, &c., and among fishes, insects, &c.), yet sex-parasitism appears among both sex forms. In certain sea-creatures, for example, the female carries about in the folds of her covering three or four minute and quite inactive males, who are entirely passive and dependent upon her.

Among termites, on the other hand, the female has so far degenerated that she has entirely lost the power of locomotion; she can no longer provide herself or her offspring with nourishment, or defend or even clean herself; she has become a mere passive, distended, bag of eggs, without intelligence or activity, she and her off-spring existing through the exertions of the slaves and workers of the community. Among other insects, such, for example, as certain ticks, another form of female parasitism prevails, and while the male remains a complex, highly active, and winged creature, the female, fastening herself by the head into the flesh of some living animal and sucking its blood, has lost wings and all activity, and power of locomotion, having become a mere distended bladder, which when filled with eggs bursts and ends a parasitic existence which has hardly been life. It is not impossible, and it appears, indeed, highly probable, that it has been this degeneration and parasitism on the part of the female which has set its limitation to the evolution of ants, creatures which, having reached a point of mental development in some respects almost as high as that of man, have yet become curiously and immovably arrested. The whole question of sex-parasitism among the lower animals is one throwing suggestive and instructive side-lights on human social problems, but is too extensive to be here entered on [Schreiner's note].

with the material goods of life that mere physical toil on the part of its own female members has become unnecessary.

It is when this point has been reached, and never before, that the symptoms of female parasitism have in the past almost invariably tended to manifest themselves, and have become a social danger. The males of the dominant class have almost always contrived to absorb to themselves the new intellectual occupations, which the absence of necessity for the old forms of physical toil made possible in their societies; and the females of the dominant class or race, for whose muscular labors there was now also no longer any need, not succeeding in grasping or attaining to these new forms of labor, have sunk into a state in which, performing no species of active social duty, they have existed through the passive performance of sexual functions alone, with how much or how little of discontent will now never be known, since no literary record has been made by the woman of the past, of her desires or sorrows. Then, in place of the active laboring woman, upholding society by her toil, has come the effete wife, concubine or prostitute, clad in fine raiment, the work of others' fingers; fed on luxurious viands, the result of others' toil, waited on and tended by the labor of others. The need for her physical labor having gone, and mental industry not having taken its place, she bedecked and scented her person, or had it bedecked and scented for her, she lay upon her sofa, or drove or was carried out in her vehicle, and, loaded with jewels, she sought by dissipations and amusements to fill up the inordinate blank left by the lack of productive activity. And the hand whitened and frame softened, till, at last, the very duties of motherhood which were all the constitution of her life left her, became distasteful, and, from the instant when her infant came damp from her womb, it passed into the hands of others, to be tended and reared by them; and from youth to age her offspring often owed nothing to her personal toil. In many cases so complete was her enervation, that at last the very joy of giving life, the glory and beatitude of a virile womanhood, became distasteful; and she sought to evade it, not because of its interference with more imperious duties to those already born of her, or to her society, but because her existence of inactivity had robbed her of all joy in strenuous exertion and endurance in any form. Finely clad, tenderly housed, life became for her merely the gratification of her own physical and sexual appetites, and the appetites of the male, through the stimulation of which she could maintain herself. And, whether as kept wife, kept mistress, or prostitute, she contributed nothing to the active and sustaining labors of her society. She had attained to the full development of that type which, whether in modern Paris or New York or London, or in ancient Greece, Assyria, or Rome, is essentially one in its features, its nature, and its results. She was the "fine lady," the human female parasite—the most deadly microbe which can make its appearance on the surface of any social organism.[4]

Wherever in the history of the past this type has reached its full development and has comprised the bulk of the females belonging to any dominant

4. The relation of female parasitism generally to the peculiar phenomenon of prostitution is fundamental. Prostitution can never be adequately dealt with, either from the moral or the scientific standpoint, unless its relation to the general phenomenon of female parasitism be fully recognized. It is the failure to do this which leaves so painful a sense of abortion on the mind, after listening to most modern utterances on the question, whether made from the emotional platform of the moral reformer, or the intellectual platform of the would-be scientist. We are left with a feeling that the matter has been handled but not dealt with: that the knife has not reached the core [Schreiner's note].

class or race, it has heralded its decay. In Assyria, Greece, Rome, Persia, as in Turkey today, the same material conditions have produced the same social disease among wealthy and dominant races; and again and again when the nation so affected has come into contact with nations more healthily constituted, this diseased condition has contributed to its destruction.

1911

CHARLOTTE PERKINS GILMAN
1860–1935

In her autobiography, *The Living of Charlotte Perkins Gilman* (1935), Charlotte Perkins Gilman described the "dark fog" that enveloped her after she gave birth to her daughter, Katherine, and was treated by the prominent physician Dr. S. Weir Mitchell. This major proponent of the so-called rest cure put her to bed, where she was fed, bathed, massaged, and advised to have her child with her at all times. Only further troubled by the treatment, the twenty-five-year-old wife and mother "made a rag baby, hung it on a doorknob and played with it. I would crawl into remote closets and under beds—to hide from the grinding pressure of that profound distress." Two years later, in the fall of 1887, she knew that she had to choose "not . . . between going and staying" with her husband and child, "but between going, insane, and staying, sane." She left her husband in 1888, but this early nervous collapse marked the rest of her life, disrupting her concentration and draining her energies. Yet it also led to the writing of her now classic short story, *The Yellow Wallpaper* (1892), and to the lecturing and publishing that would establish her reputation during her lifetime as the leading feminist-theorist in America.

Gilman's early breakdown, which might today be diagnosed as postpartum depression, probably had its origin in the emotional deprivation she suffered as a child. Born in 1860, in Hartford, Connecticut, she and her older brother were raised by their mother, Mary A. (Fitch) Perkins, after their father left the family because Mary had been warned against another pregnancy, or so Gilman suggests in her autobiography. In any case, the young girl found it difficult to sustain through letters a relationship with a father who was so remote, although she identified her own intellectual ambition with his relatives, the famous Beechers: "The word Father," she explained in her autobiography, "means nothing to me, save indeed in advice about books and the care of them—which seems more the librarian than the father." The great-niece of Catharine Beecher and Harriet Beecher Stowe, Gilman also suffered from her mother's poverty, a problem that caused the family to move nineteen times in eighteen years. Just as difficult to accept was Mary Perkins's apparently principled decision to spare her children the expectation of emotional fulfillment by refusing them any physical signs of tenderness: "She would not let me caress her, and would not caress me, unless I was asleep." Understandably, the young girl would keep herself awake, "even using pins to prevent dropping off," so as to feign sleep and gain the "raptur[ous]" enjoyment of "being gathered into her arms, held close and kissed."

For a short period of time, Gilman attended the Rhode Island School of Design, where she obtained the training that enabled her to work as an art teacher and governess. Her first husband, Charles Walter Stetson, was a Providence artist whom she married in 1884, although even during their courtship she was aware of the difficulty of combining marriage, motherhood, and work. After her breakdown, she

moved with her daughter to Pasadena, California. There she obtained a divorce and decided to send her daughter, Katherine, to live with her ex-husband and his new wife, her friend Grace Ellery Channing. The resulting publicity, generated by Massachusetts and California newspapers, condemned Gilman as unfeeling and unnatural. In spite of her anguish over both the decision and the notoriety, she struggled to support herself first in Oak and and then in San Francisco by lecturing, editing, writing, and teaching. Many of her most effective polemical poems were composed and printed in this period. *The Yellow Wallpaper*, which was published in May 1892 in *The New England Magazine* and later reprinted by William Dean Howells in *Great Modern American Stories* (1920), was followed by the feminist polemic *Women and Economics* (1898). Hailed as the Bible of the women's movement and translated into seven languages, the latter work established the argument Gilman would extend in many other publications, namely, the claim that women's economic dependency on men had arrested not only their intellectual and emotional growth but also the healthy development of the human species.

Two years after the publication of *Women and Economics*, Charlotte Perkins Stetson married George Houghton Gilman, a first cousin who had corresponded extensively with her about her doubts and desires concerning marriage. For the next three decades they lived together, first in New York and then in Norwich, Connecticut. His support, as well as the household help provided by Helen Campbell, a close friend she had made in California, allowed Gilman to develop more fully the socialist ideas of Edward Bellamy and the principles of the American sociologist Frank Ward. As in *Women and Economics*, she continued to argue that the subordination of the female sex had been necessary in the past for human evolution, but that in the twentieth century masculine assertiveness had to be complemented by a female culture grounded in cooperation and nurturance. Attacking what she called a "masculinist" society, Gilman explored alternative social organizations to free women from domestic subservience: in *Concerning Children* (1900), *The Home* (1903), and *Human Work* (1904), she suggested daycare centers, the professionalization of house cleaning, laundry, and sewing, and kitchenless houses. Later books like *Man-Made World* (1911) and *His Religion and Hers* (1923) posit the female as the primary type of the human species, arguing that women's commitment to sustaining life directly contrasts with men's engagement with war, an involvement that results in a theology of sacrificial violence. From 1909 until 1916, Gilman's editorials, poems, and fiction appeared in the *Forerunner*, the monthly magazine she edited and published. It was there that she serialized her feminist utopia, *Herland* (1915), a fantasy about a world of parthenogenetic women whose culture explicitly dramatizes the ecological and ethical superiority of matriarchy while implicitly demonstrating the inferiority of patriarchy.

Although Gilman played an important role in the feminist movement, addressing the International Suffrage Convention in Budapest in 1913 and helping to found the Woman's Peace Party in 1915, when that movement declined in the 1920s she began to lose her audience. After her husband's sudden death in 1934, she returned to California to live near her daughter. There she was joined by the widowed Grace Channing Stetson. After discovering that she was suffering from breast cancer, she ended her life with chloroform, not because of the pain she suffered, she explained, but because her career of service was over. After her death, Gilman and her work were relegated to a minor place in history. For almost fifty years, *The Yellow Wallpaper* went unprinted and unread. For more than sixty years, *Herland* was unavailable. The editorial and biographical work of Ann J. Lane, Gail Parker, Elaine R. Hedges, Carl Degler, Catherine Golden and Mary A. Hill has made possible a critical reappraisal of this socialist-feminist whose fiction furnishes a poetics for the feminist politics she developed at the turn of the century.

She Walketh Veiled and Sleeping

She walketh veiled and sleeping,
For she knoweth not her power;
She obeyeth but the pleading
Of her heart, and the high leading
Of her soul, unto this hour. 5
Slow advancing, halting, creeping,
Comes the Woman to the hour!—
She walketh veiled and sleeping,
For she knoweth not her power.

1889

False Play

"Do you love me?" asked the mother of her child,
 And the baby answered, "No!"
Great Love listened and sadly smiled;
He knew the love in the heart of the child—
 That you could not wake it so. 5

"Do not love me?" the foolish mother cried,
 And the baby answered, "No!"
He knew the worth of the trick she tried—
Great Love listened, and grieving, sighed
 That the mother scorned him so. 10

"Oh, poor mama!" and she played her part
 Till the baby's strength gave way:
He knew it was false in his inmost heart,
But he could not bear that her tears should start,
 So he joined in the lying play. 15

"Then love mama!" and the soft lips crept
 To the kiss that his love should show,—
The mouth to speak while the spirit slept!
Great Love listened, and blushed, and wept
 That they blasphemed him so. 20

1893

The Mother's Charge

She raised her head. With hot and glittering eye,
"I know," she said, "that I am going to die.
Come here, my daughter, while my mind is clear.
Let me make plain to you your duty here;
My duty once—I never failed to try— 5
But for some reason I am going to die."
She raised her head, and, while her eyes rolled wild,
Poured these instructions on the gasping child:

"Begin at once—don't iron sitting down—
Wash your potatoes wher the fat is brown—
Monday, unless it rains—it always pays 10
To get fall sewing done on the right days—
A carpet-sweeper and a little broom—
Save dishes—wash the summer dining-room
With soda—keep the children out of doors— 15
The starch is out—beeswax on all the floors—
If girls are treated like your friends they stay—
They stay, and treat you like their friends—the way
To make home happy is to keep a jar—
And save the prettiest pieces for the star 20
In the middle—blue's too dark—all silk is best—
And don't forget the corners—when they're dressed
Put them on ice—and always wash the chest
Three times a day, the windows every week—
We need more flour—the bedroom ceilings leak— 25
It's better than onion—keep the boys at home—
Gardening is good—a load, three loads of loam—
They bloom in spring—and smile, smile always, dear—
Be brave, keep on—I hope I've made it clear."

She died, as all her mothers died before. 30
Her daughter died in turn, and made one more.

1894

The Yellow Wallpaper

It is very seldom that mere ordinary people like John and myself secure ancestral halls for the summer.

A colonial mansion, a hereditary estate, I would say a haunted house and reach the height of romantic felicity—but that would be asking too much of fate!

Still I will proudly declare that there is something queer about it.

Else, why should it be let so cheaply? And why have stood so long untenanted?

John laughs at me, of course, but one expects that.

John is practical in the extreme. He has no patience with faith, an intense horror of superstition, and he scoffs openly at any talk of things not to be felt and seen and put down in figures.

John is a physician, and *perhaps*—(I would not say it to a living soul, of course, but this is dead paper and a great relief to my mind)—*perhaps* that is one reason I do not get well faster.

You see, he does not believe I am sick! And what can one do?

If a physician of high standing, and one's own husband, assures friends and relatives that there is really nothing the matter with one but temporary nervous depression—a slight hysterical[1] tendency—what is one to do?

1. *Hysteria* was, at the time, a loose term covering various kinds of "female" emotional disorders—depression, anxiety, nervousness, and so on.

My brother is also a physician, and also of high standing, and he says the same thing.

So I take phosphates or phosphites—whichever it is—and tonics, and air and exercise, and journeys, and am absolutely forbidden to "work" until I am well again.

Personally, I disagree with their ideas.

Personally, I believe that congenial work, with excitement and change, would do me good.

But what is one to do?

I did write for a while in spite of them; but it *does* exhaust me a good deal—having to be so sly about it, or else meet with heavy opposition.

I sometimes fancy that in my condition, if I had less opposition and more society and stimulus—but John says the very worst thing I can do is to think about my condition, and I confess it always makes me feel bad.

So I will let it alone and talk about the house.

The most beautiful place! It is quite alone, standing well back from the road, quite three miles from the village. It makes me think of English places that you read about, for there are hedges and walls and gates that lock, and lots of separate little houses for the gardeners and people.

There is a *delicious* garden! I never saw such a garden—large and shady, full of box-bordered paths, and lined with long grape-covered arbors with seats under them.

There were greenhouses, but they are all broken now.

There was some legal trouble, I believe, something about the heirs and co-heirs; anyhow, the place has been empty for years.

That spoils my ghostliness, I am afraid, but I don't care—there is something strange about the house—I can feel it.

I even said so to John one moonlight evening, but he said what I felt was a draught, and shut the window.

I get unreasonably angry with John sometimes. I'm sure I never used to be so sensitive. I think it is due to this nervous condition.

But John says if I feel so I shall neglect proper self-control; so I take pains to control myself—before him, at least, and that makes me very tired.

I don't like our room a bit. I wanted one downstairs that opened onto the piazza and had roses all over the window, and such pretty old-fashioned chintz hangings! But John would not hear of it.

He said there was only one window and not room for two beds, and no near room for him if he took another.

He is very careful and loving, and hardly lets me stir without special direction.

I have a schedule prescription for each hour in the day; he takes all care from me, and so I feel basely ungrateful not to value it more.

He said he came here solely on my account, that I was to have perfect rest and all the air I could get. "Your exercise depends on your strength, my dear," said he, "and your food somewhat on your appetite; but air you can absorb all the time." So we took the nursery at the top of the house.

It is a big, airy room, the whole floor nearly, with windows that look all ways, and air and sunshine galore. It was nursery first, and then playroom and gymnasium, I should judge, for the windows are barred for little children, and there are rings and things in the walls.

The paint and paper look as if a boys' school had used it. It is stripped off—the paper—in great patches all around the head of my bed, about as far as I can reach, and in a great place on the other side of the room low down. I never saw a worse paper in my life. One of those sprawling, flamboyant patterns committing every artistic sin.

It is dull enough to confuse the eye in following, pronounced enough constantly to irritate and provoke study, and when you follow the lame uncertain curves for a little distance they suddenly commit suicide—plunge off at outrageous angles, destroy themselves in unheard-of contradictions.

The color is repellent, almost revolting: a smouldering unclean yellow, strangely faded by the slow-turning sunlight. It is a dull yet lurid orange in some places, a sickly sulphur tint in others.

No wonder the children hated it! I should hate it myself if I had to live in this room long.

There comes John, and I must put this away—he hates to have me write a word.

We have been here two weeks, and I haven't felt like writing before, since that first day.

I am sitting by the window now, up in this atrocious nursery, and there is nothing to hinder my writing as much as I please, save lack of strength.

John is away all day, and even some nights when his cases are serious.

I am glad my case is not serious!

But these nervous troubles are dreadfully depressing.

John does not know how much I really suffer. He knows there is no reason to suffer, and that satisfies him.

Of course it is only nervousness. It does weigh on me so not to do my duty in any way!

I meant to be such a help to John, such a real rest and comfort, and here I am a comparative burden already!

Nobody would believe what an effort it is to do what little I am able—to dress and entertain, and order things.

It is fortunate Mary is so good with the baby. Such a dear baby!

And yet I *cannot* be with him, it makes me so nervous.

I suppose John never was nervous in his life. He laughs at me so about this wallpaper!

At first he meant to repaper the room, but afterward he said that I was letting it get the better of me, and that nothing was worse for a nervous patient than to give way to such fancies.

He said that after the wallpaper was changed it would be the heavy bedstead, and then the barred windows, and then that gate at the head of the stairs, and so on.

"You know the place is doing you good," he said, "and really, dear, I don't care to renovate the house just for a three months' rental."

"Then do let us go downstairs," I said. "There are such pretty rooms there."

Then he took me in his arms and called me a blessed little goose, and said he would go down cellar, if I wished, and have it whitewashed into the bargain.

But he is right enough about the beds and windows and things.

It is as airy and comfortable a room as anyone need wish, and, of course, I would not be so silly as to make him uncomfortable just for a whim.

I'm really getting quite fond of the big room, all but that horrid paper.

Out of one window I can see the garden—those mysterious deep-shaded arbors, the riotous old-fashioned flowers, and bushes and gnarly trees.

Out of another I get a lovely view of the bay and a little private wharf belonging to the estate. There is a beautiful shaded lane that runs down there from the house. I always fancy I see people walking in these numerous paths and arbors, but John has cautioned me not to give way to fancy in the least. He says that with my imaginative power and habit of story-making, a nervous weakness like mine is sure to lead to all manner of excited fancies, and that I ought to use my will and good sense to check the tendency. So I try.

I think sometimes that if I were only well enough to write a little it would relieve the press of ideas and rest me.

But I find I get pretty tired when I try.

It is so discouraging not to have any advice and companionship about my work. When I get really well, John says we will ask Cousin Henry and Julia down for a long visit; but he says he would as soon put fireworks in my pillow-case as to let me have those stimulating people about now.

I wish I could get well faster.

But I must not think about that. This paper looks to me as if it *knew* what a vicious influence it had!

There is a recurrent spot where the pattern lolls like a broken neck and two bulbous eyes stare at you upside down.

I get positively angry with the impertinence of it and the everlastingness. Up and down and sideways they crawl, and those absurd unblinking eyes are everywhere. There is one place where two breadths didn't match, and the eyes go all up and down the line, one a little higher than the other.

I never saw so much expression in an inanimate thing before, and we all know how much expression they have! I used to lie awake as a child and get more entertainment and terror out of blank walls and plain furniture than most children could find in a toy-store.

I remember what a kindly wink the knobs of our big old bureau used to have, and there was one chair that always seemed like a strong friend.

I used to feel that if any of the other things looked too fierce I could always hop into that chair and be safe.

The furniture in this room is no worse than inharmonious, however, for we had to bring it all from downstairs. I suppose when this was used as a playroom they had to take the nursery things out, and no wonder! I never saw such ravages as the children have made here.

The wallpaper, as I said before, is torn off in spots, and it sticketh closer than a brother—they must have had perseverance as well as hatred.

Then the floor is scratched and gouged and splintered, the plaster itself is dug out here and there, and this great heavy bed, which is all we found in the room, looks as if it had been through the wars.

But I don't mind it a bit—only the paper.

There comes John's sister. Such a dear girl as she is, and so careful of me! I must not let her find me writing.

She is a perfect and enthusiastic housekeeper, and hopes for no better profession. I verily believe she thinks it is the writing which made me sick!

But I can write when she is out, and see her a long way off from these windows.

There is one that commands the road, a lovely shaded winding road, and one that just looks off over the country. A lovely country, too, full of great elms and velvet meadows.

This wallpaper has a kind of sub-pattern in a different shade, a particularly irritating one, for you can only see it in certain lights, and not clearly then.

But in the places where it isn't faded and where the sun is just so—I can see a strange, provoking, formless sort of figure that seems to skulk about behind that silly and conspicuous front design.

There's sister on the stairs!

Well, the Fourth of July is over! The people are all gone, and I am tired out. John thought it might do me good to see a little company, so we just had Mother and Nellie and the children down for a week.

Of course I didn't do a thing. Jennie sees to everything now.

But it tired me all the same.

John says if I don't pick up faster he shall send me to Weir Mitchell[2] in the fall.

But I don't want to go there at all. I had a friend who was in his hands once, and she says he is just like John and my brother, only more so!

Besides, it is such an undertaking to go so far.

I don't feel as if it was worthwhile to turn my hand over for anything, and I'm getting dreadfully fretful and querulous.

I cry at nothing, and cry most of the time.

Of course I don't when John is here, or anybody else, but when I am alone.

And I am alone a good deal just now. John is kept in town very often by serious cases, and Jennie is good and lets me alone when I want her to.

So I walk a little in the garden or down that lovely lane, sit on the porch under the roses, and lie down up here a good deal.

I'm getting really fond of the room in spite of the wallpaper. Perhaps *because* of the wallpaper.

It dwells in my mind so!

I lie here on this great immovable bed—it is nailed down, I believe—and follow that pattern about by the hour. It is as good as gymnastics, I assure you. I start, we'll say, at the bottom, down in the corner over there where it has not been touched, and I determine for the thousandth time that I *will* follow that pointless pattern to some sort of a conclusion.

I know a little of the principle of design, and I know this thing was not arranged on any laws of radiation, or alternation, or repetition, or symmetry, or anything else that I ever heard of.

It is repeated, of course, by the breadths, but not otherwise.

Looked at in one way, each breadth stands alone; the bloated curves and flourishes—a kind of "debased Romanesque" with delirium tremens[3]—go waddling up and down in isolated columns of fatuity.

But, on the other hand, they connect diagonally, and the sprawling outlines run off in great slanting waves of optic horror, like a lot of wallowing sea-weeds in full chase.

The whole thing goes horizontally, too, at least it seems so, and I exhaust myself trying to distinguish the order of its going in that direction.

2. Silas Weir Mitchell (1829–1914), American nerve specialist, who popularized the "rest cure," and who treated Gilman herself.

3. Trembling delirium associated with alcoholism. "Romanesque": a highly decorative style of architecture.

They have used a horizontal breadth for a frieze, and that adds wonderfully to the confusion.

There is one end of the room where it is almost intact, and there, when the crosslights fade and the low sun shines directly upon it, I can almost fancy radiation after all—the interminable grotesque seems to form around a common center and rush off in headlong plunges of equal distraction.

It makes me tired to follow it. I will take a nap, I guess.

I don't know why I should write this.

I don't want to.

I don't feel able.

And I know John would think it absurd. But I *must* say what I feel and think in some way—it is such a relief!

But the effort is getting to be greater than the relief.

Half the time now I am awfully lazy, and lie down ever so much. John says I mustn't lose my strength, and has me take cod liver oil and lots of tonics and things, to say nothing of ale and wine and rare meat.

Dear John! He loves me very dearly, and hates to have me sick. I tried to have a real earnest reasonable talk with him the other day, and tell him how I wish he would let me go and make a visit to Cousin Henry and Julia.

But he said I wasn't able to go, nor able to stand it after I got there; and I did not make out a very good case for myself, for I was crying before I had finished.

It is getting to be a great effort for me to think straight. Just this nervous weakness, I suppose.

And dear John gathered me up in his arms, and just carried me upstairs and laid me on the bed, and sat by me and read to me till it tired my head.

He said I was his darling and his comfort and all he had, and that I must take care of myself for his sake, and keep well.

He says no one but myself can help me out of it, that I must use my will and self-control and not let any silly fancies run away with me.

There's one comfort—the baby is well and happy, and does not have to occupy this nursery with the horrid wallpaper.

If we had not used it, that blessed child would have! What a fortunate escape! Why, I wouldn't have a child of mine, an impressionable little thing, live in such a room for worlds.

I never thought of it before, but it is lucky that John kept me here after all; I can stand it so much easier than a baby, you see.

Of course I never mention it to them any more—I am too wise—but I keep watch for it all the same.

There are things in that wallpaper that nobody knows about but me, or ever will.

Behind that outside pattern the dim shapes get clearer every day.

It is always the same shape, only very numerous.

And it is like a woman stooping down and creeping about behind that pattern. I don't like it a bit. I wonder—I begin to think—I wish John would take me away from here!

It is so hard to talk with John about my case, because he is so wise, and because he loves me so.

But I tried it last night.

It was moonlight. The moon shines in all around just as the sun does.

I hate to see it sometimes, it creeps so slowly, and always comes in by one window or another.

John was asleep and I hated to waken him, so I kept still and watched the moonlight on that undulating wallpaper till I felt creepy.

The faint figure behind seemed to shake the pattern, just as if she wanted to get out.

I got up softly and went to feel and see if the paper did move. and when I came back John was awake.

"What is it, little girl?" he said. "Don't go walking about like that—you'll get cold."

I thought it was a good time to talk, so I told him that I really was not gaining here, and that I wished he would take me away.

"Why, darling!" said he. "Our lease will be up in three weeks, and I can't see how to leave before.

"The repairs are not done at home, and I cannot possibly leave town just now. Of course, if you were in any danger, I could and would, but you really are better, dear, whether you can see it or not. I am a doctor, dear, and I know. You are gaining flesh and color, your appetite is better, I feel really much easier about you."

"I don't weigh a bit more," said I, "nor as much; and my appetite may be better in the evening when you are here but it is worse in the morning when you are away!"

"Bless her little heart!" said he with a big hug. "She shall be as sick as she pleases! But now let's improve the shining hours[4] by going to sleep, and talk about it in the morning!"

"And you won't go away?" I asked gloomily.

"Why, how can I, dear? It is only three weeks more and then we will take a nice little trip of a few days while Jennie is getting the house ready. Really, dear, you are better!"

"Better in body perhaps—" I began, and stopped short, for he sat up straight and looked at me with such a stern, reproachful look that I could not say another word.

"My darling," said he, "I beg of you, for my sake and for our child's sake, as well as for your own, that you will never for one instant let that idea enter your mind! There is nothing so dangerous, so fascinating, to a temperament like yours. It is a false and foolish fancy. Can you not trust me as a physician when I tell you so?"

So of course I said no more on that score, and we went to sleep before long. He thought I was asleep first, but I wasn't, and lay there for hours trying to decide whether that front pattern and the back pattern really did move together or separately.

On a pattern like this, by daylight, there is a lack of sequence, a defiance of law, that is a constant irritant to a normal mind.

The color is hideous enough, and unreliable enough, and infuriating enough, but the pattern is torturing.

You think you have mastered it, but just as you get well under way in follow-

4. From the popular moral poem by Isaac Watts (1674–1748), *Against Idleness and Mischief:* "How doth the little busy bee / Improve each shining hour, / And gather honey all the day / From every opening flower!"

ing, it turns a back-somersault and there you are. It slaps you in the face, knocks you down, and tramples upon you. It is like a bad dream.

The outside pattern is a florid arabesque,[5] reminding one of a fungus. If you can imagine a toadstool in joints, an interminable string of toadstools, budding and sprouting in endless convolutions—why, that is something like it.

That is, sometimes!

There is one marked peculiarity about this paper, a thing nobody seems to notice but myself, and that is that it changes as the light changes.

When the sun shoots in through the east window—I always watch for that first long, straight ray—it changes so quickly that I never can quite believe it.

That is why I watch it always.

By moonlight—the moon shines in all night when there is a moon—I wouldn't know it was the same paper.

At night in any kind of light, in twilight, candlelight, lamplight, and worst of all by moonlight, it becomes bars! The outside pattern, I mean, and the woman behind it is as plain as can be.

I didn't realize for a long time what the thing was that showed behind, that dim sub-pattern, but now I am quite sure it is a woman.

By daylight she is subdued, quiet. I fancy it is the pattern that keeps her so still. It is so puzzling. It keeps me quiet by the hour.

I lie down ever so much now. John says it is good for me, and to sleep all I can.

Indeed he started the habit by making me lie down for an hour after each meal.

It is a very bad habit, I am convinced, for you see, I don't sleep.

And that cultivates deceit, for I don't tell them I'm awake—oh, no!

The fact is I am getting a little afraid of John.

He seems very queer sometimes, and even Jennie has an inexplicable look.

It strikes me occasionally, just as a scientific hypothesis, that perhaps it is the paper!

I have watched John when he did not know I was looking, and come into the room suddenly on the most innocent excuses, and I've caught him several times *looking at the paper!* And Jennie too. I caught Jennie with her hand on it once.

She didn't know I was in the room, and when I asked her in a quiet, a very quiet voice, with the most restrained manner possible, what she was doing with the paper, she turned around as if she had been caught stealing, and looked quite angry—asked me why I should frighten her so!

Then she said that the paper stained everything it touched, that she had found yellow smooches on all my clothes and John's and she wished we would be more careful!

Did not that sound innocent? But I know she was studying that pattern, and I am determined that nobody shall find it out but myself!

Life is very much more exciting now than it used to be. You see, I have something more to expect, to look forward to, to watch. I really do eat better, and am more quiet than I was.

John is so pleased to see me improve! He laughed a little the other day, and said I seemed to be flourishing in spite of my wallpaper.

5. An intricate pattern of interlaced lines.

I turned it off with a laugh. I had no intention of telling him it was *because* of the wallpaper—he would make fun of me. He might even want to take me away.

I don't want to leave now until I have found it out. There is a week more, and I think that will be enough.

I'm feeling so much better!

I don't sleep much at night, for it is so interesting to watch developments; but I sleep a good deal during the daytime.

In the daytime it is tiresome and perplexing.

There are always new shoots on the fungus, and new shades of yellow all over it. I cannot keep count of them, though I have tried conscientiously.

It is the strangest yellow, that wallpaper! It makes me think of all the yellow things I ever saw—not beautiful ones like buttercups, but old, foul, bad yellow things.

But there is something else about that paper—the smell! I noticed it the moment we came into the room, but with so much air and sun it was not bad. Now we have had a week of fog and rain, and whether the windows are open or not, the smell is here.

It creeps all over the house.

I find it hovering in the dining-room, skulking in the parlor, hiding in the hall, lying in wait for me on the stairs.

It gets into my hair.

Even when I go to ride, if I turn my head suddenly and surprise it—there is that smell!

Such a peculiar odor, too! I have spent hours in trying to analyze it, to find what it smelled like.

It is not bad—at first—and very gentle, but quite the subtlest, most enduring odor I ever met.

In this damp weather it is awful. I wake up in the night and find it hanging over me.

It used to disturb me at first. I thought seriously of burning the house—to reach the smell.

But now I am used to it. The only thing I can think of that it is like is the *color* of the paper! A yellow smell.

There is a very funny mark on this wall, low down, near the mopboard. A streak that runs round the room. It goes behind every piece of furniture, except the bed, a long, straight, even *smooch*, as if it had been rubbed over and over.

I wonder how it was done and who did it, and what they did it for. Round and round and round—round and round and round—it makes me dizzy!

I really have discovered something at last.

Through watching so much at night, when it changes so, I have finally found out.

The front pattern *does* move—and no wonder! The woman behind shakes it!

Sometimes I think there are a great many women behind, and sometimes only one, and she crawls around fast, and her crawling shakes it all over.

Then in the very bright spots she keeps still, and in the very shady spots she just takes hold of the bars and shakes them hard.

And she is all the time trying to climb through. But nobody could climb through that pattern—it strangles so; I think that is why it has so many heads.

They get through, and then the pattern strangles them off and turns them upside down, and makes their eyes white!

If those heads were covered or taken off it would not be half so bad.

I think that woman gets out in the daytime!

And I'll tell you why—privately—I've seen her!

I can see her out of every one of my windows!

It is the same woman, I know, for she is always creeping, and most women do not creep by daylight.

I see her in that long shaded lane, creeping up and down. I see her in those dark grape arbors, creeping all around the garden.

I see her on that long road under the trees, creeping along, and when a carriage comes she hides under the blackberry vines.

I don't blame her a bit. It must be very humiliating to be caught creeping by daylight!

I always lock the door when I creep by daylight. I can't do it at night, for I know John would suspect something at once.

And John is so queer now that I don't want to irritate him. I wish he would take another room! Besides, I don't want anybody to get that woman out at night but myself.

I often wonder if I could see her out of all the windows at once.

But, turn as fast as I can, I can only see out of one at one time.

And though I always see her, she *may* be able to creep faster than I can turn! I have watched her sometimes away off in the open country, creeping as fast as a cloud shadow in a wind.

If only that top pattern could be gotten off from the under one! I mean to try it, little by little.

I have found out another funny thing, but I shan't tell it this time! It does not do to trust people too much.

There are only two more days to get this paper off, and I believe John is beginning to notice. I don't like the look in his eyes.

And I heard him ask Jennie a lot of professional questions about me. She had a very good report to give.

She said I slept a good deal in the daytime.

John knows I don't sleep very well at night, for all I'm so quiet!

He asked me all sorts of questions, too, and pretended to be very loving and kind.

As if I couldn't see through him!

Still, I don't wonder he acts so, sleeping under this paper for three months.

It only interests me, but I feel sure John and Jennie are affected by it.

Hurrah! This is the last day, but it is enough. John is to stay in town over night, and won't be out until this evening.

Jennie wanted to sleep with me—the sly thing; but I told her I should undoubtedly rest better for a night all alone.

That was clever, for really I wasn't alone a bit! As soon as it was moonlight and that poor thing began to crawl and shake the pattern, I got up and ran to help her.

I pulled and she shook. I shook and she pulled, and before morning we had peeled off yards of that paper.

A strip about as high as my head and half around the room.

And then when the sun came and that awful pattern began to laugh at me, I declared I would finish it today!

We go away tomorrow, and they are moving all my furniture down again to leave things as they were before.

Jennie looked at the wall in amazement, but I told her merrily that I did it out of pure spite at the vicious thing.

She laughed and said she wouldn't mind doing it herself, but I must not get tired.

How she betrayed herself that time!

But I am here, and no person touches this paper but Me—not *alive*!

She tried to get me out of the room—it was too patent! But I said it was so quiet and empty and clean now that I believed I would lie down again and sleep all I could and not to wake me even for dinner—I would call when I woke.

So now she is gone, and the servants are gone, and the things are gone, and there is nothing left but that great bedstead nailed down, with the canvas mattress we found on it.

We shall sleep downstairs tonight, and take the boat home tomorrow.

I quite enjoy the room, now it is bare again.

How those children did tear about here!

This bedstead is fairly gnawed!

But I must get to work.

I have locked the door and thrown the key down into the front path.

I don't want to go out, and I don't want to have anybody come in, till John comes.

I want to astonish him.

I've got a rope up here that even Jennie did not find. If that woman does get out, and tries to get away, I can tie her!

But I forgot I could not reach far without anything to stand on!

This bed will *not* move!

I tried to lift and push it until I was lame, and then I got so angry I bit off a little piece at one corner—but it hurt my teeth.

Then I peeled off all the paper I could reach standing on the floor. It sticks horribly and the pattern just enjoys it! All those strangled heads and bulbous eyes and waddling fungus growths just shriek with derision!

I am getting angry enough to do something desperate. To jump out of the window would be admirable exercise, but the bars are too strong even to try.

Besides I wouldn't do it. Of course not. I know well enough that a step like that is improper and might be misconstrued.

I don't like to *look* out of the windows even—there are so many of those creeping women, and they creep so fast.

I wonder if they all come out of that wallpaper as I did?

But I am securely fastened now by my well-hidden rope—you don't get *me* out in the road there!

I suppose I shall have to get back behind the pattern when it comes night, and that is hard!

It is so pleasant to be out in this great room and creep around as I please!

I don't want to go outside. I won't, even if Jennie asks me to.

For outside you have to creep on the ground, and everything is green instead of yellow.

But here I can creep smoothly on the floor, and my shoulder just fits in that long smooch around the wall, so I cannot lose my way.

Why, there's John at the door!

It is no use, young man, you can't open it!

How he does call and pound!

Now he's crying to Jennie for an axe.

It would be a shame to break down that beautiful door!

"John, dear!" said I in the gentlest voice. "The key is down by the front steps, under a plantain leaf!"

That silenced him for a few moments.

Then he said, very quietly indeed, "Open the door, my darling!"

"I can't," said I. "The key is down by the front door under a plantain leaf!" And then I said it again, several times, very gently and slowly, and said it so often that he had to go and see, and he got it of course, and came in. He stopped short by the door.

"What is the matter?" he cried. "For God's sake, what are you doing!"

I kept on creeping just the same, but I looked at him over my shoulder.

"I've got out at last," said I, "in spite of you and Jane. And I've pulled off most of the paper, so you can't put me back!"

Now why should that man have fainted? But he did, and right across my path by the wall, so that I had to creep over him every time!

1892

MARY ELIZABETH COLERIDGE
1861–1907

The great-great-niece of the Romantic poet Samuel Taylor Coleridge, Mary Elizabeth Coleridge was once called "the tail of the comet S. T. C.," and she herself declared that "I have no fairy god-mother, but lay claim to a fairy great-great uncle, which is perhaps the reason that I am condemned to wander restlessly around the Gates of Fairyland, although I have never yet passed them." In fact, in a number of uncannily imaginative verses, this late Victorian woman does seem to have "passed" such gates to peer into the realm of fantasy that her Romantic ancestor inhabited. At the same time, perhaps at least in part because she was raised to be a dutiful nineteenth-century English lady, Coleridge never achieved her great-great-uncle's literary importance. Although she published several successful novels in her lifetime, she refused to release, or even discuss, most of her verse. Because a friend of the family, the poet Robert Bridges, discovered and admired some of her work, she allowed two small volumes—*Fancy's Following* and *Fancy's Guerdon*—to be privately printed in the 1890s, but the rest of her poetry remained unpublished until 1908, the year after her death.

The daughter of a charitable, domestic mother, and a literary lawyer who frequently entertained such notables as Tennyson and Browning, Coleridge lived all her life at home with her parents, and on the surface her existence was uneventful. She was exceptionally well educated, however; according to her friend Edith Sichel, "by the time she was nineteen she was well versed in [Hebrew], as well as in German, French, Italian; and a little later she became a keen reader of Greek." In addition, she undertook ambitious studies of philosophy and literature; participated in intellectual circles; traveled on the continent; wrote a number of stories and essays for *The Cornhill Magazine*, *The Times Literary Supplement*, and *The Reflector*; and during the last twelve years of her life taught English literature at a

working women's college, a job she did with passionate commitment. When she died at the early age of forty-six, she left a substantial body of work, in particular a series of luminously phrased, visionary poems. A piece like *The Other Side of a Mirror*, for instance, reminds us that despite all its comforts and satisfactions, her life may not have been as serene as it seemed.

The Other Side of a Mirror

I sat before my glass one day,
 And conjured up a vision bare,
Unlike the aspects glad and gay,
 That erst were found reflected there—
The vision of a woman, wild 5
 With more than womanly despair.

Her hair stood back on either side
 A face bereft of loveliness.
It had no envy[1] now to hide
 What once no man on earth could guess. 10
It formed the thorny aureole[2]
 Of hard unsanctified distress.

Her lips were open—not a sound
 Came through the parted lines of red.
Whate'er it was, the hideous wound 15
 In silence and in secret bled.
No sigh relieved her speechless woe,
 She had no voice to speak her dread.

And in her lurid eyes there shone
 The dying flame of life's desire, 20
Made mad because its hope was gone,
 And kindled at the leaping fire
Of jealousy, and fierce revenge,
 And strength that could not change nor tire.

Shade of a shadow in the glass, 25
 O set the crystal surface free!
Pass—as the fairer visions pass—
 Nor ever more return, to be
The ghost of a distracted hour,
 That heard me whisper, "I am she!' 30

1882 1908

Regina[1]

My Queen her scepter did lay down,
She took from her head the golden crown
Worn by right of her royal birth.

1. Desire. .. Queen (Latin).
2. Radiant light around the head.

Her purple robe she cast aside,
And the scarlet vestures of her pride, 5
That was the pride of the earth.
In her nakedness was she
Queen of the world, herself and me.

My Queen took up her scepter bright,
Her crown more radiant than the light, 10
The rubies gleaming out of the gold.
She donned her robe of purple rare,
And did a deed that none may dare,
That makes the blood run cold.
And in her bravery is she 15
Queen of herself, the world and me.

1884 1908

The Devil's Funeral

The Devil is dead, good people all!
Who are the bearers that bear the pall?

One of them thinks he has slain God too,
With the self-same sword that Satan slew.

One of them thinks he has saved God's life; 5
The Devil was ever the God of strife.

A purple pall above him spread!
A king it is that is lying dead.

The worst of kings never ruled so well
As this magnificent King of Hell. 10

What is the guerdon[1] of all his pains?
He is dead himself, but Hell remains.

He forged his coffin before he died.
'Twas made of gold that was seven times tried:[2]

The glittering golden words of those, 15
Who counted themselves his chiefest foes.

Where will you bury him? Not on earth!
In poison flowers he would come to birth.

We will not cast him into the sea.
The winds and the waves would set him free. 20

Lay him out straight on the funeral pyre!
All his life he has lived in fire.

1. Reward. 2. Tempered.

And lo! as the crackling flame burns bright,
Satan transformed to an angel of light,

That he may work more utter woe 25
Than ever he worked when he dwelt below.

1890 1908

The Witch

I have walked a great while over the snow
And I am not tall nor strong.
My clothes are wet, and my teeth are set,
And the way was hard and long.
I have wandered over the fruitful earth, 5
But I never came here before.
Oh, lift me over the threshold, and let me in at the door!

The cutting wind is a cruel foe.
I dare not stand in the blast.
My hands are stone, and my voice a groan, 10
And the worst of death is past.
I am but a little maiden still,
My little white feet are sore.
Oh, lift me over the threshold, and let me in at the door!

Her voice was the voice that women have. 15
Who plead for their heart's desire.
She came—she came—and the quivering flame
Sank and died in the fire.
It never was lit again on my hearth
Since I hurried across the floor, 20
To lift her over the threshold, and let her in at the door.

1892 1908

Doubt

Two forms of darkness are there. One is Night,
When I have been an animal, and feared
I knew not what, and lost my soul, nor dared
Feel aught save hungry longing for the light.
And one is Blindness. Absolute and bright, 5
The Sun's rays smote me till they masked the Sun;
The Light itself was by the light undone;
The day was filled with terrors and affright.

Then did I weep, compassionate of those
Who see no friend in God—in Satan's host no foes. 10

1892 1908

The White Women[1]

Where dwell the lovely, wild white women folk,
 Mortal to man?
They never bowed their necks beneath the yoke,
They dwelt alone when the first morning broke
 And Time began. 5

Taller are they than man, and very fair,
 Their cheeks are pale,
At sight of them the tiger in his lair,
The falcon hanging in the azure air,
 The eagles quail. 10

The deadly shafts their nervous hands let fly
 Are stronger than our strongest—in their form
Larger, more beauteous, carved amazingly,
And when they fight, the wild white women cry
 The war-cry of the storm. 15

Their words are not as ours. If man might go
 Among the waves of Ocean when they break
And hear them—hear the language of the snow
Falling on torrents—he might also know
 The tongue they speak. 20

Pure are they as the light; they never sinned,
 But when the rays of the eternal fire
Kindle the West, their tresses they unbind
And fling their girdles to the Western wind,
 Swept by desire. 25

Lo, maidens to the maidens then are born,
 Strong children of the maidens and the breeze,
Dreams are not—in the glory of the morn,
Seen through the gates of ivory and horn[2]—
 More fair than these. 30

And none may find their dwelling. In the shade
 Primeval of the forest oaks they hide.
One of our race, lost in an awful glade,
Saw with his human eyes a wild white maid,
 And gazing, died. 35

1900 1908

Marriage

No more alone sleeping, no more alone waking,
 Thy dreams divided, thy prayers in twain;
Thy merry sisters to-night forsaking,
 Never shall we see thee, maiden, again.

1. From a legend of Malay, told by Hugh Clifford [Coleridge's note]. 2. The two gates through which dreams pass up from the underworld, according to Greek myth.

> Never shall we see thee, thine eyes glancing, 5
> Flashing with laughter and wild in glee,
> Under the mistletoe kissing and dancing,
> Wantonly free.
>
> There shall come a matron walking sedately,
> Low-voiced, gentle, wise in reply. 10
> Tell me, O tell me, can I love her greatly?
> All for her sake must the maiden die!

1900 1908

EDITH WHARTON

1862–1937

When Edith Wharton was forty-five, at the height of her considerable personal and literary powers, her longtime mentor and friend, the American novelist Henry James, began to characterize her (as he would for the rest of his life) in a series of striking phrases: as Wharton's biographer Cynthia Griffin Wolff reports, he called her "the whirling princess, the great and glorious pendulum, the gyrator, the devil-dancer, the golden eagle, the Fire Bird, the Shining One, the angel of desolation or of devastation, the historic ravager." Already the author of twelve books—including collections of poems, essays, and short stories as well as successful major novels and novellas like *The House of Mirth* (1905) and *Madame de Treymes* (1907)— Wharton, as James understood, was well on her way to becoming a major force in American literature. Within a few decades, in fact, she would be the highest-paid novelist in the country. Yet only a few years earlier, in 1898 (when she was thirty-six), this "whirling princess" had suffered a severe mental breakdown; in the words of her biographer R. W. B. Lewis, she had experienced a "terrible and long drawn-out period . . . of paralyzing melancholy, extreme exhaustion, constant fits of nausea, and no capacity whatever to make choices and decisions."

Born in New York City to a wealthy family, Edith Newbold Jones was raised to be a decorous, even aristocratic young lady. Long established in high society, her parents summered in the elite resort community of Newport. Rhode Island, and, when Edith was three, took her to live abroad—in Italy, France, and Germany— because their income had been reduced by the economic depression that followed the American Civil War. Educated at home by a governess, the girl made her debut at seventeen.

At the same time, however, even while following the course that had been plotted for debutantes by generations of conservative forebears, this novelist-to-be was transforming herself into an artist. At sixteen, she wrote a volume of poetry that her parents, although they generally disapproved of literary activity, arranged to have privately printed. Even earlier, moreover, she had begun to read voraciously, sensing that her genteel education was inadequate to her intellectual ambitions. If she had not had "the leave to range in my father's library," she later remembered, "my mind would have starved at the age when the mental muscles are most in need of feeding," adding that "I was enthralled by *words* . . . Wherever I went, they sang to me like the birds in an enchanted forest."

Despite her consciousness of her literary "enthrallment," however, the tension between what appeared to be Edith Jones's social role and what she had gradually begun to understand were her creative aspirations continued well into her twenties and thirties. In 1885, at the age of twenty-three, she married Edward Robbins Wharton (known as Teddy), a wealthy Bostonian who was thirteen years older than she, and the couple settled into a life of conventional gentility, dividing their

time between New York, Boston, Newport, and Europe, where they moved in politely idle circles. A kind and decent but not especially intellectual man, Teddy Wharton had little sympathy for his wife's literary interests, and it soon became clear that their childless marriage was not a happy one, though they preserved a facade of compatibility for many years. In fact, what Wharton herself called "the slow, stammering beginnings" of her artistic career did not seriously manifest themselves until she and her husband returned in 1888 from a yacht tour of the Aegean. At this point, perhaps energized by new insights and experiences, the young woman began to write with fresh vigor and even to publish verses and stories in such major periodicals as *Scribner's*, *Harper's*, and the *Century*. A few years later, too, she collaborated with Ogden Codman Jr., a Boston architect, on *The Decoration of Houses* (1897). Despite her increasing productivity, however, she evidently felt conflicted about yielding herself entirely to her newly awakened ambition, for it was at about this time that she sought and received S. Weir Mitchell's "rest cure" treatment for the "paralyzing melancholy" that suddenly afflicted her.

But by 1899, when she published two collections of short stories, Wharton had recovered from her nervous illness and definitively committed herself to the world of letters. From then on, indeed, she was to publish, on the average, a book a year for the rest of her life. As the critic Louis Auchincloss observes, however, her "major period" began with her composition of *The House of Mirth*, which appeared in 1905. Tracing the decline of Lily Bart, an elegant young lady in straitened circumstances who cannot bring herself to marry for money and consequently falls into hopeless poverty and alienation, this haunting masterpiece exposes the hypocrisies of the old New York society that its author had been educated to honor and obey. In particular, the novel examines both the problems associated with the artificial construction of woman-as-ornament and the pains inflicted by the secret but often savage dynamics of the marriage market on which such a decorative creature is supposed to be an object of exchange, a realm of social trade in which even the links of Lily's bracelet seem "like manacles chaining her to her fate."

In the novels that followed *The House of Mirth*, Wharton continued to dissect the pretensions and conventions of the civilization that destroyed Lily Bart. *The Reef* (1912), *The Custom of the Country* (1913), and *The Age of Innocence* (1920), for instance, all deal in one way or another with the imprisonment of unorthodox or even rebellious women by the social "manacles chaining" them to their fates. Often considered a female Henry James, Wharton explored in these works the social and psychological nuances that were of such compelling interest to that artful novelist. At the same time, however, she also began to become a kind of modern mythologist. Studying the symbolist fictions of the Polish-born British novelist Joseph Conrad and admiring the innovative music of the Russian composer Igor Stravinsky, she wrote starkly structured, almost legendary tales of people whose fierce but forgotten lives were lived largely outside the urbane society in which she herself traveled with innate authority. *Ethan Frome* (1911) and *Summer* (1917) are her two most important novels in this mode; but she also composed a number of ghost stories, which reveal an abiding interest in the uncanny, the supernatural, the asocial.

Throughout this period of intense productivity, Wharton's marriage was slowly but inexorably deteriorating. During her middle forties, as the biographers Lewis and Wolff have revealed, she had a passionate affair with Morton Fullerton, a literary man who was also one of Henry James's protégés, an affair that may well have forced her and her husband to confront the inadequacies of their marriage. In any case, in 1910, as the relationship worsened, they sold The Mount, a lavish mansion they had built together near Lenox, Massachusetts, and moved to France, where Teddy had a nervous breakdown and was sent to a Swiss sanitorium. Then, in 1913, the couple divorced, and Wharton settled permanently in Europe, eventually purchasing two beautifully maintained French houses, where she was to spend the rest of her life.

Wharton evidently experienced her single state as a liberation Traveling indefatigably, entertaining spectacularly, and writing energetically, she formed friendships with many well-known men of letters, including—along with Henry James—the critic Percy Lubbock and the art historian Bernard Berenson. In addition, she became far more active in public affairs than she had been earlier. During World War I, in particular, she organized shelters and workrooms for refugees and did much other charitable work. In the view of some critics, however, her writings—with a few exceptions—declined in quality during the 1920s.

Nevertheless, in the last years of her life Wharton was at the peak of her fame. In 1930 she was elected to the National Institute of Arts and Letters, and in 1934 to the American Academy of Arts and Letters. When she died of a stroke at the age of seventy-five, she had produced a body of work that is extraordinarily impressive in its range and richness. Though they date from comparatively early in her career, *The Angel at the Grave* (1901) and *The Other Two* (1904) reveal in miniature the sardonic skill with which she could analyze the social pressures that had produced even her own complex personality. Each is, in a phrase she herself used to describe a successful short fiction, "a shaft driven straight into the heart of experience." Specifically, moreover, each is a dissection of the female condition: *The Angel at the Grave* examines the nature of a woman inheritor's problematic relationship to the male literary tradition she feels she has been appointed to carry on, and *The Other Two*—a tale the critic and biographer R. W. B. Lewis has called "very likely the best story Mrs. Wharton ever wrote"—explores the artifice of the supposedly romantic process by which a woman is constructed as a "perfect wife." Scholars have customarily assumed that James applied epithets like "the whirling princess" and "the Fire Bird" to Wharton because of the energy with which she traveled and entertained. Yet, despite their sometimes coolly ironic surfaces, stories like these, along with novels from *The House of Mirth* and *Ethan Frome*, to *Summer* and *The Age of Innocence*, have a fiercely subversive force that more than justifies such phrases.

The Angel at the Grave

I

The House stood a few yards back from the elm-shaded village street, in that semi-publicity sometimes cited as a democratic protest against old-world standards of domestic exclusiveness. This candid exposure to the public eye is more probably a result of the gregariousness which, in the New England bosom, oddly coexists with a shrinking from direct social contact; most of the inmates of such houses preferring that furtive intercourse which is the result of observations through shuttered windows and a categorical acquaintance with the neighboring clothes-lines. The House, however, faced its public with a difference. For sixty years it had written itself with a capital letter, had self-consciously squared itself in the eye of an admiring nation. The most searching inroads of village intimacy hardly counted in a household that opened on the universe; and a lady whose door-bell was at any moment liable to be rung by visitors from London or Vienna was not likely to flutter up-stairs when she observed a neighbor "stepping over."

The solitary inmate of the Anson House owed this induration[1] of the social texture to the most conspicuous accident in her annals: the fact that she was the only granddaughter of the great Orestes Anson.[2] She had been born, as it

1. Process of growing hard
2. Probably a reference to Orestes Brownson (1803–
1870), a prominent New England clergyman, editor, and writer who was interested in Transcendentalism.

were, into a museum, and cradled in a glass case with a label; the first founda-
tions of her consciousness being built on the rock of her grandfather's
celebrity. To a little girl who acquires her earliest knowledge of literature
through a *Reader* embellished with fragments of her ancestor's prose, that
personage necessarily fills an heroic space in the foreground of life. To com-
municate with one's past through the impressive medium of print, to have, as
it were, a footing in every library in the country, and an acknowledged kinship
with that world-diffused clan, the descendants of the great, was to be pledged
to a standard of manners that amazingly simplified the lesser relations of life.
The village street on which Paulina Anson's youth looked out led to all the
capitals of Europe; and over the roads of intercommunication unseen cara-
vans bore back to the elm-shaded House the tribute of an admiring world.

 Fate seemed to have taken a direct share in fitting Paulina for her part as the
custodian of this historic dwelling. It had long been secretly regarded as a "vis-
itation"[3] by the great man's family that he had left no son and that his daugh-
ters were not "intellectual." The ladies themselves were the first to lament
their deficiency, to own that nature had denied them the gift of making the
most of their opportunities. A profound veneration for their parent and an
unswerving faith in his doctrines had not amended their congenital incapacity
to understand what he had written. Laura, who had her moments of mute re-
bellion against destiny, had sometimes thought how much easier it would
have been if their progenitor had been a poet; for she could recite, with feel-
ing, portions of *The Culprit Fay* and of the poems of Mrs. Hemans;[4] and
Phoebe, who was more conspicuous for memory than imagination, kept an
album filled with "selections." But the great man was a philosopher; and to
both daughters respiration was difficult on the cloudy heights of metaphysic.
The situation would have been intolerable but for the fact that, while Phoebe
and Laura were still at school, their father's fame had passed from the open
ground of conjecture to the chill privacy of certitude. Dr. Anson had in fact
achieved one of those anticipated immortalities not uncommon at a time
when people were apt to base their literary judgments on their emotions, and
when to affect plain food and despise England went a long way toward estab-
lishing a man's intellectual pre-eminence. Thus, when the daughters were
called on to strike a filial attitude about their parent's pedestal, there was little
to do but to pose gracefully and point upward; and there are spines to which
the immobility of worship is not a strain. A legend had by this time crystal-
lized about the great Orestes, and it was of more immediate interest to the
public to hear what brand of tea he drank, and whether he took off his boots in
the hall, than to rouse the drowsy echo of his dialectic. A great man never
draws so near his public as when it has become unnecessary to read his books
and is still interesting to know what he eats for breakfast.

 As recorders of their parent's domestic habits, as pious scavengers of his
waste-paper basket, the Misses Anson were unexcelled. They always had an in-
teresting anecdote to impart to the literary pilgrim, and the tact with which,
in later years, they intervened between the public and the growing inaccessi-
bility of its idol, sent away many an enthusiast satisfied to have touched the

3. An affliction.
4. Felicia Hemans (1793–1835), popular English poet.

veil before the sanctuary. Still it was felt, especially by old Mrs. Anson, who survived her husband for some years, that Phoebe and Laura were not worthy of their privileges. There had been a third daughter so unworthy of hers that she had married a distant cousin, who had taken her to live in a new Western community where the *Works of Orestes Anson* had not yet become a part of the civic consciousness; but of this daughter little was said, and she was tacitly understood to be excluded from the family heritage of fame. In time, however, it appeared that the traditional penny with which she had been cut off had been invested to unexpected advantage; and the interest on it, when she died, returned to the Anson House in the shape of a granddaughter who was at once felt to be what Mrs. Anson called a "compensation." It was Mrs. Anson's firm belief that the remotest operations of nature were governed by the centripetal force of her husband's greatness and that Paulina's exceptional intelligence could be explained only on the ground that she was designed to act as the guardian of the family temple.

The House, by the time Paulina came to live in it, had already acquired the publicity of a place of worship; not the perfumed chapel of a romantic idolatry but the cold clean empty meetinghouse of ethical enthusiasms. The ladies lived on its outskirts, as it were, in cells that left the central fane[5] undisturbed. The very position of the furniture had come to have a ritual significance: the sparse ornaments were the offerings of kindred intellects, the steel engravings by Raphael Morghen marked the Via Sacra[6] of a European tour, and the black-walnut desk with its bronze inkstand modelled on the Pantheon was the altar of this bleak temple of thought.

To a child compact of enthusiasms, and accustomed to pasture them on the scanty herbage of a new social soil, the atmosphere of the old house was full of floating nourishment. In the compressed perspective of Paulina's outlook it stood for a monument of ruined civilizations, and its white portico opened on legendary distances. Its very aspect was impressive to eyes that had first sur-veyed life from the jig-saw "residence" of a raw-edged Western town. The high-ceilinged rooms, with their panelled walls, their polished mahogany, their portraits of triple-stocked[7] ancestors and of ringleted "females" in crayon, furnished the child with the historic scenery against which a young imagination constructs its vision of the past. To other eyes the cold spotless thinly-furnished interior might have suggested the shuttered mind of a maiden-lady who associates fresh air and sunlight with dust and discoloration; but it is the eye which supplies the coloring-matter, and Paulina's brimmed with the richest hues.

Nevertheless, the House did not immediately dominate her. She had her confused out-reachings toward other centers of sensation, her vague intuition of a heliocentric system; but the attraction of habit, the steady pressure of ex-ample, gradually fixed her roving allegiance and she bent her neck to the yoke. Vanity had a share in her subjugation; for it had early been discovered that she was the only person in the family who could read her grandfather's works. The fact that she had perused them with delight at an age when (even presuppos-ing a metaphysical bias) it was impossible for her to understand them, seemed to her aunts and grandmother sure evidence of predestination. Paulina was to

5. Temple 1833, Italian engraver.
6. Holy Route (Latin). Raphael Morghen (1758– 7. Wearing multiple neck cloths.

be the interpreter of the oracle, and the philosophic fumes so vertiginous to meaner minds would throw her into the needed condition of clairvoyance. Nothing could have been more genuine than the emotion on which this theory was based. Paulina, in fact, delighted in her grandfather's writings. His sonorous periods,[8] his mystic vocabulary, his bold flights into the rarefied air of the abstract, were thrilling to a fancy unhampered by the need of definitions. This purely verbal pleasure was supplemented later by the excitement of gathering up crumbs of meaning from the rhetorical board. What could have been more stimulating than to construct the theory of a girlish world out of the fragments of this Titanic cosmogony? Before Paulina's opinions had reached the stage when ossification sets in their form was fatally predetermined.

The fact that Dr. Anson had died and that his apotheosis had taken place before his young priestess's induction to the temple, made her ministrations easier and more inspiring. There were no little personal traits—such as the great man's manner of helping himself to salt, or the guttural cluck that started the wheels of speech—to distract the eye of young veneration from the central fact of his divinity. A man whom one knows only through a crayon portrait and a dozen yellowing tomes on free-will and intuition is at least secure from the belittling effects of intimacy.

Paulina thus grew up in a world readjusted to the fact of her grandfather's greatness; and as each organism draws from its surroundings the kind of nourishment most needful to its growth, so from this somewhat colorless conception she absorbed warmth, brightness and variety. Paulina was the type of woman who transmutes thought into sensation and nurses a theory in her bosom like a child.

In due course Mrs. Anson "passed away"—no one died in the Anson vocabulary—and Paulina became more than ever the foremost figure of the commemorative group. Laura and Phoebe, content to leave their father's glory in more competent hands, placidly lapsed into needlework and fiction, and their niece stepped into immediate prominence as the chief "authority" on the great man. Historians who were "getting up" the period wrote to consult her and to borrow documents; ladies with inexplicable yearnings begged for an interpretation of phrases which had "influenced" them, but which they had not quite understood; critics applied to her to verify some doubtful citation or to decide some disputed point in chronology; and the great tide of thought and investigation kept up a continuous murmur on the quiet shores of her life.

An explorer of another kind disembarked there one day in the shape of a young man to whom Paulina was primarily a kissable girl, with an afterthought in the shape of a grandfather. From the outset it had been impossible to fix Hewlett Winsloe's attention on Dr. Anson. The young man behaved with the innocent profanity of infants sporting on a tomb. His excuse was that he came from New York, a Cimmerian[9] outskirt which survived in Paulina's geography only because Dr. Anson had gone there once or twice to lecture. The curious thing was that she should have thought it worth while to find excuses for young Winsloe. The fact that she did so had not escaped the attention of the village; but people, after a gasp of awe, said it was the most natural thing in the world that a girl like Paulina Anson should think of marrying. It

8. Sentences.
9. Gloomy; from the Homeric myth of a country of perpetual fog and darkness.

would certainly seem a little odd to see a man in the House, but young Winsloe would of course understand that the Doctor's books were not to be disturbed, and that he must go down to the orchard to smoke—. The village had barely framed this *modus vivendi*[1] when it was convulsed by the announcement that young Winsloe declined to live in the House on any terms. Hang going down to the orchard to smoke! He meant to take his wife to New York. The village drew its breath and watched.

Did Persephone,[2] snatched from the warm fields of Enna, peer half-consentingly down the abyss that opened at her feet? Paulina it must be owned, hung a moment over the black gulf of temptation. She would have found it easy to cope with a deliberate disregard of her grandfather's rights; but young Winsloe's unconsciousness of that shadowy claim was as much a natural function as the falling of leaves on a grave. His love was an embodiment of the perpetual renewal which to some tender spirits seems a crueller process than decay.

On women of Paulina's mould this piety toward implicit demands, toward the ghosts of dead duties walking unappeased among usurping passions, has a stronger hold than any tangible bond. People said that she gave up young Winsloe because her aunts disapproved of her leaving them; but such disapproval as reached her was an emanation from the walls of the House, from the bare desk, the faded portraits, the dozen yellowing tomes that no hand but hers ever lifted from the shelf.

II

After that the House possessed her. As if conscious of its victory, it imposed a conqueror's claims. It had once been suggested that she should write a life of her grandfather, and the task from which she had shrunk as from a too-oppressive privilege now shaped itself into a justification of her course. In a burst of filial pantheism she tried to lose herself in the vast ancestral consciousness. Her one refuge from scepticism was a blind faith in the magnitude and the endurance of the idea to which she had sacrificed her life, and with a passionate instinct of self-preservation she labored to fortify her position.

The preparations for the *Life* led her through byways that the most scrupulous of the previous biographers had left unexplored. She accumulated her material with a blind animal patience unconscious of fortuitous risks. The years stretched before her like some vast blank page spread out to receive the record of her toil; and she had a mystic conviction that she would not die till her work was accomplished.

The aunts, sustained by no such high purpose, withdrew in turn to their respective divisions of the Anson "plot,"[3] and Paulina remained alone with her task. She was forty when the book was completed. She had travelled little in her life, and it had become more and more difficult to her to leave the House even for a day; but the dread of entrusting her document to a strange hand made her decide to carry it herself to the publisher. On the way to Boston she had a sudden vision of the loneliness to which this last parting condemned her. All her youth, all her dreams, all her renunciations lay in that neat bundle on her knee. It was not so much her grandfather's life as her own that she had

1. Way of life (Latin).
2. In Greek mythology, the queen of the underworld, stolen from earth by Hades.
3. Burial plot.

written; and the knowledge that it would come back to her in all the glorifica-
tion of print was of no more help than, to a mother's grief, the assurance that
the lad she must part with will return with epaulets.[4]

She had naturally addressed herself to the firm which had published her
grandfather's works. Its founder, a personal friend of the philosopher's, had
survived the Olympian[5] group of which he had been a subordinate member,
long enough to bestow his octogenarian approval on Paulina's pious undertak-
ing. But he had died soon afterward; and Miss Anson found herself confronted
by his grandson, a person with a brisk commercial view of his trade, who was
said to have put "new blood" into the firm.

This gentleman listened attentively, fingering her manuscript as though lit-
erature were a tactile substance; then, with a confidential twist of his revolving
chair, he emitted the verdict: "We ought to have had this ten years sooner."

Miss Anson took the words as an allusion to the repressed avidity of her
readers. "It has been a long time for the public to wait," she solemnly as-
sented.

The publisher smiled. "They haven't waited," he said.

She looked at him strangely. "Haven't waited?"

"No—they've gone off; taken another train. Literature's like a big railway-
station now, you know: there's a train starting every minute. People are not
going to hang round the waiting-room. If they can't get to a place when they
want to they go somewhere else."

The application of this parable cost Miss Anson several minutes of throb-
bing silence. At length she said: "Then I am to understand that the public is
no longer interested in—in my grandfather?" She felt as though heaven must
blast the lips that risked such a conjecture.

"Well, it's this way. He's a name still, of course. People don't exactly want to
be caught not knowing who he is; but they don't want to spend two dollars
finding out, when they can look him up for nothing in any biographical dictio-
nary."

Miss Anson's world reeled. She felt herself adrift among mysterious forces,
and no more thought of prolonging the discussion than of opposing an earth-
quake with argument. She went home carrying the manuscript like a wounded
thing. On the return journey she found herself travelling straight toward a fact
that had lurked for months in the background of her life, and that now seemed
to await her on the very threshold: the fact that fewer visitors came to the
House. She owned to herself that for the last four or five years the number had
steadily diminished. Engrossed in her work, she had noted the change only to
feel thankful that she had fewer interruptions. There had been a time when, at
the travelling season, the bell rang continuously, and the ladies of the House
lived in a chronic state of "best silks" and expectancy. It would have been im-
possible then to carry on any consecutive work; and she now saw that the si-
lence which had gathered round her task had been the hush of death.

Not of *his* death! The very walls cried out against the implication. It was the
world's enthusiasm, the world's faith, the world's loyalty that had died. A cor-
rupt generation that had turned aside to worship the brazen serpent.[6] Her
heart yearned with a prophetic passion over the lost sheep straying in the

4. Shoulder ornaments worn by soldiers. gods live.
5. I.e., godlike. Olympus is the mountain where Greek 6. I.e., false idol.

wilderness. But all great glories had their interlunar period; and in due time her grandfather would once more flash full-orbed upon a darkling world.

The few friends to whom she confided her adventure reminded her with tender indignation that there were other publishers less subject to the fluctuations of the market; but much as she had braved for her grandfather she could not again brave that particular probation. She found herself, in fact, incapable of any immediate effort. She had lost her way in a labyrinth of conjecture where her worst dread was that she might put her hand upon the clue.

She locked up the manuscript and sat down to wait. If a pilgrim had come just then the priestess would have fallen on his neck; but she continued to celebrate her rites alone. It was a double solitude; for she had always thought a great deal more of the people who came to see the House than of the people who came to see her. She fancied that the neighbors kept a keen eye on the path to the House; and there were days when the figure of a stranger strolling past the gate seemed to focus upon her the scorching sympathies of the village. For a time she thought of travelling; of going to Europe, or even to Boston; but to leave the House now would have seemed like deserting her post. Gradually her scattered energies centred themselves in the fierce resolve to understand what had happened. She was not the woman to live long in an unmapped country or to accept as final her private interpretation of phenomena. Like a traveller in unfamiliar regions she began to store for future guidance the minutest natural signs. Unflinchingly she noted the accumulating symptoms of indifference that marked her grandfather's descent toward posterity. She passed from the heights on which he had been grouped with the sages of his day to the lower level where he had come to be "the friend of Emerson," "the correspondent of Hawthorne,"[7] or (later still) "the Dr. Anson" mentioned in their letters. The change had taken place as slowly and imperceptibly as a natural process. She could not say that any ruthless hand had stripped the leaves from the tree: it was simply that, among the evergreen glories of his group, her grandfather's had proved deciduous.

She had still to ask herself why. If the decay had been a natural process, was it not the very pledge of renewal? It was easier to find such arguments than to be convinced by them. Again and again she tried to drug her solicitude with analogies; but at last she saw that such expedients were but the expression of a growing incredulity. The best way of proving her faith in her grandfather was not to be afraid of critics. She had no not on where these shadowy antagonists lurked; for she had never heard of the great man's doctrine being directly combated. Oblique assaults there must have been, however, Parthian shots[8] at the giant that none dared face; and she thirsted to close with such assailants. The difficulty was to find them. She began by re-reading the *Works*; thence she passed to the writers of the same school, those whose rhetoric bloomed perennial in *First Readers* from which her grandfather's prose had long since faded. Amid that clamor of far-off enthusiasms she detected no controversial note. The little knot of Olympians held their views in common with an early-Christian promiscuity.[9] They were continually proclaiming their admiration

7. Nathaniel Hawthorne (1804–1864), American fiction writer. Ralph Waldo Emerson (1803–1882), American essayist, founder of the Transcendentalist movement.

8. Shots delivered while retreating (after Parthian archers).

9. I.e., like the early Christians, who banded together without distinction.

for each other, the public joining as chorus in this guileless antiphon[1] of praise; and she discovered no traitor in their midst.

What then had happened? Was it simply that the main current of thought had set another way? Then why did the others survive? Why were they still marked down as tributaries to the philosophic stream? This question carried her still farther afield, and she pressed on with the passion of a champion whose reluctance to know the worst might be construed into a doubt of his cause. At length—slowly but inevitably—an explanation shaped itself. Death had overtaken the doctrines about which her grandfather had draped his cloudy rhetoric. They had disintegrated and been re-absorbed, adding their little pile to the dust drifted about the mute lips of the Sphinx.[2] The great man's contemporaries had survived not by reason of what they taught, but of what they were; and he, who had been the mere mask through which they mouthed their lesson, the instrument on which their tune was played, lay buried deep among the obsolete tools of thought.

The discovery came to Paulina suddenly. She looked up one evening from her reading and it stood before her like a ghost. It had entered her life with stealthy steps, creeping close before she was aware of it. She sat in the library, among the carefully-tended books and portraits; and it seemed to her that she had been walled alive into a tomb hung with the effigies of dead ideas. She felt a desperate longing to escape into the outer air, where people toiled and loved, and living sympathies went hand in hand. It was the sense of wasted labor that oppressed her; of two lives consumed in that ruthless process that uses generations of effort to build a single cell. There was a dreary parallel between her grandfather's fruitless toil and her own unprofitable sacrifice. Each in turn had kept vigil by a corpse.

III

The bell rang—she remembered it afterward—with a loud thrilling note. It was what they used to call the "visitor's ring"; not the tentative tinkle of a neighbor dropping in to borrow a sauce-pan or discuss parochial incidents, but a decisive summons from the outer world.

Miss Anson put down her knitting and listened. She sat upstairs now, making her rheumatism an excuse for avoiding the rooms below. Her interests had insensibly adjusted themselves to the perspective of her neighbors' lives, and she wondered—as the bell re-echoed—if it could mean that Mrs. Heminway's baby had come. Conjecture had time to ripen into certainty, and she was limping toward the closet where her cloak and bonnet hung, when her little maid fluttered in with the announcement: "A gentleman to see the house."

"The *House?*"

"Yes, m'm. I don't know what he means," faltered the messenger, whose memory did not embrace the period when such announcements were a daily part of the domestic routine.

Miss Anson glanced at the proffered card. The name it bore—*Mr. George Corby*—was unknown to her, but the blood rose to her languid cheek. "Hand me my Mechlin cap, Katy," she said, trembling a little, as she laid aside her walking stick. She put her cap on before the mirror, with rapid unsteady touches. "Did you draw up the library blinds?" she breathlessly asked.

1. Verses sung responsively.
2. In Greek mythology, a monster who killed all who could not answer her riddles; here, a figure for inscrutable mysteries.

She had gradually built up a wall of commonplace between herself and her illusions, but at the first summons of the past filial passion swept away the frail barriers of expediency.

She walked down-stairs so hurriedly that her stick clicked like a girlish heel; but in the hall she paused, wondering nervously if Katy had put a match to the fire. The autumn air was cold and she had the reproachful vision of a visitor with elderly ailments shivering by her inhospitable hearth. She thought instinctively of the stranger as a survivor of the days when such a visit was a part of the young enthusiast's itinerary.

The fire was unlit and the room forbiddingly cold. but the figure which, as Miss Anson entered, turned from a lingering scrutiny of the book-shelves, was that of a fresh-eyed sanguine youth clearly independent of any artificial caloric.[3] She stood still a moment, feeling herself the victim of some anterior impression that made this robust presence an insubstantial thing; but the young man advanced with an air of genial assurance which rendered him at once more real and more reminiscent.

"Why this, you know," he exclaimed, "is simply immense!"

The words, which did not immediately present themselves as slang to Miss Anson's unaccustomed ear, echoed with an odd familiarity through the academic silence.

"The room, you know, I mean," he explained with a comprehensive gesture. "These jolly portraits, and the books—that's the old gentleman himself over the mantelpiece, I suppose—and the elms outside, and—and the whole business. I do like a congruous background—don't you?"

His hostess was silent. No one but Hewlett Winsloe had ever spoken of her grandfather as "the old gentleman."

"It's a hundred times better than I could have hoped," her visitor continued, with a cheerful disregard of her silence. "The seclusion, the remoteness, the philosophic atmosphere—there's so little of that kind of flavor left! I should have simply hated to find that he lived over a grocery, you know.—I had the deuce of a time finding out where he *did* live," he began again, after another glance of parenthetical enjoyment. "But finally I got on the trail through some old book on Brook Farm.[4] I was bound I'd get the environment right before I did my article."

Miss Anson, by this time, had recovered sufficient self-possession to seat herself and assign a chair to her visitor.

"Do I understand," she asked slowly, following his rapid eye about the room, "that you intend to write an article about my grandfather?"

"That's what I'm here for," Mr. Corby genially responded; "that is, if you're willing to help me; for I can't get on without your help," he added with a confident smile.

There was another pause, during which Miss Anson noticed a fleck of dust on the faded leather of the writing-table and a fresh spot of discoloration in the right-hand upper corner of Raphael Morghen's "Parnassus."

"Then you believe in him?" she said, looking up. She could not tell what had prompted her; the words rushed out irresistibly.

"Believe in him?" Corby cried, springing to his feet. "Believe in Orestes

3. An imaginary fluid thought to produce and transfer heat.
4. A cooperative community (1841–1847) founded by Transcendentalist Bronson Alcott, father of Louisa May Alcott.

Anson? Why, I believe he's simply the greatest—the most stupendous—the most phenomenal figure we've got!"

The color rose to Miss Anson's brow. Her heart was beating passionately. She kept her eyes fixed on the young man's face, as though it might vanish if she looked away.

"You—you mean to say this in your article?" she asked.

"Say it? Why, the facts will say it," he exulted. "The baldest kind of a statement would make it clear. When a man is as big as that he doesn't need a pedestal!"

Miss Anson sighed. "People used to say that when I was young," she murmured. "But now—"

Her visitor stared. "When you were young? But how did they know—when the thing hung fire[5] as it did? When the whole edition was thrown back on his hands?"

"The whole edition—what edition?" It was Miss Anson's turn to stare.

"Why, of his pamphlet—*the* pamphlet—the one thing that counts, that survives, that makes him what he is! For heaven's sake," he tragically adjured her, "don't tell me there isn't a copy of it left!"

Miss Anson was trembling slightly. "I don't think I understand what you mean," she faltered, less bewildered by his vehemence than by the strange sense of coming on an unexplored region in the very heart of her dominion.

"Why, his account of the *amphioxus*,[6] of course! You can't mean that his family didn't know about it—that *you* don't know about it? I came across it by the merest accident myself, in a letter of vindication that he wrote in 1830 to an old scientific paper; but I understood there were journals—early journals; there must be references to it somewhere in the 'twenties. He must have been at least ten or twelve years ahead of Yarrell; and he saw the whole significance of it, too—he saw where it led to. As I understand it, he actually anticipated in his pamphlet Saint Hilaire's theory of the universal type, and supported the hypothesis by describing the notochord of the *amphioxus* as a cartilaginous vertebral column. The specialists of the day jeered at him, of course, as the specialists in Goethe's time jeered at the plant-metamorphosis.[7] As far as I can make out, the anatomists and zoologists were down on Dr. Anson to a man; that was why his cowardly publishers went back on their bargain. But the pamphlet must be here somewhere—he writes as though, in his first disappointment, he had destroyed the whole edition; but surely there must be at least one copy left?"

His scientific jargon was as bewildering as his slang; and there were even moments in his discourse when Miss Anson ceased to distinguish between them; but the suspense with which he continued to gaze on her acted as a challenge to her scattered thoughts.

"The *amphioxus*," she murmured, half-rising. "It's an animal, isn't it—a fish? Yes, I think I remember." She sank back with the inward look of one who retraces some lost line of association.

Gradually the distance cleared, the details started into life. In her researches for the biography she had patiently followed every ramification of her subject, and one of these overgrown paths now led her back to the episode in

7. Johann Wolfgang von Goethe (1749–1832), poet, developed a controversial botanical theory.

question. The great Orestes's title of "Doctor" had in fact not been merely the spontaneous tribute of a national admiration; he had actually studied medicine in his youth, and his diaries, as his granddaughter now recalled, showed that he had passed through a brief phase of anatomical ardor before his attention was diverted to super-sensual problems. It had indeed seemed to Paulina, as she scanned those early pages, that they revealed a spontaneity, a freshness of feeling somehow absent from his later lucubrations[8]—as though this one emotion had reached him directly, the others through some intervening medium. In the excess of her commemorative zeal she had even struggled through the unintelligible pamphlet to which a few lines in the journal had bitterly directed her. But the subject and the phraseology were alien to her and unconnected with her conception of the great man's genius; and after a hurried perusal she had averted her thoughts from the episode as from a revelation of failure. At length she rose a little unsteadily, supporting herself against the writing-table. She looked hesitatingly about the room; then she drew a key from her old fashioned reticule[9] and unlocked a drawer beneath one of the book-cases. Young Corby watched her breathlessly. With a tremulous hand she turned over the dusty documents that seemed to fill the drawer. "Is this it?" she said, holding out a thin discolored volume.

He seized it with a gasp. "Oh, by George," he said, dropping into the nearest chair.

She stood observing him strangely as his eye devoured the moldy pages.

"Is this the only copy left?" he asked at length, looking up for a moment as a thirsty man lifts his head from his glass.

"I think it must be. I found it long ago, among some old papers that my aunts were burning up after my grandmother's death. They said it was of no use—that he'd always meant to destroy the whole edition and that I ought to respect his wishes. But it was something he had written: to burn it was like shutting the door against his voice—against something he had once wished to say, and that nobody had listened to. I wanted him to feel that I was always here, ready to listen, even when others hadn't thought it worth while; and so I kept the pamphlet, meaning to carry out his wish and destroy it before my death."

Her visitor gave a groan of retrospective anguish. "And but for me—but for today—you would have?"

"I should have thought it my duty."

"Oh, by George—by George," he repeated, subdued afresh by the inadequacy of speech.

She continued to watch him in silence. At length he jumped up and impulsively caught her by both hands.

"He's bigger and bigger!" he almost shouted. "He simply leads the field! You'll help me go to the bottom of this, won't you? We must turn out all the papers—letters, journals, memoranda. He must have made notes. He must have left some record of what led up to this. We must leave nothing unexplored. By Jove," he cried, looking up at her with his bright convincing smile, "do you know you're the granddaughter of a Great Man?"

Her color flickered like a girl's. "Are you—sure of him?" she whispered, as though putting him on his guard against a possible betrayal of trust.

8. Laborious studies.　　　　　9. Woman's small handbag.

"Sure! Sure! My dear lady—" he measured her again with his quick confident glance. "Don't *you* believe in him?"

She drew back with a confused murmur. "I—used to." She had left her hands in his: their pressure seemed to send a warm current to her heart. "It ruined my life!" she cried with sudden passion. He looked at her perplexedly.

"I gave up everything," she went on wildly, "to keep *him* alive. I sacrificed myself—others—I nursed his glory in my bosom and it died—and left me—left me here alone." She paused and gathered her courage with a gasp. "Don't make the same mistake!" she warned him.

He shook his head, still smiling. "No danger of that! You're not alone, my dear lady. He's here with you—he's come back to you today. Don't you see what's happened? Don't you see that it's your love that has kept him alive? If you'd abandoned your post for an instant—let things pass into other hands— if your wonderful tenderness hadn't perpetually kept guard—this might have been—must have been—irretrievably lost." He laid his hand on the pamphlet. "And then—then he *would* have been dead!"

"Oh," she said, "don't tell me too suddenly!" And she turned away and sank into a chair.

The young man stood watching her in an awed silence. For a long time she sat motionless, with her face hidden, and he thought she must be weeping.

At length he said, almost shyly: "You'll let me come back, then? You'll help me work this thing out?"

She rose calmly and held out her hand. "I'll help you," she declared.

"I'll come tomorrow, then. Can we get to work early?"

"As early as you please."

"At eight o'clock, then," he said briskly. "You'll have the papers ready?"

"I'll have everything ready." She added with a half-playful hesitancy: "And the fire shall be lit for you."

He went out with his bright nod. She walked to the window and watched his buoyant figure hastening down the elm-shaded street. When she turned back into the empty room she looked as though youth had touched her on the lips.

1901

The Other Two[1]

I

Waythorn, on the drawing-room hearth, waited for his wife to come down to dinner.

It was their first night under his own roof, and he was surprised at his thrill of boyish agitation. He was not so old, to be sure—his glass gave him little more than the five-and-thirty years to which his wife confessed—but he had fancied himself already in the temperate zone; yet here he was listening for her step with a tender sense of all it symbolized, with some old trail of verse about the garlanded nuptial doorposts floating through his enjoyment of the pleasant room and the good dinner just beyond it.

1. First published by Scribners in the 1904 collection *The Descent of Man and Other Stories*, the source of the present text.

They had been hastily recalled from their honeymoon by the illness of Lily Haskett, the child of Mrs. Waythorn's first marriage. The little girl, at Waythorn's desire, had been transferred to his house on the day of her mother's wedding, and the doctor, on their arrival, broke the news that she was ill with typhoid, but declared that all the symptoms were favorable. Lily could show twelve years of unblemished health, and the case promised to be a light one. The nurse spoke as reassuringly and after a moment of alarm Mrs. Waythorn had adjusted herself to the situation. She was very fond of Lily— her affection for the child had perhaps been her decisive charm in Waythorn's eyes—but she had the perfectly balanced nerves which her little girl had inherited, and no woman ever wasted less tissue in unproductive worry. Waythorn was therefore quite prepared to see her come in presently, a little late because of a last look at Lily, but as serene and well-appointed as if her good-night kiss had been laid on the brow of health. Her composure was restful to him; it acted as ballast to his somewhat unstable sensibilities. As he pictured her bending over the child's bed he thought how soothing her presence must be in illness: her very step would prognosticate recovery.

His own life had been a gray one, from temperament rather than circumstance, and he had been drawn to her by the unperturbed gaiety which kept her fresh and elastic at an age when most woman's activities are growing either slack or febrile. He knew what was said about her; for, popular as she was, there had always been a faint undercurrent of detraction. When she had appeared in New York, nine or ten years earlier, as the pretty Mrs. Haskett whom Gus Varick had unearthed somewhere—was it in Pittsburgh or Utica?—society, while promptly accepting her, had reserved the right to cast a doubt on its own indiscrimination. Inquiry, however, established her undoubted connection with a socially reigning family, and explained her recent divorce as the natural result of a runaway match at seventeen; and as nothing was known of Mr. Haskett it was easy to believe the worst of him.

Alice Haskett's remarriage with Gus Varick was a passport to the set whose recognition she coveted, and for a few years the Varicks were the most popular couple in town. Unfortunately the alliance was brief and stormy, and this time the husband had his champions. Still, even Varick's stanchest supporters admitted that he was not meant for matrimony, and Mrs. Varick's grievances were of a nature to bear the inspection of the New York courts.[2] A New York divorce is in itself a diploma of virtue, and in the semi-widowhood of this second separation Mrs. Varick took on an air of sanctity, and was allowed to confide her wrongs to some of the most scrupulous ears in town. But when it was known that she was to marry Waythorn there was a momentary reaction. Her best friends would have preferred to see her remain in the role of the injured wife, which was as becoming to her as crape to a rosy complexion. True, a decent time had elapsed, and it was not even suggested that Waythorn had supplanted his predecessor. People shook their heads over him, however, and one grudging friend, to whom he affirmed that he took the step with his eyes open, replied oracularly: "Yes—and with your ears shut."

Waythorn could afford to smile at these innuendoes. In the Wall Street phrase, he had "discounted" them. He knew that society has not yet adapted itself to the consequences of divorce, and that till the adaptation takes place

2. Divorce in New York State could then be granted only on the grounds of adultery.

every woman who uses the freedom the law accords her must be her own social justification. Waythorn had an amused confidence in his wife's ability to justify herself. His expectations were fulfilled, and before the wedding took place Alice Varick's group had rallied openly to her support. She took it all imperturbably: she had a way of surmounting obstacles without seeming to be aware of them, and Waythorn looked back with wonder at the trivialities over which he had worn his nerves thin. He had the sense of having found refuge in a richer, warmer nature than his own, and his satisfaction, at the moment, was humorously summed up in the thought that his wife, when she had done all she could for Lily, would not be ashamed to come down and enjoy a good dinner.

The anticipation of such enjoyment was not, however, the sentiment expressed by Mrs. Waythorn's charming face when she presently joined him. Though she had put on her most engaging teagown she had neglected to assume the smile that went with it, and Waythorn thought he had never seen her look so nearly worried.

"What is it?" he asked. "Is anything wrong with Lily?"

"No; I've just been in and she's still sleeping." Mrs. Waythorn hesitated. "But something tiresome has happened."

He had taken her two hands, and now perceived that he was crushing a paper between them.

"This letter?"

"Yes—Mr. Haskett has written—I mean his lawyer has written."

Waythorn felt himself flush uncomfortably. He dropped his wife's hands.

"What about?"

"About seeing Lily. You know the courts—"

"Yes, yes," he interrupted nervously.

Nothing was known about Haskett in New York. He was vaguely supposed to have remained in the outer darkness from which his wife had been rescued, and Waythorn was one of the few who were aware that he had given up his business in Utica and followed her to New York in order to be near his little girl. In the days of his wooing, Waythorn had often met Lily on the doorstep, rosy and smiling, on her way "to see papa."

"I am so sorry," Mrs. Waythorn murmured.

He roused himself. "What does he want?"

"He wants to see her. You know she goes to him once a week."

"Well—he doesn't expect her to go to him now, does he?"

"No—he has heard of her illness; but he expects to come here."

"Here?"

Mrs. Waythorn reddened under his gaze. They looked away from each other.

"I'm afraid he has the right. . . . You'll see." She made a proffer of the letter.

Waythorn moved away with a gesture of refusal. He stood staring about the softly-lighted room, which a moment before had seemed so full of bridal intimacy.

"I'm so sorry," she repeated. "If Lily could have been moved—"

"That's out of the question," he returned impatiently.

"I suppose so."

Her lip was beginning to tremble, and he felt himself a brute.

"He must come, of course," he said. "When is—his day?"

"I'm afraid—to-morrow."

"Very well. Send a note in the morning."

The butler entered to announce dinner.

Waythorn turned to his wife. "Come—you must be tired. It's beastly, but try to forget about it," he said, drawing her hand through his arm.

"You're so good, dear. I'll try," she whispered back.

Her face cleared at once, and as she looked at him across the flowers, between the rosy candle-shades, he saw her lips waver back into a smile.

"How pretty everything is!" she sighed luxuriously.

He turned to the butler. "The champagne at once, please. Mrs Waythorn is tired."

In a moment or two their eyes met above the sparkling glasses. Her own were quite clear and untroubled: he saw that she had obeyed his injunction and forgotten.

II

Waythorn, the next morning, went downtown earlier than usual. Haskett was not likely to come till the afternoon, but the instinct of flight drove him forth. He meant to stay away all day—he had thoughts of dining at his club. As his door closed behind him he reflected that before he opened it again it would have admitted another man who had as much right to enter it as himself, and the thought filled him with a physical repugnance.

He caught the "elevated"[3] at the employees' hour, and found himself crushed between two layers of pendulous humanity. At Eighth Street the man facing him wriggled out, and another took his place. Waythorn glanced up and saw that it was Gus Varick. The men were so close together that it was impossible to ignore the smile of recognition on Varick's handsome overblown face. And after all—why not? They had always been on good terms, and Varick had been divorced before Waythorn's attentions to his wife began. The two exchanged a word on the perennial grievance of the congested trains, and when a seat at their side was miraculously left empty the instinct of self-preservation made Waythorn slip into it after Varick.

The latter drew the stout man's breath of relief. "Lord—I was beginning to feel like a pressed flower." He leaned back, looking unconcernedly at Waythorn. "Sorry to hear that Sellers is knocked out again."

"Sellers?" echoed Waythorn, starting at his partner's name.

Varick looked surprised. "You didn't know he was laid up with the gout?"

"No. I've been away—I only got back last night." Waythorn felt himself reddening in anticipation of the other's smile.

"Ah—yes; to be sure. And Sellers' attack came on two days ago. I'm afraid he's pretty bad. Very awkward for me, as it happens, because he was just putting through a rather important thing for me."

"Ah?" Waythorn wondered vaguely since when Varick had been dealing in "important things." Hitherto he had dabbled only in the shallow pools of speculation, with which Waythorn's office did not usually concern itself.

It occurred to him that Varick might be talking at random, to relieve the

3. Elevated railway

strain of their propinquity. That strain was becoming momentarily more apparent to Waythorn, and when, at Cortlandt Street, he caught sight of an acquaintance and had a sudden vision of the picture he and Varick must present to an initiated eye, he jumped up with a muttered excuse.

"I hope you'll find Sellers better," said Varick civilly, and he stammered back: "If I can be of any use to you—" and let the departing crowd sweep him to the platform.

At his office he heard that Sellers was in fact ill with the gout, and would probably not be able to leave the house for some weeks.

"I'm sorry it should have happened so, Mr. Waythorn," the senior clerk said with affable significance. "Mr. Sellers was very much upset at the idea of giving you such a lot of extra work just now."

"Oh, that's no matter," said Waythorn hastily. He secretly welcomed the pressure of additional business, and was glad to think that, when the day's work was over, he would have to call at his partner's on the way home.

He was late for luncheon, and turned in at the nearest restaurant instead of going to his club. The place was full, and the waiter hurried him to the back of the room to capture the only vacant table. In the cloud of cigar-smoke Waythorn did not at once distinguish his neighbors: but presently, looking about him, he saw Varick seated a few feet off. This time, luckily, they were too far apart for conversation, and Varick, who faced another way, had probably not even seen him; but there was an irony in their renewed nearness.

Varick was said to be fond of good living, and as Waythorn sat dispatching his hurried luncheon he looked across half enviously at the other's leisurely degustation of his meal. When Waythorn first saw him he had been helping himself with critical deliberation to a bit of Camembert at the ideal point of liquefaction, and now, the cheese removed, he was just pouring his *café double* from its little two-storied earthen pot. He poured slowly, his ruddy profile bent over the task, and one beringed white hand steadying the lid of the coffee-pot; then he stretched his other hand to the decanter of cognac at his elbow, filled a liqueur glass, took a tentative sip, and poured the brandy into his coffee-cup.

Waythorn watched him in a kind of fascination. What was he thinking of— only of the flavor of the coffee and the liqueur? Had the morning's meeting left no more trace in his thoughts than on his face? Had his wife so completely passed out of his life that even this odd encounter with her present husband, within a week after her remarriage, was no more than an incident in his day? And as Waythorn mused, another idea struck him: had Haskett ever met Varick as Varick and he had just met? The recollection of Haskett perturbed him, and he rose and left the restaurant, taking a circuitous way out to escape the placid irony of Varick's nod.

It was after seven when Waythorn reached home. He thought the footman who opened the door looked at him oddly.

"How is Miss Lily?" he asked in haste.

"Doing very well, sir. A gentleman—"

"Tell Barlow to put off dinner for half an hour," Waythorn cut him off, hurrying upstairs.

He went straight to his room and dressed without seeing his wife. When he reached the drawing-room she was there, fresh and radiant. Lily's day had been good; the doctor was not coming back that evening.

At dinner Waythorn told her of Sellers' illness and of the resulting compli-

cations. She listened sympathetically, adjuring him not to let himself be over-
worked, and asking vague feminine questions about the routine of the office.
Then she gave him the chronicle of Lily's day: quoted the nurse and doctor,
and told him who had called to inquire. He had never seen her more serene
and unruffled. It struck him, with a curious pang, that she was very happy in
being with him, so happy that she found a childish pleasure in rehearsing the
trivial incidents of her day.

After dinner they went to the library, and the servant put the coffee and
liqueurs on a low table before her and left the room. She looked singularly soft
and girlish in her rosy pale dress, against the dark leather of one of his bache-
lor armchairs. A day earlier the contrast would have charmed him.

He turned away now, choosing a cigar with affected deliberation.

"Did Haskett come?" he asked, with his back to her.

"Oh, yes—he came."

"You didn't see him, of course?"

She hesitated a moment. "I let the nurse see him."

That was all. There was nothing more to ask. He swung round toward her,
applying a match to his cigar. Well, the thing was over for a week, at any rate.
He would try not to think of it. She looked up at him, a trifle rosier than usual,
with a smile in her eyes.

"Ready for your coffee, dear?"

He leaned against the mantelpiece, watching her as she lifted the coffeepot.
The lamplight struck a gleam from her bracelets and tipped her soft hair with
brightness. How light and slender she was, and how each gesture flowed into
the next! She seemed a creature all compact of harmonies. As the thought of
Haskett receded, Waythorn felt himself yielding again to the joy of possessor-
ship. They were his, those white hands with their flitting motions, his the light
haze of hair, the lips and eyes. . . .

She set down the coffee-pot, and reaching for the decanter of cognac, mea-
sured off a liqueur-glass and poured it into his cup.

Waythorn uttered a sudden exclamation.

"What is the matter?" she said, startled.

"Nothing; only—I don't take cognac in my coffee."

"Oh, how stupid of me," she cried.

Their eyes met, and she blushed a sudden agonized red.

III

Ten days later, Mr. Sellers, still house-bound, asked Waythorn to call on his
way down town.

The senior partner, with his swaddled foot propped up by the fire, greeted
his associate with an air of embarrassment.

"I'm sorry, my dear fellow; I've got to ask you to do an awkward thing for
me."

Waythorn waited, and the other went on, after a pause apparently given to
the arrangement of his phrases: "The fact is, when I was knocked out I had just
gone into a rather complicated piece of business for—Gus Varick."

"Well?" said Waythorn, with an attempt to put him at his ease.

"Well—it's this way: Varick came to me the day before my attack. He had
evidently had an inside tip from somebody, and had made about a hundred

thousand. He came to me for advice, and I suggested his going in with Vanderlyn."

"Oh, the deuce!" Waythorn exclaimed. He saw in a flash what had happened. The investment was an alluring one, but required negotiation. He listened quietly while Sellers put the case before him, and, the statement ended, he said: "You think I ought to see Varick?"

"I'm afraid I can't as yet. The doctor is obdurate. And this thing can't wait. I hate to ask you, but no one else in the office knows the ins and outs of it."

Waythorn stood silent. He did not care a farthing for the success of Varick's venture, but the honor of the office was to be considered, and he could hardly refuse to oblige his partner.

"Very well," he said, "I'll do it."

That afternoon, apprised by telephone, Varick called at the office. Waythorn, waiting in his private room, wondered what the others thought of it. The newspapers, at the time of Mrs. Waythorn's marriage, had acquainted their readers with every detail of her previous matrimonial ventures, and Waythorn could fancy the clerks smiling behind Varick's back as he was ushered in.

Varick bore himself admirably. He was easy without being undignified, and Waythorn was conscious of cutting a much less impressive figure. Varick had no experience of business, and the talk prolonged itself for nearly an hour while Waythorn set forth with scrupulous precision the details of the proposed transaction.

"I'm awfully obliged to you," Varick said as he rose. "The fact is I'm not used to having much money to look after, and I don't want to make an ass of myself—" He smiled, and Waythorn could not help noticing that there was something pleasant about his smile. "It feels uncommonly queer to have enough cash to pay one's bills. I'd have sold my soul for it a few years ago!"

Waythorn winced at the allusion. He had heard it rumored that a lack of funds had been one of the determining causes of the Varick separation, but it did not occur to him that Varick's words were intentional. It seemed more likely that the desire to keep clear of embarrassing topics had fatally drawn him into one. Waythorn did not wish to be outdone in civility.

"We'll do the best we can for you," he said. "I think this is a good thing you're in."

"Oh, I'm sure it's immense. It's awfully good of you—" Varick broke off, embarrassed. "I suppose the thing's settled now—but if—"

"If anything happens before Sellers is about, I'll see you again," said Waythorn quietly. He was glad, in the end, to appear the more self-possessed of the two.

* * *

The course of Lily's illness ran smooth, and as the days passed Waythorn grew used to the idea of Haskett's weekly visit. The first time the day came round, he stayed out late, and questioned his wife as to the visit on his return. She replied at once that Haskett had merely seen the nurse downstairs, as the doctor did not wish any one in the child's sick-room till after the crisis.

The following week Waythorn was again conscious of the recurrence of the day, but had forgotten it by the time he came home to dinner. The crisis of the disease came a few days later, with a rapid decline of fever, and the little girl

was pronounced out of danger. In the rejoicing which ensued the thought of Haskett passed out of Waythorn's mind, and one afternoon, letting himself into the house with a latch-key, he went straight to his library without noticing a shabby hat and umbrella in the hall.

In the library he found a small effaced-looking man with a thinnish gray beard sitting on the edge of a chair. The stranger might have been a piano-tuner, or one of those mysteriously efficient persons who are summoned in emergencies to adjust some detail of the domestic machinery. He blinked at Waythorn through a pair of gold-rimmed spectacles and said mildly: "Mr. Waythorn, I presume? I am Lily's father."

Waythorn flushed. "Oh—" he stammered uncomfortably. He broke off, disliking to appear rude. Inwardly he was trying to adjust the actual Haskett to the image of him projected by his wife's reminiscences. Waythorn had been allowed to infer that Alice's first husband was a brute.

"I am sorry to intrude," said Haskett, with his over-the-counter politeness.

"Don't mention it," returned Waythorn, collecting himself. "I suppose the nurse has been told?"

"I presume so. I can wait," said Haskett. He had a resigned way of speaking, as though life had worn down his natural powers of resistance.

Waythorn stood on the threshold, nervously pulling off his gloves.

"I'm sorry you've been detained. I will send for the nurse," he said; and as he opened the door he added with an effort: "I'm glad we can give you a good report of Lily." He winced as the *we* slipped out, but Haskett seemed not to notice it.

"Thank you, Mr. Waythorn. It's been an anxious time for me."

"Ah, well, that's past. Soon she'll be able to go to you." Waythorn nodded and passed out.

In his own room he flung himself down with a groan. He hated the womanish sensibility which made him suffer so acutely from the grotesque chances of life. He had known when he married that his wife's former husbands were both living, and that amid the multiplied contacts of modern existence there were a thousand chances to one that he would run against one or the other, yet he found himself as much disturbed by his brief encounter with Haskett as though the law had not obligingly removed all difficulties in the way of their meeting.

Waythorn sprang up and began to pace the room nervously. He had not suffered half as much from his two meetings with Varick. It was Haskett's presence in his own house that made the situation so intolerable. He stood still, hearing steps in the passage.

"This way, please," he heard the nurse say. Haskett was being taken upstairs, then: not a corner of the house but was open to him. Waythorn dropped into another chair, staring vaguely ahead of him. On his dressing table stood a photograph of Alice, taken when he had first known her. She was Alice Varick then—how fine and exquisite he had thought her! Those were Varick's pearls about her neck. At Waythorn's instance they had been returned before her marriage. Had Haskett ever given her any trinkets—and what had become of them, Waythorn wondered? He realized suddenly that he knew very little of Haskett's past or present situation; but from the man's appearance and manner of speech he could reconstruct with curious precision the surroundings of Alice's first marriage. And it startled him to think that she had, in the back-

ground of her life, a phase of existence so different from anything with which he had connected her. Varick, whatever his faults, was a gentleman, in the conventional, traditional sense of the term: the sense which at that moment seemed, oddly enough, to have most meaning to Waythorn. He and Varick had the same social habits, spoke the same language, understood the same allusions. But this other man . . . it was grotesquely uppermost in Waythorn's mind that Haskett had worn a made-up tie attached with an elastic. Why should that ridiculous detail symbolize the whole man? Waythorn was exasperated by his own paltriness, but the fact of the tie expanded, forced itself on him, became as it were the key to Alice's past. He could see her, as Mrs. Haskett, sitting in a "front parlor" furnished in plush, with a pianola, and a copy of "*Ben Hur*"[4] on the center-table. He could see her going to the theater with Haskett—or perhaps even to a "Church Sociable"—she in a "picture hat" and Haskett in a black frock coat, a little creased, with the made-up tie on an elastic. On the way home they would stop and look at the illuminated shop windows, lingering over the photographs of New York actresses. On Sunday afternoons Haskett would take her for a walk, pushing Lily ahead of them in a white enamelled perambulator, and Waythorn had a vision of the people they would stop and talk to. He could fancy how pretty Alice must have looked, in a dress adroitly constructed from the hints of a New York fashion-paper, and how she must have looked down on the other women, chafing at her life, and secretly feeling that she belonged in a bigger place.

For the moment his foremost thought was one of wonder at the way in which she had shed the phase of existence which her marriage with Haskett implied. It was as if her whole aspect, every gesture, every inflection, every allusion, were a studied negation of that period of her life. If she had denied being married to Haskett she could hardly have stood more convicted of duplicity than in this obliteration of the self which had been his wife.

Waythorn started up, checking himself in the analysis of her motives. What right had he to create a fantastic effigy of her and then pass judgment on it? She had spoken vaguely of her first marriage as unhappy, had hinted, with becoming reticence, that Haskett had wrought havoc among her young illusions. . . . It was a pity for Waythorn's peace of mind that Haskett's very inoffensiveness shed a new light on the nature of those illusions. A man would rather think that his wife has been brutalized by her first husband than that the process has been reversed.

<div align="center">IV</div>

"Mr. Waythorn, I don't like that French governess of Lily's."

Haskett, subdued and apologetic, stood before Waythorn in the library, revolving his shabby hat in his hand.

Waythorn, surprised in his armchair over the evening paper, stared back perplexedly at his visitor.

"You'll excuse me asking to see you," Haskett continued. "But this is my last visit, and I thought if I could have a word with you it would be a better way than writing to Mrs. Waythorn's lawyer."

4. *Ben Hur, A Tale of the Christ* (1880), an immensely popular, rather melodramatic romance by Lew Wallace (1827–1905).

Waythorn rose uneasily. He did not like the French governess either; but that was irrelevant.

"I am not so sure of that," he returned stiffly; "but since you wish it I will give your message to—my wife." He always hesitated over the possessive pronoun in addressing Haskett.

The latter sighed. 'I don't know as that will help much. She didn't like it when I spoke to her."

Waythorn turned red. "When did you see her?" he asked.

"Not since the first day I came to see Lily—right after she was taken sick. I remarked to her then that I didn't like the governess."

Waythorn made no answer. He remembered distinctly that, after the first visit, he had asked his wife if she had seen Haskett. She had lied to him then, but she had respected his wishes since; and the incident cast a curious light on her character. He was sure she would not have seen Haskett that first day if she had divined that Waythorn would object, and the fact that she did not divine it was almost as disagreeable to the latter as the discovery that she had lied to him.

"I don't like the woman," Haskett was repeating with mild persistency. "She ain't straight, Mr. Waythorn—she'll teach the child to be underhand. I've noticed a change in Lily—she's too anxious to please—and she don't always tell the truth. She used to be the straightest child, Mr. Waythorn—" He broke off, his voice a little thick. "Not but what I want her to have a stylish education," he ended.

Waythorn was touched. "I'm sorry, Mr. Haskett; but frankly I don't quite see what I can do."

Haskett hesitated. Then he laid his hat on the table, and advanced to the hearth-rug, on which Waythorn was standing. There was nothing aggressive in his manner, but he had the solemnity of a timid man resolved on a decisive measure.

"There's just one thing you can do, Mr Waythorn," he said. "You can remind Mrs. Waythorn that, by the decree of the courts, I am entitled to have a voice in Lily's bringing-up." He paused, and went on more deprecatingly: "I'm not the kind to talk about enforcing my rights, Mr. Waythorn. I don't know as I think a man is entitled to rights he hasn't known how to hold on to; but this business of the child is different. I've never let go there—and I never mean to."

* * *

The scene left Waythorn deeply shaken. Shamefacedly, in indirect ways, he had been finding out about Haskett; and all that he learned was favorable. The little man, in order to be near his daughter, had sold out his share in a profitable business in Utica, and accepted a modest clerkship in a New York manufacturing house. He boarded in a shabby street and had few acquaintances. His passion for Lily filled his life. Waythorn felt that this exploration of Haskett was like groping about with a dark-lantern in his wife's past; but he saw now that there were recesses his lantern had not explored. He had never enquired into the exact circumstances of his wife's first matrimonial rupture. On the surface all had been fair. It was she who had obtained the divorce, and the court had given her the child. But Waythorn knew how many ambiguities such a verdict might cover. The mere fact that Haskett retained a right over his

daughter implied an unsuspected compromise. Waythorn was an idealist. He always refused to recognize unpleasant contingencies till he found himself confronted with them, and then he saw them followed by a spectral train of consequences. His next days were thus haunted, and he determined to try to lay the ghosts by conjuring them up in his wife's presence.

When he repeated Haskett's request a flame of anger passed over her face; but she subdued it instantly and spoke with a slight quiver of outraged motherhood.

"It is very ungentlemanly of him," she said.

The word grated on Waythorn. "That is neither here nor there. It's a bare question of rights."

She murmured: "It's not as if he could ever be a help to Lily—"

Waythorn flushed. This was even less to his taste. "The question is," he repeated, "what authority has he over her?"

She looked downward, twisting herself a little in her seat. "I am willing to see him—I thought you objected," she faltered.

In a flash he understood that she knew the extent of Haskett's claims. Perhaps it was not the first time she had resisted them.

"My objecting has nothing to do with it," he said coldly; "if Haskett has a right to be consulted you must consult him."

She burst into tears, and he saw that she expected him to regard her as a victim.

Haskett did not abuse his rights. Waythorn had felt miserably sure that he would not. But the governess was dismissed, and from time to time the little man demanded an interview with Alice. After the first outburst she accepted the situation with her usual adaptability. Haskett had once reminded Waythorn of the piano-tuner, and Mrs. Waythorn, after a month or two, appeared to class him with that domestic familiar. Waythorn could not but respect the father's tenacity. At first he had tried to cultivate the suspicion that Haskett might be "up to" something, that he had an object in securing a foothold in the house. But in his heart Waythorn was sure of Haskett's singlemindedness; he even guessed in the latter a mild contempt for such advantages as his relation with the Waythorns might offer. Haskett's sincerity of purpose made him invulnerable, and his successor had to accept him as a lien on the property.

* * *

Mr. Sellers was sent to Europe to recover from his gout, and Varick's affairs hung on Waythorn's hands. The negotiations were prolonged and complicated; they necessitated frequent conferences between the two men, and the interests of the firm forbade Waythorn's suggesting that his client should transfer his business to another office.

Varick appeared well in the transaction. In moments of relaxation his coarse streak appeared, and Waythorn dreaded his geniality; but in the office he was concise and clear-headed, with a flattering deference to Waythorn's judgment. Their business relations being so affably established, it would have been absurd for the two men to ignore each other in society. The first time they met in a drawing-room, Varick took up their intercourse in the same easy key, and his hostess's grateful glance obliged Waythorn to respond to it. After that they ran across each other frequently, and one evening at a ball

Waythorn, wandering through the remoter rooms, came upon Varick seated beside his wife. She colored a little, and faltered in what she was saying; but Varick nodded to Waythorn without rising, and the latter strolled on.

In the carriage, on the way home, he broke out nervously: "I didn't know you spoke to Varick."

Her voice trembled a little. "It's the first time—he happened to be standing near me; I didn't know what to do. It's so awkward, meeting everywhere—and he said you had been very kind about some business."

"That's different," said Waythorn.

She paused a moment. "I'll do just as you wish," she returned pliantly. "I thought it would be less awkward to speak to him when we meet."

Her pliancy was beginning to sicken him. Had she really no will of her own—no theory about her relation to these men? She had accepted Haskett—did she mean to accept Varick? It was "less awkward," as she had said, and her instinct was to evade difficulties or to circumvent them. With sudden vividness Waythorn saw how the instinct had developed. She was "as easy as an old shoe"—a shoe that too many feet had worn. Her elasticity was the result of tension in too many different directions. Alice Haskett—Alice Varick—Alice Waythorn—she had been each in turn, and had left hanging to each name a little of her privacy, a little of her personality, a little of the inmost self where the unknown god abides.

"Yes—it's better to speak to Varick," said Waythorn wearily.

V

The winter wore on, and society took advantage of the Waythorns' acceptance of Varick. Harassed hostesses were grateful to them for bridging over a social difficulty, and Mrs. Waythorn was held up as a miracle of good taste. Some experimental spirits could not resist the diversion of throwing Varick and his former wife together, and there were those who thought he found a zest in the propinquity. But Mrs. Waythorn's conduct remained irreproachable. She neither avoided Varick nor sought him out. Even Waythorn could not but admit that she had discovered the solution of the newest social problem.

He had married her without giving much thought to that problem. He had fancied that a woman can shed her past like a man. But now he saw that Alice was bound to hers both by the circumstances which forced her into continued relation with it, and by the traces it had left on her nature. With grim irony Waythorn compared himself to a member of a syndicate. He held so many shares in his wife's personality and his predecessors were his partners in the business. If there had been any element of passion in the transaction he would have felt less deteriorated by it. The fact that Alice took her change of husbands like a change of weather reduced the situation to mediocrity. He could have forgiven her for blunders, for excesses; for resisting Haskett, for yielding to Varick; for anything but her acquiescence and her tact. She reminded him of a juggler tossing knives; but the knives were blunt and she knew they would never cut her.

And then, gradually, habit formed a protecting surface for his sensibilities. If he paid for each day's comfort with the small change of his illusions, he grew daily to value the comfort more and set less store upon the coin. He had

drifted into a dulling propinquity with Haskett and Varick and he took refuge in the cheap revenge of satirizing the situation. He even began to reckon up the advantages which accrued from it, to ask himself if it were not better to own a third of a wife who knew how to make a man happy than a whole one who had lacked opportunity to acquire the art. For it *was* an art, and made up, like all others, of concessions, eliminations and embellishments; of lights judiciously thrown and shadows skillfully softened. His wife knew exactly how to manage the lights, and he knew exactly to what training she owed her skill. He even tried to trace the source of his obligations, to discriminate between the influences which had combined to produce his domestic happiness: he perceived that Haskett's commonness had made Alice worship good breeding, while Varick's liberal construction of the marriage bond had taught her to value the conjugal virtues; so that he was directly indebted to his predecessors for the devotion which made his life easy if not inspiring.

From this phrase he passed into that of complete acceptance. He ceased to satirize himself because time dulled the irony of the situation and the joke lost its humor with its sting. Even the sight of Haskett's hat on the hall table had ceased to touch the springs of epigram. The hat was often seen there now, for it had been decided that it was better for Lily's father to visit her than for the little girl to go to his boarding-house. Waythorn, having acquiesced in this arrangement, had been surprised to find how little difference it made. Haskett was never obtrusive, and the few visitors who met him on the stairs were unaware of his identity. Waythorn did not know how often he saw Alice, but with himself Haskett was seldom in contact.

One afternoon, however, he learned on entering that Lily's father was waiting to see him. In the library he found Haskett occupying a chair in his usual provisional way. Waythorn always felt grateful to him for not leaning back.

"I hope you'll excuse me, Mr. Waythorn," he said rising. "I wanted to see Mrs. Waythorn about Lily, and your man asked me to wait here till she came in."

"Of course," said Waythorn, remembering that a sudden leak had that morning given over the drawing-room to the plumbers.

He opened his cigar-case and held it out to his visitor, and Haskett's acceptance seemed to mark a fresh stage in their intercourse. The spring evening was chilly, and Waythorn invited his guest to draw up his chair to the fire. He meant to find an excuse to leave Haskett in a moment; but he was tired and cold, and after all the little man no longer jarred on him.

The two were enclosed in the intimacy of their blended cigar smoke when the door opened and Varick walked into the room. Waythorn rose abruptly. It was the first time that Varick had come to the house, and the surprise of seeing him, combined with the singular inopportuneness of his arrival, gave a new edge to Waythorn's blunted sensibilities. He stared at his visitor without speaking.

Varick seemed too preoccupied to notice his host's embarrassment.

"My dear fellow," he exclaimed in his most expansive tone, "I must apologize for tumbling in on you in this way, but I was too late to catch you downtown, and so I thought—"

He stopped short, catching sight of Haskett, and his sanguine color deepened to a flush which spread vividly under his scant blond hair. But in a moment he recovered himself and nodded slightly. Haskett returned the bow in

silence, and Waythorn was still groping for speech when the footman came in carrying a tea-table.

The intrusion offered a welcome vent to Waythorn's nerves. "What the deuce are you bringing this here for?" he said sharply.

"I beg your pardon, sir, but the plumbers are still in the drawing-room, and Mrs. Waythorn said she would have tea in the library." The footman's perfectly respectful tone implied a reflection on Waythorn's reasonableness.

"Oh, very well," said the latter resignedly, and the footman proceeded to open the folding tea-table and set out its complicated appointments. While this interminable process continued the three men stood motionless, watching it with a fascinated stare, till Waythorn, to break the silence, said to Varick: "Won't you have a cigar?"

He held out the case he had just tendered to Haskett, and Varick helped himself with a smile. Waythorn looked about for a match, and finding none, proffered a light from his own cigar. Haskett, in the background, held his ground mildly, examining his cigar-tip now and then, and stepping forward at the right moment to knock its ashes into the fire.

The footman at last withdrew, and Varick immediately began: "If I could just say half a word to you about this business—"

"Certainly," stammered Waythorn; "in the dining room—"

But as he placed his hand on the door it opened from without, and his wife appeared on the threshold.

She came in fresh and smiling, in her street dress and hat, shedding a fragrance from the boa which she loosened in advancing.

"Shall we have tea in here, dear?" she began; and then she caught sight of Varick. Her smile deepened, veiling a slight tremor of surprise.

"Why, how do you do?" she said with a distinct note of pleasure.

As she shook hands with Varick she saw Haskett standing behind him. Her smile faded for a moment, but she recalled it quickly with a scarcely perceptible side-glance at Waythorn.

"How do you do, Mr. Haskett?" she said, and shook hands with him a shade less cordially.

The three men stood awkwardly before her, till Varick, always the most self-possessed, dashed into an explanatory phrase.

"We—I had to see Waythorn a moment on business," he stammered, brick-red from chin to nape.

Haskett stepped forward with his air of mild obstinacy. "I am sorry to intrude; but you appointed five o'clock—' he directed his resigned glance to the timepiece on the mantel.

She swept aside their embarrassment with a charming gesture of hospitality.

"I'm so sorry—I'm always late, but the afternoon was so lovely." She stood drawing off her gloves, propitiatory and graceful, diffusing about her a sense of ease and familiarity in which the situation lost its grotesqueness. "But before talking business," she added brightly, "I'm sure every one wants a cup of tea."

She dropped into her low chair by the tea-table, and the two visitors, as if drawn by her smile, advanced to receive the cups she held out.

She glanced about for Waythorn, and he took the third cup with a laugh.

1904

MAY SINCLAIR
1863–1946

Through her generous literary patronage, May Sinclair helped defend and define early modernist efforts to break free of Victorian literary conventions. Not only did she protest the censorship of D. H. Lawrence's *The Rainbow*, she also was the first to use William James's phrase "stream of consciousness" to praise Dorothy Richardson's fictional technique in *Pilgrimage*. An early promoter of experimental poets like Ezra Pound and H. D. (Hilda Doolittle), Sinclair also helped Charlotte Mew publish her verse and defended T. S. Eliot's first book against detractors. In the twenty-four works she wrote between 1897 and 1927, moreover, Sinclair herself moved from realistic protests against Victorian constraints to psychological narratives that attempt to capture the inner growth of her characters' consciousness. In the best of these novels—*The Three Sisters* (1914), *Mary Olivier* (1919), and *Life and Death of Harriett Frean* (1920)—Sinclair focused on the efforts of women to escape the sexual repression and domestic confinement that clearly shaped her own early environment.

The youngest child and only girl in a family of five boys, Mary Amelia St. Clair Sinclair lived in an affluent suburb of Liverpool until the bankruptcy of her father's ship-owning business caused the family to move in the 1870s to Ilford, Essex. Sinclair's semiautobiographical novel *Mary Olivier* portrayed her father as an ineffectual alcoholic, while her mother was presented as a dogmatic Christian determined to make her children conform to her puritanical will. Like her heroine, Sinclair assimilated her mother's passionate commitment to service, but rebelled against her narrow-minded social conformity. Like Mary Olivier, Sinclair educated herself in Greek, German philosophy, and English literature by reading her brothers' books, although she did spend one year at Cheltenham Ladies' College. Like Mary Olivier, too, Sinclair witnessed the deaths of her father and brothers, and devoted her life to her aging mother. Just as Mary Olivier was inspired by her reading of Walt Whitman to translate Euripides' *Bacchae* and to compose her own poetry, Sinclair supported her mother throughout the 1890s by publishing translations, poetry, and her first novel, *Audrey Craven* (1897).

After her mother died in 1901, Sinclair went on to become a major intellectual presence in London. She worked with both the Women's Freedom League and the Women Writers' Suffrage League. When she returned to England from service in an ambulance unit in Belgium, she published *The Tree of Heaven* (1917), an exploration of feminism in the context of World War I. Founder-member of the Medico-Psychological Clinic in London, Sinclair wrote essays on the work of Sigmund Freud and C. G. Jung before psychoanalysis was widely known. Throughout the early 1920s, her London apartment and country cottage were meeting places for poets and novelists, including Pound, H. D., Robert Frost, Edith Wharton, and Ford Madox Ford. By this time, however, she was beginning to suffer from the neuromuscular deterioration that incapacitated her for more than a decade.

Besides her novels and essays, Sinclair produced two novellas and five volumes of short stories as well as a biographical study, *The Three Brontës* (1912), in which she praised Charlotte Brontë's "new voice," which, she declared, uncovered everything "that proud, decorous mid-Victorian reticence most sedulously sought to hide." Not only in her novels but also in her short stories, Sinclair contributed to the "subtler and more intimate psychology" that she believed Brontë had pioneered. Unusual in its candor about female sexual desire, *Where Their Fire Is Not Quenched* studies the psychology of loneliness and guilt in a heroine convinced that her life has been cheated of its expected pleasures.

Where Their Fire Is Not Quenched

There was nobody in the orchard. Harriott Leigh went out, carefully, through the iron gate nto the field. She had made the latch slip into its notch without a sound.

The path slanted widely up the field from the orchard gate to the stile under the elder tree. George Waring waited for her there.

Years afterwards, when she thought of George Waring she smelled the sweet, hot, wine-scent of the elder flowers. Years afterwards, when she smelled elder flowers she saw George Waring, with his beautiful, gentle face, like a poet's or a musician's, his black-blue eyes, and sleek, olive-brown hair. He was a naval lieutenant.

Yesterday he had asked her to marry him and she had consented. But her father hadn't, and she had come to tell him that and say good-bye before he left her. His ship was to sail the next day.

He was eager and excited. He couldn't believe that anything could stop their happiness, that anything he didn't want to happen could happen.

"Well?" he said.

"He's a perfect beast, George. He won't let us He says we're too young."

"I was twenty last August," he said, aggrieved.

"And I shall be seventeen in September."

"And this is June. We're quite old, really. How long does he mean us to wait?"

"Three years."

"Three years before we can be engaged even—Why, we might be dead."

She put her arms round him to make him feel safe. They kissed; and the sweet, hot, wine-scent of the elder flowers mixed with their kisses. They stood, pressed close together, under the elder tree.

Across the yellow fields of charlock[1] they heard the village clock strike seven. Up in the house a gong clanged.

"Darling, I must go," she said.

"Oh stay—Stay *five* minutes."

He pressed her close. It lasted five minutes, and five more. Then he was running fast down the road to the station, while Harriott went along the field-path, slowly, struggling with her tears.

"He'll be back in three months," she said. "I can live through three months."

But he never came back. There was something wrong with the engines of his ship, the *Alexandra*. Three weeks later she went down in the Mediterranean, and George with her.

Harriott said she didn't care how soon she died now. She was quite sure it would be soon, because she couldn't live without him.

Five years passed.

The two lines of beech trees stretched on and on, the whole length of the Park, a broad green drive between. When you came to the middle they branched off right and left in the form of a cross, and at the end of the right arm there was a white stucco pavilion with pillars and a three-cornered pedi-

1. Wild mustard.

ment like a Greek temple. At the end of the left arm, the west entrance to the Park, double gates and a side door.

Harriott, on her stone seat at the back of the pavilion, could see Stephen Philpotts the very minute he came through the side door.

He had asked her to wait for him there. It was the place he always chose to read his poems aloud in. The poems were a pretext. She knew what he was going to say. And she knew what she would answer.

There were elder bushes in flower at the back of the pavilion, and Harriott thought of George Waring. She told herself that George was nearer to her now than he could ever have been, living. If she married Stephen she would not be unfaithful, because she loved him with another part of herself. It was not as though Stephen were taking George's place. She loved Stephen with her soul, in an unearthly way.

But her body quivered like a stretched wire when the door opened and the young man came towards her down the drive under the beech trees.

She loved him; she loved his slenderness, his darkness and sallow whiteness, his black eyes lighting up with the intellectual flame, the way his black hair swept back from his forehead, the way he walked, tiptoe, as if his feet were lifted with wings.

He sat down beside her. She could see his hands tremble. She felt that her moment was coming; it had come.

"I wanted to see you alone because there's something I must say to you. I don't quite know how to begin. . . ."

Her lips parted. She panted lightly.

"You've heard me speak of Sybill Foster?"

Her voice came stammering, "N-no, Stephen. Did you?"

"Well, I didn't mean to, till I knew it was all right. I only heard yesterday."

"Heard what?"

"Why, that she'll have me. Oh, Harriott—do you know what it's like to be terribly happy?"

She knew. She had known just now, the moment before he told her. She sat there, stone-cold and stiff, listening to his raptures; listening to her own voice saying she was glad.

Ten years passed.

Harriott Leigh sat waiting in the drawing-room of a small house in Maida Vale.[2] She had lived there ever since her father's death two years before.

She was restless. She kept on looking at the clock to see if it was four, the hour that Oscar Wade had appointed. She was not sure that he would come, after she had sent him away yesterday.

She now asked herself, why, when she had sent him away yesterday, she had let him come today. Her motives were not altogether clear. If she really meant what she had said then, she oughtn't to let him come to her again. Never again.

She had shown him plainly what she meant. She could see herself, sitting very straight in her chair, uplifted by a passionate integrity, while he stood before her, hanging his head, ashamed and beaten; she could feel again the throb in her voice as she kept on saying that she couldn't, she couldn't; he must see

2. A section of northwest London.

that she couldn't; that no, nothing would make her change her mind; she couldn't forget he had a wife; that he must think of Muriel

To which he had answered savagely: "I needn't. That's all over. We only live together for the look of the thing."

And she, serenely, with great dignity: "And for the look of the thing, Oscar, we must leave off seeing each other. Please go."

"Do you mean it?"

"Yes. We must never see each other again."

And he had gone then, ashamed and beaten.

She could see him, squaring his broad shoulders to meet the blow. And she was sorry for him. She told herself she had been unnecessarily hard. Why shouldn't they see each other again, now he understood where they must draw the line? Until yesterday the line had never been very clearly drawn. Today she meant to ask him to forget what he had said to her. Once it was forgotten, they could go on being friends as if nothing had happened.

It was four o'clock. Half-past. Five. She had finished tea and given him up when, between the half-hour and six o'clock, he came.

He came as he had come a dozen times, with his measured, deliberate, thoughtful tread, carrying himself well braced with a sort of held-in arrogance, his great shoulders heaving. He was a man of about forty, broad and tall, lean-flanked and short-necked, his straight, handsome features showing small and even in the big square face and in the flush that swamped it. The close-clipped, reddish-brown moustache bristled forwards from the pushed-out upper lip. His small, flat eyes shone, reddish-brown, eager and animal.

She liked to think of him when he was not there, but always at the first sight of him she felt a slight shock. Physically, he was very far from her admired ideal. So different from George Waring and Stephen Philpotts.

He sat down, facing her.

There was an embarrassed silence, broken by Oscar Wade.

"Well, Harriott, you said I could come." He seemed to be throwing the responsibility on her.

"So I suppose you've forgiven me," he said.

"Oh, yes, Oscar, I've forgiven you."

He said she'd better show it by coming to dine with him somewhere that evening.

She could give no reason to herself for going. She simply went.

He took her to a restaurant in Soho. Oscar Wade dined well, even extravagantly, giving each dish its importance. She liked his extravagance. He had none of the mean virtues.

It was over. His flushed, embarrassed silence told her what he was thinking. But when he had seen her home he left her at her garden gate. He had thought better of it.

She was not sure whether she were glad or sorry. She had had her moment of righteous exaltation and she had enjoyed it. But there was no joy in the weeks that followed it. She had given up Oscar Wade because she didn't want him very much; and now she wanted him furiously, perversely, because she had given him up. Though he had no resemblance to her ideal, she couldn't live without him.

She dined with him again and again, till she knew Schnebler's Restaurant by heart, the white paneled walls picked out with gold; the white pillars, and

the curling gold fronds of their capitals; the Turkey carpets, blue and crimson, soft under her feet; the thick crimson velvet cushions, that clung to her skirts; the glitter of silver and glass on the innumerable white circles of the tables. And the faces of the diners, red, white, pink, brown, gray and sallow, distorted and excited; the curled mouths that twisted as they ate; the convoluted electric bulbs pointing, pointing down at them, under the red, crinkled shades. All shimmering in a thick air that the red light stained as wine stains water.

And Oscar's face, flushed with his dinner. Always, when he leaned back from the table and brooded in silence she knew what he was thinking. His heavy eyelids would lift; she would find his eyes fixed on hers, wondering, considering.

She knew now what the end would be. She thought of George Waring, and Stephen Philpotts, and of her life, cheated. She hadn't chosen Oscar, she hadn't really wanted him; but now he had forced himself on her she couldn't afford to let him go. Since George died no man had loved her, no other man ever would. And she was sorry for him when she thought of him going from her, beaten and ashamed.

She was certain, before he was, of the end. Only she didn't know when and where and how it would come. That was what Oscar knew.

It came at the close of one of their evenings when they had dined in a private sitting-room. He said he couldn't stand the heat and noise of the public restaurant.

She went before him, up a steep, red-carpeted stair to a white door on the second landing.

From time to time they repeated the furtive, hidden adventure. Sometimes she met him in the room above Schnebler's. Sometimes, when her maid was out, she received him at her house in Maida Vale. But that was dangerous, not to be risked too often.

Oscar declared himself unspeakably happy. Harriott was not quite sure. This was love, the thing she had never had, that she had dreamed of, hungered and thirsted for; but now she had it she was not satisfied. Always she looked for something just beyond it, some mystic, heavenly rapture, always beginning to come, that never came. There was something about Oscar that repelled her. But because she had taken him for her lover, she couldn't bring herself to admit that it was a certain coarseness. She looked another way and pretended it wasn't there. To justify herself, she fixed her mind on his good qualities, his generosity, his strength, the way he had built up his engineering business. She made him take her over his works and show her his great dynamos. She made him lend her the books he read. But always, when she tried to talk to him, he let her see that *that* wasn't what she was there for.

"My dear girl, we haven't time," he said. "It's waste of our priceless moments."

She persisted. "There's something wrong about it all if we can't talk to each other."

He was irritated. "Women never seem to consider that a man can get all the talk he wants from other men. What's wrong is our meeting in this unsatisfactory way. We ought to live together. It's the only sane thing. I would, only I don't want to break up Muriel's home and make her miserable."

"I thought you said she wouldn't care."

"My dear, she cares for her home and her position and the children. You forget the children."

Yes. She had forgotten the children. She had forgotten Muriel. She had left off thinking of Oscar as a man with a wife and children and a home.

He had a plan. His mother-in-law was coming to stay with Muriel in October and he would get away. He would go to Paris, and Harriott should come to him there. He could say he went on business. No need to lie about it; he *had* business in Paris.

He engaged rooms in an hotel in the rue de Rivoli. They spent two weeks there.

For three days Oscar was madly in love with Harriott and Harriott with him. As she lay awake she would turn on the light and look at him as he slept at her side. Sleep made him beautiful and innocent; it air a fine, smooth tissue over his coarseness; it made his mouth gentle; it entirely hid his eyes.

In six days reaction had set in. At the end of the tenth day, Harriott, returning with Oscar from Montmartre, burst into a fit of crying. When questioned, she answered wildly that the Hotel Saint Pierre was too hideously ugly; it was getting on her nerves. Mercifully Oscar explained her state as fatigue following excitement. She tried hard to believe that she was miserable because her love was purer and more spiritual than Oscar's; but all the time she knew perfectly well she had cried from pure boredom. She was in love with Oscar, and Oscar bored her. Oscar was in love with her, and she bored him. At close quarters, day in and day out, each was revealed to the other as an incredible bore.

At the end of the second week she began to doubt whether she had ever been really in love with him.

Her passion returned for a little while after they got back to London. Freed from the unnatural strain which Paris had put on them, they persuaded themselves that their romantic temperaments were better fitted to the old life of casual adventure

Then, gradually, the sense of danger began to wake in them. They lived in perpetual fear, face to face with all the chances of discovery. They tormented themselves and each other by imagining possibilities that they would never have considered in their first fine moments. It was as though they were beginning to ask themselves if it were, after all, worth while running such awful risks, for all they got out of it. Oscar still swore that if he had been free he would have married her. He pointed out that his intentions at any rate were regular. But she asked herself: Would I marry him? Marriage would be the Hotel Saint Pierre all over again, without any possibility of escape. But, if she wouldn't marry him, was she in love with him? That was the test. Perhaps it was a good thing he wasn't free. Then she told herself that these doubts were morbid, and that the question wouldn't arise.

One evening Oscar called to see her. He had come to tell her that Muriel was ill.

"Seriously ill?"

"I'm afraid so. It's pleurisy. May turn to pneumonia. We shall know one way or another in the next few days."

A terrible fear seized upon Harriott. Muriel might die of her pleurisy; and if Muriel died, she would have to marry Oscar. He was looking at her queerly, as if he knew what she was thinking, and she could see that the same thought had occurred to him and that he was frightened too.

Muriel got well again; but their danger had enlightened them. Muriel's life was now inconceivably precious to them both; she stood between them and

that permanent union, which they dreaded and yet would not have the courage to refuse.

After enlightenment the rupture.

It came from Oscar, one evening when he sat with her in her drawing-room.

"Harriott," he said, "do you know I'm thinking seriously of settling down?"

"How do you mean, settling down?"

"Patching it up with Muriel, poor girl. . . . Has it never occurred to you that this little affair of ours can't go on for ever?"

"You don't want it to go on?"

"I don't want to have any humbug about it. For God's sake, let's be straight. If it's done, it's done. Let's end it decently."

"I see. You want to get rid of me."

"That's a beastly way of putting it."

"Is there any way that isn't beastly? The whole thing's beastly. I should have thought you'd have stuck to it now you've made it what you wanted. When I haven't an ideal, I haven't a single illusion, when you've destroyed everything you didn't want."

"What didn't I want?"

"The clean, beautiful part of it. The part *I* wanted."

"My part at least was real. It was cleaner and more beautiful than all that putrid stuff you wrapped it up in. You were a hypocrite, Harriott, and I wasn't. You're a hypocrite now if you say you weren't happy with me."

"I was never really happy. Never for one moment. There was always something I missed. Something you didn't give me. Perhaps you couldn't."

"No. I wasn't spiritual enough," he sneered.

"You were not. And you made me what you were."

"Oh, I noticed that you were always very spiritual *after* you'd got what you wanted."

"What I wanted?" she cried. "Oh, my God—"

"If you ever knew what you wanted."

"What—I—wanted," she repeated, drawing out her bitterness.

"Come," he said, "why not be honest? Face facts. I was awfully gone on you. You were awfully gone on me—once. We got tired of each other and it's over. But at least you might own we had a good time while it lasted."

"A good time?"

"Good enough for me."

"For you, because for you love only means one thing. Everything that's high and noble in it you dragged down to that, till there's nothing left for us but that. *That's* what you made of love."

Twenty years passed.

It was Oscar who died first, three years after the rupture. He did it suddenly one evening, falling down in a fit of apoplexy.

His death was an immense relief to Harriott. Perfect security had been impossible as long as he was alive. But now there wasn't a living soul who knew her secret.

Still, in the first moment of shock Harriott told herself that Oscar dead would be nearer to her than ever. She forgot how little she had wanted him to be near her, alive. And long before the twenty years had passed she had contrived to persuade herself that he had never been near to her at all. It was in-

credible that she had ever known such a person as Oscar Wade. As for their affair, she wouldn't think of Harriott Leigh as the sort of woman to whom such a thing could happen. Schnebler's and the Hotel Saint Pierre ceased to figure among prominent images of her past. Her memories, if she had allowed herself to remember, would have clashed disagreeably with the reputation for sanctity which she had now acquired.

For Harriott at fifty-two was the friend and helper of the Reverend Clement Farmer, Vicar of St. Mary the Virgin's, Maida Vale. She worked as a deaconess in his parish, wearing the uniform of a deaconess, the semi-religious gown, the cloak, the bonnet and veil, the cross and rosary, the holy smile. She was also secretary to the Maida Vale and Kilburn Home for Fallen Girls.

Her moments of excitement came when Clement Farmer, the lean, austere likeness of Stephen Philpotts, in his cassock and lace-bordered surplice, issued from the vestry, when he mounted the pulpit, when he stood before the altar rails and lifted up his arms in the Benediction; her moments of ecstasy when she received the Sacrament from his hands. And she had moments of calm happiness when his study door closed on their communion. All these moments were saturated with a solemn holiness.

And they were insignificant compared with the moment of her dying.

She lay dozing in her white bed under the black crucifix with the ivory Christ. The basins and medicine bottles had been cleared from the table by her pillow; it was spread for the last rites. The priest moved quietly about the room, arranging the candles, the Prayer Book and the Holy Sacrament. Then he drew a chair to her bedside and watched with her, waiting for her to come up out of her doze.

She woke suddenly. Her eyes were fixed upon him. She had a flash of lucidity. She was dying, and her dying made her supremely important to Clement Farmer.

"Are you ready?" he asked.

"Not yet. I think I'm afraid. Make me not afraid."

He rose and lit the two candles on the altar. He took down the crucifix from the wall and stood it against the foot-rail of the bed.

She sighed. That was not what she had wanted.

"You will not be afraid now," he said.

"I'm not afraid of the hereafter. I suppose you get used to it. Only it may be terrible just at first."

"Our first state will depend very much on what we are thinking of at our last hour."

"There'll be my—confession," she said.

"And after it you will receive the Sacrament.[3] Then you will have your mind fixed firmly upon God and your Redeemer. . . . Do you feel able to make your confession now Sister? Everything is ready."

Her mind went back over her past and found Oscar Wade there. She wondered: Should she confess to him about Oscar Wade? One moment she thought it was possible; the next she knew that she couldn't. She could not. It wasn't necessary. For twenty years he had not been part of her life. No. She wouldn't confess about Oscar Wade. She had been guilty of other sins.

3. Here, extreme unction; the anointing of a dying person performed in the Roman Catholic and Anglican Churches.

She made a careful selection.

"I have cared too much for the beauty of this world. . . . I have failed in charity to my poor girls. Because of my intense repugnance to their sin. . . . I have thought, often, about—people I love, when I should have been thinking about God."

After that she received the Sacrament.

"Now," he said, "there is nothing to be afraid of."

"I won't be afraid if—if you would hold my hand."

He held it. And she lay still a long time, with her eyes shut. Then he heard her murmuring something. He stooped close.

"This—is—dying. I thought it would be horrible. And it's bliss. . . . Bliss."

The priest's hand slackened, as if at the bidding of some wonder. She gave a weak cry.

"Oh—don't let me go."

His grasp tightened.

"Try," he said, "to think about God. Keep on looking at the crucifix."

"If I look," she whispered, "you won't let go my hand?"

"I will not let you go."

He held it till it was wrenched from him in the last agony.

She lingered for some hours in the room where these things had happened.

Its aspect was familiar and yet unfamiliar, and slightly repugnant to her. The altar, the crucifix, the lighted candles, suggested some tremendous and awful experience the details of which she was not able to recall. She seemed to remember that they had been connected in some way with the sheeted body on the bed; but the nature of the connection was not clear; and she did not associate the dead body with herself. When the nurse came in and laid it out, she saw that it was the body of a middle-aged woman. Her own living body was that of a young woman of about thirty-two.

Her mind had no past and no future, no sharp-edged, coherent memories, and no idea of anything to be done next.

Then, suddenly, the room began to come apart before her eyes, to split into shafts of floor and furniture and ceiling that shifted and were thrown by their commotion into different planes. They leaned slanting at every possible angle; they crossed and overlaid each other with a transparent mingling of dislocated perspectives, like reflections fallen on an interior seen behind glass.

The bed and the sheeted body slid away somewhere out of sight. She was standing by the door that still remained in position.

She opened it and found herself in the street, outside a building of yellowish-gray brick and freestone, with a tall slated spire. Her mind came together with a palpable click of recognition. This object was the Church of St. Mary the Virgin, Maida Vale. She could hear the droning of the organ. She opened the door and slipped in.

She had gone back into a definite space and time, and recovered a certain limited section of coherent memory. She remembered the rows of pitch-pine benches, with their Gothic peaks and moldings; the stone-colored walls and pillars with their chocolate stenciling; the hanging rings of lights along the aisles of the nave; the high altar with its lighted candles, and the polished brass cross, twinkling. These things were somehow permanent and real, adjusted to the image that now took possession of her.

She knew what she had come there for. The service was over. The choir had gone from the chancel; the sacristan moved before the altar, putting out the candles. She walked up the middle aisle to a seat that she knew under the pulpit. She knelt down and covered her face with her hands. Peeping sideways through her fingers, she could see the door of the vestry on her left at the end of the north aisle. She watched it steadily.

Up in the organ loft the organist drew out the Recessional, slowly and softly, to its end in the two solemn, vibrating chords.

The vestry door opened and Clement Farmer came out, dressed in his black cassock. He passed before her, close, close outside the bench where she knelt. He paused at the opening. He was waiting for her. There was something he had to say.

She stood up and went towards him. He still waited. He didn't move to make way for her. She came close, closer than she had ever come to him, so close that his features grew indistinct. She bent her head back, peering, shortsightedly, and found herself looking into Oscar Wade's face.

He stood still, horribly still, and close, barring her passage.

She drew back; his heaving shoulders followed her. He leaned forward, covering her with his eyes. She opened her mouth to scream, and no sound came.

She was afraid to move lest he should move with her. The heaving of his shoulders terrified her.

One by one the lights in the side aisles were going out. The lights in the middle aisle would go next. They had gone. If she didn't get away she would be shut up with him there, in the appalling darkness.

She turned and moved towards the north aisle, groping, steadying herself by the book ledge.

When she looked back, Oscar Wade was not there.

Then she remembered that Oscar Wade was dead. Therefore, what she had seen was not Oscar; it was his ghost. He was dead; dead seventeen years ago. She was safe from him forever.

When she came out on to the steps of the church she saw that the road it stood in had changed. It was not the road she remembered. The pavement on this side was raised slightly and covered in. It ran under a succession of arches. It was a long gallery walled with glittering shop windows on one side; on the other a line of tall gray columns divided it from the street.

She was going along the arcades of the rue de Rivoli. Ahead of her she could see the edge of an immense gray pillar jutting out. That was the porch of the Hotel Saint Pierre. The revolving glass doors swung forward to receive her; she crossed the gray, sultry vestibule under the pillared arches. She knew it. She knew the porter's shining, wine-colored mahogany pen on her left, and the shining wine-colored mahogany barrier of the clerk's bureau on her right; she made straight for the great gray carpeted staircase; she climbed the endless flights that turned round and round the caged-in shaft of the well, past the latticed doors of the lift, and came up on to a landing that she knew, and into the long, ash-gray, foreign corridor lit by a dull window at one end.

It was there that the horror of the place came on her. She had no longer any memory of St. Mary's Church, so that she was unaware of her backward course through time. All space and time were here.

She remembered she had to go to the left, the left.

But there was something there; where the corridor turned by the window; at the end of all the corridors. If she went the other way she would escape it.

The corridor stopped there. A blank wall. She was driven back past the stair-head to the left.

At the corner, by the window, she turned down another long ash-gray corridor on her right, and to the right again where the night-light sputtered on the table-flap at the turn.

This third corridor was dark and secret and depraved. She knew the soiled walls and the warped door at the end. There was a sharp-pointed streak of light at the top. She could see the number on it now, 107.

Something had happened there. If she went in it would happen again.

Oscar Wade was in the room waiting for her behind the closed door. She felt him moving about in there. She leaned forward, her ear to the key-hole, and listened. She could near the measured, deliberate, thoughtful footsteps. They were coming from the bed to the door.

She turned and ran; her knees gave way under her; she sank and ran on, down the long gray corridors and the stairs, quick and blind, a hunted beast seeking for cover, hearing his feet coming after her.

The revolving doors caught her and pushed her out into the street.

The strange quality of her state was this, that it had no time. She remembered dimly that there had once been a thing called time; but she had forgotten altogether what it was like. She was aware of things happening and about to happen; she fixed them by the place they occupied, and measured their duration by the space she went through.

So now she thought: If I could only go back and get to the place where it hadn't happened.

To get back farther—

She was walking now on a white road that went between broad grass borders. To the right and left were the long raking lines of the hills, curve after curve, shimmering in a thin mist.

The road dropped to the green valley. It mounted the humped bridge over the river. Beyond it she saw the twin gables of the gray house pricked up over the high, gray garden wall. The tall iron gate stood in front of it between the ball-topped stone pillars.

And now she was in a large, low-ceilinged room with drawn blinds. She was standing before the wide double bed. It was her father's bed. The dead body, stretched out in the middle under the drawn white sheet, was her father's body.

The outline of the sheet sank from the peak of the upturned toes to the shin bone, and from the high bridge of the nose to the chin.

She lifted the sheet and folded it back across the breast of the dead man. The face she saw then was Oscar Wade's face, stilled and smoothed in the innocence of sleep, the supreme innocence of death. She stared at it, fascinated, in a cold, pitiless joy.

Oscar was dead.

She remembered how he used to lie like that beside her in the room in the Hotel Saint Pierre, on his back with his hands folded on his waist, his mouth half open, his big chest rising and falling. If he was dead, it would never happen again. She would be safe.

The dead face frightened her, and she was about to cover it up again when she was aware of a light heaving, a rhythmical rise and fall. As she drew the sheet up tighter, the hands under it began to struggle convulsively, the broad ends of the fingers appeared above the edge, clutching it to keep it down. The mouth opened; the eyes opened; the whole face stared back at her in a look of agony and horror.

Then the body drew itself forwards from the hips and sat up, its eyes peering into her eyes; he and she remained for an instant motionless, each held there by the other's fear.

Suddenly she broke away, turned and ran, out of the room, out of the house.

She stood at the gate, looking up and down the road, not knowing by which way she must go to escape Oscar. To the right, over the bridge and up the hill and across the downs she would come to the arcades of the rue de Rivoli and the dreadful gray corridors of the hotel. To the left the road went through the village.

If she could get further back she would be safe, out of Oscar's reach. Standing by her father's death-bed she had been young, but not young enough. She must get back to the place where she was younger still, to the Park and the green drive under the beech trees and the white pavilion at the cross. She knew how to find it. At the end of the village the high road ran right and left, east and west, under the Park walls; the south gate stood there at the top, looking down the narrow street.

She ran towards it through the village, past the long gray barns of Goodyer's farm, past the grocer's shop, past the yellow front and blue sign of the "Queen's Head," past the post office, with its one black window blinking under its vine, past the church and the yew-trees in the churchyard, to where the south gate made a delicate black pattern on the green grass.

These things appeared insubstantial, drawn back behind a sheet of air that shimmered over them like thin glass. They opened out, floated past and away from her; and instead of the high road and park walls she saw a London street of dingy white façades, and instead of the south gate the swinging glass doors of Schnebler's Restaurant.

The glass doors swung open and she passed into the restaurant. The scene beat on her with the hard impact of reality: the white and gold panels, the white pillars and their curling gold capitals, the white circles of the tables, glittering, the flushed faces of the diners, moving mechanically.

She was driven forward by some irresistible compulsion to a table in the corner, where a man sat alone. The table napkin he was using hid his mouth, and jaw, and chest; and she was not sure of the upper part of the face above the straight, drawn edge. It dropped; and she saw Oscar Wade's face. She came to him, dragged, without power to resist; she sat down beside him, and he leaned to her over the table; she could feel the warmth of his red, congested face; the smell of wine floated towards her on his thick whisper.

"I knew you would come."

She ate and drank with him in silence, nibbling and sipping slowly, staving off the abominable moment it would end in.

At last they got up and faced each other. His long bulk stood before her, above her; she could almost feel the vibration of its power.

"Come," he said. "Come."

And she went before him, slowly, slipping out through the maze of the tables, hearing behind her Oscar's measured, deliberate, thoughtful tread. The steep, red-carpeted staircase rose up before her.

She swerved from it, but he turned her back.

"You know the way," he said.

At the top of the flight she found the white door of the room she knew. She knew the long windows guarded by drawn muslin blinds; the gilt looking-glass over the chimney-piece that reflected Oscar's head and shoulders grotesquely between two white porcelain babies with bulbous limbs and garlanded loins, she knew the sprawling stain on the drab carpet by the table, the shabby, infamous couch behind the screen.

They moved about the room, turning and turning in it like beasts in a cage, uneasy, inimical, avoiding each other.

At last they stood still, he at the window, she at the door, the length of the room between.

"It's no good your getting away like that," he said. "There couldn't be any other end to it—to what we did."

"But that *was* ended."

"Ended there, but not here."

"Ended for ever. We've done with it for ever."

"We haven't. We've got to begin again. And go on. And go on."

"Oh, no. No. Anything but that."

"There isn't anything else."

"We can't. We can't. Don't you remember how it bored us?"

"Remember? Do you suppose I'd touch you if I could help it? . . . That's what we're here for. We must. We must."

"No. No. I shall get away—now."

She turned to the door to open it.

"You can't," he said. "The door's locked."

"Oscar—what did you do that for?"

"We always did it. Don't you remember?"

She turned to the door again and shook it; she beat on it with her hands.

"It's no use, Harriott. If you got out now you'd only have to come back again. You might stave it off for an hour or so, but what's that in an immortality?"

"Immortality?"

"That's what we're in for."

"Time enough to talk about immortality when we're dead. . . . Ah—"

They were being drawn towards each other across the room, moving slowly, like figures in some monstrous and appalling dance, their heads thrown back over their shoulders, their faces turned from the horrible approach. Their arms rose slowly, heavy with intolerable reluctance; they stretched them out towards each other, aching, as if they held up an overpowering weight. Their feet dragged and were drawn.

Suddenly her knees sank under her; she shut her eyes; all her being went down before him in darkness and terror.

It was over. She had got away, she was going back, back, to the green drive of the Park, between the beech trees, where Oscar had never been, where he would never find her. When she passed through the south gate her memory

became suddenly young and clean. She forgot the rue de Rivoli and the Hotel Saint Pierre; she forgot Schnebler's Restaurant and the room at the top of the stairs. She was back in her youth. She was Harriott Leigh going to wait for Stephen Philpotts in the pavilion opposite the west gate. She could feel herself, a slender figure moving fast over the grass between the lines of the great beech trees. The freshness of her youth was upon her.

She came to the heart of the drive where it branched right and left in the form of a cross. At the end of the right arm the white Greek temple, with its pediment and pillars, gleamed against the wood.

She was sitting on their seat at the back of the pavilion watching the side door that Stephen would come in by.

The door was pushed open; he came towards her, light and young, skimming between the beech trees with his eager, tiptoeing stride. She rose up to meet him. She gave a cry.

"Stephen!"

It had been Stephen. She had seen him coming. But the man who stood before her between the pillars of the pavilion was Oscar Wade.

And now she was walking along the field-path that slanted from the orchard door to the stile, further and further back, to where young George Waring waited for her under the older tree. The smell of the elder flowers came to her over the field. She could feel on her lips and in all her body the sweet, innocent excitement of her youth.

"George, oh, George!"

As she went along the field-path she had seen him. But the man who stood waiting for her under the elder tree was Oscar Wade.

"I told you it's no use getting away, Harriott. Every path brings you back to me. You'll find me at every turn."

"But how did you get *here?*"

"As I got into the pavilion. As I got into your father's room, on to his death bed. Because I was there. I am in all your memories."

"My memories are innocent. How could you take my father's place, and Stephen's, and George Waring's? You?"

"Because I did take them."

"Never. My love for *them* was innocent."

"Your love for me was part of it. You think the past affects the future. Has it never struck you that the future may affect the past? In your innocence there was the beginning of your sin. You *were* what you *were to be.*"

"I shall get away," she said.

"And, this time, I shall go with you."

The stile, the elder tree, and the field floated away from her. She was going under the beech trees down the Park drive towards the south gate and the village, slinking close to the right-hand row of trees. She was aware that Oscar Wade was going with her under the left-hand row, keeping even with her, step by step, and tree by tree. And presently there was gray pavement under her feet and a row of gray pillars on her right hand. They were walking side by side down the rue de Rivoli towards the hotel.

They were sitting together now on the edge of the dingy white bed. Their arms hung by their sides, heavy and limp, their heads drooped, averted. Their passion weighed on them with the unbearable, unescapable boredom of immortality.

"Oscar—how long will it last?"

"I can't tell you. I don't know whether *this* is one moment of eternity, or the eternity of one moment."

"It must end some time," she said. "Life doesn't go on for ever. We shall die."

"Die? We *have* died. Don't you know what this is? Don't you know where you are? This is death. We're dead, Harriott. We're in hell."

"Yes. There can't be anything worse than this."

"This isn't the worst. We're not quite dead yet, as long as we've life in us to turn and run and get away from each other; as long as we can escape into our memories. But when you've got back to the farthest memory of all and there's nothing beyond it—When there's no memory but this—

"In the last hell we shall not run away any longer; we shall find no more roads, no more passages, no more open doors. We shall have no need to look for each other.

"In the last death we shall be shut up in this room, behind that locked door, together. We shall lie here together, for ever and ever, joined so fast that even God can't put us asunder. We shall be one flesh and one spirit, one sin repeated for ever, and ever; spirit loathing flesh, flesh loathing spirit; you and I loathing each other."

"Why? Why?" she cried.

"Because that's all that's left us. That's what you made of love."

The darkness came down swamping, it blotted out the room. She was walking along a garden path between high borders of phlox and larkspur and lupin. They were taller than she was, their flowers swayed and nodded above her head. She tugged at the tall stems and had no strength to break them. She was a little thing.

She said to herself then that she was safe. She had gone back so far that she was a child again; she had the blank innocence of childhood. To be a child, to go small under the heads of the lupins, to be blank and innocent, without memory, was to be safe.

The walk led her out through a yew hedge on to a bright green lawn. In the middle of the lawn there was a shallow round pond in a ring of rockery cushioned with small flowers, yellow and white and purple. Gold-fish swam in the olive brown water. She would be safe when she saw the gold-fish swimming towards her. The old one with the white scales would come up first, pushing up his nose, making bubbles in the water.

At the bottom of the lawn there was a privet hedge cut by a broad path that went through the orchard. She knew what she would find there; her mother was in the orchard. She would life her up in her arms to play with the hard red balls of the apples that hung from the tree. She had got back to the farthest memory of all; there was nothing beyond it.

There would be an iron gate in the wall of the orchard. It would lead into a field.

Something was different here, something that frightened her. An ash-gray door instead of an iron gate.

She pushed it open and came into the last corridor of the Hotel Saint Pierre.

1922

MARY AUSTIN

1868–1934

Ecologist, ethnographer, feminist, fiction writer, journalist, mystic—Mary Austin wrote hundreds of articles and more than thirty books, many focused on the American West, but she was born and raised in Carlinville, Illinois. After the untimely deaths of her father and sister, the young Mary Hunter was brought up by a mother very active in the Women's Christian Temperance Union, an organization important in the nineteenth-century evolution of the women's movement. At the age of twenty, after graduating from Blackburn College, the aspiring writer moved to California with her family and began publishing her first short stories. In 1891 she married Stafford Wallace Austin, and they settled in the Owens Valley, northwest of Bakersfield, where she gave birth to a daughter, Ruth, who proved to be retarded. The Austins were divorced in 1914; Ruth died in an institution four years later.

Austin's most famous work, *The Land of Little Rain* (1903). was inspired by the Mojave Desert and her residence with her husband in a succession of desert towns. Since its publication, this collection of sketches has been celebrated as a western classic. During the years following her move to Carmel, California, Austin maintained a long and productive literary career. Some of her work focuses on American Indian legends: *The Basket Woman* (1905) is a collection of realistic short stories, and *The Arrow-Maker* (1910) is a play about a female shaman. A number of her nonfictional studies examine the influence of Indian song on written poetry (*The American Rhythm*, 1923). The problem novels she produced explore the relationship between gender and creativity; her novel *A Woman of Genius* (1912) was based on her own early conflicts about her developing imaginative energies, as was her autobiography *Earth Horizon* (1932). But Austin remains most revered for the love and respect with which she depicted the American desert as well as the Latino and Native American Indian folk arts that flourished throughout the region. *The Walking Woman*, one of her most frequently anthologized stories, captures the resonant mystery Austin found in rural solitaries attempting to follow nature's dictates in the quiet obscurity or seclusion they have chosen. An active, ardent advocate of environmental responsibility, Austin settled in Santa Fe, New Mexico, and it seems fitting that Willa Cather wrote her paean to the physical beauties of the Southwest, *Death Comes for the Archbishop* (1927), in Austin's house.

The Walking Woman

The first time of my hearing of her was at Temblor.[1] We had come all one day between blunt, whitish bluffs rising from mirage water, with a thick, pale wake of dust billowing from the wheels, all the dead wall of the foothills sliding and shimmering with heat, to learn that the Walking Woman had passed us somewhere in the dizzying dimness, going down to the Tulares on her own feet. We heard of her again in the Carrisal, and again at Adobe Station, where she had passed a week before the shearing, and at last I had a glimpse of her at the Eighteen-Mile House as I went hurriedly northward on the Mojave stage; and afterward, sheepherders at whose camps she slept, and cowboys at rodeos, told me as much of her way of life as they could understand. Like enough they

1. A town in the Mojave Desert in California. All the places named in the story are located in or near this region.

told her as much of mine. That was very little. She was the Walking Woman, and no one knew her name, but because she was a sort of whom men speak respectfully, they called her to her face Mrs. Walker, and she answered to it if she was so inclined. She came and went about our western world on no discoverable errand, and whether she had some place of refuge where she lay by in the interim, or whether between her seldom, unaccountable appearances in our quarter she went on steadily walking, was never learned. She came and went, oftenest in a kind of muse[2] of travel which the untrammelled space begets, or at rare intervals flooding wondrously with talk, never of herself, but of things she had known and seen. She must have seen some rare happenings, too—by report. She was at Maverick the time of the Big Snow, and at Tres Piños when they brought home the body of Morena; and if anybody could have told whether De Borba killed Mariana for spite or defence, it would have been she, only she could not be found when most wanted. She was at Tunawai at the time of the cloud-burst, and if she had cared for it she could have known most desirable things of the ways of trail-making, burrow-habiting small things.

All of which should have made her worth meeting, though it was not, in fact, for such things I was wishful to meet her; and as it turned out, it was not of these things we talked when at last we came together. For one thing, she was a woman, not old, who had gone about alone in a country where the number of women is as one in fifteen. She had eaten and slept at the herder's camps, and laid by for days at one-man stations whose masters had no other touch of human kind than the passing of chance prospectors, or the halting of the tri-weekly stage. She had been set on her way by teamsters[3] who lifted her out of white, hot desertness and put her down at the crossing of unnamed ways, days distant from anywhere. And through all this she passed unarmed and unoffended. I had the best testimony to this, the witness of the men themselves. I think they talked of it because they were so much surprised at it. It was not, on the whole, what they expected of themselves.

Well I understand that nature which wastes its borders with too eager burning, beyond which rim of desolation it flares forever quick and white, and have had some inkling of the isolating calm of a desire too high to stoop to satisfaction. But you could not think of these things pertaining to the Walking Woman; and if there were ever any truth in the exemption from offence residing in a frame of behavior called ladylike, it should have been inoperative here. What this really means is that you get no affront so long as your behavior in the estimate of the particular audience invites none. In the estimate of the immediate audience—conduct which affords protection in Mayfair[4] gets you no consideration in Maverick. And by no canon could it be considered ladylike to go about on your own feet, with a blanket and a black bag and almost no money in your purse, in and about the haunts of rude and solitary men.

There were other things that pointed the wish for a personal encounter with the Walking Woman. One of them was the contradiction of reports of her—as to whether she was comely, for example. Report said yes, and again, plain to the point of deformity. She had a twist to her face, some said; a hitch to one shoulder; they averred she limped as she walked. But by the distance she covered she should have been straight and young. As to sanity, equal incertitude. On the mere evidence of her way of life she was cracked; not quite broken, but

2. State of dreamy abstraction. 4. A fashionable part of London.
3. Those who drive teams of horses, mules, or oxen.

unserviceable. Yet in her talk there was both wisdom and information, and the word she brought about trails and water-holes was as reliable as an Indian's.

By her own account she had begun by walking off an illness. There had been an invalid to be taken care of for years, leaving her at last broken in body, and with no recourse but her own feet to carry her out of that predicament. It seemed there had been, besides the death of her invalid, some other worrying affairs, upon which, and the nature of her illness, she was never quite clear, so that it might very well have been an unsoundness of mind which drove her to the open, sobered and healed at last by the large soundness of nature. It must have been about that time that she lost her name. I am convinced that she never told it because she did not know it herself. She was the Walking Woman, and the country people called her Mrs. Walker. At the time I knew her, though she wore short hair and a man's boots, and had a fine down over all her face from exposure to the weather, she was perfectly sweet and sane.

I had met her occasionally at ranch-houses and road-stations, and had got as much acquaintance as the place allowed; but for the things I wished to know there wanted a time of leisure and isolation. And when the occasion came we talked altogether of other things.

It was at Warm Spring in the Little Antelope I came upon her in the heart of a clear forenoon. The spring lies off a mile from the main trail, and has the only trees about it known in that country. First you come upon a pool of waste full of weeds of a poisonous dark green, every reed ringed about with the water-level with a muddy white incrustation. Then the three oaks appear staggering on the slope, and the spring sobs and blubbers below them in ashy-colored mud. All the hills of that country have the down plunge toward the desert and back abruptly toward the Sierra. The grass is thick and brittle and bleached straw-color toward the end of the season. As I rode up the swale[5] of the spring I saw the Walking Woman sitting where the grass was deepest, with her black bag and blanket, which she carried on a stick, beside her. It was one of those days when the genius of talk flows as smoothly as the rivers of mirage through the blue hot desert morning.

You are not to suppose that in my report of a Borderer[6] I give you the words only, but the full meaning of the speech. Very often the words are merely the punctuation of thought; rather, the crests of the long waves of intercommunicative silences. Yet the speech of the Walking Woman was fuller than most.

The best of our talk that day began in some dropped word of hers from which I inferred that she had had a child. I was surprised at that, and then wondered why I should have been surprised, for it is the most natural of all experiences to have children. I said something of that purport, and also that it was one of the perquisites of living I should be least willing to do without. And that led to the Walking Woman saying that there were three things which if you had known you could cut out all the rest, and they were good any way you got them, but best if, as in her case, they were related to and grew each one out of the others. It was while she talked that I decided that she really did have a twist to her face, a sort of natural warp or skew into which it fell when it was worn merely as a countenance, but which disappeared the moment it became the vehicle of thought or feeling.

The first of the experiences the Walking Woman had found most worth

5. Low-lying and often wet stretch of land.
6. I.e., one who lives in what Austin calls the "country of lost borders."

while had come to her in a sand-storm on the south slope of Tehachapi in a dateless spring. I judged it should have been about the time she began to find herself, after the period of worry and loss in which her wandering began. She had come, in a day pricked full of intimations of a storm, to the camp of Filon Geraud, whose companion shepherd had gone a three days' *pasear*[7] to Mojave for supplies. Geraud was of great hardihood, red-blooded, of a full laughing eye, and an indubitable spark for women. It was the season of the year when there is a soft bloom on the days, but the nights are cowering cold and the lambs tender, not yet flockwise. At such times a sand-storm works incalculable disaster. The lift of the wind is so great that the whole surface of the ground appears to travel upon it slantwise, thinning out miles high in air. In the intolerable smother the lambs are lost from the ewes; neither dogs nor man make headway against it.

The morning flared through a horizon of yellow smudge, and by midforenoon the flock broke.

"There were but the two of us to deal with the trouble," said the Walking Woman. "Until that time I had not known how strong I was, nor how good it is to run when running is worth while. The flock travelled down the wind, the sand bit our faces; we called, and after a time heard the words broken and beaten small by the wind. But after a little we had not to call. All the time of our running in the yellow dusk of day and the black dark of night, I knew where Filon was. A flock-length away, I knew him. Feel? What should I feel? I knew. I ran with the flock and turned it this way and that as Filon would have.

"Such was the force of the wind that when we came together we held by one another and talked a little between pantings. We snatched and ate what we could as we ran. All that day and night until the next afternoon the camp kit was not out of the cayaques.[8] But we held the flock. We herded them under a butte[9] when the wind fell off a little, and the lambs sucked; when the storm rose they broke, but we kept upon their track and brought them together again. At night the wind quieted, and we slept by turns; at least Filon slept. I lay on the ground when my turn was and beat with the storm. I was no more tired than the earth was. The sand filled in the creases of the blanket, and where I turned, dripped back upon the ground. But we saved the sheep. Some ewes there were that would not give down their milk because of the worry of the storm, and the lambs died. But we kept the flock together. And I was not tired."

The Walking Woman stretched out her arms and clasped herself, rocking in them as if she would have hugged the recollection to her breast.

"For you see," said she, "I worked with a man, without excusing, without any burden on me of looking or seeming. Not fiddling or fumbling as women work, and hoping it will all turn out for the best. It was not for Filon to ask, Can you, or Will you. He said, Do, and I did. And my work was good. We held the flock. And that," said the Walking Woman, the twists coming in her face again, "is one of the things that make you able to do without the others."

"Yes," I said; and then, "What others?"

"Oh," she said, as if it pricked her, "the looking and the seeming."

And I had not thought until that time that one who had the courage to be the Walking Woman would have cared! We sat and looked at the pattern of

7. Walk (Spanish).
8. Saddlebags. "Camp kit": supplies.
9. Isolated hill or rocky formation.

the thick crushed grass on the slope, wavering in the fierce noon like the waterings in the coat of a tranquil beast; the ache of a world-old bitterness sobbed and whispered in the spring. At last—

"It is by the looking and the seeming," said I, "that the opportunity finds you out."

"Filon found out," said the Walking Woman. She smiled, and went on from that to tell me how, when the wind went down about four o'clock and left the afternoon clear and tender, the flock began to feed, and they had out the kit from the cayaques, and cooked a meal. When it was over and Filon had his pipe between his teeth, he came over from his side of the fire, of his own notion, and stretched himself on the ground beside her. Of his own notion. There was that in the way she said it that made it seem as if nothing of the sort had happened before to the Walking Woman, and for a moment I thought she was about to tell me one of the things I wished to know; but she went on to say what Filon had said to her of her work with the flock. Obvious, kindly things, such as any man in sheer decency would have said, so that there must have something more gone with the words to make them so treasured of the Walking Woman.

"We were very comfortable," said she, "and not so tired as we expected to be. Filon leaned up on his elbow. I had not noticed until then how broad he was in the shoulders, and how strong in the arms. And we had saved the flock together. We felt that. There was something that said together, in the slope of his shoulders toward me. It was around his mouth and on the cheek high up under the shine of his eyes. And under the shine the look—the look that said, 'We are one sort and one mind'—his eyes that were the co or of the flat water in the tulares[1]—do you know the look?"

"I know it."

"The wind was stopped and all the earth smelled of dust, and Filon understood very well that what I had done with him I could not have done so well with another. And the look—the look in the eyes—"

"Ah-ah—!"

I have always said, I will say again, I do not know why at this point the Walking Woman touched me. If it were merely a response to my unconscious throb of sympathy, or the unpremeditated way of her heart to declare that this, after all, was the best of all indispensable experiences; or if in some flash of forward vision, encompassing the unimpassioned years, the stir, the movement of tenderness were for me—but no; as often as I have thought of it, I have thought of a different reason, but no conclusive one, why the Walking Woman should have put out her hand and laid it on my arm.

"To work together, to love together," said the Walking Woman, withdrawing her hand again; "there you have two of the things; the other you know."

"The mouth at the breast," said I.

"The lips and the hands," said the Walking Woman. "The little, pushing hands and the small cry." There ensued a pause of fullest understanding, while the land before us swam in the noon, and a dove in the oaks behind the spring began to call. A little red fox came out of the hills and lapped delicately at the pool.

"I stayed with Filon until the fall," said she. "All that summer in the Sierra, until it was time to turn south on the trail. It was a good time, and longer than

1. Marshy places overgrown with bulrushes ("tules").

he could be expected to have loved one like me. And besides, I was no longer able to keep the trail. My baby was born in October."

Whatever more there was to say to this, the Walking Woman's hand said it, straying with remembering gesture to her breast. There are so many ways of loving and working, but only one way of the first-born. She added after an interval, that she did not know if she would have given up her walking to keep at home and tend him, or whether the thought of her son's small feet running beside her in the trails would have driven her to the open again. The baby had not stayed long enough for that. "And whenever the wind blows in the night," said the Walking Woman, "I wake and wonder if he is well covered."

She took up her black bag and her blanket; there was the ranch-house of Dos Palos to be made before night, and she went as outliers do, without a hope expressed of another meeting and no word of good-bye. She was the Walking Woman. That was it. She had walked off all sense of society-made values, and, knowing the best when the best came to her, was able to take it. Work—as I believed; love—as the Walking Woman had proved it; a child—as you subscribe to it. But look you: it was the naked thing the Walking Woman grasped, not dressed and tricked out, for instance, by prejudices in favor of certain occupations; and love, man love, taken as it came, not picked over and rejected if it carried no obligation of permanency; and a child; *any* way you get it, a child is good to have, say nature and the Walking Woman; to have it and not to wait upon a proper concurrence of so many decorations that the event may not come at all.

At least one of us is wrong. To work and to love and to bear children. *That* sounds easy enough. But the way we live establishes so many things of much more importance.

Far down the dim, hot valley I could see the Walking Woman with her blanket and the black bag over her shoulder. She had a queer, sidelong gait, as if in fact she had a twist all through her.

Recollecting suddenly that people called her lame, I ran down to the open space below the spring where she had passed. There in the bare, hot sand the track of her two feet bore evenly and white.

<div align="right">1909</div>

CHARLOTTE MEW
1869–1928

When Charlotte Mew died in 1928, she was so obscure that one newspaper report of her death described her as "Charlotte New [*sic*], said to be a writer." Yet in her earlier years Mew had been a well-known literary woman whose works were admired by a number of contemporaries, including such notable artists as John Masefield, Walter de la Mare, and Thomas Hardy. Even during her lifetime, however, Mew was a paradoxical figure. The author of vividly detailed dramatic monologues that were surprising in their era for their frank depictions of both female and male sexuality, she was extraordinarily rigorous in maintaining her own moral standards and would, as one scholar explains, "drop anyone whom scandal had touched." Raised by genteel parents as a typical Victorian lady, she was, according to her friend Alida Monroe, "passionately attached to another woman," and she became virtually a transvestite in middle age, dressing in a tweed topcoat, a pork pie hat, and "size-two custom-made boots."

Mew was born in London, one of four children in a comfortable middle-class family. But the pleasures of her youth were short-lived: the two younger Mew children became mentally ill and were confined to asylums, while her father's death, when she was in her late twenties, left Charlotte, her sister, and her mother nearly impoverished, for, she later recollected, he had "spent all his available capital on living." To support themselves and their mother, Charlotte and her sister attempted various odd jobs; most notably, Charlotte wrote stories and poems for *The Egoist, The English Woman, The Yellow Book,* and other journals. But despite a modicum of literary success, she always had to economize and never recaptured the gaiety of her childhood home.

Mew's most important verses appeared in a 1916 collection, *The Farmer's Bride,* whose title poem is still much anthologized. In this monologue, as in the equally powerful *The Quiet House,* she demonstrates the vitality and inventiveness that must have especially appealed to a fellow dramatic poet like Thomas Hardy. At the same time, though, both pieces suggest the intensity with which she herself may have secretly rebelled against the veneer of docility she had been taught to cultivate. When the speaker of *The Quiet House* exclaims, "I think that my soul is red / Like the soul of a sword or a scarlet flower," one feels that she may be expressing Mew's own sexual and emotional frustrations. Similarly, when the same speaker wistfully and wishfully looks forward to the day when "I *shall* not think; I shall not be," one fears that her nihilistic desire predicts the day when Mew herself, alone and impoverished, put an end to her conflicted life by drinking a bottle of Lysol.

The Farmer's Bride

Three Summers since I chose a maid,
Too young maybe—but more's to do
At harvest-time than bide and woo.
 When us was wed she turned afraid
Of love and me and all things human; 5
Like the shut of a winter's day
Her smile went out, and 'twadn't a woman—
 More like a little frightened fay.[1]
 One night, in the Fall, she runned away.

"Out 'mong the sheep, her be," they said, 10
Should properly have been abed;
But sure enough she wadn't there
Lying awake with her wide brown stare.
So over seven-acre field and up-along across the down[2]
We chased her, flying like a hare 15
Before our lanterns. To Church-Town
 All in a shiver and a scare
We caught her, fetched her home at last
 And turned the key upon her, fast.

She does the work about the house 20
As well as most, but like a mouse:
 Happy enough to chat and play
 With birds and rabbits and such as they,
 So long as men-folk keep away.

1. Fairy. 2. Meadow used for grazing.

"Not near, not near!" her eyes beseech 25
When one of us comes within reach.
 The women say that beasts in stall
 Look round like children at her call.
 I've hardly heard her speak at all.

Shy as a leveret,[3] swift as he, 30
Straight and slight as a young larch tree,
Sweet as the first wild violets, she,
To her wild self. But what to me?

The short days shorten and the oaks are brown,
 The blue smoke rises to the low gray sky, 35
One leaf in the still air falls slowly down,
 A magpie's spotted feathers lie
On the black earth spread white with rime,
The berries redden up to Christmas-time.
 What's Christmas-time without there be 40
 Some other in the house than we!

 She sleeps up in the attic there
 Alone, poor maid. 'Tis but a stair
Betwixt us. Oh! my God! the down,
The soft young down of her, the brown, 45
The brown of her—her eyes, her hair, her hair!

 1916

The Quiet House

When we were children old Nurse used to say,
The house was like an auction or a fair
Until the lot of us were safe in bed.
It has been quiet as the country-side
Since Ted and Janey and then Mother died 5
And Tom crossed[1] Father and was sent away.
After the lawsuit he could not hold up his head,
 Poor Father, and he does not care
 For people here, or to go anywhere.

To get away to Aunt's for that week-end 10
 Was hard enough; (since then, a year ago,
 He scarcely lets me slip out of his sight—)
At first I did not like my cousin's friend,
 I did not think I should remember him:
 His voice has gone, his face is growing dim 15
And if I like him now I do not know.
 He frightened me before he smiled—

3. A young hare. 1. Disobeyed.

He did not ask me if he might—
He said that he would come one Sunday night.
He spoke to me as if I were a child. 20

No year has been like this that has just gone by;
 It may be that what Father says is true,
If things are so it does not matter why:
 But everything has burned, and not quite through.
 The colors of the world have turned 25
 To flame, the blue, the gold has burned
In what used to be such a leaden sky.
When you are burned quite through you die.

 Red is the strangest pain to bear;
In Spring the leaves on the budding trees; 30
In Summer the roses are worse than these,
 More terrible than they are sweet:
 A rose can stab you across the street
 Deeper than any knife:
 And the crimson haunts you everywhere— 35
Thin shafts of sunlight, like the ghosts of reddened swords
 have struck our stair
As if, coming down, you had spilt your life

 I think that my soul is red
Like the soul of a sword or a scarlet flower: 40
 But when these are dead
 They have had their hour.

 I shall have had mine, too,
 For from head to feet
 I am burned and stabbed half through, 45
 And the pain is deadly sweet.

 The things that kill us seem
 Blind to the death they give:
 It is only in our dream
 The things that kill us live. 50

The room is shut where Mother died,
 The other rooms are as they were,
The world goes on the same outside,
 The sparrows fly across the Square,
 The children play as we four did there, 55
 The trees grow green and brown and bare,
The sun shines on the dead Church spire.
 And nothing lives here but the fire.
While Father watches from his chair
 Day follows day 60
The same, now and then a different gray,
 Till, like his hair,
Which Mother said was wavy once and bright,
 They will all turn white.

Tonight I heard a bell again— 65
Outside it was the same mist of fine rain,
The lamps just lighted down the long, dim street,
 No one for me—
I think it is myself I go to meet:
I do not care; some day I *shall* not think; I shall not be. 70

1916

HENRY HANDEL RICHARDSON
1870–1946

Named Ethel Florence Lindsay Richardson at her birth, the writer who called her-self H. H. Richardson left Australia at the age of seventeen, returning only once in 1912 for "a flying six-weeks' visit." Yet she has been claimed as one of Australia's most important novelists. Her trilogy, *The Fortunes of Richard Mahony* (1917, 1925, 1929), describes the psychological impact of colonialism on a character based on her father: a Dublin-born physician, he reestablished his practice in a se-ries of provincial Australian towns, but he eventually lost his sanity. Her mother, who supported the family as postmaster in Koroit, is sympathetically presented as resourcefully practical in *The Getting of Wisdom* (1910). This satiric novel, which was produced as a film in 1977, provides a fictional portrait of the author as she moved at the age of twelve from her home to the Presbyterian Ladies' College in Melbourne. Richardson's surrogate, Laura Ramsbotham, is a rebellious, imagina-tive adolescent who is unable—no matter how she tries—to conform to the mind-less proprieties of the school or to stifle her artistic creativity.

Laura's musical accomplishments reflect Richardson's training as a concert pi-anist in Leipzig in 1887. There she met and married J. G. Robertson, who subse-quently became a professor of German languages at the University of London. Two works—*Maurice Guest* (1908) and *The Young Cosima* (1939)—deal directly with the development of musical genius, a subject of central importance to a liter-ary artist who took Handel as her middle name. The best-selling *Ultima Thule* (1929), the final volume of the trilogy *The Fortunes of Richard Mahoney* brought Richardson international fame. After the death of her husband, Richardson sur-vived the bombings of Sussex during World War II, but she did not live to com-plete her autobiography, *Myself When Young* (1948).

Two Hanged Women portrays with economy the same competition between het-erosexuality and female bonding that *The Getting of Wisdom* traces in its divided heroine. In doing so, it offers a subtle analysis of the ways in which society discour-ages public demonstrations of affection between same-sex couples while encour-aging romantic displays between men and women. Thus it supplements the remarkably frank treatment of sexuality in *Maurice Guest* as well as in some of the other stories Richardson collected in *The End of Childhood* (1934).

Two Hanged Women

Hand in hand the youthful lovers sauntered along the esplanade. It was a night in midsummer; a wispy moon had set, and the stars glittered. The dark mass of the sea, at flood, lay tranquil, slothfully lapping the shingle.[1]

1. Beach gravel.

"Come on, let's make for the usual," said the boy.

But on nearing their favorite seat they found it occupied. In the velvety shade of the overhanging sea-wall, the outlines of two figures were visible.

"Oh, blast!" said the lad. "That's torn it. What now, Baby?"

"Why, let's stop here, Pincher, right close up, till we frighten 'em off."

And very soon loud, smacking kisses, amatory pinches and ticklings, and skittish squeals of pleasure did their work. Silently the intruders rose and moved away.

But the boy stood gaping after them, open-mouthed.

"Well, I'm damned! If it wasn't just two hanged[2] women!"

Retreating before a salvo of derisive laughter, the elder of the girls said: "We'll go out on the breakwater."[3] She was tall and thin, and walked with a long stride.

Her companion, shorter than she by a bobbed head of straight flaxen hair, was hard put to it to keep pace. As she pegged along she said doubtfully, as if in self-excuse: "Though I really ought to go home. It's getting late. Mother will be angry."

They walked with finger-tips lightly in contact; and at her words she felt what was like an attempt to get free, on the part of the fingers crooked in hers. But she was prepared for this, and held fast, gradually working her own up till she had a good half of the other hand in her grip.

For a moment neither spoke. Then, in a low, muffled voice, came the question: "Was she angry last night, too?"

The little fair girl's reply had an unlooked-for vehemence. "You know she wasn't!" And, mildly despairing: "But you never will understand. Oh, what's the good of . . . of anything!"

And on sitting down she let the prisoned hand go, even putting it from her with a kind of push. There it lay, palm upwards, the fingers still curved from her hold, looking like a thing with a separate life of its own; but a life that was ebbing.

On this remote seat, with their backs turned on lovers, lights, the town, the two girls sat and gazed wordlessly at the dark sea, over which great Jupiter was flinging a thin gold line. There was no sound but the lapping, sucking, sighing, of the ripples at the edge of the breakwater, and the occasional screech of an owl in the tall trees on the hillside.

But after a time, having stolen more than one side glance at her companion, the younger seemed to take heart of grace. With a childish toss of the head that set her loose hair swaying, she said, in a tone of meaning emphasis: "I like Fred."

The only answer was a faint, contemptuous shrug.

"I tell you I *like* him!"

"Fred? Rats!"

"No it isn't . . . that's just where you're wrong, Betty. But you think you're so wise. Always."

"I know what I know."

"Or imagine you do! But it doesn't matter. Nothing you can say makes any difference. I like him and always shall. In heaps of ways. He's so big and strong, for one thing: it gives you such a safe sort of feeling to be with him . . . as if nothing could happen while you were. Yes, it's . . . it's . . . well, I can't help it,

2. Confounded (British expletive). 3. Barrier protecting the shore from strong waves.

Betty, there's something *comfy* in having a boy to go about with—like other girls do. One they'd eat their hats to get, too! I can see it in their eyes when we pass; Fred with his great long legs and broad shoulders—I don't nearly come up to them—and his blue eyes with the black lashes, and his shiny black hair. And I like his tweeds, the Harris[4] smell of them, and his dirty old pipe, and the way he shows his teeth—he's got *topping* teeth—when he laughs and says ra-*ther!* And other people, when they see us, look … well I don't quite know how to say it, but they look sort of pleased; and they make room for us and let us into the dark corner-seats at the pictures, just as if we'd a right to them. And they never laugh. (Oh, I can't *stick*[5] being laughed at!—and that's the truth.) Yes, it's so comfy, Betty darling … such a warm cosy comfy feeling. Oh, *won't* you understand?"

"Gawd! why not make a song of it?" But a moment later, very fiercely: "And who is it's taught you to think all this? Who's hinted it and suggested it till you've come to believe it? … believe it's what you really feel."

"She hasn't! Mother's never said a word … about Fred."

"Words?—why waste words? … when she can do it with a cock of the eye. For your Fred, that!" and the girl called Betty held her fingers aloft and snapped them viciously. "But your mother's a different proposition."

"I think you're simply horrid."

To this there was no reply.

"*Why* have you such a down on her? What's she ever done to you? … except not get ratty when I stay out late with Fred. And I don't see how you can ex-pect … being what she is … and with nobody but me—after all she *is* my mother … you can't alter that. I know very well—and you know, too—I'm not *too* putrid-looking. But" —beseechingly—"I'm *nearly* twenty-five now, Betty. And other girls … well, she sees them, every one of them, with a boy of their own, even though they're ugly, or fat, or have legs like sausages—they've only got to ogle them a bit—the girls, I mean … and there they are. And Fred's a good sort—he is, really!—and he dances well, and doesn't drink, and so … so why *shouldn't* I like him? … and off my own bat … without it having to be all Mother's fault, and me nothing but a parrot, and without any will of my own?"

"Why? Because I know her too well, my child! I can read her as you'd never dare to … even if you could. She's sly, your mother is, so sly there's no coming to grips with her … one might as well try to fill one's hand with cobwebs. But she's got a hold on you, a stranglehold, that nothing'll loosen. Oh! mothers aren't fair—I mean it's not fair of nature to weigh us down with them and yet expect us to be our own true selves. The handicap's too great. All those months, when the same blood's running through two sets of veins—there's no getting away from that, ever after. Take yours. As I say, does she need to open her mouth? Not she! She's only got to let it hang at the corners, and you reek, you drip with guilt."

Something in these words seemed to sting the younger girl. She hit back. "I know what it is, you're jealous, that's what you are! … and you've no other way of letting it out. But I tell you this. If ever I marry—yes, *marry!*—it'll be to please myself, and nobody else. Can you imagine me doing it to oblige her?"

Again silence.

4. Popular type of tweed clothing made of cloth 5. Bear.
woven on an island in the Hebrides.

"If I only think what it would be like to be fixed up and settled and able to live in peace, without this eternal dragging two ways . . . just as if I was being torn in half. And see Mother smiling and happy again, like she used to be. Between the two of you I'm nothing but a punch-ball. Oh, I'm fed up with it! . . . fed up to the neck. As for you . . . And yet you can sit there as if you were made of stone! Why don't you *say* something? *Betty!* Why won't you speak?"

But no words came.

"I can *feel* you sneering. And when you sneer I hate you more than any one on earth. If only I'd never seen you!"

"Marry your Fred, and you'll never need to again."

"I will, too! I'll marry him, and have a proper wedding like other girls, with a veil and bridesmaids and bushels of flowers. And I'll live in a house of my own, where I can do as I like, and be left in peace, and there'll be no one to badger and bully me—Fred wouldn't . . . ever! Besides, he'll be away all day. And when he came back at night, he'd . . . I'd . . . I mean I'd—' But here the flying words gave out; there came a stormy breath and a cry of: "Oh, Betty, Betty! . . . I couldn't, no, I couldn't! It's when I think of *that* . . . Yes, it's quite true! I like him all right, I do indeed, but only as long as he doesn't come too near. If he even sits too close, I have to screw myself up to bear it"—and flinging herself down over her companion's lap, she hid her face. "And if he tries to touch me, Betty, or even takes my arm or puts his round me . . . And then his face . . . when it looks like it does sometimes . . . all wrong . . . as if it had gone all wrong—oh! then I feel I shall have to scream—out loud. I'm afraid of him . . . when he looks like that. Once . . . when he kissed me . . . I could have died with the horror of it. His breath . . . his breath . . . and his mouth—like fruit pulp—and the black hairs on his wrists . . . and the way he looked—and . . . and everything! No, I can't, I can't . . . nothing will make me . . . I'd rather die twice over. But what am I to do? Mother'll *never* understand. Oh, why has it got to be like this? I want to be happy, like other girls, and to make her happy, too . . . and everything's all wrong. You tell me, Betty darling, you help me you're older . . . you *know* . . . and you can help me, if you will . . . if you only will!" And locking her arms round her friend she drove her face deeper into the warmth and darkness, as if, from the very fervor of her clasp, she could draw the aid and strength she needed.

Betty had sat silent, unyielding, her sole movement being to loosen her own arms from her sides and point her elbows outwards, to hinder them touching the arms that lay round her. But at this last appeal she melted; and gathering the young girl to her breast, she held her fast.—And so for long she continued to sit, her chin resting lightly on the fair hair, that was silky and downy as an infant's, and gazing with somber eyes over the stealthily heaving sea.

1934

Early-Twentieth-Century Literature

MEN AND WOMEN IN A NEW AGE

In *Everybody's Autobiography* (1937), the experimental writer Gertrude Stein recalled a conversation with the mystery novelist Dashiell Hammett. "In the nineteenth century men were confident, the women were not," she reports Hammett as having observed, "but in the twentieth century the men have no confidence." Hammett's comment summarizes a major change in social dynamics that characterized the life and literature of almost all English-speaking countries in the era (roughly between 1914 and 1939) that is usually called the "modernist" period. More generally, however, many literary men experienced the first half of this century as what W. H. Auden was to call an "Age of Anxiety," while many of their female counterparts experienced the time—to be sure, with important qualifications—as an era of exuberance. One reason for such different reactions was the increase in female power which marked the new culture of the twentieth century. In the second two decades of the century, women on both sides of the Atlantic not only achieved the vote after a seventy-five-year struggle but also entered all the professions in ever greater numbers. "The modern young man," wrote the British novelist D. H. Lawrence in his essay *Matriarchy* (1929), talks "rather feebly about man being master again. He knows perfectly well that he will never be master again."

Between the years 1914 and 1939 in particular, of course, there were many reasons, besides the altered position of women, for both sexes, but especially men, to feel anxious about the rapidly changing world in which they lived. The phenomenon that has been called the "shock of the new" was profoundly disturbing to people who had been born and brought up in what now seemed comparatively serene late Victorian times, for "the new" in this period included a scientific revolution that virtually transformed the physical and social landscapes of England and America while producing a technology of destruction that shaped World War I, the deadliest war yet fought in Europe. In addition, because "the new" in these years also implied a complete disruption of the few traditional ideas about God and human nature that had emerged intact from the onslaughts of nineteenth-century skepticism, it was responsible for a widespread sense of intellectual doubt and social alienation. Finally, because the scientific revolution that shocked early-twentieth-century culture also meant the development of mass communication systems on a startling scale, it greatly intensified the rift between so-called high culture and so-called low (or "mass") culture, leading to what seemed an unbridgeable gulf between serious artists and popular, commercial artists. Inevitably, a number of literary figures responded with trepidation to these changes. But because women had never perceived themselves as the heirs of a stable and orderly society, it was especially male thinkers who felt themselves to be living in unprecedentedly threatening times. Assaulted in public by the machinery of a new age and haunted in private by women who would no longer to stay in their traditional places, a number of men saw themselves as increasingly marginal and powerless.

BEGINNINGS OF THE "MODERN" WORLD

The Georgian Afternoon

Despite the drastic cultural transformations that would soon become obvious to many observers, the years that were to be known as the modernist period began, at least in England, with what is often described (referring to the accession to the throne in 1910 of King George V) as a long "Georgian" afternoon, a kind of extension of the Victorian era in which large social changes were largely disguised by smug and apparently secure continuations of traditional modes and manners. Thus, while experimental painters, poets, and musicians wrote manifestos, mounted art shows, and performed concerts that clamored for attention in Paris, London, and New York, much business—in the provinces and even, to some extent, in the cities—went on as usual.

Between 1910 and 1918, for instance, traditional class stratifications persisted. The American novelists Edith Wharton and Henry James, for instance, as well as the more radical English writer Virginia Woolf, recorded the doings of an upper-class pre–World War I society that continued to be concerned with conventional tea parties and elegant libraries, while the American novelist Willa Cather, the British novelists Arnold Bennett and D. H. Lawrence, and the Irish novelists George Moore and James Joyce portrayed bourgeois and working-class figures whose motivations were no less monetary than were those of characters in middle- and late-nineteenth-century works by Dickens, Hardy, and Dreiser. At the same time, literary tastes (at least on the surface) changed very little: in England, for example, the editor Edward Marsh's *Georgian Anthologies* (1912, 1915, 1917, 1919, 1922) offered the public verses by such poets as John Masefield and Walter de la Mare that generally celebrated bucolic landscapes or recounted romantic stories.

The New Technology

Nevertheless, even while the long Georgian afternoon seemed to suggest that old customs could still be preserved, the swift growth of a new technology, a long-term consequence of the Industrial Revolution, was eroding traditional ways of life. The first decade of the century saw the invention of radio, the introduction of theaters called nickelodeons for the showing of moving pictures, the development of a viable airplane, and the production (by Henry Ford) of an inexpensive automobile that could be manufactured on what was for the first time called an "assembly line." Along with such late-nineteenth-century innovations as the phonograph, the typewriter, the telephone, and the telegraph, these new devices were to have far-reaching effects on travel, business, and communication.

To begin with, a number of artists on both sides of the Atlantic hailed the industrial inventiveness of the age in much the way that their nineteenth-century predecessors had welcomed the powers promised by, in William Wordsworth's phrase, "Steamboats, Viaducts, and Railways." It is perhaps not surprising that the best-selling British writer Rudyard Kipling, often considered an apologist for the ambitions of the Empire, should have exulted in the glamour of modern railroads ("Romance brings up the 9:15"), nor is it surprising that a wealthy novelist like Edith Wharton should have been the devoted owner of an expensive motorcar, but the early reactions to technology of a range of passionately revolutionary artists are rather more unexpected. In the June 1914 issue of the short-lived little magazine *Blast*, for instance, such rebels against the old order as the British painter-writer Wyndham Lewis and the American poet Ezra Pound signed a series of manifestos declaring that "machinery is the greatest Earth-medium." Within a decade or two, their enthusiasm would be seconded by the American poets William Carlos Williams, whose *Overture to a Dance of Locomotives* (1921) portrayed the exuberance of train travel from a perspective remarkably similar to

Kipling's, and Hart Crane, whose *The Bridge* (1930) characterized the engineering marvel of the Brooklyn Bridge as a "harp and altar" of the future. As late as 1945, moreover, the iconoclastic Gertrude Stein exuberantly proclaimed that "America began to live in the twentieth century in the [eighteen] eighties with the Ford car."

Even while many writers were eulogizing modern technology as the harbinger of a transfigured world, though, others were beginning to examine its darker implications; indeed, some of those who had originally been most optimistic were eventually to express skepticism. If mass media like radio and film turned people into mere disembodied voices or images, these thinkers argued, mass manufacturing methods like the assembly line made individuals into interchangeable parts or robots. In addition, they claimed that the capitalist system which had fostered such developments severely widened the gap between what the Victorian writer Thomas Carlyle had called the "captains of industry" and the working classes whose labor served their needs. Thus, from the teens of the century on, critiques of the effects of technology and the intentions of industrial capitalism quickened in pace, focusing both on the psychology of the economic "masters" whose business triumphs were remaking society and the sociology of the alienated masses whose lives were being remade. In *The Financier* (1912), *The Titan* (1914), and *The Stoic* (not published until 1947), for instance, three novels that he called his *Trilogy of Desire*, Theodore Dreiser examined the power of what one critic has called "the businessman as buccaneer." At around the same time the English novelist-poet D. H. Lawrence was producing a series of books that studied not only the lives of coal miners and factory workers in the industrial Midlands but also the minds of the magnates who shaped their fates. In particular, *Sons and Lovers* (1912), *Women in Love* (1921), and *Lady Chatterley's Lover* (1928) analyzed the deadened and deadening consciousness of the modern "captain of industry" while vividly dramatizing the "soulless ugliness of the coal-and-iron Midlands . . . the cruelty of iron and the smoke of coal, and the endless, endless greed that drove it all."

Even more extravagant than the hostile critiques of novelists were the attacks of poets on the alienated world produced by modern technology. Though T. S. Eliot's despairing depiction of contemporary culture is not simply confined to a portrayal of the effects of mercantile industrialism, his *The Waste Land* (1922) includes perhaps the most famous scenes of alienation that were created in this period, notably its almost hallucinatory vision of a zombielike mass of urban pedestrians ("A crowd flowed over London Bridge, so many / I had not thought death had undone so many"). Similarly, Eliot's friend and mentor Ezra Pound, who had originally joined Wyndham Lewis in welcoming the new age of the machine, soon saw the negative implications of an era of mechanization. "The age demanded chiefly a mould in plaster," he noted in his sardonic *Hugh Selwyn Mauberly* (1920), "Made with no loss of time, / A prose kinema [cinema], not, not assuredly, alabaster / Or the 'sculpture' of rhyme." Later, in his radically experimental long poem called the *Cantos* (published serially between 1925 and 1959), Pound would go on to attack the foundations of the economic system, which he identified as "Usura" (usury), that had fostered such vulgarity.

Verse attacks like those by Eliot and Pound were both anticipated and echoed by a number of other poets. As if predicting Eliot's *Waste Land* vision of a deadened London crowd, the American poet Carl Sandburg wrote in a 1916 poem called *Halsted Street Car* of the blank faces—"Tired of wishes, / Empty of dreams"—of working-class passengers on a Chicago trolley, and in a 1920 verse titled *Manual System*, he described the workday of a telephone operator: "Mary has a thingama-jig clamped on her ears / And sits all day taking plugs out and sticking plugs in," while in his brief *Modern Prayer*, D. H. Lawrence summarized the culture of greedy materialism that had fostered such alienation:

> Almighty Mammon, make me rich!
> Make me rich quickly, with never a hitch

> in my fine prosperity! Kick those in the ditch
> who hinder me, Mammon, great son of a bitch!

Finally, beginning in 1930, such English poets as W. H. Auden, Stephen Spender, and Louis MacNeice produced a rich range of work based on the apocalyptic assumption that modern technology might virtually self-destruct. Though Auden, for instance, had begged in one early poem for "new styles of architecture, a change of heart," he and his contemporaries soon saw the "new" technology as wholly pernicious.

What particularly fostered the disillusionment of the Auden group was the economic depression that had struck both England and America at around the time these writers were beginning their literary careers, a transatlantic calamity that had been precipitated, especially in America, by the perilous practice of buying stocks "on margin" (for a fraction of their real price) and that resulted in the great New York stock market crash of 1929. Though both the British and American governments struggled to counteract the effects of the "crash"—which included breadlines, soup kitchens, and "tent cities" of the unemployed—by instituting new social welfare programs (in America known as Franklin Delano Roosevelt's 1933 "New Deal"), the Great Depression persisted in both countries throughout the 1930s, and it is clearly reflected in the works of Auden, Spender, and others, who vividly depicted a ruined and ruinous industrial landscape—in Auden's words, "Smokeless chimneys, damaged bridges, rotting wharves and choked canals." At the same time, adopting a Marxist belief in the inevitability of a revolution that would replace industrial capitalism with a new order, these writers predicted the end of the "businessman as buccaneer." Auden's warning to captains of industry in *Consider This and in Our Time* (1930) was marked by a grimly prophetic exhilaration that permeated the verse of many of his contemporaries both in England and America: "Financier, leaving your little room / Where the money is made but not spent, / You'll need your typist and your boy no more; / The game is up for you and for the others."

World War I

In a sense, a technological "apocalypse"—a seeming end to the known world—*had* already occurred in Europe, for World War I, defined by leaders as "the war to end all wars" but experienced by participants as an unprecedented triumph of death-dealing military technology, functioned in these years as an extraordinary historical turning point. The critic Paul Fussell has shown that many of the young men who went to the front during World War I were imbued with almost chivalric ideals of heroism, ideals that were rapidly destroyed by the horror of the conflict, only to be replaced by the kind of pervasive irony that Ezra Pound expressed in his *Hugh Selwyn Mauberley:* "There died a myriad, / And of the best, among them, / For an old bitch gone in the teeth, / For a botched civilization." But even in the minds of those who might have thought culture still deserved defense, the new technological realities of trenches and poison gas, land mines and machine guns—devices of destruction that had been expressly invented for this "Great War" and that led to a higher fatality rate than has ever been seen in any war before or since—subverted idealism.

As the historian Eric Leed has observed, the practice of digging trenches to hold established positions left foot soldiers with the feeling that they were living in a realm of pollution. Buried beneath the soil, assaulted by the continuous rumble of big guns, threatened by mines from below and poison gas from above, these young men experienced themselves as helpless rather than heroic, and they saw the apparently empty landscape of the battlefield—a landscape that was really "saturated" with enemies who were enclosed in trenches of their own—as nightmarishly threatening, even uncanny. Moreover, because, as the war veteran and poet Robert Graves reported, "the average life expectancy of an infantry subaltern

[lieutenant] on the western front was, at some stages of the war, only about three months," the despairing anxiety of such combatants was more than justified.

Many responded with a form of nervous breakdown called "shell shock." Others became permanently embittered and alienated. Some blamed civilians, often—like the English poet Siegfried Sassoon in his *Glory of Women* (1918)—reproaching women because "you love us when we're heroes, home on leave. . . . You worship decorations. . . . You make us shells." Some—like the English poet Wilfred Owen (who was killed at the front in 1918)—held not only women civilians but "fathers" responsible for the conflict, arguing, as Owen did in his *Dulce et Decorum Est* (1920), that "if . . . you [could see] the white eyes writhing in [the] face" of a victim of poison gas, "you would not tell with such high zest / To children ardent for some desperate glory, / The old Lie: Dulce et decorum est / Pro patria mori" (It is sweet and proper to die for one's country).

As the comments of noncombatants like Pound reveal, moreover, even civilians were profoundly affected by the enormity of the catastrophe. In England, figures as diverse as the poet-suffragist Alice Meynell and the colonial apologist Rudyard Kipling shared Owen's belief that "fathers"—meaning an avaricious male ruling class—were responsible for the disaster. In *A Father of Women* (1917), Meynell reproached the "million living fathers of the war," while in *Common Form*, one of his *Epitaphs of the War* (1914–18), Kipling—whose son was killed in an early battle—imagined a dead soldier saying, "If any question why we died, / Tell them, because our fathers lied." Though the United States did not enter the war until 1917—and only then after considerable national debate about the issue—a number of American writers expressed equal revulsion toward the conflict, with pacifists like the activist-feminist writers Charlotte Perkins Gilman and Crystal Eastman holding a patriarchal system accountable for its horrors in much the way that Meynell had.

Much of the most intensely disillusioned World War I literature, however, was written not during but after the war. Works like Ernest Hemingway's *The Sun Also Rises* (1926), a portrait of an artist made impotent by a war wound, as well as Lawrence's *Lady Chatterley's Lover* and Virginia Woolf's *Mrs. Dalloway* (1925), a profile of a society lady shadowed by a portrait of a young man made mad by the war, suggest the many ways in which this apocalyptic European crisis had deadened or sickened both participants and onlookers. For many thinkers, moreover, such alienation widened into a deeper sense of cultural fragmentation. Before the war, the Viennese psychoanalyst Sigmund Freud (1856–1939) wrote in 1915, "he who was not by stress of circumstances confined to one spot, could also confer upon himself . . . a new, a wider fatherland, wherein he moved unhindered and unsuspected," but after the war, he noted, "that civilized cosmopolitan . . . stand[s] helpless in a world grown strange to him—his all-embracing patrimony disintegrated, the common estates in it laid waste, the fellow-citizens embroiled and debased!"

Intellectual Anxiety

Interestingly, Freud's own theories about the human psyche, as well as the ideas of such fellow analysts as Alfred Adler (1870–1937) and the speculations of such contemporary scientists as Albert Einstein (1879–1955), had dramatically contributed to just the alienation that Freud thought had been fostered by the war. Though Freud's and Einstein's radically disruptive scientific theories were formulated early in the twentieth century, they were to have their most powerful impact in the decades between 1910 and 1940, and we are still feeling their effects today. Specifically, Freud's concept of psychoanalysis, first definitively set out in *The Interpretation of Dreams* (1900) and then elaborated in a series of studies that were published through the 1930s, implied that what the human mind experiences as "knowable" is not necessarily all that there is of the mind: the self, argued Freud, is constituted not only by the conscious personality (the "ego") but also by such war-

ring forces as the desirous unconscious (the "id") and the moralistic, socially learned "upper"-conscious (the "superego").

More problematic still, this complex and layered self is, in Freud's view, constructed out of an interaction between the urgently voracious, primitive infant and the adult world, represented by the parents, whose repressive or seductive actions inexorably shape the child's development. Somewhat in the way that Charles Darwin's account of human evolution from animal forms (in *The Origin of Species*, 1859) had seemed to destroy the concept of human singularity, Freud's vision of an essentially amoral secret self, together with his insistence that that self was helplessly conditioned by external forces, seemed to subvert traditional beliefs in free will and morality, and this subversion was intensified by the claims of such other thinkers as Freud's former colleague Alfred Adler, who argued that the individual was driven by a "will to power" and—failing to achieve sufficient parental support—subject to disorders like the "inferiority complex."

The new physics outlined by Albert Einstein and other scientists mirrored these disturbing concepts of the "inner" world with equally troublesome visions of the "outer" world, while new philosophical ideas further fractured traditional notions of time, reality, experience, and language. Einstein's special theory of relativity (1905), for instance, followed by his general theory of relativity (1916), invited doubts about even such apparently absolute categories as space and time, implying that the physical universe was far more complex than earlier Newtonian physics had asserted it was. Diverse as they were, moreover, the questionings of received reality produced by the speculations of Henri Bergson (1859–1941), Edmund Husserl (1859–1938), and Martin Heidegger (1889–1976), the revisions of logic and mathematics undertaken by Alfred North Whitehead (1861–1947), and the linguistic analyses of Ludwig Wittgenstein (1889–1951) also tended to undercut the confidence of intellectuals in both the "knowability" of a material world and the plausibility of a moral order.

To complicate matters further, new research by ethnologists and archaeologists led to a cultural relativism that fostered skepticism about the nature of human society itself. Increasingly, such investigators of so-called primitive societies and ancient artifacts had come to the conclusion that neither the origins nor the structure of society was necessarily patriarchal and that indeed there was no one fixed social system that governed the behavior of human groups around the world. By the turn of the century, moreover, the work of figures like the British anthropologist Sir James Frazer (1854–1941) and his classicist colleague Jane Ellen Harrison (1850–1928) suggested—to the distress of many religious readers—that Western Christianity was as deeply shaped by the codes of archaic fertility cults as any supposedly primitive theology. In particular, Frazer's *The Golden Bough* (1890) implied a connection between the figure of the Christian Messiah and the "dying and rising god" of such cults. Extensively revised between 1911 and 1915 and issued in an abridged edition in 1922, the book had an enormous impact on a number of modernist writers, as did the speculations of Freud's former associate the psychoanalyst Carl Jung (1875–1961), who postulated that human thought was shaped by primitive "archetypal" images drawn from a "collective unconscious," and the work of Frazer's disciple Jessie Weston, whose *From Ritual to Romance* (1920)—a study of the relationship between fertility religions and the medieval cult of the Holy Grail—was adopted by T. S. Eliot to help provide a narrative framework for *The Waste Land*. Indeed, from Eliot's *The Waste Land* and Joyce's *Ulysses* to Hemingway's *The Sun Also Rises* and H. D.'s *Trilogy* (1944, 1945, 1946), many twentieth-century works were inspired by anthropological and mythographical research.

At the same time, a number of literary figures welcomed the annihilation of traditional faith that was brought about by all these scientific and philosophical movements. In his *Sunday Morning* (1923), for instance, the American poet Wallace Stevens celebrated "the heavenly fellowship / Of men that perish and of

summer morn," rejecting the old pieties of paradise, while in England, D. H. Lawrence vigorously redefined God as no more than ' the great urge that has not yet found a body," and in Ireland, the poet William Butler Yeats concluded that "we are blest by everything, / Everything we look upon is blest." The case of Yeats is a telling one, however, for before affirming the blessedness of material reality, this poet had struggled for years to define a redemptive spiritual reality; repudiating traditional Christian dogma, he studied the occult, engaged in psychic research, and sought to strengthen his art with images of transcendence.

In this last respect, Yeats's early career was surprisingly similar to the later careers of such disparate poets as T. S. Eliot and W. H. Auden, both of whom—after periods of skepticism—took refuge in orthodox Christianity from what seemed to them a culture of disbelief. Following the publication of *The Waste Land,* that classic of modernist despair, Eliot in particular became increasingly religious, as if proposing that the best way to allay the intellectual anxieties of the twentieth century was to revive the verities of former ages. At the same time, in keeping with his conscious orthodoxy, his politics and his social views became notably conservative, even reactionary, charting a course that would be followed in their various ways by such American writers as the poet-critics John Crowe Ransom and Allen Tate. Manifesting itself during the 1930s, the conservatism of these figures represented one major response to skepticism about reality and signaled a deep political split between two sets of twentieth-century writers, a split that would become more significant as the 1920s darkened into the 1930s, and the intellectual anxiety fueled by contemporary science and philosophy was coupled with a more specifically political anxiety fostered by a new series of critical international developments.

International Anxiety

World War I was not the only disturbing international event that marked the years between 1914 and 1939, though it was the most striking. Specifically, this period saw the continuing decline of the British Empire; the intensification of so-called isolationism in the United States; the growth of such threateningly revolutionary movements as anarchism, socialism, and communism; the worldwide trauma caused by the Russian Revolution of 1917; and the rise of international fascism, first manifested by Benito Mussolini's takeover of Italy (1928) and Adolf Hitler's accession to dictatorship in Germany (1933), and then most vividly dramatized by the Spanish civil war (1936–39).

In a sense, the slow but inexorable disintegration of the British Empire may have served as a portent of things to come, foreshadowing what the German historian Oswald Spengler was to call, in a gloomy theoretical volume, *The Decline of the West* (1922). In the once-crucial British colony of Ireland, for instance, the Easter Rising of 1916 was followed first by the so-called Irish troubles—guerrilla warfare, between British troops called "Black and Tans" and Irish rebels, that lasted from 1918 to 1920—and then by the establishment of the Irish Free State in 1921. At about the same time, agitation for freedom began in India, where Mohandas K. Gandhi returned from years spent in England and South Africa to lead an independence movement in 1915. The nation was not to achieve Gandhi's goal until 1949, but his radicalism—though manifested by "passive resistance" rather than overt violence—was so threatening that he was imprisoned by the British in 1930–31 and again from 1942 to 1944, and English anxiety about the troublesome "otherness" now asserting itself in a major colony was brilliantly represented in E. M. Forster's *A Passage to India* (1924). Other subject domains also gradually freed themselves from England in this period: Egypt achieved independence in 1923, while the establishment of the British Commonwealth in 1931 granted equal and independent status to such nations as Canada, Australia, and New Zealand.

Perhaps in part because of the monitory example of Britain's decline, the mood

in the United States became increasingly conservative and isolationist in these years. Northern anxiety about blacks, for instance, was intensified when, between 1910 and 1920, the mass migration of southern blacks to New York City made the upper-Manhattan neighborhood of Harlem one of the largest black communities in the United States and—because of poor living conditions and the under-employment of many of its citizens—the site of racial unrest throughout the 1920s and 1930s. At the same time, the white supremacist Ku Klux Klan gained strength in the South and the Midwest as well as in such northern states as Maine and Oregon. Founded in 1915, the Klan grew in membership to a peak in the mid-1920s; its power was symbolic of a widespread American racism that also led to the controversial 1931 trial of the so-called Scottsboro boys, nine young Alabama black men who were accused (unjustly, in the view of many liberals) of having raped two young white women.

Besides feeling assaulted from within, however, many conservative Americans felt threatened from without. In response to the country's isolationist mood, the government sought to stem the tide of immigration that brought thirty-eight million new citizens to the land between 1820 and 1930. In 1917, a literacy requirement was imposed on all immigrants, and in 1921 and 1924 quota systems were established, severely restricting the number of southern and eastern Europeans and Asians who could enter the country. Still, despite such measures, American anxiety about international involvement was clearly responsible for the reluctance of President Woodrow Wilson (who was elected on a platform of neutrality) to enter World War I, and it was responsible, too, for a terror of Communist infiltration—a "Red scare"—that dominated the 1920s.

It was not the American 1920s alone that were haunted by the threat of such revolutionary movements as anarchism, socialism, and communism. Significantly, however, a number of British socialists were such comparatively respected figures as the playwright George Bernard Shaw, the novelist H. G. Wells, the journalist Rebecca West, and the writer-editor Leonard Woolf (husband of Virginia Woolf), whereas in the United States, anarchism and rebellion were usually associated with immigrants who were perceived as both unsavory and lawless. Such a perception in America fostered the passage of the Volstead Act (1918), which instituted the prohibition of liquor sales in the United States until its repeal in 1933, for the consumption of alcohol was often connected with just the immigrant groups that, during the Prohibition years, bootlegged sales of "bathtub" wine and gin. More specifically, this attitude led to the persecution in America of radical immigrants like Emma Goldman, Nicola Sacco, and Bartolomeo Vanzetti.

The political agitator and free-love advocate Emma Goldman was a Russian Jew popularly called "Red Emma" and "the Queen of the Anarchists"; her *Living My Life* (1931) recorded a brilliant but controversial career as a rebel against oppression, a career for which she was deported to Russia in 1919. The Italian-born left-wing labor agitators Nicola Sacco and Bartolomeo Vanzetti, who were tried in 1920 and executed in 1927 for an alleged payroll robbery, were the focus of fierce American debate throughout the 1920s because it was believed by radicals and liberals alike that they were innocent, and that their "alien" ethnic origins and their political convictions had led to their deaths.

Even before the deportation of Emma Goldman and the Sacco-Vanzetti case had aroused American political passions, the Russian Revolution of 1917 had brought anxieties about left-wing agitation to a climax. To many thinkers, it appeared that the assassination of the czar and his family represented an apotheosis of the anarchy that had been troubling Europe for more than a century, ever since the French Revolution of 1789, and especially after Karl Marx and Friedrich Engels had produced their *Communist Manifesto* (1848). Certainly for William Butler Yeats the 1917 turmoil in Russia constituted a historical crux, a moment when he felt obliged to concede that what Spengler had called "the decline of the West" was a reality. In his famous poem *The Second Coming* (1920), Yeats sug-

gested that the historical cycle represented by Western Christianity had at last come to an end: "Things fall apart; the center cannot hold," he wrote. "Mere anarchy is loosed upon the world. / The blood-dimmed tide is loosed," and later, according to one scholar, he "accepted the poem" not only as a comment on the Russian Revolution but as "an unconscious prophecy of the rise of fascism."

Again, however, Yeats is emblematic here, for despite his later repudiation of fascism, he had actually, in 1934, written a sequence of poems that were intended to be inspiriting to the Irish fascist movement. His gesture revealed a political ambivalence that was characteristic of a number of the major modernists. In 1926, for instance, D. H. Lawrence published a novel fantasizing the redemption of Mexico by what he called a "blood-brotherhood" of revolutionaries whose common creed was based on the assumption that natural leaders must always command unquestioning loyalty from their subordinates, and in 1933, just before Hitler was to rise to power in Germany with the plan of finding a "final solution" to the "Jewish problem," T. S. Eliot gave a series of lectures (titled *After Strange Gods*) in which he declared that populations "should be homogeneous" both in race and in religion, adding that "reasons of race and religion combine to make any large number of free-thinking Jews undesirable" and that "a spirit of excessive tolerance is to be deprecated."

Even while these writers were flirting with fascism, however, another group of modernists were passionately attacking their reactionary orthodoxy. With its radical double assault on patriarchal culture and fascist ideology, *Three Guineas* (1938), by Eliot's friend and publisher Virginia Woolf, was perhaps this period's fiercest critique of the intertwined Nazi notions of leadership and the Fatherland. But during the 1930s the Englishmen W. H. Auden and George Orwell, and the Americans John Dos Passos, John Steinbeck, Langston Hughes, Edna St. Vincent Millay, and Muriel Rukeyser, also wrote novels and poems that mourned the oppression of what the poet Carl Sandburg had once called "the people, yes" while advocating strong rebellion against both fascist and capitalist domination. On both sides of the Atlantic, moreover, many younger artists—including Ernest Hemingway, George Orwell, and Virginia Woolf's nephew Julian Bell—journeyed to Spain to fight on the side of the Loyalists (Republicans) against Franco's Falangists (Fascists). Speaking for all these activists, Auden's *Spain 1937* said: "We are left alone with our day, and the time is short and / History to the defeated / May say alas but cannot help or pardon."

Artistic Innovation

Many modern artists responded to the rapid change in which they found themselves with an urgent sense that new aesthetic modes were needed to mirror the newness of the century, and many gathered into informal communities for which the creation of such modes became a kind of group project. Three intertwined phenomena were associated with the development of these radical intellectual communities. First, because the new availability and speed of steamships, railroads, and motorcars had made long-range travel easy, a number of artists chose to journey abroad: Americans became expatriates in London and Paris. English writers settled in Paris, Mexico, Berlin, and the United States; German, Russian, and Spanish artists traveled to Paris or New York; and wherever they went, these figures tended to establish cosmopolitan groups that shared innovative aesthetic ideas. Second, because so many of these groups were bonded by common artistic goals, a number of "little magazines" and anthologies sprang up in these years, journals disseminating a range of new literary views. Third, the availability of such periodicals fostered the development of the genre of the "manifesto," a statement in which groups of artists outlined their aesthetic principles, usually in revolutionary language.

Charting the movements of twentieth-century writers, painters, and musicians

can be dizzying. Ezra Pound, T. S. Eliot, Robert Frost, and H. D. (Hilda Doolittle) established themselves in London during the first two decades of the century, but though Eliot was by and large to remain in England for the rest of his life, Pound was later to travel to Italy (where he would broadcast pro-fascist propaganda for the Mussolini government), Frost was eventually to return to his New England home, and after the 1920s H. D. was to live intermittently in Switzerland. The same complexities mark the itineraries of many other writers. Though Gertrude Stein—perhaps this century's most famous expatriate—moved to Paris in 1903, where she settled permanently, as did Edith Wharton (who hardly left France after 1914), Ernest Hemingway, Sherwood Anderson, Henry Miller, Djuna Barnes, and Anaïs Nin lived in Paris during the 1920s and 1930s (where Hemingway and Anderson, in particular, were members of the "Stein circle"), but then departed for points elsewhere. Similarly, though James Joyce was ultimately to settle in Paris, he did not do so until he had spent some years living in Trieste and Zurich, while W. B. Yeats, though he was deeply identified with the so-called Irish Renaissance, actually spent most of his life journeying between London, Paris, Dublin, and western Ireland. All these travelers produced a literature that is always singularly cosmopolitan even while it expresses a deep sense of uprootedness.

To be sure, little magazines did provide writers with aesthetic "homes" of a sort. *Poetry* and *The Little Review* in Chicago, *Broom* and the *Dial* in New York, *Blast*, the *Egoist*, and the *Criterion* in London, and *transition* in Paris, along with annual anthologies like *The Imagist Anthology* (edited first by Ezra Pound, then by Amy Lowell) and *Wheels* (edited by Edith Sitwell) offered experimental writers a rich range of outlets for their talents as well as an array of pages that could be filled with manifestoes explaining the new aesthetic assumptions on which these artists operated. The *Blast* manifestoes of 1914, quoted earlier, were typical of these productions, but the *Imagist Manifesto* of 1915, written to justify the sharply chiseled free verse that had been composed from 1908 on by Pound and H. D., was more crucially influential, with its admonitions to "employ always the *exact* word," "to create new rhythms—as the expression of new moods," "to present an image," and "to produce poetry that is hard and clear" because "concentration is of the very essence of poetry."

Having slightly less impact on poetry in English, but almost equally representative in their radical repudiation of old forms and their enthusiasm for shockingly new methods, were the *Surrealist Manifesto* (1924) and *Manifesto: The Revolution of the Word*, which was published in *transition* in the early 1930s. In the first, the French poet André Breton confided that the "Secrets of the Magical/Surrealist Art"—an art based on dreams and visions, wild associations and images of the world that were "sur" (or super) real—included automatic writing, for the poet must "trust . . . the inexhaustible nature of the murmur." In the second, a series of axioms attacking linguistic and narrative "realism," such diverse figures as Kay Boyle and Hart Crane agreed that "THE LITERARY CREATOR HAS THE RIGHT TO DIS-INTEGRATE THE PRIMAL MATTER OF WORDS."

A number of individual writers produced critical statements of their own that also functioned as manifestoes of a sort. Quite early in his career, for instance, Ezra Pound had advised all his contemporaries to "make it new" and paid tribute to Walt Whitman, the nineteenth-century American poet who virtually pioneered free verse, with the words "it was you that broke the new wood." Similarly, in a lecture called *Composition as Explanation* (1926), Gertrude Stein sought both to justify her use of what she called "the continuous present" and to account for what seemed the obscurity of her avant-garde writing with the observation that "the creator of the new composition in the arts is an outlaw until he is a classic." In an article on *Modern Fiction* (1919), Virginia Woolf insisted that it is "the task of the novelist to convey" a "varying . . . unknown and uncircumscribed spirit" rather than fixed and discrete external realities, while in an analysis of *The Novel*

Démeublé ("The Unfurnished Novel," 1936) Willa Cather argued for a fiction stripped of the stuffy furniture of circumstantial detail that had cluttered the works of "naturalists" and Victorians alike. Though other modernists did not make quite such hortatory statements, their critical analyses of literature past and present often acted as equally passionate personal manifestoes. Certainly Eliot's *Tradition and the Individual Talent* or his *The Metaphysical Poets* can be read in such a way, as can William Carlos Williams's book of essays titled *In the American Grain* (1925) and his essay praising the brilliance with which the American poet Marianne Moore cut "soiled words" out of "greasy" traditional contexts.

The experimental impulses articulated in both group and personal literary manifestoes were strengthened by the intense experimentation that was being conducted by artists in other media. Since the late nineteenth century, painters from Auguste Renoir, Mary Cassatt, Marie Laurencin, and Edvard Munch to Georges Bracque and Pablo Picasso had used the techniques of impressionism, expressionism, and cubism to break down traditional modes of representing the material world, substituting for strictly pictorial images more abstract forms, forms either determined by unique individual perceptions or governed by larger principles of design. It was during the modernist period, however, that the innovations of these artists began to seem most compelling to their literary contemporaries. Picasso, in particular, became a hero of the avant-garde: Gertrude Stein, one of the first great collectors of modern art and the subject of what was perhaps the Spanish painter's most famous portrait, wrote in an ironic understatement that he was "one whom some were certainly following." Similarly exhilarating to many literary figures were the daring works of such composers as Igor Stravinsky (whose ballet *Le Sacre du Printemps*, 1913—"The Rite of Spring"—shocked even cosmopolitan Paris with its ferocious primitivism) and Arnold Schoenberg (whose theory of the "twelve-tone row" seemed to many conservatives to threaten to substitute mathematical formulas for traditional melodies).

Both the poetry and the fiction produced by writers who participated in this experimental culture were also often unnervingly controversial. To some, the Imagists' liberation of verse from traditional rhyme and rhythm, along with their turn toward such alien forms as the Japanese *haiku*, seemed to signal the end of poetry; to others, such liberation—particularly as it appeared in the beautifully crafted poems of H. D. and the early Pound—promised the beginning of a style that might, as William Carlos Williams thought, capture the inflections of the voice (and especially the American voice) more accurately than any conventional meter ever had. Similarly, to some the fragmented narratives of such ambitious works as Eliot's *The Waste Land*, Pound's *Cantos*, H. D.'s *Trilogy*, and Williams's *Paterson*, as well as the more modest poems of Marianne Moore, together with these artists' use of literary allusions—quotations from writings in a range of languages—appeared willfully obscurantist, while to others the freeing of poetry from a straightforward narrative or argumentative line promised a new richness in the art.

Equally crucial but controversial innovations marked the development of modernist fiction. Most notable perhaps was the development in this period of the so-called stream-of-consciousness novel, a genre that seemed to many readers quite as obscure as the fragmented and allusive poetry of Eliot and Pound but that was destined to become no less influential. First defined by the English writer May Sinclair, who borrowed the phrase "stream of consciousness" from the American philosopher William James, this kind of novel generally focused on the mental processes—the thoughts, responses, and interior emotional experiences—of a single central character (although sometimes the writer switched points of view among several key figures). Reflecting the concerns of an era obsessed by the hypotheses of Sigmund Freud and other psychoanalysts, the novelists who worked in this mode strove to represent not only the fluid movements of what might be con-

sidered the surface of the mind but also the irrational disruptions of thought that signaled the explosions of unconscious material into the consciousness.

James Joyce's *Ulysses* (1922) was unquestionably the most famous work in this mode; indeed, with its searching examinations of the phases of the mind of its protagonist Leopold Bloom and its equally innovative dramatizations of the thoughts of Bloom's counterhero Stephen Daedalus, the book represented a turning point in modern novelistic technique. But this important work's strategies were prepared for not only by Joyce's earlier *A Portrait of the Artist as a Young Man* (1916), a *Bildungsroman* (development novel) that traced Stephen Daedalus's growth to maturity, but also by such equally radical experimentations as Dorothy Richardson's *Pointed Roofs* (1915), the first novel in a series called *Pilgrimage* that explored the mental evolution of its heroine, Miriam Henderson. Comparable stream-of-consciousness techniques were implemented in the work of such artists as May Sinclair, whose *Mary Olivier* (1919) was only one of several fictions by this writer that explored the lights and shadows of a protagonist's mind; Virginia Woolf, whose *Mrs. Dalloway* (1925), *To the Lighthouse* (1927), and *The Waves* (1933) were particularly notable examples of what Woolf called a "tunneling" technique through which she "excavated" the dreams and desires of her characters; and William Faulkner, whose *The Sound and the Fury* (1929) and *As I Lay Dying* (1930) consisted of brilliantly sewn together "interior monologues."

Modernist fiction writers also undertook other revisionary strategies. What the critic Michael Hoffman has called Gertrude Stein's "abstractionism"—a method of emphasizing language itself rather than its narrative components—led not only to the experiment in "the continuous present" of Stein's own *Three Lives* (1909) but also, because of the force of Stein's personality and example, to the highly stylized and stripped repetitions of Ernest Hemingway's *The Sun Also Rises* (1926) and *A Farewell to Arms* (1929). In the writings of Joyce (*Dubliners*, 1916), D. H. Lawrence, and Katherine Mansfield (*The Garden Party*, 1922), moreover, this period saw what was in effect the invention of the modern short story. Influenced by the work of the continental artists Maupassant, Turgenev, and Chekhov, these writers struggled to create a genre whose plot would reflect not the complexity of an extended chain of causes and effects but the purity of what Woolf called a "timeless moment" or, in Joyce's words, an "epiphany" (a revelation) that functions as the turning point of a life. Similarly, particularly in the United States, a group of experimental dramatists—notably those associated with the Provincetown Players, headquartered both on Cape Cod and in Greenwich Village, in New York City—sought to import new life into the theater: writers like Eugene O'Neill and Susan Glaspell produced plays that were striking for such "expressionistic" techniques as the use of archaic masks and symbols (in O'Neill's *The Emperor Jones*, 1922) or for their oblique, even mysterious narrative forms (in Glaspell's *Trifles*, 1916). In her highly experimental *Machinal* (1928), Sophie Treadwell used pointedly nonrealistic scenes to present a feminist parable about an everywoman character called the Young Woman.

Even while these largely elite artists were striving to articulate manifestoes, to experiment with styles, and to pioneer new genres, however, a number of more popular literary modes and movements were developing. Perhaps the most impressive of these was the so-called Harlem Renaissance, a movement led by the American black writers Jean Toomer, Nella Larson, Langston Hughes, Countee Cullen, and Zora Neale Hurston, all of whom agreed, despite major philosophical differences among them, that it was now essential for African-Americans to become conscious of, and write about, their uniquely rich culture. In the 1920s, Harlem had in any case become, along with the bohemian quarter of Greenwich Village, a center of New York's aesthetic life: the increasingly fascinating new musical form of jazz, with its improvisational intensity, had forced many white intellectuals to pay attention to their black contemporaries. Finally, therefore, it

seemed possible for these writers to dramatize not only what Cullen called in *Heritage* (1925) the history of Africa's lost "copper sun or scarlet sea"—the history of a forgotten past—but also the distinctive pain of the black mother who represents the oppression of all her people when she tells her child in Hughes's *Mother to Son* (1926) that "life for me ain't been no crystal stair." While the work of these writers clearly had an impact on that of their white contemporaries, it was to be most dramatically carried on in the writing of their black descendants Amiri Baraka (LeRoi Jones), Ishmael Reed, Toni Morrison, Paule Marshall, Audre Lorde, and Alice Walker.

Other movements that major modernists sometimes defined as "popular" also had important effects. Joyce, Stein, Woolf, and Lawrence, for instance, may have in various ways scorned such vulgar genres as science fiction and the detective novel along with radio, musical comedy, and film. However, the rapid development of all these modes inevitably impinged on the careers of these artists as well as on the styles of their descendants. For one thing, the commercial appeal of best-selling thrillers and hit musicals contrasted sharply with the small sales achieved by the works of elite modernists, whose difficult experimental novels and poems often earned little money even when they were greeted with critical praise. Thus the gap between the aesthetically ambitious artist and the hack writer, first perceived in the nineteenth century, widened dramatically in these years, intensifying the sense of alienation experienced by many serious novelists and poets.

Modernist writers could not, however, simply ignore the rise of popular media. Some actually led double lives, supporting themselves by writing for money while doing their "real" work on the side. William Faulkner, F. Scott Fitzgerald, and Dorothy Parker, for instance, went to Hollywood to write for the movies. In addition, a number of supposedly hack writers who produced only commercial works were ultimately to be perceived as more serious than they had at first seemed. H. L. Mencken and George Jean Nathan's *Black Mask* magazine developed the talents of the powerful and influential artist Dashiell Hammett, whose style and subject matter have been frequently compared with those of Ernest Hemingway. In addition, this period—often referred to as the "Golden Age" of detective fiction—fostered the work of mystery writers like Agatha Christie and Dorothy L. Sayers, novelists whose plots and characters left indelible marks on the consciousness of the era. Ultimately, as much as the innovations of the so-called high modernists, the pioneering contributions of such artists may represent the extraordinarily transfigurative quality of the age, an era whose literary no less than its intellectual and social changes were among the most radical experienced in Western history.

MODERNIST IMAGES OF WOMEN

Perhaps because of the sense of cultural cataclysm inspired by the new technology, together with the widespread male anxiety about a female "takeover" that characterized the early years of the twentieth century, the images of women produced by modernist men (and even some produced by their female contemporaries) were largely negative. To be sure, a number of writers created attractive female characters (and a number depicted unpleasant male characters), but by and large much literature of the period is notable for its obsession with what women should—and should not—be. In particular, threatened by suffragists, immobilized and unmanned by the war, alienated from both the industrial modes and the commercial media of what seemed an increasingly hectic society, many male novelists and poets tended to blame women for the sense of lost mastery that Lawrence outlined in his essay *Matriarchy*. If man would never, in Lawrence's words, "be master again," these writers implied, that was because women had in effect conspired with the new technology to render their male contemporaries socially and even

sexually impotent. Thus, where late-nineteenth-century literary men had become obsessed by the threatening and predatory figure of the *femme fatale*, a merciless siren whose wiles were associated with the deadly potential of nature, modernist men were haunted by a new kind of destructive female: the flapper, a figure whose daunting ease with technology and unnerving sexual freedom were manifested by her short skirts and bobbed hair, her feverish dancing and wild drinking, her skill-ful driving and willful wandering.

Perhaps the most famously destructive flappers in modernist fiction were Brett Ashley, the antiheroine of Ernest Hemingway's *The Sun Also Rises* (1926), and Daisy Buchanan, the equally problematic heroine of F. Scott Fitzgerald's *The Great Gatsby* (1925). A "damned good-looking" woman whose almost mechani-cally sleek sexuality is emphasized by the narrator's notation that she "was built with curves like the hull of a racing yacht," Hemingway's Brett rules over a novel whose hero, Jake Barnes, has been rendered literally impotent by a World War I wound and whose other male characters are shown to be in one way or another fig-uratively impotent. Similarly seductive, Fitzgerald's narcissistic Daisy is a rich and faithless young married woman who incarnates the corrupted morals of the society over which she presides: her voice "was full of money—that was the inexhaustible charm that rose and fell in it, the jingle of it, the cymbals' song of it," and her mechanistic deathliness reaches a climax when she casually slams her lover's ex-pensive automobile into her husband's mistress in a hit-and-run accident that leads not only to the woman's death but later to the deaths of two men.

If few other flappers were quite as metaphorically murderous as Brett Ashley and Daisy Buchanan, many were characterized as either decadent or dangerous. In Richard Aldington's World War I novel *The Death of a Hero* (1929), for instance, the soldier-protagonist's wife and mistress—indifferent to his suffering in the trenches—are described as "terribly at ease upon the Zion of sex, abounding in masochism, Lesbianism, sodomy, etcetera," while in T. S. Eliot's *The Waste Land* the loveless and even anaesthetized sexuality of a "typist home at teatime" is echoed by the robotlike eroticism of a number of other female figures, all of whom the poet sees as having been liberated from traditional moral standards to no good end. Moreover, in countless bitterly misogynistic poems and stories written toward the close of his life, D. H. Lawrence held newly energetic women responsible for most social ills, implying that the apocalypse of modernism had been set in mo-tion by what he variously defined as "energetic women," "dominant women," and "volcanic Venuses," for, as he explained in one verse, "Vengeance is mine, saith the Lord, / but the women are my favorite vessels of wrath."

In picturing women as such "vessels of wrath," however, Lawrence was moving to a more general concept of the destructiveness implicit in all female ambition. Particularly the newly liberated intellectual or literary woman—the figure whom turn-of-the-century observers had labeled "the New Woman"—was seen by this writer and others as a flawed and potentially evil personage. Gudrun Brangwen, one of the two female protagonists of his *Women in Love*, for example, is no flapper but a serious artist, yet her commitment to her works is frequently shown to be narcissistic, while her consciousness is often characterized as coldly "glittering," and her turbulent love affair with Gerald Crich, one of the book's major male fig-ures, leads directly to his death. In creating such a deadly female intellectual Lawrence was expressing an attitude that would also permeate the writings of W. B. Yeats, Ernest Hemingway, William Faulkner, and Nathanael West.

Imagining ideal womanhood in his *A Prayer for My Daughter* (1919), for in-stance, Yeats transcribed his own ambivalence toward the activism of Maude Gonne, the Irish actress and revolutionary whom he had loved almost all his life, with the imperative "let her [his infant daughter] think opinions are accursed" and the comment "Have I not seen the loveliest woman born / Out of the mouth of Plenty's horn / Because of her opinionated mind / Barter that horn and every

good / By quiet natures understood / For an old bellows full of angry wind?" A similar ambivalence toward the female intellect appears in West's *Miss Lonelyhearts*, in which a group of male reporters curse lady writers with three names: "Mary Roberts Wilcox, Ella Wheeler Catheter... what they all needed was a good rape." As for suffragists, many were characterized as insane man-haters, and if they were not seen as mad, many—along with female intellectuals and New Women—were often labeled as lesbians. If they actually *were* lesbians, moreover, they were almost always described with horror or nervous scorn: in his *Autobiography* (1952), William Carlos Williams recalls a visit to the salon of the lesbian expatriate Natalie Barney, where women were "sneaking off together into a side room while casting surreptitious glances about them," and was reminded of the behavior of a French deputy who, confronted with the same scene, "undid his pants buttons, took out his tool and, shaking it right and left, yelled out in a rage, 'Have you never seen one of these?'"

Single women who did not define themselves as New Women or intellectuals fared little better at the hands of twentieth-century male artists, for the Victorian myth of the frustrated spinster lingered on, at least through the 1930s. Faulkner's short story *A Rose for Emily* (written 1931) told the morbid tale of an unmarried southern heiress who keeps the skeleton of her lover in her bed for decades after his death while she herself grows increasingly bloated, as if fattening on his decay. In an equally savage vein, Auden's ballad *Miss Gee* (1937) recounted the case history of a churchgoing spinster who wears "her clothes buttoned up to her neck" and gets cancer from sexual frustration; the medical men who operate on her find the sight of her sick body hilarious: "They laid her on the table, / The students began to laugh; / And Mr. Rose the surgeon / He cut Miss Gee in half." Even the images of women who had dutifully married did not necessarily escape such opprobrium, for widows were often depicted as prissy, fussy creatures. Wallace Stevens's *A High-toned Old Christian Woman* (1923), for instance, complained that the joy generated by the "supreme fiction" of poetry "will make widows wince," but defiantly contended that "fictive things / Wink as they will. Wink most when widows wince."

Nor can the male modernists' portrayals of "properly" heterosexual women—married women, mothers, mistresses, whores—have been very much more inspiriting for female readers. Perhaps the most famous female character in early twentieth-century fiction was Molly Bloom, the heroine of *Ulysses*, an insatiably lusty earth-goddess who never gets out of bed in the course of the novel, and whose last words in the book—"yes I said yes I will Yes"—express her passionate acquiescence in her purely sexual destiny. From Lawrence's desirous Lady Chatterley to the obscene female figures in Samuel Beckett's poem *Whoroscope* (1929) to the prostitutes who haunt Henry Miller's *Tropic of Cancer* (1934) and his *Tropic of Capricorn* (1938), Molly Bloom's descendants proliferated in twentieth-century fiction, frequently described in terms of body parts, with Miller's whores usually appraised as "cunts." Even the former Victorian ideals of mothers and motherhood were now castigated, moreover, for psychoanalysts increasingly tended to blame the sins of the mothers for the neuroses of the sons. By 1942, the American writer Philip Wylie was to inveigh in *Generation of Vipers* against "the destroying mother," arguing that "we must face the dynasty of the dames at once."

Finally, with perhaps a few exceptions—Mrs. Wilcox and Margaret Schlegel in Forster's *Howards End* (1912) come to mind, for instance—it began to seem that the only "good" women in male-authored modern literature were, on the one hand, little girls who had not yet *become* women, and, on the other hand, adults who were willing to sacrifice themselves completely to the imperatives of male desire and need. An example of the first group is "Littless," the prepubescent tomboy heroine of Hemingway's *The Last Good Country* (published in 1972), Nick Adams's younger sister who is beloved by the hero partly for her impassioned loy-

alty and partly for her intense innocence. Examples of the second group would include the nameless heroine of Lawrence's *The Woman Who Rode Away* (1923), a white woman who is stripped and sacrificed by American Indian priests so that their people can "regain the mastery that man must hold," and Rose of Sharon, the daughter of the Joads in John Steinbeck's *The Grapes of Wrath* (1939), who offers her milk-filled breast to a starving tramp she has never seen before. What distinguished both these groups of women was their absence of self-will, their vulnerable passivity, their dutiful instrumentality, qualities that seemed to their creators to be increasingly lacking in the real behavior of real women.

WOMEN'S NEW LIVES

When Virginia Woolf meditated in her essay *Mr. Bennett and Mrs. Brown* on the change in "human character" that took place "on or about December, 1910," her examples were telling. First, she noted that while the "Victorian cook lived like a leviathan in the lower depths . . . the Georgian cook is a creature of sunshine and fresh air." Then, she observed that contemporary readers of Aeschylus's drama *Agamemnon* will find that their "sympathies are . . . almost entirely with Clytemnestra," the rebellious wife whose betrayal of her husband was traditionally vilified. Finally, she argued that readers who study the biographies of the Victorian sage Thomas Carlyle and his wife will dislike "the horrible domestic tradition" that confined "a woman of genius" like Jane Carlyle to the kitchen. For, declared Woolf, "all human relations have shifted"—and especially, as her images of change indicate, the relations between the sexes.

Woolf's analysis was characteristically acute, for the technological and intellectual innovations of the early twentieth century had a striking impact on women of all classes. Though workers on both sides of the Atlantic continued to suffer from economic exploitation—and in particular from the effects of widespread postwar unemployment in the 1920s and of the Great Depression in the 1930s—trade unionism and social welfare programs had begun to insulate them to some extent from the horrors experienced by, for instance, Victorian women in the mines or sweatshops, while universal public education, together with new systems of mass communication, gave them access to cultural institutions from which they had earlier been excluded. Similarly, both middle- and upper-class women, no longer bound by the preceding century's ideology of femininity, entered universities and professions in ever-increasing numbers while exulting in a new intellectual and sexual freedom. Finally, after nearly a century of struggle, women of all classes in both England and America at last gained the right to vote, a right that—at least legally—for the first time acknowledged their full citizenship in the human community.

Just before England entered the Great War in the summer of 1914, suffragist militancy had reached a new intensity. In 1913, British feminists, led by the Pankhursts, engaged in hunger strikes, window smashings, and other radical actions, and five thousand American feminists, led by Alice Paul, marched on Washington. When war broke out, however, British suffrage societies immediately suspended their protests, and the government issued an amnesty to all its hunger-striking female prisoners. Although a splinter group of pacifist women, led by the socialist Sylvia Pankhurst, refused to support "this capitalist war," most suffrage workers abandoned their struggle for the vote in favor of war work on the home front, and major figures in the Women's Social and Political Union (WSPU)—most notably Sylvia Pankhurst's mother, Emmeline Pankhurst, and her sister, Christabel Pankhurst—became passionately patriotic, supporting (in the words of the historian Sheila Rowbotham) "military conscription for men, industrial conscription for women." In fact, the suffrage battle did not resume in England until 1916, when the National Union of Women's Suffrage Societies,

led by Millicent Garrett Fawcett, pressured Parliament to introduce the new Franchise Bill and managed at last to win the support of prominent politicians. By June 1917, the House of Commons had actually passed a women's suffrage bill, and by January 1918, the more conservative House of Lords had also accepted the bill.

Although the United States did not actually enter the war until 1917, events paralleled those in Great Britain to some extent. To be sure, between 1914 and 1916 the struggle for suffrage did not lapse in America as t had in England; on the contrary, two parties with rather different philosophies pressed the issue vigorously. Led by Carrie Chapman Catt, the National American Woman Suffrage Association (NAWSA) organized state referenda while also proselytizing for an amendment to the Constitution. At the same time, led by Alice Paul, the Congressional Union (later the Woman's Party) directed its energies entirely toward the passage of a constitutional amendment, and—in doing so—adopted increasingly militant tactics. As it had in England, the tide of political opinion began to turn in America in 1916 and 1917, although, again as in England, the already divided women's movement split further over the issue of America's entrance into the war: the NAWSA—like the WSPU—patriotically supported war work, and the Woman's Party—like Sylvia Pankhurst's faction—took a pacifist line. Despite these rifts, however, the Nineteenth Amendment, granting women the vote, finally came before the House of Representatives in January 1918 and, with the support of President Woodrow Wilson, passed by a two-thirds majority while cheering throngs in the galleries and corridors of the Capitol sang the hymn "Old Hundred." Although another year and a half of struggle—including elaborate maneuvers in the Senate and arduous state-by-state campaigning—was necessary before the amendment became law, thirty-six states had finally ratified it by August 1920.

Most historians agree that, in addition to decades of struggle and hard work, a major factor in achieving the right to vote was women's contributions to the war effort. For, in fact, one of the most striking discontinuities between male and female experience in the modernist period was generated by the Great War. Specifically, as young men were sent off to a front where their chances for survival were often slim and as they became increasingly immured in the muck and blood of "No Man's Land," their mothers, wives, sisters, and daughters on the home front seemed to become ever more powerful. Filling the places soldiers had left behind in mines and munitions factories, farms and railroads, women found themselves confronted for the first time with opportunities to do remunerative and meaningful work in the public sphere. By 1918, a visitor to London observed that "England was a world of women—women in uniforms," and the English poet Nina Macdonald proudly proclaimed that "Girls are doing things / They've never done before. . . . All the world is topsy-turvy / Since the War began."

That the world *was* in some sense "topsy-turvy" contributed, of course, to the soldiers' sickened sense of anxiety and exclusion from the homes they had left behind. Nevertheless, despite the massive tragedy that the conflict represented for thousands of grieving wives and mothers, such a reversal of the old order contributed enormously to the liberation—and the new exuberance—of women, who felt for the first time not only needed but appreciated. The American writer Harriot Stanton Blatch declared that war "make[s] the blood course through the veins" because, by compelling "women to work," it sends them "over the top . . . up the scaling-ladder, and out into 'All Man's Land.'" Similarly, women who were for the first time invited to work as nurses and ambulance drivers at the front itself, found their experiences exhilarating as well as painful the English novelist May Sinclair—an ambulance driver in Belgium—confided that "[you think] 'What a fool I would have been if I hadn't come. I wouldn't have missed this run for the world.'"

By the end of the war, the number of working women had increased by almost 50 percent in England, and seven hundred thousand of the women employed had directly replaced men in the work force; similar statistics obtained in the United States. In both countries, moreover, it was not only working-class women who delighted in new usefulness and prosperity; many a middle- or upper-class woman could rejoice with the English doctor Caroline Matthews, who asserted that because her medical services were needed at last, "life was worth living in those days." Prime Minister Asquith, repudiating his former opposition to women's suffrage, admitted that women "have aided in the most effective way in the prosecution of the war" while President Wilson declared that "the services of the women—services rendered in every sphere . . . wherever men have worked, and upon the very skirts and edges of the battle itself" should be rewarded with the full rights of citizenship.

There were a number of other ways in which the social disruption fostered by the war seemed also to help facilitate the liberation of women. Although nineteenth-century factory and farm workers had always had more freedom of movement than their upper-class counterparts, "war girls" were among the first "respectable" female groups in Western history who could stroll the public streets unescorted, go to theaters and dances without chaperones, and even travel on their own without incurring the suspicion that they were "fallen" women. In addition, such female workers were the first group to shed traditional women's costumes in significant numbers: though the American suffragist Amelia Bloomer had devised the divided skirt (known as "the bloomer") as early as 1850, that garment had only been a passing fad among radical freethinkers; now, however, impelled by the necessities of hard labor on the land, at the front, or in factories, most women shortened their skirts, and many took to wearing breeches or overalls. Even after the war, the trend they pioneered proved irreversible. As one historian has observed, flappers' clothing—short skirts, brassieres instead of corsets, silk stockings—"weighed one-tenth as much as [women's clothing] in the Victorian period."

To be sure, some of the most crucial social changes that marked women's lives in this era had already been set in motion by turn-of-the-century feminists; the birth-control movement as well as the free-love and child-care movements, for example, had prewar origins. Nevertheless, all three came to considerable prominence in the years between 1914 and 1921. The American nurse and birth-control advocate Margaret Sanger, for instance, founded a journal, *The Woman Rebel*, in 1914, designed to give working women advice on birth control, and in 1916 she established the first birth-control clinic in America. Also in 1916, the anarchist and free-love theorist Emma Goldman was arrested in New York for lecturing on birth control, while in England the suffragist and scientist Marie Stopes published her *Married Love*—a book offering contraceptive advice—in 1918, and in 1921 she opened a London birth-control clinic. Margaret Sanger summarized the long-standing feminist assumptions of all these women when she declared in *Woman and the New Race* (1920) that "the most far-reaching social development of modern times is the revolt of women against sex servitude."

Besides the advocacy of birth control, other elements of this revolt were agitation for communal child-care centers (and in some cases communal domestic centers) and proselytizing for free love or at least for the sort of egalitarian conjugal relationship that came to be called "companionate marriage." In 1914, the British feminist Sylvia Pankhurst opened a small nursery for the children of factory workers which became so successful that it was moved to a pub formerly called "The Gunmaker's Arms" and now renamed "The Mother's Arms." At around the same time, free-love advocates in England and the United States, ranging from the activist Emma Goldman and the writer Neith Boyce to self-proclaimed male feminists like Bertrand Russell and Floyd Dell, championed the cause of sexual liberation. In her *Hypatia* (1925), the British suffragist Dora Russell, wife of the

philosopher Bertrand Russell, declared that "sex, even without children and without marriage is . . . a thing of dignity, beauty, and delight."

Russell's view was distinctively new both in its departure from the Victorian ideal of what the scholar Nancy Cott has called female "passionlessness" and in its repudiation of the vision of male sexual brutality implicit in the writings of turn-of-the-century feminists like Charlotte Perkins Gilman. Yet this new view was quickly to become characteristic of an age marked by the publication of some of the earliest marriage manuals to emphasize female pleasure: not only Marie Stopes's *Married Love* but also Theodore Hendrik van de Velde's *Ideal Marriage: Its Physiology and Technique* (1928, trans. 1930) for the first time encouraged women, the way Dora Russell did, to experience sex as a "thing of . . . delight" rather than an act of submission, and as researchers subsequently discovered, countless women did just that. The psychologist Lewis Terman found in 1938 that among 777 middle-class wives, 74 percent of those born between 1890 and 1900 remained virgins until marriage, but only 31.7 percent of those born after 1910 did so.

What contributed to the unprecedented feelings of female autonomy that fostered such a new emphasis on women's sexual desires may, paradoxically enough, have been the fact that—in Virginia Woolf's phrase—"Professions for Women" seemed finally to have become seriously possible. The historian William Chafe has noted that in America during the first two decades of the twentieth century "female enrollment increased 1,000 per cent in public colleges and 485 per cent in private schools," and "the number of women employed in the professions increased by over 450,000 and in business by over 100,000." While the figures for England were not quite so dramatic, they were almost equally impressive to contemporary observers. Certainly, among activists, an increasing number seem to have been professional women. Of seventeen female contributors to a symposium on *These Modern Women* sponsored by *The Nation* in 1927–28, four had Ph.D.s, two were lawyers, one was an artist, one was a cartoonist, one was a politician, and three were journalists, while the editor of *The Nation*, Freda Kirchwey, was herself a successful professional woman. In addition, during these years a number of other professional women rose to national prominence on both sides of the Atlantic, including the anthropologists Margaret Mead, Ruth Benedict, and Zora Neale Hurston; the psychologists Lorine Pruette and Lillian Gilbreth; and the psychoanalysts Karen Horney, Helene Deutsch, and Melanie Klein.

Despite all these advances, however, the 1920s and 1930s saw the inauguration of, in the phrase of the literary critic Elaine Showalter, "feminism's awkward age." As Chafe has observed, the statistics representing American women's professional advances were misleading, for despite some gains, most career women tended to gravitate toward such traditionally "feminine" occupations as teaching and nursing, while the number of female medical students "actually diminished" between 1902–03 and 1926; in addition, women academicians rarely achieved the status of full professor, and "prospects for career women" actually "grew worse rather than better" during the economic difficulties of the 1930s. Similarly, many vocational opportunities for English women closed down in the postwar years, a fact for which some female workers wrongly tended to blame themselves. By 1925, moreover, the feminist movement had significantly disintegrated, for the suffragists' utopian expectation that the achievement of the vote would mark a turning point into a better world was proven wrong when most female voters either failed to register or, if they did vote, cast ballots for the candidates recommended by husbands and fathers. Many sometime suffragists discovered, too, that "anti-feminism" was, in the words of Rebecca West, "strikingly the correct fashion . . . among . . . the intellectuals" in this period.

Even the ideal of companionate marriage now appeared to collapse; a number of women realized, with Crystal Eastman, that a woman "wants work of her own"

but she also "wants husband, home, and children"—for whose care she was still obliged to bear primary responsibility—so that "how to reconcile these two desires in real life" was a perplexing question. As for the freedom of costume in which "war girls" had delighted, flappers learned that, as Sheila Rowbotham puts it, "going out to work in short skirts and fragile shoes was a problem," and the exhortations of a booming cosmetics industry along with the rise of "beauty parlors" threatened to turn even the most liberated New Woman back into a revised version of the living doll who had been the goal of her Victorian grandmother. Indeed, the masklike faces of movie stars like Mary Pickford, Jean Harlow, and Clara Bow symbolized a return to the artificial ideal of "femininity" that was rapidly replacing the assertive ideas of feminism.

Nevertheless, the dreams and demands of feminists from Mary Wollstonecraft to Elizabeth Cady Stanton still lived in some quarters. Virginia Woolf's *A Room of One's Own* (1929) was no doubt the most brilliant contemporary analysis of woman's situation, while her *Orlando* (1928)—with its portrait of a four-hundred-year-old heroine who changes her sex from male to female in the late seventeenth century—was probably the wittiest contemporary dramatization of the feminist desire to revise and reconstruct history as what some recent writers have called "herstory." But neither work was anomalous. From Elizabeth Robins's *Ancilla's Share* (1924) and Dora Russell's *Hypatia* (1925) to the feminist essays included in V. F. Calverton and Samuel Schmalhausen's *Woman's Coming of Age* (1931), women continued to express the wish for a transformed society. From Ray Strachey's *The Cause* (1928) to Mary Beard's *On Understanding Women* (1931), I. B. O'Malley's *Women in Subjection* (1933), and Winifred Holtby's *Women and a Changing Civilization* (1935), women historians—both amateurs and professionals—continued to excavate and reconstruct a feminist past. Furthermore, in spite of the setbacks that fragmented the women's movement in the 1920s and 1930s, all these thinkers would have agreed with Woolf that they *were* living astonishingly new lives. "Am I the Christian gentlewoman my mother slaved to make me?" asked the poet Genevieve Taggard, and answered her own question with vehemence: "No indeed. I am a poet, a wine-bibber, a radical; a non-churchgoer who will no longer sing in the choir or lead prayer-meeting with a testimonial." In the same vein, the politician Cornelia Bryce Pinchot declared that "my feminism tells me that woman can bear children, charm her lovers, boss a business, swim the Channel, stand at Armageddon and battle for the Lord—all in the day's work!"

FEMINISM AND MODERNISM: THE NEW WOMAN'S LITERARY HISTORY

The exuberance of feminists like Woolf and Russell, Taggard and Pinchot suggests that, although the women's movement per se had suffered a series of defeats in the 1920s, a significant number of individuals felt themselves to be in possession of a new source of strength, a source that did not entirely depend on the vagaries of contemporary politics. Given the concern with "herstory" that permeated the writings of so many theorists who continued to espouse the feminist cause in the face of increasingly widespread indifference or hostility, what seems to have functioned as a wellspring of energy was a new realization that women did have a history, and particularly a history of cultural achievement. "We think back through our mothers if we are women," wrote Virginia Woolf in *A Room of One's Own*, explaining that a crucial problem of early-nineteenth-century women novelists was "that they had no tradition behind them, or one so short and partial that it was of little help." Elsewhere, she contrasted her own situation with that of her literary ancestresses: "The road [to female literary accomplishment] was cut many years ago . . . many famous women, and many more unknown and forgotten have been before me, making the path smooth, and regulating my steps." In other words, the very existence of the nineteenth century's golden age of women's writing seems to have made a difference in Woolf's self-definition as a woman writer. For if women

had written, and written successfully, women could write, and it was no longer necessary to ask, with the eighteenth-century poet Anne Finch, "How are we fal'n? Fal'n by mistaken rules?" The poet or novelist "in" a woman was no longer what Aphra Behn had called "my masculine part"; rather, "it" was a powerful female self for whom Emily and Charlotte Brontë, Elizabeth Barrett Browning, and Emily Dickinson (as well as Finch and Behn themselves) provided patterns.

Of course, as the critic Harold Bloom has argued, the high achievements of literary precursors can in themselves constitute a source of anxiety for writers: Virginia Woolf and other literary women of her generation may well have wondered if their art could ever be as successful as the art of their great predecessors. In addition, women in Woolf's era had to contend with an intense male reaction not only against the present triumphs of suffragists but also against the past cultural achievements of women, whose history was now for the first time being adequately recounted. On balance, however, the records of women who had made the way "smooth" for Woolf and her peers seem to have been empowering rather than intimidating, and they seem to have persuaded writers of the teens, twenties, and thirties that any talented woman could be in Taggard's words, "a poet, a wine-bibber, a radical."

Perhaps, too, the distinction between women writers' exuberant recognition that they at last had a strong female past and men writers' anxiety about the turmoil of the present accounts for the subtle but significant ways in which the texts produced by the two sexes often differ in this period. To be sure, as in earlier periods, women worked in most of the same modes and genres as their male contemporaries. The popular novelists Edith Wharton, Willa Cather, Katharine Susannah Prichard, Dorothy Sayers, and Agatha Christie had their counterparts in Sinclair Lewis, F. Scott Fitzgerald, John Galsworthy, Ellery Queen, and Rex Stout. The fictional experiments of Gertrude Stein, Dorothy Richardson, Virginia Woolf, and Djuna Barnes paralleled the fictional experiments of James Joyce, D. H. Lawrence, Ernest Hemingway, and William Faulkner. Women poets who employed traditional forms and meters—Anna Wickham, Edna St. Vincent Millay, Eleanor Wylie, Ruth Pitter, and Anne Spencer—were matched by male poets who employed comparable strategies—John Masefield, Stephen Vincent Benét, Robert Frost, and Countee Cullen. Finally, women innovators in verse—H. D., Marianne Moore, and Edith Sitwell—were influenced by (and influenced) the experiments of male innovators—Ezra Pound, T. S. Eliot, and William Carlos Williams. Nevertheless, both in theme and in technique the works of modernist women in all four categories frequently swerved from the works of modernist men.

Popular women novelists and memoirists, for instance, ranging from the best-selling writers Wharton and Cather to the autobiographers Vera Brittain and the mystery writer Christie, were distinctly concerned to explore the dynamics, and often the triumphs, of female lives. In the modernist period, Wharton, who had criticized the social system that sacrificed her heroine Lily Bart in her early *The House of Mirth* (1905), moved increasingly toward an affirmation of female strength. Ellen Olenska, the heroine of Wharton's Pulitzer Prize–winning *The Age of Innocence* (1920), expatriates herself to Paris (as her author, too, did during these years) and becomes an emblem of independence for the book's self-imprisoned hero, Newland Archer. In *My Ántonia* (1918) Willa Cather—though she spoke through a male narrator and often wrote novels and stories with male protagonists (for instance, *Coming, Aphrodite!*)—explored the virtually matriarchal energies of Ántonia Shimerda Cusack, a pioneer woman whose genius for survival transforms her into a symbol of natural endurance and fertility. Working in a different mode and with entirely different materials, Vera Brittain developed a surprisingly similar theme: her *Testament of Youth* (1933), a memoir of the World War I years, recounted her discovery of her own capacities, her commitment to service in the world, and her ability to surmount the tragedies of the war. Even the detective story writers Sayers and Christie—women who might seem to have been

merely producing entertainment for a popular market—created and celebrated strong women characters: Sayers's Harriet Vane, the heroine of *Gaudy Night* (1935), a mystery set in one of Oxford's women's colleges, is at least as smart and tough as Lord Peter Wimsey, the novel's detective hero; while Christie's Miss Jane Marple, the brilliant detective heroine of a series of novels, is arguably smarter and tougher than Christie's detective hero Hercule Poirot, who is often portrayed as foppish and effete.

Women who composed more consciously experimental books elaborated similar ideas about female power. From Virginia Woolf and Katherine Mansfield to Gertrude Stein and Zora Neale Hurston, such artists excavated the lives and strengths of heroines and their ancestresses. Woolf's Clarissa Dalloway, the protagonist of her *Mrs. Dalloway*, and her Mrs. Ramsay, the mystical and mysterious mother in *To the Lighthouse* (1927), become emblems of independence and endurance as resonant as Ellen Olenska or Ántonia Cusack, while Mansfield's Mrs. Fairfield, the grandmother who presides over a group of fine stories about the author's New Zealand childhood, is equally energetic and inspiring. Similarly, the figure of St. Therese in Stein's libretto for the opera *Four Saints in Three Acts* (1927) is characterized as magically charismatic, and Janie, the heroine of Hurston's *Their Eyes Were Watching God* (1937), is depicted as a triumphant survivor. The artists who created these figures did not, however, limit themselves to portraying what we would today call "positive role models" for women. Rather, in literary essays and experiments they meditated on fundamental questions having to do with the nature of writing itself, questions that ranged from the kind of language a woman author inherited to the kinds of aesthetic traditions and conventions that were passed down to her.

In *A Room of One's Own*, for example, Woolf called for "a woman's sentence," a sentence that would be different from the "common sentence . . . [the] man's sentence" that female writers had learned from "Thackeray . . . Dickens, De Quincey," for, she observed, "the weight, the pace, the stride of a man's mind are too unlike" those of female minds for women "to lift anything substantial" from male precursors. Whether or not they had read Woolf's proposal, her contemporaries Dorothy Richardson, Gertrude Stein, and Djuna Barnes—writing in very different ways—attempted stylistic innovations that would meet the kind of need she expressed. *Pilgrimage*, Richardson's ambitious sequence of novels (published between 1915 and 1935), was composed in a freely flowing language that transcribed her heroine's stream of consciousness so effectively that Woolf thought this writer *had* "invented the psychological sentence of the feminine gender." In the meantime, Gertrude Stein, experimenting in Paris, sought to subvert the grammatical and narrative conventions of what she called "patriarchal poetry" by putting words together in an entirely unprecedented (and often enigmatic) fashion because, as she argued in *Composition as Explanation*, "composition is the difference which makes each and all of them then different from other generations." Less drastically but perhaps just as dramatically, Djuna Barnes, in *Nightwood* (1937) and other works, wrote in an ornate and archaic style, as if by doing so she could create a new ancestral past for herself and other women. In remaking language so that it might more accurately reflect female experience, while revising conventions so that female artists might, as Stein put it, "Reject" what was oppressive in tradition, "Rejoice" in what was possible for the future, and "Rejuvenate" what was stale in the present, all these writers were employing the experimental strategies of male modernists to achieve distinctively feminist goals.

Many of the women poets who were their contemporaries used a variety of techniques toward the same ends. The poets Wylie, Millay, Spencer, and Pitter, for instance—none of whom were consciously experimental—nevertheless emphasized women's experiences and female perspectives. The sonnet sequences of Millay and Wylie appropriated and revised a genre traditionally used by male writers to praise a female beloved in order to express the dreams and desires of a female

writer about a male beloved. Similarly, Spencer and Potter used apparently conventional forms to record the unconventional feelings of passionate women or to recount the case histories of obscure but unique heroines. As for the more experimental poets H. D., Marianne Moore, and Edith Sitwell, all quested with the same urgency that marked the work of writers like Woolf and Stein for styles and forms that would free them from the burdensome conventions infecting "patriarchal poetry." Each in her own way—Moore slyly and sardonically, Sitwell with jazzy exuberance, and H. D. through overt re-creations of matriarchal images as well as through inventive wordplay—sought to annihilate the inherited forms and formulas of tradition so as to release her individual talent.

Finally, then, while many feminist modernists worked to excavate a specifically female past, all modernist women, even those who were not consciously feminists, in some sense strove to bring into being what H. D. called in *Trilogy* "the unwritten book of the new." Besides manifesting itself in linguistic experimentation and in the development of uniquely female perspectives, moreover, that "book of the new" now included a number of unprecedentedly frank and forceful writings from artists working in the suddenly burgeoning lesbian tradition (including Radclyffe Hall and Amy Lowell), in a newly rich ethnic and working-class tradition (including Meridel Le Sueur and Anzia Yezierska), in a growing postcolonial tradition (including Jean Rhys and Katharine Susannah Prichard), and in a lively tradition of revisionary feminist mythmaking (including Isak Dinesen and Laura Riding Jackson).

As she so often did, Virginia Woolf summarized at least one aspect of the project on which so many of these artists were engaged. Toward the end of *A Room of One's Own*, she described a novel by an imaginary female author named Mary Carmichael, who had "broken the sequence" of traditional fiction because, instead of focusing on a conventional romance between hero and heroine, she had written about a friendship between two women: " 'Chloe liked Olivia,' I read," noted Woolf. 'And then it struck me how immense a change was there. Chloe liked Olivia perhaps for the first time in literature." Almost as significant, from Woolf's point of view, was the occupation that had fostered the new friendship of these two characters: "They shared a laboratory together." Entering the new world of the professions, as Woolf and many of her contemporaries saw, women were no longer to be primarily defined through their erotic relationships with men. Thus the task of the woman writer was, for the first time, the task of tracing the prospects and problems of an expanding female intellectual community. In 1932, in the first serious study of Virginia Woolf's work, the novelist and essayist Winifred Holtby summarized this point in a statement about the author of *A Room of One's Own* and *Mrs. Dalloway* that has resonant implications for our understanding of most female modernists: "When Virginia Woolf wrote of women," declared Holtby, "she wrote of a generation as adventurous in its exploration of experience as the Elizabethan men had been in their exploration of the globe. The women whom Mrs. Woolf knew were exploring the professional world, the political world, the world of business, discovering that they themselves had legs as well as wombs, brains as well as nerves, reason as well as sensibility; their Americas lay within themselves, and altered the map as profoundly as any added by Cabot or Columbus."

WILLA CATHER

1873–1947

Willa Cather's novels commemorate an obdurate, primordial landscape that had almost been erased by the time she began writing. Her fictional frontiers—the

shaggy midwestern plains of *O Pioneers!* (1913) or the cliffs, canyons, and caves of the Southwest in *The Professor's House* (1925)—evoke the grandeur of eternal, mysterious forces that call forth the exertions characteristic of her early settlers. But the pioneer is only one type of the determined, willful character who absorbed Cather throughout her highly successful career. Another is the artist, whom she portrayed first in the opera singer of *The Song of the Lark* (1915) and later in the actresses and vocalists of *Coming, Aphrodite!* (1920), *My Mortal Enemy* (1926), and *Lucy Gayheart* (1940). Whether she focused on pioneering settlers or pioneering artists, however, Cather was frequently drawn to powerful female figures.

Possibly the most momentous event in Cather's early life was the move from Virginia to Nebraska that her family undertook in 1883. For her first nine years, she lived in a spacious, three-story, brick farmhouse near Winchester, Virginia. Wilella Cather was the first of seven children born to Charles Cather, an easygoing farmer who turned to real estate in later life, and Mary Virginia (Boak) Cather, an imperious woman remembered with some ambivalence by her daughter. But Willie, as she liked to call herself, was primarily educated by her maternal grandmother, whose portrait she lovingly drew in the short story *Old Mrs. Harris* (1932). When the family moved to Webster County, Nebraska, Cather must have experienced the same shock at the primitive sod houses and the ice-encrusted wilderness that her narrator Jim Burden expresses in *My Ántonia* (1918). Less a country than the vast "material out of which countries are made," the land on which her family settled was, in her own words, "naked as the back of your hand."

Like Jim, too, when Cather moved with her family to neighboring Red Cloud, a town of twenty-five hundred situated on the Burlington railroad line, she identified with other uprooted immigrants: Swedish, Bohemian, and Russian settlers struggling to make a new life in the New World while preserving the cultural traditions of the old world. In school at Red Cloud, as Sharon O'Brien has shown, Cather frequently dressed in boyish clothes, dreamed of becoming William Cather, M.D., and began equating artistry with masculinity. At home she read widely in British and American literature in her parents' library and in French and German translations at her neighbors'. At the University of Nebraska in Lincoln, she began studying the classics while publishing her writing in the undergraduate literary magazine. Before and after graduation in 1895, she reviewed cultural events for the Lincoln newspaper and then moved to Pittsburgh to edit the *Home Monthly* magazine for another year.

Cather's personal life during her ten-year residence in Pittsburgh is no less shrouded in obscurity than her later life in New York, because she burned as many of her letters as she could and because in her will she forbade publication of the surviving letters. Her biographers James Woodress and Leon Edel have argued, however, that what saved Cather from loneliness in those years was her relationship with Isabelle McClung. This daughter of a conservative Pittsburgh judge invited Cather to live in her house, where the two shared a bedroom. Cather began writing her fiction in an attic room in the McClung house, but she continued to work at the *Pittsburgh Daily Leader*. As music, drama, and book reviewer, Cather wrote about the Pittsburgh symphony's performance of Dvořák's *New World Symphony*, Helen Modjeska's acting in *Mary Stuart*, and Kate Chopin's predilection for romanticism in *The Awakening*. As a freelance artist, she composed the verse that would appear in *April Twilights* (1903) and the stories collected in *The Troll Garden* (1905).

In 1906 Cather moved to New York to join the staff of *McClure's Magazine*. An assignment in Boston led to a meaningful friendship with Sarah Orne Jewett: in subsequent essays, Cather praised Jewett's sparse but evocative prose style, a style she would strive toward in her own later fiction. In New York, Cather lived in a studio apartment at 60 South Washington Square, a building that also housed the woman who would become her lifelong companion, Edith Lewis. Cather decided

to resign as managing editor of *McClure's* after her first novel, *Alexander's Bridge*, was serialized in the 1912 issues. From the architect Alexander, she moved on to the pioneer Alexandra in her next novel, *O Pioneers!*, which she dedicated to Jewett. Although Cather wrote both *O Pioneers!* and *The Song of the Lark* during stays in Isabelle McClung's house, by 1913 she had moved to 5 Bank Street with Edith Lewis. Cather was apparently extremely upset at Isabelle McClung's decision to marry in 1915. Yet she and Edith Lewis had already become close friends. Indeed, they had embarked on a series of trips to the Southwest, which would shape the writer's novels.

My *Ántonia*, the next novel Cather composed, was strongly autobiographical. Although it presents her memories of her Nebraskan childhood through a male narrator, its main subject is Ántonia, a female character who heroically survives the suicide of her father, arduous farm work, town employment as a hired girl, and an illegitimate pregnancy, to become "a rich mine of life, like the founders of early races." The tension between Ántonia's sturdy earthiness and Jim Burden's commitment to the sophistication and learning he associates with the East would inform a number of Cather's finest stories as well as later works like her Pulitzer Prize–winning war novel, *One of Ours* (1922). Yet, although she was gaining a literary reputation, Cather was becoming disillusioned with modern life. "The world was broken in two in 1922 or thereabouts," she wrote in her collected essays, *Not under Forty* (1936), expressing her distress over poor health, her disappointment about her books' receptions, and her growing contempt for contemporary values. From this point on, she would turn with nostalgia to historically remote periods.

Later novels like *The Professor's House* (1925), *Death Comes for the Archbishop* (1927), and *Shadows on the Rock* (1931) continue to explore the individual's withdrawal from society, frequently depicting a quest for integrity through male characters who are often placed in a Catholic context. Typical in this respect are the European missionaries in New Mexico of *Death Comes for the Archbishop* and the seventeenth-century French Canadian settlers of *Shadows on the Rock*. With her last novel, however, Cather returned to the questions about female identity that had absorbed her earlier in her career. *Sapphira and the Slave Girl* (1940) focuses on the Shenandoah Valley of the writer's early childhood and on the reconciliation of a domineering mother with her equally willful daughter. As in Cather's earlier fiction, romantic plot elements are far less important than suggestive tableaux in which the self is tested and shaped by experience.

Cather had already received a number of honorary degrees and literary prizes when, in 1937, she prepared a complete edition of her works for Scribner's. *Coming, Aphrodite!*, which appeared in her collection *Youth and the Bright Medusa*, integrates mythic material and social analysis to explore both the triumphs and the irrevocable personal costs of the artistic ambition that clearly propelled her own career.

Coming, Aphrodite!¹

I

Don Hedger had lived for four years on the top floor of an old house on the south side of Washington Square,² and nobody had ever disturbed him. He occupied one big room with no outside exposure except on the north, where he had built in a many-paned studio window that looked upon a court and upon the roofs and walls of other buildings. His room was very cheerless, since he never got a ray of direct sunlight; the south corners were always in shadow.

1. The Greek goddess of love. 2. In the Greenwich Village section of New York City.

In one of the corners was a clothes closet, built against the partition, in another a wide divan, serving as a seat by day and a bed by night. In the front corner, the one farther from the window, was a sink, and a table with two gas burners where he sometimes cooked his food. There, too, in the perpetual dusk, was the dog's bed, and often a bone or two for his comfort.

The dog was a Boston bull terrier, and Hedger explained his surly disposition by the fact that he had been bred to the point where it told on his nerves. His name was Caesar III, and he had taken prizes at very exclusive dog shows. When he and his master went out to prowl about University Place or to promenade along West Street, Caesar III was invariably fresh and shining. His pink skin showed through his mottled coat, which glistened as if it had just been rubbed with olive oil, and he wore a brass-studded collar, bought at the smartest saddler's. Hedger, as often as not, was hunched up in an old striped blanket coat, with a shapeless felt hat pulled over his bushy hair, wearing black shoes that had become gray, or brown ones that had become black, and he never put on gloves unless the day was biting cold.

Early in May, Hedger learned that he was to have a new neighbor in the rear apartment—two rooms, one large and one small, that faced the west. His studio was shut off from the larger of these rooms by double doors, which, though they were fairly tight, left him a good deal at the mercy of the occupant. The rooms had been leased, long before he came there, by a trained nurse who considered herself knowing in old furniture. She went to auction sales and bought up mahogany and dirty brass and stored it away here, where she meant to live when she retired from nursing. Meanwhile, she sublet her rooms, with their precious furniture, to young people who came to New York to "write" or to "paint"—who proposed to live by the sweat of the brow rather than of the hand, and who desired artistic surroundings. When Hedger first moved in, these rooms were occupied by a young man who tried to write plays,—and who kept on trying until a week ago, when the nurse had put him out for unpaid rent.

A few days after the playwright left, Hedger heard an ominous murmur of voices through the bolted double doors: the lady-like intonation of the nurse—doubtless exhibiting her treasures—and another voice, also a woman's, but very different; young, fresh, unguarded, confident. All the same, it would be very annoying to have a woman in there. The only bath-room on the floor was at the top of the stairs in the front hall, and he would always be running into her as he came or went from his bath. He would have to be more careful to see that Caesar didn't leave bones about the hall, too; and she might object when he cooked steak and onions on his gas burner.

As soon as the talking ceased and the women left, he forgot them. He was absorbed in a study of paradise fish at the Aquarium, staring out at people through the glass and green water of their tank. It was a highly gratifying idea; the incommunicability of one stratum of animal life with another,—though Hedger pretended it was only an experiment in unusual lighting. When he heard trunks knocking against the sides of the narrow hall, then he realized that she was moving in at once. Toward noon, groans and deep gasps and the creaking of ropes, made him aware that a piano was arriving. After the tramp of the movers died away down the stairs, somebody touched off a few scales and chords on the instrument, and then there was peace. Presently he heard her lock her door and go down the hall humming something; going out to

lunch, probably. He stuck his brushes in a can of turpentine and put on his hat, not stopping to wash his hands. Caesar was smelling along the crack under the bolted doors; his bony tail stuck out hard as a hickory withe, and the hair was standing up about his elegant collar.

Hedger encouraged him. "Come along, Caesar. You'll soon get used to a new smell."

In the hall stood an enormous trunk, behind the ladder that led to the roof, just opposite Hedger's door. The dog flew at it with a growl of hurt amazement. They went down three flights of stairs and out into the brilliant May afternoon.

Behind the Square, Hedger and his dog descended into a basement oyster house where there were no tablecloths on the tables and no handles on the coffee cups, and the floor was covered with sawdust, and Caesar was always welcome,—not that he needed any such precautionary flooring. All the carpets of Persia would have been safe for him. Hedger ordered steak and onions absentmindedly, not realizing why he had an apprehension that this dish might be less readily at hand hereafter. While he ate, Caesar sat beside his chair, gravely disturbing the sawdust with his tail.

After lunch Hedger strolled about the Square for the dog's health and watched the stages[3] pull out;—that was almost the very last summer of the old horse stages on Fifth Avenue. The fountain had but lately begun operations for the season and was throwing up a mist of rainbow water which now and then blew south and sprayed a bunch of Italian babies that were being supported on the outer rim by older, very little older, brothers and sisters. Plump robins were hopping about on the soil; the grass was newly cut and blindingly green. Looking up the Avenue through the Arch, one could see the young poplars with their bright, sticky leaves, and the Brevoort[4] glistening in its spring coat of paint, and shining horses and carriages,—occasionally an automobile, mis-shapen and sullen, like an ugly threat in a stream of things that were bright and beautiful and alive.

While Caesar and his master were standing by the fountain, a girl approached them, crossing the Square. Hedger noticed her because she wore a lavender cloth suit and carried in her arms a big bunch of fresh lilacs. He saw that she was young and handsome,—beautiful, in fact, with a splendid figure and good action. She, too, paused by the fountain and looked back through the Arch up the Avenue. She smiled rather patronizingly as she looked, and at the same time seemed delighted. Her slowly curving upper lip and half-closed eyes seemed to say: "You're gay, you're exciting, you are quite the right sort of thing; but you're none too fine for me!"

In the moment she tarried, Caesar stealthily approached her and sniffed at the hem of her lavender skirt, then, when she went south like an arrow, he ran back to his master and lifted a face full of emotion and alarm, his lower lip twitching under his sharp white teeth and his hazel eyes pointed with a very definite discovery. He stood thus, motionless, while Hedger watched the lavender girl go up the steps and through the door of the house in which he lived.

"You're right, my boy, it's she! She might be worse looking, you know."

When they mounted to the studio, the new lodger's door, at the back of the

3. Public horse-drawn vehicles. 4. A fashionable hotel.

hall, was a little ajar, and Hedger caught the warm perfume of lilacs just brought in out of the sun. He was used to the musty smell of the old hall carpet. (The nurse-lessee had once knocked at his studio door and complained that Caesar must be somewhat responsible for the particular flavor of that mustiness, and Hedger had never spoken to her since.) He was used to the old smell, and he preferred it to that of the lilacs, and so did his companion, whose nose was so much more discriminating. Hedger shut his door vehemently, and fell to work.

Most young men who dwell in obscure studios in New York have had a beginning, come out of something, have somewhere a home town, a family, a paternal roof. But Don Hedger had no such background. He was a foundling, and had grown up in a school for homeless boys, where book-learning was a negligible part of the curriculum. When he was sixteen, a Catholic priest took him to Greensburg, Pennsylvania, to keep house for him. The priest did something to fill in the large gaps in the boy's education,—taught him to like "Don Quixote" and "The Golden Legend,"[5] and encouraged him to mess with paints and crayons in his room up under the slope of the mansard. When Don wanted to go to New York to study at the Art League, the priest got him a night job as packer in one of the big department stores. Since then, Hedger had taken care of himself; that was his only responsibility. He was singularly unencumbered; had no family duties, no social ties, no obligations toward any one but his landlord. Since he travelled light, he had travelled rather far. He had got over a good deal of the earth's surface, in spite of the fact that he never in his life had more than three hundred dollars ahead at any one time, and he had already outlived a succession of convictions and revelations about his art.

Though he was now but twenty-six years old, he had twice been on the verge of becoming a marketable product; once through some studies of New York streets he did for a magazine, and once through a collection of pastels he brought home from New Mexico, which Remington,[6] then at the height of his popularity, happened to see, and generously tried to push. But on both occasions Hedger decided that this was something he didn't wish to carry further,—simply the old thing over again and got nowhere,—so he took enquiring dealers experiments in a "later manner," that made them put him out of the shop. When he ran short of money, he could always get any amount of commercial work; he was an expert draughtsman and worked with lightning speed. The rest of his time he spent in groping his way from one kind of painting into another, or travelling about without luggage, like a tramp, and he was chiefly occupied with getting rid of ideas he had once thought very fine.

Hedger's circumstances, since he had moved to Washington Square, were affluent compared to anything he had ever known before. He was now able to pay advance rent and turn the key on his studio when he went away for four months at a stretch. It didn't occur to him to wish to be richer than this. To be sure, he did without a great many things other people think necessary, but he didn't miss them, because he had never had them. He belonged to no clubs, visited no houses, had no studio friends, and he ate his dinner alone in some decent little restaurant, even on Christmas and New Year's. For days together he talked to nobody but his dog and the janitress and the lame oysterman.

5. A poem of medieval chivalry by Henry Wadsworth Longfellow (1807–1882). "Don Quixote": the famous novel of an aging knight longing for adventure, by Miguel de Cervantes (1547–1616).
6. Frederic Remington (1861–1909), popular American painter.

After he shut the door and settled down to his paradise fish on that first Tuesday in May, Hedger forgot all about his new neighbor. When the light failed, he took Caesar out for a walk. On the way home he did his marketing on West Houston Street, with a one-eyed Italian woman who always cheated him. After he had cooked his beans and scallopini, and drank half a bottle of Chianti, he put his dishes in the sink and went up on the roof to smoke. He was the only person in the house who ever went to the roof, and he had a secret understanding with the janitress about it. He was to have ' the privilege of the roof," as she said, if he opened the heavy trapdoor on sunny days to air out the upper hall, and was watchful to close it when rain threatened. Mrs. Foley was fat and forty and hated to climb stairs,—besides, the roof was reached by a perpendicular iron ladder, definitely inaccessible to a woman of her bulk, and the iron door at the top of it was too heavy for any but Hedger's stong arm to lift. Hedger was not above medium height, but he practiced with weights and dumb-bells, and in the shoulders he was as strong as a gorilla.

So Hedger had the roof to himself. He and Caesar often slept up there on hot nights, rolled in blankets he had brought home from Arizona. He mounted with Caesar under his left arm. The dog had never learned to climb a perpendicular ladder, and never did he feel so much his master's greatness and his own dependence upon him, as when he crept under his arm for this perilous ascent. Up there was even gravel to scratch in and a dog could do whatever he liked, so long as he did not bark. It was a kind of Heaven, which no one was strong enough to reach but his great paint-smelling master.

On this blue May night there was a slender girlish looking young moon in the west, playing with a whole company of silver stars. Now and then one of them darted away from the ground and shot off into the gauzy blue with a soft little trail of light, like laughter. Hedger and his dog were delighted when a star did this. They were quite lost in watching the glittering game, when they were suddenly diverted by a sound,—not from the stars, though it was music. It was not the Prologue to Pagliacci,[7] which rose ever and anon on hot evenings from an Italian tenement on Thompson Street. with the gasps of the corpulent baritone who got behind it; nor was it the hurdy-gurdy[8] man, who often played at the corner in the balmy twilight. No, this was a woman's voice, singing the tempestuous, over-lapping phrases of Signor Puccini,[9] then comparatively new in the world, but already so popular that even Hedger recognized his un-mistakable gusts of breath. He looked about over the roofs; all was blue and still, with the well-built chimneys that were never used now standing up dark and mournful. He moved softly toward the yellow quadrangle where the gas from the hall shone up through the half-lifted trapdoor. Oh yes! It came up through the hole like a strong draught, a big, beautiful voice, and it sounded rather like a professional's. A piano had arrived in the morning, Hedger re-membered. This might be a very great nuisance. It would be pleasant enough to listen to, if you could turn it on and off as you wished; but you couldn't. Caesar, with the gas light shining on his collar and his ugly but sensitive face, panted and looked up for information. Hedger put down a reassuring hand.

"I don't know. We can't tell yet. It may not be so bad."

He stayed on the roof until all was still below, and finally descended, with

7. Popular Italian opera by Ruggiero Leoncavallo (1858–1919).

8. Portable instrument that plays popular tunes when a crank is turned.

9. Giacomo Puccini (1858–1924), popular Italian opera composer.

quite a new feeling about his neighbor. Her voice, like her figure, inspired re-
spect,—if one did not choose to call it admiration. Her door was shut, the
transom was dark; nothing remained of her but the obtrusive trunk, unright-
fully taking up room in the narrow hall.

II

For two days Hedger didn't see her. He was painting eight hours a day just
then, and only went out to hunt for food. He noticed that she practiced scales
and exercises for about an hour in the morning; then she locked her door, went
humming down the hall, and left him in peace. He heard her getting her cof-
fee ready at about the same time he got his. Earlier still, she passed his room
on her way to her bath. In the evening she sometimes sang, but on the whole
she didn't bother him. When he was working well he did not notice anything
much. The morning paper lay before his door until he reached out for his milk
bottle, then he kicked the sheet inside and it lay on the floor until evening.
Sometimes he read it and sometimes he did not. He forgot there was anything
of importance going on in the world outside of his third floor studio. Nobody
had ever taught him that he ought to be interested in other people; in the
Pittsburgh steel strike, in the Fresh Air Fund,[1] in the scandal about the Babies'
Hospital. A gray wolf, living in a Wyoming canyon, would hardly have been
less concerned about these things than was Don Hedger.

One morning he was coming out of the bath-room at the front end of the
hall, having just given Caesar his bath and rubbed him into a glow with a
heavy towel. Before the door, lying in wait for him, as it were, stood a tall figure
in a flowing blue silk dressing gown that fell away from her marble arms. In her
hands she carried various accessories of the bath.

"I wish," she said distinctly, standing in his way, "I wish you wouldn't wash
your dog in the tub. I never heard of such a thing! I've found his hair in the
tub, and I've smelled a doggy smell, and now I've caught you at it. It's an out-
rage!"

Hedger was badly frightened. She was so tall and positive, and was fairly
blazing with beauty and anger. He stood blinking, holding on to his sponge
and dog-soap, feeling that he ought to bow very low to her. But what he actu-
ally said was:

"Nobody has ever objected before. I always wash the tub,—and, anyhow,
he's cleaner than most people."

"Cleaner than me?" her eyebrows went up, her white arms and neck and her
fragrant person seemed to scream at him like a band of outraged nymphs.
Something flashed through his mind about a man who was turned into a dog,
or was pursued by dogs, because he unwittingly intruded upon the bath of
beauty.[2]

"No, I didn't mean that," he muttered, turning scarlet under the bluish
stubble of his muscular jaws. "But I know he's cleaner than I am."

"That I don't doubt!" Her voice sounded like a soft shivering of crystal, and
with a smile of pity she drew the folds of her voluminous blue robe close about
her and allowed the wretched man to pass. Even Caesar was frightened; he

1. New York charity that sends city children to the country.
2. In Greek myth, the hunter Actaeon was punished by the goddess Artemis when he spied on her while she was bathing; he was turned into a stag and torn apart by his own hounds.

darted like a streak down the hall, through the door and to his own bed in the corner among the bones.

Hedger stood still in the doorway, listening to indignant sniffs and coughs and a great swishing of water about the sides of the tub. He had washed it; but as he had washed it with Caesar's sponge, it was quite possible that a few bristles remained; the dog was shedding now. The playwright had never objected, nor had the jovial illustrator who occupied the front apartment,—but he, as he admitted, "was usually pye-eyed,[3] when he wasn't in Buffalo." He went home to Buffalo sometimes to rest his nerves.

It had never occurred to Hedger that any one would mind using the tub after Caesar;—but then, he had never seen a beautiful girl caparisoned[4] for the bath before. As soon as he beheld her standing there, he realized the unfitness of it. For that matter, she ought not to step into a tub that any other mortal had bathed in; the illustrator was sloppy and left cigarette ends on the moulding.

All morning as he worked he was gnawed by a spiteful desire to get back at her. It rankled that he had been so vanquished by her disdain. When he heard her locking her door to go out for lunch, he stepped quickly into the hall in his messy painting coat, and addressed her.

"I don't wish to be exigent, Miss,"—he had certain grand words that he used upon occasion—"but if this is your trunk, it's rather in the way here."

"Oh, very well!" she exclaimed carelessly, dropping her keys into her handbag. "I'll have it moved when I can get a man to do it," and she went down the hall with her free, roving stride.

Her name, Hedger discovered from her letters, which the postman left on the table in the lower hall, was Eden Bower.

III

In the closet that was built against the partition separating his room from Miss Bower's, Hedger kept all his wearing apparel, some of it on hooks and hangers, some of it on the floor. When he opened his closet door now-a-days, little dust-colored insects flew out on downy wing, and he suspected that a brood of moths were hatching in his winter overcoat. Mrs. Foley, the janitress, told him to bring down all his heavy clothes and she would give them a beating and hang them in the court. The closet was in such disorder that he shunned the encounter, but one hot afternoon he set himself to the task. First he threw out a pile of forgotten laundry and tied it up in a sheet. The bundle stood as high as his middle when he had knotted the corners. Then he got his shoes and overshoes together. When he took his over-coat from its place against the partition, a long ray of yellow light shot across the dark enclosure,—a knot hole, evidently, in the high wainscoating of the west room. He had never noticed it before, and without realizing what he was doing, he stooped and squinted through it.

Yonder, in a pool of sunlight, stood his new neighbor, wholly unclad, doing exercises of some sort before a long gilt mirror. Hedger did not happen to think how unpardonable it was of him to watch her. Nudity was not improper to any one who had worked so much from the figure, and he continued to look, sim-

3. Drunk. 4. Adorned.

ply because he had never seen a woman's body so beautiful as this one,—positively glorious in action. As she swung her arms and changed from one pivot of motion to another, muscular energy seemed to flow through her from her toes to her finger-tips. The soft flush of exercise and the gold of afternoon sun played over her flesh together, enveloped her in a luminous mist which, as she turned and twisted, made now an arm, now a shoulder, now a thigh, dissolve in pure light and instantly recover its outline with the next gesture. Hedger's fingers curved as if he were holding a crayon; mentally he was doing the whole figure in a single running line, and the charcoal seemed to explode in his hand at the point where the energy of each gesture was discharged into the whirling disc of light, from a foot or shoulder, from the up-thrust chin or the lifted breasts.

He could not have told whether he watched her for six minutes or sixteen. When her gymnastics were over, she paused to catch up a lock of hair that had come down, and examined with solicitude a little reddish mole that grew under her left arm-pit. Then, with her hand on her hip, she walked unconcernedly across the room and disappeared through the door into her bed-chamber.

Disappeared—Don Hedger was crouching on his knees, staring at the golden shower which poured in through the west windows, at the lake of gold sleeping on the faded Turkish carpet. The spot was enchanted; a vision out of Alexandria, out of the remote pagan past, had bathed itself there in Helianthine fire.[5]

When he crawled out of his closet, he stood blinking at the gray sheet stuffed with laundry, not knowing what had happened to him. He felt a little sick as he contemplated the bundle. Everything here was different; he hated the disorder of the place, the gray prison light, his old shoes and himself and all his slovenly habits. The black calico curtains that ran on wires over his big window were white with dust. There were three greasy frying pans in the sink, and the sink itself— He felt desperate. He couldn't stand this another minute. He took up an armful of winter clothes and ran down four flights into the basement.

"Mrs. Foley," he began, "I want my room cleaned this afternoon, thoroughly cleaned. Can you get a woman for me right away?"

"Is it company you're having?" the fat, dirty janitress enquired. Mrs. Foley was the widow of a useful Tammany man, and she owned real estate in Flatbush.[6] She was huge and soft as a feather bed. Her face and arms were permanently coated with dust, grained like wood where the sweat had trickled.

"Yes, company. That's it."

"Well, this is a queer time of the day to be asking for a cleaning woman. It's likely I can get you old Lizzie, if she's not drunk. I'll send Willy round to see."

Willy, the son of fourteen, roused from the stupor and stain of his fifth box of cigarettes by the gleam of a quarter, went out. In five minutes he returned with old Lizzie,—she smelling strong of spirits and wearing several jackets which she had put on one over the other, and a number of skirts, long and short, which made her resemble an animated dish-clout. She had, of course, to borrow her equipment from Mrs. Foley, and toiled up the long flights, drag-

5. Fire of the sun.
6. Section of Brooklyn. "Tammany man": i.e., member of the corrupt New York political organization.

ging mop and pail and broom. She told Hedger to be of good cheer, for he had
got the right woman for the job, and showed him a great leather strap she wore
about her wrist to prevent dislocation of tendons. She swished about the
place, scattering dust and splashing soapsuds, while he watched her in ner-
vous despair. He stood over Lizzie and made her scour the sink, directing her
roughly, then paid her and got rid of her. Shutting the door on his failure, he
hurried off with his dog to lose himself among the stevedores and dock labor-
ers on West Street.

A strange chapter began for Don Hedger Day after day, at that hour in the
afternoon, the hour before his neighbor dressed for dinner, he crouched down
in his closet to watch her go through her mysterious exercises. It did not occur
to him that his conduct was detestable; there was nothing shy or retreating
about this unclad girl,—a bold body, studying itself quite coolly and evidently
well pleased with itself, doing all this for a purpose Hedger scarcely regarded
his action as conduct at all; it was something that had happened to him. More
than once he went out and tried to stay away for the whole afternoon, but at
about five o'clock he was sure to find himself among his old shoes in the dark.
The pull of that aperture was stronger than his will,—and he had always con-
sidered his will the strongest thing about him. When she threw herself upon
the divan and lay resting, he still stared, holding his breath. His nerves were so
on edge that a sudden noise made him start and brought out the sweat on his
forehead. The dog would come and tug at his sleeve, knowing that something
was wrong with his master. If he attempted a mournful whine, those strong
hands closed about his throat.

When Hedger came slinking out of his closet, he sat down on the edge of
the couch, sat for hours without moving. He was not painting at all now. This
thing, whatever it was, drank him up as ideas had sometimes done, and he
sank into a stupor of idleness as deep and dark as the stupor of work. He could
not understand it; he was no boy, he had worked from models for years, and a
woman's body was no mystery to him. Yet now he did nothing but sit and
think about one. He slept very little, and with the first light of morning he
awoke as completely possessed by this woman as if he had been with her all the
night before. The unconscious operations of life went on in him only to per-
petuate this excitement. His brain held but one image now—vibrated, burned
with it. It was a heathenish feeling; without friendliness, almost without ten-
derness.

Women had come and gone in Hedger's life. Not having had a mother to
begin with, his relations with them, whether amorous or friendly, had been ca-
sual. He got on well with janitresses and wash-women, with Indians and with
the peasant women of foreign countries. He had friends among the silk-skirt
factory girls who came to eat their lunch in Washington Square, and he some-
times took a model for a day in the country. He felt an unreasoning antipathy
toward the well-dressed women he saw coming out of big shops, or driving in
the Park. If, on his way to the Art Museum, he noticed a pretty girl standing on
the steps of one of the houses on upper Fifth Avenue, he frowned at her and
went by with his shoulders hunched up as if he were cold. He had never known
such girls, or heard them talk, or seen the inside of the houses in which they
lived; but he believed them all to be artificial and, in an aesthetic sense, per-
verted. He saw them enslaved by desire of merchandise and manufactured
articles, effective only in making life complicated and insincere and in em-

broidering it with ugly and meaningless trivialities. They were enough, he thought, to make one almost forget woman as she existed in art, in thought, and in the universe.

He had no desire to know the woman who had, for the time at least, so broken up his life,—no curiosity about her every-day personality. He shunned any revelation of it, and he listened for Miss Bower's coming and going, not to encounter, but to avoid her. He wished that the girl who wore shirt-waists and got letters from Chicago would keep out of his way, that she did not exist. With her he had naught to make. But in a room full of sun, before an old mirror, on a little enchanted rug of sleeping colors, he had seen a woman who emerged naked through a door, and disappeared naked. He thought of that body as never having been clad, or as having worn the stuffs and dyes of all the centuries but his own. And for him she had no geographical associations; unless with Crete, or Alexandria, or Veronese's[7] Venice. She was the immortal conception, the perennial theme.

The first break in Hedger's lethargy occurred one afternoon when two young men came to take Eden Bower out to dine. They went into her music room, laughed and talked for a few minutes, and then took her away with them. They were gone a long while, but he did not go out for food himself; he waited for them to come back. At last he heard them coming down the hall, gayer and more talkative than when they left. One of them sat down at the piano, and they all began to sing. This Hedger found absolutely unendurable. He snatched up his hat and went running down the stairs. Caesar leaped beside him, hoping that old times were coming back. They had supper in the oysterman's basement and then sat down in front of their own doorway. The moon stood full over the Square, a thing of regal glory; but Hedger did not see the moon; he was looking, murderously, for men. Presently two, wearing straw hats and white trousers and carrying canes, came down the steps from his house. He rose and dogged them across the Square. They were laughing and seemed very much elated about something. As one stopped to light a cigarette, Hedger caught from the other:

"Don't you think she has a beautiful talent?"

His companion threw away his match. "She has a beautiful figure." They both ran to catch the stage.

Hedger went back to his studio. The light was shining from her transom. For the first time he violated her privacy at night, and peered through that fatal aperture. She was sitting fully dressed, in the window, smoking a cigarette and looking out over the housetops. He watched her until she rose, looked about her with a disdainful, crafty smile, and turned out the light.

The next morning, when Miss Bower went out Hedger followed her. Her white skirt gleamed ahead of him as she sauntered about the Square. She sat down behind the Garibaldi[8] statue and opened a music book she carried. She turned the leaves carelessly, and several times glanced in his direction. He was on the point of going over to her, when she rose quickly and looked up at the sky. A flock of pigeons had risen from somewhere in the crowded Italian quarter to the south, and were wheeling rapidly up through the morning air, soaring and dropping, scattering and coming together, now gray, now white as

7. Paolo Veronese (1528–1588), Venetian painter.
8. Giuseppe Garibaldi (1807–1882), Italian patriot and champion of independence.

silver, as they caught or intercepted the sunlight. She put up her hand to shade her eyes and followed them with a kind of defiant delight in her face.

Hedger came and stood beside her. "You've surely seen them before?"

"Oh, yes," she replied, still looking up. "I see them every day from my windows. They always come home about five o'clock. Where do they live?"

"I don't know. Probably some Italian raises them for the market. They were here long before I came, and I've been here four years."

"In that same gloomy room? Why didn't you take mine when it was vacant?"

"It isn't gloomy. That's the best light for painting."

"Oh, is it? I don't know anything about painting. I'd like to see your pictures sometime. You have such a lot in there. Don't they get dusty, piled up against the wall like that?"

"Not very. I'd be glad to show them to you. Is your name really Eden Bower? I've seen your letters on the table."

"Well, it's the name I'm going to sing under. My father's name is Bowers, but my friend Mr. Jones, a Chicago newspaper man who writes about music, told me to drop the 's.' He's crazy about my voice."

Miss Bower didn't usually tell the whole story,—about anything. Her first name, when she lived in Huntington, Illinois was Edna, but Mr. Jones had persuaded her to change it to one which he felt would be worthy of her future. She was quick to take suggestions, though she told him she "didn't see what was the matter with 'Edna.' "

She explained to Hedger that she was going to Paris to study. She was waiting in New York for Chicago friends who were to take her over but who had been detained. "Did you study in Paris?" she asked.

"No, I've never been in Paris. But I was in the south of France all last summer, studying with C——.[9] He's the biggest man among the moderns,—at least I think so."

Miss Bower sat down and made room for him on the bench. "Do tell me about it. I expected to be there by this time, and I can't wait to find out what it's like."

Hedger began to relate how he had seen some of this Frenchman's work in an exhibition, and deciding at once that this was the man for him, he had taken a boat for Marseilles the next week going over steerage. He proceeded at once to the little town on the coast where his painter lived, and presented himself. The man never took pupils, but because Hedger had come so far he let him stay. Hedger lived at the master's house and every day they went out together to paint, sometimes on the blazing rocks down by the sea. They wrapped themselves in light woollen blankets and didn't feel the heat. Being there and working with C—— was being in Paradise, Hedger concluded; he learned more in three months than in all his life before.

Eden Bower laughed. "You're a funny fellow. Didn't you do anything but work? Are the women very beautiful? Did you have awfully good things to eat and drink?"

Hedger said some of the women were fine looking, especially one girl who went about selling fish and lobsters. About the food there was nothing remarkable,—except the ripe figs, he liked those. They drank sour wine, and

9. Perhaps a reference to French painter Paul Cézanne (1839–1906).

used goat-butter, which was strong and full of hair, as it was churned in a goat skin.

"But don't they have parties or banquets? Aren't there any fine hotels down there?"

"Yes, but they are all closed in summer, and the country people are poor. It's a beautiful country, though."

"How, beautiful?" she persisted.

"If you want to go in, I'll show you some sketches, and you'll see."

Miss Bower rose. "All right. I won't go to my fencing lesson this morning. Do you fence? Here comes your dog. You can't move but he's after you. He always makes a face at me when I meet him in the hall, and shows his nasty little teeth as if he wanted to bite me."

In the studio Hedger got out his sketches, but to Miss Bower, whose favorite pictures were Christ Before Pilate and a redhaired Magdalen of Henner,[1] these landscapes were not at all beautiful, and they gave her no idea of any country whatsoever. She was careful not to commit herself, however. Her vocal teacher had already convinced her that she had a great deal to learn about many things.

"Why don't we go out to lunch somewhere?" Hedger asked, and began to dust his fingers with a handkerchief—which he got out of sight as swiftly as possible.

"All right, the Brevoort," she said carelessly. "I think that's a good place, and they have good wine. I don't care for cocktails."

Hedger felt his chin uneasily. "I'm afraid I haven't shaved this morning. If you could wait for me in the Square? It won't take me ten minutes."

Left alone, he found a clean collar and handkerchief, brushed his coat and blacked his shoes, and last of all dug up ten dollars from the bottom of an old copper kettle he had brought from Spain. His winter hat was of such complexion that the Brevoort hall boy winked at the porter as he took it and placed it on the rack in a row of fresh straw ones.

IV

That afternoon Eden Bower was lying on the couch in her music room, her face turned to the window, watching the pigeons. Reclining thus she could see none of the neighboring roofs, only the sky itself and the birds that crossed and recrossed her field of vision, white as scraps of paper blowing in the wind. She was thinking that she was young and handsome and had had a good lunch, that a very easy-going, light-hearted city lay in the streets below her; and she was wondering why she found this queer painter chap, with his lean, bluish cheeks and heavy black eyebrows, more interesting than the smart young men she met at her teacher's studio.

Eden Bower was, at twenty, very much the same person that we all know her to be at forty, except that she knew a great deal less. But one thing she knew: that she was to be Eden Bower. She was like some one standing before a great show window full of beautiful and costly things, deciding which she will order. She understands that they will not all be delivered immediately, but one by

1. A painting of Mary Magdalen, a reformed prostitute in the New Testament, by Jean Jacques Henner (1829–1905), French painter of religious subjects. Pilate is the judge who permitted Christ's crucifixion.

one they will arrive at her door. She already knew some of the many things that were to happen to her; for instance, that the Chicago millionaire who was going to take her abroad with his sister as chaperone, would eventually press his claim in quite another manner. He was the most circumspect of bachelors, afraid of everything obvious, even of women who were too flagrantly handsome. He was a nervous collector of pictures and furniture, a nervous patron of music, and a nervous host; very cautious about his health, and about any course of conduct that might make him ridiculous. But she knew that he would at last throw all his precautions to the winds.

People like Eden Bower are inexplicable. Her father sold farming machinery in Huntington, Illinois, and she had grown up with no acquaintances or experiences outside of that prairie town. Yet from her earliest childhood she had not one conviction or opinion in common with the people about her,—the only people she knew. Before she was out of short dresses she had made up her mind that she was going to be an actress, that she would live far away in great cities, that she would be much admired by men and would have everything she wanted. When she was thirteen, and was already singing and reciting for church entertainments, she read in some illustrated magazine a long article about the late Czar of Russia, then just come to the throne or about to come to it. After that, lying in the hammock on the front porch on summer evenings, or sitting through a long sermon in the family pew, she amused herself by trying to make up her mind whether she would or would not be the Czar's mistress when she played in his Capital. Now Edna had met this fascinating word only in the novels of Ouida,[2]—her hard-worked little mother kept a long row of them in the upstairs store-room, behind the linen chest. In Huntington, women who bore that relation to men were called by a very different name, and their lot was not an enviable one; of all the shabby and poor, they were the shabbiest. But then, Edna had never lived in Huntington, not even before she began to find books like "Sapho" and "Mademoiselle de Maupin,"[3] secretly sold in paper covers throughout Illinois. It was as if she had come into Huntington, into the Bowers family, on one of the trains that puffed over the marshes behind their back fence all day long, and was waiting for another train to take her out.

As she grew older and handsomer, she had many beaux, but these small-town boys didn't interest her. If a lad kissed her when he brought her home from a dance, she was indulgent and she rather liked it. But if he pressed her further, she slipped away from him, laughing. After she began to sing in Chicago, she was consistently discreet. She stayed as a guest in rich people's houses, and she knew that she was being watched like a rabbit in a laboratory. Covered up in bed, with the lights out, she thought her own thoughts, and laughed.

This summer in New York was her first taste of freedom. The Chicago capitalist, after all his arrangements were made for sailing, had been compelled to go to Mexico to look after oil interests. His sister knew an excellent singing master in New York. Why should not a discreet, well-balanced girl like Miss Bower spend the summer there, studying quietly? The capitalist suggested

2. Pseudonym of Louise de la Ramée (1839–1908), English author of popular romantic novels.
3. *Mademoiselle de Maupin* (1835), by Théophile Gautier, and *Sapho* (1884), by Alphonse Daudet, novels whose heroines are, respectively, a bisexual cross-dresser and a courtesan (one of whose affairs is with a woman).

that his sister might enjoy a summer on Long Island; he would rent the Griffiths' place for her, with all the servants, and Eden could stay there. But his sister met this proposal with a cold stare. So it fell out, that between selfishness and greed, Eden got a summer all her own,—which really did a great deal toward making her an artist and whatever else she was afterward to become. She had time to look about, to watch without being watched; to select diamonds in one window and furs in another, to select shoulders and moustaches in the big hotels where she went to lunch. She had the easy freedom of obscurity and the consciousness of power. She enjoyed both. She was in no hurry.

While Eden Bower watched the pigeons, Don Hedger sat on the other side of the bolted doors, looking into a pool of dark turpentine, at his idle brushes, wondering why a woman could do this to him. He, too, was sure of his future and knew that he was a chosen man. He could not know, of course, that he was merely the first to fall under a fascination which was to be disastrous to a few men and pleasantly stimulating to many thousands. Each of these two young people sensed the future, but not completely. Don Hedger knew that nothing much would ever happen to him. Eden Bower understood that to her a great deal would happen. But she did not guess that her neighbor would have more tempestuous adventures sitting in his dark studio than she would find in all the capitals of Europe, or in all the latitude of conduct she was prepared to permit herself.

V

One Sunday morning Eden was crossing the Square with a spruce young man in a white flannel suit and a panama hat. They had been breakfasting at the Brevoort and he was coaxing her to let him come up to her rooms and sing for an hour.

"No, I've got to write letters. You must run along now. I see a friend of mine over there, and I want to ask him about something before I go up."

"That fellow with the dog? Where did you pick him up?" The young man glanced toward the seat under a sycamore where Hedger was reading the morning paper.

"Oh, he's an old friend from the West," said Eden easily. "I won't introduce you, because he doesn't like people. He's a recluse. Good-bye. I can't be sure about Tuesday. I'll go with you if I have time after my lesson." She nodded, left him, and went over to the seat littered with newspapers. The young man went up the Avenue without looking back.

"Well, what are you going to do today? Shampoo this animal all morning?" Eden enquired teasingly.

Hedger made room for her on the seat. "No, at twelve o'clock I'm going out to Coney Island.[4] One of my models is going up in a balloon this afternoon. I've often promised to go and see her, and now I'm going."

Eden asked if models usually did such stunts. No, Hedger told her, but Molly Welch added to her earnings in that way. "I believe," he added, "she likes the excitement of it. She's got a good deal of spirit. That's why I like to paint her. So many models have flaccid bodies."

"And she hasn't, eh? Is she the one who comes to see you? I can't help hearing her, she talks so loud."

4. Amusement park on the beach in Brooklyn.

"Yes, she has a rough voice, but she's a fine girl. I don't suppose you'd be interested in going?"

"I don't know," Eden sat tracing patterns on the asphalt with the end of her parasol. "Is it any fun? I got up feeling I'd like to do something different today. It's the first Sunday I've not had to sing in church. I had that engagement for breakfast at the Brevoort, but it wasn't very exciting. That chap can't talk about anything but himself."

Hedger warmed a little. "If you've never been to Coney Island, you ought to go. It's nice to see all the people; tailors and bar-tenders and prize-fighters with their best girls, and all sorts of folks taking a holiday."

Eden looked sidewise at him. So one ought to be interested in people of that kind, ought one? He was certainly a funny fellow. Yet he was never, somehow, tiresome. She had seen a good deal of him lately, but she kept wanting to know him better, to find out what made him different from men like the one she had just left—whether he really was as different as he seemed. "I'll go with you," she said at last, "if you'll leave that at home." She pointed to Caesar's flickering ears with her sunshade.

"But he's half the fun. You'd like to hear him bark at the waves when they come in."

"No, I wouldn't. He's jealous and disagreeable if he sees you talking to any one else. Look at him now."

"Of course, if you make a face at him. He knows what that means, and he makes a worse face. He likes Molly Welch, and she'll be disappointed if I don't bring him."

Eden said decidedly that he couldn't take both of them. So at twelve o'clock when she and Hedger got on the boat at Desbrosses street, Caesar was lying on his pallet, with a bone.

Eden enjoyed the boat-ride. It was the first time she had been on the water, and she felt as if she were embarking for France. The light warm breeze and the plunge of the waves made her very wide awake, and she liked crowds of any kind. They went to the balcony of a big, noisy restaurant and had a shore dinner, with tall steins of beer. Hedger had got a big advance from his advertising firm since he first lunched with Miss Bower ten days ago, and he was ready for anything.

After dinner they went to the tent behind the bathing beach, where the tops of two balloons bulged out over the canvas. A red-faced man in a linen suit stood in front of the tent, shouting in a hoarse voice and telling the people that if the crowd was good for five dollars more, a beautiful young woman would risk her life for their entertainment. Four little boys in dirty red uniforms ran about taking contributions in their pill-box hats. One of the balloons was bobbing up and down in its tether and people were shoving forward to get nearer the tent.

"Is it dangerous, as he pretends?" Eden asked.

"Molly says it's simple enough if nothing goes wrong with the balloon. Then it would be all over, I suppose."

"Wouldn't you like to go up with her?"

"I? Of course not. I'm not fond of taking foolish risks."

Eden sniffed. "I shouldn't think sensible risks would be very much fun."

Hedger did not answer, for just then every one began to shove the other way and shout, "Look out. There she goes!" and a band of six pieces commenced playing furiously.

As the balloon rose from its tent enclosure, they saw a girl in green tights standing in the basket, holding carelessly to one of the ropes with one hand and with the other waving to the spectators. A long rope trailed behind to keep the balloon from blowing out to sea.

As it soared, the figure in green tights in the basket diminished to a mere spot, and the balloon itself, in the brilliant light, looked like a big silver-gray bat, with its wings folded. When it began to sink, the girl stepped through the hole in the basket to a trapeze that hung below, and gracefully descended through the air, holding to the rod with both hands, keeping her body taut and her feet close together. The crowd, which had grown very large by this time, cheered vociferously. The men took off their hats and waved, little boys shouted, and fat old women, shining with the heat and a beer lunch, murmured admiring comments upon the balloonist's figure. "Beautiful legs, she has!"

"That's so," Hedger whispered. "Not many girls would look well in that position." Then, for some reason, he blushed a slow, dark, painful crimson.

The balloon descended slowly, a little way from the tent, and the red-faced man in the linen suit caught Molly Welch before her feet touched the ground, and pulled her to one side. The band struck up "Blue Bell" by way of welcome, and one of the sweaty pages ran forward and presented the balloonist with a large bouquet of artificial flowers. She smiled and thanked him, and ran back across the sand to the tent.

"Can't we go inside and see her?" Eden asked. "You can explain to the door man. I want to meet her." Edging forward, she herself addressed the man in the linen suit and slipped something from her purse into his hand.

They found Molly seated before a trunk that had a mirror in the lid and a "make-up" outfit spread upon the tray. She was wiping the cold cream and powder from her neck with a discarded chemise.

"Hello, Don," she said cordially. "Brought a friend?"

Eden liked her. She had an easy, friendly manner, and there was something boyish and devil-may-care about her.

"Yes, it's fun. I'm mad about it," she said in reply to Eden's questions. "I always want to let go, when I come down on the bar. You don't feel your weight at all, as you would on a stationary trapeze."

The big drum boomed outside, and the publicity man began shouting to newly arrived boat-loads. Miss Welch took a last pull at her cigarette. "Now you'll have to get out, Don. I change for the next act. This time I go up in a black evening dress, and lose the skirt in the basket before I start down."

"Yes, go along," said Eden. "Wait for me outside the door. I'll stay and help her dress."

Hedger waited and waited, while women of every build bumped into him and begged his pardon, and the red pages ran about holding out their caps for coins, and the people ate and perspired and shifted parasols against the sun. When the band began to play a two-step, all the bathers ran up out of the surf to watch the ascent. The second balloon bumped and rose, and the crowd began shouting to the girl in a black evening dress who stood leaning against the ropes and smiling. "It's a new girl," they called. "It ain't the Countess this time. You're a peach, girlie!"

The balloonist acknowledged these compliments, bowing and looking down over the sea of upturned faces,—but Hedger was determined she should

not see him, and he darted behind the tent-fly. He was suddenly dripping with cold sweat, his mouth was full of the bitter taste of anger and his tongue felt stiff behind his teeth. Molly Welch, in a shirt-waist and a white tam-o'-shanter cap, slipped out from the tent under his arm and laughed up in his face. "She's a crazy one you brought along. She'll get what she wants!"

"Oh, I'll settle with you, all right!" Hedger brought out with difficulty.

"It's not my fault, Donnie. I couldn't do anything with her. She bought me off. What's the matter with you? Are you soft on her? She's safe enough. It's as easy as rolling off a log, if you keep cool." Molly Welch was rather excited herself, and she was chewing gum at a high speed as she stood beside him, looking up at the floating silver cone. "Now watch," she exclaimed suddenly. "She's coming down on the bar. I advised her to cut that cut, but you see she does it first-rate. And she got rid of the skirt, too. Those black tights show off her legs very well. She keeps her feet together like I told her, and makes a good line along the back. See the light on those silver slippers,—that was a good idea I had. Come along to meet her. Don't be a grouch; she's done it fine!"

Molly tweaked his elbow, and then left him standing like a stump, while she ran down the beach with the crowd.

Though Hedger was sulking, his eye could not help seeing the low blue welter of the sea, the arrested bathers, standing in the surf, their arms and legs stained red by the dropping sun, all shading their eyes and gazing upward at the slowly falling silver star.

Molly Welch and the manager caught Eden under the arms and lifted her aside, a red page dashed up with a bouquet, and the band struck up "Blue Bell." Eden laughed and bowed, took Molly's arm, and ran up the sand in her black tights and silver slippers, dodging the friendly old women, and the gallant sports[5] who wanted to offer their homage on the spot.

When she emerged from the tent, dressed in her own clothes, that part of the beach was almost deserted. She stepped to her companion's side and said carelessly: "Hadn't we better try to catch this boat? I hope you're not sore at me. Really, it was lots of fun."

Hedger looked at his watch. "Yes, we have fifteen minutes to get to the boat," he said politely.

As they walked toward the pier, one of the pages ran up panting. "Lady, you're carrying off the bouquet," he said, aggrievedly.

Eden stopped and looked at the bunch of spotty cotton roses in her hand. "Of course. I want them for a souvenir. You gave them to me yourself."

"I give 'em to you for looks, but you can't take 'em away. They belong to the show."

"Oh, you always use the same bunch?"

"Sure we do. There ain't too much money in this business."

She laughed and tossed them back to him.

"Why are you angry?" she asked Hedger. "I wouldn't have done it if I'd been with some fellows, but I thought you were the sort who wouldn't mind. Molly didn't for a minute think you would."

"What possessed you to do such a fool thing?" he asked roughly.

"I don't know. When I saw her coming down, I wanted to try it. It looked exciting. Didn't I hold myself as well as she did?"

5. Jaunty young men.

Hedger shrugged his shoulders, but in his heart he forgave her.

The return boat was not crowded, though the boats that passed them, going out, were packed to the rails. The sun was setting. Boys and girls sat on the long benches with their arms about each other, singing. Eden felt a strong wish to propitiate her companion, to be alone with him. She had been curiously wrought up by her balloon trip; it was a lark, but not very satisfying unless one came back to something after the flight. She wanted to be admired and adored. Though Eden said nothing, and sat with her arms limp on the rail in front of her, looking languidly at the rising silhouette of the city and the bright path of the sun, Hedger felt a strange drawing near to her. If he but brushed her white skirt with his knee, there was an instant communication between them, such as there had never been before. They did not talk at all, but when they went over the gangplank she took his arm and kept her shoulder close to his. He felt as if they were enveloped in a highly charged atmosphere, an invisible network of subtle, almost painful sensibility. They had somehow taken hold of each other.

An hour later, they were dining in the back garden of a little French hotel on Ninth Street, long since passed away. It was cool and leafy there, and the mosquitoes were not very numerous. A party of South Americans at another table were drinking champagne, and Eden murmured that she thought she would like some, if it were not too expensive. "Perhaps it will make me think I am in the balloon again. That was a very nice feeling. You've forgiven me, haven't you?"

Hedger gave her a quick straight look from under his black eyebrows, and something went over her that was like a chill, except that it was warm and feathery. She drank most of the wine: her companion was indifferent to it. He was talking more to her tonight than he had ever done before. She asked him about a new picture she had seen in his room; a queer thing full of stiff, supplicating female figures. "It's Indian, isn't it?"

"Yes. I call it Rain Spirits, or maybe, Indian Rain. In the Southwest, where I've been a good deal, the Indian traditions make women have to do with the rain-fall. They were supposed to control it, somehow, and to be able to find springs and make moisture come out of the earth. You see I'm trying to learn to paint what people think and feel; to get away from all that photographic stuff. When I look at you, I don't see what a camera would see, do I?"

"How can I tell?"

"Well, if I should paint you, I could make you understand what I see." For the second time that day Hedger crimsoned unexpectedly, and his eyes fell and steadily contemplated a dish of little radishes. "That particular picture I got from a story a Mexican priest told me; he said he found it in an old manuscript book in a monastery down there, written by some Spanish Missionary, who got his stories from the Aztecs. This one he called 'The Forty Lovers of the Queen,' and it was more or less about rain-making."

"Aren't you going to tell it to me?" Eden asked.

Hedger fumbled among the radishes. "I don't know if it's the proper kind of story to tell a girl."

She smiled; "Oh, forget about that! I've been balloon riding today. I like to hear you talk."

Her low voice was flattering. She had seemed like clay in his hands ever since they got on the boat to come home. He leaned back in his chair, forgot

his food, and, looking at her intently, began to tell his story, the theme of which he somehow felt was dangerous tonight.

The tale began, he said, somewhere in Ancient Mexico, and concerned the daughter of a king. The birth of this Princess was preceded by unusual portents. Three times her mother dreamed that she was delivered of serpents, which betokened that the child she carried would have power with the rain gods. The serpent was the symbol of water. The Princess grew up dedicated to the gods, and wise men taught her the rain-making mysteries. She was with difficulty restrained from men and was guarded at all times, for it was the law of the Thunder that she be maiden until her marriage. In the years of her adolescence, rain was abundant with her people. The eldest man could not remember such fertility. When the Princess had counted eighteen summers, her father went to drive out a war party that harried his borders on the north and troubled his prosperity. The King destroyed the invaders and brought home many prisoners. Among the prisoners was a young chief, taller than any of his captors, of such strength and ferocity that the King's people came a day's journey to look at him. When the Princess beheld his great stature, and saw that his arms and breast were covered with the figures of wild animals, bitten into the skin and colored, she begged his life from her father. She desired that he should practice his art upon her, and prick upon her skin the signs of Rain and Lightning and Thunder, and stain the wounds with herb-juices, as they were upon his own body. For many days, upon the roof of the King's house, the Princess submitted herself to the bone needle, and the women with her marvelled at her fortitude. But the Princess was without shame before the Captive, and it came about that he threw from him his needles and his stains, and fell upon the Princess to violate her honor; and her women ran down from the roof screaming, to call the guard which stood at the gateway of the King's house, and none stayed to protect their mistress. When the guard came, the Captive was thrown into bonds, and he was gelded, and his tongue was torn out, and he was given for a slave to the Rain Princess.

The country of the Aztecs to the east was tormented by thirst, and their king, hearing much of the rain-making arts of the Princess, sent an embassy to her father, with presents and an offer of marriage. So the Princess went from her father to be the Queen of the Aztecs, and she took with her the Captive, who served her in everything with entire fidelity and slept upon a mat before her door.

The King gave his bride a fortress on the outskirts of the city, whither she retired to entreat the rain gods. This fortress was called the Queen's House, and on the night of the new moon the Queen came to it from the palace. But when the moon waxed and grew toward the round, because the god of Thunder had had his will of her, then the Queen returned to the King. Drout abated in the country and rain fell abundantly by reason of the Queen's power with the stars.

When the Queen went to her own house she took with her no servant but the Captive, and he slept outside her door and brought her food after she had fasted. The Queen had a jewel of great value, a turquoise that had fallen from the sun, and had the image of the sun upon it. And when she desired a young man whom she had seen in the army or among the slaves, she sent the Captive to him with the jewel, for a sign that he should come to her secretly at the Queen's House upon business concerning the welfare of all. And some, after

she had talked with them, she sent away with rewards; and some she took into her chamber and kept them by her for one night or two. Afterward she called the Captive and bade him conduct the youth by the secret way he had come, underneath the chambers of the fortress. But for the going away of the Queen's lovers the Captive took out the bar that was beneath a stone in the floor of the passage, and put in its stead a rush-reed, and the youth stepped upon it and fell through into a cavern that was the bed of an underground river, and whatever was thrown into it was not seen again. In this service nor in any other did the Captive fail the Queen.

But when the Queen sent for the Captain of the Archers, she detained him four days in her chamber, calling often for food and wine, and was greatly content with him. On the fourth day she went to the Captive outside her door and said:

"Tomorrow take this man up by the sure way, by which the King comes, and let him live."

In the Queen's door were arrows, purple and white. When she desired the King to come to her publicly, with his guard, she sent him a white arrow; but when she sent the purple, he came secretly, and covered himself with his mantle to be hidden from the stone gods at the gate. On the fifth night that the Queen was with her lover, the Captive took a purple arrow to the King, and the King came secretly and found them together. He killed the Captain with his own hand, but the Queen he brought to public trial. The Captive, when he was put to the question, told on his fingers forty men that he had let through the underground passage into the river. The Captive and the Queen were put to death by fire, both on the same day, and afterward there was scarcity of rain.

Eden Bower sat shivering a little as she listened. Hedger was not trying to please her, she thought, but to antagonize and frighten her by his brutal story. She had often told herself that his lean, big-boned lower jaw was like his bulldog's, but tonight his face made Caesar's most savage and determined expression seem an affectation. Now she was looking at the man he really was. Nobody's eyes had ever defied her like this. They were searching her and seeing everything; all she had concealed from Livingston, and from the millionaire and his friends, and from the newspaper men. He was testing her, trying her out, and she was more ill at ease than she wished to show.

"That's quite a thrilling story," she said at last, rising and winding her scarf about her throat. "It must be getting late. Almost every one has gone."

They walked down the Avenue like people who have quarrelled, or who wish to get rid of each other. Hedger did not take her arm at the street crossings, and they did not linger in the Square. At her door he tried none of the old devices of the Livingston boys. He stood like a post, having forgotten to take off his hat, gave her a harsh, threatening glance, muttered "goodnight," and shut his own door noisily.

There was no question of sleep for Eden Bower. Her brain was working like a machine that would never stop. After she undressed, she tried to calm her nerves by smoking a cigarette, lying on the divan by the open window. But she grew wider and wider awake, combating the challenge that had flamed all evening in Hedger's eyes. The balloon had been one kind of excitement, the wine another; but the thing that had roused her, as a blow rouses a proud man, was the doubt, the contempt, the sneering hostility with which the painter had looked at her when he told his savage story. Crowds and balloons were all

very well, she reflected, but woman's chief adventure is man. With a mind over active and a sense of life over strong, she wanted to walk across the roofs in the starlight, to sail over the sea and face at once a world of which she had never been afraid.

Hedger must be asleep; his dog had stopped sniffing under the double doors. Eden put on her wrapper and slippers and stole softly down the hall over the old carpet; one loose board creaked just as she reached the ladder. The trap-door was open, as always on hot nights. When she stepped out on the roof she drew a long breath and walked across it, looking up at the sky. Her foot touched something soft; she heard a low growl, and on the instant Caesar's sharp little teeth caught her ankle and waited. His breath was like steam on her leg. Nobody had ever intruded upon his roof before, and he panted for the movement or the word that would let him spring his jaw. Instead, Hedger's hand seized his throat.

"Wait a minute. I'll settle with him," he said grimly. He dragged the dog toward the manhole and disappeared. When he came back, he found Eden standing over by the dark chimney, looking away in an offended attitude.

"I caned him unmercifully," he panted. "Of course you didn't hear anything; he never whines when I beat him. He didn't nip you, did he?"

"I don't know whether he broke the skin or not," she answered aggrievedly, still looking off into the west.

"If I were one of your friends in white pants, I'd strike a match to find whether you were hurt, though I know you are not, and then I'd see your ankle, wouldn't I?"

"I suppose so."

He shook his head and stood with his hands in the pockets of his old painting jacket. "I'm not up to such boy-tricks. If you want the place to yourself, I'll clear out. There are plenty of places where I can spend the night, what's left of it. But if you stay here and I stay here—" He shrugged his shoulders.

Eden did not stir, and she made no reply. Her head drooped slightly, as if she were considering. But the moment he put his arms about her they began to talk, both at once, as people do in an opera. The instant avowal brought out a flood of trivial admissions. Hedger confessed his crime, was reproached and forgiven, and now Eden knew what it was in his look that she had found so disturbing of late.

Standing against the black chimney, with the sky behind and blue shadows before, they looked like one of Hedger's own paintings of that period; two figures, one white and one dark, and nothing whatever distinguishable about them but that they were male and female. The faces were lost, the contours blurred in shadow, but the figures were a man and a woman, and that was their whole concern and their mysterious beauty,—it was the rhythm in which they moved, at last, along the roof and down into the dark hole; he first, drawing her gently after him. She came down very slowly. The excitement and bravado and uncertainty of that long day and night seemed all at once to tell upon her. When his feet were on the carpet and he reached up to lift her down, she twined her arms about his neck as after a long separation, and turned her face to him, and her lips, with their perfume of youth and passion.

One Saturday afternoon Hedger was sitting in the window of Eden's music room. They had been watching the pigeons come wheeling over the roofs from their unknown feeding grounds.

"Why," said Eden suddenly, "don't we fix those big doors into your studio so they will open? Then, if I want you, I won't have to go through the hall. That illustrator is loafing about a good deal of late."

"I'll open them, if you wish. The bolt is on your side."

"Isn't there one on yours, too?"

"No. I believe a man lived there for years before I came in, and the nurse used to have these rooms herself. Naturally, the lock was on the lady's side."

Eden laughed and began to examine the bolt. "It's all stuck up with paint." Looking about, her eye lighted upon a bronze Buddah which was one of the nurse's treasures. Taking him by his head, she struck the bolt a blow with his squatting posteriors. The two doors creaked, sagged, and swung weakly inward a little way, as if they were too old for such escapades. Eden tossed the heavy idol into a stuffed chair. "That's better," she exclaimed exultantly. "So the bolts are always on the lady's side? What a lot society takes for granted!"

Hedger laughed, sprang up and caught her arms roughly. "Whoever takes you for granted— Did anybody, ever?"

"Everybody does. That's why I'm here. You are the only one who knows anything about me. Now I'll have to dress if we're going out for dinner."

He lingered, keeping his hold on her. "But I won't always be the only one, Eden Bower. I won't be the last."

"No, I suppose not," she said carelessly. "But what does that matter? You are the first."

As a long, despairing whine broke in the warm stillness, they drew apart. Caesar, lying on his bed in the dark corner, had lifted his head at this invasion of sunlight, and realized that the side of his room was broken open, and his whole world shattered by change. There stood his master and this woman, laughing at him! The woman was pulling the long black hair of this mightiest of men, who bowed his head and permitted it.

VI

In time they quarrelled, of course, and about an abstraction,—as young people often do, as mature people almost never do. Eden came in late one afternoon. She had been with some of her musical friends to lunch at Burton Ives' studio, and she began telling Hedger about its splendors. He listened a moment and then threw down his brushes. "I know exactly what it's like," he said impatiently. "A very good department-store conception of a studio. It's one of the show places."

"Well, it's gorgeous, and he said I could bring you to see him. The boys tell me he's awfully kind about giving people a lift,[6] and you might get something out of it."

Hedger started up and pushed his canvas out of the way. "What could I possibly get from Burton Ives? He's almost the worst painter in the world; the stupidest, I mean."

Eden was annoyed. Burton Ives had been very nice to her and had begged her to sit for him. "You must admit that he's a very successful one," she said coldly.

"Of course he is! Anybody can be successful who will do that sort of thing. I wouldn't paint his pictures for all the money in New York."

6. I.e., help.

"Well, I saw a lot of them, and I think they are beautiful.'.

Hedger bowed stiffly.

"What's the use of being a great painter if nobody knows about you?" Eden went on persuasively. "Why don't you paint the kind of pictures people can understand, and then, after you're successful, do whatever you like?"

"As I look at it," said Hedger brusquely, "I am successful."

Eden glanced about. "Well, I don't see any evidences of it," she said, biting her lip. "He has a Japanese servant and a wine cellar, and keeps a riding horse."

Hedger melted a little. "My dear, I have the most expensive luxury in the world, and I am much more extravagant than Burton Ives, for I work to please nobody but myself."

"You mean you could make money and don't? That you don't try to get a public?"

"Exactly. A public only wants what has been done over and over. I'm painting for painters—who haven't been born."

"What would you do if I brought Mr. Ives down here to see your things?"

"Well, for God's sake, don't! Before he left I'd probably tell him what I thought of him."

Eden rose. "I give you up. You know very well there's only one kind of success that's real."

"Yes, but it's not the kind you mean. So you've been thinking me a scrub painter, who needs a helping hand from some fashionable studio man? What the devil have you had anything to do with me for, then?"

"There's no use talking to you," said Eden walking slowly toward the door. "I've been trying to pull wires for you all afternoon, and this is what it comes to." She had expected that the tidings of a prospective call from the great man would be received very differently, and had been thinking as she came home in the stage how, as with a magic wand, she might gild Hedger's future, float him out of his dark hole on a tide of prosperity, see his name in the papers and his pictures in the windows on Fifth Avenue.

Hedger mechanically snapped the midsummer leash on Caesar's collar and they ran downstairs and hurried through Sullivan Street off toward the river. He wanted to be among rough, honest people, to get down where the big drays bumped over stone paving blocks and the men wore corduroy trowsers and kept their shirts open at the neck. He stopped for a drink in one of the sagging bar-rooms on the water front. He had never in his life been so deeply wounded; he did not know he could be so hurt. He had told this girl all his secrets. On the roof, in these warm, heavy summer nights, with her hands locked in his, he had been able to explain all his misty ideas about an unborn art the world was waiting for; had been able to explain them better than he had ever done to himself. And she had looked away to the chattels of this uptown studio and coveted them for him! To her he was only an unsuccessful Burton Ives.

Then why, as he had put it to her, did she take up with him? Young, beautiful, talented as she was, why had she wasted herself on a scrub? Pity? Hardly; she wasn't sentimental. There was no explaining her. But in this passion that had seemed so fearless and so fated to be, his own position now looked to him ridiculous; a poor dauber without money or fame,—it was her caprice to load him with favors. Hedger ground his teeth so loud that his dog, trotting beside him, heard him and looked up.

While they were having supper at the oysterman's, he planned his escape.

Whenever he saw her again, everything he had told her, that he should never have told any one, would come back to him; ideas he had never whispered even to the painter whom he worshipped and had gone all the way to France to see. To her they must seem his apology for not having horses and a valet, or merely the puerile boastfulness of a weak man. Yet if she slipped the bolt tonight and came through the doors and said, "Oh, weak man, I belong to you!" what could he do? That was the danger. He would catch the train out to Long Beach tonight, and tomorrow he would go on to the north end of Long Island, where an old friend of his had a summer studio among the sand dunes. He would stay until things came right in his mind. And she could find a smart painter, or take her punishment.

When he went home, Eden's room was dark; she was dining out somewhere. He threw his things into a hold-all he had carried about the world with him, strapped up some colors and canvases, and ran downstairs.

VII

Five days later Hedger was a restless passenger on a dirty, crowded Sunday train, coming back to town. Of course he saw now how unreasonable he had been in expecting a Huntington girl to know anything about pictures; here was a whole continent full of people who knew nothing about pictures and he didn't hold it against them. What had such things to do with him and Eden Bower? When he lay out on the dunes, watching the moon come up out of the sea, it had seemed to him that there was no wonder in the world like the wonder of Eden Bower. He was going back to her because she was older than art, because she was the most overwhelming thing that had ever come into his life.

He had written her yesterday, begging her to be at home this evening, telling her that he was contrite, and wretched enough.

Now that he was on his way to her, his stronger feeling unaccountably changed to a mood that was playful and tender. He wanted to share everything with her, even the most trivial things. He wanted to tell her about the people on the train, coming back tired from their holiday with bunches of wilted flowers and dirty daisies; to tell her that the fish-man, to whom she had often sent him for lobsters, was among the passengers, disguised in a silk shirt and a spotted tie, and how his wife looked exactly like a fish, even to her eyes on which cataracts were forming. He could tell her, too, that he hadn't as much as unstrapped his canvases,—that ought to convince her.

In those days passengers from Long Island came into New York by ferry. Hedger had to be quick about getting his dog out of the express car in order to catch the first boat. The East River, and the bridges, and the city to the west, were burning in the conflagration of the sunset; there was that great home-coming reach of evening in the air.

The car changes from Thirty-fourth Street were too many and too perplexing; for the first time in his life Hedger took a hansom cab for Washington Square. Caesar sat bolt upright on the worn leather cushion beside him, and they jogged off, looking down on the rest of the world.

It was twilight when they drove down lower Fifth Avenue into the Square, and through the Arch behind them were the two long rows of pale violet lights that used to bloom so beautifully against the gray stone and asphalt. Here and yonder about the Square hung globes that shed a radiance not unlike the blue

mists of evening, emerging softly when daylight died, as the stars emerged in the thin blue sky. Under them the sharp shadows of the trees fell on the cracked pavement and the sleeping grass. The first stars and the first lights were growing silver against the gradual darkening when Hedger paid his driver and went into the house,—which, thank God, was still there! On the hall table lay his letter of yesterday, unopened.

He went upstairs with every sort of fear and every sort of hope clutching at his heart; it was as if tigers were tearing him. Why was there no gas burning in the top hall? He found matches and the gas bracket. He knocked, but got no answer; nobody was there. Before his own door were exactly five bottles of milk, standing in a row. The milk-boy had taken spiteful pleasure in thus reminding him that he forgot to stop his order.

Hedger went down to the basement; it, too, was dark. The janitress was taking her evening airing on the basement steps. She sat waving a palm-leaf fan majestically, her dirty calico dress open at the neck. She told him at once that there had been "changes." Miss Bower's room was to let again, and the piano would go tomorrow. Yes, she left yesterday, she sailed for Europe with friends from Chicago. They arrived on Friday, heralded by many telegrams. Very rich people they were said to be, though the man had refused to pay the nurse a month's rent in lieu of notice,—which would have been only right, as the young lady had agreed to take the rooms until October. Mrs. Foley had observed, too, that he didn't overpay her or Willy for their trouble, and a great deal of trouble they had been put to, certainly. Yes, the young lady was very pleasant, but the nurse said there were rings on the mahogany table where she had put tumblers and wine glasses. It was just as well she was gone. The Chicago man was uppish in his ways, but not much to look at. She supposed he had poor health, for there was nothing to him inside his clothes.

Hedger went slowly up the stairs—never had they seemed so long, or his legs so heavy. The upper floor was emptiness and silence. He unlocked his room, lit the gas, and opened the windows. When he went to put his coat in the closet, he found, hanging among his clothes, a pale, flesh-tinted dressing gown he had liked to see her wear, with a perfume—oh, a perfume that was still Eden Bower! He shut the door behind him and there, in the dark, for a moment he lost his manliness. It was when he held this garment to him that he found a letter in the pocket.

The note was written with a lead pencil, in haste: She was sorry that he was angry, but she still didn't know just what she had done. She had thought Mr. Ives would be useful to him; she guessed he was too proud. She wanted awfully to see him again, but Fate came knocking at her door after he had left her. She believed in Fate. She would never forget him, and she knew he would become the greatest painter in the world. Now she must pack. She hoped he wouldn't mind her leaving the dressing gown; somehow, she could never wear it again.

After Hedger read this, standing under the gas, he went back into the closet and knelt down before the wall; the knot hole had been plugged up with a ball of wet paper,—the same blue note-paper on which her letter was written.

He was hard hit. Tonight he had to bear the loneliness of a whole lifetime. Knowing himself so well, he could hardly believe that such a thing had ever happened to him, that such a woman had lain happy and contented in his arms. And now it was over. He turned out the light and sat down on his

painter's stool before the big window. Caesar, on the floor beside him, rested his head on his master's knee. We must leave Hedger thus, sitting in his tank with his dog, looking up at the stars.

COMING, APHRODITE! This legend, in electric lights over the Lexington Opera House, had long announced the return of Eden Bower to New York after years of spectacular success in Paris. She came at last, under the management of an American Opera Company, but bringing her own *chef d'orchestre*.[7]

One bright December afternoon Eden Bower was going down Fifth Avenue in her car, on the way to her broker, in Williams Street. Her thoughts were entirely upon stocks,—Cerro de Pasco, and how much she should buy of it,—when she suddenly looked up and realized that she was skirting Washington Square. She had not seen the place since she rolled out of it in an old-fashioned four-wheeler to seek her fortune, eighteen years ago.

"*Arrêtez, Alphonse. Attendez moi*,"[8] she called, and opened the door before he could reach it. The children who were streaking over the asphalt on roller skates saw a lady in a long fur coat, and short, high-heeled shoes, alight from a French car and pace slowly about the Square, holding her muff to her chin. This spot, at least, had changed very little, she reflected; the same trees, the same fountain, the white arch, and over yonder, Garibaldi, drawing the sword for freedom. There, just opposite her, was the old red brick house.

"Yes, that is the place," she was thinking. "I can smell the carpets now, and the dog,—what was his name? That grubby bathroom at the end of the hall, and that dreadful Hedger—still, there was something about him, you know—" She glanced up and blinked against the sun. From somewhere in the crowded quarter south of the Square a flock of pigeons rose, wheeling quickly upward into the brilliant blue sky. She threw back her head, pressed her muff closer to her chin, and watched them with a smile of amazement and delight. So they still rose, out of all that dirt and noise and squalor, fleet and silvery, just as they used to rise that summer when she was twenty and went up in a balloon on Coney Island!

Alphonse opened the door and tucked her robes about her. All the way down town her mind wandered from Cerro de Pasco, and she kept smiling and looking up at the sky.

When she had finished her business with the broker, she asked him to look in the telephone book for the address of M. Gaston Jules, the picture dealer, and slipped the paper on which he wrote it into her glove. It was five o'clock when she reached the French Galleries, as they were called. On entering she gave the attendant her card, asking him to take it to M. Jules. The dealer appeared very promptly and begged her to come into his private office, where he pushed a great chair toward his desk for her and signalled his secretary to leave the room.

"How good your lighting is in here," she observed, glancing about. "I met you at Simon's studio, didn't I? Oh, no! I never forget anybody who interests me." She threw her muff on his writing table and sank into the deep chair. "I

7. Orchestra leader. *Aphrodite* (1906) is an opera by Camille Erlanger (1863–1919), based on Pierre Loüy's novel, *Aphrodite* (1896).
8. Stop, Alphonse. Wait for me (French).

have come to you for some information that's not in my line. Do you know anything about an American painter named Hedger?"

He took the seat opposite her. "Don Hedger? But, certainly! There are some very interesting things of his in an exhibition at V——'s. If you would care to—"

She held up her hand. "No, no. I've no time to go to exhibitions. Is he a man of any importance?"

"Certainly. He is one of the first men among the moderns. That is to say, among the very moderns. He is always coming up with something different. He often exhibits in Paris, you must have seen—"

"No, I tell you I don't go to exhibitions. Has he had great success? That is what I want to know."

M. Jules pulled at his short gray moustache. "But, Madame, there are many kinds of success," he began cautiously.

Madame gave a dry laugh. "Yes, so he used to say. We once quarrelled on that issue. And how would you define his particular kind?"

M. Jules grew thoughtful. "He is a great name with all the young men, and he is decidedly an influence in art. But one can't definitely place a man who is original, erratic, and who is changing all the time."

She cut him short. "Is he much talked about at home? In Paris, I mean? Thanks. That's all I want to know." She rose and began buttoning her coat. "One doesn't like to have been an utter fool, even at twenty."

"*Mais, non!*"[9] M. Jules handed her her muff with a quick, sympathetic glance. He followed her out through the carpeted show-room, now closed to the public and draped in cheesecloth, and put her into her car with words appreciative of the honor she had done him in calling.

Leaning back in the cushions, Eden Bower closed her eyes, and her face, as the street lamps flashed their ugly orange light upon it, became hard and settled, like a plaster cast; so a sail, that has been filled by a strong breeze, behaves when the wind suddenly dies. Tomorrow night the wind would blow again, and this mask would be the golden face of Aphrodite. But a "big" career takes its toll, even with the best of luck.

1920

9. No, of course not! (French).

DOROTHY RICHARDSON
1873–1957

"She has invented a sentence that we might call the psychological sentence of the feminine gender," wrote Virginia Woolf about Dorothy Richardson's fluid and flexible transcriptions of female consciousness. She is "the greatest woman genius of our time," asserted the writer John Cowper Powys. Yet though Richardson's authorship of a ground-breaking, thirteen-volume novel sequence titled *Pilgrimage* won her such acclaim from intellectuals as well as the financial patronage of the novelist Bryher (Winifred Ellerman, a shipping heiress who was the close friend of the poet H. D.), she lived and worked in comparative obscurity, and she earned minimal royalties from her books, which, after her death, were largely overlooked

except by literary historians, who regarded them as experimental curiosities. Her ambition, however, was extraordinary: in the thirteen volumes of *Pilgrimage*, each a self-contained text yet all intricately interrelated, Richardson set out to recount the subtlest details of the living-and-learning process by which her heroine, Miriam Henderson, forges an identity.

As many contemporary critics observed, Miriam Henderson *was* in some sense Dorothy Richardson, or at least a crucial "aspect" of that artist, for Richardson endowed her protagonist with a family background and an early life almost exactly the equivalent of her own. Born in Abingdon, in the English county of Berkshire, Richardson, like Miriam Henderson, was the third of four daughters. Her father was a proud, independently wealthy man who lost most of his money during the 1890s; her mother was charming but mentally fragile. In 1895, while Dorothy was staying with her in the seaside resort of Hastings, where the two had gone for the sake of Mrs. Richardson's health, the older woman committed suicide in an episode that Richardson records with hallucinatory vividness at the end of *Honeycomb* (1917), the third book of *Pilgrimage*. Even before this drastic event, however, the young writer-to-be had had to confront a number of difficulties. Because of her father's bankruptcy, she had accepted two arduous teaching jobs— one at a girls' school in Germany, another at a school in the north of London; again, both situations are described with subtlety and sensitivity in the two first books of *Pilgrimage: Pointed Roofs* (1915) and *Backwater* (1916).

After her mother's death, Richardson moved to London, where she found an inexpensive "room of her own" in Bloomsbury and worked for eight years as a dental assistant. Here she began to write sketches, articles, and reviews; she encountered a number of London intellectuals who were to be lifelong friends; she became involved in the feminist and socialist movements; and—perhaps most important— she met the rising novelist H. G. Wells. The husband of one of Richardson's schoolfriends, Wells grew intensely interested in this lively and thoughtful young woman, and soon the two had entered into a prolonged affair, which Richardson used as the basis for a later volume of *Pilgrimage*.

In 1912, Richardson embarked on the composition of what was to become *Pilgrimage*. A few years earlier, she had left her job as dental assistant and begun to eke out a thin living as a writer, publishing sketches, reviews, and social commentaries in the mode of *Women and the Future* as well as articles about dentistry in a number of journals; in addition, she produced several books about Quakerism, a subject that fascinated her throughout her career. For the most part, however, after 1912, staying sometimes in London and sometimes in country cottages lent her by friends, she devoted herself with special passion to the massive work that would take her three decades to complete. Shortly after the first volume (*Pointed Roofs*) appeared, she met and, in 1917, married the artist Allan Odle. A skillful illustrator who was widely regarded as the heir of the sardonic turn-of-the-century aesthete Aubrey Beardsley, Odle was considerably younger than Richardson and evidently almost ethereally frail, so that her feelings for him appear to have been mostly maternal. Yet—despite some ambivalence on Richardson's part—the marriage was a strong one, lasting until Odle died of a heart attack in 1948.

In an early review of *Pointed Roofs*, the novelist May Sinclair borrowed a phrase from the American philosopher William James to describe Richardson's literary technique. "Every definite image of the mind is steeped and dyed in the free water that flows around it," James had written, adding, "Let us call [that water] the stream of thought, of consciousness, or of subjective life." Though Richardson herself objected to what she called the "label" of stream of consciousness, the phrase became standard for historians of modernism seeking to characterize not only her work but also the work of such major contemporaries as James Joyce, Virginia Woolf, and Sinclair herself. As the critic Walter Allen remarks of Richardson's ambitious novel sequence, "Reading *Pilgrimage*, we are within Miriam as in life we are within ourselves; we share in her extraordinary capacity for

continuous and never-blunted response to current existence, the ultimate aston-
isher." Similarly, in *Death*—a brief tale that nevertheless demonstrates
Richardson's technique in miniature—we share in the fluidity, the ceaseless
streaming, of her protagonist's gradually lapsing consciousness, as well as in the
uncannily brilliant perceptions with which the author endows the dying woman in
her final crisis.

In 1957, Dorothy Richardson died in a nursing home in southeast London
where she had been residing for some five years. Despite the influence she had had
on novelists like Sinclair and Woolf, no one at the home had ever heard of her;
when she claimed to be a writer, the nurses, according to her biographer Gloria
Fromm, "believed at first that she had delusions." Yet in recent years critics and
scholars have begun to reread *Pilgrimage*, to recognize the significance both of its
contribution to a modernist aesthetic and of its feminist emphasis on a single
woman's mind and thus to acknowledge the importance of Dorothy Richardson.
For interestingly, in recounting the process by which Miriam Henderson forged her
identity, Richardson had also forged an indelible identity for herself: though her
given name was really Dorothy Miller Richardson, her tombstone—through an
error that seems more crucial than coincidental—was inscribed "To the Memory
of Dorothy *Miriam* Odle, Authoress D. M. Richardson."

Death

This was death this time, no mistake. Her cheeks flushed at the indecency
of being seen, dying and then dead. If only she could get it over and lay herself
out decent before anyone came in to see and meddle. Mrs. Gworsh winning,
left out there in the easy world, coming in to see her dead and lay her out and
talk about her. . . . While there's life there's hope. Perhaps she wasn't dying.
Only afraid. People can be so mighty bad and get better. But no. Not after that
feeling rolling up within, telling her in words, her whom it knew, that this time
she was going to be overwhelmed. That was the beginning, the warning and
the certainty. To be more and more next time, any minute, increasing till her
life flowed out for all to see. Her heart thumped. The rush of life beating
against the walls of her body, making her head spin, numbed the pain and
brought a mist before her eyes. Death. What she'd always feared so shocking,
and put away. But no one knows what it is, how awful beyond everything, till
they're in for it. Nobody knows death is this rush of life in all your parts.

The mist cleared. Her face was damp. The spinning in her head had ceased.
She drew a careful breath. Without pain. Some of the pain had driven through
her without feeling. But she was heavier. It wasn't gone either. Only waiting.
She saw the doctor on his way. Scorn twisted her lips against her empty gums.
Scores of times she'd waited for him. Felt him drive fear away. Joked. This
time he'd say nothing. Watch, for her secret life to come up and out. When
his turn came he'd know what it was like letting your life out; and all of them
out there. No good telling. You can't know till you're in for it. They're all in for
it, rich and poor alike. No help. The great enormous creature driving your in-
nards up, what nobody knows. What *you* don't know. . . . Life ain't worth
death.

It's got to be stuck, shame or no . . . but how do you do it?

She lay still and listened for footsteps. They knew next door by now. That
piece[1] would never milk Snowdrop dry. Less cream, less butter. Everything

1. Girl (pejorative).

going back. Slip-slop, go as you please, and never done. Where'd us be to now if I hadn't? That's it. What they don't think of. Slip-slop. Grinning and singing enough to turn the milk. I've got a tongue. I know it. You've got to keep on and keep on at them. Or nothing done. I been young, but never them silly ways. Snowdrop'll go back; for certain. . . .

But I shan't ever *see* it no more . . . the thought flew lifting through her mind. See no more. Work no more. Worry no more. Then what had been the good of it? Why had she gone on year in year out since Tom died and she began ailing, tramping all weathers up to the field, toiling and aching, and black as thunder most times. What was the good? Nobody knew her. Tom never had. And now there was only that piece downstairs, and what she did didn't matter any more. Except to herself, and she'd go on being slip-slop; not knowing she was in for death that makes it all one whatever you do. Good and bad they're all dying and don't know it's the most they've got to do.

Her mind looked back up and down her life. Tom. What a fool she'd been to think him any different. Then when he died she'd thought him the same as at first, and cried because she'd let it all all slip in the worries. Little Joe. Tearing her open, then snuggled in her arms, sucking. And all outside bright and peaceful; better than the beginning with Tom. But they'd all stop if they knew where it led. Joe, and his wife, and his little ones, in for all of it, getting the hard of it now, and death waiting for them. She could tell them all now what it was like, all of them, the squire, all the same. All going the same way, rich and poor.

The Bible was right, "Remember now thy Creator in the days of thy youth."[2] What she had always wanted. She had always wanted to be good. Now it was too late. Nothing mattering, having it all lifted away, made the inside of you come back as it was at the first, ready to begin. Too late. Shocking she had thought it when parson said prepare for death, live as if you were going to die tonight. But it's true. If every moment was your last on earth you could be yourself. You'd dare. Everybody would dare. People is themselves when they are children, and not again till they know they'm dying. But conscience knows all the time. I've a heavy bill for all my tempers. God forgive me. But why should He? He was having his turn now, anyhow, with all this dying to do. Death must be got through as life had been, just somehow. But how?

When the doctor had gone she knew she was left to do it alone. While there's life there's hope. But the life in her was too much smaller than the great weight and pain. He made her easier, numb. Trying to think and not thinking. Everything unreal. The piece coming up and downstairs like something in another world. Perhaps God would let her go easy. Then it was all over? Just fading to nothing with everything still to do. . . .

The struggle came unexpectedly. She heard her cries, and then the world leapt upon her and grappled, and even in the midst of the agony of pain was the surprise of her immense strength. The strength that struggled against the huge stifling, the body that leapt and twisted against the heavy darkness, a shape within her shape, that she had not known. Her unknown self rushing forward through all her limbs to fight. Leaping out and curving in a great sweep away from where she lay to the open sill, yet pinned back, unwrenchable from the bed. Back and back she slid, down a long tunnel at terrific speed,

2. Ecclesiastes 12:1.

cool, her brow cool and wet, with wind blowing upon it. Darkness in front. Back and back into her own young body, alone. In front on the darkness came the garden, the old garden in April, the crab-apple blossom, all as it was before she began, but brighter. . . .

1924

Women and the Future

Most of the prophecies born of the renewed moral visibility of woman, though superficially at war with each other, are united at their base. They meet and sink, in the sands of the assumption that we are, today, confronted with a new species of woman.

Nearly all of the prophets, nearly all of those who are at work constructing hells, or heavens, upon this loose foundation, are men. And their crying up, or down, of the woman of today, as contrasted to the woman of the past, is easily understood when we consider how difficult it is, even for the least prejudiced, to *think* the feminine past, to escape the images that throng the mind from the centuries of masculine expressiveness on the eternal theme: expressiveness that has so rarely reached beyond the portrayal of woman, whether Madonna, Diana, or Helen,[1] in her moments of relationship to the world as it is known to men.

Even the pioneers of feminism, Mill, Buckle,[2] and their followers, looked only to woman as she was to be in the future, making, for her past, polite, question-begging excuses. The poets, with one exception, accepted the old readings. There is little to choose between the vision of Catholic Rossetti and Swinburne the Pagan. Tennyson,[3] it is true, crowns woman, elaborately, and withal a little irritably, and with much logic-chopping. But he never escapes patronage, and leaves her leaning heavily, albeit most elegantly, upon the arm of man. Browning stands apart, and Stopford Brooke[4] will not be alone in asking what women themselves think of Browning's vision of woman as both queen and lord, outstripping man not only in the wisdom of the heart, but in that of the brain also.

And there is Meredith[5]—with his shining reputation for understanding; a legend that by far outruns his achievement. Glimpses of woman as a full cup unto herself, he certainly had. And he reveals much knowledge of men as they appear in the eyes of such women. This it is that has been accounted unto him for righteousness. He never sees that he is demanding the emancipation of that which he has shown to be independent of bonds. Hardy, his brother

1. These figures—the Virgin Mary, the Roman goddess of the moon, and Helen of Troy—stand, respectively, for the female stereotypes of mother, virgin, and whore.
2. Henry Thomas Buckle (1821–1862), British historian of civilization. John Stuart Mill (1806–1873), philosopher and economist, worked for political and social reform and wrote *The Subjection of Women* (1869).
3. Alfred, Lord Tennyson (1809–1892) showed "patronage" perhaps most clearly in *The Princess* (1850), a fantasy on women's education. Dante Gabriel Rossetti (1828–1882), in both his poetry and painting, showed

his great interest in women's beauty. Algernon Charles Swinburne (1837–1909), a "pagan" both in his rebellion against Christianity and in his interest in Greek literature, created in his poetry some memorably powerful but horrifying women.
4. Stopford Brooke (1832–1916) poses this question in his *Poetry of Robert Browning* (1902). Robert Browning (1812–1889), in whose poetry women display remarkable variety.
5. George Meredith (1828–1909), whose reputation was earned by poems such as *Modern Love* (1862) and novels such as *The Egoist* (1879).

pagan and counterpart, is Perseus[6] hastening to Andromeda, seeking the freedom of the bound.

Since the heyday of Meredith and Hardy, batallions of women have become literate and, in the incandescence of their revelations, masculine illusions are dying like flies. But, even today, most men are scarcely aware of the searchlight flung by these revelations across the past. These modern women, they say, are a new type.

It does not greatly matter to women that men cling to this idea. The truth about the past can be trusted to look after itself. There is, however, no illusion more wasteful than the illusion of beginning all over again; nothing more misleading than the idea of being divorced from the past. It is, nevertheless, quite probable that feminine insistence on exhuming hatchets is not altogether a single-hearted desire to avoid waste and error.

Many men, moreover, are thoroughly disconcerted by the "Modern Woman." They sigh for ancient mystery and inscrutability. For La Giaconda[7] . . . And the most amazing thing in the history of Leonardo's masterpiece is their general failure to recognize that Lisa stands alone in feminine portraiture because she is centered, unlike her nearest peers, those dreamful, passionately blossoming imaginations of Rossetti, neither upon humanity nor upon the consolations of religion.

The Essential Egoist

It is because she is so completely *there* that she draws men like a magnet. Never was better artistic bargain driven than between Leonardo and this lady who sat to him for years; who sat so long that she grew at home in her place, and the deepest layer of her being, her woman's enchanted domestication within the sheer marvel of existing, came forth and shone through the mobile mask of her face. Leonardo of the innocent eye, his genius concentrated upon his business of making a good picture, caught her, unawares, on a gleeful, cosmic holiday. And in seeking the highest, in going on till he got what he wanted, he reaped also the lesser things. For there is in Lisa more than the portrayal of essential womanhood. The secondary life of the lady is clearly visible. Her traffic with familiar webs, with her household and the external shapings of life. When Pater[8] said that her eyelids were a little weary, he showed himself observant. But he misinterpreted the weariness.

On the part of contemporary artists, there are, here and there, attempts to resuscitate man's ancient mystery woman, the beloved-hated abyss. The intensest and the most affrighted of these essayists are D. H. Lawrence and Augustus John.[9] Perhaps they are nearer salvation than they know.

For the essential characteristic of women is egoism. Let it at once be admitted that this is a masculine discovery. It has been offered as the worst that can be said of the sex as a whole. It is both the worst and the best. Egoism is at

6. In Greek legend, the hero Perseus rescued Andromeda, who had been bound on a rock as a sacrifice to a sea monster. Thomas Hardy (1840–1928), a poet and a novelist; in this context, see especially *Tess of the D'Urbervilles* (1891).
7. The painting (c. 1506) by Leonardo da Vinci also known as the *Mona Lisa*.
8. The observation is from Walter Pater's (1839–1894) essay on Leonardo da Vinci in *The Renaissance*

(1893).
9. British painter and etcher (1879–1961). Richardson may be alluding not only to reliance on women as muses for his art but also to his remarkably tangled personal life. D. H. Lawrence (1885–1930), British poet, essayist, and novelist, who was notoriously concerned with relationships between the sexes, and particularly with powerful women.

once the root of shameless selfishness and the ultimate dwelling place of charity. Many men, of whom Mr. Wells[1] is the chief spokesman, read the history of woman's past influence in public affairs as one long story of feminine egoism. They regard her advance with mixed feelings, and face her with a neat dilemma. Either, they say, you must go on being Helens and Cinderellas, or you must drop all that and play the game, in so far as your disabilities allow, as we play it. They look forward to the emergence of an army of civilized, docile women, following modestly behind the vanguard of males at work upon the business of reducing chaos to order.

Another group of thinkers sees the world in process of feminization, the savage wilderness, where men compete and fight, turned into a home. Over against them are those who view the opening prospect with despair. To them, feminism is the invariable accompaniment of degeneration. They draw back in horror before the oncoming flood of mediocrity. They see ahead a democratized world, overrun by hordes of inferior beings, organized by majorities for material ends; with primitive, uncivilizable woman rampant in the midst.

Serenely apart from these small camps is a large class of delightful beings, the representatives of average masculinity at its best, drawing much comfort from the spectacle of contradictory, mysterious woman at last bidding fair to become something recognizably like itself. Women, they say, are beginning to take life like men; are finding in life the things men have found. They make room for her. They are charming. Their selfishness is social, gregarious. Woman is to be the jolly companion; to co-operate with man in the great business of organizing the world for jollity. But have any of these so variously grouped males any idea of the depth and scope of feminine egoism? Do they not confound it with masculine selfishness? Do they realize anything of the vast difference between these two things?

It is upon the perception of this difference that any verdict as to the result of woman's arrival "in the world" ultimately rests. Though, it is true, certain of these masculine forecasts are being abundantly realized. There is abroad in life a growing army of man-trained women, brisk, positive, rational creatures with no nonsense about them, living from the bustling surfaces of the mind; sharing the competitive partisanships of men; subject, like men, to fear; subject to national panic; to international, and even to cosmic panic. There is also an army let loose of the daughters of the horse-leech;[2] part of the organization of the world for pleasure. These types have always existed. The world of the moment particularly favors them. But their egoism is as nothing to the egoism of the womanly woman, the beloved-hated abyss, at once the refuge and the despair of man.

For the womanly woman lives, all her life, in the deep current of eternity, an individual, self-centered. Because she is one with life, past, present, and future are together in her, unbroken. Because she thinks flowingly, with her feelings, she is relatively indifferent to the fashions of men, to the momentary arts, religions, philosophies, and sciences, valuing them only in so far as she is aware of their importance in the evolution of the beloved. It is man's incomplete individuality that leaves him at the mercy of that subtle form of despair which is called ambition, and accounts for his apparent selfishness. Only completely

1. H. G. Wells (1866–1946), writer of fiction and social criticism (whose views are more commonly seen as feminist).

2. I.e., insatiable, greedy women. See Proverbs 30:15: "The horseleech hath two daughters, crying, Give, give."

self-centered consciousness can attain to unselfishness—the celebrated un-selfishness of the womanly woman. Only a complete self, carrying all its goods in its own hands, can go out, perfectly, to others, move freely in any direction. Only a complete self can afford to man the amusing spectacle of the chameleon woman.

Apart from the saints, the womanly woman is the only human being free to try to be as good as she wants to be. And it is to this inexorable creature, whom even Nietzsche[3] was constrained to place ahead of man, that man returns from his wanderings with those others in the deserts of agnosticism. She is rare. But wherever she is found, there also are found the dependent hosts.

But is not the material of this intuitive creature strictly limited? Is she not fettered by sex? Seeking man, while man, freed by nature for his divine pur-pose, seeks God, through blood and tears, through trial and error, in every form of civilization? He for God only, she for God in him?[4] She is. She does. When man announces that the tree at the door of the cave is God, she excels him in the dark joy of the discovery. When he reaches the point of saying that God is a Spirit and they that worship him must worship him in spirit and in truth, she is there waiting for him, ready to parrot any formula that shows him aware of the amazing fact of life.

And it is this creature who is now on the way to be driven out among the practical affairs of our world, together with the "intelligent" woman; i.e., with the woman who is intelligible to men. For the first time. Unwillingly. The re-sults cannot be exactly predicted. But her gift of imaginative sympathy, her ca-pacity for vicarious living, for being simultaneously in all the warring camps, will tend to make her within the council of nations what the Quaker[5] is within the council of religions.

Women in the Future

Public concerted action must always be a compromise. But there is all the difference between having things roughly arranged *ad hoc* by father, however strong his sense of abstract justice, and having them arranged by father prompted by mother, under the unseen presidency[6] of desire to do the best re-gardless, in the woman's regardless, unprincipled, miracle-working way, for all concerned.

The world at large is swiftly passing from youthful freebooting.[7] It is on the way to find itself married. That is to say, in for startling changes. Shaken up. Led by the nose and liking it. A question arises. How will his apparently less-ened state react on man? In how far has he been dependent on his illusion of supremacy? Perhaps the answer to this is the superiority of men in talent, in constructive capacity. It is the talent of man, his capacity to *do* most things better than women, backed up by the genius of woman. The capacity to *see* that is carrying life forward to the levels opening out ahead.

1924

3. This is an unusual reading of the Germany philoso-pher Friedrich Nietzsche (1844–1900), who is gener-ally highly critical of the "eternal feminine." However, in *Beyond Good and Evil* he finds woman inspiring re-spect and "even fear" because of "her *nature*, which is more 'natural' than man's," and "the naïveté of her egoism.
4. Milton's *Paradise Lost* (1667) 4.299 (where "he" and "she" are Adam and Eve).

5. Or a member of the Society of Friends. Quakers emphasize the importance of each individual's under-standing as guided by inner light; they are pacifists who traditionally have been active in reform and phil-anthropic movements.
6. I.e., act of presiding. "*Ad hoc*": for this (Latin, literal trans.); for the particular case at hand.
7. Piracy, plundering.

AMY LOWELL

1874–1925

"I am ugly, fat, conspicuous & dull," Amy Lowell confided to her diary when she was fifteen, adding, soon after, that "I should like best of anything to be literary." Although she *was* overweight, Lowell's adolescent self-definition was otherwise quite inaccurate. As the daughter of a prominent Boston family, she had inherited a confident manner bred by generations of privilege: her grandfathers on both sides had founded important textile businesses; one of her cousins was the poet James Russell Lowell; her father was a member of the governing board of the Massachusetts Institute of Technology; her brother Percival was the founder of the Lowell Observatory at Harvard; and her brother Abbott Lawrence was a president of Harvard. She herself, moreover, was evidently a gifted child who discovered that she liked best "to be literary" mainly by ranging through her father's excellent library. By the time she was in her early teens she had begun to read the Romantic poets, and she had produced a first book titled *Dream Drops, or Stories from Fairy Land, by a Dreamer* (1887), which her mother arranged for her to sell at a charity bazaar.

To be sure, as the daughter of a distinguished family Amy Lowell was expected to lead a genteel life. After making her debut in society, she took several long trips abroad, and at one point she almost became engaged to a "proper" Bostonian. In addition, both before and after the deaths of her parents in the last years of the century, she served on numerous civic boards and committees. At the same time, however, she continued to be tormented by personal problems; she suffered from bouts of "nervous prostration" and was intransigently overweight despite countless attempts at severe dieting, even while, persistently "literary," she converted several rooms of Sevenels—the Lowell family mansion—into what one biographer has called "a baronial library."

It was during the Boston theater season of 1902 that this ambivalent former debutante first seriously defined herself as a poet. She experienced her literary awakening because of an encounter with Eleanora Duse, the Italian actress, who was appearing in a play written by her lover, the poet Gabriel D'Annunzio. Lowell attended the work's opening-night performance, where she was so overcome by Duse's dramatic presence that she returned home and wrote, as she later remembered, "seventy-one lines of bad blank verse," including a tribute to the actress's "woman's soul" and "woman's heart." After this, and after attending all the other performances of the D'Annunzio play, Lowell claimed to know that verse writing was her true vocation. Struggling to perfect her art, she read, studied, founded a little theater group, and in 1912 published her first collection, a somewhat derivative volume titled *A Dome of Many-Coloured Glass* in deference to *Adonais*, the Romantic poet Shelley's elegy for her beloved John Keats.

Shortly before *A Dome* appeared and ten years after her crucial encounter with Duse, Lowell met another woman who was to inspire her even more than the Italian celebrity had. Ada Dwyer Russell, a divorced actress eleven years Lowell's senior, was introduced to the poet at a women's "lunch club," and the attraction between the two was evidently both mutual and instantaneous. By 1914, Ada Russell had moved into Sevenels, where she was to live with Amy Lowell for the rest of the writer's life, acting—the way Alice B. Toklas did for Gertrude Stein—as beloved companion, general amanuensis, resident critic, and nurturing muse. For her, Lowell composed many of her most poignant love poems, including *Madonna of the Evening Flowers*, *The Letter*, *Venus Transiens*, and *Opal*. At the same time, the relationship between the two women was evidently so deeply collaborative

that Lowell sometimes joked that they should put up a sign above the doorway at Sevenels reading "Lowell & Russell, Makers of Fine Poems."

Also significantly influential on Lowell's evolving art was the founding in 1912 of *Poetry* magazine. Edited in Chicago by the innovative woman of letters Harriet Monroe, this journal immediately began to publish the works of Ezra Pound, T. S. Eliot, D. H. Lawrence, John Gould Fletcher, Richard Aldington, and H. D. (Hilda Doolittle), among others. Upon Lowell, H. D.'s free verse, with its irregular lines and crisp, Greek-inspired images, had the greatest impact; as one critic observes, "When in the January 1913 number [of *Poetry*] she saw the signature 'H. D., Imagiste,' she recognized in a flash her own as yet unrealized poetic identity," for she felt that she too ought to be writing verse in the deliberately stripped, cool, vividly pictorial style employed by the group of aesthetic radicals who, under the leadership of the revolutionary Ezra Pound, called themselves "Imagists." Journeying to London in 1913, Lowell and Russell met Pound; the following year, just before the outbreak of World War I, the pair returned to England to make the acquaintance of John Gould Fletcher, H. D., Henry James, D. H. Lawrence, and Robert Frost. With Lawrence and Frost, in particular, Lowell formed important, long-lasting friendships, though, as is clear in the sardonic couplets of her *A Critical Fable* (an updating of a similar poem by her uncle James Russell Lowell), her responses to other writers were not uniformly positive.

Nevertheless, no doubt encouraged by her participation in innovative aesthetic circles as well as by her relationship with Ada Russell, Lowell now began to produce and edit volumes of poetry and criticism at an increasingly energetic pace. Works like *Can Grande's Castle* (1918) and *Pictures of the Floating World* (1919) firmly established her reputation as a leader of the Imagist movement, which its founder, Ezra Pound, sarcastically renamed "Amygism." Books like *Tendencies in Modern American Poetry* (1917) gave her an equally solid reputation as a critic. Eccentric in her personal behavior—she was, for instance, famous for smoking what most people thought were "big black cigars" (really slim cigarillos)—she became a celebrity.

During her last years, Lowell's lifetime of ambitious activity combined with serious overweight led to ill health. In 1918, she had the first of a series of operations (for an umbilical hernia) that drastically weakened her. Still, she continued indefatigably writing, lecturing, reviewing, and maintaining many friendships. Her most important project in the early 1920s was a massive biography of John Keats, the Romantic poet she had admired since her youth. Published early in 1925, the book aroused much controversy, especially in England, and the author was planning to travel to London to defend it when she died of a cerebral hemorrhage in May 1925, at fifty-one. The following year her posthumously published volume of poems, *What's O'Clock*, was awarded the Pulitzer Prize. The honor, as her biographer Jean Gould observes, was fitting, for this collection featured a number of Lowell's finest verses, including her long meditation on the lot of female poets titled *The Sisters*, a work that might well stand as a vindication of the rights of women like Amy Lowell to abandon genteel New England society and, instead, create poems, compose criticism, edit anthologies, write biographies, love women like Ada Russell, and smoke slim, elegant cigarillos.

The Letter

Little cramped words scrawling all over the paper
Like draggled fly's legs,
What can you tell of the flaring moon
Through the oak leaves?
Or of my uncurtained window and the bare floor 5
Spattered with moonlight?

Your silly quirks and twists have nothing in them
Of blossoming hawthorns,
And this paper is dull, crisp, smooth, virgin of loveliness
Beneath my hand. 10

I am tired, Beloved, of chafing my heart against
The want of you,
Of squeezing it into little inkdrops,
And posting[1] it.
And I scald alone, here, under the fire 15
Of the great moon.

1919

Venus Transiens[1]

Tell me,
Was Venus more beautiful
Than you are,
When she topped
The crinkled waves, 5
Drifting shoreward
On her plaited shell?
Was Botticelli's vision[2]
Fairer than mine;
And were the painted rosebuds 10
He tossed his lady,
Of better worth
Than the words I blow about you
To cover your too great loveliness
As with a gauze 15
Of misted silver?
For me,
You stand poised
In the blue and buoyant air,
Cinctured by bright winds, 20
Treading the sunlight.
And the waves which precede you
Ripple and stir
The sands at my feet.

1919

Madonna[1] of the Evening Flowers

All day long I have been working.
Now I am tired.

1. Mailing.
1. Venus passing over (Latin). Venus is the Roman equivalent of Aphrodite, the goddess of love.
2. Sandro Botticelli (1444–1510) executed a famous painting called *The Birth of Venus*, in which the god-

dess stands on a large scalloped seashell riding on the ocean waves.
1. My lady. In Italian painting, the phrase is applied to the Virgin Mary.

I call: "Where are you?"
But there is only the oak-tree rustling in the wind.
The house is very quiet, 5
The sun shines in on your books,
On your scissors and thimble just put down,
But you are not there.
Suddenly I am lonely:
Where are you? 10
I go about searching.

Then I see you,
Standing under a spire of pale blue larkspur,
With a basket of roses on your arm.
You are cool, like silver, 15
And you smile.
I think the Canterbury bells[2] are playing little tunes.

You tell me that the peonies need spraying,
That the columbines have overrun all bounds,
That the pyrus japonica should be cut back and rounded. 20
You tell me these things.
But I look at you, heart of silver,
White heart-flame of polished silver,
Burning beneath the blue steeples of the larkspur,
And I long to kneel instantly at your feet, 25
While all about us peal the loud, sweet *Te Deums*[3] of the
 Canterbury bells.

 1919

The Weather-Cock Points South

I put your leaves aside,
One by one:
The stiff, broad outer leaves;
The smaller ones,
Pleasant to touch, veined with purple; 5
The glazed inner leaves.
One by one
I parted you from your leaves,
Until you stood up like a white flower
Swaying slightly in the evening wind. 10

White flower,
Flower of wax, of jade, of unstreaked agate;
Flower with surfaces of ice,
With shadows faintly crimson.
Where in all the garden is there such a flower? 15

2. The bells of the famous cathedral at Canterbury, 3. An ancient Christian Latin hymn: "*Te deum lau-*
England. *damus*" (We praise thee, God).

The stars crowd through the lilac leaves
To look at you.
The low moon brightens you with silver.

The bud is more than the calyx.
There is nothing to equal a white bud, 20
Of no color, and of all,
Burnished by moonlight,
Thrust upon by a softly-swinging wind.

 1919

Opal

You are ice and fire,
The touch of you burns my hands like snow.
You are cold and flame.
You are the crimson of amaryllis,
The silver of moon-touched magnolias. 5
When I am with you,
My heart is a frozen pond
Gleaming with agitated torches.

 1919

Decade

When you came, you were like red wine and honey,
And the taste of you burnt my mouth with its sweetness.
Now you are like morning bread
Smooth and pleasant.
I hardly taste you at all for I know your savour, 5
But I am completely nourished.

 1919

Summer Rain

All night our room was outer-walled with rain.
Drops fell and flattened on the tin roof,
And rang like little disks of metal.
Ping!—Ping!—and there was not a pinpoint of silence between them.
The rain rattled and clashed, 5
And the slats of the shutters danced and glittered.
But to me the darkness was red-gold and crocus-colored
With your brightness,
And the words you whispered to me
Sprang up and flamed—orange torches against the rain. 10
Torches against the wall of cool, silver rain!

 1919

From A Critical Fable

[*On T. S. Eliot and Ezra Pound*]

* * *

To start off again with my tale: "The expatriates
Come next," I began, "but the man who expatiates
Upon them must go all yclad in cold steel
Since these young men are both of them most *difficile*,[1]
And each is possessed of a gift for satire. 5
Their forked barbs would pierce any usual attire.
In order of merit, if not of publicity,
I will take Eliot first, though it smacks of duplicity
To award Ezra Pound[2] the inferior place
As he simply won't run if not first in a race. 10
Years ago, 'twould have been the other way round,
With Eliot a rather bad second to Pound.
But Pound has been woefully free with the mustard[3]
And so occupied has quite ruined his custard.
No poems from his pen, just spleen[4] on the loose, 15
And a man who goes on in that way cooks his goose.
T. S. Eliot's a very unlike proposition,
He has simply won through by process of attrition.
Where Pound played the fool, Eliot acted the wiseacre;
Eliot works in his garden, Pound stultifies his acre. 20
Eliot's always engaged digging fruit out of dust;
Pound was born in an orchard, but his trees have the rust.
Eliot's mind is perpetually fixed and alert;
Pound goes off anywhere, anyhow, like a squirt.
Pound believes he's a thinker, but he's far too romantic; 25
Eliot's sure he's a poet when he's only pedantic.
But Eliot has raised pedantry to a pitch,
While Pound has upset romance into a ditch.
Eliot fears to abandon an old masquerade;
Pound's one perfect happiness is to parade. 30
Eliot's learning was won at a very great price;
What Pound calls his learning he got in a trice.
Eliot knows what he knows, though he cannot digest it;
Pound knows nothing at all, but has frequently guessed it.
Eliot builds up his essays by a process of massing; 35
Pound's are mostly hot air, what the vulgar call 'gassing.'
Eliot lives like a snail in his shell, pen protruding;
Pound struts like a cock, self-adored, self-deluding.
Pound's darling desire is his ego's projection;
Eliot tortures his soul with a dream of perfection. 40
Pound's an ardent believer in the value of noise;
Eliot strains every nerve to attain a just poise.
Each despises his fellows, for varying reasons;
Each one is a traitor, but with different treasons.

1. Difficult (French). "Yclad": dressed (archaic).
2. The American poets T. S. Eliot (1888–1965) and Ezra Pound (1885–1972); each came to England in his twenties.
3. I.e., strong, pungent words.
4. Ill temper, spitefulness.

Each has left his own country, but Pound is quite sick of it, 45
While for Eliot's sojourn, he is just in the nick of it.
Pound went gunning for trouble, and got it, for cause;
Eliot, far more astute, has deserved his applause.
Each has more brain than heart, but while one man's a critic
The other is more than two-thirds tympanitic.[5] 50
Both of them are book-men, but where Eliot has found
A horizon in letters, Pound has only found Pound.
Each man feels himself so little complete
That he dreads the least commerce with the man in the street;
Each imagines the world to be leagued in a dim pact 55
To destroy his immaculate taste by its impact.
To conceive such a notion, one might point out slyly,
Would scarcely occur to an author more highly
Original; such men seldom bother their wits
With outsiders at all, whether fits or misfits. 60
Where they are, whom they see, is a matter of sheer
Indifference to a poet with his own atmosphere
To exist in, and such have no need to be preachy
Anent commonplaceness since they can't write a cliché—
In toto,[6] at least, and it's toto that grounds 65
All meticulous poets like the Eliots and Pounds.
Taking up Eliot's poetry, it's a blend of intensive
And elegant satire with a would-be offensive
Kind of virulent diatribe, and neither sort's lacking
In the high type of polish we demand of shoe-blacking. 70
Watteau if you like, arm in arm with Laforgue,[7]
And both of these worthies laid out in a morgue.
The poems are expert even up to a vice,
But they're chilly and dead like corpses on ice.
Now a man who's reluctant to heat his work through, 75
I submit, is afraid of what that work will do
On its own, with its muscles and sinews unfrozen.
Something, I must think, which he would not have chosen.
Is there barely a clue here that the action of heat
Might reveal him akin to the man in the street? 80
For his brain—there's no doubt that is up on a steeple,
But his heart might betray him as one of the people.
A fearful dilemma! We can hardly abuse him
For hiding the damaging fact and excuse him
If it really be so, and we've more than a hint of it, 85
Although I, for one, like him better by dint of it.
Since the poet's not the half of him, we must include
The critical anchorite of his 'Sacred Wood.'
'This slim duodecimo[8] you must have your eye on
If you'd be up to date,' say his friends. He's a sly one. 90
To have chosen this format—the book's heavy as iron
I'm acutely aware that its grave erudition

5. I.e., Pound beats his own drum.
6. On the whole (Latin). "Anent": concerning.
7. Jules L. Laforgue (1860–1887), French symbolist
poet who wrote in free verse. Antoine Watteau

(1684–1721), French painter.
8. A small book size. "Sacred Wood": a book of critical
essays (1920).

Is quite in the line of a certain tradition,
That one which is commonly known as tuition.
To read it is much like a lengthy sojourning 95
In at least two or three institutions of learning.
But, being no schoolboy, I find I'm not burning
For this sort of instruction, and vote for adjourning.
What the fellow's contrived to stuff into his skull 100
May be certainly classed as a pure miracle,
But the way he imparts it is terribly dull.
This may not be fair, for I've only begun it,
And one should not pronounce on a book till one's done it,
But I've started so often, in so many places, 105
I think, had there been any livelier spaces
I must have encountered at least one of those
Before falling, I say it with shame, in a doze.
We must take Ezra Pound from a different angle:
He's a belfry of excellent chimes run to jangle 110
By being too often and hurriedly tugged at,
And even, when more noise was wanted, just slugged at
And hammered with anything there was lying round.
Such delicate bells could not stand so much Pound.
Few men have to their credit more excellent verses 115
Than he used to write, and even his worse is
Much better than most people's good. He'd a flair
For just the one word indispensably there,
But which few could have hit on. Another distinction
Was the way he preserved fledgeling poets from extinction.[9] 120
Had he never consented to write when the urge
To produce was not on him, he'd have been on the verge
Of a great reputation by now, but his shoulder
Had always its chip, and Ezra's a scolder.
Off he flew, giving nerves and brain up to the business 125
In a crowing excitement not unmixed with dizziness,
Whenever he could get any sort of newspaper
To lend him a column and just let him vapor.
But while he was worrying his gift of invention
For adequate means to ensure the prevention 130
Of any one's getting what he had not got,
His uncherished talent succumbed to dry rot.
When, after the battle, he would have employed her,
He learnt, to his cost, that he had destroyed her.
Now he does with her ghost, and the ghosts of the hosts 135
Of troubadors, minstrels, and kings, for he boasts
An acquaintance with persons of whose very names
I am totally ignorant, likewise their fames.
The foremost, of course, is Bertrand de Born,[1]
He's a sort of pervasively huge leprecawn 140
Popping out from Pound's lines where you never expect him.

9. Pound promoted avant-garde movements, notably
Imagism and Vorticism; the writers he encouraged in-
cluded H. D. as well as Eliot.
1. Bertrans de Born (c. 1140–c. 1215), a viscount, was
a celebrated Provençal troubadour (as well as a sol-
dier). Pound wrote of him in *Sestina: Altaforte* (1909)
and *Near Perigord* (1911) and translated him in *Planh
for the Young English King* (1909) and *A War Song*
(1910).

He is our poet's chief lar,[2] so we must not neglect him.
There is Pierre de Maensac, and Pierre won the singing—
Where or how I can't guess, but Pound sets his fame ringing
Because he was *dreitz hom* (whatever that is) 145
And had De Tierci's wife; what happened to his
We don't know, in fact we know nothing quite clearly,
For Pound always treats his ghosts cavalierly.
There is John Borgia's bath, and be sure that he needed it;
Aurunculeia's shoe, but no one much heeded it. 150
There's a chap named Navighero and another Barabello,
Who prods a Pope's elephant; and one Mozarello;
Savairic Mauleon—Good Lord, what a dance
Of impossible names![3] First I think we're in France,
Then he slides in Odysseus, and Eros, and Atthis— 155
But I'm not to be fooled in my Greek, that's what that is.
Yet, look, there's Italian sticking out in italics
And French in plain type, the foreign vocalics
Do give one the feeling of infinite background,
When it's all just a trick of that consummate quack, Pound, 160
To cheat us to thinking there's something behind it.
But, when nothing's to find, it's a hard job to find it.
The tragedy lies in the fact that the man
Had a potentiality such as few can
Look back or forward to; had he but kept it, 165
There's no bar in all poetry but he might have leapt it.
Even now, I believe, if he'd let himself grow,
He might start again. . ." "We will have no 'although'
In your gamut of poets. Your man is a victim
Of expatriation, and, as usual, it's licked him. 170
It has happened more times than I care to reflect,
And the general toll is two countries' neglect."

 * * *

 1922

The Sisters

Taking us by and large, we're a queer lot
We women who write poetry. And when you think
How few of us there've been, it's queerer still.
I wonder what it is that makes us do it,
Singles us out to scribble down, man-wise, 5
The fragments of ourselves. Why are we
Already mother-creatures, double-bearing,
With matrices in body and in brain?
I rather think that there is just the reason
We are so sparse a kind of human being; 10
The strength of forty thousand Atlases[1]

2. Spirit guarding a Roman household.
3. These "impossible names" are in *Canto* 5 (1921), except Odysseus, who first appears in *Canto* 1 (a version was published in 1917).

1. In Greek mythology, one of a giant race called the Titans, who was assigned the task of holding up the earth.

Is needed for our every-day concerns.
There's Sapho,[2] now I wonder what was Sapho.
I know a single slender thing about her:
That, loving, she was like a burning birch-tree 15
All tall and glittering fire, and that she wrote
Like the same fire caught up to Heaven and held there,
A frozen blaze before it broke and fell.
Ah, me! I wish I could have talked to Sapho,
Surprised her reticences by flinging mine 20
Into the wind. This tossing off of garments
Which cloud the soul is none too easy doing
With us today. But still I think with Sapho
One might accomplish it, were she in the mood
To bare her loveliness of words and tell 25
The reasons, as she possibly conceived them,
Of why they are so lovely. Just to know
How she came at them, just to watch
The crisp sea sunshine playing on her hair,
And listen, thinking all the while 'twas she 30
Who spoke and that we two were sisters
Of a strange, isolated little family.
And she is Sapho—Sapho—not Miss or Mrs.,
A leaping fire we call so for convenience;
But Mrs. Browning[3]—who would ever think 35
Of such presumption as to call her "Ba."
Which draws the perfect line between sea-cliffs
And a close-shuttered room in Wimpole Street.
Sapho could fly her impulses like bright
Balloons tip-tilting to a morning air 40
And write about it. Mrs. Browning's heart
Was squeezed in stiff conventions. So she lay
Stretched out upon a sofa, reading Greek
And speculating, as I must suppose,
In just this way on Sapho; all the need, 45
The huge, imperious need of loving, crushed
Within the body she believed so sick.
And it was sick, poor lady, because words
Are merely simulacra after deeds
Have wrought a pattern; when they take the place 50
Of actions they breed a poisonous miasma
Which, though it leave the brain, eats up the body.
So Mrs. Browning, aloof and delicate,
Lay still upon her sofa, all her strength
Going to uphold her over-topping brain. 55
It seems miraculous, but she escaped
To freedom and another motherhood
Than that of poems. She was a very[4] woman
And needed both.
 If I had gone to call,

2. Or Sappho (600 B.C.), Greek lyric poet.
3. Elizabeth Barrett Browning (1806–1861), English poet known familiarly as "Ba"; she lived as an invalid in her father's house in Wimpole Street, until the poet Robert Browning courted and married her.
4. True.

Would Wimpole Street have been the kindlier place, 60
Or Casa Guidi,[5] in which to have met her?
I am a little doubtful of that meeting,
For Queen Victoria was very young and strong
And all-pervading in her apogee
At just that time. If we had stuck to poetry, 65
Sternly refusing to be drawn off by mesmerism
Or Roman revolutions,[6] it might have done.
For, after all, she is another sister,
But always, I rather think, an older sister
And not herself so curious a technician 70
As to admit newfangled modes of writing—
"Except, of course, in Robert, and that is neither
Here nor there for Robert is a genius."
I do not like the turn this dream is taking,
Since I am very fond of Mrs. Browning 75
And very much indeed should like to hear her
Graciously asking me to call her "Ba."
But then the Devil of Verisimilitude
Creeps in and forces me to know she wouldn't.
Convention again, and how it chafes my nerves, 80
For we are such a little family
Of singing sisters, and as if I didn't know
What those years felt like tied down to the sofa.
Confound Victoria, and the slimy inhibitions
She loosed on all us Anglo-Saxon creatures! 85
Suppose there hadn't been a Robert Browning,
No *Sonnets from the Portuguese*[7] would have been written.
They are the first of all her poems to be,
One might say, fertilized. For, after all,
A poet is flesh and blood as well as brain 90
And Mrs. Browning, as I said before,
Was very, very woman. Well, there are two
Of us, and vastly unlike that's for certain.
Unlike at least until we tear the veils
Away which commonly gird souls. I scarcely think 95
Mrs. Browning would have approved the process
In spite of what had surely been relief;
For speaking souls must always want to speak
Even when bat-eyed, narrow-minded Queens
Set prudishness to keep the keys of impulse. 100
Then do the frowning Gods invent new banes
And make the need of sofas. But Sapho was dead
And I, and others, not yet peeped above
The edge of possibility So that's an end
To speculating over tea-time talks 105
Beyond the movement of pentameters
With Mrs. Browning.

5. The house in Florence where the Brownings resided
after their marriage.
6. At the time of the Brownings' residence, Italy was
struggling for independence from foreign rule.
7. A sequence of love sonnets by Barrett Browning ad-
dressed to her husband, Robert.

But I go dreaming on,
In love with these my spiritual relations.
I rather think I see myself walk up
A flight of wooden steps and ring a bell 110
And send a card in to Miss Dickinson.[8]
Yet that's a very silly way to do.
I should have taken the dream twist-ends about
And climbed over the fence and found her deep
Engrossed in the doings of a humming-bird 115
Among nasturtiums. Not having expected strangers,
She might forget to think me one, and holding up
A finger say quite casually: "Take care.
Don't frighten him, he's only just begun."
"Now this," I well believe I should have thought, 120
"Is even better than Sapho. With Emily
You're really here, or never anywhere at all
In range of mind." Wherefore, having begun
In the strict center we could slowly progress
To various circumferences, as we pleased. 125
We could, but should we? That would quite depend
On Emily. I think she'd be exacting,
Without intention possibly, and ask
A thousand tight-rope tricks of understanding.
But, bless you, I would somersault all day 130
If by so doing I might stay with her.
I hardly think that we should mention souls
Although they might just round the corner from us
In some half-quizzical, half-wistful metaphor.
I'm very sure that I should never seek 135
To turn her parables to stated fact.
Sapho would speak, I think, quite openly,
And Mrs. Browning guard a careful silence,
But Emily would set doors ajar and slam them
And love you for your speed of observation. 140

Strange trio of my sisters, most diverse,
And how extraordinarily unlike
Each is to me, and which way shall I go?
Sapho spent and gained; and Mrs. Browning,
After a miser girlhood, cut the strings 145
Which tied her money-bags and let them run;
But Emily hoarded—hoarded—only giving
Herself to cold, white paper.[9] Starved and tortured,
She cheated her despair with games of patience[1]
And fooled herself by winning. Frail little elf, 150
The lonely brain-child of a gaunt maturity,
She hung her womanhood upon a bough
And played ball with the stars—too long—too long—
The garment of herself hung on a tree
Until at last she lost even the desire 155

8. Emily Dickinson (1830–1886), American poet.
9. This sentence relies on a sexual as well as a financial

metaphor: "to spend" also means to have an orgasm.
1. Solitaire card games.

To take it down. Whose fault? Why let us say,
To be consistent, Queen Victoria's.
But really, not to over-rate the queen,
I feel obliged to mention Martin Luther,[2]
And behind him the long line of Church Fathers 160
Who draped their prurience like a dirty cloth
About the naked majesty of God.
Good-bye, my sisters, all of you are great.
And all of you are marvellously strange,
And none of you has any word for me. 165
I cannot write like you, I cannot think
In terms of Pagan or of Christian now.
I only hope that possibly some day
Some other woman with an itch for writing
May turn to me as I have turned to you 170
And chat with me a brief few minutes. How
We lie, we poets! It is three good hours
I have been dreaming. Has it seemed so long
To you? And yet I thank you for the time
Although you leave me sad and self-distrustful, 175
For older sisters are very sobering things.
Put on your cloaks, my dears, the motor's waiting.
No, you have not seemed strange to me, but near,
Frightfully near, and rather terrifying.
I understand you all, for in myself— 180
Is that presumption? Yet indeed it's true—
We are one family. And still my answer
Will not be any one of yours, I see.
Well, never mind that now. Good night! Good night!

1925

2. German monk (1483–1546), leader of the Protestant Reformation.

GERTRUDE STEIN

1874–1946

In paintings by Pablo Picasso (1906) and Pavel Tchelitchew (1930), sculptures by Jacques Lipchitz (1920) and Jo Davidson (1920), and the many photographs by Carl Van Vechten and Cecil Beaton, Gertrude Stein sometimes looks like the Roman emperor Ernest Hemingway took her to be and sometimes like the great Jewish Buddha many of her other friends thought she resembled. Whether, in a reference to the derisively experimental movement called "dadaism," she was hailed as the "the Mama of dada" or ridiculed as "the Mother Goose of Montparnasse," Stein herself was hardly embarrassed about her growing celebrity, for she believed that "Einstein was the creative philosophic mind of the century and I have been the creative literary mind of the century." But as late in her career as 1937 she admitted, "It always did bother me that the American public were more interested in me than in my work." If her *oeuvre* has been neglected because it sometimes seems opaque or even incomprehensible, that is because it includes short stories, portraits, novels, autobiographies, dramas, and poems that develop the radical linguistic experimentation associated with modernism

Stein was a first-generation American, the youngest of seven children. In 1841, her German-Jewish father, Daniel Stein, emigrated from Bavaria to Baltimore, where he established a profitable clothing business and married Amelia (Keyser) Stein before moving to Allegheny, Pennsylvania, in 1862 to start his family. Stein's earliest memories dated from the age of four, when the family lived in Austria and Paris before settling down in Oakland, California, in 1879. Although she had prat-tled in German and French, she soon began reading English poetry and fiction, and more idiosyncratically, congressional records and constitutional histories of England. After the death of her mother in 1888 and the death of her father three years later, she and her closest sibling, Leo, traveled to Baltimore, where they were cared for by their mother's sister, Fannie Bachrach, and provided for by an inde-pendent income secured for them by their eldest brother, Michael.

Stein's identification with Leo continued to inform her early development. After Leo transferred from the University of California to Harvard, Gertrude en-rolled as a special student at the Annex that would become Radcliffe College. There she studied with the philosopher George Santayana and the psychologist William James. With the encouragement of James, she joined Leo in Baltimore in 1897 to pursue a medical education at Johns Hopkins, where her formal class training was supplemented by obstetrical work and by her friendship with Claribel and Etta Cone, two well-to-do and well-educated young women. But after two years, Stein abandoned her plans to complete the medical degree. She was proba-bly depressed by her involvement in an erotic triangle with Mabel Haynes and May Bookstaver: Stein fictionalized her sense of misery at the futility of this relation-ship in *Q.E.D. or Things as They Are*, a work published posthumously in 1950. In 1902, she joined Leo, who had been studying in Italy with the art critic Bernard Berenson. After a summer in Bloomsbury and a winter in New York, she again re-turned to Leo, who occupied rooms at 27 rue de Fleurus that would soon become famous as a center of avant-garde activity in Paris.

It was from this early period in Paris that Stein's fascination with modern art dated. Attached by a courtyard to the rooms the Steins shared was an atelier (a stu-dio), which was quickly filled with the many paintings they purchased from art dealers like Amboise Vollard. Stein herself recounted how they found Matisse's *La Femme au Chapeau* at the Petit Palais show where some viewers were so infuriated by this picture that they laughed and tried to scratch off the paint. What attracted Stein to the impressionist and postimpressionist work of Cézanne, Renoir, Rousseau, Braque, Matisse, and Picasso was their effort to use deformation to in-tensify and clarify visual effect. Soon she began her own efforts to intensify and clarify English so as to liberate language from representation. The three stories that comprise *Three Lives* (1909)—*The Good Anna, Melanctha*, and *The Gentle Lena*—were composed while the writer studied Cézanne's portrait of his wife and while she sat for Picasso's portrait of her. They are what she called "the first defi-nite step away from the nineteenth century and into the twentieth century in lit-erature." Early in her career, moreover, Stein began working in "the continuous present": derived from William James, her notion of time as a series of discrete moments, rather than a linear progression, allowed her to move toward a language drained of conventional meaning and charged, through repetition, with the insis-tent, recurrent obsessions of her characters' consciousnesses. Reliant as they are on commonplace American ethnic vocabularies, the stories have been both praised as sensitive analyses of stereotypes and criticized as insensitive promulga-tions of stereotypes.

When Stein finally found a publisher for *Three Lives*, she willingly allowed her new friend, Alice B. Toklas, to proofread the manuscript for her. Just arrived from California, Alice quickly supplanted Leo both in Gertrude's affections and in the atelier. Much later, Stein would cheerfully explain that she stopped being inter-ested in Leo when it became clear that "it was I who was the genius, there was no reason for it but I was, and he was not." For the American Diane Wakoski, Stein

and Toklas epitomize the genius and the devoted wife: Stein's "craggy, grand / stony ideas" were in some sense made possible by Toklas's embroidery, baking, and secretarial skills. Yet the Stein-Toklas relationship was not just based on Toklas's renunciatory adulation or Stein's energetic egotism. Stein's earlier depression in Baltimore was ended by the lifelong companionship of Toklas, who created the Plain Edition Press to publish Stein when she was feeling "a little better" about all her unpublished manuscripts. Even more important, Toklas helped free Stein's style. In the early experimental portraits *Ada* and *Miss Furr and Miss Skeene* as well as in the long poem *Lifting Belly*, Stein developed an encoded language to articulate the erotic and linguistic play she associated with Toklas. Indeed, in her first commercial success, Stein even wrote using Toklas's voice: in *The Autobiography of Alice B. Toklas* (1933), Gertrude's Alice describes the formative influence Stein had on younger writers like Ernest Hemingway and Sherwood Anderson, even as she provides titillating gossip about the postimpressionists and modernists who populated the Stein-Toklas salon.

The books Stein completed before and after World War I are markedly different from each other and from works produced in the realistic tradition in fiction. Her thousand-page history, *The Making of Americans* (1925), attempted to delineate every sort of American "who ever can or is or was or will be living," while the prose poems of *Tender Buttons* (1914) supplied impressionistic definitions that are sometimes sardonic ("A White Hunter: A white hunter is nearly crazy") and sometimes enigmatic ("Cream: Cream cut. Any where crumb. Left hop chambers"). Within a small circle of artists, Stein was gaining a reputation as a prolific and daring inventor of new forms. Judging from *The Autobiography*, the Great War was a great adventure for Toklas and Stein, who enlisted in an American ambulance unit in France. After the war, they reestablished their salon, which was frequented by many American expatriates and visitors. Stein continued to produce experimental poems, but she also began writing plays (*Four Saints in Three Acts*, 1934) and giving lectures at Oxford and Cambridge, speeches that issued in—among other works—*Composition as Explanation* (1926), which was published by the Woolfs' Hogarth Press. In the 1930s, Stein profited from the commercial success of both the *Autobiography of Alice B. Toklas* and Virgil Thomson's opera version of her play *Four Saints in Three Acts*, which led to a long American lecture tour and a contract that ensured her continued publication in America.

During the German occupation of France in the early 1940s, Stein and Toklas were forced to take refuge in the area around Bilignin, where they had a summer house. Always productive, Stein continued to write novels (*Ida, a Novel*, 1941), plays (*The Mother of Us All*, 1947), and memoirs (*Wars I Have Seen*, 1945). Generous and friendly to the many GIs still in Paris after 1944, she was by this time a celebrity in the American press. Two years after her return to Paris, she entered the American Hospital at Neuilly-sur-Seine because of an abdominal tumor. On her deathbed, she was said to have asked, "What is the answer?" When no one spoke, she replied to herself with characteristic aplomb: "What is the question?" Alice B. Toklas, who died twenty-one years later, was buried beside Stein in the cemetery of Père-Lachaise in Paris.

The Gentle Lena

Lena was patient, gentle, sweet and german. She had been a servant for four years and had liked it very well.

Lena had been brought from Germany to Bridgepoint by a cousin and had been in the same place there for four years.

This place Lena had found very good. There was a pleasant, unexacting mistress and her children, and they all liked Lena very well.

There was a cook there who scolded Lena a great deal but Lena's german patience held no suffering and the good incessant woman really only scolded so for Lena's good.

Lena's german voice when she knocked and called the family in the morning was as awakening, as soothing, and as appealing, as a delicate soft breeze in midday, summer. She stood in the hallway every morning a long time in her unexpectant and unsuffering german patience calling to the young ones to get up. She would call and wait a long time and then call again, always even, gentle, patient, while the young ones fell back often into that precious, tense, last bit of sleeping that gives a strength of joyous vigor in the young, over them that have come to the readiness of middle age, in their awakening.

Lena had good hard work all morning, and on the pleasant, sunny afternoons she was sent out into the park to sit and watch the little two year old girl baby of the family.

The other girls, all them that make the pleasant, lazy crowd, that watch the children in the sunny afternoons out in the park, all liked the simple, gentle, german Lena very well. They all, too, liked very well to tease her, for it was so easy to make her mixed and troubled, and all helpless, for she could never learn to know just what the other quicker girls meant by the queer things they said.

The two or three of these girls, the ones that Lena always sat with, always worked together to confuse her. Still it was pleasant, all this life for Lena.

The little girl fell down sometimes and cried, and then Lena had to soothe her. When the little girl would drop her hat, Lena had to pick it up and hold it. When the little girl was bad and threw away her playthings, Lena told her she could not have them and took them from her to hold until the little girl should need them.

It was all a peaceful life for Lena, almost as peaceful as a pleasant leisure. The other girls, of course, did tease her, but then that only made a gentle stir within her.

Lena was a brown and pleasant creature, brown as blonde races often have them brown, brown, not with the yellow or the red or the chocolate brown of sun burned countries, but brown with the clear color laid flat on the light toned skin beneath, the plain, spare brown that makes it right to have been made with hazel eyes, and not too abundant straight, brown hair, hair that only later deepens itself into brown from the straw yellow of a german childhood.

Lena had the flat chest, straight back and forward falling shoulders of the patient and enduring working woman, though her body was now still in its milder girlhood and work had not yet made these lines too clear.

The rarer feeling that there was with Lena, showed in all the even quiet of her body movements, but in all it was the strongest in the patient, old-world ignorance, and earth made pureness of her brown, flat, soft featured face. Lena had eyebrows that were a wondrous thickness. They were black, and spread, and very cool, with their dark color and their beauty, and beneath them were her hazel eyes, simple and human, with the earth patience of the working, gentle, german woman.

Yes it was all a peaceful life for Lena. The other girls, of course, did tease her, but then that only made a gentle stir within her.

"What you got on your finger Lena," Mary, one of the girls she always sat with, one day asked her. Mary was good natured, quick, intelligent and Irish.

Lena had just picked up the fancy paper made accordion that the little girl had dropped beside her, and was making it squeak sadly as she pulled it with her brown strong, awkward finger.

"Why, what is it, Mary, paint?" said Lena, putting her finger to her mouth to taste the dirt spot.

"That's awful poison Lena, don't you know?" said Mary, "that green paint that you just tasted."

Lena had sucked a good deal of the green paint from her finger. She stopped and looked hard at the finger. She did not know just how much Mary meant by what she said.

"Ain't it poison, Nellie, that green paint, that Lena sucked just now," said Mary. "Sure it is Lena, its real poison, I ain't foolin' this time anyhow."

Lena was a little troubled. She looked hard at her finger where the paint was, and she wondered if she had really sucked it.

It was still a little wet on the edges and she rubbed it off a long time on the inside of her dress, and in between she wondered and looked at the finger and thought, was it really poison that she had just tasted.

"Ain't it too bad, Nellie, Lena should have sucked that," Mary said.

Nellie smiled and did not answer. Nellie was dark and thin, and looked Italian. She had a big mass of black hair that she wore high up on her head, and that made her face look very fine.

Nellie always smiled and did not say much, and then she would look at Lena to perplex her.

And so they all three sat with their little charges in the pleasant sunshine a long time. And Lena would often look at her finger and wonder if it was really poison that she had just tasted and then she would rub her finger on her dress a little harder.

Mary laughed at her and teased her and Nellie smiled a little and looked queerly at her.

Then it came time, for it was growing cooler, for them to drag together the little ones, who had begun to wander, and to take each one back to its own mother. And Lena never knew for certain whether it was really poison, that green stuff that she had tasted.

During these four years of service, Lena always spent her Sundays out at the house of her aunt, who had brought her four years before to Bridgepoint.

This aunt, who had brought Lena, four years before, to Bridgepoint, was a hard, ambitious, well meaning, german woman. Her husband was a grocer in the town, and they were very well to do. Mrs. Haydon, Lena's aunt, had two daughters who were just beginning as young ladies, and she had a little boy who was not honest and who was very hard to manage.

Mrs. Haydon was a short, stout, hard built, german woman. She always hit the ground very firmly and compactly as she walked. Mrs. Haydon was all a compact and well hardened mass, even to her face, reddish and darkened from its early blonde, with its hearty, shiny, cheeks, and doubled chin well covered over with the up-roll from her short, square neck.

The two daughters, who were fourteen and fifteen, looked like unkneaded, unformed mounds of flesh beside her.

The elder girl, Mathilda, was blonde, and slow, and simple, and quite fat. The younger, Bertha, who was almost as tall as her sister, was dark, and quicker, and she was heavy, too, but not really fat.

These two girls the mother had brought up very firmly. They were well

taught for their position. They were always both well dressed, in the same kinds of hats and dresses, as is becoming in two german sisters. The mother liked to have them dressed in red. Their best clothes were red dresses, made of good heavy cloth, and strongly trimmed with braid of a glistening black. They had stiff, red felt hats, trimmed with black velvet ribbon, and a bird. The mother dressed matronly, in a bonnet and in black, always sat between her two big daughters, firm, directing, and repressed.

The only weak spot in this good german woman's conduct was the way she spoiled her boy, who was not honest and who was very hard to manage.

The father of this family was a decent, quiet, heavy, and uninterfering german man. He tried to cure the boy of his bad ways, and make him honest, but the mother could not make herself let the father manage, and so the boy was brought up very badly.

Mrs. Haydon's girls were now only just beginning as young ladies, and so to get her niece, Lena, married, was just then the most important thing that Mrs. Haydon had to do.

Mrs. Haydon had four years before gone to Germany to see her parents, and had taken the girls with her. This visit had been for Mrs. Haydon most successful, though her children had not liked it very well.

Mrs. Haydon was a good and generous woman, and she patronized her parents grandly, and all the cousins who came from all about to see her. Mrs. Haydon's people were of the middling class of farmers. They were not peasants, and they lived in a town of some pretension, but it all seemed very poor and smelly to Mrs. Haydon's american born daughters.

Mrs. Haydon liked it all. It was familiar, and then here she was so wealthy and important. She listened and decided, and advised all of her relations how to do things better. She arranged their present and their future for them, and showed them how in the past they had been wrong in all their methods.

Mrs. Haydon's only trouble was with her two daughters, whom she could not make behave well to her parents. The two girls were very nasty to all their numerous relations. Their mother could hardly make them kiss their grandparents, and every day the girls would get a scolding. But then Mrs. Haydon was so very busy that she did not have time to really manage her stubborn daughters.

These hard working, earth-rough german cousins were to these american born children, ugly and dirty and as far below them as were italian or negro workmen, and they could not see how their mother could ever bear to touch them, and then all the women dressed so funny, and were worked all rough and different.

The two girls stuck up their noses at them all, and always talked in english to each other about how they hated all these people and how they wished their mother would not do so. The girls could talk some german, but they never chose to use it.

It was her eldest brother's family that most interested Mrs. Haydon. Here there were eight children, and out of the eight, five of them were girls.

Mrs. Haydon thought it would be a fine thing to take one of these girls back with her to Bridgepoint and get her well started. Everybody liked that she should do so and they were all willing that it should be Lena.

Lena was the second girl in her large family. She was at this time just seventeen years old. Lena was not an important daughter in the family. She was al-

ways sort of dreamy and not there. She worked hard and went very regularly at it, but even good work never seemed to bring her near.

Lena's age just suited Mrs. Haydon's purpose. Lena could first go out to service, and learn how to do things, and then, when she was a little older, Mrs. Haydon could get her a good husband. And then Lena was so still and docile, she would never want to do things her own way. And then, too, Mrs. Haydon, with all her hardness had wisdom, and she could feel the rarer strain there was in Lena.

Lena was willing to go with Mrs. Haydon. Lena did not like her german life very well. It was not the hard work but the roughness that disturbed her. The people were not gentle, and the men when they were glad were very boisterous, and would lay hold of her and roughly tease her. They were good people enough around her, but it was all harsh and dreary for her.

Lena did not really know that she did not like it. She did not know that she was always dreamy and not there. She did not think whether it would be different for her away off there in Bridgepoint. Mrs. Haydon took her and got her different kinds of dresses, and then took her with them to the steamer. Lena did not really know what it was that had happened to her.

Mrs. Haydon, and her daughters, and Lena traveled second class on the steamer. Mrs. Haydon's daughters hated that their mother should take Lena. They hated to have a cousin, who was to them, little better than a nigger, and then everybody on the steamer there would see her. Mrs. Haydon's daughters said things like this to their mother, but she never stopped to hear them, and the girls did not dare to make their meaning very clear. And so they could only go on hating Lena hard, together. They could not stop her from going back with them to Bridgepoint.

Lena was very sick on the voyage. She thought, surely before it was over that she would die. She was so sick she could not even wish that she had not started. She could not eat, she could not moan, she was just blank and scared, and sure that every minute she would die. She could not hold herself in, nor help herself in her trouble. She just staid where she had been put, pale, and scared, and weak, and sick, and sure that she was going to die.

Mathilda and Bertha Haydon had no trouble from having Lena for a cousin on the voyage, until the last day that they were on the ship, and by that time they had made their friends and could explain.

Mrs. Haydon went down every day to Lena, gave her things to make her better, held her head when it was needful, and generally was good and did her duty by her.

Poor Lena had no power to be strong in such trouble. She did not know how to yield to her sickness nor endure. She lost all her little sense of being in her suffering. She was so scared, and then at her best, Lena, who was patient, sweet and quiet, had not self-control, nor any active courage.

Poor Lena was so scared and weak, and every minute she was sure that she would die.

After Lena was on land again a little while, she forgot all her bad suffering. Mrs. Haydon got her the good place, with the pleasant unexacting mistress, and her children, and Lena began to learn some English and soon was very happy and content.

All her Sundays out Lena spent at Mrs. Haydon's house. Lena would have liked much better to spend her Sundays with the girls she always sat with, and

who often asked her, and who teased her and made a gentle stir within her, but it never came to Lena's unexpectant and unsuffering german nature to do something different from what was expected of her, just because she would like it that way better. Mrs. Haydon had said that Lena was to come to her house every other Sunday, and so Lena always went there.

Mrs. Haydon was the only one of her family who took any interest in Lena. Mr. Haydon did not think much of her. She was his wife's cousin and he was good to her, but she was for him stupid, and a little simple, and very dull, and sure some day to need help and to be in trouble. All young poor relations, who were brought from Germany to Bridgepoint were sure, before long, to need help and to be in trouble.

The little Haydon boy was always very nasty to her. He was a hard child for any one to manage, and his mother spoiled him very badly. Mrs. Haydon's daughters as they grew older did not learn to like Lena any better. Lena never knew that she did not like them either. She did not know that she was only happy with the other quicker girls, she always sat with in the park, and who laughed at her and always teased her.

Mathilda Haydon, the simple, fat, blonde, older daughter felt very badly that she had to say that this was her cousin Lena, this Lena who was little better for her than a nigger. Mathilda was an overgrown, slow, flabby, blonde, stupid, fat girl, just beginning as a woman; thick in her speech and dull and simple in her mind, and very jealous of all her family and of other girls, and proud that she could have good dresses and new hats and learn music, and hating very badly to have a cousin who was a common servant. And then Mathilda remembered very strongly that dirty nasty place that Lena came from and that Mathilda had so turned up her nose at, and where she had been made so angry because her mother scolded her and liked all those rough cow-smelly people.

Then, too, Mathilda would get very mad when her mother had Lena at their parties, and when she talked about how good Lena was, to certain german mothers in whose sons, perhaps, Mrs. Haydon might find Lena a good husband. All this would make the dull, blonde, fat Mathilda very angry. Sometimes she would get so angry that she would, in her thick, slow way, and with jealous anger blazing in her light blue eyes, tell her mother that she did not see how she could like that nasty Lena; and then her mother would scold Mathilda, and tell her that she knew her cousin Lena was poor and Mathilda must be good to poor people.

Mathilda Haydon did not like relations to be poor. She told all her girl friends what she thought of Lena, and so the girls would never talk to Lena at Mrs. Haydon's parties. But Lena in her unsuffering and unexpectant patience never really knew that she was slighted. When Mathilda was with her girls in the street or in the park and would see Lena, she always turned up her nose and barely nodded to her, and then she would tell her friends how funny her mother was to take care of people like that Lena, and how, back in Germany, all Lena's people lived just like pigs.

The younger daughter, the dark, large, but not fat, Bertha Haydon, who was very quick in her mind, and in her ways, and who was the favorite with her father, did not like Lena, either. She did not like her because for her Lena was a fool and so stupid, and she would let those Irish and Italian girls laugh at her and tease her, and everybody always made fun of Lena, and Lena never got

mad, or even had sense enough to know that they were all making an awful
fool of her.

Bertha Haydon hated people to be fools. Her father, too, thought Lena was
a fool, and so neither the father nor the daughter ever paid any attention to
Lena, although she came to their house every other Sunday.

Lena did not know how all the Haydons felt. She came to her aunt's house
all her Sunday afternoons that she had out, because Mrs. Haydon had told her
she must do so. In the same way Lena always saved all of her wages. She never
thought of any way to spend it. The german cook, the good woman who always
scolded Lena, helped her to put it in the bank each month, as soon as she got
it. Sometimes before it got into the bank to be taken care of, somebody would
ask Lena for it. The little Haydon boy sometimes asked and would get it, and
sometimes some of the girls, the ones Lena always sat with, needed some
more money; but the german cook, who always scolded Lena, saw to it that
this did not happen very often. When it did happen she would scold Lena very
sharply, and for the next few months she would not let Lena touch her wages,
but put it in the bank for her on the same day that Lena got it.

So Lena always saved her wages, for she never thought to spend them, and
she always went to her aunt's house for her Sundays because she did not know
that she could do anything different.

Mrs. Haydon felt more and more every year that she had done right to bring
Lena back with her, for it was all coming out just as she had expected. Lena
was good and never wanted her own way, she was learning English, and saving
all her wages, and soon Mrs. Haydon would get her a good husband.

All these four years Mrs. Haydon was busy looking around among all the
german people that she knew for the right man to be Lena's husband, and now
at last she was quite decided.

The man Mrs. Haydon wanted for Lena was a young german-american tai-
lor, who worked with his father. He was good and all the family were very sav-
ing, and Mrs. Haydon was sure that this would be just right for Lena, and then
too, this young tailor always did whatever his father and his mother wanted.

This old german tailor and his wife, the father and the mother of Herman
Kreder, who was to marry Lena Mainz, were very thrifty, careful people.
Herman was the only child they had left with them, and he always did every-
thing they wanted. Herman was now twenty-eight years old, but he had never
stopped being scolded and directed by his father and his mother. And now
they wanted to see him married.

Herman Kreder did not care much to get married. He was a gentle soul and
a little fearful. He had a sullen temper, too. He was obedient to his father and
his mother. He always did his work well. He often went out on Saturday nights
and on Sundays, with other men. He liked it with them but he never became
really joyous. He liked to be with men and he hated to have women with them.
He was obedient to his mother, but he did not care much to get married.

Mrs. Haydon and the elder Kreders had often talked the marriage over.
They all three liked it very well. Lena would do anything that Mrs. Haydon
wanted, and Herman was always obedient in everything to his father and his
mother. Both Lena and Herman were saving and good workers and neither of
them ever wanted their own way.

The elder Kreders, everybody knew, had saved up all their money, and they
were hard, good german people, and Mrs. Haydon was sure that with these

people Lena would never be in any trouble. Mr. Haydon would not say anything about it. He knew old Kreder had a lot of money and owned some good houses, and he did not care what his wife did with that simple, stupid Lena, so long as she would be sure never to need help or to be in trouble.

Lena did not care much to get married. She liked her life very well where she was working. She did not think much about Herman Kreder. She thought he was a good man and she always found him very quiet. Neither of them ever spoke much to the other. Lena did not care much just then about getting married.

Mrs. Haydon spoke to Lena about it very often. Lena never answered anything at all. Mrs. Haydon thought, perhaps Lena did not like Herman Kreder. Mrs. Haydon could not believe that any girl not even Lena, really had no feeling about getting married.

Mrs. Haydon spoke to Lena very often about Herman. Mrs. Haydon sometimes got very angry with Lena. She was afraid that Lena, for once, was going to be stubborn, now when it was all fixed right for her to be married.

"Why you stand there so stupid, why don't you answer, Lena," said Mrs. Haydon one Sunday, at the end of a long talking that she was giving Lena about Herman Kreder, and about Lena's getting married to him.

"Yes ma'am," said Lena, and then Mrs. Haydon was furious with this stupid Lena. "Why don't you answer with some sense, Lena, when I ask you if you don't like Herman Kreder. You stand there so stupid and don't answer just like you ain't heard a word what I been saying to you. I never see anybody like you, Lena. If you going to burst out at all, why don't you burst out sudden instead of standing there so silly and don't answer. And here I am so good to you, and find you a good husband so you can have a place to live in all your own. Answer me, Lena, don't you like Herman Kreder? He is a fine young fellow, almost too good for you, Lena, when you stand there so stupid and don't make no answer. There ain't many poor girls that get the chance you got now to get married."

"Why, I do anything you say, Aunt Mathilda. Yes, I like him. He don't say much to me, but I guess he is a good man, and I do anything you say for me to do."

"Well then Lena, why you stand there so silly all the time and not answer when I asked you."

"I didn't hear you say you wanted I should say anything to you. I didn't know you wanted me to say nothing. I do whatever you tell me it's right for me to do. I marry Herman Kreder, if you want me."

And so for Lena Mainz the match was made.

Old Mrs. Kreder did not discuss the matter with her Herman. She never thought that she needed to talk such things over with him. She just told him about getting married to Lena Mainz who was a good worker and very saving and never wanted her own way, and Herman made his usual little grunt in answer to her.

Mrs. Kreder and Mrs. Haydon fixed the day and made all the arrangements for the wedding and invited everybody who ought to be there to see them married.

In three months Lena Mainz and Herman Kreder were to be married.

Mrs. Haydon attended to Lena's getting all the things that she needed. Lena had to help a good deal with the sewing. Lena did not sew very well. Mrs. Haydon scolded because Lena did not do it better, but then she was very good to Lena, and she hired a girl to come and help her. Lena still stayed on with her

pleasant mistress, but she spent all her evenings and her Sundays with her aunt and all the sewing.

Mrs. Haydon got Lena some nice dresses. Lena liked that very well. Lena liked having new hats even better, and Mrs. Haydon had some made for her by a real milliner who made them very pretty.

Lena was nervous these days, but she did not think much about getting married. She did not know really what it was, that, which was always coming nearer.

Lena liked the place where she was with the pleasant mistress and the good cook, who always scolded, and she liked the girls she always sat with. She did not ask if she would like being married any better. She always did whatever her aunt said and expected, but she was always nervous when she saw the Kreders with their Herman. She was excited and she liked her new hats, and everybody teased her and every day her marrying was coming nearer, and yet she did not really know what it was, this that was about to happen to her.

Herman Kreder knew more what it meant to be married and he did not like it very well. He did not like to see girls and he did not want to have to have one always near him. Herman always did everything that his father and his mother wanted and now they wanted that he should be married.

Herman had a sullen temper; he was gentle and he never said much. He liked to go out with other men, but he never wanted that there should be any women with them. The men all teased him about getting married. Herman did not mind the teasing but he did not like very well the getting married and having a girl always with him.

Three days before the wedding day, Herman went away to the country to be gone over Sunday. He and Lena were to be married Tuesday afternoon. When the day came Herman had not been seen or heard from.

The old Kreder couple had not worried much about it. Herman always did everything they wanted and he would surely come back in time to get married. But when Monday night came, and there was no Herman, they went to Mrs. Haydon to tell her what had happened.

Mrs. Haydon got very much excited. It was hard enough to work so as to get everything all ready, and then to have that silly Herman go off that way, so no one could tell what was going to happen. Here was Lena and everything all ready, and now they would have to make the wedding later so that they would know that Herman would be sure to be there.

Mrs. Haydon was very much excited, and then she could not say much to the old Kreder couple. She did not want to make them angry, for she wanted very badly now that Lena should be married to their Herman.

At last it was decided that the wedding should be put off a week longer. Old Mr. Kreder would go to New York to find Herman, for it was very likely that Herman had gone there to his married sister.

Mrs. Haydon sent word around, about waiting until a week from that Tuesday, to everybody that had been invited, and then Tuesday morning she sent for Lena to come down to see her.

Mrs. Haydon was very angry with poor Lena when she saw her. She scolded her hard because she was so foolish, and now Herman had gone off and nobody could tell where he had gone to, and all because Lena always was so dumb and silly. And Mrs. Haydon was just like a mother to her, and Lena always stood there so stupid and did not answer what anybody asked her, and Herman was so silly too, and now his father had to go and find him. Mrs.

Haydon did not think that any old people should be good to their children. Their children always were so thankless, and never paid any attention, and older people were always doing things for their good. Did Lena think it gave Mrs. Haydon any pleasure, to work so hard to make Lena happy, and get her a good husband, and then Lena was so thankless and never did anything that anybody wanted. It was a lesson to poor Mrs. Haydon not to do things any more for anybody. Let everybody take care of themselves and never come to her with any troubles; she knew better now than to meddle to make other people happy. It just made trouble for her and her husband did not like it. He always said she was too good, and nobody ever thanked her for it, and there Lena was always standing stupid and not answering anything anybody wanted. Lena could always talk enough to those silly girls she liked so much, and always sat with, but who never did anything for her except to take away her money, and here was her aunt who tried so hard and was so good to her and treated her just like one of her own children and Lena stood there, and never made any answer and never tried to please her aunt, or to do anything that her aunt wanted. "No, it ain't no use your standin' there and cryin', now, Lena. Its too late now to care about that Herman. You should have cared some before, and then you wouldn't have to stand and cry now, and be a disappointment to me, and then I get scolded by my husband for taking care of everybody, and nobody ever thankful. I am glad you got the sense to feel sorry now, Lena, anyway, and I try to do what I can to help you out in your trouble, only you don't deserve to have anybody take any trouble for you. But perhaps you know better next time. You go home now and take care you don't spoil your clothes and that new hat, you had no business to be wearin' that this morning, but you ain't got no sense at all, Lena. I never in my life see anybody be so stupid."

Mrs. Haydon stopped and poor Lena stood there in her hat, all trimmed with pretty flowers, and the tears coming out of her eyes, and Lena did not know what it was that she had done, only she was not going to be married and it was a disgrace for a girl to be left by a man on the very day she was to be married.

Lena went home all alone, and cried in the street car.

Poor Lena cried very hard all alone in the street car. She almost spoiled her new hat with her hitting it against the window in her crying. Then she remembered that she must not do so.

The conductor was a kind man and he was very sorry when he saw her crying. "Don't feel so bad, you get another feller, you are such a nice girl," he said to make her cheerful. "But Aunt Mathilda said now, I never get married," poor Lena sobbed out for her answer. "Why you really got trouble like that," said the conductor, "I just said that now to josh you. I didn't ever think you really was left by a feller. He must be a stupid feller. But don't you worry, he wasn't much good if he could go away and leave you, lookin' to be such a nice girl. You just tell all your trouble to me, and I help you." The car was empty and the conductor sat down beside her to put his arm around her, and to be a comfort to her. Lena suddenly remembered where she was, and if she did things like that her aunt would scold her. She moved away from the man into the corner. He laughed, "Don't be scared," he said, "I wasn't going to hurt you. But you just keep up your spirit. You are a real nice girl, and you'll be sure to get a real good husband. Don't you let nobody fool you. You're all right and I don't want to scare you."

The conductor went back to his platform to help a passenger get on the car. All the time Lena stayed in the street car, he would come in every little while and reassure her, about her not to feel so bad about a man who hadn't no more sense than to go away and leave her. She'd be sure yet to get a good man, she needn't be so worried, he frequently assured her.

He chatted with the other passenger who had just come in, a very well dressed old man, and then with another who came in later, a good sort of a working man, and then another who came in, a nice lady, and he told them all about Lena's having trouble, and it was too bad there were men who treated a poor girl so badly. And everybody in the car was sorry for poor Lena and the workman tried to cheer her, and the old man looked sharply at her, and said she looked like a good girl, but she ought to be more careful and not be so careless, and things like that would not happen to her, and the nice lady went and sat beside her and Lena liked it, though she shrank away from being near her.

So Lena was feeling a little better when she got off the car, and the conductor helped her, and he called out to her, "You be sure you keep up a good heart now. He wasn't no good that feller and you were lucky for to lose him. You'll get a real man yet, one that will be better for you. Don't you be worried, you're a real nice girl as I ever see in such trouble," and the conductor shook his head and went back into his car to talk it over with the other passengers he had there.

The german cook, who always scolded Lena, was very angry when she heard the story. She never did think Mrs. Haydon would do so much for Lena, though she was always talking so grand about what she could do for everybody. The good german cook always had been a little distrustful to her. People who always thought they were so much never did really do things right for anybody. Not that Mrs. Haydon wasn't a good woman. Mrs. Haydon was a real, good, german woman, and she did really mean to do well by her niece Lena. The cook knew that very well, and she had always said so, and she always had liked and respected Mrs. Haydon, who always acted very proper to her, and Lena was so backward, when there was a man to talk to, Mrs. Haydon did have hard work when she tried to marry Lena. Mrs. Haydon was a good woman, only she did talk sometimes too grand. Perhaps this trouble would make her see it wasn't always so easy to do, to make everybody do everything just like she wanted. The cook was very sorry now for Mrs. Haydon. All this must be such a disappointment, and such a worry to her, and she really had always been very good to Lena. But Lena had better go and put on her other clothes and stop with all that crying. That wouldn't do nothing now to help her, and if Lena would be a good girl, and just be real patient, her aunt would make it all come out right yet for her. "I just tell Mrs. Aldrich, Lena, you stay here yet a little longer. You know she is always so good to you, Lena, and I know she let you, and I tell her all about that stupid Herman Kreder I got no patience, Lena, with anybody who can be so stupid. You just stop now with your crying, Lena, and take off them good clothes and put them away so you don't spoil them when you need them, and you can help me with the dishes and everything will come off better for you. You see if I ain't right by what I tell you. You just stop crying now Lena quick, or else I scold you."

Lena still choked a little and was very miserable inside her but she did everything just as the cook told her.

The girls Lena always sat with were very sorry to see her look so sad with her

trouble. Mary the Irish girl sometimes got very angry with her. Mary was always very hot when she talked of Lena's aunt Mathilda, who thought she was so grand, and had such stupid, stuck up daughters. Mary wouldn't be a fat fool like that ugly tempered Mathilda Haydon, not for anything anybody could ever give her. How Lena could keep on going there so much when they all always acted as if she was just dirt to them, Mary never could see. But Lena never had any sense of how she should make people stand round for her, and that was always all the trouble with her. And poor Lena, she was so stupid to be sorry for losing that gawky fool who didn't ever know what he wanted and just said "ja"[1] to his mamma and his papa, like a baby, and was scared to look at a girl straight, and then sneaked away the last day like as if somebody was going to do something to him. Disgrace, Lena talking about disgrace! It was a disgrace for a girl to be seen with the likes of him, let alone to be married to him. But that poor Lena, she never did know how to show herself off for what she was really. Disgrace to have him go away and leave her. Mary would just like to get a chance to show him. If Lena wasn't worth fifteen like Herman Kreder, Mary would just eat her own head all up. It was a good riddance Lena had of that Herman Kreder and his stingy, dirty parents, and if Lena didn't stop crying about it,—Mary would just naturally despise her.

Poor Lena, she knew very well how Mary meant it all, this she was always saying to her. But Lena was very miserable inside her. She felt the disgrace it was for a decent german girl that a man should go away and leave her. Lena knew very well that her aunt was right when she said the way Herman had acted to her was a disgrace to everyone that knew her. Mary and Nellie and the other girls she always sat with were always very good to Lena but that did not make her trouble any better. It was a disgrace the way Lena had been left, to any decent family, and that could never be made any different to her.

And so the slow days wore on, and Lena never saw her Aunt Mathilda. At last on Sunday she got word by a boy to go and see her aunt Mathilda. Lena's heart beat quick for she was very nervous now with all this that had happened to her. She went just as quickly as she could to see her Aunt Mathilda.

Mrs. Haydon quick, as soon as she saw Lena, began to scold her for keeping her aunt waiting so long for her, and for not coming in all the week to see her, to see if her aunt should need her, and so her aunt had to send a boy to tell her. But it was easy, even for Lena, to see that her aunt was not really angry with her. It wasn't Lena's fault, went on Mrs. Haydon, that everything was going to happen all right for her. Mrs. Haydon was very tired taking all this trouble for her, and when Lena couldn't even take trouble to come and see her aunt, to see if she needed anything to tell her. But Mrs. Haydon really never minded things like that when she could do things for anybody. She was tired now, all the trouble she had been taking to make things right for Lena, but perhaps now Lena heard it she would learn a little to be thankful to her. "You get all ready to be married Tuesday. Lena, you hear me," said Mrs. Haydon to her. "You come here Tuesday morning and I have everything all ready for you. You wear your new dress I got you, and your hat with all them flowers on it, and you be very careful coming you don't get your things all dirty, you so careless all the time, Lena, and not thinking, and you act sometimes you never got no head at all on you. You go home now, and you tell your Mrs. Aldrich that you leave her

1. Yes (German).

Tuesday. Don't you go forgetting now, Lena, anything I ever told you what you should do to be careful. You be a good girl, now Lena. You get married Tuesday to Herman Kreder." And that was all Lena ever knew of what had happened all this week to Herman Kreder. Lena forgot there was anything to know about it. She was really to be married Tuesday, and her Aunt Mathilda said she was a good girl, and now there was no disgrace left upon her.

Lena now fell back into the way she always had of being always dreamy and not there, the way she always had been, except for the few days she was so excited, because she had been left by a man the very day she was to have been married. Lena was a little nervous all these last days, but she did not think much about what it meant for her to be married.

Herman Kreder was not so content about it. He was quiet and was sullen and he knew he could not help it. He knew now he just had to let himself get married. It was not that Herman did not like Lena Mainz. She was as good as any other girl could be for him. She was a little better perhaps than other girls he saw, she was so very quiet, but Herman did not like to always have to have a girl around him. Herman had always done everything that his mother and his father wanted. His father had found him in New York, where Herman had gone to be with his married sister.

Herman's father when he had found him coaxed Herman a long time and went on whole days with his complaining to him, always troubled but gentle and quite patient with him, and always he was worrying to Herman about what was the right way his boy Herman should always do, always whatever it was his mother ever wanted from him, and always Herman never made him any answer.

Old Mr. Kreder kept on saying to him, he did not see how Herman could think now, it could be any different. When you make a bargain you just got to stick right to it, that was the only way old Mr. Kreder could ever see it, and saying you would get married to a girl and she got everything all ready, that was a bargain just like one you make in business and Herman he had made it, and now Herman he would just have to do it, old Mr. Kreder didn't see there was any other way a good boy like his Herman had, to do it. And then too that Lena Mainz was such a nice girl and Herman hadn't ought to really give his father so much trouble and make him pay out all that money, to come all the way to New York just to find him, and they both lose all that time from their working, when all Herman had to do was just to stand up, for an hour, and then he would be all right married, and it would be all over for him, and then everything at home would never be any different to him.

And his father went on; there was his poor mother saying always how her Herman always did everything before she ever wanted, and now just because he got notions in him, and wanted to show people how he could be stubborn, he was making all this trouble for her, and making them pay all that money just to run around and find him. "You got no idea Herman, how bad mama is feeling about the way you been acting Herman," said old Mr. Kreder to him. "She says she never can understand how you can be so thankless Herman. It hurts her very much you been so stubborn, and she find you such a nice girl for you, like Lena Mainz who is always just so quiet and always saves up all her wages, and she never wanting her own way at all like some girls are always all the time to have it, and your mama trying so hard, just so you could be comfortable Herman to be married, and then you act so stubborn Herman. You

like all young people Herman, you think only about yourself, and what you are just wanting, and your mama she is thinking only what is good for you to have, for you in the future. Do you think your mama wants to have a girl around to be a bother, for herself, Herman. Its just for you Herman she is always thinking, and she talks always about how happy she will be, when she sees her Herman married to a nice girl, and then when she fixed it all up so good for you, so it never would be any bother to you, just the way she wanted you should like it, and you say yes all right, I do it, and then you go away like this act stubborn, and make all this trouble everybody to take for you, and we spend money, and I got to travel all round to find you. You come home now with me Herman and get married, and I tell your mama she better not say anything to you about how much it cost me to come all the way to look for you— Hey Herman," said his father coaxing, "Hey, you come home now and get married. All you got to do Herman is just to stand up for an hour Herman, and then you don't never to have any more bother to it—Hey Herman!—you come home with me to-morrow and get married. Hey Herman."

Herman's married sister liked her brother Herman, and she had always tried to help him, when there was anything she knew he wanted. She liked it that he was so good and always did everything that their father and their mother wanted, but still she wished it could be that he could have more his own way, if there was anything he ever wanted.

But now she thought Herman with his girl was very funny. She wanted that Herman should be married. She thought it would do him lots of good to get married. She laughed at Herman when she heard the story. Until his father came to find him, she did not know why it was Herman had come just then to New York to see her. When she heard the story she laughed a good deal at her brother Herman and teased him a good deal about his running away, because he didn't want to have a girl to be all the time around him.

Herman's married sister liked her brother Herman, and she did not want him not to like to be with women. He was good, her brother Herman, and it would surely do him good to get married. It would make him stand up for himself stronger. Herman's sister always laughed at him and always she would try to reassure him. "Such a nice man as my brother Herman acting like as if he was afraid of women. Why the girls all like a man like you Herman, if you didn't always run away when you saw them. It do you good really Herman to get married, and then you got somebody you can boss around when you want to. It do you good Herman to get married, you see if you don't like it, when you really done it. You go along home now with papa, Herman and get married to that Lena. You don't know how nice you like it Herman when you try once how you can do it. You just don't be afraid of nothing, Herman. You good enough for any girl to marry, Herman. Any girl be glad to have a man like you to be always with them Herman. You just go along home with papa and try it what I say, Herman. Oh you so funny Herman, when you sit there, and then run away and leave your girl behind you. I know she is crying like anything Herman for to lose you. Don't be bad to her Herman. You go along home with papa now and get married Herman. I'd be awful ashamed Herman, to really have a brother didn't have spirit enough to get married, when a girl is just dying for to have him. You always like me to be with you Herman. I don't see why you say you don't want a girl to be all the time around you. You always been good to me Herman, and I know you always be good to that Lena, and you soon feel

just like as if she had always been there with you. Don't act like as if you wasn't
a nice strong man, Herman. Really I laugh at you Herman, but you know I like
awful well to see you real happy. You go home and get married to that Lena,
Herman. She is a real pretty girl and real nice and good and quiet and she
make my brother Herman very happy. You just stop your fussing now with
Herman, papa. He go with you to-morrow papa, and you see he like it so much
to be married, he make everybody laugh just to see him be so happy. Really
truly, that's the way it will be with you Herman. You just listen to me what I
tell you Herman." And so his sister laughed at him and reassured him, and his
father kept on telling what the mother always said about her Herman, and he
coaxed him and Herman never said anything in answer, and his sister packed
his things up and was very cheerful with him, and she kissed him, and then she
laughed and then she kissed him, and his father went and brought the tick-
ets for the train, and at last late on Sunday he brought Herman back to
Bridgepoint with him.

It was always very hard to keep Mrs. Kreder from saying what she thought,
to her Herman, but her daughter had written her a letter, so as to warn her not
to say anything about what he had been doing, to him, and her husband came
in with Herman and said, "Here we are come home mama, Herman and me,
and we are very tired it was so crowded coming," and then he whispered to her.
"You be good to Herman, mama, he didn't mean to make us so much trouble,"
and so old Mrs. Kreder, held in what she felt was so strong in her to say to her
Herman. She just said very stiffly to him, "I'm glad to see you come home to-
day, Herman." Then she went to arrange it all with Mrs. Haydon.

Herman was now again just like he always had been, sullen and very good,
and very quiet, and always ready to do whatever his mother and his father
wanted. Tuesday morning came. Herman got his new clothes on and went
with his father and his mother to stand up for an hour and get married. Lena
was there in her new dress, and her hat with all the pretty flowers, and she was
very nervous for now she knew she was really very soon to be married. Mrs.
Haydon had everything all ready. Everybody was there just as they should be
and very soon Herman Kreder and Lena Mainz were married.

When everything was really over, they went back to the Kreder house to-
gether. They were all now to live together, Lena and Herman and the old fa-
ther and the old mother, in the house where Mr. Kreder had worked so many
years as a tailor, with his son Herman always there to help him.

Irish Mary had often said to Lena she never did see how Lena could ever
want to have anything to do with Herman Kreder and his dirty stingy parents.
The old Kreders were to an Irish nature, a stingy, dirty couple. They had not
the free-hearted, thoughtless, fighting, mud bespattered, ragged, peat-
smoked cabin dirt that irish Mary knew and could forgive and love. Theirs was
the german dirt of saving, of being dowdy and loose and foul in your clothes so
as to save them and yourself in washing, having your hair greasy to save it in
the soap and drying, having your clothes dirty, not in freedom, but because so
it was cheaper, keeping the house close and smelly because so it cost less to get
it heated, living so poorly not only so as to save money but so they should
never even know themselves that they had it, working all the time not only be-
cause from their nature they just had to and because it made them money but
also that they never could be put in any way to make them spend their money.

This was the place Lena now had for her home and to her it was very differ-

ent than it could be for an irish Mary. She too was german and was thrifty, though she was always so dreamy and not there. Lena was always careful with things and she always saved her money, for that was the only way she knew how to do it. She never had taken care of her own money and she never had thought how to use it.

Lena Mainz had been, before she was Mrs. Herman Kreder, always clean and decent in her clothes and in her person, but it was not because she ever thought about it or really needed so to have it, it was the way her people did in the german country where she came from, and her Aunt Mathilda and the good german cook who always scolded, had kept her on and made her, with their scoldings, always more careful to keep clean and to wash real often. But there was no deep need in all this for Lena and so, though Lena did not like the old Kreders, though she really did not know that, she did not think about their being stingy dirty people.

Herman Kreder was cleaner than the old people, just because it was his nature to keep cleaner, but he was used to his mother and his father, and he never thought that they should keep things cleaner. And Herman too always saved all his money, except for that little beer he drank when he went out with other men of an evening the way he always liked to do it, and he never thought of any other way to spend it. His father had always kept all the money for them and he always was doing business with it. And then too Herman really had no money, for he always had worked for his father, and his father had never thought to pay him.

And so they began all four to live in the Kreder house together, and Lena began soon with it to look careless and a little dirty, and to be more lifeless with it, and nobody ever noticed much what Lena wanted, and she never really knew herself what she needed.

The only real trouble that came to Lena with their living all four there together, was the way old Mrs. Kreder scolded. Lena had always been used to being scolded, but this scolding of old Mrs. Kreder was very different from the way she ever before had had to endure it.

Herman, now he was married to her, really liked Lena very well. He did not care very much about her but she never was a bother to him being there around him, only when his mother worried and was nasty to them because Lena was so careless, and did not know how to save things right for them with their eating, and all the other ways with money, that the old woman had to save it.

Herman Kreder had always done everything his mother and his father wanted but he did not really love his parents very deeply. With Herman it was always only that he hated to have any struggle. It was all always all right with him when he could just go along and do the same thing over every day with his working, and not to hear things, and not to have people make him listen to their anger. And now his marriage, and he just knew it would, was making trouble for him. It made him hear more what his mother was always saying, with her scolding. He had to really hear it now because Lena was there, and she was so scared and dull always when she heard it. Herman knew very well with his mother, it was all right if one ate very little and worked hard all day and did not learn her when she scolded, the way Herman always had done before they were so foolish about his getting married and having a girl there to be all the time around him, and now he had to help her so the girl could learn too,

not to hear it when his mother scolded, and not to look so scared, and not to
eat much, and always to be sure to save it.

Herman really did not know very well what he could do to help Lena to un-
derstand it. He could never answer his mother back to help Lena, that never
would make things any better for her, and he never could feel in himself any
way to comfort Lena, to make her strong not to hear his mother, in all the
awful ways she always scolded. It just worried Herman to have it like that all
the time around him. Herman did not know much about how a man could
make a struggle with a mother, to do much to keep her quiet, and indeed
Herman never knew much how to make a struggle against anyone who really
wanted to have anything very badly. Herman all his life never wanted anything
so badly, that he would really make a struggle against any one to get it. Herman
all his life only wanted to live regular and quiet, and not talk much and to do
the same way every day like every other with his working. And now his mother
had made him get married to this Lena and now with his mother making all
that scolding, he had all this trouble and this worry always on him.

Mrs. Haydon did not see Lena now very often. She had not lost her interest
in her niece Lena, but Lena could not come much to her house to see her, it
would not be right, now Lena was a married woman. And then too Mrs.
Haydon had her hands full just then with her two daughters, for she was get-
ting them ready to find them good husbands, and then too her own husband
now worried her very often about her always spoiling that boy of hers, so he
would be sure to turn out no good and be a disgrace to a german family, and all
because his mother always spoiled him. All these things were very worrying
now to Mrs. Haydon, but still she wanted to be good to Lena, though she
could not see her very often. She only saw her when Mrs. Haydon went to call
on Mrs. Kreder or when Mrs. Kreder came to see Mrs. Haydon, and that never
could be very often. Then too these days Mrs. Haydon could not scold Lena,
Mrs. Kreder was always there with her, and it would not be right to scold Lena
when Mrs. Kreder was there, who had now the real right to do it. And so her
aunt always said nice things now to Lena, and though Mrs. Haydon some-
times was a little worried when she saw Lena looking sad and not careful, she
did not have time just then to really worry much about it.

Lena now never any more saw the girls she always used to sit with. She had
no way now to see them and it was not in Lena's nature to search out ways to
see them, nor did she now ever think much of the days when she had been
used to see them. They never any of them had come to the Kreder house to see
her. Not even Irish Mary had ever thought to come to see her. Lena had been
soon forgotten by them. They had soon passed away from Lena and now Lena
never thought any more that she had ever known them.

The only one to her old friends who tried to know what Lena liked and what
she needed, and who always made Lena come to see her, was the good german
cook who had always scolded. She now scolded Lena hard for letting herself go
so, and going out when she was looking so untidy. "I know you going to have a
baby Lena, but that's no way for you to be looking. I am ashamed most to see
you come and sit here in my kitchen, looking so sloppy and like you never used
to Lena. I never see anybody like you Lena. Herman is very good to you, you al-
ways say so, and he don't treat you bad ever though you don't deserve to have
anybody good to you, you so careless all the time, Lena, letting yourself go like
you never had anybody tell you what was the right way you should know how

to be looking. No, Lena, I don't see no reason you should let yourself go so and look so untidy Lena, so I am ashamed to see you sit there looking so ugly, Lena. No Lena that ain't no way ever I see a woman make things come out better, letting herself go so every way and crying all the time like as if you had real trouble. I never wanted to see you marry Herman Kreder, Lena, I knew what you got to stand with that old woman always, and that old man, he is so stingy too and he don't say things out but he ain't any better in his heart than his wife with her bad ways, I know that Lena, I know they don't hardly give you enough to eat, Lena, I am real sorry for you Lena, you know that Lena, but that ain't any way to be going round so untidy Lena, even if you have got all that trouble. You never see me do like that Lena, though sometimes I got a headache so I can't see to stand to be working hardly, and nothing comes right with all my cooking, but I always see Lena, I look decent. That's the only way a german girl can make things come out right Lena. You hear me what I am saying to you Lena. Now you eat something nice Lena, I got it all ready for you, and you wash up and be careful Lena and the baby will come all right to you, and then I make your Aunt Mathilda see that you live in a house soon all alone with Herman and your baby, and then everything go better for you. You hear me what I say to you Lena. Now don't let me ever see you come looking like this any more Lena, and you just stop with that always crying. You ain't got no reason to be sitting there now with all that crying, I never see anybody have trouble it did them any good to be the way you are doing, Lena. You hear me Lena. You go home now and you be good the way I tell you Lena, and I see what I can do. I make your Aunt Mathilda make old Mrs. Kreder let you be till you get your baby all right. Now don't you be scared and so silly Lena. I don't like to see you act so Lena when really you got a nice man and so many things really any girl should be grateful to be having. Now you go home Lena to-day and you do the way I say, to you, and I see what I can do to help you."

"Yes Mrs. Aldrich" said the good german woman to her mistress later, "Yes Mrs. Aldrich that's the way it is with them girls when they want so to get married. They don't know when they got it good Mrs. Aldrich. They never know what it is they're really wanting when they got it, Mrs. Aldrich. There's that poor Lena, she just been here crying and looking so careless so I scold her, but that was no good that marrying for that poor Lena, Mrs. Aldrich. She do look so pale and sad now Mrs. Aldrich, it just break my heart to see her. She was a good girl was Lena, Mrs. Aldrich, and I never had no trouble with her like I got with so many young girls nowadays, Mrs. Aldrich, and I never see any girl any better to work right than our Lena, and now she got to stand it all the time with that old woman Mrs. Kreder. My! Mrs. Aldrich, she is a bad old woman to her. I never see Mrs. Aldrich how old people can be so bad to young girls and not have no kind of patience with them. If Lena could only live with her Herman, he ain't so bad the way men are, Mrs. Aldrich, but he is just the way always his mother wants him, he ain't got no spirit in him, and so I don't really see no help for that poor Lena. I know her aunt, Mrs. Haydon, meant it all right for her Mrs. Aldrich, but poor Lena, it would be better for her if her Herman had stayed there in New York that time he went away to leave her. I don't like it the way Lena is looking now, Mrs. Aldrich. She looks like as if she don't have no life left in her hardly, Mrs. Aldrich, she just drags around and looks so dirty and after all the pains I always took to teach her and to keep her nice in her ways and looking. It don't do no good to them, for them girls to get

married Mrs. Aldrich, they are much better when they only know it, to stay in a good place when they got it, and keep on regular with their working. I don't like it the way Lena looks now Mrs. Aldrich. I wish I knew some way to help that poor Lena, Mrs. Aldrich, but she is a bad old woman, that old Mrs. Kreder, Herman's mother. I speak to Mrs. Haydon real soon, Mrs. Aldrich, I see what we can do now to help that poor Lena."

These were really bad days for poor Lena. Herman always was real good to her and now he even sometimes tried to stop his mother from scolding Lena. "She ain't well now mama, you let her be now you hear me. You tell me what it is you want she should be doing, I tell her. I see she does it right just the way you want it mama. You let be, I say now mama, with that always scolding Lena. You let be, I say now, you wait till she is feeling better." Herman was getting really strong to struggle, for he could see that Lena with that baby working hard inside her, really could not stand it any longer with his mother and the awful ways she always scolded.

It was a new feeling Herman now had inside him that made him feel he was strong to make a struggle. It was new for Herman Kreder really to be wanting something, but Herman wanted strongly now to be a father, and he wanted badly that his baby should be a boy and healthy. Herman never had cared really very much about his father and his mother, though always all his life, he had done everything just as they wanted, and he had never really cared much about his wife, Lena, though he always had been very good to her, and had always tried to keep his mother off her, with the awful way she always scolded, but to be really a father of a little baby, that feeling took hold of Herman very deeply. He was almost ready, so as to save his baby from all trouble, to really make a strong struggle with his mother and with his father, too, if he would not help him to control his mother.

Sometimes Herman even went to Mrs. Haydon to talk all this trouble over. They decided then together, it was better to wait there all four together for the baby, and Herman could make Mrs. Kreder stop a little with her scolding, and then when Lena was a little stronger, Herman should have his own house for her, next door to his father, so he could always be there to help him in his working, but so they could eat and sleep in a house where the old woman could not control them and they could not hear her awful scolding.

And so things went on, the same way, a little longer. Poor Lena was not feeling any joy to have a baby. She was scared the way she had been when she was so sick on the water. She was scared now every time when anything would hurt her. She was scared and still and lifeless, and sure that every minute she would die. Lena had no power to be strong in this kind of trouble, she could only sit still and be scared, and dull, and lifeless, and sure that every minute she would die.

Before very long, Lena had her baby. He was a good, healthy little boy, the baby. Herman cared very much to have the baby. When Lena was a little stronger he took a house next door to the old couple, so he and his own family could eat and sleep and do the way they wanted. This did not seem to make much change now for Lena. She was just the same as when she was waiting with her baby. She just dragged around and was careless with her clothes and all lifeless, and she acted always and lived on just as if she had no feeling. She always did everything regular with the work, the way she always had had to do it, but she never got back any spirit in her. Herman was always good and kind,

and always helped her with her working. He did everything he knew to help her. He always did all the active new things in the house and for the baby. Lena did what she had to do the way she always had been taught it. She always just kept going now with her working, and she was always careless, and dirty, and a little dazed, and lifeless. Lena never got any better in herself of this way of being that she had had ever since she had been married.

Mrs. Haydon never saw any more of her niece, Lena. Mrs. Haydon had now so much trouble with her own house, and her daughters getting married, and her boy, who was growing up, and who always was getting so much worse to manage. She knew she had done right by Lena. Herman Kreder was a good man, she would be glad to get one so good, sometimes, for her own daughters, and now they had a home to live in together, separate from the old people, who had made their trouble for them. Mrs. Haydon felt she had done very well by her niece, Lena, and she never thought now she needed any more to go and see her. Lena would do very well now without her aunt to trouble herself any more about her.

The good german cook who had always scolded, still tried to do her duty like a mother to poor Lena. It was very hard now to do right by Lena. Lena never seemed to hear now what anyone was saying to her. Herman was always doing everything he could to help her. Herman always, when he was home, took good care of the baby. Herman loved to take care of his baby. Lena never thought to take him out or to do anything she didn't have to.

The good cook sometimes made Lena come to see her. Lena would come with her baby and sit there in the kitchen, and watch the good woman cooking, and listen to her sometimes a little, the way she used to, while the good german woman scolded her for going around looking so careless when now she had no trouble, and sitting there so dull, and always being just so thankless. Sometimes Lena would wake up a little and get back into her face her old, gentle, patient, and unsuffering sweetness, but mostly Lena did not seem to hear much when the good german woman scolded. Lena always liked it when Mrs. Aldrich her good mistress spoke to her kindly, and then Lena would seem to go back and feel herself to be like she was when she had been in service. But mostly Lena just lived along and was careless in her clothes, and dull, and lifeless.

By and by Lena had two more little babies. Lena was not so much scared now when she had the babies. She did not seem to notice very much when they hurt her, and she never seemed to feel very much now about anything that happened to her.

They were very nice babies, all these three that Lena had, and Herman took good care of them always. Herman never really cared much about his wife, Lena. The only things Herman ever really cared for were his babies. Herman always was very good to his children. He always had a gentle, tender way when he held them. He learned to be very handy with them. He spent all the time he was not working, with them. By the by he began to work all day in his own home so that he could have his children always in the same room with him.

Lena always was more and more lifeless and Herman now mostly never thought about her. He more and more took all the care of their three children. He saw to their eating right and their washing, and he dressed them every morning, and he taught them the right way to do things, and he put them to their sleeping, and he was now always every minute with them. Then there

was to come to them, a fourth baby. Lena went to the hospital near by to have the baby. Lena seemed to be going to have much trouble with it. When the baby was come out at last, it was like its mother lifeless. While it was coming, Lena had grown very pale and sicker. When it was all over Lena had died, too, and nobody knew just how it had happened to her.

The good german cook who had always scolded Lena, and had always to the last day tried to help her, was the only one who ever missed her. She remembered how nice Lena had looked all the time she was in service with her, and how her voice had been so gentle and sweet-sounding, and how she always was a good girl, and how she never had to have any trouble with her, the way she always had with all the other girls who had been taken into the house to help her. The good cook sometimes spoke so of Lena when she had time to have a talk with Mrs. Aldrich, and this was all the remembering there now ever was of Lena.

Herman Kreder now always lived very happy, very gentle, very quiet, very well content alone with his three children. He never had a woman any more to be all the time around him. He always did all his own work in his house, when he was through every day with the work he was always doing for his father. Herman always was alone, and he always worked alone, until his little ones were big enough to help him. Herman Kreder was very well content now and he always lived very regular and peaceful, and with every day just like the next one, always alone now with his three good, gentle children.

Finis[2]

1909

Picasso[1]

One whom some were certainly following was one who was completely charming. One whom some were certainly following was one who was charming. One whom some were following was one who was completely charming. One whom some were following was one who was certainly completely charming.

Some were certainly following and were certain that the one they were then following was one working and was one bringing out of himself then something. Some were certainly following and were certain that the one they were then following was one bringing out of himself then something that was coming to be a heavy thing, a solid thing and a complete thing.

One whom some were certainly following was one working and certainly was one bringing something out of himself then and was one who had been all his living had been one having something coming out of him.

Something had been coming out of him, certainly it had been coming out of him, certainly it was something, certainly it had been coming out of him and it had meaning, a charming meaning, a solid meaning, a struggling meaning, a clear meaning.

2. The end (Latin).
1. Stein became a friend of the Spanish artist Pablo Picasso (1881–1973) when she lived in Paris.

One whom some were certainly following and some were certainly following him, one whom some were certainly following was one certainly working.

One whom some were certainly following was one having something coming out of him something having meaning and this one was certainly working then.

This one was working and something was coming then, something was coming out of this one then. This one was one and always there was something coming out of this one and always there had been something coming out of this one. This one had never been one not having something coming out of this one. This one was one having something coming out of this one. This one had been one whom some were following. This one was one whom some were following. This one was being one whom some were following. This one was one who was working.

This one was one who was working. This one was one being one having something being coming out of him. This one was one going on having something come out of him. This one was one going on working. This one was one whom some were following. This one was one who was working.

This one always had something being coming out of this one. This one was working. This one always had been working. This one was always having something that was coming out of this one that was a solid thing, a charming thing, a lovely thing, a perplexing thing, a disconcerting thing, a simple thing, a clear thing, a complicated thing, an interesting thing, a disturbing thing, a repellant thing, a very pretty thing. This one was one certainly being one having something coming out of him. This one was one whom some were following. This one was one who was working.

This one was one who was working and certainly this one was needing to be working so as to be one being working. This one was one having something coming out of him. This one would be one all his living having something coming out of him. This one was working and then this one was working and this one was needing to be working, not to be one having something coming out of him something having meaning, but was needing to be working so as to be one working.

This one was certainly working and working was something this one was certain this one would be doing and this one was doing that thing, this one was working. This one was not one completely working. This one was not ever completely working. This one certainly was not completely working.

This one was one having always something being coming out of him, something having completely a real meaning. This one was one whom some were following. This one was one who was working. This one was one who was working and he was one needing this thing needing to be working so as to be one having some way of being one having some way of working. This one was one who was working. This one was one having something come out of him something having meaning. This one was one always having something come out of him and this thing the thing coming out of him always had real meaning. This one was one who was working. This one was one who was almost always working. This one was not one completely working. This one was one not ever completely working. This one was not one working to have anything come out of him. This one did have something having meaning that did come out of him. He always did have something come out of him. He was working, he was not ever completely working. He did have some following. They were always fol-

lowing him. Some were certainly following him. He was one who was working. He was one having something coming out of him something having meaning. He was not ever completely working.

<div align="right">1912, 1934</div>

Ada[1]

Barnes Colhard did not say he would not do it but he did not do it. He did it and then he did not do it, he did not ever think about it. He just thought some time he might do something.

His father Mr. Abram Colhard spoke about it to every one and very many of them spoke to Barnes Colhard about it and he always listened to them.

Then Barnes fell in love with a very nice girl and she would not marry him. He cried then, his father Mr. Abram Colhard comforted him and they took a trip and Barnes promised he would do what his father wanted him to be doing. He did not do the thing, he thought he would do another thing, he did not do the other thing, his father Mr. Colhard did not want him to do the other thing. He really did not do anything then. When he was a good deal older he married a very rich girl. He had thought perhaps he would not propose to her but his sister wrote to him that it would be a good thing. He married the rich girl and she thought he was the most wonderful man and one who knew everything. Barnes never spent more than the income of the fortune he and his wife had then, that is to say they did not spend more than the income and this was a surprise to very many who knew about him and about his marrying the girl who had such a large fortune. He had a happy life while he was living and after he was dead his wife and children remembered him.

He had a sister who also was successful enough in being one being living. His sister was one who came to be happier than most people come to be in living. She came to be a completely happy one. She was twice as old as her brother. She had been a very good daughter to her mother. She and her mother had always told very pretty stories to each other. Many old men loved to hear her tell these stories to her mother. Every one who ever knew her mother liked her mother. Many were sorry later that not every one liked the daughter. Many did like the daughter but not every one as every one had liked the mother. The daughter was charming inside in her, it did not show outside in her to every one, it certainly did to some. She did sometimes think her mother would be pleased with a story that did not please her mother, when her mother later was sicker the daughter knew that there were some stories she could tell her that would not please her mother. Her mother died and really mostly altogether the mother and the daughter had told each other stories very happily together.

The daughter then kept house for her father and took care of her brother. There were many relations who lived with them. The daughter did not like them to live with them and she did not like them to die with them. The daughter, Ada they had called her after her grandmother who had delightful ways of smelling flowers and eating dates and sugar, did not like it at all then as

1. The character Ada is probably based on Stein's companion Alice B. Toklas (1887–1967).

she did not like so much dying and she did not like any of the living she was doing then. Every now and then some old gentlemen told delightful stories to her. Mostly then there were not nice stories told by any one then in her living. She told her father Mr. Abram Colhard that she did not like it at all being one being living then. He never said anything. She was afraid then, she was one needing charming stories and happy telling of them and not having that thing she was always trembling. Then every one who could live with them were dead and there were then the father and the son a young man then and the daughter coming to be that one then. Her grandfather had left some money to them each one of them. Ada said she was going to use it to go away from them. The father said nothing then, then he said something and she said nothing then, then they both said nothing and then it was that she went away from them. The father was quite tender then, she was his daughter then. He wrote her tender letters then, she wrote him tender letters then, she never went back to live with him. He wanted her to come and she wrote him tender letters then. He liked the tender letters she wrote to him. He wanted her to live with him. She answered him by writing tender letters to him and telling very nice stories indeed in them. He wrote nothing and then he wrote again and there was some waiting and then he wrote tender letters again and again.

She came to be happier than anybody else who was living then. It is easy to believe this thing. She was telling some one, who was loving every story that was charming. Some one who was living was almost always listening. Some one who was loving[2] was almost always listening. That one who was loving was almost always listening. That one who was loving was telling about being one then listening. That one being loving was then telling stories having a beginning and a middle and an ending. That one was then one always completely listening. Ada was then one and all her living then one completely telling stories that were charming, completely listening to stories having a beginning and a middle and an ending. Trembling was all living, living was all loving, some one was then the other one. Certainly this one was loving this Ada then. And certainly Ada all her living then was happier in living than any one else who ever could, who was, who is, who ever will be living.

1909–10 1922

Miss Furr and Miss Skeene

Helen Furr had quite a pleasant home. Mrs. Furr was quite a pleasant woman. Mr. Furr was quite a pleasant man. Helen Furr had quite a pleasant voice a voice quite worth cultivating. She did not mind working. She worked to cultivate her voice. She did not find it gay living in the same place where she had always been living. She went to a place where some were cultivating something, voices and other things needing cultivating. She met Georgine Skeene there who was cultivating her voice which some thought was quite a pleasant one. Helen Furr and Georgine Skeene lived together then. Georgine Skeene liked travelling. Helen Furr did not care about travelling, she liked to stay in

2. Implicitly, Stein herself.

one place and be gay there. They were together then and travelled to another place and stayed there and were gay[1] there.

They stayed there and were gay there, not very gay there, just gay there. They were both gay there, they were regularly working there both of them cultivating their voices there, they were both gay there. Georgine Skeene was gay there and she was regular, regular in being gay, regular in not being gay, regular in being a gay one who was one not being gay longer than was needed to be one being quite a gay one. They were both gay then there and both working there then.

They were in a way both gay there where there were many cultivating something. They were both regular in being gay there. Helen Furr was gay there, she was gayer and gayer there and really she was just gay there, she was gayer and gayer there, that is to say she found ways of being gay there that she was using in being gay there. She was gay there, not gayer and gayer, just gay there, that is to say she was not gayer by using the things she found there that were gay things, she was gay there, always she was gay there.

They were quite regularly gay there, Helen Furr and Georgine Skeen, they were regularly gay there where they were gay. They were very regularly gay.

To be regularly gay was to do every day the gay thing that they did every day. To be regularly gay was to end every day at the same time after they had been regularly gay. They were regularly gay. They were gay every day. They ended every day in the same way, at the same time, and they had been every day regularly gay.

The voice Helen Furr was cultivating was quite a pleasant one. The voice Georgine Skeene was cultivating was, some said a better one. The voice Helen Furr was cultivating she cultivated and it was quite completely a pleasant enough one then, a cultivated enough one then. The voice Georgine Skeene was cultivating she did not cultivate too much. She cultivated it quite some. She cultivated and she would sometime go on cultivating it and it was not then an unpleasant one, it would not be then an unpleasant one, it would be a quite richly enough cultivated one, it would be quite richly enough to be a pleasant enough one.

They were gay where there were many cultivating something. The two were gay there, were regularly gay there. Georgine Skeene would have liked to do more travelling. They did some travelling, not very much travelling, Georgine Skeene would have liked to do more travelling, Helen Furr did not care about doing travelling, she liked to stay in a place and be gay there.

They stayed in a place and were gay there, both of them stayed there, they stayed together there, they were gay there, they were regularly gay there.

They went quite often, not very often, but they did go back to where Helen Furr had a pleasant enough home and then Georgine Skeene went to a place where her brother had quite some distinction. They both went, every few years, went visiting to where Helen Furr had quite a pleasant home. Certainly Helen Furr would not find it gay to stay, she did not find it gay, she said she would not stay, she said she did not find it gay, she said she would not stay where she did not find it gay, she said she found it gay where she did stay and she did stay there where very many were cultivating something. She did stay there. She always did find it gay there.

1. The use of the word *gay* to mean "homosexual" was not widespread until the middle of the 20th century

She went to see them where she had always been living and where she did not find it gay. She had a pleasant home there, Mrs. Furr was a pleasant enough woman, Mr. Furr was a pleasant enough man, Helen told them and they were not worrying, that she did not find it gay living where she had always been living.

Georgine Skeene and Helen Furr were living where they were both cultivating their voices and they were gay there. They visited where Helen Furr had come from and then they went to where they were living where they were then regularly living.

There were some dark and heavy men there then. There were some who were not so heavy and some who were not so dark. Helen Furr and Georgine Skeene sat regularly with them. They sat regularly with the ones who were dark and heavy. They sat regularly with the ones who were not so dark. They sat regularly with the ones that were not so heavy. They sat with them regularly, sat with some of them. They went with them regularly went with them. They were regular then, they were gay then, they were where they wanted to be then where it was gay to be then, they were regularly gay then. There were men there then who were dark and heavy and they sat with them with Helen Furr and Georgine Skeene and they went with them with Miss Furr and Miss Skeene, and they went with the heavy and dark men Miss Furr and Miss Skeene went with them, and they sat with them, Miss Furr and Miss Skeene sat with them, and there were other men, some were not heavy men and they sat with Miss Furr and Miss Skeene and Miss Furr and Miss Skeene sat with them, and there were other men who were not dark men and they sat with Miss Furr and Miss Skeene and Miss Furr and Miss Skeene sat with them. Miss Furr and Miss Skeene went with them and they went with Miss Furr and Miss Skeene, some who were not heavy men, some who were not dark men. Miss Furr and Miss Skeene sat regularly, they sat with some men. Miss Furr and Miss Skeene went and there were some men with them. There were men and Miss Furr and Miss Skeene went with them, went somewhere with then, went with some of them.

Helen Furr and Georgine Skeene were regularly living where very many were living and cultivating in themselves something. Helen Furr and Georgine Skeene were living very regularly then, being very regular then in being gay then. They did then learn many ways to be gay and they were then being gay being quite regular in being gay, being gay and they were learning little things, little things in ways of being gay, they were very regular then, they were learning very many little things in ways of being gay, they were being gay and using these little things they were learning to have to be gay with regularly gay with then and they were gay the same amount they had been gay. They were quite gay, they were quite regular, they were learning little things, gay little things, they were gay inside them the same amount they had been gay, they were gay the same length of time they had been gay every day.

They were regular in being gay, they learned little things that are things in being gay, they learned many little things that are things in being gay, they were gay every day, they were regular, they were gay, they were gay the same length of time every day, they were gay, they were quite regularly gay.

Georgine Skeene went away to stay two months with her brother. Helen Furr did not go then to stay with her father and her mother. Helen Furr stayed there where they had been regularly living the two of them and she would then

certainly not be lonesome, she would go on being gay. She did go on being gay. She was not any more gay but she was gay longer every day than they had been being gay when they were together being gay. She was gay then quite exactly the same way. She learned a few more little ways of being gay. She was quite gay and in the same way, the same way she had been gay and she was gay a little longer in the day, more of each day she was gay. She was gay longer every day than when the two of them had been being gay. She was gay quite in the way they had been gay, quite in the same way.

She was not lonesome then, she was not at all feeling any need of having Georgine Skeene. She was not astonished at this thing. She would have been a little astonished by this thing but she knew she was not astonished at anything and so she was not astonished at this thing not astonished at not feeling any need of having Georgine Skeene.

Helen Furr had quite a completely pleasant voice and it was quite well enough cultivated and she could use it and she did use it but then there was not any way of working at cultivating a completely pleasant voice when it has become a quite completely well enough cultivated one, and there was not much use in using it when one was not wanting it to be helping to make one a gay one. Helen Furr was not needing using her voice to be a gay one. She was gay then and sometimes she used her voice and she was not using it very often. It was quite completely enough cultivated and it was quite completely a pleasant one and she did not use it very often. She was then, she was quite exactly as gay as she had been, she was gay a little longer in the day than she had been.

She was gay exactly the same way. She was never tired of being gay that way. She had learned very many little ways to use in being gay. Very many were telling about using other ways in being gay. She was gay enough, she was always gay exactly the same way, she was always learning little things to use in being gay, she was telling about using other ways in being gay, she was telling about learning other ways in being gay, she was learning other ways in being gay, she would be using other ways in being gay, she would always be gay in the same way, when Georgine Skeene was there not so long each day as when Georgine Skeene was away.

She came to using many ways in being gay, she came to use every way in being gay. She went on living where many were cultivating something and she was gay, she had used, every way to be gay.

They did not live together then Helen Furr and Georgine Skeene. Helen Furr lived there the longer where they had been living regularly together. Then neither of them were living there any longer. Helen Furr was living somewhere else then and telling some about being gay and she was gay then and she was living quite regularly then. She was regularly gay then. She was quite regular in being gay then. She remembered all the little ways of being gay. She used all the little ways of being gay. She was quite regularly gay. She told many then the way of being gay, she taught very many then little ways they could use in being gay. She was living very well, she was gay then, she went on living then, she was regular in being gay, she always was living very well and was gay very well and was telling about little ways one could be learning to use in being gay, and later was telling them quite often, telling them again and again

 1922

ALICE DUNBAR-NELSON

1875–1935

Short-story writer, poet, teacher, and black political activist, Alice Dunbar-Nelson was born Alice Ruth Moore in New Orleans, Louisiana, the second daughter of a seaman father and a seamstress mother. After attending a two-year teachers' training program, she had her first book, *Violets and Other Tales*—a collection of twelve poems and seventeen sketches—privately printed in 1895. When one of the poems in this volume was first published in the Boston *Monthly Review*, it caught the fancy of the young black poet Paul Laurence Dunbar, who began to correspond with her. A few years later, the pair met and married, and Nelson began teaching in the New York City school system while also serving as recording secretary of the National Association of Colored Women. In 1899, her second book, *The Goodness of St. Rocque and Other Stories*, appeared, and in 1902, after she and Dunbar separated (later to divorce), she began teaching at the Howard High School in Wilmington, Delaware, where she was to be a popular instructor and the head of the English department for eighteen years.

In 1916, Alice Moore Dunbar remarried; her second husband, Robert John Nelson, was the publisher of the *Wilmington Advocate*, a weekly newspaper dedicated to the cause of black rights. Continually energetic, she edited several anthologies in these years—*Masterpieces of Negro Eloquence* (1914) and *The Dunbar Speaker and Entertainer* (1920)—and, besides working on many councils and committees, wrote a regular column for the *Washington Eagle*. In 1920, she risked—and lost—her teaching position because she insisted (despite her school district's rules forbidding employees to engage in political activity) on attending a meeting at which the presidential candidate Warren Harding's racial policies were to be formulated. From 1928 to 1931, she served as executive secretary of the American Interracial Peace Committee, a group sponsored by the American Friends Service Committee, which worked to encourage black support for world peace. Not coincidentally, *I Sit and Sew*, one of the comparatively few verses she wrote, expresses Nelson's distinctively female frustration at the "wasted fields" of a world at war, a world she consistently tried to improve. *Mr. Baptiste* captures her sympathy for the African-American and Creole characters about whom she often writes. In doing so, it illustrates a commitment to social activism that also motivated and shaped her journalism, her personal diary, and her work for antilynching as well as suffrage and educational campaigns.

Mr. Baptiste

He might have had another name: we never knew. Someone had christened him Mr. Baptiste long ago in the dim past, and it sufficed. No one had ever been known who had the temerity to ask him for another cognomen, for though he was a mild-mannered little man, he had an uncomfortable way of shutting up oyster-wise and looking disagreeable when approached concerning his personal history.

He was small: most Creole men are small when they are old. It is strange, but a fact. It must be that age withers them sooner and more effectually than those of un-Latinized extraction. Mr. Baptiste was, furthermore, very much wrinkled and lame. Like the Son of Man,[1] he had nowhere to lay his head, save

1. Jesus Christ.

when some kindly family made room for him in a garret or a barn. He subsisted by doing odd jobs, whitewashing, cleaning yards, doing errands, and the like.

The little old man was a frequenter of the levee.[2] Never a day passed that his quaint little figure was not seen moving up and down about the ships. Chiefly did he haunt the Texas and Pacific warehouses and the landing-place of the Morgan-line steamships. This seemed like madness, for these spots are almost the busiest on the levee, and the rough seamen and 'longshoremen have least time to be bothered with small weak folks. Still there was method in the madness of Mr. Baptiste. The Morgan steamships, as everyone knows, ply between New Orleans and Central and South American ports, doing the major part of the fruit trade; and many were the baskets of forgotten fruit that Mr. Baptiste took away with him unmolested. Sometimes, you know, bananas and mangoes and oranges and citrons will half spoil, particularly if it has been a bad voyage over the stormy Gulf, and the officers of the ships will give away stacks of fruit, too good to go into the river, too bad to sell to the fruit-dealers.

You could see Mr. Baptiste trudging up the street with his quaint one-sided walk, bearing his dilapidated basket on one shoulder, a nondescript headcover pulled over his eyes, whistling cheerily. Then he would slip in at the back door of one of his clients with a brisk,—

"Ah, bonjour, madame. Now here ees jus' a lil' bit fruit, some bananas. Perhaps madame would cook some for Mr. Baptiste?"

And madame, who understood and knew his ways, would fry him some of the bananas, and set it before him, a tempting dish, with a bit of madame's bread and meat and coffee thrown in for lagniappe;[3] and Mr. Baptiste would depart, filled and contented, leaving the load of fruit behind as madame's pay. Thus did he eat, and his clients were many, and never too tired or too cross to cook his meals and get their pay in baskets of fruit.

One day he slipped in at Madame Garcia's kitchen door with such a woebegone air, and slid a small sack of nearly ripe plantains on the table with such a misery-laden sigh, that madame, who was fat and excitable, threw up both hands and cried out:

"Mon Dieu, Mistare Baptiste, fo' w'y you look lak dat? What ees de mattare?"

For answer, Mr. Baptiste shook his head gloomily and sighed again. Madame Garcia moved heavily about the kitchen, putting the plantains in a cool spot and punctuating her footsteps with sundry "Mon Dieux" and "Misères."[4]

"Dose cotton!" ejaculated Mr. Baptiste, at last.

"Ah, mon Dieu!" groaned Madame Garcia, rolling her eyes heavenwards.

"Hit will drive de fruit away!" he continued.

"Misère!" said Madame Garcia.

"Hit will."

"Oui, oui" said Madame Garcia. She had carefully inspected the plantains, and seeing that they were good and wholesome, was inclined to agree with anything Mr. Baptiste said.

He grew excited. "Yaas, dose cotton-yardmans,[5] dose 'longsho mans, dey go

2. An embankment that serves as a river landing place.
3. A gratuity.
4. Misères (French). "Mon Dieux": my gods (French).
5. Those hired to load cotton.

out on one strik'. Dey t'row down dey tool an' say dey work no mo' wid niggers. Les veseaux,[6] dey lay in de river, no work, no cargo, yaas. Den de fruit ship, dey can' mak' lan, de mans, dey t'reaten an' say t'ings. Dey mak' big fight, yaas. Dere no mo' work on de levee, lak dat. Ever'body jus' walk roun' an' say cuss word, yaas!"

"Oh, mon Dieu, mon Dieu!" groaned Madame Garcia, rocking her guinea-blue-clad self to and fro.

Mr. Baptiste picked up his nondescript head-cover and walked out through the brick-reddened alley, talking excitedly to himself. Madame Garcia called after him to know if he did not want his luncheon, but he shook his head and passed on.

Down on the levee it was even as Mr. Baptiste had said. The 'longshoremen, the cotton-yardmen, and the stevedores had gone out on a strike. The levee lay hot and unsheltered under the glare of a noonday sun. The turgid Mississippi scarce seemed to flow, but gave forth a brazen gleam from its yellow bosom. Great vessels lay against the wharf, silent and unpopulated. Excited groups of men clustered here and there among bales of uncompressed cotton, lying about in disorderly profusion. Cargoes of molasses and sugar gave out a sticky sweet smell, and now and then the fierce rays of the sun would kindle tiny blazes in the cotton and splinter-mixed dust underfoot.

Mr. Baptiste wandered in and out among the groups of men, exchanging a friendly salutation here and there. He looked the picture of woe-begone misery.

"Hello, Mr. Baptiste," cried a big, brawny Irishman, "sure an' you look, as if you was about to be hanged."

"Ah, mon Dieu," said Mr. Baptiste, "dose fruit ship be ruined fo' dees strik'."

"Damn the fruit!" cheerily replied the Irishman, artistically disposing of a mouthful of tobacco juice. "It ain't the fruit we care about, it's the cotton."

"Hear! hear!" cried a dozen lusty comrades.

Mr. Baptiste shook his head and moved sorrowfully away.

"Hey, by howly St. Patrick, here's that little fruit-eater!" called the center of another group of strikers perched on cotton-bales.

"Hello! Where—" began a second; but the leader suddenly held up his hand for silence, and the men listened eagerly.

It might not have been a sound, for the levee lay quiet and the mules on the cotton-drays[7] dozed languidly, their ears pitched at varying acute angles. But the practiced ears of the men heard a familiar sound stealing up over the heated stillness.

"Oh—ho—ho—humph—humph—humph—ho—ho—ho—oh—o—o—humph!"

Then the faint rattle of chains, and the steady thump of a machine pounding.

If ever you go on the levee you'll know that sound, the rhythmic song of the stevedores heaving cotton-bales, and the steady thump, thump, of the machine compressing them within the hold of the ship.

Finnegan, the leader, who had held up his hand for silence, uttered an oath.

6. Vessels (French). 7. Carts, usually without sides, used to haul cotton.

"Scabs![8] Men, come on!"

There was no need for a further invitation. The men rose in sullen wrath and went down the levee, the crowd gathering in numbers as it passed along. Mr. Baptiste followed in its wake, now and then sighing a mournful protest which was lost in the roar of the men.

"Scabs!" Finnegan had said; and the word was passed along, until it seemed that the half of the second District knew and had risen to investigate.

"Oh—ho—ho—humph—humph—humph—oh—ho—ho—oh—o—o— humph!"

The rhythmic chorus sounded nearer, and the cause manifested itself when the curve of the levee above the French Market was passed. There rose a White Star steamer, insolently settling itself to the water as each consignment of cotton bales was compressed into her hold.

"Niggers!" roared Finnegan wrathily.

"Niggers! niggers! Kill'em, scabs!" chorused the crowd.

With muscles standing out like cables through their blue cotton shirts, and sweat rolling from glossy black skins, the Negro stevedores were at work steadily laboring at the cotton, with the rhythmic song swinging its cadence in the hot air. The roar of the crowd caused the men to look up with momentary apprehension, but at the overseer's reassuring word they bent back to work.

Finnegan was a Titan.[9] With livid face and bursting veins he ran into the street facing the French Market, and uprooted a huge block of paving stone. Staggering under its weight, he rushed back to the ship, and with one mighty effort hurled it into the hold.

The delicate poles of the costly machine tottered in the air, then fell forward with a crash as the whole iron framework in the hold collapsed.

"Damn ye," shouted Finnegan, "now yez can pack yer cotton!"

The crowd's cheers at this changed to howls, as the Negroes, infuriated at their loss, for those costly machines belong to the laborers and not to the ship-owners, turned upon the mob and began to throw brickbats, pieces of iron, chunks of wood, anything that came to hand. It was pandemonium turned loose over a turgid stream, with a malarial sun to heat the passions to fever point.

Mr. Baptiste had taken refuge behind a bread-stall on the outside of the market. He had taken off his cap, and was weakly cheering the Negroes on.

"Bravo!" cheered Mr. Baptiste.

"Will yez look at that damned fruit-eatin' Frinchman!" howled McMahon. "Cheerin' the niggers, are you?" and he let fly a brickbat in the direction of the bread-stall.

"Oh, mon Dieu, mon Dieu!" wailed the bread-woman.

Mr. Baptiste lay very still with a great ugly gash in his wrinkled brown temple. Fishmen and vegetable marchands[1] gathered around him in a quick, sympathetic mass. The individual, the concrete bit of helpless humanity, had more interest for them than the vast, vague fighting mob beyond.

The noon-hour pealed from the brazen throats of many bells, and the numerous hoarse whistles of the steam-boats called the unheeded luncheon-

8. Those who work while others (in the same jobs) are striking.

9. A giant.

1. Merchants (French).

time to the levee workers. The war waged furiously, and groans of the wounded mingled with curses and roars from the combatants.

"Killed instantly," said the surgeon, carefully lifting Mr. Baptiste into the ambulance.

Tramp, tramp, tramp, sounded the militia steadily marching down Decatur Street.

"Whist! do yez hear!" shouted Finnegan; and the conflict had ceased ere the yellow river could reflect the sun from the polished bayonets.

You remember, of course, how long the strike lasted, and how many battles were fought and lives lost before the final adjustment of affairs. It was a fearsome war, and many forgot afterwards whose was the first life lost in the struggle,—poor little Mr. Baptiste's, whose body lay at the Morgue unclaimed for days before it was finally dropped unnamed into Potter's Field.[2]

1899

I Sit and Sew

I sit and sew—a useless task it seems,
My hands grown tired, my head weighed down with dreams—
The panoply of war, the martial tread of men,
Grim-faced, stern-eyed, gazing beyond the ken[1]
Of lesser souls, whose eyes have not seen Death 5
Nor learned to hold their lives but as a breath—
But—I must sit and sew.

I sit and sew—my heart aches with desire—
That pageant terrible, that fiercely pouring fire
On wasted fields, and writhing grotesque things 10
Once men. My soul in pity flings
Appealing cries, yearning only to go
There in that holocaust of hell, those fields of woe—
But—I must sit and sew.

The little useless seam, the idle patch; 15
Why dream I here beneath my homely thatch,
When there they lie in sodden mud and rain,
Pitifully calling me, the quick[2] ones and the slain?
You need me, Christ! It is no roseate dream
That beckons me—this pretty futile seam, 20
It stifles me—God, must I sit and sew?

1920

2. Public burying place for the poor, unknown, and criminals (from Matthew 22:7).
1. Range of vision.
2. Living.

ANNA HEMPSTEAD BRANCH

1875–1937

The daughter of a comfortable professional family—her father was a lawyer, her mother a poet and writer of children's books—Anna Hempstead Branch was born in New London, Connecticut, and after graduating from Smith College in 1897, she achieved a considerable reputation in the early years of the century with two collections of verse, *The Shoes That Danced* (1905) and *Rose of the Wind* (1910), both of which were significantly influenced by the art of the English Pre-Raphaelites, especially by the poetry of Christina Rossetti. Later her reputation was enhanced by *Sonnets from a Lock Box* (1929), a volume that is generally considered her finest book. Throughout her career she was both devout and philosophical, pursuing studies of mysticism and numerology as well as more orthodox Christian theology, so that at least one critic felt some of her work was reminiscent not only of Rossetti's devotional poetry but also of the meditative verse produced by the seventeenth-century Anglican lyricist George Herbert.

Putting her religious principles into practice, Branch devoted a good deal of time and energy to social service at Christadora House, a settlement house on New York's Lower East Side. In the belief that poetry was a sacred and redemptive activity that would foster human fellowship, she organized a series of readings at the house as well as at a successful youth club; then, along with Edwin Arlington Robinson, William Rose Benét, and other notable writers, she become a founding member of the Poets' Guild, an organization whose classes, readings, and dramatic performances lent what one scholar describes as a special "intellectual aura" to the house. Yet although a number of Branch's poems brood on the "stolid, homely, visible things" that manifest divinity, pieces like the *Sonnets from a Lock Box*, excerpted here, reveal a deeply rebellious and unorthodox strain in her thinking.

From Sonnets from a Lock Box

XIV

What witchlike spell weaves here its deep design,
And sells its pattern to the ignorant buyer.
Oh lacelike cruelty with stitches fine—
Which stings the flesh with its sharp mesh of fire.
God of the Thief and Patron of the Liar, 5
I think that it is best not to inquire
Upon whose wheel was spun this mortal thread;
What dyed this curious robe so rich a red;
With shivering hues it is embroidered.
With changing colors like unsteady eyes. 10
I think the filigree is Medea's wreath.[1]
Oh, treacherous splendor! In this lustrous prize
Of gold and silver weaving, madness lies.
Who purchases this garment—Sire—buys death

1. Medea was a sorceress who helped Jason, a Greek hero, win the Golden Fleece. She became his wife and bore him two sons, but when they returned to Greece, Jason took a new wife, Creusa. In revenge, Medea sent Creusa a splendid "wreath" or tiara and wedding robes; when Creusa put them on, they clung to her flesh and killed her.

XXV

Into the void behold my shuddering flight,
Plunging straight forward through unhuman space,
My wild hair backward blown and my white face
Set like a wedge of ice. My chattering teeth
Cut like sharp knives my swiftly freezing breath. 5
Perched upon straightness I seek a wilder zone.
My Flying Self—on this black steed alone—
Drives out to God or else to utter death.
Beware straight lines which do subdue man's pride!
'Tis on a broomstick that great witches ride. 10
Wild, dangerous and holy are the runes
Which shift the whirling atoms with their tunes.
Oh like a witch accursed shall she be burned
Who having flown on straightness has returned.

XXXI

I say that words are men and when we spell
In alphabets we deal with living things;
With feet and thighs and breasts, fierce heads, strong wings;
Material Powers, great Bridals, Heaven and Hell.
There is a menace in the tales we tell. 5
From out the throne from which all language springs
Voices proceed and fires and thunderings.
Oh when we speak, Great God, let us speak well.
Beware of shapes, beware of letterings,
For in them lies such magic as alters dream, 10
Shakes cities down and moves the inward scheme.
Beware the magic of the coin that sings.
These coins are graved with supernatural powers
And magic wills that are more strong than ours.

1929

GERTRUDE BONNIN (ZITKALA ŚA)
(1876-1938)

Born at the Yankton Sioux Agency in South Dakota and given the name of her mother's second husband, Gertrude Simmons took the tribal name Zitkala Śa ("Red Bird"). She lived on the reservation until her eighth year, when she was sent to a Quaker missionary school in Wabash, Indiana. Although, after returning home, she felt dislocated by her experience, she continued to seek educational opportunities elsewhere, first traveling back to the institute, then enrolling for two years at Earlham College in Richmond, Indiana, next teaching at the Indian school at Carlisle, Pennsylvania, and finally studying violin at the Boston Conservatory of Music. Throughout this period, she felt divided between the Native American and white worlds. At the turn of the century, she began publishing her autobiographical essays and stories in the *Atlantic Monthly* and *Harper's Monthly*. Her *Old Indian Legends* (1902) attempted to "transplant the native spirit . . . into the English language."

After marriage to Raymond Talesfase Bonnin, another Yankton Sioux, in 1902 the author moved to Utah, where she raised their son, continued to teach, and become involved in Native American rights activism. In 1916 Bonnin moved with her family to Washington, D.C., eventually becoming president of the National Council of American Indians. Beside lecturing on Indian rights, she edited the *American Indian Magazine*; published another collection, *American Indian Stories* (1921); and collaborated on the composition of an opera, *Sun Dance*. A pioneering individualist, she often explained, "I will say just what I think. I fear no man— sometimes I think I do not even fear God."

The Trial Path

It was an autumn night on the plain. The smoke-lapels of the cone-shaped tepee flapped gently in the breeze. From the low night sky, with its myriad fire points, a large bright star peeped in at the smoke-hole of the wigwam between its fluttering lapels, down upon two Dakotas talking in the dark. The mellow stream from the star above, a maid of twenty summers, on a bed of sweetgrass, drank in with her wakeful eyes. On the opposite side of the tepee, beyond the center fireplace, the grandmother spread her rug. Though once she had lain down, the telling of a story has aroused her to a sitting posture.

Her eyes are tight closed. With a thin palm she strokes her wind-shorn hair.

"Yes, my grandchild, the legend says the large bright stars are wise old warriors, and the small dim ones are handsome young braves," she reiterates, in a high, tremulous voice.

"Then this one peeping in at the smoke-hole yonder is my dear old grandfather," muses the young woman, in long-drawn-out words.

Her soft rich voice floats through the darkness within the tepee, over the cold ashes heaped on the center fire, and passes into the ear of the toothless old woman, who sits dumb in silent reverie. Thence it flies on swifter wing over many winter snows, till at last it cleaves the warm light atmosphere of her grandfather's youth. From there her grandmother made answer:

"Listen! I am young again. It is the day of your grandfather's death. The elder one, I mean, for there were two of them. They were like twins, though they were not brothers. They were friends, inseparable! All things, good and bad, they shared together, save one, which made them mad. In that heated frenzy the younger man slew his most intimate friend. He killed his elder brother, for long had their affection made them kin."

The voice of the old woman broke. Swaying her stooped shoulders to and fro as she sat upon her feet, she muttered vain exclamations beneath her breath. Her eyes, closed tight against the night, beheld behind them the light of bygone days. They saw again a rolling black cloud spread itself over the land. Her ear heard the deep rumbling of a tempest in the west. She bent low a cowering head, while angry thunder-birds shrieked across the sky. "Heyá! heyá!" (No! no!) groaned the toothless grandmother at the fury she had awakened. But the glorious peace afterward, when yellow sunshine made the people glad, now lured her memory onward through the storm.

"How fast, how loud my heart beats as I listen to the messenger's horrible tale!" she ejaculates. "From the fresh grave of the murdered man he hurried to our wigwam. Deliberately crossing his bare shins, he sat down unbidden be-

side my father, smoking a long-stemmed pipe. He had scarce caught his breath when, panting, he began:

" 'He was an only son, and a much-adored brother.'

"With wild, suspecting eyes he glanced at me as if I were in league with the man-killer, my lover. My father, exhaling sweet-scented smoke, assented—'How.' Then interrupting the 'Eya' on the lips of the round-eyed talebearer, he asked, 'My friend, will you smoke?' He took the pipe by its red-stone bowl, and pointed the long slender stem toward the man. 'Yes, yes, my friend,' replied he, and reached out a long brown arm.

"For many heart-throbs he puffed out the blue smoke, which hung like a cloud between us. But even through the smoke-mist I saw his sharp black eyes glittering toward me. I longed to ask what doom awaited the young murderer, but dared not open my lips, lest I burst forth into screams instead. My father plied the question. Returning the pipe, the man replied: 'Oh, the chieftain and his chosen men have had counsel together. They have agreed it is not safe to allow a man-killer loose in our midst. He who kills one of our tribe is an enemy, and must suffer the fate of a foe.'

"My temples throbbed like a pair of hearts!

"While I listened, a crier passed by my father's tepee. Mounted, and swaying with his pony's steps, he proclaimed in a loud voice these words (hark! I hear them now!): 'Ho-po! Give ear, all you people. A terrible deed is done. Two friends—ay, brothers in heart—have quarreled together. Now one lies buried on the hill, while the other sits, a dreaded man-killer, within his dwelling. Says our chieftain: "He who kills one of our tribe commits the offense of an enemy. As such he must be tried. Let the father of the dead man choose the mode of torture or taking of life. He has suffered livid pain, and he alone can judge how great the punishment must be to avenge his wrong." It is done.

" 'Come, every one, to witness the judgment of a father upon him who was once his son's best friend. A wild pony is now lassoed. The man-killer must mount and ride the ranting beast. Stand you all in two parallel lines from the center tepee of the bereaved family to the wigwam opposite in the great outer ring. Between you, in the wide space, is the given trailway. From the outer circle the rider must mount and ride his pony toward the center tepee. If, having gone the entire distance, the man-killer gains the center tepee still sitting on the pony's back, his life is spared and pardon given. But should he fall, then he himself has chosen death.'

"The crier's words now cease. A lull holds the village breathless. Then hurrying feet tear along, swish, swish, through the tall grass. Sobbing women hasten toward the trailway. The muffled groan of the round camp-ground is unbearable. With my face hid in the folds of my blanket, I run with the crowd toward the open place in the outer circle of our village. In a moment the two long files of solemn-faced people mark the path of the public trial. Ah! I see strong men trying to lead the lassoed pony, pitching and rearing, with white foam flying from his mouth. I choke with pain as I recognize my handsome lover desolately alone, striding with set face toward the lassoed pony. 'Do not fall! Choose life and me!' I cry in my breast, but over my lips I hold my thick blanket.

"In an instant he has leaped astride the frightened beast, and the men have let go their hold. Like an arrow sprung from a strong bow, the pony, with extended nostrils, plunges halfway to the center tepee. With all his might the rider draws the strong reins in. The pony halts with wooden legs. The rider is

thrown forward by force, but does not fall. Now the maddened creature pitches, with flying heels. The line of men and women sways outward. Now it is back in place, safe from the kicking, snorting thing.

"The pony is fierce, with its large black eyes bulging out of their sockets. With humped back and nose to the ground, it leaps into the air. I shut my eyes. I can not see him fall.

"A loud shout goes up from the hoarse throats of men and women. I look. So! The wild horse is conquered My lover dismounts at the doorway of the center wigwam. The pony, wet with sweat and shaking with exhaustion, stands like a guilty dog at his master's side. Here at the entranceway of the tepee sit the bereaved father, mother, and sister. The old warrior father rises. Stepping forward two long strides, he grasps the hand of the murderer of his only son. Holding it so the people can see, he cries, with compassionate voice, 'My son!' A murmur of surprise sweeps like a puff of sudden wind along the lines.

"The mother, with swollen eyes, with her hair cut square with her shoulders, now rises. Hurrying to the young man, she takes his right hand. 'My son!' she greets him. But on the second word her voice shook, and she turned away in sobs.

"The young people rivet their eyes upon the young woman. She does not stir. With bowed head, she sits motionless. The old warrior speaks to her. 'Shake hands with the young brave, my little daughter. He was your brother's friend for many years. Now he must be both friend and brother to you.'

"Hereupon the girl rises. Slowly reaching out her slender hand, she cries, with twitching lips, 'My brother!' The trial ends."

"Grandmother!" exploded the girl on the bed of sweet-grass. ' Is this true?"

"Tosh!" answered the grandmother, with a warmth in her voice. "It is all true. During the fifteen winters of our wedded life many ponies passed from our hands, but this little winner, Ohiyesa, was a constant member of our family. At length, on that sad day your grandfather died, Ohiyesa was killed at the grave."

Though the various groups of stars which move across the sky marking the passing of time, told how the night was in its zenith, the old Dakota woman ventured an explanation of the burial ceremony.

"My grandchild, I have scarce ever breathed the sacred knowledge in my heart. Tonight I must tell you one of them. Surely you are old enough to understand.

"Our wise medicine-man said I did well to hasten Ohiyesa after his master. Perchance on the journey along the ghostpath your grandfather will weary, and in his heart wish for his pony. The creature, already bound on the spirit-trail, will be drawn by that subtle wish. Together master and beast will enter the next camp-ground."

The woman ceased her talking. But only the deep breathing of the girl broke the quiet, for now the night wind had lulled itself to sleep.

"Hinnu! hinnu! Asleep! I have been talking in the dark, unheard. I did wish the girl would plant in her heart this sacred tale," muttered she, in a querulous voice.

Nestling into her bed of sweet scented grass, she dozed away into another dream. Still the guardian star in the night sky beamed compassionately down upon the little tepee on the plain.

1901, 1921

VIRGINIA WOOLF

1882–1941

In a memoir titled A *Sketch of the Past* (1939), the mature Virginia Woolf asked "Who was I . . . ? Adeline Virginia Stephen, the second daughter of Leslie and Julia Prinsep Stephen, born on 25th January 1882, descended from a great many people, some famous, others obscure; born into a large connection, born not of rich parents, but of well-to-do parents, born into a very communicative, literate, letter writing, visiting, articulate, late-nineteenth-century world." At the height of her fame as a novelist, essayist, editor, feminist, and influential force in English life and letters, Woolf had moved far from the Victorian origins she outlined in her reminiscence, yet—as she herself understood with greater clarity than many of her contemporaries—what her first biographer, Winifred Holtby, had called "the advantages of being Virginia Stephen" had consistently shaped both her consciousness and her career.

Woolf's father, Leslie Stephen, was a distinguished literary man, the editor, first, of *The Cornhill Magazine* and, then, of *The Dictionary of National Biography* as well as the author of numerous critical, biographical, and philosophical studies. His friends, frequent visitors to the Stephen household, included the American poet and ambassador James Russell Lowell, the English novelist-poet George Meredith, and the American novelist Henry James. Woolf's lively and beautiful mother, Julia Stephen, also had important artistic connections. As a girl, Julia had spent much time at Little Holland House, the Kensington estate where the painters William Holman Hunt, Edward Burne-Jones, and G. F. Watts, the actress Ellen Terry, and the poet Alfred, Lord Tennyson frequently gathered, and as a young widow she had seriously devoted herself to the profession of nursing, about which she wrote a useful and witty little book titled *Notes from Sick Rooms* (1883).

The union of these two was the second for both. As a young man, Leslie Stephen had been married to a daughter of the Victorian novelist William Makepeace Thackeray, by whom he had one child, a retarded girl who lived at home with the Stephen family during the years when Virginia was growing up. For her part, his wife Julia had been married at the age of nineteen to a promising attorney, Herbert Duckworth, by whom she had three children—Stella, George, and Gerald—who were to figure importantly in Virginia's life. Widower and widow, the pair met and eventually wed when they were London neighbors, living in an upper-middle-class quarter near London's Hyde Park Gate. Together, they had four more children: Vanessa (who became a painter), Thoby (who died at the age of twenty-six, after a promising university career), Virginia, and Adrian (who became a physician).

Woolf's childhood at 22 Hyde Park Gate was for the most part rich and exhilarating but, at times, bewildering. As she recalled in another memoir, the house itself consisted "of innumerable small oddly shaped rooms built to accommodate not one family but three" (the two Stephen families along with the Duckworths), and here "eleven people aged between eight and sixty lived . . . and were waited upon by seven servants," so that "the place seemed tangled and matted with emotion." Nevertheless, many of the children's activities were perfectly normal for their class and era. Summers the family spent at Talland House in Cornwall, a late-nineteenth-century country home of which Woolf has left an idyllic record in her 1927 novel *To the Lighthouse*. Winters, in London, were occupied with standard Victorian pedagogical routines: the boys were sent away to school, the girls were taught at home by their mother and by a series of tutors and governesses, an inequitable education that was later to inspire considerable bitterness in Woolf. Still, despite such familial adherence to convention, the novelist's childhood was

distinctively intellectual: not only was she continually brought in touch with what she once called the "old men of recognized genius" who were her father's friends, she was also early given the freedom of her father's extraordinarily well stocked library, and she began, too, when she was quite young to demonstrate her own imaginative talents, writing stories that her mother proudly circulated to friends, and editing (at first with her brother Thoby and later alone) a family bulletin called *The Hyde Park Gate News*.

Although she had a few painful childhood experiences—evidently including bizarre sexual advances from her stepbrothers Gerald and George Duckworth—Woolf herself identified the death in 1895 of her adored mother as the first and perhaps the most significant trauma of her life, an event from which she would not recover until she had in effect exorcized her mother's ghost through her characterization of Julia Stephen as Mrs. Ramsay in *To the Lighthouse*. "With mother's death the merry, various family life which she had held in being shut for ever," Woolf later remembered. "In its place a dark cloud settled over us. . . . A finger seemed laid on one's lips." To make matters worse, the girl's older half-sister, Stella Duckworth, who had become hostess and surrogate mother in the Stephen house, married within two years of Julia Stephen's death and died, apparently from complications of pregnancy worsened by appendicitis, three months after her marriage. For the next seven years, Virginia and her sister Vanessa were to be left largely at the mercy of their lugubrious father, now a mournful and deaf old man, and their social-climbing half brother George Duckworth, the central subject of her scathing autobiographical sketch *22 Hyde Park Gate*. Perhaps because of these difficulties, or perhaps, as she herself speculated, because of inherited sensitivities, it was in this period that the novelist-to-be suffered the first of a series of mental breakdowns that were certainly to mark, and significantly to mar, the rest of her life.

In her own way, Woolf clearly loved Leslie Stephen, yet she experienced his death in 1904 as a kind of liberation. Years later, she remarked in her diary that, had her father lived, "his life would have entirely ended mine. What would have happened? No writing, no books:—inconceivable." Certainly, after Stephen's demise, the ambition manifested by "writing" and "books" became possible for her as it had never been before. Packing up the relics of 22 Hyde Park Gate that they still wished to keep, the four youngest Stephens—Thoby, Vanessa, Virginia, and Adrian—left Kensington and settled at 46 Gordon Square in Bloomsbury, where the two young women, at last freed from the constraints of the Victorian society George Duckworth had so cherished, quickly became acquainted with a group of their brother Thoby's most brilliant Cambridge friends—Lytton Strachey, Saxon Sydney-Turner, John Maynard Keynes, Clive Bell, Leonard Woolf, Duncan Grant, and, eventually, E. M. Forster.

Many of these young men had been members of a college group known as the "Apostles," and a number were to become prominent in English intellectual circles, Strachey as an iconoclastic biographer, Keynes as a groundbreaking economist, Forster as a novelist, and Leonard Woolf as a man of letters, a socialist politician, and the husband of Virginia Stephen. In these early Bloomsbury years, however, they functioned primarily as messengers of a freedom that Virginia, in particular, seems hardly to have allowed herself to imagine before she met them. From late-night discussions of beauty and truth, the group moved to frank analyses of their own sexuality, especially of the homosexuality that had characterized many of the men's public (secondary) school and college careers. For the young woman who was to become the novelist Virginia Woolf, the Victorian period, with its covert suppression of the female intellect and its overt disapproval of everybody's sexuality seems definitively to have ended.

To be sure, just before and right after the move to Gordon Square, Virginia Woolf had been actively engaged in a number of radical projects, studying Greek (still at that time an unusual undertaking for a young woman), teaching in a work-

ing women's college in South London, doing office chores for the suffrage movement, and writing reviews for the prestigious *Times Literary Supplement*. Plainly, she was already quite aware that her vocation was to be a literary one, and more, she was already quite conscious of her own deeply feminist inclinations. Yet still another trauma was to darken her life in this period: her brother Thoby's sudden death from typhoid fever on a trip that the four Stephens took to Greece in 1906. Like the loss of her mother, this family calamity may well have slowed Woolf's aesthetic growth; certainly it weakened her own mental and physical health for a time (in fact, she herself had a bad case of the illness that killed Thoby). Perhaps for this reason, it was not until after her marriage to Leonard Woolf in 1912 that she was able sufficiently to focus her energies so that she could finish her first novel, *The Voyage Out* (1915), a book on which she had been working for seven years when it was finally published.

Only a year before her wedding, Virginia Stephen had brooded on the contrast between her sister Vanessa—now married, a mother, and a productive painter—and herself: "To be 29 and unmarried—to be a failure—childless—insane too, no writer." But when she married Woolf, after the fiasco of a twenty-four-hour engagement to the homosexual Lytton Strachey, she appears to have felt that she had found a husband with whom she could be perfectly happy. Although their relationship may have been in some ways unusual—it seems hardly to have existed sexually, for example—the "Woolves," as Leonard and Virginia were called in their circle, were evidently an exceptionally compatible couple. A former colonial administrator and, in his wife's words, a "penniless Jew," Leonard Woolf was passionately devoted to the sensitive yet powerfully ambitious literary woman he had married, nursing her through periods of mental illness, guarding her time and supporting her work when she was well. As a combination of Jewish "outsider" and Cambridge "insider," moreover, he may well have provided the former Virginia Stephen with just the oblique perspective on her culture that she needed. Thus, though the fact that she and Leonard remained childless did sometimes continue to trouble her, Woolf was in most ways satisfied, indeed sustained, by her relationship with him.

In the years after her marriage, Woolf worked with increasing intensity at the craft of fiction, publishing a series of novels that made her, by the middle 1920s, one of the best-known and most innovative literary artists in England. *The Voyage Out* was followed in 1919 by *Night and Day*, an exploration of the trials of a young woman who was, like the writer herself, a kind of anxious literary heiress. Comparatively conventional in form and substance, this book gave little indication of the more profoundly experimental works that were to come: *Jacob's Room* (1922), a deliberately fragmented meditation on the life and death of a young man who seemed, like Woolf's brother Thoby, to have been a confident inheritor of the patriarchal culture represented by institutions like Cambridge and Oxford; *Mrs. Dalloway* (1925), a daringly structured analysis of post–World War I London society that shifts from one character's mind to another's even while it focuses on a single day in the life of Clarissa Dalloway, a well-born Westminister hostess, and her mad double, Septimus Warren Smith, a shell-shocked veteran, who paradoxically functions as a kind of "other self " for her; and *To the Lighthouse* (1927), partly a nostalgic memoir of Woolf's own childhood summers at Talland House and partly a critique of the Victorian mores that made Talland House both a stimulating and a suffocating environment, especially for girls like the rebellious Virginia Stephen.

In the period when she was writing these books, Woolf and her husband also undertook to found a press. The Hogarth Press, as they called it, began at first as a hobby, an attempt on Leonard Woolf's part to offer his wife a species of what would today be called "occupational therapy." But the enterprise quickly grew into a serious publishing venture; the Woolves produced editions of, among other no-

table works, the poems of T. S. Eliot, the short stories of Katherine Mansfield, and the writings of Sigmund Freud in translation. Dominating what had come to be called "the Bloomsbury Group" both with her art and with her press, Leslie Stephen's youngest daughter had become, in her own right, an intellectual force to be reckoned with.

Central as she was to London literary life, however, Woolf continued to perceive herself as, in many ways, an outsider, and specifically as an outsider because she was a woman. From the first—as the critical essays included here suggest—she had been obsessed with reconstructing a uniquely female aesthetic heritage, a heritage that she implicitly opposed to the predominantly male tradition represented by her father's *Dictionary of National Biography*, and which she herself was eventually to define as, at least in its inceptions, one of marginality. But when, in the early 1920s, Woolf met and fell in love with a younger writer named Victoria Sackville-West, her commitment to women's lives and works was dramatically intensified. The daughter of an ancient and aristocratic family, Sackville-West was a lesbian poet-novelist who had been married for some years to Harold Nicolson, a literarily inclined diplomat who was evidently an unusually congenial and sympathetic husband. The mother of two sons, she nevertheless quite frankly led what she and Woolf called a "Sapphic" life, though over the years the ambiguity of her sexual identity had given her considerable pain.

Despite the comfort of her marriage to Leonard, Woolf's relationship with Vita, as she was called, became, in one biographer's words, the "great passion" of the older novelist's career. More, it inspired at least one book: *Orlando* (1928), a parodic biography of a four-hundred-year-old character who changes from male to female in the late seventeenth century and whose fantastic, centuries-long development represents not only the history of the Sackville-West family but also the evolution of English literature from the Renaissance to the twentieth century. In addition, Woolf's feelings for Sackville-West may have energized her composition of a text that is in a sense *Orlando*'s "sister" book: *A Room of One's Own* (1929), a luminous extended essay on "women and fiction" that is, as most literary historians would agree, the first major achievement of feminist criticism in the English language.

After the exuberant blossoming represented by *Orlando* and *A Room of One's Own*, Woolf's life and work slowly darkened. Though her friendship with Vita was never completely disrupted, it gradually dissolved, never to be replaced by another truly erotic passion. In some ways, *The Waves* (1931) represents Woolf at the height of her avant-garde experimental powers. A "poem-play," as she called it, this innovative novel consists of a series of meditative-ly lyric monologues spoken by six central characters, yet the book is already notably elegiac: each figure is, in one way or another, an aspect of the central human self, and all are haunted by the untimely death of an ambiguously heroic youth named Percival, who seems significantly related to Woolf's lost brother Thoby. Following *The Waves*, Woolf achieved great popular success with what would now be called a "family chronicle" novel, *The Years* (1937), a book that traced the lives of the upper-class Pargiter clan from the Victorian 1880s to "the present moment" in the 1930s. But as Europe began to sink beneath the shadow of fascism, her own existence became increasingly painful. During the 1930s, her nephew Julian Bell, the oldest son of her sister Vanessa, was killed in the Spanish civil war, and she herself had never, in any case, struggled free of the recurrent mental illness that had tormented her since adolescence. Her last novel, *Between the Acts* (posthumously published in 1941), was written at a time when she felt herself to be precariously balanced between health and disease. A few years earlier, she had produced her most radically feminist work, *Three Guineas* (1938), whose title referred to monetary contributions she had been asked to give to various political causes. The book had taken a number of years—and three scrapbooks full of notes and clippings—to compose, and in its

examination of the modes of social oppression, it made overt what Woolf saw as the covert connections between the West's patriarchal social structures and Hitler's jackbooted Nazis marching for the Fatherland.

As German planes began to appear over the once bucolic Sussex countryside, where the Woolves had a weekend home in the small village of Rodmell, Virginia Woolf evidently became increasingly anxious, not only about her own sanity but about her society's health. Her physician brother, Adrian, had provided her and Leonard with a painless poison, in case of a German invasion (which would, of course, have been a particularly disastrous event for the couple, considering Leonard's Jewish origins). But no doctor, apparently, could offer her a cure for the "voices" she had begun to hear; no one could provide a panacea to prevent, in her words, "another of those terrible times" when she would sink into madness. On March 28, 1941, she weighted her pockets with stones and walked into the river Ouse, a stream near her cottage at Rodmell, leaving a note for Leonard that explained, "I feel certain I am going mad again," but concluded with the reassurance that "I don't think two people could have been happier than we have been."

Dramatic and disturbing as it was, Woolf's suicide should not be taken as her life's ultimate gesture. Certainly, when one sets that gray, precarious moment in 1941—a moment when the sky above Sussex was heavy with bombers and the novelist's own head buzzing with "voices"—against this artist's lifetime of energetic achievement, the sad instant dissipates. Had Woolf lived, she would surely have written more and just as well, revising *Between the Acts* and perhaps reworking even such other posthumously published works included here as *22 Hyde Park Gate*. Yet stories like *The New Dress* and *Slater's Pins Have No Points*, along with essays like *Professions for Women* or *Jane Eyre and Wuthering Heights*, demonstrate that her vitality was continually intense, while a seemingly casual sketch like *The Death of the Moth* documents her intense attentiveness to—and empathy with— even the most radical otherness. "The advantages of being Virginia Stephen," after all, had been manifold: they had taught her not only how to write but how not to think: not to think like a Victorian, not to think like an "insider," not to think like what she called "a patriarch." Instead, defining herself, the way she had in *Three Guineas*, as the founder of a "Society of Outsiders," Woolf had spent most of her life setting herself against both literal and figurative death: the death of the mind symbolized by mental illness as well as the death of the soul manifested by deadening social structures. The last line of *The Waves*, spoken by a character who is perhaps her most significant alter ego—the novelist Bernard— summarizes an attitude that informed all her finest achievements: "Against you I will fling myself, unvanquished and unyielding, O Death!"

22 Hyde Park Gate[1]

As I have said, the drawing room at Hyde Park Gate was divided by black folding doors picked out with thin lines of raspberry red. We were still much under the influence of Titian. Mounds of plush, Watts'[2] portraits, busts shrined in crimson velvet, enriched the gloom of a room naturally dark and thickly shaded in summer by showers of Virginia Creeper.

But it is of the folding doors that I wish to speak. How could family life have been carried on without them? As soon dispense with water-closets or bathrooms as with folding doors in a family of nine men and women, one of whom

1. Written by Woolf to be read aloud to the Memoir Club, a group consisting of the members of the famous Bloomsbury circle. All members of the club were expected to read memoirs characterized by "absolute frankness." This house, where Woolf was born, was in
Kensington, a prosperous part of London.
2. George Frederick Watts (1817–1904), English painter strongly influenced by Titian. "Titian": Tiziano Vercelli (c. 1490–1576), Venetian painter of rich, dark interiors.

into the bargain was an idiot.[3] Suddenly there would be a crisis—a servant dismissed, a lover rejected, pass books[4] opened, or poor Mrs. Tyndall who had lately poisoned her husband by mistake come for consolation. On one side of the door Cousin Adeline, Duchess of Bedford, perhaps would be on her knees—the Duke had died tragically at Woburn; Mrs. Dolmetsch would be telling how she had found her husband in bed with the parlor-maid or Lisa Stillman would be sobbing that Walter Headlam had chalked her nose with a billiard cue—"which," she cried, "is what comes of smoking a pipe before gentlemen"—and my mother had much ado to persuade her that Life had still to be faced, and the flower of virginity was still unplucked in spite of a chalk mark on the nose.

Though dark and agitated on one side, the other side of the door, especially on Sunday afternoons, was cheerful enough. There round the oval tea table with its pink china shell full of spice buns would be found old General Beadle, talking of the Indian Mutiny; or Mr. Haldane, or Sir Frederick Pollock—talking of all things under the sun; or old C. B. Clarke, whose name is given to three excessively rare Himalayan ferns; and Professor Wolstenholme, capable, if you interrupted him, of spouting two columns of tea not unmixed with sultanas through his nostrils; after which he would relapse into a drowsy ursine[5] torpor, the result of eating opium to which he had been driven by the unkindness of his wife and the untimely death of his son Oliver who was eaten, somewhere off the coast of Coromandel, by a shark. These gentlemen came and came again; and they were often reinforced by Mr. Frederick Gibbs, sometime tutor to the Prince of Wales, whose imperturbable common sense and fund of information about the colonies in general and Canada in particular were a perpetual irritation to my father who used to wonder whether a brain fever at college in the year 1863 had not something to do with it. These old gentlemen were generally to be found, eating very slowly, staying very late and making themselves agreeable at Christmas-time with curious presents of Indian silver work, and hand bags made from the skin of the ornithorhynchus[6]—as I seem to remember.

The tea table however was also fertilized by a ravishing stream of female beauty—the three Miss Lushingtons, the three Miss Stillmans, and the three Miss Montgomeries—all triplets, all ravishing, but of the nine the paragon for wit, grace, charm and distinction was undoubtedly the lovely Kitty Lushington—now Mrs. Leo Maxse. (Their engagement under the jackmanii in the Love Corner at St. Ives was my first introduction to the passion of love.) At the time I speak of she was in process of disengaging herself from Lord Morpeth, and had, I suspect, to explain her motives to my mother, a martinet[7] in such matters, for first promising to marry a man and then breaking it off. My mother believed that all men required an infinity of care. She laid all the blame, I feel sure, upon Kitty. At any rate I have a picture of her as she issued from the secret side of the folding doors bearing on her delicate pink cheeks two perfectly formed pear-shaped crystal tears. They neither fell nor in the least dimmed the luster of her eyes. She at once became the life and soul of the tea table—perhaps Leo Maxse was there—perhaps Ronny Norman—per-

3. An allusion to Laura Stephen, Woolf's half sister,
who eventually was sent to an asylum.
4. Bankbooks.
5. Bearlike. "Sultanas": raisins.
6. Duck-billed platypus.
7. Strict disciplinarian.

haps Esmé Howard—perhaps Arthur Studd, for the gentlemen were not all old, or all professors by any means—and when my father groaned beneath his breath but very audibly, "Oh Gibbs, what a bore you are!" it was Kitty whom my mother instantly threw into the breach. "Kitty wants to tell you how much she loved your lecture," my mother would cry, and Kitty still with the tears on her cheeks would improvise with the utmost gallantry some compliment or opinion which pacified my father who was extremely sensitive to female charm and largely depended upon female praise. Repenting of his irritation he would press poor Gibbs warmly by the hand and beg him to come soon again—which needless to say, poor Gibbs did.

And then there would come dancing into the room rubbing his hands, wrinkling his forehead, the most remarkable figure, as I sometimes think, that our household contained. I have alluded to a grisly relic of another age which we used to disinter from the nursery wardrobe—Herbert Duckworth's wig. (Herbert Duckworth had been a barrister.) Herbert Duckworth's son— George Herbert—was by no means grisly. His hair curled naturally in dark crisp ringlets; he was six foot high; he had been in the Eton Eleven; he was now cramming at Scoones[8] in the hope of passing the Foreign Office examination. When Miss Willett of Brighton saw him "throwing off his ulster" in the middle of her drawing room she was moved to write an Ode Comparing George Duckworth to the Hermes of Praxiteles[9]—which Ode my mother kept in her writing table drawer, along with a little Italian medal that George had won for saving a peasant from drowning. Miss Willett was reminded of the Hermes; but if you looked at him closely you noticed that one of his ears was pointed; and the other round; you also noticed that though he had the curls of a God and the ears of a faun he had unmistakably the eyes of a pig. So strange a compound can seldom have existed. And in the days I speak of, God, faun and pig were all in all alive, all in opposition, and in their conflicts producing the most astonishing eruptions.

To begin with the God—well, he was only a plaster cast perhaps of Miss Willett's Hermes, but I cannot deny that the benign figure of George Duckworth teaching his small half-brothers and sisters by the hour on a strip of coconut matting to play forward with a perfectly straight bat[1] had something Christlike about it. He was certainly Christian rather than Pagan in his divinity, for it soon became clear that this particular forward stroke to be applied to every ball indifferently, was a symbol of moral rectitude, and that one could neither slog nor bowl a sneak[2] without paltering rather dangerously (as poor Gerald Duckworth used to do) with the ideals of a sportsman and an English gentleman. Then, he would run miles to fetch cushions; he was always shutting doors and opening windows; it was always George who said the tactful thing, and broke bad news, and braved my father's irritation, and read aloud to us when we had the whooping cough, and remembered the birthdays of aunts, and sent turtle soup to the invalids, and attended funerals, and took children to the pantomime—oh yes, whatever else George might be he was certainly a saint.

But then there was the faun. Now this animal was at once sportive and

8. I.e., intensively preparing for examinations at a "cram school." "Eton Eleven": i.e., on the cricket team at Eton, a prestigious English boy's school.
9. A statue of Hermes, the Greek messenger god, by

Praxiteles (4th century B.C.), Greek sculptor. "Ulster": long, loose overcoat.
1. I.e., properly using a cricket bat.
2. Unsportsmanlike strategies in cricket.

demonstrative and thus often at variance with the self-sacrificing nature of the God. It was quite a common thing to come into the drawing room and find George on his knees with his arms extended, addressing my mother, who might be adding up the weekly books, in tones of fervent adoration. Perhaps he had been staying with the Chamberlains for the week-end. But he lavished caresses, endearments, enquiries and embraces as if, after forty years in the Australian bush, he had at last returned to the home of his youth and found an aged mother still alive to welcome him. Meanwhile we gathered round—the dinner bell had already rung—awkward, but appreciative. Few families, we felt, could exhibit such a scene as this. Tears rushed to his eyes with equal abandonment. For example when he had a tooth out he flung himself into the cook's arms in a paroxysm of weeping. When Judith Blunt refused him he sat at the head of the table sobbing loudly, but continuing to eat. He cried when he was vaccinated. He was fond of sending telegrams which began "My darling mother" and went on to say that he would be dining out. (I copied this style of his, I regret to say, with disastrous results on one celebrated occasion. "She is an angel" I wired, on hearing that Flora Russell had accepted him, and signed my nickname "Goat." "She is an aged Goat" was the version that arrived, at Islay, and had something to do, George said, with Flora's reluctance to ally herself with the Stephen family.) But all this exuberance of emotion was felt to be wholly to George's credit. It proved not only how deep and warm his feelings were, but how marvellously he had kept the open heart and simple manners of a child.

But when nature refused him two pointed ears and gave him only one she knew, I think, what she was about. In his wildest paroxysms of emotion, when he bellowed with grief, or danced round the room, leaping like a kid, and flung himself on his knees before the Dowager Lady Carnarvon there was always something self conscious, a little uneasy about him, as though he were not quite sure of the effect—as though the sprightly faun had somehow been hobbled together with a timid and conventional old sheep.

It is true that he was abnormally stupid. He passed the simplest examinations with incredible difficulty. For years he was crammed by Mr. Scoones; and again and again he failed to pass the Foreign Office examination. He had existed all his life upon jobs found for him by his friends. His small brown eyes seemed perpetually to be boring into something too hard for them to penetrate. But when one compares them to the eyes of a pig, one is alluding not merely to their stupidity, or to their greed—George, I have been told, had the reputation of being the greediest young man in London ball-rooms—but to something obstinate and pertinacious in their expression as if the pig were grouting for truffles with his snout and would by sheer persistency succeed in unearthing them. Never shall I forget the pertinacity with which he learned "Love in the Valley" by heart in order to impress Flora Russell; or the determination with which he mastered the first volume of *Middlemarch*[3] for the same purpose; and how immensely he was relieved when he left the second volume in a train and got my father, whose set was ruined, to declare that in his opinion one volume of *Middlemarch* was enough. Had his obstinacy been directed solely to self-improvement there would have been no call for us to complain. I myself might even have been of use to him. But it gradually became clear that

3. Long novel by George Eliot (1819–1880).

he was muddling out a scheme, a plan of campaign, a system of life—I scarcely know what to call it—and then we had every reason to feel the earth tremble beneath our feet and the heavens darken. For George Duckworth had become after my mother's death, for all practical purposes, the head of the family. My father was deaf, eccentric, absorbed in his work, and entirely shut off from the world. The management of affairs fell upon George. It was usually said that he was father and mother, sister and brother in one—and all the old ladies of Kensington and Belgravia added with one accord that Heaven had blessed those poor Stephen girls beyond belief, and it remained for them to prove that they were worthy of such devotion.

But what was George Duckworth thinking and what was there alarming in the sight of him as he sat in the red leather arm-chair after dinner, mechanically stroking the dachshund Schuster, and lugubriously glancing at the pages of George Eliot? Well, he might be thinking about the crest on the post office notepaper, and how nice it would look picked out in red (he was now Austen Chamberlain's private secretary) or he might be thinking how the Duchess of St. Albans had given up using fish knives at dinner; or how Mrs. Grenfell had asked him to stay and he had created as he thought a good impression by refusing; at the same time he was revolving in the slow whirlpool of his brain schemes of the utmost thoughtfulness—plans for sending us for treats; for providing us with riding lessons; for finding jobs for some of poor Augusta Croft's innumerable penniless children. But the alarming thing was that he looked not merely muddled and emotional but obstinate. He looked as if he had made up his mind about something and would refuse to budge an inch. At the time it was extremely difficult to say what he had made up his mind to, but after the lapse of many years I think it may be said brutally and baldly, that George had made up his mind to rise in the social scale. He had a curious in-born reverence for the British aristocracy; the beauty of our great aunts had allied us in the middle of the nineteenth century with, I think I am right in saying, two dukes and quite a number of earls and countesses. They naturally showed no particular wish to remember the connection but George did his best to live up to it. His reverence for the symbols of greatness now that he was attached to a Cabinet Minister had fuller scope. His talk was all of ivory buttons that the coachmen of Cabinet Ministers wear in their coats; of having the entrée at Court; of baronies descending in the female line; of countesses secreting the diamonds of Marie Antoinette in black boxes under their beds. His secret dreams as he sat in the red leather chair stroking Schuster were all of marrying a wife with diamonds, and having a coachman with a button, and having the entrée at Court. But the danger was that his dreams were secret even to himself. Had you told him—and I think Vanessa did once—that he was a snob, he would have burst into tears. What he liked, he explained, was to know "nice people"; Lady Jeune was nice; so were Lady Sligo, Lady Carnarvon and Lady Leitrim. Poor Mrs. Clifford, on the other hand, was not; nor was old Mr. Wolstenholme; of all our old friends, Kitty Maxse, who might have been Lady Morpeth, came nearest to his ideal. It was not a question of birth or wealth; it was—and then if you pressed him further he would seize you in his arms and cry out that he refused to argue with those he loved. "Kiss me, kiss me, you beloved", he would vociferate; and the argument was drowned in kisses. Everything was drowned in kisses. He lived in the thickest emotional haze, and as his passions increased and his desires became more vehement—

he lived, Jack Hills[4] assured me, in complete chastity until his marriage—one felt like an unfortunate minnow shut up in the same tank with an unwieldy and turbulent whale.

Nothing stood in the way of his advancement. He was a bachelor of prepossessing appearance though inclined to fat, aged about thirty years, with an independent income of something over a thousand a year. As private secretary to Austen Chamberlain he was as a matter of course invited to all the great parties of all the great peers. Hostesses had no time to remember, if they had ever known, that the Duckworths had made their money in cotton or coal, not a hundred years ago, and did not really rank, as George made out, among the ancient families of Somersetshire. For I have it on the best authority that when the original Duckworth acquired Orchardleigh about the year 1810 he filled it with casts from the Greek to which he had attached not merely fig leaves for the Gods but aprons for the Goddesses—much to the amusement of the Lords of Longleat who never forgot that old Duckworth had sold cotton by the yard and probably bought his aprons cheap. George, as I say, could have mounted alone to the highest pinnacles of London society. His mantelpiece was a gallery of invitation cards from every house in London. Why then did he insist upon cumbering himself with a couple of half-sisters who were more than likely to drag him down? It is probably useless to enquire. George's mind swam and steamed like a cauldron of rich Irish stew. He believed that aristocratic society was possessed of all the virtues and all the graces. He believed that his family had been entrusted to his care. He believed that it was his sacred duty—but when he reached that point his emotions overcame him; he began to sob; he flung himself on his knees; he seized Vanessa in his arms; he implored her in the name of her mother, of her grandmother, by all that was sacred in the female sex and holy in the traditions of our family to accept Lady Arthur Russell's invitation to dinner, to spend the week-end with the Chamberlains at Highbury.

I cannot conceal my own opinion that Vanessa was to blame; not indeed that she could help herself, but if, I sometimes think, she had been born with one shoulder higher than another, with a limp, with a squint, with a large mole on her left cheek, both our lives would have been changed for the better. As it was, George had a good deal of reason on his side. It was plain that Vanessa in her white satin dress made by Mrs. Young, wearing a single flawless amethyst round her neck, and a blue enamel butterfly in her hair—the gifts, of course, of George himself—beautiful, motherless, aged only eighteen, was a touching spectacle, an ornament for any dinner table, a potential peeress, anything might be made of such precious material as she was—outwardly at least; and to be seen hovering round her, providing her with jewels, and Arab horses, and expensive clothes, whispering encouragement, lavishing embraces which were not entirely concealed from the eyes of strangers, redounded to the credit of George himself and invested his figure with a pathos which it would not otherwise have had in the eyes of the dowagers of Mayfair. Unfortunately, what was inside Vanessa did not altogether correspond with what was outside. Underneath the necklaces and the enamel butterflies was one passionate desire—for paint and turpentine, for turpentine and paint. But poor George was no psychologist. His perceptions were obtuse. He never saw within. He was

4. Husband of Woolf's half sister Stella Duckworth.

completely at a loss when Vanessa said she did not wish to stay with the
Chamberlains at Highbury; and would not dine with Lady Arthur Russell—a
rude, tyrannical old woman, with a bloodstained complexion and the manners
of a turkey cock. He argued, he wept, he complained to Aunt Mary Fisher, who
said that she could not believe her ears. Every battery was turned upon
Vanessa. She was told that she was selfish, unwomanly, callous and incredibly
ungrateful considering the treasures of affection that had been lavished upon
her—the Arab horse she rode and the slabs of bright blue enamel which she
wore. Still she persisted. She did not wish to dine with Lady Arthur Russell. As
the season wore on, every morning brought its card of invitation for Mr.
Duckworth and Miss Stephen; and every evening witnessed a battle between
them. For the first year or so George, I suppose, was usually the victor. Off they
went, in the hansom cab of those days and late at night Vanessa would come
into my room complaining that she had been dragged from party to party,
where she knew no one, and had been bored to death by the civilities of young
men from the Foreign Office and the condescensions of old ladies of title. The
more Vanessa resisted, the more George's natural obstinacy persisted. At last
there was a crisis. Lady Arthur Russell was giving a series of select parties on
Thursday evenings in South Audley Street. Vanessa had sat through one entire
evening without opening her lips. George insisted that she must go next week
and make amends, or he said, "Lady Arthur will never ask you to her house
again." They argued until it was getting too late to dress. At last Vanessa, more
in desperation than in concession, rushed upstairs, flung on her clothes and
announced that she was ready to go. Off they went. What happened in the cab
will never be known. But whenever they reached 2 South Audley Street—and
they reached it several times in the course of the evening—one or the other
was incapable of getting out. George refused to enter with Vanessa in such a
passion; and Vanessa refused to enter with George in tears. So the cabman had
to be told to drive once more round the Park. Whether they ever managed to
alight I do not know.

But next morning as I was sitting spelling out my Greek George came into
my room carrying in his hand a small velvet box. He presented me with the
jewel it contained—a Jews' harp made of enamel with a pinkish blob of matter
swinging in the center which I regret to say only fetched a few shillings when I
sold it the other day. But his face showed that he had come upon a different er-
rand. His face was sallow and scored with innumerable wrinkles, for his skin
was as loose and flexible as a pug dog's, and he would express his anguish in
the most poignant manner by puckering lines, folds, and creases from fore-
head to chin. His manner was stern. His bearing rigid. If Miss Willett of
Brighton could have seen him then she would certainly have compared him to
Christ on the cross. After giving me the Jews' harp he stood before the fire in
complete silence. Then, as I expected, he began to tell me his version of the
preceding night—wrinkling his forehead more than ever, but speaking with a
restraint that was at once bitter and manly. Never, never again, he said, would
he ask Vanessa to go out with him. He had seen a look in her eyes which posi-
tively frightened him. It should never be said of him that he made her do what
she did not wish to do. Here he quivered, but checked himself. Then he went
on to say that he had only done what he knew my mother would have wished
him to do. His two sisters were the most precious things that remained to him.
His home had always meant more to him—more than he could say, and here

he became agitated, struggled for composure, and then burst into a statement which was at once dark and extremely lurid. We were driving Gerald from the house, he cried—when a young man was not happy at home—he himself had always been content—but if his sisters—if Vanessa refused to go out with him—if he could not bring his friends to the house—in short, it was clear that the chaste, the immaculate George Duckworth would be forced into the arms of whores. Needless to say he did not put it like that; and I could only conjure up in my virgin consciousness, dimly irradiated by having read the "Symposium"[5] with Miss Case, horrible visions of the vices to which young men were driven whose sisters did not make them happy at home. So we went on talking for an hour or two. The end of it was that he begged me, and I agreed, to go a few nights later to the Dowager Marchioness of Sligo's ball. I had already been to May Week[6] at Cambridge, and my recollections of gallopading round the room with Hawtrey, or sitting on the stairs and quizzing the dancers with Clive,[7] were such as to make me wonder why Vanessa found dances in London so utterly detestable. A few nights later I discovered for myself. After two hours of standing about in Lady Sligo's ball-room, of waiting to be introduced to strange young men, of dancing a round with Conrad Russell or with Esmé Howard, of dancing very badly, of being left without a partner, of being told by George that I looked lovely but must hold myself upright, I retired to an ante-room and hoped that a curtain concealed me. For some time it did. At length old Lady Sligo discovered me, judged the situation for herself and being a kind old peeress with a face like a rubicund sow's carried me off to the dining room, cut me a large slice of iced cake, and left me to devour it by myself in a corner.

On that occasion George was lenient. We left about two o'clock, and on the way home he praised me warmly, and assured me that I only needed practice to be a great social success. A few days later he told me that the Dowager Countess of Carnarvon particularly wished to make my acquaintance, and had invited me to dinner. As we drove across the Park he stroked my hand, and told me how he hoped that I should make friends with Elsie—for so both he and Vanessa had called her for some time at her own request—how I must not be frightened—how though she had been vice-reine of Canada and vice-reine of Ireland she was simplicity itself—always since the death of her husband dressed in black—refused to wear any of her jewels though she had inherited the diamonds of Marie Antoinette—and was the one woman, he said, with a man's sense of honor. The portrait he drew was of great distinction and bereavement. There would also be present her sister, Mrs. Popham of Littlecote, a lady also of distinction and also bereaved, for her husband, Dick Popham of Littlecote, came of an ancient unhappy race, cursed in the reign of Henry the Eighth, since which time the property had never descended from father to son. Sure enough Mary Popham was childless, and Dick Popham was in a lunatic asylum. I felt that I was approaching a house of grandeur and desolation, and was not a little impressed. But I could see nothing alarming either in Elsie Carnarvon or in Mrs. Popham of Littlecote. They were a couple of spare prim little women, soberly dressed in high black dresses, with gray hair strained off

5. Dialogue on the subject of love—heterosexual, homosexual, and the love of beauty—by the Greek philosopher Plato.

6. The festive week (in June) of intercollegiate boat races at the English universty.

7. Clive Bell, later to be Vanessa's husband.

their foreheads, rather prominent blue eyes, and slightly protruding front teeth. We sat down to dinner.

The conversation was mild and kindly. Indeed I soon felt that I could not only reply to their questions—was I fond of painting?—was I fond of reading?—did I help my father in his work?—but could initiate remarks of my own. George had always complained of Vanessa's silence. I would prove that I could talk. So off I started. Heaven knows what devil prompted me—or why to Lady Carnarvon and Mrs. Popham of Littlecote of all people in the world I, a chit of eighteen, should have chosen to discourse upon the need of expressing the emotions! That, I said, was the great lack of modern life. The ancients, I said, discussed everything in common. Had Lady Carnarvon ever read the dialogues of Plato? "We—both men and women—" once launched it was difficult to stop, nor was I sure that my audacity was not holding them spell-bound with admiration. I felt that I was earning George's gratitude for ever. Suddenly a twitch, a shiver, a convulsion of amazing expressiveness, shook the Countess by my side; her diamonds, of which she wore a chaste selection, flashed in my eyes; and stopping, I saw George Duckworth blushing crimson on the other side of the table. I realized that I had committed some unspeakable impropriety. Lady Carnarvon and Mrs. Popham began at once to talk of something entirely different; and directly dinner was over George, pretending to help me on with my cloak, whispered in my ear in a voice of agony, "They're not used to young women saying anything—." And then as if to apologize to Lady Carnarvon for my ill breeding, I saw him withdraw with her behind a pillar in the hall, and though Mrs. Popham of Littlecote tried to attract my attention to a fine specimen of Moorish metal work which hung on the wall, we both distinctly heard them kiss. But the evening was not over. Lady Carnarvon had taken tickets for the French actors, who were then appearing in some play whose name I have forgotten. We had stalls[8] of course, and filed soberly to our places in the very center of the crowded theater. The curtain went up. Snubbed, shy, indignant, and uncomfortable, I paid little attention to the play. But after a time I noticed that Lady Carnarvon on one side of me, and Mrs. Popham on the other, were both agitated by the same sort of convulsive twitching which had taken them at dinner. What could be the matter? They were positively squirming in their seats. I looked at the stage. The hero and heroine were pouring forth a flood of voluble French which I could not disentangle. Then they stopped. To my great astonishment the lady leapt over the back of a sofa; the gentleman followed her. Round and round the stage they dashed, the lady shrieking, the man groaning and grunting in pursuit. It was a fine piece of realistic acting. As the pursuit continued, the ladies beside me held to the arms of their stalls with claws of iron. Suddenly, the actress dropped exhausted upon the sofa, and the man with a howl of gratification, loosening his clothes quite visibly, leapt on top of her. The curtain fell. Lady Carnarvon, Mrs. Popham of Littlecote and George Duckworth rose simultaneously. Not a word was said. Out we filed. And as our procession made its way down the stalls I saw Arthur Cane leap up in his seat like a jack-in-the-box, amazed and considerably amused that George Duckworth and Lady Carnarvon of all people should have taken a girl of eighteen to see the French actors copulate upon the stage.

8. Expensive seats.

The brougham[9] was waiting, and Mrs. Popham of Littlecote, without speaking a word or even looking at me, immediately secreted herself inside it. Nor could Lady Carnarvon bring herself to face me. She took my hand, and said in a tremulous voice—her elderly cheeks were flushed with emotion—"I do hope, Miss Stephen, that the evening has not tired you very much." Then she stepped into the carriage, and the two bereaved ladies returned to Bruton Street. George meanwhile had secured a cab. He was much confused, and yet very angry. I could see that my remarks at dinner upon the dialogues of Plato rankled bitterly in his mind. And he told the cabman to go, not back to Hyde Park Gate as I hoped, but on to Melbury Road.

"It's quite early still," he said in his most huffy manner as he sat down. "And I think you want a little practice in how to behave to strangers. It's not your fault of course, but you have been out much less than most girls of your age." So it appeared that my education was to be continued, and that I was about to have another lesson in the art of behaviour at the house of Mrs. Holman Hunt.[1] She was giving a large evening party. Melbury Road was lined with hansoms, four-wheelers, hired flies, and an occasional carriage drawn by a couple of respectable family horses. "A very *dritte*[2] crowd," said George disdainfully as we took our place in the queue. Indeed all our old family friends were gathered together in the Moorish Hall, and directly I came in I recognized the Stillmans, the Lushingtons, the Montgomeries, the Morrises, the Burne-Joneses—Mr. Gibbs, Professor Wolstenholme and General Beadle would certainly have been there too had they not all been sleeping for many years beneath the sod. The effect of the Moorish Hall, after Bruton Street, was garish, a little eccentric, and certainly very dowdy. The ladies were intense and untidy; the gentlemen had fine foreheads and short evening trousers, in some cases revealing a pair of bright red Pre-Raphaelite socks. George stepped among them like a Prince in disguise. I soon attached myself to a little covey of Kensington ladies who were being conveyed by Gladys Holman Hunt across the Moorish Hall to the studio. There we found old Holman Hunt himself dressed in a long Jaeger dressing gown, holding forth to a large gathering about the ideas which had inspired him in painting "The Light of the World," a copy of which stood upon an easel. He sipped cocoa and stroked his flowing beard as he talked, and we sipped cocoa and shifted our shawls—for the room was chilly—as we listened. Occasionally some of us strayed off to examine with reverent murmurs other bright pictures upon other easels, but the tone of the assembly was devout, high-minded, and to me after the tremendous experiences of the evening, soothingly and almost childishly simple. George was never lacking in respect for old men of recognized genius, and he now advanced with his opera hat pressed beneath his arm; drew his feet together, and made a profound bow over Holman Hunt's hand. Holman Hunt had no notion who he was, or indeed who any of us were; but went on sipping his cocoa, stroking his beard, and explaining what ideas had inspired him in painting "The Light of the World," until we left.

At last—at last—the evening was over.

I went up to my room, took off my beautiful white satin dress, and unfas-

9. Closed carriage.
1. Wife of William Holman Hunt (1827–1910), well-known Victorian painter; one of his most famous paintings is *The Light of the World*.
2. Third (German, literal trans.); i.e., third rate.

tened the three pink carnations which had been pinned to my breast by the Jews' harp. Was it really possible that tomorrow I should open my Greek dictionary and go on spelling out the dialogues of Plato with Miss Case? I felt I knew much more about the dialogues of Plato than Miss Case could ever do. I felt old and experienced and disillusioned and angry, amused and excited, full of mystery, alarm and bewilderment. In a confused whirlpool of sensation I stood slipping off my petticoats, withdrew my long white gloves, and hung my white silk stockings over the back of a chair. Many different things were whirling round in my mind—diamonds and countesses, copulations, the dialogues of Plato, Mad Dick Popham and "The Light of the World." Ah, how pleasant it would be to stretch out in bed, fall asleep and forget them all!

Sleep had almost come to me. The room was dark. The house silent. Then, creaking stealthily, the door opened; treading gingerly, someone entered. "Who?" I cried. "Don't be frightened," George whispered. "And don't turn on the light, oh beloved. Beloved—" and he flung himself on my bed, and took me in his arms.

Yes, the old ladies of Kensington and Belgravia never knew that George Duckworth was not only father and mother, brother and sister to those poor Stephen girls; he was their lover also.

1921? 1976

Jane Eyre and Wuthering Heights[1]

Of the hundred years that have passed since Charlotte Brontë was born, she, the center now of so much legend, devotion, and literature, lived but thirty-nine. It is strange to reflect how different those legends might have been had her life reached the ordinary human span. She might have become, like some of her famous contemporaries, a figure familiarly met with in London and elsewhere, the subject of pictures and anecdotes innumerable, the writer of many novels, of memoirs possibly, removed from us well within the memory of the middle-aged in all the splendor of established fame. She might have been wealthy, she might have been prosperous. But it is not so. When we think of her we have to imagine some one who had no lot in our modern world; we have to cast our minds back to the 'fifties of the last century, to a remote parsonage upon the wild Yorkshire moors. In that parsonage, and on those moors, unhappy and lonely, in her poverty and her exaltation, she remains for ever.

These circumstances, as they affected her character, may have left their traces on her work. A novelist, we reflect, is bound to build up his structure with much very perishable material which begins by lending it reality and ends by cumbering it with rubbish. As we open Jane Eyre once more we cannot stifle the suspicion that we shall find her world of imagination as antiquated, mid-Victorian, and out of date as the parsonage on the moor, a place only to be visited by the curious, only preserved by the pious. So we open Jane Eyre; and in two pages every doubt is swept clean from our minds.

1. Two famous novels, the first by Charlotte Brontë (1816–1855), the second by her sister Emily Brontë (1818–1848).

Folds of scarlet drapery shut in my view to the right hand; to the left were the clear panes of glass, protecting, but not separating me from the drear November day. At intervals, while turning over the leaves of my book, I studied the aspect of that winter afternoon. Afar, it offered a pale blank of mist and cloud; near, a scene of wet lawn and storm-beat shrub, with ceaseless rain sweeping away wildly before a long and lamentable blast.

There is nothing there more perishable than the moor itself, or more subject to the sway of fashion than the "long and lamentable blast." Nor is this exhilaration short-lived. It rushes us through the entire volume, without giving us time to think, without letting us lift our eyes from the page. So intense is our absorption that if some one moves in the room the movement seems to take place not there but up in Yorkshire. The writer has us by the hand, forces us along her road, makes us see what she sees, never leaves us for a moment or allows us to forget her.[2] At the end we are steeped through and through with the genius, the vehemence, the indignation of Charlotte Brontë. Remarkable faces, figures of strong outline and gnarled feature have flashed upon us in passing; but it is through her eyes that we have seen them. Once she is gone, we seek for them in vain. Think of Rochester and we have to think of Jane Eyre. Think of the moor, and again, there is Jane Eyre. Think of the drawing-room, even, those "white carpets on which seemed laid brilliant garlands of flowers," that "pale Parian mantelpiece" with its Bohemia glass of "ruby red" and the "general blending of snow and fire"—what is all that except Jane Eyre?

The drawbacks of being Jane Eyre are not far to seek. Always to be a governess and always to be in love is a serious limitation in a world which is full, after all, of people who are neither one nor the other. The characters of a Jane Austen or of a Tolstoi[3] have a million facets compared with these. They live and are complex by means of their effect upon many different people who serve to mirror them in the round. They move hither and thither whether their creators watch them or not, and the world in which they live seems to us an independent world which we can visit, now that they have created it, by ourselves. Thomas Hardy[4] is more akin to Charlotte Brontë in the power of his personality and the narrowness of his vision. But the differences are vast. As we read *Jude the Obscure* we are not rushed to a finish; we brood and ponder and drift away from the text in plethoric trains of thought which build up round the characters an atmosphere of question and suggestion of which they are themselves, as often as not, unconscious. Simple peasants as they are, we are forced to confront them with destinies and questionings of the hugest import, so that often it seems as if the most important characters in a Hardy novel are those which have no names. Of this power, of this speculative curiosity, Charlotte Brontë has no trace. She does not attempt to solve the problems of human life; she is even unaware that such problems exist; all her force,

2. Charlotte and Emily Brontë had much the same sense of colour. ". . . we saw—ah! it was beautiful—a splendid place carpeted with crimson, and crimson-covered chairs and tables, and a pure white ceiling bordered by gold, a shower of glass drops hanging in silver chains from the centre, and shimmering with little soft tapers" (*Wuthering Heights*). Yet it was merely a very pretty drawing-room, and within it a boudoir, both spread with white carpets, on which seemed laid brilliant garlands of flowers; both ceiled with snowy mouldings of white grapes and vine leaves, beneath which glowed in rich contrast crimson couches and ottomans; while the ornaments on the pale Parian mantelpiece were of sparkling Bohemia glass, ruby red; and between the windows large mirrors repeated the general blending of snow and fire [Woolf's note].
3. Count Leo Tolstoi (1828–1910), Russian novelist. Jane Austen (1775–1817), English novelist.
4. Thomas Hardy (1840–1928), English novelist, author of *Jude the Obscure*.

and it is the more tremendous for being constricted, goes into the assertion, "I love," "I hate," "I suffer."

For the self-centered and self-limited writers have a power denied the more catholic and broad-minded. Their impressions are close packed and strongly stamped between their narrow walls. Nothing issues from their minds which has not been marked with their own impress. They learn little from other writers, and what they adopt they cannot assimilate. Both Hardy and Charlotte Brontë appear to have founded their styles upon a stiff and decorous journalism. The staple of their prose is awkward and unyielding. But both with labor and the most obstinate integrity by thinking every thought until it has subdued words to itself, have forged for themselves a prose which takes the mould of their minds entire; which has, into the bargain, a beauty, a power, a swiftness of its own. Charlotte Brontë, at least, owed nothing to the reading of many books. She never learned the smoothness of the professional writer, or acquired his ability to stuff and sway his language as he chooses. "I could never rest in communication with strong, discreet, and refined minds, whether male or female," she writes, as any leader-writer[5] in a provincial journal might have written; but gathering fire and speed goes on in her own authentic voice "till I had passed the outworks of conventional reserve and crossed the threshold of confidence, and won a place by their hearts' very hearthstone." It is there that she takes her seat; it is the red and fitful glow of the heart's fire which illumines her page. In other words, we read Charlotte Brontë not for exquisite observation of character—her characters are vigorous and elementary; not for comedy—hers is grim and crude; not for a philosophic view of life—hers is that of a country parson's daughter; but for her poetry. Probably that is so with all writers who have, as she has, an overpowering personality, who, as we should say in real life, have only to open the door to make themselves felt. There is in them some untamed ferocity perpetually at war with the accepted order of things which makes them desire to create instantly rather than to observe patiently. This very ardor, rejecting half shades and other minor impediments, wings its way past the daily conduct of ordinary people and allies itself with their more inarticulate passions. It makes them poets, or, if they choose to write in prose, intolerant of its restrictions. Hence it is that both Emily and Charlotte are always invoking the help of nature. They both feel the need of some more powerful symbol of the vast and slumbering passions in human nature than words or actions can convey. It is with a description of a storm that Charlotte ends her finest novel *Villette*. "The skies hang full and dark—a wrack[6] sails from the west; the clouds cast themselves into strange forms." So she calls in nature to describe a state of mind which could not otherwise be expressed. But neither of the sisters observed nature accurately as Dorothy Wordsworth observed it, or painted it minutely as Tennyson[7] painted it. They seized those aspects of the earth which were most akin to what they themselves felt or imputed to their characters, and so their storms, their moors, their lovely spaces of summer weather are not ornaments applied to decorate a dull page of display the writer's powers of observation—they carry on the emotion and light up the meaning of the book.

5. Editorial writer.
6. Wrecked ship.
7. Alfred, Lord Tennyson (1809–1892), English poet.

Dorothy Wordsworth (1771–1855), English poet and diarist.

 The meaning of a book, which lies so often apart from what happens and what is said and consists rather in some connection which things in themselves different have had for the writer, is necessarily hard to grasp. Especially this is so when, like the Brontës, the writer is poetic, and his meaning inseparable from his language, and itself rather a mood than a particular observation. *Wuthering Heights* is a more difficult book to understand than *Jane Eyre*, because Emily was a greater poet than Charlotte. When Charlotte wrote she said with eloquence and splendor and passion "I love," "I hate," "I suffer." Her experience, though more intense, is on a level with our own. But there is no "I" in *Wuthering Heights*. There are no governesses. There are no employers. There is love, but it is not the love of men and women. Emily was inspired by some more general conception. The impulse which urged her to create was not her own suffering or her own injuries. She looked out upon a world cleft into gigantic disorder and felt within her the power to unite it in a book. That gigantic ambition is to be felt throughout the novel—a struggle, half thwarted but of superb conviction, to say something through the mouths of her characters which is not merely "I love" or "I hate," but "we, the whole human race" and "you, the eternal powers . . . " the sentence remains unfinished. It is not strange that it should be so; rather it is astonishing that she can make us feel what she had it in her to say at all. It surges up in the half-articulate words of Catherine Earnshaw,[8] "If all else perished and he remained, I should still continue to be; and if all else remained and he were annihilated, the universe would turn to a mighty stranger; I should not seem part of it." It breaks out again in the presence of the dead. "I see a repose that neither earth nor hell can break, and I feel an assurance of the endless and shadowless hereafter—the eternity they have entered—where life is boundless in its duration, and love in its sympathy and joy in its fulness." It is this suggestion of power underlying the apparitions of human nature, and lifting them up into the presence of greatness that gives the book its huge stature among other novels. But it was not enough for Emily Brontë to write a few lyrics, to utter a cry, to express a creed. In her poems she did this once and for all, and her poems will perhaps outlast her novel. But she was novelist as well as poet. She must take upon herself a more laborious and a more ungrateful task. She must face the fact of other existences, grapple with the mechanism of external things, build up, in recognisable shape, farms and houses and report the speeches of men and women who existed independently of herself. And so we reach these summits of emotion not by rant or rhapsody but by hearing a girl sing old songs to herself as she rocks in the branches of a tree; by watching the moor sheep crop the turf; by listening to the soft wind breathing through the grass. The life at the farm with all its absurdities and its improbability is laid open to us. We are given every opportunity of comparing *Wuthering Heights* with a real farm and Heathcliff with a real man. How, we are allowed to ask, can there be truth or insight or the finer shades of emotion in men and women who so little resemble what we have seen ourselves? But even as we ask it we see in Heathcliff the brother that a sister of genius might have seen; he is impossible, we say, but nevertheless no boy in literature has so vivid an existence as his. So it is with the two Catherines; never could women feel as they do or act in their manner,

8. The central female character of *Wuthering Heights*; the "he" in her speech is Heathcliff, her adoptive brother and lover.

we say. All the same, they are the most lovable women in English fiction. It is as if she could tear up all that we know human beings by, and fill these unrecognizable transparences with such a gust of life that they transcend reality. Hers, then, is the rarest of all powers. She could free life from its dependence on facts; with a few touches indicate the spirit of a face so that it needs no body; by speaking of the moor make the wind blow and the thunder roar.

1925

A Woman's College from Outside

The feathery-white moon never let the sky grow dark; all night the chestnut blossoms were white in the green, and dim was the cow-parsley in the meadows. Neither to Tartary nor to Arabia went the wind of the Cambridge courts, but lapsed dreamily in the midst of gray-blue clouds over the roofs of Newnham.[1] There, in the garden, if she needed space to wander, she might find it among the trees; and as none but women's faces could meet her face, she might unveil it, blank, featureless, and gaze into rooms where at that hour, blank, featureless, eyelids white over eyes, ringless hands extended upon sheets, slept innumerable women. But here and there a light still burned.

A double light one might figure in Angela's room, seeing how bright Angela herself was, and how bright came back the reflection of herself from the square glass. The whole of her was perfectly delineated—perhaps the soul. For the glass held up an untrembling image—white and gold, red slippers, pale hair with blue stones in it, and never a ripple or shadow to break the smooth kiss of Angela and her reflection in the glass, as if she were glad to be Angela. Anyhow the moment was glad—the bright picture hung in the heart of night, the shrine hollowed in the nocturnal blackness. Strange indeed to have this visible proof of the rightness of things; this lily floating flawless upon Time's pool, fearless, as if this were sufficient—this reflection. Which meditation she betrayed by turning, and the mirror held nothing at all, or only the brass bedstead, and she, running here and there, patting, and darting, became like a woman in a house, and changed again, pursing her lips over a black book and marking with her finger what surely could not be a firm grasp of the science of economics. Only Angela Williams was at Newnham for the purpose of earning her living, and could not forget even in moments of impassioned adoration the checks of her father at Swansea: her mother washing in the scullery: pink frocks out to dry on the line; tokens that even the lily no longer floats flawless upon the pool, but has a name on a card like another.

A. Williams—one may read it in the moonlight; and next to it some Mary or Eleanor, Mildred, Sarah, Phoebe upon square cards on their doors. All names, nothing but names. The cool white light withered them and starched them until it seemed as if the only purpose of all these names was to rise martially in order should there be a call on them to extinguish a fire, suppress an insurrection, or pass an examination. Such is the power of names written upon cards pinned upon doors. Such too the resemblance, what with tiles, corridors, and bedroom doors, to dairy or nunnery, a place of seclusion or discipline, where the bowl of milk stands cool and pure and there's a great washing of linen.

1. A woman's college of Cambridge University.

At that very moment soft laughter came from behind a door. A prim-voiced clock struck the hour—one, two. Now if the clock were issuing his commands, they were disregarded. Fire, insurrection, examination, were all snowed under by laughter, or softly uprooted, the sound seeming to bubble up from the depths and gently waft away the hour, rules, discipline. The bed was strewn with cards. Sally was on the floor. Helena in the chair. Good Bertha clasping her hands by the fire-place. A. Williams came in yawning.

"Because it's utterly and intolerably damnable," said Helena.

"Damnable," echoed Bertha. Then yawned.

"We're not eunuchs."

"I saw her slipping in by the back gate with that old hat on. They don't want us to know."

"They?" said Angela. "She."

Then the laughter.

The cards were spread, falling with their red and yellow faces on the table, and hands were dabbled in the cards. Good Bertha, leaning with her head against the chair, sighed profoundly. For she would willingly have slept, but since night is free pasturage, a limitless field, since night is unmolded richness, one must tunnel into its darkness. One must hang it with jewels. Night was shared in secret, day browsed on by the whole flock. The blinds were up. A mist was on the garden. Sitting on the floor by the window (while the others played), body, mind, both together, seemed blown through the air, to trail across the bushes. Ah, but she desired to stretch out in bed and to sleep! She believed that no one felt her desire for sleep; she believed humbly—sleepily— with sudden nods and lurchings, that other people were wide awake. When they laughed all together a bird chirped in its sleep out in the garden, as if the laughter—

Yes, as if the laughter (for she dozed now) floated out much like mist and attached itself by soft elastic shreds to plants and bushes, so that the garden was vaporous and clouded. And then, swept by the wind, the bushes would bow themselves and the white vapors blow off across the world.

From all the rooms where women slept this vapor issued, attaching itself to shrubs, like mist, and then blew freely out into the open. Elderly women slept, who would on waking immediately clasp the ivory rod of office. Now smooth and colorless, reposing deeply, they lay surrounded, lay supported, by the bodies of youth recumbent or grouped at the window; pouring forth into the garden this bubbling laughter, this irresponsible laughter: this laughter of mind and body floating away rules, hours, discipline: immensely fertilising, yet formless, chaotic, trailing and straying and tufting the rose-bushes with shreds of vapor.

"Ah," breathed Angela, standing at the window in her nightgown. Pain was in her voice. She leant her head out. The mist was cleft as if her voice parted it. She had been talking, while the others played, to Alice Avery, about Bamborough Castle;[2] the color of the sands at evening; upon which Alice said she would write and settle the day, in August, and stooping, kissed her, at least touched her head with her hand, and Angela, positively unable to sit still, like one possessed of a wind-lashed sea in her heart, roamed up and down the room (the witness of such a scene) throwing her arms out to relieve this ex-

2. A medieval castle on the northeastern coast of England.

citement, this astonishment at the incredible stooping of the miraculous tree with the golden fruit at its summit—hadn't it dropped into her arms? She held it glowing to her breast, a thing not to be touched, thought of, or spoken about, but left to glow there. And then, slowly putting there her stockings, there her slippers, folding her petticoat neatly on top, Angela, her other name being Williams, realized—how could she express it?—that after the dark churning of myriad ages here was light at the end of the tunnel; life; the world. Beneath her it lay—all good; all lovable. Such was her discovery.

Indeed, how could one then feel surprise if, lying in bed, she could not close her eyes?—something irresistibly unclosed them—if in the shallow darkness chair and chest of drawers looked stately, and the looking-glass precious with its ashen hint of day? Sucking her thumb like a child (her age nineteen last November), she lay in this good world, this new world, this world at the end of the tunnel, until a desire to see it or forestall it drove her, tossing her blankets, to guide herself to the window, and there, looking out upon the garden, where the mist lay, all the windows open, one fiery-bluish, something murmuring in the distance, the world of course, and the morning coming, "Oh," she cried, as if in pain.

<div style="text-align: right">1926, 1977</div>

Moments of Being

"Slater's Pins Have No Points"

"Slater's pins have no points—don't you always find that?" said Miss Craye, turning round as the rose fell out of Fanny Wilmot's dress, and Fanny stooped, with her ears full of the music, to look for the pin on the floor.

The words gave her an extraordinary shock, as Miss Craye struck the last chord of the Bach fugue. Did Miss Craye actually go to Slater's and buy pins then, Fanny Wilmot asked herself, transfixed for a moment. Did she stand at the counter waiting like anybody else, and was she given a bill with coppers wrapped in it, and did she slip them into her purse and then, an hour later, stand by her dressing table and take out the pins? What need had she of pins? For she was not so much dressed as cased, like a beetle compactly in its sheath, blue in winter, green in summer. What need had she of pins—Julia Craye—who lived, it seemed, in the cool glassy world of Bach fugues, playing to herself what she liked, and only consenting to take one or two pupils at the Archer Street College of Music (so the Principal, Miss Kingston, said) as a special favor to herself, who had "the greatest admiration for her in every way." Miss Craye was left badly off, Miss Kingston was afraid, at her brother's death. Oh, they used to have such lovely things, when they lived at Salisbury, and her brother Julius was, of course, a very well-known man: a famous archaeologist. It was a great privilege to stay with them, Miss Kingston said ("My family had always known them—they were regular Canterbury[1] people," Miss Kingston said), but a little frightening for a child; one had to be careful not to slam the door or bounce into the room unexpectedly. Miss Kingston, who gave little character sketches like this on the first day of term while she received checks

1. A city in southern England.

and wrote out receipts for them, smiled here. Yes, she had been rather a tomboy; she had bounced in and set all those green Roman glasses and things jumping in their case. The Crayes were not used to children. The Crayes were none of them married. They kept cats; the cats, one used to feel, knew as much about the Roman urns and things as anybody.

"Far more than I did!" said Miss Kingston brightly, writing her name across the stamp in her dashing, cheerful, full-bodied hand, for she had always been practical. That was how she made her living, after all.

Perhaps then, Fanny Wilmot thought, looking for the pin, Miss Craye said that about "Slater's pins having no points," at a venture. None of the Crayes had ever married. She knew nothing about pins—nothing whatever. But she wanted to break the spell that had fallen on the house; to break the pane of glass which separated them from other people. When Polly Kingston, that merry little girl, had slammed the door and made the Roman vases jump, Julius, seeing that no harm was done (that would be his first instinct) looked, for the case was stood in the window, at Polly skipping home across the fields; looked with the look his sister often had, that lingering, driving² look.

"Stars, sun, moon," it seemed to say, "the daisy in the grass, fires, frost on the window pane, my heart goes out to you. But," it always seemed to add, "you break, you pass, you go." And simultaneously it covered the intensity of both these states of mind with "I can't reach you—I can't get at you," spoken wistfully, frustratedly. And the stars faded, and the child went. That was the kind of spell that was the glassy surface, that Miss Craye wanted to break by showing, when she had played Bach beautifully as a reward to a favorite pupil (Fanny Wilmot knew that she was Miss Craye's favorite pupil), that she, too, knew, like other people, about pins. Slater's pins had no points.

Yes, the "famous archaeologist" had looked like that too. "The famous archaeologist"—as she said that, endorsing cheques, ascertaining the day of the month, speaking so brightly and frankly, there was in Miss Kingston's voice an indescribable tone which hinted at something odd; something queer in Julius Craye; it was the very same thing that was odd perhaps in Julia too. One could have sworn, thought Fanny Wilmot, as she looked for the pin, that at parties, meetings (Miss Kingston's father was a clergyman), she had picked up some piece of gossip, or it might only have been a smile, or a tone when his name was mentioned, which had given her "a feeling" about Julius Craye. Needless to say, she had never spoken about it to anybody. Probably she scarcely knew what she meant by it. But whenever she spoke of Julius, or heard him mentioned, that was the first thing that came to mind; and it was a seductive thought; there was something odd about Julius Craye.

It was so that Julia looked too, as she sat half turned on the music stool, smiling. It's on the field, it's on the pane, it's in the sky—beauty; and I can't get at it; I can't have it—I, she seemed to add, with that little clutch of the hand which was so characteristic, who adore it so passionately, would give the whole world to possess it! And she picked up the carnation which had fallen on the floor, while Fanny searched for the pin. She crushed it, Fanny felt, voluptuously in her smooth veined hands stuck about with water-colored rings set in pearls. The pressure of her fingers seemed to increase all that was most bril-

2. The text printed here is from *A Haunted House and Other Stories* (1944), edited by Leonard Woolf. In the original version published in *Forum* (1928), this word was "desiring."

liant in the flower; to set it off; to make it more frilled, fresh, immaculate. What was odd in her, and perhaps in her brother, too, was that this crush and grasp of the finger was combined with a perpetual frustration. So it was even now with the carnation. She had her hands on it; she pressed it; but she did not possess it, enjoy it, not entirely and altogether.

None of the Crayes had married, Fanny Wilmot remembered. She had in mind how one evening when the lesson had lasted longer than usual and it was dark, Julia Craye had said "it's the use of men, surely, to protect us," smiling at her that same odd smile, as she stood fastening her cloak, which made her, like the flower, conscious to her finger tips of youth and brilliance, but, like the flower, too, Fanny suspected, made her feel awkward.

"Oh, but I don't want protection," Fanny had laughed, and when Julia Craye, fixing on her that extraordinary look, had said she was not so sure of that, Fanny positively blushed under the admiration in her eyes.

It was the only use of men, she had said. Was it for that reason then, Fanny wondered, with her eyes on the floor, that she had never married? After all, she had not lived all her life in Salisbury. "Much the nicest part of London," she had said once, "(but I'm speaking of fifteen or twenty years ago) is Kensington.[3] One was in the Gardens in ten minutes—it was like the heart of the country. One could dine out in one's slippers without catching cold. Kensington—it was like a village then, you know," she had said.

Here she broke off, to denounce acridly the draughts in the Tubes.[4]

"It was the use of men," she had said, with a queer wry acerbity. Did that throw any light on the problem why she had not married? One could imagine every sort of scene in her youth, when with her good blue eyes, her straight firm nose, her air of cool distinction, her piano playing, her rose flowering with chaste passion in the bosom of her muslin dress, she had attracted first the young men to whom such things, the china tea cups and the silver candlesticks and the inlaid table, for the Crayes had such nice things, were wonderful; young men not sufficiently distinguished; young men of the cathedral town with ambitions. She had attracted them first, and then her brother's friends from Oxford or Cambridge. They would come down in the summer; row her on the river; continue the argument about Browning[5] by letter; and arrange perhaps, on the rare occasions when she stayed in London, to show her—Kensington Gardens?

"Much the nicest part of London—Kensington (I'm speaking of fifteen or twenty years ago)," she had said once. One was in the gardens in ten minutes—in the heart of the country. One could make that yield what one liked, Fanny Wilmot thought, single out, for instance, Mr. Sherman, the painter, an old friend of hers; make him call for her, by appointment, one sunny day in June; take her to have tea under the trees. (They had met, too, at those parties to which one tripped in slippers without fear of catching cold.) The aunt or other elderly relative was to wait there while they looked at the Serpentine.[6] They looked at the Serpentine. He may have rowed her across. They compared it with the Avon.[7] She would have considered the comparison very furiously. Views of rivers were important to her. She sat hunched a little, a little angular, though she was graceful then, steering. At the critical moment, for he

3. A fashionable district of London with an elegant park.
4. The London subway.

5. Robert Browning (1812–1889), English poet.
6. An artificial body of water in Hyde Park, London.
7. An English river.

had determined that he must speak now—it was his only chance of getting her alone—he was speaking with his head turned at an absurd angle, in his great nervousness, over his shoulder—at that very moment she interrupted fiercely. He would have them into the Bridge,[8] she cried. It was a moment of horror, of disillusionment, of revelation, for both of them. I can't have it, I can't possess it, she thought. He could not see why she had come then. With a great splash of his oar he pulled the boat round. Merely to snub him? He rowed her back and said good-bye to her.

The setting of that scene could be varied as one chose, Fanny Wilmot reflected. (Where had that pin fallen?) It might be Ravenna; or Edinburgh, where she had kept house for her brother. The scene could be changed; and the young man and the exact manner of it all, but one thing was constant—her refusal, and her frown, and her anger with herself afterwards, and her argument, and her relief—yes, certainly her immense relief. The very next day, perhaps, she would get up at six, put on her cloak, and walk all the way from Kensington to the river. She was so thankful that she had not sacrificed her right to go and look at things when they are at their best—before people are up, that is to say she could have her breakfast in bed if she liked. She had not sacrificed her independence.

Yes, Fanny Wilmot smiled, Julia had not endangered her habits. They remained safe; and her habits would have suffered if she had married. "They're ogres," she had said one evening, half laughing, when another pupil, a girl lately married, suddenly bethinking her that she would miss her husband, had rushed off in haste.

"They're ogres," she had said, laughing grimly. An ogre would have interfered perhaps with breakfast in bed; with walks at dawn down to the river. What would have happened (but one could hardly conceive this) had she had children. She took astonishing precautions against chills, fatigue, rich food, the wrong food, draughts, heated rooms, journeys in the Tube, for she could never determine which of these it was exactly that brought on those terrible headaches that gave her life the semblance of a battlefield. She was always engaged in outwitting the enemy, until it seemed as if the pursuit had its interest; could she have beaten the enemy finally she would have found life a little dull. As it was, the tug-of-war was perpetual—on the one side the nightingale or the view which she loved with passion—yes, for views and birds she felt nothing less than passion; on the other the camp path or the horrid long drag up a steep hill which would certainly make her good for nothing next day and bring on one of her headaches. When, therefore, from time to time, she managed her forces adroitly and brought off a visit to Hampton Court[9] the week the crocuses—those glossy bright flowers were her favorite—were at their best, it was a victory. It was something that lasted; something that mattered for ever. She strung the afternoon on the necklace of memorable days, which was not too long for her to be able to recall this one or that one; this view, that city; to finger it, to feel it, to savour, sighing, the quality that made it unique.

"It was so beautiful last Friday," she said, "that I determined I must go there." So she had gone off to Waterloo or her great undertaking—to visit Hampton Court—alone. Naturally, but perhaps foolishly, one pitied her for the thing she never asked pity for (indeed she was reticent habitually, speaking

8. I.e., they were about to run into the bridge.
9. Former royal residence with extensive gardens located on the Thames, fifteen miles from London.

of her health only as a warrior might speak of his foe)—one pitied her for always doing everything alone. Her brother was dead. Her sister was asthmatic. She found the climate of Edinburgh good for her. It was too bleak for Julia. Perhaps, too, she found the associations painful, for her brother, the famous archæologist, had died there; and she had loved her brother. She lived in a little house off the Brompton Road entirely alone.

Fanny Wilmot saw the pin; she picked it up. She looked at Miss Craye. Was Miss Craye so lonely? No, Miss Craye was steadily, blissfully, if only for that moment, a happy woman. Fanny had surprised her in a moment of ecstasy. She sat there, half turned away from the piano, with her hands clasped in her lap holding the carnation upright, while behind her was the sharp square of the window, uncurtained, purple in the evening, intensely purple after the brilliant electric lights which burned unshaded in the bare music room. Julia Craye, sitting hunched and compact holding her flower, seemed to emerge out of the London night, seemed to fling it like a cloak behind her, it seemed, in its bareness and intensity, the effluence of her spirit, something she had made which surrounded her. Fanny stared.

All seemed transparent, for a moment, to the gaze of Fanny Wilmot, as if looking through Miss Craye, she saw the very fountain of her being spurting its pure silver drops. She saw back and back into the past behind her. She saw the green Roman vases stood in their case; heard the choristers playing cricket; saw Julia quietly descend the curving steps on to the lawn; then saw her pour out tea beneath the cedar tree; softly enclosed the old man's hand in hers; saw her going round and about the corridors of that ancient Cathedral dwelling place with towels in her hand to mark them;[1] lamenting, as she went, the pettiness of daily life; and slowly ageing, and putting away clothes when summer came, because at her age they were too bright to wear; and tending her father's sickness; and cleaving her way ever more definitely as her will stiffened towards her solitary goal; traveling frugally; counting the cost and measuring out of her tight shut purse the sum needed for this journey or for that old mirror; obstinately adhering, whatever people might say, in choosing her pleasures for herself. She saw Julia——

Julia blazed. Julia kindled. Out of the night she burnt like a dead white star. Julia opened her arms. Julia kissed her on the lips. Julia possessed it.[2]

"Slater's pins have no points," Miss Craye said, laughing queerly and relaxing her arms as Fanny Wilmot pinned the flower to her breast with trembling fingers.

1928, 1944

From A Room of One's Own

[Shakespeare's Sister][1]

It was disappointing not to have brought back in the evening some important statement, some authentic fact. Women are poorer than men because—

1. I.e., mark them for the laundry.
2. In the 1928 version, this paragraph reads: "She saw Julie open her arms; saw her blaze; saw her kindle. Out of the night she burnt like a dead white star. Julie kissed her. Julia possessed her."

1. This selection is taken from Chapter Three and the conclusion of the final chapter. In the previous chapter Woolf visits the British Museum library in an attempt to trace the different fates of men and women in history.

this or that. Perhaps now it would be better to give up seeking for the truth, and receiving on one's head an avalanche of opinion hot as lava, discolored as dishwater. It would be better to draw the curtains; to shut out distractions; to light the lamp; to narrow the inquiry and to ask the historian, who records not opinions but facts, to describe under what conditions women lived, not throughout the ages, but in England, say in the time of Elizabeth.

For it is a perennial puzzle why no woman wrote a word of that extraordinary literature when every other man, it seemed, was capable of song or sonnet. What were the conditions in which women lived, I asked myself; for fiction, imaginative work that is, is not dropped like a pebble upon the ground, as science may be; fiction is like a spider's web, attached ever so lightly perhaps, but still attached to life at all four corners. Often the attachment is scarcely perceptible; Shakespeare's plays, for instance, seem to hang there complete by themselves. But when the web is pulled askew, hooked up at the edge, torn in the middle, one remembers that these webs are not spun in midair by incorporeal creatures, but are the work of suffering human beings, and are attached to grossly material things, like health and money and the houses we live in.

I went, therefore, to the shelf where the histories stand and took down one of the latest. Professor Trevelyan's *History of England*.[2] Once more I looked up Women, found "position of," and turned to the pages indicated. "Wife-beating," I read, "was a recognized right of man, and was practiced without shame by high as well as low. . . . Similarly," the historian goes on, "the daughter who refused to marry the gentleman of her parents' choice was liable to be locked up, beaten, and flung about the room, without any shock being inflicted on public opinion. Marriage was not an affair of personal affection, but of family avarice, particularly in the 'chivalrous' upper classes . . . Betrothal often took place while one or both of the parties was in the cradle, and marriage when they were scarely out of the nurses' charge." That was about 1470, soon after Chaucer's time. The next reference to the position of women is some two hundred years later, in the time of the Stuarts. "It was still the exception for women of the upper and middle class to choose their own husbands, and when the husband had been assigned, he was lord and master, so far at least as law and custom could make him. Yet even so," Professor Trevelyan concludes, "neither Shakespeare's women nor those of authentic seventeenth-century memoirs, like the Verneys and the Hutchinsons,[3] seem wanting in personality and character." Certainly, if we consider it, Cleopatra must have had a way with her; Lady Macbeth, one would suppose, had a will of her own; Rosalind,[4] one might conclude, was an attractive girl. Professor Trevelyan is speaking no more than the truth when he remarks that Shakespeare's women do not seem wanting in personality and character. Not being a historian, one might go even further and say that women have burned like beacons in all the works of all the poets from the beginning of time—Clytemnestra, Antigone, Cleopatra, Lady Macbeth, Phèdre, Cressida, Rosalind, Desdemona, the Duchess of Malfi, among the dramatists; then among the prose writers: Millamant, Clarissa,

2. G. M. Trevelyan's *History of England* (1926), then the standard one-volume history.
3. Lucy Hutchinson wrote a biography of her husband, Colonel John Hutchinson (1616–1684). "The ideal family life of the period [1640–1650] that ended

in such tragic political division has been recorded once and for all in the *Memoirs of the Verney Family*" (Trevelyan, *History of England*).
4. Heroines of three plays by Shakespeare, *Antony and Cleopatra*, *Macbeth*, and *As You Like It*, respectively.

Becky Sharp, Anna Karenina, Emma Bovary, Madame de Guermantes[5]—the names flock to mind, nor do they recall women "lacking in personality and character." Indeed, if woman had no existence save in the fiction written by men, one would imagine her a person of the utmost importance; very various; heroic and mean; splendid and sordid; infinitely beautiful and hideous in the extreme; as great as a man, some think even greater.[6] But this is woman in fiction. In fact, as Professor Trevelyan points out, she was locked up, beaten, and flung about the room.

A very queer, composite being thus emerges. Imaginatively she is of the highest importance; practically she is completely insignificant. She pervades poetry from cover to cover; she is all but absent from history. She dominates the lives of kings and conquerors in fiction; in fact she was the slave of any boy whose parents forced a ring upon her finger. Some of the most inspired words, some of the most profound thoughts in literature fall from her lips; in real life she could hardly read, could scarcely spell, and was the property of her husband.

It was certainly an odd monster that one made up by reading the historians first and the poets afterwards—a worm winged like an eagle; the spirit of life and beauty in a kitchen chopping up suet. But these monsters, however amusing to the imagination, have no existence in fact. What one must do to bring her to life was to think poetically and prosaically at one and the same moment, thus keeping in touch with fact—that she is Mrs. Martin, aged thirty-six, dressed in blue, wearing a black hat and brown shoes; but not losing sight of fiction either—that she is a vessel in which all sorts of spirits and forces are coursing and flashing perpetually. The moment, however, that one tries this method with the Elizabethan woman, one branch of illumination fails; one is held up by the scarcity of facts. One knows nothing detailed, nothing perfectly true and substantial about her. History scarcely mentions her. And I turned to Professor Trevelyan again to see what history meant to him. I found by looking at his chapter headings that it meant—

"The Manor Court and the Methods of Open-Field Agriculture . . . The Cistercians and Sheep-Farming . . . The Crusades . . . The University . . . The House of Commons . . . The Hundred Years' War . . . The Wars of the Roses . . . The Renaissance Scholars . . . The Dissolution of the Monasteries . . . Agrarian and Religious Strife . . . The Origin of English Sea-Power . . . The Armada . . . " and so on. Occasionally an individual woman is mentioned, an Elizabeth, or a Mary; a queen or a great lady. But by no possible means could middle-class women with nothing but brains and character at

5. Characters in, respectively, Aeschylus's *Agamemnon*, Sophocles' *Antigone*; Shakespeare's *Antony and Cleopatra* and *Macbeth*; Racine's *Phèdre*; Shakespeare's *Troilus and Cressida*, *As You Like It*, and *Othello*; Webster's *The Duchess of Malfi*; Congreve's *The Way of the World*; Richardson's *Clarissa*; Thackeray's *Vanity Fair*; Tolstoy's *Anna Karenina*; Flaubert's *Madame Bovary*; and Proust's *A la recherche du temps perdu*.
6. "It remains a strange and almost inexplicable fact that in Athena's city, where women were kept in almost Oriental suppression as odalisques or drudges, the stage should yet have produced figures like Clytemnestra and Cassandra, Atossa and Antigone, Phèdre and Medea, and all the other heroines who dominate play after play of the 'misogynist' Euripides. But the paradox of this world where in real life a respectable woman could hardly show her face alone in the street, and yet on the stage woman equals or surpasses man, has never been satisfactorily explained. In modern tragedy the same predominance exists. At all events, a very cursory survey of Shakespeare's work (similarly with Webster, though not with Marlowe or Jonson) suffices to reveal how this dominance, this initiative of women, persists from Rosalind to Lady Macbeth. So too in Racine; six of his tragedies bear their heroines' names; and what male characters of his shall we set against Hermione and Andromaque, Bérénice and Roxane, Phèdre and Athalie? So again with Ibsen; what men shall we match with Solveig and Nora, Hedda and Hilda Wangel and Rebecca West?"—F. L. Lucas, *Tragedy*, pp. 114–15" [Woolf's note].

their command have taken part in any one of the great movements which, brought together, constitute the historian's view of the past. Nor shall we find her in any collection of anecdotes. Aubrey[7] hardly mentions her. She never writes her own life and scarcely keeps a diary; there are only a handful of her letters in existence. She left no plays or poems by which we can judge her. What one wants, I thought—and why does not some brilliant student at Newnham or Girton[8] supply it?—is a mass of information; at what age did she marry; how many children had she as a rule; what was her house like; had she a room to herself; did she do the cooking; would she be likely to have a servant? All these facts lie somewhere, presumably, in parish registers and account books; the life of the average Elizabethan woman must be scattered about somewhere, could one collect it and make a book of it. It would be ambitious beyond my daring, I thought, looking about the shelves for books that were not there, to suggest to the students of those famous colleges that they should rewrite history, though I own that it often seems a little queer as it is, unreal, lopsided; but why should they not add a supplement to history? calling it, of course, by some inconspicuous name so that women might figure there without impropriety? For one often catches a glimpse of them in the lives of the great, whisking away into the background, concealing, I sometimes think, a wink, a laugh, perhaps a tear. And, after all, we have lives enough of Jane Austen; it scarcely seems necessary to consider again the influence of the tragedies of Joanna Baillie upon the poetry of Edgar Allan Poe; as for myself, I should not mind if the homes and haunts of Mary Russell Mitford[9] were closed to the public for a century at least. But what I find deplorable, I continued, looking about the bookshelves again, is that nothing is known about women before the eighteenth century. I have no model in my mind to turn about this way and that. Here am I asking why women did not write poetry in the Elizabethan age, and I am not sure how they were educated; whether they were taught to write; whether they had sitting rooms to themselves; how many women had children before they were twenty-one; what, in short, they did from eight in the morning till eight at night. They had no money evidently; according to Professor Trevelyan they were married whether they liked it or not before they were out of the nursery, at fifteen or sixteen very likely. It would have been extremely odd, even upon this showing, had one of them suddenly written the plays of Shakespeare, I concluded, and I thought of that old gentleman, who is dead now, but was a bishop, I think, who declared that it was impossible for any woman, past, present, or to come, to have the genius of Shakespeare. He wrote to the papers about it. He also told a lady who applied to him for information that cats do not as a matter of fact go to heaven, though they have, he added, souls of a sort. How much thinking those old gentlemen used to save one! How the borders of ignorance shrank back at their approach! Cats do not go to heaven. Women cannot write the plays of Shakespeare.

Be that as it may, I could not help thinking, as I looked at the works of Shakespeare on the shelf, that the bishop was right at least in this; it would have been impossible, completely and entirely, for any woman to have written

7. John Aubrey (1626–1697), English diarist.
8. The two women's colleges of Cambridge University.
9. English poet and novelist (1787–1855), best known for her sketches of rural life. Jane Austen (1775–1817),

English novelist. Joanna Baillie (1787–1855), English poet and dramatist. Edgar Allan Poe (1809–1849), American poet and short-story writer.

the plays of Shakespeare in the age of Shakespeare. Let me imagine, since facts are so hard to come by, what would have happened had Shakespeare had a wonderfully gifted sister, called Judith, let us say. Shakespeare himself went, very probably—his mother was an heiress—to grammar school, where he may have learnt Latin—Ovid, Virgil, and Horace[1]—and the elements of grammar and logic. He was, it is well known, a wild boy who poached rabbits, perhaps shot a deer, and had, rather sooner than he should have done, to marry a woman in the neighborhood, who bore him a child rather quicker than was right. That escapade sent him to seek his fortune in London. He had, it seemed, a taste for the theater; he began by holding horses at the stage door. Very soon he got work in the theater, became a successful actor, and lived at the hub of the universe, meeting everybody, knowing everybody, practicing his art on the boards, exercising his wits in the streets, and even getting access to the palace of the queen. Meanwhile his extraordinarily gifted sister, let us suppose, remained at home. She was as adventurous, as imaginative, as agog to see the world as he was. But she was not sent to school. She had no chance of learning grammar and logic, let alone of reading Horace and Virgil. She picked up a book now and then, one of her brother's perhaps, and read a few pages. But then her parents came in and told her to mend the stockings or mind the stew and not moon about with books and papers. They would have spoken sharply but kindly, for they were substantial people who knew the conditions of life for a woman and loved their daughter—indeed, more likely than not she was the apple of her father's eye. Perhaps she scribbled some pages up in an apple loft on the sly, but was careful to hide them or set fire to them. Soon, however, before she was out of her teens, she was to be betrothed to the son of a neighboring wool-stapler.[2] She cried out that marriage was hateful to her, and for that she was severely beaten by her father. Then he ceased to scold her. He begged her instead not to hurt him, not to shame him in this matter of her marriage. He would give her a chain of beads or a fine petticoat, he said; and there were tears in his eyes. How could she disobey him? How could she break his heart? The force of her own gift alone drove her to it. She made up a small parcel of her belongings, let herself down by a rope one summer's night, and took the road to London. She was not seventeen. The birds that sang in the hedge were not more musical than she was. She had the quickest fancy, a gift like her brother's, for the tune of words. Like him, she had a taste for the theater. She stood at the stage door; she wanted to act, she said. Men laughed in her face. The manager—a fat, loose-lipped man—guffawed. He bellowed something about poodles dancing and women acting—no woman, he said, could possibly be an actress. He hinted—you can imagine what. She could get no training in her craft. Could she even seek her dinner in a tavern or roam the streets at midnight? Yet her genius was for fiction and lusted to feed abundantly upon the lives of men and women and the study of their ways. At last— for she was very young, oddly like Shakespeare the poet in her face, with the same gray eyes and rounded brows—at last Nick Greene the actor-manager took pity on her; she found herself with child by that gentleman and so—who shall measure the heat and violence of the poet's heart when caught and tan-

1. Three Latin poets of the Augustan age (27 B.C.–A.D. 14), whose works were part of the standard curriculum in boys' schools.

2. A dealer in wool, a "staple" product of 16th-century England.

gled in a woman's body?—killed herself one winter's night and lies buried at some crossroads where the omnibuses now stop outside the Elephant and Castle![3]

That, more or less, is how the story would run, I think, if a woman in Shakespeare's day had had Shakespeare's genius. But for my part, I agree with the deceased bishop, if such he was—it is unthinkable that any woman in Shakespeare's day should have had Shakespeare's genius. For genius like Shakespeare's is not born among laboring, uneducated, servile people. It was not born in England among the Saxons and the Britons. It is not born today among the working classes. How, then, could it have been born among women whose work began, according to Professor Trevelyan, almost before they were out of the nursery, who were forced to it by their parents and held to it by all the power of law and custom? Yet genius of a sort must have existed among women as it must have existed among the working classes. Now and again an Emily Brontë or a Robert Burns[4] blazes out and proves its presence. But certainly it never got itself on to paper. When, however, one reads of a witch being ducked, of a woman possessed by devils, of a wise woman selling herbs, or even of a very remarkable man who had a mother, then I think we are on the track of a lost novelist, a suppressed poet, of some mute and inglorious[5] Jane Austen, some Emily Brontë who dashed her brains out on the moor or mopped and mowed about the highways crazed with the torture that her gift had put her to. Indeed, I would venture to guess that Anon, who wrote so many poems without signing them, was often a woman. It was a woman Edward Fitzgerald,[6] I think, suggested who made the ballads and the folk songs, crooning them to her children, beguiling her spinning with them, or the length of the winter's night.

This may be true or it may be false—who can say?—but what is true in it, so it seemed to me, reviewing the story of Shakespeare's sister as I had made it, is that any woman born with a great gift in the sixteenth century would certainly have gone crazed, shot herself, or ended her days in some lonely cottage outside the village, half witch, half wizard, feared and mocked at. For it needs little skill in psychology to be sure that a highly gifted girl who had tried to use her gift for poetry would have been so thwarted and hindered by other people, so tortured and pulled asunder by her own contrary instincts, that she must have lost her health and sanity to a certainty. No girl could have walked to London and stood at a stage door and forced her way into the presence of actor-managers without doing herself a violence and suffering an anguish which may have been irrational—for chastity may be a fetish invented by certain societies for unknown reasons—but were none the less inevitable. Chastity had then, it has even now, a religious importance in a woman's life, and has so wrapped itself round with nerves and instincts that to cut it free and bring it to the light of day demands courage of the rarest. To have lived a free life in London in the sixteenth century would have meant for a woman who was poet and playwright a nervous stress and dilemma which might well have killed her. Had she survived, whatever she had written would have been

3. A tavern located at a busy crossroads in south London. Suicides were commonly buried at crossroads.
4. A working-class Scottish poet (1759–1796) who wrote in his native dialect. Emily Brontë (1818–1848),

English poet and novelist.
5. An echo of Thomas Gray's *Elegy Written in a Country Churchyard* (1751): "Some mute inglorious Milton here may rest."
6. English poet and translator (1809–1883).

VIRGINIA WOOLF

twisted and deformed, issuing from a strained and morbid imagination. And
undoubtedly, I thought, looking at the shelf where there are no plays by
women, her work would have gone unsigned. That refuge she would have
sought certainly. It was the relic of the sense of chastity that dictated
anonymity to women even so late as the nineteenth century. Currer Bell,
George Eliot, George Sand,[7] all the victims of inner strife as their writings
prove, sought ineffectively to veil themselves by using the name of a man.
Thus they did homage to the convention, which if not implanted by the other
sex was liberally encouraged by them (the chief glory of a woman is not to be
talked of, said Pericles,[8] himself a much-talked-of man), that publicity in
women is detestable. Anonymity runs in their blood. The desire to be veiled
still possesses them.

* * *

I told you in the course of this paper that Shakespeare had a sister; but do
not look for her in Sir Sidney Lee's[9] life of the poet. She died young—alas, she
never wrote a word. She lies buried where the omnibuses now stop, opposite
the Elephant and Castle. Now my belief is that this poet who never wrote a
word and was buried at the crossroads still lives. She lives in you and in me,
and in many other women who are not here tonight, for they are washing up
the dishes and putting the children to bed. But she lives; for great poets do not
die; they are continuing presences; they need only the opportunity to walk
among us in the flesh. This opportunity, as I think, it is now coming within
your power to give her. For my belief is that if we live another century or so—I
am talking of the common life which is the real life and not of the little sepa-
rate lives which we live as individuals—and have five hundred a year each of us
and rooms of our own; if we have the habit of freedom and the courage to
write exactly what we think; if we escape a little from the common sitting
room and see human beings not always in their relation to each other but in
relation to reality; and the sky, too, and the trees or whatever it may be in
themselves; if we look past Milton's[1] bogey, for no human being should shut
out the view; if we face the fact, for it is a fact, that there is no arm to cling to,
but that we go alone and that our relation is to the world of reality and not only
to the world of men and women, then the opportunity will come and the dead
poet who was Shakespeare's sister will put on the body which she has so often
laid down. Drawing her life from the lives of the unknown who were her fore-
runners, as her brother did before her, she will be born. As for her coming with-
out that preparation, without that effort on our part, without that
determination that when she is born again she shall find it possible to live and
write her poetry, that we cannot expect, for that would be impossible. But I
maintain that she would come if we worked for her, and that so to work, even
in poverty and obscurity, is worth while.

1929

7. Male pen names of the novelists Charlotte Brontë,
Marian Evans, and Aurore Dupin.
8. Athenian statesman and orator (495–429 B.C.); this
statement comes from his funeral oration (*Thucydides*
2.4).

9. Biographer of Shakespeare (1859–1926).
1. John Milton (1608–1674), English poet; his epic
poem *Paradise Lost* retells the story of Genesis 2–3,
and portrays Eve as morally and intellectually sec-
ondary to Adam.

Professions for Women[1]

When your secretary invited me to come here she told me that your Society is concerned with the employment of women and she suggested that I might tell you something about my own professional experiences. It is true that I am a woman; it is true I am employed; but what professional experiences have I had? It is difficult to say. My profession is literature; and in that profession there are fewer experiences for women than in any other, with the exception of the stage—fewer, I mean, that are peculiar to women. For the road was cut many years ago—by Fanny Burney, by Aphra Behn, by Harriet Martineau, by Jane Austen, by George Eliot[2]—many famous women, and many more unknown and forgotten, have been before me, making the path smooth, and regulating my steps. Thus, when I came to write, there were very few material obstacles in my way. Writing was a reputable and harmless occupation. The family peace was not broken by the scratching of a pen. No demand was made upon the family purse. For ten[3] and sixpence one can buy paper enough to write all the plays of Shakespeare—if one has a mind that way. Pianos and models, Paris, Vienna, and Berlin, masters and mistresses, are not needed by a writer. The cheapness of writing paper is, of course, the reason why women have succeeded as writers before they have succeeded in the other professions.

But to tell you my story—it is a simple one. You have only got to figure to yourselves a girl in a bedroom with a pen in her hand. She had only to move that pen from left to right—from ten o'clock to one. Then it occurred to her to do what is simple and cheap enough after all—to slip a few of those pages into a envelope, fix a penny stamp in the corner and drop the envelope into the red box at the corner. It was thus that I became a journalist; and my effort was rewarded on the first day of the following month—a very glorious day it was for me—by a letter from an editor containing a check for one pound ten shillings and sixpence. But to show you how little I deserve to be called a professional woman, how little I know of the struggles and difficulties of such lives, I have to admit that instead of spending that sum upon bread and butter, rent, shoes and stockings, or butcher's bills, I went out and bought a cat—a beautiful cat, a Persian cat, which very soon involved me in bitter disputes with my neighbors.

What could be easier than to write articles and to buy Persian cats with the profits? But wait a moment. Articles have to be about something. Mine, I seem to remember, was about a novel by a famous man. And while I was writing this review, I discovered that if I were going to review books I should need to do battle with a certain phantom. And the phantom was a woman, and when I came to know her better I called her after the heroine of a famous poem, The Angel in the House.[4] It was she who used to come between me and my paper when I was writing reviews. It was she who bothered me and wasted my time and so tormented me that at last I killed her. You who come of a younger and happier generation may not have heard of her—you may not

1. A paper read to the Women's Service League [Woolf's note].
2. English novelist (1819–1880). Frances Burney (1752–1840), English novelist. Aphra Behn (1640–1689), English poet and playwright. Harriet Martineau (1802–1876), English economist, journalist, and novelist. Jane Austen (1775–1817), English novelist.
3. I.e., ten shillings.
4. A popular Victorian poem of idealized domestic life by Coventry Patmore (1823–1896).

know what I mean by The Angel in the House. I will describe her as shortly as I can. She was intensely sympathetic. She was immensely charming. She was utterly unselfish. She excelled in the difficult arts of family life. She sacrificed herself daily. If there was chicken, she took the leg; if there was a draft she sat in it—in short she was so constituted that she never had a mind or a wish of her own, but preferred to sympathize always with the minds and wishes of others. Above all—I need not say it—she was pure. Her purity was supposed to be her chief beauty—her blushes, her great grace. In those days—the last of Queen Victoria—every house had its Angel. And when I came to write I encountered her with the very first words. The shadow of her wings fell on my page; I heard the rustling of her skirts in the room. Directly, that is to say, I took my pen in my hand to review that novel by a famous man, she slipped behind me and whispered: "My dear, you are a young woman. You are writing about a book that has been written by a man. Be sympathetic; be tender; flatter; deceive; use all the arts and wiles of our sex. Never let anybody guess that you have a mind of your own. Above all, be pure." And she made as if to guide my pen. I now record the one act for which I take some credit to myself, though the credit rightly belongs to some excellent ancestors of mine who left me a certain sum of money—shall we say five hundred pounds a year?—so that it was not necessary for me to depend solely on charm for my living. I turned upon her and caught her by the throat. I did my best to kill her. My excuse, if I were to be had up in a court of law, would be that I acted in self-defense. Had I not killed her she would have killed me. She would have plucked the heart out of my writing. For, as I found, directly I put pen to paper, you cannot review even a novel without having a mind of your own, without expressing what you think to be the truth about human relations, morality, sex. And all these questions, according to the Angel of the House, cannot be dealt with freely and openly by women; they must charm, they must conciliate, they must—to put it bluntly—tell lies if they are to succeed. Thus, whenever I felt the shadow of her wing or the radiance of her halo upon my page, I took up the inkpot and flung it at her. She died hard. Her fictitious nature was of great assistance to her. It is far harder to kill a phantom than a reality. She was always creeping back when I thought I had despatched her. Though I flatter myself that I killed her in the end, the struggle was severe; it took much time that had better have been spent upon learning Greek grammar; or in roaming the world in search of adventures. But it was a real experience; it was an experience that was bound to befall all women writers at that time. Killing the Angel in the House was part of the occupation of a woman writer.

But to continue my story. The Angel was dead; what then remained? You may sat that what remained was a simple and common object—a young woman in a bedroom with an inkpot. In other words, now that she had rid herself of falsehood, that young woman had only to be herself. Ah, but what is "herself"? I mean, what is a woman? I assure you, I do not know. I do not believe that you know. I do not believe that anybody can know until she has expressed herself in all the arts and professions open to human skill. That indeed is one of the reasons why I have come here—out of respect for you, who are in process of showing us by your experiments what a woman is, who are in process of providing us, by your failures and successes, with that extremely important piece of information.

But to continue the story of my professional experiences. I made one pound

ten and six by my first review; and I bought a Persian cat with the proceeds. Then I grew ambitious. A Persian cat is all very well, I said; but a Persian cat is not enough. I must have a motorcar. And it was thus that I became a novelist—for it is a very strange thing that people will give you a motorcar if you will tell them a story. It is a still stranger thing that there is nothing so delightful in the world as telling stories. It is far pleasanter than writing reviews of famous novels. And yet, if I am to obey your secretary and tell you my professional experiences as a novelist, I must tell you about a very strange experience that befell me as a novelist. And to understand it you must try first to imagine a novelist's state of mind. I hope I am not giving away professional secrets if I say that a novelist's chief desire is to be as unconscious as possible. He has to induce in himself a state of perpetual lethargy. He wants life to proceed with the utmost quiet and regularity. He wants to see the same faces, to read the same books, to do the same things day after day, month after month, while he is writing, so that nothing may break the illusion in which he is living—so that nothing may disturb or disquiet the mysterious nosings about, feelings around, darts, dashes, and sudden discoveries of that very shy and illusive spirit, the imagination. I suspect that this state is the same both for men and women. Be that as it may, I want you to imagine me writing a novel in a state of trance. I want you to figure to yourselves a girl sitting with a pen in her hand, which for minutes, and indeed for hours, she never dips into the inkpot. The image that comes to my mind when I think of this girl is the image of a fisherman lying sunk in dreams on the verge of a deep lake with a rod held out over the water. She was letting her imagination sweep unchecked round every rock and cranny of the world that lies submerged in the depths of our unconscious being. Now came the experience that I believe to be far commoner with women writers than with men. The line raced through the girl's fingers. Her imagination had rushed away. It had sought the pools, the depths, the dark places where the largest fish slumber. And then there was a smash. There was an explosion. There was foam and confusion. The imagination had dashed itself against something hard. The girl was roused from her dream. She was indeed in a state of the most acute and difficult distress. To speak without figure, she had thought of something, something about the body, about the passions which it was unfitting for her as a woman to say. Men, her reason told her, would be shocked. The consciousness of what men will say of a woman who speaks the truth about her passions had roused her from her artist's state of unconsciousness. She could write no more. The trance was over. Her imagination could work no longer. This I believe to be a very common experience with women writers—they are impeded by the extreme conventionality of the other sex. For though men sensibly allow themselves great freedom in these respects, I doubt that they realize or can control the extreme severity with which they condemn such freedom in women.

 These then were two very genuine experiences of my own. These were two of the adventures of my professional life. The first—killing The Angel in the House—I think I solved. She died. But the second, telling the truth about my own experiences as a body, I do not think I solved. I doubt that any woman has solved it yet. The obstacles against her are still immensely powerful—and yet they are very difficult to define. Outwardly, what is simpler than to write books? Outwardly, what obstacles are there for a woman rather than for a man? Inwardly, I think, the case is very different; she has still many ghosts to fight,

many prejudices to overcome. Indeed it will be a long time still, I think, before a woman can sit down to write a book without finding a phantom to be slain, a rock to be dashed against. And if this is so in literature, the freest of all professions for women, how is it in the new professions which you are now for the first time entering?

Those are the questions that I should like, had I time, to ask you. And indeed, if I have laid stress upon these professional experiences of mine, it is because I believe that they are, though in different forms, yours also. Even when the path is nominally open—when there is nothing to prevent a woman from being a doctor, a lawyer, a civil servant—there are many phantoms and obstacles, as I believe, looming in her way. To discuss and define them is I think of great value and importance; for thus only can the labor be shared, the difficulties be solved. But besides this, it is necessary also to discuss the ends and the aims for which we are fighting, for which we are doing battle with these formidable obstacles. Those aims cannot be taken for granted; they must be perpetually questioned and examined. The whole position, as I see it—here in this hall surrounded by women practicing for the first time in history I know not how many different professions—is one of extraordinary interest and importance. You have won rooms of your own in the house hitherto exclusively owned by men. You are able, though not without great labor and effort, to pay the rent. You are earning your five hundred pounds a year. But this freedom is only a beginning; the room is your own, but it is still bare. It has to be furnished; it has to be decorated; it has to be shared. How are you going to furnish it, how are you going to decorate it? With whom are you going to share it, and upon what terms? These, I think are questions of the utmost importance and interest. For the first time in history you are able to ask them; for the first time you are able to decide for yourselves what the answers should be. Willingly would I stay and discuss those questions and answers—but not tonight. My time is up; and I must cease.

1942

The Death of the Moth

Moths that fly by day are not properly to be called moths; they do not excite that pleasant sense of dark autumn nights and ivy-blossom which the commonest yellow-underwing asleep in the shadow of the curtain never fails to rouse in us. They are hybrid creatures, neither gay like butterflies nor somber like their own species. Nevertheless the present specimen, with his narrow hay-colored wings, fringed with a tassel of the same color, seemed to be content with life. It was a pleasant morning, mid-September, mild, benignant, yet with a keener breath than that of the summer months. The plow was already scoring the field opposite the window, and where the share[1] had been, the earth was pressed flat and gleamed with moisture. Such vigor came rolling in from the fields and the down beyond that it was difficult to keep the eyes strictly turned upon the book. The rooks too were keeping one of their annual festivities; soaring round the tree tops until it looked as if a vast net with thou-

1. Plowshare.

sands of black knots in it had been cast up into the air; which, after a few moments sank slowly down upon the trees until every twig seemed to have a knot at the end of it. Then, suddenly, the net would be thrown into the air again in a wider circle this time, with the utmost clamor and vociferation, as though to be thrown into the air and settle slowly down upon the tree tops were a tremendously exciting experience.

The same energy which inspired the rooks, the plow-men, the horses, and even, it seemed, the lean bare-backed downs, sent the moth fluttering from side to side of his square of the window-pane. One could not help watching him. One was, indeed, conscious of a queer feeling of pity for him. The possibilities of pleasure seemed that morning so enormous and so various that to have only a moth's part in life, and a day moth's at that, appeared a hard fate, and his zest in enjoying his meager opportunities to the full, pathetic. He flew vigorously to one corner of his compartment, and, after waiting there a second, flew across to the other. What remained for him but to fly to a third corner and then to a fourth? That was all he could do, in spite of the size of the downs, the width of the sky, the far-off smoke of houses, and the romantic voice, now and then, of a steamer out at sea. What he could do he did. Watching him, it seemed as if a fiber, very thin but pure, of the enormous energy of the world had been thrust into his frail and diminutive body. As often as he crossed the pane, I could fancy that a thread of vital light became visible. He was little or nothing but life.

Yet, because he was so small, and so simple a form of the energy that was rolling in at the open window and driving its way through so many narrow and intricate corridors in my own brain and in those of other human beings, there was something marvelous as well as pathetic about him. It was as if someone had taken a tiny bead of pure life and decking it as lightly as possible with down and feathers, had set it dancing and zigzagging to show us the true nature of life. Thus displayed one could not get over the strangeness of it. One is apt to forget all about life, seeing it humped and bossed[2] and garnished and cumbered so that it has to move with the greatest circumspection and dignity. Again, the thought of all that life might have been had he been born in any other shape caused one to view his simple activities with a kind of pity.

After a time, tired by his dancing apparently, he settled on the window ledge in the sun, and, the queer spectacle being at an end, I forgot about him. Then, looking up, my eye was caught by him. He was trying to resume his dancing, but seemed either so stiff or so awkward that he could only flutter to the bottom of the window-pane; and when he tried to fly across it he failed. Being intent on other matters I watched these futile attempts for a time without thinking, unconsciously waiting for him to resume his flight, as one waits for a machine, that has stopped momentarily, to start again without considering the reason of its failure. After perhaps a seventh attempt he slipped from the wooden ledge and fell, fluttering his wings, on to his back on the window sill. The helplessness of his attitude roused me. It flashed upon me that he was in difficulties; he could no longer raise himself; his legs struggled vainly. But, as I stretched out a pencil, meaning to help him to right himself, it came over me that the failure and awkwardness were the approach of death. I laid the pencil down again

2. Ornamented.

The legs agitated themselves once more. I looked as if for the enemy against which he struggled. I looked out of doors. What had happened there? Presumably it was midday, and work in the fields had stopped. Stillness and quiet had replaced the previous animation. The birds had taken themselves off to feed in the brooks. The horses stood still. Yet the power was there all the same, massed outside indifferent, impersonal, not attending to anything in particular. Somehow it was opposed to the little hay-colored moth. It was useless to try to do anything. One could only watch the extraordinary efforts made by those tiny legs against an oncoming doom which could, had it chosen, have submerged an entire city, not merely a city, but masses of human beings; nothing, I knew had any chance against death. Nevertheless after a pause of exhaustion the legs fluttered again. It was superb this last protest, and so frantic that he succeeded at last in righting himself. One's sympathies, of course, were all on the side of life. Also, when there was nobody to care or to know, this gigantic effort on the part of an insignificant little moth, against a power of such magnitude, to retain what no one else valued or desired to keep, moved one strangely. Again, somehow, one saw life, a pure bead. I lifted the pencil again, useless though I knew it to be. But even as I did so, the unmistakable tokens of death showed themselves. The body relaxed, and instantly grew stiff. The struggle was over. The insignificant little creature now knew death. As I looked at the dead moth, this minute wayside triumph of so great a force over so mean an antagonist filled me with wonder. Just as life had been strange a few minutes before, so death was now as strange. The moth having righted himself now lay most decently and uncomplainingly composed. O yes, he seemed to say, death is stronger than I am.

1942

SUSAN GLASPELL
1882–1948

Cofounder in 1915 of the Provincetown Players, Susan Glaspell was also a noted dramatist and prolific fiction writer. Her full-length play *The Verge* (1921), which experimented with the psychological portrayal of character, focused on the feminism of the New Woman, while her Pulitzer Prize–winning drama *Alison's House* (1930) presented a fictionalized portrait of a woman artist modeled on Emily Dickinson. She published ten novels and more than forty short stories. A *Jury of Her Peers*—a short-story version of her one-act play *Trifles* (1916)—was included in E. J. O'Brien's edition of *The Best Short Stories of 1917*.

The daughter of Elmer S. Glaspell, a feed dealer, and Alice (Keating) Glaspell, an emigrant from Dublin, Susan Glaspell was born and raised in Davenport, Iowa. After graduating from Drake University in 1899, she worked on the staff of the *Des Moines Daily News* until she could support herself by writing fiction. Her stories appeared in magazines like *Harper's* and the *Ladies' Home Journal,* and her early novels were popular examples of regionalism. In 1911, Glaspell moved to Greenwich Village with a friend, and two years later she married George Cram Cook, a Harvard graduate from her hometown who was soon to become known as a charismatic director. They spent their winters in the Village and their summers

in Provincetown, a small town on Cape Cod. Together they organized a group of Provincetown actors who performed one-act plays in a wharf theater (and later in Greenwich Village, in New York). Eugene O'Neill, Edna St. Vincent Millay, John Reed, Michael Gold, and Susan Glaspell were to become the leading playwrights of that group and in the Playwrights' Theater Glaspell also helped found in the Village. Determinedly anticommercial and avant-garde, Glaspell's and Cook's productions fostered the first experimental drama in America. Indeed, when their theaters grew commercially successful, Cook became disillusioned, and he and his wife lived in Greece from 1922 until his death in 1924. In 1925 she married Norman Matson, whom she was to divorce in 1932. The rest of her life was spent in Provincetown, where she wrote novels that continued to explore the major subject of *Trifles*, the confining environments that frustrate the full development of human potential as well as the impact of gender on the complex process by which we read and interpret not only literary but also social texts.

Trifles A Jury of Her Peers

CHARACTERS

GEORGE HENDERSON, *County Attorney* MRS. PETERS
HENRY PETERS, *Sheriff* MRS. HALE
LEWIS HALE, *A Neighboring Farmer*

SCENE. *The kitchen in the now abandoned farmhouse of John Wright, a gloomy kitchen, and left without having been put in order—unwashed pans under the sink, a loaf of bread outside the breadbox, a dish towel on the table—other signs of incompleted work. At the rear the outer door opens and the* SHERIFF *comes in followed by the* COUNTY ATTORNEY *and* HALE. *The* SHERIFF *and* HALE *are men in middle life, the* COUNTY ATTORNEY *is a young man; all are much bundled up and go at once to the stove. They are followed by two women—the* SHERIFF'S WIFE *first; she is a slight wiry woman, a thin nervous face.* MRS. HALE *is larger and would ordinarily be called more comfortable looking, but she is disturbed now and looks fearfully about as she enters. The women have come in slowly, and stand close together near the door.*

COUNTY ATTORNEY. [*Rubbing his hands.*] This feels good. Come up to the fire, ladies.
MRS. PETERS. [*After taking a step forward.*] I'm not—cold.
SHERIFF. [*Unbuttoning his overcoat and stepping away from the stove as if to mark the beginning of official business.*] Now, Mr. Hale, before we move things about, you explain to Mr. Henderson just what you saw when you came here yesterday morning.
COUNTY ATTORNEY. By the way, has anything been moved? Are things just as you left them yesterday?
SHERIFF. [*Looking about.*] It's just the same. When it dropped below zero last night I thought I'd better send Frank out this morning to make a fire for us—no use getting pneumonia with a big case on, but I told him not to touch anything except the stove—and you know Frank.
COUNTY ATTORNEY. Somebody should have been left here yesterday.

SHERIFF. Oh—yesterday. When I had to send Frank to Morris Center for that man who went crazy—I want you to know I had my hands full yesterday, I knew you could get back from Omaha by today and as long as I went over everything here myself—

COUNTY ATTORNEY. Well, Mr. Hale, tell just what happened when you came here yesterday morning.

HALE. Harry and I had started to town with a load of potatoes. We came along the road from my place and as I got here I said, "I'm going to see if I can't get John Wright to go in with me on a party telephone." I spoke to Wright about it once before and he put me off, saying folks talked too much anyway, and all he asked was peace and quiet—I guess you know about how much he talked himself; but I thought maybe if I went to the house and talked about it before his wife, though I said to Harry that I didn't know as what his wife wanted made much difference to John—

COUNTY ATTORNEY. Let's talk about that later, Mr. Hale. I do want to talk about that, but tell now just what happened when you got to the house.

HALE. I didn't hear or see anything; I knocked at the door, and still it was all quiet inside. I knew they must be up, it was past eight o'clock. So I knocked again, and I thought I heard somebody say, "Come in." I wasn't sure, I'm not sure yet, but I opened the door—this door [*Indicating the door by which the two women are still standing*] and there in that rocker—[*Pointing to it.*] sat Mrs. Wright.

[*They all look at the rocker.*]

COUNTY ATTORNEY. What—was she doing?

HALE. She was rockin' back and forth. She had her apron in her hand and was kind of—pleating it.

COUNTY ATTORNEY. And how did she—look?

HALE. Well, she looked queer.

COUNTY ATTORNEY. How do you mean—queer?

HALE. Well, as if she didn't know what she was going to do next. And kind of done up.

COUNTY ATTORNEY. How did she seem to feel about your coming?

HALE. Why, I don't think she minded—one way or other. She didn't pay much attention. I said, "How do, Mrs. Wright, it's cold, ain't it?" And she said, "Is it?"—and went on kind of pleating at her apron. Well, I was surprised; she didn't ask me to come up to the stove, or to set down, but just sat there, not even looking at me, so I said, "I want to see John." And then she—laughed. I guess you would call it a laugh. I thought of Harry and the team outside, so I said a little sharp: "Can't I see John?" "No," she says, kind o' dull like. "Ain't he home?" says I. "Yes," says she, "he's home." "Then why can't I see him?" I asked her, out of patience. " 'Cause he's dead," says she. "*Dead?*" says I. She just nodded her head, not getting a bit excited, but rockin' back and forth. "Why—where is he?" says I, not knowing what to say. She just pointed upstairs—like that [*Himself pointing to the room above*]. I got up, with the idea of going up there. I walked from there to here—then I says, "Why, what did he die of?" "He died of a rope round his neck," says she, and just went on pleatin' at her apron. Well, I went out and called Harry. I thought I might—need help. We went upstairs and there he was lyin'—

COUNTY ATTORNEY. I think I'd rather have you go into that upstairs, where you can point it all out. Just go on now with the rest of the story.

HALE. Well, my first thought was to get that rope off. It looked . . . [*Stops,*

his face twitches.]. . . but Harry, he went up to him, and he said, "No, he's dead all right, and we'd better not touch anything." So we went back down stairs. She was still sitting that same way. "Has anybody been notified?" I asked. "No," says she, unconcerned. "Who did this, Mrs. Wright?" said Harry. He said it businesslike—and she stopped pleatin' of her apron. "I don't know," she says. "You don't *know*?" says Harry. "No," says she. "Weren't you sleepin' in the bed with him?" says Harry. "Yes," says she, "but I was on the inside." "Somebody slipped a rope round his neck and strangled him and you didn't wake up?" says Harry. "I didn't wake up," she said after him. We must 'a looked as if we didn't see how that could be, for after a minute she said, "I sleep sound." Harry was going to ask her more questions but I said maybe we ought to let her tell her story first to the coroner, or the sheriff, so Harry went fast as he cou'd to Rivers' place, where there's a telephone.

COUNTY ATTORNEY. And what did Mrs. Wright do when she knew that you had gone for the coroner?

HALE. She moved from that chair to this one over here [*Pointing to a small chair in the corner.*] and just sat there with her hands held together and looking down. I got a feeling that I ought to make some conversation, so I said I had come in to see if John wanted to put in a telephone, and at that she started to laugh, and then she stopped and looked at me—scared. [*The* COUNTY ATTORNEY, *who has had his notebook out, makes a note.*] I dunno, maybe it wasn't scared. I wouldn't like to say it was. Soon Harry got back, and then Dr. Lloyd came, and you, Mr. Peters, and so I guess that's all I know that you don't.

COUNTY ATTORNEY. [*Looking around.*] I guess we'll go upstairs first—and then out to the barn and around there. [*To the* SHERIFF.] You're convinced that there was nothing important here—nothing that would point to any motive.

SHERIFF. Nothing here but kitchen things.

[*The* COUNTY ATTORNEY, *after again looking around the kitchen, opens the door of a cupboard closet. He gets up on a chair and looks on a shelf. Pulls his hand away, sticky.*]

COUNTY ATTORNEY. Here's a nice mess.

[*The women draw nearer.*]

MRS. PETERS. [*To the other woman.*] Oh, her fruit; it did freeze. [*To the* COUNTY ATTORNEY.] She worried about that when it turned so cold. She said the fire'd go out and her jars would break.

SHERIFF. Well, can you beat the women! Held for murder and worryin' about her preserves.

COUNTY ATTORNEY. I guess before we're through she may have something more serious than preserves to worry about.

HALE. Well, women are used to worrying over trifles.

[*The two women move a little closer together.*]

COUNTY ATTORNEY. [*With the gallantry of a young politician.*] And yet, for all their worries, what would we do without the ladies? [*The women do not unbend. He goes to the sink, takes a dipperful of water from the pail and pouring it into a basin, washes his hands. Starts to wipe them on the roller towel, turns it for a cleaner place.*] Dirty towels! [*Kicks his foot against the pans under the sink.*] Not much of a housekeeper, would you say, ladies?

MRS. HALE. [*Stiffly.*] There's a great deal of work to be done on a farm.

COUNTY ATTORNEY. To be sure. And yet [*With a little bow to her.*] I know

there are some Dickson county farmhouses which do not have such roller towels.

[*He gives it a pull to expose its full length again.*]

MRS. HALE.　Those towels get dirty awful quick. Men's hands aren't always as clean as they might be.

COUNTY ATTORNEY.　Ah, loyal to your sex, I see. But you and Mrs. Wright were neighbors. I suppose you were friends, too.

MRS. HALE.　[*Shaking her head.*]　I've not seen much of her of late years. I've not been in this house—it's more than a year.

COUNTY ATTORNEY.　And why was that? You didn't like her?

MRS. HALE.　I liked her all well enough. Farmers' wives have their hands full, Mr. Henderson. And then—

COUNTY ATTORNEY.　Yes—?

MRS. HALE.　[*Looking about.*]　It never seemed a very cheerful place.

COUNTY ATTORNEY.　No—it's not cheerful. I shouldn't say she had the homemaking instinct.

MRS. HALE.　Well, I don't know as Wright had, either.

COUNTY ATTORNEY.　You mean that they didn't get on very well?

MRS. HALE.　No, I don't mean anything. But I don't think a place'd be any cheerfuller for John Wright's being in it.

COUNTY ATTORNEY.　I'd like to talk more of that a little later. I want to get the lay of things upstairs now.

[*He goes to the left, where three steps lead to a stair door.*]

SHERIFF.　I suppose anything Mrs. Peter does'll be all right. She was to take in some clothes for her, you know, and a few little things. We left in such a hurry yesterday.

COUNTY ATTORNEY.　Yes, but I would like to see what you take, Mrs. Peters, and keep an eye out for anything that might be of use to us.

MRS. PETERS.　Yes, Mr. Henderson.

[*The women listen to the men's steps on the stairs, then look about the kitchen.*]

MRS. HALE.　I'd hate to have men coming into my kitchen, snooping around and criticizing.

[*She arranges the pans under sink which the* COUNTY ATTORNEY *had shoved out of place.*]

MRS. PETERS.　Of course it's no more than their duty.

MRS. HALE.　Duty's all right, but I guess that deputy sheriff that came out to make the fire might have got a little of this on. [*Gives the roller towel a pull.*] Wish I'd thought of that sooner. Seems mean to talk about her for not having things slicked up when she had to come away in such a hurry.

MRS. PETERS.　[*Who has gone to a small table in the left rear corner of the room, and lifted one end of a towel that covers a pan.*]　She had bread set. [*Stands still.*]

MRS. HALE.　[*Eyes fixed on a loaf of bread beside the breadbox, which is on a low shelf at the other side of the room. Moves slowly toward it.*]　She was going to put this in there. [*Picks up loaf, then abruptly drops it. In a manner of returning to familiar things.*] It's a shame about her fruit. I wonder if it's all gone. [*Gets up on the chair and looks.*] I think there's some here that's all right, Mrs. Peters. Yes—here; [*Holding it toward the window.*] this is cherries, too. [*Looking again.*] I declare I believe that's the only one. [*Gets down, bottle in her hand. Goes to the sink and wipes it off on the outside.*] She'll feel awful bad after all her hard work in the hot weather. I remember the afternoon I put up my cherries last summer.

[*She puts the bottle on the big kitchen table, center of the room With a sigh,
is about to sit down in the rocking-chair. Before she is seated realizes what
chair it is; with a slow look at it, steps back. The chair which she has touched
rocks back and forth.*]

MRS. PETERS. Well, I must get those things from the front room closet. [*She
goes to the door at the right, but after looking into the other room, steps back.*]
You coming with me, Mrs. Hale? You could help me carry them.

[*They go in the other room; reappear, MRS PETERS carrying a dress and skirt,
MRS. HALE following with a pair of shoes.*]

MRS. PETERS. My, it's cold in there.

[*She puts the clothes on the big table, and hurries to the stove.*]

MRS. HALE. [*Examining her skirt.*] Wright was close. I think maybe that's
why she kept so much to herself. She didn't even belong to the Ladies Aid.
I suppose she felt she couldn't do her part, and then you don't enjoy things
when you feel shabby. She used to wear pretty clothes and be lively, when
she was Minnie Foster, one of the town girls singing in the choir. But that—
oh, that was thirty years ago. This all you was to take in?

MRS. PETERS. She said she wanted an apron. Funny thing to want, for there
isn't much to get you dirty in jail, goodness knows. But I suppose just to
make her feel more natural. She said they was in the top drawer in this cup-
board. Yes, here. And then her little shawl that always hung behind the
door. [*Opens stair door and looks.*] Yes, here it is.

[*Quickly shuts door leading upstairs.*]

MRS. HALE. [*Abruptly moving toward her.*] Mrs. Peters?

MRS. PETERS. Yes, Mrs. Hale?

MRS. HALE. Do you think she did it?

MRS. PETERS. [*In a frightened voice.*] Oh, I don't know.

MRS. HALE. Well, I don't think she did. Asking for an apron and her little
shawl. Worrying about her fruit.

MRS. PETERS. [*Starts to speak, glances up, where footsteps are heard in the room
above. In a low voice.*] Mr. Peters says it looks bad for her Mr. Henderson is
awful sarcastic in a speech and he'll make fun of her sayin' she didn't wake
up.

MRS. HALE. Well, I guess John Wright didn't wake when they was slipping
that rope under his neck.

MRS. PETERS. No, it's strange. It must have been done awful crafty and still.
They say it was such a—funny way to kill a man, rigging it all up like that.

MRS. HALE. That's just what Mr. Hale said. There was a gun in the house. He
says that's what he can't understand.

MRS. PETERS. Mr. Henderson said coming out that what was needed for the
case was a motive; something to show anger, or—sudden feeling.

MRS. HALE. [*Who is standing by the table*] Well I don't see any signs of
anger around here. [*She puts her hand on the dish towel which lies on the
table, stands looking down at table, one half of which is clean, the other half
messy.*] It's wiped to here. [*Makes a move as if to finish work, then turns and
looks at loaf of bread outside the breadbox. Drops towel. In that voice of com-
ing back to familiar things.*] Wonder how they are finding things upstairs. I
hope she had it a little more red-up up there. You know, it seems kind of
sneaking. Locking her up in town and then coming out here and trying to
get her own house to turn against her!

MRS. PETERS. But Mrs. Hale, the law is the law.

MRS. HALE. I s'pose 'tis. [*Unbuttoning her coat.*] Better loosen up your
things, Mrs. Peters. You won't feel them when you go out.

[MRS. PETERS *takes off her fur tippet, goes to hang it on hook at back of room, stands looking at the under part of the small corner table.*]

MRS. PETERS. She was piecing a quilt.

[*She brings the large sewing basket and they look at the bright pieces.*]

MRS. HALE. It's log cabin pattern. Pretty, isn't it? I wonder if she was goin' to quilt it or just knot it?

[*Footsteps have been heard coming down the stairs. The* SHERIFF *enters followed by* HALE *and the* COUNTY ATTORNEY.]

SHERIFF. They wonder if she was going to quilt it or just knot it!

[*The men laugh; the women look abashed.*]

COUNTY ATTORNEY. [*Rubbing his hands over the stove.*] Frank's fire didn't do much up there, did it? Well, let's go out to the barn and get that cleared up.

[*The men go outside.*]

MRS. HALE. [*Resentfully.*] I don't know as there's anything so strange, our takin' up our time with little things while we're waiting for them to get the evidence. [*She sits down at the big table smoothing out a block with decision.*] I don't see as it's anything to laugh about.

MRS. PETERS. [*Apologetically.*] Of course they've got awful important things on their minds.

[*Pulls up a chair and joins* MRS. HALE *at the table.*]

MRS. HALE. [*Examining another block.*] Mrs. Peters, look at this one. Here, this is the one she was working on, and look at the sewing! All the rest of it has been so nice and even. And look at this! It's all over the place! Why, it looks as if she didn't know what she was about!

[*After she has said this they look at each other, then start to glance back at the door. After an instant* MRS. HALE *has pulled at a knot and ripped the sewing.*]

MRS. PETERS. Oh, what are you doing, Mrs. Hale?

MRS. HALE. [*Mildly.*] Just pulling out a stitch or two that's not sewed very good. [*Threading a needle.*] Bad sewing always made me fidgety.

MRS. PETERS. [*Nervously.*] I don't think we ought to touch things.

MRS. HALE. I'll just finish up this end. [*Suddenly stopping and leaning forward.*] Mrs. Peters?

MRS. PETERS. Yes, Mrs. Hale?

MRS. HALE. What do you suppose she was so nervous about?

MRS. PETERS. Oh—I don't know. I don't know as she was nervous. I sometimes sew awful queer when I'm just tired. [MRS. HALE *starts to say something, looks at* MRS. PETERS, *then goes on sewing.*] Well, I must get these things wrapped up. They may be through sooner than we think. [*Putting apron and other things together.*] I wonder where I can find a piece of paper, and string.

MRS. HALE. In that cupboard, maybe.

MRS. PETERS. [*Looking in cupboard.*] Why, here's a birdcage. [*Holds it up.*] Did she have a bird, Mrs. Hale?

MRS. HALE. Why, I don't know whether she did or not—I've not been here for so long. There was a man around last year selling canaries cheap, but I don't know as she took one; maybe she did. She used to sing real pretty herself.

MRS. PETERS. [*Glancing around.*] Seems funny to think of a bird here. But she must have had one, or why would she have a cage? I wonder what happened to it.

MRS. HALE. I s'pose maybe the cat got it.

MRS. PETERS. No, she didn't have a cat. She's got that feeling some people

have about cats—being afraid of them. My cat got in her room and she was real upset and asked me to take it out.

MRS. HALE. My sister Bessie was like that. Queer, ain't it?

MRS. PETERS. [*Examining the cage.*] Why, look at this door. It's broke. One hinge is pulled apart.

MRS. HALE. [*Looking too.*] Looks as if someone must have been rough with it.

MRS. PETERS. Why, yes.

[*She brings the cage forward and puts it on the table.*]

MRS. HALE. I wish if they're going to find any evidence they'd be about it. I don't like this place.

MRS. PETERS. But I'm awful glad you came with me, Mrs Hale. It would be lonesome for me sitting here alone.

MRS. HALE. It would, wouldn't it? [*Dropping her sewing.*] But I tell you what I do wish, Mrs. Peters. I wish I had come over sometimes when she was here. I—[*Looking around the room.*]—wish I had.

MRS. PETERS. But of course you were awful busy, Mrs. Hale—your house and your children.

MRS. HALE. I could've come. I stayed away because it weren't cheerful—and that's why I ought to have come. I—I've never liked this place. Maybe because it's down in a hollow and you don't see the road. I dunno what it is but it's a lonesome place and always was. I wish I had come over to see Minnie Foster sometimes. I can see now—

[*Shakes her head.*]

MRS. PETERS. Well, you mustn't reproach yourself, Mrs. Hale. Somehow we just don't see how it is with other folks until—something comes up.

MRS. HALE. Not having children makes less work—but it makes a quiet house, and Wright out to work all day, and no company when he did come in. Did you know John Wright, Mrs. Peters?

MRS. PETERS. Not to know him; I've seen him in town. They say he was a good man.

MRS. HALE. Yes—good; he didn't drink, and kept his word as well as most, I guess, and paid his debts. But he was a hard man, Mrs Peters. Just to pass the time of day with him—[*Shivers.*] Like a raw wind that gets to the bone. [*Pauses, her eye falling on the cage.*] I should think she would 'a wanted a bird. But what do you suppose went with it?

MRS. PETERS. I don't know, unless it got sick and died.

[*She reaches over and swings the broken door, swings it again. Both women watch it.*]

MRS. HALE. You weren't raised round here, were you? [MRS. PETERS *shakes her head.*] You didn't know—her?

MRS. PETERS. Not till they brought her yesterday.

MRS. HALE. She—come to think of it, she was kind of like a bird herself—real sweet and pretty, but kind of timid and—fluttery. How—she—did—change. [*Silence; then as if struck by a happy thought and relieved to get back to every day things.*] Tell you what, Mrs. Peters, why don't you take the quilt in with you? It might take up her mind.

MRS. PETERS. Why, I think that's a real nice idea, Mrs. Hale. There couldn't possibly be any objection to it, could there? Now, just what would I take? I wonder if her patches are in here—and her things.

[*They look in the sewing basket.*]

MRS. HALE. Here's some red. I expect this has got sewing things in it. [*Brings out a fancy box.*] What a pretty box. Looks like something somebody would

give you. Maybe her scissors are in here. [*Opens box. Suddenly puts her hand to her nose.*] Why—[MRS. PETERS *bends nearer, then turns her face away.*] There's something wrapped up in this piece of silk.

MRS. PETERS. Why, this isn't her scissors.

MRS. HALE. [*Lifting the silk.*] Oh, Mrs. Peters—it's—

[MRS. PETERS *bends closer.*]

MRS. PETERS. It's the bird.

MRS. HALE. [*Jumping up.*] But, Mrs. Peters—look at it! Its neck! Look at its neck! It's all—other side to.

MRS. PETERS. Somebody—wrung—its—neck.

[*Their eyes meet. A look of growing comprehension, of horror. Steps are heard outside.* MRS. HALE *slips box under quilt pieces, and sinks into her chair. Enter* SHERIFF *and* COUNTY ATTORNEY. MRS. PETERS *rises.*]

COUNTY ATTORNEY. [*As one turning from serious things to little pleasantries.*] Well, ladies, have you decided whether she was going to quilt it or knot it?

MRS. PETERS. We think she was going to—knot it.

COUNTY ATTORNEY. Well, that's interesting, I'm sure. [*Seeing the birdcage.*] Has the bird flown?

MRS. HALE. [*Putting more quilt pieces over the box.*] We think the—cat got it.

COUNTY ATTORNEY. [*Preoccupied.*] Is there a cat?

[MRS. HALE *glances in a quick covert way at* MRS. PETERS.]

MRS. PETERS. Well, not now. They're superstitious, you know. They leave.

COUNTY ATTORNEY. [*To* SHERIFF PETERS, *continuing an interrupted conversation.*] No sign at all of anyone having come from the outside. Their own rope. Now let's go up again and go over it piece by piece. [*They start upstairs.*] It would have to have been someone who knew just the—

[MRS. PETERS *sits down. The two women sit there not looking at one another, but as if peering into something and at the same time holding back. When they talk now it is in the manner of feeling their way over strange ground, as if afraid of what they are saying, but as if they can not help saying it.*]

MRS. HALE. She liked the bird. She was going to bury it in that pretty box.

MRS. PETERS. [*In a whisper.*] When I was a girl—my kitten—there was a boy took a hatchet, and before my eyes—and before I could get there—[*Covers her face an instant.*] If they hadn't held me back I would have—[*Catches herself, looks upstairs where steps are heard, falters weakly.*]—hurt him.

MRS. HALE. [*With a slow look around her.*] I wonder how it would seem never to have had any children around. [*Pause.*] No, Wright wouldn't like the bird—a thing that sang. She used to sing. He killed that, too.

MRS. PETERS. [*Moving uneasily.*] We don't know who killed the bird.

MRS. HALE. I knew John Wright.

MRS. PETERS. It was an awful thing was done in this house that night, Mrs. Hale. Killing a man while he slept, slipping a rope around his neck that choked the life out of him.

MRS. HALE. His neck. Choked the life out of him.

[*Her hand goes out and rests on the birdcage.*]

MRS. PETERS. [*With rising voice.*] We don't know who killed him. We don't know.

MRS. HALE. [*Her own feeling not interrupted.*] If there'd been years and years of nothing, then a bird to sing to you, it would be awful—still, after the bird was still.

MRS. PETERS. [*Something within her speaking.*] I know what stillness is.

When we homesteaded in Dakota, and my first baby died—after he was two years old, and me with no other then—

MRS. HALE. [*Moving.*] How soon do you suppose they'll be through, looking for the evidence?

MRS. PETERS. I know what stillness is. [*Pulling herself back.*] The law has got to punish crime, Mrs. Hale.

MRS. HALE. [*Not as if answering that.*] I wish you'd seen Minnie Foster when she wore a white dress with blue ribbons and stood up there in the choir and sang. [*A look around the room.*] Oh, I wish I'd come over here once in a while! That was a crime! That was a crime! Who's going to punish that?

MRS. PETERS. [*Looking upstairs.*] We mustn't—take on.

MRS. HALE. I might have known she needed help! I know how things can be—for women. I tell you, it's queer, Mrs. Peters. We live close together and we live far apart. We all go through the same things—it's all just a different kind of the same thing. [*Brushes her eyes; noticing the bottle of fruit, reaches out for it.*] If I was you I wouldn't tell her her fruit was gone. Tell her it ain't. Tell her it's all right. Take this in to prove it to her. She—she may never know whether it was broke or not.

MRS. PETERS. [*Takes the bottle, looks about for something to wrap it in; takes petticoat from the clothes brought from the other room, very nervously begins winding this around the bottle. In a false voice.*] My, it's a good thing the men couldn't hear us. Wouldn't they just laugh! Getting all stirred up over a little thing like a—dead canary. As if that could have anything to do with—with—wouldn't they laugh!

[*The men are heard coming down stairs.*]

MRS. HALE. [*Under her breath.*] Maybe they would—maybe they wouldn't.

COUNTY ATTORNEY. No, Peters, it's all perfectly clear except a reason for doing it. But you know juries when it comes to women. If there was some definite thing. Something to show—something to make a story about—a thing that would connect up with this strange way of doing it—

[*The women's eyes meet for an instant. Enter* HALE *from outer door.*]

HALE. Well, I've got the team around. Pretty cold out there.

COUNTY ATTORNEY. I'm going to stay here a while by myself. [*To the* SHERIFF.] You can send Frank out for me, can't you? I want to go over everything. I'm not satisfied that we can't do better.

SHERIFF. Do you want to see what Mrs. Peters is going to take in?

[*The* COUNTY ATTORNEY *goes to the table, picks up the apron, laughs.*]

COUNTY ATTORNEY. Oh, I guess they're not very dangerous things the ladies have picked out. [*Moves a few things about, disturbing the quilt pieces which cover the box. Steps back.*] No, Mrs. Peters doesn't need supervising. For that matter, a sheriff's wife is married to the law. Ever think of it that way, Mrs. Peters?

MRS. PETERS. Not—just that way.

SHERIFF. [*Chuckling.*] Married to the law. [*Moves toward the other room.*] I just want you to come in here a minute, George. We ought to take a look at these windows.

COUNTY ATTORNEY. [*Scoffingly.*] Oh, windows!

SHERIFF. We'll be right out, Mr. Hale.

[HALE *goes outside. The* SHERIFF *follows the* COUNTY ATTORNEY *into the other room. Then* MRS. HALE *rises, hands tight together, looking intensely at* MRS. PETERS, *whose eyes make a slow turn, finally meeting* MRS. HALE'*s. A moment* MRS. HALE *holds her, then her own eyes point the way to where the box*

is concealed. Suddenly MRS. PETERS *throws back quilt pieces and tries to put the box in the bag she is wearing. It is too big. She opens box, starts to take bird out, cannot touch it, goes to pieces, stands there helpless. Sound of a knob turning in the other room.* MRS. HALE *snatches the box and puts it in the pocket of her big coat. Enter* COUNTY ATTORNEY *and* SHERIFF.]

COUNTY ATTORNEY. [*Facetiously.*] Well, Henry, at least we found out that she was not going to quilt it. She was going to—what is it you call it, ladies?

MRS. HALE. [*Her hand against her pocket.*] We call it—knot it, Mr. Henderson.

CURTAIN

1916

MINA LOY

1882–1966

"Women," declaimed Mina Loy in her unpublished *Feminist Manifesto* (1909), "if you want to realize yourselves (for you are on the brink of a devastating psychological upheaval) all your pet illusions must be unmasked. The lies of centuries have got to be discarded." An avant-garde writer and painter at various times associated with radically innovative aesthetic movements (futurism, dadaism) as well as with the social protests of feminism, Mina Loy refused throughout her career to abide by the rules of what she elsewhere called "the rubbish heap of tradition." "Nothing short of Absolute Demolition will bring about reform," she declared, identifying herself with the experimental works produced by such contemporaries as Gertrude Stein, Djuna Barnes, and Marianne Moore.

Born Mina Gertrude Lowy in London, she shortened her name to Loy when she married the painter Stephen Haweis and moved to Paris in 1903. The couple had three children and lived for a while in Paris, for a while in Florence, moving in expatriate modernist circles. In 1916, however, Loy emigrated alone to New York, where she acted with the Provincetown Players, exhibited paintings, published in little magazines, and was defined by one newspaper as a typical "modern woman." In 1917, she divorced her first husband and soon married Arthur Craven, a somewhat shady "proto-Dadaist" and "master of disguise" who mysteriously disappeared within a year, leaving Loy pregnant. In the 1920s, after bearing Craven's child, she returned to Europe, where she resided for many years in Florence, Berlin, and Paris, painting, writing poetry, and supporting herself by designing and manufacturing lampshades. In 1953, she moved again, this time to Aspen, Colorado, where she lived in seclusion and comparative obscurity near her only surviving children (two daughters) until her death in 1966.

Loy published few books in her lifetime: *Lunar Baedecker* (1923), a collection of diverse writings, had no successor until *Lunar Baedecker and Time-Tables* appeared, virtually unnoticed, in 1958. Yet major contemporaries and descendants from Ezra Pound and T. S. Eliot to William Carlos Williams and Denise Levertov deeply admired her rigorous experimentalism, sexual frankness, and severe commitment to precisely the search for the "radium of the word" that she herself praised in the works of Gertrude Stein.

Gertrude Stein[1]

Curie[2]
of the laboratory
of vocabulary
she crushed
the tonnage 5
of consciousness
congealed to phrases
to extract
a radium of the word

 1914, 1925

From Three Moments in Paris

One O'Clock at Night

Though you have never possessed me
I have belonged to you since the beginning of time
And sleepily I sit on your chair beside you
Leaning against your shoulder
And your careless arm across my back gesticulates 5
As your indisputable male voice roars
Through my brain and my body
Arguing "Dynamic Decomposition"
Of which I understand nothing
Sleepily 10
And the only less male voice of your brother pugilist of the intellect
Booms as it seems to me so sleepy
Across an interval of a thousand miles
An interim of a thousand years
But you who make more noise than any man in the world when you
 clear your throat 15
Deafening wake me
And I catch the thread of the argument
Immediately assuming my personal mental attitude
And cease to be a woman

Beautiful halfhour of being a mere woman 20
The animal woman
Understanding nothing of man
But mastery and the security of imparted physical heat
Indifferent to cerebral gymnastics
Or regarding them as the self-indulgent play of children 25
Or the thunder of alien gods
But you wake me up
Anyhow who am I that I should criticize
 your theories of "Plastic Velocity"

1. Gertrude Stein (1874–1946), American writer whose prose and poetry reflect her interest in radical linguistic experimentation. 2. Marie Curie (1867–1934), physicist, chemist, and codiscoverer of radium.

"Let us go home she is tired and
 wants to go to bed."

1915

Omen of Victory

Women in uniform
relaxed for tea
under a shady garden tree
discover
a dove's feather 5
fallen in the sugar.

1958

Photo after Pogrom[1]

Arrangement by rage
of human rubble
the false-eternal statues of the slain
until they putrify:

Tossed on a pile of dead, 5
one woman,
her body hacked to utter beauty,
oddly, by murder,

attains the absolute smile
of dispossession: 10
the marble pause before the extinct haven.

Death's drear
erasure of fear,
the unassumed
composure, 15

the purposeless peace
sealing the faces
of corpses.

Corpses are virgin.

1961

Songge Byrd

for Isadora Duncan[2]

Gossip-blown songstress
you flew upon men

1. An organized massacre of Jews.
2. Innovator in expressionistic dance based on Greek forms (1878–1927).

caressed them
with the feathers of your eyes
seeing without the censor of surprise 5
that like yourself
descended from the skies
so many gods.

1982

Nancy Cunard[1]

Your eyes diffused with holly lights
of ancient Christmas
helmeted with masks
whose silken nostrils
point the cardinal airs 5

the vermilion[2] wall
receding as a sin
beyond your moonstone whiteness

your chiffon voice
tears with soft mystery 10
a lily loaded with a sucrose dew
of vigil carnival

Your lone fragility
of mythological queens
conjures long-vanished dragons— 15
their vast jaws
yawning in disillusion—

your drifting hands,
faint as exotic snow,
spread silver silence 20

as a fondant nun
framed in the facing profiles
of Princess Murat
and George Moore[3]

1982

Portrait of a Nun

The smile folded as a marriage-veil
hoarded in heaven

1. An heiress, poet, publisher, and later activist and journalist (1896–1965), who was an emblem of the 1920s.
2. Bright red.

3. Irish novelist and friend of Cunard's (1852–1933). "Fondant": a creamy candy. "Princess Murat": the French princess Caroline Murat (1833–1902) fled to England in 1870 at the fall of the Second Empire.

Over her abdomen
the hands crossed: consequence
of a mystic conception 5

The nostril: arched for incense—

The mourning and the starching
of her body's concealing:
a cloth coffin

Her face wrapping: a white napkin— 10

The round halo rising
through her flesh shining:
virgin apple to angels' offering

The ascensional eyes:
pointed skyward as a crown 15
or now cast down.

A nun
seeing no one
but Jesus
is gentle to us 20

 1982

Feminist Manifesto

The Feminist Movement as instituted at present is INADEQUATE.

Women, if you want to realize yourselves (for you are on the brink of a devastating psychological upheaval) all your pet illusions must be unmasked. The lies of centuries have got to be discarded. Are you prepared for the WRENCH?

There is no half measure, no scratching on the surface of the rubbish heap of tradition. Nothing short of Absolute Demolition will bring about reform. So cease to place your confidence in economic legislation, vice-crusades and uniform education. You are glossing over REALITY.

Professional and commercial careers are opening up for you. *Is that all you want?* If you honestly desire to find your level without prejudice, be brave and deny at the outset that pathetic clap-trap warcry, "Woman is the equal of man."

She is *not*.

For the man who lives a life in which his activities conform to a social code which is a protectorate of the feminine element is no longer masculine. The

woman who adapts herself to a theoretical valuation of her sex as a *relative impersonality* is not yet feminine.

Leave off looking to men to find out what you are *not*. Seek within yourselves to find out what you *are*. As conditions are at present constituted you have the choice between Parasitism, Prostitution, or Negation.

Men and women are enemies, with the enmity of the exploited for the parasite, the parasite for the exploited—at present they are at the mercy of the advantage that each can take of the others' sexual dependence. The only point at which the interests of the sexes merge is the sexual embrace.

The first illusion to demolish is the division of women into two classes: the mistress and the mother. Every well balanced and developed woman knows that no such division exists, that Nature has endowed the Complete Woman with a faculty for expressing herself through all her functions. These are *no restrictions*. The woman who is so incompletely evolved as to be unselfconscious in sex will prove a restrictive influence on the temperamental expansion of the next generation; the woman who is a poor mistress will be an incompetent mother, an inferior mentality. She will not have an adequate apprehension of LIFE.

To obtain results you must make sacrifices and the first and greatest sacrifice you have to make is of your VIRTUE.

The fictitious value of woman as identified with her physical purity is too easy a standby. It renders her lethargic in the acquisition of intrinsic merits of character by which she could obtain a concrete value. Therefore, the first self-enforced law for the female sex, as protection against the manmade bogey[1] of virtue (which is the principal instrument of her subjugation) is the *unconditional* surgical *destruction of virginity* throughout the female population at puberty.

The value of man is assessed entirely according to his use or interest to the community; the value of woman depends entirely on chance—her success or failure in manipulating a man into taking life-long responsibility for her.

The advantages of marriage are too ridiculously ample compared to all other trades, for under modern conditions a woman can accept preposterously luxurious support from a man without returning anything—even offspring—as an offering of thanks for her virginity.

The woman who has not succeeded in striking that advantageous bargain is prohibited from any but the most surreptitious reaction to life-stimuli and is entirely debarred from maternity. Every woman has a right to maternity.

Every woman of superior intelligence should realize her race-responsibility by producing children in adequate proportion to the unfit or degenerate members of her sex.

1. Source of fear.

Each child of a superior woman should be the result of a definite period of psychic development in her life and not necessarily of a possibly irksome and outworn continuance of an alliance that is spontaneously adapted for vital creation in the beginning but which becomes unbalanced as the parties of that alliance follow the individual lines of their personal evolution.

For the harmony of the race, each individual should be the expression of an easy and ample interpenetration of the male and female temperaments—free from stress.

Woman must become more responsible for the child than man.

Woman must destroy in herself the desire to be loved.

The desire for comfortable protection rather than intelligent curiosity and courage in meeting and resisting the presence of sex (or so-called love) must be reduced to its initial element. Honor, grief, sentimentality, pride, and consequently jealousy must be detached from sex.

Woman must retain her deceptive fragility of appearance, combined with indomitable will, irreducible courage, abundant health, and sound nerves.

Another great illusion that woman must use all her introspection, innate clear-sightedness, and unbiased bravery to destroy is the impurity of sex—for the sake of her self-respect.

In defiance of superstition I assert that *there is nothing impure in sex* except the mental attitude toward it. The eventual acceptance of this fact will constitute an incalculably wider social regeneration than it is possible for our generation to acquire.

1914 1982

ANNE SPENCER
1882–1975

Although she lived her entire life in relative obscurity and never collected her verse into a volume, Anne Spencer produced a number of the finest poems published during the Harlem Renaissance. Born on a Virginia plantation, Anne Bethel Scales Bannister witnessed with some dismay the incompatibility of her parents, free African-Americans whose disputes ended in a separation around 1887. Mother and daughter moved to Bramwell, West Virginia, where Anne was educated at home until she entered the Virginia Seminary at fourteen years of age. After marrying a seminary schoolmate, Edward Spencer, she resided with her husband and mother in Lynchburg, Virginia, where she raised three children, helped organize black citizens for civil rights, cultivated a beautiful garden, and corresponded with a number of prominent literary men of her time, including James Weldon Johnson. With his help, she placed her poems in such influential anthologies as Charles S. Johnson's *Ebony and Topaz* (1927) and Countee Cullen's *Caroling*

Dusk (1927) as well as in leading journals like *Crisis*. For many years, editors who anthologized her verse praised her for writing about nonracial themes with imagistic precision and economy; however, the selections printed here illustrate the subtlety of her thinking about the impact of overvaluations of whiteness and devaluations of blackness in Western culture.

White Things

Most things are colorful things—the sky, earth, and sea
 Black men are most men; but the white are free!
White things are rare things; so rare, so rare
They stole from out a silvered world—somewhere.
Finding earth-plains fair plains, save greenly grassed, 5
They strewed white feathers of cowardice,[1] as they passed;
 The golden stars with lances fine
 The hills all red and darkened pine,
They blanched with their wand of power;
And turned the blood in a ruby rose 10
To a poor white poppy-flower.

They pyred a race of black, black men,
And burned them to ashes white; then,
Laughing, a young one claimed a skull,
For the skull of a black is white, not dull, 15
 But a glistening awful thing;
 Made, it seems, for this ghoul to swing
In the face of God with all his might,
And swear by the hell that siréd him:
 "Man-maker, make white!" 20

 1923

Lady, Lady

Lady, Lady, I saw your face,
Dark as night withholding a star . . .
The chisel fell, or it might have been
You had borne so long the yoke of men.
Lady, Lady, I saw your hands 5
Twisted, awry, like crumpled roots,
Bleached poor white in a suesy tub,
Wrinkled and drawn from your rub-a-dub.
Lady, Lady, I saw your heart,
And altared there in its darksome place 10
Were the tongues of flames the ancients knew,
Where the good God sits to spangle through.

 1925

1. The association of white feathers with cowardice is traditional (from cockfighting: a white feather was seen as a sign of degenerate stock).

Letter to My Sister

It is dangerous for a woman to defy the gods;
To taunt them with the tongue's thin tip,
Or strut in the weakness of mere humanity,
Or draw a line daring them to cross;
The gods own the searing lightning, 5
The drowning waters, tormenting fears
And anger of red sins.

Oh, but worse still if you mince timidly—
Dodge this way or that, or kneel or pray,
Be kind, or sweat agony drops 10
Or lay your quick body over your feeble young;
If you have beauty or none, if celibate
Or vowed—the gods are Juggernaut,[1]
Passing over . . . over . . .

This you may do: 15
Lock your heart, then, quietly,
And lest they peer within,
Light no lamp when dark comes down
Raise no shade for sun;
Breathless must your breath come through 20
If you'd die and dare deny
The gods their god-like fun.

1927

Innocence

She tripped and fell against a star,
A lady we all have known;
Just what the villagers lusted for
To claim her one of their own;
Fallen but once the lower felt she, 5
So turned her face and died,—
With never a hounding fool to see
'Twas a star-lance in her side!

1927

1. A force that crushes everything in its path.

KATHARINE SUSANNAH PRICHARD
1883–1969

"With Henry Handel Richardson she pioneered the Australian novel as [an] art form," wrote one critic of Katharine Susannah Prichard. The author of twelve novels, a number of short-story collections, two volumes of verse, and a series of marxist political pamphlets, Prichard is still little known outside Australia, yet her

groundbreaking contribution to that nation's literary development was crucial; in addition, as *The Cooboo* reveals, her art transcended regional issues to focus on universal questions of exploitation and justice, freedom and survival.

Born in Levuka, Fiji, Prichard was the daughter of conservative middle-class parents. Her father was a Melbourne journalist who had published a novel in 1891, and the family lived in moderate comfort until his newspaper went out of business and their household goods were sold to pay debts, an event that may have fostered Prichard's later consciousness of economic inequities. Nevertheless, despite straitened circumstances, she was a precocious child who wrote and published her first story at the age of sixteen, and continued to write, even to publish, short stories thereafter. In 1908, she journeyed to England, where she spent a year studying and writing journalism, a career she continued to pursue when she returned to Australia. In 1915, her novel *The Pioneers* won a major Australian literary prize and, as one biographer reports, she "was accorded public honors unprecedented for a native born writer."

Shortly after the 1917 Russian Revolution, Prichard became a committed marxist, and in 1919, the year after she married Captain Hugo Throssell, an Australian World War I hero, she joined the Communist Party, whose ideology was to influence her worldview for the next few decades. In particular, *Working Bullocks* (1926) and *Coonardoo* (1929) were marked by her newly passionate interest in the lives of the working classes and of the Australian aborigines. Among her later novels, the so-called goldfields trilogy—*The Roaring Nineties* (1946), *Golden Miles* (1948), and *Winged Seeds* (1950)—is widely regarded as her most significant achievement, partly for its historically realistic exploration of west Australia's prospecting era and partly for its vivid portrayal of an implicitly feminist heroine, Sally Gough. But *The Cooboo*, too, suggests the skill with which this productively political artist could render the social dynamics that shadowed the lives of Australian aborigines and half-castes while shaping the society of settlers who might seem to have traveled far from the oppressions of civilization.

The Cooboo[1]

They had been mustering[2] all day on the wide plains of Murndoo station. Over the red earth, black with ironstone pebbles, through mulga and curari bush, across the ridges which make a blue wall along the horizon. And the rosy, garish light of sunset was on plains, hills, moving cattle, men and horses.

Through red dust the bullocks mooched, restless and scary still, a wild mob from the hills. John Gray, in the rear with Arra, the boy who was his shadow; Wongana, on the right with his gin,[3] Rose; Frank, the half-caste, on the left with Minni.

A steer breaking from the mob before Rose, she wheeled and went after him. Faint and wailing, a cry followed her, as though her horse had stepped on and crushed some small creature. But the steer was getting away. Arra went after him, stretched along his horse's neck, rounded the beast and rode him back to the mob, sulky and blethering.[4] The mob swayed; it had broken three times that day, but was settling to the road.

John Gray called: "Yienda (you) damn fool, Rosey. Finish!"

The gin, on her slight, rough-haired horse, pulled up scowling.

1. Baby (Australian aborigine dialect).
2. Rounding up cattle.
3. Native Australian wife or woman.
4. Muttering, grumbling.

"Tell Meetchie, Thirty Mile, to-morrow," John Gray said. "Miah, new moon."

Rose slewed[5] her horse away from the mob of men and cattle. That wailing, thin and hard as hair-string, moved with her.

"Minni!"

John Gray jerked his head towards Rose. Minni's bare heels struck her horse's belly; with a turn of the wrist she swung her horse off from the mob, turned, leaned forward, rising in her stirrups, and came up with Rose.

Thin, dark figures on their wiry station-bred horses, the gins rode into the haze of sunset towards the hills. The dull, dirty blue of the trousers wrapped round their legs was torn; their short, fairish hair tousled by the wind. But the glitter and tumult of Rose's eyes, Minni looked away from them.

At a little distance, when men and cattle were a moving cloud of red dust, Rose's anger gushed after them.

"Koo!"[6]

Fierce as the cry of a hawk flew her last note of derision and defiance.

A far-away rattle of laughter drifted back across country. Alone they would have been afraid, as darkness coming up behind, was hovering near them, secreting itself among the low, writhen trees, and bushes; afraid of the evil spirits who wander over the plains and stony ridges when the light of day is withdrawn. But together they were not so afraid. Twenty miles away, over there, below that dent in the hills where Nyedee Creek made a sandy bed for itself among white-bodied gums, was Murndoo homestead and the uloo[7] of their people.

There was no track; and in the first darkness, which would be thick as wool after the glow of sunset faded, only their instinct would keep them moving in the direction of the homestead and their own low, round huts of bagging, rusty tin and dead boughs.

Both were Wongana's women: Rose, tall, gaunt and masterful; Minni, younger, fat and jolly. Rose had been a good stockman[8] in her day: one of the best. Minni did not ride or track nearly as well as Rose.

And yet, as they rode along, Minni pattered complacently of how well she had worked that day; of how she was flashed, this way and that, heading-off breakaways, dashing after them, turning them back to the mob so smartly that John had said, "Good man, Minni!" There was the white bullock—he had rushed near the yards. Had Rose seen the chestnut mare stumble in a crab-hole and send Arra flying? But Minni had chased the white bullock, chased him for a couple of miles, and brought him back to the yards. No doubt there would be nammery for her and a new gina-gina[9] when the men came in from the muster.

She pulled a pipe from her belt, shook the ashes out, and with reins looped over one arm stuffed the bowl with tobacco from a tin tied to her belt. Stooping down, she struck a match on her stirrup-iron, guarded the flame to the pipe between her short, white teeth, and smoked contentedly.

The scowl on Rose's face deepened, darkened. That thin, fretted wailing came from her breast.

5. Swung.
6. An aborigine cry.
7. Camp.

8. Herdsman.
9. Dress. "Nammery": reward.

She unslung from her neck the rag rope by which the baby had been against her body, and gave him a sagging breast to suck. Holding him with one arm, she rode slowly, her horse picking his way over the rough, stony earth.

It had been a hard day. The gins were mustering with the men at sunrise. Camped at Nyedee well the night before, in order to get a good start, they had been riding through the timbered ridges all the morning, rounding up the wild cows, calves and young bullocks, and driving them to the yards at Nyedee, where John Gray cut out the fats, left old Jimmy and a couple of boys to brand calves, turn the cows and calves back to the ridge again while he took on the mob for trucking at Meekatharra. The bullocks were as wild as birds: needed watching all day. And all the time that small, whimpering bundle against her breast had hampered Rose's movements.

There was nothing the gins liked better than a muster, riding after cattle. And they could ride, were quicker in their movements, more alert than the men; sharper at picking up tracks. They did not go mustering very often nowadays when there was work to do at the homestead. Since John Gray had married, and there was a woman on Murndoo, she found plenty of washing, scrubbing and sweeping for the gins to do; would not spare them often to go after cattle. But John was short-handed. He had said he must have Rose and Minni to muster Nyedee. And all day her baby's crying had irritated Rose. The cooboo had wailed and wailed as she rode with him tied to her body.

The cooboo was responsible for the wrong things she had done all day. Stupid things. Rose was furious. The men had yelled at her. Wongana, her man, blackguarding her before everybody, had called her "a her who did not know where she laid her eggs." And John Gray, with his "Yienda, damn fool, Rosey. Finish!" had sent her home like a naughty child.

Now, here was Minni jabbering of the tobacco she would get and the new gina-gina. How pleased Wongana would be with her! And the cooboo, wailing, wailing. He wailed as he chewed Rose's empty breast, squirming against her; wailed and gnawed.

She cried out with hurt and impatience. Rage, irritated to madness, rushed through her; rushed like waters coming down the dry creek-beds after heavy rain. Rose wrenched the cooboo from her breast and flung him from her to the ground. There was a crack as of twigs breaking.

Minni glanced aside. "Wiah!"[1] she gasped with widening eyes. But Rose rode on, gazing ahead over the rosy, garish plains and wall of the hills, darkening from the blue to purple and indigo.

When the women came into the station kitchen, earth, hills and trees were dark; the sky heavy with stars. Minni gave John's wife his message: that he would be home with the new moon, in about a fortnight.

Meetchie, as the blacks called Mrs. John Gray, could not make out why the gins were so stiff and quiet: why Rose stalked scowling and sulky-fellow, somber eyes just glancing, and away again. Meetchie wanted to ask about the muster, what sort of condition the bullocks had on; how many were on the road; if many calves had been branded at Nyedee. But she knew them too well to ask questions when they looked like that.

Only when she had given them bread and a tin of jam, cut off hunks of corned beef for them, filled their billies[2] with strong black tea, put sugar in

1. Ho! 2. Cylindrical tin containers with close-fitting lids.

their empty tins, and they were going off to the uloo, she was surprised to see Rose without her baby.

"Why, Rose," she exclaimed, "where's the cooboo?"

Rose stalked off into the night. Minni glanced back with scared eyes, and followed Rose.

In the dawn, when a cry, remote and anguished flew through the clear air, Meetchie wondered who was dead in the camp by the creek. She remembered Rose: how she had looked the night before. And the cooboo—where was he?

Then she knew that it was Rose wailing for her cooboo in the dawn: Rose cutting herself with stones until her body bled: Rose screaming in a fury of unavailing grief.

1932

ANZIA YEZIERSKA

c. 1883–1970

Anzia Yezierska's novel *Bread Givers* (1925) dramatizes the ambivalence of a girl who confronts the misogyny of Jewish laws and learning in the Torah (the first five books of the Bible): "Women were always the curse of men," the girl's pious father proclaims, "but when they get older they're devils and witches." Angered though she is, later in the novel, after she rejects a lucrative marriage proposal that would have turned her into "another piece of property," this same daughter believes that her integrity comes from her father's "wiser-than-the-world kind of wisdom," for "he had given up worldly success to drink the wisdom of the Torah." Many of Yezierska's characters are similarly caught between the old world of their fathers, the *shtetl* (village) of Europe transplanted to the Lower East Side of New York, and the New World of America with its promise of advancement through education and economic mobility, a world that, ironically enough, inexorably isolates them from those origins that are the source of their energies. Like the heroine of *Where Lovers Dream*, Yezierska's protagonists long for the education, the language, the clothing, the manners that would make them American, but that very longing inflicts painfully acute moments of self-hatred and despair.

Born in Poland of poor parents who had nine children, Yezierska emigrated with her family to America in the early 1890s. Although her father continued to maintain the honorable poverty associated with the study of the Talmud (the ancient writings of rabbis), she sought advancement in night school. Married twice, once for a few months in 1910, and soon again for three years, she eventually decided to leave her only child, a daughter, with her second husband. Her fiction, which began appearing in 1915, won quick acclaim; *The Fat of the Land* was awarded the Edward J. O'Brien prize and her collection *Hungry Hearts* (1920) was purchased by the Hollywood producer Samuel Goldwyn for $10,000. Although she published story collections (like *Children of Loneliness*, 1923) and novels (like *Salome of the Tenements*, 1923) throughout the 1920s, her success had cut her off from the people who had inspired her writing in the first place. For all of the filth, poverty, ignorance, degrading toil, and misogyny of the ghetto, Jewish immigrant culture provided the familiar cadences of the Yiddish language and the warmth of familial customs that animated her fiction.

By the 1930s and 1940s, Yezierska had difficulties finding a publisher for her writing. She was quite poor and more than eighty years old when readers began to rediscover her work. But by the time she died, she was being recognized as a sensitive interpreter of the assimilation process.

Where Lovers Dream

For years I was saying to myself—Just so you will act when you meet him. Just so you will stand. So will you look on him. These words you will say to him.

I wanted to show him that what he had done to me could not down me; that his leaving me the way he left me, that his breaking my heart the way he broke it, didn't crush me; that his grand life and my pinched-in life, his having learning and my not having learning—that the difference didn't count so much like it seemed; that on the bottom I was the same like him.

But he came upon me so sudden, all my plannings for years smashed to the wall. The sight of him was like an earthquake shaking me to pieces.

I can't yet see nothing in front of me and can't get my head together to anything, so torn up I am from the shock.

It was at Yetta Solomon's wedding I met him again. She was after me for weeks I should only come.

"How can I come to such a swell hall?" I told her. "You know I ain't got nothing decent to wear."

"Like you are without no dressing-up, I want you to come. You are the kind what people look in your eyes and not on what you got on. Ain't you yourself the one what helped me with my love troubles? And now, when everything is turning out happy, you mean to tell me that you ain't going to be there?"

She gave me a grab over and kissed me in a way that I couldn't say "No" to her.

So I shined myself up in the best I had and went to the wedding.

I was in the middle from giving my congratulations to Yetta and her new husband, when—Gott! Gott im Himmel![1] The sky is falling to the earth! I see him—him, and his wife leaning on his arm, coming over.

I gave a fall back, like something sharp hit me. My head got dizzy, and my eyes got blind.

I wanted to run away from him, but, ach! everything in me rushed to him.

I was feeling like struck deaf, dumb, and blind all in one.

He must have said something to me, and I must have answered back something to him, but how? What? I only remember like in a dream my getting to the cloakroom. Such a tearing, grinding pain was dragging me down to the floor that I had to hold on to the wall not to fall.

All of a sudden I feel a pull on my arm. It was the janitor with the broom in his hand.

"Lady, are you sick? The wedding people is all gone, and I swept up already." But I couldn't wake up from myself.

"Lady, the lights is going out," he says, looking on me queer.

"I think I ain't well," I said. And I went out.

Ach, I see again the time when we was lovers! How beautiful the world was then!

"Maybe there never was such love like ours, and never will be," we was always telling one another.

When we was together there was like a light shining around us, the light

1 God! God in heaven! (Yiddish).

from his heart on mine, and from my heart on his. People began to look happy just looking on us.

When we was walking we didn't feel we was touching the earth but flying high up through the air. We looked on the rest of the people with pity, because it was seeming to us that we was the only two persons awake, and all the rest was hurrying and pushing and slaving and crowding one on the other without the splendidness of feeling for what it was all for, like we was feeling it.

David was learning for a doctor. Daytimes he went to college, and nights he was in a drugstore. I was working in a factory on shirt-waists. We was poor. But we didn't feel poor. The waists I was sewing flyed like white birds through my fingers, because his face was shining out of everything I touched.

David was always trying to learn me how to make myself over for an American. Sometimes he would spend out fifteen cents to buy me the "Ladies' Home Journal" to read about American life, and my whole head was put away on how to look neat and be up-to-date like the American girls. Till long hours in the night I used to stay up brushing and pressing my plain blue suit with the white collar what David liked, and washing my waists, and fixing up my hat like the pattern magazines show you.

On holidays he took me out for a dinner by a restaurant, to learn me how the Americans eat, with napkins, and use up so many plates—the butter by itself, and the bread by itself, and the meat by itself, and the potatoes by itself.

Always when the six o'clock whistle blowed, he was waiting for me on the corner from the shop to take me home.

"Ut, there waits Sara's doctor feller," the girls were nudging one to the other, as we went out from the shop. "Ain't she the lucky one!"

All the way as we walked along he was learning me how to throw off my greenhorn[2] talk, and say out the words in the American.

He used to stop me in the middle of the pavement and laugh from me, shaking me: "No t'ink or t'ank or t'ought, now. You're an American," he would say to me. And then he would fix my tongue and teeth together and make me say after him: "th-think, th-thank, th-thought; this, that, there." And if I said the words right, he kissed me in the hall when we got home. And if I said them wrong, he kissed me anyhow.

He moved next door to us, so we shouldn't lose the sweetness from one little minute that we could be together. There was only the thin wall between our kitchen and his room, and the first thing in the morning, we would knock in one to the other to begin the day together.

"See what I got for you, Hertzele,"[3] he said to me one day, holding up a grand printed card.

I gave a read. It was the ticket invitation for his graduation from college. I gave it a touch, with pride melting over in my heart.

"Only one week more, and you'll be a doctor for the world!"

"And then, heart of mine," he said, drawing me over to him and kissing me on the lips, "when I get my office fixed up, you will marry me?"

"Ach, such a happiness," I answered, "to be together all the time, and wait on you and cook for you, and do everything for you, like if I was your mother!"

"Uncle Rosenberg is coming special from Boston for my graduation."

"The one what helped out your chance for college?" I asked.

2. A new immigrant. 3. My heart (-le is an affectionate diminutive).

"Yes, and he's going to start me up the doctor's office, he says. Like his son he looks on me, because he only got daughters in his family.'

"Ach, the good heart! He'll yet have joy and good luck from us! What is he saying about me?" I ask.

"I want him to see you first, darling. You can't help going to his heart, when he'll only give a look on you.'

"Think only, Mammele—David is graduating for a doctor in a week!" I gave a hurry in to my mother that night. "And his Uncle Rosenberg is coming special from Boston and says he'll start him up in his doctor's office."

"Oi weh,[4] the uncle is going to give a come, you say? Look how the house looks! And the children in rags and no shoes on their feet!"

The whole week before the uncle came, my mother and I was busy nights buying and fixing up, and painting the chairs, and nailing together solid the table, and hanging up calendar pictures to cover up the broken plaster on the wall, and fixing the springs from the sleeping lounge so it didn't sink in, and scrubbing up everything, and even washing the windows, like before Passover.[5]

I stopped away from the shop, on the day David was graduating. Everything in the house was like for a holiday. The children shined up like rich people's children, with their faces washed clean and their hair brushed and new shoes on their feet. I made my father put away his black shirt and dress up in an American white shirt and starched collar. I fixed out my mother in a new white waist and a blue checked apron, and I blowed myself to dress up the baby in everything new, like a doll in a window. Her round, laughing face lighted up the house, so beautiful she was.

By the time we got finished the rush to fix ourselves out, the children's cheeks was red with excitement and our eyes was bulging bright, like ready to start for a picnic.

When David came in with his uncle, my father and mother and all the children gave a stand up.

But the "Boruch Chabo"[6] and the hot words of welcome, what was rushing from us to say, froze up on our lips by the stiff look the uncle throwed on us.

David's uncle didn't look like David. He had a thick neck and a red face and the breathing of a man what eats plenty.—But his eyes looked smart like David's.

He wouldn't take no seat and didn't seem to want to let go from the door.

David laughed and talked fast, and moved around nervous, trying to cover up the ice. But he didn't get no answers from nobody. And he didn't look in my eyes, and I was feeling myself ashamed, like I did something wrong which I didn't understand.

My father started up to say something to the uncle—"Our David—" But I quick pulled him by the sleeve to stop. And nobody after that could say nothing, nobody except David.

I couldn't get up the heart to ask them to give a taste from the cake and the wine what we made ready special for them on the table.

The baby started crying for a cake, and I quick went over to take her up, because I wanted to hide myself with being busy with her. But only the crying

4. Oh, pain (Yiddish); used as a general expression of distress or despair.
5. Because strict observance forbids the presence of even a speck of leaven in a Jew's house during the fes-

tival of Passover, a thorough cleaning is part of the preparations for the holiday.
6. Blessed is he who comes (Hebrew prayer), usually used in more elevated contexts.

and nothing else happening made my heart give a shiver, like bad luck was in the air.

And right away the uncle and him said goodbye and walked out.

When the door was shut the children gave a rush for the cakes, and then burst out in the street.

"Come, Schmuel," said my mother, "I got to say something with you." And she gave my father a pull in the other room and closed the door.

I felt they was trying not to look on me, and was shrinking away from the shame that was throwed on me.

"Och, what's the matter with me! Nothing can come between David and me. His uncle ain't everything," I said, trying to pull up my head.

I sat myself down by the table to cool down my nervousness. "Brace yourself up," I said to myself, jumping up from the chair and beginning to walk around again. "Nothing has happened. Stop off nagging yourself."

Just then I hear loud voices through the wall. I go nearer. Ut, it's his uncle!

The plaster from the wall was broken on our side by the door. "Lay your ear in this crack, and you can hear plain the words," I say to myself.

"What's getting over you? You ain't that kind to do such a thing," I say. But still I do it.

Oi weh, I hear the uncle plainly! "What's all this mean, these neighbors? Who's the pretty girl what made such eyes on you?"

"Ain't she beautiful? Do you like her?" I hear David.

"What? What's that matter to you?"

"I'll marry myself to her," says David.

"Marry! Marry yourself into that beggar house! Are you crazy?"

"A man could get to anywhere with such a beautiful girl."

"Koosh! Pretty faces is cheap like dirt. What has she got to bring you in for your future? An empty pocketbook? A starving family to hang over your neck?"

"You don't know nothing about her. You don't know what you're saying. She comes from fine people in Russia. You can see her father is a learned man."

"Ach! You make me a disgust with your calf talk! Poverty winking from every corner of the house! Hunger hollering from all their starved faces! I got too much sense to waste my love on beggars. And all the time I was planning for you an American family, people which are somebodies in this world, which could help you work up a practice! For why did I waste my good dollars on you?"

"Gott! Ain't David answering?" my heart cries out. "Why don't he throw him out of the house?"

"Perhaps I can't hear him," I think, and with my finger-nails I pick thinner the broken plaster.

I push myself back to get away and not to do it. But it did itself with my hands. "Don't let me hear nothing," I pray, and yet I strain more to hear.

The uncle was still hollering. And David wasn't saying nothing for me.

"Gazlen![7] You want to sink your life in a family of beggars?"

"But I love her. We're so happy together. Don't that count for something? I can't live without her."

"Koosh! Love her! Do you want to plan your future with your heart or with your head? Take for your wife an ignorant shopgirl without a cent! Can two dead people start up a dance together?"

7. Thief, swindler (Yiddish).

"So you mean not to help me with the office?"

"Yah-yah-yah! I'll run on all fours to do it! The impudence from such pen-niless nobodies wanting to pull in a young man with a future for a doctor! Nobody but such a yok[8] like you would be such an easy mark."

"Well, I got to live my own life, and I love her."

"That's all I got to say.—Where's my hat? Throw yourself away on the pretty face, make yourself to shame and to laughter with a ragged Melamid[9] for a father-in-law, and I wash my hands from you for the rest of your life."

A change came over David from that day. For the first time we was no more one person together. We couldn't no more laugh and talk like we used to. When I tried to look him in the eyes, he gave them a turn away from me.

I used to lie awake nights turning over in my head David's looks, David's words, and it made me frightened like something black rising over me and pushing me out from David's heart. I could feel he was blaming me for something I couldn't understand.

Once David asked me, "Don't you love me no more?"

I tried to tell him that there wasn't no change in my love but I couldn't no more talk out to him what was in my mind, like I used.

"I didn't want to worry you before with my worries," he said to me at last.

"Worry me, David! What am I here for?"

"My uncle is acting like a stingy grouch," he answered me, "and I can't stand no more his bossing me."

"Why didn't you speak yourself out to me what was on your mind, David?" I asked him.

"You don't know how my plans is smashed to pieces," he said, with a worried look on his face. "I don't see how I'll ever be able to open my doctor's office. And how can we get married with your people hanging on for your wages?"

"Ah, David, don't you no longer feel that love can find a way out?"

He looked on me, down and up, and up and down, till I crawed myself back, frightened.

But he grabbed me back to him. "I love you. I love you, heart of mine," he said, kissing me on the neck, on my hair and my eyes. "And nothing else mat-ters, does it, does it?" and he kissed me again and again, as if he wanted to swallow me up.

Next day I go out from the shop and down the steps to meet him, like on every day.

I give a look around.

"Gott! Where is he? He wasn't never late before," gave a knock my heart.

I waited out till all the girls was gone, and the streets was getting empty, but David didn't come yet.

"Maybe an accident happened to him, and I standing round here like a dummy," and I gave a quick hurry home.

But nobody had heard nothing.

"He's coming! He *must* come!" I fighted back my fear. But by evening he hadn't come yet.

I sent in my brother next door to see if he could find him.

"He moved to-day," comes in my brother to tell me.

8. Pejorative term for a non-Jew (Yiddish).
9. A teacher of elementary Hebrew; here someone incompetent or impractical (Yiddish).

"My God! David left me? It ain't possible!"

I walk around the house, waiting and listening. "Don't let nobody see your nervousness. Don't let yourself out. Don't break down."

It got late and everybody was gone to bed.

I couldn't take my clothes off. Any minute he'll come up the steps or knock on the wall. Any minute a telegram will come.

It's twelve o'clock. It's one. Two!

Every time I hear footsteps in the empty street, I am by the window—"Maybe it's him."

It's beginning the day.

The sun is rising. Oi weh, how can the sun rise and he not here?

Mein Gott! He ain't coming!

I sit myself down on the floor by the window with my head on the sill.

Everybody is sleeping. I can't sleep. And I'm so tired.

Next day I go, like pushed on, to the shop, glad to be swallowed up by my work.

The noise of the knocking machines is like a sleeping-medicine to the cryings inside of me. All day I watched my hands push the waists up and down the machine. I wasn't with my hands. It was like my breathing stopped and I was sitting inside of myself, waiting for David.

The six o'clock whistle blowed. I go out from the shop.

I can't help it—I look for him.

"Oi, Gott! Do something for me once! Send him only!"

I hold on to the iron fence of the shop, because I feel my heart bleeding away.

I can't go away. The girls all come out from the shops, and the streets get empty and still. But at the end of the block once in a while somebody crosses and goes out from sight.

I watch them. I begin counting, "One, two, three—"

Underneath my mind is saying, "Maybe it's him. Maybe the next one!"

My eyes shut themselves. I feel the end from everything.

"Ah, David! David! Gott! Mein Gott!"

I fall on the steps and clinch the stones with the twistings of my body. A terrible cry breaks out from me—"David! David!" My soul is tearing itself out from my body. It is gone.

Next day I got news—David opened a doctor's office uptown.

Nothing could hurt me no more. I didn't hope for nothing. Even if he wanted me back, I couldn't go to him no more. I was like something dying what wants to be left alone in darkness.

But still something inside of me wanted to see for itself how all is dead between us, and I write him:

"David Novak: You killed me. You killed my love. Why did you leave me yet living? Why must I yet drag on the deadness from me?"

I don't know why I wrote him. I just wanted to give a look on him. I wanted to fill up my eyes with him before I turned them away forever.

I was sitting by the table in the kitchen, wanting to sew, but my hands was lying dead on the table, when the door back of me burst open.

"O God! What have I done? Your face is like ashes! You look like you are dying!" David gave a rush in

His hair wasn't combed, his face wasn't shaved, his clothes was all wrinkled. My letter he was holding crushed in his hand.

"I killed you! I left you! But I didn't rest a minute since I went away! Heart of mine, forgive me!"

He gave a take my hand, and fell down kneeling by me.

"Sarale, speak to me!"

"False dog! Coward!" cried my father, breaking in on us. "Get up! Get out! Don't dare touch my child again! May your name and memory be blotted out!"

David covered up his head with his arm and fell back to the wall like my father had hit him.

"You yet listen to him?" cried my father, grabbing me by the arm and shaking me. "Didn't I tell you he's a Meshumid,¹ a denier of God?"

"Have pity! Speak to me! Give me only a word!" David begged me.

I wanted to speak to him, to stretch out my hands to him and call him over, but I couldn't move my body. No voice came from my lips no more than if I was locked in my grave.

I was dead, and the David I loved was dead.

I married Sam because he came along and wanted me, and I didn't care about nothing no more.

But for long after, even when the children began coming, my head was still far away in the dream of the time when love was. Before my eyes was always his face, drawing me on. In my ears was always his voice, but thin, like from far away.

I was like a person following after something in the dark.

For years when I went out into the street or got into a car, it gave a knock my heart— "Maybe I'll see him yet to-day."

When I heard he got himself engaged, I hunted up where she lived, and with Sammy in the carriage and the three other children hanging on to my skirts, I stayed around for hours to look up at the grand stone house where she lived, just to take a minute's look on her.

When I seen her go by, it stabbed awake in me the old days.

It ain't that I still love him, but nothing don't seem real to me no more. For the little while when we was lovers I breathed the air from the high places where love comes from, and I can't no more come down.

1920

1. An apostate (one who willingly renounces his or her faith).

ANNA WICKHAM

1884–1947

"I have to thank God I'm a woman," wrote Anna Wickham in a poem titled *The Affinity*, explaining with some irony that "in these ordered days a woman only / Is free to be very hungry, very lonely." That terse, sardonic couplet defines the difficult liberty that was achieved in verse by this distinctively feminist poet who has now been largely forgotten. Born in Wimbledon, just outside London, Wickham emigrated with her family to Australia at the age of six, where she was evidently raised in a freer environment than that of her English contemporaries. When she was twenty, she returned to Europe and studied opera singing in Paris, then entered into a marriage that seems to have been somewhat unsatisfactory, for, as one critic observes, she "was considered a 'rebellious' wife, a woman who lived by her

own rules." Yet her problematic marriage appears to have energized her art: after a few years of domesticity, she began to write poetry at an extraordinary pace. Her first collection was privately printed in 1911, and it was followed by three more volumes—*The Contemplative Quarry* (1915), *The Man with a Hammer* (1916), and *The Little Old House* (1921). All in all, in one four-year period of intense creative activity, she produced nine hundred poems.

Among London intellectuals of her era, Wickham was well known, especially in a circle that included the writers T. E. Hulme and D. H. Lawrence as well as the artists Gaudier-Brzeska and Jacob Epstein. Her poems are often as bitterly explicit about the impediments to female achievement as the critical writings of her contemporary Virginia Woolf. In *Dedication of the Cook*, for instance, she declares, "If any ask why there's no great She-Poet, / Let him come live with me, and he will know it." At the same time, a number of her works, like *The Affinity* (quoted earlier), celebrate the aesthetic freedom made possible by woman's status as what Woolf called an "outsider."

Meditation at Kew[1]

Alas! for all the pretty women who marry dull men,
Go into the suburbs and never come out again,
Who lose their pretty faces, and dim their pretty eyes,
Because no one has skill or courage to organize.

What do these pretty women suffer when they marry? 5
They bear a boy who is like Uncle Harry,
A girl, who is like Aunt Eliza, and not new,
These old, dull races must breed true.

I would enclose a common[2] in the sun,
And let the young wives out to laugh and run; 10
I would steal their dull clothes and go away,
And leave the pretty naked things to play.

Then I would make a contract with hard Fate
That they see all the men in the world and choose a mate,
And I would summon all the pipers in the town 15
That they dance with Love at a feast, and dance him down.

From the gay unions of choice
We'd have a race of splendid beauty, and of thrilling voice.
The World whips frank, gay love with rods,
But frankly, gayly shall we get the gods. 20

1915

The Affinity

I have to thank God I'm a woman,
For in these ordered days a woman only
Is free to be very hungry, very lonely.

1. A south London suburb. 2. A piece of land for public use; a park.

It is sad for Feminism, but still clear
That man, more often than woman, is pioneer. 5
If I would confide a new thought,
First to a man must it be brought.

Now, for our sins, it is my bitter fate
That such a man wills soon to be my mate,
And so of friendship is quick end: 10
When I have gained a love I lose a friend.

It is well within the order of things
That man should listen when his mate sings;
But the true male never yet walked
Who liked to listen when his mate talked. 15

I would be married to a full man,
As would all women since the world began;
But from a wealth of living I have proved
I must be silent, if I would be loved.

Now of my silence I have much wealth 20
I have to do my thinking all by stealth.
My thoughts may never see the day;
My mind is like a catacomb where early Christians pray.

And of my silence I have much pain,
But of these pangs I have great gain; 25
For I must take to drugs or drink,
Or I must write the things I think.

If my sex would let me speak,
I would be very lazy and most weak;
I should speak only, and the things I spoke 30
Would fill the air awhile, and clear like smoke.

The things I think now I write down,
And some day I will show them to the Town.
When I am sad I make thought clear;
I can re-read it all next year. 35

I have to thank God I'm a woman,
For in these ordered days a woman only
Is free to be very hungry, very lonely.

 1915

Divorce

A voice from the dark is calling me.
In the close house I nurse a fire.
Out in the dark, cold winds rush free,

To the rock heights of my desire.
I smother in the house in the valley below, 5
Let me out to the night, let me go, let me go!

Spirits that ride the sweeping blast,
Frozen in rigid tenderness,
Wait! For I leave the fire at last,
My little-love's warm loneliness. 10
I smother in the house in the valley below,
Let me out in the night, let me go, let me go!

High on the hills are beating drums,
Clear from a line of marching men
To the rock's edge the hero comes. 15
He calls me, and he calls again.
On the hill there is fighting, victory, or quick death,
In the house is the fire, which I fan with sick breath
I smother in the house in the valley below,
Let me out in the dark, let me go, let me go! 20

 1916

Dedication of the Cook

If any ask why there's no great She-Poet,
Let him come live with me, and he will know it:
If I'd indite an ode or mend a sonnet,
I must go choose a dish or tie a bonnet;
For she who serves in forced virginity 5
Since I am wedded will not have me free;
And those new flowers my garden is so rich in
Must die for clammy odors of my kitchen.

Yet had I chosen Dian's¹ barrenness
I'm not full woman, and I can't be less, 10
So could I state no certain truth for life,
Can I survive and be my good man's wife?

Yes! I will make the servant's cause my own
That she in pity leave me hours alone
So I will tend her mind and feed her wit 15
That she in time have her own joy of it;
And count it pride that not a sonnet's spoiled
Lacking her choice betwixt the baked and boiled.
So those young flowers my garden is so rich in 20
Will blossom from the ashes of my kitchen!

 1922

1. Diana, the Roman virgin goddess of the moon.

ELINOR WYLIE
1885–1928

During her lifetime, Elinor Wylie seemed to the writer Carl Van Doren like a "white queen"—pale, elegantly dressed, brilliantly successful, dominating the literary world with glittering poems and eloquent talk—while the critic Edmund Wilson regarded her as "one of the most steadily industrious and most productive writers of my acquaintance." Yet, more recently, at least one essayist has declared that her work "holds little interest; the poems include far too many references to goldfish, moonbeams, and snowflakes for modern taste." The woman who inspired such mixed opinions was born Elinor Hoyt in Somerville, New Jersey, the eldest of five children in a distinguished family, and her early life was marked by what one biographer calls "unruffled gentility." In 1905, at the age of twenty, she married Philip Hichborn, the son of a prominent admiral, but five years later she left him and her young son, Philip, to elope with Horace Wylie, a married lawyer seventeen years older than she. The ensuing scandal clearly altered the well-born young woman's sense of herself and of the world, imbuing her poetry with an enduring irony about society. Wylie's wife refused to grant him a divorce, and though the lovers sought anonymity in England, they were considered notorious for a number of years.

When the couple returned to the United States just after the outbreak of World War I, they were legally married in 1916, then settled in 1919 in Washington, D.C., where Horace had a government job and where Elinor began seriously to write and publish poetry with the sponsorship of a group of new friends, including the novelist Sinclair Lewis and the poet William Rose Benét. In 1912, she had had a small collection of verse, *Incidental Numbers*, privately printed in England, but she herself regarded the book as marred by "incredible immaturity." Her first really ambitious volume, therefore, was *Nets to Catch the Wind* (1921), a book that achieved instantaneous success with what the anthologist Louis Untermeyer called its "brilliance of moonlight coruscating on a plain of ice." It was followed in 1923 by an equally notable collection, *Black Armour*, and by a well-received first novel, *Jennifer Lorn: A Sedate Extravaganza*.

At around the time that *Nets to Catch the Wind* appeared, Wylie had moved to New York, where she became increasingly close to William Rose Benét, now the editor of the prestigious *Saturday Review of Literature*. In 1923, she divorced Wylie and married Benét. Though later she was to travel to England, where she resided for long periods in the late 1920s and where, as she confided to the critic Carl Van Doren, she found someone she really loved "for the first time" (the mysterious lover to whom her *Sonnets to One Person* are addressed), her marriage to Benét seems on the whole to have been a good one. She had returned to live with him just before she died of a stroke on the very day that she had finished correcting the proofs for her last collection of verse, *Angels and Earthly Creatures* (posthumously published in 1929). In addition, her years in New York had been both triumphant and productive: publishing three novels after *Jennifer Lorn*, one of which—*The Orphan Angel* (1926)—was a Book-of-the-Month Club selection, and several other collections of verse, she had become a literary personage; wealthy, beautiful, and fashionably dressed, she had also become a public personality, a friend of many key intellectuals and almost a patron saint to such younger writers as the poet Edna St. Vincent Millay, who wrote a series of moving elegies on her death.

Despite such success, however, Wylie's best poetry is marked by an austere lyricism that suggests a deeply pessimistic cast of mind. "I was, being human, born alone," she confesses in one verse, adding "I am, being woman, hard beset."

Elsewhere, moreover, she reveals a bitterly ironic consciousness that her admirers may be mythologizing her, musing that "the woman [might be] moulded by your wish." Perhaps some of the recent rejection of her work as disfigured by "too many references to goldfish [and] moonbeams" is the consequence of such mythologizing, an inability to separate the worldly glamour of the woman from the aesthetic severity of the poet.

The Eagle and the Mole

Avoid the reeking herd,
Shun the polluted flock,
Live like that stoic bird,
The eagle of the rock.

The huddled warmth of crowds 5
Begets and fosters hate;
He keeps, above the clouds,
His cliff inviolate.

When flocks are folded warm,
And herds to shelter run, 10
He sails above the storm,
He stares into the sun.

If in the eagle's track
Your sinews cannot leap,
Avoid the lathered pack, 15
Turn from the steaming sheep.

If you would keep your soul
From spotted sight or sound,
Live like the velvet mole;
Go burrow underground. 20

And there hold intercourse
With roots of trees and stones,
With rivers at their source,
And disembodied bones.

1921

Atavism[1]

I always was afraid of Somes's Pond:
Not the little pond, by which the willow stands,
Where laughing boys catch alewives[2] of in their hands
In brown, bright shallows; but the one beyond.
There, when the frost makes all the birches burn 5
Yellow as cow-lilies, and the pale sky shines

1. Recurrence in a person of genetic traits occurring several generations in the past. 2. An Atlantic fish of the herring family.

Like a polished shell between black spruce and pines,
Some strange thing tracks us, turning where we turn.

You'll say I dream it, being the true daughter
Of those who in old times endured this dread. 10
Look! Where the lily-stems are showing red
A silent paddle moves below the water,
A sliding shape has stirred them like a breath:
Tall plumes surmount a painted mask of death.

1921

Wild Peaches

1

When the world turns completely upside down
You say we'll emigrate to the Eastern Shore[1]
Aboard a river-boat from Baltimore;
We'll live among wild peach trees, miles from town,
You'll wear a coonskin cap, and I a gown 5
Homespun, dyed butternut's dark gold color.
Lost, like your lotus-eating[2] ancestor,
We'll swim in milk and honey till we drown.

The winter will be short, the summer long,
The autumn amber-hued, sunny and hot, 10
Tasting of cider and of scuppernong;[3]
All seasons sweet, but autumn best of all.
The squirrels in their silver fur will fall
Like falling leaves, like fruit, before your shot.

2

The autumn frosts will lie upon the grass 15
Like bloom on grapes of purple-brown and gold.
The misted early mornings will be cold;
The little puddles will be roofed with glass.
The sun, which burns from copper into brass,
Melts these at noon, and makes the boys unfold 20
Their knitted mufflers; full as they can hold,
Fat pockets dribble chestnuts as they pass.

Peaches grow wild, and pigs can live in clover;
A barrel of salted herrings lasts a year;
The spring begins before the winter's over. 25
By February you may find the skins
Of garter snakes and water moccasins
Dwindled and harsh, dead-white and cloudy-clear.

1. I.e., of Maryland, east of the Chesapeake Bay
2. In Homer's *Odyssey* the lotus-eaters remain in a
state of drugged contentment due to the fruit they
consume.
3. A sweet golden wine made from grapes native to
America.

3

When April pours the colors of a shell
Upon the hills, when every little creek 30
Is shot with silver from the Chesapeake
In shoals new-minted by the ocean swell,
When strawberries go begging, and the sleek
Blue plums lie open to the blackbird's beak,
We shall live well—we shall live very well. 35

The months between the cherries and the peaches
Are brimming cornucopias which spill
Fruits red and purple, somber-bloomed and black;
Then, down rich fields and frosty river beaches
We'll trample bright persimmons, while you kill 40
Bronze partridge, speckled quail, and canvasback.

4

Down to the Puritan marrow of my bones
There's something in this richness that I hate.
I love the look, austere, immaculate,
Of landscapes drawn in pearly monotones. 45
There's something in my very blood that owns
Bare hills, cold silver on a sky of slate,
A thread of water, churned to milky spate[4]
Streaming through slanted pastures fenced with stones.
I love those skies, thin blue or snowy gray, 50
Those fields sparse-planted, rendering meager sheaves:
That spring, briefer than apple-blossom's breath,
Summer, so much too beautiful to stay,
Swift autumn, like a bonfire of leaves,
And sleepy winter, like the sleep of death. 55

1921

Full Moon

My bands of silk and miniver[1]
Momently grew heavier;
The black gauze was beggarly thin;
The ermine muffled mouth and chin;
I could not suck the moonlight in. 5

Harlequin in lozenges
Of love and hate, I walked in these
Striped and ragged rigmaroles;
Along the pavement my footsoles
Trod warily on living coals. 10

4. Flood or freshet. 1. A white fur.

Shouldering the thoughts I loathed,
In their corrupt disguises clothed,
Mortality I could not tear
From my ribs, to leave them bare
Ivory in silver air. 15

There I walked, and there I raged;
The spiritual savage caged
Within my skeleton, raged afresh
To feel, behind a carnal mesh,
The clean bones crying in the flesh. 20

 1923

Let No Charitable Hope

Now let no charitable hope
Confuse my mind with images
Of eagle and of antelope:
I am in nature none of these.

I was, being human, born alone; 5
I am, being woman, hard beset;
I live by squeezing from a stone
The little nourishment I get.

In masks outrageous and austere
The years go by in single file;[1] 10
But none has merited my fear,
And none has quite escaped my smile.

 1923

From One Person[1]

XII

In our content, before the autumn came
To shower sallow droppings on the mold,
Sometimes you have permitted me to fold
Your grief in swaddling-bands, and smile to name
Yourself my infant, with an infant's claim 5
To utmost adoration as of old,
Suckled with kindness, fondled from the cold,
And loved beyond philosophy or shame.

I dreamt I was the mother of a son
Who had deserved a manger for a crib; 10

1. Possibly an echo of Ralph Waldo Emerson's poem
Days (1857): "Daughters of Time, the hypocritic
Days, / Muffled and dumb like barefoot dervishes, /
And marching single in an endless file."
1. A sonnet sequence.

Torn from your body, furbished from your rib,[2]
I am the daughter of your skeleton,
Born of your bitter and excessive pain:
I shall not dream you are my child again.

1929

To a Lady's Countenance

This unphilosophic sight;
This silly mask of silken white;
This thing which has, to hide its grief,
Less than a rose's lesser leaf;
This web a spider might have spun 5
With patience and precision;
This veil concealing sorrow's face,
Arranged with coquetry and grace,
Which shall remain, when all is said,
After sorrow itself is dead; 10
In color, a camellia flower;
In shape, a whim of the glass-blower;
The mind's eye hollowed and made blind,
But not the brow above the mind;
And, whatsoever may be starved, 15
The little lips uncut, uncarved;
God's power has disdained to mold
This clay so delicate and cold;
Perchance he took it for the flesh
Of mushrooms, or the silkworm's mesh; 20
Stuff too slight to bear the fine
Finger-tip of the divine
In lines of noble heritage;
And so, you do not show your age.

1929

Pastiche

Is not the woman molded by your wish
A cockatrice[1] of a most intricate kind?
You have, my friend, the high fantastic mind
To clasp the cold enamel of a fish
As breastplate for a bosom tigerish; 5
To make a dove a dragon; or to bind
A panther skin upon the escaping hind:
You mix ambiguous spices in your dish.

2. In the Bible God fashions Eve from one of Adam's 1. Legendary monster with the head, wings, and legs
ribs (Genesis 2:21–22). The son with a manger for a of a cock and the tail of a serpent.
crib was Jesus.

Will there remain, when thus embellished I
Sprout wings, or am by cloven heels improved, 10
An atom of the lady that you loved?
Does Christ or Lucifer seal this alchemy?
Is there not lacking from your synthesis
Someone you may occasionally miss?

1932

ISAK DINESEN
1885–1962

Isak Dinesen's writing career did not begin until she reached her late forties, when she believed that she had left her real life behind, although she would survive another thirty years to produce several brilliant volumes of short stories, as well as a fascinating autobiography, a novel, and a collection of essays. She had lost her coffee plantation in Africa, her husband, her health, and her lover when she returned to what she considered the stultifying confinement of her mother's house at Rungstedlund in Denmark. "All sorrows," she believed, "can be borne if you put them into a story or tell a story about them." And she was, by her own admission, *"une conteuse, et rien qu'une conteuse"* (a storyteller and nothing but a storyteller). As a storyteller who transformed the sorrows of her life through the sorcery of her art, she could see herself in her past youth and her future old age as a magical witch or wise sibyl.

Christened Karen Christentze Dinesen in 1885, Dinesen viewed her matrilineage with dislike, associating her mother, Ingeborg (Westenholz) Dinesen, with bourgeois practicality and puritanical morality. Tanne, as she was called, condescended to her mother and romanticized her father, Wilhelm Dinesen, as the representative of adventurous, aristocratic ancestors, erotically daring in their restless search for intense experiences in love and war. The author of *Letters from the Hunt*, Wilhelm Dinesen had fought in the Dano-Prussian War of 1864, suffered the death of his first "great passion," an eighteen-year-old cousin, and wandered as far as America. Tanne was the second of five children in the family, all of whom must have been shocked by Wilhelm Dinesen's suicide in 1895. Her father left a note admitting that, while he knew his other two daughters would fend for themselves, "my heart aches for Tanne." Certainly, the nine-year-old Tanne felt herself to be especially bereaved, and as her biographer Judith Thurman has shown, by fifteen Dinesen was obsessed with a fantasy of union with her father that would inform not only her subsequent relationships with men but also her sense of herself as an artist.

Educated in the schoolroom at Rungstedlund with her two sisters while her brothers were sent to boarding school, Dinesen wrote witty essays on Danish proverbs and the French Revolution, plays in which she took the part of Pierrot, and fantasies in which she was a romantic Lord Byron. In 1899, she went with her sisters and mother to Switzerland, where the girls entered the École Bénét and where Dinesen began painting. Although after this her formal education was supposed to be complete, back at home she read the plays of Shakespeare, the poetry of Heine and Shelley, and the novels of Laurence Sterne, as well as Danish writers like the novelist Meïr Aaron Goldschmidt, the lyricist Johannes Ewald, and the storyteller Hans Christian Andersen. Over the objections of her family, moreover, she left for Copenhagen to enroll in the private art classes girls had to take for admission into the Royal Academy of Fine Arts. In 1904, she began work on a group

of tales called *Likely Stories*, two of which were published in the Danish journal *Tilskueren* under the pseudonym Osceola, chosen to commemorate a rebellious leader of the Seminole Indians.

After five semesters at the Royal Academy, Dinesen returned home and fell in love with Hans Blixen-Finecke, a distant and dashing cousin on her father's side. When he did not respond, she married his twin brother, Bror, and convinced her family to support Bror's purchase of several hundred acres of land for a coffee plantation near Nairobi. Embarking in 1913 on the thirteen-day passage to British East Africa, neither Bror nor Tanne knew that the acreage was too acidic and too high in altitude for successful coffee growing. In *Out of Africa* (1937), Dinesen described the beauty of the Ngong hills around Nairobi, the dignified customs of the Masai and the Somali, her passionate love of safari life, and her enjoyment at playing the role of the aristocratic baroness to intelligent servants like Farah Aden, her steward. "Here I am where I ought to be," she explained. But, as a pastoral, *Out of Africa* is reticent about the personal problems she confronted on the farm.

The worst of these presented itself as a recurrent malady that she diagnosed as malaria, although it turned out to be syphilis contracted from her husband. Though she managed to treat her symptoms during a trip to Copenhagen in 1910, the disease would recur throughout her life, causing her repeated "lumbago," shooting pains "like a toothache" in her ears, and spinal degeneration. While she had no desire to separate from Bror, she soon fell in love with another adventurous aristocrat, the handsome, thirty-two-year-old Denys Finch-Hatton. Son of the earl of Winchilsea and Nottingham, Finch-Hatton had become a farmer, trader, flyer, and safari leader in East Africa in 1912, after an Eton and Oxford education. For a while, her lover and her husband shared a bedroom at Ngong, each using it while the other was on safari. But Bror began an affair with a woman he would eventually marry, and by 1922 Tanne had to agree to the divorce he wanted. For ten years, the woman who relished being called "The Lioness" managed the farm alone, although her visiting brother Thomas helped her face the droughts, fires, and disappointing harvests that eventually made it impossible for her to stay. Just before Dinesen's departure, in 1931, Finch-Hatton died in a plane crash and was buried in the Ngong hills.

Dinesen had begun reading Rudyard Kipling, Oscar Wilde, and Robert Louis Stevenson on the African farm, where she also wrote romances for her lover. On her return to Denmark, when she had to rescue herself from bankruptcy, she chose to write in Finch-Hatton's language to distance herself from her Danish surroundings, just as she used the pseudonym Isak, "the one who laughs," to cope with her sorrow. In *Seven Gothic Tales* (1934) and *Winter Tales* (1942), she focused with ironic wit on the charades and masquerades that liberate the self from the constraints of a fixed identity. Similarly, she created a myth of herself through her extravagant costumes, a gown that she named Sappho, for example, or a suit she called Sober Truth. Identifying her disease with her fallen father, whose suicide, she had reason to believe, was related to a case of syphilis, she considered "it was worth while having syphilis in order to become a Baroness." As one of the last representatives of the aristocratic spirit, then, she saw herself as a quixotic rebel opposed to a dreary bourgeois realism. In her later years, she was active in Danish intellectual life as a patroness of avant-garde artists, as a hostess of a lively salon, and as a speaker on the radio. Like many of the characters in her parables and fables, Dinesen delighted in her personal and artistic power even in the bleakest of historical moments.

Between the appearance of her thriller *The Angelic Avengers* (1944), published under the pseudonym Pierre Andrezel, and her next volume of stories, *Last Tales* (1957), Dinesen suffered from the syphilis, which was now beyond treatment. Nevertheless, with the help of her companion and secretary, Clara Svendsen, she continued to travel—to America in 1959, for instance, where her books were

greeted enthusiastically by admirers like Carson McCullers. After an operation on her spinal cord, and another on her stomach, however, Dinesen would never again weigh more than eighty-five pounds. "The doctor tells me that I have all the symptoms of a concentration camp prisoner," she explained during the time she lived on asparagus, fruit juice, oysters, and dry biscuits. She died of malnutrition.

The Blank Page

By the ancient city gate sat an old coffee-brown, black-veiled woman who made her living by telling stories.

She said:

"You want a tale, sweet lady and gentleman? Indeed I have told many tales, one more than a thousand,[1] since that time when I first let young men tell me, myself, tales of a red rose, two smooth lily buds, and four silky, supple, deadly entwining snakes. It was my mother's mother, the black-eyed dancer, the often-embraced, who in the end—wrinkled like a winter apple and crouching beneath the mercy of the veil—took upon herself to teach me the art of story-telling. Her own mother's mother had taught it to her, and both were better story-tellers than I am. But that, by now, is of no consequence, since to the people they and I have become one, and I am most highly honored because I have told stories for two hundred years."

Now if she is well paid and in good spirits, she will go on.

"With my grandmother," she said, "I went through a hard school. 'Be loyal to the story,' the old hag would say to me. 'Be eternally and unswervingly loyal to the story.' 'Why must I be that, Grandmother?' I asked her. 'Am I to furnish you with reasons, baggage?' she cried. 'And you mean to be a story-teller! Why, you are to become a story-teller, and I shall give you my reasons! Hear then: Where the story-teller is loyal, eternally and unswervingly loyal to the story, there, in the end, silence will speak. Where the story has been betrayed, silence is but emptiness. But we, the faithful, when we have spoken our last word, will hear the voice of silence. Whether a small snotty lass understands it or not.'

"Who then," she continues, "tells a finer tale than any of us? Silence does. And where does one read a deeper tale than upon the most perfectly printed page of the most precious book? Upon the blank page. When a royal and gallant pen, in the moment of its highest inspiration, has written down its tale with the rarest ink of all—where, then, may one read a still deeper, sweeter, merrier and more cruel tale than that? Upon the blank page."

The old beldame[2] for a while says nothing, only giggles a little and munches with her toothless mouth.

"We," she says at last, "the old women who tell stories, we know the story of the blank page. But we are somewhat averse to telling it, for it might well, among the uninitiated, weaken our own credit. All the same, I am going to make an exception with you, my sweet and pretty lady and gentleman of the generous hearts. I shall tell it to you."

1. A reference to *The Thousand and One Nights*, a collection of Arabian tales told by Scheherezade, a bride trying to delay her execution at the hands of her husband, the Sultan.
2. Woman.

High up in the blue mountains of Portugal there stands an old convent for sisters of the Carmelite order, which is an illustrious and austere order. In ancient times the convent was rich, the sisters were all noble ladies, and miracles took place there. But during the centuries highborn ladies grew less keen on fasting and prayer, the great dowries flowed scantily into the treasury of the convent, and today the few portionless[3] and humble sisters live in but one wing of the vast crumbling structure, which looks as if it longed to become one with the gray rock itself. Yet they are still a blithe and active sisterhood. They take much pleasure in their holy meditations, and will busy themselves joyfully with that one particular task which did once, long, long ago, obtain for the convent a unique and strange privilege: they grow the finest flax and manufacture the most exquisite linen of Portugal.

The long field below the convent is plowed with gentle-eyed, milk-white bullocks, and the seed is skillfully sown out by labor-hardened virginal hands with mold under the nails. At the time when the flax field flowers, the whole valley becomes air-blue, the very color of the apron which the blessed virgin put on to go out and collect eggs within St. Anne's poultry yard, the moment before the Archangel Gabriel in mighty wing-strokes lowered himself onto the threshold of the house, and while high, high up a dove, neck-feathers raised and wings vibrating, stood like a small clear silver star in the sky. During this month the villagers many miles round raise their eyes to the flax field and ask one another: "Has the convent been lifted into heaven? Or have our good little sisters succeeded in pulling down heaven to them?"

Later in due course the flax is pulled, scutched and hackled;[4] thereafter the delicate thread is spun, and the linen woven, and at the very end the fabric is laid out on the grass to bleach, and is watered time after time, until one may believe that snow has fallen round the convent walls. All this work is gone through with precision and piety and with such sprinklings and litanies as are the secret of the convent. For these reasons the linen, baled high on the backs of small gray donkeys and sent out through the convent gate, downwards and ever downwards to the towns, is as flower-white, smooth and dainty as was my own little foot when, fourteen years old, I had washed it in the brook to go to a dance in the village.

Diligence, dear Master and Mistress, is a good thing, and religion is a good thing, but the very first germ of a story will come from some mystical place outside the story itself. Thus does the linen of the Convento Velho draw its true virtue from the fact that the very first linseed was brought home from the Holy Land itself by a crusader.

In the Bible, people who can read may learn about the lands of Lecha and Maresha, where flax is grown. I myself cannot read, and have never seen this book of which so much is spoken. But my grandmother's grandmother as a little girl was the pet of an old Jewish rabbi, and the learning she received from him has been kept and passed on in our family. So you will read, in the book of Joshua, of how Achsah the daughter of Caleb lighted from her ass and cried unto her father: "Give me a blessing! For thou hast now given me land; give me also the blessing of springs of water!" And he gave her the upper springs and the nether springs.[5] And in the fields of Lecha and Maresha lived, later on,

3. Without dowries.
4. Beaten and combed.
5. Joshua 15:18–19.

the families of them that wrought the finest linen of all. Our Portuguese crusader, whose own ancestors had once been great linen weavers of Tomar, as he rode through these same fields was struck by the quality of the flax, and so tied a bag of seeds to the pommel of his saddle.

From this circumstance originated the first privilege of the convent, which was to procure bridal sheets for all the young princesses of the royal house.

I will inform you, dear lady and gentleman, that in the country of Portugal in very old and noble families a venerable custom has been observed. On the morning after the wedding of a daughter of the house, and before the morning gift had yet been handed over, the Chamberlain or High Steward from a balcony of the palace would hang out the sheet of the night and would solemnly proclaim: *Virginem eam tenemus*—"we declare her to have been a virgin." Such a sheet was never afterwards washed or again lain on.

This time-honored custom was nowhere more strictly upheld than within the royal house itself, and it has there subsisted till within living memory.

Now for many hundred years the convent in the mountains, in appreciation of the excellent quality of the linen delivered, has held its second high privilege: that of receiving back that central piece of the snow-white sheet which bore witness to the honor of a royal bride.

In the tall main wing of the convent, which overlooks an immense landscape of hills and valleys, there is a long gallery with a black-and-white marble floor. On the walls of the gallery, side by side, hangs a long row of heavy, gilt frames, each of them adorned with a coroneted plate of pure gold, on which is engraved the name of a princess: Donna Christina, Donna Ines, Donna Jacintha Lenora, Donna Maria. And each of these frames encloses a square cut from a royal wedding sheet.

Within the faded markings of the canvases people of some imagination and sensibility may read all the signs of the zodiac: the Scales, the Scorpion, the Lion, the Twins. Or they may there find pictures from their own world of ideas: a rose, a heart, a sword—or even a heart pierced through with a sword.

In days of old it would occur that a long, stately, richly colored procession wound its way through the stone-gray mountain scenery, upwards to the convent. Princesses of Portugal, who were now queens or queen dowagers of foreign countries, Archduchesses, or Electresses, with their splendid retinue, proceeded here on a pilgrimage which was by nature both sacred and secretly gay. From the flax field upwards the road rises steeply; the royal-lady would have to descend from her coach to be carried this last bit of the way in a palanquin[6] presented to the convent for the very same purpose.

Later on, up to our own day, it has come to pass—as it comes to pass when a sheet of paper is being burnt, that after all other sparks have run along the edge and died away, one last clear little spark will appear and hurry along after them—that a very old highborn spinster undertakes the journey to Convento Velho. She has once, a long long time ago, been playmate, friend and maid-of-honor to a young princess of Portugal. As she makes her way to the convent she looks round to see the view widen to all sides. Within the building a sister conducts her to the gallery and to the plate bearing the name of the princess she has once served, and there takes leave of her, aware of her wish to be alone.

Slowly, slowly a row of recollections passes through the small, venerable,

6. Enclosed litter carried on poles.

skull-like head under its mantilla[7] of black lace, and it nods to them in amicable recognition. The loyal friend and confidante looks back upon the young bride's elevated married life with the elected royal consort. She takes stock of happy events and disappointments—coronations and jubilees, court intrigues and wars, the birth of heirs to the throne, the alliances of younger generations of princes and princesses, the rise or decline of dynasties. The old lady will remember how once, from the markings on the canvas, omens were drawn; now she will be able to compare the fulfillment to the omen, sighing a little and smiling a little. Each separate canvas with its coroneted name-plate has a story to tell, and each has been set up in loyalty to the story.

But in the midst of the long row there hangs a canvas which differs from the others. The frame of it is as fine and as heavy as any, and as proudly as any carries the golden plate with the royal crown. But on this one plate no name is inscribed, and the linen within the frame is snow-white from corner to corner, a blank page.

I beg of you, you good people who want to hear stories told: look at this page, and recognize the wisdom of my grandmother and of all old story-telling women!

For with what eternal and unswerving loyalty has not this canvas been inserted in the row! The story-tellers themselves before it draw their veils over their faces and are dumb. Because the royal papa and mama who once ordered this canvas to be framed and hung up, had they not had the tradition of loyalty in their blood, might have left it out.

It is in front of this piece of pure white linen that the old princesses of Portugal—worldly wise, dutiful, long-suffering queens, wives and mothers—and their noble old playmates, bridesmaids and maids-of-honor have most often stood still.

It is in front of the blank page that old and young nuns, with the Mother Abbess herself, sink into deepest thought.

1957

7. A light shawl (mantle).

RADCLYFFE HALL
1886–1943

Una, Lady Troubridge, who was Radclyffe Hall's lover for twenty-seven years, supplied in her biography (1945) most of the scanty facts we have about the early life of this pioneering lesbian novelist. Marguerite Radclyffe-Hall was born in Bournemouth, Hampshire. She was neglected by her father, who left the family when she was three, and alienated from her American-born mother, who remarried an Italian singing teacher as insensitive to her daughter as she was. By the time she attended day schools and, for one year, King's College, Radclyffe Hall was calling herself "Peter" or "John," as if to express her desire to forge a new sexual identity for herself. At twenty-one, she inherited a fortune from the Radclyffe-Hall Trust, and moved to Kensington with the only affectionate relative she had ever known, her maternal grandmother. Six years later, she began the affair that would really provide her education. Mabel Veronica Batten ("Ladye") was a cultivated patroness of music. Twenty-three years older than Hall, she encouraged her young

lover to relinquish sports for more intellectual pursuits, horses and dogs for books. After the death of Ladye in 1916, Hall turned to Una Troubridge for consolation, and they lived together for the rest of Hall's life.

Handsome in her tweed suits and cropped hair, Radclyffe Hall had published several volumes of verse and two novels before *Adam's Breed* (1926) won the Femina Vie Heureuse Prize and the James Tait Black Memorial Book Prize. But she became famous because of the trial and scandal that greeted her next book, *The Well of Loneliness* (1928). Introduced by the psychologist Havelock Ellis, Radclyffe Hall's novel focused on a heroine named Stephen Gordon, a girl brought up by a father who wanted a boy. Stephen lives and loves heroically, engaging in passionate affairs with other women and working in the London Ambulance Column during World War I. Feeling herself to be a man trapped in a female body, however, she suffers the frustrations of the "congenital invert." Through its reliance on this concept of the "invert," *The Well of Loneliness* presents lesbianism as a biological tragedy and has, therefore, been criticized by a number of contemporary historians of lesbian culture. Yet it nevertheless protests against the persecution of lesbians with unusual explicitness, even as it presents a broodingly attractive portrait of a young woman who aspires to the courage and verve she associates with masculinity. Although Radclyffe Hall responded to the banning of *The Well of Loneliness* in England by going on to write several religious novels, her contribution to literary history is still measured by her portrait of the conflicted but androgynous Stephen, who seems "to combine the strength of a man with the gentler and more subtle strength of a woman." *Miss Ogilvy Finds Herself* meditates on the same themes that inform Hall's lesbian classic.

Miss Ogilvy Finds Herself

Miss Ogilvy stood on the quay at Calais and surveyed the disbanding of her Unit, the Unit that together with the coming of war[1] had completely altered the complexion of her life, at all events for three years.

Miss Ogilvy's thin, pale lips were set sternly and her forehead was puckered in an effort of attention, in an effort to memorize every small detail of every old war-weary battered motor on whose side still appeared the merciful emblem[2] that had set Miss Ogilvy free.

Miss Ogilvy's mind was jerking a little, trying to regain its accustomed balance, trying to readjust itself quickly to this sudden and paralyzing change. Her tall, awkward body with its queer look of strength, its broad, flat bosom and thick legs and ankles, as though in response to her jerking mind, moved uneasily, rocking backwards and forwards. She had this trick of rocking on her feet in moments of controlled agitation. As usual, her hands were thrust deep into her pockets, they seldom seemed to come out of her pockets unless it were to light a cigarette, and as though she were still standing firm under fire while the wounded were placed in her ambulances, she suddenly straddled her legs very slightly and lifted her head and listened. She was standing firm under fire at that moment, the fire of a desperate regret.

Some girls came towards her, young, tired-looking creatures whose eyes were too bright from long strain and excitement. They had all been members of that glorious Unit, and they still wore the queer little forage-caps[3] and the

1. World War I, in 1914.
2. A Red Cross symbol of the ambulance corps.
3. Caps worn by infantry soldiers

short, clumsy tunics of the French Militaire. They still slouched in walking and smoked Caporals in emulation of the Poilus.[4] Like their founder and leader these girls were all English, but like her they had chosen to serve England's ally, fearlessly thrusting right up to the trenches in search of the wounded and dying. They had seen some fine things in the course of three years, not the least fine of which was the cold, hard-faced woman who, commanding, domineering, even hectoring at times, had yet been possessed of so dauntless a courage and of so insistent a vitality that it vitalized the whole Unit.

"It's rotten!" Miss Ogilvy heard someone saying. "It's rotten, this breaking up of our Unit!" And the high, rather childish voice of the speaker sounded perilously near to tears.

Miss Ogilvy looked at the girl almost gently, and it seemed, for a moment, as though some deep feeling were about to find expression in words. But Miss Ogilvy's feelings had been held in abeyance so long that they seldom dared become vocal, so she merely said "Oh?" on a rising inflection—her method of checking emotion.

They were swinging the ambulance cars in midair, those of them that were destined to go back to England, swinging them up like sacks of potatoes, then lowering them with much clanging of chains to the deck of the waiting steamer. The porters were shoving and shouting and quarreling, pausing now and again to make meaningless gestures; while a pompous official was becoming quite angry as he pointed at Miss Ogilvy's own special car—it annoyed him, it was bulky and difficult to move.

"Bon Dieu! Mais dépêchez-vous donc!"[5] he bawled, as though he were bullying the motor.

Then Miss Ogilvy's heart gave a sudden, thick thud to see this undignified, pitiful ending; and she turned and patted the gallant old car as though she were patting a well-beloved horse, as though she would say: "Yes, I know how it feels—never mind, we'll go down together."

2

Miss Ogilvy sat in the railway carriage on her way from Dover to London. The soft English landscape sped smoothly past: small homesteads, small churches, small pastures, small lanes with small hedges; all small like England itself, all small like Miss Ogilvy's future. And sitting there still arrayed in her tunic, with her forage-cap resting on her knees, she was conscious of a sense of complete frustration; thinking less of those glorious years at the Front and of all that had gone to the making of her, than of all that had gone to the marring of her from the days of her earliest childhood.

She saw herself as a queer little girl, aggressive and awkward because of her shyness; a queer little girl who loathed sisters and dolls, preferring the stable-boys as companions, preferring to play with footballs and tops, and occasional catapults. She saw herself climbing the tallest beech trees, arrayed in old breeches illicitly come by. She remembered insisting with tears and some temper that her real name was William and not Wilhelmina. All these childish pretences and illusions she remembered, and the bitterness that came after.

4. French soldiers.　　　　　　5. Good God! Move along, then! (French).

For Miss Ogilvy had found as her life went on that in this world it is better to be one with the herd, that the world has no wish to understand those who cannot conform to its stereotyped pattern. True enough, in her youth she had gloried in her strength, lifting weights, swinging clubs and developing muscles, but presently this had grown irksome to her; it had seemed to lead nowhere, she being a woman, and then as her mother had often protested: muscles looked so appalling in evening dress—a young girl ought not to have muscles.

Miss Ogilvy's relation to the opposite sex was unusual and at that time added much to her worries, for no less than three men had wished to propose, to the genuine amazement of the world and her mother. Miss Ogilvy's instinct made her like and trust men, for whom she had a pronounced fellow-feeling; she would always have chosen them as her friends and companions in preference to girls or women; she would dearly have loved to share in their sports, their business, their ideas and their wide-flung interests. But men had not wanted her, except the three who had found in her strangeness a definite attraction, and those would-be suitors she had actually feared, regarding them with aversion. Towards young girls and women she was shy and respectful, apologetic and sometimes admiring. But their fads and their foibles, none of which she could share, while amusing her very often in secret, set her outside the sphere of their intimate lives, so that in the end she must blaze a lone trail through the difficulties of her nature.

"I can't understand you," her mother had said, "you're a very odd creature—now when I was your age . . ."

And her daughter had nodded, feeling sympathetic. There were two younger girls who also gave trouble, though in their case the trouble was fighting for husbands who were scarce enough even in those days. It was finally decided, at Miss Ogilvy's request, to allow her to leave the field clear for her sisters. She would remain in the country with her father when the others went up for the Season.[6]

Followed long, uneventful years spent in sport, while Sarah and Fanny toiled, sweated and gambled in the matrimonial market. Neither ever succeeded in netting a husband, and when the Squire died leaving very little money, Miss Ogilvy found to her great surprise that they looked upon her as a brother. They had so often jibed at her in the past, that at first she could scarcely believe her senses, but before very long it became all too real: she it was who must straighten out endless muddles, who must make the dreary arrangements for the move, who must find a cheap but genteel house in London and, once there, who must cope with the family accounts which she only, it seemed, could balance.

It would be: "You might see to that, Wilhelmina; you write, you've got such a good head for business." Or: "I wish you'd go down and explain to that man that we really can't pay his account till next quarter." Or: "This money for the grocer is five shillings short. Do run over my sum, Wilhelmina."

Her mother, grown feeble, discovered in this daughter a staff upon which she could lean with safety. Miss Ogilvy genuinely loved her mother, and was therefore quite prepared to be leaned on; but when Sarah and Fanny began to lean too with the full weight of endless neurotic symptoms incubated in resentful virginity, Miss Ogilvy found herself staggering a little. For Sarah and

6. The social season.

Fanny were grown hard to bear, with their mania for telling their symptoms to doctors, with their unstable nerves and their acrid tongues and the secret dislike they now felt for their mother. Indeed, when old Mrs. Ogilvy died, she was unmourned except by her eldest daughter who actually felt a void in her life— the unforeseen void that the ailing and weak will not infrequently leave behind them.

At about this time an aunt also died, bequeathing her fortune to her niece Wilhelmina who, however, was too weary to gird up her loins and set forth in search of exciting adventure—all she did was to move her protesting sisters to a little estate she had purchased in Surrey. This experiment was only a partial success, for Miss Ogilvy failed to make friends of her neighbors; thus at fifty-five she had grown rather dour, as is often the way with shy, lonely people.

When the war came she had just begun settling down—people do settle down in their fifty-sixth year—she was feeling quite glad that her hair was gray, that the garden took up so much of her time, that, in fact, the beat of her blood was slowing. But all this was changed when war was declared; on that day Miss Ogilvy's pulses throbbed wildly.

"My God! If only I were a man!" she burst out, as she glared at Sarah and Fanny, "if only I had been born a man!" Something in her was feeling deeply defrauded.

Sarah and Fanny were soon knitting socks and mittens and mufflers and Jaeger trench-helmets.[7] Other ladies were busily working at depots, making swabs at the Squire's, or splints at the Parson's; but Miss Ogilvy scowled and did none of these things—she was not at all like other ladies.

For nearly twelve months she worried officials with a view to getting a job out in France—not in their way but in hers, and that was the trouble. She wished to go up to the front-line trenches, she wished to be actually under fire, she informed the harassed officials.

To all her enquiries she received the same answer: "We regret that we cannot accept your offer." But once thoroughly roused she was hard to subdue, for her shyness had left her as though by magic.

Sarah and Fanny shrugged angular shoulders: "There's plenty of work here at home," they remarked, "though of course it's not quite so melodramatic!"

"Oh . . . ?" queried their sister on a rising note of impatience—and she promptly cut off her hair: "That'll jar them!" she thought with satisfaction.

Then she went up to London, formed her admirable unit and finally got it accepted by the French, despite renewed opposition.

In London she had found herself quite at her ease, for many another of her kind was in London doing excellent work for the nation. It was really surprising how many cropped heads had suddenly appeared as it were out of space; how many Miss Ogilvies, losing their shyness, had come forward asserting their right to serve, asserting their claim to attention.

There followed those turbulent years at the front, full of courage and hardship and high endeavor; and during those years Miss Ogilvy forgot the bad joke that Nature seemed to have played her. She was given the rank of a French lieutenant and she lived in a kind of blissful illusion; appalling reality lay on all sides and yet she managed to live in illusion. She was competent, fearless, devoted and untiring. What then? Could any man hope to do better?

7. Woolen caps worn in the trenches, where much of World War I was fought.

She was nearly fifty-eight, yet she walked with a stride, and at times she even swaggered a little.

Poor Miss Ogilvy sitting so glumly in the train with her manly trench-boots and her forage-cap! Poor all the Miss Ogilvies back from the war with their tunics, their trench-boots, and their childish illusions. Wars come and wars go but the world does not change: it will always forget an indebtedness which it thinks it expedient not to remember.

3

When Miss Ogilvy returned to her home in Surrey it was only to find that her sisters were ailing from the usual imaginary causes, and this to a woman who had seen the real thing was intolerable, so that she looked with distaste at Sarah and then at Fanny. Fanny was certainly not prepossessing, she was suffering from a spurious attack of hay fever.

"Stop sneezing!" commanded Miss Ogilvy, in the voice that had so much impressed the Unit. But as Fanny was not in the least impressed, she naturally went on sneezing.

Miss Ogilvy's desk was piled mountain-high with endless tiresome letters and papers: circulars, bills, months-old correspondence, the gardener's accounts, an agent's report on some fields that required land-draining. She seated herself before this collection; then she sighed, it all seemed so absurdly trivial.

"Will you let your hair grow again?" Fanny enquired . . . she and Sarah had followed her into the study. "I'm certain the Vicar would be glad if you did."

"Oh?" murmured Miss Ogilvy, rather too blandly.

"Wilhelmina!"

"Yes?"

"You will do it, won't you?"

"Do what?"

"Let your hair grow; we all wish you would."

"Why should I?"

"Oh, well, it will look less odd, especially now that the war is over—in a small place like this people notice such things."

"I entirely agree with Fanny," announced Sarah.

Sarah had become very self-assertive, no doubt through having mismanaged the estate during the years of her sister's absence. They had quite a heated dispute one morning over the south herbaceous border.

"Whose garden is this?" Miss Ogilvy asked sharply. "I insist on auricula-eyed sweet Williams! I even took the trouble to write from France, but it seems that my letter has been ignored."

"Don't shout," rebuked Sarah, "you're not in France now!"

Miss Ogilvy could gladly have boxed her ears: "I only wish to God I were," she muttered.

Another dispute followed close on its heels, and this time it happened to be over the dinner. Sarah and Fanny were living on weeds—at least that was the way Miss Ogilvy put it.

"We've become vegetarians," Sarah said grandly.

"You've become two damn tiresome cranks!" snapped their sister.

Now it never had been Miss Ogilvy's way to indulge in acid recriminations,

but somehow, these days, she forgot to say: "Oh?" quite so often as expediency demanded. It may have been Fanny's perpetual sneezing that had got on her nerves; or it may have been Sarah, or the gardener, or the Vicar, or even the canary; though it really did not matter very much what it was just so long as she found a convenient peg upon which to hang her growing irritation.

"This won't do at all," Miss Ogilvy thought sternly, "life's not worth so much fuss, I must pull myself together." But it seemed this was easier said than done; not a day passed without her losing her temper and that over some trifle: "No, this won't do at all—it just mustn't be," she thought sternly.

Everyone pitied Sarah and Fanny: "Such a dreadful, violent old thing," said the neighbors.

But Sarah and Fanny had their revenge: "Poor darling, it's shell shock,[8] you know," they murmured.

Thus Miss Ogilvy's prowess was whittled away until she herself was beginning to doubt it. Had she ever been that courageous person who had faced death in France with such perfect composure? Had she ever stood tranquilly under fire, without turning a hair, while she issued her orders? Had she ever been treated with marked respect? She herself was beginning to doubt it.

Sometimes she would see an old member of the Unit, a girl who, more faithful to her than the others, would take the trouble to run down to Surrey. These visits, however, were seldom enlivening.

"Oh, well . . . here we are . . ." Miss Ogilvy would mutter.

But one day the girl smiled and shook her blond head: "I'm not—I'm going to be married."

Strange thoughts had come to Miss Ogilvy, unbidden, thoughts that had stayed for many an hour after the girl's departure. Alone in her study she had suddenly shivered, feeling a sense of complete desolation. With cold hands she had lighted a cigarette.

"I must be ill or something," she had mused, as she stared at her trembling fingers.

After this she would sometimes cry out in her sleep, living over in dreams God knows what emotions; returning, maybe to the battlefield of France. Her hair turned snow-white; it was not unbecoming yet she fretted about it.

"I'm growing very old," she would sigh as she brushed her thick mop before the glass; and then she would peer at her wrinkles.

For now that it had happened she hated being old; it no longer appeared such an easy solution of those difficulties that had always beset her. And this she resented most bitterly, so that she became the prey of self-pity, and of other undesirable states in which the body will torment the mind, and the mind, in its turn, the body. Then Miss Ogilvy straightened her ageing back, in spite of the fact that of late it had ached with muscular rheumatism, and she faced herself squarely and came to a resolve.

"I'm off!" she announced abruptly one day; and that evening she packed her kit-bag.

4

Near the south coast of Devon there exists a small island that is still very little known to the world, but which nevertheless can boast an hotel, the only

8. A mental illness suffered by some soldiers during World War I, brought on by combat experience (i.e., post-traumatic stress disorder).

building upon it. Miss Ogilvy had chosen this place quite at random, it was marked on her map by scarcely more than a dot, but somehow she had liked the look of that dot and had set forth alone to explore it.

She found herself standing on the mainland one morning looking at a vague blur of green through the mist, a vague blur of green that rose out of the Channel like a tidal wave suddenly suspended. Miss Ogilvy was filled with a sense of adventure; she had not felt like this since the ending of war.

"I was right to come here, very right indeed. I'm going to shake off all my troubles," she decided.

A fisherman's boat was parting the mist, and before it was properly beached, in she bundled.

"I hope they're expecting me?" she said gaily.

"They du be expecting you," the man answered.

The sea, which is generally rough off that coast, was indulging itself in an oily ground-swell; the broad, glossy swells struck the side of the boat, then broke and sprayed over Miss Ogilvy's ankles.

The fisherman grinned: "Feeling all right?" he queried. "It du be tiresome most times about these parts." But the mist had suddenly drifted away and Miss Ogilvy was staring wide-eyed at the island.

She saw a long shoal of jagged black rocks, and between them the curve of a small sloping beach, and above that the lift of the island itself, and above that again, blue heaven. Near the beach stood the little two-storied hotel which was thatched, and built entirely of timber; for the rest she could make out no signs of life apart from a host of white sea-gulls.

Then Miss Ogilvy said a curious thing. She said: "On the south-west side of that place there was once a cave—a very large cave. I remember that it was some way from the sea."

"There du be a cave still," the fisherman told her, "but it's just above high-water level."

"A-ah," murmured Miss Ogilvy thoughtfully, as though to herself; then she looked embarrassed.

The little hotel proved both comfortable and clean, the hostess both pleasant and comely. Miss Ogilvy started unpacking her bag, changed her mind and went for a stroll round the island. The island was covered with turf and thistles and traversed by narrow green paths thick with daisies. It had four rock-bound coves of which the south-western was by far the most difficult of access. For just here the island descended abruptly as though it were hurtling down to the water; and just here the shale was most treacherous and the tide-swept rocks most aggressively pointed. Here it was that the seagulls, grown fearless of man by reason of his absurd limitations, built their nests on the ledges and reared countless young who multiplied, in their turn, every season. Yes, and here it was that Miss Ogilvy, greatly marveling, stood and stared across at a cave; much too near the crumbling edge for her safety, but by now completely indifferent to caution.

"I remember . . . I remember . . ." she kept repeating. Then: "That's all very well, but what do I remember?"

She was conscious of somehow remembering all wrong, of her memory being distorted and colored—perhaps by the endless things she had seen since her eyes had last rested upon that cave. This worried her sorely, far more than the fact that she should be remembering the cave at all, she who had never set foot on the island before that actual morning. Indeed, except for the sense of

wrongness when she struggled to piece her memories together, she was steeped in a very profound contentment which surged over her spirit, wave upon wave.

"It's extremely odd," pondered Miss Ogilvy. Then she laughed, so pleased did she feel with its oddness.

<div align="center">5</div>

That night after supper she talked to her hostess who was only too glad, it seemed, to be questioned. She owned the whole island and was proud of the fact, as she very well might be, decided her boarder. Some curious things had been found on the island, according to comely Mrs. Nanceskivel: bronze arrow-heads, pieces of ancient stone celts;[9] and once they had dug up a man's skull and thigh-bone—this had happened while they were sinking a well. Would Miss Ogilvy care to have a look at the bones? They were kept in a cupboard in the scullery.

Miss Ogilvy nodded.

"Then I'll fetch him this moment," said Mrs. Nanceskivel, briskly.

In less than two minutes she was back with the box that contained those poor remnants of a man, and Miss Ogilvy, who had risen from her chair, was gazing down at those remnants. As she did so her mouth was sternly compressed, but her face and her neck flushed darkly.

Mrs. Nanceskivel was pointing to the skull: "Look, miss, he was killed," she remarked rather proudly, "and they tell me that the axe that killed him was bronze. He's thousands and thousands of years old, they tell me. Our local doctor knows a lot about such things and he wants me to send these bones to an expert; they ought to belong to the Nation, he says. But I know what would happen, they'd come digging up my island, and I won't have people digging up my island, I've got enough worry with the rabbits as it is." But Miss Ogilvy could no longer hear the words for the pounding of the blood in her temples.

She was filled with a sudden, inexplicable fury against the innocent Mrs. Nanceskivel: "You . . . you . . ." she began, then checked herself, fearful of what she might say to the woman.

For her sense of outrage was overwhelming as she stared at those bones that were kept in the scullery; moreover, she knew how such men had been buried, which made the outrage seem all the more shameful. They had buried such men in deep, well-dug pits surmounted by four stout stones at their corners— four stout stones there had been and a covering stone. And all this Miss Ogilvy knew as by instinct, having no concrete knowledge on which to draw. But she knew it right down in the depths of her soul, and she hated Mrs. Nanceskivel.

And now she was swept by another emotion that was even more strange and more devastating: such a grief as she had not conceived could exist; a terrible unassuageable grief, without hope, without respite, without palliation, so that with something akin to despair she touched the long gash in the skull. Then her eyes, that had never wept since her childhood, filled slowly with large, hot, difficult tears. She must blink very hard, then close her eyelids, turn away from the lamp and say rather loudly:

"Thanks, Mrs. Nanceskivel. It's past eleven—I think I'll be going upstairs."

9. Prehistoric stone axes.

6

Miss Ogilvy closed the door of her bedroom, after which she stood quite still to consider: "Is it shell shock?" she muttered incredulously. "I wonder, can it be shell shock?"

She began to pace slowly about the room, smoking a Caporal. As usual her hands were deep in her pockets; she could feel small, familiar things in those pockets and she gripped them, glad of their presence. Then all of a sudden she was terribly tired, so tired that she flung herself down on the bed, unable to stand any longer.

She thought that she lay there struggling to reason, that her eyes were closed in the painful effort, and that as she closed them she continued to puff the inevitable cigarette. At least that was what she thought at one moment— the next, she was out in a sunset evening, and a large red sun was sinking slowly to the rim of a distant sea.

Miss Ogilvy knew that she was herself, that is to say she was conscious of her being, and yet she was not Miss Ogilvy at all, nor had she a memory of her. All that she now saw was very familiar, all that she now did was what she should do, and all that she now was seemed perfectly natural. Indeed, she did not think of these things; there seemed no reason for thinking about them.

She was walking with bare feet on turf that felt springy and was greatly enjoying the sensation; she had always enjoyed it, ever since as an infant she had learned to crawl on this turf. On either hand stretched rolling green uplands, while at her back she knew that there were forests; but in front, far away, lay the gleam of the sea towards which the big sun was sinking. The air was cool and intensely still, with never so much as a ripple or bird song. It was wonderfully pure—one might almost say young—but Miss Ogilvy thought of it merely as air. Having always breathed it she took it for granted, as she took the soft turf and the uplands.

She pictured herself as immensely tall; she was feeling immensely tall at the moment. As a matter of fact she was five feet eight which, however, was quite a considerable height when compared to that of her fellow tribesmen. She was wearing a single garment of pelts which came to her knees and left her arms sleeveless. Her arms and her legs, which were closely tattooed with blue zigzag lines, were extremely hairy. From a leathern thong twisted about her waist there hung a clumsily made stone weapon, a celt, which in spite of its clumsiness was strongly hafted and useful for killing.

Miss Ogilvy wanted to shout aloud from a glorious sense of physical well-being, but instead she picked up a heavy, round stone which she hurled with great force at some distant rocks.

"Good! Strong!" she exclaimed. "See how far it goes!"

"Yes, strong. There is no one so strong as you. You are surely the strongest man in our tribe," replied her little companion.

Miss Ogilvy glanced at this little companion and rejoiced that they two were all alone together. The girl at her side had a smooth brownish skin, oblique black eyes and short, sturdy limbs. Miss Ogilvy marveled because of her beauty. She also was wearing a single garment of pelts, new pelts, she had made it that morning. She had stitched at it diligently for hours with short lengths of gut and her best bone needle. A strand of black hair hung over her bosom, and this she was constantly stroking and fondling, then she lifted the strand and examined her hair.

"Pretty," she remarked with childish complacence.

"Pretty," echoed the young man at her side.

"For you," she told him, "all of me is for you and none other. For you this body has ripened."

He shook back his own coarse hair from his eyes; he had sad brown eyes like those of a monkey. For the rest he was lean and steel-strong of loin, broad of chest, and with features not too uncomely. His prominent cheekbones were set rather high, his nose was blunt, his jaw somewhat bestial; but his mouth, though full-lipped, contradicted his jaw, being very gentle and sweet in expression. And now he smiled, showing big, square, white teeth.

"You . . . woman," he murmured contentedly, and the sound seemed to come from the depths of his being.

His speech was slow and lacking in words when it came to expressing a vital emotion, so one word must suffice and this he now spoke, and the word that he spoke had a number of meanings. It meant: "Little spring of exceedingly pure water." It meant: "Hut of peace for a man after battle." It meant: "Ripe red berry sweet to the taste." It meant: "Happy small home of future generations." All these things he must try to express by a word, and because of their loving she understood him.

They paused, and lifting her up he kissed her. Then he rubbed his large shaggy head on her shoulder; and when he released her she knelt at his feet.

"My master; blood of my body," she whispered. For with her it was different, love had taught her love's speech, so that she might turn her heart into sounds that her primitive tongue could utter.

After she had pressed her lips to his hands, and her cheek to his hairy and powerful forearm, she stood up and they gazed at the setting sun, but with bowed heads, gazing under their lids, because this was very sacred.

A couple of mating bears padded toward them from a thicket, and the female rose to her haunches. But the man drew his celt and menaced the beast, so that she dropped down noiselessly and fled, and her mate also fled, for here was the power that few dared to withstand by day or by night, on the uplands or in the forests. And now from across to the left where a river would presently lose itself in the marshes, came a rhythmical thudding, as a herd of red deer with wide nostrils and starting eyes thundered past, disturbed in their drinking by the bears.

After this the evening returned to its silence, and the spell of its silence descended on the lovers, so that each felt very much alone, yet withal more closely united to the other. But the man became restless under that spell, and he suddenly laughed; then grasping the woman he tossed her above his head and caught her. This he did many times for his own amusement and because he knew that his strength gave her joy. In this manner they played together for a while, he with his strength and she with her weakness. And they cried out, and made many guttural sounds which were meaningless save only to themselves. And the tunic of pelts slipped down from her breasts, and her two little breasts were pear-shaped.

Presently, he grew tired of their playing, and he pointed toward a cluster of huts and earthworks that lay to the eastward. The smoke from these huts rose in thick straight lines, bending neither to right nor left in its rising, and the thought of sweet burning rushes and brushwood touched his consciousness, making him feel sentimental.

"Smoke," he said.

And she answered: "Blue smoke."

He nodded: "Yes, blue smoke—home."

Then she said: "I have ground much corn since the full moon. My stones are too smooth. You make me new stones."

"All you have need of, I make," he told her.

She stole closer to him, taking his hand: "My father is sti l a black cloud full of thunder. He thinks that you wish to be head of our tribe in his place, because he is now very old. He must not hear of these meetings of ours, if he did I think he would beat me!"

So he asked her: "Are you unhappy, small berry?"

But at this she smiled: "What is being unhappy? I do not know what that means any more."

"I do not either," he answered.

Then as though some invisible force had drawn him, his body swung around and he stared at the forests where they lay and darkened, fold upon fold; and his eyes dilated with wonder and terror, and he moved his head quickly from side to side as a wild thing will do that is held between bars and whose mind is pitifully bewildered.

"Water!" he cried hoarsely, "great water—look, look! Over there. This land is surrounded by water!"

"What water?" she questioned

He answered: "The sea." And he covered his face with his hands.

"Not so," she consoled, "big forests, good hunting. Big forests in which you hunt boar and aurochs.[1] No sea over there but only the trees."

He took his trembling hands from his face: "You are right . . . only trees," he said dully.

But now his face had grown heavy and brooding and he started to speak of a thing that oppressed him: "The Roundheaded-ones, they are devils," he growled, while his bushy black brows met over his eyes, and when this happened it changed his expression which became a little sub-human.

"No matter," she protested, for she saw that he forgot her and she wished him to think an talk only of love. "No matter. My father laughs at your fears. Are we not friends with the Roundheaded-ones? We are friends, so why should we fear them?"

"Our forts, very old, very weak," he went on, "and the Roundheaded-ones have terrible weapons. Their weapons are not made of good stone like ours, but of some dark, devilish substance."

"What of that?" she said lightly. "They would fight on our side, so why need we trouble about their weapons?"

But he looked away, not appearing to hear her. "We must barter all, all for their celts and arrows and spears, and then we must learn their secret. They lust after our women, they lust after our lands. We must barter all, all for their sly brown celts."

"Me . . . bartered?" she queried, very sure of his answer, otherwise she had not dared to say this.

"The Roundheaded-ones may destroy my tribe and yet I will not part with you," he told her. Then he spoke very gravely: "But I think they desire to slay

1. Extinct long-horned wild oxen.

us, and me they will try to slay first because they well know how much I mistrust them—they have seen my eyes fixed many times on their camps."

She cried: "I will bite out the throats of these people if they so much as scratch your skin!"

And at this his mood changed and he roared with amusement: "You . . . woman!" he roared. "Little foolish white teeth. Your teeth were made for nibbling wild cherries, not for tearing the throats of the Roundheaded-ones!"

"Thoughts of war always make me afraid," she whimpered, still wishing him to talk about love.

He turned his sorrowful eyes upon her, the eyes that were sad even when he was merry, and although his mind was often obtuse, yet he clearly perceived how it was with her then. And his blood caught fire from the flame in her blood, so that he strained her against his body.

"You . . . mine . . ." he stammered.

"Love," she said, trembling, "this is love."

And he answered: "Love."

Then their faces grew melancholy for a moment, because dimly, very dimly in their dawning souls, they were conscious of a longing for something more vast than their earthly passion could compass.

Presently, he lifted her like a child and carried her quickly southward and westward till they came to a place where a gentle descent led down to a marshy valley. Far away, at the line where the marshes ended, they discerned the misty line of the sea; but the sea and the marshes were become as one substance, merging, blending, folding together; and since they were lovers they also would be one, even as the sea and the marshes.

And now they reached the mouth of a cave that was set in the quiet hillside. There was bright green verdure beside the cave, and a number of small, pink, thick-stemmed flowers that when they were crushed smelt of spices. And within the cave there was bracken newly gathered and heaped together for a bed; while beyond, from some rocks, came a low liquid sound as a spring dripped out through a crevice. Abruptly, he set the girl on her feet, and she knew that the days of her innocence were over. And she thought of the anxious virgin soil that was rent and sown to bring forth fruit in season, and she gave a quick little gasp of fear:

"No . . . no . . ." she gasped. For, divining his need, she was weak with the longing to be possessed, yet the terror of love lay heavy upon her. "No . . . no . . ." she gasped.

But he caught her wrist and she felt the great strength of his rough, gnarled fingers, the great strength of the urge that leapt in his loins, and again she must give the quick gasp of fear, the while she clung close to him lest he should spare her.

The twilight was engulfed and possessed by darkness, which in turn was transfigured by the moonrise, which in turn was fulfilled and consumed by dawn. A mighty eagle soared up from his eyrie,[2] cleaving the air with his masterful wings, and beneath him from the rushes that harbored their nests, rose other great birds, crying loudly. Then the heavy-horned elks appeared on the uplands, bending their burdened heads to the sod; while beyond in the forests the fierce wild aurochs stamped as they bellowed their love songs.

But within the dim cave the lord of these creatures had put by his weapon

2. Nest on a cliff or mountaintop.

and his instinct for slaying. And he lay there defenseless with tenderness, thinking no longer of death but of life as he murmured the word that had so many meanings. That meant: "Little spring of exceedingly pure water." That meant: "Hut of peace for a man after battle." That meant: "Ripe red berry sweet to the taste." That meant: "Happy small home of future generations."

<p style="text-align:center">7</p>

They found Miss Ogilvy the next morning; the fisherman saw her and climbed to the ledge. She was sitting at the mouth of the cave. She was dead, with her hands thrust deep into her pockets.

<p style="text-align:right">1926, 1934</p>

H. D. (HILDA DOOLITTLE)
1886–1961

"Take care, do not know me," H. D. warned her readers in her book-length poem *Trilogy*; "shun me; for this reality / is infectious—ecstasy." The infectious ecstasy that H. D. dared to express was an alternative to what she considered the senseless violence of the modern world. Writing, in her periods of greatest productivity, during the two world wars, H. D. rejected the nightmare of history, substituting for it a personal, spiritual quest for resurrection. In search of "what men say is-not," she recovered eternal, mythic patterns in everyday events through what she called "spiritual realism." At their most problematic, H. D.'s equivalencies can be dizzyingly associative, for she traced the multiple meanings of related words, decoding such words as if they were hieroglyphs. At their most powerful, the images of her poetry transformed her own life and the life of her times into a palimpsest, a record that retains traces of a still visible and viable ancient script.

Until recently, H. D. has been remembered for a handful of short, intense poems that helped define the literary movement the modernist poet Ezra Pound dubbed Imagism. But the pioneering works of the critic Norman Holmes Pearson, Susan Stanford Friedman, and Louis Martz have illuminated the later development of this major modernist. The early Imagist lyrics written at the beginning of this century were followed by long poetic narratives composed at midcentury. In part, H. D.'s development as a poet was the result of the Greek translations, prose fiction, and film criticism she produced throughout the 1920s and 1930s. In part, too, it was indebted to a series of illustrious men who functioned as "initiators" for the poet. If, as the literary critic Rachel Blau DuPlessis has shown, H. D. sometimes seemed inextricably drawn to a relationship of "romantic thralldom" with such men, what she took away from them was transformed into a revisionary mythology that reflected her lifelong effort to understand her identity as a woman and a poet.

The only surviving daughter in a prominent family that included five sons, Hilda Doolittle lived the first eight years of her life in Bethlehem Pennsylvania. Her father, Charles Doolittle, was professor of mathematics and astronomy at Lehigh University. In her autobiographical prose, H. D. recurrently associated him with authority and knowledge, for he charted the course of the stars in his study, where the maps and instruments impressed her as sacred symbols. Artistically talented, H. D.'s mother, Helen (Wolle) Doolittle, was a member of the Moravian brotherhood, a Protestant sect noted for its mysticism, and she maintained a close relationship with her own mother and with her father, who was the head of the

Moravian seminary. The community had brought with them from Germany a doctrine that taught faith in a direct, sensuous illumination of God. Indeed, for H. D., the "gift" of vision and spiritual wisdom that the Moravians traced from generation to generation was an aspect of her own poetic gift.

In 1895, when H. D.'s father became Flower Professor of Astronomy and director of the Flower Observatory at the University of Pennsylvania, the family moved to a suburb of Philadelphia. Hilda lived at home while attending first the Gordon School, then the Friends Central School, and, finally, Bryn Mawr. She soon left college, however, after failing English and suffering from a breakdown. In her autobiographical novel *HERmione* (1923, published 1981), she analyzed the conflict she experienced at this time between her relationship with the young Ezra Pound, to whom she became engaged, and her growing attachment to a girlfriend, Frances Gregg. An early admirer, the poet William Carlos Williams has described the beauty of the youthful H. D. (which Pound celebrated in his *Is-Hilda Book*) as well as her nervous isolation within her family (which H. D. attributed to her relationship with Frances). By 1911, she had decided to sail to Europe with Frances and Mrs. Gregg, a trip that resulted in her reunion with Pound in London and the beginning of a lifelong expatriation.

Through Pound, H. D. met D. H. Lawrence, William Butler Yeats, May Sinclair, and the poet-translator Richard Aldington. It was at Pound's suggestion, too, that she submitted her first poems to Harriet Monroe's magazine, *Poetry*. Indeed, in the tea room of the British Museum in August 1912, Pound signed Hilda Doolittle's poems with the pseudonym "H. D. Imagiste." As the promoter of early Imagism, he defined the poetic principles he saw embodied in H. D.'s verse: direct treatment of the subject, no inessential words, and musical (rather than strictly regular) rhythms. H. D.'s strikingly minimalist poems from this period were collected in her first volume of verse, *Sea Garden* (1916). Before this happened, however, her relationship with Pound had become troubled by his magisterial willfulness and his infidelities. Influenced by Aldington, who had succeeded Pound as the editor of *The New Freewoman* (soon to become *The Egoist*), H. D. had begun to concentrate on her own poetic education, studying Greek lyrics, the French symbolists, and the troubadours of medieval Provence. In 1913, she married Aldington.

While Pound went on from Imagism to another experimental movement, Vorticism, and from H. D. to Dorothy Shakespear, whom he married in 1914, H. D. and Aldington were befriended by the wealthy American poet Amy Lowell, who published three anthologies and a critical book publicizing both Imagism and H. D. in America. At this time, too, the couple became intimate with D. H. and Frieda Lawrence. Much has been written about this relationship: Lawrence fictionalized H. D. as the bohemian Julia in *Aaron's Rod* (1922); H. D. portrayed Lawrence in the unpublished "Pilate's Wife" (1924–29) and in *Bid Me to Live* (1939, published 1960); and Aldington wrote a biography of D. H. Lawrence titled *Portrait of a Genius, But* . . . (1950). Lawrence and H. D., who met on the eve of World War I, shared a common revulsion against the war. Both were convinced of the necessity for spiritual rebirth, which they sought to attain through writing that drew on esoteric mythology and imagery grounded in the physical details of a natural world. From H. D.'s point of view, however, Lawrence sometimes seemed to represent an oppressively masculine smugness. Whether or not Lawrence withdrew from the sexual relationship H. D. was led to expect, as she implied in *Bid Me to Live*, she continued to wrestle in writing with her admiration and fear of his creative potency.

By 1915, when H. D. suffered a miscarriage, the catastrophes she identified with World War I had begun. In 1917, when the Lawrences lived in H. D.'s London flat, Aldington, who was training to become an army officer, began an affair with one of H. D.'s acquaintances. In 1918, he was sent to the French front, and at about the same time, H. D.'s brother Gilbert was killed in the war. The next year her father

died, and she found herself pregnant after a trip to Cornwall with Cecil Gray, a wealthy young man who would go on to become a well-known music critic. After she contracted double pneumonia, H. D. was terrified that either she or her child would die. As she explains in the novel *Palimpsest* (1926), which fictionalizes much of this autobiographical material, she was "saved" from this crisis by the intercession of the twenty-four-year-old woman who would befriend her for the rest of her life, the writer Winifred Ellerman—or "Bryher," as she called herself (after one of the Scilly Islands).

Bryher was the illegitimate daughter of the richest of England's shipping magnates, a rebellious girl who wanted to be a boy and grew up to write historical adventure novels about boys. She had memorized all of *Sea Garden* before she met H. D.; subsidized the publication of *Hymen* (1921), H. D.'s next volume of verse; continued to pay many of H. D.'s bills; and eventually adopted H. D.'s daughter, Perdita. In 1919 and 1920, Bryher fulfilled a promise to take H. D. to Greece, where H. D. had one of her first psychic or visionary experiences. She saw what she later called "writing on the wall" projected in her hotel room, pictographic images of the helmeted face of a dead airman, a tripod, and then the winged figure of Niké, goddess of victory. When H. D. was too exhausted to sustain her concentration, Bryher described the last vision, the union of Niké with the god of the sun, Helios. The two women felt they had glimpsed a narrative line that, moving beyond the destruction of modern culture to a vision of female regeneration, would inform H. D.'s later poetry. The visit to Corfu was the most dramatic of a series of trips that took them to Egypt (1923), Paris (1924), and America (1921, 1926).

Although H. D. published *Heliodora and Other Poems* in 1924, her *Collected Poems* in 1925, *Red Roses for Bronze* in 1931, and several novels, short stories, and Greek translations during the late 1930s, she was troubled by what she considered a decline in her creativity, a decline that she related both to her personal problems and to the confusion of the times. While H. D. resided, for the most part, in London and Switzerland, Bryher twice embarked on marriages of convenience. H. D., who had an affair with Bryher's second husband, Kenneth MacPherson, became interested in film through his journal *Close-Up*; however, her tremulous performance in MacPherson's movie *Borderline* (1930) seems to dramatize her sense of anxiety during this period. Already acquainted with the psychologists Hans Sachs and Havelock Ellis, H. D. decided to confront her writing difficulties and her dread of an impending world war by journeying to 19 Bergasse in Vienna, where she would undergo the still relatively new process of psychoanalysis with the famous psychotherapist Sigmund Freud.

H. D.'s 1933 and 1934 sessions with Freud are brilliantly portrayed in her impressionistic *Tribute to Freud* (1944, 1956). As *The Master* indicates, the poet accepted Freud's insights into the associative, imagistic workings of the unconscious, as well as his conviction about the importance of the childhood of the individual and the infancy of the race. But she viewed herself as more intuitive, more attuned to spiritual realities, than Freud was. Analyzing visions like those she had seen in Greece, he diagnosed H. D.'s "symptoms" in terms of her unresolved attachment to her mother, implying that she was a victim of penis envy; however, she went on to explore the "inspiration" she associated with her mother to forge a poetry dedicated to the daughter's excavation of the maternal principle.

After surviving the bombings of London in World War II, H. D. composed two major epics about war, *Trilogy* (1944–46) and *Helen in Egypt* (1961). The former begins with the wasteland of war-torn London in *The Walls Do Not Fall* and moves backward first in *Tribute to the Angels* and then in *The Flowering of the Rod* to the birth of Christ, which is understood as a miracle of female creativity, for in the last of these books H. D. meditates on the crucial roles of the prostitute Mary Magdalene and the virgin mother Mary. Similarly, *Helen in Egypt* focuses on Helen of Troy as the scapegoat of a war that reveals the nihilism of a culture based on masculine values. Helen, who has been reviled as the cause of the war, must re-

cover a less punitive sense of her self. H. D.'s two Marys and her Helen are each helped in their quests by mentors who resemble Freud: Kaspar, one of the three Wise Men to visit the Christ child in *Trilogy*, and Theseus, in *Helen in Egypt*, provide the ancient wisdom that empowers female rebirth.

After the war, H. D. suffered a mental breakdown and moved from London to Küsnacht, Switzerland, but she continued to work on *Helen in Egypt* and on a coda to it titled *Hermetic Definition* (1972). She also wrote a number of prose and verse narratives that remain unpublished. Neither her interest in spiritualism nor her propensity for "romantic thralldom" was diminished in her later years. She continued working on occult material, specifically with Tarot cards, Moravian rituals, and astrology. During World War II, she had become emotionally attached to Sir Hugh Carswell Dowding, chief air marshal of the Royal Air Force Fighter Command, and in her seventies she fell in love with Lionel Durand, a Haitian journalist. Yet, as her memoir of her earlier relationship with Pound, *End to Torment* (1979), indicates, she had come to believe that, while "there was always a challenge" in the creativity of the men whom she admired or even adored, "the mother is the Muse, the Creator." The pseudonym H. D., which had begun as Pound's invention, had transformed itself into the mirror image of D. H. (Lawrence) and the replication of H(ugh) D(owding); however, by the end of the artist's life it seems to have stood for the hermetic definition of Hermes, for her mother, Helen, and for the spirit of Hellas.

In 1960, H. D. visited the United States for the last time, to accept the Award of Merit Medal for Poetry from the American Academy of Arts and Letters. The poets Robert Duncan and Denise Levertov were among her earliest admirers because, as Levertov succinctly explained, H. D.'s poetry offers "doors, ways in, tunnels through" the "hiddenness before which man must shed his arrogance."

Orchard[1]

I saw the first pear
as it fell—
the honey-seeking, golden-banded,
the yellow swarm
was not more fleet than I, 5
(spare us from loveliness)
and I fell prostrate
crying:
you have flayed us
with your blossoms, 10
spare us the beauty
of fruit-trees.

The honey-seeking
paused not,
the air thundered their song, 15
and I alone was prostrate.

O rough-hewn
god of the orchard,
I bring you an offering—

1. When first published in *Poetry* (1913), this poem was entitled *Priapus / Keeper of Orchards*.

do you, alone unbeautiful, 20
son of the god,
spare us from loveliness:

these fallen hazel-nuts,
stripped late of their green sheaths,
grapes, red-purple, 25
their berries
dripping with wine,
pomegranates already broken,
and shrunken figs
and quinces untouched, 30
I bring you as offering.

1913, 1916

Oread[1]

Whirl up, sea—
whirl your pointed pines,
splash your great pines
on our rocks,
hurl your green over us, 5
cover us with your pools of fir.

1914, 1925

Sea Poppies

Amber husk
fluted with gold,
fruit on the sand
marked with a rich grain,

treasure 5
spilled near the shrub-pines
to bleach on the boulders:

your stalk has caught root
among wet pebbles
and drift flung by the sea 10
and grated shells
and split conch-shells.

Beautiful, wide-spread,
fire upon leaf,
what meadow yields 15
so fragrant a leaf
as your bright leaf?

1916

1. A mountain nymph.

Garden

I

You are clear
O rose, cut in rock,
hard as the descent of hail.

I could scrape the color
from the petals 5
like spilt dye from a rock.

If I could break you
I could break a tree.

If I could stir
I could break a tree— 10
I could break you.

II

O wind, rend open the heat,
cut apart the heat,
rend it to tatters.

Fruit cannot drop 15
through this thick air—
fruit cannot fall into heat
that presses up and blunts
the points of pears
and rounds the grapes. 20

Cut the heat—
plough through it,
turning it on either side
of your path.

 1916

Eurydice[1]

I

So you have swept me back,
I who could have walked with the live souls
above the earth,
I who could have slept among the live flowers
at last; 5

1. According to Greek myth, the wife of the poet
Orpheus, who died and was carried to Hades. Orpheus
managed to win her back through the power of his
song, but then lost her again when he glanced back as
she followed him up from the underworld.

so for your arrogance
and your ruthlessness
I am swept back
where dead lichens drip
dead cinders upon moss of ash; 10

so for your arrogance
I am broken at last,
I who had lived unconscious,
who was almost forgot;

if you had let me wait 15
I had grown from listlessness into peace,
if you had let me rest with the dead,
I had forgot you
and the past.

II

Here only flame upon flame 20
and black among the red sparks,
streaks of black and light
grown colorless;

why did you turn back,
that hell should be reinhabited 25
of myself thus
swept into nothingness?

why did you turn?
why did you glance back?
why did you hesitate for that moment? 30
why did you bend your face
caught with the flame of the upper earth,
above my face?

what was it that crossed my face
with the light from yours 35
and your glance?
what was it you saw in my face?
the light of your own face,
the fire of your own presence?

What had my face to offer 40
but reflex of the earth,
hyacinth color
caught from the raw fissure in the rock
where the light struck,
and the color of azure crocuses 45
and the bright surface of gold crocuses
and of the wind-flower,
swift in its veins as lightning
and as white.

III

Saffron from the fringe of the earth, 50
wild saffron that has bent
over the sharp edge of earth,
all the flowers that cut through the earth,
all, all the flowers are lost;

everything is lost, 55
everything is crossed with black,
black upon black
and worse than black,
this colorless light.

IV

Fringe upon fringe 60
of blue crocuses,
crocuses, walled against blue of themselves,
blue of that upper earth,
blue of the depth upon depth of flowers,
lost; 65

flowers,
if I could have taken once my breath of them,
enough of them,
more than earth,
even than of the upper earth, 70
had passed with me
beneath the earth;

if I could have caught up from the earth,
the whole of the flowers of the earth,
if once I could have breathed into myself 75
the very golden crocuses
and the red,
and the very golden hearts of the first saffron,
the whole of the golden mass,
the whole of the great fragrance, 80
I could have dared the loss.

V

So for your arrogance
and your ruthlessness
I have lost the earth
and the flowers of the earth, 85
and the live souls above the earth,
and you who passed across the light
and reached
ruthless;

you who have your own light, 90
who are to yourself a presence,
who need no presence;

yet for all your arrogance
and your glance,
I tell you this: 95

such loss is no loss,
such terror, such coils and strands and pitfalls
of blackness,
such terror
is no loss; 100

hell is no worse than your earth
above the earth,
hell is no worse,
no, nor your flowers
nor your veins of light 105
nor your presence,
a loss;

my hell is no worse than yours
though you pass among the flowers and speak
with the spirits above earth. 110

VI

Against the black
I have more fervor
than you in all the splendor of that place,
against the blackness
and the stark gray 115
I have more light;

and the flowers,
if I should tell you,
you would turn from your own fit paths
toward hell, 120
turn again and glance back
and I would sink into a place
even more terrible than this.

VIII

At least I have the flowers of myself,
and my thoughts, no god 125
can take that;
I have the fervor of myself for a presence
and my own spirit for light;

and my spirit with its loss
knows this; 130

though small against the black,
small against the formless rocks,
hell must break before I am lost;

before I am lost,
hell must open like a red rose 135
for the dead to pass.

<div align="right">1917, 1925</div>

Fragment Thirty-six

I know not what to do: my mind is divided.
—Sappho.[1]

I know not what to do,
my mind is reft:
is song's gift best?
is love's gift loveliest?
I know not what to do, 5
now sleep has pressed
weight on your eyelids.

Shall I break your rest,
devouring, eager?
is love's gift best? 10
nay, song's the loveliest:
yet were you lost,
what rapture
could I take from song?
what song were left? 15

I know not what to do:
to turn and slake
the rage that burns,
with my breath burn
and trouble your cool breath? 20
so shall I turn and take
snow in my arms?
(is love's gift best?)
yet flake on flake
of snow were comfortless, 25
did you lie wondering,
wakened yet unawake.

Shall I turn and take
comfortless snow within my arms?
press lips to lips 30
that answer not,

1. This fragment by Sappho (c. 600 B.C.), Greek woman poet, has, as H. D. states, been "reworked freely" in the poem.

press lips to flesh
that shudders not nor breaks?

Is love's gift best?
shall I turn and slake 35
all the wild longing?
O I am eager for you!
as the Pleiads[2] shake
white light in whiter water
so shall I take you? 40

My mind is quite divided,
my minds hesitate,
so perfect matched,
I know not what to do:
each strives with each 45
as two white wrestlers
standing for a match,
ready to turn and clutch
yet never shake muscle nor nerve nor tendon;
so my mind waits 50
to grapple with my mind,
yet I lie quiet,
I would seem at rest.

I know not what to do:
strain upon strain, 55
sound surging upon sound
makes my brain blind;
as a wave-line may wait to fall
yet (waiting for its falling)
still the wind may take 60
from off its crest,
white flake on flake of foam,
that rises,
seeming to dart and pulse
and rend the light, 65
so my mind hesitates
above the passion
quivering yet to break,
so my mind hesitates
above my mind, 70
listening to song's delight.

I know not what to do:
will the sound break,
rending the night
with rift on rift of rose 75
and scattered light?

2. Seven sister nymphs who, according to Greek legend, were turned into stars (in the constellation Taurus).

will the sound break at last
as the wave hesitant,
or will the whole night pass
and I lie listening awake? 80

1924

Helen[1]

All Greece hates
the still eyes in the white face,
the lustre as of olives
where she stands,
and the white hands. 5

All Greece reviles
the wan face when she smiles,
hating it deeper still
when it grows wan and white,
remembering past enchantments 10
and past ills.

Greece sees unmoved,
God's daughter, born of love,
the beauty of cool feet
and slenderest knees, 15
could love indeed the maid,
only if she were laid,
white ash amid funereal cypresses.

1924

The Master[1]

I

He was very beautiful,
the old man,
and I knew wisdom,
I found measureless truth
in his words, 5
his command
was final;

(how did he understand?)

when I traveled to Miletus[2]
to get wisdom, 10

1. The beautiful wife of the Greek leader Menelaus, who was given to the Trojan prince Paris by Aphrodite, and blamed for the Trojan War waged to regain her.
1. Identified with Sigmund Freud (1856–1939), the founder of psychoanalysis, with whom H. D. underwent analysis (see headnote, p. 1409).
2. Ancient city on the west coast of Asia Minor (modern Turkey).

I left all else behind,
I fasted,
I worked late,
rose early;
whether I wore simple garments 15
or intricate
nothing was lost,
each vestment had meaning,
"every gesture is wisdom,"
he taught; 20
"nothing is lost,"[3]
he said;
I went late to bed
or early,
I caught the dream 25
and rose dreaming,
and we wrought philosophy on the dream content,[4]
I was content;

nothing was lost
for God is all 30
and the dream is God;
only to us,
to us
is small wisdom,
but great enough 35
to know God everywhere;

O he was fair,
even when I flung his words in his teeth,
he said,
"I will soon be dead 40
I must learn from the young";

his tyranny was absolute,
for I had to love him then,
I had to recognize that he was beyond all men,
nearer to God 45
(he was so old)
I had to claim
pardon,
which he granted
with his old head 50
so wise,
so beautiful
with his mouth so young
and his eyes—

O God, 55
let there be some surprise in heaven for him,

3. An allusion to the Freudian notion that what seems
to be forgotten has actually been repressed and re-
mains in the unconscious.

4. Analysis of the contents of dreams is central to
Freud's methods.

for no one but you could devise
anything suitable
for him,
so beautiful. 60

II

I don't know what to suggest,
I can hardly suggest things to God
who with a nod
says, "rise Olympos,
sink into the sea, 65
O Pelion,
Ossa,[5]
be still";

I do not know what to say to God,
for the hills 70
answer his nod,
and the sea
when he tells his daughter,
white Mother
of green 75
leaves
and green rills
and silver,
to still
tempest 80
or send peace
and surcease of peril
when a mountain has spit fire:

I did not know how to differentiate
between volcanic desire, 85
anemones like embers
and purple fire
of violets
like red heat,
and the cold 90
silver
of her feet:

I had two loves separate;
God who loves all mountains,
alone knew why 95
and understood
and told the old man
to explain

5. All mountains in Greece.

the impossible,

which he did.[6] 100

III

What can God give the old man,
who made this possible?

for a woman
breathes fire
and is cold, 105
a woman sheds snow from ankles
and is warm;
white heat
melts into snow-flake
and violets 110
turn to pure amethysts,
water-clear:

no,
I did not falter,
I saw the whole miracle, 115
I knew that the old man made this tenable,
but how could he have foreseen
the impossible?

how could he have known
how each gesture of this dancer 120
would be hieratic?[7]
words were scrawled on papyrus,
words were written most carefully,
each word was separate
yet each word led to another word, 125
and the whole made a rhythm
in the air,
till now unguessed at,
unknown.

IV

I was angry at the old man, 130
I wanted an answer,
a neat answer,
when I argued and said, "well, tell me,
you will soon be dead,
the secret lies with you," 135
he said,
"you are a poet";

6. H. D. wrote to Bryher of Freud's "terribly exciting" that all-but extinct phenomena, the perfect bi-."
explanation of her writer's block: "It appears that I am 7. Highly stylized; also, priestly.

I do not wish to be treated like a child, a weakling,
so I said,
(I was angry) 140
"you can not last forever,
the fire of wisdom dies with you,
I have traveled far to Miletus,
you can not stay long now with us,
I came for an answer"; 145

I was angry with the old man
with his talk of the man-strength,
I was angry with his mystery, his mysteries,
I argued till day-break;

O, it was late, 150
and God will forgive me, my anger,
but I could not accept it.

I could not accept from wisdom
what love taught,
woman is perfect. 155

<center>V</center>

She is a woman,
yet beyond woman,
yet in woman,
her feet are the delicate pulse of the narcissus bud,
pushing from earth 160
(ah, where is your man-strength?)
her arms are the waving of the young
male,
tentative,
reaching out 165
that first evening
alone in a forest;

she is woman,
her thighs are frail yet strong,
she leaps from rock to rock 170
(it was only a small circle for her dance)

and the hills dance,

she conjures the hills;
"rhododendrons[8]
awake," 175
her feet
pulse,
the rhododendrons

8. In Greek, the word *rhodon* has the primary meaning "rose"; it can also refer to female genitalia.

wake
there is purple flower 180
between her marble, her birch-tree white
thighs,
or there is a red flower,

there is a rose flower
parted wide, 185
as her limbs fling wide in dance
ecstatic
Aphrodite,[9]
there is a frail lavender flower
hidden in grass; 190

O God, what is it,
this flower
that in itself had power over the whole earth?
for she needs no man,
herself 195
is that dart and pulse of the male,
hands, feet, thighs,
herself perfect.

VI

Let the old man lie in the earth
(he has troubled men's thought long enough) 200
let the old man die,
let the old man be of the earth
he is earth,
Father,
O beloved 205
you are the earth,
he is the earth, Saturn, wisdom,
rock, (O his bones are hard, he is strong, that old man)
let him create a new earth,
and from the rocks of this re-birth 210
the whole world
must suffer,
only we
who are free,

may foretell, 215
may prophesy,
he,
(it is he the old man
who will bring a new world to birth)
it is he, 220
it is he
who already has formed a new earth.

9. Greek goddess of love.
1. Roman deity identified with the Greek Titan Cronos, father of Zeus.

VII

He will trouble the thoughts of men
yet for many an aeon,
they will travel far and wide, 225
they will discuss all his written words,
his pen will be sacred
they will build a temple
and keep all his sacred writings safe,
and men will come 230
and men will quarrel
but he will be safe;

they will found temples in his name,
his fame
will be so great 235
that anyone who has known him
will also be hailed as master,
seer,
interpreter;

only I, 240
I will escape.

VIII

And it was he himself, he who set me free
to prophesy,

he did not say
"stay, 250
my disciple,"
he did not say,
"write,
each word I say is sacred,"
he did not say, "teach" 255
he did not say,
"heal
or seal
documents in my name,"

no, 260
he was rather casual,
"we won't argue about that"
(he said)
"you are a poet."

IX

So I went forth 265
blinded a little with the sort of terrible tears
that won't fall;

I said good-bye
and saw his old head
as he turned, 270
as he left the room
leaving me alone
with all his old trophies,[2]
the marbles, the vases, the stone Sphynx,
the old, old jars from Egypt; 275
he left me alone with these things
and his old back was bowed;

O God,
those tears didn't come,
how could they? 280
I went away,
I said,
"I won't have this tyranny
of an old man
he is too old, 285
I will die,
if I love him;

I can not love him
he is too near,
too precious to God." 290

X

But one does not forget him
who makes all things feasible,
one does not forgive him
who makes God-in-all
possible, 295
for that is unbearable.

XI

Now can I bear even God,
for a woman's laughter
prophesies
happiness: 300
(not man, not men,
only one, the old man,
sacred to God);

no man will be present in those mysteries,
yet all men will kneel, 305
no man will be potent,
important,
yet all men will feel

2. Freud had an extensive collection of antiquities; in his study and consulting room were over more than two thousand Egyptian, Greek, Roman, Near Eastern, and Asian objects.

what it is to be a woman,
will yearn, 310
burn,
turn from easy pleasure
to hardship
of the spirit,

men will see how long they have been blind, 315
poor men
poor man-kind
how long
how long
this thought of the man-pulse has tricked them, 320
has weakened them,
shall see woman,
perfect.

XII

And they did;
I was not the only one that cried 325
madly,
madly,
we were together,
we were one;

we were together 330
we were one;
sun-worshipers,
we flung
as one voice
our cry 335
Rhodocleia;[3]

Rhodocleia,
near to the sun,
we did not say
"pity us," 340
we did not say, "look at us,"
we cried,
"O heart of the sun
rhododendron,
Rhodocleia, 350
we are unworthy your beauty,

you are near beauty the sun,
you are that Lord become woman."

1934–35 1981

3. H. D. seems to be making a number of allusions with this made-up name: to Rhodos, daughter of Aphrodite and wife of Helios (the sun); to *rhodon* (see n. 8, p. 1422); to the Greek noun *kleis*, "a key"; and to the verb *kleien*, "to praise or announce."

From Tribute to the Angels

To Osbert Sitwell
. . possibly we will reach haven
heaven.

[1]

Hermes Trismegistus[2]
is patron of alchemists;

his province is thought,
inventive, artful and curious;

his metal is quicksilver, 5
his clients, orators, thieves and poets;

steal then, O orator,
plunder, O poet,

take what the old-church
found in Mithra's[3] tomb, 10

candle and script and bell,[4]
take what the new-church spat upon

and broke and shattered;
collect the fragments of the splintered glass

and of your fire and breath, 15
melt down and integrate,

re-invoke, re-create
opal, onyx, obsidian,

now scattered in the shards
men tread upon. 20

[2]

Your walls do not fall, he said,
because your walls are made of jasper;[5]

but not four-square, I thought,
another shape (octahedron?)

1. An echo of the last lines of *The Walls Do Not Fall*, the first part of *Trilogy*. In *Tribute to the Angels*, the second book of *Trilogy*, H. D. revises the biblical Book of Revelation while invoking a series of symbolic angels; in the midst of this invocation the poet has a vision of "a Lady."
2. Supposed author of the Hermetic Books, dealing with magic, astrology, and alchemy, the Greek name for the Egyptian Thoth, god of the dead and originator of culture. Hermes was the Greek messenger god, god

of science and invention, and conductor of the souls of the dead to the underworld.
3. A chief god of the ancient Persians, associated with the sun.
4. An allusion to the phrase "bell, book, and candle"; here meaning the articles accompanying religious ceremonies.
5. The first line echoes the title of the first part of *Trilogy*; in Revelation 21:18, the City of God is described as having a wall of jasper.

slipped into the place 25
reserved by rule and rite

for the *twelve foundations,*
for the *transparent glass,*

for *no need of the sun*
nor *moon to shine;*[6] 30

for the vision as we see
or have seen or imagined it

or in the past invoked
or conjured up or had conjured

by another, was usurped; 35
I saw the shape

which might have been of jasper,
but it was not four-square.

<center>[3]</center>

I John saw.[7] *I testify;*
if any man shall add 40

God shall add unto him the plagues,
but he that sat upon the throne said,

I make all things new.
I John saw. I testify,

but *I make all things new,* 45
said He of the seven stars,

he of the seventy-times-seven[8]
passionate, bitter wrongs,

He of the seventy-times-seven
bitter, unending wars. 50

<center>* * *</center>

<center>[8]</center>

Now polish the crucible
and in the bowl distill

a word most bitter, *marah,*
a word bitterer still, *mar,*[9] 120

6. Other allusions to the City of God in Revelation
21:14–23: the City has "twelve foundations"; its
streets are of gold like "transparent glass"; and there is
"no need of the sun" or the "moon to shine" because it
is lighted by the "glory of God."

7. An echo of Revelation 22:8.
8. When asked how many times to forgive a person
who sins against you, Jesus replied, "Until seventy
times seven" (Matthew 18:22).
9. Ocean. "Marah": bitter (Hebrew).

sea, brine, breaker, seducer,
giver of life, giver of tears;

now polish the crucible
and set the jet of flame

under, till *marah-mar*
are melted, fuse and join 125

and change and alter,
mer, mere, mère, mater, Maia, Mary,[1]

Star of the Sea,
Mother. 130

[9]

Bitter, bitter jewel
in the heart of the bowl,

what is your color?
what do you offer

to us who rebel? 135
what were we had you loved other?

what is this mother-father
to tear at our entrails?

what is this unsatisfied duality
which you can not satisfy? 140

[10]

In the field-furrow
the rain-water

showed splintered edge
as of a broken mirror,

and in the glass 145
as in a polished spear,

glowed the star Hesperus,[2]
white, far and luminous,

incandescent and near,
Venus, Aphrodite, Astarte,[3] 150

1. H. D. here plays on the common etymologies of words for "ocean" and "mother" in French and Latin: Maia, mother of Hermes; Mary, mother of Jesus.
2. The evening star.

3. Semitic goddess of fecundity and love, identified with the crescent moon. Venus is the Roman name for Aphrodite, also the morning star. Aphrodite was the Greek goddess of love.

star of the east,
star of the west,

Phosphorus[4] at sun-rise,
Hesperus at sun-set.

[11]

O swiftly, re-light the flame 155
before the substance cool,

for suddenly we saw your name
desecrated; knaves and fools

have done you impious wrong,
Venus, for venery stands for impurity 160

and Venus as desire
is venereous, lascivious,

while the very root of the word shrieks
like a mandrake when foul witches pull

its stem at midnight, 165
and rare mandragora[5] itself

is full, they say, of poison,
food for the witches' den.

[12]

Swiftly re-light the flame,
Aphrodite, holy name, 170

Astarte, hull and spar
of wrecked ships lost your star,

forgot the light at dusk,
forgot the prayer at dawn;

return, O holiest one, 175
Venus whose name is kin

to venerate,
venerator.

[13]

"What is the jewel color?"
green-white, opalescent, 180

4. I.e., light bearing.
5. Mandrake, so-called for the resemblance of its forked root to a human body; used in witchcraft.

with under-layer of changing blue,
with rose-vein; a white agate

with a pulse uncooled that beats yet,
faint blue-violet;

it lives, it breathes, 185
it gives off—fragrance?

I do not know what it gives,
a vibration that we can not name

for there is no name for it;
my patron said, "name it"; 190

I said, I can not name it,
there is no name;

he said,
"invent it."

 [14]

I can not invent it, 195
I said it was agate,

I said it lived, it gave—
fragrance—was near enough

to explain that quality
for which there is no name; 200

I do not want to name it,
I want to watch its faint

heart-beat, pulse-beat
as it quivers, I do not want

to talk about it, 205
I want to minimize thought,

concentrate on it
till I shrink,

dematerialize
and am drawn into it. 210

 * * *

 [24]

Every hour, every moment
has its specific attendant Spirit;

the clock-hand, minute by minute,
ticks round its prescribed orbit;

but this curious mechanical perfection 350
should not separate but relate rather,

our life, this temporary eclipse
to that other. . . .

 [25]

. . . of the *no need*
of the moon to shine in it, 355

for it was ticking minute by minute
(the clock at my bed-head,

with its dim, luminous disc)
when the Lady knocked;

I was talking casually 360
with friends in the other room,

when we saw the outer hall
grow lighter—then we saw where the door was,

there was no door
(this was a dream, of course), 365

and she was standing there,
actually, at the turn of the stair.

 [26]

One of us said, how odd,
she is actually standing there,

I wonder what brought her? 370
another of us said,

have we some power between us,
we three together,

that acts as a sort of magnet,
that attracts the super-natural? 375

(yet it was all natural enough,
we agreed);

I do not know what I said
or if I said anything,

for before I had time to speak, 380
I realized I had been dreaming,

that I lay awake now on my bed,
that the luminous light

was the phosphorescent face
of my little clock 385

and the faint knocking
was the clock ticking.

[27]

And yet in some very subtle way,
she was there more than ever,

as if she had miraculously 390
related herself to time here,

which is no easy trick, difficult
even for the experienced stranger,

of whom we must *be not forgetful*
for *some have entertained angels unawares* 395

[28]

I had been thinking of Gabriel,[7]
of the moon-cycle, of the moon-shell,

of the moon-crescent
and the moon at full:

I had been thinking of Gabriel, 400
the moon-regent, the Angel,

and I had intended to recall him
in the sequence of candle and fire

and the law of the seven;
I had not forgotten 405

his special attribute
of annunciator; I had thought

to address him as I had the others,
Uriel, Annael;[8]

how could I imagine 410
the Lady herself would come instead?

6. "Be not forgetful to entertain strangers: for thereby some have entertained angels unawares" (Hebrews 13:2).
7. One of the seven archangels in Christian tradition; thought to be the angel of mercy. He announced the coming of Christ to Mary.
8. Two of the seven archangels.

[29]

We have seen her
the world over,

Our Lady of the Goldfinch,
Our Lady of the Candelabra, 415

Our Lady of the Pomegranate,
Our Lady of the Chair;[9]

we have seen her, an empress,
magnificent in pomp and grace,

and we have seen her 420
with a single flower

or a cluster of garden-pinks
in a glass beside her;

we have seen her snood[1]
drawn over her hair, 425

or her face set in profile
with the blue hood and stars;

we have seen her head bowed down
with the weight of a domed crown,

or we have seen her, a wisp of a girl 430
trapped in a golden halo;

we have seen her with arrow, with doves
and a heart like a valentine;

we have seen her in fine silks imported
from all over the Levant, 435

and hung with pearls brought
from the city of Constantine;[2]

we have seen her sleeve
of every imaginable shade

of damask and figured brocade; 440
it is true,

the painters did very well by her;
it is true, they missed never a line

9. Titles of different iconographic representations of
Mary.
1. Hair net.
2. Constantinople, the new name given to the ancient
city of Byzantium by the great Roman emperor
Constantine. "The Levant": countries of the eastern
Mediterranean noted for their rich goods.

of the suave turn of the head
or subtle shade of lowered eye-lid 445

or eye-lids half-raised; you find
her everywhere (or did find),

in cathedral, museum, cloister,
at the turn of the palace stair.

<p align="center">* * *</p>

<p align="center">[35]</p>

So she must have been pleased with us,
who did not forge our heritage

at the grave-edge. 515
she must have been pleased

with the straggling company of the brush and quill
who did not deny their birthright;

she must have been pleased with us,
for she looked so kindly at us 520

under her drift of veils,
and she carried a book.

<p align="center">[36]</p>

Ah (you say), this is Holy Wisdom,
Santa Sophia, the SS of the Sanctus Spiritus,[3]

so by facile reasoning, logically 525
the incarnate symbol of the Holy Ghost;

your Holy Ghost was an apple-tree
smoldering—or rather now bourgeoning

with flowers; the fruit of the Tree?[4]
this is the new Eve who comes 530

clearly to return, to retrieve
what she lost the race,

given over to sin, to death;
she brings the Book of Life, obviously.

3. Holy Ghost. "Santa Sophia": holy wisdom, as well
as the name of an important church in Constan-
tinople.

4. A reference to the Tree of Knowledge in Genesis
2–3.

[37]

This is a symbol of beauty (you continue), 535
she is Our Lady universally,

I see her as you project her,
not out of place

flanked by Corinthian capitals,
or in a Coptic nave,[5] 540

or frozen above the center door
of a Gothic cathedral;

you have done very well by her
(to repeat your own phrase),

you have carved her tall and unmistakable, 545
a hieratic figure, the veiled Goddess,

whether of the seven delights,
whether of the seven spear-points.

[38]

O yes—you understand, I say,
this is all most satisfactory, 550

but she wasn't hieratic, she wasn't frozen,
she wasn't very tall;

she is the Vestal
from the days of Numa,[6]

she carries over the cult 555
of the *Bona Dea*,[7]

she carries a book but it is not
the tome of the ancient wisdom,

the pages, I imagine, are the blank pages
of the unwritten volume of the new; 560

all you say, is implicit,
all that and much more;

but she is not shut up in a cave
like a Sibyl;[8] she is not

5. I.e., a nave in an Egyptian Christian church. "Corinthian capitals": the upper ends of Greek pillars, carved in the lightest and most ornate "Corinthian" style.
6. Legendary King of Rome associated with ceremonial laws and religious honored institutions, including appointing the first virgin priestesses of Vesta, goddess of hearth and home.
7. Good goddess (Italian), Italian deity whose secret festival was forbidden to men.
8. Female prophet.

imprisoned in leaden bars 565
in a colored window;

she is Psyche,[9] of the butterfly,
out of the cocoon.

[39]

But nearer than Guardian Angel
or good Daemon.[1] 570

she is the counter-coin-side
of primitive terror;

she is not-fear, she is not-war,
but she is no symbolic figure

of peace, charity, chastity, goodness, 575
faith, hope, reward;

she is not Justice with eyes
blindfolded like Love's;[2]

I grant you the dove's symbolic purity,[3]
I grant you her face was innocent 580

and immaculate and her veils
like the Lamb's[4] Bride,

but the Lamb was not with her,
either as Bridegroom or Child;

her attention is undivided, 585
we are her bridegroom and lamb;

her book is our book; written
or unwritten, its pages will reveal

a tale of a Fisherman,
a tale of a jar or jars,[5] 590

the same—different—the same attributes,
different yet the same as before.

9. Human lover of the Greek god of love, Cupid or
Eros, who was eventually deified after performing a
number of apparently impossible tasks, including a de-
scent to Hades. Her name means "soul" in Greek; the
butterfly is her symbol because its career parallels her
own.
1. Indwelling spirit or genius.
2. Both Justice and Cupid ("Love") are traditionally

depicted as blindfolded.
3. The spiritual purity of the dove is an important
Christian theme.
4. I.e., Christ's. His bride is traditionally the church.
5. Anticipates the last book of Trilogy, The Flowering
of the Rod, which retells the Gospel story of the wise
men's gift of a jar of myrrh to the Christ child.
"Fisherman": a reference to Christ.

[40]

This is no rune[6] nor symbol,
what I mean is—it is so simple

yet no trick of the pen or brush 595
could capture that impression;

what I wanted to indicate was
a new phase, a new distinction of color;

I wanted to say, I did say
there was no sheen, no reflection, 600

no shadow; when I said white,
I did not mean sculptor's or painter's white,

nor porcelain; dim-white could
not suggest it, for when

is fresh-fallen snow (or snow 605
in the act of falling) dim?

yet even now, we stumble, we are lost—
what can we say?

she was not impalpable like a ghost,
she was not awe-inspiring like a Spirit, 610

she was not even over-whelming
like an Angel.

[41]

She carried a book, either to imply
she was one of us, with us,

or to suggest she was satisfied 615
with our purpose, a tribute to the Angels;

yet though the campanili[7] spoke,
Gabriel, Azrael,

though the campanili answered,
Raphael, Uriel, 620

though a distant note over-water
chimed *Annael,* and *Michael*[8]

6. A character in the runic alphabet, associated with 8. All archangels previously invoked in the poem
mysticism. (some in passages not printed here).
7. Bell tower.

was implicit from the beginning,
another, deep, un-named, resurging bell

answered, sounding through them all: 625
remember, where there was

no need of the moon to shine. . . .
I saw no temple.

[42]

Some call that deep-deep bell
Zadkiel,[9] the righteousness of God, 630

he is regent of Jupiter
or Zeus-pater[1] or Theus-pater,

Theus, God; God-the-father, father-god
or the Angel god-father,

himself, heaven yet at home in a star 635
whose color is amethyst,

whose candle burns deep-violet
with the others.

[43]

And the point in the spectrum
where all lights become one, 640

is white and white is not no-color,
as we were told as children,

but all-color;
where the flames mingle

and the wings meet, when we gain 645
the arc of perfection,

we are satisfied, we are happy,
we begin again;

I John saw. I testify
to rainbow feathers, to the span of heaven 650

and walls of color,
the colonnades of jasper;

9. An archangel. most powerful of the Roman gods and patriarch of the
1. Father (Latin). Jupiter (Zeus in Greek) was the pantheon.

but when the jewel
melts in the crucible

we find not ashes, not ash-of-rose, 655
not a tall vase and a staff of lilies,

not *vas spirituale*,
not *rosa mystica*[2] even,

but a cluster of garden-pinks
or a face like a Christmas-rose. 660

This is the flowering of the rod,[3]
this is the flowering of the burnt-out wood,

where, Zadkiel, we pause to give
thanks that we rise again from death and live.

London 1945
May 17–31, 1944

2. Mystic rose (Latin). "*Vas spirituale*": spiritual ves- 3. The title of the next and last book of *Trilogy*.
sel.

EDITH SITWELL

1887–1964

The daughter of an aristocratic English family, brought up in a sumptuous home, Edith Sitwell nevertheless began her life by feeling that "I was unpopular with my parents from the moment of my birth." Tall and slim, with a markedly aquiline nose for which a London orthopedist provided a special "contraption [turning] the organ in question . . . very firmly to the opposite way which Nature had intended," she must as a girl have seemed an unlikely candidate for the glamorous reputation she later achieved. Yet, with the help of a supportive grandmother, a kind nurse, and an encouraging governess, Sitwell began early to read and write poetry, dismissing her eccentric, scholarly father as a foolish man and her elegant but unloving mother as a woman who cared only about a "silly daily life of bridge and watching the golfers on the golf course." Despite financial difficulties—including a series of debts that at one point sent the extravagant Lady Ida Sitwell to prison—Edith Sitwell settled in London in 1914, sharing a flat with her former governess, and in 1916 began editing *Wheels*, an avant-garde literary anthology featuring experimental writings that shocked conservative critics who might have expected greater decorum from an upper-class heiress.

Sitwell had from the first enjoyed the admiration and respect of her younger brothers, Osbert and Sacheverell, each of whom became a distinguished literary man in his own right, and such powerful ties with her siblings also clearly energized her. Yet that she was innately strong willed, vigorous, and imaginative is plain from the innovative verse she began to publish during her *Wheels* period. *Clown's Houses* (1918), *The Wooden Pegasus* (1920), and *Façade* (1922) followed each other in rapid succession, proposing surprising alternatives to the more traditional work included in the comparatively sedate *Georgian Anthology* (1911–20)—an annual collection of poems by such writers as Rupert Brooke, Walter de la Mare,

and John Masefield—against which Sitwell was reacting with some violence. Deliberately stylized, even rebelliously artificial, these early works seemed, according to a contemporary critic, to be composed for "the xylophone," written by "a virtuoso in the communication of a half-wooden, half-glassy tone which is seldom without brilliance." The musical analogy is apt, for *Façade* is a jazzy poem sequence whose syncopated linguistic rhythms are echoed by the background music that the British composer Sir William Walton wrote for it: when the pair first performed this joint production in public—Walton conducting the orchestra, Sitwell reading the poems from behind a screen—the controversial work was, according to one observer, a "sensation."

In her later years, Edith Sitwell became an increasingly dramatic figure on the London literary and artistic scene. As an aristocratic infant she had been painted in a Sitwell family portrait by the renowned American artist John Singer Sargent, but as a more compellingly aquiline adult she was the subject of photographs by Cecil Beaton and paintings by Roger Fry, Alvaro Guevara, Wyndham Lewis, Felix Topolski, and her close friend Pavel Tchelitchew; the Guevara hangs today in London's Tate Gallery. More important, she continued to move—determinedly unmarried and fiercely independent—in major British aesthetic circles, discovering and befriending the young Dylan Thomas and associating with such writers as Virginia Woolf. During the grim years of World War II, when London was being blitzed by German planes, she began to write poems that were less sardonically stylized, more bitterly macabre than any of her earlier works. Yet pieces like *Lullaby* and *Serenade: Any Man to Any Woman* retain the metallic edge—the "xylophone" quality—that had marked even the verses of the lighthearted *Façade*, as if Sitwell had decided, when she was quite young, that her supposedly privileged world was no more and no less than, in the words of *Façade*'s Sir Beelzebub, a "hotel in Hell."

En Famille[1]

In the early springtime, after their tea.
Through the young fields of the springing Bohea,[2]
Jemima, Jocasta, Dinah, and Deb
Walked with their father Sir Joshua Jebb—
An admiral red, whose only notion 5
(A butterfly poised on a pigtailed ocean),
Is of the peruked[3] sea whose swell
Breaks on the flowerless rocks of Hell.
Under the thin trees, Deb and Dinah,
Jemima, Jocasta walked, and finer 10
Their black hair seemed (flat-sleek to see)
Than the young leaves of the springing Bohea;
Their cheeks were like nutmeg-flowers when swells
The rain into foolish silver bells.
They said, "If the door you would only slam, 15
Or if, Papa, you would once say 'Damn'—
Instead of merely roaring 'Avast'
Or boldly invoking the nautical Blast—
We should now stand in the street of Hell

1 As a family (French). 3. Wearing 18th-century periwigs.
2 A black Chinese tea.

Watching siesta shutters that fell 20
With a noise like amber softly sliding;
Our moon-like glances through these gliding
Would see at her table preened and set
Myrrhina[4] sitting at her toilette
With eyelids closed as soft as the breeze 25
That flows from gold flowers on the incense-trees."

The Admiral said, "You could never call—
I assure you it would not do at all!
She gets down from table without saying 'Please,'
Forgets her prayers and to cross her T's, 30
In short, her scandalous reputation
Has shocked the whole of the Hellish nation;
And every turbaned Chinoiserie,[5]
With whom we should sip our black Bohea,
Would stretch out her simian fingers thin 35
To scratch you, my dears, like a mandoline;
For Hell is just as properly proper
As Greenwich, or as Bath, or Joppa!"[6]

 1922

Sir Beelzebub[1]

When
Sir
Beelzebub called for his syllabub[2] in the hotel in Hell
 Where Proserpine[3] first fell,
Blue as the gendarmerie[4] were the waves of the sea 5

 (Rocking and shocking the bar-maid).

Nobody comes to give him his rum but the
Rim of the sky hippopotamus-glum
Enhances the chances to bless with a benison
Alfred Lord Tennyson crossing the bar[5] laid 10
With cold vegetation from pale deputations
Of temperance workers (all signed In Memoriam[6])
Hoping with glory to trip up the Laureate's[7] feet

 (Moving in classical meters) . . .

4. Possibly a variation on "Myrrha," who in Greek myth was transformed into a myrrh tree by the gods because of her incestuous love for her father (their son was Adonis).
5. A term denoting European adaptations of Chinese forms and customs; though here it may simply refer to Chinese people.
6. The ancient name of the Israeli city of Jaffa, the center of many religious battles. Greenwich and Bath are cities in England.
1. One of the fallen angels who was cast into hell with Satan.
2. A dessert made of sweetened cream and wine or liquor.
3. Wife of Hades and goddess of the underworld in Greek myth.
4. The French police force.
5. A narrow ridge of sand near a harbor or beach. Tennyson (1809–1892) wrote a late poem called *Crossing the Bar,* in which he said that he hoped "to see [his] Pilot face to face."
6. The title of Tennyson's long elegy for his friend Arthur Hallam.
7. Tennyson succeeded Wordsworth as Poet Laureate, an honorific title bestowed on English poets by the Crown.

Like Balaclava,[8] the lava came down from the 15
Roof, and the sea's blue wooden gendarmerie
Took them in charge while Beelzebub roared for his rum.

 . . . None of them come!

 1922

Aubade[1]

Jane, Jane,
Tall as a crane,
The morning light creaks down again;

Comb your cockscomb-ragged hair,
Jane, Jane, come down the stair. 5

Each dull blunt wooden stalactite
Of rain creaks, hardened by the light,

Sounding like an overtone
From some lonely world unknown.

But the creaking empty light 10
Will never harden into sight,

Will never penetrate your brain
With overtones like the blunt rain.

The light would show (if it could harden)
Eternities of kitchen garden,[2] 15

Cockscomb flowers that none will pluck,
And wooden flowers that 'gin to cluck.

In the kitchen you must light
Flames as staring, red and white,

As carrots or as turnips, shining 20
Where the cold dawn light lies whining.

Cockscomb hair on the cold wind
Hangs limp. turns the milk's weak mind. . . .

Jane, Jane,
Tall as a crane, 25
The morning light creaks down again!

 1923

8. Site of a battle during the Crimean War in 1854, described by Tennyson in *The Charge of the Light Brigade*.

1. Dawn poem.
2. Small back gardens used by cooks to grow herbs and vegetables.

Lullaby[1]

Though the world has slipped and gone,
Sounds my loud discordant cry
Like the steel birds' song on high:
"Still one thing is left—the Bone!"
Then out danced the Babioun.[2] 5

She sat in the hollow of the sea—
A socket whence the eye's put out—
She sang to the child a lullaby
(The steel birds' nest was thereabout).

"Do, do, do, do— 10
Thy mother's hied to the vaster race:
The Pterodactyl made its nest
And laid a steel egg in her breast—
Under the Judas[3]-colored sun.
She'll work no more, nor dance, nor moan, 15
And I am come to take her place
Do, do.

There's nothing left but earth's low bed—
(The Pterodactyl fouls its nest):
But steel wings fan thee to thy rest, 20
And wingless truth and larvae lie
And eyeless hope and handless fear—
All these for thee as toys are spread,
Do—do—

Red is the bed of Poland, Spain,[4] 25
And thy mother's breast, who has grown wise
In that fouled nest. If she could rise.
Give birth again,
In wolfish pelt she'd hide thy bones
To shield thee from the world's long cold, 30
And down on all fours shouldst thou crawl
For thus from no height canst thou fall—
Do, do.

She'd give no hands: there's nought to hold
And nought to make: there's dust to sift, 35
But no food for the hands to lift.
Do, do.

Heed my ragged lullaby,
Fear not living, fear not chance;
All is equal—blindness, sight, 40

1. Written in reaction to World War II.
2. The phrase "out-dance the Babioun" occurs in an Epigram by Ben Jonson [Sitwell's note].
3. The apostle who betrayed Jesus. "Pterodactyl": pre- historic flying reptile.
4. Countries that had recently, after many battles, come under fascist rule.

There is no depth, there is no height:
Do, do.

The Judas-colored sun is gone,
And with the Ape thou art alone—
Do, 45

 Do.'

 1942

Serenade: Any Man to Any Woman

Dark angel who art clear and straight
As cannon shining in the air,
Your blackness doth invade my mind,
And thunderous as the armored wind
That rained on Europe is your hair; 5

And so I love you till I die—
(Unfaithful I, the cannon's mate):
Forgive my love of such brief span.
But fickle is the flesh of man,
And death's cold puts the passion out. 10

I'll woo you with a serenade—
The wolfish howls the starving made;
And lies shall be your canopy
To shield you from the freezing sky.

Yet when I clasp you in my arms— 15
Who are my sleep, the zero hour
That clothes, instead of flesh, my heart—
You in my heaven have no part,
For you, my mirage broken in flower,

Can never see what dead men know! 20
Then die with me and be my love [1]
The grave shall be your shady grove,
And in your pleasaunce[2] rivers flow

(To ripen this new Paradise)
From a more universal Flood 25
Than Noah knew: but yours is blood.

Yet still you will imperfect be
That in my heart like death's chill grows,

1 An ironic variation of a line from Christopher
Marlowe's (1564–1593) poem *The Passionate Sheb-*
herd to His Love: "Come live with me, and be my love."
2. Pleasure ground.

—A rainbow[3] shining in the night,
Born of my tears . . . your lips, the bright 30
Summer-old folly of the rose.

1942

Song

to Alberto de Lacerda[1]

Where is all the bright company gone—
The Trojan Elaine and the Knight Sir Gawaine?[2]
Why have they glided out of the rain?
The Queens were bright as the waters' sheen,
Beautiful, bountiful as the grain; 5
The Knights were brighter than stars in the sky
(The moons thick as roses in hot July)—
As bright as the raindrops and roses in June,
And many and merry as notes in a tune.
Alas, they are gone and I am alone, 10
For all they glided out of the rain.
And now I sit under the bright apple tree
And weep that ever the speech was spoken
That the false angel said unto me.
For had I never the apple-branch broken, 15
Death had not fallen on mankind and me.[3]

1954

3. The rainbow was the sign God gave to Noah of the
Covenant after the Flood (Genesis 9:12).
1. A Portuguese poet.
2. Sir Gawaine was one of the knights of the Round
Table in Arthurian legend. Elaine is Helen of Troy,
whose beauty was the cause of the Trojan War.
3. "Lines 13–14 are from Eva's Lament in the
Coventry Plays" [Sitwell's note]. Eve brought death
into the world when she and Adam ate fruit from the
Tree of Knowledge (Genesis 3:6).

MARIANNE MOORE
1887–1972

"I, too, dislike it," Marianne Moore once remarked about poetry, explaining, "There are things that are important beyond all this fiddle." Yet even as she wrote these words, this reserved and obscure sometime librarian was beginning to earn a distinctive reputation as a poet, and by the end of her career she had become one of the most famous—and famously eccentric—American writers of her generation. Wearing her legendary three-cornered hat, she appeared at baseball games, of which she was notoriously fond, like some character out of a fairytale. Brooding in her Brooklyn apartment, she thought up names for a new Ford car—"The Resilient Bullet," "Mongoose Civique," "Turcotingo," "Utopian Turtletop"—that was eventually, despite her fanciful suggestions, to be called the "Edsel," in honor of one of the company's presidents. Even as a somewhat austere young writer, moreover, she had been praised by such major literary men as William Carlos Williams and T. S. Eliot, and praised not for public idiosyncrasies but for private inspiration. In a way, the contradictions in Moore's history—between early reti-

cence and later reputation, between impassioned aesthetic rigor and ironically eccentric self-presentation—are emblematic of both her life and art

Born in Kirkwood, Missouri, near St. Louis, Moore moved with her mother and brother to Carlisle, Pennsylvania, in 1894, when her father abandoned the family because of financial and personal problems. After studying at the Metzger Institute, where her mother taught, and graduating in 1908 from Bryn Mawr College, where she found biology classes particularly "exhilarating' and where the poet H. D. (Hilda Doolittle) was a fellow student, she took courses in business at the Carlisle Commercial College, traveled to Europe with her mother, and from 1911 to 1915 taught shorthand, typing, and commercial law at the U.S. Industrial Indian School at Carlisle. In 1915, her verse began to appear in *The Egoist* in London and *Poetry* in Chicago, and by the end of the decade she had won a small but distinguished reputation.

Unassuming and shy, Moore continued to live with her mother, as she would throughout most of her life, and the pair moved first to New Jersey, then to Greenwich Village, and finally to Brooklyn, so that they could be near the poet's brother, a Presbyterian minister to whom she was also exceptionally close. Yet, even this early, friends could perceive the paradoxes in her personality. Presenting herself as a kind of anachronism—a dutiful, neo-Victorian daughter, an old-fashioned "lady"—she nevertheless struck William Carlos Williams as "a rafter holding up the superstructure of our uncompleted building a caryatid, her red hair plaited and wound twice about the fine skull . . . she was surely one of the main supports of the new order." And indeed, though Moore earned her living at conventional jobs—secretary in a girls' school, part-time assistant in a New York City branch library—she was mingling socially with a group of avant-garde painters and writers who were connected with the experimental little magazine *Others*; more important, she was herself composing the disruptive verse, with lines consistently organized into unusual stanza forms and language frequently freed from traditional associations, that would demonstrate her commitment to "the new order." Nevertheless, her first book appeared only because her former schoolmate H. D. and H. D.'s close friend the writer Bryher (Winifred Ellerman) conspired without her knowledge to have the volume, simply tit ed *Poems*, issued in London in 1921. After that, Moore herself arranged the publication of *Observations* (1924), which won the prestigious *Dial* award for that year, and the following year she herself became editor of *The Dial*, a position she held from 1925 to 1929.

A major New York literary magazine, *The Dial* brought Moore even further into touch with a number of important figures, including Ezra Pound (whose work she printed in the same issue with work by the neo-Victorian essayist George Saintsbury), Hart Crane (whose poems she attempted rigorously to edit), and James Joyce (portions of whose *Finnegans Wake* she rejected because they seemed to her to be morally and linguistically "offensive"). Although she largely abandoned her own verse writing during her period with this journal, her editorial experience strengthened her aesthetic self-confidence and enriched her imagination. When she began to write and publish again, she produced one of her most significant books, *Selected Poems* (1935), a volume that appeared with a laudatory introduction from T. S. Eliot and that included among other major works *The Jerboa* and *Poetry*.

Shortly before the publication of *Selected Poems*, Marianne Moore was sought out by a young poet, Elizabeth Bishop, then a student at Vassar, who was to become a lifelong friend and who later remembered the older writer as "not very tall and not in the least intimidating." It was at this time, however, that Moore was composing some of her most formidable verse, carefully constructed stanzas bristling with erudite allusions, which were soon to strike the editor Louis Untermeyer as "frankly puzzling" because they "seem to erect a barrier of jagged

clauses [and] barbed quotations ... between herself and her audience." About her characteristic, even notorious, use of quotations, however, Moore herself explained that "I was just trying to be honorable and not to steal things," and about her apparently "jagged" stanza forms, she insisted that "words cluster like chromosomes, determining the procedure [though] I may influence an arrangement or thin it, then try to have successive stanzas identical with the first."

Moore had perhaps more forthrightly formulated her personal aesthetic in her poem *To a Snail* (1924), where, defining " 'compression [as] the first grace of style,' " she added that "contractility is a virtue / as modesty is a virtue," a motto that seems eminently suitable to the quasi-Victorian spinster she so often pretended to be. Still, self-consciously "modest" and compressed as many of Moore's most ambitious early- and middle-period poems are, their serious implications become clear on close reading. Many, for instance, take animals, often quite exotic ones, as their overt subjects. But this poet appears deeply to identify with the ironically "humble" creatures who constitute her distinctive bestiary, especially with those who are in their way as carefully camouflaged or fancifully armored as her own verse.

Moore's later years were increasingly characterized by honors—including the Pulitzer Prize in 1951 and the Bollingen Prize in 1953—and by the kind of public adulation that led to her being asked, at one point, to throw out the ball that would open the Brooklyn Dodgers' baseball season. During World War II, her poetry had become more frankly passionate; pieces like *The Paper Nautilus* openly addressed themselves to issues of love and survival that she might earlier have treated more obliquely. After her mother died in 1947, she continued living in the Brooklyn apartment that the pair had shared since the late 1920s, indomitably active to the end and enjoying, as Elizabeth Bishop put it, "an unusually fortunate old age." Even for a close friend like Bishop, however, the contradictions represented by the career and personality of this radically innovative old-fashioned "lady" who made such a mark on modern poetry continued to be haunting. "When I try to summarize her life," confessed the younger woman, "I become foolishly bemused: I have a sort of subliminal glimpse of the capital letter *M* multiplying ... Marianne's monogram; mother; manners; morals; and I catch myself murmuring, 'Manners and morals; manners *as* morals? or is it morals *as* manners?' "

Sojourn in the Whale[1]

Trying to open locked doors with a sword, threading
 the points of needles, planting shade trees
 upside down; swallowed by the opaqueness of one whom the
 seas
love better than they love you, Ireland[2]—

you have lived and lived on every kind of shortage. 5
 You have been compelled by hags to spin
 gold thread from straw[3] and have heard men say:
"There is a feminine temperament in direct contrast to ours

1. Moore alludes to the biblical story of Jonah, who was swallowed by a whale because he disobeyed God, but was then released after praying for help (Jonah 1–2). Text and format follow *Selected Poems* (1935).
2. Ireland had long been politically and economically exploited by England; it had also been the victim of numerous famines.
3. In the folk tale *Rumplestiltskin*, collected by the brothers Grimm, a maiden is commanded by a king to spin straw into gold.

which makes her do these things. Circumscribed by a
 heritage of blindness and native 10
 incompetence, she will become wise and will be forced to
 give in.
Compelled by experience, she will turn back;

water seeks its own level":
 and you have smiled. "Water in motion is far
 from level."[4] You have seen it, when obstacles happened
 to bar 15
the path, rise automatically.

<div align="right">

1917, 1967

</div>

Those Various Scalpels,

those
various sounds consistently indistinct, like intermingled echoes
 struck from thin glasses successively at random—
 the inflection disguised: your hair, the tails of two
fighting-cocks head to head in stone— 5
 like sculptured scimitars repeating the curve of your ears in
 reverse order:
 your eyes, flowers of ice and snow

sown by tearing winds on the cordage of disabled ships; your
 raised hand,
 an ambiguous signature: your cheeks, those rosettes 10
 of blood on the stone floors of French châteaux.[1]
 with regard to which the guides are so affirmative—
 your other hand,

a bundle of lances all alike, partly hid by emeralds from Persia
 and the fractional magnificence of Florentine 15
 goldwork—a collection of little objects—
sapphires set with emeralds, and pearls with a moonstone,
 made fine
 with enamel in gray, yellow, and dragonfly blue;
 a lemon, a pear 20

and three bunches of grapes, tied with silver: your dress, a
 magnificent square
 cathedral tower of uniform
 and at the same time diverse appearance—a
species of vertical vineyard rustling in the storm 25
 of conventional opinion. Are they weapons or scalpels?
 Whetted to brilliance

by the hard majesty of that sophistication which is superior to
 opportunity,

4. *Literary Digest* [Moore's note]. 1. Castles

these things are rich instruments with which to experiment. 30
 But why dissect destiny with instruments
 more highly specialized than components of destiny itself?

<div align="right">1917, 1967</div>

Poetry[1]

 I, too, dislike it: there are things that are important beyond all
 this fiddle.
 Reading it, however, with a perfect contempt for it, one
 discovers in
 it after all, a place for the genuine. 5
 Hands that can grasp, eyes
 that can dilate, hair that can rise
 if it must, these things are important not because a

high-sounding interpretation can be put upon them but because
 they are 10
useful. When they become so derivative as to become
 unintelligible,
the same thing may be said for all of us, that we
 do not admire what
 we cannot understand: the bat 15
 holding on upside down or in quest of something to

eat, elephants pushing, a wild horse taking a roll, a tireless
 wolf under
a tree, the immovable critic twitching his skin like a horse
 that feels a flea, the base-
ball fan, the statistician— 20
 nor is it valid
 to discriminate against 'business documents and

school-books';[2] all these phenomena are important. One must
 make a distinction
however: when dragged into prominence by half poets, the 25
 result is not poetry,
nor till the poets among us can be
 'literalists of
 the imagination'[3]—above
 insolence and triviality and can present 30

 for inspection, imaginary gardens with real toads in them, shall
 we have

1. Moore revised this poem a number of times after its first publication in 1921. In her *Complete Poems* it is reduced to the first two sentences. The version printed here is that of *Selected Poems* (1935).
2. "*Diary of Tolstoy* (Dutton), p. 84. 'Where the boundary between prose and poetry lies, I shall never be able to understand. The question is raised in manuals of style, yet the answer to it lies beyond me. Poetry is verse; prose is not verse. Or else poetry is everything with the exception of business documents and school books' " [Moore's note]. Count Leo Tolstoi (1828–1910), Russian novelist and mystic.
3. "Yeats: *Ideas of Good and Evil* (A. H. Bullen), p. 182. 'The limitation of his view was from the very intensity of his vision; he was a too literal realist of the imagination, as others are of nature; and because he believed that the figures seen by the mind's eye, when exalted by inspiration, were "eternal essences," symbols of divine essences, he hated every grace of style that might obscure their lineaments' " [Moore's note]. William Butler Yeats (1865–1939), Irish poet.

it. In the meantime, if you demand on the one hand,
the raw material of poetry in
 all its rawness and 35
 that which is on the other hand
 genuine, then you are interested in poetry.

1919, 1935

To a Snail

If "compression is the first grace of style,"[1]
you have it. Contractility is a virtue
as modesty is a virtue.
It is not the acquisition of any one thing
that is able to adorn, 5
or the incidental quality that occurs
as a concomitant of something well said,
that we value in style,
but the principle that is hid:
in the absence of feet, "a method of conclusions"; 10
"a knowledge of principles,"
in the curious phenomenon of your occipital[2] horn.

1921, 1967

Sea Unicorns and Land Unicorns

with their respective lions—
"mighty monoceroses with immeasured tayles"[1]—
these are those very animals
described by the cartographers of 1539,
defiantly revolving 5
in such a way that
the long keel of white exhibited in tumbling,
disperses giant weeds
and those sea snakes whose forms, looped in the foam, "disquiet
 shippers."[2]
Knowing how a voyager obtained the horn of a sea unicorn 10
to give to Queen Elizabeth,
who thought it worth a hundred thousand pounds,
they persevere in swimming where they like,
finding the place where sea-lions live in herds,
strewn on the beach like stones with lesser stones— 15

1. "The very first grace of style is that which comes
from compression." *Demetrius on Style*, translated by
W. Hamilton Fyfe. Heinemann, 1932 [Moore's note].
2. I.e., located near the back of the head.
1. An echo of Edmund Spenser (1552–1599, English
poet.
2. Violet A. Wilson, in *Queen Elizabeth's Maids of
Honour* (Dutton, 1922), quotes Olaus Magnus,
History of the Goths and Swedes, with regard to the sea

serpent; says of Cavendish as a voyager, "He sailed up
the Thames in splendour, the sails of his ship being
cloth of gold and his seamen clad in rich silks. Many
were the curiosities which the explorers brought home
as presents for the ladies. The Queen naturally had
first choice and to her fell the unicorn's horn valued at
a hundred thousand pounds, which became one of the
treasures of Windsor" [Moore's note].

and bears are white;
discovering Antarctica, its penguin kings and icy spires,
and Sir John Hawkins' Florida
"abounding in land unicorns and lions;
since where the one is, 20
its arch-enemy cannot be missing."[3]
Thus personalities by nature much opposed,
can be combined in such a way
that when they do agree, their unanimity is great,
 "in politics, in trade, law, sport, religion, 25
china-collecting, tennis, and church-going."[4]
You have remarked this fourfold combination of strange animals,
upon embroideries
enwrought with "polished garlands" of agreeing difference—
 thorns, "myrtle rods, and shafts of bay,"[5] 30
"cobwebs, and knotts, and mulberries"[6]
of lapis lazuli and pomegranate and malachite—
Britannia's sea unicorn with its rebellious child
now ostentatiously indigenous to the new English coast;
and its land lion oddly tolerant of those pacific counterparts to it, 35
the water lions of the west.
This is a strange fraternity—these sea lions and land lions,
land unicorns and sea unicorns:
the lion civilly rampant,
tame and concessive like the long-tailed bear of Ecuador[7]— 40
the lion standing up against this screen of woven air
which is the forest:
the unicorn also, on its hind legs in reciprocity.
A puzzle to the hunters, is this haughtiest of beasts,
to be distinguished from those born without a horn, 45
in use like Saint Jerome's tame lion,[8] as domestics;
rebelling proudly at the dogs
which are dismayed by the chain lightning
playing at them from its horn—
the dogs persistent in pursuit of it as if it could be caught, 50
"deriving agreeable terror" from its "moonbeam throat"[9]
on fire like its white coat and unconsumed as if of salamander's
 skin.[1]

3. Sir John Hawkins "affirmed the existence of land unicorns in the forests of Florida, and from their presence deduced abundance of lions because of the antipathy between the two animals, so that 'where the one is, the other cannot be missing' " [Moore's note].
4. An echo of the American novelist Henry James's (1843–1916) book *English Hours* (1905).
5. Moore takes these phrases from the English poet J. A. Symonds (1840–1893).
6. Apropos Queen Elizabeth's dresses, "cobwebs, and knotts and mulberries." "A petticoat embroidered all over slightly with snakes of Venice gold and silver and some O's, with a faire border embroidered like seas, cloudes, and rainbowes" [Moore's note].
7. *The long-tailed bear.* C. H. Prodgers in *Adventures in Bolivia* (Dodd, Mead, 1922), p. 193, tells of a strange animal that he bought: "It was stuffed with long grass and cost me ten shillings, turning out even-

tually to be a bear with a tail. In his book on wild life, Rowland Ward says, 'Amongst the rarest animals is a bear with a tail; this animal is known to exist, is very rare, and only to be found in the forests of Ecuador,' and this was where the man who sold it to me said he got it" [Moore's note].
8. St. Jerome (4th century), a Church father traditionally thought to have spent a night unharmed in a lion's den.
9. "The lover of reading will derive agreeable terror from Sir Bertram and the Haunted Chamber." Leigh Hunt's *Autobiography.* Lines 52, 80, 82: "Moonbeam throat," "with pavon high," "upon her lap." "Mediaeval," an anonymous poem in *Punch,* April 25, 1923 [Moore's notes].
1. Salamanders are traditionally reputed to be immune to flames.

So wary as to disappear for centuries and reappear,
yet never to be caught,
the unicorn has been preserved 55
by an unmatched device[2]
wrought like the work of expert blacksmiths,
this animal of that one horn
throwing itself upon which head foremost from a cliff,
it walks away unharmed; 60
proficient in this feat which, like Herodotus,[3]
I have not seen except in pictures.
Thus this strange animal with its miraculous elusiveness,
has come to be unique,
"impossible to take alive,"[4] 65
tamed only by a lady inoffensive like itself—
as curiously wild and gentle;
"as straight and slender as the crest,
or antlet of the one-beam'd beast."[5]
Upon the printed page, 70
also by word of mouth,
we have a record of it all
and how, unfearful of deceit,
etched like an equine monster of an old celestial map,
beside a cloud or dress of Virgin-Mary blue, 75
improved "all over slightly with snakes of Venice gold,
and silver, and some O's,"
the unicorn "with pavon high," approaches eagerly;
until engrossed by what appears of this strange enemy,
upon the map, "upon her lap," 80
its "mild wild head doth lie."

 1921, 1967

An Egyptian Pulled Glass Bottle in the Shape of a Fish

Here we have thirst
and patience, from the first,
 and art, as in a wave held up for us to see
 in its essential perpendicularity;

not brittle but 5
intense—the spectrum, that
 spectacular and nimble animal the fish,
 whose scales turn aside the sun's sword by their polish.

 1921, 1967

2. Bulfinch's *Mythology*, under "Unicorn" [Moore's note].
3. "Herodotus says of the phoenix, 'I have not seen it myself except in a picture'" [Moore's note]. Herodotus (5th century B.C.), Greek historian.
4. Moore quotes Pliny the Elder (1st century A.D.), Roman naturalist.
5. "Charles Cotton, *An Epitaph on M. H.*: 'As soft, and snow, as that down / Adorns the Blow-ball's frizzled crown; / As straight and slender as the crest / Or antlet of the one-beam'd beast'" [Moore's note]. Charles Cotton (1630–1687), English poet and translator.

Silence

My father used to say,
"Superior people never make long visits,
have to be shown Longfellow's grave
or the glass flowers at Harvard.[1]
Self-reliant like the cat— 5
that takes it prey to privacy,
the mouse's limp tail hanging like a shoelace from its mouth—
they sometimes enjoy solitude,
and can be robbed of speech
by speech which has delighted them. 10
The deepest feeling always shows itself in silence;
not in silence, but restraint."
Nor was he insincere in saying, "Make my house your inn."[2]
Inns are not residences.

 1921, 1967

No Swan So Fine

"No water so still as the
 dead fountains of Versailles."[1] No swan,
with swart blind look askance
and gondoliering legs, so fine
 as the chintz china one with fawn- 5
brown eyes and toothed gold
collar on to show whose bird it was.

Lodged in the Louis Fifteenth
 candelabrum-tree of cockscomb-
tinted buttons, dahlias, 10
sea urchins, and everlastings,
 it perches on the branching foam
of polished sculptured
flowers—at ease and tall. The king is dead.

 1932, 1967

The Jerboa[1]

Too Much

A Roman had an
artist, a freedman,

1. "My father used to say, 'Superior people never make
long visits. When I am visiting, I like to go about by
myself. I never had to be shown Longfellow's grave or
the glass flowers at Harvard.' Miss A. M. Homans"
[Moore's note]. The Botanical Museum of Harvard
began its famous glass flower collection in 1887.
2. Edmund Burke, in *Burke's Life*, by Sir James Prior
(1872). " 'Throw yourself into a coach,' said he. 'Come
down and make my house your inn' " [Moore's note].

1. "A pair of Louis XV candelabra with Dresden figures
of swans belonging to Lord Balfour. 'There is no water
so still as in the dead fountains of Versailles.' Percy
Phillip, *New York Times Magazine*, May 10, 1931"
[Moore's note]. Louis XV, the king of France, held
court at the opulent palace of Versailles in the 18th
century.
1. A nocturnal jumping rodent.

contrive a cone—pine cone
or fir cone-with holes for a fountain. Placed on
 the Prison of St. Angelo,[2] this cone 5
 of the Pompeys which is known

now as the Popes', passed
for art. A huge cast
 bronze, dwarfing the peacock
 statue in the garden of the Vatican, 10
 it looks like a work of art made to give
 to a Pompey, or native

of Thebes[3] Others could
build, and understood
 making colossi[4] and 15
 how to use slaves, and kept crocodiles and put
 baboons on the necks of giraffes to pick
 fruit, and used serpent magic.

They had their men tie
hippopotami 20
 and bring out dappled dog-
 cats to course antelopes, dikdik, and ibex;[5]
 or used small eagles. They looked on as theirs,
 impalas and onigers,[6]

the wild ostrich herd 25
with hard feet and bird
 necks rearing back in the
 dust like a serpent preparing to strike, cranes,
 mongooses, storks, anoas,[7] Nile geese;
 and there were gardens for these— 30

combining planes, dates,
limes, and pomegranates,
 in avenues—with square
 pools of pink flowers, tame fish, and small frogs. Besides
 yarns dyed with indigo, and red cotton,
 they had a flax which they spun 35

into fine linen
cordage for yachtsmen.
 These people liked small things;
 they gave to boys little paired playthings such as
 nests of eggs, ichneumon[8] and snake, paddle
 and raft, badger and camel; 40

2. A prison in Rome.
3. Greek city. Pompey (1st century A.D.), Roman general.
4. Huge statues of human forms.
5. Wild goats. "Dikdik": a variety of antelope.
6. African antelopes.
7. Small wild oxen.
8. Mongoose; a small ferretlike animal that eats snakes.

and made toys for them-
selves: the royal totem;
 and toilet boxes marked
 with the contents. Lords and ladies put goose-grease 45
 paint in round bone boxes—the pivoting
 lid incised with a duck-wing

or reverted duck-
head; kept in a buck
 or rhinoceros horn, 50
 the ground horn; and locust oil in stone locusts.[9]
 It was a picture with a fine distance;
 of drought, and of assistance

in time, from the Nile
rising slowly, while 55
 the pig-tailed monkeys on
 slab hands, with arched-up slack-slung gait, and the brown
 dandy looked at the jasmine two-leafed twig
 and bud, cactus pads, and fig.

Dwarfs here and there, lent 60
to an evident
 poetry of frog grays,
 duck-egg greens, and eggplant blues, a fantasy
 and a verisimilitude that were
 right to those with, everywhere, 65

power over the poor.
The bees' food is your
 food. Those who tended flower-
 beds and stables were like the king's cane[1] in the
 form of a hand, or the folding bedroom[2] 70
 made for his mother of whom

he was fond. Princes
clad in queens' dresses,
 calla or petunia
 white, that trembled at the edge, and queens in a 75
 king's underskirt of fine-twilled thread like silk-
 worm gut, as bee-man and milk-

maid, kept divine cows
and bees; limestone brows,
 and gold-foil wings. They made 80
 basalt serpents and portraits of beetles; the
 king gave his name to them and he was named
 for them. He feared snakes, and tamed

9. Toilet box dating from about the twenty-second Egyptian Dynasty. *Illustrated London News*, July 26, 1930 [Moore's note].
1. Description by J. D. S. Pendlebury, *Illustrated London News*, March 19, 1932 [Moore's note].

2. The portable bedchamber of Queen Hetepheres presented to her by her son, Cheops. Described by Dr. G. A. Reisner, *Illustrated London News*, May 7, 1932 [Moore's note].

Pharaoh's rat, the rust-
backed mongoose. No bust 85
 of it was made, but there
 was pleasure for the rat. Its restlessness was
 its excellence; it was praised for its wit;
 and the jerboa,[3] like it,

a small desert rat, 90
and not famous, that
 lives without water, has
 happiness. Abroad seeking food, or at home
 in its burrow, the Sahara fieldmouse
 has a shining silver house 95

of sand. O rest and
joy, the boundless sand,
 the stupendous sandspout,
 no water, no palm trees, no ivory bed,
 tiny cactus; but one would not be he 100
 who has nothing but plenty.

Abundance

Africanus[4] meant
the conqueror sent
 from Rome. It should mean the
 untouched: the sand-brown jumping-rat—free-born; and 105
 the blacks, that choice race with an elegance
 ignored by one's ignorance.

Part terrestrial,
and part celestial,
 Jacob saw,[5] of cudgel staff 110
 in claw hand—steps of air and air angels; his
 friends were the stones. The translucent mistake
 of the desert, does not make

hardship for one who
can rest and then do 115
 the opposite—launching
 as if on wings, from its match-thin hind legs, in
 daytime or at night, with the tail as a weight,
 undulated out by speed, straight.

Looked at by daylight, 120
the underside's white,
 though the fur on the back

3. "There are little rats called jerboas which run on long hindlegs as thin as a match. The forelimbs are mere tiny hands." Dr. R. L. Ditmars, *Strange Animals I Have Known* (New York: Harcourt Brace, 1931), p. 274 [Moore's note].
4. An honorary name bestowed on Roman generals who made conquests in Africa, such as the two Scipios who fought against Carthage.
5. During a journey through the desert, Jacob dreams he sees a ladder rising to heaven, carrying God's angels (Genesis 28:12).

 is buff-brown like the breast of the fawn-breasted
 bower-bird. It hops like the fawn-breast, but has
 chipmunk contours—perceived as 125

it turns its bird head—
the nap directed
 neatly back and blending
 with the ear which reiterates the slimness
 of the body. The fine hairs on the tail, 130
 repeating the other pale

markings, lengthen until
at the tip they fill
 out in a tuft—black and
 white; strange detail of the simplified creature, 135
 fish-shaped and silvered to steel by the force
 of the large desert moon. Course

the jerboa, or
plunder its food store,
 and you will be cursed. It 140
 honors the sand by assuming its color;
 closed upper paws seeming one with the fur
 in its flight from a danger.

By fifths and sevenths,[6]
in leaps of two lengths, 145
 like the uneven notes
 of the Bedouin flute, it stops its gleaning
 on little wheel castors, and makes fern-seed
 footprints with kangaroo speed.

Its leaps should be set 150
to the flageolet;[7]
 pillar body erect
 on a three-cornered smooth-working Chippendale[8]
 claw—propped on hind legs, and tail as third toe,
 between leaps to its burrow. 155

 1932, 1967

The Paper Nautilus[1]

For authorities whose hopes
are shaped by mercenaries?
Writers entrapped by

6. Wide melodic intervals in music.
7. A small flute.
8. An English manufacturer of furniture, often featuring clawlike feet.
1. A fish related to the octopus, also known as the Argonaut. The female builds a fragile shell to contain her eggs, carrying it on the surface of the water with two of her eight tentacles, once thought to serve as sails; hence the name, which means "sailor."

 teatime fame and by
commuters' comforts? Not for these 5
 the paper nautilus
 constructs her thin glass shell

 Giving her perishable
souvenir of hope, a dull
 white outside and smooth- 10
 edged inner surface
glossy as the sea, the watchful
 maker of it guards it
 day and night; she scarcely

 eats until the eggs are hatched. 15
Buried eightfold in her eight
 arms, for she is in
 a sense a devil-
fish, her glass ram's-horn-cradled freight
 is hid but is not crushed; 20
 as Hercules, bitten

 by a crab loyal to the hydra,[2]
was hindered to succeed.
 the intensively
 watched eggs coming from 25
the shell free it when they are freed—
 leaving its wasp-nest flaws
 of white on white, and close-

 laid Ionic chiton[3]-folds
like the lines in the mane of 30
 a Parthenon horse.[4]
 round which the arms had
wound themselves as if they knew love
 is the only fortress
 strong enough to trust to. 35

 1941

His Shield

The pin-swin or spine-swine
 (the edgehog miscalled hedgehog) with all his edges out,
 echidna and echinoderm[1] in distressed-
pin-cushion thorn-fur coats, the spiny pig or porcupine,
 the rhino with horned snout— 5
 everything is battle-dressed.

2. In Greek myth, a many-headed monster subdued
by the hero Hercules As he fought the monster, a crab
bit him, and he crushed it underfoot.
3. Ancient Greek tunic.

4. I.e., represented in the frieze at the Parthenon, a
temple in Athens
1. I.e., spiny-skin. "Echidna": another species of por-
cupine.

Pig-fur won't do, I'll wrap
 myself in salamander-skin like Presbyter John.[2]
 A lizard in the midst of flames, a firebrand
that is life, asbestos-eyed asbestos-eared, with tattooed nap 10
 and permanent pig on
 the instep; he can withstand

fire and won't drown. In his
 unconquerable country of unpompous gusto,
 gold was so common none considered it; greed 15
and flattery were unknown. Though rubies large as tennis
 balls conjoined in streams so
 that the mountain seemed to bleed,

the inextinguishable
 salamander styled himself but presbyter. His shield 20
 was his humility. In Carpasian
linen coat, flanked by his household lion cubs and sable
 retinue, he revealed
 a formula safer than

an armorer's: the power of relinquishing 25
 what one would keep; that is freedom. Become dinosaur-
 skulled, quilled or salamander-wooled, more ironshod
and javelin-dressed than a hedgehog battalion of steel, but be
 dull. Don't be envied or
 armed with a measuring-rod. 30

<div align="right">1951</div>

O to Be a Dragon[1]

 If I, like Solomon,[2]. . .
 could have my wish—

 my wish . . . O to be a dragon,
 a symbol of the power of Heaven—of silkworm
 size or immense; at times invisible. 5
 Felicitous phenomenon!

<div align="right">1957</div>

2. A legendary Christian monarch (12th century), who was said to perform marvels of all kinds. The salamander was traditionally thought to be immune to fire. "Presbyter": priest.
1. See secondary symbols, Volume II of *The Tao of Painting*, translated and edited by Mai-mai Sze, Bollingen Series 49 (New York: Pantheon, 1956; Modern Library edition, p. 57) [Moore's note].
2. Solomon's wish: "an understanding heart." 1 Kings 3:9 [Moore's note].

KATHERINE MANSFIELD

1888–1923

When she was thirty years old, Katherine Mansfield described the two motives of what she called her "writing game" with striking clarity and conviction: "*One* is joy," she explained in a letter to her husband, the critic J. Middleton Murry, adding that in this state of being "in some perfectly blissful way *at peace*," something like a flower "seems to open before my eyes." The other "kick off" consisted of "*a cry against corruption*" that she associated with the hopeless sense that "everything [is] doomed to disaster." It is hardly surprising that the New Zealand–born Kathleen Beauchamp should have felt divided about her identity as a London literary figure called Katherine Mansfield. She came from a conventional Victorian family, but she lived the bohemian life of a New Woman. She referred to herself as a "child" and liked to play with dolls, kittens, and imaginary babies, but she suffered from gonorrhea, had one miscarriage, and seems to have had an abortion. She repeatedly protested that she wanted nothing more than a home of her own, but she spent her life restlessly traveling from England to France and Italy, and back again. She said she adored her husband, but she never relinquished her close ties to her "wife," Ida Baker. Finally, and most tragically, while she searched for spiritual health, she suffered the debilitating consequences of the tuberculosis that killed her at the age of thirty-five.

Kathleen Beauchamp's father, Harold Beauchamp, was an enterprising Wellington businessman who would go on to become a prominent director of the Bank of New Zealand. Her mother, Annie (Dyer) Beauchamp, was a delicate woman who brought her own mother to live in the household. This grandmother provided the affectionate protection Kathleen's self-absorbed, frail mother and upwardly mobile father could not supply. After the birth of her only brother, Kathleen was sent with her sisters to a series of New Zealand schools; then, at fifteen, she traveled with her family to London, where she studied for three years at Queen's College. By the time she unwillingly returned to New Zealand, she was reading the fiction of Oscar Wilde, Elizabeth Robins, the Brontës, and Leo Tolstoi, and she was beginning to receive payment for vignettes appearing in *The Native Companion*, a New Zealand journal. This sign of success was sufficient to convince her father to allow her to go back to London.

Kathleen had already begun to establish the divided emotional loyalties that would inform the rest of her life. On the one hand, she was writing love letters to the son of her Wellington music teacher, Tom Trowell, whose twin, Garnet, would become her fiancé when she finally managed to return to England. On the other hand, an early journal entry indicates that she felt guilty about her passion for a Wellington schoolfriend, Maata Mahupuku a Maori (native New Zealand) heiress. At Queen's College, moreover, she met Ida Constance Baker, a motherless girl whose father was to become the model for the tyrannical paterfamilias in *The Daughters of the Late Colonel*. Ida eventually became known as L. M. (Leslie Moore) and Kathleen called herself Katherine Mansfield. When Katherine was rejected by Garnet Trowell's parents and decided on the spur of the moment to marry a new acquaintance, George Bowden, it was L. M. who accompanied the twenty-one-year-old bride, dressed all in black, to the Registry Office; it was also to L. M. that the bride fled on her wedding night. At this point, however, Mrs. Beauchamp arrived in London and packed Katherine off to a German hotel. There, according to her biographer Antony Alpers, she was "treated" for her lesbianism with cold baths, and she suffered a miscarriage.

Mansfield's early stories were first published individually in A. R. Orage's *New Age* and then collected in the caustic volume titled *In a German Pension* (1911).

After she sent one tale, *The Woman at the Store*, to a new review, *Rhythm*, she was visited by its literary editor, J. Middleton Murry, an Oxford undergraduate who came from what Alpers calls "the very bottom of the lower middle class." One year younger than Mansfield, he became in 1912 first a lodger in her flat and then her lover. Although *Rhythm* would soon go bankrupt, Mansfield continued to publish stories to supplement the modest allowance provided by her father, and Murry began earning money from critical essays and reviews.

Their lives, like everyone else's, were shattered by World War I. While L. M. worked as a machinist in an airplane factory, Murry took a job in military intelligence. For Mansfield, however, the reality of the war was brought home by the death of her brother, Leslie, who was "blown to bits" in France. In *Prelude* (1918) and *At the Bay* (1921), Mansfield went on to reconstruct the "undiscovered country" she had shared with Leslie Beauchamp in stories that depart from conventional narration to convey the mysterious radiance of childhood as it is perceived by a community of women and children. Near the end of her life, moreover, she wrote the startling antiwar story *The Fly* (1922) to express her outrage at the sacrifice of a generation of sons by their fathers, the architects of the war.

When she was not traveling or living on the Continent, Mansfield was befriended by a number of literary celebrities in London, including, most importantly, the novelists D. H. Lawrence and Virginia Woolf. These last two relationships illuminate the tensions in the writer's literary career. Throughout her journal and her numerous letters, Mansfield expressed her admiration for Lawrence, her sense that they were "unthinkably alike" not only in temperament but in their artistic efforts to capture the sensuous feeling of life. Yet she was horrified by the violent, public bickering in which Lawrence and his wife, Frieda, engaged, and she may have also understood that Lawrence was really searching for what he called a "blood brotherhood" with Murry, to whom he was greatly attracted. Even if she did not recognize herself and Murry in Lawrence's portraits of the self-conscious miniaturist Gudrun and her masterfully attractive but flawed lover Gerald in *Women in Love* (1920), Mansfield had been alienated by a shocking letter Lawrence wrote her in 1920: "You revolt me, stewing in your consumption."

Significant as Mansfield's relationship with Lawrence was, her friendship with Virginia Woolf was perhaps equally crucial. In 1917, the "Woolves" published *Prelude* at their Hogarth Press, and Mansfield and Woolf began visiting and writing each other. Sometimes the older, wealthier Woolf criticized Mansfield's bohemian promiscuity, but she nevertheless admitted that beyond Mansfield's "commonness" was an "inscrutable" intelligence. Analyzing their similar literary aims, Mansfield wrote Woolf, "We have the same job, Virginia." After Mansfield died, moreover, Woolf recorded in her diary that Mansfield had produced "the only writing I have ever been jealous of." Although Woolf did not understand why their relationship deteriorated, it is clear from Mansfield's letters that the younger writer envied a woman who had her own home, her own possessions, and her own man within call, for Mansfield's rootlessness was related to her uneasy alliance with Murry.

Mansfield sustained a relationship with Murry from the time she was twenty-four until her death. While she admired the critical intelligence shown in his book on Dostoevsky, she knew the "sham" side of Murry's personality, when he seemed "to uncover" himself "and quiver" in an ecstasy of self-pity. Mansfield was also aware of Murry's physical revulsion against and impatience with her tuberculosis, a reaction she presents brilliantly in her short story *The Man Without a Temperament* (1920). Mansfield's continual search for a healthy place to recuperate meant long separations, and her letters complain of her husband's monetary and emotional stinginess as well as of her loneliness. The sicker she became, the more she relied on L. M.'s services as a traveling companion, a home nurse, and a cook, but her dependence bred resentment, and L. M. came to seem like "The Albatross" or "a revolting hysterical ghoul." Mansfield's letters from this period re-

main difficult to interpret, for they were, like her *Journal*, heavily edited by Murry.

After 1918, Mansfield increasingly suffered from night terrors, insomnia, difficulty walking, pains in the chest, and a nausea that made it difficult for her to eat. The complex relationship between illness and creativity in Mansfield's career has been the source of much critical attention, most recently by Mary Burgan. At the onset of her physical problems Mansfield began writing the stories that would be published in *Bliss and Other Stories* (1920) as well as many reviews for Murry's journal, the *Atheneum*. Always short of money, she nevertheless began a series of cures that included stays in nursing homes, radium treatments, and x-rays. By 1922, when *The Garden Party and Other Stories* was published to critical acclaim, she was reading P. D. Ouspensky's *Cosmic Anatomy* and contemplating spiritual cures for the physical problems her physicians could not alleviate. Then she became acquainted through Orage with the Caucasian Greek spiritualist George Ivanovich Gurdjieff. He was just establishing his Institute for the Harmonious Development of Man at Fontainebleau, where he recommended drastic shifts in habit, unsettling alterations in living conditions, and rhythmic exercises and dances to accomplish a "centering" that would result in a new self and a new way of seeing. In 1922, Mansfield secretly joined Gurdjieff's community, but soon she invited Murry to visit her. By that time, she had been installed in a hayloft where she could breathe the exhalation of cows, drink fresh milk, and gaze at the ceiling and walls, which were decorated with paintings of flowers, birds, and animals. On the night of Murry's visit, Mansfield suffered a hemorrhage and died almost instantly.

During her short lifetime, the former Kathleen Beauchamp had been recognized for the sardonic, often cynical stories that she wrote as a cry against the corruption of modern English society. But, midway in her career, she had also begun composing joyous narratives, peaceful memories of a blissful New Zealand childhood. For the last few years of her life, moreover, she brilliantly integrated her satiric and sympathetic impulses in portraits of impoverished, single women and imaginative children that transformed the art of the short story. Frequently compared with Anton Chekhov, whom she greatly admired, Mansfield practiced her art with strenuous discipline for it was a reprieve from the pain of her life.

The Daughters of the Late Colonel

1

The week after was one of the busiest weeks of their lives. Even when they went to bed it was only their bodies that lay down and rested; their minds went on, thinking things out, talking things over, wondering, deciding, trying to remember where . . .

Constantia lay like a statue, her hands by her sides, her feet just overlapping each other, the sheet up to her chin. She stared at the ceiling.

"Do you think father would mind if we gave his top-hat to the porter?"[1]

"The porter?" snapped Josephine. "Why ever the porter? What a very extraordinary idea!"

"Because," said Constantia slowly, "he must often have to go to funerals. And I noticed at—at the cemetery that he only had a bowler." She paused. "I thought then how very much he'd appreciate a top-hat. We ought to give him a present, too. He was always very nice to father."

"But," cried Josephine, flouncing on her pillow and staring across the dark at Constantia, "father's head!" And suddenly, for one awful moment, she

1. In England, a male servant; originally a gatekeeper.

nearly giggled. Not, of course, that she felt in the least like giggling. It must have been habit. Years ago, when they had stayed awake at night talking, their beds had simply heaved. And now the porter's head, disappearing, popped out, like a candle, under father's hat. . . . The giggle mounted, mounted; she clenched her hands; she fought it down; she frowned fiercely at the dark and said "Remember" terribly sternly.

"We can decide tomorrow," she sighed.

Constantia had noticed nothing; she sighed.

"Do you think we ought to have our dressing-gowns dyed as well?"

"Black?" almost shrieked Josephine.

"Well, what else?" said Constantia. "I was thinking—it doesn't seem quite sincere, in a way, to wear black out of doors and when we're fully dressed, and then when we're at home—"

"But nobody sees us," said Josephine. She gave the bedclothes such a twitch that both her feet became uncovered, and she had to creep up the pillows to get them well under again.

"Kate does," said Constantia. "And the postman very well might."

Josephine thought of her dark-red slippers, which matched her dressing-gown, and of Constantia's favorite indefinite green ones which went with hers. Black! Two black dressing-gowns and two pairs of black woolly slippers, creeping off to the bathroom like black cats.

"I don't think it's absolutely necessary," said she.

Silence. Then Constantia said, "We shall have to post the papers with the notice in them tomorrow to catch the Ceylon mail. . . . How many letters have we had up till now?"

"Twenty-three."

Josephine had replied to them all, and twenty-three times when she came to "We miss our dear father so much" she had broken down and had to use her handkerchief, and on some of them even to soak up a very light-blue tear with an edge of blotting-paper. Strange! She couldn't have put it on—but twenty-three times. Even now, though, when she said over to herself sadly. "We miss our dear father *so* much" she could have cried if she'd wanted to.

"Have you got enough stamps?" came from Constantia.

"Oh, how can I tell?" said Josephine crossly. "What's the good of asking me that now?"

"I was just wondering," said Constantia mildly.

Silence again. There came a little rustle, a scurry, a hop.

"A mouse," said Constantia.

"It can't be a mouse because there aren't any crumbs," said Josephine.

"But it doesn't know there aren't," said Constantia.

A spasm of pity squeezed her heart. Poor little thing! She wished she'd left a tiny piece of biscuit on the dressing-table. It was awful to think of it not finding anything. What would it do?

"I can't think how they manage to live at all," she said slowly.

"Who?" demanded Josephine.

And Constantia said more loudly than she meant to, "Mice."

Josephine was furious. "Oh, what nonsense, Con!" she said. "What have mice got to do with it? You're asleep."

"I don't think I am," said Constantia. She shut her eyes to make sure. She was.

Josephine arched her spine, pulled up her knees, folded her arms so that her fists came under her ears, and pressed her cheek hard against the pillow.

2

Another thing which complicated matters was they had Nurse Andrews staying on with them that week. It was their own fault; they had asked her. It was Josephine's idea On the morning—well, on the last morning, when the doctor had gone, Josephine had said to Constantia, 'Don't you think it would be rather nice if we asked Nurse Andrews to stay on for a week as our guest?"

"Very nice," said Constantia.

"I thought," went on Josephine quickly, "I should just say this afternoon, after I've paid her, 'My sister and I would be very pleased, after all you've done for us, Nurse Andrews, if you would stay on for a week as our guest.' I'd have to put that in about being our guest in case—"

"Oh, but she could hardly expect to be paid!" cried Constantia.

"One never knows," said Josephine sagely.

Nurse Andrews had, of course, jumped at the idea. But it was a bother. It meant they had to have regular sit-down meals at the proper times, whereas if they'd been alone they could just have asked Kate if she wouldn't have minded bringing them a tray wherever they were. And meal-times now that the strain was over were rather a trial.

Nurse Andrews was simply fearful about butter. Really they couldn't help feeling that about butter, at least, she took advantage of their kindness. And she had that maddening habit of asking for just an inch more bread to finish what she had on her plate, and then, at the last mouthful, absent-mindedly— of course it wasn't absent-mindedly—taking another helping. Josephine got very red when this happened, and she fastened her small, bead-like eyes on the tablecloth as if she saw a minute strange insect creeping through the web of it. But Constantia's long, pale face lengthened and set, and she gazed away— away—far over the desert, to where that line of camels unwound like a thread of wool. . . .

"When I was with Lady Tukes," said Nurse Andrews, "she had such a dainty little contrayvance for the buttah. It was a silvah Cupid balanced on the—on the bordah of a glass dish, holding a tayny fork. And when you wanted some buttah you simply pressed his foot and he bent down and speared you a piece. It was quite a gayme."

Josephine could hardly bear that. But "I think those things are very extravagant" was all she said.

"But whey?" asked Nurse Andrews, beaming through her eye-glasses. "No one, surely, would take more buttah than one wanted—would one?"

"Ring, Con," cried Josephine. She couldn't trust herself to reply.

And proud young Kate, the enchanted princess, came in to see what the old tabbies wanted now. She snatched away their plates of mock something or other and slapped down a white, terrified blancmange.[2]

"Jam, please, Kate," said Josephine kindly.

Kate knelt and burst open the sideboard, lifted the lid of the jam-pot, saw it was empty, put it on the table, and stalked off.

2. A sweet pudding.

"I'm afraid," said Nurse Andrews a moment later, "there isn't any."

"Oh, what a bother!" said Josephine. She bit her lip. "What had we better do?"

Constantia looked dubious. "We can't disturb Kate again," she said softly.

Nurse Andrews waited, smiling at them both. Her eyes wandered, spying at everything behind her eye-glasses. Constantia in despair went back to her camels. Josephine frowned heavily—concentrated. If it hadn't been for this idiotic woman she and Con would, of course, have eaten their blancmange without. Suddenly the idea came.

"I know," she said. "Marmalade. There's some marmalade in the sideboard. Get it, Con."

"I hope," laughed Nurse Andrews, and her laugh was like a spoon tinkling against a medicine-glass—"I hope it's not very bittah marmalayde."

3

But, after all, it was not long now, and then she'd be gone for good. And there was no getting over the fact that she had been very kind to father. She had nursed him day and night at the end. Indeed, both Constantia and Josephine felt privately she had rather overdone the not leaving him at the very last. For when they had gone in to say good-bye Nurse Andrews had sat beside his bed the whole time, holding his wrist and pretending to look at her watch. It couldn't have been necessary. It was so tactless, too. Supposing father had wanted to say something—something private to them. Not that he had. Oh, far from it! He lay there, purple, a dark angry purple in the face, and never even looked at them when they came in. Then, as they were standing there, wondering what to do, he had suddenly opened one eye. Oh, what a difference it would have made, what a difference to their memory of him, how much easier to tell people about it, if he had only opened both! But no—one eye only. It glared at them a moment and then . . . went out.

4

It had made it very awkward for them when Mr. Farolles, of St. John's, called the same afternoon.

"The end was quite peaceful, I trust?" were the first words he said as he glided towards them through the dark drawing-room.

"Quite," said Josephine faintly. They both hung their heads. Both of them felt certain that eye wasn't at all a peaceful eye.

"Won't you sit down?" said Josephine.

"Thank you, Miss Pinner," said Mr. Farolles gracefully. He folded his coat-tails and began to lower himself into father's armchair, but just as he touched it he almost sprang up and slid into the next chair instead.

He coughed. Josephine clasped her hands; Constantia looked vague.

"I want you to feel, Miss Pinner," said Mr. Farolles, "and you Miss Constantia, that I'm trying to be helpful. I want to be helpful to you both, if you will let me. These are the times," said Mr. Farolles, very simple and earnestly, "when God means us to be helpful to one another."

"Thank you very much, Mr. Farolles," said Josephine and Constantia.

"Not at all," said Mr. Farolles gently. He drew his kid gloves through his fin-

gers and leaned forward. "And if either of you would like a little Communion,[3] either or both of you, here *and* now, you have only to tell me. A little Communion is often very help—a great comfort," he added tenderly.

But the idea of a little Communion terrified them. What! In the drawing-room by themselves—with no—no altar or anything! The piano would be much too high, thought Constantia, and Mr. Farolles could not possibly lean over it with the chalice. And Kate would be sure to come bursting in and interrupt them, thought Josepine. And supposing the bell rang in the middle? It might be somebody important—about their mourning. Would they get up reverently and go out, or would they have to wait . . . in torture?

"Perhaps you will send round a note by your good Kate if you would care for it later," said Mr. Farolles.

"Oh yes, thank you very much!" they both said.

Mr. Farolles got up and took his black straw hat from the round table.

"And about the funeral," he said softly. "I may arrange that—as your dear father's old friend and yours, Miss Pinner—and Miss Constantia?"

Josephine and Constantia got up too.

"I should like it to be quite simple," said Josephine firmly, "and not too expensive. At the same time, I should like—"

"A good one that will last," thought dreamy Constantia, as if Josephine were buying a nightgown. But of course Josephine didn't say that. "One suitable to our father's position." She was very nervous.

"I'll run round to our good friend Mr. Knight," said Mr. Farolles soothingly. "I will ask him to come and see you. I am sure you will find him very helpful indeed."

<center>5</center>

Well, at any rate, all that part of it was over, though neither of them could possibly believe that father was never coming back. Josephine had had a moment of absolute terror at the cemetery, while the coffin was lowered, to think that she and Constantia had done this thing without asking his permission. What would father say when he found out? For he was bound to find out sooner or later. He always did. "Buried. You two girls had me *buried!*" She heard his stick thumping. Oh, what would they say? What possible excuse could they make? It sounded such an appallingly heartless thing to do. Such a wicked advantage to take of a person because he happened to be helpless at the moment. The other people seemed to treat it all as a matter of course. They were strangers; they couldn't be expected to understand that father was the very last person for such a thing to happen to. No, the entire blame for it all would fall on her and Constantia. And the expense, she thought, stepping into the tight-buttoned cab. When she had to show him the bills. What would he say then?

She heard him absolutely roaring. "And do you expect me to pay for this gimcrack excursion of yours?"

"Oh," groaned poor Josephine aloud, "we shouldn't have done it, Con!"

And Constantia, pale as a lemon in all that blackness, said in a frightened whisper, "Done what, Jug?"

3. The Anglican ceremony in which sacramental wine and bread are consumed, symbolizing the Blood and Body of Christ.

"Let them bu-bury father like that," said Josephine, breaking down and crying into her new, queer-smelling mourning handkerchief.

"But what else could we have done?" asked Constantia wonderingly. "We couldn't have kept him, Jug—we couldn't have kept him unburied. At any rate, not in a flat that size."

Josephine blew her nose; the cab was dreadfully stuffy.

"I don't know," she said forlornly. "It is all so dreadful. I feel we ought to have tried to, just for a time at least. To make perfectly sure. One thing's certain"—and her tears sprang out again—"father will never forgive us for this—never!"

6

Father would never forgive them. That was what they felt more than ever when, two mornings later, they went into his room to go through his things. They had discussed it quite calmly. It was even down on Josephine's list of things to be done. *Go through father's things and settle about them.* But that was a very different matter from saying after breakfast:

"Well, are you ready, Con?"

"Yes, Jug—when you are."

"Then I think we'd better get it over."

It was dark in the hall. It had been a rule for years never to disturb father in the morning, whatever happened. And now they were going to open the door without knocking even. . . . Constantia's eyes were enormous at the idea; Josephine felt weak in the knees.

"You—you go first," she gasped, pushing Constantia.

But Constantia said, as she always had said on those occasions, "No, Jug, that's not fair. You're eldest."

Josephine was just going to say—what at other times she wouldn't have owned to for the world—what she kept for her very last weapon, "But you're tallest," when they noticed that the kitchen door was open, and there stood Kate. . . .

"Very stiff," said Josephine, grasping the door-handle and doing her best to turn it. As if anything ever deceived Kate!

It couldn't be helped. That girl was . . . Then the door was shut behind them, but—but they weren't in father's room at all. They might have suddenly walked through the wall by mistake into a different flat altogether. Was the door just behind them? They were too frightened to look. Josephine knew that if it was it was holding itself tight shut; Constantia felt that, like the doors in dreams, it hadn't any handle at all. It was the coldness which made it so awful. Or the whiteness—which? Everything was covered. The blinds were down, a cloth hung over the mirror, a sheet hid the bed; a huge fan of white paper filled the fireplace. Constantia timidly put out her hand; she almost expected a snowflake to fall. Josephine felt a queer tingling in her nose, as if her nose was freezing. Then a cab klop-klopped over the cobbles below, and the quiet seemed to shake into little pieces.

"I had better pull up a blind," said Josephine bravely.

"Yes, it might be a good idea," whispered Constantia.

They only gave the blind a touch, but it flew up and the cord flew after, rolling round the blindstick, and the little tassel tapped as if trying to get free. That was too much for Constantia.

"Don't you think—don't you think we might put it off for another day?" she whispered.

"Why?" snapped Josephine, feeling, as usual, much better now that she knew for certain that Constantia was terrified. "It's got to be done. But I do wish you wouldn't whisper, Con."

"I didn't know I was whispering," whispered Constantia.

"And why do you keep on staring at the bed?" said Josephine, raising her voice almost defiantly. "There's nothing on the bed."

"Oh, Jug, don't say so!" said poor Connie. "At any rate, not so loudly."

Josephine felt herself that she had gone too far. She took a wide swerve over to the chest of drawers, put out her hand, but quickly drew it back again.

"Connie!" she gasped, and she wheeled round and leaned with her back against the chest of drawers.

"Oh, Jug—what?"

Josephine could only glare. She had the most extraordinary feeling that she had just escaped something simply awful. But how could she explain to Constantia that father was in the chest of drawers? He was in the top drawer with his handkerchiefs and neckties, or in the next with his shirts and pyjamas, or in the lowest of all with his suits. He was watching there, hidden away—just behind the door-handle—ready to spring.

She pulled a funny old-fashioned face at Constantia, just as she used to in the old days when she was going to cry.

"I can't open," she nearly wailed.

"No, don't, Jug," whispered Constantia earnestly. "It's much better not to. Don't let's open anything. At any rate, not for a long time."

"But—but it seems so weak," said Josephine, breaking down.

"But why not be weak for once, Jug?" argued Constantia, whispering quite fiercely. "If it is weak." And her pale stare flew from the locked writing-table—so safe—to the huge glittering wardrobe, and she began to breathe in a queer, panting way. "Why shouldn't we be weak for once in our lives, Jug? It's quite excusable. Let's be weak—be weak, Jug. It's much nicer to be weak than to be strong."

And then she did one of those amazingly bold things that she'd done about twice before in their lives; she marched over to the wardrobe, turned the key, and took it out of the lock. Took it out of the lock and held it up to Josephine, showing Josephine by her extraordinary smile that she knew what she'd done, she'd risked deliberately father being in there among his overcoats.

If the huge wardrobe had lurched forward, had crashed down on Constantia, Josephine wouldn't have been surprised. On the contrary, she would have thought it the only suitable thing to happen. But nothing happened. Only the room seemed quieter than ever, and bigger flakes of cold air fell on Josephine's shoulders and knees. She began to shiver.

"Come, Jug," said Constantia, still with that awful callous smile, and Josephine followed just as she had that last time, when Constantia had pushed Benny into the round pond.

7

But the strain told on them when they were back in the dining-room. They sat down, very shaky, and looked at each other.

"I don't feel I can settle to anything," said Josephine, "until I've had something. Do you think we could ask Kate for two cups of hot water?"

"I really don't see why we shouldn't," said Constantia carefully. She was quite normal again. "I won't ring. I'll go to the kitchen door and ask her."

"Yes, do," said Josephine, sinking down into a chair. "Tell her, just two cups, Con, nothing else—on a tray."

"She needn't even put the jug on, need she?" said Constantia, as though Kate might very well complain if the jug had been there.

"Oh no, certainly not! The jug's not at all necessary. She can pour it direct out of the kettle," cried Josephine, feeling that would be a labor-saving indeed.

Their cold lips quivered at the greenish brims. Josephine curved her small red hands round the cup; Constantia sat up and blew on the wavy stream, making it flutter from one side to the other.

"Speaking of Benny," said Josephine.

And though Benny hadn't been mentioned Constantia immediately loked as though he had.

"He'll expect us to sent him something of father's, of course. But it's so difficult to know what to send to Ceylon."

"You mean things get unstuck so on the voyage," murmured Constantia.

"No, lost," said Josephine sharply. "You know there's no post. Only runners."

Both paused to watch a black man in white linen drawers running through the pale fields for dear life, with a large brown-paper parcel in his hands. Josephine's black man was tiny; he scurried along glistening like an ant. But there was something blind and tireless about Constantia's tall, thin fellow, which made him, she decided, a very unpleasant person indeed. . . . On the veranda, dressed all in white and wearing a cork helmet, stood Benny. His right hand shook up and down, as father's did when he was impatient. And behind him, not in the least interested, sat Hilda, the unknown sister-in-law. She swung in a cane rocker and flicked over the leaves of the *Tatler*.

"I think his watch would be the most suitable present," said Josephine.

Constantia looked up; she seemed surprised.

"Oh, would you trust a gold watch to a native?"

"But of course I'd disguise it," said Josephine. "No one would know it was a watch." She liked the idea of having to make a parcel such a curious shape that no one could posssibly guess what it was. She even thought for a moment of hiding the watch in a narrow cardboard corset-box that she'd kept by her for a long time, waiting for it to come in for something. It was such beautiful firm cardboard. But, no, it wouldn't be appropriate for this occasion. It had lettering on it: *Medium Women's 28. Extra Firm Busks.*[4] It would be almost too much of a surprise for Benny to open that and find father's watch inside.

"And of course it isn't as though it would be going—ticking, I mean," said Constantia, who was still thinking of the native love of jewelry. "At least," she added, "it would be very strange if after all that time it was."

8

Josephine made no reply. She had flown off on one of her tangents. She had suddenly thought of Cyril. Wasn't it more usual for the only grandson to have

4. Ridged strips that stiffen a corset.

the watch? And then dear Cyril was so appreciative, and a gold watch meant so much to a young man. Benny, in all probability, had quite got out of the habit of watches; men so seldom wore waistcoats in those hot climates. Whereas Cyril in London wore them from year's end to year's end. And it would be so nice for her and Constantia, when he came to tea, to know it was there. "I see you've got on grandfather's watch, Cyril." It would be somehow so satisfactory.

Dear boy! What a blow his sweet, sympathetic little note had been! Of course they quite understood; but it was most unfortunate.

"It would have been such a point, having him," said Josephine

"And he would have enjoyed it so," said Constantia, not thinking what she was saying.

However, as soon as he got back he was coming to tea with his aunties. Cyril to tea was one of their rare treats.

"Now, Cyril, you must't be frightened of our cakes. Your Auntie Con and I bought them at Buszard's this morning. We know what a man's appetite is. So don't be ashamed of making a good tea."

Josephine cut recklessly into the rich dark cake that stood for her winter gloves or the soling and heeling of Constantia's only respectable shoes. But Cyril was most unmanlike in appetite.

"I say, Aunt Josephine, I simply can't. I've only just had lunch, you know."

"Oh, Cyril, that can't be true! It's after four," cried Josephine. Constantia sat with her knife poised over the chocolate-roll.

"It is all the same," said Cyril. "I had to meet a man at Victoria⁵ and he kept me hanging about till . . . there was only time to get lunch and to come on here. And he gave me—phew"—Cyril put his hand to his forehead—"a terrific blow-out," he said.

It was disappointing—today of all days. But still he couldn't be expected to know.

"But you'll have a meringue, won't you, Cyril?" said Aunt Josephine. "These meringues were bought specially for you. Your dear father was so fond of them. We were sure you are, too."

"I am, Aunt Josephine," cried Cyril ardently. "Do you mind if I take half to begin with?"

"Not at all, dear boy; but we mustn't let you off with that."

"Is your dear father still so fond of meringues?" asked Auntie Con gently. She winced faintly as she broke through the shell of hers.

"Well, I don't quite know, Auntie Con," said Cyril breezily.

At that they both looked up.

"Don't know?" almost snapped Josephine. "Don't know a thing like that about your own father, Cyril?"

"Surely," said Auntie Con softly.

Cyril tried to laugh it off. "Oh well," he said, "it's such a long time since—" He faltered. He stopped. Their faces were too much for him.

"Even so," said Josephine.

And Auntie Con looked.

Cyril put down his teacup. "Wait a bit," he cried. "Wait a bit, Aunt Josephine. What am I thinking of?"

5. A railroad station in London.

He looked up. They were beginning to brighten. Cyril slapped his knee.

"Of course," he said, "it was meringues. How could I have forgotten? Yes, Aunt Josephine, you're perfectly right. Father's most frightfully keen on meringues."

They didn't only beam. Aunt Josephine went scarlet with pleasure; Auntie Con gave a deep, deep sigh.

"And now, Cyril, you must come and see father," said Josephine. "He knows you were coming to-day."

"Right," said Cyril, very firmly and heartily. He got up from his chair; suddenly he glanced at the clock.

"I say, Auntie Con, isn't your clock a bit slow? I've got to meet a man at—at Paddington[6] just after five. I'm afraid I shan't be able to stay very long with grandfather."

"Oh, he won't expect you to stay *very* long!" said Aunt Josephine.

Constantia was still gazing at the clock. She couldn't make up her mind if it was fast or slow. It was one or the other, she felt almost certain of that. At any rate, it had been.

Cyril still lingered. "Aren't you coming along, Auntie Con?"

"Of course," said Josephine, "we shall all go. Come on, Con."

<p style="text-align:center">9</p>

They knocked at the door, and Cyril followed his aunts into grandfather's hot, sweetish room.

"Come on," said Grandfather Pinner. "Don't hang about. What is it? What've you been up to?"

He was sitting in front of the roaring fire, clasping his stick. He had a thick rug over his knees. On his lap there lay a beautiful pale yellow silk handkerchief.

"It's Cyril, father," said Josephine shyly. And she took Cyril's hand and led him forward.

"Good afternoon, grandfather," said Cyril, trying to take his hand out of Aunt Josephine's. Grandfather Pinner shot his eyes at Cyril in the way he was famous for. Where was Auntie Con? She stood on the other side of Aunt Josephine; her long arms hung down in front of her; her hands were clasped. She never took her eyes off grandfather.

"Well," said Grandfather Pinner, beginning to thump, "what have you got to tell me?"

What had he, what had he got to tell him? Cyril felt himself smiling like a perfect imbecile. The room was stifling, too.

But Aunt Josephine came to the rescue. She cried brightly, "Cyril says his father is still very fond of meringues, father dear."

"Eh?" said Grandfather Pinner, curving his hand like a purple meringue-shell over one ear.

Josephine repeated, "Cyril says his father is still very fond of meringues."

"Can't hear," said old Colonel Pinner. And he waved Josephine away with his stick, then pointed with his stick to Cyril. "Tell me what she's trying to say," he said.

(My God) "Must I?" said Cyril, blushing and staring at Aunt Josephine.

6. Another London railroad station.

"Do, dear," she smiled. "It will please him so much."

"Come on, out with it!" cried Colonel Pinner testily, beginning to thump again.

And Cyril leaned forward and yelled, "Father's still very fond of meringues."

At that Grandfather Pinner jumped as though he had been shot.

"Don't shout!" he cried. "What's the matter with the boy? *Meringues!* What about 'em?"

"Oh, Aunt Josephine, must we go on?" groaned Cyril desperately.

"It's quite all right, dear boy," said Aunt Josephine, as though he and she were at the dentist's together. "He'll understand in a minute." And she whispered to Cyril, "He's getting a bit deaf, you know." Then she leaned forward and really bawled at Grandfather Pinner, "Cyril only wanted to tell you, father dear, that *his* father is still very fond of meringues."

Colonel Pinner heard that time, heard and brooded, looking Cyril up and down.

"What an esstrordinary thing!" said old Grandfather Pinner. "What an esstrordinary thing to come all this way here to tell me!"

And Cyril felt it *was*.

"Yes, I shall send Cyril the watch," said Josephine.

"That would be very nice," said Constantia. "I seem to remember last time he came there was some little trouble about the time."

<center>10</center>

They were interrupted by Kate bursting through the door in her usual fashion, as though she had discovered some secret panel in the wall.

"Fried or boiled?" asked the bold voice.

Fried or boiled? Josephine and Constantia were quiet bewildered for the moment. They could hardly take it in.

"Fried or boiled what, Kate?" asked Josephine, trying to begin to concentrate.

Kate gave a loud sniff. "Fish."

"Well, why didn't you say so immediately?" Josephine reproached her gently. "How could you expect us to understand, Kate? There are a great many things in this world, you know, which are fried or boiled." And after such a display of courage she said quite brightly to Constantia, "Which do you prefer, Con?"

"I think it might be nice to have it fried," said Constantia. "On the other hand, of course boiled fish is very nice. I think I prefer both equally well . . . Unless you . . . In that case—"

"I shall fry it," said Kate, and she bounced back, leaving their door open and slamming the door of her kitchen.

Josephine gazed at Constantia; she raised her pale eyebrows until they rippled away into her pale hair. She got up. She said in a very lofty, imposing way, "Do you mind following me into the drawing-room, Constantia? I've something of great importance to discuss with you."

For it was always to the drawing-room they retired when they wanted to talk over Kate.

Josephine closed the door meaningly. "Sit down, Constantia," she said, still very grand. She might have been receiving Constantia for the first time. And

Con looked round vaguely for a chair, as though she felt indeed quite a stranger.

"Now the question is," said Josephine, bending forward, "whether we shall keep her or not."

"That is the question," agreed Constantia.

"And this time," said Josephine firmly. "we must come to a definite decision."

Constantia looked for a moment as though she might begin going over all the other times, but she pulled herself together and said, "Yes, Jug."

"You see, Con," explained Josephine, "everything is so changed now." Constantia looked up quickly. "I mean," went on Josephine, "we're not dependent on Kate as we were." And she blushed faintly. "There's not father to cook for."

"That is perfectly true," agreed Constantia. "Father certainly doesn't want any cooking now, whatever else—"

Josephine broke in sharply. "You're not sleepy, are you, Con?"

"Sleepy, Jug?" Constantia was wide-eyed.

"Well, concentrate more," said Josephine sharply, and she returned to the subject. "What it comes to is, if we did"—and this she barely breathed, glancing at the door—"give Kate notice"—she raised her voice again—"we could manage our own food."

"Why not?" cried Constantia. She couldn't help smiling. The idea was so exciting. She clasped her hands. "What should we live on, Jug?"

"Oh, eggs in various forms!" said Jug, lofty again. "And, besides, there are all the cooked foods."

"But I've always heard," said Constantia, "they are considered so very expensive."

"Not if one buys them in moderation," said Josephine. But she tore herself away from this fascinating bypath and dragged Constantia after her.

"What we've got to decide now, however, is whether we really do trust Kate or not."

Constantia leaned back. Her flat little laugh flew from her lips.

"Isn't it curious, Jug," said she, "that just on this one subject I've never been able to quite make up my mind?"

11

She never had. The whole difficulty was to prove anything. How did one prove things, how could one? Suppose Kate had stood in front of her and deliberately made a face. Mightn't she very well have been in pain? Wasn't it impossible, at any rate, to ask Kate if she was making a face at her? If Kate answered "No"—and of course she would say "No"—what a position! How undignified! Then again Constantia suspected, she was almost certain that Kate went to her chest of drawers when she and Josephine were out, not to take things but to spy. Many times she had come back to find her amethyst cross in the most unlikely places, under her lace ties or on top of her evening Bertha.[7] More than once she had laid a trap for Kate. She had arranged things in a special order and then called Josephine to witness.

7. A detachable lace collar for low-necked dresses.

"You see, Jug?"

"Quite, Con."

"Now we shall be able to tell."

But, oh dear, when she did go to look, she was as far off from a proof as ever! If anything was displaced, it might so very well have happened as she closed the drawer; a jolt might have done it so easily.

"You come, Jug, and decide. I really can't. It's too difficult."

But after a pause and a long glare Josephine would sigh, "Now you've put the doubt into my mind, Con, I'm sure I can't tell myself."

"Well, we can't postpone it again," said Josephine. "If we postpone it this time—"

12

But at that moment in the street below a barrel-organ struck up. Josephine and Constantia sprang to their feet together.

"Run, Con," said Josephine. "Run quickly. There's sixpence on the—"

Then they remembered. It didn't matter. They would never have to stop the organ-grinder again. Never again would she and Constantia be told to make that monkey take his noise somewhere else. Never would sound that loud, strange bellow when father thought they were not hurrying enough. The organ-grinder might play there all day and the stick would not thump.

> It never will thump again.
> It never will thump again,

played the barrel-organ.

What was Constantia thinking? She had such a strange smile; she looked different. She couldn't be going to cry.

"Jug, Jug," said Constantia softly, pressing her hands together. "Do you know what day it is? It's Saturday. It's a week to-day, a whole week."

> A week since father died,
> A week since father died,

cried the barrel-organ. And Josephine, too, forgot to be practical and sensible; she smiled faintly, strangely. On the Indian carpet there fell a square of sunlight, pale red; it came and went and came—and stayed, deepened—until it shone almost golden.

"The sun's out," said Josephine, as though it really mattered.

A perfect fountain of bubbling notes shook from the barrel-organ, round, bright notes, carelessly scattered.

Constantia lifted her big, cold hands as if to catch them, and then her hands fell again. She walked over to the mantelpiece to her favorite Buddha. And the stone and gilt image, whose smile always gave her such a queer feeling, almost a pain and yet a pleasant pain, seemed today to be more than smiling. He knew something; he had a secret. "I know something that you don't know," said her Buddah. Oh, what was it, what could it be? And yet she had always felt there was . . . something.

The sunlight pressed through the windows, thieved its way in, flashed its light over the furniture and the photographs. Josephine watched it. When it

came to mother's photograph, the enlargement over the piano, it lingered as though puzzled to find so little remained of mother, except the earrings shaped like tiny pagodas and a black feather boa. Why did the photographs of dead people always fade so? wondered Josephine. As soon as a person was dead their photograph died too. But, of course, this one of mother was very old. It was thirty-five years old. Josephine remembered standing on a chair and pointing out that feather boa to Constantia and telling her that it was a snake that had killed their mother in Ceylon. . . . Would everything have been different if mother hadn't died? She didn't see why. Aunt Florence had lived with them until they had left school, and they had moved three times and had their yearly holiday and . . . and there'd been changes of servants, of course.

Some little sparrows, young sparrows they sounded, chirped on the window-ledge. *Yeep—eyeep—yeep.* But Josephine felt they were not sparrows, not on the window-ledge. It was inside her, that queer little crying noise. *Yeep—eyeep—yeep.* Ah, what was it crying, so weak and forlorn?

If mother had lived, might they have married? But there had been nobody for them to marry. There had been father's Anglo-Indian friends before he quarreled with them. But after that she and Constantia never met a single man except clergymen. How did one meet men? Or even if they'd met them, how could they have got to know men well enough to be more than strangers? One read of people having adventures, being followed, and so on. But nobody had ever followed Constantia and her. Oh yes, there had been one year at Eastbourne[8] a mysterious man at their boarding-house who had put a note on the jug of hot water outside their bedroom door! But by the time Connie had found it the steam had made the writing too faint to read; they couldn't even make out to which of them it was addressed. And he had left next day. And that was all. The rest had been looking after father, and at the same time keeping out of father's way. But now? But now? The thieving sun touched Josephine gently. She lifted her face. She was drawn over to the window by gentle beams. . . .

Until the barrel-organ stopped playing Constantia stayed before the Buddha, wondering, but not as usual, not vaguely. This time her wonder was like longing. She remembered the times she had come in here, crept out of bed in her nightgown when the moon was full, and lain on the floor with her arms outstretched, as though she was crucified. Why? The big, pale moon had made her do it. The horrible dancing figures on the carved screen had leered at her and she hadn't minded. She remembered too how, whenever they were at the seaside, she had gone off by herself and got as close to the sea as she could, and sung something, something she had made up, while she gazed all over that restless water. There had been this other life, running out, bringing things home in bags, getting things on approval, discussing them with Jug, and taking them back to get more things on approval, and arranging father's trays and trying not to annoy father. But it all seemed to have happened in a kind of tunnel. It wasn't real. It was only when she came out of the tunnel into the moonlight or by the sea or into a thunderstorm that she really felt herself. What did it mean? What was it she was always wanting? What did it all lead to? Now? Now?

She turned away from the Buddha with one of her vague gestures. She went

8. A seaside resort in Sussex.

over to where Josephine was standing. She wanted to say something to Josephine, something frightfully important, about—about the future and what . . .

"Don't you think perhaps—" she began.

But Josephine interrupted her. "I was wondering if now—" she murmured. They stopped; they waited for each other.

"Go on, Con," said Josephine.

"No, no, Jug; after you," said Constantia.

"No, say what you were going to say. You began," said Josephine.

"I . . . I'd rather hear what you were going to say first," said Constantia.

"Don't be absurd, Con."

"Really, Jug."

"Connie!"

"Oh, Jug!"

A pause. Then Constantia said faintly, "I can't say what I was going to say, Jug, because I've forgotten what it was . . . that I was going to say."

Josephine was silent for a moment. She stared at a big cloud where the sun had been. Then she replied shortly, "I've forgotten too."

 1922

The Fly

"Y'are very snug in here," piped old Mr. Woodifield, and he peered out of the great, green-leather armchair by his friend the boss's desk as a baby peers out of its pram. His talk was over; it was time for him to be off. But he did not want to go. Since he had retired, since his . . . stroke, the wife and the girls kept him boxed up in the house every day of the week except Tuesday. On Tuesday he was dressed and brushed and allowed to cut back to the City[1] for the day. Though what he did there the wife and girls couldn't imagine. Made a nuisance of himself to his friends, they supposed. . . . Well, perhaps so. All the same, we cling to our last pleasures as the tree clings to its last leaves. So there sat old Woodifield, smoking a cigar and staring almost greedily at the boss, who rolled in his office chair, stout, rosy, five years older than he, and still going strong, still at the helm. It did one good to see him.

Wistfully, admiringly, the old voice added, "It's snug in here, upon my word!"

"Yes, it's comfortable enough," agreed the boss, and he flipped the *Financial Times* with a paper-knife. As a matter of fact he was proud of his room; he liked to have it admired, especially by old Woodifield. It gave him a feeling of deep, solid satisfaction to be planted there in the midst of it in full view of that frail old figure in the muffler.

"I've had it done up lately," he explained, as he had explained for the past— how many?—weeks. "New carpet," and he pointed to the bright red carpet with a pattern of large white rings. "New furniture," and he nodded towards the massive bookcase and the table with legs like twisted treacle.[2] "Electric

1. I.e., the City of London; used more generally of 2. A thick syrup.
London's business and financial interests

heating!" He waved almost exultantly towards the five transparent, pearly sausages glowing so softly in the tilted copper pan.

But he did not draw old Woodifield's attention to the photograph over the table of a grave-looking boy in uniform standing in one of those spectral photographers' parks with photographers' storm-clouds behind him. It was not new. It had been there for over six years.

"There was something I wanted to tell you," said old Woodifield, and his eyes grew dim remembering. "Now what was it? I had it in my mind when I started out this morning." His hands began to tremble, and patches of red showed above his beard.

Poor old chap, he's on his last pins, thought the boss. And, feeling kindly, he winked at the old man, and said jokingly, "I tell you what. I've got a little drop of something here that'll do you good before you go out into the cold again. It's beautiful stuff. It wouldn't hurt a child." He took a key off his watch-chain, unlocked a cupboard below his desk, and drew forth a dark, squat bottle. "That's the medicine," said he. "And the man from whom I got it told me on the strict Q.T.[3] it came from the cellars at Windsor Castle."

Old Woodifield's mouth fell open at the sight. He couldn't have looked more surprised if the boss had produced a rabbit.

"It's whisky, ain't it?" he piped feebly.

The boss turned the bottle and lovingly showed him the label. Whisky it was.

"D'you know," said he, peering up at the boss wonderingly, "they won't let me touch it at home." And he looked as though he was going to cry.

"Ah, that's where we know a bit more than the ladies," cried the boss, swooping across for two tumblers that stood on the table with the water-bottle, and pouring a generous finger into each. "Drink it down. It'll do you good. And don't put any water with it. It's sacrilege to tamper with stuff like this. Ah!" He tossed off his, pulled out his handkerchief, hastily wiped his moustaches, and cocked an eye at old Woodifield, who was rolling his in his chaps.

The old man swallowed, was silent a moment, and then said faintly, "It's nutty!"

But it warmed him; it crept into his chill old brain—he remembered.

"That was it," he said, heaving himself out of his chair. "I thought you'd like to know. The girls were in Belgium last week having a look at poor Reggie's grave, and they happened to come across your boy's. They're quite near each other, it seems."

Old Woodifield paused, but the boss made no reply. Only a quiver in his eyelids showed that he heard.

"The girls were delighted with the way the place is kept," piped the old voice. "Beautifully looked after. Couldn't be better if they were at home. You've not been across, have yer?"

"No, no!" For various reasons the boss had not been across.

"There's miles of it," quavered old Woodifield, "and it's all as neat as a garden. Flowers growing on all the graves. Nice broad paths." It was plain from his voice how much he liked a nice broad path.

3. With complete secrecy ("Q.T." stands for "quiet").

The pause came again. Then the old man brightened wonderfully.

"D'you know what the hotel made the girls pay for a pot of jam?" he piped. "Ten francs! Robbery, I call it. It was a little pot, so Gertrude says, no bigger than a half-crown. And she hadn't taken more than a spoonful when they charged her ten francs. Gertrude brought the pot away with her to teach 'em a lesson. Quite right, too; it's trading on our feelings. They think because we're over there having a look round we're ready to pay anything. That's what it is." And he turned towards the door.

"Quite right, quite right!" cried the boss, though what was quite right he hadn't the least idea. He came round by his desk, followed the shuffling footsteps to the door, and saw the old fellow out. Woodifield was gone.

For a long moment the boss stayed, staring at nothing, while the gray-haired office messenger, watching him, dodged in and out of his cubby-hole like a dog that expects to be taken for a run. Then: "I'll see nobody for half an hour, Macey," said the boss. "Understand? Nobody at all."

"Very good, sir."

The door shut, the firm heavy steps recrossed the bright carpet, the fat body plumped down in the spring chair, and leaning forward, the boss covered his face with his hands. He wanted, he intended, he had arranged to weep. . . .

It had been a terrible shock to him when old Woodifield sprang that remark upon him about the boy's grave. It was exactly as though the earth had opened and he had seen the boy lying there with Woodifield's girls staring down at him. For it was strange. Although over six years had passed away, the boss never thought of the boy except as lying unchanged, unblemished in his uniform, asleep for ever. "My son!" groaned the boss. But no tears came yet. In the past, in the first months and even years after the boy's death, he had only to say those words to be overcome by such grief that nothing short of a violent fit of weeping could relieve him. Time, he had declared then, he had told everybody, could make no difference. Other men perhaps might recover, might live their loss down, but not he. How was it possible? His boy was an only son. Ever since his birth the boss had worked at building up this business for him; it had no other meaning if it was not for the boy. Life itself had come to have no other meaning. How on earth could he have slaved, denied himself, kept going all those years without the promise for ever before him of the boy's stepping into his shoes and carrying on where he left off?

And that promise had been so near being fulfilled. The boy had been in the office learning the ropes for a year before the war. Every morning they had started off together; they had come back by the same train. And what congratulations he had received as the boy's father! No wonder; he had taken to it marvelously. As to his popularity with the staff, every man jack of them down to old Macey couldn't make enough of the boy. And he wasn't in the least spoilt. No, he was just his bright natural self, with the right word for everybody, with that boyish look and his habit of saying, "Simply splendid!"

But that was all over and done with as though it never had been. The day had come when Macey had handed him the telegram that brought the whole place crashing about his head. "Deeply regret to inform you . . ." And he had left the office a broken man, with his life in ruins.

Six years ago, six years. . . . How quickly time passed! It might have happened yesterday. The boss took his hands from his face; he was puzzled. Something seemed to be wrong with him. He wasn't feeling as he wanted

to feel. He decided to get up and have a look at the boy's photograph. But it wasn't a favorite photograph of his; the expression was unnatural. It was cold, even stern-looking. The boy had never looked like that.

At that moment the boss noticed that a fly had fallen into his broad inkpot, and was trying feebly but desperately to clamber out again. Help! help! said those struggling legs. But the sides of the inkpot were wet and slippery; it fell back again and began to swim. The boss took up a pen, picked the fly out of the ink, and shook it on to a piece of blotting-paper. For a fraction of a second it lay still on the dark patch that oozed round it. Then the front legs waved, took hold, and, pulling its small, sodden body up, it began the immense task of cleaning the ink from its wings. Over and under, over and under, went a leg along a wing as the stone goes over and under the scythe. Then there was a pause, while the fly, seeming to stand on the tips of its toes, tried to expand first one wing and then the other. It succeeded at last, and, sitting down, it began, like a minute cat, to clean its face. Now one could imagine that the little front legs rubbed against each other lightly, joyfully. The horrible danger was over; it had escaped; it was ready for life again.

But just then the boss had an idea. He plunged his pen back into the ink, leaned his thick wrist on the blotting-paper, and as the fly tried its wings down came a great heavy blot. What would it make of that? What indeed! The little beggar seemed absolutely cowed, stunned, and afraid to move because of what would happen next. But then, as if painfully, it dragged itself forward. The front legs waved, caught hold, and, more slowly this time, the task began from the beginning.

He's a plucky little devil, thought the boss, and he felt a real admiration for the fly's courage. That was the way to tackle things; that was the right spirit. Never say die; it was only a question of . . . But the fly had again finished its laborious task, and the boss had just time to refill his pen, to shake fair and square on the new-cleaned body yet another dark drop. What about it this time? A painful moment of suspense followed. But behold, the front legs were again waving; the boss felt a rush of relief. He leaned over the fly and said to it tenderly, "You artful little b" And he actually had the brilliant notion of breathing on it to help the drying process. All the same, there was something timid and weak about its efforts now, and the boss decided that this time should be the last, as he dipped the pen deep into the inkpot.

It was. The last blot fell on the soaked blotting-paper, and the draggled fly lay in it and did not stir. The back legs were stuck to the body; the front legs were not to be seen.

"Come on," said the boss. "Look sharp!" And he stirred it with his pen—in vain. Nothing happened or was likely to happen. The fly was dead.

The boss lifted the corpse on the end of the paper-knife and flung it into the waste-paper basket. But such a grinding feeling of wretchedness seized him that he felt positively frightened. He started forward and pressed the bell for Macey.

"Bring me some fresh blotting-paper," he said sternly, "and look sharp about it." And while the old dog padded away he fell to wondering what it was he had been thinking about before. What was it? It was . . . He took out his handkerchief and passed it inside his collar. For the life of him he could not remember.

1922 1923

KATHERINE ANNE PORTER

c. 1890–1980

Writing in her journal, Katherine Anne Porter observed in 1935 that the "constant exercise of memory seems to be the chief occupation of my mind, and all my experience seems to be simply memory, with continuity, marginal notes, constant revision and comparison of one thing with another." When "thousands of memories converge, harmonize, arrange themselves around a central ideal in a coherent form," she continued, "I write a story." Through the memories that are transformed in her twenty-seven works of short fiction and her one novel, *Ship of Fools* (1962), Porter established herself as a fine stylist who could convey what she called "the thumbprint"—the distinctive individuality—of characters "who populate all these enormous migrations, calamities; who fight wars and furnish life for the future; these beings without which, one by one, all the 'broad movements of history' could never take place." Curiously, however, despite her "constant exercise of memory," the episodes from the past that Porter recalled in interviews and autobiographical sketches contain contradictory evidence about her birth date, her family's religion, her medical history, and even her literary career.

Porter's parents and siblings lived in a small log house in Indian Creek, Texas, but before she was two years old her mother died and the family moved to Kyle, into the household of her paternal grandmother, Catherine Anne Porter. According to this strong-willed woman, the young Callie Russell Porter (as she was called then) was "precocious nervous rebellious, unteachable, and made life very uncomfortable" for everyone. Porter's biographer Joan Givner has described the house as disorderly and cramped; however, Porter's grandmother was a storyteller who, in Givner's words, "laid the foundation for Porter's literary gifts." When her grandmother died in 1901, the destitute family eventually settled in San Antonio. Although Porter disliked the convent schools she attended, she later boasted that already at this point in her life she was reading Shakespeare, Dante, and Homer as well as French poetry in translation. At sixteen, she ran away, married John Henry Koontz, a railroad clerk, and converted to her husband's religion, Catholicism. Eight years later, she left Koontz to try an acting career in the movies, and in 1915 they divorced.

For several years, Porter worked on newspapers in Chicago, Fort Worth, Texas, and Denver, Colorado, and she also traveled around the South singing ballads and acting in little theater groups. After a long bout with tuberculosis in 1915 and a transformative trip to Mexico City in 1919, Porter produced her first published story while living in Greenwich Village; *María Concepción* was published in *Century* magazine in 1922. Fascinated by Mexican folk art, Porter would return to Mexico in such stories as *The Mexican Trinity* (1921), *Flowering Judas* (1930), and *Hacienda* (1934), where she studied the "chance of salvation" in Mexican culture as well as the dissolution of that chance for expatriated Americans.

Although throughout the 1920s and 1930s Porter traveled, wrote book reviews for *The New Republic* and *The Nation*, and collected her stories in the volume *Flowering Judas* (1930), a succession of unsatisfying love affairs and brief marriages made her personal life tormenting. *Noon Wine* (1937), *Pale Horse, Pale Rider* (1939), and *The Leaning Tower, and Other Stories* (1944) firmly established her reputation as a cosmopolitan writer of brilliant short stories, one who drew on her travels throughout New England, Bermuda, New York, Mexico, and Europe. After several years living in Paris, Porter returned to the United States in 1936. When her novel *Ship of Fools* was published in 1962, it was an instant best-seller. Soon after, Porter received the National Book Award and the Pulitzer Prize for her *Collected Stories* (1954). In 1970, she published an expanded version of her essays.

Influenced by Willa Cather, Katherine Mansfield, James Joyce, and Virginia Woolf, Porter produced fictionalized accounts of herself and her childhood memories of her grandmother in such stories as *The Source, The Grave, Old Mortality*, and *The Jilting of Granny Weatherall. The Jilting of Granny Weatherall* is less overtly autobiographical than those stories in which Porter figures as the character Miranda; however, it presents a strong-willed, older woman who has reared a large family. And, as in so much of her fiction, Porter manages here to convey how past and present events mingle in the consciousness of a character who experiences an epiphany that is linked to her confrontation with death.

The Jilting of Granny Weatherall

She flicked her wrist neatly out of Doctor Harry's pudgy careful fingers and pulled the sheet up to her chin. The brat ought to be in knee breeches. Doctoring around the country with spectacles on his nose! "Get along now, take your schoolbooks and go. There's nothing wrong with me."

Doctor Harry spread a warm paw like a cushion on her forehead where the forked green vein danced and made her eyelids twitch. "Now, now, be a good girl, and we'll have you up in no time."

"That's no way to speak to a woman nearly eighty years old just because she's down. I'd have you respect your elders, young man."

"Well, Missy, excuse me." Doctor Harry patted her cheek. "But I've got to warn you, haven't I? You're a marvel, but you must be careful or you're going to be good and sorry."

"Don't tell me what I'm going to be. I'm on my feet now, morally speaking. It's Cornelia. I had to go to bed to get rid of her."

Her bones felt loose, and floated around in her skin, and Doctor Harry floated like a balloon around the foot of the bed. He floated and pulled down his waistcoat and swung his glasses on a cord. "Well, stay where you are, it certainly can't hurt you."

"Get along and doctor your sick," said Granny Weatherall. "Leave a well woman alone. I'll call for you when I want you. . . . Where were you forty years ago when I pulled through milk-leg[1] and double pneumonia? You weren't even born. Don't let Cornelia lead you on," she shouted, because Doctor Harry appeared to float up to the ceiling and out. "I pay my own bills, and I don't throw my money away on nonsense!"

She meant to wave good-by, but it was too much trouble. Her eyes closed of themselves, it was like a dark curtain drawn around the bed. The pillow rose and floated under her, pleasant as a hammock in a light wind. She listened to the leaves rustling outside the window. No, somebody was swishing newspapers: no, Cornelia and Doctor Harry were whispering together. She leaped broad awake, thinking they whispered in her ear.

"She was never like this, never like this!" "Well, what can we expect?" "Yes, eighty years old. . . ."

Well, and what if she was? She still had ears. It was like Cornelia to whisper around doors. She always kept things secret in such a public way. She was always being tactful and kind. Cornelia was dutiful; that was the trouble with

1. Swelling of the legs after childbirth.

her. Dutiful and good: "So good and dutiful," said Granny, "that I'd like to spank her." She saw herself spanking Cornelia and making a fine job of it.

"What'd you say, Mother?"

Granny felt her face tying up in hard knots.

"Can't a body think, I'd like to know?"

"I thought you might want something."

"I do. I want a lot of things. First off, go away and don't whisper."

She lay and drowsed, hoping in her sleep that the children would keep out and let her rest a minute. It had been a long day. Not that she was tired. It was always pleasant to snatch a minute now and then. There was always so much to be done, let me see: tomorrow.

Tomorrow was far away and there was nothing to trouble about. Things were finished somehow when the time came; thank God there was always a little margin over for peace: then a person could spread out the plan of life and tuck in the edges orderly. It was good to have everything clean and folded away, with the hair brushes and tonic bottles sitting straight on the white embroidered linen: the day started without fuss and the pantry shelves laid out with rows of jelly glasses and brown jugs and white stone-china jars with blue whirligigs and words painted on them: coffee, tea, sugar, ginger, cinnamon, allspice: and the bronze clock with the lion on top nicely dusted off. The dust that lion could collect in twenty-four hours! The box in the attic with all those letters tied up, well, she'd have to go through that tomorrow. All those letters—George's letters and John's letters and her letters to them both—lying around for the children to find afterwards made her uneasy. Yes, that would be tomorrow's business. No use to let them know how silly she had been once.

While she was rummaging around she found death in her mind and it felt clammy and unfamiliar. She had spent so much time preparing for death there was no need for bringing it up again. Let it take care of itself now. When she was sixty she had felt very old, finished, and went around making farewell trips to see her children and grandchildren, with a secret in her mind: This is the very last of your mother, children! Then she made her will and came down with a long fever. That was all just a notion like a lot of other things, but it was lucky too, for she had once for all got over the idea of dying for a long time. Now she couldn't be worried. She hoped she had better sense now. Her father had lived to be one hundred and two years old and had drunk a noggin of strong hot toddy on his last birthday. He told the reporters it was his daily habit, and he owed his long life to that. He had made quite a scandal and was very pleased about it. She believed she'd just plague Cornelia a little.

"Cornelia! Cornelia!" No footsteps, but a sudden hand on her cheek. "Bless you, where have you been?"

"Here, Mother."

"Well, Cornelia, I want a noggin of hot toddy."

"Are you cold, darling?"

"I'm chilly, Cornelia. Lying in bed stops the circulation. I must have told you that a thousand times."

Well, she could just hear Cornelia telling her husband that Mother was getting a little childish and they'd have to humor her. The thing that most annoyed her was that Cornelia thought she was deaf, dumb, and blind. Little hasty glances and tiny gestures tossed around her and over her head saying, "Don't cross her, let her have her way, she's eighty years old," and she sitting

there as if she lived in a thin glass cage. Sometimes Granny almost made up her mind to pack up and move back to her own house where nobody could remind her every minute that she was old. Wait, wait, Cornelia, till your own children whisper behind your back!

In her day she had kept a better house and had got more work done. She wasn't too old yet for Lydia to be driving eighty miles for advice when one of the children jumped the track, and Jimmy still dropped in and talked things over: "Now, Mammy, you've a good business head, I want to know what you think of this? . . . " Old. Cornelia couldn't change the furniture around without asking. Little things, little things! They had been so sweet when they were little. Granny wished the old days were back again with the children young and everything to be done over. It had been a hard pull, but not too much for her. When she thought of all the food she had cooked, and all the clothes she had cut and sewed, and all the gardens she had made—well, the children showed it. There they were, made out of her, and they couldn't get away from that. Sometimes she wanted to see John again and point to them and say, Well, I didn't do so badly, did I? But that would have to wait. That was for tomorrow. She used to think of him as a man, but now all the children were older than their father, and he would be a child beside her if she saw him now. It seemed strange and there was something wrong in the idea. Why, he couldn't possibly recognize her. She had fenced in a hundred acres once, digging the post holes herself and clamping the wires with just a negro boy to help. That changed a woman. John would be looking for a young woman with the peaked Spanish comb in her hair and the painted fan. Digging post holes changed a woman. Riding country roads in the winter when women had their babies was another thing: sitting up nights with sick horses and sick negroes and sick children and hardly ever losing one. John, I hardly ever lost one of them! John would see that in a minute, that would be something he could understand, she wouldn't have to explain anything!

It made her feel like rolling up her sleeves and putting the whole place to rights again. No matter if Cornelia was determined to be everywhere at once, there were a great many things left undone on this place. She would start tomorrow and do them. It was good to be strong enough for everything, even if all you made melted and changed and slipped under your hands, so that by the time you finished you almost forgot what you were working for. What was it I set out to do? she asked herself intently, but she could not remember. A fog rose over the valley, she saw it marching across the creek swallowing the trees and moving up the hill like an army of ghosts. Soon it would be at the near edge of the orchard, and then it was time to go in and light the lamps. Come in, children, don't stay out in the night air.

Lighting the lamps had been beautiful. The children huddled up to her and breathed like little calves waiting at the bars[2] in the twilight. Their eyes followed the match and watched the flame rise and settle in a blue curve, then they moved away from her. The lamp was lit, they didn't have to be scared and hang on to Mother any more. Never, never never more. God, for all my life I thank Thee. Without Thee, my God, I could never have done it. Hail, Mary, full of grace.

2. Pasture gates.

I want you to pick all the fruit this year and see that nothing is wasted. There's always someone who can use it. Don't let good things rot for want of using. You waste life when you waste good food. Don't let things get lost. It's bitter to lose things. Now, don't let me get to thinking, not when I am tired and taking a little nap before supper. . . .

The pillow rose about her shoulders and pressed against her heart and the memory was being squeezed out of it: oh, push down the pillow, somebody; it would smother her if she tried to hold it. Such a fresh breeze blowing and such a green day with no threats in it. But he had not come, just the same. What does a woman do when she has put on the white veil and set out the white cake for a man and he doesn't come? She tried to remember. No, I swear he never harmed me but in that. He never harmed me but in that . . . and what if he did? There was the day, the day, but a whirl of dark smoke rose and covered it, crept up and over into the bright field where everything was planted so carefully in orderly rows. That was hell, she knew hell when she saw it. For sixty years she had prayed against remembering him and against losing her soul in the deep pit of hell, and now the two things were mingled in one and the thought of him was a smoky cloud from hell that moved and crept in her head when she had just got rid of Doctor Harry and was trying to rest a minute. Wounded vanity, Ellen, said a sharp voice in the top of her mind. Don't let your wounded vanity get the upper hand of you. Plenty of girls get jilted. You were jilted, weren't you? Then stand up to it. Her eyelids wavered and let in streamers of blue-gray light like tissue paper over her eyes. She must get up and pull the shades down or she'd never sleep. She was in bed again and the shades were not down. How could that happen? Better turn over, hide from the light, sleeping in the light gave you nightmares. "Mother, how do you feel now?" and a stinging wetness on her forehead. But I don't like having my face washed in cold water!

Hapsy? George? Lydia? Jimmy? No, Cornelia, and her features were swollen and full of little puddles. "They're coming, darling, they'll all be here soon." Go wash your face, child, you look funny.

Instead of obeying, Cornelia knelt down and put her head on the pillow. She seemed to be talking but there was no sound. "Well, are you tongue-tied? Whose birthday is it? Are you going to give a party?"

Cornelia's mouth moved urgently in strange shapes. "Don't do that, you bother me, daughter."

"Oh, no, Mother. Oh, no. . . . "

Nonsense. It was strange about children. They disputed your every word. "No what, Cornelia?"

"Here's Doctor Harry."

"I won't see that boy again. He just left five minutes ago."

"That was this morning, Mother. It's night now. Here's the nurse."

"This is Doctor Harry, Mrs. Weatherall. I never saw you look so young and happy!"

"Ah, I'll never be young again—but I'd be happy if they'd let me lie in peace and get rested."

She thought she spoke up loudly, but no one answered. A warm weight on her forehead, a warm bracelet on her wrist, and a breeze went on whispering, trying to tell her something. A shuffle of leaves in the everlasting hand of God, He blew on them and they danced and rattled. "Mother, don't mind, we're

going to give you a little hypodermic." "Look here, daughter, how do ants get in this bed? I saw sugar ants yesterday." Did you send for Hapsy too?

It was Hapsy she really wanted. She had to go a long way back through a great many rooms to find Hapsy standing with a baby on her arm. She seemed to herself to be Hapsy also, and the baby on Hapsy's arm was Hapsy and himself and herself, all at once, and there was no surprise in the meeting. Then Hapsy melted from within and turned flimsy as gray gauze and the baby was a gauzy shadow, and Hapsy came up close and said, "I thought you'd never come," and looked at her very searchingly and said, "You haven't changed a bit!" They leaned forward to kiss, when Cornelia began whispering from a long way off, "Oh, is there anything you want to tell me? Is there anything I can do for you?"

Yes, she had changed her mind after sixty years and she would like to see George. I want you to find George. Find him and be sure to tell him I forgot him. I want him to know I had my husband just the same and my children and my house like any other woman. A good house too and a good husband that I loved and fine children out of him. Better than I hoped for even. Tell him I was given back everything he took away and more. Oh, no, oh, God, no, there was something else besides the house and the man and the children. Oh, surely they were not all? What was it? Something not given back. . . . Her breath crowded down under her ribs and grew into a monstrous frightening shape with cutting edges; it bored up into her head, and the agony was unbelievable: Yes, John, get the Doctor now, no more talk, my time has come.

When this one was born it should be the last. The last. It should have been born first, for it was the one she had truly wanted. Everything came in good time. Nothing left out, left over. She was strong, in three days she would be as well as ever. Better. A woman needed milk in her to have her full health.

"Mother, do you hear me?"

"I've been telling you—"

"Mother, Father Connolly's here."

"I went to Holy Communion only last week. Tell him I'm not so sinful as all that."

"Father just wants to speak to you."

He could speak as much as he pleased. It was like him to drop in and inquire about her soul as if it were a teething baby, and then stay on for a cup of tea and a round of cards and gossip. He always had a funny story of some sort, usually about an Irishman who made his little mistakes and confessed them, and the point lay in some absurd thing he would blurt out in the confessional showing his struggles between native piety and original sin. Granny felt easy about her soul. Cornelia, where are your manners? Give Father Connolly a chair. She had her secret comfortable understanding with a few favorite saints who cleared a straight road to God for her. All as surely signed and sealed as the papers for the new Forty Acres. Forever . . . heirs and assigns forever. Since the day the wedding cake was not cut, but thrown out and wasted. The whole bottom dropped out of the world, and there she was blind and sweating with nothing under her feet and the walls falling away. His hand had caught her under the breast, she had not fallen, there was the freshly polished floor with the green rug on it, just as before. He had cursed like a sailor's parrot and said, "I'll kill him for you." Don't lay a hand on him, for my sake leave something to God. "Now, Ellen, you must believe what I tell you. . . ."

So there was nothing, nothing to worry about any more, except sometimes in the night one of the children screamed in a nightmare, and they both hustled out shaking and hunting for the matches and calling, "There, wait a minute, here we are!" John, get the doctor now, Hapsy's time has come. But there was Hapsy standing by the bed in a white cap. "Cornelia, tell Hapsy to take off her cap. I can't see her plain."

Her eyes opened very wide and the room stood out like a picture she had seen somewhere. Dark colors with the shadows rising towards the ceiling in long angles. The tall black cresser gleamed with nothing on it but John's picture enlarged from a little one, with John's eyes very black when they should have been blue. You never saw him, so how do you know how he looked? But the man insisted the copy was perfect, it was very rich and handsome. For a picture, yes, but it's not my husband. The table by the bed had a linen cover and a candle and a crucifix. The light was blue from Cornelia's silk lampshades. No sort of light at all, just frippery. You had to live forty years with kerosene lamps to appreciate honest electricity. She felt very strong and she saw Doctor Harry with a rosy nimbus around him.

"You look like a saint, Doctor Harry, and I vow that's as near as you'll ever come to it."

"She's saying something."

"I heard you, Cornelia. What's all this carrying-on?"

"Father Connolly's saying—"

Cornelia's voice staggered and bumped like a cart in a bad road. It rounded corners and turned back again and arrived nowhere. Granny stepped up in the cart very lightly and reached for the reins, but a man sat beside her and she knew him by his hands, driving the cart. She did not look in his face, for she knew without seeing, but looked instead down the road where the trees leaned over and bowed to each other and a thousand birds were singing a Mass. She felt like singing too, but she put her hand in the bosom of her dress and pulled out a rosary, and Father Connolly murmured Latin in a very solemn voice and tickled her feet. My God, will you stop that nonsense? I'm a married woman. What if he did run away and leave me to face the priest by myself? I found another a whole world better. I wouldn't have exchanged my husband for anybody except St. Michael himself, and you may tell him that for me with a thank you in the bargain.

Light flashed on her closed eyelids, and a deep roaring shook her. Cornelia, is that lightning? I hear thunder. There's going to be a storm. Close all the windows. Call the children in. . . . "Mother, here we are, all of us." "Is that you, Hapsy?" "Oh, no, I'm Lydia. We drove as fast as we could." Their faces drifted above her, drifted away. The rosary fell out of her hands and Lydia put it back. Jimmy tried to help, their hands fumbled together, and Granny closed two fingers around Jimmy's thumb. Beads wouldn't do, it must be something alive. She was so amazed her thoughts ran round and round. So, my dear Lord, this is my death and I wasn't even thinking about it. My children have come to see me die. But I can't, it's not time Oh, I always hated surprises. I wanted to give Cornelia the amethyst set—Cornelia, you're to have the amethyst set, but Hapsy's to wear it when she wants, and, Doctor Harry, do shut up. Nobody sent for you. Oh, my dear Lord, do wait a minute. I meant to do something about the Forty Acres, Jimmy doesn't need it and Lydia will later on, with that worthless husband of hers. I meant to finish the altar cloth and send six bot-

tles of wine to Sister Borgia for her dyspepsia. I want to send six bottles of wine to Sister Borgia, Father Connolly, now don't let me forget.

Cornelia's voice made short turns and tilted over and crashed. "Oh, Mother, oh, Mother, oh, Mother. . . . "

"I'm not going, Cornelia. I'm taken by surprise. I can't go."

You'll see Hapsy again. What about her? "I thought you'd never come." Granny made a long journey outward, looking for Hapsy. What if I don't find her? What then? Her heart sank down and down, there was no bottom to death, she couldn't come to the end of it. The blue light from Cornelia's lampshade drew into a tiny point in the center of her brain, it flickered and winked like an eye, quietly it fluttered and dwindled. Granny lay curled down within herself, amazed and watchful, staring at the point of light that was herself; her body was now only a deeper mass of shadow in an endless darkness and this darkness would curl around the light and swallow it up. God, give a sign!

For the second time there was no sign. Again no bridegroom and the priest in the house.[3] She could not remember any other sorrow because this grief wiped them all away. Oh, no, there's nothing more cruel than this—I'll never forgive it. She stretched herself with a deep breath and blew out the light.

1930

3. In Christ's parable of the wise and foolish virgins, salvation is compared to the arrival of a bridegroom (Matthew 25:1–13).

ZORA NEALE HURSTON

1891–1960

Zora Neale Hurston once claimed that she had escaped punishment when arrested for crossing against a red light by explaining to the authorities that "I had seen white folks pass on green and therefore assumed the red light was for me." Both the humor and the audacity of this incident were typical of her. Like a number of her female characters, Hurston was a strong woman, determined to "wrassle me up a future, or die trying," and she was encouraged by another strong woman, her mother, who advised her to "jump at de sun." Not only did Hurston profit from a mother who refused to "squinch" the girl's spirits, she also gained self-confidence from her hometown, the first incorporated, self-governing, all-black town in the United States. Her father, John Hurston, a Baptist preacher, was elected to three terms as the mayor of Eatonville, Florida. Although Eatonville later inspired Hurston to preserve the linguistic exuberance, the protective community, and the spiritual traditions of southern black culture, when her mother died the nine-year-old girl saw herself as a wanderer. Alienated by her father's remarriage, she worked at fourteen as a wardrobe girl in a traveling Gilbert and Sullivan troupe until—with one dress and one change of underwear—she enrolled at Morgan Academy in Baltimore. There, and later at Howard University in Washington, D.C., she supported herself in jobs ranging from manicurist to maid.

After 1925, when Hurston moved to New York City, she became a frequent guest at the writer Carl Van Vechten's parties, where many distinguished Harlem artists mingled with wealthy whites. She worked first as a secretary and then as a chauffeur and companion to the popular white novelist Fannie Hurst. Early writings at Howard had brought her to the attention of Alain Locke, whose anthology *The New Negro* (1925) hailed the coming of a "new soul" for black America.

Hurston contributed a story to Locke's influential volume, and she also helped edit the quarterly *Fire!!*, which the authors Langston Hughes and Wallace Thurman created in 1926. In addition, a number of her plays and stories won literary awards. Although Hughes and Hurston quarreled in 1931 after they tried to collaborate on the play *Mule Bone*, during the two and a half years that Hurston actively participated in the Harlem Renaissance she was appreciated by Hughes and his friends as a flamboyant dresser and a great teller of folk tales.

During her early New York years, Hurston also enrolled at Barnard College, where she studied anthropology on a scholarship. Barnard's only black student, she received her degree in 1928 after working with the noted anthropologist Franz Boas. One year earlier, however, she had already embarked on folklore research in her hometown of Eatonville, research sponsored by Mrs. R. Osgood Mason, a white patron who subsidized a number of other artists besides Hurston. Generous though Mrs. Mason was, both Hurston's biographer Robert Hemenway and the literary critic Mary Helen Washington have shown that Hurston was placed in a situation of childlike dependency on a "godmother" who prohibited the young writer and scholar from publishing both her fiction and her anthropological findings. In addition, Hurston had to write her patroness adulatory letters to get her to agree even to the purchase of a much needed pair of shoes In 1932, when Mrs. Mason claimed ownership of the material Hurston had collected, the relationship collapsed.

During the period in which she published her most important work, Hurston taught at Bethune-Cookman College (1934), enrolled at Columbia University on a fellowship for graduate study in anthropology (1935), did dramatic coaching for the Federal Theater Project in New York (1935–36), traveled in the Caribbean on Guggenheim Fellowships (1936 and 1937), and worked as an editor for the Federal Writers' Project in Florida. In 1927, she was briefly married to Herbert Sheen, a medical student she had met at Howard University, and, at the end of the 1930s, she was again briefly married to Albert Price, a younger man. Among the most successful of the works she composed in this time, her collection of folklore *Mules and Men* (1935) and her novel *Their Eyes Were Watching God* (1937) have recently been reissued after years of critical neglect.

These two books established Hurston as an important twentieth-century writer. *Mules and Men* was based on Hurston's anthropological studies in Florida and Louisiana. During her earlier travels, Hurston had participated in hoodoo initiation ceremonies in New Orleans, spending sixty-nine hours, on one occasion, nude on a conjurer's couch, with her navel touching a snakeskin. Hoodoo ceremonies and tall-tale sessions reappear, vividly dramatized, in *Mules and Men*, along with descriptions of such hoodoo rites as *Eulalia—Ritual to Get a Man*. Through her recounting of initiation, cursing, and conjuring ceremonies, Hurston demonstrated that hoodoo was "a suppressed religion" and not "just superstition," even while she rescued black expression from ridicule by illustrating its metaphoric inventiveness. Similarly, *Their Eyes Were Watching God* celebrated the uniqueness of black cultural roots. Hurston's heroine, Janie Woods, is warned by her grandmother that "de nigger woman is de mule uh de world." Yet Janie manages to live the text of a sermon her grandmother had wanted to preach, "a great sermon about colored women sittin' on high." Through her heroine's progress, then, Hurston charted the evolution of African-American culture from subjugation through identification with whites and, finally, into autonomous racial identity and self-celebration.

Hurston received remarkably good reviews not only for these two books but for her novel *Jonah's Gourd Vine* (1934), for her play *Singing Steel* (1934), which attempted to debunk "the current mammy-song-Jolson conception of the Southern Negro," and for her autobiography *Dust Tracks on a Road* (1942); however, she came under attack throughout the 1940s and 1950s. As early as 1937, the celebrated black novelist Richard Wright had criticized *Their Eyes Were Watching God*

as a "minstrel" novel intended to make white people laugh at blacks. Her former teacher and friend Alain Locke called *Moses, Man of the Mountain* (1939)—a novel that takes Moses out of the Judeo-Christian tradition by portraying him as an African—"caricature instead of portraiture." Such critics were also opposed to the conservative cast of the political and social essays Hurston published in predominantly white magazines. Yet the basis for Hurston's rejection of northern liberalism was clarified by a letter she wrote to the editor of a Florida newspaper, in which she attacked the Supreme Court school desegregation decision (1954), for Hurston argued that integration denied the value of already-existing black institutions. By the 1950s, like many other journalists Hurston was publishing anticommunist essays. While Hemenway has attributed Hurston's growing conservatism to her inability "to admit that one could both celebrate Afro-American culture and deplore many of the conditions that helped shape it," Washington has associated Hurston's decision to ignore the brutal side of black experience with a refusal to submit to political pressures on black writers, who were expected throughout this period to protest against racism by portraying blacks as degraded or victimized.

In any case, by the time Hurston published her last novel, *Seraph on the Suwanee* (1948), she was beginning to experience the insecurity and pain that would characterize the rest of her life. Although she continued to teach and travel, she began to suffer from gallbladder attacks and an ulcer. In 1948, she was accused in New York of impairing the morals of a minor, a charge that was dismissed but that nevertheless horrified her. In 1950, she was working as a maid in Miami until the woman who employed her discovered an article Hurston had published in the *Saturday Evening Post*. Subsequent freelance writing earned her some savings, and she managed to spend several years in a house in Eau Gallie, Florida, during the early 1950s. But her fiction was being rejected by publishing houses, and in 1956, she was evicted after her landlord decided to sell the property. After a stroke in 1959, she entered the St. Lucie County Welfare Home. Three months later she died penniless, and her body was placed in an unmarked grave.

Both *How It Feels to Be Colored Me* and *Sweat* were published before Hurston attained national visibility as a folklorist and a novelist. Their vitality is typical, however, and helps explain why the contemporary black writer Alice Walker—the editor of a Zora Neale Hurston reader—admires Hurston's vision of "racial health—a sense of black people as complete, complex, *undiminished* human beings."

Sweat

It was eleven o'clock of a Spring night in Florida. It was Sunday. Any other night, Delia Jones would have been in bed for two hours by this time. But she was a washwoman, and Monday morning meant a great deal to her. So she collected the soiled clothes on Saturday when she returned the clean things. Sunday night after church, she sorted them and put the white things to soak. It saved her almost a half day's start. A great hamper in the bedroom held the clothes that she brought home. It was so much neater than a number of bundles lying around.

She squatted in the kitchen floor beside the great pile of clothes, sorting them into small heaps according to color, and humming a song in a mournful key, but wondering through it all where Sykes, her husband, had gone with her horse and buckboard.[1]

1. An open wagon.

Just then something long, round, limp and black fell upon her shoulders and slithered to the floor beside her. A great terror took hold of her. It softened her knees and dried her mouth so that it was a full minute before she could cry out or move. Then she saw that it was the big bull whip her husband liked to carry when he drove.

She lifted her eyes to the door and saw him standing there bent over with laughter at her fright. She screamed at him.

"Sykes, what you throw dat whip on me like dat? You know it would skeer me—looks just like a snake, an' you knows how skeered Ah is of snakes."

"Course Ah knowed it! That's how come Ah done it." He slapped his leg with his hand and almost rolled on the ground in his mirth. "If you such a big fool dat you got to have a fit over a earth worm or a string, Ah don't keer how bad Ah skeer you."

"You aint got no business doing it. Gawd knows it's a sin. Some day Ah'm gointuh drop dead from some of yo' foolishness. 'Nother thing, where you been wid mah rig? Ah feeds dat pony. He aint fuh you to be drivin' wid no bull whip."

"You sho is one aggravatin' nigger woman!" he declared and stepped into the room. She resumed her work and did not answer him at once. "Ah done tole you time and again to keep them white folks' clothes outa dis house."

He picked up the whip and glared down at her. Delia went on with her work. She went out into the yard and returned with a galvanized tub and set it on the washbench. She saw that Sykes had kicked all of the clothes together again, and now stood in her way truculently, his whole manner hoping, *praying*, for an argument. But she walked calmly around him and commenced to re-sort the things.

"Next time, Ah'm gointer kick 'em outdoors," he threatened as he struck a match along the leg of his corduroy breeches.

Delia never looked up from her work, and her thin, stooped shoulders sagged further.

"Ah aint for no fuss t'night, Sykes. Ah just come from taking sacrament at the church house."

He snorted scornfully. "Yeah, you just come from de church house on a Sunday night, but heah you is gone to work on them clothes. You ain't nothing but a hypocrite. One of them amen-corner Christians—sing, whoop, and shout, then come home and wash white folks' clothes on the Sabbath."

He stepped roughly upon the whitest pile of things, kicking them helter-skelter as he crossed the room. His wife gave a little scream of dismay, and quickly gathered them together again.

"Sykes, you quit grindin' dirt into these clothes! How can Ah git through by Sat'day if Ah don't start on Sunday?"

"Ah don't keer if you never git through. Anyhow, Ah done promised Gawd and a couple of other men, Ah aint gointer have it in mah house. Don't gimme no lip neither, else Ah'll throw 'em out and put mah fist up side yo' head to boot."

Delia's habitual meekness seemed to slip from her shoulders like a blown scarf. She was on her feet; her poor little body, her bare knuckly hands bravely defying the strapping hulk before her.

"Looka heah, Sykes, you done gone too fur. Ah been married to you fur fifteen years, and Ah been takin' in washin' fur fifteen years. Sweat, sweat, sweat! Work and sweat, cry and sweat, pray and sweat!"

"What's that got to do with me?" he asked brutally.

"What's it got to do with you, Sykes? Mah tub of suds is filled yo' belly with vittles more times than yo' hands is filled it. Mah sweat is done paid for this house and Ah reckon Ah kin keep on sweatin' in it."

She seized the iron skillet from the stove and struck a defensive pose, which act surprised him greatly, coming from her. It cowed him and he did not strike her as he usually did.

"Naw you won't," she panted, "that ole snaggle-toothed black woman you runnin' with aint comin' heah to pile up on mah sweat and blood. You aint paid for nothin' on this place, and Ah'm gointer stay right heah till Ah'm toted out foot foremost."

"Well, you better quit gittin' me riled up, else they'll be totin' you out sooner than you expect. Ah'm so tired of you Ah don't know whut to do. Gawd! how Ah hates skinny wimmen!"

A little awed by this new Delia, he sidled out of the door and slammed the back gate after him. He did not say where he had gone, but she knew too well. She knew very well that he would not return until nearly daybreak also. Her work over, she went on to bed but not to sleep at once. Things had come to a pretty pass!

She lay awake, gazing upon the debris that cluttered their matrimonial trail. Not an image left standing along the way. Anything like flowers had long ago been drowned in the salty stream that had been pressed from her heart. Her tears, her sweat, her blood. She had brought love to the union and he had brought a longing after the flesh. Two months after the wedding, he had given her the first brutal beating. She had the memory of his numerous trips to Orlando[2] with all of his wages when he had returned to her penniless, even before the first year had passed. She was young and soft then, but now she thought of her knotty, muscled limbs, her harsh knuckly hands, and drew herself up into an unhappy little ball in the middle of the big feather bed. Too late now to hope for love, even if it were not Bertha it would be someone else. This case differed from the others only in that she was bolder than the others. Too late for everything except her little home. She had built it for her old days, and planted one by one the trees and flowers there. It was lovely to her, lovely.

Somehow, before sleep came, she found herself saying aloud: "Oh well, whatever goes over the Devil's back, is got to come under his belly. Sometime or ruther, Sykes, like everybody else, is gointer reap his sowing." After that she was able to build a spiritual earthworks[3] against her husband. His shells could no longer reach her. Amen. She went to sleep and slept until he announced his presence in bed by kicking her feet and rudely snatching the covers away.

"Gimme some kivah heah, an' git yo' damn foots over on yo' own side! Ah oughter mash you in yo' mouf fuh drawing dat skillet on me."

Delia went clear to the rail without answering him. A triumphant indifference to all that he was or did.

The week was as full of work for Delia as all other weeks, and Saturday found her behind her little pony, collecting and delivering clothes.

It was a hot, hot day near the end of July. The village men on Joe Clarke's porch even chewed cane listlessly. They did not hurl the caneknots as usual.

2. City in Florida.
3. An embankment of earth of the kind used as a fortification.

They let them dribble over the edge of the porch. Even conversation had collapsed under the heat.

"Heah come Delia Jones," Jim Merchant said, as the shaggy pony came 'round the bend of the road toward them. The rusty buckboard was heaped with baskets of crisp, clean laundry.

"Yep," Joe Lindsay agreed. "Hot or col', rain or shine, es ez reg'lar ez de weeks roll roun' Delia carries 'em an' fetches 'em on Sat'day."

"She better if she wanter eat," said Moss. "Syke Jones aint wuth de shot an' powder hit would tek tuh kill 'em. Not to huh he aint."

"He sho' aint," Walter Thomas chimed in. "It's too bad, too, cause she wuz a right pritty lil trick when he got huh. Ah'd uh mah'ied huh mahseff if he hadnter beat me to it."

Delia nodded briefly at the men as she drove past.

"Too much knockin' will ruin any 'oman. He done beat huh 'nough tuh kill three women, let 'lone change they looks," said Elijah Moseley. "How Syke kin stommuck dat big black greasy Mogul he's 'avin' roun' wid, gits me. Ah swear dat eight-rock[4] couldn't kiss a sardine can Ah done thowed out de back do 'way las' yeah."

"Aw, she's fat, thass how come. He's allus been crazy 'bout fat women," put in Merchant. "He'd a' been tied up wid one long time ago f he could a' found one tuh have him. Did Ah tell yuh 'bout him come sidlin' roun' *mah* wife—bringin' her a basket uh peecans outa his yard fuh a present? Yessir, mah wife! She tol' him tuh take em right straight back home, cause Delia works so hard ovah dat wash tub she reckon everything on de place taste lak sweat an' soap-suds. Ah jus' wisht Ah'd a caught 'im roun' dere! Ah'd a' made his hips ketch on fiah down dat shell road."

"Ah know he done it, too. Ah sees 'im grinnin' at every 'oman dat passes," Walter Thomas said. "But even so, he useter eat some mighty big hunks uh humble pie tuh git dat lil' 'oman he got. She wuz ez pritty ez a speckled pup! Dat wuz fifteen yeahs ago. He useter be so skeered uh losin' huh, she could make him do some parts of a husband's duty. Dey never wuz de same in de mind."

"There oughter be a law about him," said Lindsay. "He aint fit tuh carry guts tuh a bear."

Clarke spoke for the first time. "Taint no law on earth dat kin make a man be decent if it aint in 'im. There's plenty men dat takes a wife lak dey do a joint uh sugar-cane. It's round, juicy an' sweet when dey gits it. But dey squeeze an' grind, squeeze an' grind an' wring tell dey wring every drop uh pleasure dat's in 'em out. When dey's satisfied dat dey is wrung dry, dey treats 'em jes lak dey do a cane-chew. Dey thows 'em away. Dey knows whut dey is doin' while dey is at it, an' hates theirselves fuh it but they keeps on hangin' after huh tell she's empty. Den dey hates huh fuh bein' a cane-chew an' in de way."

"We oughter take Syke an' dat stray 'oman uh his'n down in Lake Howell swamp an' lay on de rawhide till they cain't say Lawd a' mussy' He allus wuz uh ovahbearin' niggah, but since dat white 'oman from up north done teached 'im how to run a automobile, he done got too biggety[5] to live—an' we oughter kill 'im." Old Man Anderson advised.

4. Derogatory term for a very dark-skinned black person. "Mogul": i.e., big woman. 5. I.e., full of himself.

A grunt of approval went around the porch. But the heat was melting their civic virtue and Elijah Moseley began to bait Joe Clarke.

"Come on, Joe, git a melon outa dere an' slice it up for yo' customers. We'se all sufferin' wid de heat. De bear's done got *me!*"

"Thass right, Joe, a watermelon is jes' whut Ah needs tuh cure de eppizu-dicks,"[6] Walter Thomas joined forces with Moseley. "Come on dere, Joe. We all is steady customers an' you aint set us up in a long time. Ah chooses dat long, bowlegged Floridy favorite."

"A god, an' be dough. You all gimme twenty cents and slice way," Clarke re-torted. "Ah needs a col' slice m'self. Heah, everybody chip in. Ah'll lend y'll mah meat knife."

The money was quickly subscribed and the huge melon brought forth. At that moment, Sykes and Bertha arrived. A determined silence fell on the porch and the melon was put away again.

Merchant snapped down the blade of his jackknife and moved toward the store door.

"Come on in, Joe, an' gimme a slab uh sow belly an' uh pound uh coffee—almost fuhgot 'twas Sat'day. Got to git on home." Most of the men left also.

Just then Delia drove past on her way home, as Sykes was ordering magnifi-cently for Bertha. It pleased him for Delia to see.

"Git whutsoever yo' heart desires, Honey. Wait a minute, Joe. Give huh two bottles uh strawberry soda-water, uh quart uh parched ground-peas, an' a block uh chewin' gum."

With all this they left the store, with Sykes reminding Bertha that this was his town and she could have it if she wanted it.

The men returned soon after they left, and held their watermelon feast.

"Where did Syke Jones git da 'oman from nohow?" Lindsay asked.

"Ovah Apopka. Guess dey musta been cleanin' out de town when she lef'. She don't look lak a thing but a hunk uh liver wid hair on it."

"Well, she sho' kin squall," Dave Carter contributed. "When she gits ready tuh laff, she jes' opens huh mouf an' latches it back tuh de las' notch. No ole grandpa alligator down in Lake Bell ain't got nothin' on huh."

Bertha had been in town three months now. Sykes was still paying her room rent at Della Lewis'—the only house in town that would have taken her in. Sykes took her frequently to Winter Park to "stomps."[7] He still assured her that he was the swellest man in the state.

"Sho' you kin have dat lil' ole house soon's Ah kin git dat 'oman outa dere. Everything b'longs tuh me an' you sho' kin have it. Ah sho' 'bominates uh skinny 'oman. Lawdy, you sho' is got one portly shape on you! You kin git *any-thing* you wants. Dis is mah town an' you sho' kin have it."

Delia's work-worn knees crawled over the earth in Gethsemane and up the rocks of Calvary[8] many, many times during these months. She avoided the vil-lagers and meeting places in her efforts to be blind and deaf. But Bertha nulli-fied this to a degree, by coming to Delia's house to call Sykes out to her at the gate.

6. I.e., "epizootic," used of a disease that attacks a large number of animals at once.
7. Jazz dances.

8. The hill where Jesus was crucified. Gethsemane is the garden where he was betrayed (Matthew 26:36–47).

Delia and Sykes fought all the time now with no peaceful interludes. They slept and ate in silence. Two or three times Delia had attempted a timid friendliness, but she was repulsed each time. It was plain that the breaches must remain agape.

The sun had burned July to August. The heat streamed down like a million hot arrows, smiting all things living upon the earth. Grass withered, leaves browned, snakes went blind in shedding and men and dogs went mad. Dog days!

Delia came home one day and found Sykes there before her. She wondered, but started to go on into the house without speaking, even though he was standing in the kitchen door and she must either stoop under his arm or ask him to move. He made no room for her. She noticed a soap box beside the steps, but paid no particular attention to it, knowing that he must have brought it there. As she was stooping to pass under his outstretched arm, he suddenly pushed her backward, laughingly

"Look in de box dere Delia, Ah done brung yuh somethin'!"

She nearly fell upon the box in her stumbling, and when she saw what it held, she all but fainted outright.

"Syke! Syke, mah Gawd! You take dat rattlesnake 'way from heah! You got-tuh. Oh, Jesus, have mussy!"

"Ah aint gut tuh do nuthin' uh de kin'—fact is Ah aint got tuh do nothin' but die. Taint no use uh you puttin' on airs makin' out lak you skeered uh dat snake—he's gointer stay right heah tell he die. He wouldn't bite me cause Ah knows how tuh handle 'im. Nohow he wouldn't risk breakin' out his fangs 'gin yo' skinny laigs."

"Naw, now Syke, don't keep dat thing 'roun' heah tuh skeer me tuh death. You knows Ah'm even feared uh earth worms. Thass de biggest snake Ah evah did see. Kill 'im Syke, please."

"Doan ast me tuh do nothin' fuh yuh. Goin' 'roun' tryin' tuh be so damn asterperious.[9] Naw, Ah aint gonna kill it. Ah think uh damn sight mo' uh him dan you! Dat's a nice snake an' anybody doan lak 'im kin jes' hit de grit."

The village soon heard that Sykes had the snake, and came to see and ask questions.

"How de hen-fire did you ketch dat six-foot rattler, Syke?" Thomas asked.

"He's full uh frogs so he caint hardly move, thass how Ah eased up on 'm. But Ah'm a snake charmer an' knows how tuh handle 'em. Shux, dat aint nothin'. Ah could ketch one eve'y day if Ah so wanted tuh."

"Whut he needs is a heavy hick'ry club leaned real heavy on his head. Dat's de bes 'way tuh charm a rattlesnake."

"Naw, Walt, y'll jes' don't understand dese diamon' backs lak Ah do," said Sykes in a superior tone of voice.

The village agreed with Walter, but the snake stayed on. His box remained by the kitchen door with its screen wire covering. Two or three days later it had digested its meal of frogs and literally came to life. It rattled at every movement in the kitchen or the yard. One day as Delia came down the kitchen steps she saw his chalky-white fangs curved like scimitars hung in the wire meshes. This time she did not run away with averted eyes as usual. She stood

9. I.e., obstreperous (unruly).

for a long time in the doorway in a red fury that grew bloodier for every second that she regarded the creature that was her torment.

That night she broached the subject as soon as Sykes sat down to the table.

"Syke, Ah wants you tuh take dat snake 'way fum heah. You done starved me an' Ah put up widcher, you done beat me an Ah took dat, but you done kilt all mah insides bringin' dat varmint heah."

Sykes poured out a saucer full of coffee and drank it deliberately before he answered her.

"A whole lot Ah keer 'bout how you feels inside uh out. Dat snake aint goin' no damn wheah till Ah gits ready fuh'im tuh go. So fur as beatin' is concerned, yuh aint took near all dat you gointer take ef yuh stay 'roun' me."

Delia pushed back her plate and got up from the table. "Ah hates you, Sykes," she said calmly. "Ah hates you tuh de same degree dat Ah useter love yuh. Ah done took an' took till mah belly is full up tuh mah neck. Dat's de reason Ah got mah letter fum de church an' moved mah membership tuh Woodbridge—so Ah don't haftuh take no sacrament wid yuh. Ah don't wantuh see yuh 'roun' me atall. Lay 'roun' wid dat 'oman all yuh wants tuh, but gwan 'way fum me an' mah house. Ah hates yuh lak uh suck-egg dog."

Sykes almost let the huge wad of corn bread and collard greens he was chewing fall out of his mouth in amazement. He had a hard time whipping himself up to the proper fury to try to answer Delia.

"Well, Ah'm glad you does hate me. Ah'm sho' tiahed uh you hangin' ontuh me. Ah don't want yuh. Look at yuh stringey ole neck! Yo' rawbony laigs an' arms is enough tuh cut uh man tuh death. You looks jes' lak de devvul's doll-baby tuh me. You cain't hate me no worse dan Ah hates you. Ah been hatin' you fuh years."

"Yo' ole black hide don't look lak nothin' tuh me, but uh passle uh wrinkled up rubber, wid yo' big ole yeahs flappin' on each side lak uh paih uh buzzard wings. Don't think Ah'm gointuh be run 'way fum mah house neither. Ah'm goin' tuh de white folks bout you, mah young man, de very nex' time you lay yo' han's on me. Mah cup is done run ovah."

Delia said this with no signs of fear and Sykes departed from the house, threatening her, but made not the slightest move to carry out any of them.

That night he did not return at all, and the next day being Sunday, Delia was glad she did not have to quarrel before she hitched up her pony and drove the four miles to Woodbridge.

She stayed to the night service—"love feast"—which was very warm and full of spirit. In the emotional winds her domestic trials were borne far and wide so that she sang as she drove homeward,

> "Jurden water,[1] black an' col'
> Chills de body, not de soul
> An' Ah wantah cross Jurden in uh calm time."

She came from the barn to the kitchen door and stopped.

"Whut's de mattah, ol' satan, you aint kickin' up yo' racket?" She addressed

1. The Jordan River, the eastern border of Israel, which the Israelites had to cross to reach the promised land (Joshua 3).

the snake's box. Complete silence. She went on into the house with a new hope in its birth struggles. Perhaps her threat to go to the white folks had frightened Sykes! Perhaps he was sorry! Fifteen years of misery and suppression had brought Delia to the place where she would hope *anything* that looked towards a way over or through her wall of inhibitions.

She felt in the match safe behind the stove at once for a match. There was only one there.

"Dat niggah wouldn't fetch nothin' heah tuh save his rotten neck, but he kin run thew whut Ah brings quick enough. Now he done toted off nigh on tuh haff uh box uh matches. He done had dat 'oman heah in mah house too."

Nobody but a woman could tell how she knew this even before she struck the match. But she did and it put her into a new fury.

Presently she brought in the tubs to put the white things to soak. This time she decided she need not bring the hamper out of the bedroom she would go in there and do the sorting. She picked up the pot-bellied lamp and went in. The room was small and the hamper stood hard by the foot of the white iron bed. She could sit and reach through the bedposts—resting as she worked.

"Ah wantah cross Jurden in uh calm time." She was singing again. The mood of the "love feast" had returned. She threw back the lid of the basket almost gaily. Then, moved by both horror and terror, she sprang back toward the door. *There lay the snake in the basket!* He moved sluggishly at first, but even as she turned round and round, jumped up and down in an insanity of fear, he began to stir vigorously. She saw him pouring his awful beauty from the basket upon the bed, then she seized the lamp and ran as fast as she could to the kitchen. The wind from the open door blew out the light and the darkness added to her terror. She sped to the darkness of the yard, slamming the door after her before she thought to set down the lamp. She did not feel safe even on the ground, so she climbed up in the hay barn.

There for an hour or more she lay sprawled upon the hay a gibbering wreck.

Finally she grew quiet, and after that, coherent thought. With this, stalked through her a cold, bloody rage. Hours of this. A period of introspection, a space of retrospection, then a mixture of both. Out of this an awful calm.

"Well, Ah done de bes' Ah could. If things aint right, Gawd knows taint mah fault."

She went to sleep—a twitch sleep—and woke up to a faint gray sky. There was a loud hollow sound below. She peered out. Sykes was at the wood-pile, demolishing a wire-covered box.

He hurried to the kitchen door, but hung outside there some minutes before he entered, and stood some minutes more inside before he closed it after him.

The gray in the sky was spreading. Delia descended without fear now, and crouched beneath the low bedroom window. The drawn shade shut out the dawn, shut in the night. But the thin walls held back no sound.

"Dat ol' scratch is woke up now!" She mused at the tremendous whirr inside, which every woodsman knows, is one of the sound illusions The rattler is a ventriloquist. His whirr sounds to the right, to the left, straight ahead, behind, close under foot—everywhere but where it is. Woe to him who guesses wrong unless he is prepared to hold up his end of the argument! Sometimes he strikes without rattling at all.

Inside, Sykes heard nothing until he knocked a pot lid off the stove while

trying to reach the match safe in the dark. He had emptied his pockets at Bertha's.

The snake seemed to wake up under the stove and Sykes made a quick leap into the bedroom. In spite of the gin he had had, his head was clearing now.

"Mah Gawd!" he chattered, "ef Ah could on'y strack uh light!"

The rattling ceased for a moment as he stood paralyzed. He waited. It seemed that the snake waited also.

"Oh, fuh de light! Ah thought he'd be too sick"—Sykes was muttering to himself when the whirr began again, closer, right underfoot this time. Long before this, Sykes' ability to think had been flattened down to primitive instinct and he leaped—onto the bed.

Outside Delia heard a cry that might have come from a maddened chimpanzee, a stricken gorilla. All the terror, all the horror, all the rage that man possibly could express, without a recognizable human sound.

A tremendous stir inside there, another series of animal screams, the intermittent whirr of the reptile. The shade torn violently down from the window, letting in the red dawn, a huge brown hand seizing the window stick, great dull blows upon the wooden floor punctuating the gibberish of sound long after the rattle of the snake had abruptly subsided. All this Delia could see and hear from her place beneath the window, and it made her ill. She crept over to the four-o'clocks[2] and stretched herself on the cool earth to recover.

She lay there. "Delia, Delia!" She could hear Sykes calling in a most despairing tone as one who expected no answer. The sun crept on up, and he called. Delia could not move—her legs were gone flabby. She never moved, he called, and the sun kept rising.

"Mah Gawd!" She heard him moan, "Mah Gawd fum Heben!" She heard him stumbling about and got up from her flower-bed. The sun was growing warm. As she approached the door she heard him call out hopefully, "Delia, is dat you Ah heah?"

She saw him on his hands and knees as soon as she reached the door. He crept an inch or two toward her—all that he was able, and she saw his horribly swollen neck and his one open eye shining with hope. A surge of pity too strong to support bore her away from that eye that must, could not, fail to see the tubs. He would see the lamp. Orlando with its doctors was too far. She could scarcely reach the Chinaberry tree, where she waited in the growing heat while inside she knew the cold river was creeping up and up to extinguish that eye which must know by now that she knew.

1926

How It Feels to Be Colored Me

I am colored but I offer nothing in the way of extenuating circumstances except the fact that I am the only Negro in the United States whose grandfather on the mother's side was not an Indian chief.

I remember the very day that I became colored. Up to my thirteenth year I lived in the little Negro town of Eatonville, Florida. It is exclusively a colored

2. A tropical plant with tubular flowers.

town. The only white people I knew passed through the town going to or coming from Orlando. The native whites rode dusty horses, the Northern tourists chugged down the sandy village road in automobiles. The town knew the Southerners and never stopped cane chewing[1] when they passed. But the Northerners were something else again. They were peered at cautiously from behind curtains by the timid. The more venturesome would come out on the porch to watch them go past and got just as much pleasure out of the tourists as the tourists got out of the village.

The front porch might seem a daring place for the rest of the town, but it was a gallery seat for me. My favorite place was atop the gate-post Proscenium box for a born first-nighter. Not only did I enjoy the show, but I didn't mind the actors knowing that I liked it. I usually spoke to them in passing. I'd wave at them and when they returned my salute, I would say something like this: "Howdy-do-well-I-thank-you-where-you-goin'?" Usually automobile or the horse paused at this, and after a queer exchange of compliments, I would probably "go a piece of the way" with them, as we say in farthest Florida. If one of my family happened to come to the front in time to see me, of course negotiations would be rudely broken off. But even so, it is clear that I was the first "welcome-to-our-state" Floridian, and I hope the Miami Chamber of Commerce will please take notice.

During this period, white people differed from colored to me only in that they rode through town and never lived there. They liked to hear me "'speak pieces" and sing and wanted to see me dance the parse-me-la, and gave me generously of their small silver for doing these things, which seemed strange to me for I wanted to do them so much that I needed bribing to stop. Only they didn't know it. The colored people gave no dimes. They deplored any joyful tendencies in me, but I was their Zora nevertheless. I belonged to them, to the nearby hotels, to the county—everybody's Zora.

But changes came in the family when I was thirteen, and I was sent to school in Jacksonville. I left Eatonville, the town of the oleanders, as Zora. When I disembarked from the river-boat at Jacksonville, she was no more. It seemed that I had suffered a sea change. I was not Zora of Orange County any more, I was now a little colored girl. I found it out in certain ways. In my heart as well as in the mirror, I became a fast brown—warranted not to rub nor run.

But I am not tragically colored. There is no great sorrow dammed up in my soul, nor lurking behind my eyes. I do not mind at all. I do not belong to the sobbing school of Negrohood who hold that nature somehow has given them a lowdown dirty deal and whose feelings are all hurt about it. Even in the helter-skelter skirmish that is my life, I have seen that the world is to the strong regardless of a little pigmentation more or less. No, I do not weep at the world—I am too busy sharpening my oyster knife.[2]

Someone is always at my elbow reminding me that I am the granddaughter of slaves. It fails to register depression with me. Slavery is sixty years in the past. The operation was successful and the patient is doing well, thank you. The terrible struggle that made me an American out of a potential slave said "On the line!" The Reconstruction[3] said "Get set!"; and the generation before

<hr />

1. Chewing sugar cane.
2. A reference to the popular expression "The world is my oyster."
3. The period immediately following the Civil War

("the terrible struggle") when federal control of the South brought the newly freed slaves economic, political, and educational opportunities.

said "Go!" I am off to a flying start and I must not halt in the stretch to look behind and weep. Slavery is the price I paid for civilization, and the choice was not with me. It is a bully adventure and worth all that I have paid through my ancestors for it. No one on earth ever had a greater chance for glory. The world to be won and nothing to be lost. It is thrilling to think—to know that for any act of mine, I shall get twice as much praise or twice as much blame. It is quite exciting to hold the center of the national stage, with the spectators not knowing whether to laugh or to weep.

The position of my white neighbor is much more difficult. No brown specter pulls up a chair beside me when I sit down to eat. No dark ghost thrusts its leg against mine in bed. The game of keeping what one has is never so exciting as the game of getting.

I do not always feel colored. Even now I often achieve the unconscious Zora of Eatonville before the Hegira.[4] I feel most colored when I am thrown against a sharp white background.

For instance at Barnard. "Beside the waters of the Hudson"[5] I feel my race. Among the thousand white persons, I am a dark rock surged upon, and overswept, but through it all, I remain myself. When covered by the waters, I am; and the ebb but reveals me again.

Sometimes it is the other way around. A white person is set down in our midst, but the contrast is just as sharp for me. For instance, when I sit in the drafty basement that is The New World Cabaret with a white person, my color comes. We enter chatting about any little nothing that we have in common and are seated by the jazz waiters. In the abrupt way that jazz orchestras have, this one plunges into a number. It loses no time in circumlocutions, but gets right down to business. It constricts the thorax and splits the heart with its tempo and narcotic harmonies. This orchestra grows rambunctious, rears on its hind legs and attacks the tonal veil with primitive fury, rending it, clawing it until it breaks through to the jungle beyond. I follow those heathen—follow them exultingly. I dance wildly inside myself; I yell within, I whoop; I shake my assegai[6] above my head, I hurl it true to the mark yeeeeooww! I am in the jungle and living in the jungle way. My face is painted red and yellow and my body is painted blue. My pulse is throbbing like a war drum. I want to slaughter something—give pain, give death to what, I do not know. But the piece ends. The men of the orchestra wipe their lips and rest their fingers. I creep back slowly to the veneer we call civilization with the last tone and find the white friend sitting motionless in his seat, smoking calmly.

"Good music they have here," he remarks, drumming the table with his fingertips.

Music. The great blobs of purple and red emotion have not touched him. He has only heard what I felt. He is far away and I see him but dimly across the ocean and the continent that have fallen between us. He is so pale with his whiteness then and I am so colored.

At certain times I have no race, I am me. When I set my hat at a certain angle and saunter down Seventh Avenue, Harlem City, feeling as snooty as the lions in front of the Forty-Second Street Library, for instance. So far as my

4. Flight of Muhammed from Mecca in A.D. 622; any journey, especially one undertaken to escape from a dangerous or undesirable situation.
5. Compare Psalm 137: "By the rivers of Babylon," where the exiled Israelites wept. Barnard is a women's college in New York City.
6. A light spear used by tribesmen in southern Africa.

feelings are concerned, Peggy Hopkins Joyce on the Boule Mich[7] with her gorgeous raiment, stately carriage, knees knocking together in a most aristocratic manner, has nothing on me. The cosmic Zora emerges. I belong to no race nor time. I am the eternal feminine with its string of beads.

I have no separate feeling about being an American citizen and colored. I am merely a fragment of the Great Soul that surges within the boundaries. My country, right or wrong.

Sometimes, I feel discriminated against, but it does not make me angry. It merely astonishes me. How can any deny themselves the pleasure of my company? It's beyond me.

But in the main, I feel like a brown bag of miscellany propped against a wall. Against a wall in company with other bags, white, red and yellow. Pour out the contents, and there is discovered a jumble of small things priceless and worthless. A first-water diamond, an empty spool, bits of broken glass, lengths of string, a key to a door long since crumbled away, a rusty knife-blade, old shoes saved for a road that never was and never will be, a nail bent under the weight of things too heavy for any nail, a dried flower or two still a little fragrant. In your hand is the brown bag. On the ground before you is the jumble it held— so much like the jumble in the bags, could they be emptied, that all might be dumped in a single heap and the bags refilled without altering the content of any greatly. A bit of colored glass more or less would not matter. Perhaps that is how the Great Stuffer of Bags filled them in the first place—who knows?

<div align="right">1928</div>

7. The Boulevard Saint-Michel, a street in Paris's student quarter. Peggy Hopkins Joyce was an American beauty and fashion setter in the 1920s.

EDNA ST. VINCENT MILLAY
1892–1950

In the late 1950s, the poet Anne Sexton worried that she might be a "reincarnation" of Edna St. Vincent Millay, and at around the same time Sexton's friend Sylvia Plath was expressing similar fears, insisting to her mother that she would not write "simple lyrics like Millay." At least in part, such anxieties were the result of the enormous success that Edna St. Vincent Millay—poet, playwright, feminist, and political activist—achieved, especially in her early youth, by producing fluent and inventive sonnet cycles, verse dramas, and dramatic poems. For indeed, even while Sexton was troubled by the thought that she might be seriously compared with Millay, she was candidly admitting that "2 years ago I had never heard of any poet but Edna St. Vincent."

Born in Rockland, Maine, Edna St. Vincent Millay was the oldest of three daughters whose father deserted them and their mother, a practical nurse, when the child—called "Vincent" in the family—was eight. According to one biographer, her mother "taught" her to write verse at the age of four; in any case, she soon exhibited a precocious talent, and, when she was only twenty, one of her most famous poems, *Renascence*, was a prize winner in an important contest sponsored by *The Lyric Year*, an anthology of contemporary poetry. Almost immediately, her ability brought her to the attention of a number of older intellectuals, one of whom, Caroline Dow, the executive secretary of the YWCA's national training

school in New York, urged her to attend Vassar College, where she had a lively career as a notable undergraduate poet, actress, and playwright.

After graduation from Vassar in 1917, Edna St. Vincent Millay lived a bohemian life in Greenwich Village. Writing articles for popular magazines and innovative plays (for example, *Aria da Capo*) as well as acting in the Provincetown Players, a radical little theater group, she seemed to be an incarnation of what was in the 1920s called "the Jazz Age." Passionately independent, red haired, green eyed, she was a celebrity of sorts among artists and intellectuals, with, according to the critic Edmund Wilson (who proposed marriage to her), "an intoxicating effect on people." For her part, she mythologized such intoxication from the heroine's point of view, writing poems that extolled sexual and emotional liberation, poems that would be memorized by generations of young women from her own day to Anne Sexton's. "My candle burns at both ends," she rebelliously proclaimed; "It will not last the night; / But ah, my foes, and oh, my friends— / It gives a lovely light!"

Millay was also undertaking more ambitious tasks. Though financial difficulties drove her to hackwork for magazines, which she wrote under the name "Nancy Boyd," she produced a number of quite serious volumes of verse: *Ballad of the Harp-Weaver* won the Pulitzer Prize in 1923. In addition, she presented herself as, in the words of her friend the writer Floyd Dell, "very much a revolutionary in all her sympathies, and a whole-hearted Feminist." In 1923—in keeping with this self-definition—she married the widower of the prominent American feminist Inez Milholland, a Dutch businessman named Eugen Jan Boissevain.

After her marriage to Boissevain, Millay's career continued to flourish for a while. In 1925, she was awarded an honorary degree by Tufts College, the first of many such degrees, and in 1927, she became intensely involved in the crusade to stay the execution of the alleged anarchists Sacco and Vanzetti, about whom she wrote a number of passionate verses. In the 1930s, however, her reputation began to wane, perhaps because her art did not seem as innovative as the work of modernist contemporaries like T. S. Eliot, Wallace Stevens, and Marianne Moore, writers whose rugged and sometimes seemingly ragged forms appeared to be far in advance of the more traditional modes and meters Millay employed. Although during World War II she continued to work actively for public causes and to write intensely political poetry, she became increasingly isolated. In 1944, she suffered a nervous breakdown, and in 1950, a year after her husband died, she too died of a heart attack while living alone on their country place at Austerlitz, New York. Yet despite the obscurity into which her work fell in the 1950s and 1960s—decades when former acolytes like Plath and Sexton felt it necessary to repudiate her as an old-fashioned "poetess"—Millay's art has endured and seems, sometimes, surprisingly fresh: indeed, not too long ago one prominent editor remarked that her *Childhood Is the Kingdom* reads like "a twenty-first-century poem."

First Fig[1]

My candle burns at both ends;
 It will not last the night;
But ah, my foes, and oh, my friends—
 It gives a lovely light!

1920

1. From *A Few Figs from Thistles*, a title that refers to Matthew 7:16: "Do men gather grapes of thorns, or figs of thistles?"

Second Fig[2]

Safe upon the solid rock the ugly houses stand
Come and see my shining palace built upon the sand!

1920

[Oh, oh, you will be sorry for that word!]

Oh, oh, you will be sorry for that word!
Give back my book and take my kiss instead.
Was it my enemy or my friend I heard,
"What a big book for such a little head!"
Come, I will show you now my newest hat, 5
And you may watch me purse my mouth and drink![3]
Oh, I shall love you still, and all of that.
I never again shall tell you what I think.
I shall be sweet and crafty, soft and sly;
You will not catch me reading any more: 10
I shall be called a wife to pattern by;
And some day when you knock and push the door,
Some sane day, not too bright and not too stormy,
I shall be gone, and you may whistle for me.

1923

[I, being born a woman and distressed]

I, being born a woman and distressed
By all the needs and notions of my kind,
Am urged by your propinquity to find
Your person fair, and feel a certain zest
To bear your body's weight upon my breast: 5
So subtly is the fume of life designed,
To clarify the pulse and cloud the mind,
And leave me once again undone, possessed.
Think not for this, however, the poor treason
Of my stout blood against my staggering brain, 10
I shall remember you with love, or season
My scorn with pity,—let me make it plain:
I find this frenzy insufficient reason
For conversation when we meet again.

1923

2. See note for *First Fig*; see also Matthew 7:26–27, upon the sand."
which criticizes "a foolish man, which built his house 3. Primp.

Sonnets from an Ungrafted Tree[4]

I

So she came back into his house again
And watched beside his bed until he died,
Loving him not at all. The winter rain
Splashed in the painted butter-tub outside,
Where once her red geraniums had stood, 5
Where still their rotted stalks were to be seen;
The thin log snapped; and she went out for wood,
Bareheaded, running the few steps between
The house and shed; there, from the sodden eaves
Blown back and forth on ragged ends of twine, 10
Saw the dejected creeping-jinny vine,
(And one, big-aproned, blithe, with stiff blue sleeves
Rolled to the shoulder that warm day in spring,
Who planted seeds, musing ahead to their far blossoming).

II

The last white sawdust on the floor was grown
Gray as the first, so long had he been ill;
The axe was nodding in the block; fresh-blown
And foreign came the rain across the sill,
But on the roof so steadily it drummed 5
She could not think a time it might not be—
In hazy summer, when the hot air hummed
With mowing, and locusts rising raspingly,
When that small bird with iridescent wings
And long incredible sudden silver tongue 10
Had just flashed (and yet maybe not!) among
The dwarf nasturtiums—when no sagging springs
Of shower were in the whole bright sky, somehow
Upon this roof the rain would drum as it was drumming now.

III

She filled her arms with wood, and set her chin
Forward, to hold the highest stick in place,
No less afraid than she had always been
Of spiders up her arms and on her face,
But too impatient for a careful search 5
Or a less heavy loading, from the heap
Selecting hastily small sticks of birch,
For their curled bark, that instantly will leap
Into a blaze, nor thinking to return
Some day, distracted, as of old, to find 10
Smooth, heavy, round, green logs with a wet, gray rind
Only, and knotty chunks that will not burn,
(That day when dust is on the wood-box floor,
And some old catalogue, and a brown, shriveled apple core).

4. A tree to which new branches or cuttings have not been attached.

IV

The white bark writhed and sputtered like a fish
Upon the coals, exuding odorous smoke.
She knelt and blew, in a surging desolate wish
For comfort; and the sleeping ashes woke
And scattered to the hearth, but no thin fire 5
Broke suddenly, the wood was wet with rain.
Then, softly stepping forth from her desire,
(Being mindful of like passion hurled in vain
Upon a similar task, in other days)
She thrust her breath against the stubborn coal, 10
Bringing to bear upon its hilt the whole
Of her still body . . . there sprang a little blaze . . .
A pack of hounds, the flame swept up the flue!—
And the blue night stood flattened against the window, staring through.

V

A wagon stopped before the house; she heard
The heavy oilskins of the grocer's man
Slapping against his legs. Of a sudden whirred
Her heart like a frightened partridge, and she ran
And slid the bolt, leaving his entrance free; 5
Then in the cellar way till he was gone
Hid, breathless, praying that he might not see
The chair sway she had laid her hand upon
In passing. Sour and damp from that dark vault
Arose to her the well-remembered chill; 10
She saw the narrow wooden stairway still
Plunging into the earth, and the thin salt
Crusting the crocks; until she knew him far,
So stood, with listening eyes upon the empty doughnut jar.

VI

Then cautiously she pushed the cellar door
And stepped into the kitchen—saw the track
Of muddy rubber boots across the floor,
The many paper parcels in a stack
Upon the dresser; with accustomed care 5
Removed the twine and put the wrappings by,
Folded, and the bags flat, that with an air
Of ease had been whipped open skillfully,
To the gape of children. Treacherously dear
And simple was the dull, familiar task. 10
And so it was she came at length to ask:
How came the soda there? The sugar here?
Then the dream broke. Silent, she brought the mop,
And forced the trade-slip[5] on the nail that held his razor strop.

5. Receipt.

VII

One way there was of muting in the mind
A little while the ever-clamorous care;
And there was rapture, of a decent kind,
In making mean and ugly objects fair:
Soft-sooted kettle-bottoms, that had been 5
Time after time set in above the fire,
Faucets, and candlesticks, corroded green,
To mine again from quarry; to attire
The shelves in paper petticoats, and tack
New oilcloth in the ringed-and-rotten's place, 10
Polish the stove till you could see your face,
And after nightfall rear an aching back
In a changed kitchen, bright as a new pin,
An advertisement, far too fine to cook a supper in.

VIII

She let them leave their jellies at the door
And go away, reluctant, down the walk.
She heard them talking as they passed before
The blind, but could not quite make out their talk
For noise in the room—the sudden heavy fall 5
And roll of a charred log, and the roused shower
Of snapping sparks; then sharply from the wall
The unforgivable crowing of the hour.
One instant set ajar, her quiet ear
Was stormed and forced by the full rout of day: 10
The rasp of a saw, the fussy cluck and bray
Of hens, the wheeze of a pump, she needs must hear;
She inescapably must endure to feel
Across her teeth the grinding of a backing wagon wheel.

IX

Not over-kind nor over-quick in study
Nor skilled in sports nor beautiful was he,
Who had come into her life when anybody
Would have been welcome, so in need was she.
They had become acquainted in this way: 5
He flashed a mirror in her eyes at school;
By which he was distinguished; from that day
They went about together, as a rule.
She told, in secret and with whispering,
How he had flashed a mirror in her eyes; 10
And as she told, it struck her with surprise
That this was not so wonderful a thing.
But what's the odds?—It's pretty nice to know
You've got a friend to keep you company everywhere you go.

X

She had forgotten how the August night
Was level as a lake beneath the moon,
In which she swam a little, losing sight
Of shore; and how the boy, who was at noon
Simple enough, not different from the rest, 5
Wore now a pleasant mystery as he went,
Which seemed to her an honest enough test
Whether she loved him, and she was content.
So loud, so loud the million crickets' choir . . .
So sweet the night, so long-drawn-out and late . . . 10
And if the man were not her spirit's mate,
Why was her body sluggish with desire?
Stark on the open field the moonlight fell,
But the oak tree's shadow was deep and black and secret as a well.

XI

It came into her mind, seeing how the snow
Was gone, and the brown grass exposed again,
And clothes-pins, and an apron—long ago,
In some white storm that sifted through the pane
And sent her forth reluctantly at last 5
To gather in, before the line gave way,
Garments, board-stiff, that galloped on the blast
Clashing like angel armies in a fray,
An apron long ago in such a night
Blown down and buried in the deepening drift, 10
To lie till April thawed it back to sight,
Forgotten, quaint and novel as a gift—
It struck her, as she pulled and pried and tore,
That here was spring, and the whole year to be lived through once more.

XII

Tenderly, in those times, as though she fed
An ailing child—with sturdy propping up
Of its small, feverish body in the bed,
And steadying of its hands about the cup—
She gave her husband of her body's strength, 5
Thinking of men, what helpless things they were,
Until he turned and fell asleep at length,
And stealthily stirred the night and spoke to her.
Familiar, at such moments, like a friend,
Whistled far off the long, mysterious train, 10
And she could see in her mind's vision plain
The magic World, where cities stood on end . . .
Remote from where she lay—and yet—between,
Save for something asleep beside her, only the window screen.

XIII

From the wan dream that was her waking day,
Wherein she journeyed, borne along the ground
Without her own volition in some way,
Or fleeing, motionless, with feet fast bound,
Or running silent through a silent house 5
Sharply remembered from an earlier dream,
Upstairs, down other stairs, fearful to rouse,
Regarding him, the wide and empty scream
Of a strange sleeper on a malignant bed,
And all the time not certain if it were 10
Herself so doing or some one like to her,
From this wan dream that was her daily bread,
Sometimes, at night, incredulous, she would wake—
A child, blowing bubbles that the chairs and carpet did not break!

XIV

She had a horror he would die at night.
And sometimes when the light began to fade
She could not keep from noticing how white
The birches looked—and then she would be afraid,
Even with a lamp, to go about the house 5
And lock the windows; and as night wore on
Toward morning, if a dog howled, or a mouse
Squeaked in the floor, long after it was gone
Her flesh would sit awry on her. By day
She would forget somewhat, and it would seem 10
A silly thing to go with just this dream
And get a neighbor to come at night and stay.
But it would strike her sometimes, making the tea:
She had kept that kettle boiling all night long, for company.

XV

There was upon the sill a pencil mark,
Vital with shadow when the sun stood still
At noon, but now, because the day was dark,
It was a pencil mark upon the sill.
And the mute clock, maintaining ever the same 5
Dead moment, blank and vacant of itself,
Was a pink shepherdess, a picture frame,
A shell marked Souvenir, there on the shelf.
Whence it occurred to her that he might be,
The mainspring being broken in his mind, 10
A clock himself, if one were so inclined,
That stood at twenty minutes after three—
The reason being for this, it might be said,
That things in death were neither clocks nor people, but only dead.

XVI

The doctor asked her what she wanted done
With him, that could not lie there many days.
And she was shocked to see how life goes on
Even after death, in irritating ways;
And mused how if he had not died at all 5
'Twould have been easier—then there need not be
The stiff disorder of a funeral
Everywhere, and the hideous industry,
And crowds of people calling her by name
And questioning her, she'd never seen before, 10
But only watching by his bed once more
And sitting silent if a knocking came . . .
She said at length, feeling the doctor's eyes,
"I don't know what you do exactly when a person dies."

XVII

Gazing upon him now, severe and dead,
It seemed a curious thing that she had lain
Beside him many a night in that cold bed,
And that had been which would not be again.
From his desirous body the great heat 5
Was gone at last, it seemed, and the taut nerves
Loosened forever. Formally the sheet
Set forth for her today those heavy curves
And lengths familiar as the bedroom door.
She was as one who enters, sly, and proud, 10
To where her husband speaks before a crowd,
And sees a man she never saw before—
The man who eats his victuals at her side,
Small, and absurd, and hers: for once, not hers, unclassified.

1923

The Buck in the Snow

White sky, over the hemlocks bowed with snow,
Saw you not at the beginning of evening the antlered buck and his doe
Standing in the apple-orchard? I saw them. I saw them suddenly go,
Tails up, with long leaps lovely and slow,
Over the stone-wall into the wood of hemlocks bowed with snow. 5

Now lies he here, his wild blood scalding the snow.

How strange a thing is death, bringing to his knees, bringing to his antlers
The buck in the snow.
How strange a thing,—a mile away by now, it may be,

Under the heavy hemlocks that as the moments pass 10
Shift their loads a little, letting fall a feather of snow—
Life, looking out attentive from the eyes of the doe.

 1928

To Inez Milholland[6]

Read in Washington, November eighteenth, 1923, at the unveiling of a
statue of three leaders in the cause of Equal Rights for Women

Upon this marble bust that is not I
Lay the round, formal wreath that is not fame;
But in the forum of my silenced cry
Root ye the living tree whose sap is flame.
I, that was proud and valiant, am no more;— 5
Save as a dream that wanders wide and late,
Save as a wind that rattles the stout door,
Troubling the ashes in the sheltered grate.
The stone will perish; I shall be twice dust.
Only my standard on a taken hill 10
Can cheat the mildew and the red-brown rust
And make immortal my adventurous will.
Even now the silk is tugging at the staff:
Take up the song; forget the epitaph.

 1928

[Women have loved before as I love now][7]

Women have loved before as I love now;
At least, in lively chronicles of the past—
Of Irish waters by a Cornish prow
Or Trojan waters by a Spartan mast[8]
Much to their cost invaded—here and there, 5
Hunting the amorous line, skimming the rest,
I find some woman bearing as I bear
Love like a burning city in the breast.
I think however that of all alive
I only in such utter, ancient way 10
Do suffer love; in me alone survive
The unregenerate passions of a day
When treacherous queens, with death upon the tread,
Heedless and wilful, took their knights to bed.

 1931

6. Socialist reformer and activist (1886–1916) who
started the women's suffrage movement at Vassar,
where Millay was a student, and died from her overex-
ertions on behalf of the women's vote.

7. From the sonnet sequence *Fatal Interview*.
8. An allusion to Isolde, the Irish lover of her Cornish
captor, Tristan, and Helen, taken from Greece to Troy
by Paris.

[Oh, sleep forever in the Latmian cave]

Oh, sleep forever in the Latmian cave,
Mortal Endymion, darling of the Moon![9]
Her silver garments by the senseless wave
Shouldered and dropped and on the shingle strewn,
Her fluttering hand against her forehead pressed, 5
Her scattered looks that trouble all the sky,
Her rapid footsteps running down the west—
Of all her altered state, oblivious lie!
Whom earthen you, by deathless lips adored,
Wild-eyed and stammering to the grasses thrust, 10
And deep into her crystal body poured
The hot and sorrowful sweetness of the dust:
Whereof she wanders mad, being all unfit
For mortal love, that might not die of it.

 1931

Childhood Is the Kingdom Where Nobody Dies

Childhood is not from birth to a certain age and at a certain age
The child is grown, and puts away childish things.
Childhood is the kingdom where nobody dies.

Nobody that matters, that is. Distant relatives of course
Die, whom one never has seen or has seen for an hour, 5
And they gave one candy in a pink-and-green striped bag, or a jack-knife,
And went away, and cannot really be said to have lived at all.

And cats die. They lie on the floor and lash their tails,
And their reticent fur is suddenly all in motion
With fleas that one never knew were there, 10
Polished and brown, knowing all there is to know,
Trekking off into the living world.
You fetch a shoe-box, but it's much too small, because she won't curl up
 now:
So you find a bigger box, and bury her in the yard, and weep.

But you do not wake up a month from then, two months, 15
A year from then, two years, in the middle of the night
And weep, with your knuckles in your mouth, and say Oh, God! Oh, God!
Childhood is the kingdom where nobody dies that matters,— mothers and
 fathers don't die.

And if you have said, "For Heaven's sake, must you always be kissing a
 person?"
Or, "I do wish to gracious you'd stop tapping on the window with your
 thimble!" 20

9. According to Greek myth, Endymion was a beauti- moon, Selene.
ful youth who fell asleep in a cave on Mount Latmos; 1. Pebbly beach
there he was visited by the personification of the

Tomorrow, or even the day after tomorrow if you're busy having fun,
Is plenty of time to say, "I'm sorry, mother."

To be grown up is to sit at the table with people who have died, who
 neither listen nor speak;
Who do not drink their tea, though they always said
Tea was such a comfort. 25

Run down into the cellar and bring up the last jar of raspberries; they are
 not tempted.
Flatter them, ask them what was it they said exactly
That time, to the bishop, or to the overseer, or to Mrs. Mason;
They are not taken in.
Shout at them, get red in the face, rise, 30
Drag them up out of their chairs by their stiff shoulders and shake them
 and yell at them;
They are not startled, they are not even embarrassed; they slide back into
 their chairs.

Your tea is cold now.
You drink it standing up,
And leave the house. 35

 1934

Apostrophe to Man

(on reflecting that the world is ready to go to war again)[2]

Detestable race, continue to expunge yourself, die out.
Breed faster, crowd, encroach, sing hymns, build bombing airplanes;
Make speeches, unveil statues, issue bonds, parade;
Convert again into explosives the bewildered ammonia and the
 distracted cellulose;
Convert again into putrescent matter drawing flies 5
The hopeful bodies of the young; exhort,
Pray, pull long faces, be earnest, be all but overcome, be photographed;
Confer, perfect your formulae, commercialize
Bacteria harmful to human tissue,
Put death on the market; 10
Breed, crowd, encroach, expand, expunge yourself, die out,
Homo called *sapiens*.[3]

 1934

Rendezvous

Not for these lovely blooms that prank[4] your chambers did I come. Indeed,
I could have loved you better in the dark;

2. Written in the decade before World War II. here, "man called intelligent."
"Apostrophe": address to a person or personification. 4. Adorn.
3. The scientific Latin name for the human species;

That is to say, in rooms less bright with roses, rooms more casual, less
 aware
Of History in the wings about to enter with benevolent air
On ponderous tiptoe, at the cue "Proceed." 5
Not that I like the ash-trays over-crowded and the place in a mess,
Or the monastic cubicle too unctuously austere and stark,
But partly that these formal garlands for our Eighth Street Aphrodite[5] are a
 bit too Greek,
And partly that to make the poor walls rich with our unaided loveliness
Would have been more *chic*. 10
Yet here I am, having told you of my quarrel with the taxi-driver over a line
 of Milton, and you laugh; and you are you, none other.
Your laughter pelts my skin with small delicious blows.
But I am perverse; I wish you had not scrubbed—with pumice, I
 suppose—
The tobacco stains from your beautiful fingers. And I wish I did not feel
 like your mother.

1939

The Fitting

The fitter said, "*Madame, vous avez maigri*,"[6]
And pinched together a handful of skirt at my hip.
"*Tant mieux*,"[7] I said, and looked away slowly, and took my under-lip
Softly between my teeth.

Rip—rip! 5

Out came the seam, and was pinned together in another place.
She knelt before me, a hardworking woman with a familiar and unknown
 face,
Dressed in linty black, very tight in the arm's-eye and smelling of sweat.
She rose, lifting my arm, and set her cold shears against me,—snip-snip;
Her knuckles gouged my breast. My drooped eyes lifted to my guarded
 eyes in the glass, and glanced away as from someone they had never
 met. 10
"Ah, *que madame a maigri!*" cried the *vendeuse*,[8] coming in with dresses
 over her arm.
"*C'est la chaleur*,"[9] I said, looking out into the sunny tops of the horse-
 chestnuts—and indeed it was very warm.

I stood for a long time so, looking out into the afternoon, thinking of the
 evening and you. . . .
While they murmured busily in the distance, turning me, touching my
 secret body, doing what they were paid to do.

1939

5. Greek goddess of love.
6. Madame, you have grown thin. (French).
7. So much the better.

8. Saleswoman. "Ah, how madame has grown thin!"
9. It's the heat.

[I too beneath your moon, almighty Sex]

I too beneath your moon, almighty Sex,
Go forth at nightfall crying like a cat,
Leaving the lofty tower I labored at
For birds to foul and boys and girls to vex
With tittering chalk; and you, and the long necks 5
Of neighbours sitting where their mothers sat
Are well aware of shadowy this and that
In me, that's neither noble nor complex.
Such as I am, however, I have brought
To what it is, this tower; it is my own; 10
Though it was reared To Beauty, it was wrought
From what I had to build with: honest bone
Is there, and anguish; pride; and burning thought;
And lust is there, and nights not spent alone.

1939

[The courage that my mother had]

The courage that my mother had
Went with her, and is with her still:
Rock from New England quarried;
Now granite in a granite hill.

The golden brooch my mother wore 5
She left behind for me to wear;
I have no thing I treasure more:
Yet, it is something I could spare.

Oh, if instead she'd left to me
The thing she took into the grave!— 10
That courage like a rock, which she
Has no more need of, and I have.

1954

An Ancient Gesture

I thought, as I wiped my eyes on the corner of my apron:
Penelope[1] did this too.
And more than once: you can't keep weaving all day
And undoing it all through the night;
Your arms get tired, and the back of your neck gets tight; 5
And along towards morning, when you think it will never be light,
And your husband has been gone, and you don't know where, for years,

1. The wife of Odysseus (Ulysses) in Homer's *Odyssey*, who waited twenty years for her husband to return from the Trojan Wars. She wove all day but tore out the weaving at night to keep away the suitors for her hand.

Suddenly you burst into tears;
There is simply nothing else to do.

And I thought, as I wiped my eyes on the corner of my apron: 10
This is an ancient gesture, authentic, antique,
In the very best tradition. classic, Greek;
Ulysses did this too.
But only as a gesture,—a gesture which implied
To the assembled throng that he was much too moved to speak. 15
He learned it from Penelope . . .
Penelope, who really cried.

1954

Aria da Capo

A *Play in One Act*

PERSONS

PIERROT
COLUMBINE
COTHURNUS, MASQUE OF TRAGEDY
THYRSIS } *Shepherds*
CORYDON

SCENE: *A Stage*

The curtain rises on a stage set for a Harlequinade,[1] *a merry
black and white interior. Directly behind the footlights, and
running parallel with them, is a long table, covered with a gay
black and white cloth, on which is spread a banquet. At the op-
posite ends of this table, seated on delicate thin-legged chairs
with high backs, are* PIERROT *and* COLUMBINE, *dressed accord-
ing to the tradition. excepting that* PIERROT *is in lilac, and*
COLUMBINE *in pink. They are dining.*

COLUMBINE. Pierrot, a macaroon! I cannot *live* without a macaroon!
PIERROT. My only love,
 You are *so* intense! . . . Is it Tuesday, Columbine?—
 I'll kiss you if it's Tuesday.
COLUMBINE. It is Wednesday,
 If you must know. . . . Is this my artichoke,
 Or yours?
PIERROT. Ah, Columbine,—as if it mattered!
 Wednesday. . . . Will it be Tuesday, then, tomorrow,
 By any chance?
COLUMBINE. Tomorrow will be—Pierrot,
 That isn't funny!

1. A play in which Harlequin, a stock comic character,
has a leading role; he is often invisible to all but his
sweetheart Columbine, a frivolous, coquettish young
woman. His rival is Pierrot, a kind of idealized clown,
who traditionally wears a white costume with very long
sleeves and big buttons; the costume of Columbine is
more variable. "Da capo": from the beginning
(Italian); a musical term. meaning to repeat the piece
from the beginning to the point so marked.

PIERROT. I thought it rather nice.
 Well, let us drink some wine and lose our heads
 And love each other.
COLUMBINE. Pierrot, don't you love
 Me now?
PIERROT. La, what a woman!—how should I know?
 Pour me some wine: I'll tell you presently.
COLUMBINE. Pierrot, do you know, I think you drink too much.
PIERROT. Yes, I dare say I do. . . . Or else too little.
 It's hard to tell. You see, I am always wanting
 A little more than what I have,—or else
 A little less. There's something wrong. My dear,
 How many fingers have you?
COLUMBINE. La, indeed,
 How should I know?—It always takes me one hand
 To count the other with. It's too confusing.
 Why?
PIERROT. Why?—I am a student, Columbine;
 And search into all matters.
COLUMBINE. La, indeed?—
 Count them yourself, then!
PIERROT. No. Or, rather, *nay*.
 'Tis of no consequence. . . . I am become
 A painter, suddenly,—and you impress me—
 Ah, yes!—six orange bull's eyes, four green pinwheels,
 And one magenta jelly-roll,—the title
 As follows: *Woman Taking in Cheese from Fire-Escape.*
COLUMBINE. Well, I like that! So that is all I've meant
 To you!
PIERROT. Hush! All at once I am become
 A pianist. I will image you in sound. . . .
 On a new scale. . . . Without tonality. . . .
 Vivace senza tempo senza tutto.[2]. . .
 Title: *Uptown Express at Six O'Clock.*
 Pour me a drink.
COLUMBINE. Pierrot, you work too hard.
 You need a rest. Come on out into the garden,
 And sing me something sad.
PIERROT. Don't stand so near me!
 I am become a socialist. I love
 Humanity; but I hate people. Columbine,
 Put on your mittens, child; your hands are cold.
COLUMBINE. My hands are *not* cold!
PIERROT. Oh, I am sure they are.
 And you must have a shawl to wrap about you,
 And sit by the fire.
COLUMBINE. Why, I'll do no such thing!
 I'm hot as a spoon in a teacup!
PIERROT. Columbine,
 I'm a philanthropist. I know I am,

2. Lively, wholly without time (Italian); in the style of tempo instructions for music.

Because I feel so restless Do not scream,
Or it will be the worse for you!
COLUMBINE. Pierrot,
 My vinaigrette! I cannot *live* without
 My vinaigrette!
PIERROT. My only love, you are
 So fundamental! . . . How would you like to be
 An actress, Columbine?—I am become
 Your manager.
COLUMBINE. Why, Pierrot, I can't act.
PIERROT. Can't act! Can't act La, listen to the woman!
 What's that to do with the price of furs?—You're blonde,
 Are you not?—you have no education, have you?—
 Can't act! You underrate yourself, my dear!
COLUMBINE. Yes, I suppose I do.
PIERROT. As for the rest,
 I'll teach you how to cry, and how to die,
 And other little tricks; and the house will love you.
 You'll be a star by five o'clock . . . that is,
 If you will let me pay for your apartment
COLUMBINE. *Let* you?—well, that's a good one!
 Ha! Ha! Ha!
 But why?
PIERROT. But why?—well, as to that, my dear,
 I cannot say. It's just a matter of form.
COLUMBINE. Pierrot, I'm getting tired of caviar
 And peacocks' livers. Isn't there something else
 That people eat?—some humble, vegetable,
 That grows in the ground?
PIERROT. Well, there are mushrooms.
COLUMBINE. Mushrooms!
 That's so! I had forgotten . . . mushrooms . . . mushrooms. . . .
 I cannot *live* with . . . How do you like this gown?
PIERROT. Not much. I'm tired of gowns that have the waist-line
 About the waist, and the hem around the bottom,—
 And women with their breasts in front of them!—
 Zut and ehè![3] Where does one go from here!
COLUMBINE. Here's a persimmon, love. You always like them.
PIERROT. I am become a critic; there is nothing
 I can enjoy. . . . However set it aside;
 I'll eat it between meals.
COLUMBINE. Pierrot, do you know,
 Sometimes I think you're making fun of me.
PIERROT. My love, by yon black moon, you wrong us both.
COLUMBINE. There isn't a sign of a moon, Pierrot.
PIERROT. Of course not.
 There never was. "Moon's" just a word to swear by.
 "Mutton!"—now *there's* a thing you can lay the hands on,
 And set the tooth in! Listen, Columbine:

3. Interjections (French) expressing disgust or surprise.

I always lied about the moon and you.
Food is my only lust.
COLUMBINE. Well, eat it, then,
For heaven's sake, and stop your silly noise!
I haven't heard the clock tick for an hour.
PIERROT. It's ticking all the same. If you were a fly,
You would be dead by now. And if I were a parrot,
I could be talking for a thousand years!
[*Enter* COTHURNUS.[4]]
PIERROT. Hello, what's this, for God's sake?—
What's the matter?
Say, whadda you mean?—get off the stage, my friend,
And pinch yourself,—you're walking in your sleep!
COTHURNUS. I never sleep.
PIERROT. Well, anyhow, clear out.
You don't belong on here. Wait for your own scene!
Whadda you think this is,—a dress-rehearsal?
COTHURNUS. Sir, I am tired of waiting. I will wait
No longer.
PIERROT. Well, but whadda you going to do?
The scene is set for me!
COTHURNUS. True, sir; yet I
Can play the scene.
PIERROT. Your scene is down for later!
COTHURNUS. That, too, is true, sir; but I play it now.
PIERROT. Oh, very well!—Anyway, I am tired
Of black and white. At least, I think I am.
[*Exit* COLUMBINE.]
Yes, I am sure I am. I know what I'll do!—
I'll go and strum the moon, that's what I'll do. . . .
Unless, perhaps . . . you never can tell . . . I may be,
You know, tired of the moon. Well, anyway,
I'll go find Columbine. . . . And when I find her,
I will address her thus: "*Ehè*, Pierrette!"—
There's something in that.
[*Exit* PIERROT.]
COTHURNUS. You, Thyrsis! Corydon![5]
Where are you!
THYRSIS. [*Off stage.*] Sir, we are in our dressing-room!
COTHURNUS. Come out and do the scene.
CORYDON. [*Off stage.*] You are mocking us!—
The scene is down for later.
COTHURNUS. That is true;
But we will play it now. I am the scene.
[*Seats himself on high place in back of stage.*]
[*Enter* CORYDON *and* THYRSIS.]
CORYDON. Sir, we are counting on this little hour.
We said, "Here is an hour,—in which to think
A mighty thought, and sing a trifling song,

4. The thick-soled high boot worn by actors in Greek
tragedies.

5. Conventional names of rustics, used in pastoral po-
etry.

And look at nothing."—And, behold! the hour,
Even as we spoke, was over, and the act begun,
Under our feet!

THYRSIS. Sir, we are not in the fancy
To play the play. We had thought to play it later.

CORYDON. Besides, this is the setting for a farce.
Our scene requires a wall; we cannot build
A wall of tissue-paper!

THYRSIS. We cannot act
A tragedy with comic properties!

COTHURNUS. Try it and see. I think you'll find you can.
One wall is like another. And regarding
The matter of your insufficient mood,
The important thing is that you speak the lines.
And make the gestures. Wherefore I shall remain
Throughout, and hold the prompt-book. Are you ready?

CORYDON *and* THYRSIS [*Sorrowfully.*] Sir, we are always ready.

COTHURNUS. Play the play!

[CORYDON *and* THYRSIS *move the table and chairs to one side out of the way,
and seat themselves in a half-reclining position on the floor.*]

THYRSIS. How gently in the silence, Corydon,
Our sheep go up the bank. They crop a grass
That's yellow where the sun is out, and black
Where the clouds drag their shadows. Have you noticed
How steadily, yet with what a slanting eye
They graze?

CORYDON. As if they thought of other things.
What say you, Thyrsis, do they only question
Where next to pull?—Or do their far minds draw them
Thus vaguely north of west and south of east?

THYRSIS. One cannot say. . . . The black lamb wears its burdocks[6]
As if they were a garland,—have you noticed?
Purple and white—and drinks the bitten grass
As if it were a wine.

CORYDON. I've noticed that.
What say you, Thyrsis, shall we make a song
About a lamb that thought himself a shepherd?

THYRSIS. Why, yes!—that is, why,—no. (I have forgotten my line.)

COTHURNUS. [*Prompting.*] "I know a game worth two of that!"

THYRSIS. Oh, yes. . . . I know a game worth two of that!
Let's gather rocks, and build a wall between us;
And say that over there belongs to me,
And over here to you!

CORYDON. Why,—very well.
And say you may not come upon my side
Unless I say you may!

THYRSIS. Nor you on mine!
And if you should, 'twould be the worse for you!

6. Weedy plants with burrs.

[*They weave a wall of colored crêpe paper ribbons from the center front to the center back of the stage, fastening the ends to* COLUMBINE'S *chair in front and to* PIERROT's *chair in the back.*]

CORYDON. Now there's a wall a man may see across,
 But not attempt to scale.

THYRSIS. An excellent wall.

CORYDON. Come, let us separate, and sit alone
 A little while, and lay a plot whereby
 We may outdo each other.
 [*They seat themselves on opposite sides of the wall.*]

PIERROT. [*Off stage.*] Ehè, Pierrette!

COLUMBINE. [*Off stage.*] My name is Columbine!
 Leave me alone!

THYRSIS. [*Coming up to the wall.*]
 Corydon, after all, and in spite of the fact
 I started it myself, I do not like this
 So very much. What is the sense of saying
 I do not want you on my side the wall?
 It is a silly game. I'd much prefer
 Making the little song you spoke of making,
 About the lamb, you know, that thought himself
 A shepherd!—what do you say?
 [*Pause.*]

CORYDON. [*At wall.*] (I have forgotten the line.)

COTHURNUS. [*Prompting.*] "How do I know this isn't a trick?"

CORYDON. Oh, yes. . . . How do I know this isn't a trick
 To get upon my land?

THYRSIS. Oh, Corydon,
 You *know* it's not a trick. I do not like
 The game, that's all. Come over here, or let me
 Come over there.

CORYDON. It is a clever trick
 To get upon my land. [*Seats himself as before.*]

THYRSIS. Oh, very well! [*Seats himself as before.*]
 [*To himself.*] I think I never knew a sillier game.

CORYDON. [*Coming to wall.*]
 Oh. Thyrsis, just a minute!—all the water
 Is on your side the wall, and the sheep are thirsty.
 I hadn't thought of that.

THYRSIS. Oh, hadn't you?

CORYDON. Why, what do you mean?

THYRSIS. What do I mean?—I mean
 That I can play a game as well as you can.
 And if the pool is on my side, it's on
 My side, that's all.

CORYDON. You mean you'd let the sheep
 Go thirsty?

THYRSIS. Well, they're not my sheep. My sheep
 Have water enough.

CORYDON. *Your* sheep! You are mad, to call them
 Yours—mine—they are all one flock! Thyrsis, you can't mean
 To keep the water from them, just because

They happened to be grazing over here
Instead of over there, when we set the wall up?
THYRSIS. Oh, can't I?—wait and see!—and if you try
To lead them over here, you'll wish you hadn't!
CORYDON. I wonder how it happens all the water
Is on your side. . . . I'll say you had an eye out
For lots of little things, my innocent friend,
When I said, "Let us make a song," and you said,
"I know a game worth two of that!"
COLUMBINE. [*Off stage.*] Pierrot,
D'you know, I think you must be getting old,
Or fat, or something,—stupid, anyway!—
Can't you put on some other kind of collar?
THYRSIS. You know as well as I do, Corydon,
I never thought anything of the kind.
Don't you?
CORYDON. I *do* not.
THYRSIS. Don't you?
CORYDON. Oh, I suppose so.
Thyrsis, let's drop this,—what do you say?—it's only
A game, you know . . . we seem to be forgetting
It's only a game . . . a pretty serious game
It's getting to be, when one of us is willing
To let the sheep go thirsty for the sake of it.
THYRSIS. I know it, Corydon.
[*They reach out their arms to each other across the wall.*]
COTHURNUS. [*Prompting.*] "But how do I know—"
THYRSIS. Oh, yes. . . . But how do I know this isn't a trick
To water your sheep, and get the laugh on me?
CORYDON. You can't know, that's the difficult thing about it,
Of course,—you can't be sure You have to take
My word for it. And I know just how you feel.
But one of us has to take a risk, or else,
Why, don't you see?—the game goes on forever!
It's terrible, when you stop to think of it. . . .
Oh, Thyrsis, now for the first time I feel
This wall is actually a wall, a thing
Come up between us, shutting you away
From me. . . . I do not know you any more!
THYRSIS. No, don't say that! Oh, Corydon, I'm willing
To drop it all, if you will! Come on over
And water your sheep! It is an ugly game.
I hated it from the first. . . . How did it start?
CORYDON. I do not know . . . I do not know . . . I think
I am afraid of you!—you are a stranger!
I never set eyes on you before! "Come over
And water my sheep," indeed!—They'll be more thirsty
Than they are now before I bring them over
Into your land, and have you mixing them up
With yours, and calling them yours, and trying to keep them!
[*Enter* COLUMBINE.]
COLUMBINE. [*To* COTHURNUS.] Glummy, I want my hat.

THYRSIS. Take it, and go.
COLUMBINE. Take it and go, indeed. Is it my hat,
 Or isn't it? Is this my scene, or not?
 Take it and go! Really, you know, you two
 Are awfully funny!
 [*Exit* COLUMBINE.]
THYRSIS. Corydon, my friend,
 I'm going to leave you now, and whittle me
 A pipe or sing a song, or go to sleep.
 When you have come to your senses, let me know.
 [*Goes back to where he has been sitting, lies down and sleeps.*]
 [CORYDON, *in going back to where he has been sitting, stumbles over bowl of*
 colored confetti and colored paper ribbons.]
CORYDON. Why, what is this?—Red stones—and purple stones—
 And stones stuck full of gold!—The ground is full
 Of gold and colored stones! . . . I'm glad the wall
 Was up before I found them!—Otherwise,
 I should have had to share them. As it is,
 They all belong to me. . . . Unless—[*He goes to wall and digs up and down the*
 length of it, to see if there are jewels on the other side.] None here—
 None here—none here—They all belong to me!
 [*Sits.*]
THYRSIS. [*Awakening.*] How curious! I thought the little black lamb
 Came up and licked my hair; I saw the wool
 About its neck as plain as anything!
 It must have been a dream. The little black lamb
 Is on the other side of the wall, I'm sure. [*Goes to wall and looks over.*
 CORYDON *is seated on the ground, tossing the confetti up into the air and*
 catching it.]
 Hello, what's that you've got there, Corydon?
CORYDON. Jewels.
THYRSIS. Jewels?—And where did you ever get them?
CORYDON. Oh, over here.
THYRSIS. You mean to say you found them,
 By digging around in the ground for them?
CORYDON. [*Unpleasantly.*] No, Thyrsis,
 By digging down for water for my sheep.
THYRSIS. Corydon, come to the wall a minute, will you?
 I want to talk to you.
CORYDON. I haven't time.
 I'm making me a necklace of red stones.
THYRSIS. I'll give you all the water that you want,
 For one of those red stones,—if it's a good one.
CORYDON. Water?—what for?—what do I want of water?
THYRSIS. Why, for your sheep!
CORYDON. My sheep?—I'm not a shepherd!
THYRSIS. Your sheep are dying of thirst.
CORYDON. Man, haven't I told you
 I can't be bothered with a few untidy
 Brown sheep all full of burdocks?—I'm a merchant.
 That's what I am!—And if I set my mind to it
 I dare say I could be an emperor!
 [*To himself.*] Wouldn't I be a fool to spend my time

Watching a flock of sheep go up a hill,
When I have these to play with?—when I have these
To think about?—I can't make up my mind
Whether to buy a city, and have a thousand
Beautiful girls to bathe me, and be happy
Until I die, or build a bridge, and name it
The Bridge of Corydon,—and be remembered
After I'm dead.

THYRSIS. Corydon come to the wall,
Won't you?—I want to tell you something.

CORYDON. Hush!
Be off! Be off! Go finish your nap, I tell you!

THYRSIS. Corydon, listen: if you don't want your sheep,
Give them to me.

CORYDON. Be off! Go finish your nap.
A red one—and a blue one—and a red one—
And a purple one—give you my sheep, did you say?—
Come, come! What do you take me for, a fool?
I've a lot of thinking to do,—and while I'm thinking,
The sheep might just as well be over here
As over there. . . . A blue one—and a red one—

THYRSIS. But they will die!

CORYDON. And a green one—and a couple
Of white ones, for a change.

THYRSIS. Maybe I have
Some jewels on my side.

CORYDON. And another green one—
Maybe, but I don't think so. You see, this rock
Isn't so very wide. It stops before
It gets to the wall. It seems to go quite deep,
However.

THYRSIS. [With hatred.] I see.

COLUMBINE. [Off stage.] Look, Pierrot, there's the moon.

PIERROT. [Off stage.] Nonsense!

THYRSIS. I see.

COLUMBINE. [Off stage.] Sing me an old song, Pierrot,—
Something I can remember.

PIERROT. [Off stage.] Columbine.
Your mind is made of crumbs,—like an escallop
Of oysters,—first layer of crumbs, and then
An oystery taste, and then a layer of crumbs.

THYRSIS. [Searching.] I find no jewels . . . but I wonder what
The root of this black weed would do to a man
If he should taste it. . . . I have seen a sheep die,
With half the stalk still drooling from its mouth.
'Twould be a speedy remedy, I should think,
For a festered pride and a feverish ambition.
It has a curious root. I think I'll hack it
In little pieces. . . . First I'll get me a drink;
And then I'll hack that root in little pieces
As small as dust, and see what the color is
Inside. [Goes to bowl on floor.]
 The pool is very clear. I see

A shepherd standing on the brink, with a red cloak
About him, and a black weed in his hand. . . .
 'Tis I. [*Kneels and drinks.*]
CORYDON. [*Coming to wall.*] Hello, what are you doing, Thyrsis?
THYRSIS. Digging for gold.
CORYDON. I'll give you all the gold
You want, if you'll give me a bowl of water.
If you don't want too much, that is to say.
THYRSIS. Ho, so you've changed your mind?—It's different,
Isn't it, when you want a drink yourself?
CORYDON. Of course it is.
THYRSIS. Well, let me see . . . a bowl
Of water,—come back in an hour, Corydon.
I'm busy now.
CORYDON. Oh, Thyrsis, give me a bowl
Of water!—and I'll fill the bowl with jewels,
And bring it back!
THYRSIS. Be off, I'm busy now.
[*He catches sight of the weed, picks it up and looks at it, unseen by*
CORYDON.]
Wait!—Pick me out the finest stones you have . . .
I'll bring you a drink of water presently.
CORYDON. [*Goes back and sits down, with the jewels before him.*]
A bowl of jewels is a lot of jewels.
THYRSIS. [*Chopping up the weed.*] I wonder if it has a bitter taste.
CORYDON. There's sure to be a stone or two among them
I have grown fond of, pouring them from one hand
Into the other.
THYRSIS. I hope it doesn't taste
Too bitter, just at first.
CORYDON. A bowl of jewels
Is far too many jewels to give away
And not get back again.
THYRSIS. I don't believe
He'll notice. He's too thirsty. He'll gulp it down
And never notice.
CORYDON. There ought to be some way
To get them back again. . . . I could give him a necklace,
And snatch it back, after I'd drunk the water,
I suppose. . . . Why, as for that, of course a *necklace*. . . .
[*He puts two or three of the colored tapes together and tries their strength by
pulling them, after which he puts them around his neck and pulls them,
gently, nodding to himself. He gets up and goes to the wall, with the colored
tapes in his hands.*]
[THYRSIS *in the meantime has poured the powdered root—black confetti—
into the pot which contained the flower and filled it up with wine from the
punch-bowl on the floor. He comes to the wall at the same time, holding the
bowl of poison.*]
THYRSIS. Come, get your bowl of water, Corydon.
CORYDON. Ah, very good!—and for such a gift as that
I'll give you more than a bowl of unset stones.
I'll give you three long necklaces, my friend.
Come closer. Here they are. [*Puts the ribbons about* THYRSIS' *neck.*]

THYRSIS. [*Putting bowl to* CORYDON's *mouth.*]
 I'll hold the bowl
 Until you've drunk it all.
CORYDON. Then hold it steady.
 For every drop you spill I'll have a stone back
 Out of this chain.
THYRSIS. I shall not spill a drop.
 [CORYDON *drinks, meanwhile beginning to strangle* THYRSIS.]
THYRSIS. Don't pull the string so tight.
CORYDON. You're spilling the water.
THYRSIS. You've had enough—you've had enough—stop pulling
 The string so tight!
CORYDON. Why, that's not tight at all . . .
 How's this?
THYRSIS. [*Drops bowl.*] You're strangling me! Oh, Corydon!
 It's only a game!—and you are strangling me!
CORYDON. It's only a game, is it?—Yet I believe
 You've poisoned me in earnest! [*Writhes and pulls the strings tighter, wind-
 ing them about* THYRSIS' *neck.*]
THYRSIS. Corydon! [*Dies.*]
CORYDON. You've poisoned me in earnest. . . . I feel so cold. . . .
 So cold. . . . this is a very silly game. . . .
 Why do we play it?—let's not play this game
 A minute more . . . let's make a little song
 About a lamb. . . . I'm coming over the wall,
 No matter what you say,—I want to be near you. . . .
 [*Groping his way, with arms wide before him, he strides through the frail pa-
 pers of the wall without knowing it, and continues seeking for the wall straight
 across the stage.*]
 Where is the wall? [*Gropes his way back, and stands very near* THYRSIS *with-
 out seeing him; he speaks slowly.*]
 There isn't any wall,
 I think. [*Takes a step forward, his foot touches* THYRSIS' *body, and he falls
 down beside him.*]
 Thyrsis, where is your cloak?—just give me
 A little bit of your cloak! . . . [*Draws corner of* THYRSIS' *cloak over his shoul-
 ders, falls across* THYRSIS' *body, and dies.*]
 [COTHURNUS *closes the prompt-book with a bang, arises matter-of-factly,
 comes down stage, and places the table over the two bodies, drawing down the
 cover so that they are hidden from any actors on the stage, but visible to the
 audience, pushing in their feet and hands with his boot. He then turns his
 back to the audience, and claps his hands twice.*]
COTHURNUS. Strike the scene! [*Exit* COTHURNUS.] [*Enter* PIERROT *and*
 COLUMBINE.]
PIERROT. Don't puff so, Columbine!
COLUMBINE. Lord, what a mess
 This set is in! If there's one thing I hate
 Above everything else,—even more than getting my feet wet—
 It's clutter!—He might at least have left the scene
 The way he found it . . . don't you say so, Pierrot?
 [*She picks up punch bowl. They arrange chairs as before at ends of table.*]
PIERROT. Well, I don't know. I think it rather diverting
 The way it is. [*Yawns, picks up confetti bowl.*] Shall we begin?

COLUMBINE. [*Screams.*] My God!
 What's that there under the table?
PIERROT. It is the bodies
 Of the two shepherds from the other play.
COLUMBINE. [*Slowly.*] How curious to strangle him like that,
 With colored paper ribbons.
PIERROT. Yes, and yet
 I dare say he is just as dead. [*Pauses. Calls.*] Cothurnus!
 Come drag these bodies out of here! We can't
 Sit down and eat with two dead bodies lying
 Under the table! . . . The audience wouldn't stand for it!
COTHURNUS. [*Off stage.*] What makes you think so?—
 Pull down the tablecloth
 On the other side, and hide them from the house,
 And play the farce. The audience will forget.
PIERROT. That's so. Give me a hand there, Columbine.
 [PIERROT *and* COLUMBINE *pull down the table cover in such a way that the*
 two bodies are hidden from the house, then merrily set their bowls back on the
 table, draw up their chairs, and begin the play exactly as before.]
COLUMBINE. Pierrot, a macaroon,—I cannot *live* without a macaroon!
PIERROT. My only love,
 You are so intense! . . . Is it Tuesday, Columbine?—
 I'll kiss you if it's Tuesday. [*Curtains begin to close slowly.*]
COLUMBINE. It is Wednesday,
 If you must know. . . . Is this my artichoke
 Or yours?
PIERROT. Ah, Columbine, as if it mattered!
 Wednesday. . . . Will it be Tuesday, then, tomorrow,
 By any chance? . . .
 [*Curtain.*]

 1920

DJUNA BARNES

1892–1982

Few writers have remained as elusive to literary critics, historians, and biographers
as Djuna Barnes. Throughout this century, Barnes published journalism, plays,
and stories as well as two novels, one of which, *Nightwood* (1937), has been con-
sidered a classic. She also played a major role in two expatriate groups: the mod-
ernist movement associated with James Joyce and T. S. Eliot, and the circle of
lesbians who frequented the salons of Natalie Barney and Gertrude Stein. Yet,
from 1919, when she refused to answer any questions about herself in *The Little
Review*, through her return from Europe to America in 1940 to her subsequent life
in Greenwich Village, she rejected publicity and lived an ever more reclusive life.

 Barnes was raised in upstate New York, near Cornwall-on-Hudson, until her fa-
ther moved the family to Long Island, where he purchased a 105–acre farm. Wald
Barnes, who rejected his father's surname in preference for his mother's, was ded-
icated to an independent, private, and eccentric life. Little is known about
Elizabeth (Chappell) Barnes, Wald Barnes's British-born wife and Djuna Barnes's
mother. The major source of Barnes's private education was her father's mother,

Zadel Barnes, who was both a feminist and a published journalist. After a brief stint studying art at Pratt Institute and at the Art Students League. Barnes quickly became active in the New York literary world: she wrote journalism for the *Brooklyn Daily Eagle* as well as fiction for *Vanity Fair*; a slim volume of drawings and poems, *The Book of Repulsive Women* (1915), was published as a chapbook; and she joined the Provincetown Players. Supporting herself as a newspaper-woman, she produced reviews of theatrical events along with stunt stories that required her to be hugged by a gorilla or forcibly fed, as in the lively (never before anthologized) article that we have reprinted here. After the 1919–20 season, when three of Barnes's plays were produced by the Provincetown Players, she left for Europe on assignment for *McCall's* magazine.

In Europe, whether she was interviewing the filmmaker D. W. Griffith, describing "the Jungle folk" at the circus, or depicting her meetings with James Joyce (who later presented her with the original manuscript of *Ulysses*), Barnes continued to make a reputation for herself as a witty, unconventional reporter. Just as she had earlier relished the bohemian sexual freedom of Greenwich Village, in Paris and later in Berlin and London she had a number of affairs; her most important and tempestuous relationship (for seventeen years) was with the sculptor Thelma Wood. Befriended by such figures as the poet Mina Loy and the wealthy art patron Peggy Guggenheim, Barnes began to write the stories for which she quickly became famous. Earlier, in *The Book of Repulsive Women*, she had produced macabre portraits of victimized females. In her next volume, *A Book* (1923), and in its 1929 reprint, *A Night Among the Horses*, she depicted the baffling instability of relationships among characters who are estranged not only from all societal and religious traditions but also from each other and from themselves.

Barnes's next two books marked the beginning of her fascination with anachronistic literary models. Using Elizabethan diction, the *Ladies Almanack* (1928) records the life story of Dame Evangeline Musset, who had "developed in the Womb of her most gentle Mother to be a Boy," but "came forth an Inch or so less than this." Determined to "do it without the Tools for the Trade," Dame Musset embarks on the affairs that turn her into a lesbian saint or crusader. With its use of elaborate puns and fables, the *Ladies Almanack* presents fictionalized portraits of the expatriate writer Natalie Barney and the members of her salon. *Ryder* (1928), which Barnes described as a 'female *Tom Jones*," focuses on the comic arrogance of a man who wants to establish himself as the father of the whole world.

The linguistic exuberance of these two books, along with their emphasis on female sexuality, also characterized Barnes's major work, *Nightwood*, an experimental novel that explores the love affair between two women and records the meditations on that affair furnished by the sage but derelict Dr. O'Connor, a character who made his first appearance in *Ryder*. But in this work Barnes presented a more tragic view of what she called the "stop[s] the mind makes between uncertainties," for all of her expatriated characters are lost to themselves and to each other. T. S. Eliot's introduction established the reputation of the novel, which was, he said, closer to Elizabethan poetry than modern prose. 'Uncle Tom," as she called him, was Barnes's editor at Faber & Faber during the composition of *Nightwood* and *The Antiphon* (1958), a fact that may explain why the latter has been considered a response to Eliot's *Family Reunion*. A blank verse tragedy, *The Antiphon* is even more gothic than *Nightwood* in its dramatization of the anguished confusion experienced by a mother and daughter during the reunion of a family that is in the process of destroying itself. Scholars from Louis F. Kannenstine to Louise DeSalvo have interpreted the play as an encoded confession of the pain the author endured from early sexual abuse.

Although Eliot, like the critic Edwin Muir, continued to support Barnes after her return to America, she isolated herself in her apartment on Patchin Place, and retreated into decades of silence that were punctuated by quarrels, breakdowns,

and hospitalizations or by the inquiries of her neighbor the poet E. E. Cummings, who would occasionally yell out of his window, "—Are ya still alive, Djuna?!" The writer Samuel Beckett, Peggy Guggenheim, Natalie Barney, and, eventually, the National Endowment for the Arts supplemented Barnes's meager income, and the novelists Anaïs Nin and John Hawkes acknowledged her influence on their own work, but according to her biographer, Andrew Field, she was alienated from her native country, holding the only partly comic belief that most Americans were "—A *fierce sadistic race crouching behind radiators.*"

How It Feels to
Be Forcibly Fed[1]

I have been forcibly fed!

In just what relation to the other incidents in my life does this one stand? For me it was an experiment. It was only tragic in my imagination. But it offered sensations sufficiently poignant to compel comprehension of certain of the day's phenomena.

The hall they took me down was long and faintly lighted. I could hear the doctor walking ahead of me, stepping as all doctors step, with that little confiding gait that horses must have returning from funerals. It is not a sad or mournful step; perhaps it suggests suppressed satisfaction.

Every now and then one of the four men that followed turned his head to look at me; a woman by the stairs gazed wonderingly—or was it contemptuously—as I passed.

They brought me into a great room. A table loomed before me; my mind sensed it pregnant with the pains of the future—it was the table whereon I must lie.

The doctor opened his bag, took out a heavy, white gown, a small white cap, a sheet, and laid them all upon the table.

Out across the city, in a flat, frail, coherent yet incoherent monotone, resounded the song of a million machines doing their bit in the universal whole. And the murmur was vital and confounding, for what was before me knew no song.

I shall be strictly professional, I assured myself. If it be an ordeal, it is familiar to my sex at this time; other women have suffered it in acute reality. Surely I have as much nerve as my English sisters? Then I held myself steady. I thought so, and I caught sight of my face in the glass. It was quite white; and I was swallowing convulsively.

And then I knew my soul stood terrified before a little yard of red rubber tubing.

The doctor was saying, "Help her upon the table."

He was tying thin, twisted tapes about his arm; he was testing his instruments. He took the loose end of the sheet and began to bind me: he wrapped it round and round me, my arms tight to my sides, wrapped it up to my throat so that I couldn't move. I lay in as long and unbroken lines as any corpse—unbroken, definite lines that stretched away beyond my vision, for I saw only the skylight. My eyes wandered, outcasts in a world they knew.

1. In their effort to get the vote, British women adopted the tactic of hunger striking while in prison. Many became ill, and the Home Office ordered that hunger strikers be forcibly fed by prison officials. The feeding method used in Britain differed somewhat from Barnes's description, employing a steel gag to allow a tube between the teeth, thus damaging the teeth and jaws as well as the throat.

It was the most concentrated moment of my life.

Three of the men approached me. The fourth stood at a distance, looking at the slow, crawling hands of a watch. The three took me not unkindly, but quite without compassion, one by the head, one by the feet; one sprawled above me, holding my hands down at my hips.

All life's problems had now been reduced to one simple act—to swallow or to choke. As I lay in passive revolt, a quizzical thought wandered across my beleaguered mind: This, at least, is one picture that will never go into the family album.

Oh, this ridiculous perturbation!—I reassured myself. Yet how imagination can obsess! It is the truth that the lights of the windows—pictures of a city's skyline—the walls, the men, all went out into a great blank as the doctor leaned down. Then suddenly the dark broke into a blotch of light, as he trailed the electric bulb up and down and across my face, stopping to examine my throat to make sure I was fully capable of swallowing.

He sprayed both nostrils with a mixture of cocaine and disinfectant. As it reached my throat, it burned and burned.

There was no progress on this pilgrimage. Now I abandoned myself. I was in the valley, and it seemed years that I lay there watching the pitcher as it rose in the hand of the doctor and hung, a devilish, inhuman menace. In it was the liquid food I was to have. It was milk, but I could not tell what it was, for all things are alike when they reach the stomach by a rubber tube.

He had inserted the red tubing, with the funnel at the end, through my nose into the passages of the throat. It is utterly impossible to describe the anguish of it.

The hands above my head tightened into a vise, and like answering vises the hands at my hips and those at my feet grew rigid and secure.

Unbidden visions of remote horrors danced madly through my mind. There arose the hideous thought of being gripped in the tentacles of some monster devil fish in the depths of a tropic sea, as the liquid slowly sensed its way along innumerable endless passages that seemed to traverse my nose, my ears, the inner interstices of my throbbing head. Unsuspected nerves thrilled pain tidings that racked the area of my face and bosom. They seared along my spine. They set my heart at catapultic[2] plunging.

An instant that was an hour, and the liquid had reached my throat. It was ice cold, and sweat as cold broke out upon my forehead.

Still my heart plunged on with the irregular, meaningless motion that sunlight reflected from a mirror casts upon a wall. A dull ache grew and spread from my shoulders into the whole area of my back and through my chest.

The pit of my stomach had lapsed long ago, had gone out into absolute vacancy. Things around began to move lethargically; the electric light to my left took a hazy step or two toward the clock, which lurched forward to meet it; the windows could not keep still. I, too, was detached and moved as the room moved. The doctor's eyes were always just before me. And I knew then that I was fainting. I struggled against surrender. It was the futile defiance of nightmare. My utter hopelessness was a pain. I was conscious only of head and feet and that spot where someone was holding me by the hips.

Still the liquid trickled irresistibly down the tubing into my throat; every drop seemed a quart, and every quart slid over and down into space. I had

2. I.e., with the force of a catapult.

lapsed into a physical mechanism without power to oppose or resent the out-
rage to my will.

The spirit was betrayed by the body's weakness. There it is—the outraged
will. If I, playacting, felt my being burning with revolt at this brutal usurpation
of my own functions, how they who actually suffered the ordeal in its acutest
horror must have flamed at the violation of the sanctuaries of their spirits.

I saw in my hysteria a vision of a hundred women in grim prison hospitals,
bound and shrouded on tables just like this, held in the rough grip of callous
warders while white-robed doctors thrust rubber tubing into the delicate in-
terstices of their nostrils and forced into their helpless bodies the crude fuel to
sustain the life they longed to sacrifice.

Science had at last, then, deprived us of the right to die.

Still the liquid trickled irresistibly down the tubing into my throat.

Was my body so inept, I asked myself, as to be incapable of further struggle?
Was the will powerless to so constrict that narrow passage to the life reservoir
as to dam the hated flow? The thought flashed a defiant command to supine
muscles. They gripped my throat with strangling bonds. Ominous shivers
shook my body.

"Be careful—you'll choke," shouted the doctor in my ear.

One could still choke, then. At least one could if the nerves did not betray.

And if one insisted on choking—what then? Would they—the callous
warders and the servile doctors—ruthlessly persist, even with grim death at
their elbow?

Think of the paradox: those white robes assumed for the work of prolonging
life would then be no better than shrouds; the linen envelope encasing the de-
fiant victim a winding sheet.

Limits surely there are to the subservience even of those who must sternly
execute the law. At least I have never heard of a militant choking herself into
eternity.

It was over. I stood up, swaying in the returning light; I had shared the great-
est experience of the bravest of my sex. The torture and outrage of it burned in
my mind; a dull, shapeless, wordless anger arose to my lips, but I only smiled.
The doctor had removed the towel about his face. The little, red mustache
upon his upper lip was drawn out in a line of pleasant understanding. He had
forgotten all but the play. The four men, having finished their minor roles in
one minor tragedy, were already filing out at the door.

"Isn't there any other way of tying a person up?" I asked. "That thing looks
like ——"

"Yes, I know," he said, gently.

1914

Cassation[1]

"Do you know Germany, Madame, Germany in the spring? It is charming
then, do you not think so? Wide and clean, the Spree[2] winding thin and

1. An annullment or cancellation; also the dismissal
of a soldier. The story was originally published under
the title A Little Girl Tells a Story to a Lady in A Night
Among the Horses (1929); it was reprinted under the
present title in Spillway (1972).
2. A small German river south of Berlin.

dark—and the roses! the yellow roses in the windows; and the bright talkative Americans passing through groups of German men staring over their *steins*, at the light and laughing women.

"It was such a spring, three years ago, that I came into Berlin from Russia. I was just sixteen, and my heart was a dancer's heart. It is that way sometimes; one's heart is all one thing for months, then—altogether another thing, *nicht wahr?*[3] I used to sit in the café at the end of the Zelten, eating eggs and drinking coffee, watching the sudden rain of sparrows. Their feet struck the table all together, and all together they cleared the crumbs, and all together they flew into the sky, so that the café was as suddenly without birds as it had been suddenly full of birds.

"Sometimes a woman came here, at about the same hour as myself, around four in the afternoon; once she came with a little man, quite dreamy and uncertain. But I must explain how she looked: *temperamentvoll* and tall, *kraftvoll*[4] and thin. She must have been forty then, dressed richly and carelessly. It seemed as though she could hardly keep her clothes on; her shoulders were always coming out, her skirt would be hanging on a hook, her pocket book would be mislaid, but all the time she was savage with jewels, and something purposeful and dramatic came in with her, as if she were the center of a whirlpool, and her clothes a temporary debris.

"Sometimes she clucked the sparrows, and sometimes she talked to the *weinschenk*,[5] clasping her fingers together until the rings stood out and you could see through them, she was so vital and so wasted. As for her dainty little man, she would talk to him in English, so that I did not know where they came from.

"Then one week I stayed away from the café because I was trying out for the *Schauspielhaus*,[6] I heard they wanted a ballet dancer, and I was very anxious to get the part, so of course I thought of nothing else. I would wander, all by myself, through the *Tiergarten*, or I would stroll down the *Sieges-Allee*[7] where all the great German emperors' statues are, looking like widows. Then suddenly I thought of the *Zelten*, and of the birds, and of that tall odd woman and so I went back there, and there she was, sitting in the garden sipping beer and chuck-chucking the sparrows.

"When I came in, she got up at once and came over to me and said: 'Why, how do you do, I have missed you. Why did you not tell me that you were going away? I should have seen what I could do about it.' "

"She talked like that; a voice that touched the heart because it was so unbroken and clear. 'I have a house', she said, 'just on the Spree. You could have stayed with me. It is a big, large house, and you could have the room just off my room. It is difficult to live in, but it is lovely—Italian you know, like the interiors you see in Venetian paintings, where young girls lie dreaming of the Virgin. You could find that you could sleep there because you have dedication.'

"Somehow it did not seem at all out of the way that she should come to me and speak to me. I said I would meet her again some day in the garden, and we could go 'home' together, and she seemed pleased but did not show surprise.

3. Isn't it true? (German, idiomatic)
4. Powerful. *"Temperamentvoll"*: temperamental.
5. Wine steward.
6. Theater.
7. "Tiergarten": zoo. Victory Lane

"Then one evening we came into the garden at the same moment. It was late and the fiddles were already playing. We sat together without speaking, just listening to the music, and admiring the playing of the only woman member of the orchestra. She was very intent on the movement of her fingers, and seemed to be leaning over her chin to watch. Then suddenly the lady got up, leaving a small rain of coin, and I followed her until we came to a big house and she let herself in with a brass key. She turned to the left and went into a dark room and switched on the lights and sat down and said: 'This is where we sleep; this is how it is.'

"Everything was disorderly, and expensive and melancholy. Everything was massive and tall, or broad and wide. A chest of drawers rose above my head. The china stove was enormous and white, enamelled in blue flowers. The bed was so high that you could only think of it as something that might be overcome. The walls were all bookshelves, and all the books were bound in red morocco, on the back of each, in gold, was stamped a coat of arms, intricate and oppressive. She rang for tea and began taking off her hat.

"A great painting hung over the bed; the painting and the bed ran together in encounter, the huge rumps of the stallions reined into the pillows. The generals, with foreign helmets and dripping swords, raging through rolling smoke and the bleeding ranks of the dying, seemed to be charging the bed, so large, so rumpled, so devastated. The sheets were trailing, the counterpane hung torn, and the feathers shivered along the floor, trembling in the slight wind from the open window. The lady was smiling in a sad grave way, but she said nothing, and it was not until some moments later that I saw a child, not more than three years old, a small child, lying in the center of the pillows, making a thin noise, like the buzzing of a fly, and I thought it was a fly.

"She did not talk to the child, indeed she paid no attention to it, as if it were in her bed and she did not know it. When the tea was brought in she poured it, but she took none, instead she drank small glasses of Rhine wine.

" 'You have seen Ludwig,' she said in her faint and grieving voice, 'we were married a long time ago, he was just a boy then. I? Me? I am an Italian, but I studied English and German because I was with a travelling company. You,' she said abruptly, 'you must give up the ballet—the theatre—acting.' Somehow I did not think it odd that she should know of my ambition, though I had not mentioned it. 'And', she went on, 'you are not for the stage; you are for something quieter, more withdrawn. See here, I like Germany very much, I have lived here a good many years. You will stay and you will see. You have seen Ludwig, you have noticed that he is not strong; he is always declining, you must have noticed it yourself; he must not be distressed, he can't bear anything. He has his room to himself.' She seemed suddenly tired, and she got up and threw herself across the bed, at the foot, and fell asleep, almost instantly, her hair all about her. I went away then, but I came back that night and tapped at the window. She came to the window and signed to me, and presently appeared at another window to the right of the bedroom, and beckoned with her hand, and I came up and climbed in, and did not mind that she had not opened the door for me. The room was dark except for the moon, and two thin candles burning before the Virgin.

"It was a beautiful room, Madame, *'traurig'*[8] as she said. Everything was im-

8. Sad.

portant and old and gloomy. The curtains about the bed were red velvet, Italian you know, and fringed in gold bullion. The bed cover was a deep red velvet with the same gold fringe: on the floor, beside the bed, a stand on which was a tasselled red cushion, on the cushion a Bible in Italian, lying open.

"She gave me a long nightgown, it came below my feet and came back up again almost to my knees. She loosened my hair, it was long then, and yellow. She plaited it in two plaits; she put me down at her side and said a prayer in German, then in Italian, and ended, 'God bless you', and I got into bed. I loved her very much because there was nothing between us but this strange preparation for sleep. She went away then. In the night I heard the child crying, but I was tired.

"I stayed a year. The thought of the stage had gone out of my heart. I had become a *religieuse*; a gentle religion that began with the prayer I had said after her the first night, and the way I had gone to sleep, though we never repeated the ceremony. It grew with the furniture and the air of the whole room, and with the Bible lying open at a page that I could not read; a religion, Madame, that was empty of need, therefore it was not holy perhaps, and not as it should have been in its manner. It was that I was happy, and I lived there for one year. I almost never saw Ludwig, and almost never Valentine, for that was her child's name, a little girl.

"But at the end of that year I knew there was trouble in other parts of the house. I heard her walking in the night, sometimes Ludwig would be with her, I could hear him crying and talking, but I could not hear what was said. It sounded like a sort of lesson, a lesson for a child to repeat, but if so, there would have been no answer, for the child never uttered a sound, except that buzzing cry.

"Sometimes it is wonderful in Germany, Madame, *nicht wahr?* There is nothing like a German winter. She and I used to walk about the Imperial Palace, and she stroked the cannon, and said they were splendid. We talked about philosophy, for she was troubled with too much thinking, but she always came to the same conclusion, that one must be, or try to be, like everyone else. She explained that to be like everyone, all at once, in your own person, was to be holy. She said that people did not understand what was meant by 'Love thy neighbor as thyself.' It meant, she said, that one should be like all people and oneself, then, she said, one was both ruined and powerful.

"Sometimes it seemed that she was managing it, that she was all Germany, at least in her Italian heart. She seemed so irreparably collected and yet distressed, that I was afraid of her, and not afraid.

"That is the way it was, Madame, she seemed to wish it to be that way, though at night she was most scattered and distraught, I could hear her pacing in her room.

"Then she came in one night and woke me and said that I must come into her room. It was in a most terrible disorder. There was a small cot bed that had not been there before. She pointed to it and said that it was for me.

"The child was lying in the great bed against a large lace pillow. Now it was four years old and yet it did not walk, and I never heard it say a thing, or make a sound, except that buzzing cry. It was beautiful in the corrupt way of idiot children; a sacred beast without a taker, tainted with innocence and waste time; honey-haired and failing, like those dwarf angels on holy prints and valentines, if you understand me, Madame, something saved for a special day

that would not arrive, not for life at all: and my lady was talking quietly, but I did not recognize any of her former state.

" 'You must sleep here now,' she said, 'I brought you here for this if I should need you, and I need you. You must stay, you must stay forever.' Then she said, 'Will you?' And I said no, I could not do that.

"She took up the candle and put it on the floor beside me, and knelt beside it, and put her arms about my knees. 'Are you a traitor?' she said, 'have you come into my house, Ludwig's house, the house of my child, to betray us?' And I said, no, I had not come to betray. 'Then', she said, 'you will do as I tell you. I will teach you slowly, slowly; it will not be too much for you, but you must begin to forget, you must forget *everything*. You must forget all the things people have told you. You must forget arguments and philosophy. I was wrong in talking of such things; I thought it would teach you how to lag with her mind, to undo time for her as it passes, to climb into her bereavement and her dispossession. I brought you up badly; I was vain. You will do better. Forgive me.' She put the palms of her hands on the floor, her face to my face. 'You must never see any other room than this room. It was a great vanity that I took you out walking. Now you will stay here safely, and you will see. You will like it, you will learn to like it the very best of all. I will bring you breakfast, and luncheon, and supper. I will bring it to you both, myself. I will hold you on my lap, I will feed you like the birds. I will rock you to sleep. You must not argue with me—above all we must have no arguments, no talk about man and his destiny—man has no destiny—that is my secret—I have been keeping it from you until today, this very hour. Why not before? Perhaps I was jealous of the knowledge, yes, that must be it, but now I give it to you, I share it with you. I am an old woman,' she said, still holding me by the knees. 'When Valentine was born, Ludwig was only a boy.' She got up and stood behind me. 'He is not strong, he does not understand that the weak are the strongest things in the world, because he is one of them. He cannot help her, they are adamant together. I need you, it must be you.' Suddenly she began talking to me as she talked with the child, and I did not know which of us she was talking to. 'Do not repeat anything after me. Why should children repeat what people say? The whole world is nothing but a noise, as hot as the inside of a tiger's mouth. They call it civilization—that is a lie! But some day you may have to go out, someone will try to take you out, and you will not understand them or what they are saying, unless you understand nothing, absolutely nothing, then you will manage.' She moved around so that she faced us, her back against the wall. 'Look,' she said, 'it is all over, it has gone away, you do not need to be afraid; there is only you. The stars are out, and the snow is falling down and covering the world, the hedges, the houses and the lamps. No, no!' she said to herself, 'wait. I will put you on your feet and tie you up in ribbons, and we will go out together, out into the garden where the swans are, and the flowers and the bees and small beasts. And the students will come because it will be summer, and they will read in their books. . . .' She broke off, then took her wild speech up again, this time as though she were really speaking to the child, 'Katya will go with you. She will instruct you, she will tell you there are no swans, no flowers, no beasts, no boys—nothing, nothing at all, just as you like it. No mind no thought, nothing whatsoever else. No bells will ring, no people will talk, no birds will fly, no boys will move, there'll be no birth and no death; no sorrow, no laughing, no kissing, no crying, no terror, no joy; no eating, no

drinking, no games, no dancing; no father, no mother, no sisters, no brothers—only you, only you!'

"I stopped her and I said, 'Gaya, why is it that you suffer so. and what am I to do?' I tried to put my arms around her. but she struck them down crying, 'Silence!' Then she said, bringing her face close to my face, 'She has no claws to hang by; she has no hunting foot; she has no mouth for the meat—*vacancy!*'

"Then, Madame, I got up. It was very cold in the room. I went to the window and pulled the curtain, it was a bright and starry night, and I stood leaning my head against the frame, saying nothing. When I turned around, she was regarding me, her hands held apart, and I knew that I had to go away and leave her. So I came up to her and said, 'Good-bye. my Lady.' And I went and put on my street clothes, and when I came back she was leaning against the battle picture, her hands hanging. I said to her, without approaching her, 'Good-bye, my love,' and went away.

"Sometimes it is beautiful in Berlin, Madame, *nicht wahr?* There was something new in my heart, a passion to see Paris, so it was natural that I said *lebe wohl*[9] to Berlin.

"I went for the last time to the café in the Zelten, ate my eggs, drank my coffee and watched the birds coming and going just as they used to come and go—altogether here then altogether gone. I was happy in my spirit, for that is the way it is with my spirit, Madame, when I am going away.

"But I went back to her house just once. I went in quite easily by the door, for all the doors and windows were open—perhaps they were sweeping that day. I came to the bedroom door and knocked, but there was no answer. I pushed, and there she was, sitting up in the bed with the child, and she and the child were making that buzzing cry, and no human sound between them, and as usual, everything was in disorder. I came up to her, but she did not seem to know me. I said. 'I am going away. I am going to Paris. There is a longing in me to be in Paris. So I have come to say farewell.'

"She got down off the bed and came to the door with me. She said, 'Forgive me—I trusted you—I was mistaken. I did not know that I could do it myself, but you see, I can do it myself.' Then she got back on to the bed and said, 'Go away,' and I went.

"Things are like that, when one travels, *nicht wahr*, Madame?"

<div align="right">1929, 1972</div>

9. Farewell.

REBECCA WEST
1892–1983

"Ladies of Great Britain," Rebecca West exclaimed in 1912, "we are clever, we are trustworthy, we are twice the women that our grandmothers were, but we have not enough evil in us." But West herself published caustic journalism and fiction that led a number of her contemporaries to condemn her as demonically rebellious. Her choice of a pseudonym was part of the rebellion she fomented for women's economic and sexual freedom. Born Cicily Isabel Fairfield, the youngest of three daughters of Isabella McKenzie, a Scots pianist, and Captain Charles Fairfield, an

impoverished Irish journalist, West went to school in Edinburgh, but left at sixteen for the London stage. Though her theatrical career was short-lived, it gave her the name that she would quickly make famous: one script she read was Henrik Ibsen's *Rosmersholm* (1886), a play about a radical feminist named Rebecca West. Writing in the feminist journal *The Freewoman* and the socialist weekly *The Clarion*, the nineteen-year-old who now called herself Rebecca West reviewed books by antisuffragists like Mrs. Humphrey Ward and suffragists like Olive Schreiner, even as she argued for free love and women's trade unions and against imperialism and conservative divorce laws.

To an unfortunate extent, West's part in the journalistic radicalism preceding World War I has been obscured in literary history by the attention paid to her ten-year affair with the novelist H. G. Wells and by her son Anthony West's public attacks on her. As the critic Gordon Ray has shown in his *H. G. Wells and Rebecca West*, West at twenty was understandably drawn to the forty-six-year-old spokesman for societal reform, but she was also convinced that she was right in the review she wrote about the antifeminism of Wells's early novels, an essay that first attracted him to her in 1912. In any case, when West gave birth to Wells's son in 1914, she became responsive to the cause of unwed mothers. Her novel *The Judge* (1922) was the most direct expression of this concern, placing the issues of rape, illegitimacy, and motherhood in the context of the suffrage struggle, but an early war novel like *The Return of the Soldier* (1918) also described the sham conventionalities and desexualization of traditional marriage.

Throughout the 1920s West wrote a series of literary reviews for the *New Statesman*, and during the 1930s she produced more novels. Moreover, from her study of Henry James (1916) to her biography of St. Augustine (1933), she exploited the insights of psychology, a fact that helps explain her early enthusiasm for the fiction of Virginia Woolf and D. H. Lawrence. In 1930, she married a banker, Henry Maxwell Andrews, and moved with him to a country house in Buckinghamshire. During World War II, she published *Black Lamb and Grey Falcon* (1941), a travel book that was also a powerful attack on Nazism. By the 1950s, however, West had been converted from a feminist-socialist to a conservative anti-Communist. In 1959, the year before her husband died, she was created a dame commander of the British Empire, a strange fate for the woman who had written forty-seven years earlier that "there are two kinds of imperialists—imperialists and bloody imperialists." Nevertheless, despite her political turnabout, Dame Rebecca never lost sight of the fact that, "like all terrible and wicked things, sex-antagonism has a sound logical basis," and it is the nature of sex-antagonism that she analyzed in *Indissoluble Matrimony*, a story that the scholar Jane Marcus recovered from critical neglect in the early eighties.

Indissoluble Matrimony

When George Silverton opened the front door he found that the house was not empty for all its darkness. The spitting noise of the striking of damp matches and mild, growling exclamations of annoyance told him that his wife was trying to light the dining-room gas. He went in and with some short, hostile sound of greeting lit a match and brought brightness into the little room. Then, irritated by his own folly in bringing private papers into his wife's presence, he stuffed the letters he had brought from the office deep into the pockets of his overcoat. He looked at her suspiciously, but she had not seen them, being busy in unwinding her orange motor-veil.[1] His eyes remained on her

1. A scarf worn in open automobiles.

face to brood a little sourly on her moving loveliness, which he had not been sure of finding: for she was one of those women who create an illusion alternately of extreme beauty and extreme ugliness. Under her curious dress, designed in some pitifully cheap and worthless stuff by a successful mood of her indiscreet taste—she had black blood in her—her long body seemed pulsing with some exaltation. The blood was coursing violently under her luminous yellow skin, and her lips, dusky with fatigue, drooped contentedly over her great humid black eyes. Perpetually she raised her hand to the mass of black hair that was coiled on her thick golden neck and stroked it with secretive enjoyment, as a cat licks its fur. And her large mouth smiled frankly, but abstractedly, at some digested pleasure.

There was a time when George would have looked on this riot of excited loveliness with suspicion. But now he knew it was almost certainly caused by some trifle—a long walk through stinging weather, the report of a socialist victory at a by-election, or the intoxication of a waltz refrain floating from the municipal bandstand across the flats of the local recreation ground. And even if it had been caused by some amorous interlude he would not have greatly cared. In the ten years since their marriage he had lost the quality which would have made him resentful. He now believed that quality to be purely physical. Unless one was in good condition and responsive to the messages sent out by the flesh Evadne could hardly concern one. He turned the bitter thought over in his heart and stung himself by deliberately gazing unmoved upon her beautiful joyful body.

"Let's have supper now!" she said rather greedily.

He looked at the table and saw she had set it before she went out. As usual she had been in an improvident hurry: it was carelessly done. Besides what an absurd supper to set before a hungry solicitor's[2] clerk! In the center, obviously intended as the principal dish, was a bowl of plums, softly red, soaked with the sun, glowing like jewels in the downward stream of the incandescent light. Beside them was a great yellow melon, its sleek sides fluted with rich growth, and a honeycomb glistening on a willow-pattern dish. The only sensible food to be seen was a plate of tongue laid at his place.

"I can't sit down to supper without washing my hands!"

While he splashed in the bathroom upstairs he heard her pull a chair to the table and sit down to her supper. It annoyed him. There was no ritual about it. While he was eating the tongue she would be crushing honey on new bread, or stripping a plum of its purple skin and holding the golden globe up to the gas to see the light filter through. The meal would pass in silence. She would innocently take his dumbness for a sign of abstraction and forbear to babble. He would find the words choked on his lips by the weight of dullness that always oppressed him in her presence. Then, just about the time when he was beginning to feel able to formulate his obscure grievances against her, she would rise from the table without a word and run upstairs to her work, humming in that uncanny, Negro way of hers.

And so it was. She ate with an appalling catholicity of taste, with a nice child's love of sweet foods, and occasionally she broke into that hoarse, beautiful croon. Every now and then she looked at him with too obvious speculations as to whether his silence was due to weariness or uncertain temper.

2. Lawyer's.

Timidly she cut him an enormous slice of the melon, which he did not want. Then she rose abruptly and flung herself into the rocking-chair on the hearth. She clasped her hands behind her head and strained backwards so that the muslin stretched over her strong breasts. She sang softly to the ceiling.

There was something about the fantastic figure that made him feel as though they were not properly married.

"Evadne?"

"'S?"

"What have you been up to this evening?"

"I was at Milly Stafordale's."

He was silent again. That name brought up the memory of his courting days. It was under the benign eyes of blonde, plebeian Milly that he had wooed the distracting creature in the rocking-chair.

Ten years before, when he was twenty-five, his firm had been reduced to hysteria over the estates of an extraordinarily stupid old woman, named Mrs. Mary Ellerker. Her stupidity, grappling with the complexity of the sources of the vast income which rushed in spate from the properties of four deceased husbands, demanded oceans of explanations even over her weekly rents. Silverton alone in the office, by reason of a certain natural incapacity for excitement, could deal calmly with this marvel of imbecility. He alone could endure to sit with patience in the black-paneled drawing-room amidst the jungle of shiny mahogany furniture and talk to a mass of darkness, who rested heavily in the window-seat and now and then made an idiotic remark in a bright, hearty voice. But it shook even him. Mrs. Mary Ellerker was obscene. Yet she was perfectly sane and although of that remarkable plainness noticeable in most oft-married women, in good enough physical condition. She merely presented the loathsome spectacle of an ignorant mind, contorted by the artificial idiocy of coquetry, lack of responsibility and hatred of discipline, stripped naked by old age. That was the real horror of her. One feared to think how many women were really like Mrs. Ellerker under their armor of physical perfection or social grace. For this reason he turned eyes of hate on Mrs. Ellerker's pretty little companion, Milly Stafordale, who smiled at him over her embroidery with wintry northern brightness. When she was old she too would be obscene.

This horror obsessed him. Never before had he feared anything. He had never lived more than half an hour from a police station and, as he had by some chance missed the melancholy clairvoyance of adolescence, he had never conceived of any horror with which the police could not deal. This disgust of women revealed to him that the world is a place of subtle perils. He began to fear marriage as he feared death. The thought of intimacy with some lovely, desirable and necessary wife turned him sick as he sat at his lunch. The secret obscenity of women! He talked darkly of it to his friends. He wondered why the Church did not provide a service for the absolution of men after marriage. Wife desertion seemed to him a beautiful return of the tainted body to cleanliness.

On his fifth visit to Mrs. Ellerker he could not begin his business at once. One of Milly Stafordale's friends had come in to sing to the old lady. She stood by the piano against the light, so that he saw her washed with darkness. And before he had time to apprehend the sleepy wonder of her beauty, she had begun to sing. Now he knew that her voice was a purely physical attribute,

built in her as she lay in her mother's womb, and no index of her spiritual values. But then, as it welled up from the thick golden throat and clung to her lips, it seemed a sublime achievement of the soul. It was a smoldering contralto such as only those of black blood can possess. As she sang her great black eyes lay on him with the innocent shamelessness of a young animal, and he remembered hopefully that he was good-looking. Suddenly she stood in silence, playing with her heavy black plait. Mrs. Ellerker broke into silly thanks. The girl's mother, who had been playing the accompaniment, rose and stood rolling up her music. Silverton, sick with excitement, was introduced to them. He noticed that the mother was a little darker than the conventions permit. Their name was Hannan—Mrs. Arthur Hannan and Evadne. They moved lithely and quietly out of the room, the girl's eyes still lingering on his face.

The thought of her splendor and the rolling echoes of her voice disturbed him all night. Next day, going to his office, he travelled with her on the horse-car that bound his suburb to Petrick. One of the horses fell lame, and she had time to tell him that she was studying at a commercial college. He quivered with distress. All the time he had a dizzy illusion that she was nestling up against him. They parted shyly. During the next few days they met constantly. He began to go and see them in the evening at their home—a mean flat crowded with cheap glories of bead curtains and Oriental hangings that set off the women's alien beauty. Mrs Hannan was a widow and they lived alone, in a wonderful silence. He talked more than he had ever done in his whole life before. He took a dislike to the widow, she was consumed with fiery passions, no fit guardian for the tender girl.

Now he could imagine with what silent rapture Evadne had watched his agitation. Almost from the first she had meant to marry him. He was physically attractive, though not strong. His intellect was gently stimulating like a mild white wine. And it was time she married. She was ripe for adult things. This was the real wound in his soul. He had tasted of a divine thing created in his time for dreams out of her rich beauty, her loneliness, her romantic poverty, her immaculate youth. He had known love. And Evadne had never known anything more than a magnificent physical adventure which she had secured at the right time as she would have engaged a cab to take her to the station in time for the cheapest excursion train. It was a quick way to light-hearted living. With loathing he remembered how in the days of their engagement she used to gaze purely into his blinking eyes and with her unashamed kisses incite him to extravagant embraces. Now he cursed her for having obtained his spiritual revolution on false pretences. Only for a little time had he had his illusion, for their marriage was hastened by Mrs. Hannan's sudden death. After three months of savage mourning Evadne flung herself into marriage, and her excited candor had enlightened him very soon.

That marriage had lasted ten years. And to Evadne their relationship was just the same as ever. Her vitality needed him as it needed the fruit on the table before him. He shook with wrath and a sense of outraged decency.

"Oh George!" She was yawning widely.

"What's the matter?" he said without interest.

"It's so beastly dull."

"I can't help that, can I?"

"No." She smiled placidly at him. "We're a couple of dull dogs, aren't we? I wish we had children."

After a minute she suggested, apparently as an alternative amusement, "Perhaps the post hasn't passed."

As she spoke there was a rat-tat and the slither of a letter under the door. Evadne picked herself up and ran out of the lobby. After a second or two, during which she made irritating inarticulate exclamations, she came in reading the letter and stroking her bust with a gesture of satisfaction.

"They want me to speak at Longton's meeting on the nineteenth," she purred.

"Longton? What's he up to?"

Stephen Longton was the owner of the biggest iron-works in Petrick, a man whose refusal to adopt the livery of busy oafishness thought proper to commercial men aroused the gravest suspicions.

"He's standing as socialist candidate for the town council."

" . . . Socialist!" he muttered.

He set his jaw. That was a side of Evadne he considered as little as possible. He had never been able to assimilate the fact that Evadne had, two years after their marriage, passed through his own orthodox radicalism to a passionate socialism, and that after reading enormously of economics she had begun to write for the socialist Press and to speak successfully at meetings. In the jaundiced recesses of his mind he took it for granted that her work would have the lax fiber of her character: that it would be infected with her Oriental crudities. Although once or twice he had been congratulated on her brilliance, he mistrusted this phase in her activity as a caper of the sensualist. His eyes blazed on her and found the depraved, over-sexed creature, looking milder than a gazelle, holding out a handbill to him.

"They've taken it for granted!"

He saw her name—his name—MRS. EVADNE SILVERTON.

It was at first the blaze of stout scarlet letters on the dazzling white ground that made him blink. Then he was convulsed with rage.

"Georgie dear!"

She stepped forward and caught his weak body to her bosom. He wrenched himself away. Spiritual nausea made him determined to be a better man than her.

"A pair of you! You and Longton!" he snarled scornfully. Then seeing her startled face, he controlled himself.

"I thought it would please you," said Evadne, a little waspishly.

"You mustn't have anything to do with Longton," he stormed.

A change passed over her. She became ugly. Her face was heavy with intellect, her lips coarse with power. He was at arms with a socialist leader. Much would he have preferred the bland sensualist again.

"Why?"

"Because," his lips stuck together like blotting paper "he's not the sort of man my wife should—should—."

With movements which terrified him by their rough energy, she folded up the bills and put them back in the envelope.

"George. I suppose you mean that he's a bad man." He nodded. "I know quite well that the girl who used to be his typist is his mistress." She spoke it sweetly, as if reasoning with an old fool. "But she's got consumption.[3] She'll be

3. Tuberculosis.

dead in six months. In fact. I think it's rather nice of him. To look after her and all that."

"My God!" He leapt to his feet, extending a shaking forefinger. As she turned to him, the smile dying on her lips, his excited weakness wrapped him in a paramnesic illusion:[4] it seemed to him that he had been through all this before—a long, long time ago. "My God, you talk like a woman off the streets!"

Evadne's lips lifted over her strong teeth. With clever cruelty she fixed his eyes with hers, well knowing that he longed to fall forward and bury his head on the table in a transport of hysterical sobs. After a moment of this torture she turned away, herself distressed by a desire to cry.

"How can you say such dreadful, dreadful things " she protested, chokingly.

He sat down again. His eyes looked little and red, but they blazed on her. "I wonder if you are," he said softly.

"Are what?" she asked petulantly, a tear rolling down her nose.

"You know," he answered, nodding.

"George, George, George!" she cried.

"You've always been keen on kissing and making love, haven't you, my precious. At first you startled me, you did. I didn't know women were like that." From that morass he suddenly stepped on to a high peak of terror. Amazed to find himself sincere, he cried, "I don't believe good women are!"

"Georgie, how can you be so silly!" exclaimed Evadne shrilly. "You know quite well I've been as true to you as any woman could be." She sought his eyes with a liquid glance of reproach. He averted his gaze, sickened at having put himself in the wrong. For even while he degraded his tongue his pure soul fainted with loathing of her fleshliness.

"I . . . I'm sorry."

Too wily to forgive him at once, she showed him a lowering profile with downcast lids. Of course, he knew it was a fraud. An imputation against her chastity was no more poignant than a reflection on the cleanliness of her nails—rude and spiteful, but that was all. But for a time they kept up the deception, while she cleared the table in steely silence.

"Evadne, I'm sorry. I'm tired." His throat was dry. He could not bear the discord of a row added to the horror of their companionship. "Evadne, do forgive me—I don't know what I meant by. . . ."

"That's all right, silly!" she said suddenly and bent over the table to kiss him. Her brow was smooth. It was evident from her splendid expression that she was preoccupied. Then she finished clearing up the dishes and took them into the kitchen. While she was out of the room he rose from his seat and sat down in the armchair by the fire, setting his bulldog pipe alight. For a very short time he was free of her voluptuous presence. But she ran back soon, having put the kettle on and changed her blouse for a loose dressing-jacket, and sat down on the arm of his chair. Once or twice she bent and kissed his brow, but for the most part she lay back with his head drawn to her bosom, rocking herself rhythmically Silverton, a little disgusted by their contact, sat quite motionless and passed into a doze. He revolved in his mind the incidents of his day's routine and remembered a snub from a superior. So he opened his eyes and tried to think of something else. It was then that he became con-

4. I.e., a feeling of déjà vu.

scious that the rhythm of Evadne's movement was not regular. It was broken
as though she rocked in time to music. Music? His sense of hearing crept up to
hear if there was any sound of music in the breaths she was emitting rather
heavily, every now and then. At first he could hear nothing. Then it struck him
that each breath was a muttered phrase. He stiffened, and hatred flamed
through his veins. The words came clearly through her lips. . . . "The present
system of wage-slavery. . . . "

"Evadne!" He sprang to his feet. "You're preparing your speech!"

She did not move. "I am," she said.

"Damn it, you shan't speak!"

"Damn it, I will!"

"Evadne, you shan't speak! If you do I swear to God above I'll turn you out
into the streets." She rose and came towards him. She looked black and dan-
gerous. She trod softly like a cat with her head down. In spite of himself, his
tongue licked his lips in fear and he cowered a moment before he picked up a
knife from the table. For a space she looked down on him and the sharp blade.

"You idiot, can't you hear the kettle's boiling over?"

He shrank back, letting the knife fall on the floor. For three minutes he
stood there controlling his breath and trying to still his heart. Then he fol-
lowed her into the kitchen. She was making a noise with a basinful of dishes.

"Stop that row."

She turned round with a dripping dishcloth in her hand and pondered
whether to throw it at him. But she was tired and wanted peace; so that she
could finish the rough draft of her speech. So she stood waiting.

"Did you understand what I said then? If you don't promise me here and
now. . . . "

She flung her arms upwards with a cry and dashed past him. He made to run
after her upstairs, but stumbled on the threshold of the lobby and sat with his
ankle twisted under him, shaking with rage. In a second she ran downstairs
again, clothed in a big cloak with a black bundle clutched to her breast. For the
first time in their married life she was seized with a convulsion of sobs. She
dashed out the front door and banged it with such passion that a glass pane
shivered to fragments behind her.

"What's this? What's this?" he cried stupidly, standing up. He perceived
with an insane certainty that she was going to meet some unknown lover. "I'll
come and tell him what a slut you are!" he shouted after her and stumbled to
the door. It was jammed now and he had to drag at it.

The night was flooded with the yellow moonshine of midsummer; it
seemed to drip from the lacquered leaves of the shrubs in the front garden. In
its soft clarity he could see her plainly, although she was now two hundred
yards away. She was hastening to the north end of Sumatra Crescent, an end
that curled up the hill like a silly kitten's tail and stopped abruptly in green
fields. So he knew that she was going to the young man who had just bought
the Georgian manor, whose elm trees crowned the hill. Oh, how he hated her!
Yet he must follow her, or else she would cover up her adulteries so that he
could not take his legal revenge. So he began to run—silently, for he wore his
carpet-slippers. He was only a hundred yards behind her when she slipped
through a gap in the hedge to tread a field-path. She still walked with pride, for
though she was town-bred, night in the open seemed not at all fearful to her.
As he shuffled in pursuit his carpet-slippers were engulfed in a shining pool of
mud. He raised one with a squelch, the other was left. This seemed the last

humiliation. He kicked the other one off his foot and padded on in his socks, snuffling in anticipation of a cold. Then physical pain sent him back to the puddle to pluck out the slippers. It was a dirty job. His heart battered his breast as he saw that Evadne had gained the furthest hedge and was crossing the stile into the lane that ran up to the manor gates.

"Go on, you beast!" he muttered. "Go on, go on!" After a scamper he climbed the stile and thrust his lean neck beyond a mass of wilted hawthorn bloom that crumbled into vagrant petals at his touch.

The lane mounted yellow as cheese to where the moon lay on the iron tracery of the manor gates. Evadne was not there. Hardly believing his eyes he hobbled over into the lane and looked in the other direction. There he saw her disappearing round the bend of the road. Gathering himself up to a run, he tried to think out his bearings. He had seldom passed this way, and like most people without strong primitive instincts he had no sense of orientation. With difficulty he remembered that after a mile's mazy wanderings between high hedges this lane sloped suddenly to the bowl of heather overhung by the moorlands, in which lay the Petrick reservoirs, two untamed lakes.

"Eh! She's going to meet him by the water!" he cursed to himself. He remembered the withered ash tree, seared by lightning to its root, that stood by the road at the bare frontier of the moor. "May God strike her like that," he prayed, "as she fouls the other man's lips with her kisses. Oh God! Let me strangle her. Or bury a knife deep in her breast." Suddenly he broke into a lolloping run. "Oh my Lord, I'll be able to divorce her. I'll be free. Free to live alone. To do my day's work and sleep my night's sleep without her. I'll get a job somewhere else and forget her. I'll bring her to the dogs. No clean man or woman in Petrick will look at her now. They won't have her to speak at that meeting now!" His throat swelled with joy, he leapt high in the air.

"I'll lie about her. If I can prove that she's wrong with this man they'll believe me if I say she's a bad woman and drinks. I'll make her name a joke. And then. . . ."

He flung wide his arms in ecstasy: the left struck against stone. More pain than he had thought his body could hold convulsed him, so that he sank on the ground hugging his aching arm. He looked backwards as he writhed and saw that the hedge had stopped; above him was the great stone wall of the county asylum. The question broke on him—was there any lunatic in its confines so slavered with madness as he himself? Nothing but madness could have accounted for the torrent of ugly words, the sea of uglier thoughts that was now a part of him. "Oh God, for me to turn like this!" he cried, rolling over full-length on the grassy bank by the roadside. That the infidelity of his wife, a thing that should have brought out the stern manliness of his true nature, should have discovered him as lecherous-lipped as any pot-house[5] lounger, was the most infamous accident of his married life. The sense of sin descended on him so that his tears flowed hot and bitterly. "Have I gone to the Unitarian chapel every Sunday morning and to the Ethical Society every evening for nothing?" his spirit asked itself in its travail. "All those Browning lectures[6] for nothing. . . ." He said the Lord's Prayer several times and lay for a minute quietly crying. The relaxation of his muscles brought him a sense of rest which seemed forgiveness falling from God. The tears dried on his cheeks.

5. Tavern.
6. Lectures given under the auspices of the Browning Society, a popular literary society devoted chiefly to the works of the English poet Robert Browning (1812–1889).

His calmer consciousness heard the sound of rushing waters mingled with the beating of blood in his ears. He got up and scrambled round the turn of the road that brought him to the withered ash tree.

He walked forward on the parched heatherland to the mound whose scarred sides, heaped with boulders, tufted with mountain grasses, shone before him in the moonlight. He scrambled up to it hurriedly and hoisted himself from ledge to ledge till he fell on his knees with a squeal of pain. His ankle was caught in a crevice of the rock. Gulping down his agony at this final physical humiliation he heaved himself upright and raced on to the summit, and found himself before the Devil's Caldron, filled to the brim with yellow moonshine and the fiery play of summer lightning. The rugged crags opposite him were a low barricade against the stars to which the mound where he stood shot forward like a bridge. To the left of this the long Lisbech pond lay like a trailing serpent; its silver scales glittered as the wind swept down from the vaster moorlands to the east. To the right under a steep drop of twenty feet was the Whimsey pond, more sinister, shaped in an unnatural oval, sheltered from the wind by the high ridge so that the undisturbed moonlight lay across it like a sharp-edged sword.

He looked about for some sign of Evadne. She could not be on the land by the margin of the lakes, for the light blazed so strongly that each reed could be clearly seen like a black dagger stabbing the silver. He looked down Lisbech and saw far east a knot of red and green and orange lights. Perhaps for some devilish purpose Evadne had sought Lisbech railway station. But his volcanic mind had preserved one grain of sense that assured him that, subtle as Evadne's villainy might be, it would not lead her to walk five miles out of her way to a terminus which she could have reached in fifteen minutes by taking a train from the station down the road. She must be under cover somewhere here. He went down the gentle slope that fell from the top of the ridge to Lisbech pond in a disorder of rough heather, unhappy patches of cultivated grass and coppices of silver birch, fringed with flaming broom that seemed faintly tarnished in the moonlight. At the bottom was a roughly hewn path which he followed in hot aimless hurry. In a little he approached a riot of falling waters. There was a slice ten feet broad carved out of the ridge, and to this narrow channel of black shining rock the floods of Lisbech leapt some feet and raced through to Whimsey. The noise beat him back. The gap was spanned by a gaunt thing of paint-blistered iron, on which he stood dizzily and noticed how the wide step that ran on each side of the channel through to the other pond was smeared with sinister green slime. Now his physical distress reminded him of Evadne, whom he had almost forgotten in contemplation of these lonely waters. The idea of her had been present but obscured, as sometimes toothache may cease active torture. His blood-lust set him on and he staggered forward with covered ears. Even as he went something caught his eye in a thicket high up on the slope near the crags. Against the slender pride of some silver birches stood a gnarled hawthorn tree, its branches flattened under the stern moorland winds so that it grew squat like an opened umbrella. In its dark shadows, faintly illumined by a few boughs of withered blossom, there moved a strange bluish light. Even while he did not know what it was it made his flesh stir.

The light emerged. It was the moonlight reflected from Evadne's body. She was clad in a black bathing-dress, and her arms and legs and the broad streak

of flesh laid bare by a rent down the back shone brilliantly white, so that she seemed like a grotesquely patterned wild animal as she ran down to the lake. Whirling her arms above her head she trampled down into the water and struck out strongly. Her movements were full of brisk delight and she swam quickly. The moonlight made her the center of a little feathery blur of black and silver, with a comet's tail trailing in her wake.

Nothing in all his married life had ever staggered Silverton so much as this. He had imagined his wife's adultery so strongly that it had come to be. It was now as real as their marriage; more real than their courtship. So this seemed to be the last crime of the adulteress. She had dragged him over those squelching fields and these rough moors and changed him from a man of irritations, but no passions, into a cold designer of murderous treacheries, so that he might witness a swimming exhibition! For a minute he was stunned. Then he sprang down to the rushy edge and ran along in the direction of her course, crying, "Evadne! Evadne!" She did not hear him. At last he achieved a chest-note and shouted, "Evadne! Come here!" The black-and-silver feather shivered in mid-water. She turned immediately and swam back to shore. He suspected sullen-ness in her slowness, but was glad of it, for after the shock of this extraordinary incident he wanted to go to sleep. Drowsiness lay on him like lead. He shook himself like a dog and wrenched off his linen collar, winking at the bright moon to keep himself awake. As she came quite near he was exasperated by the happy, snorting breaths she drew, and strolled a pace or two up the bank. To his enragement the face she lifted as she waded to dry land was placid, and she scrambled gaily up the bank to his side.

"Oh George, why did you come!" she exclaimed quite affectionately, laying a damp hand on his shoulder.

"Oh damn it, what does this mean?" he cried, committing a horrid tenor squeak. "What are you doing?"

"Why, George," she said, "I came here for a bathe."

He stared into her face and could make nothing of it. It was only sweet sur-faces of flesh, soft radiances of eye and lip, a lovely lie of comeliness. He forgot this present grievance in a cold search for the source of her peculiar hateful-ness. Under this sick gaze she pouted and turned away with a peevish gesture. He made no sign and stood silent, watching her saunter to that gaunt iron bridge. The roar of the little waterfall did not disturb her splendid nerves and she drooped sensuously over the hand-rail, sniffing up the sweet night smell; too evidently trying to abase him to another apology.

A mosquito whirred into his face. He killed it viciously and strode off to-wards his wife, who showed by a common little toss of the head that she was conscious of his coming.

"Look here, Evadne!" he panted. "What did you come here for? Tell me the truth and I promise I'll not . . . I'll not. . . ."

"Not *what*, George?"

"Oh please, please tell me the truth, do Evadne!" he cried pitifully.

"But, dear, what is there to carry on about so? You went on so queerly about my meeting that my head felt fit to split, and I thought the long walk and the dip would do me good." She broke off, amazed at the wave of horror that passed over his face.

His heart sank. From the loose-lipped hurry in the telling of her story, from the bigness of her eyes and the lack of subtlety in her voice, he knew that this

was the truth. Here was no adulteress whom he could accuse in the law courts and condemn into the street, no resourceful sinner whose merry crimes he could discover. Here was merely his good wife, the faithful attendant of his hearth, relentless wrecker of his soul.

She came towards him as a cat approaches a displeased master, and hovered about him on the stone coping of the noisy sluice.

"Indeed!" he found himself saying sarcastically. "Indeed!"

"Yes, George Silverton, indeed!" she burst out, a little frightened. "And why shouldn't I? I used to come here often enough on summer nights with poor Mamma.'

"Yes!" he shouted. It was exactly the sort of thing that would appeal to that weird half-black woman from the back of beyond. "Mamma!" he cried tauntingly, "Mamma!"

There was a flash of silence between them before Evadne, clutching her breast and balancing herself dangerously on her heels on the stone coping, broke into gentle shrieks. "You dare talk of my Mamma, my poor Mamma, and she cold in her grave! I haven't been happy since she died and I married you, you silly little misery, you!" Then the rage was suddenly wiped off her brain by the perception of a crisis.

The trickle of silence overflowed into a lake, over which their spirits flew, looking at each other's reflection in the calm waters: in the hurry of their flight they had never before seen each other. They stood facing one another with dropped heads, quietly thinking.

The strong passion which filled them threatened to disintegrate their souls as a magnetic current decomposes the electrolyte,[7] so they fought to organize their sensations. They tried to arrange themselves and their lives for comprehension, but beyond sudden lyric visions of old incidents of hatefulness—such as a smarting quarrel of six years ago as to whether Evadne had or had not cheated the railway company out of one-and-eightpence on an excursion ticket—the past was intangible. It trailed behind this intense event as the pale hair trails behind the burning comet. They were preoccupied with the moment. Quite often George had found a mean pleasure in the thought that by never giving Evadne a child he had cheated her out of one form of experience, and now he paid the price of this unnatural pride of sterility. For now the spiritual offspring of their intercourse came to birth. A sublime loathing was between them. For a little time it was a huge perilous horror, but afterwards, like men aboard a ship whose masts seek the sky through steep waves, they found a drunken pride in the adventure. This was the very absolute of hatred. It cheapened the memory of the fantasias of irritation and ill-will they had performed in the less boring moments of their marriage, and they felt dazed, as amateurs who had found themselves creating a masterpiece. For the first time they were possessed by a supreme emotion and they felt a glad desire to strip away restraint and express it nakedly. It was ecstasy; they felt tall and full of blood.

Like people who, bewitched by Christ, see the whole earth as the breathing body of God, so they saw the universe as the substance and the symbol of their hatred. The stars trembled overhead with wrath. A wind from behind the angry crags set the moonlight on Lisbech quivering with rage, and the squat

7. A substance that conducts electricity.

hawthorn tree creaked slowly like the irritation of a dull little man. The dry moors, parched with harsh anger, waited thirstily and, sending out the murmur of rustling mountain grass and the cry of wakening fowl, seemed to huddle closer to the lake. But this sense of the earth's sympathy slipped away from them and they loathed all matter as the dull wrapping of their flame-like passion. At their wishing matter fell away and they saw sarcastic visions. He saw her as a toad squatting on the clean earth, obscuring the stars and pressing down its hot moist body or the cheerful fields. She felt his long boneless body coiled round the roots of the lovely tree of life. They shivered fastidiously. With an uplifting sense of responsibility they realized that they must kill each other.

A bird rose over their heads with a leaping flight that made it seem as though its black body was bouncing against the bright sky. The foolish noise and motion precipitated their thoughts. They were broken into a new conception of life. They perceived that God is war and his creatures are meant to fight. When dogs walk through the world cats must climb trees. The virgin must snare the wanton, the fine lover must put the prude to the sword. The gross man of action walks, spurred on by the bloodless bodies of the men of thought, who lie quiet and cunningly do not tell him where his grossness leads him. The flesh must smother the spirit, the spirit must set the flesh on fire and watch it burn. And those who were gentle by nature and shrank from the ordained brutality were betrayers of their kind, surrendering the earth to the seed of their enemies. In this war there is no discharge. If they succumbed to peace now, the rest of their lives would be dishonorable, like the exile of a rebel who has begged his life as the reward of cowardice. It was their first experience of religious passion, and they abandoned themselves to it so that their immediate personal qualities fell away from them. Neither his weakness nor her prudence stood in the way of the event.

They measured each other with the eye. To her he was a spidery thing against the velvet blackness and hard silver surfaces of the pond. The light soaked her bathing-dress so that she seemed, against the jagged shadows of the rock cutting, as though she were clad in a garment of dark polished mail. Her knees were bent so clearly, her toes gripped the coping so strongly. He understood very clearly that if he did not kill her instantly she would drop him easily into the deep riot of waters. Yet for a space he could not move, but stood expecting a degrading death. Indeed, he gave her time to kill him. But she was without power too, and struggled weakly with a hallucination. The quarrel in Sumatra Crescent with its suggestion of vast and unmentionable antagonisms; her swift race through the moon-drenched countryside, all crepitant with night noises; the swimming in the wine-like lake; their isolation on the moor, which was expressedly hostile to them, as nature always is to lonely man; and this stark contest face to face, with their resentments heaped between them like a pile of naked swords—these things were so strange that her civilized self shrank back appalled. There entered into her the primitive woman who is the curse of all women: a creature of the most utter femaleness, useless, save for childbirth, with no strong brain to make her physical weakness a light accident, abjectly and corruptingly afraid of man. A squaw, she dared not strike her lord.

The illusion passed like a moment of faintness and left her enraged at having forgotten her superiority even for an instant. In the material world she had

a thousand times been defeated into making prudent reservations and practicing unnatural docilities. But in the world of thought she had maintained unfalteringly her masterfulness in spite of the strong yearning of her temperament towards voluptuous surrenders. That was her virtue. Its violation whipped her to action and she would have killed him at once, had not his moment come a second before hers. Sweating horribly, he had dropped his head forward on his chest; his eyes fell on her feet and marked the plebeian molding of her ankle, which rose thickly over a crease of flesh from the heel to the calf. The woman was coarse in grain and pattern.

He had no instinct for honorable attack, so he found himself striking her in the stomach. She reeled from pain, not because his strength overcame hers. For the first time her eyes looked into his candidly open, unveiled by languor or lust; their hard brightness told him how she despised him for that unwarlike blow. He cried out as he realized that this was another of her despicable victories and that the whole burden of the crime now lay on him, for he had begun it. But the rage was stopped on his lips as her arms, flung wildly out as she fell backwards, caught him about the waist with abominable justness of eye and evil intention. So they fell body to body into the quarrelling waters.

The feathery confusion had looked so soft, yet it seemed the solid rock they struck. The breath shot out of him and suffocation warmly stuffed his ears and nose. Then the rock cleft and he was swallowed by a brawling blackness in which whirled a vortex that flung him again and again on a sharp thing that burned his shoulder. All about him fought the waters, and they cut his flesh like knives. His pain was past belief. Though God might be war, he desired peace in his time, and he yearned for another God—a child's God, an immense arm coming down from the hills and lifting him to a kindly bosom. Soon his body would burst for breath, his agony would smash in his breastbone. So great was his pain that his consciousness was strained to apprehend it, as a too tightly stretched canvas splits and rips.

Suddenly the air was sweet on his mouth. The starlight seemed as hearty as a cheer. The world was still there, the world in which he had lived, so he must be safe. His own weakness and lovableness induced enjoyable tears, and there was a delicious moment of abandonment to comfortable whining before he realized that the water would not kindly buoy him up for long, and that even now a hostile current clasped his waist. He braced his flaccid body against the sucking blackness and flung his head back so that the water should not bubble so hungrily against the cords of his throat. Above him the slime of the rock was sticky with moonbeams, and the leprous light brought to his mind a newspaper paragraph, read years ago, which told him that the dawn had discovered floating in some oily Mersey dock, under walls as infected with wet growth as this, a corpse whose blood-encrusted finger-tips were deeply cleft. On the instant his own fingertips seemed hot with blood and deeply cleft from clawing at the impregnable rock. He screamed gaspingly, and beat his hands through the strangling flood. Action, which he had always loathed and dreaded, had broken the hard mold of his self-possession, and the dry dust of his character was blown hither and thither by fear. But one sharp fragment of intelligence which survived this detrition of his personality perceived that a certain gleam on the rock about a foot above the water was not the cold putrescence of the slime, but certainly the hard and merry light of a moon-ray striking on solid metal. His left hand clutched upwards at it, and he swung from a rounded pro-

jection. It was, his touch told him, a leaden ring hanging obliquely from the rock, to which his memory could visualize precisely in some past drier time when Lisbech sent no flood to Whimsey, a waterman mooring a boat strewn with pale-bellied perch. And behind the stooping waterman he remembered a flight of narrow steps that led up a buttress to a stone shelf that ran through the cutting. Unquestionably he was safe. He swung in a happy rhythm from the ring, his limp body trailing like a caterpillar through the stream to the foot of the steps, while he gasped in strength. A part of him was in agony, for his arm was nearly dragged out of its socket, and a part of him was embarrassed because his hysteria shook him with a deep rumbling chuckle that sounded as though he meditated on some unseemly joke; the whole was pervaded by a twilight atmosphere of unenthusiastic gratitude for his rescue, like the quietly cheerful tone of a Sunday evening sacred concert. After a minute's deep breathing he hauled himself up by the other hand and prepared to swing himself on to the steps.

But first, to shake off the wet worsted rags, once his socks, that now stuck uncomfortably between his toes, he splashed his feet outwards to midstream. A certain porpoise-like surface met his left foot. Fear dappled his face with goose-flesh. Without turning his head he knew what it was. It was Evadne's fat flesh rising on each side of her deep-furrowed spine through the rent in her bathing-dress.

Once more hatred marched through his soul like a king: a compelling service by his godhead and, like all gods, a little hatred for his harsh len on his worshiper. He saw his wife as the curtain of flesh between him and celibacy, and solitude and all those delicate abstentions from life which his soul desired. He saw her as the invisible worm destroying the rose of the world with her dark secret love.[8] Now he knelt on the lowest stone step watching her wet seal-smooth head bobbing nearer on the waters. As her strong arms, covered with little dark points where her thick hairs were clotted with moisture, stretched out towards safety he bent forward and laid his hands on her head. He held her face under water. Scornfully he noticed the bubbles that rose to the surface from her protesting mouth and nostrils, and the foam raised by her arms and her thick ankles. To the end the creature persisted in turmoil, in movement, in action. . . .

She dropped like a stone. His hands, with nothing to resist them, slapped the water foolishly and he nearly overbalanced forward into the stream. He rose to his feet very stiffly. "I must be a very strong man," he said, as he slowly climbed the steps. "I must be a very strong man," he repeated, a little louder, as with hot and painful rigidity of the joints he stretched himself out at full length along the stone shelf. Weakness closed him in like a lead coffin. For a little time the wetness of his clothes persisted in being felt; then the sensation oozed out of him and his body fell out of knowledge. There was neither pain nor joy nor any other reckless ploughing of the brain by nerves. He knew unconsciousness, or rather the fullest consciousness he had ever known. For the world became nothingness, and nothingness which is free from the yeasty nuisance of matter and the ugliness of generation was the law of his being. He was

8. An echo of a poem by William Blake (1757–1827), *The Sick Rose:* "O Rose thou art sick. / The invisible worm / That flies in the night / In the howling storm: / Has found out thy bed / Of crimson joy: / And his dark secret love / Does thy life destroy."

absorbed into vacuity, the untamed substance of the universe, round which he conceived passion and thought to circle as straws caught up by the wind. He saw God and lived.

In Heaven a thousand years are a day. And this little corner of time in which he found happiness shrank to a nutshell as he opened his eyes again. This peace was hardly printed on his heart, yet the brightness of the night was blurred by the dawn. With the grunting carefulness of a man drunk with fatigue, he crawled along the stone shelf to the iron bridge, where he stood with his back to the roaring sluice and rested. All things seemed different now and happier. Like most timid people he disliked the night, and the commonplace hand which the dawn laid on the scene seemed to him a sanctification. The dimmed moon sank to her setting behind the crags. The jewel lights of Lisbech railway station were weak, cheerful twinklings. A steaming bluish milk of morning mist had been spilt on the hard silver surface of the lake, and the reeds no longer stabbed it like little daggers, but seemed a feathery fringe, like the pampas grass in the front garden in Sumatra Crescent. The black crags became brownish, and the mist disguised the sternness of the moor. This weakening of effects was exactly what he had always thought the extinction of Evadne would bring the world. He smiled happily at the moon.

Yet he was moved to sudden angry speech. "If I had my time over again," he said, "I wouldn't touch her with the tongs." For the cold he had known all along he would catch had settled in his head, and his handkerchief was wet through.

He leaned over the bridge and looked along Lisbech and thought of Evadne. For the first time for many years he saw her image without spirits, and wondered without indignation why she had so often looked like the cat about to steal the cream. What was the cream? And did she ever steal it? Now he would never know. He thought of her very generously and sighed over the perversity of fate in letting so much comeliness.

"If she had married a butcher or a veterinary surgeon she might have been happy," he said, and shook his head at the glassy black water that slid under the bridge to that boiling sluice.

A gust of ague[9] reminded him that wet clothes clung to his fevered body and that he ought to change as quickly as possible, or expect to be laid up for weeks. He turned along the path that led back across the moor to the withered ash tree, and was learning the torture of bare feet on gravel when he cried out to himself: "I shall be hanged for killing my wife." It did not come as a trumpet-call, for he was one of those people who never quite hear what is said to them, and this deafishness extended in him to emotional things. It stole on him calmly, like a fog closing on a city. When he first felt hemmed in by this certainty he looked over his shoulder to the crags, remembering tales of how Jacobite[1] fugitives had hidden on the moors for many weeks. There lay at least another day of freedom. But he was the kind of man who always goes home. He stumbled on, not very unhappy, except for his feet. Like many people of weak temperament he did not fear death. Indeed, it had a peculiar appeal to him; for while it was important, exciting, it did not, like most important and exciting things, try to create action. He allowed his imagination the vanity of

9. A fit of shivering.
1. Supporters of the Stuarts (James II was deposed in the Glorious Revolution of 1688), who were defeated fighting for Bonnie Prince Charlie at Culloden (1746).

painting pictures. He saw himself standing in their bedroom, plotting this last event, with the white sheet and the high lights of the mahogany wardrobe shining ghostly at him through the darkness. He saw himself raising a thin hand to the gas bracket and turning on the tap. He saw himself staggering to their bed while death crept in at his nostrils. He saw his corpse lying in full daylight, and for the first time knew himself certainly, unquestionably dignified.

He threw back his chest in pride; but at that moment the path stopped and he found himself staggering down the mound of heatherland and boulders with bleeding feet. Always he had suffered from sore feet, which had not exactly disgusted but, worse still, disappointed Evadne. A certain wistfulness she had always evinced when she found herself the superior animal had enraged and humiliated him many times. He felt that sting him now, and flung himself down the mound cursing. When he stumbled up to the withered ash tree he hated her so much that it seemed as though she were alive again, and a sharp wind blowing down from the moor terrified him like her touch.

He rested there. Leaning against the stripped gray trunk, he smiled up at the sky, which was now so touched to ineffectiveness by the dawn that it looked like a tent of faded silk. There was the peace of weakness in him, which he took to be spiritual, because it had no apparent physical justification, but he lost it as his dripping clothes chilled his tired flesh. His discomfort reminded him that the phantasmic night was passing from him. Daylight threatened him; the daylight in which for so many years he had worked in the solicitor's office and been snubbed and ignored. "The garish day,"[2] he murmured disgustedly, quoting the blasphemy of some hymn-writer. He wanted his death to happen in this phantasmic night.

So he limped his way along the road. The birds had not yet begun to sing, but the rustling noises of the night had ceased. The silent highway was consecrated to his proud progress. He staggered happily like a tired child returning from a lovely birthday walk: his death in the little bedroom, which for the first time he would have to himself, was a culminating treat to be gloated over like the promise of a favorite pudding for supper. As he walked he brooded dozingly on large and swelling thoughts. Like all people of weak passions and enterprise he loved to think of Napoleon, and in the shadow of the great asylum wall he strutted a few steps of his advance from murder to suicide, with arms crossed on his breast and thin legs trying to strut massively. He was so happy. He wished that a military band went before him, and pretended that the high hedges were solemn lines of men, stricken in awe to silence as their king rode out to some nobly self-chosen doom. Vast he seemed to himself, and magnificent like music, and solemn like the Sphinx. He had saved the earth from corruption by killing Evadne, for whom he now felt the unremorseful pity a conqueror might bestow on a devastated empire. He might have grieved that his victory brought him death, but with immense pride he found that the occasion was exactly described by a text. "He saved others, Himself He could not save."[3] He had missed the stile in the field above Sumatra Crescent and had to go back and hunt for it in the hedge. So quickly had his satisfaction borne him home.

2. From the hymn *Lead Kindly Light*, by John Henry Cardinal Newman (1801–1890): "I loved the garish day, and, spite of fears, / Pride ruled my will: remember not past years."
3. I.e., Christ (Matthew 27:42).

The field had the fantastic air that jerry-builders[4] give to land poised on the knife-edge of town and country, so that he walked in romance to his very door. The unmarred grass sloped to a stone-hedge of towers of loose brick, trenches and mounds of shining clay, and the fine intentful spires of the scaffolding round the last unfinished house. And he looked down on Petrick. Though to the actual eye it was but a confusion of dark instances through the twilight, a breaking of velvety perspectives, he saw more intensely than ever before its squalid walls and squalid homes where mean men and mean women enlaced their unwholesome lives. Yet he did not shrink from entering for his great experience, as Christ did not shrink from being born in a stable. He swaggered with humility over the trodden mud of the field and the new white flags of Sumatra Crescent. Down the road before him there passed a dim figure, who paused at each lamp-post and raised a long wand to behead the yellow gasflowers that were now wilting before the dawn; a ghostly herald preparing the world to be his deathbed. The crescent curved in quiet darkness, save for one house, where blazed a gas-lit room with undrawn blinds. The brightness had the startled quality of a scream. He looked in almost anxiously as he passed, and met the blank eyes of a man in evening clothes who stood by the window shaking a medicine bottle. His face was like a wax mask softened by heat: the features were blurred with the suffering which comes from the spectacle of suffering. His eyes lay unshiftingly on George's face as he went by and he went on shaking the bottle. It seemed as though he would never stop.

In the hour of his grandeur George was not forgetful of the griefs of the little human people, but interceded with God for the sake of this stranger. Everything was beautiful, beautiful, beautiful.

His own little house looked solemn as a temple. He leaned against the lamp-post at the gate and stared at its empty windows and neat bricks. The disorder of the shattered pane of glass could be overlooked by considering a sign that this house was a holy place, like the Passover blood on the lintel.[5] The propriety of the evenly drawn blind pleased him enormously. He had always known that this was how the great tragic things of the world had accomplished themselves: quietly. Evadne's raging activity belonged to trivial or annoying things like spring-cleaning or thunderstorms. Well, the house belonged to him now. He opened the gate and went up the asphalt path, sourly noticing that Evadne had as usual left out the lawnmower, though it might very easily have rained, with the wind coming up as it was. A stray cat that had been sleeping in the tuft of pampas grass in the middle of the lawn was roused by his coming, and fled insolently close to his legs. He hated all wild homeless things, and bent for a stone to throw at it. But instead his fingers touched a slug, which reminded him of the feeling of Evadne's flesh through the slit in her bathing-dress. And suddenly the garden was possessed by her presence; she seemed to amble there as she had so often done, sowing seeds unwisely and tormenting the last days of an ailing geranium by insane transplantation, exclaiming absurdly over such mere weeds as morning glory. He caught the very clucking of her voice. . . . The front door opened at his touch.

The little lobby with its closed doors seemed stuffed with expectant silence.

4. Builders whose work is cheap and careless.
5. The blood on the door was a sign to God on the eve of the Exodus to pass over the houses of the Israelites while killing the first-born children of the Egyptians (Exodus 12:13).

He realized that he had come to the theatre of his great adventure. Then panic seized him. Because this was the home where he and she had lived together so horribly he doubted whether he could do this splendid momentous thing, for here he had always been a poor thing with the habit of failure. His heart beat in him more quickly than his raw feet could pad up the oil-clothed stairs. Behind the deal door at the end of the passage was death. Nothingness! It would escape him, even the idea of it would escape him if he did not go to it at once. When he burst at last into its presence he felt so victorious that he sank back against the door waiting for death to come to him without turning on the gas. He was so happy. His death was coming true.

But Evadne lay on his deathbed. She slept there soundly, with her head flung back on the pillows so that her eyes and brow seemed small in shadow, and her mouth and jaw huge above her thick throat in the light. Her wet hair straggled across the pillow on to a broken cane chair covered with her tumbled clothes. Her breast, silvered with sweat, shone in the ray of the street lamp that had always disturbed their nights. The counterpane rose enormously over her hips in rolls of glazed linen. Out of mere innocent sleep her sensuality was distilling a most drunken pleasure.

Not for one moment did he think this a phantasmic appearance. Evadne was not the sort of woman to have a ghost.

Still leaning against the door he tried to think it all out, but his thoughts came brokenly, because the dawnlight flowing in at the window confused him by its pale glare and that lax figure on the bed held his attention. It must have been that when he laid his murderous hands on her head she had simply dropped below the surface and swum a few strokes under water as any expert swimmer can. Probably he had never even put her into danger, for she was a great lusty creature and the weir[6] was a little place. He had imagined the wonder and peril of the battle as he had imagined his victory. He sneezed exhaustingly, and from his physical distress realized how absurd it was ever to have thought that he had killed her. Bodies like his do not kill bodies like hers.

Now his soul was naked and lonely as though the walls of his body had fallen in at death, and the grossness of Evadne's sleep made him suffer more unlovely a destitution than any old beggarwoman squatting by the roadside in the rain. He had thought he had had what every man most desires: one night of power over a woman for the business of murder or love. But it had been a lie. Nothing beautiful had ever happened to him. He would have wept, but the hatred he had learnt on the moors obstructed all tears in his throat. At least this night had given him passion enough to put an end to it all.

Quietly he went to the window and drew down the sash. There was no fireplace, so that sealed the room. Then he crept over to the gas bracket and raised his thin hand, as he had imagined in his hour of vain glory by the lake. He had forgotten Evadne's thrifty habit of turning off the gas at the main to prevent leakage when she went to bed.

He was beaten. He undressed and got into bed; as he had done every night for ten years, and as he would do every night until he died. Still sleeping, Evadne caressed him with warm arms.

1914, 1982

6. A dam or a fenced enclosure in the water for catching fish.

DOROTHY PARKER
1893–1967

"Brevity is the soul of Lingerie," Dorothy Parker announced in a *Vogue* advertisement that captured the witty brevity that would make her famous in the 1920s and 1930s. Whether in conversation she dubbed a young man "a rhinestone in the rough" or, as "Constant Reader" in *The New Yorker*, reviewed *The House at Pooh Corner* by protesting that "Tonstant Weader Fwowed Up," the wisecracking Parker epitomized style in New York, but she also managed, through an unfailing sense of humor and an uncanny ear for dialogue, to express her dissatisfaction with herself and with the society she so flamboyantly inhabited.

Dorothy Rothschild was the daughter of a Scottish mother, who died when the writer was a young child, and a Jewish garment manufacturer, who remarried a woman Dorothy disliked as much as she disliked her father. She grew up on the Upper West Side of Manhattan, and attended first a Catholic convent school and then Miss Dana's School in Morristown, New Jersey. After a brief stint writing captions for fashion photographs at *Vogue*, she was hired as a drama critic by Frank Crowninshield, the editor of *Vanity Fair*. Friendly with the playwright Robert Sherwood, the humorist Robert Benchley, and the newspaper writer Harold Ross, she became a prominent member of the Algonquin Hotel's Round Table (a lively lunch group) and, through her sketches and dialogues, she helped shape the character of *The New Yorker*, which Ross founded in 1925.

She had married Edwin Pond Parker II, a Wall Street businessman, in 1917, but they separated soon after his return from World War I and divorced in 1928. Parker's love life was never simple. After an abortion in 1923, she tried unsuccessfully to commit suicide. In the 1930s, she married Alan Campbell, a bisexual writer eleven years her junior, and they subsequently divorced (1947), remarried (1950), separated (1953), and reunited (1956) until his death in 1963. Throughout this time, however, Parker continued to produce successful criticism, fiction, and verse. Her reviews and stories appeared in *The New Yorker* at irregular intervals from 1926 until 1955. In 1926, her first collection of verse, *Enough Rope*, was a smash success. Volumes like *Sunset Gun* (1928), *Death and Taxes* (1931), and *Not So Deep as a Well* (1936) were received just as favorably. Parker's protests against the execution of the anarchists Sacco and Vanzetti and her work against fascism during the Spanish Civil War made her conspicuous when she and Campbell earned $5,000 a week in Hollywood during the late 1930s; by the 1940s the couple were blacklisted for their political views. Her last years were sadly marked by self-doubt about her literary accomplishments and by her reliance on alcohol. Yet in stories like *The Waltz* and in poems like those in *A Pig's-Eye View of Literature*, she had satirized literary, social, and sexual pieties with sardonic exuberance.

Résumé[1]

Razors pain you;
Rivers are damp;
Acids stain you;
And drugs cause cramp.
Guns aren't lawful; 5

1. Summary.

Nooses give;
Gas smells awful;
You might as well live

1926

One Perfect Rose

A single flow'r he sent me, since we met.
 All tenderly his messenger he chose;
Deep-hearted, pure, with scented dew still wet—
 One perfect rose.

I knew the language of the flowers; 5
 "My fragile leaves," it said, "his heart enclose."
Love long has taken for his amulet
 One perfect rose.

Why is it no one ever sent me yet
 One perfect limousine, do you suppose? 10
Ah no, it's always just my luck to get
 One perfect rose.

1926

News Item

Men seldom make passes
At girls who wear glasses.

1926

Song of One of the Girls

Here in my heart I am Helen;
 I'm Aspasia and Hero, at least.
I'm Judith, and Jael, and Madame de Staël;
 I'm Salome,¹ moon of the East.

Here in my soul I am Sappho; 5
 Lady Hamilton am I, as well.
In me Recamier vies with Kitty O'Shea,
 With Dido, and Eve, and poor Nell.²

1. The beautiful daughter of Queen Herodias who demanded that the head of John the Baptist be brought to her. Helen of Troy was a Greek woman renowned for her beauty. Aspasia was the consort of the Greek statesman Pericles. Hero was a Greek woman whose lover, Leander, swam the Hellespont nightly to see her. Judith was a courageous Jewish woman who killed Israel's enemy Holofernes singlehandedly; Jael was a Jewish woman who similarly killed the enemy general Sisera. Madame de Staël (1766–1817), French writer.
2. A girl who dies in Charles Dickens's novel *The Old Curiosity Shop* (1840–41). Sappho (c. 600 B.C.), Greek lyric poet. Lady Hamilton (1765–1815), mistress of the English admiral Lord Nelson. Madame Récamier (1777–1849), French beauty and friend of Madame de Staël. Kitty O'Shea was the wife of an Irish patriot; her adultery with Charles Parnell (1845–1891), the charismatic Irish leader, brought about his downfall. Dido was the queen of ancient Carthage, abandoned by her lover Aeneas in Virgil's *Aeneid*. Eve was the first woman created by God in the Book of Genesis.

I'm of the glamorous ladies
 At whose beckoning history shook.
But you are a man, and see only my pan,[3] 10
 So I stay at home with a book.

1926

From A Pig's-Eye View of Literature

The Lives and Times of John Keats, Percy Bysshe Shelley, and George Gordon Noel, Lord Byron[1]

Byron and Shelley and Keats
Were a trio of lyrical treats.
The forehead of Shelley was cluttered with curls
And Keats never was a descendant of earls,
And Byron walked out with a number of girls, 5
 But it didn't impair the poetical feats
 Of Byron and Shelley,
 Of Byron and Shelley,
Of Byron and Shelley and Keats.

Oscar Wilde[2]

If, with the literate, I am
Impelled to try an epigram,
I never seek to take the credit;
We all assume that Oscar said it.

Harriet Beecher Stowe[3]

The pure and worthy Mrs. Stowe
Is one we all are proud to know
As mother, wife, and authoress—
Thank God, I am content with less!

D. G. Rossetti[4]

Dante Gabriel Rossetti
Buried all of his *libretti*,[5]
Thought the matter over—then
Went and dug them up again.

Thomas Carlyle[6]

Carlyle combined the lit'ry life
With throwing teacups at his wife,

3. Face.
1. Keats (1795–1821), Shelley (1792–1822), and Byron (1788–1824), major Romantic poets. Keats was of working-class descent, and Byron was notorious for his philandering.
2. Irish writer (1854–1900), famous for his wit.
3. American novelist and activist (1811–1896), the author of the antislavery novel *Uncle Tom's Cabin*.
4. English poet and painter (1828–1882).
5. Books (Italian). Rossetti actually buried his manuscripts in his wife's coffin in 1862, then recovered them eight years later.
6. Scottish essayist and historian (1795–1881).

Remarking, rather testily,
"Oh, stop your dodging, Mrs. C.!"

Alfred, Lord Tennyson[7]

Should Heaven send me any son,
I hope he's not like Tennyson.
I'd rather have him play a fiddle
Than rise and bow and speak an idyll.[8]

Walter Savage Landor[9]

Upon the work of Walter Landor
I am unfit to write with candor.
If you can read it, well and good;
But as for me, I never could.

George Sand[1]

What time the gifted lady took
Away from paper, pen, and book,
She spent in amorous dalliance
(They do those things so well in France).

1928

The Waltz

Why, thank you so much. I'd adore to.

I don't want to dance with him. I don't want to dance with anybody. And
even if I did, it wouldn't be him. He'd be well down among the last ten. I've
seen the way he dances; it looks likes something you do on Saint Walpurgis
Night.[1] Just think, not a quarter of an hour ago, here I was sitting, feeling so
sorry for the poor girl he was dancing with. And now *I'm* going to be the poor
girl. Well, well. Isn't it a small world?

And a peach of a world, too. A true little corker. Its events are so fascinat-
ingly unpredictable, are not they? Here I was, minding my own business, not
doing a stitch of harm to any living soul. And then he comes into my life, all
smiles and city manners, to sue me for the favor of one memorable mazurka.[2]
Why, he scarcely knows my name, let alone what it stands for. It stands for
Despair, Bewilderment, Futility, Degradation, and Premeditated Murder, but
little does he wot. I don't wot his name, either; I haven't any idea what it is.
Jukes,[3] would be my guess from the look in his eyes. How do you do, Mr. Jukes?
And how is that dear little brother of yours, with the two heads?

Ah, now why did he have to come around me, with his low requests? Why
can't he let me lead my own life? I ask so little—just to be left alone in my

7. English poet (1809–1892).
8. A poem describing a scene or episode. Tennyson wrote a long Arthurian poem called *Idylls of the King.*
9. English lyric poet (1775–1843).
1. The pen name of Aurore Dupin (1804–1876), French novelist.
1. The eve of May Day is the feast of St. Walpurga,

traditionally thought to be a witches' sabbat.
2. A Polish folk dance that, like the waltz, is in three/four time.
3. The name given to a much-studied, inbred 19th-century New York family characterized by criminality, disease, and feeblemindedness.

quiet corner of the table, to do my evening brooding over all my sorrows. And he must come, with his bows and his scrapes and his may-I-have-this ones. And I had to go and tell him that I'd adore to dance with him. I cannot understand why I wasn't struck right down dead. Yes, and being struck dead would look like a day in the country, compared to struggling out a dance with this boy. But what could I do? Everyone else at the table had got up to dance, except him and me. There was I, trapped. Trapped like a trap in a trap.

What can you say, when a man asks you to dance with him? I most certainly will *not* dance with you, I'll see you in hell first. Why, thank you, I'd like to awfully, but I'm having labor pains. Oh, yes, *do* let's dance together—it's so nice to meet a man who isn't a scaredy-cat about catching my beri-beri.[4] No. There was nothing for me to do, but say I'd adore to. Well, we might as well get it over with. All right, Cannonball, let's run out on the field. You won the toss; you can lead.

Why, I think it's more of a waltz, really. Isn't it? We might just listen to the music a second. Shall we? Oh, yes, it's a waltz. Mind? Why, I'm simply thrilled. I'd love to waltz with you.

I'd love to waltz with you. I'd love to waltz with you. I'd love to have my tonsils out, I'd love to be in a midnight fire at sea. Well, it's too late now. We're getting under way. *Oh.* Oh, dear. Oh, dear, dear, dear. Oh, this is even worse than I thought it would be. I suppose that's the one dependable law of life—everything is always worse than you thought it was going to be. Oh, if I had any real grasp of what this dance would be like, I'd have held out for sitting it out. Well, it will probably amount to the same thing in the end.We'll be sitting it out on the floor in a minute, if he keeps this up.

I'm so glad I brought it to his attention that this is a waltz they're playing. Heaven knows what might have happened, if he had thought it was something fast; we'd have blown the sides right out of the building. Why does he always want to be somewhere that he isn't? Why can't we stay in one place just long enough to get acclimated? It's this constant rush, rush, rush, that's the curse of American life. That's the reason that we're all of us so—*Ow!* For God's sake, don't *kick*, you idiot; this is only second down. Oh, my shin. My poor, poor shin, that I've had ever since I was a little girl!

Oh, no, no, no. Goodness, no. It didn't hurt the least little bit. And anyway it was my fault. Really it was. Truly. Well, you're just being sweet, to say that. It really was all my fault.

I wonder what I'd better do—kill him this instant, with my naked hands, or wait and let him drop in his traces. Maybe it's best not to make a scene. I guess I'll just lie low, and watch the pace get him. He can't keep this up indefinitely—he's only flesh and blood. Die he must, and die he shall, for what he did to me. I don't want to be of the over-sensitive type, but you can't tell me that kick was unpremeditated. Freud says there are no accidents.[5] I've led no cloistered life, I've known dancing partners who have spoiled my slippers and torn my dress; but when it come to kicking, I am Outraged Womanhood. When you kick me in the shin, *smile*.

Maybe he didn't do it maliciously. Maybe it's just his way of showing his

4. A vitamin deficiency disease that causes muscle weakness, especially in the legs.
5. Sigmund Freud (1856–1939), the founder of psy-choanalysis, argued that slips of the tongue and other "mistakes" actually reveal suppressed wishes and ideas.

high spirits. I suppose I ought to be glad that one of us is having such a good time. I suppose I ought to think myself lucky if he brings me back alive. Maybe it's captious to demand of a practically strange man that he leave your shins as he found them. After all, the poor boy's doing the best he can. Probably he grew up in the hill country, and never had no larnin'. I bet they had to throw him on his back to get shoes on him.

Yes, it's lovely, isn't it? It's simply lovely. It's the loveliest waltz. Isn't it? Oh, I think it's lovely, too.

Why, I'm getting positively drawn to the Triple Threat here. He's my hero. He has the heart of a lion, and the sinews of a buffalo. Look at him—never a thought of the consequences, never afraid of his face, hurling himself into every scrimmage, eyes shining, checks ablaze. And shall it be said that I hung back? No, a thousand times no. What's it to me if I have to spend the next couple of years in a plaster cast? Come on, Butch, right through them! Who wants to live forever?

Oh. Oh, dear. Oh, he's all right, thank goodness. For a while I thought they'd have to carry him off the field. Ah, I couldn't bear to have anything happen to him. I love him. I love him better than anybody in the world. Look at the spirit he gets into a dreary, commonplace waltz; how effete the other dancers seem, beside him. He is youth and vigor and courage, he is strength and gaiety and—Ow! Get off my instep, you hulking peasant! What do you think I am, anyway—a gangplank? Ow!

No, of course it didn't hurt. Why, it didn't a bit. Honestly. And it was all my fault. You see, that little step of yours—well, it's perfectly lovely, but it's just a tiny bit tricky to follow at first. Oh, did you work it up yourself? You really did? Well, aren't you amazing! Oh, now I think I've got it. Oh, I think it's lovely. I was watching you do it when you were dancing before. It's awfully effective when you look at it.

It's awfully effective when you look at it. I bet I'm awfully effective when you look at me. My hair is hanging along my cheeks, my skirt is swaddled about me, I can feel the cold damp of my brow. I must look like something out of the "Fall of the House of Usher." This sort of thing takes a fearful toll of a woman my age. And he worked up his little step himself, he with his degenerate cunning. And it was just a tiny bit tricky at first, but now I think I've got it. Two stumbles, slip, and a twenty-yard dash; yes. I've got it. I've got several other things, too, including a split shin and a bitter heart. I hate this creature I'm chained to. I hated him the moment I saw his leering, bestial face. And here I've been locked in his noxious embrace for the thirty-five years this waltz has lasted. Is that orchestra never going to stop playing? Or must this obscene travesty of a dance go on until hell burns out?

Oh, they're going to play another encore. Oh, goody. Oh, that's lovely. Tired? I should say I'm not tired. I'd like to go on like this forever.

I should say I'm not tired. I'm dead, that's all I am. Dead, and in what a cause! And the music is never going to stop playing, and we're going on like this, Double-Time Charlie and I, throughout eternity. I suppose I won't care any more, after the first hundred thousand years. I suppose nothing will matter then, not heat nor pain nor broken heart nor cruel, aching weariness. Well. It can't come too soon for me.

I wonder why I didn't tell him I was tired. I wonder why I didn't suggest going back to the table. I could have said let's just listen to the music. Yes, and

if he would, that would be the first bit of attention he has given it all evening. George Jean Nathan[6] said that the lovely rhythms of the waltz should be listened to in stillness and not be accompanied by strange gyrations of the human body. I think that's what he said. I think it was George Jean Nathan. Anyhow, whatever he said whoever he was and whatever he's doing now, he's better off than I am. That's safe. Anybody who isn't waltzing with this Mrs. O'Leary's cow[7] I've got here is having a good time.

Still if we were back at the table, I'd probably have to talk to him. Look at him—what could you say to a thing like that! Did you go to the circus this year, what's your favorite kind of ice cream, how do you spell cat? I guess I'm as well off here. As well off as if I were in a cement mixer in full action.

I'm past all feeling now. The only way I can tell when he steps on me is that I can hear the splintering of bones. And all the events of my life are passing before my eyes. There was the time I was in a hurricane in the West Indies, there was the day I got my head cut open in the taxi smash, there was the night the drunken lady threw a bronze ash-tray at her own true love and got me instead, there was that summer that the sailboat kept capsizing. Ah, what an easy, peaceful time was mine, until I fell in with Swifty, here. I didn't know what trouble was, before I got drawn into this *danse macabre*.[8] I think my mind is beginning to wander. It almost seems to me as if the orchestra were stopping. It couldn't be, of course; it could never, never be. And yet in my ears there is a silence like the sound of angel voices. . . .

Oh, they've stopped, the mean things. They're not going to play any more. Oh darn. Oh, do you think they would? Do you really think so, if you gave them twenty dollars? Oh, that would be lovely. And look, do tell them to play the same thing. I'd simply adore to go on waltzing.

1930

6. American editor, writer, and dramatic critic (1882–1958).
7. The legendary cause (by kicking over a lantern) of
the devastating 1871 Chicago fire.
8. Dance of death (French).

JEAN RHYS
1894?–1979

Described by one friend as "a shy, gentle and almost fatally impractical person," the novelist Jean Rhys was nevertheless thought by her mentor and sometime lover, Ford Madox Ford, to have "a terrifying insight, and a terrific . . . passion for stating the case of the underdog." Ford's comment, made early in Rhys's career, was an acute one, for, in five novels and a number of short stories, Rhys established a reputation for subtlety and style; more specifically, exploring the pain of wounded or abandoned women, she created a haunting landscape of anxiety that provides a kind of female equivalent to the wastelands of metaphysical despair constructed by such male contemporaries as the playwright Samuel Beckett and the poet T. S. Eliot.

Like the protagonist of *Wide Sargasso Sea* (1966), one of her most celebrated novels, Rhys was born and raised in Roseau, Dominica, in the West Indies. The girl who was originally named Ella Gwendolyn Rhys Williams was educated at a convent school in Roseau. She traveled to London at the age of sixteen, where she studied for a term at the Royal Academy of Dramatic Art, then toured England as

a chorus girl in a musical comedy during the years of World War I. Married for a time to the poet Max Hamer, she had one child. Much of her life, however, was spent in Paris and in travels on the Continent, an expatriation whose alienating implications she captured in, for instance, her portrait of the numbed and lonely heroine of *Good Morning, Midnight* (1939).

According to one commentator, Rhys "had always kept 'a sort of diary,'" but she didn't think seriously of writing until a time when she was desperate for money, which fortunately coincided with her 'discovery' by . . . Ford." Once she began to write, though, she quickly became a serious professional: throughout her years of wandering, she was producing her poignant yet coolly understated novels and tales, and when she returned to settle in England—chiefly in London and Cornwall—she continued to write, although her reputation fell into an eclipse for some years. After *Good Morning, Midnight* was broadcast in England in 1957, Rhys was "rediscovered," however, and the subsequent publication of *Wide Sargasso Sea* was defined as "a magnificent comeback."

Whether or not *Wide Sargasso Sea* was a "comeback," it continued and elaborated a mode of psychological analysis that Rhys had already pioneered in earlier works. In particular, it developed a technique of literary allusion hinted at in the title of *Good Morning, Midnight*—a line drawn from one of Emily Dickinson's poems ("Good Morning—Midnight— / I'm coming Home— / Day—got tired of Me—," no. 425), for *Wide Sargasso Sea* is a disturbing yet brilliantly revisionary retelling of the story of *Jane Eyre* from the point of view of Bertha Mason Rochester, the madwoman sequestered in Thornfield's attic. Describing Bertha's experience as a repressed daughter and an oppressed wife, Rhys continued the delineation of a landscape of female despair that she had begun in her earlier novels, but now she located that countryside of anguish more specifically in the context of the women's literary tradition. Acknowledging the affinity between the anxieties of her protagonists and the pain articulated by such precursors as Dickinson and Brontë, Rhys elaborated what Ford had called her "terrifying insight" into the lives of "underdogs"—forgotten women imprisoned by self or society in attics and rooming houses, rebellious women whose stories she recounted with sympathy and sensitivity. In *The Insect World*, for example, Rhys illuminates the physical and psychological suffering of the character called "the girl they left behind" during World War II—i.e., the female civilians "left behind" on the home front, where they endured the terror of nightly bombings and daily scarcities.

The Insect World

Audrey began to read. Her book was called *Nothing So Blue*. It was set in the tropics. She started at the paragraph which described the habits of an insect called the jigger.[1]

Almost any book was better than life, Audrey thought. Or rather, life as she was living it. Of course, life would soon change, open out, become quite different. You couldn't go on if you didn't hope that, could you? But for the time being there was no doubt that it was pleasant to get away from it. And books could take her away.

She could give herself up to the written word as naturally as a good dancer to music or a fine swimmer to water. The only difficulty was that after finishing the last sentence she was left with a feeling at once hollow and uncomfortably full. Exactly like indigestion. It was perhaps for this reason that she never forgot that books were one thing and that life was another.

1. I.e., the chigger.

When it came to life Audrey was practical. She accepted all she was told to accept. And there had been quite a lot of it. She had been in London for the last five years but for one short holiday. There had been the big blitz, then the uneasy lull, then the little blitz, now the fly bombs.[2] But she still accepted all she was told to accept, tried to remember all she was told to remember. The trouble was that she could not always forget all she was told to forget. She could not forget, for instance, that on her next birthday she would be twenty-nine years of age. Not a Girl any longer. Not really. The war had already gobbled up several years and who knew how long it would go on. Audrey dreaded growing old. She disliked and avoided old people and thought with horror of herself as old. She had never told anyone her real and especial reason for loathing the war. She had never spoken of it—even to her friend Monica.

Monica, who was an optimist five years younger than Audrey, was sure that the war would end soon.

"People always think that wars will end soon. But they don't," said Audrey. "Why, one lasted for a hundred years. What about that?"

Monica said: "But that was centuries ago and quite different. Nothing to do with Now."

But Audrey wasn't at all sure that it was so very different.

"It's as if I'm twins," she had said to Monica one day in an attempt to explain herself. "Do you ever feel like that ?" But it seemed that Monica never did feel like that or if she did she didn't want to talk about it.

Yet there it was. Only one of the twins accepted. The other felt lost, betrayed, forsaken, a wanderer in a very dark wood. The other told her that all she accepted so meekly was quite mad, potty. And here even books let her down, for no book—at least no book that Audrey had ever read—even hinted at this essential wrongness or pottiness.

Only yesterday, for instance, she had come across it in *Nothing So Blue*. *Nothing So Blue* belonged to her, for she often bought books—most of them Penguins, but some from second-hand shops. She always wrote her name on the fly-leaf and tried to blot out any signs of previous ownership. But this book had been very difficult. It had taken her more than an hour to rub out the pencil marks that had been found all through it. They began harmlessly, "Read and enjoyed by Charles Edwin Roofe in this Year of our Salvation MCMXLII,[3] which, being interpreted is Thank You Very Much," continued Blue? Rather pink, I think" and, throughout the whole of the book, the word "blue"—which of course often occurred—was underlined and in the margin there would be a question mark, a note of exclamation, or "Ha, ha." "Nauseating," he had written on the page which began "I looked her over and decided she would do." Then came the real love affair with the beautiful English girl who smelt of daffodils and Mr Roofe had relapsed into "Ha, ha—sez you!" But it was on page 166 that Audrey had a shock. He had written "Women are an unspeakable abomination" with such force that the pencil had driven through the paper. She had torn the page out and thrown it into the fireplace. Fancy that! There was no fire, of course, so she was able to pick it up, smooth it out and stick it back.

2. The Blitz, the German night bombing raids on London and other British cities, lasted from September 1940 to May 1941. In the "little blitz" of January to April 1944 were the heaviest bombing raids since 1941. The "flying bombs" were the V-1 (and then V-2) rockets, which began to be used in June 1944.
3. I.e., 1942.

"Why should I spoil my book ?" she had thought. All the same she felt terribly down for some reason. And yet, she told herself, "I bet if you met that man he would be awfully ordinary, just like everybody else." It was something about his small, neat, precise handwriting that made her think so. But it was always the most ordinary things that suddenly turned round and showed you another face, a terrifying face. That was the hidden horror, the horror everybody pretended did not exist, the horror that was responsible for all the other horrors.

The book was not so cheering, either. It was about damp, moist heat, birds that did not sing, flowers that had no scent. Then there was this horrible girl whom the hero simply had to make love to, though he didn't really want to, and when the lovely, cool English girl heard about it she turned him down.

The natives were surly. They always seemed to be jeering behind your back. And they were stupid. They believed everything they were told, so that they could be easily worked up against somebody. Then they became cruel—so horribly cruel, you wouldn't believe . . .

And the insects. Not only the rats, snakes and poisonous spiders, scorpions, centipedes, millions of termites in their earth-colored nests from which branched out yards of elaborately built communication lines leading sometimes to a smaller nest, sometimes to an untouched part of the tree on which they were feeding, while sometimes they just petered out, empty. It was no use poking at a nest with a stick. It seemed vulnerable, but the insects would swarm, whitely horrible, to its defense, and would rebuild it in a night. The only thing was to smoke them out. Burn them alive-oh. And even then some would escape and at once start building somewhere else.

Finally, there were the minute crawling unseen things that got at you as you walked along harmlessly. Most horrible of all these was the Jigger.

Audrey stopped reading. She had a headache. Perhaps that was because she had not had anything to eat all day; unless you can count a cup of tea at eight in the morning as something to eat. But she did not often get a weekday off and when she did not a moment must be wasted. So from ten to two, regardless of sirens wailing, she went shopping in Oxford Street, and she skipped lunch. She bought stockings, a nightgown and a dress. It was buying the dress that had taken it out of her. The assistant had tried to sell her a print dress a size too big and, when she did not want it, had implied that it was unpatriotic to make so much fuss about what she wore. "But the colors are so glaring and it doesn't fit. It's much too short," Audrey said.

"You could easily let it down."

Audrey said: "But there's nothing to let down. I'd like to try on that dress over there."

"It's a very small size."

"Well, I'm thin enough," said Audrey defiantly. "How much thinner d'you want me to be?"

"But that's a dress for a girl," the assistant said.

And suddenly, what with the pain in her back and everything, Audrey had wanted to cry. She nearly said "I work just as hard as you," but she was too dignified.

"The gray one looks a pretty shape," she said. "Not so drear Drear," she repeated, because that was a good word and if the assistant knew anything she would place her by it. But the woman, not at all impressed, stared over her head.

"The dresses on that rail aren't your size. You can try one on if you like but it wouldn't be any use. You could easily let down the print one," she repeated maddeningly.

Audrey had felt like a wet rag after her defeat by the shop assistant, for she had ended by buying the print dress. It would not be enough to go and spruce up in the Ladies' Room on the fifth floor—which would be milling full of Old Things—so she had gone home again, back to the flat she shared with Monica. There had not been time to eat anything, but she had put on the new dress and it looked even worse than it had looked in the shop. From the neck to the waist it was enormous, or shapeless. The skirt, on the other hand, was very short and skimpy and two buttons came off in her hand; she had to wait and sew them on again.

It had all made her very tired. And she would be late for tea at Roberta's....

"I wish I lived here," she thought when she came out of the Tube[4] station. But she often thought that when she went to a different part of London. "It's nicer here," she'd think, "I might be happier here."

Her friend Roberta's house was painted green and had a small garden. Audrey felt envious as she pressed the bell. And still more envious when Roberta came to the door wearing a flowered house coat, led the way into a pretty sitting-room and collapsed onto her sofa in a filmstar attitude. Audrey's immediate thought was "What right has a woman got to be lolling about like that in wartime, even if she is going to have a baby?" But when she noticed Roberta's deep-circled eyes, her huge, pathetic stomach, her spoilt hands, her broken nails, and realized that her house coat had been made out of a pair of old curtains ("not half so pretty as she was. Looks much older") she said the usual things, warmly and sincerely.

But she hoped that, although it was nearly six by the silver clock, Roberta would offer her some tea and cake. Even a plain slice of bread—she could have wolfed that down.

"Why are you so late?" Roberta asked. "I suppose you've had tea," and hurried on before Audrey could open her mouth. "Have a chocolate biscuit."[5]

So Audrey ate a biscuit slowly. She felt she did not know Roberta well enough to say "I'm ravenous. I must have something to eat." Besides that was the funny thing. The more ravenous you grew, the more impossible it became to say "I'm ravenous."

"Is that a good book?" Roberta asked.

"I brought it to read on the Tube. It isn't bad."

Roberta flicked through the pages of *Nothing So Blue* without much interest. And she said "English people always mix up tropical places. My dear, I met a girl the other day who thought Moscow was the capital of India! Really, I think it's dangerous to be as ignorant as that, don't you?"

Roberta often talked about "English" people in that way. She had acquired the habit, Audrey thought, when she was out of England for two years before the war. She had lived for six months in New York. Then she had been to Miami, Trinidad, Bermuda—all those places—and no expense spared, or so she said. She had brought back all sorts of big ideas. Much too big. Gadgets for the kitchen. An extensive wardrobe. Expensive makeup. Having her hair and

4. The London underground (the city's subway system). 5. Cookie.

nails looked after every week at the hairdresser's. There was no end to it. Anyway, there was one good thing about the war. It had taken all that right off. Right off.

"Read what he says about jiggers," Audrey said.

"My dear," said Roberta, "he *is* piling it on."

"Do you mean that there aren't such things as jiggers?"

"Of course there are such things," Roberta said, "but they're only sand fleas. It's better not to go barefoot if you're frightened of them."

She explained about jiggers. They had nasty ways—the man wasn't so far wrong. She talked about tropical insects for some time after that she seemed to remember them more vividly than anything else. Then she read out bits of *Nothing So Blue*, laughing at it.

"If you must read all the time, you needn't believe everything you read."

"I don't," said Audrey. "if you knew how little I really believe you'd be surprised. Perhaps he doesn't see it the way you do. It all depends on how people see things. If someone wanted to write a horrible book about London, couldn't he write a horrible book? I wish somebody would. I'd buy it."

"You dope!" said Roberta affectionately.

When the time came to go Audrey walked back to the Tube station in a daze, and in a daze sat in the train until a jerk of the brain warned her that she had passed Leicester Square and now had to change at King's Cross. She felt very bad when she got out, as if she could flop any minute. There were so many people pushing, you got bewildered.

She tried to think about Monica, about the end of the journey, above all about food—warm, lovely food—but something had happened inside her head and she couldn't concentrate. She kept remembering the termites. Termites running along one of the covered ways that peter out and lead to nothing. When she came to the escalator she hesitated, afraid to get on it. The people clinging to the sides looked very like large insects. No, they didn't *look* like large insects: they were insects.

She got onto the escalator and stood staidly on the right-hand side. No running up for her tonight. She pressed her arm against her side and felt the book. That started her thinking about jiggers again. Jiggers got in under your skin when you didn't know it and laid eggs inside you. Just walking along, as you might be walking along the street to a Tube station, you caught a jigger as easily as you bought a newspaper or turned on the radio. And there you were—infected—and not knowing a thing about it.

In front of her stood an elderly woman with dark hair and mean-looking clothes. It was funny how she hated women like that. It was funny how she hated most women anyway. Elderly women ought to stay at home. They oughtn't to walk about. Depressing people! Jutting out, that was what the woman was doing. Standing right in the middle, instead of in line. So that you could hardly blame the service girl, galloping up in a hurry, for giving her a good shove and saying under her breath "Oh get out of the way!" But she must have shoved too hard for the old thing tottered. She was going to fall. Audrey's heart jumped sickeningly into her mouth as she shut her eyes. She didn't want to see what it would look like, didn't want to hear the scream.

But no scream came and when Audrey opened her eyes she saw that the old woman had astonishingly saved herself. She had only stumbled down a couple of steps and clutched the rail again. She even managed to laugh and say "Now

1566

JEAN RHYS

I know where all the beef goes to!" Her face, though, was very white. So was Audrey's. Perhaps her heart kept turning over. So did Audrey's.

Even when she got out of the Tube the nightmare was not over. On the way home she had to walk up a little street which she hated and it was getting dark now. It was one of those streets which are nearly always empty. It had been badly blitzed and Audrey was sure that it was haunted. Weeds and wild-looking flowers were growing over the skeleton houses, over the piles of rubble. There were front doorsteps which looked as though they were hanging by a thread, and near one of them lived a black cat with green eyes. She liked cats but not this one, not this one. She was sure it wasn't a cat really.

Supposing the siren went? "If the siren goes when I'm in this street it'll mean that it's all U.P. with me." Supposing a man with a strange blank face and no eyebrows like that one who got into the Ladies at the cinema the other night and stood there grinning at them and nobody knew what to do so everybody pretended he wasn't there. Perhaps he was not there, either—supposing a man like that were to come up softly behind her, touch her shoulder, speak to her, she wouldn't be able to struggle, she would just lie down and die of fright, so much she hated that street. And she had to walk slowly because if she ran she would give whatever it was its opportunity and it would run after her. However, even walking slowly, it came to an end at last. Just round the corner in a placid ordinary street where all the damage had been tidied up was the third floor flat which she shared with Monica, also a typist in a government office.

The radio was on full tilt. The smell of cabbage drifted down the stairs. Monica, for once, was getting the meal ready. They ate out on Mondays, Wednesdays and Fridays, in on Tuesdays, Thursdays, Saturdays and Sundays. Audrey usually did the housework and cooking and Monica took charge of the ration books, stood in long queues to shop and lugged the laundry back and forwards every week because the van didn't call any longer.

"Hullo," said Monica.

Audrey answered her feebly, "Hullo."

Monica, a dark, pretty girl, put the food on the table and remarked at once, "You're a bit green in the face. Have you been drinking mock gin?"

"Oh, don't be funny. I haven't had much to eat today that's all."

After a few minutes Monica said impatiently, "Well why don't you eat then?"

"I think I've gone past it," said Audrey, fidgeting with the sausage and cabbage on her plate.

Monica began to read from the morning paper. She spoke loudly above the music on the radio.

"Have you seen this article about being a woman in Germany? It says they can't get any scent or eau-de-cologne or nail polish."

"Fancy that!" Audrey said. "Poor things!"

"It says the first thing Hitler stopped was nail polish. He began that way. I wonder why. He must have had a reason, mustn't he?"

"Why must he have had a reason?" said Audrey.

"Because," said Monica, "if they've got a girl thinking she isn't pretty, thinking she's shabby, they've got her where they want her, as a rule. And it might start with nail polish, see? And it says: 'All the old women and the middle-aged women look most terribly unhappy. They simply *slink* about,' it says."

"You surprise me," Audrey said. "Different in the Isle of Dogs, isn't it?"

She was fed up now and she wanted to be rude to somebody. "Oh *do* shut up," she said. "I'm not interested. Why should I have to cope with German women as well as all the women over here? What a nightmare!"

Monica opened her mouth to answer sharply; then shut it again. She was an even-tempered girl. She piled the plates onto a tray, took it into the kitchen and began to wash up.

As soon as she had gone Audrey turned off the radio and the light. Blissful sleep, lovely sleep, she never got enough of it. . . . On Sunday mornings, long after Monica was up, she would lie unconscious. A heavy sleeper, you might call her, except that her breathing was noiseless and shallow and that she lay so still, without tossing or turning. And then *She (who?) sent the gentle sleep from Heaven that slid into my soul. That slid into my soul. Sleep, Nature's sweet, something-or-the-other. The sleep that knits up the ravelled.*[6] . . .

It seemed that she had hardly shut her eyes when she was awake again. Monica was shaking her.

"What's the matter? Is it morning?" Audrey said. "What is it? What is it?"

"Oh, nothing at all," Monica said sarcastically. "You were only shrieking the place down."

"Was I?" Audrey said, interested. "What was I saying?"

"I don't know what you were saying and I don't care. But if you're trying to get us turned out, that's the way to do it. You know perfectly well that the woman downstairs is doing all she can to get us out because she says we are too noisy. You said something about jiggers. What are jiggers anyway?"

"It's slang for people in the Tube," Audrey answered glibly to her great surprise. "Didn't you know that?"

"Oh is it? No, I never heard that."

"The name comes from a tropical insect," Audrey said, "that gets in under your skin when you don't know it. It lays eggs and hatches them out and you don't know it. And there's another sort of tropical insect that lives in enormous cities. They have railways, Tubes, bridges, soldiers, wars, everything we have. And they have big cities, and smaller cities with roads going from one to another. Most of them are what they call workers. They never fly because they've lost their wings and they never make love either. They're just workers. Nobody quite knows how this is done, but they think it's the food. Other people say it's segregation. Don't you believe me?" she said, her voice rising. "Do you think I'm telling lies?"

"Of course I believe you," said Monica soothingly, "But I don't see why you should shout about it."

Audrey drew a deep breath. The corners of her mouth quivered. Then she said "Look I'm going to bed. I'm awfully tired. I'm going to take six aspirins and then go to bed. If the siren goes don't wake me up. Even if one of those things seems to be coming very close, don't wake me up. I don't want to be woken up whatever happens."

"Very well," Monica said. "All right, old girl."

<hr>

6. Compare with the following: Coleridge's *The Rime of the Ancient Mariner* (1798), part 5: "She sent the gentle sleep from Heaven / That slid into my soul"; Shakespeare's *2 Henry IV* 3.1.5–6: "O sleep! O gentle sleep! / Nature's soft nurse"; Shakespeare's *Macbeth* 2.2 33–34: "Sleep that knits up the ravell'd sleave of care."

Audrey rushed at her with clenched fists and began to shriek again. "Damn you, don't call me that. Damn your soul to everlasting hell *don't call me that....*"

1976

LOUISE BOGAN
1897–1970

"Women have no wilderness in them, / They are provident instead," wrote Louise Bogan in a famous poem entitled *Women*. Yet this scrupulous artist, who was from 1931 to 1969 the influential and fiercely independent poetry critic for *The New Yorker*, herself wrote poems that constituted rigorous and fearless explorations of an interior "wilderness," poems that—in the words of W. H. Auden, a fellow writer whom she much admired—"wrested beauty and truth out of dark places." Born in Livermore Falls, Maine, Bogan described herself as "the highly charged and neurotically inclined product of an extraordinary childhood and an unfortunate early marriage, into which last state I had rushed to escape the first." Her parents were genteelly impoverished and unhappily married, often separating for long periods, so that she later confessed that "I cannot bring myself to describe the horrors of the pre–1914 lower-middle-class life, in which they found themselves."

The family had moved to Boston in 1909, where the young Bogan entered Girls' Latin School and began to write poetry. In 1915, she enrolled as a freshman at Boston University, where two of her verses were printed in the literary magazine. But though she had been offered a scholarship to Radcliffe for the following year, she decided instead to marry Curt Alexander, a professional soldier, so that she could get away from the turmoil in her home. While living on an army base in the Panama Canal Zone, the couple had a daughter in 1917, but the marriage was indeed, in other ways, "unfortunate," and Bogan left her husband in 1919. The next year he died, and she received a small widow's pension, which enabled her to travel to Vienna in 1922, where she studied piano.

In 1923, after she had returned to New York, Bogan met Raymond Holden, a novelist and minor poet, whom she was to marry in 1925. Supporting herself at various odd jobs, she began seriously to write and publish; her work in this period included film criticism and poetry reviews as well as two well-received volumes of verse, *Body of This Death* (1923) and *Dark Summer* (1929). In 1931, just after she had begun her career as a poetry reviewer for *The New Yorker*, Bogan had the first of a series of nervous breakdowns that were to acquaint her with what Auden called "dark places." Recovering, she separated from Holden in 1934 and entered into a relationship with the poet Theodore Roethke, who became her lifelong friend and partisan. Her new collections appeared at regular intervals—*The Sleeping Fury* in 1937 and *Poems and New Poems* in 1941—and a growing number of prizes recognized the nature of her aesthetic achievement. After serving in 1945 as a Consultant in Poetry to the Library of Congress, she was awarded visiting professorships and literary residencies at several major institutions, including the University of Washington and Brandeis University. Her last book of verse, *The Blue Estuaries: Poems, 1923–1968*, appeared shortly before she resigned from her job as poetry reviewer for *The New Yorker* and a year before she died of a heart attack.

Throughout her successful and productive career, Bogan had remained an intensely private woman: she made few pronouncements on public events and, as the poem *Women* suggests, did not particularly identify herself as a feminist. Yet in a late essay on women poets she reminded her audience that "the word feminism

. . . is a word which has its own honor and radiance," and—though she had once claimed that she disliked "other women poets (jealousy!)"—she catalogued in some detail the achievements of literary women from Sappho to Virginia Woolf. What may seem at first like a puzzling inconsistency in her thought becomes easier to understand when one sets the bitterness this writer expresses in *Women* against the powerful reimagining of mythology that she undertakes in such poems as *Medusa* and *Cassandra*.

Medusa[1]

I had come to the house, in a cave of trees,
Facing a sheer sky.
Everything moved,—a bell hung ready to strike,
Sun and reflection wheeled by.

When the bare eyes were before me 5
And the hissing hair,
Held up at a window, seen through a door.
The stiff bald eyes, the serpents on the forehead
Formed in the air.

This is a dead scene forever now. 10
Nothing will ever stir.
The end will never brighten it more than this,
Nor the rain blur.

The water will always fall, and will not fall,
And the tipped bell make no sound. 15
The grass will always be growing for hay
Deep on the ground.

And I shall stand here like a shadow
Under the great balanced day,
My eyes on the yellow dust, that was lifting in the wind, 20
And does not drift away.

 1923

The Crows

The woman who has grown old
And knows desire must die,
Yet turns to love again,
Hears the crows' cry.

She is a stem long hardened, 5
A weed that no scythe mows.

1. In Greek myth, one of three snake-haired sisters called the Gorgons, the sight of whom turned all who looked at them to stone.

The heart's laughter will be to her
The crying of the crows.

Who slide in the air with the same voice
Over what yields not, and what yields, 10
Alike in spring, and when there is only bitter
Winter-burning in the fields.

<div style="text-align: right">1923</div>

Women

Women have no wilderness in them,
They are provident instead,
Content in the tight hot cell of their hearts
To eat dusty bread.

They do not see cattle cropping red winter grass, 5
They do not hear
Snow water going down under culverts
Shallow and clear.

They wait, when they should turn to journeys,
They stiffen, when they should bend. 10
They use against themselves that benevolence
To which no man is friend.

They cannot think of so many crops to a field
Or of clean wood cleft by an axe.
Their love is an eager meaninglessness 15
Too tense, or too lax.

They hear in every whisper that speaks to them
A shout and a cry.
As like as not, when they take life over their door-sills
They should let it go by. 20

<div style="text-align: right">1923</div>

Cassandra[1]

To me, one silly task is like another.
I bare the shambling tricks of lust and pride.
This flesh will never give a child its mother,—
Song, like a wing, tears through my breast, my side,
And madness chooses out my voice again, 5
Again. I am the chosen no hand saves:
The shrieking heaven lifted over men,
Not the dumb earth, wherein they set their graves.

<div style="text-align: right">1929</div>

1. Trojan princess with the gift of prophecy, but believed by no one.

The Crossed Apple

I've come to give you fruit from out my orchard,
Of wide report.
I have trees there that bear me many apples
Of every sort:

Clear, strekèd; red and russet; green and golden; 5
Sour and sweet.
This apple's from a tree yet unbeholden,
Where two kinds meet,—

So that this side is red without a dapple,
And this side's hue 10
Is clear and snowy. It's a lovely apple.
It is for you.

Within are five black pips as big as peas,
As you will find,
Potent to breed you five great apple trees 15
Of varying kind:

To breed you wood for fire, leaves for shade,
Apples for sauce
Oh, this is a good apple for a maid,
It is a cross, 20

Fine on the finer, so the flesh is tight,
And grained like silk.
Sweet Burning gave the red side, and the white
Is Meadow Milk.

Eat it; and you will taste more than the fruit; 25
The blossom, too,
The sun, the air, the darkness at the root,
The rain, the dew,

The earth we came to, and the time we flee,
The fire and the breast. 30
I claim the white part, maiden, that's for me.
You take the rest.

1929

Evening in the Sanitarium[1]

The free evening fades, outside the windows fastened with decorative
 iron grilles.
The lamps are lighted; the shades drawn; the nurses are watching a little.

1. Originally published with the subtitle *Imitated from Auden* (W. H. Auden, 1907–1973, English poet).

It is the hour of the complicated knitting on the safe bone needles; of the
 games of anagrams and bridge;
The deadly game of chess; the book held up like a mask.

The period of the wildest weeping, the fiercest delusion, is over. 5
The women rest their tired half-healed hearts; they are almost well.
Some of them will stay almost well always: the blunt-faced woman whose
 thinking dissolved
Under academic discipline; the manic-depressive girl
Now leveling off; one paranoiac afflicted with jealousy.
Another with persecution. Some alleviation has been possible. 10

O fortunate bride, who never again will become elated after childbirth!
O lucky older wife, who has been cured of feeling unwanted!
To the suburban railway station you will return, return,
To meet forever Jim home on the 5:35.
You will be again as normal and selfish and heartless as anybody else. 15

There is life left: the piano says it with its octave smile.
The soft carpets pad the thump and splinter of the suicide to be.
Everything will be splendid: the grandmother will not drink habitually.
The fruit salad will bloom on the plate like a bouquet
And the garden produce the blue-ribbon aquilegia.[2] 20
The cats will be glad; the fathers feel justified; the mothers relieved.
The sons and husbands will no longer need to pay the bills.
Childhoods will be put away, the obscene nightmare abated.

At the ends of the corridors the baths are running.
Mrs. C. again feels the shadow of the obsessive idea. 25
Miss R. looks at the mantel-piece, which must mean something.

 1941

Several Voices out of a Cloud

 Come, drunks and drug-takers; come, perverts unnerved!
 Receive the laurel,[1] given, though late, on merit; to whom and
 wherever deserved.

 Parochial punks, trimmers, nice people, joiners true-blue,
 Get the hell out of the way of the laurel. It is deathless[2] 5
 And it isn't for you.

 1941

The Dream

 O God, in the dream the terrible horse began
 To paw at the air, and make for me with his blows.

2. Columbine.

1. In classical Greece, a laurel wreath crowned the vic- tor in an athletic or poetic contest.

2. Because laurel is an evergreen.

Fear kept for thirty-five years poured through his mane,
And retribution equally old, or nearly, breathed through his nose.

Coward complete, I lay and wept on the ground 5
When some strong creature appeared, and leapt for the rein.
Another woman, as I lay half in a swound,
Leapt in the air, and clutched at the leather and chain.

Give him, she said, something of yours as a charm.
Throw him, she said, some poor thing you alone claim. 10
No, no, I cried, he hates me; he's out for harm,
And whether I yield or not, it is all the same.

But, like a lion in a legend, when I flung the glove
Pulled from my sweating, my cold right hand,
The terrible beast, that no one may understand 15
Came to my side, and put down his head in love.

1941

RUTH PITTER

1897–1992

"My purpose has never varied," wrote Ruth Pitter in a foreword to her *Collected Poems* (1969). "It has been simply to capture . . . some of the secret meanings which haunt life and language." Despite years of poverty and obscurity, Pitter did this in verses that were acclaimed by a range of literary figures, including the poet Hilaire Belloc and the critic Lord David Cecil, and that won the Hawthornden Prize, the Heinemann Award, and the Queen's Gold Medal for Poetry. Born in the East End of London, Pitter was the daughter of middle-class parents who, she once recalled, "loved poetry and were determined to impart it to their children." She herself began to write poems at the age of five, publishing her first book when she was in her early twenties but later acknowledging that "I produced little that I now think worth keeping until about the age of thirty."

After a comparatively sketchy education, Pitter worked in the British War Office during World War I, then studied various handicrafts and opened a shop where she sold hand-painted trays. Her major collections of verse include *A Mad Lady's Garland* (1935), *A Trophy of Arms* (1936), *The Spirit Watches* (1939), and *Collected Poems*. Her best work oscillates between grave meditation and sardonic wit, but throughout her career she consistently sought to express what she termed "the silent music, the dance in stillness . . . of which everything is full."

The Military Harpist

Strangely assorted, the shape of song and the bloody man.

Under the harp's gilt shoulder and rainlike strings,
Prawn-eyed, with prawnlike bristle, well-waxed moustache,
With long tight cavalry legs, and the spurred boot

Ready upon the swell, the Old Sweat waits. 5

Now dies, and dies hard, the stupid, well-relished fortissimo,
Wood-wind alone inviting the liquid tone,
The voice of the holy and uncontending, the harp.

Ceasing to ruminate interracial fornications,
He raises his hands, and his wicked old mug is David's,[1] 10
Pastoral, rapt, the king and the poet in innocence,
Singing Saul in himself asleep, and the ancient Devil
Clean out of countenance, as with an army of angels.

He is now where his bunion has no existence.
Breathing an atmosphere free of pipeclay[2] and swearing, 15
He wears the starched nightshirt of the hereafter, his halo
Is plain manly brass with a permanent polish,
Requiring no oily rag and no Soldier's Friend.[3]

His place is with the beloved poet of Israel,
With the wandering minnesinger[4] and the loves of Provence, 20
With Blondel[5] footsore and heartsore, the voice in the darkness
Crying like beauty bereaved beneath many a donjon,[6]
O Richard! O king! where is the lion of England?
With Howell, Llewellyn,[7] and far in the feral north
With the savage fame of the hero in glen and in ben, 25
At the morning discourse of saints in the island Eire,[8]
And at nameless doings in the stone-circle, the dreadful grove.

Thus far into the dark do I delve for his likeness:
He harps at the Druid[9] sacrifice, where the golden string
Sings to the golden knife and the victim's shriek. 30
Strangely assorted, the shape of song and the bloody man.

 1939

The Irish Patriarch

He bathes his soul in women's wrath;
His whiskers twinkle, and it seems
As if he trod some airy path
In that young land of warriors' dreams;

1. Ancient king of Israel, both a musician and military leader. As a youth, David sang and played before the previous king, Saul, who later turned against him.
2. A whitener, for sprucing up military uniforms.
3. A popular brand of metal polish.
4. Traveling poet and musician of the Middle Ages in Germany and Provence.
5. A French troubadour poet (12th century), companion to the English king Richard the Lion-Hearted. According to legend, Blondel discovered Richard imprisoned in the castle of Dürnstein while singing a song they had written together, to which the king sang back.
6. Massive tower in medieval castles.
7. Prince of northern Wales in the Middle Ages who revolted against the English king.
8. Ireland.
9. Ancient Celtic priest.
1. I.e., cold shower of water.

As if he took a needle-bath 5
In mountain falls, in tingling streams.

The man whom nagging drives to drink
Should learn from him, whom female rage
Seems but to make a precious link
With some sweet ancient heritage, 10
With women saying—huh!—what they think!
To the amusement of the sage.

O women, what a boon it is,
With workday worries at their worst,
When hordes of little miseries 15
Force us to speak our mind or burst,
To be Rich-angered Mistresses,[2]
Not Shrews and Vixens, Cross and Curst!

1966

Old Nelly's Birthday

She knows where to get cracked eggs, does Nelly.
Knows where to get them cheap:
Ninepence a dozen from that Mrs. Kelly.
Of course they will not keep,
But Nelly will make them into a jam sandwich[1] 5
Of most portentous size.
Now this jam sandwich is her secret language,
And sacred in her eyes;
And to go with this sandwich, her love, her treasure,
She'll make a pot of tea, 10
Her urn, her cauldron of almost unholy pleasure,
For in that tea will be
Never a drop of shivering starving water,
But milk with all its cream;
A boiling foaming snow, by pleasure's daughter, 15
Obedient to the dream,
Brewed and kept hot and poured out and dejected,
This once of all the year,
Most cordial to the hearts of those selected,
Those delicate, those dear, 20
Mystical inmost friends of fervent Nelly,
Who will consume with glee
And blessings on the decent Mrs. Kelly,
That sandwich and that tea.

But this year it was really extra special; 25
For when old Nelly went

2. An echo of John Keats's *Ode on Melancholy* (1819):
"Or if thy mistress some rich anger shows, / Imprison
her soft hand, and let her rave, / And feed deep, deep
upon her peerless eyes."
1. I.e., a layer cake.

Down to the dairy, she beheld a vessel
Of marvelous extent,
Full of fine milk soured by the spring thunder,
With cream on top galore: 30
And Mrs. Kelly, who really is the world's wonder,
Skimmed her a quart and more;
And Nelly with light heart and little trouble
Beat it and made it turn
Into lovely butter that made the pleasure double: 35
Her sandwich and her urn,
Flanked by the light new loaf and heavenly butter,
Home-made from magic cream,
Ravished the creature till words could not utter
The glory of the dream.[2] 40

 1966

Yorkshire Wife's Saga

War was her life, with want and the wild air;
Not for life only; she was out to win.
Houses and ground were cheap, out on the bare
Moor, and the land not bad; they could begin,
Now that the seven sons were mostly men. 5

Two acres and a sow, on hard-saved brass;[1]
Men down the mine, and mother did the rest.
Pity, with all those sons, they had no lass;
No help, no talk, no mutual interest,
Made fourteen slaving hours empty at best. 10

Fierce winter mornings, up at three or four;
Men bawl, pigs shriek against the raving beck.[2]
Off go the eight across the mile of moor,
With well-filled dinner-pail and sweat-ragged neck;
But pigs still shriek, and wind blows door off sneck.[3] 15

Of course they made it; what on earth could stop
People like that? Marrying one by one,
This got a farm, the other got a shop;
Now she was left with but the youngest son,
But she could look about and feel she'd won. 20

Doctor had told her she was clean worn out.
All pulled to bits, and nowt[4] that he could do.
But plenty get that way, or die, without
Having a ruddy ten-quid[5] note to show.
She'd got seven thriving sons all in a row. 25

2. An echo of William Wordsworth's *Ode: Intimations*
of Immortality (1807): "Where is it now, the glory and
the dream?"
1. Money.

2. Brook.
3. Latch.
4. Nothing.
5. English currency: £10.

And grandchildren. She liked going by bus
Or train, to stay a bit in those snug homes.
They were her colonies, fair glorious.
"Sit by the fire, ma, till the dinner comes.
Sit by the fire and cuddle little lass." 30

1968

MARITA BONNER
1899–1971

By the time Marita Bonner's collected works, *Frye Street & Environs*, appeared in 1987, this gifted artist had been largely forgotten, perhaps because she had ceased to publish after 1941. But the book quickly garnered accolades as well as new readers. Bonner—who was born in Boston and educated at Radcliffe College—was teaching high school in Washington, D.C., when she began her literary career at the salon of the playwright Georgia Douglas Johnson. At that time, too, Bonner met and married William Almy Occomy, a native of Rhode Island and graduate of Brown University. Before and after her move with her husband to Chicago, where she resided the rest of her life, Bonner published many of her prize-winning stories, essays, and reviews in *Crisis* and *Opportunity*, two of the most influential black journals of the Harlem Renaissance. Of the three plays she composed, *The Purple Flower* (1928) is deemed her most ambitious, allegorical effort to represent a black quest for "Life-At-Its-Fullest." Throughout the 1930s, Bonner worked on a series of narratives about the relationship between children and parents in Chicago families coping with poverty, prejudice, and violence.

The selection printed here comes from the early stage of Bonner's career. As an autobiographical study, *On Being Young—a Woman—and Colored* complements Zora Neale Hurston's analysis of herself in *How It Feels to Be Colored Me*. Like Bonner's stories, it exemplifies the sensitivity with which she repeatedly examined the psychosexual conflicts bequeathed by a racist society.

On Being Young—a Woman—and Colored

You start out after you have gone from kindergarten to sheepskin covered with sundry Latin phrases.

At least you know what you want life to give you. A career as fixed and as calmly brilliant as the North Star. The one real thing that money buys. Time. Time to do things. A house that can be as delectably out of order and as easily put in order as the doll-house of "playing house" days. And of course, a husband you can look up to without looking down on yourself.

Somehow you feel like a kitten in a sunny catnip field that sees sleek, plump brown field mice and yellow baby chicks sitting coyly, side by side, under each leaf. A desire to dash three or four ways seizes you.

That's Youth.

But you know that things learned need testing—acid testing—to see if they are really after all, an interwoven part of you. All your life you have heard of the

1. I.e., other blacks.

debt you owe "Your People"[1] because you have managed to have the things they have not largely had.

So you find a spot where there are hordes of them—of course below the Line[2]—to be your catnip field while you close your eyes to mice and chickens alike.

If you have never lived among your own, you feel prodigal. Some warm untouched current flows through them—through you—and drags you out into the deep waters of a new sea of human foibles and mannerisms; of a peculiar psychology and prejudices. And one day you find yourself entangled—enmeshed—pinioned in the seaweed of a Black Ghetto.

Not a Ghetto, placid like the Strasse[3] that flows, outwardly unperturbed and calm in a stream of religious belief, but a peculiar group. Cut off, flung together, shoved aside in a bundle because of color and with no more in common.

Unless color is, after all, the real bond.

Milling around like live fish in a basket. Those at the bottom crushed into a sort of stupid apathy by the weight of those on top. Those on top leaping, leaping; leaping to scale the sides; to get out.

There are two "colored" movies, innumerable parties—and cards. Cards played so intensely that it fascinates and repulses at once.

Movies.

Movies worthy and worthless—but not even a low-caste spoken stage.

Parties, plentiful. Musk and dancing and much that is wit and color and gaiety. But they are like the richest chocolate; stuffed costly chocolates that make the taste go stale if you have too many of them. That make plain whole bread taste like ashes.

There are all the earmarks of a group within a group. Cut off all around from ingress from or egress to other groups. A sameness of type. The smug self-satisfaction of an inner measurement; a measurement by standards known within a limited group and not those of an unlimited, seeing, world. . . . Like the blind, blind mice. Mice whose eyes have been blinded.

Strange longing seizes hold of you. You wish yourself back where you can lay your dollar down and sit in a dollar seat to hear voices, strings, reeds that have lifted the World out, up, beyond things that have bodies and walls. Where you can marvel at new marbles and bronzes and flat colors that will make men forget that things exist in a flesh more often than in spirit. Where you can sink your body in a cushioned seat and sink your soul at the same time into a section of life set before you on the boards[4] for a few hours.

You hear that up at New York this is to be seen; that, to be heard.

You decide the next train will take you there.

You decide the next second that that train will not take you, nor the next— nor the next for some time to come.

For you know that—being a woman—you cannot twice a month or twice a year, for that matter, break away to see or hear anything in a city that is supposed to see and hear too much.

That's being a woman. A woman of any color.

You decide that something is wrong with a world that stifles and chokes;

2. The Mason-Dixon Line; the boundary between Pennsylvania and Maryland that popularly divides the North from the South.

3. Street (German). "Ghetto": originally that section of a European city where Jews were forced to live.

4. I.e., on a stage.

that cuts off and stunts; hedging in, pressing down on eyes, ears and throat. Somehow all wrong.

You wonder how it happens there that—say five hundred miles from the Bay State[5]—Anglo Saxon intelligence is so warped and stunted

How judgment and discernment are bred out of the race. And what has become of discrimination? Discrimination of the right sort. Discrimination that the best minds have told you weighs shadows and nuances and spiritual differences before it catalogues. The kind they have taught you all of your life was best: that looks clearly past generalization and past appearance to dissect, to dig down to the real heart of matters. That casts aside rapid summary conclusions, drawn from primary inference, as Daniel did the spiced meats.[6]

Why can't they then perceive that there is a difference in the glance from a pair of eyes that look, mildly docile, at "white ladies" and those that, impersonally and perceptively—aware of distinctions—see only women who happen to be white?

Why do they see a colored woman only as a gross collection of desires, all uncontrolled, reaching out for their Apollos and the Quasimodos[7] with avid indiscrimination?

Why unless you talk in staccato squawks—brittle as seashells—unless you "champ" gum—unless you cover two yards square when you laugh—unless your taste runs to violent colors—impossible perfumes and more impossible clothes—are you a feminine Caliban craving to pass for Ariel?[8]

An empty imitation of an empty invitation. A mime; a sham; a copy-cat. A hollow re-echo. A froth, a foam. A fleck of the ashes of superficiality?

Everything you touch or taste now is like the flesh of an unripe persimmon.[9] . . . Do you need to be told what that is being . . . ?

Old ideas, old fundamentals seem worm-eaten, out-grown, worthless, bitter; fit for the scrap-heap of Wisdom.

What you had thought tangible and practical has turned out to be a collection of "blue flower"[1] theories.

If they have not discovered how to use their accumulation of facts, they are useless to you in Their world.

Every part of you becomes bitter.

But—"In Heaven's name, do not grow bitter. Be bigger than they are"—exhort white friends who have never had to draw breath in a Jim Crow[2] train. Who have never had petty putrid insult dragged over them—drawing blood— like pebbled sand on your body where the skin is tenderest. On your body where the skin is thinnest and tenderest.

You long to explode and hurt everything white; friendly; unfriendly. But you know that you cannot live with a chip on your shoulder even if you can manage a smile around your eyes—without getting steely and brittle and losing the softness that makes you a woman.

For chips make you bend your body to balance them. And once you bend,

5. Massachusetts, here meant as a place of relative racial enlightenment.

6. Daniel, a prisoner of the king of Babylon, refused to eat the king's meat (Daniel 1).

7. I.e., the most perfect and highly deformed men. Apollo was the Greek god of the sun. Quasimodo was the hunchback in Victor Hugo's *Hunchback of Notre Dame* (1831).

8. A monster wishing to pass for a spirit (from characters in Shakespeare's *Tempest*).

9. Until thoroughly ripe, persimmons are extremely astringent.

1. An expression for something rare or unheard of.

2. The legal and extralegal system enforcing segregation of blacks and whites.

you lose your poise, your balance, and the chip gets into you. The real you. You get hard.

 . . . And many things in you can ossify . . .

 And you know, being a woman, you have to go about it gently and quietly, to find out and to discover just what is wrong. Just what can be done.

 You see clearly that they have acquired things.

 Money; money. Money to build with, money to destroy. Money to swim in. Money to drown in. Money.

 An ascendancy of wisdom. An incalculable hoard of wisdom in all fields, in all things collected from all quarters of humanity.

 A stupendous mass of things.

 Things.

 So, too, the Greeks . . . Things.

 And the Romans. . . .

 And you wonder and wonder why they have not discovered how to handle deftly and skillfully, Wisdom, stored up for them—like the honey for the Gods on Olympus[3]—since time unknown.

 You wonder and you wonder until you wander out into Infinity, where—if it is to be found anywhere—Truth really exists.

 The Greeks had possessions, culture. They were lost because they did not understand.

 The Romans owned more than anyone else. Trampled under the heel of Vandals[4] and Civilization, because they would not understand.

 Greeks. Did not understand.

 Romans. Would not understand.

 "They." Will not understand.

 So you find they have shut Wisdom up and have forgotten to find the key that will let her out. They have trapped, trammeled, lashed her to themselves with thews and thongs and theories. They have ransacked sea and earth and air to bring every treasure to her. But she sulks and will not work for a world with a whitish hue because it has snubbed her twin sister, Understanding.

 You see clearly—off there is Infinity—Understanding. Standing alone, waiting for someone to really want her.

 But she is so far out there is no way to snatch at her and really drag her in.

 So—being a woman—you can wait.

 You must sit quietly without a chip. Not sodden—and weighted as if your feet were cast in the iron of your soul. Not wasting strength in enervating gestures as if two hundred years of bonds and whips had really tricked you into nervous uncertainty.

 But quiet; quiet. Like Buddha—who brown like I am—sat entirely at ease, entirely sure of himself; motionless and knowing, a thousand years before the white man knew there was so very much difference between feet and hands.

 Motionless on the outside. But on the inside?

 Silent.

 Still . . . "Perhaps Buddha is a woman."

 So you too. Still; quiet; with a smile, ever so slight, at the eyes so that Life will flow into and not by you. And you can gather, as it passes, the essences, the overtones, the tints, the shadows; draw understanding to yourself.

3. The mountaintop home of the Greek gods. 4. The Germanic peoples who sacked Rome in A.D. 455.

And then you can, when Time is ripe, swoop to your feet—at your full
height—at a single gesture.
 Ready to go where?
 Why . . . Wherever God motions.

 1925

ELIZABETH BOWEN

1899–1973

Elizabeth Bowen was born in Dublin and identified her early childhood with her
family's estate near Kildorrery, County Cork. Of Welsh extraction, the Bowens
had acquired Bowen's Court in the seventeenth century, and her father wanted a
male heir to inherit it. When he realized that Elizabeth was to be his only child, he
suffered a nervous breakdown, and the child was taken away to England with her
mother and governess. Leading a nomadic existence, the ten-year-old witnessed
her mother's suffering from a fatal cancer. From the ages of fifteen to eighteen, she
attended Downe House School in Kent, the only Bowen to be educated in
England and increasingly self-conscious about belonging neither in England nor in
Ireland. In 1918, after nursing shell-shocked veterans of World War I in Dublin,
she went to live in London, and in 1923 she married Alan C Cameron, an educa-
tor in the Oxford city school system. Seven years later, the death of her father
made Elizabeth Bowen the first female owner of Bowen's Court. But she did not
return to live there until 1952, and in that year her husband died. Seven years later,
she was forced to sell the house. In 1963, it was pulled down.
 Bowen herself attributed her thematic focus on the insecurity of childhood to
her Anglo-Irish personal history. "Motherless since I was thirteen," she wrote in a
preface (1948), "I was in and out of the homes of my different relatives—and, as
constantly, shuttling between two countries: Ireland and England." An Irish out-
sider in England and a guilty English landowner in Ireland, she nevertheless used
her acute sense of "submerged fear" to depict the vulnerability of child-heroines
like the orphaned Portia of *The Death of the Heart* (1938) or to describe the sinis-
ter menace of war-torn London in *The Heat of the Day* (1949). As in *The Demon
Lover*, moreover, that sense of fear is often conveyed through descriptions of phys-
ically damaged or psychically damaging houses. Bowen wrote most of her fiction
first in Northampton and then in London, where she worked for the Ministry of
Information during the bombings of the early 1940s. After a prolific career, in
which she published more than twenty novels and collections of short stories, she
died at seventy-four, having been made a commander of the British Empire and
having received honorary degrees from Trinity College, Dublin, and from Oxford
University.

The Demon Lover

Towards the end of her day in London Mrs. Drover went round to her shut-
up house to look for several things she wanted to take away. Some belonged to
herself, some to her family, who were by now used to their country life. It was
late August; it had been a steamy, showery day: at the moment the trees down
the pavement glittered in an escape of humid yellow afternoon sun. Against
the next batch of clouds, already piling up ink-dark, broken chimneys and

parapets stood out. In her once familiar street, as in any unused channel, an unfamiliar queerness had silted up; a cat wove itself in and out of railings, but no human eye watched Mrs. Drover's return. Shifting some parcels under her arm, she slowly forced round her latchkey in an unwilling lock, then gave the door, which had warped, a push with her knee. Dead air came out to meet her as she went in.

The staircase window having been boarded up, no light came down into the hall. But one door, she could just see, stood ajar, so she went quickly through into the room and unshuttered the big window in there. Now the prosaic woman, looking about her, was more perplexed than she knew by everything that she saw, by traces of her long former habit of life—the yellow smoke-stain up the white marble mantelpiece, the ring left by a vase on the top of the es-critoire;[1] the bruise in the wallpaper where, on the door being thrown open widely, the china handle had always hit the wall. The piano, having gone away to be stored, had left what looked like claw-marks on its part of the parquet. Though not much dust had seeped in, each object wore a film of another kind; and, the only ventilation being the chimney, the whole drawing room smelled of the cold hearth. Mrs. Drover put down her parcels on the escritoire and left the room to proceed upstairs; the things she wanted were in the bedroom chest.

She had been anxious to see how the house was—the part-time caretaker she shared with some neighbors was away this week on his holiday, known to be not yet back. At the best of times he did not look in often, and she was never sure that she trusted him. There were some cracks in the structure, left by the last bombing, on which she was anxious to keep an eye. Not that one could do anything—

A shaft of refracted daylight now lay across the hall. She stopped dead and stared at the hall table—on this lay a letter addressed to her.

She thought first—then the caretaker must be back. All the same, who, see-ing the house shuttered, would have dropped a letter in at the box? It was not a circular, it was not a bill. And the post office redirected, to the address in the country, everything for her that came through the post. The caretaker (even if he were back) did not know she was due in London today—her call here had been planned to be a surprise—so his negligence in the matter of this letter, leaving it to wait in the dusk and dust, annoyed her. Annoyed, she picked up the letter, which bore no stamp. But it cannot be important, or they would know. . . . She took the letter rapidly upstairs with her, without a stop to look at the writing till she reached what had been her bedroom, where she let in light. The room looked over the garden and other gardens: the sun had gone in; as the clouds sharpened and lowered, the trees and rank lawns seemed al-ready to smoke with dark. Her reluctance to look again at the letter came from the fact that she felt intruded upon—and by someone contemptuous of her ways. However, in the tenseness preceding the fall of rain she read it: it was a few lines.

> Dear Kathleen,
> You will not have forgotten that today is our anniversary, and the
> day we said. The years have gone by at once slowly and fast. In

1. Writing desk.

view of the fact that nothing has changed, I shall rely upon you to keep your promise. I was sorry to see you leave London, but was satisfied that you would be back in time. You may expect me, therefore, at the hour arranged.

<div align="right">

Until then

K.

</div>

Mrs. Drover looked for the date: it was today's. She dropped the letter on to the bedsprings, then picked it up to see the writing again—her lips, beneath the remains of lipstick, beginning to go white. She felt so much the change in her own face that she went to the mirror, polished a clear patch in it and looked at once urgently and stealthily in. She was confronted by a woman of forty-four, with eyes staring out under a hat brim that had been rather carelessly pulled down. She had not put on any more powder since she left the shop where she ate her solitary tea. The pearls her husband had given her on their marriage hung loose round her now rather thinner throat, slipping into the V of the pink wool jumper her sister knitted last autumn as they sat round the fire. Mrs. Drover's most normal expression was one of controlled worry, but of assent. Since the birth of the third of her little boys, attended by a quite serious illness, she had had an intermittent muscular flicker to the left of her mouth, but in spite of this she could always sustain a manner that was at once energetic and calm.

Turning from her own face as precipitately as she had gone to meet it, she went to the chest where the things were, unlocked it, threw up the lid and knelt to search. But as the rain began to come crashing down she could not keep from looking over her shoulder at the stripped bed on which the letter lay. Behind the blanket of rain the clock of the church that still stood struck six—with rapidly heightening apprehension she counted each of the slow strokes. "The hour arranged. . . . My God," she said, "*what* hour? How should I . . . ? After twenty-five years. . ."

The young girl talking to the soldier in the garden had not ever completely seen his face. It was dark; they were saying goodbye under a tree. Now and then—for it felt, from not seeing him at this intense moment, as though she had never seen him at all—she verified his presence for these few moments longer by putting out a hand, which he each time pressed, without very much kindness, and painfully, on to one of the breast buttons of his uniform. That cut of the button on the palm of her hand was, principally, what she was to carry away. This was so near the end of a leave from France that she could only wish him already gone. It was August 1916. Being not kissed, being drawn away from and looked at intimidated Kathleen till she imagined spectral glitters in the place of his eyes. Turning away and looking back up the lawn she saw, through branches of trees, the drawing room window alight: she caught a breath for the moment when she could go running back there into the safe arms of her mother and sister, and cry: "What shall I do, what shall I do? He has gone."

Hearing her catch her breath, her fiancé said, without feeling: "Cold?"

"You're going away such a long way."

"Not so far as you think."

"I don't understand?"

"You don't have to," he said. "You will. You know what we said."

"But that was—suppose you—I mean, suppose."

"I shall be with you," he said, "sooner or later. You won't forget that. You need do nothing but wait."

Only a little more than a minute later she was free to run up the silent lawn. Looking in through the window at her mother and sister, who did not for the moment perceive her, she already felt that unnatural promise drive down between her and the rest of all human kind. No other way of having given herself could have made her feel so apart, lost and forsworn. She could not have plighted a more sinister troth.

Kathleen behaved well when, some months later, her fiancé was reported missing, presumed killed. Her family not only supported her but were able to praise her courage without stint because they could not regret, as a husband for her, the man they knew almost nothing about. They hoped she would, in a year or two, console herself—and had it been only a question of consolation things might have gone much straighter ahead. But her trouble, behind just a little grief, was a complete dislocation from everything. She did not reject other lovers, for these failed to appear: for years she failed to attract men—and with the approach of her thirties she became natural enough to share her family's anxiousness on this score. She began to put herself out, to wonder; and at thirty-two she was very greatly relieved to find herself being courted by William Drover. She married him, and the two of them settled down in this quiet, arboreal part of Kensington:[2] in this house the years piled up, her children were born and they all lived till they were driven out by the bombs of the next war. Her movements as Mrs. Drover were circumscribed, and she dismissed any idea that they were still watched.

As things were—dead or living the letter-writer sent her only a threat. Unable, for some minutes, to go on kneeling with her back exposed to the empty room, Mrs. Drover rose from the chest to sit on an upright chair whose back was firmly against the wall. The desuetude[3] of her former bedroom, her married London home's whole air of being a cracked cup from which memory, with its reassuring power, had either evaporated or leaked away, made a crisis—and at just this crisis the letter-writer had, knowledgeably, struck. The hollowness of the house this evening cancelled years on years of voices, habits and steps. Through the shut windows she only heard rain fall on the roofs around. To rally herself, she said she was in a mood—and, for two or three seconds shutting her eyes, told herself that she had imagined the letter. But she opened them—there it lay on the bed.

On the supernatural side of the letter's entrance she was not permitting her mind to dwell. Who, in London, knew she meant to call at the house today? Evidently, however, this had been known. The caretaker, had he come back, had had no cause to expect her: he would have taken the letter in his pocket, to forward it, at his own time, through the post. There was no other sign that the caretaker had been in—but, if not? Letters dropped in at doors of deserted houses do not fly or walk to tables in halls. They do not sit on the dust of empty tables with the air of certainty that they will be found. There is needed some human hand—but nobody but the caretaker had a key. Under circum-

2. Fashionable neighborhood in London. 　　　3. Disuse.

stances she did not care to consider, a house can be entered without a key. It was possible that she was not alone now. She might be being waited for, downstairs. Waited for—until when? Until "the hour arranged." At least that was not six o'clock: six had struck.

She rose from the chair and went over and locked the door.

The thing was, to get out. To fly? No, not that: she had to catch her train. As a woman whose utter dependability was the keystone of her family life she was not willing to return to the country, to her husband, her little boys and her sister, without the objects she had come up to fetch. Resuming work at the chest she set about making up a number of parcels in a rapid, fumbling-decisive way. These, with her shopping parcels, would be too much to carry; these meant a taxi—at the thought of the taxi her heart went up and her normal breathing resumed. I will ring up the taxi now; the taxi cannot come too soon: I shall hear the taxi out there running its engine, till I walk calmly down to it through the hall. I'll ring up—But no: the telephone is cut off . . . She tugged at a knot she had tied wrong.

The idea of flight . . . He was never kind to me, not really. I don't remember him kind at all. Mother said he never considered me. He was set on me, that was what it was—not love. Not love, not meaning a person well. What did he do, to make me promise like that? I can't remember.—But she found that she could.

She remembered with such dreadful acuteness that the twenty-five years since then dissolved like smoke and she instinctively looked for the weal left by the button on the palm of her hand. She remembered not only all that he said and did but the complete suspension of her existence during that August week. I was not myself—they all told me so at the time. She remembered—but with one white burning blank as where acid has dropped on a photograph: *under no conditions* could she remember his face.

So, wherever he may be waiting, I shall not know him. You have no time to run from a face you do not expect.

The thing was to get to the taxi before any clock struck what could be the hour. She would slip down the street and round the side of the square to where the square gave on the main road. She would return in the taxi, safe, to her own door, and bring the solid driver into the house with her to pick up the parcels from room to room. The idea of the taxi driver made her decisive, bold: she unlocked her door, went to the top of the staircase and listened down.

She heard nothing—but while she was hearing nothing the *passé*[4] air of the staircase was disturbed by a draught that travelled up to her face. It emanated from the basement: down there a door or window was being opened by someone who chose this moment to leave the house.

The rain had stopped; the pavements steamily shone as Mrs. Drover let herself out by inches from her own front door into the empty street. The unoccupied houses opposite continued to meet her look with their damaged stare. Making towards the thoroughfare and the taxi, she tried not to keep looking behind. Indeed, the silence was so intense—one of those creeks of London silence exaggerated this summer by the damage of war—that no tread could have gained on hers unheard. Where her street debouched on the square

4. I.e., foul, stuffy.

where people went on living she grew conscious of and checked her unnatural pace. Across the open end of the square two buses impassively passed each other; women, a perambulator, cyclists, a man wheeling a barrow signalized, once again, the ordinary flow of life. At the square's most populous corner should be—and was—the short taxi rank. This evening, only one taxi—but this, although it presented its blank rump, appeared already to be alertly waiting for her. Indeed, without looking round the driver started his engine as she panted up from behind and put her hand on the door. As she did so, the clock struck seven. The taxi faced the main road: to make the trip back to her house it would have to turn—she had settled back on the seat and the taxi had turned before she, surprised by its knowing movement, recollected that she had not "said where." She leaned forward to scratch at the glass panel that divided the driver's head from her own.

The driver braked to what was almost a stop, turned round and slid the glass panel back: the jolt of this flung Mrs. Drover forward till her face was almost into the glass. Through the aperture driver and passenger, not six inches between them, remained for an eternity eye to eye. Mrs. Drover's mouth hung open for some seconds before she could issue her first scream. After that she continued to scream freely and to beat with her gloved hands on the glass all round as the taxi, accelerating without mercy, made off with her into the hinterland of deserted streets.

1945

MERIDEL LE SUEUR
1900–1996

During the Great Depression, Meridel Le Sueur recorded the stories of midwestern women, insisting that "their lives were not defeated, trashed, defenseless but that we as woman contained the real and only seed, and were the granary of the people." She had begun to consider herself a "village scribe" for Native Americans and immigrant farm and factory workers when she was a young girl traveling throughout the Midwest and Southwest with her socialist parents. Born in Iowa, Le Sueur dropped out of high school to devote herself to political activism as well as a career in various types of performance. She lived in a New York anarchist commune with Emma Goldman, acted in the early movies produced in Hollywood, and directed the Little Theater of Sacramento, California. Married to Harry Rice, a labor organizer, she gave birth to two daughters in the late 1920s, the period in which she began to publish the work she had been recording in her journals.

Le Sueur's fifty-year career was shaped by her association with prairie populists (who advocated an equitable redistribution of wealth to help farmers and laborers) and Marxists. During the 1930s, both her prize-winning stories and the articles she wrote for left-wing periodicals documented the struggle of working people. According to the critic Elaine Hedges, *Salute to Spring* (1940), a collection of Le Sueur's stories and articles, marked both the high point of Le Sueur's reputation and the beginning of her critical neglect. The first draft of her novel *The Girl* was written in 1939, but the book remained unpublished until 1978. When national sentiment against communism arose during the so-called red scare of the 1950s, Le Sueur was informally blacklisted, and she turned to writing children's stories—about Abraham Lincoln's mother, for example, and about Native

American–white relationships. In her later publication, *Rites of Ancient Ripening* (1975), Le Sueur created what the critic Blanche Gelphant calls "assertive, drumming chants, 'renderings' of Native American oral poetry." An early work, *Annunciation* (1935) looks forward to *Rites of Ancient Ripening*, for it demonstrates Le Sueur's fascination with the myths and realities of motherhood; originally written in the form of notes to her first, unborn child, it was, she explained, "the bud of a new flower within the time of the old."

Annunciation[1]

For Rachel

Ever since I have known I was going to have a child I have kept writing things down on these little scraps of paper. There is something I want to say, something I want to make clear for myself and others. One lives all one's life in a sort of way, one is alive and that is about all that there is to say about it. Then something happens.

There is the pear tree I can see in the afternoons as I sit on this porch writing these notes. It stands for something. It has had something to do with what has happened to me. I sit here all afternoon in the autumn sun and then I begin to write something on this yellow paper; something seems to be going on like a buzzing, a flying and circling within me, and then I want to write it down in some way. I have never felt this way before, except when I was a girl and was first in love and wanted then to set things down on paper so that they would not be lost. It is something perhaps like a farmer who hears the swarming of a host of bees and goes out to catch them so that he will have honey. If he does not go out right away, they will go, and he will hear the buzzing growing more distant in the afternoon.

My sweater pocket is full of scraps of paper on which I have written. I sit here many afternoons while Karl is out looking for work, writing on pieces of paper, unfolding, reading what I have already written.

We have been here two weeks at Mrs. Mason's boarding house. The leaves are falling and there is a golden haze over everything. This is the fourth month for me and it is fall. A rich powerful haze comes down from the mountains over the city. In the afternoon I go out for a walk. There is a park just two blocks from here. Old men and tramps lie on the grass all day. It is hard to get work. Many people beside Karl are out of work. People are hungry just as I am hungry. People are ready to flower and they cannot. In the evenings we go there with a sack of old fruit we can get at the stand across the way quite cheap, bunches of grapes and old pears. At noon there is a hush in the air and at evening there are stirrings of wind coming from the sky, blowing in the fallen leaves, or perhaps there is a light rain, falling quickly on the walk. Early in the mornings the sun comes up hot in the sky and shines all day through the mist. It is strange, I notice all these things, the sun, the rain falling, the blowing of the wind. It is as if they had a meaning for me as the pear tree has come to have.

In front of Mrs. Mason's house there is a large magnolia tree with its blossoms yellow, hanging over the steps almost within reach. Its giant leaves are

1. The angel Gabriel's announcement to Mary that she is to give birth to the son of God (Luke 1:26–38).

motionless and shining in the heat, occasionally as I am going down the steps towards the park one falls heavily on the walk.

This house is an old wooden one, that once was quite a mansion I imagine. There are glass chandeliers in the hall and fancy tile in the bathrooms. It was owned by the rich once and now the dispossessed live in it with the rats. We have a room three flights up. You go into the dark hallway and up the stairs. Broken settees and couches sit in the halls. About one o'clock the girls come down stairs to get their mail and sit on the front porch. The blinds go up in the old wooden house across the street. It is always quite hot at noon.

Next to our room lies a sick woman in what is really a kind of closet with no windows. As you pass you see her face on the pillow and a nauseating odor of sickness comes out the door. I haven't asked her what is the matter with her but everyone knows she is waiting for death. Somehow it is not easy to speak to her. No one comes to see her. She has been a housemaid all her life tending other people's children; now no one comes to see her. She gets up sometimes and drinks a little from the bottle of milk that is always sitting by her bed covered with flies.

Mrs. Mason, the landlady, is letting us stay although we have only paid a week's rent and have been here over a week without paying. But it is a bad season and we may be able to pay later. It is better perhaps for her than having an empty room. But I hate to go out and have to pass her door and I am always fearful of meeting her on the stairs. I go down as quietly as I can but it isn't easy, for the stairs creak frightfully.

The room we have on the top floor is a back room, opening out onto an old porch which seems to be actually tied to the wall of the house with bits of wire and rope. The floor of it slants downward to a rickety railing. There is a box perched on the railing that has geraniums in it. They are large, tough California geraniums. I guess nothing can kill them. I water them since I have been here and a terribly red flower has come. It is on this porch I am sitting. Just over the banisters stand the top branches of a pear tree.

Many afternoons I sit here. It has become a kind of alive place to me. The room is dark behind me, with only the huge walnut tree scraping against the one window over the kitchenette. If I go to the railing and look down I can see far below the back yard which has been made into a garden with two fruit trees and I can see where a path has gone in the summer between a small bed of flowers, now only dead stalks. The ground is bare under the walnut tree where little sun penetrates. There is a dog kennel by the round trunk but there doesn't ever seem to be a dog. An old wicker chair sits outdoors in rain or shine. A woman in an old wrapper comes out and sits there almost every afternoon. I don't know who she is, for I don't know anybody in this house, having to sneak downstairs as I do.

Karl says I am foolish to be afraid of the landlady. He comes home drunk and makes a lot of noise. He says she's lucky in these times to have anybody in her house, but I notice in the mornings he goes down the stairs quietly and often goes out the back way.

I'm alone all day so I sit on this rickety porch. Straight out from the rail so that I can almost touch it is the radiating frail top of the pear tree that has opened a door for me. If the pears were still hanging on it each would be alone and separate with a kind of bloom upon it. Such a bloom is upon me at this moment. Is it possible that everyone, Mrs. Mason who runs this boarding

house, the woman next door, the girls downstairs, all in this dead wooden house have hung at one time, each separate in a mist and bloom upon some invisible tree? I wonder if it is so.

I am in luck to have this high porch to sit on and this tree swaying before me through the long afternoons and the long nights. Before we came here, after the show broke up in S.F.[2] we were in an old hotel, a foul smelling place with a dirty chambermaid and an old cat in the halls, and night and day we could hear the radio going in the office. We had a room with a window looking across a narrow way into another room where a lean man stood in the mornings looking across, shaving his evil face. By leaning out and looking up I could see straight up the sides of the tall building and above the smoky sky.

Most of the time I was sick from the bad food we ate. Karl and I walked the streets looking for work. Sometimes I was too sick to go. Earl would come in and there would be no money at all. He would go out again to perhaps borrow something. I know many times he begged although we never spoke of it, but I could tell by the way he looked when he came back with a begged quarter. He went in with a man selling Mexican beans but he didn't make much. I lay on the bed bad days feeling sick and hungry, sick too with the stale odor of the foul walls. I would lie there a long time listening to the clang of the city outside. I would feel thick with this child. For some reason I remember that I would sing to myself and often became happy as if mesmerised there in the foul room. It must have been because of this child. Karl would come back perhaps with a little money and we would go out to a dairy lunch[3] and there have food I could not relish. The first alleyway I must give it up with the people all looking at me.

Karl would be angry. He would walk on down the street so people wouldn't think he was with me. Once we walked until evening down by the docks. "Why don't you take something?" he kept saying. "Then you wouldn't throw up your food like that. Get rid of it. That's what everybody does nowadays. This isn't the time to have a child. Everything is rotten. We must change it." He kept on saying, "Get rid of it. Take something why don't you?" And he got angry when I didn't say anything but just walked along beside him. He shouted so loud at me that some stevedores loading a boat for L.A. laughed at us and began kidding us, thinking perhaps we were lovers having a quarrel.

Some time later, I don't know how long it was, for I hadn't any time except the nine months I was counting off, but one evening Karl sold enough Mexican jumping beans at a carnival to pay our fare, so we got on a river boat and went up the river to a delta town. There might be a better chance of a job. On this boat you can sit up all night if you have no money to buy a berth. We walked all evening along the deck and then when it got cold we went into the saloon because we had pawned our coats. Already at that time I had got the habit of carrying slips of paper around with me and writing on them, as I am doing now. I had a feeling then that something was happening to me of some kind of loveliness I would want to preserve in some way. Perhaps that was it. At any rate I was writing things down. Perhaps it had something to do with Karl wanting me all the time to take something. "Everybody does it," he kept telling me. "It's nothing, then it's all over." I stopped talking to him much.

2. San Francisco.
3. In Jewish dietary custom, a meal containing only fish and dairy products.

Everything I said only made him angry. So writing was a kind of conversation I carried on with myself and with the child.

Well, on the river boat that night after we had gone into the saloon to get out of the cold, Karl went to sleep right away in a chair. But I couldn't sleep. I sat watching him. The only sound was the churning of the paddle wheel and the lap of the water. I had on then this sweater and the notes I wrote are still in the breast pocket. I would look up from writing and see Karl sleeping like a young boy.

"Tonight, the world into which you are coming"—then I was speaking to the invisible child—"is very strange and beautiful. That is, the natural world is beautiful. I don't know what you will think of man, but the dark glisten of vegetation and the blowing of the fertile land wind and the delicate strong step of the sea wind, these things are familiar to me and will be familiar to you. I hope you will be like these things. I hope you will glisten with the glisten of ancient life, the same beauty that is in a leaf or a wild rabbit, wild sweet beauty of limb and eye. I am going on a boat between dark shores, and the river and the sky are so quiet that I can hear the scurryings of tiny animals on the shores and their little breathings seem to be all around. I think of them, wild, carrying their young now, crouched in the dark underbrush with the fruit-scented land wind in their delicate nostrils, and they are looking out at the moon and the fast clouds. Silent, alive, they sit in the dark shadow of the greedy world. There is something wild about us too, something tender and wild about my having you as a child, about your crouching so secretly here. There is something very tender and wild about it. We, too, are at the mercy of many hunters. On this boat I act like the other human beings, for I do not show that I have you, but really I know we are as helpless, as wild, as at bay as some tender wild animals who might be on the ship.

"I put my hand where you lie so silently. I hope you will come glistening with life power, with it shining upon you as upon the feathers of birds. I hope you will be a warrior and fierce for change, so all can live."

Karl woke at dawn and was angry with me for sitting there looking at him. Just to look at me makes him angry now. He took me out and made me walk along the deck although it was hardly light yet. I gave him the "willies" he said, looking at him like that. We walked round and round the decks and he kept talking to me in a low voice, trying to persuade me. It was hard for me to listen. My teeth were chattering with cold, but anyway I found it hard to listen to anyone talking, especially Karl. I remember I kept thinking to myself that a child should be made by machinery now, then there would be no fuss. I kept thinking of all the places I had been with this new child, traveling with the show from Tia Juana to S.F. In trains, over mountains, through deserts, in hotels and rooming houses, and myself in a trance of wonder. There wasn't a person I could have told it to, that I was going to have a child. I didn't want to be pitied. Night after night we played in the tent and the faces were all dust to me, but traveling, through the window the many vistas of the earth meant something—the bony skeleton of the mountains, like the skeleton of the world jutting through its flowery flesh. My child too would be made of bone. There were the fields of summer, the orchards fruiting, the berry fields and the pickers stooping, the oranges and the grapes. Then the city again in September and the many streets I walk looking for work, stopping secretly in doorways to feel beneath my coat.

It is better in this small town with the windy fall days and the sudden rain falling out of a sunny sky. I can't look for work any more. Karl gets a little work washing dishes at a wienie place.[4] I sit here on the porch as if in a deep sleep waiting for this unknown child. I keep hearing this far flight of strange birds going on in the mysterious air about me. This time has come without warning. How can it be explained? Everything is dead and closed, the world a stone, and then suddenly everything comes alive as it has for me, like an anemone on a rock, opening itself, disclosing itself, and the very stones themselves break open like bread. It has all got something to do with the pear tree too. It has come about some way as I have sat here with this child so many afternoons, with the pear tree murmuring in the air.

The pears are all gone from the tree but I imagine them hanging there, ripe curves within the many scimitar leaves, and within them many pears of the coming season. I feel like a pear. I hang secret within the curling leaves, just as the pear would be hanging on its tree. It seems possible to me that perhaps all people at some time feel this, round and full. You can tell by looking at most people that the world remains a stone to them and a closed door. I'm afraid it will become like that to me again. Perhaps after this child is born, then everything will harden and become small and mean again as it was before. Perhaps I would even have a hard time remembering this time at all and it wouldn't seem wonderful. That is why I would like to write it down.

How can it be explained? Suddenly many movements are going on within me, many things are happening, there is an almost unbearable sense of sprouting, of bursting encasements, of moving kernels, expanding flesh. Perhaps it is such an activity that makes a field come alive with millions of sprouting shoots of corn or wheat. Perhaps it is something like that that makes a new world.

I have been sitting here and it seems as if the wooden houses around me had become husks that suddenly as I watched began to swarm with livening seed. The house across becomes a fermenting seed alive with its own movements. Everything seems to be moving along a curve of creation. The alley below and all the houses are to me like an orchard abloom, shaking and trembling, moving outward with shouting. The people coming and going seem to hang on the tree of life, each blossoming from himself. I am standing here looking at the blind windows of the house next door and suddenly the walls fall away, the doors open, and within I see a young girl making a bed from which she had just risen having dreamed of a young man who became her lover . . . she stands before her looking-glass in love with herself.

I see in another room a young man sleeping, his bare arm thrown over his head. I see a woman lying on a bed after her husband has left her. There is a child looking at me. An old woman sits rocking. A boy leans over a table reading a book. A woman who has been nursing a child comes out and hangs clothes on the line, her dress in front wet with milk. A young woman comes to an open door looking up and down the street waiting for her young husband. I get up early to see this young woman come to the door in a pink wrapper and wave to her husband. They have only been married a short time, she stands waving until he is out of sight and even then she stands smiling to herself, her hand upraised.

4. Hotdog stand.

Why should I be excited? Why should I feel this excitement, seeing a woman waving to her young husband, or a woman who has been nursing a child, or a young man sleeping? Yet I am excited. The many houses have become like an orchard blooming soundlessly. The many people have become like fruits to me, the young girl in the room alone before her mirror, the young man sleeping, the mother, all are shaking with their inward blossoming, shaken by the windy blooming, moving along a future curve.

I do not want it all to go away from me. Now many doors are opening and shutting, light is falling upon darkness, closed places are opening, still things are now moving. But there will come a time when the doors will close again, the shouting will be gone, the sprouting and the movement and the wondrous opening out of everything will be gone. I will be only myself. I will come to look like the women in this house. I try to write it down on little slips of paper, trying to preserve this time for myself so that afterwards when everything is the same again I can remember what all must have.

This is the spring there should be in the world, so I say to myself, "Lie in the sun with the child in your flesh shining like a jewel. Dream and sing, pagan, wise in your vitals. Stand still like a fat budding tree, like a stalk of corn athrob and aglisten in the heat. Lie like a mare panting with the dancing feet of colts against her sides. Sleep at night as the spring earth. Walk heavily as a wheat stalk at its full time bending towards the earth waiting for the reaper. Let your life swell downward so you become like a vase, a vessel. Let the unknown child knock and knock against you and rise like a dolphin within."

I look at myself in the mirror. My legs and head hardly make a difference, just a stem my legs. My hips are full and tight in back as if bracing themselves. I look like a pale and shining pomegranate, hard and tight, and my skin shines like crystal with the veins showing beneath blue and distended. Children are playing outside and girls are walking with young men along the walk. All that seems over for me. I am a pomegranate hanging from an invisible tree with the juice and movement of seed within my hard skin. I dress slowly. I hate the smell of clothes. I want to leave them off and just hang in the sun ripening . . . ripening.

It is hard to write it down so that it will mean anything. I've never heard anything about how a woman feels who is going to have a child, or about how a pear tree feels bearing its fruit. I would like to read these things many years from now, when I am barren and no longer trembling like this, when I get like the women in this house, or like the woman in the closed room, I can hear her breathing through the afternoon.

When Karl has no money he does not come back at night. I go out on the street walking to forget how hungry I am. This is an old town and along the streets are many old strong trees. Night leaves hang from them ready to fall, dark and swollen with their coming death. Trees, dark, separate, heavy with their down hanging leaves, cool surfaces hanging on the dark. I put my hand among the leaf sheaves. They strike with a cool surface, their glossy surfaces surprising me in the dark. I feel like a tree swirling upwards too, muscular sap alive, with rich surfaces hanging from me, flaring outward rocket-like and falling to my roots, a rich strong power in me to break through into a new life. And dark in me as I walk the streets of this decayed town are the buds of my child. I walk alone under the dark flaring trees. There are many houses with the lights shining out but you and I walk on the skirts of the lawns amidst the

downpouring darkness. Houses are not for us. For us many kinds of hunger, for us a deep rebellion.

Trees come from a far seed walking the wind, my child too from a far seed blowing from last year's rich and revolutionary dead. My child budding secretly from far walking seed, budding secretly and dangerously in the night.

The woman has come out and sits in the rocker, reading, her fat legs crossed. She scratches herself, cleans her nails, picks her teeth. Across the alley lying flat on the ground is a garage. People are driving in and out. But up here it is very quiet and the movement of the pear tree is the only movement and I seem to hear its delicate sound of living as it moves upon itself silently, and outward and upward.

The leaves twirl and twirl all over the tree, the delicately curving tinkling leaves. They twirl and twirl on the tree and the tree moves far inward upon its stem, moves in an invisible wind, gently swaying. Far below straight down the vertical stem like a stream, black and strong into the ground, runs the trunk; and invisible, spiraling downward and outwards in powerful radiation, lie the roots. I can see it spiraling upwards from below, its stem straight, and from it, spiraling the branches season by season, and from the spiraling branches moving out in quick motion, the forked stems, and from the stems twirling fragilely the tinier stems holding outward until they fall, the half curled pear leaves.

Far below lies the yard, lying flat and black beneath the body of the up-shooting tree, for the pear tree from above looks as if it had been shot instantaneously from the ground, shot upward like a rocket to break in showers of leaves and fruits twirling and falling. Its movement looks quick, sudden and rocketing. My child when grown can be looked at in this way as if it suddenly existed . . . but I know the slow time of making. The pear tree knows.

Far inside the vertical stem there must be a movement a river of sap rising from below and radiating outward in many directions clear to the tips of the leaves. The leaves are the lips of the tree speaking in the wind or they move like many tongues. The fruit of the tree you can see has been a round speech, speaking in full tongue on the tree, hanging in ripe body, the fat curves hung within the small curves of the leaves. I imagine them there. The tree has shot up like a rocket, then stops in midair and its leaves flow out gently and its fruit curves roundly and gently in a long slow curve. All is gentle on the pear tree after its strong upward shooting movement.

I sit here all the afternoon as if in its branches, midst the gentle and curving body of the tree. I have looked at it until it has become more familiar to me than Karl. It seems a strange thing that a tree might come to mean more to one than one's husband. It seems a shameful thing even. I am ashamed to think of it but it is so. I have sat here in the pale sun and the tree has spoken to me with its many tongued leaves, speaking through the afternoon of how to round a fruit. And I listen through the slow hours. I listen to the whisperings of the pear tree, speaking to me, speaking to me. How can I describe what is said by a pear tree? Karl did not speak to me so. No one spoke to me in any good speech.

There is a woman coming up the stairs, slowly. I can hear her breathing. I can hear her behind me at the screen door.

She came out and spoke to me. I know why she was looking at me so closely. "I hear you're going to have a child," she said. "It's too bad." She is the same color as the dead leaves in the park. Was she once alive too?

I am writing on a piece of wrapping paper now. It is about ten o'clock. Karl didn't come home and I had no supper. I walked through the streets with their heavy, heavy trees bending over the walks and the lights shining from the houses and over the river the mist rising.

Before I came into this room I went out and saw the pear tree standing motionless, its leaves curled in the dark, its radiating body falling darkly, like a stream far below into the earth.

1935

Later-Twentieth-Century
Literature

THE CONTEMPORARY WORLD

Meditating on the woman of the future, the American poet Adrienne Rich mused in *Snapshots of a Daughter-in-Law* (1958–60) that "she's long about her coming, who must be / more merciless to herself than history." Yet, added Rich in a moment of visionary certitude, "I see her plunge / breasted and glancing through the currents / . . . at least as beautiful as any boy / or helicopter." Rich's vision reflects a major cultural shift that—in a sense reiterating and reemphasizing the moments of change that ushered in turn-of-the-century and modernist crises—occurred in the years between 1940 and the end of the twentieth century, a shift suggesting to many writers and thinkers all over the world that, whether it meant apocalyptic annihilation or ecstatic transformation, the future had at last definitively arrived.

On the one hand, contemporary thinkers brooded on what the novelist James Joyce had earlier called "the nightmare of history," diagnosing social ills in terms of the crises they associated with the rise of totalitarianism and the threat of nuclear catastrophe. On the other hand, these thinkers dwelled on the metamorphic possibilities implicit in what the poet Hart Crane (echoing Walt Whitman) had called *Years of the Modern!*, prescribing and predicting new and more harmonious relationships between mind and body, culture and nature, as well as among nations, classes, races, and sexes. From the modernist novelist Virginia Woolf to the French feminist theorist Simone de Beauvoir to Adrienne Rich herself, women writers expressed both attitudes toward the contemporary world, but—as the women's movement strengthened during the 1960s—the hopes of many feminists became increasingly utopian.

To begin with, pessimistic speculations were fostered in both sexes by a period that saw such major global calamities as the Holocaust (the genocide of millions of Jews and other prisoners during World War II) and the dropping of the first atomic bomb on Hiroshima (in 1945, at the end of that war). Later, however, optimistic speculations were encouraged by an era that witnessed such dramatic impulses toward liberation as those that impelled the rise of many third world countries and the formation of the international peace movement as well as the development of the civil rights, ecological, feminist, and gay rights movements. Difficult as it is to generalize about a period characterized by radical extremes and rapid change, an era whose deepest implications are still unclear, it is nevertheless true that in the years from 1940 to the present almost all the traditional categories through which the Western mind had understood reality were questioned or annihilated. As geographic markers bounding nations shifted, boundary lines between disciplines and genres blurred and traditional explanatory narratives disintegrated. Not only conventional concepts of space, time, authority, and morality but also received ideas about class, race, and gender were dissolved and revised in a world reeling from what the social observer Alvin Toffler has called *Future Shock*.

TOWARD THE TWENTY-FIRST CENTURY

The Impact of World War II

One of the first systems to be traumatically shaken in this period was the system of capitalism itself, for international crises in the 1930s indicated to many observers on both sides of the Atlantic that a free market economy might no longer be viable. The 1929 New York stock market crash, followed by the Great Depression and serious crop failures (the "Dust Bowl") in America and crippling monetary inflation in Germany, along with business slumps as well as bread lines in England, posed problems that seemed impossible to solve despite the efforts of such a leader as President Franklin Delano Roosevelt, whose "New Deal" constituted an unprecedented social welfare program. The widespread disillusionment that marked the era was vividly recorded in such American novels as John Steinbeck's Pulitzer Prize–winning *The Grapes of Wrath* (1939) and Tillie Olsen's *Yonnondio: From the Thirties* (1974), both of which described the grim lives of agricultural and industrial workers as well as the miseries of the unemployed in the 1930s. In addition, the skepticism about capitalism manifested in books like these fostered a disbelief in the efficacy of government in general. Centered in cities like London, Chicago, and New York, for instance, political unrest in England and America resulted in strikes, riots, marches, and demonstrations.

Similar economic and political discontent on the Continent led to the strengthening of the powers of Benito Mussolini, *Il Duce* ("the leader"), whose blackshirted *Fascisti* had established him as ruler of Italy in 1922, and to the rise of Adolf Hitler, the so-called *Fuehrer* ("leader"), whose goose-stepping Nazis took over Germany and elevated him to absolute dictatorship in 1933. Dreaming of a new Roman Empire, Mussolini annexed Ethiopia in 1936 and Albania in 1939 while advocating the supreme authority of the strong leader and ruthlessly suppressing dissent. Similarly, arguing for the "natural superiority" of Aryans (Nordic-Germanic peoples) and for their right to *Lebensraum* ("living space"), Hitler invaded Austria and the Sudetenland (a province of Czechoslovakia) in 1938 and Poland in 1939. At the same time, he put into practice the brutally totalitarian principles he had outlined in *Mein Kampf* ("My Battle," 1925) and implemented what would be called the "final solution" to "the Jewish problem" as well as to the "problem" of other aliens or dissenters by setting up concentration camps, in whose gas ovens millions would die during his reign.

In Japan and Russia, totalitarian dictatorships had also formed. In 1926, Hirohito became emperor of Japan and began to pursue an aggressively militaristic policy of international expansion, while in 1927 Joseph Stalin rose to power in the former Soviet Union and began liquidating opponents in a series of purges. By 1939, the world had been divided into hostile camps by a series of treaties and alliances, including the formation of an Axis (1936), which aligned Fascist Italy, Nazi Germany, and imperialist Japan; the Munich Pact (1938), in which England and France followed a policy of appeasement toward Hitler; and the short-lived Hitler-Stalin pact (1939), in which Germany and Russia entered into a nonaggression treaty. On the brink of World War II, citizens of many countries felt not only disillusioned about government but anxiously at the mercy of the authoritarian men who controlled so many lives.

War broke out in Europe during 1939, and the United States entered the conflict when Japanese planes bombed the American naval base at Pearl Harbor (in Hawaii) in 1941. Although the mortality rate for combatants was not nearly as high as it had been in World War I, enormous numbers of noncombatants were for the first time profoundly vulnerable to attack from the air in homes, schools, and workplaces. What made possible the destruction of whole cities was the swift development of a technology of death even more sinister than that used in the earlier

war. While armored tanks and submarines provided some protection to soldiers and sailors, civilians in urban centers like London, Dresden, and Tokyo huddled in shelters or tube (subway) stations that offered little security against blitzes (rains of bombs) and fire bombings. A number of the most significant participants in World War II were aviators who bombed immobilized populations of women, children, and old people. After the Battle of Britain (1941), planes were no longer the kinds of fragile two-seaters in which chivalric pilots had dueled during World War I. Intricate and often large machines, protected by the newly developed device of radar, bombers and transport aircraft insulated their crews and often alienated them from the targets they mapped, surveyed, and destroyed. James Dickey's *The Fire Bombing* (1964) recalled the poet's anesthetized sense of distance from humanity on a bombing run over Japan in terms echoing the infamous remark of Mussolini's pilot son that the flames of a bombed Ethiopian city looked "like a rose unfolding."

To be sure, airmen were also subject to ferocious attacks by antiaircraft guns or other planes, and the poet Randall Jarrell, who was himself in the air force during the war, described the terrible vulnerability of the ball turret gunner, a man who, wrote Jarrell in a note, had to "hunch upside-down . . . like a foetus in the womb" to operate machine guns set into the plexiglass belly of a B-17 or B-24 bomber: "When I died they washed me out of the turret with a hose," explains the dead speaker of *The Death of the Ball Turret Gunner* (1945). In addition, as Jarrell's poem also implied, these men—subject to a universal conscription system that reduced them to mere cyphers—had been assimilated into a gigantic military bureaucracy that sought to deprive them of their individuality by making them standardized and interchangeable parts of what seemed a monstrous whole. "From my mother's sleep I fell into the State," Jarrell's gunner confesses. Similarly, the hero of Joseph Heller's satiric *Catch-22* (1961) discovers that he is helplessly entangled in a logically absurd army hierarchy whose rules contradict and confound each other and him.

Nevertheless, to civilians the assaults by such military men seemed virtually apocalyptic. The American poet H. D., who lived through the blitz of London in the 1940s, saw England as "an island of wounds," while the expatriate poet T. S. Eliot, a British air raid warden during the same years characterized an attacking plane as a "dark dove with [a] flickering tongue." Even in the supposedly safe and stable United States, Japanese-American citizens, called *Nisei*, were suspected of collusion with the enemy and imprisoned in camps in California, a development that proved—as if working off the title of Sinclair Lewis's dystopian (anti-utopian) novel *It Can't Happen Here* (1935)—that "it" could happen here. As the critic Susan Schweik has shown, the war widened the gulf between soldiers and civilians (and therefore also between men and women).

But despite the difficulties recounted by H. D. and T. S. Eliot, the civilians who suffered the most dramatically during the war and whose experiences were destined to become emblematic of the apocalypse that had engulfed an entire generation were those who endured either the Holocaust in Germany or the American atomic bombing of Hiroshima, the latter a cataclysm that culminated and concluded World War II on the Pacific front. Both these events, too, were facilitated or created by recent technological innovations and by the construction of elaborate bureaucracies which so depersonalized the decision-making process that moral responsibility was obscured for individuals who claimed they were only "following orders." The demonic efficiency with which the Nazis conducted Jews to death factories was documented by victims of the Holocaust like Anne Frank, a thirteen-year-old girl whose *Diary* became famous when it was published after her death in a concentration camp at the age of fifteen, and by survivors like the expatriate Rumanian-Jewish novelist Eli Wiesel and the German-Jewish poet Nelly

Sachs, both of whom paradoxically explained how the moral implications of such a mass cultural descent into hell were so drastic that the existence of death camps could never be explained away.

The destruction of most of the inhabitants of Hiroshima and Nagasaki and the debilitation of those who survived were not the result of the same sort of genocidal program, but they nevertheless had similarly resonant implications, not only for citizens of Japan but for a number of Americans, who were distressed by the Truman administration's decision actually to drop the bomb. Later, however, it was not so much this one decision that haunted the whole world as it was the concept of the bomb itself, whose characteristic mushroom cloud began to symbolize a science harnessed to death rather than to life. Only a hundred years after nineteenth-century poets as diverse as Tennyson and Whitman had extolled the virtues of technological progress, the poet Karl Shapiro could write in *The Progress of Faust* (1947) that the sinister scientist-magician of legend had appeared "in an American desert at war's end / Where, at his back, a dome of atoms rose."

It was perhaps inevitable that intellectuals should have responded to such events with writings based on nihilistic assumptions about the world. Existentialism, a philosophical movement led by the French thinkers Jean-Paul Sartre and Albert Camus, posited a meaningless cosmos from which human beings could only derive significance through acts of engagement willed in and for themselves. The movement's theories issued in a number of major works, including Sartre's treatise *Being and Nothingness* (1943) and Camus's novel *The Stranger* (1942), while shaping the spirit of the age in which Samuel Beckett depicted in his play *Waiting for Godot* (1952) the tragicomic fate of two tramps who are pointlessly waiting for a no one who never arrives. But many other writers of this period also expressed sardonic disillusionment: from Norman Mailer's *The Naked and the Dead* (1948) to Katherine Anne Porter's *Ship of Fools* (1962) and Thomas Pynchon's *Gravity's Rainbow* (1973), their works explored the irrationality of both culture and nature in a world at war.

The Cold War

It can be argued that the so-called cold war began at the Yalta Conference of 1945, when the British prime minister Winston Churchill and the American president Franklin Delano Roosevelt allowed the Soviet premier Joseph Stalin to claim portions of conquered Germany as the spoils of war. In a sense, the division of Germany into what were to become two separate states—East and West Germany—represented a splitting of the world into two opposed ideological camps that deeply affected every phase of the life of this period. Internationally, the so-called iron curtain—physically symbolized by the Berlin wall that the Soviets built to keep East Berliners from escaping to the West—shut western Europe off from the eastern sphere of Hungary, Poland, and East Germany, which had been annexed by the U.S.S.R. The Korean War in the early 1950s, followed by the Suez Canal and Cuban crises, dramatized the struggle between Soviet and American powers while manifesting the decline of Great Britain as an imperial force. At the same time, in the United States, citizens anxious about nuclear attack built basement bomb shelters and stockpiled canned goods while anti-Communist sentiment grew in intensity.

During the late 1940s in Hollywood and New York, "left-wing" writers like Dashiell Hammett and Lillian Hellman, together with prominent film directors and actors, were "blacklisted"—deprived of jobs and reputations—by producers worried about political respectability. By 1953, Senator Joseph McCarthy was acting as, in the words of one historian, an "inquisitor," accusing such diverse figures as the former diplomat Alger Hiss and the American president Dwight Eisenhower of being Communists or Communist sympathizers, while members of the House

Un-American Activities Committee promoted patriotism and inveighed against the supposedly subversive doings of liberal intellectuals. From the loyalty oaths that many civic employees were now obliged to sign to retain their jobs to the execution in 1953 of Julius and Ethel Rosenberg, a Jewish couple convicted of conspiring to commit espionage in behalf of the Soviet Union, the 1950s were permeated by the anxiety of "ordinary" citizens that they were threatened by Communists and by intellectuals' fear that they might be charged with being Communists or Communist sympathizers. "A savage servility / slides by on grease," wrote the poet Robert Lowell about the spirit of the age in *For the Union Dead* (1960).

In a number of other poems that were to become crucially influential on contemporary verse, Lowell further characterized the era with remarks such as, "These are the tranquilized *Fifties,* / and I am forty." It was not only Lowell who felt himself and his age to be middle-aged, for the conservatism of the 1950s, as many writers perceived, was social as well as political. In England, to be sure, the years from 1945 to 1951 had seen the ascendancy of a strong Labour government that nationalized major industries and introduced a program of socialized medicine. But by the early 1950s, England had reinstated the Conservative Party, which, led by Winston Churchill, ruled the country throughout the decade. On both sides of the Atlantic, then, but perhaps more in the newly prosperous United States than in still war-devastated England, this was the era of the "man in the gray flannel suit," the title of a 1955 best-seller by Sloan Wilson. The phrase perfectly captured the conformity and materialism that characterized the middle-class suburban culture which arose in this period.

Largely created by and for a postwar population exhausted by the calamities of the 1940s, the suburbs of the 1950s were enclaves of nuclear families in a newly nuclear age. Ambitious commuting husbands and dutifully domestic wives produced a record number of children who constituted the so-called baby boom of the period. The workplace was still located in urban centers, but as the bourgeois ideal of home-ownership sent more and more young couples into affordable out-of-town subdivisions, inner cities began to decay and to be associated with the poverty and violence of ghettos—usually slum districts—where many blacks, Chicanos, Puerto Ricans, and other disadvantaged groups were obliged to live. Among the middle classes, an ideology of "togetherness" permeated the age, as did an ethic of "adjustment' and "maturity." Television shows like *I Love Lucy, Ozzie and Harriet,* and *Leave It to Beaver* might celebrate the charmingly nutty antics of middle-class wives and children, but in the end everyone professed to agree that, as the title of another series put it, *Father Knows Best.* For those who did not acquiesce in such an idea, a new breed of professionals—psychiatrists, psychologists, advice columnists, and guidance counselors—arose to explain the virtues of "normalcy": to be "well adjusted," they argued, was to "fit in" to a system that was morally right and emotionally healthful.

In a more sophisticated form, this popular ideology of adjustment affected even the increasingly conservative intellectual and literary life of the age. Paralleling the rise of corporations, public universities grew in size and number, aided by monies for education that the government had provided returning veterans through the G.I. Bill, as well as by other federal grants. In the United States, in particular, higher education became a major industry, offering jobs to countless intellectuals. Just at this point, too, an effort to elevate the study of literature to the status already achieved by the sciences resulted in what was called the "New Criticism." Detaching the literary text from its cultural context—its author, its audience, and its historical setting—the New Critics analyzed the ironic and metaphorical complexities within poems that were now considered well-wrought, autonomous objects. Developing sophisticated techniques of reading, these thinkers saw themselves as rebels against the naïveté of traditional scholarship. Yet, signifi-

cantly, their efforts to divorce art and criticism from culture and society were essentially conservative. Such theorists as Cleanth Brooks and R. P. Blackmur insisted that the literary analyst should adopt a position of political neutrality, while writers like T. S. Eliot, Allan Tate, and John Crowe Ransom actually defined themselves as "reactionaries."

A similar academic professionalization marked the careers of a number of creative writers in this period, some of whom were themselves also practicing critics and many of whom now accepted positions in newly established university creative writing programs. From Tate and Ransom to Theodore Roethke, Robert Lowell, John Berryman, and Randall Jarrell, most of the major American poets of the age were associated with English departments, and many British writers, including Donald Davie and Phillip Larkin, were also connected with universities. Novels such as C. P. Snow's *The Masters* (1951), Mary McCarthy's *The Groves of Academe* (1952), and Randall Jarrell's *Pictures from an Institution* (1954) all dealt with the so-called ivory tower of academia, while the school of poets known as "the Movement," which arose in England in the 1950s, produced work that was both stylistically conservative and thematically modest.

Nevertheless, despite the overt decorum of what Lowell called "the tranquilized *Fifties*," a number of dissenting voices were raised throughout the period. In America, for instance, even during the McCarthy investigations, radical folksingers like the Weavers continued to play to large audiences, and left-wing students circulated the so-called Stockholm Peace Petition—a demand for world peace sponsored by a set of radical organizations—while in England the British philosopher Bertrand Russell presided over a series of mass demonstrations demanding nuclear disarmament. Among poets, too, the *dicta* of orthodoxy and depersonalization promulgated by a leader like T. S. Eliot were challenged, first by the flamboyant behavior and neo-Romantic verse of the Welsh poet Dylan Thomas, whose influence was at least as great in America as it was in England; then by the so-called Beat writers; and finally by the group of artists known as the "confessional" poets—most notably, W. D. Snodgrass, Robert Lowell, and John Berryman, but later also Sylvia Plath and Anne Sexton—all of whom insisted, in their different ways, on defying the values of maturity, adjustment, and normalcy.

In addition, during this period the "Southern Gothic" writers Carson McCullers, Truman Capote, Tennessee Williams, and Flannery O'Connor constructed grotesque fantasies to reveal the immaturity, maladjustment, and perversity endemic to apparently ordinary small-town communities. At the same time, a set of English playwrights known as "Angry Young Men" were producing realistic dramas like John Osborne's *Look Back in Anger* (1956), which attacked the complacency of the welfare state. The rebellious young Allen Ginsberg, a leader of the American Beat movement that would help shape the verse of the 1960s, spoke for many such dissenters in his poem *America* (1956), when, referring to left-wing anti-Stalinists, he asked, "America when will you be worthy of your million Trotskyites?," and he cursed the age that produced the cold war as well as his own country's complicity in it, telling "America" to "go fuck yourself with your atom bomb."

The Third World

Even as he excoriated the United States in *America*, Ginsberg mockingly identified with his culture in the line "Asia is rising against me." Parodic though his comment was, it referred to the increasing anxiety with which many American and British citizens responded to the emergence of third world countries and peoples that began in the late 1940s and continued throughout the 1960s and 1970s. As early as 1945, when the United Nations was established, granting responsibility in world councils to a number of small powers, a process of global redefinition had been initiated. When two years later, in 1947, Mohandas Gandhi finally achieved

his goal of national independence for India, the final disintegration of the British Empire was under way. In 1948, Burma also achieved independence, and in that year the new state of Israel was established. During the late fifties and sixties, a growing number of African states—Ghana (1957), Nigeria (1960), and Kenya (1963)—won autonomy from Britain, and their victories, paralleled earlier by the liberation of North Vietnam from French rule (1945), were now paralleled by the liberation in 1960 of the French colonies Chad, the Congo Republic, Mali, and Senegal. Counterpointing the emergence of new African, Middle Eastern, and Asian nations was the rise of China to prominence as a world power. In 1949, the Communist Party chairman Mao Tse-tung established the Chinese People's Republic, and though the new state was not officially recognized by the American government until the 1970s, it became ever more important on the international scene, complicating the plot of the cold war with interventions in Korea, Africa, Cuba, and, ultimately, Vietnam.

At least in part inspired by the theorizing of radical critics of imperialism like the black political writer Frantz Fanon, these new nations struggled to recover lost national traditions, and their efforts were reflected in the literature that native artists—Chinua Achebe, Amos Tutuola, Kamala Das, Bessie Head, and Ama Ata Aidoo—began to produce. Although frequently writing in English to ensure an international audience, poets and novelists of former British colonies or possessions nevertheless often drew heavily on local myths and legends while recording the conflicts of identity experienced by people inhabiting cultures in transition, cultures that were no longer colonized yet still not free from Western influence. At the same time, the struggle of these countries was also recorded by the African-born white writers Alan Paton, Doris Lessing, and Nadine Gordimer and by the expatriate women writers Buchi Emecheta, Bharati Mukherjee, and Jamaica Kincaid.

Meanwhile, in Latin America, the Chilean poet Pablo Neruda wrote such passionate poems as *The United Fruit Company*, attacking American exploitation, as well as vividly surrealistic works like *The Heights of Macchu Pichu*, recovering legends of the Andes. Mining similar veins were the Peruvian poet César Vallejo, the Mexican writer Octavio Paz, and the Colombian novelist Gabriel García Márquez, all authors whose work was to become extraordinarily influential in the United States during the 1960s and 1970s. In Australia and Canada, moreover, the poet Judith Wright and the poet-novelist Margaret Atwood were only two among many who sought to memorialize what Wright in *South of My Days* called "my blood's country." Atwood, in particular, epitomized this effort of self-definition in white English-speaking lands resisting engulfment by England and the United States. In *Survival* (1972), for instance, she offered a "thematic guide to Canadian literature," while in her *Oxford Anthology of Canadian Literature* (1982) she established her literary inheritance.

It was not just abroad, however, that oppressed or subordinated peoples sought to claim lost cultural identities and win political power. In the United States, Native Americans became newly conscious of their own traditions and, supported by the reissuing of such classics as *Black Elk Speaks*, a shaman's memoir translated and edited by John Neihardt in 1932, writers like Scott Momaday, Leslie Marmon Silko, and Paula Gunn Allen struggled to reclaim their aesthetic legacy. But perhaps the most important of the libertarian struggles that gained momentum between the 1950s and the 1970s was the black civil rights movement in America.

Most prominently led by the Nobel Prize–winning clergyman Martin Luther King Jr., who advocated nonviolent resistence to white racism, this movement began with so-called freedom riders, who helped register African American voters in the South, and progressed to sit-ins, marches, and mass demonstrations in the North, events that helped pass the sweeping Civil Rights Act of 1964, outlawing segregation in public places and guaranteeing legal equality to blacks. More mili-

tant than King was the black Muslim leader Malcolm X, who began his career, arguing that whites were inherently evil, by seeking to convert blacks to a revised form of the Islamic religion. Both represented the new passion for self-affirmation that swept black communities in these years. From Rosa Parks, who fought to integrate buses in 1955, to Representative Shirley Chisolm, who ran for the presidency in 1972, to the prisoner-turned-writer Eldridge Cleaver and the group of revolutionaries who called themselves the Black Panthers, black activists struggled against social, economic, legal, and psychological oppression. Yet their battle was marked by tragedy, for Malcolm X and Martin Luther King Jr. were assassinated in, respectively, 1965 and 1968, while four children killed in a bombed Birmingham, Alabama, Sunday school were just a few among many victims of a violent white backlash.

The civil rights movement produced a rich proliferation of black writing, work marked by a confidence and energy that had not been seen since the Harlem Renaissance of the 1920s. From Richard Wright, whose prize-winning novel *Native Son* was published in 1940, to Ralph Ellison, whose novel *Invisible Man* won the National Book Award in 1952, James Baldwin, whose impassioned essay *The Fire Next Time* was widely read when it appeared in 1963, and Toni Morrison, whose *The Bluest Eye* was published in 1970, a new generation of black prose writers arose to express what Baldwin defined as "the sorrow, the rage, and the murderous bitterness which was eating up my life and the lives of those about me." Similarly, from Margaret Walker and Gwendolyn Brooks to Imamu Amiri Baraka (Le Roi Jones), Ishmael Reed, Mari Evans, June Jordan, Audre Lorde, Nikki Giovanni, Lucille Clifton, and Sonia Sanchez, two new generations of black poets appeared to proclaim that—in the words of Lorde's *Coal*—"I / is the total black, being spoken / from the earth's inside" and to demand that the reader "now take my word for jewel in the open light." Their project would inspire a generation of Chicano writers—Gloria Anzaldúa, Lorna Dee Cervantes, Sandra Cisneros, Gary Soto—to forge an aesthetic identity in the 1980s.

The Sixties

Not insignificantly, the styles and strategies of Baraka, Reed, and Lorde were influenced by and influenced a new literary movement that developed on the Lower East Side of New York City and in San Francisco: called the Beats, a term coined by the novelist Jack Kerouac and conflating the words "beaten" and "beatified," writers in this group attained national notoriety early in the 1960s, in part because of the impact of Kerouac's *On the Road* (1957) and Allen Ginsberg's long poem *Howl* (1956). With its violent assault on the bourgeois materialism of the 1950s, *Howl*, in particular, spoke for a disaffected and rebellious generation. Writing in Whitmanesque lines and in a visionary mode shaped by his studies of the late-eighteenth-century prophetic poet William Blake, Ginsberg exclaimed that "I saw the best minds of my generation destroyed by madness, starving hysterical naked," and excoriated the modern world: "Robot apartments! invisible suburbs! skeleton treasuries! blind capitals! demonic industries! spectral nations! invincible madhouses! granite cocks! monstrous bombs!" He and his followers earned the label "beatniks," a term that implied that these unorthodox young people were Soviet sympathizers. At the same time, however, this poet defined the characteristic stance of a decade that was to be marked by what often seemed like one long howl of protest.

Politically, such protests, which were in part the result of early civil rights activism, took the form of rebellion against censorship, poverty, war, and the destruction of natural resources. As early as 1959, the complaints of publishers and intellectuals had led to the rescinding of bans against the distribution of such supposedly pornographic novels as D. H. Lawrence's *Lady Chatterley's Lover* and Henry Miller's *Tropic of Capricorn*. In the early sixties, however, students at the

University of California, Berkeley, led by Mario Savio, organized "sit-ins," conducted rallies, and made speeches to force university authorities to let them use whatever language they pleased in newspapers and journals. Their tactics were adopted by such other groups as Students for a Democratic Society (SDS) and the California Diggers, who tried to draw attention to poverty by demonstrating against what President Eisenhower once called the "military-industrial complex" and by distributing free food to impoverished sections of the population.

Though brief, the tradition of student leafleting, picketing, marching, and meeting that these groups pioneered laid the groundwork for what became a nationwide phenomenon: the antiwar movement. Under the leadership of John Kennedy and then of Lyndon Johnson, the United States had intervened in South Vietnam to support a series of conservative, even dictatorial, governments against both the revolutionary guerrilla forces of the Viet Cong and the Communist troops marshaled by Ho Chi Minh, leader of North Vietnam. The outrage of young people at this intervention, and especially of draft-eligible young men, grew into a mass disaffection that was exacerbated when the Ohio National Guard fired on demonstrators at Kent State University, killing four students.

Not only had such protesters adopted the tactics of the Free Speech movement and the SDS, they had also employed more theatrical strategies: burning draft cards, pouring blood on military files, and organizing "read-ins" to which famous writers drew large audiences. Among the poets who performed on such occasions were Robert Bly and Denise Levertov. "You who go out on schedule / to kill," Levertov exclaimed, "do you know there are eyes that watch you, / eyes whose lids you burned off [?]" "It's because the aluminum window shade business is doing so well in the U.S. that we roll fire over entire villages," noted Bly sardonically. "It's because we have new packaging for smoked oysters that bomb holes appear in the rice paddies."

Because, as Bly's line suggests, the militancy of the 1960s involved a critique of Western culture in general, it rigidly evolved from political to social protest. The period, in any case, was marked by a general loosening of authoritarian hierarchies; with the accession in 1958 of Pope John XXIII, and the convening of the Second Vatican Council, even the traditionally conservative Catholic Church had relaxed old rules and substituted services in the vernacular for masses in Latin. But in England and America, as the sixties wore on, popular trends also dramatized change. The Beats gave way to the Beatles, and beatniks became hippies. The rock movement of the fifties, picked up in England and popularized by the Rolling Stones as well as the Beatles, issued in such diverse phenomena as miniskirts, unisex clothes, long hair (for both sexes), and psychedelic drugs. Some British youths defined themselves as "mods" or "rockers," while others became disciples of the radical psychologist R. D. Laing, who preached that the sane were mad and the mad, sane. Some Americans dreamed of running away to the Haight Ashbury district of San Francisco and becoming hippies. What the historian Theodore Roszak called the "counterculture" may have at first seemed juvenile and narcissistic, with its emphasis on flower children and hedonistic self-development, but it was to result in a serious ecology movement, whose spokespersons included the poet Gary Snyder (Earth House Hold, 1969), the feminist writer Susan Griffin (Woman and Nature, 1978), and the feminist theologian Mary Daly (Gyn/Ecology, 1978).

But Griffin and Daly spoke for another growing constituency, too, for the activism of the sixties functioned, paradoxically, in two ways for women: on the one hand, many women participated with passion in all phases of the political and social movements prevalent in the period; on the other hand, the very intensity of their participation forced them to confront their marginalization both in the reigning culture and in the counterculture. Performing as coffee makers, secretaries, or sex objects for male rebels, radical women soon became disillusioned and, like the nineteenth-century women who had worked for abolition but discovered that their male contemporaries held them in as low esteem as the oppressive

slave system held blacks, they formed a movement of their own. In turn, the women's liberation movement, stressing sexual freedom, fostered the development of the gay (homosexual) rights movement, for gay men and lesbians now began organizing to combat the legal and moral strictures that had ostracized them in the past.

Inevitably, so much ferment had its effect on the entertainment and literature of the era. The disillusionment expressed by Allen Ginsberg, for instance, was picked up and popularized by the stand-up comedians Lenny Bruce, Woody Allen, and Joan Rivers, even as it evolved into the genre of "black humor" (grotesque comedy) produced in the United States by Terry Southern, Donald Barthelme, Thomas Pynchon, Vladimir Nabokov, and Stanley Elkin, and matched in England by the witty novels of Kingsley Amis, John Wain, and Iris Murdoch. Similarly comic, but more self-consciously ethnic, were the writings of the Jewish-American writers Philip Roth, Grace Paley, Saul Bellow, Bernard Malamud, and Cynthia Ozick, while the realistic novels of social criticism produced by the British authors Doris Lessing and Margaret Drabble expressed the same disaffection with the status quo.

Irreverent, sometimes vulgar, and often nihilistic, the work of both "black humorists" and Jewish writers was paralleled by the experimental, "guerrilla," and "street" theater that developed in these years, led by such figures as Julian Beck and Judith Malina, whose "Living Theater" attempted through radically disruptive methods to bridge the distance between author, actor, and audience. Finally, a similar comic nihilism also characterized the ironic and sometimes surrealistic verse of the "New York poets" Frank O'Hara, Kenneth Koch, and John Ashbery; and if poets like those who belonged to the so-called Black Mountain school (Charles Olson, Robert Creeley, Denise Levertov, Robert Duncan) were less comic, they were equally rebellious and experimental, as were the Americans Robert Bly, James Wright, and W. S. Merwin, along with the English Ted Hughes. Hughes's *Crow* (1970), for instance, was a poem sequence that drew on Native American trickster legends and summarized the spirit of the age in a bleak catechism: "Who owns the whole rainy, stony earth? *Death*."

Future Shock

The distinction between Hughes's gloom and the hopeful passion that impelled the activists of the 1960s symbolizes the thin line that separated dystopian and utopian thinkers in this period. Approaching and passing 1984, the year that George Orwell in 1949 used to date the death of "the whole rainy, stony earth," many people all over the globe must have wondered whether, if one is living in the future, one has any future. Certainly, the threats posed by neutron bombs, ICBMs (intercontinental ballistic missiles), nuclear power plants, and industrial pollution seemed to imply a future that might be merely deathly. In particular, a war of the worlds became an increasingly haunting possibility when more nations joined the race to build atomic bombs, many of them countries that were involved in intense border disputes. As the 1990s began, the end of the cold war—signaled by the disintegration of nation-states like the U.S.S.R. and Yugoslavia—brought internecine violence, often chillingly labeled "ethnic cleansing." In addition, with chemical waste accumulating and with nuclear engineering errors multiplying, apocalypse seemed in any case to be a random accident that could happen now. More, the deaths of countless victims of the AIDS pandemic horrified a world that remained baffled by the relentless spread of the disease. In the United States and England, a society based on what Orwell would have called "newspeak" and "doublethink," exemplified by advertising language and political euphemisms, presented a particular problem to observers who no longer felt they had a viable language through which to define any of these problems.

At the same time, however, a number of scientific and social breakthroughs in the years just before and after 1984 seemed to belie Orwell's pessimistic prognoses. Moon landings, space shuttles, and communications satellites promised new horizons for the world, while medical innovations, from polio vaccine to heart transplants, suggested new leases on life for humanity. Home appliances, convenience foods, and computers all offered the possibilities of liberation from drudgery, and the concept of equality implicit not only in large-scale welfare programs but also in humanitarian movements hinted at new societal steps toward moral responsibility.

Finally, though, the future that had arrived was shocking because to many it seemed almost impossible to diagnose the divergent implications of the more than new. DNA research (biochemical investigations of the nature of the cell) might yield either deadly mutations or new life. Similarly, such pioneering surgical procedures as sex-change operations and such obstetrical procedures as artificial insemination and conception outside the womb promised either to allow women to control their own reproductive functions or else to replace real women with artificial wombs. No wonder, then, that experimental writers from the French novelist Alain Robbe-Grillet to the Argentinian writer Jorge Luis Borges and writers of speculative fiction from Isaac Asimov to Ursula K. Le Guin described a world of radical instability. Just as postmodernist theorists claimed that the "grand narratives" earlier used to explain historical change only camouflaged the discontinuities and contradictions of reality, the French thinker Jacques Derrida emphasized the indeterminacy of all systems of meaning. Interestingly, Derrida decided to identify himself in *Spurs* (1978) as "a woman," an extreme self-definition suggesting that, not unlike so different a contemporary as the lesbian feminist Adrienne Rich, this male intellectual associated modernity with the coming of a woman. But that Derrida should attempt such an identification revealed how deeply what had been traditionally called the "woman question" was intertwined with the future shock experienced and expressed by so many thinkers in this period. After four decades of social turmoil and intellectual upheaval, not only were the validity of government, the boundaries of the earth, and the integrity of the cell being questioned but even the biological determinacy of gender—the deepest structure through which the self has traditionally been defined and society organized—no longer seemed inevitable.

CONTEMPORARY IMAGES OF WOMEN

Though some thinkers in the 1980s and 1990s were to arrive at radically antibiological positions like that of Derrida, by many other writers and artists from 1940 to, say, 1980, images of women were biologized and sexualized as never before. Indeed, the traditional polarities of angel and monster, virgin and whore, lady and madwoman were consistently eroticized in this period. The nineteenth century had praised women for purity and decorum while blaming them for passion and desire, but the second half of the twentieth century virtually reversed those moral priorities; contemporary writers usually blamed women for frigidity and praised them for sexiness. The scarlet letter A that Hawthorne had used in the nineteenth century to emblematize the crime of the adulteress now dissolved into the pornographic letter O that signified both the emptiness and the openness of an obediently serviceable woman in Pauline Réage's *The Story of O* (1954, 1964). To be sure, many thinkers resisted this cultural tendency to eroticize the female, creating women characters who were autonomous and intelligent, yet for many others popular pressures were hard to overcome, and the images constructed in the works of those writers posed particular problems for women readers.

Certainly from the World War II pin-up girl to the *Playboy* playmate of the 1960s, from the nymphet of Vladimir Nabokov's *Lolita* (1955) to the nymphoma-

niac of Terry Southern and Mason Hoffenberg's *Candy* (1964), representations of women often became blatantly titillating to men; indeed, the current male argot objectified the deliciously willing heroine as a cupcake, a muffin, a cookie, a tomato, a honey, a tootsie, a real sugar, a cherry, a sweetie pie, a tart, or a peach while metamorphosing all women into sexy or repellent animals (foxes, birds, chicks, beavers, kittens, pussies, bitches, dogs, pigs). Though there are, of course, distinctions among the attitudes toward women manifested in the texts produced during World War II, during the "tranquillized *Fifties*," and during the rebellious sixties, it is extraordinary how consistently most novelists and poets of the era focused their attention on the female body and its willingness to function as a receptacle for male desire. Even when contemporary male writers seemed to be contemplating such seemingly noneretic figures as the mother or the literary woman, they tended to sexualize both their dreams and their dreads about femininity.

Even before 1939, a process of frank eroticization of women had begun with the development of a cultural atmosphere whose ideology was both more permissive and more promiscuous than ever before. The dissemination of birth control information and devices, the publication of sex manuals, new divorce laws, short skirts, silk stockings, brassieres—all these diverse phenomena transformed woman from an untouchable object in a hoop skirt or a bustle to a willing and easily accessible body. By World War II, it was possible, as it had not been during World War I, for armies of sex-starved men to decorate barracks, tanks, and planes with clippings of naked or scantily dressed movie stars or models. Countless war novels and movies recorded the joys of lust and the pleasures of casual sexual encounters, especially with prostitutes and foreigners.

At the same time, the pinning-up of female nudity led to a fetishizing of body parts; breasts, buttocks, and legs were often appraised separately, as if the ideal woman could be put together like a jigsaw puzzle. Such fetishizing was perhaps most dramatically expressed in the quasi-theology of the "cunt" that permeated the writings of the American novelist Henry Miller, who had even before the war published such sexually explicit books as *Tropic of Capricorn* (1939). "The body is hers, but the cunt's yours," Miller was to observe in *Sexus* (1949), but in *Tropic of Capricorn* he had already outlined his credo in a description of "the best fuck" he ever had: the object of his desire was a "simpleton" about whom he noted that "above the belt . . . she was batty. . . . Perhaps that was what made her cunt so marvellously impersonal. It was one cunt out of a million."

But of course besides being seductive, those "millions" of "cunts" were threatening: for example, governments constantly urged fighting men to protect themselves against the danger of VD posed by whores and foreigners, a peril that, according to official propagandists, implicitly involved all women. Moreover, just as many World War I soldiers had blamed women for their suffering, combatants in World War II sometimes tended to associate the devastation of war with unleashed female energies. The American poet Stanley Kunitz's *Careless Love* (1944) actually personified the event as an insatiable female, who contaminates and destroys men: "for what / This nymphomaniac enjoys," Kunitz wrote about the machinery of destruction, "Inexhaustibly is boys."

Even while the horror of the war was metaphorized as female, however, fighting men were continually reminded and constantly reminded themselves that they were struggling to preserve both the "girl back home" and the values she represented. In countless movies and popular songs, this good girl was kissed and reluctantly left in railroad stations and on wharves. Karl Shapiro's *V Letter* (1944), perhaps the most famous war poem of the period, was addressed to this girl and summarized both her virtues ("I love you first because your face is fair . . . I love you first because you wait. . . . You are my home and in your spacious love / I dream to march as under flaring flags . . .") and the poet's commitment to die for her, if

necessary ("I love you first because your years / Lead to my matter-of-fact and simple death / or to our open marriage").

Yet though Shapiro's poem suggests that his beloved simply waits while he risks death, not every stay-at-home sweetheart was wholly passive. Dutiful and patriotic, many a lady in waiting became Rosie the Riveter and went to work in a munitions factory, for, as the war progressed, government propagandists in both England and America transformed the image of the good girl from that of a wistful dreamer to that of an energetic partner doing her share for the boys abroad. As soon as the conflict was over, however, this image faded; Rosie was turned back into a cheerful housewife or a clean-cut girl-next-door and admonished in such works as Ferdinand Lundberg and Marynia Farnham's *Modern Woman, the Lost Sex* (1947) that she would lose her sexiness and her sex life if she insisted on continuing to compete with men outside the home.

As "pioneers of the sex frontier," wrote David Riesman, Nathan Glazer, and Reuel Denney in their influential sociological study *The Lonely Crowd* (1950), women "must foster aggressiveness and simulate modesty . . . if they have a profession, both men and women are apt to think that their skill detracts from their sexual life or that their sexual life detracts from their skill." Besides reemphasizing Lundberg and Farnham's point, their comment reminds us that these researchers were writing in the age of the Kinsey report and the sex manual, the sex goddess and the high school date. Whether male writers during these years portrayed women as involuntarily animal or expertly sensual, they frequently saw the women they described as less than fully conscious human beings. In his well-known poem *A Girl in a Library* (1951), for instance, Randall Jarrell depicted his subject as "an object among dreams," and remarked that "one sees in your blurred eyes / The 'uneasy half-soul' Kipling saw in dogs"; and in a long story titled *The Making of Ashenden* (1973), Stanley Elkin's protagonist finds a consummation he devoutly wishes in the luxurious lap of a hairy bear, while both the English writer Kingsley Amis and the American poet Kenneth Koch characterized women as dreamy parts of a dream world: in *A Dream of Fair Women* (1957) Amis imagined a horde of "Lime-lighted dolls guttering in their brain," each one begging him "to sign / Her body's autograph-book," and in *Sleeping with Women* (1969), Koch created a surrealistic landscape in which he could be "Asleep with women, awake with man." Clearly the popular cultural equivalents of all these sexy somnambulists were such stars as Marilyn Monroe and Jayne Mansfield, whose tantalizingly exposed bosoms and thighs revealed them as mindlessly voluptuous embodiments of bodily pleasure even while the artifice of their glamour defined them as no more than fantasy figures.

From the Beat poets of the fifties to the "black humorists" of the sixties and seventies, many writers continued the tendency of earlier artists to reduce females to collections of body parts. As if elaborating on what we earlier called Henry Miller's theology of the "cunt," Allen Ginsberg in *Sather Gate Illumination* (1956) proclaimed of his friend Neal Cassady that "Neal sees all girls / as visions of their inner cunts," and Gary Snyder in *For a Far-out Friend* (1955) told a woman whom, he confessed, he had once beaten up that "visions of your body / kept me high for weeks," and, in particular, visions of her with "a little golden belt, just above / your naked snatch." Interestingly these celebrations of women's body parts implicitly characterized the male speaker as a voyeur, pruriently peering at female mysteries that the male must master.

For some writers in this period, however, such distancing techniques sometimes collapsed and were replaced by frank and frankly comic acknowledgments of male helplessness about the female body. Not only did Philip Roth in *The Breast* (1971) bemusedly imagine a male narrator's terrified transformation into a female breast, but both the American novelist John Barth in *Night Sea Journey* (1966) and the American filmmaker Woody Allen in *Everything You Wanted to Know about Sex*

(1972) recounted the hapless expeditions of nervous sperm up the cavernous labyrinth of the birth canal toward the heart of darkness where female power lurks. Perhaps it was because the distancing strategy of voyeurism did not always work to defuse anxiety about such engulfing femininity that contemporaries of Roth, Barth, and Allen also turned to other defensive strategies, and particularly to a strategy of domesticating female sexuality. In his *Wife Wooing* (1962), for instance, the American writer John Updike praised the dutifully passive wife as "the Wide W, the receptive O. Womb," while in *The Lingam and the Yoni* (1955) the Australian poet A. D. Hope used the Sanskrit words for phallus and vulva to satirize a society that does "the Lingam honor" by keeping "the Yoni in" a cute suburban cottage.

Even this strategy, however, backfired for a number of writers in the era. Novels and stories of suburban sexual intrigue like those of Philip Roth (*Goodbye, Columbus*, 1959) and John Updike (*Couples*, 1969) often depicted the domesticated heroine as spoiled and idle, indeed as so bored that she is driven to plot pointlessly promiscuous or merely pragmatic romantic conquests. Perhaps the paradigm of these banal, bed-hopping predators is Brenda Patimkin in Roth's *Goodbye, Columbus*, a "Jewish-American princess" whose narcissism, heartlessness, and materialism lead her to seduce and abandon her impoverished and ardent lover. In the same vein, for beleaguered mates like the speaker of Robert Creeley's *Ballad of the Despairing Husband* (1955) and protesting prospective mates like the speaker of Gregory Corso's *Marriage* (1959), the woman who is a wife became the traditional "battle axe." Looking for "the darling I did love," Creeley's speaker encounters instead a ferocious female who declares, "I'm free of you, you little prick, / and I'm the one can make it stick," and Corso's speaker, fantasizing "a fat Reichian wife screeching over potatoes Get a job!," argues that "I never wanted to marry a girl who was like my mother, / And Ingrid Bergman was always impossible."

When women characters in contemporary literary texts were perceived as both "real" and "good," they were often defined as "good" because they were willing to be sacrificed by men and for male purposes. In a tradition that goes back to D. H. Lawrence's *The Woman Who Rode Away* (1926), a fisherman-artist in the Welsh poet Dylan Thomas's *Ballad of the Long-Legged Bait* (1942) "throw[s] to the swift flood / A girl alive with his hooks through her lips" so that he can "catch" the inspiration that he seeks, while in a mode that goes back even further, to the self-immolations of martyrs like St. Cecelia, Celia Coplestone, the heroine of T. S. Eliot's play *The Cocktail Party* (1950), proves her virtue by allowing herself to be "crucified / Very near an ant hill" in the service of a "handful of plague-stricken natives / Who would have died anyway." A number of male writers brought to the surface the hostility implicit in works like those by Thomas and Eliot, constructing revenge fantasies in which autonomous females were punished for their supposed sins. In the British poet Roger McGough's *The Newly Pressed Suit* (1971), for example, the speaker first takes the role of the hero, placing his heroine "gently upon the *bed* / like a *newly pressed suit*," but then "step[s] into the poem" as the villain, to knock out the hero "and with a cruel laugh / Rape the *heroine* / (The raping continues for several stanzas)."

While McGough plainly intended to be sardonic, fictions by Norman Mailer, Hubert Selby, and Thomas Pynchon enacted visions of rape that were also murderous. Mailer's *An American Dream* (1964) not only told the story of a homicidal assault on a wife but associated that assault with a brutal act of anal intercourse; as the critic Kate Millett has observed, "The reader is given to understand that by murdering one woman and buggering another, Rojack [Mailer's hero] became a 'man.' " More grotesquely, male revenge on the "dumb" but desirous female was enacted in Selby's *Last Exit to Brooklyn* (1957), where the whorish Tra La La is gang-raped and finally murdered by being impaled on broomsticks and beer-

bottles. Even a brilliantly metaphysical comedy like Pynchon's *V* (1963) turned on comparable vengeance dreams. V's lesbian actress-lover Melanie is skewered by a pole in an onstage act in which she has failed to protect herself with a prop chastity belt, while the supposedly charismatic body of V herself is disassembled by children who steal her wooden legs, false teeth, and wig. As the critic Mary Allan has pointed out, "V" is clearly a virgin who thrives on both violence and vulgarity; at the same time, however, she incarnates the vulva, the vagina, and the horrifying void that these female body parts seemed ultimately to epitomize for many contemporary male artists.

Some of this period's fiercest conflicts among men similarly issued in literal as well as literary acts of aggression toward women. The revolt of male rock 'n' roll culture against bourgeois conventionality was often dramatized through record albums and posters flaunting images of enchained, semi-naked women, while racial battles between black and white males seem to have been fought out, over, and on the body of the female. Although the black prisoner-writer Eldridge Cleaver conceded in his memoir *Soul on Ice* (1968) that he "could not approve the act of rape," he explained that for him sexual assalts on white women had been "insurrectionary act[s]." "I was very resentful over the historical fact of how the white man has used the black woman. I felt I was getting revenge." Precisely such revenge was imagined in *Babylon Revisited* (1969), a curse poem by the black writer Imamu Amiri Baraka (Le Roi Jones), which damns the whorish white woman as "a vast puschamber / of pus(sy) memories / with no organs / nothing to make babies," and prays that "this bitch and her sisters, all of them, / receive my word / in all their orifices / like lye mixed with / cocola and alaga syrup." As if to establish and explain a relationship between *Soul on Ice* and *Babylon Revisited*, moreover, Cleaver quoted from *The Dead Lecturer* (1965), one of Baraka's earlier books: "Rape the white girls. Rape their fathers. Cut the mothers' throats."

Despite, or perhaps because of, its use of a black colloquialism ("mother" for "mother-fucker"), Baraka's last phrase highlighted an anxiety that may underlie a good deal of degrading contemporary rhetoric about women specifically an anxiety about a generation of viperous and vituperative mothers who were no longer experienced as being the selfless nurturers that their sons wanted them to be. With its definition of the pernicious American disease of "momism," Philip Wylie's *Generation of Vipers* (1942) definitively described the malaise that some men had begun to feel. Arguing that "the male is an attachment of the female in our civilization," Wylie excoriated a "dynasty of the dames," whom he saw as "five-and-ten-cent-store Lilith[s]"—that is, as modern equivalents of the monstrous first woman and first witch in Jewish legend. Ostensibly writing in a more scientific vein, the social historian Ferdinand Lundberg and the psychiatrist Marynia Farnham declared a few years later in *Modern Woman, the Lost Sex* that research had shown "the traditional 'Mom'" to be "the mother of [a] deficient male" and, rhetorically asking "Just what have these women done to their sons?," they replied "They have stripped them of their male powers—that is, they have castrated them."

As late as 1962, a character like "Big Nurse" in Ken Kesey's *One Flew Over the Cuckoo's Nest* was portrayed as embodying exactly the maternal flaws described by Wylie, Lundberg, and Farnham: Kesey's hero seemed to speak for the author when he exclaimed that Big Nurse "may be a mother, but she's big as a damn barn and tough as a knife metal . . . she's a bitch and a buzzard and a ball-cutter." In this period, moreover, even mothers apparently dedicated to the good of their growing boys were pictured as guilty and guilt-inducing. The stereotypical Jewish mother who reigns over Philip Roth's *Portnoy's Complaint* (1970) reveals her love for her son by threatening him with a knife in order to make him eat. Finally, even mothers who were neither castrating nor guilt-inducing often seemed horrifyingly weak and hence grotesquely pathetic. In *Kaddish* (1960), Allen Ginsberg lamented the

death of his mad mother, ritually telling her "farewell / with your old dress and a long black beard around the vagina / farewell / with your sagging belly," while in *Sailing Home from Rapallo* (1959) Robert Lowell described bringing his mother's body home from Italy, noting that "Mother travelled first-class in the hold," and adding that "the corpse / was wrapped like *panettone* [a Milanese Christmas bread] in Italian tinfoil."

Perhaps what informed depictions of both maternal power and maternal pathos in this period was a mythology of the mother goddess that can be traced back to the nineteenth century and that was outlined in the mid-twentieth century by the English poet-novelist Robert Graves, the German psychoanalyst Erich Neumann, and the American poet Robert Bly. For Graves, the enduring feminine ideal was a figure he called the "White Goddess," while for both Neumann and Bly she was the four-faceted "Great Mother." In all these cases, however, her differing aspects corresponded significantly with just the aspects of women, and especially mothers, that were praised or blamed by many contemporary male artists. Though such mythological schema and the ideology of sexuality on which they were based might have seemed only indirectly relevant to literary women, these ideals and ideas in fact reverberated through male definitions of female writing that had considerable impact on women of letters.

In *The White Goddess* (1948), Graves claimed that "a woman who concerns herself with poetry" should either be "a Silent Muse" or should "be the Muse in a complete sense . . . and should write . . . with antique authority." If most other writers did not mystify the literary woman as Graves did, many either scornfully trivialized or melodramatically aggrandized her. Theodore Roethke claimed in a glowing review of Louise Bogan's verse that most women poets were guilty of "running between the boudoir and the altar; stamping a tiny foot against God or lapsing into . . . sententiousness," while W. H. Auden praised Adrienne Rich's volume of verse *A Change of World* with the faintly patronizing comment that "the poems are neatly and modestly dressed, speak quietly but do not mumble, respect their elders but are not cowed by them, and do not tell fibs." Similarly, Robert Lowell introduced the first American edition of Sylvia Plath's *Ariel* (1965) by proclaiming that its author had here become "hardly a person at all, or a woman, certainly not another 'poetess,' but one of those super-real, hypnotic, great classical heroines." More generally, the British novelist-critic Anthony Burgess declared in 1966 that Jane Austen's novels failed because her writing "lacks a strong male thrust," and the American philosopher-novelist William Gass asserted in 1976 that literary women "lack that blood congested genital drive which energizes every great style." Given the impulse simultaneously to sexualize and dehumanize women that seems to have permeated much male thinking in the second half of the twentieth century, how was it possible for women writers—indeed for women generally—to accomplish anything of importance in this period?

CONTEMPORARY WOMEN'S LIVES

The pervasive eroticizing of women characteristic of so much contemporary male culture may have been in part a reaction against many personal and professional options that had just become open to women of all ages, classes, and races. For with newly granted legal, economic, social, political, and educational rights, women were in fact able to accomplish a great deal in these years. At the same time, however, it is no doubt true that many of these new rights were not equally available to all women, that all these new rights were controversial and continually threatened by conservative social movements, and finally, that a number of these new rights often presented problems to those who were supposedly benefiting from them.

During the second half of the twentieth century the legal status of women im-

proved in most English-speaking countries. Throughout the twentieth century, divorce had become increasingly common and simple to obtain, with the introduction of a "no-fault" divorce law in California in the 1970s representing perhaps the most dramatic symbol of the way in which the Victorian double standard of morality had been reversed: where in the past a woman could be chastised and divorced for adultery (while, often enough, a man could not), now either partner could dissolve a marriage for any or no reason whatsoever. Nor could a divorced woman's children be taken from her by their father—as they could have been in the nineteenth and early twentieth centuries—without elaborate court battles. In addition, the Abortion Act (1967) in Great Britain, and the landmark Supreme Court decision in the case of *Roe v. Wade* (1973) in the United States, gave women in both countries an unprecedented control over their own reproductive systems, and though in some English-speaking nations abortion remained illegal, the British and American models were powerful ones, implying that, in the words of the historian Carl Degler, "the law and society [had given] women final authority over the size of the family." Finally, throughout the 1960s and 1970s, equal-pay acts were passed and equal-opportunity commissions established in a number of English-speaking countries, seeking to rectify traditionally large differentials between male and female wages. The American Equal Pay Act of 1963 formulated for the first time the principle that women should not be paid less money for doing exactly the same work as men, and the Civil Rights Act of 1964 outlawed job discrimination on the basis of gender as well as race. During the 1980s and 1990s, an unprecedented number of women entered law schools, graduated to take on highly visible legal positions in the judiciary, and moved into political prominence.

Yet all these transformations in women's legal status were in one way or another problematic in their consequences. Not only did the ease of divorce lead to unprecedentedly high divorce rates, it was associated with a weakening of alimony and child support arrangements so that, as Degler reports, "in 1970, some 77 per cent of white women and 85 per cent of black women with children but without husbands maintained their own households. Yet as recently as 1940 only 45 per cent of white women and 40 per cent of black women did." A divorcée, therefore, was frequently impoverished and solely responsible for the welfare of her children. As for abortion legislation, because the so-called right to life of the developing fetus rapidly evolved in many countries from an ethical and religious question to a political issue, such legislation was continually being challenged. Moreover, women's wages remained significantly inferior to those of male counterparts; at present in the United States women workers earn seventy-six cents for every dollar earned by men, while in Great Britain and Canada working women receive seventy percent of the amount received by men. Worse still, in Australia in the late 1970s/early 1980s, the law established minimum wages for women that were lower than those for men performing identical tasks. By the mid-1990s, moreover, the American press reported widespread public suspicions about the affirmative action policies that had put some women and minorities into improved professional and political positions.

The issue of wages for women's work became an increasingly critical one in this period, precisely because women now found that they had increasing economic opportunities. To begin with—as the prize-winning documentary film *Rosie the Riveter* illustrated—World War II brought enormous numbers of women into the job market. By 1960, as the historian William Chafe has shown, "twice as many women were at work as in 1940, and 40 per cent of all women over sixteen held a job." In addition, he notes, between 1940 and 1960, "the number of mothers at work leaped 400 per cent—from 1.5 million to 6.6 million—and 39 per cent of women with children ages six to seventeen had jobs." Once again, though, the gains achieved by contemporary women were problematic. First, women workers tended to be clustered in low-status, low-paying, or service-oriented jobs: as the

sociologists Juanita Kreps and R. John Leaper put it, in 1976 "the working woman [was] a typist, maid, teacher, nurse, cashier, or saleswoman." Second, few married women workers were defined as primary breadwinners even when they were in fact the sole supporters of themselves or their families. Third, working women had few support systems to help them cope with what had traditionally been considered as the unique female responsibilities of child-care and housework. Though nursery school and day-care enrollments rose radically in this period, child-care facilities were often either inadequate or expensive, while working wives found themselves performing two jobs, one paid and one unpaid.

As if to underline the contradictions implicit in the history of women's gains during this period, Degler observes that "the proportion of women graduating from college was higher than ever" while Chafe remarks that "the proportion of women in business and the professions . . . changed hardly at all." Perhaps this paradox reflects a debate over the nature of women's education that goes back at least to the nineteenth century but that intensified in these years when female students flooded into universities, colleges, community colleges, and vocational training programs in every English-speaking country. The nature of this debate was succinctly summarized in 1955 by Lynn White Jr., then president of Mills College, in California. In a book called *Educating Our Daughters*, he proposed a "distinctively feminine curriculum," and speculated that "a beginning course in foods"—perhaps focusing on "the theory and preparation of Basque paella"—might be "as exciting . . . as a course in post-Kantian philosophy." Such ideas had an effect on female students, with a number of studies revealing that many young women who were ambitious to get A's in classes nevertheless felt obliged to "play dumb" on dates. The psychologist Matina Horner's classic essay *Fail: Bright Women* (1969) documented the consequences of such a conflict: precisely the young women who had been the most dutiful students in early life were least likely to succeed later.

Of course, the fact remains that Horner herself, president of Radcliffe College from 1972 to 1989, represented a group of women intellectuals who had *not* failed. After World War II, a range of female thinkers gained prominence in virtually every profession. To name only a few of them: in the United States, the philosopher Hannah Arendt, the critic Susan Sontag, the political theorist Angela Davis, and the biologist Barbara McClintock; in England, the crystallographer Rosalind Franklin, the philosopher-novelist Iris Murdoch, and the critic Helen Gardiner. At the same time, such women politicians as Indira Gandhi, Margaret Thatcher, Golda Meir, and Benazir Bhutto came to power. Moreover, although in these years women achievers might have seemed "singular anomalies," by the 1970s female enrollments in graduate and professional schools had risen so sharply that it was possible that Degler and Chafe's contradiction might be resolved.

The shifts in fashionable styles that can be traced from the forties through the eighties and nineties might function as an index of the enormous social changes that marked these years. From the utilitarian suits of the forties, with their padded shoulders and severe lines, to the "New Look" of the fifties, with its long, full, aggressively feminine skirts and decorous Peter Pan blouses, the revealing miniskirts and flowing Indian prints of the sixties, the unisex costumes and pantsuits of the late sixties and early seventies, and the dress-for-success costumes of the eighties, women's fashions illustrated, successively, the austerity of the forties' war effort, the domestic conservatism of the fifties, the new sexual freedom of the sixties, and the emergence of reactions in the seventies and eighties against the eroticizing of women in the sixties. No wonder, then, that an awareness of the rapidity of fashion's changes led to so-called "retro" dressing in the nineties as women adopted and parodied styles from the past.

What intensified, perhaps even triggered, the debate about female sexual liberation that was enacted through these changes in costume was a series of major ad-

vances in birth control techniques. Beginning with the repeal in the forties and fifties of laws forbidding the public dissemination of contraceptive information, birth control devices like the condom and the diaphragm had become more widely available. The development in the sixties of the birth control pill and the IUD (intrauterine device) meant that for unmarried women a new morality no longer grounded in the threat of pregnancy was now imaginable, while for married women a new control over family size was now feasible. In addition, even seemingly minor inventions such as tampons and beltless sanitary pads allowed women far greater flexibility in their activities. Particularly in the sixties, then, women may have seemed to be on the brink of an age of utopian sexuality in which desire could at last be expressed without dread.

Yet the new emphasis on sex was often in its own way puritanical: "coming" together was *de rigueur*; "good girls" always said yes; and proliferating sex manuals propounded efficient techniques for amorous encounters that reduced life between the sheets to a series of athletic events. As Barbara Ehrenreich has shown, with the legalization of pornography in the late 1950s, the sexual revolution began to seem like a specifically male revolution which, through such popular magazines as *Playboy* and *Penthouse*, expounded a hedonistic philosophy that turned women into consumable luxury goods. When hardcore pornographic films, journals, and books in the 1970s began to emphasize bondage and discipline of women along with "kiddy porn," a number of female thinkers became radically disaffected. Their alienation was increased by their recognition that, despite the apparently enlightened rhetoric of the era, social problems such as child abuse, wife beating, and rape continued unabated. During the 1980s and 1990s, when the AIDS pandemic took its tragic toll, sexual liberation was no longer identical with women's liberation.

As early as 1963, Betty Friedan's *The Feminine Mystique* had begun to define the difficulties fostered by the cult of suburban domesticity that marked the fifties. Describing "the problem that has no name," Friedan excavated the feelings of almost metaphysical emptiness that were associated with the roles of housewife and consumer. At around the same time, moreover, women involved in the civil rights movement (and not too much later in the peace movement) were discovering that their revolutionary energies were mainly taken up by making coffee and love. These women turned not only to Friedan's book but also to earlier works—notably Simone de Beauvoir's *The Second Sex* (1949)—and began to produce theoretical writings of their own. Together, Mary Ellmann's *Thinking about Women* (1968), Kate Millett's *Sexual Politics* (1969), Shulamith Firestone's *The Dialectic of Sex* (1970), and Germaine Greer's *The Female Eunuch* (1970) sought to rescue liberationist arguments for female freedom from the sexual exploitation their authors believed implicit in male-dominated radical movements.

At the same time, activists who gained societal recognition through public demonstrations began to issue manifestoes, even as they helped popularize socalled consciousness-raising groups (small gatherings of women who met to discuss the effects of gender on their lives). In England, militants articulated "the 7 demands of The Women's Liberation Movement": "1. Equal pay, 2. Equal education and job opportunities, 3. Free contraception and abortion on demand, 4. Free twenty-four-hour nurseries under community control, 5. Legal and financial independence, 6. An end to discrimination against lesbians, 7. Freedom from intimidation by . . . assumptions and institutions that perpetuate male dominance." In America, similar demands were formulated by groups like Red Stockings, SCUM (Society for Cutting Up Men), and the Feminists, while more moderate women joined the new movement when Betty Friedan organized the National Organization for Women (NOW) in 1966, and when the magazine *Ms.* was founded under the editorship of the journalist Gloria Steinem in 1972. In addition, in many English-speaking countries, grass-roots projects were founded in these years: child-

care centers, women's health collectives, abortion clinics, rape crisis hotlines and centers, as well as shelters for battered women and abused children.

Politically, of course, this sort of activity had a long history. In the United States, the League of Women Voters had evolved out of the National Woman's Suffrage Association shortly after women gained the vote in 1920. But the first significant political gesture made by feminists and their supporters since the passage of the Nineteenth Amendment was the campaign for congressional approval and state ratification of the Equal Rights Amendment, an amendment to the Constitution declaring that "equality of rights under the law shall not be denied or abridged by the United States or by any State on account of sex." Until 1970, both organized labor and women's leaders had opposed this amendment on the grounds that it threatened protective legislation for working women. But in 1970, Elizabeth B. Koontz, the first black woman to head the Women's Bureau in Washington, arranged for the Bureau to support the amendment; it was easily passed by Congress in 1972 and shortly thereafter ratified by several dozen states. However, at this point the ERA encountered powerful opposition from very different quarters. Led by Phyllis Schlafly, a conservative Republican, women anxious about their rights as wives and their protection as members of the second sex joined with religious fundamentalists and other upholders of traditional familial structures to claim that the amendment would bring about social chaos. Despite prolonged and arduous efforts by feminists, the ERA had not been approved by the necessary minimum of thirty-eight states in 1982, the deadline year by which it would have had to be ratified to become law.

That so many women were mobilized to oppose what had been defined as their own liberation dramatizes the anxieties raised by the women's movement. A conservative like Schlafly spoke not only for women who wished to preserve the prerogatives of suburban consumerism but also for women who felt empowered by precisely the fetishizing of female sexuality that characterized this era. The seductive wife described in Marabel Morgan's *The Total Woman* (1973) sought to guarantee her own emotional and material security through strategies of submissiveness and enticement. Moreover, even world leaders like Evita Perón, Indira Gandhi, and Margaret Thatcher—women who had managed what seemed astonishing rises to political power in this era—publicly endorsed Schlafly's ways of thinking, if not Morgan's. As for working-class women, in most English-speaking countries a significant percentage could not see any special advantage in feminist ideals of female autonomy. The American sociologists Louise Kapp Howe and Lillian Rubin have pointed out that many blue-collar women tended to agree with a seventies homemaker who insisted that "a lot of women are much better off married and at home than they would be at some low-paying job and they know this; they've usually worked before, after all. So when they hear some feminist writers or lawyers or something like that say that jobs are so terrific, they know that for the average woman that's a lot of baloney."

Despite these controversies, however, the awareness of women's complex cultural situation manifested in such research as that by Howe and Rubin points to another significant phenomenon in this period: the development of women's studies as an area of intellectual concern in colleges and universities. Humanists (historians, literary critics, and philosophers), social scientists (anthropologists, psychologists, sociologists, linguists, and economists), and scholars of the fine arts (art historians, musicologists, theater historians, and film critics) joined during the 1970s and 1980s to undertake interdisciplinary investigations of women's role in history and society, analyses that sought to transform traditional disciplines and curricula. Founding such journals as *Signs, Feminist Studies*, and the *International Journal of Women's Studies*, they explored not only the gender pressures all women seemed to share but also the distinctive perspectives that marked the lives of disparate groups and cultures—blacks, lesbians, Chicanas, working-class women, and

others. To be sure, many experienced themselves as marginalized, fearing in particular that their effort to widen the scope of scholarly inquiry from a study of man's culture to a study of human culture would have only a fleeting influence on intellectual institutions. Yet by the 1990s they had set in place major and minor programs for undergraduates in many colleges and universities as well as a number of graduate degrees. Their academic endeavors coincided with an era when women were striving to bring about a number of other large social and ideological changes. In literary criticism, for instance, feminist scholars unearthed and analyzed a tradition of female artistic achievement at just the moment when contemporary women writers were sometimes consciously and sometimes unconsciously extending that tradition into the future.

WOMEN'S WRITING

Whether they defined themselves as feminists or not, women writers after 1940 wrote out of a double consciousness: on the one hand a newly intense awareness of their role as female artists who had inherited an increasingly strong tradition and, on the other hand, a newly protective sense of their vulnerability as women who inhabited a culture hostile to female ambition and haunted by eroticized images of women. Certainly both these strands of thought came together in Adrienne Rich's *Writing as Re-Vision* (1971), an essay that might be said to have functioned as a kind of manifesto for both female writers and feminist critics in these years. Criticizing "the use that the male artist and thinker . . . has made of women, in his life and in his work," Rich resurrected foremothers from Virginia Woolf to Marianne Moore, explaining that "re-vision" of both male imperatives and female ancestresses was 'for us more than a chapter in cultural history: it is an act of survival."

In their various ways, many contemporaries of this notable American feminist were engaged in exactly such acts of survival. Essays like Tillie Olsen's *One Out of Twelve* (1972) and Joanna Russ's *What Can a Heroine Do?* (1972); poems like Muriel Rukeyser's *Myth*, Denise Levertov's *Hypocrite Women*, and Sylvia Plath's *Stings*; as well as stories like Doris Lessing's *One off the Short List* articulate or enact a deep resistance to male-created social strictures and structures. At the same time, essays like Alice Walker's *In Search of Our Mothers' Gardens* (1974) and Paule Marshall's *Poets in the Kitchen* (1983), poems like May Sarton's *My Sisters, O My Sisters* and Kamala Das's *An Introduction*, as well as stories like Edna O'Brien's *A Rose in the Heart* and Ursula K. Le Guin's *Sur* articulate or enact a deep identification with either literal or literary mothers. In coming to terms with both the male and female forces that shaped them, contemporary writers were consistently struggling to define the cultural forces that had formed their personal and artistic identities.

Such a search for the roots of selfhood was perhaps especially urgent for women writers in third world and Commonwealth countries, and for writers who inhabited racial, ethnic, and lesbian subcultures in England or America. Though all these authors had in common the medium of the English language, with its comparatively fixed grammatical and lexical conventions, they were influenced by distinctive traits and traditions to use English in very different ways and for notably different ends. Tillie Olsen captured the inflections of an immigrant Russian Jew in *Tell Me a Riddle*; Lucille Clifton used a modified black dialect to retell the story of the Virgin Mary in her "Mary Poems"; the Anglo-Indian poet Kamala Das confronted head-on her conflicted but nevertheless definitive decision to write in English in *The Introduction*; and Gloria Anzaldúa composed an English infused by Spanish rhythms as well as Mexican images. Writers with such disparate backgrounds as the African Ama Ata Aidoo, the Asian American Maxine Hong Kingston, the black lesbian Audre Lorde, and the Native American Leslie Marmon

Silko filtered their stories of significant ethnicity through an English language that registered diverse cultural and sexual heritages. Indeed, artists with what came to be called hyphenated identities—Bharati Mukherjee, Buchi Emecheta, Jamaica Kincaid, Lorna Dee Cervantes, Louise Erdrich, Cathy Song—attained extraordinary prominence and, in the process, altered the conventional demarcations used to map the aesthetic geography of the West.

By simultaneously defining or redefining both themselves and their worlds, such women indicated the general parameters of female writing in this period, for the motivating impulse behind the works of contemporary women of letters can often be located along a continuum that reaches from self-definition to social criticism. Taking the real or figurative self as a subject, the writers whose work depended on processes of self-definition tended to explore not only the dynamics but the dreams of subjectivity itself. Remembering in *In the Waiting Room* how she had learned "I was an Elizabeth," Elizabeth Bishop can stand as a model for the poets Sylvia Plath, Diane Wakoski, Denise Levertov, Audre Lorde, and Ruth Stone, all of whom struggled to articulate—in Levertov's words—"what, woman, and who, myself, I am." Clearly, the diarists and memoirists Anaïs Nin, Maya Angelou, and Mary McCarthy shared this project, but, less obviously, so did fiction writers as diverse as Margaret Laurence and Carson McCullers.

In a quite different mode, those artists who took a real or imagined society as their subject set out, often in a strikingly realistic manner, to describe the world that circumscribes the self. Gwendolyn Brooks's Chicago "bean-eaters," Flannery O'Connor's Georgia country people, Stevie Smith's cartoon Britons, Rita Dove's nineteenth-century slaves, and Nadine Gordimer's South African liberals inhabit markedly different landscapes, yet all their authors explored the everyday worlds in which such characters were situated to construct an almost sociological analysis of the relationship between the individual and her community.

To be sure, most contemporary writers oscillated between both these modes, for—as most would have agreed—to know the society *is* to know the self. Even a tale of black culture like Toni Morrison's *Sula* (1973), with its implicit indictment of the ways in which white dominance cripples black men and maddens black women, can be said also to constitute a fable of identity, an act of self-examination as well as of social analysis. For, as Morrison herself remarked, "I do feel a strong connection to 'ancestors.' . . . What is uppermost in my mind . . . is that my life seems to be dominated by information about black women. . . . I feel the authority of those women more than I do my own." The fact that Morrison has perceived her exploration of the black female community as a kind of analysis of her own (as well as its) "authority" implies an interdependency between the sociological and the psychological modes of writing. In this respect, Morrison is representative of her peers, although contemporary writers are a highly diverse group.

"Diversity," in fact, became a feminist theme in the eighties and nineties, with many women writers exploring and dramatizing their national, economic, linguistic, regional, ethnic, religious, and political divergences along with their differing sexual preferences, their disparate stances regarding earlier aesthetic traditions, their attractions to a broad spectrum of genres, and their complicated attitudes toward various feminist projects. During the 1980s and 1990s, this emphasis among literary women on their distinctive backgrounds paralleled (and was sometimes associated with) the evolution of a range of innovative academic disciplines and methodologies, including African American, Asian American, Latino, and Native American studies, as well as postcolonial criticism and gay studies. The increasingly significant presence of such new interdisciplinary fields shifted the emphases of many feminist critics, a number of whom began examining multiple aspects of women's cultural experiences. At the same time, the very term "woman" came under scrutiny, as some gender theorists debated the notion that the female role should be understood as a fictive or artificial concept, with "femininity" itself merely a performance of societal stereotypes.

With the year 2001 approaching, such phrases as "postmodernism" or "generation X" might seem to have implied widespread cultural feelings of belatedness or at least confusion, yet as the often heated discussions of feminists suggest and as the writings of women around the world reveal female literary traditions remained vital and were often characterized by exciting experimentation. Long and interconnected poetic sequences, prose that slides into poetry, autobiography with the features of fiction, fairy tales written in the Gothic mode: many women's productions manifest a transgressive exuberance. What critics and artists continued to share is Morrison's ethical determination to examine the interdependence of the private female self and the public world. From this last perspective, Adrienne Rich's celebration of a woman as an icon of the future—her vision of the woman "who must be more merciless to herself than history"—is significant because it draws on a dream of social transformation to create an image of a transformed self. As Rich herself tells us in a number of her poems, it was her reading of feminist analyses of society that enabled her to convert the eroticized body of the fifties and sixties into a luminous figure fully self-aware and self-possessed. Perhaps, too, Rich's vision was made possible by her consciousness that she herself belonged to a community of women artists, even as that same consciousness empowered her to produce her ambitious long poem titled *An Atlas of the Difficult World* (1991).

If we compare the section of this anthology in which Rich's work appears with the first section of the book, we cannot fail to be struck by the complexity and energy of the voices raised in recent years to address questions that only a few medieval and Renaissance women had been able to formulate. Yet we have included here merely a representative selection of authors whose works reveal the new authority with which women are writing today. Nevertheless, the vigorous line of development we have been able to trace from the Middle Ages to the present suggests the ways in which by the end of the twentieth century women of letters no longer believed themselves to be what May Sarton in *My Sisters, O My Sisters* called "strange monsters." Instead, many female artists had already, in Sarton's words, "come to the deep place where poet becomes woman" while rejoicing in "that great sanity, that sun, the feminine power."

STEVIE SMITH

1902–1971

"Who and what is Stevie Smith? / Is she woman? Is she myth?" asked the American poet-humorist Ogden Nash in 1964, expressing awe at the ways in which this English writer was able "to sing at Man's expense / Songs of deadly innocence." Nash's praise is not surprising, for as a sardonic versifier Smith wrote comic poems significantly akin to his famously witty couplets; at the same time, both more mordant and (occasionally) more morbid than her American counterpart, she frequently achieved what the poet Robert Lowell called a "unique and cheerfully gruesome voice."

Born Florence Margaret Smith in Hull, Yorkshire. Smith (subsequently nicknamed "Stevie" after the famous jockey Steve Donohue, because she was very short) moved to London with her mother and sister when she was only three. There, in the unfashionable suburb of Palmers Green, she and her sister Molly were largely raised by an aunt (whom Smith affectionately called "Auntie Lion") because their father was frequently away, and their mother's health was bad. After graduating from the North London Collegiate School for Girls, Smith became a secretary in the magazine publishing house of George Newnes, where she was to work for thirty years, from 1923 to 1953. Continuing to live, as she would all her

life, with Auntie Lion, she began to publish both poetry and fiction when she was in her early thirties. *Novel on Yellow Paper; or, Work It Out for Yourself* appeared in 1936, succeeded by her first volume of verse, *A Good Time Was Had by All* (1937), and later followed by two more novels and more than ten other collections of poetry, including *Not Waving but Drowning* (1957) and *The Frog Prince and Other Poems* (1966).

Ranging from satiric melancholy to ferocious irony, Smith's work both celebrated and criticized the customs of a slowly declining British Empire. Perhaps for this reason, it was some years before her American audience grew as large as her English readership. Yet by the time she was awarded the Queen's Gold Medal for Poetry in 1969, her "cheerfully gruesome voice" had been noted and appreciated in the United States. "Across the world I hear her still," declared Ogden Nash, "singing underneath the hill."

Papa Love Baby

My mother was a romantic girl
So she had to marry a man with his hair in curl
Who subsequently became my unrespected papa,
But that was a long time ago now.

What folly it is that daughters are always supposed to be 5
In love with papa. It wasn't the case with me
I couldn't take to him at all.
But he took to me
What a sad fate to befall
A child of three. 10
I sat upright in my baby carriage
And wished mama hadn't made such a foolish marriage.
I tried to hide it, but it showed in my eyes unfortunately
And a fortnight later papa ran away to sea.

He used to come home on leave 15
It was always the same
I could not grieve
But I think I was somewhat to blame.

 1937

This Englishwoman

This Englishwoman is so refined
She has no bosom and no behind.

 1937

Lord Barrenstock

Lord Barrenstock and Epicene,[1]
What's it to me that you have been

1. A sexless or effeminate man. "Barrenstock": i.e., unable to produce children.

In your pursuit of interdicted[2] joys
Seducer of a hundred little boys?

Your sins are red about your head 5
And many people wish you dead.

You trod the widow in the mire
Wronged the son, deceived the sire.

You put a fence about the land
And made the people's cattle graze on sand. 10

Ratted from many a pool and forced amalgamation[3]
And dealt in shares which never had a stock exchange quotation.

Non flocci facio,[4] I do not care
For wrongs you made the other fellow bear:
'Tis not for these unsocial acts not these 15
I wet my pen. I would not have you tease,
With a repentance smug and overdue
For all the things you still desire to do,
The ears of an outraged divinity:
But oh your tie is crooked and I see 20
Too plain you had an éclair for your tea.

It is this nonchalance about your person—
That is the root of my profound aversion.

You are too fat. In spite of stays[5]
Your shape is painful to the polished gaze; 25
Your uncombed hair grows thin and daily thinner,
In fact you're far too ugly to be such a sinner.

Lord Barrenstock and Epicene, consider all that you have done
Lord Epicene and Barrenstock, yet not two Lords but one,
I think you are an object not of fear but pity 30
Be good, my Lord, since you cannot be pretty.

 1937

Dear Female Heart

Dear Female Heart, I am sorry for you,
You must suffer, that is all that you can do.
But if you like, in common with the rest of the human race,
You may also look most absurd with a miserable face.

 1938

2. Forbidden.
3. I.e., cheated business associates.

4. I don't give a straw, I don't care (Latin).
5. Corsets.

Souvenir de Monsieur Poop[1]

I am the self-appointed guardian of English literature,
I believe tremendously in the significance of age;
I believe that a writer is wise at 50,
Ten years wiser at 60, at 70 a sage.
I believe that juniors are lively, to be encouraged with discretion
 and snubbed, 5
I believe also that they are bouncing, communistic, ill mannered
 and, of course, young.
But I never define what I mean by youth
Because the word undefined is more useful for general purposes
 of abuse.
I believe that literature is a school where only those who apply
 themselves diligently to their tasks acquire merit.
And only they after the passage of a good many years (see above). 10
But then I am an old fogey.
I always write more in sorrow than in anger.
I am, after all, devoted to Shakespeare, Milton,
And, coming to our own times,
Of course 15
Housman.[2]
I have never been known to say a word against the established
 classics,
I am in fact devoted to the established classics.
In the service of literature I believe absolutely in the principle
 of division;
I divide into age groups and also into schools. 20
This is in keeping with my scholastic mind, and enables me to
 trounce
Not only youth
(Which might be thought intellectually frivolous by pedants)
 but also periodical tendencies,
To ventilate, in a word, my own political and moral philosophy.
(When I say that I am an old fogey, I am, of course, joking.) 25
English literature, as I see it, requires to be defended
By a person of integrity and essential good humor
Against the forces of fanaticism, idiosyncrasy and anarchy.
I perfectly apprehend the perilous nature of my convictions
And I am prepared to go to the stake 30
For Shakespeare, Milton,
And, coming to our own times,
Of course
Housman.
I cannot say more than that, can I? 35
And I do not deem it advisable, in the interests of the editor
 to whom I am spatially contracted,
To say less.

1938

1. Memory of Mister Poop (French).
2. A. E. Housman (1859–1936), English poet, writer of ballads and other traditional forms, and classical scholar.

Human Affection

Mother, I love you so.
Said the child, I love you more than I know.
She laid her head on her mother's arm,
And the love between them kept them warm.

<div align="right">1942</div>

The Wanderer[1]

Twas the voice of the Wanderer, I heard her exclaim,
You have weaned me too soon, you must nurse me again,
She taps as she passes at each window pane,
Pray, does she not know that she taps in vain?

Her voice flies away on the midnight wind, 5
But would she be happier if she were within?
She is happier far where the night winds fall,
And there are no doors and no windows at all.

No man has seen her, this pitiful ghost,
And no woman either, but heard her at most, 10
Sighing and tapping and sighing again,
You have weaned me too soon, you must nurse me again.

<div align="right">1950</div>

Lightly Bound

You beastly child, I wish you had miscarried,
You beastly husband, I wish I had never married.
You hear the north wind riding fast past the window? He calls me.
Do you suppose I shall stay when I can go so easily?

<div align="right">1950</div>

Not Waving but Drowning

Nobody heard him, the dead man,
But still he lay moaning:
I was much further out than you thought
And not waving but drowning.

Poor chap, he always loved larking 5
And now he's dead

1. Compare the moral poem by Isaac Watts (1674–1748), *The Sluggard*: "'Tis the voice of the sluggard; I heard him complain, / 'You have waked me too soon, I must slumber again.' / As the door on its hinges, so he on his bed, / Turns his sides and his shoulders and his heavy head." See also Lewis Carroll's parody of Watts, *'Twas the Voice of the Lobster*, in *Alice in Wonderland*.

It must have been too cold for him his heart gave way,
They said.

Oh, no no no, it was too cold always
(Still the dead one lay moaning)
I was much too far out all my life
And not waving but drowning.

1957

How Cruel Is the Story of Eve[1]

How cruel is the story of Eve
What responsibility
It has in history
For cruelty.

Touch, where the feeling is most vulnerable, 5
Unblameworthy—ah reckless—desiring children,
Touch there with a touch of pain?
Abominable.

Ah what cruelty,
In history 10
What misery.

Put up to barter
The tender feelings
Buy her a husband to rule her
Fool her to marry a master 15
She must or rue it
The Lord said it.

And man, poor man,
Is he fit to rule,
Pushed to it? 20
How can he carry it, the governance,
And not suffer for it
Insuffisance?

He must make woman lower then
So he can be higher then. 25
Oh what cruelty,
In history what misery.

Soon woman grows cunning
Masks her wisdom,
How otherwise will he 30

1. According to the Old Testament, Eve was the first woman, created by God from a rib belonging to Adam, the first man. There is a long tradition of blaming Eve for the Fall, because first she, then Adam ate the for- bidden fruit of the Tree of Knowledge. God punished them by bringing death into the world as well as pain in childbirth, male work, and female submission (Genesis 3).

Bring food and shelter, kill enemies?
If he did not feel superior
It would be worse for her
And for the tender children
Worse for them. 35

Oh what cruelty,
In history what misery
Of falsity.

It is only a legend
You say? But what 40
Is the meaning of the legend
If not
To give blame to women most
And most punishment?

This is the meaning of a legend that colors 45
All human thought; it is not found among animals.

How cruel is the story of Eve,
What responsibility it has
In history
For misery. 50

Yet there is this to be said still:
Life would be over long ago
If men and women had not loved each other
Naturally, naturally,
Forgetting their mythology 55
They would have died of it else
Long ago, long ago,
And all would be emptiness now
And silence.

Oh dread Nature, for your purpose, 60
To have made them love so.

 1966

ANAÏS NIN

1903–1977

In a passage from her critical book *The Novel of the Future* (1963), which typifies the introspective quality of her famous *Diary*, Anaïs Nin analyzed the origins of her creativity: the "traumatic genesis" occurred when she was nine years old and what later turned out to be an incorrect medical diagnosis that she would never walk again turned her to writing as a pastime; the "artistic genesis" of her *Diary* was her separation from her father, for she recorded her impressions "to persuade my absent father to return." The self-absorption of much of Nin's work reflects her lifelong effort to explore her sense of difference and of separation. Her father, a

Spanish pianist and composer, had taken her with him on his concert tours throughout Europe. But when her parents separated, the eleven-year-old girl and her two brothers left their native Paris for New York, where they lived with their mother, a French-Danish singer. Nin did not return to Paris until the 1930s, after her marriage to the banker Hugh Guiler. Under the name Ian Hugo, her husband later became an illustrator of her books, but she remained surprisingly reticent about him and their relationship. Indeed, for all of the self-scrutiny of her work, Nin fashioned an image of her life to demonstrate that "it is not only the woman Anaïs who has to speak, but I who have to speak for many women."

Nin's first book, a critical evaluation of the novelist D. H. Lawrence, displayed the emotional sensitivity that would continue to characterize her writing. While composing it, the twenty-eight-year-old met Henry Miller, who was drafting both *Tropic of Cancer* (1934) and his own essay on D. H. Lawrence. Like Lawrence, Nin and Miller perceived themselves as pioneers in a sexual revolution and, while Nin explored how—as a woman—she could not accept Miller's male-dominated perspective, both artists produced fiction about the nature of eroticism. Nin's other friends were just as fascinated by the relationship between identity and sexuality: they included Henry Miller's wife, June Miller, the surrealist poet Antonin Artaud, the novelist Lawrence Durrell, and the well-known psychiatrist Dr. Otto Rank, with whom Nin studied.

Although she was forced to leave Europe at the outbreak of World War II, Nin continued her journal in America, where she responded to the difficulty she experienced in getting her work published by buying a printing press. The *Diary* first received serious critical attention in 1966, when it began to be printed by Alan Swallow. It constitutes an extraordinary effort "to capture the living moments" of her emotional reactions to experience, an effort that Miller had earlier compared to the literary self-revelations of St. Augustine, Petronius, Abelard, Rousseau, and Proust. The *Diaries* were significantly complemented and supplemented, moreover, by a series of lyrical prose fictions in which Nin reworked and objectified much of her personal experience. In particular, the sequence of novels called *Cities of the Interior* (1959)—*Ladders to Fire, Children of the Albatross, The Four-Chambered Heart, A Spy in the House of Love*, and *Seduction of the Minotaur*—extended her exploration of the female psyche in lyrical language that attempts to capture the fluid formations and reformations of the self. With unusual candor, *Birth* recounts the painful consciousness born during a labor destined never to give birth to life.

Birth

"The child," said the doctor, "is dead."

I lay stretched on a table. I had no place on which to rest my legs. I had to keep them raised. Two nurses leaned over me. In front of me stood the doctor with the face of a woman and eyes protruding with anger and fear. For two hours I had been making violent efforts. The child inside of me was six months old and yet it was too big for me. I was exhausted, the veins in me were swelling with the strain. I had pushed with my entire being. I had pushed as if I wanted this child out of my body and hurled into another world.

"Push, push with all your strength!"

Was I pushing with all my strength? All my strength?

No. A part of me did not want to push out the child. The doctor knew it. That is why he was angry, mysteriously angry. He knew. A part of me lay passive, did not want to push out anyone, not even this dead fragment of myself,

out in the cold, outside of me. All in me which chose to keep, to lull, to em-
brace, to love, all in me which carried, preserved, and protected, all in me
which imprisoned the whole world in its passionate tenderness, this part of
me would not thrust out the child, even though it had died in me. Even
though it threatened my life, I could not break, tear out, separate, surrender,
open and dilate and yield up a fragment of a life like a fragment of the past,
this part of me rebelled against pushing out the child, or anyone, out in the
cold, to be picked up by strange hands, to be buried in strange places, to be
lost, lost, lost. . . . He knew, the doctor. A few hours before he adored me,
served me. Now he was angry. And I was angry with a black anger at this part of
me which refused to push, to separate, to lose.

"Push! Push! Push with all your strength!"

I pushed with anger, with despair, with frenzy, with the feeling that I would
die pushing, as one exhales the last breath, that I would push out everything
inside of me, and my soul with all the blood around it, and the sinews with my
heart inside of them, choked, and that my body itself would open and smoke
would rise, and I would feel the ultimate incision of death.

The nurses leaned over me and they talked to each other while I rested.
Then I pushed until I heard my bones cracking, until my veins swelled. I
closed my eyes so hard I saw lightning and waves of red and purple. There was
a stir in my ears, a beating as if the tympanum[1] would burst. I closed my lips so
tightly the blood was trickling. My legs felt enormously heavy, like marble
columns, like immense marble columns crushing my body. I was pleading for
someone to hold them. The nurse laid her knee on my stomach and shouted:
"Push! Push! Push!" Her perspiration fell on me.

The doctor paced up and down angrily, impatiently. "We will be here all
night. Three hours now. . . ."

The head was showing, but I had fainted. Everything was blue, then black.
The instruments were gleaming before my eyes. Knives sharpened in my ears.
Ice and silence. Then I heard voices, first talking too fast for me to understand.
A curtain was parted, the voices still tripped over each other, falling fast like a
waterfall, with sparks, and cutting into my ears. The table was rolling gently,
rolling. The women were lying in the air. Heads. Heads hung where the enor-
mous white bulbs of the lamps were hung. The doctor was still walking, the
lamps moved, the heads came near, very near, and the words came more
slowly.

They were laughing. Once nurse was saying: "When I had my first child I
was all ripped to pieces. I had to be sewn up again, and then I had another, and
had to be sewn up, and then I had another. . . ."

The other nurse said: "Mine passed like an envelope through a letter box.
But afterwards the bag would not come out. The bag would not come out.
Out. Out. . . ." Why did they keep repeating themselves. And the lamps turn-
ing. And the steps of the doctor very fast, very fast.

"She can't labor any more, at six months nature does not help. She should
have another injection."

I felt the needle thrust. The lamps were still. The ice and the blue that was
all around came into my veins. My heart beat wildly. The nurses talked: "Now
that baby of Mrs. L. last week, who would have thought she was too small, a

1. Eardrum.

big woman like that, a big woman like that, a big woman like that. . . ." The words kept turning, as on a disk. They talked, they talked, they talked. . . .

Please hold my legs! Please hold my legs! Please hold my legs! PLEASE HOLD MY LEGS! I am ready again. By throwing my head back I can see the clock. I have been struggling four hours. It would be better to die. Why am I alive and struggling so desperately? I could not remember why I should want to live. I could not remember anything. Everything was blood and pain. I have to push. I have to push. That is a black fixed point in eternity. At the end of a long dark tunnel. I have to push. A voice saying: "Push! Push! Push!" A knee on my stomach and the marble of my legs crushing me and the head so large and I have to push.

Am I pushing or dying? The light up there, the immense round blazing white light is drinking me. It drinks me slowly, inspires me into space. If I do not close my eyes it will drink all of me. I seep upward, in long icy threads, too light, and yet inside there is a fire too, the nerves are twisted, there is no rest from this long tunnel dragging me, or am I pushing myself out of the tunnel, or is the child being pushed out of me, or is the light drinking me. Am I dying? The ice in the veins, the cracking of the bones, this pushing in darkness, with a small shaft of light in the eyes like the edge of a knife, the feeling of a knife cutting the flesh, the flesh somewhere is tearing as if it were burned through by a flame, somewhere my flesh is tearing and the blood is spilling out. I am pushing in the darkness, in utter darkness. I am pushing until my eyes open and I see the doctor holding a long instrument which he swiftly thrusts into me and the pain makes me cry out. A long animal howl. That will make her push, he says to the nurse. But it does not. It paralyzes me with pain. He wants to do it again. I sit up with fury and I shout at him: "Don't you dare do that again, don't you dare!"

The heat of my anger warms me, all the ice and pain are melted in the fury. I have an instinct that what he has done is unnecessary, that he has done it because he is in a rage, because the hands on the clock keep turning, the dawn is coming and the child does not come out, and I am losing strength and the injection does not produce the spasm.

I look at the doctor pacing up and down, or bending to look at the head which is barely showing. He looks baffled, as before a savage mystery, baffled by this struggle. He wants to interfere with his instruments, while I struggle with nature, with myself, with my child and with the meaning I put into it all, with my desire to give and to hold, to keep and to lose, to live and to die. No instrument can help me. His eyes are furious. He would like to take a knife. He has to watch and wait.

I want to remember all the time why I should want to live. I am all pain and no memory. The lamp has ceased drinking me. I am too weary to move even towards the light, or to turn my head and look at the clock. Inside of my body there are fires, there are bruises, the flesh is in pain. The child is not a child, it is a demon strangling me. The demon lies inert at the door of the womb, blocking life, and I cannot rid myself of it.

The nurses begin to talk again. I say: let me alone. I put my two hands on my stomach and very softly, with the tips of my fingers, I drum drum drum drum drum drum on my stomach in circles. Around, around, softly, with eyes open in great serenity. The doctor comes near with amazement on his face. The nurses are silent. Drum drum drum drum drum drum in soft circles, soft quiet

circles. Like a savage. The mystery. Eyes open, nerves begin to shiver, . . . a
mysterious agitation. I hear the ticking of the clock . . . inexorably, separately.
The little nerves awake, stir. But my hands are so weary, so weary, they will fall
off. The womb is stirring and dilating. Drum drum drum drum drum. I am
ready! The nurse presses her knee on my stomach. There is blood in my eyes.
A tunnel. I push into this tunnel. I bite my lips and push. There is a fire and
flesh ripping and no air. Out of the tunnel! All my blood is spilling out. Push!
Push! Push! It is coming! It is coming! It is coming! I feel the slipperiness, the
sudden deliverance, the weight is gone. Darkness. I hear voices. I open my
eyes. I hear them saying: "It was a little girl. Better not show it to her." All my
strength returns. I sit up. The doctor shouts: "Don't sit up!"

"Show me the child!"

"Don't show it," says the nurse, "it will be bad for her."

The nurses try to make me lie down. My heart is beating so loud I can hardly
hear myself repeating: "Show it to me." The doctor holds it up. It looks dark
and small, like a diminutive man. But it is a little girl. It has long eyelashes on
its closed eyes, it is perfectly made, and all glistening with the waters of the
womb.

1938

DILYS LAING

1906–1960

"To be a woman and a writer / is double mischief," declared Dilys Laing in the sym-
pathetic *Sonnet to a Sister in Error* that she addressed to the seventeenth-century
poet Anne, countess of Winchilsea, adding, in a gesture of affiliation with the fe-
male literary tradition that would be repeated by countless women writers in the
decades after her death, "Separate in time, we mutiny together." A pacifist as well
as a protofeminist, Laing mutinied in many ways throughout her literary career.
Born in Wales, raised in Canada, and educated in London, she married in 1936
and settled in Vermont, where she published poetry and fiction in such volumes of
social protest as *Birth Is Farewell* (1944), *The Great Year* (1948), and *Walk Through
Two Landscapes* (1949). Appearing posthumously, her *Poems from a Cage* (1961)
and *Collected Poems* (1967) further elaborate her sense of a God who is "woman-
shaped" and who inspires the women "created . . . in Her own image" to "war on
war."

Sonnet to a Sister in Error

> Whilst the dull manage of a servile house
> Is held by some our utmost art and use.
> —Anne, Countess of Winchilsea (1661–1720)[1]

Sweet Anne of Winchilsea, you were no hellion
intent on setting the broad world to rocking.

1. Quoted from *The Introduction* (see p. 168).

The long court dress concealed the long blue stocking,[2]
the easy manner masked the hard rebellion.
With light foot stirruped on the Muses' stallion[3] 5
you ambled privately, afraid of shocking
the Maids of Honor[4] who excelled at mocking
the matchless rose with stitches small and million.

Staunch Anne! I know your trouble. The same tether
galls us. To be a woman and a writer 10
is double mischief, for the world will slight her
who slights "the servile house," and who would rather
make odes than beds. Lost lady! Gentle fighter!
Separate in time, we mutiny together.

 1949

The Double Goer

The woman took a train
away away from herself.
She thought: I need a change
and wheels make revolutions.
I'm half a century old 5
and must be getting somewhere.
And so she futured on
away from her own presence.

The landscape boiled around her
like a pan of beans. 10
A man without a face
made her ticket holy.
Adventure thrilled her nerves
restless rapture shook her.
Love is in the next seat, 15
she mused, and strength and glory
are over the hill, and I
grow younger as I leave
my me behind.

The telephone wires were staves[1] 20
of a quintet score.
The hills were modulations
through the circle of keys.
Freedom is music, she thought,
smiling at the conductor. 25
This is your station, lady,
he snapped, and on the downbeat
she stepped to the vita nuova.[2]

2. *Bluestocking* is a disparaging term for an intellec-
tual or literary woman.
3. Pegasus; here a symbol of poetry.
4. Anne was maid of honor (an attendant) to the
duchess of York.
1. Horizontal lines on which music is written.
2. The new life (Italian); also the title of a narrative
by Dante (1265–1321), telling of his love for Beatrice.

A crowd had come to meet her
and they were fond in greeting: 30
husband, child, and father,
mother, and all the neighbors.

They travel as fast as I do,
she thought, and turned to climb
back to freedom's flying. 35
The door was shut. The train
streamed off like spilled water.

She faced the crowd and cried:
I love you all but one:
the one who wears my face. 40
She is the one I fled from.

They said: You took her with you
and brought her back again.
You look sick. Welcome home.

 1952

Let Them Ask Their Husbands

And if they will learn anything let them ask their husbands at home: for it is a
shame for women to speak in the church.
—I Corinthians 14:35

In human need
of the familiar
I see God
woman-shaped

for God created
woman in Her own image
and I have
my Pauline[1] pride.

 1957

Prayer of an Ovulating Female

I bring no throat-slit kid
no heart-scooped victim
no captive decapitated
and no self-scourged flesh.

I bring you, Domina, 5
Mother of women,

1. St. Paul wrote I Corinthians.

a calendula[1] in a pot
a candle and a peach
an egg and a
split condom. 10

Ave Mater
Mulierum![2]
may no blood flow
nec in caelo
nec in terra[3] 15
except according
to the calendar.

c. 1958

1. An herb. "Domina": lady. 3. Neither in heaven nor on Earth (Latin).
2. Hail Mother of Women! (Latin).

M. F. K. FISHER
1908–1992

Both praised and dismissed as a "food writer," Mary Frances Kennedy Fisher examined the nuances of her own life as well as the history of her society with an almost Proustian eloquence in numerous volumes of recipes and memoirs, some collected in *The Art of Eating* (1954) and others in *The Gastronomical Me* (1943). Born in Michigan and raised in California, she was married three times, first to Alfred Young Fisher, whose name she took for much of her professional work, second to Dillwyn Parrish, called "Chexbres" in the selection included here, who died in 1942, and finally to Donald Friede, whom she divorced in 1951 but with whom she had two daughters.

In addition to writing about what Virginia Woolf lovingly called "the little art of cookery," Fisher produced novels, poems, a screenplay, a travel book, a translation of the French gastronome Brillat-Savarin, and several confessional analyses of the aging process, notably *Sister Age* (1983). Trying to account for her long-term literary focus on culinary matters, however, she observed that "Anything can be a lodestar in a person's life, I suppose . . . the Kitchen serves well." For her, indeed, the kitchen, dining room, and restaurant were stages where high theater—some tragic, some comic—was often performed, as the understated yet painful drama of *The Flaw* suggests.

The Flaw

There was a train, not a particularly good one, that stopped at Vevey about ten in the morning on the way to Italy. Chexbres and I used to take it to Milano.

It had a restaurant car, an old-fashioned one with the agreeable austerity of a third-class station café about it: brown wooden walls and seats, bare tables unless you ordered the highest-priced lunch, and a few faded advertisements for Aspirina Bayer and "*Visitez le Maroc*" permanently crooked above the windows.

There was one table, next to the galley, where the cooks and waiters sat. In the morning they would be talking and sorting greens for salad and cutting the tops off radishes for the *hors d'oeuvres*, and in the early afternoon they would eat enormously of some things that had been on the menu and some that certainly had not. There was always a big straw-wrapped flask of red wine with them.

Sometimes the head chef smoked while he drank, or read parts of a newspaper aloud, but usually he worked with his helpers. And if one of the two waiters sat there, he worked too.

We liked to go into the restaurant partly because of the cooks, who after a polite salute ignored us, and partly because of the waiters, who were always the same ones.

Of course, it is impossible that they were on every train that went to Milano through Vevey at ten in the morning. But they were on that train every time we took it, so that very soon they knew us and laughed and even patted Chexbres' shoulder delightedly when we appeared.

We always went into their car a few minutes after we started . . . after we had been seen by the conductor and what few travelers there were on the unfashionable train. The restaurant would be empty at that hour, of course, except for the table of amiably chattering cooks.

We would order a large bottle of Asti Spumanti. That delighted the waiters, whether it was the young smooth one or the old sour withered one. We would sit drinking it, slightly warm, from the thick train-goblets, talking and watching the flat floor of the Valais grow narrower and wilder, waiting as always with a kind of excited dread for the first plunge in to the Simplon.[1]

The champagne would stay us, in that familiar ordeal. We'd drink gratefully, feeling the train sway, knowing a small taste of death and rebirth, as all men do in swift passage through a tunnel.

When we came out finally, into the light again and the high mountains, we'd lift our glasses silently to each other, and feel less foolish to see that the cooks too had known the same nameless stress as we.

Then people would begin to come in for lunch, and we'd go back to our compartment. The younger waiter would always call us when there were only a few more people to serve, in an hour or so.

Usually both waiters took care of us; they seemed to find us strange, and interesting enough to crack their cosmic ennui, and in some way fragile, so that they protected us. They would come swaying down the aisle as we ate, crying to us, "There will be a few bumps! Hold tight! Hold tight, M'sieu'-'dame! I will help you!"

Then they would grasp the wine, and usually my arm, and we would, it is true, make a few mild grating noises over some repairs in the road. Then they would gasp with relief, and scuttle away . . . one more crisis safely past.

It made us feel a little silly, as if we were imbeciles of royal blood, or perhaps children who only *thought* they had gray hairs and knew how to survive train trips alone. It was fun, too; almost everyone likes to feel pampered by public servants.

The young waiter with the smooth almond face was more given to the protective gestures, equally lavished on Chexbres or me to avoid any sexual mis-

1. A pass in the Alps between Switzerland and Italy, whose railway tunnels are the longest in the world.

understandings, but the older one, whose body was bent and whose face was truly the most cynical I have ever seen, was the one who watched our eating.

He hovered like an evil-visaged hawk while we ordered, and we soon found that instead of advising changes then, he would simply substitute in the kitchen what he preferred to have us enjoy that day. After the first surprise it was fun, but we always kept up the bluff of looking at the menu and then watching him pretend to memorize our order.

One thing he permitted us: simplicity. The people who traveled on that train were the kind who liked plain food and plenty of it. The menu might or might not list meat or fish, but it always had *pasti*[2] of some kind, and lentils or beans cooked with herbs, and of course fine honest garden salad. Then there would be one or two *antipasti*: the radishes we had watched being fixed, and butter for them in rather limp and sooty curls, and hardboiled eggs and sliced salami. There would be cheese for dessert, with fruit . . . fat cherries or peaches or grapes or oranges, according to the season, and always green almonds in the spring.

The people ate well, and even if they were very poor, and brought their own bread and wine into the restaurant, they ordered a plate of beans or a one-egg omelet with dignity which was no rebuke to the comparative prodigality around them. The two waiters served them with nonchalant skill, and everyone seemed to agree that Chexbres and I should be watched and fed and smiled at with extra care.

"Why are they like that? Why are they so good to us, all the people?" we would ask each other. I knew reasons for him, and he knew some for me, but for the two of us it was probably because we had a sort of palpable trust in each other.

Simple people are especially conscious of that. Sometimes it is called love, or good will. Whatever it was in us, the result was mysterious and warming, and we felt it very strongly in places like the restaurant car to Milano, always until the last time.

That was in the summer of 1939.

We were two ghosts, then. Our lives as normal living humans had ended in the winter, in Delaware, with Chexbres' illness. And when we got word that we should go back to our old home in Switzerland and save what we could before war started, we went not so much for salvage, because possessions had no meaning any more to us, but because we were helpless to do anything else. We returned to the life that had been so real like fog, or smoke, caught in a current of air.

We were very live ghosts, and drank and ate and saw and felt and made love better than ever before, with an intensity that seemed to detach us utterly from life.

Everywhere there was a little of that feeling; the only difference was that we were safely dead, and all the other people, that summer, were laughing and singing and drinking wine in a kind of catalepsy,[3] or like cancerous patients made happy with a magic combination of opiate before going into the operating theater. We had finished with all that business, and they had it still to go through.

They looked at us with a kind of envious respect, knowing that war was

2. Pastas (Italian). 3. I.e., rigid unconsciousness.

coming to them, but that we were past it; and everywhere we went, except the one time on the Milano train, we moved beatifically incommunicado, archangels on leave. None could touch us, just as none could be harmed by our knowledge of pain yet to be felt.

The train was the same. By then we had grown almost used to miracles, and when the young almond-faced waiter stood in the door of the compartment and gaped helplessly at us, we laughed at him. He stammered and sputtered, all the time shaking our hands and laughing too, and it was plain that he had buried us long since.

When he saw what had happened to Chexbres, he turned very red, and then said quickly, trying not to stare, "But the Asti! At once! It will be very chic to drink it here!"

And before we could tell him how much we wanted to drink it in the old restaurant car, and look once more at the faded aspirin signs and listen to the cooks, he was gone. It was necessary for him to disappear. we were used by then to having people do impetuous things when they first saw us, ghosts come back so far. . . . We sighed, and laughed, because even that seemed funny.

The boy brought the champagne, wrapped elegantly in a red-checked napkin for the first time. He was suave and mischievous again, and it was plain that he felt like something in a paper-bound novel, serving fair wine that way at eleven in the morning in a first-class compartment. He swayed with exaggerated grace to the rocking of the car, and flicked soot from the little wall table like the headwaiter at the Café de la Paix, at least, with his flat black eyes dancing.

We saluted him with our first taste, hiding our regret at having to be "gentry" and drink where it was chic. The wine was the same, warm and almost sickish, and we looked quietly at each other, with delight . . . one more miracle.

But at Sion, before the tunnel, three Strength-through-Joyers got on, bulbous with knapsacks and a kind of sweaty health that had nothing to do with us. We huddled against the windows, not invisible enough, and I wondered how we could ever get past all those strong brown hairy legs to the corridor.

But there in the doorway, almost before the train started again, stood the little waiter. His face was impassive, but his eyes twinkled and yet were motherly.

"Pardon, pardon," he murmured. "Entschuldigen Sie, bitte[4] . . . bitte . . ."

And before we knew it the German tourists were standing, trying to squeeze themselves small, and the boy was whisking us expertly, nonchalantly, out of the compartment, down the rocking aisle, and into our familiar hard brown seats in the restaurant.

It was all the same. We looked about us with a kind of wonder.

The old waiter saw us from the end of the car. His face did not change, but he put down his glass of wine and came to our table. The boy started to say something to him in an Italian dialect . . . it was like Niçois . . . but the old man motioned him briskly aside.

His face was still the most cynical I had ever seen, but his eyes were over-full of tears. They ran slowly down his cheeks for a few minutes, into the evil old wrinkles, and he did not wipe them away. He stood by the table, flicking his

4. Pardon, pardon . . . beg your pardon (French and German).

napkin and asking crankily if we had made a good trip and if we planned to stay long in Milano. We answered the same way . . . things about traveling and the weather.

We were not embarrassed, any more than he was, by his tears; like all ghosts, I suppose, we had grown used to seeing them in other people's eyes, and along with them we saw almost always a kind of gratitude, as if people were thanking us for coming back and for being so trustful together. We seemed to reassure them, in a mysterious way . . . that summer more than ever.

While the old man was standing there, talking with his own gruff eagerness about crops and storms, flicking the table, he had to step in behind my chair for a minute while three men walked quickly through the car.

Two were big, not in uniform but with black shirts[5] under their hot mussy coats, and stubble on their faces. The man between them was thinner and younger, and although they went single file and close together, we saw that he was handcuffed to each of them.

Before that summer such a thing would have shocked us, so that our faces would be paler and our eyes wider, but now we only looked up at the old waiter. He nodded, and his own eyes got very hot and dried all the tears.

"Political prisoner," he said, flicking the table, and his face was no more bitter than usual. "Escaped. They are bringing him back to Italy."

Then the chef with the highest bonnet saw us, and beamed and raised his glass, and the others turned around from their leafy table and saluted us too, and the door slammed behind the three dark men.

We got through the tunnel, that time, without feeling our palms grow sticky. It was the only difference: the train was the same, the people were the same. We were past the pain and travail, that was all. We were inviolate.

We drank the rest of the Asti, and as people began to come in to lunch, we made the signal to the suddenly active boy that we would be back later.

Just then there were shouts and thuds, and the sound of shattering glass. A kind of silence fell all about us, in spite of the steady rattle of the train. The old waiter ran down the car, not bumping a single table, and the door at the end closed sharply behind him. People looked strangely at one another.

Gradually the air settled, as if the motors inside all the travelers had started to hum again, and the young waiter took orders for lunch. When he got to us he said without looking at us, in his bad French, "I suggest that M'sieu'-'dame attend a moment the restaurant is not crowded today."

As a suggestion it had the icy command of a policeman or a guardian angel about it, and we sat meekly. There was no more champagne. It did not really bother us.

Finally the old man came hurriedly back into the car. His face was furious, and he clutched his shoulder. The travelers stared at him, still chewing. He stopped for a minute by our table. He was panting, and his voice was very low.

"He tried to jump through the window," he said, and we knew he was talking about the refugee. "The bastards! They tore my coat! My only coat! The dirty bastards . . . look at that!"

He flapped the ripped shoulder of his greasy old black jacket at us, and then went madly down to the galley, muttering and trembling.

5. Members of the Italian Fascist Party wore black shirts.

We stood up to go, and the smooth almond-faced waiter hurried toward us, swaying with the downhill rush of the train under a big tray of hot vegetables. "I am bringing M'sieu'-'dame's order at once," he called.

We sat down obediently. We were being bullied, but it was because he was trying to protect us, and it was kind of him. He brought two glasses of a dark vermouth, and as he put them in front of us he said confiding, "A special bottle we carry for the chef . . . very appetizing. There is a little muss on the platform. It will be swept up when M'sieu'-'dame have finished. *Santé!*"[6]

As we lifted our glasses, willy-nilly, he cleared his throat, and then said in English, "Cheerio!" He smiled at us encouragingly, like an over-attentive nurse, and went back to serving the other people. The vermouth was bitterer than any we had ever tasted, almost like a Swiss gentian-drink, but it tasted good after the insipid wine.

When we went through to our compartment, there was indeed a neat pile of broken glass on the platform between the cars, and the window of the door that opened when the train stopped was only half filled: the top part of the pane was gone, and the edge of the rest curved like ice in a smooth fine line, almost invisible.

The Strength-through-Joyers leaped politely to attention when we got back to our compartment, and subsided in a series of small waves of questions in English . . . did smoke bother me, did we mind the door open, did we feel a draft. . . .

I forget the name of the town now where the train stops and the passport men come on. Is it Domodossola? How strange, not to know! It is as if I have deliberately wiped from my mind a great many names. Some of them I thought would stay there forever, whether I wanted them or not, like old telephone numbers that suddenly come between you and the sound of a new love's voice. I never thought to disremember this town, that man, such and such a river. Was it Domodossola?

That day we were there a long time. There seemed more policemen than usual, but it was always that way in Italy. We got the questions of visas and money straightened out; that used to upset me, and I'd feel like a blushing diamond-smuggler when the hard-eyed customs man would look at me. This time it was easy, unimportant.

I kept thinking it would be a good idea to walk back to the restaurant car while the train was quiet, but Chexbres said no, we should wait for the boy to call us.

Finally we started, very slowly. We went past a lot of roadwork. Men were building beds for new tracks with great blocks of gray stone, and the Germans looked at them with a grudging fascination, leaning over us to see better and exclaiming softly.

We were glad when the young waiter came to the door. "Your table is ready, M'sieu'-'dame," he announced loftily, and the men stood up hastily to let us out.

When we got to the end of the car, the boy turned back. "Take care, please," he said to Chexbres. "There is a little humidity on the platform."

6. Health! (French).

And the place was wet, right enough. The curved piece of glass was still in the window, but it and the walls and the floor were literally dripping with water. We went carefully through it, and into the almost empty restaurant.

The chef rested at the end, reading a paper, but got up and went back to the galley as we came in. Our table was nicely laid, with fresh linen, and there were two or three little square dishes of pickled onions and salami and butter. We felt very hungry, and quite gay.

The boy brought us some good wine, a fairly expensive red Chianti we always drank on that train, and we began to eat bread and salami with it. I remember there were some of those big white beans, the kind Italians peel and eat with salt when they are fresh and tender in the early summer. They tasted delicious, so fresh and cold. . . .

It was good to be eating and drinking there on that train, free forever from the trouble of life, surrounded with a kind of insulation of love. . . .

The old waiter came through the car. He was going to pass our table without looking at us. Chexbres spoke to him. "Stop a minute," he said. "Your coat . . . how is it?"

The man turned without answering, so that we could see the neat stitches that held his sleeve in place. I said something banal about the sewing . . . how good it was . . . and Chexbres asked quietly, "The man . . . the prisoner . . . did he get away?"

The old man suddenly looked at us, and his eyes were hateful, as if he loathed us. He said something foul, and then spat, "It's none of my business!" He hurried away, and we could not turn to watch him.

It was so shocking that we sat without any movement for quite a time. I could feel my heart beat heavily, and my throat was as if an iron collar hung around it, the way it used to be when Chexbres was first ill. Finally I looked at the few people still eating, and it seemed to me as if they met my eyes with a kind of hatred too, not as awful as the old man's but still crouching there. There was fear in it, and fear all around me.

Chexbres' face was full of pain. It was the first time it had come through for weeks, the first time since we started to drift like two happy ghosts along the old current of our lives together. The iron collar tightened to see it there. I tried to drink some wine, but I couldn't swallow more than once.

The young waiter hurried past us without looking, and Chexbres stopped him firmly. "Please," he said. "What is wrong? What has happened?"

The boy looked impassively at us, and for a minute I thought he was going to be rude. Then he whispered, still protecting us, "Eat, M'sieu'-'dame. I will tell you in a minute." And he hurried off to the galley, bending supplely under the last great tray of emptied plates.

"Yes, you'd better eat something," Chexbres said coldly to me. "You've drunk rather a lot, you know." He picked up his fork, and I did too. The spaghetti was like ashes, because I felt myself coming to life again, and knew he did.

When we were the only ones left in the car, the boy came back. He stood leaning against the table across the aisle, still swaying with the motion of the train but now as if he were terribly tired, and talked to us so softly that we could hardly hear him. There was no friendliness in his voice, but not any hatred.

He said that when the train stopped at Domodossola, or wherever the bor-

der was, the political prisoner was being taken off, and suddenly he laughed and pressed his throat down on the edge of the broken windowpane. The old waiter saw it.

"That was probably the plan in the first place," the boy said. "The poor bastard was chained to the cops. There was no escaping. It was a good job," he said. "The border police helped clean up the platform. That was why the train stopped so long.

"We're making up time now all right," the boy said, looking admiringly at the rocky valleys flashing past us. "The old man keeps fussing about his coat. He's nuts anyway."

By the time we got to Milano everything was almost all right again, but for a few minutes the shell cracked. The world seeped in. We were not two ghosts, safe in our own immunity from the pain of living. Chexbres was a man with one leg gone, the other and the two arms soon to go . . . a small wracked man with snowy hair and eyes large with suffering. And I was a woman condemned, plucked at by demons, watching her true love die too slowly.

There in the train, hurrying across the ripe fields, feeling the tranced waiting of the people everywhere, we knew for a few minutes that we had not escaped. We knew no knife of glass, no distillate of hatred, could keep the pain of war outside.

I felt illimitably old, there in the train, knowing that escape was not peace, ever.

 1939

DOROTHY LIVESAY

1909–

Dorothy Livesay's mother, Florence (Randal) Livesay, was a writer, and her father, John F. B. Livesay, was a general manager of the Canadian Press. After receiving a B.A. from the University of Toronto and a Diplôme d'Études Supérieures from the Sorbonne, she studied social science at Toronto. Before and after she married Duncan Macnair in 1937, she was a social worker in Vancouver, but she has more recently worked as a correspondent for the *Toronto Daily Star*, as a documentary scriptwriter for the Canadian Broadcasting Corporation, as a UNESCO English specialist in Paris, as an English teacher in Northern Rhodesia as an editor of Canadian literary journals and anthologies, and as a lecturer and writer-in-residence in many Canadian universities.

A widow with two children, Livesay has described her work as "the evocation of the Canadian scene through the writing of lyrical and documentary poetry." For more than six decades, she has published prize-winning volumes of verse that combine frankly sensual and personal poems with more public, polemical works. Her early Imagistic volumes (*Green Pitcher*, 1928, and *Signpost*, 1932) were followed by the political poems in *Day and Night* (1944), verse that analyzed the threats of poverty and fascism. By the 1950s and 1960s, however, Livesay had established herself as a lyricist of intimacy. Many of the pieces in her *Collected Poems* (1972) focus, as she has explained, on "love, marriage and its bonds, childbirth, childhood" and on "the need for peace in the world to give children a growing place." Continuing in this vein, she has most recently published *The Self-Completing Tree: Selected Poems* (1986) and *The Woman I Am* (1991).

Green Rain

I remember long veils of green rain
Feathered like the shawl of my grandmother—
Green from the half-green of the spring trees
Waving in the valley.

I remember the road 5
Like the one which leads to my grandmother's house,
A warm house, with green carpets,
Geraniums, a trilling canary
And shining horse-hair chairs;
And the silence, full of the rain's falling 10
Was like my grandmother's parlor
Alive with herself and her voice, rising and falling—
Rain and wind intermingled.

I remember on that day
I was thinking only of my love 15
And of my love's house.
But now I remember the day
As I remember my grandmother.
I remember the rain as the feathery fringe of her shawl.

1932 1972

Eve[1]

Beside the highway
at the motel door
 it roots
the last survivor of a pioneer
 orchard 5
miraculously still
 bearing.

A thud another apple falls
 I stoop and O
that scent, gnarled, ciderish 10
 with sun in it
that woody pulp
 for teeth and tongue
 to bite and curl around
that spurting juice 15
 earth-sweet!

In fifty seconds, fifty summers sweep
 and shake me—
I am alive! can stand
 up still 20

1. According to the Bible, Eve, the first woman, disobeyed God by eating a fruit (often identified with the apple)
from the Tree of Knowledge.

hoarding this apple
 in my hand.

1967 1972

The Three Emily's[1]

These women crying in my head
Walk alone, uncomforted:
The Emily's, these three
Cry to be set free—
And others whom I will not name 5
Each different, each the same.

Yet they had liberty!
Their kingdom was the sky:
They batted clouds with easy hand,
Found a mountain for their stand; 10
From wandering lonely they could catch
The inner magic of a heath—
A lake their palette, any tree
Their brush could be.

And still they cry to me 15
As in reproach—
I, born to hear their inner storm
Of separate man in woman's form,
I yet possess another kingdom, barred
To them, these three, this Emily. 20
I move as mother in a frame,
My arteries
Flow the immemorial way
Towards the child, the man;
And only for brief span 25
Am I an Emily on mountain snows
And one of these.

And so the whole that I possess
Is still much less—
They move triumphant through my head: 30
I am the one
Uncomforted.

 1972

The Children's Letters

They are my secret food
consumed in the most hushed corners

1. Emily Brontë (1818–1848), English novelist and poet. Emily Dickinson (1830–886), American poet. Emily Carr (1871–1945), Canadian painter.

of my room
when no one's looking
I hold them up to sunlight 5
at the window
to see aright
to hear behind the spindly words
a child's tentative
 first footsteps 10
a small voice stuttering
 at the sky
"bird . . . bird. . . ."

Whether these be
my children or my grandchildren 15
they're ghostly visitors
food of a solitary kind—
they leap on shafts of sunlight
through the mind's
shutters. 20

 1972

EUDORA WELTY

1909–

"Without the love and belief my family gave me, I could not have become a writer to begin with," confessed Eudora Welty in an introduction to her *Collected Short Stories* (1980), adding, as if to argue that love begets further love, "I have been told, both in approval and in accusation, that I seem to love all my characters." In fact, her work has been consistently marked by a celebratory warmth—a sympathy for the deformed, the distorted, and even the demonic in human life, along with a loving insight into the trials and triumphs of daily living. From her earliest to her most recent stories, moreover, Welty has been particularly notable for her creation of powerfully engaging women characters: such tales as *Why I Live at the P.O.* (1941), *A Worn Path* (1941), and *The Wide Net* (1943), along with later stories like *The Bride of the Innisfallen* (1955) and *Circe* (1955), explore the varieties of female experience with grace and wit.

The daughter of an Ohio-born father and a mother who was a native West Virginian, Welty was born and raised in Jackson, Mississippi, where she has continued to live all her life, in a rural Southern setting whose customs and convictions have been as central to her work as they were to the writing of such other southern regionalists as William Faulkner and Flannery O'Connor. After attending Mississippi State College for Women from 1925 to 1927, Welty earned a B.A. in 1929 from the University of Wisconsin, then studied advertising for a year at Columbia University. Following her father's death in 1931, however, she resettled permanently in Jackson, where, throughout the 1930s, she worked for local newspapers, for the Jackson radio station, and for the WPA (the federally funded Works Progress Administration, which was created to give people jobs during the Great Depression). Her first collection of short fiction, *A Curtain of Green, and Other Stories*, was published in 1941, with an introduction by Katherine Anne Porter, whose "shining bounty," Welty has written, "nourished my life." Subsequent vol-

umes included the short-story collections *The Wide Net, and Other Stories* (1943) and *The Bride of the Innisfallen* (1955) as well as the novels *The Robber Bridegroom* (1942), *Delta Wedding* (1946), *The Ponder Heart* (1954), *The Optimist's Daughter* (for which Welty won the Pulitzer Prize in 1972), and, most recently, the memoir *One Writer's Beginnings* (1984).

Though she has sometimes been accused of—in the words of one critic—not having "often taken the South's social turmoil as subject matter," her long-standing concern for the crises of her culture is clearly revealed in *One Time, One Place* (1971), a collection of photographs of black and white sharecroppers and other workers in the Mississippi countryside that she took during her time with the WPA in the 1930s, as well as in her delineation of Phoenix Jackson, the heroic black grandmother of *A Worn Path*, who might well have stepped out of one of those pictures, and in her portrayal of the white assassin of Medgar Evers, who narrates the bitter story *Where Is the Voice Coming From?* (1963). Consistently sensitive and sympathetic to "the mind, heart, and skin of" human beings who are "not myself," Welty proves in all her sometimes sorrowful, sometimes amused, but always loving fictions the intensity with which she adheres to her central belief: "It is the act of a writer's imagination that I set most high."

A Worn Path

It was December—a bright frozen day in the early morning. Far out in the country there was an old Negro woman with her head tied in a red rag, coming along a path through the pinewoods. Her name was Phoenix Jackson. She was very old and small and she walked slowly in the dark pine shadows, moving a little from side to side in her steps, with the balanced heaviness and lightness of a pendulum in a grandfather clock. She carried a thin, small cane made from an umbrella, and with this she kept tapping the frozen earth in front of her. This made a grave and persistent noise in the still air that seemed meditative like the chirping of a solitary little bird.

She wore a dark striped dress reaching down to her shoe tops, and an equally long apron of bleached sugar sacks, with a full pocket: all neat and tidy, but every time she took a step she might have fallen over her shoelaces, which dragged from her unlaced shoes. She looked straight ahead. Her eyes were blue with age. Her skin had a pattern all its own of numberless branching wrinkles and as though a whole little tree stood in the middle of her forehead, but a golden color ran underneath, and the two knobs of her cheeks were illumined by a yellow burning under the dark. Under the red rag her hair came down on her neck in the frailest of ringlets, still black, and with an odor like copper.

Now and then there was a quivering in the thicket. Old Phoenix said, "Out of my way, all you foxes, owls, beetles, jack rabbits, coons and wild animals! . . . Keep out from under these feet, little bobwhites. . . . Keep the big wild hogs out of my path. Don't let none of those come running my direction. I got a long way." Under her small black-freckled hand her cane, limber as a buggy whip, would switch at the brush as if to rouse up any hiding things.

On she went. The woods were deep and still. The sun made the pine needles almost too bright to look at, up where the wind rocked. The cones dropped as light as feathers. Down in the hollow was the mourning dove—it was not too late for him.

The path ran up a hill. "Seem like there is chains about my feet, time I get this far," she said, in the voice of argument old people keep to use with themselves. "Something always take a hold of me on this hill—pleads I should stay."

After she got to the top she turned and gave a full, severe look behind her where she had come. "Up through pines," she said at length. "Now down through oaks."

Her eyes opened their widest, and she started down gently. But before she got to the bottom of the hill a bush caught her dress.

Her fingers were busy and intent, but her skirts were full and long, so that before she could pull them free in one place they were caught in another. It was not possible to allow the dress to tear. "I in the thorny bush," she said. "Thorns, you doing your appointed work. Never want to let folks pass, no sir. Old eyes thought you was a pretty little *green* bush."

Finally, trembling all over, she stood free, and after a moment dared to stoop for her cane.

"Sun so high!" she cried, leaning back and looking, while the thick tears went over her eyes. "The time getting all gone here."

At the foot of this hill was a place where a log was laid across the creek.

"Now comes the trial," said Phoenix.

Putting her right foot out, she mounted the log and shut her eyes. Lifting her skirt, leveling her cane fiercely before her, like a festival figure in some parade, she began to march across. Then she opened her eyes and she was safe on the other side.

"I wasn't as old as I thought," she said.

But she sat down to rest. She spread her skirts on the bank around her and folded her hands over her knees. Up above her was a tree in a pearly cloud of mistletoe. She did not dare to close her eyes, and when a little boy brought her a plate with a slice of marble-cake on it she spoke to him. "That would be acceptable," she said. But when she went to take it there was just her own hand in the air.

So she left that tree, and had to go through a barbed-wire fence. There she had to creep and crawl, spreading her knees and stretching her fingers like a baby trying to climb the steps. But she talked loudly to herself: she could not let her dress be torn now, so late in the day, and she could not pay for having her arm or her leg sawed off if she got caught fast were she was.

At last she was safe through the fence and risen up out in the clearing. Big dead trees, like black men with one arm, were standing in the purple stalks of the withered cotton field. There sat a buzzard.

"Who you watching?"

In the furrow she made her way along.

"Glad this not the season for bulls," she said, looking sideways, "and the good Lord made his snakes to curl up and sleep in the winter. A pleasure I don't see no two-headed snake coming around that tree, where it come once. It took a while to get by him, back in the summer."

She passed through the old cotton and went into a field of dead corn. It whispered and shook and was taller than her head. "Through the maze now," she said, for there was no path.

There was something tall, black, and skinny there, moving before her.

At first she took it for a man. It could have been a man dancing in the field. But she stood still and listened, and it did not make a sound. It was as silent as a ghost.

"Ghost," she said sharply, "who be you the ghost of? For I have heard of nary death close by."

But there was no answer—only the ragged dancing in the wind.

She shut her eyes, reached out her hand, and touched a sleeve. She found a coat and inside that an emptiness, cold as ice.

"You scarecrow," she said. Her face lighted. "I ought to be shut up for good," she said with laughter. "My senses is gone. I too old. I the oldest people I ever know. Dance, old scarecrow," she said, "while I dancing with you."

She kicked her foot over the furrow, and with mouth drawn down, shook her head once or twice in a little strutting way. Some husks blew down and whirled in streamers about her skirts.

Then she went on, parting her way from side to side with the cane, through the whispering field. At last she came to the end, to a wagon track where the silver grass blew between the red ruts. The quail were walking around like pullets, seeming all dainty and unseen.

"Walk pretty," she said. "This the easy place. This the easy going."

She followed the track, swaying through the quiet bare fields, through the little strings of trees silver in their dead leaves, past cabins silver from weather, with the doors and windows boarded shut, all like old women under a spell sitting there. "I walking in their sleep," she said, nodding her head vigorously.

In a ravine she went where a spring was silently flowing through a hollow log. Old Phoenix bent and drank. "Sweet-gum makes the water sweet," she said, and drank more. "Nobody know who made this well, for it was here when I was born."

The track crossed a swampy part where the moss hung as white as lace from every limb. "Sleep on, alligators, and blow your bubbles." Then the track went into the road.

Deep, deep the road went down between the high green-colored banks. Overhead the live-oaks met, and it was as dark as a cave.

A black dog with a lolling tongue came up out of the weeds by the ditch. She was meditating, and not ready, and when he came at her she only hit him a little with her cane. Over she went in the ditch, like a little puff of milkweed.

Down there, her senses drifted away. A dream visited her, and she reached her hand up, but nothing reached down and gave her a pull. So she lay there and presently went to talking. "Old woman," she said to herself, "that black dog come up out of the weeds to stall you off, and now there he sitting on his fine tail, smiling at you."

A white man finally came along and found her—a hunter, a young man, with his dog on a chain.

"Well, Granny!" he laughed. "What are you doing there?"

"Lying on my back like a June-bug waiting to be turned over, mister," she said, reaching up her hand.

He lifted her up, gave her a swing in the air, and set her down. "Anything broken, Granny?"

"No sir, them old dead weeds is springy enough," said Phoenix, when she had got her breath. "I thank you for your trouble."

"Where do you live, Granny?" he asked, while the two dogs were growling at each other.

"Away back yonder, sir, behind the ridge. You can't even see it from here."

"On your way home?"

"No sir, I going to town."

"Why, that's too far! That's as far as I walk when I come out myself, and I get something for my trouble." He patted the stuffed bag he carried, and there hung down a little closed claw. It was one of the bob-whites, with its beak hooked bitterly to show it was dead. "Now you go on home, Granny!"

"I bound to go to town, mister," said Phoenix. "The time come around."

He gave another laugh, filling the whole landscape. "I know you old colored people! Wouldn't miss going to town to see Santa Claus!"

But something held old Phoenix very still. The deep lines in her face went into a fierce and different radiation. Without warning, she had seen with her own eyes a flashing nickel fall out of the man's pocket onto the ground.

"How old are you, Granny?" he was saying.

"There is no telling, mister," she said, "no telling."

Then she gave a little cry and clapped her hand and said, "Git on away from here, dog! Look! Look at that dog!" She laughed as if in admiration. "He ain't scared of nobody. He a big black dog." She whispered, "Sic him!"

"Watch me get rid of that cur," said the man. "Sic him, Pete! Sic him!"

Phoenix heard the dogs fighting, and heard the man running and throwing sticks. She even heard a gunshot. But she was slowly bending forward by that time, further and further forward, the lids stretched down over her eyes, as if she were doing this in her sleep. Her chin was lowered almost to her knees. The yellow palm of her hand came out from the fold of her apron. Her fingers slid down and along the ground under the piece of money with the grace and care they would have in lifting an egg from under a setting hen. Then she slowly straightened up, she stood erect, and the nickel was in her apron pocket. A bird flew by. Her lips moved. "God watching me the whole time. I come to stealing."

The man came back, and his own dog panted about them. "Well, I scared him off that time," he said, and then he laughed and lifted his gun and pointed it at Phoenix.

She stood straight and faced him.

"Doesn't the gun scare you?" he said, still pointing it.

"No, sir, I seen plenty go off closer by, in my day, and for less than what I done," she said, holding utterly still.

He smiled, and shouldered the gun. "Well, Granny," he said, "you must be a hundred years old, and scared of nothing. I'd give you a dime if I had any money with me. But you take my advice and stay home, and nothing will happen to you."

"I bound to go on my way, mister," said Phoenix. She inclined her head in the red rag. Then they went in different directions, but she could hear the gun shooting again and again over the hill.

She walked on. The shadows hung from the oak trees to the road like curtains. Then she smelled wood-smoke, and smelled the river, and she saw a steeple and the cabins on their steep steps. Dozens of little black children whirled around her. There ahead was Natchez shining. Bells were ringing. She walked on.

In the paved city it was Christmas time. There were red and green electric lights strung and crisscrossed everywhere, and all turned on in the daytime. Old Phoenix would have been lost if she had not distrusted her eyesight and depended on her feet to know where to take her.

She paused quietly on the sidewalk where people were passing by. A lady

came along in the crowd, carrying an armful of red-, green- and silver-wrapped presents; she gave off perfume like the red roses in hot summer, and Phoenix stopped her.

"Please, missy, will you lace up my shoe?" She held up her foot.

"What do you want, Grandma?"

"See my shoe," said Phoenix. "Do all right for out in the country, but wouldn't look right to go in a big building."

"Stand still then, Grandma," said the lady. She put her packages down on the sidewalk beside her and laced and tied both shoes tightly.

"Can't lace 'em with a cane," said Phoenix. "Thank you, missy. I doesn't mind asking a nice lady to tie up my shoe, when I gets out on the street."

Moving slowly and from side to side, she went into the big building, and into a tower of steps, where she walked up and around and around until her feet knew to stop.

She entered a door, and there she saw nailed up on the wall the document that had been stamped with the gold seal and framed in the gold frame, which matched the dream that was hung up in her head.

"Here I be," she said. There was a fixed and ceremonial stiffness over her body.

"A charity case, I suppose," said an attendant who sat at the desk before her.

But Phoenix only looked above her head. There was sweat on her face, the wrinkles in her skin shone like a bright net.

"Speak up, Grandma," the woman said. "What's your name? We must have your history, you know. Have you been here before? What seems to be the trouble with you?"

Old Phoenix only gave a twitch to her face as if a fly were bothering her.

"Are you deaf?" cried the attendant.

But then the nurse came in.

"Oh, that's just old Aunt Phoenix," she said. "She doesn't come for herself—she has a little grandson. She makes these trips just as regular as clockwork. She lives away back off the Old Natchez Trace."[1] She bent down. "Well, Aunt Phoenix, why don't you just take a seat? We won't keep you standing after your long trip." She pointed.

The old woman sat down, bolt upright in the chair.

"Now, how is the boy?" asked the nurse.

Old Phoenix did not speak.

"I said, how is the boy?"

But Phoenix only waited and stared straight ahead, her face very solemn and withdrawn into rigidity.

"Is his throat any better?" asked the nurse. "Aunt Phoenix, don't you hear me? Is your grandson's throat any better since the last time you came for the medicine?"

With her hands on her knees, the old woman waited, silent, erect and motionless, just as if she were in armor.

"You mustn't take up our time this way, Aunt Phoenix," the nurse said. "Tell us quickly about your grandson, and get it over. He isn't dead, is he?"

At last there came a flicker and then a flame of comprehension across her face, and she spoke.

1. A 19th-century pioneer road between Natchez, Mississippi, and Nashville, Tennessee.

"My grandson. It was my memory had left me. There I sat and forgot why I made my long trip."

"Forgot?" The nurse frowned. "After you came so far?"

Then Phoenix was like an old woman begging a dignified forgiveness for waking up frightened in the night. "I never did go to school, I was too old at the Surrender,"[2] she said in a soft voice. "I'm an old woman without an education. It was my memory fail me. My little grandson, he is just the same, and I forgot it in the coming."

"Throat never heals, does it?" said the nurse, speaking in a loud, sure voice to old Phoenix. By now she had a card with something written on it, a little list. "Yes. Swallowed lye. When was it?—January—two, three years ago—"

Phoenix spoke unasked now. "No, missy, he not dead, he just the same. Every little while his throat begin to close up again, and he not able to swallow. He not get his breath. He not able to help himself. So the time come around, and I go on another trip for the soothing medicine."

"All right. The doctor said as long as you came to get it, you could have it," said the nurse. "But it's an obstinate case."

"My little grandson, he sit up there in the house all wrapped up, waiting by himself," Phoenix went on. "We is the only two left in the world. He suffer and it don't seem to put him back at all. He got a sweet look. He going to last. He wear a little patch quilt and peep out holding his mouth open like a little bird. I remembers so plain now. I not going to forget him again, no, the whole enduring time. I could tell him from all the others in creation."

"All right." The nurse was trying to hush her now. She brought her a bottle of medicine. "Charity," she said, making a check mark in a book.

Old Phoenix held the bottle close to her eyes, and then carefully put it into her pocket.

"I thank you," she said.

"It's Christmas time, Grandma," said the attendant. "Could I give you a few pennies out of my purse?"

"Five pennies is a nickel," said Phoenix stiffly.

"Here's a nickel," said the attendant.

Phoenix rose carefully and held out her hand. She received the nickel and then fished the other nickel out of her pocket and laid it beside the new one. She stared at her palm closely, with her head on one side.

Then she gave a tap with her cane on the floor.

"This is what come to me to do," she said. "I going to the store and buy my child a little windmill they sells, made out of paper. He going to find it hard to believe there such a thing in the world. I'll march myself back where he waiting, holding it straight up in this hand."

She lifted her free hand, gave a little nod, turned around, and walked out of the doctor's office. Then her slow step began on the stairs, going down.

1941

2. I.e., the surrender of Robert E. Lee at Appomattox in 1865, which ended the Civil War.

ELIZABETH BISHOP

1911–1979

"You sound like Lope de Vega and I sound like Jacob Abbot or Peter Rabbit," wrote the poet Marianne Moore in 1959 to her friend and admirer the poet Elizabeth Bishop. Self-deprecatingly comparing herself to a nineteenth-century American clergyman (Abbot) and a children's book character, Moore glowingly imagined Bishop as Spain's greatest Renaissance playwright: her compliment, if hyperbolical, was a measure of the esteem in which this writer was held by many contemporaries. The friend of—besides Moore—the poets Robert Lowell, Pablo Neruda, and Frank Bidart, Bishop achieved in her lifetime a distinctive reputation as, in the words of the critic Sibyl Estess, a "virtuoso of descriptive poetry." Since her death, however, her work has been increasingly seen as visionary and meditative, acute in its understated but powerful transcription of inner reality as well as accurate in its attention to external objects

Born in Worcester, Massachusetts, Elizabeth Bishop was raised by two sets of grandparents in Nova Scotia and New England. Her father died when she was eight months old, and not long after that, her mother had to be hospitalized for mental illness; though at one point Bishop's maternal grandparents had hoped to bring their daughter home to recover, the poet's mother experienced a final breakdown when Elizabeth was five, an event that is recorded in the poignant story *In the Village* (1953), Bishop's semifictionalized account of her last encounter with her mother. A frail child, the poet did not attend school regularly until she was sixteen, when she entered Walnut Hill School. By the time she enrolled at Vassar College at nineteen, however, she was a voracious reader and an aspiring writer. With several other undergraduates, including the novelist-to-be Mary McCarthy, she founded a literary magazine, *Con Spirito*; in addition, she began publishing poems and stories, some of them in nationally known periodicals; and perhaps most important, the year before her graduation she met and was befriended by Marianne Moore, who encouraged her to devote herself entirely to her writing rather than, as she had planned, attending medical school.

After graduation from Vassar, Bishop traveled extensively, pursuing what one biographer has called a "nomadic" way of life that was to define the rest of her career and provide central metaphors for such volumes of poetry as *North & South* (1946), *Questions of Travel* (1965), and *Geography III* (1976). Her journeys were interrupted, however, for one long and quite significant period: between 1951 and 1966, she settled in Brazil, sharing a house in the mountains and an apartment in Rio de Janeiro with Lota Costellat de Macedo Soares, a Brazilian friend; translating Brazilian poetry; and producing a book about the country—*Brazil* (1962)—for the *Life* World Library series. After leaving Brazil, Bishop returned to the United States, where she taught, first, at the University of Washington and then, from 1969 until her retirement in 1977, at Harvard University.

Throughout, Bishop's career was marked by numerous honors, including the Pulitzer Prize in 1956 and the National Book Award in 1970. Despite the acclaim she received, however, she always maintained an ironically understated yet passionately exact perspective on both her self and her society. Her commitments, both to friends and to ideas, were keen: though she had long defined herself as a feminist, for instance, she consistently refused what she considered the ghettoization implied by inclusion in anthologies of women's writing. (With the permission of Alice Methfessel, her literary executrix, we reprint here a quotation from a letter Bishop wrote in 1977, a passage that clarifies the poet's position on this matter.) Yet, as poems like *Roosters* and *Pink Dog* reveal, Bishop was capable of composing fiercely sardonic feminist critiques of her society, and as *Invitation to Miss*

Marianne Moore suggests, she was intensely loyal to her major female literary mentor.

The works reprinted here document the range as well as the precision of Bishop's art. Moving easily from the poignantly witty fantasy of *The Man-Moth* to the visionary realism of *The Fish* and the autobiographical introspection of *In the Waiting Room*, she demonstrates her mastery not only of lyric forms but also, in the memoir *Gwendolyn*, of the techniques of prose narrative.

The Man-Moth[1]

Here, above,
cracks in the buildings are filled with battered moonlight.
The whole shadow of Man is only as big as his hat.
It lies at his feet like a circle for a doll to stand on,
and he makes an inverted pin, the point magnetized to the moon.　5
He does not see the moon; he observes only her vast properties,
feeling the queer light on his hands, neither warm nor cold,
of a temperature impossible to record in thermometers.

But when the Man-Moth
pays his rare, although occasional, visits to the surface,　10
the moon looks rather different to him. He emerges
from an opening under the edge of one of the sidewalks
and nervously begins to scale the faces of the buildings.
He thinks the moon is a small hole at the top of the sky,
proving the sky quite useless for protection.　15
He trembles, but must investigate as high as he can climb.

Up the façades,
his shadow dragging like a photographer's cloth behind him,
he climbs fearfully, thinking that this time he will manage
to push his small head through that round clean opening　20
and be forced through, as from a tube, in black scrolls on the light.
(Man, standing below him, has no such illusions.)
But what the Man-Moth fears most he must do, although
he fails, of course, and falls back scared but quite unhurt.

Then he returns　25
to the pale subways of cement he calls his home. He flits,
he flutters, and cannot get aboard the silent trains
fast enough to suit him. The doors close swiftly.
The Man-Moth always seats himself facing the wrong way
and the train starts at once at its full, terrible speed,　30
without a shift in gears or a gradation of any sort.
He cannot tell the rate at which he travels backwards.

Each night he must
be carried through artificial tunnels and dream recurrent dreams.
Just as the ties recur beneath his train, these underlie　35
his rushing brain. He does not dare look out the window,

1. Newspaper misprint for "mammoth" [Bishop's note].

for the third rail,[2] the unbroken draught of poison,
runs there beside him. He regards it as a disease
he has inherited the susceptibility to. He has to keep
his hands in his pockets, as others must wear mufflers. 40

 If you catch him,
hold up a flashlight to his eye. It's all dark pupil,
an entire night itself, whose haired horizon tightens
as he stares back, and closes up the eye. Then from the lids
one tear, his only possession, like the bee's sting, slips. 45
Slyly he palms it, and if you're not paying attention
he'll swallow it. However, if you watch, he'll hand it over,
cool as from underground springs and pure enough to drink.

 1946

Roosters

 At four o'clock
 in the gun-metal blue dark
 we hear the first crow of the first cock

 just below
 the gun-metal blue window
 and immediately there is an echo 5

 off in the distance,
 then one from the backyard fence,
 then one, with horrible insistence,

 grates like a wet match 10
 from the broccoli patch,
 flares, and all over town begins to catch.

 Cries galore
 come from the water-closet[1] door,
 from the dropping-plastered henhouse floor, 15

 where in the blue blur
 their rustling wives admire,
 the roosters brace their cruel feet and glare

 with stupid eyes
 while from their beaks there rise 20
 the uncontrolled, traditional cries.

 Deep from protruding chests
 in green-gold medals dressed,
 planned to command and terrorize the rest,

2. Allusion to the exposed electrified source of power 1. A room containing a toilet.
on modern subways

the many wives 25
who lead hens' lives
of being courted and despised;

deep from raw throats
a senseless order floats
all over town. A rooster gloats 30

over our beds
from rusty iron sheds
and fences made from old bedsteads,

over our churches
where the tin rooster perches, 35
over our little wooden northern houses,

making sallies
from all the muddy alleys,
marking out maps like Rand McNally's:[2]

glass-headed pins, 40
oil-golds and copper greens,
anthracite blues, alizarins,[3]

each one an active
displacement in perspective;
each screaming, "This is where I live!" 45

Each screaming
"Get up! Stop dreaming!"
Roosters,[4] what are you projecting?

You, whom the Greeks elected
to shoot at on a post, who struggled 50
when sacrificed, you whom they labeled

"Very combative . . ."
what right have you to give
commands and tell us how to live,

cry "Here!" and "Here!" 55
and wake us here where are
unwanted love, conceit and war?

The crown of red
set on your little head
is charged with all your fighting blood. 60

2. Rand McNally publishes road maps and atlases.
3. Orange or red dyes.
4. In classical Greece, used in target practice, for sacri-
fice to the gods, and in highly popular cockfighting
contests.

Yes, the excrescence
makes a most virile presence,
plus all that vulgar beauty of iridescence.

Now in mid-air
by twos they fight each other. 65
Down comes a first flame-feather,

and one is flying,
with raging heroism defying
even the sensation of dying.

And one has fallen, 70
but still above the town
his torn-out, bloodied feathers drift down;

and what he sung
no matter. He is flung
on the gray ash-heap, lies in dung 75

with his dead wives
with open, bloody eyes,
while those metallic feathers oxidize.

St. Peter's sin
was worse than that of Magdalen[5] 80
whose sin was of the flesh alone;

of spirit, Peter's,
falling, beneath the flares,
among the "servants and officers."

Old holy sculpture[6] 85
could set it all together
in one small scene, past and future

Christ stands amazed,
Peter, two fingers raised
to surprised lips, both as if dazed. 90

But in between
a little cock is seen
carved on a dim column in the travertine,

5. A prostitute who reformed under the influence of Christ's teaching. Peter was one of Christ's Twelve Apostles; shortly before his crucifixion. Christ prophesied that Peter would deny knowing him three times before the cock crowed (Luke 22:34) This prophecy was fulfilled after Christ had been seized by the Romans; three witnesses claimed that Peter was one of Christ's associates, and three times he denied the accusation. After the third denial, a cock was heard crowing. Peter later became the founder of the Christian Church, again in fulfillment of Christ's word.
6. This sculpture was carved in c. A.D. 400 and is now in the Vatican.

explained by *gallus canit*;
flet Petrus[7] underneath it. 95
There is inescapable hope, the pivot;

yes, and there Peter's tears
run down our chanticleer's[8]
sides and gem his spurs.

Tear-encrusted thick 100
as a medieval relic
he waits. Poor Peter, heart-sick,

still cannot guess
those cock-a-doodles yet might bless,
his dreadful rooster come to mean forgiveness, 105

a new weathervane
on basilica and barn,
and that outside the Lateran[9]

there would always be
a bronze cock on a porphyry 110
pillar so the people and the Pope might see

that even the Prince
of the Apostles long since
had been forgiven, and to convince

all the assembly 115
that "Deny deny deny"
is not all the roosters cry.

In the morning
a low light is floating
in the backyard, and gilding 120

from underneath
the broccoli, leaf by leaf;
how could the night have come to grief?

gilding the tiny
floating swallow's belly 125
and lines of pink cloud in the sky,

the day's preamble
like wandering lines in marble.
The cocks are now almost inaudible.

7. The cock crows; Peter weeps (Latin). The "old holy
sculpture" described in these lines was carved c. A.D.
400 and is now in the Vatican.

8. I.e., rooster's.
9. The cathedral in Rome where the Pope presides.
"Basilica": church.

The sun climbs in, 130
following "to see the end,"[1]
faithful as enemy, or friend.

 1946

The Fish

I caught a tremendous fish
and held him beside the boat
half out of water, with my hook
fast in a corner of his mouth.
He didn't fight. 5
He hadn't fought at all.
He hung a grunting weight,
battered and venerable
and homely. Here and there
his brown skin hung in strips 10
like ancient wallpaper,
and its pattern of darker brown
was like wallpaper:
shapes like full-blown roses
stained and lost through age. 15
He was speckled with barnacles,
fine rosettes of lime,
and infested
with tiny white sea-lice,
and underneath two or three 20
rags of green weed hung down
While his gills were breathing in
the terrible oxygen
—the frightening gills,
fresh and crisp with blood, 25
that can cut so badly—
I thought of the coarse white flesh
packed in like feathers,
the big bones and the little bones,
the dramatic reds and blacks 30
of his shiny entrails,
and the pink swim bladder
like a big peony.
I looked into his eyes
which were far larger than mine 35
but shallower, and yellowed,
the irises backed and packed
with tarnished tinfoil
seen through the lenses
of old scratched isinglass.[1] 40

1. Probably not a quotation from any particular source but an expression akin to our "to stay to the bitter end."

1. Semitransparent substance, originally obtained from the swim bladder of some freshwater fishes, used for windows.

They shifted a little, but not
to return my stare.
—It was more like the tipping
of an object toward the light.
I admired his sullen face, 45
the mechanism of his jaw,
and then I saw
that from his lower lip
—if you could call it a lip—
grim, wet, and weaponlike, 50
hung five old pieces of fish-line,
or four and a wire leader
with the swivel still attached,
with all their five big hooks
grown firmly in his mouth. 55
A green line, frayed at the end
where he broke it, two heavier lines,
and a fine black thread
still crimped from the strain and snap
when it broke and he got away. 60
Like medals with their ribbons
frayed and wavering,
a five-haired beard of wisdom
trailing from his aching jaw.
I stared and stared 65
and victory filled up
the little rented boat,
from the pool of bilge
where oil had spread a rainbow
around the rusted engine 70
to the bailer rusted orange,
the sun-cracked thwarts,
the oarlocks on their strings,
the gunnels—until everything
was rainbow, rainbow, rainbow! 75
And I let the fish go.

 1946

Invitation to Miss Marianne Moore[1]

From Brooklyn, over the Brooklyn Bridge, on this fine morning,
 please come flying.
In a cloud of fiery pale chemicals,
 please come flying.
to the rapid rolling of thousands of small blue drums 5
descending out of the mackerel sky
over the glittering grandstand of harbor-water,
 please come flying.

1. American poet (1887–1972).

Whistles, pennants and smoke are blowing. The ships
are signaling cordially with multitudes of flags 10
rising and falling like birds all over the harbor.
Enter: two rivers, gracefully bearing
countless little pellucid jellies
in cut-glass epergnes[2] dragging with silver chains.
The flight is safe; the weather is all arranged 15
The waves are running in verses this fine morning.
 Please come flying.

Come with the pointed toe of each black shoe
trailing a sapphire highlight,
with a black capeful of butterfly wings and bon-mots,[3] 20
with heaven knows how many angels all riding
on the broad black brim of your hat,
 please come flying.

Bearing a musical inaudible abacus,
a slight censorious frown, and blue ribbons, 25
 please come flying.
Facts and skyscrapers glint in the tide; Manhattan
is all awash with morals this fine morning,
 so please come flying.

Mounting the sky with natural heroism, 30
above the accidents, above the malignant movies,
the taxicabs and injustices at large,
while horns are resounding in your beautiful ears
that simultaneously listen to
a soft uninvented music, fit for the musk deer, 35
 please come flying.

For whom the grim museums will behave
like courteous male bower birds,
for whom the agreeable lions lie[4] in wait
on the steps of the Public Library, 40
eager to rise and follow through the doors
up into the reading rooms,
 please come flying.

We can sit down and weep; we can go shopping,
or play at a game of constantly being wrong 45
with a priceless set of vocabularies,
or we can bravely deplore, but please
 please come flying.

With dynasties of negative constructions
darkening and dying around you, 50
with grammar that suddenly turns and shines
like flocks of sandpipers flying,
 please come flying.

2. Compartmented serving dishes.
3. Clever remarks.

4. Large stone lions flank the entrance to the main
branch of the New York Public Library.

Come like a light in the white mackerel sky,
come like a daytime comet 55
with a long unnebulous train of words,
from Brooklyn, over the Brooklyn Bridge, on this fine morning,
 please come flying.

 1955

In the Waiting Room

In Worcester, Massachusetts,
I went with Aunt Consuelo
to keep her dentist's appointment
and sat and waited for her
in the dentist's waiting room. 5
It was winter. It got dark
early. The waiting room
was full of grown-up people,
arctics[1] and overcoats,
lamps and magazines. 10
My aunt was inside
what seemed like a long time
and while I waited I read
the *National Geographic*
(I could read) and carefully 15
studied the photographs:
the inside of a volcano,
black, and full of ashes;
then it was spilling over
in rivulets of fire. 20
Osa and Martin Johnson[2]
dressed in riding breeches,
laced boots, and pith helmets.
A dead man slung on a pole
—"Long Pig,"[3] the caption said. 25
Babies with pointed heads
wound round and round with string;
black, naked women with necks
wound round and round with wire
like the necks of light bulbs. 30
Their breasts were horrifying.
I read it right straight through.
I was too shy to stop.
And then I looked at the cover:
the yellow margins, the date. 35

Suddenly, from inside,
came an *oh!* of pain

1. Thick, waterproof winter overshoes.
2. Married team of American explorers and travel writers.
3. I.e., human flesh; term used by some Polynesian groups.

—Aunt Consuelo's voice—
not very loud or long.
I wasn't at all surprised;　　　　　　　　　　40
even then I knew she was
a foolish, timid woman.
I might have been embarrassed,
but wasn't. What took me
completely by surprise　　　　　　　　　　　45
was that it was *me*:
my voice, in my mouth.
Without thinking at all
I was my foolish aunt,
I—we—were falling, falling,　　　　　　　　50
our eyes glued to the cover
of the *National Geographic*,
February, 1918.

I said to myself: three days
and you'll be seven years old.　　　　　　　55
I was saying it to stop
the sensation of falling off
the round, turning world
into cold, blue-black space.
But I felt: you are an *I*,　　　　　　　　　　60
you are an *Elizabeth*,
you are one of *them*.
Why should you be one, too?
I scarcely dared to look
to see what it was I was.　　　　　　　　　　65
I gave a sidelong glance
—I couldn't look any higher—
at shadowy gray knees,
trousers and skirts and boots
and different pairs of hands　　　　　　　　70
lying under the lamps.
I knew that nothing stranger
had ever happened, that nothing
stranger could ever happen.
Why should I be my aunt,　　　　　　　　　75
or me, or anyone?
What similarities—
boots, hands, the family voice
I felt in my throat, or even
the *National Geographic*　　　　　　　　　80
and those awful hanging breasts—
held us all together
or made us all just one?
How—I didn't know any
word for it—how "unlikely" . . .　　　　　　85
How had I come to be here,
like them, and overhear
a cry of pain that could have
got loud and worse but hadn't?

The waiting room was bright 90
and too hot. It was sliding
beneath a big black wave,
another, and another.

Then I was back in it.
The War[4] was on. Outside, 95
in Worcester, Massachusetts,
were night and slush and cold,
and it was still the fifth
of February, 1918.

 1976

One Art

The art of losing isn't hard to master;
so many things seem filled with the intent
to be lost that their loss is no disaster.

Lose something every day. Accept the fluster
of lost door keys, the hour badly spent. 5
The art of losing isn't hard to master.

Then practice losing farther, losing faster:
places, and names and where it was you meant
to travel. None of these will bring disaster.

I lost my mother's watch. And look! my last, or 10
next-to-last, of three loved houses went.
The art of losing isn't hard to master.

I lost two cities, lovely ones. And, vaster,
some realms I owned, two rivers, a continent.
I miss them, but it wasn't a disaster. 15

—Even losing you (the joking voice, a gesture
I love) I shan't have lied. It's evident
the art of losing's not too hard to master
though it may look like (Write it!) like disaster.

 1976

Pink Dog

[Rio de Janeiro]

The sun is blazing and the sky is blue.
Umbrellas clothe the beach in every hue.
Naked, you trot across the avenue.

4. I.e., World War I.

Oh, never have I seen a dog so bare!
Naked and pink, without a single hair . . . 5
Startled, the passersby draw back and stare.

Of course they're mortally afraid of rabies.
You are not mad; you have a case of scabies[1]
but look intelligent. Where are your babies?

(A nursing mother, by those hanging teats.) 10
In what slum have you hidden them, poor bitch,
while you go begging, living by your wits?

Didn't you know? It's been in all the papers,
to solve this problem, how they deal with beggars?
They take and throw them in the tidal rivers. 15

Yes, idiots, paralytics, parasites
go bobbing in the ebbing sewage, nights
out in the suburbs, where there are no lights

If they do this to anyone who begs,
drugged, drunk, or sober, with or without legs, 20
what would they do to sick, four-legged dogs?

In the cafés and on the sidewalk corners
the joke is going round that all the beggars
who can afford them now wear life preservers.

In your condition you would not be able 25
even to float, much less to dog-paddle.
Now look, the practical, the sensible

solution is to wear a *fantasia*.[2]
Tonight you simply can't afford to be a-
n eyesore. But no one will ever see a 30

dog in *mascara* this time of year.
Ash Wednesday'll come but Carnival[3] is here.
What sambas[4] can you dance? What will you wear?

They say that Carnival's degenerating
—radios, Americans, or something, 35
have ruined it completely. They're just talking.

Carnival is always wonderful!
A depilated dog would not look well.
Dress up! Dress up and dance at Carnival!

1979

1. A skin disease that causes severe itching.
2. Carnival costume [Bishop's note].
3. "Ash Wednesday": In the Christian calendar, the Wednesday before Lent (the forty-day period that precedes the anniversary of Christ's Crucifixion and
Resurrection), a day when devout Catholics place a smudge of ash on their foreheads. "Carnival": on Shrove Tuesday, the day before Ash Wednesday.
4. Popular Brazilian dances.

Gwendolyn

My Aunt Mary was eighteen years old and away in "the States," in Boston, training to be a nurse. In the bottom bureau drawer in her room, well wrapped in soft pink tissue paper, lay her best doll. That winter, I had been sick with bronchitis for a long time, and my grandmother finally produced it for me to play with, to my amazement and delight, because I had never even known of its existence before. It was a girl doll, but my grandmother had forgotten her name.

She had a large wardrobe, which my Aunt Mary had made, packed in a toy steamer trunk of green tin embossed with all the proper boards, locks, and nailheads. The clothes were wonderful garments, beautifully sewn, looking old-fashioned even to me. There were long drawers trimmed with tiny lace, and a corset cover, and a corset with little bones. These were exciting, but best of all was the skating costume. There was a red velvet coat, and a turban and muff of some sort of moth-eaten brown fur, and, to make it almost unbearably thrilling, there was a pair of laced white glacé-kid boots, which had scalloped tops and a pair of too small, dull-edged, but very shiny skates loosely attached to their soles by my Aunt Mary with stitches of coarse white thread.

The looseness of the skates didn't bother me. It went very well with the doll's personality, which in turn was well suited to the role of companion to an invalid. She had lain in her drawer so long that the elastic in her joints had become weakened; when you held her up, her head fell gently to one side, and her outstretched hand would rest on yours for a moment and then slip wearily off. She made the family of dolls I usually played with seem rugged and childish: the Campbell Kid doll, with a childlike scar on her forehead where she had fallen against the fender; the two crudely felt-dressed Indians, Hiawatha and Nokomis; and the stocky "baby doll," always holding out his arms to be picked up.

My grandmother was very nice to me when I was sick. During this same illness, she had already given me her button basket to play with, and her scrap bag, and the crazy quilt was put over my bed in the afternoons. The button basket was large and squashed and must have weighed ten pounds, filled with everything from the metal snaps for men's overalls to a set of large cut-steel buttons with deer heads with green glass eyes on them. The scrap bag was interesting because in it I could find pieces of my grandmother's dresses that she was wearing right then, and pieces of my grandfather's Sunday shirts. But the crazy quilt was the best entertainment. My grandmother had made it long before, when such quilts had been a fad in the little Nova Scotian village where we lived. She had collected small, irregularly shaped pieces of silk or velvet of all colors and got all her lady and gentleman friends to write their names on them in pencil—their names, and sometimes a date or word or two as well. Then she had gone over the writing in chain stitch with silks of different colors, and then put the whole thing together on maroon flannel, with featherstitching joining the pieces. I could read well enough to make out the names of people I knew, and then my grandmother would sometimes tell me that that particular piece of silk came from Mrs. So-and-So's "going-away" dress, forty years ago, or that that was from a necktie of one of her brothers, since dead and buried in London, or that that was from India, brought back by another brother, who was a missionary.

When it grew dark—and this, of course, was very early—she would take me out of bed, wrap me in a blanket, and, holding me on her knees, rock me vigorously in the rocking chair. I think she enjoyed this exercise as much as I did, because she would sing me hymns, in her rather affectedly lugubrious voice, which suddenly thinned out to half its ordinary volume on the higher notes. She sang me "There is a green hill far away," "Will there be any stars in my crown?" and "In the sweet bye-and-bye." Then there were more specifically children's hymns, such as:

> Little children, little children,
> Who love their Redeemer,
> Are the jewels, precious jewels,
> Bright gems for his crown . . .

And then, perhaps because we were Baptists—nice watery ones—all the saints casting down their crowns (in what kind of a tantrum?) "around the glassy sea"; "Shall we gather at the river?"; and her favorite, "Happy day, happy day, when Jesus washed my sins away."

This is preliminary. The story of Gwendolyn did not begin until the following summer, when I was in my usual summer state of good health and had forgotten about the bronchitis, the realistic cat-and-kitten family in my chest, and the doctor's cold stethoscope.

Gwendolyn Appletree was the youngest child and only daughter of a large, widely spaced family that lived away out, four or five miles, on a lonely farm among the fir trees. She was a year or so older than I—that is, about eight—and her five or six brothers. I suppose in their teens seemed like grown men to me. But Gwendolyn and I, although we didn't see each other very often, were friends, and to me she stood for everything that the slightly repellent but fascinating words "little girl" should mean. In the first place, her beautiful name. Its dactyl[1] trisyllables could have gone on forever as far as I was concerned. And then, although older, she was as small as I was, and blond, and pink and white, exactly like a blossoming apple tree. And she was "delicate," which, in spite of the bronchitis, I was not. She had diabetes. I had been told this much and had some vague idea that it was because of "too much sugar," and that in itself made Gwendolyn even more attractive, as she would prove to be solid candy if you bit her, and her pure-tinted complexion would taste exactly like the icing-sugar Easter eggs or birthday-candle holders, held to be inedible, except that I knew better.

I don't know what the treatment for diabetes was at that time—whether, for example, Gwendolyn was given insulin or not, but I rather think not. My grandparents, however, often spoke disapprovingly of the way her parents would not obey the doctor's orders and gave her whatever she wanted to eat, including two pieces of cake for tea, and of how, if they weren't more sensible, they would never keep her. Every once in a while, she would have a mysterious attack of some sort, "convulsions" or a "coma," but a day or two later I would see her driving with her father to the store right next door to our house, look-

1. Metrical foot, or unit, composed of a long and two short syllables or of a stressed syllable and two unstressed ones.

ing the same as ever and waving to me. Occasionally, she would be brought to spend the day or afternoon with me while her parents drove down the shore to visit relatives.

These were wonderful occasions. She would arrive carrying a doll or some other toy; her mother would bring a cake or a jar of preserves for my grandmother. Then I would have the opportunity of showing her all my possessions all over again. Quite often, what she brought was a set of small blocks that exactly fitted in a shallow cardboard box. These blocks were squares cut diagonally across, in clear reds, yellows, and blues, and we arranged them snugly together in geometric designs. Then, if we were careful, the whole thing could be lifted up and turned over, revealing a similar brilliant design in different colors on the other side. These designs were completely satisfying in their forthrightness, like the Union Jack. We played quietly together and did not quarrel.

Before her mother and father drove off in their buggy, Gwendolyn was embraced over and over, her face was washed one last time, her stockings were pulled up, her nose was wiped, she was hoisted up and down and swung around and around by her father and given some white pills by her mother. This sometimes went on so long that my grandfather would leave abruptly for the barn and my grandmother would busy herself at the sink and start singing a hymn under her breath, but it was nothing to the scenes of tenderness when they returned a few hours later. Then her parents almost ate her up, alternately, as if she really were made of sugar, as I half suspected. I watched these exciting scenes with envy until Mr. and Mrs. Appletree drove away, with Gwendolyn standing between them in her white dress, her pale-gold hair blowing, still being kissed from either side. Although I received many demonstrations of affection from my grandparents, they were nothing like this. My grandmother was disgusted. "They'll kiss that child to death if they're not careful," she said. "Oh, lallygagging, lallygagging!" said my grandfather, going on about his business.

I remember clearly three episodes of that summer in which Gwendolyn played the role of beautiful heroine—the role that grew and grew until finally it had grown far beyond the slight but convincing talents she had for acting it.

Once, my grandparents and I went to a church picnic. As I said, we were Baptists, but most of the village, including the Appletrees, were Presbyterians. However, on social occasions I think the two sects sometimes joined forces, or else we were broad-minded enough to go to a Presbyterian picnic—I'm not sure. Anyway, the three of us, dressed in our second-best, took a huge picnic supper and drove behind Nimble II to the picnic grounds beside the river. It was a beautiful spot; there were large spruce and pine trees right to the edge of the clear brown water and mossy terra-cotta-colored rocks; the ground was slippery with brown pine needles. Pans of beans and biscuits and scalloped potatoes were set out on long tables, and all our varieties of pickles and relishes (chowchows and piccalillis), conserves and preserves, cakes and pies, parkins and hermits—all glistening and gleaming in the late sunshine—and water for tea was being brought to the boil over two fires. My grandmother settled herself on a log to talk to her friends, and I went wading in the river with mine. My cousin Billy was there, and Seth Hill, and the little McNeil twins, but Gwendolyn was missing. Later, I joined my family for supper, or as all

Nova Scotians call their suppers, "tea." My grandmother spoke to one of the Appletree boys, filling his plate beside us, and asked him where his father and mother were, and how Gwendolyn was.

"Pretty poorly," he answered, with an imitative elderly-man shake of his head. "Ma thought we'd lost her yesterday morning. I drove down and got the doctor. She's resting better today, though."

We went on drinking our tea and eating in silence, and after a while my grandfather started talking about something else. But just before we finished, when it was beginning to get gray, and a sweet, dank, fresh-water smell had suddenly started to come up off the river, a horse and buggy turned rapidly in to the picnic grounds and pulled up beside us. In it were Mr. and Mrs. Appletree, and Gwendolyn—standing between them, as usual—wearing one of her white dresses, with a little black-and-white-checked coat over it. A great fuss was made over them and her, and my grandfather lifted her down and held her on his knee, sitting on one of the rough benches beside the picnic tables. I leaned against him, but Gwendolyn wouldn't speak to me; she just smiled as if very pleased with everything. She looked prettier and more delicate than ever, and her cheeks were bright pink. Her mother made her a cup of weak tea, and I could see my grandmother's look as the sugar went into it. Gwendolyn had wanted to come so badly, her mother said, so they thought they'd bring her just for a little while.

Some time after this, Gwendolyn was brought to visit me again, but this time she was to spend the whole day and night and part of the next day. I was very excited, and consulted with my grandmother endlessly as to how we should pass the time—if I could jump with her in the barn or take her swimming in the river. No, both those sports were too strenuous for Gwendolyn, but we could play at filling bottles with colored water (made from paints in my paintbox), my favorite game at the moment, and in the afternoon we could have a dolls' tea party.

Everything went off very well. After dinner, Gwendolyn went and lay on the sofa in the parlor, and my grandmother put a shawl over her. I wanted to pretend to play the piano to her, but I was made to stop and go outside by myself. After a while, Gwendolyn joined me in the flower garden and we had the tea party. After that, I showed her how to trap bumblebees in the foxgloves, but that was also put a stop to by my grandmother as too strenuous and dangerous. Our play was not without a touch of rustic corruption, either. I can't remember what happened, if anything, but I do remember being ordered out of the whitewashed privy in the barn after we had locked ourselves in and climbed on the seats and hung out the little window, with its beautiful view of the elm-studded "interval" in back of us. It was just getting dark; my grandmother was very stern with me and said we must never lock ourselves in there, but she was objectionably kind to Gwendolyn, who looked more angelic than ever.

After tea, we sat at the table with the oil lamp hanging over it for a while, playing with the wonderful blocks, and then it was bedtime. Gwendolyn was going to sleep in my bed with me. I was so overwrought with the novelty of this that it took me a long time to get ready for bed, but Gwendolyn was ready in a jiffy and lay on the far side of the bed with her eyes shut, trying to make me think she was asleep, with the lamplight shining on her blond, blond hair. I

asked her if she didn't say her prayers before she got into bed and she said no, her mother let her say them in bed, "because I'm going to die."

At least, that was what I thought she said. I couldn't quite believe I had really heard her say it and I certainly couldn't ask her if she had said it. My heart pounding, I brushed my teeth with the icy well water, and spat in the china pot. Then I got down on my knees and said my own prayers, half aloud, completely mechanically, while the pounding went on and on. I couldn't seem to make myself get into my side of the bed, so I went around and picked up Gwendolyn's clothes. She had thrown them on the floor. I put them over the back of a chair—the blue-and-white-striped dress, the waist, the long brown stockings. Her drawers had lace around the legs, but they were very dirty. This fact shocked me so deeply that I recovered my voice and started asking her more questions.

"I'm asleep," said Gwendolyn, without opening her eyes.

But after my grandmother had turned out the lamp, Gwendolyn began to talk to me again. We told each other which colors we liked best together, and I remember the feeling of profound originality I experienced when I insisted, although it had just occurred to me, that I had always like black and brown together best. I saw them floating in little patches of velvet, like the crazy quilt, or smooth little rectangles of enamel, like the paint-sample cards I was always begging for at the general store.

Two days after this visit, Gwendolyn did die. One of her brothers came in to tell my grandmother—and I was there in the kitchen when he told her—with more of the elderly-man headshakes and some sad and ancient phrases. My grandmother wept and wiped her eyes with her apron, answering him with phrases equally sad and ancient. The funeral was to be two days later, but I was not going to be allowed to go.

My grandfather went, but not my grandmother. I wasn't even supposed to know what was taking place, but since the Presbyterian church was right across the village green from our house, and I could hear the buggies driving up over the gravel, and then the bell beginning to ring, I knew quite well, and my heart began to pound again, apparently as loudly as the bell was ringing. I was sent out to play in the yard at the far side of the house, away from the church. But through one of the kitchen windows—the kitchen was an ell that had windows on both sides—I could see my curious grandmother drawing up her rocking chair, as she did every Sunday morning, just behind a window on the other side of the ell, to watch the Presbyterians going to church. This was the unacknowledged practice of the Baptists who lived within sight of the church and later, when they met at their own afternoon service, they would innocently say to each other things like "They had a good turnout this morning" and "Is Mrs. Peppard still laid up? I missed her this morning."

But today it was quite different, and when I peeked in at my grandmother at one side of the ell, she was crying and crying between her own peeks at the mourners out the other side. She had a handkerchief already very wet, and was rocking gently.

It was too much for me. I sneaked back into the house by the side door and into the shut-up parlor, where I could look across at the church, too. There were long lace curtains at the window and the foxgloves and bees were just outside, but I had a perfectly clear, although lace-patterned, view of every-

thing. The church was quite large—a Gothic structure made of white clapboards, with non-flying buttresses, and a tall wooden steeple—and I was as familiar with it as I was with my grandmother. I used to play hide-and-seek among the buttresses with my friends. The buggy sheds, now all filled, were at the back, and around the large grass plot were white wooden pillars with double chains slung slackly between them, on which my cousin Billy, who lived right next door to the church, and I liked to clamber and swing.

At last, everyone seemed to have gone inside, and an inner door shut. No, two men in black stood talking together in the open outside doorway. The bell suddenly stopped ringing and the two men vanished, and I was afraid of being in the parlor alone, but couldn't leave now. Hours seemed to go by. There was some singing, but I didn't recognize the hymns, either because I was too nervous or because, as they sometimes did, the Presbyterians sang hymns unfamiliar to me.

I had seen many funerals like this before, of course, and I loved to go with my grandfather when he went to the graveyard with a scythe and a sickle to cut the grass on our family's graves. The graveyard belonging to the village was surely one of the prettiest in the world. It was on the bank of the river, two miles below us, but where the bank was high. It lay small and green and white, with its firs and cedars and gravestones balancing against the dreaming lavender-red Bay of Fundy.[2] The headstones were mostly rather thin, coarse white marble slabs, frequently leaning slightly, but there was a scattering of small urns and obelisks and broken columns. A few plots were lightly chained in, like the Presbyterian church, or fenced in with wood or iron, like little gardens, and wild rosebushes grew in the grass. Blueberries grew there, too, but I didn't eat them, because I felt I "never knew," as people said, but once when I went there, my grandmother had given me a teacup without a handle and requested me to bring her back some teaberries,[3] which "grew good" on the graves, and I had.

And so I used to play while my grandfather, wearing a straw hat, scythed away, and talked to me haphazardly about the people lying there. I was, of course, particularly interested in the children's graves, their names, what ages they had died at—whether they were older than I or younger. The favorite memorial for small children was a low rectangle of the same coarse white marble as the larger stones, but with a little lamb recumbent on top. I adored these lambs, and counted them and caressed them and sat on them. Some were almost covered by dry, bright-gold lichen, some with green and gold and gray mixed together, some were almost lost among the long grass and roses and blueberries and teaberries.

But now, suddenly, as I watched through the window, something happened at the church across the way. Something that could not possibly have happened, so that I must, in reality, have seen something like it and imagined the rest; or my concentration on the one thing was so intense that I could see nothing else.

The two men in black appeared again, carrying Gwendolyn's small white coffin between them. Then—this was the impossibility—they put it down just outside the church door, one end on the grass and the other lifted up a lit-

2. Atlantic inlet between New Brunswick and Nova 3. Fruits of the American wintergreen.
Scotia

tle, to lean at a slight angle against the wall. Then they disappeared inside again. For a minute, I stared straight through my lace curtain at Gwendolyn's coffin, with Gwendolyn shut invisibly inside it forever, there, completely alone on the grass by the church door.

Then I ran howling to the back door, out among the startled white hens, with my grandmother, still weeping, after me.

If I care to, I can bring back the exact sensation of that moment today, but then, it is also one of those that from time to time are terrifyingly thrust upon us. I was familiar with it and recognized it; I had already experienced it once, shortly before the bronchitis attack of the previous winter. One evening, we were all sitting around the table with the lamp hanging above it; my grandfather was dozing in the Morris chair,[4] my grandmother was crocheting, and my Aunt Mary, who had not yet gone away to Boston, was reading *Maclean's Magazine.* I was drawing pictures when suddenly I remembered something, a present that had been given to me months before and that I had forgotten all about. It was a strawberry basket half filled with new marbles—clay ones, in the usual mottled shades of red, brown, purple, and green. However, in among them were several of a sort I have never seen before: fine, unglazed, cream-colored clay, with purple and pink lines around them. One or two of the larger ones of this sort even had little sprigs of flowers on them. But the most beautiful of all, I thought, was a really big one, probably an inch and a half in diameter, or a roughly shiny glazed pink, like crockery. It moved me almost to tears to look at it; it "went right through me."

Anyway, I started thinking about these marbles—wondering where they had been all this time, where I had put them, if they had got lost—until at last it became unbearable and I had to go and find them. I went out to the kitchen in the dark and groped around on the floor of a cupboard where I kept some of my belongings. I felt the edges of riffled old books and sharp mechanical toys, and then, at the back, I did feel the strawberry basket. I dragged it out and carried it into the sitting room.

My relatives paid no attention. I stared into the basket and took out a few of the marbles. But what could have happened? They were covered with dirt and dust, nails were lying mixed in with them, bits of string, cobwebs, old horse chestnuts blue with mildew, their polish gone. The big pink marble was there, but I hardly recognized it, all covered with dirt. (Later, when my grandmother washed it off, it was as good as new, of course.) The broad lamp flame started to blur; my aunt's fair hair started to blur; I put my head down on top of the marbles and cried aloud. My grandfather woke up with a jerk and said, "Heavens, what ails the child now?" Everyone tried to comfort me—for what, they had no idea.

A month or so after the funeral—it was still summer—my grandparents went away for the day to visit Cousin Sophy, "over the mountain." I was supposed to stay with another aunt, the mother of my cousin Billy, and to play with him while they were gone. But we soon left his yard and wandered back to mine, which was larger and more interesting, and where we felt the additional charm of being all alone and unwatched. Various diversions, quarrels, and rec-

4. Easy chair.

onciliations made up the long, sunny afternoon. We sucked water from jelly glasses through chive straws until we reeked of them, and fought for the possession of insects in matchboxes. To tease me, Billy deliberately stepped on one of the boxes and crushed its inhabitant flat. When we had made up after this violence, we sat and talked for a while, desultorily, about death in general, and going to heaven, but we were growing a little bored and reckless, and finally I did something really bad: I went in the house and upstairs to my Aunt Mary's bedroom and brought down the tissue-paper-wrapped, retired doll. Billy had never seen her before and was as impressed with her as I had been.

We handled her carefully. We took off her hat and shoes and stockings, and examined every stitch of her underclothes. Then we played vaguely at "operating" on her stomach, but we were rather too much in awe of her for that to be a success. Then we had the idea of adorning her with flowers. There was a clump of Johnny-jump-ups that I thought belonged to me; we picked them and made a wreath for the nameless doll. We laid her out in the garden path and outlined her body with Johnny-jump-ups and babies'-breath and put a pink cosmos in one limp hand. She looked perfectly beautiful. The game was more exciting than "operation." I don't know which one of us said it first, but one of us did, with wild joy—that it was Gwendolyn's funeral, and that the doll's real name, all this time, was Gwendolyn.

But then my grandparents drove into the yard and found us, and my grandmother was furious that I had dared to touch Aunt Mary's doll. Billy was sent straight home and I don't remember now what awful thing happened to me.

 1953

[Gender and Art][1]

Undoubtedly gender does play an important part in the making of any art, but art is art and to separate writings, paintings, musical compositions, etc., into two sexes is to emphasize values in them that are *not* art.

 1977

1. From a letter to Joan Keefe, June 8, 1977.

MARY LAVIN
1912–1996

"Mary Lavin's characters . . . speak directly from the spiritual setting of Joyce's *Dubliners*," the writer Kay Boyle has commented, linking Lavin with one of Ireland's greatest men of letters. "But this time," Boyle adds, "it is a woman's voice telling us . . . of other women's love, and pride, and courage, and despair." Born in Massachusetts to Irish parents who returned with her to their native country when she was nine, Lavin started her career not as a creative writer but as a literary critic, studying at University College, Dublin. After producing a master's thesis on Jane Austen and an unfinished Ph.D. dissertation on Virginia Woolf, however, she turned her intellectual energies to fiction.

In 1942, Lavin married William Walsh, a lawyer with whom she had three

daughters; he died in 1954, and after some years of widowhood—an experience that may well be reflected in the poignant *In a Café*—she remarried in 1969. She published several novels, notably *The House on Clewe Street* (1945) and *Mary O'Grady* (1950), but is best known for seventeen collections of powerful short stories, including many on distinctively Irish subjects as well as many that explore the nuances of women's lives with strength and subtlety. "Short-story writing," she explained, "is only looking closer than normal into the human heart."

In a Café

The café was in a back street. Mary's ankles ached and she was glad Maudie had not got there before her. She sat down at a table near the door.

It was a place she had only recently found, and she dropped in often, whenever she came up to Dublin. She hated to go anywhere else now. For one thing, she knew that she would be unlikely ever to have set foot in it if Richard were still alive. And this knowledge helped to give her back a semblance of the identity she lost willingly in marriage, but lost doubly, and unwillingly, in widowhood.

Not that Richard would have disliked the café. It was the kind of place they went to when they were students. Too much water had gone under the bridge since those days, though. Say what you liked, there was something faintly snobby about a farm in Meath,[1] and together she and Richard would have been out of place here. But it was a different matter to come here alone. There could be nothing—oh, nothing—snobby about a widow. Just by being one, she fitted into this kind of café. It was an unusual little place. She looked around.

The walls were distempered red above and the lower part was boarded, with the boards painted white. It was probably the boarded walls that gave it the peculiarly functional look you get in the snuggery of a public house[2] or in the confessional of a small and poor parish church. For furniture there were only deal tables and chairs, with black-and-white checked tablecloths that were either unironed or badly ironed. But there was a decided feeling that money was not so much in short supply as dedicated to other purposes—as witness the paintings on the walls, and a notice over the fire-grate to say that there were others on view in a studio overhead, in rather the same way as pictures in an exhibition. The paintings were for the most part experimental in their technique.

The café was run by two students from the Art College. They often went out and left the place quite empty—as now—while they had a cup of coffee in another café—across the street. Regular clients sometimes helped themselves to coffee from the pot on the gas-ring, behind a curtain at the back; or, if they only came in for company and found none, merely warmed themselves at the big fire always blazing in the little black grate that was the original grate when the café was a warehouse office. Today, the fire was banked up with coke.[3] The coffee was spitting on the gas-ring.

Would Maudie like the place? That it might not be exactly the right place to have arranged to meet her, above all under the present circumstances, oc-

1. County in Ireland close to Dublin.
2. The bar-parlor.

3. Fuel made from coal.

curred vaguely to Mary, but there was nothing that could be done about it now. When Maudie got there, if she didn't like it, they could go somewhere else. On the other hand, perhaps she might like it? Or perhaps she would be too upset to take notice of her surroundings? The paintings might interest her. They were certainly stimulating. There were two new ones today, which Mary herself had not seen before: two flower paintings, just inside the door. From where she sat she could read the signature, Johann van Stiegler. Or at least they suggested flowers. They were nameable as roses surely in spite of being a bit angular. She knew what Richard would have said about them. But she and Richard were no longer one. So what would *she* say about them? She would say—she would say—

But what was keeping Maudie? It was all very well to be glad of a few minutes' time in which to gather herself together; it was a different thing altogether to be kept a quarter of an hour.

Mary leaned back against the boarding. She was less tired that when she came in, but she was still in no way prepared for the encounter in front of her.

What had she to say to a young widow recently bereaved? Why on earth had she arranged to meet her? The incongruity of their both being widowed came forcibly upon her. Would Maudie, too, be in black with touches of white? Two widows! It was like two magpies: one for sorrow, two for joy. The absurdity of it was all at once so great she had an impulse to get up and make off out of the place. She felt herself vibrating all over with resentment at being coupled with anyone, and urgently she began to sever them, seeking out their disparities.

Maudie was only a year married! And her parents had been only too ready to take care of her child, greedily possessing themselves of it. Maudie was as free as a girl. Then—if it mattered—?—she had a nice little income in her own right too, apart from all Michael had left her. So?

But what was keeping her? Was she not coming at all?

Ah! the little iron bell that was over the door—it too, since the warehouse days—tinkled to tell there was another customer coming into the café.

It wasn't Maudie though. It was a young man—youngish anyway—and Mary would say that he was an artist. Yet his hands at which, when he sat down, he began to stare, were not like the hands of an artist. They were peculiarly plump soft-skinned hands, and there was something touching in the relaxed way in which, lightly clasped one in the other, they rested on the table. Had they a womanish look perhaps? No; that was not the word, but she couldn't for the life of her find the right word to describe them. And her mind was teased by trying to find it. Fascinated, her eyes were drawn to those hands, time and again, no matter how resolutely she tore them away. It was almost as if it was by touch, not sight, that she knew their warm fleshiness.

Even when she closed her eyes—as she did—she could still see them. And so, innocent of where she was being led, she made no real effort to free her thoughts from them, and not until it was too late did she see before her the familiar shape of her recurring nightmare. All at once it was Richard's hands she saw, so different from those others, wiry, supple, thin. There they were for an instant in her mind, limned by love and anguish, before they vanished.

It happened so often. In her mind she would see a part of him, his hand—his arm, his foot perhaps, in the finely worked leather shoes he always wore—and from it, frantically, she would try to build up the whole man. Sometimes she succeeded better than others, built him up from foot to shoulder, seeing

his hands, his gray suit, his tie, knotted always in a slightly special way, his neck, even his chin that was rather sharp, a little less attractive than his other features—

—But always at that point she would be defeated. Never once voluntarily since the day he died had she been able to see his face again.

And if she could not remember him, at will, what meaning had time at all? What use was it to have lived the past, if behind us it fell away so sheer?

In the hour of his death, for her it was part of the pain that she knew this would happen. She was standing beside him when, outside the hospital window, a bird called out with a sweet, clear whistle, and hearing it she knew that he was dead, because not for years had she really heard bird-song or bird-call, so loud was the noise of their love in her ears. When she looked down it was a strange face, the look of death itself, that lay on the pillow. And after that brief moment of silence that let in the bird-song for an instant, a new noise started in her head; the noise of a nameless panic that did not always roar, but never altogether died down.

And now—here in the little café—she caught at the table-edge—for the conflagration had started again and her mind was a roaring furnace.

It was just then the man at the end of the table stood up and reached for the menu-card on which, as a matter of fact, she was leaning—breasts and elbows—with her face in her hands. Hastily, apologetically, she pushed it towards him, and at once the roar died down in her mind. She looked at him. Could he have known? Her heart was filled with gratitude, and she saw that his eyes were soft and gentle. But she had to admit that he didn't look as if he were much aware of her. No matter! She still was grateful to him.

"Don't you want this too?" she cried, thankful, warm, as she saw that the small slip of paper with the specialty for the day that had been clipped to the menu card with a paper-pin, had come off and remained under the elbow, caught on the rough sleeve of her jacket. She stood up and leant over the table with it.

"Ah! thank you!" he said, and bowed. She smiled. There was such gallantry in a bow. He was a foreigner, of course. And then, before she sat down again she saw that he had been sketching, making little pencil sketches all over a newspaper on the table, in the margins and in the spaces between the newsprint. Such intricate minutely involuted little figures—she was fascinated, but of course she could not stare.

Yet, when she sat down, she watched him covertly, and every now and then she saw that he made a particular flourish: it was his signature, she felt sure, and she tried to make it out from where she sat. A disproportionate, a ridiculous excitement rushed through her, when she realized it was Johann van Stiegler, the name on the new flower paintings that had preoccupied her when she first came into the place.

But it's impossible, she thought. The sketches were so meticulous; the painting so—

But the little bell tinkled again.

"Ah! Maudie!"

For all her waiting, taken by surprise in the end, she got to her feet in her embarrassment, like a man.

"Maudie, my dear!" She had to stare fixedly at her in an effort to convey the sympathy, which, tongue-tied, she could express in no other way.

They shook hands, wordlessly.

"I'm deliberately refraining from expressing sympathy—you know that?" said Mary then, as they sat down at the checkered table.

"Oh, I do!" cried Maudie. And she seemed genuinely appreciative. "It's so awful trying to think of something to say back!—Isn't it? It has to come right out of yourself, and sometimes what comes is something you can't even say out loud when you do think of it!"

It was so true. Mary looked at her in surprise. Her mind ran back over the things people had said to her, and the replies.

Them: It's a good thing it wasn't one of the children.

Her: I'd give them all for him.

Them: Time is a great healer.

Her: Thief would be more like: taking away even my memory of him.

Them: God's ways are wonderful. Some day you'll see His plan in all this.

Her: Do you mean, some day I'll be glad he's dead?

So Maudie apprehended these subtleties too? Mary looked hard at her. "I know, I know," she said. "In the end you have to say what is expected of you—and you feel so cheapened by it."

"Worse still, you cheapen the dead!" said Maudie.

Mary looked really hard at her now. Was it possible for a young girl—a simple person at that—to have wrung from one single experience so much bitter knowledge? In spite of herself, she felt she was being drawn into complicity with her. She drew back resolutely.

"Of course, you were more or less expecting it, weren't you?" she said, spitefully.

Unrepulsed, Maudie looked back at her. "Does that matter?" she asked, and then, unexpectedly, she herself put a rift between them. "You have the children, of course!" she said, and then, hastily, before Mary could say anything, she rushed on. "Oh, I know I have my baby, but there seems so little link between him and his father! I just can't believe that it's me sometimes, wheeling him round the park in his pram; it's like as if he was illegitimate. No! I mean it really. I'm not just trying to be shocking. It must be so different when there has been time for a relationship to be started between children and their father, like there was in your case."

"Oh, I don't know that that matters," said Mary. "And you'll be glad to have him some day." This time she spoke with deliberate malice, for she knew so well how those same words had lacerated her. She knew what they were meant to say: the children would be better than nothing.

But the poison of her words did not penetrate Maudie. And with another stab she knew why this was so. Maudie was so young; so beautiful. Looking at her, it seemed quite inaccurate to say that she had lost her husband: it was Michael who had lost her, fallen out, as it were, while she perforce went outward. She didn't even look like a widow. There was nothing about her to suggest that she was in any way bereft or maimed.

"You'll marry again, Maudie," she said, impulsively. "Don't mind my saying it," she added quickly, hastily. "It's not a criticism. It's because I know how you're suffering that I say it. Don't take offense."

Maudie didn't really look offended though, she only looked on the defensive. Then she relaxed.

"Not coming from you," she said. "You know what it's like." Mary saw

she was trying to cover up the fact that she simply could not violently refute
the suggestion. "Not that I think I will," she added, but weakly, "After all, you
didn't!"

It was Mary who was put upon the defensive now.

"After all, it's only two years—less even," she said stiffly.

"Oh, it's not altogether a matter of time," said Maudie, seeing she had
erred, but not clear how or where. "It's the kind of person you are, I think. I ad-
mire you so much! It's what I'd want to be like myself if I had the strength.
With remarriage it is largely the effect on oneself that matters I think, don't
you? I don't think it really matters to—to the dead! Do you? I'm sure Michael
would want me to marry again if he were able to express a wish. After all, peo-
ple say it's a compliment to a man if his widow marries again, did you ever hear
that?"

"I did," said Mary, curtly. "But I wouldn't pay much heed to it. A fat lot the
dead care about compliments."

So Maudie *was* already thinking about remarriage? Mary's irritation was
succeeded by a vague feeling of envy, and then the irritation returned tenfold.

How easily it was accepted that *she* would not marry again. This girl regards
me as too old, of course. And she's right—or she ought to be right! She re-
membered the way, even two years ago, people had said she "had" her chil-
dren. They meant, even then, that it was unlikely, unlooked for, that she'd
remarry.

Other things that had been said crowded back into her mind as well. So
many people had spoken of the special quality of her marriage—hers and
Richard's—their remarkable suitability one for the other, and the uniqueness
of the bond between them. She was avid to hear this said at the time.

But suddenly, in this little café, the light that had played over those words
flickered and went out. Did they perhaps mean that if Richard had not ap-
peared when he did, no one else would have been interested in her?

Whereas Maudie—! If she looked so attractive now, when she must still be
suffering from shock, what would she be like a year from now, when she would
be "out of mourning," as it would be put? Why, right now, she was so fresh
and—looking at her there was no other word for it—virginal. Of course she
was only a year married! A year! You could hardly call it being married at all.

But Maudie knew a thing or two about men for all that. There was no deny-
ing it. And in her eyes at that moment there was a strange expression. Seeing
it, Mary remembered at once that they were not alone in the café. She won-
dered urgently how much the man at the other end of the table had heard and
could hear of what they were saying. But it was too late to stop Maudie.

"Oh Mary," cried Maudie, leaning forward, "it's not what they give us—I've
got over wanting things like a child—it's what we have to give them! It's some-
thing—" and she pressed her hands suddenly to her breasts, "something in
here!"

"Maudie!"

Sharply, urgently, Mary tried to make her lower her voice, and with a quick
movement of her head she did manage at last to convey some caution to her.

"In case you might say something," she said, in a low voice.

"Oh, there was no fear," said Maudie. "I was aware all the time." She didn't
speak quite so low as Mary, but did lower her voice. "I was aware of him *all the
time*," she said. "It was *him* that put it into my mind—about what we have to

give." She pressed her hands to her breasts again. "He looks so lonely, don't you think? He is a foreigner, isn't he? I always think it's sad for them; they don't have many friends, and even when they do, there is always a barrier, don't you agree?"

But Mary was too embarrassed to let her go on. Almost frantically she made a diversion.

"What are you going to have, Maudie?" she said loudly. "Coffee? Tea? And is there no one to take an order?"

Immediately she felt a fool. To whom had she spoken? She looked across at Johann van Stiegler. As if he were waiting to meet her glance, his mild and patient eyes looked into hers.

"There is no one there," he said, nodding at the curtained gas-ring, "but one can serve oneself. Perhaps you would wish that I—"

"Oh, not at all," cried Mary. "Please, don't trouble! We're in absolutely no hurry! Please don't trouble yourself," she said, "not on our account."

But she saw at once that he was very much a foreigner, and that he was at a disadvantage, not knowing if he had not perhaps made a gaffe. "I have perhaps intruded?" he said, miserably.

"Oh, not at all," cried Mary, and he was so serious she had to laugh.

The laugh was another mistake though. His face took on a look of despair that could come upon a foreigner, it seemed, at the slightest provocation, as if suddenly everything was obscure to him—everything.

"Please," she murmured, and then vaguely, "—your work," meaning that she did not wish to interrupt his sketching.

"Ah, you know my work?" he said, brightening immediately, pleased with a small and quite endearing vanity. "We have met before? Yes?"

"Oh no, we haven't met," she said quickly, and she sat down, but of course after that it was impossible to go on acting as if he were a complete stranger. She turned to see what Maudie would make of the situation. It was then she felt the full force of her irritation with Maudie. She could have given her a slap in the face. Yes: a slap right in the face! For there she sat, remotely, her face indeed partly averted from them.

Maudie was waiting to be introduced! To be *introduced*, as if she, Mary, did not need any conventional preliminaries. As if it was all right that she, Mary, should begin an unprefaced conversation with a strange man in a café because—and of course that was what was so infuriating, that she knew Maudie's unconscious thought—it was all right for a woman of *her* age to strike up a conversation like that, but that it wouldn't have done for a young woman. Yet, on her still partly averted face, Mary could see the quickened look of interest. She had a good mind not to make any gesture to draw her into the conversation at all, but she had the young man to consider. She had to bring them together whether she liked it or not.

"Maudie, this is—" she turned back and smiled at van Stiegler, "this is—" But she was confused and she had to abandon the introduction altogether. Instead, she broke into a direct question.

"Those are your flower pictures, aren't they?" she asked.

It was enough for Maudie—more than enough you might say.

She turned to the young man, obviously greatly impressed; her lips apart, her eyes shining. My God, how attractive she was!

"Oh, no, not really?" she cried "How marvelous of you!"

But Johann van Stiegler was looking at Mary.

"You are sure we have not met before?"

"Oh no, but you were scribbling your signature all over that newspaper," she looked around to show it to him, but it had fallen on to the floor.

"Ah, yes," he said, and—she couldn't be certain, of course—but she thought he was disappointed.

"Ah, yes, you saw my signature," he said, flatly. He looked dejected. Mary felt helpless. She turned to Maudie. It was up to her to say something now.

Just then the little warehouse bell tinkled again, and this time it was one of the proprietors who came in, casually, like a client.

"Ah good!" said van Stiegler. "Coffee," he called out. Then he turned to Mary. "Coffee for you too?"

"Oh yes, coffee for us," said Mary, but she couldn't help wondering who was going to pay for it, and simultaneously she couldn't help noticing the shabbiness of his jacket. Well—they'd see! Meanwhile, she determined to ignore the plate of cakes that was put down with the coffee. And she hoped Maudie would too. She pushed the plate aside as a kind of hint to her, but Maudie leaned across and took a large bun filled with cream.

"Do you mind my asking you something—about your work—?" said Mary.

But Maudie interrupted.

"You are living in Ireland? I mean, you are not just here on a visit?"

There was intimacy and intimacy, and Mary felt nervous in case the young man might resent this question.

"I teach art in a college here," he said, and he did seem a little surprised, but Mary could see, too, that he was not at all displeased. He seemed to settle more comfortably into the conversation.

"It is very good for a while to go to another country," he said, "and this country is cheap. I have a flat in the next street to here, and it is very private. If I hang myself from the ceiling, it is all right—nobody knows; nobody cares. That is a good way to live when you paint."

Mary was prepared to ponder. "Do you think so?"

Maudie was not prepared to ponder. "How odd," she said, shortly, and then she looked at her watch. "I'll have to go," she said inexplicably.

They had finished the coffee. Immediately Mary's thought returned to the problem of who was to pay for it. It was a small affair for which to call up all one's spiritual resources, but she felt enormously courageous and determined when she heard herself ask in a loud voice for her bill.

"My bill, please," she called out, over the sound of spitting coffee on the gas stove.

Johann van Stiegler made no move to ask for his bill, and yet he was buttoning his jacket and folding his newspaper as if to leave too. Would his coffee go on her bill? Mary wondered.

It was all settled, however, in a second. The bill was for two eight-penny coffees, and one bun, and there was no charge for van Stiegler's coffee. He had some understanding with the owners, she supposed. Or perhaps he was not really going to leave then at all?

As they stood up, however, gloved and ready to depart, the young man bowed.

"Perhaps we go the same way?" They could see he was anxious to be polite.

"Oh, not at all," they said together, as if he had offered to escort them, and Maudie even laughed openly.

Then there was, of course, another ridiculous situation. Van Stiegler sat down again. Had they been too brusque? Had they hurt his feelings?

Oh, if only he wasn't a foreigner, thought Mary, and she hesitated. Maudie already had her hand on the door.

"I hope I will see some more of your work sometime," said Mary. It was not a question, merely a compliment.

But van Stiegler sprung to his feet again.

"Tonight after my classes I am bringing another picture to hang here," he said. "You would like to see it? I would be here—" he pulled out a large, old-fashioned watch, "—at ten minutes past nine."

"Oh, not tonight—I couldn't come back tonight," said Mary. "I live in the country, you see," she said, explaining and excusing herself. "Another time perhaps? It will be here for how long?"

She wasn't really listening to what he said. She was thinking that he had not asked if Maudie could come. Perhaps it was that, of the two of them, she looked the most likely to buy a picture, whereas Maudie, although in actual fact more likely to do so, looked less so. Or was it that he coupled them so that he thought if one came, both came. Or was it really Maudie he'd like to see again, and that he regarded her as a chaperone? Or was it—?

There was no knowing, however, and so she said goodbye again, and the next minute the little bell had tinkled over the door and they were in the street. In the street they looked at each other.

"Well! if ever there was—" began Maudie, but she didn't get time to finish her sentence. Behind them the little bell tinkled yet again, and their painter was out in the street with them.

"I forgot to give you the address of my flat—it is also my studio," he said. "I would be glad to show you my paintings at any time." He pulled out a notebook and tore out a sheet. "I will write it down," he said, concisely. And he did. But when he went to hand it to them, it was Maudie who took it. "I am nearly always there, except when I am at my classes," he said. And bowing, he turned and went back into the café.

They dared not laugh until they had walked some distance away, until they turned into the next street in fact.

"Well, I never!" said Maudie, and she handed the paper to Mary.

"Chatham Row," Mary read, "number 8."

"Will you go to see them?" asked Maudie.

Mary felt outraged.

"What do you take me for?" she asked. "I may be a bit unconventional, but can you see me presenting myself at his place? Would you go?"

"Oh, it's different for me," said Maudie, enigmatically. "And anyway, it was you he asked. But I see your point—it's a pity. Poor fellow!—he must be very lonely. I wish there was something we could do for him—someone to whom we could introduce him."

Mary looked at her. It had never occurred to her that he might be lonely! How was it that the obvious always escaped her?

They were in Grafton Street by this time.

"Well, I have some shopping to do. I suppose it's the same with you," said

Maudie. "I am glad I had that talk with you. We must have another chat soon."

"Oh yes," said Mary, over-readily, replying to her adieux though, and not to the suggestion of their meeting again! She was anxious all at once to be rid of Maudie.

And yet, as she watched her walk away from her, making her passage quickly and expertly through the crowds in the street, Mary felt a sudden terrible aimlessness descend upon herself like a physical paralysis. She walked along, pausing to look in the shop windows.

It was the evening hour when everyone in the streets was hurrying home, purposeful and intent. Even those who paused to look into the shop windows did so with direction and aim, darting their bright glances keenly, like birds. Their minds were all intent upon substantives; tangibles, while her mind was straying back to the student café, and the strange flower pictures on the walls; to the young man who was so vulnerable in his vanity: the legitimate vanity of his art.

It was so like Maudie to laugh at him. What did she know of an artist's mind? If Maudie had not been with her, it would have been so different. She might, for one thing, have got him to talk about his work, to explain the discrepancy between the loose style of the pictures on the wall and the exact, small sketches he'd been drawing on the margins of the paper.

She might even have taken up his invitation to go and see his paintings. Why had that seemed so unconventional—so laughable? Because of Maudie, that was why.

How ridiculous their scruples would have seemed to the young man. She could only hope he had not guessed them. She looked up at a clock. Supposing, right now, she were to slip back to the café and suggest that after all she found she would have time for a quick visit to his studio? Or would he have left the café? Better perhaps to call around to the studio? He would surely be back there now!

For a moment she stood debating the arguments for and against going back. Would it seem odd to him? Would he be surprised? But as if it were Maudie who put the questions, she frowned them down and all at once purposeful as anyone in the street, began to go back, headlong, you might say, towards Chatham Street.

At the point where two small streets crossed each other she had to pause, while a team of Guinness's dray horses turned with difficulty in the narrow cube of the intersection. And, while she waited impatiently, she caught sight of herself in the gilded mirror of a public house. For a second, the familiar sight gave her a misgiving of her mission, but as the dray horses moved out of the way, she told herself that her dowdy, lumpish, and unromantic figure vouched for her spiritual integrity. She pulled herself away from the face in the glass and hurried across the street.

Between two lock-up shops, down a short alley—roofed by the second story of the premises overhead, till it was like a tunnel—was his door. Away at the end of the tunnel the door could clearly be seen even from the middle of the street, for it was painted bright yellow. Odd that she had never seen it in the times she had passed that way. She crossed the street.

Once across the street, she ran down the tunnel, her footsteps echoing loud in her ears. And there on the door, tied to the latchet of the letter-box, was a

piece of white cardboard with his name on it. Grabbing the knocker, she gave three clear hammer-strokes on the door.

The little alley was a sort of cul-de-sac; except for the street behind her and the door in front of her, it had no outlet. There was not even a skylight or an aperture of any kind. As for the premises into which the door led, there was no way of telling its size or its extent, or anything at all about it, until the door was opened.

Irresponsibly, she giggled. It was like the mystifying doors in the trunks of trees that beguiled her as a child in fairy tales and fantasies. Did this door, too, like those fairy doors, lead into rooms of impossible amplitude, or would it be a cramped and poky place?

As she pondered upon what was within, seemingly so mysteriously sealed, she saw that—just as in a fairy tale—after all there was an aperture. The letter-box had lost its shutter or lid, and it gaped open, a vacant hole in the wood, re-minding her of a sleeping doll whose eyeballs had been poked back in its head, and creating an expression of vacancy and emptiness.

Impulsively, going down on one knee, she peered in through the slit.

At first she could see only segments of the objects within, but by moving her head, she was able to identify things; an unfinished canvas up against the splattered white wainscot, a bicycle-pump flat on the floor, the leg of a table, black iron bed-legs and, to her amusement, dangling down by the leg of the table, dripping their moisture in a pool on the floor, a pair of elongated, gray wool socks. It was, of course, only possible to see the lower portion of the room, but it seemed enough to infer conclusively that this was indeed a little room in a tree, no bigger than the bulk of the outer trunk, leading nowhere, and—sufficient or no—itself its own end.

There was just one break in the wainscot, where a door ran down to the floor, but this was so narrow and made of roughly jointed boards, that she took it to be the door of a press. And then, as she started moving, she saw some-thing else, an intricate segment of fine wire spokes. It was a second before she realized it was the wheel of a bicycle.

So, a bicycle, too, lived here, in this little room in a tree-trunk!

Oh, poor young man, poor painter: poor foreigner, inept at finding the good lodgings in a strange city. Her heart went out to him.

It was just then that the boarded door—it couldn't have been a press after all—opened into the room, and she found herself staring at two feet. They were large feet, shoved into unlaced shoes, and they were bare to the white an-kles. For, of course, she thought wildly, focusing her thoughts, his socks are washed! But her power to think clearly only lasted an instant. She sprang to her feet.

"Who iss that?" asked a voice. "Did someone knock?"

It was the voice of the man in the café. But where was she to find a voice with which to reply? And who was she to say what she was? Who—to this stranger—was she?

And if he opened the door, what then? All the thoughts and words that had, like a wind, blown her down this tunnel, subsided suddenly, and she stood, ap-palled, at where they had brought her.

"Who iss that?" came the voice within, troubled

Staring at those white feet, thrust into the unlaced shoes, she felt that she would die on the spot if they moved an inch. She turned.

Ahead of her, bright, shining and clear, as if it were at the end of a powerful telescope, was the street. Not caring if her feet were heard, volleying and echoing as if she ran through a mighty drain-pipe, she kept running till she reached the street, kept running even then, jostling surprised shoppers, hitting her ankles off the wheel-knobs of push-cars and prams. Only when she came to the junction of the streets again, did she stop, as in the pub mirror she caught sight again of her familiar face. That face steadied her. How absurd to think that anyone would sinisterly follow this middle-aged woman?

But suppose he had been in the outer room when she knocked! If he had opened the door? What would have happened then? What would she have said? A flush spread over her face. The only true words that she could have uttered were those that had sunk into her mind in the café; put there by Maudie.

"I'm lonely!" That was all she could have said. "I'm lonely. Are you?"

A deep shame came over her with this admission and, guiltily, she began to walk quickly onward again, towards Grafton Street. If anyone had seen her, there in that dark alleyway! If anyone could have looked into her mind, her heart!

And yet, was it so unnatural? Was it so hard to understand? So unforgivable?

As she passed the open door of the Carmelite Church she paused. Could she rid herself of her feeling of shame in the dark of the confessional? To the sin-accustomed ears of the wise old fathers her story would be lightweight; a tedious tale of scrupulosity. Was there no one, no one who'd understand?

She had reached Grafton Street once more, and stepped into its crowded thoroughfare. It was only a few minutes since she left it, but in the street the evasion of light had begun. Only the bustle of people, and the activity of traffic, made it seem that it was yet day. Away at the top of the street, in Stephen's Green, to which she turned, although the tops of the trees were still clear, branch for branch, in the last of the light, mist muted the outline of the bushes. If one were to put a hand between the railings now, it would be with a slight shock that the fingers would feel the little branches, like fine bones, under the feathers of mist. And in their secret nests the smaller birds were making faint avowals in the last of the day. It was the time at which she used to meet Richard.

"Oh Richard!" she cried, almost out loud, as she walked along by the railings to where the car was parked. "Oh Richard! it's you I want."

And as she cried out, her mind presented him to her, as she so often saw him, coming towards her: tall, handsome, and with his curious air of apartness from those around him. He had his hat in his hand, down by his side, as on a summer day he might trail a hand in water from the side of a boat. She wanted to preserve that picture of him for ever in an image, and only as she struggled to hold on to it did she realize there was no urgency in the search. She had a sense of having all the time in the world to look and look and look at him. That was the very way he used to come to meet her—indolently trailing the old felt hat, glad to be done with the day; and when they got nearer to each other she used to take such joy in his unsmiling face, with its happiness integral to it in all its features. It was the first time in the two years he'd been gone from her that she'd seen his face.

Not till she had taken out the key of the car, and gone straight around to the driver's side, not stupidly, as so often, to the passenger seat—not till then did she realize what she had achieved. Yet she had no more than got back her

rights. No more. It was not a subject for amazement. By what means exactly had she got them back though—in that little café? That was the wonder.

1961

MARY McCARTHY

1912–1989

Sardonically associating "the kind of woman writer who's a capital W, capital W" with the production of literature that focuses on decor and drapery, Mary McCarthy claimed in a *Paris Review* interview in 1962 that Jane Austen and George Eliot were not "Women Writers." Should she divide literary women into the categories of "Sense and Sensibility," she explained, "I *am* for the ones who represent sense, and so was Jane Austen." As an accomplished journalist, McCarthy was hailed for politically astute essays on Vietnam and the Watergate crisis as well as for intelligent criticism of contemporary drama and fiction. Her reputation as a creative writer rests, however, on the work that illuminates her growth from an emotional sensibility to the tolerant but ironic common sense that so frequently animated her prose style.

The oldest child of parents who were killed in the influenza epidemic of 1918, McCarthy was raised in Minneapolis by a series of relatives, some of whom enjoyed tormenting her and her siblings. In *Memories of a Catholic Girlhood* (1957), she explored her grief at the loss of her parents as well as her development into "a lapsed Catholic," first in the homes of her Catholic, Protestant, and Jewish relatives, and later at the convent school she attended in Seattle. She began publishing fiction after graduating from Vassar College and divorcing her first husband. While married to the literary critic Edmund Wilson, with whom she had a child, McCarthy wrote *The Company She Keeps* (1942), a successful series of satiric stories. After the marriage broke up in 1945, McCarthy traveled and published extensively. From *The Groves of Academe* (1952) to *Cannibals and Missionaries* (1979), McCarthy delineated the limits and liabilities of modern liberalism. In addition, the novels *A Charmed Life* (1955) and *The Group* (1963) focused with wit and intelligence on the restricted options and sensibilities of well-educated middle-class women. Later in her career, *Mary McCarthy's Theatre Chronicles* (1936–62), *Venice Observed* (1956), *On the Contrary* (1961), *The Writing on the Wall* (1970), and *The Seventeenth Degree* (1974) established her reputation as a drama critic, social commentator, travel writer, arts observer, and political journalist. Like her fiction and her essays, McCarthy's autobiographical writing is marked by scrupulous detachment; in *Names*, for instance, she meditates on the disjunction between her sense of herself as an adolescent and the sometimes baffling, sometimes degrading identities she was given by teachers and fellow students.

From Memories of a Catholic Girlhood

Names

Anna Lyons, Mary Louise Lyons, Mary von Phul, Emilie von Phul, Eugenia McLellan, Marjorie McPhail, Marie-Louise L'Abbé, Mary Danz, Julia Dodge, Mary Fordyce Blake, Janet Preston—these were the names (I can still tell them

over like a rosary[1]) of some of the older girls in the convent: the Virtues and Graces. The virtuous ones wore wide blue or green moire good-conduct ribbons, bandoleer-style,[2] across their blue serge uniforms; the beautiful ones wore rouge and powder or at least were reputed to do so. Our class, the eighth grade, wore pink ribbons (I never got one myself) and had names like Patricia ("Pat") Sullivan, Eileen Donohoe, and Joan Kane. We were inelegant even in this respect; the best name we could show, among us, was Phyllis ("Phil") Chatham, who boasted that her father's name, Ralph, was pronounced "Rafe" as in England.

Names had a great importance for us in the convent, and foreign names, French, German, or plain English (which, to us, were foreign, because of their Protestant sound), bloomed like prize roses among a collection of spuds. Irish names were too common in the school to have any prestige either as surnames (Gallagher, Sheehan, Finn, Sullivan, McCarthy) or as Christian names (Kathleen, Eileen). Anything exotic had value: an "olive" complexion, for example. The pet girl of the convent was a fragile Jewish girl named Susie Lowenstein, who had pale red-gold hair and an exquisite retroussé[3] nose, which, if we had had it, might have been called "pug." We liked her name too and the name of a child in the primary grades: Abbie Stuart Baillargeon. My favorite name, on the whole, though, was Emilie von Phul (pronounced "Pool"); her oldest sister, recently graduated, was called Celeste. Another name that appealed to me was Genevieve Albers, Saint Genevieve being the patron saint of Paris who turned back Attila[4] from the gates of the city.

All these names reflected the still-pioneer character of the Pacific Northwest. I had never heard their like in the parochial school in Minneapolis, where "foreign" extraction, in any case, was something to be ashamed of, the whole drive being toward Americanization of first name and surname alike. The exceptions to this were the Irish, who could vaunt such names as Catherine O'Dea and the name of my second cousin, Mary Catherine Anne Rose Violet McCarthy, while an unfortunate German boy named Manfred was made to suffer for his. But that was Minneapolis. In Seattle, and especially in the convent of the Ladies of the Sacred Heart, foreign names suggested not immigration but emigration—distinguished exile. Minneapolis was a granary; Seattle was a port, which had attracted a veritable Foreign Legion[5] of adventurers—soldiers of fortune, younger sons, gamblers, traders, drawn by the fortunes to be made in virgin timber and shipping and by the Alaska Gold Rush. Wars and revolutions had sent the defeated out to Puget Sound, to start a new life; the latest had been the Russian Revolution, which had shipped us, via Harbin, a Russian colony, complete with restaurant, on Queen Anne Hill. The English names in the convent, when they did not testify to direct English origin, as in the case of "Rafe" Chatham, had come to us from the South and represented a kind of internal exile; such girls as Mary Fordyce Blake and Mary McQueen Street (a class ahead of me; her sister was named Francesca) bore their double-barreled first names like titles of aristocracy from the antebellum South. Not all our girls, by any means, were Catholic; some of the very prettiest ones—Julia Dodge and Janet Preston, if I remember rightly—were

1. A series of Catholic prayers that are often counted on a string of special beads.
2. Across the chest.
3. Turned up.

4. Attila the Hun (A.D.406?–453), notorious invader of Europe.
5. International volunteer army corps that does not inquire into its enlistees' backgrounds.

Protestants. The nuns had taught us to behave with special courtesy to these strangers in our midst, and the whole effect was of some superior hostel for refugees of all the lost causes of the past hundred years. Money could not count for much in such an atmosphere; the fathers and grandfathers of many of our "best" girls were ruined men.

Names, often, were freakish in the Pacific Northwest, particularly girls' names. In the Episcopal boarding school I went to later, in Tacoma, there was a girl called De Vere Utter, and there was a girl called Rocena and another called Hermoine. Was Rocena a mistake for Rowena and Hermoine for Hermione? And was Vere, as we called her, Lady Clara Vere de Vere? Probably. You do not hear names like those often, in any case, east of the Cascade Mountains; they belong to the frontier, where books and libraries were few and memory seems to have been oral, as in the time of Homer.[6]

Names have more significance for Catholics than they do for other people; Christian names are chosen for the spiritual qualities of the saints they are taken from; Protestants used to name their children out of the Old Testament and now they name them out of novels and plays, whose heroes and heroines are perhaps the new patron saints of a secular age. But with Catholics it is different. The saint a child is named for is supposed to serve, literally, as a model or pattern to imitate; your name is your fortune and it tells you what you are or must be. Catholic children ponder their names for a mystic meaning, like birthstones; my own, I learned, besides belonging to the Virgin and Saint Mary of Egypt, originally meant "bitter" or "star of the sea." My second name, Therese, could dedicate me either to Saint Theresa or to the saint called the Little Flower, Soeur Thérèse of Lisieux, on whom God was supposed to have descended in the form of a shower of roses. At Confirmation,[7] I had added a third name (for Catholics then rename themselves, as most nuns do, yet another time, when they take orders); on the advice of a nun, I had taken "Clementina," after Saint Clement, an early pope—a step I soon regretted on account of "My Darling Clementine"[8] and her number nine shoes. By the time I was in the convent, I would no longer tell anyone what my Confirmation name was. The name I had nearly picked was "Agnes," after a little Roman virgin martyr, always shown with a lamb, because of her purity. But Agnes would have been just as bad, I recognized in Forest Ridge Convent—not only because of the possibility of "Aggie," but because it was subtly, indefinably wrong, in itself. Agnes would have made me look like an ass.

The fear of appearing ridiculous first entered my life, as a governing motive, during my second year in the convent. Up to then, a desire for prominence had decided many of my actions and, in fact, still persisted. But in the eighth grade, I became aware of mockery and perceived that I could not seek prominence without attracting laughter. Other people could, but I couldn't. This laughter was proceeding, not from my classmates, but from the girls of the class just above me, in particular from two boon companions, Elinor Heffernan and Mary Harty, a clownish pair—oddly assorted in size and shape, as teams of clowns generally are, one short, plump, and baby-faced, the other tall, lean, and owlish—who entertained the high-school department by calling attention to the oddities of the younger girls. Nearly every school has such a

6. Homer's Iliad and Odyssey were originally oral, not written, epics.
7. In the Catholic church, a ceremony admitting
adolescents to full membership in the church.
8. A popular American folk song.

pair of satirists, whose marks are generally low and who are tolerated just be-
cause of their laziness and non-conformity; one of them (in this case, Mary
Harty, the plump one) usually appears to be half asleep. Because of their low
standing, their indifference to appearances, the sad state of their uniforms,
their clowning is taken to be harmless, which, on the whole, it is, their object
being not to wound but to divert; such girls are bored in school. We in the
eighth grade sat directly in front of the two wits in study hall, so that they had
us under close observation; yet at first I was not afraid of them, wanting, if
anything, to identify myself with their laughter, to be initiated into the joke.
One of their specialties was giving people nicknames, and it was considered an
honor to be the first in the eighth grade to be let in by Elinor and Mary on
their latest invention. This often happened to me; they would tell me, on the
playground, and I would tell the others. As their intermediary, I felt myself al-
most their friend and it did not occur to me that I might be next on their list.

I had achieved prominence not long before by publicly losing my faith and
regaining it at the end of a retreat. I believe Elinor and Mary questioned me
about this on the playground, during recess, and listened with serious, re-
spectful faces while I told them about my conversations with the Jesuits.
Those serious faces ought to have been an omen, but if the two girls used what
I had revealed to make fun of me, it must have been behind my back. I never
heard any more of it, and yet just at this time I began to feel something, like a
cold breath on the nape of my neck, that made me wonder whether the new
position I had won for myself in the convent was as secure as I imagined. I
would turn around in study hall and find the two girls looking at me with spec-
ulation in their eyes.

It was just at this time, too, that I found myself in a perfectly absurd situa-
tion, a very private one, which made me live, from month to month, in horror
of discovery. I had waked up one morning, in my convent room, to find a few
small spots of blood on my sheet; I had somehow scratched a trifling cut on
one of my legs and opened it during the night. I wondered what to do about
this, for the nuns were fussy about bedmaking, as they were about our white
collars and cuffs, and if we had an inspection those spots might count against
me. It was best, I decided, to ask the nun on dormitory duty, tall, stout Mother
Slattery, for a clean bottom sheet, even though she might scold me for having
scratched my leg in my sleep and order me to cut my toenails. You never know
what you might be blamed for. But Mother Slattery, when she bustled in to
look at the sheet, did not scold me at all; indeed, she hardly seemed to be lis-
tening as I explained to her about the cut. She told me to sit down: she would
be back in a minute. "You can be excused from athletics today," she added,
closing the door. As I waited, I considered this remark, which seemed to me
strangely munificent, in view of the unimportance of the cut. In a moment,
she returned, but without the sheet. Instead, she produced out of her big
pocket a sort of cloth girdle and a peculiar flannel object which I first took to
be a bandage, and I began to protest that I did not need or want a bandage; all
I needed was a bottom sheet. "The sheet can wait," said Mother Slattery, suc-
cinctly, handing me two large safety pins. It was the pins that abruptly en-
lightened me; I saw Mother Slattery's mistake, even as she was instructing me
as to how this flannel article, which I now understood to be a sanitary napkin,
was to be put on.

"Oh, no, Mother," I said, feeling somewhat embarrassed. "You don't under-

stand. It's just a little cut, on my leg." But Mother, again, was not listening; she appeared to have grown deaf, as the nuns had a habit of doing when what you were saying did not fit in with their ideas. And now that I knew what was in her mind, I was conscious of a funny constraint; I did not feel it proper to name a natural process, in so many words, to a nun. It was like trying not to think of their going to the bathroom or trying not to see the straggling iron-grey hair coming out of their coifs (the common notion that they shaved their heads was false). On the whole, it seemed better just to show her my cut. But when I offered to do so and unfastened my black stocking, she only glanced at my leg, cursorily. "That's only a scratch, dear," she said. "Now hurry up and put this on or you'll be late for chapel. Have you any pain?" "No, no, Mother!" I cried. "You don't understand!" "Yes, yes, I understand," she replied soothingly, "and you will too, a little later. Mother Superior will tell you about it some time during the morning. There's nothing to be afraid of. You have become a woman."

"I know all about that," I persisted. "Mother, please listen. I just cut my leg. On the athletic field. Yesterday afternoon." But the more excited I grew, the more soothing, and yet firm, Mother Slattery became. There seemed to be nothing for it but to give up and do as I was bid. I was in the grip of a higher authority, which almost had the power to persuade me that it was right and I was wrong. But of course I was not wrong; that would have been too good to be true. While Mother Slattery waited, just outside my door, I miserably donned the equipment she had given me, for there was no place to hide it, on account of drawer inspection. She led me down the hall to where there was a chute and explained how I was to dispose of the flannel thing by dropping it down the chute into the laundry. (The convent arrangements were very old-fashioned, dating back, no doubt, to the days of Louis Philippe.[9])

The Mother Superior, Madame MacIllvra, was a sensible woman, and all through my early morning classes, I was on pins and needles, chafing for the promised interview with her which I trusted would clear things up. "*Ma Mère*,"[1] I would begin, "Mother Slattery thinks . . . " Then I would tell her about the cut and the athletic field. But precisely the same impasse confronted me when I was summoned to her office at recess-time. *I* talked about my cut, and *she* talked about becoming a woman. It was rather like a round, in which she was singing "Scotland's burning, Scotland's burning," and I was singing "Pour on water, pour on water." Neither of us could hear the other, or, rather, I could hear her, but she could not hear me. Owing to our different positions in the convent, she was free to interrupt me, whereas I was expected to remain silent until she had finished speaking. When I kept breaking in, she hushed me, gently, and took me on her lap. Exactly like Mother Slattery, she attributed all my references to the cut to a blind fear of this new, unexpected reality that had supposedly entered my life. Many young girls, she reassured me, were frightened if they had not been prepared. "And you, Mary, have lost your dear mother, who could have made this easier for you." Rocked on Madame MacIllvra's lap, I felt paralysis overtake me and I lay, mutely listening, against her bosom, my face being tickled by her white, starched, fluted wimple, while she explained to me how babies were born all of which I had heard before.

There was no use fighting the convent. I had to pretend to have become a

9. King of France (1773–1850). 1. My mother (French).

woman, just as, not long before, I had had to pretend to get my faith back—for the sake of peace. This pretense was decidedly awkward. For fear of being found out by the lay sisters downstairs in the laundry (no doubt an imaginary contingency, but the convent was so very thorough), I reopened the cut on my leg, so as to draw a little blood to stain the napkins, which were issued me regularly, not only on this occasion, but every twenty-eight days thereafter. Eventually, I abandoned this bloodletting, for fear of lockjaw, and trusted to fate. Yet I was in awful dread of detection; my only hope, as I saw it, was either to be released from the convent or to become a woman in reality, which might take a year, at least, since I was only twelve. Getting out of athletics once a month was not sufficient compensation for the farce I was going through. It was not my fault; they had forced me into it; nevertheless, it was I who would look silly—worse than silly; half mad—if the truth ever came to light.

I was burdened with this guilt and shame when the nickname finally found me out. "Found me out," in a general sense, for no one ever did learn the particular secret I bore about with me, pinned to the linen band. "We've got a name for you," Elinor and Mary called out to me, one day on the playground. "What is it?" I asked, half hoping, half fearing, since not all their sobriquets were unfavorable. "Cye," they answered, looking at each other and laughing. " 'Si'?" I repeated, supposing that it was based on Simple Simon. Did they regard me as a hick? "C.Y.E.," they elucidated, spelling it out in chorus. "The letters stand for something. Can you guess?" I could not and I cannot now. The closest I could come to it in the convent was "Clean Your Ears." Perhaps that was it, though in later life I have wondered whether it did not stand, simply, for "Clever Young Egg" or "Champion Young Eccentric." But in the convent I was certain that it stood for something horrible, something even worse than dirty ears (as far as I knew, my ears were clean), something I could never guess because it represented some aspect of myself that the world could see and I couldn't, like a sign pinned on my back. Everyone in the convent must have known what the letters stood for, but no one would tell me. Elinor and Mary had made them promise. It was like halitosis; not even my best friend, my deskmate, Louise, would tell me, no matter how much I pleaded. Yet everyone assured me that it was "very good," that is, very apt. And it made everyone laugh.

This name reduced all my pretensions and solidified my sense of *wrongness*. Just as I felt I was beginning to belong to the convent, it turned me into an outsider, since I was the only pupil who was not in the know. I liked the convent, but it did not like me, as people say of certain foods that disagree with them. By this, I do not mean that I was actively unpopular, either with the pupils or with the nuns. The Mother Superior cried when I left and predicted that I would be a novelist, which surprised me. And I had finally made friends; even Emilie von Phul smiled upon me softly out of her bright blue eyes from the far end of the study hall. It was just that I did not fit into the convent pattern; the simplest thing I did, like asking for a clean sheet, entrapped me in consequences that I never could have predicted. I was not bad; I did not consciously break the rules; and yet I could never, not even for a week, get a pink ribbon, and this was something I could not understand, because I was trying as hard as I could. It was the same case as with the hated name; the nuns, evidently, saw something about me that was invisible to me.

The oddest part was all that pretending. There I was, a walking mass of lies,

pretending to be a Catholic and going to confession while really I had lost my faith, and pretending to have monthly periods by cutting myself with nail scissors; yet all this had come about without my volition and even contrary to it. But the basest pretense I was driven to was the acceptance of the nickname. Yet what else could I do? In the convent, I could not live it down. To all those girls, I had become "Cye McCarthy." That was who I was. That was how I had to identify myself when telephoning my friends during vacations to ask them to the movies: "Hello, this is Cye." I loathed myself when I said it, and yet I succumbed to the name totally, making myself over into a sort of hearty to go with it—the kind of girl I hated. "Cye" was my new patron saint. This false personality stuck to me, like the name, when I entered public high school, the next fall, as a freshman, having finally persuaded my grandparents to take me out of the convent, although they could never get to the bottom of my reasons, since, as I admitted, the nuns were kind, and I had made many nice new friends. What I wanted was a fresh start, a chance to begin life over again, but the first thing I heard in the corridors of the public high school was that name called out to me, like the warmest of welcomes: "Hi, there, Si." That was the way they thought it was spelled. But this time I was resolute. After the first weeks, I dropped the hearties who called me "Si" and I never heard it again. I got my own name back and sloughed off Clementina and even Therese—the names that did not seem to me any more to be mine but to have been imposed on me by others. And I preferred to think that Mary meant "bitter" rather than "star of the sea."

1957

MAY SARTON

1912–1995

The woman artist in May Sarton's novel *Mrs. Stevens Hears the Mermaids Singing* (1965) explains about herself that "we are all monsters . . . we women who have chosen to be something more and something less than women!" Yet, as a novelist, a memoirist, and a poet, Sarton described the everyday and often prosaic details that fill the life of the single and sometimes singular woman writer. For, like Mrs. Stevens, Sarton clearly believed that "we have to dare to be ourselves, however frightening or strange that self may prove to be."

Born in Belgium and raised in Cambridge, Massachusetts, Sarton was the only child of an eminent historian of science, George Sarton, and an English portrait painter, Mabel (Elwes) Sarton. She attended the Shady Hill School in Cambridge and the Institut Belge de Culture Française in Brussels before joining Eva Le Gallienne's Civic Repertory Theatre in New York and experimenting with her own theatrical company. In *I Knew a Phoenix* (1959), Sarton also described her early trips to England, where she met the writers Elizabeth Bowen and Virginia Woolf. In spite of the gregarious personality that emerges from this autobiography, Sarton became famous for the journals that described her solitary life in Nelson, New Hampshire, and for such novels as *The Small Room* (1961), *Joanna and Ulysses* (1963), and *Kinds of Love* (1970) which depict the female friendships and love affairs that save women from loneliness.

Remarkably prolific, she worked in many genres, producing near the end of her

life *After the Stroke: A Journal* (1988) and *Encore: A Journal of the Eightieth Year* (1993) as well as—among other volumes—*The Education of Harriet Hatfield: A Novel* (1989) and *Collected Poems, 1930–1993* (1993). Nonetheless, for many years her publications received little critical attention. Yet few writers dealt as sensitively with such subjects as the roots of identity (*The House by the Sea*, 1977), aging and death (*As We Are Now*, 1973), and the different forms female creativity takes. In her *Journal of a Solitude* (1973), wondering why "poetry always seems to me so much more a true work of the soul than prose," Sarton explained that it is "because the poem is primarily a dialogue with the self." Significantly, however, both *Letter from Chicago* and *My Sisters, O My Sisters* analyze her own creativity through dialogues with other literary women.

My Sisters, O My Sisters

> Nous qui voulions poser, image ineffaceable
> Comme un delta divin notre main sur le sable
> Anna de Noailles[1]

I

Dorothy Wordsworth,[2] dying, did not want to read,
"I am too busy with my own feelings," she said.

And all women who have wanted to break out
Of the prison of consciousness to sing or shout

Are strange monsters who renounce the treasure 5
Of their silence for a curious devouring pleasure.

Dickinson, Rossetti, Sappho[3]—they all know it,
Something is lost, strained, unforgiven in the poet.

She abdicates from life or like George Sand[4]
Suffers from the mortality in an immortal hand, 10

Loves too much, spends a whole life to discover
She was born a good grandmother, not a good lover.

Too powerful for men: Madame de Stael. Too sensitive:
Madame de Sévigné[5] who burdened where she meant to give.

Delicate as that burden was and so supremely lovely, 15
It was too heavy for her daughter, much too heavy.

Only when she built inward in a fearful isolation
Did any one succeed or learn to fuse emotion

1. We who wanted to leave in an ineffaceable image / Like a divine delta, our hand on the sand (French). Anna-Elisabeth, comtesse de Noailles (1876–1933), French poet and novelist
2. English poet and diarist.
3. Emily Dickinson (1830–1886), Christina Rossetti (1830–1894), and Sappho (c.600 B.C.) were three female lyric poets, American, English and Greek, respectively.
4. Pen name of Aurore Dupin (1804–1876), French novelist known for her many love affairs.
5. Marie de Sévigné (1626-1696), French noblewoman and prolific letter-writer. Germaine de Staël (1766–1817), French woman of letters.

With thought. Only when she renounced did Emily
Begin in the fierce lonely light to learn to be. 20

Only in the extremity of spirit and the flesh
And in renouncing passion did Sappho come to bless.

Only in the farewells or in old age does sanity
Shine through the crimson stains of their mortality.

And now we who are writing women and strange monsters 25
Still search our hearts to find the difficult answers,

Still hope that we may learn to lay our hands
More gently and more subtly on the burning sands.

To be through what we make more simply human,
To come to the deep place where poet becomes woman, 30

Where nothing has to be renounced or given over
In the pure light that shines out from the lover,

In the pure light that brings forth fruit and flower
And that great sanity, that sun, the feminine power.

II

Let us rejoice in 35
The full curve of breast,
The supple thigh
And all riches in
A woman's keeping
For man's comfort and rest 40
(Crimson and ivory)
For children's nourishment
(Magic fruits and flowers)
But when they are sleeping,
The children, the men, 45
Fed by these powers,
We know what is meant
By the wise serpent,
By the gentle dove,
And remember then 50
How we wish to love,

Let us rejoice now
In these great powers
Which are ours alone.
And trust what we know: 55
First the green hand
That can open flowers
In the deathly bone,
And the magic breast
That can feed the child, 60

And is under a hand
A rose of fire in snow
So tender, so wild
All fires come to rest,
All lives can be blest— 65
So sighs the gentle dove,
Wily the serpent so,
Matched in a woman's love.

III

Eve and Mary[6] the mother are our stem;
All our centuries go back to them. 70
And delicate the balance lies
Between the passionate and wise:
Of man's rib, one, and cleaves to him;
And one bears man and then frees him.
This double river has created us, 75
Always the rediscovered, always the cherished.
(But many fail in this. Many have perished.)

Hell is the loss of balance when woman is destroyer.
Each of us has been there.
Each of us knows what the floods can do. 80
How many women mother their husbands
Out of all strength and secret *Virtu*;[7]
How many women love an only son
As a lover loves, binding the free hands.
How many yield up their true power 85
Out of weakness, the moment of passion
Betrayed by years of confused living—
For it is surely a lifetime work,
This learning to be a woman.
Until at the end what is clear 90
Is the marvelous skill to make
Life grow in all its forms.

Is knowing where to ask, where to yield,
Where to sow, where to plough the field,
Where to kill the heart or let it live; 95
To be Eve, the giver of knowledge, the lover;
To be Mary, the shield, the healer and the mother.
The balance is eternal whatever we may wish;
The law can be broken but we cannot change
What is supremely beautiful and strange. 100
Where find the root? Where re-join the source?
The fertile feminine goddess, double river?

6. In the Book of Genesis, Eve was the first woman, made from the rib of Adam, with whom she was responsible for the Fall. In the New Testament, Mary was the mother of Jesus Christ, whose Crucifixion redeemed humanity from sin.
7. Strength or power (Italian).

IV

We think of all the women hunting for themselves,
Turning and turning to each other with a driving
Need to learn to understand, to live in charity, 105
And above all to be used fully, to be giving
From wholeness, wholeness back to love's deep clarity.
O, all the burning hearts of women unappeased
Shine like great stars, like flowers of fire,
As the sun goes and darkness opens all desire— 110
And we are with a fierce compassion seized.
How lost, how far from home, how parted from
The earth, my sisters, O my sisters, we have come!

For so long asked so little of ourselves and men,
And let the Furies[8] have their way—our treasure, 115
The single antidote to all our world's confusion
A few gifts to the poor small god of pleasure.
The god of passion has gone back into the mountain,
Is sleeping in the dark, deep in the earth.

We have betrayed a million times the holy fountain, 120
The potent spirit who brings his life to birth,
The masculine and violent joy of pure creation—
And yielded up the sacred fires to sensation.
But we shall never come home to the earth
Until we bring the great god and his mirth 125
Back from the mountain, until we let the stranger
Plough deep into our hearts his joy and anger,[9]
For we shall never find ourselves again
Until we ask men's greatness back from men,
And we shall never find ourselves again 130
Until we match mens' greatness with our own.

 1948

Letter from Chicago

For Virginia Woolf[1]

Four years ago I met your death here,
Heard it where I had never been before
In a city of departures, streets of wind,
Soft plumes of smoke dissolving—
City of departures beside an aloof lake. 5
Here where you never were, they said,
"Virginia Woolf is dead."

8. In Greek myth, female avenging spirits
9. Dionysus, Greek god of wine, was associated with
tragedy, comedy, and the mountains; in the story of
Pentheus, he disguises himself as a stranger.
1. English novelist and essayist (1882–1941).

The city died. I died in the city,
Witness of unreal tears, my own,
For experience involves time 10
And time was gone
The world arrested at the instant of death.
I wept wildly like a child
Who cannot give his present after all:
I met your death and did not recognize you. 15

Now you are dead four years
And there are no more private tears.
The city of departure is the city of arrival,
City of triumphant wind lifting people,
City of spring: yesterday I found you. 20
Wherever I looked was love.
Wherever I went I had presents in my hands.
Wherever I went I recognized you.

You are not, never to be again,
Never, never to be dead, 25
Never to be dead again in this city,
Never to be mourned again,
But to come back yearly,
Hourly, with the spring, with the wind,
Fresh as agony or resurrection; 30
A plume of smoke dissolving,
Remaking itself, never still,
Never static, never lost:
The place where time flows again.

I speak to you and meet my own life. 35
Is it to be poised as the lake beside the city,
Aloof, but given still to air and wind,
Detached from time, but given to the moment—
Is it to be a celebration always?

I send you love forward into the past. 40

 1953

The Muse as Medusa[1]

I saw you once, Medusa; we were alone.
I looked you straight in the cold eye, cold.
I was not punished, was not turned to stone—
How to believe the legends I am told?

I came as naked as any little fish, 5
Prepared to be hooked, gutted, caught;

1. A female monster with snakes for hair, the sight of whom turns men to stone, according to Greek myth.
"Muse": a goddess of arts and learning, prayed to for inspiration.

But I saw you, Medusa, made my wish,
And when I left you I was clothed in thought. . . .

Being allowed, perhaps, to swim my way
Through the great deep and on the rising tide, 10
Flashing wild streams, as free and rich as they,
Though you had power marshaled on your side.

The fish escaped to many a magic reef;
The fish explored many a dangerous sea—
The fish, Medusa, did not come to grief, 15
But swims still in a fluid mystery.

Forget the image: your silence is my ocean,
And even now it teems with life. You chose
To abdicate by total lack of motion,
But did it work, for nothing really froze? 20

It is all fluid still, that world of feeling
Where thoughts, those fishes, silent, feed and rove;
And, fluid, it is also full of healing,
For love is healing, even rootless love.

I turn your face around! It is my face. 25
That frozen rage is what I must explore—
Oh secret, self-enclosed, and ravaged place!
This is the gift I thank Medusa for.

 1971

MURIEL RUKEYSER

1913–1980

"Breathe-in experience, breathe-out poetry": Muriel Rukeyser opened the first
poem of her first volume of verse, *Theory of Flight* (1935), with a vow to eschew all
that might be construed as artificially poetic in favor of a lyrical articulation of per-
sonal experience. That those experiences would be shaped by political realities is
evidenced later in the poem, when Rukeyser exclaims, "Not Sappho, Sacco."
Rejecting the erotic verse of ancient Greece for poetry focusing on the racial, po-
litical, and economic issues that led to the execution of the anarchist-immigrants
Sacco and Vanzetti, Rukeyser placed herself in the expansive tradition of
American verse established by Walt Whitman as well as in the school of modern
political poetry led by W. H. Auden, and she thereby dedicated herself throughout
her distinguished career to breathing in the ordinary expressions of the victimized
and breathing out the songs that linked their lives to her own.
 Rukeyser was born and lived most of her life in New York. Her parents were af-
fluent, and she attended the Fieldston School, Vassar College, and Columbia
University. But most of her friends were socialists, labor organizers, or artists. At
Vassar, she began publishing her work, and in the early 1930s, along with Elizabeth
Bishop and Mary McCarthy, she founded a literary magazine to protest the poli-
cies of the *Vassar Review*. *Theory of Flight*, published in the Yale Series of Younger

Poets, was quickly followed by *Mediterranean* (1938), *A Turning Wind* (1939), *The Soul and Body of John Brown* (1940), *Wake Island* (1942), *Beast in View* (1944), and *The Green Wave* (1948). A number of these volumes deal directly with social injustice in America and with the atrocities of World War II, a subject of passionate concern to Rukeyser because of her Jewishness and because of her earlier involvement in the fight against fascism in Spain.

After the war, Rukeyser lived briefly in Berkeley, where she taught at the California Labor School, but she spent much of her time "pushing a baby carriage" after the birth of her child in 1947. Although the biographical details of her relationship with the baby's father are obscure, it is clear that Rukeyser remained a single parent. An anonymous benefactor, who turned out to be the wealthy Californian Henriette Durham, helped finance Rukeyser's return to New York, where she began teaching part-time at Sarah Lawrence College and serving as vice president of the House of Photography. During the 1950s, few of Rukeyser's publications were new compositions, a fact that the critic Louise Kertesz attributes to Rukeyser's childcare responsibilities. In such later volumes as *Body of Waking* (1958), *The Speed of Darkness* (1968), *Breaking Open* (1973), and *The Gates* (1976), giving birth became a major source of her imagery, sometimes providing the only solace against the violence she witnessed and protested both in Korea and in Vietnam. In 1978, Rukeyser's *Collected Poems* appeared, and in 1992, Kate Daniels produced a selection titled *Out of Silence*, which was followed in 1994 by a collection of poetry and prose, *A Muriel Rukeyser Reader*, edited by Jan Heller Levi.

Although, from her early training in aviation to her later biographies of scientists, Rukeyser never relinquished her fascination with technological and rational quests for transcendence, she increasingly turned to mythic and historical female figures to trace an ancestry for herself that could counter the destructiveness she associated with American capitalism. While she was faulted by some literary critics for both her optimism and her philosophizing, toward the end of her life she had clearly found an audience through her teaching and in the younger generation of emerging women writers. The poet Anne Sexton wrote "Muriel, mother of everyone," to thank her for a copy of *The Speed of Darkness*; Sexton added that the volume remained on her desk, "flow[ing] out like an infusion of blood into the body."

Boy with His Hair Cut Short

Sunday shuts down on this twentieth-century evening.
The El[1] passes. Twilight and bulb define
the brown room, the overstuffed plum sofa,
the boy, and the girl's thin hands above his head.
A neighbor radio sings stocks, news, serenade. 5

He sits at the table, head down, the young clear neck exposed,
watching the drugstore sign from the tail of his eye;
tattoo, neon, until the eye blears, while his
solicitous tall sister, simple in blue, bending
behind him, cuts his hair with her cheap shears. 10

The arrow's electric red always reaches its mark,
successful neon! He coughs, impressed by that precision.

1. The elevated train, part of the New York transit system that used to run above the street.

His child's forehead, forever protected by his cap,
is bleached against the lamplight as he turns head
and steadies to let the snippets drop. 15

Erasing the failure of weeks with level fingers,
she sleeks the fine hair, combing: "You'll look fine tomorrow!
You'll surely find something, they can't keep turning you down;
the finest gentleman's not so trim as you!" Smiling, he raises
the adolescent forehead wrinkling ironic now. 20

He sees his decent suit laid out, new-pressed,
his carfare on the shelf. He lets his head fall, meeting
her earnest hopeless look, seeing the sharp blades splitting,
the darkened room, the impersonal sign, her motion,
the blue vein, bright on her temple, pitifully beating. 25

 1938

More of a Corpse than a Woman

Give them my regards when you go to the school reunion;
and at the marriage-supper, say that I'm thinking about them.
They'll remember my name; I went to the movies with that one,
feeling the weight of their death where she sat at my elbow;
 she never said a word, 5
 but all of them were heard.

all of them alike, expensive girls, the leaden friends:
one used to play the piano, one of them once wrote a sonnet,
one even seemed awakened enough to photograph wheatfields—
the dull girls with the educated minds and technical passions— 10
 pure love was their employment,
 they tried it for enjoyment.

Meet them at the boat: they've brought the souvenirs of boredom,
a seashell from the faltering monarchy;
the nose of a marble saint; and from the battlefield, 15
an empty shell divulged from a flower-bed.
 The lady's wealthy breath
 perfumes the air with death.

The leaden lady faces the fine, voluptuous woman,
faces a rising world bearing its gifts in its hands. 20
Kisses her casual dreams upon the lips she kisses,
risen, she moves away; takes others; moves away.
 Inadequate to love,
 supposes she's enough.

Give my regards to the well-protected woman. 25
I knew the ice-cream girl, we went to school together.
There's something to bury, people, when you begin to bury

When your women are ready and rich in their wish for the world,
 destroy the leaden heart,
 we've a new race to start. 30

 1938

Who in One Lifetime

Who in one lifetime sees all causes lost,
Herself dismayed and helpless, cities down,
Love made monotonous fear and the sad-faced
Inexorable armies and the falling plane,
Has sickness, sickness. Introspective and whole, 5
She knows how several madnesses are born,
Seeing the integrated never fighting well,
The flesh too vulnerable, the eyes tear-torn.

She finds a pre-surrender on all sides:
Treaty before the war, ritual impatience turn 10
The camps of ambush to chambers of imagery.
She holds belief in the world, she stays and hides
Life in her own defeat, stands, though her whole world burn,
A childless goddess of fertility.

June 1941 1944

From Letter to the Front

VII

To be a Jew in the twentieth century
Is to be offered a gift. If you refuse,
Wishing to be invisible, you choose
Death of the spirit, the stone insanity.
Accepting, take full life. Full agonies: 5
Your evening deep in labyrinthine blood
Of those who resist, fail, and resist; and God
Reduced to a hostage among hostages.

The gift is torment. Not alone the still
Torture, isolation; or torture of the flesh. 10
That may come also. But the accepting wish,
The whole and fertile spirit as guarantee
For every human freedom, suffering to be free,
Daring to live for the impossible.

 1944

Night Feeding

Deeper than sleep but not so deep as death
I lay there sleeping and my magic head

remembered and forgot. On first cry I
remembered and forgot and did believe.
I knew love and I knew evil: 5
woke to the burning song and the tree burning blind,
despair of our days and the calm milk-giver who
knows sleep, knows growth, the sex of fire and grass,
and the black snake with gold bones.

Black sleeps, gold burns; on second cry I woke 10
fully and gave to feed and fed on feeding.
Gold seed, green pain, my wizards in the earth
walked through the house, black in the morning dark.
Shadows grew in my veins, my bright belief,
my head of dreams deeper than night and sleep. 15
Voices of all black animals crying to drink,
cries of all birth arise, simple as we,
found in the leaves, in clouds and dark, in dream,
deep as this hour, ready again to sleep

1951

The Birth of Venus[1]

Risen in a
welter of waters.

Not as he saw her
standing upon a frayed and lovely surf
clean-riding the graceful leafy breezes 5
clean-poised and easy. Not yet.

But born in a
tidal wave of the father's overthrow,
the old rule killed and its mutilated sex.

The testicles of the father-god, father of fathers, 10
sickled off by his son, the next god Time.
Sickled off. Hurled into the ocean.
In all that blood and foam.
among raving and generation,
of semen and the sea born, the 15
great goddess rises.

However, possibly,
on the long worldward voyage flowing,
horror gone down in birth, the curse, being changed,
being used, is translated far at the margin into 20
our rose and saving image, curling toward a shore
early and April, with certainly shells, certainly blossoms.

1. The Roman name for the Greek goddess of love and beauty, Aphrodite, who was born from the ocean after Uranus was castrated by his son, Cronos (*chronos* means "time"). This newly born goddess, standing in a shell, is depicted in a famous painting by Sandro Botticelli (1444?–1510).

And the girl, the wellborn, goddess, human love—
young-known, new-knowing, mouth flickering, sure eyes—
rides shoreward, from death to us as we are at this moment on 25
the crisp delightful Botticellian wave.

1958

The Power of Suicide[1]

The potflower on the windowsill says to me
In words that are green-edged red leaves:
Flower flower flower flower
Today for the sake of all the dead Burst into flower.

1963 1968

The Poem as Mask

Orpheus[2]

When I wrote of the women in their dances and wildness,
 it was a mask,
on their mountain, gold-hunting, singing, in orgy,
it was a mask; when I wrote of the god,
fragmented, exiled from himself, his life, the love gone down
 with song,
it was myself, split open, unable to speak, in exile from myself. 5

There is no mountain, there is no god, there is memory
of my torn life, myself split open in sleep, the rescued child
beside me among the doctors, and a word
of rescue from the great eyes.

No more masks! No more mythologies! 10

Now, for the first time, the god lifts his hand,
the fragments join in me with their own music.

1968

Käthe Kollwitz[1]

I

Held between wars
my lifetime

1. This poem has been read as a response to the sui-
cide of American poet Sylvia Plath (1932–1963).
2. The subject of the poem is the mythical Greek
singer and poet whose music had magical powers over
humans and animals, and who was torn to pieces by
the Maenads, a band of wild women worshipping
Dionysus, god of wine. He was the son of Apollo, the
god of poetry and the sun.
1. German graphic artist and sculptor (1867–1945),
famous for her searing drawings and prints of workers,
mothers and children, and the horrors of war. The
poem quotes her words and recalls a number of her
works.

 among wars, the big hands of the world of death
my lifetime
listens to yours. 5

The faces of the sufferers
in the street, in dailiness,
their lives showing
through their bodies
a look as of music 10
the revolutionary look
that says I am in the world
to change the world
my lifetime
is to love to endure to suffer the music 15
to set its portrait
up as a sheet of the world
the most moving the most alive
Easter and bone
and Faust[2] walking among the flowers of the world 20
and the child alive within the living woman, music of man,
and death holding my lifetime between great hands
the hands of enduring life
that suffers the gifts and madness of full life, on earth, in our time,
and through my life, through my eyes, through my arms and hands 25
may give the face of this music in portrait waiting for
the unknown person
held in the two hands, you.

 II

 Woman as gates, saying:
 "The process is after all like music, 30
 like the development of a piece of music.
 The fugues come back and
 again and again
 interweave.
 A theme may seem to have been put aside, 35
 but it keeps returning—
 the same thing modulated,
 somewhat changed in form.
 Usually richer.
 And it is very good that this is so." 40

 A woman pouring her opposites.
 "After all there are happy things in life too.
 Why do you show only the dark side?"
 "I could not answer this. But I know—
 in the beginning my impulse to know 45
 the working life

2. The questing intellectual hero of Johann Wolfgang von Goethe's epic poem *Faust*. In one scene, Faust is up-
lifted when he hears the church bells and children's choir on Easter morning

 had little to do with
pity or sympathy.
 I simply felt
that the life of the workers was beautiful." 50

She said, "I am groping in the dark."

She said, "When the door opens, of sensuality,
then you will understand it too. The struggle begins.
Never again to be free of it,
often you will feel it to be your enemy. 55
Sometimes
you will almost suffocate,
such joy it brings."

Saying of her husband: "My wish
is to die after Karl. 60
I know no person who can love as he can,
with his whole soul.
Often this love has oppressed me;
I wanted to be free.
But often too it has made me 65
so terribly happy."[3]

She said: "We rowed over to Carrara[4] at dawn,
climbed up to the marble quarries
and rowed back at night. The drops of water
fell like glittering stars 70
from our oars."

She said: "As a matter of fact,
I believe
 that bisexuality
is almost a necessary factor 75
in artistic production; at any rate,
the tinge of masculinity within me
helped me
 in my work."

She said: "The only technique I can still manage. 80
It's hardly a technique at all, lithography.
In it
 only the essentials count."

A tight-lipped man in a restaurant last night saying to me: 85
"Kollwitz? She's too black-and-white."[5]

3. Karl Kollowitz, a pioneering doctor for the poor, was 5. Kollwitz worked almost exclusively in black-and-
deeply supportive of his wife's work. white.
4. City in central Italy, center of the marble industry.

III

Held among wars, watching
 all of them
 all these people
 weavers,
 Carmagnole[6] 90

Looking at
 all of them
 death, the children
 patients in waiting-rooms
 famine 95
 the street
 the corpse with the baby
floating, on the dark river

A woman seeing
 the violent, inexorable 100
 movement of nakedness
 and the confession of No
 the confession of great weakness, war,
 all streaming to one son killed, Peter;[7]
 even the son left living; repeated, 105
 the father, the mother; the grandson
 another Peter killed in another war:[8] firestorm;
 dark, light, as two hands,
 this pole and that pole as the gates.

What would happen if one woman told the truth about her life? 110
 The world would split open

IV / Song : The Calling-Up

Rumor, stir of ripeness
rising within this girl
sensual blossoming
of meaning, its light and form. 115

The birth-cry summoning
out of the male, the father
from the warm woman
a mother in response.

The word of death 120
calls up the fight with stone
wrestle with grief with time

6. Revolution (Italian); the title of a famous series of prints.
7. Kollwitz's younger son, Peter, was killed in World War I.

8 Her grandson Peter was killed in Russia during World War II.

from the material make
an art harder than bronze.

V / *Self-Portrait*[9]

Mouth looking directly at you 125
eyes in their inwardness looking
directly at you
half light half darkness
woman, strong, German, young artist
flows into 130
wide sensual mouth meditating
looking right at you
eyes shadowed with brave hand
looking deep at you
flows into 135
wounded brave mouth
grieving and hooded eyes
alive, German, in her first War
flows into
strength of the worn face 140
a skein of lines
broods, flows into
mothers among the war graves
bent over death
facing the father 145
stubborn upon the field
flows into
the marks of her knowing—
Nie Wieder Krieg[1]
repeated in the eyes 150
flows into
"Seedcorn must not be ground"[2]
and the grooved cheek
lips drawn fine
the down-drawn grief 155
face of our age
flows into
Pieta,[3] mother and
between her knees
life as her son in death 160
pouring from the sky of
one more war
flows into
face almost obliterated
hand over the mouth forever 165
hand over one eye now

9. Kollwitz drew self-portraits throughout her life.
1. No More War (German); the title of another famous set of prints.
2. Title of her last work, depicting a mother protecting her young children; the title means that the youth who will provide the next generation must not be destroyed in war.
3. Pity (Italian); a term traditionally applied to representations of the Virgin Mary sorrowing over the dead body of Christ, which was used by Kollwitz as the title for drawings of mothers mourning their dead children.

the other great eye
closed

1968

Myth

Long afterward, Oedipus,[1] old and blinded, walked the
roads. He smelled a familiar smell. It was
the Sphinx. Oedipus said, "I want to ask one question.
Why didn't I recognize my mother?' "You gave the
wrong answer," said the Sphinx. "But that was what 5
made everything possible," said Oedipus. "No," she said.
"When I asked What walks on four legs in the morning,
two at noon, and three in the evening, you answered,
Man. You didn't say anything about woman."
"When you say Man," said Oedipus, "you include women 10
too. Everyone knows that." She said, "That's what
you think."

1973

Along History

Along history, forever
 some woman dancing,
 making shapes on the air;
 forever a man
 riding a good horse, 5
 sitting the dark horse well,
 his penis erect with
 fantasy

1973

1. According to Greek myth, a king of Thebes who saved the city from plague by answering a riddle posed by a monster called the Sphinx, then discovered that he had unknowingly killed his father and married his mother. Horrified by his deeds, he put out his eyes and went into exile.

TILLIE OLSEN

c. 1913–

"In the twenty years I bore and reared my children, usually had to work on a paid job as well, the simplest circumstances for creation did not exist," wrote Tillie Olsen in *Silences* (1962), an essay in which she explored the "relationship of circumstances—including class, color, sex" to "the unnatural thwarting of what struggles to come into being." Later, in an equally important essay, *One Out of Twelve: Women Who Are Writers in Our Century* (1971), Olsen made the connection between gender and silence even more direct: "We [women] who write are survivors, 'only's,' " she declared, defining a *survivor* as "one who must bear witness

for those who foundered," and explaining again the "cost of 'discontinuity' " in her own life. Yet despite the pressures of such discontinuity, Olsen herself has managed to produce a significant group of extraordinarily accomplished tales.

Born in Nebraska, Olsen dropped out of high school in the eleventh grade to enter the world of what she calls "everyday" jobs. A member of the Depression generation, she began early to work for social and political causes. She struggled to organize packinghouse workers in Omaha and Kansas City, joined the Young Communist League, and was involved in the San Francisco labor movement, including the general strike of 1934. Even while she was engaged in such activism, however, Olsen had begun to write. A chapter of a novel appeared in the *Partisan Review* in 1934, and for several more years she continued to work on the book. At last, however, "it had," as she herself tells us, "to be set aside, never to come to completion," though a "rewoven" version of it was finally published as *Yonnondio: From the Thirties* (1974).

Married in 1943 to Jack Olsen, a printer and, like herself, an activist passionately committed to the labor movement, Olsen had four children and did not begin to write again until the 1950s, when her youngest daughter was five years old. In eight years, she produced the four stories that were collected in her distinguished volume *Tell Me a Riddle* (1961), a book whose title novella, with its searching examination of the mind and memories of a dying woman, received the O. Henry Award as the best American story in the year when it was published. A prodigious reader ("public libraries were my college") whose interest in women's writing was rekindled by the resurgence of feminism in the 1960s, Olsen has been instrumental in bringing important forgotten books back into print. An afterword of hers appears with Rebecca Harding Davis's *Life in the Iron-Mills* (rpt. 1971), while her meticulously documented critical volume *Silences* (1978) further explores the crucial power of circumstance.

Between 1969 and 1974, Olsen taught at Amherst, Stanford, M.I.T., and the University of Massachusetts at Boston. More recently, she has received fellowships from the Guggenheim Foundation and the National Endowment for the Humanities, as well as several honorary degrees. Throughout this period, mindful of her "hatred for all that, societally rooted . . . slows, impairs, silences writers," she has continued her struggle to "re-dedicate and encourage" other women to the powers and possibilities of their own creativity. A 1994 collection of essays edited by Elaine Hedges and Shelley Fisher Fishkin, *Listening to Silences*, attests to · Olsen's success.

Tell Me a Riddle

"These Things Shall Be"

1

For forty-seven years they had been married. How deep back the stubborn, gnarled roots of the quarrel reached, no one could say—but only now, when tending to the needs of others no longer shackled them together, the roots swelled up visible, split the earth between them, and the tearing shook even to the children, long since grown.

Why now, why now? wailed Hannah.

As if when we grew up weren't enough, said Paul.

Poor Ma. Poor Dad. It hurts so for both of them, said Vivi. They never had very much; at least in old age they should be happy.

Knock their heads together, insisted Sammy; tell 'em: you're too old for this kind of thing; no reason not to get along now.

Lennie wrote to Clara: They've lived over so much together; what could possibly tear them apart?

Something tangible enough.

Arthritic hands, and such work as he got, occasional. Poverty all his life, and there was little breath left for running. He could not, could not turn away from this desire: to have the troubling of responsibility, the fretting with money, over and done with to be free, to be *carefree* where success was not measured by accumulation, and there was use for the vitality still in him.

There was a way. They could sell the house, and with the money join his lodge's Haven, co-operative for the aged. Happy communal life, and was he not already an official; had he not helped organize it, raise funds, served as a trustee?

But she—would not consider it.

"What do we need all this for?" he would ask loudly, for her hearing aid was turned down and the vacuum was shrilling. "Five rooms" (pushing the sofa so she could get into the corner) "furniture" (smoothing down the rug) "floors and surfaces to make work. Tell me, why do we need it?" And he was glad he could ask in a scream.

"Because I'm use't."

"Because you're use't. This is a reason, Mrs. Word Miser? Used to can get unused!"

"Enough unused I have to get used to already. . . . Not enough words?" turning off the vacuum a moment to hear herself answer. "Because soon enough we'll need only a little closet, no windows, no furniture, nothing to make work for but worms. Because now I want room . . Screech and blow like you're doing, you'll need that closet even sooner . . . Ha, again!" For the vacuum bag wailed, puffed half up, hung stubbornly limp. "This time fix it so it stays; quick before the phone rings and you get too important-busy."

But while he struggled with the motor, it seethed in him. Why fix it? Why have to bother? And if it can't be fixed, have to wring the mind with how to pay the repair? At the Haven they come in with their own machines to clean your room or your cottage; you fish, or play cards, or make jokes in the sun, not with knotty fingers fight to mend vacuums.

Over the dishes, coaxingly: "For once in your life, to be free, to have everything done for you, like a queen."

"I never liked queens."

"No dishes, no garbage, no towel to sop, no worry what to buy, what to eat."

"And what else would I do with my empty hands? Better to eat at my own table when I want, and to cook and eat how I want."

"In the cottages they buy what you ask, and cook it how you like. You are the one who always used to say: better mankind born without mouths and stomachs than always to worry for money to buy, to shop, to fix, to cook, to wash, to clean."

"How cleverly you hid that you heard. I said it then because eighteen hours a day I ran. And you never scraped a carrot or knew a dish towel sops. Now— for you and me—who cares? A herring out of a jar is enough. But when I want, and nobody to bother." And she turned off her ear button, so she would not have to hear.

But as *he* had no peace, juggling and rejuggling the money to figure: how will I pay for this now?; prying out the storm windows (there they take care of this); jolting in the streetcar on errands (there I would not have to ride to take care of this or that); fending the patronizing relatives just back from Florida (there it matters what one is, not what one can afford), he gave her no peace.

"Look! In their bulletin. A reading circle. Twice a week it meets."

"Haumm," her answer of not listening.

"A reading circle. Chekhov they read that you like, and Peretz.[1] Cultured people at the Haven that you would enjoy."

"Enjoy!" She tasted the word. "Now, when it pleases you, you find a reading circle for me. And forty years ago when the children were morsels and there was a Circle, did you stay home with them once so I could go? Even once? You trained me well. I do not need others to enjoy. Others!" Her voice trembled. "Because you want to be there with others. Already it makes me sick to think of you always around others. Clown, grimacer, floormat, yesman, entertainer, whatever they want of you."

And now it was he who turned on the television loud so he need not hear.

Old scar tissue ruptured and the wounds festered anew. Chekhov indeed. She thought without softness of that young wife, who in the deep night hours while she nursed the current baby, and perhaps held another in her lap, would try to stay awake for the only time there was to read. She would feel again the weather of the outside on his cheek when, coming late from a meeting, he would find her so, and stimulated and ardent, sniffing her skin, coax: "I'll put the baby to bed, and you—put the book away, don't read, don't read."

That had been the most beguiling of all the "don't read, put your book away" her life had been. Chekhov indeed!

"Money?" She shrugged him off. "Could we get poorer than once we were? And in America, who starves?"

But as still he pressed:

"Let me alone about money. Was there ever enough? Seven little ones—for every penny I had to ask—and sometimes, remember, there was nothing. But always I had to manage. No *you* manage. Rub your nose in it good."

But from those years she had had to manage, old humiliations and terrors rose up, lived again, and forced her to relive them. The children's needings; that grocer's face or this merchant's wife she had had to beg credit from when credit was a disgrace, the scenery of the long blocks walked around when she could not pay; school coming, and the desperate going over the old to see what could yet be remade; the soups of meat bones begged "for-the-dog" one winter. . . .

Enough. Now they had no children. Let him wrack his head for how they would live. She would not exchange her solitude for anything. *Never again to be forced to move to the rhythms of others.*

For in this solitude she had won to a reconciled peace.

Tranquillity from having the empty house no longer an enemy, for it stayed clean—not as in the days when it was her family, the life in it, that had seemed

1. I.L. Peretz (1852–1915), Russian author of poems, plays, and stories in Yiddish. Anton Chekov (1860–1904), Russian writer.

the enemy: tracking, smudging, littering, dirtying, engaging her in endless defeating battle—and on whom her endless defeat had been spewed.

The few old books, memorized from rereading; the pictures to ponder (the magnifying glass superimposed on her heavy eye-glasses). Or if she wishes, when he is gone, the phonograph, that if she turns up very loud and strains, she can hear: the ordered sounds and the struggling.

Out in the garden, growing things to nurture. Birds to be kept out of the pear tree, and when the pears are heavy and ripe, the old fury of work, for all must be canned, nothing wasted.

And her one social duty (for she will not go to luncheons or meetings) the boxes of old clothes left with her, as with a life-practiced eye for finding what is still wearable within the worn (again the magnifying glass superimposed on the heavy glasses) she scans and sorts—this for rag or rummage, that for mending and cleaning, and this for sending abroad.

Being able at last to live within, and not move to the rhythms of others, as life had helped her to: denying; removing; isolating; taking the children one by one; then deafening, half-blinding—and at last presenting her solitude.

And in it she had won to a reconciled peace.

Now he was violating it with his constant campaigning: *Sell the house and move to the Haven.* (You sit, you sit—there too you could sit like a stone.) He was making of her a battleground where old grievances tore. (Turn on your ear button—I am talking.) And stubbornly she resisted—so that from wheedling, reasoning, manipulation, it was bitterness he now started with.

And it came to where every happening lashed up a quarrel.

"I will sell the house anyway," he flung at her one night. "I am putting it up for sale. There will be a way to make you sign."

The television blared, as always it did on the evenings he stayed home, and as always it reached her only as noise. She did not know if the tumult was in her or outside. Snap! she turned the sound off. "Shadows," she whispered to him, pointing to the screen, "look, it is only shadows." And in a scream: "Did you say that you will sell the house? Look at me, not at that. I am no shadow. You cannot sell without me."

"Leave on the television. I am watching."

"Like Paulie, like Jenny, a four-year-old. Staring at shadows. *You cannot sell the house.*"

"I will. We are going to the Haven. There you would not hear the television when you do not want it. I could sit in the social room and watch. You could lock yourself up to smell your unpleasantness in a room by yourself—for who would want to come near you?"

"No, no selling." A whisper now.

"The television is shadows. Mrs. Enlightened! Mrs. Cultured! A world comes into your house—and it is shadows. People you would never meet in a thousand lifetimes. Wonders. When you were four years old, yes, like Paulie, like Jenny, did you know of Indian dances, alligators, how they use bamboo in Malaya? No, you scratched in your dirt with the chickens and thought Olshana[2] was the world. Yes, Mrs. Unpleasant, I will sell the house, for there better can we be rid of each other than here."

2. Village in Russia.

She did not know if the tumult was outside, or in her. Always a ravening in-side, a pull to the bed, to lie down, to succumb.

"Have you thought maybe Ma should let a doctor have a look at her?" asked their son Paul after Sunday dinner, regarding his mother crumpled on the couch, instead of, as was her custom, busying herself in Nancy's kitchen.

"Why not the President too?"

"Seriously, Dad. This is the third Sunday she's lain down like that after din-ner. Is she that way at home?"

"A regular love affair with the bed. Every time I start to talk to her."

Good protective reaction, observed Nancy to herself. The workings of hos-tility.

"Nancy could take her. I just don't like how she looks. Let's have Nancy arrange an appointment."

"You think she'll go?" regarding his wife gloomily. "All right, we have to have doctor bills, we have to have doctor bills." Loudly: "Something hurts you?"

She startled, looked to his lips. He repeated: "Mrs. Take It Easy, something hurts?"

"Nothing. . . . Only you."

"A woman of honey. That's why you're lying down?"

"Soon I'll get up to do the dishes, Nancy."

"Leave them, Mother, I like it better this way."

"Mrs. Take It Easy, Paul says you should start ballet. You should go to see a doctor and ask: how soon can you start ballet?"

"A doctor?" she begged. "Ballet?"

"We were talking, Ma," explained Paul, "you don't seem any too well. It would be a good idea for you to see a doctor for a checkup."

"I get up now to do the kitchen. Doctors are bills and foolishness, my son. I need no doctors."

"At the Haven," he could not resist pointing out, "a doctor is *not* bills. He lives beside you. You start to sneeze, he is there before you open up a Kleenex. You can be sick there for free, all you want."

"Diarrhea of the mouth, is there a doctor to make you dumb?"

"Ma. Promise me you'll go. Nancy will arrange it."

"It's all of a piece when you think of it," said Nancy, "the way she attacks my kitchen, scrubbing under every cup hook, doing the inside of the oven so I can't enjoy Sunday dinner, knowing that half-blind or not, she's going to find every speck of dirt. . . ."

"Don't Nancy, I've told you—it's the only way she knows to be useful. What did the *doctor* say?"

"A real fatherly lecture. Sixty-nine is young these days. Go out, enjoy life, find interests. Get a new hearing aid, this one is antiquated. Old age is sick-ness only if one makes it so. Geriatrics, Inc."

"So there was nothing physical."

"Of course there was. How can you live to yourself like she does without there being? Evidence of a kidney disorder, and her blood count is low. He gave her a diet, and she's to come back for follow-up and lab work. . . . But he was clear enough: Number One prescription—start living like a human being. When I think of your dad, who could really play the invalid with that arthritis of his as active as a teenager, and twice as much fun. . . ."

"You didn't tell me the doctor says your sickness is in you, how you live." He pushed his advantage. "Life and enjoyments you need better than medicine. And this diet, how can you keep it? To weigh each morsel and scrape away the bits of fat to make this soup, that pudding. There, at the Haven, they have a dietician, they would do it for you."

She is silent.

"You would feel better there, I know it," he says gently. "There there is life and enjoyments all around."

"What is the matter, Mr. Importantbusy, you have no card game or meeting you can go to?"—turning her face to the pillow.

For a while he cut his meetings and going out, fussed over her diet, tried to wheedle her into leaving the house, brought in visitors:

"I should come to a fashion tea. I should sit and look at pretty babies in clothes I cannot buy. This is pleasure?"

"Always you are better than everyone else. The doctor said you should go out. Mrs. Brem comes to you with goodness and you turn her away."
"Because you asked her to, she asked me."

"They won't come back. People you need, the doctor said. Your own cousins I asked; they were willing to come and make peace as if nothing had happened. . . ."
"No more crushers of people, pushers, hypocrites, around me. No more in my house. You go to them if you like."

"Kind he is to visit. And you, like ice."
"A babbler. All my life around babblers Enough!"

"She's even worse, Dad? Then let her stew a while," advised Nancy. "You can't let it destroy you; it's a psychological thing, maybe too far gone for any of us to help."

So he let her stew. More and more she lay silent in bed, and sometimes did not even get up to make the meals. No longer was the tongue-lashing inevitable if he left the coffee cup where it did not belong, or forgot to take out the garbage or mislaid the broom. The birds grew bold that summer and for once pecked the pears, undisturbed.

A bellyful of bitterness and every day the same quarrel in a new way and a different old grievance the quarrel forced her to enter and relive. And the new torment: I am not really sick, the doctor said it, then why do I feel so sick?

One night she asked him: "You have a meeting tonight? Do not go. Stay . . . with me."

He had planned to watch "This Is Your Life"[3] anyway, but half sick himself from the heavy heat, and sickering therefore the more after the brooks and woods of the Haven, with satisfaction he grated:

"Hah, Mrs. Live Alone And Like It wants company all of a sudden. It doesn't seem so good the time of solitary when she was a girl exile in Siberia. 'Do not go. Stay with me.' A new song for Mrs. Free As A Bird. Yes, I am going

3. A popular 1950s television program.

out, and while I am gone chew this aloneness good, and think how you keep us both from where if you want people you do not need to be alone."

"Go, go. All your life you have gone without me."

After him she sobbed curses he had not heard in years, old-country curses from their childhood: Grow, oh shall you grow like an onion, with your head in the ground. Like the hide of a drum shall you be, beaten in life, beaten in death. Oh shall you be like a chandelier, to hang, and to burn. . . .

She was not in their bed when he came back. She lay on the cot on the sun-porch. All week she did not speak or come near him; nor did he try to make peace or care for her.

He slept badly, so used to her next to him. After all the years, old harmonies and dependencies deep in their bodies; she curled to him, or he coiled to her each warmed, warming, turning as the other turned, the nights a long embrace.

It was not the empty bed or the storm that woke him, but a faint singing. *She* was singing. Shaking off the drops of rain, the lightning riving her lifted face, he saw her so; the cot covers on the floor.

"This is a private concert?" he asked. "Come in, you are wet."

"I can breathe now," she answered; "my lungs are rich." Though indeed the sound was hardly a breath.

"Come in, come in." Loosing the bamboo shades.

"Look how wet you are." Half helping, half carrying her, still faint-breathing her song.

A Russian love song of fifty years ago.

He had found a buyer, but before he told her, he called together those children who were close enough to come. Paul, of course, Sammy from New Jersey, Hannah from Connecticut, Vivi from Ohio.

With a kindling of energy for her beloved visitors, she arrayed the house, cooked and baked. She was not prepared for the solemn after-dinner conclave, they too probing in and tearing. Her frightened eyes watched from mouth to mouth as each spoke.

His stories were eloquent and funny of her refusal to go back to the doctor; of the scorned invitations; of her stubborn silences or the bile "Like a Niagara"; of her contrariness: "If I clean it's no good how I cleaned; if I don't clean, I'm still a master who thinks he has a slave."

("Vinegar he poured on me all his life; I am well marinated; how can I be honey now?")

Deftly he marched in the rightness for moving to the Haven; their money from social security free for visiting the children; not sucked into daily needs and into the house; the activities in the Haven for him; but mostly the Haven for *her*: her health, her need of care, distraction, amusement, friends who shared her interests.

"This does offer an outlet for Dad," said Paul; "he's always been an active person. And economic peace of mind isn't to be sneezed at, either. I could use a little of that myself."

But when they asked: "And you, Ma, how do you feel about it?" could only whisper:

"For him it is good. It is not for me. I can no longer live between people."

"You lived all your life *for* people," Vivi cried.

"Not with." Suffering doubly for the unhappiness on her children's faces.

"You have to find some compromise," Sammy insisted. "Maybe sell the house and buy a trailer. After forty-seven years there's surely some way you can find to live in peace."

"There's no help, my children. Different things we need."

"Then live alone!" He could control himself no longer. "I have a buyer for the house. Half the money for you, half for me. Either alone or with me to the Haven. You think I can live any longer as we are doing now?"

"Ma doesn't have to make a decision this minute, however you feel, Dad," Paul said quickly, "and you wouldn't want her to. Let's let it lay a few months, and then talk some more."

"I think I can work it out to take Mother home with me for a while," Hannah said. "You both look terrible, but especially you, Mother. I'm going to ask Phil to have a look at you."

"Sure," cracked Sammy. "What's the use of a doctor husband if you can't get free service out of him once in a while for the family? And absence might make the heart . . . you know."

"There was something after all," Paul told Nancy in a colorless voice. "That was Hannah's Phil calling. Her gall bladder. . . . Surgery."

"Her *gall* bladder. If that isn't classic. 'Bitter as gall'—talk of psychosom
——"

He stepped closer, put his hand over her mouth and said in the same colorless, plodding voice. "We have to get Dad. They operated at once. The cancer was everywhere, surrounding the liver, everywhere. They did what they could . . . at best she has a year. Dad . . . we have to tell him."

II

Honest in his weakness when they told him, and that she was not to know. "I'm not an actor. She'll know right away by how I am. Oh that poor woman. I am old too, it will break me into pieces. Oh that poor woman. She will spit on me: 'So my sickness was how I live.' Oh Paulie, how she will be, that poor woman. Only she should not suffer. . . . I can't stand sickness, Paulie, I can't go with you."

But went. And play-acted.

"A grand opening and you did not even wait for me. . . . A good thing Hannah took you with her."

"Fashion teas I needed. They cut out what tore in me; just in my throat something hurts yet. . . . Look! so many flowers, like a funeral. Vivi called, did Hannah tell you? And Lennie from San Francisco, and Clara; and Sammy is coming." Her gnome's face pressed happily into the flowers.

It is impossible to predict in these cases, but once over the immediate effects of the operation, she should have several months of comparative well-being.

The money, where will come the money?

Travel with her, Dad. Don't take her home to the old associations. The other children will want to see her.

The money, where will I wring the money?

Whatever happens, she is not to know. No, you can't ask her to sign

papers to sell the house; nothing to upset her. Borrow instead. Then, after. . . .

 I had wanted to leave you each a few dollars to make life easier, as other fathers do. There will be nothing left now. (Failure! you and your "business is exploitation." Why didn't you make it when it could be made?—Is that what you're thinking, Sammy?)

 Sure she's unreasonable, Dad—but you have to stay with her. If there's to be any happiness in what's left of her life, it depends on you.

 Prop me up, children, think of me, too. Shuffled, chained with her, bitter woman. No Haven, and the little money going. . . . How happy she looks, poor creature.

The look of excitement. The straining to hear everything (the new hearing aid turned full). Why are you so happy, dying woman?

How the petals are, fold on fold, and the gladioli color. The autumn air.

Stranger grandsons, tall above the little gnome grandmother, the little spry grandfather. Paul in a frenzy of picture-taking before going.

She, wandering the great house. Feeling the books; laughing at the maple shoemaker's bench of a hundred years ago used as a table. The ear turned to music.

"Let us go home. See how good I walk now." "One step from the hospital," he answers, "and she wants to fly. Wait till Doctor Phil says."

"Look—the birds too are flying home. Very good Phil is and will not show it, but he is sick of sickness by the time he comes home."

"Mrs. Telepathy, to read minds," he answers; "read mine what it says: when the trunks of medicines become a suitcase, then we will go."

The grandboys, they do not know what to say to us. . . . Hannah, she runs around here, there, when is there time for herself?

Let us go home. Let us go home.

Musing; gentleness—*but for the incidents of the rabbi in the hospital, and of the candles of benediction.*

Of the rabbi in the hospital:

 Now tell me what happened, Mother.

 From the sleep I awoke, Hannah's Phil, and he stands there like a devil in a dream and calls me by name. I cannot hear. I think he prays. Go away, please, I tell him, I am not a believer. Still he stands, while my heart knocks with fright.

 You scared *him*, Mother. He thought you were delirious.

 Who sent him? Why did he come to me?

 It is a custom. The men of God come to visit those of their religion they might help. The hospital makes up the list for them—race, religion—and you are on the Jewish list.

 Not for rabbis. At once go and make them change. Tell them to write: Race, human; Religion, none.

And of the candles of benediction:

 Look how you have upset yourself, Mrs. Excited Over Nothing. Pleasant memories you should leave.

 Go in, go back to Hannah and the lights. Two weeks I saw candles and said nothing. But she asked me.

So what was so terrible? She forgets you never did, she asks you to light the Friday candles and say the benediction like Phil's mother when she visits. If the candles give her pleasure, why shouldn't she have the pleasure?

Not for pleasure she does it. For emptiness. Because his family does. Because all around her do.

That is not a good reason too? But you did not hear her. For heritage, she told you. For the boys, from the past they should have tradition.

Superstition! From our ancestors, savages, afraid of the dark, of themselves: mumbo words and magic lights to scare away ghosts.

She told you: how it started does not take away the goodness. For centuries, peace in the house it means.

Swindler! does she look back on the dark centuries? Candles bought instead of bread and stuck into a potato for a candlestick? Religion that stifled and said: in Paradise, woman, you will be the footstool of your husband, and in life—poor chosen Jew—ground under, despised, trembling in cellars. And cremated. And cremated.

This is religion's fault? You think you are still an orator of the 1905 revolution?[4] Where are the pills for quieting? Which are they?

Heritage. How have we come from our savage past, how no longer to be savages—this to teach. To look back and learn what humanizes—this to teach. To smash all ghettos that still divide us—not to go back, not to go back—this to teach. Learned books in the house, will man live or die, and she gives to her boys—superstition.

Hannah that is so good to you. Take your pill, Mrs. Excited For Nothing, swallow.

Heritage! But when did I have time to teach? Of Hannah I asked only hands to help.

Swallow.

Otherwise—musing; gentleness.

Not to travel. To go home.

The children want to see you. We have to show them you are as thorny a flower as ever.

Not to travel.

Vivi wants you should see her new baby. She sent the tickets—airplane tickets—a Mrs. Roosevelt[5] she wants to make of you. To Vivi's we have to go.

A new baby. How many warm, seductive babies. She holds him stiffly, *away* from her, so that he wails. And a long shudder begins, and the sweat beads on her forehead.

"Hush, shush," croons the grandfather, lifting him back. "You should forgive your grandmamma, little prince, she has never held a baby before, only seen them in glass cases. Hush, shush."

"You're tired, Ma," says Vivi. "The travel and the noisy dinner. I'll take you to lie down."

(*A long travel from, to, what the feel of a baby evokes.*)

4. Protests, strikes, and military mutinies in czarist Russia, bloodily suppressed by the last emperor and czar, Nicholas II.

5. Eleanor Roosevelt (1884–1962), wife of President Franklin D. Roosevelt, was famous for extensive, frequent travels in the days when airplane travel was unusual.

In the airplane, cunningly designed to encase from motion (no wind, no feel of flight), she had sat severely and still, her face turned to the sky through which they cleaved and left no scar.

So this was how it looked, the determining, the crucial sky, and this was how man moved through it, remote above the dwindled earth, the concealed human life. Vulnerable life, that could scar.

There was a steerage ship[6] of memory that shook across a great, circular sea: clustered, ill human beings; and through the thick-stained air, tiny fretting waters in a window round like the airplane's—sun round, moon round. (The round thatched roofs of Olshana.) Eye round—like the smaller window that framed distance the solitary year of exile when only her eyes could travel, and no voice spoke. And the polar winds hurled themselves across snow trackless and endless and white—like the clouds which had closed together below and hidden the earth.

Now they put a baby in her lap. Do not ask me, she would have liked to beg. Enough the worn face of Vivi, the remembered grandchildren, I cannot, cannot. . . .

Cannot what? Unnatural grandmother, not able to make herself embrace a baby.

She lay there in the bed of the two little girls, her new hearing aid turned full, listening to the sound of the children going to sleep, the baby's fretful crying and hushing, the clatter of dishes being washed and put away. They thought she slept. Still she rode on.

It was not that she had not loved her babies, her children. The love—the passion of tending—had risen with the need like a torrent; and like a torrent drowned and immolated all else. But when the need was done—oh the power that was lost in the painful damming back and drying up of what still surged, but had nowhere to go. Only the thin pulsing left that could not quiet, suffering over lives one felt, but could no longer hold nor help.

On that torrent she had borne them to their own lives, and the river-bed was desert long years now. Not there would she dwell, a memoried wraith. Surely that was not all, surely there was more. Still the springs, the springs were in her seeking. Somewhere an older power that beat for life. Somewhere coherence, transport, meaning. If they would but leave her in the air now stilled of clamor, in the reconciled solitude, to journey on.

And they put a baby in her lap. Immediacy to embrace, and the breath of *that* past: warm flesh like this that had claims and nuzzled away all else and with lovely mouths devoured; hot-living like an animal—intensely and now; the turning maze; the long drunkenness; the drowning into needing and being needed. Severely she looked back—and the shudder seized her again, and the sweat. Not that way. Not there, not now could she, not yet. . . .

And all that visit, she could not touch the baby.

"Daddy, is it the . . . sickness she's like that?" asked Vivi. "I was so glad to be having the baby—for her. I told Tim, it'll give her more happiness than anything, being around a baby again. And she hasn't played with him once."

He was not listening, "Aahh little seed of life, little charmer," he crooned, "Hollywood should see you. A heart of ice you would melt. Kick, kick. The future you'll have for a ball. In 2050 still kick. Kick for your grandaddy then."

6. I.e., a ship having only the lowest class of accommodations, often used by immigrants.

Attentive with the older children; sat through their performances (command performance; we command you to be the audience); helped Ann sort autumn leaves to find the best for a school program; listened gravely to Richard tell about his rock collection, while her lips mutely formed the words to remember: *igneous, sedimentary, metamorphic;*[7] looked for missing socks, books and bus tickets; watched the children whoop after their grandfather who knew how to tickle, chuck, lift, toss, do tricks, tell secrets, make jokes, match riddle for riddle. (Tell me a riddle, Grammy. I know no riddles, child.) Scrubbed sills and woodwork and furniture in every room; folded the laundry; straightened drawers; emptied the heaped baskets waiting for ironing (while he or Vivi or Tim nagged: You're supposed to rest here, you've been sick) but to none tended or gave food—and could not touch the baby.

After a week she said: "Let us go home. Today call about the tickets."

"You have important business, Mrs. Inahurry? The President waits to consult with you?" He shouted, for the fear of the future raced in him. "The clothes are still warm from the suitcase, your children cannot show enough how glad they are to see you, and you want home. There is plenty of time for home. We cannot be with the children at home."

"Blind to around you as always: the little ones sleep four in a room because we take their bed. We are two more people in a house with a new baby, and no help."

"Vivi is happy so. The children should have their grandparents a while, she told to me. I should have my mommy and daddy. . . ."

"Babbler and blind. Do you look at her so tired? How she starts to talk and she cries? I am not strong enough yet to help. Let us go home."

(To reconciled solitude.)

For it seemed to her the crowded noisy house was listening to her, listening for her. She could feel it like a great ear pressed under her heart. And everything knocked: quick constant raps: let me in, let me in.

How was it that soft reaching tendrils also became blows that knocked?

C'mon, Grandma, I want to show you. . . .

Tell me a riddle, Grandma. (*I know no riddles.*)

Look, Grammy, he's so dumb he can't even find his hands. (Dody and the baby on a blanket over the fermenting autumn mould.)

I made them—for you. (Ann) (Flat paper dolls with aprons that lifted on scalloped skirts that lifted on flowered pants; hair of yarn and great ringed questioning eyes.)

Watch me, Grandma. (Richard snaking up the tree, hanging exultant, free, with one hand at the top. Below Dody hunching over in pretend-cooking.)

(*Climb too, Dody, climb and look*)

Be my nap bed, Grammy. (The "No!" too late.) Morty's abandoned heaviness, while his fingers ladder up and down her hearing-aid cord to his drowsy chant: eentsiebeentsiespider. (*Children trust.*)

It's to start off your own rock collection, Grandma.

That's a trilobite fossil, 200 million years old (millions of years on a boy's mouth) and that one's obsidian, black glass.

7. Basic types of rocks.

Knocked and knocked.

 Mother, I *told* you the teacher said we had to bring it back all filled out this morning. Didn't you even ask Daddy? Then tell *me* which plan and I'll check it: evacuate or stay in the city or wait for you to come and take me away. (Seeing the look of straining to hear.) It's for Disaster,[8] Grandma. (*Children trust.*)

 Vivi in the maze of the long, the lovely drunkenness. The old old noises: baby sounds; screaming of a mother flayed to exasperation; children quarreling; children playing; singing; laughter.

And Vivi's tears and memories, spilling so fast, half the words not understood.

She had started remembering out loud deliberately, so her mother would know the past was cherished, still lived in her.

Nursing the baby: My friends marvel, and I tell them, oh it's easy to be such a cow. I remember how beautiful my mother seemed nursing my brother, and the milk just flows. . . . Was that Davy? It must have been Davy. . . .

Lowering a hem: How did you ever . . . when I think how you made everything we wore . . . Tim, just think, seven kids and Mommy sewed everything . . . do I remember you sang while you sewed? That white dress with the red apples on the skirt you fixed over for me, was it Hannah's or Clara's before it was mine?

Washing sweaters: Ma, I'll never forget, one of those days so nice you washed clothes outside; one of the first spring days it must have been. The bubbles just danced up and down while you scrubbed, and we chased after, and you stopped to show us how to blow our own bubbles with green onion stalks . . . you always. . . .

"Strong onion, to still make you cry after so many years," her father said, to turn the tears into laughter.

While Richard bent over his homework: Where is it now, do we still have it, the Book of the Martyrs? It always seemed so, well—exalted, when you'd put it on the round table and we'd all look at it together; there was even a halo from the lamp. The lamp with the beaded fringe you could move up and down; they're in style again, pulley lamps like that, but without the fringe. You know the book I'm talking about, Daddy, the Book of the Martyrs, the first picture was a bust of Spartacus? . . . Socrates? I wish there was something like that for the children, Mommy, to give them what you. . . . (And the tears splashed again.)

(What I intended and did not? Stop it, daughter, stop it, leave that time. And he, the hypocrite, sitting there with tears in his eyes—it was nothing to you then, nothing.)

 . . . The time you came to school and I almost died of shame because of your accent and because I knew you knew I was ashamed; how could I? . . . Sammy's harmonica and you danced to it once, yes you did, you and Davy squealing in your arms. . . . That time you bundled us up and walked us down to the railway station to stay the night 'cause it was heated and we didn't have

8. During the 1950s, with the encouragement of the federal government, a number of American communities built fallout shelters and drew up evacuation ("Disaster") plans to be used in a nuclear attack.

any coal, that winter of the strike, you didn't think I remembered that, did you, Mammy? . . . How you'd call us out to see the sunsets. . . .

Day after day, the spilling memories. Worse now, questions, too. Even the grandchildren: Grandma, in the olden days, when you were little. . . .

It was the afternoons that saved.

While they thought she napped, she would leave the mosaic on the wall (of children's drawings, maps, calendars, pictures, Ann's cardboard dolls with their great ringed questioning eyes) and hunch in the girls' closet, on the low shelf where the shoes stood, and the girls' dresses covered.

For that while she would painfully sheathe against the listening house, the tendrils and noises that knocked, and Vivi's spilling memories. Sometimes it helped to braid and unbraid the sashes that dangled, or to trace the pattern on the hoop slips.

Today she had jacks and children under jet trails to forget. Last night, Ann and Dody silhouetted in the window against a sunset of flaming man-made clouds of jet trail, their jacks ball accenting the peaceful noise of dinner being made. Had she told them, yes she had told them of how they played jacks in her village though there was no ball, no jacks. Six stones, round and flat, toss them out, the seventh on the back of the hand, toss, catch and swoop up as many as possible, toss again. . . .

Of stones (repeating Richard) there are three kinds: earth's fire jetting; rock of layered centuries; crucibled new out of the old (*igneous, sedimentary, metamorphic*). But there was that other—frozen to black glass, never to transform or hold the fossil memory . . . (let not my seed fall on stone). There was an ancient one who fought to heights a great rock that crashed back down eternally[9]—eternal labor, freedom, labor . . . (stone will perish, but the word remain). And you, David,[1] who with a stone slew, screaming: Lord, take my heart of stone and give me flesh.

Who was screaming? Why was she back in the common room of the prison, the sun motes dancing in the shafts of light, and the informer being brought in, a prisoner now, like themselves. And Lisa leaping, yes, Lisa, the gentle and tender, biting at the betrayer's jugular. Screaming and screaming.

No, it is the children screaming. Another of Paul and Sammy's terrible fights?

In Vivi's house. Severely: you are in Vivi's house.

Blows, screams, a call: "Grandma!" For her? Oh please not for her. Hide, hunch behind the dresses deeper. But a trembling little body hurls itself beside her—surprised, smothered laughter, arms surround her neck, tears rub dry on her cheek, and words too soft to understand whisper into her ear (Is this where you hide too, Grammy? It's my secret place, we have a secret now).

And the sweat beads, and the long shudder seizes.

It seemed the great ear pressed inside now, and the knocking. "We have to go home," she told him, "I grow ill here."

9. An allusion to the myth of Sisyphus, who was punished in Tartarus (below Hades) by having to roll a huge stone uphill; each time he approached the top, the stone would roll back.

1. Future king of Israel, who killed the great Philistine champion Goliath with a stone from a slingshot (1 Samuel 17).

"It is your own fault, Mrs. Bodybusy, you do not rest, you do too much." He raged, but the fear was in his eyes. "It was a serious operation, they told you to take care. . . . All right, we will go to where you can rest."

But where? Not home to death, not yet. He had thought to Lennie's, to Clara's; beautiful visits with each of the children. She would have to rest first, be stronger. If they could but go to Florida—it glittered before him, the never-realized promise of Florida. California: of course. (The money, the money, dwindling!) Los Angeles first for sun and rest, then to Lennie's in San Francisco.

He told her the next day, "You saw what Nancy wrote: snow and wind back home, a terrible winter. And look at you—all bones and a swollen belly. I called Phil: he said: 'A prescription, Los Angeles sun and rest.'"

She watched the words on his lips. "You have sold the house," she cried, "that is why we do not go home. That is why you talk no more of the Haven. Why there is money for travel. After the children you will drag me to the Haven."

"The Haven! Who thinks of the Haven any more? Tell her, Vivi, tell Mrs. Suspicious: a prescription, sun and rest, to make you healthy. . . . And how could I sell the house without *you?*"

At the place of farewells and greetings, of winds of coming and winds of going, they say their good-byes.

They look back at her with the eyes of others before them: Richard with her own blue blaze; Ann with the Nordic eyes of Tim; Morty's dreaming brown of a great-grandmother he will never know; Dody with the laughing eyes of him who had been her springtide love (who stands beside her now); Vivi's, all tears.

The baby's eyes are closed in sleep.

Good-bye, my children.

III

It is to the back of the great city he brought her, to the dwelling places of the cast-off old. Bounded by two lines of amusement piers to the north and to the south, and between a long straight paving rimmed with black benches facing the sand—sands so wide the ocean is only a far fluting.

In the brief vacation season, some of the boarded stores fronting the sands open, and families, young people and children, may be seen. A little tasseled tram shuttles between the piers, and the lights of roller coasters prink and tweak over those who come to have sensation made in them.

The rest of the year it is abandoned to the old, all else boarded up and still; seemingly empty, except the occasional days and hours when the sun, like a tide, sucks them out of the low rooming houses, casts them on to the benches and sandy rim of the walk—and sweeps them into decaying enclosures back again.

A few newer apartments glint among the low bleached squares. It is in one of these Lennie's Jeannie has arranged their rooms. "Only a few miles north and south people pay hundreds of dollars a month for just this gorgeous air, Grandaddy, just this ocean closeness."

She had been ill on the plane, lay ill for days in the unfamiliar room. Several times the doctor came by—left medicine she would not take. Several times

Jeannie drove in the twenty miles from work still in her Visiting Nurse uniform, the lightness and brightness of her like a healing.

"Who can believe it is winter?" he asked one morning. "Beautiful it is outside like an ad. Come, Mrs. Invalid, come to taste it. You are well enough to sit in here, you are well enough to sit outside. The doctor said it too."

But the benches were encrusted with people, and the sands at the sidewalk's edge. Besides, she had seen the far ruffle of the sea: "there take me," and though she leaned against him, it was she who led.

Plodding and plodding, sitting often to rest he grumbling. Patting the sand so warm. Once she scooped up a handful, cradling it close to her better eye; peered, and flung it back. And as they came almost to the brink and she could see the glistening wet, she sat down, pulled off her shoes and stockings, left him and began to run. "You'll catch cold," he screamed, but the sand in his shoes weighed him down—he who had always been the agile one—and already the white spray creamed her feet.

He pulled her back, took a handkerchief to wipe off the wet and the sand. "Oh no," she said, "the sun will dry," seized the square and smoothed it flat, dropped on it a mound of sand, knotted the kerchief corners and tied it to a bag—"to look at with the strong glass" (for the first time in years explaining an action of hers)—and lay down with the little bag against her cheek, looking toward the shore that nurtured life as it first crawled toward consciousness the millions of years ago.

He took her one Sunday in the evil-smelling bus, past flat miles of blister houses, to the home of relatives. Oh what is this? she cried as the light began to smoke and the houses to dim and recede. Smog, he said, everyone knows but you . . . Outside he kept his arms about her, but she walked with hands pushing the heavy air as if to open it, whispered: who has done this? sat down suddenly to vomit at the curb and for a long while refused to rise.

One's age as seen on the altered face of those known in youth. Is this they he has come to visit? This Max and Rose, smooth and pleasant, introducing them to polite children, disinterested grandchildren, "the whole family, once a month on Sundays. And why not? We have the room, the help, the food."

Talk of cars, of houses, of success: this son that, that daughter this. And your children? Hastily skimped over, the intermarriages, the obscure work—"my doctor son-in-law, Phil"—all he has to offer. She silent in a corner. (Car-sick like a baby, he explains.) Years since he has taken her to visit anyone but the children, and old apprehensions prickle: "no incidents," he silently begs, "no incidents." He itched to tell them. "A very sick woman," significantly, indicating her with his eyes, "a very sick woman." Their restricted faces did not react. "Have you thought maybe she'd do better at Palm Springs?" Rose asked. "Or at least a nicer section of the beach, nicer people, a pool." Not to have to say "money" he said instead: "would she have sand to look at through a magnifying glass?" and went on, detail after detail, the old habit betraying of parading the queerness of her for laughter.

After dinner—the others into the living-room in men- or women-clusters, or into the den to watch TV—the four of them alone. She sat close to him, and did not speak. Jokes, stories, people they had known, beginning of reminiscence, Russia fifty-sixty years ago. Strange words across the Duncan Phyfe table: *hunger; secret meetings; human rights; spies; betrayals; prison; escape—*

interrupted by one of the grandchildren: "Commercial's on; any Coke left? Gee, you're missing a real hair-raiser." And then a granddaughter (Max proudly: "look at her, an American queen") drove them home on her way back to U.C.L.A. No incident—except that there had been no incidents.

The first few mornings she had taken with her the magnifying glass, but he would sit only on the benches, so she rested at the foot, where slatted bench shadows fell, and unless she turned her hearing aid down, other voices invaded.

Now on the days when the sun shone and she felt well enough, he took her on the tram to where the benches ranged in oblongs, some with tables for draughts or cards. Again the blanket on the sand in the striped shadows, but she no longer brought the magnifying glass. He played cards, and she lay in the sun and looked towards the waters; or they walked—two blocks down to the scaling hotel, two blocks back—past chili-hamburger stands, open-doored bars, Next to New and Perpetual Rummage Sale stores.

Once, out of the aimless walkers, slow and shuffling like themselves, someone ran unevenly towards them, embraced, kissed, wept: "dear friends, old friends." A friend of *hers*, not his: Mrs. Mays who had lived next door to them in Denver when the children were small.

Thirty years are compressed into a dozen sentences; and the present, not even in three. All is told: the children scattered; the husband dead; she lives in a room two blocks up from the sing hall—and points to the domed auditorium jutting before the pier. The leg? phlebitis; the heavy breathing? that, one does not ask. She, too, comes to the benches each day to sit. And tomorrow, tomorrow, are they going to the community sing? Of course he would have heard of it, everybody goes—the big doings they wait for all week. They have never been? She will come for them to dinner tomorrow and they will all go together.

So it is that she sits in the wind of the singing, among the thousand various faces of age.

She had turned off her hearing aid at once they came into the auditorium—as she would have wished to turn off sight.

One by one they streamed by and imprinted on her—and though the savage zest of their singing came voicelessly soft and distant, the faces still roared—the faces densened the air—chorded into

children-chants, mother-croons, singing of the chained
love serenades, Beethoven storms, mad Lucia's[2] scream
drunken joy-songs, keens for the dead, work-singing

> *while from floor to balcony to dome a bare-footed sore-covered little girl threaded the sound-thronged tumult, danced her ecstasy of grimace to flutes that scratched at a cross-roads village wedding.*

Yes, faces became sound, and the sound became faces; and faces and sound became weight—pushed, pressed

2. The heroine of the 19th-century opera *Lucia di Lammermoor,* who goes mad.

"Air"—her hand claws his.

"Whenever I enjoy myself. . . ." Then he saw the gray sweat on her face. "Here. Up. Help me, Mrs. Mays," and they support her out to where she can gulp the air in sob after sob.

"A doctor, we should get for her a doctor."

"Tch, it's nothing," says Ellen Mays, "I get it all the time. You've missed the tram; come to my place. Fix your hearing aid, honey . . . close . . . tea. My view. See, she *wants* to come. Steady now, that's how." Adding mysteriously: "Remember your advice, easy to keep your head above water, empty things float. Float."

The singing a fading march for them, tall woman with a swollen leg weaving little man, and the swollen thinness they help between.

The stench in the hall: mildew? decay? "We sit and rest then climb. My gorgeous view. We help each other and here we are."

The stench along into the slab of room. A wash stand for a sink, a box with oilcloth tacked around for a cupboard, a three-burner gas plate. Artificial flowers, colorless with dust. Everywhere pictures foaming: wedding, baby, party, vacation, graduation, family pictures. From the narrow couch under a slit of window, sure enough the view: lurching rooftops and a scallop of ocean heaving, preening, twitching under the moon.

"While the water heats. Excuse me . . . down the hall." Ellen Mays has gone.

"You'll live?" he asks mechanically, sat down to feel his fright; tried to pull her alongside.

She pushed him away. "For air," she said, stood clinging to the dresser. Then, in a terrible voice:

After a lifetime of room. Of many rooms.

Shhh.

You remember how she lived. Eight children. And now one room like a coffin.

She pays rent!

Shrinking the life of her into one room like a coffin
Rooms and rooms like this. I lie on the quilt and hear them talk.

Please, Mrs. Orator-without-Breath.

Once you went for coffee I walked I saw A Balzac[3] a Chekhov to write it Rummage Alone On scraps

Better old here than in the old country!

On scraps Yet they sang like . . . ike . . Wondrous. *Humankind one has to believe.* So strong for what? To rot not grow?

Your poor lungs beg you. They sob between each word.

Singing. Unused the life in them. She in this poor room with her pictures. Max You The children Everywhere unused the life And who has meaning? Century after century still all in us not to grow?

Coffins, rummage, plants: sick woman. Oh lay down. We will get for you the doctor.

"And when will it end. Oh, *the end.*" *That* nightmare thought, and this time she writhed, crumpled beside him, seized his hand (for a moment again the

3. Honoré de Balzac (1799–1850), French writer

weight, the soft distant roaring of humanity) and on the strangled-for breath, begged: "Man . . . we'll destroy ourselves?"

And looking for answer—in the helpless pity and fear for her (for *her*) that distorted his face—she understood the last months, and knew that she was dying.

IV

"Let us go home," she said after several days.

"You are in training for a cross-country run? That is why you do not even walk across the room? Here, like a prescription Phil said, till you are stronger from the operation. You want to break doctor's orders?"

She saw the fiction was necessary to him, was silent; then: "At home I will get better. If the doctor here says?"

"And winter? And the visits to Lennie and to Clara? All right," for he saw the tears in her eyes, "I will write Phil, and talk to the doctor."

Days passed. He reported nothing. Jeannie came and took her out for air, past the boarded concessions, the hooded and tented amusement rides, to the end of the pier. They watched the spent waves feeding the new, the gulls in the clouded sky; even up where they sat, the wind-blown sand stung.

She did not ask to go down the crooked steps to the sea.

Back in her bed, while he was gone to the store, she said: "Jeannie, this doctor, he is not one I can ask questions. Ask him for me, can I go home?"

Jeannie looked at her, said quickly: "Of course, poor Granny. You want your own things around you, don't you? I'll call him tonight. . . . Look, I've something to show you," and from her purse unwrapped a large cookie, intricately shaped like a little girl. "Look at the curls—can you hear me well, Granny?— and the darling eyelashes. I just came from a house where they were baking them."

"The dimples," she marveled, "there in the knees," holding it to the better light, turning, studying, "like art. Each singly they cut, or a mold?"

"Singly," said Jeannie, "and if it is a child only the mother can make them. Oh Granny, it's the likeness of a real little girl who died yesterday—Rosita. She was three years old. *Pan del Muerto*, the Bread of the Dead. It was the custom in the part of Mexico they came from."

Still she turned and inspected. "Look, the hollow in the throat, the little cross necklace. . . . I think for the mother it is a good thing to be busy with such bread. You know the family?"

Jeannie nodded. "On my rounds. I nursed. . . . Oh Granny, it is like a party; they play songs she liked to dance to. The coffin is lined with pink velvet and she wears a white dress. There are candles. . . ."

"In the house?" Surprised, "They keep her in the house?"

"Yes," said Jeannie, "and it is against the health law. I think she is . . . prepared there. The father said it will be sad to bury her in this country; in Oaxaca they have a feast night with candles each year; everyone picnics on the graves of those they loved until dawn."

"Yes, Jeannie, the living must comfort themselves." And closed her eyes.

"You want to sleep, Granny?"

"Yes, tired from the pleasure of you. I may keep the Rosita? There stand it, on the dresser, where I can see; something of my own around me."

In the kitchenette, helping her grandfather unpack the groceries, Jeannie said in her light voice:

"I'm resigning my job, Grandaddy."

"Ah, the lucky young man. Which one is he?"

"Too late. You're spoken for." She made a pyramid of cans, unstacked, and built again.

"Something is wrong with the job?"

"With me. I can't be"—she searched for the word—"What they call professional enough. I let myself feel things. And tomorrow I have to report a family. . . ." The cans clicked again. "It's not that, either. I just don't know what I want to do, maybe go back to school, maybe go to art school. I thought if you went to San Francisco I'd come along and talk it over with Mommy and Daddy. But I don't see how you can go. She wants to go home. She asked me to ask the doctor."

The doctor told her himself. "Next week you may travel, when you are a little stronger." But next week there was the fever of an infection, and by the time that was over, she could not leave the bed—a rented hospital bed that stood beside the double bed he slept in alone now.

Outwardly the days repeated themselves. Every other afternoon and evening he went out to his newfound cronies to talk and play cards. Twice a week, Mrs. Mays came. And the rest of the time, Jeannie was there.

By the sickbed stood Jeannie's FM radio. Often into the room the shapes of music came. She would lie curled on her side, her knees drawn up, intense in listening (Jeannie sketched her so, coiled, convoluted like an ear), then thresh her hand out and abruptly snap the radio mute—still to lie in her attitude of listening, concealing tears.

Once Jeannie brought in a young Marine to visit, a friend from high-school days she had found wandering near the empty pier. Because Jeannie asked him to, gravely, without self-consciousness, he sat himself cross-legged on the floor and performed for them a dance of his native Samoa.

Long after they left, a tiny thrumming sound could be heard where, in her bed, she strove to repeat the beckon, flight, surrender of his hands, the fluttering footbeats, and his low plaintive calls.

Hannah and Phil sent flowers. To deepen her pleasure he placed one in her hair. "Like a girl," he said, and brought the hand mirror so she could see. She looked at the pulsing red flower, the yellow skull face; a desolate, excited laugh shuddered from her, and she pushed the mirror away—but let the flower burn.

The week Lennie and Helen came, the fever returned. With it the excited laugh, and incessant words. She, who in her life had spoken but seldom and then only when necessary (never having learned the easy, social uses of words), now in dying, spoke incessantly.

In a half-whisper: "Like Lisa she is, your Jeannie. Have I told you of Lisa, she who taught me to read? Of the highborn she was, but noble in herself. I was sixteen; they beat me; my father beat me so I would not go to her. It was forbidden, she was a Tolstoyan.[4] At night, past dogs that howled, terrible dogs, my son, in the snows of winter to the road, I to ride in her carriage like a lady, to books. To her, life was holy, knowledge was holy, and she taught me to read.

4. I.e., a follower of Leo Tolstoy (1828–1910), Russian novelist, social reformer, and teacher of nonviolence.

They hung her. Everything that happens one must try to understand why. She killed one who betrayed many. Because of betrayal, betrayed all she lived and believed. In one minute she killed, before my eyes (there is so much blood in a human being, my son), in prison with me. All that happens, one must try to understand.

"The name?" Her lips would work. "The name that was their pole star; the doors of the death houses fixed to open on it; I read of it my year of penal servitude. Thuban!" very excited, "Thuban, in ancient Egypt the pole star. Can you see, look out to see it, Jeannie, if it swings around *our* pole star that seems to us not to move.

"Yes, Jeannie, at your age my mother and grandmother had already buried children . . . yes, Jeannie, it is more than oceans between Olshana and you . . . yes, Jeannie, they danced, and for all the bodies they had they might as well be chickens, and indeed, they scratched and flapped their arms and hopped.

"And Andrei Yefimitch, who was twenty years had never known of it and never wanted to know, said as if he wanted to cry: but why my dear friend this malicious laughter?" Telling to herself half-memorized phrases from her few books. "Pain I answer with tears and cries, baseness with indignation, meanness with repulsion . . . for life may be hated or wearied of, but never despised."

Delirious: "Tell me, my neighbor, Mrs. Mays, the pictures never lived, but what of the flowers? Tell them who ask: no rabbis, no ministers, no priests, no speeches, no ceremonies: ah, false—let the living comfort themselves. Tell Sammy's boy, he who flies, tell him to go to Stuttgart[5] and see where Davy has no grave. And what? And what? where millions have no graves save air."

In delirium or not, wanting the radio on; not seeming to listen, the words still jetting, wanting the music on. Once, silencing it abruptly as of old, she began to cry, unconcealed tears this time. "You have pain, Granny?" Jeannie asked.

"The music," she said, "still it is there and we do not hear; knocks, and our poor human ears too weak. What else, what else we do not hear?"

Once she knocked his hand aside as he gave her a pill, swept the bottles from her bedside table: "no pills, let me feel what I feel," and laughed as on his hands and knees he groped to pick them up.

Nighttimes her hand reached across the bed to hold his.

A constant retching began. Her breath was too faint for sustained speech now, but still the lips moved:

> When no longer necessary to injure others
> Pick pick pick Blind chicken
> As a human being responsibility for

"David!" imperious, "Basin!" and she would vomit, rinse her mouth, the wasted throat working to swallow, and begin the chant again.

She will be better off in the hospital now, the doctor said.

He sent the telegrams to the children, was packing her suitcase, when her hoarse voice startled. She had roused, was pulling herself to sitting.

5. City in Germany, which figured in World War II.

"Where now?" she asked. "Where now do you drag me?"

"You do not even have to have a baby to go this time," he soothed, looking for the brush to pack. "Remember, after Davy you told me—worthy to have a baby for the pleasure of the ten-day rest in the hospital?"

"Where now? Not home yet?" Her voice mourned. "Where *is* my home?"

He rose to ease her back. "The doctor, the hospital," he started to explain, but deftly, like a snake, she had slithered out of bed and stood swaying, propped behind the night table.

"Coward," she hissed, "runner."

"You stand," he said senselessly.

"To take me there and run. Afraid of a little vomit."

He reached her as she fell. She struggled against him, half slipped from his arms, pulled herself up again.

"Weakling," she taunted, "to leave me there and run. Betrayer. All your life you have run."

He sobbed, telling Jeannie. "A Marilyn Monroe to run for her virtue. Fifty-nine pounds she weighs, the doctor said, and she beats at me like a Dempsey.[6] Betrayer, she cries, and I running like a dog when she calls; day and night, running to her, her vomit, the bedpan. . . ."

"She needs you, Grandaddy," said Jeannie. "Isn't that what they call love? I'll see if she sleeps, and if she does, poor worn-out darling, we'll have a party, you and I; I brought us rum babas."

They did not move her. By her bed now stood the tall hooked pillar that held the solutions—blood and dextrose—to feed her veins. Jeannie moved down the hall to take over the sickroom, her face so radiant, her grandfather asked her once: "you are in love?" (Shameful the joy, the pure overwhelming joy from being with her grandmother, the peace, the serenity that breathed.) "My darling escape," she answered incoherently, "my darling Granny"—as if that explained.

Now one by one the children came, those that were able Hannah, Paul, Sammy. Too late to ask: and what did you learn with your living, Mother, and what do we need to know?

Clara, the eldest, clenched:

> Pay me back, Mother, pay me back for all you took from me. Those others you crowded into your heart. The hands I needed to be for you, the heaviness, the responsibility.
>
> Is this she? Noises the dying make, the crablike hands crawling over the covers. The ethereal singing.
>
> She hears that music, that singing from childhood; forgotten sound—not heard since, since. . . . And the hardness breaks like a cry: Where did we lose each other, first mother, singing mother?
>
> Annulled: the quarrels, the gibing, the harshness between; the fall into silence and the withdrawal.
>
> I do not know you, Mother. Mother, I never knew you.

6. Jack Dempsey (1895–1983), world heavyweight champion boxer in the 1920s.

Lennie, suffering not alone for her who was dying, but for that in her which never lived (for that which in him might never live). From him too, unspoken words: *good-bye Mother who taught me to mother myself.*

Not Vivi, who must stay with her children; not Davy, but he is already here, having to die again with *her* this time, for the living take their dead with them when they die.

Light she grew, like a bird, and, like a bird, sound bubbled in her throat while the body fluttered in agony. Night and day, asleep or awake (though indeed there was no difference now) the songs and the phrases leaping.

And he, who had once dreaded a long dying (from fear of himself, from horror of the dwindling money) now desired her quick death profoundly, for *her* sake. He no longer went out, except when Jeannie forced him; no longer laughed, except when, in the bright kitchenette, Jeannie coaxed his laughter (and she, who seemed to hear nothing else, would laugh too, conspiratorial wisps of laughter).

Light, like a bird, the fluttering body, the little claw hands, the beaked shadow on her face; and the throat, bubbling, straining.

He tried not to listen, as he tried not to look on the face in which only the forehead remained familiar, but trapped with her the long nights in that little room, the sounds worked themselves into his consciousness, with their punctuation of death swallows, whimpers, gurglings.

Even in reality (swallow) *life's lack of it*
Slaveships deathtrains clubs enough
The bell Summon what enables
78,000[7] *in one minute* (whisper of a scream) 78,000 *human beings we'll destroy ourselves?*

"Aah, Mrs. Miserable," he said, as if she could hear, "all your life working, and now in bed you lie, servants to tend, you do not even need to call to be tended, and still you work. Such hard work it is to die? Such hard work?"

The body threshed, her hand clung in his. A melody, ghost-thin, hovered on her lips, and like a guilty ghost, the vision of her vent in listening to it, silencing the record instantly he was near. Now, heedless of his presence, she floated the melody on and on.

"Hid it from me," he complained, "how many times you listened to remember it so?" And tried to think when she had first played it, or first begun to silence her few records when he came near—but could reconstruct nothing. There was only this room with its tall hooked pillar and its swarm of sounds.

No man one except through others
Strong with the not yet in the now
Dogma dead war dead one country

"It helps, Mrs. Philosopher, words from books? It helps?" And it seemed to him that for seventy years she had hidden a tape recorder, infinitely microscopic, within her, that it had coiled infinite mile on mile, trapping every song, every melody, every word read, heard and spoken—and that maliciously she was playing back only what said nothing of him, of the children, of their intimate life together.

7. The number killed in Hiroshima by the first atomic bomb.

"Left us indeed, Mrs. Babbler," he reproached, "you who called others babbler and cunningly saved your words. A lifetime you tended and loved, and now not a word of us, for us. Left us indeed? Left me."

And he took out his solitaire deck, shuffled the cards loudly, slapped them down.

Lift high banner of reason (tatter of an orator's voice) *justice freedom-light*

Humankind life worthy capacities

Seeks (blur of shudder) *belong human being*

"Words, words," he accused, "and what human beings did *you* seek around you, Mrs. Live Alone, and what mankind think worthy?"

Though even as he spoke, he remembered she had not always been isolated, had not always to be alone (as he knew there had been a voice before this gossamer one; before the hoarse voice that broke from silence to lash, make incidents, shame him—a girl's voice of eloquence that spoke their holiest dreams). But again he could reconstruct, image, nothing of what had been before, or when, or how, it had changed.

Ace, queen, jack. The pillar shadow fell, so, in two tracks; in the mirror depths glistened a moonlike blob, the empty solution bottle. And it worked in him: *reason and justice and freedom. Dogma dead*· he remembered the full quotation, laughed bitterly. "Hah, good you do not know what you say; good Victor Hugo[8] died and did not see it, his twentieth century."

Deuce, ten, five. Dauntlessly she began a song of their youth of belief:

These things shall be.[9] A loftier race
than e'er the world hath known shall rise
with flame of freedom in their souls
and light of knowledge in their eyes

King, four, jack. "In the twentieth century, hah!"

They shall be gentle, brave and strong
to spill no drop of blood, but dare
all . . .

on earth and fire and sea and air

"To spill no drop of blood, hah! So, cadaver, and you too, cadaver Hugo, 'in the twentieth century ignorance will be dead, prejudice will be dead, war will be dead, and for all mankind one country—of fulfillment.' Hah!"

And every life (long strangling cough) *shall be a song*

The cards fell from his fingers. Without warning, the bereavement and betrayal he had sheltered—compounded through the years—hidden even from himself—revealed itself,

8. Victor Hugo (1802–1885), French writer and champion of liberty; he prophesied the triumph of peace and liberty in the 20th century.

9. Century-old socialist song, now a United Nations hymn. The first line is a translation of the French Revolutionary slogan *Ça ira*.

uncoiled,
released,
sprung

and with it the monstrous shapes of what had actually happened in the century.

A ravening hunger or thirst seized him. He groped into the kitchenette, switched on all three lights, piled a tray—"you have finished your night snack, Mrs. Cadaver, now I will have mine." And he was shocked at the tears that splashed on the tray.

"Salt tears. For free. I forgot to shake on salt?"

Whispered: "Lost, how much I lost."

Escaped to the grandchildren whose childhoods were childish, who had never hungered, who lived unravaged by disease in warm houses of many rooms, had all the school for which they cared, could walk on any street, stood a head taller than their grandparents, towered above—beautiful skins, straight backs, clear straightforward eyes. "Yes, you in Olshana," he said to the town of sixty years ago, "they would be nobility to you."

And was this not the dream then, come true in ways undreamed? he asked.

And are there no other children in the world? he answered, as if in her harsh voice.

And the flame of freedom, the light of knowledge?

And the drop, to spill no drop of blood?

And he thought that at six Jeannie would get up and it would be his turn to go to her room and sleep, that he could press the buzzer and she would come now; that in the afternoon Ellen Mays was coming, and this time they would play cards and he could marvel at how rouge can stand half an inch on the cheek; that in the evening the doctor would come, and he could beg him to be merciful, to stop the feeding solutions, to let her die.

To let her die, and with her their youth of belief out of which her bright, betrayed words foamed; stained words, that on her working lips came stainless.

Hours yet before Jeannie's turn. He could press the buzzer and wake her to come now; he could take a pill, and with it sleep; he could pour more brandy into his milk glass, though what he had poured was not yet touched.

Instead he went back, checked her pulse, gently tended with his knotty fingers as Jeannie had taught.

She was whimpering; her hand crawled across the covers for his. Compassionately he enfolded it, and with his free hand gathered up the cards again. Still was there thirst or hunger ravening in him.

That world of their youth—dark, ignorant, terrible with hate and disease—how was it that living in it, in the midst of corruption, filth, treachery, degradation, they had not mistrusted man nor themselves; had believed so beautifully, so . . . falsely?

"Aaah, children," he said out loud, "how we believed, how we belonged." And he yearned to package for each of the children, the grandchildren, for everyone, *that joyous certainty, that sense of mattering, of moving and being moved, of being one and indivisible with the great of the past, with all that freed, ennobled.* Package it, stand on corners, in front of stadiums and on crowded beaches, knock on doors, give it as a fabled gift.

"And why not in cereal boxes, in soap packages?" he mocked himself. "Aah. You have taken my senses, cadaver."

Words foamed, died unsounded. Her body writhed; she made kissing motions with her mouth. (Her lips moving as she read, poring over the Book of the Martyrs the magnifying glass superimposed over the heavy eyeglasses.) *Still she believed?* "Eva!" he whispered. "Still you believed? You lived by it? These Things Shall Be?"

"One pound soup meat," she answered distinctly, "one soup bone."

"My ears heard you. Ellen Mays was witness 'Man . . . one has to believe.' " Imploringly: "Eva!"

"Bread, day-old." She was mumbling. "Please, in a wooden box . . . for kindling. The thread, hah, the thread breaks. Cheap thread"—and a gurgling, enormously loud, began in her throat.

"I ask for stone; she gives me bread—day-old." He pulled his hand away, shouted: "Who wanted questions? Everything you have to wake?" Then dully, "Ah, let me help you turn, poor creature."

Words jumbled, cleared. In a voice of crowded terror:

"Paul, Sammy, don't fight.

"Hannah, have I ten hands?

"How can I give it, Clara, how can I give it if I don't have?"

"You lie," he said sturdily, "there was joy too." Bitterly: "Ah how cheap you speak of us at the last."

As if to rebuke him, as if her voice had no relationship with her flailing body, she sang clearly, beautifully, a school song the children had taught her when they were little; begged:

"Not look my hair where they cut. . ."

(The crown of braids shorn.) And instantly he left the mute old woman poring over the Book of the Martyrs; went past the mother treadling at the sewing machine, singing with the children; past the girl in her wrinkled prison dress, hiding her hair with scarred hands, lifting to him her awkward, shamed, imploring eyes of love; and took her in his arms, dear, personal, fleshed, in all the heavy passion he had loved to rouse from her.

"Eva!"

Her little claw hand beat the covers. How much, how much can a man stand? He took up the cards, put them down, circled the beds, walked to the dresser, opened, shut drawers, brushed his hair, moved his hand bit by bit over the mirror to see what of the reflection he could blot out with each move, and felt that at any moment he would die of what was unendurable. Went to press the buzzer to wake Jeannie, looked down, saw on Jeannie's sketch pad the hospital bed, with *her*; the double bed alongside, with him; the tall pillar feeding into her veins, and their hands, his and hers, clasped, feeding each other. And as if he had been instructed he went to his bed, lay down, holding the sketch as if it could shield against the monstrous shapes of loss, of betrayal, of death—and with his free hand took hers back into his.

So Jeannie found them in the morning.

That last day the agony was perpetual. Time after time it lifted her almost off the bed, so they had to fight to hold her down. He could not endure and left the room; wept as if there never would be tears enough.

Jeannie came to comfort him. In her light voice she said: Grandaddy, Grandaddy don't cry. She is not there, she promised me. On the last day, she said she would go back to when she first heard music, a little girl on the road of the village where she was born. She promised me. It is a wedding and they

dance, while the flutes so joyous and vibrant tremble in the air. Leave her
there, Grandaddy, it is all right. She promised me. Come back, come back and
help her poor body to die.

> *For two of that generation*
> *Seevya and Genya*
>
> *Infinite, Dauntless, Incorruptible*
>
> *Death deepens the wonder*
>
> 1961

RUTH STONE

1915–

"I found that poems came with this mysterious feeling, and it was a kind of pecu-
liar ecstasy," the poet Ruth Stone once explained to an interviewer, noting that
"my mother read poetry—Tennyson—to me from the time, apparently, she
started suckling me at her breasts." Sometimes exuberant, often elegiac, and al-
ways elegant, Stone works with notable integrity and intensity to shape the "pecu-
liar ecstasy" of such aesthetic visions. Born in Roanoke, Virginia, she was raised in
Indiana and Illinois. After graduating from the University of Illinois, she married
twice—her second husband was the critic-novelist Walter Stone, who died in
1958—and she is the mother of three daughters. The winner of several
Guggenheim fellowships, she has published five collections of poetry: *In an
Iridescent Time* (1958), *Topography* (1970), *Cheap* (1975), *Second-Hand Coat:
New and Selected Poems* (1987), and *Simplicity* (1995). Supporting herself as a
teacher and poet-in-residence at such institutions as the University of Illinois, the
University of Wisconsin, Indiana University, the University of California at Davis,
Brandeis University, and SUNY Binghamton, she has consistently concentrated
her attention on the situations of women as different as the stubborn survivor of
Absinthe Granny and the acquiescent housewife of *Second-Hand Coat*. At the
same time, in such metaphysical meditations as *Periphery* and *Things I Say to
Myself While Hanging Laundry*, she addresses major philosophical questions—the
mind-body problem, the self in the cosmos—from a distinctly feminist perspective.

In an Iridescent Time

My mother, when young, scrubbed laundry in a tub,
She and her sisters on an old brick walk
Under the apple trees, sweet rub-a-dub.
The bees came round their heads, the wrens made talk.
Four young ladies each with a rainbow board 5
Honed their knuckles, wrung their wrists to red,
Tossed back their braids and wiped their aprons wet.
The Jersey calf beyond the back fence roared;
And all the soft day, swarms about their pet
Buzzed at his big brown eyes and bullish head. 10

Four times they rinsed, they said. Some things they starched,
Then shook them from the baskets two by two,
And pinned the fluttering intimacies of life
Between the lilac bushes and the yew:
Brown gingham, pink, and skirts of Alice blue.[1] 15

 1958

Periphery

You are not wanted
I said to the older body
Who was listening near the cupboards.
But outside on the porch
They were all eating. 5
The body dared not
Put its fingers in its mouth.
Behave, I whispered,
You have a wart on your cheek
And everyone knows you drink. 10
But that's all right, I relented,
It isn't generally known
How clever you are.
I know you aren't appreciated.
The body hunted for something good to eat, 15
But the food had all been eaten by the others.
They laughed together carelessly outside the kitchen.
The body hid in the pantry near the refrigerator.
After a while it laughed, too. 20
It listened to all the jokes and it laughed.

 1975

The Song of Absinthe[1] Granny

Among some hills there dwelt in parody
A young woman; me.
I was that gone with child
That before I knew it I had three
And they hung whining and twisting. 5
Why I wasn't more than thirty-nine
And sparse as a runt fruit tree.
Three pips[2] that plagued the life out of me.
Ah me. It wore me down,
The grubs, the grubbing. 10
We were two inches thick in dust
For lack of scrubbing.
Diapers and panty-shirts and yolk of eggs.
One day in the mirror I saw my stringy legs

1. A pale shade of blue. 2. Small seeds; anything small.
1. A strong liqueur made from wormwood.

And I looked around 15
And saw string on the floor,
And string on the chair
And heads like wasps' nests
Full of stringy hair.
"Well," I said, "if you have string, knit. 20
Knit something, don't just sit."
We had the orchard drops,[3]
But they didn't keep.
The milk came in bottles.
It came until the bottles were that deep 25
We fell over the bottles.
The milk dried on the floor.
"Drink it up," cried their papa,
And they all began to roar, "More!"
Well, time went on, 30
Not a bone that wasn't frayed.
Every chit was knicked[4] and bit,
And nothing was paid.
We had the dog spayed.
"It looks like a lifetime," 35
Their papa said.
"It's a good life, it's a good wife,
It's a good bed."
So I got the rifle out
To shoot him through the head. 40
But he went on smiling and sitting
And I looked around for a piece of string
To do some knitting.
Then I picked at the tiling
And the house fell down. 45
"Now you've done it," he said.
"I'm going to town.
Get them up out of there,
Put them to bed."
"I'm afraid to look," I whimpered, 50
"They might be dead."
"We're here, mama, under the shed."
Well, the winters wore on.
We had cats that hung around.
When I fed them they scratched. 55
How the little nippers loved them.
Cats and brats.
I couldn't see for my head was thatched
But they kept coming in when the door unlatched.
"I'll shave my head," I promised, 60
"I'll clip my mop.
This caterwauling has got to stop."
Well, all that's finished,
It's all been done.

3. Fruit fallen from trees.
4. Snapped. "Chit": voucher of a small debt, especially for food.

Those were high kick summers, 65
It was bald galled fun.
Now the daft time's over
And the string is spun.
I'm all alone
To cull[5] and be furry. 70
Not an extra page in the spanking story
The wet britches dried
And the teeth came in.
The last one cried
And no new began. 75
Those were long hot summers,
Now the sun won't tarry.
My birds have flocked,
And I'm old and wary.
I'm old and worn and a cunning sipper, 80
And I'll outlive every little nipper.
And with what's left I'm chary,
And with what's left I'm chary.

 1975

Second-Hand Coat

I feel
in her pockets; she wore nice cotton gloves,
kept a handkerchief box, washed her undies,
ate at the Holiday Inn, had a basement freezer,
belonged to a bridge club. 5
I think when I wake in the morning
that I have turned into her.
She hangs in the hall downstairs,
a shadow with pulled threads.
I slip her over my arms, skin of a matron. 10
Where are you? I say to myself, to the orphaned body,
and her coat says,
Get your purse, have you got your keys?

 1931

Names

My grandmother's name was Nora Swan.
Old Aden Swan was her father. But who was her mother?
I don't know my great-grandmother's name.
I don't know how many children she bore.
Like rings of a tree the years of woman's fertility. 5
Who were my great-aunt Swans?
For every year a child; diphtheria, dropsy, typhoid.

5. Gather, collect.

Who can bother naming all those women churning butter,
leaning on scrub boards, holding to iron bedposts,
sweating in labor? My grandmother knew the names 10
of all the plants on the mountain. Those were the names
she spoke of to me. Sorrel, lamb's ear, spleenwort, heal-all;
never go hungry, she said, when you can gather a pot of greens.
She had a finely drawn head under a smooth cap of hair
pulled back to a bun. Her deep-set eyes were quick to notice 15
in love and anger. Who are the women who nurtured her for me?
Who handed her in swaddling flannel to my great-grandmother's breast?
Who are the women who brought my great-grandmother tea
and straightened her bed? As anemone in midsummer, the air
cannot find them and grandmother's been at rest for forty years. 20
In me are all the names I can remember—pennyroyal, boneset,
bedstraw, toadflax[1]—from whom I did descend in perpetuity.

 1987

Things I Say to Myself While Hanging Laundry

If an ant, crossing on the clothesline
from apple tree to apple tree,
would think and think,
it probably could not dream up Albert Einstein.
Or even his sloppy mustache; 5
or the wrinkled skin bags under his eyes
that puffed out years later,
after he dreamed up that maddening relativity.[1]
Even laundry is three dimensional.
The ants cross its great fibrous forests 10
from clothespin to clothespin
carrying the very heart of life in their sacs or mandibles,
the very heart of the universe in their formic acid molecules.
And how refreshing the linens are,
lying in the clean sheets at night, 15
when you seem to be the only one on the mountain,
and your body feels the smooth touch of the bed
like love against your skin;
and the heavy sac of yourself relaxes into its embrace.
When you turn out the light, 20
you are blind in the dark
as perhaps the ants are blind,
with the same abstract leap out of this limiting dimension.
So that the very curve of light,
as it is pulled in the dimple of space,[2] 25
is relative to your own blind pathway across the abyss.
And there in the dark is Albert Einstein

1. All herbs.
1. The idea that time and motion are relative to the
observer, if the speed of light is constant in all frames
of reference. Albert Einstein (1879–1955) was only in
his twenties when he published his papers on the spe-
cial theory of relativity.
2. I.e., by gravity. According to Einstein's general the-
ory of relativity, which predicted such curvature of
light, gravity is a curved field created by mass.

with his clever formula[3] that looks like little mandibles
digging tunnels into the earth
and bringing it up, grain by grain, 30
the crystals of sand exploding
into white hot radiant turbulence,
smiling at you, his shy bushy smile,
along an imaginary line from here to there.

1995

3. Expressing the equivalence of mass and energy in the famous equation $E = mc^2$.

MARGARET WALKER

1915–

The dedication of Margaret Walker's *For My People*, a volume that was chosen for the Yale Series of Younger Poets in 1942, acknowledged her indebtedness to and her sense of responsibility for "my people everywhere singing their slave songs repeatedly: their dirges and their ditties and their blues and jubilees." In many of the poems she included in this book, moreover, Walker used jazz rhythms and blues meters to present the grace and daring of such folk characters as Stagolee, Molly Means, Poppa Chicken, Kissie Lee, and Yalluh Hammuh. Caught in a culture oblivious to the "black and poor and small and different," Walker's characters reflect her effort "to fashion a world that will hold all the people, all the faces, all the adams and eves and their countless generations."

One of four children of Sigismund Walker, a Methodist minister, and Marion Dozier Walker, a musicologist, Margaret Walker was born in Birmingham, Alabama. Educated at church schools in Mississippi, Alabama, and Louisiana, she began composing verse at thirteen years of age. During her undergraduate days at Northwestern University, she "went hungry unless friends fed me." Yet she received her B.A. in 1935, and her M.A. and Ph.D. from the University of Iowa in 1940 and 1965. After she married in 1943, she began teaching at Livingstone College in Salisbury, North Carolina. Now retired, she was a professor of English at Jackson State College in Mississippi, where she supported a disabled husband and four children on a salary that remained for many years well under $5,000. She also established a black studies program at Jackson. In both her academic life and her literary career, Walker has self-consciously attempted to nurture the growth of black culture. *Prophets for a New Day* (1970) and *October Journey* (1973) include a number of sonnets and ballads about the human rights struggle, just as her historical novel *Jubilee* (1966), which won the Houghton Mifflin Literary Fellowship, uses the traditional genre of the slave narrative to celebrate a heroic woman who simultaneously moves into maturity and freedom. In her mid-seventies, Walker produced a biography of Richard Wright, *The Daemonic Genius of Richard Wright* (1989), as well as a collection of autobiographical essays, *How I Wrote Jubilee and Other Essays on Life and Literature* (1990).

Dark Blood

There were bizarre beginnings in old lands for the making of me. There were
 sugar sands and islands of fern and pearl, palm jungles and stretches of
 a never-ending sea.

There were the wooing nights of tropical lands and the cool discretion of flow-
 ering plains between two stalwart hills. They nurtured my coming with
 wanderlust. I sucked fevers of adventure through my veins with my
 mother's milk.

Someday I shall go to the tropical lands of my birth, to the coasts of continents
 and the tiny wharves of island shores. I shall roam the Balkans[1] and the
 hot lanes of Africa and Asia. I shall stand on mountain tops and gaze on
 fertile homes below.

And when I return to Mobile I shall go by the way of Panama and Bocas del
 Toro[2] to the littered streets and the one-room shacks of my old poverty,
 and blazing suns of other lands may struggle then to reconcile the pride
 and pain in me.

 1942

Lineage

My grandmothers were strong.
They followed plows and bent to toil.
They moved through fields sowing seed.
They touched earth and grain grew.
They were full of sturdiness and singing. 5
My grandmothers were strong.

My grandmothers are full of memories
Smelling of soap and onions and wet clay
With veins rolling roughly over quick hands
They have many clean words to say. 10
My grandmothers were strong.
Why am I not as they?

 1942

Molly Means

Old Molly Means was a hag and a witch;
Chile of the devil, the dark, and sitch.
Her heavy hair hung thick in ropes
And her blazing eyes was black as pitch.
Imp at three and wench at 'leben 5
She counted her husbands to the number seben.
 O Molly, Molly, Molly Means
 There goes the ghost of Molly Means.

Some say she was born with a veil[1] on her face
So she could look through unnatchal space 10

1. Mountain range in Bulgaria.
2. A town in Panama. Mobile is a city in Alabama.
1. I.e., a caul. Being born with a membrane covering
one's face was thought to be a sign of supernatural
powers.

Through the future and through the past
And charm a body or an evil place
And every man could well despise
The evil look in her coal black eyes.
 Old Molly, Molly, Molly Means 15
 Dark is the ghost of Molly Means.

And when the tale begun to spread
Of evil and of holy dread:
Her black-hand arts and her evil powers
How she cast her spells and called the dead, 20
The younguns was afraid at night
And the farmers feared their crops would blight.
 Old Molly, Molly, Molly Means
 Cold is the ghost of Molly Means.

Then one dark day she put a spell 25
On a young gal-bride just come to dwell
In the lane just down from Molly's shack
And when her husband come riding back
His wife was barking like a dog
And on all fours like a common hog. 30
 O Molly, Molly, Molly Means
 Where is the ghost of Molly Means?

The neighbors come and they went away
And said she'd die before break of day
But her husband held her in his arms 35
And swore he'd break the wicked charms;
He'd search all up and down the land
And turn the spell on Molly's hand.
 O Molly, Molly, Molly Means
 Sharp is the ghost of Molly Means. 40

So he rode all day and he rode all night
And at the dawn he come in sight
Of a man who said he could move the spell
And cause the awful thing to dwell
On Molly Means, to bark and bleed 45
Till she died at the hands of her evil deed.
 Old Molly, Molly, Molly Means
 This is the ghost of Molly Means.

Sometimes at night through the shadowy trees
She rides along on a winter breeze. 50
You can hear her holler and whine and cry.
Her voice is thin and her moan is high,
And her cackling laugh or her barking cold
Bring terror to the young and old.
 O Molly, Molly, Molly Means 55
 Lean is the ghost of Molly Means.

1942

Kissie Lee

Toughest gal I ever did see
Was a gal by the name of Kissie Lee;
The toughest gal God ever made
And she drew a dirty, wicked blade.

Now this here gal warn't always tough 5
Nobody dreamed she'd turn out rough
But her Grammaw Mamie had the name
Of being the town's sin and shame.

When Kissie Lee was young and good
Didn't nobody treat her like they should 10
Allus gettin' beat by a no-good shine[1]
An' allus quick to cry and whine.

Till her Grammaw said, "Now listen to me,
I'm tiahed of yoah whinin', Kissie Lee.
People don't never treat you right, 15
An' you allus scrappin' or in a fight.

"Whin I was a gal wasn't no soul
Could do me wrong an' still stay whole.
Ah got me a razor to talk for me
An' aftah that they let me be." 20

Well Kissie Lee took her advice
And after that she didn't speak twice
'Cause when she learned to stab and run
She got herself a little gun.

And from that time that gal was mean, 25
Meanest mama you ever seen.
She could hold her likker and hold her man
And she went thoo life jus' raisin' san'.[2]

One night she walked in Jim's saloon 30
And seen a guy what spoke too soon;
He done her dirt long time ago
When she was good and feeling low.

Kissie bought her drink and she paid her dime
Watchin' this guy what beat her time
And he was making for the outside door 35
When Kissie shot him to the floor.

Not a word she spoke but she switched her blade
And flashing that lil ole baby paid:

1. Person with jet-black skin. 2. I.e., raising dust, moving briskly

Evvy livin' guy got out of her way
Because Kissie Lee was drawin' her pay 40

She could shoot glass doors offa the hinges,
She could take herself on the wildest binges.
And she died with her boots on switching blades
On Talladega Mountain in the likker raids.[3]

1942

Whores

When I grew up I went away to work
where painted whores were fascinating sights.
They came on like whole armies through the nights—
their sullen eyes on mine, their mouths a smirk,
and from their hands keys hung suggestively. 5
Old women working by an age-old plan
to make their bread in ways as best they can
would hobble past and beckon tirelessly.

Perhaps one day they'll all die in the streets
or be surprised by bombs in each wide bed; 10
learning too late in unaccustomed dread
that easy ways, like whores on special beats,
no longer have the gift to harbor pride
or bring men peace, or leave them satisfied.

1942

3. Police raids made during Prohibition on people manufacturing illegal, "bootleg," liquor.

JUDITH WRIGHT

1915–

Lamenting that "the song is gone; the dance / is secret with the dancers in the earth," the Australian poet Judith Wright mourned in *Bora Ring*, an early poem, the dispersal and destruction of the aborigines who inhabited her native land before it was conquered by the British. In part, those lines predicted one major direction her artistic career would take: in producing more than a dozen volumes of verse and a number of collections of essays on criticism and articles on conservation, as well as editing several anthologies of Australian poetry, this prolific writer has memorialized Australia as "my blood's country . . . the high lean country / full of old stories that still go walking in my sleep." At the same time, however, much of her poetry has spoken of such matters from a distinctively female perspective, a point of view explicitly summarized by the title of her second book, *Woman to Man* (1949).

The descendant of what one commentator calls "pioneering rural stock," Wright was born in Armidale, New South Wales, and educated at New England Girls School, Armidale, and the University of Sydney. Married to J. P. McKinney,

and the mother of one daughter, she worked for some time as a secretary and civil servant before taking up a position as honors tutor in English at the University of Queensland. In recent years, she has become increasingly involved in political action, including both the antiwar movement of the 1960s and Australia's conservationist movement. Cofounder and former president of the Wild Life Preservation Society of Queensland, she now lives in a wildlife sanctuary near Braidwood.

Such poems as *Ishtar* and *Eve to Her Daughters* suggest the connections that Wright sees between female power and the forces of nature, even while they explore the relationship between Adam's fear that "outside Eden the earth was imperfect" and the twentieth century's assault on the environment. That this poet identifies deeply with women's literary tradition is also made clear in these works, as well as in her "*Rosina Alcona to Julius Brenzaida*," a piece whose title is taken from a poem by another female acolyte of nature—the Victorian poet-novelist Emily Brontë.

Half-Caste[1] Girl

Little Josie buried under the bright moon
is tired of being dead, death lasts too long.
She would like to push death aside, and stand on the hill
and beat with a waddy[2] on the bright moon like a gong.

Across the hills, the hills that belong to no people 5
and so to none are foreign,
once she climbed high to find the native cherry;
the lithe darkhearted lubra[3]
who in her beads like blood
dressed delicately for love 10
moves her long hands among the strings of the wind,
singing the songs of women,
the songs of love and dying.

Against the world's stone walls she thrust her heart—
endless the strength of its beating— 15
atom of flesh that cannot move a stone.
She used her love for lever;
but the wall is cunningly made.
Not even the strong break jail.
So she is restless still under her rootwarm cover, 20
hearing the noise of living,
forgetting the pain of dying.

Little Josie buried under the bright sun
would like to open her eyes and dance in the light.
Who is it has covered the sun and the beautiful moon 25
with a wallaby[4] skin, and left her alone in the night?

1946

1. Of mixed racial descent.
2. A club used as a weapon by Australian aborigines.
3. Aboriginal Australian woman.
4. Small kangaroo.

The Sisters

In the vine-shadows on the veranda,
under the yellow leaves, in the cooling sun
sit the two sisters. Their slow voices run
like little winter creeks dwindled by frost and wind,
and the square of sunlight moves on the veranda. 5

They remember the gay young men on their tall horses
who came courting; the dancing and the smells of leather
and wine, the girls whispering by the fire together:
even their dolls and ponies, all they have left behind
moves in the yellow shadows on the veranda. 10

Thinking of their lives apart and the men they married,
thinking of the marriage-bed and the birth of the first child,
they look down smiling. "My life was wide and wild,
and who can know my heart? There in that golden jungle
I walk alone," say the old sisters on the veranda. 15

1949

Ishtar[1]

When I first saw a woman after childbirth
the room was full of your glance who had just gone away.
And when the mare was bearing her foal
you were with her but I did not see your face.

When in fear I became a woman 5
I first felt your hand.
When the shadow of the future first fell across me
it was your shadow, my grave and hooded attendant.

It is all one whether I deny or affirm you;
it is not my mind you are concerned with. 10
It is no matter whether I submit or rebel
the event will still happen.

You neither know nor care for the truth of my heart;
but the truth of my body has all to do with you.
You have no need of my thoughts or my hopes. 15
living in the realm of the absolute event.

Then why is it that when I at last see your face
under that hood of slate-blue, so calm and dark,
so worn with the burden of an inexpressible knowledge—
why is it that I begin to worship you with tears? 20

1953

1. Babylonian goddess of love and fertility.

Request to a Year

If the year is meditating a suitable gift,
I should like it to be the attitude
of my great-great-grandmother,
legendary devotee of the arts,

who, having had eight children 5
and little opportunity for painting pictures,
sat one day on a high rock
beside a river in Switzerland

and from a difficult distance viewed
her second son, balanced on a small ice-floe, 10
drift down the current towards a waterfall
that struck rock-bottom eighty feet below,

while her second daughter, impeded,
no doubt, by the petticoats of the day,
stretched out a last-hope alpenstock[1] 15
(which luckily later caught him on his way).

Nothing, it was evident, could be done;
and with the artist's isolating eye
my great-great-grandmother hastily sketched the scene.
The sketch survives to prove the story by. 20

Year, if you have no Mother's Day present planned,
reach back and bring me the firmness of her hand.

 1955

To Another Housewife

Do you remember how we went,
on duty bound, to feed the crowd
of hungry dogs your father kept
as rabbit-hunters? Lean and loud,
half-starved and furious, how they leapt 5
against their chains, as though they meant
in mindless rage for being fed,
to tear our childish hands instead!

With tomahawk and knife we hacked
the flyblown tatters of old meat, 10
gagged at their carcass-smell, and threw
the scraps and watched the hungry eat.
Then turning faint, we made a pact,
(two greensick girls), crossed hearts and swore
to touch no meat forever more. 15

1. A walking stick used in mountain climbing.

How many cuts of choice and prime
our housewife hands have dressed since then—
these hands with love and blood imbrued—
for daughters, sons, and hungry men!
How many creatures bred for food 20
we've raised and fattened for the time
they met at last the steaming knife
that serves the feast of death-in-life!

And as the evening meal is served
we hear the turned-down radio 25
begin to tell the evening news
just as the family joint[1] is carved.
O murder, famine, pious wars. . . .
Our children shrink to see us so,
in sudden meditation, stand 30
with knife and fork in either hand

 1966

Eve[1] to Her Daughters

It was not I who began it.
Turned out into drafty caves,
hungry so often, having to work for our bread,
hearing the children whining,
I was nevertheless not unhappy. 5
Where Adam went I was fairly contented to go.
I adapted myself to the punishment: it was my life.

But Adam, you know . . . !
He kept on brooding over the insult,
over the trick They had played on us, over the scolding. 10
He had discovered a flaw in himself
and he had to make up for it.

Outside Eden the earth was imperfect,
the seasons changed, the game was fleet-footed,
he had to work for our living, and he didn't like it. 15
He even complained of my cooking
(it was hard to compete with Heaven).

So he set to work.
The earth must be made a new Eden
with central heating, domesticated animals, 20
mechanical harvesters, combustion engines,
escalators, refrigerators,
and modern means of communication
and multiplied opportunities for safe investment

1. I.e., joint of roast meat.
1. The first woman, created by God as a companion for
Adam in the Garden of Eden; tempted by the serpent
into eating the forbidden fruit of the Tree of
Knowledge, which she gave to Adam; this precipitated
the Fall, their expulsion from Eden, and the introduc-
tion of work, pain, and death into the world (Genesis 3).

and higher education for Abel and Cain[2] 25
and the rest of the family.
You can see how his pride had been hurt.

In the process he had to unravel everything,
because he believed that mechanism
was the whole secret—he was always mechanical-minded. 30
He got to the very inside of the whole machine
exclaiming as he went, So this is how it works!
And now that I know how it works, why, I must have invented it.
As for God and the Other, they cannot be demonstrated,
and what cannot be demonstrated 35
doesn't exist.
You see, he had always been jealous.

Yes, he got to the center
where nothing at all can be demonstrated.
And clearly he doesn't exist; but he refuses 40
to accept the conclusion.
You see, he was always an egotist.

It was warmer than this in the cave;
there was none of this fall-out.
I would suggest, for the sake of the children, 45
that it's time you took over.

But you are my daughters, you inherit my own faults of character;
you are submissive, following Adam
even beyond existence.
Faults of character have their own logic 50
and it always works out.
I observed this with Abel and Cain.

Perhaps the whole elaborate fable
right from the beginning
is meant to demonstrate this; perhaps it's the whole secret. 55
Perhaps nothing exists but our faults?
At least they can be demonstrated.

But it's useless to make
such a suggestion to Adam.
He has turned himself into God, 60
who is faultless, and doesn't exist.

 1966

Naked Girl and Mirror

This is not I. I had no body once—
only what served my need to laugh and run

2. The first two sons of Adam and Eve; Cain murdered Abel out of jealousy because God preferred Abel's offerings.

and stare at stars and tentatively dance
on the fringe of foam and wave and sand and sun.
Eyes loved, hands reached for me, but I was gone 5
on my own currents, quicksilver, thistledown.
Can I be trapped at last in that soft face?

I stare at you in fear, dark brimming eyes.
Why do you watch me with that immoderate plea—
"Look under these curled lashes, recognize 10
that you were always here; know me—be me."
Smooth once-hermaphrodite[1] shoulders, too tenderly
your long slope runs, above those sudden shy
curves furred with light that spring below your space.

No, I have been betrayed. If I had known 15
that this girl waited between a year and a year,
I'd not have chosen her bough to dance upon.
Betrayed, by that little darkness here, and here
this swelling softness and that frightened stare
from eyes I will not answer; shut out here 20
from my own self, by its new body's grace—

for I am betrayed by someone lovely. Yes,
I see you are lovely, hateful naked girl.
Your lips in the mirror tremble as I refuse
to know or claim you. Let me go—let me be gone. 25
You are half of some other who may never come.
Why should I tend you? You are not my own;
you seek that other—he will be your home.

Yet I pity your eyes in the mirror, misted with tears;
I lean to your kiss. I must serve you; I will obey. 30
Some day we may love. I may miss your going, some day,
though I shall always resent your dumb and fruitful years.
Your lovers shall learn better, and bitterly too,
if their arrogance dares to think I am part of you.

 1966

"Rosina Alcona to Julius Bremzaida"[1]

Living long is containing
archaean[2] levels,
buried yet living.
Greek urns, their lovely tranquillity
still and yet moving, 5
directing, surviving.

So driving homewards
full of my present

1. With both female and male characteristics.
1. The title of a poem by Emily Brontë (1819–1848), quoted in lines 38–39 and echoed in line 54 (see p. 794).
2. Belonging to the earliest geological periods.

along the new freeway,
carved straight, rushing forward, 10
I see suddenly there still
that anachronism, the old wooden pub
stranded at the crossways.

Where you and I once
in an absolute present 15
drank laughing
in a day still living,
still laughing, still permanent.

Present crossed past
synchronized, at the junction. 20
The daylight of one day
was deepened, was darkened
by the light of another.

Three faces met,
your vivid face in life, 25
your face of dead marble
touched mine simultaneously.

Holding the steering-wheel
my hands freeze. Out of my eyes
jump these undryable tears 30
from artesian pressures,
from the strata that cover you,
the silt-sift of time.

These gulping dry lines
are not my song for you. 35
That's made already.
Come in, dead Emily.

Have I forgot, my only Love, to love thee,
Severed at last by time's all-wearing wave?

A work of divinest anguish, 40
a Greek urn completed.
I grip the steering-wheel.
No other star has ever shone for me.

The pure poem rises
in lovely tranquillity, 45
as the Greek urn rises
from the soil of the past,
as the lost face rises
and the tears return.

I move through my present 50
gripping the steering-wheel,
repeating, repeating it.

The crossways fade; the freeway rushes forward.
"These days obscure but cannot do thee wrong."

 1971

Some Words

Unless

Had a whole dream once
full of nothing else

A bottomless pit,
eyes bulged out 5
across it,
neck stretched out
over it.

A whole life I know of
fell into it 10
once;
and never came back.

Therefore

Three white lines
joining exactly, 15
all the angles
equal.[1]

Inside it—
symmetrical
cross-legged, 20
one finger up,
expounding a simple fact
sits Nobody.

A perfect confined space;
not one star 25
shines in.

Enough

No use, we'll never catch it.
It's just ahead,
a puff 30
of flying light.

Want it! want it!
Wake up at night

1. In mathematical proofs, the symbol for *therefore* is three dots, placed as if at the points of an equilateral triangle (∴).

crying for it,
walk round all day 35
needing it.

Till one day
it's there.

Not needed any more,
not even wanted. 40

Look at it without a smile.
Turn away.

 1973

Counting in Sevens

Seven ones are seven.
I can't remember that year
or what presents I was given.

Seven twos are fourteen.
That year I found my mind, 5
swore not to be what I had been.

Seven threes are twenty-one.
I was sailing my own sea,
first in love, the knots undone.

Seven fours are twenty-eight; 10
three false starts had come and gone;
my true love came, and not too late.

Seven fives are thirty-five.
In her cot my daughter lay,
real, miraculous, alive. 15

Seven sixes are forty-two.
I packed her sandwiches for school,
I loved my love and time came true.

Seven sevens are forty-nine.
Fruit loaded down my apple-tree, 20
near fifty years of life were mine.

Seven eights are fifty-six.
My lips still cold from a last kiss,
my fire was ash and charcoal-sticks.

Seven nines are sixty-three; seven tens are seventy. 25
Who would that old woman be?
She will remember being me,

but what she is I cannot see.
Yet with every added seven,
some strange present I was given. 30

1976

CARSON McCULLERS

1917–1967

Mick Kelly, the would-be musician of *The Heart Is a Lonely Hunter* (1940), and
Frankie Addams, the would-be poet of *The Member of the Wedding* (1946), are
probably among Carson McCullers's most famous characters, adolescents who
dream of being wedded to a new world where the children, the blacks, and the ho-
mosexuals of their hometowns would no longer be misbegotten mutes or loners.
Because of her sympathy for such figures along with sometimes grotesque or vio-
lent plots, McCullers has been placed in the so-called "Southern Gothic" tradition
of writing associated with her friend the playwright Tennessee Williams. Yet, as
Virginia Spencer Carr's biography demonstrates, the macabre atmosphere of
McCullers's art reflected the confusion of her life.

The first child of Lamar Smith, a watch repairman and jewelry store owner, and
Vera Marguerite (Waters) Smith, McCullers was born Lula Carson Smith in
Columbus, Georgia. Like many of her adolescent heroines, Lula was an imagina-
tive child, devoted to music in general and the piano in particular. When she was
fifteen, however, an attack of rheumatic fever forced her to relinquish the strenu-
ous demands of a musical career for a future in writing, and she began to produce
for her family plays that were, in her own words, "thick with incest, lunacy, and
murder." At seventeen, she arrived in New York, where she worked as a waitress and
typist while studying music at the Juilliard School and taking writing courses at
Columbia University. But at this point, her rheumatic fever had recurred, sending
her back to Georgia to recuperate.

McCullers became something of a prodigy after the publication of *The Heart Is
a Lonely Hunter*. The twenty-three-year-old author was immediately celebrated as
a brilliant regionalist and supported by friendships with such established writers as
W. H. Auden, Richard Wright, and Jane Bowles. Although *Reflections in a Golden
Eye* (1941) was less successful than her first novel, she received fellowships from
the Yaddo colony (a retreat for writers), the Guggenheim Foundation, and the
American Academy of Arts and Letters. Yet both McCullers's personal friends and
her professional acquaintances commented on the insecurity and neediness that
made her emotionally demanding and compulsively moody.

Just before the publication of *The Heart Is a Lonely Hunter*, she had married
Reeves McCullers, a would-be writer recently released from the army. But their re-
lationship was strained when Carson, as she now called herself, fell in love with
Annemarie Clarac-Schwarzenbach, a Swiss writer. Although Schwarzenbach did
not reciprocate McCullers's feelings, the McCullerses divorced in 1941, remarried
in 1945, broke up again in 1948, and reunited in 1949. Throughout this period,
McCullers's literary success was remarkable. *The Ballad of the Sad Café* was cho-
sen for Best American Stories in 1944, *The Member of the Wedding* received rave
reviews in 1946, and four years later it was hailed as a dramatic triumph when it
opened as a play in New York starring Ethel Waters and Julie Harris. Yet in 1948
McCullers tried to commit suicide, and in 1953 Reeves McCullers killed himself.

During her forties, McCullers suffered a heart attack, pneumonia, and breast
cancer. With her cropped hair and whimsical smile, however, she looks in photo-

graphs from this period like the tormented but gallant adolescents who dominated her fiction. After several strokes, she died at the age of fifty. In her last two publications—the novel *Clock without Hands* (1961) and the play *The Square Root of Wonderful* (1958)—McCullers continued to explore the loneliness of adults chafing from their childhood griefs. Typical of her work in its portrayal of alienated but imaginative individuals in search of their own albeit eccentric truths, *The Ballad of the Sad Café* brilliantly delineates the punishment meted out to a female character who arrogantly supposes that she can live a life of physical power, intellectual authority, and personal autonomy.

The Ballad of the Sad Café

The town itself is dreary; not much is there except the cotton mill, the two-room houses where the workers live, a few peach trees, a church with two colored windows, and a miserable main street only a hundred yards long. On Saturdays the tenants from the nearby farms come in for a day of talk and trade. Otherwise the town is lonesome, sad, and like a place that is far off and estranged from all other places in the world. The nearest train stop is Society City, and the Greyhound and White Bus Lines use the Forks Falls Road which is three miles away. The winters here are short and raw, the summers white with glare and fiery hot.

If you walk along the main street on an August afternoon there is nothing whatsoever to do. The largest building, in the very center of the town, is boarded up completely and leans so far to the right that it seems bound to collapse at any minute. The house is very old. There is about it a curious, cracked look that is very puzzling until you suddenly realize that at one time, and long ago, the right side of the front porch had been painted, and part of the wall—but the painting was left unfinished and one portion of the house is darker and dingier than the other. The building looks completely deserted. Nevertheless, on the second floor there is one window which is not boarded; sometimes in the late afternoon when the heat is at its worst a hand will slowly open the shutter and a face will look down on the town. It is a face like the terrible dim faces known in dreams—sexless and white, with two gray crossed eyes which are turned inward so sharply that they seem to be exchanging with each other one long and secret gaze of grief. The face lingers at the window for an hour or so, then the shutters are closed once more, and as likely as not there will not be another soul to be seen along the main street. These August afternoons—when your shift is finished there is absolutely nothing to do; you might as well walk down to the Forks Falls Road and listen to the chain gang.

However, here in this very town there was once a café. And this old boarded-up house was unlike any other place for many miles around. There were tables with cloths and paper napkins, colored streamers from the electric fans, great gatherings on Saturday nights. The owner of the place was Miss Amelia Evans. But the person most responsible for the success and gaiety of the place was a hunchback called Cousin Lymon. One other person had a part in the story of this café—he was the former husband of Miss Amelia, a terrible character who returned to the town after a long term in the penitentiary, caused ruin, and then went on his way again. The café has long since been closed, but it is still remembered.

The place was not always a café. Miss Amelia inherited the building from her father, and it was a store that carried mostly feed, guano[1], and staples such as meal and snuff. Miss Amelia was rich. In addition to the store she operated a still three miles back in the swamp, and ran out the best liquor in the county. She was a dark, tall woman with bones and muscles like a man. Her hair was cut short and brushed back from the forehead, and there was about her sun-burned face a tense, haggard quality. She might have been a handsome woman if, even then, she was not slightly cross-eyed. There were those who would have courted her, but Miss Amelia cared nothing for the love of men and was a solitary person. Her marriage had been unlike any other marriage ever contracted in this county—it was a strange and dangerous marriage, last-ing only for ten days, that left the whole town wondering and shocked. Except for this queer marriage Miss Amelia had lived her life alone. Often she spent whole nights back in her shed in the swamp, dressed in overalls and gum boots, silently guarding the low fire of the still.

With all things which could be made by the hands Miss Amelia prospered. She sold chitterlins and sausage in the town near-by. On fine autumn days she ground sorghum[2] and the syrup from her vats was dark golden and delicately flavored. She built the brick privy behind her store in only two weeks and was skilled in carpentering. It was only with people that Miss Amelia was not at ease. People, unless they are nilly-willy or very sick, cannot be taken into the hands and changed overnight to something more worth-while and profitable. So that the only use that Miss Amelia had for other people was to make money out of them. And in this she succeeded. Mortgages on crops and property, a sawmill, money in the bank—she was the richest woman for miles around. She would have been rich as a congressman if it were not for her one great fail-ing, and that was her passion for lawsuits and the courts. She would involve herself in long and bitter litigation over just a trifle. It was said that if Miss Amelia so much as stumbled over a rock in the road she would glance around instinctively as though looking for something to sue about it. Aside from these lawsuits she lived a steady life and every day was very much like the day that had gone before. With the exception of her ten-day marriage, nothing hap-pened to change this until the spring of the year that Miss Amelia was thirty years old.

It was toward midnight on a soft quiet evening in April. The sky was the color of a blue swamp iris, the moon clear and bright. The crops that spring promised well and in the past weeks the mill had run a night shift. Down by the creek, the square brick factory was yellow with light, and there was the faint, steady hum of the looms. It was such a night when it is good to hear from faraway, across the dark fields, the slow song of a Negro on his way to make love. Or when it is pleasant to sit quietly and pick up a guitar, or simply to rest alone and think of nothing at all. The street that evening was deserted, but Miss Amelia's store was lighted and on the porch outside were five people. One of these was Stumpy MacPhail, a foreman with a red face and dainty, pur-plish hands. On the top step were two boys in overalls, the Rainey twins—both of them lanky and slow, with white hair and sleepy green eyes. The other man was Henry Macy, a shy and timid person with gentle manners and ner-

1. Fertilizer (usually made of bat or seafowl excre- 2. A tropical grass whose sweet juice yields sugar
ment). syrup.

vous ways, who sat on the edge of the bottom step. Miss Amelia herself stood leaning against the side of the open door, her feet crossed in their big swamp boots, patiently untying knots in a rope she had come across. They had not talked for a long time.

One of the twins, who had been looking down the empty road, was the first to speak. "I see something coming," he said.

"A calf got loose," said his brother.

The approaching figure was still too distant to be clearly seen. The moon made dim, twisted shadows of the blossoming peach trees along the side of the road. In the air the odor of blossoms and sweet spring grass mingled with the warm, sour smell of the near-by lagoon.

"No. It's somebody's youngun," said Stumpy MacPhail.

Miss Amelia watched the road in silence. She had put down her rope and was fingering the straps of her overalls with her brown bony hand. She scowled, and a dark lock of hair fell down on her forehead. While they were waiting there, a dog from one of the houses down the road began a wild, hoarse howl that continued until a voice called out and hushed him. It was not until the figure was quite close, within the range of the yellow light from the porch, that they saw clearly what had come.

The man was a stranger, and it is rare that a stranger enters the town on foot at that hour. Besides, the man was a hunchback. He was scarcely more than four feet tall and he wore a ragged, dusty coat that reached only to his knees. His crooked little legs seemed too thin to carry the weight of his great warped chest and the hump that sat on his shoulders. He had a very large head, with deep-set blue eyes and a sharp little mouth. His face was both soft and sassy— at the moment his pale skin was yellowed by dust and there were lavender shadows beneath his eyes. He carried a lopsided old suitcase which was tied with a rope.

"Evening," said the hunchback, and he was out of breath.

Miss Amelia and the men on the porch neither answered his greeting nor spoke. They only looked at him.

"I am hunting for Miss Amelia Evans."

Miss Amelia pushed back her hair from her forehead and raised her chin. "How come?"

"Because I am kin with her," the hunchback said.

The twins and Stumpy MacPhail looked up at Miss Amelia.

"That's me," she said. "How do you mean 'kin'?"

"Because—" the hunchback began. He looked uneasy, almost as though he was about to cry. He rested the suitcase on the bottom step, but did not take his hand from the handle. "My mother was Fanny Jesup and she come from Cheehaw. She left Cheehaw some thirty years ago when she married her first husband. I remember hearing her tell how she had a half-sister named Martha. And back in Cheehaw today they tell me that was your mother."

Miss Amelia listened with her head turned slightly aside. She ate her Sunday dinners by herself; her place was never crowded with a flock of relatives, and she claimed kin with no one. She had had a great-aunt who owned the livery stable in Cheehaw, but that aunt was now dead. Aside from her there was only one double first cousin who lived in a town twenty miles away, but this cousin and Miss Amelia did not get on so well, and when they chanced to pass each other they spat on the side of the road. Other people had tried very

hard, from time to time, to work out some kind of far-fetched connection with Miss Amelia, but with absolutely no success.

The hunchback went into a long rigmarole, mentioning names and places that were unknown to the listeners on the porch and seemed to have nothing to do with the subject. "So Fanny and Martha Jesup were half-sisters. And I am the son of Fanny's third husband. So that would make you and I—" He bent down and began to unfasten his suitcase. His hands were like dirty sparrow claws and they were trembling. The bag was full of all manner of junk—ragged clothes and odd rubbish that looked like parts out of a sewing machine, or something just as worthless. The hunchback scrambled among these belongings and brought out an old photograph. "This is a picture of my mother and her half-sister."

Miss Amelia did not speak. She was moving her jaw slowly from side to side, and you could tell from her face what she was thinking about. Stumpy MacPhail took the photograph and held it out toward the light. It was a picture of two pale, withered-up little children of about two and three years of age. The faces were tiny white blurs, and it might have been an old picture in anyone's album.

Stumpy MacPhail handed it back with no comment. "Where you come from?" he asked.

The hunchback's voice was uncertain. "I was traveling."

Still Miss Amelia did not speak. She just stood leaning against the side of the door, and looked down at the hunchback. Henry Macy winked nervously and rubbed his hands together. Then quietly he left the bottom step and disappeared. He is a good soul, and the hunchback's situation had touched his heart. Therefore he did not want to wait and watch Miss Amelia chase the newcomer off her property and run him out of town. The hunchback stood with his bag open on the bottom step; he sniffled his nose, and his mouth quivered. Perhaps he began to feel his dismal predicament. Maybe he realized what a miserable thing it was to be a stranger in the town with a suitcase full of junk, and claiming kin with Miss Amelia. At any rate he sat down on the steps and suddenly began to cry.

It was not a common thing to have an unknown hunchback walk to the store at midnight and then sit down and cry. Miss Amelia rubbed back her hair from her forehead and the men looked at each other uncomfortably. All around the town was very quiet.

At last one of the twins said: "I'll be damned if he ain't a regular Morris Finestein."

Everyone nodded and agreed, for that is an expression having a certain special meaning. But the hunchback cried louder because he could not know what they were talking about. Morris Finestein was a person who had lived in the town years before. He was only a quick, skipping little Jew who cried if you called him Christkiller, and ate light bread and canned salmon every day. A calamity had come over him and he had moved away to Society City. But since then if a man were prissy in any way, or if a man ever wept, he was known as a Morris Finestein.

"Well, he is afflicted," said Stumpy MacPhail. "There is some cause."

Miss Amelia crossed the porch with two slow, gangling strides. She went down the steps and stood looking thoughtfully at the stranger. Gingerly, with one long brown forefinger, she touched the hump on his back. The hunchback

still wept, but he was quieter now. The night was silent and the moon still shone with a soft, clear light—it was getting colder. Then Miss Amelia did a rare thing; she pulled out a bottle from her hip pocket and after polishing off the top with the palm of her hand she handed it to the hunchback to drink. Miss Amelia could seldom be persuaded to sell her liquor on credit, and for her to give so much as a drop away free was almost unknown.

"Drink," she said. "It will liven your gizzard."

The hunchback stopped crying, neatly licked the tears from around his mouth, and did as he was told. When he was finished, Miss Amelia took a slow swallow, warmed and washed her mouth with it, and spat. Then she also drank. The twins and the foreman had their own bottle they had paid for.

"It is smooth liquor," Stumpy MacPhail said. "Miss Amelia, I have never known you to fail."

The whisky they drank that evening (two big bottles of it) is important. Otherwise, it would be hard to account for what followed. Perhaps without it there would never have been a café. For the liquor of Miss Amelia has a special quality of its own. It is clean and sharp on the tongue, but once down a man it glows inside him for a long time afterward. And that is not all. It is known that if a message is written with lemon juice on a clean sheet of paper there will be no sign of it. But if the paper is held for a moment to the fire then the letters turn brown and the meaning becomes clear. Imagine that the whisky is the fire and that the message is that which is known only in the soul of a man—then the worth of Miss Amelia's liquor can be understood. Things that have gone unnoticed, thoughts that have been harbored far back in the dark mind, are suddenly recognized and comprehended. A spinner who has thought only of the loom, the dinner pail, the bed, and then the loom again—this spinner might drink some on a Sunday and come across a marsh lily. And in his palm he might hold this flower, examining the golden dainty cup, and in him suddenly might come a sweetness keen as pain. A weaver might look up suddenly and see for the first time the cold, weird radiance of midnight January sky, and a deep fright at his own smallness stop his heart. Such things as these, then, happen when a man has drunk Miss Amelia's liquor. He may suffer, or he may be spent with joy—but the experience has shown the truth; he has warmed his soul and seen the message hidden there.

They drank until it was past midnight, and the moon was clouded over so that the night was cold and dark. The hunchback still sat on the bottom steps, bent over miserably with his forehead resting on his knee. Miss Amelia stood with her hands in her pockets, one foot resting on the second step of the stairs. She had been silent for a long time. Her face had the expression often seen in slightly cross-eyed persons who are thinking deeply, a look that appears to be both very wise and very crazy. At last she said: "I don't know your name."

"I'm Lymon Willis," said the hunchback.

"Well, come on in," she said. "Some supper was left in the stove and you can eat."

Only a few times in her life had Miss Amelia invited anyone to eat with her, unless she was planning to trick them in some way, or make money out of them. So the men on the porch felt there was something wrong. Later, they said among themselves that she must have been drinking back in the swamp the better part of the afternoon. At any rate she left the porch, and Stumpy

MacPhail and the twins went on off home. She bolted the front door and looked all around to see that her goods were in order. Then she went to the kitchen, which was at the back of the store. The hunchback followed her, dragging his suitcase, sniffing and wiping his nose on the sleeve of his dirty coat.

"Sit down," said Miss Amelia. "I'll just warm up what's here."

It was a good meal they had together on that night. Miss Amelia was rich and she did not grudge herself food. There was fried chicken (the breast of which the hunchback took on his own plate), mashed rootabeggars, collard greens, and hot, pale golden, sweet potatoes. Miss Amelia ate slowly and with the relish of a farm hand. She sat with both elbows on the table, bent over the plate, her knees spread wide apart and her feet braced on the rungs of the chair. As for the hunchback, he gulped down his supper as though he had not smelled food in months. During the meal one tear crept down his dingy cheek—but it was just a little leftover tear and meant nothing at all. The lamp on the table was well-trimmed, burning blue at the edges of the wick, and casting a cheerful light in the kitchen. When Miss Amelia had eaten her supper she wiped her plate carefully with a slice of light bread and then poured her own clear, sweet syrup over the bread. The hunchback did likewise—except that he was more finicky and asked for a new plate. Having finished, Miss Amelia tilted back her chair, tightened her fist, and felt the hard, supple muscles of her right arm beneath the clean, blue cloth of her shirtsleeves—an unconscious habit with her, at the close of a meal. Then she took the lamp from the table and jerked her head toward the staircase as an invitation for the hunchback to follow after her.

Above the store there were the three rooms where Miss Amelia had lived during all of her life—two bedrooms with a large parlor in between. Few people had even seen these rooms, but it was generally known that they were well-furnished and extremely clean. And now Miss Amelia was taking up with her a dirty little hunchbacked stranger, come from God knows where. Miss Amelia walked slowly, two steps at a time, holding the lamp high. The hunchback hovered so close behind her that the swinging light made on the staircase wall one great, twisted shadow of the two of them. Soon the premises above the store were dark as the rest of the town.

The next morning was serene, with a sunrise of warm purple mixed with rose. In the fields around the town the furrows were newly plowed, and very early the tenants were at work setting out the young, deep green tobacco plants. The wild crows flew down close to the fields, making swift blue shadows on the earth. In town the people set out early with their dinner pails, and the windows of the mill were blinding gold in the sun. The air was fresh and the peach trees light as March clouds with their blossoms.

Miss Amelia came down at about dawn, as usual. She washed her head at the pump and very shortly set about her business. Later in the morning she saddled her mule and went to see about her property, planted with cotton, up near the Forks Falls Road. By noon, of course, everybody had heard about the hunchback who had come to the store in the middle of the night. But no one as yet had seen him. The day soon grew hot and the sky was a rich, midday blue. Still no one had laid an eye on this strange guest. A few people remembered that Miss Amelia's mother had had a half-sister—but there was some difference of opinion as to whether she had died or had run off with a tobacco

stringer. As for the hunchback's claim, everyone thought it was a trumped-up business. And the town, knowing Miss Amelia, decided that surely she had put him out of the house after feeding him. But toward evening, when the sky had whitened, and the shift was done, a woman claimed to have seen a crooked face at the window of one of the rooms up over the store. Miss Amelia herself said nothing. She clerked in the store for a while, argued for an hour with a farmer over a plow shaft, mended some chicken wire, locked up near sundown, and went to her rooms. The town was left puzzled and talkative.

The next day Miss Amelia did not open the store, but stayed locked up inside her premises and saw no one. Now this was the day that the rumor started—the rumor so terrible that the town and all the country about were stunned by it. The rumor was started by a weaver called Merlie Ryan. He is a man of not much account—sallow, shambling, and with no teeth in his head. He has the three-day malaria, which means that every third day the fever comes on him. So on two days he is dull and cross, but on the third day he livens up and sometimes has an idea or two, most of which are foolish. It was while Merlie Ryan was in his fever that he turned suddenly and said:

"I know what Miss Amelia done. She murdered that man for something in that suitcase."

He said this in a calm voice, as a statement of fact. And within an hour the news had swept through the town. It was a fierce and sickly tale the town built up that day. In it were all the things which cause the heart to shiver—a hunchback, a midnight burial in the swamp, the dragging of Miss Amelia through the streets of the town on the way to prison, the squabbles over what would happen to her property—all told in hushed voices and repeated with some fresh and weird detail. It rained and women forgot to bring in the washing from the lines. One or two mortals, who were in debt to Miss Amelia, even put on Sunday clothes as though it were a holiday. People clustered together on the main street, talking and watching the store.

It would be untrue to say that all the town took part in this evil festival. There were a few sensible men who reasoned that Miss Amelia, being rich, would not go out of her way to murder a vagabond for a few trifles of junk. In the town there were even three good people, and they did not want this crime, not even for the sake of the interest and the great commotion it would entail; it gave them no pleasure to think of Miss Amelia holding to the bars of the penitentiary and being electrocuted in Atlanta. These good people judged Miss Amelia in a different way from what the others judged her. When a person is as contrary in every single respect as she was and when the sins of a person have amounted to such a point that they can hardly be remembered all at once—then this person plainly requires a special judgment. They remembered that Miss Amelia had been born dark and somewhat queer of face, raised motherless by her father who was a solitary man, that early in youth she had grown to be six feet two inches tall which in itself is not natural for a woman, and that her ways and habits of life were too peculiar ever to reason about. Above all, they remembered her puzzling marriage, which was the most unreasonable scandal ever to happen in this town.

So these good people felt toward her something near to pity. And when she was out on her wild business, such as rushing in a house to drag forth a sewing machine in payment for a debt, or getting herself worked up over some matter concerning the law—they had toward her a feeling which was a mixture of ex-

asperation, a ridiculous little inside tickle, and a deep, unnamable sadness. But enough of the good people, for there were only three of them; the rest of the town was making a holiday of this fancied crime the whole of the afternoon.

Miss Amelia herself, for some strange reason, seemed unaware of all this. She spent most of her day upstairs. When down in the store, she prowled around peacefully, her hands deep in the pockets of her overalls and head bent so low that her chin was tucked inside the collar of her shirt. There was no bloodstain on her anywhere. Often she stopped and just stood somberly looking down at the cracks in the floor, twisting a lock of her short-cropped hair, and whispering something to herself. But most of the day was spent upstairs.

Dark came on. The rain that afternoon had chilled the air, so that the evening was bleak and gloomy as in wintertime. There were no stars in the sky, and a light, icy drizzle had set in. The lamps in the houses made mournful, wavering flickers when watched from the street. A wind had come up, not from the swamp side of the town but from the cold black pinewoods to the north.

The clocks in the town struck eight. Still nothing had happened. The bleak night, after the gruesome talk of the day, put a fear in some people, and they stayed home close to the fire. Others were gathered in groups together. Some eight or ten men had convened on the porch of Miss Amelia's store. They were silent and were indeed just waiting about. They themselves did not know what they were waiting for, but it was this: in times of tension, when some great action is impending, men gather and wait in this way. And after a time there will come a moment when all together they will act in unison, not from thought or from the will of any one man, but as though their instincts had merged together so that the decision belongs to no single one of them, but to the group as a whole. At such a time no individual hesitates. And whether the matter will be settled peaceably, or whether the joint action will result in ransacking, violence, and crime, depends on destiny. So the men waited soberly on the porch of Miss Amelia's store, not one of them realizing what they would do, but knowing inwardly that they must wait, and that the time had almost come.

Now the door to the store was open. Inside it was bright and natural-looking. To the left was the counter where slabs of white meat, rock candy, and tobacco were kept. Behind this were shelves of salted white meat and meal. The right side of the store was mostly filled with farm implements and such. At the back of the store, to the left, was the door leading up the stairs, and it was open. And at the far right of the store there was another door which led to a little room that Miss Amelia called her office. This door was also open. And at eight o'clock that evening Miss Amelia could be seen there sitting before her rolltop desk, figuring with a fountain pen and some pieces of paper.

The office was cheerfully lighted, and Miss Amelia did not seem to notice the delegation on the porch. Everything around her was in great order, as usual. This office was a room well-known, in a dreadful way, throughout the country. It was there Miss Amelia transacted all business. On the desk was a carefully covered typewriter which she knew how to run, but used only for the most important documents. In the drawers were literally thousands of papers, all filed according to the alphabet. This office was also the place where Miss Amelia received sick people, for she enjoyed doctoring and did a great deal of it. Two whole shelves were crowded with bottles and various paraphernalia. Against the wall was a bench where the patients sat. She could sew up a wound

with a burnt needle so that it would not turn green. For burns she had a cool, sweet syrup. For unlocated sickness there were any number of different medicines which she had brewed herself from unknown recipes. They wrenched loose the bowels very well, but they could not be given to small children, as they caused bad convulsions; for them she had an entirely separate draught, gentler and sweet-flavored. Yes, all in all, she was considered a good doctor. Her hands, though very large and bony, had a light touch about them. She possessed great imagination and used hundreds of different cures. In the face of the most dangerous and extraordinary treatment she did not hesitate, and no disease was so terrible but what she would undertake to cure it. In this there was one exception. If a patient came with a female complaint she could do nothing. Indeed at the mere mention of the words her face would slowly darken with shame, and she would stand there craning her neck against the collar of her shirt, or rubbing her swamp boots together, for all the world like a great, shamed, dumb-tongued child. But in other matters people trusted her. She charged no fees whatsoever and always had a raft of patients.

On this evening Miss Amelia wrote with her fountain pen a good deal. But even so she could not be forever unaware of the group waiting out there on the dark porch, and watching her. From time to time she looked up and regarded them steadily. But she did not holler out to them to demand why they were loafing around her property like a sorry bunch of gabbies.[3] Her face was proud and stern, as it always was when she sat at the desk of her office. After a time their peering in like that seemed to annoy her. She wiped her cheek with a red handkerchief, got up, and closed the office door.

Now to the group on the porch this gesture acted as a signal. The time had come. They had stood for a long while with the night raw and gloomy in the street behind them. They had waited long and just at that moment the instinct to act came on them. All at once, as though moved by one will, they walked into the store. At that moment the eight men looked very much alike—all wearing blue overalls, most of them with whitish hair, all pale of face, and all with a set, dreaming look in the eye. What they would have done next no one knows. But at that instant there was a noise at the head of the staircase. The men looked up and then stood dumb with shock. It was the hunchback, whom they had already murdered in their minds. Also, the creature was not at all as had been pictured to them—not a pitiful and dirty little chatterer, alone and beggared in this world. Indeed, he was like nothing any man among them had ever beheld until that time. The room was still as death.

The hunchback came down slowly with the proudness of one who owns every plank of the floor beneath his feet. In the past days he had greatly changed. For one thing he was clean beyond words. He still wore his little coat, but it was brushed off and neatly mended. Beneath this was a fresh red and black checkered shirt belonging to Miss Amelia. He did not wear trousers such as ordinary men are meant to wear, but a pair of tight-fitting little knee-length breeches. On his skinny legs he wore black stockings, and his shoes were of a special kind, being queerly shaped, laced up over the ankles, and newly cleaned and polished with wax. Around his neck, so that his large, pale ears were almost completely covered, he wore a shawl of lime-green wool, the fringes of which almost touched the floor.

3. I.e., gabbers.

The hunchback walked down the store with his stiff little strut and then stood in the center of the group that had come inside. They cleared a space about him and stood looking with hands loose at their sides and eyes wide open. The hunchback himself got his bearings in an odd manner. He regarded each person steadily at his own eye-level, which was about belt line for an ordinary man. Then with shrewd deliberation he examined each man's lower regions—from the waist to the sole of the shoe. When he had satisfied himself he closed his eyes for a moment and shook his head, as though in his opinion what he had seen did not amount to much. Then with assurance, only to confirm himself, he tilted back his head and took in the halo of faces around him with one long, circling stare. There was a half-filled sack of guano on the left side of the store, and when he had found his bearings in this way, the hunchback sat down upon it. Cozily settled, with his little legs crossed, he took from his coat pocket a certain object.

Now it took some moments for the men in the store to regain their ease. Merlie Ryan, he of the three-day fever who had started the rumor that day, was the first to speak. He looked at the object which the hunchback was fondling, and said in a hushed voice:

"What is it you have there?"

Each man knew well what it was the hunchback was handling. For it was the snuffbox which had belonged to Miss Amelia's father. The snuffbox was of blue enamel with a dainty embellishment of wrought gold on the lid. The group knew it well and marveled. They glanced warily at the closed office door, and heard the low sound of Miss Amelia whistling to herself.

"Yes, what is it, Peanut?"

The hunchback looked up quickly and sharpened his mouth to speak. "Why, this is a lay-low to catch meddlers."

The hunchback reached in the box with his scrambly little fingers and ate something, but he offered no one around him a taste. It was not even proper snuff which he was taking, but a mixture of sugar and cocoa. This he took, though, as snuff, pocketing a little wad of it beneath his lower lip and licking down neatly into this with a flick of his tongue which made a frequent grimace come over his face.

"The very teeth in my head have always tasted sour to me," he said in explanation. "This is the reason why I take this kind of sweet snuff."

The group still clustered around, feeling somewhat gawky and bewildered. This sensation never quite wore off, but it was soon tempered by another feeling—an air of intimacy in the room and a vague festivity. Now the names of the men of the group there on that evening were as follows: Hasty Malone, Robert Calvert Hale, Merlie Ryan, Reverend T. M. Willin, Rosser Cline, Rip Wellborn, Henry Ford Crimp, and Horace Wells. Except for Reverend Willin, they are all alike in many ways as has been said—all having taken pleasure from something or other, all having wept and suffered in some way, most of them tractable unless exasperated. Each of them worked in the mill, and lived with others in a two- or three-room house for which the rent was ten dollars or twelve dollars a month. All had been paid that afternoon, for it was Saturday. So, for the present, think of them as a whole.

The hunchback, however, was already sorting them out in his mind. Once comfortably settled he began to chat with everyone, asking questions such as if a man was married, how old he was, how much his wages came to in an average week, et cetera—picking his way along to inquiries which were downright

intimate. Soon the group was joined by others in the town, Henry Macy, idlers who had sensed something extraordinary, women come to fetch their men who lingered on, and even one loose, towhead child who tiptoed into the store, stole a box of animal crackers, and made off very quietly. So the premises of Miss Amelia were soon crowded, and she herself had not yet opened her office door.

There is a type of person who has a quality about him that sets him apart from other and more ordinary human beings. Such a person has an instinct which is usually found only in small children, an instinct to establish immediate and vital contact between himself and all things in the world. Certainly the hunchback was of this type. He had only been in the store half an hour before an immediate contact had been established between him and each other individual. It was as though he had lived in the town for years, was a well-known character, and had been sitting and talking there on that guano sack for countless evenings. This, together with the fact that it was Saturday night, could account for the air of freedom and illicit gladness in the store. There was a tension, also, partly because of the oddity of the situation and because Miss Amelia was still closed off in her office and had not yet made her appearance.

She came out that evening at ten o'clock. And those who were expecting some drama at her entrance were disappointed. She opened the door and walked in with her slow, gangling swagger. There was a streak of ink on one side of her nose, and she had knotted the red handkerchief about her neck. She seemed to notice nothing unusual. Her gray, crossed eyes glanced over to the place where the hunchback was sitting, and for a moment lingered there. The rest of the crowd in her store she regarded with only a peaceable surprise.

"Does anyone want waiting on?" she asked quietly.

There were a number of customers, because it was Saturday night, and they all wanted liquor. Now Miss Amelia had dug up an aged barrel only three days past and had siphoned it into bottles back by the still. This night she took the money from the customers and counted it beneath the bright light. Such was the ordinary procedure. But after this what happened was not ordinary. Always before, it was necessary to go around to the dark back yard, and there she would hand out your bottle through the kitchen door. There was no feeling of joy in the transaction. After getting his liquor the customer walked off into the night. Or, if his wife would not have it in the home, he was allowed to come back around to the front porch of the store and guzzle there or in the street. Now, both the porch and the street before it were the property of Miss Amelia, and no mistake about it—but she did not regard them as premises; the premises began at the front door and took in the entire inside of the building. There she had never allowed liquor to be opened or drunk by anyone but herself. Now for the first time she broke this rule. She went to the kitchen, with the hunchback close at her heels, and she brought back the bottles into the warm, bright store. More than that she furnished some glasses and opened two boxes of crackers so that they were there hospitably in a platter on the counter and anyone who wished could take one free.

She spoke to no one but the hunchback, and she only asked him in a somewhat harsh and husky voice: "Cousin Lymon, will you have yours straight, or warmed in a pan with water on the stove?"

"If you please, Amelia," the hunchback said. (And since what time had anyone presumed to address Miss Amelia by her bare name, without a title of re-

spect?—Certainly not her bridegroom and her husband of ten days. In fact, not since the death of her father, who for some reason had always called her Little, had anyone dared to address her in such a familiar way.) "If you please, I'll have it warmed."

Now, this was the beginning of the café. It was as simple as that. Recall that the night was gloomy as in wintertime, and to have sat around the property outside would have made a sorry celebration. But inside there was company and a genial warmth. Someone had rattled up the stove in the rear, and those who bought bottles shared their liquor with friends. Several women were there and they had twists of licorice, a Nehi,[4] or even a swallow of the whisky. The hunchback was still a novelty and his presence amused everyone. The bench in the office was brought in, together with several extra chairs. Other people leaned against the counter or made themselves comfortable on barrels and sacks. Nor did the opening of liquor on the premises cause any rambunctiousness, indecent giggles, or misbehavior whatsoever. On the contrary the company was polite even to the point of a certain timidness. For people in this town were then unused to gathering together for the sake of pleasure. They met to work in the mill. Or on Sunday there would be an all-day camp meeting—and though that is a pleasure, the intention of the whole affair is to sharpen your view of Hell and put into you a keen fear of the Lord Almighty. But the spirit of a café is altogether different. Even the richest, greediest old rascal will behave himself, insulting no one in a proper café. And poor people look about them gratefully and pinch up the salt in a dainty and modest manner. For the atmosphere of a proper café implies these qualities: fellowship, the satisfactions of the belly, and a certain gaiety and grace of behavior. This had never been told to the gathering in Miss Amelia's store that night. But they knew it of themselves, although never, of course, until that time had there been a café in the town.

Now, the cause of all this, Miss Amelia, stood most of the evening in the doorway leading to the kitchen. Outwardly she did not seem changed at all. But there were many who noticed her face. She watched all that went on, but most of the time her eyes were fastened lonesomely on the hunchback. He strutted about the store, eating from his snuffbox, and being at once sour and agreeable. Where Miss Amelia stood, the light from the chinks of the stove cast a glow, so that her brown, long face was somewhat brightened. She seemed to be looking inward. There was in her expression pain, perplexity, and uncertain joy. Her lips were not so firmly set as usual, and she swallowed often. Her skin had paled and her large empty hands were sweating. Her look that night, then, was the lonesome look of the lover.

This opening of the café came to an end at midnight. Everyone said goodbye to everyone else in a friendly fashion. Miss Amelia shut the front door of her premises, but forgot to bolt it. Soon everything—the main street with its three stores, the mill, the houses—all the town, in fact—was dark and silent. And so ended three days and nights in which had come an arrival of a stranger, an unholy holiday, and the start of the café.

Now time must pass. For the next four years are much alike. There are great changes, but these changes are brought about bit by bit, in simple steps which

4. A brand of soft drink.

in themselves do not appear to be important. The hunchback continued to live with Miss Amelia. The café expanded in a gradual way. Miss Amelia began to sell her liquor by the drink, and some tables were brought into the store. There were customers every evening, and on Saturday a great crowd. Miss Amelia began to serve fried catfish suppers at fifteen cents a plate. The hunchback cajoled her into buying a fine mechanical piano. Within two years the place was a store no longer, but had been converted into a proper café, open every evening from six until twelve o'clock.

Each night the hunchback came down the stairs with the air of one who has a grand opinion of himself. He always smelled slightly of turnip greens, as Miss Amelia rubbed him night and morning with pot liquor to give him strength. She spoiled him to a point beyond reason, but nothing seemed to strengthen him; food only made his hump and his head grow larger while the rest of him remained weakly and deformed. Miss Amelia was the same in appearance. During the week she still wore swamp boots and overalls, but on Sunday she put on a dark red dress that hung on her in a most peculiar fashion. Her manners, however, and her way of life were greatly changed. She still loved a fierce lawsuit, but she was not so quick to cheat her fellow man and to exact cruel payments. Because the hunchback was so extremely sociable she even went about a little—to revivals, to funerals, and so forth. Her doctoring was as successful as ever, her liquor even finer than before, if that were possible. The café itself proved profitable and was the only place of pleasure for many miles around.

So for the moment regard these years from random and disjointed views. See the hunchback marching in Miss Amelia's footsteps when on a red winter morning they set out for the pinewoods to hunt. See them working on her properties—with Cousin Lymon standing by and doing absolutely nothing, but quick to point out any laziness among the hands. On autumn afternoons they sat on the back steps chopping sugar cane. The glaring summer days they spent back in the swamp where the water cypress is a deep black green, where beneath the tangled swamp trees there is a drowsy gloom. When the path leads through a bog or a stretch of blackened water see Miss Amelia bend down to let Cousin Lymon scramble on her back—and see her wading forward with the hunchback settled on her shoulders, clinging to her ears or to her broad forehead. Occasionally Miss Amelia cranked up the Ford which she had bought and treated Cousin Lymon to a picture-show in Cheehaw, or to some distant fair or cockfight; the hunchback took a passionate delight in spectacles. Of course, they were in their café every morning, they would often sit for hours together by the fireplace in the parlor upstairs. For the hunchback was sickly at night and dreaded to lie looking into the dark. He had a deep fear of death. And Miss Amelia would not leave him by himself to suffer with this fright. It may even be reasoned that the growth of the café came about mainly on this account; it was a thing that brought him company and pleasure and that helped him through the night. So compose from such flashes an image of these years as a whole. And for a moment let it rest.

Now some explanation is due for all this behavior. The time has come to speak about love. For Miss Amelia loved Cousin Lymon. So much was clear to everyone. They lived in the same house together and were never seen apart. Therefore, according to Mrs. MacPhail, a warty-nosed old busybody who is continually moving her sticks of furniture from one part of the front room to

another; according to her and to certain others, these two were living in sin. If they were related, they were only a cross between first and second cousins, and even that could in no way be proved. Now, of course Miss Amelia was a powerful blunderbuss of a person, more than six feet tall—and Cousin Lymon a weakly little hunchback reaching only to her waist. But so much the better for Mrs. Stumpy MacPhail and her cronies, for they and their kind glory in conjunctions which are ill-matched and pitiful. So let them be. The good people thought that if those two had found some satisfaction of the flesh between themselves, then it was a matter concerning them and God alone. All sensible people agreed in their opinion about this conjecture—and their answer was a plain, flat *no*. What sort of thing, then, was this love?

First of all, love is a joint experience between two persons—but the fact that it is a joint experience does not mean that it is a similar experience to the two people involved. There are the lover and the beloved, but these two come from different countries. Often the beloved is only a stimulus for the stored-up love which has lain quiet within the lover for a long time hitherto. And somehow every lover knows this. He feels in his soul that his love is a solitary thing. He comes to know a new, strange loneliness and it is this knowledge which makes him suffer. So there is only one thing for the lover to do. He must house his love within himself as best he can; he must create for himself a whole new inward world—a world intense and strange, complete in himself. Let it be added here that this lover about whom we speak need not necessarily be a young man saving for a wedding ring—this lover can be man, woman, child, or indeed any human creature on this earth.

Now, the beloved can also be of any description. The most outlandish people can be the stimulus for love. A man may be a doddering great-grandfather and still love only a strange girl he saw in the streets of Cheehaw one afternoon two decades past. The preacher may love a fallen woman. The beloved may be treacherous, greasy-headed, and given to evil habits. Yes, and the lover may see this as clearly as anyone else—but that does not affect the evolution of his love one whit. A most mediocre person can be the object of a love which is wild, extravagant, and beautiful as the poison lilies of the swamp. A good man may be the stimulus for a love both violent and debased, or a jabbering madman may bring about in the soul of someone a tender and simple idyll. Therefore, the value and quality of any love is determined solely by the lover himself.

It is for this reason that most of us would rather love than be loved. Almost everyone wants to be the lover. And the curt truth is that, in a deep secret way, the state of being beloved is intolerable to many. The beloved fears and hates the lover, and with the best of reasons. For the lover is forever trying to strip bare his beloved. The lover craves any possible relation with the beloved, even if this experience can cause him only pain.

It has been mentioned before that Miss Amelia was once married. And this curious episode might as well be accounted for at this point. Remember that it all happened long ago, and that it was Miss Amelia's only personal contact, before the hunchback came to her, with this phenomenon—love.

The town then was the same as it is now, except there were two stores instead of three and the peach trees along the street were more crooked and smaller than they are now. Miss Amelia was nineteen years old at the time, and

her father had been dead many months. There was in the town at that time a
loom-fixer named Marvin Macy. He was the brother of Henry Macy, although
to know them you would never guess that those two could be kin. For Marvin
Macy was the handsomest man in this region—being six feet one inch tall,
hard-muscled, and with slow gray eyes and curly hair. He was well off, made
good wages, and had a gold watch which opened in the back to a picture of a
waterfall. From the outward and worldly point of view Marvin Macy was a for-
tunate fellow; he needed to bow and scrape to no one and always got just what
he wanted. But from a more serious and thoughtful viewpoint Marvin Macy
was not a person to be envied, for he was an evil character. His reputation was
as bad, if not worse, than that of any young man in the county. For years, when
he was a boy, he had carried about with him the dried and salted ear of a man
he had killed in a razor fight. He had chopped off the tails of squirrels in the
pinewoods just to please his fancy, and in his left hip pocket he carried forbid-
den marijuana weed to tempt those who were discouraged and drawn toward
death. Yet in spite of his well-known reputation he was the beloved of many
females in this region—and there were at the time several young girls who
were clean-haired and soft-eyed, with tender sweet little buttocks and charm-
ing ways. These gentle young girls he degraded and shamed. Then finally, at
the age of twenty-two, this Marvin Macy chose Miss Amelia. That solitary,
gangling, queer-eyed girl was the one he longed for. Nor did he want her be-
cause of her money, but solely out of love.

And love changed Marvin Macy. Before the time when he loved Miss
Amelia it could be questioned if such a person had within him a heart and
soul. Yet there is some explanation for the ugliness of his character, for Marvin
Macy had had a hard beginning in this world. He was one of seven unwanted
children whose parents could hardly be called parents at all; these parents were
wild younguns who liked to fish and roam around the swamp. Their own chil-
dren, and there was a new one almost every year, were only a nuisance to them.
At night when they came home from the mill they would look at the children
as though they did not know wherever they had come from. If the children
cried they were beaten, and the first thing they learned in this world was to
seek the darkest corner of the room and try to hide themselves as best they
could. They were as thin as little whitehaired ghosts, and they did not speak,
not even to each other. Finally, they were abandoned by their parents alto-
gether and left to the mercies of the town. It was a hard winter, with the mill
closed down almost three months, and much misery everywhere. But this is
not a town to let white orphans perish in the road before your eyes. So here is
what came about: the eldest child, who was eight years old, walked into
Cheehaw and disappeared—perhaps he took a freight train somewhere and
went out into the world, nobody knows. Three other children were boarded
out amongst the town, being sent around from one kitchen to another, and as
they were delicate they died before Easter time. The last two children were
Marvin Macy and Henry Macy, and they were taken into a home. There was a
good woman in the town named Mrs. Mary Hale, and she took Marvin Macy
and Henry Macy and loved them as her own. They were raised in her house-
hold and treated well.

But the hearts of small children are delicate organs. A cruel beginning in
this world can twist them into curious shapes. The heart of a hurt child can
shrink so that forever afterward it is hard and pitted as the seed of a peach. Or

again, the heart of such a child may fester and swell until it is a misery to carry within the body, easily chafed and hurt by the most ordinary things. This last is what happened to Henry Macy, who is so opposite to his brother, is the kindest and gentlest man in town. He lends his wages to those who are unfortunate, and in the old days he used to care for the children whose parents were at the café on Saturday night. But he is a shy man, and he has the look of one who has a swollen heart and suffers. Marvin Macy, however, grew to be bold and fearless and cruel. His heart turned tough as the horns of Satan, and until the time when he loved Miss Amelia he brought to his brother and the good woman who raised him nothing but shame and trouble.

But love reversed the character of Marvin Macy. For two years he loved Miss Amelia, but he did not declare himself. He would stand near the door of her premises, his cap in his hand, his eyes meek and longing and misty gray. He reformed himself completely. He was good to his brother and foster mother, and he saved his wages and learned thrift. Moreover, he reached out toward God. No longer did he lie around on the floor of the front porch all day Sunday, singing and playing his guitar; he attended church services and was present at all religious meetings. He learned good manners: he trained himself to rise and give his chair to a lady, and he quit swearing and fighting and using holy names in vain. So for two years he passed through this transformation and improved his character in every way. Then at the end of the two years he went one evening to Miss Amelia, carrying a bunch of swamp flowers, a sack of chitterlins, and a silver ring—that night Marvin Macy declared himself.

And Miss Amelia married him. Later everyone wondered why. Some said it was because she wanted to get herself some wedding presents. Others believed it came about through the nagging of Miss Amelia's great-aunt in Cheehaw, who was a terrible old woman. Anyway, she strode with great steps down the aisle of the church wearing her dead mother's bridal gown, which was of yellow satin and at least twelve inches too short for her. It was a winter afternoon and the clear sun shone through the ruby windows of the church and put a curious glow on the pair before the altar. As the marriage lines were read Miss Amelia kept making an odd gesture—she would rub the palm of her right hand down the side of her satin wedding gown. She was reaching for the pocket of her overalls, and being unable to find it her face became impatient, bored, and exasperated. At last when the lines were spoken and the marriage prayer was done Miss Amelia hurried out of the church, not taking the arm of her husband, but walking at least two paces ahead of him.

The church is no distance from the store so the bride and groom walked home. It is said that on the way Miss Amelia began to talk about some deal she had worked up with a farmer over a load of kindling wood. In fact, she treated her groom in exactly the same manner she would have used with some customer who had come into the store to buy a pint from her. But so far all had gone decently enough; the town was gratified, as people had seen what this love had done to Marvin Macy and hoped that it might also reform his bride. At least, they counted on the marriage to tone down Miss Amelia's temper, to put a bit of bride-fat on her, and to change her at last into a calculable woman.

They were wrong. The young boys who watched through the window on that night said that this is what actually happened: The bride and groom ate a grand supper prepared by Jeff, the old Negro who cooked for Miss Amelia. The bride took second servings of everything, but the groom picked with his food.

Then the bride went about her ordinary business—reading the newspaper, finishing an inventory of the stock in the store, and so forth. The groom hung about in the doorway with a loose, foolish, blissful face and was not noticed. At eleven o'clock the bride took a lamp and went upstairs. The groom followed close behind her. So far all had gone decently enough, but what followed after was unholy.

Within half an hour Miss Amelia had stomped down the stairs in breeches and a khaki jacket. Her face had darkened so that it looked quite black. She slammed the kitchen door and gave it an ugly kick. Then she controlled herself. She poked up the fire, sat down, and put her feet up on the kitchen stove. She read the Farmer's Almanac, drank coffee, and had a smoke with her father's pipe. Her face was hard, stern, and had now whitened to its natural color. Sometimes she paused to jot down some information from the Almanac on a piece of paper. Toward dawn she went into her office and uncovered her typewriter, which she had recently bought and was only just learning how to run. That was the way in which she spent the whole of her wedding night. At daylight she went out to her yard as though nothing whatsoever had occurred and did some carpentering on a rabbit hutch which she had begun the week before and intended to sell somewhere.

A groom is in a sorry fix when he is unable to bring his well-beloved bride to bed with him, and when the whole town knows it. Marvin Macy came down that day still in his wedding finery, and with a sick face. God knows how he had spent the night. He moped about the yard, watching Miss Amelia, but keeping some distance away from her. Then toward noon an idea came to him and he went off in the direction of Society City. He returned with presents—an opal ring, a pink enamel doreen of the sort which was then in fashion, a silver bracelet with two hearts on it, and a box of candy which had cost two dollars and a half. Miss Amelia looked over these fine gifts and opened the box of candy, for she was hungry. The rest of the presents she judged shrewdly for a moment to sum up their value—then she put them in the counter out for sale. The night was spent in much the same manner as the preceding one—except that Miss Amelia brought her feather mattress to make a pallet by the kitchen stove, and she slept fairly well.

Things went on like this for three days. Miss Amelia went about her business as usual, and took great interest in some rumor that a bridge was to be built some ten miles down the road. Marvin Macy still followed her about around the premises, and it was plain from his face how he suffered. Then on the fourth day he did an extremely simple-minded thing: he went to Cheehaw and came back with a lawyer. Then in Miss Amelia's office he signed over to her the whole of his worldly goods, which was ten acres of timberland which he had bought with the money he had saved. She studied the paper sternly to make sure there was no possibility of a trick and filed it soberly in the drawer of her desk. That afternoon Marvin Macy took a quart bottle of whisky and went with it alone out in the swamp while the sun was still shining. Toward evening he came in drunk, went up to Miss Amelia with wet wide eyes, and put his hand on her shoulder. He was trying to tell her something, but before he could open his mouth she had swung once with her fist and hit his face so hard that he was thrown back against the wall and one of his front teeth was broken.

The rest of this affair can only be mentioned in bare outline. After this first blow Miss Amelia hit him whenever he came within arm's reach of her, and whenever he was drunk. At last she turned him off the premises altogether,

and he was forced to suffer publicly. During the day he hung around just outside the boundary line of Miss Amelia's property and sometimes with a drawn crazy look he would fetch his rifle and sit there clearing it, peering at Miss Amelia steadily. If she was afraid she did not show it, but her face was sterner than ever, and often she spat on the ground. His last foolish effort was to climb in the window of her store one night and to sit there in the dark, for no purpose whatsoever, until she came down the stairs next morning. For this Miss Amelia set off immediately to the courthouse in Cheehaw with some notion that she could get him locked in the penitentiary for trespassing. Marvin Macy left the town that day, and no one saw him go, or knew just where he went. On leaving he put a long curious letter, partly written in pencil and partly with ink, beneath Miss Amelia's door. It was a wild love letter—but in it were also included threats, and he swore that in his life he would get even with her. His marriage had lasted for ten days. And the town felt the special satisfaction that people feel when someone has been thoroughly done in by some scandalous and terrible means.

Miss Amelia was left with everything that Marvin Macy had ever owned—his timberwood, his gilt watch, every one of his possessions. But she seemed to attach little value to them and that spring she cut up his Klansman's robe to cover her tobacco plants. So all that he had ever done was to make her richer and to bring her love. But, strange to say, she never spoke of him but with a terrible and spiteful bitterness. She never once referred to him by name but always mentioned him scornfully as "that loom-fixer I was married to."

And later, when horrifying rumors concerning Marvin Macy reached the town, Miss Amelia was very pleased. For the true character of Marvin Macy finally revealed itself, once he had freed himself of his love. He became a criminal whose picture and whose name were in all the papers in the state. He robbed three filling stations and held up the A&P store of Society City with a sawed-off gun. He was suspected of the murder of Slit-Eye Sam who was a noted highjacker. All these crimes were connected with the name of Marvin Macy, so that his evil became famous through many counties. Then finally the law captured him, drunk, on the floor of a tourist cabin, his guitar by his side, and fifty-seven dollars in his right shoe. He was tried, sentenced, and sent off to the penitentiary near Atlanta. Miss Amelia was deeply gratified.

Well, all this happened a long time ago, and it is the story of Miss Amelia's marriage. The town laughed a long time over this grotesque affair. But though the outward facts of this love are indeed sad and ridiculous, it must be remembered that the real story was that which took place in the soul of the lover himself. So who but God can be the final judge of this or any other love? On the very first night of the café there were several who suddenly thought of this broken bridegroom, locked in the gloomy penitentiary many miles away. And in the years that followed, Marvin Macy was not altogether forgotten in the town. His name was never mentioned in the presence of Miss Amelia or the hunchback. But the memory of his passion and his crimes, and the thought of him trapped in his cell in the penitentiary, was like a troubling undertone beneath the happy love of Miss Amelia and the gaiety of the café. So do not forget this Marvin Macy, as he is to act a terrible part in the story which is yet to come.

During the four years in which the store became a café the rooms upstairs were not changed. This part of the premises remained exactly as it had been

all of Miss Amelia's life, as it was in the time of her father, and most likely his father before him. The three rooms, it is already known, were immaculately clean. The smallest object had its exact place, and everything was wiped and dusted by Jeff, the servant of Miss Amelia, each morning. The front room belonged to Cousin Lymon—it was the room where Marvin Macy had stayed during the few nights he was allowed on the premises, and before that it was the bedroom of Miss Amelia's father. The room was furnished with a large chifforobe, a bureau covered with a stiff white linen cloth crocheted at the edges, and a marble-topped table. The bed was immense, an old fourposter made of carved, dark rosewood. On it were two feather mattresses, bolsters, and a number of handmade comforts. The bed was so high that beneath it were two wooden steps—no occupant had ever used these steps before, but Cousin Lymon drew them out each night and walked up in state. Beside the steps, but pushed modestly out of view, there was a china chamberpot painted with pink roses. No rug covered the dark, polished floor and the curtains were of some white stuff, also crocheted at the edges.

On the other side of the parlor was Miss Amelia's bedroom, and it was smaller and very simple. The bed was narrow and made of pine. There was a bureau for her breeches, shirts, and Sunday dress, and she had hammered two nails in the closet wall on which to hang her swamp boots. There were no curtains, rugs, or ornaments of any kind.

The large middle room, the parlor, was elaborate. The rosewood sofa, upholstered in threadbare green silk, was before the fireplace. Marble-topped tables, two Singer sewing machines, a big vase of pampas grass—everything was rich and grand. The most important piece of furniture in the parlor was a big, glass-doored cabinet in which was kept a number of treasures and curios. Miss Amelia had added two objects to this collection—one was a large acorn from a water oak, the other a little velvet box holding two small, grayish stones. Sometimes when she had nothing much to do, Miss Amelia would take out this velvet box and stand by the window with the stones in the palm of her hand, looking down at them with a mixture of fascination, dubious respect, and fear. They were the kidney stones of Miss Amelia herself, and had been taken from her by the doctor in Cheehaw some years ago. It had been a terrible experience, from the first minute to the last, and all she had got out of it were those two little stones; she was bound to set great store by them, or else admit to a mighty sorry bargain. So she kept them and in the second year of Cousin Lymon's stay with her she had them set as ornaments in a watch chain which she gave to him. The other object she had added to the collection, the large acorn, was precious to her—but when she looked at it her face was always saddened and perplexed.

"Amelia, what does it signify?" Cousin Lymon asked her.

"Why, it's just an acorn," she answered. "Just an acorn I picked up on the afternoon Big Papa died."

"How do you mean?" Cousin Lymon insisted.

"I mean it's just an acorn I spied on the ground that day. I picked it up and put it in my pocket. But I don't know why."

"What a peculiar reason to keep it," Cousin Lymon said.

The talks of Miss Amelia and Cousin Lymon in the rooms upstairs, usually in the first few hours of the morning when the hunchback could not sleep, were many. As a rule, Miss Amelia was a silent woman, not letting her tongue

run wild on any subject that happened to pop into her head. There were certain topics of conversation, however, in which she took pleasure. All these subjects had one point in common—they were interminable. She liked to contemplate problems which could be worked over for decades and still remain insoluble. Cousin Lymon, on the other hand, enjoyed talking on any subject whatsoever, as he was a great chatterer. Their approach to any conversation was altogether different. Miss Amelia always kept to the broad, rambling generalities of the matter, going on endlessly in a low, thoughtful voice and getting nowhere—while Cousin Lymon would interrupt her suddenly to pick up, magpie fashion, some detail which, even if unimportant, was at least concrete and bearing on some practical facet close at hand. Some of the favorite subjects of Miss Amelia were: the stars, the reason why Negroes are black, the best treatment for cancer, and so forth. Her father was also an interminable subject which was dear to her.

"Why, Law," she would say to Lymon. "Those days I slept. I'd go to bed just as the lamp was turned on and sleep—why, I'd sleep like I was drowned in warm axle grease. Then come daybreak Big Papa would walk in and put his hand down on my shoulder. 'Get stirring, Little,' he would say. Then later he would holler up the stairs from the kitchen when the stove was hot. 'Fried grits,' he would holler. 'White meat and gravy. Ham and eggs.' And I'd run down the stairs and dress by the hot stove while he was out washing at the pump. Then off we'd go to the still or maybe—"

"The grits we had this morning was poor," Cousin Lymon said. "Fried too quick so that the inside never heated."

"And when Big Papa would run off the liquor in those days—" The conversation would go on endlessly, with Miss Amelia's long legs stretched out before the hearth; for winter or summer there was always a fire in the grate, as Lymon was cold-natured. He sat in a low chair across from her, his feet not quite touching the floor and his torso usually well-wrapped in a blanket or the green wool shawl. Miss Amelia never mentioned her father to anyone else except Cousin Lymon.

That was one of the ways in which she showed her love for him. He had her confidence in the most delicate and vital matters. He alone knew where she kept the chart that showed where certain barrels of whisky were buried on a piece of property near-by. He alone had access to her bankbook and the key to the cabinet of curios. He took money from the cash register, whole handfuls of it, and appreciated the loud jingle it made inside his pockets. He owned almost everything on the premises, for when he was cross Miss Amelia would prowl about and find him some present—so that now there was hardly anything left close at hand to give him. The only part of her life that she did not want Cousin Lymon to share with her was the memory of her ten-day marriage. Marvin Macy was the one subject that was never, at any time, discussed between the two of them.

So let the slow years pass and come to a Saturday evening six years after the time when Cousin Lymon came first to the town. It was August and the sky had burned above the town like a sheet of flame all day. Now the green twilight was near and there was a feeling of repose. The street was coated an inch deep with dry golden dust and the little children ran about half-naked, sneezed often, sweated, and were fretful. The mill had closed down at noon. People in

the houses along the main street sat resting on their steps and the women had palmetto fans. At Miss Amelia's there was a sign at the front of the premises saying CAFÉ. The back porch was cool with latticed shadows and there Cousin Lymon sat turning the ice-cream freezer—often he unpacked the salt and ice and removed the dasher to lick a bit and see how the work was coming on. Jeff cooked in the kitchen. Early that morning Miss Amelia had put a notice on the wall of the front porch reading: Chicken Dinner—Twenty Cents Tonite. The café was already open and Miss Amelia had just finished a period of work in her office. All the eight tables were occupied and from the mechanical piano came a jingling tune.

In a corner, near the door and sitting at a table with a child, was Henry Macy. He was drinking a glass of liquor, which was unusual for him, as liquor went easily to his head and made him cry or sing. His face was very pale and his left eye worked constantly in a nervous tic, as it was apt to do when he was agitated. He had come into the café sidewise and silent, and when he was greeted he did not speak. The child next to him belonged to Horace Wells, and he had been left at Miss Amelia's that morning to be doctored.

Miss Amelia came out from her office in good spirits. She attended to a few details in the kitchen and entered the café with the pope's nose of a hen[5] between her fingers, as that was her favorite piece. She looked about the room, saw that in general all was well, and went over to the corner table by Henry Macy. She turned the chair around and sat straddling the back, as she only wanted to pass the time of day and was not yet ready for her supper. There was a bottle of Kroup[6] Kure in the hip pocket of her overalls—a medicine made from whisky, rock candy, and a secret ingredient. Miss Amelia uncorked the bottle and put it to the mouth of the child. Then she turned to Henry Macy and, seeing the nervous winking of his left eye, she asked:

"What ails you?"

Henry Macy seemed on the point of saying something difficult, but, after a long look into the eyes of Miss Amelia, he swallowed and did not speak.

So Miss Amelia returned to her patient. Only the child's head showed above the table top. His face was very red, with the eyelids half-closed and the mouth partly open. He had a large, hard, swollen boil on his thigh, and had been brought to Miss Amelia so that it could be opened. But Miss Amelia used a special method with children; she did not like to see them hurt, struggling, and terrified. So she had kept the child around the premises all day, giving him licorice and frequent doses of the Kroup Kure, and toward evening she tied a napkin around his neck and let him eat his fill of the dinner. Now as he sat at the table his head wobbled slowly from side to side and sometimes as he breathed there came from him a little worn-out grunt.

There was a stir in the café and Miss Amelia looked around quickly. Cousin Lymon had come in. The hunchback strutted into the café as he did every night, and when he reached the exact center of the room he stopped short and looked shrewdly around him, summing up the people and making a quick pattern of the emotional material at hand that night. The hunchback was a great mischief-maker. He enjoyed any kind of to-do, and without saying a word he could set people at each other in a way that was miraculous. It was due to him

5. Fleshy projection on the rump of a cooked fowl.
6. Croup is an attack of difficult breathing, with a hoarse, metallic cough.

that the Rainey twins had quarreled over a jackknife two years past, and had not spoken one word to each other since. He was present at the big fight between Rip Wellborn and Robert Calvert Hale, and every other fight for that matter since he had come into the town. He nosed around everywhere, knew the intimate business of everybody, and trespassed every waking hour. Yet, queerly enough, in spite of this it was the hunchback who was most responsible for the great popularity of the café. Things were never so gay as when he was around. When he walked into the room there was always a quick feeling of tension, because with this busybody about there was never any telling what might descend on you, or what might suddenly be brought to happen in the room. People are never so free with themselves and so recklessly glad as when there is some possibility of commotion or calamity ahead. So when the hunchback marched into the café everyone looked around at him and there was a quick outburst of talking and a drawing of corks.

Lymon waved his hand to Stumpy MacPhail who was sitting with Merlie Ryan and Henry Ford Crimp. "I walked to Rotten Lake today to fish," he said. "And on the way I stepped over what appeared at first to be a fallen tree. But then as I stepped over I felt something stir and I taken this second look and there I was straddling this here alligator long as from the front door to the kitchen and thicker than a hog."

The hunchback chattered on. Everyone looked at him from time to time, and some kept track of his chattering and others did not. There were times when every word he said was nothing but lying and bragging. Nothing he said tonight was true. He had lain in bed with a summer quinsy[7] all day long, and had only got up in the late afternoon in order to turn the ice-cream freezer. Everybody knew this, yet he stood there in the middle of the café and held forth with such lies and boasting that it was enough to shrivel the ears.

Miss Amelia watched him with her hands in her pockets and her head turned to one side. There was a softness about her gray, queer eyes and she was smiling gently to herself. Occasionally she glanced from the hunchback to the other people in the café—and then her look was proud, and there was in it the hint of a threat, as though daring anyone to try to hold him to account for all his foolery. Jeff was bringing in the suppers, already served on the plates, and the new electric fans in the café made a pleasant stir of coolness in the air.

"The little youngun is asleep," said Henry Macy finally.

Miss Amelia looked down at the patient beside her, and composed her face for the matter in hand. The child's chin was resting on the table edge and a trickle of spit or Kroup Kure had bubbled from the corner of his mouth. His eyes were quite closed, and a little family of gnats had clustered peacefully in the corners. Miss Amelia put her hand on his head and shook it roughly, but the patient did not awake. So Miss Amelia lifted the child from the table, being careful not to touch the sore part of his leg, and went into the office. Henry Macy followed after her and they closed the office door.

Cousin Lymon was bored that evening. There was not much going on, and in spite of the heat the customers in the café were good-humored. Henry Ford Crimp and Horace Wells sat at the middle table with their arms around each other, sniggering over some long joke—but when he approached them he could make nothing of it as he had missed the beginning of the story. The

7. Attack of tonsillitis.

moonlight brightened the dusty road, and the dwarfed peach trees were black and motionless: there was no breeze. The drowsy buzz of swamp mosquitoes was like an echo of the silent night. The town seemed dark, except far down the road to the right there was the flicker of a lamp. Somewhere in the darkness a woman sang in a high wild voice and the tune had no start and no finish and was made up of only three notes which went on and on and on. The hunchback stood leaning against the banister of the porch, looking down the empty road as though hoping that someone would come along.

There were footsteps behind him, then a voice: "Cousin Lymon, your dinner is set out upon the table."

"My appetite is poor tonight," said the hunchback, who had been eating sweet snuff all the day. "There is a sourness in my mouth."

"Just a pick," said Miss Amelia. "The breast, the liver, and the heart."

Together they went back into the bright café, and sat down with Henry Macy. Their table was the largest one in the café, and on it there was a bouquet of swamp lilies in a Coca-Cola bottle. Miss Amelia had finished with her patient and was satisfied with herself. From behind the closed office door there had come only a few sleepy whimpers, and before the patient could wake up and become terrified it was all over. The child was now slung across the shoulder of his father, sleeping deeply, his little arms dangling loose along his father's back and his puffed-up face very red—they were leaving the café to go home.

Henry Macy was still silent. He ate carefully, making no noise when he swallowed, and was not a third as greedy as Cousin Lymon who had claimed to have no appetite and was now putting down helping after helping of the dinner. Occasionally Henry Macy looked across at Miss Amelia and again held his peace.

It was a typical Saturday night. An old couple who had come in from the country hesitated for a moment at the doorway, holding each other's hand, and finally decided to come inside. They had lived together so long, this old country couple, that they looked as similar as twins. They were brown, shriveled, and like two little walking peanuts. They left early, and by midnight most of the other customers were gone. Rosser Cline and Merlie Ryan still played checkers, and Stumpy MacPhail sat with a liquor bottle on his table (his wife would not allow it in the home) and carried on peaceable conversations with himself. Henry Macy had not yet gone away, and this was unusual, as he almost always went to bed soon after nightfall. Miss Amelia yawned sleepily, but Lymon was restless and she did not suggest that they close up for the night.

Finally, at one o'clock, Henry Macy looked up at the corner of the ceiling and said quietly to Miss Amelia: "I got a letter today."

Miss Amelia was not one to be impressed by this, because all sorts of business letters and catalogues came addressed to her.

"I got a letter from my brother," said Henry Macy.

The hunchback, who had been goose-stepping about the café with his hands clasped behind his head, stopped suddenly. He was quick to sense any change in the atmosphere of a gathering. He glanced at each face in the room and waited.

Miss Amelia scowled and hardened her right fist. "You are welcome to it," she said.

"He is on parole. He is out of the penitentiary."

The face of Miss Amelia was very dark, and she shivered although the night was warm. Stumpy MacPhail and Merlie Ryan pushed aside their checker game. The café was very quiet.

"Who?" asked Cousin Lymon. His large, pale ears seemed to grow on his head and stiffen. "What?"

Miss Amelia slapped her hands palm down on the table. "Because Marvin Macy is a—" But her voice hoarsened and after a few moments she only said: "He belongs to be in that penitentiary the balance of his life."

"What did he do?" asked Cousin Lymon.

There was a long pause, as no one knew exactly how to answer this. "He robbed three filling stations," said Stumpy MacPhail. But his words did not sound complete and there was a feeling of sins left unmentioned.

The hunchback was impatient. He could not bear to be left out of anything, even a great misery. The name Marvin Macy was unknown to him, but it tantalized him as did any mention of subjects which others knew about and of which he was ignorant—such as any reference to the old sawmill that had been torn down before he came, or a chance word about poor Morris Finestein, or the recollection of any event that had occurred before his time. Aside from this inborn curiosity, the hunchback took a great interest in robbers and crimes of all varieties. As he strutted around the table he was muttering the words "released on parole" and "penitentiary" to himself. But although he questioned insistently, he was unable to find anything, as nobody would dare to talk about Marvin Macy before Miss Amelia in the café.

"The letter did not say very much," said Henry Macy. "He did not say where he was going."

"Humph!" said Miss Amelia, and her face was still hardened and very dark. "He will never set his split hoof[8] on my premises."

She pushed back her chair from the table, and made ready to close the café. Thinking about Marvin Macy may have set her to brooding, for she hauled the cash register back to the kitchen and put it in a private place. Henry Macy went off down the dark road. But Henry Ford Crimp and Merlie Ryan lingered for a time on the front porch. Later Merlie Ryan was to make certain claims, to swear that on that night he had a vision of what was to come. But the town paid no attention, for that was just the sort of thing that Merlie Ryan would claim. Miss Amelia and Cousin Lymon talked for a time in the parlor. And when at last the hunchback thought that he could sleep she arranged the mosquito netting over his bed and waited until he had finished with his prayers. Then she put on her long nightgown, smoked two pipes and only after a long time went to sleep.

That autumn was a happy time. The crops around the countryside were good, and over at the Forks Falls market the price of tobacco held firm that year. After the long hot summer the first cool days had a clean bright sweetness. Goldenrod grew along the dusty roads, and the sugar cane was ripe and purple. The bus came each day from Cheehaw to carry off a few of the younger children to the consolidated school to get an education. Boys hunted foxes in the pinewoods, winter quilts were aired out on the wash lines, and sweet potatoes bedded in the ground with straw against the colder months to come. In

8. I.e., to Miss Amelia, Marvin Macy is a devil.

the evening, delicate shreds of smoke rose from the chimneys, and the moon was round and orange in the autumn sky. There is no stillness like the quiet of the first cold nights in the fall. Sometimes, late in the night when there was no wind, there could be heard in the town the thin wild whistle of the train that goes through Society City on its way far off to the North.

For Miss Amelia Evans this was a time of great activity. She was at work from dawn until sundown. She made a new and bigger condenser for her still, and in one week ran off enough liquor to souse the whole country. Her old mule was dizzy from grinding so much sorghum, and she scalded her Mason jars and put away pear preserves. She was looking forward greatly to the first frost, because she had traded for three tremendous hogs, and intended to make much barbecue, chitterlins, and sausage.

During these weeks there was a quality about Miss Amelia that many people noticed. She laughed often, with a deep ringing laugh, and her whistling had a sassy, tuneful trickery. She was forever trying out her strength, lifting up heavy objects, or poking her tough biceps with her finger. One day she sat down to her typewriter and wrote a story—a story in which there were foreigners, trap doors, and millions of dollars. Cousin Lymon was with her always, traipsing along behind her coat-tails, and when she watched him her face had a bright, soft look, and when she spoke his name there lingered in her voice the undertone of love.

The first cold spell came at last. When Miss Amelia awoke one morning there were frost flowers on the windowpanes, and rime had silvered the patches of grass in the yard. Miss Amelia built a roaring fire in the kitchen stove, then went out of doors to judge the day. The air was cold and sharp, the sky pale green and cloudless. Very shortly people began to come in from the country to find out what Miss Amelia thought of the weather; she decided to kill the biggest hog, and word got round the countryside. The hog was slaughtered and a low oak fire started in the barbecue pit. There was the warm smell of pig blood and smoke in the back yard, the stamp of footsteps, the ring of voices in the winter air. Miss Amelia walked around giving orders and soon most of the work was done.

She had some particular business to do in Cheehaw that day, so after making sure that all was going well, she cranked up her car and got ready to leave. She asked Cousin Lymon to come with her, in fact, she asked him seven times, but he was loath to leave the commotion and wanted to remain. This seemed to trouble Miss Amelia, as she always liked to have him near to her, and was prone to be terribly homesick when she had to go any distance away. But after asking him seven times, she did not urge him any further. Before leaving she found a stick and drew a heavy line all around the barbecue pit, about two feet back from the edge, and told him not to trespass beyond that boundary. She left after dinner and intended to be back before dark.

Now, it is not so rare to have a truck or an automobile pass along the road and through the town on the way from Cheehaw to somewhere else. Every year the tax collector comes to argue with rich people such as Miss Amelia. And if somebody in the town, such as Merlie Ryan, takes a notion that he can connive to get a car on credit, or to pay down three dollars and have a fine electric icebox such as they advertise in the store windows of Cheehaw, then a city man will come out asking meddlesome questions, finding out all his troubles, and ruining his chances of buying anything on the installment plan. Some-

times, especially since they are working on the Forks Falls highway, the cars hauling the chain gang come through the town. And frequently people in automobiles get lost and stop to inquire how they can find the right road again. So, late that afternoon it was nothing unusual to have a truck pass the mill and stop in the middle of the road near the café of Miss Amelia. A man jumped down from the back of the truck, and the truck went on its way.

The man stood in the middle of the road and looked about him. He was a tall man, with brown curly hair, and slow-moving, deep-blue eyes. His lips were red and he smiled the lazy, half-mouthed smile of the braggart. The man wore a red shirt, and a wide belt of tooled leather; he carried a tin suitcase and a guitar. The first person in the town to see this newcomer was Cousin Lymon, who had heard the shifting of gears and come around to investigate. The hunchback stuck his head around the corner of the porch, but did not step out altogether into full view. He and the man stared at each other, and it was not the look of two strangers meeting for the first time and swiftly summing up each other. It was a peculiar stare they exchanged between them, like the look of two criminals who recognize each other. Then the man in the red shirt shrugged his left shoulder and turned away. The face of the hunchback was very pale as he watched the man go down the road, and after a few moments he began to follow along carefully, keeping many paces away.

It was immediately known throughout the town that Marvin Macy had come back again. First, he went to the mill, propped his elbows lazily on a window sill and looked inside. He liked to watch others hard at work, as do all born loafers. The mill was thrown into a sort of numb confusion. The dyers left the hot vats, the spinners and weavers forgot about their machines, and even Stumpy MacPhail, who was foreman, did not know exactly what to do. Marvin Macy still smiled his wet half-mouthed smiles, and when he saw his brother, his bragging expression did not change. After looking over the mill Marvin Macy went down the road to the house where he had been raised, and left his suitcase and guitar on the front porch. Then he walked around the millpond, looked over the church, the three stores, and the rest of the town. The hunchback trudged along quietly at some distance behind him, his hands in his pockets, and his little face still very pale.

It had grown late. The red winter sun was setting, and to the west the sky was deep gold and crimson. Ragged chimney swifts flew to their nests; lamps were lighted. Now and then there was the smell of smoke, and the warm rich odor of the barbecue slowly cooking in the pit behind the café. After making the rounds of the town Marvin Macy stopped before Miss Amelia's premises and read the sign above the porch. Then, not hesitating to trespass, he walked through the side yard. The mill whistle blew a thin, lonesome blast, and the day's shift was done. Soon there were others in Miss Amelia's back yard beside Marvin Macy—Henry Ford Crimp, Merlie Ryan, Stumpy MacPhail, and any number of children and people who stood around the edges of the property and looked on. Very little was said. Marvin Macy stood by himself on one side of the pit, and the rest of the people clustered together on the other side. Cousin Lymon stood somewhat apart from everyone, and he did not take his eyes from the face of Marvin Macy.

"Did you have a good time in the penitentiary?" asked Merlie Ryan, with a silly giggle.

Marvin Macy did not answer. He took from his hip pocket a large knife,

opened it slowly, and honed the blade on the seat of his pants. Merlie Ryan grew suddenly very quiet and went to stand directly behind the broad back of Stumpy MacPhail.

Miss Amelia did not come home until almost dark. They heard the rattle of her automobile while she was still a long distance away, then the slam of the door and a bumping noise as though she were hauling something up the front steps of her premises. The sun had already set, and in the air there was the blue smoky glow of early winter evenings. Miss Amelia came down the back steps slowly, and the group in her yard waited very quietly. Few people in this world could stand up to Miss Amelia, and against Marvin Macy she had this special bitter hate. Everyone waited to see her burst into a terrible holler, snatch up some dangerous object, and chase him altogether out of town. At first she did not see Marvin Macy, and her face had the relieved and dreamy expression that was natural to her when she reached home after having gone some distance away.

Miss Amelia must have seen Marvin Macy and Cousin Lymon at the same instant. She looked from one to the other, but it was not the wastrel from the penitentiary on whom she finally fixed her gaze of sick amazement. She, and everyone else, was looking at Cousin Lymon, and he was a sight to see.

The hunchback stood at the end of the pit, his pale face lighted by the soft glow from the smoldering oak fire. Cousin Lymon had a very peculiar accomplishment, which he used whenever he wished to ingratiate himself with someone. He would stand very still, and with just a little concentration, he could wiggle his large pale ears with marvelous quickness and ease. This trick he always used when he wanted to get something special out of Miss Amelia, and to her it was irresistible. Now as he stood there the hunchback's ears were wiggling furiously on his head, but it was not Miss Amelia at whom he was looking this time. The hunchback was smiling at Marvin Macy with an entreaty that was near to desperation. At first Marvin Macy paid no attention to him, and when he did finally glance at the hunchback it was without any appreciation whatsoever.

"What ails this Brokeback?" he asked with a rough jerk of his thumb.

No one answered. And Cousin Lymon, seeing that his accomplishment was getting him nowhere, added new efforts of persuasion. He fluttered his eyelids, so that they were like pale, trapped moths in his sockets. He scraped his feet around on the ground, waved his hands about, and finally began doing a little trotlike dance. In the last gloomy light of the winter he resembled the child of a swamp-haunt.

Marvin Macy, alone of all the people in the yard, was unimpressed.

"Is the runt throwing a fit?" he asked, and when no one answered he stepped forward and gave Cousin Lymon a cuff on the side of his head. The hunchback staggered, then fell back on the ground. He sat where he had fallen, still looking up at Marvin Macy, and with great effort his ears managed one last forlorn little flap.

Now everyone turned to Miss Amelia to see what she would do. In all these years no one had so much as touched a hair of Cousin Lymon's head, although many had had the itch to do so. If anyone even spoke crossly to the hunchback, Miss Amelia would cut off this rash mortal's credit and find ways of making things go hard for him a long time afterward. So now if Miss Amelia had

split open Marvin Macy's head with the ax on the back porch no one would have been surprised. But she did nothing of the kind.

There were times when Miss Amelia seemed to go into a sort of trance. And the cause of these trances was usually known and understood. For Miss Amelia was a fine doctor, and did not grind up swamp roots and other untried ingredients and give them to the first patient who came along; whenever she invented a new medicine she always tried it out first on herself. She would swallow an enormous dose and spend the following day walking thoughtfully back and forth from the café to the brick privy. Often, when there was a sudden keen gripe,[9] she would stand quite still, her queer eyes staring down at the ground and her fists clenched; she was trying to decide which organ was being worked upon, and what misery the new medicine might be most likely to cure. And now as she watched the hunchback and Marvin Macy, her face wore this same expression, tense with reckoning some inward pain, although she had taken no new medicine that day.

"That will learn you, Brokeback," said Marvin Macy.

Henry Macy pushed back his limp whitish hair from his forehead and coughed nervously. Stumpy MacPhail and Merlie Ryan shuffled their feet, and the children and black people on the outskirts of the property made not a sound. Marvin Macy folded the knife he had been honing, and after looking about him fearlessly he swaggered out of the yard. The embers in the pit were turning to gray feathery ashes and it was now quite dark.

That was the way Marvin Macy came back from the penitentiary. Not a living soul in all the town was glad to see him. Even Mrs. Mary Hale, who was a good woman and had raised him with love and care—at the first sight of him even this old foster mother dropped the skillet she was holding and burst into tears. But nothing could faze that Marvin Macy. He sat on the back steps of the Hale house, lazily picking his guitar, and when the supper was ready, he pushed the children of the household out of the way and served himself a big meal, although there had been barely enough hoecakes and white meat to go round. After eating he settled himself in the best and warmest sleeping place in the front room and was untroubled by dreams.

Miss Amelia did not open the café that night. She locked the doors and all the windows very carefully, nothing was seen of her and Cousin Lymon, and a lamp burned in her room all the night long.

Marvin Macy brought with him bad fortune, right from the first, as could be expected. The next day the weather turned suddenly, and it became hot. Even in the early morning there was a sticky sultriness in the atmosphere, the wind carried the rotten smell of the swamp, and delicate shrill mosquitoes webbed the green millpond. It was unseasonable, worse than August, and much damage was done. For nearly everyone in the county who owned a hog had copied Miss Amelia and slaughtered the day before. And what sausage could keep in such weather as this? After a few days there was everywhere the smell of slowly spoiling meat, and an atmosphere of dreary waste. Worse yet, a family reunion near the Forks Falls highway ate pork roast and died, every one of them. It was plain that their hog had been infected—and who could tell whether the rest of

9. Pinching intestinal pain

the meat was safe or not? People were torn between the longing for the good taste of pork, and the fear of death. It was a time of waste and confusion.

The cause of all this, Marvin Macy, had no shame in him. He was seen everywhere. During work hours he loafed about the mill, looking in at the windows, and on Sundays he dressed in his red shirt and paraded up and down the road with his guitar. He was still handsome—with his brown hair, his red lips, and his broad strong shoulders; but the evil in him was now too famous for his good looks to get him anywhere. And this evil was not measured only by the actual sins he had committed. True, he had robbed those filling stations. And before that he had ruined the tenderest girls in the county and laughed about it. Any number of wicked things could be listed against him, but quite apart from these crimes there was about him a secret meanness that clung to him almost like a smell. Another thing—he never sweated, not even in August, and that surely is a sign worth pondering over.

Now it seemed to the town that he was more dangerous than he had ever been before, as in the penitentiary in Atlanta he must have learned the method of laying charms. Otherwise how could his effect on Cousin Lymon be explained? For since first setting eyes on Marvin Macy the hunchback was possessed by an unnatural spirit. Every minute he wanted to be following along behind this jailbird, and he was full of silly schemes to attract attention to himself. Still Marvin Macy either treated him hatefully or failed to notice him at all. Sometimes the hunchback would give up, perch himself on the banister of the front porch much as a sick bird huddles on a telephone wire, and grieve publicly.

"But why?" Miss Amelia would ask, staring at him with her crossed, gray eyes, and her fists closed tight.

"Oh, Marvin Macy," groaned the hunchback, and the sound of the name was enough to upset the rhythm of his sobs so that he hiccuped. "He has been to Atlanta."

Miss Amelia would shake her head and her face was dark and hardened. To begin with she had no patience with any traveling; those who had made the trip to Atlanta or traveled fifty miles from home to see the ocean—those restless people she despised. "Going to Atlanta does no credit to home."

"He has been to the penitentiary," said the hunchback, miserable with longing.

How are you going to argue against such envies as these? In her perplexity Miss Amelia did not herself sound any too sure of what she was saying. "Been to the penitentiary, Cousin Lymon? Why, a trip like that is no travel to brag about."

During these weeks Miss Amelia was closely watched by everyone. She went about absent-mindedly, her face remote as though she had lapsed into one of her gripe trances. For some reason, after the day of Marvin Macy's arrival, she put aside her overalls and wore always the red dress she had before this time reserved for Sundays, funerals, and sessions of the court. Then as the weeks passed she began to take some steps to clear up the situation. But her efforts were hard to understand. If it hurt her to see Cousin Lymon follow Marvin Macy about the town, why did she not make the issues clear once and for all, and tell the hunchback that if he had dealings with Marvin Macy she would turn him off the premises? That would have been simple, and Cousin Lymon would have had to submit to her, or else face the sorry business of finding him-

self loose in the world. But Miss Amelia seemed to have lost her will; for the first time in her life she hesitated as to just what course to pursue. And, like most people in such a position of uncertainty, she did the worst thing possible—she began following several courses at once, all of them contrary to each other.

The café was opened every night as usual, and, strangely enough, when Marvin Macy came swaggering through the door, with the hunchback at his heels, she did not turn him out. She even gave him free drinks and smiled at him in a wild, crooked way. At the same time she set a terrible trap for him out in the swamp that surely would have killed him if he had got caught. She let Cousin Lymon invite him to Sunday dinner, and then tried to trip him up as he went down the steps. She began a great campaign of pleasure for Cousin Lymon—making exhausting trips to various spectacles being held in distant places, driving the automobile thirty miles to Chautauqua, taking him to Forks Falls to watch a parade. All in all it was a distracting time for Miss Amelia. In the opinion of most people she was well on her way in the climb up fools' hill, and everyone wanted to see how it would all turn out.

The weather turned cold again, the winter was upon the town, and night came before the last shift in the mill was done. Children kept on all their garments when they slept, and women raised the backs of their skirts to toast themselves dreamily at the fire. After it rained, the mud in the road made hard frozen ruts, there were faint flickers of lamplight from the windows of the houses, the peach trees were scrawny and bare. In the dark, silent nights of wintertime the café was the warm center point of the town, the lights shining so brightly that they could be seen a quarter of a mile away. The great iron stove at the back of the room roared, crackled, and turned red. Miss Amelia had made red curtains for the windows, and from a salesman who passed through the town she bought a great bunch of paper roses that looked very real.

But it was not only the warmth, the decorations, and the brightness, that made the café what it was. There is a deeper reason why the café was so precious to this town. And this deeper reason has to do with a certain pride that had not hitherto been known in these parts. To understand this new pride the cheapness of human life must be kept in mind. There were always plenty of people clustered around a mill—but it was seldom that every family had enough meal, garments, and fat back to go the rounds. Life could become one long dim scramble just to get the things needed to keep alive. And the confusing point is this: all useful things have a price, and are bought only with money, as that is the way the world is run. You know without having to reason about it the price of a bale of cotton, or a quart of molasses. But no value has been put on human life; it is given to us free and taken without being paid for. What is it worth? If you look around, at times the value may seem to be little or nothing at all. Often after you have sweated and tried and things are not better for you, there comes a feeling deep down in the soul that you are not worth much.

But the new pride that the café brought to this town had an effect on almost everyone, even the children. For in order to come to the café you did not have to buy the dinner, or a portion of liquor. There were cold bottled drinks for a nickel. And if you could not even afford that, Miss Amelia had a drink called Cherry Juice which sold for a penny a glass, and was pink-colored and very sweet. Almost everyone, with the exception of Reverend T. M. Willin,

came to the café at least once during the week. Children love to sleep in houses other than their own, and to eat at a neighbor's table; on such occasions they behave themselves decently and are proud. The people in the town were likewise proud when sitting at the tables in the café. They washed before coming to Miss Amelia's, and scraped their feet very politely on the threshold as they entered the café. There, for a few hours at least, the deep bitter knowing that you are not worth much in this world could be laid low.

The café was a special benefit to bachelors, unfortunate people, and consumptives.[1] And here it may be mentioned that there was some reason to suspect that Cousin Lymon was consumptive. The brightness of his gray eyes, his insistence, his talkativeness, and his cough—these were all signs. Besides, there is generally supposed to be some connection between a hunched spine and consumption. But whenever this subject had been mentioned to Miss Amelia she had become furious; she denied these symptoms with bitter vehemence, but on the sly she treated Cousin Lymon with hot chest plasters, Kroup Kure, and such. Now this winter the hunchback's cough was worse, and sometimes even on cold days he would break out in a heavy sweat. But this did not prevent him from following along after Marvin Macy.

Early every morning he left the premises and went to the back door of Mrs. Hale's house, and waited and waited—as Marvin Macy was a lazy sleeper. He would stand there and call out softly. His voice was just like the voices of children who squat patiently over those tiny little holes in the ground where doodlebugs[2] are thought to live, poking the hole with a broom straw, and calling plaintively: "Doodlebug, Doodlebug—fly away home. Mrs. Doodlebug, Mrs. Doodlebug. Come out, come out. Your house is on fire and all your children are burning up." In just such a voice—at once sad, luring, and resigned—would the hunchback call Marvin Macy's name each morning. Then when Marvin Macy came out for the day, he would trail him about the town, and sometimes they would be gone for hours together out in the swamp.

And Miss Amelia continued to do the worst thing possible: that is, to try to follow several courses at once. When Cousin Lymon left the house she did not call him back, but only stood in the middle of the road and watched lonesomely until he was out of sight. Nearly every day Marvin Macy turned up with Cousin Lymon at dinnertime, and ate at her table. Miss Amelia opened the pear preserves, and the table was well-set with ham or chicken, great bowls of hominy grits, and winter peas. It is true that on one occasion Miss Amelia tried to poison Marvin Macy—but there was a mistake, the plates were confused, and it was she herself who got the poisoned dish. This she quickly realized by the slight bitterness of the food, and that day she ate no dinner. She sat tilted back in the chair, feeling her muscle, and looking at Marvin Macy.

Every night Marvin Macy came to the café and settled himself at the best and largest table, the one in the center of the room. Cousin Lymon brought him liquor, for which he did not pay a cent. Marvin Macy brushed the hunchback aside as if he were a swamp mosquito, and not only did he show no gratitude for these favors, but if the hunchback got in his way he would cuff him with the back of his hand, or say: "Out of my way, Brokeback—I'll snatch you bald-headed." When this happened Miss Amelia would come out from be-

1. Those with tuberculosis. Tuberculosis can affect bones and other tissues, not just the lungs. 2. Larvae of lion ants.

hind her counter and approach Marvin Macy very slowly, her fists clenched, her peculiar red dress hanging awkwardly around her bony knees. Marvin Macy would also clench his fists and they would walk slowly and meaningfully around each other. But, although everyone watched breathlessly, nothing ever came of it. The time for the fight was not yet ready.

There is one particular reason why this winter is remembered and still talked about. A great thing happened. People woke up on the second of January and found the whole world about them altogether changed. Little ignorant children looked out of the windows, and they were so puzzled that they began to cry. Old people harked back and could remember nothing in these parts to equal the phenomenon. For in the night it had snowed. In the dark hours after midnight the dim flakes started falling softly on the town. By dawn the ground was covered, and the strange snow banked the ruby windows of the church, and whitened the roofs of the houses. The snow gave the town a drawn, bleak look. The two-room houses near the mill were dirty, crooked, and seemed about to collapse, and somehow everything was dark and shrunken. But the snow itself—there was a beauty about it few people around here had ever known before. The snow was not white, as Northerners had pictured it to be; in the snow there were soft colors of blue and silver, the sky was a gentle shining gray. And the dreamy quietness of falling snow—when had the town been so silent?

People reacted to the snowfall in various ways. Miss Amelia, on looking out of her window, thoughtfully wiggled the toes of her bare feet, gathered close to her neck the collar of her nightgown. She stood there for some time, then commenced to draw the shutters and lock every window on the premises. She closed the place completely, lighted the lamps, and sat solemnly over her bowl of grits. The reason for this was not that Miss Amelia feared the snowfall. It was simply that she was unable to form an immediate opinion of this new event, and unless she knew exactly and definitely what she thought of a matter (which was nearly always the case) she preferred to ignore it. Snow had never fallen in this county in her lifetime, and she had never thought about it one way or the other. But if she admitted this snowfall she would have to come to some decision, and in those days there was enough distraction in her life as it was already. So she poked about the gloomy, lamp-lighted house and pretended that nothing had happened. Cousin Lymon, on the contrary, chased around in the wildest excitement, and when Miss Amelia turned her back to dish him some breakfast he slipped out of the door.

Marvin Macy laid claim to the snowfall. He said that he knew snow, had seen it in Atlanta, and from the way he walked about the town that day it was as though he owned every flake. He sneered at the little children who crept timidly out of the houses and scooped up handfuls of snow to taste. Reverend Willin hurried down the road with a furious face, as he was thinking deeply and trying to weave the snow into his Sunday sermon. Most people were humble and glad about this marvel; they spoke in hushed voices and said "thank you" and "please" more than was necessary. A few weak characters, of course, were demoralized and got drunk—but they were not numerous. To everyone this was an occasion and many counted their money and planned to go to the café that night.

Cousin Lymon followed Marvin Macy about all day, seconding his claim to the snow. He marveled that snow did not fall as does rain, and stared up at the

dreamy, gently falling flakes until he stumbled from dizziness. And the pride he took on himself, basking in the glory of Marvin Macy—it was such that many people could not resist calling out to him: " 'Oho,' said the fly on the chariot wheel. 'What a dust we do raise.' "

Miss Amelia did not intend to serve a dinner. But when, at six o'clock, there was the sound of footsteps on the porch she opened the front door cautiously. It was Henry Ford Crimp, and though there was no food, she let him sit at a table and served him a drink. Others came. The evening was blue, bitter, and though the snow fell no longer there was a wind from the pine trees that swept up delicate flurries from the ground. Cousin Lymon did not come until after dark, with him Marvin Macy, and he carried his tin suitcase and his guitar.

"So you mean to travel?" said Miss Amelia quickly.

Marvin Macy warmed himself at the stove. Then he settled down at his table and carefully sharpened a little stick. He picked his teeth, frequently taking the stick out of his mouth to look at the end and wipe it on the sleeve of his coat. He did not bother to answer.

The hunchback looked at Miss Amelia, who was behind the counter. His face was not in the least beseeching; he seemed quite sure of himself. He folded his hands behind his back and perked up his ears confidently. His cheeks were red, his eyes shining, and his clothes were soggy wet. "Marvin Macy is going to visit a spell with us," he said.

Miss Amelia made no protest. She only came out from behind the counter and hovered over the stove, as though the news had made her suddenly cold. She did not warm her backside modestly, lifting her skirt only an inch or so, as do most women when in public. There was not a grain of modesty about Miss Amelia, and she frequently seemed to forget altogether that there were men in the room. Now she stood warming herself, her red dress was pulled up quite high in the back so that a piece of her strong, hairy thigh could be seen by anyone who cared to look at it. Her head was turned to one side; and she had begun talking with herself, nodding and wrinkling her forehead, and there was the tone of accusation and reproach in her voice although the words were not plain. Meanwhile, the hunchback and Marvin Macy had gone upstairs—up to the parlor with the pampas grass and the two sewing machines, to the private rooms where Miss Amelia had lived the whole of her life. Down in the café you could hear them bumping around, unpacking Marvin Macy, and getting him settled.

That is the way Marvin Macy crowded into Miss Amelia's home. At first Cousin Lymon, who had given Marvin Macy his own room, slept on the sofa in the parlor. But the snowfall had a bad effect on him; he caught a cold that turned into a winter quinsy, so Miss Amelia gave up her bed to him. The sofa in the parlor was much too short for her, her feet lapped over the edges, and often she rolled off onto the floor. Perhaps it was this lack of sleep that clouded her wits; everything she tried to do against Marvin Macy rebounded on herself. She got caught in her own tricks, and found herself in many pitiful positions. But still she did not put Marvin Macy off the premises, as she was afraid that she would be left alone. Once you have lived with another, it is a great torture to have to live alone. The silence of a firelit room when suddenly the clock stops ticking, the nervous shadows in an empty house—it is better to take in your mortal enemy than face the terror of living alone.

The snow did not last. The sun came out and within two days the town was just as it had always been before. Miss Amelia did not open her house until

every flake had melted. Then she had a big house cleaning and aired everything out in the sun. But before that, the very first thing she did on going out again into her yard, was to tie a rope to the largest branch of the chinaberry tree. At the end of the rope she tied a crocus sack tightly stuffed with sand. This was the punching bag she made for herself and from that day on she would box with it out in her yard every morning. Already she was a fine fighter—a little heavy on her feet, but knowing all manner of mean holds and squeezes to make up for this.

Miss Amelia, as has been mentioned, measured six feet two inches in height. Marvin Macy was one inch shorter. In weight they were about even—both of them weighing close to a hundred and sixty pounds. Marvin Macy had the advantage in slyness of movement, and in toughness of chest. In fact from the outward point of view the odds were altogether in his favor. Yet almost everybody in the town was betting on Miss Amelia; scarcely a person would put up money on Marvin Macy. The town remembered the great fight between Miss Amelia and a Forks Falls lawyer who had tried to cheat her. He had been a huge strapping fellow, but he was left three-quarters dead when she had finished with him. And it was not only her talent as a boxer that had impressed everyone—she could demoralize her enemy by making terrifying faces and fierce noises, so that even the spectators were sometimes cowed. She was brave, she practiced faithfully with her punching bag, and in this case she was clearly in the right. So people had confidence in her, and they waited. Of course there was no set date for this fight. There were just the signs that were too plain to be overlooked.

During these times the hunchback strutted around with a pleased little pinched-up face. In many delicate and clever ways he stirred up trouble between them. He was constantly plucking at Marvin Macy's trouser leg to draw attention to himself. Sometimes he followed in Miss Amelia's footsteps—but these days it was only in order to imitate her awkward long-legged walk; he crossed his eyes and aped her gestures in a way that made her appear to be a freak. There was something so terrible about this that even the silliest customers of the café, such as Merlie Ryan, did not laugh. Only Marvin Macy drew up the left corner of his mouth and chuckled. Miss Amelia, when this happened, would be divided between two emotions. She would look at the hunchback with a lost, dismal reproach—then turn toward Marvin Macy with her teeth clamped.

"Bust a gut!" she would say bitterly.

And Marvin Macy, most likely, would pick up the guitar from the floor beside his chair. His voice was wet and slimy, as he always had too much spit in his mouth. And the tunes he sang glided slowly from his throat like eels. His strong fingers picked the strings with dainty skill, and everything he sang both lured and exasperated. This was usually more than Miss Amelia could stand.

"Bust a gut!" she would repeat, in a shout.

But always Marvin Macy had the answer ready for her. He would cover the strings to silence the quivering leftover tones, and reply with slow, sure insolence.

"Everything you holler at me bounces back on yourself. Yah! Yah!"

Miss Amelia would have to stand there helpless, as no one has ever invented a way out of this trap. She could not shout out abuse that would bounce back on herself. He had the best of her, there was nothing she could do.

So things went on like this. What happened between the three of them during the nights in the rooms upstairs nobody knows. But the café became more and more crowded every night. A new table had to be brought in. Even the Hermit, the crazy man named Rainer Smith, who took to the swamp years ago, heard something of the situation and came one night to look in at the window and brood over the gathering in the bright café. And the climax each evening was the time when Miss Amelia and Marvin Macy doubled their fists, squared up, and glared at each other. Usually this did not happen after any especial argument, but it seemed to come about mysteriously, by means of some instinct on the part of both of them. At these times the café would become so quiet that you could hear the bouquet of paper roses rustling in the draft. And each night they held this fighting stance a little longer than the night before.

The fight took place on Ground Hog Day, which is the second of February. The weather was favorable, being neither rainy nor sunny, and with a neutral temperature. There were several signs that this was the appointed day, and by ten o'clock the news spread all over the county. Early in the morning Miss Amelia went out and cut down her punching bag. Marvin Macy sat on the back step with a tin can of hog fat between his knees and carefully greased his arms and his legs. A hawk with a bloody breast flew over the town and circled twice around the property of Miss Amelia. The tables in the café were moved out to the back porch, so that the whole big room was cleared for fight. There was every sign. Both Miss Amelia and Marvin Macy ate four helpings of half-raw roast for dinner, and then lay down in the afternoon to store up strength. Marvin Macy rested in the big room upstairs, while Miss Amelia stretched herself out on the bench in her office. It was plain from her white stiff face what a torment it was for her to be lying still and doing nothing, but she lay there quiet as a corpse with her eyes closed and her hands crossed on her chest.

Cousin Lymon had a restless day, and his little face was drawn and tightened with excitement. He put himself up a lunch, and set out to find the ground hog—within an hour he returned, the lunch eaten, and said that the ground hog had seen his shadow and there was to be bad weather ahead. Then, as Miss Amelia and Marvin Macy were both resting to gather strength, and he was left to himself, it occurred to him that he might as well paint the front porch. The house had not been painted for years—in fact, God knows if it had ever been painted at all. Cousin Lymon scrambled around, and soon he had painted half the floor of the porch a gay bright green. It was a loblolly job, and he smeared himself all over. Typically enough he did not even finish the floor, but changed over to the walls, painting as high as he could reach and then standing on a crate to get up a foot higher. When the paint ran out, the right side of the floor was bright green and there was a jagged portion of wall that had been painted. Cousin Lymon left it at that.

There was something childish about his satisfaction with his painting. And in this respect a curious fact should be mentioned. No one in the town, not even Miss Amelia, had any idea how old the hunchback was. Some maintained that when he came to town he was about twelve years old, still a child—others were certain that he was well past forty. His eyes were blue and steady as a child's, but there were lavender crepy shadows beneath these blue eyes that hinted of age. It was impossible to guess his age by his hunched queer body. And even his teeth gave no clue—they were all still in his head (two were bro-

ken from cracking a pecan), but he had stained them with so much sweet snuff that it was impossible to decide whether they were old teeth or young teeth. When questioned directly about his age the hunchback professed to know absolutely nothing—he had no idea how long he had been on the earth, whether for ten years or a hundred! So his age remained a puzzle.

Cousin Lymon finished his painting at five-thirty o'clock in the afternoon. The day had turned colder and there was a wet taste in the air. The wind came up from the pinewoods, rattling windows, blowing an old newspaper down the road until at last it caught upon a thorn tree. People began to come in from the country; packed automobiles that bristled with the poked-out heads of children, wagons drawn by old mules who seemed to smile in a weary, sour way and plodded along with their tired eyes half-closed. Three young boys came from Society City. All three of them wore yellow rayon shirts and caps put on backward—they were as much alike as triplets, and could always be seen at cockfights and camp meetings.[3] At six o'clock the mill whistle sounded the end of the day's shift and the crowd was complete. Naturally, among the newcomers there were some riffraff, unknown characters, and so forth—but even so the gathering was quiet. A hush was on the town and the faces of people were strange in the fading light. Darkness hovered softly; for a moment the sky was a pale clear yellow against which the gables of the church stood out in dark and bare outline, then the sky died slowly and the darkness gathered into night.

Seven is a popular number, and especially it was a favorite with Miss Amelia. Seven swallows of water for hiccups, seven runs around the millpond for cricks in the neck, seven doses of Amelia Miracle Mover as a worm cure—her treatment nearly always hinged on this number. It is a number of mingled possibilities, and all who love mystery and charms set store by it. So the fight was to take place at seven o'clock. This was known to everyone, not by announcement or words, but understood in the unquestioning way that rain is understood, or an evil odor from the swamp. So before seven o'clock everyone gathered gravely around the property of Miss Amelia. The cleverest got into the café itself and stood lining the walls of the room. Others crowded onto the front porch, or took a stand in the yard.

Miss Amelia and Marvin Macy had not yet shown themselves. Miss Amelia, after resting all afternoon on the office bench, had gone upstairs. On the other hand Cousin Lymon was at your elbow every minute, threading his way through the crowd, snapping his fingers nervously, and batting his eyes. At one minute to seven o'clock he squirmed his way into the café and climbed up on the counter. All was very quiet.

It must have been arranged in some manner beforehand. For just at the stroke of seven Miss Amelia showed herself at the head of the stairs. At the same instant Marvin Macy appeared in front of the café and the crowd made way for him silently. They walked toward each other with no haste, their fists already gripped and their eyes like the eyes of dreamers. Miss Amelia had changed her red dress for her old overalls, and they were rolled up to the knees. She was barefooted and she had an iron strengthband around her right wrist. Marvin Macy had also rolled his trouser legs—he was naked to the waist and heavily greased; he wore the heavy shoes that had been issued him when he

3. Series of evangelistic meetings.

left the penitentiary. Stumpy MacPhail stepped forward from the crowd and slapped their hip pockets with the palm of his right hand to make sure there would be no sudden knives. They were alone in the cleared center of the bright café.

There was no signal, but they both struck out simultaneously. Both blows landed on the chin, so that the heads of Miss Amelia and Marvin Macy bobbed back and they were left a little groggy. For a few seconds after the first blows they merely shuffled their feet around on the bare floor, experimenting with various positions, and making mock fists. Then, like wildcats, they were suddenly on each other. There was the sound of knocks, panting, and thumpings on the floor. They were so fast that it was hard to take in what was going on—but once Miss Amelia was hurled backward so that she staggered and almost fell, and another time Marvin Macy caught a knock on the shoulder that spun him round like a top. So the fight went on in this wild violent way with no sign of weakening on either side.

During a struggle like this, when the enemies are as quick and strong as these two, it is worth-while to turn from the confusion of the fight itself and observe the spectators. The people had flattened back as close as possible against the walls. Stumpy MacPhail was in a corner, crouched over and with his fists tight in sympathy, making strange noises. Poor Merlie Ryan had his mouth so wide open that a fly buzzed into it, and was swallowed before Merlie realized what had happened. And Cousin Lymon—he was worth watching. The hunchback still stood on the counter, so that he was raised above everyone else in the café. He had his hands on his hips, his big head thrust forward, and his little legs bent so that the knees jutted outward. The excitement had made him break out in a rash, and his pale mouth shivered.

Perhaps it was half an hour before the course of the fight shifted. Hundreds of blows had been exchanged, and there was still a deadlock. Then suddenly Marvin Macy managed to catch hold of Miss Amelia's left arm and pinion it behind her back. She struggled and got a grasp around his waist; the real fight was now begun. Wrestling is the natural way of fighting in this country—as boxing is too quick and requires much thinking and concentration. And now that Miss Amelia and Marvin were locked in a hold together the crowd came out of its daze and pressed in closer. For a while the fighters grappled muscle to muscle, their hipbones braced against each other. Backward and forward, from side to side, they swayed in this way. Marvin Macy still had not sweated, but Miss Amelia's overalls were drenched and so much sweat had trickled down her legs that she left wet footprints on the floor. Now the test had come, and in these moments of terrible effort, it was Miss Amelia who was the stronger. Marvin Macy was greased and slippery, tricky to grasp, but she was stronger. Gradually she bent him over backward, and inch by inch she forced him to the floor. It was a terrible thing to watch and their deep hoarse breaths were the only sound in the café. At last she had him down, and straddled; her strong big hands were on his throat.

But at that instant, just as the fight was won, a cry sounded in the café that caused a shrill bright shiver to run down the spine. And what took place has been a mystery ever since. The whole town was there to testify what happened, but there were those who doubted their own eyesight. For the counter on which Cousin Lymon stood was at least twelve feet from the fighters in the center of the café. Yet at the instant Miss Amelia grasped the throat of Marvin

Macy the hunchback sprang forward and sailed through the air as though he had grown hawk wings. He landed on the broad strong back of Miss Amelia and clutched at her neck with his clawed little fingers.

The rest is confusion. Miss Amelia was beaten before the crowd could come to their senses. Because of the hunchback the fight was won by Marvin Macy, and at the end Miss Amelia lay sprawled on the floor, her arms flung outward and motionless. Marvin Macy stood over her, his face somewhat popeyed, but smiling his old half-mouthed smile. And the hunchback, he had suddenly disappeared. Perhaps he was frightened about what he had done, or maybe he was so delighted that he wanted to glory with himself alone—at any rate he slipped out of the café and crawled under the back steps. Someone poured water on Miss Amelia, and after a time she got up slowly and dragged herself into her office. Through the open door the crowd could see her sitting at her desk, her head in the crook of her arm, and she was sobbing with the last of her grating, winded breath. Once she gathered her right fist together and knocked it three times on the top of her office desk, then her hand opened feebly and lay palm upward and still. Stumpy MacPhail stepped forward and closed the door.

The crowd was quiet, and one by one the people left the café. Mules were waked up and untied, automobiles cranked, and the three boys from Society City roamed off down the road on foot. This was not a fight to hash over and talk about afterward; people went home and pulled the covers up over their heads. The town was dark, except for the premises of Miss Amelia, but every room was lighted there the whole night long.

Marvin Macy and the hunchback must have left the town an hour or so before daylight. And before they went away this is what they did:

They unlocked the private cabinet of curios and took everything in it.

They broke the mechanical piano.

They carved terrible words on the café tables.

They found the watch that opened in the back to show a picture of a waterfall and took that also.

They poured a gallon of sorghum syrup all over the kitchen floor and smashed the jars of preserves.

They went out in the swamp and completely wrecked the still, ruining the big new condenser and the cooler, and setting fire to the shack itself.

They fixed a dish of Miss Amelia's favorite food, grits with sausage, seasoned it with enough poison to kill off the county, and placed this dish temptingly on the café counter.

They did everything ruinous they could think of without actually breaking into the office where Miss Amelia stayed the night. Then they went off together, the two of them.

That was how Miss Amelia was left alone in the town. The people would have helped her if they had known how, as people in this town will as often as not be kindly if they have a chance. Several housewives nosed around with brooms and offered to clear up the wreck. But Miss Amelia only looked at them with lost crossed eyes and shook her head. Stumpy MacPhail came in on the third day to buy a plug of Queenie tobacco, and Miss Amelia said the price was one dollar. Everything in the café had suddenly risen in price to be worth one dollar. And what sort of café is that? Also, she changed very queerly as a

doctor. In all the years before she had been much more popular than the Cheehaw doctor. She had never monkeyed with a patient's soul, taking away from him such real necessities as liquor, tobacco, and so forth. Once in a great while she might carefully warn a patient never to eat fried watermelon or some such dish it had never occurred to a person to want in the first place. Now all this wise doctoring was over. She told one-half of her patients that they were going to die outright, and to the remaining half she recommended cures so farfetched and agonizing that no one in his right mind would consider them for a moment.

Miss Amelia let her hair grow ragged, and it was turning gray. Her face lengthened, and the great muscles of her body shrank until she was thin as old maids are thin when they go crazy. And those gray eyes—slowly day by day they were more crossed, and it was as though they sought each other to exchange a little glance of grief and lonely recognition. She was not pleasant to listen to; her tongue had sharpened terribly.

When anyone mentioned the hunchback she would say only this: "Ho! If I could lay hand to him I would rip out his gizzard and throw it to the cat!" But it was not so much the words that were terrible, but the voice in which they were said. Her voice had lost its old vigor; there was none of the ring of vengeance it used to have when she would mention "that loom-fixer I was married to," or some other enemy. Her voice was broken, soft, and sad as the wheezy whine of the church pump-organ.

For three years she sat out on the front steps every night, alone and silent, looking down the road and waiting. But the hunchback never returned. There were rumors that Marvin Macy used him to climb into windows and steal, and other rumors that Marvin Macy had sold him into a side show. But both these reports were traced back to Merlie Ryan. Nothing true was ever heard of him. It was in the fourth year that Miss Amelia hired a Cheehaw carpenter and had him board up the premises, and there in those closed rooms she has remained ever since.

Yes, the town is dreary. On August afternoons the road is empty, white with dust, and the sky above is bright as glass. Nothing moves—there are no children's voices, only the hum of the mill. The peach trees seem to grow more crooked every summer, and the leaves are dull gray and of a sickly delicacy. The house of Miss Amelia leans so much to the right that it is now only a question of time when it will collapse completely, and people are careful not to walk around the yard. There is no good liquor to be bought in the town; the nearest still is eight miles away, and the liquor is such that those who drink it grow warts on their livers the size of goobers, and dream themselves into a dangerous inward world. There is absolutely nothing to do in the town. Walk around the millpond, stand kicking at a rotten stump, figure out what you can do with the old wagon wheel by the side of the road near the church. The soul rots with boredom. You might as well go down to the Forks Falls highway and listen to the chain gang.

1944

GWENDOLYN BROOKS

1917–

In an important response to an interviewer's question, Gwendolyn Brooks declared that "what I'm fighting for now in my work [is] an *expression* relevant to all manner of blacks poems I could take into a tavern, into the street, into the halls of a housing project." Her impassioned statement holds true not only in the highly politicized work she wrote under the influence of the civil rights movement in the late 1960s but also in her earlier compositions. Indeed, the poetry Brooks produced during World War II remains pioneering in its effort to democratize the subject matter of verse in technically complex works clearly worthy of the Pulitzer Prize she earned in 1950; she was the first African American to win the award.

Born in Topeka, Kansas, Gwendolyn Brooks was only five weeks old when her parents brought her to live in the area with which she would always be identified, the south side of Chicago. Her mother's belief that she might become the "lady Paul Laurence Dunbar" encouraged the young writer, as did her visits to poetry readings by such African-American writers as Langston Hughes and James Weldon Johnson. After graduating from Chicago's Wilson Junior College in 1936, Brooks entered a poetry workshop at the South Side Community Art Center, where, with the guidance of Inez Cunningham Stark, a Chicago socialite, she studied the major modernists and, in the words of one biographer, was "introduced to the rigors of poetic technique."

The early work that resulted from this education revealed extraordinary verbal skill, particularly an interest in what Brooks herself has called "word play," as well as exceptional accomplishment in the handling of intricate verse forms. Like the writers of the Harlem Renaissance whose voices she had heard as a child, Brooks combined black idioms, jazz rhythm, and street slang with the traditional "high style" of English poetry. Married in 1939 to Henry Blakely, and the mother of two children, she produced in this period a series of volumes of verse—notably *A Street in Bronzeville* (1945), *Annie Allen* (1949), and *The Bean Eaters* (1960)—which offered vivid depictions of the lives and losses of people in Chicago's black neighborhoods, together with a novel, *Maud Martha* (1953), about a young black girl's growth to adulthood. Yet though she dealt brilliantly—sometimes poignantly and sometimes sardonically—with Bronzeville (the name given by journalists to Chicago's black ghetto), exploring the lives of both men (e.g., *Satin-Legs Smith*) and women (*Woman in a Red Hat*), Brooks has herself explained that "I wasn't writing consciously with the idea that blacks *must address* blacks."

In 1967, when she attended the second Black Writers' Conference at Fisk University, Brooks met a number of young black poets who persuaded her that "black poets should write as blacks, about blacks, and address themselves to blacks." Revitalized by their commitment, she began to teach a verse-writing workshop for a group of Chicago teenagers called the Blackstone Rangers, and becoming herself an activist leader, she sought to "*clarify* [her] language" so that she could reach out to wider audiences—specifically "to all manner of blacks." Exploring the tragedies of American racism as well as the triumphs of black endurance, her later works in this mode include several important volumes of verse—notably *In the Mecca* (1968), a book-length poetic sequence examining the diversity of existence in a Chicago housing project; *Riot* (1969); and *Beckonings* (1975)—along with an autobiography, *Report from Part I* (1972), and several books of poetry for children.

Though Brooks does not define herself as a feminist, believing that racial issues must take priority over gender questions, she has always written with extraordinary

sympathy about the dilemmas of female characters like those in *Bronzeville Woman in a Red Hat* and *the mother*. In addition, she has frequently attempted to analyze the roots of what she calls "woman rage," asking, for example, "Why in the world has it been that our men have preferred either white or that pigmentation which is as close to white as possible?" Courageously exploring the real choices that real women confront, she has nevertheless also insisted that, even if "black women have got some problems with black men and vice versa, . . . these are family matters. They must be worked out within the family."

the mother

Abortions will not let you forget.
You remember the children you got that you did not get,
The damp small pulps with a little or with no hair,
The singers and workers that never handled the air.
You will never neglect or beat 5
Them, or silence or buy with a sweet.
You will never wind up the sucking-thumb
Or scuttle off ghosts that come.
You will never leave them, controlling your luscious sigh,
Return for a snack of them, with gobbling mother-eye 10

I have heard in the voices of the wind the voices of my dim
 killed children.
I have contracted. I have eased
My dim dears at the breasts they could never suck.
I have said, Sweets, if I sinned, if I seized
Your luck 15
And your lives from your unfinished reach,
If I stole your births and your names,
Your straight baby tears and your games,
Your stilted or lovely loves, your tumults, your marriages,
 aches, and your deaths,
If I poisoned the beginnings of your breaths, 20
Believe that even in my deliberateness I was not deliberate.
Though why should I whine,
Whine that the crime was other than mine?—
Since anyhow you are dead.
Or rather, or instead, 25
You were never made.

But that too, I am afraid,
Is faulty: oh, what shall I say, how is the truth to be said?
You were born, you had body, you died.
It is just that you never giggled or planned or cried 30

Believe me, I loved you all.
Believe me, I knew you, though faintly, and I loved, I loved you
All.

1945

a song in the front yard

I've stayed in the front yard all my life,
I want a peek at the back
Where it's rough and untended and hungry weed grows.
A girl gets sick of a rose.

I want to go in the back yard now 5
And maybe down the alley,
To where the charity children play.
I want a good time today.

They do some wonderful things.
They have some wonderful fun. 10
My mother sneers, but I say it's fine
How they don't have to go in at quarter to nine.
My mother, she tells me that Johnnie Mae
Will grow up to be a bad woman.
That George'll be taken to Jail soon or late 15
(On account of last winter he sold our back gate.)

But I say it's fine. Honest, I do.
And I'd like to be a bad woman, too,
And wear the brave stockings of night-black lace
And strut down the streets with paint on my face. 20

1945

The Sundays
of Satin-Legs Smith

Inamoratas,[1] with an approbation,
Bestowed his title. Blessed his inclination.)

He wakes, unwinds, elaborately: a cat
Tawny, reluctant, royal. He is fat
And fine this morning. Definite. Reimbursed. 5

He waits a moment, he designs his reign,
That no performance may be plain or vain.
Then rises in a clear delirium.

He sheds, with his pajamas, shabby days,
And his desertedness, his intricate fear, the 10
Postponed resentments and the prim precautions.

1. Women whom he loves.

Now, at his bath, would you deny him lavender
Or take away the power of his pine?
What smelly substitute, heady as wine,
Would you provide? life must be aromatic. 15
There must be scent, somehow there must be some.
Would you have flowers in his life? suggest
Asters? a Really Good geranium?
A white carnation? would you prescribe a Show
With the cold lilies, formal chrysanthemum 20
Magnificence, poinsettias, and emphatic
Red of prize roses? might his happiest
Alternative (you muse) be, after all,
A bit of gentle garden in the best
Of taste and straight tradition? Maybe so. 25
But you forget, or did you ever know,
His heritage of cabbage and pigtails,
Old intimacy with alleys, garbage pails,
Down in the deep (but always beautiful) South
Where roses blush their blithest (it is said) 30
And sweet magnolias put Chanel to shame.

No! He has not a flower to his name.
Except a feather one, for his lapel.
Apart from that, if he should think of flowers
It is in terms of dandelions or death. 35
Ah, there is little hope. You might as well—
Unless you care to set the world a-boil
And do a lot of equalizing things,
Remove a little ermine, say, from kings,
Shake hands with paupers and appoint them men, 40
For instance—certainly you might as well
Leave him his lotion, lavender and oil.

Let us proceed. Let us inspect, together
With his meticulous and serious love,
The innards of this closet. Which is a vault 45
Whose glory is not diamonds, not pearls,
Not silver plate with just enough dull shine.
But wonder-suits in yellow and in wine,
Sarcastic green and zebra-striped cobalt.
All drapes. With shoulder padding that is wide 50
And cocky and determined as his pride;
Ballooning pants that taper off to ends
Scheduled to choke precisely.

 Here are hats
Like bright umbrellas; and hysterical ties 55
Like narrow banners for some gathering war.

People are so in need, in need of help.
People want so much that they do not know.

Below the tinkling trade of little coins
The gold impulse not possible to show 50
Or spend. Promise piled over and betray.

These kneaded limbs receive the kiss of silk.
Then they receive the brave and beautiful
Embrace of some of that equivocal wool.
He looks into his mirror, loves himself— 65
The neat curve here; the angularity
That is appropriate at just its place;
The technique of a variegated grace.

Here is all his sculpture and his art
And all his architectural design. 70
Perhaps you would prefer to this a fine
Value of marble, complicated stone.
Would have him think with horror of baroque,
Rococo.[2] You forget and you forget.

He dances down the hotel steps that keep 75
Remnants of last night's high life and distress.
As spat-out purchased kisses and spilled beer.
He swallows sunshine with a secret yelp.
Passes to coffee and a roll or two. 80
Has breakfasted.

 Out. Sounds about him smear,
Become a unit. He hears and does not hear
The alarm clock meddling in somebody's sleep;
Children's governed Sunday happiness;
The dry tone of a plane; a woman's oath; 85
Consumption's spiritless expectoration;[3]
An indignant robin's resolute donation
Pinching a track through apathy and din;
Restaurant vendors weeping; and the L[4]
That comes on like a slightly horrible thought. 90

Pictures, too, as usual, are blurred.
He sees and does not see the broken windows
Hiding their shame with newsprint; little girl
With ribbons decking wornness, little boy
Wearing the trousers with the decentest patch, 95
To honor Sunday; women on their way
From "service," temperate holiness arranged
Ably on asking faces; men estranged
From music and from wonder and from joy
But far familiar with the guiding awe 100
Of foodlessness.
 He loiters.
 Restaurant vendors
Weep, or out of them rolls a restless glee.
The Lonesome Blues, the Long-lost Blues, I Want A 105

2. Two artistic styles, both elaborate and ornate. 4. I.e., the elevated train
3. I.e., the cough of one with tuberculosis.

Big Fat Mama. Down these sore avenues
Comes no Saint-Saëns, no piquant elusive Grieg,
And not Tschaikovsky's wayward eloquence
And not the shapely tender drift of Brahms.[5]
But could he love them? Since a man must bring 110
To music what his mother spanked him for
When he was two: bits of forgotten hate,
Devotion: whether or not his mattress hurts:
The little dream his father humored: the thing
His sister did for money: what he ate 115
For breakfast—and for dinner twenty years
Ago last autumn: all his skipped desserts.

The pasts of his ancestors lean against
Him. Crowd him. Fog out his identity.
Hundreds of hungers mingle with his own, 120
Hundreds of voices advise so dexterously
He quite considers his reactions his,
Judges he walks most powerfully alone,
That everything is—simply what it is.

But movie-time approaches, time to boo 125
The hero's kiss, and boo the heroine
Whose ivory and yellow it is sin
For his eye to eat of. The Mickey Mouse,
However, is for everyone in the house.

Squires his lady to dinner at Joe's Eats. 130
His lady alters as to leg and eye,
Thickness and height, such minor points as these,
From Sunday to Sunday. But no matter what
Her name or body positively she's
In Queen Lace stockings with ambitious heels 135
That strain to kiss the calves, and vivid shoes
Frontless and backless, Chinese fingernails,
Earrings, three layers of lipstick, intense hat
Dripping with the most voluble of veils.
Her affable extremes are like sweet bombs 140
About him, whom no middle grace or good
Could gratify. He had no education
In quiet arts of compromise. He would
Not understand your counsels on control, nor
Thank you for your late trouble. 145

 At Joe's Eats
You get your fish or chicken on meat platters.
With coleslaw, macaroni, candied sweets,
Coffee and apple pie. You go out full.
(The end is—isn't it?—all that really matters.) 150

5. All symphonic composers: Charles Camille Saint-Saëns (1835–1921), French; Edvard Grieg (1843–1907), Norwegian; Pyotr Tchaikovsky (1840–1893), Russian; Johannes Brahms (1833–1897), German.

And even and intrepid come
The tender boots of night to home.

He- body is like new brown bread
Under the Woolworth mignonette.[6]
He- body is a honey bowl 155
Whose waiting honey is deep and not.
He- body is like summer earth,
Receptive, soft, and absolute . . .

1945

From The Womanhood

3

Stand off, daughter of the dusk,
And do not wince when the bronzy lads
Hurry to cream-yellow shining.
It is plausible. The sun is a lode.

True, there is silver under 5
The veils of the darkness.
But few care to dig in the night
For the possible treasure of stars.

1949

The Bean Eaters

They eat beans mostly, this old yellow pair.
Dinner is a casual affair.
Plain chipware on a plain and creaking wood,
Tin flatware.

Two who are Mostly Good. 5
Two who have lived their day,
But keep on putting on their clothes
And putting things away.

And remembering . . .
Remembering, with twinklings and twinges, 10
As they lean over the beans in their rented back room
 that is full of beads and receipts and dolls and
 cloths, tobacco crumbs, vases and fringes.

1960

6. Perfume made from the mignonette flower.

We Real Cool

The Pool Players.
Seven at the Golden Shovel

We real cool. We
Left school. We

Lurk late. We
Strike straight. We

Sing sin. We 5
Thin gin. We

Jazz June. We
Die soon.

1960

Bronzeville[1] Woman in a Red Hat

hires out to Mrs. Miles

I

They had never had one in the house before.
The strangeness of it all. Like unleashing
A lion, really. Poised
To pounce. A puma. A panther. A black
Bear. 5
There it stood in the door,
Under a red hat that was rash, but refreshing—
In a tasteless way, of course—across the dull dare,
The semi-assault of that extraordinary blackness.
The slackness 10
Of that light pink mouth told little. The eyes told
 of heavy care. . . .
But that was neither here nor there,
And nothing to a wage-paying mistress as should
Be getting her due whether life had been good
For her slave, or bad. 15
There it stood
In the door. They had never had
One in the house before.

But the Irishwoman had left!
A message had come. 20
Something about a murder at home.
A daughter's husband—"berserk," that was the phrase:
The dear man had "gone berserk"

1. Name given to a Chicago black ghetto.

And short work—
With a hammer—had been made 25
Of this daughter and her nights and days.
The Irishwoman (underpaid,
Mrs. Miles remembered with smiles),
Who was a perfect jewel, a red-faced tramp,
A good old sort, a baker 30
Of rum cake, a maker
Of Mustard, would never return.
Mrs. Miles had begged the bewitched woman
To finish, at least, the biscuit blending,
To tarry till the curry was done, 35
To show some concern
For the burning soup, to attend to the tending
Of the tossed salad. "Inhuman,"
Patsy Houlihan had called Mrs. Miles.
"Inhuman." And "a fool." 40
And "a cool
One."

The Alert Agency had leafed through its files—
On short notice could offer
Only this dusky duffer[2] 45
That now made its way to her kitchen and sat on her
 kitchen stool.

II

Her creamy child kissed by the black maid! square on the mouth!
World yelled, world writhed, world turned to light and rolled
Into her kitchen, nearly knocked her down.

Quotations, of course, from baby books were great 50
Ready armor: (but her animal distress
Wore, too and under, a subtler metal dress,
Inheritance of approximately hate.)
Say baby shrieked to see his finger bleed.
Wished human humoring—there was a kind 55
Of unintimate love, a love more of the mind
To order the nebulousness of that need.
—This was the way to put it, this the relief.
This sprayed a honey upon marvelous grime.
This told it possible to postpone the reef. 60
Fashioned a huggable darling out of crime.
Made monster personable in personal sight
By cracking mirrors down the personal night.

Disgust crawled through her as she chased the theme.
She, quite supposing purity despoiled, 65
Committed to sourness, disordered, soiled,
Went in to pry the ordure[3] from the cream.

2. Dense or clumsy person 3. Excrement.

Cooing, "Come." (Come out of the cannibal wilderness,
Dirt, dark, into the sun and bloomful air.
Return to freshness of your right world, wear　　　　　70
Sweetness again. Be done with beast, duress.)

Child with continuing cling issued his No in final fire,
　　　　Kissed back the colored maid,
　　　　Not wise enough to freeze or be afraid.
　　　　Conscious of kindness, easy creature bond.　　　　　75
　　　　Love had been handy and rapid to respond.

Heat at the hairline, heat between the bowels,
Examining seeming coarse unnatural scene,
She saw all things except herself serene:
Child, big black woman, pretty kitchen towels.　　　　　80

　　　　　　　　　　　　　　　　　　　　　1960

The Last Quatrain of the Ballad of Emmett Till[1]

　　　　　　　　　　after the murder,
　　　　　　　　　　after the burial

　　　Emmett's mother is a pretty-faced thing;
　　　　　　　the tint of pulled taffy.
　　　She sits in a red room,　　　　　　　　　　5
　　　　　　　drinking black coffee.
　　　She kisses her killed boy.
　　　　　　　And she is sorry.
　　　Chaos in windy grays
　　　　　　　through a red prairie.　　　　　10

　　　　　　　　　　　　　　　　　　　　　1960

To the Diaspora[1]

you did not know you were Afrika

When you set out for Afrika
you did not know you were going.
Because
you did not know you were Afrika.
You did not know the Black continent　　　　　5
that had to be reached
was you.

I could not have told you then that some sun
would come,

1. An African-American boy, fourteen years old, who
was lynched in Mississippi in 1955 for allegedly "leer-
ing" at a white woman.
1. People settled far from their ancestral homelands.

somewhere over the road, 10
would come evoking the diamonds
of you, the Black continent—
somewhere over the road.
You would not have believed my mouth.

When I told you, meeting you somewhere close 15
to the heat and youth of the road,
liking my loyalty, liking belief,
you smiled and you thanked me but very little believed me.

Here is some sun. Some.
Now off into the places rough to reach. 20
Though dry, though drowsy, all unwillingly a-wobble,
into the dissonant and dangerous crescendo.
Your work, that was done, to be done to be done to be done.

 1981

The Coora Flower

Today I learned the *coora* flower
grows high in the mountains of Itty-go-luba Bésa.
Province Meechee.
Pop. 39.

Now I am coming home. 5
This, at least, is Real, and what I know.

It was restful, learning nothing necessary.
School is tiny vacation. At least you can sleep
At least you can think of love or feeling your boy friend against you
(which is not free from grief). 10

But now it's Real Business.
I am Coming Home.

My mother will be screaming in an almost dirty dress.
The crack is gone. So a Man will be in the house.

I must watch myself. 15
I must not dare to sleep.

 1991

MURIEL SPARK

1918–

When she was an adolescent, Muriel Camberg composed torrid love letters that she signed with men's names and concealed around the house in the hope of giving her mother a good shock. This fictional gesture forecasts the witty impersonation characteristic of Spark's later writing in novels and short stories that frequently deal with blackmail, literary espionage, and the mysterious interconnections between illusion and reality.

Muriel Camberg was brought up in a prosperous Edinburgh neighborhood by a Presbyterian mother and a Jewish father. After attending James Gillespie's School for Girls, she traveled to South Africa, where she married S. O. Spark and gave birth to a son. The marriage ended quickly and several years later Spark returned to Great Britain, where she worked for the Political Intelligence Department until the end of World War II. Then she supported herself as a freelance writer and editor, publishing several books collaboratively with Derek Stanford, including lives of the Brontës and of Mary Shelley. After converting to Catholicism at the age of thirty-six, Spark completed her first novel, *The Comforters* (1957). Her subsequent stories and novels, set for the most part in England or in Africa, often unmask the hypocrisies of professional Catholics even as they dramatize the dilemmas of authentic spiritual conversions. It was, however, the grotesque comedy of *Memento Mori* (1959) that established Spark's reputation. Later novels—*The Prime of Miss Jean Brodie* (1961), *The Girls of Slender Means* (1963), and *The Abbess of Crewe* (1974), in particular—turn her irony toward the delusions and deceits of communities of women. In *The Black Madonna*, she slyly satirizes not only the spiritual bankruptcy of characters who congratulate themselves on their moral correctness but also the mythologizing of a so-called maternal instinct.

The Black Madonna

When the Black Madonna was installed in the Church of the Sacred Heart the Bishop himself came to consecrate it. His long purple train was upheld by the two curliest of the choir. The day was favored suddenly with thin October sunlight as he crossed the courtyard from the presbytery[1] to the church, as the procession followed him chanting the Litany of the Saints: five priests in vestments of white heavy silk interwoven with glinting threads, four lay officials with straight red robes, then the confraternities and the tangled columns of the Mothers' Union.

The new town of Whitney Clay had a large proportion of Roman Catholics, especially among the nurses at the new hospital; and at the paper mills, too, there were many Catholics, drawn inland from Liverpool by the new housing estate; likewise, with the canning factories.

The Black Madonna had been given to the church by a recent convert. It was carved out of bog oak.

"They found the wood in the bog. Had been there hundreds of years. They sent for the sculptor right away by phone. He went over to Ireland and carved it there and then. You see, he had to do it while it was still wet."

"Looks a bit like contemporary art."

1. The house of the parish priest.

"Nah, that's not contemporary art, it's old-fashioned. If you'd ever seen contemporary work you *know* it was old-fashioned."

"Looks like contemp—"

"It's old-*fashioned*. Else how'd it get sanctioned to be put up?"

"It's not so nice as the Immaculate Conception at Lourdes.[2] That lifts you up."

Everyone got used, eventually, to the Black Madonna with her square hands and straight carved draperies. There was a movement to dress it up in vestments, or at least a lace veil.

"She looks a bit gloomy, Father, don't you think?"

"No," said the priest, "I think it looks fine. If you start dressing it up in cloth you'll spoil the line."

Sometimes people came from London especially to see the Black Madonna, and these were not Catholics; they were, said the priest, probably no religion at all, poor souls, though gifted with faculties. They came, as if to a museum, to see the line of the Black Madonna which must not be spoiled by vestments.

The new town of Whitney Clay had swallowed up the old village. One or two cottages with double dormer windows, an inn called "The Tyger," a Methodist chapel and three small shops represented the village; the three small shops were already threatened by the Council;[3] the Methodists were fighting to keep their chapel. Only the double dormer cottages and the inn were protected by the Nation and so had to be suffered by the Town Planning Committee.

The town was laid out like geometry in squares, arcs (to allow for the bypass) and isosceles triangles, breaking off, at one point, to skirt the old village which, from the aerial view, looked like a merry doodle on the page.

Manders Road was one side of a parallelogram of green-bordered streets. It was named after one of the founders of the canning concern, Manders' Figs in Syrup, and it comprised a row of shops and a long high block of flats named Cripps House after the late Sir Stafford Cripps who had laid the foundation stone. In flat twenty-two on the fifth floor of Cripps House lived Raymond and Lou Parker. Raymond Parker was a foreman at the motor works, and was on the management committee. He had been married for fifteen years to Lou, who was thirty-seven at the time that the miraculous powers of the Black Madonna came to be talked of.

Of the twenty-five couples who live in Cripps House five were Catholics. All, except Raymond and Lou Parker, had children. A sixth family had recently been moved by the Council into one of the six-roomed houses because of the seven children besides the grandfather.

Raymond and Lou were counted lucky to have obtained their three-roomed flat although they had no children. People with children had priority; but their name had been on the waiting list for years, and some said Raymond had a pull with one of the Councilors who was a director of the motor works.

The Parkers were among the few tenants of Cripps House who owned a motor car. They did not, like most of their neighbors, have a television receiver, for being childless they had been able to afford to expand themselves in

2. A town in France that is the site of one of the most famous shrines of the Virgin Mary, associated with miraculous cures.

3. Local authority, which is responsible for housing.

the way of taste, so that their habits differed slightly and their amusements considerably, from those of their neighbors. The Parkers went to the pictures only when *The Observer*[4] had praised the film; they considered television not their sort of thing; they adhered to their religion; they voted Labour; they believed that the twentieth century was the best so far; they assented to the doctrine of original sin;[5] they frequently applied the word "Victorian" to ideas and people they did not like—for instance, when a local Town Councilor resigned his office Raymond said, "He had to go. He's Victorian. And far too young for the job"; and Lou said Jane Austen's[6] books were too Victorian; and anyone who opposed the abolition of capital punishment was Victorian. Raymond took the *Reader's Digest*, a magazine called *Motoring* and *The Catholic Herald*. Lou took *The Queen*, *Woman's Own* and *Life*. Their daily paper was *The News Chronicle*. They read two books apiece each week. Raymond preferred travel books; Lou liked novels.

For the first five years of their married life they had been worried about not having children. Both had submitted themselves to medical tests as a result of which Lou had a course of injections. These were unsuccessful. It had been a special disappointment since both came from large sprawling Catholic families. None of their married brothers and sisters had less than three children. One of Lou's sisters, now widowed, had eight; they sent her a pound a week.

Their flat in Cripps House had three rooms and a kitchen. All round them their neighbors were saving up to buy houses. A council flat, once obtained, was a mere platform in space to further the progress of the rocket. This ambition was not shared by Raymond and Lou; they were not only content, they were delighted, with these civic chambers, and indeed took something of an aristocratic view of them, not without a self-conscious feeling of being free, in this particular, from the prejudices of that middle class to which they as good as belonged. "One day," said Lou, "it will be the thing to live in a council flat."

They were eclectic as to their friends. Here, it is true, they differed slightly from each other. Raymond was for inviting the Ackleys to meet the Farrells. Mr. Ackley was an accountant at the Electricity Board. Mr. and Mrs. Farrell were respectively a sorter at Manders' Figs in Syrup and an usherette at the Odeon.

"After all," argued Raymond, "they're all Catholics."

"Ah well," said Lou, "but now, their interests are different. The Farrells wouldn't know what the Ackleys were talking about. The Ackleys like politics. The Farrells like to tell jokes. I'm not a snob, only sensible."

"Oh, please yourself." For no-one could call Lou a snob, and everyone knew she was sensible.

Their choice of acquaintance was wide by reason of their active church membership:" that is to say, they were members of various guilds and confraternities. Raymond was a sidesman,[7] and he also organized the weekly football lottery in aid of the Church Decoration Fund. Lou felt rather out of things when the Mothers' Union met and had special Masses, for the Mothers' Union was the only group she did not qualify for. Having been a nurse before her marriage she was, however, a member of the Nurses' Guild.

4. A liberal national paper.
5. The doctrine that all human beings, as a result of the Fall of Adam and Eve from divine grace, are born in a state of sin.

6. English novelist (1775–1817), whose writings do not fall into the Victorian period (1837–1903).
7. Elected assistant to a parish churchwarden.

Thus, most of their Catholic friends came from different departments of life. Others, connected with the motor works where Raymond was a foreman, were of different social grades to which Lou was more alive than Raymond. He let her have her way, as a rule, when it came to a question of which would mix with which.

A dozen Jamaicans were taken on at the motor works. Two came into Raymond's department. He invited them to the flat one evening to have coffee. They were unmarried, very polite and black. The quiet one was called Henry Pierce and the talkative one, Oxford St. John. Lou, to Raymond's surprise and pleasure, decided that all their acquaintance, from top to bottom, must meet Henry and Oxford. All along he had known she was not a snob, only sensible, but he had rather feared she would consider the mixing of their new black and their old white friends not sensible.

"I'm glad you like Henry and Oxford," he said. "I'm glad we're able to introduce them to so many people." For the dark pair had, within a month, spent nine evenings at Cripps House; they had met accountants, teachers, packers and sorters. Only Tina Farrell, the usherette, had not seemed to understand the quality of these occasions: "Quite nice chaps, them darkies, when you get to know them."

"You mean Jamaicans," said Lou. "Why shouldn't they be nice? They're no different from anyone else."

"Yes, yes, that's what I mean," said Tina.

"We're all equal," stated Lou. "Don't forget there are black Bishops."

"Jesus, I never said we were the equal of a Bishop," Tina said, very bewildered.

"Well, don't call them darkies."

Sometimes, on summer Sunday afternoons Raymond and Lou took their friends for a run in their car, ending up at a riverside road-house. The first time they turned up with Oxford and Henry they felt defiant; but there were no objections, there was no trouble at all. Soon the dark pair ceased to be a novelty. Oxford St. John took up with a pretty red-haired bookkeeper, and Henry Pierce, missing his companion, spent more of his time at the Parkers' flat.[8] Lou and Raymond had planned to spend their two weeks' summer holiday in London. "Poor Henry," said Lou. "He'll miss us."

Once you brought him out he was not so quiet as you thought at first. Henry was twenty-four, desirous of knowledge in all fields, shining very much in eyes, skin, teeth, which made him seem all the more eager. He called out the material in Lou, and to some extent the avuncular in Raymond. Lou used to love him when he read out lines from his favorite poems which he had copied into an exercise book.

> Haste thee, nymph, and bring with thee
> Jest and youthful jollity,
> Sport that[9] . . .

Lou would interrupt: "You should say jest, jollity—not yest, yollity."

"Jest," he said carefully. "And laughter holding both his sides," he continued. "*Laughter*—hear that, Lou? —*laughter*. That's what the human race was made for. Those folks that go round gloomy. Lou, they . . ."

8. Apartment. 9. Slightly misquoted from Milton's *L'Allegro* (1631).

Lou loved this talk. Raymond puffed his pipe benignly. After Henry had gone Raymond would say what a pity it was such an intelligent young fellow had lapsed. For Henry had been brought up in a Roman Catholic mission. He had, however, abandoned religion. He was fond of saying, "The superstition of today is the science of yesterday."

"I can't allow," Raymond would say, "that the Catholic Faith is superstition. I can't allow that."

"He'll return to the Church one day"—this was Lou's contribution, whether Henry was present or not. If she said it in front of Henry he would give her an angry look. These were the only occasions when Henry lost his cheerfulness and grew quiet again.

Raymond and Lou prayed for Henry, that he might regain his faith. Lou said her rosary[1] three times a week before the Black Madonna.

"He'll miss us when we go on our holidays."

Raymond telephoned to the hotel in London. "Have you a single room for a young gentleman accompanying Mr. and Mrs. Parker?" He added, " a colored gentleman." To his pleasure a room was available, and to his relief there was no objection to Henry's color.

They enjoyed their London holiday, but it was somewhat marred by a visit to that widowed sister of Lou's to whom she allowed a pound a week towards the rearing of her eight children. Lou had not seen her sister Elizabeth for nine years.

They went to her one day towards the end of their holiday. Henry sat at the back of the car beside a large suitcase stuffed with old clothes for Elizabeth. Raymond at the wheel kept saying, "Poor Elizabeth—eight kids," which irritated Lou, though she kept her peace.

Outside the underground[2] station at Victoria Park, where they stopped to ask the way, Lou felt a strange sense of panic. Elizabeth lived in a very downward quarter of Bethnal Green,[3] and in the past nine years since she had seen her Lou's memory of the shabby ground-floor rooms with their peeling walls and bare boards, had made a kinder nest for itself. Sending off the postal order to her sister each week she had gradually come to picture the habitation at Bethnal Green in an almost monastic light; it would be bare but well-scrubbed, spotless, and shining with Brasso and holy poverty. The floor boards gleamed. Elizabeth was gray-haired, lined, but neat. The children well behaved, sitting down betimes to their broth in two rows along an almost refectory table. It was not till they had reached Victoria Park that Lou felt the full force of the fact that everything would be different from what she had imagined. "It may have gone down since I was last there," she said to Raymond who had never visited Elizabeth before.

"What's gone down?"

"Poor Elizabeth's place."

Lou had not taken much notice of Elizabeth's dull little monthly letters, almost illiterate, for Elizabeth, as she herself always said, was not much of a scholar. "James is at another job I hope that's the finish of the bother I had my blood presiure there was a Health visitor very nice. Also the assistance they sent my Dinner all the time and for the kids at home they call it meals on

1. A series of Catholic prayers, which are often counted with the help of a string of special beads.
2. Subway.
3. Factory district in London's East End.

Wheels. I pray to the Almighty that James is well out of his bother he never lets on at sixteen their all the same never open his mouth but Gods eyes are not shut. Thanks for P.O.[4] you will be rewarded your affect sister Elizabeth."

Lou tried to piece together in her mind the gist of nine years' such letters. James was the eldest; she supposed he had been in trouble.

"I ought to have asked Elizabeth about young James," said Lou. "She wrote to me last year that he was in a bother, there was talk of him being sent away, but I didn't take it in at the time, I was busy."

"You can't take everything on your shoulders," said Raymond. "You do very well by Elizabeth." They had pulled up outside the house where Elizabeth lived on the ground floor. Lou looked at the chipped paint, the dirty windows and torn gray-white curtains and was reminded with startling clarity of her hopeless childhood in Liverpool from which, miraculously, hope had lifted her, and had come true. for the nuns had got her that job; and she had trained as a nurse among white-painted beds, and white shining walls, and tiles, hot water everywhere and Dettol without stint. When she had first married she had wanted all white-painted furniture that you could wash and liberate from germs; but Raymond had been for oak he did not understand the pleasure of hygiene and new enamel paint, for his upbringing had been orderly, he had been accustomed to a lounge suite and autumn tints in the front room all his life. And now Lou stood and looked at the outside of Elizabeth's place and felt she had gone right back.

On the way back to the hotel Lou chattered with relief that it was over. 'Poor Elizabeth, she hasn't had much of a chance. I liked little Francis, what did you think of little Francis, Ray?"

Raymond did not like being called Ray, but he made no objection for he knew that Lou had been under a strain. Elizabeth had not been very pleasant. She had expressed admiration for Lou's hat, bag, gloves and shoes which were all navy blue, but she had used an accusing tone. The house had been smelly and dirty. "I'll show you round," Elizabeth had said in a tone of mock refinement, and they were forced to push through a dark narrow passage behind her skinny form till they came to the big room where the children slept. A row of old iron beds each with a tumble of dark blanket rugs, no sheets. Raymond was indignant at the sight and hoped that Lou was not feeling upset. He knew very well Elizabeth had a decent living income from a number of public sources, and was simply a slut, one of those who would not help themselves.

"Ever thought of taking a job, Elizabeth?" he had said, and immediately realized his stupidity. But Elizabeth took her advantage. "What d'you mean? *I'm* not going to leave my kids in no nursery. *I'm* not going to send them to no home. What kids need these days is a good home life and that's what they get." And she added, 'God's eyes are not shut," in a tone which was meant for him, Raymond, to get at him for doing well in life.

Raymond distributed half-crowns to the younger children and deposited on the table half-crowns for those who were out playing in the street.

"Goin' already?" said Elizabeth in her tone of reproach. But she kept eyeing Henry with interest, and the reproachful tone was more or less a routine affair.

"You from the States?" Elizabeth said to Henry.

4. Postal orders.

Henry sat on the edge of his sticky chair and answered, no, from Jamaica, while Raymond winked at him to cheer him.

"During the war there was a lot of boys like you from the States," Elizabeth said, giving him a sideways look.

Henry held out his hand to the second youngest child, a girl of seven, and said, "Come talk to me."

The child said nothing, only dipped into the box of sweets which Lou had brought.

"Come talk," said Henry.

Elizabeth laughed. "If she does talk you'll be sorry you ever asked. She's got a tongue in her head, that one. You should hear her cheeking up to the teachers." Elizabeth's bones jerked with laughter among her loose clothes. There was a lopsided double bed in the corner, and beside it a table cluttered with mugs, tins, a comb and brush, a number of hair curlers, a framed photograph of the Sacred Heart, and also Raymond noticed what he thought erroneously to be a box of contraceptives. He decided to say nothing to Lou about this; he was quite sure she must have observed other things which he had not; possibly things of a more distressing nature.

Lou's chatter on the way back to the hotel had a touch of hysteria. "Raymond, dear," she said in her most chirpy west-end[5] voice. "I simply *had* to give the poor dear *all* my next week's housekeeping money. We shall have to starve, darling, when we get home. That's *simply* what we shall have to do."

"O.K.," said Raymond.

"I ask you," Lou shrieked, "what else could I do, what *could* I do?"

"Nothing at all," said Raymond, "but what you've done."

"My own *sister*, my dear," said Lou; "and did you see the way she had her hair bleached?—All streaky, and she used to have a lovely head of hair."

"I wonder if she tries to raise herself?" said Raymond. "With all those children she could surely get better accommodation if only she—"

"That sort," said Henry, leaning forward from the back of the car, "never moves. It's the slum mentality, man. Take some folks I've seen back home—"

"There's no comparison," Lou snapped suddenly, "this is quite a different case."

Raymond glanced at her in surprise; Henry sat back, offended. Lou was thinking wildly, what a cheek *him* talking like a snob. At least Elizabeth's white.

Their prayers for the return of faith to Henry Pierce were so far answered in that he took a tubercular turn which was followed by a religious one. He was sent off to a sanatorium in Wales with a promise from Lou and Raymond to visit him before Christmas. Meantime, they applied themselves to Our Lady for the restoration of Henry's health.

Oxford St. John, whose love affair with the red-haired girl had come to grief, now frequented their flat, but he could never quite replace Henry in their affections. Oxford was older and less refined than Henry. He would stand in front of the glass in their kitchen and tell himself, "Man, you just a big black bugger." He kept referring to himself as black, which of course he was, Lou thought, but it was not the thing to say. He stood in the doorway with his arms

and smile thrown wide: "I am black but comely, O ye daughters of Jerusalem."[6] And once, when Raymond was out, Oxford brought the conversation round to that question of being black *all over*, which made Lou very uncomfortable and she kept looking at the clock and dropped stitches in her knitting.

Three times a week when she went to the black Our Lady with her rosary to ask for the health of Henry Pierce, she asked also that Oxford St. John would get another job in another town, for she did not like to make objections, telling her feelings to Raymond; there were no objections to make that you could put your finger on. She could not very well complain that Oxford was common; Raymond despised snobbery, and so did she, it was a very delicate question. She was amazed when, within three weeks, Oxford announced that he was thinking of looking for a job in Manchester.

Lou said to Raymond "Do you know, there's something *in* what they say about the bog oak statue in the church."

"There may be," said Raymond. "People say so."

Lou could not tell him how she had petitioned the removal of Oxford St. John. But when she got a letter from Henry Pierce to say he was improving, she told Raymond, "You see, we asked for Henry to get back the Faith, and so he did. Now we ask for his recovery and he's improving."

"He's having good treatment at the sanatorium," Raymond said. But he added, "Of course we'll have to keep up the prayers." He himself, though not a rosary man, knelt before the Black Madonna every Saturday evening after Benediction to pray for Henry Pierce.

Whenever they saw Oxford he was talking of leaving Whitney Clay. Raymond said, "He's making a big mistake going to Manchester. A big place can be very lonely. I hope he'll change his mind."

"He won't," said Lou, so impressed was she now by the powers of the Black Madonna. She was good and tired of Oxford St. John with his feet up on her cushions, and calling himself a nigger.

"We'll miss him," said Raymond, "he's such a cheery big soul."

"We will," said Lou. She was reading the parish magazine, which she seldom did, although she was one of the voluntary workers who sent them out, addressing hundreds of wrappers every month. She had vaguely noticed, in previous numbers, various references to the Black Madonna, how she had granted this or that favor. Lou had heard that people sometimes came from neighboring parishes to pray at the Church of the Sacred Heart because of the statue. Some said they came from all over England, but whether this was to admire the art-work or to pray, Lou was not sure. She gave her attention to the article in the parish magazine:

> While not wishing to make excessive claims . . . many prayers answered and requests granted to the Faithful in an exceptional way . . . two remarkable cures effected, but medical evidence is, of course, still in reserve, a certain lapse of time being necessary to ascertain permanency of cure. The first of these cases was a child of twelve suffering from leukemia. . . . The second . . . While not desiring to create a *cuitus* where none is due, we must remember it is always our duty to honor Our Blessed Lady, the dispenser of all graces, to whom we owe . . .

6. Song of Solomon 1 5.

Another aspect of the information received by the Father Rector concerning our "Black Madonna" is one pertaining to childless couples of which three cases have come to his notice. In each case the couple claim to have offered constant devotion to the "Black Madonna" and in two of the cases specific requests were made for the favor of a child. In *all* cases the prayers were answered. The proud parents.... It should be the loving duty of every parishioner to make a special thanksgiving.... The Father Rector will be grateful for any further information....

"Look, Raymond," said Lou. "Read this."

They decided to put in for a baby to the Black Madonna.

The following Saturday, when they drove to the church for Benediction Lou jangled her rosary. Raymond pulled up outside the church. "Look here, Lou," he said, "do you want a baby in any case?"—for he partly thought she was only putting the Black Madonna to the test—"Do you want a child, after all these years?"

This was a new thought to Lou. She considered her neat flat and tidy routine, the entertaining with her good coffee cups, the weekly papers and the library books, the tastes which they would not have been able to cultivate had they had a family of children. She thought of her nice young looks which everyone envied, and her freedom of movement.

"Perhaps we should try," she said. "God won't give us a child if we aren't meant to have one."

"We have to make some decisions for ourselves," he said. "And to tell you the truth if *you* don't want a child, *I* don't."

"There's no harm in praying for one," she said.

"You have to be careful what you pray for," he said. "You mustn't tempt Providence."

She thought of her relatives, and Raymond's, all married with children. She thought of her sister Elizabeth with her eight, and remembered that one who cheeked up to the teachers, so pretty and sulky and shabby, and she remembered the fat baby Francis sucking his dummy[7] and clutching Elizabeth's bony neck.

"I don't see why I shouldn't have a baby," said Lou.

Oxford St. John departed at the end of the month. He promised to write, but they were not surprised when weeks passed and they had no word. "I don't suppose we shall ever hear from him again," said Lou. Raymond thought he detected satisfaction in her voice, and would have thought she was getting snobbish as women do as they get older, losing sight of their ideals, had she not gone on to speak of Henry Pierce. Henry had written to say he was nearly cured, but had been advised to return to the West Indies.

"We must go and see him," said Lou. "We promised. What about the Sunday after next?"

"O.K.," said Raymond.

It was the Saturday before that Sunday when Lou had her first sick turn. She struggled out of bed to attend Benediction, but had to leave suddenly during the service and was sick behind the church in the presbytery yard. Raymond took her home, though she protested against cutting out her rosary to the Black Madonna.

7. Pacifier.

"After only six weeks!" she said, and she could hardly tell whether her sickness was due to excitement or nature. "Only six weeks ago," she said—and her voice had a touch of its old Liverpool—"did we go to that Black Madonna and the prayer's answered, see."

Raymond looked at her in awe as he held the bowl for her sickness. "Are you sure?" he said.

She was well enough next day to go to visit Henry in the sanatorium. He was fatter and, she thought, a little coarser and tough in his manner, as if once having been nearly disembodied he was not going to let it happen again. He was leaving the country very soon. He promised to come and see them before he left. Lou barely skimmed through his next letter before handing it over to Raymond.

Their visitors, now, were ordinary white ones. "Not so colorful," Raymond said, "as Henry and Oxford were." Then he looked embarrassed lest he should seem to be making a joke about the word colored.

"Do you miss the niggers?" said Tina Farrell, and Lou forgot to correct her.

Lou gave up most of her church work in order to sew and knit for the baby. Raymond gave up the *Reader's Digest*. He applied for promotion and got it; he became a departmental manager. The flat was now a waiting-room for next summer, after the baby was born, when they would put down the money for a house. They hoped for one of the new houses on a building site on the outskirts of the town.

"We shall need a garden," Lou explained to her friends. "I'll join the Mothers' Union," she thought. Meantime the spare bedroom was turned into a nursery. Raymond made a cot, regardless that some of the neighbors complained of the hammering. Lou prepared a cradle, trimmed it with frills. She wrote to her relatives; she wrote to Elizabeth, sent her five pounds, and gave notice that there would be no further weekly payments, seeing that they would now need every penny.

"She doesn't require it anyway," said Raymond. "The Welfare State looks after people like Elizabeth." And he told Lou about the contraceptives he thought he had seen on the table by the double bed. Lou became very excited about this. "How did you know they were contraceptives? What did they look like? Why didn't you tell me before? What a cheek, calling herself a Catholic, do you think she has a man, then?"

Raymond was sorry he had mentioned the subject.

"Don't worry, dear, don't upset yourself, dear."

"And she told me she goes to Mass every Sunday, and all the kids go excepting James. No wonder he's got into trouble with an example like that. I might have known, with her peroxide hair. A pound a week I've been sending up to now, that's fifty-two pounds a year. I would never have done it, calling herself a Catholic with birth control by her bedside."

"Don't upset yourself, dear."

Lou prayed to the Black Madonna three times a week for a safe delivery and a healthy child. She gave her story to the Father Rector who announced it in the next parish magazine. "Another case has come to light of the kindly favor of our 'Black Madonna' towards a childless couple ..." Lou recited her rosary before the statue until it was difficult for her to kneel, and, when she stood, could not see her feet. The Mother of God with her black bog-oaken drapery, her high black cheekbones and square hands looked more virginal than ever to Lou as she stood counting her beads in front of her stomach.

She said to Raymond, "If it's a girl we must have Mary as one of the names. But not the first name, it's too ordinary."

"Please yourself, dear," said Raymond. The doctor had told him it might be a difficult birth.

"Thomas, if it's a boy," she said, "after my uncle. But if it's a girl I'd like something fancy for a first name."

He thought, Lou's slipping, she didn't used to say that word, fancy.

"What about Dawn?" she said. "I like the sound of Dawn. Then Mary for a second name. Dawn Mary Parker, it sounds sweet."

"Dawn! That's not a Christian name," he said. Then he told her, "Just as you please, dear."

"Or Thomas Parker," she said.

She had decided to go into the maternity wing of the hospital like everyone else. But near the time she let Raymond change her mind, since he kept saying, "At your age, dear, it might be more difficult than for the younger women. Better book a private ward, we'll manage the expense."

In fact, it was a very easy birth, a girl. Raymond was allowed in to see Lou in the late afternoon. She was half asleep. "The nurse will take you to see the baby in the nursery ward," she told him. "She's lovely, but terribly red."

"They're always red at birth," said Raymond.

He met the nurse in the corridor. "Any chance of seeing the baby? My wife said . . ."

She looked flustered. "I'll get the Sister," she said.

"Oh, I don't want to give any trouble, only my wife said—"

"That's all right. Wait here, Mr. Parker."

The Sister appeared, a tall grave woman. Raymond thought her to be short-sighted for she seemed to look at him fairly closely before she bade him follow her.

The baby was round and very red, with dark curly hair.

"Fancy her having hair. I thought they were born bald," said Raymond.

"They sometimes have hair at birth," said the Sister.

"She's very red in color." Raymond began comparing his child with those in the other cots. "Far more so than the others."

"Oh, that will wear off."

Next day he found Lou in a half-stupor. She had been given a strong sedative following an attack of screaming hysteria. He sat by her bed, bewildered. Presently a nurse beckoned him from the door. "Will you have a word with the Matron?"

"Your wife is upset about her baby," said the matron. "You see, the color. She's a beautiful baby, perfect. It's a question of the color."

"I noticed the baby was red," said Raymond, "but the nurse said—"

"Oh, the red will go. It changes, you know. But the baby will certainly be brown, if not indeed black, as indeed we think she will be. A beautiful healthy child."

"Black?" said Raymond.

"Yes, indeed we think so, indeed I must say, certainly so," said the matron. "We did not expect your wife to take it so badly when we told her. We've had plenty of dark babies here, but most of their mothers expect it."

"There must be a mix-up. You must have mixed up the babies," said Raymond.

"There's no question of mix-up," said the matron sharply. "We'll soon settle that. We've had some of *that* before."

"But neither of us are dark," said Raymond. "You've seen my wife. You see me—"

"That's something you must work out for yourselves. I'd have a word with the doctor if I were you. But whatever conclusion you come to, please don't upset your wife at this stage. She has already refused to feed the child, says it isn't hers, which is ridiculous."

"Was it Oxford St. John?" said Raymond.

"Raymond, the doctor told you not to come here upsetting me. I'm feeling terrible."

"Was it Oxford St. John?"

"Clear out of here, you swine, saying things like that."

He demanded to be taken to see the baby, as he had done every day for a week. The nurses were gathered round it, neglecting the squalling whites in the other cots for the sight of their darling black. She was indeed quite black, with a woolly crop and tiny negroid nostrils. She had been baptized that morning, thought not in her parents' presence. One of the nurses had stood as godmother.

The nurses dispersed in a flurry as Raymond approached. He looked hard at the baby. It looked back with its black button eyes. He saw the nametab round its neck, "Dawn Mary Parker."

He got hold of a nurse in the corridor. "Look here, you just take that name Parker off that child's neck. The name's not Parker, it isn't my child."

The nurse said, "Get away, we're busy."

"There's just a chance," said the doctor to Raymond, "that if there's ever been black blood in your family or your wife's, it's coming out now. It's a very long chance. I've never known it happen in my experience, but I've heard of cases, I could read them up."

"There's nothing like that in my family," said Raymond. He thought of Lou, the obscure Liverpool antecedents. The parents had died before he had met Lou.

"It could be several generations back," said the doctor.

Raymond went home, avoiding the neighbors who would stop him to inquire after Lou. He rather regretted smashing up the cot in his first fury. That was something low coming out in him. But again, when he thought of the tiny black hands of the baby with their pink fingernails he did not regret smashing the cot.

He was successful in tracing the whereabouts of Oxford St. John. Even before he heard the result of Oxford's blood test he said to Lou, "Write and ask your relations if there's been any black blood in the family."

"Write and ask *yours*," she said.

She refused to look at the black baby. The nurses fussed round it all day, and come to report its progress to Lou.

"Pull yourself together, Mrs. Parker, she's a lovely child."

"You must care for your infant," said the priest.

"You don't know what I'm suffering," Lou said.

"In the name of God," said the priest, "if you're a Catholic Christian you've got to expect to suffer."

"I can't go against my nature," said Lou. "I can't be expected to—"

Raymond said to her one day in the following week, "The blood tests are all right, the doctor says."

"What do you mean, all right?"

"Oxford's blood and the baby's don't tally, and—"

"Oh, shut up," she said. "The baby's black and your blood tests can't make it white."

"No," he said. He had fallen out with his mother, through his inquiries whether there had been colored blood in his family. "The doctor says," he said, "that these black mixtures sometimes occur in seaport towns. It might have been generations back."

"One thing," said Lou. "I'm not going to take that child back to the flat."

"You'll have to," he said.

Elizabeth wrote her a letter which Raymond intercepted:

"Dear Lou Raymond is asking if we have any blacks in the family well thats funny you have a colored God is not asleep. There was that Flinn cousin Tommy at Liverpool he was very dark they put it down to the past a nigro off a ship that would be before our late Mothers Time God rest her soul she would turn in her grave you shoud have kept up your bit to me whats a pound a Week to you. It was on our fathers side the color and Mary Flinn you remember at the dairy was dark remember her hare was like nigro hare it must be back in the olden days the nigro some ansester but it is only nature. I thank the almighty it has missed my kids and your hubby must think it was that nigro you was showing off when you came to my place. I wish you all the best as a widow with kids you shoud send my money as per usual you affec sister Elizabeth."

"I gather from Elizabeth," said Raymond to Lou, "that there *was* some element of color in your family. Of course, you couldn't be expected to know about it. I do think, though, that some kind of record should be kept."

"Oh, shut *up*," said Lou. "The baby's black and nothing can make it white."

Two days before Lou left the hospital she had a visitor, although she had given instructions that no-one except Raymond should be let in to see her. This lapse she attributed to the nasty curiosity of the nurses, for it was Henry Pierce come to say goodbye before embarkation. He stayed less than five minutes.

"Why, Mrs. Parker, your visitor didn't stay long," said the nurse.

"No, I soon got rid of him. I thought I made it clear to you that I didn't want to see anyone. You shouldn't have let him in."

"Oh, sorry, Mrs. Parker, but the young gentleman looked so upset when we told him so. He said he was going abroad and it was his last chance, he might never see you again. He said, 'How's the baby?' and we said, 'Tip-top.'"

"I know what's in your mind," said Lou. "But it isn't true. I've got the blood tests."

"Oh, Mrs. Parker, I wouldn't suggest for a minute . . ."

"She must have went with one of they niggers that used to come."

Lou could never be sure if that was what she heard from the doorways and landings as she climbed the stairs of Cripps House, the neighbors hushing their conversation as she approached.

"I can't take to the child. Try as I do, I simply can't even like it."

"Nor me," said Raymond. "Mind you, if it was anyone else's child I would

think it was all right. It's just the thought of it being mine, and people thinking it isn't."

"That's just it," she said.

One of Raymond's colleagues had asked him that day how his friends Oxford and Henry were getting on. Raymond had to look twice before he decided that the question was innocent. But one never knew. . . . Already Lou and Raymond had approached the adoption society. It was now only a matter of waiting for word.

"If that child was mine," said Tina Farrell, "I'd never part with her. I wish we could afford to adopt another. She's the loveliest little darkie in the world."

"You wouldn't think so," said Lou, "if she really was yours. Imagine it for yourself, waking up to find you've had a black baby that everyone thinks has a nigger for its father."

"It *would* be a shock," Tina said, and tittered.

"We've got the blood test," said Lou quickly.

Raymond got a transfer to London. They got word about the adoption very soon.

"We've done the right thing," said Lou. "Even the priest had to agree with that, considering how strongly we felt against keeping the child."

"Oh, he said it was a good thing?"

"No, not a *good* thing. In fact he said it would have been a good thing if we could have kept the baby. But failing that, we did the *right* thing. Apparently, there's a difference."

1960

DORIS LESSING
1919–

Doris Lessing has had a remarkably productive and influential career, a career which continues to show signs of developing through yet another of the shifts in fictional technique that have marked its several stages. Her autobiographical tetralogy *Children of Violence* (1952–69) was praised for its social realism in depicting the growth of a heroine, Martha Quest, who comes to terms with her own identity by confronting the racism of Africa and the class stratifications of England. When Lessing published *The Golden Notebook* (1962), a number of feminists took the novel's analysis of female socialization to be, in Lessing's words, "a useful weapon in the sex war." But, in a preface (1971), the author warned that the book was really about the threat of compartmentalization in the intellectual and moral climate of the mid-twentieth century. While the issues of female identity and aging were at the center of *The Summer before the Dark* (1973), Lessing also published two moral fables: both *Briefing for a Descent into Hell* (1971) and *The Memoirs of a Survivor* (1975) move from realistic portrayals of psychological and cultural entropy to speculative allegories that seek to explain the causes and effects of the illness she associates with the modern world. In her most recent books, those fantasies have transformed themselves into science-fiction novels in which Lessing envisions other life forms on alternative worlds.

Lessing was born Doris Tayler in Kermanshah, which is in what is now Iran. Her father had gone to work in the Imperial Bank of Persia after he had been wounded in World War I and married his nurse. But, when his daughter was five, he moved

the family to a three-thousand-acre farm in Southern Rhodesia. Doris Tayler studied at a Catholic convent school and at Girls' High School in the small city of Salisbury, while her parents farmed maize with the help of cheap native laborers. She read and reread the classics of European and American literature but left school at fourteen years of age to work as a nursemaid and a secretary. After she had given birth to two children in her first marriage to Frank Charles Wisdom and one child in her second marriage to Gottfried Anton Lessing, she decided that marriage was not one of her "talents." In 1949, she left Africa for England, where she briefly joined the Communist Party, obtained a divorce, and began earning her living as a professional writer.

While Lessing has moved from social realism to science fiction, she has maintained a strong sense of moral responsibility as a writer. A self-described "architect of the soul," she believes that the writer must be especially inventive during this age which is, she claims, "one of the great turning points of history." As a socialist, Lessing has always criticized the inequalities of capitalism. Given the destructive capabilities of technology today, moreover, Lessing believes that only an extraordinary effort of imagination can free humanity so that it will become capable of surviving. Therefore, all of her books study what she analyzed in the *Children of Violence* novels, namely, "the individual conscience in its relation with the collective." Like Martha Quest, then, Lessing is searching for a vision of unity that can empower the individual to survive the fragmentation of modern life, whether that fragmentation is associated with antagonism among races, competition between nations, the battle between men and women, the conflicts of a divided psyche, or the dualistic thinking that sets "them" against "us." In the 1970s, such fantastic novels as *Briefing for a Descent into Hell* and *The Memoirs of a Survivor* led to a five-volume work of science fiction called *Canopus in Argus* (1979–85); however, Lessing continued to produce realistic fiction under the pseudonym Jane Somers.

The short story *One off the Short List* was written several years before *The Golden Notebook* and *The Four-Gated City* (1969), the last novel in the *Children of Violence* series. In both of these books, Lessing focused on the problems creativity and solitude pose for women. Anna Wulf, the heroine of *The Golden Notebook*, struggles against her fear of being alone, her dread of her own destructive impulses, and her divided political allegiances, to get beyond a writing block. Like Anna, many of the female characters in *Four-Gated City* experience the so-called normal patterns of women's lives as a maddening form of self-censorship. Also concerned with gender roles, *One off the Short List* depicts the degradation of sexuality when power plays and ploys turn the relationship between men and women into a contest of wills.

One off the Short List

When he had first seen Barbara Coles, some years before, he only noticed her because someone said: "That's Johnson's new girl." He certainly had not used of her the private erotic formula: *Yes, that one.* He even wondered what Johnson saw in her. "She won't last long," he remembered thinking, as he watched Johnson, a handsome man, but rather flushed with drink, flirting with some unknown girl while Barbara stood by a wall looking on. He thought she had a sullen expression.

She was a pale girl, not slim, for her frame was generous, but her figure could pass as good. Her straight yellow hair was parted on one side in a way that struck him as gauche. He did not notice what she wore. But her eyes were all right, he remembered: large, and solidly green, square-looking because of

some trick of the flesh at their corners. Emeraldlike eyes in the face of a schoolgirl, or young schoolmistress who was watching her lover flirt and would later sulk about it.

Her name sometimes cropped up in the papers. She was a stage decorator, a designer, something on those lines.

Then a Sunday newspaper had a competition for stage design and she won it. Barbara Coles was one of the "names" in the theater, and her photograph was seen about. It was always serious. He remembered having thought her sullen.

One night he saw her across the room at a party. She was talking with a well-known actor. Her yellow hair was still done on one side, but now it looked sophisticated. She wore an emerald ring on her right hand that seemed deliberately to invite comparison with her eyes. He walked over and said: "We have met before, Graham Spence." He noted, with discomfort, that he sounded abrupt. "I'm sorry, I don't remember, but how do you do?" she said, smiling. And continued her conversation.

He hung around a bit, but soon she went off with a group of people she was inviting to her home for a drink. She did not invite Graham. There was about her an assurance, a carelessness, that he recognized as the signature of success. It was then, watching her laugh as she went off with her friends, that he used the formula: *"Yes, that one."* And he went home to his wife with enjoyable expectation, as if his date with Barbara Coles were already arranged.

His marriage was twenty years old. At first it had been stormy, painful, tragic—full of partings, betrayals and sweet reconciliations. It had taken him at least a decade to realize that there was nothing remarkable about this marriage that he had lived through with such surprise of the mind and the senses. On the contrary, the marriages of most of the people he knew, whether they were first, second, or third attempts, were just the same. His had run true to form even to the serious love affair with the young girl for whose sake he had *almost* divorced his wife—yet at the last moment had changed his mind, letting the girl down so that he must have her for always (not unpleasurably) on his conscience. It was with humiliation that he had understood that this drama was not at all the unique thing he had imagined. It was nothing more than the experience of everyone in his circle. And presumably in everybody else's circle too?

Anyway, round about the tenth year of his marriage he had seen a good many things clearly, a certain kind of emotional adventure went from his life, and the marriage itself changed.

His wife had married a poor youth with a great future as a writer. Sacrifices had been made, chiefly by her, for that future. He was neither unaware of them, nor ungrateful; in fact he felt permanently guilty about it. He at last published a decently successful, book, then a second which now, thank God, no one remembered. He had drifted into radio, television, book reviewing.

He understood he was not going to make it; that he had become—not a hack, no one could call him that—but a member of that army of people who live by their wits on the fringes of the arts. The moment of realization was when he was in a pub one lunchtime near the B.B.C. where he often dropped in to meet others like himself: he understood that was why he went there—they *were* like him. Just as that melodramatic marriage had turned out to be like everyone else's—except that it had been shared with one woman instead of with two or three—so it had turned out that his unique talent, his struggles

as a writer had led him here, to this pub and the half dozen pubs like it, where all the men in sight had the same history. They all had their novel, their play, their book of poems, a moment of fame, to their credit. Yet here they were, running television programs about which they were cynical (to each other or to their wives) or writing reviews about other people's books. Yes, that's what he had become, an impressario of other people's talent. These two moments of clarity, about his marriage and about his talent, had roughly coincided; and (perhaps not by chance) had coincided with his wife's decision to leave him for a man younger than himself who had a future, she said, as a playwright. Well, he had talked her out of it. For her part she had to understand he was not going to be the T. S. Eliot or Graham Greene of our time—but after all, how many were? She must finally understand this, for he could no longer bear her awful bitterness. For his part he must stop coming home drunk at five in the morning, and starting a new romantic affair every six months which he took so seriously that he made her miserable because of her implied deficiencies. In short he was to be a good husband. (He had always been a dutiful father.) And she a good wife. And so it was: the marriage became stable, as they say.

The formula: Yes, *that one* no longer implied a necessarily sexual relationship. In its more mature form, it was far from being something he was ashamed of. On the contrary, it expressed a humorous respect for what he was, for his real talents and flair, which had turned out to be not artistic after all, but to do with emotional life, hard-earned experience. It expressed an ironical dignity, a proving to himself not only: I can be honest about myself, but also: I have earned the best in *that* field whenever I want it.

He watched the field for the women who were well known in the arts, or in politics; looked out for photographs, listened for bits of gossip. He made a point of going to see them act, or dance, or orate. He built up a not unshrewd picture of them. He would either quietly pull strings to meet her or—more often, for there was a gambler's pleasure in waiting—bide his time until he met her in the natural course of events, which was bound to happen sooner or later. He would be seen out with her a few times in public, which was in order, since his work meant he had to entertain well-known people, male and female. His wife always knew, he told her. He might have a brief affair with this woman, but more often than not it was the appearance of an affair. Not that he didn't get pleasure from other people envying him—he would make a point, for instance, of taking this woman into the pubs where his male colleagues went. It was that his real pleasure came when he saw her surprise at how well she was understood by him. He enjoyed the atmosphere he was able to set up between an intelligent woman and himself: a humorous complicity which had in it much that was unspoken, and which almost made sex irrelevant.

Onto the list of women with whom he planned to have this relationship went Barbara Coles. There was no hurry. Next week, next month, next year, they would meet at a party. The world of well-known people in London is a small one. Big and little fishes, they drift around, nose each other, flirt their fins, wriggle off again. When he bumped into Barbara Coles, it would be time to decide whether or not to sleep with her.

Meanwhile he listened. But he didn't discover much. She had a husband and children, but the husband seemed to be in the background. The children were charming and well brought up, like everyone else's children. She had af-

fairs, they said; but while several men he met sounded familiar with her, it was hard to determine whether they had slept with her, because none directly boasted of her. She was spoken of in terms of her friends, her work, her house, a party she had given, a job she had found someone. She was liked, she was respected, and Graham Spence's self-esteem was flattered because he had chosen her. He looked forward to saying in just the same tone: "Barbara Coles asked me what I thought about the set and I told her quite frankly. . . ."

Then by chance he met a young man who did boast about Barbara Coles; he claimed to have had the great love affair with her, and recently at that; and he spoke of it as something generally known. Graham realized how much he had already become involved with her in his imagination because of how perturbed he was now, on account of the character of this youth, Jack Kennaway. He had recently become successful as a magazine editor—one of those young men who, not as rare as one might suppose in the big cities, are successful from sheer impertinence, effrontery. Without much talent or taste, yet he had the charm of his effrontery. "Yes, I'm going to succeed, because I've decided to; yes, I may be stupid, but not so stupid that I don't know my deficiencies. Yes, I'm going to be successful because you people with integrity, etc., etc., simply don't believe in the possibility of people like me. You are too cowardly to stop me. Yes, I've taken your measure and I'm going to succeed because I've got the courage, not only to be unscrupulous, but to be quite frank about it. And besides, you admire me, you must, or otherwise you'd stop me. . . ." Well, that was young Jack Kennaway, and he shocked Graham. He was a tall, languishing young man, handsome in a dark melting way, and, it was quite clear, he was either asexual or homosexual. And this youth boasted of the favors of Barbara Coles; boasted, indeed, of her love. Either she was a raving neurotic with a taste for neurotics; or Jack Kennaway was a most accomplished liar; or she slept with anyone. Graham was intrigued. He took Jack Kennaway out to dinner in order to hear him talk about Barbara Coles. There was no doubt the two were pretty close—all those dinners, theatres, weekends in the country—Graham Spence felt he had put his finger on the secret pulse of Barbara Coles; and it was intolerable that he must wait to meet her; he decided to arrange it.

It became unnecessary. She was in the news again, with a run of luck. She had done a successful historical play, and immediately afterwards a modern play, and then a hit musical. In all three, the sets were remarked on. Graham saw some interviews in newspapers and on television. These all centered around the theme of her being able to deal easily with so many different styles of theater; but the real point was, of course, that she was a woman, which naturally added piquancy to the thing. And now Graham Spence was asked to do a half-hour radio interview with her. He planned the questions he would ask her with care, drawing on what people had said of her, but above all on his instinct and experience with women. The interview was to be at nine-thirty at night; he was to pick her up at six from the theater where she was currently at work, so that there would be time, as the letter from the B.B.C. had put it, "for you and Miss Coles to get to know each other."

At six he was at the stage door, but a message from Miss Coles said she was not quite ready, could he wait a little. He hung about, then went to the pub opposite for a quick one, but still no Miss Coles. So he made his way backstage, directed by voices, hammering, laughter. It was badly lit, and the group of people at work did not see him. The director, James Poynter, had his arm

around Barbara's shoulders. He was newly well-known, a carelessly good-looking young man reputed to be intelligent. Barbara Coles wore a dark blue overall, and her flat hair fell over her face so that she kept pushing it back with the hand that had the emerald on it. These two stood close, side by side. Three young men, stagehands, were on the other side of a trestle which had sketches and drawings on it. They were studying some sketches. Barbara said, in a voice warm with energy: "Well, so I thought if we did *this*—do you see, James? What do you think, Steven?" "Well, love," said the young man she called Steven, "I see your idea, but I wonder if..." "I think you're right, Babs," said the director. "Look," said Barbara, holding one of the sketches towards Steven, "look, let me show you." They all leaned forward, the five of them, absorbed in the business.

Suddenly Graham couldn't stand it. He understood he was shaken to his depths. He went off stage, and stood with his back against a wall in the dingy passage that led to the dressing rooms. His eyes were filled with tears. He was seeing what a long way he had come from the crude, uncompromising, admirable young egomaniac he had been when he was twenty. That group of people there—working, joking, arguing, yes, that's what he hadn't known for years. What bound them was the democracy of respect for each other's work, a confidence in themselves and in each other. They looked like people banded together against a world which they—no, not despised, but which they measured, understood, would fight to the death, out of respect for what *they* stood for, for what *it* stood for. It was a long time since he felt part of that balance. And he understood that he had seen Barbara Coles when she was most herself, at ease with a group of people she worked with. It was then, with the tears drying on his eyelids, which felt old and ironic, that he decided he would sleep with Barbara Coles. It was a necessity for him. He went back through the door onto the stage, burning with this single determination.

The five were still together. Barbara had a length of blue gleaming stuff which she was draping over the shoulder of Steven, the stagehand. He was showing it off, and the others watched. "What do you think, James?" she asked the director. "We've got that sort of dirty green, and I thought..." "Well," said James, not sure at all, "well, Babs, well..."

Now Graham went forward so that he stood beside Barbara, and said: "I'm Graham Spence, we've met before." For the second time she smiled socially and said: "Oh, I'm sorry, I don't remember." Graham nodded at James, whom he had known, or at least had met off and on, for years. But it was obvious James didn't remember him either.

"From the B.B.C.," said Graham to Barbara, again sounding abrupt, against his will. "Oh, I'm sorry, I'm so sorry, I forgot all about it. I've got to be interviewed," she said to the group. "Mr. Spence is a journalist." Graham allowed himself a small smile ironical of the word journalist, but she was not looking at him. She was going on with her work. "We should decide tonight," she said. "Steven's right." "Yes, I am right," said the stagehand. "She's right, James, we need that blue with that sludge-green everywhere." "James," said Barbara, "James, what's wrong with it? You haven't said." She moved forward to James, passing Graham. Remembering him again, she became contrite. "I'm sorry," she said, "we can none of us agree. Well, look"—she turned to Graham—"you advise us, we've got so involved with it that..." At which James laughed, and so did the stagehands. "No, Babs," said James, "of course Mr. Spence can't ad-

vise. He's just this moment come in. We've got to decide. Well I'll give you till tomorrow morning. Time to go home, it must be six by now."

"It's nearly seven," said Graham, taking command.

"It isn't!" said Barbara, dramatic. "My God, how terrible, how appalling, how could I have done such a thing...." She was laughing at herself. "Well, you'll have to forgive me, Mr. Spence, because you haven't got any alternative."

They began laughing again: this was clearly a group joke. And now Graham took his chance. He said firmly, as if he were her director, in fact copying James Poynter's manner with her: "No, Miss Coles, I won't forgive you, I've been kicking my heels for nearly an hour." She grimaced, then laughed and accepted it. James said: "There, Babs, that's how you ought to be treated. We spoil you." He kissed her on the cheek, she kissed him on both his, the stagehands moved off. "Have a good evening, Babs," said James, going, and nodding to Graham. Who stood concealing his pleasure with difficulty. He knew, because he had had the courage to be firm, indeed, peremptory, with Barbara, that he had saved himself hours of maneuvering. Several drinks, a dinner—perhaps two or three evenings of drinks and dinners—had been saved because he was now on this footing with Barbara Coles, a man who could say: "No, I won't forgive you, you've kept me waiting."

She said: "I've just got to..." and went ahead of him. In the passage she hung her overall on a peg. She was thinking, it seemed, of something else, but seeing him watching her, she smiled at him, companionably: he realized with triumph it was the sort of smile she would offer one of the stagehands, or even James. She said again: "Just one second..." and went to the stage-door office. She and the stage doorman conferred. There was some problem. Graham said, taking another chance: "What's the trouble, can I help?"—as if he could help, as if he expected to be able to. "Well..." she said, frowning. Then, to the man: "No, it'll be all right. Good night." She came to Graham. "We've got ourselves into a bit of a fuss because half the set's in Liverpool and half's here and—but it will sort itself out." She stood, at ease, chatting to him, one colleague to another. All this was admirable, he felt; but there would be a bad moment when they emerged from the special atmosphere of the theater into the street. He took another decision, grasped her arm firmly, and said: "We're going to have a drink before we do anything at all, it's a terrible evening out." Her arm felt resistant, but remained within his. It was raining outside, luckily. He directed her, authoritative: "No, not that pub, there's a nicer one around the corner." "Oh, but I like this pub," said Barbara, "we always use it."

"Of course you do," he said to himself. But in that pub there would be the stagehands, and probably James, and he'd lose contact with her. He'd become a *journalist* again. He took her firmly out of danger around two corners, into a pub he picked at random. A quick look around—no, they weren't there. At least, if there were people from the theater, she showed no sign. She asked for a beer. He ordered her a double Scotch, which she accepted. Then, having won a dozen preliminary rounds already he took time to think. Something was bothering him—what? Yes, it was what he had observed backstage, Barbara and James Poynter. Was she having an affair with him? Because if so, it would all be much more difficult. He made himself see the two of them together, and thought with a jealousy surprisingly strong: *Yes, that's it.* Meantime he sat looking at her, seeing himself look at her, *a man gazing in calm appreciation at*

a woman: waiting for her to feel it and respond. She was examining the pub. Her white woollen suit was belted, and had a not unprovocative suggestion of being a uniform. Her flat yellow hair, hastily pushed back after work, was untidy. Her clear white skin, without any color, made her look tired. Not very exciting, at the moment, thought Graham, but maintaining his appreciative pose for when she would turn and see it. He knew what she would see: he was relying not only on the "warm kindly" beam of his gaze, for this was merely a reinforcement of the impression he knew he made. He had black hair, a little grayed. His clothes were loose and bulky—masculine. His eyes were humorous and appreciative. He was not, never had been, concerned to lessen the impression of being settled, dependable: the husband and father. On the contrary, he knew women found it reassuring.

When she at last turned she said, almost apologetic: "Would you mind if we sat down? I've been lugging great things around all day." She had spotted two empty chairs in a corner. So had he, but rejected them, because there were other people at the table. "But my dear, of course!" They took the chairs, and then Barbara said: "If you'll excuse me a moment." She had remembered she needed makeup. He watched her go off, annoyed with himself. She was tired; and he could have understood, protected, sheltered. He realized that in the other pub, with the people she had worked with all day, she would not have thought: "I must make myself up, I must be on show." That was for outsiders. She had not, until now, considered Graham an outsider, because of his taking his chance to seem one of the working group in the theater; but now he had thrown this opportunity away. She returned armored. Her hair was sleek, no longer defenseless. And she had made up her eyes. Her eyebrows were untouched, pale gold streaks above the brilliant green eyes whose lashes were blackened. Rather good, he thought, the contrast. Yes, but the moment had gone when he could say: Did you know you had a smudge on your cheek? Or— my dear girl!—pushing her hair back with the edge of a brotherly hand. In fact, unless he was careful, he'd be back at starting point.

He remarked: "That emerald is very cunning"—smiling into her eyes.

She smiled politely, and said: "It's not cunning, it's an accident, it was my grandmother's." She flirted her hand lightly by her face, though, smiling. But that was something she had done before, to a compliment she had had before, and often. It was all social, she had become social entirely. She remarked: "Didn't you say it was half past nine we had to record?"

"My dear Barbara, we've got two hours. We'll have another drink or two, then I'll ask you a couple of questions, then we'll drop down to the studio and get it over, and then we'll have a comfortable supper."

"I'd rather eat now, if you don't mind. I had no lunch, and I'm really hungry."

"But my dear, of course." He was angry. Just as he had been surprised by his real jealousy over James, so now he was thrown off balance by his anger: he had been counting on the long quiet dinner afterwards to establish intimacy. "Finish your drink and I'll take you to Nott's." Nott's was expensive. He glanced at her assessingly as he mentioned it. She said: "I wonder if you know Butler's? It's good and it's rather close." Butler's was good, and it was cheap, and he gave her a good mark for liking it. But Nott's it was going to be. "My dear, we'll get into a taxi and be at Nott's in a moment, don't worry."

She obediently got to her feet: the way she did it made him understand how badly he had slipped. She was saying to herself: Very well, he's like that, then all right, I'll do what he wants and get it over with....

Swallowing his own drink he followed her, and took her arm in the pub doorway. It was polite within his. Outside it drizzled. No taxi. He was having bad luck now. They walked in silence to the end of the street. There Barbara glanced into a side street where a sign said: BUTLER'S. Not to remind him of it, on the contrary, she concealed the glance. And here she was, entirely at his disposal, they might never have shared the comradely moment in the theater.

They walked half a mile to Nott's. No taxis. She made conversation: this was, he saw, to cover any embarrassment he might feel because of a half-mile walk through rain when she was tired. She was talking about some theory to do with the theater, with designs for theater building. He heard himself saying, and repeatedly: Yes, yes, yes. He thought about Nott's, how to get things right when they reached Nott's. There he took the headwaiter aside, gave him a pound, and instructions. They were put in a corner. Large Scotches appeared. The menus were spread. "And now, my dear," he said, "I apologize for dragging you here, but I hope you'll think it's worth it."

"Oh, it's charming, I've always liked it. It's just that ..." She stopped herself saying: it's such a long way. She smiled at him, raising her glass, and said: "It's one of my very favorite places, and I'm glad you dragged me here." Her voice was flat with tiredness. All this was appalling; he knew it; and he sat thinking how to retrieve his position. Meanwhile she fingered the menu. The headwaiter took the order, but Graham made a gesture which said: Wait a moment. He wanted the Scotch to take effect before she ate. But she saw his silent order; and, without annoyance or reproach, leaned forward to say, sounding patient: "Graham, please, I've got to eat, you don't want me drunk when you interview me, do you?"

"They are bringing it as fast as they can," he said, making it sound as if she were greedy. He looked neither at the headwaiter nor at Barbara. He noted in himself, as he slipped further and further away from contact with her, a cold determination growing in him; one apart from, apparently, any conscious act of will, that come what may, if it took all night, he'd be in her bed before morning. And now, seeing the small pale face, with the enormous green eyes, it was for the first time that he imagined her in his arms. Although he had said: Yes, that one, weeks ago, it was only now that he imagined her as a sensual experience. Now he did, so strongly that he could only glance at her, and then away towards the waiters who were bringing food.

"Thank the Lord," said Barbara, and all at once her voice was gay and intimate. "Thank heavens. Thank every power that is...." She was making fun of her own exaggeration; and, as he saw, because she wanted to put him at his ease after his boorishness over delaying the food. (She hadn't been taken in, he saw, humiliated, disliking her.) "Thank all the gods of Nott's," she went on, "because if I hadn't eaten inside five minutes I'd have died, I tell you." With which she picked up her knife and fork and began on her steak. He poured wine, smiling with her, thinking that *this* moment of closeness he would not throw away. He watched her frank hunger as she ate, and thought: Sensual— it's strange I hadn't wondered whether she would be or not.

"Now," she said, sitting back, having taken the edge off her hunger: "Let's get to work."

He said: "I've thought it over very carefully—how to present you. The first thing seems to me, we must get away from that old chestnut: Miss Coles, how extraordinary for a woman to be so versatile in her work ... I hope you agree?" This was his trump card. He had noted, when he had seen her on television,

her polite smile when this note was struck. (The smile he had seen so often tonight.) This smile said: All right, if you *have* to be stupid, what can I do?

Now she laughed and said: "What a relief. I was afraid you were going to do the same thing."

"Good, now you eat and I'll talk."

In his carefully prepared monologue he spoke of the different styles of theater she had shown herself mistress of, but not directly: he was flattering her on the breadth of her experience; the complexity of her character, as shown in her work. She ate, steadily, her face showing nothing. At last she asked: "And how did you plan to introduce this?"

He had meant to spring that on her as a surprise, something like: Miss Coles, a surprisingly young woman for what she has accomplished (she was thirty? thirty-two?) and a very attractive one.... "Perhaps I can give you an idea of what she's like if I say she could be taken for the film star Marie Carletta...." The Carletta was a strong earthy blonde, known to be intellectual. He now saw he could not possibly say this: he could imagine her cool look if he did. She said: "Do you mind if we get away from all that—my manifold talents, et cetera...." He felt himself stiffen with annoyance; particularly because this was not an accusation, he saw she did not think him worth one. She had assessed him: This is the kind of man who uses this kind of flattery and therefore.... It made him angrier that she did not even trouble to say: Why did you do exactly what you promised you wouldn't? She was being invincibly polite, trying to conceal her patience with his stupidity.

"After all," she was saying, "it is a stage designer's job to design what comes up. Would anyone take, let's say Johnnie Cranmore" (another stage designer) "onto the air or television and say: How very versatile you are because you did that musical about Java last month and a modern play about Irish laborers this?"

He battened down his anger. "My dear Barbara, I'm sorry. I didn't realize that what I said would sound just like the mixture as before. So what shall we talk about?"

"What I was saying as we walked to the restaurant: can we get away from the personal stuff?"

Now he almost panicked. Then, thank God, he laughed from nervousness, for she laughed and said: "You didn't hear one word I said."

"No, I didn't. I was frightened you were going to be furious because I made you walk so far when you were tired."

They laughed together, back to where they had been in the theater. He leaned over, took her hand, kissed it. He said: "Tell me again." He thought: Damn, now she's going to be earnest and intellectual.

But he understood he had been stupid. He had forgotten himself at twenty—or, for that matter, at thirty; forgotten one could live inside an idea, a set of ideas, with enthusiasm. For in talking about her ideas (also the ideas of the people she worked with) for a new theater, a new style of theater, she was as she had been with her colleagues over the sketches or the blue material. She was easy, informal, almost chattering. This was how, he remembered, one talked about ideas that were a breath of life. The ideas, he thought, were intelligent enough; and he would agree with them, with her, if he believed it mattered a damn one way or another, if any of these enthusiasms mattered a damn. But at least he now had the key, he knew what to do. At the end of not more than half an hour, they were again two professionals, talking about ideas

they shared, for he remembered caring about all this himself once. *When?
How many years ago was it that he had been able to care?*

At last he said: "My dear Barbara, do you realize the impossible position
you're putting me in? Margaret Ruyen who runs this program is determined to
do you personally, the poor woman hasn't got a serious thought in her head."

Barbara frowned. He put his hand on hers, teasing her for the frown: "No,
wait, trust me, we'll circumvent her." She smiled. In fact Margaret Ruyen had
left it all to him, had said nothing about Miss Coles.

"They aren't very bright—the brass," he said. "Well, never mind: we'll work
out what we want, do it, and it'll be a *fait accompli.*"

"Thank you, what a relief. How lucky I was to be given you to interview me."
She was relaxed now, because of the whiskey, the food, the wine, above all be-
cause of this new complicity against Margaret Ruyen. It would all be easy.
They worked out five or six questions, over coffee, and took a taxi through rain
to the studios. He noted that the cold necessity to have her, to make her, to
beat her down, had left him. He was even seeing himself, as the evening
ended, kissing her on the cheek and going home to his wife. This comradeship
was extraordinarily pleasant. It was balm to the wound he had not known he
carried until that evening, when he had had to accept the justice of the word
journalist. He felt he could talk forever about the state of the theater, its fi-
nances, the stupidity of the government, the philistinism of ...

At the studios he was careful to make a joke so that they walked in on the
laugh. He was careful that the interview began at once, without conversation
with Margaret Ruyen; and that from the moment the green light went on, his
voice lost its easy familiarity. He made sure that not one personal note was
struck during the interview. Afterwards, Margaret Ruyen, who was pleased,
came forward to say so: but he took her aside to say that Miss Coles was tired
and needed to be taken home at once for he knew this must look to Barbara as
if he were squaring a producer who had been expecting a different interview.
He led Barbara off, her hand held tight in his against his side. "Well," he said,
"we've done it, and I don't think she knows what hit her."

"Thank you," she said, "it really was pleasant to talk about something sensi-
ble for once."

He kissed her lightly on the mouth. She returned it, smiling. By now he felt
sure that the mood need not slip again, he could hold it.

"There are two things we can do," he said. "You can come to my club and
have a drink. Or I can drive you home and you can give me a drink. I have to go
past you."

"Where do you live?"

"Wimbledon." He lived, in fact, at Highgate; but she lived in Fulham. He
was taking another chance, but by the time she found out, they would be in a
position to laugh over his ruse.

"Good," she said. "You can drop me home then. I have to get up early." He
made no comment. In the taxi he took her hand; it was heavy in his, and he
asked: "Does James slave-drive you?"

"I didn't realize you knew him—no, he doesn't."

"Well, I don't know him intimately. What's he like to work with?"

"Wonderful," she said at once. "There's no one I enjoy working with more."

Jealousy spurted in him. He could not help himself: "Are you having an af-
fair with him?"

She looked: what's it to do with you? but said: "No, I'm not."

"He's very attractive," he said, with a chuckle of worldly complicity. She said nothing, and he insisted: "If I were a woman I'd have an affair with James."

It seemed she might very well say nothing. But she remarked: "He's married."

His spirits rose in a swoop. It was the first stupid remark she had made. It was a remark of such staggering stupidity that ... he let out a humoring snort of laughter, put his arm around her, kissed her, said: "My dear little Babs."

She said: "Why Babs?"

"Is that the prerogative of James? And of the stagehands?" he could not prevent himself adding.

"I'm only called that at work." She was stiff inside his arm.

"My dear Barbara, then ..." He waited for her to enlighten and explain, but she said nothing. Soon she moved out of his arm, on the pretext of lighting a cigarette. He lit it for her. He noted that his determination to lay her, and at all costs, had come back. They were outside her house. He said quickly: "And now, Barbara, you can make me a cup of coffee and give me a brandy." She hesitated; but he was out of the taxi, paying, opening the door for her. The house had no lights on, he noted. He said: "We'll be very quiet so as not to wake the children."

She turned her head slowly to look at him. She said, flat, replying to his real question: "My husband is away. As for the children, they are visiting friends tonight." She now went ahead of him to the door of the house. It was a small house, in a terrace of small and not very pretty houses. Inside a little, bright, intimate hall, she said: "I'll go and make some coffee. Then, my friend, you must go home because I'm very tired."

The *my friend* struck him deep, because he had become vulnerable during their comradeship. He said, gabbling: "You're annoyed with me—oh, please don't, I'm sorry."

She smiled, from a cool distance. He saw, in the small light from the ceiling, her extraordinary eyes. "Green" eyes are hazel, are brown with green flecks, are even blue. Eyes are checkered, flawed, changing. Hers were solid green, but really, he had never seen anything like them before. They were like very deep water. They were like—well, emeralds; or the absolute clarity of green in the depths of a tree in summer. And now, as she smiled almost perpendicularly up at him, he saw a darkness come over them. Darkness swallowed the clear green. She said: "I'm not in the least annoyed." It was as if she had yawned with boredom. "And now I'll get the things ... in there." She nodded at a white door and left him. He went into a long, very tidy white room, that had a narrow bed in one corner, a table covered with drawings, sketches, pencils. Tacked to the walls with drawing pins were swatches of colored stuffs. Two small chairs stood near a low round table: an area of comfort in the working room. He was thinking: I wouldn't like it if my wife had a room like this. I wonder what Barbara's husband ...? He had not thought of her till now in relation to her husband, or to her children. Hard to imagine her with a frying pan in her hand, or for that matter, cosy in the double bed.

A noise outside: he hastily arranged himself, leaning with one arm on the mantelpiece. She came in with a small tray that had cups, glasses, brandy, coffeepot. She looked abstracted. Graham was on the whole flattered by this: it probably meant she was at ease in his presence. He realized he was a little tight and rather tired. Of course, she was tired too, that was why she was vague. He remembered that earlier that evening he had lost a chance by not using her tiredness. Well now, if he were intelligent ... She was about to pour

coffee. He firmly took the coffeepot out of her hand, and nodded at a chair. Smiling, she obeyed him. "That's better," he said. He poured coffee, poured brandy, and pulled the table towards her. She watched him. Then he took her hand, kissed it, patted it, laid it down gently. Yes, he thought, I did that well.

Now, a problem. He wanted to be closer to her, but she was fitted into a damned silly little chair that had arms. If he were to sit by her on the floor…? But no, for him, the big bulky reassuring man, there could be no casual gestures, no informal postures. Suppose I scoop her out of the chair onto the bed? He drank his coffee as he plotted. Yes, he'd carry her to the bed, but not yet.

"Graham," she said, setting down her cup. She was, he saw with annoyance, looking tolerant. "Graham, in about half an hour I want to be in bed and asleep."

As she said this, she offered him a smile of amusement at this situation— man and woman maneuvering, the great comic situation. And with part of himself he could have shared it. Almost, he smiled with her, laughed. (Not till days later he exclaimed to himself: Lord what a mistake I made, not to share the joke with her then: that was where I went seriously wrong.) But he could not smile. His face was frozen, with a stiff pride. Not because she had been watching him plot; the amusement she now offered him took the string out of that; but because of his revived determination that he was going to have his own way, he was going to have her. He was not going home. But he felt that he held a bunch of keys, and did not know which one to choose.

He lifted the second small chair opposite to Barbara, moving aside the coffee table for this purpose. He sat in this chair, leaned forward, took her two hands, and said: "My dear, don't make me go home yet, don't, I beg you." The trouble was, nothing had happened all evening that could be felt to lead up to these words and his tone—simple, dignified, human being pleading with human being for surcease. He saw himself leaning forward, his big hands swallowing her small ones; he saw his face, warm with the appeal. And he realized he had meant the words he used. They were nothing more than what he felt. He wanted to stay with her because she wanted him to, because he was her colleague, a fellow worker in the arts. He needed this desperately. But she was examining him, curious rather than surprised and from a critical distance. He heard himself saying: "If James were here, I wonder what you'd do?" His voice was aggrieved; he saw the sudden dark descend over her eyes, and she said: "Graham, would you like some more coffee before you go?"

He said "I've been wanting to meet you for years. I know a good many people who know you."

She leaned forward, poured herself a little more brandy, sat back, holding the glass between her two palms on her chest. An odd gesture: Graham felt that this vessel she was cherishing between her hands was herself. A patient, long-suffering gesture. He thought of various men who had mentioned her. He thought of Jack Kennaway, wavered, panicked, said: "For instance, Jack Kennaway."

And now, at the name, an emotion lit her eyes—what was it? He went on, deliberately testing this emotion, adding to it: "I had dinner with him last week—oh, quite by chance!—and he was talking about you."

"Was he?"

He remembered he had thought her sullen, all those years ago. Now she seemed defensive, and she frowned. He said "In fact he spent most of the evening talking about you."

She said in short, breathless sentences, which he realized were due to anger:

"I can very well imagine what he says. But surely you can't think I enjoy being reminded that . . ." She broke off, resenting him, he saw, because he forced her down onto a level she despised. But it was not his level either: it was all her fault, all hers! He couldn't remember not being in control of a situation with a woman for years. Again he felt like a man teetering on a tightrope. He said, trying to make good use of Jack Kennaway, even at this late hour: "Of course, he's a charming boy, but not a man at all."

She looked at him, silent, guarding her brandy glass against her breasts.

"Unless appearances are totally deceptive, of course." He could not resist probing, even though he knew it was fatal.

She said nothing.

"Do you know you are supposed to have had the great affair with Jack Kennaway?" he exclaimed, making this an amused expostulation against the fools who could believe it.

"So I am told." She set down her glass. "And now," she said, standing up, dismissing him. He lost his head, took a step forward, grabbed her in his arms, and groaned: "Barbara!"

She turned her face this way and that under his kisses. He snatched a diagnostic look at her expression—it was still patient. He placed his lips against her neck, groaned "Barbara" again, and waited. She would have to do something. Fight free, respond, something. She did nothing at all. At last she said: "For the Lord's sake, Graham!" She sounded amused: he was again being offered amusement. But if he shared it with her, it would be the end of this chance to have her. He clamped his mouth over hers, silencing her. She did not fight him off so much as blow him off. Her mouth treated his attacking mouth as a woman blows and laughs in water, puffing off waves or spray with a laugh, turning aside her head. It was a gesture half annoyance, half humor. He continued to kiss her while she moved her head and face about under the kisses as if they were small attacking waves.

And so began what, when he looked back on it afterwards, was the most embarrassing experience of his life. Even at the time he hated her for his ineptitude. For he held her there for what must have been nearly half an hour. She was much shorter than he, he had to bend, and his neck ached. He held her rigid, his thighs on either side of hers, her arms clamped to her side in a bear's hug. She was unable to move, except for her head. When his mouth ground hers open and his tongue moved and writhed inside it, she still remained passive. And he could not stop himself. While with his intelligence he watched this ridiculous scene, he was determined to go on, because sooner or later her body must soften in wanting his. And he could not stop because he could not face the horror of the moment when he set her free and she looked at him. And he hated her more, every moment. Catching glimpses of her great green eyes, open and dismal beneath his, he knew he had never disliked anything more than those "jeweled" eyes. They were repulsive to him. It occurred to him at last that even if by now she wanted him, he wouldn't know it, because she was not able to move at all. He cautiously loosened his hold so that she had an inch or so leeway. She remained quite passive. As if, he thought derisively, she had read or been told that the way to incite men maddened by lust was to fight them. He found he was thinking: Stupid cow, so you imagine I find you attractive, do you? You've got the conceit to think that!

The sheer, raving insanity of this thought hit him, opened his arms, his

thighs, and lifted his tongue out of her mouth. She stepped back, wiping her mouth with the back of her hand, and stood dazed with incredulity. The embarrassment that lay in wait for him really engulfed him, but he let anger postpone it. She said positively apologetic, even, at this moment, humorous: "You're crazy, Graham. What's the matter, are you drunk? You don't seem drunk. You don't even find me attractive."

The blood of hatred went to his head and he gripped her again. Now she had got her face firmly twisted away so that he could not reach her mouth, and she repeated steadily as he kissed the parts of her cheeks and neck that were available to him: "Graham, let me go, do let me go, Grahahm." She went on saying this; he went on squeezing, grinding, kissing and licking. It might go on all night: it was a sheer contest of wills, nothing else. He thought: It's only a really masculine woman who wouldn't have given in by now out of sheer decency of the flesh! One thing he knew, however: that she would be in that bed, in his arms, and very soon. He let her go, but said: "I'm going to sleep with you tonight, you know that, don't you?"

She leaned with hand on the mantelpiece to steady herself. Her face was colorless, since he had licked all the makeup off. She seemed quite different: small and defenseless with her large mouth pale now, her smudged green eyes fringed with gold. And now, for the first time, he felt what it might have been supposed (certainly by her) he felt hours ago. Seeing the small damp flesh of her face, he felt kinship, intimacy with her, he felt intimacy of the flesh, the affection and good humor of sensuality. He felt she was flesh of his flesh, his sister in the flesh. He felt desire for her, instead of the will to have her; and because of this, was ashamed of the farce he had been playing. Now he desired simply to take her into bed in the affection of his senses.

She said: "What on earth am I supposed to do? Telephone for the police, or what?" He was hurt that she still addressed the man who had ground her into sulky apathy; she was not addressing *him* at all.

She said: "Or scream for the neighbors, is that what you want?"

The gold-fringed eyes were almost black, because of the depth of the shadow of boredom over them. She was bored and weary to the point of falling to the floor, he could see that.

He said: "I'm going to sleep with you."

"But how can you possibly want to?"—a reasonable, a civilized demand addressed to a man who (he could see) she believed would respond to it. She said: "You know I don't want to, and I know you don't really give a damn one way or the other."

He was stung back into being the boor because she had not the intelligence to see that the boor no longer existed; because she could not see that this was a man who wanted her in a way which she must respond to.

There she stood, supporting herself with one hand, looking small and white and exhausted, and utterly incredulous. She was going to turn and walk off out of simple incredulity, he could see that. "Do you think I don't mean it?" he demanded, grinding this out between his teeth. She made a movement—she was on the point of going away. His hand shot out on its own volition and grasped her wrist. She frowned. His other hand grasped her other wrist. His body hove up against hers to start the pressure of a new embrace. Before it could, she said: "Oh Lord, no, I'm not going through all that again. Right, then."

"What do you mean—right, then?" he demanded.

She said: "You're going to sleep with me. O.K. Anything rather than go through that again. Shall we get it over with?"

He grinned, saying in silence: "No darling, oh no you don't, I don't care what words you use, I'm going to have you now and that's all there is to it."

She shrugged. The contempt, the weariness of it, had no effect on him, because he was now again hating her so much that wanting her was like needing to kill something or someone.

She took her clothes off, as if she were going to bed by herself: her jacket, skirt, petticoat. She stood in white bra and panties, a rather solid girl, brown-skinned still from the summer. He felt a flash of affection for the brown girl with her loose yellow hair as she stood naked. She got into bed and lay there, while the green eyes looked at him in civilized appeal: Are you really going through with this? Do you have to? Yes, his eyes said back: I do have to. She shifted her gaze aside, to the wall, saying silently: Well, if you want to take me without any desire at all on my part, then go ahead, if you're not ashamed. He was not ashamed, because he was maintaining the flame of hate for her which he knew quite well was all that stood between him and shame. He took off his clothes, and got into bed beside her. As he did so, knowing he was putting himself in the position of raping a woman who was making it elaborately clear he bored her, his flesh subsided completely, sad, and full of reproach because a few moments ago it was reaching out for his sister whom he could have made happy. He lay on his side by her, secretly at work on himself, while he supported himself across her body on his elbow, using the free hand to manipulate her breasts. He saw that she gritted her teeth against his touch. At least she could not know that after all this fuss he was not potent.

In order to incite himself, he clasped her again. She felt his smallness, writhed free of him, sat up and said: "Lie down."

While she had been lying there, she had been thinking: The only way to get this over with is to make him big again, otherwise I've got to put up with him all night. His hatred of her was giving him a clairvoyance: he knew very well what went on through her mind. She had switched on, with the determination to *get it all over with*, a sensual good humor, a patience. He lay down. She squatted beside him, the light from the ceiling blooming on her brown shoulders, her flat fair hair falling over her face. But she would not look at his face. Like a bored, skilled wife, she was; or like a prostitute. She administered to him, she was setting herself to please him. Yes, he thought, she's sensual, or she could be. Meanwhile she was succeeding in defeating the reluctance of his flesh, which was the tender token of a possible desire for her, by using a cold skill that was the result of her contempt for him. Just as he decided: Right, it's enough, now I shall have her properly, she made him come. It was not a trick, to hurry or cheat him, what defeated him was her transparent thought: Yes, that's what he's worth.

Then, having succeeded, and waited for a moment or two, she stood up, naked, the fringes of gold at her loins and in her armpits speaking to him a language quite different from that of her green, bored eyes. She looked at him and thought, showing it plainly: What sort of man is it who . . . ? He watched the slight movement of her shoulders: a just-checked shrug. She went out of the room: then the sound of running water. Soon she came back in a white dressing gown, carrying a yellow towel. She handed him the towel, looking

away in politeness as he used it. "Are you going home now?" she enquired hopefully, at this point.

"No, I'm not." He believed that now he would have to start fighting her again, but she lay down beside him, not touching him (he could feel the distaste of her flesh for his) and he thought: Very well, my dear, but there's a lot of the night left yet. He said aloud: "I'm going to have you properly tonight." She said nothing, lay silent, yawned. Then she remarked consoling y, and he could have laughed outright from sheer surprise: "Those were hardly conducive circumstances for making love." She was consoling him. He hated her for it. A proper little slut: I force her into bed, she doesn't want me, but she still has to make me feel good, like a prostitute. But even while he hated her he responded in kind, from the habit of sexual generosity. "It's because of my admiration for you, because... after all, I was holding in my arms one of the thousand women."

A pause. "The thousand?" she enquired, carefully.

"The thousand especial women."

"In Britain or in the world? You choose them for their brains, their beauty—what?"

"Whatever it is that makes them outstanding," he said, offering her a compliment.

"Well," she remarked at last, inciting him to be amused again: "I hope that at least there's a short list you can say I am on for politeness' sake."

He did not reply for he understood he was sleepy. He was still telling himself that he must stay awake when he was slowly waking and it was morning. It was about eight. Barbara was not there. He thought: My God! What on earth shall I tell my wife? Where was Barbara? He remembered the ridiculous scenes of last night and nearly succumbed to shame. Then he thought, reviving anger: If she didn't sleep beside me here I'll never forgive her.... He sat up, quietly, determined to go through the house until he found her and, having found her, to possess her, when the door opened and she came in. She was fully dressed in a green suit, her hair done, her eyes made up. She carried a tray of coffee, which she set down beside the bed. He was conscious of his big loose hairy body, half uncovered. He said to himself that he was not going to lie in bed, naked, while she was dressed. He said: "Have you got a gown of some kind?" She handed him, without speaking, a towel, and said: "The bathroom's second on the left." She went out. He followed, the towel around him. Everything in this house was gay, intimate—not at all like her efficient working room. He wanted to find out where she had slept, and opened the first door. It was the kitchen, and she was in it, putting a brown earthenware dish into the oven. "The next door," said Barbara. He went hastily past the second door, and opened (he hoped quietly) the third. It was a cupboard full of linen. "This door," said Barbara, behind him.

"So all right then, where did you sleep?"

"What's it to do with you? Upstairs, in my own bed. Now, if you have everything, I'll say goodbye, I want to get to the theater."

"I'll take you," he said at once.

He saw again the movement of her eyes, the dark swallowing the light in deadly boredom. "I'll take you," he insisted.

"I'd prefer to go by myself," she remarked. Then she smiled: "However,

you'll take me. Then you'll make a point of coming right in, so that James and everyone can see—that's what you want to take me for, isn't it?"

He hated her, finally, and quite simply, for her intelligence; that not once had he got away with anything, that she had been watching, since they had met yesterday, every movement of his campaign for her. However, some fate or inner urge over which he had no control made him say sentimentally: "My dear, you must see that I'd like at least to take you to your work."

"Not at all, have it on me," she said, giving him the lie direct. She went past him to the room he had slept in. "I shall be leaving in ten minutes," she said.

He took a shower, fast. When he returned, the workroom was already tidied, the bed made, all signs of the night gone. Also, there were no signs of the coffee she had brought in for him. He did not like to ask for it, for fear of an outright refusal. Besides, she was ready, her coat on, her handbag under her arm. He went, without a word, to the front door, and she came after him, silent.

He could see that every fiber of her body signaled a simple message: Oh God, for the moment when I can be rid of this boor! She was nothing but a slut, he thought.

A taxi came. In it she sat as far away from him as she could. He thought of what he should say to his wife.

Outside the theater she remarked: "You could drop me here, if you liked." It was not a plea, she was too proud for that. "I'll take you in," he said, and saw her thinking: Very well, I'll go through with it to shame him. He was determined to take her in and hand her over to her colleagues, he was afraid she would give him the slip. But far from playing it down, she seemed determined to play it his way. At the stage door, she said to the doorman: "This is Mr. Spence, Tom—do you remember, Mr. Spence from last night?" "Good morning, Babs," said the man, examining Graham, politely, as he had been ordered to do.

Barbara went to the door to the stage, opened it, held it open for him. He went in first, then held it open for her. Together they walked into the cavernous, littered, badly lit place and she called out: "James, James!" A man's voice called out from the front of the house: "Here, Babs, why are you so late?"

The auditorium opened before them, darkish, silent, save for an early-morning busyness of charwomen. A vacuum cleaner roared, smally, somewhere close. A couple of stagehands stood looking up at a drop which had a design of blue and green spirals. James stood with his back to the auditorium, smoking. "You're late, Babs," he said again. He saw Graham behind her, and nodded. Barbara and James kissed. Barbara said, giving allowance to every syllable: "You remember Mr. Spence from last night?" James nodded: How do you do? Barbara stood beside him, and they looked together up at the blue-and-green backdrop. Then Barbara looked again at Graham, asking silently: All right now, isn't that enough? He could see her eyes, sullen with boredom.

He said: "Bye, Babs. Bye, James. I'll ring you, Babs." No response, she ignored him. He walked off slowly, listening for what might be said. For instance: "Babs, for God's sake, what are you doing with him?" Or she might say: "Are you wondering about Graham Spence? Let me explain."

Graham passed the stagehands who, he could have sworn, didn't recognize him. Then at last he heard James's voice to Barbara: "It's no good, Babs, I know you're enamored of that particular shade of blue, but do have another look at it, there's a good girl. . . ." Graham left the stage, went past the office where

the stage doorman sat reading a newspaper. Graham went to find a taxi, think-ing: I'd better think up something convincing, then I'll telephone my wife.

Luckily he had an excuse not to be at home that day, for this evening he had to interview a young man (for television) about his new novel.

1958

MAY SWENSON
1919–1989

Born and raised in Logan, Utah, where her father was a professor of mechanical en-gineering at the state university, the poet May Swenson worked as a reporter for the Salt Lake City *Desert News*, then settled in New York City, where she became an editor for New Directions in 1959. In 1966, after publishing a number of well-received collections of verse—including *Another Animal* (1954) and *To Mix with Time: New Selected Poems* (1963)—she resigned to devote herself completely to her writing. After that, with the assistance of Guggenheim and Rockefeller fellow-ships among other awards, Swenson produced a considerable body of poetry, most notably the imaginative and innovative volume of "concrete" poetry *Iconographs* (1970), a book of verses that were all, like *Women* and *Bleeding*, arranged in typo-graphical forms whose shapes reflect the nature of their subject, for her intention, as she herself explained, was "to make an existence in space, as well as time, for the poem."

About Swenson's early work, the poet Elizabeth Bishop remarked in a letter (1962) that this artist is "one of the few good poets who write good poems about nature . . . not just comparing it to states of mind or society." As the poet-critic Alicia Ostriker has observed, in Swenson's later work the scrupulous vision that Bishop was describing evolved into more radical and metaphysical "shapes of spec-ulation." Posthumously published volumes include *The Love Poems of May Swenson* (1991) and *Nature: Poems Old and New* (1994).

Women

Women
should be
pedestals
moving
pedestals
moving
to the
motions
of men

Or they
should be
little horses
those wooden
sweet 5
oldfashioned
painted
rocking
horses

the gladdest things in the toyroom 10

The
pegs
of their
ears
so similar
and dear

feelingly
and then
unfeelingly
To be
joyfully 15
ridden

<div style="text-align:center">

to the trusting rockingly
fists ridden until
To be chafed the restored

egos dismount and the legs stride away 20

Immobile willing
sweetlipped to be set
sturdy into motion
and smiling Women
women should be 25
should always pedestals
be waiting to men

1968, 1970

</div>

Bleeding

Stop bleeding said the knife
I would if I could said the cut.
Stop bleeding you make me messy with this blood.
I'm sorry said the cut.
Stop or I will sink in farther said the knife. 5
Don't said the cut.
The knife did not say it couldn't help it but it sank in farther.
If only you didn't bleed said the knife I wouldn't have to do this.
I know said the cut I bleed too easily I hate that I can't
help it I wish I were a knife like you and didn't have to bleed. 10
Meanwhile stop bleeding will you said the knife.
Yes you are a mess and sinking in farther said the cut I will
have to stop.
Have you stopped by now said the knife.
I've almost stopped I think 15
Why must you bleed in the first place said the knife.
For the reason maybe that you must do what you must do said the cut.
I can't stand bleeding said the knife and sank in father.
I hate it too said the cutI know it isn't you it's me
you're lucky to be a knife you ought to be glad about that. 20
Too many cuts around said the knife they're messy I don't know
how they stand themselves
They don't said the cut.
You're bleeding again.
No I've stopped said the cut. See you're coming out now the 25
blood is drying it will rub off you'll be shiny again and clean.
If only cuts wouldn't bleed so much said the knife coming out a little.
But then knives might become dull said the cut.
Aren't you bleeding a little said the knife.
I hope not said the cut. 30
I feel you are just a little.
Maybe just a little but I can stop now.
I feel a little wetness still said the knife sinking in
a little but then coming out a little.
Just a little maybe just enough said the cut. 35

That's encugh now stop now do you feel better said the knife.
I feel I have to bleed to feel I think said the cut.
I don't I don't have to feel said the knife drying now becoming shiny.

<div align="right">1970</div>

GWEN HARWOOD

1920–

One of Australia's finest poets, Gwen Harwood has received many awards during
her publishing career, including the Meanjir Poetry Prize (1958, 1959), the Grace
Leven Prize (1975), the Robert Frost Award (1977), the Patrick White Award
(1978), and the Victorian Premier's Literary Award (1989) Not until 1991, how-
ever, did Oxford University Press issue the first of her books to appear outside
Australia, her *Collected Poems*. Yet this neglect cannot be attributed to the re-
gional focus of her poetry, which eschews national concerns to address instead mu-
sical and philosophical issues.

Born in Taringa, Queensland, and educated at Brisbane Girls' Grammar School,
Harwood has described her youth as a time of such happiness that "in a sense it
left me without ambition. I refer everything in my life to the radiance of that time
in my childhood." Music—piano and composition—became her "first love." After
being discouraged from a concertizing career, she became a teacher and served as
organist at the Anglican Church of All Saints in Brisbane. In 1945, she married the
linguist F. W. Harwood and moved with him to Tasmania, where he had a univer-
sity lectureship and where she began an intellectually stimulating friendship with
the philosopher Ludwig Wittgenstein. Indeed, Harwood later believed that read-
ing Wittgenstein's sentence "Not how the world is, is the mystical, but that it is"
caused her to take her first steps toward becoming a poet.

Attributing her late publishing career to the decision she made to devote herself
primarily to the raising of her four children, Harwood kept her poems "a secret
vice" until the late 1950s, when her work began appearing in anthologies and mag-
azines, sometimes under various pseudonyms. She maintained her link to the
world of music by composing five opera librettos for the Australian composer Larry
Sitsky. By 1981 and 1989, when she published *The Lion's Bride* and *Bone Scan*, she
had established herself as a major artist.

In the Park

She sits in the park. Her clothes are out of date.
Two children whine and bicker, tug her skirt.
A third draws aimless patterns in the dirt.
Someone she loved once passes by—too late

to feign indifference to that casual nod. 5
"How nice," et cetera. "Time holds great surprises."
From his neat head unquestionably rises
a small balloon . . . "but for the grace of God . . ."

They stand a while in flickering light, rehearsing
the children's names and birthdays. "It's so sweet 10
to hear their chatter, watch them grow and thrive,"

she says to his departing smile. Then, nursing
the youngest child, sits staring at her feet.
To the wind she says, "They have eaten me alive."

1963

The Sea Anemones

Gray mountains, sea and sky. Even the misty
seawind is gray. I walk on lichened rock
in a kind of late assessment, call it peace.
Then the anemones, scarlet, gouts of blood.
There is a word I need, and earth was speaking. 5
I cannot hear. These seaflowers are too bright.
Kneeling on rock, I touch them through cold water.
My fingers meet some hungering gentleness.
A newborn child's lips moved so at my breast.
I woke, once, with my palm across your mouth. 10
 The word is: *ever*. Why add salt to salt?
 Blood drop by drop among the rocks they shine.
 Anemos,[1] wind. The spirit, where it will.
Not flowers, no, animals[2] that must eat or die.

1981

Mother Who Gave Me Life

Mother who gave me life
I think of women bearing
women. Forgive me the wisdom
I would not learn from you.

It is not for my children I walk 5
on earth in the light of the living.
It is for you, for the wild
daughters becoming women,

anguish of seasons burning
backward in time to those other 10
bodies, your mother, and hers
and beyond, speech growing stranger

on thresholds of ice, rock, fire,
bones changing, heads inclining
to monkey bosom, lemur breast, 15
guileless milk of the word.

I prayed you would live to see
Halley's Comet a second time.[1]

1. Wind (Greek).
2. Sea anemones, whose bright-colored tentacles and
general fixity of position make them somewhat resem-
ble flowers, are in fact animals.
1. The most recent approaches of this periodic comet
were in 1910 and 1985–86.

The Sister said, When she died
she was folding a little towel. 20

You left the world so, having lived
nearly thirty thousand days:
a fabric of marvels folded
down to a little space.

At our last meeting I closed 25
the ward door of heavy glass
between us, and saw your face
crumple, fine threadbare linen

worn, still good to the last,
then, somehow, smooth to a smile 30
so I should not see your tears.
Anguish: remembered hours:

a lamp on embroidered linen,
my supper set out, your voice
calling me in as darkness 35
falls on my father's house.

 1981

Mid-Channel

The days shall come upon you, that he will take you away with hooks, and
your posterity with fishhooks.
—Amos, IV, 2

Cod inert as an old boot,
tangling dance of the little shark,
perch nibble, flathead jerk—
blindfold I'd know them on my line.

Fugitive gleam on scale and fin, 5
lustrous eye, opalescent belly
dry and die in the undesired
element. A day will come,

matter-of-fact as knife and plate,
with death's hook in my jaw, and language 10
unspeakable, the line full out.
I'll tire you with my choking weight

old monster anchored in the void.
My God, you'll wonder what you've caught.
Land me in hell itself at last 15
I'll stab and swell your wounds with poison.

Not here, not now. Water's my kingdom
tonight, my line makes starspecks tremble.

The dinghy's decked with golden eyes
and still the cod boil round my bait.　　　　　20

1988

HISAYE YAMAMOTO

1921–

The daughter of Issei parents (immigrants from Japan), Hisaye Yamamoto explores her complicated identity as a Nisei, a member of the second American generation, in her most frequently anthologized story, *Seventeen Syllables.* Her central character, the sexually awakening Rosie, feels estranged from her mother not only because of their different languages but also because of the mystery in which the mother's life in Japan remains shrouded.

That immigration and assimilation would serve as the mainspring of Yamamoto's imagination seems apt given her attendence in Japanese schools for the first twelve years of her growing up in California. During World War II, when many Japanese-American citizens were forced to live in concentration camps, she was interned in Poston, Arizona, where she wrote for the camp newspaper. Her stint working at the socially conscious *Catholic Worker* in New York during the 1950s kept her involved with issues of disenfranchisement. Married, the mother of five children, and the grandmother of two, Yamamoto resides in southern California.

Seventeen Syllables

The first Rosie knew that her mother had taken to writing poems was one evening when she finished one and read it aloud for her daughter's approval. It was about cats, and Rosie pretended to understand it thoroughly and appreciate it no end, partly because she hesitated to disillusion her mother about the quantity and quality of Japanese she had learned in all the years now that she had been going to Japanese school every Saturday (and Wednesday, too, in the summer). Even so, her mother must have been skeptical about the depth of Rosie's understanding, because she explained afterwards about the kind of poem she was trying to write.

See, Rosie, she said, it was a *haiku*, a poem in which she must pack all her meaning into seventeen syllables only, which were divided into three lines of five, seven, and five syllables. In the one she had just read, she had tried to capture the charm of a kitten, as well as comment on the superstition that owning a cat of three colors meant good luck.

"Yes, yes, I understand. How utterly lovely," Rosie said, and her mother, either satisfied or seeing through the deception and resigned, went back to composing.

The truth was that Rosie was lazy; English lay ready on the tongue but Japanese had to be searched for and examined, and even then put forth tentatively (probably to meet with laughter). It was so much easier to say yes, yes, even when one meant no, no. Besides, this was what was in her mind to say: I was looking through one of your magazines from Japan last night, Mother, and

towards the back I found some *haiku* in English that delighted me. There was one that made me giggle off and on until I fell asleep—

> *It is morning, and lo!*
> *I lie awake, comme il faut,*
> *sighing for some dough.*

Now, how to reach her mother, how to communicate the melancholy song? Rosie knew formal Japanese by fits and starts, her mother had even less English, no French. It was much more possible to say yes. yes.

It developed that her mother was writing the *haiku* for a daily newspaper, the *Mainichi Shimbun*, that was published in San Francisco. Los Angeles, to be sure, was closer to the farming community in which the Hayashi family lived and several Japanese vernaculars were printed there, but Rosie's parents said they preferred the tone of the northern paper. Once a week, the *Mainichi* would have a section devoted to *haiku*, and her mother became an extravagant contributor, taking for herself the blossoming pen name, Ume Hanazono.

So Rosie and her father lived for awhile with two women, her mother and Ume Hanazono. Her mother (Tome Hayashi by name) kept house, cooked, washed, and, along with her husband and the Carrascos, the Mexican family hired for the harvest, did her ample share of picking tomatoes out in the sweltering fields and boxing them in tidy strata in the cool packing shed. Ume Hanazono, who came to life after the dinner dishes were done, was an earnest, muttering stranger who often neglected speaking when spoken to and stayed busy at the parlor table as late as midnight scribbling with pencil on scratch paper or carefully copying characters on good paper with her fat, pale green Parker.

The new interest had some repercussions on the household routine. Before, Rosie had been accustomed to her parents and herself taking their hot baths early and going to bed almost immediately afterwards, unless her parents challenged each other to a game of flower cards or unless company dropped in. Now if her father wanted to play cards, he had to resort to solitaire (at which he always cheated fearlessly), and if a group of friends came over, it was bound to contain someone who was also writing *haiku*, and the small assemblage would be split in two, her father entertaining the non-literary members and her mother comparing ecstatic notes with the visiting poet.

If they went out, it was more of the same thing. But Ume Hanazono's life span, even for a poet's, was very brief—perhaps three months at most.

One night they went over to see the Hayano family in the neighboring town to the west, an adventure both painful and attractive to Rosie. It was attractive because there were four Hayano girls, all lovely and each one named after a season of the year (Haru, Natsu, Aki, Fuyu),[1] painful because something had been wrong with Mrs. Hayano ever since the birth of her first child. Rosie would sometimes watch Mrs. Hayano, reputed to have been the belle of her native village, making her way about a room, stooped, slowly shuffling, violently trembling (*always* trembling), and she would be reminded that this woman, in this same condition, had carried and given issue to three babies.

1. The girls' names are Spring, Summer, Autumn, and Winter, respectively.

She would look wonderingly at Mr. Hayano, handsome, tall, and strong, and she would look at her four pretty friends. But it was not a matter she could come to any decision about.

On this visit, however, Mrs. Hayano sat all evening in the rocker, as motionless and unobtrusive as it was possible for her to be, and Rosie found the greater part of the evening practically anaesthetic. Too, Rosie spent most of it in the girls' room, because Haru, the garrulous one, said almost as soon as the bows and other greetings were over, "Oh, you must see my new coat!"

It was a pale plaid of grey, sand, and blue, with an enormous collar, and Rosie, seeing nothing special in it, said, "Gee, how nice."

"Nice?" said Haru, indignantly. "Is that all you can say about it? It's gorgeous! And so cheap, too. Only seventeen-ninety-eight, because it was a sale. The saleslady said it was twenty-five dollars regular."

"Gee," said Rosie. Natsu, who never said much and when she said anything said it shyly, fingered the coat covetously and Haru pulled it away.

"Mine," she said, putting it on. She minced in the aisle between the two large beds and smiled happily. "Let's see how your mother likes it."

She broke into the front room and the adult conversation and went to stand in front of Rosie's mother, while the rest watched from the door. Rosie's mother was properly envious. "May I inherit it when you're through with it?"

Haru, pleased, giggled and said yes, she could, but Natsu reminded gravely from the door, "You promised me, Haru."

Everyone laughed but Natsu, who shamefacedly retreated into the bedroom. Haru came in laughing, taking off the coat. "We were only kidding, Natsu," she said. "Here, you try it on now."

After Natsu buttoned herself into the coat, inspected herself solemnly in the bureau mirror, and reluctantly shed it, Rosie, Aki, and Fuyu got their turns, and Fuyu, who was eight, drowned in it while her sisters and Rosie doubled up in amusement. They all went into the front room later, because Haru's mother quaveringly called to her to fix the tea and rice cakes and open a can of sliced peaches for everybody. Rosie noticed that her mother and Mr. Hayano were talking together at the little table—they were discussing a *haiku* that Mr. Hayano was planning to send to the *Mainichi*, while her father was sitting at one end of the sofa looking through a copy of *Life*, the new picture magazine. Occasionally, her father would comment on a photograph, holding it toward Mrs. Hayano and speaking to her as he always did—loudly, as though he thought someone such as she must surely be at least a trifle deaf also.

The five girls had their refreshments at the kitchen table, and it was while Rosie was showing the sisters her trick of swallowing peach slices without chewing (she chased each slippery crescent down with a swig of tea) that her father brought his empty teacup and untouched saucer to the sink and said, "Come on, Rosie, we're going home now."

"Already?" asked Rosie.

"Work tomorrow," he said.

He sounded irritated, and Rosie, puzzled, gulped one last yellow slice and stood up to go, while the sisters began protesting, as was their wont.

"We have to get up at five-thirty," he told them, going into the front room quickly, so that they did not have their usual chance to hang onto his hands and plead for an extension of time.

Rosie, following, saw that her mother and Mr. Hayano were sipping tea and still talking together, while Mrs. Hayano concentrated, quivering, on raising

the handleless Japanese cup to her lips with both her hands and lowering it
back to her lap. Her father, saying nothing, went out the door, onto the bright
porch, and down the steps. Her mother looked up and asked, "Where is he
going?"

"Where is he going?" Rosie said. "He said we were going home now."

"Going home?" Her mother looked with embarrassment at Mr. Hayano and
his absorbed wife and then forced a smile. "He must be tired," she said.

Haru was not giving up yet. "May Rosie stay overnight?" she asked, and
Natsu, Aki, and Fuyu came to reinforce their sister's plea by helping her make
a circle around Rosie's mother. Rosie, for once having no desire to stay, was re-
lieved when her mother, apologizing to the perturbed Mr. and Mrs. Hayano
for her father's abruptness at the same time, managed to shake her head no at
the quartet, kindly but adamant, so that they broke their circle and let her go.

Rosie's father looked ahead into the windshield as the two joined him. "I'm
sorry," her mother said. "You must be tired." Her father, stepping on the
starter, said nothing. "You know how I get when it's *haiku*," she continued, "I
forget what time it is." He only grunted.

As they rode homeward silently, Rosie, sitting between, felt a rush of hate
for both—for her mother for begging, for her father for denying her mother. I
wish this old Ford would crash, right now, she thought, then immediately, no,
no, I wish my father would laugh, but it was too late: already the vision had
passed through her mind of the green pick-up crumpled in the dark against
one of the mighty eucalyptus trees they were just riding past, of the three con-
torted, bleeding bodies, one of them hers.

Rosie ran between two patches of tomatoes, her heart working more ram-
bunctiously than she had ever known it to. How lucky it was that Aunt Taka
and Uncle Gimpachi had come tonight, though, how very lucky. Otherwise
she might not have really kept her half-promise to meet Jesus Carrasco. Jesus
was going to be a senior in September at the same school she went to, and his
parents were the ones helping with the tomatoes this year. She and Jesus, who
hardly remembered seeing each other at Cleveland High where there were so
many other people and two whole grades between them, had become great
friends this summer—he always had a joke for her when he periodically drove
the loaded pick-up up from the fields to the shed where she was usually sort-
ing while her mother and father did the packing, and they laughed a great deal
together over infinitesimal repartee during the afternoon break for chilled wa-
termelon or ice cream in the shade of the shed.

What she enjoyed most was racing him to see which could finish picking a
double row first. He, who could work faster, would tease her by slowing down
until she thought she would surely pass him this time, then speeding up furi-
ously to leave her several sprawling vines behind. Once he had made her
screech hideously by crossing over, while her back was turned, to place atop
the tomatoes in her green-stained bucket a truly monstrous, pale green worm
(it had looked more like an infant snake). And it was when they had finished a
contest this morning, after she had pantingly pointed a green finger at the im-
mature tomatoes evident in the lugs[2] at the end of his row and he had re-
turned the accusation (with justice), that he had startlingly brought up the

2. Shipping containers for produce.

matter of their possibly meeting outside the range of both their parents' dubious eyes.

"What for?" she had asked.

"I've got a secret I want to tell you," he said.

"Tell me now," she demanded.

"It won't be ready till tonight," he said.

She laughed. "Tell me tomorrow then."

"It'll be gone tomorrow," he threatened.

"Well, for seven hakes,[3] what is it?" she had asked, more than twice, and when he had suggested that the packing shed would be an appropriate place to find out, she had cautiously answered maybe. She had not been certain she was going to keep the appointment until the arrival of mother's sister and her husband. Their coming seemed a sort of signal of permission, of grace, and she had definitely made up her mind to lie and leave as she was bowing them welcome.

So as soon as everyone appeared settled back for the evening, she announced loudly that she was going to the privy outside, "I'm going to the *benjo!*" and slipped out the door. And now that she was actually on her way, her heart pumped in such an undisciplined way that she could hear it with her ears. It's because I'm running, she told herself, slowing to a walk. The shed was up ahead, one more patch away, in the middle of the fields. Its bulk, looming in the dimness, took on a sinisterness that was funny when Rosie reminded herself that it was only a wooden frame with a canvas roof and three canvas walls that made a slapping noise on breezy days.

Jesus was sitting on the narrow plank that was the sorting platform and she went around to the other side and jumped backwards to seat herself on the rim of a packing stand. "Well, tell me," she said without greeting, thinking her voice sounded reassuringly familiar.

"I saw you coming out the door," Jesus said: "I heard you running part of the way, too."

"Uh-huh," Rosie said. "Now tell me the secret."

"I was afraid you wouldn't come," he said.

Rosie delved around on the chicken-wire bottom of the stall for number two tomatoes, ripe, which she was sitting beside, and came up with a left-over that felt edible. She bit into it and began sucking out the pulp and seeds. "I'm here," she pointed out.

"Rosie, are you sorry you came?"

"Sorry? What for?" she said. "You said you were going to tell me something."

"I will, I will," Jesus said, but his voice contained disappointment, and Rosie fleetingly felt the older of the two, realizing a brand-new power which vanished without category under her recognition.

"I have to go back in a minute," she said. "My aunt and uncle are here from Wintersburg. I told them I was going to the privy."

Jesus laughed. "You funny thing," he said. "You slay me!"

"Just because you have a bathroom *inside*," Rosie said. "Come on, tell me."

3. I.e., for heaven's sake.

Chuckling, Jesus came around to lean on the stand facing her. They still could not see each other very clearly, but Rosie noticed that Jesus became very sober again as he took the hollow tomato from her hand and dropped it back into the stall. When he took hold of her empty hand, she could find no words to protest; her vocabulary had become distressingly constricted and she thought desperately that all that remained intact now was yes and no and oh, and even these few sounds would not easily out. Thus, kissed by Jesus, Rosie fell for the first time entirely victim to a helplessness delectable beyond speech. But the terrible, beautiful sensation lasted no more than a second, and the reality of Jesus' lips and tongue and teeth and hands made her pull away with such strength that she nearly tumbled.

Rosie stopped running as she approached the lights from the windows of home. How long since she had left? She could not guess, but gasping yet, she went to the privy in back and locked herself in. Her own breathing deafened her in the dark, close space, and she sat and waited until she could hear at last the nightly calling of the frogs and crickets. Even then, all she could think to say was oh, my, and the pressure of Jesus' face against her face would not leave.

No one had missed her in the parlor, however, and Rosie walked in and through quickly, announcing that she was next going to take a bath. "Your father's in the bathhouse," her mother said, and Rosie, in her room, recalled that she had not seen him when she entered. There had been only Aunt Taka and Uncle Gimpachi with her mother at the table, drinking tea. She got her robe and straw sandals and crossed the parlor again to go outside. Her mother was telling them about the *haiku* competition in the *Mainichi* and the poem she had entered.

Rosie met her father coming out of the bathhouse. "Are you through, Father?" she asked. "I was going to ask you to scrub my back."

"Scrub your own back," he said shortly, going toward the main house.

"What have I done now?" she yelled at him. She suddenly felt like doing a lot of yelling. But he did not answer, and she went into the bathhouse. Turning on the dangling light, she removed her denims and T-shirt and threw them in the big carton for dirty clothes standing next to the washing machine. Her other things she took with her into the bath compartment to wash after her bath. After she had scooped a basin of hot water from the square wooden tub, she sat on the grey cement of the floor and soaped herself at exaggerated leisure, singing "Red Sails in the Sunset" at the top of her voice and using da-da-da where she suspected her words. Then, standing up, still singing, for she was possessed by the notion that any attempt now to analyze would result in spoilage and she believed that the larger her volume the less she would be able to hear herself think, she obtained more hot water and poured it on until she was free of lather. Only then did she allow herself to step into the steaming vat, one leg first, then the remainder of her body inch by inch until the water no longer stung and she could move around at will.

She took a long time soaking, afterwards remembering to go around outside to stoke the embers of the tin-lined fireplace beneath the tub and to throw on a few more sticks so that the water might keep its heat for her mother, and when she finally returned to the parlor, she found her mother still talking *haiku* with her aunt and uncle, the three of them on another round of tea. Her father was nowhere in sight.

At Japanese school the next day (Wednesday, it was), Rosie was grave and giddy by turns. Preoccupied at her desk in the row for students on Book Eight, she made up for it at recess by performing wild mimicry for the benefit of her friend Chizuko. She held her nose and whined a witticism or two in what she considered was the manner of Fred Allen; she assumed intoxication and a British accent to go over the climax of the Rudy Vallee recording of the pub conversation about William Ewart Gladstone; she was the child Shirley Temple piping, "On the Good Ship Lollipop"; she was the gentleman soprano of the Four Inkspots trilling, "If I Didn't Care."[4] And she felt reasonably satisfied when Chizuko wept and gasped, "Oh, Rosie, you ought to be in the movies!"

Her father came after her at noon, bringing her sandwiches of minced ham and two nectarines to eat while she rode, so that she could pitch right into the sorting when they got home. The lugs were piling up, he said, and the ripe tomatoes in them would probably have to be taken to the cannery tomorrow if they were not ready for the produce haulers tonight. "This heat's not doing them any good. And we've got no time for a break today."

It *was* hot, probably the hottest day of the year, and Rosie's blouse stuck damply to her back even under the protection of the canvas. But she worked as efficiently as a flawless machine and kept the stalls heaped, with one part of her mind listening in to the parental murmuring about the heat and the tomatoes and with another part planning the exact words she would say to Jesus when he drove up with the first load of the afternoon. But when at last she saw that the pick-up was coming, her hands went berserk and the tomatoes started falling in the wrong stalls, and her father said, "Hey, hey! Rosie, watch what you're doing!"

"Well, I have to go to the *benjo*," she said, hiding panic.

"Go in the weeds over there," he said, only half-joking.

"Oh, Father!" she protested.

"Oh, go on home," her mother said. "We'll make out for awhile."

In the privy Rosie peered through a knothole toward the fields, watching as much as she could of Jesus. Happily she thought she saw him look in the direction of the house from time to time before he finished unloading and went back toward the patch where his mother and father worked. As she was heading for the shed, a very presentable black car purred up the dirt driveway to the house and its driver motioned to her. Was this the Hayashi home, he wanted to know. She nodded. Was she a Hayashi? Yes, she said, thinking that he was a good-looking man. He got out of the car with a huge, flat package and she saw that he warmly wore a business suit. "I have something here for your mother then," he said, in a more elegant Japanese than she was used to.

She told him where her mother was and he came along with her, patting his face with an immaculate white handkerchief and saying something about the coolness of San Francisco. To her surprised mother and father, he bowed and introduced himself as, among other things, the *haiku* editor of the *Mainichi Shimbun*, saying that since he had been coming as far as Los Angeles anyway, he had decided to bring her the first prize she had won in the recent contest.

"First prize?" her mother echoed, believing and not believing, pleased and

4. She is imitating enormously popular figures of the 1930s. Fred Allen (1894–1956), radio comedian. Rudy Vallee (1901–1986), a singer who became one of America's first pop culture idols in the 1920s. William E. Gladstone (1809–1898), one of the greatest political figures of the Victorian age and a leader of the Liberal Party. Shirley Temple (1928–), child film star; she sang the hit song "The Good Ship Lollipop" in the movie *Bright Eyes* (1934). The Ink Spots was a jazz vocal quartet.

overwhelmed. Handed the package with a bow, she bobbed her head up and down numerous times to express her utter gratitude.

"It is nothing much," he added, "but I hope it will serve as a token of our great appreciation for your contributions and our great admiration of your considerable talent."

"I am not worthy," she said, falling easily into his style. "It is I who should make some sign of my humble thanks for being permitted to contribute."

"No, no, to the contrary," he said, bowing again.

But Rosie's mother insisted, and then saying that she knew she was being unorthodox, she asked if she might open the package because her curiosity was so great. Certainly she might. In fact, he would like her reaction to it, for personally, it was one of his favorite *Hiroshiges*.[5]

Rosie thought it was a pleasant picture, which looked to have been sketched with delicate quickness. There were pink clouds, containing some graceful calligraphy, and a sea that was a pale blue except at the edges, containing four sampans[6] with indications of people in them. Pines edged the water and on the far-off beach there was a cluster of thatched huts towered over by pine-dotted mountains of grey and blue. The frame was scalloped and gilt.

After Rosie's mother pronounced it without peer and somewhat prodded her father into nodding agreement, she said Mr. Kuroda must at least have a cup of tea after coming all this way, and although Mr. Kuroda did not want to impose, he soon agreed that a cup of tea would be refreshing and went along with her to the house, carrying the picture for her.

"Ha, your mother's crazy!" Rosie's father said, and Rosie laughed uneasily as she resumed judgment on the tomatoes. She had emptied six lugs when he broke into an imaginary conversation with Jesus to tell her to go and remind her mother of the tomatoes, and she went slowly.

Mr. Kuroda was in his shirtsleeves expounding some *haiku* theory as he munched a rice cake, and her mother was rapt. Abashed in the great man's presence, Rosie stood next to her mother's chair until her mother looked up inquiringly, and then she started to whisper the message, but her mother pushed her gently away and reproached, "You are not being very polite to our guest."

"Father says the tomatoes . . ." Rosie said aloud, smiling foolishly.

"Tell him I shall only be a minute," her mother said, speaking the language of Mr. Kuroda.

When Rosie carried the reply to her father, he did not seem to hear and she said again, "Mother says she'll be back in a minute."

"All right, all right," he nodded, and they worked again in silence. But suddenly, her father uttered an incredible noise, exactly like the cork of a bottle popping, and the next Rosie knew, he was stalking angrily toward the house, almost running in fact, and she chased after him crying, "Father! Father! What are you going to do?"

He stopped long enough to order her back to the shed. "Never mind!" he shouted. "Get on with the sorting!"

And from the place in the fields where she stood, frightened and vacillating, Rosie saw her father enter the house. Soon Mr. Kuroda came out alone,

5. Andō Hiroshige (1797–1858), a great Japanese 6. Flat-bottomed Chinese skiffs.
landscape artist.

putting on his coat. Mr. Kuroda got into his car and backed out down the driveway onto the highway. Next her father emerged, also alone, something in his arms (it was the picture, she realized), and, going over to the bathhouse woodpile, he threw the picture on the ground and picked up the axe. Smashing the picture, glass and all (she heard the explosion faintly), he reached over for the kerosene that was used to encourage the bath fire and poured it over the wreckage. I am dreaming, Rosie said to herself, I am dreaming, but her father, having made sure that his act of cremation was irrevocable, was even then returning to the fields.

Rosie ran past him and toward the house. What had become of her mother? She burst into the parlor and found her mother at the back window watching the dying fire. They watched together until there remained only a feeble smoke under the blazing sun. Her mother was very calm.

"Do you know why I married your father?" she said without turning.

"No," said Rosie. It was the most frightening question she had ever been called upon to answer. Don't tell me now, she wanted to say, tell me tomorrow, tell me next week, don't tell me today. But she knew she would be told now, that the telling would combine with the other violence of the hot afternoon to level her life, her world to the very ground.

It was like a story out of the magazines illustrated in sepia,[7] which she had consumed so greedily for a period until the information had somehow reached her that those wretchedly unhappy autobiographies, offered to her as the testimonials of living men and women, were largely inventions: Her mother, at nineteen, had come to America and married her father as an alternative to suicide.

At eighteen she had been in love with the first son of one of the well-to-do families in her village. The two had met whenever and wherever they could, secretly, because it would not have done for his family to see him favor her— her father had no money; he was a drunkard and a gambler besides. She had learned she was with child; an excellent match had already been arranged for her lover. Despised by her family, she had given premature birth to a stillborn son, who would be seventeen now. Her family did not turn her out, but she could no longer project herself in any direction without refreshing in them the memory of her indiscretion. She wrote to Aunt Taka, her favorite sister in America, threatening to kill herself if Aunt Taka would not send for her. Aunt Taka hastily arranged a marriage with a young man of whom she knew, but lately arrived from Japan, a young man of simple mind, it was said, but of kindly heart. The young man was never told why his unseen betrothed was so eager to hasten the day of meeting.

The story was told perfectly, with neither groping for words nor untoward passion. It was as though her mother had memorized it by heart, reciting it to herself so many times over that its nagging vileness had long since gone.

"I had a brother then?" Rosie asked, for this was what seemed to matter now; she would think about the other later, she assured herself, pushing back the illumination which threatened all that darkness that had hitherto been merely mysterious or even glamorous. "A half-brother?"

"Yes."

"I would have liked a brother," she said.

Suddenly, her mother knelt on the floor and took her by the wrists. "Rosie,"

7. Brown ink used for both prints and photographs.

she said urgently, "Promise me you will never marry" Shocked more by the request than the revelation, Rosie stared at her mother's face. Jesus, Jesus, she called silently, not certain whether she was invoking the help of the son of the Carrascos or of God, until there returned sweetly the memory of Jesus' hand, how it had touched her and where. Still her mother waited for an answer, holding her wrists so tightly that her hands were going numb. She tried to pull free. Promise, her mother whispered fiercely, promise. Yes, yes, I promise, Rosie said. But for an instant she turned away, and her mother, hearing the familiar glib agreement, released her. Oh, you, you, you, her eyes and twisted mouth said, you fool. Rosie, covering her face, began at last to cry, and the embrace and consoling hand came much later than she expected.

1949

GRACE PALEY

1922–

Grace Paley was born in New York into a family of socialist Russian Jews, and she grew up listening to the stories of her father, her mother, and her aunts, stories that were recounted sometimes in English and sometimes in Russian or Yiddish. For this reason, she explained in a *Shenandoah* interview (1981), she did not consider herself a writer until she managed to get beyond "me—me—me" through "hear[ing] other people's voices" that she recorded by writing "with an accent." Although Paley composed poetry in the style of W. H. Auden while she attended Hunter College, she did not begin publishing fiction until after she was thirty. Encouraged by her husband and fascinated by the community of women and children who lived separate lives in the army camps she knew during World War II, she produced the stories that eventually appeared in *The Little Disturbances of Man* (1959); the volume immediately established her as a funny and irreverent urban chronicler, a reputation strengthened by the appearance of her second collection of stories, *Enormous Changes at the Last Minute* (1974). *Later the Same Day* (1985) has sustained her reputation as a humorous and humane writer who produces strikingly compassionate portraits of city life.

The mother of two children, Paley captures the everyday cadences and causes of the immigrant Jews, impoverished African-Americans, and displaced Irish Catholics who inhabit neighborhood playgrounds and P.T.A.s, Brooklyn's Coney Island, and Manhattan's subways. In her short story *A Conversation with My Father*, she explains that her father's insistence on the somber relentlessness of plotted "Tragedy! Plain tragedy!" conflicted with her own sense that "it's a funny world nowadays." This comic yet affirmative vision, along with her determination to tell stories "in order to . . . save a few lives," has animated not only Paley's activism in antiwar and antihunger movements and her teaching at Syracuse University and Sarah Lawrence College, but also those stories where—against all odds—her characters seize the opportunity to make "enormous changes at the last minute."

Enormous Changes at the Last Minute

A young man said he wanted to go to bed with Alexandra because she had an interesting mind. He was a cabdriver and she *had* admired the curly back of his head. Still, she was surprised. He said he would pick her up again in about

an hour and a half. Because she was fair and a responsible person, she placed
between them a barrier of truthful information. She said, I suppose you don't
know many middle-aged women.

You don't look so middle-aged to me. I mean, everyone likes what they like.
That is, I'm interested in your point of view, your way of life. Anyway, he said,
peering into the mirror, your face is nice and your eyebrows are out of sight!

Make it two hours, she said. I'm visiting my father whom I happen to love.

I love mine too, he said. He just doesn't love me. Too too bad.

O.K. That's enough, she said. Because they had already *had* the following
factual and introductory conversation.

How old are your kids?

I have none.

Sorry. Then what do you do for a living?

Children. Early teenage. Adoptions, foster homes. Probation. Troubles—
well . . .

Where'd you go to school?

City colleges. What about you?

Oh, me. Lots of places. Antioch. Wisconsin. California. I might go back
someday. Some place else though. Maybe Harvard. Why not?

He leaned on his horn to move a sixteen-wheel trailer truck delivering
Kleenex to the A & P.

I wish you'd stop that, she said. I hate that kind of driving.

Why? Oh! You're an idealist! He looked through his rearview mirror straight
into her eyes. But were you married? Ever?

Once. For years.

Who to?

It's hard to describe. A revolutionist.

Really? Could I know him? What's his name? We say revolutionary nowa-
days.

Oh?

By the way, my name's Dennis. I probably like you, he said.

You do, do you? Well, why should you? And let me ask you something.
What do you mean by nowadays?

By the birdseed of St. Francis,[1] he said, taking a tiny brogue to the tip of his
tongue. I meant no harm.

Nowadays! she said. What does that mean? I guess you think you're kind of
brand-new. You're not so brand-new. The telephone was brand-new. The air-
plane was brand-new. *You've* been seen on earth before.

Wow! he said. He stopped the cab just short of the hospital entrance. He
turned to look at her and make decisions. But you're right, he said sweetly. You
know the mind *is* an astonishing, long-living, erotic thing.

Is it? she asked. Then she wondered: What is the life expectancy of the
mind?

Eighty years, said her father, glad to be useful. Once he had explained elec-
trical storms before you could find the Book of Knowledge. Now in the cave of
old age, he continued to amass wonderful information. But he was sick with

1. St. Francis of Assisi (1182?–1226) is traditionally depicted preaching to birds.

oldness. His arteries had a hopeless future, and conversation about all that obsolescent tubing often displaced very interesting subjects.

One day he said, Alexandra! Don't show me the sunset again. I'm not interested any more. You know that. She had just pointed to a simple sunset happening outside his hospital window. It was a red ball—all alone, without its evening streaking clouds—a red ball falling hopelessly west, just missing the Hudson River, Jersey City, Chicago, the Great Plains, the Golden Gate—falling, falling.

Then in Russian he sighed some Pushkin.[2] Not for me, the spring. *Nye dyla menya. . . .* He slept. She read the large-print edition of *The Guns of August.*[3] A half hour later, he opened his eyes and told her how, in that morning's *Times,* the Phoenicians had sailed to Brazil in about 500 B.C. A remarkable people. The Vikings too were remarkable. He spoke well of the Chinese, the Jews, the Greeks, the Indians—all the old commercial people. Actually he had never knocked an entire nation. International generosity had been started in him during the late nineteenth century by his young mother and father, candleholders inside the dark tyranny of the czars. It was childhood training. Thoughtfully, he passed it on.

In the hospital bed next to him, a sufferer named John feared the imminent rise of the blacks of South Africa, the desperate blacks of Chicago, the yellow Chinese, and the Ottoman Turks. He had more reason than Alexandra's father to dread the future because his heart was strong. He would probably live to see it all. He believed the Turks when they came would bring to New York City diseases like cholera, virulent scarlet fever, and particularly leprosy.

Leprosy! for God's sakes! said Alexandra. John! Upset yourself with reality for once! She read aloud from the *Times* about the bombed, burned lepers' colonies in North Vietnam. Her father said, Please, Alexandra, today, no propaganda. Why do you constantly pick on the United States? He remembered the first time he'd seen the American flag on wild Ellis Island. Under its protection and working like a horse, he'd read Dickens,[4] gone to medical school, and shot like a surface-to-air missile right into the middle class.

Then he said, But they shouldn't put a flag in the middle of the chocolate pudding. It's ridiculous.

It's Memorial Day, said the nurse's aide, removing his tray.

In the early evening Dennis stood at the door of each room of Alexandra's apartment. He looked this way and that. Underuse in a time of population stress, he muttered. He entered the kitchen and sniffed the kitchen air. It doesn't matter, he said aloud. He took a fingerful of gravy out of the pot on the stove. Beef stew, he whispered. Then he opened the door to the freezer compartment and said, Sweet Jesus! because there were eleven batches of the same, neatly stacked and frozen. They were for Alexandra's junkies, whose methadone required lots of protein and carbohydrates.

I wouldn't have them in my house. It's a wonder you got a cup and saucer left. Creeps, said Dennis. However, yes indeed, I will eat this stuff. Why? Does it make me think of home or of something else? he asked. I think, a movie I once saw.

2. Aleksandr Pushkin (1799–1837), Russian poet.
3. A history of the beginning of World War I by Barbara Tuchman, published in 1962.

4. Charles Dickens (1812–1870), English novelist. Ellis Island, in the harbor of New York City, where new immigrants were processed.

Apple turnovers! You know I have to admit it, our commune isn't working too well. Probably because it's in Brooklyn and the food coop[5] isn't together. But it's cool, they've accepted the criticism.

You have lots of junk in here, he pointed out after dinner. He had decided to give the place some respectful attention. He meant armchairs, lamps, desk sets, her grandmother's wedding portrait, and an umbrella stand with two of her father's canes.

Um, said Alexandra, it's rent-controlled.[6]

You know what I like to do, Alexandra? I like to sit with a girl and look at a late movie, he said. It's an experience common to Americans at this hour. It's important to be like others, to dig the average dude, you have to be him. Be HIM. It's groovier than a lot of phony gab. You'd be surprised how friendly you get.

I'm not against friendliness, she said, I'm not even against Americans.

They watched half of A Day at the Races.[7] This is very relaxing, he said. It's kind of long though, isn't it? Then he began to undress. He held out his arms. He said, Alexandra I really can't wait any more. I'm a sunrise person. I like to go to bed early. Can I stay a few days?

He gave reasons: 1. It was a Memorial Day weekend, and the house in Brooklyn was full of tripping visitors. 2. He was disgusted with them anyway because they'd given up the most beautiful batik work for fashionable tie-dying. 3. He and Alexandra could take some good walks in the morning because all the parks to walk in were the lightest green. He had noticed that the tree on the corner though dying of buses was green at the beginning of many twigs. 4. He could talk to her about the kids, help her to understand their hangups, their incredible virtues. He had missed being one of them by about seven useless years.

So many reasons are not essential, Alexandra said. She offered him a brandy. Holy toads! he said furiously. You *know* I'm not into that. Touched by gloom, he began to remove the heavy shoes he wore for mountain walking. He dropped his pants and stamped on them a couple of times to make sure he and they were disengaged.

Alexandra, in the first summer dress of spring, stood still and watched. She breathed deeply because of having been alone for a year or two. She put her two hands over her ribs to hold her heart in place and also out of modesty to quiet its immodest thud. Then they went to bed in the bedroom and made love until that noisy disturbance ended. She couldn't hear one interior sound. Therefore they slept.

In the morning she became interested in reality again, which she had always liked. She wanted to talk about it. She began with a description of John, her father's neighbor in the hospital.

Turks? Far out! Well he's right. And another thing. Leprosy *is* coming. It's coming to the Forest Hills County Fair, the Rikers Island Jamboree, the Fillmore East, and the Ecolocountry Gardens in Westchester.[8] In August.

Reality? A lesson in reality? Am I a cabdriver? No. I drive a cab but I am not a cabdriver. I'm a song hawk. A songmaker. I'm a poet, in other words. Do you

5. Organization for the cooperative purchase of food.
6. An apartment whose rent is controlled by the city government.

7. A 1936 comedy starring the Marx Brothers.
8. All locations in the New York area.

know that every black man walking down the street today is a poet? But only one white honky devil in ten. One in ten

Nowadays I write for the Lepers all the time. Fuck poetry. The Lepers dig me. I dig them.

The Lepers? Alexandra said.

Cool! You know them? No? Well, you may have known them under their old name. They used to be called The Split Atom. But they became too popular and their thing is anonymity. That's what they're known for. They'll probably change their name after the summer festivals. They might move to the country and call themselves Winter Moss.

Do you really make a living now?

Oh yes. I do. I do. Among technicians like myself I do.

Now: I financially carry one third of a twelve-person, three-children commune. I only drive a cab to keep on top of the world of illusion, you know, Alexandra, to rap with the bourgeoisies, the fancy whores, the straight ladies visiting their daddies. Oh, excuse me, he said.

Now, Alexandra, imagine this: two bass guitars, a country violin, one piccolo, and drums. The Lepers' theme song! He sat up in bed. The sun shone on his chest. He had begun to think of breakfast, but he sang so that Alexandra could know him better and dig his substantialness.

ooooh
first my finger goes goes goes
then my nose
 then baby my toes

if you love me this way anyway any day
I'll go your way
 my Little Neck[9] rose

Well? he asked. He looked at Alexandra. Was she going to cry? I thought you were such a reality freak. Alexandra. That's the way it is in the real world. Anyway! He then said a small prose essay to explain and buttress the poem:

The kids! the kids! Though terrible troubles hang over them, such as the absolute end of the known world quickly by detonation or slowly through the easygoing destruction of natural resources, they are still, even now, optimistic, humorous, and brave. In fact, they intend enormous changes at the last minute.

Come on, said Alexandra, hardhearted, an enemy of generalization, there are all kinds. My boys aren't like that.

Yes, they are, he said, angry. You bring them around. I'll prove it. Anyway I love them. He tried for about twenty minutes, forgetting breakfast, to show Alexandra how to look at things in this powerful last-half-of-the-century way. She tried. She had always had a progressive if sometimes reformist disposition, but at that moment, listening to him talk, she could see straight ahead over the thick hot rod of love to solitary age and lonesome death.

9. A residential section of Queens (in New York City).

But there's nothing to fear my dear girl, her father said. When you get there you will not want to live a hell of a lot. Nothing to fear at all. You will be used up. You are like a coal burning, smoldering. Then there's nothing left to burn. Finished. Believe me, he said, although he hadn't been there yet himself, at that moment you won't mind. Alexandra's face was a bit rumpled, listening.

Don't look at me like that! he said. He was too sensitive to her appearance. He hated her to begin to look older the way she'd had to in the last twenty years. He said, Now *I* have seen people die. A large number. Not one or two. Many. They are good and ready. Pain. Despair. Unconsciousness, nightmares. Perfectly good comas, wrecked by nightmares. They are ready. You will be too, Sashka.[1] Don't worry so much.

Ho ho ho, said John in the next bed listening through the curtains. Doc, I'm not ready. I feel terrible, I got lousy nightmares. I don't sleep a wink. But I'm not ready. I can't piss without this tube. Lonesomeness! Boy! Did you ever see *one* of my kids visiting? No! Still I am *not* ready NOT READY. He spelled it out, looking at the ceiling or through it, to the roof garden for incurables, and from there to God.

The next morning Dennis said, I would rather die than go to the hospital.

For God's sakes why?

Why? Because I hate to be in the hands of strangers. They don't let you take the pills you got that you know work, then if you need one of their pills, even if you buzz, they don't come. The nurse and three interns are making out in the information booth. I've seen it. It's a high counter, she's answering questions, and they're taking turns banging her from behind.

Dennis! You're too dumb. You sound like some superstitious old lady with rape dreams.

That's cool, he said. I *am* an old lady about my health. I mean I like it. I want my teeth to go right on. Right on sister. He began to sing, then stopped. Listen! Your destiny's in their hands. It's up to them. Do you live? Or are you a hippie crawling creep from their point of view? Then die!

Really. Nobody ever decides to let you die. In fact, that's what's wrong. They decide to keep people alive for years after death has set in.

You mean like your father?

Alexandra leaped out of bed stark naked. My father! Why he's got twenty times your zip.

Cool it! he said. Come back. I was just starting to fuck you and you get so freaked.

And another thing. Don't use that word. I hate it. When you're with a woman you have to use the language that's right for her.

What do you want me to say?

I want you to say, I was just starting to make love to you, etc.

Well, that's true, said Dennis, I was. When she returned to him, he only touched the tips of her fingers, though all of her was present. He kissed each finger and said right after each kiss, I want to make love to you. He did this sweetly, not sarcastically.

Dennis, Alexandra said in an embarrassment of recognition, you look like one of my placements, in fact you look like a kid, Billy Platoon. His real name

<hr>

1. Russian diminutive for Alexandra.

is Platon but he calls himself Platoon so he can go to Vietnam and get killed like his stepbrother. He's a dreamy boy.

Alexandra, you talk a lot, now hush, no politics.

Alexandra continued for a sentence or two. He carries a stick with a ball full of nails attached, like some medieval weapon, in case an enemy from Suffolk Street CIA's him. That's what they call it.

Never heard that before. Besides I'm jealous. And also I'm the enemy from Suffolk Street.

No, no, said Alexandra. Then she noticed in her mother's bedroom bureau mirror across the room a small piece of her naked self. She said, Ugh!

There, there! said Dennis lovingly, caressing what he thought she'd looked at, a couple of rippled inches between her breast and belly. It's natural, Alexandra. Men don't change as much as women. Among all the animals, human females are the only ones to lose estrogen as they get older.

Is that it? she said.

Then there was nothing to talk about for half an hour.

But how come you knew that? she asked. The things you know, Dennis. What for?

Why—for my art, he said. And despite his youth he rested from love the way artists often do in order to sing. He sang:

Camp out
 out in the forest daisy
 under the gallows tree
with the
 ace of pentacles[2]
 and me.
 daisy flower
What of the
 earth's ecology
you're drivin too fast
Daisy you're drivin alone
 Hey Daisy cut the ignition
 let the oil
 back in the stone.

Oh, I like that one. I admire it! Alexandra said. But in fact, is ecology a good word for a song? It's technical. . . .

Any word is good, it's the big word today anyway, said Dennis. It's what you do with the word. The language and the idea, they work it out together.

Really? Where do you get most of your ideas.

I don't know if I want to eat or sleep, he said. I think I just want to nuzzle your titty. Talk talk talk. Most? Well, I would say the majority are from a magazine, the *Scientific American*.

During breakfast, language remained on his mind. Because of this, he was silent. After the pancakes, he said, Actually Alexandra, I *can* use any words I want. And I have. I proved it last week in a conversation just like this one. I asked these blue-eyed cats to give me a dictionary. I just flipped the pages and

2. Card in the mystical Tarot deck.

jabbed and the word I hit was *ophidious*.[3] But I did it, because the word does the dreaming for you. The WORD.

To a tune that was probably "On Top of Old Smoky" he sang:

The ophidious garden
was invented by Freud

 where three ladies murdered
 oh three ladies murdered

the pricks of the birds

the cobra is buried
the rattlesnake writhes

 in the black snaky garden
 in the blue snaky garden

in the hairs of my wives.[4]

More coffee, please, he said with pride and modesty.

It's better than most of your songs, Alexandra said. It's a poem, isn't it? It *is* better.

What? What? It is *not* better, it is not, goddamn. It is not. . . . It just isn't . . . oh, excuse me for losing my cool like that.

Forget it sonny, Alexandra said respectfully. I only meant I liked it, but I know, I'm too frank from living alone so much I think. Anyway, how come you always think about wives? Wives, mothers?

Because that's me, said peaceful Dennis. Haven't you noticed it yet? That's my bag. I'm a motherfucker.

Oh, she said, I see. But I'm not a mother, Dennis.

Yes, you are, Alexandra. I've figured out a lot about you. I know. I act like the weekend stub sometimes. But I wrote you a song. Just last night in the cab. I think about you. The Lepers'll never dig it. They don't know too much about life. They're still baby bees trying to make it to the next flower, but some old-timer'll tape it, some sore dude who's been out of it for a couple of years who wants to grow. He'll smell the shit in it.

 Oh
I know something about you baby

 that's sad
 don't be mad
 baby
That you will never have children at
 rest

3. Involving snakes.
4. An allusion to the Gorgons, three sisters in Greek mythology with snakes for hair. Sigmund Freud (1856–1939) interprets this myth as containing phallic symbolism.

> *at that beautiful breast*
> > *my love*

But see
> *everywhere you go, children follow you*
> *for more*
> > *many more*
> *are the children of your life*
> *than the children of the married wife.*

That one is out of the Bible, he said.[5] Pa, Alexandra said, don't you think a woman in this life ought to have at least one child?

No doubt about it, he said. You should have when you were married to Granofsky, the Communist. We disagreed. He had no sense of humor. He's probably boring the Cubans to death this minute. But he was an intelligent person otherwise. I would have brilliant grandchildren. They would not necessarily have the same politics.

Then he looked at her, her age and possibilities. He softened. You don't look so bad. You could still marry, dear girl. Then he softened further, thinking of hopeless statistics he had just read about the ratio of women to men. Actually! So what! It's not important, Alexandra. According to the Torah,[6] only the man is commanded to multiply. You are not commanded. You have a child, you don't have, God doesn't care. You don't have one, you call in the maid. You say to your husband, Sweetie, get my maid with child.[7] O.K. Well, your husband has anyway been fooling around with the maid for a couple of years, but now it's a respectable business. Good. You don't have to go through the whole thing, nine months, complications, maybe a Caesarean, no no pronto, a child for the Lord, Hosanna.

Pa, she said, several weeks later, but what if I did have a baby?

Don't be a fool, he said. Then he gave her a terrible long medical look, which included her entire body. He said, Why do you ask this question? He became red in the face, which had never happened. He took hold of his chest with his right hand, the hospital buzzer with the left. First, he said, I want the nurse! Now! Then he ordered Alexandra: marry!

Dennis said, I don't know how I got into this shit. It's not right, but because your habits and culture are different, I will compromise. What I suggest is this, Alexandra. The three children in our commune belong to us all. No one knows who the father is. It's far out. I swear—by the cock of our hard-up gods, I swear it's beautiful. One of them might be mine. But she doesn't have any distinguishing marks. Why don't you come and live with us and we'll all raise that kid up to be a decent human and humane being in this world. We need a slightly older person, we really do, with a historic sense. We lack that.

Thank you, Alexandra replied. No.

Her father said, Explain it to me, please. For what purpose did you act out

5. "Sing, O barren, thou that didst not bear; break forth into singing, and cry aloud, thou that didst not travail with child: for more are the children of the desolate than the children of the married wife" (Isaiah 54:1).

5. The first five books of the Bible; i.e., according to Judaic law.

7. A brief retelling of the story of Sarah, Abraham, and Hagar (Genesis 16:1–3).

this nonsense? For love? At your age. Money? Some conniver flattered you. You probably made him supper. Some starving ne'er-do-well probably wanted a few meals and said, Why not? This middle-aged fool is an easy mark. She'll give me pot roast at night, bacon and eggs in the morning.

No Pa, no, Alexandra said. Please, you'll get sicker.

John in the next bed dying with a strong heart wrote a little note to him. Doc, you're crazy. Don't leave enemies. That girl is loyal! She hasn't missed a Tues., Thurs., or Sat. Did you ever see one of my kids visit? Something else. I feel worse and worse. But I'm still *not ready.*

I want to tell you one more thing, her father said. You are going to embitter my last days and ruin my life.

After that, Alexandra hoped every day for her father's death, so that she could have a child without ruining his interesting life at the very end of it when ruin is absolutely retroactive.

Finally, Dennis said, Then let me at least share the pad with you. It'll be to *your* advantage.

No, Alexandra said. Please, Dennis. I've got to go to work early. I'm sleepy.

I dig. I've been a joke to you. You've used me in a bad way. That's not cool. That smells under heaven.

No, Alexandra said. Please, shut up. Anyway, how do you know you're the father?

Come on, he said, who else would be?

Alexandra smiled, bit her lip to the edge of blood to show pain politely. She was thinking about the continuity of her work, how to be proud and not lose a productive minute. She thought about the members of her case load one by one.

She said, Dennis, I know exactly what I'm going to do.

In that case, this is it, I'm splitting.

This is what Alexandra did in order to make good use of the events of her life. She invited three pregnant clients who were fifteen and sixteen years old to live with her. She visited each one and explained to them that she was pregnant too, and that her apartment was very large. Although they had disliked her because she'd always worried more about the boys, they moved out of the homes of their bad-tempered parents within a week. At the very first evening meal they began to give Alexandra good advice about men, which she did appreciate years later. She ensured their health and her own and she took notes as well. She established a precedent in social work which would not be followed or even mentioned in state journals for about five years.

Alexandra's father's life was not ruined, nor did he have to die. Shortly before the baby's birth, he fell hard on the bathroom tiles, cracked his skull, dipped the wires of his brain into his heart's blood. Short circuit! He lost twenty, thirty years in the flood, the faces of nephews, in-laws, the names of two Presidents, and a war. His eyes were rounder, he was often awestruck, but he was smart as ever, and able to begin again with fewer scruples to notice and appreciate.

The baby was born and named Dennis for his father. Of course his last name was Granofsky because of Alexandra's husband, Granofsky the Communist.

The Lepers, who had changed their name to the Edible Amanita, taped the following song in his tiny honor. It was called "Who? I."

The lyrics are simple. They are:

Who is the father?
Who is the father
Who is the father

 I! I! I! I!

I am the father
I am the father
I am the father

Dennis himself sang the solo which was I! I! I! I! in a hoarse enraged prophetic voice. He had been brave to acknowledge the lyrics. After a thirty-eight-hour marathon encounter at his commune, he was asked to leave. The next afternoon he moved to a better brownstone about four blocks away where occasional fatherhood was expected.

On the baby's third birthday, Dennis and the Fair Fields of Corn produced a folk-rock album because that was the new sound and exciting. It was called *For Our Son.* Tuned-in listeners could hear how taps played by the piccolo about forty times a verse flitted in and out of the long dark drum rolls, the ordinary banjo chords, and the fiddle tune which was something but not exactly like "Lullaby and Good Night."

Will you come to see me Jack
 When I'm old and very shaky?
Yes I will for you're my dad
 And you've lost your last old lady
 Though you traveled very far
To the highlands and the badlands
 And ripped off the family car
Still, old dad, I won't forsake you.

Will you come to see me Jack?
 Though I'm really not alone.
Still I'd like to see my boy
 For we're lonesome for our own.
 Yes I will for you're my dad
Though you dumped me and my brothers
 And you sizzled down the road
Loving other fellows' mothers.

Will you come to see me Jack?
 Though I look like time boiled over.
Growing old is not a lark.
 Yes I will for you're my dad
 Though we never saw a nickel
As we struggled up life's ladder
 I will call you and together
We will cuddle up and see

> What the weather's like in Key West
> On the old-age home TV.

This song was sung coast to coast and became famous from the dark Maine woods to Texas's shining gulf. It was responsible for a statistical increase in visitors to old-age homes by the apprehensive middle-aged and the astonished young.

1974

NADINE GORDIMER
1923–

In 1991, Nadine Gordimer was awarded the Nobel Prize for literature, an honor that recognized the important role her fiction played in the contemporary evolution of racial doctrines and international policies. Until quite recently, the government of the Union of South Africa had endorsed a legal system of "apartheid" that barred native blacks from full human and civil rights. Since Gordimer's novels and stories offered a scathing critique of the effects of apartheid, it is hardly surprising that a number of her books were banned for several years in her native country. Gordimer, who was born and raised in South Africa, continues to live in Johannesburg, although she travels widely to give lectures and readings.

The daughter of Isidore and Nan Gordimer, both Jewish immigrants, the youthful Gordimer attended private schools and, for one year, the University of Witwatersrand. After a brief marriage and divorce, she remarried Reinhold H. Cassirer, the director of the Johannesburg branch of Sotheby Parke Bernet. She is the mother of two children, one from each marriage.

From her earliest fiction, *The Lying Days* (1953), to the novels that brought her critical acclaim—*A Guest of Honour* (1970), *Burger's Daughter* (1970), and *July's People* (1981)—Gordimer has written with sensitivity and intelligence about the conventional roles and ways of thinking that distinguish and divide blacks and whites in a society shaped by imperialist history. In such collections of stories as *A Soldier's Embrace* (1980), *Six Feet of the Country* (1982), and *Something Out There* (1984), she has become what the critic Maxwell Geismar calls "a luminous symbol of at least one white person's understanding of the black man's burden." Her most recent work charts the challenges of South Africa's transition into a postapartheid culture. The selection printed here, *Town and Country Lovers*, illustrates Gordimer's astute understanding of the burdens borne by African women. Writing, as she often does, from the male perspective, Gordimer hints at the ways in which South African apartheid shared certain state procedures and practices with those of Nazi Germany.

Town and Country Lovers[1]

Dr. Franz-Josef von Leinsdorf is a geologist absorbed in his work; wrapped up in it, as the saying goes—year after year the experience of this work enfolds him, swaddling him away from the landscapes, the cities and the people, wherever he lives: Peru, New Zealand, the United States. He's always been like

1. This is the first of two stories that Gordimer published as a sequence, under the title *Town and Country Lovers, One and Two*; this selection originally appeared in *The New Yorker* as *City Lovers*.

that, his mother could confirm from their native Austria. There, even as a handsome small boy he presented only his profile to her: turned away to his bits of rock and stone. His few relaxations have not changed much since then. An occasional skiing trip, listening to music, reading poetry—Rainer Maria Rilke[2] once stayed in his grandmother's hunting lodge in the forests of Styria and the boy was introduced to Rilke's poems while very young.

Layer upon layer, country after country, wherever his work takes him—and now he has been almost seven years in Africa. First the Côte d'Ivoire, and the past five years, South Africa. The shortage of skilled manpower brought about his recruitment here. He has no interest in the politics of the countries he works in. His private preoccupation-within-the-preoccupation of his work has been research into underground water-courses, but the mining company that employs him in a senior though not executive capacity is interested only in mineral discovery. So he is much out in the field—which is the veld,[3] here—seeking new gold, copper, platinum and uranium deposits. When he is at home—on this particular job, in this particular country, this city—he lives in a two-roomed flat in a suburban block with a landscaped garden, and does his shopping at a supermarket conveniently across the street. He is not married—yet. That is how his colleagues, and the typists and secretaries at the mining company's head office, would define his situation. Both men and women would describe him as a good-looking man, in a foreign way, with the lower half of the face dark and middle-aged (his mouth is thin and curving, and no matter how close-shaven his beard shows like fine shot embedded in the skin round mouth and chin) and the upper half contradictorily young, with deep-set eyes (some would say gray, some black), thick eyelashes and brows. A tangled gaze: through which concentration and gleaming thoughtfulness perhaps appear as fire and languor. It is this that the women in the office mean when they remark he's not unattractive. Although the gaze seems to promise, he has never invited any one of them to go out with him. There is the general assumption he probably has a girl who's been picked for him, he's bespoken by one of his own kind, back home in Europe where he comes from. Many of these well-educated Europeans have no intention of becoming permanent immigrants; neither the remnant of white colonial life nor idealistic involvement with Black Africa appeals to them.

One advantage, at least, of living in underdeveloped or half-developed countries is that flats are serviced. All Dr. von Leinsdorf has to do for himself is buy his own supplies and cook an evening meal if he doesn't want to go to a restaurant. It is simply a matter of dropping in to the supermarket on his way from his car to his flat after work in the afternoon. He wheels a trolley up and down the shelves, and his simple needs are presented to him in the form of tins, packages, plastic-wrapped meat, cheeses, fruit and vegetables, tubes, bottles. . . . At the cashiers' counters where customers must converge and queue[4] there are racks of small items uncategorized, for last-minute purchase. Here, as the colored girl cashier punches the adding machine, he picks up cigarettes and perhaps a packet of salted nuts or a bar of nougat. Or razor-blades, when he remembers he's running short. One evening in winter he saw that the cardboard display was empty of the brand of blades he preferred, and he drew

2. German poet (1875–1926).
3. Open grassland in southern Africa.

4. Form lines.

the cashier's attention to this. These young colored girls are usually pretty un-helpful, taking money and punching their machines in a manner that asserts with the time-serving obstinacy of the half-literate the limit of any responsi-bility towards customers, but this one ran an alert glance over the selection of razor-blades, apologized that she was not allowed to leave her post, and said she would see that the stock was replenished "next time." A day or two later she recognized him, gravely, as he took his turn before her counter—"I ahssed them, but it's out of stock. You can't get it. I did ahss about it." He said this didn't matter. "When it comes in, I can keep a few packets for you." He thanked her.

He was away with the prospectors the whole of the next week. He arrived back in town just before nightfall on Friday, and was on his way from car to flat with his arms full of briefcase, suitcase and canvas bags when someone stopped him by standing timidly in his path. He was about to dodge round un-seeingly on the crowded pavement but she spoke. "We got the blades in now. I didn't see you in the shop this week, but I kept some for when you come. So . . ."

He recognized her. He had never seen her standing before, and she was wearing a coat. She was rather small and finely-made, for one of them. The coat was skimpy but no big backside jutted. The cold brought an apricot-graining of warm color to her cheekbones, beneath which a very small face was quite delicately hollowed, and the skin was smooth, the subdued satiny color of certain yellow wood. That crêpey hair, but worn drawn back flat and in a lit-tle knot pushed into one of the cheap wool chignons that (he recognized also) hung in the miscellany of small goods along with the razor-blades, at the su-permarket. He said thanks, he was in a hurry, he'd only just got back from a trip—shifting the burdens he carried, to demonstrate. "Oh shame." She ac-knowledged his load. "But if you want I can run in and get it for you quickly. If you want."

He saw at once it was perfectly clear that all the girl meant was that she would go back to the supermarket, buy the blades and bring the packet to him there where he stood, on the pavement. And it seemed that it was this cer-tainty that made him say, in the kindly tone of assumption used for an oblig-ing underling, "I live just across there—*Atlantis*—that flat building. Could you drop them by, for me—number seven-hundred-and-eighteen, seventh floor—"

She had not before been inside one of these big flat buildings near where she worked. She lived a bus- and train-ride away to the West of the city, but this side of the black townships, in a township for people her tint. There was a pool with ferns, not plastic, and even a little waterfall pumped electrically over rocks, in the entrance of the building *Atlantis*; she didn't wait for the lift marked goods but took the one meant for whites and a white woman with one of those sausage-dogs on a lead got in with her but did not pay her any atten-tion. The corridors leading to the flats were nicely glassed-in, not draughty.

He wondered if he should give her a twenty-cent piece for her trouble—ten cents would be right for a black; but she said, "Oh no—please, here—" stand-ing outside his open door and awkwardly pushing back at his hand the change from the money he'd given her for the razor-blades. She was smiling, for the first time, in the dignity of refusing a tip. It was difficult to know how to treat these people, in this country; to know what they expected. In spite of her em-

barrassing refusal o the coin, she stood there, completely unassuming, fists thrust down the pockets of her cheap coat against the cold she'd come in from, rather pretty thin legs neatly aligned, knee to knee, ankle to ankle.

"Would you like a cup of coffee or something?"

He couldn't very well take her into his study-cum-living-room and offer her a drink. She followed him to his kitchen, but at the sight of her pulling out the single chair to drink her cup of coffee at the kitchen table, he said, "No—bring it in here—" and led the way into the big room where, among his books and his papers, his files of scientific correspondence (and the cigar boxes of stamps from the envelopes) his racks of records, his specimens of minerals and rocks, he lived alone.

It was no trouble to her; she saved him the trips to the supermarket and brought him his groceries two or three times a week. All he had to do was to leave a list and the key under the doormat, and she would come up in her lunch-hour to collect them, returning to put his supplies in the flat after work. Sometimes he was home and sometimes not. He bought a box of chocolates and left it, with a note, for her to find; and that was acceptable, apparently, as a gratuity.

Her eyes went over everything in the flat although her body tried to conceal its sense of being out of place by remaining as still as possible, holding its contours in the chair offered her as a stranger's coat is set aside and remains exactly as left until the owner takes it up to go. "You collect?"

"Well, these are specimens—connected with my work."

"My brother used to collect. Miniatures. With brandy and whisky and that, in them. From all over. Different countries."

The second time she watched him grinding coffee for the cup he had offered her she said, "You always do that? Always when you make coffee?"

"But of course. Is it no good, for you? Do I make it too strong?"

"Oh it's just I'm not used to it. We buy it ready—you know, it's in a bottle, you just add a bit to the milk or water."

He laughed, instructive: "That's not coffee, that's a synthetic flavoring. In my country we drink only real coffee, fresh, from the beans—you smell how good it is as it's being ground?"

She was stopped by the caretaker and asked what she wanted in the building. Heavy with the *bona fides*[5] of groceries clutched to her body, she said she was working at number 718, on the seventh floor. The caretaker did not tell her not to use the whites' lift; after all, she was not black; her family was very light-skinned.

There was the item "gray button for trousers" on one of his shopping lists. She said as she unpacked the supermarket carrier, "Give me the pants, so long, then," and sat on his sofa that was always gritty with fragments of pipe tobacco, sewing in and out through the four holes of the button with firm, fluent movements of the right hand, gestures supplying the articulacy missing from her talk. She had a little yokel's, peasant's (he thought of it) gap between her two front teeth when she smiled that he didn't much like, but, face ellipsed to three-quarter angle, eyes cast down in concentration with soft lips almost closed, this didn't matter. He said, watching her sew, "You're a good girl"; and touched her.

5. In good faith (Latin, literal trans.); evidence of qualifications or genuineness.

She remade the bed every late afternoon when they left it and she dressed again before she went home. After a week there was a day when late afternoon became evening, and they were still in the bed.

"Can't you stay the night?"

"My mother," she said.

"Phone her. Make an excuse." He was a foreigner. He had been in the country five years, but he didn't understand that people don't usually have telephones in their houses, where she lived. She got up to dress. He didn't want that tender body to go out in the night cold and kept hindering her with the interruption of his hands; saying nothing. Before she put on her coat, when the body had already disappeared, he spoke. "But you must make some arrangement."

"Oh my mother!" Her face opened to fear and vacancy he could not read.

He was not entirely convinced the woman would think of her daughter as some pure and unsullied virgin. . . . "Why?"

The girl said, "S'e'll be scared. S'e'll be scared we get caught."

"Don't tell her anything. Say I'm employing you." In this country he was working in now there were generally rooms on the roofs of flat buildings for tenants' servants.

She said: "That's what I told the caretaker."

She ground fresh coffee beans every time he wanted a cup while he was working at night. She never attempted to cook anything until she had watched in silence while he did it the way he liked, and she learned to reproduce exactly the simple dishes he preferred. She handled his pieces of rock and stone, at first admiring the colors—"It'd make a beautiful ring or a necklace, ay." Then he showed her the striations, the formation of each piece, and explained what each was, and how, in the long life of the earth, it had been formed. He named the mineral it yielded, and what that was used for. He worked at his papers, writing, writing, every night, so it did not matter that they could not go out together to public places. On Sundays she got into his car in the basement garage and they drove to the country and picnicked away up in the Magaliesberg, where there was no one. He read or poked about among the rocks; they climbed together, to the mountain pools. He taught her to swim. She had never seen the sea. She squealed and shrieked in the water, showing the gap between her teeth, as—it crossed his mind—she must do when among her own people. Occasionally he had to go out to dinner at the houses of colleagues from the mining company; she sewed and listened to the radio in the flat and he found her in the bed, warm and already asleep, by the time he came in. He made his way into her body without speaking; she made him welcome without a word. Once he put on evening dress for a dinner at his country's consulate; watching him brush one or two fallen hairs from the shoulders of the dark jacket that sat so well on him, she saw a huge room, all chandeliers and people dancing some dance from a costume film—stately, hand-to-hand. She supposed he was going to fetch, in her place in the car, a partner for the evening. They never kissed when either left the flat; he said, suddenly, kindly, pausing as he picked up cigarettes and keys, "Don't be lonely." And added, "Wouldn't you like to visit your family sometimes, when I have to go out?"

He had told her he was going home to his mother in the forests and mountains of his country near the Italian border (he showed her on the map) after

Christmas. She had not told him how her mother, not knowing there was any other variety, assumed he was a medical doctor, so she had talked to her about the doctor's children and the doctor's wife who was a very kind lady, glad to have someone who could help out in the surgery as well as the flat.

She remarked wonderingly on his ability to work until midnight or later, after a day at work. She was so tired when she came home from her cash register at the supermarket that once dinner was eaten she could scarcely keep awake. He explained in a way she could understand that while the work she did was repetitive, undemanding of any real response from her intelligence, requiring little mental or physical effort and therefore unrewarding, his work was his greatest interest, it taxed his mental capacities to their limit, exercised all his concentration, and rewarded him constantly as much with the excitement of a problem presented as with the satisfaction of a problem solved. He said later, putting away his papers, speaking out of a silence: "Have you done other kinds of work?" She said, "I was in a clothing factory before. Sportbeau shirts; you know? But the pay's better in the shop."

Of course. Being a conscientious newspaper-reader in every country he lived in, he was aware that it was only recently that the retail consumer trade in this one had been allowed to employ coloreds as shop assistants; even punching a cash register represented advancement. With the continuing shortage of semi-skilled whites a girl like this might be able to edge a little farther into the white-collar category. He began to teach her to type. He was aware that her English was poor, even though, as a foreigner, in his ears her pronounciation did not offend, nor categorize her as it would in those of someone of his education whose mother tongue was English. He corrected her grammatical mistakes but missed the less obvious ones because of his own sometimes exotic English usage—she continued to use the singular pronoun "it" when what was required was the plural "they." Because he was a foreigner (although so clever, as she saw) she was less inhibited than she might have been by the words she knew she misspelled in her typing. While she sat at the typewriter she thought how one day she would type notes for him, as well as making coffee the way he liked it, and taking him inside her body without saying anything, and sitting (even if only through the empty streets of quiet Sundays) beside him in his car, like a wife.

On a summer night near Christmas—he had already bought and hidden a slightly showy but nevertheless good watch he thought she would like—there was a knocking at the door that brought her out of the bathroom and him to his feet, at his work-table. No one ever came to the flat at night; he had no friends intimate enough to drop in without warning. The summons was an imperious banging that did not pause and clearly would not stop until the door was opened.

She stood in the open bathroom doorway gazing at him across the passage into the living-room; her bare feet and shoulders were free of a big bath-towel. She said nothing did not even whisper. The flat seemed to shake with the strong unhurried blows.

He made as if to go to the door, at last, but now she ran and clutched him by both arms. She shook her head wildly; her lips drew back but her teeth were clenched. she didn't speak. She pulled him into the bedroom, snatched some clothes from the clean laundry laid out on the bed and got into the wall-cupboard, thrusting the key at his hand. Although his arms and calves felt weakly

cold he was horrified, distastefully embarrassed at the sight of her pressed back crouching there under his suits and coat; it was horrible and ridiculous. *Come out!* he whispered. *No! Come out!* She hissed: *Where? Where can I go?*
Never mind! Get out of there!

He put out his hand to grasp her. At bay, she said with all the force of her terrible whisper, baring the gap in her teeth: *I'll throw myself out the window.*

She forced the key into his hand like the handle of a knife. He closed the door on her face and drove the key home in the lock, then dropped it among coins in his trouser pocket.

He unslotted the chain that was looped across the flat door. He turned the serrated knob of the Yale lock. The three policemen, two in plain clothes, stood there without impatience although they had been banging on the door for several minutes. The big dark one with an elaborate moustache held out in a hand wearing a plaited gilt ring some sort of identity card.

Dr. von Leinsdorf said quietly, the blood coming strangely back to legs and arms, "What is it?"

The sergeant told him they knew there was a colored girl in the flat. They had had information; "I been watching this flat three months, I know."

"I am alone here." Dr. von Leinsdorf did not raise his voice.

"I know, I know who is here. Come—" And the sergeant and his two assistants went into the living-room, the kitchen, the bathroom (the sergeant picked up a bottle of after-shave cologne, seemed to study the French label) and the bedroom. The assistants removed the clean laundry that was laid upon the bed and then turned back the bedding, carrying the sheets over to be examined by the sergeant under the lamp. They talked to one another in Afrikaans, which the Doctor did not understand. The sergeant himself looked under the bed, and lifted the long curtains at the window. The wall cupboard was of the kind that has no knobs; he saw that it was locked and began to ask in Afrikaans, then politely changed to English, "Give us the key."

Dr. von Leinsdorf said, "I'm sorry, I left it at my office—I always lock and take my keys with me in the mornings."

"It's no good, man, you better give me the key."

He smiled a little, reasonably. "It's on my office desk."

The assistants produced a screwdriver and he watched while they inserted it where the cupboard doors met, gave it quick, firm but not forceful leverage. He heard the lock give.

She had been naked, it was true, when they knocked. But now she was wearing a long-sleeved T-shirt with an appliquéd butterfly motif on one breast, and a pair of jeans. Her feet were still bare; she had managed, by feel, in the dark, to get into some of the clothing she had snatched from the bed, but she had no shoes. She had perhaps been weeping behind the cupboard door (her cheeks looked stained) but now her face was sullen and she was breathing heavily, her diaphragm contracting and expanding exaggeratedly and her breasts pushing against the cloth. It made her appear angry; it might simply have been that she was half-suffocated in the cupboard and needed oxygen. She did not look at Dr. von Leinsdorf. She would not reply to the sergeant's questions.

They were taken to the police station where they were at once separated and in turn led for examination by the district surgeon. The man's underwear was taken away and examined, as the sheets had been, for signs of his seed. When

the girl was undressed, it was discovered that beneath her jeans she was wear-ing a pair of men's briefs with his name on the neatly-sewn laundry tag; in her haste, she had taken the wrong garment to her hiding-place.

Now she cried, standing there before the district surgeon in a man's under-wear.

He courteously pretended not to notice. He handed briefs, jeans and T-shirt round the door, and motioned her to lie on a white-sheeted high table where he placed her legs apart, resting in stirrups, and out into her where the other had made his way so warmly a cold hard instrument that expanded wider and wider. Her thighs and knees trembled uncontrollably while the doctor looked into her and touched her deep inside with more hard instruments, carrying wafers of gauze.

When she came out of the examining room back to the charge office, Dr. von Leinsdorf was not there; they must have taken him somewhere else. She spent what was left of the night in a cell, as he must be doing; but early in the morning she was released and taken home to her mother's house in the col-ored township by a white man who explained he was the clerk of the lawyer who had been engaged for her by Dr. von Leinsdorf. Dr. von Leinsdorf, the clerk said, had also been bailed out that morning. He did not say when, or if, she would see him again.

A statement made by the girl to the police was handed in to Court when she and the man appeared to meet charges of contravening the Immorality Act in a Johannesburg flat on the night of — December, 19—. *lived with the white man in his flat. He had intercourse with me sometimes. He gave me tablets to take to prevent me becoming pregnant.*

Interviewed by the Sunday papers, the girl said, "I'm sorry for the sadness brought to my mother." She said she was one of nine children of a female laundry worker. She had left school in Standard Three[6] because there was no money at home for gym clothes or a school blazer. She had worked as a ma-chinist in a factory and a cashier in a supermarket. Dr. von Leinsdorf taught her to type his notes.

Dr. Franz-Josef von Leinsdorf, described as the grandson of a baroness, a cultured man engaged in international minera ogical research, said he ac-cepted social distinctions between people but didn't think they should be legally imposed. "Even in my own country it's difficult for a person from a higher class to marry one from a lower class."

The two accused gave no evidence. They did not greet or speak to each other in Court. The Defense argued that the sergeant's evidence that they had been living together as man and wife was hearsay. (The woman with the dachshund, the caretaker?) The magistrate acquitted them because the State failed to prove carnal intercourse had taken place on the night of — December, 19—.

The girl's mother was quoted, with photograph, in the Sunday papers: "I won't let my daughter work as a servant for a white man again."

1980

6. South African equivalent of eighth grade.

DENISE LEVERTOV

1923–

Born and brought up in Ilford, Essex, England, Denise Levertov has paradoxically become one of the most American of writers, a self-defined disciple of many of the aesthetic ideas of the American poets William Carlos Williams and H. D. (Hilda Doolittle). About Williams, for example, Levertov has observed that "he made available to us the whole range of the language, he showed us the rhythms of speech as *poetry*," adding that "it is a mistake to suppose that Williams's insistence on 'the American idiom' ever implied a reduction; on the contrary, it means the recognition of wide resources." Similarly, about H. D., she has remarked that the author of *Trilogy* offered "doors, ways in, tunnels through," noting that H. D. "showed a way to penetrate mystery; which means, not to flood darkness with light so that darkness is destroyed, but to *enter into* darkness, mystery, so that it is experienced." In her own work, moreover, Levertov has consistently employed such "natural" speech-rhythms to open the gates of mystery and enter what she defines in *The Goddess* and *Song to Ishtar* as the sacred precincts of the Muse.

The younger of two daughters of a Welsh mother and a Russian Jewish father (who later became a clergyman in the Church of England), Levertov was educated mostly at home; in several memoirs, she has described her English childhood as bucolic, paying special attention to the influence of her older sister, Olga, about whose death she wrote a poignant elegiac sequence, *The Sorrow Dance*. During World War II, she became a nurse, and in 1947 she married the writer Mitchell Goodman (from whom she was divorced in the early 1970s). The couple have one son, about whose childhood and adolescence Levertov has also written several moving poems. Emigrating to the United States in 1948, Levertov became an American citizen in 1955, and began to publish the suavely cadenced collections of verse on which her reputation is based. In England, she had already produced one book—*The Double Image* (1946)—but her American volumes, based on a radical commitment to the idea that "a poem *is* a sonic, sensuous event and not a statement or a string of ideas," are more characteristic. Over a dozen in number, they include such influential and widely read collections as *The Jacob's Ladder* (1961), *O Taste and See* (1964), *The Sorrow Dance* (1967), *Relearning the Alphabet* (1970), *The Freeing of the Dust* (1975), *Candles in Babylon* (1982), *Breathing the Water* (1987), and *Evening Train* (1993) as well as three books of essays, *The Poet in the World* (1973), *Light Up the Cave* (1981), and *Tesserae: Memories and Suppositions* (1995).

In recent years, Levertov has taught at a number of universities, including Tufts and Stanford, and she has served as poetry editor of the liberal journal *The Nation*. Perhaps most important, she was a notable activist in the peace movement of the 1960s and 1970s (protesting the Vietnam War) and in the antinuclear and peace movements of the 1980s (protesting nuclear proliferation and American intervention in El Salvador). Though she does not define herself as a feminist, her poetry frequently expresses a distinctively female perspective on the world, celebrating the values of nature and nurture while drawing on the details of domesticity to dramatize a mystical reality whose radiance she often sees (for instance, in *Abel's Bride*) as illuminating even the most apparently ordinary objects. In addition, in such poems as *Hypocrite Women, In Mind,* and *Stepping Westward,* Levertov turns again and again to questions of female self-definition, exploring the complexity of her own character as an example of the complexity of a woman's being. More generally, however, in their Romantic commitment to both an imagining of moral justice and an intuition of mystical truth, her finest verses consistently reflect her belief that "the written poem" is at its best a "record" of an "inner song."

The Goddess

She in whose lipservice
I passed my time,
whose name I knew, but not her face,
came upon me where I lay in Lie Castle!

Flung me across the room and 5
room after room (hitting the walls, re-
bounding—to the last
sticky wall—wrenching away from it
pulled hair out!)
till I lay 10
outside the outer walls!

There in cold air
lying still where her hand had thrown me,
I tasted the mud that splattered my lips:
the seeds of a forest were in it, 15
asleep and growing! I tasted
her power!

The silence was answering my silence,
a forest was pushing itself
out of sleep between my submerged fingers. 20

I bit on a seed and it spoke on my tongue
of day that shone already among stars
in the water-mirror of low ground,

and a wind rising ruffled the lights:
she passed near me returning from the encounter, 25
she who plucked me from the close rooms

without whom nothing
flowers, fruits, sleeps in season,
without whom nothing
speaks in its own tongue, but returns 30
lie for lie!

 1960

Song for Ishtar

The moon is a sow
and grunts in my throat
Her great shining shines through me
so the mud of my hollow gleams
and breaks in silver bubbles 5

1. Babylonian goddess of love and fertility.

She is a sow
and I a pig and a poet

When she opens her white
lips to devour me I bite back
and laughter rocks the moon 10

In the black of desire
we rock and grunt, grunt and
shine

 1964

Hypocrite Women

Hypocrite women, how seldom we speak
of our own doubts, while dubiously
we mother man in his doubt!

And if at Mill Valley[1] perched in the trees
the sweet rain drifting through western air 5
a white sweating bull of a poet told us

our cunts are ugly—why didn't we
admit we have thought so too? (And
what shame? They are not for the eye!)

No, they are dark and wrinkled and hairy, 10
caves of the Moon . . . And when a
dark humming fills us, a

coldness towards life,
we are too much women to
own to such unwomanliness. 15

Whorishly with the psychopomp[2]
we play and plead—and say
nothing of this later. And our dreams,

with what frivolity we have pared them
like toenails, clipped them like ends of 20
split hair.

 1964

In Mind

There's in my mind a woman
of innocence, unadorned but

1. Town in northern California, location of Marin 2. The soul's guide, usually to the place of the dead.
College.

fair-featured, and smelling of
apples or grass. She wears

a utopian smock or shift, her hair 5
is light brown and smooth, and she

is kind and very clean without
ostentation—
 but she has
no imagination. 10
 And there's a
turbulent moon-ridden girl

or old woman, or both,
dressed in opals and rags, feathers

and torn taffeta, 15
who knows strange songs—

but she is not kind.

 1964

The Ache of Marriage

The ache of marriage:

thigh and tongue, beloved,
are heavy with it,
it throbs in the teeth

We look for communion 5
and are turned away beloved,
each and each

It is leviathan[1] and we
in its belly
looking for joy, some joy 10
not to be known outside it

two by two in the ark[2] of
the ache of it.

 1964

Eros[1] at Temple Stream

The river in its abundance
many-voiced

1. A reference to the story of Jonah, who was swal-
lowed by a sea monster, or leviathan (Book of Jonah).
2. A reference to Noah's ark, in which animals of every
species were preserved from the flood that destroyed
all other life (Genesis 7).
1. The Greek god of love; also the Greek word for
"love."

all about us as we stood
on a warm rock to wash

slowly 5
smoothing in long
 sliding strokes
our soapy hands along each other's
slippery cool bodies

quiet and slow in the midst of 10
the quick of the
sounding river

our hands were
flames
stealing upon quickened flesh until 15

no part of us but was
sleek and
on fire.

 1964

Abel's Bride[1]

Woman fear for man, he goes
out alone to his labors. No mirror
nests in his pocket. His face
opens and shuts with his hopes.
His sex hangs unhidden 5
or rises before him
blind and questing.

She thinks herself
lucky. But sad. When she goes out
she looks in the glass, she remembers 10
herself. Stones, coal,
the hiss of water upon the kindled
branches—her being
is a cave, there are bones at the hearth.

 1967

The Son

i The Disclosure

He-who-came-forth was
it turned out
a man—

1. According to the Bible, Abel was the second son of Adam and Eve, and was murdered by his brother Cain (Genesis 4). No mention is made of Abel's wife in the Bible.

Moves among us from room to room of our life
in boots, in jeans, in a cloak of flame 5
pulled out of his pocket along with
old candywrappers, where it had lain
transferred from pants to pants,
folded small as a curl of dust,
from the beginning— 10

uncurled now.

The fine flame
almost unseen in common light.

ii *The Woodblock*

He cuts into a slab of wood,
engrossed, violently precise. 15
Thus, yesterday, the day before yesterday,
engines of fantasy were evolved
in poster paints. Tonight
a face forms under the knife,
slashed with stern 20
crisscrosses of longing, downstrokes
of silence endured—
 his visioned

own face!—
down which from one eye 25

rolls a tear.
 His own face
drawn from the wood,

deep in the manhood his childhood
so swiftly led to, a small brook rock-leaping 30
into the rapt, imperious, seagoing river.

 1967

Stepping Westward[1]

What is green in me
darkens, muscadine.

If woman is inconstant,
good, I am faithful to

ebb and flow, I fall 5
in season and now

is a time of ripening.
If her part

1. Title of an 1807 poem by William Wordsworth in which two male travelers meet two local women.

is to be true,
a north star, 10

good, I hold steady
in the black sky

and vanish by day,
yet burn there

in blue or above 15
quilts of cloud.

There is no savor
more sweet, more salt

than to be glad to be
what, woman, 20

and who, myself,
I am, a shadow

that grows longer as the sun
moves, drawn out

on a thread of wonder. 25
If I bear burdens

they begin to be remembered
as gifts, goods, a basket

of bread that hurts
my shoulders but closes me 30

in fragrance. I can
eat as I go.

1967

The Mutes

Those groans men use
passing a woman on the street
or on the steps of the subway

to tell her she is a female
and their flesh knows it, 5

are they a sort of tune,
an ugly enough song, sung
by a bird with a slit tongue

but meant for music?

Or are they the muffled roaring 10
of deafmutes trapped in a building that is
slowly filling with smoke?

Perhaps both.

Such men most often
look as if groan were all they could do, 15
yet a woman, in spite of herself,

knows it's a tribute:
if she were lacking all grace
they'd pass her in silence:

so it's not only to say she's 20
a warm hole. It's a word

in grief-language, nothing to do with
primitive, not an ur-language;
language stricken, sickened, cast down

in decrepitude. She wants to 25
throw the tribute away, dis-
gusted, and can't,

it goes on buzzing in her ear,
it changes the pace of her walk,
the torn posters in echoing corridors 30

spell it out, it
quakes and gnashes as the train comes in.
Her pulse sullenly

had picked up speed,
but the cars slow down and 35
jar to a stop while her understanding

keeps on translating:
"Life after life after life goes by

without poetry,
without seemliness, 40
without love."

 1967

Canción[1]

When I am the sky
a glittering bird
slashes at me with the knives of song.

1. Song or lyric poem (Spanish).

When I am the sea
fiery clouds plunge into my mirrors, 5
fracture my smooth breath with crimson sobbing.

When I am the earth
I feel my flesh of rock wearing down:
pebbles, grit, finest dust, nothing.

When I am a woman—O, when I am 10
a woman,
my wells of salt brim and brim,
poems force the lock of my throat.

 1975

Divorcing

One garland
of flowers, leaves, thorns
was twined round our two necks.
Drawn tight, it could choke us,
yet we loved its scratchy grace, 5
our fragrant yoke.

We were Siamese twins.
Our blood's not sure
if it can circulate,
now we are cut apart. 10
Something in each of us is waiting
to see if we can survive,
severed.

 1975

The Dragonfly-Mother

I was setting out from my house
to keep my promise

but the Dragonfly-Mother stopped me.

I was to speak to a multitude
for a good cause, but at home 5

the Dragonfly-Mother was listening
not to a speech but to the creak of
 stretching tissue,
tense hum of leaves unfurling.

Who is the Dragonfly-Mother? 10
What does she do?

She is the one who hovers
on stairways of air,
 sometimes almost
grazing your cheekbone, 15
she is the one who darts unforeseeably
into unsuspected dimensions.

who sees in water
her own blue fire zigzag, and lifts
her self in laughter 20
into the tearful pale sky

that sails blurred clouds in the stream.

 •

She sat at my round table,
we told one another dreams,
I stayed home breaking my promise. 25

When she left I slept
three hours, and arose

and wrote. I remember the cold
Waterwoman, in dragonfly dresses

and blue shoes, long ago.[1] 30
She is the same,

whose children were thin,
left at home when she went out dancing.
She is the Dragonfly-Mother.

that cold 35
is only the rush of air

swiftness brings.
There is a summer
over the water, over

the river mirrors 40
where she hovers, a summer
fertile, abundant, where dreams
grow into acts and journeys.

Her children
are swimmers, nymphs[2] and newts, metamorphic 45
 When she tells

1. This description appears in Levertov's *The* 2. Dragonfly nymphs are aquatic.
Earthwoman and the Waterwoman (1957).

her stories she listens; when she listens
she tells you the story you utter.

 •

When I broke my promise,
and slept, and later 50

cooked and ate the food she had bought
and left in my kitchen,

I kept a tryst with myself,
a long promise that can be fulfilled
only poem by poem, 55
broken over and over.

 I too,
a creature, grow among reeds,
 in mud, in air,
in sunbright cold, in fever
of blue-gold zenith, winds 60
of passage.

 Dragonfly-Mother's
a messenger,
if I don't trust her
I can't keep the faith. 65

 There is a summer
in the sleep
of broken promises, fertile dreams,
acts of passage, hovering
journeys over the fathomless waters. 70

 1982

Ancient Airs and Dances

I

I knew too well
what had befallen me
when, one night, I put my lips to his wineglass
after he left—an impulse I thought was locked away with a smile
into memory's museum. 5

When he took me to visit friends and the sea, he lay
asleep in the next room's dark where the fire
rustled all night; and I, from a warm bed, sleepless,
watched through the open door
that glowing hearth, and heard, 10
drumming the roof, the rain's
insistent heartbeat.

Greyhaired, I have not grown wiser,
unless to perceive absurdity
is wisdom. A powerless wisdom. 15

II

Shameless heart! Did you not vow to learn
 stillness from the heron,
 quiet from the mists of fall,
 and from the mountain—what was it?
 Pride? Remoteness? 20
You have forgotten already!
And now you clamor again
like an obstinate child demanding attention,
interrupting study and contemplation.
You try my patience. Bound as we are 25
together for life, must you now,
so late in the day, go bounding sideways,
trying to drag me with you?

 1992

Dyptich[1]

1 Mysterious Movement

Though no wind is blowing, the lake.
 as if to reënact the remote day
 when, as a journeying river it first flowed
 into the long hollow of its bed
 and met the embracing shores 5
 and could go no further,
is pressing strongly, darkly,
southward in fading light, this waning hour
near the close of the year—

although it can go no further. 10

2 Midwinter

A sky stained
even at midmorning
with the water and blood of daybreak . . .

And the mountain,
strangely approachable 15
this winter day,
has moved forward into the middle distance,
humbly letting valleys and dark
seams of rock be perceived,
like a woman not trying to hide 20

1. A work that is made up of two parts.

her loss of youth from the light.
Her snows are gray.

1992

Evening Train

An old man sleeping in the evening train,
face upturned, mouth discreetly closed,
hands clasped, with fingers interlaced.
Those large hands
lie on the fur lining of his wife's coat 5
he's holding for her, and the fur
looks like a limp dog, docile and affectionate.
The man himself is a peasant
in city clothes, moderately prosperous—
rich by the standards of his youth; 10
one can read that in his hands,
his sleeping features.
How tired he is, how tired.
I called him old, but then I remember
my own age, and acknowledge he's likely 15
no older than I. But in the dimension
that moves with us but itself keeps still
like the bubble in a carpenter's level,
I'm fourteen, watching the faces I saw each day
on the train going in to London, 20
and never spoke to; or guessing
from a row of shoes what sort of faces
I'd see if I raised my eyes.
Everyone has an unchanging age (or sometimes two)
carried within them, beyond expression. 25
This man perhaps
is ten, putting in a few hours most days
in a crowded schoolroom, and a lot more
at work in the fields; a boy who's always
making plans to go fishing his first free day. 30
The train moves through the dark quite swiftly
(the Italian dark, as it happens)
with its load of people, each
with a conscious destination, each
with a known age and that other, 35
the hidden one—except for those
still young, or not young but slower to focus,
who haven't reached yet that state of being
which will become
not a point of arrest but a core 40
around which the mind develops, reflections circle,
events accrue—a center.
 A girl with braids
sits in this corner seat, invisible,
pleased with her solitude. And across from her 45
an invisible boy, dreaming. She knows

she cannot imagine his dreams. Quite swiftly
we move through our lives; swiftly, steadily the train
rocks and bounces onward through sleeping fields,
our unknown stillness 50
holding level as water sealed in glass.

1992

PATRICIA BEER

1924–

Patricia Beer's *Reader, I Married Him* (1974), a critical examination of works by
nineteenth-century women novelists in England, was one of the first studies of the
female literary tradition to appear in the 1970s, when the so-called second wave of
feminism began to crest. A former lecturer in English at the University of Padua
and at London University, Beer was a graduate of St. Hugh's College, Oxford, and
herself a poet and novelist. Born in Devon, she began writing early and has pub-
lished almost a dozen collections of verse, including *The Loss of the Magyar*
(1959), *The Survivors* (1963), *Selected Poems* (1975), and *The Lie of the Land*
(1983) as well as a memoir, *Mrs. Beer's House* (1968), a novel, *Moon's Ottery*
(1978), several anthologies, and a study of the Metaphysical poets. Herself a dis-
tinguished woman of letters, in poems as well as in criticism, she records the
dilemmas that she and other literary women have experienced with wry wit and
technical precision, as her sardonic depiction of *Transvestism in the Novels of
Charlotte Brontë* reveals.

Witch

I shall see justice done.
I shall protect time
From monkish, cowardly men
Who say this life is not all
And do not respect the clock 5

On those who will not escape
I shall see justice done.
I have courage to use
Wax and the killing pin[1]
On behalf of prisoners. 10

I cut off the pilot's thumb
Because his compass failed.
I shall see justice done
Whenever the homeward bound
Mistake their true home. 15

In my black pointed heart
I cherish the good of all.

1. I.e., use a voodoo doll.

With storms, potions and blood
I shall see justice done
For I know goodness well. 20

Never shall bogus love—
Habit, duty or weakness—
Win any mercy from me.
By the light of my long burning
I shall see justice done. 25

1963

Brunhild[1]

My father laid me in a ring
Of fire, and then like thunder rolled
Away, though I had been more close
To him than in his arms. He told
Me I should never see his face 5
Now he had voiced me like a song,

Made me a separate thing, no more
His warrior daughter but a woman.
But I do see his face, I see
It all the time. Though I am human 10
He can still rule. He promised me
That a brave man should break the fire,

A man he would approve of, no
Tentative weakling. He will have
My father's dominant beard and mighty 15
Shoulders, and instead of love
This obligation to be doughty.
I wait for the entrance of the hero

Dressed up in my father's fashion.
If I were free to love I would 20
Decide on someone thin and shaven.
But in the ring I lie like wood
Or soil, that cannot yield or even
Be raped except with his permission.

1967

The Bull

The bull on the poster speaks
Trunkless but not just a head.
Up in London to be sold

1. Warrior maiden of Germanic mythology. In Richard Wagner's opera *Die Walküre* (1870), the second in his *Ring* cycle, Brunhild's father (the god Wotan) deprives her of her immortality.

His white face that all his sons wear
Is a man's fortune. 5

He was once a danger.
Even across three meadows
His walk gave him away,
Bred stories and giggling fright.
Without any rage he was 10
Thunder in a field.

Nobody except me seems
To notice him by day
But one night after the rush hour
Someone must have done, 15

Someone who felt the need
To draw a loop out of his mouth
Saying I AM A BULL.

1971

In Memory of Constance Markiewicz[1]

The kind of woman that men poets
Hope their own and their friends' daughters
Will not resemble, a rarity.

Stepping from silk into uniform,
From earth to dirt, she lit out and left 5
The green country where her father ruled

Then left her husband and child also
Like an evangelist with a wilder
Calling or a painter feeling trapped.

Women do not usually do this. 10
She calls to mind Mrs. Jellyby[2]
That pretty monster who looked over

Her children's heads into Africa
Though she would not have died, I suppose,
For the good of Borrioboola. 15

Constance felt the value of bloodshed
As deeply as Pearse and Connolly.[3]
She bespoke a priest to see her through

1. Irish nationalist and Sinn Fein politician (1884–1927), who took part in the Easter uprising of 1916 in Dublin.
2. A character in Charles Dickens's *Bleak House* (1852–53) who thought only of a project to aid the inhabitants of "Borrioboola-Gha" in Africa.
3. James Connolly (1870–1916), Irish nationalist and socialist, who helped organize Irish labor; he was wounded in the 1916 rebellion, captured, and subsequently shot. Patrick Pearse (1879–1916) commanded the Irish forces in the Easter uprising and was executed by the English.

The bullets, but did not require him
For eleven years and then bloodlessly, 20
Having gone far past disappointment.

Yes, she became opinionated
And shrill, but had a longer funeral
Procession than most of us will have.

 1971

Mating Calls

It is not so much the song
Of the hump-backed whale, reaching
Through a hundred miles of sea
To his love that strikes us. We
Can be heard farther than he. 5

It is not the albatross
Either, with his strident voice
Promising the most tender
"Always" in tones of thunder.
Our vows may well go under. 10

Some kind of magpie keeps on
Singing, when his mate has gone,
Not only his notes but hers.
This moves us to pride and tears
That love should make us such bores. 15

 1975

Transvestism in the Novels of Charlotte Brontë

When reading *Villette*, *Shirley* and *Jane Eyre*,
Though never somehow *The Professor*[1]
Which was all too clear,
I used to overlook
The principal point of each book 5
As it now seems to me: what the characters wore.

Mr. Rochester[2] dressed up as the old crone
That perhaps he should have been,
De Hamal[3] as a nun.
There was no need 10
For this. Each of them could
Have approached his woman without becoming one.

Not all heroines were as forthright.

1. Brontë's first novel, *The Professor* (not published 2. A character in *Jane Eyre* (1847).
until 1857), has her only male narrator. 3. A character in *Villette* (1853).

Shirley[4] in particular was a cheat.
With rakish hat 15
She strode like a man
But always down the lane
Where the handsome mill-owner lived celibate.

Lucy,[5] however, knew just what she was doing.
And cast herself as a human being. 20
Strutting and wooing
In the school play
She put on a man's gilet,[6]
Kept her own skirt, for fear of simplifying.

Their lonely begetter was both sister and brother. 25
In her dark wood trees do not scan each other
Yet foregather,
Branched or split,
Whichever they are not,
Whichever they are, and rise up together. 30

1983

4. A character in *Shirley* (1849). 6. Vest, jacket (French).
5. A character in *Villette*.

FLANNERY O'CONNOR

1925–1964

Because Flannery O'Connor believed that "the novelist with Christian concerns will find in modern life distortions" that are "repugnant" to the writer but "natural" to the reader, in a posthumously published volume of collected essays titled *Mystery and Manners* (1969), she advocated "violent means" to get her vision across: with a "hostile audience," the writer must make her "vision apparent by shock—to the hard of hearing you shout, and for the almost blind you draw large and startling figures." Christ-haunted prophets, religious hucksters, and visionary farm hands, many of the characters in O'Connor's stories and novels inhabit a South that she associated with the urgency of faith: "The South," she explained in a letter (1957), "still believes that man has fallen and that he is only perfectible by God's grace, not by his own unaided efforts." Her characters are, therefore, often caught in the grip of a violent spiritual struggle in which they are ultimately saved or lost. Few fiction writers have so successfully resisted religious sentimentality while dramatizing the cost of redemption.

The only child of Regina and Edward Francis O'Connor, Mary Flannery O'Connor grew up in Savannah, Georgia, until her father became ill and the family moved to Milledgeville, Georgia, her mother's hometown. At fifteen, when her father died of lupus erythematosus, an incurable blood disease, she was already committed to Roman Catholicism, the religion of her parents. After graduating in 1942 from Peabody High School, she attended Georgia State College for Women, where she contributed stories and cartoons to the literary magazine. After graduation, she attended the Writers' Workshop at the University of Iowa, where she won

the Rinehart-Iowa prize for a work-in-progress, which she completed first at Yaddo (a writers' retreat) and then in the Connecticut home of two friends, Sally and Robert Fitzgerald. A comic masterpiece, this book—*Wise Blood* (1952)—focused on Hazel Motes, the would-be founder of a "church without Christ, where the blind stay blind, the lame stay lame and them that's dead stays that way."

Both the grotesque humor and the rural, southern dialect of *Wise Blood* characterize the fiction O'Connor later went on to write under difficult circumstances. Two years before the publication of her first novel, she had discovered that she was suffering from the disease that had killed her father. With the aid of cortisone treatments and with her mother's care, she managed to control the disease. Mother and daughter lived on a farm near Milledgeville, where O'Connor raised peacocks and chickens and wrote her second novel, *The Violent Bear It Away* (1960), as well as the stories that appeared in *A Good Man Is Hard to Find and Others* (1955) and in the posthumous collection *Everything That Rises Must Converge* (1965). She was befriended by the poet Robert Lowell, the editor Robert Giroux, and the short-story writer Caroline Gordon, but the cortisone weakened her bones and made it difficult for her to travel or lecture. When an operation reactivated her lupus, she died at the age of thirty-nine.

Good Country People

Besides the neutral expression that she wore when she was alone, Mrs. Freeman had two others, forward and reverse, that she used for all her human dealings. Her forward expression was steady and driving like the advance of a heavy truck. Her eyes never swerved to left or right but turned as the story turned as if they followed a yellow line down the center of it. She seldom used the other expression because it was not often necessary for her to retract a statement, but when she did, her face came to a complete stop, there was an almost imperceptible movement of her black eyes, during which they seemed to be receding, and then the observer would see that Mrs. Freeman, though she might stand there as real as several grain sacks thrown on top of each other, was no longer there in spirit. As for getting anything across to her when this was the case, Mrs. Hopewell had given it up. She might talk her head off. Mrs. Freeman could never be brought to admit herself wrong on any point. She would stand there and if she could be brought to say anything, it was something like, "Well, I wouldn't of said it was and I wouldn't of said it wasn't," or letting her gaze range over the top kitchen shelf where there was an assortment of dusty bottles, she might remark, "I see you ain't ate many of them figs you put up last summer."

They carried on their most important business in the kitchen at breakfast. Every morning Mrs. Hopewell got up at seven o'clock and lit her gas heater and Joy's. Joy was her daughter, a large blonde girl who had an artificial leg. Mrs. Hopewell thought of her as a child though she was thirty-two years old and highly educated. Joy would get up while her mother was eating and lumber into the bathroom and slam the door, and before long, Mrs. Freeman would arrive at the back door. Joy would hear her mother call, "Come on in," and then they would talk for a while in low voices that were indistinguishable in the bathroom. By the time Joy came in, they had usually finished the weather report and were on one or the other of Mrs. Freeman's daughters, Glynese or Carramae, Joy called them Glycerin and Caramel. Glynese, a red-

head, was eighteen and had many admirers; Carramae, a blonde, was only fifteen but already married and pregnant. She could not keep anything on her stomach. Every morning Mrs. Freeman told Mrs. Hopewell how many times she had vomited since the last report.

Mrs. Hopewell liked to tell people that Glynese and Carramae were two of the finest girls she knew and that Mrs. Freeman was a *lady* and that she was never ashamed to take her anywhere or introduce her to anybody they might meet. Then she would tell how she had happened to hire the Freemans in the first place and how they were a godsend to her and how she had had them four years. The reason for her keeping them so long was that they were not trash. They were good country people. She had telephoned the man whose name they had given as a reference and he had told her that Mr. Freeman was a good farmer but that his wife was the nosiest woman ever to walk the earth. "She's got to be into everything," the man said. "If she don't get there before the dust settles, you can bet she's dead, that's all. She'll want to know all your business. I can stand him real good," he had said, "but me nor my wife neither could have stood that woman one more minute on this place." That had put Mrs. Hopewell off for a few days.

She had hired them in the end because there were no other applicants but she had made up her mind beforehand exactly how she would handle the woman. Since she was the type who had to be into everything, then, Mrs. Hopewell had decided, she would not only let her be into everything, she would *see to it* that she was into everything—she would give her the responsibility of everything, she would put her in charge. Mrs. Hopewell had no bad qualities of her own but she was able to use other people's in such a constructive way that she never felt the lack. She had hired the Freemans and she had kept them four years.

Nothing is perfect. This was one of Mrs. Hopewell's favorite sayings. Another was: that is life! And still another, the most important, was: well, other people have their opinions too. She would make these statements, usually at the table, in a tone of gentle insistence as if no one held them but her, and the large hulking Joy, whose constant outrage had obliterated every expression from her face, would stare just a little to the side of her, her eyes icy blue, with the look of someone who has achieved blindness by an act of will and means to keep it.

When Mrs. Hopewell said to Mrs. Freeman that life was like that, Mrs. Freeman would say, "I always said so myself." Nothing had been arrived at by anyone that had not first been arrived at by her. She was quicker than Mr. Freeman. When Mrs. Hopewell said to her after they had been on the place a while, "You know, you're the wheel behind the wheel," and winked, Mrs. Freeman had said, "I know it. I've always been quick. It's some that are quicker than others."

"Everybody is different," Mrs. Hopewell said.

"Yes, most people is," Mrs. Freeman said.

"It takes all kinds to make the world."

"I always said it did myself."

The girl was used to this kind of dialogue for breakfast and more of it for dinner; sometimes they had it for supper too. When they had no guest they ate in the kitchen because that was easier. Mrs. Freeman always managed to arrive at some point during the meal and to watch them finish it. She would

stand in the doorway if it were summer but in the winter she would stand with one elbow on top of the refrigerator and look down on them, or she would stand by the gas heater, lifting the back of her skirt slightly. Occasionally she would stand against the wall and roll her head from side to side. At no time was she in any hurry to leave. All this was very trying on Mrs. Hopewell but she was a woman of great patience. She realized that nothing is perfect and that in the Freemans she had good country people and that if, in this day and age, you get good country people, you had better hang onto them.

She had had plenty of experience with trash. Before the Freemans she had averaged one tenant family a year. The wives of these farmers were not the kind you would want to be around you for very long. Mrs. Hopewell, who had divorced her husband long ago, needed someone to walk over the fields with her; and when Joy had to be impressed for these services, her remarks were usually so ugly and her face so glum that Mrs. Hopewell would say, "If you can't come pleasantly, I don't want you at all," to which the girl, standing square and rigid-shouldered with her neck thrust slightly forward, would reply, "If you want me, here I am—LIKE I AM."

Mrs. Hopewell excused this attitude because of the leg (which had been shot off in a hunting accident when Joy was ten). It was hard for Mrs. Hopewell to realize that her child was thirty-two now and that for more than twenty years she had had only one leg. She thought of her still as a child because it tore her heart to think instead of the poor stout girl in her thirties who had never danced a step or had any *normal* good times. Her name was really Joy but as soon as she was twenty-one and away from home, she had had it legally changed. Mrs. Hopewell was certain that she had thought and thought until she had hit upon the ugliest name in any language. Then she had gone and had the beautiful name, Joy, changed without telling her mother until after she had done it. Her legal name was Hulga.

When Mrs. Hopewell thought of the name, Hulga, she thought of the broad blank hull of a battleship. She would not use it. She continued to call her Joy to which the girl responded but in a purely mechanical way.

Hulga had learned to tolerate Mrs. Freeman who saved her from taking walks with her mother. Even Glynese and Carramae were useful when they occupied attention that might otherwise have been directed at her. At first she had thought she could not stand Mrs. Freeman for she had found that it was not possible to be rude to her. Mrs. Freeman would take on strange resentments and for days together she would be sullen but the source of her displeasure was always obscure; a direct attack, a positive leer, blatant ugliness to her face—these never touched her. And without warning one day, she began calling her Hulga.

She did not call her that in front of Mrs. Hopewell who would have been incensed but when she and the girl happened to be out of the house together, she would say something and add the name Hulga to the end of it, and the big spectacled Joy-Hulga would scowl and redden as if her privacy had been intruded upon. She considered the name her personal affair. She had arrived at it first purely on the basis of its ugly sound and then the full genius of its fitness had struck her. She had a vision of the name working like the ugly sweating Vulcan[1] who stayed in the furnace and to whom, presumably, the goddess

1. Roman god of fire whom Venus, goddess of love, "presumably" (a few words later) obeyed as her consort.

had to come when called. She saw it as the name of her highest creative act. One of her major triumphs was that her mother had not been able to turn her dust into Joy, but the greater one was that she had been able to turn it herself into Hulga. However, Mrs. Freeman's relish for using the name only irritated her. It was as if Mrs. Freeman's beady steel-pointed eyes had penetrated far enough behind her face to reach some secret fact. Something about her seemed to fascinate Mrs. Freeman and then one day Hulga realized that it was the artificial leg. Mrs. Freeman had a special fondness for the details of secret infections, hidden deformities, assaults upon children. Of diseases, she preferred the lingering or incurable. Hulga had heard Mrs. Hopewell give her the details of the hunting accident, how the leg had been literally blasted off, how she had never lost consciousness. Mrs. Freeman could listen to it any time as if it had happened an hour ago.

When Hulga stumped into the kitchen in the morning (she could walk without making the awful noise but she made it—Mrs. Hopewell was certain—because it was ugly-sounding), she glanced at them and did not speak. Mrs. Hopewell would be in her red kimono with her hair tied around her head in rags. She would be sitting at the table, finishing her breakfast and Mrs. Freeman would be hanging by her elbow outward from the refrigerator, looking down at the table. Hulga always put her eggs on the stove to boil and then stood over them with her arms folded, and Mrs. Hopewell would look at her— a kind of indirect gaze divided between her and Mrs. Freeman—and would think that if she would only keep herself up a little, she wouldn't be so bad looking. There was nothing wrong with her face that a pleasant expression wouldn't help. Mrs. Hopewell said that people who looked on the bright side of things would be beautiful even if they were not.

Whenever she looked at Joy this way, she could not help but feel that it would have been better if the child had not taken the Ph.D. It had certainly not brought her out any and now that she had it, there was no more excuse for her to go to school again. Mrs. Hopewell thought it was nice for girls to go to school to have a good time but Joy had "gone through." Anyhow, she would not have been strong enough to go again. The doctors had told Mrs. Hopewell that with the best of care, Joy might see forty-five. She had a weak heart. Joy had made it plain that if it had not been for this condition, she would be far from these red hills and good country people. She would be in a university lecturing to people who knew what she was talking about. And Mrs. Hopewell could very well picture her there, looking like a scarecrow and lecturing to more of the same. Here she went about all day in a six-year-old skirt and a yellow sweat shirt with a faded cowboy on a horse embossed on it. She thought this was funny; Mrs. Hopewell thought it was idiotic and showed simply that she was still a child. She was brilliant but she didn't have a grain of sense. It seemed to Mrs. Hopewell that every year she grew less like other people and more like herself—bloated, rude, and squint-eyed. And she said such strange things! To her own mother she had said—without warning, without excuse, standing up in the middle of a meal with her face purple and her mouth half full—"Woman! do you ever look inside? Do you ever look inside and see what you are *not*? God!" she had cried sinking down again and staring at her plate, "Malebranche[2] was right: we are not our own light. We are not our own light!"

2. Nicolas Malebranche, French philosopher (1638–1715).

Mrs. Hopewell had no idea to this day what brought that on. She had only made the remark, hoping Joy would take it in, that a smile never hurt anyone.

The girl had taken the Ph.D. in philosophy and this left Mrs. Hopewell at a complete loss. You could say, "My daughter is a nurse," or "My daughter is a schoolteacher," or even, "My daughter is a chemical engineer." You could not say, "My daughter is a philosopher." That was something that had ended with the Greeks and Romans. All day Joy sat on her neck in a deep chair, reading. Sometimes she went for walks but she didn't like dogs or cats or birds or flowers or nature or nice young men. She looked at nice young men as if she could smell their stupidity.

One day Mrs. Hopewell had picked up one of the books the girl had just put down and opening it at random, she read, "Science, on the other hand, has to assert its soberness and seriousness afresh and declare that it is concerned solely with what-is. Nothing—how can it be for science anything but a horror and a phantasm? If science is right, then one thing stands firm: science wishes to know nothing of nothing. Such is after all the strictly scientific approach to Nothing. We know it by wishing to know nothing of Nothing." These words had been underlined with a blue pencil and they worked on Mrs. Hopewell like some evil incantation in gibberish. She shut the book quickly and went out of the room as if she were having a chill.

This morning when the girl came in, Mrs. Freeman was on Carramae. "She thrown up four times after supper," she said, "and was up twict in the night after three o'clock. Yesterday she didn't do nothing but ramble in the bureau drawer. All she did. Stand up there and see what she could run up on."

"She's got to eat," Mrs. Hopewell muttered, sipping her coffee, while she watched Joy's back at the stove. She was wondering what the child had said to the Bible salesman. She could not imagine what kind of a conversation she could possibly have had with him.

He was a tall gaunt hatless youth who had called yesterday to sell them a Bible. He had appeared at the door, carrying a large black suitcase that weighted him so heavily on one side that he had to brace himself against the door facing. He seemed on the point of collapse but he said in a cheerful voice, "Good morning, Mrs. Cedars!" and set the suitcase down on the mat. He was not a bad-looking young man though he had on a bright blue suit and yellow socks that were not pulled up far enough. He had prominent face bones and a streak of sticky-looking brown hair falling across his forehead.

"I'm Mrs. Hopewell," she said.

"Oh!" he said, pretending to look puzzled but with his eyes sparkling, "I saw it said 'The Cedars' on the mailbox so I thought you was Mrs. Cedars!" and he burst out in a pleasant laugh. He picked up the satchel and under cover of a pant, he fell forward into her hall. It was rather as if the suitcase had moved first, jerking him after it. "Mrs. Hopewell!" he said and grabbed her hand. "I hope you are well!" and he laughed again and then all at once his face sobered completely. He paused and gave her a straight earnest look and said, "Lady, I've come to speak of serious things."

"Well, come in," she muttered, none too pleased because her dinner was almost ready. He came into the parlor and sat down on the edge of a straight chair and put the suitcase between his feet and glanced around the room as if he were sizing her up by it. Her silver gleamed on the two sideboards; she decided he had never been in a room as elegant as this.

"Mrs. Hopewell," he began, using her name in a way that sounded almost intimate, "I know you believe in Christian service."

"Well yes," she murmured.

"I know," he said and paused, looking very wise with his head cocked on one side, "that you're a good woman. Friends have told me."

Mrs. Hopewell never liked to be taken for a fool. "What are you selling?" she asked.

"Bibles," the young man said and his eye raced around the room before he added, "I see you have no family Bible in your parlor. I see that is the one lack you got!"

Mrs. Hopewell could not say, "My daughter is an atheist and won't let me keep the Bible in the parlor." She said, stiffening slightly, "I keep my Bible by my bedside." This was not the truth. It was in the attic somewhere.

"Lady," he said, "the word of God ought to be in the parlor."

"Well, I think that's a matter of taste," she began. "I think. . . ."

"Lady," he said, "for a Christian, the word of God ought to be in every room in the house besides in his heart. I know you're a Christian because I can see it in every line of your face."

She stood up and said, "Well, young man, I don't want to buy a Bible and I smell my dinner burning."

He didn't get up. He began to twist his hands and looking down at them, he said softly, "Well lady, I'll tell you the truth—not many people want to buy one nowadays and besides, I know I'm real simple. I don't know how to say a thing but to say it. I'm just a country boy." He glanced up into her unfriendly face. "People like you don't like to fool with country people like me!"

"Why!" she cried, "good country people are the salt of the earth! Besides, we all have different ways of doing, it takes all kinds to make the world go 'round. That's life!"

"You said a mouthful," he said.

"Why, I think there aren't enough good country people in the world!" she said, stirred. "I think that's what's wrong with it!"

His face had brightened. "I didn't introduce myself," he said. "I'm Manley Pointer from out in the country around Willohobie, not even from a place, just from near a place."

"You wait a minute," she said. "I have to see about my dinner." She went out to the kitchen and found Joy standing near the door where she had been listening.

"Get rid of the salt of the earth," she said, "and let's eat."

Mrs. Hopewell gave her a pained look and turned the heat down under the vegetables. "I can't be rude to anybody," she murmured and went back into the parlor.

He had opened the suitcase and was sitting with a Bible on each knee.

"You might as well put those up," she told him. "I don't want one."

"I appreciate your honesty," he said. "You don't see any more real honest people unless you go away out in the country."

"I know," she said, "real genuine folks!" Through the crack in the door she heard a groan.

"I guess a lot of boys come telling you they're working their way through college," he said, "but I'm not going to tell you that. Somehow," he said, "I don't want to go to college. I want to devote my life to Christian service. See,"

he said, lowering his voice, "I got this heart condition. I may not live long. When you know it's something wrong with you and you may not live long, well then, lady . . . " He paused, with his mouth open, and stared at her.

He and Joy had the same condition! She knew that her eyes were filling with tears but she collected herself quickly and murmured, "Won't you stay for dinner? We'd love to have you!" and was sorry the instant she heard herself say it.

"Yes mam," he said in an abashed voice, "I would sher love to do that!"

Joy had given him one look on being introduced to him and then through-out the meal had not glanced at him again. He had addressed several remarks to her, which she had pretended not to hear. Mrs. Hopewell could not under-stand deliberate rudeness, although she lived with it, and she felt she had al-ways to overflow with hospitality to make up for Joy's lack of courtesy. She urged him to talk about himself and he did. He said he was the seventh child of twelve and that his father had been crushed under a tree when he himself was eight year old. He had been crushed very badly, in fact, almost cut in two and was practically not recognizable. His mother had got along the best she could by hard working and she had always seen that her children went to Sunday School and that they read the Bible every evening. He was now nine-teen year old and he had been selling Bibles for four months. In that time he had sold seventy-seven Bibles and had the promise of two more sales. He wanted to become a missionary because he thought that was the way you could do most for people. "He who losest his life shall find it,"[3] he said simply and he was so sincere, so genuine and earnest that Mrs. Hopewell would not for the world have smiled. He prevented his peas from sliding onto the table by blocking them with a piece of bread which he later cleaned his plate with. She could see Joy observing sidewise how he handled his knife and fork and she saw too that every few minutes, the boy would dart a keen appraising glance at the girl as if he were trying to attract her attention.

After dinner Joy cleared the dishes off the table and disappeared and Mrs. Hopewell was left to talk with him. He told her again about his childhood and his father's accident and about various things that had happened to him. Every five minutes or so she would stifle a yawn. He sat for two hours until fi-nally she told him she must go because she had an appointment in town. He packed his Bibles and thanked her and prepared to leave, but in the doorway he stopped and wrung her hand and said that not on any of his trips had he met a lady as nice as her and he asked if he could come again. She had said she would always be happy to see him.

Joy had been standing in the road, apparently looking at something in the distance, when he came down the steps toward her, bent to the side with his heavy valise. He stopped where she was standing and confronted her directly. Mrs. Hopewell could not hear what he said but she trembled to think what Joy would say to him. She could see that after a minute Joy said something and that then the boy began to speak again, making an excited gesture with his free hand. After a minute Joy said something else at which the boy began to speak once more. Then to her amazement, Mrs. Hopewell saw the two of them walk off together, toward the gate. Joy had walked all the way to the gate

3. Quoting Jesus (Matthew 16:25).

with him and Mrs. Hopewell could not imagine what they had said to each other, and she had not yet dared to ask.

Mrs. Freeman was insisting upon her attention. She had moved from the refrigerator to the heater so that Mrs. Hopewell had to turn and face her in order to seem to be listening. "Glynese gone out with Harvey Hill again last night," she said. "She had th s sty."

"Hill," Mrs. Hopewell said absently, "is that the one who works in the garage?"

"Nome, he's the one that goes to chiropracter school," Mrs. Freeman said. "She had this sty. Been had it two days. So she says when he brought her in the other night he says, 'Lemme get rid of that sty for you,' and she says, 'How?' and he says, 'You just lay yourself down acrost the seat of that car and I'll show you.' So she done it and he popped her neck. Kept on a-popping it several times until she made him quit. This morning," Mrs. Freeman said, "she ain't got no sty. She ain't got no traces of a sty."

"I never heard of that before," Mrs. Hopewell said.

"He ast her to marry him before the Ordinary,"[4] Mrs. Freeman went on, "and she told him she wasn't going to be married in no *office*."

"Well, Glynese is a fine girl," Mrs. Hopewell said. "Glynese and Carramae are both fine girls."

"Carramae said when her and Lyman was married Lyman said it sure felt sacred to him. She said he said he wouldn't take five hundred dollars for being married by a preacher."

"How much would he take?" the girl asked from the stove.

"He said he wouldn't take five hundred dollars," Mrs. Freeman repeated.

"Well we all have work to do," Mrs. Hopewell said.

"Lyman said it just felt more sacred to him," Mrs. Freeman said. "The doctor wants Carramae to eat prunes. Says instead of medicine. Says them cramps is coming from pressure. You know where I think it is?"

"She'll be better in a few weeks," Mrs. Hopewell said.

"In the tube,"[5] Mrs. Freeman said. "Else she wouldn't be as sick as she is."

Hulga had cracked her two eggs into a saucer and was bringing them to the table along with a cup of coffee that she had filled too full. She sat down carefully and began to eat, meaning to keep Mrs Freeman there by questions if for any reason she showed an inclination to leave. She could perceive her mother's eye on her. The first round-about question would be about the Bible salesman and she did not wish to bring it on. "How did he pop her neck?" she asked.

Mrs. Freeman went into a description of how he had popped her neck. She said he owned a 55 Mercury but that Glynese said she would rather marry a man with only a '36 Plymouth who would be married by a preacher. The girl asked what if he had a '32 Plymouth and Mrs. Freeman said what Glynese had said was a '36 Plymouth.

Mrs. Hopewell said there were not many girls with Glynese's common sense. She said what she admired in those girls was their common sense. She said that reminded her that they had had a nice visitor yesterday, a young man selling Bibles. "Lord" she said, "he bored me to death but he was so sincere

4. Justice of the peace who performs the marriage ceremony in his or her chambers rather than in public. 5. I.e., in the fallopian tube (an ectopic pregnancy).

and genuine I couldn't be rude to him. He was just good country people, you know," she said, "—just the salt of the earth."

"I seen him walk up," Mrs. Freeman said, "and then later—I seen him walk off," and Hulga could feel the slight shift in her voice, the slight insinuation, that he had not walked off alone, had he? Her face remained expressionless but the color rose into her neck and she seemed to swallow it down with the next spoonful of egg. Mrs. Freeman was looking at her as if they had a secret together.

"Well, it takes all kinds of people to make the world go 'round," Mrs. Hopewell said. "It's very good we aren't all alike."

"Some people are more alike than others," Mrs. Freeman said.

Hulga got up and stumped, with about twice the noise that was necessary, into her room and locked the door. She was to meet the Bible salesman at ten o'clock at the gate. She had thought about it half the night. She had started thinking of it as a great joke and then she had begun to see profound implications in it. She had lain in bed imagining dialogues for them that were insane on the surface but that reached below to depths that no Bible salesman would be aware of. Their conversation yesterday had been of this kind.

He had stopped in front of her and had simply stood there. His face was bony and sweaty and bright, with a little pointed nose in the center of it, and his look was different from what it had been at the dinner table. He was gazing at her with open curiosity, with fascination, like a child watching a new fantastic animal at the zoo, and he was breathing as if he had run a great distance to reach her. His gaze seemed somehow familiar but she could not think where she had been regarded with it before. For almost a minute he didn't say anything. Then on what seemed an insuck of breath, he whispered, "You ever ate a chicken that was two days old?"

The girl looked at him stonily. He might have just put this question up for consideration at the meeting of a philosophical association. "Yes," she presently replied as if she had considered it from all angles.

"It must have been mighty small!" he said triumphantly and shook all over with little nervous giggles, getting very red in the face, and subsiding finally into his gaze of complete admiration, while the girl's expression remained exactly the same.

"How old are you?" he asked softly.

She waited some time before she answered. Then in a flat voice she said, "Seventeen."

His smiles came in succession like waves breaking on the surface of a little lake. "I see you got a wooden leg," he said. "I think you're brave. I think you're real sweet."

The girl stood blank and solid and silent.

"Walk to the gate with me," he said. "You're a brave sweet little thing and I liked you the minute I seen you walk in the door."

Hulga began to move forward.

"What's your name?" he asked, smiling down on the top of her head.

"Hulga," she said.

"Hulga," he murmured, "Hulga. Hulga. I never heard of anybody name Hulga before. You're shy, aren't you, Hulga?" he asked.

She nodded, watching his large red hand on the handle of the giant valise.

"I like girls that wear glasses," he said. "I think a lot. I'm not like these people that a serious thought don't ever enter their heads. It's because I may die."

"I may die too," she said suddenly and looked up at him. His eyes were very small and brown, glittering feverishly.

"Listen," he said, "don't you think some people was meant to meet on account of what all they got in common and all? Like they both think serious thoughts and all?" He shifted the valise to his other hand so that the hand nearest her was free. He caught hold of her elbow and shook it a little. "I don't work on Saturday," he said. "I like to walk in the woods and see what Mother Nature is wearing. O'er the hills and far away. Pic-nics and things. Couldn't we go on a pic-nic tomorrow? Say yes, Hulga," he said and gave her a dying look as if he felt his insides about to drop out of him. He had even seemed to sway slightly toward her.

During the night she had imagined that she seduced him. She imagined that the two of them walked on the place until they came to the storage barn beyond the two back fields and there, she imagined, that things came to such a pass that she very easily seduced him and that then, of course, she had to reckon with his remorse. True genius can get an idea across even to an inferior mind. She imagined that she took his remorse in hand and changed it into a deeper understanding of life. She took all his shame away and turned it into something useful.

She set off for the gate at exactly ten o'clock, escaping without drawing Mrs. Hopewell's attention. She didn't take anything to eat, forgetting that food is usually taken on a picnic. She wore a pair of slacks and a dirty white shirt, and as an afterthought, she had put some Vapex on the collar of it since she did not own any perfume. When she reached the gate no one was there.

She looked up and down the empty highway and had the furious feeling that she had been tricked, that he had only meant to make her walk to the gate after the idea of him. Then suddenly he stood up, very tall, from behind a bush on the opposite embankment. Smiling, he lifted his hat which was new and wide-brimmed. He had not worn it yesterday and she wondered if he had bought it for the occasion. It was toast-colored with a red and white band around it and was slightly too large for him. He stepped from behind the bush still carrying the black valise. He had on the same suit and the same yellow socks sucked down in his shoes from walking. He crossed the highway and said, "I knew you'd come!"

The girl wondered acidly how he had known this. She pointed to the valise and asked, "Why did you bring your Bibles?"

He took her elbow, smiling down on her as if he could not stop. "You can never tell when you'll need the word of God, Hulga," he said. She had a moment in which she doubted that this was actually happening and then they began to climb the embankment. They went down into the pasture toward the woods. The boy walked lightly by her side, bouncing on his toes. The valise did not seem to be heavy today; he even swung it. They crossed half the pasture without saying anything and then, putting his hand easily on the small of her back, he asked softly, "Where does your wooden leg join on?"

She turned an ugly red and glared at him and for an instant the boy looked abashed. "I didn't mean you no harm," he said. "I only meant you're so brave and all. I guess God takes care of you."

"No," she said, looking forward and walking fast, "I don't even believe in God."

At this he stopped and whistled. "No!" he exclaimed as if he were too astonished to say anything else.

She walked on and in a second he was bouncing at her side, fanning with his hat. "That's very unusual for a girl," he remarked, watching her out of the corner of his eye. When they reached the edge of the wood, he put his hand on her back again and drew her against him without a word and kissed her heavily.

The kiss, which had more pressure than feeling behind it, produced that extra surge of adrenalin in the girl that enables one to carry a packed trunk out of a burning house, but in her, the power went at once to the brain. Even before he released her, her mind, clear and detached and ironic anyway, was regarding him from a great distance, with amusement but with pity. She had never been kissed before and she was pleased to discover that it was an unexceptional experience and all a matter of the mind's control. Some people might enjoy drain water if they were told it was vodka. When the boy, looking expectant but uncertain, pushed her gently away, she turned and walked on, saying nothing as if such business, for her, were common enough.

He came along panting at her side, trying to help her when he saw a root that she might trip over. He caught and held back the long swaying blades of thorn vine until she had passed beyond them. She led the way and he came breathing heavily behind her. Then they came out on a sunlit hillside, sloping softly into another one a little smaller. Beyond, they could see the rusted top of the old barn where the extra hay was stored.

The hill was sprinkled with small pink weeds. "Then you ain't saved?" he asked suddenly, stopping.

The girl smiled. It was the first time she had smiled at him at all. "In my economy," she said, "I'm saved and you are damned but I told you I didn't believe in God."

Nothing seemed to destroy the boy's look of admiration. He gazed at her now as if the fantastic animal at the zoo had put its paw through the bars and given him a loving poke. She thought he looked as if he wanted to kiss her again and she walked on before he had the chance.

"Ain't there somewheres we can sit down sometime?" he murmured, his voice softening toward the end of the sentence.

"In that barn," she said.

They made for it rapidly as if it might slide away like a train. It was a large two-story barn, cool and dark inside. The boy pointed up the ladder that led into the loft and said, "It's too bad we can't go up there."

"Why can't we?" she asked.

"Yer leg," he said reverently.

The girl gave him a contemptuous look and putting both hands on the ladder, she climbed it while he stood below, apparently awe-struck. She pulled herself expertly through the opening and then looked down at him and said, "Well, come on if you're coming," and he began to climb the ladder, awkwardly bringing the suitcase with him.

"We won't need the Bible," she observed.

"You never can tell," he said, panting. After he had got into the loft, he was a few seconds catching his breath. She had sat down in a pile of straw. A wide sheath of sunlight, filled with dust particles, slanted over her. She lay back against a bale, her face turned away, looking out the front opening of the barn where hay was thrown from a wagon into the loft. The two pink-speckled hillsides lay back against a dark ridge of woods. The sky was cloudless and cold

blue. The boy dropped down by her side and put one arm under her and the other over her and began methodically kissing her face, making little noises like a fish. He did not remove his hat but it was pushed far enough back not to interfere. When her glasses got in his way, he took them off of her and slipped them into his pocket.

The girl at first did not return any of the kisses but presently she began to and after she had put several on his cheek, she reached his lips and remained there, kissing him again and again as if she were trying to draw all the breath out of him. His breath was clear and sweet like a child's and the kisses were sticky like a child's. He mumbled about loving her and about knowing when he first seen her that he loved her, but the mumbling was like the sleepy fretting of a child being put to sleep by his mother. Her mind, throughout this, never stopped or lost itself for a second to her feelings. "You ain't said you loved me none," he whispered finally, pulling back from her. "You got to say that."

She looked away from him off into the hollow sky and then down at a black ridge and then down farther into what appeared to be two green swelling lakes. She didn't realize he had taken her glasses but this landscape could not seem exceptional to her for she seldom paid any close attention to her surroundings.

"You got to say it," he repeated. "You got to say you love me."

She was always careful how she committed herself. "In a sense," she began, "if you use the word loosely, you might say that. But it's not a word I use. I don't have illusions. I'm one of those people who see through to nothing."

The boy was frowning. "You got to say it. I said it and you got to say it," he said.

The girl looked at him almost tenderly. "You poor baby," she murmured. "It's just as well you don't understand," and she pulled him by the neck, facedown, against her. "We are all damned," she said, "but some of us have taken off our blindfolds and see that there's nothing to see. It's a kind of salvation."

The boy's astonished eyes looked blankly through the ends of her hair. "Okay," he almost whined, "but do you love me or don'tcher?"

"Yes," she said and added, "in a sense. But I must tell you something. There mustn't be anything dishonest between us." She lifted his head and looked him in the eye. "I am thirty years old," she said. "I have a number of degrees."

The boy's look was irritated but dogged. "I don't care," he said. "I don't care a thing about what all you done. I just want to know if you love me or don'tcher?" and he caught her to him and wildly planted her face with kisses until she said, "Yes, yes."

"Okay then," he said, letting her go. "Prove it."

She smiled, looking dreamily out on the shifty landscape. She had seduced him without even making up her mind to try. "How?" she asked, feeling that he should be delayed a little.

He leaned over and put his lips to her ear. "Show me where your wooden leg joins on," he whispered.

The girl uttered a sharp little cry and her face instantly drained of color. The obscenity of the suggestion was not what shocked her. As a child she had sometimes been subject to feelings of shame but education had removed the last traces of that as a good surgeon scrapes for cancer; she would no more have felt it over what he was asking than she would have believed in his Bible. But she was as sensitive about the artificial leg as a peacock about his tail. No

one ever touched it but her. She took care of it as someone else would his soul, in private and almost with her own eyes turned away. "No," she said.

"I known it," he muttered, sitting up. "You're just playing me for a sucker."

"Oh no no!" she cried. "It joins on at the knee. Only at the knee. Why do you want to see it?"

The boy gave her a long penetrating look. "Because," he said, "it's what makes you different. You ain't like anybody else."

She sat staring at him. There was nothing about her face or her round freezing-blue eyes to indicate that this had moved her; but she felt as if her heart had stopped and left her mind to pump her blood. She decided that for the first time in her life she was face to face with real innocence. This boy, with an instinct that came from beyond wisdom, had touched the truth about her. When after a minute, she said in a hoarse high voice, "All right," it was like surrendering to him completely. It was like losing her own life and finding it again, miraculously, in his.

Very gently he began to roll the slack leg up. The artificial limb, in a white sock and brown flat shoe, was bound in a heavy material like canvas and ended in an ugly jointure where it was attached to the stump. The boy's face and his voice were entirely reverent as he uncovered it and said, "Now show me how to take it off and on."

She took it off for him and put it back on again and then he took it off himself, handling it as tenderly as if it were a real one. "See!" he said with a delighted child's face. "Now I can do it myself!"

"Put it back on," she said. She was thinking that she would run away with him and that every night he would take the leg off and every morning put it back on again. "Put it back on," she said.

"Not yet," he murmured, setting it on its foot out of her reach. "Leave it off for a while. You got me instead."

She gave a little cry of alarm but he pushed her down and began to kiss her again. Without the leg she felt entirely dependent on him. Her brain seemed to have stopped thinking altogether and to be about some other function that it was not very good at. Different expressions raced back and forth over her face. Every now and then the boy, his eyes like two steel spikes, would glance behind him where the leg stood. Finally she pushed him off and said, "Put it back on me now."

"Wait," he said. He leaned the other way and pulled the valise toward him and opened it. It had a pale blue spotted lining and there were only two Bibles in it. He took one of these out and opened the cover of it. It was hollow and contained a pocket flask of whiskey, a pack of cards, and a small blue box with printing on it. He laid these out in front of her one at a time in an evenly-spaced row, like one presenting offerings at the shrine of a goddess. He put the blue box in her hand. THIS PRODUCT TO BE USED ONLY FOR THE PREVENTION OF DISEASE,[6] she read, and dropped it. The boy was unscrewing the top of the flask. He stopped and pointed, with a smile, to the deck of cards. It was not an ordinary deck but one with an obscene picture on the back of each card. "Take a swig," he said, offering her the bottle first. He held it in front of her, but like one mesmerized, she did not move.

6. Label once commonly found on condom boxes.

Her voice when she spoke had an almost pleading sound. "Aren't you," she murmured, "aren't you just good country people?"

The boy cocked his head. He looked as if he were just beginning to understand that she might be trying to insult him. "Yeah," he said, curling his lip slightly, "but it ain't held me back none. I'm as good as you any day in the week."

"Give me my leg," she said.

He pushed it farther away with his foot. "Come on now, let's begin to have us a good time," he said coaxingly. "We ain't got to know one another good yet."

"Give me my leg!" she screamed and tried to lunge for it but he pushed her down easily.

"What's the matter with you all of a sudden?" he asked, frowning as he screwed the top on the flask and put it quickly back inside the Bible. "You just a while ago said you didn't believe in nothing. I thought you was some girl!"

Her face was almost purple. "You're a Christian!" she hissed. "You're a fine Christian! You're just like them all—say one thing and do another. You're a perfect Christian, you're . . ."

The boy's mouth was set angrily. "I hope you don't think," he said in a lofty indignant tone, "that I believe in that crap! I may sell Bibles but I know which end is up and I wasn't born yesterday and I know where I'm going!"

"Give me my leg!" she screeched. He jumped up so quickly that she barely saw him sweep the cards and the blue box into the Bible and throw the Bible into the valise. She saw him grab the leg and then she saw it for an instant slanted forlornly across the inside of the suitcase with a Bible at either side of its opposite ends. He slammed the lid shut and snatched up the valise and swung it down the hole and then stepped through himself.

When all of him had passed but his head he turned and regarded her with a look that no longer had any admiration in it. "I've gotten a lot of interesting things," he said. "One time I got a woman's glass eye this way. And you needn't to think you'll catch me because Pointer ain't really my name. I use a different name at every house I call at and don't stay nowhere long. And I'll tell you another thing, Hulga," he said, using the name as if he didn't think much of it, "you ain't so smart. I been believing in nothing ever since I was born!" and then the toast-colored hat disappeared down the hole and the girl was left, sitting on the straw in the dusty sunlight. When she turned her churning face toward the opening, she saw his blue figure struggling successfully over the green speckled lake.

Mrs. Hopewell and Mrs. Freeman, who were in the back pasture, digging up onions, saw him emerge a little later from the woods and head across the meadow toward the highway. "Why, that looks like that nice dull young man that tried to sell me a Bible yesterday," Mrs. Hopewell said, squinting. "He must have been selling them to the Negroes back in there. He was so simple," he said, "but I guess the world would be better off if we were all that simple."

Mrs. Freeman's gaze drove forward and just touched him before he disappeared under the hill. Then she returned her attention to the evil-smelling onion shoot she was lifting from the ground. "Some can't be that simple," she said. "I know I never could."

CAROLYN KIZER

1925–

"From Sappho to myself, consider the fate of women," wrote Carolyn Kizer in 1963, adding, with characteristically acerbic irony, "How unwomanly to discuss it!" Yet "discuss it" Kizer has, in six volumes—*The Ungrateful Garden* (1961), *Knock upon Silence* (1965), *Midnight Was My Cry* (1971), *Yin* (1984), *Mermaids in the Basement* (1984), and *The Nearness of You* (1986)—that are marked by keen attention to the vicissitudes experienced by women who, like Kizer herself, "must act as handmaidens / To our own goddess." More recently she has produced a book of translations, *Carrying Over: Poems from the Chinese, Urdu, Macedonian, Yiddish, and French African* (1988); a volume of essays, *Proses: On Poems and Poets* (1993); and an anthology, *One Hundred Great Poems by Women* (1995).

Born in Spokane, Washington, in 1925, Kizer graduated from Sarah Lawrence College in 1945. Subsequently, she traveled widely in China and Japan, translating Tu Fu and other Chinese poets whose terse urbanity was an important influence on her style. Married and the mother of three children, she helped found the prestigious verse journal *Poetry Northwest* in 1959, then was for seven years its editor in chief. In 1966, she was director of literary programs for the National Endowment for the Arts. More recently, she has taught verse writing at many colleges and universities throughout the country, and in 1985, she won the Pulitzer Prize for *Yin*. Throughout her crowded career, she has spoken often and frankly about women of letters, explaining that "I'm in the racket." Sometimes jauntily colloquial in its phrasing, sometimes suavely elegant in its formulation, her tough wisdom is consistently based on the knowledge that women writers "are the custodians of the world's best-kept secret: / Merely the private lives of one-half of humanity."

From Pro Femina[1]

Three

I will speak about women of letters, for I'm in the racket.
Our biggest successes to date? Old maids to a woman.
And our saddest conspicuous failures? The married spinsters
On loan to the husbands they treated like surrogate fathers.
Think of that crew of self-pitiers, not-very-distant, 5
Who carried the torch for themselves and got first-degree burns.
Or the sad sonneteers, toast-and-teasdales[2] we loved at thirteen;
Middle-aged virgins seducing the puerile anthologists
Through lust-of-the-mind; barbiturate-drenched Camilles[3]
With continuous periods, murmuring softly on sofas 10
When poetry wasn't a craft but a sickly effluvium,
The air thick with incense, musk, and emotional blackmail.

I suppose they reacted from an earlier womanly modesty
When too many girls were scabs[4] to their stricken sisterhood,

1. For the woman (Latin).
2. Punning reference to Sara Teasdale (1844–1933), American poet who wrote slight, sensitive verses.
3. Camille is the repentant courtesan in *La Dame aux Camellias*, (1852), by the younger Alexandre Dumas.
4. Those who work while others (in the same jobs) are striking.

Impugning our sex to stay in good with the men, 15
Commencing their insecure bluster. How they must have swaggered
When women themselves indorsed their own inferiority!
Vestals, vassals[5] and vessels, rolled into several,
They took notes in rolling syllabics, in careful journals,
Aiming to please a posterity that despises them. 20
But we'll always have traitors who swear that a woman surrenders
Her Supreme Function, by equating Art with aggression
And failure with Femininity. Still, it's just as unfair
To equate Art with Femininity, like a prettily-packaged commodity
When we are the custodians of the world's best-kept secret: 25
Merely the private lives of one-half of humanity.

But even with masculine dominance, we mares and mistresses
Produced some sleek saboteuses, making their cracks
Which the porridge-brained males of the day were too thick to perceive.
Mistaking young hornets for perfectly harmless bumblebees. 30
Being thought innocuous rouses some women to frenzy;
They try to be ugly by aping the ways of the men
And succeed. Swearing, sucking cigars and scorching the bedspread,
Slopping straight shots, eyes blotted, vanity-blown
In the expectation of glory: *she writes like a man!* 35
This drives other women mad in a mist of chiffon
(one poetess draped her gauze over red flannels, a practical feminist).

But we're emerging from all that, more or less,
Except for some lady-like laggards and Quarterly[6] priestesses
Who flog men for fun, and kick women to maim competition. 40
Now, if we struggle abnormally, we may almost seem normal;
If we submerge our self-pity in disciplined industry;
If we stand up and be hated, and swear not to sleep with editors;
If we regard ourselves formally, respecting our true limitations
Without making an unseemly show of trying to unfreeze our assets; 45
Keeping our heads and our pride while remaining unmarried
And if wedded, kill guilt in its tracks when we stack up the dishes
And defect to the typewriter. And if mothers, believe in the luck of
 our children,
Whom we forbid to devour us, whom we shall not devour,
And the luck of our husbands and lovers, who keep free women. 50

 1963, 1965

Semele[1] Recycled

After you left me forever,
I was broken into pieces,
and all the pieces flung into the river.

5. Person in service to a feudal lord. "Vestals": Roman
virgin priestesses
6. I.e., literary magazine.

1. In Greek myth, the beloved of Zeus and the mother
of Dionysus; she requested Zeus to appear in his radi-
ant divinity; when he did, she burned to death

Then the legs crawled ashore
and aimlessly wandered the dusty cow-track. 5
They became, for a while, a simple roadside shrine:
A tiny table set up between the thighs
held a dusty candle, weed, and fieldflower chains
placed reverently there by children and old women.
My knees were hung with tin triangular medals 10
to cure all forms of hysterical disease.

After I died forever in the river,
my torso floated, bloated in the stream,
catching on logs or stones among the eddies.
White water foamed around it, then dislodged it; 15
after a whirlwind trip, it bumped ashore.
A grizzled old man who scavenged along the banks
had already rescued my arms and put them by,
knowing everything has its uses, sooner or later.

When he found my torso, he called it his canoe, 20
and, using my arms as paddles,
he rowed me up and down the scummy river.
When catfish nibbled my fingers, he scooped them up
and blessed his re-usable bait.
Clumsy but serviceable, that canoe! 25
The trail of blood that was its wake
attracted the carp and eels, and the river turtle,
easily landed, dazed by my tasty red.

A young lad found my head among the rushes
and placed it on a dry stone. 30
He carefully combed my hair with a bit of shell
and set small offerings before it
which the birds and rats obligingly stole at night,
so it seemed I ate.
And the breeze wound through my mouth and empty sockets 35
so my lungs would sigh and my dead tongue mutter.

Attached to my throat like a sacred necklace
was a circlet of small snails.
Soon the villagers came to consult my oracular head
with its waterweed crown. 40
Seers found occupation, interpreting sighs,
and their papyrus rolls accumulated.

Meanwhile, young boys retrieved my eyes
they used for marbles in a simple game
—till somebody's pretty sister snatched at them 45
and set them, for luck, in her bridal diadem.
Poor girl! When her future groom caught sight of her,
all eyes, he crossed himself in horror,
and stumbled away in haste
through her dowered meadows. 50

What then of my heart and organs,
my sacred slit
which loved you best of all?
They were caught in a fisherman's net
and tossed at night into a pen for swine. 55
But they shone so by moonlight that the sows stampeded,
trampled each other in fear, to get away.
And the fisherman's wife, who had 13 living children
and was contemptuous of holy love,
raked the rest of me onto the compost heap. 60

Then in their various places and helpful functions,
the altar, oracle, offal, canoe, and oars
learned the wild rumor of your return.
The altar leapt up and ran to the canoe,
scattering candle grease and wilted grasses. 65
Arms sprang to their sockets, blind hands with nibbled nails
groped their way, aided by loud lamentation,
to the bed of the bride, snatched up those unlucky eyes
from her discarded veil and diadem,
and rammed them home. O what a bright day it was! 70
This empty body danced on the river bank.
Hollow, it called and searched among the fields
for those parts that steamed and simmered in the sun,
and never would have found them.

But then your great voice rang out under the skies 75
my name!—and all those private names
for the parts and places that had loved you best.
And they stirred in their nest of hay and dung.
The distraught old ladies chasing their lost altar,
and the seers pursuing my skull, their lost employment, 80
and the tumbling boys, who wanted the magic marbles,
and the runaway groom, and the fisherman's 13 children
set up such a clamor, with their cries of "Miracle!"
that our two bodies met like a thunderclap
in mid-day—right at the corner of that wretched field 85
with its broken fenceposts and startled, skinny cattle.
We fell in a heap on the compost heap
and all our loving parts made love at once,
while the bystanders cheered and prayed and hid their eyes
and then went decently about their business. 90

And here it is, moonlight again; we've bathed in the river
and are sweet and wholesome once more.
We kneel side by side in the sand;
we worship each other in whispers.
But the inner parts remember fermenting hay, 95
the comfortable odor of dung, the animal incense,
and passion, its bloody labor,
its birth and rebirth and decay.

 1984

MAXINE W. KUMIN

1925–

"Even though she is fascinated by and preoccupied with the irrational unconscious," the critic Sybil Estess has written of Maxine Kumin, "sanity and a conscious choice within and for life are essential keys to [her] voice." The observation is apt, for though she was the longtime best friend and poetic coworker of the troubled, "confessional" artist Anne Sexton—the two frequently analyzed and revised their poems together and collaborated on several children's books—Kumin is a very different sort of writer from Sexton. While she sometimes writes poems about pain and suffering, Kumin has a notable drive for survival along with a deep commitment to memorialize those elements of everyday life that enrich the existence of the artist and make survival possible. Children and kitchens, animals and vegetables, friends and family—these are the stuff of the poems in which she makes a redemptive choice for sanity.

Born in Philadelphia, Pennsylvania, Kumin earned B.A. and M.A. degrees from Radcliffe College and was married young to Victor M. Kumin, an engineering consultant, with whom she has had three children. At present, she and her husband live on a farm in New Hampshire, where she grows vegetables and breeds Arabian and quarter horses while writing both poetry and fiction. Her first collection, *Halfway*, appeared in 1961 and was followed in rapid succession by a number of other volumes, including five novels, three children's books coauthored with Sexton, the collection of poems—*Up Country* (1972)—for which she won the Pulitzer Prize in 1973, and more recently, *Looking for Luck* (1992). For two years a fellow at the Radcliffe Institute for Independent Study, she has also taught verse writing at a number of universities, including Columbia, Brandeis, and Princeton. Throughout this varied career, she has found ways to formulate a hopeful if skeptical vision: "Wherever we're going / is Monday morning. / Wherever we're coming from / is Mother's lap."

Making the Jam without You

for Judy

Old daughter, small traveler
asleep in a German featherbed
under the eaves in a postcard town
of turrets and towers,
I am putting a dream in your head. 5

Listen! Here it is afternoon.
The rain comes down like bullets.
I stand in the kitchen,
that harem of good smells
where we have bumped hips and 10
cracked the cupboards with our talk
while the stove top danced with pots
and it was not clear who did
the mothering. Now I am
crushing blackberries 15

to make the annual jam
in a white cocoon of steam.

Take it, my sleeper. Redo it
in any of your three
languages and nineteen years. 20
Change the geography.
Let there be a mountain,
the fat cows on it belled
like a cathedral. Let
there be someone beside you 25
as you come upon the ruins
of a schloss,[1] all overgrown
with a glorious thicket,
its brambles soft as wool.
Let him bring the buckets 30
crooked on his angel arms
and may the berries, vaster
than any forage in
the mild hills of New Hampshire,
drop in your pail, plum size, 35
heavy as the eyes
of an honest dog
and may you bear them
home together to a square
white unreconstructed kitchen 40
not unlike this one.

Now may your two heads
touch over the kettle,
over the blood of the berries
that drink up sugar and sun, 45
over that tar-thick boil
love cannot stir down.
More plainly than
the bric-a-brac of shelves
filling with jelly glasses, 50
more surely than
the light driving through them
trite as rubies, I see him
as pale as paraffin beside you.
I see you cutting 55
fresh baked bread to spread it
with the bright royal fur.

At this time
I lift the flap of your dream
and slip out thinner than a sliver 60
as your two mouths open
for the sweet stain of purple.

1970

1. Castle (German)

The Envelope

It is true, Martin Heidegger,[1] as you have written,
I *fear to cease*, even knowing that at the hour
of my death my daughters will absorb me, even
knowing they will carry me about forever
inside them, an arrested fetus, even as I carry 5
the ghost of my mother under my navel, a nervy
little androgynous person, a miracle
folded in lotus position.

Like those old pear-shaped Russian dolls that open
at the middle to reveal another and another, down 10
to the pea-sized, irreducible minim,
may we carry our mothers forth in our bellies.
May we, borne onward by our daughters, ride
in the Envelope of Almost-Infinity,
that chain letter good for the next twenty-five 15
thousand days of their lives.

1978

How It Is[2]

Shall I say how it is in your clothes?
A month after your death I wear your blue jacket.
The dog at the center of my life recognizes
you've come to visit, he's ecstatic.
In the left pocket, a hole. 5
In the right, a parking ticket
delivered up last August on Bay State Road.
In my heart, a scatter like milkweed,
a flinging from the pods of the soul.
My skin presses your old outline. 10
It is hot and dry inside.

I think of the last day of your life,
old friend, how I would unwind it, paste
it together in a different collage,
back from the death car idling in the garage, 15
back up the stairs, your praying hands unlaced,
reassembling the bits of bread and tuna fish
into a ceremony of sandwich,
running the home movie backward to a space
we could be easy in, a kitchen place 20
with vodka and ice, our words like living meat.

Dear friend, you have excited crowds
with your example. They swell

1. German existentialist philosopher (1889–1976), who wrote extensively on the fear of death.
2. The poem is addressed to Anne Sexton (1928–1974), poet and close friend of Kumin's who commited suicide by inhaling carbon monoxide fumes from her car.

like w ne bags, straining at your seams.
I will be years gathering up our words, 25
fishing out letters, snapshots, stains,
leaning my ribs against this durable cloth
to put on the dumb blue blazer of your death.

1978

MARGARET LAURENCE
1926–1987

One of Canada's foremost novelists, Margaret Laurence frequently set her fiction in a prairie town similar to the one in which she grew up, Neepawa, Manitoba. The granddaughter of Irish and Scottish settlers, Jean Margaret Wemyss lost her mother when she was four years old and her father when she was nine. Brought up by her mother's sister and her autocratic grandfather, John Simpson, she witnessed the devastating effects of the Depression and of World War II on the lives of her neighbors In 1944, a scholarship enabled her to leave for the United College in Winnipeg, where she majored in English and wrote for the college paper. After a brief st nt working as a reporter for *The Winnipeg Citizen*, she married Jack Laurence, a civil engineer, and they moved first to England and then to Africa. A *Tree for Poverty* (1954), *The Prophet's Camel Bell* (1963), and *The Tomorrow-Tar er* (1963), her earliest publications, reflect Laurence's seven years in Somali and Ghana: the first is a collection and translation of African folk tales; the second, a record of her life in British Somaliland; the third, a collection of short stories.

Although the Laurences returned to Canada just before Ghana achieved independence, five years later Margaret Laurence separated from her husband and moved with her daughter and son to England. By this time, she had established her reputation as a writer with her first novel, *This Side Jordan* (1960), and a number of prize-winning stories. Like expatriated writers from H. H. Richardson to Doris Lessing, Laurence began to mythologize her native land while she was living in another country, although in 1972 she did return to Canada, and in 1974, she settled permanently in Lakefield, Ontario, having accepted a writer-in-residence position at Trent University. Her series of interrelated novels and stories—*The Stone Angel* (1964), *The Fire-Dwellers* (1969), *A Bird in the House* (1970), and *The Diviners* (1974)—are set in the mythical Manitoba town of Manawaka. Laurence's characters—the ninety-year-old Hagar in *The Stone Angel*, for example, or the middle-aged single schoolteacher Rachel Cameron in *A Jest of God* (1966)—confront the crippling provincialism of small-town life with a courage that lends them a capacity for increased self-knowledge and for joy. A volume of personal and literary essays, *The Heart of a Stranger* (1976), was followed by a memoir, *Dance on the Earth* (1989), which was completed by her daughter after Laurence's death. *The Loons* is part of A *Bird in the House*, a series of autobiographical stories.

The Loons

Just below Manawaka, where the Wachakwa River ran brown and noisy over the pebbles, the scrub oak and gray-green willow and chokecherry bushes grew in a dense thicket. In a clearing at the center of the thicket stood the Tor nerre

family's shack. The basis of this dwelling was a small square cabin made of poplar poles and chinked with mud, which had been built by Jules Tonnerre some fifty years before, when he came back from Batoche with a bullet in his thigh, the year that Riel was hung and the voices of the Metis[1] entered their long silence. Jules had only intended to stay the winter in the Wachakwa Valley, but the family was still there in the thirties, when I was a child. As the Tonnerres had increased, their settlement had been added to, until the clearing at the foot of the town hill was a chaos of lean-tos, wooden packing cases, warped lumber, discarded car tires, ramshackle chicken coops, tangled strands of barbed wire and rusty tin cans.

The Tonnerres were French half-breeds, and among themselves they spoke a *patois* that was neither Cree[2] nor French. Their English was broken and full of obscenities. They did not belong among the Cree of the Galloping Mountain reservation, further north, and they did not belong among the Scots-Irish and Ukrainians of Manawaka, either. They were, as my Grandmother MacLeod would have put it, neither flesh, fowl, nor good salt herring. When their men were not working at odd jobs or as section hands on the C.P.R.,[3] they lived on relief. In the summers, one of the Tonnerre youngsters, with a face that seemed totally unfamiliar with laughter, would knock at the doors of the town's brick houses and offer for sale a lard-pail full of bruised wild strawberries, and if he got as much as a quarter he would grab the coin and run before the customer had time to change her mind. Sometimes old Jules, or his son Lazarus, would get mixed up in a Saturday-night brawl, and would hit out at whoever was nearest, or howl drunkenly among the offended shoppers on Main Street, and then the Mountie would put them for the night in the barred cell underneath the Court House, and the next morning they would be quiet again.

Piquette Tonnerre, the daughter of Lazarus, was in my class at school. She was older than I, but she had failed several grades, perhaps because her attendance had always been sporadic and her interest in schoolwork negligible. Part of the reason she had missed a lot of school was that she had had tuberculosis of the bone, and had once spent many months in hospital. I knew this because my father was the doctor who had looked after her. Her sickness was almost the only thing I knew about her, however. Otherwise, she existed for me only as a vaguely embarrassing presence, with her hoarse voice and her clumsy limping walk and her grimy cotton dresses that were always miles too long. I was neither friendly nor unfriendly towards her. She dwelt and moved somewhere within my scope of vision, but I did not actually notice her very much until that peculiar summer when I was eleven.

"I don't know what to do about that kid," my father said at dinner one evening. "Piquette Tonnerre, I mean. The damn bone's flared up again. I've had her in hospital for quite a while now, and it's under control all right, but I hate like the dickens to send her home again."

"Couldn't you explain to her mother that she has to rest a lot?" my mother said.

1. Persons of mixed American Indian and European, especially French, descent. Louis Riel (1844–1885), Canadian insurgent who was tried and hanged for treason in Saskatchewan.

2. The language of a native Indian group formerly living in Ontario.
3. Canada Pacific Railroad.

"The mother's not there," my father replied. "She took off a few years back. Can't say I blame her. Piquette cooks for them, and she says Lazarus would never do anything for himself as long as she's there. Anyway, I don't think she'd take much care of herself, once she got back. She's only thirteen, after all. Beth, I was thinking—what about taking her up to Diamond Lake with us this summer? A couple of months rest would give that bone a much better chance."

My mother looked stunned.

"But Ewen—what about Roddie and Vanessa?"

"She's not contagious," my father said. "And it would be company for Vanessa."

"Oh dear," my mother said in distress. "I'll bet anything she has nits[4] in her hair."

"For Pete's sake," my father said crossly, "do you think Matron would let her stay in the hospital for all this time like that? Don't be silly, Beth."

Grandmother MacLeod, her delicately featured face as rigid as a cameo, now brought her mauve-veined hands together as though she were about to begin a prayer.

"Ewen, if that half-breed youngster comes along to Diamond Lake, I'm not going," she announced. "I'll go to Morag's for the summer."

I had trouble in stifling my urge to laugh, for my mother brightened visibly and quickly tried to hide it. If it came to a choice between Grandmother MacLeod and Piquette, Piquette would win hands down, nits or not.

"It might be quite nice for you, at that," she mused. "You haven't seen Morag for over a year, and you might enjoy being in the city for a while. Well, Ewen dear, you do what you think best. If you think it would do Piquette some good, then we'll be glad to have her, as long as she behaves herself."

So it happened that several weeks later, when we all piled into my father's old Nash, surrounded by suit-cases and boxes of provisions and toys for my ten-month-old brother, Piquette was with us and Grandmother MacLeod, miraculously, was not. My father would only be staying at the cottage for a couple of weeks, for he had to get back to his practice, but the rest of us would stay at Diamond Lake until the end of August.

Our cottage was not named, as many were, "Dew Drop Inn" or "Bide-a-Wee," or "Bonnie Doon." The sign on the roadway bore in austere letters only our name, MacLeod. It was not a large cottage, but it was on the lakefront. You could look out the windows and see, through the filigree of the spruce trees, the water glistening greenly as the sun caught it. All around the cottage were ferns, and sharp-branched raspberry bushes, and moss that had grown over fallen tree trunks. If you looked carefully among the weeds and grass, you could find wild strawberry plants which were in white flower now and in another month would bear fruit, the fragrant globes hanging like miniature scarlet lanterns on the thin hairy stems. The two gray squirrels were still there, gossiping at us from the tall spruce beside the cottage, and by the end of the summer they would again be tame enough to take pieces of crust from my hands. The broad moose antlers that hung above the back door were a little more bleached and fissured after the winter, but otherwise everything was the same. I raced joyfully around my kingdom, greeting all the places I had not

4. The eggs of lice.

seen for a year. My brother, Roderick, who had not been born when we were here last summer, sat on the car rug in the sunshine and examined a brown spruce cone, meticulously turning it round and round in his small and curious hands. My mother and father toted the luggage from car to cottage, exclaiming over how well the place had wintered, no broken windows, thank goodness, no apparent damage from storm-felled branches or snow.

Only after I had finished looking around did I notice Piquette. She was sitting on the swing, her lame leg held stiffly out, and her other foot scuffing the ground as she swung slowly back and forth. Her long hair hung black and straight around her shoulders, and her broad coarse-featured face bore no expression—it was blank, as though she no longer dwelt within her own skull, as though she had gone elsewhere. I approached her very hesitantly.

"Want to come and play?"

Piquette looked at me with a sudden flash of scorn.

"I ain't a kid," she said.

Wounded, I stamped angrily away, swearing I would not speak to her for the rest of the summer. In the days that followed, however, Piquette began to interest me, and I began to want to interest her. My reasons did not appear bizarre to me. Unlikely as it may seem, I had only just realized that the Tonnerre family, whom I had always heard called half-breeds, were actually Indians, or as near as made no difference. My acquaintance with Indians was not extensive. I did not remember ever having seen a real Indian, and my new awareness that Piquette sprang from the people of Big Bear and Poundmaker, of Tecumseh, of the Iroquois who had eaten Father Brebeufs'[5] heart—all this gave her an instant attraction in my eyes. I was a devoted reader of Pauline Johnson at this age, and sometimes would orate aloud and in an exalted voice, *West Wind, blow from your prairie nest; Blow from the mountains, blow from the west*[6]—and so on. It seemed to me that Piquette must be in some way a daughter of the forest, a kind of junior prophetess of the wilds, who might impart to me, if I took the right approach, some of the secrets which she undoubtedly knew—where the whippoorwill made her nest, how the coyote reared her young, or whatever it was that it said in Hiawatha.[7]

I set about gaining Piquette's trust. She was not allowed to go swimming, with her bad leg, but I managed to lure her down to the beach—or rather, she came because there was nothing else to do. The water was always icy, for the lake was fed by springs, but I swam like a dog, thrashing my arms and legs around at such speed and with such an output of energy that I never grew cold. Finally, when I had had enough, I came out and sat beside Piquette on the sand. When she saw me approaching, her hand squashed flat the sand castle she had been building, and she looked at me sullenly, without speaking.

"Do you like this place?" I asked, after a while, intending to lead on from there into the question of forest lore.

Piquette shrugged. "It's okay. Good as anywhere."

"I love it," I said. "We come here every summer."

"So what?" Her voice was distant, and I glanced at her uncertainly, wondering what I could have said wrong.

5. Jean de Brebeuf (1593–1649), French missionary in North America, killed by Indians. Big Bear (1825–1888) and Poundmaker (1842–1886), leaders of the Cree. Tecumseh (1768?–1813), chief of the Shawnee.
6. The first two lines from *The Song My Paddle Sings* by Pauline Johnson (1861–1913), Canadian poet who was the daughter of an English woman and a Mohawk chief.
7. *The Song of Hiawatha*, a poem about the lives of American Indians by the American poet Henry Wadsworth Longfellow (1807–1882).

"Do you want to come for a walk?" I asked her. "We wouldn't need to go far. If you walk just around the point there, you come to a bay where great big reeds grow in the water, and all kinds of fish hang around there. Want to? Come on."

She shook her head.

"Your dad said I ain't supposed to do no more walking than I got to."

I tried another line.

"I bet you know a lot about the woods and all that, eh?" I began respectfully.

Piquette looked at me from her large dark unsmiling eyes.

"I don't know what in hell you're talkin' about," she replied. "You nuts or somethin'? If you mean where my old man, and me, and all them live, you better shut up, by Jesus, you hear?"

I was startled and my feelings were hurt, but I had a kind of dogged perserverance. I ignored her rebuff.

"You know something, Piquette? There's loons here, on this lake. You can see their nests just up the shore there, behind those logs. At night, you can hear them even from the cottage, but it's better to listen from the beach. My dad says we should listen and try to remember how they sound, because in a few years when more cottages are built at Diamond Lake and more people come in, the loons will go away."

Piquette was picking up stones and snail shells and then dropping them again.

"Who gives a good goddamn?" she said.

It became increasingly obvious that, as an Indian, Piquette was a dead loss. That evening I went out by myself, scrambling through the bushes that overhung the steep path, my feet slipping on the fallen spruce needles that covered the ground. When I reached the shore, I walked along the firm damp sand to the small pier that my father had built, and sat down there. I heard someone else crashing through the undergrowth and the bracken, and for a moment I thought Piquette had changed her mind, but it turned out to be my father. He sat beside me on the pier and we waited, without speaking.

At night the lake was like black glass with a streak of amber which was the path of the moon. All around, the spruce trees grew tall and close-set, branches blackly sharp against the sky, which was lightened by a cold flickering of stars. Then the loons began their calling. They rose like phantom birds from the nests on the shore, and flew out onto the dark still surface of the water.

No one can ever describe that ululating sound, the crying of the loons, and no one who has heard it can ever forget it. Plaintive, and yet with a quality of chilling mockery, those voices belonged to a world separated by aeons from our neat world of summer cottages and the lighted lamps of home.

"They must have sounded just like that," my father remarked, "before any person ever set foot here."

Then he laughed. "You could say the same, of course, about sparrows, or chipmunks, but somehow it only strikes you that way with the loons."

"I know," I said.

Neither of us suspected that this would be the last time we would ever sit here together on the shore, listening. We stayed for perhaps half an hour, and then we went back to the cottage. My mother was reading beside the fireplace. Piquette was looking at the burning birch log, and not doing anything.

"You should have come along," I said, although in fact I was glad she had not.

"Not me," Piquette said. "You wouldn' catch me walkin' way down there jus' for a bunch of squawkin' birds."

Piquette and I remained ill at ease with one another. I felt I had somehow failed my father, but I did not know what was the matter, nor why she would not or could not respond when I suggested exploring the woods or playing house. I thought it was probably her slow and difficult walking that held her back. She stayed most of the time in the cottage with my mother, helping her with the dishes or with Roddie, but hardly ever talking. Then the Duncans arrived at their cottage, and I spent my days with Mavis, who was my best friend. I could not reach Piquette at all, and I soon lost interest in trying. But all that summer she remained as both a reproach and a mystery to me.

That winter my father died of pneumonia, after less than a week's illness. For some time I saw nothing around me, being completely immersed in my own pain and my mother's. When I looked outward once more, I scarcely noticed that Piquette Tonnerre was no longer at school. I do not remember seeing her at all until four years later, one Saturday night when Mavis and I were having Cokes in the Regal Café. The jukebox was booming like tuneful thunder, and beside it, leaning lightly on its chrome and its rainbow glass, was a girl.

Piquette must have been seventeen then, although she looked about twenty. I stared at her, astounded that anyone could have changed so much. Her face, so stolid and expressionless before, was animated now with a gaiety that was almost violent. She laughed and talked very loudly with the boys around her. Her lipstick was bright carmine, and her hair was cut short and frizzily permed. She had not been pretty as a child, and she was not pretty now, for her features were still heavy and blunt. But her dark and slightly slanted eyes were beautiful, and her skin-tight skirt and orange sweater displayed to enviable advantage a soft and slender body.

She saw me, and walked over. She teetered a little, but it was not due to her once-tubercular leg, for her limp was almost gone.

"Hi, Vanessa." Her voice still had the same hoarseness. "Long time no see, eh?"

"Hi," I said. "Where've you been keeping yourself, Piquette?"

"Oh, I been around," she said. "I been away almost two years now. Been all over the place—Winnipeg, Regina, Saskatoon. Jesus, what I could tell you! I come back this summer, but I ain't stayin'. You kids goin' to the dance?"

"No," I said abruptly, for this was a sore point with me. I was fifteen, and thought I was old enough to go to the Saturday-night dances at the Flamingo. My mother, however, thought otherwise.

"Y'oughta come," Piquette said. "I never miss one. It's just about the on'y thing in this jerkwater town that's any fun. Boy, you couldn' catch me stayin' here. I don' give a shit about this place. It stinks."

She sat down beside me, and I caught the harsh over-sweetness of her perfume.

"Listen, you wanna know something, Vanessa?" she confided, her voice only slightly blurred. "Your dad was the only person in Manawaka that ever done anything good to me."

I nodded speechlessly. I was certain she was speaking the truth. I knew a little more than I had that summer at Diamond Lake, but I could not reach her now any more than I had then. I was ashamed, ashamed of my own timidity, the frightened tendency to look the other way. Yet I felt no real warmth to-

wards her—I only felt that I ought to, because of that distant summer and because my father had hoped she would be company for me, or perhaps that I would be for her, but it had not happened that way. At this moment, meeting her again, I had to admit that she repelled and embarrassed me, and I could not help despising the self-pity in her voice. I wished she would go away. I did not want to see her. I did not know what to say to her. It seemed that we had nothing to say to one another.

"I'll tell you something else," Piquette went on. "All the old bitches an biddies in this town will sure be surprised. I'm gettin' married this fall—my boyfriend, he's an English fella, works in the stockyards in the city there, a very tall guy, got blond wavy hair. Gee, is he ever handsome. Got this real classy name. Alvin Gerald Cummings—some handle, eh? They call him Al."

For the merest instant, then, I saw her. I really did see her, for the first and only time in all the years we had both lived in the same town. Her defiant face, momentarily, became unguarded and unmasked, and in her eyes there was a terrifying hope.

"Gee, Piquette—" I burst out awkwardly, "that's swell. That's really wonderful. Congratulations—good luck—I hope you'll be happy—"

As I mouthed the conventional phrases, I could only guess how great her need must have been, that she had been forced to seek the very things she so bitterly rejected.

When I was eighteen, I left Manawaka and went away to college. At the end of my first year, I came back home for the summer. I spent the first few days in talking non-stop with my mother, as we exchanged all the news that somehow had not found its way into letters—what had happened in my life and what had happened here in Manawaka while I was away. My mother searched her memory for events that concerned people I knew.

"Did I ever write you about Piquette Tonnerre, Vanessa?" she asked one morning.

"No, I don't think so," I replied. "Last I heard of her, she was going to marry some guy in the city. Is she still there?"

My mother looked perturbed, and it was a moment before she spoke, as though she did not know how to express what she had to tell and wished she did not need to try.

"She's dead," she said at last. Then, as I stared at her, "Oh, Vanessa, when it happened, I couldn't help thinking of her as she was that summer—so sullen and gauche and badly dressed. I couldn't help wondering if we could have done something more at that time—but what could we do? She used to be around in the cottage there with me all day, and honestly, it was all I could do to get a word out of her. She didn't even talk to your father very much, although I think she liked him, in her way."

"What happened?" I asked.

"Either her husband left her, or she left him," my mother said. "I don't know which. Anyway, she came back here with two youngsters, both only babies—they must have been born very close together. She kept house, I guess, for Lazarus and her brothers, down in the valley there, in the old Tonnerre place. I used to see her on the street sometimes, but she never spoke to me. She'd put on an awful lot of weight, and she looked a mess, to tell you the truth, a real slattern, dressed any old how. She was up in court a couple of times—drunk and disorderly, of course. One Saturday night last winter, dur-

ing the coldest weather, Piquette was alone in the shack with the children. The Tonnerres made home brew all the time, so I've heard, and Lazarus said later she'd been drinking most of the day when he and the boys went out that evening. They had an old woodstove there—you know the kind, with exposed pipes. The shack caught fire. Piquette didn't get out, and neither did the children."

I did not say anything. As so often with Piquette, there did not seem to be anything to say. There was a kind of silence around the image in my mind of the fire and the snow, and I wished I could put from my memory the look that I had seen once in Piquette's eyes.

I went up to Diamond Lake for a few days that summer, with Mavis and her family. The MacLeod cottage had been sold after my father's death, and I did not even go to look at it, not wanting to witness my long-ago kingdom possessed now by strangers. But one evening I went down to the shore by myself.

The small pier which my father had built was gone, and in its place there was a large and solid pier built by the government, for Galloping Mountain was now a national park, and Diamond Lake had been re-named Lake Wapakata, for it was felt that an Indian name would have a greater appeal to tourists. The one store had become several dozen, and the settlement had all the attributes of a flourishing resort—hotels, a dance-hall, cafés with neon signs, the penetrating odors of potato chips and hot dogs.

I sat on the government pier and looked out across the water. At night the lake at least was the same as it had always been, darkly shining and bearing within its black glass the streak of amber that was the path of the moon. There was no wind that evening, and everything was quiet all around me. It seemed too quiet, and then I realized that the loons were no longer here. I listened for some time, to make sure, but never once did I hear that long-drawn call, half mocking and half plaintive, spearing through the stillness across the lake.

I did not know what had happened to the birds. Perhaps they had gone away to some far place of belonging. Perhaps they had been unable to find such a place, and had simply died out, having ceased to care any longer whether they lived or not.

I remembered how Piquette had scorned to come along, when my father and I sat there and listened to the lake birds. It seemed to me now that in some unconscious and totally unrecognized way, Piquette might have been the only one, after all, who had heard the crying of the loons.

1970

ANNE SEXTON

1928–1974

According to her best friend, the poet Maxine Kumin, at their first meeting Anne Sexton "looked every inch the fashion model"—a job she had once briefly held: she was "tall, blue-eyed, stunningly slim, her carefully coifed dark hair decorated with flowers, her face skillfully made up." Yet, as Kumin also notes, this artfully lovely and theatrical woman led a "troubled and chaotic life." By the time she met Kumin in the late winter of 1957, she had had several nervous collapses and been

intermittently hospitalized, seeking "sanctuary" from "voices that urged her to die." Described by one biographer as "a demanding, rebellious child who felt rejected by her upper-middle-class parents," she had had emotional problems since girlhood. Now the mother of two young daughters, she had married Alfred Sexton in 1948, but the couple's home in a Boston suburb was not a happy one, no doubt in part because of her persistent breakdowns Nevertheless, though Anne Sexton did not consider herself a good student and had dropped out of Garland Junior College after only a year, she had just enrolled, at the suggestion of her psychiatrist, in a verse-writing workshop taught by the poet John Holmes at the Boston Center for Adult Education.

As Kumin reports, Sexton's literary progress was astonishing once she began to understand that she could write poetry. Her first book, *To Bedlam and Part Way Back*, appeared in 1960. Including such searching (if partly disguised) self-explorations as *The Moss of His Skin*, it was influenced not only by the "workshopping" this swiftly developing artist did with Kumin and Holmes but also by the self-examinations of the poet W. D. Snodgrass and by the writings of Robert Lowell (with whom Sexton studied at Boston University) and Sylvia Plath (who was a fellow student of Sexton's in Lowell's class). Later described as "confessional poets," these last three artists had begun to use the details of their personal lives as exemplary images of larger social and metaphysical problems, and their experiments offered Sexton a fruitful mode in which she, too, could work, while her innovative self-analyses also provided models for further "confessional" verse by Lowell and Plath. Fiercely productive, Sexton published a number of volumes in rapid succession, including *All My Pretty Ones* (1962), *Live or Die* (which won the Pulitzer Prize in 1967), *Love Poems* (1969), *Transformations* (1971), *The Book of Folly* (1972), and *The Death Notebooks* (1974). Almost always marked by imaginative and often surrealistic verve and frequently characterized by sardonic wit, her poems struggled against the pain of her past to sing "in celebration of the woman I am."

Despite the honors and awards Sexton received, however, and the dramatic impression she evidently made at the poetry readings she gave, her work inspired much the sort of controversy aroused by the quite different verse of Sylvia Plath, with whom Sexton was often associated. "It would be hard to find a writer who dwells more insistently on the pathetic and disgusting aspects of bodily experience," protested the poet James Dickey in *The New York Times Book Review*, while the poet Muriel Rukeyser, taking precisely the opposite position, declared that Sexton's In *Celebration of My Uterus* was "one of the few poems in which a woman has come to the fact as symbol, the center, after many years of silence and taboo." In part, at least, such conflicting opinions arose because, as Kumin observes, Sexton "wrote openly about menstruation, abortion, masturbation, incest, adultery, and drug addiction at a time when the proprieties embraced none of these as proper topics for poetry."

That Sexton did write with unusual frankness and intensity reflected not only her commitment to her art (she was a tireless reviser and a passionate participant in workshops) but also the extremity of her personal situation. Throughout the years when she was winning prizes and fellowships, she was still under psychiatric care and gradually growing dependent on alcohol and sedatives, besides being dosed with the tranquilizing drug Thorazine, which caused her to gain weight and feel "so overwhelmed with lassitude that she could not write." At the same time, probably because of her persistent problems, she became increasingly obsessed with what the title of a posthumously published volume called *The Awful Rowing toward God* (1975). In the fall of 1974, just a month before her birthday—a time of year when the "voices" urging her to die had always been particularly insistent— Sexton gassed herself in her garage, perhaps influenced by the suicide method her friend Sylvia Plath had chosen some eleven years earlier. Yet though the story of

this prolific writer's metamorphosis from model and housewife to famous poet ended tragically, her career, like Plath's, had been marked by extraordinary aesthetic vitality.

Her Kind

I have gone out, a possessed witch,
haunting the black air, braver at night;
dreaming evil, I have done my hitch
over the plain houses, light by light:
lonely thing, twelve-fingered, out of mind. 5
A woman like that is not a woman, quite.
I have been her kind.

I have found the warm caves in the woods,
filled them with skillets, carvings, shelves,
closets, silks, innumerable goods; 10
fixed the suppers for the worms and the elves:
whining, rearranging the disaligned.
A woman like that is misunderstood.
I have been her kind.

I have ridden in your cart, driver, 15
waved my nude arms at villages going by,
learning the last bright routes, survivor
where your flames still bite my thigh
and my ribs crack where your wheels wind.
A woman like that is not ashamed to die. 20
I have been her kind.

1960

The Moss of His Skin

Young girls in old Arabia were often buried alive next to their dead
fathers, apparently as sacrifice to the goddesses of the tribes. . . .
Harold Feldman, "Children of the Desert,"
Psychoanalysis and Psychoanalytic Review, Fall 1958

It was only important
to smile and hold still,
to lie down beside him
and to rest awhile,
to be folded up together 5
as if we were silk,
to sink from the eyes of mother
and not to talk.
The black room took us
like a cave or a mouth 10
or an indoor belly.
I held my breath

and daddy was there,
his thumbs, his fat skull,
his teeth, his hair growing 15
like a field or a shawl
I lay by the moss
of his skin until
it grew strange. My sisters
will never know that I fall 20
out of myself and pretend
that Allah will not see
how I hold my daddy
like an old stone tree.

 1960

Housewife

Some women marry houses.
It's another kind of skin; it has a heart,
a mouth, a liver and bowel movements.
The walls are permanent and pink.
See how she sits on her knees all day, 5
faithfully washing herself down.
Men enter by force, drawn back like Jonah
into their fleshy mothers.[1]
A woman *is* her mother.
That's the main thing 10

 1962

Somewhere in Africa

Must you leave, John Holmes,[1] with the prayers and psalms
you never said, said over you? Death with no rage
to weigh you down? Praised by the mild God, his arm
over the pulpit, leaving you timid, with no real age,

whitewashed by belief, as dull as the windy preacher! 5
Dead of a dark thing, John Holmes, you've been lost
in the college chapel, mourned as father and teacher,
mourned with piety and grace under the University Cross.

Your last book unsung, your last hard words unknown,
abandoned by science, cancer blossomed in your throat, 10
rooted like bougainvillea into your gray backbone,
ruptured your pores until you wore it like a coat.

The thick petals, the exotic reds, the purples and whites
covered up your nakedness and bore you up with all

1. In the Bible, the prophet Jonah is swallowed by a
sea monster.

1. An American poet in whose workshop Sexton had
studied.

their blind power. I think of your last June nights 15
in Boston, your body swollen but light, your eyes small

as you let the nurses carry you into a strange land.
. . . If this is death and God is necessary let him be hidden
from the missionary, the well-wisher and the glad hand.
Let God be some tribal female who is known but forbidden. 20

Let there be this God who is a woman who will place you
upon her shallow boat, who is a woman naked to the waist,
moist with palm oil and sweat, a woman of some virtue
and wild breasts, her limbs excellent, unbruised and chaste.

Let her take you. She will put twelve strong men at the oars 25
for you are stronger than mahogany and your bones fill
the boat high as with fruit and bark from the interior.
She will have you now, you whom the funeral cannot kill.

John Holmes, cut from a single tree, lie heavy in her hold
and go down that river with the ivory, the copra[2] and the gold. 30

July 1, 1962 1966

Consorting with Angels

I was tired of being a woman,
tired of the spoons and the pots,
tired of my mouth and my breasts,
tired of the cosmetics and the silks.
There were still men who sat at my table, 5
circled around the bowl I offered up.
The bowl was filled with purple grapes
and the flies hovered in for the scent
and even my father came with his white bone.
But I was tired of the gender of things. 10

Last night I had a dream
and I said to it . . .
"You are the answer.
You will outlive my husband and my father."
In that dream there was a city made of chains 15
where Joan was put to death in man's clothes[1]
and the nature of the angels went unexplained,
no two made in the same species,
one with a nose, one with an ear in its hand,
one chewing a star and recording its orbit, 20
each one like a poem obeying itself,
performing God's functions,
a people apart.

2. Coconut oil.
1. An allusion to Joan of Arc, the early-15th-century
peasant girl who, at the behest of her angelic voices,
dressed in men's clothes and led the French to victory;
later she was captured and put to death.

"You are the answer,"
I said, and entered, 25
lying down on the gates of the city.
Ther the chains were fastened around me
and I lost my common gender and my final aspect.
Adam was on the left of me
and Eve was on the right of me, 30
both thoroughly inconsistent with the world of reason.
We wove our arms together
and rode under the sun.
I was not a woman anymore,
not one thing or the other. 35

O daughters of Jerusalem,
the king has brought me into his chamber.
I am black and I am beautiful.
I've been opened and undressed.
I have no arms or legs. 40
I'm all one skin like a fish.
I'm no more a woman
than Christ was a man.

February 1963 1966

Sylvia's Death

for Sylvia Plath[1]

O Sylvia, Sylvia,
with a dead box of stones and spoons,

with two children, two meteors
wandering loose in the tiny playroom.

with your mouth into the sheet, 5
into the roofbeam, into the dumb prayer,

(Sylvia, Sylvia,
where did you go
after you wrote me
from Devonshire[2] 10
about raising potatoes
and keeping bees?)

what did you stand by,
just how did you lie down into?

Thief!— 15
how did you crawl into,

2. The first man and the first woman (Genesis) 1963.
1. American poet who committed suicide (1932– 2. County in England.

crawl down alone
into the death I wanted so badly and for so long,

the death we said we both outgrew,
the one we wore on our skinny breasts, 20

the one we talked of so often each time
we downed three extra dry martinis in Boston,

the death that talked of analysts and cures,
the death that talked like brides with plots,

the death we drank to, 25
the motives and then the quiet deed?

(In Boston
the dying
ride in cabs,
yes death again, 30
that ride home
with *our* boy.)

O Sylvia, I remember the sleepy drummer
who beat on our eyes with an old story,

how we wanted to let him come 35
like a sadist or a New York fairy

to do his job,
a necessity, a window in a wall or a crib,

and since that time he waited
under our heart, our cupboard, 40

and I see now that we store him up
year after year, old suicides

and I know at the news of your death,
a terrible taste for it, like salt.

(And me, 45
me too.
And now, Sylvia,
you again
with death again,
that ride home 50
with *our* boy.)

And I say only
with my arms stretched out into that stone place,

what is your death
but an old belonging, 55

a mole that fell out
of one of your poems?

(O friend,
while the moon's bad,
and the king's gone, 60
and the queen's at her wit's end
the bar fly ought to sing!)

O tiny mother,
you too!
O funny duchess! 65
O blonde thing!

February 17, 1963 1966

In Celebration of My Uterus

Everyone in me is a bird.
I am beating all my wings.
They wanted to cut you out
but they will not.
They said you were immeasurably empty 5
but you are not.
They said you were sick unto dying
but they were wrong.
You are singing like a school girl.
You are not torn. 10

Sweet weight,
in celebration of the woman I am
and of the soul of the woman I am
and of the central creature and its delight
I sing for you. I dare to live. 15
Hello, spirit. Hello, cup.
Fasten, cover. Cover that does contain.
Hello to the soil of the fields.
Welcome, roots.

Each cell has a life. 20
There is enough here to please a nation.
It is enough that the populace own these goods.
Any person, any commonwealth would say of it,
"It is good this year that we may plant again
and think forward to a harvest. 25
A blight had been forecast and has been cast out."
Many women are singing together of this:
one is in a shoe factory cursing the machine,
one is at the aquarium tending a seal,
one is dull at the wheel of her Ford, 30
one is at the toll gate collecting,
one is tying the cord of a calf in Arizona,

one is straddling a cello in Russia,
one is shifting pots on the stove in Egypt,
one is painting her bedroom walls moon color, 35
one is dying but remembering a breakfast,
one is stretching on her mat in Thailand,
one is wiping the ass of her child,
one is staring out the window of a train
in the middle of Wyoming and one is 40
anywhere and some are everywhere and all
seem to be singing, although some can not
sing a note.

Sweet weight,
in celebration of the woman I am 45
let me carry a ten-foot scarf,
let me drum for the nineteen-year-olds,
let me carry bowls for the offering
(if that is my part).
Let me study the cardiovascular tissue, 50
let me examine the angular distance of meteors,
let me suck on the stems of flowers
(if that is my part).
Let me make certain tribal figures
(if that is my part). 55
For this thing the body needs
let me sing
for the supper,
for the kissing,
for the correct 60
yes.

1969

MAYA ANGELOU

1928–

At the beginning of her best-selling autobiography *I Know Why the Caged Bird Sings* (1970), Maya Angelou explained that "if growing up is painful for the Southern Black girl, being aware of her displacement is the rust on the razor that threatens the throat. It is an unnecessary insult." Later in the book, Angelou described the insult of displacement associated with her childhood move from her native St. Louis to Stamps, Arkansas, with the sexual abuse she received from her mother's boyfriend, and with the "pride and prejudice" she encountered as a streetcar conductor in San Francisco. But *I Know Why the Caged Bird Sings* also recorded her affectionate respect for the grandmother, Ann Henderson, who raised her in Stamps, as well as Angelou's relish for black religious and social traditions, and her joy in the birth of her son.

A self-described six-foot, black southwesterner, Angelou toured Europe as an entertainer, resided briefly in Ghana, performed on and off Broadway, and worked in cinema as well as television. She published her first book, *I Know Why the Caged*

Bird Sings, to remarkable critical acclaim. In part, her achievement extended the genre of the black autobiography by thinkers such as Frederick Douglass, W. E. B. Du Bois, Richard Wright, and Malcolm X by using it to express the struggle toward independence and self-expression of a decidedly female subject. Since its publication, she has followed it with a number of sequels: *Gather Together in My Name* (1974), *Singin' and Swingin' and Gettin' Merry Like Christmas* (1976), *The Heart of a Woman* (1981), and *All God's Children Need Traveling Shoes* (1986). In 1982, Angelou became Reynolds Professor of American Studies at Wake Forest University in Winston-Salem, North Carolina. Between 1971 and 1993, she also produced seven books of verse. Her poem *On the Pulse of Morning* was written for, and recited at, the inauguration of President Bill Clinton in January 1993.

From I Know Why the Caged Bird Sings

[The Peckerwood Dentist and Momma's Incredible Powers]

The Angel of the candy counter had found me out at last, and was exacting excruciating penance for all the stolen Milky Ways, Mounds, Mr. Goodbars and Hersheys with Almonds. I had two cavities that were rotten to the gums. The pain was beyond the bailiwick of crushed aspirins or oil of cloves. Only one thing could help me, so I prayed earnestly that I'd be allowed to sit under the house and have the building collapse on my left jaw. Since there was no Negro dentist in Stamps,[1] nor doctor either, for that matter, Momma had dealt with previous toothaches by pulling them out (a string tied to the tooth with the other end looped over her fist), pain killers and prayer. In this particular instance the medicine had proved ineffective; there wasn't enough enamel left to hook a string on, and the prayers were being ignored because the Balancing Angel was blocking their passage.

I lived a few days and nights in blinding pain, not so much toying with as seriously considering the idea of jumping in the well, and Momma decided I had to be taken to a dentist. The nearest Negro dentist was in Texarkana, twenty-five miles away, and I was certain that I'd be dead long before we reached half the distance. Momma said we'd go to Dr. Lincoln right in Stamps, and he'd take care of me. She said he owed her a favor.

I knew there were a number of whitefolks in town that owed her favors. Bailey and I had seen the books which showed how she had lent money to Blacks and whites alike during the Depression, and most still owed her. But I couldn't aptly remember seeing Dr. Lincoln's name, nor had I ever heard of a Negro's going to him as a patient. However, Momma said we were going, and put water on the stove for our baths. I had never been to a doctor, so she told me that after the bath (which would make my mouth feel better) I had to put on freshly starched and ironed underclothes from inside out. The ache failed to respond to the bath, and I knew then that the pain was more serious than that which anyone had ever suffered.

Before we left the Store, she ordered me to brush my teeth and then wash my mouth with Listerine. The idea of even opening my clamped jaws increased the pain, but upon her explanation that when you go to a doctor you have to clean yourself all over, but most especially the part that's to be examined, I screwed up my courage and unlocked my teeth. The cool air in my

1. The town in Arkansas where Angelou grew up.

mouth and the jarring of my molars dislodged what little remained of my reason. I had frozen to the pain, my family nearly had to tie me down to take the toothbrush away. It was no small effort to get me started on the road to the dentist. Momma spoke to all the passers-by, but didn't stop to chat. She explained over her shoulder that we were going to the doctor and she'd "pass the time of day" on our way home.

Until we reached the pond the pain was my world, an aura that haloed me for three feet around. Crossing the bridge into whitefolks' country, pieces of sanity pushed themselves forward. I had to stop moaning and start walking straight. The white towel, which was drawn under my chin and tied over my head, had to be arranged. If one was dying, it had to be done in style if the dying took place in whitefolks' part of town.

On the other side of the bridge the ache seemed to lessen as if a whitebreeze blew off the whitefolks and cushioned everything in their neighborhood—including my jaw. The gravel road was smoother, the stones smaller and the tree branches hung down around the path and nearly covered us. If the pain didn't diminish then, the familiar yet strange sights hypnotized me into believing that it had.

But my head continued to throb with the measured insistence of a bass drum, and how could a toothache pass the calaboose,[2] hear the songs of the prisoners, their blues and laughter, and not be changed? How could one or two or even a mouthful of angry tooth roots meet a wagonload of powhitetrash[3] children, endure their idiotic snobbery and not feel less important?

Behind the building which housed the dentist's office ran a small path used by servants and those tradespeople who catered to the butcher and Stamps' one restaurant. Momma and I followed that lane to the backstairs of Dentist Lincoln's office. The sun was bright and gave the day a hard reality as we climbed up the steps to the second floor.

Momma knocked on the back door and a young white girl opened it to show surprise at seeing us there. Momma said she wanted to see Dentist Lincoln and to tell him Annie was there. The girl closed the door firmly. Now the humiliation of hearing Momma describe herself as if she had no last name to the young white girl was equal to the physical pain. It seemed terribly unfair to have a toothache and a headache and have to bear at the same time the heavy burden of Blackness.

It was always possible that the teeth would quiet down and maybe drop out of their own accord. Momma said we would wait. We leaned in the harsh sunlight on the shaky railings of the dentist's back porch for over an hour.

He opened the door and looked at Momma. "Well, Annie, what can I do for you?"

He didn't see the towel around my jaw or notice my swollen face.

Momma said, "Dentist Lincoln. It's my grandbaby here. She got two rotten teeth that's giving her a fit."

She waited for him to acknowledge the truth of her statement. He made no comment, orally or facially.

"She had this toothache purt' near four days now, and today I said, 'Young lady, you going to the Dentist.' "

"Annie?"

"Yes, sir, Dentist Lincoln."

He was choosing words the way people hunt for shells. "Annie, you know I don't treat nigra colored people."

"I know, Dentist Lincoln. But this here is just my little grandbaby, and she ain't gone be no trouble to you. . . ."

"Annie, everybody has a policy. In this world you have to have a policy. Now, my policy is I don't treat colored people."

The sun had baked the oil out of Momma's skin and melted the Vaseline in her hair. She shone greasily as she leaned out of the dentist's shadow.

"Seem like to me, Dentist Lincoln, you might look after her, she ain't nothing but a little mite. And seems like maybe you owe me a favor or two."

He reddened slightly. "Favor or no favor. The money has all been repaid to you and that's the end of it. Sorry, Annie." He had his hand on the doorknob. "Sorry." His voice was a bit kinder on the second "Sorry," as if he really was.

Momma said, "I wouldn't press on you like this for myself but I can't take No. Not for my grandbaby. When you come to borrow my money you didn't have to beg. You asked me, and I lent it. Now, it wasn't my policy. I ain't no moneylender, but you stood to lose this building and I tried to help you out."

"It's been paid, and raising your voice won't make me change my mind. My policy . . ." He let go of the door and stepped nearer Momma. The three of us were crowded on the small landing. "Annie, my policy is I'd rather stick my hand in a dog's mouth than in a nigger's."

He had never once looked at me. He turned his back and went through the door into the cool beyond. Momma backed up inside herself for a few minutes. I forgot everything except her face which was almost a new one to me. She leaned over and took the doorknob, and in her everyday soft voice she said, "Sister, go on downstairs. Wait for me. I'll be there directly."

Under the most common of circumstances I knew it did no good to argue with Momma. So I walked down the steep stairs, afraid to look back and afraid not to do so. I turned as the door slammed, and she was gone.

Momma walked in that room as if she owned it. She shoved that silly nurse aside with one hand and strode into the dentist's office. He was sitting in his chair, sharpening his mean instruments and putting extra sting into his medicines. Her eyes were blazing like live coals and her arms had doubled themselves in length. He looked up at her just before she caught him by the collar of his white jacket.

"Stand up when you see a lady, you contemptuous scoundrel." Her tongue had thinned and the words rolled off well enunciated. Enunciated and sharp like little claps of thunder.

The dentist had no choice but to stand at R.O.T.C.[4] attention. His head dropped after a minute and his voice was humble. "Yes, ma'am, Mrs. Henderson."

"You knave, do you think you acted like a gentleman, speaking to me like that in front of my granddaughter?" She didn't shake him, although she had the power. She simply held him upright.

"No, ma'am, Mrs. Henderson."

"No, ma'am, Mrs. Henderson, what?" Then she did give him the tiniest of shakes, but because of her strength the action set his head and arms to shaking

4. Reserve Officers' Training Corps, a program that gives high school and college students military training.

loose on the ends of his body. He stuttered much worse than Uncle Willie. "No, ma'am, Mrs. Henderson, I'm sorry."

With just an edge of her disgust showing, Momma slung him back in his dentist's chair. "Sorry is as sorry does, and you're about the sorriest dentist I ever laid my eyes on." (She could afford to slip into the vernacular because she had such eloquent command of English.)

"I didn't ask you to apologize in front of Marguerite, because I don't want her to know my power, but I order you, now and herewith. Leave Stamps by sundown."

"Mrs. Henderson, I can't get my equipment. . . ." He was shaking terribly now.

"Now, that brings me to my second order. You will never again practice dentistry. Never! When you get settled in your next place, you will be a vegetarian caring for dogs with the mange, cats with the cholera and cows with the epizootic.[5] Is that clear?"

The saliva ran down his chin and his eyes filled with tears. "Yes, ma'am. Thank you for not killing me. Thank you, Mrs. Henderson."

Momma pulled herself back from being ten feet tall with eight-foot arms and said, "You're welcome for nothing, you varlet, I wouldn't waste a killing on the likes of you."

On her way out she waved her handkerchief at the nurse and turned her into a crocus sack of chicken feed.

Momma looked tired when she came down the stairs, but who wouldn't be tired if they had gone through what she had. She came close to me and adjusted the towel under my jaw (I had forgotten the toothache; I only knew that she made her hands gentle in order not to awaken the pain). She took my hand. Her voice never changed. "Come on, Sister."

I reckoned we were going home where she would concoct a brew to eliminate the pain and maybe give me new teeth too. New teeth that would grow overnight out of my gums. She led me toward the drugstore, which was in the opposite direction from the Store. "I'm taking you to Dentist Baker in Texarkana."

I was glad after all that that I had bathed and put on Mum and Cashmere Bouquet talcum powder. It was a wonderful surprise. My toothache had quieted to solemn pain, Momma had obliterated the evil white man, and we were going on a trip to Texarkana, just the two of us.

On the Greyhound she took an inside seat in the back, and I sat beside her. I was so proud of being her granddaughter and sure that some of her magic must have come down to me. She asked if I was scared. I only shook my head and leaned over on her cool brown upper arm. There was no chance that a dentist, especially a Negro dentist, would dare hurt me then. Not with Momma there. The trip was uneventful, except that she put her arm around me, which was very unusual for Momma to do.

The dentist showed me the medicine and the needle before he deadened my gums, but if he hadn't I wouldn't have worried. Momma stood right behind him. Her arms were folded and she checked on everything he did. The teeth were extracted and she bought me an ice cream cone from the side window of a drug counter. The trip back to Stamps was quiet, except that I had to

5. A disease that attacks a large number of animals at once.

spit into a very small empty snuff can which she had gotten for me and it was difficult with the bus humping and jerking on our country roads.

At home I was given a warm salt solution, and when I washed out my mouth I showed Bailey the empty holes, where the clotted blood sat like filling in a pie crust. He said I was quite brave, and that was my cue to reveal our confrontation with the peckerwood[6] dentist and Momma's incredible powers.

I had to admit that I didn't hear the conversation, but what else could she have said than what I said she said? What else done? He agreed with my analysis in a lukewarm way, and I happily (after all, I'd been sick) flounced into the Store. Momma was preparing our evening meal and Uncle Willie leaned on the door sill. She gave her version.

"Dentist Lincoln got right uppity. Said he'd rather put his hand in a dog's mouth. And when I reminded him of the favor, he brushed it off like a piece of lint. Well, I sent Sister downstairs and went inside. I hadn't never been in his office before, but I found the door to where he takes out teeth, and him and the nurse was in there thick as thieves. I just stood there till he caught sight of me." Crash bang the pots on the stove. "He jumped just like he was sitting on a pin. He said, 'Annie, I done tole you, I ain't gonna mess around in no niggah's mouth.' I said, 'Somebody's got to do it then,' and he said, 'Take her to Texarkana to the colored dentist' and that's when I said, 'If you paid me my money I could afford to take her.' He said, 'It's all been paid.' I tole him everything but the interest been paid. He said, 'Twasn't no interest.' I said ''Tis now. I'll take ten dollars as payment in full.' You knew, Willie, it wasn't no right thing to do, 'cause I lent that money without thinking about it.

"He tole that little snippity nurse of his'n to give me ten dollars and make me sign a 'paid in full' receipt. She gave it to me and I signed the papers. Even though by rights he was paid up before, I figger, he gonna be that kind of nasty, he gonna have to pay for it."

Momma and her son laughed and laughed over the white man's evilness and her retributive sin.

I preferred, much preferred, my version.

1969

6. Originally, very poor southern white; later, any white person.

CYNTHIA OZICK

1928–

Although Cynthia Ozick has claimed that she "became Henry James" at the age of seventeen and "remained" him for years and years, she eventually decried the effects of being "an Extreme and Hideous Example of Premature Exposure to Henry James." Indeed, after the publication of her first, very Jamesian novel *Trust* (1966), Ozick became convinced that she had confused the relative merits of life and art, even misunderstanding her predecessor's own position on the matter. After that book, her stylistic virtuosity melded with a deeply ethical commitment to produce stories that not only interpret but also judge the world. Like her novels, *The Cannibal Galaxy* (1983) and *The Messiah of Stockholm* (1987), such collections as *The Pagan Rabbi and Other Stories* (1972), *Bloodshed and Three Novellas* (1976),

and *Levitation: Five Fictions* (1982) explore the sometimes mundane, sometimes mystical conundrums faced by characters seeking to negotiate between spiritual and material realities. Many of her prize-winning stories also deal with the alienating experiences of assimilation encountered by Jewish immigrants not very different from the family into which she was born.

Working at their Park View Pharmacy in the Bronx, Ozick's parents had to mediate between the economics of the New World and the intellectual inheritance of the Old: her father was a pharmacist as well as a scholar of Yiddishized Hebrew while her mother was related to the Hebrew poet Abraham Regelson. After attending a public grade school, Hunter College, and New York University, Ozick did graduate work at Ohio State University, where she devoted her master's thesis to James. She married a lawyer, Bernard Hallote, in 1952, worked briefly as an advertising copywriter, gave birth to a daughter, and settled in New Rochelle, New York, to devote herself to articulating the ways in which she and the characters about whom she writes remain unassimilated into English. Almost a prose poem in its evocative effort to convey the unspeakable horror of the suffering inflicted on Jews by Nazism, *The Shawl* asks readers to confront their own relationship to the evil made manifest in the Holocaust, and it does so by foregrounding the figures of mother and child.

The Shawl

Stella, cold, cold, the coldness of hell. How they walked on the roads together, Rosa with Magda curled up between sore breasts, Magda wound up in the shawl. Sometimes Stella carried Magda. But she was jealous of Magda. A thin girl of fourteen, too small, with thin breasts of her own, Stella wanted to be wrapped in a shawl, hidden away, asleep, rocked by the march, a baby, a round infant in arms. Magda took Rosa's nipple, and Rosa never stopped walking, a walking cradle. There was not enough milk; sometimes Magda sucked air; then she screamed. Stella was ravenous. Her knees were tumors on sticks, her elbows chicken bones.

Rosa did not feel hunger; she felt light, not like someone walking but like someone in a faint, in trance, arrested in a fit, someone who is already a floating angel, alert and seeing everything, but in the air, not there, not touching the road. As if teetering on the tips of her fingernails. She looked into Magda's face through a gap in the shawl: a squirrel in a nest, safe, no one could reach her inside the little house of the shawl's windings. The face, very round, a pocket mirror of a face: but it was not Rosa's bleak complexion, dark like cholera, it was another kind of face altogether, eyes blue as air, smooth feathers of hair nearly as yellow as the Star sewn into Rosa's coat. You could think she was one of *their* babies.[1]

Rosa, floating, dreamed of giving Magda away in one of the villages. She could leave the line for a minute and push Magda into the hands of any woman on the side of the road. But if she moved out of line they might shoot. And even if she fled the line for half a second and pushed the shawl-bundle at a stranger, would the woman take it? She might be surprised, or afraid; she might drop the shawl, and Magda would fall out and strike her head and die. The little round head. Such a good child, she gave up screaming, and sucked

1. The Nazi "Aryan" ideal of beauty included blond hair and blue eyes. Under the Nazis, Jews in Germany and German-occupied countries were made to wear yellow Stars of David.

now only for the taste of the drying nipple itself. The neat grip of the tiny gums. One mite of a tooth tip sticking up in the bottom gum, how shining, an elfin tombstone of white marble gleaming there. Without complaining, Magda relinquished Rosa's teats, first the left, then the right; both were cracked, not a sniff of milk. The duct-crevice extinct, a dead volcano, blind eye, chill hole, so Magda took the corner of the shawl and milked it instead. She sucked and sucked, flooding the threads with wetness. The shawl's good flavor, milk of linen.

It was a magic shawl, it could nourish an infant for three days and three nights. Magda did not die, she stayed alive, although very quiet. A peculiar smell, of cinnamon and almonds, lifted out of her mouth. She held her eyes open every moment, forgetting how to blink or nap, and Rosa and sometimes Stella studied their blueness. On the road they raised one burden of a leg after another and studied Magda's face. "Aryan," Stella said, in a voice grown as thin as a string; and Rosa thought how Stella gazed at Magda like a young cannibal. And the time that Stella said "Aryan," it sounded to Rosa as if Stella had really said "Let us devour her."

But Magda lived to walk. She lived that long, but she did not walk very well, partly because she was only fifteen months old, and partly because the spindles of her legs could not hold up her fat belly. It was fat with air, full and round. Rosa gave almost all her food to Magda, Stella gave nothing; Stella was ravenous, a growing child herself, but not growing much. Stella did not menstruate. Rosa did not menstruate. Rosa was ravenous, but also not; she learned from Magda how to drink the taste of a finger in one's mouth. They were in a place without pity, all pity was annihilated in Rosa, she looked at Stella's bones without pity. She was sure that Stella was waiting for Magda to die so she could put her teeth into the little thighs.

Rosa knew Magda was going to die very soon; she should have been dead already, but she had been buried away deep inside the magic shawl, mistaken there for the shivering mound of Rosa's breasts; Rosa clung to the shawl as if it covered only herself. No one took it away from her. Magda was mute. She never cried. Rosa hid her in the barracks, under the shawl, but she knew that one day someone would inform; or one day someone, not even Stella, would steal Magda to eat her. When Magda began to walk Rosa knew that Magda was going to die very soon, something would happen. She was afraid to fall asleep; she slept with the weight of her thigh on Magda's body; she was afraid she would smother Magda under her thigh. The weight of Rosa was becoming less and less; Rosa and Stella were slowly turning into air.

Magda was quiet, but her eyes were horribly alive, like blue tigers. She watched. Sometimes she laughed—it seemed a laugh, but how could it be? Magda had never seen anyone laugh. Still, Magda laughed at her shawl when the wind blew its corners, the bad wind with pieces of black in it, that made Stella's and Rosa's eyes tear. Magda's eyes were always clear and tearless. She watched like a tiger. She guarded her shawl. No one could touch it; only Rosa could touch it. Stella was not allowed. The shawl was Magda's own baby, her pet, her little sister. She tangled herself up in it and sucked on one of the corners when she wanted to be very still.

Then Stella took the shawl away and made Magda die.

Afterward Stella said: "I was cold."

And afterward she was always cold, always. The cold went into her heart:

Rosa saw that Stella's heart was cold. Magda flopped onward with her little pencil legs scribbling this way and that, in search of the shawl; the pencils faltered at the barracks opening, where the light began. Rosa saw and pursued. But already Magda was in the square outside the barracks, in the jolly light. It was the roll-call arena. Every morning Rosa had to conceal Magda under the shawl against a wall of the barracks and go out and stand in the arena with Stella and hundreds of others, sometimes for hours, and Magda, deserted, was quiet under the shawl, sucking on her corner. Every day Magda was silent, and so she did not die. Rosa saw that today Magda was going to die, and at the same time a fearful joy ran in Rosa's two palms, her fingers were on fire, she was astonished, febrile: Magda, in the sunlight, swaying on her pencil legs, was howling. Ever since the drying up of Rosa's nipples, ever since Magda's last scream on the road, Magda had been devoid of any syllable; Magda was a mute. Rosa believed that something had gone wrong with her vocal cords, with her windpipe, with the cave of her larynx; Magda was defective, without a voice; perhaps she was deaf; there might be something amiss with her intelligence; Magda was dumb. Even the laugh that came when the ash-stippled wind made a clown out of Magda's shawl was only the air-blown showing of her teeth. Even when the lice, head lice and body lice, crazed her so that she became as wild as one of the big rats that plundered the barracks at daybreak looking for carrion, she rubbed and scratched and kicked and bit and rolled without a whimper. But now Magda's mouth was spilling a long viscous rope of clamor.

"Maaaa—"

It was the first noise Magda had ever sent out from her throat since the drying up of Rosa's nipples.

"Maaaa . . . aaa!"

Again! Magda was wavering in the perilous sunlight of the arena, scribbling on such pitiful little bent shins. Rosa saw. She saw that Magda was grieving for the loss of her shawl, she saw that Magda was going to die. A tide of commands hammered in Rosa's nipples: Fetch, get, bring! But she did not know which to go after first, Magda or the shawl. If she jumped out into the arena to snatch Magda up, the howling would not stop, because Magda would still not have the shawl; but if she ran back into the barracks to find the shawl, and if she found it, and if she came after Magda holding it and shaking it, then she would get Magda back, Magda would put the shawl in her mouth and turn dumb again.

Rosa entered the dark. It was easy to discover the shawl. Stella was heaped under it, asleep in her thin bones. Rosa tore the shawl free and flew—she could fly, she was only air—into the arena. The sunheat murmured of another life, of butterflies in summer. The light was placid, mellow. On the other side of the steel fence, far away, there were green meadows speckled with dandelions and deep-colored violets; beyond them, even farther, innocent tiger lilies, tall, lifting their orange bonnets. In the barracks they spoke of "flowers," of "rain": excrement, thick turd-braids, and the slow stinking maroon waterfall that slunk down from the upper bunks, the stink mixed with a bitter fatty floating smoke that greased Rosa's skin. She stood for an instant at the margin of the arena. Sometimes the electricity inside the fence would seem to hum; even Stella said it was only an imagining, but Rosa heard real sounds in the wire: grainy sad voices. The farther she was from the fence, the more clearly

the voices crowded at her. The lamenting voices strummed so convincingly, so passionately it was impossible to suspect them of being phantoms. The voices told her to hold up the shawl, high; the voices told her to shake it, to whip with it, to unfurl it like a flag. Rosa lifted, shook, whipped, unfurled. Far off, very far, Magda leaned across her air-fed belly, reaching out with the rods of her arms. She was high up, elevated, riding someone's shoulder. But the shoulder that carried Magda was not coming toward Rosa and the shawl, it was drifting away, the speck of Magda was moving more and more into the smoky distance. Above the shoulder a helmet glinted. The light tapped the helmet and sparkled it into a goblet. Below the helmet a black body like a domino and a pair of black boots hurled themselves in the direction of the electrified fence. The electric voices began to chatter wildly. "Maamaa, maaa-maaa," they all hummed together. How far Magda was from Rosa now, across the whole square, past a dozen barracks, all the way on the other side! She was no bigger than a moth.

All at once Magda was swimming through the air. The whole of Magda traveled through loftiness. She looked like a butterfly touching a silver vine. And the moment Magda's feathered round head and her pencil legs and balloonish belly and zigzag arms splashed against the fence, the steel voices went mad in their growling, urging Rosa to run and run to the spot where Magda had fallen from her flight against the electrified fence; but of course Rosa did not obey them. She only stood, because if she ran they would shoot, and if she tried to pick up the sticks of Magda's body they would shoot, and if she let the wolf's screech ascending now through the ladder of her skeleton break out, they would shoot; so she took Magda's shawl and filled her own mouth with it, stuffed it in and stuffed it in, until she was swallowing up the wolf's screech and tasting the cinnamon and almond depth of Magda's saliva; and Rosa drank Magda's shawl until it dried.

1980

URSULA FANTHORPE
1929–

"*Now at last I know / Why I was brought here / And what I have to do*": Ursula Fanthorpe imagines the representative woman writer speaking these words at the conclusion of her *From the Third Storey*, with its succinct depiction of the constraints confronted by literary women from Jane Austen to Virginia Woolf and their descendants. Born in London, Fanthorpe herself has lectured on English literature and been a writer-in-residence at a number of institutions, but she has also earned her living as a school counselor and a hospital clerk. Her first collection of poems, *Side Effects* (1978), investigates life on a psychiatric ward, while other books document student experiences, women's lives, and the world of "ordinary" labor. No matter what her theme, Fanthorpe frequently emphasizes what, in her note to *Only Here for the Bier*, she calls the "woman's angle," and often, too, she celebrates the liberation of female joy, as in her portrayal of the laughter of "Old women, unmanned, free / Of children, embarrassment, desire to please, / Hooting grossly, without explanation."

For Saint Peter[1]

I have a good deal of sympathy for you, mate,
Because I reckon that, like me, you deal with the outpatients.

Now the inpatients are easy, they're cowed by the nurses
(In your case, the angels) and they know what's what in the set-up.

They know about God (in my case Dr. Snow) and all His little fads, 5
And if there's any trouble with them, you can easily scare them rigid

Just by mentioning His name. But outpatients are different.
They bring their kids with them, for one thing, and that creates a wrong
 atmosphere.

They have shopping baskets, and buses to catch. They cry, or knit,
Or fall on the floor in convulsions. In fact, Saint Peter, 10

If you know what I mean, they haven't yet learned
How to be reverent.

<div align="right">1978</div>

After Visiting Hours

Like gulls they are still calling—
*I'll come again Tuesday. Our Dad
Sends his love.* They diminish, are gone.
Their world has received them,

As our world confirms us. Their debris 5
Is tidied into vases, lockers, minds.
We become pulses; mouthpieces
Of thermometers and bowels.

The trolley's rattle dispatches
The last lover. Now we can relax 10
Into illness, and reliably abstracted
Nurses will straighten our sheets,

Reorganize our symptoms. Outside,
Darkness descends like an eyelid.
It rains on our nearest and dearest 15
In car-parks, at bus-stops.

Now the bed-bound rehearse
Their repertoire of movements,
The dressing-gowned shuffle, clutching
Their glass bodies. 20

1. The most prominent of Jesus' twelve disciples, St. Peter traditionally is pictured as the gatekeeper of heaven (see Matthew 16:19).

Now siren voices whisper
From headphones, and vagrant
Doctors appear, wreathed in stethoscopes
Like South Sea dancers.

All's well, all's quiet as the great 25
Ark noses her way into night,
Caulked, battened, blessed for her trip,
And behind, the gulls crying.

1978

From Only Here for the Bier

I wrote these four poems because I was interested to see how the masculine world of Shakespeare's tragedies would look from the woman's angle. In fact, women exist in this world only to be killed, as sacrificial victims. So I imagined Gertrude (mother-in-law), Regan (king's daughter), Emilia (army wife) and the un-named waiting gentlewoman in *Macbeth* having a chat with some usual female confidante, like a hairdresser or a telephone.

1. Mother-in-Law

Such a nice girl. Just what I wanted
For the boy. Not top drawer, you know,
But so often, in our position, that
Turns out to be a mistake. They get
The ideas of their station, and that upsets 5
So many applecarts. The lieges, of course,
Are particularly hidebound, and the boy
For all his absentminded ways, is a great one
For convention. Court mourning, you know . . .
Things like that. We don't want a Brunhilde[2] 10
Here. But she was so suitable. Devoted
To her father and brother, and,
Of course, to the boy. And a very
Respectable, loyal family. Well, loyal
To number two,[3] at any rate. Number one, 15
I remember, never quite trusted . . . Yes,
And had just the right interests. Folk song, for instance,
(Such a sweet little voice), and amateur
Dramatics. Inherited *that* taste
From her father. Dear old fellow, he'd go on 20
For hours about his college drama group
And the boy's so keen on the stage. It's nice
When husband and wife have a shared interest,
Don't you think? Then botany. Poor little soul,
She was really keen. We'd go for trips 25

1. Only two of the four poems are printed here.
2. Great female warrior in Germanic mythology and literature.

3. I.e., Claudius, Gertrude's second husband, who murdered number one, Hamlet's father.

With the vasculum,[4] and have such fun
Asking the lieges their country names for flowers.
Some of them, my dear, were scarcely delicate
(The names, I mean), but the young nowadays
Don't seem to notice. Marriage 30
Would have made her more innocent, of course.
I can't think who will do for the boy now.
I seem to be the only woman left round here.

2. *King's Daughter*

Being the middle sister is tiresome.
The rawboned heroics of the eldest
Are out of reach; so is the youngest's
Gamine[5] appeal. It is impossible for the second child
To be special. One must just cultivate 5
One's own garden, neatly. For neatness and order
Matter in the world of the middle daughter,
The even number. Disorderly lives
Are distasteful. Adultery is untidy;
Servants should be accurate and invisible. 10
Individuals should have two eyes, or none;[6]
One eye is unacceptable. I enjoy the beauty
Of formality, and have no objection
To offering father the elaborate rhetoric
He expects. There is a certain correctness 15
In the situation. One must object, however,
To the impropriety of those who propose
Different rules. One is no innovator:
Innovation is unfeminine. It is important
That ashtrays should be emptied, and always 20
In the same place, that meals be punctual.
One depends on one's servants to supply
Visual and temporal symmetry. Equally,
One relies on one's family to support
The proper structure of relationships. It is a pity 25
That one's father is so eccentric, that his friends
Are the sort of people one tries not to know,
That one's sisters are, in their different ways,
Both so unwomanly. One would never dream
Of asserting oneself in public, as they do. 30
One tries to cultivate the woman's touch.

1982

Women Laughing

Gurgles, genderless,
Inside the incurious womb.

4. Special case for carrying botanical specimens.
5. Female street urchin.
6. When Gloucester is being blinded, Regan urges, "One side will mock another; th'other, too" (*King Lear* 3.7.71).

Random soliloquies of babies
Ticked by everything.

Undomesticated shrieks 5
Of small girls. Mother prophesies
You'll be crying in a minute.

Adolescents wearing giggles
Like chain-mail, against embarrassment,
Giggles formal in shape as 10
Butterpats, or dropped stitches.

Young women anxious to please,
Laughing eagerly before the punchline
(Being too naïve to know which it is).

Wives gleaming sleekly in public at 15
Husbandly jokes, masking
All trace of old acquaintance.

Mums obliging with rhetorical
Guffaws at the children's riddles
That bored their parents. 20

Old women, unmanned, free
Of children, embarrassment, desire to please,
Hooting grossly, without explanation.

1984

From the Third Storey

(for Hazel Medd)

"You have to be selfish to be a writer."
"Monstrously selfish?"
"Monstrously selfish," she said
 Jean Rhys in David Plante's *Difficult Women*

Aunt Jane scribbles in the living-room.
When visitors come, she stuffs her work
Under the blotter, and joins in the chat.[1]

(In the third storey, a curious
Laugh; distinct, formal, mirthless.)[2] 5

Daughter Charlotte's[3] first care is to discharge
Her household and filial duties. Only then
May she admit herself to her own bright sphere.

1. This story is told of the novelist Jane Austen (1775–1817) by her nephew.
2. The description is quoted from *Jane Eyre* (1847), Chapter 11; the laughter comes from Rochester's mad wife Bertha Mason, who is locked in the upper story.
3. Novelist Charlotte Brontë (1816–1855), author of *Jane Eyre*.

(There were days when she was quite silent;
Others when I could not account for 10
The sounds she made.)

Home duties are a small part of
The Reverend William's life. Reverently
Elizabeth,[4] wife and mother, furnishes his study,
And writes in the dining-room 15
Which has three doors.

(A vague murmur, peculiar
And lugubrious. Something
Gurgled and moaned.)

George is Agnes's husband. He and 20
Mistress Marian[5] *(what do people call her?)*
Write in one room at their desks, drudging
To pay off his marriage's debts.

(A savage, a sharp, a shrilly sound.
The thing delivering such utterance must rest 25
Ere it repeat the effort. It came
Out of the third storey.)

Sister Virginia,[6] childless wife,
Fathoms the metaphor of room.
But who is One? The upstairs lunatic— 30
Might she not be Oneself?

(A snarling, snatching sound,
Almost like a dog quarreling.)

Between affairs, before marriages,
Jean[7] (*I have called myself so many* 35
Different names) buys twelve technicolored
Quill pens to cheer her bare table
In bedsit Fulham.[8] And writes,

(She was standing, waving her arms,
Above the battlements, and shouting out 40
Till they could hear her a mile off.)

And sets the mad wife free to tell
Truth of mistress, divorcée, mother,
Aunt, daughter, sister, wife:

4. Elizabeth Gaskell (1810–1865), novelist and Brontë's biographer.
5. The philosopher and critic George Lewes (1817–1878) was unable to divorce his wife, Agnes; from 1854 until his death, he lived with Marian Evans (1819–1890), whose novels—written under the name George Eliot—were extremely popular and profitable.
6. Virginia Woolf (1882–1941), novelist and author of *A Room of One's Own* (1929).
7. Novelist Jean Rhys (1894–1979); in *Wide Sargasso Sea* (1966), she retells the story of *Jane Eyre* from Bertha Mason's point of view.
8. Section of London. "Bedsit": a small apartment consisting of a bedroom and sitting room; similar to an efficiency apartment.

Now at last I know 45
Why I was brought here
And what I have to do.

1984

URSULA K. LE GUIN

1929–

The daughter of the distinguished anthropologist Alfred L. Kroeber and the writer-folklorist Theodora Kroeber, the science-fiction writer Ursula K. Le Guin has sometimes compared her own work to that of an anthropologist. "Science fiction allows a fiction writer to make up cultures, to invent—not only a new world, but a new culture," she told an interviewer for the California Quarterly in 1978, adding that "my father preferred to go find [other civilizations]; I prefer to invent them." Imaginatively elaborating new possibilities for human society and personality while incisively commenting on the "real" world, Le Guin's invented cultures are described and dramatized in an impressive range of volumes, including the novels Rocannon's World (1966), The Left Hand of Darkness (1969), and The Dispossessed (1974); the short-story collections The Wind's Twelve Quarters (1975) and The Compass Rose (1982); and the three fantasies for children—A Wizard of Earthsea (1968), The Tombs of Atuan (1971), and The Farthest Shore (1972)—which make up the prize-winning Earthsea trilogy. In Always Coming Home (1985), created with composer Todd Barton, artist Margaret Chodos, and "geomancer" George Hersh, Le Guin initiated a series of multimedia productions, and in Dancing at the Edge of the World (1989), she began collecting her essays on women, language, and space. Such volumes as Wild Oats and Firewood (1988) and Going Out With Peacocks (1994) collect Le Guin's most recent poems.

Born and raised in Berkeley, California, Le Guin attended Radcliffe College and Columbia University. In 1953, while studying in Paris on a Fulbright scholarship, she married the historian Charles A. Le Guin, with whom she eventually settled in Portland, Oregon. From the start, she has explained, her writing always had "what you'd have to call a fantasy element. . . . It took place in an imaginary country or something like that," but it was not until she "got back to reading science fiction in [her] late twenties" that she realized "I could call my stuff science fiction." From that time on, even while working and raising three children, she became a productive and distinguished writer of what might be labeled "speculative fiction" as well as "science fiction." Extending the boundaries of her genre so that science fiction could explore the problems and possibilities of human society with a new intensity, she created imaginary creatures who allowed her to raise important questions about the modes and morals of her own world. Particularly in such works as The Left Hand of Darkness (which won the Hugo and Nebula awards from the Science Fiction Writers of America in 1969 and 1970) and Sur (1982), she examined the pressures and possibilities of gender with subtlety and wit. What would it "be like to be a man-woman, or a woman-man," she asks in The Left Hand of Darkness, a fantasy of life on a planet whose inhabitants are biologically bisexual, and what would it mean if women had discovered the South Pole, she wonders in Sur. Her answers to such questions are invariably both brilliant and surprising. Equally thought provoking, She Unnames Them responds to traditional myths about male linguistic priority. What would have happened if Eve, not Adam, were given the knowledge and responsibility of determining the uses of language?

Sur[1]

A *Summary Report of the* Yelcho *Expedition to the Antarctic,*
1909–1910

Although I have no intention of publishing this report, I think it would be nice if a grandchild of mine, or somebody's grandchild, happened to find it some day; so I shall keep it in the leather trunk in the attic, along with Rosita's christening dress and Juanito's silver rattle and my wedding shoes and finneskos.[2]

The first requisite for mounting an expedition—money—is normally the hardest to come by. I grieve that even in a report destined for a trunk in the attic of a house in a very quiet suburb of Lima[3] I dare not write the name of the generous benefactor, the great soul without whose unstinting liberality the *Yelcho* Expedition would never have been more than the idlest excursion into daydream. That our equipment was the best and most modern—that our provisions were plentiful and fine—that a ship of the Chilean Government, with her brave officers and gallant crew, was twice sent halfway round the world for our convenience: all this is due to that benefactor whose name, alas! I must not say, but whose happiest debtor I shall be till death.

When I was little more than a child my imagination was caught by a newspaper account of the voyage of the *Belgica*, which, sailing south from Tierra del Fuego, became beset by ice in the Bellingshausen Sea and drifted a whole year with the floe, the men aboard her suffering a great deal from want of food and from the terror of the unending winter darkness. I read and reread that account, and later followed with excitement the reports of the rescue of Dr. Nordenskjold from the South Shetland Isles by the dashing Captain Irizar of the *Uruguay*, and the adventures of the *Scotia* in the Weddell Sea. But all these exploits were to me but forerunners of the British National Antarctic Expedition of 1902–1904, in the *Discovery*, and the wonderful account of that expedition by Captain Scott.[4] This book, which I ordered from London and reread a thousand times, filled me with longing to see with my own eyes that strange continent, last Thule[5] of the South, which lies on our maps and globes like a white cloud, a void, fringed here and there with scraps of coastline, dubious capes, supposititious islands, headlands that may or may not be there: Antarctica. And the desire was as pure as the polar snows: to go, to see—no more, no less. I deeply respect the scientific accomplishments of Captain Scott's expedition, and have read with passionate interest the findings of physicists, meteorologists, biologists, etc.; but having had no training in any science, nor any opportunity for such training, my ignorance obliged me to forego any thought of adding to the body of scientific knowledge concerning Antarctica; and the same is true for all the members of my expedition. It seems a pity; but there was nothing we could do about it. Our goal was limited to observation and exploration. We hoped to go a little farther, perhaps, and see a little more; if not, simply to go and to see. A simple ambition, I think, and essentially a modest one.

1. South (Spanish).
2. Boots made of reindeer skin.
3. Largest city of Peru.
4. Robert Falcon Scott (1868–1912), British naval officer and Antarctic explorer, commanded an expedi-

tion to explore the Ross Sea region in 1901–04. The other expeditions mentioned are also genuine.
5. Ultima Thule, the northernmost lands of the ancient world.

THE MAP IN THE ATTIC

Yet it would have remained less than an ambition, no more than a longing, but for the support and encouragement of my dear cousin and friend Juana——(I use no surnames, lest this report fall into strangers' hands at last, and embarrassment or unpleasant notoriety thus be brought upon unsuspecting husbands, sons, etc.) I had lent Juana my copy of *The Voyage of the Discovery*, and it was she who, as we strolled beneath our parasols across the Plaza de Armas after Mass one Sunday in 1908, said, "Well, if Captain Scott can do it, why can't we?"

It was Juana who proposed that we write Carlota—in Valparaiso. Through Carlota we met our benefactor, and so obtained our money, our ship, and even the plausible pretext of going on retreat in a Bolivian convent, which some of us were forced to employ (while the rest of us said we were going to Paris for the winter season). And it was my Juana who in the darkest moments remained resolute, unshaken in her determination to achieve our goal.

And there were dark moments, especially in the early months of 1909—times when I did not see how the Expedition would ever become more than a quarter ton of pemmican[6] gone to waste and a lifelong regret. It was so very hard to gather our expeditionary force together! So few of those we asked even knew what we were talking about—so many thought we were mad, or wicked, or both! And of those few who shared our folly, still fewer were able, when it came to the point, to leave their daily duties and commit themselves to a voyage of at least six months, attended with not inconsiderable uncertainty and danger. An ailing parent; an anxious husband beset by business cares; a child at home with only ignorant or incompetent servants to look after it: these are not responsibilities lightly to be set aside. And those who wished to evade such claims were not the companions we wanted in hard work, risk, and privation.

But since success crowned our efforts, why dwell on the setbacks and delays, or the wretched contrivances and downright lies that we all had to employ? I look back with regret only to those friends who wished to come with us but could not, by any contrivance, get free—those we had to leave behind to a life without danger, without uncertainty, without hope.

On the seventeenth of August, 1909, in Punta Arenas, Chile, all the members of the Expedition met for the first time: Juana and I, the two Peruvians; from Argentina, Zoe, Berta, and Teresa; and our Chileans, Carlota and her friends Eva, Pepita, and Dolores. At the last moment I had received word that Maria's husband, in Quito, was ill, and she must stay to nurse him, so we were nine, not ten. Indeed, we had resigned ourselves to being but eight, when, just as night fell, the indomitable Zoe arrived in a tiny pirogue[7] manned by Indians, her yacht having sprung a leak just as it entered the Strait of Magellan.

That night before we sailed we began to get to know one another; and we agreed, as we enjoyed our abominable supper in the abominable seaport inn of Punta Arenas, that if a situation arose of such urgent danger that one voice must be obeyed without present question, the unenviable honor of speaking with that voice should fall first upon myself: if I were incapacitated, upon Carlota: if she, then upon Berta. We three were then toasted as "Supreme Inca," "La Araucana,"[8] and "The Third Mate," among a lot of laughter and

6. A food originally made by American Indians from dried meat and fruit.
7. Canoe made from a hollow tree trunk.
8. The Araucanian Indians occupied present-day Chile before the Spanish Conquest; like the Incas they were subjugated by the Spanish, but only after much resistance.

cheering. As it came out, to my very great pleasure and relief, my qualities as a "leader" were never tested; the nine of us worked things out amongst us from beginning to end without any orders being given by anybody, and only two or three times with recourse to a vote by voice or show of hands. To be sure, we argued a good deal. But then, we had time to argue. And one way or another the arguments always ended up in a decision, upon which action could be taken. Usually at least one person grumbled about the decision, sometimes bitterly. But what is life without grumbling, and the occasional opportunity to say, "I told you so"? How could one bear housework, or looking after babies, let alone the rigors of sledge-hauling in Antarctica, without grumbling? Officers—as we came to understand aboard the *Yelcho*—are forbidden to grumble; but we nine were, and are, by birth and upbringing, unequivocally and irrevocably, all crew.

Though our shortest course to the southern continent, and that originally urged upon us by the captain of our good ship, was to the South Shetlands and the Bellingshausen Sea, or else by the South Orkneys into the Weddell Sea, we planned to sail west to the Ross Sea, which Captain Scott had explored and described, and from which the brave Ernest Shackleton[9] had returned only the previous autumn. More was known about this region than any other portion of the coast of Antarctica, and though that more was not much, yet it served as some insurance of the safety of the ship, which we felt we had no right to imperil. Captain Pardo had fully agreed with us after studying the charts and our planned itinerary; and so it was westward that we took our course out of the Strait next morning.

Our journey half round the globe was attended by fortune. The little *Yelcho* steamed cheerily along through gale and gleam, climbing up and down those seas of the Southern Ocean that run unbroken round the world. Juana, who had fought bulls and the far more dangerous cows on her family's *estancia*, called the ship *"la vaca valiente,"*[1] because she always returned to the charge. Once we got over being seasick we all enjoyed the sea voyage, though oppressed at times by the kindly but officious protectiveness of the captain and his officers, who felt that we were only "safe" when huddled up in the three tiny cabins which they had chivalrously vacated for our use.

We saw our first iceberg much farther south than we had looked for it, and saluted it with Veuve Clicquot[2] at dinner. The next day we entered the ice pack, the belt of floes and bergs, broken loose from the land ice and winter-frozen seas of Antarctica, which drifts northward in the spring. Fortune still smiled on us: our little steamer, incapable with her unreinforced metal hull, of forcing a way into the ice, picked her way from lane to lane without hesitation, and on the third day we were through the pack, in which ships have sometimes struggled for weeks and been obliged to turn back at last. Ahead of us now lay the dark grey waters of the Ross Sea, and beyond that, on the horizon, the remote glimmer, the cloud-reflected whiteness of the Great Ice Barrier.

Entering the Ross Sea a little east of Longitude West 160°, we came in sight of the Barrier at the place where Captain Scott's party, finding a bight[3] in the vast wall of ice, had gone ashore and sent up their hydrogen-gas balloon for reconnaissance and photography. The towering face of the Barrier, its sheer cliffs

9. Sir Ernest Harry Shackleton (1874–1922), British Antarctic explorer, member of the Scott expedition.
1. The courageous cow (Spanish). "Estancia": cattle ranch (Spanish).
2. An expensive French champagne.
3. A bend in a shoreline, forming a bay.

and azure and violet water-worn caves, all were as described, but the location had changed: instead of a narrow bight there was a considerable bay, full of the beautiful and terrific orca whales playing and spouting in the sunshine of that brilliant southern spring.

Evidently masses of ice many acres in extent had broken away from the Barrier (which—at least for most of its vast extent—does not rest on land but floats on water) since the *Discovery's* passage in 1902. This put our plan to set up camp on the Barrier itself in a new light; and while we were discussing alternatives, we asked Captain Pardo to take the ship west along the Barrier face towards Ross Island and McMurdo Sound. As the sea was clear of ice and quite calm, he was happy to do so, and, when we sighted the smoke plume of Mount Erebus, to share in our celebration—another half case of Veuve Clicquot.

The *Yelcho* anchored in Arrival Bay, and we went ashore in the ship's boat. I cannot describe my emotions when I set foot on the earth, on that earth, the barren, cold gravel at the foot of the long volcanic slope. I felt elation, impatience, gratitude, awe, familiarity. I felt that I was home at last. Eight Adélie penguins immediately came to greet us with many exclamations of interest not unmixed with disapproval. "Where on earth have you been? What took you so long? The Hut is around this way. Please come this way. Mind the rocks!" They insisted on our going to visit Hut Point, where the large structure built by Captain Scott's party stood, looking just as in the photographs and drawings that illustrate his book. The area about it, however, was disgusting— a kind of graveyard of seal skins, seal bones, penguin bones, and rubbish, presided over by the mad, screaming skua gulls. Our escorts waddled past the slaughterhouse in all tranquility, and one showed me personally to the door, though it would not go in.

The interior of the hut was less offensive, but very dreary. Boxes of supplies had been stacked up into a kind of room within the room; it did not look as I had imagined it when the *Discovery* party put on their melodramas and minstrel shows in the long winter night. (Much later, we learned that Sir Ernest had rearranged it a good deal when he was there just a year before us.) It was dirty, and had about it a mean disorder. A pound tin of tea was standing open. Empty meat tins lay about; biscuits were spilled on the floor; a lot of dog turds were underfoot—frozen, of course, but not a great deal improved by that. No doubt the last occupants had had to leave in a hurry, perhaps even in a blizzard. All the same, they could have closed the tea tin. But housekeeping, the art of the infinite, is no game for amateurs.

Teresa proposed that we use the hut as our camp. Zoe counterproposed that we set fire to it. We finally shut the door and left it as we had found it. The penguins appeared to approve, and cheered us all the way to the boat.

McMurdo Sound was free of ice, and Captain Pardo now proposed to take us off Ross Island and across to Victoria Land, where we might camp at the foot of the Western Mountains, on dry and solid earth. But those mountains, with their storm-darkened peaks and hanging cirques and glaciers, looked as awful as Captain Scott had found them on his western journey, and none of us felt much inclined to seek shelter among them.

Aboard the ship that night we decided to go back and set up our base as we had originally planned, on the Barrier itself. For all available reports indicated that the clear way south was across the level Barrier surface until one could as-

cend one of the confluent glaciers to the high plateau which appears to form the whole interior of the continent. Captain Pardo argued strongly against this plan, asking what would become of us if the Barrier "calved"—if our particular acre of ice broke away and started to drift northward. "Well," said Zoe, "then you won't have to come so far to meet us." But he was so persuasive on this theme that he persuaded himself into leaving one of the *Yelcho*'s boats with us when we camped, as a means of escape. We found it useful for fishing, later on.

My first steps on Antarctic soil, my only visit to Ross Island, had not been pleasure unalloyed. I thought of the words of the English poet:

> Though every prospect pleases,
> And only Man is vile.[4]

But then, the backside of heroism is often rather sad; women and servants know that. They know also that the heroism may be no less real for that. But achievement is smaller than men think. What is large is the sky, the earth, the sea, the soul. I looked back as the ship sailed east again that evening. We were well into September now, with ten hours or more of daylight. The spring sunset lingered on the twelve-thousand-foot peak of Erebus and shone rosy gold on her long plume of steam. The steam from our own small funnel faded blue on the twilit water as we crept along under the towering pale wall of ice.

On our return to "Orca Bay"—Sir Ernest. we learned years later, had named it the Bay of Whales—we found a sheltered nook where the Barrier edge was low enough to provide fairly easy access from the ship. The *Yelcho* put out her ice anchor, and the next long, hard days were spent in unloading our supplies and setting up our camp on the ice, a half kilometer in from the edge: a task in which the *Yelcho*'s crew lent us invaluable aid and interminable advice. We took all the aid gratefully, and most of the advice with salt.

The weather so far had been extraordinarily mild for spring in this latitude; the temperature had not yet gone below –20° Fahrenheit, and there was only one blizzard while we were setting up camp. But Captain Scott had spoken feelingly of the bitter south winds on the Barrier, and we had planned accordingly. Exposed as our camp was to every wind, we built no rigid structures above ground. We set up tents to shelter in while we dug out a series of cubicles in the ice itself, lined them with hay insulation and pine boarding, and roofed them with canvas over bamboo poles, covered with snow for weight and insulation. The big central room was instantly named Buenos Aires by our Argentineans, to whom the center, wherever one is, is always Buenos Aires. The heating and cooking stove was in Buenos Aires. The storage tunnels and the privy (called Punta Arenas) got some back heat from the stove. The sleeping cubicles opened off Buenos Aires, and were very small, mere tubes into which one crawled feet first; they were lined deeply with hay and soon warmed by one's body warmth. The sailors called them "coffins" and "wormholes," and looked with horror on our burrows in the ice. But our little warren or prairie-dog village served us well, permitting us as much warmth and privacy as one could reasonably expect under the circumstances. If the *Yelcho* was unable to get through the ice in February, and we had to spend the winter in Antarctica, we certainly could do so, though on very limited rations. For this

4. From the hymn *From Greenland's Icy Mountains* by Bishop Reginald Heber (1783–1826).

coming summer, our base—Sudamérica del Sur, South South America, but we generally called it the Base—was intended merely as a place to sleep, to store our provisions, and to give shelter from blizzards.

To Berta and Eva, however, it was more than that. They were its chief architect-designers, its most ingenious builder-excavators, and its most diligent and contented occupants, forever inventing an improvement in ventilation, or learning how to make skylights, or revealing to us a new addition to our suite of rooms, dug in the living ice. It was thanks to them that our stores were stowed so handily, that our stove drew and heated so efficiently, and that Buenos Aires, where nine people cooked, ate, worked, conversed, argued, grumbled, painted, played the guitar and banjo, and kept the Expedition's library of books and maps, was a marvel of comfort and convenience. We lived there in real amity; and if you simply had to be alone for a while, you crawled into your sleeping hole head first.

Berta went a little farther. When she had done all she could to make South South America livable, she dug out one more cell just under the ice surface, leaving a nearly transparent sheet of ice like a greenhouse roof; and there, alone, she worked at sculptures. They were beautiful forms, some like a blending of the reclining human figure with the subtle curves and volumes of the Weddell seal, others like the fantastic shapes of ice cornices and ice caves. Perhaps they are there still, under the snow, in the bubble in the Great Barrier. There where she made them they might last as long as stone. But she could not bring them north. That is the penalty for carving in water.

Captain Pardo was reluctant to leave us, but his orders did not permit him to hang about the Ross Sea indefinitely, and so at last, with many earnest injunctions to us to stay put—make no journeys—take no risks—beware of frostbite—don't use edge tools—look out for cracks in the ice—and a heartfelt promise to return to Orca Bay on the twentieth of February, or as near that date as wind and ice would permit, the good man bade us farewell, and his crew shouted us a great goodbye cheer as they weighed anchor. That evening, in the long orange twilight of October, we saw the topmast of the *Yelcho* go down the north horizon, over the edge of the world, leaving us to ice, and silence, and the Pole.

That night we began to plan the Southern Journey.

The ensuing month passed in short practice trips and depotlaying.[5] The life we had led at home, though in its own way strenuous, had not fitted any of us for the kind of strain met with in sledge-hauling at ten or twenty degrees below freezing. We all needed as much working-out as possible before we dared undertake a long haul.

My longest exploratory trip, made with Dolores and Carlota, was southwest towards Mount Markham, and it was a nightmare—blizzards and pressure ice[6] all the way out, crevasses and no view of the mountains when we got there, and white weather and sastrugi[7] all the way back. The trip was useful, however, in that we could begin to estimate our capacities; and also in that we had started out with a very heavy load of provisions, which we depoted at 100 and 130 miles SSW of Base. Thereafter other parties pushed on farther, till we had

5. Depositing supplies of food along the route to be taken.
6. Ridges formed in the Antarctic seas by the pres-
sures of sea ice.
7. Long wavelike ridges of snow.

a line of snow cairns and depots right down to Latitude 83° 43′, where Juana
and Zoe, on an exploring trip, had found a kind of stone gateway opening on a
great glacier leading south. We established these depots to avoid, if possible,
the hunger that had bedeviled Captain Scott's Southern Party, and the conse-
quent misery and weakness. And we also established to our own satisfaction—
intense satisfaction—that we were sledge haulers at least as good as Captain
Scott's husky dogs. Of course we could not have expected to pull as much or
as fast as his men. That we did so was because we were favored by much better
weather than Captain Scott's party ever met on the Barrier; and also the quan-
tity and quality of our food made a very considerable difference. I am sure that
the fifteen percent of dried fruits in our pemmican helped prevent scurvy; and
the potatoes, frozen and dried according to an ancient Andean Indian
method, were very nourishing yet very light and compact—perfect sledging
rations. In any case, it was with considerable confidence in our capacities that
we made ready at last for the Southern Journey.

The Southern Party consisted of two sledge teams: Juana, Dolores, and my-
self; Carlota, Pepita, and Zoe. The support team of Berta, Eva, and Teresa set
out before us with a heavy load of supplies, going right up onto the glacier to
prospect routes and leave depots of supplies for our return journey. We fol-
lowed five days behind them, and met them returning between Depot Ercilla
and Depot Miranda (see map). That "night"—of course there was no real
darkness—we were all nine together in the heart of the level plain of ice. It was
the fifteenth of November, Dolores's birthday. We celebrated by putting eight
ounces of pisco[8] in the hot chocolate, and became very merry. We sang. It is
strange now to remember how thin our voices sounded in that great silence. It
was overcast, white weather, without shadows and without visible horizon or
any feature to break the level; there was nothing to see at all. We had come to
that white place on the map, that void, and there we flew and sang like spar-
rows.

After sleep and a good breakfast the Base Party continued north, and the
Southern Party sledged on. The sky cleared presently. High up, thin clouds
passed over very rapidly from southwest to northeast, but down on the Barrier
it was calm and just cold enough, five or ten degrees below freezing, to give a
firm surface for hauling.

On the level ice we never pulled less than eleven miles, seventeen kilome-
ters, a day, and generally fifteen or sixteen miles, twenty-five kilometers. (Our
instruments, being British made, were calibrated in feet, miles, degrees
Fahrenheit, etc., but we often converted miles to kilometers because the
larger numbers sounded more encouraging.) At the time we left South
America, we knew only that Mr. Shackleton had mounted another expedition
to the Antarctic in 1908, had tried to attain the Pole but failed, and had re-
turned to England in June of the current year, 1909. No coherent report of his
explorations had yet reached South America when we left; we did not know
what route he had gone, or how far he had got. But we were not altogether
taken by surprise when, far across the featureless white plain, tiny beneath the
mountain peaks and the strange silent flight of the rainbow-fringed cloud
wisps, we saw a fluttering dot of black. We turned west from our course to visit
it: a snow heap nearly buried by the winter's storms—a flag on a bamboo pole,

8. A Peruvian brandy.

a mere shred of threadbare cloth—an empty oilcan—and a few footprints standing some inches above the ice. In some conditions of weather the snow compressed under one's weight remains when the surrounding soft snow melts or is scoured away by the wind; and so these reversed footprints had been left standing all these months, like rows of cobbler's lasts[9]—a queer sight.

We met no other such traces on our way. In general I believe our course was somewhat east of Mr. Shackleton's. Juana, our surveyor, had trained herself well and was faithful and methodical in her sightings and readings, but our equipment was minimal—a theodolite on tripod legs, a sextant[1] with artificial horizon, two compasses, and chronometers. We had only the wheel meter on the sledge to give distance actually traveled.

In any case, it was the day after passing Mr. Shackleton's waymark that I first saw clearly the great glacier among the mountains to the southwest, which was to give us a pathway from the sea level of the Barrier up to the altiplano,[2] ten thousand feet above. The approach was magnificent: a gateway formed by immense vertical domes and pillars of rock. Zoe and Juana had called the vast ice river that flowed through that gateway the Florence Nightingale[3] Glacier, wishing to honor the British, who had been the inspiration and guide of our expedition; that very brave and very peculiar lady seemed to represent so much that is best, and strangest, in the island race. On maps, of course, this glacier bears the name Mr. Shackleton gave it, the Beardmore.

The ascent of the Nightingale was not easy. The way was open at first, and well marked by our support party, but after some days we came among terrible crevasses, a maze of hidden cracks, from a foot to thirty feet wide and from thirty to a thousand feet deep. Step by step we went, and step by step, and the way always upward now. We were fifteen days on the glacier. At first the weather was hot, up to 20° F., and the hot nights without darkness were wretchedly uncomfortable in our small tents. And all of us suffered more or less from snowblindness just at the time when we wanted clear eyesight to pick our way among the ridges and crevasses of the tortured ice, and to see the wonders about and before us. For at every day's advance more great, nameless peaks came into view in the west and southwest, summit beyond summit, range beyond range, stark rock and snow in the unending noon.

We gave names to these peaks, not very seriously, since we did not expect our discoveries to come to the attention of geographers. Zoe had a gift for naming, and it is thanks to her that certain sketch maps in various suburban South American attics bear such curious features as "Bolívar's Big Nose," "I Am General Rosas,"[4] "The Cloudmaker," "Whose Toe?," and "Throne of Our Lady of the Southern Cross." And when at last we got up onto the altiplano, the great interior plateau, it was Zoe who called it the pampa, and maintained that we walked there among vast herds of invisible cattle, transparent cattle pastured on the spindrift snow, their gauchos[5] the restless, merciless winds. We were by then all a little crazy with exhaustion and the great altitude—

9. Foot-shaped blocks used in shoemaking.
1. An instrument that measures the altitude of stars. "Theodolite": an instrument that measures angles. Both are used for surveying and navigation.
2. High plateau.
3. Florence Nightingale (1820–1910), British nursing pioneer and feminist writer.

4. Juan Manuel de Rosas (1793–1877), Argentine dictator. Simon Bolívar (1783–1830), South American soldier and activist who led the revolution against Spain.
5. South American cattlemen. "Pampa": South American grazing land.

twelve thousand feet—and the cold and the wind blowing and the luminous circles and crosses surrounding the suns, for often there were three or four suns in the sky, up there.

That is not a place where people have any business to be. We should have turned back; but since we had worked so hard to get there, it seemed that we should go on, at least for a while.

A blizzard came with very low temperatures, so we had to stay in the tents, in our sleeping bags, for thirty hours, a rest we all needed; though it was warmth we needed most, and there was no warmth on that terrible plain anywhere at all but in our veins. We huddled close together all that time. The ice we lay on is two miles thick.

It cleared suddenly and became, for the plateau, good weather: twelve below zero and the wind not very strong. We three crawled out of our tent and met the others crawling out of theirs. Carlota told us then that her group wished to turn back. Pepita had been feeling very ill; even after the rest during the blizzard, her temperature would not rise above 90°. Carlota was having trouble breathing. Zoe was perfectly fit, but much preferred staying with her friends and lending them a hand in difficulties to pushing on towards the Pole. So we put the four ounces of pisco which we had been keeping for Christmas into the breakfast cocoa, and dug out our tents, and loaded our sledges, and parted there in the white daylight on the bitter plain.

Our sledge was fairly light by now. We pulled on to the south. Juana calculated our position daily. On the twenty-second of December, 1909, we reached the South Pole. The weather was, as always, very cruel. Nothing of any kind marked the dreary whiteness. We discussed leaving some kind of mark or monument, a snow cairn, a tent pole and flag; but there seemed no particular reason to do so. Anything we could do, anything we were, was insignificant, in that awful place. We put up the tent for shelter for an hour and made a cup of tea, and then struck "90° Camp."[6] Dolores, standing patient as ever in her sledging harness, looked at the snow; it was so hard frozen that it showed no trace of our footprints coming, and she said, "Which way?"

"North," said Juana.

It was a joke, because at that particular place there is no other direction. But we did not laugh. Our lips were cracked with frostbite and hurt too much to let us laugh. So we started back, and the wind at our backs pushed us along, and dulled the knife edges of the waves of frozen snow.

All that week the blizzard wind pursued us like a pack of mad dogs. I cannot describe it. I wished we had not gone to the Pole. I think I wish it even now. But I was glad even then that we had left no sign there, for some man longing to be first might come some day, and find it, and know then what a fool he had been, and break his heart.

We talked, when we could talk, of catching up to Carlota's party, since they might be going slower than we. In fact they had used their tent as a sail to catch the following wind and had got far ahead of us. But in many places they had built snow cairns or left some sign for us; once Zoe had written on the lee side of a ten-foot sastruga, just as children write on the sand of the beach at Miraflores, "This Way Out!" The wind blowing over the frozen ridge had left the words perfectly distinct.

6. The South Pole is at latitude 90 degrees and longitude 0 degrees.

In the very hour that we began to descend the glacier, the weather turned warmer, and the mad dogs were left to howl forever tethered to the Pole. The distance that had taken us fifteen days going up we covered in only eight days going down. But the good weather that had aided us descending the Nightingale became a curse down on the Barrier ice, where we had looked forward to a kind of royal progress from depot to depot, eating our fill and taking our time for the last three hundred-odd miles. In a tight place on the glacier I lost my goggles—I was swinging from my harness at the time in a crevasse— and then Juana had broken hers when we had to do some rock climbing coming down to the Gateway. After two days in bright sunlight with only one pair of snow goggles to pass amongst us, we were all suffering badly from snowblindness. It became acutely painful to keep lookout for landmarks or depot flags, to take sightings, even to study the compass, which had to be laid down on the snow to steady the needle. At Concolorcorvo Depot, where there was a particularly good supply of food and fuel, we gave up, crawled into our sleeping bags with bandaged eyes, and slowly boiled alive like lobsters in the tent exposed to the relentless sun. The voices of Berta and Zoe were the sweetest sound I ever heard. A little concerned about us, they had skied south to meet us. They led us home to Base.

We recovered quite swiftly, but the altiplano left its mark. When she was very little, Rosita asked if a dog "had bitted Mama's toes." I told her Yes, a great, white, mad dog named Blizzard! My Rosita and my Juanito heard many stories when they were little, about that fearful dog and how it howled, and the transparent cattle of the invisible gauchos, and a river of ice eight thousand feet high called Nightingale, and how Cousin Juana drank a cup of tea standing on the bottom of the world under seven suns, and other fairy tales.

We were in for one severe shock when we reached Base at last. Teresa was pregnant. I must admit that my first response to the poor girl's big belly and sheepish look was anger—rage—fury. That one of us should have concealed anything, and such a thing, from the others! But Teresa had done nothing of the sort. Only those who had concealed from her what she most needed to know were to blame. Brought up by servants, with four years' schooling in a convent, and married at sixteen, the poor girl was still so ignorant at twenty years of age that she had thought it was "the cold weather" that made her miss her periods. Even this was not entirely stupid, for all of us on the Southern Journey had seen our periods change or stop altogether as we experienced increasing cold, hunger, and fatigue. Teresa's appetite had begun to draw general attention; and then she had begun, as she said pathetically, "to get fat." The others were worried at the thought of all the sledge-hauling she had done, but she flourished, and the only problem was her positively insatiable appetite. As well as could be determined from her shy references to her last night on the hacienda with her husband, the baby was due at just about the same time as the *Yelcho*, the twentieth of February. But we had not been back from the Southern Journey two weeks when, on February 14, she went into labor.

Several of us had borne children and had helped with deliveries, and anyhow most of what needs to be done is fairly self-evident; but a first labor can be long and trying, and we were all anxious, while Teresa was frightened out of her wits. She kept calling for her José till she was as hoarse as a skua.[7] Zoe lost

7. Predatory seabird.

all patience at last and said, "By God, Teresa, if you say 'José!' once more I hope you have a penguin!" But what she had, after twenty long hours, was a pretty little red-faced girl.

Many were the suggestions for that child's name from her eight proud mid-wife-aunts: Polita, Penguina, McMurdo, Victoria. . . . But Teresa announced, after she had had a good sleep and a large serving of pemmican, "I shall name her Rosa—Rosa del Sur," Rose of the South. That night we drank the last two bottles of Veuve Clicquot (having finished the pisco at 88° 30′ South) in toasts to our little Rose.

On the nineteenth of February, a day early, my Juana came down into Buenos Aires in a hurry. "The ship," she said, "the ship has come," and she burst into tears—she who had never wept in all our weeks of pain and weariness on the long haul.

Of the return voyage there is nothing to tell. We came back safe.

In 1912 all the world learned that the brave Norwegian Amundsen[8] had reached the South Pole; and then, much later, came the accounts of how Captain Scott and his men had come there after him, but did not come home again.

Just this year, Juana and I wrote to the captain of the *Yelcho*, for the newspapers have been full of the story of his gallant dash to rescue Sir Ernest Shackleton's men from Elephant Island, and we wished to congratulate him, and once more to thank him. Never one word has he breathed of our secret. He is a man of honor, Luis Pardo.

I add this last note in 1929. Over the years we have lost touch with one another. It is very difficult for women to meet, when they live so far apart as we do. Since Juana died, I have seen none of my old sledge-mates, though sometimes we write. Our little Rosa del Sur died of the scarlet fever when she was five years old. Teresa had many other children. Carlota took the veil[9] in Santiago ten years ago. We are old women now, with old husbands, and grown children, and grandchildren who might some day like to read about the Expedition. Even if they are rather ashamed of having such a crazy grandmother, they may enjoy sharing in the secret. But they must not let Mr. Amundsen know. He would be terribly embarrassed and disappointed. There is no need for him or anyone else outside the family to know. We left no footprints, even.

1982

She Unnames Them

Most of them accepted namelessness with the perfect indifference with which they had so long accepted and ignored their names. Whales and dolphins, seals and sea otters consented with particular grace and alacrity, sliding into anonymity as into their element. A faction of yaks, however, protested. They said that "yak" sounded right, and that almost everyone who knew they existed called them that. Unlike the ubiquitous creatures such as rats and

8. Roald Amundsen (1872–1928), Norwegian explorer, first man to reach the South Pole. 9. I.e., became a nun.

fleas, who had been called by hundreds or thousands of different names since Babel, the yaks could truly say, they said, that they had a *name*. They discussed the matter all summer. The councils of the elderly females finally agreed that though the name might be useful to others it was so redundant from the yak point of view that they never spoke it themselves and hence might as well dispense with it. After they presented the argument in this light to their bulls, a full consensus was delayed only by the onset of severe early blizzards. Soon after the beginning of the thaw, their agreement was reached and the designation "yak" was returned to the donor.

Among the domestic animals, few horses had cared what anybody called them since the failure of Dean Swift's[1] attempt to name them from their own vocabulary. Cattle, sheep, swine, asses, mules, and goats, along with chickens, geese, and turkeys, all agreed enthusiastically to give their names back to the people to whom—as they put it—they belonged.

A couple of problems did come up with pets. The cats, of course, steadfastly denied ever having had any name other than those self-given, unspoken, ineffably personal names which, as the poet named Eliot[2] said, they spend long hours daily contemplating—though none of the contemplators has ever admitted that what they contemplate is their names and some onlookers have wondered if the object of that meditative gaze might not in fact be the Perfect, or Platonic, Mouse.[3] In any case, it is a moot point now. It was with the dogs, and with some parrots, lovebirds, ravens, and mynahs, that the trouble arose. These verbally talented individuals insisted that their names were important to them, and flatly refused to part with them. But as soon as they understood that the issue was precisely one of individual choice, and that anybody who wanted to be called Rover, or Froufrou, or Polly, or even Birdie in the personal sense, was perfectly free to do so, not one of them had the least objection to parting with the lowercase (or, as regards German creatures, uppercase) generic appellations "poodle," "parrot," "dog," or "bird," and all the Linnaean[4] qualifiers that had trailed along behind them for two hundred years like tin cans tied to a tail.

The insects parted with their names in vast clouds and swarms of ephemeral[5] syllables buzzing and stinging and humming and flitting and crawling and tunneling away.

As for the fish of the sea, their names dispersed from them in silence throughout the oceans like faint, dark blurs of cuttlefish ink, and drifted off on the currents without a trace.

None were left now to unname, and yet how close I felt to them when I saw one of them swim or fly or trot or crawl across my way or over my skin, or stalk me in the night, or go along beside me for a while in the day. They seemed far closer than when their names had stood between myself and them like a clear barrier: so close that my fear of them and their fear of me became one same fear. And the attraction that many of us felt, the desire to smell one another's

1. The last section of *Gulliver's Travels* (1726) by Jonathan Swift (1667–1745), dean of St. Patrick's, Dublin, describes the country and language of the Houyhnhnms, who were rational horses.
2. T. S. Eliot, in *The Naming of Cats* (1939).
3. The Greek philosopher Plato (4th century B.C.) argued that there exist ideal forms or archetypes of all

material things (these perfect Ideas guarantee the existence of the phenomenal world).
4. Swiss botanist Karl Linnaeus (1701–1778) devised the modern system of binomial scientific nomenclature for plants and animals.
5. Existing only for a day.

smells, feel or rub or caress one another's scales or skin or feathers or fur, taste one another's blood or flesh, keep one another warm—that attraction was now all one with the fear, and the hunter could not be told from the hunted, nor the eater from the food.

This was more or less the effect I had been after. It was somewhat more powerful than I had anticipated, but I could not now, in all conscience, make an exception for myself. I resolutely put anxiety away, went to Adam,[6] and said, "You and your father lent me this—gave it to me, actually. It's been really useful, but it doesn't exactly seem to fit very well lately. But thanks very much! It's really been very useful."

It is hard to give back a gift without sounding peevish or ungrateful, and I did not want to leave him with that impression of me. He was not paying much attention, as it happened, and said only, "Put it down over there, O.K.?" and went on with what he was doing.

One of my reasons for doing what I did was that talk was getting us nowhere, but all the same I felt a little let down. I had been prepared to defend my decision. And I thought that perhaps when he did notice he might be upset and want to talk. I put some things away and fiddled around a little, but he continued to do what he was doing and to take no notice of anything else. At last I said, "Well, goodbye, dear. I hope the garden key turns up."

He was fitting parts together, and said, without looking around, "O.K., fine, dear. When's dinner?"

"I'm not sure,' I said. "I'm going now. With the—" I hesitated, and finally said, "With them, you know," and went on out. In fact, I had only just then realized how hard it would have been to explain myself. I could not chatter away as I used to do, taking it all for granted. My words now must be as slow, as new, as single, as tentative as the steps I took going down the path away from the house, between the dark-branched, tall dancers motionless against the winter shining.

1985

6. In Genesis 2:19, God brings all the beasts to Adam for naming; in Genesis 3:20, shortly before their expulsion from the Garden of Eden, Adam gives his wife the name Eve.

PAULE MARSHALL

1929–

Taken together, *Brown Girl, Brownstones* (1959), *Soul Clap Hands and Sing* (1961), *The Chosen Place, the Timeless People* (1969), *Praisesong for the Widow* (1983), *Reema and Other Short Stories* (1983), and *Daughters* (1991) constitute Paule Marshall's lyrical story about the hybridity of American culture and in particular her appreciation of the enriching traditions possessed by people from African and Caribbean backgrounds. Whether her setting is New York City, British Guiana, Brazil, Grenada, or Barbados, her characters experience the competing values, linguistic practices, spiritual ties, and social mores of mixed ancestries that enable Marshall to examine not only the personal toll histories of colonization take but also paradoxically the intertwined heritages they generate.

The daughter of emigrants from Barbados, West Indies, Marshall grew up in

Brooklyn, New York, and was educated first at Hunter, then at Brooklyn College. During the 1950s, she worked as a librarian and as the only female staff member of *Our World*, a black magazine. She currently teaches English and creative writing at Virginia Commonwealth University. Although her fiction has been shaped by her early, extensive reading in the works of Thomas Mann, Joseph Conrad, Ralph Ellison, and James Baldwin, the essay printed here makes clear how indebted she remains to the verbal creativity she encountered amid the "ordinary housewives" who chatted daily in what she calls "the wordshop" of her mother's kitchen.

Poets in the Kitchen

Some years ago, when I was teaching a graduate seminar in fiction at Columbia University, a well known male novelist visited my class to speak on his development as a writer. In discussing his formative years, he didn't realize it but he seriously endangered his life by remarking that women writers are luckier than those of his sex because they usually spend so much time as children around their mothers and their mothers' friends in the kitchen.

What did he say that for? The women students immediately forgot about being in awe of him and began readying their attack for the question and answer period later on. Even I bristled. There again was that awful image of women locked away from the world in the kitchen with only each other to talk to, and their daughters locked in with them.

But my guest wasn't really being sexist or trying to be provocative or even spoiling for a fight. What he meant—when he got around to explaining himself more fully—was that, given the way children are (or were) raised in our society, with little girls kept closer to home and their mothers, the women writer stands a better chance of being exposed, while growing up, to the kind of talk that goes on among women, more often than not in the kitchen; and that this experience gives her an edge over her male counterpart by instilling in her an appreciation for ordinary speech.

It was clear that my guest lecturer attached great importance to this, which is understandable. Common speech and the plain, workaday words that make it up are, after all, the stock in trade of some of the best fiction writers. They are the principal means by which characters in a novel or story reveal themselves and give voice sometimes to profound feelings and complex ideas about themselves and the world. Perhaps the proper measure of a writer's talent is skill in rendering everyday speech—when it is appropriate to the story—as well as the ability to tap, to exploit, the beauty, poetry and wisdom it often contains.

"If you say what's on your mind in the language that comes to you from your parents and your street and your friends you'll probably say something beautiful." Grace Paley[1] tells this, she says, to her students at the beginning of every writing course.

It's all a matter of exposure and a training of the ear for the would-be writer in those early years of apprenticeship. And, according to my guest lecturer, this training, the best of it, often takes place in as unglamorous a setting as the kitchen.

He didn't know it, but he was essentially describing my experience as a little

1. American poet and short-story writer (1922–).

girl. I grew up among poets. Now they didn't look like poets—whatever that breed is supposed to look like. Nothing about them suggested that poetry was their calling. They were just a group of ordinary housewives and mothers, my mother included, who dressed in a way (shapeless housedresses, dowdy felt hats and long, dark, solemn coats) that made it impossible for me to imagine they had ever been young.

Nor did they do what poets were supposed to do—spend their days in an attic room writing verses. They never put pen to paper except to write occasionally to their relatives in Barbados. "I take my pen in hand hoping these few lines will find you in health as they leave me fair for the time being," was the way their letters invariably began. Rather, their day was spent "scrubbing floor," as they described the work they did.

Several mornings a week these unknown bards would put an apron and a pair of old house shoes in a shopping bag and take the train or streetcar from our section of Brooklyn out to Flatbush.[2] There, those who didn't have steady jobs would wait on certain designated corners for the white housewives in the neighborhood to come along and bargain with them over pay for a day's work cleaning their houses. This was the ritual even in the winter.

Later, armed with the few dollars they had earned, which in their vocabulary became "a few raw-mouth pennies," they made their way back to our neighborhood, where they would sometimes stop off to have a cup of tea or cocoa together before going home to cook dinner for their husbands and children.

The basement kitchen of the brownstone house where my family lived was the usual gathering place. Once inside the warm safety of its walls the women threw off the drab coats and hats, seated themselves at the large center table, drank their cups of tea or cocoa, and talked. While my sister and I sat at a smaller table over in a corner doing our homework, they talked—endlessly, passionately, poetically, and with impressive range. No subject was beyond them. True, they would indulge in the usual gossip: whose husband was running with whom, whose daughter looked slightly "in the way" (pregnant) under her bridal gown as she walked down the aisle. That sort of thing. But they also tackled the great issues of the time. They were always, for example, discussing the state of the economy. It was the mid and late 30's then, and the aftershock of the Depression, with its soup lines and suicides on Wall Street, was still being felt.

Some people, they declared, didn't know how to deal with adversity. They didn't know that you had to "tie up your belly" (hold in the pain, that is) when things got rough and go on with life. They took their image from the belly-band that is tied around the stomach of a newborn baby to keep the navel pressed in.

They talked politics. Roosevelt was their hero. He had come along and rescued the country with relief and jobs, and in gratitude they christened their sons Franklin and Delano and hoped they would live up to the names.

If F.D.R. was their hero, Marcus Garvey[3] was their God. The name of the fiery, Jamaican-born black nationalist of the 20's was constantly invoked around the table. For he had been their leader when they first came to the

2. Another section of Brooklyn.
3. Leader of the Back to Africa movement (1887–1940).

United States from the West Indies shortly after World War I. They had contributed to his organization, the United Negro Improvement Association
(UNIA), out of their meager salaries, bought shares in his ill-fated Black Star
Shipping Line, and at the height of the movement they had marched as members of his "nurses' brigade" in their white uniforms up Seventh Avenue in
Harlem during the great Garvey Day parades. Garvey: He lived on through the
power of their memories.

And their talk was of war and rumors of wars. They raged against World War
II when it broke out in Europe, blaming it on the politicians. "It's these politicians. They're the ones always starting up all this lot of war. But what they
care? It's the poor people got to suffer and mothers with their sons." If it was
their sons, they swore they would keep them out of the Army by giving them
soap to eat each day to make their hearts sound defective. Hitler? He was for
them "the devil incarnate."

Then there was home. They reminisced often and at length about home.
The old country. Barbados—or Bimshire, as they affectionately called it. The
little Caribbean island in the sun they loved but had to leave. "Poor—poor but
sweet" was the way they remembered it.

And naturally they discussed their adopted home. America came in for
both good and bad marks. They lashed out at it for the racism they encountered. They took to task some of the people they worked for, especially those
who gave them only a hard-boiled egg and a few spoonfuls of cottage cheese
for lunch. "As if anybody can scrub floor on an egg and some cheese that don't
have no taste to it!"

Yet although they caught H in "this man country," as they called America, it
was nonetheless a place where "you could at least see your way to make a dollar." That much they acknowledged. They might even one day accumulate
enough dollars, with both them and their husbands working, to buy the
brownstone houses which, like my family, they were only leasing at that period. This was their consuming ambition: to "buy house" and to see the children through.

There was no way for me to understand it at the time, but the talk that filled
the kitchen those afternoons was highly functional. It served as therapy, the
cheapest kind available to my mother and her friends. Not only did it help
them recover from the long wait on the corner that morning and the bargaining over their labor, it restored them to a sense of themselves and reaffirmed
their self-worth. Through language they were able to overcome the humiliations of the work-day.

But more than therapy, that freewheeling, wide-ranging, exuberant talk
functioned as an outlet for the tremendous creative energy they possessed.
They were women in whom the need for self-expression was strong, and since
language was the only vehicle readily available to them they made of it an art
form that—in keeping with the African tradition in which art and life are
one—was an integral part of their lives.

And their talk was a refuge. They never really ceased being baffled and overwhelmed by America—its vastness, complexity and power. Its strange customs and laws. At a level beyond words they remained fearful and in awe.
Their uneasiness and fear were even reflected in their attitude toward the children they had given birth to in this country. They referred to those like myself,

the little Brooklyn-born Bajans (Barbadians), as "these New York children" and complained that they couldn't discipline us properly because of the laws here. "You can't beat these children as you would like, you know, because the authorities in this place will dash you in jail for them. After all, these is New York children." Not only were we different, American, we had, as they saw it, escaped their ultimate authority.

Confronted therefore by a world they could not encompass, which even limited their rights as parents, and at the same time finding themselves permanently separated from the world they had known, they took refuge in language. "Language is the only homeland," Czeslaw Milosz, the emigré Polish writer and Nobel Laureate, has said. This is what it became for the women at the kitchen table.

It served another purpose also, I suspect. My mother and her friends were after all the female counterpart of Ralph Ellison's invisible man.[4] Indeed, you might say they suffered a triple invisibility, being black, female and foreigners. They really didn't count in American society except as a source of cheap labor. But given the kind of women they were, they couldn't tolerate the fact of their invisibility, their powerlessness. And they fought back, using the only weapon at their command: the spoken word.

Those late afternoon conversations on a wide range of topics were a way for them to feel they exercised some measure of control over their lives and the events that shaped them. "Soully-gal, talk yuh talk!" they were always exhorting each other. "In this man world you got to take yuh mouth and make a gun!" They were in control, if only verbally and if only for the two hours or so that they remained in our house.

For me, sitting over in the corner, being seen but not heard, which was the rule for children in those days, it wasn't only what the women talked about—the content—but the way they put things—their style. The insight, irony, wit and humor they brought to their stories and discussions and their poet's inventiveness and daring with language—which of course I could only sense but not define back then.

They had taken the standard English taught them in the primary schools of Barbados and transformed it into an idiom, an instrument that more adequately described them—changing around the syntax and imposing their own rhythm and accent so that the sentences were more pleasing to their ears. They added the few African sounds and words that had survived, such as the derisive suck-teeth sound and the word "yam," meaning to eat. And to make it more vivid, more in keeping with their expressive quality, they brought to bear a raft of metaphors, parables, Biblical quotations, sayings and the like:

"The sea ain' got no back door," they would say, meaning that it wasn't like a house where if there was a fire you could run out the back. Meaning that it was not to be trifled with. And meaning perhaps in a larger sense that man should treat all of nature with caution and respect.

"I has read hell by heart and called every generation blessed!" They sometimes went in for hyperbole.

A woman expecting a baby was never said to be pregnant. They never used that word. Rather, she was "in the way" or, better yet, "tumbling big." "Guess who I butt up on in the market the other day tumbling big again!"

4. The hero of Ellison's 1952 novel, *Invisible Man*.

And a woman with a reputation of being too free with her sexual favors was known in their book as a "thoroughfare"—the sense of men like a steady stream of cars moving up and down the road of her life. Or she might be dubbed "a free-bee," which was my favorite of the two. I liked the image it conjured up of a woman scandalous perhaps but independent, who flitted from one flower to another in a garden of male beauties, sampling their nectar, taking her pleasure at will, the roles reversed.

And nothing, no matter how beautiful, was ever described as simply beautiful. It was always "beautiful-ugly": the beautiful-ugly dress, the beautiful-ugly house, the beautiful-ugly car. Why the word "ugly," I used to wonder, when the thing they were referring to was beautiful, and they knew it. Why the antonym, the contradiction, the linking of opposites? It used to puzzle me greatly as a child.

There is the theory in linguistics which states that the idiom of a people, the way they use language, reflects not only the most fundamental views they hold of themselves and the world but their very conception of reality. Perhaps in using the term "beautiful-ugly" to describe nearly everything, my mother and her friends were expressing what they believed to be a fundamental dualism in life: the idea that a thing is at the same time its opposite, and that these opposites, these contradictions make up the whole. But theirs was not a Manichaean brand of dualism that sees matter, flesh, the body, as inherently evil, because they constantly addressed each other as "soully-gal"—soul: spirit; gal: the body, flesh, the visible self. And it was clear from their tone that they gave one as much weight and importance as the other. They had never heard of the mind/body split.

As for God, they summed up His essential attitude in a phrase. "God," they would say, "don't love ugly and He ain' stuck on pretty."

Using everyday speech, the simple commonplace words—but always with imagination and skill—they gave voice to the most complex ideas. Flannery O'Connor[5] would have approved of how they made ordinary language work, as she put it, "double-time," stretching, shading, deepening its meaning. Like Joseph Conrad[6] they were always trying to infuse new life in the "old words worn thin . . . by . . . careless usage." And the goals of their oral art were the same as his: "to make you hear, to make you feel . . . to make you *see*." This was their guiding esthetic.

By the time I was 8 or 9, I graduated from the corner of the kitchen to the neighborhood library, and thus from the spoken to the written word. The Macon Street Branch of the Brooklyn Public Library was an imposing half block long edifice of heavy gray masonry, with glass-paneled doors at the front and two tall metal torches symbolizing the light that comes of learning flanking the wide steps outside.

The inside was just as impressive. More steps—of pale marble with gleaming brass railings at the center and sides—led up to the circulation desk, and a great pendulum clock gazed down from the balcony stacks that faced the entrance. Usually stationed at the top of the steps like the guards outside Buckingham Palace[7] was the custodian, a stern-faced West Indian type who

5. American fiction writer (1925–1964), who wrote that the aim of the short-story writer is "to make the concrete work double time" (*Mystery and Manners*).
6. Polish-born writer of fiction (1857–1924); the quo-

tation is from the preface to *The Nigger of the "Narcissus"* (1897).
7. The London residence of British sovereigns; its guards are the famous "Beefeaters."

for years, until I was old enough to obtain an adult card, would immediately shoo me with one hand into the Children's Room and with the other threaten me into silence, a finger to his lips. You would have thought he was the chief librarian and not just someone whose job it was to keep the brass polished and the clock wound. I put him in a story called "Barbados" years later and had terrible things happen to him at the end.

I sheltered from the storm of adolescence in the Macon Street library, reading voraciously, indiscriminately, everything from Jane Austen to Zane Grey,[8] but with a special passion for the long, full-blown, richly detailed 18th- and 19th-century picaresque tales: "Tom Jones," "Great Expectations," "Vanity Fair."[9]

But although I loved nearly everything I read and would enter fully into the lives of the characters—indeed, would cease being myself and become them—I sensed a lack after a time. Something I couldn't quite define was missing. And then one day, browsing in the poetry section, I came across a book by someone called Paul Laurence Dunbar[1] and opening it I found the photograph of a wistful, sad-eyed poet who to my surprise was black. I turned to a poem at random. "Little brown-baby wif spa'klin' eyes / Come to yo' pappy an' set on his knee." Although I had a little difficulty at first with the words in dialect, the poem spoke to me as nothing I had read before of the closeness, the special relationship I had had with my father, who by then had become an ardent believer in Father Divine[2] and gone to live in Father's "Kingdom" in Harlem. Reading it helped to ease somewhat the tight knot of sorrow and longing I carried around in my chest that refused to go away. I read another poem. " 'Lias! 'Lias! Bless de Lawd! / Don' you know de day's / erbroad? / Ef you don't get up, you scamp / Dey'll be trouble in dis camp." I laughed. It reminded me of the way my mother sometimes yelled at my sister and me to get out of bed in the mornings.

And another: "Seen my lady home las' night / Jump back, honey, jump back. / Hel' huh han' an' sque'z it tight . . ." About love between a black man and a black woman. I had never seen that written about before and it roused in me all kinds of delicious feelings and hopes

And I began to search then for books and stories and poems about "The Race" (as it was put back then), about my people. While not abandoning Thackeray, Fielding, Dickens and the others, I started asking the reference librarian, who was white, for books by Negro writers, although I must admit I did so at first with a feeling of shame—the shame I and many others used to experience in those days whenever the word "Negro" or "colored" came up.

No grade school literature teacher of mine had ever mentioned Dunbar or James Weldon Johnson or Langston Hughes. I didn't know that Zora Neale Hurston existed and was busy writing and being published during those years. Nor was I made aware of people like Frederick Douglass and Harriet Tubman[3]—their spirit and example—or the great 19th-century abolitionist and feminist Sojourner

8. American writer of westerns (1875–1939). Jane Austen (1775–1817), English novelist.
9. Novels by the English authors Henry Fielding (1707–1754), Charles Dickens (1812–1870), and William Thackeray (1811–1863), respectively.
1. American poet (1872–1906).
2. Born George Baker (1880?–1965), he became the most popular Harlem religious leader of the 1930s, gaining much wealth and many followers of his cult-

like Peace Mission movement.
3. A fugitive slave (1820?–1913), who rescued many other slaves. Johnson (1871–1938), lyricist, writer, and civil rights activist who became secretary of the NAACP. Hughes (1902–1967) wrote poetry, fiction, and plays. Hurston (1891–1960), writer and anthropologist. Douglass (1817–1896), orator, author, abolitionist, and supporter of women's rights.

Truth. There wasn't even Negro History Week when I attended P.S. 35 on Decatur Street!

What I needed, what all the kids—West Indian and native black American alike—with whom I grew up needed, was an equivalent of the Jewish shul,[4] someplace where we could go after school—the schools that were shortchanging us—and read works by those like ourselves and learn about our history.

It was around that time that I began harboring the dangerous thought of someday trying to write myself. Perhaps a poem about an apple tree, although I had never seen one. Or the story of a girl who could magically transplant herself to wherever she wanted to be in the world—such as Father Divine's kingdom in Harlem. Dunbar—his dark, eloquent face, his large volume of poems—permitted me to dream that I might someday write, and with something of the power with words my mother and her friends possessed.

When people at readings and writers' conferences ask me who my major influences were, they are sometimes a little disappointed when I don't immediately name the usual literary giants. True, I am indebted to those writers, white and black, whom I read during my formative years and still read for instruction and pleasure. But they were preceded in my life by another set of giants whom I always acknowledge before all others: the group of women around the table long ago. They taught me my first lessons in the narrative art. They trained my ear. They set a standard of excellence. This is why the best of my work must be attributed to them; it stands as testimony to the rich legacy of language and culture they so freely passed on to me in the wordshop of the kitchen.

1983

4. School, synagogue (Yiddish).

ADRIENNE RICH

1929–

"I am an instrument," wrote Adrienne Rich in her poem *Planetarium* (1968), "in the shape / of a woman trying to translate pulsations / into images for the relief of the body / and the reconstruction of the mind." How she began to change herself into such an "instrument" is the subject of her famous autobiographical essay, *When We Dead Awaken: Writing as Re-Vision* (1972, 1976, 1978). Her life—first as "faculty wife" and mother, then as civil rights and antiwar activist, then as lesbian in the women's liberation movement, teacher and lecturer—and her books—sixteen of poetry, four of prose—all demonstrate that, as the critic David Kalstone has said, work, for her, "is a jagged present, always pitched toward the future and change." It is this commitment to change, as much as the example of her life, that has made her a crucial figure in contemporary feminist experience.

"*From where does your strength come, you Southern Jew? / split at the root, raised in a castle of air?*" Rich asked in her poem *Sources* (1983). She was born in Baltimore on May 16, 1929, the elder of two sisters; the family was intellectual and well-off ("a castle of air"), but aware of being apart as Jews. She began to write carefully crafted poetry at an early age, above all for her taskmaster father. Her mother, who had studied to be a musician, gave over her life to her husband and children. Rich graduated from Radcliffe in 1951, "where I did not see a woman teacher for four years," and where, as she tells us in *When We Dead Awaken*, she

studied exclusively the work of male poets. She also published her first book, *A Change of World*, in the prestigious Yale Younger Poets series. The volume was introduced by the British poet W. H. Auden, who admired her command of diction and meter: the poems, he says, "are neatly and modestly dressed, speak quietly but do not mumble, respect their elders but are not cowed by them, and do not tell fibs." Four years later, when she published *The Diamond Cutters*, the poet Randall Jarrell observed that "the poet whom we see behind" the poems "cannot help seeming to us a sort of princess in a fairy tale."

Meanwhile, "determined to have a 'full' woman's life," Rich married Alfred Conrad, an economist at Harvard, in 1953, and had three sons before she was thirty—"a radicalizing experience," as she later called it. Of this period she has said (in *Of Woman Born*, 1976), "I *knew* I had to remake my life; I did not then understand that we—the women of that academic community—as in so many middle-class communities of the period—were expected to fill both the part of the Victorian Lady of Leisure, the Angel in the House, and also of the Victorian cook, scullery maid, laundress, governess, and nurse." In *When We Dead Awaken*, she describes the long struggle to confront, for the first time, her condition as a woman, which resulted in *Snapshots of a Daughter-in-Law*, the title poem of her next book, eight difficult years later. The "modest princess," as Jarrell had defined her, was beginning to change.

In 1966, the Conrads moved to New York, where Alfred had taken a post at City College. There they both became increasingly involved in resistance activities against the Vietnam War. Rich taught in the SEEK Program for disadvantaged young people, and her poems as well as her view of her audience changed. Her vivid political concerns were the subject of many of the verses in *Leaflets* (1969) and *The Will to Change* (1971), while transformations in her poetic style reflected the continuing evolution of her political attitudes. Writing with a new urgency, she broke away from the tight verse forms and neat metrics that had marked much of her early work and began to produce poems that were characterized by a kind of improvisational intensity. As Kalstone usefully reminds us, Rich has also—ever since *Snapshots*—been dating each of her poems, "like entries in a journal where feelings are subject to continual revision." In this respect the title of her 1971 volume is significant: whereas she had called her first book *A Change of World*, as if dependent on changes outside of herself, now she took her title from the poet Charles Olson's line, "What does not change / is the will to change," for "the moment of change," as she wrote, "is the only poem." Rich's life was changing, too: in 1970 she left her marriage, "to do something very common, in my own way" (*A Valediction Forbidding Mourning*). Later that year, Alfred Conrad committed suicide.

In *Diving into the Wreck* (1973), Rich continued her explorations into both the exterior world and the interior self, as the title poem makes clear. The book also contains a poem called *The Phenomenology of Anger* which articulates the way Rich has worked, in this and previous poems, to use the anger aroused by her political and cultural concerns for positive ends "anger," as she told her friends the critics Barbara Charlesworth Gelpi and Albert Gelpi, "can be a kind of genius if it's acted on."

Diving into the Wreck received the National Book Award in 1974; Rich rejected the prize as an individual but accepted it, in a statement written with Audre Lorde and Alice Walker, two other nominees, in the name of all women. That same year, she became professor of English at City College and began the research for *Of Woman Born: Motherhood as Experience and Institution*. This prose work, published in 1975, employs personal journals, anthropology, political and medical history, as a background for meditation on a subject that, she said, she had not chosen: "it had, long ago, chosen me." The book examines the experience of motherhood, along with the myths that have been projected on that experience.

In 1977, Rich published *Twenty-one Love Poems*, a verse sequence whose form recalls that of Elizabethan sonnet cycles in which male poets wrote hyperbolically of their lady-loves: these poems, however, record and explore a lesbian relationship. But the term *lesbian*, for Rich, was "nothing so simple and dismissible as the fact that two women might go to bed together," as she wrote in *It Is the Lesbian in Us* (1976). Lesbianism, for her,

> was a sense of desiring oneself, choosing oneself; it was also a primary intensity between women, an intensity which in the world at large was trivialized, caricatured, or invested with evil.

> Even before I wholly knew I was a lesbian, it was the lesbian in me who pursued that elusive configuration. And I believe it is the lesbian in every woman who is compelled by female energy, who gravitates toward strong women, who seeks a literature that will express that energy and strength. It is the lesbian in us who drives us to feel imaginatively, render in language, grasp, the full connection between woman and woman.

Characteristically, for Rich, the points of view expressed in the *Love Poems* and in this essay are significantly interrelated.

In the late seventies, Rich taught for a time at Douglass College in New Jersey. Then for several years she left the academy and moved to western Massachusetts, where with Michelle Cliff she edited the lesbian-feminist journal *Sinister Wisdom*. Most recently, she has been professor of English at Stanford University in California, where she now resides.

Recently, too, Rich has moved into comparatively new poetic styles and subjects. In the eighties, her impassioned and sometimes severe commitment to personal exploration and analysis compelled her—in *Sources* (1982) and other works—to re-examine both her complex relationships with her dead father and husband and what they represent of her Jewish heritage. In the nineties, she produced what may be her most daring work to date, the ambitious long poem *An Atlas of the Difficult World* (1991), the title piece of an impressive collection, and she has published as well the poignant volume *Dark Fields of the Republic* (1995).

From *The Will to Change* (1971), *Diving into the Wreck* (1973), and *The Dream of a Common Language* (1978) onward, Rich has functioned as a sort of unofficial poet laureate of feminism's "second wave," tracing the interactions between past and present along with those between men and women, in (to use her own words) "a succession of brief, amazing movements / each one making possible the next." But in *An Atlas* she has in a sense transformed herself into the bard of her country, a woman who speaks *as* a woman but *for* the United States with prophetic sureness and intensity.

Specifically, the thirteen-part sequence that constitutes Rich's *Atlas* is a geography of America which, with passion, clarity, and uncanny detail, extends and expands the political, cultural, and intellectual explorations that were begun in the nineteenth century by the self-consciously American poet Walt Whitman, who is perhaps Rich's most crucial precursor here. Yet Rich's Whitmanesque cadences in this work bespeak not belatedness but a simultaneously proud and humble acquiescence in the task of personal as well as communal self-definition that ultimately brought Whitman himself to the battlefield of Gettysburg and the hospital wards of Washington during the Civil War, as well as to *When Lilacs Last in the Dooryard Bloom'd*, his great elegy for Abraham Lincoln. "I am bent on fathoming what it means to love my country," Rich confesses, then persists in the intrepid stocktaking that empowers the famous catalogs of *Leaves of Grass*: "The history of this earth and the bones within it? / Soils and cities, promises made and mocked ... Loyalties, symbols, murmers extinguished and echoing? ... Minerals,

traces, rumors I am made from, morsel, miniscule fibre. one woman / like and un-
like so many, fooled as to her destiny, the scope of her task?"

Like Whitman, too, Rich has an evangelical need to speak not just *for* but *to* her
readers. Part XIII ("Dedications") of *Atlas* offers some of the work's most poignant
passages, reminiscent of Whitman's confident "I step somewhere waiting for
you": "I know you are reading this poem / late, before leaving your office," notes
Rich, adding in a series of Whitmanesque variations, "I know you are reading this
poem / standing up in a bookstore … I know you are reading this poem / in a room
where too much has happened … I know you are reading this poem … torn be-
tween bitterness and hope / turning back once again to the task you cannot
refuse."

"The task you cannot refuse," Rich writes in *Two Arts*, the aesthetic statement
by which she herself defines her project, that when you "Raise it up there—raise
up the task of vision or revision—it will / loom, the gaunt original thing / gristle and
membrane of your life … but you have to raise it up there, you / have a brutal thing
to do." Worse, she adds in *Final Notations*, her book's powerful concluding poem
(as much a meditation on death as on art and politics), "it will not be simple, it will
not be long / it will take little time, it will take all your thought." Yet *it*—the work,
the living and the dying—must be done, must "become your will. "

For nearly half a century, since the publication of her first collection in 1951,
such an impressive and absorbing task has been wholly Adrienne Rich's will.

Aunt Jennifer's Tigers

> Aunt Jennifer's tigers prance across a screen,
> Bright topaz denizens of a world of green.
> They do not fear the men beneath the tree;
> They pace in sleek chivalric certainty.
>
> Aunt Jennifer's fingers fluttering through her wool 5
> Find even the ivory needle hard to pull.
> The massive weight of Uncle's wedding band
> Sits heavily upon Aunt Jennifer's hand.
>
> When Aunt is dead, her terrified hands will lie
> Stil ringed with ordeals she was mastered by. 10
> The tigers in the panel that she made
> Will go on prancing, proud and unafraid.

1951

Snapshots of a Daughter-in-Law

1

> You, once a belle in Shreveport,
> with henna-colored hair, skin like a peachbud,
> sti have your dresses copied from that time,
> and play a Chopin prelude
> called by Cortot: "*Delicious recollections* 5
> *float like perfume through the memory.*"[1]

1. A remark made by Alfred Cortot (1877–1962), a well-known French pianist, in his *Chopin: 24 Preludes* (1930); he is referring specifically to Chopin's Prelude No. 7, Andantino, A Major. Frederic François Chopin 1810–1849), Polish composer and pianist who settled in Paris in 1831.

Your mind now, moldering like wedding-cake,
heavy with useless experience, rich
with suspicion, rumor, fantasy,
crumbling to pieces under the knife-edge 10
of mere fact. In the prime of your life.

Nervy, glowering, your daughter
wipes the teaspoons, grows another way.

2

Banging the coffee-pot into the sink
she hears the angels chiding, and looks out 15
past the raked gardens to the sloppy sky.
Only a week since They said: *Have no patience.*

The next time it was: *Be insatiable.*
Then: *Save yourself; others you cannot save,*
Sometimes she's let the tapstream scald her arm, 20
a match burn to her thumbnail,

or held her hand above the kettle's snout
right in the woolly steam. They are probably angels,
since nothing hurts her anymore, except
each morning's grit blowing into her eyes. 25

3

A thinking woman sleeps with monsters.
The beak that grips her, she becomes. And Nature,
that sprung-lidded, still commodious
steamer-trunk of *tempora* and *mores*[2]
gets stuffed with it all: the mildewed orange-flowers, 30
the female pills,[3] the terrible breasts
of Boadicea[4] beneath flat foxes' heads and orchids.

Two handsome women, gripped in argument,
each proud, acute, subtle, I hear scream
across the cut glass and majolica 35
like Furies[5] cornered from their prey:
The argument *ad feminam,*[6] all the old knives
that have rusted in my back, I drive in yours,
ma semblable, ma soeur![7]

2. Times and customs (Latin, literal trans.); alluding to the Roman orator Cicero's famous phrase, "O Tempora! O Mores!" (i.e., Alas for the degeneracy of our times and the low standard of our morals!).
3. Remedies for menstrual pain.
4. British queen in the time of the emperor Nero; she led her people in a large though ultimately unsuccessful revolt against Roman rule.
5. Greek female spirits of vengeance.

6. Feminine version of the phrase *ad hominem* (against the man; Latin, literal trans.), referring to an argument directed not to reason but to personal prejudices and emotions.
7. Like me, my sister (French). From the last line of Charles Baudelaire's poem *Au Lecteur,* which addresses "*Hypocrite lecteur!—mon semblable—mon frère!*" (Hypocrite reader, like me, my brother); Rich here instead addresses "my sister."

> Thus wrote
a woman, partly brave and partly good,
who fought with what she partly understood.
Few men about her would or could do more, 75
hence she was labeled harpy, shrew and whore.

8

"You all die at fifteen," said Diderot,[6]
and turn part legend, part convention.
Still, eyes inaccurately dream
behind closed windows blankening with steam. 80
Deliciously, all that we might have been,
all that we were—fire, tears,
wit, taste, martyred ambition—
stirs like the memory of refused adultery
the drained and flagging bosom of our middle years. 85

9

*Not that it is done well, but
that it is done at all?*[7] Yes, think
of the odds! or shrug them off forever.
This luxury of the precocious child,
Time's precious chronic invalid,— 90
would we, darlings, resign it if we could?
Our blight has been our sinecure:
mere talent was enough for us—
glitter in fragments and rough drafts.

Sigh no more, ladies. 95
> Time is male

and in his cups drinks to the fair.
Bemused by gallantry, we hear
our mediocrities over-praised,
indolence read as abnegation, 100
slattern thought styled intuition,
every lapse forgiven, our crime
only to cast too bold a shadow
or smash the mold straight off.

For that, solitary confinement, 105
tear gas, attrition shelling.
Few applicants for that honor.

10

> Well,
she's long about her coming, who must be

6. Denis Diderot (1713–1784), French philosopher, encyclopedist, playwright, and critic. " 'You all die at fifteen': 'Vous mourez toutes a quinze ans,' from the *Lettres à Sophie Volland*, quoted by Simone de Beauvoir in *Le Deuxième Sexe*, Vol. II, pp. 123–24" [Rich's note].
7. An allusion to Samuel Johnson's remark to Boswell: "Sir, a woman's preaching is like a dog's walking on his hinder legs. It is not done well; but you are surprised to find it done at all" (July 31, 1763).

more merciless to herself than history. 110
Her mind full to the wind, I see her plunge
breasted and glancing through the currents,
taking the light upon her
at least as beautiful as any boy
or helicopter,[8] 115

 poised, still coming,

her fine blades making the air wince

but her cargo
no promise then:
delivered 120
palpable
ours.

1958–60 1963

"I Am in Danger—Sir—"[1]

"Half-cracked"[2] to Higginson, living,
afterward famous in garbled versions,
your hoard of dazzling scraps a battlefield,
now your old snood

mothballed at Harvard[3] 5
and you in your variorum monument[4]
equivocal to the end—
who are you?

Gardening the day-lily,
wiping the wine-glass stems, 10
your thought pulsed on behind
a forehead battered paper-thin,

you, woman, masculine
in single-mindedness,
for whom the word was more 15
than a symptom—

a condition of being.
Till the air buzzing with spoiled language

8. "She comes down from the remoteness of ages, from Thebes, from Crete, from Chichén-Itzá; and she is also the totem set deep in the African jungle, she is a helicopter and she is a bird; and there is this, the greatest wonder of all: under her tinted hair the forest murmur becomes a thought, and words issue from her breasts" (Simone de Beauvoir, *The Second Sex*, trans. H. M. Parshley, New York, 1953, p. 729). [A translation of the passage from *Le Deuxième Sexe*, Vol. 2, p. 574, cited in French by Rich.]
1. "See the *Letters of Emily Dickinson*. T. H. Johnson, ed., Vol. II, p. 409" [Rich's note]. In one of her letters to her "mentor," the editor Thomas Wentworth Higginson, Dickinson wrote, "You think my gait 'spasmodic'—I am in danger—Sir—You think me 'uncontrolled'—I have no Tribunal."
2. Higginson described Dickinson, in a letter, as "my partially cracked poetess at Amherst."
3. The Rare Books Library at Harvard has a collection of Dickinson manuscripts and memorabilia, including her "snood" (hairnet).
4. I.e., Thomas H. Johnson's three-volume *Poems of Emily Dickinson* (1955). A "variorum" edition contains all the variant readings of a text.

 sang in your ears
 of Perjury 20

 and in your half-cracked way you chose
 silence for entertainment,
 chose to have it out at last
 on your own premises.

1964 1966

Diving into the Wreck

 First having read the book of myths,
 and loaded the camera,
 and checked the edge of the knife-blade,
 I put on
 the body-armor of black rubber 5
 the absurd flippers
 the grave and awkward mask.
 I am having to do this
 not like Cousteau[1] with his
 assiduous team 10
 aboard the sun-flooded schooner
 but here alone.

 There is a ladder.
 The ladder is always there
 hanging innocently 15
 close to the side of the schooner.
 We know what it is for,
 we who have used it.
 Otherwise
 it's a piece of maritime floss 20
 some sundry equipment.

 I go down.
 Rung after rung and still
 the oxygen immerses me
 the blue light 25
 the clear atoms
 of our human air.
 I go down.
 My flippers cripple me,
 I crawl like an insect down the ladder 30
 and there is no one
 to tell me when the ocean
 will begin.

 First the air is blue and then
 it is bluer and then green and then 35

1. Jacques Cousteau (1910–), French underwater explorer, author, and filmmaker.

black I am blacking out and yet
my mask is powerful
it pumps my blood with power
the sea is another story
the sea is not a question of power 40
I have to learn alone
to turn my body without force
in the deep element.

And now: it is easy to forget
what I came for 45
among so many who have always
lived here
swaying their crenellated[2] fans
between the reefs
and besides 50
you breathe differently down here.

I came to explore the wreck.
The words are purposes.
The words are maps.
I came to see the damage that was done 55
and the treasures that prevail.
I stroke the beam of my lamp
slowly along the flank
of something more permanent
than fish or weed 60

the thing I came for:
the wreck and not the story of the wreck
the thing itself and not the myth
the drowned face always staring
toward the sun 65
the evidence of damage
worn by salt and sway into this threadbare beauty
the ribs of the disaster
curving their assertion
among the tentative haunters. 70

This is the place.
And I am here, the mermaid whose dark hair
streams black, the merman in his armored body
We circle silently
about the wreck 75
we dive into the hold.
I am she: I am he

whose drowned face sleeps with open eyes
whose breasts still bear the stress
whose silver, copper, vermeil[3] cargo lies 80

2. Notched with rounded or scalloped projections. 3. Gilded silver or bronze.

obscurely inside barrels
half-wedged and left to rot
we are the half-destroyed instruments
that once held to a course
the water-eaten log 85
the fouled compass

We are, I am, you are
by cowardice or courage
the one who find our way
back to this scene 90
carrying a knife, a camera
a book of myths
in which
our names do not appear.

1972 1973

Power

Living in the earth-deposits of our history

Today a backhoe divulged out of a crumbling flank of earth
one bottle amber perfect a hundred-year-old
cure for fever or melancholy a tonic
for living on this earth in the winters of this climate 5

Today I was reading about Marie Curie:[1]
she must have known she suffered from radiation sickness
her body bombarded for years by the element
she had purified
It seems she denied to the end 10
the source of the cataracts on her eyes
the cracked and suppurating skin of her finger-ends
till she could no longer hold a test-tube or a pencil

She died a famous woman denying
her wounds
denying 15
her wounds came from the same source as her power

1974 1978

From Twenty-one Love Poems

XI

Every peak is a crater. This is the law of volcanoes,
making them eternally and visibly female.

1. Physicist and chemist (1867–1934) who, with her husband, Pierre, discovered radium.

No height without depth, without a burning core,
though our straw soles shred on the hardened lava.
I want to travel with you to every sacred mountain 5
smoking within like the sibyl stooped over her tripod,[1]
I want to reach for your hand as we scale the path,
to feel your arteries glowing in my clasp,
never failing to note the small, jewel-like flower
unfamiliar to us, nameless till we rename her, 10
that clings to the slowly altering rock—
that detail outside ourselves that brings us to ourselves,
was here before us, knew we would come, and sees beyond us. 15

(The Floating Poem, Unnumbered)

Whatever happens with us, your body
will haunt mine—tender, delicate
your lovemaking, like the half-curled frond
of the fiddlehead fern in forests
just washed by sun. Your traveled, generous thighs 5
between which my whole face has come and come—
the innocence and wisdom of the place my tongue
 has found there—
the live, insatiate dance of your nipples in my mouth—
your touch on me, firm, protective, searching 10
me out, your strong tongue and slender fingers
reaching where I had been waiting years for you
in my rose-wet cave—whatever happens, this is.

XXI

The dark lintels, the blue and foreign stones
of the great round rippled by stone implements
the midsummer night light rising from beneath
the horizon—when I said "a cleft of light"
I meant this. And this is not Stonehenge[2] 5
simply nor any place but the mind
casting back to where her solitude,
shared, could be chosen without loneliness,
not easily nor without pains to stake out
the circle, the heavy shadows, the great light. 10
I choose to be a figure in that light,
half-blotted by darkness, something moving
across that space, the color of stone
greeting the moon, yet more than stone:
a woman. I choose to walk here. And to draw this circle. 15

1974–76 1976, 1978

1. At Delphi, the priestess sat on a tripod when she gave oracles. "Sibyl": a Greek prophetess. 2. A great prehistoric structure of stones set in a circle on Salisbury Plain in England.

Phantasia for Elvira Shatayev

(leader of a women's climbing team, all of whom died in a storm on
Lenin Peak, August 1974. Later, Shatayev's husband found and buried
the bodies.)

The cold felt cold until our blood
grew colder then the wind
died down and we slept

If in this sleep I speak
it's with a voice no longer personal 5
(I want to say *with voices*)
When the wind tore our breath from us at last
we had no need of words
For months for years each one of us
had felt her own *yes* growing in her 10
slowly forming as she stood at windows waited
for trains mended her rucksack combed her hair
What we were to learn was simply what we had
up here as out of all words that *yes* gathered
its forces fused itself and only just in time 15
to meet a *No* of no degrees
the black hole sucking the world in

I feel you climbing toward me
your cleated bootsoles leaving their geometric bite
colossally embossed on microscopic crystals 20
as when I trailed you in the Caucasus
Now I am further
ahead than either of us dreamed anyone would be
I have become
the white snow packed like asphalt by the wind 25
the women I love lightly flung against the mountain
that blue sky
our frozen eyes unribboned through the storm
we could have stitched that blueness together like a quilt

You come (I know this) with your love your loss 30
strapped to your body with your tape-recorder camera
ice-pick against advisement
to give us burial in the snow and in your mind
While my body lies out here
flashing like a prism into your eyes 35
how could you sleep You climbed here for yourself
we climbed for ourselves

When you have buried us told your story
ours does not end we stream
into the unfinished the unbegun 40
the possible
Every cell's core of heat pulsed out of us
into the thin air of the universe

the armature of rock beneath these snows
this mountain which has taken the imprint of our minds 45
through changes elemental and minute
as those we underwent
to bring each other here
choosing ourselves each other and this life
whose every breath and grasp and further foothold 50
is somewhere still enacted and continuing

In the diary I wrote: *Now we are ready*
and each of us knows it I have never loved
like this I have never seen
my own forces so taken up and shared 55
and given back
After the long training the early sieges
we are moving almost effortlessly in our love

In the diary as the wind began to tear
at the tents over us I wrote: 60
We know now we have always been in danger
down in our separateness
and now up here together but till now
we had not touched our strength

In the diary torn from my fingers I had written: 65
What does love mean
what does it mean "to survive"
A cable of blue fire ropes our bodies
burning together in the snow We will not live
to settle for less We have dreamed of this 70
all of our lives

1974 1978

An Atlas of the Difficult World

I

A dark woman, head bent, listening for something
—a woman's voice, a man's voice or
voice of the freeway, night after night, metal streaming downcoast
past eucalyptus, cypress, agribusiness empires
THE SALAD BOWL OF THE WORLD, gurr of small planes 5
dusting the strawberries, each berry picked by hand
in close communion, strawberry blood on the wrist.
Malathion[1] in the throat, communion,
the hospital at the edge of the fields,
prematures slipping from unsafe wombs, 10
the labor and delivery nurse on her break watching
planes dusting rows of pickers.

1. A pesticide that has been criticized for harming those working in the fields where it is applied.

Elsewhere declarations are made: at the sink
rinsing strawberries flocked and gleaming, fresh from market
one says: "On the pond this evening is a light 15
finer than my mother's handkerchief
received from her mother, hemmed and initialed
by the nuns in Belgium."
One says: "I can lie for hours
reading and listening to music. But sleep comes hard. 20
I'd rather lie awake and read." One writes:
"Mosquitoes pour through the cracks
in this cabin's walls, the road
in winter is often impassable,
I live here so I don't have to go out and act, 25
I'm trying to hold onto my life, it feels like nothing."
One says: "I never knew from one day to the next
where it was coming from: I had to make my life happen
from day to day. Every day an emergency.
Now I have a house, a job from year to year. 30
What does that make me?"

In the writing workshop a young man's tears
wet the frugal beard he's grown to go with his poems
hoping they have redemption stored
in their lines, maybe will get him home free. In the classroom 35
eight-year-old faces are grey. The teacher knows which children
have not broken fast that day,
remembers the Black Panthers[2] spooning cereal.

 •

I don't want to hear how he beat her after the earthquake,
tore up her writing, threw the kerosene 40
lantern into her face waiting
like an unbearable mirror of his own. I don't
want to hear how she finally ran from the trailer
how he tore the keys from her hands, jumped into the truck
and backed it into her. I don't want to think 45
how her guesses betrayed her—that he meant well, that she
was really the stronger and ought not to leave him
to his own apparent devastation. I don't want to know
wreckage, dreck[3] and waste, but these are the materials
and so are the slow lift of the moon's belly 50
over wreckage, dreck, and waste, wild treefrogs calling in
another season, light and music still pouring over
our fissured, cracked terrain.

 •

Within two miles of the Pacific rounding
this long bay, sheening the light for miles 55

2. A black militant organization of the 1960s and early pousing violent revolution.
1970s; the group did community work as well as es- 3. Trash (Yiddish).

inland, floating its fog through redwood rifts and over
strawberry and artichoke fields, its bottomless mind
returning always to the same rocks, the same cliffs, with
ever-changing words, always the same language
—this is where I live now. If you had known me 50
once, you'd still know me now though in a different
light and life This is no place you ever knew me.
But it would not surprise you
to find me here, walking in fog, the sweep of the great ocean
eluding me, even the curve of the bay, because as always 55
I fix on the land I am stuck to earth. What I love here
is old ranches, leaning seaward, lowroofed spreads between rocks
small canyons running through pitched hillsides
liveoaks twisted on steepness, the eucalyptus avenue leading
to the wrecked homestead, the fogwreathed heavy-chested cattle 70
on their blond hills. I drive inland over roads
closed in wet weather, past shacks hunched in the canyons
roads that crawl down into darkness and wind into light
where trucks have crashed and riders of horses tangled
to death with lowstruck boughs. These are not the roads 75
you knew me by. But the woman driving, walking, watching
for life and death, is the same.

<center>II</center>

Here is a map of our country:
here is the Sea of Indifference, glazed with salt
This is the haunted river flowing from brow to groin 80
we dare not taste its water
This is the desert where missiles are planted like corms[4]
This is the breadbasket of foreclosed farms
This is the birthplace of the rockabilly boy
This is the cemetery of the poor 85
who died for democracy This is a battlefield
from a nineteenth-century war the shrine is famous
This is the sea-town of myth and story when the fishing fleets
went bankrupt here is where the jobs were on the pier
processing frozen fishsticks hourly wages and no shares 90
These are other battlefields Centralia Detroit
here are the forests primeval[5] the copper the silver lodes
These are the suburbs of acquiescence silence rising fumelike from the
 streets
This is the capital of money and dolor whose spires
flare up through air inversions whose bridges are crumbling 95
whose children are drifting blind alleys pent
between coiled rolls of razor wire
I promised to show you a map you say but this is a mural
then yes let it be these are small distinctions
where do we see it from is the question 100

4. Bulblike stems from which some plants reproduce.
5. Recalls the opening words of Henry Wadsworth
Longfellow's *Evangeline* (1847): "This is the forest
primeval." Centralia was a town in Pennsylvania that
was virtually destroyed in the 1980s by a devastating
decades-old underground mine fire.

III

Two five-pointed star-shaped glass candleholders, bought at the Ben
 Franklin,[6] Barton, twenty-three years ago, one chipped
—now they hold half-burnt darkred candles, and in between
a spider is working, the third point of her filamental passage
a wicker basket-handle. All afternoon I've sat
at this table in Vermont, reading, writing, cutting an apple in slivers 105
and eating them, but mostly gazing down through the windows
at the long scribble of lake due south
where the wind and weather come from. There are bottles set in the
 windows
that children dug up in summer woods or bought for nickels and dimes
in dark shops that are no more, gold-brown, foam-green or cobalt glass,
 blue that gave way to the cobalt bomb.[7] The woods 110
are still on the hill behind the difficult unknowable
incommensurable barn. The wind's been working itself up
in low gusts gnashing the leaves left chattering on branches
or drifting over still-green grass; but it's been a warm wind.
An autumn without a killing frost so far, still warm 115
feels like a time of self-deception, a memory of pushing
limits in youth, that intricate losing game of innocence long overdue.
Frost is expected tonight, gardens are gleaned, potplants taken in, there is
 talk of withering, of wintering-over.

 •

North of Willoughby the back road to Barton
turns a right-hand corner on a high plateau 120
bitten by wind now and rimed[8] grey-white
—farms of rust and stripping paint, the shortest growing season
south of Quebec, a place of sheer unpretentious hardship, dark pines
 stretching away
toward Canada. There was a one-room schoolhouse
by a brook where we used to picnic, summers, a little world 125
of clear bubbling water, cowturds, moss, wild mint, wild mushrooms under
 the pines.
One hot afternoon I sat there reading Gaskell's *Life of Charlotte Brontë*[9]—
 the remote
upland village where snow lay long and late, the deep-rutted roads, the dun
 and grey moorland
—trying to enfigure such a life, how genius
unfurled in the shortlit days, the meager means of that house. I never
 thought 130
of lives at that moment around me, what girl dreamed
and was extinguished in the remote back-country I had come to love,
reader reading under a summer tree in the landscape
of the rural working poor.

6. A chain of retail stores, featuring textiles, notions, and arts and crafts supplies.
7. A proposed thermonuclear bomb designed to produce large amounts of deadly radioactive fallout.
Cobalt oxide helps give some glass a blue color.
8. Frosted.
9. The novelist Elizabeth Gaskell was a friend of Brontë and published this biography in 1857.

Now the panes are black and from the south the wind still staggers,
 creaking the house: 135
brown milkweeds toss in darkness below but I cannot see them
the room has lost the window and turned into itself: two corner shelves of
 things
both useful and unused, things arrived here by chance or choice, two tea-
 pots, one broken-spouted, red and blue
came to me with some books from my mother's mother, my grandmother
 Mary
who traveled little, loved the far and strange, bits of India, Asia
and this teapot of hers was Chinese or she thought it was 140
—the other given by a German Jew, a refugee who killed herself:
Midlands[1] flowered ware, and this too cannot be used because coated in
 side—why?—with flaking paint:
"You will always use it for flowers," she instructed when she gave it.
In a small frame, under glass, my father's bookplate, engraved in his ardent
 youth. the cleft tree-trunk and the wintering ants:
Without labor, no sweetness—motto I breathed in from him and learned in
 grief and rebellion to take and use 145
—and later learned that not all labor ends in sweetness.
A little handwrought iron candlestick, given by another German woman
who hidden survived the Russian soldiers beating the walls in 1945,
emigrated, married a poet. I sat many times at their table. They are now
 long apart.
Some odd glasses for wine or brandy, from an ignorant, passionate time—
 we were in our twenties— 150
with the father of the children who dug for old medicine bottles in the
 woods
—afternoons listening to records, reading Karl Shapiro's Poems of a Jew and
 Auden's "In Sickness and in Health"[2] aloud, using the poems to talk
 to each other
—now it's twenty years since last I heard that intake
of living breath, as if language were too much to bear,
that voice overcast like klezmer[3] with echoes, uneven, edged, torn,
 Brooklyn street crowding Harvard Yard 155
—I'd have known any syllable anywhere.

Stepped out onto the night-porch. That wind has changed, though still
 from the south
it's blowing up hard now, no longer close to earth but driving high
into the crowns of the maples, into my face
almost slamming the stormdoor into me. But it's warm, warm, 160
pneumonia wind, death of innocence wind, unwinding wind,
time-hurtling wind. And it has a voice in the house. I hear
conversations that can't be happening, overhead in the bedrooms
and I'm not talking of ghosts. The ghosts are here of course but they
 speak plainly
—haven't I offered food and wine, listened well for them all these years, 165

1. I.e., from the central counties of England. Shapiro's volume was published in 1958.
2. W. H. Auden's poem was published in 1948. 3. The traditional music of eastern European Jews.

not only those known in life but those before our time
of self-deception, our intricate losing game of innocence long overdue?

<center>•</center>

The spider's decision is made, her path cast, candle-wick to wicker handle
 to candle,
in the air, under the lamp, she comes swimming toward me
(have I been sitting here so long?) she will use everything, nothing comes
 without labor, she is working so hard and I know 170
nothing all winter can enter this house or this web, not all labor ends in
 sweetness.
But how do I know what she needs? Maybe simply
to spin herself a house within a house, on her own terms
in cold, in silence.

<center>IV</center>

Late summers, early autumns, you can see something that binds 175
the map of this country together: the girasol, orange gold-petaled
with her black eye, laces the roadsides from Vermont to California
runs the edges of orchards, chain-link fences
milo[4] fields and malls, schoolyards and reservations
truckstops and quarries, grazing ranges, graveyards 180
of veterans, graveyards of cars hulked and sunk, her tubers the jerusalem
 artichoke
that has fed the Indians, fed the hobos, could feed us all.
Is there anything in the soil, cross-country, that makes for
a plant so generous? *Spendthrift* we say, as if
accounting nature's waste. Ours darkens 185
the states to their strict borders, flushes
down borderless streams, leaches from lakes to the curdled foam
down by the riverside.

Waste. Waste. The watcher's eye put out, hands of the builder severed,
 brain of the maker starved
those who could bind, join, reweave, cohere, replenish 190
now at risk in this segregate republic
locked away out of sight and hearing, out of mind, shunted aside
those needed to teach, advise, persuade, weigh arguments
those urgently needed for the work of perception
work of the poet, the astronomer, the historian, the architect of new
 streets 195
work of the speaker who also listens
meticulous delicate work of reaching the heart of the desperate woman,
 the desperate man
—never-to-be-finished, still unbegun work of repair—it cannot be done
 without them
and where are they now?

4. A cultivated grain.

V

Catch if you can your country's moment, begin 200
where any calendar's ripped-off: Appomattox
Wounded Knee, Los Alamos, Selma, the last airlift from Saigon[5]
the ex-Army nurse hitch-hiking from the debriefing center; medal of spit
 on the veteran's shoulder
—catch if you can this unbound land these states without a cause
earth of despoiled graves and grazing these embittered brooks 205
these pilgrim ants pouring out from the bronze eyes, ears, nostrils,
the mouth of Liberty
 over the chained bay waters[6]
 San Quentin:[7]
once we lost our way and drove in under the searchlights to the gates 210
end of visiting hours, women piling into cars
the bleak glare aching over all
 Where are we moored? What are the bind-
 ings? What behooves us?

Driving the San Francisco–Oakland Bay Bridge
no monument's in sight but fog 215
prowling Angel Island muffling Alcatraz[8]
poems in Cantonese inscribed on fog
no icon lifts a lamp here[9]
history's breath blotting the air
over Gold Mountain[1] a transfer, 220
of patterns like the transfer of African appliqué
to rural Alabama voices alive in legends, curses
tongue-lashings
 poems on a weary wall

And when light swivels off Angel Island and Alcatraz 225
when the bays leap into life
 views of the Palace of Fine Arts, Trans-
 America[2]
when sunset bathes the three bridges
 still
old ghosts crouch hoarsely whispering 230
under Gold Mountain

5. These all mark critical moments in U.S. history. Appomattox, Virginia, where Robert E. Lee surrendered to Ulysses S. Grant to end the Civil War (1865). Wounded Knee, South Dakota, the site of the last major battle of the so-called Indian Wars (1890), a massacre by the U.S. troops. Los Alamos, New Mexico, where the atomic bomb was designed and first produced. Selma, Alabama, the center of a black voter registration drive led by Martin Luther King Jr. (1965). After the city of Saigon surrendered to North Vietnamese Communists, the last Americans were evacuated by helicopter from the roof of the U.S. embassy.
6. From Hart Crane, "To Brooklyn Bridge," in The *Poems of Hart Crane*, ed. Marc Simon (New York and London: Liveright, 1989; poem originally published in 1930) [Rich's note].
7. A prison in California.
8. A rocky island in San Francisco Bay used for a prison (1858–1963). Angel Island, also in San Francisco Bay, was used as an army base (1863–1946); enemy prisoners of war were confined there during World War II.
9. I.e., unlike the Statue of Liberty in New York's harbor.
1. Chinese immigrants' name for California.
2. Well-known buildings in San Francisco.

North and east of the romantic headlands there are roads into tule fog
places where life is cheap poor quick unmonumented
Rukeyser[3] would have guessed it coming West for the opening
of the great red bridge *There are roads to take* she wrote 235
when you think of your country[4] driving south
to West Virginia Gauley Bridge silicon mines the flakes of it heaped like
 snow, death-angel white[5]
—poet journalist pioneer mother
uncovering her country: *there are roads to take*

I don't want to know how he tracked them 240
along the Appalachian Trail, hid close
by their tent, pitched as they thought in seclusion
killing one woman, the other
dragging herself into town his defense they had teased his loathing
of what they were I don't want to know 245
but this is not a bad dream of mine[6] these are the materials
and so are the smell of wild mint and coursing water remembered
and the sweet salt darkred tissue I lay my face
upon, my tongue within.
 A crosshair against the pupil of an eye 250
could blow my life from hers
a cell dividing without maps, sliver of ice beneath a wheel
could do the job. Faithfulness isn't the problem.

VI

A potato explodes in the oven. Poetry and famine:
the poets who never starved, whose names we know 255
the famished nameless taking ship with their hoard of poetry
Annie Sullivan[7] half-blind in the workhouse enthralling her childmates
with lore her father had borne in his head from Limerick along with the
 dream of work
and *hatred of England smouldering like a turf-fire.*[8] But a poetry older than
 hatred. Poetry
in the workhouse, laying of the rails, a potato splattering oven walls 260
poetry of cursing and silence, bitter and deep, shallow and drunken
poetry of priest-talk, of I.R.A.-talk, kitchen-talk, dream-talk, tongues de
 spised
in cities where in a mere fifty years language has rotted to jargon, *lingua
 franca*[9] of inclusion

3. Muriel Rukeyser (1913–1980), American poet.
4. From Muriel Rukeyser, *U.S. 1* (New York: Covici Friede, 1938); see also Muriel Rukeyser, *The Collected Poems* (New York: McGraw-Hill, 1978) [Rich's note].
5. When inhaled over time, silicon can cause deadly fibrosis of the lungs.
6. On May 13, 1988, Stephen Roy Carr shot and killed Rebecca Wight, one of two lesbians camping on the Appalachian Trail in Pennsylvania. Her lover, Claudia Brenner, suffered five bullet wounds. She dragged herself two miles along the trail to a road, where she flagged a car to take her to the police. In October of that year, Carr was found guilty of first-degree murder and sentenced to life in prison without parole. During the legal proceedings, it became clear that Carr had attacked the women because they were lesbians [Rich's note].
7. Educator (1866–1936), usually remembered only in connection with her famous successful student who had seemed unteachable, the deaf and blind Helen Keller (1880–1968).
8. See Nella Braddy, *Anne Sullivan Macy: The Story behind Helen Keller* (Garden City, N.Y.: Doubleday, Doran & Company, 1933), p. 13 [Rich's note].
9. Common language. "I.R.A.": Irish nationalist organization whose goal is the unification of the country.

from turns of speech ancient as the potato, muttered at the coals by
 women and men
rack-rented,[1] harshened, numbered by labor ending 265
in root-harvest rotted in field. 1847. No relief. No succor.
America. Meat three times a day,[2] they said. Slaves—You would not be
 that.

VII (The Dream-Site)

Some rooftop, water-tank looming, street-racket strangely quelled
and others known and unknown there, long sweet summer evening on the
 tarred roof:
leaned back your head to the nightvaults warming with stars 270
the Pleiades[3] broken loose, not seven but thousands
every known constellation flinging out fiery threads
and you could distinguish all
—cobwebs, tendrils, anatomies of stars
coherently hammocked, blueblack avenues between 275
—you knew your way among them, knew you were part of them
until neck aching, you sat straight up and saw:

It was New York, the dream-site
the lost city the city of dreadful light[4]
where once as the sacks of garbage rose 280
like barricades around us we
stood listening to riffs from Pharaoh Sanders' window
on the brownstone steps
went striding the avenues in our fiery hair
in our bodies young and ordinary riding the subways reading 285
or pressed against other bodies
feeling in them the maps of Brooklyn Queens Manhattan
The Bronx unscrolling in the long breakneck
express plunges
 as darkly we felt our own blood 290
streaming a living city overhead
coherently webbed and knotted bristling
we and all the others
 known and unknown
living its life 295

VIII

He thought there would be a limit and that it would stop him. He depended
 on that:
the cuts would be made by someone else, the direction
come from somewhere else, arrows flashing on the freeway.
That he'd end somewhere gazing
straight into It was what he imagined and nothing beyond. 300

1 Paying excessively high rent. The great potato
famine, which sparked massive emigration to the
United States, was in 1846-47.
2. See Frank Murray, "The Irish and Afro-Americans
in U.S. History," Freedomways: A Quarterly Review of
the Freedom Movement 22, no. 1 (1982): 22 [Rich's

note].
3. In Greek mythology, the seven daughters of Atlas
turned into this group of stars.
4. An allusion to James Thomson's The City of
Dreadful Night (1874), a long poem centering on a
half-ruined city.

That he'd end facing as limit a thing without limits and so he flung
and burned and hacked and bled himself toward that (if I understand
this story at all). What he found: FOR SALE: DO NOT DISTURB
OCCUPANT on some cliffs; some ill-marked, ill-kept roads
ending in warnings about shellfish in Vietnamese, Spanish and English. 305
But the spray was any color he could have dreamed
—gold, ash, azure, smoke, moonstone—
and from time to time the ocean swirled up through the eye of a rock and
 taught him
limits. Throwing itself backward, singing and sucking, no teacher, only
 its violent 310
self, the Pacific, dialectical waters rearing
their wild calm constructs, momentary, ancient.

 •

If your voice could overwhelm those waters, what would it say?
What would it cry of the child swept under, the mother
on the beach then, in her black bathing suit, walking straight out 315
into the glazed lace as if she never noticed, what would it say of the father
facing inland in his shoes and socks at the edge of the tide,
what of the lost necklace glittering twisted in foam?
If your voice could crack in the wind hold its breath still as the rocks
what would it say to the daughter searching the tidelines for a bottled
 message 320
from the sunken slaveships? what of the huge sun slowly defaulting into
 the clouds
what of the picnic stored in the dunes at high tide, full of the moon, the
 basket
with sandwiches, eggs, paper napkins, can-opener, the meal
packed for a family feast, excavated now by scuttling
ants, sandcrabs, dune-rats, because no one understood 325
all picnics are eaten on the grave?

 IX

On this earth, in this life, as I read your story, you're lonely.
Lonely in the bar, on the shore of the coastal river
with your best friend, his wife, and your wife, fishing
lonely in the prairie classroom with all the students who love you. You
 know some ghosts 330
come everywhere with you yet leave them unaddressed
for years. You spend weeks in a house
with a drunk, you sober, whom you love, feeling lonely.
You grieve in loneliness, and if I understand you fuck in loneliness.

I wonder if this is a white man's madness. 335
I honor your truth and refuse to leave it at that.

What have I learned from stories of the hunt, of lonely men in gangs?
But there were other stories:
one man riding the Mohave Desert
another man walking the Grand Canyon. 340
I thought those solitary men were happy, as ever they had been.

Indio's long avenues
of Medjool date-palm and lemon sweep to the Salton Sea
in Yucca Flats the high desert reaches higher, bleached and spare of talk
At Twentynine Palms[5] I found the grave 345
of Maria Eleanor Whallon, eighteen years, dead at the watering-hole in
 1903, under the now fire-branded palms
Her mother traveled on alone to cook in the mining camps.

X

Soledad. = f.[5] Solitude, loneliness, homesickness; lonely retreat.
Winter sun in the rosetrees. 350
An old Mexican with a white moustache prunes them back, spraying
the cut branches with dormant oil. The old paper-bag-brown adobe walls
stretch apart from the rebuilt mission, in their own time. It is lonely here
in the curve of the road winding through vast brown fields machine-
 engraved in furrows
of relentless precision. In the small chapel 355
La Nuestra Señora de la Soledad[7] dwells in her shallow arch
painted on either side with columns. She is in black lace crisp as cinders
from head to foot. Alone. solitary, homesick
in her lonely retreat. Outside black olives fall and smash
littering and staining the beaten path. The gravestones of the padres 360
are weights pressing down on the Indian artisans. It is the sixth day of
 another war.[8]

 •

Across the freeway stands another structure
from the other side of the mirror *it destroys*
the logical processes of the mind, a man's thoughts
become completely disorganized, madness streaming from every throat 365
frustrated sounds from the bars, metallic sounds from the walls
the steel trays, iron beds bolted to the wall, the smells, the human waste.
To determine how men will behave once they enter prison
it is of first importance to know that prison.[9] (From the freeway
gun-turrets planted like water-towers in another garden, out-buildings
 spaced in winter sun 370
and the concrete mass beyond: who now writes letters deep inside that
 cave?)

If my instructor tells me that the world and its affairs
are run as well as they possibly can be, that I am governed
by wise and judicious men, that I am free and should be happy,
and if when I leave the instructor's presence and encounter 375
the exact opposite, if I actually sense or see confusion, war,
recession, depression, death and decay, is it not reasonable
that I should become perplexed?

5. These towns are all located in southern California, east of Los Angeles; the Salton Sea is a large lake.
6. Feminine (i.e., the gender of this Spanish noun). Soledad is also a prison in California.
7. Our Lady of Solitude (Spanish).
8. An allusion to the 1967 Six-Day War (Israel's suc-cessful preemptive attack on Syria and Egypt and subsequent counterattack on Jordan).
9. The passages in italics are quoted from *Soledad Brother: The Prison Letters of George Jackson* (New York: Bantam, 1970), pp. 24, 26, 93, 245 [Rich's note].

 From eighteen to twenty-eight of his
 years
a young man schools himself, argues, 380
debates, trains, lectures to himself,
teaches himself Swahili, Spanish, learns
five new words of English every day,
chainsmokes, reads, writes letters.
In this college of force he wrestles bitterness, 385
self-hatred, sexual anger, cures his own nature.
Seven of these years in solitary. Soledad.

But the significant feature of the desperate man reveals itself
when he meets other desperate men, directly or vicariously;
and he experiences his first kindness, someone to strain with him, 390
to strain to see him as he strains to see himself.
someone to understand, someone to accept the regard,
the love, that desperation forces into hiding.
Those feelings that find no expression in desperate times
store themselves up in great abundance, ripen, strengthen, 395
and strain the walls of their repository to the utmost;
where the kindred spirit touches this wall it crumbles—
no one responds to kindness, no one is more sensitive to it
than the desperate man.

 XI

One night on Monterey Bay the death-freeze of the century: 400
a precise, detached calliper-grip holds the stars and the quarter-moon
in arrest: the hardiest plants crouch shrunken, a "killing frost"
on bougainvillea, Pride of Madeira, roseate black-purple succulents bowed
juices sucked awry in one orgy of freezing
slumped on their stems like old faces evicted from cheap hotels 405
—*into the streets of the universe, now!*

Earthquake and drought followed by freezing followed by war.
Flags are blossoming now where little else is blossoming
and I am bent on fathoming what it means to love my country.
The history of this earth and the bones within it? 410
Soils and cities, promises made and mocked, plowed contours of shame
 and of hope?
Loyalties, symbols, murmurs extinguished and echoing?
Grids of states stretching westward, underground waters?
Minerals, traces, rumors I am made from, morsel, minuscule fiber, one
 woman
like and unlike so many, fooled as to her destiny, the scope of her task? 415
One citizen like and unlike so many, touched and untouched in passing
—each of us now a driven grain, a nucleus, a city in crisis
some busy constructing enclosures, bunkers, to escape the common fate
some trying to revive dead statues to lead us, breathing their breath against
 marble lips
some who try to teach the moment, some who preach the moment 420
some who aggrandize, some who diminish themselves in the face of half-
 grasped events

—power and powerlessness run amuck, a tape reeling backward in jeering,
 screeching syllables—
some for whom war is new, others for whom it merely continues the old
 paroxysms of time
some marching for peace who for twenty years did not march for justice
some for whom peace is a white man's word and a white man's privilege 425
some who have learned to handle and contemplate the shapes of power-
 lessness and power
as the nurse learns hip and thigh and weight of the body he has to lift and
 sponge, day upon day
as she blows with her every skill on the spirit's embers still burning by their
 own laws in the bed of death.
A patriot is not a weapon.[1] A patriot is one who wrestles for the soul of
 her country
as she wrestles for her own being, for the soul of his country 430
(gazing through the great circle at Window Rock into the sheen of the Viet
 Nam Wall[2])
as he wrestles for his own being. A patriot is a citizen trying to wake
from the burnt-out dream of innocence, the nightmare
of the white general and the Black general[3] posed in their camouflage,
to remember her true country, remember his suffering land: remember 435
that blessing and cursing are born as twins and separated at birth to meet
 again in mourning
that the internal emigrant is the most homesick of all women and of all
 men
that every flag that flies today is a cry of pain.
 Where are we moored?
 What are the bindings? 440
 What behooves us?

XII

What homage will be paid to a beauty built to last
from inside out, executing the blueprints of resistance and mercy
drawn up in childhood, in that little girl, round-faced with clenched fists,
 already acquainted with mourning
in the creased snapshot you gave me? What homage will be paid to
 beauty 445
that insists on speaking truth, knows the two are not always the same,
beauty that won't deny, is itself an eye, will not rest under contemplation?
Those low long clouds we were driving under a month ago in New Mexico,
 clouds an arm's reach away
were beautiful and we spoke of it but I didn't speak then
of your beauty at the wheel beside me, dark head steady, eyes drinking the
 space 450
of crimson, indigo, Indian distance, Indian presence,

1. The ballistic-missile defense system made up of Patriot missiles was deployed during the 1991 Gulf War.
2. The Vietnam Veterans' Memorial in Washington, D.C., which comprises two black granite walls inscribed with the names of that war's dead and missing

"Window Rock" a stone formation in Arches National Park in Utah.
3. Colin Powell, chairman of the Joint Chiefs of Staff during the Gulf War. "The white general": H. Norman Schwarzkopf, the American commander during the Gulf War.

your spirit's gaze informing your body, impatient to mark what's possible,
 impatient to mark
what's lost, deliberately destroyed, can never any way be returned,
your back arched against all icons, simulations, dead letters
your woman's hands turning the wheel or working with shears, torque
 wrench, knives, with salt pork, onions, ink and fire 455
your providing sensate hands, your hands of oak and silk, of blackberry
 juice and drums
—I speak of them now.

(FOR M.)

XIII (Dedications)

I know you are reading this poem
late, before leaving your office 460
of the one intense yellow lamp-spot and the darkening window
in the lassitude of a building faded to quiet
long after rush-hour. I know you are reading this poem
standing up in a bookstore far from the ocean
on a grey day of early spring, faint flakes driven 465
across the plains' enormous spaces around you.
I know you are reading this poem
in a room where too much has happened for you to bear
where the bedclothes lie in stagnant coils on the bed
and the open valise speaks of flight 470
but you cannot leave yet. I know you are reading this poem
as the underground train loses momentum and before running up the
 stairs
toward a new kind of love
your life has never allowed.
I know you are reading this poem by the light 475
of the television screen where soundless images jerk and slide
while you wait for the newscast from the *intifada*.[4]
I know you are reading this poem in a waiting-room
of eyes met and unmeeting, of identity with strangers.
I know you are reading this poem by fluorescent light 480
in the boredom and fatigue of the young who are counted out,
count themselves out, at too early an age. I know
you are reading this poem through your failing sight, the thick
lens enlarging these letters beyond all meaning yet you read on
because even the alphabet is precious. 485
I know you are reading this poem as you pace beside the stove
warming milk, a crying child on your shoulder, a book in your hand
because life is short and you too are thirsty.
I know you are reading this poem which is not in your language
guessing at some words while others keep you reading 490
and I want to know which words they are.

4. Shaking off (Arabic, literal trans.); the Palestinian uprising against Israeli occupation of the West Bank of Jordan and the Gaza Strip, which began in 1987 and which is meant to be ended by the interim accord between Israel and the Palestine Liberation Organization, signed in September 1993.

I know you are reading this poem listening for something, torn between
 bitterness and hope
turning back once again to the task you cannot refuse.
I know you are reading this poem because there is nothing else left to read
there where you have landed, stripped as you are. 495

1990–91 1991

Final Notations

it will not be simple, it will not be long
it will take little time, it will take all your thought
it will take all your heart, it will take all your breath
it will be short, it will not be simple

it will touch through your ribs, it will take all your heart 5
it will not be long, it will occupy your thought
as a city is occupied, as a bed is occupied
it will take all your flesh, it will not be simple

You are coming into us who cannot withstand you
you are coming into us who never wanted to withstand you 10
you are taking parts of us into places never planned
you are going far away with pieces of our lives

it will be short, it will take all your breath
it will not be simple, it will become your will

1991 1991

In Those Years

In those years, people will say, we lost track
of the meaning of *we*, of *you*
we found ourselves
reduced to *I*
and the whole thing became 5
silly, ironic, terrible:
we were trying to live a personal life
and, yes, that was the only life
we could bear witness to

But the great dark birds of history screamed and plunged 10
into our personal weather
They were headed somewhere else but their beaks and pinions drove
along the shore, through the rags of fog
where we stood, saying *I*

1991 1995

To the Days

From you I want more than I've ever asked,
all of it—the newscasts' terrible stories
of life in my time, the knowing it's worse than that,
much worse—the knowing what it means to be lied to.

Fog in the mornings, hunger for clarity, 5
coffee and bread with sour plum jam.
Numbness of soul in placid neighborhoods.
Lives ticking on as if.

A typewriter's torrent, suddenly still.
Blue soaking through fog, two dragonflies wheeling. 10
Acceptable levels of cruelty, steadily rising.
Whatever you bring in your hands, I need to see it.

Suddenly I understand the verb without tenses.
To smell another woman's hair, to taste her skin.
To know the bodies drifting underwater. 15
To be human, said Rosa[1]—I can't teach you that.

A cat drinks from a bowl of marigolds—his moment.
Surely the love of life is never-ending,
the failure of nerve, a charred fuse?
I want more from you than I ever knew to ask. 20

Wild pink lilies erupting, tasseled stalks of corn
in the Mexican gardens, corn and roses.
Shortening days, strawberry fields in ferment
with tossed-aside, bruised fruit.

1991 1995

When We Dead Awaken: Writing as Re-Vision (1971)[1]

The Modern Language Association is both marketplace and funeral parlor for
the professional study of Western literature in North America. Like all gather-
ings of the professions, it has been and remains a "procession of the sons of edu-

1. Rosa Luxemburg (1871–1919) was a Polish-born middle-class Jew. Early in her abbreviated life she entered the currents of European socialist revolutionary thinking and action. She became one of the most influential and controversial figures in the social-democratic movements of Eastern Europe and Germany. Besides her political essays, she left hundreds of vivid letters to friends and comrades. Imprisoned during World War I for her strongly internationalist and anticapitalist beliefs, she was murdered in Berlin in 1919 by right-wing soldiers, with the passive collusion of a faction from her own party. Her body was thrown into a canal.

On December 28, 1916, from prison, she wrote a New Year letter to friends she feared were both backsliding and complaining: "Then see to it that you remain a *Mensch!* [Yiddish/German for human being]

. . . . Being a *Mensch* means happily throwing one's life 'on fate's great scale' if necessary, but, at the same time, enjoying every bright day and every beautiful cloud. Oh, I can't write you a prescription for being a *Mensch.* I only know how one is a *Mensch,* and you used to know it too when we went walking for a few hours in the Südende fields with the sunset's red light falling on the wheat. The world is so beautiful even with all its horrors" (*The Letters of Rosa Luxemburg,* ed., trans., and with an intro. by Stephen Eric Bronner [Atlantic Highlands, N.J.: Humanities Press, 1993], p. 173.) [Rich's note].

1. As Rich explains, this essay—written in 1971—was first published in 1972 and then included in her volume *On Lies, Secrets, and Silence* (1978). At that time she added the introductory note reprinted here, as well as some notes beginning, "A.R., 1978."

cated men" (*Virginia Woolf*):[2] a congeries of old-boys' networks, academicians rehearsing their numb canons in sessions dedicated to the literature of white males, junior scholars under the lash of "publish or perish" delivering papers in the bizarrely lit drawing-rooms of immense hotels: a ritual competition veering between cynicism and desperation.

However, in the interstices of these gentlemanly rites (or, in Mary Daly's words, on the boundaries of this patriarchal space),[3] some feminist scholars, teachers, and graduate students, joined by feminist writers, editors, and publishers, have for a decade been creating more subversive occasions, challenging the sacredness of the gentlemanly canon, sharing the rediscovery of buried works by women, asking women's questions, bringing literary history and criticism back to life in both senses. The Commission on the Status of Women in the Profession was formed in 1969 and held its first public event in 1970. In 1971 the Commission asked Ellen Peck Killoh, Tillie Olsen, Elaine Reuben, and myself, with Elaine Hedges as moderator, to talk on "The Woman Writer in the Twentieth Century." The essay that follows was written for that forum, and later published, along with the other papers from the forum and workshops, in an issue of College English edited by Elaine Hedges ("Women Writing and Teaching," vol. 34, no. 1, October 1972). With a few revisions, mainly updating, it was reprinted in American Poets in 1976, edited by William Heyen (New York: Bobbs-Merrill, 1976). That later text is the one published here.

The challenge flung by feminists at the accepted literary canon, at the methods of teaching it, and at the biased and astigmatic view of male "literary scholarship," has not diminished in the decade since the first Women's Forum; it has become broadened and intensified more recently by the challenges of black and lesbian feminists pointing out that feminist literary criticism itself has overlooked or held back from examining the work of black women and lesbians. The dynamic between a political vision and the demand for a fresh vision of literature is clear: without a growing feminist movement, the first inroads of feminist scholarship could not have been made; without the sharpening of a black feminist consciousness, black women's writing would have been left in limbo between misogynist black male critics and white feminists still struggling to unearth a white women's tradition; without an articulate lesbian/feminist movement, lesbian writing would still be lying in that closet where many of us used to sit reading forbidden books "in a bad light."

Much, much more is yet to be done; and university curricula have of course changed very little as a result of all this. What *is* changing is the availability of knowledge, of vital texts, the visible effects on women's lives of seeing, hearing our wordless or negated experience affirmed and pursued further in language.

Ibsen's[4] *When We Dead Awaken* is a play about the use that the male artist and thinker—in the process of creating culture as we know it—has made of women, in his life and in his work; and about a woman's slow struggling awakening to the use to which her life has been put. Bernard Shaw wrote in 1900 of this play:

2. The phrase is a quote from Woolf's *Three Guineas* (1938).

3. Mary Daly, *Beyond God the Father* (Boston: Beacon,

1971), pp. 40–41 [Rich's note].

4. Henrik Ibsen (1828–1906), Norwegian poet and playwright.

[Ibsen] shows us that no degradation ever devized or permitted is as disastrous as this degradation; that through it women can die into luxuries for men and yet can kill them; that men and women are becoming conscious of this; and that what remains to be seen as perhaps the most interesting of all imminent social developments is what will happen "when we dead awaken."[5]

It's exhilarating to be alive in a time of awakening consciousness; it can also be confusing, disorienting, and plainful. This awakening of dead or sleeping consciousness has already affected the lives of millions of women, even those who don't know it yet. It is also affecting the lives of men, even those who deny its claims upon them. The argument will go on whether an oppressive economic class system is responsible for the oppressive nature of male/female relations, or whether, in fact, patriarchy—the domination of males—is the original model of oppression on which all others are based. But in the last few years the women's movement has drawn inescapable and illuminating connections between our sexual lives and our political institutions. The sleepwalkers are coming awake, and for the first time this awakening has a collective reality; it is no longer such a lonely thing to open one's eyes.

Re-vision—the act of looking back, of seeing with fresh eyes, of entering an old text from a new critical direction—is for women more than a chapter in cultural history: it is an act of survival. Until we can understand the assumptions in which we are drenched we cannot know ourselves. And this drive to self-knowledge, for women, is more than a search for identity: it is part of our refusal of the self-destructiveness of male-dominated society. A radical critique of literature, feminist in its impulse, would take the work first of all as a clue to how we live, how we have been living, how we have been led to imagine ourselves, how our language has trapped as well as liberated us, how the very act of naming has been till now a male prerogative, and how we can begin to see and name—and therefore live—afresh. A change in the concept of sexual identity is essential if we are not going to see the old political order reassert itself in every new revolution. We need to know the writing of the past, and know it differently than we have ever known it; not to pass on a tradition but to break its hold over us.

For writers, and at this moment for women writers in particular, there is the challenge and promise of a whole new psychic geography to be explored. But there is also a difficult and dangerous walking on the ice, as we try to find language and images for a consciousness we are just coming into, and with little in the past to support us. I want to talk about some aspect of this difficulty and this danger.

Jane Harrison, the great classical anthropologist, wrote in 1914 in a letter to her friend Gilbert Murray:

By the by, about "Women," it has bothered me often—why do women never want to write poetry about Man as a sex—why is Woman a dream and a terror to man and not the other way around? . . . Is it mere convention and propriety, or something deeper?[6]

5. G. B. Shaw, *The Quintessence of Ibsenism* (New York: Hill & Wang, 1922), p. 139 [Rich's note].

6. J. G. Stewart, *Jane Ellen Harrison: A Portrait from Letters* (London: Merlin, 1959), p. 140 [Rich's note].

I think Jane Harrison's question cuts deep into the myth-making tradition, the romantic tradition; deep into what women and men have been to each other; and deep into the psyche of the woman writer. Thinking about that question, I began thinking of the work of two twentieth-century women poets, Sylvia Plath and Diane Wakoski. It strikes me that in the work of both Man appears as, if not a dream, a fascination and a terror; and that the source of the fascination and the terror is, simply, Man's power—to dominate, tyrannize, choose, or reject the woman. The charisma of Man seems to come purely from his power over her and his control of the world by force, not from anything fertile or life-giving in him. And, in the work of both these poets, it is finally the woman's sense of *herself*—embattled, possessed—that gives the poetry its dynamic charge, its rhythms of struggle, need, will, and female energy. Until recently this female anger and this furious awareness of the Man's power over her were not available materials to the female poet, who tended to write of Love as the source of her suffering, and to view that victimization by Love as an almost inevitable fate. Or, like Marianne Moore and Elizabeth Bishop,[7] she kept sexuality at a measured and chiseled distance in her poems.

One answer to Jane Harrison's question has to be that historically men and women have played very different parts in each others' lives. Where woman has been a luxury for man, and has served as the painter's model and the poet's muse, but also as comforter, nurse, cook, bearer of his seed, secretarial assistant, and copyist of manuscripts, man has played a quite different role for the female artist. Henry James repeats an incident which the writer Prosper Mérimée described, of how, while he was living with George Sand,

> he once opened his eyes, in the raw winter dawn, to see his companion, in a dressing-gown, on her knees before the domestic hearth, a candle-stick beside her and a red *madras* round her head, making bravely, with her own hands the fire that was to enable her to sit down betimes to urgent pen and paper. The story represents him as having felt that the spectacle chilled his ardor and tried his taste; her appearance was unfortunate, her occupation an inconsequence, and her industry a reproof—the result of all which was a lively irritation and an early rupture.[8]

The specter of this kind of male judgment, along with the misnaming and thwarting of her needs by a culture controlled by males, has created problems for the woman writer: problems of contact with herself, problems of language and style, problems of energy and survival.

In rereading Virginia Woolf's *A Room of One's Own* (1929) for the first time in some years, I was astonished at the sense of effort, of pains taken, of dogged tentativeness, in the tone of that essay. And I recognized that tone. I had heard it often enough, in myself and in other women. It is the tone of a woman almost in touch with her anger, who is determined not to appear angry, who is *willing* herself to be calm, detached, and even charming in a roomful of men where things have been said which are attacks on her very integrity. Virginia Woolf is addressing an audience of women, but she is acutely conscious—as

7. Plath, Wakoski, Moore, and Bishop are all included in this anthology.
8. Henry James, "Notes on Novelists," in *Selected*

Literary Criticism of Henry James, Morris Shapira, ed. (London: Heinemann, 1963), pp. 157–58 [Rich's note]

she always was—of being overheard by men: by Morgan and Lytton and Maynard Keynes[9] and for that matter by her father, Leslie Stephen.[1] She drew the language out into an exacerbated thread in her determination to have her own sensibility yet protect it from those masculine presences. Only at rare moments in that essay do you hear the passion in her voice; she was trying to sound as cool as Jane Austen, as Olympian as Shakespeare, because that is the way the men of the culture thought a writer should sound.

No male writer has written primarily or even largely for women, or with the sense of women's criticism as a consideration when he chooses his materials, his theme, his language. But to a lesser or greater extent, every woman writer has written for men even when, like Virginia Woolf, she was supposed to be addressing women. If we have come to the point when this balance might begin to change, when women can stop being haunted, not only by "convention and propriety" but by internalized fears of being and saying themselves, then it is an extraordinary moment for the woman writer—and reader.

I have hesitated to do what I am going to do now, which is to use myself as an illustration. For one thing, it's a lot easier and less dangerous to talk about other women writers. But there is something else. Like Virginia Woolf, I am aware of the women who are not with us here because they are washing the dishes and looking after the children. Nearly fifty years after she spoke, that fact remains largely unchanged. And I am thinking also of women whom she left out of the picture altogether—women who are washing other people's dishes and caring for other people's children, not to mention women who went on the streets last night in order to feed their children. We seem to be special women here, we have liked to think of ourselves as special, and we have known that men would tolerate, even romanticize us as special, as long as our words and actions didn't threaten their privilege of tolerating or rejecting us and our work according to *their* ideas of what a special woman ought to be. An important insight of the radical women's movement has been how divisive and how ultimately destructive is this myth of the special woman, who is also the token woman. Every one of us here in this room has had great luck—we are teachers, writers, academicians; our own gifts could not have been enough, for we all know women whose gifts are buried or aborted. Our struggles can have meaning and our privileges—however precarious under patriarchy—can be justified only if they can help to change the lives of women whose gifts—and whose very being—continue to be thwarted and silenced.

My own luck was being born white and middle-class into a house full of books, with a father who encouraged me to read and write. So for about twenty years I wrote for a particular man, who criticized and praised me and made me feel I was indeed "special." The obverse side of this, of course, was that I tried for a long time to please him, or rather, not to displease him. And then of course there were other men—writers, teachers—the Man, who was not a terror or a dream but a literary master and a master in other ways less

9. I.e., E. M. Forster, Lytton Strachey, and John Maynard Keynes, all members of Woolf's Bloomsbury circle.
1. "A. R., 1978: This intuition of mine was corroborated when, early in 1978, I read the correspondence between Woolf and Dame Ethel Smyth (Henry W. and Albert A. Berg Collection, The New York Public Library, Astor, Lenox and Tilden Foundations); in a letter dated June 8, 1933, Woolf speaks of having kept her own personality out of *A Room of One's Own* lest she not be taken seriously: '. . . how personal, so will they say, rubbing their hands with glee, women always are; *I even hear them as I write.*' (Italics mine.)" [Rich's note]. Leslie Stephen (1832–1904), a distinguished man of letters.

easy to acknowledge. And there were all those poems about women, written by men: it seemed to be a given that men wrote poems and women frequently inhabited them. These women were almost always beautiful, but threatened with the loss of beauty, the loss of youth—the fate worse than death. Or, they were beautiful and died young, like Lucy and Lenore. Or, the woman was like Maud Gonne[2] cruel and disastrously mistaken, and the poem reproached her because she had refused to become a luxury for the poet.

A lot is being said today about the influence that the myths and images of women have on all of us who are products of culture. I think it has been a peculiar confusion to the girl or woman who tries to write because she is peculiarly susceptible to language. She goes to poetry or fiction looking for *her* way of being in the world, since she too has been putting words and images together; she is looking eagerly for guides, maps, possibilities; and over and over in the "words' masculine persuasive force" of literature she comes up against something that negates everything she is about: she meets the image of Woman in books written by men. She finds a terror and a dream, she finds a beautiful pale face, she finds La Belle Dame Sans Merci, she finds Juliet or Tess or Salomé,[3] but precisely what she does not find is that absorbed, drudging, puzzled, sometimes inspired creature, herself, who sits at a desk trying to put words together.

So what does she do? What did I do? I read the older women poets with their peculiar keenness and ambivalence: Sappho, Christina Rossetti, Emily Dickinson, Elinor Wylie, Edna Millay, H. D.[4] I discovered that the woman poet most admired at the time (by men) was Marianne Moore, who was maidenly, elegant, intellectual, discreet. But even in reading these women I was looking in them for the same things I had found in the poetry of men, because I wanted women poets to be the equals of men, and to be equal was still confused with sounding the same.

I know that my style was formed first by male poets: by the men I was reading as an undergraduate—Frost, Dylan Thomas, Donne, Auden, MacNeice, Stevens, Yeats. What I chiefly learned from them was craft.[5] But poems are like dreams: in them you put what you don't know you know. Looking back at poems I wrote before I was twenty-one, I'm startled because beneath the conscious craft are glimpses of the split I even then experienced between the girl who wrote poems, who defined herself in writing poems, and the girl who was to define herself by her relationships with men. "Aunt Jennifer's Tigers" (1951), written while I was a student, looks with deliberate detachment at this split.[6] In writing this poem, composed and apparently cool as it is, I thought I was creating a portrait of an imaginary woman. But this woman suffers from the opposition of her imagination, worked out in tapestry, and her life-style, "ringed with ordeals she was mastered by." It was important to me that Aunt

2. Irish revolutionary activist (1865–1953), beautiful beloved of William Butler Yeats, and subject of many of his poems. "Lucy and Lenore": in poems written by William Wordsworth and Edgar Allan Poe.
3. Dancer responsible for killing John the Baptist in Oscar Wilde's play. "La Belle Dame Sans Merci": title of a poem by John Keats (the beautiful lady without pity; French). "Juliet": tragic heroine of Shakespeare's *Romeo and Juliet.* "Tess": doomed heroine in Thomas Hardy's *Tess of the D'Urbervilles.*
4. Rossetti, Dickinson, Wylie, Millay, and H. D. are included in this anthology. Sappho (c. 600 B.C.), Greek poet.
5. A. R., 1978: Yes: I spent months, at sixteen, memorizing and writing imitations of Millay's sonnets; and in notebooks of that period I find what are obviously attempts to imitate Dickinson's metrics and verbal compression. I knew H. D. only through anthologized lyrics; her epic poetry was not then available to me. [Rich's note].

6. For the text of the poem, see p. 1955.

Jennifer was a person as distinct from myself as possible—distanced by the
formalism of the poem, by its objective, observant tone—even by putting the
woman in a different generation.

 In those years formalism was part of the strategy—like asbestos gloves, it al-
lowed me to handle materials I couldn't pick up bare-handed. A later strategy
was to use the persona of a man, as I did in "The Loser" (1958):

> *A man thinks of the woman he once loved: first, after her*
> *wedding, and then nearly a decade later.*

I

I kissed you, bride and lost, and went
home from that bourgeois sacrament,
your cheek still tasting cold upon
my lips that gave you benison
with all the swagger that they knew—
as losers somehow learn to do.

Your wedding made my eyes ache; soon
the world would be worse off for one
more golden apple dropped to ground
without the least protesting sound,
and you would windfall lie, and we
forget your shimmer on the tree.

Beauty is always wasted: if
not Mignon's song[7] sung to the deaf,
at all events to the unmoved.
A face like yours cannot be loved
long or seriously enough.
Almost, we seem to hold it off.

II

Well, you are tougher than I thought.
Now when the wash with ice hangs taut
this morning of St. Valentine,
I see you strip the squeaking line,
your body weighed against the load,
and all my groans can do no good.

Because you are still beautiful,
though squared and stiffened by the pull
of what nine windy years have done.
You have three daughters, lost a son.
I see all your intelligence
flung into that unwearied stance.

My envy is of no avail.
I turn my head and wish him well
who chafed your beauty into use

7. From Ambroise Thomas's *Mignon* (1866), an opera based on Goethe's *Wilhelm Meister.*

and lives forever in a house
lit by the friction of your mind.
You stagger in against the wind.

I finished college, published my first book by a fluke, as it seemed to me, and broke off a love affair. I took a job, lived alone, went on writing, fell in love. I was young, full of energy, and the book seemed to mean that others agreed I was a poet. Because I was also determined to prove that as a woman poet I could also have what was then defined as a "full" woman's life, I plunged in my early twenties into marriage and had three children before I was thirty. There was nothing overt in the environment to warn me: these were the fifties, and in reaction to the earlier wave of feminism, middle-class women were making careers of domestic perfection, working to send their husbands through professional schools, then retiring to raise large families. People were moving out to the suburbs, technology was going to be the answer to everything, even sex; the family was in its glory. Life was extremely private; women were isolated from each other by the loyalties of marriage. I have a sense that women didn't talk to each other much in the fifties—not about their secret emptinesses, their frustrations. I went on trying to write; my second book and first child appeared in the same month. But by the time that book came out I was already dissatisfied with those poems, which seemed to me mere exercises for poems I hadn't written. The book was praised, however, for its "gracefulness"; I had a marriage and a child. If there were doubts, if there were periods of null depression or active despairing, these could only mean that I was ungrateful, insatiable, perhaps a monster.

About the time my third child was born, I felt that I had either to consider myself a failed woman and a failed poet, or to try to find some synthesis by which to understand what was happening to me. What frightened me most was the sense of drift, of being pulled along on a current which called itself my destiny, but in which I seemed to be losing touch with whoever I had been, with the girl who had experienced her own will and energy almost ecstatically at times, walking around a city or riding a train at night or typing in a student room. In a poem about my grandmother I wrote (of myself): "A young girl, thought sleeping, is certified dead" ("Halfway"). I was writing very little, partly from fatigue, that female fatigue of suppressed anger and loss of contact with my own being; partly from the discontinuity of female life with its attention to small chores, errands, work that others constantly undo, small children's constant needs. What I did write was unconvincing to me; my anger and frustration were hard to acknowledge in or out of poems because in fact I cared a great deal about my husband and my children. Trying to look back and understand that time I have tried to analyze the real nature of the conflict. Most, if not all, human lives are full of fantasy—passive day-dreaming which need not be acted on. But to write poetry or fiction, or even to think well, is not to fantasize, or to put fantasies on paper. For a poem to coalesce, for a character or an action to take shape, there has to be an imaginative transformation of reality which is no way passive. And a certain freedom of the mind is needed—freedom to press on, to enter the currents of your thought like a glider pilot, knowing that your motion can be sustained, that the buoyancy of your attention will not be suddenly snatched away. Moreover, if the imagination is to transcend and transform experience it has to question, to

challenge, to conceive of alternatives, perhaps to the very life you are living at that moment. You have to be free to play around with the notion that day might be night, love might be hate; nothing can be too sacred for the imagination to turn into its opposite or to call experimentally by another name. For writing is re-naming. Now, to be maternally with small children all day in the old way, to be with a man in the old way of marriage, requires a holding-back, a putting-aside of that imaginative activity, and demands instead a kind of conservatism. I want to make it clear that I am *not* saying that in order to write well, or think well, it is necessary to become unavailable to others, or to become a devouring ego. This has been the myth of the masculine artist and thinker; and I do not accept it. But to be a female human being trying to fulfill traditional female functions in a traditional way *is* in direct conflict with the subversive function of the imagination. The word traditional is important here. There must be ways, and we will be finding out more and more about them, in which the energy of creation and the energy of relation can be united. But in those years I always felt the conflict as a failure of love in myself. I had thought I was choosing a full life: the life available to most men, in which sexuality, work, and parenthood could coexist. But I felt, at twenty-nine, guilt toward the people closest to me, and guilty toward my own being.

I wanted, then, more than anything, the one thing of which there was never enough: time to think, time to write. The fifties and early sixties were years of rapid revelations: the sit-ins and marches in the South, the Bay of Pigs,[8] the early antiwar movement, raised large questions—questions for which the masculine world of the academy around me seemed to have expert and fluent answers. But I needed to think for myself—about pacifism and dissent and violence, about poetry and society, and about my own relationship to all these things. For about ten years I was reading in fierce snatches, scribbling in notebooks, writing poetry in fragments; I was looking desperately for clues, because if there were no clues then I thought I might be insane. I wrote in a notebook about this time:

> Paralyzed by the sense that there exists a mesh of relationships—e.g., between my anger at the children, my sensual life, pacifism, sex (I mean sex in its broadest significance, not merely sexual desire)—an interconnectedness which, if I could see it, make it valid, would give me back myself, make it possible to function lucidly and passionately. Yet I grope in and out among these dark webs.

I think I began at this point to feel that politics was not something "out there" but something "in here" and of the essence of my condition.

In the late fifties I was able to write, for the first time, directly about experiencing myself as a woman. The poem was jotted in fragments during children's naps, brief hours in a library, or at 3:00 A.M. after rising with a wakeful child. I despaired of doing any continuous work at this time. Yet I began to feel that my fragments and scraps had a common consciousness and a common theme, one which I would have been very unwilling to put on paper at an ear-

8. A 1961 abortive invasion of Cuba by CIA-trained anti-Castro exiles—financed and supported by the U.S. government—which was a fiasco. Like the other "revelations" mentioned, it fed the growing distrust of the government among some Americans.

lier time because I had been taught that poetry should be "universal," which meant, of course, nonfemale. Until then I had tried very much *not* to identify myself as a female poet. Over two years I wrote a ten-part poem called "Snapshots of a Daughter-in-Law" (1958–1960), in a longer looser mode than I'd ever trusted myself with before. It was an extraordinary relief to write that poem. It strikes me now as too literary, too dependent on allusion; I hadn't found the courage yet to do without authorities, or even to use the pronoun "I"—the woman in the poem is always ' she." One section of it, No. 2, concerns a woman who thinks she is going mad; she is haunted by voices telling her to resist and rebel, voices which she can hear but not obey.

> 2.
> Banging the coffee-pot into the sink
> she hears the angels chiding, and looks out
> past the raked gardens to the sloppy sky.
> Only a week since They said: *Have no patience.*
>
> The next time it was: *Be insatiable.*
> Then: *Save yourself; others you cannot save.*
> Sometimes she's let the tapstream scald her arm,
> a match burn to her thumbnail,
>
> or held her hand above the kettle's snout
> right in the woolly steam. They are probably angels,
> since nothing hurts her anymore, except
> each morning's grit blowing into her eyes.

The poem "Orion," written five years later, is a poem of reconnection with a part of myself I had felt I was losing—the active principle, the energetic imagination, the "half-brother" whom I projected, as I had for many years, into the constellation Orion. It's no accident that the words "cold and egotistical" appear in this poem, and are applied to myself.

> Far back when I went zig-zagging
> through tamarack[9] pastures
> you were my genius, you
> my cast-iron Viking, my helmed
> lion-heart king in prison.
> Years later now you're young
>
> my fierce half-brother, staring
> down from that simplified west
> your breast open, your belt dragged down
> by an oldfashioned thing, a sword
> the last bravado you won't give over
> though it weighs you down as you stride
>
> and the stars in it are dim
> and maybe have stopped burning.
> But you burn, and I know it;

9. Larch.

as I throw back my head to take you in
an old transfusion happens again:
divine astronomy is nothing to it.

Indoors I bruise and blunder,
break faith, leave ill enough
alone, a dead child born in the dark.
Night cracks up over the chimney,
pieces of time, frozen geodes
come showering down in the grate.

A man reaches behind my eyes
and finds them empty
a woman's head turns away
from my head in the mirror
children are dying my death
and eating crumbs of my life.

Pity is not your forte.
Calmly you ache up there
pinned aloft in your crow's nest,
my speechless pirate!
You take it all for granted
and when I look you back

it's with a starlike eye
shooting its cold and egotistical spear
where it can do least damage.
Breathe deep! No hurt, no pardon
out here in the cold with you
you with your back to the wall.

The choice still seemed to be between "love"—womanly, maternal love, altru-
istic love—a love defined and ruled by the weight of an entire culture; and
egotism—a force directed by men into creation, achievement, ambition,
often at the expense of others, but justifiably so. For weren't they men, and
wasn't that their destiny as womanly, selfless love was ours? We know now that
the alternatives are false ones—that the word "love" is itself in need of re-
vision.

There is a companion poem to "Orion," written three years later, in which
at last the woman in the poem and the woman writing the poem become the
same person. It is called "Planetarium," and it was written after a visit to a real
planetarium, where I read an account of the work of Caroline Herschel, the as-
tronomer, who worked with her brother William, but whose name remained
obscure, as his did not.

A woman in the shape of a monster
a monster in the shape of a woman
the skies are full of them

a woman 'in the snow
among the Clocks and instruments
or measuring the ground with poles'

in her 98 years to discover
8 comets

she whom the moon ruled
like us
levitating into the night sky
riding the polished lenses

Galaxies of women, there
doing penance for impetuousness
ribs chilled
in those spaces of the mind

An eye,

 'virile, precise and absolutely certain'
 from the mad webs of Uranusborg

 encountering the NOVA

every impulse of light exploding
from the core
as life flies out of us

 Tycho whispering at last
 'Let me not seem to have lived in vain'

What we see, we see
and seeing is changing

the light that shrivels a mountain
and leaves a man alive

Heartbeat of the pulsar
heart sweating through my body

The radio impulse
pouring in from Taurus

 I am bombarded yet I stand

I have been standing all my life in the
direct path of a battery of signals
the most accurately transmitted most
untranslatable language in the universe
I am a galactic cloud so deep so invo-
luted that a light wave could take 15
years to travel through me And has
taken I am an instrument in the shape
of a woman trying to translate pulsations
into images for the relief of the body
and the reconstruction of the mind.

In closing I want to tell you about a dream I had last summer. I dreamed I was asked to read my poetry at a mass women's meeting, but when I began to read, what came out were the lyrics of a blues song. I share this dream with you because it seemed to me to say something about the problems and the future of the woman writer, and probably of women in general. The awakening of consciousness is not like the crossing of a frontier—one step and you are in another country. Much of woman's poetry has been of the nature of the blues song: a cry of pain, of victimization, or a lyric of seduction.[1] And today, much poetry by women—and prose for that matter—is charged with anger. I think we need to go through that anger, and we will betray our own reality if we try, as Virginia Woolf was trying, for an objectivity, a detachment, that would make us sound more like Jane Austen or Shakespeare. We know more than Jane Austen or Shakespeare knew: more than Jane Austen because our lives are more complex, more than Shakespeare because we know more about the lives of women—Jane Austen and Virginia Woolf included.

Both the victimization and the anger experienced by women are real, and have real sources, everywhere in the environment, built into society, language, the structures of thought. They will go on being tapped and explored by poets, among others. We can neither deny them, nor will we rest there. A new generation of women poets is already working out of the psychic energy released when women begin to move out towards what the feminist philosopher Mary Daly has described as the "new space" on the boundaries of patriarchy.[2] Women are speaking to and of women in these poems, out of a newly released courage to name, to love each other, to share risk and grief and celebration.

To the eye of a feminist, the work of Western male poets now writing reveals a deep, fatalistic pessimism as to the possibilities of change, whether societal or personal, along with a familiar and threadbare use of women (and nature) as redemptive on the one hand, threatening on the other; and a new tide of phallocentric sadism and overt woman-hating which matches the sexual brutality of recent films. "Political" poetry by men remains stranded amid the struggles for power among male groups; in condemning U.S. imperialism or the Chilean junta the poet can claim to speak for the oppressed while remaining, as male, part of a system of sexual oppression. The enemy is always outside the self, the struggle somewhere else. The mood of isolation, self-pity, and self-imitation that pervades "nonpolitical" poetry suggests that a profound change in masculine consciousness will have to precede any new male poetic—or other—inspiration. The creative energy of patriarchy is fast running out; what remains is its self-generating energy for destruction. As women, we have our work cut out for us.

<div align="right">1972, 1976, 1978</div>

1. A. R., 1978: When I dreamed that dream, was I wholly ignorant of the tradition of Bessie Smith and other women's blues lyrics which transcended victimization to sing of resistance and independence? [Rich's note].

2. Mary Daly, *Beyond God the Father: Towards a Philosophy of Women's Liberation* (Boston: Beacon, 1973) [Rich's note].

PARIAH?

TONI MORRISON

1931–

When Toni Morrison received the Pulitzer Prize in 1988 and the Nobel Prize for literature in 1993, it became clear that she had established herself as one of America's foremost writers. An exceptionally popular novelist, Morrison has enthralled readers all over the world. At the same time, she has been critically celebrated not only for her incisive analyses of the dynamics of race and gender but also for the lyricism of her language and the inventive originality of her plots. Verbal magic and fantastic, sometimes even mystic events combine in Morrison's six published novels to engage readers in often hauntingly elusive but always ethically crucial questions about American culture, past and present.

Morrison, who frequently focuses on black, midwestern communities in her fiction, was born Chloe Anthony Wofford and was raised by working-class parents in the small town of Lorain, Ohio. Because Ohio is bordered by a southern state, Kentucky, as well as Lake Erie, which is in turn one of Canada's borders, Morrison views it as a crucial boundary between North and South. With a history of underground railroad stations and cross burnings, abolitionist activism and Ku Klux Klan persecution, Ohio is, in Morrison's phrase, "neither plantation nor ghetto," and so it provides an ideal site for her analysis of the struggle for freedom in which so many of her characters engage.

After graduating from Howard University in 1953, Morrison went north to Cornell University, where she earned a master's degree for a thesis on the theme of suicide in the fiction of William Faulkner and Virginia Woolf. While she was teaching at Howard University, she married Harold Morrison, a Jamaican architect, and gave birth to two sons, Harold Ford and Slade. In 1964, she separated from her husband and moved with her children first to Syracuse, New York, and then to New York City, where she worked as a senior editor at Random House. There she helped shape such autobiographies as those by the activist Angela Davis and the boxer Muhammad Ali, as well as an anthology titled *The Black Book* (1974), a collection that reflects the breadth of the "anonymous Black man's" experience in America. Recently, she has taught at Yale, Rutgers, and (currently) Princeton universities.

Morrison's novels—*The Bluest Eye* (1970), *Sula* (1973), *Song of Solomon* (1977), *Tar Baby* (1981), *Beloved* (1987), and *Jazz* (1992)—have been widely acclaimed as evocative meditations on African-American cultural identity in contemporary America. Like Lucille Clifton and Toni Cade Bambara, artists she praises, Morrison has managed to convey racial pain without losing a sense of joy. She does this, in part at least, by exploring the unique cultural inheritance of black Americans in terms of universal moral issues, namely, the tension between the individual and society and the problem of good and evil. Typical in her work, then, are "outlaw" figures, wild characters like Cholly Breedlove in *The Bluest Eye*, Sula in *Sula*, Guitar in *Song of Solomon*, and Sethe in *Beloved*. Rebellious and defiant, such characters are often castigated as evil by the community and cast out as pariahs. For Morrison, however, their energy and verve can never be wholly rejected, for "evil is not an alien force." Just as important, Morrison sees the pariah as a paradigm of the black community, which is, she claims, "a pariah community" in white America.

Many scholars of the aesthetic achievements of African-American women have regarded *Sula* as a touchstone or breakthrough work. Hortense Spillers, for example, views Morrison's second novel as "the single most important irruption of black

women's writing in our era." What intrigues critics like Spillers is not only the friendship between two female characters as different as Nel and Sula but also the ways in which Sula herself departs from conventional definitions of feminine service or servitude to live for herself and only by standards she has herself set. Neither a wife nor a mother, Sula is never "woman-for-the-other" and always "woman-for-self." The "badness" of Sula thus engages readers in questions pertaining to the sources and limits of a community's ethics, the nature and extent of social responsibility. In addition, the historical framework of Morrison's novel brackets its events in the context of two world wars, exploring their impact on the lives of African-Americans.

That Morrison's characters in *Sula* inhabit an inhospitable public culture adds to their particularized, private burdens. As in her other novels, Morrison examines the excruciating legacy of slavery by focusing on the lives of individuals living within unique social networks. *Beloved*, the story of an ex-slave mother grieving over the loss of one of her children, most directly addresses that inheritance; however, all of Morrison's works explore the effects that the stereotyping and discrimination against African-Americans have on whites as well as on blacks. Her critical book, *Playing in the Dark: Whiteness and the Literary Imagination* (1992), analyzes American authors from Edgar Allan Poe and Willa Cather to Ernest Hemingway to explain the important functions fulfilled by what Morison calls "the Africanist presence." In her powerful fictional prose, Morrison's analysis of race illuminates her characters' familial, erotic, and moral situations, helping her to pay tribute to the resiliency and richness of African-American culture and to fulfill the task she has set for herself throughout her career, to study "how and why we learn to live this life intensely and well."

Sula

Part One

In that place, where they tore the nightshade and blackberry patches from their roots to make room for the Medallion City Golf Course, there was once a neighborhood. It stood in the hills above the valley town of Medallion and spread all the way to the river. It is called the suburbs now, but when black people lived there it was called the Bottom. One road, shaded by beeches, oaks, maples and chestnuts, connected it to the valley. The beeches are gone now, and so are the pear trees where children sat and yelled down through the blossoms to passersby. Generous funds have been allotted to level the stripped and faded buildings that clutter the road from Medallion up to the golf course. They are going to raze the Time and a Half Pool Hall, where feet in long tan shoes once pointed down from chair rungs. A steel ball will knock to dust Irene's Palace of Cosmetology, where women used to lean their heads back on sink trays and doze while Irene lathered Nu Nile into their hair. Men in khaki work clothes will pry loose the slats of Reba's Grill, where the owner cooked in her hat because she couldn't remember the ingredients without it.

There will be nothing left of the Bottom (the footbridge that crossed the river is already gone), but perhaps it is just as well, since it wasn't a town anyway: just a neighborhood where on quiet days people in valley houses could hear singing sometimes, banjos sometimes, and, if a valley man happened to have business up in those hills—collecting rent or insurance payments—he might see a dark woman in a flowered dress doing a bit of cakewalk, a bit of

black bottom,[1] a bit of "messing around" to the lively notes of a mouth organ. Her bare feet would raise the saffron dust that floated down on the coveralls and bunion-split shoes of the man breathing music in and out of his harmonica. The black people watching her would laugh and rub their knees, and it would be easy for the valley man to hear the laughter and not notice the adult pain that rested somewhere under the eyelids, somewhere under their head rags and soft felt hats, somewhere in the palm of the hand, somewhere behind the frayed lapels, somewhere in the sinew's curve. He'd have to stand in the back of Greater Saint Matthew's and let the tenor's voice dress him in silk, or touch the hands of the spoon carvers (who had not worked in eight years) and let the fingers that danced on wood kiss his skin. Otherwise the pain would escape him even though the laughter was part of the pain.

A shucking, knee-slapping, wet-eyed laughter that could even describe and explain how they came to be where they were.

A joke. A nigger joke. That was the way it got started. Not the town, of course, but that part of town where the Negroes lived, the part they called the Bottom in spite of the fact that it was up in the hills. Just a nigger joke. The kind white folks tell when the mill closes down and they're looking for a little comfort somewhere. The kind colored folks tell on themselves when the rain doesn't come, or comes for weeks, and they're looking for a little comfort somehow.

A good white farmer promised freedom and a piece of bottom land to his slave if he would perform some very difficult chores. When the slave completed the work, he asked the farmer to keep his end of the bargain. Freedom was easy—the farmer had no objection to that. But he didn't want to give up any land. So he told the slave that he was very sorry that he had to give him valley land. He had hoped to give him a piece of the Bottom. The slave blinked and said he thought valley land was bottom land. The master said, "Oh, no! See those hills? That's bottom land, rich and fertile."

"But it's high up in the hills," said the slave.

"High up from us," said the master, "but when God looks down, it's the bottom. That's why we call it so. It's the bottom of heaven—best land there is."

So the slave pressed his master to try to get him some. He preferred it to the valley. And it was done. The nigger got the hilly land, where planting was backbreaking, where the soil slid down and washed away the seeds, and where the wind lingered all through the winter.

Which accounted for the fact that white people lived on the rich valley floor in that little river town in Ohio, and the blacks populated the hills above it, taking small consolation in the fact that every day they could literally look down on the white folks.

Still, it was lovely up in the Bottom. After the town grew and the farm land turned into a village and the village into a town and the streets of Medallion were hot and dusty with progress, those heavy trees that sheltered the shacks up in the Bottom were wonderful to see. And the hunters who went there sometimes wondered in private if maybe the white farmer was right after all. Maybe it was the bottom of heaven.

1. A dance, viewed by some as indecent that was popular in the late 1920s. "Cakewalk" (p. 1994): stage dance devised by black entertainers.

The black people would have disagreed, but they had no time to think about it. They were mightily preoccupied with earthly things—and each other, wondering even as early as 1920 what Shadrack was all about, what that little girl Sula who grew into a woman in their town was all about, and what they themselves were all about, tucked up there in the Bottom.

1919

Except for World War II, nothing ever interfered with the celebration of National Suicide Day. It had taken place every January third since 1920, although Shadrack,[2] its founder, was for many years the only celebrant. Blasted and permanently astonished by the events of 1917, he had returned to Medallion handsome but ravaged, and even the most fastidious people in the town sometimes caught themselves dreaming of what he must have been like a few years back before he went off to war. A young man of hardly twenty, his head full of nothing and his mouth recalling the taste of lipstick, Shadrack had found himself in December, 1917, running with his comrades across a field in France. It was his first encounter with the enemy and he didn't know whether his company was running toward them or away. For several days they had been marching, keeping close to a stream that was frozen at its edges. At one point they crossed it, and no sooner had he stepped foot on the other side than the day was adangle with shouts and explosions. Shellfire was all around him, and though he knew that this was something called *it*, he could not muster up the proper feeling—the feeling that would accommodate *it*. He expected to be terrified or exhilarated—to feel *something* very strong. In fact, he felt only the bite of a nail in his boot, which pierced the ball of his foot whenever he came down on it. The day was cold enough to make his breath visible, and he wondered for a moment at the purity and whiteness of his own breath among the dirty, gray explosions surrounding him. He ran, bayonet fixed, deep in the great sweep of men flying across this field. Wincing at the pain in his foot, he turned his head a little to the right and saw the face of a soldier near him fly off. Before he could register shock, the rest of the soldier's head disappeared under the inverted soup bowl of his helmet. But stubbornly, taking no direction from the brain, the body of the headless soldier ran on, with energy and grace, ignoring altogether the drip and slide of brain tissue down its back.

When Shadrack opened his eyes he was propped up in a small bed. Before him on a tray was a large tin plate divided into three triangles. In one triangle was rice, in another meat, and in the third stewed tomatoes. A small round depression held a cup of whitish liquid. Shadrack stared at the soft colors that filled these triangles: the lumpy whiteness of rice, the quivering blood tomatoes, the grayish-brown meat. All their repugnance was contained in the neat balance of the triangles—a balance that soothed him, transferred some of its equilibrium to him. Thus reassured that the white, the red and the brown would stay where they were—would not explode or burst forth from their restricted zones—he suddenly felt hungry and looked around for his hands. His glance was cautious at first, for he had to be very careful—anything could be

2. The name given to a captive Judean by Nebuchadnezzar, king of Babylon (Daniel 1:1–7). Because he and his companions refused to worship the golden image, they were thrown into the fiery furnace, where they were not burned (3:13–27).

anywhere. Then he noticed two lumps beneath the beige blanket on either side of his hips. With extreme care he lifted one arm and was relieved to find his hand attached to his wrist. He tried the other and found it also. Slowly he directed one hand toward the cup and, just as he was about to spread his fingers, they began to grow in higgledy-piggledy fashion like Jack's beanstalk all over the tray and the bed. With a shriek he closed his eyes and thrust his huge growing hands under the covers. Once out of sight they seemed to shrink back to their normal size. But the yell had brought a male nurse.

"Private? We're not going to have any trouble today, are we? Are we, Private?"

Shadrack looked up at a balding man dressed in a green-cotton jacket and trousers. His hair was parted low on the right side so that some twenty or thirty yellow hairs could discreetly cover the nakedness of his head.

"Come on. Pick up that spoon. Pick it up, Private. Nobody is going to feed you forever."

Sweat slid from Shadrack's armpits down his sides. He could not bear to see his hands grow again and he was frightened of the voice in the apple-green suit.

"Pick it up. I said. There's no point to this . . ." The nurse reached under the cover for Shadrack's wrist to pull out the monstrous hand. Shadrack jerked it back and overturned the tray. In panic he raised himself to his knees and tried to fling off and away his terrible fingers, but succeeded only in knocking the nurse into the next bed.

When they bound Shadrack into a straitjacket, he was both relieved and grateful, for his hands were at last hidden and confined to whatever size they had attained

Laced and silent in his small bed, he tried to tie the loose cords in his mind. He wanted desperately to see his own face and connect it with the word "private"—the word the nurse (and the others who helped bind him) had called him. "Private" he thought was something secret, and he wondered why they looked at him and called him a secret. Still, if his hands behaved as they had done, what might he expect from his face? The fear and longing were too much for him, so he began to think of other things. That is, he let his mind slip into whatever cave mouths of memory it chose.

He saw a window that looked out on a river which he knew was full of fish. Someone was speaking softly just outside the door . . .

Shadrack's earlier violence had coincided with a memorandum from the hospital executive staff in reference to the distribution of patients in high-risk areas. There was clearly a demand for space. The priority or the violence earned Shadrack his release, $217 in cash, a full suit of clothes and copies of very official-looking papers.

When he stepped out of the hospital door the grounds overwhelmed him: the cropped shrubbery, the edged lawns, the undeviating walks. Shadrack looked at the cement stretches: each one leading clearheadedly to some presumably desirable destination. There were no fences, no warnings, no obstacles at all between concrete and green grass, so one could easily ignore the tidy sweep of stone and cut out in another direction—a direction of one's own.

Shadrack stood at the foot of the hospital steps watching the heads of trees tossing ruefully but harmlessly, since their trunks were rooted too deeply in

the earth to threaten him. Only the walks made him uneasy. He shifted his weight, wondering how he could get to the gate without stepping on the concrete. While plotting his course—where he would have to leap, where to skirt a clump of bushes—a loud guffaw startled him. Two men were going up the steps. Then he noticed that there were many people about, and that he was just now seeing them, or else they had just materialized. They were thin slips, like paper dolls floating down the walks. Some were seated in chairs with wheels, propelled by other paper figures from behind. All seemed to be smoking, and their arms and legs curved in the breeze. A good high wind would pull them up and away and they would land perhaps among the tops of the trees.

Shadrack took the plunge. Four steps and he was on the grass heading for the gate. He kept his head down to avoid seeing the paper people swerving and bending here and there, and he lost his way. When he looked up, he was standing by a low red building separated from the main building by a covered walkway. From somewhere came a sweetish smell which reminded him of something painful. He looked around for the gate and saw that he had gone directly away from it in his complicated journey over the grass. Just to the left of the low building was a graveled driveway that appeared to lead outside the grounds. He trotted quickly to it and left, at last, a haven of more than a year, only eight days of which he fully recollected.

Once on the road, he headed west. The long stay in the hospital had left him weak—too weak to walk steadily on the gravel shoulders of the road. He shuffled, grew dizzy, stopped for breath, started again, stumbling and sweating but refusing to wipe his temples, still afraid to look at his hands. Passengers in dark, square cars shuttered their eyes at what they took to be a drunken man.

The sun was already directly over his head when he came to a town. A few blocks of shaded streets and he was already at its heart—a pretty, quietly regulated downtown.

Exhausted, his feet clotted with pain, he sat down at the curbside to take off his shoes. He closed his eyes to avoid seeing his hands and fumbled with the laces of the heavy high-topped shoes. The nurse had tied them into a double knot, the way one does for children, and Shadrack, long unaccustomed to the manipulation of intricate things, could not get them loose. Uncoordinated, his fingernails tore away at the knots. He fought a rising hysteria that was not merely anxiety to free his aching feet; his very life depended on the release of the knots. Suddenly without raising his eyelids, he began to cry. Twenty-two years old, weak, hot, frightened, not daring to acknowledge the fact that he didn't even know who or what he was . . . with no past, no language, no tribe, no source, no address book, no comb, no pencil, no clock, no pocket handkerchief, no rug, no bed, no can opener, no faded postcard, no soap, no key, no tobacco pouch, no soiled underwear and nothing nothing nothing to do . . . he was sure of one thing only: the unchecked monstrosity of his hands. He cried soundlessly at the curbside of a small Midwestern town wondering where the window was, and the river, and the soft voices just outside the door . . .

Through his tears he saw the fingers joining the laces, tentatively at first, then rapidly. The four fingers of each hand fused into the fabric, knotted themselves and zigzagged in and out of the tiny eyeholes.

By the time the police drove up, Shadrack was suffering from a blinding headache, which was not abated by the comfort he felt when the policemen

pulled his hands away from what he thought was a permanent entanglement with his shoelaces. They took him to jail, booked him for vagrancy and intoxication, and locked him in a cell. Lying on a cot, Shadrack could only stare helplessly at the wall, so paralyzing was the pain in his head. He lay in this agony for a long while and then realized he was staring at the painted-over letters of a command to fuck himself. He studied the phrase as the pain in his head subsided.

Like moonlight stealing under a window shade an idea insinuated itself: his earlier desire to see his own face. He looked for a mirror; there was none. Finally, keeping his hands carefully behind his back he made his way to the toilet bowl and peeped in. The water was unevenly lit by the sun so he could make nothing out. Returning to his cot he took the blanket and covered his head, rendering the water dark enough to see his reflection. There in the toilet water he saw a grave black face. A black so definite, so unequivocal, it astonished him. He had been harboring a skittish apprehension that he was not real—that he didn't exist at all. But when the blackness greeted him with its indisputable presence, he wanted nothing more. In his joy he took the risk of letting one edge of the blanket drop and glanced at his hands. They were still. Courteously still.

Shadrack rose and returned to the cot, where he fell into the first sleep of his new life. A sleep deeper than the hospital drugs; deeper than the pits of plums, steadier than the condor's wing; more tranquil than the curve of eggs.

The sheriff looked through the bars at the young man with the matted hair. He had read through his prisoner's papers and hailed a farmer. When Shadrack awoke, the sheriff handed him back his papers and escorted him to the back of a wagon. Shadrack got in and in less than three hours he was back in Medallion, for he had been only twenty-two miles from his window, his river, and his soft voices just outside the door.

In the back of the wagon, supported by sacks of squash and hills of pumpkins, Shadrack began a struggle that was to last for twelve days, a struggle to order and focus experience. It had to do with making a place for fear as a way of controlling it. He knew the smell of death and was terrified of it, for he could not anticipate it. It was not death or dying that frightened him, but the unexpectedness of both. In sorting it all out, he hit on the notion that if one day a year were devoted to it, everybody could get it out of the way and the rest of the year would be safe and free. In this manner he instituted National Suicide Day.

On the third day of the new year, he walked through the Bottom down Carpenter's Road with a cowbell and a hangman's rope calling the people together. Telling them that this was their only chance to kill themselves or each other.

At first the people in the town were frightened; they knew Shadrack was crazy but that did not mean that he didn't have any sense or, even more important, that he had no power. His eyes were so wild, his hair so long and matted, his voice was so full of authority and thunder that he caused panic on the first, or Charter, National Suicide Day in 1920. The next one, in 1921, was less frightening but still worrisome. The people had seen him a year now in between. He lived in a shack on the riverbank that had once belonged to his grandfather long time dead. On Tuesday and Friday he sold the fish he had

caught that morning, the rest of the week he was drunk, loud, obscene, funny and outrageous. But he never touched anybody, never fought, never caressed. Once the people understood the boundaries and nature of his madness, they could fit him, so to speak, into the scheme of things.

Then, on subsequent National Suicide Days, the grown people looked out from behind curtains as he rang his bell; a few stragglers increased their speed, and little children screamed and ran. The tetter heads tried goading him (although he was only four or five years older then they) but not for long, for his curses were stingingly personal.

As time went along, the people took less notice of these January thirds, or rather they thought they did, thought they had no attitudes or feelings one way or another about Shadrack's annual solitary parade. In fact they had simply stopped remarking on the holiday because they had absorbed it into their thoughts, into their language, into their lives.

Someone said to a friend, "You sure was a long time delivering that baby. How long was you in labor?"

And the friend answered, " 'Bout three days. The pains started on Suicide Day and kept up till the following Sunday. Was borned on Sunday. All my boys is Sunday boys."

Some lover said to his bride-to-be, "Let's do it after New Years, 'stead of before. I get paid New Year's Eve."

And his sweetheart answered, "OK, but make sure it ain't on Suicide Day. I ain't 'bout to be listening to no cowbells whilst the weddin's going on."

Somebody's grandmother said her hens always started a laying of double yolks right after Suicide Day.

Then Reverend Deal took it up, saying the same folks who had sense enough to avoid Shadrack's call were the ones who insisted on drinking themselves to death or womanizing themselves to death. "May's well go on with Shad and save the Lamb the trouble of redemption."

Easily, quietly, Suicide Day became a part of the fabric of life up in the Bottom of Medallion, Ohio.

1920

It had to be as far away from the Sundown House as possible. And her grandmother's middle-aged nephew who lived in a Northern town called Medallion was the one chance she had to make sure it would be. The red shutters had haunted both Helene Sabat and her grandmother for sixteen years. Helene was born behind those shutters, daughter of a Creole[3] whore who worked there. The grandmother took Helene away from the soft lights and flowered carpets of the Sundown House and raised her under the dolesome eyes of a multicolored Virgin Mary, counseling her to be constantly on guard for any sign of her mother's wild blood.

So when Wiley Wright came to visit his Great Aunt Cecile in New Orleans, his enchantment with the pretty Helene became a marriage proposal—under the pressure of both women. He was a seaman (or rather a lakeman, for he was a ship's cook on one of the Great Lakes lines), in port only three days out of every sixteen.

3. Person of mixed French and black descent.

He took his bride to his home in Medallion and put her in a lovely house with a brick porch and real lace curtains at the window. His long absences were quite bearable for Helene Wright, especially when, after some nine years of marriage, her daughter was born.

Her daughter was more comfort and purpose than she had ever hoped to find in this life. She rose grandly to the occasion of motherhood—grateful, deep down in her heart, that the child had not inherited the great beauty that was hers: that her skin had dusk in it, that her lashes were substantial but not undignified in their length, that she had taken the broad flat nose of Wiley (although Helene expected to improve it somewhat) and his generous lips.

Under Helene's hand the girl became obedient and polite. Any enthusiasms that little Nel showed were calmed by the mother until she drove her daughter's imagination underground.

Helene Wright was an impressive woman, at least in Medallion she was. Heavy hair in a bun, dark eyes arched in a perpetual query about other people's manners. A woman who won all social battles with presence and a conviction of the legitimacy of her authority. Since there was no Catholic church in Medallion then, she joined the most conservative black church. And held sway. It was Helene who never turned her head in church when latecomers arrived; Helene who established the practice of seasonal altar flowers; Helene who introduced the giving of banquets of welcome to returning Negro veterans. She lost only one battle—the pronunciation of her name. The people in the Bottom refused to say Helene. They called her Helen Wright and left it at that.

All in all her life was a satisfactory one. She loved her house and enjoyed manipulating her daughter and her husband. She would sigh sometimes just before falling asleep, thinking that she had indeed come far enough away from the Sundown House.

So it was with extremely mixed emotions that she read a letter from Mr. Henri Martin describing the illness of her grandmother, and suggesting she come down right away. She didn't want to go, but could not bring herself to ignore the silent plea of the woman who had rescued her.

It was November. November, 1920. Even in Medallion there was a victorious swagger in the legs of white men and a cull-eyed excitement in the eyes of colored veterans.

Helene thought about the trip South with heavy misgiving but decided that she had the best protection: her manner and her bearing, to which she would add a beautiful dress. She bought some deep-brown wool and three-fourths of a yard of matching velvet. Out of this she made herself a heavy but elegant dress with velvet collar and pockets.

Nel watched her mother cutting the pattern from newspapers and moving her eyes rapidly from a magazine model to her own hands. She watched her turn up the kerosene lamp at sunset to sew far into the night.

The day they were ready Helene cooked a smoked ham, left a note for her lake-bound husband, in case he docked early, and walked head high and arms stiff with luggage ahead of her daughter to the train depot.

It was a longer walk than she remembered, and they saw the train steaming up just as they turned the corner. They ran along the track looking for the coach pointed out to them by the colored porter. Even at that they made a mistake. Helene and her daughter entered a coach peopled by some twenty

white men and women. Rather than go back and down the three wooden steps again, Helene decided to spare herself some embarrassment and walk on through to the colored car. She carried two pieces of luggage and a string purse; her daughter carried a covered basket of food.

As they opened the door marked COLORED ONLY, they saw a white conductor coming toward them. It was a chilly day but a light skim of sweat glistened on the woman's face as she and the little girl struggled to hold the door open, hang on to their luggage and enter all at once. The conductor let his eyes travel over the pale yellow woman and then stuck his little finger into his ear, jiggling it free of wax. "What you think you doin', gal?"

Helene looked up at him.

So soon. So soon. She hadn't even begun the trip back. Back to her grandmother's house in the city where the red shutters glowed, and already she had been called "gal." All the old vulnerabilities, all the old fears of being somehow flawed gathered in her stomach and made her hands tremble. She had heard only that one word; it dangled above her wide-brimmed hat, which had slipped, in her exertion, from its carefully leveled placement and was now tilted in a bit of a jaunt over her eye.

Thinking he wanted her tickets, she quickly dropped both the cowhide suitcase and the straw one in order to search for them in her purse. An eagerness to please and an apology for living met in her voice. "I have them. Right here somewhere, sir . . ."

The conductor looked at the bit of wax his fingernail had retrieved. "What was you doin' back in there? What was you doin' in that coach yonder?"

Helene licked her lips. "Oh . . . I" Her glance moved beyond the white man's face to the passengers seated behind him. Four or five black faces were watching, two belonging to soldiers still in their shit-colored uniforms and peaked caps. She saw their closed faces, their locked eyes, and turned for compassion to the gray eyes of the conductor.

"We made a mistake, sir. You see, there wasn't no sign. We just got in the wrong car, that's all. Sir."

"We don't 'low no mistakes on this train. Now git your butt on in there."

He stood there staring at her until she realized that he wanted her to move aside. Pulling Nel by the arm, she pressed herself and her daughter into the foot space in front of a wooden seat. Then, for no earthly reason, at least no reason that anybody could understand, certainly no reason that Nel understood then or later, she smiled. Like a street pup that wags its tail at the very doorjamb of the butcher shop he has been kicked away from only moments before, Helene smiled. Smiled dazzlingly and coquettishly at the salmon-colored face of the conductor.

Nel looked away from the flash of pretty teeth to the other passengers. The two black soldiers, who had been watching the scene with what appeared to be indifference, now looked stricken. Behind Nel was the bright and blazing light of her mother's smile; before her the midnight eyes of the soldiers. She saw the muscles of their faces tighten, a movement under the skin from blood to marble. No change in the expression of the eyes, but a hard wetness that veiled them as they looked at the stretch of her mother's foolish smile.

As the door slammed on the conductor's exit, Helene walked down the aisle to a seat. She looked about for a second to see whether any of the men would help her put the suitcases in the overhead rack. Not a man moved. Helene sat

down, fussily, her back toward the men. Nel sat opposite, facing both her mother and the soldiers, neither of whom she could look at. She felt both pleased and ashamed to sense that these men, unlike her father, who worshipped his graceful beautiful wife, were bubbling with a hatred for her mother that had not been there in the beginning but had been born with the dazzling smile. In the silence that preceded the train's heave, she looked deeply at the folds of her mother's dress. There in the fall of the heavy brown wool she held her eyes. She could not risk letting them travel upward for fear of seeing that the hooks and eyes in the placket of the dress had come undone and exposed the custard-colored skin underneath. She stared at the hem, wanting to believe in its weight but knowing that custard was all that it hid. If this tall, proud woman, this woman who was very particular about her friends, who slipped into church with unequaled elegance, who could quell a roustabout[4] with a look, if *she* were really custard, then there was a chance that Nel was too.

It was on that train, shuffling toward Cincinnati, that she resolved to be on guard—always. She wanted to make certain that no man ever looked at her that way. That no midnight eyes or marbled flesh would ever accost her and turn her into jelly.

For two days they rode; two days of watching sleet turn to rain, turn to purple sunsets, and one night knotted on the wooden seats (their heads on folded coats), trying not to hear the snoring soldiers. When they changed trains in Birmingham for the last leg of the trip, they discovered what luxury they had been in through Kentucky and Tennessee, where the rest stops had all had colored toilets. After Birmingham there were none. Helene's face was drawn with the need to relieve herself, and so intense was her distress she finally brought herself to speak about her problem to a black woman with four children who had got on in Tuscaloosa.

"Is there somewhere we can go to use the restroom?"

The woman looked up at her and seemed not to understand. "Ma'am?" Her eyes fastened on the thick velvet collar, the fair skin, the high-tone voice.

"The restroom," Helene repeated. Then, in a whisper, "The toilet."

The woman pointed out the window and said, "Yes, ma'am. Yonder."

Helene looked out of the window halfway expecting to see a comfort station in the distance; instead she saw gray-green trees leaning over tangled grass. "Where?"

"Yonder," the woman said. "Meridian. We be pullin' in direc'lin." Then she smiled sympathetically and asked, "Kin you make it?"

Helene nodded and went back to her seat trying to think of other things—for the surest way to have an accident would be to remember her full bladder.

At Meridian the woman got out with their children. While Helene looked about the tiny stationhouse for a door that said COLORED WOMEN, the other woman stalked off to a field of high grass on the far side of the track. Some white men were leaning on the railing in front of the stationhouse. It was not only their tongues curling around toothpicks that kept Helene from asking information of them. She looked around for the other woman and, seeing just the top of her head rag in the grass, slowly realized where "yonder" was. All of them, the fat woman and her four children, three boys and a girl, Helene and

4. A longshoreman or an unskilled worker.

her daughter, squatted there in the four o'clock Meridian sun. They did it again in Ellisville, again in Hattiesburg, and by the time they reached Slidell, not too far from Lake Pontchartrain, Helene could not only fold leaves as well as the fat woman, she never felt a stir as she passed the muddy eyes of the men who stood like wrecked Dorics[5] under the station roofs of those towns.

The lift in spirit that such an accomplishment produced in her quickly disappeared when the train finally pulled into New Orleans.

Cecile Sabat's house leaned between two others just like it on Elysian Fields.[6] A Frenchified shotgun house, it sported a magnificent garden in the back and a tiny wrought-iron fence in the front. On the door hung a black crepe wreath with purple ribbon. They were too late. Helene reached up to touch the ribbon, hesitated, and knocked. A man in a collarless shirt opened the door. Helene identified herself and he said he was Henri Martin and that he was there for the settin'-up. They stepped into the house. The Virgin Mary clasped her hands in front of her neck three times in the front room and once in the bedroom where Cecile's body lay. The old woman had died without seeing or blessing her granddaughter.

No one other than Mr. Martin seemed to be in the house, but a sweet odor as of gardenias told them that someone else had been. Blotting her lashes with a white handkerchief, Helene walked through the kitchen to the back bedroom where she had slept for sixteen years. Nel trotted along behind, enchanted with the smell, the candles and the strangeness. When Helene bent to loosen the ribbons of Nel's hat, a woman in a yellow dress came out of the garden and onto the back porch that opened into the bedroom. The two women looked at each other. There was no recognition in the eyes of either. Then Helene said, "This is your . . . grandmother, Nel." Nel looked at her mother and then quickly back at the door they had just come out of.

"No. That was your great-grandmother. This is your grandmother. My . . . mother."

Before the child could think, her words were hanging in the gardenia air. "But she looks so young."

The woman in the canary-yellow dress laughed and said she was forty-eight, "an old forty-eight."

Then it was she who carried the gardenia smell. This tiny woman with the softness and glare of a canary. In that somber house that held four Virgin Marys, where death sighed in every corner and candles sputtered, the gardenia smell and canary-yellow dress emphasized the funeral atmosphere surrounding them.

The woman smiled, glanced in the mirror and said, throwing her voice toward Helene, "That your only one?"

"Yes," said Helene.

"Pretty. A lot like you."

"Yes. Well, She's ten now."

"Ten? Vrai?[7] Small for her age, no?"

Helene shrugged and looked at her daughter's questioning eyes. The woman in the yellow dress leaned forward. "Come. Come, chere."

5. I.e., like columns holding the roofs up.
6. A section of New Orleans; also, in classical mythol-
ogy, the abode of the blessed after death.
7. True? (French).

Helene interrupted. "We have to get cleaned up. We been three days on the train with no chance to wash or . . ."

"Comment t'appelle?"

"She doesn't talk Creole."

"Then you ask her."

"She wants to know your name, honey."

With her head pressed into her mother's heavy brown dress, Nel told her and then asked, "What's yours?"

"Mine's Rochelle. Well. I must be going on." She moved closer to the mirror and stood there sweeping hair up from her neck back into its halo-like roll, and wetting with spit the ringlets that fell over her ears. "I been here, you know, most of the day. She pass on yesterday. The funeral tomorrow. Henri takin' care." She struck a match, blew it out and darkened her eyebrows with the burnt head. All the while Helene and Nel watched her. The one in a rage at the folded leaves she had endured, the wooden benches she had slept on, all to miss seeing her grandmother and seeing instead that painted canary who never said a word of greeting or affection or . . .

Rochelle continued. "I don't know what happen to de house. Long time paid for. You be thinkin' on it? Oui?"[8] Her newly darkened eyebrows queried Helene.

"Oui." Helene's voice was chilly. "I be thinkin' on it."

"Oh, well. Not for me to say . . ."

Suddenly she swept around and hugged Nel—a quick embrace tighter and harder than one would have imagined her thin soft arms capable of.

"'Voir![9] 'Voir!" and she was gone.

In the kitchen, being soaped head to toe by her mother, Nel ventured an observation. "She smelled so nice. And her skin was so soft."

Helene rinsed the cloth. "Much handled things are always soft."

"What does 'vwah' mean?"

"I don't know," her mother said. "I don't talk Creole." She gazed at her daughter's wet buttocks. "And neither do you."

When they got back to Medallion and into the quiet house they saw the note exactly where they had left it and the ham dried out in the icebox.

"Lord, I've never been so glad to see this place. But look at the dust. Get the rags, Nel. Oh, never mind. Let's breathe awhile first. Lord, I never thought I'd get back here safe and sound. Whoo. Well, it's over. Good and over. Praise His name. Look at that. I told that old fool not to deliver any milk and there's the can curdled to beat all. What gets into people? I told him not to. Well, I got other things to worry 'bout. Got to get a fire started. I left it ready so I wouldn't have to do nothin' but light it. Lord, it's cold. Don't just sit there, honey. You could be pulling your nose . . ."

Nel sat on the red-velvet sofa listening to her mother but remembering the smell and the tight, tight hug of the woman in yellow who rubbed burned matches over her eyes.

Late that night after the fire was made, the cold supper eaten, the surface dust removed, Nel lay in bed thinking of her trip. She remembered clearly the urine running down and into her stockings until she learned how to squat

<hr />

8. Yes (French). 9. Good-bye (French).

properly; the disgust on the face of the dead woman and the sound of the funeral drums. It had been an exhilarating trip but a fearful one. She had been frightened of the soldiers' eyes on the train, the black wreath on the door, the custard pudding she believed lurked under her mother's heavy dress, the feel of unknown streets and unknown people. But she had gone on a real trip, and now she was different. She got out of bed and lit the lamp to look in the mirror. There was her face, plain brown eyes, three braids and the nose her mother hated. She looked for a long time and suddenly a shiver ran through her.

"I'm me," she whispered. "Me."

Nel didn't know quite what she meant, but on the other hand she knew exactly what she meant.

"I'm me. I'm not their daughter. I'm not Nel. I'm me. Me."

Each time she said the word *me* there was a gathering in her like power, like joy, like fear. Back in bed with her discovery, she stared out the window at the dark leaves of the horse chestnut.

"Me," she murmured. And then, sinking deeper into the quilts, "I want . . . I want to be . . . wonderful. Oh, Jesus, make me wonderful."

The many experiences of her trip crowded in on her. She slept. It was the last as well as the first time she was ever to leave Medallion.

For days afterward she imagined other trips she would take, alone though, to faraway places. Contemplating them was delicious. Leaving Medallion would be her goal. But that was before she met Sula, the girl she had seen for five years at Garfield Primary but never played with, never knew, because her mother said that Sula's mother was sooty. The trip, perhaps, or her new found me-ness, gave her the strength to cultivate a friend in spite of her mother.

When Sula first visited the Wright house, Helene's curdled scorn turned to butter. Her daughter's friend seemed to have none of the mother's slackness. Nel, who regarded the oppressive neatness of her home with dread, felt comfortable in it with Sula, who loved it and would sit on the red-velvet sofa for ten to twenty minutes at a time—still as dawn. As for Nel, she preferred Sula's woolly house, where a pot of something was always cooking on the stove; where the mother, Hannah, never scolded or gave directions; where all sorts of people dropped in; where newspapers were stacked in the hallway, and dirty dishes left for hours at a time in the sink, and where a one-legged grandmother named Eva handed you goobers from deep inside her pockets or read you a dream.

1921

Sula Peace lived in a house of many rooms that had been built over a period of five years to the specifications of its owner, who kept on adding things: more stairways—there were three sets to the second floor—more rooms, doors and stoops. There were rooms that had three doors, others that opened out on the porch only and were inaccessible from any other part of the house; others that you could get to only by going through somebody's bedroom. The creator and sovereign of this enormous house with the four sickle-pear trees in the front yard and the single elm in the back yard was Eva Peace, who sat in a wagon on the third floor directing the lives of her children, friends, strays, and a constant stream of boarders. Fewer than nine people in the town remembered when Eva had two legs, and her oldest child, Hannah, was not one of them. Unless

Eva herself introduced the subject, no one ever spoke of her disability; they pretended to ignore it, unless, in some mood of fancy, she began some fearful story about it—generally to entertain children. How the leg got up by itself one day and walked on off. How she hobbled after it but it ran too fast. Or how she had a corn on her toe and it just grew and grew and grew until her whole foot was a corn and then it traveled on up her leg and wouldn't stop growing until she put a red rag at the top but by that time it was already at her knee.

Somebody said Eva stuck it under a train and made them pay off. Another said she sold it to a hospital for $10,000—at which Mr. Reed opened his eyes and asked, "Nigger gals legs goin' for $10,000 a *piece*?" as though he could understand $10,000 a *pair*—but for one?

Whatever the fate of her lost leg, the remaining one was magnificent. It was stockinged and shod at all times and in all weather. Once in a while she got a felt slipper for Christmas or her birthday, but they soon disappeared, for Eva always wore a black laced-up shoe that came well above her ankle. Nor did she wear overlong dresses to disguise the empty place on her left side. Her dresses were mid-calf so that her one glamorous leg was always in view as well as the long fall of space below her left thigh. One of her men friends had fashioned a kind of wheelchair for her: a rocking-chair top fitted into a large child's wagon. In this contraption she wheeled around the room, from bedside to dresser to the balcony that opened out the north side of her room or to the window that looked out on the back yard. The wagon was so low that children who spoke to her standing up were eye level with her, and adults, standing or sitting, had to look down at her. But they didn't know it. They all had the impression that they were looking up at her, up into the open distances of her eyes, up into the soft black of her nostrils and up at the crest of her chin.

Eva had married a man named BoyBoy and had three children: Hannah, the eldest, and Eva, whom she named after herself but called Pearl, and a son named Ralph, whom she called Plum.

After five years of a sad and disgruntled marriage BoyBoy took off. During the time they were together he was very much preoccupied with other women and not home much. He did whatever he could that he liked, and he liked womanizing best, drinking second, and abusing Eva third. When he left in November, Eva had $1.65, five eggs, three beets and no idea of what or how to feel. The children needed her; she needed money, and needed to get on with her life. But the demands of feeding her three children were so acute she had to postpone her anger for two years until she had both the time and the energy for it. She was confused and desperately hungry. There were very few black families in those low hills then. The Suggs, who lived two hundred yards down the road, brought her a warm bowl of peas, as soon as they found out, and a plate of cold bread. She thanked them and asked if they had a little milk for the older ones. They said no, but Mrs. Jackson, they knew, had a cow still giving. Eva took a bucket over and Mrs. Jackson told her to come back and fill it up in the morning, because the evening milking had already been done. In this way, things went on until near December. People were very willing to help, but Eva felt she would soon run her welcome out; winters were hard and her neighbors were not that much better off. She would lie in bed with the baby boy, the two girls wrapped in quilts on the floor, thinking. The oldest child, Hannah, was five and too young to take care of the baby alone, and any house-

work Eva could find would keep her away from them from five thirty or earlier in the morning until dark—way past eight. The white people in the valley weren't rich enough then to want maids; they were small farmers and tradesmen and wanted hard-labor help if anything. She thought also of returning to some of her people in Virginia, but to come home dragging three young ones would have to be a step one rung before death for Eva. She would have to scrounge around and beg through the winter, until her baby was at least nine months old, then she could plant and maybe hire herself out to valley farms to weed or sow or feed stock until something steadier came along at harvest time. She thought she had probably been a fool to let BoyBoy haul her away from her people, but it had seemed so right at the time. He worked for a white carpenter and toolsmith who insisted on BoyBoy's accompanying him when he went West and set up in a squinchy little town called Medallion. BoyBoy brought his new wife and built them a one-room cabin sixty feet back from the road that wound up out of the valley, on up into the hills and was named for the man he worked for. They lived there a year before they had an outhouse.

Sometime before the middle of December, the baby, Plum, stopped having bowel movements. Eva massaged his stomach and gave him warm water. Something must be wrong with my milk, she thought. Mrs. Suggs gave her castor oil, but even that didn't work. He cried and fought so they couldn't get much down his throat anyway. He seemed in great pain and his shrieks were pitched high in outrage and suffering. At one point, maddened by his own crying, he gagged, choked and looked as though he was strangling to death. Eva rushed to him and kicked over the earthen slop jar, washing a small area of the floor with the child's urine. She managed to soothe him, but when he took up the cry again late that night, she resolved to end his misery once and for all. She wrapped him in blankets, ran her finger around the crevices and sides of the lard can and stumbled to the outhouse with him. Deep in its darkness and freezing stench she squatted down, turned the baby over on her knees, exposed his buttocks and shoved the last bit of food she had in the world (besides three beets) up his ass. Softening the insertion with the dab of lard, she probed with her middle finger to loosen his bowels. Her fingernail snagged what felt like a pebble; she pulled it out and others followed. Plum stopped crying as the black hard stools ricocheted onto the frozen ground. And now that it was over, Eva squatted there wondering why she had come all the way out there to free his stools, and what was she doing down on her haunches with her beloved baby boy warmed by her body in the almost total darkness, her shins and teeth freezing, her nostrils assailed. She shook her head as though to juggle her brains around, then said aloud, "Uh uh. Nooo." Thereupon she returned to the house and her bed. As the grateful Plum slept, the silence allowed her to think.

Two days later she left all of her children with Mrs. Suggs, saying she would be back the next day.

Eighteen months later she swept down from a wagon with two crutches, a new black pocketbook, and one leg. First she reclaimed her children, next she gave the surprised Mrs. Suggs a ten-dollar bill, later she started building a house on Carpenter's Road, sixty feet from BoyBoy's one-room cabin, which she rented out.

When Plum was three years old, BoyBoy came back to town and paid her a visit. When Eva got the word that he was on his way, she made some lemonade. She had no idea what she would do or feel during that encounter. Would she cry, cut his throat, beg him to make love to her? She couldn't imagine. So she just waited to see. She stirred lemonade in a green pitcher and waited.

BoyBoy danced up the steps and knocked on the door.

"Come on in," she hollered.

He opened the door and stood smiling, a picture of prosperity and good will. His shoes were a shiny orange, and he had on a citified straw hat, a light-blue suit, and a cat's-head stickpin in his tie. Eva smiled and told him to sit himself down. He smiled too.

"How you been, girl?"

"Pretty fair. What you know good?" When she heard those words come out of her own mouth she knew that their conversation would start off polite. Although it remained to be seen whether she would still run the ice pick through the cat's-head pin.

"Have some lemonade."

"Don't mind if I do." He swept his hat off with a satisfied gesture. His nails were long and shiny. "Sho is hot, and I been runnin' around all day."

Eva looked out of the screen door and saw a woman in a pea-green dress leaning on the smallest pear tree. Glancing back at him, she was reminded of Plum's face when he managed to get the meat out of a walnut all by himself. Eva smiled again, and poured the lemonade.

Their conversation was easy: she catching him up on all the gossip, he asking about this one and that one, and like everybody else avoiding any reference to her leg. It was like talking to somebody's cousin who just stopped by to say howdy before getting on back to wherever he came from. BoyBoy didn't ask to see the children, and Eva didn't bring them into the conversation.

After a while he rose to go. Talking about his appointments and exuding an odor of new money and idleness, he danced down the steps and strutted toward the pea-green dress. Eva watched. She looked at the back of his neck and the set of his shoulders. Underneath all of that shine she saw defeat in the stalk of his neck and the curious tight way he held his shoulders. But still she was not sure what she felt. Then he leaned forward and whispered into the ear of the woman in the green dress. She was still for a moment and then threw back her head and laughed. A high-pitched big-city laugh that reminded Eva of Chicago. It hit her like a sledge hammer, and it was then that she knew what to feel. A liquid trail of hate flooded her chest.

Knowing that she would hate him long and well filled her with pleasant anticipation, like when you know you are going to fall in love with someone and you wait for the happy signs. Hating BoyBoy, she could get on with it, and have the safety, the thrill, the consistency of that hatred as long as she wanted or needed it to define and strengthen her or protect her from routine vulnerabilities. (Once when Hannah accused her of hating colored people, Eva said she only hated one, Hannah's father BoyBoy, and it was hating him that kept her alive and happy.)

Happy or not, after BoyBoy's visit she began her retreat to her bedroom, leaving the bottom of the house more and more to those who lived there: cousins who were passing through, stray folks, and the many, many newly mar-

ried couples she let rooms to with housekeeping privileges, and after 1910 she didn't willingly set foot on the stairs but once and that was to light a fire, the smoke of which was in her hair for years.

Among the tenants in that big old house were the children Eva took in. Operating on a private scheme of preference and prejudice, she sent off for children she had seen from the balcony of her bedroom or whose circumstances she had heard about from the gossipy old men who came to play checkers or to read the *Courier*, or write her number.[1] In 1921, when her granddaughter Sula was eleven, Eva had three such children. They came with woolen caps and names given to them by their mothers, or grandmothers, or somebody's best friend. Eva snatched the caps off their heads and ignored their names. She looked at the first child closely, his wrists, the shape of his head and the temperament that showed in his eyes and said, "Well. Look at Dewey. My my mymymy." When later that same year she sent for a child who kept falling down off the porch across the street, she said the same thing. Somebody said, "But, Miss Eva, you calls the other one Dewey."

"So? This here's another one."

When the third one was brought and Eva said "Dewey" again, everybody thought she had simply run out of names or that her faculties had finally softened.

"How is anybody going to tell them apart?" Hannah asked her.

"What you need to tell them apart for? They's all deweys."

When Hannah asked the question it didn't sound very bright, because each dewey was markedly different from the other two. Dewey one was a deeply black boy with a beautiful head and the golden eyes of chronic jaundice. Dewey two was light-skinned with freckles everywhere and a head of tight red hair. Dewey three was half Mexican with chocolate skin and black bangs. Besides, they were one and two years apart in age. It was Eva saying things like, "Send one of them deweys out to get me some Garret, if they don't have Garret, get Buttercup,"[2] or, "Tell them deweys to cut out that noise," or, "Come here, you dewey you," and, "Send me a dewey," that gave Hannah's question its weight.

Slowly each boy came out of whatever cocoon he was in at the time his mother or somebody gave him away, and accepted Eva's view, becoming in fact as well as in name a dewey—joining with the other two to become a trinity with a plural name . . . inseparable, loving nothing and no one but themselves. When the handle from the icebox fell off, all the deweys got whipped, and in dry-eyed silence watched their own feet as they turned their behinds high up into the air for the stroke. When the golden-eyed dewey was ready for school he would not go without the others. He was seven, freckled dewey was five, and Mexican dewey was only four. Eva solved the problem by having them all sent off together. Mr. Buckland Reed said, "But one of them's only four."

"How you know? They all come here the same year," Eva said.

"But that one there was one year old when he came, and that was three years ago."

1. Eva played the numbers, an illegal form of lottery in which one wagers on a certain combination of digits. 2. Brands of snuff.

"You don't know how old he was when he come here and neither do the teacher. Send 'em."

The teacher was startled but not unbelieving, for she had long ago given up trying to fathom the ways of the colored people in town. So when Mrs. Reed said that their names were Dewey King, that they were cousins, and all were six years old, the teacher gave only a tiny sigh and wrote them in the record book for the first grade. She too thought she would have no problem distinguishing among them, because they looked nothing alike, but like everyone else before her, she gradually found that she could not tell one from the other. The deweys would not allow it. They got all mixed up in her head, and finally she could not literally believe her eyes. They spoke with one voice, thought with one mind, and maintained an annoying privacy. Stouthearted, surly, and wholly unpredictable, the deweys remained a mystery not only during all of their lives in Medallion but after as well.

The deweys came in 1921, but the year before Eva had given a small room off the kitchen to Tar Baby, a beautiful, slight, quiet man who never spoke above a whisper. Most people said he was half white, but Eva said he was all white. That she knew blood when she saw it, and he didn't have none. When he first came to Medallion, the people called him Pretty Johnnie, but Eva looked at his milky skin and cornsilk hair and out of a mixture of fun and meanness called him Tar Baby. He was a mountain boy who stayed to himself, bothering no one, intent solely on drinking himself to death. At first he worked in a poultry market, and after wringing the necks of chickens all day, he came home and drank until he slept. Later he began to miss days at work and frequently did not have his rent money. When he lost his job altogether, he would go out in the morning, scrounge around for money doing odd jobs, bumming or whatever, and come home to drink. Because he was no bother, ate little, required nothing, and was a lover of cheap wine, no one found him a nuisance. Besides, he frequently went to Wednesday-night prayer meetings and sang with the sweetest hill voice imaginable "In the Sweet By-and-By." He sent the deweys out for his liquor and spent most of his time in a heap on the floor or sitting in a chair staring at the wall.

Hannah worried about him a little, but only a very little. For it soon became clear that he simply wanted a place to die privately but not quite alone. No one thought of suggesting to him that he pull himself together or see a doctor or anything. Even the women at prayer meeting who cried when he sang "In the Sweet By-and-By" never tried to get him to participate in the church activities. They just listened to him sing, wept and thought very graphically of their own imminent deaths. The people either accepted his own evaluation of his life, or were indifferent to it. There was, however, a measure of contempt in their indifference, for they had little patience with people who took themselves that seriously. Seriously enough to try to die. And it was natural that he, after all, became the first one to join Shadrack—Tar Baby and the deweys—on National Suicide Day.

Under Eva's distant eye, and prey to her idiosyncrasies, her own children grew up stealthily: Pearl married at fourteen and moved to Flint, Michigan, from where she posted frail letters to her mother with two dollars folded into the writing paper. Sad little nonsense letters about minor troubles, her husband's job and who the children favored. Hannah married a laughing man

named Rekus who died when their daughter Sula was about three years old, at which time Hannah moved back into her mother's big house prepared to take care of it and her mother forever.

With the exception of BoyBoy, those Peace women loved all men. It was manlove that Eva bequeathed to her daughters. Probably, people said, because there were no men in the house, no men to run it. But actually that was not true. The Peace women simply loved maleness, for its own sake. Eva, old as she was, and with one leg, had a regular flock of gentleman callers, and although she did not participate in the act of love, there was a good deal of teasing and pecking and laughter. The men wanted to see her lovely calf, that neat shoe, and watch the focusing that sometimes swept down out of the distances in her eyes. They wanted to see the joy in her face as they settled down to play checkers, knowing that even when she beat them, as she almost always did, somehow, in her presence, it was they who had won something. They would read the newspaper aloud to her and make observations on its content, and Eva would listen feeling no obligation to agree and, in fact, would take them to task about their interpretation of events. But she argued with them with such an absence of bile, such a concentration of manlove, that they felt their convictions solidified by her disagreement.

With other people's affairs Eva was equally prejudiced about men. She fussed interminably with the brides of the newly wed couples for not getting their men's supper ready on time; about how to launder shirts, press them, etc. "Yo' man be here direc'lin. Ain't it 'bout time you got busy?"

"Aw, Miss Eva. It'll be ready. We just having spaghetti."

"Again?" Eva's eyebrows fluted up and the newlywed pressed her lips together in shame.

Hannah simply refused to live without the attentions of a man, and after Rekus' death had a steady sequence of lovers, mostly the husbands of her friends and neighbors. Her flirting was sweet, low and guileless. Without ever a pat of the hair, a rush to change clothes or a quick application of paint, with no gesture whatsoever, she rippled with sex. In her same old print wraparound, barefoot in the summer, in the winter her feet in a man's leather slippers with the backs flattened under her heels, she made men aware of her behind, her slim ankles, the dew-smooth skin and the incredible length of neck. Then the smile-eyes, the turn of the head—all so welcoming, light and playful. Her voice trailed, dipped and bowed; she gave a chord to the simplest words. Nobody, but nobody, could say "hey sugar" like Hannah. When he heard it, the man tipped his hat down a little over his eyes, hoisted his trousers and thought about the hollow place at the base of her neck. And all this without the slightest confusion about work and responsibilities. While Eva tested and argued with her men, leaving them feeling as though they had been in combat with a worthy, if amiable, foe, Hannah rubbed no edges, made no demands, made the man feel as though he were complete and wonderful just as he was—he didn't need fixing—and so he relaxed and swooned in the Hannah-light that shone on him simply because he was. If the man entered and Hannah was carrying a coal scuttle up from the basement, she handled it in such a way that it became a gesture of love. He made no move to help her with it simply because he wanted to see how her thighs looked when she bent to put it down, knowing that she wanted him to see them too.

But since in that crowded house there were no places for private and spon-

taneous lovemaking, Hannah would take the man down into the cellar in the
summer where it was cool back behind the coal bin and the newspapers, or in
the winter they would step into the pantry and stand up against the shelves
she had filled with canned goods, or lie on the flour sack just under the rows of
tiny green peppers. When those places were not available, she would slip into
the seldom-used parlor, or even up to her bedroom. She liked the last place
least, not because Sula slept in the room with her but because her love mate's
tendency was always to fall asleep afterward and Hannah was fastidious about
whom she slept with. She would fuck practically anything, but sleeping with
someone implied for her a measure of trust and a definite commitment. So
she ended up a daylight lover, and it was only once actually that Sula came
home from school and found her mother in the bed, curled spoon in the arms
of a man.

Seeing her step so easily into the pantry and emerge looking precisely as she
did when she entered, only happier, taught Sula that sex was pleasant and fre-
quent, but otherwise unremarkable. Outside the house, where children gig-
gled about underwear, the message was different. So she watched her
mother's face and the face of the men when they opened the pantry door and
made up her own mind.

Hannah exasperated the women in the town—the "good" women who said,
"One thing I can't stand is a nasty woman"; the whores, who were hard put to
find trade among black men anyway and who resented Hannah's generosity;
the middling women, who had both husbands and affairs, because Hannah
seemed too unlike them, having no passion attached to her relationships and
being wholly incapable of jealousy. Hannah's friendships with women were, of
course, seldom and short-lived, and the newly married couples whom her
mother took in soon learned what a hazard she was. She could break up a mar-
riage before it had even become one—she would make love to the new groom
and wash his wife's dishes all in an afternoon. What she wanted, after Rekus
died, and what she succeeded in having more often than not, was some touch-
ing every day.

The men, surprisingly, never gossiped about her. She was unquestionably a
kind and generous woman and that, coupled with her extraordinary beauty
and funky elegance of manner, made them defend her and protect her from
any vitriol that newcomers or their wives might spill.

Eva's last child, Plum, to whom she hoped to bequeath everything, floated
in a constant swaddle of love and affection, until 1917 when he went to war.
He returned to the States in 1919 but did not get back to Medallion until
1920. He wrote letters from New York, Washington, D.C., and Chicago full of
promises of homecomings, but there was obviously something wrong. Finally
some two or three days after Christmas, he arrived with just the shadow of his
old dip-down walk. His hair had been neither cut nor combed in months, his
clothes were pointless and he had no socks. But he did have a black bag, a
paper sack, and a sweet, sweet smile. Everybody welcomed him and gave him
a warm room next to Tar Baby's and waited for him to tell them whatever it
was he wanted them to know. They waited in vain for his telling but not long
for the knowing. His habits were much like Tar Baby's but there were no bot-
tles, and Plum was sometimes cheerful and animated. Hannah watched and
Eva waited. Then he began to steal from them, take trips to Cincinnati and
sleep for days in his room with the record player going. He got even thinner,

since he ate only snatches of things at beginnings or endings of meals. It was Hannah who found the bent spoon black from steady cooking.[3]

So late one night in 1921, Eva got up from her bed and put on her clothes. Hoisting herself up on her crutches, she was amazed to find that she could still manage them, although the pain in her armpits was severe. She practiced a few steps around the room, and then opened the door. Slowly, she manipulated herself down the long flights of stairs, two crutches under her left arm, the right hand grasping the banister. The sound of her foot booming in comparison to the delicate pat of the crutch tip. On each landing she stopped for breath. Annoyed at her physical condition, she closed her eyes and removed the crutches from under her arms to relieve the unaccustomed pressure. At the foot of the stairs she redistributed her weight between the crutches and swooped on through the front room, to the dining room, to the kitchen, swinging and swooping like a giant heron, so graceful sailing about in its own habitat but awkward and comical when it folded its wings and tried to walk. With a swing and a swoop she arrived at Plum's door and pushed it open with the tip of one crutch. He was lying in bed barely visible in the light coming from a single bulb. Eva swung over to the bed and propped her crutches at its foot. She sat down and gathered Plum into her arms. He woke, but only slightly.

"Hey, man. Hey. You holdin' me, Mamma?" His voice was drowsy and amused. He chuckled as though he had heard some private joke. Eva held him closer and began to rock. Back and forth she rocked him, her eyes wandering around his room. There in the corner was a half-eaten store-bought cherry pie. Balled-up candy wrappers and empty pop bottles peeped from under the dresser. On the floor by her foot was a glass of strawberry crush and a *Liberty* magazine. Rocking, rocking, listening to Plum's occasional chuckles, Eva let her memory spin, loop and fall. Plum in the tub that time as she leaned over him. He reached up and dripped water into her bosom and laughed. She was angry, but not too, and laughed with him.

"Mamma, you so purty. You so purty, Mamma."

Eva lifted her tongue to the edge of her lip to stop the tears from running into her mouth. Rocking, rocking. Later she laid him down and looked at him a long time. Suddenly she was thirsty and reached for the glass of strawberry crush. She put it to her lips and discovered it was blood-tainted water and threw it to the floor. Plum woke up and said, "Hey, Mamma, whyn't you go on back to bed? I'm all right. Didn't I tell you? I'm all right. Go on, now."

"I'm going, Plum," she said. She shifted her weight and pulled her crutches toward her. Swinging and swooping, she left his room. She dragged herself to the kitchen and made grating noises.

Plum on the rim of a warm light sleep was still chuckling. Mamma. She sure was somethin'. He felt twilight. Now there seemed to be some kind of wet light traveling over his legs and stomach with a deeply attractive smell. It wound itself—this wet light—all about him, splashing and running into his skin. He opened his eyes and saw what he imagined was the great wing of an eagle pouring a wet lightness over him. Some kind of baptism, some kind of

3. I.e., heating powdered heroin in water to make an injectable solution.

blessing, he thought. Everything is going to be all right, it said. Knowing that it was so he closed his eyes and sank back into the bright hole of sleep.

Eva stepped back from the bed and let the crutches rest under her arms. She rolled a bit of newspaper into a tight stick about six inches long, lit it and threw it onto the bed where the kerosene-soaked Plum lay in snug delight. Quickly, as the *whoosh* of flames engulfed him, she shut the door and made her slow and painful journey back to the top of the house.

Just as she got to the third landing she could hear Hannah and some child's voice. She swung along, not even listening to the voices of alarm and the cries of the deweys. By the time she got to her bed someone was bounding up the stairs after her. Hannah opened the door. "Plum! Plum! He's burning, Mamma! We can't even open the door! Mamma!"

Eva looked into Hannah's eyes. "Is? My baby? Burning?" The two women did not speak, for the eyes of each were enough for the other. Then Hannah closed hers and ran toward the voices of neighbors calling for water.

1922

It was too cool for ice cream. A hill wind was blowing dust and empty Camels wrappers about their ankles. It pushed their dresses into the creases of their behinds then lifted the hems to peek at their cotton underwear. They were on their way to Edna Finch's Mellow House, an ice-cream parlor catering to nice folks—where even children would feel comfortable, you know, even though it was right next to Reba's Grill and just one block down from the Time and a Half Pool Hall. It sat in the curve of Carpenter's Road, which, in four blocks, made up all the sporting life available in the Bottom. Old men and young ones draped themselves in front of the Elmira Theater, Irene's Palace of Cosmetology, the pool hall, the grill and the other sagging business enterprises that lined the street. On sills, on stoops, on crates and broken chairs they sat tasting their teeth and waiting for something to distract them. Every passerby, every motorcar, every alteration in stance caught their attention and was commented on. Particularly they watched women. When a woman approached, the older men tipped their hats; the younger ones opened and closed their thighs. But all of them, whatever their age, watched her retreating view with interest.

Nel and Sula walked through this valley of eyes chilled by the wind and heated by the embarrassment of appraising stares. The old men looked at their stalklike legs, dwelled on the cords in the backs of their knees and remembered old dance steps they had not done in twenty years. In their lust, which age had turned to kindness, they moved their lips as though to stir up the taste of young sweat on tight skin.

Pig meat. The words were in all their minds. And one of them, one of the young ones, said it aloud. Softly but definitively and there was no mistaking the compliment. His name was Ajax, a twenty-one-year-old pool haunt of sinister beauty. Graceful and economical in every movement, he held a place of envy with men of all ages for his magnificently foul mouth. In fact he seldom cursed, and the epithets he chose were dull, even harmless. His reputation was derived from the way he handled the words. When he said "hell" he hit the *h* with his lungs and the impact was greater than the achievement of the most imaginative foul mouth in the town. He could say "shit" with a nastiness im-

possible to imitate. So, when he said "pig meat" as Nel and Sula passed, they guarded their eyes lest someone see their delight.

It was not really Edna Finch's ice cream that made them brave the stretch of those panther eyes. Years later their own eyes would glaze as they cupped their chins in remembrance of the inchworm smiles, the squatting haunches, the track-rail legs straddling broken chairs. The cream-colored trousers marking with a mere seam the place where the mystery curled. Those smooth vanilla crotches invited them; those lemon-yellow gabardines beckoned to them.

They moved toward the ice-cream parlor like tightrope walkers, as thrilled by the possibility of a slip as by the maintenance of tension and balance. The least sideways glance, the merest toe stub, could pitch them into those creamy haunches spread wide with welcome. Somewhere beneath all of that daintiness, chambered in all that neatness, lay the thing that clotted their dreams.

Which was only fitting, for it was in dreams that the two girls had first met. Long before Edna Finch's Mellow House opened, even before they marched through the chocolate halls of Garfield Primary School out onto the playground and stood facing each other through the ropes of the one vacant swing ("Go on." "No. You go."), they had already made each other's acquaintance in the delirium of their noon dreams. They were solitary little girls whose loneliness was so profound it intoxicated them and sent them stumbling into Technicolored visions that always included a presence, a someone, who, quite like the dreamer, shared the delight of the dream. When Nel, an only child, sat on the steps of her back porch surrounded by the high silence of her mother's incredibly orderly house, feeling the neatness pointing at her back, she studied the poplars and fell easily into a picture of herself lying on a flowered bed, tangled in her own hair, waiting for some fiery prince. He approached but never quite arrived. But always, watching the dream along with her, were some smiling sympathetic eyes. Someone as interested as she herself in the flow of her imagined hair, the thickness of the mattress of flowers, the voile[4] sleeves that closed below her elbows in gold-threaded cuffs.

Similarly, Sula, also an only child, but wedged into a household of throbbing disorder constantly awry with things, people, voices and the slamming of doors, spent hours in the attic behind a roll of linoleum galloping through her own mind on a gray-and-white horse tasting sugar and smelling roses in full view of a someone who shared both the taste and the speed.

So when they met, first in those chocolate halls and next through the ropes of the swing, they felt the ease and comfort of old friends. Because each had discovered years before that they were neither white nor male, and that all freedom and triumph was forbidden to them, they had set about creating something else to be. Their meeting was fortunate, for it let them use each other to grow on. Daughters of distant mothers and incomprehensible fathers (Sula's because he was dead; Nel's because he wasn't), they found in each other's eyes the intimacy they were looking for.

Nel Wright and Sula Peace were both twelve in 1922, wishbone thin and easy-assed. Nel was the color of wet sandpaper—just dark enough to escape the blows of the pitch-black truebloods and the contempt of old women who worried about such things as bad blood mixtures and knew that the origins of

4. A fine, sheer fabric.

a mule and a mulatto were one and the same.[5] Had she been any lighter-skinned she would have needed either her mother's protection on the way to school or a streak of mean to defend herself. Sula was a heavy brown with large quiet eyes, one of which featured a birthmark that spread from the middle of the lid toward the eyebrow, shaped something like a stemmed rose. It gave her otherwise plain face a broken excitement and blue-blade threat like the keloid scar[6] of the razored man who sometimes played checkers with her grand-mother. The birthmark was to grow darker as the years passed, but now it was the same shade as her gold-flecked eyes, which, to the end, were as steady and clean as rain.

Their friendship was as intense as it was sudden. They found relief in each other's personality. Although both were unshaped, formless things, Nel seemed stronger and more consistent than Sula, who could hardly be counted on to sustain any emotion for more than three minutes. Yet there was one time when that was not true, when she held on to a mood for weeks, but even that was in defense of Nel.

Four white boys in their early teens, sons of some newly arrived Irish people, occasionally entertained themselves in the afternoon by harassing black schoolchildren. With shoes that pinched and woolen knickers that made red rings on their calves, they had come to this valley with their parents believing as they did that it was a promised land—green and shimmering with welcome. What they found was a strange accent, a pervasive fear of their religion and firm resistance to their attempts to find work. With one exception the older residents of Medallion scorned them. The one exception was the black community. Although some of the Negroes had been in Medallion before the Civil War (the town didn't even have a name then), if they had any hatred for these newcomers it didn't matter because it didn't show. As a matter of fact, baiting them was the one activity that the white Protestant residents concurred in. In part their place in this world was secured only when they echoed the old residents' attitude toward blacks.

These particular boys caught Nel once, and pushed her from hand to hand until they grew tired of the frightened helpless face. Because of that incident, Nel's route home from school became elaborate. She, and then Sula, managed to duck them for weeks until a chilly day in November when Sula said, "Let's us go on home the shortest way."

Nel blinked, but acquiesced. They walked up the street until they got to the bend of Carpenter's Road where the boys lounged on a disused well. Spotting their prey, the boys sauntered forward as though there were nothing in the world on their minds but the gray sky. Hardly able to control their grins, they stood like a gate blocking the path. When the girls were three feet in front of the boys, Sula reached into her coat pocket and pulled out Eva's paring knife. The boys stopped short, exchanged looks and dropped all pretense of inno-cence. This was going to be better than they thought. They were going to try and fight back, and with a knife. Maybe they could get an arm around one of their waists, or tear . . .

Sula squatted down in the dirt road and put everything down on the ground: her lunchpail, her reader, her mittens, her slate. Holding the knife in

<hr />

her right hand, she pulled the slate toward her and pressed her left forefinger down hard on its edge. Her aim was determined but inaccurate. She slashed off only the tip of her finger. The four boys stared open-mouthed at the wound and the scrap of flesh, like a button mushroom, curling in the cherry blood that ran into the corners of the slate.

Sula raised her eyes to them. Her voice was quiet. "If I can do that to myself, what you suppose I'll do to you?"

The shifting dirt was the only way Nel knew that they were moving away; she was looking at Sula's face, which seemed miles and miles away.

But toughness was not their quality—adventuresomeness was—and a mean determination to explore everything that interested them, from one-eyed chickens highstepping in their penned yards to Mr. Buckland Reed's gold teeth, from the sound of sheets flapping in the wind to the labels on Tar Baby's wine bottles. And they had no priorities. They could be distracted from watching a fight with mean razors by the glorious smell of hot tar being poured by roadmen two hundred yards away.

In the safe harbor of each other's company they could afford to abandon the ways of other people and concentrate on their own perceptions of things. When Mrs. Wright reminded Nel to pull her nose, she would do it enthusiastically but without the least hope in the world.

"While you sittin' there, honey, go 'head and pull your nose."

"It hurts, Mamma."

"Don't you want a nice nose when you grow up?"

After she met Sula, Nel slid the clothespin under the blanket as soon as she got in the bed. And although there was still the hateful hot comb to suffer through each Saturday evening, its consequences—smooth hair—no longer interested her.

Joined in mutual admiration they watched each day as though it were a movie arranged for their amusement. The new theme they were now discovering was men. So they met regularly, without even planning it, to walk down the road to Edna Finch's Mellow House, even though it was too cool for ice cream.

Then summer came. A summer limp with the weight of blossomed things. Heavy sunflowers weeping over fences; iris curling and browning at the edges far away from their purple hearts; ears of corn letting their auburn hair wind down to their stalks. And the boys. The beautiful, beautiful boys who dotted the landscape like jewels, split the air with their shouts in the field, and thickened the river with their shining wet backs. Even their footsteps left a smell of smoke behind.

It was in that summer, the summer of their twelfth year, the summer of the beautiful black boys, that they became skittish, frightened and bold—all at the same time.

In that mercury mood in July, Sula and Nel wandered about the Bottom barefoot looking for mischief. They decided to go down by the river where the boys sometimes swam. Nel waited on the porch of 7 Carpenter's Road while Sula ran into the house to go to the toilet. On the way up the stairs, she passed the kitchen where Hannah sat with two friends, Patsy and Valentine. The two women were fanning themselves and watching Hannah put down some

dough, all talking casually about one thing and another, and had gotten around, when Sula passed by, to the problems of child rearing.

"They a pain."

"Yeh. Wish I'd listened to mamma. She told me not to have 'em too soon."

"Any time atall is too soon for me."

"Oh, I don't know. My Rudy minds his daddy. He just wild with me. Be glad when he growed and gone."

Hannah smiled and said, "Shut your mouth. You love the ground he pee on."

"Sure I do. But he still a pain. Can't help loving your own child. No matter what they do."

"Well, Hester grown now and I can't say love is exactly what I feel."

"Sure you do. You love her, like I love Sula. I just don't like her. That's the difference."

"Guess so. Likin' them is another thing."

"Sure. They different people, you know . . ."

She only heard Hannah's words, and the pronouncement sent her flying up the stairs. In bewilderment, she stood at the window fingering the curtain edge, aware of a sting in her eye. Nel's call floated up and into the window, pulling her away from dark thoughts back into the bright, hot daylight.

They ran most of the way.

Heading toward the wide part of the river where trees grouped themselves in families darkening the earth below. They passed some boys swimming and clowning in the water, shrouding their words in laughter.

They ran in the sunlight, creating their own breeze, which pressed their dresses into their damp skin. Reaching a kind of square of four leaf-locked trees which promised cooling, they flung themselves into the four-cornered shade to taste their lip sweat and contemplate the wildness that had come upon them so suddenly. They lay in the grass, their foreheads almost touching, their bodies stretched away from each other at a 180-degree angle. Sula's head rested on her arm, an undone braid coiled around her wrist. Nel leaned on her elbows and worried long blades of grass with her fingers. Underneath their dresses flesh tightened and shivered in the high coolness, their small breasts just now beginning to create some pleasant discomfort when they were lying on their stomachs.

Sula lifted her head and joined Nel in the grass play. In concert, without ever meeting each other's eyes, they stroked the blades up and down, up and down. Nel found a thick twig and, with her thumbnail, pulled away its bark until it was stripped to a smooth, creamy innocence. Sula looked about and found one too. When both twigs were undressed Nel moved easily to the next stage and began tearing up rooted grass to make a bare spot of earth. When a generous clearing was made, Sula traced intricate patterns in it with her twig. At first Nel was content to do the same. But soon she grew impatient and poked her twig rhythmically and intensely into the earth, making a small neat hole that grew deeper and wider with the least manipulation of her twig. Sula copied her, and soon each had a hole the size of a cup. Nel began a more strenuous digging and, rising to her knee, was careful to scoop out the dirt as she made her hole deeper. Together they worked until the two holes were one and

the same. When the depression was the size of a small dishpan, Nel's twig broke. With a gesture of disgust she threw the pieces into the hole they had made. Sula threw hers in too. Nel saw a bottle cap and tossed it in as well. Each then looked around for more debris to throw into the hole: paper, bits of glass, butts of cigarettes, until all of the small defiling things they could find were collected there. Carefully they replaced the soil and covered the entire grave with uprooted grass.

Neither one had spoken a word.

They stood up, stretched, then gazed out over the swift dull water as an unspeakable restlessness and agitation held them. At the same instant each girl heard footsteps in the grass. A little boy in too big knickers was coming up from the lower bank of the river. He stopped when he saw them and picked his nose.

"Your mama tole you to stop eatin' snot, Chicken," Nel hollered at him through cupped hands.

"Shut up," he said, still picking.

"Come up here and say that."

"Leave him 'lone, Nel. Come here, Chicken. Lemme show you something."

"Naw."

"You scared we gone take your bugger away?"

"Leave him 'lone, I said. Come on, Chicken. Look. I'll help you climb a tree."

Chicken looked at the tree Sula was pointing to—a big double beech with low branches and lots of bends for sitting.

He moved slowly toward her.

"Come on, Chicken, I'll help you up."

Still picking his nose, his eyes wide, he came to where they were standing. Sula took him by the hand and coaxed him along. When they reached the base of the beech, she lifted him to the first branch, saying, "Go on. Go on. I got you." She followed the boy, steadying him, when he needed it, with her hand and her reassuring voice. When they were as high as they could go, Sula pointed to the far side of the river.

"See? Bet you never saw that far before, did you?"

"Uh uh."

"Now look down there." They both leaned a little and peered through the leaves at Nel standing below, squinting up at them. From their height she looked small and foreshortened.

Chicken Little laughed.

"Y'all better come on down before you break your neck," Nel hollered.

"I ain't never coming down," the boy hollered back.

"Yeah. We better. Come on, Chicken."

"Naw. Lemme go."

"Yeah, Chicken. Come on, now."

Sula pulled his leg gently.

"Lemme go."

"OK, I'm leavin' you." She started on.

"Wait!" he screamed.

Sula stopped and together they slowly worked their way down.

Chicken was still elated. "I was way up there, wasn't I? Wasn't I? I'm a tell my brovver."

Sula and Nel began to mimic him: "I'm a tell my brovver; I'm a tell my brovver."

Sula picked him up by his hands and swung him outward then around and around. His knickers ballooned and his shrieks of frightened joy startled the birds and the fat grasshoppers. When he slipped from her hands and sailed away out over the water they could still hear his bubbly laughter.

The water darkened and closed quickly over the place where Chicken Little sank. The pressure of his hard and tight little fingers was still in Sula's palms as she stood looking at the closed place in the water. They expected him to come back up, laughing. Both girls stared at the water.

Nel spoke first. "Somebody saw." A figure appeared briefly on the opposite shore.

The only house over there was Shadrack's. Sula glanced at Nel. Terror widened her nostrils. Had he seen?

The water was so peaceful now. There was nothing but the baking sun and something newly missing. Sula cupped her face for an instant, then turned and ran up to the little plank bridge that crossed the river to Shadrack's house. There was no path. It was as though neither Shadrack nor anyone else ever came this way.

Her running was swift and determined, but when she was close to the three little steps that led to his porch, fear crawled into her stomach and only the something newly missing back there in the river made it possible for her to walk up the three steps and knock at the door.

No one answered. She started back, but thought again of the peace of the river. Shadrack would be inside, just behind the door ready to pounce on her. Still she could not go back. Ever so gently she pushed the door with the tips of her fingers and heard only the hinges weep. More. And then she was inside. Alone. The neatness, the order startled her, but more surprising was the restfulness. Everything was so tiny, so common, so unthreatening. Perhaps this was not the house of the Shad. The terrible Shad who walked about with his penis out, who peed in front of ladies and girl-children, the only black who could curse white people and get away with it, who drank in the road from the mouth of the bottle, who shouted and shook in the streets. This cottage? This sweet old cottage? With its made-up bed? With its rag rug and wooden table? Sula stood in the middle of the little room and in her wonder forgot what she had come for until a sound at the door made her jump. He was there in the doorway looking at her. She had not heard his coming and now he was looking at her.

More in embarrassment than terror she averted her glance. When she called up enough courage to look back at him, she saw his hand resting upon the door frame. His fingers, barely touching the wood, were arranged in a graceful arc. Relieved and encouraged (no one with hands like that, no one with fingers that curved around wood so tenderly could kill her), she walked past him out of the door, feeling his gaze turning, turning with her.

At the edge of the porch, gathering the wisps of courage that were fast leaving her, she turned once more to look at him, to ask him . . . had he . . . ?

He was smiling, a great smile, heavy with lust and time to come. He nodded his head as though answering a question, and said, in a pleasant conversational tone, a tone of cooled butter, "Always."

Sula fled down the steps, and shot through the greenness and the baking

sun back to Nel and the dark closed place in the water. There she collapsed in tears.

Nel quieted her. "Sh, sh. Don't, don't. You didn't mean it. It ain't your fault. Sh. Sh. Come on, le's go, Sula. Come on, now. Was he there? Did he see? Where's the belt to your dress?"

Sula shook her head while she searched her waist for the belt.

Finally she stood up and allowed Nel to lead her away. "He said, 'Always. Always.'"

"What?"

Sula covered her mouth as they walked down the hill. Always. He had answered a question she had not asked, and its promise licked at her feet.

A bargeman, poling away from the shore, found Chicken late that afternoon stuck in some rocks and weeds, his knickers ballooning about his legs. He would have left him there but noticed that it was a child, not an old black man, as it first appeared, and he prodded the body loose, netted it and hauled it aboard. He shook his head in disgust at the kind of parents who would drown their own children. When, he wondered, will those people ever be anything but animals, fit for nothing but substitutes for mules, only mules didn't kill each other the way niggers did. He dumped Chicken Little into a burlap sack and tossed him next to some egg crates and boxes of wool cloth. Later, sitting down to smoke on an empty lard tin, still bemused by God's curse and the terrible burden his own kind had of elevating Ham's sons,[7] he suddenly became alarmed by the thought that the corpse in this heat would have a terrible odor, which might get into the fabric of his woolen cloth. He dragged the sack away and hooked it over the side, so that the Chicken's body was half in and half out of the water.

Wiping the sweat from his neck he reported his find to the sheriff at Porter's Landing, who said they didn't have no niggers in their county, but that some lived in those hills 'cross the river, up above Medallion. The bargeman said he couldn't go all the way back there, it was every bit of two miles. The sheriff said whyn't he throw it on back into the water. The bargeman said he never shoulda taken it out in the first place. Finally they got the man who ran the ferry twice a day to agree to take it over in the morning.

That was why Chicken Little was missing for three days and didn't get to the embalmer's until the fourth day, by which time he was unrecognizable to almost everybody who once knew him, and even his mother wasn't deep down sure, except that it just had to be him since nobody could find him. When she saw his clothes lying on the table in the basement of the mortuary, her mouth snapped shut, and when she saw his body her mouth flew wide open again and it was seven hours before she was able to close it and make the first sound.

So the coffin was closed.

The Junior Choir, dressed in white, sang "Nearer My God to Thee" and "Precious Memories," their eyes fastened on the songbooks they did not need, for this was the first time their voices had presided at a real-life event.

Nel and Sula did not touch hands or look at each other during the funeral. There was a space, a separateness, between them. Nel's legs had turned to

7. Blacks (Ham, which means "swarthy" in Hebrew, was a son of Noah held to be the ancestor of Egyptians and Nubians).

granite and she expected the sheriff or Reverend Deal's pointing finger at any moment. Although she knew she had "done nothing," she felt convicted and hanged right there in the pew—two rows down from her parents in the children's section.

Sula simply cried. Soundlessly and with no heaving and gasping for breath, she let the tears roll into her mouth and slide down her chin to dot the front of her dress.

As Reverend Deal moved into his sermon, the hands of the women unfolded like pairs of raven's wings and flew high above their hats in the air. They did not hear all of what he said; they heard the one word, or phrase, or inflection that was for them the connection between the event and themselves. For some it was the term "Sweet Jesus." And they saw the Lamb's eye and the truly innocent victim: themselves. They acknowledged the innocent child hiding in the corner of their hearts, holding a sugar-and-butter sandwich. That one. The one who lodged deep in their fat, thin, old, young skin, and was the one the world had hurt. Or they thought of their son newly killed and remembered his legs in short pants and wondered where the bullet went in. Or they remembered how dirty the room looked when their father left home and wondered if that is the way the slim, young Jew[8] felt, he who for them was both son and lover and in whose downy face they could see the sugar-and-butter sandwiches and feel the oldest and most devastating pain there is: not the pain of childhood, but the remembrance of it.

Then they left their pews. For with some emotions one has to stand. They spoke, for they were full and needed to say. They swayed, for the rivulets of grief or of ecstasy must be rocked. And when they thought of all that life and death locked into that little closed coffin they danced and screamed, not to protest God's will but to acknowledge it and confirm once more their conviction that the only way to avoid the Hand of God is to get in it.

In the colored part of the cemetery, they sank Chicken Little in between his grandfather and an aunt. Butterflies flew in and out of the bunches of field flowers now loosened from the top of the bier and lying in a small heap at the edge of the grave. The heat had gone, but there was still no breeze to lift the hair of the widows.

Nel and Sula stood some distance away from the grave, the space that had sat between them in the pews had dissolved. They held hands and knew that only the coffin would lie in the earth; the bubbly laughter and the press of fingers in the palm would stay aboveground forever. At first, as they stood there, their hands were clenched together. They relaxed slowly until during the walk back home their fingers were laced in as gentle a clasp as that of any two young girlfriends trotting up the road on a summer day wondering what happened to butterflies in the winter.

1923

The second strange thing was Hannah's coming into her mother's room with an empty bowl and a peck of Kentucky Wonders[9] and saying, "Mamma, did you ever love us?" She sang the words like a small child saying a piece at Easter, then knelt to spread a newspaper on the floor and set the basket on it;

8. I.e., Jesus. 9. A variety of string bean.

the bowl she tucked in the space between her legs. Eva, who was just sitting there fanning herself with the cardboard fan from Mr. Hodges' funeral parlor, listened to the silence that followed Hannah's words, then said, "Scat!" to the deweys who were playing chain gang near the window. With the shoelaces of each of them tied to the laces of the others, they stumbled and tumbled out of Eva's room.

"Now," Eva looked up across from her wagon at her daughter. "Give me that again. Flat out to fit my head."

"I mean, did you? You know. When we was little."

Eva's hand moved snail-like down her thigh toward her stump, but stopped short of it to realign a pleat. "No. I don't reckon I did. Not the way you thinkin'."

"Oh, well. I was just wonderin'." Hannah appeared to be through with the subject.

"An evil wonderin' if I ever heard one." Eva was not through.

"I didn't mean nothing by it, Mamma."

"What you mean you didn't *mean* nothing by it? How you gone not mean something by it?"

Hannah pinched the tips off the Kentucky Wonders and snapped their long pods. What with the sound of the cracking and snapping and her swift-fingered movements, she seemed to be playing a complicated instrument. Eva watched her a moment and then said, "You gone can them?"

"No. They for tonight."

"Thought you was gone can some."

"Uncle Paul ain't brought me none yet. A peck ain't enough to can. He say he got two bushels for me."

"Triflin'."

"Oh, he all right."

"Sho he all right. Everybody all right. 'Cept Mamma. Mamma the only one ain't all right. Cause she didn't *love* us."

"Awww, Mamma."

"Awww, Mamma? Awww, Mamma? You settin' here with your healthy-ass self and ax me did I love you? Them big old eyes in your head would a been two holes full of maggots if I hadn't."

"I didn't mean that, Mamma. I know you fed us and all. I was talkin' 'bout something else. Like. Like. Playin' with us. Did you ever, you know, play with us?"

"Play? Wasn't nobody playin' in 1895. Just 'cause you got it good now you think it was always this good? 1895 was a killer, girl. Things was bad. Niggers was dying like flies. Stepping tall, ain't you? Uncle Paul gone bring me *two* bushels. Yeh. And they's a melon downstairs, ain't they? And I bake every Saturday, and Shad brings fish on Friday, and they's a pork barrel full of meal, and we float eggs in a crock of vinegar . . ."

"Mamma, what you talkin' 'bout?"

"I'm talking' 'bout 18 and 95 when I set in that house five days with you and Pearl and Plum and three beets, you snake-eyed ungrateful hussy. What would I look like leapin' 'round that little old room playin' with youngins with three beets to my name?"

"I know 'bout them beets, Mamma. You told us that a million times."

"Yeah? Well? Don't that count? Ain't that love? You want me to tinkle you

under the jaw and forget 'bout them sores in your mouth? Pearl was shittin' worms and I was supposed to play rang-around-the-rosie?"

"But Mamma, they had to be some time when you wasn't thinkin' 'bout . . ."

"No time. They wasn't no time. Not none. Soon as I got one day done here come a night. With you all coughin' and me watchin' so TB wouldn't take you off and if you was sleepin' quiet I thought, O Lord, they dead and put my hand over your mouth to feel if the breath was comin' what you talkin' 'bout did I love you girl I stayed alive for you can't you get that through your thick head or what is that between your ears, heifer?"

Hannah had enough beans now. With some tomatoes and hot bread, she thought, that would be enough for everybody, especially since the deweys didn't eat vegetables no how and Eva never made them and Tar Baby was living off air and music these days. She picked up the basket and stood with it and the bowl of beans over her mother. Eva's face was still asking her last question. Hannah looked into her mother's eyes.

"But what about Plum? What'd you kill Plum for, Mamma?"

It was a Wednesday in August and the ice wagon was coming and coming. You could hear bits of the driver's song. Now Mrs. Jackson would be tipping down her porch steps. "Jes a piece. You got a lil ole piece layin' 'round in there you could spare?" And as he had since the time of the pigeons, the iceman would hand her a lump of ice saying, "Watch it now, Mrs. Jackson. That straw'll tickle your pretty neck to death."

Eva listened to the wagon coming and thought about what it must be like in the icehouse. She leaned back a little and closed her eyes trying to see the insides of the icehouse. It was a dark, lovely picture in this heat, until it reminded her of that winter night in the outhouse holding her baby in the dark, her fingers searching for his asshole and the last bit of lard scooped from the sides of the can, held deliberately on the tip of her middle finger, the last bit of lard to keep from hurting him when she slid her finger in and all because she had broken the slop jar and the rags had frozen. The last food staple in the house she had rammed up her baby's behind to keep from hurting him too much when she opened up his bowels to pull the stools out. He had been screaming fit to kill, but when she found his hole at last and stuck her finger up in it, the shock was so great he was suddenly quiet. Even now on the hottest day anyone in Medallion could remember—a day so hot flies slept and cats were splaying their fur like quills a day so hot pregnant wives leaned up against trees and cried, and women remembering some three-month-old hurt put ground glass in their lovers' food and the men looked at the food and wondered if there was glass in it and ate it anyway because it was too hot to resist eating it—even on this hottest of days in the hot spell, Eva shivered from the biting cold and stench of that outhouse.

Hannah was waiting. Watching her mother's eyelids. When Eva spoke at last it was with two voices. Like two people were talking at the same time, saying the same thing, one a fraction of a second behind the other.

"He give me such a time. Such a time. Look like he didn't even want to be born. But he come on out. Boys is hard to bear. You wouldn't know that but they is. It was such a carryin' on to get him born and to keep him alive. Just to keep his little heart beating and his little old lungs cleared and look like when he came back from that war he wanted to git back in. After all that carryin' on,

just gettin' him out and keepin' him alive, he wanted to crawl back in my womb and well . . . I ain't got the room no more even if he could do it. There wasn't space for him in my womb. And he was crawlin' back. Being helpless and thinking baby thoughts and dreaming baby dreams and messing up his pants again and smiling all the time. I had room enough in my heart, but not in my womb, not no more. I birthed him once. I couldn't do it again. He was growed, a big old thing. Godhavemercy, I couldn't birth him twice. I'd be laying here at night and he be downstairs in that room, but when I closed my eyes I'd see him . . . six feet tall smilin' and crawlin' up the stairs quietlike so I wouldn't hear and opening the door soft so I wouldn't hear and he'd be creepin' to the bed trying to spread my legs trying to get back up in my womb. He was a man, girl, a big old growed-up man. I didn't have that much room. I kept on dreaming it. Dreaming it and I knowed it was true. One night it wouldn't be no dream. It'd be true and I would have done it, would have let him if I'd've had the room but a big man can't be a baby all wrapped up inside his mamma no more; he suffocate. I done everything I could to make him leave me and go on and live and be a man but he wouldn't and I had to keep him out so I just thought of a way he could die like a man not all scrunched up inside my womb, but like a man."

Eva couldn't see Hannah clearly for the tears, but she looked up at her anyway and said, by way of apology or explanation or perhaps just by way of neatness, "But I held him close first. Real close. Sweet Plum. My baby boy."

Long after Hannah turned and walked out of the room, Eva continued to call his name while her fingers lined up the pleats in her dress.

Hannah went off to the kitchen, her old man's slippers plopping down the stairs and over the hardwood floors. She turned the spigot on, letting water break up the tight knots of Kentucky Wonders and float them to the top of the bowl. She swirled them about with her fingers, poured the water off and repeated the process. Each time the green tubes rose to the surface she felt elated and collected whole handfuls at a time to drop in twos and threes back into the water.

Through the window over the sink she could see the deweys still playing chain gang; their ankles bound one to the other, they tumbled, struggled back to their feet and tried to walk single file. Hens strutted by with one suspicious eye on the deweys, another on the brick fireplace where sheets and mason jars[1] were boiled. Only the deweys could play in this heat. Hannah put the Kentucky Wonders over the fire and, struck by a sudden sleepiness, she went off to lie down in the front room. It was even hotter there, for the windows were shut to keep out the sunlight. Hannah straightened the shawl that draped the couch and lay down. She dreamed of a wedding in a red bridal gown until Sula came in and woke her.

But before the second strange thing, there had been the wind, which was the first. The very night before the day Hannah had asked Eva if she had ever loved them, the wind tore over the hills rattling roofs and loosening doors. Everything shook, and although the people were frightened they thought it meant rain and welcomed it. Windows fell out and trees lost arms. People waited up half the night for the first crack of lightning. Some had even uncovered barrels to catch the rain water, which they loved to drink and cook in.

1. I.e., for canning.

They waited in vain, for no lightning no thunder no rain came. The wind just swept through, took what dampness there was out of the air, messed up the yards, and went on. The hills of the Bottom, as always, protected the valley part of town where the white people lived, and the next morning all the people were grateful because there was a dryer heat. So they set about their work early, for it was canning time, and who knew but what the wind would come back this time with a cooling rain. The men who worked in the valley got up at four thirty in the morning and looked at the sky where the sun was already rising like a hot white bitch. They beat the brims of their hats against their legs before putting them on and trudged down the road like old promises nobody wanted kept.

On Thursday, when Hannah brought Eva her fried tomatoes and soft scrambled eggs with the white left out for good luck, she mentioned her dream of the wedding in the red dress. Neither one bothered to look it up for they both knew the number was 522.[2] Eva said she'd play it when Mr. Buckland Reed came by. Later she would remember it as the third strange thing. She had thought it odd even then, but the red in the dream confused her. But she wasn't certain that it was third or not because Sula was acting up, fretting the deweys and meddling the newly married couple. Because she was thirteen, everybody supposed her nature was coming down, but it was hard to put up with her sulking and irritation. The birthmark over her eye was getting darker and looked more and more like a stem and rose. She was dropping things and eating food that belonged to the newly married couple and started in to worrying everybody that the deweys needed a bath and she was going to give it to them. The deweys, who went wild at the thought of water, were crying and thundering all over the house like colts.

"We ain't got to, do we? Do we got to do what she says? It ain't Saturday." They even woke up Tar Baby, who came out of his room to look at them and then left the house in search of music.

Hannah ignored them and kept on bringing mason jars out of the cellar and washing them. Eva banged on the floor with her stick but nobody came. By noon it was quiet. The deweys had escaped, Sula was either in her room or gone off somewhere. The newly married couple, energized by their morning lovemaking, had gone to look for a day's work happily certain that they would find none.

The air all over the Bottom got heavy with peeled fruit and boiling vegetables. Fresh corn, tomatoes, string beans, melon rinds. The women, the children and the old men who had no jobs were putting up for a winter they understood so well. Peaches were stuffed into jars and black cherries (later, when it got cooler, they would put up jellies and preserves). The greedy canned as many as forty-two a day even though some of them, like Mrs. Jackson, who ate ice, had jars from 1920.

Before she trundled her wagon over to the dresser to get her comb, Eva looked out the window and saw Hannah bending to light the yard fire. And that was the fifth (or fourth, if you didn't count Sula's craziness) strange thing. She couldn't find her comb. Nobody moved stuff in Eva's room except to clean and then they put everything right back. But Eva couldn't find it any-

<hr>

2. I.e., in a dream book, which assigns numbers to particular dreams (the appropriate number can then be played).

where. One hand pulling her braids loose, the other searching the dresser drawers, she had just begun to get irritated when she felt it in her blouse drawer. Then she trundled back to the window to catch a breeze, if one took a mind to come by, while she combed her hair. She rolled up to the window and it was then she saw Hannah burning. The flames from the yard fire were licking the blue cotton dress, making her dance. Eva knew there was time for nothing in this world other than the time it took to get there and cover her daughter's body with her own. She lifted her heavy frame up on her good leg, and with fists and arms smashed the windowpane. Using her stump as a support on the window sill, her good leg as a lever, she threw herself out of the window. Cut and bleeding she clawed the air trying to aim her body toward the flaming, dancing figure. She missed and came crashing down some twelve feet from Hannah's smoke. Stunned but still conscious, Eva dragged herself toward her firstborn, but Hannah, her senses lost, went flying out of the yard gesturing and bobbing like a sprung jack-in-the-box.

Mr. and Mrs. Suggs, who had set up their canning apparatus in their front yard, saw her running, dancing toward them. They whispered, "Jesus, Jesus," and together hoisted up their tub of water in which tight red tomatoes floated and threw it on the smoke-and-flame-bound woman. The water did put out the flames, but it also made steam, which seared to sealing all that was left of the beautiful Hannah Peace. She lay there on the wooden sidewalk planks, twitching lightly among the smashed tomatoes, her face a mask of agony so intense that for years the people who gathered 'round would shake their heads at the recollection of it.

Somebody covered her legs with a shirt. A woman unwrapped her head rag and placed it on Hannah's shoulder. Somebody else ran to Dick's Fresh Food and Sundries to call the ambulance. The rest stood there as helpless as sunflowers leaning on a fence. The deweys came and stepped in the tomatoes, their eyes raked with wonder. Two cats sidled through the legs of the crowd, sniffing the burned flesh. The vomiting of a young girl finally broke the profound silence and caused the women to talk to each other and to God. In the midst of calling Jesus they heard the hollow clang of the ambulance bell struggling up the hill, but not the "Help me, ya'll" that the dying woman whispered. Then somebody remembered to go and see about Eva. They found her on her stomach by the forsythia bushes calling Hannah's name and dragging her body through the sweet peas and clover that grew under the forsythia by the side of the house. Mother and daughter were placed on stretchers and carried to the ambulance. Eva was wide awake. The blood from her face cuts filled her eyes so she could not see, could only smell the familiar odor of cooked flesh.

Hannah died on the way to the hospital. Or so they said. In any case, she had already begun to bubble and blister so badly that the coffin had to be kept closed at the funeral and the women who washed the body and dressed it for death wept for her burned hair and wrinkled breasts as though they themselves had been her lovers.

When Eva got to the hospital they put her stretcher on the floor, so preoccupied with the hot and bubbling flesh of the other (some of them had never seen so extreme a burn case before) they forgot Eva, who would have bled to death except Old Willy Fields, the orderly, saw blood staining his just-mopped floors and went to find out where it was coming from. Recognizing Eva at once

he shouted to a nurse, who came to see if the bloody one-legged black woman was alive or dead. From then on Willy boasted that he had saved Eva's life—an indisputable fact which she herself admitted and for which she cursed him every day for thirty-seven years thereafter and would have cursed him for the rest of her life except by then she was already ninety years old and forgot things.

Lying in the colored ward of the hospital, which was a screened corner of a larger ward, Eva mused over the perfection of the judgment against her. She remembered the wedding dream and recalled that weddings always meant death. And the red gown, well that was the fire, as she should have known. She remembered something else too, and try as she might to deny it, she knew that as she lay on the ground trying to drag herself through the sweet peas and clover to get to Hannah, she had seen Sula standing on the back porch just looking. When Eva, who was never one to hide the faults of her children, mentioned what she thought she'd seen to a few friends, they said it was natural. Sula was probably struck dumb, as anybody would be who saw her own mamma burn up. Eva said yes, but inside she disagreed and remained convinced that Sula had watched Hannah burn not because she was paralyzed, but because she was interested.

1927

Old people were dancing with little children. Young boys with their sisters, and the church women who frowned on any bodily expression of joy (except when the hand of God commanded it) tapped their feet. Somebody (the groom's father, everybody said) had poured a whole pint jar of cane liquor into the punch, so even the men who did not sneak out the back door to have a shot, as well as the women who let nothing stronger than Black Draught enter their blood, were tipsy. A small boy stood at the Victrola turning its handle and smiling at the sound of Bert Williams' "Save a Little Dram for Me."

Even Helene Wright had mellowed with the cane, waving away apologies for drinks spilled on her rug and paying no attention whatever to the chocolate cake lying on the arm of her red-velvet sofa. The tea roses above her left breast had slipped from the brooch that fastened them and were hanging heads down. When her husband called her attention to the children wrapping themselves into her curtains, she merely smiled and said, "Oh, let them be." She was not only a little drunk, she was weary and had been for weeks. Her only child's wedding—the culmination of all she had been, thought or done in this world—had dragged from her energy and stamina even she did not know she possessed. Her house had to be thoroughly cleaned, chickens had to be plucked, cakes and pies made, and for weeks she, her friends and her daughter had been sewing. Now it was all happening and it took only a little cane juice to snap the cords of fatigue and damn the white curtains that she had pinned on the stretcher only the morning before. Once this day was over she would have a lifetime to rattle around in that house and repair the damage.

A real wedding in a church, with a real reception afterward, was rare among the people of the Bottom. Expensive for one thing, and most newlyweds just went to the courthouse if they were not particular, or had the preacher come in and say a few words if they were. The rest just "took up" with one another. No invitations were sent. There was no need for that formality. Folks just

came, bringing a gift if they had one, none if they didn't. Except for those who worked in valley houses, most of them had never been to a big wedding; they simply assumed it was rather like a funeral except afterward you didn't have to walk all the way out to Beechnut Cemetery.

This wedding offered a special attraction, for the bridegroom was a handsome, well-liked man—the tenor of Mount Zion's Men's Quartet, who had an enviable reputation among the girls and a comfortable one among men. His name was Jude Greene, and with the pick of some eight or ten girls who came regularly to services to hear him sing, he had chosen Nel Wright.

He wasn't really aiming to get married. He was twenty then, and although his job as a waiter at the Hotel Medallion was a blessing to his parents and their seven other children, it wasn't nearly enough to support a wife. He had brought the subject up first on the day the word got out that the town was building a new road, tarmac, that would wind through Medallion on down to the river, where a great new bridge was to be built to connect Medallion to Porter's Landing, the town on the other side. The war over, a fake prosperity was still around. In a state of euphoria, with a hunger for more and more, the council of founders cast its eye toward a future that would certainly include trade from cross-river towns. Towns that needed more than a house raft to get to the merchants of Medallion. Work had already begun on the New River Road (the city had always meant to name it something else, something wonderful, but ten years later when the bridge idea was dropped for a tunnel it was still called the New River Road).

Along with a few other young black men, Jude had gone down to the shack where they were hiring. Three old colored men had already been hired, but not for the road work, just to do the picking up, food bringing and other small errands. These old men were close to feeble, not good for much else, and everybody was pleased they were taken on; still it was a shame to see those white men laughing with the grandfathers but shying away from the young black men who could tear that road up. The men like Jude who could do real work. Jude himself longed more than anybody else to be taken. Not just for the good money, more for the work itself. He wanted to swing the pick or kneel down with the string or shovel the gravel. His arms ached for something heavier than trays, for something dirtier than peelings; his feet wanted the heavy work shoes, not the thin-soled black shoes that the hotel required. More than anything he wanted the camaraderie of the road men: the lunch buckets, the hollering, the body movement that in the end produced something real, something he could point to. "I built that road," he could say. How much better sundown would be than the end of a day in the restaurant, where a good day's work was marked by the number of dirty plates and the weight of the garbage bin. "I built that road." People would walk over his sweat for years. Perhaps a sledge hammer would come crashing down on his foot, and when people asked him how come he limped, he could say, "Got that building the New Road."

It was while he was full of such dreams, his body already feeling the rough work clothes, his hands already curved to the pick handle, that he spoke to Nel about getting married. She seemed receptive but hardly anxious. It was after he stood in lines for six days running and saw the gang boss pick out thin-armed white boys from the Virginia hills and the bull-necked Greeks and Italians and heard over and over, "Nothing else today. Come back tomorrow,"

that he got the message. So it was rage, rage and a determination to take on a man's role anyhow that made him press Nel about settling down. He needed some of his appetites filled, some posture of adulthood recognized, but mostly he wanted someone to care about his hurt, to care very deeply. Deep enough to hold him, deep enough to rock him, deep enough to ask, "How you feel? You all right? Want some coffee?" And if he were to be a man, that someone could no longer be his mother. He chose the girl who had always been kind, who had never seemed hell-bent to marry, who made the whole venture seem like his idea, his conquest.

The more he thought about marriage, the more attractive it became. Whatever his fortune, whatever the cut of his garment, there would always be the hem—the tuck and fold that hid his raveling edges; a someone sweet, industrious and loyal to shore him up. And in return he would shelter her, love her, grow old with her. Without that someone he was a waiter hanging around a kitchen like a woman. With her he was head of a household pinned to an unsatisfactory job out of necessity. The two of them together would make one Jude.

His fears lest his burst dream of road building discourage her were never realized. Nel's indifference to his hints about marriage disappeared altogether when she discovered his pain. Jude could see himself taking shape in her eyes. She actually wanted to help, to soothe, and was it true what Ajax said in the Time and a Half Pool Hall? That "all they want, man, is they own misery. Ax em to die for you and they yours for life."

Whether he was accurate in general, Ajax was right about Nel. Except for an occasional leadership role with Sula, she had no aggression. Her parents had succeeded in rubbing down to a dull glow any sparkle or splutter she had. Only with Sula did that quality have free reign, but their friendship was so close, they themselves had difficulty distinguishing one's thoughts from the other's. During all of her girlhood the only respite Nel had had from her stern and undemonstrative parents was Sula. When Jude began to hover around, she was flattered—all the girls liked him—and Sula made the enjoyment of his attentions keener simply because she seemed always to want Nel to shine. They never quarreled, those two, the way some girlfriends did over boys, or competed against each other for them. In those days a compliment to one was a compliment to the other, and cruelty to one was a challenge to the other.

Nel's response to Jude's shame and anger selected her away from Sula. And greater than her friendship was this new feeling of being needed by someone who saw her singly. She didn't even know she had a neck until Jude remarked on it, or that her smile was anything but the spreading of her lips until he saw it as a small miracle.

Sula was no less excited about the wedding. She thought it was the perfect thing to do following their graduation from general school. She wanted to be the bridesmaid. No others. And she encouraged Mrs. Wright to go all out, even to borrowing Eva's punch bowl. In fact, she handled most of the details very efficiently, capitalizing on the fact that most people were anxious to please her since she had lost her mamma only a few years back and they still remembered the agony in Hannah's face and the blood on Eva's.

So they danced up in the Bottom on the second Saturday in June, danced at the wedding where everybody realized for the first time that except for their

magnificent teeth, the deweys would never grow. They had been forty-eight inches tall for years now, and while their size was unusual it was not unheard of. The realization was based on the fact that they remained boys in mind. Mischievous, cunning, private and completely unhousebroken, their games and interests had not changed since Hannah had them all put into the first grade together.

Nel and Jude, who had been the stars all during the wedding, were forgotten finally as the reception melted into a dance, a feed, a gossip session, a playground and a love nest. For the first time that day they relaxed and looked at each other, and liked what they saw. They began to dance, pressed in among the others, and each one turned his thoughts to the night that was coming on fast. They had taken a housekeeping room with one of Jude's aunts (over the protest of Mrs. Wright, who had rooms to spare, but Nel didn't want to make love to her husband in her mother's house) and were getting restless to go there.

As if reading her thoughts, Jude leaned down and whispered, "Me too." Nel smiled and rested her cheek on his shoulder. The veil she wore was too heavy to allow her to feel the core of the kiss he pressed on her head. When she raised her eyes to him for one more look of reassurance, she saw through the open door a slim figure in blue, gliding, with just a hint of a strut, down the path toward the road. One hand was pressed to the head to hold down the large hat against the warm June breeze. Even from the rear Nel could tell that it was Sula and that she was smiling; that something deep down in that litheness was amused. It would be ten years before they saw each other again, and their meeting would be thick with birds.

Part Two

1937

Accompanied by a plague of robins, Sula came back to Medallion. The little yam-breasted shuddering birds were everywhere, exciting very small children away from their usual welcome into a vicious stoning. Nobody knew why or from where they had come. What they did know was that you couldn't go anywhere without stepping in their pearly shit, and it was hard to hang up clothes, pull weeds or just sit on the front porch when robins were flying and dying all around you.

Although most of the people remembered the time when the sky was black for two hours with clouds and clouds of pigeons, and although they were accustomed to excesses in nature—too much heat, too much cold, too little rain, rain to flooding—they still dreaded the way a relatively trivial phenomenon could become sovereign in their lives and bend their minds to its will.

In spite of their fear, they reacted to an oppressive oddity, or what they called evil days, with an acceptance that bordered on welcome. Such evil must be avoided, they felt, and precautions must naturally be taken to protect themselves from it. But they let it run its course, fulfill itself, and never invented ways either to alter it, to annihilate it or to prevent its happening again. So also were they with people.

What was taken by outsiders to be slackness, slovenliness or even generosity was in fact a full recognition of the legitimacy of forces other than good

ones. They did not believe doctors could heal—for them, none ever had done so. They did not believe death was accidental—life might be, but death was deliberate. They did not believe Nature was ever askew—only inconvenient. Plague and drought were as "natural" as springtime. If milk could curdle, God knows robins could fall. The purpose of evil was to survive it and they determined (without ever knowing they had made up their minds to do it) to survive floods, white people, tuberculosis, famine and ignorance. They knew anger well but not despair, and they didn't stone sinners for the same reason they didn't commit suicide—it was beneath them.

Sula stepped off the Cincinnati Flyer[3] into the robin shit and began the long climb up into the Bottom. She was dressed in a manner that was as close to a movie star as anyone would ever see. A black crepe dress splashed with pink and yellow zinnias, foxtails, a black felt hat with the veil of net lowered over one eye. In her right hand was a black purse with a beaded clasp and in her left a red leather traveling case, so small, so charming—no one had seen anything like it ever before, including the mayor's wife and the music teacher, both of whom had been to Rome.

Walking up the hill toward Carpenter's Road the heels and sides of her pumps edged with crying bird shit, she attracted the glances of old men sitting on stone benches in front of the courthouse, housewives throwing buckets of water on their sidewalks, and high school students on their way home for lunch. By the time she reached the Bottom, the news of her return had brought the black people out on their porches or to their windows. There were scattered hellos and nods but mostly stares. A little boy ran up to her saying, "Carry yo' bag, ma'am?" Before Sula could answer his mother had called him, "You, John. Get back in here."

At Eva's house there were four dead robins on the walk. Sula stopped and with her toe pushed them into the bordering grass.

Eva looked at Sula pretty much the same way she had looked at BoyBoy that time when he returned after he'd left her without a dime or a prospect of one. She was sitting in her wagon, her back to the window she had jumped out of (now all boarded up) setting fire to the hair she had combed out of her head. When Sula opened the door she raised her eyes and said, "I might have knowed them birds meant something. Where's your coat?"

Sula threw herself on Eva's bed. "The rest of my stuff will be on later."

"I should hope so. Them little old furry tails ain't going to do you no more good than they did the fox that was wearing them."

"Don't you say hello to nobody when you ain't seen them for ten years?"

"If folks let somebody know where they is and when they coming, then other folks can get ready for them. If they don't—if they just pop in all sudden like—then they got to take whatever mood they find."

"How you been doing, Big Mamma?"

"Gettin' by. Sweet of you to ask. You was quick enough when you wanted something. When you needed a little change or . . ."

"Don't talk to me about how much you gave me, Big Mamma, and how much I owe you or none of that."

"Oh? I ain't supposed to mention it?"

3. A train.

"OK. Mention it." Sula shrugged and turned over on her stomach, her buttocks toward Eva.

"You ain't been in this house ten seconds and already you starting something."

"Takes two, Big Mamma."

"Well, don't let your mouth start nothing that your ass can't stand. When you gone to get married? You need to have some babies. It'll settle you."

"I don't want to make somebody else. I want to make myself."

"Selfish. Ain't no woman got no business floatin' around without no man."

"You did."

"Not by choice."

"Mama did."

"Not by choice, I said. It ain't right for you to want to stay off by yourself. You need . . . I'm a tell you what you need."

Sula sat up. "I need you to shut your mouth."

"Don't nobody talk to me like that. Don't nobody . . ."

"This body does. Just 'cause you was bad enough to cut off your own leg you think you got a right to kick everybody with the stump."

"Who said I cut off my leg?"

"Well, you stuck it under a train to collect insurance."

"Hold on, you lyin' heifer!"

"I aim to."

"Bible say honor thy father and thy mother that thy days may be long upon the land thy God giveth thee."

"Mamma must have skipped that part. Her days wasn't too long."

"Pus mouth! God's going to strike you!"

"Which God? The one watched you burn Plum?"

"Don't talk to me about no burning. You watched your own mamma. You crazy roach! You the one should have been burnt!"

"But I ain't. Got that? I ain't. Any more fires in this house, I'm lighting them!"

"Hellfire don't need lighting and it's already burning in you . . ."

"Whatever's burning in me is mine!"

"Amen!"

"And I'll split this town in two and everything in it before I'll let you put it out!"

"Pride goeth before a fall."

"What the hell do I care about falling?"

"Amazing Grace."

"You sold your life for twenty-three dollars a month."

"You throwed yours away."

"It's mine to throw."

"One day you gone need it."

"But not you. I ain't never going to need you. And you know what? Maybe one night when you dozing in that wagon flicking flies and swallowing spit, maybe I'll just tip on up here with some kerosene and—who knows—you may make the brightest flame of them all."

So Eva locked her door from then on. But it did no good. In April two men came with a stretcher and she didn't even have time to comb her hair before they strapped her to a piece of canvas.

When Mr. Buckland Reed came by to pick up the number, his mouth sagged at the sight of Eva being carried out and Sula holding some papers against the wall, at the bottom of which, just above the word "guardian," she very carefully wrote Miss Sula Mae Peace.

Nel alone noticed the peculiar quality of the May that followed the leaving of the birds. It had a sheer, a glimmering as of green, rain-soaked Saturday nights (lit by the excitement of newly installed street lights); of lemon-yellow afternoons bright with iced drinks and splashes of daffodils. It showed in the damp faces of her children and the river-smoothness of their voices. Even her own body was not immune to the magic. She would sit on the floor to sew as she had done as a girl, fold her legs up under her or do a little dance that fitted some tune in her head. There were easy sun-washed days and purple dusks in which Tar Baby sang "Abide With Me" at prayer meetings, his lashes darkened by tears, his silhouette limp with regret against the whitewashed walls of Greater Saint Matthew's. Nel listened and was moved to smile. To smile at the sheer loveliness that pressed in from the windows and touched his grief, making it a pleasure to behold.

Although it was she alone who saw this magic, she did not wonder at it. She knew it was all due to Sula's return to the Bottom. It was like getting the use of an eye back, having a cataract removed. Her old friend had come home. Sula. Who made her laugh, who made her see old things with new eyes, in whose presence she felt clever, gentle and a little raunchy. Sula, whose past she had lived through and with whom the present was a constant sharing of perceptions. Talking to Sula had always been a conversation with herself. Was there anyone else before whom she could never be foolish? In whose view inadequacy was mere idiosyncrasy, a character trait rather than a deficiency? Anyone who left behind that aura of fun and complicity? Sula never competed; she simply helped others define themselves. Other people seemed to turn their volume on and up when Sula was in the room. More than any other thing, humor returned. She could listen to the crunch of sugar underfoot that the children had spilled without reaching for the switch; and she forgot the tear in the living-room window shade. Even Nel's love for Jude, which over the years had spun a steady gray web around her heart, became a bright and easy affection, a playfulness that was reflected in their lovemaking.

Sula would come by of an afternoon, walking along with her fluid stride, wearing a plain yellow dress the same way her mother, Hannah, had worn those too-big house dresses—with a distance, an absence of a relationship to clothes which emphasized everything the fabric covered. When she scratched the screen door, as in the old days, and stepped inside, the dishes piled in the sink looked as though they belonged there; the dust on the lamps sparkled; the hair brush lying on the "good" sofa in the living room did not have to be apologetically retrieved, and Nel's grimy intractable children looked like three wild things happily insouciant in the May shine.

"Hey, girl." The rose mark over Sula's eye gave her glance a suggestion of startled pleasure. It was darker than Nel remembered.

"Hey yourself. Come on in here."

"How you doin'?" Sula moved a pile of ironed diapers from a chair and sat down.

"Oh, I ain't strangled nobody yet so I guess I'm all right."

"Well, if you change your mind call me."

"Somebody need killin'?"

"Half this town need it."

"And the other half?"

"A drawn-out disease."

"Oh, come on. Is Medallion that bad?"

"Didn't nobody tell you?"

"You been gone too long, Sula."

"Not too long, but maybe too far."

"What's that supposed to mean?" Nel dipped her fingers into the bowl of water and sprinkled a diaper.

"Oh, I don't know."

"Want some cool tea?"

"Mmmm. Lots of ice, I'm burnin' up."

"Iceman don't come yet, but it's good and cold."

"That's fine."

"Hope I didn't speak too soon. Kids run in and out of here so much." Nel bent to open the icebox.

"You puttin' it on, Nel. Jude must be wore out."

"*Jude* must be wore out? You don't care nothin' 'bout my back, do you?"

"Is that where it's at, in your back?"

"Hah! Jude thinks it's everywhere."

"He's right, it is everywhere. Just be glad he found it, wherever it is. Remember John L.?"

"When Shirley said he got her down by the well and tried to stick it in her hip?" Nel giggled at the remembrance of that teen-time tale. "She should have been grateful. Have you seen her since you been back?"

"Mmm. Like a ox."

"That was one dumb nigger, John L."

"Maybe. Maybe he was just sanitary."

"Sanitary?"

"Well. Think about it. Suppose Shirley was all splayed out in front of you. Wouldn't you go for the hipbone instead?"

Nel lowered her head onto crossed arms while tears of laughter dripped into the warm diapers. Laughter that weakened her knees and pressed her bladder into action. Her rapid soprano and Sula's dark sleepy chuckle made a duet that frightened the cat and made the children run in from the back yard, puzzled at first by the wild free sounds, then delighted to see their mother stumbling merrily toward the bathroom, holding on to her stomach, fairly singing through the laughter: "Aw. Aw. Lord. Sula. Stop." And the other one, the one with the scary black thing over her eye, laughing softly and egging their mother on: "Neatness counts. You know what cleanliness is next to . . ."

"Hush." Nel's plea was clipped off by the slam of the bathroom door.

"What y'all laughing at?"

"Old time-y stuff. Long gone, old time-y stuff."

"Tell us."

"Tell *you*?" The black mark leaped.

"Uh huh. Tell us."

"What tickles us wouldn't tickle you."

"Uh huh, it would."

"Well, we was talking about some people we used to know when we was little."

"Was my mamma little?"

"Of course."

"What happened?"

"Well, some old boy we knew named John L. and a girl name . . ."

Damp-faced, Nel stepped back into the kitchen. She felt new soft and new. It had been the longest time since she had had a rib-scraping laugh. She had forgotten how deep and down it could be. So different from the miscellaneous giggles and smiles she had learned to be content with these past few years.

"O Lord, Sula. You haven't changed none." She wiped her eyes. "What was all that about, anyway? All that scramblin' we did trying to do it and not do it at the same time?"

"Beats me. Such a simple thing."

"But we sure made a lot out of it, and the boys were dumber than we were."

"Couldn't nobody be dumber than I was."

"Stop lying. All of 'em liked you best."

"Yeah? Where are they?"

"They still here. You the one went off."

"Didn't I, though?"

"Tell me about it. The big city."

"Big is all it is. A big Medalion."

"No. I mean the life. The nightclubs, and parties . . ."

"I was in college, Nellie. No nightclubs on campus."

"Campus? That what they call it? Well. You wasn't in no college for—what—ten years now? And you didn't write to nobody. How come you never wrote?"

"You never did either."

"Where was I going to write to? All I knew was that you was in Nashville. I asked Miss Peace about you once or twice."

"What did she say?"

"I couldn't make much sense out of her. You know she been gettin' stranger and stranger after she come out the hospital. How is she anyway?"

"Same, I guess. Not so hot."

"No? Laura I know, was doing her cooking and things. Is she still?"

"No. I put her out."

"Put her out? What for?"

"She made me nervous."

"But she was doing it for nothing, Sula."

"That's what you think. She was stealing right and left."

"Since when did you get froggy[4] about folks' stealing?"

Sula smiled. "OK. I lied. You wanted a reason."

"Well, give me the real one."

"I don't know the real one. She just didn't belong in that house. Digging around in the cupboards, picking up pots and ice picks . . ."

"You sure have changed. That house was always full of people digging in cupboards and carrying on."

"That's the reason, then."

4. Nervous, jumpy.

"Sula. Come on, now."

"You've changed too. I didn't used to have to explain everything to you."

Nel blushed. "Who's feeding the deweys and Tar Baby? You?"

"Sure me. Anyway Tar Baby don't eat and the deweys still crazy."

"I heard one of 'em's mamma came to take him back but didn't know which was hern."

"Don't nobody know."

"And Eva? You doing the work for her too?"

"Well, since you haven't heard it, let me tell you. Eva's real sick. I had her put where she could be watched and taken care of."

"Where would that be?"

"Out by Beechnut."

"You mean that home the white church run? Sula! That ain't no place for Eva. All them women is dirt poor with no people at all. Mrs. Wilkens and them. They got dropsy and can't hold their water—crazy as loons. Eva's odd, but she got sense. I don't think that's right, Sula."

"I'm scared of her, Nellie. That's why . . ."

"Scared? Of Eva?"

"You don't know her. Did you know she burnt Plum?"

"Oh, I heard that years ago. But nobody put no stock in it."

"They should have. It's true. I saw it. And when I got back here she was planning to do it to me too."

"Eva? I can't hardly believe that. She almost died trying to get to your mother."

Sula leaned forward, her elbows on the table. "You ever known me to lie to you?"

"No. But you could be mistaken. Why would Eva . . ."

"All I know is I'm scared. And there's no place else for me to go. We all that's left, Eva and me. I guess I should have stayed gone. I didn't know what else to do. Maybe I should have talked to you about it first. You always had better sense than me. Whenever I was scared before, you knew just what to do."

The closed place in the water spread before them. Nel put the iron on the stove. The situation was clear to her now. Sula, like always, was incapable of making any but the most trivial decisions. When it came to matters of grave importance, she behaved emotionally and irresponsibly and left it to others to straighten out. And when fear struck her, she did unbelievable things. Like that time with her finger. Whatever those hunkies[5] did, it wouldn't have been as bad as what she did to herself. But Sula was so scared she had mutilated herself, to protect herself.

"What should I do, Nellie? Take her back and sleep with my door locked again?"

"No. I guess it's too late anyway. But let's work out a plan for taking care of her. So she won't be messed over."

"Anything you say."

"What about money? She got any?"

Sula shrugged. "The checks come still. It's not much, like it used to be. Should I have them made over to me?"

5. A disparaging term for Hungarians, or for any whites.

"Can you? Do it, then. We can arrange for her to have special comforts. That place is a mess, you know. A doctor don't never set foot in there. I ain't figured out yet how they stay alive in there as long as they do."

"Why don't I have the checks made over to you, Nellie? You better at this than I am."

"Oh no. People will say I'm scheming. You the one to do it. Was there insurance from Hannah?"

"Yes. Plum too. He had all that army insurance."

"Any of it left?"

"Well I went to college on some. Eva banked the rest. I'll look into it, though."

". . . and explain it all to the bank people."

"Will you go down with me?"

"Sure. It's going to be all right."

"I'm glad I talked to you 'bout this. It's been bothering me."

"Well, tongues will wag, but so long as we know the truth, it don't matter."

Just at that moment the children ran in announcing the entrance of their father. Jude opened the back door and walked into the kitchen. He was still a very good-looking man, and the only difference Sula could see was the thin pencil mustache under his nose, and a part in his hair.

"Hey, Jude. What you know good?"

"White man running it—nothing good."

Sula laughed while Nel, high-tuned to his moods, ignored her husband's smile saying, "Bad day, honey?"

"Same old stuff," he replied and told them a brief tale of some personal insult done him by a customer and his boss—a whiney tale that peaked somewhere between anger and a lapping desire for comfort. He ended it with the observation that a Negro man had a hard row to hoe in this world. He expected his story to dovetail into milkwarm commiseration, but before Nel could excrete it, Sula said she didn't know about that—it looked like a pretty good life to her.

"Say what?" Jude's temper flared just a bit as he looked at this friend of his wife's, this slight woman, not exactly plain, but not fine either, with a copperhead over her eye. As far as he could tell, she looked like a woman roaming the country trying to find some man to burden down with a lot of lip and a lot of mouths.

Sula was smiling. "I mean, I don't know what the fuss is about. I mean, everything in the world loves you. White men love you. They spend so much time worrying about your penis they forget their own. The only thing they want to do is cut off a nigger's privates. And if that ain't love and respect I don't know what is. And white women? They chase you all to every corner of the earth, feel for you under every bed. I knew a white woman wouldn't leave the house after 6 o'clock for fear one of you would snatch her. Now ain't that love? They think rape soon's they see you, and if they don't get the rape they looking for, they scream it anyway just so the search won't be in vain. Colored women worry themselves into bad health just trying to hang on to your cuffs. Even little children—white and black, boys and girls—spend all their childhood eating their hearts out 'cause they think you don't love them. And if that ain't enough, you love yourselves. Nothing in this world loves a black man more than another black man. You hear of solitary white men, but niggers?

Can't stay away from one another a whole day. So. It looks to me like you the envy of the world."

Jude and Nel were laughing, he saying, "Well, if that's the only way they got to show it—cut off my balls and throw me in jail—I'd just as soon they left me alone." But thinking that Sula had an odd way of looking at things and that her wide smile took some of the sting from that rattlesnake over her eye. A funny woman, he thought, not that bad-looking. But he could see why she wasn't married; she stirred a man's mind maybe, but not his body.

He left his tie. The one with the scriggly yellow lines running lopsided across the dark-blue field. It hung over the top of the closet door pointing steadily downward while it waited with every confidence for Jude to return.

Could he be gone if his tie is still here? He will remember it and come back and then she would . . . uh. Then she could . . . tell him. Sit down quietly and tell him. "But Jude," she would say, "you *knew* me. All those days and years, Jude, you *knew* me. My ways and my hands and how my stomach folded and how we tried to get Mickey to nurse and how about that time when the landlord said . . . but you said . . . and I cried, Jude. You knew me and had listened to the things I said in the night, and heard me in the bathroom and laughed at my raggedy girdle and I laughed too because I knew you too, Jude. So how could you leave me when you knew me?"

But they had been down on all fours naked, not touching except their lips right down there on the floor where the tie is pointing to, on all fours like (uh huh, go on, say it) like dogs. Nibbling at each other, not even touching, not even looking at each other, just their lips, and when I opened the door they didn't even look for a minute and I thought the reason they are not looking up is because they are not doing that. So it's all right. I am just standing here. They are not doing that. I am just standing here and seeing it, but they are not really doing it. But then they did look up. Or you did. You did, Jude. And if only you had not looked at me the way the soldiers did on the train, the way you look at the children when they come in while you are listening to Gabriel Heatter[6] and break your train of thought—not focusing exactly but giving them an instant, a piece of time, to remember what they are doing, what they are interrupting, and to go on back to wherever they were and let you listen to Gabriel Heatter. And I did not know how to move my feet or fix my eyes or what. I just stood there seeing it and smiling, because maybe there was some explanation, something important that I did not know about that would have made it all right. I waited for Sula to look up at me any minute and say one of those lovely college words like *aesthetic* or *rapport,* which I never understood but which I loved because they sounded so comfortable and firm. And finally you just got up and started putting on clothes and your privates were hanging down, so soft, and you buckled your pants belt but forgot to button the fly and she was sitting on the bed not even bothering to put on her clothes because actually she didn't need to because somehow she didn't look naked to me, only you did. Her chin was in her hand and she sat like a visitor from out of town waiting for the hosts to get some quarreling done and over with so the

6. Popular radio journalist (1890–1972).

card game could continue and me wanting her to leave so I could tell you privately that you had forgotten to button your fly because I didn't want to say it in front of her, Jude. And even when you began to talk, I couldn't hear because I was worried about you not knowing that your fly was open and scared too because your eyes looked like the soldiers' that time on the train when my mother turned to custard.

Remember how big that bedroom was? Jude? How when we moved here we said, Well, at least we got us a real big bedroom, but it was small then, Jude, and so shamely, and maybe it was that way all along but it would have been better if I had gotten the dust out from under the bed because I was ashamed of it in that small room. And then you walked past me saying, "I'll be back for my things." And you did but you left your tie.

The clock was ticking. Nel looked at it and realized that it was two thirty, only forty-five minutes before the children would be home and she hadn't even felt anything right or sensible and now there was no time or wouldn't be until nighttime when they were asleep and she could get into bed and maybe she could do it then. Think. But who could think in that bed where *they* had been and where they *also* had been and where only she was now?

She looked around for a place to be. A small place. The closet? No. Too dark. The bathroom. It was both small and bright, and she wanted to be in a very small, very bright place. Small enough to contain her grief. Bright enough to throw into relief the dark things that cluttered her. Once inside, she sank to the tile floor next to the toilet. On her knees, her hand on the cold rim of the bathtub, she waited for something to happen . . . inside. There was a stirring, a movement of mud and dead leaves. She thought of the women at Chicken Little's funeral. The women who shrieked over the bier and at the lip of the open grave. What she had regarded since as unbecoming behavior seemed fitting to her now; they were screaming at the neck of God, his giant nape, the vast back-of-the-head that he had turned on them in death. But it seemed to her now that it was not a fist-shaking grief they were keening but rather a simple obligation to say something, do something, feel something about the dead. They could not let that heart-smashing event pass unrecorded, unidentified. It was poisonous, unnatural to let the dead go with a mere whimpering, a slight murmur, a rose bouquet of good taste. Good taste was out of place in the company of death, death itself was the essence of bad taste. And there must be rage and saliva in its presence. The body must move and throw itself about, the eyes must roll, the hands should have no peace, and the throat should release all the yearning, despair and outrage that accompany the stupidity of loss.

"The real hell of Hell is that it is forever." Sula said that. She said doing anything forever and ever was hell. Nel didn't understand it then, but now in the bathroom, trying to feel, she thought, "If I could be sure that I could stay here in this small white room with the dirty tile and water gurgling in the pipes and my head on the cool rim of this bathtub and never have to go out the door, I would be happy. If I could be certain that I never had to get up and flush the toilet, go in the kitchen, watch my children grow up and die, see my food chewed on my plate . . . Sula was wrong. Hell ain't things lasting forever. Hell is change." Not only did men leave and children grew up and die, but even the misery didn't last. One day she wouldn't even have that. This very grief that

had twisted her into a curve on the floor and flayed her would be gone. She would lose that too.

"Why, even in hate here I am thinking of what Sula said."

Hunched down in the small bright room Nel waited. Waited for the oldest cry. A scream not for others, not in sympathy for a burnt child, or a dead father, but a deeply personal cry for one's own pain. A loud, strident: "Why me?" She waited. The mud shifted, the leaves stirred, the smell of overripe green things enveloped her and announced the beginnings of her very own howl.

But it did not come.

The odor evaporated; the leaves were still, the mud settled. And finally there was nothing, just a flake of something dry and nasty in her throat. She stood up frightened. There was something just to the right of her, in the air, just out of view. She could not see it, but she knew exactly what it looked like. A gray ball hovering just there. Just there. To the right. Quiet, gray, dirty. A ball of muddy strings, but without weight, fluffy but terrible in its malevolence. She knew she could not look, so she closed her eyes and crept past it out of the bathroom, shutting the door behind her. Sweating with fear, she stepped to the kitchen door and onto the back porch. The lilac bushes preened at the railing, but there were no lilacs yet. Wasn't it time? Surely it was time. She looked over the fence to Mrs. Rayford's yard. Hers were not in bloom either. Was it too late? She fastened on this question with enthusiasm, all the time aware of something she was not thinking. It was the only way she could get her mind off the flake in her throat.

She spent a whole summer with the gray ball, the little ball of fur and string and hair always floating in the light near her but which she did not see because she never looked. But that was the terrible part, the effort it took not to look. But it was there anyhow, just to the right of her head and maybe further down by her shoulder, so when the children went to a monster movie at the Elmira Theater and came home and said, "Mamma, can you sleep with us tonight?" she said all right and got into bed with the two boys, who loved it, but the girl did not. For a long time she could not stop getting in the bed with her children and told herself each time that they might dream a dream about dragons and would need her to comfort them. It was so nice to think about their scary dreams and not about a ball of fur. She even hoped their dreams would rub off on her and give her the wonderful relief of a nightmare so she could stop going around scared to turn her head this way or that lest she see it. That was the scary part—seeing it. It was not coming at her; it never did that, or tried to pounce on her. It just floated there for the seeing, if she wanted to, and O my God for the touching if she wanted to. But she didn't want to see it, ever, for if she saw it, who could tell but what she might actually touch it, or want to, and then what would happen if she actually reached out her hand and touched it? Die probably, but no worse than that. Dying was OK because it was sleep and there wasn't no gray ball in death, was there? Was there? She would have to ask somebody about that, somebody she could confide in and who knew a lot of things, like Sula, for Sula would know or if she didn't she would say something funny that would make it all right. Ooo no, not Sula. Here she was in the midst of it, hating it, scared of it, and again she thought of Sula as though they were still friends and talked things over. That was too much. To lose Jude and not have Sula to talk to about it because it was Sula that he had left her for.

Now her thighs were really empty. And it was then that what those women

said about never looking at another man made some sense to her, for the real
point, the heart of what they said, was the word *looked*. Not to promise never
to make love to another man, not to refuse to marry another man, but to
promise and know that she could never afford to look again, to see and accept
the way in which their heads cut the air or see moons and tree limbs framed by
their necks and shoulders . . . never to look, for now she could not risk look-
ing—and anyway, so what? For now her thighs were truly empty and dead too,
and it was Sula who had taken the life from them and Jude who smashed her
heart and the both of them who left her with no thighs and no heart just her
brain raveling away.

And what am I supposed to do with these old thighs now, just walk up and
down these rooms? What good are they, Jesus? They will never give me the
peace I need to get from sunup to sundown, what good are they, are you trying
to tell me that I am going to have to go all the way through these days all the
way, O my god, to that box with four handles with never nobody settling down
between my legs even if I sew up those old pillow cases and rinse down the
porch and feed my children and beat the rugs and haul the coal up out of the
bin even then nobody, O Jesus, I could be a mule or plow the furrows with my
hands if need be or hold these rickety walls up with my back if need be if I
knew that somewhere in this world in the pocket of some night I could open
my legs to some cowboy lean hips but you are trying to tell me no and O my
sweet Jesus what kind of cross is that?

1939

When the word got out about Eva being put in Sunnydale, the people in
the Bottom shook their heads and said Sula was a roach. Later, when they saw
how she took Jude, then ditched him for others, and heard how he bought a
bus ticket to Detroit (where he bought but never mailed birthday cards to his
sons), they forgot all about Hannah's easy ways (or their own) and said she was
a bitch. Everybody remembered the plague of robins that announced her re-
turn, and the tale about her watching Hannah burn was stirred up again.

But it was the men who gave her the final label, who fingerprinted her for all
time. They were the ones who said she was guilty of the unforgivable thing—
the thing for which there was no understanding, no excuse, no compassion.
The route from which there was no way back, the dirt that could not ever be
washed away. They said that Sula slept with white men. It may not have been
true, but it certainly could have been. She was obviously capable of it. In any
case, all minds were closed to her when that word was passed around. It made
the old women draw their lips together; made small children look away from
her in shame; made young men fantasize elaborate torture for her—just to get
the saliva back in their mouths when they saw her.

Every one of them imagined the scene, each according to his own predilec-
tions—Sula underneath some white man—and it filled them with choking
disgust. There was nothing lower she could do, nothing filthier. The fact that
their own skin color was proof that it had happened in their own families was
no deterrent to their bile. Nor was the willingness of black men to lie in the
beds of white women a consideration that might lead them toward tolerance.
They insisted that all unions between white men and black women be rape;

for a black woman to be willing was literally unthinkable. In that way, they re-
garded integration with precisely the same venom that white people did.

So they laid broomsticks across their doors at night and sprinkled salt on
porch steps.[7] But aside from one or two unsuccessful efforts to collect the dust
from her footsteps, they did nothing to harm her. As always the black people
looked at evil stoney-eyed and let it run.

Sula acknowledged none of their attempts at counter-conjure or their gos-
sip and seemed to need the services of nobody. So they watched her far more
closely than they watched any other roach or bitch in the town, and their alert-
ness was gratified. Things began to happen.

First off, Teapot knocked on her door to see if she had any bottles. He was
the five-year-old son of an indifferent mother, all of whose interests sat around
the door of the Time and a Half Pool Hall. Her name was Betty but she was
called Teapot's Mamma because being his mamma was precisely her major
failure. When Sula said no, the boy turned around and fell down the steps. He
couldn't get up right away and Sula went to help him. His mother, just then
tripping home, saw Sula bending over her son's pained face. She flew into a fit
of concerned, if drunken, motherhood, and dragged Teapot home. She told
everybody that Sula had pushed him, and talked so strongly about it she was
forced to abide by the advice of her friends and take him to the county hospi-
tal. The two dollars she hated to release turned out to be well spent, for Teapot
did have a fracture, although the doctor said poor diet had contributed sub-
stantially to the daintiness of his bones. Teapot's Mamma got a lot of atten-
tion anyway and immersed herself in a role she had shown no inclination for:
motherhood. The very idea of a grown woman hurting her boy kept her teeth
on edge. She became the most devoted mother: sober, clean and industrious.
No more nickels for Teapot to go to Dick's for a breakfast of Mr. Goodbars and
soda pop: no more long hours of him alone or wandering the roads while she
was otherwise engaged. Her change was a distinct improvement, although lit-
tle Teapot did miss those quiet times at Dick's.

Other things happened. Mr. Finley sat on his porch sucking chicken bones,
as he had done for thirteen years, looked up, saw Sula, choked on a bone and
died on the spot. That incident, and Teapot's Mamma, cleared up for every-
body the meaning of the birthmark over her eye; it was not a stemmed rose, or
a snake, it was Hannah's ashes marking her from the very beginning.

She came to their church suppers without underwear, bought their steam-
ing platters of food and merely picked at it—relishing nothing, exclaiming
over no one's ribs or cobbler. They believed that she was laughing at their God.

And the fury she created in the women of the town was incredible—for she
would lay their husbands once and then no more. Hannah had been a nui-
sance, but she was complimenting the women, in a way, by wanting their hus-
bands. Sula was trying them out and discarding them without any excuse the
men could swallow. So the women, to justify their own judgment, cherished
their men more, soothed the pride and vanity Sula had bruised.

Among the weighty evidence piling up was the fact that Sula did not look
her age. She was near thirty and, unlike them, had lost no teeth, suffered no
bruises, developed no ring of fat at the waist or pocket at the back of her neck.
It was rumored that she had had no childhood diseases, was never known to

7. These are both traditional methods of keeping witches away.

have chicken pox, croup or even a runny nose. She had played rough as a child—where were the scars? Except for a funny-shaped finger and that evil birthmark, she was free of any normal signs of vulnerability. Some of the men, who as boys had dated her, remembered that on picnics neither gnats nor mosquitoes would settle on her. Patsy, Hannah's one-time friend, agreed and said not only that, but she had witnessed the fact that when Sula drank beer she never belched.

The most damning evidence, however, came from Dessie, who was a big Daughter Elk[8] and knew things. At one of the social meetings she revealed something to her friends.

"Yeh, well I noticed something long time ago. Ain't said nothing 'bout it 'cause I wasn't sure what it meant. Well . . . I did mention it to Ivy but not nobody else. I disremember how long ago. 'Bout a month or two I guess 'cause I hadn't put down my new linoleum yet. Did you see it, Cora? It's that kind we saw in the catalogue."

"Naw."

"Get on with it, Dessie."

"Well, Cora was with me when we looked in the catalogue . . . "

"We all know 'bout your linoleum. What we don't know is . . ."

"OK. Let me tell it, will you? Just before the linoleum come I was out front and seed Shadrack carryin' on as usual . . . up by the well . . . walkin' 'round it salutin' and carryin' on. You know how he does . . . hollerin' commands and . . ."

"Will you get on with it?"

"Who's tellin' this? Me or you?"

"You."

"Well, let me tell it then. Like I say, he was just cuttin' up as usual when Miss Sula Mae walks by on the other side of the road. And quick as that"—she snapped her fingers—"he stopped and cut on over 'cross the road, steppin' over to her like a tall turkey in short corn. And guess what? He tips his hat."

"Shadrack don't wear no hat."

"I know that but he tipped it anyway. You know what I mean. He acted like he had a hat and reached up for it and tipped it at her. Now you know Shadrack ain't civil to nobody!"

"Sure ain't."

"Even when you buyin' his fish he's cussin'. If you ain't got the right change he cussin' you. If you act like a fish ain't too fresh he snatch it out of your hand like he doin' you the favor."

"Well, everybody know he a reprobate."

"Yeh, so how come he tip his hat to Sula? How come he don't cuss her?"

"Two devils."

"Exactly!"

"What'd she do when he tipped it? Smile and give him a curtsey?"

"No, and that was the other thing. It was the first time I see her look anything but hateful. Like she smellin' you with her eyes and don't like your soap. When he tipped his hat she put her hand on her throat for a minute and cut out. Went runnin on up the road to home. And him still standin' there tippin' away. And—this the point I was comin' to—when I went back in the house a big sty come on my eye. And I ain't never had no sty before. Never!"

8. I.e., she held a prominent office in the Elks, a benevolent and fraternal organization.

"That's 'cause you saw it."

"Exactly."

"Devil all right."

"No two ways about it," Dessie said, and she popped the rubber band off the deck of cards to settle them down for a nice long game of bid whist.

Their conviction of Sula's evil changed them in accountable yet mysterious ways. Once the source of their personal misfortune was identified, they had leave to protect and love one another. They began to cherish their husbands and wives, protect their children, repair their homes and in general band together against the devil in their midst. In their world, aberrations were as much a part of nature as grace. It was not for them to expel or annihilate it. They would no more run Sula out of town than they would kill the robins that brought her back, for in their secret awareness of Him, He was not the God of three faces[9] they sang about. They knew quite well that He had four, and that the fourth explained Sula. They had lived with various forms of evil all their days, and it wasn't that they believed God would take care of them. It was rather that they knew God had a brother and that brother hadn't spared God's son, so why should he spare them?

There was no creature so ungodly as to make them destroy it. They could kill easily if provoked to anger, but not by design, which explained why they could not "mob kill" anyone. To do so was not only unnatural, it was undignified. The presence of evil was something to be first recognized, then dealt with, survived, outwitted, triumphed over.

Their evidence against Sula was contrived, but their conclusions about her were not. Sula was distinctly different. Eva's arrogance and Hannah's self-indulgence merged in her and, with a twist that was all her own imagination, she lived out her days exploring her own thoughts and emotions, giving them full reign, feeling no obligation to please anybody unless their pleasure pleased her. As willing to feel pain as to give pain, to feel pleasure as to give pleasure, hers was an experimental life—ever since her mother's remarks sent her flying up those stairs, ever since her one major feeling of responsibility had been exorcised on the bank of a river with a closed place in the middle. The first experience taught her there was no other that you could count on; the second that there was no self to count on either. She had no center, no speck around which to grow. In the midst of a pleasant conversation with someone she might say, "Why do you chew with your mouth open?" not because the answer interested her but because she wanted to see the person's face change rapidly. She was completely free of ambition, with no affection for money, property or things, no greed, no desire to command attention or compliments—no ego. For that reason she felt no compulsion to verify herself—be consistent with herself.

She had clung to Nel as the closest thing to both an other and a self, only to discover that she and Nel were not one and the same thing. She had no thought at all of causing Nel pain when she bedded down with Jude. They had always shared the affection of other people: compared how a boy kissed, what line he used with one and then the other. Marriage, apparently, had changed all that, but having had no intimate knowledge of marriage, having lived in a

9. I.e., the Father, the Son, and the Holy Spirit.

house with women who thought all men available, and selected from among them with a care only for their tastes, she was ill prepared for the possessiveness of the one person she felt close to. She knew well enough what other women said and felt, or said they felt. But she and Nel had always seen through them. They both knew that those women were not jealous of other women; that they were only afraid of losing their jobs. Afraid their husbands would discover that no uniqueness lay between their legs.

Nel was the one person who had wanted nothing from her, who had accepted all aspects of her. Now she wanted everything, and all because of *that*. Nel was the first person who had been real to her, whose name she knew, who had seen as she had the slant of life that made it possible to stretch it to its limits. Now Nel was one of *them*. One of the spiders whose only thought was the next rung of the web, who dangled in dark dry places suspended by their own spittle, more terrified of the free fall than the snake's breath below. Their eyes so intent on the wayward stranger who trips into their net, they were blind to the cobalt on their own backs, the moonshine fighting to pierce their corners. If they were touched by the snake's breath, however fatal, they were merely victims and knew how to behave in that role (just as Nel knew how to behave as the wronged wife). But the free fall, oh no, that required—demanded—invention: a thing to do with the wings, a way of holding the legs and most of all a full surrender to the downward flight if they wished to taste their tongues or stay alive. But alive was what they, and now Nel, did not want to be. Too dangerous. Now Nel belonged to the town and all of its ways. She had given herself over to them, and the flick of their tongues would drive her back into her little dry corner where she would cling to her spittle high above the breath of the snake and the fall.

It had surprised her a little and saddened her a good deal when Nel behaved the way the others would have. Nel was one of the reasons she had drifted back to Medallion, that and the boredom she found in Nashville, Detroit, New Orleans, New York, Philadelphia, Macon and San Diego. All those cities held the same people, working the same mouths, sweating the same sweat. The men who took her to one or another of those places had merged into one large personality: the same language of love, the same entertainments of love, the same cooling of love. Whenever she introduced her private thoughts into their rubbings or goings, they hooded their eyes. They taught her nothing but love tricks, shared nothing but worry, gave nothing but money. She had been looking all along for a friend, and it took her a while to discover that a lover was not a comrade and could never be—for a woman. And that no one would ever be that version of herself which she sought to reach out to and touch with an ungloved hand. There was only her own mood and whim, and if that was all there was, she decided to turn the naked hand toward it, discover it and let others become as intimate with their own selves as she was.

In a way, her strangeness, her naïveté, her craving for the other half of her equation was the consequence of an idle imagination. Had she paints, or clay, or knew the discipline of the dance, or strings; had she anything to engage her tremendous curiosity and her gift for metaphor, she might have exchanged the restlessness and preoccupation with whim for an activity that provided her with all she yearned for. And like any artist with no art form, she became dangerous.

She had lied only once in her life—to Nel about the reason for putting Eva

out, and she could lie to her only because she cared about her. When she had come back home, social conversation was impossible for her because she could not lie. She could not say to those old acquaintances, "Hey, girl, you looking good," when she saw how the years had dusted their bronze with ash, the eyes that had once opened wide to the moon bent into grimy sickles of concern. The narrower their lives, the wider their hips. Those with husbands had folded themselves into starched coffins, their sides bursting with other people's skinned dreams and bony regrets. Those without men were like sour-tipped needles featuring one constant empty eye. Those with men had had the sweetness sucked from their breath by ovens and steam kettles. Their children were like distant but exposed wounds whose aches were no less intimate because separate from their flesh. They had looked at the world and back at their children, back at the world and back again at their children, and Sula knew that one clear young eye was all that kept the knife away from the throat's curve.

She was pariah, then, and knew it. Knew that they despised her and believed that they framed their hatred as disgust for the easy way she lay with men. Which was true. She went to bed with men as frequently as she could. It was the only place where she could find what she was looking for: misery and the ability to feel deep sorrow. She had not always been aware that it was sadness that she yearned for. Lovemaking seemed to her, at first, the creation of a special kind of joy. She thought she liked the sootiness of sex and its comedy; she laughed a great deal during the raucous beginnings, and rejected those lovers who regarded sex as healthy or beautiful. Sexual aesthetics bored her. Although she did not regard sex as ugly (ugliness was boring also), she liked to think of it as wicked. But as her experiences multiplied she realized that not only was it not wicked, it was not necessary for her to conjure up the idea of wickedness in order to participate fully. During the lovemaking she found and needed to find the cutting edge. When she left off cooperating with her body and began to assert herself in the act, particles of strength gathered in her like steel shavings drawn to a spacious magnetic center, forming a tight cluster that nothing, it seemed, could break. And there was utmost irony and outrage in lying under someone, in a position of surrender, feeling her own abiding strength and limitless power. But the cluster did break, fall apart, and in her panic to hold it together she leaped from the edge into soundlessness and went down howling, howling in a stinging awareness of the endings of things: an eye of sorrow in the midst of all that hurricane rage of joy. There, in the center of that silence was not eternity but the death of time and a loneliness so profound the word itself had no meaning. For loneliness assumed the absence of other people. She wept then. Tears for the deaths of the littlest things: the castaway shoes of children; broken stems of marsh grass battered and drowned by the sea; prom photographs of dead women she never knew; wedding rings in pawnshop windows; the tidy bodies of Cornish hens in a nest of rice.

When her partner disengaged himself, she looked up at him in wonder trying to recall his name; and he looked down at her, smiling with tender understanding of the state of tearful gratitude to which he believed he had brought her. She waiting impatiently for him to turn away and settle into a wet skim of satisfaction and light disgust, leaving her to the postcoital privateness in which she met herself, welcomed herself, and joined herself in matchless harmony.

At twenty-nine she knew it would be no other way for her, but she had not counted on the footsteps on the porch, and the beautiful black face that stared at her through the blue-glass window. Ajax.

Looking for all the world as he had seventeen years ago when he had called her pig meat. He was twenty-one then, she twelve. A universe of time between them. Now she was twenty-nine, he thirty-eight, and the lemon-yellow haunches seemed not so far away after all.

She opened the heavy door and saw him standing on the other side of the screen door with two quarts of milk tucked into his arms like marble statues. He smiled and said, "I been lookin' all over for you."

"Why?" she asked.

"To give you these," and he nodded toward one of the quarts of milk.

"I don't like milk," she said.

"But you like bottles don't you?" He held one up. "Ain't that pretty?"

And indeed it was. Hanging from his fingers, framed by a slick blue sky, it looked precious and clear and permanent. She had the distinct impression that he had done something dangerous to get them.

Sula ran her fingernails over the screen thoughtfully for a second and then, laughing, she opened the screen door.

Ajax came in and headed straight for the kitchen. Sula followed slowly. By the time she got to the door he had undone the complicated wire cap and was letting the cold milk run into his mouth.

Sula watched him—or rather the rhythm in his throat—with growing interest. When he had had enough, he poured the rest into the sink, rinsed the bottle out and presented it to her. She took the bottle with one hand and his wrist with the other and pulled him into the pantry. There was no need to go there, for not a soul was in the house, but the gesture came to Hannah's daughter naturally. There in the pantry, empty now of flour sacks, void of row upon row of canned goods, free forever of strings of tiny green peppers, holding the wet milk bottle tight in her arm she stood wide-legged against the wall and pulled from his track-lean hips all the pleasure her thighs could hold.

He came regularly then, bearing gifts: clusters of black berries still on their branches, four meal-fried porgies[1] wrapped in a salmon-colored sheet of the Pittsburgh *Courier*, a handful of jacks, two boxes of lime Jell-Well, a hung of ice-wagon ice, a can of Old Dutch Cleanser with the bonneted woman chasing dirt with her stick; a page of Tillie the Toiler comics, and more gleaming white bottles of milk.

Contrary to what anybody would have suspected from just seeing him lounging around the pool hall, or shooting at Mr. Finley for beating his own dog, or calling filthy compliments to passing women, Ajax was very nice to women. His women, of course, knew it, and it provoked them into murderous battles over him in the streets, brawling thick-thighed women with knives disturbed many a Friday night with their bloodletting and attracted whooping crowds. On such occasions Ajax stood, along with the crowd, and viewed the fighters with the same golden-eyed indifference with which he watched old men playing checkers. Other than his mother, who sat in her shack with six

1. Fish.

younger sons working roots,[2] he had never met an interesting woman in his life.

His kindness to them in general was not due to a ritual of seduction (he had no need for it) but rather to the habit he acquired in dealing with his mother, who inspired thoughtfulness and generosity in all her sons.

She was an evil conjure woman, blessed with seven adoring children whose joy it was to bring her the plants, hair, underclothing, fingernail parings, white hens, blood, camphor, pictures, kerosene and footstep dust that she needed, as well as to order Van Van, High John the Conqueror, Little John to Chew, Devil's Shoe String, Chinese Wash, Mustard Seed and the Nine Herbs from Cincinnati.[3] She knew about the weather, omens, the living, the dead, dreams and all illnesses and made a modest living with her skills. Had she any teeth or ever straightened her back, she would have been the most gorgeous thing alive, worthy of her sons' worship for her beauty alone, if not for the absolute freedom she allowed them (known in some quarters as neglect) and the weight of her hoary knowledge.

This woman Ajax loved, and after her—airplanes. There was nothing in between. And when he was not sitting enchanted listening to his mother's words, he thought of airplanes, and pilots, and the deep sky that held them both. People thought that those long trips he took to large cities in the state were for some sophisticated good times they could not imagine but only envy; actually he was leaning against the barbed wire of airports, or nosing around hangars just to hear the talk of the men who were fortunate enough to be in the trade. The rest of the time, the time he was not watching his mother's magic or thinking of airplanes, he spent in the idle pursuits of bachelors without work in small towns. He had heard all the stories about Sula, and they aroused his curiosity. Her elusiveness and indifference to established habits of behavior reminded him of his mother, who was as stubborn in her pursuits of the occult as the women of Greater Saint Matthew's were in the search for redeeming grace. So when his curiosity was high enough he picked two bottles of milk off the porch of some white family and went to see her, suspecting that this was perhaps the only other woman he knew whose life was her own, who could deal with life efficiently, and who was not interested in nailing him.

Sula, too, was curious. She knew nothing about him except the word he had called out to her years ago and the feeling he had excited in her then. She had grown quite accustomed to the clichés of other people's lives as well as her own increasing dissatisfaction with Medallion. If she could have thought of a place to go, she probably would have left, but that was before Ajax looked at her through the blue glass and held the milk aloft like a trophy.

But it was not the presents that made her wrap him up in her thighs. They were charming, of course (especially the jar of butterflies he let loose in the bedroom), but her real pleasure was the fact that he talked to her. They had genuine conversations. He did not speak down to her or at her, nor content himself with puerile questions about her life or monologues of his own activities. Thinking she was possibly brilliant, like his mother, he seemed to expect brilliance from her, and she delivered. And in all of it, he listened more than he spoke. His clear comfort at being in her presence, his lazy willingness to tell

2. Performing witchcraft, conjuring. 3. Roots and powders for the conjure work.

her all about fixes[4] and the powers of plants, his refusal to baby or protect her, his assumption that she was both tough and wise—all of that coupled with a wide generosity of spirit only occasionally erupting into vengeance sustained Sula's interest and enthusiasm.

His idea of bliss (on earth as opposed to bliss in the sky) was a long bath in piping-hot water—his head on the cool white rim, his eyes closed in reverie.

"Soaking in hot water give you a bad back." Sula stood in the doorway looking at his knees glistening just at the surface of the soap-gray water.

"Soaking in Sula give me a bad back."

"Worth it?"

"Don't know yet. Go 'way."

"Airplanes?"

"Airplanes."

"Lindbergh know about you?"

"Go 'way."

She went and waited for him in Eva's high bed, her head turned to the boarded-up window. She was smiling, thinking how like Jude's was his craving to do the white man's work, when two deweys came in with their beautiful teeth and said, "We sick."

Sula turned her head slowly and murmured, "Get well."

"We need some medicine."

"Look in the bathroom."

"Ajax in there."

"Then wait."

"We sick now."

Sula leaned over the bed, picked up a shoe and threw it at them.

"Cocksucker!" they screamed, and she leaped out of the bed naked as a yard dog. She caught the redheaded dewey by his shirt and held him by the heels over the banister until he wet his pants. The other dewey was joined by the third, and they delved into their pockets for stones, which they threw at her. Sula, ducking and tottering with laughter, carried the wet dewey to the bedroom and when the other two followed her, deprived of all weapons except their teeth, Sula had dropped the first dewey on the bed and was fishing in her purse. She gave each of them a dollar bill which they snatched and then scooted off down the stairs to Dick's to buy the catarrh remedy they loved to drink.

Ajax came sopping wet into the room and lay down on the bed to let the air dry him. They were both still for a long time until he reached out and touched her arm.

He liked for her to mount him so he could see her towering above him and call soft obscenities up into her face. As she rocked there, swayed there, like a Georgia pine on its knees, high above the slipping, falling smile, high above the golden eyes and the velvet helmet of hair, rocking, swaying, she focused her thoughts to bar the creeping disorder that was flooding her hips. She looked down, down from what seemed an awful height at the head of the man whose lemon-yellow gabardines had been the first sexual excitement she'd known. Letting her thoughts dwell on his face in order to confine, for just a while longer, the drift of her flesh toward the high silence of orgasm.

4 Spells.

If I take a chamois and rub real hard on the bone, right on the ledge of your cheek bone, some of the black will disappear. It will flake away into the chamois and underneath there will be gold leaf. I can see it shining through the black. I know it is there . . .

How high she was over his wand-lean body, how slippery was his sliding sliding smile.

And if I take a nail file or even Eva's old paring knife—that will do—and scrape away at the gold, it will fall away and there will be alabaster. The alabaster is what gives your face its planes, its curves. That is why your mouth smiling does not reach your eyes. Alabaster is giving it a gravity that resists a total smile.

The height and the swaying dizzied her, so she bent down and let her breasts graze his chest.

Then I can take a chisel and small tap hammer and tap away at the alabaster. It will crack then like ice under the pick, and through the breaks I will see the loam, fertile, free of pebbles and twigs. For it is the loam that is giving you that smell.

She slipped her hands under his armpits, for it seemed as though she would not be able to dam the spread of weakness she felt under her skin without holding on to something.

I will put my hand deep into your soil, lift it, sift it with my fingers, feel its warm surface and dewy chill below.

She put her head under his chin with no hope in the world of keeping anything at all at bay.

I will water your soil, keep it rich and moist. But how much? How much water to keep the loam moist? And how much loam will I need to keep my water still? And when do the two make mud?

He swallowed her mouth just as her thighs had swallowed his genitals, and the house was very, very quiet.

Sula began to discover what possession was. Not love, perhaps, but possession or at least the desire for it. She was astounded by so new and alien a feeling. First there was the morning of the night before when she actually wondered if Ajax would come by that day. Then there was an afternoon when she stood before the mirror finger-tracing the laugh lines around her mouth and trying to decide whether she was good-looking or not. She ended this deep perusal by tying a green ribbon in her hair. The green silk made a rippling whisper as she slid it into her hair—a whisper that could easily have been Hannah's chuckle, a soft slow nasal hiss she used to emit when something amused her. Like women sitting for two hours under the marcelling irons[5] only to wonder two days later how soon they would need another appointment. The ribbon-tying was followed by other activity, and when Ajax came that evening, bringing her a reed whistle he had carved that morning, not only was the green ribbon still in her hair, but the bathroom was gleaming, the bed was made, and the table was set for two.

He gave her the reed whistle, unlaced his shoes and sat in the rocking chair in the kitchen.

Sula walked toward him and kissed his mouth. He ran his fingers along the nape of her neck.

5. Heated curling irons for making deep, soft waves in hair.

"I bet you ain t even missed Tar Baby, have you?" he asked.

"Missed? No. Where is he?"

Ajax smiled at he- delicious ind:fference. "Jail."

"Since when?"

"Last Saturday."

"Picked up for drunk?"

"Little bit more than that," he answered and went ahead to tell her about his own involvement in another of Tar Baby's misfortunes.

On Saturday afternoon Tar Baby had stumbled drunk into traffic on the New River Road. A woman driver swerved to avoid him and hit another car. When the police came, they recognized the woman as the mayor's niece and arrested Tar Baby. Later, after the word got out, Ajax and two other men went to the station to see about him. At first they wouldn't let them in. But they relented after Ajax and the other two just stood around for one hour and a half and repeated their request at regular intervals. When they finally got permission to go in and looked in at him in the cell, he was twisted up in a corner badly beaten and dressed in nothing but extremely soiled underwear. Ajax and the other men asked the officer why Tar Baby couldn't have back his clothes. "It ain't right," they said, "to let a grown man lay around in his own shit."

The policeman, obviously in agreement with Eva, who had always maintained that Tar Baby was white, said that if the prisoner didn't like to live in shit, he should come down out of those hills, and live like a decent white man.

More words were exchanged, hot words and dark, and the whole thing ended with the arraignment of the three black men, and an appointment to appear in civil court Thursday next.

Ajax didn't seem too bothered by any of it. More annoyed and inconvenienced than anything else. He had had several messes with the police, mostly in gambling raids, and regarded them as the natural hazards of Negro life.

But Sula, the green ribbon shining in her hair, was flooded with an awareness of the impact of the outside world on Ajax. She stood up and arranged herself on the arm of the rocking chair. Putting her fingers deep into the velvet of his hair, she murmured, "Come on. Lean on me."

Ajax blinked. Then he looked swiftly into her face. In her words, in her voice, was a sound he knew well. For the first time he saw the green ribbon. He looked around and saw the gleaming kitchen and the table set for two and detected the scent of the nest. Every hackle on his body rose, and he knew that very soon she would, like all of her sisters before her, put to him the death-knell question "Where you been?" His eyes dimmed with a mild and momentary regret.

He stood and mounted the stairs with her and entered the spotless bathroom where the dust had been swept from underneath the claw-foot tub. He was trying to remember the date of the air show in Dayton. As he came into the bedroom, he saw Sula lying on fresh white sheets, wrapped in the deadly odor of freshly applied cologne.

He dragged her under him and made love to her with the steadiness and the intensity of a man about to leave for Dayton.

Every now and then she looked around for tangible evidence of his having ever been there. Where were the butterflies? the blueberries? the whistling reed? She could find nothing, for he had left nothing but his stunning ab-

sence. An absence so decorative, so ornate, it was difficult for her to under-stand how she had ever endured, without falling dead or being consumed, his magnificent presence.

The mirror by the door was not a mirror by the door, it was an altar where he stood for only a moment to put on his cap before going out. The red rocking chair was a rocking of his own hips as he sat in the kitchen. Still, there was nothing of his—his own—that she could find. It was as if she were afraid she had hallucinated him and needed proof to the contrary. His absence was everywhere, stinging everything, giving the furnishings primary colors, sharp outlines to the corners of rooms and gold light to the dust collecting on table tops. When he was there he pulled everything toward himself. Not only her eyes and all her senses but also inanimate things seemed to exist because of him, backdrops to his presence. Now that he had gone, these things, so long subdued by his presence, were glamorized in his wake.

Then one day, burrowing in a dresser drawer, she found what she had been looking for: proof that he had been there, his driver's license. It contained just what she needed for verification—his vital statistics: Born 1901, height 5'11", weight 152 lbs., eyes brown, hair black, color black. Oh yes, skin black. Very black. So black that only a steady careful rubbing with steel wool would re-move it, and as it was removed there was the glint of gold leaf and under the gold leaf the cold alabaster and deep, deep down under the cold alabaster more black only this time the black of warm loam.

But what was this? Albert Jacks? His name was Albert Jacks? A. Jacks. She had thought it was Ajax. All those years. Even from the time she walked by the pool hall and looked away from him sitting astride a wooden chair, looked away to keep from seeing the wide space of intolerable orderliness between his legs; the openness that held no sign, no sign at all, of the animal that lurked in his trousers; looked away from the insolent nostrils and the smile that kept slipping and falling, falling, falling so she wanted to reach out with her hand to catch it before it fell to the pavement and was sullied by the cigarette butts and bottle caps and spittle at his feet and the feet of other men who sat or stood around outside the pool hall, calling, singing out to her and Nel and grown women too with lyrics like *pig meat* and *brown sugar* and *jailbait* and *O Lord, what have I done to deserve the wrath*, and *Take me, Jesus, I have seen the promised land*, and *Do, Lord, remember me* in voices mellowed by hopeless pas-sion into gentleness. Even then, when she and Nel were trying hard not to dream of him and not to think of him when they touched the softness in their underwear or undid their braids as soon as they left home to let the hair bump and wave around their ears, or wrapped the cotton binding around their chests so the nipples would not break through their blouses and give him cause to smile his slipping, falling smile, which brought the blood rushing to their skin. And even later, when for the first time in her life she had lain in bed with a man and said his name involuntarily or said it truly meaning *him*, the name she was screaming and saying was not his at all.

Sula stood with a worn slip of paper in her fingers and said aloud to no one, "I didn't even know his name. And if I didn't know his name, then there is nothing I did know and I have known nothing ever at all since the one thing I wanted was to know his name so how could he help but leave me since he was making love to a woman who didn't even know his name.

"When I was a little girl the heads of my paper dolls came off, and it was a

long time before I discovered that my own head would not fall off if I bent my neck. I used to walk around holding it very stiff because I thought a strong wind or a heavy push would snap my neck. Nel was the one who told me the truth. But she was wrong. I did not hold my head stiff enough when I met him and so I lost it just like the dolls.

"It's just as well he left. Soon I would have torn the flesh from his face just to see if I was right about the gold and nobody would have understood that kind of curiosity. They would have believed that I wanted to hurt him just like the little boy who fell down the steps and broke his leg and the people think I pushed him just because I looked at it."

Holding the driver's license she crawled into bed and fell into a sleep full of dreams of cobalt blue.

When she awoke, there was a melody in her head she could not identify or recall ever hearing before. "Perhaps I made it up," she thought. Then it came to her—the name of the song and all its lyrics just as she had heard it many times before. She sat on the edge of the bed thinking, "There aren't any more new songs and I have sung all the ones there are. I have sung them all. I have sung all the songs there are." She lay down again on the bed and sang a little wandering tune made up of the words *I have sung all the songs all the songs I have sung all the songs there are* until, touched by her own lullaby, she grew drowsy, and in the hollow of near-sleep she tasted the acridness of gold, left the chill of alabaster and smelled the dark, sweet stench of loam.

1940

"I heard you was sick. Anything I can do for you?"

She had practiced not just the words but the tone, the pitch of her voice. It should be calm, matter-of-fact, but strong in sympathy—for the illness though, not for the patient.

The sound of her voice as she heard it in her head betrayed no curiosity, no pride, just the inflection of any good woman come to see about a sick person who, incidentally, had such visits from nobody else.

For the first time in three years she would be looking at the stemmed rose that hung over the eye of her enemy. Moreover, she would be doing it with the taste of Jude's exit in her mouth, with the resentment and shame that even yet pressed for release in her stomach. She would be facing the black rose that Jude had kissed and looking at the nostrils of the woman who had twisted her love for her own children into something so thick and monstrous she was afraid to show it lest it break loose and smother them with its heavy paw. A cumbersome bear-love that, given any rein, would suck their breath away in its crying need for honey.

Because Jude's leaving was so complete, the full responsibility of the household was Nel's. There were no more fifty dollars in brown envelopes to count on, so she took to cleaning rather than fret away the tiny seaman's pension her parents lived on. And just this past year she got a better job working as a chambermaid in the same hotel Jude had worked in. The tips were only fair, but the hours were good—she was home when the children got out of school.

At thirty her hot brown eyes had turned to agate, and her skin had taken on the sheen of maple struck down, split and sanded at the height of its green. Virtue, bleak and drawn, was her only mooring. It brought her to Number 7

Carpenter's Road and the door with the blue glass; it helped her to resist scratching the screen as in days gone by; it hid from her the true motives for her charity, and, finally, it gave her voice the timbre she wanted it to have: free of delight or a lip-smacking "I told you so" with which the news of Sula's illness had been received up in the Bottom—free of the least hint of retribution.

Now she stood in Eva's old bedroom, looking down at that dark rose, aware of the knife-thin arms sliding back and forth over the quilt and the boarded-up window Eva had jumped out of.

Sula looked up and without a second's pause followed Nel's example of leaving out the greeting when she spoke.

"As a matter of fact, there is. I got a prescription. Nathan usually goes for me but he . . . school don't let out till three. Could you run it over to the drugstore?"

"Where is it?" Nel was glad to have a concrete errand. Conversation would be difficult. (Trust Sula to pick up a relationship exactly where it lay.)

"Look in my bag. No. Over there."

Nel walked to the dresser and opened the purse with the beaded clasp. She saw only a watch and the folded prescription down inside. No wallet, no change purse. She turned to Sula: "Where's your . . ."

But Sula was looking at the boarded-up window. Something in her eye right there in the corner stopped Nel from completing her question. That and the slight flare of the nostrils—a shadow of a snarl. Nel took the piece of paper and picked up her own purse, saying, "OK. I'll be right back."

As soon as the door was shut, Sula breathed through her mouth. While Nel was in the room the pain had increased. Now that this new pain killer, the one she had been holding in reserve, was on the way her misery was manageable. She let a piece of her mind lay on Nel. It was funny, sending Nel off to that drugstore right away like that, after she had not seen her to speak to for years. The drugstore was where Edna Finch's Mellow House used to be years back when they were girls. Where they used to go, the two of them, hand in hand, for the 18-cent ice-cream sundaes, past the Time and a Half Pool Hall, where the sprawling men said "pig meat," and they sat in that cool room with the marble-top tables and ate the first ice-cream sundaes of their lives. Now Nel was going back there alone and Sula was waiting for the medicine the doctor said not to take until the pain got really bad. And she supposed "really bad" was now. Although you could never tell. She wondered for an instant what Nellie wanted; why she had come. Did she want to gloat? Make up? Following this line of thought required more concentration than she could muster. Pain was greedy; it demanded all of her attention. But it was good that this new medicine, the reserve, would be brought to her by her old friend. Nel, she remembered, always thrived on a crisis. The closed place in the water; Hannah's funeral. Nel was the best. When Sula imitated her, or tried to, those long years ago, it always ended up in some action noteworthy not for its coolness but mostly for its being bizarre. The one time she tried to protect Nel, she had cut off her own finger tip and earned not Nel's gratitude but her disgust. From then on she had let her emotions dictate her behavior.

She could hear Nel's footsteps long before she opened the door and put the medicine on the table near the bed.

As Sula poured the liquid into a sticky spoon, Nel began the sickroom conversation.

"You look fine, Sula."

"You lying, Nellie. I look bad." She gulped the medicine.

"No. I haven't seen you for a long time, but you look . . ."

"You don't have to do that, Nellie. It's going to be all right."

"What ails you? Have they said?"

Sula licked the corners of her lips. "You want to talk about that?"

Nel smiled, slightly, at the bluntness she had forgotten. "No. No, I don't, but you sure you should be staying up here alone?"

"Nathan comes by. The deweys sometimes, and Tar Baby . . ."

"That ain't help, Sula. You need to be with somebody grown. Somebody who can . . ."

"I'd rather be here, Nellie."

"You know you don't have to be proud with me."

"Proud?" Sula's laughter broke through the phlegm. "What you talking about? I like my own dirt, Nellie. I'm not proud. You sure have forgotten me."

"Maybe. Maybe not. But you a woman and you alone."

"And you? Ain't you alone?"

"I'm not sick. I work."

"Yes. Of course you do. Work's good for you, Nellie. It don't do nothing for me."

"You never *had* to."

"I never would."

"There's something to say for it, Sula. 'Specially if you don't want people to have to do for you."

"Neither one, Nellie. Neither one."

"You can't have it all, Sula." Nel was getting exasperated with her arrogance, with her lying at death's door still smart-talking.

"Why? I can do it all, why can't I have it all?"

"You *can't* do it all. You a woman and a colored woman at that. You can't act like a man. You can't be walking around all independent-like, doing whatever you like, taking what you want, leaving what you don't."

"You repeating yourself."

"How repeating myself?"

"You say I'm a woman and colored. Ain't that the same as being a man?"

"I don't think so and you wouldn't either if you had children."

"Then I really would act like what you call a man. Every man I ever knew left his children."

"Some were taken."

"Wrong, Nellie. The word is 'left.' "

"You still going to know everything, ain't you?"

"I don't know everything, I just do everything."

"Well, you don't do what I do."

"You think I don't know what your life is like just because I ain't living it? I know what every colored woman in this country is doing."

"What's that?"

"Dying. Just like me. But the difference is they dying like a stump. Me, I'm going down like one of those redwoods. I sure did live in this world."

"Really? What have you got to show for it?"

"Show? To who? Girl, I got my mind. And what goes on in it. Which is to say, I got me."

"Lonely, ain't it?"

"Yes. But my lonely is *mine*. Now your lonely is somebody else's. Made by

somebody else and handed to you. Ain't that something? A secondhand lonely."

Nel sat back on the little wooden chair. Anger skipped but she realized that Sula was probably just showing off. No telling what shape she was really in, but there was no point in saying anything other than what was the truth. "I always understood how you could take a man. Now I understand why you can't keep none."

"Is that what I'm supposed to do? Spend my life keeping a man?"

"They worth keeping, Sula."

"They ain't worth more than me. And besides, I never loved no man because he was worth it. Worth didn't have nothing to do with it."

"What did?"

"My mind did. That's all."

"Well I guess that's it. You own the world and the rest of us is renting. You ride the pony and we shovel the shit. I didn't come up here for this kind of talk, Sula . . ."

"No?"

"No. I come to see about you. But now that you opened it up, I may as well close it." Nel's fingers closed around the brass rail of the bed. Now she would ask her. "How come you did it, Sula?"

There was a silence but Nel felt no obligation to fill it.

Sula stirred a little under the covers. She looked bored as she sucked her teeth. "Well, there was this space in front of me, behind me, in my head. Some space. And Jude filled it up. That's all. He just filled up the space."

"You mean you didn't even love him?" The feel of the brass was in Nel's mouth. "It wasn't even loving him?"

Sula looked toward the boarded-up window again. Her eyes fluttered as if she were about to fall off into sleep.

"But . . ." Nel held her stomach in. "But what about me? What about me? Why didn't you think about me? Didn't I count? I never hurt you. What did you take him for if you didn't love him and why didn't you think about me?" And then, "I was good to you, Sula, why don't that matter?"

Sula turned her head away from the boarded window. Her voice was quiet and the stemmed rose over her eye was very dark. "It matters, Nel, but only to you. Not to anybody else. Being good to somebody is just like being mean to somebody. Risky. You don't get nothing for it."

Nel took her hands from the brass railing. She was annoyed with herself. Finally when she had gotten the nerve to ask the question, the right question, it made no difference. Sula couldn't give her a sensible answer because she didn't know. Would be, in fact, the last to know. Talking to her about right and wrong was like talking to the deweys. She picked at the fringe on Sula's bedspread and said softly, "We were friends."

"Oh, yes. Good friends," Sula said.

"And you didn't love me enough to leave him alone. To let him love me. You had to take him away."

"What you mean take him away? I didn't kill him, I just fucked him. If we were such good friends, how come you couldn't get over it?"

"You laying there in that bed without a dime or a friend to your name having done all the dirt you did in this town and you still expect folks to love you?"

Sula raised herself up on her elbows. Her face glistened with the dew of fever. She opened her mouth as though to say something, then fell back on the

pillows and sighed. "Oh, they'll love me all right. It will take time, but they'll love me." The sound of her voice was as soft and distant as the look in her eyes. "After the old women have lain with teen-agers; when all the young girls have slept with their old drunken uncles; after all the black men fuck all the white ones; when all the white women kiss all the black ones; when the guards have raped all the jailbirds and after all the whores make love to their grannies; after all the faggots get their mothers' trim; when Lindbergh sleeps with Bessie Smith and Norma Shearer makes it with Stepin Fetchit,[6] after all the dogs have fucked all the cats and every weathervane on every barn flies off the roof to mount the hogs . . . then there'll be a little love left over for me. And I know just what it will feel like."

She closed her eyes then and thought of the wind pressing her dress between her legs as she ran up the bank of the river to four leaf-locked trees and the digging of holes in the earth.

Embarrassed, irritable and a little bit ashamed, Nel rose to go. "Goodbye, Sula. I don't reckon I'll be back."

She opened the door and heard Sula's low whisper. "Hey, girl." Nel paused and turned her head but not enough to see her.

"How you know?" Sula asked.

"Know what?" Nel still wouldn't look at her.

"About who was good. How you know it was you?"

"What you mean?"

"I mean maybe it wasn't you. Maybe it was me."

Nel took two steps out the door and closed it behind her. She walked down the hall and down the four flights of steps. The house billowed around her light then dark, full of presences without sounds. The deweys, Tar Baby, the newly married couples, Mr Buckland Reed Patsy, Valentine, and the beautiful Hannah Peace. Where were they? Eva out at the old folks' home, the deweys living anywhere, Tar Baby steeped in wine, and Sula upstairs in Eva's bed with a boarded-up window and an empty pocketbook on the dresser.

When Nel closed the door, Sula reached for more medicine. Then she turned the pillow over to its cool side and thought about her old friend. "So she will walk on down that road, her back so straight in that old green coat, the strap of her handbag pushed back all the way to the elbow, thinking how much I have cost her and never remember the days when we were two throats and one eye and we had no price."

Pictures drifted through her head as lightly as dandelion spores the blue eagle that swallowed the E of the Sherman's Mellowe wine that Tar Baby drank; the pink underlid of Hannah's eye as she probed for a fleck of coal dust or a lash. She thought of looking out of the windows of all those trains and buses, looking at the feet and backs of all those people. Nothing was ever different. They were all the same. All of the words and all of the smiles, every tear and every gag just something to do.

"That's the same sun I looked at when I was twelve, the same pear trees. If I live a hundred years my urine will flow the same way, my armpits and breath will smell the same. My hair will grow from the same holes. I didn't mean any-

<hr/>

6. Actor (born Lincoln Perry) (1902–1985), who played stereotypical Hollywood blacks (lazy, stupid, and so forth) in films from the 1920s through the 1950s. Charles Lindbergh (1902–1974), white aviator. Bessie Smith (1894?–1937), black blues singer Norma Shearer (1900–1983), white actress of the 1920s and 1930s.

thing. I never meant anything. I stood there watching her burn and was thrilled. I wanted her to keep on jerking like that, to keep on dancing."

Then she had the dream again. The Clabber Girl Baking Powder lady was smiling and beckoning to her, one hand under her apron. When Sula came near she disintegrated into white dust, which Sula was hurriedly trying to stuff into the pockets of her blue-flannel housecoat. The disintegration was awful to see, but worse was the feel of the powder—its starchy slipperiness as she tried to collect it by handfuls. The more she scooped, the more it billowed. At last it covered her, filled her eyes, her nose, her throat, and she woke gagging and overwhelmed with the smell of smoke.

Pain took hold. First a fluttering as of doves in her stomach, then a kind of burning, followed by a spread of thin wires to other parts of her body. Once the wires of liquid pain were in place, they jelled and began to throb. She tried concentrating on the throbs, identifying them as waves, hammer strokes, razor edges or small explosions. Soon even the variety of the pain bored her and there was nothing to do, for it was joined by fatigue so great she could not make a fist or fight the taste of oil at the back of her tongue.

Several times she tried to cry out, but the fatigue barely let her open her lips, let alone take the deep breath necessary to scream. So she lay there wondering how soon she would gather enough strength to lift her arm and push the rough quilt away from her chin and whether she should turn her cheek to the cooler side of the pillow now or wait till her face was thoroughly soaked and the move would be more refreshing. But she was reluctant to move her face for another reason. If she turned her head, she would not be able to see the boarded-up window Eva jumped out of. And looking at those four wooden planks with the steel rod slanting across them was the only peace she had. The sealed window soothed her with its sturdy termination, its unassailable finality. It was as though for the first time she was completely alone—where she had always wanted to be—free of the possibility of distraction. It would be here, only here, held by this blind window high above the elm tree, that she might draw her legs up to her chest, close her eyes, put her thumb in her mouth and float over and down the tunnels, just missing the dark walls, down, down until she met a rain scent and would know the water was near, and she would curl into its heavy softness and it would envelop her, carry her, and wash her tired flesh always. Always. Who said that? She tried hard to think. Who was it that had promised her a sleep of water always? The effort to recall was too great; it loosened a knot in her chest that turned her thoughts again to the pain.

While in this state of weary anticipation, she noticed that she was not breathing, that her heart had stopped completely. A crease of fear touched her breast, for any second there was sure to be a violent explosion in her brain, a gasping for breath. Then she realized, or rather she sensed, that there was not going to be any pain. She was not breathing because she didn't have to. Her body did not need oxygen. She was dead.

Sula felt her face smiling. "Well, I'll be damned," she thought, "it didn't even hurt. Wait'll I tell Nel."

1941

The death of Sula Peace was the best news folks up in the Bottom had had since the promise of work at the tunnel. Of the few who were not afraid to wit-

ness the burial of a witch and who had gone to the cemetery, some had come just to verify her being put away but stayed to sing "Shall We Gather at the River" for politeness' sake, quite unaware of the bleak promise of their song. Others came to see that nothing went awry, that the shallow-minded and small-hearted kept their meanness at bay, and that the entire event be characterized by that abiding gentleness of spirit to which they themselves had arrived by the simple determination not to let anything—anything at all: not failed crops, not rednecks, lost jobs, sick children, rotten potatoes, broken pipes, bug-ridden flour, third-class coal, educated social workers, thieving insurance men, garlic-ridden hunkies, corrupt Catholics, racist Protestants, cowardly Jews, slaveholding Moslems, jackleg nigger preachers, squeamish Chinamen, cholera, dropsy or the Black Plague, let alone a strange woman—keep them from their God

In any case, both the raw-spirited and the gentle who came—not to the white funeral parlor but to the colored part of the Beechnut Cemetery—felt that either *because* Sula was dead or just *after* she was dead a brighter day was dawning. There were signs. The rumor that the tunnel spanning the river would use Negro workers became an announcement. Planned, abandoned and replanned for years, this project had finally begun in 1937. For three years there were rumors that blacks would work it, and hope was high in spite of the fact that the River Road leading to the tunnel had encouraged similar hopes in 1927 but had ended up being built entirely by white labor—hillbillies and immigrants taking even the lowest jobs. But the tunnel itself was another matter. The craft work—no, they would not get that. But it was a major job, and the government seemed to favor opening up employment to black workers. It meant black men would not have to sweep Medallion to eat, or leave the town altogether for the steel mills in Akron and along Lake Erie.

The second sign was the construction begun on an old people's home. True, it was more renovation than construction, but the blacks were free, or so it was said, to occupy it. Some said that the very transfer of Eva from the ramshackle house that passed for a colored women's nursing home to the bright new one was a clear sign of the mystery of God's ways, His mighty thumb having been seen at Sula's throat.

So it was with a strong sense of hope that the people in the Bottom watched October close.

Then Medallion turned silver. It seemed sudden, but actually there had been days and days of no snow—just frost—when, late one afternoon, a rain fell and froze. Way down Carpenter's Road, where the concrete sidewalks started, children hurried to the sliding places before shopkeepers and old women sprinkled stove ashes, like ancient onyx, onto the new-minted silver. They hugged trees simply to hold for a moment all that life and largeness stilled in glass, and gazed at the sun pressed against the gray sky like a worn doubloon, wondering all the while if the world were coming to an end. Grass stood blade by blade, shocked into separateness by an ice that held for days.

Late-harvesting things were ruined, of course, and fowl died of both chill and rage. Cider turned to ice and split the jugs, forcing the men to drink their cane liquor too soon. It was better down in the valley, since, as always, the hills protected it, but up in the Bottom black folks suffered heavily in their thin houses and thinner clothes. The ice-cold wind bled what little heat they had through windowpanes and ill-fitting doors. For days on end they were virtually

housebound, venturing out only to coalbins or right next door for the trading of vital foodstuffs. Never to the stores. No deliveries were being made anyway, and when they were, the items were saved for better-paying white customers. Women could not make it down the icy slopes and therefore missed days of wages they sorely needed.

The consequence of all that ice was a wretched Thanksgiving of tiny tough birds, heavy pork cakes, and pithy sweet potatoes. By the time the ice began to melt and the first barge was seen shuddering through the ice skim on the river, everybody under fifteen had croup, or scarlet fever, and those over had chilblains, rheumatism, pleurisy,[7] earaches and a world of other ailments.

Still it was not those illnesses or even the ice that marked the beginning of the trouble, that self-fulfilled prophecy that Shadrack carried on his tongue. As soon as the silvering began, long before the cider cracked the jugs, there was something wrong. A falling away, a dislocation was taking place. Hard on the heels of the general relief that Sula's death brought a restless irritability took hold. Teapot, for example, went into the kitchen and asked his mother for some sugar-butter-bread. She got up to fix it and found that she had no butter, only oleomargarine. Too tired to mix the saffron-colored powder into the hard cake of oleo, she simply smeared the white stuff on the bread and sprinkled the sugar over it. Teapot tasted the difference and refused to eat it. This keenest of insults that a mother can feel, the rejection by a child of her food, bent her into fury and she beat him as she had not done since Sula knocked him down the steps. She was not alone. Other mothers who had defended their children from Sula's malevolence (or who had defended their positions as mothers from Sula's scorn for the role) now had nothing to rub up against. The tension was gone and so was the reason for the effort they had made. Without her mockery, affection for others sank into flaccid disrepair. Daughters who had complained bitterly about the responsibilities of taking care of their aged mothers-in-law had altered when Sula locked Eva away, and they began cleaning those old women's spittoons without a murmur. Now that Sula was dead and done with, they returned to a steeping resentment of the burdens of old people. Wives uncoddled their husbands; there seemed no further need to reinforce their vanity. And even those Negroes who had moved down from Canada to Medallion, who remarked every chance they got that they had never been slaves, felt a loosening of the reactionary compassion for Southern-born blacks Sula had inspired in them. They returned to their original claims of superiority.

The normal meanness that the winter brought was compounded by the small-spiritedness that hunger and scarlet fever produced. Even a definite and witnessed interview of four colored men (and the promise of more in the spring) at the tunnel site could not break the cold vise of that lean and bitter year's end.

Christmas came one morning and haggled everybody's nerves like a dull ax—too shabby to cut clean but too heavy to ignore. The children lay wall-eyed on creaking beds or pallets near the stove, sucking peppermint and oranges in between coughs while their mothers stomped the floors in rage at the

7. An infection around the lungs. "Croup" (an inflammation of the larynx) and "scarlet fever" (a contagious bacterial disease) were once common childhood diseases. "Chilblains": sores (usually on the feet or hands) caused by exposure to cold.

cakes that did not rise because the stove fire had been so stingy; at the curled bodies of men who chose to sleep the day away rather than face the silence made by the absence of Lionel trains, drums, crybaby dolls and rocking horses. Teen-agers sneaked into the Elmira Theater in the afternoon and let Tex Ritter[8] free them from the recollection of their fathers' shoes, yawning in impotence under the bed. Some of them had a bottle of wine, which they drank at the feet of the glittering Mr. Ritter, making such a ruckus the manager had to put them out. The white people who came with Christmas bags of rock candy and old clothes were hard put to get a *Yes'm, thank you,* out of those sullen mouths.

Just as the ice lingered in October, so did the phlegm of December—which explained the enormous relief brought on by the first three days of 1941. It was as though the season had exhausted itself, for on January first the temperature shot up to sixty-one degrees and slushed the whiteness overnight. On January second drab patches of grass could be seen in the fields. On January third the sun came out—and so did Shadrack with his rope, his bell and his childish dirge.

He had spent the night before watching a tiny moon. The people, the voices that kept him company, were with him less and less. Now there were long periods when he heard nothing except the wind in the trees and the plop of buckeyes on the earth. In the winter, when the fish were too hard to get to, he did picking-up jobs for small businessmen (nobody would have him in or even near their homes), and thereby continued to have enough money for liquor. Yet the drunk times were becoming deeper but more seldom. It was as though he no longer needed to drink to forget whatever it was he could not remember. Now he could not remember that he had ever forgotten anything. Perhaps that was why for the first time after that cold day in France he was beginning to miss the presence of other people. Shadrack had improved enough to feel lonely. If he was lonely before, he didn't know it because the noise he kept up, the roaring, the busyness, protected him from knowing it. Now the compulsion to activity, to filling up the time when he was not happily fishing on the riverbank, had dwindled. He sometimes fell asleep before he got drunk; sometimes spent whole days looking at the river and the sky; and more and more he relinquished the military habits of cleanliness in his shack. Once a bird flew into his door—one of the robins during the time there was a plague of them. It stayed, looking for an exit, for the better part of an hour. When the bird found the window and flew away, Shadrack was grieved and actually waited and watched for its return. During those days of waiting, he did not make his bed, or sweep, or shake out the little rag-braid rug, and almost forgot to slash with his fish knife the passing day on his calendar. When he did return to housekeeping, it was not with the precision he had always insisted upon. The messier his house got, the lonelier he felt, and it was harder and harder to conjure up sergeants, and orderlies, and invading armies; harder and harder to hear the gunfire and keep the platoon marching in time. More frequently now he looked at and fondled the one piece of evidence that he once had a visitor in his house: a child's purple-and-white belt. The one the little girl left behind when she came to see him. Shadrack remembered the scene clearly. He had

8. The "singing cowboy" (1906–1974), actor and singer on radio, screen, television, and stage.

stepped into the door and there was a tear-stained face turning, turning to-
ward him; eyes hurt and wondering; mouth parted in an effort to ask a ques-
tion. She had wanted something—from him. Not fish, not work, but
something only he could give. She had a tadpole over her eye (that was how he
knew she was a friend—she had the mark of the fish he loved), and one of her
braids had come undone. But when he looked at her face he had seen also the
skull beneath, and thinking she saw it too—knew it was there and was afraid—
he tried to think of something to say to comfort her, something to stop the
hurt from spilling out of her eyes. So he had said "always," so she would not
have to be afraid of the change—the falling away of skin, the drip and slide of
blood, and the exposure of bone underneath. He had said "always" to con-
vince her, assure her, of permanency.

It worked, for when he said it her face lit up and the hurt did leave. She ran
then, carrying his knowledge, but her belt fell off and he kept it as a memento.
It hung on a nail near his bed—unfrayed, unsullied after all those years, with
only the permanent bend in the fabric made by its long life on a nail. It was
pleasant living with that sign of a visitor, his only one. And after a while he was
able to connect the belt with the face, the tadpole-over-the-eye-face that he
sometimes saw up in the Bottom. His visitor, his company, his guest, his social
life, his woman, his daughter, his friend—they all hung there on a nail near his
bed.

Now he stared at the tiny moon floating high over the ice-choked river. His
loneliness had dropped down somewhere around his ankles. Some other feel-
ing possessed him. A feeling that touched his eyes and made him blink. He
had seen her again months? weeks? ago. Raking leaves for Mr. Hodges, he had
gone into the cellar for two bushel baskets to put them in. In the hallway he
passed an open door leading to a small room. She lay on a table there. It was
surely the same one. The same little-girl face, same tadpole over the eye. So he
had been wrong. Terribly wrong. No "always" at all. Another dying away of
someone whose face he knew.

It was then he began to suspect that all those years of rope hauling and bell
ringing were never going to do any good. He might as well sit forever on his
riverbank and stare out of the window at the moon.

By his day-slashed calendar he knew that tomorrow was the day. And for the
first time he did not want to go. He wanted to stay with the purple-and-white
belt. Not go. Not go.

Still, when the day broke in an incredible splash of sun, he gathered his
things. In the early part of the afternoon, drenched in sunlight and certain
that this would be the last time he would invite them to end their lives neatly
and sweetly, he walked over the rickety bridge and on into the Bottom. But it
was not heartfelt this time, not loving this time, for he no longer cared
whether he helped them or not. His rope was improperly tied; his bell had a
tinny unimpassioned sound. His visitor was dead and would come no more.

Years later people would quarrel about who had been the first to go. Most
folks said it was the deweys, but one or two knew better, knew that Dessie and
Ivy had been first. Said that Dessie had opened her door first and stood there
shielding her eyes from the sun while watching Shadrack coming down the
road. She laughed.

Maybe the sun; maybe the clots of green showing in the hills promising so

much; maybe the contrast between Shadrack's doomy, gloomy bell glinting in all that sweet sunshine. Maybe just a brief moment, for once, of not feeling fear, of looking at death in the sunshine and being unafraid. She laughed.

Upstairs, Ivy heard her and looked to see what caused the thick music that rocked her neighbor's breasts. Then Ivy laughed too. Like the scarlet fever that had touched everybody and worn them down to gristle, their laughter infected Carpenter's Road. Soon children were jumping about giggling and men came to the porches to chuckle. By the time Shadrack reached the first house, he was facing a line of delighted faces.

Never before had they laughed. Always they had shut their doors, pulled down the shades and called their children out of the road. It frightened him, this glee, but he stuck to his habit—singing his song, ringing his bell and holding fast to his rope. The ceweys with their magnificent teeth ran out from Number 7 and danced a little jig around the befuddled Shadrack, then cut into a wild aping of his walk, his song and his bell-ringing. By now women were holding their stomachs, and the men were slapping their knees. It was Mrs. Jackson, who ate ice, who tripped down off her porch and marched—actually marched—along behind him. The scene was so comic the people walked into the road to make sure they saw it all. In that way the parade started.

Everybody, Dessie, Tar Baby, Patsy, Mr. Buckland Reed, Teapot's Mamma, Valentine, the deweys, Mrs. Jackson, Irene, the proprietor of the Palace of Cosmetology, Reba, the Herrod brothers and flocks of teen-agers got into the mood and, laughing, dancing, calling to one another, formed a pied piper's band[9] behind Shadrack. As the initial group of about twenty people passed more houses, they called to the people standing in doors and leaning out of windows to join them; to help them open further this slit in the veil, this respite from anxiety, from dignity, from gravity, from the weight of that very adult pain that had undergirded them all those years before. Called to them to come out and play in the sunshine—as though the sunshine would last, as though there really was hope. The same hope that kept them picking beans for other farmers; kept them from finally leaving as they talked of doing; kept them knee-deep in other people's dirt; kept them excited about other people's wars; kept them solicitous of white people's children; kept them convinced that some magic "government" was going to lift them up, out and away from that dirt, those beans, those wars.

Some, of course, like Helene Wright, would not go. She watched the ruckus with characteristic scorn. Others, who understood the Spirit's touch which made them dance, who understood whole families bending their backs in a field while singing as from one throat, who understood the ecstasy of river baptisms under suns just like this one, did not understand this curious disorder, this headless display and so refused also to go.

Nevertheless, the sun splashed on a larger and larger crowd that strutted, skipped, marched, and shuffled down the road. When they got down to where the sidewalk started, some of them stopped and decided to turn back, too embarrassed to enter the white part of town whooping like banshees.[1] But except for three or four, the fainthearted were put to shame by the more aggressive and abandoned, and the parade danced down Main Street past Woolworth's

9. In the story of the Pied Piper of Hamlin, the piper (because he wasn't paid for freeing the town of rats) charmed the town's children into following him away forever.

1. In Gaelic folklore, female spirits whose wailing portends a coming death.

and the old poultry house, turned right and moved on down the New River Road.

At the mouth of the tunnel excavation, in a fever pitch of excitement and joy, they saw the timber, the bricks, the steel ribs and the tacky wire gate that glittered under ice struck to diamond in the sun. It dazzled them, at first, and they were suddenly quiet. Their hooded eyes swept over the place where their hope had lain since 1927. There was the promise: leaf-dead. The teeth unrepaired, the coal credit cut off, the chest pains unattended, the school shoes unbought, the rush-stuffed mattresses, the broken toilets, the leaning porches, the slurred remarks and the staggering childish malevolence of their employers. All there in blazing sunlit ice rapidly becoming water.

Like antelopes they leaped over the little gate—a wire barricade that was never intended to bar anything but dogs, rabbits and stray children—and led by the tough, the enraged and the young they picked up the lengths of timber and thin steel ribs and smashed the bricks they would never fire in yawning kilns, split the sacks of limestone they had not mixed or even been allowed to haul; tore the wire mesh, tipped over wheelbarrows and rolled forepoles down the bank, where they sailed far out on the icebound river.

Old and young, women and children, lame and hearty, they killed, as best they could, the tunnel they were forbidden to build.

They didn't mean to go in, to actually go down into the lip of the tunnel, but in their need to kill it all, all of it, to wipe from the face of the earth the work of the thin-armed Virginia boys, the bull-necked Greeks and the knife-faced men who waved the leaf-dead promise, they went too deep, too far . . .

A lot of them died there. The earth, now warm, shifted; the first forepole slipped; loose rock fell from the face of the tunnel and caused a shield to give way. They found themselves in a chamber of water, deprived of the sun that had brought them there. With the first crack and whoosh of water, the clamber to get out was so fierce that others who were trying to help were pulled to their deaths. Pressed up against steel ribs and timber blocks young boys strangled when the oxygen left them to join the water. Outside, others watched in terror as ice split and earth shook beneath their feet. Mrs. Jackson, weighing less than 100 pounds, slid down the bank and met with an open mouth the ice she had craved all her life. Tar Baby, Dessie, Ivy, Valentine, the Herrod boys, some of Ajax's younger brothers and the deweys (at least it was supposed; their bodies were never found)—all died there. Mr. Buckland Reed escaped, so did Patsy and her two boys, as well as some fifteen or twenty who had not gotten close enough to fall, or whose timidity would not let them enter an unfinished tunnel.

And all the while Shadrack stood there. Having forgotten his song and his rope, he just stood there high up on the bank ringing, ringing his bell.

1965

Things were so much better in 1965. Or so it seemed. You could go downtown and see colored people working in the dime store behind the counters, even handling money with cash-register keys around their necks. And a colored man taught mathematics at the junior high school. The young people had a look about them that everybody said was new but which reminded Nel of the deweys, whom nobody had ever found. Maybe, she thought, they had

gone off and seeded the land and growed up in these young people in the dime store with the cash-register keys around their necks.

They were so different, these young people. So different from the way she remembered them forty years ago.

Jesus, there were some beautiful boys in 1921! Look like the whole world was bursting at the seams with them. Thirteen, fourteen, fifteen years old. Jesus, they were fine. L. P., Paul Freeman and his brother Jake, Mrs. Scott's twins—and Ajax had a whole flock of younger brothers. They hung out of attic windows, rode on car fenders, delivered the coal, moved into Medallion and moved out, visited cousins, plowed, hoisted, lounged on the church steps, careened on the school playground. The sun heated them and the moon slid down their backs. God, the world was *full* of beautiful boys in 1921.

Nothing like these kids. Everything had changed. Even the whores were better then: tough, fat, laughing women with burns on their cheeks and wit married to their meanness; or widows couched in small houses in the woods with eight children to feed and no man. These modern-day whores were pale and dull before those women. These little clothes-crazy things were always embarrassed. Nasty but shamed. They didn't know what shameless was. They should have known those silvery widows in the woods who would get up from the dinner table and walk into the trees with a customer with as much embarrassment as a calving mare.

Lord, how time flies. She hardly recognized anybody in the town any more. Now there was another old people's home. Look like this town just kept on building homes for old people. Every time they built a road they built a old folks' home. You'd think folks was living longer, but the fact of it was, they was just being put out faster.

Nel hadn't seen the insides of this most recent one yet, but it was her turn in Circle Number 5 to visit some of the old women there. The pastor visited them regularly, but the circle thought private visits were nice too. There were just nine colored women out there, the same nine that had been in the other one. But a lot of white ones. White people didn't fret about putting their old ones away. It took a lot for black people to let them go, and even if somebody was old and alone, others did the dropping by, the floor washing, the cooking. Only when they got crazy and unmanageable were they let go. Unless it was somebody like Sula, who put Eva away out of meanness. It was true that Eva was foolish in the head, but not so bad as to need locking up.

Nel was more than a little curious to see her. She had been really active in church only a year or less, and that was because the children were grown now and took up less time and less space in her mind. For over twenty-five years since Jude walked out she had pinned herself into a tiny life. She spent a little time trying to marry again, but nobody wanted to take her on with three children, and she simply couldn't manage the business of keeping boyfriends. During the war she had had a rather long relationship with a sergeant stationed at the camp twenty miles down river from Medallion, but then he got called away and everything was reduced to a few letters—then nothing. Then there was a bartender at the hotel. But now she was fifty-five and hard put to remember what all that had been about.

It didn't take long, after Jude left, for her to see what the future would be. She had looked at her children and knew in her heart that that would be all.

That they were all she would ever know of love. But it was a love that, like a pan of syrup kept too long on the stove, had cooked out, leaving only its odor and a hard, sweet sludge, impossible to scrape off. For the mouths of her children quickly forgot the taste of her nipples, and years ago they had begun to look past her face into the nearest stretch of sky.

In the meantime the Bottom had collapsed. Everybody who had made money during the war moved as close as they could to the valley, and the white people were buying down river, cross river, stretching Medallion like two strings on the banks. Nobody colored lived much up in the Bottom any more. White people were building towers for television stations up there and there was a rumor about a golf course or something. Anyway, hill land was more valuable now, and those black people who had moved down right after the war and in the fifties couldn't afford to come back even if they wanted to. Except for the few blacks still huddled by the river bend, and some undemolished houses on Carpenter's Road, only rich white folks were building homes in the hills. Just like that, they had changed their minds and instead of keeping the valley floor to themselves, now they wanted a hilltop house with a river view and a ring of elms. The black people, for all their new look, seemed awfully anxious to get to the valley, or leave town, and abandon the hills to whoever was interested. It was sad, because the Bottom had been a real place. These young ones kept talking about the community, but they left the hills to the poor, the old, the stubborn—and the rich white folks. Maybe it hadn't been a community, but it had been a place. Now there weren't any places left, just separate houses with separate televisions and separate telephones and less and less dropping by.

These were the same thoughts she always had when she walked down into the town. One of the last true pedestrians, Nel walked the shoulder road while cars slipped by. Laughed at by her children, she still walked wherever she wanted to go, allowing herself to accept rides only when the weather required it.

Now she went straight through the town and turned left at its farthest end, along a tree-lined walk that turned into a country road farther on and passed the cemetery, Beechnut Park.

When she got to Sunnydale, the home for the aged, it was already four o'clock and turning chill. She would be glad to sit down with those old birds and rest her feet.

A red-haired lady at the desk gave her a pass card and pointed to a door that opened onto a corridor of smaller doors. It looked like what she imagined a college dormitory to be. The lobby was luxurious—modern—but the rooms she peeped into were sterile green cages. There was too much light everywhere; it needed some shadows. The third door, down the hall, had a little name tag over it that read EVA PEACE. Nel twisted the knob and rapped a little on the door at the same time, then listened a moment before she opened it.

At first she couldn't believe it. She seemed so small, sitting at that table in a black-vinyl chair. All the heaviness had gone and the height. Her once beautiful leg had no stocking and the foot was in a slipper. Nel wanted to cry—not for Eva's milk-dull eyes or her floppy lips, but for the once proud foot accustomed for over a half century to a fine well-laced shoe, now stuffed gracelessly into a pink terrycloth slipper.

"Good evening, Miss Peace. I'm Nel Greene come to pay a call on you. You remember me, don't you?"

Eva was ironing and dreaming of stairwells. She had neither iron nor clothes but did not stop her fastidious lining up of pleats or pressing out of wrinkles even when she acknowledged Nel's greeting.

"Howdy. Sit down."

"Thank you." Nel sat on the edge of the little bed. "You've got a pretty room, a real pretty room, Miss Peace."

"You eat something funny today?"

"Ma'am?"

"Some chop suey? Think back."

"No, ma'am."

"No? Well you gone be sick later on."

"But I didn't have no chop suey."

"You think I come all the way over here for you to tell me that? I can't make visits too often. You should have some respect for old people."

"But Miss Peace, I'm visiting you. This is your room." Nel smiled.

"What you say your name was?"

"Nel Greene."

"Wiley Wright's girl?"

"Uh huh. You do remember. That makes me feel good, Miss Peace. You remember me and my father."

"Tell me how you killed that little boy."

"What? What little boy?"

"The one you threw in the water. I got oranges. How did you get him to go in the water?"

"I didn't throw no little boy in the river. That was Sula."

"You. Sula. What's the difference? You was there. You watched, didn't you? Me, I never would've watched."

"You're confused, Miss Peace. I'm Nel. Sula's dead."

"It's awful cold in the water. Fire is warm. How did you get him in?" Eva wet her forefinger and tested the iron's heat.

"Who told you all these lies? Miss Peace? Who told you? Why are you telling lies on me?"

"I got oranges. I don't drink they old orange juice. They puts something in it."

"Why are you trying to make out like I did it?"

Eva stopped ironing and looked at Nel. For the first time her eyes looked sane.

"You think I'm guilty?" Nel was whispering.

Eva whispered back, "Who would know that better than you?"

"I want to know who you been talking to." Nel forced herself to speak normally.

"Plum. Sweet Plum. He tells me things." Eva laughed a light, tinkly giggle—girlish.

"I'll be going now, Miss Peace." Nel stood.

"You ain't answered me yet."

"I don't know what you're talking about."

"Just alike. Both of you. Never was no difference between you. Want some oranges? It's better for you than chop suey. Sula? I got oranges."

Nel walked hurriedly down the hall, Eva calling after her, "Sula?" Nel couldn't see the other women today. That woman had upset her. She handed her pass back to the lady, avoiding her look of surprise.

Outside she fastened her coat against the rising wind. The top button was missing so she covered her throat with her hand. A bright space opened in her head and memory seeped into it.

Standing on the riverbank in a purple-and-white dress, Sula swinging Chicken Little around and around. His laughter before the hand-slip and the water closing quickly over the place. What had she felt then, watching Sula going around and around and then the little boy swinging out over the water? Sula had cried and cried when she came back from Shadrack's house. But Nel had remained calm.

"Shouldn't we tell?"

"Did he see?"

"I don't know. No."

"Let's go. We can't bring him back."

What did old Eva mean by *you watched*? How could she help seeing it? She was right there. But Eva didn't say *see*, she said *watched*. "I did not watch it. I just saw it." But it was there anyway, as it had always been, the old feeling and the old question. The good feeling she had had when Chicken's hands slipped. She hadn't wondered about that in years. "Why didn't I feel bad when it happened? How come it felt so good to see him fall?"

All these years she had been secretly proud of her calm, controlled behavior when Sula was uncontrollable, her compassion for Sula's frightened and shamed eyes. Now it seemed that what she had thought was maturity, serenity and compassion was only the tranquillity that follows a joyful stimulation. Just as the water closed peacefully over the turbulence of Chicken Little's body, so had contentment washed over her enjoyment.

She was walking too fast. Not watching where she placed her feet, she got into the weeds by the side of the road. Running almost, she approached Beechnut Park. Just over there was the colored part of the cemetery. She went in. Sula was buried there along with Plum, Hannah and now Pearl. With the same disregard for name changes by marriage that the black people of Medallion always showed, each flat slab had one word carved on it. Together they read like a chant: PEACE 1895–1921, PEACE 1890–1923, PEACE 1910–1940, PEACE 1892–1959.

They were not dead people. They were words. Not even words. Wishes, longings.

All these years she had been harboring good feelings about Eva; sharing, she believed, her loneliness and unloved state as no one else could or did. She, after all, was the only one who really understood why Eva refused to attend Sula's funeral. The others thought they knew; thought the grandmother's reasons were the same as their own—that to pay respect to someone who had caused them so much pain was beneath them. Nel, who did go, believed Eva's refusal was not due to pride or vengeance but to a plain unwillingness to see the swallowing of her own flesh into the dirt, a determination not to let the eyes see what the heart could not hold.

Now, however, after the way Eva had just treated her, accused her, she wondered if the townspeople hadn't been right the first time. Eva *was* mean. Sula had even said so. There was no good reason for her to speak so. Feeble-minded or not. Old. Whatever. Eva knew what she was doing. Always had. She had stayed away from Sula's funeral and accused Nel of drowning Chicken Little for spite. The same spite that galloped all over the Bottom. That made every gesture an offense, every off-center smile a threat, so that even the bubbles of

relief that broke in the chest of practically everybody when Sula died did not soften their spite and allow them to go to Mr. Hodges' funeral parlor or send flowers from the church or bake a yellow cake.

She thought about Nathan opening the bedroom door the day she had visited her, and finding the body. He said he knew she was dead right away not because her eyes were open but because her mouth was. It looked to him like a giant yawn that she never got to finish. He had run across the street to Teapot's Mamma, who, when she heard the news, said, "Ho!" like the conductor on the train when it was about to take off except louder, and then did a little dance. None of the women left their quilt patches in disarray to run to the house. Nobody left the clothes halfway through the wringer to run to the house. Even the men just said "uhn," when they heard. The day passed and no one came. The night slipped into another day and the body was still lying in Eva's bed gazing at the ceiling trying to complete a yawn. It was very strange, this stubbornness about Sula. For even when China, the most rambunctious whore in the town, died (whose black son and white son said, when they heard she was dying, "She ain't dead yet?"), even then everybody stopped what they were doing and turned out in numbers to put the fallen sister away.

It was Nel who finally called the hospital, then the mortuary, then the police, who were the ones to come. So the white people took over. They came in a police van and carried the body down the steps past the four pear trees and into the van for all the world as with Hannah. When the police asked questions nobody gave them any information. It took them hours to find out the dead woman's first name. The call was for a Miss Peace at 7 Carpenter's Road. So they left with that: a body, a name and an address. The white people had to wash her, dress her, prepare her and finally lower her. It was all done elegantly, for it was discovered that she had a substantial death policy. Nel went to the funeral parlor, but was so shocked by the closed coffin she stayed only a few minutes.

The following day Nel walked to the burying and found herself the only black person there, steeling her mind to the roses and pulleys. It was only when she turned to leave that she saw the cluster of black folk at the lip of the cemetery. Not coming in, not dressed for mourning, but there waiting. Not until the white folks left—the gravediggers, Mr. and Mrs. Hodges, and their young son who assisted them—did those black people from up in the Bottom enter with hooded hearts and filed eyes to sing "Shall We Gather at the River" over the curved earth that cut them off from the most magnificent hatred they had ever known. Their question clotted the October air, Shall We Gather at the River? The beautiful, the beautiful river? Perhaps Sula answered them even then, for it began to rain, and the women ran in tiny leaps through the grass for fear their straightened hair would beat them home.

Sadly, heavily, Nel left the colored part of the cemetery. Further along the road Shadrack passed her by. A little shaggier, a little older, still energetically mad, he looked at the woman hurrying along the road with the sunset in her face.

He stopped. Trying to remember where he had seen her before. The effort of recollection was too much for him and he moved on. He had to haul some trash out at Sunnydale and it would be good and dark before he got home. He hadn't sold fish in a long time now. The river had killed them all. No more silver-gray flashes, no more flat, wide, unhurried look. No more slowing down of gills. No more tremor on the line.

Shadrack and Nel moved in opposite directions, each thinking separate thoughts about the past. The distance between them increased as they both remembered gone things.

Suddenly Nel stopped. Her eye twitched and burned a little.

"Sula?" she whispered, gazing at the tops of trees. "Sula?"

Leaves stirred; mud shifted; there was the smell of overripe green things. A soft ball of fur broke and scattered like dandelion spores in the breeze.

"All that time, all that time, I thought I was missing Jude." And the loss pressed down on her chest and came up into her throat. "We was girls together," she said as though explaining something. "O Lord, Sula," she cried, "girl, girl, girlgirlgirl."

It was a fine cry—loud and long—but it had no bottom and it had no top, just circles and circles of sorrow.

1973

ALICE MUNRO

1931–

Fashioning an art that, in the words of the novelist-critic Joyce Carol Oates, "works to conceal itself, in order to celebrate its subject," Alice Munro has published several prize-winning volumes of short stories and two story-sequences that have been read as novels, *Lives of Girls and Women* (1971) and *Who Do You Think You Are?* (1978). The latter, issued in the United States as *The Beggar Maid: Stories of Flo and Rose,* is typical of Munro's work, focusing, as it does, on the relationship of a stepmother (Flo) and a stepdaughter (Rose), who confront their emotionally subtle responses to each other and to the banal people and everyday events that nevertheless continue to surprise them. More recently, Munro has published *The Moons of Jupiter* (1982), *The Progress of Love* (1986), and *Open Secrets* (1994). The subjects celebrated in many of these works are the small-town Canadians who inhabit the southwestern Ontario of her own childhood. Born in Wingham, Ontario, the daughter of farmers, Alice Laidlaw attended the University of Western Ontario before marrying the bookseller James Munro in 1951. Although she brought up her three daughters in Vancouver and Victoria, Munro returned in 1972 to western Ontario. After a divorce in 1976, she married Gerald Fremlin, a geographer. As a reader, Munro has explained, she can "go into [a story], and move back and forth and settle here and there, and stay in it for a while." As a writer, too, she meditates on the enigmatic interrelationships of past and present in a landscape evocative enough to sustain her vision. Whether she writes about piano recitals, high school dances, chance sexual encounters, or fox farming, that vision frequently centers on the lives of girls and women. In *Wild Swans* she broods on a recurring theme, namely what she calls "the pain of human contact . . . the fascinating pain; the humiliating necessity."

Wild Swans

Flo said to watch for White Slavers. She said this was how they operated: an old woman, a motherly or grandmotherly sort, made friends while riding beside you on a bus or train. She offered you candy, which was drugged. Pretty

soon you began to droop and mumble, were in no condition to speak for yourself. Oh, help, the woman said, my daughter (granddaughter) is sick, please somebody help me get her off so that she can recover in the fresh air. Up stepped a polite gentleman, pretending to be a stranger, offering assistance. Together, at the next stop, they hustled you off the train or bus, and that was the last the ordinary world ever saw of you. They kept you a prisoner in the White Slave place (to which you had been transported drugged and bound so you wouldn't even know where you were), until such time as you were thoroughly degraded and in despair, your insides torn up by drunken men and invested with vile disease, your mind destroyed by drugs, your hair and teeth fallen out. It took about three years, for you to get to this state. You wouldn't want to go home, then, maybe couldn't remember home, or find your way if you did. So they let you out on the streets.

Flo took ten dollars and put it in a little cloth bag which she sewed to the strap of Rose's slip. Another thing likely to happen was that Rose would get her purse stolen.

Watch out, Flo said as well, for people dressed up as ministers. They were the worst. That disguise was commonly adopted by White Slavers, as well as those after your money.

Rose said she didn't see how she could tell which ones were disguised.

Flo had worked in Toronto once. She had worked as a waitress in a coffee shop in Union Station. That was how she knew all she knew. She never saw sunlight, in those days, except on her days off. But she saw plenty else. She saw a man cut another man's stomach with a knife, just pull out his shirt and do a tidy cut, as if it was a watermelon not a stomach. The stomach's owner just sat looking down surprised, with no time to protest. Flo implied that that was nothing, in Toronto. She saw two bad women (that was what Flo called whores, running the two words together, like badminton) get into a fight, and a man laughed at them, other men stopped and laughed and egged them on, and they had their fists full of each other's hair. At last the police came and took them away, still howling and yelping.

She saw a child die of a fit, too. Its face was black as ink.

"Well I'm not scared," said Rose provokingly. "There's the police, anyway."

"Oh, them! They'd be the first ones to diddle you!"

She did not believe anything Flo said on the subject of sex. Consider the undertaker.

A little bald man, very neatly dressed, would come into the store sometimes and speak to Flo with a placating expression.

"I only wanted a bag of candy. And maybe a few packages of gum. And one or two chocolate bars. Could you go to the trouble of wrapping them?"

Flo in her mock-deferential tone would assure him that she could. She wrapped them in heavy-duty white paper, so they were something like presents. He took his time with the selection, humming and chatting, then dawdled for a while. He might ask how Flo was feeling. And how Rose was, if she was there.

"You look pale. Young girls need fresh air." To Flo he would say, "You work too hard. You've worked hard all your life."

"No rest for the wicked," Flo would say agreeably.

When he went out she hurried to the window. There it was—the old black hearse with its purple curtains.

"He'll be after them today!" Flo would say as the hearse rolled away at a
gentle pace, almost a funeral pace. The little man had been an undertaker, but
he was retired now. The hearse was retired too. His sons had taken over the un-
dertaking and bought a new one. He drove the old hearse all over the country,
looking for women. So Flo said. Rose could not believe it. Flo said he gave
them the gum and the candy. Rose said he probably ate them himself. Flo said
he had been seen, he had been heard. In mild weather he drove with the win-
dows down, singing, to himself or to somebody out of sight in the back.

> Her brow is like the snowdrift
> Her throat is like the swan

Flo imitated him singing. Gently overtaking some woman walking on a back
road, or resting at a country crossroads. All compliments and courtesy and
chocolate bars, offering a ride. Of course every woman who reported being
asked said she had turned him down. He never pestered anybody, drove po-
litely on. He called in at houses, and if the husband was home he seemed to
like just as well as anything to sit and chat. Wives said that was all he ever did
anyway but Flo did not believe it.

"Some women are taken in," she said. "A number." She liked to speculate on
what the hearse was like inside. Plush. Plush on the walls and the roof and the
floor. Soft purple, the color of the curtains, the color of dark lilacs.

All nonsense, Rose thought. Who could believe it, of a man that age?

Rose was going to Toronto on the train for the first time by herself. She had
been once before, but that was with Flo, long before her father died. They
took along their own sandwiches and bought milk from the vendor on the
train. It was sour. Sour chocolate milk. Rose kept taking tiny sips, unwilling to
admit that something so much desired could fail her. Flo sniffed it, then
hunted up and down the train until she found the old man in his red jacket,
with no teeth and the tray hanging around his neck. She invited him to sam-
ple the chocolate milk. She invited people nearby to smell it. He let her have
some ginger ale for nothing. It was slightly warm.

"I let him know," Flo said looking around after he had left. "You have to let
them know."

A woman agreed with her but most people looked out the window. Rose
drank the warm ginger ale. Either that, or the scene with the vendor, or the
conversation Flo and the agreeing woman now got into about where they
came from, why they were going to Toronto, and Rose's morning constipation
which was why she was lacking color, or the small amount of chocolate milk
she had got inside her, caused her to throw up in the train toilet. All day long
she was afraid people in Toronto could smell vomit on her coat.

This time Flo started the trip off by saying, "Keep an eye on her, she's never
been away from home before!" to the conductor, then looking around and
laughing, to show that was jokingly meant. Then she had to get off. It seemed
the conductor had no more need for jokes than Rose had, and no intention of
keeping an eye on anybody. He never spoke to Rose except to ask for her ticket.
She had a window seat, and was soon extraordinarily happy. She felt Flo re-
ceding, West Hanratty flying away from her, her own wearying self discarded
as easily as everything else. She loved the towns less and less known. A woman

was standing at her back door in her nightgown, not caring if everybody on the train saw her. They were traveling south, out of the snow belt, into an earlier spring, a tenderer sort of landscape. People could grow peach trees in their backyards.

Rose collected in her mind the things she had to look for in Toronto. First, things for Flo. Special stockings for her varicose veins. A special kind of cement for sticking handles on pots. And a full set of dominoes.

For herself Rose wanted to buy hair-remover to put on her arms and legs, and if possible an arrangement of inflatable cushions, supposed to reduce your hips and thighs. She thought they probably had hair-remover in the drugstore in Hanratty, but the woman in there was a friend of Flo's and told everything. She told Flo who bought hair dye and slimming medicine and French safes.[1] As for the cushion business, you could send away for it but there was sure to be a comment at the Post Office, and Flo knew people there as well. She also planned to buy some bangles, and an angora sweater. She had great hopes of silver bangles and powder-blue angora. She thought they could transform her, make her calm and slender and take the frizz out of her hair, dry her underarms and turn her complexion to pearl.

The money for these things, as well as the money for the trip, came from a prize Rose had won, for writing an essay called "Art and Science in the World of Tomorrow." To her surprise, Flo asked if she could read it, and while she was reading it, she remarked that they must have thought they had to give Rose the prize for swallowing the dictionary. Then she said shyly, "It's very interesting."

She would have to spend the night at Cela McKinney's. Cela McKinney was her father's cousin. She had married a hotel manager and thought she had gone up in the world. But the hotel manager came home one day and sat down on the dining room floor between two chairs and said, "I am never going to leave this house again." Nothing unusual had happened, he had just decided not to go out of the house again, and he didn't, until he died. That had made Cela McKinney odd and nervous. She locked her doors at eight o'clock. She was also very stingy. Supper was usually oatmeal porridge, with raisins. Her house was dark and narrow and smelled like a bank.

The train was filling up. At Brantford a man asked if she would mind if he sat down beside her.

"It's cooler out than you'd think," he said. He offered her part of his newspaper. She said no thanks.

Then lest he think her rude she said it really was cooler. She went on looking out the window at the spring morning. There was no snow left, down here. The trees and bushes seemed to have a paler bark than they did at home. Even the sunlight looked different. It was as different from home, here, as the coast of the Mediterranean would be, or the valleys of California.

"Filthy windows, you'd think they'd take more care," the man said. "Do you travel much by train?"

She said no.

Water was lying in the fields. He nodded at it and said there was a lot this year.

1. Condoms.

"Heavy snows."

She noticed his saying *snows*, a poetic-sounding word. Anyone at home would have said *snow*.

"I had an unusual experience the other day. I was driving out in the country. In fact I was on my way to see one of my parishioners, a lady with a heart condition—"

She looked quickly at his collar. He was wearing an ordinary shirt and tie and a dark blue suit.

"Oh, yes," he said. "I'm a United Church minister. But I don't always wear my uniform. I wear it for preaching in. I'm off duty today."

"Well as I said I was driving through the country and I saw some Canada geese down on a pond, and I took another look, and there were some swans down with them. A whole great flock of swans. What a lovely sight they were. They would be on their spring migration, I expect, heading up north. What a spectacle. I never saw anything like it."

Rose was unable to think appreciatively of the wild swans because she was afraid he was going to lead the conversation from them to Nature in general and then to God, the way a minister would feel obliged to do. But he did not, he stopped with the swans.

"A very fine sight. You would have enjoyed them."

He was between fifty and sixty years old, Rose thought. He was short, and energetic-looking, with a square ruddy face and bright waves of gray hair combed straight up from his forehead. When she realized he was not going to mention God she felt she ought to show her gratitude.

She said they must have been lovely.

"It wasn't even a regular pond, it was only some water lying in a field. It was just luck the water was lying there and they came down and I came driving by at the right time. Just luck. They come in at the east end of Lake Erie, I think. But I never was lucky enough to see them before."

She turned by degrees to the window, and he returned to his paper. She remained slightly smiling, so as not to seem rude, not to seem to be rejecting conversation altogether. The morning really was cool, and she had taken down her coat off the hook where she put it when she first got on the train, she had spread it over herself, like a lap robe. She had set her purse on the floor when the minister sat down, to give him room. He took the sections of the paper apart, shaking and rustling them in a leisurely, rather showy, way. He seemed to her the sort of person who does everything in a showy way. A ministerial way. He brushed aside the sections he didn't want at the moment. A corner of newspaper touched her leg, just at the edge of her coat.

She thought for some time that it was the paper. Then she said to herself, what if it is a hand? That was the kind of thing she could imagine. She would sometimes look at men's hands, at the fuzz on their forearms, their concentrating profiles. She would think about everything they could do. Even the stupid ones. For instance the driver-salesman who brought the bread to Flo's store. The ripeness and confidence of manner, the settled mixture of ease and alertness with which he handled the bread truck. A fold of mature belly over the belt did not displease her. Another time she had her eye on the French teacher at school. Not a Frenchman at all, really, his name was McLaren, but Rose thought teaching French had rubbed off on him, made him look like one. Quick and sallow; sharp shoulders; hooked nose and sad eyes. She saw

him lapping and coiling his way through slow pleasures, a perfect autocrat of indulgences. She had a considerable longing to be somebody's object. Pounded, pleasured, reduced, exhausted.

But what if it was a hand? What if it really was a hand? She shifted slightly, moved as much as she could toward the window. Her imagination seemed to have created this reality, a reality she was not prepared for at all. She found it alarming. She was concentrating on that leg, that bit of skin with the stocking over it. She could not bring herself to look. Was there a pressure, or was there not? She shifted again. Her legs had been, and remained, tightly closed. It was. It was a hand. It was a hand's pressure.

Please don't. That was what she tried to say. She shaped the words in her mind, tried them out, then couldn't get them past her lips. Why was that? The embarrassment, was it, the fear that people might hear? People were all around them, the seats were full.

It was not only that.

She did manage to look at him, not raising her head but turning it cautiously. He had tilted his seat back and closed his eyes. There was his dark blue suit sleeve, disappearing under the newspaper. He had arranged the paper so that it overlapped Rose's coat. His hand was underneath, simply resting, as if flung out in sleep.

Now, Rose could have shifted the newspaper and removed her coat. If he was not asleep, he would have been obliged to draw back his hand. If he was asleep, if he did not draw it back, she could have whispered, *Excuse me,* and set his hand firmly on his own knee. This solution, so obvious and foolproof, did not occur to her. And she would have to wonder, why not? The minister's hand was not, or not yet, at all welcome to her. It made her feel uncomfortable, resentful, slightly disgusted, trapped and wary. But she could not take charge of it, to reject it. She could not insist that it was there, when he seemed to be insisting that it was not. How could she declare him responsible, when he lay there so harmless and trusting, resting himself before his busy day, with such a pleased and healthy face? A man older than her father would be, if he were living, a man used to deference, an appreciator of Nature, delighter in wild swans. If she did say *Please don't* she was sure he would ignore her, as if overlooking some silliness or impoliteness on her part. She knew that as soon as she said it she would hope he had not heard.

But there was more to it than that. Curiosity. More constant, more imperious, than any lust. A lust in itself, that will make you draw back and wait, wait too long, risk almost anything, just to see what will happen. *To see what will happen.*

The hand began, over the next several miles, the most delicate, the most timid, pressures and investigations. Not asleep. Or if he was, his hand wasn't. She did feel disgust. She felt a faint, wandering nausea. She thought of flesh: lumps of flesh, pink snouts, fat tongues, blunt fingers, all on their way trotting and creeping and lolling and rubbing, looking for their comfort. She thought of cats in heat rubbing themselves along the top of board fences, yowling with their miserable complaint. It was pitiful, infantile, this itching and shoving and squeezing. Spongy tissues, inflamed membranes, tormented nerve-ends, shameful smells; humiliation.

All that was starting. His hand, that she wouldn't ever have wanted to hold, that she wouldn't have squeezed back, his stubborn patient hand was able,

after all, to get the ferns to rustle and the streams to flow, to waken a sly luxuriance.

Nevertheless, she would rather not. She would still rather not. Please remove this, she said out the window. Stop it, please, she said to the stumps and barns. The hand moved up her leg past the top of her stocking to her bare skin, had moved higher, under her suspender, reached her underpants and the lower part of her belly. Her legs were still crossed, pinched together. While her legs stayed crossed she could lay claim to innocence, she had not admitted anything. She could still believe that she would stop this in a minute. Nothing was going to happen, nothing more. Her legs were never going to open.

But they were. They were. As the train crossed the Niagra Escarpment above Dundas, as they looked down at the preglacial valley, the silver-wooded rubble of little hills, as they came sliding down to the shores of Lake Ontario, she would make this slow, and silent, and definite, declaration, perhaps disappointing as much as satisfying the hand's owner. He would not lift his eyelids, his face would not alter, his fingers would not hesitate, but would go powerfully and discreetly to work. Invasion, and welcome, and sunlight flashing far and wide on the lake water; miles of bare orchards stirring round Burlington.

This was disgrace, this was beggary. But what harm in that, we say to ourselves at such moments, what harm in anything, the worse the better, as we ride the cold wave of greed, of greedy assent. A stranger's hand, or root vegetables or humble kitchen tools that people tell jokes about; the world is tumbling with innocent-seeming objects ready to declare themselves, slippery and obliging. She was careful of her breathing. She could not believe this. Victim and accomplice she was borne past Glassco's Jams and Marmalades, past the big pulsating pipes of oil refineries. They glided into suburbs where bedsheets, and towels used to wipe up intimate stains, flapped leeringly on the clotheslines, where even the children seemed to be frolicking lewdly in the schoolyards, and the very truckdrivers stopped at the railway crossings must be thrusting their thumbs gleefully into curled hands. Such cunning antics now, such popular visions. The gates and towers of the Exhibition Grounds came into view, the painted domes and pillars floated marvelously against her eyelids' rosy sky. Then flew apart in celebration. You could have had such a flock of birds, wild swans, even, wakened under one big dome together, exploding from it, taking to the sky.

She bit the edge of her tongue. Very soon the conductor passed through the train, to stir the travelers, warn them back to life.

In the darkness under the station the United Church minister, refreshed, opened his eyes and got his paper folded together, then asked if she would like some help with her coat. His gallantry was self-satisfied, dismissive. No, said Rose, with a sore tongue. He hurried out of the train ahead of her. She did not see him in the station. She never saw him again in her life. But he remained on call, so to speak, for years and years, ready to slip into place at a critical moment, without even any regard, later on, for husband or lovers. What recommended him? She could never understand it. His simplicity, his arrogance, his perversely appealing lack of handsomeness, even of ordinary grown-up masculinity? When he stood up she saw that he was shorter even than she had thought, that his face was pink and shiny, that there was something crude and pushy and childish about him.

Was he a minister, really, or was that only what he said? Flo had mentioned

people who were not ministers, dressed up as if they were. Not real ministers dressed as if they were not. Or, stranger still, men who were not real ministers pretending to be real but dressed as if they were not. But that she had come as close as she had, to what could happen, was an unwelcome thing. Rose walked through Union Station feeling the little bag with the ten dollars rubbing at her, knew she would feel it all day long, rubbing its reminder against her skin.

She couldn't stop getting Flo's messages, even with that. She remembered, because she was in Union Station, that there was a girl named Mavis working here, in the Gift Shop, when Flo was working in the coffee shop. Mavis had warts on her eyelids that looked like they were going to turn into sties but they didn't, they went away. Maybe she had them removed, Flo didn't ask. She was very good-looking, without them. There was a movie star in those days she looked a lot like. The movie star's name was Frances Farmer.

Frances Farmer. Rose had never heard of her.

That was the name. And Mavis went and bought herself a big hat that dipped over one eye and a dress entirely made of lace. She went off for the weekend to Georgian Bay, to a resort up there. She booked herself in under the name of Florence Farmer. To give everybody the idea she was really the other one, Frances Farmer, but calling herself Florence because she was on holiday and didn't want to be recognized. She had a little cigarette holder that was black and mother-of-pearl. She could have been arrested, Flo said. For the *nerve*.

Rose almost went over to the Gift Shop, to see if Mavis was still there and if she could recognize her. She thought it would be an especially fine thing, to manage a transformation like that. To care it; to get away with it, to enter on preposterous adventures in your own, but newly named, skin.

1978

SYLVIA PLATH
1932–1963

"I am afraid of getting older," wrote the seventeen-year-old Sylvia Plath in 1949, "I am afraid of getting married. Spare me from cooking three meals a day—spare me from the relentless cage of routine and rote. I want to be free. . . . I want, I think, to be ominiscient I think I would like to call myself The girl who wanted to be God.' " Plath's adolescent anxieties were prophetic, for, fourteen years after she wrote these words, the failure of her marriage and the "relentless cage of routine and rote" in which she felt imprisoned as she struggled alone in London to care for two young children appear to have led directly to her suicide, an event that continues to arouse controversy. Equally controversial, however, is the poetry that she wrote shortly before she died. Published posthumously in *Ariel* (1965), her last verses are fiercely innovative and sometimes ferociously vituperative, exulting in their own aesthetic liberation as if to remind us of the early ambitions of this "girl who wanted to be God." Excoriated by some critics for—in the words of the British psychoanalyst David Holbrook—seducing "us to taste of [their] poisoned chalice," they have also been praised as—in the phrase of the American poet Robert Lowell—the productions of "one of those super-real, hypnotic, great classical heroines."

The girl who was to end her life as the center of both a personal and a public melodrama was born and brought up in comparatively quiet, middle-class circumstances. Her parents, German immigrants, were ambitious, hardworking professionals: Otto Plath, an entomologist, taught at Boston University, where Aurelia Plath was also to become a faculty member, teaching secretarial skills. The older of two children, Sylvia Plath herself exhibited an early precocity as well as a penchant for hard work. With her mother's encouragement, she began to write stories and poems when she was quite young, and by the time she confided to her diary that she wanted to be "omniscient" she had already published some of this work in *Seventeen* and other periodicals. What might have been simply a prosperous and productive girlhood had been darkened, however, by her father's death (from a gangrenous leg, to which she refers in *Daddy*) when she was eight. In the myth into which she increasingly transformed her life throughout her later work—for example, the sardonic curse-poem *Daddy* (1963) and the autobiographical novel *The Bell Jar* (1963)—this event consistently played a central part, marking a fall from childhood innocence to adult experience, from grace to loss.

In 1950, Plath won a scholarship to Smith College, where for several years she continued her career as a "superachiever," accumulating a steady string of honors and prizes along with high grades and accolades from her teachers. But the distinction that made the greatest difference in her career at the time (as well as in her later life) proved problematic: in 1953, Plath became one of a dozen "Guest Editors" of the New York fashion magazine *Mademoiselle* and traveled to the city to work on the journal's staff for a month. Thinly fictionalized, her feelings and experiences there are recounted in some detail in *The Bell Jar*, where she records the ambivalences that marked her initiation into the Madison Avenue world of female glamour and professional high style. Returning to her mother's home in Wellesley, Massachusetts, she suffered a serious breakdown and she attempted suicide—an attempt that she would later record not only in *The Bell Jar* but also in such poems as *Daddy* and *Lady Lazarus*.

Following her breakdown, Plath was institutionalized for a year and given (among other therapies) electric shock treatments, treatments whose intensity may inform some of her most violent metaphors of physical and spiritual transformation. When she returned to Smith in 1954, however, she seems easily to have resumed her successful academic career. In 1955, she graduated *summa cum laude* and won a Fulbright to Cambridge University, where she studied for a graduate degree in English literature and where, in 1956, she met and married the poet Ted Hughes, an ambitious and energetic artist whose intellectual and emotional support significantly aided her development during their early years together. In the late 1950s, the couple traveled to the United States, and Plath taught for a year at Smith, but, passionately committed to her literary vocation, she ultimately rejected academic ambition. Instead, she and Hughes settled first in London, then in a farmhouse in Devon, where Plath devoted herself to writing and to her two children—Frieda and Nicholas—born in the early 1960s.

After her marriage broke up in the summer of 1962, Plath moved back to London and struggled to continue her work while caring for her children through the coldest winter England had seen in decades. Her letters to her mother from this period (edited in *Letters Home*, by Aurelia Schober Plath) are characterized by intense bitterness over the collapse of her marriage and mounting anxiety about her future and her children's. At the same time, they are marked by extraordinary exultation, for Plath was now producing—sometimes at the rate of two or three a day—the poems that would later appear in *Ariel*, and she knew their value. "I am a writer . . . I am a genius of a writer . . . I am writing the best poems of my life; they will make my name," she told her mother. Nevertheless, despite her awareness of the nature of her achievement, there is considerable evidence that she was again experiencing a breakdown not unlike the one that had led to her suicide attempt

in 1953. Early in the morning of February 11, 1963, she left mugs of milk next to her children's cribs, carefully stuffed towels into the cracks around her kitchen door, and gassed herself in the oven of her stove.

The mythologizing of self and family that energizes Plath's later poems, as well as earlier works like *The Colossus* and *The Disquieting Muses*, has almost certainly led to much of the critical misunderstanding that continues to surround her poetry with controversy. About *Daddy* for instance, the critic Elizabeth Hardwick has complained that Plath's real father "died of a long illness, but there is no pity for *his* lost life," adding that he "did not kill anyone and 'the fat black heart' [of the poem] is really [Plath's] own," and concluding that to bring "strangers, the town . . . into the punishment of her father . . . is somehow the most biting and ungenerous thought of all." The problem with such remarks, which are representative of a good many attacks that have been mounted against Plath, is that the literary figure of "Daddy" in the poem of that name (like the father figure in *The Colossus*) is not identical with, but rather *generalized* from, Plath's literal father.

Similarly, though late poems like *Ariel, Fever 103,* and *Edge* are death-haunted, they cannot be said to "predict" Plath's suicide, despite Robert Lowell's comment that these verses 'are playing Russian roulette with six cartridges in the cylinder." Rather, it is important to understand that Plath's demise, far from being the consequence of fearfully unleashed imaginative forces, was the result of a series of personal calamities. Lately, some feminists have worried that because this artist was not a "survivor" she does not offer younger women who study her life a "positive role model." Yet, as Plath's own poems show, the works that would "make [her] name" were inspired by yearning to endure and overcome the ice of circumstance. *Wintering,* the poem with which she herself had planned to end *Ariel,* concludes with a question and answer that express just such longing. "Will the hive survive, . . . / To enter another year?' the poet wonders, and replies to her own query with an affirmation of certainty: "The bees are flying. They taste the spring." Sylvia Plath herself may not have lasted out her struggle to "taste" another spring, but her poems record her will to triumph.

The Disquieting Muses[1]

Mother, mother, what illbred aunt
Or what disfigured and unsightly
Cousin did you so unwisely keep
Unasked to my christening,[2] that she
Sent these ladies in her stead 5
With heads like darning-eggs to nod
And nod and nod at foot and head
And at the left side of my crib?

Mother, who made to order stories
Of Mixie Blackshort the heroic bear, 10
Mother, whose witches always, always
Got baked into gingerbread,[3] I wonder
Whether you saw them, whether you said

1. Greek goddesses of the arts and learning, and sources of inspiration.
2. An allusion to the fairy tale *Sleeping Beauty* in which a young princess is cast into a deep sleep by a spiteful aunt who was not invited to the girl's christen-ing.
3. An allusion to the story of Hansel and Gretel, who baked the murderous witch who lived in a gingerbread house.

Words to rid me of those three ladies
Nodding by night around my bed, 15
Mouthless, eyeless, with stitched bald head.

In the hurricane, when father's twelve
Study windows bellied in
Like bubbles about to break, you fed
My brother and me cookies and Ovaltine 20
And helped the two of us to choir:
"Thor[4] is angry: boom boom boom!
Thor is angry: we don't care!"
But those ladies broke the panes.

When on tiptoe the schoolgirls danced, 25
Blinking flashlights like fireflies
And singing the glowworm song, I could
Not lift a foot in the twinkle-dress
But, heavy-footed, stood aside
In the shadow cast by my dismal-headed 30
Godmothers, and you cried and cried:
And the shadows stretched, the lights went out.

Mother, you sent me to piano lessons
And praised my arabesques and trills
Although each teacher found my touch 35
Oddly wooden in spite of scales
And the hours of practicing, my ear
Tone-deaf and yes, unteachable.
I learned, I learned, I learned elsewhere,
From muses unhired by you, dear mother. 40

I woke one day to see you, mother,
Floating above me in bluest air
On a green balloon bright with a million
Flowers and bluebirds that never were
Never, never, found anywhere. 45
But the little planet bobbed away
Like a soap-bubble as you called: Come here!
And I faced my traveling companions.

Day now, night now, at head, side, feet,
They stand their vigil in gowns of stone, 50
Faces blank as the day I was born,
Their shadows long in the setting sun
That never brightens or goes down.
And this is the kingdom you bore me to,
Mother, mother. But no frown of mine 55
Will betray the company I keep.

1957 1960

4. The Norse god of war and thunder.

The Colossus[1]

I shall never get you put together entirely,
Pieced, glued, and properly jointed.
Mule-bray, pig-grunt and bawdy cackles
Proceed from your great lips.
It's worse than a barnyard. 5

Perhaps you consider yourself an oracle,
Mouthpiece of the dead, or of some god or other.
Thirty years now I have labored
To dredge the silt from your throat.
I am none the wiser. 10

Scaling little ladders with gluepots and pails of Lysol
I crawl like an ant in mourning
Over the weedy acres of your brow
To mend the immense skull-plates and clear
The bald, white tumuli[2] of your eyes. 15

A blue sky out of the Oresteia[3]
Arches above us. O father, all by yourself
You are pithy and historical as the Roman Forum.[4]
I open my lunch on a hill of black cypress.
Your fluted bones and acanthine[5] hair are littered 20

In their old anarchy to the horizon-line.
It would take more than a lightning-stroke
To create such a ruin.
Nights, I squat in the cornucopia
Of your left ear, out of the wind, 25

Counting the red stars and those of plum-color.
The sun rises under the pillar of your tongue.
My hours are married to shadow.
No longer do I listen for the scrape of a keel
On the blank stones of the landing. 30

1959 1960

You're

Clownlike, happiest on your hands,
Feet to the stars, and moon-skulled,
Gilled like a fish. A common-sense
Thumbs-down on the dodo's mode.

1. A gigantic statue that stood at the entrance to the harbor of Rhodes, Greece in the 3rd century B.C.
2. Grave mounds.
3. A cycle of three plays by Aeschylus (525–456 B.C.) that recount the story of the young Greek prince Orestes' efforts to avenge the murder of his father, Agamemnon

4. The public square in ancient Rome, where legal and political proceedings took place.
5. I.e., sculptured (as in Greek columns) like the leaves of the acanthus plant. "Fluted": grooved (again, as in columns).

Wrapped up in yourself like a spool, 5
Trawling your dark as owls do.
Mute as a turnip from the Fourth
Of July to All Fools' Day,[1]
O high-riser, my little loaf.

Vague as fog and looked for like mail. 10
Farther off than Australia.
Bent-backed Atlas,[2] our traveled prawn.
Snug as a bud and at home
Like a sprat in a pickle jug.
A creel of eels, all ripples. 15
Jumpy as a Mexican bean.
Right, like a well-done sum.
A clean slate, with your own face on.

 1960

Mirror

I am silver and exact. I have no preconceptions.
Whatever I see I swallow immediately
Just as it is, unmisted by love or dislike.
I am not cruel, only truthful—
The eye of a little god, four-cornered. 5
Most of the time I meditate on the opposite wall.
It is pink, with speckles. I have looked at it so long
I think it is part of my heart. But it flickers.
Faces and darkness separate us over and over.

Now I am a lake. A woman bends over me, 10
Searching my reaches for what she really is.
Then she turns to those liars, the candles or the moon.
I see her back, and reflect it faithfully.
She rewards me with tears and an agitation of hands.
I am important to her. She comes and goes. 15
Each morning it is her face that replaces the darkness.
In me she has drowned a young girl, and in me an old woman
Rises toward her day after day, like a terrible fish.

 1961

The Bee Meeting

Who are these people at the bridge to meet me? They are the villagers—
The rector, the midwife, the sexton, the agent for bees.
In my sleeveless summery dress I have no protection,
And they are all gloved and covered, why did nobody tell me?
They are smiling and taking out veils tacked to ancient hats. 5

1. I.e., April Fool's Day.
2. In Greek mythology, the Titan Atlas was con-
demned by Zeus to uphold the heavens on his shoul-
ders.

I am nude as a chicken neck, does nobody love me?
Yes, here is the secretary of bees with her white shop smock,
Buttoning the cuffs at my wrists and the slit from my neck to my knees.
Now I am milkweed silk, the bees will not notice.
They will not smell my fear, my fear, my fear. 10

Which is the rector now, is it that man in black?
Which is the midwife, is that her blue coat?
Everybody is nodding a square black head, they are knights in visors,
Breastplates of cheesecloth knotted under the armpits.
Their smiles and their voices are changing. I am led through a beanfield. 15

Strips of tinfoil winking like people,
Feather dusters fanning their hands in a sea of bean flowers,
Creamy bean flowers with black eyes and leaves like bored hearts.
Is it blood clots the tendrils are dragging up that string?
No, no, it is scarlet flowers that will one day be edible. 20

Now they are giving me a fashionable white straw Italian hat
And a black veil that molds to my face, they are making me one of them.
They are leading me to the shorn grove, the circle of hives.
Is it the hawthorn that smells so sick?
The barren body of hawthorn, etherizing its children. 25

Is it some operation that is taking place?
It is the surgeon my neighbors are waiting for,
This apparition in a green helmet,
Shining gloves and white suit.
Is it the butcher, the grocer, the postman, someone I know? 30

I cannot run, I am rooted, and the gorse hurts me
With its yellow purses, its spiky armory.
I could not run without having to run forever.
The white hive is snug as a virgin,
Sealing off her brood cells, her honey, and quietly humming. 35

Smoke rolls and scarves in the grove.
The mind of the hive thinks this is the end of everything.
Here they come, the outriders, on their hysterical elastics.
If I stand very still, they will think I am cow-parsley.
A gullible head untouched by their animosity, 40

Not even nodding, a personage in a hedgerow.
The villagers open the chambers, they are hunting the queen.[1]
Is she hiding, is she eating honey? She is very clever.
She is old, old, old, she must live another year, and she knows it.
While in their finger-joint cells the new virgins 45

Dream of a duel they will win inevitably,
A curtain of wax dividing them from the bride flight,
The upflight of the murderess into a heaven that loves her.

1. I.e., the queen bee.

The villagers are moving the virgins, there will be no killing.
The old queen does not show herself, is she so ungrateful? 50

I am exhausted, I am exhausted—
Pillar of white in a blackout of knives.
I am the magician's girl who does not flinch.
The villagers are untying their disguises, they are shaking hands.
Whose is that long white box in the grove, what have they accomplished,
 why am I cold. 55

October 3, 1962 1963

The Arrival of the Bee Box

I ordered this, this clean wood box
Square as a chair and almost too heavy to lift.
I would say it was the coffin of a midget
Or a square baby
Were there not such a din in it. 5

The box is locked, it is dangerous.
I have to live with it overnight
And I can't keep away from it.
There are no windows, so I can't see what is in there.
There is only a little grid, no exit. 10

I put my eye to the grid.
It is dark, dark,
With the swarmy feeling of African hands
Minute and shrunk for export,
Black on black, angrily clambering. 15

How can I let them out?
It is the noise that appalls me most of all,
The unintelligible syllables.
It is like a Roman mob,[1]
Small, taken one by one, but my god, together! 20

I lay my ear to furious Latin.
I am not a Caesar.[2]
I have simply ordered a box of maniacs.
They can be sent back.
They can die, I need feed them nothing, I am the owner. 25

I wonder how hungry they are.
I wonder if they would forget me
If I just undid the locks and stood back and turned into a tree.
There is the laburnum, its blond colonnades,
And the petticoats of the cherry. 30

1. Thought of (as in Shakespeare's *Julius Caesar*) as 2. I.e., Roman ruler, emperor.
being unruly and unmanageable.

They might ignore me immediately
In my moon suit and funeral veil.
I am no source of honey
So why should they turn on me?
Tomorrow I will be sweet God, I will set them free. 35

The box is only temporary.

October 4, 1962 1963

Stings

Bare-handed, I hand the combs.
The man in white smiles, bare-handed.
Our cheesecloth gauntlets neat and sweet,
The throats of our wrists brave lilies.
He and I 5

Have a thousand clean cells between us,
Eight combs of yellow cups,
And the hive itself a teacup,
White with pink flowers on it,
With excessive love I enameled it 10

Thinking "Sweetness, sweetness."
Brood cells gray as the fossils of shells
Terrify me, they seem so old.
What am I buying, wormy mahogany?
Is there any queen at all in it? 15

If there is, she is old,
Her wings torn shawls, her long body
Rubbed of its plush—
Poor and bare and unqueenly and even shameful.
I stand in a column 20

Of winged, unmiraculous women,
Honey-drudgers.[1]
I am no drudge
Though for years I have eaten dust
And dried plates with my dense hair. 25

And seen my strangeness evaporate,
Blue dew from dangerous skin.
Will they hate me,
These women who only scurry,
Whose news is the open cherry, the open clover? 30

It is almost over.
I am in control.

1. I.e., the female worker bees who produce the hive's honey.

Here is my honey-machine,
It will work without thinking,
Opening, in spring, like an industrious virgin 35

To scour the creaming crests
As the moon, for its ivory powders, scours the sea.
A third person is watching.
He has nothing to do with the bee-seller or with me.
Now he is gone 40

In eight great bounds, a great scapegoat.
Here is his slipper, here is another,
And here the square of white linen
He wore instead of a hat.
He was sweet, 45

The sweat of his efforts a rain
Tugging the world to fruit.
The bees found him out,
Molding onto his lips like lies,
Complicating his features. 50

They thought death was worth it, but I
Have a self to recover, a queen.
Is she dead, is she sleeping?
Where has she been,
With her lion-red body, her wings of glass? 55

Now she is flying
More terrible than she ever was, red
Scar in the sky, red comet
Over the engine that killed her—
The mausoleum, the wax house. 60

October 6, 1962 1965

The Swarm

Somebody is shooting at something in our town—
A dull pom, pom in the Sunday street.
Jealousy can open the blood,
It can make black roses.
Who are they shooting at? 5

It is you the knives are out for
At Waterloo, Waterloo, Napoleon,
The hump of Elba[1] on your short back,
And the snow, marshaling its brilliant cutlery
Mass after mass, saying Shh! 10

1. Napoleon Bonaparte (1769–1821) was France's
emperor (1804–14) and military leader of his "Grand
Army." Forced into exile on the island of Elba, off the
western coast of Italy, he escaped, reassembled his fol-
lowers, and was finally defeated by the British at the
battle of Waterloo in 1815.

Shh! These are chess people you play with,
Still figures of ivory.
The mud squirms with throats,
Stepping stones for French bootsoles.
The gilt and pink domes of Russia melt and float off 15

In the furnace of greed. Clouds, clouds.
So the swarm balls and deserts
Seventy feet up, in a black pine tree.
It must be shot down. Pom! Pom!
So dumb it thinks bullets are thunder. 20

It thinks they are the voice of God
Condoning the beak, the claw, the grin of the dog
Yellow-haunched, a pack-dog,
Grinning over its bone of ivory
Like the pack, the pack, like everybody. 25

The bees have got so far. Seventy feet high
Russia, Poland and Germany![2]
The mild hills, the same old magenta
Fields shrunk to a penny
Spun into a river, the river crossed. 30

The bees argue, in their black ball,
A flying hedgehog, all prickles.
The man with gray hands stands under the honeycomb
Of their dream, the hived station
Where trains, faithful to their steel arcs, 35

Leave and arrive, and there is no end to the country.
Pom! Pom! They fall
Dismembered, to a tod[3] of ivy.
So much for the charioteers, the outriders, the Grand Army!
A red tatter, Napoleon! 40

The last badge of victory.
The swarm is knocked into a cocked straw hat.
Elba, Elba, bleb[4] on the sea!
The white busts of marshals, admirals, generals
Worming themselves into niches. 45

How instructive this is!
The dumb, banded bodies
Walking the plank draped with Mother France's upholstery
Into a new mausoleum,
An ivory palace, a crotch pine. 50

The man with gray hands smiles—
The smile of a man of business, intensely practical.

2. Three countries that Napoleon attempted to con- 3. A clump (British).
quer. 4. A small blister.

They are not hands at all
But asbestos receptacles.
Pom! Pom! "They would have killed *me*." 55

Stings big as drawing pins!
It seems bees have a notion of honor,
A black intractable mind.
Napoleon is pleased, he is pleased with everything.
O Europe! O ton of honey! 60

October 7, 1962 1965

Wintering

This is the easy time, there is nothing doing.
I have whirled the midwife's extractor,[1]
I have my honey,
Six jars of it,
Six cat's eyes in the wine cellar, 5

Wintering in a dark without window
At the heart of the house
Next to the last tenant's rancid jam
And the bottles of empty glitters—
Sir So-and-so's gin. 10

This is the room I have never been in
This is the room I could never breathe in.
The black bunched in there like a bat,
No light
But the torch and its faint 15

Chinese yellow on appalling objects—
Black asininity. Decay.
Possession.
It is they who own me.
Neither cruel nor indifferent, 20

Only ignorant.
This is the time of hanging on for the bees—the bees
So slow I hardly know them,
Filing like soldiers
To the syrup tin 25

To make up for the honey I've taken.
Tate and Lyle[2] keeps them going,
The refined snow.
It is Tate and Lyle they live on, instead of flowers.
They take it. The cold sets in. 30

1. A device used for removing honey from beehives. 2. A common brand of syrup.

Now they ball in a mass,
Black
Mind against all that white.
The smile of the snow is white.
It spreads itself out, a mile-long body of Meissen,[3] 35

Into which, on warm days,
They can only carry their dead.
The bees are all women,
Maids and the long royal lady.
They have got rid of the men,[4] 40

The blunt, clumsy stumblers, the boors.
Winter is for women—
The woman, still at her knitting,
At the cradle of Spanish walnut,
Her body a bulb in the cold and too dumb to think. 45

Will the hive survive, will the gladiolas
Succeed in banking their fires
To enter another year?
What will they taste of, the Christmas roses?
The bees are flying. They taste the spring. 50

October 9, 1962 1965

Daddy

You do not do, you do not do
Any more, black shoe
In which I have lived like a foot
For thirty years, poor and white,
Barely daring to breathe or Achoo. 5

Daddy, I have had to kill you.
You died before I had time—
Marble-heavy, a bag full of God,
Ghastly statue with one gray toe[1]
Big as a Frisco seal 10

And a head in the freakish Atlantic
Where it pours bean green over blue
In the waters off beautiful Nauset.[2]
I used to pray to recover you.
Ach, du.[3] 15

In the German tongue, in the Polish town[4]
Scraped flat by the roller

3. A kind of porcelain made in Germany.
4. There are no male drones in bee colonies in the winter.
1. Plath's father's toe turned black from gangrene.
2. Beach north of Boston.

3. Ah, you (German); the first of a series of references to her father's German origins.
4. Grabow, the birthplace of Otto Plath, the poet's father.

Of wars, wars, wars.
But the name of the town is common.
My Polack friend 20

Says there are a dozen or two.
So I never could tell where you
Put your foot, your root,
I never could talk to you.
The tongue stuck in my jaw. 25

It stuck in a barb wire snare.
Ich,[5] ich, ich, ich,
I could hardly speak.
I thought every German was you.
And the language obscene 30

An engine, an engine
Chuffing me off like a Jew.
A Jew to Dachau, Auschwitz, Belsen.[6]
I began to talk like a Jew.
I think I may well be a Jew. 35

The snows of the Tyrol,[7] the clear beer of Vienna
Are not very pure or true.
With my gipsy ancestress and my weird luck
And my Taroc pack[8] and my Taroc pack
I may be a bit of a Jew. 40

I have always been scared of you,
With your Luftwaffe,[9] your gobbledygoo.
And your neat mustache
And your Aryan eye, bright blue.
Panzer[1]-man, panzer-man, O You— 45

Not God but a swastika
So black no sky could squeak through.
Every woman adores a Fascist,
The boot in the face, the brute
Brute heart of a brute like you. 50

You stand at the blackboard, daddy,
In the picture I have of you,
A cleft in your chin instead of your foot
But no less a devil for that, no not
Any less the black man who 55

Bit my pretty red heart in two.
I was ten when they buried you.

5. I.
6. German concentration camps, where millions of Jews were murdered during World War II.
7. Austrian Alpine region.
8. I.e., Tarot, ancient fortune-telling cards.
9. The German air force.
1. Armor or tank (German). Adolf Hitler, who had a neat moustache, preached the superiority of the Aryan race—persons with blond hair and blue eyes, as opposed to those with darker, Semitic characteristics.

At twenty I tried to die[2]
And get back, back, back to you.
I thought even the bones would do. 60

But they pulled me out of the sack
And they stuck me together with glue.
And then I knew what to do.
I made a model of you,
A man in black with a Meinkampf[3] look 65

And a love of the rack and the screw.
And I said I do, I do.
So daddy, I'm finally through.
The black telephone's off at the root,
The voices just can't worm through. 70

If I've killed one man, I've killed two—
The vampire who said he was you
And drank my blood for a year,
Seven years, if you want to know.
Daddy, you can lie back now. 75

There's a stake in your fat black heart
And the villagers never liked you.
They are dancing and stamping on you.
They always knew it was you
Daddy, daddy, you bastard, I'm through. 80

October 12, 1962 1965

Medusa[1]

Off that landspit of stony mouth-plugs,
Eyes rolled by white sticks,
Ears cupping the sea's incoherences,
You house your unnerving head—God-ball,
Lens of mercies, 5

Your stooges
Plying their wild cells in my keel's shadow,
Pushing by like hearts,
Red stigmata[2] at the very center,
Riding the rip tide to the nearest point of departure, 10

Dragging their Jesus hair.
Did I escape, I wonder?
My mind winds to you

2. An allusion to Plath's first suicide attempt.
3. A reference to Hitler's political autobiography, *Mein Kampf* ("My Struggle"), written and published before his rise to power, in which the future dictator outlined his plans for world conquest.

1. A jellyfish; also a mythological woman with snakes for hair, whose look has the power to turn men to stone.
2. Signs on the body resembling Christ's wounds.

Old barnacled umbilicus, Atlantic cable,[3]
Keeping itself, it seems, in a state of miraculous repair. 15

In any case, you are always there,
Tremulous breath at the end of my line,
Curve of water upleaping
To my water rod, dazzling and grateful,
Touching and sucking. 20

I didn't call you.
I didn't call you at all.
Nevertheless, nevertheless
You steamed to me over the sea,
Fat and red, a placenta 25

Paralysing the kicking lovers.
Cobra light
Squeezing the breath from the blood bells
Of the fuchsia. I could draw no breath,
Dead and moneyless, 30

Overexposed, like an X-ray.
Who do you think you are?
A Communion wafer? Blubbery Mary?[4]
I shall take no bite of your body,
Bottle in which I live, 35

Ghastly Vatican.[5]
I am sick to death of hot salt.
Green as eunuchs, your wishes
Hiss at my sins.
Off, off, eely tentacle! 40

There is nothing between us.

October 16, 1962 1965

Ariel[1]

Stasis in darkness.
Then the substanceless blue
Pour of tor[2] and distances.

God's lioness,
How one we grow,
Pivot of heels and knees!—The furrow 5

3. A telephone cable, laid on the ocean floor, which connects America and Europe.
4. A pun on *Bloody Mary*, the title given to Mary Tudor (1516–1558), the queen of England and Ireland from 1553 to 1558, renowned for her slaughtering of Protestant dissidents. The Communion wafer is part of the Catholic Mass, where it is believed to incarnate the body of Christ.
5. The residence of the pope in Rome.
1. The name of the horse Plath frequently rode; also the name of a fairy or spirit in Shakespeare's *The Tempest*.
2. Craggy hill.

Splits and passes, sister to
The brown arc
Of the neck I cannot catch,

Nigger-eye 10
Berries cast dark
Hooks—

Black sweet blood mouthfuls,
Shadows.
Something else 15

Hauls me through air—
Thighs, hair;
Flakes from my heels.

White
Godiva,[3] I unpeel— 20
Dead hands, dead stringencies.

And now I
Foam to wheat, a glitter of seas.
The child's cry

Melts in the wall. 25
And I
Am the arrow,

The dew that flies
Suicidal, at one with the drive
Into the red 30

Eye, the cauldron of morning.

October 27, 1962 1965

Nick and the Candlestick[1]

I am a miner. The light burns blue.
Waxy stalactites
Drip and thicken, tears

The earthen womb
Exudes from its dead boredom. 5
Black bat airs

Wrap me, raggy shawls,
Cold homicides.
They weld to me like plums.

3. According to legend Lady Godiva (1010?–1067) rode naked through the streets of Coventry to persuade her husband the local lord, to lower heavy taxes.

1. Plath's son, Nicholas, was less than a year old when this poem was written.

Old cave of calcium 10
Icicles, old echoer.
Even the newts are white,

Those holy Joes.[2]
And the fish, the fish—
Christ! they are panes of ice, 15

A vice of knives,
A piranha
Religion, drinking

Its first communion out of my live toes.
The candle 20
Gulps and recovers its small altitude,

Its yellows hearten.
O love, how did you get here?
O embryo

Remembering, even in sleep, 25
Your crossed position.
The blood blooms clean

In you, ruby.
The pain
You wake to is not yours. 30

Love, love,
I have hung our cave with roses,
With soft rugs—

The last of Victoriana.[3]
Let the stars 35
Plummet to their dark address,

Let the mercuric
Atoms that cripple drip
Into the terrible well,

You are the one 40
Solid the spaces lean on, envious.
You are the baby in the barn.[4]

October 29, 1962 1965

2. A pious person or clergyman (British slang). 4. An allusion to the infant Jesus, who was nursed in a
3. I.e., the rich furnishings and decor associated with manger.
the Victorian age.

Lady Lazarus[1]

I have done it again.
One year in every ten
I manage it—

A sort of walking miracle, my skin
Bright as a Nazi lampshade,[2] 5
My right foot

A paperweight,
My face a featureless, fine
Jew linen.

Peel off the napkin 10
O my enemy.
Do I terrify?—

The nose, the eye pits, the full set of teeth?
The sour breath
Will vanish in a day. 15

Soon, soon the flesh
The grave cave ate will be
At home on me

And I a smiling woman.
I am only thirty. 20
And like the cat I have nine times to die.

This is Number Three.
What a trash
To annihilate each decade.

What a million filaments 25
The peanut-crunching crowd
Shoves in to see

Them unwrap me hand and foot—
The big strip tease.
Gentlemen, ladies 30

These are my hands
My knees.
I may be skin and bone,

Nevertheless, I am the same, identical woman.
The first time it happened I was ten. 35
It was an accident.

1. Lazarus, the brother of Mary and Martha, was raised by Jesus from the dead (John 11 1–44).
2. The Nazis made use of the corpses of Jews whom they had killed by turning their skin into lampshades and their bodies into soap.

The second time I meant
To last it out and not come back at all.
I rocked shut

As a seashell. 40
They had to call and call
And pick the worms off me like sticky pearls.

Dying
Is an art, like everything else.
I do it exceptionally well. 45

I do it so it feels like hell.
I do it so it feels real.
I guess you could say I've a call.

It's easy enough to do it in a cell.
It's easy enough to do it and stay put. 50
It's the theatrical

Comeback in broad day
To the same place, the same face, the same brute
Amused shout:

"A miracle!" 55
That knocks me out.
There is a charge

For the eyeing of my scars, there is a charge
For the hearing of my heart—
It really goes. 60

And there is a charge, a very large charge
For a word or a touch
Or a bit of blood

Or a piece of my hair or my clothes.
So, so, Herr Doktor. 65
So, Herr Enemy.

I am your opus,
I am your valuable,
The pure gold baby

That melts to a shriek. 70
I turn and burn.
Do not think I underestimate your great concern.

Ash, ash—
You poke and stir.
Flesh, bone, there is nothing there— 75

A cake of soap,
A wedding ring.
A gold filling.

Herr God, Herr Lucifer[3]
Beware 80
Beware.

Out of the ash
I rise with my red hair
And I eat men like air.

October 23–29, 1962 1965

Words

Axes
After whose stroke the wood rings,
And the echoes!
Echoes traveling
Off from the center like horses. 5

The sap
Wells like tears, like the
Water striving
To re-establish its mirror
Over the rock 10

That drops and turns,
A white skull,
Eaten by weedy greens.
Years later I
Encounter them on the road— 15

Words dry and riderless,
The indefatigable hoof-taps.
While
From the bottom of the pool, fixed stars
Govern a life. 20

February 1, 1963 1965

Edge

The woman is perfected.
Her dead

Body wears the smile of accomplishment,
The illusion of a Greek necessity[1]

3. The devil. "Herr": mister (German) 1. The Greek idea of necessity or *ananke*.

Flows in the scrolls of her toga, 5
Her bare

Feet seem to be saying:
We have come so far, it is over.

Each dead child coiled, a white serpent,
One at each little 10

Pitcher of milk, now empty.
She has folded

Them back into her body as petals
Of a rose close when the garden

Stiffens and odors bleed 15
From the sweet, deep throats of the night flower.

The moon has nothing to be sad about,
Staring from her hood of bone.

She is used to this sort of thing.
Her blacks crackle and drag. 20

February 5, 1963 1965

EDNA O'BRIEN

1932–

After Edna O'Brien completed a trilogy of novels (composed of *The Country Girls, The Lonely Girl,* and *Girls in Their Married Bliss,* 1960–64), she explained to an interviewer that, while women can become high-court judges, "the high-court judge will still have to come home and make the evening meal." Her skepticism about women's social progress, like her rejection of her own Catholic upbringing, is based on the belief that most human beings feel themselves to be engaged in a struggle to ensure their own survival. O'Brien's fiction is characterized, on the one hand, by her robust handling of explicitly sexual themes and, on the other, by her indictment of what she perceives as the poverty and fanaticism of her cultural roots. Born in a small village in the west of Ireland, O'Brien attended Pharmaceutical College in Dublin. At the age of twenty, she married and, after the birth of two sons, she moved to London, where she currently resides. Besides the trilogy, she has composed several novels, a play, some television scripts, and a number of short stories. *A Fanatic Heart: Selected Stories of Edna O'Brien* appeared in 1984; *Lantern Slides: Short Stories* was published in 1990; other later works include *Time and Tide* (1992) and *House of Splendid Isolation* (1994).

Like Irish fiction writers from James Joyce to Julia O'Faolain, O'Brien captures the spiritual and social atmosphere of Irish family life. In addition, *A Rose in the Heart* explores the dynamics of mother-daughter bonding that the psychologist Nancy Chodorow has associated with the origins of female psychosexual development, a bonding that Chodorow sees as related to the "fluid" boundaries of female identity.

A Rose in the Heart[1]

December night. Jack Frost in scales along the outside of the windows giving to the various rooms a white filtered light. The ice like bits of mirror beveling the puddles of the potholes. The rooms were cold inside, and for the most part identically furnished. The room with no furniture at all—save for the apples gathered in the autumn—was called The Vacant Room. The apples were all over the floor and in rows along the curb of the tiled fireplace. Their smell was heady, many of them having begun to rot. Rooms into which no-one had stepped for days and yet these rooms and their belongings would become part of the remembered story. A solemn house, set in its own grounds, away from the lazy bustle of the village. A lonesome house it would prove to be, and with a strange lifelikeness as if it was not a house at all but a person observing and breathing, a presence amid a cluster of trees and sturdy wind-shorn hedges.

The overweight midwife hurried up the drive, her serge cape blowing behind her. She was puffing. She carried her barrel-shaped leather bag in which were disinfectant, forceps, instruments and a small bottle of holy water[2] lest the new child should prove to be in danger of death. More infants died around Christmas time than in any other month of the year. When she passed the little sycamore tree that was halfway up she began to hear the roaring and beseeching to God. Poor mother, she thought, poor poor mother. She was not too early, had come more or less at the correct time, even though she had been summoned hours before by Donal the serving boy who worked on the farm. She had brought most of the children of that parish into the world yet had neither kith nor kin of her own. Coming in the back door she took off her bonnet and then attached it to the knob by means of its elastic string.

It was a blue room—walls of dark wet morose blue, furniture made of walnut, including the bed on which the event was taking place. Fronting the fireplace was a huge lid of a chocolate box with the representation of a saucy-looking lady. The tassel of the blind kept bobbing against the frosted windowpane. There was a washstand, a basin and ewer of off-white with big roses splashed throughout the china itself, and a huge lumbering beast of a wardrobe. The midwife recalled once going to a house up the mountain, and finding the child smothered by the time she arrived; the fatherless child had been stuffed in a drawer. The moans filled that room and went beyond the distempered walls out into the cold hall outside, where the black felt doggie with the amber eyes stood sentinel on a tall varnished whatnot.[3] At intervals the woman apologized to the midwife for the untoward commotion, said sorry in a gasping whisper, and then was seized again by a pain, that at different times she described as being a knife, a dagger, a hell on earth. It was her fourth labor. The previous child had died two days after being born. An earlier child, also a daughter, had died of whooping cough. Her womb was sick unto death. Why be a woman. Oh cruel life, oh merciless fate, oh heartless man, she sobbed. Gripping the coverlet and remembering that between those self-same, much-patched sheets, she had been pried apart, again and again, with not a word to her, not a little endearment, only rammed through and told to open up.

1. This story has also appeared under the titles *There's a Rose in the Heart of New York* and *A Rose in the Heart of New York*.
2. In the Catholic Church, water that has been
blessed by a priest and is used in religious ceremonies such as baptism.
3. An open stand with shelves.

When she married she had escaped the life of a serving girl, the possible experience of living in some grim institution but as time went on and the trousseau[4] drawer was emptied of its gifts, she saw that she was made to serve in an altogether other way. When she wasn't screaming she was grinding her head into the pillow, and praying for it to be all over. She dreaded the bloodshed long before they saw any. The midwife made her ease up as she put an old sheet under her and over that a bit of oilcloth. The midwife said it was no joke and repeated the hypothesis that if men had to give birth there would not be a child born in the whole wide world.

The husband was downstairs getting paralytic. Earlier, when his wife had announced that she would have to go upstairs because of her labor, he said, looking for the slightest pretext for a celebration, that if there was any homemade wine or altar wine[5] stacked away, to get it out, to produce it, and also the cut glasses. She said there was none and well he knew it since they could hardly afford tea and sugar. He started to root and to rummage, to empty cupboards of their contents of rags, garments and provisions, even to put his hand inside the bolster case, to delve into pillows; on he went, rampaging until he found a bottle in the wardrobe, in the very room into which she delivered her moans and exhortations. She begged of him not to, but all he did was to wield the amber-colored bottle in her direction, and then put it to his head so that the spirit started to go glug-glug. It was intoxicating stuff. By a wicked coincidence a crony of his had come to sell them another stove, most likely another crock, a thing that would have to be coaxed alight with constant attention and puffing, to create a draft. The other child was with a neighbor, the dead ones in a graveyard six or seven miles away, among strangers and distant relatives, without their names being carved on the crooked rain-soaked tomb.

"Oh Jesus," she cried out as he came back to ask for the knitting needle to skewer out the bit of broken cork.

"Blazes," he said to her as she coiled into a knot and felt the big urgent ball—that would be the head—as it pressed on the base of her bowels, and battered at her insides.

Curses and prayers combined to issue out of her mouth, and as time went on, they became most pitiful and were interrupted with screams. The midwife put a facecloth on her forehead and told her to push, in the name of the Lord to push. She said she had no strength left, but the midwife went on enjoining her, and simulating a hefty breath. It took over an hour. The little head showing its tonsure would recoil, would reshow itself, each time a fraction more, although in between it was seeming to shrink from the world that it was hurtling towards. She said to the nurse that she was being burst apart, and that she no longer cared if she died, or if they drank themselves to death. In the kitchen they were sparring over who had the best grayhound, who had the successor to Mick the Miller. The crucifix that had been in her hand had fallen out, and her hands themselves felt bony and skinned because of the way they wrenched one another.

"In the name of God push, Missus."

She would have pushed everything out of herself, her guts, her womb, her craw, her lights[6] and her liver but the center of her body was holding on and

this center seemed to be the governor of her. She wished to be nothing, a shell, devoid of everything and everyone and she was announcing that, and roaring and raving when the child came hurtling out, slowly at first as if its neck could not wring its way through, then the shoulder—that was the worst bit—carving a straight course, then the hideous turnabout, and a scream other than her own, and an urgent presage of things, as the great gouts of blood and lymph followed upon the mewling creature itself. Her last bit of easiness was then torn from her, and she was without hope. It had come into the world lopsided and the first announcement from the midwife was a fatality, was that it had clubbed feet. Its little feet she ventured to say, were like two stumps adhering to one another, and the blasted cord was bound around its neck. The result was a mewling piece of screwed-up, inert, dark, purple misery.

The men subsided a little when the announcement was shouted down and they came to say congrats. The father waved a strip of pink flesh on a fork that he was carrying and remarked on its being unappetizing. They were cooking a goose downstairs and he said in future he would insist on turkey as goose was only for gobs and goms.[7] The mother felt green and disgusted, asked them to leave her alone. The salesman said was it a boy or a child, although he had just been told that it was a daughter. The mother could feel the blood gushing out of her, like water at a weir.[8] The midwife told them to go down and behave like gentlemen.

Then she got three back numbers of the weekly paper, a shoe box with a lid, and into it she stuffed the mess and the unnecessaries. She hummed as she prepared to do the stitching down the line of torn flesh that was gaping and coated with blood. The mother roared again and said this indeed was her vinegar and gall. She bit into the crucifix, and dented it further. She could feel her mouth and her eyelids being stitched too, she was no longer a lovely body, she was a vehicle for pain and for insult. The child was so quiet it scarcely breathed. The afterbirth was placed on the stove, where the dog Shep sniffed at it through its layers of paper and for his curiosity got a kick in the tail. The stove had quenched and the midwife said to the men that it was a crying shame to leave a good goose like that, neither cooked nor uncooked. The men had torn off bits of the breast so that the goose looked wounded, like the woman upstairs who was then tightening her heart and soul, tightening inside the array of catgut stitches and regarding her whole life as a vast disappointment. The midwife carried the big bundle up to the cellar, put an oil rag to it, set a match to it and knew that she would have to be off soon to do the same task elsewhere. She would have liked to stay and swaddle the infant, and comfort the woman and drink hot sweet tea but there was not enough time. There was never enough time and she hadn't even cleaned out the ashes or the cinders in her grate that morning.

The child was in a corner of the room in a brown cot with the slats that rattled because of the racket they had received from the previous children. The mother was not proud, far from it. She fed the child its first bottle, looked down at its wizened face and thought where have you come from and why. She had no choice of a name. In fact she said to her first visitor, a lieutenant from the army, not to tell her a pack of lies because this child had the ugliest face that had ever seen the light of day. That Christmas the drinking and sparring

7. Gluttons and fools. 8. Dam.

went on, the odd neighbor called, the mother got up on the third day and staggered down to do something about the unruly kitchen. Each evening at nightfall she got a bit of a candle to have handy and re-oiled the Sacred Heart lamp for when the child cried. They both contracted bronchitis and the child was impounded in masses of flannel and flannelette.

Things changed. The mother came to idolize the child, because it was so quiet, never bawling, never asking for anything, just covert, in its pram, the dog watching over it, its eyes staring out at whatever happened to loom in. Its very ugliness disappeared. Its feet were all right. It seemed to drink them all in with its huge, contemplating, slightly hazed-over, navy eyes. They shone at whatever they saw. The mother would look in the direction of the pram and say a little prayer for it, or smile, and often at night she held the candle shielded by her hand to see the face, to say pet, or tush, to say nonsenses to it. It ate whatever it was given but as time went on it knew what it liked and had a sweet tooth. The food was what united them, eating off the same plate using the same spoon, watching one another's chews, feeling the food as it went down the other's gullet. The child was slow to crawl and slower still to walk but it knew everything, it perceived everything. When it ate blancmange or junket[9] it was eating part of the lovely substance of its mother.

They were together, always together. If its mother went to the post office the child stood in the middle of the drive praying until its mother returned safely. The child cut the ridges of four fingers, along the edge of a razor blade that had been wedged upright in the wood of the dresser, and seeing these four deep horizontal identical slits the mother took the poor fingers into her own mouth and sucked them, to lessen the pain, and licked them to abolish the blood, and kept saying soft things until the child was stilled again. Her mother's knuckles were her knuckles, her mother's veins were her veins, her mother's lap was a second heaven, her mother's forehead a copybook onto which she traced A B C D, her mother's body was a recess that she would wander inside for ever and ever, a sepulcher growing deeper and deeper. When she saw other people, especially her pretty sister, she would simply wave from that safe place, she would not budge, would not be lured out.

Her father took a hatchet to her mother and threatened that he would split open the head of her. The child watched through the kitchen window because this assault took place out of doors on a hillock under the three beech trees where the clothes line stretched, then sagged. The mother had been hanging out the four sheets washed that morning, the two off each bed. The child was engaged in twisting her hair, looping it around bits of white rag, to form ringlets, decking herself in the kitchen mirror, and then every other minute running across to the window to reconnoiter, wondering what she ought to do, jumping up and down as if she had a pain, not knowing what to do, running back to the mirror, hoping that the terrible scene would pass, that the ground would open up and swallow her father, that the hatchet would turn into a magic wand, that her mother would come through the kitchen door and say, "Fear Not," that travail would all be over. Later she heard a verbatim account of what had happened. Her father demanded money, her mother refused same on the grounds that she had none, but added that if she had it she would hang

9. Puddinglike desserts.

sooner than give it to him. That did it. It was then he really got bucking. grit-
ted his teeth and his muscles, said that he would split the head of her and the
mother said that if he did so there was a place for him. That place was the lu-
natic asylum. It was twenty or thirty miles away, a big gray edifice, men and
women lumped in together, some in strait jackets, some in padded cells, some
blindfolded because of having sacks thrown over their heads, some strapped
across the chest to quell and impede them. Those who did not want to go
there were dragged by relatives, or by means of rope, some being tied onto the
end of a plough or a harrow and brought in on all fours like beasts of the earth.
Then when they were not so mad, not so rampaging, they were let home again
where they were very peculiar, and given to smiling and to chattering to them-
selves and in no time they were ripe to go off again or to be dragged off. March
was the worst month, when everything went askew, even the wind, even the
March hares.

Her father did not go there. He went off on a batter[1] and then went to a
monastery, and then was brought home and shook in the bed chair for five
days eating bread and milk, and asking who would convey him over the fields,
until he saw his yearlings, and when no one volunteered to, it fell to her be-
cause she was the youngest. Over in the fields he patted the yearlings and said
soppy things that he'd never say indoors, or to a human, and he cried and said
he'd never touch a drop again, and there was a dribble on his pewter-brown
moustache, that was the remains of the mush that he had been eating, and the
bay yearling herself became fidgety and fretful as if she might bolt or stamp
the ground to smithereens. The girl and her mother took walks on Sundays—
strolls, picked blackberries, consulted them for worms, made preserve, and
slept side by side, entwined like twigs of trees or the ends of the sugar tongs.

When she wakened and found that her mother had got up and was already
mixing meal for the hens or stirabout for the young pigs she hurried down car-
rying her clothes under her arm and dressed in whatever spot that she could
feast on the sight of her mother, most. Always an egg for breakfast. An egg a
day and she would grow strong. Her mother never ate an egg but topped the
girl's egg and fed her it off the tarnished eggy spoon and gave her little sups of
tea with which to wash it down. She had her own mug, red enamel and with
not a chip. The girl kept looking back as she went down the drive for school,
and as time went on she mastered the knack of walking backwards to be able
to look all the longer, look at the aproned figure waving or holding up a potato
pounder or a colander or whatever happened to be in her hand.

The girl came home once and the mother was missing. Her mother had ac-
tually fulfilled her promise of going away one day and going to a spot where
she would not be found. That threatened spot was the bottom of the lake. But
in fact her mother had gone back to her own family because the father had
taken a shotgun to her and had shot her but was not a good aim like William
Tell,[2] had missed, had instead made a hole in the Blue Room wall. What were
they doing upstairs in the middle of the day, an ascent they never made except
the mother alone to dress the two beds. She could guess. She slept in a neigh-
bor's house, slept in a bed with two old people who reeked of eucalyptus. She

1. A binge. "March hares": hares were thought to go 2. Legendary Swiss patriot who successfully shot an
mad in March, during their mating season. apple off his son's head.

kept most of her clothes on, and shriveled into herself, not wanting to touch or be touched by these two old people buried in their various layers of skin and hair and winceyette.[3] Outside the window was a climbing rose with three or four red flowers along the bow of it, and looking at the flowers and thinking of the wormy clay she would try to shut out what these two old people were saying, in order that she could remember the mother whom she despaired of ever seeing again.

Not far away was their own house with the back door wide open so that any stranger or tinker could come in or out. The dog was probably lonely and bloodied from hunting rabbits, the hens were forgotten about, and were probably in their coops, hysterical, and picking at each other's feathers because of their nerves. Eggs would rot. Her father could be anywhere. If she stood on the low whitewashed wall that fronted the cottage she could see over the high limestone wall that bounded their fields and then look to the driveway that led to the abandoned house itself. To her it was like a kind of castle where strange things had happened and would go on happening. She loved it and she feared it. The sky behind and above gave it mystery, sometimes made it broody[4] and gave it a kind of splendor when the red streaks in the heavens were like torches that betokened the performance of a gory play. All of a sudden standing there, with a bit of grass between her front teeth, looking at her home and imagining this future drama she heard the nearby lich[5] gate open, and then shut with a clang, and saw her father appear, and jumped so clumsily she thought she had broken everything, particularly her ribs. She felt she was in pieces. She would be like Humpty Dumpty, and all the king's horses and all the king's men would not be able to put her together again.

Dismemberment did happen, a long time before, the time when her neck swelled out into a big fleshed balloon. She could only move her neck on one side, because the other side was like a ball and full of fluid that made gluggles when touched with the fingers. They were going to lance it. They placed her on a kitchen chair. Her mother boiled a saucepan of water. Her mother stood on another chair and reached far into the rear of a cupboard and hauled out a new towel. Everything was in that cupboard, sugar and tea, and round biscuits and white flour and linen and must and mice. First one man, then another man, then another man, then a last man who was mending the chimney, and then last of all her father, each took a hold of her—an arm, another arm, a shoulder, a waist and her two flying legs that were doing everything possible not to be there. The lady doctor said nice things and cut into the big football of her neck and it was like a pig's bladder bursting all over, the waters flowing out, and then it was not like that at all, it was like a sword on the bone of her neck sawing, cutting into the flesh, deeper and deeper, the men pressing upon her with all their might saying that she was a demon and the knife went into her swallow or where she thought of forever more as her swallow, and the lady doctor said "drat it," because she had done the wrong thing—had cut too deep and had to start scraping now and her elder sister danced a jig out in the flag,[6] so that neighbors going down the road would not get the impression that someone was being murdered to death. Long afterwards she came back to the

world of voices, muffled voices, and their reassurances, and a little something sweet to help her get over it all and the lacy doctor putting on her brown fur coat and hurrying to her next important work of mercy.

When she slept with the neighbors the old man asked the old woman were they ever going to be rid of her, were they going to have this dunce off their hands, were they saddled with her for the rest of their blooming lives. She declined the milk they gave her because it was goat's milk and too yellow and there was dust in it. She would answer them in single syllables, just yes or no, mostly no. She was learning to frown so that she too would have ABCs. Her mother's forehead and hers would meet in heaven, salute, and all their lines would coincide. She refused food. She pined. In all it was about a week.

The day her mother returned home—it was still January—the water pipes had burst and when she got to the neighbors, and was told she could go on up home, she ran with all her might and resolution so that her windpipes ached and then stopped aching when she found her mother down on her knees dealing with pools of water that had gushed from the red pipes. The brown rag was wet every other second and had to be wrung out, and squeezed in the big chapped basin, the one she was first bathed in. The lodges[7] of water were everywhere, lapping back and forth, threatening to expand, to discolor the tiles, and it was of this hazard they talked and fretted over rather than the mother's disappearance, or the dire cause of it, or the reason for her return. They went indoors and got the ingredients and the utensils and the sieve so as to make an orange cake with orange filling and orange and lemon icing. She never tasted anything so wonderful in all her life. She ate three big hunks and her mother put her hand around her and said if she ate any more she would have a little corporation.[8]

The father came from the hospital, cried again, said that sure he wouldn't hurt a fly and predicted that he would never break his pledge or go outside the gate again, only to Mass, never leave his own sweet acres.

As before, the girl slept with her mother, recited the rosary[9] with her, and shared the small cubes of dark raisin-filled chocolate, then trembled while her mother went along to her father's bedroom, for a tick, to stop him bucking.[1] The consequences of those visits were deterred by the bits of tissue paper, a protection between herself and any emission. No other child got conceived and there was no further use for the baggy napkins, the bottle, and the dark-brown mottled teat. The cot itself was sawn up and used to back two chairs, and they constituted something of the furniture in the big upstairs landing, where the felt dog still lorded it, but now had an eye missing because a visiting child had poked wire at it. The chairs were painted ox-blood red and had the sharp end of a nail dragged along the varnish to give a wavering effect. Also on the landing there was a bowl with a bit of wire inside to hold a profusion of artificial tea roses. These tea roses were a two-toned color, were red and yellow plastic and the point of each petal was seared like the point of a thorn. Cloth flowers were softer. She had seen some once, very pale pink and purple, tumbling roses made of voile,[2] in another house, in a big jug, on a lady's bureau. In

7. Reservoirs.
8. I.e., a protruding belly.
9. A series of Catholic prayers, often counted on a

string of special beads.
1. Complaining "For a tick": briefly.
2. A sheer, fine fabric.

the landing at home too was the speared head of Christ that assayed on all the proceedings with endless patience, endless commiseration. Underneath Christ was a pussy cat of black papier mâché which originally had sweets stuffed into its middle, sweets the exact image of strawberries and even with a little leaf at the base, a leaf made of green glazed angelica.[3] They liked the same things—apple sauce and beetroot and tomato sausages and angelica. They cleaned the windows, one the inside, the other the outside, they sang duets, they put newspapers over the newly washed dark-red tiles so as to keep them safe from the muck and trampalations[4] of the men. About everything they agreed, or almost everything.

In the dark nights the wind used to sweep through the window and out on the landing and into the other rooms, and into the Blue Room, by now uninhabited. The wardrobe door would open of its own accord, or the ewer would rattle, or the lovely buxom Our Lady of Limerick[5] picture would fall onto the marble washstand and there was a rumpus followed by prognostications of bad luck for seven years.

When the other child came back from secretarial school the girl was at first excited, prepared lovingly for her, made cakes, and soon after, was plunged into a state of wretchedness. Her mother was being taken away from her, or worse was gladly giving her speech, her attention, her hands, and all of her gaze to this intruder. Her mother and her elder sister would go up-stairs where her mother would have some little treat for her, a hanky or a hanky sachet,[6] and once a remnant that had been got at the mill at reduced price, due to a fire there. Beautiful, a flecked salmon pink.

Downstairs *she* had to stack dishes onto the tray. She banged the cups, she put a butter knife into the two-pound pot of blackcurrant jam and hauled out a big helping, then stuck the greasy plates one on top of the other whereas normally she would have put a fork in between to protect the undersides. She dreamt that her mother and her rival sister were going for a walk and she asked to go too but they sneaked off. She followed on a bicycle, but once outside the main gate could not decide whether to go to the left or the right, and then having decided, made the wrong choice and stumbled on a herd of bullocks, all butting one another and endeavouring to get up into one another's backsides. She turned back and there they were strolling up on the drive, like two sedate ladies linking and laughing, and the salmon-flecked remnant was already a garment, a beautiful swagger coat[7] which her sister wore with a dash.

"I wanted to be with you," she said, and one said to the other, "She wanted to be with us," and then no matter what she said, no matter what the appeal, they repeated it as if she wasn't there. In the end she knew that she would have to turn away from them because she was not wanted, she was in their way. As a result of that dream, or rather the commotion that she made in her sleep, it was decided that she had worms and the following morning they gave her a dose of turpentine and castor oil the same as they gave the horses. When her sister went back to the city happiness was restored again. Her mother consulted her about the design on a leather bag which she was making. Her mother wanted a very old design, something concerning the history of their

3. A candied herb used in baking.
4. Trampling.
5. A picture of the Virgin Mary associated with the

cathedral at Limerick, Ireland.
6. A little bag containing dried herbs or flowers.
7. A coat for going out.

country. She said there would have to be atrocious battles and then peace and wonderful lace-like scenes from nature. Her mother said that there must be a lot of back history to a land and that education was a very fine thing. Finer than the bog her mother said. She said when she grew up that she would get a very good job and bring her mother to America. Her mother mentioned the street in Brooklyn where she had lodged and said that it had adjoined a park. They would go there one day. Her mother said maybe.

The growing girl began to say the word "backside" to herself and knew that her mother would be appalled. The girl laughed at bullocks and the sport they had. Then she went one further and jumped up and down and said "Jumping Jack" as if some devil were inside her, touching and tickling the lining of her. It was creepy. It was done out of doors, far from the house, out in the fields, in a grove, or under a canopy of rhododendrons. The buds of the rhododendrons were sticky and oozed with life and everything along with herself was soaking wet and she was given to wandering flushes, and then fits of untoward laughter so that she had to scold herself into some state of normality and this she did by slapping both cheeks vehemently. As a dire punishment she took cups of glauber salts[8] three times a day, choosing to drink it when it was lukewarm and at its most nauseating. She would be told by her father to get out, to stop hatching, to get out from under her mother's apron strings, and he would send her for a spin on the woeful brakeless bicycle. She would go to the chapel finding it empty of all but herself and the lady sacristan who spent her life in there, polishing and rearranging the artificial flowers; or she would go down into a bog and make certain unattainable wishes, but always at the end of every day, and at the end of every thought, and at the beginning of sleep, and the precise moment of wakening it was of her mother and for her mother she existed and her prayers and her good deeds and her ringlets and the ire on her legs[9]—created by the serge of her gym frock—were for her mother's intention, and on and on. Only death could part them and not even that because she resolved that she would take her own life if some disease or some calamity snatched her mother away. Her mother's three-quarter length jacket she would don, sink her hands into the deep pockets and say the name "Delia," her mother's, say it in different tones of voice, over and over again, always in a whisper and a note of conspiracy.

A lovely thing happened. Her mother and father went on a journey by hire car to do a transaction whereby they could get some credit on his lands, and her father did not get drunk but ordered a nice pot of tea, and then sat back gripping his braces and gave her mother a few bob,[1] with which her mother procured a most beautiful lipstick in a ridged gold case. It was like fresh fruit so moist was it, and dark red in color. Her mother and she tried it on over and over again, were comical with it, trying it on, then wiping it off, trying it on again, making cupids[2] so that her mother expostulated and said what scatterbrains they were, and even the father joined in the hilarity and daubed down the mother's cheek and said Fannie Annie and the mother said that was enough, as the lipstick was liable to get broken. With her thumb nail she pressed on the little catch pushing the lipstick down into its case, into its bed.

8. A medicine used as a laxative. 1. Shillings, small British currency.
9. A rash. 2. Bow-shaped lips.

As the years went on it dried out, and developed a peculiar shape and they read somewhere that a lady's character could be told by that particular shape, and they wished that they could discover whether the mother was the extrovert or the shy violet.

The girl had no friends, she didn't need any. Her cup was full. Her mother was the cup, the cupboard, the press[3] with all the things in it, the tabernacle with God in it, the lake with the legends in it, the bog with the wishing wells in it, the sea with the oyster and the corpses in it, her mother a gigantic sponge, a habitation in which she longed to sink and disappear for ever and ever. Yet she was afraid to sink; caught in that hideous trap between fear of sinking and fear of swimming, she moved like a flounderer through this and that; through school, through inoculation, through a man who put his white handkerchief between naked her and naked him, and against a galvanized boway door came, gruntling and disgruntling like a tethered beast upon her; through a best friend, a girl friend who tried to clip the hairs of her vagina with a shears. The hairs of her vagina were mahogany colored and her best friend said that that denoted mortal sin. She agonized over it.

Then came a dreadful blow. Two nuns called and her mother and her father said that she was to stay outside in the kitchen and see that the kettle boiled and then lift it off so that the water would not boil over. She went on tiptoe through the hall and listened at the door of the room. She got it in snatches. She was being discussed. She was being sent away to school. A fee was being discussed and her mother was asking if they could make a reduction. She ran out of the house in a dreadful state. She ran to the chicken run and went inside to cry and to go berserk. The floor was full of damp and gray-green mottled droppings. The nests were full of sour sops of hay. She thought she was going out of her mind. When they found her later her father said to cut out the bull but her mother tried to comfort her by saying they had a prospectus[4] and that she would have to get a whole lot of new clothes in navy blue. But where would the money come from?

In the convent to which they sent her she eventually found solace. A nun became her new idol. A nun with a dreadfully pale face, and a Master's Degree in Science. This nun and herself worked out codes with the eyelids, and the flutter of the lashes, so they always knew each other's moods and feelings, so that the slightest hurt imposed by one was spotted by the other and responded to with a cough. The nun gave another girl more marks at the midterm examination, and did it solely to hurt her, to wound her pride; the nun addressed her briskly in front of the whole class, said her full name and asked her a theological conundrum that was impossible to answer. In turn she let one of the nun's holy pictures fall on the chapel floor where of course it was found by the cleaning nun who gave it back to the nun who gave it to her with a "This seems to have got mislaid." They exchanged Christmas presents and notes that contained blissful innuendos. She had given chocolates with a kingfisher on the cover and she had received a prayer book with gilt edging and it was as tiny as her middle finger. She could not read the print but she held it to herself like a talisman, like a secret scroll in which love was mentioned.

3. An upright closet or case.　　　　4. Description of the school.

Home on holiday it was a different story. Now *she* did the avoiding, the shunning. All the little treats and the carrageen soufflé[5] that her mother had prepared were not gloated over. Then the pink crêpe-de-chine apron that her mother had made from an old dance dress, did not receive the acclamation that the mother expected It was fitted on and at once taken off, and flung over the back of a chair with no praise except to remark on the braiding which was cleverly done.

"These things are not to be sniffed at," her mother said, passing the plate of scones[6] for the third or fourth time. The love of the nun dominated all her thoughts and the nun's pale face got between her and the visible world that she was supposed to be seeing. At times she could taste it. It interfered with her studies, her other friendships, it got known about. She was called to see the Reverend Mother. The nun and herself never had a tête-à-tête again and never swapped holy pictures. The day she was leaving for ever they made an illicit date to meet in the summer-house, out in the grounds, but neither of them turned up. They each sent a message with an apology and it was in fact the messengers who met, a junior girl and a postulant[7] carrying the same sentence on separate lips—"So-and-so is sorry—she wishes to say she can't . . ." They might have broken down or done anything, they might have kissed.

Out of school, away from the spell of nuns and gods and flower gardens and acts of contrition, away from the chapel with its incense and its brimstone sermons, away from surveillance, she met a bakery man who was also a notable hurley[8] player and they started up that kind of courtship common to their sort—a date at the pillar two evenings a week, then to a café to have coffee and cream cakes, to hold hands under the table, to take a bus to her digs, to kiss against a railing and devour each other's faces, as earlier they had devoured the mock cream and the sugar-dusted sponge cakes. But these orgies only increased her hunger, made it into something that could not be appeased. She would recall her mother from the very long ago, in the three-quarter-length jacket of salmon tweed, the brooch on the lapel, the smell of face powder, the lipstick hurriedly put on so that a little of it always smudged on the upper or the lower lip and appeared like some kind of birthmark. Recall that they even had the same mole on the back of the left hand, a mole that did not alter winter or summer and was made to seem paler when the fist was clenched. But she was recalling someone whom she wanted to banish. The bakery man got fed-up, wanted more than a cuddle, hopped it.[9]

Then there was no-one; just a long stretch, doing novenas,[1] working in the library, and her mother's letters arriving, saying the usual things, how life was hard, how inclement the weather, how she'd send a cake that day or the next day as soon as there were enough eggs to make it with. The parcels arrived once a fortnight, bound in layers of newspaper, and then a strong outer layer of brown paper, all held with hideous assortments of twines—binding twine, very white twine, and colored plastic string from the stools that she had taken to making; then great spatters of sealing wax adorning it. Always a registered parcel, always a cake, a pound of butter, and a chicken that had to be cooked at once, because of its being nearly putrid from the four-day journey. It was not

5. An egg dish made with seaweed.
6. British pastries.
7. A novice, applicant for admission to a religious order.

8. Irish version of hockey.
9. Left.
1. A nine-day recitation of prayers.

difficult to imagine the kitchen table, the bucket full of feathers, the moled hand picking away at the pin feathers, the other hand plunging in and drawing out all the undesirables, tremulous, making sure not to break a certain little pouch, which if broken its tobacco-colored contents would taint the flavour of the bird itself. Phow. Always the same implications in each letter, the same cry—"Who knows what life brings. Your father is not hardboiled despite his failings. It makes me sad to think of the little things that I used to be able to do for you." She hated those parcels despite the fact that they were most welcome.

She married. Married in haste. Her mother said from the outset that he was as odd as two left shoes. He worked on an encyclopedia and was a mine of information on certain subjects. His theme was vegetation in pond life. The family lived to themselves. She learned to do chores, to bottle and preserve, to comply, to be a wife, to undress neatly at night, to fold her clothes, to put them on a cane chair making sure to put her corset and her underthings respectfully under her dress or her skirt. It was like being at school again. The mother did not visit, being at odds with the censuring husband. Mother and daughter would meet in a market town midway between each of their rural homes and when they met they sat in some hotel lounge, ordered tea and discussed things that can easily be discussed—recipes, patterns for knitting, her sister, items of furniture that they envisaged buying.

Her mother was getting older, had developed a slight stoop and held up her hands to show the rheumatism in her joints. Then all of a sudden, as if she had just remembered it, she spoke about the cataracts and her journey to the specialist and how the specialist had asked her if she remembered anything about her eyes and how she had to tell him that she had lost her sight for five or six minutes one morning and that then it came back. He told her how lucky it was because in some instances it does not come back at all. She said yes that the shades of life were closing in on her.

The daughter knew that her marriage would not last but she dared not say so. Things were happening such as that they had separate meals, that he did not speak for weeks on end, and yet she defended him, talked of the open pine dresser he had made and her mother rued the fact that she never had a handyman to do odd things for her. She said the window had broken in a storm and that there was still a bit of cardboard in it. She said she had her eye on two armchairs with a slight rock. The daughter longed to give them to her and thought that she might steal from her husband when he was asleep, steal the deposit that is, and pay for them on hire purchase.[2] But they said none of the things that they should have said.

"You didn't get any new style," the mother said, restating her particular dislike for a tweed coat.

"I don't want it," the girl said tersely.

"You were always a softie," the mother said, and inherent in this was disapproval for a man who allowed his wife to be dowdy. Perhaps she thought that her daughter's marriage might have amended for her own.

When her marriage did end the girl wrote and said that it was all over and the mother wrote post-haste exacting two dire promises—the girl must write

2. Renting toward eventual purchase.

back on her oath and promise her that she would never touch an alcoholic drink as long as she lived and she would never again have to do with any man in body or soul. High commands. At the time the girl was walking the streets in a daze and stopping strangers in her plight. One day in a park she met a man who was very sympathetic, a sort of tramp. She told him her story and then all of a sudden he told her this terrible dream. He had wakened up and he was swimming in water and the water kept changing color, it was blue and red and green and these changing colors terrified him. She saw that he was not all there and invented an excuse to be somewhere.

In time she sold her bicycle and pawned a gold bracelet and a gold watch and chain. She fled to England. She wanted to go somewhere where she knew no one. She was trying to start afresh to wipe out the previous life. She was staggered by the assaults of memory—a bowl with her mother's menstrual cloth soaking in it and her sacrilegious idea that if lit it could resemble the heart of Christ, the conical wick of the aladdin lamp[3] being lit too high and disappearing into a jet of black, the roses, the five freakish winter roses that were in bloom when the pipes burst, the mice that came out of the shoes, then out of the shoe closet itself, onto the floor where the newspapers had been laid to prevent the muck and manure of the trampling men, the little box of rouge that almost asked to be licked so dry and rosy was it, the black range whose temperature could be tested by just spitting on it and watching the immediate jig and trepidation of the spit, the pancakes on Shrove Tuesday[4] (if there wasn't a row), the flitches of bacon hanging to smoke, the forgotten jam jars with inevitably the bit of moldy jam in the bottom, and always, like an overseeing spirit, the figure of the mother who was responsible for each and every one of these facets, and always the pending doom in which the mother would perhaps be struck with the rim of a bucket or a sledgehammer, or some improvised weapon, struck by the near-crazed father. It would be something as slight as that the mother had a splinter under her nail and the girl felt her own nail being lifted up, felt hurt to the quick, or felt her mother's sputum, could taste it like a dish.

She was possessed by these thoughts, in the library where she worked day in and day out, filing and cataloging and handing over books. They were more than thoughts, they were the presence of this woman whom she resolved to kill. Yes she would have to kill. She would have to take up arms and commit a murder. She thought of choking or drowning. Certainly the method had to do with suffocation, and she foresaw herself holding big suffocating pillows or a bolster, in the secrecy of the Blue Room where it had all began. Her mother turned into the bursting red pipes, into the brown dishcloths, into swamps of black-brown blooded water. Her mother turned into a streetwalker, and paraded. Her mother was taking down her knickers in public, squatting to do awful things, left little piddles, small as puppies' piddles, her mother was drifting down a well in a big bucket, crying for help but no help was forthcoming. The oddest dream came along. Her mother was on her deathbed, having just given birth to her—the little tonsured head jutted above the sheet—and had a neck rash, and was busy trying to catch a little insect, trying to cup it in the palms of her hands and was saying that in the end "all there is, is yourself and

3. An oil-burning lamp like that from which Aladdin summoned a genie in *The Arabian Nights*. 4. The Tuesday preceding Ash Wednesday.

this little insect that you're trying to kill." The word kill was everywhere, on the hoardings, in the evening air, on the tip of her thoughts.

But life goes on. She bought a yellow two-piece, worsted, and wrote home and said, "I must be getting cheerful, I wear less black." Her mother wrote, "I have only one wish now and it is that we will be buried together." The more she tried to kill the more potent the advances became. Her mother was taking out all old souvenirs, the brown scapulars[5] salvaged from the hurtful night in December, a mug, with their similar initials on it, a tablecloth that the girl had sent from her first earnings when she qualified as a librarian. The mother's letters began to show signs of wander. They broke off in mid-sentence, one was written on blotting paper and almost indecipherable, they contained snatches of information such as "So-and-so died, there was a big turn-out at the funeral," "I could do with a copper bracelet for rheumatism," "You know life gets lonelier."

She dreaded the summer holidays but still she went. The geese and the gander would be trailing by the river bank, the cows would gape at her as if an alien had entered their terrain. It was only the horses she avoided—always on the nervy side as if ready to bolt. The fields themselves as beguiling as ever, fields full of herbage and meadowsweet, fields adorned with spangles of gold as the buttercups caught the shafts of intermittent sunshine. If only she could pick them up and carry them away. They sat indoors. The dog had a deep cut in his paw and it was thought that a fox did it, that the dog and the fox had tussled one night. As a result of this he was admitted to the house. The mother and the dog spoke although not a word passed between them. The father asked pointed questions such as would it rain or was it tea-time. For a pastime they then discussed all the dogs that they had had. The mother especially remembered Monkey and said that he was a queer one, that he'd know what you were thinking of. The father and daughter remembered further back to Shep the big collie who guarded the child's pram and drove thoroughbred horses off the drive, causing risk to his own person. Then there were the several pairs of dogs all of whom sparred and quarreled throughout their lives, yet all of whom died within a week of one another, the surviving dog dying of grief for his pal. No matter how they avoided it, death crept into the conversation. The mother said unconvincingly how lucky they were never to have been crippled, to have enjoyed good health and enough to eat. The curtains behind her chair were a warm red velveteen and gave a glow to her face. A glow that was reminiscent of her lost beauty.

She decided on a celebration. She owed it to her mother. They would meet somewhere else, away from that house, and its skeletons and its old cunning tug at the heart strings. She planned it a year in advance, a holiday in a hotel, set in beautiful woodland surroundings and on the verge of the Atlantic Ocean. Their first hours were happily and most joyfully passed as they looked at the rooms, the view, the various tapestries, found where things were located, looked at the games room and then at the display cabinets where there was cut glass and marble souvenirs on sale. The mother said that everything was "Poison, dear." They took a walk by the seashore and remarked one to the other on the different stripes of color on the water, how definite they were,

5. Garments worn by monks and nuns.

each color claiming its surface of sea, just like oats or grass or a plowed land. The brown plaits of seaweed slapped and slathered over rocks, long-legged birds let out their lonesome shrieks and the mountains that loomed beyond seemed to hold the specter of continents inside them so vast were they, so old. They dined early. Afterwards there was a singsong and the mother whispered that money wasn't everything. She said, "Look at the hard-boiled faces."

Something snapped inside of the girl and forgetting that this was her errand of mercy, she thought instead how this mother had a whole series of grudges, bitter grudges concerning love, happiness, and her hard inpecunious fate. The angora jumpers, the court shoes,[6] the brown and the fawn garments, the milk complexion, the auburn tresses, the little breathlessnesses, the hands worn by toil, the sore feet, these were but the trimmings and behind them lay the real person who demanded her pound of flesh from life. They sat on a sofa. The mother sipped tea and she her whiskey. They said cheers.

The girl tried to get the conversation back, to before she was born, or before other children were born, to the dances and the annual race-day and the courtship that pre-empted the marriage. The mother refused to speak, baulked, had no story to tell, said that even if she had a story she would not tell it. Said she hated raking up the past. The girl tweezed it out of her in scraps. The mother said yes, that as a young girl she was bold and obstinate and she did have fancy dreams but soon learned to toe the line. Then she burst out laughing and said she climbed up a ladder once in to the chapel, and into the confessional so as to be the first person there to have her confession heard by the missioner.[7] The missioner nearly lost his life because he didn't know how anyone could possibly have got in, since the door was bolted and he had simply come to sit in the confessional to compose himself, when there she was spouting sins. What sins? The mother said, "Oh I forget, love, I forget everything now."

The girl said, "No you don't."

They said good-night and arranged to meet in the dining room the following morning.

The mother didn't sleep a wink, complained that her eyes and her nose were itchy, and she feared she was catching a cold. She drank tea noisily, slugged it down. They walked by the sea that was now the color of gun-metal and the mountains were no longer a talking point. They visited a ruined monastery where the nettles, the sorrel, the clover and the seedy dock grew high in a rectangle. Powder shed from walls that were built of solid stone. The mother said that probably it was a chapel or a chancery, a seat of sanctity down through the centuries and she genuflected. To the girl it was just a ruin, unhallowed, full of weeds and buzzing with wasps and insects. Outside there was a flock of noisy starlings. She could feel the trouble brewing. She said that there was a lovely smell, that it was most likely some wild herb and she got down on her knees to locate it. Peering with eyes and fingers among the low grass she came upon a nest of ants that were crawling over a tiny bit of ground with an amazing amount of energy and will. She felt barely in control.

6. Pumps. "Jumpers": sweaters.
7. One who conducts or is in charge of a parochial mission.

They trailed back in time for coffee. The mother said hotel life was demoralizing as she bit into an iced biscuit.[8] The porter fetched the paper. Two strange little puppies lapped at the mother's feet, and the porter said they would have to be drowned if they were not claimed before dusk. The mother said what a shame and recalled her own little pups who didn't eat clothes on the line during the day but when night came got down to work on them.

"You'd be fit to kill them, but of course you couldn't," she said lamely.

She was speaking of puppies from ten or fifteen years back.

He asked if she was enjoying it and the mother said, "I quote the saying 'See Naples and Die,' the same applies to this."

The daughter knew that the mother wanted to go home there and then, but they had booked for four days and it would be an admission of failure to cut it short. She asked the porter to arrange a boat trip to the island inhabited by seabirds, then a car drive to the lakes of Killarney and another to see the home of the liberator, Daniel O'Connell,[9] the man who had asked to have his dead heart sent to Rome, to the Holy See. The porter said certainly and made a great to-do about accepting the tip she gave him. It was he who told them where Daniel O'Connell's heart lay, and the mother said it was the most rending thing she had ever heard, and the most devout. Then she said yes that a holiday was an uplift, but that it came too late as she wasn't used to the spoiling. The girl did not like that. The girl showed the porter a photograph of a gouged torso, said that was how she felt, that was the state of her mind. The mother said later she didn't think the girl should have said such a thing and wasn't it a bit extreme. Then the mother wrote a six-page letter to her friend Molly and the girl conspired to be the one to post it so that she could read it and find some clue to the chasm that stretched between them. As it happened she could not bring herself to read it, because the mother gave it to her unsealed, as if she had guessed those thoughts and the girl bit her lower lip and said "How's Molly doing?"

The mother became very sentimental and said "Poor creature, blind as a bat," but added that people were kind and how when they saw her with the white cane, they knew. The letter would be read to her by a daughter who was married and overweight and who suffered with her nerves. The girl recalled an autograph book, the mother's, with its confectionery-colored pages and its likewise rhymes and ditties. The mother recalled ice creams that she had eaten in Brooklyn long before. The mother remembered the embroidery she had done, making the statement in stitches that there was a rose in the heart of New York. The girl said stitches played such an important role in life and said, "A stitch in time saves nine." They tittered. They were getting nearer.

The girl delicately inquired into the name and occupation of the mother's previous lover, in short the father's rival. The mother would not divulge, except to say that he loved his mother, loved his sister, was most thoughtful, and that was that. Another long silence. Then the mother stirred in her chair, coughed, confided, said that in fact she and this thoughtful man, fearing, somehow sensing that they would not be man and wife, had made each other a solemn pact one Sunday afternoon in Coney Island[1] over an ice. They swore

8. Frosted cookie.
9. Irish Catholic political leader (1775–1847).

1. Amusement park in Brooklyn, New York.

that they would get in touch with each other towards the end of their days. Lo and behold after fifty-five years the mother wrote that letter!

The girl's heart quickened, and her blood danced to the news of this tryst, this long sustained clandestine passion. She felt that something momentous was about to get uttered. They could be true at last, they need not hide from one another's gaze. Her mother would own up. Her own life would not be one of curtained shame. She thought of the married man who was waiting for her in London, the one who took her for delicious weekends and she shivered. The mother said that her letter had been returned and probably his sister had refused it, always being jealous. The girl begged to know the contents of the letter. The mother said it was harmless. The girl said go on. She tried to revive the spark but the mother's mind was made up. The mother said that there was no such thing as love between the sexes and that it was all bull. She reaffirmed that there was only one kind of love and that was a mother's love for her child.

There passed between them then such a moment, not a moment of sweetness, not a moment of reaffirmation but a moment dense with hate—one hating and the other receiving it like rays, and then it was glossed over by the mother's remark about the grandeur of the ceiling. The girl gritted her teeth and resolved that they would not be buried in the same grave, and vehemently lit a cigarette although they had hardly tasted the first course.

"I think you're very unsettled," her mother said.

"I didn't get that from the ground," the daughter said.

The mother bridled, stood up to leave, but was impeded by a waiter who was carrying a big chafing dish, over which a bright blue flame riotously spread. She sat down as if pushed down and said that that remark was the essence of cruelty. The girl said sorry. The mother said she had done all she could and that, without maid, or car or cheque book or any of life's luxuries. Life's dainties had not dropped on her path, she had to knit her own sweaters, cut and sew her own skirts, be her own hairdresser. The girl said for God's sake to let them enjoy it. The mother said that at seventy-eight one had time to think.

"And at thirty-eight," the girl said.

She wished then that her mother's life had been happier, and had not exacted so much from her and she felt she was being milked emotionally. With all her heart she pitied this woman, pitied her for having her dreams pupped and for betrothing herself to a life of suffering. But also she blamed her. They were both wild with emotion. They were speaking out of turn and eating carelessly, the very food seemed to taunt them. The mother wished that one of those white-coated waiters would tactfully take her plate of dinner away and replace it with a nice warm pot of tea, or better still that she could be home in her own house by her own fireside, and furthermore she wished that her daughter had never grown into the cruel feelingless hussy that she was.

"What else could I have done?" the mother said.

"A lot," the girl said, and gulped at once.

The mother excused herself. "When I pass on, I won't be sorry," she said.

Up in the room she locked and bolted the door, and lay curled up on the bed, knotted as a fetus, with a clump of paper handkerchiefs in front of her mouth. Downstairs she left behind her a grown girl, remembering a woman she most bottomlessly loved, then unloved, and cut off from herself in the

middle of a large dining room while confronting a plate of undercooked lamb strewn with mint.

 Death in its way comes just as much of a surprise as birth. We know we will die, just as the mother knows that she is primed to deliver around such and such a time, yet there is a fierce inner exclamation from her at the first onset of labor and when the water breaks she is already a shocked woman. So it was. The reconciliation that she had hoped for, and indeed intended to instigate never came. She was abroad at a conference when her mother died and when she arrived through her own front door the phone was ringing with the news of her mother's death. The message though clear to her ears was incredulous to herself. How had her mother died and why? In a hospital, as a result of a heart attack. Straight away she set back for the airport hoping to get a seat on a late-night flight.

 The last plane had gone but she decided to sit there until dawn and thought to herself that she might be sitting up at her mother's wake. The tube lighting[2] drained the color from all the other waiting faces and though she could not cry she longed to tell someone that something incalculable had happened to her. They seemed as tired and as inert as she did. Coffee, bread, whiskey, all tasted the same, tasted of nothing, or at best of blotting paper. There was no man in her life at the moment, no one to ring up and tell the news to. Even if there was, she thought that lovers never know the full story of one another, only know the bit they meet, never know the iceberg of hurts, that have gone before, and therefore are always strangers, or semi-strangers, even in the folds of love. She could not cry. She asked herself if perhaps her heart had turned to lead. Yet she dreaded that on impulse she might break down, and that an attendant might have to lead her away.

 When she arrived at the hospital next day the remains had been removed and was now on its way through the center of Ireland. Through Joyce's[3] Ireland as she always called it, and thought of the great central plain open to the elements, the teeming rain, the drifting snow, the winds that gave chapped faces to farmers and cattle dealers and sometimes croup to the young calves. She passed the big towns and the lesser towns, recited snatches of recitation that she remembered and hoped that no one could consider her disrespectful because the hire car was a bright ketchup red. When she got to her own part of the world the sign of the mountains moved her as they had always done—solemn, beautiful, unchanging except for different streaks of color. Solid and timeless. She had bought a sandwich at the airport and now removed the glacé paper[4] with her teeth and bit into it. The two days ahead would be awful. There would be her father's wild grief, there would be her aunt's grief, there would be cousins and friends, and strays and workmen, there would be a grave wide open and as they walked to it they would walk over other graves under hawthorn stamping the nettles as they went. She knew the graveyard very well, since childhood. She knew the tombs, the headstones and the hidden vaults. She used to play there alone and both challenge and cower from ghosts. The inside of the grave was always a rich broody brown and the gravedigger would probably lace it with a trellis of ivy or convolvulus leaf.

2. Fluorescent lighting. 4. Waxed paper.
3. The novelist James Joyce (1882–1941).

At that very moment she found that she had just caught up with the funeral cortege but she could hardly believe that it would be her mother's. Too much of a coincidence. They drove at a great pace and without too much respect for the dead. She kept up with them. The light was fading, the bushes were like blurs, the air bat-black, the birds had ceased and the mountains were dark bulks. If the file of cars took a right from the main road towards the lake town then it must certainly be her mother's. It did. The thought of catching up with it was what made her cry. She cried with such a delight, cried like a child who has done something good and is being praised for it and yet cannot bear the weight of emotion. She cried the whole way through the lakeside town and sobbed as they crossed the old bridge towards the lovely dark leafy country road that led towards home. She cried like a homing bird. She was therefore seen as a daughter deeply distressed when she walked past the file of mourners outside the chapel gate, and when she shook the hand or touched the sleeves of those who had come forward to meet her. Earlier a friend had left flowers at the car-hire desk and she carried them as if she had specially chosen them. She thought they think it is grief but it is not the grief they think it is. It is emptiness more than grief. It is a grief at not being able to be whole-hearted again. It is not a false grief but it is unyielding, it is blood from a stone.

Inside the chapel she found her father howling, and in the first rows closest to the altar and to the coffin the chief mourners, both men and women, were sobbing, or having just sobbed were drying their eyes. As she shook hands with each one of them she heard the same condolence—"Sorry for your trouble, sorry for your trouble, sorry for your trouble."

That night in her father's house, people supped and ate and reminisced. As if in mourning a huge branch of a nearby tree had fallen down. Its roots were like a hand stuck up in the air. The house already reeked of neglect. She kept seeing her mother's figure coming through the door with a large tray, laden down with dainties. The undertaker called her out. He said since she had not seen the remains he would bring her to the chapel and unscrew the lid. She shrank from it but she went because to say no would have wrought her disgrace. The chapel was cold, the wood creaked and even the flowers at night seemed to have departed from themselves, like ghost flowers. Just as he lifted the lid he asked her to please step away and she thought something fateful has happened, the skin has turned black or a finger moves or, the worst or, she is not dead, she has merely visited the other world. Then he called her and she walked solemnly over and she almost screamed. The mouth was trying to speak. She was sure of it. One eyelid was not fully shut. It was unfinished. She kissed the face and felt a terrible pity.

"Oh soul," she said, "where are you, on your voyaging and oh soul, are you immortal?"

Suddenly she was afraid for her mother's fate and afraid for the fact that one day she too would have to make it. She longed to hold the face and utter consolations to it but she was unable. She thought of the holiday that had been such a fiasco and the love that she had first so cravenly and so rampantly given and the love that she had so callously and so conclusively taken back. She thought why did she have to withdraw, why do people have to withdraw, why?

After the funeral she went around the house tidying and searching—as if for some secret. In the Blue Room damp had seeped through the walls and

there were little burrs of fungus that clung like bobbins on a hat veiling.[5] In the drawers she found bits of her mother's life. Wishes. Dreams contained in such things as a gauze rose of the darkest drenchingest red. Perfume bottles, dance shoes, boxes of handkerchiefs and the returned letter. It was from the man called Vincent, the man her mother had intended to marry but whom she had forsaken when she left New York and came back to Ireland, back to her destiny. For the most part it was a practical letter outlining the size of her farm, the crops they grew, asking about mutual friends, his circumstances and so forth. It seems he worked in a meat factory. There was only one little leak— "I think of you, you would not believe how often." The envelope had marked on the outside—"Return to Sender." The words seemed brazen as if he himself had written them.

There were so many hats, hats with flowers, hats with veiling, all of pastel colour, hats conceived for summer outings and meant for rainless climes. Ah the garden parties she must have conceived. Never having had the money for real style her mother had invested in imitation things—an imitation crocodile handbag and an imitation fur bolero.[6] It felt light as if made of hair. There were, too, pink embroidered corsets, long bloomers and three unworn cardigans.

For some reason she put her hand above the mantelpiece to the place where they hid shillings when she was young. There wrapped in cobweb was an envelope addressed to herself in her mother's handwriting. It sent shivers through her and she prayed that it did not bristle with accusations. Inside there were some trinkets, a gold sovereign and some money. The notes were dirty, crumpled and folded many times. How long had the envelope lain there? How had her mother managed to save? There was no letter, yet in her mind she concocted little tendernesses that her mother might have written—words such as "Buy yourself a jacket," or "Have a night out," or "Don't spend this on masses." She wanted something, some communiqué. But there was no such thing.

A new wall had arisen, stronger and sturdier than before. Their life together and all those exchanges were like so many split feelings and she looked to see some sign, or hear some murmur. Instead a silence filled the room and there was a vaster silence beyond as if the house itself had died or had been carefully put down to sleep.

1978

5. I.e., like knots in a veil that hangs from a hat. 6. A short jacket.

FLEUR ADCOCK

1934–

Karen Fleur Adcock was born in Papakura, New Zealand, and educated at Victoria University in Wellington. Twice briefly married and the mother of two children, she has worked mainly as a librarian, first in New Zealand and then in London, where she joined the Foreign and Commonwealth Office in 1963. A year later, her first volumes of poetry began to appear in print: *The Eye of the Hurricane* (1964) was followed by *Tigers* (1967), *High Tide in the Garden* (1971), *The Scenic Route*

(1974), *The Inner Harbour* (1979), *Selected Poems* (1983), *The Incident Book* (1986), and *Time-Zones* (1991). Characterized by a disconcerting juxtaposition of the mundane with the bizarre, her poems have earned her a number of awards in her native New Zealand. While she has been praised for the "suballegory" she makes out of domesticity in elegantly wrought poems, Adcock has also been recognized for dream poems in which "something angry, or nightmarish, or discomfiting leaps out." Perhaps it is what one reviewer called her "well-bred, genteel air" that allows Adcock to write a poem like *Against Coupling* on the previously unmentionable subject of "the solitary act."

For a Five-Year-Old

A snail is climbing up the window-sill
Into your room, after a night of rain.
You call me in to see, and I explain
That it would be unkind to leave it there:
It might crawl to the floor; we must take care 5
That no one squashes it. You understand,
And carry it outside, with careful hand,
To eat a daffodil.

I see, then, that a kind of faith prevails:
Your gentleness is molded still by words 10
From me, who have trapped mice and shot wild birds,
From me, who drowned your kittens, who betrayed
Your closest relatives, and who purveyed
The harshest kind of truth to many another.
But that is how things are: I am your mother, 15
And we are kind to snails.

1967

Miss Hamilton in London

It would not be true to say she was doing nothing:
She visited several bookshops, spent an hour
In the Victoria and Albert Museum (Indian section),
And walked carefully through the streets of Kensington[1]
Carrying five mushrooms in a paper bag, 5
A tin of black pepper, a literary magazine,
And enough money to pay the rent for two weeks.
The sky was cloudy, leaves lay on the pavements.

Nor did she lack human contacts: she spoke
To three shop-assistants and a newsvendor, 10
And returned the "Goodnight" of a museum attendant.
Arriving home, she wrote a letter to someone
In Canada, as it might be, or in New Zealand,

1. The middle-class London borough in which the Victoria and Albert Museum is located.

Listened to the news as she cooked her meal,
And conversed for five minutes with the landlady. 15
The air was damp with the mist of late autumn.

A full day, and not unrewarding.
Night fell at the usual seasonal hour.
She drew the curtains, switched on the electric fire,
Washed her hair and read until it was dry, 20
Then went to bed; where, for the hours of darkness,
She lay pierced by thirty black spears
And felt her limbs numb, her eyes burning,
And dark rust carried along her blood.

 1967

Against Coupling

I write in praise of the solitary act:
of not feeling a trespassing tongue
forced into one's mouth, one's breath
smothered, nipples crushed against the
ribcage, and that metallic tingling 5
in the chin set off by a certain odd nerve:

unpleasure. Just to avoid those eyes would help—
such eyes as a young girl draws life from,
listening to the vegetal
rustle within her, as his gaze 10
stirs polypal[1] fronds in the obscure
sea-bed of her body, and her own eyes blur.

There is much to be said for abandoning
this no longer novel exercise—
for not "participating in 15
a total experience"—when
one feels like the lady in Leeds who
had seen *The Sound of Music*[2] eighty-six times;

or more, perhaps, like the school drama mistress
producing *A Midsummer Night's Dream*[3] 20
for the seventh year running, with
yet another cast from 5B.
Pyramus and Thisbe are dead, but
the hole in the wall can still be troublesome.

1. Like the tiny organism the polyp, which has a mouth surrounded by tentacles.
2. A very popular sentimental musical film (1965) by Rodgers and Hammerstein, starring Julie Andrews.
3. A comedy (1595) by William Shakespeare, which includes a short burlesque of the story of Pyramus and Thisbe, two doomed lovers who had to communicate through a hole in a wall because their families forbade them to meet.

I advise you, then, to embrace it without 25
encumbrance. No need to set the scene,
dress up (or undress), make speeches.
Five minutes of solitude are
enough—in the bath, or to fill
that gap between the Sunday papers and lunch. 30

<div align="right">1971</div>

The Voyage Out

The weekly dietary scale
per adult: pork and Indian beef,
three pounds together; one of sugar
two of potatoes, three and a half
of flour; a gill of vinegar; 5
salt, pepper, a pint of oatmeal;
coffee, two ounces, likewise tea;
six of butter, suet, treacle,[1]
and, in the tropics, of lime-juice;
grudging grants of mustard and pickle; 10
split peas, raisins, currants, rice,
and half a pound of biscuit a day.
A diet for the young and fit:
monotonous, but not starvation—
and Martha traded half her ration 15
for extra lime-juice from the crew
Their quarters, also, adequate.
So not the middle passage;[2] no.
But not a pleasure-cruise, either.
A hundred days of traveling steerage 20
under capricious canvas; Martha
newly pregnant, struggling to manage
the first four (Tom, Eliza, Joe,
Annie); to keep them cool and clean
from a two-gallon can of water; 25
to calm their sleeping; to stay awake,
so heavy, herself; to protect the daughter
she rocked unborn in the swaying hammock
below her ribs (who would be Jane).
True, the family was together. 30
But who could envy Martha? Sick
with salt meat; thirsty; and gazing on
a sky huge as the whole Atlantic,
storm-waves like Sieve Gallion,[3]
and no more Ireland than went with her. 35

<div align="right">1974</div>

1. A thick syrup.
2. I.e., the passage of slaves from West Africa to the
West Indies.

3. A hill in Londonderry, northern Ireland.

On the Border

Dear posterity, it's 2 a.m.
and I can't sleep for the smothering heat,
or under mosquito nets. The others
are swathed in theirs, humid and sweating,
long white packets on rows of chairs 5
(no bunks. The building isn't finished).

I prowled in the dark back room for water
and came outside for a cigarette
and a pee in waist-high leafy scrub.
The moon is brilliant: the same moon, 10
I have to believe, as mine in England
or theirs in the places where I'm not.

Knobbly trees mark the horizon,
black and angular, with no leaves:
blossoming flame-trees; and behind them 15
soft throbbings come from the village.
Birds or animals croak and howl;
the river rustles; there could be snakes.

I don't care. I am standing here,
posterity, on the face of the earth, 20
letting the breeze blow up my nightdress,
writing in English, as I do,
in all this tropical non-silence.
Now let me tell you about the elephants.

1983

Street Song

Pink Lane, Strawberry Lane, Pudding Chare:
someone is waiting, I don't know where;
hiding among the nursery names,
he wants to play peculiar games.

In Leazes Terrace or Leazes Park 5
someone is loitering in the dark,
feeling the giggles rise in his throat
and fingering something under his coat.

He could be sidling along Forth Lane
to stop some girl from catching her train, 10
or stalking the grounds of the RVI
to see if a student nurse goes by.

In Belle Grove Terrace or Fountain Row
or Hunter's Road he's raring to go—

unless he's the quiet shape you'll meet 15
on the cobbles in Back Stowell Street.

Monk Street, Friars Street, Gallowgate
are better avoided when it's late.
Even in Sandhill and the Side
there are shadows where a man could hide. 20

So don't go lightly along Darn Crock
because the Ripper's been brought to book.[1]
Wear flat shoes, and be ready to run:
remember, sisters, there's more than one.

1983

1. Brought to account. The so-called Yorkshire Ripper, held responsible for a series of thirteen murders that began in 1975, was arrested in January 1981; most of the women he attacked were prostitutes. He took his name from Jack the Ripper, the never-identified murderer of at least seven women in London's East End in 1888.

KAMALA DAS

1934–

Kamala Das has traced her love of poetry back to her grand-uncle Nalapat Narayana Menon, a philosopher, to her mother, Nalapat Balamani Amma, a poet, and to the matriarchal community of Nayars, with its four-hundred-year-old ancestral house that contained a number of ancient manuscripts and books of mantras. She was born in Malabar, south India, and privately educated. At fifteen years of age, she married K. Madhava Das, and the couple had three sons. Several volumes of verse—*Summer in Calcutta: Fifty Poems* (1965), *The Descendants* (1967), and *The Old Playhouse and Other Poems* (1973)—have established her reputation as a lyricist who defies the traditional taboos placed on upper-class married Indian women, specifically the taboo against candid sexual expression. In addition, she has published a novel, *Alphabet of Lust* (1977), many volumes of short stories, including *Mathilukah* (*Walls*, 1972) and *A Doll for the Child Prostitute* (1977), and an autobiography, *My Story* (1978). *Kamala Das: A Selection with Essays on Her Work* appeared in 1986 and *The Best of Kamala Das*, in 1991.

According to Das her novel, stories, and autobiography were "tor[n] . . . to shreds" by critics who viewed her works as eccentric or naïve. Yet, together with her verse, they also established her effort "to be real and honest to my readers." Composed, for the most part, in an English fashioned to retain Indian cadences and concerns, Das's poetry also reflects the "Indo-Anglian" inheritance she analyzes in *An Introduction*.

An Introduction

I don't know politics but I know the names
Of those in power, and can repeat them like
Days of the week, or names of months, beginning with

KAMALA DAS

Nehru.[1] I am Indian, very brown, born in
Malabar, I speak three languages, write in 5
Two, dream in one. Don't write in English, they said,
English is not your mother-tongue. Why not leave
Me alone, critics, friends, visiting cousins,
Every one of you? Why not let me speak in
Any language I like? The language I speak 10
Becomes mine, its distortions, its queernesses
All mine, mine alone. It is half English, half
Indian, funny perhaps, but it is honest,
It is as human as I am human, don't
You see? It voices my joys, my longings, my 15
Hopes, and it is useful to me as cawing
Is to crows or roaring to the lions, it
Is human speech, the speech of the mind that is
Here and not there, a mind that sees and hears and
Is aware. Not the deaf, blind speech 20
Of trees in storm or of monsoon clouds or of rain or the
Incoherent mutterings of the blazing
Funeral pyre. I was child, and later they
Told me I grew, for I became tall, my limbs
Swelled and one or two places sprouted hair. When 25
I asked for love, not knowing what else to ask
For, he drew a youth of sixteen into the
Bedroom and closed the door. He did not beat me
But my sad woman-body felt so beaten.
The weight of my breasts and womb crushed me. I shrank 30
Pitifully. Then . . . I wore a shirt and my
Brother's trousers, cut my hair short and ignored
My womanliness. Dress in saris,[2] be girl,
Be wife, they said. Be embroiderer, be cook,
Be a quarreller with servants. Fit in. Oh, 35
Belong, cried the categorizers. Don't sit
On walls or peep in through our lace-draped windows.
Be Amy, or be Kamala. Or, better
Still, be Madhavikutty.[3] It is time to
Choose a name, a role. Don't play pretending games. 40
Don't play at schizophrenia or be a
Nympho. Don't cry embarrassingly loud when
Jilted in love . . . I met a man, loved him. Call
Him not by any name, he is every man
Who wants a woman, just as I am every 45
Woman who seeks love. In him . . . the hungry haste
Of rivers, in me . . . the ocean's tireless
Waiting. Who are you, I ask each and everyone,
The answer is, it is I. Anywhere and
Everywhere, I see the one who calls himself 50
I; in this world, he is tightly packed like the
Sword in its sheath. It is I who drink lonely

1. Jawaharlal Nehru (1889–1964), India's first prime
minister after it gained independence.
2. Traditional dress of Indian women.

3. Madhavikutty is the pseudonym I use when I write
stories in Malayalam, the language spoken here in
Kerala State [Das's note].

Drinks at twelve, midnight, in hotels of strange towns.
It is I who laugh, it is I who make love
And then feel shame, it is I who lie dying 55
With a rattle in my throat. I am sinner,
I am saint. I am the beloved and the
Betrayed. I have no joys which are not yours, no
Aches which are not yours. I too call myself I.

1962 1962, 1965

AUDRE LORDE
1934–1992

Audre Lorde once described herself as a "black lesbian feminist warrior poet," adding that "when I say myself, I mean not only the Audre who inhabits my body but all those feisty, incorrigible black women who insist on standing up and saying '*I am* and you cannot wipe me out, no matter how irritating I am, how much you fear what I might represent.' " Of West Indian descent, Lorde was born and educated in New York City, receiving a B.A from Hunter College and an M.L.S. from Columbia University. After some years as a librarian for the City University of New York, she became a teacher of creative writing, first at Tougaloo College in Mississippi and later at John Jay College and Hunter College in New York. Her books include numerous collections of verse, among them *The First Cities* (1968), *Cables to Rage* (1970), *Coal* (1976), *The Black Unicorn* (1978), *Our Dead Behind Us* (1986), *Undersong: Chosen Poems, Old and New* (1992), and *The Marvelous Arithmetics of Distance* (1992); along with an account of her struggle with breast cancer—*The Cancer Journals* (1980)—and a fictionalized memoir of her development as an artist and coming of age as a lesbian—*Zami: A New Spelling of My Name* (1982), which she calls a "biomythography."

Lorde explained that her work owes much to the "legends of . . . struggle and survival" embedded in the writings of such African-American artists as Toni Morrison and Ralph Ellison, and to similar legends recounted by African writers ranging from Chinua Achebe and Amos Tutuola to Flora Nwapa and Ama Ata Aidoo; in addition, she was fascinated by the matriarchal myths and goddesses of Africa and of the West Indian island Carriacou, where her mother was born. As the title *Cables to Rage* indicates, however, she was conscious of the roots of her own anger at North American racism and sexism from early in her career, and the poem *Coal* suggests the strength through which she transformed rage at racism into triumphant self-assertion.

In an essay titled *The Uses of the Erotic*, Lorde indicated that for her "love [is] a source of tremendous power," while in a late interview she declared, "I speak of the erotic as the deepest life force, a force which moves us toward living in a fundamental way. And when I say living I mean it as that force which moves us toward what will accomplish real positive change." Her own life force was extraordinarily strong, sustaining her through a battle with cancer that lasted for more than a dozen years; she finally succumbed to the disease in 1992.

Coal

I
is the total black, being spoken
from the earth's inside.
There are many kinds of open
how a diamond comes into a knot of flame
how sound comes into a word, colored 5
by who pays what for speaking.

Some words are open like a diamond
on glass windows
singing out within the passing crash of sun
Then there are words like stapled wagers 10
in a perforated book,—buy and sign and tear apart—
and come whatever wills all chances
the stub remains
an ill-pulled tooth with a ragged edge.
Some words live in my throat 15
breeding like adders. Others know sun
seeking like gypsies over my tongue
to explode through my lips
like young sparrows bursting from shell.
Some words 20
bedevil me.

Love is a word, another kind of open.
As the diamond comes into a knot of flame
I am Black because I come from the earth's inside
now take my word for jewel in the open light. 25

 1976

On a Night of the Full Moon

I

Out of my flesh that hungers
and my mouth that knows
comes the shape I am seeking
for reason.
The curve of your waiting body 5
fits my waiting hand
your breasts warm as sunlight
your lips quick as young birds
between your thighs the sweet
sharp taste of limes. 10

Thus I hold you
frank in my heart's eye
in my skin's knowing
as my fingers conceive your flesh

I feel your stomach 15
moving against me.

Before the moon wanes again
we shall come together.

II

And I would be the moon
spoken over your beckoning flesh 20
breaking against reservations
beaching thought
my hands at your high tide
over and under inside you
and the passing of hungers 25
attended, forgotten.

Dark.y risen
the moon speaks
my eyes
judging your roundness 30
delightful.

 1976

Now That I Am Forever with Child

How the days went
while you were blooming within me
I remember each upon each—
the swelling changed planes of my body
and how you first fluttered, then jumped 5
and I thought it was my heart.

How the days wound down
and the turning of winter
I recall, with you growing heavy
against the wind. I thought 10
now her hands
are formed, and her hair
has started to curl
now her teeth are done
now she sneezes. 15
Then the seed opened
I bore you one morning just before spring
My head rang like a fiery piston
my legs were towers between which
a new world was passing. 20

Since then
I can only distinguish
one thread within running hours

You, flowing through selves
toward You. 25

<div align="right">1976</div>

From the House of Yemanjá[1]

My mother had two faces and a frying pot
where she cooked up her daughters
into girls
before she fixed our dinner.
My mother had two faces 5
and a broken pot
where she hid out a perfect daughter
who was not me
I am the sun and moon and forever hungry
for her eyes. 10

I bear two women upon my back
one dark and rich and hidden
in the ivory hungers of the other
mother
pale as a witch 15
yet steady and familiar
brings me bread and terror
in my sleep
her breasts are huge exciting anchors
in the midnight storm. 20

All this has been
before
in my mother's bed
time has no sense
I have no brothers 25
and my sisters are cruel.

Mother I need
mother I need
mother I need your blackness now
as the august earth needs rain. 30

I am
the sun and moon and forever hungry
the sharpened edge
where day and night shall meet

1. Mother of the other *Orisha* [goddesses and gods of the Yoruba people of Western Nigeria], Yemanjá is also the goddess of oceans. Rivers are said to flow from her breasts. One legend has it that a son tried to rape her. She fled until she collapsed, and from her breasts, the rivers flowed. Another legend says that a husband insulted Yemanjá's long breasts, and when she fled with her pots he knocked her down. From her breasts flowed the rivers, and from her body then sprang forth all the other *Orisha*. River-smooth stones are Yemanjá's symbol, and the sea is sacred to her followers. Those who please her are blessed with many children [Lorde's note].

and not be 35
one.

 1978

The Women of Dan[1] Dance with Swords in Their Hands to Mark the Time When They Were Warriors

I did not fall from the sky
I
nor descend like a plague of locusts
to drink color and strength from the earth
and I do not come like rain 5
as a tribute or symbol for earth's becoming
I come as a woman
dark and open
some times I fall like night
softly 10
and terrible
only when I must die
in order to rise again.

I do not come like a secret warrior
with an unsheathed sword in my mouth 15
hidden behind my tongue
slicing my throat to ribbons
of service with a smile
while the blood runs
down and out 20
through holes in the two sacred mounds
on my chest.

I come like a woman
who I am
spreading out through nights 25
laughter and promise
and dark heat
warming whatever I touch
that is living
consuming 30
only
what is already dead.

 1978

Kitchen Linoleum

The cockroach
who is dying

1. An ancient name for the kingdom of Dahomey [Lorde's note].

and the woman
who is blind
agree 5
not to notice
each other's shame.

1993

The Electric Slide Boogie

New Year's Day 1:16 AM
and my body is weary beyond
time to withdraw and rest
ample room allowed me in everyone's head
but community calls 5
right over the threshold
drums beating through the walls
children playing their truck dramas
under the collapsible coatrack
in the narrow hallway outside my room 10

The TV lounge next door is wide open
it is midnight in Idaho
and the throb easy subtle spin
of the electric slide boogie
step-stepping 15
around the corner of the parlor
past the sweet clink
of dining room glasses
and the edged aroma of slightly overdone
dutch-apple pie 20
all laced together
with the rich dark laughter
of Gloria
and her higher-octave sisters

How hard it is to sleep 25
in the middle of life.

January 3, 1992 1993

From Zami: A New Spelling of My Name

[Origins]

To whom do I owe the power behind my voice, what strength I have become, yeasting up like sudden blood from under the bruised skin's blister?

My father leaves his psychic print upon me, silent, intense, and unforgiving. But his is a distant lightning. Images of women flaming like torches adorn and define the borders of my journey, stand like dykes between me and the chaos. It is the images of women, kind and cruel, that lead me home.

To whom do I owe the symbols of my survival?

Days from pumpkin until the year's midnight, when my sisters and I hovered indoors, playing potsy on holes in the rosy linoleum that covered the living-room floor. On Saturdays we fought each other for the stray errand out of doors, fought each other for the emptied Quaker Oats boxes, fought each other for the last turn in the bathroom at nightfall, and for who would be the first one of us to get chickenpox.

The smell of the filled Harlem streets during summer, after a brief shower or the spraying drizzle of the watering trucks released the rank smell of the pavements back to the sun. I ran to the corner to fetch milk and bread from the Short-Neck Store-Man, stopping to search for some blades of grass to bring home for my mother. Stopping to search for hidden pennies winking like kittens under the subway gratings. I was always bending over to tie my shoes, delaying, trying to figure out something. How to get at the money, how to peep out the secret that some women carried like a swollen threat, under the gathers of their flowered blouses.

To whom do I owe the woman I have become?

DeLois lived up the block on 142nd Street and never had her hair done, and all the neighborhood women sucked their teeth as she walked by. Her crispy hair twinkled in the summer sun as her big proud stomach moved her on down the block while I watched, not caring whether or not she was a poem. Even though I tied my shoes and tried to peep under her blouse as she passed by, I never spoke to DeLois, because my mother didn't. But I loved her, because she moved like she felt she was somebody special, like she was somebody I'd like to know someday. She moved like how I thought god's mother must have moved, and my mother, once upon a time, and someday maybe me.

Hot noon threw a ring of sunlight like a halo on the top of DeLois's stomach, like a spotlight, making me sorry that I was so fat and could only feel the sun on my head and shoulders. I'd have to lie down on my back before the sun could shine down like that on my belly.

I loved DeLois because she was big and Black and special and seemed to laugh all over. I was scared of DeLois for those very same reasons. One day I watched DeLois step off the curb of 142nd Street against the light, slow and deliberate. A high yaller dude in a white Cadillac passed by and leaned out and yelled at her, "Hurry up, you fat-footed, nappy-headed, funny-looking bitch!" The car almost knocked her down. DeLois kept right on about her leisurely business and never so much as looked around.

To Louise Briscoe who died in my mother's house as a tenant in a furnished room with cooking privileges—no linens supplied. I brought her a glass of warm milk that she wouldn't drink, and she laughed at me when I wanted to change her sheets and call a doctor. "No reason to call him unless he's real cute," said Miz Briscoe. "Ain't nobody sent for me to come, I got here all by myself. And I'm going back the same way. So I only need him if he's cute real cute." And the room smelled like she was lying.

"Miz Briscoe," I said, "I'm really worried about you."

She looked up at me out of the corner of her eyes, like I was making her a proposition which she had to reject, but which she appreciated all the same. Her huge bloated body was quiet beneath the gray sheet, as she grinned knowingly.

"Why, that's all right, honey. I don't hold it against you. I know you can't help it, it's just in your nature, that's all."

To the white woman I dreamed standing behind me in an airport, silently watching while her child deliberately bumps into me over and over again. When I turn around to tell this woman that if she doesn't restrain her kid I'm going to punch her in the mouth, I see that she's been punched in the mouth already. Both she and her child are battered, with bruised faces and blackened eyes. I turn, and walk away from them in sadness and fury.

To the pale girl who ran up to my car in a Staten Island midnight with only a nightgown and bare feet, screaming and crying, "Lady, please help me oh please take me to the hospital, lady. . ." Her voice was a mixture of overripe peaches and doorchimes; she was the age of my daughter, running along the woody curves of Van Duzer Street.

I stopped the car quickly, and leaned over to open the door. It was high summer. "Yes, yes, I'll try to help you," I said. "Get in."

And when she saw my face in the streetlamp her own collapsed into terror.

"Oh no!" she wailed. "Not you!" then whirled around and started to run again.

What could she have seen in my Black face that was worth holding onto such horror? Wasting me in the gulf between who I was and her vision of me. Left with no help.

I drove on.

In the rear-view mirror I saw the substance of her nightmare catch up with her at the corner—leather jacket and boots, male and white.

I drove on, knowing she would probably die stupid.

To the first woman I ever courted and left. She taught me that women who want without needing are expensive and sometimes wasteful, but women who need without wanting are dangerous—they suck you in and pretend not to notice.

To the battalion of arms where I often retreated for shelter and sometimes found it. To the others who helped, pushing me into the merciless sun—I, coming out blackened and whole.

To the journeywoman pieces of myself.
Becoming.
Afrekete.[1]

1982

1. In the epilogue to *Zami*, Lorde identifies Afrekete as the youngest daughter of "MawuLisa, thunder, sky, sun, the great mother of us all; [she is] the mischievous lingoist, trickster, best-beloved, whom we must all become." There she also explains that *Zami* is a "name for women who work together as friends and lovers."

LUCILLE CLIFTON

1936–

Lucille Clifton's daring and exuberance as a poet stand in marked contrast to what in one poem she characterizes as her own mother's anxious reticence: "She got us almost through the high grass / then seemed like she turned around and ran / right back in / right back on in." At the same time, however, Clifton's irreverence echoes what she describes as the feistiness of her father, a man who changed his name from Sayle to Sayles because he knew that "there will be more than one of me." Whether she speaks as her parents' daughter or as the mother of six children, Clifton presents herself as a woman linked to history through her family, an ordinary woman trying to deal with the fears and joys of everyday life.

She was born in Depew, New York, and attended Howard University and Fredonia State Teachers College. In 1958, she married Fred J. Clifton, an educator and writer. Three volumes of verse—*Good Times* (1969), *Good News about the Earth* (1972), and *An Ordinary Woman* (1974)—were followed by a memoir, *Generations* (1976), in which she recounts the genealogical stories that animate so much of her writing. The author of numerous books for children, Clifton has also published many other collections, including *Two-Headed Woman* (1980), *Next* (1987), *Quilting* (1991), and *The Book of Light* (1993). Although she strenuously rejects what she calls "white ways," her work is never marked by rancor. In poems that focus on the activist Angela Davis or on the biblical figure of the Virgin Mary, she extends the invitation explicit in her *After Kent State*, an invitation to "come into the / Black / and live."

admonitions

boys
i don't promise you nothing
but this
what you pawn
i will redeem 5
what you steal
i will conceal
my private silence to
your public guilt
is all i got 10

girls
first time a white man
opens his fly
like a good thing
we'll just laugh 15
laugh real loud my
black women

children
when they ask you
why is your mama so funny 20
say

she is a poet
she don't have no sense

<div align="right">1969</div>

the astrologer predicts at mary's birth[1]

this one lie down on grass.
this one old men will follow
calling Mother Mother.
she womb will blossom then die.
this one she hide from evening. 5
at a certain time when she hear something
it will burn her ear.
at a certain place when she see something
it will break her eye.

<div align="right">1980</div>

anna speaks of the childhood of mary her daughter

we rise up early and
we work. work is the medicine
for dreams.
 that dream
i am having again; 5
she washed in light,
whole world bowed to its knees,
she on a hill looking up,
face all long tears.
 and shall i give her up 10
to dreaming then? i fight this thing.
all day we scrubbing scrubbing.

<div align="right">1980</div>

mary's dream

winged women was saying
"full of grace" and like.
was light beyond sun and words
of a name and a blessing.
winged women to only i. 5
i joined them, whispering
yes.

<div align="right">1980</div>

1. This sequence of poems concerns the life of Mary, the mother of Jesus Christ. According to the New Testament of the Bible, Mary was a virgin, and Jesus' father was God. Mary's mother was St. Anne or Anna; her husband was Joseph. An angel foretold the birth of Jesus to her (the Annunciation). When Jesus was born he was laid in a manger, a trough filled with straw for feeding animals in a barn.

how is he coming then

like a pot turned on the straw
nuzzled by cows and an old man
dressed like a father. like a loaf
a poor baker sets in the haystack to cool.
like a shepherd who hears in his herding 5
his mother whisper my son my son.

1980

holy night

joseph, i afraid of stars,
their brilliant seeing.
so many eyes. such light.
joseph, i cannot still these limbs,
i hands keep moving toward i breasts, 5
so many stars. so bright.
joseph, is wind burning from east
joseph, i shine, oh joseph. oh
illuminated night.

1980

a song of mary

somewhere it being yesterday.
i a maiden in my mother's house.
the animals silent outside.
is morning.
princes sitting on thrones in the east 5
studying the incomprehensible heavens.
joseph carving a table somewhere
in another place.
watching my mother.
smiling an ordinary smile. 10

1980

island mary

after the all been done and i
one old creature carried on
another creature's back, i wonder
could i have fought these thing?
surrounded by no son of mine save 5
old men calling Mother like in the tale
the astrologer tell, i wonder
could i have walk away when voices

singing in my sleep? i one old woman.
always i seem to worrying now for 10
another young girl asleep
in the plain evening.
what song around her ear?
what star still choosing?

1980

move

On May 13, 1985 Wilson Goode, Philadelphia's first Black mayor, authorized
the bombing of 6221 Osage Avenue after the complaints of neighbors, also
Black, about the Afrocentric back-to-nature group headquartered there and
calling itself Move. All the members of the group wore dreadlocks and had
taken the surname Africa. In the bombing eleven people, including children,
were killed and sixty-one homes in the neighborhood were destroyed.

they had begun to whisper
among themselves hesitant
to be branded neighbor to the wild
haired women the naked children
reclaiming a continent 5
away

move

he hesitated
then turned his smoky finger
toward africa toward the house 10
he might have lived in might have
owned or saved had he not turned
away

move

the helicopter rose at the command 15
higher at first then hesitating
then turning toward the center
of its own town only a neighborhood
away

move 20

she cried as the child stood
hesitant in the last clear sky
he would ever see the last
before the whirling blades the whirling smoke
and sharp debris carried all clarity 25
away

move

if you live in a mind
that would destroy itself
to comfort itself 30
if you would stand fire
rather than difference
do not hesitate
move
away 35

1987

if our grandchild be a girl

i wish for her
fantastic hands,
twelve spiky fingers
symbols of our tribe.
she will do magic 5
with them,
she will turn personal
abracadabra
remembered from
dahomean[1] women 10
wearing
extravagant gloves.

1987

my dream about being white

hey music and
me
only white,
hair a flutter of
fall leaves 5
circling my perfect
line of a nose,
no lips,
no behind, hey
white me 10
and i'm wearing
white history
but there's no future
in those clothes
so i take them off and 15
wake up
dancing.

1987

1. Dahomey, now known as Benin, is a country of west Africa on the Gulf of Guinea (as well as one of the major ethnic groups constituting its population); there is a tradition of Dahomean warrior women

BESSIE HEAD

1937–1986

Born in a mental hospital, Bessie Amelia Emery Head believed that "the only honor South African officials ever did me" was to name her after her mother, a "lovely, and unpredictable woman." The tragic irony of Head's remark is clarified by her mother's fate: this young white woman had been committed by her wealthy family to a mental hospital and labeled insane after she was found to have conceived a child with a Zulu stable worker; she committed suicide when her daughter was still a young girl. A *Question of Power* (1973), Head's only autobiographical work, describes the mental anguish of a protagonist haunted by a sense of psychic disintegration intensified by racial bigotry.

Brought up by a black foster family and then at thirteen given an education in a mission orphanage in South Africa, Bessie Head married a journalist in 1961, but divorced soon after. Horrified by apartheid in South Africa, the twenty-seven-year-old woman left for Botswana in 1964 to live with her son as a refugee at Bamangwato Development Farm. Typing by the light of candles because she had no electricity and making money by selling jams and vegetables, Head attributed her writing career to the sense of community she received even in this impoverished setting. Her first two novels—*When Rain Clouds Gather* (1969) and *Maru* (1971)—and her story collection—*The Collector of Treasures* (1977)—often revolve around the repercussions of apartheid and other forms of racism, as do the two historical chronicles she published in the 1980s: *Serowe: Village of the Rain Wind* (1981) and *A Bewitched Crossroad: An African Saga* (1984) contain sociological accounts, personal interviews, and narrative histories as well as folklore about African native history. Throughout her career, Head examined the personal dilemmas faced by new arrivals, outsiders, and refugees residing within Third World countries and coping with the competitions and contradictions between traditional and modern systems of values.

Haunted by her mother's mental illness and her own breakdown in 1971, Head died of hepatitis in 1986. In "her concern for women and madness," noted one critic, she "almost single-handedly brought about the inward turning of the African novel."

Snapshots of a Wedding

Wedding days always started at the haunting, magical hour of early dawn when there was only a pale crack of light on the horizon. For those who were awake, it took the earth hours to adjust to daylight. The cool and damp of the night slowly arose in shimmering waves like water and even the forms of the people who bestirred themselves at this unearthly hour were distorted in the haze; they appeared to be dancers in slow motion, with fluid, watery forms. In the dim light, four men, the relatives of the bridegroom, Kegoletile, slowly herded an ox before them towards the yard of MmaKhudu, where the bride, Neo, lived. People were already astir in MmaKhudu's yard, yet for a while they all came and peered closely at the distorted fluid forms that approached, to ascertain if it were indeed the relatives of the bridegroom. Then the ox, who was a rather stupid fellow and unaware of his sudden and impending end as meat for the wedding feast, bellowed casually his early morn-

ing yawn. At this, the beautiful ululating of the women rose and swelled over the air like water bubbling rapidly and melodiously over the stones of a clear, sparkling stream. In between ululating all the while, the women began to weave about the yard in the wedding dance; now and then they bent over and shook their buttocks in the air. As they handed over the ox, one of the bridegroom's relatives joked:

"This is going to be a modern wedding." He meant that a lot of the traditional courtesies had been left out of the planning for the wedding day; no one had been awake all night preparing diphiri or the traditional wedding breakfast of pounded meat and samp;[1] the bridegroom said he had no church and did not care about such things; the bride was six months pregnant and showing it, so there was just going to be a quick marriage ceremony at the police camp.

"Oh, we all have our own ways," one of the bride's relatives joked back. "If the times are changing, we keep up with them." And she weaved away ululating joyously.

Whenever there was a wedding the talk and gossip that preceded it were appalling, except that this time the relatives of the bride, Neo, kept their talk a strict secret among themselves. They were anxious to be rid of her; she was an impossible girl with haughty, arrogant ways. Of all her family and relatives, she was the only one who had completed her "O" levels[2] and she never failed to rub in this fact. She walked around with her nose in the air; illiterate relatives were beneath her greeting—it was done in a clever way, she just turned her head to one side and smiled to herself or when she greeted it was like an insult; she stretched her hand out, palm outspread, swung it down laughing with a gesture that plainly said: "Oh, that's you!" Only her mother seemed bemused by her education. At her own home Neo was waited on hand and foot. Outside her home nasty remarks were passed. People bitterly disliked conceit and pride.

"That girl has no manners!" the relatives would remark. "What's the good of education if it goes to someone's head so badly they have no respect for the people? Oh, she is not a person."

Then they would nod their heads in that fatal way, with predictions that one day life would bring her down. Actually, life had treated Neo rather nicely. Two months after completing her "O' levels she became pregnant by Kegoletile with their first child. It soon became known that another girl, Mathata, was also pregnant by Kegoletile. The difference between the two girls was that Mathata was completely uneducated; the only work she would ever do was that of a housemaid, while Neo had endless opportunities before her—typist, book-keeper, or secretary. So Neo merely smiled; Mathata was no rival. It was as though the decision had been worked out by circumstance because when the families converged on Kegoletile at the birth of the children—he was rich in cattle and they wanted to see what they could get—he of course immediately proposed marriage to Neo; and for Mathata, he agreed to a court order to pay a maintenance of R10.00[3] a month until the child was twenty years old. Mathata merely smiled too. Girls like her offered no resistance to the approaches of men; when they lost them, they just let things ride.

1. Corn mush, hominy.
2. " 'O' levels", the lowest level ("ordinary") of standardized examinations in secondary-school subjects.

3. Ten rands; one rand is worth about twenty-eight cents.

"He is of course just running after the education and not the manners," Neo's relatives commented, to show they were not fooled by human nature. "He thinks that since she is as educated as he is they will both get good jobs and be rich in no time . . ."

Educated as he was, Kegoletile seemed to go through a secret conflict during that year he prepared a yard for his future married life with Neo. He spent most of his free time in the yard of Mathata. His behavior there wasn't too alarming but he showered Mathata with gifts of all kinds—food, fancy dresses, shoes and underwear. Each time he came, he brought a gift and each time Mathata would burst out laughing and comment: "Ow, Kegoletile, how can I wear all these dresses? It's just a waste of money! Besides, I manage quite well with the R10.00 you give every month for the child . . ."

She was a very pretty girl with black eyes like stars; she was always smiling and happy; immediately and always her own natural self. He knew what he was marrying—something quite the opposite, a new kind of girl with false postures and acquired, grand-madame ways. And yet, it didn't pay a man these days to look too closely into his heart. They all wanted as wives, women who were big money-earners and they were so ruthless about it! And yet it was as though the society itself stamped each of its individuals with its own particular brand of wealth and Kegoletile had not yet escaped it; he had about him an engaging humility and eagerness to help and please that made him loved and respected by all who knew him. During those times he sat in Mathata's yard, he communicated nothing of the conflict he felt but he would sit on a chair with his arms spread out across its back, turn his head sideways and stare at what seemed to be an empty space beside him. Then he would smile, stand up and walk away. Nothing dramatic. During the year he prepared the huts in his new yard, he frequently slept at the home of Neo.

Relatives on both sides watched this division of interest between the two yards and one day when Neo walked patronizingly into the yard of an aunt, the aunt decided to frighten her a little.

"Well aunt," she said, with the familiar careless disrespect which went with her so-called, educated, status. "Will you make me some tea? And how's things?"

The aunt spoke very quietly.

"You may not know it, my girl, but you are hated by everyone around here. The debate we have going is whether a nice young man like Kegoletile should marry bad-mannered rubbish like you. He would be far better off if he married a girl like Mathata, who though uneducated, still treats people with respect."

The shock the silly girl received made her stare for a terrified moment at her aunt. Then she stood up and ran out of the house. It wiped the superior smile off her face and brought her down a little. She developed an anxiety to greet people and also an anxiety about securing Kegoletile as a husband—that was why she became pregnant six months before the marriage could take place. In spite of this, her own relatives still disliked her and right up to the day of the wedding they were still debating whether Neo was a suitable wife for any man. No one would have guessed it though with all the dancing, ululating and happiness expressed in the yard and streams of guests gaily ululated themselves along the pathways with wedding gifts precariously balanced on their heads. Neo's maternal aunts, all sedately decked up in shawls, sat in a select group by themselves in a corner of the yard. They sat on the bare ground with their legs

stretched out before them but they were served like queens the whole day long. Trays of tea, dry white bread, plates of meat, rice, and salad were constantly placed before them. Their important task was to formally hand over the bride to Kegoletile's maternal aunts when they approached the yard at sunset. So they sat the whole day with still, expressionless faces, waiting to fulfill this ancient rite.

Equally still and expressionless were the faces of the long column of women, Kegoletile's maternal aunts who appeared outside the yard just as the sun sank low. They walked slowly into the yard indifferent to the ululating that greeted them and seated themselves in a group opposite Neo's maternal aunts. The yard became very silent while each group made its report. Kegoletile had provided all the food for the wedding feast and a maternal aunt from his side first asked:

"Is there any complaint? Has all gone well?"

"We have no complaint," the opposite party replied.

"We have come to ask for water," Kegoletile's side said, meaning that from times past the bride was supposed to carry water at her in-law's home.

"It is agreed to," the opposite party replied.

Neo's maternal aunts then turned to the bridegroom and counseled him: "Son, you must plow and supply us with corn each year."

Then Kegoletile's maternal aunts turned to the bride and counseled her: "Daughter, you must carry water for your husband. Beware, that at all times, he is the owner of the house and must be obeyed. Do not mind if he stops now and then and talks to other ladies. Let him feel free to come and go as he likes . . ."

The formalities over, it was now time for Kegoletile's maternal aunts to get up, ululate and weave and dance about the yard. Then, still dancing and ululating, accompanied by the bride and groom they slowly wound their way to the yard of Kego etile where another feast had been prepared. As they approached his yard, an old woman suddenly dashed out and chopped at the ground with a hoe. It was all only a formality. Neo would never be the kind of wife who went to the lands to plow. She already had a well-paid job in an office as a secretary. Following on this another old woman took the bride by the hand and led her to a smeared and decorated courtyard wherein had been placed a traditional animal-skin Tswana[4] mat. She was made to sit on the mat and a shawl and kerchief were placed before her. The shawl was ceremonially wrapped around her shoulders; the kerchief tied around her head—the symbols that she was now a married woman.

Guests quietly moved forward to greet the bride. Then two girls started to ululate and dance in front of the bride. As they both turned and bent over to shake their buttocks in the air, they bumped into each other and toppled over. The wedding guests roared with laughter. Neo, who had all this time been stiff, immobile, and rigid, bent forward and her shoulders shook with laughter.

The hoe, the mat, the shawl, the kerchief, the beautiful flute-like ululating of the women seemed in itself a blessing on the marriage but all the guests were deeply moved when out of the crowd, a woman of majestic, regal bearing slowly approached the bride. It was the aunt who had scolded Neo for her bad manners and modern ways. She dropped to her knees before the bride,

4. The Tswana are an African people of the region between the Orange and Zambezi rivers and the dominant ethnic group of Botswana.

clenched her fists together and pounded the ground hard with each clenched fist on either side of the bride's legs. As she pounded her fists she said loudly: "Be a good wife! Be a good wife!"

1977

DIANE WAKOSKI

1937–

"I write in the first person because I have always wanted to make my life more interesting than it was," explained the poet Diane Wakoski in 1974, adding that in her work "I created a Diane whose real experiences were dramatized and exaggerated" as a way of "inventing myself into a new life." In more than twenty volumes of poetry, Wakoski has succeeded in accomplishing exactly the self-transformation she describes in this statement. Born in Whittier, California, she has deliberately allowed her "real" origins to remain obscure, refusing to include biographical statements in her books and implying in her poems a personal history that cannot be definitively verified. (According to the critic Estella Lauter, her "poems indicate that she and one sister were born to poor Polish-American parents and were deserted by their father in early childhood." In addition, she "may have borne two children and given them up for adoption before 1971, and she has experienced at least two cycles of marriage and divorce.")

Educated at the University of California, Berkeley, Wakoski settled in New York City in the early 1960s, where she worked in a bookstore and taught junior high school English while writing and publishing such volumes as *Coins and Coffins* (1962), *The George Washington Poems* (1967), and *Inside the Blood Factory* (1968). More recently, she has supported herself with university teaching and by giving poetry readings and conducting verse-writing workshops. She is currently professor of English and writer-in-residence at Michigan State University.

Wakoski's many later collections include *Waiting for the King of Spain* (1976), *The Man Who Shook Hands* (1978), *Emerald Ice: Selected Poems* (1988), and *Medea the Sorceress* (1991). As the fantastic leaps and surrealistic images of *Blue Monday* indicate, her life as an "invented" person has continually taken precedence over ordinary existence. Whether disguised as an acolyte of George Washington, of Beethoven, of the "motorcycle betrayer," or of "the King of Spain"—all figures who play prominent parts in the poems that constitute her imaginary autobiography—Wakoski has devoted herself to the construction of what the modernist American poet Wallace Stevens once called "a Supreme Fiction."

Blue Monday

Blue of the heaps of beads poured into her breasts
and clacking together in her elbows;
blue of the silk
that covers lily-town at night;
blue of her teeth
that bite cold toast
and shatter on the streets;
blue of the dyed flower petals with gold stamens

5

hanging like tongues
over the fence of her dress
at the opera/ opals clasped under her lips 10
and the moon breaking over her head a
gush of blood-red lizards.

Blue Monday. Monday at 3:00 and
Monday at 5. Monday at 7:30 and 15
Monday at 10:00. Monday passed under the rippling
California fountain. Monday alone
a shark in the cold blue waters.

 You are dead: wound round like a paisley shawl.
 I cannot shake you out of the sheets. Your name 20
 is still wedged in every corner of the sofa.

 Monday is the first of the week,
 and I think of you all week.
 I beg Monday not to come
 so that I will not think of you 25
 all week.

You paint my body blue. On the balcony
in the soft muddy night, you paint me
with bat wings and the crystal
the crystal 30
the crystal
the crystal in your arm cuts away
the night, folds back ebony whale skin
and my face, the blue of new rifles,
and my neck, the blue of Egypt, 35
and my breast, the blue of sand,
and my arms, bass-blue,
and my stomach, arsenic;

there is electricity dripping from me like cream;
there is love dripping from me I cannot use—like acacia or 40
jacaranda[1]—fallen blue and gold flowers, crushed into the street.

 Love passed me in a blue business suit
 and fedora.
 His glass cane, hollow and filled with
 sharks and whales . . . 45
 He wore black
 patent leather shoes
 and had a mustache. His hair was so black
 it was almost blue.

 "Love," I said. 50
 "I beg your pardon," he said.

1. A tree with pale purple flowers. "Acacia": a tree with small yellow or white flowers.

"Mr. Love," I said.
"I beg your pardon," he said.

So I saw there was no use bothering him on the street.

Love passed me on the street in a blue 55
business suit. He was a banker
I could tell.

So blue trains rush by in my sleep.
Blue herons fly overhead.
Blue paint cracks in my 60
arteries and sends titanium[2]
floating into my bones.
Blue liquid pours down
my poisoned throat and blue veins
rip open my breast. Blue daggers tip 65
and are juggled on my palms.
Blue death lives in my fingernails.

If I could sing one last song
with water bubbling through my lips
I would sing with my throat torn open, 70
the blue jugular spouting that black shadow pulse,
and on my lips
I would balance volcanic rock
emptied out of my veins. At last
my children strained out 75
of my body. At last my blood
solidified and tumbling into the ocean.
It is blue.
It is blue.
It is blue. 80

1968

Ringless

I cannot stand the man who wears
a ring
on his little finger/ a white peacock walking on the moon
and splinters of silver dust his body;
but the great man, George, cracked in half in my living room 5
one day and I saw he was made of marble
with black veins. It does not justify the ring to say
someone gave it to you and the little finger is the only one
it will fit;
it does not justify to say Cocteau wore one 10
and still made the man burst silently through the mirror[1]—

2. A strong white metal sometimes used as a paint pigment.
1. A reference, perhaps, to scenes in the film *Orphée* (1950), by the French director Jean Cocteau (1889–1963), in which the poet Orphée returns from the underworld through a mirror.

many beautiful
poems have been made with rings worn on the little finger.
That
isn't the point. [15]
Flaubert had jasper; Lorca had jade; Dante had
amber; and Browning had carnelian;
George Washington had solid gold—even Kelly[2] once wore a scarab there;
but I am telling you I cannot stand the man
who wears a ring [20]
on his little finger. He may indeed
run the world;
that does not make him any better in
my needlepoint eyes.
Why [25]
is a story.
 There were heaps of fish lying, shimmering in the sun
 with red gashes still heaving
 and the mouths of medieval lovers.
 There were gold and green glass balls bobbing in their [30]
 nets on the waves.
 There were black-eyed men with hair all over their bodies
 There were black-skirted ladies baking bread
 and there were gallons and gallons of red wine.
 A girl spilled one drop of hot wax on her lover's neck [35]
 as she glanced at his white teeth and thick arms.
 There were red and silver snakes coiling around the legs
 of the dancers.
 There was hot sun and there was no talk.
 How do I reconcile these images with our cool president, [40]
 George Washington, walking the streets? Every bone
 in my body is ivory and has the word, "America"
 carved on it, but
 my head takes me away from furniture and pewter
 to the sun tugging at my nipples and trying to squeeze [45]
 under my toes.
 The sun appeared in the shape of a man and he had
 a ring made of sun around his little finger.
 "It will burn up your hand," I said.
 But he made motions in the air and passed by. [50]
 The moon appeared in the shape of a young negro boy,
 and he had a ring made of dew around his little finger.
 "You'll lose it," I said,
 but he touched my face,
 not losing a drop and passed away. Then I saw [55]
 Alexander Hamilton,[3] whom I loved,
 and he had a ring on his little finger,
 but he wouldn't touch me.
 And Lorca had rings around both little fingers,

2. Robert Kelly, a poet and friend of Wakoski's. Gustave Flaubert (1821–1880), French novelist. Federico García Lorca (1899–1938), Spanish poet. Dante (1265–1321), author of The Divine Comedy. Robert Browning (1812–1889), English poet.
3. Alexander Hamilton (1755–1804), American statesman.

and suddenly everyone I knew appeared, 60
and they all had rings on their little fingers,
and I was the only one in the world left without any
rings
on any
of my fingers whatsoever. 65
And worst of all,
there was George Washington
walking down the senate aisles
with a ring on his little finger—managing
the world, 70
managing *my* world.
This is what I mean—you wear a ring on your
 little finger
 and you manage the world,
 and I am ringless 75
 ringless . . .
I cannot stand the man who wears
a ring
on his little finger;

not even if it is you. 80

 1968

My Trouble

 my trouble
 is that I have the spirit of Gertrude Stein
 but the personality of Alice B. Toklas;[1]
 craggy, grand
 stony ideas 5
 but
 all I can do
 is embroider Picasso's drawings
 and bake hashish fudge.[2]
 I am poor 10
 and don't have very much to say
 am usually taken for
 somebody's
 secretary.

 1972

The Mirror of a Day Chiming Marigold

Astronomer,
I strike my gong for you.
It is gold.

1. Companion (1877–1967) to the expatriate
American writer Stein (1874–1946).
2. A recipe for this appears in *The Alice B. Toklas*
Cookbook (1954). The Spanish painter Pablo Picasso
(1881–1973) was championed early by Stein.

Ancient.
Engraved with a calendar 5
of my heart.
And I strike it.
It rings
loud and melodious,
the sound of seashells, 10
the shouting of marigolds,
the angry book of dragonflies,
thunder,
an erupting volcano,
my heart pounding in exhaustion. 15

I strike it,
and it sounds for you.
As all of us are instruments
recording the heart,
playing its jealous and beautiful sounds, 20
the mirror breaking and shattering
past our tongues
when the fire burns our skins.

The astronomer looks at the sky and sees
all the phenomena of light. 25
This one gives himself a solar corona
while I stand in the shade of the moon.

There is
an ancient priestess
whose tears make the spiderlilies grow. 30
She knows my name is darkness.
We are sisters.
As my tears are the blue lilies of the nile themselves,
my tongue,
a stamen waiting to be touched by the breath of insects 35
my life, a rock;
I look for a poet,
an astronomer,
one who studies
my moon. 40

1973

The Photos

My sister in her well-tailored silk blouse hands me
the photo of my father
in naval uniform and white hat.
I say, "Oh, this is the one which Mama used to have on her dresser."

My sister controls her face and furtively looks at my mother, 5
a sad rag bag of a woman, lumpy and sagging everywhere,

like a mattress at the Salvation Army, though with no holes or tears,
and says, "No."

I look again,
and see that my father is wearing a wedding ring, 10
which he never did
when he lived with my mother. And that there is a legend on it,
"To my dearest wife,
 Love
 Chief" 15
And I realize the photo must have belonged to his second wife,
whom he left our mother to marry.

My mother says, with her face as still as the whole unpopulated part of the
state of North Dakota,
"May I see it too?" 20
She looks at it.

I look at my tailored sister
and my own blue-jeaned self. Have we wanted to hurt our mother,
sharing these pictures on this, one of the few days I ever visit or
spend with family? For her face is curiously haunted, 25
not now with her usual viperish bitterness,
but with something so deep it could not be spoken.

I turn away and say I must go on, as I have a dinner engagement with
 friends.
But I drive all the way to Pasadena from Whittier,
thinking of my mother's face; how I could never love her; how my father 30
could not love her either. Yet knowing I have inherited
the rag-bag body,
stony face with bulldog jaws.

I drive, thinking of that face.
Jeffers'[1] California Medea who inspired me to poetry. 35
I killed my children,
but there as I am changing lanes on the freeway, necessarily glancing in the
rearview mirror, I see the face,
not even a ghost, but always with me, like a photo in a beloved's wallet.

How I hate my destiny. 40

 1976

Medea[1] the Sorceress

She is in the Home for Unwed Mothers in
Pasadena, the only girl who reads poetry. He

1. Robinson Jeffers (1887–1962), American poet whose work centered on California; his stage adaptation of Euripides' *Medea* was highly successful in the 1940s.

1. According to Greek myth, Medea, daughter of the king of Colchis and granddaughter of the sun, loved and aided Jason; when he left her for another princess, she killed his new bride as well as her own two children

writes to her from his prep school, and she memorizes
the sonnets of Shakespeare as she takes her exercise
on the dusty, scrubby grounds of 5
The Home.

No enchantment changes her life.
She is told by the Social Worker that she has
FAILED because
 she still loves J 10
 she doesn't regret doing anything for love.
 she doesn't believe she is bad
 she doesn't regret giving up her child
 she believes her life will go on, the same as it has always gone on
 she won't talk about her mistakes. 15

This is the same as being on the desert,
this life in the linoleum-floored room,
eating with girls who have been raped by their fathers,
and girls who got caught but didn't know with what man
and girls who were only 13 20
and girls who were nurses sleeping with doctors
and girls who wanted to forget everything and join the army,
girls who were all pregnant and ashamed and who knew they were
wandering some desert, though most of them, most
of us, didn't know 25
the names of desert rattlers, or moths like the Dusty Silverwing, or
about the tiny burrowing owls, or the lingering scent of sagebrush
when the night was pure, pure as we knew we still were.

So, as if she were Medea, when the letters came
talking casually about his dates with other girls, un-pregnant girls, 30
she decided that she would have no choice. She
would kill him and her children, and like the Sorceress
leave for another world, in her chariot drawn by dragons.

She gave up her baby. No regrets. Only the weak
have regrets. 35
She went to Berkeley, and she told him
to go away. No regrets. Only the weak have
regrets. She flew in her chariot
with all her dragonlady power to Berkeley,
then New York then the Midwest, and finally to this Cafe 40
where she sits telling the tale, not of the tribe,
but of herself, and in spite of what others say, she knows
that the song this Silvery Moon Questing Lady of Dragonlight sings,
is the tale for at least half
of the tribe. 45

by Jason, escaping in a winged chariot. In one of the
prose sections of her book of the same title, Wakosk
notes, "When I was young, I fell in love with the story

of Medea. I identified completely with the betrayed
sorceress."

Strum, Gunslinger.
Hail, Maximus,
Ascent is descent, Dr. Paterson,[2]
O, Love, one-eyed poet, where are you leading me now. No one should
be at the Home for Unwed Mothers. That is the real Wasteland.[3] 50
These epistles, not Cantos[4] or songs will be for Craig, Knight of
Hummingbird Light,
for Jonathan[5] who understands the myth of the woman "Sleeping In
Flame,"
for Steel Man, my husband, who loves me at night in his invisible Cap of 55
Darkness,[6]
and for all women, the other half of the tribe,
for Eve who dared to eat the apple,
I write this letter, and sign myself
Diane,[7] 60

The Lady of Light.

 1991

2. I.e., William Carlos Williams (1883–1963), American physician-poet whose best-known work is the autobiographical epic *Paterson*.
3. An allusion to the poet T. S. Eliot (1888–1965), author of *The Waste Land*.
4. An allusion to Ezra Pound (1885–1972) and his *Cantos*.
5. Letters to Craig Cotter and Jonathan Carroll, friends of Wakoski, are interspersed with the poems in

her book *Medea the Sorceress*. Carroll is the author of the novel *Sleeping in Flame* (1990).
6. *Medea the Sorceress* includes a poem about Wakoski's husband titled *Robert's Caps*; it begins: "He wears / the cap of darkness / to bed each night."
7. The goddess Diana is identified with Artemis, the moon, who is the sister of Apollo, the sun. Eve, of course, "dared" to eat the fruit of the Tree of Knowledge (Genesis 3).

CARYL CHURCHILL

1938–

A remarkably theatrical episode opens Caryl Churchill's play *Top Girls*, providing a visual and dramatic contrast with the rest of the action and posing crucial questions about the impact of history on women's lives. The first scene, a pointedly unrealistic, even surrealistic dinner party, brings together women from different periods, various regions, and distinct states of being, for while two are actual historical persons, one is a character in a narrative, another a figure in a painting, and yet another a personage who is very likely apocryphal. On stage, the pageantry of the oddly dissimilar constumes displayed by, among others, Chaucer's Patient Griselda, Brueghel's Dull Gret, and the Japanese courtesan Lady Nijo makes the beginning of *Top Girls* almost seem like a kind of carnival. But all the other scenes focus on the everyday lives of an executive in an employment agency in contemporary London as well as on the ordinary existences of several members of her family. Structurally as well as thematically, therefore, Churchill's play asks, what is the relationship between women's past—as represented in literature, painting, and legend or in the lives of prominent women from earlier periods— and the situation in which women find themselves today? Has our history evolved, gaining women greater freedom, or has it devolved, generating more calamitous constrictions, or has there been no real change at all? More specifically, what transformations has the women's movement brought about for those notable women Churchill calls "top girls"? Just as important to the playwright, what modifications has the movement brought about for those women at the bottom of the class system?

Not simply experimental in its use of characters, *Top Girls* also deploys a host of other formally fascinating techniques: speeches are typographically marked, for example, to indicate interruptions as well as simultaneous talking; the actors who play legendary female characters in the first scene reappear in the roles of contemporary women in later scenes—and such double-casting can be used by a director to draw connections between the past and the present; the time line of the play is not strictly chronological, since the last scene in Act Two occurs a year before the scene that precedes it. These unconventional techniques may make the play a challenge to the reader who does not actually see it on stage, but they also typify the brilliant strategies Caryl Churchill has used since her early radio play, *The Ants* (1962), and her early major stage plays, *Owners* (1972) and *Objections to Sex and Violence* (1975). As these works indicate, from the beginning of her career this artist has tied formal experimentation to her interest in feminism and socialism in order to address such issues as state violence, economic dispossession, and sexual politics.

An only child and London born, Churchill has attributed her attraction to show business to her parents' occupations. Her father was a political cartoonist, and she has explained that "Cartoons are really so much like plays. An image with somebody saying something." Her mother was a secretary, a model, and a minor film actress. From 1948 to 1956, the family lived in Canada, where Churchill attended the Trafalgar School, Montreal. During her English studies at Lady Margaret Hall, Oxford, Churchill began writing plays, although after her marriage to David Harter in 1961 and the birth of her three children, as well as a succession of miscarriages, she found herself leading a solitary life "of being a barrister's wife and just being at home." Her husband's decision to leave private practice to work for a legal aid group in 1972 and their subsequent travels helped shape her almost instantaneously successful writing career.

Two productions in 1976—*Light Shining in Buckinghamshire* and *Vinegar Tom*—demonstrate both Churchill's fascination with history and her collaborative interaction with experimental theater workshops. But it was the satirical farce *Cloud Nine* (1979) that first brought her success outside of London; when the play opened off-Broadway in New York, it was welcomed by critics as "the most rewarding surprise of the theatrical season," ran for two years, and won three Obie awards. With its first act set in Victorian Africa and its second in contemporary London, its black character played by a white, and its cross-sex casting (male roles played by women and female roles played by men), *Cloud Nine* continued to explore what Churchill called her "two preoccupations": "people's internal states of being and the external political structures which affect them, which make them insane." Possibly her best-known play, *Top Girls* (1982) was followed by such productions as *Fen* (1983), *Serious Money* (1987). *Ice Cream* (1989), and *Mad Forest* (1990). Taken together, they explain why Churchill has been praised by so many audiences for the audacity and wit with which she addresses the psychological, sexual, social, and economic complexities of modern life.

Top Girls

Top Girls was first performed at the Royal Court Theatre, London, on 28 August 1982 with the following cast:

MARLENE	Gwen Taylor
ISABELLA BIRD	
JOYCE	Deborah Findlay
MRS. KIDD	
LADY NIJO	
WIN	Lindsay Duncan

DULL GRET ANGIE	}	Carole Hayman
POPE JOAN LOUISE	}	Selina Cadell
PATIENT GRISELDA NELL JEANINE	}	Lesley Manville
WAITRESS KIT SHONA	}	Lou Wakefield

Directed by Max Stafford Clark
Designed by Peter Hartwell

This production transferred to Joe Papp's Public Theatre, New York, later the same year, and returned to the Royal Court early in 1983.

ACT ONE

Scene One: Restaurant. Saturday night.
Scene Two: "Top Girls" Employment agency. Monday morning.
Scene Three: Joyce's back yard. Sunday afternoon.

ACT TWO

Scene One: Employment agency. Monday morning.
Scene Two: Joyce's kitchen. Sunday evening, a year earlier.

Note on Characters

ISABELLA BIRD (1831–1904) lived in Edinburgh, traveled extensively between the ages of 40 and 70.

LADY NIJO (b. 1258), Japanese, was an Emperor's courtesan and later a Buddhist nun who traveled on foot through Japan.

DULL GRET is the subject of the Brueghel painting, *Dulle Griet*,[1] in which a woman in an apron and armor leads a crowd of women charging through hell and fighting the devils.

POPE JOAN, disguised as a man, is thought to have been Pope between 854–856.

PATIENT GRISELDA is the obedient wife whose story is told by Chaucer in The Clerk's Tale of *The Canterbury Tales*.

Note on Layout

A speech usually follows the one immediately before it BUT:

1. When one character starts speaking before the other has finished, the point of interruption is marked /.

e.g., ISABELLA. This is the Emperor of Japan? / I once met the Emperor of Morocco.

NIJO. In fact he was the ex-Emperor.

2. A character sometimes continues speaking right through another's speech:

e.g., ISABELLA. When I was forty I thought my life was over. / Oh I was pitiful. I was

NIJO. I didn't say I felt it for twenty years. Not every minute.

1. This 1562 painting by Pieter Brueghel the Elder is also known as *Mad Meg*.

ISABELLA. sent on a cruise for my health and I felt even worse. Pains in my bones, pins and needles . . . etc.

3. Sometimes a speech follows on from a speech earlier than the one immediately before it, and continuity is marked *.

e.g., GRISELDA. I'd seen him riding by, we all had. And he'd seen me in the fields with the sheep*.
ISABELLA. I would have been well suited to minding sheep.
NIJO. And Mr. Nugent riding by.
ISABELLA. Of course not, Nijo, I mean a healthy life in the open air.
JOAN. *He just rode up while you were minding the sheep and asked you to marry him?

where "in the fields with the sheep" is the cue to both "I would have been" and "He just rode up."

Act One

SCENE ONE

Restaurant. Table set for dinner with white tablecloth. Six places. MARLENE *and* WAITRESS.

MARLENE. Excellent, yes, table for six. One of them's going to be late but we won't wait. I'd like a bottle of Frascati straight away if you've got one really cold.
[*The* WAITRESS *goes.* ISABELLA BIRD *arrives.*]
Here we are. Isabella.
ISABELLA. Congratulations, my dear.
MARLENE. Well, it's a step. It makes for a party. I haven't time for a holiday. I'd like to go somewhere exotic like you but I can't get away. I don't know how you could bear to leave Hawaii. / I'd like to lie in the sun forever, except of course I
ISABELLA. I did think of settling.
MARLENE. can't bear sitting still.
ISABELLA. I sent for my sister Hennie to come and join me. I said, Hennie we'll live here forever and help the natives. You can buy two sirloins of beef for what a pound of chops costs in Edinburgh. And Hennie wrote back, the dear, that yes, she would come to Hawaii if I wished, but I said she had far better stay where she was. Hennie was suited to life in Tobermory.
MARLENE. Poor Hennie.
ISABELLA. Do you have a sister?
MARLENE. Yes in fact.
ISABELLA. Hennie was happy. She was good. I did miss its face, my own pet. But I couldn't stay in Scotland. I loathed the constant murk.
MARLENE. Ah! Nijo!
[*She sees* LADY NIJO *arrive. The* WAITRESS *enters with wine.*]
NIJO. Marlene!
MARLENE. I think a drink while we wait for the others. I think a drink anyway. What a week.
[*The* WAITRESS *pours wine.*]
NIJO. It was always the men who used to get so drunk. I'd be one of the maidens, passing the sake.
ISABELLA. I've had sake. Small hot drink. Quite fortifying after a day in the wet.

NIJO. One night my father proposed three rounds of three cups, which was
normal, and then the Emperor should have said three rounds of three cups,
but he said three rounds of nine cups, so you can imagine. Then the
Emperor passed his sake cup to my father and said, "Let the wild goose
come to me this spring."

MARLENE. Let the what?

NIJO. It's a literary allusion to a tenth-century epic,[2] / His Majesty was very
cultured.

ISABELLA. This is the Emperor of Japan? / I once met the Emperor of
Morocco.

NIJO. In fact he was the ex-Emperor.

MARLENE. But he wasn't old? / Did you, Isabella?

NIJO. Twenty-nine.

ISABELLA. Oh it's a long story.

MARLENE. Twenty-nine's an excellent age.

NIJO. Well I was only fourteen and I knew he meant something but I didn't
know what. He sent me an eight-layered gown and I sent it back. So when
the time came I did nothing but cry. My thin gowns were badly ripped. But
even that morning when he left /—he'd a green robe with a scarlet lining
and

MARLENE. Are you saying he raped you?

NIJO. very heavily embroidered trousers, I already felt different about him. It
made me uneasy. No, of course not, Marlene, I belonged to him, it was what
I was brought up for from a baby. I soon found I was sad if he stayed away. It
was depressing day after day not knowing when he would come. I never en-
joyed taking other women to him.

ISABELLA. I certainly never saw my father drunk. He was a clergyman. / And
I didn't get married till I was fifty.

[*The* WAITRESS *brings menus.*]

NIJO. Oh, my father was a very religious man. Just before he died he said to
me, "Serve His Majesty, be respectful, if you lose his favor enter holy or-
ders."

MARLENE. But he meant stay in a convent, not go wandering round the
country.

NIJO. Priests were often vagrants, so why not a nun? You think I shouldn't? /
I still did what my father wanted.

MARLENE. No no, I think you should. / I think it was wonderful.

[DULL GRET *arrives.*]

ISABELLA. I tried to do what my father wanted.

MARLENE. Gret, good. Nijo. Gret. / I know Griselda's going to be late, but
should we wait for Joan? / Let's get you a drink.

ISABELLA. Hello Gret! [*Continues to* NIJO.] I tried to be a clergyman's
daughter. Needlework, music, charitable schemes. I had a tumor removed
from my spine and spent a great deal of time on the sofa. I studied the
metaphysical poets and hymnology. / I thought I enjoyed intellectual pur-
suits.

NIJO. Ah, you like poetry. I come of a line of eight generations of poets.
Father had a poem / in the anthology.

ISABELLA. My father taught me Latin although I was a girl. / But

MARLENE. They didn't have Latin at my school.

2. The reference is to a poem in the *Kokinshū*, the first of the anthologies of Japanese poetry compiled by Imperial order.

ISABELLA. really I was more suited to manual work. Cooking, washing, mending, riding horses. / Better than reading books,

NIJO. Oh but I m sure you're very clever.

ISABELLA. eh Gret? A rough life in the open air.

NIJO. I can t say I enjoyed my rough life. What I enjoyed most was being the Emperor's favorite / and wearing thin silk.

ISABELLA. Did you have any horses, Gret?

GRET. Pig.

[POPE JOAN arrives.]

MARLENE. Oh Joan, thank God, we can order. Do you know everyone? We were just talking about learning Latin and being clever girls. Joan was by way of an infant prodigy. Of course you were. What excited you when you were ten?

JOAN. Because angels are without matter they are not individuals. Every angel is a species.

MARLENE. There you are.

[They laugh. They look at menus.]

ISABELLA. Yes, I forgot all my Latin. But my father was the mainspring of my life and when he died I was so grieved. I'll have the chicken, please, / and the soup.

NIJO. Of course you were grieved. My father was saying his prayers and he dozed off in the sun. So I touched his knee to rouse him. "I wonder what will happen," he said, and then he was dead before he finished the sentence. / If he'd died saying

MARLENE. What a shock.

NIJO. his prayers he would have gone straight to heaven. / Waldorf salad.

JOAN. Death is the return of all creatures to God.

NIJO. I shouldn't have woken him.

JOAN. Damnat on only means ignorance of the truth. I was always attracted by the teachings of John the Scot, though he was inclined to confuse / God and the world.

ISABELLA. Grief always overwhelmed me at the time.

MARLENE. What I fancy is a rare steak. Gret?

ISABELLA. I am of course a member of the / Church of England.*

GRET. Potatoes.

MARLENE. *I haven't been to church for years. / I like Christmas carols.

ISABELLA. Good works matter more than church attendance.

MARLENE. Make that two steaks and a lot of potatoes. Rare. But I don't do good works either.

JOAN. Cane lor i, please, / and a salad.

ISABELLA. Well, I tried, but oh dear. Hennie did good works.

NIJO. The first half of my life was all sin and the second / all repentance.*

MARLENE. Oh what about starters?

GRET. Soup.

JOAN. *And which did you like best?

MARLENE. Were your travels just a penance? Avocado vinaigrette. Didn't you / enjoy yourself?

JOAN. Nothing to start with for me, thank you.

NIJO. Yes, but I was very unhappy. / It hurt to remember

MARLENE. And the wine list.

NIJO. the past. I think that was repentance.

MARLENE. Well I wonder.

NIJO. I might have just been homesick.

MARLENE. Or angry.

NIJO. Not angry, no, / why angry?

GRET. Can we have some more bread?

MARLENE. Don't you get angry? I get angry.

NIJO. But what about?

MARLENE. Yes let's have two more Frascati. And some more bread, please.
 [*The* WAITRESS *exits.*]

ISABELLA. I tried to understand Buddhism when I was in Japan but all this
 birth and death succeeding each other through eternities just filled me with
 the most profound melancholy. I do like something more active.

NIJO. You couldn't say I was inactive. I walked every day for twenty years.

ISABELLA. I don't mean walking. / I mean in the head.

NIJO. I vowed to copy five Mahayana sutras. / Do you know how

MARLENE. I don't think religious beliefs are something we have in common.
 Activity yes.

NIJO. long they are? My head was active. / My head ached.

JOAN. It's no good being active in heresy.

ISABELLA. What heresy? She's calling the Church of England / a heresy.

JOAN. There are some very attractive / heresies.

NIJO. I had never heard of Christianity. Never / heard of it. Barbarians.

MARLENE. Well I'm not a Christian. / And I'm not a Buddhist.

ISABELLA. You have heard of it?

MARLENE. We don't all have to believe the same.

ISABELLA. I knew coming to dinner with a pope we should keep off religion.

JOAN. I always enjoy a theological argument. But I won't try to convert you,
 I'm not a missionary. Anyway I'm a heresy myself.

ISABELLA. There are some barbaric practices in the east.

NIJO. Barbaric?

ISABELLA. Among the lower classes.

NIJO. I wouldn't know.

ISABELLA. Well theology always made my head ache.

MARLENE. Oh good, some food.

 [WAITRESS *is bringing the first course.*]

NIJO. How else could I have left the court if I wasn't a nun? When father
 died I had only His Majesty. So when I fell out of favor I had nothing.
 Religion is a kind of nothing / and I dedicated what was left of me to noth-
 ing.

ISABELLA. That's what I mean about Buddhism. It doesn't brace.

MARLENE. Come on, Nijo, have some wine.

NIJO. Haven't you ever felt like that? Nothing will ever happen again. I am
 dead already. You've all felt / like that.

ISABELLA. You thought your life was over but it wasn't.

JOAN. You wish it was over.

GRET. Sad.

MARLENE. Yes, when I first came to London I sometimes . . . and when I got
 back from America I did. But only for a few hours. Not twenty years.

ISABELLA. When I was forty I thought my life was over. / Oh I

NIJO. I didn't say I felt it for twenty years. Not every minute.

ISABELLA. was pitiful. I was sent on a cruise for my health and I felt even
 worse. Pains in my bones, pins and needles in my hands, swelling behind the
 ears, and—oh, stupidity. I shook all over, indefinable terror. And Australia
 seemed to me a hideous country, the acacias stank like drains. / I had a

NIJO. You were homesick.

ISABELLA. photograph for Hennie but I told her I wouldn't send it, my hair had fallen out and my clothes were crooked, I looked completely insane and suicidal.

NIJO. So did I, exactly, dressed as a nun. I was wearing walking shoes for the first time.

ISABELLA. I longed to go home, / but home to what? Houses

NIJO. I longed to go back ten years.

ISABELLA. are so perfectly dismal.

MARLENE. I thought traveling cheered you both up.

ISABELLA. Oh it did / of course. It was on the trip from

NIJO. I'm not a cheerful person, Marlene. I just laugh a lot.

ISABELLA. Australia to the Sandwich Isles, I fell in love with the sea. There were rats in the cabin and ants in the food but suddenly it was like a new world. I woke up every morning happy, knowing there would be nothing to annoy me. No nervousness. No dressing.

NIJO. Don't you like getting dressed? I adored my clothes. / When I was chosen to give sake to His Majesty's brother,

MARLENE. You had prettier colors than Isabella.

NIJO. the Emperor Kameyama, on his formal visit, I wore raw silk pleated trousers and a seven-layered gown in shades of red, and two outer garments, / yellow lined with green and a light

MARLENE. Yes, all that silk must have been very . . .

[*The* WAITRESS *starts to clear the first course.*]

JOAN. I dressed as a boy when I left home.*

NIJO. green jacket. Lady Betto had a five-layered gown in shades of green and purple.

ISABELLA. *You dressed as a boy?

MARLENE. Of course, / for safety.

JOAN. It was easy, I was only twelve. / Also women weren't allowed in the library. We wanted to study in Athens.

MARLENE. You ran away alone?

JOAN. No, not alone, I went with my friend. / He was sixteen

NIJO. Ah, an elopement.

JOAN. but I thought I knew more science than he did and almost as much philosophy.

ISABELLA. Well I always traveled as a lady and I repudiated strongly any suggestion in the press that I was other than feminine.

MARLENE. I don't wear trousers in the office. / I could but I don't.

ISABELLA. There was no great danger to a woman of my age and appearance.

MARLENE. And you got away with it, Joan?

JOAN. I did then

[*The* WAITRESS *starts to bring the main course.*]

MARLENE. And nobody noticed anything?

JOAN. They noticed I was a very clever boy. * And when I

MARLENE. I couldn't have kept pretending for so long.

JOAN. shared a bed with my friend, that was ordinary—two poor students in a lodging house. I think I forgot I was pretending.

ISABELLA. Rocky Mountain Jim, Mr. Nugent,[3] showed me no disrespect. He found it interesting, I think, that I could make scones and also lasso cattle. Indeed he declared his love for me, which was most distressing.

NIJO. What did he say? / We always sent poems first.

3. Irish-born trapper (d. 1874), who lived in the Colorado Rockies.

MARLENE. What did you say?

ISABELLA. I urged him to give up whisky, / but he said it was too late.

MARLENE. Oh Isabella.

ISABELLA. He had lived alone in the mountains for many years.

MARLENE. But did you—?

[*The* WAITRESS *goes.*]

ISABELLA. Mr. Nugent was a man that any woman might love but none could marry. I came back to England.

NIJO. Did you write him a poem when you left? / Snow on the

MARLENE. Did you never see him again?

ISABELLA. No, never.

NIJO. mountains. My sleeves are wet with tears. In England no tears, no snow.

ISABELLA. Well, I say never. One morning very early in Switzerland, it was a year later, I had a vision of him as I last saw him / in his trapper's clothes with his hair round his face,

NIJO. A ghost!

ISABELLA. and that was the day, / I learned later, he died with a

NIJO. Ah!

ISABELLA. bullet in his brain. / He just bowed to me and vanished.

MARLENE. Oh Isabella.

NIJO. When your lover dies—One of my lovers died. / The priest Ariake.

JOAN. My friend died. Have we all got dead lovers?

MARLENE. Not me, sorry.

NIJO. [*To* ISABELLA.] I wasn't a nun, I was still at court, but he was a priest, and when he came to me he dedicated his whole life to hell. / He knew that when he died he would fall into one of the three lower realms. And he died, he did die.

JOAN. [*To* MARLENE.] I'd quarreled with him over the teachings of John the Scot,[4] who held that our ignorance of God is the same as his ignorance of himself. He only knows what he creates because he creates everything he knows but he himself is above being—do you follow?

MARLENE. No, but go on.

NIJO. I couldn't bear to think / in what shape would he be reborn.*

JOAN. St. Augustine[5] maintained that the Neo-Platonic Ideas[6] are indivisible from God, but I agreed with John that the created

ISABELLA. *Buddhism is really most uncomfortable.

JOAN. world is essences derived from Ideas which derived from God. As Denys the Areopagite[7] said—the pseudo-Denys—first we give God a name, then deny it / then reconcile the

NIJO. In what shape would he return?

JOAN. contradiction by looking beyond / those terms—

MARLENE. Sorry, what? Denys said what?

JOAN. Well we disagreed about it, we quarreled. And next day he was ill, / I was so annoyed with him, all the time I was

NIJO. Misery in this life and worse in the next, all because of me.

4. John ("Irish John born in Ireland") Scotus Erigena (c. 810–c. 880), the earliest scholastic philosopher, whose beliefs were pantheistic and Neoplatonic in spirit.
5. The first great theologian of Christianity (354–430) turned to the religion after studying Plato.
6. Neoplatonic philosophy, as founded by Plotinus (3rd century A.D.), opposed materialism and intro-

duced the religious conception of "Ideas" (Plato's eternal paradigms) as the thoughts of God.
7. Dionysius the Areopagite was converted by Paul (Acts 17:34) and, according to tradition, was a martyr and the first bishop of Athens; famous philosophical works attributed to him (as "pseudo-Dionysius"), written in the 5th or 6th century, brought Neoplatonism into Western Christian thought.

JOAN. nursing him I kept going over the arguments in my mind. Matter is not a means of knowing the essence. The source of the species is the Idea. But then I realized he'd never understand my arguments again, and that night he died. John the Scot held that the individual disintegrates / and there is no personal immortality.

ISABELLA. I wouldn't have you think I was in love with Jim Nugent. It was yearning to save him that I felt.

MARLENE. [To JOAN.] So what did you do?

JOAN. First I decided to stay a man. I was used to it. And I wanted to devote my life to learning. Do you know why I went to Rome? Italian men didn't have beards.

ISABELLA. The loves of my life were Hennie, my own pet, and my dear husband the doctor, who nursed Hennie in her last illness. I knew it would be terrible when Hennie died but I didn't know how terrible. I felt half of myself had gone. How could I go on my travels without that sweet soul waiting at home for my letters? It was Doctor Bishop's devotion to her in her last illness that made me decide to marry him. He and Hennie had the same sweet character. I had not.

NIJO. I thought his majesty had sweet character because when he found out about Ariake he was so kind. But really it was because he no longer cared for me. One night he even sent me out to a man who had been pursuing me. / He lay awake on the other side of the screens and listened.

ISABELLA. I did wish marriage had seemed more of a step. I tried very hard to cope with the ordinary drudgery of life. I was ill again with carbuncles on the spine and nervous prostration. I ordered a tricycle, that was my idea of adventure then. And John himself fell ill, with erysipelas and anaemia. I began to love him with my whole heart but it was too late. He was a skeleton with transparent white hands. I wheeled him on various seafronts in a bathchair. And he faded and left me. There was nothing in my life. The doctors said I had gout / and my heart was much affected.

NIJO. There was nothing in my life, nothing, without the Emperor's favor. The Empress had always been my enemy, Marlene, she said I had no right to wear three-layered gowns. / But I was the adopted daughter of my grandfather the Prime Minister. I had been publicly granted permission to wear thin silk.

JOAN. There was nothing in my life except my studies. I was obsessed with pursuit of the truth. I taught at the Greek School in Rome, which St. Augustine had made famous. I was poor, I worked hard. I spoke apparently brilliantly, I was still very young, I was a stranger; suddenly I was quite famous, I was everyone's favorite. Huge crowds came to hear me. The day after they made me cardinal I fell ill and lay two weeks without speaking, full of terror and regret. / But then I got up

MARLENE. Yes, success is very . . .

JOAN. determined to go on. I was seized again / with a desperate longing for the absolute.

ISABELLA. Yes, yes, to go on. I sat in Tobermory among Hennie's flowers and sewed a complete outfit in Jaeger flannel. / I was fifty-six years old.

NIJO. Out of favor but I didn't die. I left on foot, nobody saw me go. For the next twenty years I walked through Japan.

GRET. Walking is good.

[The WAITRESS enters.]

JOAN. Pope Leo died and I was chosen. All right then. I would be Pope. I would know God. I would know everything.

ISABELLA. I determined to leave my grief behind and set off for Tibet.

MARLENE. Magnificent all of you. We need some more wine, please, two bottles I think, Griselda isn't even here yet, and I want to drink a toast to you all.

ISABELLA. To yourself surely, / we're here to celebrate your success.

NIJO. Yes, Marlene.

JOAN. Yes, what is it exactly, Marlene?

MARLENE. Well it's not Pope but it is managing director.*

JOAN. And you find work for people.

MARLENE. Yes, an employment agency.

NIJO. *Over all the women you work with. And the men.

ISABELLA. And very well deserved too. I'm sure it's just the beginning of something extraordinary.

MARLENE. Well it's worth a party.

ISABELLA. To Marlene.*

MARLENE. And all of us.

JOAN. *Marlene.

NIJO. Marlene.

GRET. Marlene.

MARLENE. We've all come a long way. To our courage and the way we changed our lives and our extraordinary achievements.
[*They laugh and drink a toast.*]

ISABELLA. Such adventures. We were crossing a mountain pass at seven thousand feet, the cook was all to pieces, the muleteers suffered fever and snow blindness. But even though my spine was agony I managed very well.

MARLENE. Wonderful.

NIJO. Once I was ill for four months lying alone at an inn. Nobody to offer a horse to Buddha. I had to live for myself, and I did live.

ISABELLA. Of course you did. It was far worse returning to Tobermory. I always felt dull when I was stationary. / That's why I could never stay anywhere.

NIJO. Yes, that's it exactly. New sights. The shrine by the beach, the moon shining on the sea. The goddess had vowed to save all living things. / She would even save the fishes. I was full of hope.

JOAN. I had thought the Pope would know everything. I thought God would speak to me directly. But of course he knew I was a woman.

MARLENE. But nobody else even suspected?
[*The* WAITRESS *brings more wine.*]

JOAN. In the end I did take a lover again.*

ISABELLA. In the Vatican?

GRET. *Keep you warm.

NIJO. *Ah, lover.

MARLENE. *Good for you.

JOAN. He was one of my chamberlains. There are such a lot of servants when you're a Pope. The food's very good. And I realized I did know the truth. Because whatever the Pope says, that's true.

NIJO. What was he like, the chamberlain?*

GRET. Big cock.

ISABELLA. Oh Gret.

MARLENE. *Did he fancy you when he thought you were a fella?

NIJO. What was he like?

JOAN. He could keep a secret.

MARLENE. So you did know everything.

JOAN. Yes, I enjoyed being Pope. I consecrated bishops and let people kiss
my feet. I received the King of England when he came to submit to the
church. Unfortunately there were earthquakes, and some village reported it
had rained blood, and in France there was a plague of giant grasshoppers,
but I don't think that can have been my fault, do you?*
[Laughter.]
The grasshoppers fell on the English Channel / and were

NIJO. I once went to sea. It was very lonely. I realized it made very little dif-
ference where I went.

JOAN. washed up on shore and their bodies rotted and poisoned the air and
everyone in those parts died.
[Laughter.]

ISABELLA. *Such superstition! I was nearly murdered in China by a howling
mob. They thought the barbarians ate babies and put them under railway
sleepers to make the tracks steady, and ground up their eyes to make the
lenses of cameras. / So

MARLENE. And you had a camera!

ISABELLA. And they were shouting, "child-eater, child-eater." Some people
tried to sell girl babies to Europeans for cameras or stew!
[Laughter.]

MARLENE. So apart from the grasshoppers it was a great success.

JOAN. Yes, if it hadn't been for the baby I expect I'd have lived to an old age
like Theodora of Alexandria,⁸ who lived as a monk. She was accused by a girl
/ who fell in love with her of being the father of her child and—

NIJO. But tell us what happened to your baby. I had some babies.

MARLENE. Didn't you think of getting rid of it?

JOAN. Wouldn't that be a worse sin than having it? / But a Pope with a child
was about as bad as possible.

MARLENE. I don't know, you're the Pope.

JOAN. But I wouldn't have known how to get rid of it.

MARLENE. Other Popes had children, surely.

JOAN. They didn't give birth to them.

NIJO. Well you were a woman.

JOAN. Exactly and I shouldn't have been a woman. Women, children and lu-
natics can't be Pope.

MARLENE. So the only thing to do / was to get rid of it somehow.

NIJO. You had to have it adopted secretly.

JOAN. But I didn't know what was happening. I thought I was getting fatter,
but then I was eating more and sitting about, the life of a Pope is quite lux-
urious. I don't think I'd spoken to a woman since I was twelve. The cham-
berlain was the one who realized.

MARLENE. And by then it was too late.

JOAN. Oh I didn't want to pay attention. It was easier to do nothing.

NIJO. But you had to plan for having it. You had to say you were ill and go
away.

JOAN. That's what I should have done I suppose.

MARLENE. Did you want them to find out?

NIJO. I too was often in embarrassing situations, there's no need for a scan-
dal. My first child was His Majesty's, which unfortunately died, but my sec-
ond was Akebono's. I was seventeen. He was in love with me when I was

8. Wife of a prefect of Egypt, who, according to legend, left him to do penance for a sin and lived for the rest of her
life as a monk; her sex was discovered only on her death at the monastery.

thirteen, he was very upset when I had to go to the Emperor, it was very ro-
mantic, a lot of poems. Now His Majesty hadn't been near me for two
months so he thought I was four months pregnant when I was really six, so
when I reached the ninth month / I

JOAN. I never knew what month it was.

NIJO. announced I was seriously ill, and Akebono announced he had gone on
a religious retreat. He held me round the waist and lifted me up as the baby
was born. He cut the cord with a short sword, wrapped the baby in white
and took it away. It was only a girl but I was sorry to lose it. Then I told the
Emperor that the baby had miscarried because of my illness, and there you
are. The danger was past.

JOAN. But Nijo, I wasn't used to having a woman's body.

ISABELLA. So what happened?

JOAN. I didn't know of course that it was near the time. It was Rogation
Day,[9] there was always a procession. I was on the horse dressed in my robes
and a cross was carried in front of me, and all the cardinals were following,
and all the clergy of Rome, and a huge crowd of people. / We set off from

MARLENE. Total Pope.

JOAN. St. Peter's to go to St. John's. I had felt a slight pain earlier, I thought
it was something I'd eaten, and then it came back, and came back more
often. I thought when this is over I'll go to bed. There were still long gaps
when I felt perfectly all right and I didn't want to attract attention to myself
and spoil the ceremony. Then I suddenly realized what it must be. I had to
last out till I could get home and hide. Then something changed, my breath
started to catch, I couldn't plan things properly any more. We were in a lit-
tle street that goes between St. Clement's and the Colosseum, and I just
had to get off the horse and sit down for a minute. Great waves of pressure
were going through my body, I heard sounds like a cow lowing, they came
out of my mouth. Far away I heard people screaming, "The Pope is ill, the
Pope is dying." And the baby just slid out onto the road.*

MARLENE. The cardinals / won't have known where to put themselves.

NIJO. Oh dear, Joan, what a thing to do! In the street!

ISABELLA. *How embarrassing.

GRET. In a field, yah.

[They are laughing.]

JOAN. One of the cardinals said, "The Antichrist!" and fell over in a faint.

[They all laugh.]

MARLENE. So what did they do? They weren't best pleased.

JOAN. They took me by the feet and dragged me out of town and stoned me
to death.

[They stop laughing.]

MARLENE. Joan, how horrible.

JOAN. I don't really remember.

NIJO. And the child died too?

JOAN. Oh yes, I think so, yes.

[Pause. The WAITRESS enters to clear the plates. They start talking quietly.]

ISABELLA. [To JOAN.] I never had any children. I was very fond of horses.

NINJO. [To MARLENE.] I saw my daughter once. She was three years old. She
wore a plum-red / small-sleeved gown. Akebono's

9. One of four days on which there are solemn processions and litanies to invoke God's mercies (the Major
Rogation is April 25).

ISABELLA. Birdie was my favorite. A little Indian bay mare I rode in the Rocky Mountains.

NIJO. wife had taken the child because her own died. Everyone thought I was just a visitor. She was being brought up carefully so she could be sent to the palace like I was.

ISABELLA. Legs of iron and always cheerful and such a pretty face. If a stranger led her she reared up like a bronco.

NIJO. I never saw my third child after he was born, the son of Ariake the priest. Ariake held him on his lap the day he was born and talked to him as if he could understand, and cried. My fourth child was Ariake's too. Ariake died before he was born. I didn't want to see anyone, I stayed alone in the hills. It was a boy again, my third son. But oddly enough I felt nothing for him.

MARLENE. How many children did you have, Gret?

GRET. Ten.

ISABELLA. Whenever I came back to England I felt I had so much to atone for. Hennie and John were so good. I did no good in my life. I spent years in self-gratification. So I hurled myself into committees, I nursed the people of Tobermory in the epidemic of influenza, I lectured the Young Women's Christian Association on Thrift. I talked and talked explaining how the East was corrupt and vicious. My travels must do good to someone beside myself. I wore myself out with good causes.

MARLENE. Oh God, why are we all so miserable?

JOAN. The process on never went down that street again.

MARLENE. They rerouted it specially?

JOAN. Yes they had to go all round to avoid it. And they introduced a pierced chair.

MARLENE. A pierced chair?

JOAN. Yes, a chair made out of solid marble with a hole in the seat / and it was in the Chapel of the Savior, and after he was

MARLENE. You're not serious.

JOAN. elected the Pope had to sit in it.

MARLENE. And someone looked up his skirts? / Not really?

ISABELLA. What an extraordinary thing.

JOAN. Two of the clergy / made sure he was a man.

NIJO. On their hands and knees!

MARLENE. A pierced chair!

GRET. Balls!

[GRISELDA arrives unnoticed.]

NIJO. Why couldn't he just pull up his robe?

JOAN. He had to sit there and look dignified.

MARLENE. You could have made all your chamberlains sit in it.*

GRET. Big one, small one.

NIJO. Very useful chair at court.

ISABELLA. *Or the laird of Tobermory in his kilt.

[They are quite drunk. They get the giggles. MARLENE notices GRISELDA.]

MARLENE. Griselda / There you are. Do you want to eat?

GRISELDA. I'm sorry I'm so late. No, no, don't bother.

MARLENE. Of course it's no bother. / Have you eaten?

GRISELDA. No really, I'm not hungry.

MARLENE. Well have some pudding.[1]

1. A general term meaning dessert.

GRISELDA. I never eat pudding.

MARLENE. Griselda, I hope you're not anorexic. We're having pudding, I am, and getting nice and fat.

GRISELDA. Oh if everyone is. I don't mind.

MARLENE. Now who do you know? This is Joan who was Pope in the ninth century, and Isabella Bird, the Victorian traveler, and Lady Nijo from Japan, Emperor's concubine and Buddhist nun, thirteenth century, nearer your own time, and Gret who was painted by Brueghel. Griselda's in Boccaccio and Petrarch and Chaucer because of her extraordinary marriage. I'd like profiteroles because they're disgusting.

JOAN. Zabaglione, please.

ISABELLA. Apple pie / and cream.

NIJO. What's this?

MARLENE. Zabaglione, it's Italian, it's what Joan's having, / it's delicious.

NIJO. A Roman Catholic / dessert? Yes please.

MARLENE. Gret?

GRET. Cake.

GRISELDA. Just cheese and biscuits, thank you.

MARLENE. Yes, Griselda's life is like a fairy-story, except it starts with marrying the prince.

GRISELDA. He's only a marquis, Marlene.

MARLENE. Well everyone for miles around is his liege and he's absolute lord of life and death and you were the poor but beautiful peasant girl and he whisked you off. / Near enough a prince.

NIJO. How old were you?

GRISELDA. Fifteen.

NIJO. I was brought up in court circles and it was still a shock. Had you ever seen him before?

GRISELDA. I'd seen him riding by, we all had. And he'd seen me in the fields with the sheep.*

ISABELLA. I would have been well suited to minding sheep.

NIJO. And Mr. Nugent riding by.

ISABELLA. Of course not, Nijo, I mean a healthy life in the open air.

JOAN. *He just rode up while you were minding the sheep and asked you to marry him?

GRISELDA. No, no, it was on the wedding day. I was waiting outside the door to see the procession. Everyone wanted him to get married so there'd be an heir to look after us when he died, / and at last he announced a day for the wedding but

MARLENE. I don't think Walter wanted to get married. It is Walter? Yes.

GRISELDA. nobody knew who the bride was, we thought it must be a foreign princess, we were longing to see her. Then the carriage stopped outside our cottage and we couldn't see the bride anywhere. And he came and spoke to my father.

NIJO. And your father told you to serve the Prince.

GRISELDA. My father could hardly speak. The Marquis said it wasn't an order, I could say no, but if I said yes I must always obey him in everything.

MARLENE. That's when you should have suspected.

GRISELDA. But of course a wife must obey her husband. / And of course I must obey the Marquis.*

ISABELLA. I swore to obey dear John, of course, but it didn't seem to arise. Naturally I wouldn't have wanted to go abroad while I was married.

MARLENE. *Then why bother to mention it at all? He'd got a thing about it, that's why.

GRISELDA. I'd rather obey the Marquis than a boy from the village.

MARLENE. Yes, that's a point.

JOAN. I never obeyed anyone. They all obeyed me.

NIJO. And what did you wear? He didn't make you get married in your own clothes? That would be perverse.*

MARLENE. Oh, you wait.

GRISELDA. *He had ladies with him who undressed me and they had a white silk dress and jewels for my hair.

MARLENE. And at first he seemed perfectly normal?

GRISELDA. Marlene, you're always so critical of him. / Of course he was normal, he was very kind.

MARLENE. But Griselda, come on, he took your baby.

GRISELDA. Walter found it hard to believe I loved him. He couldn't believe I would always obey him. He had to prove it.

MARLENE. I don't think Walter likes women.

GRISELDA. I'm sure he loved me, Marlene, all the time.

MARLENE. He just had a funny way / of showing it

GRISELDA. It was hard for him too.

JOAN. How do you mean he took away your baby?

NIJO. Was it a boy?

GRISELDA. No, the first one was a girl.

NIJO. Even so it's hard when they take it away. Did you see it at all?

GRISELDA. Oh yes, she was six weeks old.

NIJO. Much better to do it straight away.

ISABELLA. But why did your husband take the child?

GRISELDA. He said all the people hated me because I was just one of them. And now I had a child they were restless. So he had to get rid of the child to keep them quiet. But he said he wouldn't snatch her, I had to agree and obey and give her up. So when I was feeding her a man came in and took her away. I thought he was going to kill her even before he was out of the room.

MARLENE. But you let him take her? You didn't struggle?

GRISELDA. I asked him to give her back so I could kiss her. And I asked him to bury her where no animals could dig her up. / It

ISABELLA. Oh my dear.

GRISELDA. was Walter's child to do what he liked with.*

MARLENE. Walter was bonkers.

GRET. Bastard.

ISABELLA. *But surely, murder.

GRISELDA. I had promised.

MARLENE. I can't stand this. I'm going for a pee.

[MARLENE goes out. The WAITRESS brings dessert.]

NIJO. No, I understand. Of course you had to, he was your life. And were you in favor after that?

GRISELDA. Oh yes, we were very happy together. We never spoke about what had happened.

ISABELLA. I can see you were doing what you thought was your duty. But didn't it make you ill?

GRISELDA. No, I was very well, thank you.

NIJO. And you had another child?

GRISELDA. Not for four years, but then I did, yes a boy.

NIJO. Ah a boy. / So it all ended happily.

GRISELDA. Yes he was pleased. I kept my son till he was two years old. A peasant's grandson. It made the people angry. Walter explained.

ISABELLA. But surely he wouldn't kill his children / just because—

GRISELDA. Oh it wasn't true. Walter would never give in to the people. He wanted to see if I loved him enough.

JOAN. He killed his children / to see if you loved him enough?

NIJO. Was it easier the second time or harder?

GRISELDA. It was always easy because I always knew I would do what he said. [Pause. They start to eat.]

ISABELLA. I hope you didn't have any more children.

GRISELDA. Oh no, no more. It was twelve years till he tested me again.

ISABELLA. So whatever did he do this time? / My poor John, I never loved him enough, and he would never have dreamed . . .

GRISELDA. He sent me away. He said the people wanted him to marry someone else who'd give him an heir and he'd got special permission from the Pope. So I said I'd go home to my father. I came with nothing / so I went with nothing. I

NIJO. Better to leave if your master doesn't want you.

GRISELDA. took off my clothes. He let me keep a slip so he wouldn't be shamed. And I walked home barefoot. My father came out in tears. Everyone was crying except me.

NIJO. At least your father wasn't dead. / I had nobody.

ISABELLA. Well it can be a relief to come home. I loved to see Hennie's sweet face again.

GRISELDA. Oh yes, I was perfectly content. And quite soon he sent for me again.

JOAN. I don't think I would have gone.

GRISELDA. But he told me to come. I had to obey him. He wanted me to help prepare his wedding. He was getting married to a young girl from France / and nobody except me knew how to arrange things the way he liked them.

NIJO. It's always hard taking him another woman. [MARLENE comes back.]

JOAN. I didn't live a woman's life. I don't understand it.

GRISELDA. The girl was sixteen and far more beautiful than me. I could see why he loved her. / She had her younger brother with her as a page. [The WAITRESS enters.]

MARLENE. Oh God, I can't bear it. I want some coffee. Six coffees. Six brandies. / Double brandies. Straightaway.

GRISELDA. They all went in to the feast I'd prepared. And he stayed behind and put his arms round me and kissed me. / I felt half asleep with the shock.

NIJO. Oh, like a dream.

MARLENE. And he said, "This is your daughter and your son."

GRISELDA. Yes.

JOAN. What?

NIJO. Oh. Oh I see. You got them back.

ISABELLA. I did think it was remarkably barbaric to kill them but you learn not to say anything. / So he had them brought up secretly I suppose.

MARLENE. Walter's a monster. Weren't you angry? What did you do?

GRISELDA. Well I fainted. Then I cried and kissed the children. / Everyone was making a fuss of me.

NIJO. But did you feel anything for them?

GRISELDA. What?

NIJO. Did you feel anything for the children?

GRISELDA. Of course, I loved them.

JOAN. So you forgave him and lived with him?

GRISELDA. He suffered so much all those years.

ISABELLA. Hennie had the same sweet nature.

NIJO. So they dressed you again?

GRISELDA. Cloth of gold.

JOAN. I can't forgive anything.

MARLENE. You really are exceptional, Griselda.

NIJO. Nobody gave me back my children

[NIJO cries. The WAITRESS brings brandies.]

ISABELLA. I can never be like Hennie. I was always so busy in England, a kind of business I detested. The very presence of people exhausted my emotional reserves. I could not be like Hennie however I tried. I tried and was as ill as could be. The doctor suggested a steel net to support my head, the weight of my own head was too much for my diseased spine. / It is dangerous to put oneself in depressing circumstances. Why should I do it?

JOAN. Don't cry.

NIJO. My father and the Emperor both died in the autumn. So much pain.

JOAN. Yes, but don't cry.

NIJO. They wouldn't let me into the palace when he was dying. I hid in the room with his coffin, then I couldn't find where I'd left my shoes, I ran after the funeral procession in bare feet, I couldn't keep up. When I got there it was over, a few wisps of smoke in the sky, that's all that was left of him. What I want to know is, if I'd still been at court, would I have been allowed to wear full mourning?

MARLENE. I'm sure you would.

NIJO. Why do you say that? You don't know anything about it. Would I have been allowed to wear full mourning?

ISABELLA. How can people live in this dim pale island and wear our hideous clothes? I cannot and will not live the life of a lady.

NIJO. I'll tell you something that made me angry. I was eighteen, at the Full Moon Ceremony. They make a special rice gruel and stir it with their sticks, and then they beat their women across the loins so they'll have sons and not daughters. So the Emperor beat us all / very hard as usual—that's not it,

MARLENE. What a sod.

NIJO. Marlene, that's normal, what made us angry, he told his attendants they could beat us too. Well they had a wonderful time. / So Lady Genki and I made a plan, and the ladies all hid

[The WAITRESS has entered with coffees.]

MARLENE. I'd like another brandy please. Better make it six.

NIJO. in his rooms, and Lady Mashimizu stood guard with a stick at the door, and when His Majesty came in Genki seized him and I beat him till he cried out and promised he would never order anyone to hit us again. Afterwards there was a terrible fuss. The nobles were horrified. "We wouldn't even dream of stepping on your Majesty's shadow." And I had hit him with a stick. Yes, I hit him with a stick.

JOAN. Suave, mari magno turbantibus aequora ventis,
e terra magnum alterius spectare laborem:
non quia vexari quemquamst iucunda voluptas,
sed quibus ipse malis careas quia cernere suave est.
Suave etiam belli certamina magna tueri

per campos instructa tua sine parte pericli.
Sed nil dulcius est, bene quam munita tenere
edita doctrina sapientum templa serena, /
despicere unde queas alios passimque videre
errare atque viam palantis quaerere vitae,[2]

GRISELDA. I do think—I do wonder—it would have been nicer if Walter hadn't had to.

ISABELLA. Why should I? Why should I?

MARLENE. Of course not.

NIJO. I hit him with a stick.

JOAN. certare ingenio, contendere nobilitate,
noctes atque dies niti praestante labore
ad summas emergere opes rerumque potiri.
O miseras / hominum mentis, o pectora caeca!*

ISABELLA. Oh miseras!

NIJO. *Pectora caeca.

JOAN. qualibus in tenebris vitae quantisque periclis
degitur hoc aevi quodcumquest! / nonne videre
nil aliud sibi naturam latrare, nisi utqui
corpore seiunctus dolor absit, mente fruatur
[JOAN subsides.]

GRET. We come into hell through a big mouth. Hell's black and red. / It's like the village where I come from. There's a river and

MARLENE. [To JOAN.] Shut up, pet.

ISABELLA. Listen, she's been to hell.

GRET. a bridge and houses. There's places on fire like when the soldiers come. There's a big devil sat on a roof with a big hole in his arse and he's scooping stuff out of it with a big ladle and it's falling down on us, and it's money, so a lot of the women stop and get some. But most of us is fighting the devils. There's lots of little devils, our size, and we get them down all right and give them a beating. There's lots of funny creatures round your feet, you don't like to look, like rats and lizards, and nasty things, a bum with a face, and fish with legs, and faces on things that don't have faces on. But they don't hurt, you just keep going. Well we'd all had worse, you see, we'd had the Spanish. We'd all had family killed. My big son die on a wheel. Birds eat him. My baby, a soldier run her through with a sword. I'd had enough, I was mad, I hate the bastards. I come out my front door that morning and shout till my neighbors come out and I said, "Come on, we're going where the evil come from and pay the bastards out." And they all come out just as they was / from baking or washing in their

NIJO. All the ladies come.

GRET. aprons, and we push down the street and the ground opens up and we go through a big mouth into a street just like ours but in hell. I've got a

2. Joan quotes Lucretius's (c. 96–c. 55 B.C.) philosophical poem *On the Nature of Things* 2.1–18 (the translation is broken where other dialogue interrupts): "It is pleasant, when over a great sea the winds are roiling the waters, to look out from land at another's great labor; not because it is so delightful that anyone be troubled, but because it is sweet to understand from what ills you yourself are free. It is also pleasant to watch great contests of war arrayed on the plains when you have no share of the danger. But nothing is sweeter than to hold tranquil, high sanctuaries, well fortified by the teaching of the wise, from which you may look down and see others wandering all about without direction as they seek a way of life, as they compete with wit, fight for precedence, struggle night and day with remarkable effort to rise to the heights of wealth and to possess things. Oh wretched minds of humans, oh blind hearts! [Isabella repeats, "O wretched!"; Nijo repeats, "Blind hearts."] In what darkness of life, in how great dangers this brief lifetime is passed! Don't you see that nature clamors for nothing except this, that the body be freed from pain, and that the mind enjoy [delight]?"

sword in my hand from somewhere and I fill a basket with gold cups they drink out of down there You just keep running on and fighting / you didn't stop for nothing. Oh we give them devils such a beating.

NIJO. Take that, take that.

JOAN. Something something something mortisque timores
tum vacuum pectus—damn.
Quod si ridicula—
something something on and on and on and something
splendorem purpurea.[3]

ISABELLA. I thought I would have a last jaunt up the west river in China. Why not? But the doctors were so very grave. I just went to Morocco. The sea was so wild I had to be landed by ship's crane in a coal bucket. / My horse was a terror to me a

GRET. Coal bucket, good.

JOAN. nos in luce timemus
something
terrorem.[4]

ISABELLA. powerful black charger.
[NIJO *is laughing and crying.* JOAN *gets up and is sick in a corner.* MARLENE *is drinking* ISABELLA's *brandy.*]
So off I went to visit the Berber sheikhs in full blue trousers and great brass spurs. I was the only European woman ever to have seen the Emperor of Morocco. I was seventy years old. What lengths to go to for a last chance of joy. I knew my return of vigor was only temporary, but how marvelous while it lasted.

SCENE TWO

Employment Agency. MARLENE *and* JEANINE.

MARLENE. Right Jeanine, you are Jeanine aren't you? Let's have a look. Os and As.[5] / No As, all those Os you probably

JEANINE. Six Cs.

MARLENE. could have got an A. / Speeds, not brilliant, not too bad.

JEANINE. I wanted to go to work.

MARLENE. Well, Jeanine, what's your present job like?

JEANINE. I'm a secretary.

MARLENE. Secretary or typist?

JEANINE. I did start as a typist but the last six months I've been a secretary.

MARLENE. To?

JEANINE. To three of them, really, they share me. There's Mr. Ashford, he's the office manager, and Mr. Philby / is sales, and—

MARLENE. Quite a small place?

JEANINE. A bit small.

MARLENE. Friendly?

JEANINE. Oh it's friendly enough.

MARLENE. Prospects?

JEANINE. I don't think so, that's the trouble. Miss Lewis is secretary to the managing director and she's been there forever, and Mrs. Bradford/ is—

3. Also from Lucretius: "then fears of death [leave your heart empty" [2.45–46); "But if [we see] these things [to be] ridiculous" (2.47); "the magnificence of purple" (2.52).
4. Lucretius 2.54. 59: "We are afraid in the light"
something "terror."
5. O ("Ordinary") levels are the lowest level of standardized examinations in secondary school subjects, and A ("Advanced") levels are used in applying to universities

MARLENE. So you want a job with better prospects?
JEANINE. I want a change.
MARLENE. So you'll take anything comparable?
JEANINE. No, I do want prospects. I want more money.
MARLENE. You're getting—?
JEANINE. Hundred.
MARLENE. It's not bad you know. You're what? Twenty?
JEANINE. I'm saving to get married.
MARLENE. Does that mean you don't want a long-term job, Jeanine?
JEANINE. I might do.
MARLENE. Because where do the prospects come in? No kids for a bit?
JEANINE. Oh no, not kids, not yet.
MARLENE. So you won't tell them you're getting married?
JEANINE. Had I better not?
MARLENE. It would probably help.
JEANINE. I'm not wearing a ring. We thought we wouldn't spend on a ring.
MARLENE. Saves taking it off.
JEANINE. I wouldn't take it off.
MARLENE. There's no need to mention it when you go for an interview. /
 Now Jeanine do you have a feel for any particular
JEANINE. But what if they ask?
MARLENE. kind of company?
JEANINE. I thought advertising.
MARLENE. People often do think advertising. I have got a few vacancies but
 I think they're looking for something glossier.
JEANINE. You mean how I dress? / I can dress different. I
MARLENE. I mean experience.
JEANINE. dress like this on purpose for where I am now.
MARLENE. I have a marketing department here of a knitwear manufacturer.
 / Marketing is near enough advertising. Secretary
JEANINE. Knitwear?
MARLENE. to the marketing manager, he's thirty-five, married, I've sent him
 a girl before and she was happy, left to have a baby, you won't want to men-
 tion marriage there. He's very fair I think, good at his job, you won't have to
 nurse him along. Hundred and ten, so that's better than you're doing now.
JEANINE. I don't know.
MARLENE. I've a fairly small concern here, father and two sons, you'd have
 more say potentially, secretarial and reception duties, only a hundred but
 the job's going to grow with the concern and then you'll be in at the top
 with new girls coming in underneath you.
JEANINE. What is it they do?
MARLENE. Lampshades. / This would be my first choice for you.
JEANINE. Just lampshades?
MARLENE. There's plenty of different kinds of lampshade. So we'll send you
 there, shall we, and the knitwear second choice. Are you free to go for an in-
 terview any day they call you?
JEANINE. I'd like to travel.
MARLENE. We don't have any foreign clients. You'd have to go elsewhere.
JEANINE. Yes I know. I don't really . . . I just mean . . .
MARLENE. Does your fiancé want to travel?
JEANINE. I'd like a job where I was here in London and with him and every-
 thing but now and then—I expect it's silly. Are there jobs like that?
MARLENE. There's personal assistant to a top executive in a multinational.

If that's the idea you need to be planning ahead. Is that where you want to be in ten years?

JEANINE. I might not be alive in ten years.

MARLENE. Yes but you will be. You'll have children.

JEANINE. I can't think about ten years.

MARLENE. You haven't got the speeds anyway. So I'll send you to these two shall I? You haven't been to any other agency? Just so we don't get crossed wires. Now Jeanine I want you to get one of these jobs, all right? If I send you that means I'm putting myself on the line for you. Your presentation's OK, you look fine, just be confident and go in there convinced that this is the best job for you and you're the best person for the job. If you don't believe it they won't believe it.

JEANINE. Do you believe it?

MARLENE. I think you could make me believe it if you put your mind to it.

JEANINE. Yes, all right.

SCENE THREE

JOYCE's *back yard. The house with back door is upstage. Downstage a shelter made of junk, made by children. Two girls,* ANGIE *and* KIT, *are in it, squashed together.* ANGIE *is 16,* KIT *is 12. They cannot be seen from the house.* JOYCE *calls from the house.*

JOYCE. Angie. Angie are you out there?

[*Silence. They keep still and wait. When nothing else happens they relax.*]

ANGIE. Wish she was dead.

KIT. Wanna watch *The Exterminator*?

ANGIE. You're sitting on my leg.

KIT. There's nothing on telly. We can have an ice cream. Angie?

ANGIE. Shall I tell you something?

KIT. Do you wanna watch *The Exterminator*?

ANGIE. It's X, innit.

KIT. I can get into Xs.

ANGIE. Shall I tell you something?

KIT. We'll go to something else. We'll go to Ipswich. What's on the Odeon?

ANGIE. She won't let me, will she?

KIT. Don't tell her.

ANGIE. I've no money.

KIT. I'll pay.

ANGIE. She'll moan though, won't she?

KIT. I'll ask her for you if you like.

ANGIE. I've no money, I don't want you to pay.

KIT. I'll ask her.

ANGIE. She don't like you

KIT. I still got three pounds birthday money. Did she say she don't like me? I'll go by myself then.

ANGIE. Your mum don't let you. I got to take you.

KIT. She won't know.

ANGIE. You'd be scared who'd sit next to you.

KIT. No I wouldn't.

She does like me anyway.

Tell me then.

ANGIE. Tell you what?

KIT. It's you she doesn't like.

ANGIE. Well I don't like her so tough shit.

JOYCE. [*Off.*] Angie. Angie. Angie. I know you're out there. I'm not coming out after you. You come in here.

[*Silence. Nothing happens.*]

ANGIE. Last night when I was in bed. I been thinking yesterday could I make things move. You know, make things move by thinking about them without touching them. Last night I was in bed and suddenly a picture fell down off the wall.

KIT. What picture?

ANGIE. My gran, that picture. Not the poster. The photograph in the frame.

KIT. Had you done something to make it fall down?

ANGIE. I must have done.

KIT. But were you thinking about it?

ANGIE. Not about it, but about something.

KIT. I don't think that's very good.

ANGIE. You know the kitten?

KIT. Which one?

ANGIE. There only is one. The dead one.

KIT. What about it?

ANGIE. I heard it last night.

KIT. Where?

ANGIE. Out here. In the dark. What if I left you here in the dark all night?

KIT. You couldn't. I'd go home.

ANGIE. You couldn't.

KIT. I'd / go home.

ANGIE. No you couldn't, not if I said.

KIT. I could.

ANGIE. Then you wouldn't see anything. You'd just be ignorant.

KIT. I can see in the daytime.

ANGIE. No you can't. You can't hear it in the daytime.

KIT. I don't want to hear it.

ANGIE. You're scared that's all.

KIT. I'm not scared of anything.

ANGIE. You're scared of blood.

KIT. It's not the same kitten anyway. You just heard an old cat, / you just heard some old cat.

ANGIE. You don't know what I heard. Or what I saw. You don't know nothing because you're a baby.

KIT. You're sitting on me.

ANGIE. Mind my hair / you silly cunt.

KIT. Stupid fucking cow, I hate you.

ANGIE. I don't care if you do.

KIT. You're horrible.

ANGIE. I'm going to kill my mother and you're going to watch.

KIT. I'm not playing.

ANGIE. You're scared of blood.

[KIT *puts her hand under her dress, brings it out with blood on her finger.*]

KIT. There, see, I got my own blood, so.

[ANGIE *takes* KIT'*s hand and licks her finger.*]

ANGIE. Now I'm a cannibal. I might turn into a vampire now.

KIT. That picture wasn't nailed up right.

ANGIE. You'll have to do that when I get mine.

KIT. I don't have to.

ANGIE. You're scared.

KIT. I'll do it, I might do it. I don't have to just because you say. I'll be sick on you.

ANGIE. I don't care if you are sick on me, I don't mind sick. I don't mind blood. If I don't get away from here I'm going to die.

KIT. I'm going home.

ANGIE. You can't go through the house. She'll see you.

KIT. I won't tell her.

ANGIE. Oh great, fine.

KIT. I'll say I was by myself. I'll tell her you're at my house and I'm going there to get you.

ANGIE. She knows I'm here, stupid.

KIT. Then why can't I go through the house?

ANGIE. Because I said not.

KIT. My mum don't like you anyway.

ANGIE. I don't want her to like me. She's a slag

KIT. She is not.

ANGIE. She does it with everyone.

KIT. She does not.

ANGIE. You don't even know what it is.

KIT. Yes I do.

ANGIE. Tell me then.

KIT. We get it all at school, cleverclogs. It's on television. You haven't done it.

ANGIE. How do you know?

KIT. Because I know you haven't.

ANGIE. You know wrong then because I have.

KIT. Who with?

ANGIE. I'm not telling you / who with.

KIT. You haven't anyway.

ANGIE. How do you know?

KIT. Who with?

ANGIE. I'm not telling you.

KIT. You said you told me everything.

ANGIE. I was lying wasn't I?

KIT. Who with? You can't tell me who with because / you never—

ANGIE. Sh.

[JOYCE *has come out of the house. She stops half way across the yard and listens. They listen*]

JOYCE. You there Angie? Kit? You there Kitty? Want a cup of tea? I've got some chocolate biscuits. Come on now I'll put the kettle on. Want a choccy biccy, Angie?

[*They all listen and wait.*]

Fucking rotten little cunt. You can stay there and die. I'll lock the back door.

[*They all wait.* JOYCE *goes back to the house.* ANGIE *and* KIT *sit in silence for a while.*]

KIT. When there's a war, where's the safest place?

ANGIE. Nowhere

KIT. New Zealand is, my mum said. Your skin's burned right off. Shall we go to New Zealand?

ANGIE. I'm not staying here.

KIT. Shall we go to New Zealand?

ANGIE. You're not old enough.

KIT. You're not old enough.

ANGIE. I'm old enough to get married.

KIT. You don't want to get married.

ANGIE. No but I'm old enough.

KIT. I'd find out where they were going to drop it and stand right in the place.

ANGIE. You couldn't find out.

KIT. Better than walking round with your skin dragging on the ground. Eugh. / Would you like walking round with your skin dragging on the ground?

ANGIE. You couldn't find out, stupid, it's a secret.

KIT. Where are you going?

ANGIE. I'm not telling you.

KIT. Why?

ANGIE. It's a secret.

KIT. But you tell me all your secrets.

ANGIE. Not the true secrets.

KIT. Yes you do.

ANGIE. No I don't.

KIT. I want to go somewhere away from the war.

ANGIE. Just forget the war.

KIT. I can't.

ANGIE. You have to. It's so boring.

KIT. I'll remember it at night.

ANGIE. I'm going to do something else anyway.

KIT. What? Angie come on. Angie.

ANGIE. It's a true secret.

KIT. It can't be worse than the kitten. And killing your mother. And the war.

ANGIE. Well I'm not telling you so you can die for all I care.

KIT. My mother says there's something wrong with you playing with someone my age. She says why haven't you got friends your own age. People your own age know there's something funny about you. She says you're a bad influence. She says she's going to speak to your mother.

[ANGIE *twists* KIT'*s arm till she cries out.*]

ANGIE. Say you're a liar.

KIT. She said it not me.

ANGIE. Say you eat shit.

KIT. You can't make me.

[ANGIE *lets go.*]

ANGIE. I don't care anyway. I'm leaving.

KIT. Go on then.

ANGIE. You'll all wake up one morning and find I've gone.

KIT. Good.

ANGIE. I'm not telling you when.

KIT. Go on then.

ANGIE. I'm sorry I hurt you.

KIT. I'm tired.

ANGIE. Do you like me?

KIT. I don't know.

ANGIE. You do not like me.

KIT. I'm going home.

[KIT *gets up.*]

ANGIE. No you're not.

KIT. I'm tired
ANGIE. She'll see you.
KIT. She'll give me a chocolate biscuit.
ANGIE. Kitty.
KIT. Tell me where you're going.
ANGIE. Sit down.
 [KIT *sits in the hut again.*]
KIT. Go on then.
ANGIE. Swear?
KIT. Swear.
ANGIE. I'm going to London. To see my aunt.
KIT. And what?
ANGIE. That's it.
KIT. I see my aunt all the time.
ANGIE. I don't see my aunt.
KIT. What's so special?
ANGIE. It is special. She's special.
KIT. Why?
ANGIE. She is.
KIT. Why?
ANGIE. She is.
KIT. Why?
ANGIE. My mother hates her.
KIT. Why?
ANGIE. Because she does.
KIT. Perhaps she's not very nice.
ANGIE. She is nice.
KIT. How do you know?
ANGIE. Because I know her.
KIT. You said you never see her.
ANGIE. I saw her last year. You saw her.
KIT. Did I?
ANGIE. Never mind.
KIT. I remember her. That aunt. What's so special?
ANGIE. She gets people jobs.
KIT. What's so special?
ANGIE. I think I'm my aunt's child. I think my mother's really my aunt.
KIT. Why?
ANGIE. Because she goes to America, now shut up.
KIT. I've been to London.
ANGIE. Now give us a cuddle and shut up because I'm sick.
KIT. You're sitting on my arm.
 [*Silence. JOYCE comes out and comes up to them quietly*]
JOYCE. Come on.
KIT. Oh hello.
JOYCE. Time you went home.
KIT. We want to go to the Odeon.
JOYCE. What time?
KIT. Don't know.
JOYCE. Don't know much do you?
KIT. That all right then?
JOYCE. Angie's got to clean her room first.
ANGIE. No I don't.

JOYCE. Yes you do, it's a pigsty.

ANGIE. Well I'm not.

JOYCE. Then you're not going. I don't care.

ANGIE. Well I am going.

JOYCE. You've no money, have you?

ANGIE. Kit's paying anyway.

JOYCE. No she's not.

KIT. I'll help you with your room.

JOYCE. That's nice.

ANGIE. No you won't. You wait here.

KIT. Hurry then.

ANGIE. I'm not hurrying. You just wait.

[ANGIE *goes into the house. Silence.*]

JOYCE. I don't know.

[*Silence.*]

How's school then?

KIT. All right.

JOYCE. What are you now? Third year?

KIT. Second year.

JOYCE. Your mum says you're good at English.

[*Silence.*]

Maybe Angie should've stayed on.

KIT. She didn't like it.

JOYCE. I didn't like it. And look at me. If your face fits at school it's going to fit other places too. It wouldn't make no difference to Angie. She's not going to get a job when jobs are hard to get. I'd be sorry for anyone in charge of her. She'd better get married. I don't know who'd have her, mind. She's one of those girls might never leave home. What do you want to be when you grow up, Kit?

KIT. Physicist.

JOYCE. What?

KIT. Nuclear physicist.

JOYCE. Whatever for?

KIT. I could, I'm clever.

JOYCE. I know you're clever, pet.

[*Silence.*]

I'll make a cup of tea.

[*Silence.*]

Looks like it's going to rain.

[*Silence.*]

Don't you have friends your own age?

KIT. Yes.

JOYCE. Well then.

KIT. I'm old for my age.

JOYCE. And Angie's simple is she? She's not simple.

KIT. I love Angie.

JOYCE. She's clever in her own way.

KIT. You can't stop me.

JOYCE. I don't want to.

KIT. You can't, so.

JOYCE. Don't be cheeky, Kitty. She's always kind to little children.

KIT. She's coming so you better leave me alone.

[ANGIE *comes out. She has changed into an old best dress, slightly small for her.*]

JOYCE. What you put that on for? Have you done your room? You can't clean your room in that.

ANGIE. I looked in the cupboard and it was there.

JOYCE. Of course it was there, it's meant to be there. Is that why it was a surprise, finding something in the right place? I should think she's surprised, wouldn't you Kit, to find something in her room in the right place.

ANGIE. I decided to wear it.

JOYCE. Not today, why? To clean your room? You're not going to the pictures till you've done your room. You can put your dress on after if you like.

[ANGIE *picks up a brick.*]

Have you done your room? You're not getting out of it, you know.

KIT. Angie, let's go.

JOYCE. She's not going till she's done her room.

KIT. It's starting to rain.

JOYCE. Come on, come on then. Hurry and do your room, Angie, and then you can go to the cinema with Kit. Oh it's wet, come on. We'll look up the time in the paper. Does your mother know, Kit, it's going to be a late night for you, isn't it? Hurry up, Angie. You'll spoil your dress. You make me sick.

[JOYCE *and* KIT *run in.* ANGIE *stays where she is. Sound of rain.* KIT *comes out of the house and shouts.*]

KIT. Angie. Angie, come on, you'll get wet.

[KIT *comes back to* ANGIE.]

ANGIE. I put on this dress to kill my mother.

KIT. I suppose you thought you'd do it with a brick.

ANGIE. You can kill people with a brick.

KIT. Well you didn't, so.

Act Two

SCENE ONE

Office of "Top Girls" Employment Agency. Three desks and a small interviewing area. Monday morning. WIN *and* NELL *have just arrived for work.*

NELL. Coffee coffee coffee coffee / coffee.

WIN. The roses were smashing. / Mermaid.

NELL. Ohhh.

WIN. Iceberg. He taught me all their names.

[NELL *has some coffee now.*]

NELL. Ah. Now then.

WIN. He has one of the finest rose gardens in West Sussex. He exhibits.

NELL. He what?

WIN. His wife was visiting her mother. It was like living together.

NELL. Crafty, you never said.

WIN. He rang on Saturday morning.

NELL. Lucky you were free.

WIN. That's what I told him.

NELL. Did you hell.

WIN. Have you ever seen a really beautiful rose garden?

NELL. I don't like flowers. / I like swimming pools.

WIN. Marilyn. Esther's Baby. They're all called after birds.

NELL. Our friend's late. Celebrating all weekend I bet you.

WIN. I'd call a rose Elvis. Or John Conteh.[6]

NELL. Is Howard in yet?

WIN. If he is he'll be bleeping us with a problem.

NELL. Howard can just hang onto himself.

WIN. Howard's really cut up.

NELL. Howard thinks because he's a fella the job was his as of right. Our Marlene's got far more balls than Howard and that's that.

WIN. Poor little bugger.

NELL. He'll live.

WIN. He'll move on.

NELL. I wouldn't mind a change of air myself.

WIN. Serious?

NELL. I've never been a staying put lady. Pastures new.

WIN. So who's the pirate?

NELL. There's nothing definite.

WIN. Inquiries?

NELL. There's always inquiries. I'd think I'd got bad breath if there stopped being inquiries. Most of them can't afford me. Or you.

WIN. I'm all right for the time being. Unless I go to Australia.

NELL. There's not a lot of room upward.

WIN. Marlene's filled it up.

NELL. Good luck to her. Unless there's some prospects moneywise.

WIN. You can but ask.

NELL. Can always but ask.

WIN. So what have we got? I've got a Mr. Holden I saw last week.

NELL. Any use?

WIN. Pushy. Bit of a cowboy.

NELL. Good-looker?

WIN. Good dresser.

NELL. High flyer?

WIN. That's his general idea certainly but I'm not sure he's got it up there.

NELL. Prestel wants six high flyers and I've only seen two and a half.

WIN. He's making a bomb on the road but he thinks it's time for an office. I sent him to IBM but he didn't get it.

NELL. Prestel's on the road.

WIN. He's not overbright.

NELL. Can he handle an office?

WIN. Provided his secretary can punctuate he should go far.

NELL. Bear Prestel in mind then, I might put my head round the door. I've got that poor little nerd I should never have said I could help. Tender heart me.

WIN. Tender like old boots. How old?

NELL. Yes well forty-five.

WIN. Say no more.

NELL. He knows his place, he's not after calling himself a manager, he's just a poor little bod wants a better commission and a bit of sunshine.

WIN. Don't we all.

NELL. He's just got to relocate. He's got a bungalow in Dymchurch.

6. English boxer (b. 1951).

WIN. And his wife says.

NELL. The lady wife wouldn't care to relocate. She's going through the change.

WIN. It's his funeral, don't waste your time.

NELL. I don't waste a lot.

WIN. Good weekend you?

NELL. You could say.

WIN. Which one?

NELL. One Friday, one Saturday.

WIN. Aye—aye.

NELL. Sunday night I watched telly.

WIN. Which of them do you like best really?

NELL. Sunday was best, I liked the Ovaltine.

WIN. Holden, Barker, Gardner, Duke.

NELL. I've a lady here thinks she can sell.

WIN. Taking her on?

NELL. She's had some jobs.

WIN. Services?

NELL. No, quite heavy stuff, electric.

WIN. Tough bird like us.

NELL. We could do with a few more here.

WIN. There's nothing going here.

NELL. No but I always want the tough ones when I see them. Hang onto them.

WIN. I think we're plenty

NELL. Derek asked me to marry him again.

WIN. He doesn't know when he's beaten.

NELL. I told him I'm not going to play house, not even in Ascot.

WIN. Mind you, you could play house.

NELL. If I chose to play house I would play house ace.

WIN. You could marry him and go on working.

NELL. I could go on working and not marry him.

[MARLENE *arrives*.]

MARLENE. Morning ladies.

[WIN *and* NELL *cheer and whistle*.]

Mind my head

NELL. Coffee coffee coffee.

WIN. We're tactfully not mentioning you're late.

MARLENE. Fucking tube.

WIN. We've heard that one.

NELL. We've used that one.

WIN. It's the top executive doesn't come in as early as the poor working girl.

MARLENE. Pass the sugar and shut your pace, pet.

WIN. Well I'm delighted.

NELL. Howard's looking sick.

WIN. Howard is sick. He's got ulcers and heart. He told me.

NELL. He'll have to stop then won't he?

WIN. Stop what?

NELL. Smoking, drinking, shouting. Working.

WIN. Well, working.

NELL. We're just looking through the day.

MARLENE. I'm doing some of Pam's ladies. They've been piling up while she's away.

NELL. Half a dozen little girls and an arts graduate who can't type.

WIN. I spent the whole weekend at his place in Sussex.

NELL. She fancies his rose garden.

WIN. I had to lie down in the back of the car so the neighbors wouldn't see me go in.

NELL. You're kidding.

WIN. It was funny.

NELL. Fuck that for a joke.

WIN. It was funny.

MARLENE. Anyway they'd see you in the garden.

WIN. The garden has extremely high walls.

NELL. I think I'll tell the wife.

WIN. Like hell.

NELL. She might leave him and you could have the rose garden.

WIN. The minute it's not a secret I'm out on my ear.

NELL. Don't know why you bother.

WIN. Bit of fun.

NELL. I think it's time you went to Australia.

WIN. I think it's pushy Mr. Holden time.

NELL. If you've any really pretty bastards, Marlene, I want some for Prestel.

MARLENE. I might have one this afternoon. This morning it's all Pam's secretarial.

NELL. Not long now and you'll be upstairs watching over us all.

MARLENE. Do you feel bad about it?

NELL. I don't like coming second.

MARLENE. Who does?

WIN. We'd rather it was you than Howard. We're glad for you, aren't we Nell.

NELL. Oh yes. Aces.

INTERVIEW

WIN *and* LOUISE.

WIN. Now Louise, hello, I have your details here. You've been very loyal to the one job I see.

LOUISE. Yes I have.

WIN. Twenty-one years is a long time in one place.

LOUISE. I feel it is. I feel it's time to move on.

WIN. And you are what age now?

LOUISE. I'm in my early forties.

WIN. Exactly?

LOUISE. Forty-six.

WIN. It's not necessarily a handicap, well it is of course we have to face that, but it's not necessarily a disabling handicap, experience does count for something.

LOUISE. I hope so.

WIN. Now between ourselves is there any trouble, any reason why you're leaving that wouldn't appear on the form?

LOUISE. Nothing like that.

WIN. Like what?

LOUISE. Nothing at all.

WIN. No long-term understandings come to a sudden end, making for an insupportable atmosphere?

LOUISE. I've always completely avoided anything like that at all.

WIN. No personality clashes with your immediate superiors or inferiors?

LOUISE. I've always taken care to get on very well with everyone.

WIN. I only ask because it can affect the reference and it also affects your motivation, I want to be quite clear why you're moving on. So I take it the job itself no longer satisfies you. Is it the money?

LOUISE. It's partly the money. It's not so much the money.

WIN. Nine thousand is very respectable. Have you dependants?

LOUISE. No, no dependants. My mother died.

WIN. So why are you making a change?

LOUISE. Other people make changes.

WIN. But why are you, now, after spending most of your life in the one place?

LOUISE. There you are, I've lived for that company, I've given my life really you could say because I haven't had a great deal of social life, I've worked in the evenings. I haven't had office entanglements for the very reason you just mentioned and if you are committed to your work you don't move in many other circles. I had management status from the age of twenty-seven and you'll appreciate what that means. I've built up a department. And there it is it works extremely well, and I feel I'm stuck there. I've spent twenty years in middle management. I've seen young men who I trained go on, in my own company or elsewhere, to higher things. Nobody notices me, I don't expect it, I don't attract attention by making mistakes, everybody takes it for granted that my work is perfect. They will notice me when I go, they will be sorry I think to lose me, they will offer me more money of course, I will refuse. They will see when I've gone what I was doing for them.

WIN. If they offer you more money you won't stay?

LOUISE. No I won't.

WIN. Are you the only woman?

LOUISE. Apart from the girls of course, yes. There was one, she was my assistant, it was the only time I took on a young woman assistant, I always had my doubts. I don't care greatly for working with women, I think I pass as a man at work. But I did take on this young woman, her qualifications were excellent, and she did well, she got a department of her own, and left the company for a competitor where she's now on the board and good luck to her. She has a different style, she's a new kind of attractive well-dressed—I don't mean I don't dress properly. But there is a kind of woman who is thirty now who grew up in a different climate. They are not so careful. They take themselves for granted. I have had to justify my existence every minute, and I have done so, I have proved—well.

WIN. Let's face it, vacancies are going to be ones where you'll be in competition with younger men. And there are companies that will value your experience enough you'll be in with a chance. There are also fields that are easier for a woman, there is a cosmetic company here where your experience might be relevant. It's eight and a half, I don't know if that appeals.

LOUISE. I've proved I can earn money. It's more important to get away. I feel it's now or never. I sometimes think—

WIN. You shouldn't talk too much at an interview.

LOUISE. I don't. I don't normally talk about myself. I know very well how to handle myself in an office situation. I only talk to you because it seems to me this is different, it's your job to understand me, surely. You asked the questions.

WIN. I think I understand you sufficiently.

LOUISE. Well good, that's good.

WIN.　Do you drink?

LOUISE.　Certainly not. I'm not a teetotaler, I think that's very suspect, it's seen as being an alcoholic if you're teetotal. What do you mean? I don't drink. Why?

WIN.　I drink.

LOUISE.　I don't.

WIN.　Good for you.

MAIN OFFICE

MARLENE *and* ANGIE.

[ANGIE *arrives*.]

ANGIE.　Hello.

MARLENE.　Have you an appointment?

ANGIE.　It's me. I've come.

MARLENE.　What? It's not Angie?

ANGIE.　It was hard to find this place. I got lost.

MARLENE.　How did you get past the receptionist? The girl on the desk, didn't she try to stop you?

ANGIE.　What desk?

MARLENE.　Never mind.

ANGIE.　I just walked in. I was looking for you.

MARLENE.　Well you found me.

ANGIE.　Yes.

MARLENE.　So where's your mum? Are you up in town for the day?

ANGIE.　Not really.

MARLENE.　Sit down. Do you feel all right?

ANGIE.　Yes thank you.

MARLENE.　So where's Joyce?

ANGIE.　She's at home.

MARLENE.　Did you come up on a school trip then?

ANGIE.　I've left school.

MARLENE.　Did you come up with a friend?

ANGIE.　No. There's just me.

MARLENE.　You came up by yourself, that's fun. What have you been doing? Shopping? Tower of London?

ANGIE.　No, I just come here. I come to you.

MARLENE.　That's very nice of you to think of paying your aunty a visit. There's not many nieces make that the first port of call. Would you like a cup of coffee?

ANGIE.　No thank you.

MARLENE.　Tea, orange?

ANGIE.　No thank you.

MARLENE.　Do you feel all right?

ANGIE.　Yes thank you.

MARLENE.　Are you tired from the journey?

ANGIE.　Yes, I'm tired from the journey.

MARLENE.　You sit there for a bit then. How's Joyce?

ANGIE.　She's all right.

MARLENE.　Same as ever.

ANGIE.　Oh yes.

MARLENE.　Unfortunately you've picked a day when I'm rather busy, if there's ever a day when I'm not, or I'd take you out to lunch and we'd go to

Madame Tussaud's. We could go shopping. What time do you have to be back? Have you got a day return?

ANGIE. No

MARLENE. So what train are you going back on?

ANGIE. I came on the bus.

MARLENE. So what bus are you going back on? Are you staying the night?

ANGIE. Yes.

MARLENE. Who are you staying with? Do you want me to put you up for the night, is that it?

ANGIE. Yes please

MARLENE. I haven't got a spare bed.

ANGIE. I can sleep on the floor.

MARLENE. You can sleep on the sofa.

ANGIE. Yes please

MARLENE. I do think Joyce might have phoned me. It's like her.

ANGIE. This is where you work is it?

MARLENE. It's where I have been working the last two years but I'm going to move into another office.

ANGIE. It's lovely.

MARLENE. My new office is nicer than this. There's just the one big desk in it for me.

ANGIE. Can I see it?

MARLENE. No now, no, there's someone else in it now. But he's leaving at the end of next week and I'm going to do his job.

ANGIE. Is that good?

MARLENE. Yes, it's very good.

ANGIE. Are you going to be in charge?

MARLENE. Yes I am.

ANGIE. I knew you would be.

MARLENE. How did you know?

ANGIE. I knew you'd be in charge of everything

MARLENE. Not quite everything.

ANGIE. You will be.

MARLENE. Well we'll see.

ANGIE. Can I see it next week then?

MARLENE. Will you still be here next week?

ANGIE. Yes

MARLENE. Don't you have to go home?

ANGIE. No

MARLENE. Why not?

ANGIE. It's all right.

MARLENE. Is it all right?

ANGIE. Yes, don't worry about it.

MARLENE. Does Joyce know where you are?

ANGIE. Yes of course she does.

MARLENE. Well does she?

ANGIE. Don't worry about it.

MARLENE. How long are you planning to stay with me then?

ANGIE. You know when you came to see us last year?

MARLENE. Yes, that was nice wasn't it?

ANGIE. That was the best day of my whole life.

MARLENE. So how long are you planning to stay?

ANGIE. Don't you want me?

MARLENE. Yes yes, I just wondered.

ANGIE. I won't stay if you don't want me.

MARLENE. No, of course you can stay.

ANGIE. I'll sleep on the floor. I won't be any bother.

MARLENE. Don't get upset.

ANGIE. I'm not, I'm not. Don't worry about it.
 [MRS. KIDD *comes in.*]

MRS. KIDD. Excuse me.

MARLENE. Yes.

MRS. KIDD. Excuse me.

MARLENE. Can I help you?

MRS. KIDD. Excuse me bursting in on you like this but I have to talk to you.

MARLENE. I am engaged at the moment. / If you could go to reception—

MRS. KIDD. I'm Rosemary Kidd, Howard's wife, you don't recognize me but
 we did meet, I remember you of course / but you wouldn't—

MARLENE. Yes of course, Mrs. Kidd, I'm sorry, we did meet. Howard's about
 somewhere I expect, have you looked in his office?

MRS. KIDD. Howard's not about, no. I'm afraid it's you I've come to see if I
 could have a minute or two.

MARLENE. I do have an appointment in five minutes.

MRS. KIDD. This won't take five minutes. I'm very sorry. It is a matter of
 some urgency.

MARLENE. Well of course. What can I do for you?

MRS. KIDD. I just wanted a chat, an informal chat. It's not something I can
 simply—I'm sorry if I'm interrupting your work. I know office work isn't like
 housework / which is all interruptions.

MARLENE. No no, this is my niece. Angie. Mrs. Kidd.

MRS. KIDD. Very pleased to meet you.

ANGIE. Very well thank you.

MRS. KIDD. Howard's not in today.

MARLENE. Isn't he?

MRS. KIDD. He's feeling poorly.

MARLENE. I didn't know. I'm sorry to hear that.

MRS. KIDD. The fact is he's in a state of shock. About what's happened.

MARLENE. What has happened?

MRS. KIDD. You should know if anyone. I'm referring to you being ap-
 pointed managing director instead of Howard. He hasn't been at all well all
 weekend. He hasn't slept for three nights. I haven't slept.

MARLENE. I'm sorry to hear that, Mrs. Kidd. Has he thought of taking sleep-
 ing pills?

MRS. KIDD. It's very hard when someone has worked all these years.

MARLENE. Business life is full of little setbacks. I'm sure Howard knows
 that. He'll bounce back in a day or two. We all bounce back.

MRS. KIDD. If you could see him you'd know what I'm talking about. What's
 it going to do to him working for a woman? I think if it was a man he'd get
 over it as something normal.

MARLENE. I think he's going to have to get over it.

MRS. KIDD. It's me that bears the brunt. I'm not the one that's been pro-
 moted. I put him first every inch of the way. And now what do I get? You
 women this, you women that. It's not my fault. You're going to have to be
 very careful how you handle him. He's very hurt.

MARLENE. Naturally I'll be tactful and pleasant to him, you don't start
 pushing someone round. I'll consult him over any decisions affecting his

department. But that's no different, Mrs. Kidd, from any of my other col-
leagues.

MRS. KIDD. I think it is different, because he's a man.

MARLENE. I'm not quite sure why you came to see me.

MRS. KIDD. I had to do something.

MARLENE. Well you've done it, you've seen me. I think that's probably all
we've time for. I'm sorry he's been taking it out on you. He really is a shit,
Howard.

MRS. KIDD. But he's got a family to support. He's got three children. It's
only fair.

MARLENE. Are you suggesting I give up the job to him then?

MRS. KIDD. It had crossed my mind if you were unavailable after all for some
reason, he would be the natural second choice I think, don't you? I'm not
asking.

MARLENE. Good.

MRS. KIDD. You mustn't tell him I came. He's very proud.

MARLENE. If he doesn't like what's happening here he can go and work
somewhere else.

MRS. KIDD. Is that a threat?

MARLENE. I'm sorry but I do have some work to do.

MRS. KIDD. It's not that easy, a man of Howard's age. You don't care. I
thought he was going too far but he's right. You're one of these ballbreakers
/ that's what you are. You'll end up

MARLENE. I'm sorry but I do have some work to do.

MRS. KIDD. miserable and lonely. You're not natural.

MARLENE. Could you please piss off?

MRS. KIDD. I thought if I saw you at least I'd be doing something.
 [MRS. KIDD goes.]

MARLENE. I've got to go and do some work now. Will you come back later?

ANGIE. I think you were wonderful.

MARLENE. I've got to go and do some work now.

ANGIE. You told her to piss off.

MARLENE. Will you come back later?

ANGIE. Can't I stay here?

MARLENE. Don't you want to go sightseeing?

ANGIE. I'd rather stay here.

MARLENE. You can stay here I suppose, if it's not boring.

ANGIE. It's where I most want to be in the world.

MARLENE. I'll see you later then.
 [MARLENE goes. ANGIE sits at WIN's desk.]

INTERVIEW

NELL and SHONA.

NELL. Is this right? You are Shona?

SHONA. Yeh.

NELL. It says here you're twenty-nine.

SHONA. Yeh.

NELL. Too many late nights, me. So you've been where you are for four
years. Shona, you're earning six basic and three commission. So what's the
problem?

SHONA. No problem.

NELL. Why do you want a change?

SHONA. Just a change.
NELL. Change of product, change of area?
SHONA. Both.
NELL. But you're happy on the road?
SHONA. I like driving.
NELL. You're not after management status?
SHONA. I would like management status.
NELL. You'd be interested in titular management status but not come off the road?
SHONA. I want to be on the road, yeh.
NELL. So how many calls have you been making a day?
SHONA. Six.
NELL. And what proportion of those are successful?
SHONA. Six.
NELL. That's hard to believe.
SHONA. Four.
NELL. You find it easy to get the initial interest do you?
SHONA. Oh yeh, I get plenty of initial interest.
NELL. And what about closing?
SHONA. I close, don't I?
NELL. Because that's what an employer is going to have doubts about with you a lady as I needn't tell you, whether she's got the guts to push through to a closing situation. They think we're too nice. They think we listen to the buyer's doubts. They think we consider his needs and his feelings.
SHONA. I never consider people's feelings.
NELL. I was selling for six years, I can sell anything, I've sold in three continents, and I'm jolly as they come but I'm not very nice.
SHONA. I'm not very nice.
NELL. What sort of time do you have on the road with the other reps? Get on all right? Handle the chat?
SHONA. I get on. Keep myself to myself.
NELL. Fairly much of a loner are you?
SHONA. Sometimes.
NELL. So what field are you interested in?
SHONA. Computers.
NELL. That's a top field as you know and you'll be up against some very slick fellas there, there's some very pretty boys in computers, it's an American-style field.
SHONA. That's why I want to do it.
NELL. Video systems appeal? That's a high-flying situation.
SHONA. Video systems appeal OK.
NELL. Because Prestel have half a dozen vacancies I'm looking to fill at the moment. We're talking in the area of ten to fifteen thousand here and upwards.
SHONA. Sounds OK.
NELL. I've half a mind to go for it myself. But it's good money here if you've got the top clients. Could you fancy it do you think?
SHONA. Work here?
NELL. I'm not in a position to offer, there's nothing officially going just now, but we're always on the lookout. There's not that many of us. We could keep in touch.
SHONA. I like driving.
NELL. So the Prestel appeals?

SHONA. Yeh.

NELL. What about ties?

SHONA. No ties.

NELL. So relocation wouldn't be a problem.

SHONA. No problem.

NELL. So just fill me in a bit more could you about what you've been doing.

SHONA. What I've been doing. It's all down there.

NELL. The bare facts are down here but I've got to present you to an employer.

SHONA. I'm twenty-nine years old.

NELL. So it says here.

SHONA. We look young. Youngness runs in the family in our family.

NELL. So just describe your present job for me.

SHONA. My present job at present. I have a car. I have a Porsche. I go up the M1[7] a lot. Burn up the M1 a lot. Straight up the M1 in the fast lane to where the clients are, Staffordshire, Yorkshire, I do a lot in Yorkshire. I'm selling electric things Like dishwashers, washing machines, stainless steel tubs are a feature and the reliability of the program. After sales service, we offer a very good after sales service, spare parts, plenty of spare parts. And fridges, I sell a lot of fridges specially in the summer. People want to buy fridges in the summer because of the heat melting the butter and you get fed up standing the milk in a basin of cold water with a cloth over, stands to reason people don't want to do that in this day and age. So I sell a lot of them. Big ones with big freezers. Big freezers. And I stay in hotels at night when I'm away from home. On my expense account. I stay in various hotels. They know me, the ones I go to. I check in, have a bath, have a shower. Then I go down to the bar, have a gin and tonic, have a chat. Then I go into the dining room and have dinner. I usually have fillet steak and mushrooms, I like mushrooms. I like smoked salmon very much I like having a salad on the side. Green salad. I don't like tomatoes.

NELL. Christ what a waste of time.

SHONA. Beg your pardon?

NELL. Not a word of this is true is it?

SHONA. How do you mean?

NELL. You just filled in the form with a pack of lies.

SHONA. Not exactly.

NELL. How old are you?

SHONA. Twenty-nine.

NELL. Nineteen?

SHONA. Twenty-one.

NELL. And what jobs have you done? Have you done any?

SHONA. I could though, I bet you.

MAIN OFFICE

ANGIE *sitting as before.*
[WIN *comes in.*]

WIN. Who's sitting in my chair?

ANGIE. What? Sorry.

WIN. Who's been eating my porridge?

ANGIE. What?

7. A major highway leading north from London.

WIN. It's all right, I saw Marlene. Angie isn't it? I'm Win. And I'm not going
out for lunch because I'm knackered. I'm going to set me down here and
have a yoghurt. Do you like yoghurt?

ANGIE. No.

WIN. That's good because I've only got one. Are you hungry?

ANGIE. No.

WIN. There's a cafe on the corner.

ANGIE. No thank you. Do you work here?

WIN. How did you guess?

ANGIE. Because you look as if you might work here and you're sitting at the
desk. Have you always worked here?

WIN. No I was headhunted. That means I was working for another outfit like
this and this lot came and offered me more money. I broke my contract,
there was a hell of a stink. There's not many top ladies about. Your aunty's a
smashing bird.

ANGIE. Yes I know.

MARLENE. Fan are you? Fan of your aunty's?

ANGIE. Do you think I could work here?

WIN. Not at the moment.

ANGIE. How do I start?

WIN. What can you do?

ANGIE. I don't know. Nothing.

WIN. Type?

ANGIE. Not very well. The letters jump up when I do capitals. I was going to
do a CSE[8] in commerce but I didn't.

WIN. What have you got?

ANGIE. What?

WIN. CSE's, O's.

ANGIE. Nothing, none of that. Did you do all that?

WIN. Oh yes, all that, and a science degree funnily enough. I started out
doing medical research but there's no money in it. I thought I'd go abroad.
Did you know they sell Coca-Cola in Russia and Pepsi-cola in China? You
don't have to be qualified as much as you might think. Men are awful bull-
shitters, they like to make out jobs are harder than they are. Any job I ever
did I started doing it better than the rest of the crowd and they didn't like it.
So I'd get unpopular and I'd have a drink to cheer myself up. I lived with a
fella and supported him for four years, he couldn't get work. After that I
went to California. I like the sunshine. Americans know how to live. This
country's too slow. Then I went to Mexico, still in sales, but it's no country
for a single lady. I came home, went bonkers for a bit, thought I was five dif-
ferent people, got over that all right, the psychiatrist said I was perfectly
sane and highly intelligent. Got married in a moment of weakness and he's
inside now, he's been inside four years, and I've not been to see him too
much this last year. I like this better than sales, I'm not really that aggres-
sive. I started thinking sales was a good job if you want to meet people, but
you're meeting people that don't want to meet you. It's no good if you like
being liked. Here your clients want to meet you because you're the one
doing them some good. They hope.

[ANGIE *has fallen asleep*. NELL *comes in.*]

NELL. You're talking to yourself, sunshine.

WIN. So what's new?

8. Certificate of Secondary Education.

NELL. Who is this?

WIN. Marlene's little niece.

NELL. What's she got, brother, sister? She never talks about her family.

WIN. I was telling her my life story.

NELL. Violins?

WIN. No, success story.

NELL. You've heard Howard's had a heart attack?

WIN. No, when?

NELL. I heard just now. He hadn't come in, he was at home, he's gone to hospital. He's not dead. His wife was here, she rushed off in a cab.

WIN. Too much butter, too much smoke. We must send him some flowers.
 [MARLENE *comes in.*]
 You've heard about Howard?

MARLENE. Poor sod.

NELL. Lucky he didn't get the job if that's what his health's like.

MARLENE. Is she asleep?

WIN. She wants to work here.

MARLENE. Packer in Tesco more like.

WIN. She's a nice kid. Isn't she?

MARLENE. She's a bit thick. She's a bit funny.

WIN. She thinks you're wonderful.

MARLENE. She's not going to make it.

SCENE TWO

A *year earlier. Sunday evening.* JOYCE's *kitchen.* JOYCE, ANGIE, MARLENE. MARLENE *is taking presents out of a bright carrier bag.* ANGIE *has already opened a box of chocolates.*

MARLENE. Just a few little things. / I've no memory for

JOYCE. There's no need.

MARLENE. birthdays have I, and Christmas seems to slip by. So I think I owe Angie a few presents.

JOYCE. What do you say?

ANGIE. Thank you very much. Thank you very much, Aunty Marlene.
 [*She opens a present. It is the dress from Act One, new.*]

ANGIE. Oh look, Mum, isn't it lovely?

MARLENE. I don't know if it's the right size. She's grown up since I saw her. / I knew she was always tall for her age.

ANGIE. Isn't it lovely?

JOYCE. She's a big lump.

MARLENE. Hold it up, Angie, let's see.

ANGIE. I'll put it on, shall I?

MARLENE. Yes, try it on.

JOYCE. Go on to your room then, we don't want / a strip show thank you.

ANGIE. Of course I'm going to my room. what do you think? Look Mum, here's something for you. Open it, go on. What is it? Can I open it for you?

JOYCE. Yes you open it, pet.

ANGIE. Don't you want to open it yourself? / Go on.

JOYCE. I don't mind, you can do it.

ANGIE. It's something hard. It's—what is it? A bottle. Drink is it? No, it's what? Perfume, look. What a lot. Open it, look, let's smell it. Oh it's strong. It's lovely. Put it on me. How do you do it? Put it on me.

JOYCE. You're too young.

ANGIE. I can play wearing it like dressing up.

JOYCE. And you're too old for that. Here, give it here, I'll do it, you'll tip the whole bottle over yourself / and we'll have you smelling all summer.

ANGIE. Put it on you. Do I smell? Put it on Aunty too. Put it on Aunty too. Let's all smell.

MARLENE. I didn't know what you'd like.

JOYCE. There's no danger I'd have it already, / that's one thing.

ANGIE. Now we all smell the same.

MARLENE. It's a bit of nonsense.

JOYCE. It's very kind of you Marlene, you shouldn't.

ANGIE. Now I'll put on the dress and then we'll see.

 [ANGIE *goes.*]

JOYCE. You've caught me on the hop with the place in a mess. / If you'd let me know you was coming I'd have got

MARLENE. That doesn't matter.

JOYCE. something in to eat. We had our dinner dinnertime. We're just going to have a cup of tea. You could have an egg.

MARLENE. No, I'm not hungry. Tea's fine.

JOYCE. I don't expect you take sugar.

MARLENE. Why not?

JOYCE. You take care of yourself.

MARLENE. How do you mean you didn't know I was coming?

JOYCE. You could have written. I know we're not on the phone but we're not completely in the dark ages, / we do have a postman.

MARLENE. But you asked me to come.

JOYCE. How did I ask you to come?

MARLENE. Angie said when she phoned up.

JOYCE. Angie phoned up, did she?

MARLENE. Was it just Angie's idea?

JOYCE. What did she say?

MARLENE. She said you wanted me to come and see you. / It was a couple of weeks ago. How was I to know that's a

JOYCE. Ha.

MARLENE. ridiculous idea? My diary's always full a couple of weeks ahead so we fixed it for this weekend. I was meant to get here earlier but I was held up. She gave me messages from you.

JOYCE. Didn't you wonder why I didn't phone you myself?

MARLENE. She said you didn't like using the phone. You're shy on the phone and can't use it. I don't know what you're like, do I.

JOYCE. Are there people who can't use the phone?

MARLENE. I expect so.

JOYCE. I haven't met any.

MARLENE. Why should I think she was lying?

JOYCE. Because she's like what she's like.

MARLENE. How do I know / what she's like?

JOYCE. It's not my fault you don't know what she's like. You never come and see her.

MARLENE. Well I have now / and you don't seem over the moon.*

JOYCE. Good.

 *Well I'd have got a cake if she'd told me.

 [*Pause.*]

MARLENE. I did wonder why you wanted to see me.

JOYCE. I didn't want to see you.

MARLENE. Yes, I know. Shall I go?

JOYCE. I don't mind seeing you.

MARLENE. Great, I feel really welcome.

JOYCE. You can come and see Angie any time you like, I'm not stopping you. / You know where we are. You're the

MARLENE. Ta ever so.

JOYCE. one went away, not me. I'm right here where I was. And will be a few years yet I shouldn't wonder.

MARLENE. All right. All right.

[JOYCE *gives* MARLENE *a cup of tea.*]

JOYCE. Tea.

MARLENE. Sugar?

[JOYCE *passes* MARLENE *the sugar.*]

It's very quiet down here.

JOYCE. I expect you'd notice it.

MARLENE. The air smells different too.

JOYCE. That's the scent.

MARLENE. No, I mean walking down the lane.

JOYCE. What sort of air you get in London then?

[ANGIE *comes in, wearing the dress. It fits*]

MARLENE. Oh very pretty. / You do look pretty, Angie.

JOYCE. That fits all right

MARLENE. Do you like the color?

ANGIE. Beautiful. Beautiful.

JOYCE. You better take it off, / you'll get it dirty.

ANGIE. I want to wear it. I want to wear it.

MARLENE. It is for wearing after all. You can't just hang it up and look at it.

ANGIE. I love it.

JOYCE. Well if you must you must.

ANGIE. If someone asks me what's my favorite color I'll tell them it's this. Thank you very much, Aunty Marlene.

MARLENE. You didn't tell your mum you asked me down.

ANGIE. I wanted it to be a surprise.

JOYCE. I'll give you a surprise / one of these days.

ANGIE. I thought you'd like to see her. She hasn't been here since I was nine. People do see their aunts.

MARLENE. Is it that long? Doesn't time fly?

ANGIE. I wanted to.

JOYCE. I'm not cross.

ANGIE. Are you glad?

JOYCE. I smell nicer anyhow, don't I?

[KIT *comes in without saying anything, as if she lived there.*]

MARLENE. I think it was a good idea, Angie, about time. We are sisters after all. It's a pity to let that go.

JOYCE. This is Kitty, / who lives up the road. This is Angie's Aunty Marlene.

KIT. What's that?

ANGIE. It's a present. Do you like it?

KIT. It's all right. / Are you coming out?*

MARLENE. Hello, Kitty.

ANGIE. *No.

KIT. What's that smell?

ANGIE. It's a present.

KIT. It's horrible. Come on.*
MARLENE. Have a chocolate.
ANGIE. *No, I'm busy.
KIT. Coming out later?
ANGIE. No.
KIT. [*To* MARLENE.] Hello.
 [KIT *goes without a chocolate.*]
JOYCE. She's a little girl Angie sometimes plays with because she's the only
 child lives really close. She's like a little sister to her really. Angie's good with
 little children.
MARLENE. Do you want to work with children, Angie? / Be a teacher or a
 nursery nurse?
JOYCE. I don't think she's ever thought of it.
MARLENE. What do you want to do?
JOYCE. She hasn't an idea in her head what she wants to do. / Lucky to get
 anything.
MARLENE. Angie?
JOYCE. She's not clever like you.
 [*Pause.*]
MARLENE. I'm not clever, just pushy.
JOYCE. True enough.
 [MARLENE *takes a bottle of whisky out of the bag.*]
 I don't drink spirits.
ANGIE. You do at Christmas.
JOYCE. It's not Christmas, is it?
ANGIE. It's better than Christmas.
MARLENE. Glasses?
JOYCE. Just a small one then.
MARLENE. Do you want some, Angie?
ANGIE. I can't, can I?
JOYCE. Taste it if you want. You won't like it.
MARLENE. We got drunk together the night your grandfather died.
JOYCE. We did not get drunk.
MARLENE. I got drunk. You were just overcome with grief.
JOYCE. I still keep up the grave with flowers.
MARLENE. Do you really?
JOYCE. Why wouldn't I?
MARLENE. Have you seen Mother?
JOYCE. Of course I've seen Mother.
MARLENE. I mean lately.
JOYCE. Of course I've seen her lately, I go every Thursday.
MARLENE. [*To* ANGIE.] Do you remember your grandfather?
ANGIE. He got me out of the bath one night in a towel.
MARLENE. Did he? I don't think he ever gave me a bath. Did he give you a
 bath, Joyce? He probably got soft in his old age. Did you like him?
ANGIE. Yes of course.
MARLENE. Why?
ANGIE. What?
MARLENE. So what's the news? How's Mrs. Paisley? Still going crazily? / And
 Dorothy. What happened to Dorothy?*
ANGIE. Who's Mrs. Paisley?
JOYCE. *She went to Canada.
MARLENE. Did she? What to do?

JOYCE. I don't know. She just went to Canada.

MARLENE. Well / good for her.

ANGIE. Mr. Connolly killed his wife.

MARLENE. What, Connolly at Whitegates?

ANGIE. They found her body in the garden. / Under the cabbages.

MARLENE. He was always so proper.

JOYCE. Stuck up git. Connolly. Best lawyer money could buy but he couldn't get out of it. She was carrying on with Matthew.

MARLENE. How old's Matthew then?

JOYCE. Twenty-one. / He's got a motorbike.

MARLENE. I think he's about six.

ANGIE. How can he be six? He's six years older than me. / If he was six I'd be nothing, I'd be just born this minute.

JOYCE. Your aunty knows that, she's just being silly. She means it's so long since she's been here she's forgotten about Matthew.

ANGIE. You were here for my birthday when I was nine. I had a pink cake. Kit was only five then, she was four, she hadn't started school yet. She could read already when she went to school. You remember my birthday? / You remember me?

MARLENE. Yes, I remember the cake.

ANGIE. You remember me?

MARLENE. Yes, I remember you.

ANGIE. And Mum and Dad was there, and Kit was.

MARLENE. Yes, how is your dad? Where is he tonight? Up the pub?

JOYCE. No, he's not here.

MARLENE. I can see he's not here.

JOYCE. He moved out.

MARLENE. What? When did he? / Just recently?*

ANGIE. Didn't you know that? You don't know much.

JOYCE. *No, it must be three years ago. Don't be rude, Angie.

ANGIE. I'm not, am I Aunty? What else don't you know?

JOYCE. You was in America or somewhere. You sent a postcard.

ANGIE. I've got that in my room. It's the Grand Canyon. Do you want to see it? Shall I get it? I can get it for you.

MARLENE. Yes, all right.

[ANGIE goes.]

JOYCE. You could be married with twins for all I know. You must have affairs and break up and I don't need to know about any of that so I don't see what the fuss is about.

MARLENE. What fuss?

[ANGIE comes back with the postcard.]

ANGIE. "Driving across the states for a new job in L.A. It's a long way but the car goes very fast. It's very hot. Wish you were here. Love from Aunty Marlene."

JOYCE. Did you make a lot of money?

MARLENE. I spent a lot.

ANGIE. I want to go to America. Will you take me?

JOYCE. She's not going to America, she's been to America, stupid.

ANGIE. She might go again, stupid. It's not something you do once. People who go keep going all the time, back and forth on jets. They go on Concorde and Laker and get jet lag. Will you take me?

MARLENE. I'm not planning a trip.

ANGIE. Will you let me know?

JOYCE. Angie, / you're getting silly.

ANGIE. I want to be American.

JOYCE. It's time you were in bed.

ANGIE. No it's not. / I don't have to go to bed at all tonight.

JOYCE. School in the morning.

ANGIE. I'll wake up.

JOYCE. Come on now, you know how you get.

ANGIE. How do I get? / I don't get anyhow.

JOYCE. Angie.
 Are you staying the night?

MARLENE. Yes, if that's all right. / I'll see you in the morning.

ANGIE. You can have my bed. I'll sleep on the sofa.

JOYCE. You will not, you'll sleep in your bed. / Think I can't

ANGIE. Mum.

JOYCE. see through that? I can just see you going to sleep / with us talking.

ANGIE. I would, I would go to sleep, I'd love that.

JOYCE. I'm going to get cross, Angie.

ANGIE. I want to show her something.

JOYCE. Then bed.

ANGIE. It's a secret.

JOYCE. Then I expect it's in your room so off you go. Give us a shout when
 you're ready for bed and your aunty'll be up and see you.

ANGIE. Will you?

MARLENE. Yes of course.
 [ANGIE *goes. Silence.*]
 It's cold tonight.

JOYCE. Will you be all right on the sofa? You can / have my bed.

MARLENE. The sofa's fine.

JOYCE. Yes the forecast said rain tonight but it's held off.

MARLENE. I was going to walk down to the estuary but I've left it a bit late.
 Is it just the same?

JOYCE. They cut down the hedges a few years back. Is that since you were
 here?

MARLENE. But it's not changed down the end, all the mud? And the reeds?
 We used to pick them when they were bigger than us. Are there still lap-
 wings?

JOYCE. You get strangers walking there on a Sunday. I expect they're looking
 at the mud and the lapwings, yes.

MARLENE. You could have left.

JOYCE. Who says I wanted to leave?

MARLENE. Stop getting at me then, you're really boring.

JOYCE. How could I have left?

MARLENE. Did you want to?

JOYCE. I said how, / how could I?

MARLENE. If you'd wanted to you'd have done it.

JOYCE. Christ.

MARLENE. Are we getting drunk?

JOYCE. Do you want something to eat?

MARLENE. No, I'm getting drunk.

JOYCE. Funny time to visit, Sunday evening.

MARLENE. I came this morning. I spent the day.

ANGIE. [*Off.*] Aunty! Aunty Marlene!

MARLENE. I'd better go.

JOYCE. Go on then.

MARLENE. All right.

ANGIE. [Off.] Aunty! Can you hear me? I'm ready.

[MARLENE goes. JOYCE goes on sitting. MARLENE comes back.]

JOYCE. So what's the secret?

MARLENE. It's a secret.

JOYCE. I know what it is anyway.

MARLENE. I bet you don't. You always said that.

JOYCE. It's her exercise book.

MARLENE. Yes, but you don't know what's in it.

JOYCE. It's some game, some secret society she has with Kit.

MARLENE. You don't know the password. You don't know the code.

JOYCE. You're really in it, aren't you. Can you do the handshake?

MARLENE. She didn't mention a handshake.

JOYCE. I thought they'd have a special handshake. She spends hours writing that but she's useless at school. She copies things out of books about black magic, and politicians out of the paper. It's a bit childish.

MARLENE. I think it's a plot to take over the world.

JOYCE. She's been in the remedial class the last two years.

MARLENE. I came up this morning and spent the day in Ipswich. I went to see mother.

JOYCE. Did she recognize you?

MARLENE. Are you trying to be funny?

JOYCE. No, she does wander.

MARLENE. She wasn't wandering at all, she was very lucid thank you.

JOYCE. You were very lucky then

MARLENE. Fucking awful life she's had.

JOYCE. Don't tell me.

MARLENE. Fucking waste.

JOYCE. Don't talk to me.

MARLENE. Why shouldn't I talk? Why shouldn't I talk to you? / Isn't she my mother too?

JOYCE. Look, you've left, you've gone away, / we can do without you.

MARLENE. I left home, so what, I left home. People do leave home / it is normal.

JOYCE. We understand that, we can do without you.

MARLENE. We weren't happy. Were you happy?

JOYCE. Don't come back.

MARLENE. So it's just your mother is it, your child, you never wanted me round, / you were jealous of me because I was the

JOYCE. Here we go.

MARLENE. little one and I was clever.

JOYCE. I'm not clever enough for all this psychology / if that's what it is.

MARLENE. Why can't I visit my own family / without all this?*

JOYCE. Aah.

Just don't go on about Mum's life when you haven't been to see her for how many years. / I go and see her every week.

MARLENE. It's up to me.

*Then don't go and see her every week.

JOYCE. Somebody has to.

MARLENE. No they don't. / Why do they?

JOYCE. How would I feel if I didn't go?

MARLENE. A lot better.

JOYCE. I hope you feel better.

MARLENE. It's up to me.

JOYCE. You couldn't get out of here fast enough.

MARLENE. Of course I couldn't get out of here fast enough. What was I going to do? Marry a dairyman who'd come home pissed? / Don't you fucking this fucking that fucking bitch

JOYCE. Christ.

MARLENE. fucking tell me what to fucking do fucking.

JOYCE. I don't know how you could leave your own child.

MARLENE. You were quick enough to take her.

JOYCE. What does that mean?

MARLENE. You were quick enough to take her.

JOYCE. Or what? Have her put in a home? Have some stranger / take her would you rather?

MARLENE. You couldn't have one so you took mine.

JOYCE. I didn't know that then.

MARLENE. Like hell, / married three years.

JOYCE. I didn't know that. Plenty of people / take that long.

MARLENE. Well it turned out lucky for you, didn't it?

JOYCE. Turned out all right for you by the look of you. You'd be getting a few less thousand a year.

MARLENE. Not necessarily.

JOYCE. You'd be stuck here / like you said.

MARLENE. I could have taken her with me.

JOYCE. You didn't want to take her with you. It's not good coming back now, Marlene, / and saying—

MARLENE. I know a managing director who's got two children, she breast feeds in the board room, she pays a hundred pounds a week on domestic help alone and she can afford that because she's an extremely high-powered lady earning a great deal of money.

JOYCE. So what's that got to do with you at the age of seventeen?

MARLENE. Just because you were married and had somewhere to live—

JOYCE. You could have lived at home. / Or live with me

MARLENE. Don't be stupid.

JOYCE. and Frank. / You said you weren't keeping it. You

MARLENE. You never suggested.

JOYCE. shouldn't have had it / if you wasn't going to keep it.

MARLENE. Here we go.

JOYCE. You was the most stupid, / for someone so clever you was the most stupid, get yourself pregnant, not go to the doctor, not tell.

MARLENE. You wanted it, you said you were glad, I remember the day, you said I'm glad you never got rid of it, I'll look after it, you said that down by the river. So what are you saying, sunshine, you don't want her?

JOYCE. Course I'm not saying that.

MARLENE. Because I'll take her, / wake her up and pack now.

JOYCE. You wouldn't know how to begin to look after her.

MARLENE. Don't you want her?

JOYCE. Course I do, she's my child.

MARLENE. Then what are you going on about / why did I have her?

JOYCE. You said I got her off you / when you didn't—

MARLENE. I said you were lucky / the way it—

JOYCE. Have a child now if you want one. You're not old.

MARLENE. I might do.

JOYCE. Good.

[*Pause.*]

MARLENE. I've been on the pill so long / I'm probably sterile.

JOYCE. Listen when Angie was six months I did get pregnant and I lost it because I was so tired looking after your fucking baby / because she cried so much—yes I did tell

MARLENE. You never told me.

JOYCE. you—/ and the doctor said if I'd sat down all day with

MARLENE. Well I forgot.

JOYCE. my feet up I'd've kept it / and that's the only chance I ever had because after that—

MARLENE. I've had two abortions, are you interested? Shall I tell you about them? Well I won't, it's boring, it wasn't a problem. I don't like messy talk about blood / and what a bad

JOYCE. If I hadn't had your baby. The doctor said.

MARLENE. time we all had. I don't want a baby. I don't want to talk about gynecology.

JOYCE. Then stop trying to get Angie off of me.

MARLENE. I come down here after six years. All night you've been saying I don't come often enough. If I don't come for another six years she'll be twenty-one, will that be OK?

JOYCE. That'll be fine, yes, six years would suit me fine.

[*Pause.*]

MARLENE. I was afraid of this.

I only came because I thought you wanted . . .

I just want . . .

[MARLENE *cries.*]

JOYCE. Don't grizzle, Marlene, for God's sake.

Marly? Come on, pet. Love you really.

Fucking stop it, will you?

MARLENE. No let me cry. I like it.

[*They laugh.* MARLENE *begins to stop crying.*]

I knew I'd cry if I wasn't careful.

JOYCE. Everyone's always crying in this house. Nobody takes any notice.

MARLENE. You've been wonderful looking after Angie.

JOYCE. Don't get carried away.

MARLENE. I can't write letters but I do think of you.

JOYCE. You're getting drunk. I'm going to make some tea.

MARLENE. Love you.

[JOYCE *gets up to make tea.*]

JOYCE. I can see why you'd want to leave. It's a dump here.

MARLENE. So what's this about you and Frank?

JOYCE. He was always carrying on, wasn't he? And if I wanted to go out in the evening he'd go mad, even if it was nothing, a class, I was going to go to an evening class. So he had this girlfriend, only twenty-two poor cow, and I said go on, off you go, hoppit. I don't think he even likes her.

MARLENE. So what about money?

JOYCE. I've always said I don't want your money.

MARLENE. No, does he send you money?

JOYCE. I've got four different cleaning jobs. Adds up. There's not a lot round here.

MARLENE. Does Angie miss him?

JOYCE. She doesn't say.

MARLENE. Does she see him?

JOYCE. He was never that fond of her to be honest.

MARLENE. He tried to kiss me once. When you were engaged.

JOYCE. Did you fancy him?

MARLENE. No, he looked like a fish.

JOYCE. He was lovely then.

MARLENE. Ugh.

JOYCE. Well I fancied him. For about three years.

MARLENE. Have you got someone else?

JOYCE. There's not a lot round here. Mind you, the minute you're on your own, you'd be amazed how your friends' husbands drop by. I'd sooner do without.

MARLENE. I don't see why you couldn't take my money.

JOYCE. I do, so don't bother about it.

MARLENE. Only got to ask.

JOYCE. So what about you? Good job?

MARLENE. Good for a laugh. / Got back from the US of A a bit

JOYCE. Good for more than a laugh I should think.

MARLENE. wiped out and slotted into this speedy employment agency and still there.

JOYCE. You can always find yourself work then.

MARLENE. That's right.

JOYCE. And men?

MARLENE. Oh there's always men.

JOYCE. No one special?

MARLENE. There's fellas who like to be seen with a high-flying lady. Shows they've got something really good in their pants. But they can't take the day to day. They're waiting for me to turn into the little woman. Or maybe I'm just horrible of course.

JOYCE. Who needs them?

MARLENE. Who needs them? Well I do. But I need adventures more. So on on into the sunset. I think the eighties are going to be stupendous.

JOYCE. Who for?

MARLENE. For me. / I think I'm going up up up.

JOYCE. Oh for you. Yes, I'm sure they will.

MARLENE. And for the country, come to that. Get the economy back on its feet and whoosh. She's a tough lady, Maggie.[9] I'd give her a job. / She just needs to hang in there. This country

JOYCE. You voted for them, did you?

MARLENE. needs to stop whining. / Monetarism is not stupid.

JOYCE. Drink your tea and shut up, pet.

MARLENE. It takes time, determination. No more slop. / And

JOYCE. Well I think they're filthy bastards.

MARLENE. who's got to drive it on? First woman prime minister. Terrifico. Aces. Right on. / You must admit. Certainly gets my vote.

JOYCE. What good's first woman if it's her? I suppose you'd have liked Hitler if he was a woman. Ms. Hitler. Got a lot done, Hitlerina. / Great adventures.

MARLENE. Bosses still walking on the workers' faces? Still Dadda's little parrot? Haven't you learned to think for yourself? I believe in the individual. Look at me.

JOYCE. I am looking at you.

9. Margaret Thatcher, Conservative prime minister (1979–90).

MARLENE. Come on, Joyce, we're not going to quarrel over politics.

JOYCE. We are though.

MARLENE. Forget I mentioned it. Not a word about the slimy unions will cross my lips.

[Pause.]

JOYCE. You say Mother had a wasted life.

MARLENE. Yes I do. Married to that bastard.

JOYCE. What sort of life did he have? / Working in the fields like

MARLENE. Violent life?

JOYCE. an animal. / Why wouldn't he want a drink?

MARLENE. Come off it.

JOYCE. You want a drink. He couldn't afford whisky.

MARLENE. I don't want to talk about him.

JOYCE. You started, I was talking about her. She had a rotten life because she had nothing. She went hungry.

MARLENE. She was hungry because he drank the money. / He used to hit her.

JOYCE. It's not all down to him. / Their lives were rubbish. They

MARLENE. She didn't hit him.

JOYCE. were treated like rubbish. He's dead and she'll die soon and what sort of life / did they have?

MARLENE. I saw him one night. I came down.

JOYCE. Do you think I didn't? / They didn't get to America and

MARLENE. I still have dreams.

JOYCE. drive across it in a fast car. / Bad nights, they had bad days.

MARLENE. America, America, you're jealous. / I had to get out,

JOYCE. Jealous?

MARLENE. I knew when I was thirteen, out of their house, out of them, never let that happen to me, / never let him, make my own way, out.

JOYCE. Jealous of what you've done, you're ashamed of me if I came to your office, your smart friends, wouldn't you, I'm ashamed of you, think of nothing but yourself, you've got on, nothing's changed for most people / has it?

MARLENE. I hate the working class / which is what you're going

JOYCE. Yes you do.

MARLENE. to go on about now, it doesn't exist any more, it means lazy and stupid. / I don't like the way they talk. I don't

JOYCE. Come on, now we're getting it.

MARLENE. like beer guts and football vomit and saucy tits / and brothers and sisters—

JOYCE. I spit when I see a Rolls Royce, scratch it with my ring / Mercedes it was.

MARLENE. Oh very mature—

JOYCE. I hate the cows I work for / and their dirty dishes with blanquette of fucking veau.[1]

MARLENE. and I will not be pulled down to their level by a flying picket[2] and I won't be sent to Siberia / or a loony bin

JOYCE. No, you'll be on a yacht, you'll be head of Coca-Cola and you wait, the eighties is going to be stupendous all right because we'll get you lot off our backs—

MARLENE. just because I'm original. And I support Reagan even if he is a lousy movie star because the reds are swarming up his map and I want to be free in a free world—

1. Veal stew.
2. Mobile picket available to reinforce local pickets during a strike.

JOYCE. What? / What?

MARLENE. I know what I mean / by that—not shut up here.

JOYCE. So don't be round here when it happens because if someone's kicking you I'll just laugh.

[*Silence.*]

MARLENE. I don't mean anything personal. I don't believe in class. Anyone can do anything if they've got what it takes.

JOYCE. And if they haven't?

MARLENE. If they're stupid or lazy or frightened, I'm not going to help them get a job, why should I?

JOYCE. What about Angie?

MARLENE. What about Angie?

JOYCE. She's stupid, lazy and frightened, so what about her?

MARLENE. You run her down too much. She'll be all right.

JOYCE. I don't expect so, no. I expect her children will say what a wasted life she had. If she has children. Because nothing's changed and it won't with them in.

MARLENE. Them, them. / Us and them?

JOYCE. And you're one of them.

MARLENE. And you're us, wonderful us, and Angie's us / and Mum and Dad's us.

JOYCE. Yes, that's right, and you're them.

MARLENE. Come on, Joyce, what a night. You've got what it takes.

JOYCE. I know I have.

MARLENE. I didn't really mean all that.

JOYCE. I did.

MARLENE. But we're friends anyway.

JOYCE. I don't think so, no.

MARLENE. Well it's lovely to be out in the country. I really must make the effort to come more often.

I want to go to sleep.

I want to go to sleep.

[JOYCE *gets blankets for the sofa.*]

JOYCE. Goodnight then. I hope you'll be warm enough.

MARLENE. Goodnight. Joyce—

JOYCE. No, pet. Sorry.

[JOYCE *goes.* MARLENE *sits wrapped in a blanket and has another drink.* ANGIE *comes in.*]

ANGIE. Mum?

MARLENE. Angie? What's the matter?

ANGIE. Mum?

MARLENE. No, she's gone to bed. It's Aunty Marlene.

ANGIE. Frightening.

MARLENE. Did you have a bad dream? What happened in it? Well you're awake now, aren't you pet?

ANGIE. Frightening.

1982

JOYCE CAROL OATES

1938–

Whether her characters are situated in contemporary urban centers or in the towns of a Victorian past, Joyce Carol Oates has established her reputation as a psychologist of what she has called "the human soul caught in the stampede of time." In a remarkably prolific career, Oates has produced many novels, short stories, books of essays, and volumes of poems. The violence associated with some of her fiction is a result of her sense that ordinary people cannot always articulate or even understand the ways in which they are trapped in the convulsions of history.

Oates was born to Irish-Catholic, working-class parents in Lockport, New York. After graduating Phi Beta Kappa from Syracuse University and receiving an M.A. in English from the University of Wisconsin, she began an academic career that moved her from the University of Detroit and the University of Windsor, Ontario, to Princeton, New Jersey, where she currently resides with her husband, the scholar Raymond Smith. Whether, as in *Expensive People* (1968), she focuses on a murderous child, or, as in *them* (1969), on prostitution and male aggression, Oates documents the sometimes grotesque violence of contemporary family life. While in *Wonderland* (1971) and *Do with Me What You Will* (1973), she deals with the psychological tactics individuals use to avoid reality, in works like *Bellefleur* (1980) and *A Bloodsmoor Romance* (1982) she focuses on the situation of women in social history and on the aesthetic dimensions of the novel form. However, many of Oates's most successful works—from the short story collections *By the North Gate* (1963) and *Haunted: Tales of the Grotesque* (1994) to the novels *You Must Remember This* (1987) and *Foxfire: Confessions of a Girl Gang* (1993)—characteristically dramatize unsettling, unpleasant, even macabre subjects. *The Profane Act* (1983) and *On Boxing* (1987) demonstrate Oates's critical skills, while *You Must Remember* (1987) exemplifies her ongoing fascination with the violence of American culture. Defending herself against critics who fault her analyses of pain, Oates has explained that "the more violent the murders in *Macbeth,* the more relief one can feel at *not* having to perform them. Great art," she continued, "is cathartic; it is always moral."

Where Are You Going, Where Have You Been?

For Bob Dylan[1]

Her name was Connie. She was fifteen and she had a quick, nervous giggling habit of craning her neck to glance into mirrors or checking other peoples faces to make sure her own was all right. Her mother, who noticed everything and knew everything and who hadn't much reason any longer to look at her own face, always scolded Connie about it. "Stop gawking at yourself. Who are you? You think you're so pretty?" she would say. Connie would raise her eyebrows at these familiar old complaints and look right through her mother, into a shadowy vision of herself as she was right at that moment: she knew she was pretty and that was everything. Her mother had been pretty once too, if you could believe those old snapshots in the album, but now her looks were gone and that was why she was always after Connie.

1. Popular American folk and rock singer, a symbol of youth protest during the 1960s.

"Why don't you keep your room clean like your sister? How've you got your hair fixed—what the hell stinks? Hair spray? You don't see your sister using that junk."

Her sister June was twenty-four and still lived at home. She was a secretary in the high school Connie attended, and if that wasn't bad enough—with her in the same building—she was so plain and chunky and steady that Connie had to hear her praised all the time by her mother and her mother's sisters. June did this, June did that, she saved money and helped clean the house and cooked and Connie couldn't do a thing, her mind was all filled with trashy daydreams. Their father was away at work most of the time and when he came home he wanted supper and he read the newspaper at supper and after supper he went to bed. He didn't bother talking much to them, but around his bent head Connie's mother kept picking at her until Connie wished her mother was dead and she herself was dead and it was all over. "She makes me want to throw up sometimes," she complained to her friends. She had a high, breathless, amused voice that made everything sound a little forced, whether it was sincere or not.

There was one good thing: June went places with girl friends of hers, girls who were just as plain and steady as she, and so when Connie wanted to do that her mother had no objections. The father of Connie's best girl friend drove the girls the three miles to town and left them at a shopping plaza so they could walk through the stores or go to a movie, and when he came to pick them up again at eleven he never bothered to ask what they had done.

They must have been familiar sights, walking around the shopping plaza in their shorts and flat ballerina slippers that always scuffed on the sidewalk, with charm bracelets jingling on their thin wrists; they would lean together to whisper and laugh secretly if someone passed who amused or interested them. Connie had long dark blond hair that drew anyone's eye to it, and she wore part of it pulled up on her head and puffed out and the rest of it she let fall down her back. She wore a pull-over jersey blouse that looked one way when she was at home and another way when she was away from home. Everything about her had two sides to it, one for home and one for anywhere that was not home: her walk, which could be childlike and bobbing, or languid enough to make anyone think she was hearing music in her head; her mouth, which was pale and smirking most of the time, but bright and pink on these evenings out; her laugh, which was cynical and drawling at home— "Ha, ha, very funny,"— but high-pitched and nervous anywhere else, like the jingling of the charms on her bracelet.

Sometimes they did go shopping or to a movie, but sometimes they went across the highway, ducking fast across the busy road, to a drive-in restaurant where older kids hung out. The restaurant was shaped like a big bottle, though squatter than a real bottle, and on its cap was a revolving figure of a grinning boy holding a hamburger aloft. One night in midsummer they ran across, breathless with daring, and right away someone leaned out a car window and invited them over, but it was just a boy from high school they didn't like. It made them feel good to be able to ignore him. They went up through the maze of parked and cruising cars to the bright-lit, fly-infested restaurant, their faces pleased and expectant as if they were entering a sacred building that loomed up out of the night to give them what haven and blessing they yearned for. They sat at the counter and crossed their legs at the ankles, their thin

shoulders rigid with excitement, and listened to the music that made every-
thing so good: the music was always in the background, like music at a church
service; it was something to depend upon.

A boy named Eddie came in to talk with them. He sat backwards on his
stool, turning himself jerkily around in semicircles and then stopping and
turning back again, and after a while he asked Connie if she would like some-
thing to eat. She said she would so she tapped her friend's arm on her way
out—her friend pulled her face up into a brave, droll look—and Connie said
she would meet her at eleven across the way. "I just hate to leave her like that,"
Connie said earnestly, but the boy said that she wouldn't be alone for long. So
they went out to his car, and on the way Connie couldn't help but let her eyes
wander over the windshields and faces all around her, her face gleaming with a
joy that had nothing to do with Eddie or even this place; it might have been
the music. She drew her shoulders up and sucked in her breath with the pure
pleasure of being alive, and just at that moment she happened to glance at a
face just a few feet away from hers. It was a boy with shaggy black hair, in a
convertible jalopy painted gold. He stared at her and then his lips widened
into a grin. Connie slit her eyes at him and turned away, but she couldn't help
glancing back and there he was, still watching her. He wagged a finger and
laughed and said, "Gonna get you, baby," and Connie turned away again with-
out Eddie noticing anything.

She spent three hours with him, at the restaurant where they ate hamburg-
ers and drank Cokes in wax cups that were always sweating, and then down an
alley a mile or so away, and when he left her off at five to eleven only the movie
house was still open at the plaza. Her girl friend was there, talking with a boy.
When Connie came up, the two girls smiled at each other and Connie said,
"How was the movie?" and the girl said, "you should know." They rode off with
the girl's father, sleepy and pleased, and Connie couldn't help but look back at
the darkened shopping plaza with its big empty parking lot and its signs that
were faded and ghostly now, and over at the drive-in restaurant where cars
were still circling tirelessly. She couldn't hear the music at this distance.

Next morning June asked her how the movie was and Connie said, "So-so."

She and that girl and occasionally another girl went out several times a
week, and the rest of the time Connie spent around the house—it was sum-
mer vacation—getting in her mother's way and thinking, dreaming about the
boys she met. But all the boys fell back and dissolved into a single face that was
not even a face but an idea, a feeling, mixed up with the urgent insistent
pounding of the music and the humid night air of July. Connie's mother kept
dragging her back to the daylight by finding things for her to do or saying sud-
denly, "What's this about the Pettinger girl?"

And Connie would say nervously, "Oh, her. That dope." She always drew
thick clear lines between herself and such girls, and her mother was simple
and kind enough to believe it. Her mother was so simple, Connie thought,
that it was maybe cruel to fool her so much. Her mother went scuffling around
the house in old bedroom slippers and complained over the telephone to one
sister about the other, then the other called up and the two of them com-
plained about the third one. If June's name was mentioned her mother's tone
was approving, and if Connie's name was mentioned it was disapproving. This
did not really mean she disliked Connie, and actually Connie thought that her
mother preferred her to June just because she was prettier, but the two of

them kept up a pretense of exasperation, a sense that they were tugging and struggling over something of little value to either of them. Sometimes, over coffee, they were almost friends, but something would come up—some vexation that was like a fly buzzing suddenly around their heads—and their faces went hard with contempt.

One Sunday Connie got up at eleven—none of them bothered with church—and washed her hair so that it could dry all day long in the sun. Her parents and sister were going to a barbecue at an aunt's house and Connie said no, she wasn't interested, rolling her eyes to let her mother know just what she thought of it. "Stay home alone then," her mother said sharply. Connie sat out back in a lawn chair and watched them drive away, her father quiet and bald, hunched around so that he could back the car out, her mother with a look that was still angry and not at all softened through the windshield, and in the back seat poor old June, all dressed up as if she didn't know what a barbecue was, with all the running yelling kids and the flies. Connie sat with her eyes closed in the sun, dreaming and dazed with the warmth about her as if this were a kind of love, the caresses of love, and her mind slipped over onto thoughts of the boy she had been with the night before and how nice he had been, how sweet it always was, not the way someone like June would suppose but sweet, gently, the way it was in movies and promised in songs; and when she opened her eyes she hardly knew where she was, the back yard ran off into weeds and a fence-like line of trees and behind it the sky was perfectly blue and still. The asbestos "ranch house" that was now three years old startled her—it looked small. She shook her head as if to get awake.

It was too hot. She went inside the house and turned on the radio to drown out the quiet. She sat on the edge of her bed, barefoot, and listened for an hour and a half, to a program called XYZ Sunday Jamboree, record after record of hard, fast, shrieking songs she sang along with, interspersed by exclamations from "Bobby King": "An' look here, you girls at Napoleon's—Son and Charley want you to pay real close attention to this song coming up!"

And Connie paid close attention herself, bathed in a glow of slow-pulsed joy that seemed to rise mysteriously out of the music itself and lay languidly about the airless little room, breathed in and breathed out with each gentle rise and fall of her chest.

After a while she heard a car coming up the drive. She sat up at once, startled, because it couldn't be her father so soon. The gravel kept crunching all the way in from the road—the driveway was long—and Connie ran to the window. It was a car she didn't know. It was an open jalopy, painted a bright gold that caught the sunlight opaquely. Her heart began to pound and her fingers snatched at her hair, checking it, and she whispered, "Christ, Christ," wondering how she looked. The car came to a stop at the side door and the horn sounded four short taps, as if this were a signal Connie knew.

She went into the kitchen and approached the door slowly, then hung out the screen door, her bare toes curling down off the step. There were two boys in the car and now she recognized the driver: he had shaggy black hair that looked crazy as a wig and he was grinning at her.

"I ain't late, am I?" he said.

"Who the hell do you think you are?" Connie said.

"Toldja I'd be out, didn't I?"

"I don't even know who you are."

She spoke sullenly, careful to show no interest or pleasure, and he spoke in a fast, bright monotone. Connie looked past him to the other boy, taking her time. He had fair brown hair, with a lock that fell onto his forehead. His sideburns gave him a fierce, embarrassed look, but so far he hadn't even bothered to glance at her. Both boys wore sunglasses. The driver's glasses were metallic and mirrored everything in miniature.

"You wanta come for a ride?" he said.

Connie smirked and let her hair fall loose over one shoulder.

"Dont'cha like my car? New paint job," he said. "Hey."

"What?"

"You're cute."

She pretended to fidget, chasing flies away from the door.

"Don'tcha believe me, or what?" he said.

"Look, I don't even know who you are," Connie said in disgust.

"Hey, Ellie's got a radio, see. Mine broke down." He lifted his friend's arm and showed her the little transistor radio the boy was holding, and now Connie began to hear the music. It was the same program that was playing inside the house.

"Bobby King?" she said.

"I listen to him all the time. I think he's great."

"He's kind of great," Connie said reluctantly.

"Listen, that guy's *great*. He knows where the action is."

Connie blushed a little, because the glasses made it impossible for her to see just what this boy was looking at. She couldn't decide if she liked him or if he was a jerk, and so she dawdled in the doorway and wouldn't come down or go back inside. She said, "What's all that stuff painted on your car?"

"Can'tcha read it?" He opened the door very carefully, as if he were afraid it might fall off. He slid out just as carefully, planting his feet firmly on the ground, the tiny metallic world in his glasses slowing down like gelatine hardening, and in the midst of it Connie's bright green blouse. "This here is my name, to begin with," he said. ARNOLD FRIEND was written in tarlike black letters on the side, with a drawing of a round, grinning face that reminded Connie of a pumpkin, except it wore sunglasses. "I wanta introduce myself. I'm Arnold Friend and that's my real name and I'm gonna be your friend, honey, and inside the car's Ellie Oscar, he's kinda shy." Ellie brought his transistor radio up to his shoulder and balanced it there. "Now, these numbers are a secret code, honey," Arnold Friend explained. He read off the numbers 33, 19, 17 and raised his eyebrows at her to see what she thought of that, but she didn't think much of it. The left rear fender had been smashed and around it was written, on the gleaming gold background: DONE BY CRAZY WOMAN DRIVER. Connie had to laugh at that. Arnold Friend was pleased at her laughter and looked up at her. "Around the other side's a lot more—you wanta come and see them?"

"No."

"Why not?"

"Why should I?"

"Don'tcha wanta see what's on the car? Don'tcha wanta go for a ride?"

"I don't know."

"Why not?"

"I got things to do."

"Like what?"

"Things."

He laughed as if she had said something funny. He slapped his thighs. He was standing in a strange way, leaning back against the car as if he were balancing himself. He wasn't tall, only an inch or so taller than she would be if she came down to him. Connie liked the way he was dressed, which was the way all of them dressed: tight faded jeans stuffed into black, scuffed boots, a belt that pulled his waist in and showed how lean he was, and a white pull-over shirt that was a little soiled and showed the hard small muscles of his arms and shoulders. He looked as if he probably did hard work, lifting and carrying things. Even his neck looked muscular. And his face was a familiar face, somehow; the jaw and chin and cheeks slightly darkened because he hadn't shaved for a day or two, and the nose long and hawklike, sniffing as if she were a treat he was going to gobble up and it was all a joke.

"Connie, you ain't telling the truth. This is your day set aside for a ride with me and you know it," he said, still laughing. The way he straightened and recovered from his fit of laughing showed that it had been all fake.

"How do you know what my name is?" she said suspiciously.

"It's Connie."

"Maybe and maybe not."

"I know my Connie," he said, wagging his finger. Now she remembered him even better, back at the restaurant, and her cheeks warmed at the thought of how she had sucked in her breath just at the moment she passed him—how she must have looked to him. And he had remembered her. "Ellie and I come out here especially for you," he said. "Ellie can sit in back. How about it?"

"Where?"

"Where what?"

"Where're we going?"

He looked at her. He took off the sunglasses and she saw how pale the skin around his eyes was, like holes that were not in shadow but instead in light. His eyes were like chips of broken glass that catch the light in an amiable way. He smiled. It was as if the idea of going for a ride somewhere, to someplace, was a new idea to him.

"Just for a ride, Connie sweetheart."

"I never said my name was Connie," she said.

"But I know what it is. I know your name and all about you, lots of things," Arnold Friend said. He had not moved yet but stood still leaning back against the side of his jalopy. "I took a special interest in you, such a pretty girl, and found out all about you—like I know your parents and sister are gone somewheres and I know where and how long they're going to be gone, and I know who you were with last night, and your best girl friend's name is Betty. Right?"

He spoke in a simple lilting voice, exactly as if he were reciting the words to a song. His smile assured her that everything was fine. In the car Ellie turned up the volume on his radio and did not bother to look around at them.

"Ellie can sit in the back seat," Arnold Friend said. He indicated his friend with a casual jerk of his chin, as if Ellie did not count and she should not bother with him.

"How'd you find out all that stuff?" Connie said.

"Listen: Betty Schultz and Tony Fitch and Jimmy Pettinger and Nancy Pettinger," he said in a chant. "Raymond Stanley and Bob Hutter—"

"Do you know all those kids?"

"I know everybody."

"Look, you're kidding. You're not from around here."

"Sure."

"But—how come we never saw you before?"

"Sure you saw me before," he said. He looked down at his boots, as if he were a little offended. "You just don't remember."

"I guess I'd remember you," Connie said.

"Yeah?" He looked up at this, beaming. He was pleased. He began to mark time with the music from Ellie's radio, tapping his fists lightly together. Connie looked away from his smile to the car, which was painted so bright it almost hurt her eyes to look at it. She looked at that name, ARNOLD FRIEND. And up at the front fender was an expression that was familiar—MAN THE FLYING SAUCERS. It was an expression kids had used the year before but didn't use this year. She looked at it for a while as if the words meant something to her that she did not yet know.

"What're you thinking about? Huh?" Arnold Friend demanded. "Not worried about your hair blowing around in the car, are you?"

"No."

"Think I maybe can't drive good?"

"How do I know?"

"You're a hard girl to handle. How come?" he said. "Don't you know I'm your friend? Didn't you see me put my sign in the air when you walked by?"

"What sign?"

"My sign." And he drew an X in the air, leaning out toward her. They were maybe ten feet apart. After his hand fell back to his side the X was still in the air, almost visible. Connie let the screen door close and stood perfectly still inside it, listening to the music from her radio and the boy's blend together. She stared at Arnold Friend. He stood there so stiffly relaxed, pretending to be relaxed, with one hand idly on the door handle as if he were keeping himself up that way and had no intention of ever moving again. She recognized most things about him, the tight jeans that showed his thighs and buttocks and the greasy leather boots and tight shirt, and even that slippery friendly smile of his, that sleepy dreamy smile that all the boys used to get across ideas they didn't want to put into words. She recognized all this and also the sing-song way he talked, slightly mocking, kidding, but serious and a little melancholy, and she recognized the way he tapped one fist against the other in homage to the perpetual music behind him. But all these things did not come together.

She said suddenly, "Hey, how old are you?"

His smile faded. She could see then that he wasn't a kid, he was much older—thirty, maybe more. At this knowledge her heart began to pound faster.

"That's a crazy thing to ask. Can'tcha see I'm your own age?"

"Like hell you are."

"Or maybe a coupla years older. I'm eighteen."

"Eighteen?" she said doubtfully.

He grinned to reassure her and lines appeared at the corners of his mouth. His teeth were big and white. He grinned so broadly his eyes became slits and she saw how thick the lashes were, thick and black as if painted with a black tarlike material. Then, abruptly, he seemed to become embarrassed and looked over his shoulder at Ellie. "Him, he's crazy," he said. "Ain't he a riot?

He's a nut, a real character." Ellie was still listening to the music. His sunglasses told nothing about what he was thinking. He wore a bright orange shirt unbuttoned halfway to show his chest, which was a pale, bluish chest and not muscular like Arnold Friend's. His shirt collar was turned up all around and the very tips of the collar pointed out past his chin as if they were protecting him. He was pressing the transistor radio up against his ear and sat there in a kind of daze, right in the sun.

"He's kinda strange," Connie said.

"Hey, she says you're kinda strange! Kinda strange!" Arnold Friend cried. He pounded on the car to get Ellie's attention. Ellie turned for the first time and Connie saw with shock that he wasn't a kid either—he had a fair, hairless face, cheeks reddened slightly as if the veins grew too close to the surface of his skin, the face of a forty-year-old baby. Connie felt a wave of dizziness rise in her at this sight and she stared at him as if waiting for something to change the shock of the moment, make it all right again. Ellie's lips kept shaping words, mumbling along with the words blasting in his ear.

"Maybe you two better go away," Connie said faintly.

"What? How come?" Arnold Friend cried. "We come out here to take you for a ride. It's Sunday." He had the voice of the man on the radio now. It was the same voice, Connie thought. "Don'tcha know it's Sunday all day? And honey, no matter who you were with last night, today you're with Arnold Friend and don't you forget it! Maybe you better step out here," he said, and this last was in a different voice. It was a little flatter, as if the heat was finally getting to him.

"No. I got things to do."

"Hey."

"You two better leave."

"We ain't leaving until you come with us."

"Like hell I am—"

"Connie, don't fool around with me. I mean—I mean, don't fool *around*," he said, shaking his head. He laughed incredulously. He placed his sunglasses on top of his head, carefully, as if he were indeed wearing a wig, and brought the stems down behind his ears. Connie stared at him, another wave of dizziness and fear rising in her so that for a moment he wasn't even in focus but was just a blur standing there against his gold car, and she had the idea that he had driven up the driveway all right but had come from nowhere before that and belonged nowhere and that everything about him and even about the music that was so familiar to her was only half real.

"If my father comes and sees you—"

"He ain't coming. He's at a barbecue."

"How do you know that?"

"Aunt Tillie's. Right now they're—uh—they're drinking. Sitting around," he said vaguely, squinting as if he were staring all the way to town and over to Aunt Tillie's back yard. Then the vision seemed to get clear and he nodded energetically. "Yeah. Sitting around. There's your sister in a blue dress, huh? And high heels, the poor sad bitch—nothing like you, sweetheart! And your mother's helping some fat woman with the corn, they're cleaning the corn—husking the corn—"

"What fat woman?" Connie cried.

"How do I know what fat woman, I don't know every goddamn fat woman in the world!" Arnold Friend laughed.

"Oh, that's Mrs. Hornsby Who invited her?" Connie said. She felt a little lightheaded. Her breath was coming quickly.

"She's too fat. I don't like them fat. I like them the way you are, honey," he said, smiling sleepily at her. They stared at each other for a while through the screen door. He said softly. "Now, what you're going to do is this: you're going to come out that door. You're going to sit up front with me and Ellie's going to sit in the back, the hell with Ellie, right? This isn't Ellie's date. You're my date. I'm your lover, honey."

"What? You're crazy—"

"Yes. I'm your lover. You don't know what that is but you will," he said. "I know that too. I know all about you. But look: it's real nice and you couldn't ask for nobody better than me, or more polite. I always keep my word. I'll tell you how it is, I'm always nice at first, the first time. I'll hold you so tight you won't think you have to try to get away or pretend anything because you'll know you can't. And I'll come inside you where it's all secret and you'll give in to me and you'll love me—"

"Shut up! You're crazy!" Connie said. She backed away from the door. She put her hands up against her ears as if she'd heard something terrible, something not meant for her. "People don't talk like that, you're crazy," she muttered. Her heart was almost too big now for her chest and its pumping made sweat break out all over her. She looked out to see Arnold Friend pause and then take a step toward the porch, lurching. He almost fell. But, like a clever drunken man, he managed to catch his balance. He wobbled in his high boots and grabbed hold of one of the porch posts.

"Honey?" he said. "You still listening?"

"Get the hell out of here!"

"Be nice, honey. Listen."

"I'm going to call the police—"

He wobbled again and out of the side of his mouth came a fast spat curse, an aside not meant for her to hear. But even this "Christ!" sounded forced. Then he began to smile again. She watched this smile come, awkward as if he were smiling from inside a mask. His whole face was a mask, she thought wildly, tanned down to his throat but then running out as if he had plastered makeup on his face but had forgotten about his throat.

"Honey—? Listen, here's how it is. I always tell the truth and I promise you this: I ain't coming in that house after you."

"You better not! I'm going to call the police if you—if you don't—"

"Honey," he said, talking right through her voice, "honey, I'm not coming in there but you are coming out here. You know why?"

She was panting. The kitchen looked like a place she had never seen before, some room she had run inside but that wasn't good enough, wasn't going to help her. The kitchen window had never had a curtain, after three years, and there were dishes in the sink for her to do—probably—and if you ran your hand across the table you'd probably feel something sticky there.

"You listening, honey? Hey?"

"—going to call the police—"

"Soon as you touch the phone I don't need to keep my promise and can come inside. You won't want that."

She rushed forward and tried to lock the door. Her fingers were shaking. "But why lock it," Arnold Friend said gently, talking right into her face. "It's just a screen door. It's just nothing." One of his boots was at a strange angle, as

if his foot wasn't in it. It pointed out to the left, bent at the ankle. "I mean, anybody can break through a screen door and glass and wood and iron or anything else if he needs to, anybody at all, and specially Arnold Friend. If the place got lit up with a fire, honey, you'd come runnin' out into my arms, right into my arms an' safe at home—like you knew I was your lover and'd stopped fooling around. I don't mind a nice shy girl but I don't like no fooling around." Part of those words were spoken with a slight rhythmic lilt, and Connie somehow recognized them—the echo of a song from last year, about a girl rushing into her boy friend's arms and coming home again—

Connie stood barefoot on the linoleum floor, staring at him. "What do you want?" she whispered.

"I want you," he said.

"What?"

"Seen you that night and thought, that's the one, yes sir. I never needed to look anymore."

"But my father's coming back. He's coming to get me. I had to wash my hair first—" She spoke in a dry, rapid voice, hardly raising it for him to hear.

"No, your daddy is not coming and yes, you had to wash your hair and you washed it for me. It's nice and shining and all for me. I thank you sweetheart," he said with a mock bow, but again he almost lost his balance. He had to bend and adjust his boots. Evidently his feet did not go all the way down; the boots must have been stuffed with something so that he would seem taller. Connie stared out at him and behind him at Ellie in the car, who seemed to be looking off toward Connie's right, into nothing. Then Ellie said, pulling the words out of the air one after another as if he were just discovering them, "You want me to pull out the phone?"

"Shut your mouth and keep it shut," Arnold Friend said, his face red from bending over or maybe from embarrassment because Connie had seen his boots. "This ain't none of your business."

"What—what are you doing? What do you want?" Connie said. "If I call the police they'll get you, they'll arrest you—"

"Promise was not to come in unless you touch that phone, and I'll keep that promise," he said. He resumed his erect position and tried to force his shoulders back. He sounded like a hero in a movie, declaring something important. But he spoke too loudly and it was as if he were speaking to someone behind Connie. "I ain't made plans for coming in that house where I don't belong but just for you to come out to me, the way you should. Don't you know who I am?"

"You're crazy," she whispered. She backed away from the door but did not want to go into another part of the house, as if this would give him permission to come through the door. "What do you ... you're crazy, you...."

"Huh? What're you saying, honey?"

Her eyes darted everywhere in the kitchen. She could not remember what it was, this room.

"This is how it is, honey: you come out and we'll drive away, have a nice ride. But if you don't come out we're gonna wait till your people come home and then they're all going to get it."

"You want that telephone pulled out?" Ellie said. He held the radio away from his ear and grimaced, as if without the radio the air was too much for him.

"I toldja shut up, Ellie," Arnold Friend said, "you're deaf, get a hearing aid, right? Fix yourself up This little girl's no trouble and's gonna be nice to me, so Ellie keep to yourself, this ain't your date—right? Don't hem in on me, don't hog, don't crush, don't bird dog, don't trail me," he said in a rapid, meaningless voice, as if he were running through all the expressions he'd learned but was no longer sure which of them was in style, then rushing on to new ones, making them up with his eyes closed. "Don't crawl under my fence, don't squeeze in my chipmunk hole, don't sniff my glue, suck my popsicle, keep your own greasy fingers on yourself!" He shaded his eyes and peered in at Connie, who was backed against the kitchen table. "Don't mind him, honey, he's just a creep. He's a dope. Right? I m the boy for you and like I said, you come out here nice like a lady and give me your hand, and nobody else gets hurt, I mean, your nice old bald-headed daddy and your mummy and your sister in her high heels. Because listen: why bring them in this?"

"Leave me alone," Connie whispered.

"Hey, you know that old woman down the road, the one with the chickens and stuff—you know her?"

"She's dead!"

"Dead? What? You know her?" Arnold Friend said.

"She's dead—"

"Don't you like her?"

"She's dead—she's—she isn't here any more—"

"But don't you like her, I mean, you got something against her? Some grudge or something?" Then his voice dipped as if he were conscious of a rudeness. He touched the sunglasses perched up on top of his head as if to make sure they were still there. "Now, you be a good girl."

"What are you going to do?"

"Just two things, or maybe three," Arnold Friend said. "But I promise it won't last long and you'll like me the way you get to like people you're close to. You will. It's all over for you here, so come on out. You don't want your people in any trouble, do you?"

She turned and bumped against a chair or something, hurting her leg, but she ran into the back room and picked up the telephone. Something roared in her ear, a tiny roaring, and she was so sick with fear that she could do nothing but listen to it—the telephone was clammy and very heavy and her fingers groped down to the dial but were too weak to touch it. She began to scream into the phone, into the roaring. She cried out, she cried for her mother, she felt her breath start jerking back and forth in her lungs as if it were something Arnold Friend was stabbing her with again and again with no tenderness. A noisy sorrowful wailing rose all about her and she was locked inside it the way she was locked inside this house.

After a while she could hear again. She was sitting on the floor with her wet back against the wall.

Arnold Friend was saying from the door, "That's a good girl. Put the phone back"

She kicked the phone away from her.

"No, honey. Pick it up. Put it back right.'

She picked it up and put it back. The dial tone stopped.

"That's a good girl. Now, you come outside."

She was hollow with what had been fear but what was now just an empti-

ness. All that screaming had blasted it out of her. She sat, one leg cramped under her, and deep inside her brain was something like a pinpoint of light that kept going and would not let her relax. She thought, I'm not going to see my mother again. She thought, I'm not going to sleep in my bed again. Her bright green blouse was all wet.

Arnold Friend said, in a gentle-loud voice that was like a stage voice, "The place where you come from ain't there any more, and where you had in mind to go is cancelled out. This place you are now—inside your daddy's house—is nothing but a cardboard box I can knock down any time. You know that and always did know it. You hear me?"

She thought, I have got to think. I have got to know what to do.

"We'll go out to a nice field, out in the country here where it smells so nice and it's sunny," Arnold Friend said. "I'll have my arms tight around you so you won't need to try to get away and I'll show you what love is like, what it does. The hell with this house! It looks solid all right," he said. He ran his fingernail down the screen and the noise did not make Connie shiver, as it would have the day before. "Now, put your hand on your heart, honey. Feel that? That feels solid too but we know better. Be nice to me, be sweet like you can because what else is there for a girl like you but to be sweet and pretty and give in?—and get away before her people get back?"

She felt her pounding heart. Her hand seemed to enclose it. She thought for the first time in her life that it was nothing that was hers, that belonged to her, but just a pounding, living thing inside this body that wasn't really hers either.

"You don't want them to get hurt," Arnold Friend went on. "Now, get up, honey. Get up all by yourself."

She stood.

"Now, turn this way. That's right. Come over here to me.—Ellie, put that away, didn't I tell you? You dope. You miserable creepy dope," Arnold Friend said. His words were not angry but only part of an incantation. The incantation was kindly. "Now, come out through the kitchen to me, honey, and let's see a smile, try it, you're a brave, sweet little girl and now they're eating corn and hot dogs cooked to bursting over an outdoor fire, and they don't know one thing about you and never did and honey, you're better than them because not a one of them would have done this for you."

Connie felt the linoleum under her feet; it was cool. She brushed her hair back out of her eyes. Arnold Friend let go of the post tentatively and opened his arms for her, his elbows pointing in toward each other and his wrists limp, to show that this was an embarrassed embrace and a little mocking, he didn't want to make her self-conscious.

She put out her hand against the screen. She watched herself push the door slowly open as if she were back safe somewhere in the other doorway, watching this body and his head of long hair moving out into the sunlight where Arnold Friend waited.

"My sweet little blue-eyed girl," he said in a half-sung sigh that had nothing to do with her brown eyes but was taken up just the same by the vast sunlit reaches of the land behind him and on all sides of him—so much land that Connie had never seen before and did not recognize except to know that she was going to it.

1970

MARGARET ATWOOD

1939–

Although Margaret Atwood has explained that she grew up singing *Rule, Britannia*, drawing the Union Jack, and reading stacks of Captain Marvel and Batman comic books, she has helped disengage Canada's cultural identity from both English and American influences. Most directly, she did this by working as an editor for the House of Anansi Press, by writing what she called "a map" for the uncharted territory of Canadian literature *Survival* (1972), and by compiling *The Oxford Book of Canadian Verse* (1982). Just as important, as if to elaborate on the significance of her thesis that the central image for Canadians is survival, Atwood has produced a number of influential volumes of poems, stories, and novels that meditate on the impediments Canadians, and often Canadian women, encounter in their efforts to stay alive.

Married to the novelist Graeme Gibson and the mother of a daughter, Atwood was born and raised in Ottawa, Ontario, but her formal schooling there was frequently interrupted by extensive family trips in the northern Ontario and Quebec bush, where her father did entomological research. In the year when she graduated from the University of Toronto, she published her first book of poems, *Double Persephone* (1962). After receiving a master's degree from Radcliffe College and studying Victorian fantasy at Harvard, she took a series of positions in the English departments of several Canadian universities. Six volumes of verse appeared between 1966 and 1974, as well as two novels, both of them hailed by critics for their sometimes comic, sometimes grim analyses of the mysteries of the self when, in isolation, it confronts a fractured or distorted image of itself.

In many of her poems, Atwood is similarly concerned with the splitting up of the self as it does "tricks with mirrors," or with the "power politics" between lovers, or with the need to revise mythic stories, like those of Homer's Odysseus, to retell them from the silenced perspective of the female who has been seduced and abandoned. In such novels as *The Edible Woman* (1969), *Surfacing* (1972), *Lady Oracle* (1976), *Life before Man* (1979), *Bodily Harm* (1981), and *Cat's Eye* (1988), moreover, she presents individuals questing for personal integrity and for a more harmonious relationship with the natural world. Atwood's poetry and fiction often attempt to provide what she calls, in one book title, *Procedures for Underground* (1970), where the underground is understood as the unconscious or the other side of what has been defined as normal by a given culture. Frequently this journey into the interior offers a visionary solution to the psychosexual problems Atwood associates with modern technological society. Whether her central character is a pioneer woman or an author of Gothic romances, she seeks some form of control over an environment that is seen as alien or alienating.

A number of Atwood's characters are moving toward the conclusion of the heroine of *Surfacing*: "This above all, to refuse to be a victim." Because, in Atwood's view, Canadians have viewed themselves as victims of either English or American imperialism, and because women have perceived themselves as victims of masculine privilege, Atwood implies that cultural colonization and sexual subordination are parallel, if not identical, situations. Both the humor and the tenderness of her most recent work indicate how writing continues to empower Atwood herself to defy colonization. In such volumes of prose fiction as *Bluebeard's Egg and Other Stories* (1986), *The Handmaid's Tale* (1987), *Good Bones* (1992), and *The Robber Bride* (1993), she exploits fantastic, futuristic and fairy-tale techniques to examine both feminist ideology and women's biological, familial, and social experi-

ences, while in such poems as those collected in the elegiac *Morning in the Burned House* (1995) she reimagines a "Mothertongue" that seeks to "speak both cherishing and farewell."

This Is a Photograph of Me

It was taken some time ago.
At first it seems to be
a smeared
print: blurred lines and gray flecks
blended with the paper; 5

then, as you scan
it, you see in the left-hand corner
a thing that is like a branch: part of a tree
(balsam or spruce) emerging
and, to the right, halfway up 10
what ought to be a gentle
slope, a small frame house.

In the background there is a lake,
and beyond that, some low hills.

(The photograph was taken 15
the day after I drowned.

I am in the lake, in the center
of the picture, just under the surface.

It is difficult to say where
precisely, or to say 20
how large or small I am:
the effect of water
on light is a distortion

but if you look long enough,
eventually 25
you will be able to see me.)

1966

Spelling

My daughter plays on the floor
with plastic letters,
red, blue & hard yellow,
learning how to spell,
spelling, 5
how to make spells

*

and I wonder how many women
denied themselves daughters,

closed themselves in rooms,
drew the curtains 10
so they could mainline words.

 *

A child is not a poem,
a poem is not a child.
There is no either/or.
However. 15

 *

I return to the story
of the woman caught in the war
& in labor, her thighs tied
together by the enemy
so she could not give birth. 20
Ancestress: the burning witch,
her mouth covered by leather
to strangle words.

A word after a word
after a word is power. 25

 *

At the point where language falls away
from the hot bones, at the point
where the rock breaks open and darkness
flows out of it like blood, at
the melting point of granite 30
when the bones know
they are hollow & the word
splits & doubles & speaks
the truth & the body
itself becomes a mouth. 35

 *

This is a metaphor.

 *

How do you learn to spell?
Blood, sky & the sun,
your own name first,
your first naming, your first name, 40
your first word.

 1981

Waiting

Here it is then, the dark thing,
the dark thing you have waited for so long.
You have made such melodramas.

You thought it would carry its own mist,
obscuring you in a damp enfolding, like the mildew 5
shroud on bread. Or you thought it would hide
in your closet, among the clothes you outgrew years ago,
nesting in dustballs and fallen hair, shedding
one of your fabricated skins
after another and growing bigger, 10
honing its teeth on your discarded
cloth lives, and then it would pounce
from the inside out, and your heart
would be filled with roaring

or else that it would come swiftly and without sound, 15
but with one pitiless glaring eye, like a high-speed train,
and a single blow on the head and the blackout.

Instead it is strangely like home.
Like your own home, fifty years ago,
in December, in the early evening 20
when the indoor light changed, from clear to clouded,
a clouded thick yellow, like a sulphury eggyolk,

and the reading lamp was turned on
with its brown silk shade, its aroma
of hot copper, the living 25
room flickering in the smells of cooking dinner,

and you crouched on the hardwood floor, smudged elbows
and scaly winter knees on the funny papers,
listening to the radio, news of disasters
that made you feel safe, 30
like the voice of your mother
urging you yet again to set the table
you are doing your best to ignore,
and you realized for the first time
in your life that you would be old 35

some day, you would some day be
as old as you are now,
and the home you were reading the funnies in
by the thick yellow light, would be gone
with all the people in it, even you, 40
even you in your young, smudgy body
with its scent of newsprint and dirty
knees and washed cotton,
and you would have a different body
by then, an old murky one, 45
a stranger's body you could not even imagine,
and you would be lost and alone.

And now it is now
and the dark thing is here,

and after all it is nothing new; 50
it is only a memory, after all:
a memory of a fear,
a yellowing paper child's fear
you have long since forgotten
and that has now come true. 55

1995

Asparagus

This afternoon a man leans over
the hard rolls and the curled
butter, and tells me everything: two
women love him, he loves them, what
should he do? 5

 The sun
sifts down through the imperceptibly
brownish urban air. I'm going to
suffer for this: turn red, get
blisters or else cancer. I eat 10
asparagus with my fingers, he
plunges into description.
He's at his wit's end, sewed
up in his own frenzy. He has
breadcrumbs in his beard. 15
 I wonder
if I should let my hair go gray
so my advice will be better.
I could wrinkle up my eyelids,
look wise. I could get a pet lizard. 20
You're not crazy, I tell him.
Others have done this. Me too.
Messy love is better than none,
I guess. I'm no authority
on sane living. 25

Which is all true
and no help at all, because
this form of love is like the pain
of childbirth: so intense
it's hard to remember afterwards, 30
of what kind of screams and grimaces
it pushed you into.

The shrimp arrive on their skewers,
the courtyard trees unroll
their yellowy caterpillars, 35
pollen powders our shoulders.
He wants them both, he relates

tortures, the coffee
arrives, and altogether I am amazed
at his stupidities. 40

I sit looking at him
with a sort of wonder,
or is it envy?

Listen, I say to him,
you're very lucky. 45

 1995

Marsh Languages

The dark soft languages are being silenced:
Mothertongue Mothertongue Mothertongue
falling one by one back into the moon.

Language of marshes,
language of the roots of rushes tangled 5
together in the ooze,
marrow cells twinning themselves
inside the warm core of the bone:
pathways of hidden light in the body fade and wink out.

The sibilants and gutturals, 10
the cave language, the half-light
forming at the back of the throat,
the mouth's damp velvet molding
the lost syllable for "I" that did not mean separate,
all are becoming sounds no longer 15
heard because no longer spoken,
and everything that could once be said in them has ceased to exist.

The languages of the dying suns
are themselves dying,
but even the word for this has been forgotten. 20
The mouth against skin, vivid and fading,
can no longer speak both cherishing and farewell.
It is now only a mouth, only skin.
There is no more longing.

Translation was never possible. 25
Instead there was always only
conquest, the influx
of the language of hard nouns,
the language of metal,
the language of either/or, 30
the one language that has eaten all the others.

 1995

Morning in the Burned House

In the burned house I am eating breakfast.
You understand: there is no house, there is no breakfast,
yet here I am.

The spoon which was melted scrapes against
the bowl which was melted also. 5
No one else is around.

Where have they gone to, brother and sister,
mother and father? Off along the shore,
perhaps. Their clothes are still on the hangers,

their dishes piled beside the sink, 10
which is beside the woodstove
with its grate and sooty kettle,

every detail clear,
tin cup and rippled mirror.
The day is bright and songless, 15

the lake is blue, the forest watchful.
In the east a bank of cloud
rises up silently like dark bread.

I can see the swirls in the oilcloth,
I can see the flaws in the glass, 20
those flares where the sun hits them.

I can't see my own arms and legs
or know if this is a trap or blessing,
finding myself back here, where everything

in this house has long been over, 25
kettle and mirror, spoon and bowl,
including my own body,

including the body I had then,
including the body I have now
as I sit at this morning table, alone and happy, 30

bare child's feet on the scorched floorboards
(I can almost see)
in my burning clothes, the thin green shorts

and grubby yellow T-shirt
holding my cindery, non-existent, 35
radiant flesh Incandescent.

1995

Rape Fantasies

The way they're going on about it in the magazines you'd think it was just invented, and not only that but it's something terrific, like a vaccine for cancer. They put it in capital letters on the front cover, and inside they have these questionnaires like the ones they used to have about whether you were a good enough wife or an endomorph or an ectomorph,[1] remember that? with the scoring upside down on page 73, and then these numbered do-it-yourself dealies, you know? RAPE, TEN THINGS TO DO ABOUT IT, like it was ten new hairdos or something. I mean, what's so new about it?

So at work they all have to talk about it because no matter what magazine you open, there it is, staring you right between the eyes, and they're beginning to have it on the television, too. Personally I'd prefer a June Allyson[2] movie anytime but they don't make them any more and they don't even have them that much on the Late Show. For instance, day before yesterday, that would be Wednesday, thank god it's Friday as they say, we were sitting around in the women's lunch room—the *lunch* room, I mean you'd think you could get some peace and quiet in there—and Chrissy closes up the magazine she's been reading and says, "How about it, girls, do you have rape fantasies?"

The four of us were having our game of bridge the way we always do, and I had a bare twelve points counting the singleton with not that much of a bid in anything. So I said one club, hoping Sondra would remember about the one club convention, because the time before when I used that she thought I really meant clubs and she bid us up to three, and all I had was four little ones with nothing higher than a six, and we went down two and on top of that we were vulnerable. She is not the world's best bridge player. I mean, neither am I but there's a limit.

Darlene passed but the damage was done, Sondra's head went round like it was on ball bearings and she said, "*What* fantasies?"

"Rape fantasies," Chrissy said. She's a receptionist and she looks like one; she's pretty but cool as a cucumber, like she's been painted all over with nail polish, if you know what I mean. Varnished. "It says here all women have rape fantasies."

"For Chrissake, I'm eating an egg sandwich," I said, "and I bid one club and Darlene passed."

"You mean, like some guy jumping you in an alley or something," Sondra said. She was eating her lunch, we all eat our lunches during the game, and she bit into a piece of that celery she always brings and started to chew away on it with this thoughtful expression in her eyes and I knew we might as well pack it in as far as the game was concerned.

"Yeah, sort of like that," Chrissy said. She was blushing a little, you could see it even under her makeup.

"I don't think you should go out alone at night," Darlene said, "you put yourself in a position," and I may have been mistaken but she was looking at me. She's the oldest, she's forty-one though you wouldn't know it and neither does she, but I looked it up in the employees' file. I like to guess a person's age and then look it up to see if I'm right. I let myself have an extra pack of ciga-

1. I.e., possessing a short and wide body structure or a tall and narrow one.

2. She portrayed smiling small-town girls in many musical-comedy films of the 1940s and 1950s.

rettes if I am, though I'm trying to cut down. I figure it's harmless as long as you don't tell. I mean, not everyone has access to that file, it's more or less confidential. But it's all right if I tell you, I don't expect you'll ever meet her, though you never know, it's a small world. Anyway.

"For *heaven's* sake, it's only *Toronto*," Greta said. She worked in Detroit for three years and she never lets you forget it, it's like she thinks she's a war hero or something, we should all admire her just for the fact that she's still walking this earth, though she was really living in Windsor the whole time, she just worked in Detroit Which for me doesn't really count. It's where you sleep, right?

"Well, do you?" Chrissy said. She was obviously trying to tell us about hers but she wasn't about to go first, she's cautious, that one.

"I certainly don't," Darlene said, and she wrinkled up her nose, like this, and I had to laugh. "I think it's disgusting." She's divorced, I read that in the file too, she never talks about it. It must've been years ago anyway. She got up and went over to the coffee machine and turned her back on us as though she wasn't going to have anything more to do with it.

"Well," Greta said. I could see it was going to be between her and Chrissy. They're both blondes, I don't mean that in a bitchy way but they do try to outdress each other. Greta would like to get out of Filing, she'd like to be a receptionist too so she could meet more people. You don't meet much of anyone in Filing except other people in Filing. Me, I don't mind it so much, I have outside interests.

"Well," Greta said, "I sometimes think about, you know my apartment? It's got this little balcony, I like to sit out there in the summer and I have a few plants out there. I never bother that much about locking the door to the balcony, it's one of those sliding glass ones, I'm on the eighteenth floor for heaven's sake, I've got a good view of the lake and the CN Tower and all. But I'm sitting around one night in my house-coat, watching TV with my shoes off, you know how you do, and I see this guy's feet, coming down past the window, and the next thing you know he's standing on the balcony, he's let himself down by a rope with a hook on the end of it from the floor above, that's the nineteenth, and before I can even get up off the chesterfield he's inside the apartment. He's all dressed in black with black gloves on"—I knew right away what show she got the black gloves off because I saw the same one—"and then he, well, you know."

"You know what?" Chrissy said, but Greta said, "And afterwards he tells me that he goes all over the outside of the apartment building like that, from one floor to another, with his rope and his hook . . . and then he goes out to the balcony and tosses his rope, and he climbs up it and disappears."

"Just like Tarzan," I said, but nobody laughed.

"Is that all?" Chrissy said. "Don't you ever think about, well, I think about being in the bathtub, with no clothes on . . . "

"So who takes a bath in their clothes?" I said, you have to admit it's stupid when you come to think of it, but she just went on, " . . . with lots of bubbles, what I use is Vitabath, it's more expensive but it's so relaxing, and my hair pinned up, and the door opens and this fellow's standing there. . . . "

"How'd he get in?" Greta said.

"Oh, I don't know, through a window or something. Well, I can't very well get out of the bathtub, the bathroom's too small and besides he's blocking the

doorway, so I just *lie* there, and he starts to very slowly take his own clothes off, and then he gets into the bathtub with me."

"Don't you scream or anything?" said Darlene. She'd come back with her cup of coffee, she was getting really interested. "I'd scream like bloody murder."

"Who'd hear me?" Chrissy said. "Besides, all the articles say it's better not to resist, that way you don't get hurt."

"Anyway you might get bubbles up your nose," I said, "from the deep breathing," and I swear all four of them looked at me like I was in bad taste, like I'd insulted the Virgin Mary or something. I mean, I don't see what's wrong with a little joke now and then. Life's too short, right?

"Listen," I said, "those aren't *rape* fantasies. I mean, you aren't getting *raped*, it's just some guy you haven't met formally who happens to be more attractive than Derek Cummins"—he's the Assistant Manager, he wears elevator shoes or at any rate they have these thick soles and he has this funny way of talking, we call him Derek Duck—"and you have a good time. Rape is when they've got a knife or something and you don't want to."

"So what about you, Estelle," Chrissy said, she was miffed because I laughed at her fantasy, she thought I was putting her down. Sondra was miffed too, by this time she'd finished her celery and she wanted to tell about hers, but she hadn't got in fast enough.

"All right, let me tell you one," I said. "I'm walking down this dark street at night and this fellow comes up and grabs my arm. Now it so happens that I have a plastic lemon in my purse, you know how it always says you should carry a plastic lemon in your purse? I don't really do it, I tried it once but the darn thing leaked all over my checkbook, but in this fantasy I have one, and I say to him, 'You're intending to rape me, right?' and he nods, so I open my purse to get the plastic lemon, and I can't find it! My purse is full of all this junk, Kleenex and cigarettes and my change purse and my lipstick and my driver's licence, you know the kind of stuff; so I ask him to hold out his hands, like this, and I pile all this junk into them and down at the bottom there's the plastic lemon, and I can't get the top off. So I hand it to him and he's very obliging, he twists the top off and hands it back to me, and I squirt him in the eye."

I hope you don't think that's too vicious. Come to think of it, it is a bit mean, especially when he was so polite and all.

"*That's* your rape fantasy?" Chrissy says. "I don't believe it."

"She's a card," Darlene says, she and I are the ones that've been here the longest and she never will forget the time I got drunk at the office party and insisted I was going to dance under the table instead of on top of it, I did a sort of Cossack number[3] but then I hit my head on the bottom of the table—actually it was a desk—when I went to get up, and I knocked myself out cold. She's decided that's the mark of an original mind and she tells everyone new about it and I'm not sure that's fair. Though I did do it.

"I'm being totally honest," I say. I always am and they know it. There's no point in being anything else, is the way I look at it, and sooner or later the truth will out so you might as well not waste the time, right? "You should hear the one about the Easy-Off Oven Cleaner."

3. I.e., a folk dance called the *kazatzka*, performed in a squatting position by Cossacks, a people of southern Russia.

But that was the end of the lunch hour, with one bridge game shot to hell, and the next day we spent most of the time arguing over whether to start a new game or play out the hands we had left over from the day before, so Sondra never did get a chance to tell about her rape fantasy.

It started me thinking though, about my own rape fantasies. Maybe I'm abnormal or something, I mean I have fantasies about handsome strangers coming in through the window too, like Mr. Clean,[4] I wish one would, please god somebody without flat feet and big sweat marks on his shirt, and over five feet five, believe me being tall is a handicap though it's getting better, tall guys are starting to like someone whose nose reaches higher than their belly button. But if you're being totally honest you can't count those as rape fantasies. In a real rape fantasy, what you should feel is this anxiety, like when you think about your apartment building catching on fire and whether you should use the elevator or the stairs or maybe just stick your head under a wet towel, and you try to remember everything you've read about what to do but you can't decide.

For instance, I'm walking along this dark street at night and this short, ugly fellow comes up and grabs my arm, and not only is he ugly, you know, with a sort of puffy nothing face, like those fellows you have to talk to in the bank when your account's overdrawn—of course I don't mean they're all like that—but he's absolutely covered in pimples. So he gets me pinned against the wall, he's short but he's heavy, and he starts to undo himself and the zipper gets stuck. I mean, one of the most significant moments in a girl's life, it's almost like getting married or having a baby or something, and he sticks the zipper.

So I say, kind of disgusted, "Oh for Chrissake," and he starts to cry. He tells me he's never been able to get anything right in his entire life, and this is the last straw, he's going to go jump off a bridge.

"Look," I say, I feel so sorry for him, in my rape fantasies I always end up feeling sorry for the guy, I mean there has to be something *wrong* with them, if it was Clint Eastwood[5] it'd be different but worse luck it never is. I was the kind of little girl who buried dead robins, know what I mean? It used to drive my mother nuts, she didn't like me touching them, because of the germs I guess. So I say, "Listen, I know how you feel. You really should do something about those pimples, if you got rid of them you'd be quite good looking, honest; then you wouldn't have to go around doing stuff like this. I had them myself once," I say, to comfort him, but in fact I did, and it ends up I give him the name of my old dermatologist, the one I had in high school, that was back in Leamington, except I used to go to St. Catharine's for the dermatologist. I'm telling you, I was really lonely when I first came here; I thought it was going to be such a big adventure and all, but it's a lot harder to meet people in a city. But I guess it's different for a guy.

Or I'm lying in bed with this terrible cold, my face is all swollen up, my eyes are red and my nose is dripping like a leaky tap, and this fellow comes in through the window and *he* has a terrible cold too, it's a new kind of flu that's been going around. So he says, "I'b goig do rabe you"—I hope you don't mind me holding my nose like this but that's the way I imagine it—and he lets out this terrific sneeze, which slows him down a bit, also I'm no object of beauty

myself, you'd have to be some kind of pervert to want to rape someone with a cold like mine, it'd be like raping a bottle of LePages mucilage the way my nose is running. He's looking wildly around the room, and I realize it's because he doesn't have a piece of Kleenex! "Id's ride here," I say, and I pass him the Kleenex, god knows why he even bothered to get out of bed, you'd think if you were going to go around climbing in windows you'd wait till you were healthier, right? I mean, that takes a certain amount of energy. So I ask him why doesn't he let me fix him a Neo-Citran[6] and scotch, that's what I always take, you still have the cold but you don't feel it, so I do and we end up watching the Late Show together. I mean, they aren't all sex maniacs, the rest of the time they must lead a normal life. I figure they enjoy watching the Late Show just like anybody else.

I do have a scarier one though . . . where the fellow says he's hearing angel voices that're telling him he's got to kill me, you know, you read about things like that all the time in the papers. In this one I'm not in the apartment where I live now, I'm back in my mother's house in Leamington and the fellow's been hiding in the cellar, he grabs my arm when I go downstairs to get a jar of jam and he's got hold of the axe too, out of the garage, that one is really scary. I mean, what do you say to a nut like that?

So I start to shake but after a minute I get control of myself and I say, is he sure the angel voices have got the right person, because I hear the same angel voices and they've been telling me for some time that I'm going to give birth to the reincarnation of St. Anne[7] who in turn has the Virgin Mary and right after that comes Jesus Christ and the end of the world, and he wouldn't want to interfere with that, would he? So he gets confused and listens some more, and then he asks for a sign and I show him my vaccination mark, you can see it's sort of an odd-shaped one, it got infected because I scratched the top off, and that does it, he apologizes and climbs out the coal chute again, which is how he got in in the first place, and I say to myself there's some advantage in having been brought up a Catholic even though I haven't been to church since they changed the service into English, it just isn't the same, you might as well be a Protestant. I must write to Mother and tell her to nail up that coal chute, it always has bothered me. Funny, I couldn't tell you at all what this man looks like but I know exactly what kind of shoes he's wearing, because that's the last I see of him, his shoes going up the coal chute, and they're the old-fashioned kind that lace up the ankles, even though he's a young fellow. That's strange, isn't it?

Let me tell you though I really sweat until I see him safely out of there and I go upstairs right away and make myself a cup of tea. I don't think about that one much. My mother always said you shouldn't dwell on unpleasant things and I generally agree with that, I mean, dwelling on them doesn't make them go away. Though not dwelling on them doesn't make them go away either, when you come to think of it.

Sometimes I have these short ones where the fellow grabs my arm but I'm really a Kung-Fu expert, can you believe it, in real life I'm sure it would just be a conk on the head and that's that, like getting your tonsils out, you'd wake up and it would be all over except for the sore places, and you'd be lucky if your neck wasn't broken or something, I could never even hit the volleyball in gym

6. Citrus-flavored cold medicine.

7. Mother of Mary, the mother of Jesus Christ.

and a volleyball is fairly large, you know?—and I just go *zap* with my fingers into his eyes and that's it, he falls over, or I flip him against a wall or something. But I could never really stick my fingers in anyone's eyes, could you? It would feel like hot jello and I don't even like cold jello, just thinking about it gives me the creeps. I feel a bit guilty about that one, I mean how would you like walking around knowing someone's been blinded for life because of you?

But maybe it's different for a guy.

The most touching one I have is when the fellow grabs my arm and I say, sad and kind of dignified, "You'd be raping a corpse." That pulls him up short and I explain that I've just found out I have leukaemia and the doctors have only given me a few months to live. That's why I'm out pacing the streets alone at night, I need to think, you know, come to terms with myself. I don't really have leukaemia but in the fantasy I do, I guess I chose that particular disease because a girl in my grade four class died of it, the whole class sent her flowers when she was in the hospital. I didn't understand then that she was going to die and I wanted to have leukaemia too so I could get flowers. Kids are funny, aren't they? Well, it turns out that he has leukaemia himself, and *he* only has a few months to live, that's why he's going around raping people, he's very bitter because he's so young and his life is being taken from him before he's really lived it. So we walk along gently under the street lights, it's spring and sort of misty, and we end up going for coffee, we're happy we've found the only other person in the world who can understand what we're going through, it's almost like fate, and after a while we just sort of look at each other and our hands touch, and he comes back with me and moves into my apartment and we spend our last months together before we die, we just sort of don't wake up in the morning, though I've never decided which one of us gets to die first. If it's him I have to go on and fantasize about the funeral, if it's me I don't have to worry about that, so it just about depends on how tired I am at the time. You may not believe this but sometimes I even start crying. I cry at the ends of movies, even the ones that aren't all that sad, so I guess it's the same thing. My mother's like that too.

The funny thing about these fantasies is that the man is always someone I don't know, and the statistics in the magazines, well, most of them anyway, they say it's often someone you do know, at least a little bit, like your boss or something—I mean, it wouldn't be my boss, he's over sixty and I'm sure he couldn't rape his way out of a paper bag, poor old thing, but it might be someone like Derek Duck, in his elevator shoes, perish the thought—or someone you just met, who invites you up for a drink, it's getting so you can hardly be sociable any more, and how are you supposed to meet people if you can't trust them even that basic amount? You can't spend your whole life in the Filing Department or cooped up in your own apartment with all the doors and windows locked and the shades down. I'm not what you would call a drinker but I like to go out now and then for a drink or two in a nice place, even if I am by myself, I'm with Women's Lib on that even though I can't agree with a lot of the other things they say. Like here for instance, the waiters all know me and if anyone, you know, bothers me . . . I don't know why I'm telling you all this, except I think it helps you get to know a person, especially at first, hearing some of the things they think about. At work they call me the office worry wart, but it isn't so much like worrying, it's more like figuring out what you should do in an emergency, like I said before.

Anyway, another thing about it is that there's a lot of conversation, in fact I spend most of my time, in the fantasy that is, wondering what I'm going to say and what he's going to say, I think it would be better if you could get a conversation going. Like, how could a fellow do that to a person he's just had a long conversation with, once you let them know you're human, you have a life too, I don't see how they could go ahead with it, right? I mean, I know it happens but I just don't understand it, that's the part I really don't understand.

<div align="right">1977</div>

There Was Once

—There was once a poor girl, as beautiful as she was good, who lived with her wicked stepmother in a house in the forest.

—Forest? *Forest* is passé, I mean, I've had it with all this wilderness stuff. It's not a right image of our society, today. Let's have some *urban* for a change.

—There was once a poor girl, as beautiful as she was good, who lived with her wicked stepmother in a house in the suburbs.

—That's better. But I have to seriously query this word *poor*.

—But she *was* poor!

—Poor is a relative. She lived in a house, didn't she?

—Yes.

—Then socioeconomically speaking, she was not poor.

—But none of the money was *hers!* The whole point of the story is that the wicked stepmother makes her wear old clothes and sleep in the fireplace—

—Aha! They had a *fireplace!* With *poor*, let me tell you, there's no fireplace. Come down to the park, come to the subway stations after dark, come down to where they sleep in cardboard boxes, and I'll show you *poor!*

—There was once a middle-class girl, as beautiful as she was good—

—Stop right there. I think we can cut the *beautiful*, don't you? Women these days have to deal with too many intimidating physical role models as it is, what with those bimbos in the ads. Can't you make her, well, more average?

—There was once a girl who was a little overweight and whose front teeth stuck out, who—

—I don't think it's nice to make fun of people's appearances. Plus you're encouraging anorexia.

—I wasn't making fun! I was just describing—

—Skip the description. Description oppresses. But you can say what color she was.

—What color?

—You know. Black, white, red, brown, yellow. Those are the choices. And I'm telling you right now, I've had enough of white. Dominant culture this, dominant culture that—

—I don't know what color.

—Well, it would probably be *your* color, wouldn't it?

—But this isn't *about* me! It's about this girl—

—Everything is about you.

—Sounds to me like you don't want to hear this story at all.

—Oh well, go on. You could make her ethnic. That might help.

—There was once a girl of indeterminate descent, as average-looking as she was good, who lived with her wicked—

—Another thing. *Good* and *wicked*. Don't you think you should transcend those puritanical judgmental moralistic epithets? I mean, so much of that is conditioning, isn't it?

—There was once a girl, as average-looking as she was well-adjusted, who lived with her stepmother, who was not a very open and loving person because she herself had been abused in childhood.

—Better. But I am so *tired* of negative female images! And stepmothers— they always get it in the neck! Change it to step*father*, why don't you? That would make more sense anyway, considering the bad behavior you're about to describe. And throw in some whips and chains. We all know what those twisted, repressed, middle-aged men are like—

—*Hey, just a minute!* I'm *a middle-aged*—

—Stuff it Mister Nosy Parker. Nobody asked you to stick in your oar,[1] or whatever you want to call that thing. This is between the two of us. Go on.

—There was once a girl—

—How old was she?

—I don't know. She was young.

—This ends with a marriage, right?

1. I.e., to interfere in someone else's affairs.

—Well, not to blow the plot, but—yes.

—Then you can scratch the condescending paternalistic terminology. It's *woman*, pal. *Woman.*

—There was once—

—What's this *was, once?* Enough of the dead past. Tell me about *now.*

—There—

—So?

—So, what?

—So, why not *here?*

1992

The Little Red Hen Tells All

Everyone wants in on it. Everyone! Not just the cat, the pig and the dog. The horse too, the cow, the rhinoceros, the orangutang, the horned toad, the wombat, the duck-billed platypus, you name it. There's no peace any more and all because of that goddamn loaf of bread.

It's not easy, being a hen.

You know my story. Probably you had it told to you as a shining example of how you yourself ought to behave. Sobriety and elbow grease. Do it yourself. Then invest your capital. Then collect. I'm supposed to be an illustration of *that?* Don't make me laugh.

I found the grain of wheat, true. So what? There are lots of grains of wheat lying around. Keep your eyes to the grindstone and you could find a grain of wheat, too. I saw one and picked it up. Nothing wrong with that. Finders keepers. A grain of wheat saved is a grain of wheat earned. Opportunity is bald behind.[1]

Who will help me plant this grain of wheat? I said. *Who? Who?* I felt like a goddamn owl.

Not me, not me, they replied. *Then I'll do it myself,* I said, as the nun quipped to the vibrator. Nobody was listening, of course. They'd all gone to the beach.

Don't think it didn't hurt, all that rejection. Brooding in my nest of straw, I cried little red hen tears. Tears of chicken blood. You know what that looks like, you've eaten enough of it. Makes good gravy.

So, what were my options? I could have eaten that grain of wheat right away. Done myself a nutritional favor. But instead I planted it. Watered it. Stood guard over it night and day with my little feathered body.

So it grew. Why not? So it made more grains of wheat. So I planted those. So I watered those. So I ground them into flour. So I finally got enough for a loaf of bread. So I baked it. You've seen the pictures, me in my little red hen

1. These are incomplete or slightly altered clichés: "Keep your nose to the grindstone"; "Finders keepers, losers weepers"; and "A penny saved is a penny earned." However, "Opportunity is bald behind" accurately quotes from a distich of Cato (c. 175 B.C.).

apron, holding the loaf with its plume of aroma in between the tips of my wings, smiling away. I smile in all the pictures, as much as you can smile, with a beak. Whenever they said *Not me,* I smiled. I never lost my temper.

Who will help me eat this loaf of bread? I said. *I will,* said the cat, the dog and the pig. *I will,* said the antelope. *I will,* said the yak. *I will,* said the five-lined skink. *I will,* said the pubic louse. They meant it, too. They held out their paws, hooves, tongues, claws, mandibles, prehensile tails. They drooled at me with their eyes. They whined. They shoved petitions through my mail slot. They became depressed. They accused me of selfishness. They developed symptoms. They threatened suicide. They said it was my fault, for having a loaf of bread when they had none. Every single one of them, it seemed, needed that godcamn loaf of bread more than I did.

You can bake more, they said.

So then what? I know what the story says, what I'm supposed to have said: *I'll eat it myself, so kiss off.* Don't believe a word of it. As I've pointed out, I'm a hen, not a rooster.

Here, I said. *I apologize for having the idea in the first place. I apologize for luck. I apologize for self-denial. I apologize for being a good cook. I apologize for that crack about nuns. I apologize for that crack about roosters. I apologize for smiling, in my smug hen apron, with my smug hen beak. I apologize for being a hen.*

Have some more.

Have mine.

<div align="right">1992</div>

ANGELA CARTER

1940–1992

Angela Carter claimed "witch blood on her father's side; solid radical trade-unionists on mother's." In the essays she published in many British magazines and in book form, she wrote with fierce irreverence about such diverse subjects as the eighteenth-century French pornographer the Marquis de Sade and contemporary movie stars. A self-proclaimed leftist in politics, she was born Angela Stalker in London and attended the University of Bristol, from which she graduated in 1965. Married for twelve years, Carter published her first novel at the age of twenty-six. It was quickly followed by such children's books as *The Magic Toyshop* (1967), *Miss Z, The Dark Young Lady* (1970) and *The Donkey Prince* (1970), and by a number of adult novels, including *Love* (1971), *The Infernal Desire Machines of Doctor Hoffman* (1972), and *The Passion of New Eve* (1977). Before her untimely death, Carter turned to magical realism in *Nights at the Circus* (1984) and *Wise Children* (1992); her essays and journalism were collected in *Nothing Sacred* (1982). In *The Bloody Chamber* (1979), a book whose title refers to the Bluebeard story, Carter brought together her fascination with the dynamics of female desire and her work on children's literature, for in this collection the grim quality of many fairy tales is fully explored in surrealistic meditations on such traditional fantasies. The screenplay for the British film of *The Company of Wolves* was coauthored by Carter, and it testifies (along with the tale itself) to this author's fascination with issues revolving around domination and physical desire.

The Company of Wolves[1]

One beast and only one howls in the woods by night.

The wolf is carnivore incarnate and he's as cunning as he is ferocious; once he's had a taste of flesh, then nothing else will do.

At night, the eyes of wolves shine like candle flames, yellowish, reddish, but that is because the pupils of their eyes fatten on darkness and catch the light from your lantern to flash it back to you—red for danger; if a wolf's eyes reflect only moonlight, then they gleam a cold and unnatural green, a mineral, a piercing color. If the benighted traveler spies those luminous, terrible sequins stitched suddenly on the black thickets, then he knows he must run, if fear has not struck him stock-still.

But those eyes are all you will be able to glimpse of the forest assassins as they cluster invisibly round your smell of meat as you go through the wood unwisely late. They will be like shadows, they will be like wraiths, gray members of a congregation of nightmare. Hark! his long, wavering howl . . . an aria of fear made audible.

The wolfsong is the sound of the rending you will suffer, in itself a murdering.

It is winter and cold weather. In this region of mountain and forest, there is now nothing for the wolves to eat. Goats and sheep are locked up in the byre,[2] the deer departed for the remaining pasturage on the southern slopes— wolves grow lean and famished. There is so little flesh on them that you could count the starveling ribs through their pelts, if they gave you time before they pounced. Those slavering jaws; the lolling tongue; the rime[3] of saliva on the grizzled chops—of all the teeming perils of the night and the forest, ghosts, hobgoblins, ogres that grill babies upon gridirons, witches that fatten their captives in cages for cannibal tables, the wolf is worst, for he cannot listen to reason.

You are always in danger in the forest, where no people are. Step between the portals of the great pines where the shaggy branches tangle about you, trapping the unwary traveler in nets as if the vegetation itself were in a plot with the wolves who live there, as though the wicked trees go fishing on behalf of their friends—step between the gateposts of the forest with the greatest trepidation and infinite precautions, for if you stray from the path for one instant, the wolves will eat you. They are gray as famine, they are as unkind as plague.

The grave-eyed children of the sparse villages always carry knives with them when they go out to tend the little flocks of goats that provide the homesteads with acrid milk and rank, maggoty cheeses. Their knives are half as big as they are; the blades are sharpened daily.

But the wolves have ways of arriving at your own hearthside. We try and try but sometimes we cannot keep them out. There is no winter's night the cottager does not fear to see a lean, gray, famished snout questing under the door, and there was a woman once bitten in her own kitchen as she was straining the macaroni.

Fear and flee the wolf; for worst of all, the wolf may be more than he seems.

1. The story is based on the children's folk tale *Little Red Riding Hood*, in which a young girl goes through the woods to visit her grandmother and meets a wolf, who rushes ahead and eats the grandmother, then tries to pass himself off as the old woman so as to eat Little Red Riding Hood. A passing woodsman rescues the girl.
2. Barn.
3. Coating of frost.

There was a hunter once, near here, that trapped a wolf in a pit. This wolf had massacred the sheep and goats; eaten up a mad old man who used to live by himself in a hut halfway up the mountain and sing to Jesus all day; pounced on a girl looking after the sheep, but she made such a commotion that men came with rifles and scared him away and tried to track him into the forest but he was cunning and easily gave them the slip. So this hunter dug a pit and put a duck in it, for bait, all alive-oh; and he covered the pit with straw smeared with wolf dung. Quack, quack! went the duck and a wolf came slinking out of the forest, a big one, a heavy one, he weighed as much as a grown man and the straw gave way beneath him—into the pit he tumbled. The hunter jumped down after him, slit his throat, cut off all his paws for a trophy.

And then no wolf at all lay in front of the hunter but the bloody trunk of a man, headless, footless, dying, dead.

A witch from up the valley once turned an entire wedding party into wolves because the groom had settled on another girl. She used to order them to visit her, at night, from spite, and they would sit and howl around her cottage for her, serenading her with their misery.

Not so very long ago, a young woman in our village married a man who vanished clean away on her wedding night. The bed was made with new sheets and the bride lay down in it; the groom said he was going out to relieve himself, insisted on it, for the sake of decency, and she drew the coverlet up to her chin and she lay there. And she waited and she waited and then she waited again—surely he's been gone a long time? Until she jumps up in bed and shrieks to hear a howling, coming on the wind from the forest.

That long-drawn, wavering howl has, for all its fearful resonance, some inherent sadness in it, as if the beasts would love to be less beastly if only they knew how and never cease to mourn their own condition. There is a vast melancholy in the canticles[4] of the wolves, melancholy infinite as the forest, endless as these long nights of winter and yet that ghastly sadness, that mourning for their own, irremediable appetites, can never move the heart, for not one phrase in it hints at the possibility of redemption; grace could not come to the wolf from its own despair, only through some external mediator, so that, sometimes, the beast will look as if he half welcomes the knife that dispatches him.

The young woman's brothers searched the outhouses and the haystacks but never found any remains, so the sensible girl dried her eyes and found herself another husband, not too shy to piss into a pot, who spent the nights indoors. She gave him a pair of bonny babies and all went right as a trivet until, one freezing night, the night of the solstice, the hinge of the year when things do not fit together as well as they should, the longest night, her first good man came home again.

A great thump on the door announced him as she was stirring the soup for the father of her children and she knew him the moment she lifted the latch to him although it was years since she'd worn black for him and now he was in rags and his hair hung down his back and never saw a comb, alive with lice.

"Here I am again, missis," he said. "Get me my bowl of cabbage and be quick about it."

Then her second husband came in with wood for the fire and when the first

4. Songs, especially hymns.

one saw she'd slept with another man and, worse, clapped his red eyes on her little children, who'd crept into the kitchen to see what all the din was about, he shouted: "I wish I were a wolf again, to teach this whore a lesson!" So a wolf he instantly became and tore off the eldest boy's left foot before he was chopped up with the hatchet they used for chopping logs. But when the wolf lay bleeding and gasping its last, the pelt peeled off again and he was just as he had been, years ago, when he ran away from his marriage bed, so that she wept and her second husband beat her.

They say there's an ointment the Devil gives you that turns you into a wolf the minute you rub it on. Or that he was born feet first and had a wolf for his father and his torso is a man's but his legs and genitals are a wolf's. And he has a wolf's heart.

Seven years is a werewolf's natural span, but if you burn his human clothing you condemn him to wolfishness for the rest of his life, so old wives here-abouts think it some protection to throw a hat or an apron at the werewolf, as if clothes made the man. Yet by the eyes, those phosphorescent eyes, you know him in all his shapes; the eyes alone unchanged by metamorphosis.

Before he can become a wolf, the lycanthrope[5] strips stark naked. If you spy a naked man among the pines, you must run as if the Devil were after you.

It is midwinter and the robin, the friend of man, sits on the handle of the gardener's spade and sings. It is the worst time in all the year for wolves, but this strong-minded child insists she will go off through the wood. She is quite sure the wild beasts cannot harm her although, well-warned, she lays a carving knife in the basket her mother has packed with cheeses. There is a bottle of harsh liquor distilled from brambles; a batch of flat oat cakes baked on the hearthstone; a pot or two of jam. The flaxen-haired girl will take these deli-cious gifts to a reclusive grandmother so old the burden of her years is crush-ing her to death. Granny lives two hours' trudge through the winter woods; the child wraps herself up in her thick shawl, draws it over her head. She steps into her stout wooden shoes; she is dressed and ready and it is Christmas Eve. The malign door of the solstice still swings upon its hinges, but she has been too much loved ever to feel scared.

Children do not stay young for long in this savage country. There are no toys for them to play with, so they work hard and grow wise, but this one, so pretty and the youngest of her family, a little latecomer, had been indulged by her mother and the grandmother who'd knitted her the red shawl that, today, has the ominous if brilliant look of blood on snow. Her breasts have just begun to swell; her hair is like lint, so fair it hardly makes a shadow on her pale forehead; her cheeks are an emblematic scarlet and white and she has just started her woman's bleeding, the clock inside her that will strike, henceforward, once a month.

She stands and moves within the invisible pentacle[6] of her own virginity. She is an unbroken egg; she is a sealed vessel; she has inside her a magic space the entrance to which is shut tight with a plug of membrane; she is a closed system; she does not know how to shiver. She has her knife and she is afraid of nothing.

5. Werewolf. 6. Five-pointed star, an occult symbol.

Her father might forbid her, if he were home, but he is away in the forest, gathering wood, and her mother cannot deny her.

The forest closed upon her like a pair of jaws

There is always something to look at in the forest, even in the middle of winter—the huddled mounds of birds, succumbed to the lethargy of the season, heaped on the creaking boughs and too forlorn to sing; the bright frills of the winter fungi on the blotched trunks of the trees; the cuneiform[7] slots of rabbits and deer, the herringbone tracks of the birds, a hare as lean as a rasher of bacon streaking across the path where the thin sunlight dapples the russet brakes of last year's bracken.

When she heard the freezing howl of a distant wolf, her practiced hand sprang to the handle of her knife, but she saw no sign of a wolf at all, nor of a naked man, neither, but then she heard a clattering among the brushwood and there sprang onto the path a fully clothed one, a very handsome young one, in the green coat and wide-awake hat of a hunter, laden with carcasses of game birds. She had her hand on her knife at the first rustle of twigs, but he laughed with a flash of white teeth when he saw her and made her a comic yet flattering little bow; she'd never seen such a fine fellow before, not among the rustic clowns[8] of her native village. So on they went together, through the thickening light of the afternoon.

Soon they were laughing and joking like old friends. When he offered to carry her basket, she gave it to him although her knife was in it because he told her his rifle would protect them. As the day darkened, it began to snow again; she felt the first flakes settle on her eyelashes, but now there was only half a mile to go and there would be a fire, and hot tea, and a welcome, a warm one, surely, for the dashing huntsman as well as for herself.

This young man had a remarkable object in his pocket. It was a compass. She looked at the little round glass face in the palm of his hand and watched the wavering needle with a vague wonder. He assured her this compass had taken him safely through the wood on his hunting trip because the needle always told him with perfect accuracy where the north was. She did not believe it; she knew she should never leave the path or the way through the wood or else she would be lost instantly. He laughed at her again; gleaming trails of spittle clung to his teeth. He said if he plunged off the path into the forest that surrounded them, he could guarantee to arrive at her grandmother's house a good quarter of an hour before she did, plotting his way through the undergrowth with his compass, while she trudged the long way, along the winding path.

I don't believe you. Besides, aren't you afraid of the wolves?

He only tapped the gleaming butt of his rifle and grinned

Is it a bet? he asked her. Shall we make a game of it? What will you give me if I get to your grandmother's house before you?

What would you like? she asked disingenuously.

A kiss.

Commonplaces of a rustic seduction: she lowered her eyes and blushed.

He went through the undergrowth and took her basket with him, but she forgot to be afraid of the beasts, although now the moon was rising, for she

7. Wedge shaped, like ancient Babylonian and Assyrian writing.

8. Here, country folk.

wanted to dawdle on her way to make sure the handsome gentleman would win his wager.

Grandmother's house stood by itself a little way out of the village. The freshly falling snow blew in eddies about the kitchen garden and the young man stepped delicately up the snowy path to the door as if he were reluctant to get his feet wet, swinging his bundle of game and the girl's basket and humming a little tune to himself.

There is a faint trace of blood on his chin; he has been snacking on his catch.

He rapped upon the panels with his knuckles.

Aged and frail, granny is three-quarters succumbed to the mortality the ache in her bones promises her and almost ready to give in entirely. A boy came out from the village to build up her hearth for the night an hour ago and the kitchen crackles with busy firelight. She has her Bible for company; she is a pious old woman. She is propped up on several pillows in the bed set into the wall peasant fashion, wrapped up in the patchwork quilt she made before she was married, more years ago than she cares to remember. Two china spaniels with liver-colored blotches on their coats and black noses sit on either side of the fireplace. There is a bright rug of woven rags on the pantiles. The grandfather clock ticks away her eroding time.

We keep the wolves outside by living well.

He rapped upon the panels with his hairy knuckles.

It is your granddaughter, he mimicked in a high soprano.

Lift up the latch and walk in, my darling.

You can tell them by their eyes, eyes of a beast of prey, nocturnal, devastating eyes as red as a wound; you can hurl your Bible at him and your apron after, granny; you thought that was a sure prophylactic against these infernal vermin. . . . Now call on Christ and his mother and all the angels in heaven to protect you, but it won't do you any good.

His feral muzzle is sharp as a knife; he drops his golden burden of gnawed pheasant on the table and puts down your dear girl's basket, too. Oh, my God, what have you done with her?

Off with his disguise, that coat of forest-colored cloth, the hat with the feather tucked into the ribbon; his matted hair streams down his white shirt and she can see the lice moving in it. The sticks in the hearth shift and hiss; night and the forest has come into the kitchen with darkness tangled in its hair.

He strips off his shirt. His skin is the color and texture of vellum. A crisp stripe of hair runs down his belly, his nipples are ripe and dark as poison fruit, but he's so thin you could count the ribs under his skin if only he gave you the time. He strip off his trousers and she can see how hairy his legs are. His genitals, huge. Ah! huge.

The last thing the old lady saw in all this world was a young man, eyes like cinders, naked as a stone, approaching her bed.

The wolf is carnivore incarnate.

When he had finished with her, he licked his chops and quickly dressed himself again, until he was just as he had been when he came through her door. He burned the inedible hair in the fireplace and wrapped the bones up in a napkin that he hid away under the bed in the wooden chest in which he found a clean pair of sheets. These he carefully put on the bed instead of the

telltale stained ones he stowed away in the laundry basket. He plumped up the pillows and shook out the patchwork quilt, he picked up the Bible from the floor, closed it and laid it on the table. All was as it had been before except that grandmother was gone. The sticks twitched in the grate, the clock ticked and the young man sat patiently, deceitfully beside the bed in granny's nightcap.

Rat-a-tap-tap.

Who's there, he quavers in granny's antique falsetto.

Only your granddaughter.

So she came in, bringing with her a flurry of snow that melted in tears on the tiles, and perhaps she was a little disappointed to see only her grandmother sitting beside the fire. But then he flung off the blanket and sprang to the door, pressing his back against it so that she could not get out again.

The girl looked round the room and saw there was not even the indentation of a head on the smooth cheek of the pillow and how, for the first time she'd seen it so, the Bible lay closed on the table. The tick of the clock cracked like a whip. She wanted her knife from her basket but she did not dare reach for it because his eyes were fixed upon her—huge eyes that now seemed to shine with a unique, interior light, eyes the size of saucers, saucers full of Greek fire,[9] diabolic phosphorescence.

What big eyes you have.

All the better to see you with.

No trace at all of the old woman except for a tuft of white hair that had caught in the bark of an unburned log. When the girl saw that, she knew she was in danger of death.

Where is my grandmother?

There's nobody here but we two, my darling.

Now a great howling rose up all around them, near, very near, as close as the kitchen garden, the howling of a multitude of wolves; she knew the worst wolves are hairy on the inside and she shivered, in spite of the scarlet shawl she pulled more closely round herself as if it could protect her, although it was as red as the blood she must spill.

Who has come to sing us carols? she said.

Those are the voices of my brothers, darling; I love the company of wolves. Look out of the window and you'll see them.

Snow half-caked the lattice and she opened it to look into the garden. It was a white night of moon and snow; the blizzard whirled round the gaunt, gray beasts who squatted on their haunches among the rows of winter cabbage, pointing their sharp snouts to the moon and howling as if their hearts would break. Ten wolves; twenty wolves—so many wolves she could not count them, howling in concert as if demented or deranged. Their eyes reflected the light from the kitchen and shone like a hundred candles.

It is very cold, poor things, she said; no wonder they howl so.

She closed the window on the wolves' threnody[1] and took off her scarlet shawl, the color of poppies, the color of sacrifices, the color of her menses, and since her fear did her no good, she ceased to be afraid.

What shall I do with my shawl?

Throw it on the fire, dear one. You won't need it again.

She bundled up her shawl and threw it on the blaze, which instantly con-

9. Flammable mixture that burns on wetting. 1 Song of lamentation for the dead.

sumed it. Then she drew her blouse over her head; her small breasts gleamed as if the snow had invaded the room.

What shall I do with my blouse?

Into the fire with it, too, my pet.

The thin muslin went flaring up the chimney like a magic bird and now off came her skirt, her woolen stockings, her shoes, and onto the fire they went, too, and were gone for good. The firelight shone through the edges of her skin; now she was clothed only in her untouched integument of flesh. Thus dazzling, naked, she combed out her hair with her fingers; her hair looked white as the snow outside. Then went directly to the man with red eyes in whose unkempt mane the lice moved; she stood up on tiptoe and unbottoned the collar of his shirt.

What big arms you have.

All the better to hug you with.

Every wolf in the world now howled a prothalamion[2] outside the window as she freely gave the kiss she owed him.

What big teeth you have!

She saw how his jaw began to slaver and the room was full of the clamor of the forest's *Liebestod*,[3] but the wise child never flinched, even when he answered:

All the better to eat you with.

The girl burst out laughing; she knew she was nobody's meat. She laughed at him full in the face, she ripped off his shirt for him and flung it into the fire, in the fiery wake of her own discarded clothing. The flames danced like dead souls on Walpurgisnacht[4] and the old bones under the bed set up a terrible clattering, but she did not pay them any heed.

Carnivore incarnate, only immaculate flesh appeases him.

She will lay his fearful head on her lap and she will pick out the lice from his pelt and perhaps she will put the lice into her mouth and eat them, as he will bid her, as she would do in a savage marriage ceremony.

The blizzard will die down.

The blizzard died down, leaving the mountains as randomly covered with snow as if a blind woman had thrown a sheet over them, the upper branches of the forest pines limed, creaking, swollen with the fall.

Snowlight, moonlight, a confusion of pawprints.

All silent, all still.

Midnight; and the clock strikes. It is Christmas Day, the werewolves' birthday; the door of the solstice stands wide open; let them all sink through.

See! Sweet and sound she sleeps in granny's bed, between the paws of the tender wolf.

 1979

2. Song before marriage.
3. Love-death (German); applied to the closing scene of Richard Wagner's opera *Tristan and Isolde* (1865),

in which Isolde joyfully dies to join her lover, Tristan.
4. Witches' celebration.

MAXINE HONG KINGSTON

1940–

The daughter of Chinese immigrants who operated a laundry in Stockton, California, Maxine Hong Kingston recorded the mysteries and marvels of "a girl-hood among ghosts" in *The Woman Warrior* (1975), a book that combines auto-biography and fiction to counterpoint memories of a Chinese-American childhood with fantasies about Chinese history and culture. Educated at the University of California, Berkeley, Kingston married the actor Earll Kingston in 1962, and in 1967 she settled in Honolulu with him and their son, Joseph. There she taught English at the Mid-Pacific Institute, a private high school, and at the University of Hawaii, while continuing to explore the dynamics of Chinese-American society in *China Men* (1980), a reconstruction of her grandfather's and her father's pilgrimages to America, the "Gold Mountain" of Chinese legend. More recently, she has returned to Berkeley, where she teaches at the University of California and has published a novel, *Tribmaster Monkey: His Fake Book* (1989).

The "ghosts" who haunted Kingston's girlhood are both the alien Caucasian-Americans with whom she went to school and the mystifying Asian ancestors whose stories her mother told her—often, in particular, damned or glamorous fe-male characters like "No Name Woman" and the "Woman Warrior." No doubt be-cause this artist has so brilliantly illuminated the intricate processes by which "femininity" is constructed in a culture different from our own, the novelist Kay Boyle has written with delight that *The Woman Warrior* is "a woman's book that has the vitality to take one far, . . . from the domestic grievances of American sub-urbia, . . . into the wit, and the love, and grief of another place entirely."

No Name Woman

"You must not tell anyone," my mother said, "what I am about to tell you. In China your father had a sister who killed herself. She jumped into the fam-ily well. We say that your father has all brothers because it is as if she had never been born.

"In 1924 just a few days after our village celebrated seventeen hurry-up weddings—to make sure that every young man who went 'out on the road' would responsibly come home—your father and his brothers and your grand-father and his brothers and your aunt's new husband sailed for America, the Gold Mountain. It was your grandfather's last trip. Those lucky enough to get contracts waved good-bye from the decks. They fed and guarded the stow-aways and helped them off in Cuba, New York, Bali, Hawaii. 'We'll meet in California next year,' they said. All of them sent money home.

"I remember looking at your aunt one day when she and I were dressing; I had not noticed before that she had such a protruding melon of a stomach. But I did not think, 'She's pregnant,' until she began to look like other preg-nant women, her shirt pulling and the white tops of her black pants showing. She could not have been pregnant, you see, because her husband had been gone for years. No one said anything. We did not discuss it. In early summer she was ready to have the child, long after the time when it could have been possible.

"The village had also been counting. On the night the baby was to be born the villagers raided our house. Some were crying. Like a great saw, teeth strung with lights, files of people walked zigzag across our land, tearing the rice. Their lanterns doubled in the disturbed black water, which drained away through the broken bunds.[1] As the villagers closed in, we could see that some of them, probably men and women we knew well, wore white masks. The people with long hair hung it over their faces. Women with short hair made it stand up on end. Some had tied white bands around their foreheads, arms, and legs.

"At first they threw mud and rocks at the house. Then they threw eggs and began slaughtering our stock. We could hear the animals scream their deaths—the roosters, the pigs, a last great roar from the ox. Familiar wild heads flared in our night windows; the villagers encircled us. Some of the faces stopped to peer at us, their eyes rushing like searchlights. The hands flattened against the panes, framed heads, and left red prints.

"The villagers broke in the front and the back doors at the same time, even though we had not locked the doors against them. Their knives dripped with the blood of our animals. They smeared blood on the doors and walls. One woman swung a chicken, whose throat she had slit, splattering blood in red arcs about her. We stood together in the middle of our house, in the family hall with the pictures and tables of the ancestors around us, and looked straight ahead.

"At that time the house had only two wings. When the men came back, we would build two more to enclose our courtyard and a third one to begin a second courtyard. The villagers pushed through both wings, even your grandparents' rooms, to find your aunt's, which was also mine until the men returned. From this room a new wing for one of the younger families would grow. They ripped up her clothes and shoes and broke her combs, grinding them underfoot. They tore her work from the loom. They scattered the cooking fire and rolled the new weaving in it. We could hear them in the kitchen breaking our bowls and banging the pots. They overturned the great waist-high earthenware jugs; duck eggs, pickled fruits, vegetables burst out and mixed in acrid torrents. The old woman from the next field swept a broom through the air and loosed the spirits-of-the-broom over our heads. 'Pig.' 'Ghost.' 'Pig,' they sobbed and scolded while they ruined our house.

"When they left, they took sugar and oranges to bless themselves. They cut pieces from the dead animals. Some of them took bowls that were not broken and clothes that were not torn. Afterward we swept up the rice and sewed it back up into sacks. But the smells from the spilled preserves lasted. Your aunt gave birth in the pigsty that night. The next morning when I went for the water, I found her and the baby plugging up the family well.

"Don't let your father know that I told you. He denies her. Now that you have started to menstruate, what happened to her could happen to you. Don't humiliate us. You wouldn't like to be forgotten as if you had never been born. The villagers are watchful."

Whenever she had to warn us about life, my mother told stories that ran like this one, a story to grow up on. She tested our strength to establish realities. Those in the emigrant generations who could not reassert brute survival died young and far from home. Those of us in the first American generations

1. Embankments.

have had to figure out how the invisible world the emigrants built around our childhoods fit in solid America.

The emigrants confused the gods by diverting their curses, misleading them with crooked streets and false names. They must try to confuse their offspring as well, who, I suppose, threaten them in similar ways—always trying to get things straight, always trying to name the unspeakable. The Chinese I know hide their names; sojourners take new names when their lives change and guard their real names with silence.

Chinese-Americans, when you try to understand what things in you are Chinese, how do you separate what is peculiar to childhood, to poverty, insanities, one family, your mother who marked your growing with stories, from what is Chinese? What is Chinese tradition and what is the movies?

If I want to learn what clothes my aunt wore, whether flashy or ordinary, I would have to begin, "Remember Father's drowned-in-the-well sister?" I cannot ask that. My mother has told me once and for all the useful parts. She will add nothing unless powered by Necessity, a riverbank that guides her life. She plants vegetable gardens rather than lawns; she carries the odd-shaped tomatoes home from the fields and eats food left for the gods.

Whenever we did frivolous things, we used up energy; we flew high kites. We children came up off the ground over the melting cones our parents brought home from work and the American movie on New Year's Day—*Oh, You Beautiful Doll* with Betty Grable one year, and *She Wore a Yellow Ribbon* with John Wayne another year. After the one carnival ride each, we paid in guilt; our tired father counted his change on the dark walk home.

Adultery is extravagance. Could people who hatch their own chicks and eat the embryos and the heads for delicacies and boil the feet in vinegar for party food, leaving only the gravel, eating even the gizzard lining—could such people engender a prodigal aunt? To be a woman, to have a daughter in starvation time was a waste enough. My aunt could not have been the lone romantic who gave up everything for sex. Women in the old China did not choose. Some man had commanded her to lie with him and be his secret evil. I wonder whether he masked himself when he joined the raid of her family.

Perhaps she encountered him in the fields or on the mountain where the daughters-in-law collected fuel. Or perhaps he first noticed her in the marketplace. He was not a stranger because the village housed no strangers. She had to have dealings with him other than sex. Perhaps he worked an adjoining field, or he sold her the cloth for the dress she sewed and wore. His demand must have surprised, then terrified her. She obeyed him; she always did as she was told.

When the family found a young man in the next village to be her husband, she stood tractably beside the best rooster, his proxy, and promised before they met that she would be his forever. She was lucky that he was her age and she would be the first wife, an advantage secure now. The night she first saw him, he had sex with her. Then he left for America. She had almost forgotten what he looked like. When she tried to envision him, she only saw the black and white face in the group photograph the men had had taken before leaving.

The other man was not, after all, much different from her husband. They both gave orders: she followed. "If you tell your family, I'll beat you. I'll kill you. Be here again next week." No one talked sex, ever. And she might have separated the rapes from the rest of living if only she did not have to buy her

oil from him or gather wood in the same forest. I want her fear to have lasted just as long as rape lasted so that the fear could have been contained. No drawn-out fear. But women at sex hazarded birth and hence lifetimes. The fear did not stop but permeated everywhere. She told the man, "I think I'm pregnant." He organized the raid against her.

On nights when my mother and father talked about their life back home, sometimes they mentioned an "outcast table" whose business they still seemed to be settling, their voices tight. In a commensal[2] tradition, where food is precious, the powerful older people made wrongdoers eat alone. Instead of letting them start separate new lives like the Japanese, who could become samurais and geishas, the Chinese family, faces averted but eyes glowering sideways, hung on to the offenders and fed them leftovers. My aunt must have lived in the same house as my parents and eaten at an outcast table. My mother spoke about the raid as if she had seen it, when she and my aunt, a daughter-in-law to a different household, should not have been living together at all. Daughters-in-law lived with their husbands' parents, not their own; a synonym for marriage in Chinese is "taking a daughter-in-law." Her husband's parents could have sold her, mortgaged her, stoned her. But they had sent her back to her own mother and father, a mysterious act hinting at disgraces not told me. Perhaps they had thrown her out to deflect the avengers.

She was the only daughter; her four brothers went with her father, husband, and uncles "out on the road" and for some years became western men. When the goods were divided among the family, three of the brothers took land, and the youngest, my father, chose an education. After my grandparents gave their daughter away to her husband's family, they had dispensed all the adventure and all the property. They expected her alone to keep the traditional ways, which her brothers, now among the barbarians, could fumble without detection. The heavy, deep-rooted women were to maintain the past against the flood, safe for returning. But the rare urge west had fixed upon our family, and so my aunt crossed boundaries not delineated in space.

The work of preservation demands that the feelings playing about in one's guts not be turned into action. Just watch their passing like cherry blossoms. But perhaps my aunt, my forerunner, caught in a slow life, let dreams grow and fade and after some months or years went toward what persisted. Fear at the enormities of the forbidden kept her desires delicate, wire and bone. She looked at a man because she liked the way the hair was tucked behind his ears, or she liked the question-mark line of a long torso curving at the shoulder and straight at the hip. For warm eyes or a soft voice or a slow walk—that's all—a few hairs, a line, a brightness, a sound, a pace, she gave up family. She offered us up for a charm that vanished with tiredness, a pigtail that didn't toss when the wind died. Why, the wrong lighting could erase the dearest thing about him.

It could very well have been, however, that my aunt did not take subtle enjoyment of her friend, but, a wild woman, kept rollicking company. Imagining her free with sex doesn't fit, though. I don't know any women like that, or men either. Unless I see her life branching into mine, she gives me no ancestral help.

2. Eating together, at the same table.

To sustain her being in love, she often worked at herself in the mirror, guessing at the colors and shapes that would interest him, changing them frequently in order to hit on the right combination. She wanted him to look back.

On a farm near the sea, a woman who tended her appearance reaped a reputation for eccentricity. All the married women blunt-cut their hair in flaps about their ears or pulled it back in tight buns. No nonsense. Neither style blew easily into heart-catching tangles. And at their weddings they displayed themselves in their long hair for the last time. "It brushed the backs of my knees," my mother tells me. "It was braided, and even so, it brushed the backs of my knees."

At the mirror my aunt combed individuality into her bob. A bun could have been contrived to escape into black streamers blowing in the wind or in quiet wisps about her face, but only the older women in our picture album wear buns. She brushed her hair back from her forehead, tucking the flaps behind her ears. She looped a piece of thread, knotted into a circle between her index fingers and thumbs, and ran the double strand across her forehead. When she closed her fingers as if she were making a pair of shadow geese bite, the string twisted together catching the little hairs. Then she pulled the thread away from her skin, ripping the hairs out neatly, her eyes watering from the needles of pain. Opening her fingers, she cleaned the thread, then rolled it along her hairline and the tops of her eyebrows. My mother did the same to me and my sisters and herself. I used to believe that the expression "caught by the short hairs" meant a captive held with a depilatory string. It especially hurt at the temples, but my mother said we were lucky we didn't have to have our feet bound when we were seven. Sisters used to sit on their beds and cry together, she said, as their mothers or their slaves removed the bandages for a few minutes each night and let the blood gush back into their veins. I hope that the man my aunt loved appreciated a smooth brow, that he wasn't just a tits-and-ass man.

Once my aunt found a freckle on her chin, at a spot that the almanac said predestined her for unhappiness. She dug it out with a hot needle and washed the wound with peroxide.

More attention to her looks than these pullings of hairs and pickings at spots would have caused gossip among the villagers. They owned work clothes and good clothes, and they wore good clothes for feasting the new seasons. But since a woman combing her hair hexes beginnings, my aunt rarely found an occasion to look her best. Women looked like great sea snails—the corded wood, babies, and laundry they carried were the whorls on their backs. The Chinese did not admire a bent back; goddesses and warriors stood straight. Still there must have been a marvelous freeing of beauty when a worker laid down her burden and stretched and arched.

Such commonplace loveliness, however, was not enough for my aunt. She dreamed of a lover for the fifteen days of New Year's, the time for families to exchange visits, money, and food. She plied her secret comb. And sure enough she cursed the year, the family, the village, and herself.

Even as her hair lured her imminent lover, many other men looked at her. Uncles, cousins, nephews, brothers would have looked, too, had they been home between journeys. Perhaps they had already been restraining their curiosity, and they left, fearful that their glances, like a field of nesting birds,

might be startled and caught. Poverty hurt, and that was their first reason for leaving. But another, final reason for leaving the crowded house was the never-said.

She may have been unusually beloved, the precious only daughter, spoiled and mirror gazing because of the affection the family lavished on her. When her husband left, they welcomed the chance to take her back from the in-laws; she could live like the little daughter for just a while longer. There are stories that my grandfather was different from other people, "crazy ever since the little Jap bayoneted him in the head." He used to put his naked penis on the dinner table, laughing. And one day he brought home a baby girl, wrapped up inside his brown western-style greatcoat. He had traded one of his sons, probably my father, the youngest, for her. My grandmother made him trade back. When he finally got a daughter of his own, he doted on her. They must have all loved her, except perhaps my father, the only brother who never went back to China, having once been traded for a girl.

Brothers and sisters, newly men and women, had to efface their sexual color and present plain miens. Disturbing hair and eyes, a smile like no other threatened the ideal of five generations living under one roof. To focus blurs, people shouted face to face and yelled from room to room. The immigrants I know have loud voices, unmodulated to American tones even after years away from the village where they called their friendships out across the fields. I have not been able to stop my mother's screams in public libraries or over telephones. Walking erect (knees straight, toes pointed forward, not pigeon-toed, which is Chinese-feminine) and speaking in an inaudible voice, I have tried to turn myself American-feminine. Chinese communication was loud, public. Only sick people had to whisper. But at the dinner table, where the family members came nearest one another, no one could talk, not the outcasts nor any eaters. Every word that falls from the mouth is a coin lost. Silently they gave and accepted food with both hands. A preoccupied child who took his bowl with one hand got a sideways glare. A complete moment of total attention is due everyone alike. Children and lovers have no singularity here, but my aunt used a secret voice, a separate attentiveness.

She kept the man's name to herself throughout her labor and dying; she did not accuse him that he be punished with her. To save her inseminator's name she gave silent birth.

He may have been somebody in her own household, but intercourse with a man outside the family would have been no less abhorrent. All the village were kinsmen, and the titles shouted in loud country voices never let kinship be forgotten. Any man within visiting distance would have been neutralized as a lover—"brother," "younger brother, "older brother"—one hundred and fifteen relationship titles. Parents researched birth charts probably not so much to assure good fortune as to circumvent incest in a population that has but one hundred surnames. Everybody has eight million relatives. How useless then sexual mannerisms, how dangerous.

As if it came from an atavism deeper than fear, I used to add "brother" silently to boys' names. It hexed the boys who would or would not ask me to dance, and made them less scary and as familiar and deserving of benevolence as girls.

But, of course, I hexed myself also—no dates. I should have stood up, both arms waving, and shouted out across libraries, "Hey, you! Love me back." I had

no idea, though, how to make attraction selective, how to control its direction and magnitude. If I made myself American-pretty so that the five or six Chinese boys in the class fell in love with me, everyone else—the Caucasian, Negro, and Japanese boys—would too. Sisterliness, dignified and honorable, made much more sense.

Attraction eludes control so stubbornly that whole societies designed to organize relationships among people cannot keep order, not even when they bind people to one another from childhood and raise them together. Among the very poor and the wealthy, brothers married their adopted sisters, like doves. Our family allowed some romance, paying adult brides' prices and providing dowries so that their sons and daughters could marry strangers. Marriage promises to turn strangers into friendly relatives—a nation of siblings.

In the village structure, spirits shimmered among the live creatures, balanced and held in equilibrium by time and land. But one human being flaring up into violence could open up a black hole, a maelstrom that pulled in the sky. The frightened villagers, who depended on one another to maintain the real, went to my aunt to show her a personal, physical representation of the break she had made in the "roundness." Misallying couples snapped off the future, which was to be embodied in true offspring. The villagers punished her for acting as if she could have a private life, secret and apart from them.

If my aunt had betrayed the family at a time of large grain yields and peace, when many boys were born, and wings were being built on many houses, perhaps she might have escaped such severe punishment. But the men—hungry, greedy, tired of planting in dry soil, cuckolded—had had to leave the village in order to send food-money home. There were ghost plagues, bandit plagues, wars with the Japanese, floods. My Chinese brother and sister had died of an unknown sickness. Adultery, perhaps only a mistake during good times, became a crime when the village needed food.

The round moon cakes and round doorways, the round tables of graduated size that fit one roundness inside another, round windows and rice bowls—these talismen had lost their power to warn this family of the law: a family must be whole, faithfully keeping the descent line by having sons to feed the old and the dead, who in turn look after the family. The villagers came to show my aunt and her lover-in-hiding a broken house. The villagers were speeding up the circling of events because she was too shortsighted to see that her infidelity had already harmed the village, that waves of consequences would return unpredictably, sometimes in disguise, as now, to hurt her. This roundness had to be made coin-sized so that she would see its circumference: punish her at the birth of her baby. Awaken her to the inexorable. People who refused fatalism because they could invent small resources insisted on culpability. Deny accidents and wrest fault from the stars.

After the villagers left, their lanterns now scattering in various directions toward home, the family broke their silence and cursed her. "Aiaa, we're going to die. Death is coming. Death is coming. Look what you've done. You've killed us. Ghost! Dead ghost! Ghost! You've never been born." She ran out into the fields, far enough from the house so that she could no longer hear their voices, and pressed herself against the earth, her own land no more. When she felt the birth coming, she thought that she had been hurt. Her body seized together. "They've hurt me too much," she thought. "This is gall, and it will kill

me." Her forehead and knees against the earth, her body convulsed and then released her onto her back. The black well of sky and stars went out and out and out forever; her body and her complexity seemed to disappear. She was one of the stars, a bright dot in blackness, without home, without a companion, in eternal cold and silence. An agoraphobia rose in her, speeding higher and higher, bigger and bigger; she would not be able to contain it; there would be no end to fear.

Flayed, unprotected against space, she felt pain return, focusing her body. This pain chilled her—a cold, steady kind of surface pain. Inside, spasmodically, the other pain, the pain of the child, heated her. For hours she lay on the ground, alternately body and space. Sometimes a vision of nomal comfort obliterated reality: she saw the family in the evening gambling at the dinner table, the young people massaging their elders' backs. She saw them congratulating one another, high joy on the mornings the rice shoots came up. When these pictures burst, the stars drew yet further apart. Black space opened.

She got to her feet to fight better and remembered that old-fashioned women gave birth in their pigsties to fool the jealous, pain-dealing gods, who do not snatch piglets. Before the next spasms could stop her, she ran to the pigsty, each step a rushing out into emptiness. She climbed over the fence and knelt in the dirt. It was good to have a fence enclosing her, a tribal person alone.

Laboring, this woman who had carried her child as a foreign growth that sickened her every day, expelled it at last. She reached down to touch the hot, wet, moving mass, surely smaller than anything human, and could feel that it was human after all—fingers, toes, nails, nose. She pulled it up on to her belly, and it lay curled there, butt in the air, feet precisely tucked one under the other. She opened her loose shirt and buttoned the child inside. After resting, it squirmed and thrashed and she pushed it up to her breast. It turned its head this way and that until it found her nipple. There, it made little snuffling noises. She clenched her teeth at its preciousness, lovely as a young calf, a piglet, a little dog.

She may have gone to the pigsty as a last act of responsibility: she would protect this child as she had protected its father. It would look after her soul, leaving supplies on her grave. But how would this tiny child without family find her grave when there would be no marker for her anywhere, neither in the earth nor the family hall? No one would give her a family hall name. She had taken the child with her into the wastes. At its birth the two of them had felt the same raw pain of separation, a wound that only the family pressing tight could close. A child with no descent line would not soften her life but only trail after her, ghostlike, begging her to give it purpose. At dawn the villagers on their way to the fields would stand around the fence and look.

Full of milk, the little ghost slept. When it awoke, she hardened her breasts against the milk that crying loosens. Toward morning she picked up the baby and walked to the well.

Carrying the baby to the well shows loving. Otherwise abandon it. Turn its face into the mud. Mothers who love their children take them along. It was probably a girl; there is some hope of forgiveness for boys.

"Don't tell anyone you had an aunt. Your father does not want to hear her name. She has never been born." I have believed that sex was unspeakable and

words so strong and fathers so frail that "aunt" would do my father mysterious harm. I have thought that my family, having settled among immigrants who had also been their neighbors in the ancestral land, needed to clean their name, and a wrong word would incite the kinspeople even here. But there is more to this silence: they want me to participate in her punishment. And I have.

In the twenty years since I heard this story I have not asked for details nor said my aunt's name; I do not know it. People who can comfort the dead can also chase after them to hurt them further—a reverse ancestor worship. The real punishment was not the raid swiftly inflicted by the villagers, but the family's deliberately forgetting her. Her betrayal so maddened them, they saw to it that she would suffer forever, even after death. Always hungry, always needing, she would have to beg food from other ghosts, snatch and steal it from those whose living descendants give them gifts. She would have to fight the ghosts massed at crossroads for the buns a few thoughtful citizens leave to decoy her away from village and home so that the ancestral spirits could feast unharassed. At peace, they could act like gods, not ghosts, their descent lines providing them with paper suits and dresses, spirit money, paper houses, paper automobiles, chicken, meat, and rice into eternity[3]—essences delivered up in smoke and flames, steam and incense rising from each rice bowl. In an attempt to make the Chinese care for people outside the family, Chairman Mao[4] encourages us now to give our paper replicas to the spirits of outstanding soldiers and workers, no matter whose ancestors they may be. My aunt remains forever hungry. Goods are not distributed evenly among the dead.

My aunt haunts me—her ghost drawn to me because now, after fifty years of neglect, I alone devote pages of paper to her, though not origamied[5] into houses and clothes. I do not think she always means me well. I am telling on her, and she was a spite suicide, drowning herself in the drinking water. The Chinese are always very frightened of the drowned one, whose weeping ghost, wet hair hanging and skin bloated, waits silently by the water to pull down a substitute.

1976

3. According to Chinese custom, these objects are periodically left as offerings at the graves of dead ancestors.
4. Mao T'se-tung (1893–1976), leader of the Chinese

Communist Party and head of state from 1949 to 1959.
5. Origami is the Asian art of folding paper to produce sculptures of animals and other objects.

BOBBIE ANN MASON

1940–

Everyday details drawn from television, popular music, fast-food ads, and brand-name supermarket products; working-class characters; the cadences of rural Kentucky: these are what readers have come to expect from the fiction of Bobbie Ann Mason, narratives that teach us to confront the disparity between culture as it is defined in the canon or the curriculum and the popular culture in which most people live their lives. In her story collections, *Shiloh and Other Stories* (1982) and *Love Life: Stories* (1988), as in her novels, *In Country* (1985), *Spence and Lila* (1988), and *Feather Crowns* (1994), Mason has examined incongruous juxtaposi-

tions between events of historical magnitude (like the Vietnam War or the urban-ization of agrarian mid-America) and ordinary occurrences (like a trip to church or a card party). Partly, she has been coming to terms with her own origins, for she grew up on a farm near Mayfield, Kentucky, and graduated from the University of Kentucky before moving east to graduate school.

First at the State University of New York, Binghamton, and then at the University of Connecticut, Mason gained the distance she needed to write about her roots. Apprentice work of the 1970s included a guide to young women's novels and another to Nabokov's fiction as well as numerous stories sent to *The New Yorker* but rejected, until the breakthrough acceptance of *Shiloh* in 1982 that launched her publishing career. What seems remarkable about Mason's stories is the empathy she creates for characters whose eccentricities defy rational explana-tion and whose mundane existences rarely achieve heroic proportions but who nevertheless exhibit an integrity of being that humanizes them and us as well.

Wish

Sam tried to hold his eyes open. The preacher, a fat-faced boy with a college degree, had a curious way of pronouncing his *r*'s. The sermon was about pollu-tion of the soul and started with a news item about an oil spill. Sam drifted into a dream about a flock of chickens scratching up a bed of petunias. His sis-ter Damson, beside him, knifed him in the ribs with her bony elbow. Snoring, she said with her eyes.

Every Sunday after church, Sam and Damson visited their other sister, Hortense, and her husband, Cecil. Ordinarily, Sam drove his own car, but today Damson gave him a ride because his car was low on gas. Damson lived in town, but Hort and Cecil lived out in the country, not far from the old home-place, which had been sold twenty years before, when Pap died. As they drove past the old place now, Sam saw Damson shudder. She had stopped saying "Trash" under her breath when they passed by and saw the junk cars that had accumulated around the old house. The yard was bare dirt now, and the large elm in front had split. Many times Sam and his sisters had wished the new in-terstate had gone through the homeplace instead. Sam knew he should have bought out his sisters and kept it.

"How are you, Sam?" Hort asked when he and Damson arrived. Damson's husband, Porter, had stayed home today with a bad back.

"About dead." Sam grinned and knuckled his chest, pretending heart trou-ble and exaggerating the arthritis in his hands.

"Not again!" Hort said, teasing him. "You just like to growl, Sam. You've been that way all your life."

"You ain't even knowed me that long! Why, I remember the night you was born. You come in mad at the world, with your stinger out, and you've been like that ever since."

Hort patted his arm. "Your barn door's open, Sam," she said as they went into the living room.

He zipped up his fly unself-consciously. At his age, he didn't care.

Hort steered Damson off into the kitchen, murmuring something about a blue dish, and Sam sat down with Cecil to discuss crops and the weather. It was their habit to review the week's weather, then their health, then local news—in that order. Cecil was a small, amiable man who didn't like to argue.

A little later, at the dinner table, Cecil jokingly asked Sam, "Are you sending any money to Jimmy Swaggart?"[1]

"Hell, no! I ain't sending a penny to that bastard."

"Sam never gave them preachers nothing," Hort said defensively as she sent a bowl of potatoes au gratin Sam's way. "That was Nova."

Nova. Sam's wife, had been dead eight and a half years. Nova was always buying chances on Heaven, Sam thought. There was something squirrelly in her, like the habit she had of saving out extra seed from the garden or putting up more preserves than they could use.

Hort said, "I still think Nova wanted to build on that ground she heired so she could have a house in her own name."

Damson nodded vigorously. "She didn't want you to have your name on the new house, Sam. She wanted it in her name."

"Didn't make no sense, did it?" Sam said, reflecting a moment on Nova. He could see her plainly, holding up a piece of fried chicken like a signal for attention. The impression was so vivid he almost asked her to pass the peas.

Hort said, "You already had a nice house with shade trees and a tobacco patch, and it was close to your kinfolks, but she just *had* to move toward town."

"She told me if she had to get to the hospital the ambulance would get there quicker," said Damson, taking a second biscuit. "Hort, these biscuits ain't as good as you usually make."

"I didn't use self-rising," said Hort.

"It wouldn't make much difference, with that new highway," said Cecil, speaking of the ambulance.

On the day they moved to the new house, Sam stayed in bed with the covers pulled up around him and refused to budge. He was still there at four o'clock in the evening, after his cousins had moved out all the furniture. Nova ignored him until they came for the bed. She laid his clothes on the bed and rattled the car keys in his face. She had never learned to drive. That was nearly fifteen years ago. Only a few years after that, Nova died and left him in that brick box she called a dream house. There wasn't a tree in the yard when they built the house. Now there were two flowering crab apples and a flimsy little oak.

After dinner, Hort and Cecil brought out new pictures of their great-grandchildren. The children had changed, and Sam couldn't keep straight which ones belonged to Linda and which ones belonged to Donald. He felt full. He made himself comfortable among the crocheted pillows on Hort's high-backed couch. For ten minutes, Hort talked on the telephone to Linda, in Louisiana, and when she hung up she reported that Linda had a new job at a finance company. Drowsily, Sam listened to the voices rise and fall. Their language was so familiar; his kinfolks never told stories or reminisced when they sat around on a Sunday. Instead, they discussed character. "He's the stingiest man alive." "She was nice to talk to on the street but H[2] to work with." "He never would listen when you tried to tell him anything." "She'd do anything for you."

Now, as Sam stared at a picture of a child with a Depression-style bowl hair-

1. American televangelist (b. 1935). 2. I.e., hell.

cut, Damson was saying, "Old Will Stone always referred to himself as 'me.' *Me* did this. *Me* wants that.' "

Hort said, "The Stones were always trying to get you to do something for them. Get around one of them and they'd think of something they wanted you to do." The Stones were their mother's people.

"I never would let 'em tell me what to do," Damson said with a laugh. "I'd say, 'I can't! I've got the nervous trembles.' "

Damson was little then, and her aunt Rue always complained of nervous trembles. Once, Damson had tried to get out of picking English peas by claiming she had nervous trembles, too. Sam remembered that. He laughed—a hoot so sudden they thought he hadn't been listening and was laughing about something private.

Hort fixed a plate of fried chicken, potatoes, field peas, and stewed apples for Sam to take home. He set it on the back seat of Damson's car, along with fourteen eggs and a sack of biscuits. Damson spurted out of the driveway backward, scaring the hound dog back to his hole under a lilac bush.

"Hort and Cecil's having a time keeping up this place," Sam said, noticing the weed-clogged pen where they used to keep hogs.

Damson said, "Hort's house always smelled so good, but today it smelled bad. It smelled like fried fish."

"I never noticed it," said Sam, yawning.

"Ain't you sleeping good, Sam?"

"Yeah, but when my stomach sours I get to yawning."

"You ain't getting old on us, are you?"

"No, I ain't old. Old is in your head."

Damson invited herself into Sam's house, saying she wanted to help him put the food away. His sisters wouldn't leave him alone. They checked on his housekeeping, searched for ruined food, made sure his commode was flushed. They had fits when he took in a stray dog one day, and they would have taken her to the pound if she hadn't got hit on the road first.

Damson stored the food in the kitchen and snooped in his refrigerator. Sam was itching to get into his bluejeans and watch something on Ted Turner's channel that he had meant to watch. He couldn't remember now what it was, but he knew it came on at four o'clock. Damson came into the living room and began to peer at all his pictures, exclaiming over each great-grandchild. All Sam's kids and grandkids were scattered around. His son worked in the tire industry in Akron, Ohio, and his oldest granddaughter operated a frozen-yogurt store in Florida. He didn't know why anybody would eat yogurt in any form. His grandson Bobby had arrived from Arizona last year with an Italian woman who spoke in a sharp accent. Sam had to hold himself stiff to keep from laughing. He wouldn't let her see him laugh, but her accent tickled him. Now Bobby had written that she'd gone back to Italy.

Damson paused over an old family portrait—Pap and Mammy and all six children, along with Uncle Clay and Uncle Thomas and their wives, Rosie and Zootie, and Aunt Rue. Sam's three brothers were dead now. Damson, a young girl in the picture, wore a lace collar, and Hort was in blond curls and a pinafore. Pap sat in the center on a chair with his legs set far apart, as if to anchor himself to hold the burden of this wild family. He looked mean and willful, as though he were about to whip somebody.

Suddenly Damson blurted out, "Pap ruined my life."

Sam was surprised. Damson hadn't said exactly that before, but he knew what she was talking about. There had always been a sadness about her, as though she had had the hope knocked out of her years ago.

She said, "He ruined my life—keeping me away from Lyle."

"That was near sixty years ago, Damson. That don't still bother you now, does it?"

She held the picture close to her breast and said, "You know how you hear on the television nowadays about little children getting beat up or treated nasty and it makes such a mark on them? Nowadays they know about that, but they didn't back then. They never knowed how something when you're young can hurt you so long."

"None of that happened to you."

"Not that, but it was just as bad."

"Lyle wouldn't have been good to you," said Sam.

"But I loved him, and Pap wouldn't let me see him."

"Lyle was a drunk and Pap didn't trust him no further than he could throw him."

"And then I married Porter, for pure spite," she went on. "You know good and well I never cared a thing about him."

"How come you've stayed married to him all these years then? Why don't you do like the kids do nowadays—like Bobby out in Arizona? Him and that Italian. They've done quit!"

"But she's a foreigner. I ain't surprised," said Damson, blowing her nose with a handkerchief from her pocketbook. She sat down on Sam's divan. He had towels spread on the upholstery to protect it, a habit of Nova's he couldn't get rid of. That woman was so practical she had even orchestrated her deathbed. She had picked out her burial clothes, arranged for his breakfast. He remembered holding up hangers of dresses from her closet for her to choose from.

"Damson," he said, "if you could do it over, you'd do it different, but it might not be no better. You're making Lyle out to be more than he would have been."

"He wouldn't have shot hisself," she said calmly.

"It was an accident."

She shook her head. "No, I think different."

Damson had always claimed he killed himself over her. That night, Lyle had come over to the homeplace near dark. Sam and his brothers had helped Pap put in a long day suckering[3] tobacco. Sam was already courting Nova, and Damson was just out of high school. The neighborhood boys came over on Sundays after church like a pack of dogs after a bitch. Damson had an eye for Lyle because he was so daresome, more reckless than the rest. That Saturday night when Lyle came by for her, he had been into some moonshine, and he was frisky, like a young bull. Pap wouldn't let her go with him. Sam heard Damson in the attic, crying, and Lyle was outside, singing at the top of his lungs, calling her. "Damson! My fruit pie!" Pap stepped out onto the porch then, and Lyle slipped off into the darkness.

Damson set the family picture back on the shelf and said, "He was different

3. I.e., removing suckers from.

from all the other boys. He knew a lot, and he'd been to Texas once with his daddy—for his daddy's asthma. He had a way about him."

"I remember when Lyle come back late that night," Sam said. "I heard him on the porch. I knowed it must be him. He was loud and acted like he was going to bust in the house after you."

"I heard him," she said. "From my pallet up there at the top. It was so hot I had a bucket of water and a washrag and I'd wet my face and stand in that little window and reach for a breeze. I heard him come, and I heard him thrashing around down there on the porch. There was a loose board you always had to watch out for."

"I remember that!" Sam said. He hadn't thought of that warped plank in years.

"He fell over it," Damson said. "But then he got up and backed down the steps. I could hear him out in the yard. Then—" She clasped her arms around herself and bowed her head. "Then he yelled out, 'Damson!' I can still hear that."

A while later, they had heard the gunshot. Sam always remembered hearing a hollow thump and a sudden sound like cussing, then the explosion. He and his brother Bob rushed out in the dark, and then Pap brought a coal-oil lantern. They found Lyle sprawled behind the barn, with the shotgun kicked several feet away. There was a milk can turned over, and they figured that Lyle had stumbled over it when he went behind the barn. Sam had never forgotten Damson on the living-room floor, bawling. She lay there all the next day, screaming and beating her heavy work shoes against the floor, and people had to step around her. The women fussed over her, but none of the men could say anything.

Sam wanted to say something now. He glared at that big family in the picture. The day the photographer came, Sam's mother made everyone dress up, and they had to stand there as still as stumps for about an hour in that August heat. He remembered the kink in Damson's hair, the way she had fixed it so pretty for Lyle. A blurred chicken was cutting across the corner of the picture, and an old bird dog named Obadiah was stretched out in front, holding a pose better than the fidgety people. In the front row, next to her mother, Damson's bright, upturned face sparkled with a smile. Everyone had admired the way she could hold a smile for the camera.

Pointing to her face in the picture, he said, "Here you are, Damson—a young girl in love."

Frowning, she said, "I just wish life had been different."

He grabbed Damson's shoulders and stared into her eyes. To this day, she didn't even wear glasses and was still pretty, still herself in there, in that puffed-out old face. He said, "You wish! Well, wish in one hand and shit in the other one and see which one fills up the quickest!"

He got her. She laughed so hard she had to catch her tears with her handkerchief. "Sam, you old hound. Saying such as that—and on a Sunday."

She rose to go. He thought he'd said the right thing, because she seemed lighter on her feet now. "You've got enough eggs and bacon to last you all week," she said. "And I'm going to bring you some of that popcorn cake my neighbor makes. You'd never guess it had popcorn in it."

She had her keys in her hand, her pocketbook on her arm. She was wearing a pretty color of pink, the shade of baby pigs. She said, "I know why you've

lived so long, Sam. You just see what you want to see. You're like Pap, just as hard and plain."

"That ain't the whole truth," he said, feeling a mist of tears come.

That night he couldn't get to sleep. He went to bed at eight-thirty, after a nature special on the television—grizzly bears. He lay in bed and replayed his life with Nova. The times he wanted to leave home. The time he went to a lawyer to inquire about a divorce. (It turned out to cost too much, and anyway he knew his folks would never forgive him.) The time she hauled him out of bed for the move to this house. He had loved their old place, a wood-frame house with a porch and a swing, looking out over tobacco fields and a strip of woods. He always had a dog then, a special dog, sitting on the porch with him. Here he had no porch, just some concrete steps, where he would sit sometimes and watch the traffic. At night, drunk drivers zoomed along, occasionally plowing into somebody's mailbox.

She had died at three-thirty in the morning, and toward the end she didn't want anything—no food, no talk, no news, nothing soft. No kittens to hold, no memories. He stayed up with her in case she needed him, but she went without needing him at all. And now he didn't need her. In the dim light of the street lamp, he surveyed the small room where he had chosen to sleep—the single bed, the bare walls, his jeans hanging up on a nail, his shoes on a shelf, the old washstand that had belonged to his grandmother, the little rag rug beside the bed. He was happy. His birthday was two months from today. He would be eighty-four. He thought of that bird dog, Obadiah, who had been with him on his way through the woods the night he set out to meet someone—the night he first made love to a girl. Her name was Nettie, and at first she had been reluctant to lie down with him, but he had brought a quilt, and he spread it out in the open pasture. The hay had been cut that week, and the grass was damp and sweet-smelling. He could still feel the clean, soft, cool cotton of that quilt, the stubble poking through and the patterns of the quilting pressing into his back. Nettie lay there beside him, her breath blowing on his shoulder as they studied the stars far above the field—little pinpoint holes punched through the night sky like the needle holes around the tiny stitches in the quilting. Nettie. Nettie Slade. Her dress had self-covered buttons, hard like seed corn.

1988

BHARATI MUKHERJEE
1940–

Born a Bengali Brahmin in Calcutta, Bharati Mukherjee refuses to play the role of "a Third World woman writer" because to do so would be "to confine oneself to a narrow, airless, tightly roofed arena." Certainly, her early education in the English-speaking Loreto Convent School and the University of Calcutta as well as her graduate work at the University of Iowa Writer's Workshop, her subsequent marriage to the novelist Clark Blaise, and their expatriation in Canada with their two

children as well as the family's subsequent return to the United States suggest the cosmopolitan, international flair of a highly individuated existence.

Nevertheless, Mukherjee's narratives capture the tensions at work in lives stereotyped by national prejudices and permeated by what she calls the "broken identities and discarded languages" spawned by geographical dislocation. Her first two novels, *The Tiger's Daughter* (1972) and *Wife* (1975), examine the social conflicts and psychological tensions experienced by displaced Indian women seeking to negotiate between the shock of an alien (often alienating) American culture and the equally depersonalizing violence permeating Calcutta's society. Two collaborative works composed with her husband, *Days and Nights in Calcutta* (1977, rev. 1986) and *The Sorrow and the Terror: The Haunting Legacy of the Air India Tragedy* (1987), reveal her skepticism about bankrupt discourses of multiculturalism actually saturated by racist assumptions. The stories published in *Darkness* (1985) and *The Middleman* (1988) brilliantly capture the impact of international events on the lives of ordinary people.

The Management of Grief

A woman I don't know is boiling tea the Indian way in my kitchen. There are a lot of women I don't know in my kitchen, whispering, and moving tactfully. They open doors, rummage through the pantry, and try not to ask me where things are kept. They remind me of when my sons were small, on Mother's Day or when Vikram and I were tired, and they would make big, sloppy omelets. I would lie in bed pretending I didn't hear them.

Dr. Sharma, the treasurer of the Indo-Canada Society, pulls me into the hallway. He wants to know if I am worried about money. His wife, who has just come up from the basement with a tray of empty cups and glasses, scolds him. "Don't bother Mrs. Bhave with mundane details." She looks so monstrously pregnant her baby must be days overdue. I tell her she shouldn't be carrying heavy things. "Shaila," she says, smiling, "this is the fifth." Then she grabs a teenager by his shirttails. He slips his Walkman off his head. He has to be one of her four children, they have the same domed and dented foreheads. "What's the official word now?" she demands. The boy slips the headphones back on. "They're acting evasive, Ma. They're saying it could be an accident or a terrorist bomb."

All morning, the boys have been muttering, Sikh Bomb, Sikh Bomb. The men, not using the word, bow their heads in agreement. Mrs. Sharma touches her forehead at such a word. At least they've stopped talking about space debris and Russian lasers.

Two radios are going in the dining room. They are tuned to different stations. Someone must have brought the radios down from my boys' bedrooms. I haven't gone into their rooms since Kusum came running across the front lawn in her bathrobe. She looked so funny, I was laughing when I opened the door.

The big TV in the den is being whizzed through American networks and cable channels.

"Damn!" some man swears bitterly. "How can these preachers carry on like nothing's happened?" I want to tell him we're not that important. You look at the audience, and at the preacher in his blue robe with his beautiful white

hair, the potted palm trees under a blue sky, and you know they care about nothing.

The phone rings and rings. Dr. Sharma's taken charge. "We're with her," he keeps saying. "Yes, yes, the doctor has given calming pills. Yes, yes, pills are having necessary effect." I wonder if pills alone explain this calm. Not peace, just a deadening quiet. I was always controlled, but never repressed. Sound can reach me, but my body is tensed, ready to scream. I hear their voices all around me. I hear my boys and Vikram cry, "Mommy, Shaila!" and their screams insulate me, like headphones.

The woman boiling water tells her story again and again. "I got the news first. My cousin called from Halifax before six A.M., can you imagine? He'd gotten up for prayers and his son was studying for medical exams and he heard on a rock channel that something had happened to a plane. They said first it had disappeared from the radar, like a giant eraser just reached out. His father called me, so I said to him, what do you mean, 'something bad'? You mean a hijacking? And he said, behn, there is no confirmation of anything yet, but check with your neighbors because a lot of them must be on that plane.[1] So I called poor Kusum straightaway. I knew Kusum's husband and daughter were booked to go yesterday."

Kusum lives across the street from me. She and Satish had moved in less than a month ago. They said they needed a bigger place. All these people, the Sharmas and friends from the Indo-Canada Society, had been there for the housewarming. Satish and Kusum made homemade tandoori on their big gas grill and even the white neighbors piled their plates high with that luridly red, charred, juicy chicken. Their younger daughter had danced, and even our boys had broken away from the Stanley Cup telecast to put in a reluctant appearance. Everyone took pictures for their albums and for the community newspapers—another of our families had made it big in Toronto—and now I wonder how many of those happy faces are gone. "Why does God give us so much if all along He intends to take it away?" Kusum asks me.

I nod. We sit on carpeted stairs, holding hands like children. "I never once told him that I loved him," I say. I was too much the well brought up woman. I was so well brought up I never felt comfortable calling my husband by his first name.

"It's all right," Kusum says. "He knew. My husband knew. They felt it. Modern young girls have to say it because what they feel is fake."

Kusum's daughter, Pam, runs in with an overnight case. Pam's in her McDonald's uniform. "Mummy! You have to get dressed!" Panic makes her cranky. "A reporter's on his way here."

"Why?"

"You want to talk to him in your bathrobe?" She starts to brush her mother's long hair. She's the daughter whose always in trouble. She dates Canadian boys and hangs out in the mall, shopping for tight sweaters. The younger one, the goody-goody one according to Pam, the one with a voice so sweet that when she sang bhajans[2] for Ethiopian relief even a frugal man like my husband wrote out a hundred dollar check, she was on that plane. She was

1. In June 1985, an Air India flight from Toronto to Bombay crashed off the coast of Ireland, apparently as the result of an explosion caused by a bomb. All 329 people on board were killed.
2. Devotional songs, hymns (Hindi).

going to spend July and August with grandparents because Pam wouldn't go. Pam said she'd rather waitress at McDonald's. "If it's a choice between Bombay and Wonderland, I'm picking Wonderland," she'd said.

"Leave me alone," Kusum yells. "You know what I want to do? If I didn't have to look after you now, I'd hang myself."

Pam's young face goes blotchy with pain. "Thanks," she says, "don't let me stop you."

"Hush," pregnant Mrs. Sharma scolds Pam. "Leave your mother alone. Mr. Sharma will tackle the reporters and fill out the forms. He'll say what has to be said."

Pam stands her ground. "You think I don't know what Mummy's thinking? *Why her?* that's what. That's sick! Mummy wishes my little sister were alive and I were dead."

Kusum's hand in mine is trembly hot. We continue to sit on the stairs.

She calls before she arrives, wondering if there's anything I need. Her name is Judith Templeton and she's an appointee of the provincial government. "Multiculturalism?" I ask, and she says, "partially," but that her mandate is bigger. "I've been told you knew many of the people on the flight," she says. "Perhaps if you'd agree to help us reach the others . . . ?"

She gives me time at least to put on tea water and pick up the mess in the front room. I have a few *samosas*[3] from Kusum's housewarming that I could fry up, but then I think, Why prolong this visit?

Judith Templeton is much younger than she sounded. She wears a blue suit with a white blouse and a polka dot tie. Her blond hair is cut short, her only jewelry is pearl drop earrings. Her briefcase is new and expensive looking, a gleaming cordovan leather. She sits with it across her lap. When she looks out the front windows onto the street, her contact lenses seem to float in front of her light blue eyes.

"What sort of help do you want from me?" I ask. She has refused the tea, out of politeness, but I insist, along with some slightly stale biscuits.

"I have no experience," she admits. "That is, I have an MSW and I've worked in liaison with accident victims, but I mean I have no experience with a tragedy of this scale—"

"Who could?" I ask.

"—and with the complications of culture, language, and customs. Someone mentioned that Mrs. Bhave is a pillar—because you've taken it more calmly."

At this, perhaps, I frown, for she reaches forward, almost to take my hand. "I hope you understand my meaning, Mrs. Bhave. There are hundreds of people in Metro directly affected, like you, and some of them speak no English. There are some widows who've never handled money or gone on a bus, and there are old parents who still haven't eaten or gone outside their bedrooms. Some houses and apartments have been looted. Some wives are still hysterical. Some husbands are in shock and profound depression. We want to help, but our hands are tied in so many ways. We have to distribute money to some people, and there are legal documents—these things can be done. We have interpreters, but we don't always have the human touch, or maybe the right human

3. Deep fried pastries filled with vegetables or meat.

touch. We don't want to make mistakes, Mrs. Bhave, and that's why we'd like to ask you to help us."

"More mistakes, you mean," I say.

"Police matters are not in my hands," she answers.

"Nothing I can do will make any difference," I say. "We must all grieve in our own way."

"But you are coping very well. All the people said, Mrs. Bhave is the strongest person of all. Perhaps if the others could see you, talk with you, it would help them."

"By the standards of the people you call hysterical, I am behaving very oddly and very badly, Miss Templeton." I want to say to her, *I wish I could scream, starve, walk into Lake Ontario, jump from a bridge.* "They would not see me as a model. I do not see myself as a model."

I am a freak. No one who has ever known me would think of me reacting this way. This terrible calm will not go away.

She asks me if she may call again, after I get back from a long trip that we all must make. "Of course," I say. "Feel free to call, anytime."

Four days later, I find Kusum squatting on a rock overlooking a bay in Ireland. It isn't a big rock, but it juts sharply out over water. This is as close as we'll ever get to them. June breezes balloon out her sari and unpin her knee-length hair. She has the bewildered look of a sea creature whom the tides have stranded.

It's been one hundred hours since Kusum came stumbling and screaming across my lawn. Waiting around the hospital, we've heard many stories. The police, the diplomats, they tell us things thinking that we're strong, that knowledge is helpful to the grieving, and maybe it is. Some, I know, prefer ignorance, or their own versions. The plane broke into two, they say. Unconsciousness was instantaneous. No one suffered. My boys must have just finished their breakfasts. They loved eating on planes, they loved the smallness of plates, knives, and forks. Last year they saved the airline salt and pepper shakers. Half an hour more and they would have made it to Heathrow.

Kusum says that we can't escape our fate. She says that all those people— our husbands, my boys, her girl with the nightingale voice, all those Hindus, Christians, Sikhs, Muslims, Parsis, and atheists on that plane—were fated to die together off this beautiful bay. She learned this from a swami in Toronto.

I have my Valium.

Six of us "relatives"—two widows and four widowers—choose to spend the day today by the waters instead of sitting in a hospital room and scanning photographs of the dead. That's what they call us now: relatives. I've looked through twenty-seven photos in two days. They're very kind to us, the Irish are very understanding. Sometimes understanding means freeing a tourist bus for this trip to the bay, so we can pretend to spy our loved ones through the glassiness of waves or in sun-speckled cloud shapes.

I could die here, too, and be content.

"What is that, out there?" She's standing and flapping her hands and for a moment I see a head shape bobbing in the waves. She's standing in the water, I, on the boulder. The tide is low, and a round, black, head-sized rock has just risen from the waves. She returns, her sari end dripping and ruined and her face is a twisted remnant of hope, the way mine was a hundred hours ago, still

laughing but inwardly knowing that nothing but the ultimate tragedy could bring two women together at six o'clock on a Sunday morning. I watch her face sag into blankness.

"That water felt warm, Shaila," she says at length.

"You can't," I say. "We have to wait for our turn to come."

I haven't eaten in four days, haven't brushed my teeth.

"I know," she says. "I tell myself I have no right to grieve. They are in a better place than we are. My swami says I should be thrilled for them. My swami says depression is a sign of our selfishness."

Maybe I'm selfish. Selfishly I break away from Kusum and run, sandals slapping against stones, to the water's edge. What if my boys aren't lying pinned under the debris? What if they aren't stuck a mile below that innocent blue chop? What if, given the strong currents. . . .

Now I've ruined my sari, one of my best. Kusum has joined me, knee-deep in water that feels to me like a swimming pool. I could settle in the water, and my husband would take my hand and the boys would slap water in my face just to see me scream.

"Do you remember what good swimmers my boys were, Kusum?"

"I saw the medals," she says.

One of the widowers, Dr. Ranganathan from Montreal, walks out to us, carrying his shoes in one hand. He's an electrical engineer. Someone at the hotel mentioned his work is famous around the world, something about the place where physics and electricity come together. He has lost a huge family, something indescribable. "With some luck," Dr. Ranganathan suggests to me, "a good swimmer could make it safely to some island. It is quite possible that there may be many, many microscopic islets scattered around."

"You're not just saying that?" I tell Dr. Ranganathan about Vinod, my elder son. Last year he took diving as well.

"It's a parent's duty to hope," he says. "It is foolish to rule out possibilities that have not been tested. I myself have not surrendered hope."

Kusum is sobbing once again. "Dear lady," he says, laying his free hand on her arm, and she calms down.

"Vinod is how old?" he asks me. He's very careful, as we all are. *Is*, not was.

"Fourteen. Yesterday he was fourteen. His father and uncle were going to take him down to the Taj and give him a big birthday party. I couldn't go with them because I couldn't get two weeks off from my stupid job in June." I process bills for a travel agent. June is a big travel month.

Dr. Ranganathan whips the pockets of his suit jacket inside out. Squashed roses, in darkening shades of pink, float on the water. He tore the roses off creepers in somebody's garden. He didn't ask anyone if he could pluck the roses, but now there's been an article about it in the local papers. When you see an Indian person, it says, please give him or her flowers.

"A strong youth of fourteen," he says, "can very likely pull to safety a younger one."

My sons, though four years apart, were very close. Vinod wouldn't let Mithun drown. *Electrical engineering*, I think, foolishly perhaps: this man knows important secrets of the universe, things closed to me. Relief spins me lightheaded. No wonder my boys' photographs haven't turned up in the gallery of photos of the recovered dead. "Such pretty roses," I say.

"My wife loved pink roses. Every Friday I had to bring a bunch home. I used to say, Why? After twenty odd years of marriage you're still needing proof pos-

itive of my love?" He has identified his wife and three of his children. Then others from Montreal, the lucky ones, intact families with no survivors. He chuckles as he wades back to shore. Then he swings around to ask me a question. "Mrs. Bhave, you are wanting to throw in some roses for your loved ones? I have two big ones left."

But I have other things to float: Vinod's pocket calculator; a half-painted model B-52 for my Mithun. They'd want them on their island. And for my husband? For him I let fall into the calm, glassy waters a poem I wrote in the hospital yesterday. Finally he'll know my feelings for him

"Don't tumble, the rocks are slippery," Dr. Ranganathan cautions. He holds out a hand for me to grab.

Then it's time to get back on the bus, time to rush back to our waiting posts on hospital benches.

Kusum is one of the lucky ones. The lucky ones flew here, identified in multiplicate their loved ones, then will fly to India with the bodies for proper ceremonies. Satish is one of the few males who surfaced. The photos of faces we saw on the walls in an office at Heathrow and here in the hospital are mostly of women. Women have more body fat, a nun said to me matter-of-factly. They float better.

Today I was stopped by a young sailor on the street. He had loaded bodies, he'd gone into the water when—he checks my face for signs of strength— when the sharks were first spotted. I don't blush, and he breaks down. "It's all right," I say. "Thank you." I had heard about the sharks from Dr. Ranganathan. In his orderly mind, science brings understanding, it holds no terror. It is the shark's duty. For every deer there is a hunter, for every fish a fisherman.

The Irish are not shy; they rush to me and give me hugs and some are crying. I cannot imagine reactions like that on the streets of Toronto. Just strangers, and I am touched. Some carry flowers with them and give them to any Indian they see.

After lunch, a policeman I have gotten to know quite well catches hold of me. He says he thinks he has a match for Vinod. I explain what a good swimmer Vinod is.

"You want me with you when you look at photos?" Dr. Ranganathan walks ahead of me into the picture gallery. In these matters, he is a scientist, and I am grateful. It is a new perspective. "They have performed miracles," he says. "We are indebted to them."

The first day or two the policemen showed us relatives only one picture at a time; now they're in a hurry, they're eager to lay out the possibles, and even the probables.

The face on the photo is of a boy much like Vinod; the same intelligent eyes, the same thick brows dipping into a V. But this boy's features, even his cheeks, are puffier, wider, mushier.

"No." My gaze is pulled by other pictures. There are five other boys who look like Vinod.

The nun assigned to console me rubs the first picture with a fingertip. "When they've been in the water for a while, love, they look a little heavier." The bones under the skin are broken, they said on the first day—try to adjust your memories. It's important.

"It's not him. I'm his mother. I'd know."

"I know this one!" Dr. Ranganathan cries out suddenly from the back of the gallery. "And this one!" I think he senses that I don't want to find my boys. "They are the Kutty brothers. They were also from Montreal." I don't mean to be crying. On the contrary, I am ecstatic. My suitcase in the hotel is packed heavy with dry clothes for my boys.

The policeman starts to cry. "I am so sorry, I am so sorry, ma'am. I really thought we had a match."

With the nun ahead of us and the policeman behind, we, the unlucky ones without our children's bodies, file out of the makeshift gallery.

From Ireland most of us go on to India. Kusum and I take the same direct flight to Bombay, so I can help her clear customs quickly. But we have to argue with a man in uniform. He has large boils on his face. The boils swell and glow with sweat as we argue with him. He wants Kusum to wait in line and he refuses to take authority because his boss is on a tea break. But Kusum won't let her coffins out of sight, and I shan't desert her though I know that my parents, elderly and diabetic, must be waiting in a stuffy car in a scorching lot.

"You bastard!" I scream at the man with the popping boils. Other passengers press closer. "You think we're smuggling contraband in those coffins!"

Once upon a time we were well brought up women; we were dutiful wives who kept our heads veiled, our voices shy and sweet.

In India, I become, once again, an only child of rich, ailing parents. Old friends of the family come to pay their respects. Some are Sikh, and inwardly, involuntarily, I cringe. My parents are progressive people; they do not blame communities for a few individuals.

In Canada it is a different story now.

"Stay longer," my mother pleads. "Canada is a cold place. Why would you want to be all by yourself?" I stay.

Three months pass. Then another.

"Vikram wouldn't have wanted you to give up things!" they protest. They call my husband by the name he was born with. In Toronto he'd changed to Vik so the men he worked with at his office would find his name as easy as Rod or Chris. "You know, the dead aren't cut off from us!"

My grandmother, the spoiled daughter of a rich *zamindar*,[4] shaved her head with rusty razor blades when she was widowed at sixteen. My grandfather died of childhood diabetes when he was nineteen, and she saw herself as the harbinger of bad luck. My mother grew up without parents, raised indifferently by an uncle, while her true mother slept in a hut behind the main estate house and took her food with the servants. She grew up a rationalist. My parents abhor mindless mortification.

The zamindar's daughter kept stubborn faith in Vedic rituals;[5] my parents rebelled. I am trapped between two modes of knowledge. At thirty-six, I am too old to start over and too young to give up. Like my husband's spirit, I flutter between worlds.

Courting aphasia, we travel. We travel with our phalanx of servants and poor relatives. To hill stations and to beach resorts. We play contract bridge in

4. Landholder.　　　　　　　　5. The *Vedas* are the oldest scriptures in Hinduism.

dusty gymkhana clubs.[6] We ride stubby ponies up crumbly mountain trails. At tea dances, we let ourselves be twirled twice round the ballroom. We hit the holy spots we hadn't made time for before. In Varanasi, Kalighat, Rishikesh, Hardwar, astrologers and palmists seek me out and for a fee offer me cosmic consolations.

Already the widowers among us are being shown new bride candidates. They cannot resist the call of custom, the authority of their parents and older brothers. They must marry; it is the duty of a man to look after a wife. The new wives will be young widows with children, destitute but of good family. They will make loving wives, but the men will shun them. I've had calls from the men over crackling Indian telephone lines. "Save me," they say, these substantial, educated, successful men of forty. "My parents are arranging a marriage for me." In a month they will have buried one family and returned to Canada with a new bride and partial family.

I am comparatively lucky. No one here thinks of arranging a husband for an unlucky widow.

Then, on the third day of the sixth month into this odyssey, in an abandoned temple in a tiny Himalayan village, as I make my offering of flowers and sweetmeats to the god of a tribe of animists, my husband descends to me. He is squatting next to a scrawny *sadhu*[7] in moth-eaten robes. Vikram wears the vanilla suit he wore the last time I hugged him. The *sadhu* tosses petals on a butter-fed flame, reciting Sanskrit mantras[8] and sweeps his face of flies. My husband takes my hands in his.

You're beautiful, he starts. Then, *What are you doing here?*

Shall I stay? I ask. He only smiles, but already the image is fading. *You must finish alone what we started together.* No seaweed wreathes his mouth. He speaks too fast just as he used to when we were an envied family in our pink split-level. He is gone.

In the windowless altar room, smoky with joss[9] sticks and clarified butter lamps, a sweaty hand gropes for my blouse. I do not shriek. The *sadhu* arranges his robe. The lamps hiss and sputter out.

When we come out of the temple, my mother says, "Did you feel something weird in there?"

My mother has no patience with ghosts, prophetic dreams, holy men, and cults.

"No," I lie. "Nothing."

But she knows that she's lost me. She knows that in days I shall be leaving.

Kusum's put her house up for sale. She wants to live in an ashram[1] in Hardwar. Moving to Hardwar was her swami's idea. Her swami runs two ashrams, the one in Hardwar and another here in Toronto.

"Don't run away," I tell her.

"I'm not running away," she says. "I'm pursuing inner peace. You think you or that Ranganathan fellow are better off?"

Pam's left for California. She wants to do some modeling, she says. She says when she comes into her share of the insurance money she'll open a yoga-cum-aerobics studio in Hollywood. She sends me postcards so naughty I

6. Athletic facilities.
7. A Hindu holy man (a mendicant ascetic).
8. Mystic words used in ritual and meditation.

9. Incense.
1. Hindu religious retreat.

daren't leave them on the coffee table. Her mother has withdrawn from her and the world.

The rest of us don't lose touch, that's the point. Talk is all we have, says Dr. Ranganathan, who has also resisted his relatives and returned to Montreal and to his job, alone. He says, whom better to talk with than other relatives? We've been melted down and recast as a new tribe.

He calls me twice a week from Montreal. Every Wednesday night and every Saturday afternoon. He is changing jobs, going to Ottawa. But Ottawa is over a hundred miles away, and he is forced to drive two hundred and twenty miles a day. He can't bring himself to sell his house. The house is a temple, he says; the king-sized bed in the master bedroom is a shrine. He sleeps on a folding cot. A devotee.

There are still some hysterical relatives. Judith Templeton's list of those needing help and those who've "accepted" is in nearly perfect balance. Acceptance means you speak of your family in the past tense and you make active plans for moving ahead with your life. There are courses at Seneca and Ryerson we could be taking. Her gleaming leather briefcase is full of college catalogs and lists of cultural societies that need our help. She has done impressive work, I tell her.

"In the textbooks on grief management," she replies—I am her confidante, I realize, one of the few whose grief has not sprung bizarre obsessions—"there are stages to pass through: rejection, depression, acceptance, reconstruction." She has compiled a chart and finds that six months after the tragedy, none of us still reject reality, but only a handful are reconstructing. "Depressed Acceptance" is the plateau we've reached. Remarriage is a major step in reconstruction (though she's a little surprised, even shocked, over *how* quickly some of the men have taken on new families). Selling one's house and changing jobs and cities is healthy.

How do I tell Judith Templeton that my family surrounds me, and that like creatures in epics, they've changed shapes? She sees me as calm and accepting but worries that I have no job, no career. My closest friends are worse off than I. I cannot tell her my days, even my nights, are thrilling.

She asks me to help with families she can't reach at all. An elderly couple in Agincourt whose sons were killed just weeks after they had brought their parents over from a village in Punjab. From their names, I know they are Sikh. Judith Templeton and a translator have visited them twice with offers of money for air fare to Ireland, with bank forms, power-of-attorney forms, but they have refused to sign, or to leave their tiny apartment. Their sons' money is frozen in the bank. Their sons' investment apartments have been trashed by tenants, the furnishings sold off. The parents fear that anything they sign or any money they receive will end the company's or the country's obligations to them. They fear they are selling their sons for two airline tickets to a place they've never seen.

The high-rise apartment is a tower of Indians and West Indians, with a sprinkling of Orientals. The nearest bus stop kiosk is lined with women in saris. Boys practice cricket in the parking lot. Inside the building, even I wince a bit from the ferocity of onion fumes, the distinctive and immediate Indianness of frying *ghee*,[2] but Judith Templeton maintains a steady flow of

2. Clarified butter.

information. These poor old people are in imminent danger of losing their place and all their services.

I say to her, "They are Sikh. They will not open up to a Hindu woman." And what I want to add is, as much as I try not to, I stiffen now at the sight of beards and turbans. I remember a time when we all trusted each other in this new country, it was only the new country we worried about.

The two rooms are dark and stuffy. The lights are off, and an oil lamp sputters on the coffee table. The bent old lady has let us in, and her husband is wrapping a white turban over his oiled, hip-length hair. She immediately goes to the kitchen, and I hear the most familiar sound of an Indian home, tap water hitting and filling a teapot.

They have not paid their utility bills, out of fear and the inability to write a check. The telephone is gone; electricity and gas and water are soon to follow. They have told Judith their sons will provide. They are good boys, and they have always earned and looked after their parents.

We converse a bit in Hindi. They do not ask about the crash and I wonder if I should bring it up. If they think I am here merely as a translator, then they may feel insulted. There are thousands of Punjabi-speakers, Sikhs, in Toronto to do a better job. And so I say to the old lady, "I too have lost my sons, and my husband, in the crash."

Her eyes immediately fill with tears. The man mutters a few words which sound like a blessing. "God provides and God takes away," he says.

I want to say, But only men destroy and give back nothing. "My boys and my husband are not coming back," I say. "We have to understand that."

Now the old woman responds. "But who is to say? Man alone does not decide these things." To this her husband adds his agreement.

Judith asks about the bank papers, the release forms. With a stroke of the pen, they will have a provincial trustee to pay their bills, invest their money, send them a monthly pension.

"Do you know this woman?" I ask them.

The man rises his hand from the table, turns it over and seems to regard each finger separately before he answers. "This young lady is always coming here, we make tea for her and she leaves papers for us to sign." His eyes scan a pile of papers in the corner of the room. "Soon we will be out of tea, then will she go away?"

The old lady adds, "I have asked my neighbors and no one else gets *angrezi*[3] visitors. What have we done?"

"It's her job," I try to explain. "The government is worried. Soon you will have no place to stay, no lights, no gas, no water."

"Government will get its money. Tell her not to worry, we are honorable people."

I try to explain the government wishes to give money, not take. He raises his hand. "Let them take," he says. "We are accustomed to that. That is no problem."

"We are strong people," says the wife. "Tell her that."

"Who needs all this machinery?" demands the husband. "It is unhealthy, the bright lights, the cold air on a hot day, the cold food, the four gas rings. God will provide, not government."

3. An English speaker, a Westerner.

"When our boys return," the mother says. Her husband sucks his teeth. "Enough talk," he says.

Judith breaks in. "Have you convinced them?" The snaps on her cordovan briefcase go off like firecrackers in that quiet apartment. She lays the sheaf of legal papers on the coffee table. "If they can't write their names, an X will do— I've told them that."

Now the old lady has shuffled to the kitchen and soon emerges with a pot of tea and two cups. "I think my bladder will go first on a job like this," Judith says to me, smiling. "If only there was some way of reaching them. Please thank her for the tea. Tell her she's very kind."

I nod in Judith's direction and tell them in Hindi, "She thanks you for the tea. She thinks you are being very hospitable but she doesn't have the slightest idea what it means."

I want to say, Humor her. I want to say, My boys and my husband are with me too, more than ever. I look in the old man's eyes and I can read his stubborn, peasant's message: *I have protected this woman as best I can. She is the only person I have left. Give to me or take from me what you will, but I will not sign for it. I will not pretend that I accept.*

In the car, Judith says, "You see what I'm up against? I'm sure they're lovely people, but their stubbornness and ignorance are driving me crazy. They think signing a paper is signing their sons' death warrants, don't they?"

I am looking out the window. I want to say, *In our culture, it is a parent's duty to hope.*

"Now Shaila, this next woman is a real mess. She cries day and night, and she refuses all medical help. We may have to—"

"—Let me out at the subway," I say.

"I beg your pardon?" I can feel those blue eyes staring at me.

It would not be like her to disobey. She merely disapproves, and slows at a corner to let me out. Her voice is plaintive. "Is there anything I said? Anything I did?"

I could answer her suddenly in a dozen ways, but I choose not to. "Shaila? Let's talk about it," I hear, then slam the door.

A wife and mother begins her new life in a new country, and that life is cut short. Yet her husband tells her: Complete what we have started. We who stayed out of politics and came halfway around the world to avoid religious and political feuding have been the first in the New World to die from it. I no longer know what we started, nor how to complete it. I write letters to the editors of local papers and to members of Parliament. Now at least they admit it was a bomb. One MP answers back, with sympathy, but with a challenge. You want to make a difference? Work on a campaign. Work on mine. Politicize the Indian voter.

My husband's old lawyer helps me set up a trust. Vikram was a saver and a careful investor. He had saved the boys' boarding school and college fees. I sell the pink house at four times what we paid for it and take a small apartment downtown. I am looking for a charity to support.

We are deep in the Toronto winter, gray skies, icy pavements. I stay indoors, watching television. I have tried to assess my situation, how best to live my life, to complete what we began so many years ago. Kusum has written me from Hardwar that her life is now serene. She has seen Satish and has heard

her daughter sing again. Kusum was on a pilgrimage, passing through a village when she heard a young girl's voice, singing one of her daughter's favorite *bhajans*. She followed the music through the squalor of a Himalayan village, to a hut where a young girl, an exact replica of her daughter, was fanning coals under the kitchen fire. When she appeared, the girl cried out, "Ma!" and ran away. What did I think of that?

I think I can only envy her.

Pam didn't make it to California, but writes me from Vancouver. She works in a department store, giving make-up hints to Indian and Oriental girls. Dr. Ranganathan has given up his commute, given up his house and job, and accepted an academic position in Texas where no one knows his story and he has vowed not to tell it. He calls me now once a week.

I wait, I listen and I pray, but Vikram has not returned to me. The voices and the shapes and the nights filled with visions ended abruptly several weeks ago.

I take it as a sign.

One rare, beautiful, sunny day last week, returning from a small errand on Yonge Street, I was walking through the park from the subway to my apartment. I live equidistant from the Ontario Houses of Parliament and the University of Toronto. The day was not cold, but something in the bare trees caught my attention. I looked up from the gravel, into the branches and the clear blue sky beyond. I thought I heard the rustling of larger forms, and I waited a moment for voices. Nothing.

"What?" I asked.

Then as I stood in the path looking north to Queen's Park and west to the university, I heard the voices of my family one last time. *Your time has come,* they said. *Go, be brave.*

I do not know where this voyage I have begun will end. I do not know which direction I will take. I dropped the package on a park bench and started walking.

1988

AMA ATA AIDOO
1942–

"Things are working out towards their dazzling conclusions," begins Christina Ama Ata Aidoo's characteristically wry yet hopeful epigraph for *Our Sister Killjoy, or Reflections from a Black-Eyed Squint* (1966), her first novel. Born near Dominase, in the center of Ghana, Aidoo has been one of Africa's most productive and talented younger writers: she is the author of two plays (*Dilemma of a Ghost*, 1964, and *Anowa*, 1970) as well as a collection of poems, *An Angry Letter in January and Other Poems* (1992), two collections of short stories, *No Sweetness Here* (1970) and *The Eagle and the Chicken* (1989), and most recently *Changes: A Love Story* (1992). Her work, the American writer Alice Walker once remarked, has "reaffirmed my faith in the power of the written word to reach, to teach, to empower and encourage."

After graduation from the University of Ghana and a period as a research fellow at that university's Institute of African Studies, Aidoo studied creative writing at

Stanford University, in California, and she has subsequently taught English and African literature at the University of Ghana, Cape Coast branch. In much of her fiction, she explores with poignancy, verve, and wit the dissonance between Western culture and the civilization of an Africa just emerging from colonization, even while she seeks to imagine the ways in which, particularly for African women, things might work out toward a surprising and "dazzling" conclusion.

The Message

"Look here my sister, it should not be said but they say they opened her up."

"They opened her up?"

"Yes, opened her up."

"And the baby removed?"

"Yes, the baby removed."

"Yes the baby removed."

"I say. . . ."

"They do not say, my sister."

"Have you heard it?"

"What?"

"This and this and that. . . ."

"A-a-ah! that is it. . . ."

"*Meewuo!*"[1]

"They don't say *meewuo*. . . ."

"And how is she?"

"Am I not here with you? Do I know the highway which leads to Cape Coast?"[2]

"Hmmm. . . ."

"And anyway how can she live? What is it like even giving birth with a stomach which is whole . . . eh? . . . I am asking you. And if you are always standing on the brink of death who go to war with a stomach that is whole, then how would she do whose stomach is open to the winds?"

"Oh, *poo*,[3] pity. . . ."

"I say. . . ."

My little bundle, come. You and I are going to Cape Coast today.

I am taking one of her own cloths with me, just in case. These people on the coast do not know how to do a thing and I am not going to have anybody mishandling my child's body. I hope they give it to me. Horrible things I have heard done to people's bodies. Cutting them up and using them for instructions. Whereas even murderers still have decent burials.

I see Mensima coming. . . . And there is Nkama too . . . and Adwoa Meenu. . . . Now they are coming to . . . "*poo* pity" me. Witches, witches, witches . . . they have picked mine up while theirs prosper around them, children, grandchildren and great-grandchildren—theirs shoot up like mushrooms.

"Esi, we have heard of your misfortune. . . ."

"That our little lady's womb has been opened up. . . ."

1. "I'm going to die!" We are indebted to Dan Avorgbedor for his invaluable help in translating Ghanaian words and phrases.

2. A principal city in Ghana.

3. An exclamation.

"And her baby removed. . . ."

Thank you very much.

"Has she lived through it?"

I do not know.

"Esi, bring her here, back home whatever happens."

Yoo,[4] thank you. If the government's people allow it, I shall bring her home.

"And have you got ready your things?"

Yes. . . . No.

I cannot even think well.

It feels so nosy in my head. . . . Oh my little child. . . . I am wasting time. . . . And so I am going. . . .

Yes, to Cape Coast.

No, I do not know anyone there now but do you think no one would show me the way to this big hospital . . . if I asked around?

Hmmm . . . it's me has ended up like this. I was thinking that everything was alright now. . . . Yoo. And thank you too. Shut the door for me when you are leaving. You may stay too long outside if you wait for me, so go home and be about your business. I will let you know when I bring her in.

"Maami Amfoa, where are you going?"

My daughter, I am going to Cape Coast.

"And what is our old mother going to do with such swift steps? Is it serious?"

My daughter, it is very serious.

"Mother, may God go with you."

Yoo, my daughter.

"Eno, and what calls at this hour of the day?"

They want me at Cape Coast.

"Does my friend want to go and see how much the city has changed since we went there to meet the new Wesleyan Chairman,[5] twenty years ago?"

My sister, do you think I have knees to go parading on the streets of Cape Coast?

"Is it heavy?"

Yes, very heavy indeed. They have opened up my grandchild at the hospital, hi, hi, hi. . . .

"Eno due, due, due.[6] . . . I did not know. May God go with you. . . ."

Thank you Yaa.

"O, the world!"

"It's her grandchild. The only daughter of her only son. Do you remember Kojo Amisa who went to sodja[7] and fell in the great war, overseas?"

"Yes, it's his daughter. . . ."

. . . O, poo, pity.

"Kobina, run to the street, tell Draba Anan to wait for Nana Amfoa."

". . . Draba Anan, Draba, my mother says I must come and tell you to wait for Nana Amfoa."

"And where is she?"

"There she comes."

"Just look at how she hops like a bird . . . does she think we are going to be here all day? And anyway we are full already. . . ."

4. Yes.
5. Official in the Wesleyan mission, which was active in Ghana.
6. An expression of lamentation.
7. I.e., soldier.

O, you drivers!

"What have drivers done?"

"And do you think it shows respect when you speak in this way? It is only that things have not gone right; but she could, at least have been your mother. . . ."

"But what have I said? I have not insulted her. I just think that only Youth must be permitted to see Cape Coast, the town of the Dear and Expensive. . . ."

"And do you think she is going on a peaceful journey? The only daughter of her only son has been opened up and her baby removed from her womb."

O . . . God.

O

O

O

Poo, pity.

"Me . . . poo—pity, I am right about our modern wives. I always say they are useless as compared with our mothers."

"You drivers!"

"Now what have your modern wives done?"

"Am I not right what I always say about them?"

"You go and watch them in the big towns. All so thin and dry as sticks—you can literally blow them away with your breath. No decent flesh anywhere. Wooden chairs groan when they meet with their hard exteriors."

"O you drivers. . . ."

"But of course all drivers. . . ."

"What have I done? Don't all my male passengers agree with me? These modern girls. . . . Now here is one who cannot even have a baby in a decent way. But must have the baby removed from her stomach. *Tchiaa!*"[8]

"What. . . ."

"Here is the old woman."

"Whose grandchild. . . . ?"

"Yes."

"Nana, I hear you are coming to Cape Coast with us."

Yes my master.

"We nearly left you behind but we heard it was you and that it is a heavy journey you are making."

Yes my master . . . thank you my master.

"Push up please . . . push up. Won't you push up? Why do you all sit looking at me with such eyes as if I was a block of wood?"

"It is not that there is nowhere to push up to. Five fat women should go on that seat, but look at you!

And our own grandmother here is none too plump herself. . . . Nana, if they won't push, come to the front seat with me."

". . . Hei,[9] scholar, go to the back. . . .

. . . And do not scowl on me. I know your sort too well. Something tells me you do not have any job at all. As for that suit you are wearing and looking so grand in, you hired or borrowed it. . . ."

"Oh you drivers!"

Oh you drivers. . . .

8. Expression of the absurdity of things. 9. Hey there, or keep quiet!

The scholar who read this tengram[1] thing, said it was made about three days ago. My lady's husband sent it. . . . Three days. . . . God—that is too long ago. Have they buried her . . . where? Or did they cut her up . . . I should not think about it . . . or something will happen to me. Eleven or twelve . . . Efua Panyin, Okuma, Kwame Gyasi and who else? But they should not have left me here. Sometimes . . . ah, I hate this nausea. But it is this smell of petrol. Now I have remembered I never could travel in a lorry.[2] I always was so sick. But now I hope at least that will not happen. These young people will think it is because I am old and they will laugh. At least if I knew the child of my child was alive, it would have been good. And the little things she sent me. . . . Sometimes some people like Mensima and Nkansa make me feel as if I had been a barren woman instead of only one with whom infant-morality pledged friendship. . . .

I will give her that set of earrings, bracelet and chair which Odwumfo Ata made for me. It is the most beautiful and the most expensive thing I have. . . . It does not hurt me to think that I am going to die very soon and have them and their children gloating over my things. After all what did they they swallow my children for? It does not hurt me at all If I had been someone else, I would have given them all away before I died. But it does not matter. They can share their own curse. Now, that is the end of me and my roots. . . . Eternal death has worked like a warrior rat, with diabolical sense of duty, to gnaw my bottom. Everything is finished now. The vacant lot is swept and the scraps of old sugar-cane pulp, dry sticks and bunches of hair burnt . . . how it reeks, the smoke!

"O, Nana do not weep. . . ."

"Is the old woman weeping?"

"If the only child of your only child died, won't you weep?"

"Why do you ask me? Did I know her grandchild is dead?"

"Where have you been, not in this lorry? Where were your ears when we were discussing it?"

"I do not go putting my mouth in other people's affairs. . . ."

"So what?"

"So go and die."

"*Hei, hei,* it is prohibited to quarrel in my lorry."

"Draba, here is me, sitting quiet and this lady of muscles and bones being cheeky to me."

"Look, I can beat you."

"Beat me . . . beat me . . . let's see."

"*Hei,* you are not civilized, eh?"

"Keep quiet and let us think, both of you, or I will put you down."

"Nana, do not weep. There is God above."

Thank you my master.

"But we are in Cape Coast already."

Meewuo! My God, hold me tight or something will happen to me.

My master, I will come down here.

"O Nana, I thought you said you were going to the hospital. . . . We are not there yet."

I am saying maybe I will get down here and ask my way around.

1. I.e., telegram. 2. Truck or bus.

"Nana, you do not know these people, eh? They are very impudent here. They have no use for old age. So they do not respect it. Sit down, I will take you there."

Are you going there, my master?

"No, but I will take you there."

Ah, my master, your old mother thanks you. Do not shed a tear when you hear of my death . . . my master, your old mother thanks you.

I hear there is somewhere where they keep corpses until their owners claim them . . . if she has been buried, then I must find her husband . . . Esi Amfoa, what did I come to do under this sky? I have buried all my children and now I am going to bury my only grandchild!

"Nana we are there."

Is this the hospital?

"Yes, Nana. What is your child's name?"

Esi Amfoa. His father named her after me.

"Do you know her European name?"

No, my master.

"What shall we do?"

" . . . Ei lady, Lady Nurse, we are looking for somebody."

"You are looking for somebody and can you read? If you cannot, you must ask someone what the rules in the hospital are. You can only come and visit people at three o'clock."

Lady, please. She was my only grandchild. . . .

"Who? And anyway, it is none of our business."

Nana, you must be patient . . . and not cry. . . .

"Old woman, why are you crying, it is not allowed here. No one must make any noise. . . ."

My lady, I am sorry but she was all I had.

"Who? Oh, are you the old woman who is looking for somebody?"

Yes.

"Who is he?"

She was my granddaughter—the only child of my only son.

"I mean, what was her name?"

Esi Amfoa.

"Esi Amfoa . . . Esi Amfoa. I am sorry, we do not have anyone whom they call like that here."

Is that it?

"Nana, I told you they may know only her European name here."

My master, what shall we do then?

"What is she ill with?"

She came here to have a child. . . .

" . . . And they say, they opened her stomach and removed the baby. Oh . . . oh, I see."

My Lord, hold me tight so that nothing will happen to me now.

"I see. It is the Caesarean case."

"Nurse, you know her?"

And when I take her back, Anona Ebusuafo will say that I did not wait for them to come with me. . . .

"Yes. Are you her brother?"

"No. I am only the driver who brought the old woman."

"Did she bring all her clan?"

"No. She came alone."

"Strange thing for a villager to do."

I hope they have not cut her up already.

"Did she bring a whole bag full of cassava and plantain and kenkey?"[3]

"No. She has only her little bundle."

"Follow me. But you must not make any noise This is not the hour for coming here. . . ."

My master, does she know her?

"Yes."

I hear it is very cold where they put them. . .

It was feeding time for new babies. When old Esi Amfoa saw young Esi Amfoa, the latter was all neat and nice. White sheets and all. She did not see the beautiful stitches under the sheets. "This woman is a tough bundle," Dr. Gyamfi had declared after the identical twins had been removed, the last stitches had been threaded off and Mary Koomson, alias Esi Amfoa, had come to.

The old woman somersaulted into the room and lay groaning, not screaming, by the bed. For was not her last pot broken? So they lay them in state even in hospitals and not always cut them up for instruction?

The Nursing Sister was furious. Young Esi Amfoa spoke. And this time old Esi Amfoa wept loud and hard—wept all her tears.

Scrappy nurse-under-training, Jessy Treeson, second-generation-Cape Coaster-her-grandmother-still-remembered-at-Egyaa No. 7 said, "As for these villagers," and giggled.

Draba Anan looked hard at Jessy Treeson, looked hard at her, all of her: her starched uniform, apron and cap . . . and then dismissed them all. . . . "Such a cassava stick . . but maybe I will break my toe if I kicked at her buttocks," he thought.

And by the bed the old woman was trying hard to rise and look at the only pot which had refused to get broken.

1970

3. A staple food made from fermented corn; "cassava": another staple food.

GLORIA ANZALDÚA

1942–

"I think Chicano families can be really hard on women and maybe they are hard on men, too. Very early on you start being taught how to be a man and being taught how to be a little woman and the divisions are pretty rigid": with characteristic candor, Gloria Anzaldúa describes her refusal to conform to dictates that would force girls to drop out of school so they could devote their time to cooking or sewing or cleaning and that in particular would limit her fierce love of reading. The daughter of Urbano and Amalia Garcia, Anzaldúa was born on a ranch settlement called Jésus Maria of the Valley of South Texas, but at eleven she moved with her family to Hargill, Texas. After the death of her father when she was fifteen, she

worked with her family as an agricultural laborer until she became the first woman from her region to go to college, earning her B.A. from Pan American University in 1969 and then her M.A. in English and education from the University of Texas, Austin. While subsequently lecturing at San Francisco State University, the University of California, Santa Cruz, and Vermont College, Anzaldúa devoted her attention to Chicana women and culture at least in part because of her keen awareness of the fragility of the advances Third World women of color have made.

To some extent, Anzaldúa's goals met early resistence. In her undergraduate and graduate classes, Anzaldúa found it difficult to pursue Chicano and feminist studies since programs in those areas did not yet exist. Her collaborative work on the multicultural anthology *This Bridge Called My Back* (1981) brought a measure of recognition, but also the censure of her mother and sister, who objected to her disclosures about the family and in particular to her essay *La Prieta* ("The Dark One"), a piece describing her vision of a coalition between Third World women, feminists, and lesbians. While teaching at Vermont and experiencing herself as a foreigner, Anzaldúa conceived her plan for *Borderlands* (1987), an ambitious book prefaced by her description of herself as "a border woman" who "grew up between two cultures, the Mexican (with a heavy Indian influence) and the Anglo (as a member of a colonized people in our own territory)." Combining historical scholarship with poetry, linguistics with mythology, the text is as preoccupied by formal boundaries as by geographical lines of demarcation. Anzaldúa's most recent publication, *Making Face, Making Soul/Haciendo Caras* (1990), reveals her continuing fascination with crossing aesthetic and physical states of mind and matter.

Tlilli, Tlapalli[1] / The Path of the Red and Black Ink

Out of poverty, poetry;
out of suffering, song.
—a Mexican saying

When I was seven, eight, nine, fifteen, sixteen years old, I would read in bed with a flashlight under the covers, hiding my self-imposed insomnia from my mother. I preferred the world of the imagination to the death of sleep. My sister, Hilda, who slept in the same bed with me, would threaten to tell my mother unless I told her a story.

I was familiar with *cuentos*[2]—my grandmother told stories like the one about her getting on top of the roof while down below rabid coyotes were ravaging the place and wanting to get at her. My father told stories about a phantom giant dog that appeared out of nowhere and sped along the side of the pickup no matter how fast he was driving.

Nudge a Mexican and she or he will break out with a story. So, huddling under the covers, I made up stories for my sister night after night. After a while she wanted two stories per night. I learned to give her installments, building up the suspense with convoluted complications until the story climaxed several nights later. It must have been then that I decided to put stories on paper. It

1. Annotations and translations by Lee-Ann Laffey, Margalida Pons, and Chris Sindt. Nahuatl is the language primarily spoken by the Aztec; in Nahuatl the word *Nahuatl* means "that which is near, or that which is plainly audible." *Tlilli*: black or red ink. *Tlapalli*:

dyed, usually with blood. Anzaldúa defines it later in the text as "(the black and red ink painted on codices) [which] were colors symbolizing escrituras y sabiduría (writing and wisdom)."
2. Stories or tales (Spanish).

must have been then that working with images and writing became connected to night.

Invoking Art

In the ethno-poetics and performance of the shaman, my people, the Indians, did not split the artistic from the functional, the sacred from the secular, art from everyday life. The religious, social and aesthetic purposes of art were all intertwined. Before the Conquest, poets gathered to play music, dance, sing and read poetry in open-air places around the *Xochicuahuitl*,[3] *el Árbol Florido*, Tree-in-Flower. (The *Coaxihuitl*[4] or morning glory is called the snake plant and its seeds, known as *ololiuhqui*, are hallucinogenic.) The ability of story (prose and poetry) to transform the storyteller and the listener into something or someone else is shamanistic. The writer, as shape-changer, is a *nahual*,[5] a shaman.

In looking at this book that I'm almost finished writing, I see a mosaic pattern (Aztec-like) emerging, a weaving pattern, thin here, thick there. I see a preoccupation with the deep structure, the underlying structure, with the gesso[6] underpainting that is red earth, black earth. I can see the deep structure, the scaffolding. If I can get the bone structure right, then putting flesh on it proceeds without too many hitches. The problem is that the bones often do not exist prior to the flesh, but are shaped after a vague and broad shadow of its form is discerned or uncovered during beginning, middle and final stages of the writing. Numerous overlays of paint, rough surfaces, smooth surfaces make me realize I am preoccupied with texture as well. Too, I see the barely contained color threatening to spill over the boundaries of the object it represents and into other "objects" and over the borders of the frame. I see a hybridization of metaphor, different species of ideas popping up here, popping up there, full of variations and seeming contradictions, though I believe in an ordered, structured universe where all phenomena are interrelated and imbued with spirit. This almost finished product seems an assemblage, a montage, a beaded work with several leitmotifs and with a central core, now appearing, now disappearing in a crazy dance. The whole thing has had a mind of its own, escaping me and insisting on putting together the pieces of its own puzzle with minimal direction from my will. It is a rebellious, willful entity, a precocious girl-child forced to grow up too quickly, rough, unyielding, with pieces of feather sticking out here and there, fur, twigs, clay. My child, but not for much longer. This female being is angry, sad, joyful, is *Coatlicue*,[7] dove, horse, serpent, cactus. Though it is a flawed thing—a clumsy, complex, groping blind thing—for me it is alive, infused with spirit. I talk to it; it talks to me.

I make my offerings of incense and cracked corn, light my candle. In my head I sometimes will say a prayer—an affirmation and a voicing of intent. Then I run water, wash the dishes or my underthings, take a bath, or mop the kitchen floor. This "induction" period sometimes takes a few minutes, some-

3. Nahuatl. The tree located in the other world "decorated with flowers"—the source of God. Defined by Anzaldúa as *el Arbol Florido*, Spanish for "the Tree in Flower."

4. Nahuatl. (Nahuatl and Spanish words defined in the text will not be annotated.)

5. Nahuatl. Usually *nahualli*, shaman, sorcerer, one who uses spells and incantations.

6. A plaster of Paris preparation used as a base for low-relief or as a surface for painting.

7. Nahuatl. Snake-Skirted One; a fertility goddess. The *coatl* is a snake, and *icue* means "it is her skirt."

times hours. But always I go against a resistance. Something in me does not want to do this writing. Yet once I'm immersed in it, I can go fifteen to seventeen hours in one sitting and I don't want to leave it.

My "stories" are acts encapsulated in time, "enacted" every time they are spoken aloud or read silently. I like to think of them as performances and not as inert and "dead" objects (as the aesthetics of Western culture think of art works). Instead, the work has an identity; it is a "who" or a "what" and contains the presences of persons, that is, incarnations of gods or ancestors or natural and cosmic powers. The work manifests the same needs as a person, it needs to be "fed," *la tengo que bañar y vestir*.[8]

When invoked in rite, the object/event is "present;" that is, "enacted," it is both a physical thing and the power that infuses it. It is metaphysical in that it "spins its energies between gods and humans" and its task is to move the gods. This type of work dedicates itself to managing the universe and its energies. I'm not sure what it is when it is at rest (not in performance). It may or may not be a "work" then. A mask may only have the power of presence during a ritual dance and the rest of the time it may merely be a "thing." Some works exist forever invoked, always in performance. I'm thinking of totem poles, cave paintings. Invoked art is communal and speaks of everyday life. It is dedicated to the validation of humans; that is, it makes people hopeful, happy, secure, and it can have negative effects as well, which propel one towards a search for validation.

The aesthetic of virtuosity, art typical of Western European cultures, attempts to manage the energies of its own internal system such as conflicts, harmonies, resolutions and balances. It bears the presences of qualities and internal meanings. It is dedicated to the validation of itself. Its task is to move humans by means of achieving mastery in content, technique, feeling. Western art is always whole and always "in power." It is individual (not communal). It is "psychological" in that it spins its energies between itself and its witness.

Western cultures behave differently toward works of art than do tribal cultures. The "sacrifices" Western cultures make are in housing their art works in the best structures designed by the best architects; and in servicing them with insurance, guards to protect them, conservators to maintain them, specialists to mount and display them, and the educated and upper classes to "view" them. Tribal cultures keep art works in honored and sacred places in the home and elsewhere. They attend them by making sacrifices of blood (goat or chicken), libations of wine. They bathe, feed, and clothe them. The works are treated not just as objects, but also as persons. The "witness" is a participant in the enactment of the work in a ritual, and not a member of the privileged classes.

Ethnocentrism is the tyranny of Western aesthetics. An Indian mask in an American museum is transposed into an alien aesthetic system where what is missing is the presence of power invoked through performance ritual. It has become a conquered thing, a dead "thing" separated from nature and, therefore, its power.

8. I have to bathe it and dress it (Spanish).

Modern Western painters have "borrowed," copied, or otherwise extrapolated the art of tribal cultures and called it cubism, surrealism, symbolism. The music, the beat of the drum, the Blacks' jive talk. All taken over. Whites, along with a good number of our own people, have cut themselves off from their spiritual roots, and they take our spiritual art objects in an unconscious attempt to get them back. If they're going to do it, I'd like them to be aware of what they are doing and to go about doing it the right way. Let's all stop importing Greek myths and the Western Cartesian split point of view and root ourselves in the mythological soil and soul of this continent. White America has only attended to the body of the earth in order to exploit it, never to succor it or to be nurtured in it. Instead of surreptitiously ripping off the vital energy of people of color and putting it to commercial use, whites could allow themselves to share and exchange and learn from us in a respectful way. By taking up *curanderismo*, Santeria, shamanism, Taoism, Zen[9] and otherwise delving into the spiritual life and ceremonies of multi-colored people, Anglos would perhaps lose the white sterility they have in their kitchens, bathrooms, hospitals, mortuaries and missile bases. Though in the conscious mind, black and dark may be associated with death, evil and destruction, in the subconscious mind and in our dreams, white is associated with disease, death and hopelessness. Let us hope that the left hand, that of darkness, of femaleness, of "primitiveness," can divert the indifferent, right-handed, "rational" suicidal drive that, unchecked, could blow us into acid rain in a fraction of a millisecond.

Ni cuicani: *I, the Singer*

For the ancient Aztecs, *tlilli, tlapalli, la tinta negra y roja de sus códices* (the black and red ink painted on codices) were the colors symbolizing *escritura y sabiduría* (writing and wisdom). They believed that through metaphor and symbol, by means of poetry and truth, communication with the Divine could be attained, and *topan* (that which is above—the gods and spirit world) could be bridged with *mictlán* (that which is below—the underworld and the region of the dead).

Poet: she pours water from the mouth of the pump, lowers the handle then lifts it, lowers, lifts. Her hands begin to feel the pull from the entrails, the live animal resisting. A sigh rises up from the depths, the handle becomes a wild thing in her hands, the cold sweet water gushes out, splashing her face, the shock of nightlight filling the bucket.

An image is a bridge between evoked emotion and conscious knowledge; words are the cables that hold up the bridge. Images are more direct, more immediate than words, and closer to the unconscious. Picture language precedes thinking in words; the metaphorical mind precedes analytical consciousness.

The Shamanic State

When I create stories in my head, that is, allow the voices and scenes to be projected in the inner screen of my mind, I "trance." I used to think I was

9 A school of Buddhism which originated in Japan and China and asserts that enlightenment is achieved through meditation, self-contemplation, and intuition. *Curanderismo*: the study of curing (Spanish). *Santeria*: religion practiced originally in Cuba which identifies Yoruba deities with Roman Catholic saints.

going crazy or that I was having hallucinations. But now I realize it is my job, my calling, to traffic in images. Some of these film-like narratives I write down; most are lost, forgotten. When I don't write the images down for several days or weeks or months, I get physically ill. Because writing invokes images from my unconscious, and because some of the images are residues of trauma which I then have to reconstruct, I sometimes get sick when I *do* write. I can't stomach it, become nauseous, or burn with fever, worsen. But, in reconstructing the traumas behind the images, I make "sense" of them, and once they have "meaning" they are changed, transformed. It is then that writing heals me, brings me great joy.

To facilitate the "movies" with soundtracks, I need to be alone, or in a sensory-deprived state. I plug up my ears with wax, put on my black cloth eye-shades, lie horizontal and unmoving, in a state between sleeping and waking, mind and body locked into my fantasy. I am held prisoner by it. My body is experiencing events. In the beginning it is like being in a movie theater, as pure spectator. Gradually I become so engrossed with the activities, the conversations, that I become a participant in the drama. I have to struggle to "disengage" or escape from my "animated story," I have to get some sleep so I can write tomorrow. Yet I am gripped by a story which won't let me go. Outside the frame, I am film director, screenwriter, camera operator. Inside the frame, I am the actors—male and female—I am desert sand, mountain, I am dog, mosquito. I can sustain a four- to six-hour "movie." Once I am up, I can sustain several "shorts" of anywhere between five and thirty minutes. Usually these "narratives" are the offspring of stories acted out in my head during periods of sensory deprivation.

My "awakened dreams" are about shifts. Thought shifts, reality shifts, gender shifts: one person metamorphoses into another in a world where people fly through the air, heal from mortal wounds. I am playing with my Self, I am playing with the world's soul, I am the dialogue between my Self and *el espíritu del mundo.*[1] I change myself, I change the world.

Sometimes I put the imagination to a more rare use. I choose words, images, and body sensations and animate them to impress them on my consciousness, thereby making changes in my belief system and reprogramming my consciousness. This involves looking my inner demons in the face, then deciding which I want in my psyche. Those I don't want, I starve; I feed them no words, no images, no feelings. I spend no time with them, share not my home with them. Neglected, they leave. This is harder to do than to merely generate "stories." I can only sustain this activity for a few minutes.

I write the myths in me, the myths I am, the myths I want to become. The word, the image and the feeling have a palatable energy, a kind of power. *Con imagenes domo mi miedo, cruzo los abismos que tengo por dentro. Con palabras me hago piedra, pájaro, puente de serpientes arrastrando a ras del suelo todo lo que soy, todo lo que algún día seré.*[2]

> *Los que están mirando (leyendo),*
> *los que cuentan (o refieren lo que leen).*

1. The spirit of the world (Spanish).
2. With images I control my fear, I cross the abyss inside me. With words I become stone, bird, bridge of snakes dragging to the ground all that I am, all that some day I will be (Spanish).

Los que vuelven ruidosamente las hojas de los códices.
Los que tienen en su poder
la tinta negra y roja (la sabiduría)
y lo pintado,
ellos nos llevan, nos guían,
nos dicen el camino.[3]

Writing Is a Sensuous Act

Tallo mi cuerpo como si estuviera lavando un trapo. Toco las saltadas venas de
mis manos, mis chichis adormecidas como pájaros a la anochecer. Estoy encor-
bada sobre la cama. Las imagenes aletean alrededor de mi cama como murciéla-
gos, la sábana como que tuviese alas. El ruido de los trenes subterráneos en mi
sentido como conchas. Parece que las paredes del cuarto se me arriman cada vez
más cerquita.[4]

Picking out images from my soul's eye, fishing for the right words to recre-
ate the images. Words are blades of grass pushing past the obstacles, sprouting
on the page; the spirit of the words moving in the body is as concrete as flesh
and as palpable; the hunger to create is as substantial as fingers and hand.

I look at my fingers, see plumes growing there. From the fingers, my feath-
ers, black and red ink drips across the page. *Escribo con la tinta de mi sangre.*[5] I
write in red. Ink. Intimately knowing the smooth touch of paper, its speech-
lessness before I spill myself on the insides of trees. Daily, I battle the silence
and the red. Daily, I take my throat in my hands and squeeze until the cries
pour out, my larynx and soul sore from the constant struggle.

Something to Do with the Dark

Quien canta, sus males espanta.
—*un dicho*[6]

The toad comes out of its hiding place inside the lobes of my brain. It's
going to happen again. The ghost of the toad that betrayed me—I hold it in
my hand. The toad is sipping the strength from my veins, it is sucking my pale
heart. I am a dried serpent skin, wind scuttling me across the hard ground,
pieces of me scattered over the countryside. And there in the dark I meet the
crippled spider crawling in the gutter, the day-old newspaper fluttering in the
dirty rain water.

Musa bruja, venga. Cubrese con
una sábana y espante mis demonios que a rempujones y a cachetadas me roban la
pluma me rompen el sueño. Musa, ¡misericordia!

3. Those who are watching (reading), / those who re-
late (or recount what they read). / Those who loudly
turn the pages of the manuscripts. / Those who have in
their power / the black and red ink (the wisdom) / and
that which is painted, / those are the ones who lead us,
guide us, and tell us the way (Spanish; from Miguel
Leon-Portilla's *Los Antiguos Mexicanos: A través de sus
cronicas y canveves*, p 125).
4. I carve my body as if I were a washing rag. I touch
my hands' bulging veins, my sleepy breasts like birds at
nightfall I am bent over my bed Images fly around my
bed like bats, the sheet flutters as if it had wings. The
noise of the underground trains like shells in my
senses. I seems that the walls of the room move to-
ward me coming closer and closer (Spanish).
5. I write with the dye of my blood (Spanish).
6. He who sings throws away his troubles—a saying
(Spanish)

> *Óigame, musa bruja. ¿Porqué*
> *huye uste' en mi cara? Su grito me desarrolla de mi caracola, me sacude el alma.*
> *Vieja, quítese de aquí con sus alas de navaja. Ya no me despedaze mi cara. Vaya*
> *con sus pinche uñas que me desgarran de los ojos hasta los talones. Váyese a la*
> *tiznada. Que no me coman, le digo. Que no me coman sus nueve dedos caníbales.*
> *Hija negra de la noche, carnala,*
> *¿Porqué me sacas las tripas, porqué cardas mis entrañas? Este hilvanando pal-*
> *abras con tripas me está matando. Jija de la noche ivete a la chingada!*[7]

Writing produces anxiety. Looking inside myself and my experience, look-
ing at my conflicts, engenders anxiety in me. Being a writer feels very much
like being a Chicana, or being queer—a lot of squirming, coming up against
all sorts of walls. Or its opposite: nothing defined or definite, a boundless,
floating state of limbo where I kick my heels, brood, percolate, hibernate and
wait for something to happen.

Living in a state of psychic unrest, in a Borderland, is what makes poets
write and artists create. It is like a cactus needle embedded in the flesh. It wor-
ries itself deeper and deeper, and I keep aggravating it by poking at it. When it
begins to fester I have to do something to put an end to the aggravation and to
figure out why I have it. I get deep down into the place where it's rooted in my
skin and pluck away at it, playing it like a musical instrument—the fingers
pressing, making the pain worse before it can get better. Then out it comes.
No more discomfort, no more ambivalence. Until another needle pierces the
skin. That's what writing is for me, an endless cycle of making it worse, making
it better, but always making meaning out of the experience, whatever it may
be.

> My flowers shall not cease to live;
> my songs shall never end:
> I, a singer, intone them;
> they become scattered, they are spread about.
> —*Cantares mexicanos*[8]

To write, to be a writer, I have to trust and believe in myself as a speaker, as
a voice for the images. I have to believe that I can communicate with images
and words and that I can do it well. A lack of belief in my creative self is a lack
of belief in my total self and vice versa—I cannot separate my writing from any
part of my life. It is all one.

When I write it feels like I'm carving bone. It feels like I'm creating my own
face, my own heart—a Nahuatl concept. My soul makes itself through the cre-
ative act. It is constantly remaking and giving birth to itself through my body.
It is this learning to live with *la Coatlicue* that transforms living in the
Borderlands from a nightmare into a numinous experience. It is always a
path/state to something else.

7. Come, witch-muse. Cover yourself with a sheet and
expel my demons which push and slap me, and steal
my pen, and interrupt my sleep. Muse, have mercy!
 Listen to me, witch-muse. Why do you flee in front
of me? Your scream unwinds me from my shell, it
moves my soul. Get out of here with your knife-like
wings, old hag. Don't cut my face into pieces. Go with
your wretched fingernails that rip me from my eyes to
my heels. Get lost. Don't let them eat me, I say to her.
Don't let your cannibal fingers eat me.
 Lustful daughter of the night, why do you remove
my guts, wrapping up my innards? This tacking of
words to guts is killing me. Daughter of the night, go to
hell! (Spanish).
8. Mexican songs (Spanish).

In Xóchilt in Cuícatl[9]

She writes while other people
sleep. Something is trying to come out. She fights the words, pushes them
down, down, a woman with morning sickness in the middle of the night. How
much easier it would be to carry a baby for nine months and then expel it per-
manently. These continuous multiple pregnancies are going to kill her. She is
the battlefield for the pitched fight between the inner image and the words
trying to recreate it. *La musa bruja*[1] has no manners. Doesn't she know, nights
are for sleeping?

She is getting too close to the
mouth of the abyss. She is teetering on the edge, trying to balance while she
makes up her mind whether to jump in or to find a safer way down. That's why
she makes herself sick—to postpone having to jump blindfolded into the
abyss of her own being and there in the depths confront her face, the face un-
derneath the mask.

To be a mouth—the cost is too
high—her whole life enslaved to that devouring mouth. *Todo pasaba por esa
boca, el viento, e' fuego, los mares y la Tierra.*[2] Her body, a crossroads, a fragile
bridge, cannot support the tons of cargo passing through it. She wants to in-
stall "stop" and "go" signal lights, instigate a curfew, police Poetry. But some-
thing wants to come out.

Blocks (*Coatl cue* states) are related to my cultural identity. The painful pe-
riods of confusion that I suffer from are symptomatic of a larger creative
process: cultural shifts. The stress of living with cultural ambiguity both com-
pels me to write and blocks me. It isn't until I'm almost at the end of the
blocked state that I remember and recognize it for what it is. As soon as this
happens, the piercing light of awareness melts the block and I accept the deep
and the darkness and I hear one of my voices saying, "I am tired of fighting. I
surrender. I give up, let go, let the walls fall. On this night of the hearing of
faults, *Tlazolteotl, diosa de la cara negra*,[3] let fall the cockroaches that live in
my hair, the rats that nestle in my skull. Gouge out my lame eyes, rout my
demon from its nocturnal cave. Set torch to the tiger that stalks me. Loosen
the dead faces gnawing my cheekbones. I am tired of resisting. I surrender. I
give up, let go, let the walls fall."

And in descending to the depths I realize that down is up, and I rise up from
and into the deep. And once again I recognize that the internal tension of op-
positions can propel (if it doesn't tear apart) the *mestiza*[4] writer out of the
metate[5] where she is being ground with corn and water, eject her out as *nahual*,

9. Nahuatl. Defined by Anzaldúa in a note as "Flower
and Song."
1. The witch-muse, or the poor muse (Spanish).
2. All that passes through this mouth, the wind, the
fire, the seas of the earth (Spanish).
3. *Tlazolteotle* is a Nahuatl word, defined here by
Anzaldúa as, in Spanish, goddess of the black face.
4. A woman of mixed European and Native American
ancestry. This term has special significance for
Anzaldúa, who explains earlier in *Borderlands / La
Frontera* that "our Spanish, Indian, and mestizo ances-
tors explored and settled parts of the U.S. Southwest

as early as the sixteenth century. For every gold-hungry
conquistador and soul-hungry missionary who came
from North Mexico, ten to twenty Indians and *mesti-
zos* went along as porters or in other capacities. For the
Indians, this constituted a return to the place of origin,
Aztlán, thus making Chicanos originally or secondarily
indigenous to the Southwest. Indians and *mestizos*
from central Mexico intermarried with North
American Indians. The continual intermarriage be-
tween Mexicans and American Indians formed an
even greater *mestizaje*."
5. Flat stone used for grinding corn (Spanish).

an agent of transformation, able to modify and shape primordial energy and therefore able to change herself and others into turkey, coyote, tree, or human.

 I sit here before my computer, *Amiguita*,[6] my altar on top of the monitor with the *Virgen de Coatlalopeuh* candle and copal incense burning. My companion, a wooden serpent staff with feathers, is to my right while I ponder the ways metaphor and symbol concretize the spirit and etherealize the body. The Writing is my whole life, it is my obsession. This vampire which is my talent does not suffer other suitors. Daily I court it, offer my neck to its teeth. This is the sacrifice that the act of creation requires, a blood sacrifice. For only through the body, through the pulling of flesh, can the human soul be transformed. And for images, words, stories to have this transformative power, they must arise from the human body—flesh and bone—and from the Earth's body—stone, sky, liquid, soil. This work, these images, piercing tongue or ear lobes with cactus needle, are my offerings, are my Aztecan blood sacrifices.

<div align="right">1987</div>

6. Play on words referring to the computer brand known as Amigo—literally, in Spanish, friend.

MARILYN HACKER
1942–

"Where are the expatriate *salonnières?*" Marilyn Hacker asks with wry humor as she celebrates the sometimes lost, sometimes (re)found lesbian literary tradition in her high-spirited *Ballad of Ladies Lost and Found.* Both a deeply committed feminist and an artist of extraordinary technical accomplishment, Hacker deploys a range of forms—sestinas, sonnets, villanelles, ballades—to produce a poetry that is simultaneously tough and tender in a style characterized by one critic as "the colloquial sublime."

 Born and brought up in New York City, Hacker married the science fiction writer Samuel Delaney in 1961; they had one daughter and were divorced in 1980. She has been a teacher and a bookseller as well as the editor of such prestigious journals as *Thirteenth Moon* and the *Kenyon Review.* Her collections of verse include *Presentation Piece*, for which she won the National Book Award in 1974, *Assumptions* (1985), *Love, Death and the Changing of the Seasons* (1986), *The Hang-Glider's Daughter* (1990), *Winter Numbers* (1994), and *Selected Poems, 1965–1990* (1994). In recent years, she has lived part of the time in Paris, ironically describing herself in the refrain of one poem as "another Jewish lesbian in France."

Almost Aubade[1]

The little hours: two lovers herd upstairs
two children, one of whom is one of theirs.
Past them, two of the other sex lope down,
dressed for mid-winter cruising bars in brown
bomber-jackets—their lives as uncluttered 5

1. A morning love song.

as their pink shaven cheeks, one of us muttered.
fumbling with keys. Yes, they did look alike.
Fooling their scarves and parkas on the bike,
the seven-year-old women shuck a heap
of ve vet jeans and Mary Janes. They sleep 10
diagonal, instantly, across the top
bunk, while their exhausted elders drop,
not to the bliss breasts melt to against breasts
yet, but to kitchen chairs. One interests
herself in omelets, listening anyhow. 15
It's certain that fine women pick at food.
A loaf of bread, a jug of wine, and thou[2]
shalt piecemeal total both. gripped in that mood
whose hunger makes a contrapunta. stutter
across connectives. Unwrap cheese, find butter, 20
dip bread crusts in a bowl of pasta sauce
saved from the children's supper. Tired because
of all we should stay up to say. we keep
awake together often as we sleep
together. I'll clear the plates. Leave your cup. 25
Lie in my arms until the kids get up.

 1981

Ballad of Ladies[1] Lost and Found

for Julia Álvarez

Where are the women who, *entre deux guerres*,[2]
came out on college-graduation trips,
came to New York on football scholarships,
came to town meeting in a decorous pair?
Where are the expatriate *salonnières*,[3] 5
the gym teacher, the math-department head?
Do nieces follow where their odd aunts led?
The elephants die off in Cagnes-sur-Mer.
H. D., whose "nature was bisexual,"[4]
and plain old Margaret Fuller died as well. 10

Where are the single-combat champions:
the Chevalier d'Eon with curled peruke,[5]
Big Sweet who ran with Zora in the jook,[6]
open-handed Winifred Ellerman,[7]

2. Quoting Edward FitzGerald's *Rubáiyát of Omar Khayyám* (1859), which continues: "Beside me singing in the Wilderness— / Oh, Wilderness were Paradise enow!" (stanza 11).
1. Most of the "ladies" mentioned in the poem appear in this anthology; the others are identified in footnotes.
2. Between two wars (French); i.e., World Wars I and II.
3. Frequenters of salons (French); gatherings both fashionable and intellectual.

4. H. D.'s "bisexual nature" came out in her analysis with Sigmund Freud. Cagnes-sur-Mer is a town on the southern coast of France frequented for years by French writers.
5. Wig. Charles d'Eon de Beaumont (1728–1810), French writer, spy, and female impersonator.
6. A dive, for drinking, dancing, and music. Big Sweet befriended Zora Neal Hurston; see *Dust Tracks on a Road* (1942).
7. Better known as Bryher (1894–1983), the author and heiress supported H. D. for much of her life.

Colette,[8] who hedged her bets and always won?　　15
Sojourner's sojourned where she need not pack
decades of whitegirl conscience on her back.
The spirit gave up Zora; she lay down
under a weed field miles from Eatonville,
and plain old Margaret Fuller died as well.　　20

Where's Stevie, with her pleated schoolgirl dresses,
and Rosa, with her permit to wear pants?[9]
Who snuffed Clara's *mestiza*[1] flamboyance
and bled Frida[2] onto her canvases?
Where are the Niggerati[3] hostesses,　　25
the kohl-eyed ivory poets with severe
chignons,[4] the rebels who grew out their hair,
the bulldaggers with marceled processes?[5]
Conglomerates co-opted Sugar Hill,[6]
and plain old Margaret Fuller died as well.　　30

Anne Hutchinson,[7] called witch, termagant, whore,
fell to the long knives, having tricked the noose.
Carolina María de Jesús'[8]
tale from the slag heaps of the landless poor
ended on a straw mat on a dirt floor.　　35
In action thirteen years after fifteen
in prison, Eleanor of Aquitaine[9]
accomplished half of Europe and fourscore
anniversaries for good or ill,
and plain old Margaret Fuller died as well.　　40

Has Ida B. persuaded Susan B.[1]
to pool resources for a joint campaign?
(Two Harriets act a pageant by Lorraine,
cheered by the butch drunk on the IRT[2]
who used to watch me watch her watching me.)　　45
We've notes by Angelina Grimké Weld[3]
for choral settings drawn from the *Compiled
Poems* of Angelina Weld Grimké.[4]
There's no such tense as Past Conditional,
and plain old Margaret Fuller died as well.　　50

8. Sidonie-Gabrielle Colette (1873–1954), French author.
9. It was illegal for women to wear trousers. Rosa Bonheur (1822–1899), French painter.
1. Spanish term for mixed blood, especially European and American Indian.
2. Frida Kahlo (1907–1954), Mexican painter.
3. Mocking term for black literary intellectuals of the Harlem Renaissance, used particularly by Hurston and the author Wallace Thurman (1902–1934).
4. Knot of hair at the nape of the neck. "Kohl": preparation used to darken the eyelids.
5. Lesbians, with hair straightened into deep, soft waves.
6. The most fashionable residential area of Harlem.
7. Religious liberal (1591–1643) banished from the Massachusetts Bay Colony who became a founder of Rhode Island.
8. Brazilian diarist (1913–1977).
9. Wife (1122?–1204) of Henry II, who imprisoned her from 1173 until his death in 1189. Under her son, Richard I, she administered the French lands and acted as regent of England.
1. Susan B. Anthony (1820–1906), a leader of the American women's suffrage movement. Ida B. Wells-Barnett (1862–1931), black journalist best known for her crusade against lynching.
2. One of the three formerly distinct subway systems in New York City. Lorraine Hansberry (1930–1965), black American playwright.
3. American abolitionist (1805–1879).
4. Black poet (1880–1958) of the Harlem Renaissance.

Who was Sappho's protégée,[5] and when did
we lose Hrotsvitha,[6] dramaturge and nun?
What did bibulous Suzanne Valadon[7]
think about Artemisia,[8] who tended
to make a life-size murderess look splendid? 55
Where's Aphra, fond of dalliance and the pun?
Where's Jane,[9] who didn't indulge in either one?
Whoever knows how Ende, Pintrix, ended
is not teaching Art History at Yale,
and plain old Margaret Fuller died as well. 60

Is Beruliah[2] upstairs behind the curtain
debating Juana Inés de la Cruz?[3]
Where's savante Anabella, Augusta-Goose,[4]
Fanny, Maude, Lidian, Freda and Caitlin,[5]
"without whom this could never have been written"? 65
Louisa[6] who wrote, scrimped, saved, sewed, and nursed,
Malinche,[7] who's, like all translators, cursed,
Bessie,[8] whose voice was hemp and steel and satin,
outside a segregated hospital,
and plain old Margaret Fuller died as well. 70

Where's Amy, who kept Ada[9] in cigars
and love, requited, both country and courtly,
although quinquagenarian and portly?
Where's Emily?[1] It's very still upstairs.
Where's Billie, whose strange fruit ripened in bars? 75
Where's the street-scavenging Little Sparrow?[2]
Too poor, too mean, too weird, too wide, too narrow:
Marie Curie,[3] examining her scars,
was not particularly beautiful;
and plain old Margaret Fuller died as well. 80

5. Poet (6th century B.C.) traditionally described as a teacher or mentor of younger women, sometimes identified with those named in her surviving poems (Atthis is the most frequently mentioned).
6. German poet, dramatist, and historian (935?–1002?).
7. French painter (1865–1938).
8. Artemisia Gentileschi, French painter; one of her most famous works is *Judith Decapitating Holofernes* (1615–1620).
9. I.e., Jane Austen.
1. The earliest illuminated manuscript attributed to a woman, the *Gerona Apocalypse* produced in Spain around 975, was so signed (or "Ende regirix").
2. Perhaps Beruliah (2nd century) scholar who is mentioned in the Talmud as learned in Jewish law, wife of the sage Rabbi Meir.
3. Mexican nun and poet (1651–1695), famous for her learning and her feminist ideas.
4. Augusta Leigh (1784–1851), the poet Byron's half-sister, affectionately called "Goose," Annabella Milbanke (1792–1860) the poet Byron's wife.
5. All best known for their connection with famous male writers. Fanny Brawne [Lindon] (1800–1865), whom the English poet John Keats loved. Maude Gonne [MacBride] (1866–1953), loved by the Irish poet William Butler Yeats. Lydia Jackson Emerson (1802–1892), second wife of the American essayist and poet Ralph Waldo Emerson. Frieda von Richthofen Lawrence (1879–1956), wife of English writer D. H. Lawrence. Caitlin Macnamara Thomas (1913–1994), wife of Welsh poet Dylan Thomas.
6. I.e., Louisa May Alcott.
7. Also known as Malintzin or Doña Marina (1501?–1550), an Aztec given as a slave to Cortés who acted as translator and helped him defeat Moctezuma (to Mexicans. *Malinche* became synonymous with "traitor").
8. Bessie Smith (1894–1937), American blues singer and songwriter, said (probably inaccurately) to have died while trying to be admitted to a whites-only hospital after an automobile accident.
9. The actress Ada Dwyer Russell (1863–1952) left the stage and lived with Amy Lowell from 1914 until Lowell died in 1925.
1. I.e., Emily Dickinson.
2. Edith Piaf (1915–1963), French singer. Billie Holiday (1915–1959), American jazz singer, who in 1939 recorded "Strange Fruit," a song about lynching.
3. Polish-born physicist (1867–1934), who codiscovered radium (and died of radiation-caused leukemia).

Who was the grandmother of Frankenstein?[4]
The Vindicatrix of the Rights of Woman.
Madame de Sévigné[5] said prayers to summon
the postman just as eloquent as mine,
though my Madame de Grignan's only nine. 85
But Mary Wollstonecraft had never known
that daughter, nor did Paula Modersohn.[6]
The three-day infants blinked in the sunshine.
The mothers turned their faces to the wall;
and plain old Margaret Fuller died as well. 90

Tomorrow night the harvest moon will wane
that's floodlighting the silhouetted wood.
Make your own footnotes; it will do you good.
Emeritae[7] have nothing to explain.
She wasn't very old, or really plain— 95
my age exactly, volumes incomplete.
"The life, the life, will it never be sweet?"[8]
She wrote it once; I quote it once again
midlife at midnight when the moon is full
and I can almost hear the warning bell 100
offshore, sounding through starlight like a stain
on waves that heaved over what she began
and truncated a woman's chronicle,
and plain old Margaret Fuller died as well.

 1985

Runaways Café I

You hailed a cab outside the nondescript
yuppie bar on Lexington[1] to go
downtown. Hug; hug: this time I brushed my lips
just across yours, and fire down below
in February flared. O bless and curse 5
what's waking up no wiser than it was.
I will not go to bed with you because
I want to very much. If that's perverse,
there are, you'll guess, perversions I'd prefer:
fill the lacunae[2] in: one; two; three; four . . . 10
I did, cab gone. While my late bus didn't come,
desire ticked over like a metronome.
For you, someone was waiting up at home.
For me, I might dare more if someone were.

 1986

4. I.e., Mary Wollstonecraft.
5. Marie de Rabutin-Chantal, marquise de Sévigné (1626–1695), French letter writer; most of her witty letters on fashionable and everyday life were to her daughter, Madame de Grignan (1646–1705) (line 85).
6. German painter (1876–1907), who died two weeks after childbirth.

7. Those [women] who have served out their terms (Latin, literal trans.); retired women holding an honorary title, used most often of professors.
8. From Fuller's *Memoirs* (1852) 1.237: "The life, the life! O, my God! shall the life never be sweet?"
1. I.e., Lexington Avenue in Manhattan.
2. Gaps.

Runaways Café II

For once, I hardly noticed what I ate
(salmon and broccoli and Saint-Véran[1]).
My elbow twitched like jumping beans; sweat ran
into my shirtsleeves. Could I concentrate
on anything but your leg against mine 5
under the table? It was difficult,
but I impersonated an adult
looking at you, and knocking back the wine.
Now that we both want to know what we want,
now that we both want to know what we know, 10
it still behooves us to know what to do:
be circumspect, be generous, be brave,
be honest, be together, and behave.
At least I didn't get white sauce down my front.

1986

From Orient Point

The art of living isn't hard to muster:[2]
Enjoy the hour, not what it might portend.
When someone makes you promises, don't trust her

unless they're in the here and now, and just her
willing largesse free-handed to a friend 5
The art of living isn't hard to muster:

groom the old dog, her coat gets back its luster;
take brisk walks so you're hungry at the end.
When someone makes you promises, don't trust her

to know she can afford what they will cost her 10
to keep until they're kept. Till then, pretend
the art of living isn't hard to muster.

Cooking, eating and drinking are a cluster
of pleasures. Next time, don't go round the bend
when someone makes you promises. Don't trust her 15

past where you'd trust yourself, and don't adjust her
words to mean more to you than she'd intend.
The art of living isn't hard to muster.

You never had her, so you haven't lost her
like spare house keys. Whatever *she* opens, 20
when someone makes you promises, don't. Trust your
art; go on living: that's not hard to muster.

1990

1. A wine.
2. An allusion to Elizabeth Bishop's *One Art* (p. 1658), which begins "The art of losing isn't hard to master."

From Cancer Winter

I woke up, and the surgeon said, "You're cured."
Strapped to the gurney, in the cotton gown
and pants I was wearing when they slid me down
onto the table, made new straps secure
while I stared at the hydra-headed O.R. 5
lamp, I took in the tall, confident, brown-
skinned man, and the ache I couldn't quite call pain
from where my right breast wasn't anymore
to my armpit. A not-yet-talking head,
I bit dry lips. What else could he have said? 10
And then my love was there in a hospital coat;
then my old love, still young and very scared.
Then I, alone, graphed clock hands' asymptote[1]
to noon, when I would be wheeled back upstairs.

 * * *

The odd and even numbers of the street 15
I live on are four thousand miles away
from an Ohio February day
snow-blanketed, roads iced over, with sleet
expected later, where I'm incomplete
as my abbreviated chest. I weigh 20
less—one breast less—since the Paris-gray
December evening, when a neighbor's feet
coming up ancient stairs, the feet I counted
on paper were the company I craved.
My calm right breast seethed with a grasping tumor. 25
The certainty of my returns amounted
to nothing. After terror, being brave
became another form of gallows humor.

 * * *

At noon, an orderly wheeled me upstairs
via an elevator hung with Season's 30
Greetings streamers, bright and false as treason.
The single room the surgeon let us share
the night before the knife was scrubbed and bare
except for blush-pink roses in a vase on
the dresser. Veering through a morphine haze on 35
the cranked bed, I was avidly aware
of my own breathing, my thirst, that it was over—
the week that ended on this New Year's Eve.
A known hand held, while I sipped, icewater,
afloat between ache, sleep, lover and lover. 40
The one who stayed would stay; the one would leave.
The hand that held the cup next was my daughter's.

1. I.e., their approach that never reaches noon.

* * *

It's become a form of gallows humor
to reread the elegies I wrote
at that pine table, with their undernote 45
of cancer as death's leitmotiv,[2] enumer-
ating my dead, the unknown dead, the rumor
of random and pandemic deaths. I thought
I was a witness, a survivor, caught
in a maelstrom and brought forth who knew more 50
of pair than some, but learned it loving others.
I need to find another metaphor
while I eat up stories of people's mothers
who had mastectomies. "She's eighty-four
this year, and *fine!*" Cell-shocked, I brace to do 55
what I can, an unimportant exiled Jew.

1994

2. Lead motif (German, literal trans.); dominant recurring theme.

SHARON OLDS

1942–

Boldly staking her claim to a place in the tradition of American poetry shaped by
such charismatic male speakers as Whitman and Ginsberg, Sharon Olds redefines
heroism as she proclaims the power of maternity, declaring in *The Language of the
Brag* that "I have done what you wanted to do, Walt Whitman, / Allan Ginsberg
. . . / . . . this exceptional / act with the exceptional heroic body, / this giving birth,
this glistening verb." Olds was born in San Francisco, and educated at Stanford
and Columbia, where she earned a Ph.D. in 1972. Married and the mother of two,
she has taught at a number of institutions, most recently New York University. A
poet who excavates the metaphysical significance of the physical and gives power-
ful public voice to the supposedly private and personal, she has examined the
erotics and politics of family life in four sometimes shockingly explicit collections
of verse, from *Satan Says* (1980) to *The Father* (1992), for which she has won a
number of prizes.

The Language of the Brag

I have wanted excellence in the knife-throw,
I have wanted to use my exceptionally strong and accurate arms
and my straight posture and quick electric muscles
to achieve something at the center of a crowd,
the blade piercing the bark deep, 5
the haft slowly and heavily vibrating like the cock.

I have wanted some epic use for my excellent body,
some heroism, some American achievement
beyond the ordinary for my extraordinary self,

magnetic and tensile, I have stood by the sandlot 10
and watched the boys play.

I have wanted courage, I have thought about fire
and the crossing of waterfalls, I have dragged around

my belly big with cowardice and safety,
my stool black with iron pills, 15
my huge breasts oozing mucus,
my legs swelling, my hands swelling,
my face swelling and darkening, my hair
falling out, my inner sex
stabbed again and again with terrible pain like a knife. 20
I have lain down.

I have lain down and sweated and shaken
and passed blood and feces and water and
slowly alone in the center of a circle I have
passed the new person out 25
and they have lifted the new person free of the act
and wiped the new person free of that
language of blood like praise all over the body.

I have done what you wanted to do, Walt Whitman,
Allen Ginsberg,[1] I have done this thing, 30
I and the other women this exceptional
act with the exceptional heroic body,
this giving birth, this glistening verb,
and I am putting my proud American boast
right here with the others. 35

 1980

Rite of Passage

As the guests arrive at my son's party
they gather in the living room—
short men, men in first grade
with smooth jaws and chins.
Hands in pockets, they stand around 5
jostling, jockeying for place, small fights
breaking out and calming. One says to another
How old are you? Six. I'm seven. So?
They eye each other, seeing themselves
tiny in the other's pupils. They clear their 10
throats a lot, a room of small bankers,
they fold their arms and frown. *I could beat you
up*, a seven says to a six,
the dark cake, round and heavy as a
turret, behind them on the table. My son, 15

<hr>

1. Both Whitman (1819–1892) and Ginsberg (b. 1926) are American poets known for celebrating themselves in
their writing.

freckles like specks of nutmeg on his cheeks.
chest narrow as the balsa keel of a
model boat, long hands
cool and thin as the day they guided him
out of me, speaks up as a host 20
for the sake of the group.
We could easily kill a two-year-old,
he says in his clear voice. The other
men agree, they clear their throats
like Generals they relax and get down to 25
playing war, celebrating my son's life.

 1984

The One Girl at the Boys' Party

When I take my girl to the swimming party
I set her down among the boys. They tower and
bristle she stands there smooth and sleek,
her math scores unfolding in the air around her.
They will strip to their suits, her body hard and 5
indivisible as a prime number,
they'll plunge in the deep end, she'll subtract
her height from ten feet, divide it into
hundreds of gallons of water, the numbers
bouncing in her mind like molecules of chlorine 10
in the bright blue pool. When they climb out,
her ponytail will hang its pencil lead
down her back, her narrow silk suit
with hamburgers and french fries printed on it
will glisten in the brilliant air, and they will 15
see her sweet face, solemn and
sealed, a factor of one, and she will
see their eyes, two each,
their legs, two each, and the curves of their sexes,
one each, and in her head she'll be doing her 20
wild multiplying, as the drops
sparkle and fall to the power of a thousand from her body.

 1984

This

Maybe if I did not have this
I would call myself my mother's daughter
or identify my soul with the blue bowl
that stood on the table, or with the gold wall, or the field.
I would call myself Cobb, Stuart, Torrance, 5
McLean, I would wear the plaid[1] at all times,

1. I.e., the wool garment worn by men of the Scottish Highlands, patterned in tartans that came distinctively to identify each clan.

clan green, blood red,
fine line of the purple vein,
if I did not have this. Or I would wrap my life in the
flag, in its wide swaths of blood, its 10
stars like broken bowls on that table,
or the cupped curve of my father's cereal-bowl forehead
here above my brows, or my mother's bad vein
running up the inside of my leg
like a river under the land. 15
 But I have this,
so this is who I am, this body
white as yellowish dough brushed with dry flour
pressed to his body. I am these breasts that
crush against him like collapsible silver 20
travel cups that telescope into themselves,
and the nipples that float in the center like hard
raspberries in bright sunlight, they
are my life, the dark sex that
takes him in as anyone in summer will 25
open their throat to the hose held up
hot on the edge of the sandlot—don't
ask me about my country or who my
father was or even what I do, if you
want to know who I am, I am this, *this*. 30

 1989

The Mortal One

All my life I had seen that long
glazed yellow narrow body,
not like Christ but like one of his saints,
or a hermit in gilt, all knees and raw ribs—
the ones who died of nettles, bile, 5
the one who died roasted over a fire.
I am glad we burned my father before
the bloom of mold could grow from him,
maybe it had begun in his bowels but we burned his bowels,
cleansing them with fire. Now I am learning 10
to think of his corpse without shock,
almost without grief, to take
the thought of it into each day, the way
when a loom parts the vertical threads,
half to the left half to the right, one can 15
throw the shuttlecock through with the warp-thread
tied to its feet, that small gold figure of my father—
how often I saw him in paintings and did not know him,
the tiny naked dead one in the corner,
the mortal one. 20

 1992

LOUISE GLÜCK

1943–

The critic Helen Vendler observed some time ago that Louise Glück's "cryptic narratives" are in some ways "far removed from the more circumstantial poetry written by many women poets . . . but they remain poems chiefly about childhood, family life, love, and motherhood." Recently, however, her long-standing concern with more general metaphysical questions has become clear—in, for instance, the brilliant theological meditations included in *The Wild Iris* (1992).

Born in New York City, Louise Glück attended Sarah Lawrence College and Columbia University. The mother of one son, she has been twice married and at present lives in Vermont with her husband, John Dranow. Her well-received collections of poetry include *Firstborn* (1968), *Descending Figure* (1980), *The Triumph of Achilles* (1985), *Ararat* (1990), and *The Wild Iris* (1992), for which she won the Pulitzer Prize. She has been awarded Rockefeller and Guggenheim fellowships; has taught verse writing at such institutions as Columbia University, the University of Iowa, and Williams College, and has also produced a volume of criticism, *Proofs and Theories: Essays on Poetry* (1994).

Throughout her career, as both the style and the subject of her *Illuminations* reveal, Glück has been intensely attentive to the sun that "rises / cold and single over the map of language." Whether stripped and chill or ecstatically pure, her beautifully crafted lines evoke essence more than circumstance. Yet, as Vendler argues, in their precise attention to such subjects as anorexia, motherhood, and marriage, Glück's words imply the details as well as the desires of femininity. At the same time, as a poem like *Vespers* demonstrates, Glück consistently sets the dramas of womanhood, including its familiar family romance, in a resonant spiritual context.

Illuminations[1]

1

My son squats in the snow in his blue snowsuit.
All around him stubble, the brown
degraded bushes. In the morning air
they seem to stiffen into words.
And, between, the white steady silence. 5
A wren hops on the airstrip
under the sill, drills
for sustenance, then spreads
its short wings, shadows
dropping from them. 10

2

Last winter he could barely speak
I moved his crib to face the window:
in the dark mornings
he would stand and grip the bars
until the walls appeared. 15

1. The title of a sequence of visionary prose poems by the French Symbolist poet Arthur Rimbaud (1854–1891).

calling *light, light,*
that one syllable, in
demand or recognition.

<div align="center">3</div>

He sits at the kitchen window
with his cup of apple juice.　　　　　　　　　　　　20
Each tree forms where he left it,
leafless, trapped in his breath.
How clear their edges are,
no limb obscured by motion,
as the sun rises　　　　　　　　　　　　　　　　25
cold and single over the map of language.

<div align="right">1980</div>

<div align="center">

From Dedication to Hunger

4 The Deviation [1]

</div>

It begins quietly
in certain female children:
the fear of death, taking as its form
dedication to hunger,
because a woman's body　　　　　　　　　　　　5
is a grave;[2] it will accept
anything. I remember
lying in bed at night
touching the soft, digressive breasts,
touching, at fifteen,　　　　　　　　　　　　　10
the interfering flesh
that I would sacrifice
until the limbs were free
of blossom and subterfuge: I felt
what I feel now, aligning these words　　　　　15
it is the same need to perfect,
of which death is the mere byproduct.

<div align="right">1980</div>

<div align="center">

Widows

</div>

My mother's playing cards with my aunt,
Spite and Malice, the family pastime, the game
my grandmother taught all her daughters.

Midsummer: too hot to go out.
Today, my aunt's ahead; she's getting the good cards.　　　　5

1. Glück is referring to *anorexia nervosa,* an eating disorder.
2. An allusion to the saying of Greek Orphic philosophers (6th century B.C.): "the body is a tomb" (*sōma sēma*).

My mother's dragging, having trouble with her concentration.
She can't get used to her own bed this summer.
She had no trouble last summer,
getting used to the floor. She learned to sleep there
to be near my father. 10
He was dying; he got a special bed.

My aunt doesn't give an inch, doesn't make
allowance for my mother's weariness.
It's how they were raised: you show respect by fighting.
To let up insults the opponent. 15

Each player has one pile to the left, five cards in the hand.
It's good to stay inside on days like this,
to stay where it's cool.
And this is better than other games, better than solitaire.

My grandmother thought ahead; she prepared her daughters. 20
They have cards they have each other.
They don't need any more companionship.

All afternoon the game goes on, but the sun doesn't move.
It just keeps bearing down, turning the grass yellow.
That's how it must seem to my mother. 25
And then, suddenly, something is over.

My aunt's been at it longer; maybe that's why she's playing better.
Her cards evaporate; that's what you want, that's the object: in the end,
the one who has nothing wins.

 1990

Terminal Resemblance

When I saw my father for the last time, we both did the same thing.
He was standing in the doorway to the living room,
waiting for me to get off the telephone.
That he wasn't also pointing to his watch
was a signal he wanted to talk. 5

Talk for us always meant the same thing.
He'd say a few words. I'd say a few back.
That was about it.

It was the end of August, very hot, very humid.
Next door, workmen dumped new gravel on the driveway. 10

My father and I avoided being alone;
we didn't know how to connect, to make small talk—
there didn't seem to be
any other possibilities.
So this was special: when a man's dying, 15
he has a subject.

It must have been early morning. Up and down the street
sprinklers started coming on. The gardener's truck
appeared at the end of the block,
then stopped, parking. 20
My father wanted to tell me what it was like to be dying.
He told me he wasn't suffering.
He said he kept expecting pain, waiting for it, but it never came.
All he felt was a kind of weakness.
I said I was glad for him, that I thought he was lucky. 25

Some of the husbands were getting in their cars, going to work.
Not people we knew anymore. New families,
families with young children.
The wives stood on the steps, gesturing or calling.

We said goodbye in the usual way, 30
no embrace, nothing dramatic.
When the taxi came, my parents watched from the front door,
arm in arm, my mother blowing kisses as she always does,
because it frightens her when a hand isn't being used.
But for a change, my father didn't just stand there. 35
This time, he waved.

That's what I did, at the door to the taxi.
Like him, waved to disguise my hand's trembling.

1990

First Memory

Long ago, I was wounded. I lived
to revenge myself
against my father, not
for what he was—
for what I was: from the beginning of time, 5
in childhood, I thought
that pain meant
I was not loved.
It meant I loved.

1990

Vespers[1]

End of August. Heat
like a tent over
John's garden. And some things
have the nerve to be getting started,
clusters of tomatoes, stands 5

1. A service of evening worship.

of late lilies—optimism
of the great stalks—imperial
gold and silver: but why
start anything
so close to the end? 10
Tomatoes that will never ripen, lilies
winter will kill, that won't
come back in spring. Or
are you thinking
I spend too much time 15
looking ahead, like
an old woman wearing
sweaters in summer;
are you saying I can
flourish, having 20
no hope
of enduring? Blaze of the red cheek, glory
of the open throat, white,
spotted with crimson.

 1992

Lullaby[1]

Time to rest now; you have had
enough excitement for the time being.

Twilight, then early evening. Fireflies
in the room, flickering here and there, here and there,
and summer's deep sweetness filling the open window. 5

Don't think of these things anymore.
Listen to my breathing, your own breathing
like the fireflies, each small breath
a flare in which the world appears.

I've sung to you long enough in the summer night. 10
I'll win you over in the end; the world can't give you
this sustained vision.

You must be taught to love me. Human beings must be taught to love
silence and darkness.

 1992

The Gold Lily

As I perceive
I am dying now and know

1. *Lullaby* is one of a number of poems in *The Wild Iris* that are spoken by a voice outside the human, presumably by the spirit traditionally defined as "God."

I will not speak again, will not
survive the earth, be summoned
out of it again, not 5
a flower yet, a spine only, raw dirt
catching my ribs, I call you,
father and master: all around,
my companions are failing, thinking
you do not see. How 10
can they know you see
unless you save us?
In the summer twilight, are you
close enough to hear
your child's terror? Or 15
are you not my father,
you who raised me?

 1992

EAVAN BOLAND

1944–

Yearning "to be a sibyl / able to sing the past / in pure syllables . . . / able to speak at
last / my mother tongue," the Irish poet Eavan Boland examines what she has
called the "domestic interiors" of women's lives with wit and grace, sometimes
celebrating the powers of maternity, sometimes mourning the defeats inflicted by
anorexia, mastectomy, conjugal violence. Born in Dublin, Boland studied at
Trinity College and at the Iowa Writers' Workshop. In 1969, she married the nov-
elist Kevin Casey, with whom she has two daughters. From *Poetry* (1963) and *New
Territory* (1967) to *Night Feed* (1982), *The Journey* (1986), and *Outside History*
(1990), her collections of verse have explored both the dilemmas of Ireland,
caught between "Dublin reverence and Belfast irony," and the situation of women,
especially the circumstances of those who are painfully or pleasurably "settled / in
the sort of light / jugs and kettles / grow important by."

In His Own Image

I was not myself, myself.
The celery feathers,
the bacon flitch,[1]
the cups deep on the shelf
and my cheek 5
coppered and shone
in the kettle's paunch,
my mouth
blubbed in the tin of the pan—
they were all I had to go on. 10

1. Side of bacon.

How could I go on
with such meagre proofs of myself?
I woke day after day.
Day after day I was gone
from the self I was last night. 15

And then he came home tight.[2]

Such a simple definition!
How did I miss it?
Now I see
that all I needed 20
was a hand
to mould my mouth,
to scald my cheek,
was this concussion
by whose lights I find 25
my self possession,
where I grow complete.

He splits my lip with his fist,
shadows my eye with a blow,
knuckles my neck to its proper angle. 30
What a perfectionist!

His are a sculptor's hands:
they summon
form from the void,
they bring 35
me to myself again.
I am a new woman.

 1980

Anorexic

Flesh is heretic.
My body is a witch.
I am burning it.

Yes I am torching
her curves and paps[1] and wiles. 5
They scorch in my self denials.

How she meshed my head
in the half-truths
of her fevers

till I renounced 10
milk and honey
and the taste of lunch.

2. Drunk 1. Nipples.

I vomited
her hungers.
Now the bitch is burning. 15

I am starved and curveless.
I am skin and bone.
She has learned her lesson.

Thin as a rib
I turn in sleep. 20
My dreams probe

a claustrophobia
a sensuous enclosure.
How warm it was and wide
once by a warm drum, 25
once by the song of his breath
and in his sleeping side.

Only a little more,
only a few more days
sinless, foodless, 30

I will slip
back into him again
as if I had never been away.

Caged so
I will grow 35
angular and holy

past pain,
keeping his heart
such company

as will make me forget 40
in a small space
the fall

into forked dark,
into python needs
heaving to hips and breasts 45
and lips and heat
and sweat and fat and greed.

 1980

The Muse Mother

My window pearls wet.
The bare rowan tree
berries rain.

I can see
from where I stand 5
a woman hunkering—
her busy hand
worrying a child's face,

working a nappy[1] liner
over his sticky, loud 10
round of a mouth.

Her hand's a cloud
across his face
making light and rain,
smiles and a frown, 15
a smile again.

She jockeys him to her hip,
pockets the nappy liner,
collars rain on her nape
and moves away, 20
but my mind stays fixed:

If I could only decline[2] her—
lost noun
out of context,
stray figure of speech— 25
from this rainy street
again to her roots,
she might teach me
a new language:

to be a sibyl[3] 30
able to sing the past
in pure syllables,
limning hymns sung
to belly[4] wheat or a woman,

able to speak at last 35
my mother tongue.

1982

Degas's Laundresses[1]

You rise, you dawn
roll-sleeved Aphrodites,
out of a camisole[2] brine,

1. Diaper.
2. Boland is punning on the grammatical sense of *decline*, as used regarding languages whose nouns have different case endings to give the grammatical forms of a noun (or pronoun or adjective) in a fixed order.
3. A Greek prophetess
4. To cause to swell out. "Limning": delineating, portraying.

1. Degas (1835–1917) is best known for his paintings of contemporary life on a wide variety of subjects from different classes; the painting alluded to here is *Two Laundresses*.
2. Woman's short, sleeveless garment. Aphrodite, the Greek goddess of love, was born from the sea.

a linen pit of stitches
silking the fitted sheets 5
away from you like waves.

You seam dreams in the folds
of wash from which freshes
the whiff and reach of fields
where it bleached and stiffened. 10
Your chat's sabbatical:[3]
brides, wedding outfits,

a pleasure of leisured women
are sweated into the folds,
the neat heaps of linen. 15
Now the drag of the clasp.
Your wrists basket your waist.
You round to the square weight.

Wait. There. Behind you.
A man. There behind you. 20
Whatever you do don't turn.
Why is he watching you?
Whatever you do don't turn.
Whatever you do don't turn.

See he takes his ease, 25
staking his easel so,
slowly sharpening charcoal,
closing his eyes just so,
slowly smiling as if
so slowly he is 30

unbandaging his mind.
Surely a good laundress
would understand its twists,
its white turns,
its blind designs: 35

it's your winding sheet.[4]

 1982

3. I.e., pertaining to rest or leisure. 4. The sheet in which a corpse is wrapped.

BUCHI EMECHETA
1944–

Enmeshed in the history of the Nigerian shift from a preindustrial tribal culture to an industrialized urban society, the heroine of Buchi Emecheta's ironically titled *Joys of Motherhood* (1979) asks God, "when will you create a woman who will be fulfilled in herself, a full human being, not anybody's appendage?" Arranged mar-

riages, polygamy, the stigma associated with barrenness, the psychological reper-cussions of the devaluation of girl children, the economic and educational privi-leging of boys, wife abuse: these are the forms of sexual inequality with which Emecheta's novels often deal and which she witnessed firsthand in her life as well.

Born in Yaba, a small village near Lagos, Nigeria, and orphaned at an early age, Florence Onye Buchi was educated in a Methodist girls' high school where she was instructed to ask God's forgiveness for wanting to be a writer. After she married a man to whom she had been betrothed since the age of eleven, she followed her husband to England in 1962. His burning of the manuscript of her first novel, *The Bride Price* (1976), caused her to pack up her "four siblings and pregnant self and face the streets of London." The work she began composing in what John Updike has termed an "English being reinvented" explores women's quest for identity in alien and alienating circumstances. Both *In the Ditch* (1972) and *Second-Class Citizen* (1974), for example, describe the lonely struggle she herself experienced setting out to write in a foreign language. A sociology graduate of London University, Emecheta has produced a column for the *New Statesman*, radio and television plays, and an autobiography titled *Head Above Water* (1986) as well as numerous children's books and nine novels. That Emecheta named her own pub-lishing house Ogwugwu Afor Co., after a strong Ibo goddess and that she believes "Women are born storytellers, We keep the history" reflect her effort to conserve a past that will preserve women's creativity.

The Mother's Mother, the second chapter of *The Joys of Motherhood*, functions as a flashback to describe the origins of its heroine "in a little Ibo town called Ibuza"; yet, read on its own, it stands as a self-contained story about the tensions between traditional tribal customs and the disruptive passions of highly individual men and women.

From The Joys of Motherhood

The Mother's Mother

Nwokocha Agbadi was a very wealthy local chief. He was a great wrestler, and was glib and gifted in oratory. His speeches were highly spiced with sharp anecdotes and thoughtful proverbs. He was taller than most and, since he was born in an age when physical prowess determined one's role in life, people nat-urally accepted him as a leader. Like most handsome men who are aware of their charismatic image, he had many women in his time. Whenever they raided a neighboring village, Agbadi was sure to come back with the best-looking women. He had a soft spot for those from big houses, daughters of chiefs and rich men. He knew from experience that such women had an extra confidence and sauciness even in captivity. And that type of arrogance, which even captivity could not diminish, seemed to excite some wicked trait in him. In his young days, a woman who gave in to a man without first fighting for her honor was never respected. To regard a woman who is quiet and timid as de-sirable was something that came after his time, with Christianity and other changes. Most of the women Nwokocha Agbadi chose as his wives and even slaves were those who could match his arrogance, his biting sarcasm, his painful jokes, and also, when the mood called, his human tenderness.

He married a few women in the traditional sense, but as he watched each of them sink into domesticity and motherhood he was soon bored and would go further afield for some other exciting, tall and proud female. This predilection of his extended to his mistresses as well.

Agbadi was from Ogboli, a village of people who, legend said, had lived in that part of what is now Ibuza before the Eastern Ibo people from Isu came and settled there with them. The Ogboli people allowed the founder of Ibuza to stay, and bestowed titles on him and his descendants. They also inherited most of the widows of the newcomers. This was the arrangement for a long time, until the people of Ibuza grew in number and strength, and those of Ogboli somehow diminished. It is still not known why this was so, though some claim that many of them emigrated to neighboring towns like Asaba. But that is by the way. The Ibuza people, who came from the eastern part of Nigeria, fought and won many civil battles against their hosts. They won their freedom of movement to the extent that they started crowning themselves and refused to send their wives to the Ogboli people again.

During the time of Nwokocha Agbadi the town had become known as Ibuza, and Ogboli was then one of the villages that made up the town. The glory was still there, and the Ogboli people still regarded themselves as the sons of the soil, even though the soil had long been taken away from under their feet. Two of Agbadi's wives came from Ibuza, two from his own village of Ogboli, three were slaves he had captured during his wanderings; and he also had two mistresses.

One of these mistresses was a very beautiful young woman who managed to combine stubbornness with arrogance. So stubborn was she that she refused to live with Agbadi. Men being what they are, he preferred spending his free time with her, with this woman who enjoyed humiliating him by refusing to be his wife. Many a night she would send him away, saying she did not feel like having anything to do with him, even though Agbadi was not supposed to be the kind of man women should say such things to. But she refused to be dazzled by his wealth, his name or his handsomeness. People said that Nwokocha Agbadi spent all his life on this earth courting his Ona.

Ona was Agbadi's name for her, not the name originally given to her. Her father was a chief, too, and Agbadi had seen her as a child following her father about. People used to find it strange that a chief like Obi Umunna would go about unashamedly pulling a tiny toddler with him. But her father told people that his little girl was his ornament. Agbadi then said, jokingly, "Why don't you wear her round your neck like an *ona*, a 'priceless jewel'?" People had laughed. But the name stuck. It never occurred to him that he would be one of the men to ask for her when she grew up. Her father, despite having several wives, had few children, and in fact no living son at all, but Ona grew to fill her father's expectation. He had maintained that she must never marry; his daughter was never going to stoop to any man. She was free to have men, however, and if she bore a son, he would take her father's name, thereby rectifying the omission nature had made.

She was of medium height, and had skin like that of half-ripe palm nuts, smooth, light coffee in color. Her hair, closely cropped, fitted her skull like a hat atop a head that seemed to be thrust out of her shoulders by a strong, long powerful neck. When she walked her expensive waist-beads, made of the best coral, murmured, and for men raised in that culture, who knew the sound of each bead, this added to her allurement. She had been used all her life to walking in bush paths, so she knew the tricks of avoiding thorns, using the balls of her feet rather than putting her full weight on her soles. This gave her movement the air of a mysterious and yet exciting cat. She had a trick of pointing

her chin forward, as if she saw with it instead of her eyes, which were black-rimmed and seemed sunken into her head. Like most of her people, she had little patience for walking and as she ran, in the same way as young girls would run to the stream or run out of their homesteads to find out what was going on, she would cup her hands to support her breasts, which swung with bare health. She seldom wore any tops, neither did she tie her lappa[1] over her breasts like the old women. But she had many waist lappas, and expensive changes of coral beads for her neck and waist. Greenish-black tattoos stood out richly against her brown skin. Though she was always scantily dressed, she frequently made people aware of being a conservative, haughty presence, cold as steel and remote as any woman royally born. When she sat, and curled her long legs together in feminine modesty, one knew that she had style, this only daughter of Obi Umunna.

Nwokocha Agbadi would not have minded sending all his wives away just to live with this one woman. But that was not to be. People said she had him bewitched, that she had a kind of power over him; what person in his right mind would leave his big spacious household and women who were willing to worship and serve him in all things to go after a rude, egocentric woman who had been spoiled by her father? This story gained credence particularly when Agbadi's young wives showed signs of sexual neglect. He would be reminded to do his duty by them, then when they became pregnant he would not be seen in their huts until the time came for him to mate them again. But whenever he returned from his many wanderings he would go and stay with his Ona.

It was during one rainy season that Nwokocha Agbadi went to hunt some elephants which he and his age-group knew would be crossing the bush marshes called Ude. He came too near one of the heavy creatures on this occasion, and that single slip almost led to a terrible disaster. He was thrown with a mighty tusk into a nearby wild sugar-cane bush and he landed in the bubbly black mud. The animal was so enraged that, uncharacteristically for a big elephant, it chased after him blindly, bellowing like a great locomotive, so that the very ground seemed about to give way at its heavy approach. Agbadi reacted quickly. He was pinned to the sugar-cane bush unable to move his body, none the less with a practiced hand he aimed his spear and threw it under the belly of the angry animal. It roared, but still made a determined assault on Agbadi, almost tearing his arm from his shoulder, attacking him with a fury increased by the painful spear under it. The elephant roared and fell, but not before it had wounded Agbadi so badly that he himself suspected he was nearing his end. The other hunters, hearing the commotion, rushed to the scene and quickly finished off the elephant, which was still very alive and kicking furiously. They saw Nwokocha Agbadi bleeding to death. His shoulder bone was thrust out of his skin, and the elephant's tusks had indented his side. The men gathered and with bamboo splints tied the twisted shoulder, though they could do little about the bleeding side; judging from the pool of blood that was fast forming around him, they doubted that he would last long. Agbadi soon passed out and it seemed to all that he had died. The oldest man of the group took his otuogwu cloth which he had left in a dry hilly place by the stream, rolled Agbadi in it as if he were a dead person, then the anxious

1. A woman's shawl or skirt.

hunters carried him in a bigger bamboo crate which they had quickly con-
structed, and made their way gradually and sadly home.

The procession of dignified men emerging from the belly of the bush into
the town was a moving spectacle. It was obvious to those farmers on their way
to their lands that something was very wrong, but if they suspected the truth,
they could not yet show grief: Nwokocha Agbadi was not only a chief but an
important one, therefore the disclosure of his death would have to comply
with certain cultural laws—there must be gun shots, and two or three goats
must be slaughtered before the announcement. Anyone who started grieving
before the official proclamation would be made to pay fines equivalent to
three goats. So people watched the hunters' approach in awe, wondering who
it was that had been so mummified. Women and children ran from their
homesteads to witness the sight, and observant people noticed that the only
chief missing among the returning hunters was Nwokocha Agbadi. His carriers
were followed by four hefty male slaves dragging the dead elephant, groaning
and sweating with the weight of the beast. People knew then that Agbadi had
either been badly wounded or killed while hunting the elephant! Word circu-
lated in whispers.

When Ona heard of it, the more vulnerable personality underneath her
daily steely mask came out. She dashed out from where she was sitting by her
father and soon caught up with the carriers.

"Tell me, please say something, is my lover dead?" she asked anxiously as
she galloped after them on the balls of her feet, her waist-beads rumbling to
the rhythm of her movements.

She held on first to this man, asking the same question, then to that one,
begging him to say something. She pestered Agbadi's closest and oldest friend
Obi Idayi, so much so that he lost his temper. He had ignored her for some
time, and never had any love for this wild uncontrolled woman. He did not
know what Agbadi found in her. Now he stopped in his heavy stride and
snapped.

"In life you tortured him, teased him with your body. Now that he is dead,
you cry for his manhood."

Ona was stunned. She held her hands over her head and spoke like someone
hypnotized: "It can't be. It just can't be."

Some older women standing by hushed her, saying, "He may be your lover,
girl, but don't forget that he is Nwokocha Agbadi. Watch you tongue."

With fear and apprehension lightening her brain, Ona followed the carriers
to Ogboli.

Agbadi was placed in the center of his courtyard. The medicine man was
able to detect a very faint life in him, although his breathing was toilsome and
indicated that he was a dying man. They had to massage his heart into activity
again. All his wives were shooed away, but Ona fought and clawed to be al-
lowed to stay and would let no one touch Agbadi except herself. His people
did not much like her, yet they respected her as the only woman who could
make Agbadi really happy, so the medicine man let her attend to him. So
frightened was she in the aftermath of the accident that, together with the
men sitting around Agbadi, she forgot that food was meant to be eaten and
that night was meant for sleep.

Goats were slaughtered every day to appease Agbadi's *chi*;[2] others were left

2. One's personal god or spiritual essence.

alive by river banks and at Ude to appease the other gods. The thought of going home never occurred to Ona, not even on the fourth day. Nor did her possessive father call for her, for he understood her plight: hers were civilized people and they trusted her. For the first time, she realized how attached she was to this man Nwokocha Agbadi, though he was cruel in his imperiousness. His tongue was biting like the edge of a circumcision blade. He ruled his family and children as if he were a god. Yet he gave her his love without reservation, and she enjoyed it; she suspected, however, that her fate would be the same as that of his other women should she consent to become one of his wives. No, maybe the best way to keep his love was not to let that happen. But if he were to die now . . . God, she would will herself to death too! All the same, she would rather have her tongue pulled out of her head than let that beast of a man know how much she cared. That, she decided, would be his lot for being so domineering and having such a foul temper. She watched over him closely and told herself that she would go if he should start showing signs of being on the mend.

On the fifth day he opened his eyes without any help from the medicine man. Ona was so surprised that she simply stared back at him. Her first impulsive act was to scream in her joy; then she remembered her self control. Agbadi looked at her for a split second, his eyes unfocused. For that small time, he looked so dependent that Ona felt like gathering him in her arms and singing to him, as one would do to a baby. He started to chew the side of his mouth, a habit of his which she knew from experience was normally the prelude to a hurtful remark. He looked at her sitting there cross-legged beside him, one of her knees almost touching his head which was supported by a wooden headrest. He said nothing but his sharp mind had taken in the whole situation. Still biting the corner of his lower lip, he allowed his eyes to wander over her from head to toe. Then he simply rolled away and closed his eyes again. She did not doubt that the light in the open courtyard where he was lying was too strong for his eyes, since he had not opened them for five long days, but she had not missed his look of derision. What a way to thank her for all her help!

She did not tell anyone that Agbadi had regained consciousness; she watched hopefully, yet with fear, for further signs of recovery. That evening while she was trying to ease the bamboo splints that had been fixed to straighten his shoulder, two men had to hold his strong long legs to prevent him from kicking. He groaned in pain, and she was told to mop up the fresh blood oozing from the wound. She heard herself saying, "You have borne the pain like a man. The bones are set now; you only have the wound, and this will heal in a day or two."

Agbadi's eyes flew open, and this time they were clear and evil. His white teeth flashed in a sardonic smile. He chuckled wickedly, then said roughly, "What would you have done without your lover, Ona?"

"If you don't stop talking that way, I shall throw this calabash of medicine at you and walk out of Lere back to my father's compound. You're much better now, judging from the sharpness of your tongue."

Her eyes burned with hot tears, but she controlled and never shed them, sensing that nothing would please her lover more than to see her face awash with tears of frustration. She got up from Agbadi's goatskin rug and began to make her way out of the compound.

"You can't go now. You have to finish what you started," Agbadi observed.

She whirled round. "Who is going to stop me? Who cares to stop me? You?"

she wailed, very near hysteria. "Bah! You think you have the right to play God, just because you are Agbadi? You have your wives—they can look after you. You have your slaves—let them mop up your stinking blood!"

"My wives are too much in love with me to stand by and see me in pain. I need a heartless woman like you . . . a woman whose heart is made of stone to stay and watch men remove my splints and not drown me with tears. I will die if you go."

"You will die if I go?" Ona sneered, jutting her pointed chin into the air and throwing back her head in feigned amusement. "A statement like that coming from the great Agbadi! So you are just an ordinary person after all—no, not an ordinary man but a spoiled child who cries when his mother leaves him. Nwokocha Agbadi, hurry up and die, because I'm going back to my father's compound. My heart is not made of stone but I would rather die than let it soften for the like of you."

"I did not say I am dying because you are so indispensable . . ." This was followed by his low, mocking laughter. He was joined by his close friend Idayi, and they seemed to be enjoying her discomfiture.

Then Idayi coughed gently. "Look, Agbadi," he warned, "if you don't stop chuckling you'll start to bleed again. As for you, our Ona, you have lain there by him these five days, when he had lost his power of speech. Now that he can talk, you want him to kneel down and say 'thank you,' eh?"

"Yes, why not? Haven't I done enough for that? I left my father's compound to come here—"

"I didn't ask you to come, remember," Agbadi put in, determined to be the proud hunter till death.

"Oh, you have nerve!"

"All right, all right," Idayi intervened again, seeing that Ona was becoming more and more angry. If her self-control was allowed to snap she might well throw the calabash as she threatened. "In a day or two he will get better, Ona. Then you can go back to your people. We are grateful to you and to your father, I assure you. If Agbadi were to lower himself to thank you, I am sure you would stop caring for him. You need a man, Ona, not a snail. We all know you. For a while I thought we were losing our giant forever. Well, don't worry, he is still too weak to bother any woman for many days, but what he needs is the comfort of your nearness, though he won't admit it. The sun is going down now; he needs to be brought his blood meal, if you want him to heal properly," Idayi said with his usual studied calmness.

Ona went to do as she was told, thinking to herself how unfair it was that Agbadi should accuse her of having a heart of stone. How else could she behave since she could not marry him? Because her father had no son, she had been dedicated to the gods to produce children in his name, not that of any husband. Oh, how torn she was between two men: she had to be loyal to her father, as well as to her lover Agbadi.

There were many friends and well-wishers in Agbadi's compound when she brought the meal from the medicine man's hut, knelt down and silently began to feed Agbadi.

Then the familiar salutation "He who keeps peace" could be heard from people outside, and Ona knew that her father Obi Umunna had come to pay Agbadi a visit. Agbadi looked at her in silent appeal and the message was clear: he did not want her to leave yet.

"How can you be so strong and yet so soft, Agbadi?" she asked him in a low voice so that the well-wishers would not hear.

In answer, he simply smiled non-committally.

Obi Umunna approached and said airily: "So how is the lucky man? You are very lucky, my friend. Bring your best drink and kolanuts and let us pray for long life and thank your *chi* for rescuing you."

"You are right," Idayi agreed "I was just telling your daughter that for a while we thought we would lose him. But, my friend, I hope you are not here to take her home. She is not ready yet."

"And how is my Ona?" Obi Umunna asked after watching her for a few moments.

"He who keeps peace," she replied, "I am being well looked after, Father."

"Good; but remember that you are not married to Agbadi. I don't want his money. You must come home as soon as he is better."

"Why do you not turn her into a man?" Agbadi said bitingly. "Clinging to your daughter as if—"

"I am not here to argue with you, Agbadi; you are sick. And we have gone through this argument so many times before. My daughter will marry no one."

Ona purposely spooned some of the meal near Agbadi's nose, as a way of telling him not to insult her father in her presence.

Agbadi coughed and remarked: "A daughter who you have not even taught how to feed a sick man . . ."

"Oh, Agbadi!" Ona gasped.

"Kolanut and palm wine are here," Idayi said as one of Agbadi's children brought in the wooden tray with refreshments. "Let us pray to our ancestors."

Being the oldest man in the courtyard, Idayi said the prayers. He prayed to the almighty Olisa to cure his good friend Nwokocha Agbadi and begged him to give them all good health. Agbadi lay silently on his back on the goatskin, sometimes gazing at the bamboo ceiling, sometimes letting out grunts in agreement with the many prayers being said. For most of the time his eyes were closed, and the sweat on his matted chest had to be mopped with cold water time and time again.

Agbadi had slept so much in the day that, now he was feeling better, he was finding it difficult to sleep the night through. He must have dozed for a while, none the less, for when he opened his eyes, the whole compound was quiet. Cool night air blew in through the open roof window and he could hear his goats grunting. He heard a light breathing nearby on a separate goatskin. Now he remembered—Ona was there lying beside him. He watched her bare breasts rising and falling as she breathed, and noted with amusement how she made sure to stay as far away from him as possible, though in unconscious defiance, like everything else she did, her leg was thrust out so that it was almost touching him. "The heartless bitch," he thought, "I will teach her." He winced as his still-sore shoulder protested, but he managed to turn fully on to his side and gazed his fill at her. To think that in that proud head, held high even in sleep, and to think that in those breasts, two beautiful firm mounds on her chest looking like calabashes turned upside-down, there was some tenderness was momentarily incredible to him. He felt himself burn.

Then the anger came to him again as he remembered how many times this young woman had teased him and demeaned him sexually. He felt like jumping on her, clawing at her, hurting her. Then again the thought that she

needed him and was there just for his sake came uppermost in his mind and won against the vengeful impulse. He found himself rolling towards her, giving her nipples gentle lover's bites, letting his tongue glide down the hollow in the center of her breasts and then back again. He caressed her thigh with his good hand, moving to her small night lappa and fingering her coral waist-beads. Ona gasped and opened her eyes. She wanted to scream. But Agbadi was faster, more experienced. He slid on his belly, like a big black snake, and covered her mouth with his. He did not let her mouth free for a very long time. She struggled fiercely like a trapped animal, but Agbadi was becoming himself again. He was still weak, but not weak enough to ignore his desire. He worked on her, breaking down all her resistance. He stroked and explored with his perfect hand, banking heavily on the fact that Ona was a woman, a mature woman, who had had him many a time. And he was right. Her struggling and kicking lessened. She started to moan and groan instead, like a woman in labor. He kept on, and would not let go, so masterful was he in this art. He knew he had reduced her to longing and craving for him. He knew he had won. He wanted her completely humiliated in her burning desire. And Ona knew. So she tried to counteract her feelings in the only way she guessed would not give her away.

"I know you are too ill to take me," she murmured.

"No, my Ona, I am waiting for you to be ready."

She felt like screaming to let free the burning of her body. How could one's body betray one so! She should have got up and run out, but something was holding her there; she did not know what and she did not care. She wanted to be relieved of the fire inside her. "Please, I am in pain."

"Yes," came his confident reply. "I want you to be."

She melted and could say no more. She wept and the sobs she was trying to suppress shook her whole being. He felt it, chuckled, and remarked thickly, "Please, Ona, don't wake the whole household."

Either she did not hear, or he wanted her to do just that, for he gave her two painful bites in between her breasts, and she in desperation clawed at him, and was grateful when at least she felt him inside her.

He came deceptively gently, and so unprepared was she for the passionate thrust which followed that she screamed, so piercingly she was even surprised at her own voice: "Agbadi, you are splitting me into two!"

Suddenly the whole courtyard seemed to be filled with moving people. A voice, a male voice, which later she recognized to be that of Agbadi's friend Obi Idayi, shouted from the corner of the open courtyard: "Agbadi! Agbadi! Are you all right?"

Again came that low laughter Ona loved and yet loathed so much. "I am fine, my friend. You go to sleep. I am only giving my woman her pleasures."

Grunting like an excited animal with a helpless prey, he left her abruptly, still unsatiated, and rolled painfully to the other side of the goatskin. Having hurt her on purpose for the benefit of his people sleeping in the courtyard, he had had his satisfaction.

She hated him at that moment. "All this show just for your people, Agbadi?" she whispered. Unable to help herself, she began to cry quietly.

Then he was sorry for her. He moved her closer to him and, letting her curl up to him, encouraged her to get the bitterness off her chest. He felt her hot

tears flowing, but he said nothing, just went on tracing the contours of those offending nipples.

Agbadi's senior wife, Agunwa, became ill that very night. Some said later that she sacrificed herself for her husband; but a few had noticed that it was bad for her morale to hear her husband giving pleasure to another woman in the same courtyard where she slept, and to such a woman who openly treated the man they all worshipped so badly. A woman who was troublesome and impetuous, who had the audacity to fight with her man before letting him have her: a bad woman.

Agbadi and Ona were still sleeping the following morning when the alarm was raised by one of the children.

"Wake up, Father wake up! Our mother is having a seizure."

"What?" Agbadi barked. "What is the matter with her? She was all right last night." Momentarily he forgot himself and made as if to get up; Ona, wide awake now, restrained him. "Damn this shoulder," he grumbled. "But what is the matter with Agunwa?"

"That's what we are trying to find out," said the reassuring voice of Idayi, who had been keeping vigil over his friend.

"Lie still, Agbadi," other voices advised.

He watched helplessly as they took his senior wife away to her hut in her own part of the compound. "Send her my medicine man. What is the matter with the woman?" he fumed.

Soon his friend came from Agunwa's hut and told him, "Your chief wife is very ill. Your *dibia*[3] is doing all he can for her, but I don't think she will survive."

"Why, Idayi, why at this time?"

"Nobody knows when their time will come. Your wife Agunwa is no exception. The strain of your illness . . . since the day we brought you back from Ude, she has watched over you from that corner of your courtyard. She was even here last night."

"Oh, come, my friend. What are you trying to tell me? She's my chief wife, I took her to Ude the day I became an Obi. She is the mother of my grown sons. You are wrong, Idayi, to suggest she might be sore or bitter just because last night with Ona I amused myself a little. Agunwa is too mature to mind that. Why, if she behaved like that what kind of example would that be to the younger wives?"

"You talk of last night as only a little amusement. But it kept all of us awake. You and your Ona woke the very dead . . ."

Goats and hens were sacrificed in an attempt to save Agunwa. When, on the eighteenth day, Agbadi was able to get up and move about with the help of one of his male slaves and a stick, the first place he visited was his senior wife's hut. He was shocked to see her. She was too far gone to even know of his presence.

He looked around and saw two of his grown sons watching him. "Your mother is a good woman. So unobtrusive, so quiet. I don't know who else will help me keep an eye on those young wives of mine, and see to the smooth running of my household."

3. Doctor (Igbo).

Two days later, Agunwa died and Agbadi sent a big cow to her people to an-
nounce her death. Having died a "complete woman," she was to be buried in
her husband's compound.

"Make sure that her slave and her cooking things go with her. We must all
mourn her."

Ona moved about like a quiet wife. She knew that people blamed her for
Agunwa's death though no one had the courage to say so openly. That night,
after she had given Agbadi his meal and helped his men rub life into his stiff
side and shoulder, she curled up to him and asked: "Would you like me to go
now? My father will be worrying, wondering what your people are saying."

"And what are my people saying, woman? That I took my mistress in my
own courtyard, and that I take her every night as I see fit? Is that it? Haven't I
got enough to worry about without you adding your bit? Go to sleep, Ona,
you're tired and you don't look too well to me. Tomorrow is going to be a busy
day. The burial of a chief's wife is not a small thing in Ibuza."

The funeral dancing and feasting started very early in the morning and
went on throughout the day. Different groups of people came and went and
had to be entertained. In the evening it was time to put Agunwa in her grave.
All the things that she would need in her after-life were gathered and arranged
in her wooden coffin which was made of the best mahogany Agbadi could
find. Then her personal slave was ceremoniously called in a loud voice by the
medicine man: she must be laid inside the grave first. A good slave was sup-
posed to jump into the grave willingly, happy to accompany her mistress; but
this young and beautiful woman did not wish to die yet.

She kept begging for her life, much to the annoyance of many of the men
standing around. The women stood far off for this was a custom they found re-
volting. The poor slave was pushed into the shallow grave, but she struggled
out, fighting and pleading, appealing to her owner Agbadi.

Then Agbadi's eldest son cried in anger: "So my mother does not even de-
serve a decent burial? Now we are not to send her slave down with her, just be-
cause the girl is beautiful?" So saying, he gave the woman a sharp blow with the
head of the cutlass he was carrying. "Go down like a good slave!" he shouted.

"Stop that at once!" Agbadi roared, limping up to his son. "What do you
call this, bravery? You make my stomach turn."

The slave woman turned her eyes, now glazed with approaching death,
towards him. "Thank you for this kindness, Nwokocha the son of Agbadi. I
shall come back to your household, but as a legitimate daughter. I shall come
back . . ."

Another relative gave her a final blow to the head, and at last she fell into
the grave, silenced forever. As her blood spurted, splashing the men standing
round, there was a piercing scream from the group of mourning women stand-
ing a little way off. But it was not their feelings for the dead woman that
caused this reaction, Agbadi saw; they were holding Ona up.

"Now what is happening?" Agbadi said hoarsely. "My friend Idayi, take the
burial kolanut and finish the ceremony. I think Umunna's daughter Ona
wants to die on me, too. She has been ill all day, I don't know why. I must take
her inside." He limped over to her with his stick as fast as he could.

Ona was lain on a goatskin in Agbadi's courtyard while the medicine man
went on praying and performing in the center of the compound. For a while
that night Ona went hot and cold, but before dawn it was clear that although

the illness was tiring and weakening her she could bear it. Agbadi's early fear had been that it might be *iba*, the malaria which killed anyone in a short time.

Obi Umunna came in the morning and said to Agbadi without preamble: "I think there is something in your family killing everyone. First you barely escaped death, then your Agunwa was taken, now my healthy daughter who came to look after you—"

"My friend, if you were not an Obi like me, and not Ona's father, I would tell you a few home truths. If she is ill because of a curse in my household, would it not be right for you to leave her with me until she gets better? I will look after her myself."

Over the next few days Agbadi's practiced eyes noted the pattern of the sickness, and he said to Ona one morning as she sat beside him, "Ona, the daughter of Umunna, I think I am making you into a mother. You are carrying our love child."

He said it so lightly that she was too surprised to say a word.

"Well, it is true. What are you going to say to your father?"

"Oh, please, Agbadi, don't take my joy away. You know I like staying here with you, but I am my father's daughter. He has no son. Your house is full of children. Please, Nwokocha the son of Agbadi, your bravery is known afar and so is your tenderness. Don't complicate this for me—the greatest joy of my life."

"But what of me? You and your father are using me as a tool to get what you wanted."

"We did not force you, remember," Ona said, anger rising in her. "Is it my fault that you decided to treat me as a wife and not a lover? You knew of my father's determination before you came to me. We did not use you. You used me, yet I don't regret it. If you want to regret it, well, that is up to you."

"So when are you leaving me?" Agbadi asked eventually.

"As soon as I feel stronger. You are getting better every day, ready to go back to your farm."

"Forget about my farm. Hurry up and get well, and go back to your shameless father."

"Don't call him names," she cried, and felt very weak.

"You see, you won't even allow yourself to be a woman. You are in the first weeks of motherhood, and all you can do is to think like a man, raising male issue for your father, just because he cannot do it himself."

"I am not going to quarrel with you," Ona declared.

That day, for the first time since the accident, Agbadi went to his farm, much to everybody's surprise. "I want to see how the work is going," he replied to questions people put to him.

Ona felt lonely during his absence. But she sent word to her father to come for her the next day.

On that last night she tried to reason with Agbadi, but he gave her his stiff back. "All right," she said in compromise, "my father wants a son and you have many sons. But you do not have a girl yet. Since my father will not accept any bride price from you, if I have a son he will belong to my father, but if a girl, she will be yours. That is the best I can do for you both."

They made it up before morning. Agbadi being tender and loving the rest of the night.

The next day, the women from Obi Umunna's compound came with pre-

sents for Agbadi's household. They were all very polite to each other, and Ona was relieved to note that her father had not come; she could not stand another argument between the two men, though she supposed she should regard herself as lucky for two men to want to own her.

Nwokocha Agbadi visited her often in her hut, and slept there many an Eke[4] night when he did not have to go to the farm or hunting. People had thought that after a while he would get fed up with her, but that was not so. Each parting was painful, just as if they were young people playing by the moonlight.

Some days when he could not come to her, she knew he was with his other wives. Being Agbadi, however, he never talked about them to her, and she respected him for it. It was on such a night that she came into labor. She cried quietly as she agonized alone through the long hours of darkness. Only when the pain became unbearable did she enlist the help of the women in her father's compound.

Her baby daughter was very merciful to her. "She simply glided into the world," the women around told her.

Ona was dazed with happiness. Agbadi had won, she thought to herself, at the same time feeling pity for her poor father.

Agbadi came the very second day and was visibly overjoyed. "Well, you have done well, Ona. A daughter, eh?"

He bent down and peeped at the day-old child wrapped and kept warm by the fireside and remarked: "This child is priceless, more than twenty bags of cowries. I think that should really be her name, because she is a beauty and she is mine. Yes, 'Nnu Ego': twenty bags of cowries."

He called in the men who came with him and they brought enough yams and drinks to last Ona a long time, for custom did not allow him to go near her again until after twenty-five days.

Obi Umunna came in and for a while the two men toasted and prayed for the happiness of the new child.

"Did Ona tell you of our compromise? She agreed that if she bore a baby girl, she would be mine, if a boy, he would be yours," Agbadi said coolly.

"That may be true, my friend. I am not a man who can take seriously talks lovers have on their love mat. She was your guest, and you were a sick man then."

"What are you trying to say, Umunna? That your daughter should go back on her promise?"

"She is a woman so I don't see why not. However, because she is my daughter, I am not asking her to violate her word. Yes, the baby is yours, but my daughter remains here. I have not accepted any money from you."

"How much do you want for her? What else do you expect? Is it her fault that you have no son?" Agbadi was beginning to roar like the wild animals he was wont to hunt and kill.

"Please, please, aren't you two happy that I have survived the birth? It seems nobody is interested in that part of it. I made a promise to Agbadi, yes; but, dear Agbadi, I am still my father's daughter. Since he has not taken a bride price from you, do you think it would be right for me to stay with you permanently? You know our custom does not permit it. I am still my father's daughter," Ona intoned sadly.

4. The first Igbo market day.

Agbadi drew himself up from the mud pavement where he had been sitting and said, "I have never forced a woman to come to me. Never, and I am not going to start now. The only women I captured were slaves. All my wives are happy to be such. You want to stay with your father? So be it." And he left her alone.

For months, Ona did not see Agbadi. She heard from people that he more or less lived in thick, swampy Ude where game was plentiful. Ona missed him, yet she knew that, according to the way things were, she was doing the right thing.

A year after the birth of Nnu Ego, Obi Umunna died, and Ona cried for days for him, especially as he had gone without her producing the wanted son. Agbadi relented when he heard of it, for he knew how close Ona was to her father.

For over two years, he persisted in trying to persuade her to come and live in his compound. ' You are no longer bound by your father's hopes. He is dead. But we are still living. Come and stay with me. You are all alone here among your extended relatives. Please, Ona, don't let us waste our lives longing for each other."

"You know my father would not have liked it, so stop talking like that, Agbadi. I refuse to be intimidated by your wealth and your position."

Yet Agbadi went on visiting Ona.

Nnu Ego was the apple of her parents' eyes. She was a beautiful child, fair-skinned like the women from the Aboh and Itsekiri areas. At her birth it was noticed that there was a lump on her head, which in due course was covered with thick, curly, black hair. But suddenly one evening she started to suffer from a strange headache that held her head and shoulder together. In panic, Ona sent for Agbadi who came tearing down from Ogboli with a *dibia*.

The *dibia* touched the child's head and drew in his breath, feeling how much hotter the lump was than the rest of her body. He quickly set to work, arranging his pieces of kolanut and snail shells and cowries on the mud floor. He soon went into a trance and began to speak in a far-off voice, strange and unnatural: "This child is the slave woman who died with your senior wife Agunwa. She promised to come back as a daughter. Now here she is. That is why this child has the fair skin of the water people, and the painful lump on her head is from the beating your men gave her before she fell into the grave. She will always have trouble with that head. If she has a fortunate life, the head will not plug up. But if she is unhappy, it will trouble her both physically and emotionally. My advice is that you go and appease the slave woman."

"Ona, you must leave this place," Agbadi ordered, "you have to leave your father's house, otherwise I am taking my daughter from you. She can't worship her *chi* from a foreign place; she must be where her *chi* is until all the sacrifices have been made."

So Ona finally had to leave her people, not because she allowed her love for Agbadi to rule her actions but because she wanted the safety of her child. As soon as they arrived at Ogboli, Nnu Ego got better. The slave woman was properly buried in a separate grave, and an image of her was made for Nnu Ego to carry with her.

Soon after that, Ona became pregnant again. From the very beginning she was ill, so that it was not a surprise to Agbadi's household when she came into premature labor. After the birth, Ona was weak but her head was clear. She knew she was dying.

"Agbadi," she called hoarsely, "you see that I was not destined to live with you. But you are stubborn, my father was stubborn, and I am stubborn too. Please don't mourn me for long; and see that however much you love our daughter Nnu Ego you allow her to have a life of her own, a husband if she wants one. Allow her to be a woman."

Not long after this, Ona died; and her weak new-born son followed her only a day later. So all Nwokocha Agbadi had to remind him of his great passion for Ona was their daughter, Nnu Ego.

1979

ALICE WALKER
1944–

Alice Walker's father, Willie Lee Walker, farmed as a sharecropper in Georgia. Her mother, Minnie Grant Walker, "labored beside—not behind" her husband when she was not caring for her eight children. "As I remember it," Alice Walker—her youngest child—has reminisced, "we were really not allowed to be discouraged. Discouragement couldn't hold out against her faith." It is characteristic of Walker to be proud of her origins, for she believes that "the grace with which we embrace life, in spite of the pain, the sorrows, is always a measure of what has gone before." In her autobiographical essay *In Search of Our Mothers' Gardens*, Walker explores the dynamics of the empowerment she gained through her own matrilineage.

Walker attended Spelman College in Atlanta, Georgia, and Sarah Lawrence in New York before she began publishing poetry that was influenced by her involvement in the voter registration movement in Georgia and the welfare rights movement in Mississippi and New York. Her first volume of verse, *Once* (1968), appeared when she was teaching at Jackson State University in Mississippi. Sardonic and lyrical by turns, the poems recount not only her experiences in civil rights work but also her travels in Africa. Her next volume of poetry, *Revolutionary Petunias* (1973), describes the rural Georgia of her childhood. While both books were well received, Walker has achieved national prominence through her work as the editor of an anthology of Zora Neale Hurston's writings (*I Love Myself When I Am Laughing*, 1979), as a contributing editor to the magazine *Ms.*, and even more important, through her own fiction.

From *The Third Life of Grange Copeland* (1970) to *In Love and Trouble* (1973), *Meridian* (1976), *The Color Purple* (1982), and *The Temple of My Familiar* (1989), Walker analyzes the effect of racism on black men and celebrates the resiliency of black women. *Meridian*, which documents the struggles of several civil rights workers during the 1960s, is no less focused on black women's survival skills than *The Color Purple*, which won the National Book Award, the Pulitzer Prize, and the American Book Award. *The Color Purple* experiments with epistolary form to present the linguistic strategies of characters who struggle to articulate their feelings about divinity, sexuality, and identity from the complex perspective of African-American experience. In this novel, as in her earlier stories, Walker extends the fictional techniques of her two favorite authors: Zora Neale Hurston and Jean Toomer. Not only does Walker portray the impact of racism on the relationships between black men and women and the importance of female networks of support, she also captures the humor and the pathos of her characters' erotic entanglements. Her first volume of essays, *In Search of Our Mothers' Gardens* (1983), offers insight into the achievements of such black women as the mystical writer

Rebecca Cox Jackson and Coretta Scott King, the widow of the civil rights advocate Martin Luther King Jr., providing, too, a portrait of the artist herself as she reconciles her commitment to writing with the responsibilities of motherhood. Walker's second volume of essays, *Warrior Masks: Female Genital Mutilation and the Sexual Bindings of Women* (1993), was coauthored with Pratibha Parmar and extends her feminist concerns to some of the problems faced by women in African countries.

In Search of Our Mothers' Gardens

> I described her own nature and temperament. Told how they needed a larger life for their expression . . . I pointed out that in lieu of proper channels, her emotions had overflowed into paths that dissipated them. I talked, beautifully I thought, about an art that would be born, an art that would open the way for women the likes of her. I asked her to hope, and build up an inner life against the coming of that day. . . . I sang, with a strange quiver in my voice, a promise song.
>
> —Jean Toomer, "Avey," *Cane*[1]

> The poet speaking to a prostitute who falls asleep while he's talking—

When the poet Jean Toomer walked through the South in the early twenties, he discovered a curious thing: black women whose spirituality was so intense, so deep, so unconscious, that they were themselves unaware of the richness they held. They stumbled blindly through their lives: creatures so abused and mutilated in body, so dimmed and confused by pain, that they considered themselves unworthy even of hope. In the selfless abstractions their bodies became to the men who used them, they became more than "sexual objects," more even than mere women: they became "Saints." Instead of being perceived as whole persons, their bodies became shrines: what was thought to be their minds became temples suitable for worship. These crazy Saints stared out at the world, wildly, like lunatics—or quietly, like suicides; and the "God" that was in their gaze was as mute as a great stone.

Who were these Saints? These crazy, loony, pitiful women?

Some of them without a doubt, were our mothers and grandmothers.

In the still heat of the post-Reconstruction South,[2] this is how they seemed to Jean Toomer: exquisite butterflies trapped in an evil honey, toiling away their lives in an era, a century, that did not acknowledge them, except as "the *mule* of the world."[3] They dreamed dreams that no one knew—not even themselves, in any coherent fashion—and saw visions no one could understand. They wandered or sat about the countryside crooning lullabies to ghosts, and drawing the mother of Christ in charcoal on courthouse walls.

They forced their minds to desert their bodies and their striving spirits sought to rise, like frail whirlwinds from the hard red clay. And when those frail whirlwinds fell, in scattered particles, upon the ground, no one mourned. Instead, men lit candles to celebrate the emptiness that remained, as people do who enter a beautiful but vacant space to resurrect a God.

1. The major work of Jean Toomer (1894–1967), one of the writers of the Harlem Renaissance; the book is a mixture of narrative prose and lyric poetry.
2. I.e., the South after home rule (and thus while supremacy) was restored following the Confederacy's so-
cial and political "reconstruction" (1865–77).
3. An allusion to a statement in Zora Neale Hurston's (1891–1960) *Their Eyes Were Watching God* (1937): "De nigger woman is de mule uh de world."

Our mothers and grandmothers, some of them: moving to music not yet written. And they waited.

They waited for a day when the unknown thing that was in them would be made known; but guessed, somehow in their darkness, that on the day of their revelation they would be long dead. Therefore to Toomer they walked, and even ran, in slow motion. For they were going nowhere immediate, and the future was not yet within their grasp. And men took our mothers and grandmothers, "but got no pleasure from it." So complex was their passion and their calm.

To Toomer, they lay vacant and fallow as autumn fields, with harvest time never in sight: and he saw them enter loveless marriages, without joy; and become prostitutes, without resistance; and become mothers of children, without fulfillment.

For these grandmothers and mothers of ours were not Saints, but Artists; driven to a numb and bleeding madness by the springs of creativity in them for which there was no release. They were Creators, who lived lives of spiritual waste, because they were so rich in spirituality—which is the basis of Art— that the strain of enduring their unused and unwanted talent drove them insane. Throwing away this spirituality was their pathetic attempt to lighten the soul to a weight their work-worn, sexually abused bodies could bear.

What did it mean for a black woman to be an artist in our grandmothers' time? In our great-grandmothers' day? It is a question with an answer cruel enough to stop the blood.

Did you have a genius of a great-great-grandmother who died under some ignorant and depraved white overseer's lash? Or was she required to bake biscuits for a lazy backwater tramp, when she cried out in her soul to paint watercolors of sunsets, or the rain falling on the green and peaceful pasturelands? Or was her body broken and forced to bear children (who were more often than not sold away from her)—eight, ten, fifteen, twenty children—when her one joy was the thought of modeling heroic figures of rebellion, in stone or clay?

How was the creativity of the black woman kept alive, year after year and century after century, when for most of the years black people have been in America, it was a punishable crime for a black person to read or write? And the freedom to paint, to sculpt, to expand the mind with action did not exist. Consider, if you can bear to imagine it, what might have been the result if singing, too, had been forbidden by law. Listen to the voices of Bessie Smith, Billie Holiday, Nina Simone, Roberta Flack, and Aretha Franklin,[4] among others, and imagine those voices muzzled for life. Then you may begin to comprehend the lives of our "crazy," "Sainted" mothers and grandmothers. The agony of the lives of women who might have been Poets, Novelists, Essayists, and Short-Story Writers (over a period of centuries), who died with their real gifts stifled within them.

And, if this were the end of the story, we would have cause to cry out in my paraphrase of Okot p'Bitek's great poem:[5]

> O, my clanswomen
> Let us all cry together!

4. All female black American singers from the 1920s to the present.

5. The African poet's (b. 1931) *Song of Lawino*

(1966). Walker has changed the original's masculine nouns to feminine equivalents.

Come,
Let us mourn the death of our mother,
The death of a Queen
The ash that was produced
By a great fire!
O, this homestead is utterly dead
Close the gates
With *lacari* thorns,
For our mother
The creator of the Stool is lost!
And all the young women
Have perished in the wilderness.

But this is not the end of the story, for all the young women—our mothers and grandmothers, *ourselves*—have not perished in the wilderness. And if we ask ourselves why, and search for and find the answer, we will know beyond all efforts to erase it from our minds, just exactly who, and of what, we black American women are.

One example perhaps the most pathetic, most misunderstood one, can provide a backdrop for our mothers' work Phillis Wheatley,[6] a slave in the 1700s.

Virginia Woolf,[7] in her book A *Room of One's Own*, wrote that in order for a woman to write fiction she must have two things, certainly: a room of her own (with key and lock) and enough money to support herself.

What then are we to make of Phillis Wheatley, a slave, who owned not even herself? This sickly, frail black girl who required a servant of her own at times—her health was so precarious—and who, had she been white, would have been easily considered the intellectual superior of all the women and most of the men in the society of her day.

Virginia Woolf wrote further, speaking of course not of our Phillis, that "any woman born with a great gift in the sixteenth century [insert "eighteenth century," insert "black woman," insert "born or made a slave"] would certainly have gone crazed, shot herself, or ended her days in some lonely cottage outside the village, half witch, half wizard [insert "Saint"], feared and mocked at. For it needs little skill and psychology to be sure that a highly gifted girl who had tried to use her gift for poetry would have been so thwarted and hindered by contrary instincts [add "chains, guns, the lash, the ownership of one's body by someone else, submission to an alien religion"], that she must have lost her health and sanity to a certainty."

The key words as they relate to Phillis, are "contrary instincts." For when we read the poetry of Phillis Wheatley—as when we read the novels of Nella Larsen[8] or the oddly false-sounding autobiography of that freest of all black women writers, Zora Hurston—evidence of "contrary instincts" is everywhere. Her loyalties were completely divided, as was, without question, her mind.

But how could this be otherwise? Captured at seven, a slave of wealthy, doting whites who instilled in her the savagery ' of the Africa they "rescued" her

6. Highly educated black slave (1753–1784), who wrote formal neoclassical poems.
7. British novelist and essayist (1882–1941); A *Room*

was published in 1929.
8. Black woman novelist of the Harlem Renaissance (1893–1964).

from . . . one wonders if she was even able to remember her homeland as she had known it, or as it really was.

Yes, because she did try to use her gift for poetry in a world that made her a slave, she was "so thwarted and hindered by . . . contrary instincts, that she . . . lost her health. . . ." In the last years of her brief life, burdened not only with the need to express her gift but also with a penniless, friendless "freedom" and several small children for whom she was forced to do strenuous work to feed, she lost her health, certainly. Suffering from malnutrition and neglect and who knows what mental agonies, Phillis Wheatley died.

So torn by "contrary instincts" was black, kidnapped, enslaved Phillis that her description of "the Goddess"—as she poetically called the Liberty she did not have—is ironically, cruelly humorous. And, in fact, has held Phillis up to ridicule for more than a century. It is usually read prior to hanging Phillis's memory as that of a fool. She wrote:

> The Goddess comes, she moves divinely fair,
> Olive and laurel binds her *golden* hair.
> Wherever shines this native of the skies,
> Unnumber'd charms and recent graces rise. [My italics][9]

It is obvious that Phillis, the slave, combed the "Goddess's" hair every morning; prior, perhaps, to bringing in the milk, or fixing her mistress's lunch. She took her imagery from the one thing she saw elevated above all others.

With the benefit of hindsight we ask, "How could she?"

But at last, Phillis, we understand. No more snickering when your stiff, struggling, ambivalent lines are forced on us. We know now that you were not an idiot or a traitor; only a sickly little black girl, snatched from your home and country and made a slave; a woman who still struggled to sing the song that was your gift, although in a land of barbarians who praised you for your bewildered tongue. It is not so much what you sang, as that you kept alive, in so many of our ancestors, *the notion of song*.

Black women are called, in the folklore that so aptly identifies one's status in society, "the *mule* of the world," because we have been handed the burdens that everyone else—*everyone* else—refused to carry. We have also been called "Matriarchs," "Superwomen," and "Mean and Evil Bitches." Not to mention "Castraters" and "Sapphire's[1] Mama." When we have pleaded for understanding, our character has been distorted; when we have asked for simple caring, we have been handed empty inspirational appellations, then stuck in the farthest corner. When we have asked for love, we have been given children. In short, even our plainer gifts, our labors of fidelity and love, have been knocked down our throats. To be an artist and a black woman, even today, lowers our status in many respects, rather than raises it: and yet, artists we will be.

Therefore we must fearlessly pull out of ourselves and look at and identify with our lives the living creativity some of our great-grandmothers were not allowed to know. I stress *some* of them because it is well known that the majority of our great-grandmothers knew, even without "knowing" it, the reality of

9. From *To His Excellency General Washington* (1775).

1. Wife of "the Kingfish" in *Amos and Andy*, a popular early radio and television show.

their spirituality, even if they didn't recognize it beyond what happened in the singing at church—and they never had any intention of giving it up.

How they did it—those millions of black women who were not Phillis Wheatley, or Lucy Terry or Frances Harper or Zora Hurston or Nella Larsen or Bessie Smith; or Elizabeth Catlett, or Katherine Dunham,[2] either—brings me to the title of this essay, "In Search of Our Mothers' Gardens," which is a personal account that is yet shared, in its theme and its meaning, by all of us. I found, while thinking about the far-reaching world of the creative black woman, that often the truest answer to a question that really matters can be found very close.

In the late 1920s my mother ran away from home to marry my father. Marriage, if not running away, was expected of seventeen-year-old girls. By the time she was twenty, she had two children and was pregnant with a third. Five children later, I was born. And this is how I came to know my mother: she seemed a large, soft, loving-eyed woman who was rarely impatient in our home. Her quick, violent temper was on view only a few times a year, when she battled with the white landlord who had the misfortune to suggest to her that her children did not need to go to school.

She made all the clothes we wore, even my brothers' overalls. She made all the towels and sheets we used. She spent the summers canning vegetables and fruits. She spent the winter evenings making quilts enough to cover all our beds.

During the "working" day, she labored beside—not behind—my father in the fields. Her day began before sunup, and did not end until late at night. There was never a moment for her to sit down, undisturbed, to unravel her own private thoughts; never a time free from interruption—by work or the noisy inquiries of her many children. And yet, it is to my mother—and all our mothers who were not famous—that I went in search of the secret of what has fed that muzzled and often mutilated, but vibrant, creative spirit that the black woman has inherited, and that pops out in wild and unlikely places to this day.

But when, you will ask, did my overworked mother have time to know or care about feeding the creative spirit?

The answer is so simple that many of us have spent years discovering it. We have constantly looked high, when we should have looked high—and low.

For example: in the Smithsonian Institution in Washington, D.C., there hangs a quilt unlike any other in the world. In fanciful, inspired, and yet simple and identifiable figures, it portrays the story of the Crucifixion. It is considered rare, beyond price. Though it follows no known pattern of quilt-making, and though it is made of bits and pieces of worthless rags, it is obviously the work of a person of powerful imagination and deep spiritual feeling. Below this quilt I saw a note that says it was made by "an anonymous Black woman in Alabama, a hundred years ago."

If we could locate this "anonymous" black woman from Alabama, she

2. Black American dancer and choreographer (b. 1910). Lucy Terry (1730–1821), black poet and fictionist. Frances E. W. Harper (1825–1911), black woman poet. Elizabeth Catlett (b. 1915?), black educator and sculptor.

would turn out to be one of our grandmothers—an artist who left her mark in the only materials she could afford, and in the only medium her position in society allowed her to use.

As Virginia Woolf wrote further, in *A Room of One's Own*:

> Yet genius of a sort must have existed among women as it must have existed among the working class. [Change this to "slaves" and "the wives and daughters of sharecroppers."] Now and again an Emily Brontë or a Robert Burns [change this to "a Zora Hurston or a Richard Wright"[3]] blazes out and proves its presence. But certainly it never got itself on to paper. When, however, one reads of a witch being ducked, of a woman possessed by devils [or "Sainthood"], of a wise woman selling herbs [our root workers], or even a very remarkable man who had a mother, then I think we are on the track of a lost novelist, a suppressed poet, of some mute and inglorious Jane Austen. . . . Indeed, I would venture to guess that Anon, who wrote so many poems without signing them, was often a woman. . . .

And so our mothers and grandmothers have, more often than not anonymously, handed on the creative spark, the seed of the flower they themselves never hoped to see: or like a sealed letter they could not plainly read.

And so it is, certainly, with my own mother. Unlike "Ma" Rainey's[4] songs, which retained their creator's name even while blasting forth from Bessie Smith's mouth, no song or poem will bear my mother's name. Yet so many of the stories that I write, that we all write, are my mother's stories. Only recently did I fully realize this: that through years of listening to my mother's stories of her life, I have absorbed not only the stories themselves, but something of the manner in which she spoke, something of the urgency that involves the knowledge that her stories—like her life—must be recorded. It is probably for this reason that so much of what I have written is about characters whose counterparts in real life are so much older than I am.

But the telling of these stories, which came from my mother's lips as naturally as breathing, was not the only way my mother showed herself as an artist. For stories, too, were subject to being distracted, to dying without conclusion. Dinners must be started, and cotton must be gathered before the big rains. The artist that was and is my mother showed itself to me only after many years. This is what I finally noticed:

Like Mem, a character in *The Third Life of Grange Copeland*,[5] my mother adorned with flowers whatever shabby house we were forced to live in. And not just your typical straggly country stand of zinnias, either. She planted ambitious gardens—and still does—with over fifty different varieties of plants that bloom profusely from early March until late November. Before she left home for the fields, she watered her flowers, chopped up the grass, and laid out new beds. When she returned from the fields she might divide clumps of bulbs, dig a cold pit, uproot and replant roses, or prune branches from her taller bushes or trees—until night came and it was too dark to see.

Whatever she planted grew as if by magic, and her fame as a grower of flowers spread over three counties. Because of her creativity with her flowers, even

3. Black American novelist (1908–1960). Emily Brontë (1819–1848), English novelist and poet. Robert Burns (1759–1796), Scottish poet.

4. Gertrude Pridgett Rainey (1886–1939), black blues singer and songwriter.
5. Walker's first novel.

my memories of poverty are seen through a screen of blooms—sunflowers, petunias, roses, dahlias, forsythia, spirea, delphiniums, verbena . . . and on and on.

And I remember people coming to my mother's yard to be given cuttings from her flowers; I hear again the praise showered on her because whatever rocky soil she landed on, she turned into a garden. A garden so brilliant with colors, so original in its design, so magnificent with life and creativity, that to this day people drive by our house in Georgia—perfect strangers and imperfect strangers—and ask to stand or walk among my mother's art.

I notice that it is only when my mother is working in her flowers that she is radiant, almost to the point of being invisible—except as Creator: hand and eye. She is involved in work her soul must have. Ordering the universe in the image of her personal conception of Beauty.

Her face, as she prepared the Art that is her gift, is a legacy of respect she leaves to me, for all that illuminates and cherishes life. She has handed down respect for the possibilities—and the will to grasp them.

For her, so hindered and intruded upon in so many ways, being an artist has still been a daily part of her life. This ability to hold on, even in very simple ways, is work black women have done for a very long time.

This poem is not enough, but it is something, for the woman who literally covered the holes in our walls with sunflowers:

> They were women then
> My mama's generation
> Husky of voice—Stout of
> Step
> With fists as well as
> Hands
> How they battered down
> Doors
> And ironed
> Starched white
> Shirts
> How they led
> Armies
> Headragged Generals
> Across mined
> Fields
> Booby-trapped
> Kitchens
> To discover books
> Desks
> A place for us
> How they knew what we
> *Must* know
> Without knowing a page
> Of it
> Themselves.

Guided by my heritage of a love of beauty and a respect for strength—in search of my mother's garden, I found my own.

And perhaps in Africa over two hundred years ago, there was just such a mother; perhaps she painted vivid and daring decorations in oranges and yel-

lows and greens on the walls of her hut; perhaps she sang—in a voice like Roberta Flack's—*sweetly* over the compounds of her village; perhaps she wove the most stunning mats or told the most ingenious stories of all the village storytellers. Perhaps she was herself a poet—though only her daughter's name is signed to the poems that we know.

Perhaps Phillis Wheatley's mother was also an artist.

Perhaps in more than Phillis Wheatley's biological life is her mother's signature made clear.

<div align="right">1974, 1983</div>

ANNIE DILLARD

1945–

The spirit of Thoreau hovers over the writings of Annie Dillard, or so the titles and subjects of her books suggest. *Tickets for a Prayer Wheel* (1974), a collection of poems about the mysterious details of the natural world and the poet's quest for spiritual knowledge of its creator, was overshadowed by *Pilgrim at Tinker Creek* (1976), which became a best-seller and won the Pulitzer Prize for general non-fiction. Touted as "a *Walden* for the 1970s," the book recounts Dillard's years in seclusion, camping along the Roanoke creek banks and the Blue Ridge Mountains. Whether stalking a muskrat or watching the migration of monarch butterflies, Dillard uses the naturalist's task—to scrutinize even the most minute aspects of the physical world—to affirm the goodness of nature, its ability to enable human beings at least for a few moments to evade solipsism and self-consciousness. *Holy the Firm* (1977) and *Teaching a Stone to Talk* (1982) sustain her attempt to join naturalism and personal introspection with mysticism and even with theology, as do Dillard's most recent publications: the autobiography *An American Childhood* (1987) and the novel *The Living* (1992).

Born in Pittsburgh, Annie (Doak) Dillard has described her childhood environment as affluent and ordinary, inflected by the racial tensions and social conformity of the 1950s. After she began writing poetry in the private girls' schools she attended, she enrolled in the writing program at Hollins College in Virginia, where she received both her bachelor's and her master's degrees in English. In 1965, she married one of her teachers, the writer R. H. W. Dillard. The success of *Pilgrim at Tinker Creek* led to her becoming a contributing editor of *Harper's* magazine as well as a columnist for the *Living Wilderness*. After a divorce in 1974, she taught at Western Washington University. In 1979 she relocated to Wesleyan University in Connecticut and in 1980 she married the novelist Gary Clevidence. The selection printed here, besides typifying her attentiveness to the natural world, points through its analysis of the death of a moth to one of Dillard's less obvious precursors in the essay form, namely Virginia Woolf, who wrote an essay entitled *The Death of the Moth* (1942).

From Holy the Firm

[*The Death of a Moth*]

I live on northern Puget Sound, in Washington State, alone. I have a gold cat, who sleeps on my legs, named Small. In the morning I joke to her blank

face, Do you remember last night? Do you remember? I throw her out before breakfast, so I can eat.

There is a spider, too, in the bathroom, with whom I keep a sort of company. Her little outfit always reminds me of a certain moth I helped to kill. The spider herself is of uncertain lineage, bulbous at the abdomen and drab. Her six-inch mess of a web works, works somehow, works miraculously, to keep her alive and me amazed. The web itself is in a corner behind the toilet, connecting tile wall to tile wall and floor, in a place where there is, I would have thought, scant traffic. Yet under the web are sixteen or so corpses she has tossed to the floor.

The corpses appear to be mostly sow bugs, those little armadillo creatures who live to travel flat out in houses, and die round. There is also a new shred of earwig, three old spider skins crinkled and clenched, and two moth bodies, wingless and huge and empty, moth bodies I drop to my knees to see.

Today the earwig shines darkly and gleams, what there is of him: a dorsal curve of thorax and abdomen, and a smooth pair of cerci[1] by which I knew his name. Next week, if the other bodies are any indication, he will be shrunken and gray, webbed to the floor with dust. The sow bugs beside him are hollow and empty of color, fragile, a breath away from brittle fluff. The spider skins lie on their sides, translucent and ragged, their legs drying in knots. And the moths, the empty moths, stagger against each other, headless, in a confusion of arcing strips of chitin[2] like peeling varnish, like a jumble of buttresses for cathedral domes, like nothing resembling moths, so that I should hesitate to call them moths, except that I have had some experience with the figure Moth reduced to a nub.

Two summers ago I was camping alone in the Blue Ridge Mountains in Virginia. I had hauled myself and gear up there to read, among other things, James Ramsey Ullman's *The Day on Fire*, a novel about Rimbaud[3] that had made me want to be a writer when I was sixteen; I was hoping it would do it again. So I read, lost, every day sitting under a tree by my tent, while warblers swung in the leaves overhead and bristle worms trailed their inches over the twiggy dirt at my feet; and I read every night by candlelight, while barred owls called in the forest and pale moths massed round my head in the clearing, where my light made a ring.

Moths kept flying into the candle. They would hiss and recoil, lost upside down in the shadows among my cooking pans. Or they would singe their wings and fall, and their hot wings, as if melted, would stick to the first thing they touched—a pan, a lid, a spoon—so that the snagged moths could flutter only in tiny arcs, unable to struggle free. These I could release by a quick flip with a stick; in the morning I would find my cooking stuff gilded with torn flecks of moth wings, triangles of shiny dust here and there on the aluminum. So I read, and boiled water, and replenished candles, and read on.

One night a moth flew into the candle, was caught, burnt dry, and held. I must have been staring at the candle, or maybe I looked up when a shadow

1. Posterior appendages that act as sensory organs.
2. The hard outer covering of an insect.
3. Arthur Rimbaud (1854–1891), French poet who strongly influenced the later Symbolist writers. *The Day on Fire* was published in 1958.

crossed my page; at any rate, I saw it all. A golden female moth, a biggish one with a two-inch wingspan, flapped into the fire, dropped her abdomen into the wet wax, stuck, flamed, frazzled and fried in a second. Her moving wings ignited like tissue paper, enlarging the circle of light in the clearing and creating out of the darkness the sudden blue sleeves of my sweater, the green leaves of jewelweed by my side, the ragged red trunk of a pine. At once the light contracted again and the moth's wings vanished in a fine, foul smoke. At the same time her six legs clawed, curled, blackened, and ceased, disappearing utterly. And her head jerked in spasms, making a splattering noise; her antennae crisped and burned away and her heaving mouth parts crackled like pistol fire. When it was all over, her head was, so far as I could determine, gone, gone the long way of her wings and legs. Had she been new, or old? Had she mated and laid her eggs, had she done her work? All that was left was the glowing horn shell of her abdomen and thorax—a fraying, partially collapsed gold tube jammed upright in the candle's round pool.

And then this moth-essence, this spectacular skeleton, began to act as a wick. She kept burning. The wax rose in the moth's body from her soaking abdomen to her thorax to the jagged hole where her head should be, and widened into flame, a saffron-yellow flame that robed her to the ground like any immolating monk. That candle had two wicks, two flames of identical height, side by side. The moth's head was fire. She burned for two hours, until I blew her out.

She burned for two hours without changing, without bending or leaning— only glowing within, like a building fire glimpsed through silhouetted walls, like a hollow saint, like a flame-faced virgin gone to God, while I read by her light, kindled, while Rimbaud in Paris burnt out his brains in a thousand poems, while night pooled wetly at my feet.

And that is why I believe those hollow crisps on the bathroom floor are moths. I think I know moths, and fragments of moths, and chips and tatters of utterly empty moths, in any state. How many of you, I asked the people in my class, which of you want to give your lives and be writers? I was trembling from coffee, or cigarettes, or the closeness of faces all around me. (Is this what we live for? I thought; is this the only final beauty: the color of any skin in any light, and living, human eyes?) All hands rose to the question. (You, Nick? Will you? Margaret? Randy? Why do I want them to mean it?) And then I tried to tell them what the choice must mean: you can't be anything else. You must go at your life with a broadax. . . .They had no idea what I was saying. (I have two hands, don't I? And all this energy, for as long as I can remember. I'll do it in the evenings, after skiing, or on the way home from the bank, or after the children are asleep. . . .) They thought I was raving again. It's just as well.

I have three candles here on the table which I disentangle from the plants and light when visitors come. Small usually avoids them, although once she came too close and her tail caught fire; I rubbed it out before she noticed. The flames move light over everyone's skin, draw light to the surface of the faces of my friends. When the people leave I never blow the candles out, and after I'm asleep they flame and burn.

1977

LINDA HOGAN

1947–

A poet, novelist, playwright, and screenwriter, Linda Hogan has explained that "My writing comes from and goes back to the community, both the human and the global community," because, she adds, "I am interested in the deepest questions, those of spirit, of shelter, of growth and movement toward peace and liberation, inner and outer." Throughout her career she has addressed such issues in an art that draws on Native American culture to emphasize the mystical coherence of all life forms, the vitality of the natural world, and the reverence with which human beings should approach the powerful otherness of that world.

A member of the Chickasaw tribe, Hogan was born to Charles and Cleona Henderson in Denver, Colorado, and raised in that state, where she attended the University of Colorado, Boulder, the school at which she now teaches English after stints at Colorado Women's College, Rocky Mountain Women's Institute, the University of Minnesota, and other institutions. Divorced from Pat Hogan, she is the mother of two daughters, Sandra Dawn Protector and Tanya Thunder Horse, and has authored more than six collections of poetry, including *Calling Myself Home* (1979), *Daughters, I Love You* (1981), *Savings* (1988), and most recently *The Book of Medicines* (1993). In addition, she has produced such prose works as the novel *Mean Spirit* (1990, 1992) and the essay collection *Dwellings: Reflections on the Natural World* (1995), as well as a play entitled *A Piece of Moon* (1981) and a number of screenplays—*Mean Spirit* and *Aunt Moon* (both 1986). Bringing the places and people about which she writes "to life with quick, spare phrases," as one reviewer puts it, Hogan has also consistently dramatized a healing vision of what in *Germinal* she herself calls "the older world / with its pale, thin roots of grass / and all things saved and growing."

The Avalanche

Just last month
the avalanches like good women
were headed for a downfall. I saw one
throw back her head
and let go of the world. 5

No more free soup bones for that one.
No more faces of friends at the door
with doilies and lace,
with ivory charms
carved of the elephant's great collapse. 10

Once an avalanche makes up her mind
not to cling,
there's no more covering up the cliff face
and hiding the truth,
and in her breakdown 15
she knows everything

and knows what she knows
about the turning wheel of earth,
love, markets, and even the spring
coming soon with its wildflowers. 20

1988

Germinal

Downstairs, things are growing.
Down stairs to the cellar
guinea eggs have quickened
and grapes have turned to wine.
Lye is burning through its tub 5
near potatoes with pale shoots,
and the molds are dividing
in jellies beneath wax,
that underworld
beneath the house with its bad family, 10
that world below
drumming
like old women
and blood stirring in the neck,
the older world 15
with its pale, thin roots of grass
and all things saved and growing.

1988

The Hands

The poor hands, overworked and dry,
dressing the body like maids
who button the lady's silk shirt
and fan her with their palms.

The poor palms 5
with their geography of lines.
One is broken,
another tells us, short life.

It is just like the hands
to tell their stories without shame. 10
Even held down, the white knucklebones
assert themselves through the skin.

1988

Bamboo

First woman was made of slender bones
like these that stand upright together
in the rich, green world of daylight.

As night, they are a darkened forest
of sisters who grow quickly 5
in moving water
and talk in the clattering breeze
as if each is an open throat, rising
to peak.

I tell a man about this beautiful, 10
creaking world, how it flowers all
at once. He has been to war. He says
with bamboo they do terrible things
to men and women.

I look at this bamboo. 15
It did not give permission to soldiers.
It is imprisoned in its own skin.
The stalks are restless about this.
They have lived too long in the world of men.
They are hollow inside. 20

Lord, are you listening to this?
Plants are climbing to heaven
to talk to you.

1993

LESLIE MARMON SILKO
1948–

"It's stories that make this a community," Leslie Marmon Silko has remarked about the Native American world of Laguna Pueblo, New Mexico, in which she grew up, and in five books—*Laguna Woman* (1974), *Ceremony* (1977), *Storyteller* (1981), *Almanac of the Dead* (1991), and *Yellow Woman* (1993)—she has told and retold the tales that, she believes, make her people who they are. Of mixed Native American, Mexican, and Caucasian descent, Leslie Marmon attended Bureau of Indian Affairs schools at Laguna until entering high school, then studied at the University of New Mexico and later matriculated in law school before deciding to do graduate work in English and devote herself to a literary career. Divorced from John Silko, she has taught at Navajo Community College in Arizona and at the University of New Mexico, is the mother of two sons, and has been the recipient of a MacArthur Foundation fellowship. Her ceremonial impulse to tell stories that are both self-defining and celebratory of her community has issued in an art that

employs many forms: poetry, short stories, legendary tales, a novel, and most recently, film scripts. *Yellow Woman* illustrates the haunting power with which she blends the real and the mythic in resonant fictions about the places and people of the Southwest she knows so well.

Yellow Woman

I

My thigh clung to his with dampness, and I watched the sun rising up through the tamaracks and willows. The small brown water birds came to the river and hopped across the mud, leaving brown scratches in the alkali-white crust. They bathed in the river silently. I could hear the water, almost at our feet where the narrow fast channel bubbled and washed green ragged moss and fern leaves. I looked at him beside me, rolled in the red blanket on the white river sand. I cleaned the sand out of the cracks between my toes, squinting because the sun was above the willow trees. I looked at him for the last time, sleeping on the white river sand.

I felt hungry and followed the river south the way we had come the afternoon before, following our footprints that were already blurred by lizard tracks and bug trails. The horses were still lying down, and the black one whinnied when he saw me but he did not get up—maybe it was because the corral was made out of thick cedar branches and the horses had not yet felt the sun like I had. I tried to look beyond the pale red mesas to the pueblo.[1] I knew it was there, even if I could not see it, on the sandrock hill above the river, the same river that moved past me now and had reflected the moon last night.

The horse felt warm underneath me. He shook his head and pawed the sand. The bay whinnied and leaned against the gate trying to follow, and I remembered him asleep in the red blanket beside the river. I slid off the horse and tied him close to the other horse. I walked north with the river again, and the white sand broke loose in footprints over footprints.

"Wake up."

He moved in the blanket and turned his face to me with his eyes still closed. I knelt down to touch him.

"I'm leaving."

He smiled now, eyes still closed. "You are coming with me, remember?" He sat up now with his bare dark chest and belly in the sun.

"Where?"

"To my place."

"And will I come back?"

He pulled his pants on. I walked away from him, feeling him behind me and smelling the willows.

"Yellow Woman," he said.

I turned to face him. "Who are you?" I asked.

He laughed and knelt on the low, sandy bank, washing his face in the river. "Last night you guessed my name, and you knew why I had come."

I stared past him at the shallow moving water and tried to remember the

1. Communal dwelling of grouped houses.

night, but I could only see the moon in the water and remember his warmth around me.

"But I only said that you were him and that I was Yellow Woman—I'm not really her—I have my own name and I come from the pueblo on the other side of the mesa. Your name is Silva and you are a stranger I met by the river yesterday afternoon."

He laughed softly. "What happened yesterday has nothing to do with what you will do today Yellow Woman."

"I know—that's what I'm saying—the old stories about the ka'tsina spirit and Yellow Woman can't mean us."

My old grandpa liked to tell those stories best. There is one about Badger and Coyote who went hunting and were gone all day, and when the sun was going down they found a house. There was a girl living there alone, and she had light hair and eyes and she told them that they could sleep with her. Coyote wanted to be with her all night so he sent Badger into a prairie-dog hole, telling him he thought he saw something in it. As soon as Badger crawled in, Coyote blocked up the entrance with rocks and hurried back to Yellow Woman.

"Come here," he said gently.

He touched my neck and I moved close to him to feel his breathing and to hear his heart. I was wondering if Yellow Woman had known who she was—if she knew that she would become part of the stories. Maybe she'd had another name that her husband and relatives called her so that only the ka'tsina from the north and the storytellers would know her as Yellow Woman. But I didn't go on; I felt him all around me, pushing me down into the white river sand.

Yellow Woman went away with the spirit from the north and lived with him and his relatives. She was gone for a long time, but then one day she came back and she brought twin boys.

"Do you know the story?"

"What story?" He smiled and pulled me close to him as he said this. I was afraid lying there on the red blanket. All I could know was the way he felt, warm, damp, his body beside me. This is the way it happens in the stories, I was thinking, with no thought beyond the moment she meets the ka'tsina spirit and they go.

"I don't have to go. What they tell in stories was real only then, back in time immemorial, like they say."

He stood up and pointed at my clothes tangled in the blanket. "Let's go," he said.

I walked beside him, breathing hard because he walked fast, his hand around my wrist. I had stopped trying to pull away from him, because his hand felt cool and the sun was high, drying the river bed into alkali. I will see someone, eventually I will see someone, and then I will be certain that he is only a man—some man from nearby—and I will be sure that I am not Yellow Woman. Because she is from out of time past and I live now and I've been to school and there are highways and pickup trucks that Yellow Woman never saw.

It was an easy ride north on horseback. I watched the change from the cottonwood trees along the river to the junipers that brushed past us in the foothills, and finally there were only piñons, and when I looked up at the rim of the mountain plateau I could see pine trees growing on the edge. Once I

stopped to look down, but the pale sandstone had disappeared and the river was gone and the dark lava hills were all around. He touched my hand, not speaking, but always singing softly a mountain song and looking into my eyes.

I felt hungry and wondered what they were doing at home now—my mother, my grandmother, my husband, and the baby. Cooking breakfast, saying "Where did she go?—maybe kidnapped," and Al going to the tribal police with the details: "She went walking along the river."

The house was made with black lava rock and red mud. It was high above the spreading miles of arroyos[2] and long mesas. I smelled a mountain smell of pitch and buck brush. I stood there beside the black horse, looking down on the small, dim country we had passed, and I shivered.

"Yellow Woman, come inside where it's warm."

II

He lit a fire in the stove. It was an old stove with a round belly and an enamel coffeepot on top. There was only the stove, some faded Navajo blankets, and a bedroll and cardboard box. The floor was made of smooth adobe plaster, and there was one small window facing east. He pointed at the box.

"There's some potatoes and the frying pan." He sat on the floor with his arms around his knees pulling them close to his chest and he watched me fry the potatoes, I didn't mind him watching me because he was always watching me—he had been watching me since I came upon him sitting on the river bank trimming leaves from a willow twig with his knife. We ate from the pan and he wiped the grease from his fingers on his Levis.

"Have you brought women here before?" He smiled and kept chewing, so I said, "Do you always use the same tricks?"

"What tricks?" He looked at me like he didn't understand.

"The story about being a ka'tsina from the mountains. The story about Yellow Woman."

Silva was silent; his face was calm.

"I don't believe it. Those stories couldn't happen now," I said.

He shook his head and said softly, "But someday they will talk about us, and they will say, 'Those two lived long ago when things like that happened.' "

He stood up and went out. I ate the rest of the potatoes and thought about things—about the noise the stove was making and the sound of the mountain wind outside. I rememberd yesterday and the day before, and then I went outside.

I walked past the corral to the edge where the narrow trail cut through the black rim rock. I was standing in the sky with nothing around me but the wind that came down from the blue mountain peak behind me. I could see faint mountain images in the distance miles across the vast spread of mesas and valleys and plains. I wondered who was over there to feel the mountain wind on those sheer blue edges—who walks on the pine needles in those blue mountains.

"Can you see the pueblo?" Silva was standing behind me.

I shook my head. "We're too far away."

"From here I can see the world." He stepped out on the edge. "The Navajo

2. Water-carved gulleys.

reservation begins over there." He pointed to the east. "The Pueblo bound-
aries are over here." He looked below us to the south, where the narrow trail
seemed to come from. "The Texans have their ranches over there, starting
with that valley, the Concho Valley. The Mexicans run some cattle over there
too."

"Do you ever work for them?"

"I steal from them," Silva answered. The sun was dropping behind us and
shadows were filling the land below. I turned away from the edge that dropped
forever into the valleys below.

"I'm cold," I said; "I'm going inside." I started wondering about this man
who could speak the Pueblo language so well but who lived on a mountain and
rustled cattle. I decided that this man Silva must be Navajo, because Pueblo
men didn't do things like that.

"You must be a Navajo."

Silva shook his head gently. "Little Yellow Woman," he said, "you never give
up, do you? I have told you who I am. The Navajo people know me, too." He
knelt down and unrolled the bedroll and spread the extra blankets out on a
piece of canvas. The sun was down, and the only light in the house came from
outside—the dim orange light from sundown.

I stood there and waited for him to crawl under the blankets.

"What are you waiting for?" he said, and I lay down beside him. He un-
dressed me slowly like the night before beside the river—kissing my face gen-
tly and running his hands up and down my belly and legs. He took off my
pants and then he laughed.

"Why are you laughing?"

"You are breathing so hard."

I pulled away from him and turned my back to him.

He pulled me around and pinned me down with his arms and chest. "You
don't understand, do you, little Yellow Woman? You will do what I want."

And again he was all around me with his skin slippery against mine, and I
was afraid because I understood that his strength could hurt me. I lay under-
neath him and I knew that he could destroy me. But later, while he slept be-
side me, I touched his face and I had a feeling—the kind of feeling for him
that overcame me that morning along the river. I kissed him on the forehead
and he reached out for me.

When I woke up in the morning he was gone. It gave me a strange feeling
because for a long time I sat there on the blankets and looked around the little
house for some object of his—some proof that he had been there or maybe
that he was coming back. Only the blankets and the cardboard box remained.
The .30-30 that had been leaning in the corner was gone, and so was the knife
I had used the night before. He was gone, and I had my chance to go now. But
first I had to eat, because I knew it would be a long walk home.

I found some dried apricots in the cardboard box, and I sat down on a rock
at the edge of the plateau rim. There was no wind and the sun warmed me. I
was surrounded by silence. I drowsed with apricots in my mouth, and I didn't
believe that there were highways or railroads or cattle to steal.

When I woke up, I stared down at my feet in the black mountain dirt. Little
black ants were swarming over the pine needles around my foot. They must
have smelled the apricots. I thought about my family far below me. They
would be wondering about me, because this had never happened to me be-

fore. The tribal police would file a report. But if old Grandpa weren't dead he would tell them what happened—he would laugh and say, "Stolen by a ka'tsina, a mountain spirit. She'll come home—they usually do." There are enough of them to handle things. My mother and grandmother will raise the baby like they raised me. Al will find someone else, and they will go on like before, except that there will be a story about the day I disappeared while I was walking along the river. Silva had come for me; he said he had. I did not decide to go. I just went. Moonflowers blossom in the sand hills before dawn, just as I followed him. That's what I was thinking as I wandered along the trail through the pine trees.

It was noon when I got back. When I saw the stone house I remembered that I had meant to go home. But that didn't seem important any more, maybe because there were little blue flowers growing in the meadow behind the stone house and the gray squirrels were playing in the pines next to the house. The horses were standing in the corral, and there was a beef carcass hanging on the shady side of a big pine in front of the house. Flies buzzed around the clotted blood that hung from the carcass. Silva was washing his hands in a bucket full of water. He must have heard me coming because he spoke to me without turning to face me.

"I've been waiting for you."

"I went walking in the big pine trees."

I looked into the bucket full of bloody water with brown-and-white animal hairs floating in it. Silva stood there letting his hands drip, examining me intently.

"Are you coming with me?"

"Where?" I asked him.

"To sell the meat in Marquez."

"If you're sure it's O.K."

"I wouldn't ask you if it wasn't," he answered.

He sloshed the water around in the bucket before he dumped it out and set the bucket upside down near the door. I followed him to the corral and watched him saddle the horses. Even beside the horses he looked tall, and I asked him again if he wasn't Navajo. He didn't say anything; he just shook his head and kept cinching up the saddle.

"But Navajos are tall."

"Get on the horse," he said, "and let's go."

The last thing he did before we started down the steep trail was to grab the .30-30 from the corner. He slid the rifle into the scabbard that hung from his saddle.

"Do they ever try to catch you?" I asked.

"They don't know who I am."

"Then why did you bring the rifle?"

"Because we are going to Marquez where the Mexicans live."

III

The trail leveled out on a narrow ridge that was steep on both sides like an animal spine. On one side I could see where the trail went around the rocky gray hills and disappeared into the southeast where the pale sandrock mesas stood in the distance near my home. On the other side was a trail that went

west, and as I looked far into the distance I thought I saw the little town. But
Silva said no, that I was looking in the wrong place, that I just thought I saw
houses. After that I quit looking off into the distance; it was hot and the wild-
flowers were closing up their deep-yellow petals. Only the waxy cactus flowers
bloomed in the bright sun, and I saw every color that a cactus blossom can be;
the white ones and the red ones were still buds, but the purple and the yellow
were blossoms, open full and the most beautiful of all.

Silva saw him before I did. The white man was riding a big gray horse, com-
ing up the trail toward us. He was traveling fast and the gray horse's feet sent
rocks rolling off the trail into the dry tumbleweeds. Silva motioned for me to
stop and we watched the white man. He didn't see us right away, but finally his
horse whinnied at our horses and he stopped. He looked at us briefly before he
loped the gray horse across the three hundred yards that separated us. He
stopped his horse in front of Silva, and his young fat face was shadowed by the
brim of his hat. He didn't look mad, but his small, pale eyes moved from the
blood-soaked gunny sacks hanging from my saddle to Silva's face and then
back to my face.

"Where did you get the fresh meat?" the white man asked.

"I've been hunting," Silva said, and when he shifted his weight in the saddle
the leather creaked.

"The hell you have, Indian. You've been rustling cattle. We've been looking
for the thief for a long time."

The rancher was fat, and sweat began to soak through his white cowboy
shirt and the wet cloth stuck to the thick rolls of belly fat. He almost seemed
to be panting from the exertion of talking, and he smelled rancid, maybe be-
cause Silva scared him.

Silva turned to me and smiled. "Go back up the mountain, Yellow
Woman."

The white man got angry when he heard Silva speak in a language he
couldn't understand. "Don't try anything, Indian. Just keep riding to Mar-
quez. We'll call the state police from there."

The rancher must have been unarmed because he was very frightened and
if he had a gun he would have pulled it out then. I turned my horse around and
the rancher yelled, "Stop!" I looked at Silva for an instant and there was some-
thing ancient and dark—something I could feel in my stomach—in his eyes,
and when I glanced at his hand I saw his finger on the trigger of the .30-30 that
was still in the saddle scabbard. I slapped my horse across the flank and the
sacks of raw meat swung against my knees as the horse leaped up the trail. It
was hard to keep my balance, and once I thought I felt the saddle slipping
backward; it was because of this that I could not look back.

I didn't stop until I reached the ridge where the trail forked. The horse was
breathing deep gasps and there was a dark film of sweat on its neck. I looked
down in the direction I had come from, but I couldn't see the place. I waited.
The wind came up and pushed warm air past me. I looked up at the sky, pale
blue and full of thin clouds and fading vapor trails left by jets.

I think four shots were fired—I remember hearing four hollow explosions
that reminded me of deer hunting. There could have been more shots after
that, but I couldn't have heard them because my horse was running again and
the loose rocks were making too much noise as they scattered around his feet.

Horses have a hard time running downhill, but I went that way instead of

uphill to the mountain because I thought it was safer. I felt better with the horse running southeast past the round gray hills that were covered with cedar trees and black lava rock. When I got to the plain in the distance I could see the dark green patches of tamaracks that grew along the river; and beyond the river I could see the beginning of the pale sandrock mesas. I stopped the horse and looked back to see if anyone was coming; then I got off the horse and turned the horse around, wondering if it would go back to its corral under the pines on the mountain. It looked back at me for a moment and then plucked a mouthful of green tumbleweeds before it trotted back up the trail with its ears pointed forward, carrying its head daintily to one side to avoid stepping on the dragging reins. When the horse disappeared over the last hill, the gunny sacks full of meat were still swinging and bouncing.

IV

I walked toward the river on a wood-hauler's road that I knew would eventually lead to the paved road. I was thinking about waiting beside the road for someone to drive by, but by the time I got to the pavement I had decided it wasn't very far to walk if I followed the river back the way Silva and I had come.

The river water tasted good, and I sat in the shade under a cluster of silvery willows. I thought about Silva, and I felt sad at leaving him; still, there was something strange about him, and I tried to figure it out all the way back home.

I came back to the place on the river bank where he had been sitting the first time I saw him. The green willow leaves that he had trimmed from the branch were still lying there, wilted in the sand. I saw the leaves and I wanted to go back to him—to kiss him and to touch him—but the mountains were too far away now. And I told myself, because I believe it, he will come back sometime and be waiting again by the river.

I followed the path up from the river into the village. The sun was getting low, and I could smell supper cooking when I got to the screen door of my house. I could hear their voices inside—my mother was telling my grandmother how to fix the Jell-O and my husband, Al, was playing with the baby. I decided to tell them that some Navajo had kidnapped me, but I was sorry that old Grandpa wasn't alive to hear my story because it was the Yellow Woman stories he liked to tell best.

1992

JAMAICA KINCAID

1949–

Girl, the first of many contributions Jamaica Kincaid has made to *The New Yorker*, was reprinted in her prize-winning collection *At the Bottom of the River* (1983) and epitomizes her evocative style. Almost liturgical in its rhythms, it juxtaposes sensory, everyday images in a style more reminiscent of poetry than prose to portray a character who seems mysteriously like a paradigmatic everygirl, rather than an individuated personality. *Annie John* (1985) and *Lucy* (1990), Kincaid's next publications, move toward more traditional methods of narration in their autobiographical

account of a young Antiguan girl's separation from her family and her home. Yet both books articulate Kincaid's responses to the island she left at sixteen, her sense of the beauty of Antigua as well as her indictment of its colonial past. This last is the subject of her passionately argued essay *A Small Place* (1988), which Kincaid has described as a book written with a lot of anger and one that radicalized her

Kincaid, who attributes her love of reading and writing to her mother's early influence, was named Elaine Potter Richardson by her parents. After leaving Antigua in 1965, she worked as a live-in baby-sitter and a receptionist before she began publishing in magazines. She took her first name Jamaica, because it evoked the West Indies and the second, Kincaid, because it went well with the first. Although Jamaica Kincaid believes that she would not have become a writer if it had not been for the interest and support of *The New Yorker* and in particular of its editor William Shawn, she has come to feel "less interested in the approval of the First World." She currently resides in North Bennington, Vermont, where she lives with her husband, the composer Allen Shawn, and their two children.

Girl

Wash the white clothes on Monday and put them on the stone heap; wash the color clothes on Tuesday and put them on the clothesline to dry; don't walk barehead in the hot sun; cook pumpkin fritters in very hot sweet oil; soak your little cloths right after you take them off; when buying cotton to make yourself a nice blouse, be sure that it doesn't have gum on it, because that way it won't hold up well after a wash; soak salt fish overnight before you cook it; is it true that you sing benna[1] in Sunday school?; always eat your food in such a way that it won't turn someone else's stomach; on Sundays try to walk like a lady and not like the slut you are so bent on becoming; don't sing benna in Sunday school; you mustn't speak to wharf-rat boys, not even to give directions; don't eat fruits on the street—flies will follow you; *but I don't sing benna on Sundays at all and never in Sunday school*; this is how to sew on a button; this is how to make a buttonhole for the button you have just sewed on; this is how to hem a dress when you see the hem coming down and so to prevent yourself from looking like the slut I know you are so bent on becoming; this is how you iron your father's khaki shirt so that it doesn't have a crease; this is how you iron your father's khaki pants so they don't have a crease; this is how you grow okra—far from the house, because okra tree harbors red ants; when you are growing dasheen,[2] make sure it gets plenty of water or else it makes your throat itch when you are eating it; this is how you sweep a corner; this is how you sweep a whole house; this is how you sweep a yard; this is how you smile to someone you don't like too much; this is how you smile to someone you don't like at all; this is how you smile to someone you like completely; this is how you set a table for tea; this is how you set a table for dinner; this is how you set a table for dinner with an important guest; this is how you set a table for lunch; this is how you set a table for breakfast; this is how to behave in the presence of men who don't know you very well, and this way they won't recognize immediately the slut I have warned you against becoming; be sure to wash every day, even if it is with your own spit; don't squat down to play marbles—you are not a boy, you know; don't pick people's flowers—you might catch something; don't throw stones at blackbirds, because it might not be a

1. Calypso music. 2. A variety of taro.

blackbird at all; this is how to make a bread pudding; this is how to make doukona;[3] this is how to make pepper pot; this is how to make a good medicine for a cold; this is how to make a good medicine to throw away a child before it even becomes a child; this is how to catch a fish; this is how to throw back a fish you don't like, and that way something bad won't fall on you; this is how to bully a man; this is how a man bullies you; this is how to love a man, and if this doesn't work there are other ways, and if they don't work don't feel too bad about giving up; this is how to spit up in the air if you feel like it, and this is how to move quick so that it doesn't fall on you; this is how to make ends meet; always squeeze bread to make sure it's fresh; *but what if the baker won't let me feel the bread?*; you mean to say that after all you are really going to be the kind of woman who the baker won't let near the bread?

1984

3. A kind of pudding.

JORIE GRAHAM
1951–

Situating herself under a "sky that keeps / sliding away," in an atmosphere "married to hurry / and grim song," Jorie Pepper Graham has produced five collections of elegantly formulated, subtly nuanced, elliptical verse. Educated at New York University and the University of Iowa, she is married and has one child. At present the director of the Iowa Writers' Workshop, she is the recipient of a MacArthur fellowship as well as many other honors and awards. From *Hybrids of Plants and of Ghosts* (1980) to *The End of Beauty* (1987) and *Materialism* (1993), her often elegiac volumes focus on modes of perception and understanding, on the many ways in which lived experience "unfastens itself / from the deep ocean of the given." At the same time, as she has noted in one of her poems, she sees an aesthetic based on the sexual exploitation and oppression of women as a reason to "weep / for the moral nature / of this world." With characteristic thoughtfulness, both *Orpheus and Eurydice* and *Concerning the Right to Life* meditate on such painful issues.

Orpheus and Eurydice[1]

Up ahead, I know, he felt it stirring in himself already, the glance,
the darting thing in the pile of rocks,

already in him, there, shiny in the rubble, hissing Did you want to remain
completely unharmed?—

the point-of-view darting in him, shiny head in the ash-heap, 5

hissing Once upon a time, and then Turn now darling give me that look,

1. According to Greek myth, Eurydice, the wife of the poet Orpheus, died after being bitten by a snake; Orpheus's song temporarily won her back from the underworld, but he could not keep his promise not to look back at her until they had reached the lands above.

that perfect shot, give me that place where I'm erased . . .

The thing, he must have wondered, could it be put to rest, there, in the
 glance,

could it lie back down into the dustyness, giving its outline up? 10

When we turn to them—limbs, fields, expanses of dust called meadow and
 avenue—

will they be freed then to slip back in?

Because you see he could not be married to it anymore, this field with
 minutes in it 15

called woman, its presence in him the thing called

future—could not be married to it anymore, expanse tugging his mind out
 into it,

tugging the wanting-to-finish out.

 What he dreamed of was this road (as he walked on it), this dustyness, 20
but without their steps on it, their prints, without
song—

What she dreamed, as she watched him turning with the bend in the road
 (can you

understand this?)—what she dreamed 25

was of disappearing into the seen

not of disappearing, lord, into the real—

And yes she could feel it in him already, up ahead, that wanting-to-turn-and-
cast-the-outline-over-her

by his glance, 30

sealing the edges down,

saying I know you from somewhere darling, don't I,
saying You're the kind of woman who etcetera—

(Now the cypress are swaying) (Now the lake in the distance)
(Now the view-from-above, the aerial attack of *do you* 35
remember?)—

now the glance reaching her shoreline wanting only to be recalled,
now the glance reaching her shoreline wanting only to be taken in,

(somewhere the castle above the river)

(somewhere you holding this piece of paper) 40

(what will you do next?) (—feel it beginning?)

now she's raising her eyes, as if pulled from above,

now she's looking back into it, into the poison the beginning,

giving herself to it, looking back into the eyes,

feeling the dry soft grass beneath her feet for the first time now the mind 45

looking into that which sets the —————— in motion and seeing in there

a doorway open nothing on either side
(a slight wind now around them, three notes from up the hill)

through which morning creeps and the first true notes—

For they were deep in the earth and what is possible swiftly took hold. 50

1987

Concerning the Right to Life

1

As I rounded the corner—noiselessly—as if wide unseeable
 doors slid open—*intelligent*—almost a halo with
hinges—almost a split where something
 overripens—
I came upon the rose 5
 tall as a man
on its senseless stem,
 thorns like equal-signs all the way up—
each tip looking as if the air were cut

 open right there by its
idea— 10
 all round it the invisible
scent,
 rough muscle,
drenched veil—As I 15
 rounded the corner, the possible
sprung from
 possibility

 into whipped red
choice. 20
 I looked into its face—its authorship—accretion of
discardings
 all whispering at once—
looked for the *living* in there—half-awake—
 sultry, a fellow destiny to mine— 25
courage here not the issue

or what is good—
only the form that
 matters—
how at the core, at the end, there is 30
 a thrashing forking red, and how
around it—shuddering—the invisible
 ripens, parent . . .
I touched it. My fate

crossed out along my silly white extended arm—five 35

 fingers flared
to somehow prolong desire
 out past the sticky glove of
matter—Touched

 its lip—thin and resilient as my sleeping child's, 40
barely trembling—Stopped
 and tried to look at it—
A long distance—

 my shadow from the time of day upon it—
on Tuesday— 45
 remembering then those locked in the cattlecars[1]—
remembering them with my hand as I run my finger on the tip—

 those waving goodbye as the doors close—
The shutting doors sliding loomlike
 across the stiff even rows of faces— 50

 and then this one face in the dusk my hand upon it—
Pity us, dusk light—
 Judge us, red rose—do not let us pass unjudged—

 2

The clinic's layers of glass door glide open. Tiny hiss.

 Outside the protest continues— 55

from inside a muffling
 sound, making us feel, in the waiting room,
ourselves unborn . . .

 I try to feel it, beneath my
magazine, 60
 the immaculate spot within—the freedom of
choice, illustrious
 sleep, bloody spot. . . .
 Now I lay me 65
 down to

1. I.e., those being transported to the concentration camps of the Holocaust.

sleep—tick tock—I pray thee Lord
 to make these words have
materiality—
 make there be a tiny draft
just underneath them—there—make them displace something to 70
 be—something that opens—sliding

back—firm
 over the fault—a *subject*—indifferent to rot as matter,
 rotting, is
indifferent. . . . Out there (framed by the gleaming levelors[2]) some 75
 voices screaming *right to life*, some others screaming
choice choice—

 placards above bodies—an old man
 (suit and tie) screaming *pseudo-christians* at the photos of 80
fetuses blossoming
 bloody
at the tops of their stems—one nun

staring out
 at some orphaned perfection undressed before her—
above her (in magic-marker): *the other* 85
 holocaust: don't kill
your children—
 all round her the bodies lying down (it's
crowded), the young policeman's

 shy angelic face, his glittering new 90
uniform—
 (*home* behind him, *home* before him)
(and the immanence of day)
 leaves blowing across as

 one girl's red dress 95
wraps suddenly round her—terra
 infidel—(if only we could rid ourselves
of pity)—acacias on fire in
 the parking lot—

 "let the mother die but save the child" 100
the huge man screams—
 as the
siren—
 its one intransigent mythology, high-pitched,
clean as a knife—(oh glitzy splendor of the shiny *me*)— 105
 kicks in—

What can happen?
 What is the worst that can happen?

2. Window blinds.

3

The storm has struck, the weather channel says
 the worst has passed. 110
I sponge your sleeping brow—
 trying not to wake your
pain again—104 and holding—when does the
 medicine kick in?—I want
your blood to cool, my blood is shrieking that your 115
 blood, there on its path inside, *must cool!*—
Cicadas will begin again now that the storm
 has done— it will be

 normal—we will
fore- 120
 see
tomorrow and tomorrow and tomorrow's
 weather—I read the label on the medicine.
How many hours have passed (I count again)—
 It seems the shadows of your room 125
ring round—*there is no choice*—and yet your yellow
 lion winks, your horse leans
softly to the wall—

your 3 *1st prizes* (on the shelf)—
 a note you got from a *best friend*— 130

It is a mountain. And then it is a sea.

4

 What is it, the spot inside Mary,[3] the punched-out spot of
blood which is *not her?*—
 to whom does it belong?—immaculate[4]
garden—red idea; truth held *self-* 135
 evident—
through which the crowd can cross

 and *take possession*
of the earth—
 So she is a shore, a *vulgar ocean* which round the *idea of* 140
 ocean

roils—

5[5]

 ... for I see a thousand kinds of trees (Tuesday October 23)
each of which has its own kind of fruit (1492)
 and they are green now as in Spain in the month of 145

3. I.e., Mary, mother of Jesus.
4. Recalls the Immaculate Conception, the doctrine
that she was conceived and born without original sin.
5. This section is a slightly abridged but generally lit-
eral translation of the October 23, 1492, entry in
Christopher Columbus's *Diario*, the diary of his first
voyage to America (1492–93).

May and June
 and the same with flower and with
everything—but that I do not
 recognize them
burdens me with the greatest sorrow 150

in the world—
 nothing was recognized,
nothing!—
 except the red aloe
of which today I have ordered great quantities 155
 brought to the ship
to take to Your
 Highness—

and it is raining a lot
 and yesterday it rained a lot without being cold— 160
rather the day is hot and the nights temperate
 as in May in Spain in Andalusia. . . .

 1993

RITA DOVE

1952—

Rita Dove was born in Akron, Ohio, the second of four children and the oldest daughter. Her father was the first black chemist at the Goodyear Tire and Rubber Company, her mother a housekeeper. She believes that belonging to a "first-generation middle-class family" helped to shape both her early insecurities and her feeling of privilege. After graduating summa cum laude from Miami University in Ohio in 1973, she attended the University of Tubingen on a Fulbright scholarship and received a master of fine arts from the University of Iowa Writers' Workshop in 1977. Attributing her interest in poetry to a fascination with "the ways in which language can change your perceptions," Dove published *The Yellow House on the Corner* (1980) and *Museum* (1983) to critical acclaim. Here, Dove's poetry exhibits a technical acumen and a fascination with history that enable her to move between familiar themes ("the yellow house") and sophisticated, aesthetic subjects (the nature of the "museum").

Dove's subsequent work also negotiates between national and personal concerns. In *Thomas and Beulah* (1986), winner of the Pulitzer Prize in 1987, she produced an ambitious sequence about her grandparents' courtship and marriage that melded public and private narratives. Continuing to move into autobiography, many of the poems in *Grace Notes* (1989) deal with her personal experiences as a daughter and as a mother of a daughter. The youngest poet named Poet Laureate and the first African-American, Dove, who is married to Fred Viebahn and currently teaches at the University of Virginia, has also published a collection of stories, *Fifth Sunday* (1985), as well as a play, *The Siberian Village* (1991), and a novel, *Through the Ivory Gate* (1992). Her most recent collection of verse, *Mother Love* (1995), focuses on themes and images of the maternal. Whether she examines her own adolescence or her grandfather's courtship, a Haitian dictator or an African-American mother, Dove avoids didacticism by entering into the unique subjectivity of the diverse cast of characters who haunt her imagination.

The House Slave

The first horn lifts its arm over the dew-lit grass
and in the slave quarters there is a rustling—
children are bundled into aprons, cornbread

and water gourds grabbed, a salt pork breakfast taken.
I watch them driven into the vague before-dawn 5
while their mistress sleeps like an ivory toothpick

and Massa dreams of asses, rum and slave-funk.
I cannot fall asleep again. At the second horn,
the whip-curls across the backs of the laggards—

sometimes my sister's voice, unmistaken, among them. 10
"Oh! pray," she cries. 'Oh! pray!" Those days
I lie on my cot, shivering in the early heat,

and as the fields unfold to whiteness,
and they spill like bees among the fat flowers.
I weep. It is not yet daylight. 15

1980

From Thomas and Beulah

The Great Palaces of Versailles[1]

Nothing nastier than a white person!
She mutters as she irons alterations
in the backroom of Charlotte's Dress Shoppe.
The steam rising from a cranberry wool
comes alive with perspiration 5
and stale Evening of Paris.
*Swamp she born from, swamp
she swallow, swamp she got to sink again.*

The iron shoves gently
into a gusset, waits until 10
the puckers bloom away. Beyond
the curtain, the white girls are all
wearing shoulder pads to make their faces
delicate. That laugh would be Autumn,
tossing her hair in imitation of Bacall.[2] 15

Beulah had read in the library
how French ladies at court would tuck
their fans in a sleeve
and walk in the gardens for air. Swaying
among lilies, lifting shy layers of silk, 20

1. A French city that contain not only Louis XIV's
large palace, now also called Versailles, but two smaller
places (the Grande Trianon and the Petit Trianon) in
its park.
2. Lauren Bacall (b. 1924), one of the most glamorous
film stars of the 1940s and 1950s.

they dropped excrement as daintily
as handkerchieves. Against all rules

she had saved the lining from a botched coat
to face last year's gray skirt. She knows
whenever she lifts a knee 25
she flashes crimson. That seems legitimate;
but in the book she had read
how the *cavaliere* amused themselves
wearing powder and perfume and spraying
yellow borders knee-high on the stucco 30
of the *Orangerie*.[3]

A hanger clatters
in the front of the shoppe.
Beulah remembers how
even Autumn could lean into a settee 35
with her ankles crossed, sighing
I need a man who'll protect me
while smoking her cigarette down to the very end.

Wingfoot Lake

(INDEPENDENCE DAY, 1964)

On her 36th birthday, Thomas had shown her
her first swimming pool. It had been 40
his favorite color, exactly—just
so much of it, the swimmers' white arms jutting
into the chevrons[4] of high society.
She had rolled up her window
and told him to drive on, fast. 45

Now this *act of mercy:* four daughters
dragging her to their husbands' company picnic,
white families on one side and them
on the other, unpacking the same
squeeze bottles of Heinz, the same 50
waxy beef patties and Salem potato chip bags.
So he was dead for the first time
on Fourth of July—ten years ago

had been harder, waiting for something to happen,
and ten years before that, the girls 55
like young horses eyeing the track.
Last August she stood alone for hours
in front of the T.V. set
as a crow's wing moved slowly through
the white streets of government. 60
That brave swimming

3. The greenhouse of the Tuileries Gardens in Paris. 4. I.e., the swimmers' arms meet at an angle like a
"Cavaliere": horsewoman (French). chevron (which is also a badge indicating rank).

scared her, like Joanna saying
Mother, we're Afro-Americans now!
What did she know about Africa?
Were there lakes like this one 65
with a rowboat pushed under the pier?
Or Thomas' Great Mississippi
with its sullen silks? (There was
the Nile but the Nile belonged

to God.) Where she came from 70
was the past, 12 miles into town
where nobody had locked their back door,
and Goodyear hadn't begun to dream of a park
under the company symbol, a white foot
sprouting two small wings. 75

1986

Persephone, Falling[1]

One narcissus among the ordinary beautiful
flowers, one unlike all the others! She pulled,
stooped to pull harder—
when, sprung out of the earth
on his glittering terrible 5
carriage, he claimed his due.
It is finished. No one heard her.
No one! She had strayed from the herd.

(Remember to straight to school.
This is important, stop fooling around! 10
Don't answer to strangers. Stick
with your playmates. Keep your eyes down.)
This is how easily the pit
opens. This is how one foot sinks into the ground.

1995

Sonnet in Primary Colors

This is for the woman with one black wing
perched over her eyes: lovely Frida,[1] erect
among parrots, in the stern petticoats of the peasant,
who painted herself a present—
wildflowers entwining the plaster corset 5
her spine resides in that flaming pillar—
this priestess in the romance of mirrors.

1. In Greek mythology, Persephone, the daughter of
Zeus and Demeter, was abducted by Pluto, who held
her captive in Hades and allowed her to return each
spring and summer.

1. Frida Kahlo (1907–1954), Mexican painter famous
for her self-portraits. Kahlo was married to Diego
Rivera (1886–1957) (line 12).

Each night she lay down in pain and rose
to the celluloid butterflies of her Beloved Dead,
Lenin and Marx and Stalin arrayed at the footstead. 10
And rose to her easel, the hundred dogs panting
like children along the graveled walks of the garden, Diego's
love a skull in the circular window
of the thumbprint searing her immutable brow.

1995

LUCI TAPAHONSO
1953–

Born and raised on the Navajo Nation in Shiprock, New Mexico, Luci Tapahonso grew up speaking both Navajo and English, a linguistic counterpoint that characterizes much of the work she has published in four collections of poetry, including *Seasonal Woman* (1982), *A Breeze Swept Through* (1987), and *Saani Dahataal: The Women Are Singing* (1993). Twice married and the mother of two daughters as well as several stepchildren, she was educated at the University of New Mexico and currently teaches at the University of Kansas, Lawrence.

While she was still in college, Tapahonso has explained, her work was nurtured by support and encouragement from the Native American author Leslie Marmon Silko, who became a kind of mentor for her. At the same time, she sees herself as having been inspired to write by both the social oppression and the cultural plenitude experienced by her people. "For an Indian person," she insists, "the land is rich with memories, stories, and sacred songs that ensure survival in this country. The huge rocks in Utah, near Kayenta, Shiprock pinnacle, and the various others are strong places and exist for spiritual purposes. The desert is vast and expansive yet full of power and a strength that few can comprehend."

Blue Horses Rush In

For Chamisa Bah Edmo,
who was born March 6, 1991

Before the birth, she moved and pushed inside her mother.
Her heart pounded quickly and we recognized the sound of horses running:

the thundering of hooves on the desert floor.

Her mother clenched her fists and gasped.
She moans ageless pain and pushes: This is it! 5

Chamisa slips out, glistening wet and takes her first breath.
The wind outside swirls small leaves
and branches in the dark.
Her father's eyes are wet with gratitude.
He prays and watches both mother and baby—stunned. 10

This baby arrived amid a herd of horses,
 horses of different colors.

White horses r de n on the breath of the wind.
White horses from the west
where plants of golden chamisa shimmer in the moonlight. 15

She arrived amid a herd of horses.
Yellow horses enter from the east
bringing the scent of prairie grasses from the small hills outside.

She arrived amid a herd of horses.

Blue horses rush in, snorting from the desert in the south. 20
It is possible to see across the entire valley to Niist'áá from Tó.[1]
Bah, from here your grandmothers went to war long ago.

She arrived amid a herd of horses.

Black horses came from the north.
They are the lush summers of Montana and still white winters of Idaho 25

Chamisa, Chamisa Bah. It is all this that you are.
You will grow: laughing, crying,
and we will celebrate each change you live.

You will grow strong like the horses of your past.
You will grow strong like the horses of your birth. 30

 1993

Leda[1] and the Cowboy

A few months back, when the night sky was darker
than Leda had ever seen, she stepped through
the worn door frame of the Q lounge.
The suddenness of thick smoky air left her slightly faint.
After that, it was easy enough, Leda saw him across 5
the damp just-wiped bar—she did nothing
but hold the glance a second too long.
Sure enough, as if she had called out his name,
he walked over—a slight smile and straw hat.

Even then, as they danced, the things he told her 10
were fleeting. Leda smiled and a strange desperation
engulfed him. "I have to leave," she said,
remembering the clean, empty air outside.
He followed her, holding her shoulder lightly,

1. One of the names for Shiprock, New Mexico.
Niist 'áá: the Navajo name of Oaksprings, a small com-
munity on the western slope of the Carriso Mountains
in New Mexico.

1. In Greek mythology, Leda was a Spartan queen,
wife of Tyndareus, and mother of Clytemnestra, Helen
of Troy, and Castor and Pollux. She was raped by Zeus,
who came to her in the image of a swan.

and outside, he bent over: his body an arc in the street light, 15
and it was clear he didn't know the raw music she lived.

But for now, he is leaning across the table, smiling,
and telling Leda things: he wants to take her on a picnic,
 it might rain tonight,
 and she can phone him anytime. 20
He thinks he is leaving for a rodeo 400 miles to the north
in a few hours. His pickup is loaded with saddles, clothes,
and a huge ice chest. Leda notices the parking lot outside
is stained with oil, twisted cigarettes, and small bits of
colored glass. He leans toward her, hat tilted, and in that 25
low morning voice says he has been tracking her all night.

In this desert city of half a million people, he drove
over cooled asphalt trails searching smoky dance halls,
small Indian bars, the good Mexican place that serves
until 12 and when he found her at a table near 30
the dance floor, she was laughing. But Leda saw his
straw hat and half-smile as he watched from the bar.
When they danced, it was flawless.
He thinks he has done this many times before.
His shirt carried the scent of the hot night breezes outside. 35

East of here, above the dry fields of the Hoohookamki,[2]
the stars are sparse, and as he follows Leda through
the stark beauty of the old stories,

 he has already left his own life behind.

 1993

2. The original Oohdam name for their ancestors, sometimes referred to as Hohokam. Their land is located in what is now Phoenix, Arizona.

LORNA DEE CERVANTES

1954–

A native Californian of Mexican and Native American ancestry, Lorna Dee Cervantes funneled political energies into literary activism during the 1970s, when she edited a magazine called *Mango* and established a small press, Mango Publications, to publish the work of Chicano writers. Before graduating from California State University at San Jose in 1984, she received several grants from the National Endowment for the Arts and completed two collections of her own verse. After attending the History of Consciousness program at the University of California at Santa Cruz, she began teaching at the University of Colorado, Boulder, and editing the multicultural magazine *Red Dirt*.

In *Emplumada* (1981), winner of the 1982 American Book Award, and *Cables of Genocide: Poems on Love and Hunger* (1991), Cervantes combines Spanish and English to communicate the complexity of Chicana identity. Both titles illuminate the nature of her project. *Pluma*, meaning "pen" and "feather" in Spanish, al-

lows Cervantes to conceive of herself as imaginatively *emplumada*, feathered like a bird or an Indian, armed for song like an epic warrior or poet. Referring to the second title, the Native American poet Joy Harjo has declared, "Lorna Dee Cervantes is a daredevil braving the cables of genocide. . . . There is no net." Because, as Cervantes puts it, she is deluged every day "with reminders / that this is not / my land // and this is my land," she speaks for and about internal exiles, indigenous aliens, natives with dual citizenship, common people with divided allegiances, all of whom try to learn the tricks of survival her poems seek to enact or encourage.

Cannery Town in August

All night it humps the air.
Speechless, the steam rises
from the cannery columns. I hear
the night bird rave about work
or lunch, or sing the swing shift[1] 5
home. I listen, while bodyless
uniforms and spinach specked shoes
drift in monochrome down the dark
moon-possessed streets. Women
who smell of whiskey and tomatoes, 10
peach fuzz reddening their lips and eyes—
I imagine them not speaking, dumbed
by the can's clamor and drop
to the trucks that wait, grunting
in their headlights below. 15
They spotlight those who walk
like a dream, with no one
waiting in the shadows
to palm them back to living.

1981

For Virginia Chavez

It was never in the planning,
in the life we thought
we'd live together, two fast
women living cheek to cheek,
still teasing the dog's 5
breath of boys in our testy
new awakening.
We were never the way
they had it planned.
Their wordless tongues we stole 10
and tased the power
that comes of that.
We were never what they wanted
but we were bold. We could take

1. Work shift between day and night shifts.

something of life and not 15
give it back. We could utter
the rules, mark the lines
and cross them ourselves—we two
women using our fists, we thought,
our wits, our tunnels. They were such 20
dumb hunks of warm fish
swimming inside us,
but this was love,
we knew, love, and that was all
we were ever offered. 25

You were always alone
so *another lonely life*
wouldn't matter.
In the still house
your mother left you, 30
when the men were gone
and the television droned
into test patterns, with our cups
of your mother's whiskey
balanced between the brown thighs 35
creeping out of our shorts, I read
you the poems of Lord Byron, Donne,
the Brownings:[1] all about love,
explaining the words
before realizing that you knew 40
all that the kicks in your belly
had to teach you. You were proud
of the woman blooming out of your
fourteen lonely years, but you cried
when you read that poem I wrote you, 45
something about our "waning moons"
and the child in me
I let die that summer.

In the years that separate,
in the tongues that divide 50
and conquer, in the love
that was a language
in itself, you never spoke,
never regret. Even
that last morning 55
I saw you with blood
in your eyes, blood
on your mouth, the blood
pushing out of you
in purple blossoms. 60

1. All English poets: Byron (1788–1824), John Donne (1572–1631), Elizabeth Barrett Browning (1806–1861), and Robert Browning (1812–1889).

He did this.
When I woke, the kids
were gone. They told me
I'd never get them back.

With our arms holding 65
each other's waists, we walked
the waking streets
back to your empty flat,
ignoring the horns and catcalls
behind us, ignoring what 70
the years had brought between us:
my diploma and the bare bulb
that always lit your bookless room.

1981

Emplumada[1]

When summer ended
the leaves of snapdragons withered
taking their shrill-colored mouths with them.
They were still, so quiet. They were
violet where umber now is. She hated 5
and she hated to see
them go. Flowers

born when the weather was good—this
she thinks of, watching the branch of peaches
daring their ways above the fence, and further, 10
two hummingbirds, hovering, stuck to each other,
arching their bodies in grim determination
to find what is good, what is
given to them to find. These are warriors

distancing themselves from history. 15
They find peace
in the way they contain the wind
and are gone.

1981

On Touring Her Hometown

I'm going away to where I'm from
I'm fleeing from visions, fences
grinning from the post. Give me
a hole with a past to it. Fill up

1. Cervantes has two epigraphs to her first book, which takes its title from this poem: "Em-plu-ma-do v.m., feathered; in plumage, as after molting" and "plu-ma-da n.f., pen flourish."

this mess with your wicked engines. 5
Give me the gun of holidays, calendar
shards, disarray on the avenues
unending as the streets of my vast
memory. There are marigolds six feet
under. They eat the names of the dead. 10
There are hovels under these caverns
where liquids marry and paint themselves
a mauve display. There's a place
in the mists of this city where a silence,
lean as ghosts, beckons, is archaic 15
in the workclothes of my otherness.
There is cedar, ash sage, an owl
on the grave of this town the width
of sin. And crying's like hating,
it won't ever pay. I'm going away 20
to where I'm from. I'm leaving,
last condor, last chance.

 1991

Y Volver[1]

Who is to say Love
with her battered face
won't come? Who's to know
she won't rise and run
her comb through clotted 5
hair and spray the scent
of mysterious apples
between her breasts?

She rises with the strength
of seeds and the rule of roots 10
riddling the sidewalk.
She is the hag who cries
for hours in the mewing
of lovers. She's the catch
in their sweaty breath, 15
the blush of rose wine
on the magnolia in winter.

She is her best in ice
when her swelling abides
and small mirrors litter 20
the lawns. She is the face
you casually scuff through
in the refuse of a storm.
She can't ever hear you
but she sings. She feeds 25

1. And to come back (Spanish).

the blooming magpie
death until he's bloated
with the feast of her
leaving. She is the dried
blood gracing his wings. 30
Vengeful and forgiving,
her honor weighs in a few
blown stars, in the halo
that lingers in the west
when the launched nightship 35

explodes, in the one lie
she espouses in her heat,
the beat between her thighs,
the veldt[2] where she holds
you when you mean to go
free. Love, in her candor,
can't explain the attraction
but nuzzles the wild
horse's mane, and rides.

1991

2. Grassland of southern Africa.

LOUISE ERDRICH

1954–

The daughter of a Chippewa Indian mother and a German-American father, Louise Erdrich was raised near Turtle Mountain Chippewa Reservation in North Dakota. Both of her parents worked in the Bureau of Indian Affairs boarding school in Wahpeton. 'My father used to give me a nickel for every story I wrote," she once explained, "and my mother wove strips of construction paper together and stapled them into book covers. So at an early age I felt myself to be a published author earning substantial royalties." And when she was in her twenties, a story collaboratively composed with Michael Dorris won $5,000, leading her to expand it into the novel *Love Medicine* (1984), which earned her the National Book Critics Circle Award when she was thirty.

Erdrich had met Dorris when attending Dartmouth College as an undergraduate. After earning a master's degree in creative writing from Johns Hopkins University, she returned to Dartmouth to become a writer in residence and in 1981 married Dorris, himself a highly respected writer. Over the next decade, she continued producing her fictional portraits of several interrelated characters living in North Dakota from 1912 to the 1980s. *The Beet Queen* (1986), *Tracks* (1988), and *The Bingo Palace* (1994) counterpoint short stories told by a number of different narrators to chronicle three generations of Native American and immigrant families, lyrically exploring the economic, social, and psychological pressures exerted on dislocated people. Besides publishing two books of poetry—*Jacklight* (1984) and *Baptism of Fire* 1989)—Erdrich has produced a collaborative work with Dorris titled *The Crown of Columbus* (1991).

Saint Marie, which was chosen for *Prize Stories 1985: The O. Henry Awards*

(1985) and became the second chapter of *Love Medicine*, stands on its own as a disturbing portrait of the uses to which religion has been put. Its Gothic plot raises questions about the confusion of goodness with masochism, of spiritual discipline with sadism in a community purportedly dedicated to spiritual sanctuary and sanctity.

Saint Marie

(1934)

MARIE LAZARRE

So when I went there, I knew the dark fish must rise. Plumes of radiance had soldered on me. No reservation girl had ever prayed so hard. There was no use in trying to ignore me any longer. I was going up there on the hill with the black robe women.[1] They were not any lighter than me. I was going up there to pray as good as they could. Because I don't have that much Indian blood. And they never thought they'd have a girl from this reservation as a saint they'd have to kneel to. But they'd have me. And I'd be carved in pure gold. With ruby lips. And my toenails would be little pink ocean shells which they would have to stoop down off their high horse to kiss.

I was ignorant. I was near age fourteen. The length of sky is just about the size of my ignorance. Pure and wide. And it was just that —the pure and wideness of my ignorance—that got me up the hill to Sacred Heart Convent and brought me back down alive. For maybe Jesus did not take my bait, but them Sisters tried to cram me right down whole.

You ever see a walleye strike so bad the lure is practically out its back end before you reel it in? That is what they done with me. I don't like to make that low comparison, but I have seen a walleye do that once. And it's the same attempt as Sister Leopolda made to get me in her clutch.

I had the mail-order Catholic soul you get in a girl raised out in the bush, whose only thought is getting into town. For Sunday Mass is the only time my father brought his children in except for school, when we were harnessed. Our soul went cheap. We were so anxious to get there we would have walked in on our hands and knees. We just craved going to the store, slinging bottle caps in the dust, making fool eyes at each other. And of course we went to church.

Where they have the convent is on top of the highest hill, so that from its windows the Sister can be looking into the marrow of the town. Recently a windbreak was planted before the bar "for the purposes of tornado insurance." Don't tell me that. That poplar stand was put up to hide the drinkers as they get the transformation. As they are served into the beast of their burden. While they're drinking, that body comes upon them, and then they stagger or crawl out the bar door, pulling a weight they can't move past the poplars. They don't want no holy witness to their fall.

Anyway, I climbed. That was a long-ago day. There was a road then for wagons that wound in ruts to the top of the hill where they had their buildings of painted brick. Gleaming white. So white the sun glanced off in dazzling display to set forms whirling behind your eyelids. The face of God you could hardly look at. But that day it drizzled, so I could look all I wanted. I saw the

1. I.e., nuns.

homelier side. The cracked whitewash and swallows nesting in the busted ends of eaves. I saw the boards sawed the size of broken windowpanes and the fruit trees, stripped. Only the tough wild rhubarb flourished. Goldenrod rubbed up their walls. It was a poor convent. I didn't see that then but I know that now. Compared to others it was humble, ragtag, out in the middle of no place. It was the end of the world to some. Where the maps stopped. Where God had only half a hand in the creation. Where the Dark One had put in thick bush, liquor, wild dogs, and Indians.

I heard later that the Sacred Heart Convent was a catchall place for nuns that don't get along elsewhere. Nuns that complain too much or lose their mind. I'll always wonder now, after hearing that, where they picked up Sister Leopolda. Perhaps she had scarred someone else, the way she left a mark on me. Perhaps she was just sent around to test her Sister's faith, here and there, like the spot-checker in a factory. For she was the definite most-hard trial to anyone's endurance even when they started out with veils of wretched love upon their eyes.

I was that girl who thought the black hem of her garment would help me rise. Veils of love which was only hate petrified by longing—that was me. I was like those bush Indians who stole the holy black hat of a Jesuit and swallowed little scraps of it to cure their fevers. But the hat itself carried smallpox and was killing them with belief. Veils of faith! I had this confidence in Leopolda. She was different. The other Sisters had long ago gone blank and given up on Satan. He slept for them. They never noticed his comings and goings. But Leopolda kept track of him and knew his habits, minds he burrowed in, deep spaces where he hid. She knew as much about him as my grandma, who called him by other names and was not afraid.

In her class, Sister Leopolda carried a long oak pole for opening high windows. It had a hook made of iron on one end that could jerk a patch of your hair out or throttle you by the collar—all from a distance. She used this deadly hook-pole for catching Satan by surprise. He could have entered without your knowing it—through your lips or your nose or any one of your seven openings—and gained your mind. But she would see him. That pole would brain you from behind. And he would gasp, dazzled, and take the first thing she offered, which was pain.

She had a stringer of children who could only breathe if she said the word. I was the worst of them. She always said the Dark One wanted me most of all, and I believed this. I stood out. Evil was a common thing I trusted. Before sleep sometimes he came and whispered conversation in the old language of the bush. I listened. He told me things he never told anyone but Indians. I was privy to both words of his knowledge. I listened to him, but I had confidence in Leopolda. She was the only one of the bunch he even noticed.

There came a day, though, when Leopolda turned the tide with her hook-pole.

It was a quiet day with everyone working at their desks, when I heard him. He had sneaked into the closets in the back of the room. He was scratching around, tasting crumbs in our pockets, stealing buttons, squirting his dark juice in the linings and the boots. I was the only one who heard him, and I got bold. I smiled. I glanced back and smiled and looked up at her sly to see if she had noticed. My heart jumped. For she was looking straight at me. And she sniffed. She had a big stark bony nose stuck to the front of her face for

smelling out brimstone and evil thoughts. She had smelled him on me. She stood up. Tall, pale, a blackness leading into the deeper blackness of the slate wall behind her. Her oak pole had flown into her grip. She had seen me glance at the closet. Oh, she knew. She knew just where he was. I watched her watch him in her mind's eye. The whole class was watching now. She was staring, sizing, following his scuffle. And all of a sudden she tensed down, posed on her bent kneesprings, cocked her arm back. She threw the oak pole singing over my head, through my braincloud. It cracked through the thin wood door of the back closet, and the heavy pointed hook drove through his heart. I turned. She'd speared her own black rubber overboot where he'd taken refuge in the tip of her darkest toe.

Something howled in my mind. Loss and darkness. I understood. I was to suffer for my smile.

He rose up hard in my heart. I didn't blink when the pole cracked. My skull was tough. I didn't flinch when she shrieked in my ear. I only shrugged at the flowers of hell. He wanted me. More than anything he craved me. But then she did the worst. She did what broke my mind to her. She grabbed me by the collar and dragged me, feet flying, through the room and threw me in the closet with her dead black overboot. And I was there. The only light was a crack beneath the door. I asked the Dark One to enter into me and boost my mind. I asked him to restrain my tears, for they was pushing behind my eyes. But he was afraid to come back there. He was afraid of her sharp pole. And I was afraid of Leopolda's pole for the first time, too. I felt the cold hook in my heart. How it could crack through the door at any minute and drag me out, like a dead fish on a gaff, drop me on the floor like a gutshot squirrel.

I was nothing. I edged back to the wall as far as I could. I breathed the chalk dust. The hem of her full black cloak cut against my cheek. He had left me. Her spear could find me any time. Her keen ears would aim the hook into the beat of my heart.

What was that sound?

It filled the closet, filled it up until it spilled over, but I did not recognize the crying wailing voice as mine until the door cracked open, brightness, and she hoisted me to her camphor-smelling lips.

"He *wants* you," she said. "That's the difference. I give you love."

Love. The black hook. The spear singing through the mind. I saw that she had tracked the Dark One to my heart and flushed him out into the open. So now my heart was an empty nest where she could lurk.

Well, I was weak. I was weak when I let her in, but she got a foothold there. Hard to dislodge as the year passed. Sometimes I felt him—the brush of dim wings—but only rarely did his voice compel. It was between Marie and Leopolda now, and the struggle changed. I began to realize I had been on the wrong track with the fruits of hell. The real way to overcome Leopolda was this: I'd get to heaven first. And then, when I saw her coming, I'd shut the gate. She'd be out! That is why, besides the bowing and the scraping I'd be dealt, I wanted to sit on the altar as a saint.

To this end, I went up on the hill. Sister Leopolda was the consecrated nun who had sponsored me to come there.

"You're not vain," she said. "You're too honest, looking into the mirror, for that. You're not smart. You don't have the ambition to get clear. You have two choices. One, you can marry a no-good Indian, bear his brats, die like a dog. Or two, you can give yourself to God."

"I'll come up there," I said, "but not because of what you think."

I could have had any damn man on the reservation at the time. And I could have made him treat me like his own life. I looked good. And I looked white. But I wanted Sister Leopolda's heart. And here was the thing: sometimes I wanted her heart in love and admiration. Sometimes. And sometimes I wanted her heart to roast on a black stick.

She answered the back door where they had instructed me to call. I stood there with my bundle. She looked me up and down.

"All right," she said finally. "Come in."

She took my hand. Her fingers were like a bundle of broom straws, so thin and dry, but the strength of them was unnatural. I couldn't have tugged loose if she was leading me into rooms of white-hot coal. Her strength was a kind of perverse miracle, for she got it from fasting herself thin. Because of this hunger practice her lips were a wounded brown and her skin deadly pale. Her eye sockets were two deep lashless hollows in a taut skull. I told you about the nose already. It stuck out far and made the place her eyes moved even deeper, as if she stared out the wrong end of a gun barrel. She took the bundle from my hands and threw it in the corner.

"You'll be sleeping behind the stove, child."

It was immense, like a great furnace. There was a small cot close behind it.

"Looks like it could get warm there," I said.

"Hot. It does."

"Do I get a habit?"

I wanted something like the thing she wore. Flowing black cotton. Her face was strapped in white bandages, and a sharp crest of starched white cardboard hung over her forehead like a glaring beak. If possible, I wanted a bigger, longer, whiter beak than hers.

"No," she said, grinning her great skull grin. "You don't get one yet. Who knows, you might not like us. Or we might not like you."

But she had loved me, or offered me love. And she had tried to hunt the Dark One down. So I had this confidence.

"I'll inherit your keys from you," I said.

She looked at me sharply, and her grin turned strange. She hissed, taking in her breath. Then she turned to the door and took a key from her belt. It was a giant key, and it unlocked the larder where the food was stored.

Inside there was all kinds of good stuff. Things I'd tasted only once or twice in my life. I saw sticks of dried fruit, jars of orange peel, spice like cinnamon. I saw tins of crackers with ships painted on the side. I saw pickles. Jars of herring and the rind of pigs. There was cheese, a big brown block of it from the thick milk of goats. And besides that there was the everyday stuff, in great quantities, the flour and the coffee.

It was the cheese that got to me. When I saw it my stomach hollowed. My tongue dripped. I loved that goat-milk cheese better than anything I'd ever ate. I stared at it. The rich curve in the buttery cloth.

"When you inherit my keys," she said sourly, slamming the door in my face, "you can eat all you want of the priest's cheese."

Then she seemed to consider what she'd done. She looked at me. She took the key from her belt and went back, sliced a hunk off, and put it in my hand.

"If you're good you'll taste this cheese again. When I'm dead and gone," she said.

Then she dragged out the big sack of flour. When I finished that heaven stuff she told me to roll my sleeves up and begin doing God's labor. For a while we worked in silence, mixing up the dough and pounding it out on stone slabs.

"God's work," I said after a while. "If this is God's work, then I've done it all my life.

"Well, you've done it with the Devil in your heart then," she said. "Not God."

"How do you know?" I asked. But I knew she did. And I wished I had not brought up the subject.

"I see right into you like a clear glass," she said. "I always did."

"You don't know it," she continued after a while, "but he's come around here sulking. He's come around here brooding. You brought him in. He knows the smell of me, and he's going to make a last ditch try to get you back. Don't let him." She glared over at me. Her eyes were cold and lighted. "Don't let him touch you. We'll be a long time getting rid of him."

So I was careful. I was careful not to give him an inch. I said a rosary, two rosaries, three, underneath my breath. I said the Creed.[2] I said every scrap of Latin I knew while we punched the dough with our fists. And still, I dropped the cup. It rolled under that monstrous iron stove, which was getting fired up for baking.

And she was on me. She saw he'd entered my distraction.

"Our good cup," she said. "Get it out of there, Marie."

I reached for the poker to snag it out from beneath the stove. But I had a sinking feel in my stomach as I did this. Sure enough, her long arm darted past me like a whip. The poker lighted in her hand.

"Reach," she said. "Reach with your arm for that cup. And when your flesh is hot, remember that the flames you feel are only one fraction of the heat you will feel in his hellish embrace."

She always did things this way, to teach you lessons. So I wasn't surprised. It was playacting, anyway, because a stove isn't very hot underneath right along the floor. They aren't made that way. Otherwise a wood floor would burn. So I said yes and got down on my stomach and reached under. I meant to grab it quick and jump up again, before she could think up another lesson, but here it happened. Although I groped for the cup, my hand closed on nothing. That cup was nowhere to be found. I heard her step toward me, a slow step. I heard the creak of thick shoe leather, the little *plat* as the folds of her heavy skirts met, a trickle of fine sand sifting, somewhere, perhaps in the bowels of her, and I was afraid. I tried to scramble up, but her foot came down lightly behind my ear, and I was lowered. The foot came down more firmly at the base of my neck, and I was held.

"You're like I was," she said. "He wants you very much."

"He doesn't want me no more," I said. "He had his fill. I got the cup!"

I heard the valve opening, the hissed intake of breath, and knew that I should not have spoke.

"You lie," she said. "You're cold. There is a wicked ice forming in your blood. You don't have a shred of devotion for God. Only wild cold dark lust. I know it.

2. The Nicene Creed, the official creed of the Roman Catholic Church. "Rosaries": series of Catholic prayers, often counted on a string of special beads.

I know how you feel. I see the beast . . . the beast watches me out of your eyes sometimes. Cold."

The urgent scrape of metal. It took a moment to know from where. Top of the stove. Kettle. Lessons. She was steadying herself with the iron poker. I could feel it like pure certainty, driving into the wood floor. I would not remind her of pokers. I heard the water as it came, tipped from the spout, cooling as it fell but still scalding as it struck. I must have twitched beneath her foot, because she steadied me, and then the poker nudged up beside my arm as if to guide. "To warm your cold ash heart," she said. I felt how patient she would be. The water came. My mind went dead blank. Again. I could only think the kettle would be cooling slowly in her hand. I could not stand it. I bit my lip so as not to satisfy her with a sound. She gave me more reason to keep still.

"I will boil him from your mind if you make a peep," she said, "by filling up your ear."

Any sensible fool would have run back down the hill the minute Leopolda let them up from under her heel. But I was snared in her black intelligence by then. I could not think straight. I had prayed so hard I think I broke a cog in my mind. I prayed even when I heard the wind come through, shrieking in the busted bird nests. I didn't stop when pure light fell, turning slowly behind my eyelids. God's face. Even that did not disrupt my continued praise. Words came. Words came from nowhere and flooded my mind.

Now I could pray much better than any one of them. Than all of them full force. This was proved. I turned to her in a daze when she let me up. My thoughts were gone, and yet I remember how surprised I was. Tears glittered in her eyes, deep down, like the sinking reflection in a well.

"It was so hard, Marie," she gasped. Her hands were shaking. The kettle clattered against the stove. "But I have used all the water up now. I think he is gone."

"I prayed," I said foolishly. "I prayed very hard."

"Yes," she said. "My dear one, I know."

We sat together quietly because we had no more words. We let the dough rise and punched it down once. She gave me a bowl of mush, unlocked the sausage from a special cupboard, and took that in to the Sisters. They sat down the hall, chewing their sausage, and I could hear them. I could hear their teeth bite through their bread and meat. I couldn't move. My shirt was dry but the cloth stuck to my back, and I couldn't think straight. I was losing the sense to understand how her mind worked. She'd gotten past me with her poker and I would never be a saint. I despaired. I felt I had no inside voice, nothing to direct me, no darkness, no Marie. I was about to throw that cornmeal mush out to the birds and make a run for it, when the vision rose up blazing in my mind.

I was rippling gold. My breasts were bare and my nipples flashed and winked. Diamonds tipped them. I could walk through panes of glass. I could walk through windows. She was at my feet, swallowing the glass after each step I took. I broke through another and another. The glass she swallowed ground and cut until her starved insides were only a subtle dust. She coughed. She coughed a cloud of dust. And then she was only a black rag that flapped off, snagged in bobwire, hung there for an age, and finally rotted into the breeze.

I saw this, mouth hanging open, gazing off into the flagged boughs of trees.

"Get up!" she cried. "Stop dreaming. It is time to bake."

Two other Sisters had come in with her, wide women with hands like pad-
dles. They were evening and smoothing out the fire box beneath the great jaws
of the oven.

"Who is this one?" they asked Leopolda. "Is she yours?"

"She is mine," said Leopolda. "A very good girl."

"What is your name?" one asked me.

"Marie."

"Marie. Star of the Sea."[3]

"She will shine," said Leopolda, "when we have burned off the dark corro-
sion."

The others laughed, but uncertainly. They were mild and sturdy French,
who did not understand Leopolda's twisted jokes, although they muttered re-
spectfully at things she said. I knew they wouldn't believe what she had done
with the kettle. There was no question. So I kept quiet.

"*Elle est docile*,"[4] they said approvingly as they left to starch the linens.

"Does it pain?" Leopolda asked me as soon as they were out the door.

I did not answer. I felt sick with the hurt.

"Come along," she said.

The building was wholly quiet now. I followed her up the narrow staircase
into a hall of little rooms, many doors. Her cell was the quietest, at the very
end. Inside, the air smelled stale, as if the door had not been opened for years.
There was a crude straw mattress, a tiny bookcase with a picture of Saint
Francis hanging over it, a ragged palm, a stool for sitting on, a crucifix. She
told me to remove my blouse and sit on the stool. I did so. She took a pot of
salve from the bookcase and began to smooth it upon my burns. Her hands
made slow, wide circles, stopping the pain. I closed my eyes. I expected to see
blackness. Peace. But instead the vision reared up again. My chest was still
tipped with diamonds. I was walking through windows. She was chewing up
the broken litter I left behind.

"I am going," I said, "Let me go."

But she held me down.

"Don't go," she said quickly. "Don't. We have just begun."

I was weakening. My thoughts were whirling pitifully. The pain had kept me
strong, and as it left me I began to forget; I couldn't hold on. I began to won-
der if she'd really scalded me with the kettle. I could not remember. To re-
member this seemed the most important thing in the world. But I was losing
the memory. The scalding. The pouring. It began to vanish. I felt like my mind
was coming off its hinge, flapping in the breeze, hanging by the hair of my own
pain. I wrenched out of her grip.

"He was always in you," I said. "Even more than in me. He wanted you even
more. And now he's got you. Get thee behind me!"[5]

I shouted that, grabbed my shirt, and ran through the door throwing it on
my body. I got down the stairs and into the kitchen, even, but no matter what
I told myself, I couldn't get out the door. It wasn't finished. And she knew I
would not leave. Her quiet step was immediately behind me.

"We must take the bread from the oven now," she said.

3. *Maria* is related to the Latin word for "sea," *mare*. 5. I.e., get thee behind me, Satan.
4. She is compliant (French).

She was pretending nothing happened. But for the first time I had gotten through some chink she'd left in her darkness. Touched some doubt. Her voice was so low and brittle it cracked off at the end of her sentence.

"Help me, Marie," she said slowly.

But I was not going to help her, even though she had calmly buttoned the back of my shirt up and put the big cloth mittens in my hands for taking out the loaves. I could have bolted for it then. But I didn't. I knew that something was nearing completion. Something was about to happen. My back was a wall of singing flame. I was turning. I watched her take the long fork in one hand, to tap the loaves. In the other hand she gripped the black poker to hook the pans.

"Help me," she said again, and I thought, Yes, this is part of it. I put the mittens on my hands and swung the door open on its hinges. The oven gaped. She stood back a moment, letting the first blast of heat rush by. I moved behind her. I could feel the heat at my front and at my back. Before, behind. My skin was turning to beaten gold. It was coming quicker than I thought. The oven was like the gate of a personal hell. Just big enough and hot enough for one person, and that was her. One kick and Leopolda would fly in headfirst. And that would be one-millionth of the heat she would feel when she finally collapsed in his hellish embrace.

Saints know these numbers.

She bent forward with her fork held out. I kicked her with all my might. She flew in. But the outstretched poker hit the back wall first, so she rebounded. The oven was not so deep as I had thought.

There was a moment when I felt a sort of thin, hot disappointment, as when a fish slips off the line. Only I was the one going to be lost. She was fearfully silent. She whirled. Her veil had cutting edges. She had the poker in one hand. In the other she held that long sharp fork she used to tap the delicate crusts of loaves. Her face turned upside down on her shoulders. Her face turned blue. But saints are used to miracles. I felt no trace of fear.

If I was going to be lost, let the diamonds cut! Let her eat ground glass!

"Bitch of Jesus Christ!" I shouted. "Kneel and beg! Lick the floor!"

That was when she stabbed me through the hand with the fork, then took the poker up alongside my head, and knocked me out.

It must have been a half an hour later when I came around. Things were so strange. So strange I can hardly tell it for delight at the remembrance. For when I came around this was actually taking place. I was being worshipped. I had somehow gained the altar of a saint.

I was laying back on the stiff couch in the Mother Superior's office. I looked around me. It was as though my deepest dream had come to life. The Sisters of the convent were kneeling to me. Sister Bonaventure. Sister Dympna. Sister Cecilia Saint-Claire. The two French with hands like paddles. They were down on their knees. Black capes were slung over some of their heads. My name was buzzing up and down the room, like a fat autumn fly lighting on the tips of their tongues between Latin, humming up the heavy blood-dark curtains, circling their little cosseted heads. Marie! Marie! A girl thrown in a closet. Who was afraid of a rubber overboot. Who was half overcome. A girl who came in the back door where they threw their garbage. Marie! Who never found the cup. Who had to eat their cold mush. Marie! Leopolda had her face

buried in her knuckles. Saint Marie of the Holy Slops! Saint Marie of the Bread Fork! Saint Marie of the Burnt Back and Scalded Butt!

I broke out and laughed.

They looked up. All holy hell burst loose when they saw I'd woke. I still did not understand what was happening. They were watching, talking, but not to me.

"The marks . . ."

"She has her hand closed."

"*Je ne peux pas voir.*"[6]

I was not stupid enough to ask what they were talking about. I couldn't tell why I was laying in white sheets. I couldn't tell why they were praying to me. But I'll tell you this: it seemed entirely natural. It was me. I lifted up my hand as in my dream. It was completely limp with sacredness.

"Peace be with you."

My arm was dried blood from the wrist down to the elbow. And it hurt. Their faces turned like flat flowers of adoration to follow that hand's movements. I let it swing through the air, imparting a saint's blessing. I had practiced. I knew exactly how to act.

They murmured. I heaved a sigh, and a golden beam of light suddenly broke through the clouded window and flooded down directly on my face. A stroke of perfect luck! They had to be convinced.

Leopolda still knelt in the back of the room. Her knuckles were crammed halfway down her throat. Let me tell you, a saint has senses honed keen as a wolf. I knew that she was over my barrel now. How it happened did not matter. The last thing I remembered was how she flew from the oven and stabbed me. That one thing was most certainly true.

"Come forward, Sister Leopolda." I gestured with my heavenly wound. Oh, it hurt. It bled when I reopened the slight heal. "Kneel beside me," I said.

She kneeled, but her voice box evidently did not work, for her mouth opened, shut, opened, but no sound came out. My throat clenched in noble delight I had read of as befitting a saint. She could not speak. But she was beaten. It was in her eyes. She stared at me now with all the deep hate of the wheel of devilish dust that rolled wild within her emptiness.

"What is it you want to tell me?" I asked. And at last she spoke.

"I have told my Sisters of your passion," she managed to choke out. "How the stigmata . . . the marks of the nails . . . appeared in your palm and you swooned at the holy vision. . . ."

"Yes," I said curiously.

And then, after a moment, I understood.

Leopolda had saved herself with her quick brain. She had witnessed a miracle. She had hid the fork and told this to the others. And of course they believed her, because they never knew how Satan came and went or where he took refuge.

"I saw it from the first," said the large one who put the bread in the oven. "Humility of the spirit. So rare in these girls."

"I saw it too," said the other one with great satisfaction. She sighed quietly. "If only it was me."

6. I can't see (French).

Leopolda was kneeling bolt upright, face blazing and twitching, a barely held fountain of blasting poison.

"Christ has marked me," I agreed.

I smiled the saint's smirk into her face. And then I looked at her. That was my mistake.

For I saw her kneeling there. Leopolda with her soul like a rubber overboot. With her face of a starved rat. With the desperate eyes drowning in the deep wells of her wrongness. There would be no one else after me. And I would leave. I saw Leopolda kneeling within the shambles of her love.

My heart had been about to surge from my chest with the blackness of my joyous heat. Now it dropped. I pitied her. I pitied her. Pity twisted in my stomach like that hook-pole was driven through me. I was caught. It was a feeling more terrible than any amount of boiling water and worse than being forked. Still, still, I could not help what I did. I had already smiled in a saint's mealy forgiveness. I heard myself speaking gently.

"Receive the dispensation of my sacred blood," I whispered

But there was no heart in it. No joy when she bent to touch the floor. No dark leaping. I fell back into the white pillows. Blank dust was whirling through the light shafts. My skin was dust. Dust my lips. Dust the dirty spoons on the ends of my feet.

Rise up! I thought. Rise up and walk! There is no limit to this dust!

1984

CATHY SONG

1955–

Cathy Song has said that her subject is "the mind in the diamond pinpoint light of concentration tunneling into memory, released by the imagination." At that moment, she adds, 'squares of light form, like windows you pass at night, like photographs developing in the dark." In her scrupulously detailed poems, she herself offers just such fleeting glimpses of people and places: "squares of light" surrounding the half-rebellious, half-resigned "youngest daughter," the aging mother with her 'graveled" breathing, the little boy who thinks that China and heaven are the same. Born in Hawaii, Song earned degrees from Wellesley College and Boston University. She is married, with two children, and currently lives and teaches in Hawaii. Her first collection, *Picture Bride* (1983), won the Yale Younger Poets prize. It was followed by *Frameless Windows, Squares of Light* (1988) and *School Figures* (1994), all marked by "concentration tunneling into memory."

The Youngest Daughter

The sky has been dark
for many years.
My skin has become as damp
and pale as rice paper[1]

1. Thin papery material made from the pith of an Asian shrub.

and feels the way 5
mother's used to before the drying sun
parched it out there in the fields.

 Lately, when I touch my eyelids,
my hands react as if
I had just touched something 10
hot enough to burn.
My skin, aspirin colored,
tingles with migraine. Mother
has been massaging the left side of my face
especially in the evening 15
when the pain flares up.

This morning
her breathing was graveled,
her voice gruff with affection
when I wheeled her into the bath, 20
She was in a good humor,
making jokes about her great breasts,
floating in the milky water
like two walruses,
flaccid and whiskered around the nipples. 25
I scrubbed them with a sour taste
in my mouth, thinking
six children and an old man
have sucked from these brown nipples.

I was almost tender 30
when I came to the blue bruises
that freckle her body,
places where she has been injecting insulin[2]
for thirty years. I soaped her slowly,
she sighed deeply, her eyes closed. 35
It seems it has always
been like this: the two of us
in this sunless room,
the splashing of the bathwater.

In the afternoons 40
when she has rested,
she prepares our ritual of tea and rice,
garnished with a shred of gingered fish,
a slice of pickled turnip,
a token for my white body. 45
We eat in the familiar silence.
She knows I am not to be trusted,
even now planning my escape.
As I toast to her health

2. A hormone used in treating diabetes.

with the tea she has poured, 50
a thousand cranes[3] curtain the window,
fly up in a sudden breeze.

1983

Heaven

He thinks when we die we'll go to China.
Think of it—a Chinese heaven.
where except for his blond hair,
the part that belongs to his father.
everyone will look like him. 5
China, that blue flower on the map,
bluer than the sea
his hand must span like a bridge
to reach it.
An octave away. 10

I've never seen it.
It's as if I can't sing that far.
But look—
on the map, this black dot.
Here is where we live, 15
on the pancake plains
just east of the Rockies,
on the other side of the clouds.
A mile above the sea,
the air is so thin, you can starve on it. 20
No bamboo trees
but the alpine equivalent,
reedy aspen with light fluttering leaves.
Did a boy in Guangzhou[1] dream of this
as his last stop? 25

I've heard the trains at night
whistling past our yards,
what we've come to own,
the broken fences, the whiny dog, the rattletrap cars.
It's still the wild west, 30
mean and grubby,
the shootouts and fistfights in the back alley.
With my son the dreamer
and my daughter, who is too young to walk,
I've sat in this spot 35
and wondered why here?
Why in this short life,
this town, this creek they call a river?

3. According to Chinese myth, white cranes carry im- 1. Large port city in southeastern China (also known
mortals and those journeying between this world and as Canton).
the next.

He had never planned to stay,
the boy who helped to build 40
the railroads for a dollar a day.[2]
He had always meant to go back.
When did he finally know
that each mile of track led him further away,
that he would die in his sleep, 45
dispossessed,
having seen Gold Mountain[3]
the icy wind tunneling through it,
these landlocked, makeshift ghost towns?

It must be in the blood, 50
this notion of returning.
It skipped two generations, lay fallow,
the garden an unmarked grave.
On a spring sweater day
it's as if we remember him. 55
I call to the children.
We can see the mountains
shimmering blue above the air.
If you look really hard
says my son the dreamer, 60
leaning out from the laundry's rigging,
the work shirts fluttering like sails,
you can see all the way to heaven.

 1988

Frameless Windows,
Squares of Light

1

Everything changed the summer your sister was born.
Your mother, suddenly slim but asymmetrical
(with your sister slung on one hip),
regained her figure and lost her sense of humor.
She snapped easily like the beans 5
she snipped for supper,
a succession of little flare-ups
that came and went, efficient and clean.
Her hands would pass over you in transit,
preoccupied, on their way somewhere else. 10
You watched them fly

the way you'd watch the birds in the evening
when a slight ruffling of the air
would lift your face toward their flight.
You'd watch them skim over rooftops, 15

2. Thousands of ill-paid Chinese laborers worked in roads.
the West to complete the U.S. transcontinental rail- 3. The name Chinese immigrants gave California.

still pools in the darkening light,
and wave after wave of trees
and feel alone in your body,
wind filling your shoes, your clothes
with the hollow sound of water. 20

<center>2</center>

Once it had been just the two of you
cloistered in your infancy.
Days when not only winter locked you in.
The days had the solemn expectation
of a child who today opens another window, 25
an advent calendar's[1] blue paper window.
Each window a wafer of light
you could carry like a snowflake
to the darkest part of the house.

Her face, unadorned as a kitchen clock, 30
surveyed the white feathery weather,
measuring the distance between each hour
as carefully as she counted the cups of flour.
She'd wipe her hand across the window
so that you too could look out; 35
like a schoolteacher erasing a cluttered blackboard,
she'd leave a clearing,
a window framed within another,
a space for your name.

It remained, the wooden syllables, 40
scattered, unclaimed on the bureau
while you watched her sift the flour,
lulled into silence like a paperweight
(the cottage, the pine tree, the falling snow).
And it would be snowing on both sides of the glass, 45
snow sifting through her hands,
blowing across the kitchen table.

<center>3</center>

You are smiling in all the pictures,
standing in the foreground
while the backdrop shifted; 50
like musical chairs,
places were relinquished and exchanged
until every combination was snapped.
The nurses came and went.
Flowers appeared. The baby slept on its mother's lap. 55
Time like a temperature was taken.

1. Advent is the four weeks immediately before Christmas. Advent calendars begin on December 1 and have flaps numbered for every day until Christmas. The appropriate flap is opened each day, revealing a seasonal picture, the last being of the baby Jesus.

You watched the scene changes in slow motion,
the distance of figures
trudging through a falling snow.

You are smiling in the pictures 60
but your heart is not in it.
Your mouth forms a big O,
sweet and empty as the doughnuts
you were not allowed to eat.
You can eat anything now. 65
You are smiling but your heart is not in it.
You snatched it out of the picture
and gave it to the boy
who sits under the trees
(frameless windows, squares of light 70
float upward in the dark like luminous kites)
waiting for the words to come in.

 1988

REBECCA BROWN

1956–

Possessed of an impassioned, sardonic, and sometimes gothic imagination, the novelist and short-story writer Rebecca Brown has been compared to the great lesbian feminist-modernist Djuna Barnes, whose *Nightwood* (1936) prefigures the grotesque fantasies that often haunt Brown's fictions. Yet as the critic Victoria A. Brownworth has put it, Brown's work "is brutal and bizarre—but with a kind of dark beauty and even humor that compel."

Born in San Diego, California, to Vergil Neal Brown, Jr., a military officer, and Barbara Ann Brown, a social worker, the writer was raised on the move, as the family followed her father from place to place—a childhood partly reflected in the plot of her first novel, *The Haunted House* (1987). Brown earned a B.A. at George Washington University and an M.F.A. at the University of Virginia; has worked as a teacher, carpenter, freelance journalist, and rock music critic; and currently resides some of the time in Seattle, Washington, and some of the time in London, England. Her latest publications include *The Terrible Girls* (1992), a collection of eight linked stories from which *Forgiveness*, reprinted here, is drawn, as well as, more recently, *Annie Oakley's Girl* (1993) and *The Gifts of the Body* (1994). Of these intermittently comic and unnerving works, she herself has admitted that, "though the surreal and fantastical elements . . . aren't autobiographical, I think of them as emotionally autobiographical: real late-night-sweating-blood kind of stuff."

Forgiveness

When I said I'd give my right arm for you, I didn't think you'd ask me for it, but you did.
You said, Give it to me.
And I said OK.

There were lots of reasons I gave it to you.

First of all, I didn't want to be made a liar of. (I had never lied to you.) So when you reminded me that I'd said it and asked me if I really meant it, I didn't want to seem like I was copping out by saying that I'd only spoken figuratively. (It is and old saying, after all.) Also, I had the feeling you didn't think I would really do it, that you were testing me to see if I would, and I wanted you to know I would.

Also, I believed you wouldn't have asked me for it unless you really wanted it, and needed it.

But then, when you got it, you bronzed it and put it on the mantel over the fireplace in the den.

The night you took it, I dreamt of arms. I slept on the couch in the den because I was still bleeding, even through the bandages, and I knew I'd stir during the night and need to put on more bandages and we didn't want me to wake you up. So I stayed on the couch and when I slept, I dreamt of arms: red arms, blue arms, golden arms. And arms made out of jade. Arms with tattoos, arms with stripes. Arms waving, sleeping, holding. Arms that rested up against my ribs.

We kept my arm in the bathtub, bleeding like a fish. When I went to bed, the water was the color of rose water, with thick red lines like strings. And when I woke up the first time to change my bandages, it was colored like salmon. Then it was carnation red, and then maroon, then burgundy, then purple, thick, and almost black by morning.

In the morning, you took it out. I watched you pat it dry with my favorite big fat terry cloth towel and wrap it in saran wrap and take it out to get it bronzed.

I learned to do things differently. To button my shirts, to screw and unscrew the toothpaste cap, to tie my shoes. We didn't think of this. Together, we were valiant, brave and stoic. Though I couldn't quite keep up with you at tennis anymore.

In a way, it was fun. Things I once took for granted became significant. Cutting a steak with a knife and fork, or buttoning my fly, untying a knot around a bag, adding milk while stirring.

After a while, I developed a scab and you let me come back to bed. But sometimes in the night, I'd shift or have a nightmare, jolt, and suddenly, I'd open up again, and bleed all over uncontrollably. The first time this happened neither of us could go back to sleep. But after a while, you got used to it and you'd be back asleep in a minute. It didn't seem to bother you at all.

But I guess after a while it started bothering you, because one day when I was washing out the sheets I'd bloodied the night before, you said, You sleep too restless. I don't like it when your bleeding wakes me up. I think you're sick I think it's sick to cut off your own arm.

I looked at you, your sweet brown eyes, innocent as a puppy. But you cut it off, I said. You did it. You didn't blink. You asked me for it, so I said OK.

Don't try to make me feel guilty, you said, your pretty brown eyes looking at me. It was your arm.

You didn't blink.

I closed my eyes.

That night I bled again. I woke up and the bed was red, all full of blood and wet. I reached over to touch you and to wake you up and tell you I was sorry, but you were not there.

I learned more. To cook and clean, to eat a quarter pounder with one fist, to balance my groceries on my knee while my hand fumbled with the front door key.

My arm got strong. My left sleeve on my shirts got tight and pinched. My right shirt sleeve was lithe and open, carefree, like a pretty girl.

But then the novelty wore off. I had to convince myself. I read about those valiant cases, one-legged heroes who run across the continent to raise money for causes, and paraplegic mothers of four, one-eyed pool sharks. I wanted these stories to inspire me, but they didn't. I didn't want to be like those people. I didn't want to be cheery and valiant. I didn't want to have to rise above my situation. What I wanted was my arm.

Because I missed it. I missed everything about it. I missed the long solid weight of it in my sleeve. I missed clapping and waving and putting my hand in my pocket. I missed waking up at night with it twisted behind my head, asleep and heavy and tingling.

And then I realized that I had missed these things all along, the whole time my arm had been over the mantel, but that I'd never said anything or even let myself feel anything bad because I didn't want to dwell on those feelings because I didn't want to make you feel bad and I didn't want you to think I wanted you to feel bad.

I decided to look for it. Maybe you'd sold it. You were always good with things like that.

I hit the pawnshops. I walked into them and they'd ask me could they help me and I'd say, I'm looking for an arm. And they'd stare at me, my empty sleeve pinned to my shirt, or flapping in the air. I never have liked acting like things aren't the way they are.

When I searched all the local pawnshops, I started going to ones further away. I saw a lot of the country. It was nice. And I got good at it. The more I did, the more I learned to do. The braver ones would look at me directly in the eye. They'd give me the names and addresses of outlets selling artificial limbs, or reconstructive surgeons. But I didn't want another one, I wanted mine. And then, the more I looked for it, the more I wondered if I wasn't looking more for something else besides my severed arm. I wondered was I really searching for you?

It all came clear to me. Like something hacked away from me: you'd done this to me as a test. To show me things. To show me what things meant to me, how much my arm was part of me, but how I could learn to live without it. How, if I was forced to, I could learn to get by with only part of me, with next to nothing. You'd done this to me to teach me something.

And then I thought how, if you were testing me, you must be watching me, to see if I was passing.

So I started acting out my life for you. And then I felt you watching all my actions. I whistled with bravado, jaunted, rather than walked. I had a confident swagger. I slapped friendly pawnshop keepers on their shoulders and told them jokes. I was fun, an inspiration they'd remember after I'd passed through.

I acted like I couldn't care less about my old arm. Like I liked the breezes in my sleeve.

I began to think in perfect sentences, as if you were listening to me. I thought clear sentences inside myself. I said, I get along just fine without my arm. I think that I convinced myself, in trying to convince you, that I had never had an arm I'd lost.

Soon I didn't think the word inside me any more. I didn't think about the right hand gloves buried in my bottom drawer.

I made myself not miss it. I tested myself. I sat in the den and stared at the empty space above the mantel. I spent the night on the couch. I went into the bathroom and looked in the tub. I felt nothing. I went to bed.

I thought my trips to pawnshops, my wanderlust, were only things I did to pass the time. I thought of nothing almost happily.

I looked at my shoulder. The tissue was smooth. I ran my fingers over it. Round and slightly puffed, pink and shiny and slick. As soft as pimento, as cool as a spoon, the tenderest flesh of my body.

My beautiful empty sleeve and I were friends, like intimates.

So everything was fine.
For a while.
Then you came back.
Then everything did.

But I was careful. It had been a long time. I had learned how to live. Why, hadn't I just forgotten what used to fill my empty sleeve entirely? I was very careful. I acted like nothing had ever been different, that you had never ripped it out of me, then bronzed it, put it on the mantel, left with it.

I wanted things to stay forgot.

And besides, it was so easy, so familiar having you around. It was nice.

I determined to hold on to what I'd learned. About the strength of having only one.

Maybe I should have told you then. Maybe I should have told you then. But then, I told myself, if you knew to leave it alone, then good. And if you didn't know, we needed to find that out.

So we were sitting in the den. You looked at me with your big sweet pretty brown eyes and you said, you whispered it softly like a little girl, you said, Oh, I'm so sorry. You started crying softly, your lips quivering. Can you ever forgive me? You said it slow and sweet like a foreign language. I watched you, knowing you knew the way I was watching you. You leaned into me and pulled my arm around you and ran your pretty fingers down the solid muscle in my sleeve. Just hold me darling, you said. Just hold me again.

I ran my wet palm, shaking, on your gorgeous back. Your hair smelled sweet.

I looked at your beautiful tear-lined face and tried to pretend that I had never seen you before in my life.

Why did you do it? I whispered.

You looked at me, your eyes all moist and sweet like you could melt anything in the world. You didn't answer.

What did you do with it?

You shrugged your shoulders, shook your head and smiled at me sweeter than an angel.

Say something, I whispered into your pretty hair. Say something, god-dammit.

You looked up at me and your sweet brown eyes welled up with tears again. You put your head against my breast and sobbed.

You made me rock you and I did and then you cried yourself to sleep as innocent as a baby. When you were asleep I walked you to the bedroom and put you to bed. You slept. I watched you all night. You remembered nothing in the morning.

In the morning we had coffee. You chatted to me about your adventures. You cocked your head at just the right places, the way I remembered you did. You told me you'd worked hard in the time you'd been away. You told me how much you had learned about the world, about yourself, about honor, faith and trust, etc. You looked deep into my eyes and said, I've changed. You said how good and strong and true and truly different you were. How you had learned that it is not our acts, but our intents, that make us who we are.

I watched your perfect teeth.

I felt your sweet familiar hands run up my body, over the empty sleeve that rumpled on the exposed side of me. I closed my eyes and couldn't open them. My mouth was closed. I couldn't tell you anything.

I couldn't tell you that you can't re-do a thing that's been undone. I couldn't tell you anything that you would understand. I couldn't tell you that it wasn't just the fact that you had ripped it out of me and taken it and mounted it, then left with it then lost it, how it wasn't only that, but it was more. How it was that when you asked me, I believed you and I told you yes. How, though I had tried a long time to replace what you had hacked away from me, I never could undo the action of your doing so, that I had, and only ever would have, more belief in your faulty memory, your stupid sloppy foresight, than in you claims of change. How I believed, yes, I believed with all my heart, that given time, you'd do something else again, some new and novel variant to what you'd done to me, again. And then I thought, but this was only half a thought, that even if you had changed, no *really* changed, truly and at last, and even if you knew me better than I know myself, and even if I'm better off than I've ever been, and even if this was the only way we could have gotten to this special place where we are now, and even if there's a reason, darling, something bigger than both of us, and even if all these even if's are true, that I would never believe you again, never forget what I know of you, never forget what you've done to me, what you will do. I'll never believe the myth of forgiveness between us.

1990

Selected Bibliographies

For ease of reference, all the authors are listed in alphabetical order. Parentheses around dates indicate first publication of primary sources or periodical publication.

Abigail Adams

Adams's published correspondence consists of *Letters of Mrs. Adams* (1840) and *Familiar Letters of John Adams and His Wife, during the Revolution* (1876), both edited by her grandson Charles Adams; *The Book of Abigail and John*, 1975, ed. L. H. Butterfield, who restored the original spelling and content that Charles Adams had edited; *New Letters of Abigail Adams*, 1973, ed. Stewart Mitchell; and *The Adams Family Correspondence*, 1964–73, ed. L. H. Butterfield. Two useful biographies are Phyllis Lee Levin, *Abigail Adams, A Biography*, 1987; and Edith Belle Gelles, *Portia: The World of Abigail Adams*, 1992. Helpful critical essays are Edith B. Gelles, "The Abigail Industry," *William and Mary Quarterly* 45(1988); and Frank Shuffleton, "In Different Voices: Gender in the American Republic of Letters," *Early American Literature* 25 (1990). A recent and valuable full-length study is Rosemary Skinner Keller, *Patriotism and the Female Sex: Abigail Adams and the American Revolution*, 1994.

Fleur Adcock

Adcock's poetry includes *Tigers* (1967), *High Tide in the Garden* (197), *The Scenic Route* (1974), *The Inner Harbour* (1979), *Selected Poems* (1983), *The Incident Book* (1986), *Meeting the Comet* (1988), and *Time-Zones* (1991). She translated *The Virgin and the Nightingale: Medieval Poems*, 1983, and edited *The Faber Book of Twentieth-Century Women's Poetry*, 1987. She is also the author of several texts and libretti for musical works by the composer Gillian Whitehead. An autobiographical essay, "Rural Blitz: Fleur Adcock's English Childhood," appears in *Poetry Review* 74 (1984), and an interview with Adcock is included in *Talking About Ourselves*, 1986, ed. Harry Ricketts. An interesting recent study on

Adcock's poetry is Ian Gregson, "Your Voice Speaking in My Poems: Polyphony in Fleur Adcock," *English* 42 (1993).

Ama Ata Aidoo

Aidoo's works include the book of short stories *No Sweetness Here* (1969), the plays *Dilemma of a Ghost* (1965) and *Anowa* (1970), and the novel *Our Sister Killjoy, or, Reflections from a Black-Eyed Squint* (1979). Her recent work includes a collection of children's stories, *The Eagle and the Chickens and Other Stories* (1986); a novel, *Changes: A Love Story* (1991); and two books of poetry: *Someone Talking to Sometime* (1985) and *An Angry Letter in January and Other Poems* (1992). An interesting interview is Rosemary Marangoly George and Helen Scott, " 'A New Tail to an Old Tale': An Interview with Ama Ata Aidoo," *Novel* 26 (1993).

For critical material, see Dapo Adelugba, "Language and Drama: Ama Ata Aidoo," *African Literature Today* 3 (1976); Marion Kilson, "Women and African Literature," *Journal of African Studies* 4 (1977); Kathleen McCaffrey, "Images of the Mother in the Stories of Ama Ata Aidoo," *Africa Women* 23 (1979); and Karen C. Chapman " 'Introduction' to Ama Ata Aidoo's *Dilemma of a Ghost*," in *Sturdy Black Bridges: Visions of Black Women in Literature*, 1979, ed. Roseann P. Bell, Bettye J. Parker, and Beverly Guy-Sheftall. Alice Walker includes a discussion of Aidoo in *In Search of Our Mothers' Gardens*, 1984. See also Chimalum Nwanko, "The Feminist Impulse and Social Realism in Ama Ata Aidoo's *No Sweetness Here* and *Our Sister Killjoy*," in *Nganbika: Studies of Women in African Literature*, 1986, ed. Carole Boyce Davies and Anne Adams Graves; Caroline Rooney, "Dangerous Knowledge and the Poetics of

Survival: A Reading of *Our Sister Killjoy* and *A Question of Power*," in *Motherlands: Black Women's Writing from Africa, the Caribbean, and South Asia*, 1992, ed. Susheila Nasta; and Chikwenye Okonjo Ogunyemi, "Womanism: The Dynamics of the Contemporary Black Female Novel in English," in *Revising the Word and the World: Essays in Feminist Literary Criticism*, 1993, ed. VeVe Clark, Ruth-Ellen B. Joeres, and Madelon Sprengnether.

Louisa May Alcott

Besides Alcott's famous children's novels— *Little Women* (1869), *Little Men* (1871), *Eight Cousins* (1875), *Jo's Boys* (1886), and many others, all currently available in many editions—a number of other Alcott works have been republished, including *Hospital Sketches* (1863), 1960, ed. Bessie Z. Jones; *Behind a Mask: The Unknown Thrillers of Louisa May Alcott*, 1975, ed. and with an introduction by Madeline Stern; *Plots and Counterplots: More Unknown Thrillers of Louisa May Alcott* (1976) and *A Double Life: Newly Discovered Thrillers of Louisa May Alcott* (1988), both ed. Stern; *Louisa May Alcott: Selected Fiction*, 1990, ed. Madeline Stern and Daniel Shealy; *Work: A Story of Experience* (1873), 1977, with an introduction by Elizabeth Hardwick; and *Alternative Alcott*, 1988, ed. and with an introduction by Elaine Showalter.

Valuable background information is included in *Louisa May Alcott, Her Life, Letters, and Journals*, 1889, ed. Ednah D. Cheney; and *The Journals of Louisa May Alcott*, 1989, ed. Joel Myerson and Daniel Shealy. The many biographies of Alcott include Katharine Susan Anthony, *Louisa May Alcott*, 1939; Marjorie Worthington, *Miss Alcott of Concord, a Biography*, 1958; and Martha Sexton, *Louisa May: A Modern Biography of Louisa May Alcott*, 1977.

Critical studies include Cornelia Lynde Meigs, *Louisa May Alcott and the American Family Story*, 1970; Ruth K. McDonald, *Louisa May Alcott*, 1983; Sarah Elber, *Hunger for Home: Louisa May Alcott's Place in American Culture*, 1987; and Elizabeth Lennox Keyser, *Whispers in the Dark: The Fiction of Louisa May Alcott*, 1993. Important short analyses are Carolyn Heilbrun, "Louisa May Alcott: The Influence of *Little Women*," in *Women, the Arts, and the 1920's in Paris and New York*, 1982, ed. Kenneth Wheeler and Virginia Lee Dussier; Nina Auerbach's discussion of *Little Women* in *Communities of Women*, 1979; and Elaine Showalter, "*Little Women*: The American Female Myth," in her *Sister's Choice: Tradition and Change in American Women's Writing*, 1991. Two bibliographies—Alma J. Payne,

Louisa May Alcott, a Reference Guide, 1980; and Ruth K. McDonald, "Recent Alcott Criticism," *Children's Literature* 9 (1981)—are helpful, though somewhat outdated. Other useful articles are Janet S. Zehr, "The Response of Nineteenth-Century Audiences to Louisa May Alcott's Fiction," *American Transcendental Quarterly* 1 (1987); and Glenn Hendler, "The Limits of Sympathy: Louisa May Alcott and the Sentimental Novel," *American Literary History* 3 (1991).

Maya Angelou

Angelou's works are *I Know Why the Caged Bird Sings* (1970), *Just Give Me a Cool Drink of Water 'Fore I Diiie* (1971), *Georgia, Georgia* (1972), *Gather Together in My Name* (1974), *Oh Pray My Wings Are Gonna Fit Me Well* (1975), *Singin' and Swingin' and Gettin' Merry Like Christmas* (1976), *And Still I Rise* (1978), and *The Heart of a Woman* (1981). *The Complete Poems of Maya Angelou* appeared in 1994. Useful interviews appear in "The Black Scholar Interviews Maya Angelou," *Black Scholar* 8 (1977); and in *Black Women Writers at Work*, 1984, ed. Claudia Tate. Critical essays on her achievement include Sidonie A. Smith, "The Song of a Caged Bird: Maya Angelou's Quest after Self-Acceptance," *Southern Humanities Review* 7 (1973); George E. Kent, "Maya Angelou's *I Know Why the Caged Bird Sings* and Black Autobiographical Tradition," *Kansas Quarterly* 7 (1975); Myra K. McMurry, "Role-Playing as Art in Maya Angelou's *Caged Bird*," *South Atlantic Bulletin* 41 (1976); and R. B. Stepto, "The Phenomenal Woman and the Severed Daughter," *Parnassus* (1980). Two useful essays—Selwyn R. Cudjoe, "Maya Angelou and the Autobiographical Statement," and Sandra O'Neale, "Reconstruction of the Composite Self"—appear in *Black Women Writers (1950–1980)*, 1984, ed. Mari Evans. See also the recent discussions of Angelou in *Notable Black Women*, 1992, ed. Jessie Carney Smith; and by Kathleen Thompson in *Black Women in America*, 1993, ed. Darlene Clark Hine.

Gloria Anzaldúa

Anzaldúa is the author of *Borderlands/La Frontera* (1987) and *Friends from the Other Side*, with pictures by Consuelo Mendez (1993). She is the editor of *This Bridge Called My Back: Writings by Radical Women of Color* (1981) and *Making Face, Making Soul / Hacienda Caras: Creative and Critical Perspectives by Feminists of Color* (1990). Critical work on Anzaldúa includes Y. Yarbrobejarano, "Gloria Anzaldúa, *Borderlands/La Frontera*: Cultural Studies, Difference, and the Non-

Unitary Subject," *Cultural Critique* 28 (1994); and A. L. Keating, "Writing, Politics, and *Las Lesberadas—Platicando—con Gloria Anzaldúa*," *Frontiers—A Journal of Women's Studies* 14 (1994).

Mary Astell

Besides *A Serious Proposal to the Ladies* (1694), Astell's works include *Letters Concerning the Love of God* (1695), *Some Reflections on Marriage* (1700), *Moderation Truly Stated* (1704), and *The Christian Religion as Professed by a Daughter of the Church of England* (1705). The most useful critical study to date is Ruth Perry's *The Celebrated Mary Astell: An Early English Feminist*, 1986. The only other full-length study is the early *Mary Astell*, 1916, by Florence M. Smith. Astell is discussed in Hilda Smith, *Reason's Disciples*, 1982; and Joan Kinnaird writes about Astell in *Feminist Theorists*, 1984, ed. Dale Spender.

Margaret Atwood

Two excellent introductions to Atwood's poetry are *Selected Poems* (1976) and *Selected Poems II: Poems Selected and New, 1976–1986* (1987). Her novels include *The Edible Woman* (1969), *Surfacing* (1972) *Lady Oracle* (1976), *Life before Man* (1979), *Bodily Harm* (1982), *The Handmaid's Tale* (1985), *Cat's Eye* (1989), and *The Robber Bride* (1993). She has also published volumes of short stories, including *True Stories* (1982), *Wilderness Tips* (1991), and *Good Bones and Simple Murders* (1994). In addition, she has written plays, books for children, and literary criticism. There are many published interviews with Atwood, including one by Joyce Carol Oates in the *New York Times Book Review*, May 21, 1978. Useful full-length studies are Sherrill Grace, *Violent Duality: A Study of Margaret Atwood*, 1980; Jerome H. Rosenburg, *Margaret Atwood*, 1984; Kathryn VanSpanckeren and Jan Garden Castro, *Margaret Atwood: Vision and Form*, 1988; J. Brooks Bouson, *Brutal Choreographies: Oppositional Strategies and Narrative Design in the Novels of Margaret Atwood*, 1993; and Sharon Rose Wilson, *Margaret Atwood's Fairy-Tale Sexual Politics*, 1993 Helpful collections of critical essays on Atwood are *Margaret Atwood: A Symposium*, ed. Linda Sandler in *The Malahat Review* (1977); *The Art of Margaret Atwood: Essays in Criticism*, 1981, ed. Arnold E. Davidson and Cathy N. Davidson; *Margaret Atwood: Language, Text, and System*, 1983, ed. Sherrill E. Grace and Lorraine Weir; *Critical Essays on Margaret Atwood*, 1988, ed. Judith McCombs; and *Margaret Atwood, Writing, and Subjectivity: New Critical Essays*, 1994, ed. Colin Nicholson.

Jane Austen

The standard edition of Austen's work—including *Sense and Sensibility* (1811), *Pride and Prejudice* (1813), *Mansfield Park* (1814), *Emma* (1816), *Persuasion* (1818), and *Northanger Abbey* (1818)—is *The Works of Jane Austen*, ed. R. W. Chapman, first published in the 1920s and reprinted in the 1970s with revisions by Mary Lascelles. Chapman also collected and edited *Jane Austen's Letters*, 1979, and *Selected Letters, 1796–1817*, 1985. The recently issued *Jane Austen's Manuscript Letters in Facsimile*, 1990, ed. Jo Modert, includes Austen's every known letter; and *My Dear Cassandra: The Letters of Jane Austen*, 1991, ed. Penelope Hughes-Hellet, contains a selection. Norton Critical Editions of *Emma*, ed. Stephen M. Parrish, *Pride and Prejudice*, ed. Donald J. Gray, and *Persuasion*, ed. Patricia Meyer Spacks, contain valuable secondary material. Useful biographical information can be found in William and Richard Austen-Leigh, *Jane Austen: Her Life and Letters*, 1913; Mary A. Austen-Leigh, *Personal Aspects of Jane Austen*, 1920; and James Edward Austen-Leigh, *Memoir of Jane Austen*, 1926. Other biographies include R.W. Chapman, *Jane Austen, Facts and Problems*, 1948; Margaret Kennedy, *Jane Austen*, 1950; Marghanita Laski, *Jane Austen and Her World*, 1969; Margaret Llewelyn, *Jane Austen: A Character Study*, 1977; George H. Tucker, *A Goodly Heritage: A History of Jane Austen's Family*, 1983; John Halperin, *The Life of Jane Austen*, 1984; and Park Honan, *Jane Austen: Her Life*, 1987.

Full-length critical studies of Austen's novels are numerous. Among the more influential are Mary Lascelles, *Jane Austen and Her Art*, 1938; Marvin Mudrick, *Jane Austen: Irony as Defense and Discovery*, 1952; Andrew H. Wright, *Jane Austen's Novels*, 1957; A. Walton Litz, *Jane Austen*, 1965; Joseph Wiesenfarth, *The Errand of Form*, 1967; Alistair M. Duckworth, *The Improvement of the Estate*, 1971; and Stuart M. Tave, *Some Words of Jane Austen*, 1973. Other helpful studies are Julia P. Brown, *Jane Austen's Novels: Social Change and Literary Form*, 1979; Susan Morgan, *In the Meantime: Character and Perception in Jane Austen's Fiction*, 1980; John Odmark, *An Understanding of Jane Austen's Novels: Character, Value, and Ironic Perspective*, 1981; P. J. M. Scott, *Jane Austen, A Reassessment*, 1982; Laura G. Mooneyham, *Romance, Language, and Education in Jane Austen's Novels*, 1986; James Thompson, *Between Self and World: The Novels of Jane Austen*, 1988; Roger Gard, *Jane Austen's Novels: The Art of Clarity*, 1992; and Maaja A. Stewart, *Domestic Realities and Imperial Fictions: Jane Austen's Novels in Eighteenth-Century Contexts*, 1993. Collections of essays include *Jane Austen*

Today, 1975, ed. Joel Weinscheimer; and *Jane Austen: New Perspectives,* 1983, ed. Janet Todd, a feminist collection. Feminist approaches to Austen's work can be found in Jean Kennard, *Victims of Convention,* 1977; Sandra M. Gilbert and Susan Gubar, *The Madwoman in the Attic,* 1979; Mary Poovey, *The Proper Lady and the Woman Writer,* 1984; Claudia L. Johnson, *Jane Austen: Women, Politics, and the Novel,* 1988; and Alison Sulloway, *Jane Austen and the Province of Womanhood,* 1989. Interesting recent critical essays are Janet Todd, "Jane Austen, Politics and Sensibility," in *Feminist Criticism: Theory and Practice,* 1991, ed. Linda Hutcheon and Paul Perron; and Christine Marshall, " 'Dull Elves' and Feminists: A Summary of Feminist Criticism of Jane Austen," *Persuasions* 14 (1992). For further references, see David Gibson's useful, though somewhat dated, *A Bibliography of Jane Austen,* 1982.

Mary Austin

Among Austin's numerous publications are four nature works, *One Hundred Miles on Horseback* (1889), *The Land of Little Rain* (1903), *The Flock* (1909), and *Land of Journey's Ending* (1923); two collections of short stories, *The Basket Woman* (1904) and *Lost Borders* (1909); and many novels, including *Isidro* (1905), *A Woman of Genius* (1912), *Santa Lucia* (1908), *No. 26 Jayme Street* (1920), and *Starry Adventure* (1931). The title story from *The Mother of Felipe and Other Early Stories* (1950) was Austin's first publication. Two nonfiction works are *The Young Woman Citizen* (1918), a meditation on women's legal rights in the United States, and *Can Prayer Be Answered?* (1934). The short story collections, *Stories from the Country of Lost Borders,* ed. Marjorie Pryse, and *Western Trails: A Collection of Short Stories,* ed. Melody Graulich, both appeared in 1987. Austin's autobiography, *Earth Horizon,* was originally printed in 1932 and reissued in 1991. Her letters, collected in *Literary America, 1903–1934: The Mary Austin Letters,* were printed in 1979.

Two full-length studies containing valuable biographical material are Augusta Fink, *I—Mary: A Biography of Mary Austin,* 1983; and Esther Lanigan Stineman, *Mary Austin: Song of a Maverick,* 1989. James Ruppert has two useful essays on Austin: "Discovering America: Mary Austin and Imagism," in *Studies in American Indian Literature: Critical Essays and Course Designs,* 1983, ed. Paula Gunn Allen; and "Mary Austin's Landscape Line in Native American Literature," *Southwest Review* 68 (1983). Other helpful articles include David Wyatt, "Mary Austin: Nature and Nurturance," in his *The Fall into Eden,* 1986; Lois Rudnick, "Re-Naming the Land: Anglo-

Expatriate Women in the Southwest," in *The Desert Is No Lady,* 1987, ed. Vera Norwood and Janice Monk; and Esther Lanigan Stineman, "Mary Austin Rediscovered," *Journal of the Southwest* 30 (1988).

Anna Letitia Barbauld

Barbauld's complete poems—only recently available in a modern edition—are assembled chronologically in *The Poems of Anna Laetitia Barbauld,* 1994, ed. William McCarthy and Elizabeth Kraft, a collection that includes an informative introduction and meticulous textual notes. Barbauld's important prose works (not available in a modern edition) include *Lessons for Children* (1778) and *Hymns in Prose for Children* (1781) as well as two works written in collaboration with John Aiken: *Miscellaneous Pieces in Prose* (1773) and *Evenings at Home; or, the Juvenile Budget Opened,* 6 vols. (1792–96). Barbauld edited the six-volume *Correspondence of Samuel Richardson* (1804); a fifty-volume anthology, *British Novelists* (1810); and a collection of passages by English poets and prose writers, *The Female Speaker* (1811). The two-volume *Works of Anna Laetitia Barbauld,* ed. Lucy Aikin, was published posthumously in 1825, and *Letters of Maria Edgeworth and Anna Laetitia Barbauld,* ed. Sir Walter Sidney Scott, appeared in 1953.

Betsy Rodgers's valuable biography, *Georgian Chronicle: Barbauld and Her Family,* 1958, contains previously unpublished letters. More recent studies of Barbauld include Marilyn L. Williamson, "Who's Afraid of Mrs. Barbauld? The Blue-Stockings and Feminism," *International Journal of Women's Studies* 3 (1980); Ann Messenger, "Heroics and Mock-Heroics: John Milton, Alexander Pope, and Anna Laetitia Barbauld," in her *His and Hers: Essays in Restoration and Eighteenth-Century Literature,* 1986; Catherine Moore, " 'Ladies . . . Taking the Pen in Hand': Mrs. Barbauld's Criticism of Eighteenth-Century Women Novelists," in *Fetter'd or Free? British Women Novelists, 1670–1815,* 1986, ed. Mary Ann Schofield and Cecilia Macheski; Katherine Rogers, "Anna Barbauld's Criticism of Fiction: Johnsonian Mode, Female Vision," *Studies in Eighteenth-Century Culture* 21 (1991); and John M. Anderson, " 'The First Fire': Barbauld Rewrites the Greater Romantic Lyric," *Studies in English Literature, 1500–1900* 34 (1994).

Djuna Barnes

Known primarily for her novel *Nightwood* (1937), Barnes wrote many other works, which are now receiving critical attention. They include *The Book of Repulsive Women, Eight Rhythms and Five Drawings* (1915), *Ladies' Almanack* (1928), *Ryder* (1928), *The Antiphon* (1958), *Spillway* (1962), and *Creatures in an*

Alphabet (1982). Recently, Philip F. Herring presented "'Behind the Heart': An Unpublished Story by Djuna Barnes," *Library Chronicle of the University of Texas* 23 (1993). There is a 1962 edition of *The Selected Works of Djuna Barnes*. *Smoke and Other Early Stories*, ed. and with an introduction by Douglas Messerli, was published in 1982. Alyce Barry has edited two collections of Barnes's works: *Interviews*, 1985, and *New York*, 1989. A volume of correspondence, *Selected Letters of Djuna Barnes*, appeared in 1993.

Full-length biographies and critical studies include James B. Scott, *Djuna Barnes*, 1976; Louis F. Kannenstine, *The Art of Djuna Barnes: Duality and Damnation*, 1977; Andrew Field, *Djuna, The Formidable Miss Barnes*, 1985, a revision of his *Djuna. The Life and Time of Djuna Barnes*, 1983; and *Silence and Power: A Reevaluation of Djuna Barnes*, 1991, ed. Mary Lynn Broe and with an afterword by Catharine Stimpson. Critical essays include Carolyn Allen, "'Dressing the Unknowable in the Garments of the Known': The Style of Djuna Barnes in *Nightwood*," in *Women's Language and Style*, 1978, ed. Douglas Butturff and Edmund L. Epstein; Susan Sniader Lanser, "Speaking in Tongues: *Ladies' Almanack* and the Language of Celebration," *Frontiers* 4 (1979); Lynn DeVore, "The Background of *Nightwood*: Robin, Felix, and Nora," *Journal of Modern Literature* 10 (1983); Carolyn J. Allen, "Sexual Narrative in the Fiction of Djuna Barnes," in *Sexual Practice, Textual Theory: Lesbian Cultural Criticism*, 1993, ed. Susan J. Wolfe and Julian Penelope; and Frann Michael, "'I Just Loved Thelma': Djuna Barnes and the Construction of Bisexuality," *The Review of Contemporary Fiction* 13 (1993). Douglas Messerli compiled *Djuna Barnes: A Bibliography*, 1975, and Jamie Stevens recently published "Djuna Barnes: An Updated Bibliography," *The Review of Contemporary Fiction* 13 (1993).

Patricia Beer

Beer's books of poetry are *Loss of the Magrar and Other Poems* (1959), *The Survivors* (1963), *Just Like the Resurrection* (1967), *The Estuary* (1971), *Driving West* (1975), *Selected Poems* (1979), *The Lie of the Land* (1983), and *Friend of Heraclitus* (1993). Her *Collected Poems* (1988) includes some previously unpublished poems as well as most of the contents of her seven earlier volumes. Beer's influential critical study of nineteenth-century women novelists, *Reader: I Married Him*, appeared in 1974. Other important prose works include the autobiographical *Mrs. Beer's House* (1968) and the novel *Moon's Ottery* (1978). Poems by Beer appear in *The Faber Book of Twentieth-Century Women's Poetry*, 1987, ed. Fleur Adcock; and

The Things That Matter: An Anthology of Women's Spiritual Poetry, 1992, ed. Julia Neuberger. Anne Stevenson discusses Beer's poetry (along with that of five other contemporary women poets) in "Houses of Choice," *Poetry Review* 70 (1980).

Aphra Behn

The four-volume edition of *The Works of Aphra Behn*, 1992, ed. Janet M. Todd, is arranged as follows: I, poetry; II, *Love-Letters Between a Nobleman and His Sister*; III, *The Fair Jilt and Other Stories*; IV, *Seneca Unmasked and Other Prose Translations*. *Oronooko, The Rover, and Other Stories*, ed. Maureen Duffy, was published in 1992. *Five Plays*, selected and introduced by Maureen Duffy, appeared in 1990. The following editions of Behn's works are part of a Garland series called "Satire and Sense": A *Critical Old-Spelling Edition of Aphra Behn's The City Heiress*, 1987, and *Aphra Behn's The Luckey Chance* (1687): A Critical Edition, 1987, ed. Stephen Orgel. Malcolm Hicks edited and wrote an introduction to *Selected Poems*, 1993. Mary Ann O'Donnell has conducted a useful bibliographical study in *Aphra Behn: An Annotated Bibliography of Primary and Secondary Sources*, 1986. Good introductions are Laura Brown, "The Romance of Empire: Oronooko and the Trade in Slaves," in *The New Eighteenth Century: Theory, Politics English Literature*, 1987, eds. Brown and Felicity Nussbaum; Rosalind Ballaster, *Seductive Forms: Women's Amatory Fiction from 1684–1740: with Particular Reference to Aphra Behn, Delarvier Manley, and Eliza Haywood*, 1992, and *Rereading Aphra Behn: History, Theory, and Criticism*, 1993, ed. Heidi Hutner. In addition, two biographies have appeared over the last two decades: *The Passionate Shepherdess: Aphra Behn, 1640–1689*, 1977, by Maureen Duffy, and *Reconstructing Aphra: A Social Biography of Aphra Behn*, 1980, by Angeline Goreau. Articles of interest are Judith Kegan Gardiner, "Aphra Behn: Sexuality and Self-Respect," *Women's Studies* 7 (1980), and in the same journal, 7, Robert Adams Day, "Muses in the Mud: The Female Wits Anthropologically Considered." Behn is also discussed by Fidelis Morgan in *The Female Wits*, 1981, and by Angeline Goreau in *Feminist Theorists*, 1984, ed. Dale Spender.

Juliana Berners

Although there is no complete modernized edition of the *Book of Saint Albans* (1468), originally published by the "Schoolmaster of St Albans," Middle English editions include *The Boke of Saint Albans by Dame Juliana Berners*, (1901), a large facsimile of the 1468 edition, with an introduction by William Blades;

Julians Barnes: Boke of Huntyng, 1964, ed. Gunnar Tilander; and *English Hawking and Hunting in "The Boke of St Albans,"* 1975, ed. Rachel Hands, which has a helpful critical introduction and textual notes. Berners is also discussed in E. F. Jacob, "The Book of St Albans," *BJRL* 28 (1944); A. L. Binns, "A Manuscript Source of *The Book of St Albans*," *BJRL* 33 (1950); Rachel Hands, "Juliana Berners and the *Boke of St. Albans*," *Review of English Studies* 18 (1967); and, most recently, Alexandra Barratt, ed., *Women's Writing in Middle English*, 1992.

Elizabeth Bishop

The Complete Poems of Elizabeth Bishop, 1927–1979, was published in 1983, and *The Collected Prose* in 1984. A collection of Bishop's correspondence, *One Art: Letters*, ed. Robert Giroux, was issued in 1994. Anne Stevenson's biographical and critical study, *Elizabeth Bishop*, appeared in 1966; Brett C. Miller's *Elizabeth Bishop: Life and the Memory of It* in 1993; and Gary Fountain and Peter Brazeau's *Remembering Elizabeth Bishop: An Oral Biography* was released in 1994. Useful critical essays on Bishop's poetry appear in the issue of *World Literature Today* (1976) devoted to her; in David Kalstone's *Five Temperaments*, 1977; and in two recent books: Victoria Harrison's *Elizabeth Bishop's Poetics of Intimacy*, 1993; and Marilyn May Lombardi, ed., *Elizabeth Bishop: The Geography of Gender*, 1993. A valuable collection of essays, *Elizabeth Bishop and Her Art*, ed. Lloyd Schwartz and Sybil P. Estess, was published in 1983.

Helpful critical essays are Richard Mullen, "Elizabeth Bishop's Surrealist Inheritance," *American Literature* 54 (1982); Kathleen Brogan, "Lyric Voice and Sexual Difference in Elizabeth Bishop," in *Writing the Woman Artist: Essays on Poetics, Politics, and Portraiture*, 1991, ed. Suzanne Jones; and Marilyn May Lombardi, "The Closet of Breath: Elizabeth Bishop, Her Body and Her Art," *Twentieth-Century Literature* 38 (1992). Two useful full-length studies are Robert Parker Dale, *The Unbeliever: The Poetry of Elizabeth Bishop*, 1988; and Lorrie Goldensohn, *Elizabeth Bishop: The Biography of a Poetry*, 1991. Though somewhat outdated, *Elizabeth Bishop: A Bibliography, 1927–1979*, 1980, comp. Candace W. McMahon; *Elizabeth Bishop and Howard Nemerov: A Reference Guide*, 1983, Diana E. Wyllie; and *A Concordance to Elizabeth Bishop's Poetry*, 1985, Anne Merrill Greenhalgh, are still useful reference books.

Louise Bogan

Among the collections of Bogan's poetry are *Collected Poems, 1923–1953* (1954) and *The*

Blue Estuaries: Poems, 1923–1968 (1968). Her *Selected Criticism* was published in 1955. William Jay Smith edited a lecture delivered at the Library of Congress, *Louise Bogan: A Woman's Words*, 1971; and Ruth Limmer edited the selected letters of 1920–70, *What the Woman Lived*, 1973, as well as a series of passages from her work put together to constitute a memoir, *Journey around My Room: The Autobiography of Louise Bogan: A Mosaic*, 1980. Elizabeth Frank's important biography, *Louise Bogan: A Portrait*, appeared in 1985. Also valuable are *Critical Essays on Louise Bogan*, 1984, ed. Martha Collins; and *Louise Bogan's Aesthetic of Limitation*, 1987, by Gloria Bowles. In addition, see the interesting discussions of Bogan in Alicia Ostriker, *Stealing the Language: The Emergence of Women's Poetry in America*, 1986; and Elizabeth Dodd, *The Veiled Mirror and the Woman Poet: H. D., Louise Bogan, Elizabeth Bishop, and Louise Gluck*, 1992. Other useful studies include Patrick Moore, "Symbol, Mask, and Meter in the Poetry of Louise Bogan," *Woman and Literature* 1 (1980); Mary De Shazer, "'My Scourge, My Sister': Louise Bogan's Muse," in *Coming to Light: American Poets in the Twentieth Century*, 1985, ed. Diane Wood Middlebrook and Marilyn Yalom; John P. Muller, "Light and the Wisdom of the Dark: Aging and the Language of Desire in the Texts of Louise Bogan," in *Memory and Desire: Aging, Literature, Psychoanalysis*, 1986, ed. Kathleen Woodward and Murray M. Schwartz; Suzanne Clark, "Medusa and Melancholy: The Fatal Allure of Beauty in Louise Bogan's Poetry," in her *Sentimental Modernism: Women Writers and the Revolution of the Word*, 1991; Cheryl Walker, "Woman and the Retreat of the Mind: Louise Bogan and the Stoic Persona," in her *Masks Outrageous and Austere: Culture, Psyche, and Persona in Modern Women Poets*, 1991; and Marcia Aldrich, "Lethal Brevity: Louise Bogan's Lyric Career," in *Aging and Gender in Literature: Studies in Creativity*, 1993, ed. Anne M. Wyatt-Brown and Janice Rossen. A useful bibliography is Claire E. Knox, *Louise Bogan: A Reference Source*, 1990.

Eavan Boland

Boland's works include *New Territory: Poems* (1967), *The War Horse: Poems* (1975), *In Her Own Image* (1980), *Night Feed* (1982), *The Journey* (1983), *Outside History: Selected Poems, 1980–1990* (1990), *In a Time of Violence* (1994), and *An Origin Like Water* (1996). She has also written three critical studies concerning women's poetic and political place in Ireland: *A Kind of Scar: The Woman Poet in a National Tradition* (1989), *A Dozen LIPS* (1994), and *Object Lessons: The Life of the*

Woman and the Poet in Our Time (1995). An interview with Boland by Deborah McWilliams Conslavo appears in Studies: An Irish Quarterly Review 81 (1992). Helpful critical essays include Sheila C. Conboy, "'What You Have Seen Is Beyond Speech': Female Journeys in the Poetry of Eavan Boland and Eilean Ni Chuilleanain," Canadian Journal of Irish Studies 16 (1990); Patricia L. Hagen and Thomas W. Zelman, "'We Were Never on the Scene of the Crime': Eavan Boland's Repossession of History," Twentieth-Century Literature 37 (1991); and David Wheatley, "'An Origin like Water': The Poetry of Eavan Boland and Modernist Critiques of Irish Literature," Irishness and (Post)Modernism, 1994, ed. John S. Rickard.

Marita Bonner

Bonner's essays, plays, and short stories are collected in Frye Street & Environs: The Collected Works of Marita Bonner, 1987, ed. Joyce Flynn and Joyce Occomy Stricklin. This includes a prefatory essay by Stricklin, "A Portrait of My Mother," and an introduction by Flynn.

Gertrude Bonnin (Zitkala Sá)

Bonnin's works include Old Indian Legends (1901) and American Indian Stories (1921). With William Hanson, she wrote the libretto for Sundance (1913), an opera, and she also coauthored Okla's Poor Rich Indians: An Orgy of Graft and Exploitation of the Five Civilized Tribes—Legalized Robbery (1924). She also published three essays: "Impressions of an Indian Childhood" and "An Indian Teacher among Indians," both in Atlantic Monthly (Jan.–Mar. 1900), and "Why I Am a Pagan," Atlantic Monthly 90 (Dec. 1902) Biographical information is included in Hazel W. Hertzberg, The Search for an American Indian Identity, 1971; and Marion E. Gridley, American Indian Women, 1974. Useful critical articles are Dexter Fisher, "Zitkala-Sa: The Evolution of a Writer," American Indian Quarterly 5 (1979); Mary Stout, "Zitkala-Sa: The Literature of Politics" in Coyote Was Here: Essays on Contemporary Native American Literary and Political Mobilization, 1984, ed. Bo Scholer; Fisher, "The Transformation of Tradition: A Study of Zitkala-Sa and Mourning Dove, Two Transitional American Indian Writers" in Critical Essays on American Literature, 1985, ed. Andrew Wiget; and Dorothea M. Susag, "Zitkala-Sa (Gertrude Simmons Bonnin): A Powerful Literary Voice," Studies in American Indian Literature 5 (1993).

Elizabeth Bowen

An edition of The Collected Stories of Elizabeth Bowen, with an introduction by Angus Wilson, was published in 1989. Among her best-known novels are The Hotel (1927), The House in Paris (1935), The Death of the Heart (1938), The Heat of the Day (1949), The Little Girls (1964), and Eva Trout or Changing Scenes (1968), all of which are available in paperback editions. She also wrote many nonfiction works, including Collected Impressions (1950) and Pictures and Conversations (1975), a posthumous collection. The Mulberry Tree: Writings of Elizabeth Bowen, appeared in 1986. Two useful biographies are Victoria Glendenning, Elizabeth Bowen: Portrait of a Writer, 1977; and Patricia Craig, Elizabeth Bowen, 1986. Full-length critical studies include William W. Heath, Elizabeth Bowen: An Introduction to Her Novels, 1961; Allen E. Austin, Elizabeth Bowen, 1989; Harriet Blodgett, Patterns of Reality: Elizabeth Bowen's Novels, 1975; Hermione Lee, Elizabeth Bowen: An Estimation, 1981; Phyllis Lassner, Elizabeth Bowen, 1989, and Elizabeth Bowen: A Study of the Short Fiction, 1991; Heather Bryant Jordan, How Will the Heart Endure: Elizabeth Bowen and the Landscape of War, 1992; Renee C. Hoogland, Elizabeth Bowen: A Reputation in Writing, 1994; and Andrew Bennett, Elizabeth Bowen and the Dissolution of the Novel: Still Lives, 1994. Useful critical articles are Harriet S. Chessman "Women and Language in the Fiction of Elizabeth Bowen," Twentieth-Century Literature 29 (1983); Thomas Dukes, "The Unorthodox Plots of Elizabeth Bowen," Studies in the Humanities 16 (1989); and Sandra Kemp, "'But How Describe a World Seen without a Self': Feminism, Fiction, and Modernism," Critical Quarterly 32 (1990). Harold Bloom edited the essay collection Elizabeth Bowen, 1987. J'nan Sellery and William O. Harris compiled the valuable Elizabeth Bowen: A Bibliography, 1981.

Anne Bradstreet

Jeannine Hensley's edition The Works of Anne Bradstreet, 1967, has an introduction by Adrienne Rich this essay also appears, with a later preface, in Rich's On Lies, Secrets, and Silence, 1979. The Complete Works of Anne Bradstreet, ed. Joseph McElrath and Allan Robb, came out in 1981; and Charles E. Hambrick-Stowe's edited collection Early New England Meditative Poetry: Anne Bradstreet and Edward Taylor, was printed in 1988. Useful critical discussion may be found in Josephine Piercy, Anne Bradstreet, 1965; Elizabeth W. White, Anne Bradstreet: The Tenth Muse, 1971; Ann Stanford, Anne Bradstreet: The Worldly Puritan, 1977; Albert J. Von Frank, The Sacred Game: Provincialism and Frontier Consciousness in American Literature, 1630–1860, 1985; Douglas R. Anderson, A House Undivided:

Domesticity and Community in American Literature, 1990; Rob Wilson, *American Sublime: The Genealogy of a Poetic Genre,* 1991; and Amanda Porterfield, *Female Piety in Puritan New England: The Emergence of Religious Humanism,* 1992. An interesting recent study is Jeffrey A. Hammond, *Sinful Self, Saintly Self: The Puritan Experience of Poetry,* 1993. Feminist work appears in Wendy Martin, "Anne Bradstreet's Poetry: A Study of Subversive Piety," in *Shakespeare's Sisters,* 1979, ed. Sandra M. Gilbert and Susan Gubar; and, also by Martin, *An American Triptych,* 1984. Other helpful articles include Emily Stipes Watts, "'The Posy Unity': Anne Bradstreet's Search for Order," in *Puritan Influences in American Literature,* 1979, ed. Emory Elliott; Ellen B. Brandt, "Anne Bradstreet: The Erotic Component in Puritan Poetry," *Women's Studies* 7 (1980); and Eileen Margerum, "Anne Bradstreet's Public Poetry and the Tradition of Humility," *Early American Literature* 17 (1982). Also of interest are Beth M. Doriani, "'Then Have I... Said with David': Anne Bradstreet's Andover Manuscript Poems and the Influence of the Psalm Tradition," *Early American Literature* 24 (1989); Jane D. Eberwein, "Civil War and Bradstreet's 'Monarchies,'" *Early American Literature* 26 (1991); and Robert Boschman, "Anne Bradstreet and Elizabeth Bishop: Nature, Culture, and Gender in 'Contemplations' and 'At the Fishhouses,'" *Journal of American Studies* 26 (1992). A useful bibliography is Raymond F. Dalle, *Anne Bradstreet: A Reference Guide,* 1990.

Anna Hempstead Branch

Besides *Sonnets from a Lock Box* (1929), Branch's verse collections include *The Shoes That Danced, and Other Poems* (1905), *Rose of the Wind, and Other Poems* (1910), and *Last Poems of Anna Hempstead Branch,* 1944, ed. and with a foreword by Ridgely Torrence. Poems by Branch appear in *American Mystical Verse: An Anthology,* 1925, ed. Irene Hunter; and in *The World Split Open: Four Centuries of Women Poets in England and America, 1552–1950,* 1974, ed. Louise Bernikow.

Charlotte Brontë

The standard edition of Brontë's work—including *Jane Eyre* (1847), *Shirley* (1849), *Villette* (1853), and *The Professor* (1857)—is *The Shakespeare Head Brontë,* 1931–38, ed. Thomas James Wise and John Alexander Symington. The same editors also produced *The Brontës: Their Lives, Friendships, and Correspondence,* 4 vols., 1932. Brontë's juvenilia is included in *Legends of Angria,* 1933, ed. Fannie E. Ratchford, with the collaboration of William Clyde DeVane; and *An Edition of the*

Early Writings of Charlotte Brontë, II: The Rise of Angria, 1833–1835, 2 vols., 1991, ed. Christine Alexander. In addition, numerous editions of Brontë's individual novels exist, including a Penguin series, with valuable introductions, and a Norton Critical Edition of *Jane Eyre,* 1987, ed. Richard J. Dunn, with a number of critical articles and a bibliography. See also *Five Novelettes,* 1971, ed. Winifred Gérin; and *The Secret and Lily Hart: Two Tales,* 1979, ed. William Holtz. *Poems by the Brontë Sisters,* 1948, has an introduction by M. R. D. Seaward; *The Poems of Charlotte Brontë,* 1985, has a new text and commentary by Victor A. Neufeldt; Christine Alexander edited *Something about Arthur,* 1981; and *The Unfinished Novels* was published in 1993.

The best biographies are Elizabeth Gaskell's justly famous *The Life of Charlotte Brontë,* 1857; and Winifred Gérin's *Charlotte Brontë: The Evolution of Genius,* 1967; but Helene Moglen's critical biography, *Charlotte Brontë: The Self Conceived,* 1976, also offers useful psychological insights. In addition, Lyndall Gordon's recent biography, *Charlotte Brontë: A Passionate Life,* 1994, is a valuable resource. Critical works include Robert Bernard Martin, *The Accents of Persuasion,* 1966; Earl A. Knies, *The Art of Charlotte Brontë,* 1969; Margot Peters, *Charlotte Brontë: Style in the Novel,* 1973; Lawrence Jay Dessner, *The Homely Web of Truth: A Study of Charlotte Brontë's Novels,* 1973; Charles Burkhart, *Charlotte Brontë: A Psychosexual Study of Her Novels,* 1973; Patricia Beer, *Reader, I Married Him,* 1974; Terence Eagleton, *Myths of Power: A Marxist Study of the Brontës,* 1975; and Christine Alexander, *The Early Writings of Charlotte Brontë,* 1983. Feminist approaches can be found in Elaine Showalter, *A Literature of Their Own,* 1977; Barbara Hill Rigney, *Madness and Sexual Politics in the Feminist Novel,* 1978; Sandra M. Gilbert and Susan Gubar, *The Madwoman in the Attic,* 1979; Judith Lowder Newton, *Women, Power, and Subversion,* 1981; and Dianne F. Sadoff, *Monsters of Affection: Dickens, Eliot, and Brontë on Fatherhood,* 1982. Essay collections include *The Brontës: The Critical Heritage,* 1974, ed. Miriam Allot; *The Brontës: A Collection of Critical Essays,* 1970, ed. Ian Gregor; and *Critical Essays on Charlotte Brontë,* 1990, Barbara Timm Gates. Also useful is Rebecca Crump, *Charlotte and Emily Brontë: A Reference Guide,* 1982.

Emily Brontë

A definitive edition of Brontë's *The Complete Poems* was produced by C. W. Hatfield in 1941, while her Gondal narrative was reconstructed in Fannie E. Ratchford, *The Brontës' Web of Childhood,* 1941, and in Ratchford, *Gondal's Queen: A Novel in Verse,* 1955. A useful edition

of *Wuthering Heights* (1847) is the No ton Critical Edition, ed. William M. Sale Jr. An excellent biography is Winifred Gérin, *Emily Brontë*, 1971; and two recent biographies are Edward Chitham, *A Life of Emily Brontë*, 1987; and Katherine Frank, *A Chainless Soul: A Life of Emily Brontë*, 1990.

Full-length critical studies include Margaret Lane, *The Drug-like Brontë Dream*, 1980; Mary Visick, *The Genesis of Wuthering Heights*, 1980; Stevie Davis, *Emily Brontë: The Artist as a Free Man*, 1983; Meg Harris Williams, *A Strange Way of Killing: The Poetic Structure of Wuthering Heights*, 1987; Stevie Davis, *Emily Brontë*, 1988; Maureen Peck-O'Toole, *Aspects of Lyric in the Poetry of Emily Brontë*, 1988; Carol Jacobs, *Uncontainable Romanticism: Shelley, Brontë Kleist*, 1989; Irene Taylor, *Holy Ghosts: The Male Muses of Emily and Charlotte Brontë*, 1990; and Virginia Jill Dix Ghnassia, *Metaphysical Rebellion in the Works of Emily Brontë: A Reinterpretation*, 1994. Feminist analyses appear in Sandra M. Gilbert and Susan Gubar, *The Madwoman in the Attic*, 1979; Margaret Homans, *Women Writers and Poetic Identity*, 1980; Christine Gallant, "The Archetypal Feminine in Emily Brontë's Poetry," *Women's Studies* 7 (1980); Nina Auerbach, *Romantic Imprisonment: Women and Other Glorified Outcasts*, 1985 Homans, *Bearing the Word: Language and Female Experience in Nineteenth-Century Women's Writing*, 1986; Judith Weissman, *Half Savage and Hardy and Free: Women and Rural Radicalism in the Nineteenth-Century Novel*, 1987; Patricia Yaeger, *Honey-Mad Women: Emancipatory Strategies in Women's Writing*, 1988; and Elsie B. Michie, *Outside the Pale: Cultural Exclusion, Gender Difference, and the Victorian Woman Writer*, 1993. Three valuable collections of critical essays are *The Art of Emily Brontë*, 1977, ed. Anne Smith; *The Brontës: Modern Critical Views*, 1987, ed. Harold Bloom; *Emily Brontë's Wuthering Heights: Modern Critical Interpretations*, 1987. Also helpful, though somewhat dated, is Janet M. Barclay, *Emily Brontë Criticism, 1900–1982: An Annotated Checklist*, 1984.

Gwendolyn Brooks

Gwendolyn Brooks's volumes include *A Street in Bronzeville* (1945), *Annie Allen* (1949), *Bronzeville Boys and Girls* (1956), *The Bean Eaters* (1960), *Selected Poems* (1963), *In the Mecca* (1968), *Riot* (1969), *Family Pictures* (1970), *The World of Gwendolyn Brooks* (1971), *Aloneness* (1972), *Beckonings* (1975), *To Disembark* (1981), *The Near-Johannesburg Boy and Other Poems* (1986) *Gottschalk and the Grand Toranbelle* (1988), *Winnie* (1988), and *Children Coming Home* (1992). *Blacks* (1987) is a collection of her prose and poetry. She has

also written novels, including *Maud Martha* (1953), and an autobiographical work, *Report from Part One* (1972).

Useful biographical, critical, and bibliographical studies are George E. Kent, *A Life of Gwendolyn Brooks*, 1990, and *A Life Distilled: Gwendolyn Brooks: Her Poetry and Fiction*, 1987, ed. Maria K. Mootry and Gary Smith, which includes a biographical chronology and a good bibliography. Haki Madhubuti edited *Say That the River Turns: The Impact of Gwendolyn Brooks*, 1987, a tribute to Brooks in honor of her seventieth birthday, containing essays by more than seventy writers.

Rebecca Brown

Brown's works of fiction include *The Evolution of Darkness and Other Stories* (1984), *The Haunted House* (1990), *The Children's Crusade* (1991), *The Terrible Girls* (1992), and *Annie Oakley's Girl* (1993). Her most recent work is the autobiographical *The Gifts of the Body* (1994). Short stories have appeared in two anthologies: *Mae West Is Dead: Recent Lesbian and Gay Fiction*, 1983, ed. Adam Mars-Jones; and *Women on Women 2: An Anthology of America n Lesbian Short Fiction*, 1993, ed. Joan Nestle and Naomi Holoch.

Elizabeth Barrett Browning

Barrett Browning's works—including *An Essay on Mind, with Other Poems* (1826), *The Seraphim, and Other Poems* (1838), *Poems* (1844), *Sonnets from the Portuguese* (1850). *Casa Guidi Windows* (1851), *Aurora Leigh* (1857), *Poems before Congress* (1860), and *Last Poems* (1862)—have been collected in the standard *Complete Works of Elizabeth Barrett Browning*, 6 vols., 1900, ed. Charlotte Porter and Helen Clarke. In addition, Julia Markus's edition of *Casa Guidi Windows*, 1977; Cora Kaplan's edition of *Aurora Leigh and Other Poems*, 1978; and Margaret Forster's edition of *Selected Poems of Elizabeth Barrett Browning*, 1988, are useful texts. Volumes of letters include *The Letters of Elizabeth Barrett Browning*, 1899, ed. Frederic G. Kenyon; *Elizabeth Barrett to Mr. Boyd*, 1955, ed. Barbara McCarthy; *The Letters of Robert Browning and Elizabeth Barrett, 1845–1846*, 2 vols., 1969; and *The Letters of Elizabeth Barrett Browning to Mary Russell Mitford, 1836–1854*, 1983, ed. Meredith Raymond and Mary Rose Sullivan. Volumes 1 and 2 of *The Brownings' Correspondence*, ed. Philip Kelley and Ronald Hudson, appeared in 1984, and volume 3 in 1985. Other collections of correspondence include *Woman of Letters: Selected Letters of Elizabeth Barrett Browning and Mary Russell Mitford*, 1987, ed. Meredith B. Raymond and Mary Rose Sullivan; and *Robert Browning and Elizabeth Barrett: The Courtship Correspon-*

dence, 1845–1846: A Selection, 1989, ed. Daniel Karlin.

Among biographies and biographical studies, the most helpful are Gardner B. Taplin, *The Life of Elizabeth Barrett Browning*, 1957; Alethea Hayter, *Elizabeth Barrett Browning*, 1965; Edward C. McAlzer, *The Brownings at Casa Guidi*, 1979; Rosalie Mander, *Mrs. Browning: The Story of Elizabeth Barrett*, 1980; Roy E. Gridley, *The Brownings and France: A Chronicle with Commentary*, 1982; Margaret Forster, *Elizabeth Barrett Browning: A Biography*, 1988; Daniel Karlin, *The Courtship of Robert Browning and Elizabeth Barrett*, 1985; Joanna Richardson, *The Brownings: A Biography*, 1986; and Peter Dally, *Elizabeth Barrett Browning: A Psychological Portrait*, 1989. Full-length critical studies include Angela Leighton, *Elizabeth Barrett Browning*, 1986; Helen Cooper, *Elizabeth Barrett Browning: Woman and Artist*, 1988; Dorothy Mermin, *Elizabeth Barrett Browning: The Origins of a New Poetry*, 1989; and Glennis Stephenson, *Elizabeth Barrett Browning and the Poetry of Love*, 1989. A valuable feminist study is Deirdre David, *Intellectual Women and Victorian Patriarchy: Harriet Martineau, Elizabeth Barrett Browning, George Eliot*, 1987. In addition, a number of essays have appeared in journals: Flavia Alaya, "The Ring, the Rescue and the Risorgimento: Reunifying the Brownings' Italy," *Browning Institute Studies* 6 (1978); Virginia Steinmetz, "Beyond the Sun: Patriarchal Images in *Aurora Leigh*," *Studies in Browning and His Circle* 9 (1981); Barbara Gelpi, "*Aurora Leigh*: The Vocation of the Woman Poet," *Victorian Poetry* 19 (1981); Dorothy Mermin, "The Female Poet and the Embarrassed Reader: Elizabeth Barrett Browning's *Sonnets from the Portuguese*," *ELH* (1981); Dolores Rosenblum, "Face to Face: Elizabeth Barrett Browning's *Aurora Leigh* and 19th-Century Poetry," *Victorian Studies* 26 (1983); and Sandra M. Gilbert, "From Patria to Matria: Elizabeth Barrett Browning's Risorgimento," *PMLA* (1984). Helpful reference guides are Joseph Magoon, *A Bibliography of Writings about the Brownings: Robert Browning and Elizabeth Barrett Browning from 1980 to 1989*, 1990; and Sandra Donaldson, *Elizabeth Barrett Browning: An Annotated Bibliography of the Commentary and Criticism, 1826–1990*, 1993.

Frances Burney

Burney's works include *Evelina* (1778), *Cecilia* (1782), *Camilla* (1796), *The Wanderer; or, Female Difficulties* (1814), and *The Memoirs of Dr. Burney* (1832). Eight volumes of her *Journals and Letters* have been edited by Joyce Hemlow, 1972–80; *Fanny Burney, Selected Letters and Journals*, edited by Hemlow, was published in 1986, and the three-volume work *The Early Journals and Letters of Fanny Burney*, ed. Lars Troide, was published in 1988. The most useful biography is Margaret Anne Doody's *Frances Burney: The Life in the Works*, 1988; many other biographies have been published, including Emily Hahn, *A Degree of Prudery*, 1950; Winifred Gérin, *The Young Fanny Burney*, 1961; and Michael E. Adelstein, *Fanny Burney*, 1968. Recent critical studies include Kristina Straub, *Divided Fictions: Fanny Burney and Feminine Strategy*, 1987; Julia Epstein, *The Iron Pen: Frances Burney and the Politics of Women's Writing*, 1989; Tracy Daugherty, *Narrative Techniques in the Novels of Fanny Burney*, 1989; Katharine M. Rogers, *Frances Burney: The World of "Female Difficulties,"* 1990; and Joanne Cutting-Gray, *Woman as "Nobody" and the Novels of Fanny Burney*, 1992. Also useful is Joseph A. Grau, *Fanny Burney: An Annotated Bibliography*, 1981.

Angela Carter

Carter's fiction includes *Shadow Dance* (1965), *The Magic Toyshop* (1967), *Several Perceptions* (1968), *Heroes and Villains* (1969), *Love* (1971), *The Infernal Desire Machine of Doctor Hoffman* (1972), and *The Passion of New Eve* (1977). She translated Charles Perrault's fairy tales and published three collections of stories: *Fireworks* (1974), *The Bloody Chamber* (1979), and *Wayward Girls & Wicked Women: An Anthology of Stories* (1986). She also published two collections of other writings: *Nothing Sacred: Selected Writings* (1982), and *Expletives Deleted: Selected Writings* (1992). *The Sadeian Woman: An Exercise in Cultural History* appeared in 1979, and *American Ghosts and Old World Wonders* appeared in 1993. For useful critical essays, see the collection *Flesh and the Mirror: Essays on the Art of Angela Carter*, 1994, ed. Lorna Sage; and Robert Wilson, "SLIP PAGE: Angela Carter, In/Out/In the Post-Modern Nexus," in *Past the Last Post: Theorizing Post-Colonialism and Post-Modernism*, 1990, ed. Ian Adam and Helen Tiffin. Carter is also discussed in Ellen Rose, "Through the Looking Glass: When Women Tell Fairy Tales," in *The Voyage In: Fictions of Female Development*, 1983, ed. Elizabeth Abel and Marianne Hirsch; and Sally Robinson, *Engendering the Subject: Gender and Self-Representation in Contemporary Women's Fiction*, 1991.

Elizabeth Cary

Cary's dramas include *The Tragedy of Mariam, the Fair Queen of Jewry* (1613). A 1994 reprint, edited by Barry Weller and Margaret W.

Ferguson, also includes *The Lady Falkland: Her Life*, a biography written by either Anne or Mary, Cary's daughters, as well as a valuable introduction, textual notes, and bibliography. Cary also composed *The History of Edward II* (1627), religious poetry saints lives, and translated Catholic polemical texts. An interesting biography is Kenneth B. Murdock's *The Sun at Noon*, 1939.

A recent essay collection is *Renaissance Women: The Plays of Elizabeth Cary and the Poems of Aemilia Lanier*, 1993, ed. Diane Purkiss. For critical essays, see Sandra K. Fischer, "Elizabeth Cary and Tyranny, Domestic and Religious," in *Silent but for the Word: Tudor Women as Patrons, Translators, and Writers of Religious Works*, 1985, ed. Margaret Patterson Hannay; Betty S. Travitsky, "The Feme Covert in Elizabeth Cary's *Mariam*," in *Ambiguous Realities: Women in the Middle Ages and Renaissance*, 1987, ed. Carole Levin and Jeanie Watson. Tina Krontiris, "Style and Gender in Elizabeth Cary's *Edward II*," in *The Renaissance Englishwoman in Print*, 1990, ed. Anne M. Haselkorn and Betty S. Travitsky; Margaret W. Ferguson "Running On with Almost Public Voice: The Case of 'E. C.,'" in *Tradition and the Talents of Women*, 1991, ed. Florence Howe; Maureen Quilligan, "Staging Gender: William Shakespeare and Elizabeth Cary," in *Sexuality and Gender in Early Modern Europe: Institutions, Texts, Images*, 1993, ed. James Grantham Turner and Louise Schleiner, "Lady Falkland's Reentry into Writing: Anglo-Catholic Consensual Discourse and Her *Edward II* as Historical Fiction," in *The Witness of Times: Manifestations of Ideology in Seventeenth-Century England*, 1993, ed. Katherine Keller and Gerald Schifflhorst.

Willa Cather

Cather's collection of poems, *April Twilights* (1903), and her book of essays, *Not under Forty* (1936), supplement the standard edition of her fiction, *The Novels and Stories of Willa Cather*, 1937–41, which includes such works as *O Pioneers!* (1913), *The Song of the Lark* (1915), *My Antonia* (1918), *Youth and the Bright Medusa* (1920), *A Lost Lady* (1923), *The Professor's House* (1925), *Death Comes for the Archbishop* (1927), and *Shadows on the Rock* (1931). Other texts include *The Old Beauty and Others*, posthumously collected short stories (1948); *Willa Cather on Writing*, 1949; *Writings from Willa Cather's Campus Years*, 1950, ed. James Shively; *Collected Short Fiction, 1892–1912*, 1965, ed. Virginia Faulkner; and *The Kingdom of Art: Willa Cather's First Principles and Critical Statements*, 1967, ed. Bernice Slote. L. Brent Bohlke selected and edited *Willa Cather in Person: Interviews, Speeches, and Letters*, 1986.

Personal memoirs include Edith Lewis, *Willa Cather Living*, 1953, and Elizabeth Sergeant, *Willa Cather: A Memoir*, 1953. Among biographies and critical studies are David Daiches, *Willa Cather*, 1951; E. K. Brown, *Willa Cather*, 1953; Dorothy Van Ghent, *Willa Cather*, 1964; James Woodress, *Willa Cather*, 1970; Philip Gerber, *Willa Cather*, 1975; David Stouck, *Willa Cather's Imagination*, 1975; Phyllis C. Robinson, *Willa: The Life of Willa Cather*, 1983; James Woodress, *Willa Cather: A Literary Life*, 1987; Sharon O'Brien, *Willa Cather: The Emerging Voice*, 1987; and Hermione Lee, *Willa Cather: Double Lives*, 1991. Commentaries on Cather are gathered in *Willa Cather and Her Critics*, 1967, ed. James Schroeter; *The Art of Willa Cather*, 1974, ed. Bernice Slote and Virginia Faulkner; and *Women Writing in America*, 1985, Blanche Gelfant. Joan Crane compiled the valuable *Willa Cather: A Bibliography*, 1982.

Margaret Cavendish, Duchess of Newcastle

There is no modern edition of Cavendish's work, but some of her writings are *Poems and Fancies* (1653), *Nature's Pictures* (1656), *The Description of a New World* (1666), *Grounds of Natural Philosophy* (1668), and *Letters* (1676). She is discussed in Reverend J. Granger, *Biographical History of England*, 1824, and Louisa Costello, *Memoirs of Eminent Englishwomen*, 1844. Critical studies of her life and work are Douglas Grant, *Margaret the First*, 1957, and Kathleen Jones, *A Glorious Fame: The Life of Margaret Cavendish, Duchess of Newcastle, 1623–1673*, 1988. Useful critical essays on Cavendish include Moira Ferguson, "A 'Wise, Witte and Learned Lady': Margaret Lucas Cavendish," in *Women Writers of the Seventeenth Century*, 1989, ed. Katharina M. Wilson; and Linda Payne, "Dramatic Dreamscape: Women's Dreams and Utopian Vision in the Works of Margaret Cavendish, Duchess of Newcastle," in *Curtain Calls: British and American Women and the Theater, 1660–1820*, 1991, ed. Mary Anne Schofield. Journal articles of interest are Patricia A. Sullivan, "Female Writing beside the Rhetorical Tradition," *International Journal of Women's Studies* 3 (1981); and Catherine Gallagher, "Embracing the Absolute: The Politics of the Female Subject in Seventeenth-Century England," *Genders* 1 (1989).

Lorna Dee Cervantes

Cervantes's books of poetry are *Emplumada* (1981) and *From the Cables of Genocide: Poems on Love and Hunger* (1991). For an interesting interview, see Bernadette Monda, "Interview

with Lorna Dee Cervantes," *Third Woman* 2
(1984). Cervantes is also discussed in Marta
Ester Sánchez, "The Chicana as Scribe:
Harmonizing Gender and Culture in Lorna
Dee Cervantes' 'Beneath the Shadow of the
Freeway,'" in her *Contemporary Chicana
Poetry: A Critical Approach to an Emerging
Literature*, 1985; Yvonne Yarbro-Bejarano,
"Chicana Literature from a Chicana Feminist
Perspective," in *Chicana Creativity and
Criticism: Charting New Frontiers in American
Literature*, 1988, ed. Maria Herrera-Sobek and
Helena Maria Viramontes; John F. Crawford,
"Notes toward a New Multicultural Criticism:
Three Works by Women of Color" in A *Gift of
Tongues: Critical Challenges in Contemporary
American Poetry*, 1987, ed. Marie Harris and
Kathleen Aguero; Lynette Seator, "Emplu-
mada: Chicana Rites-of-Passage," *MELUS* 11
(1984); and Tey Diana Rebolledo, "Soothing
Restless Serpents: The Dreaded Creation and
Other Inspirations in Chicana Poetry," *Third
Woman* 2 (1984).

Kate Chopin
Chopin's works include *At Fault* (1890), *Bayou
Folk* (1894), *A Night in Acadie* (1897), *The
Awakening* (1899), and *A Vocation and a Voice:
Stories* (1991), originally cancelled by her pub-
lisher and just recently issued. A new Norton
Critical Edition of *The Awakening* appeared in
1994. A definitive *Complete Works of Kate
Chopin*, 1969, appeared in two volumes edited
by Per Seyersted, who is also the author of *Kate
Chopin: A Critical Biography*, 1969; in addi-
tion, with Emily Toth, Seyersted edited A *Kate
Chopin Miscellany*, 1979. An early critical biog-
raphy is Daniel Rankin, *Kate Chopin and Her
Creole Stories*, 1932; and a recent biography is
Emily Toth, *Kate Chopin*, 1994.

Among important articles are Robert
Cantwell, "The Awakening by Kate Chopin,"
Georgia Review 10 (1956); Larzer Ziff, "An
Abyss of Inequality: Sarah Orne Jewett, Mary
Wilkins Freeman, Kate Chopin," in *The
American 1890s*, 1966; George Spangler, "Kate
Chopin's The Awakening: A Partial Dissent,"
Novel 3 (1970); Cynthia Griffin Wolff,
"Thanatos and Eros: Kate Chopin's The
Awakening," *American Quarterly* 25 (1973);
Ruth Sullivan and Stewart Smith, "Narrative
Stance in Kate Chopin's The Awakening,"
Studies in American Fiction 1 (1973); Otis B.
Wheeler, "The Five Awakenings of Edna
Pontellier," *The Southern Review* 11 (1975);
Jane P. Tompkins, "The Awakening: An
Evaluation," *Feminist Studies* 3 (1976); Emily
Toth, "Kate Chopin's The Awakening as
Feminist Criticism," *Louisiana Studies* 15
(1976); Priscilla Allen, "Old Critics and New:
The Treatment of Chopin's The Awakening," in

The Authority of Experience, 1977, ed. Arlyn
Diamond and Lee R. Edwards; Lawrence
Thornton, "*The Awakening*: A Political
Romance," *American Literature* 52 (1980);
Anne Goodwyn Jones, "Kate Chopin: The Life
Behind the Mask," in *Tomorrow Is Another Day*
by Jones, 1981; and Sandra M. Gilbert, "The
Second Coming of Aphrodite: Kate Chopin's
Fantasy of Desire," *Kenyon Review* 5 (1983). A
recent collection of critical essays, *Kate Chopin
Reconsidered: Beyond the Bayou*, 1992, ed.
Lynda S. Boren and Sara deSaussure Davis, is a
useful volume. Valuable, though now out-
dated, is Marlene Springer, *Edith Wharton and
Kate Chopin: A Reference Guide*, 1976. A more
recent helpful resource is Linda Wagner
Martin, "Recent Books on Kate Chopin,"
Mississippi Quarterly 42 (1989).

Lady Mary Chudleigh
Chudleigh's works include *The Female
Advocate; or, A Plea for the Just Liberty of the
Tender Sex and Particularly of Married Women*
(1701), *The Ladies Defence; or, "The Bride-
Woman's Counseller" Answer'd* (1701), and
Poems on Several Occasions (1703). A new col-
lection, *The Poems and Prose of Mary, Lady
Chudleigh*, ed. Margaret J. M. Ezell, appeared
in 1993.

Caryl Churchill
Among Churchill's many plays are *Traps*
(1978), *Cloud Nine* (1979), *Top Girls* (1982),
Vinegar Tom (1982), *Fen* (1983), *Softcops*
(1984), *A Mouthful of Birds* (written with
David Lan, 1986), *Serious Money* (1987), *Ice
Cream with Hot Fudge* (1990), and *The Skriker*
(1994). Several of her plays are collected in
Plays: Two, 1990, and *Churchill Shorts: Short
Plays*, 1990. She has also composed a libretto,
Lives of the Great Poisoners (1993). A biography
is Geraldine Cousin, *Churchill, the Playwright*,
1989.

A collection containing valuable critical es-
says is *Caryl Churchill: A Casebook*, 1988, ed.
Phyllis R. Randall. For a recent book-length
study of Churchill's work, see Amelia Howe
Kritzer, *The Plays of Caryl Churchill: Theatre of
Empowerment*, 1991. Linda Fitzsimmons's *File
on Churchill*, 1989, provides a useful bibliogra-
phy and synopses of Churchill's plays as well as
their performance history. Three essays from a
feminist perspective are Alisa Solomon,
"Witches, Ranters, and the Middle Class: The
Plays of Caryl Churchill," *Theater* 12 (1981);
Linda Fitzsimmons, "'I Won't Turn Back for
You or Anyone': Caryl Churchill's Socialist-
Feminist Theatre," *Essays in Theatre* 6 (1987);
and Austin E. Quigley, "Stereotype and
Prototype: Character in the Plays of Caryl
Churchill," in *Feminine Focus: The New Women*

Playwrights, 1989, ed. Enoch Brater. Other useful critical articles are Helene Keyssar, "The Dramas of Caryl Churchill: The Politics of Possibility," *Massachusetts Review* 24 (1983), and Amelia Howe Kitzer, "Madness and Political Change in the Plays of Caryl Churchill," in *Madness in Drama*, 1993, ed. James Redmond.

Lucille Clifton

Besides numerous books for children, Clifton's works include *Good Times* (1969), *Good News about the Earth* (1972), *An Ordinary Woman* (1974), *Generations: A Memoir* (1976), *Two-Headed Woman* (1980), *Sonora Beautiful* (1981), *Good Woman: Poems and a Memoir, 1969–1980* (1987), *Next: New Poems* (1987), and *Quilting: Poems, 1987–1990* (1991). Audrey McCluskey, "Tell the Good News: A View of the Works of Lucille Clifton," and Haki Madhubuti, "Lucille Clifton: Warm Water, Greased Legs, and Dangerous Poetry," appear in *Black Women Writers (1950–1980)*, 1984, ed. Mari Evans. Andrea Benton Rushing, "Lucille Clifton: A Changing Voice for Changing Times," was published in *Coming to Light: American Women Poets in the Twentieth Century*, 1985, ed. Diane Wood Middlebrook.

Mary Elizabeth Coleridge

Theresa Whistler edited and introduced Coleridge's *Collected Poems*, 1954, which includes verse from *Poems* (1908) and additional, previously unpublished material. Poems by Coleridge have appeared in a number of collections and anthologies: *Bread and Roses: Women's Poetry of the Nineteenth and Twentieth Centuries*, 1982, ed. Diana Scott; *Sound the Deep Waters: Women's Romantic Poetry in the Victorian Age*, 1991, ed. Pamela Norris; *Faith in Her Words: Six Centuries of Women's Poetry*, 1991, ed. Veronica Zundel; *The Things That Matter: An Anthology of Women's Spiritual Poetry*, 1992, ed. Julia Neuberger; and *Winged Words: Victorian Women's Poetry and Verse*, 1994, ed. Catherine Reilly. Edith Schel wrote a memoir that is included in *Gathered Leaves from the Prose of Mary E. Coleridge*, 1910. Among Coleridge's other works are a novel, *The Seven Sleepers of Ephesus* (1893), and a biographical study, *Holmen Hunt* (1908).

Kamala Das

Among Das's works are a novel, *Alphabet of Lust* (1977); several books of short stories, including *A Doll for the Child Prostitute* (1977); and a number of collections of poetry, including *Summer in Calcutta* (1965) and *The Descendants* (1967). Most of Das's recent work is in Malayalam, but *The Best of Kamala Das* (1991) is a collection of poems in English. She

has also published an autobiography, *My Story* (1976). Full-length studies of her career include Devendra Kohl, *Virgin Whiteness, the Poetry of Kamala Das*, 1968, and *Kamala Das*, 1975; Anisur Rahman, *Expressive Form in the Poetry of Kamala Das*, 1981; and Vrinda Nabar, *The Endless Female Hungers: A Study of Kamala Das*, 1994. Useful essays are Anne Brewster, " 'The Freedom to Decompose': The Poetry of Kamala Das," *Journal of Indian Writing in English* 8 (1980); Eunice de Souza, "Kamala Das," in *Indian Poetry in English: A Critical Assessment*, 1981, ed. Vasant A. Shahane; Mohamed Elias, "The Short Stories of Kamala Das," *World Literature Written in English* 25 (1985); Marilla North, "Watching Herself/Watching Her Self: Kamala Das's Split Texts," *New Literature Review* 21 (1991); Ranjama Ash, "The Search for Freedom in Indian Women's Writing," in *Motherlands: Black Women's Writing from America, the Caribbean, and South Asia*, 1991, ed. Susheila Nasta; and Shirley Goek-Lin Lim, "Terms of Empowerment in Kamala Das's *My Story*," in *De/Colonizing the Subject: The Politics of Gender in Women's Autobiography*, 1992, ed. Sidonie Smith and Julia Watson.

Rebecca Harding Davis

Davis's most famous story, *Life in the Iron-Mills; or, The Korl Woman* (1861), was reissued by the Feminist Press in 1972, with a biographical interpretation by Tillie Olsen. Other works by Davis include *Margaret Howth* (1862), *Waiting for the Verdict* (1868), *Pro Aris et Focis—A Plea for Our Altars and Hearths* (1870), *John Andross* (1874), *Doctor Warrick's Daughters* (1896), and *Frances Waldeaux* (1899). For biographical information, see Jean Pfaelzer, "Legacy Profile: Rebecca Harding Davis (1831–1910)," *Legacy* 7 (1990).

The increasing interest in Davis is generating many critical articles, including Walter Hesford, "The Literary Context of *Life in the Iron-Mills*," *American Literature* 49 (1977); Jean Pfaelzer, "Rebecca Harding-Davis: Domesticity, Social Order, and the Industrial Novel," *International Journal of Women's Studies* 4 (1981); Jean Fagan Yellin, "The 'Feminization' of Rebecca Harding Davis," *American Literary History* 2 (1990); Jane Atteridge Rose, "The Artist Manqué in the Fiction of Rebecca Harding Davis," in *Writing the Woman Artist: Essays on Poetics, Politics, and Portraiture*, 1991, ed. Suzanne W. Jones; and Amy Schrager Lang, "Class and the Strategies of Sympathy," *The Culture of Sentiment: Race, Gender, and Sentimentality in Nineteenth-Century America*, 1992, ed. Shirley Samuels, which compares Davis and Harriet

Beecher Stowe. Two full-length studies are Sharon M. Harris, *Rebecca Harding Davis and American Realism*, 1991; and Jane Attenridge Rose, *Rebecca Harding Davis*, 1993. A valuable resource is Jane Attenridge Rose, "A Bibliography of Fiction and Non-Fiction by Rebecca Harding Davis," *American Literary Realism, 1870–1910* 22 (1990).

Emily Dickinson

The Poems of Emily Dickinson, 1955, was edited by Thomas H. Johnson, and he and Theodora Ward edited the three companion volumes *The Letters of Emily Dickinson*, 1958. More recently, Ralph W. Franklin has edited *The Manuscript Books of Emily Dickinson*, 1981, and *The Master Letters of Emily Dickinson*, 1986. *New Poems of Emily Dickinson*, 1993, ed. William H. Shurr, Anna Dunlap, and Emily Grey Shurr, is a collection of poems gathered from Dickinson's letters. In addition, Jay Leyda's compendious *The Years and Hours of Emily Dickinson*, 1960, provides documents about the poet's life and time. Richard B. Sewall, *The Life of Emily Dickinson*, 1974, is probably the most definitive biography, but Thomas H. Johnson, *Emily Dickinson: An Interpretive Biography*, 1955, is also an important one. John Cody, *After Great Pain: The Inner Life of Emily Dickinson*, 1971, is an interesting but controversial psychoanalytic study. Cynthia Griffin Wolff's biography, *Emily Dickinson*, appeared in 1986.

Full-length critical works include Albert J. Gelpi, *Emily Dickinson: The Mind of the Poet*, 1965; Brita Lindberg-Seyersted, *The Voice of the Poet: Aspects of Style in the Poetry of Emily Dickinson*, 1968; Ruth Miller, *The Poetry of Emily Dickinson*, 1968; Rebecca Patterson, *Emily Dickinson's Imagery*, 1974; Robert Weisbuch, *Emily Dickinson's Poetry*, 1975; Christopher E. G. Benfrey, *Emily Dickinson and the Problem of Others*, 1985; Jane Donahue Eberwein, *Emily Dickinson: Strategies of Limitation*, 1985; Wendy Barker, *Lunacy of Light: Emily Dickinson and the Experience of Metaphor*, 1987; Christianne Miller, *Emily Dickinson: A Poet's Grammar*, 1987; Elizabeth Phillips, *Emily Dickinson: Personae and Performance*, 1988; Joanne Dobson, *Emily Dickinson and the Strategies of Reticence*, 1989; Judy Jo Small, *Positive as Sound: Emily Dickinson's Rhyme*, 1990; Gary Lee Stonum, *The Dickinson Sublime*, 1990; and Sharon Cameron, *Choosing Not Choosing: Dickinson's Fascicles*, 1992. See also Margaret Dickie, *Lyric Contingencies: Emily Dickinson and Wallace Stevens*, 1991, and James Olney, *The Language(s) of Poetry: Walt Whitman, Emily Dickinson, Gerard Manley Hopkins*, 1993. Other studies include Paul J. Ferlazzo, *Emily Dickinson*, 1976; Sharon Cameron, *Lyric Time*, 1979; Karl Keller, *The Only Kangaroo among the Beauty: Emily Dickinson and America*, 1979; and David Porter, *Dickinson: The Modern Idiom*, 1981.

Feminist analyses of Dickinson's work are represented by Joanne Feit Diehl, *Dickinson and the Romantic Imagination*, 1981; Barbara Clarke Mossberg, *Emily Dickinson: When a Writer Is a Daughter*, 1982; Suzanne Juhasz, *The Undiscovered Continent: Emily Dickinson and the Space of the Mind*, 1983; Vivian R. Pollak, *Dickinson: The Anxiety of Gender*, 1984; Paula Bennett, *Emily Dickinson: Woman Poet*, 1990; Mary Leoffelholz, *Dickinson and the Boundaries of Feminist Theory*, 1990; Judith Farr, *The Passion of Emily Dickinson*, 1992; and Martha Nell Smith, *Rowing in Eden: Rereading Emily Dickinson*, 1992. Two valuable collections of critical essays are *Emily Dickinson: Modern Critical Views*, 1985, ed. Harold Bloom; and *On Dickinson: The Best from American Literature*, 1990, ed. Edwin H. Cady and Louis J. Budd. Recent useful reference guides are Karen Dandurand, *Dickinson Scholarship: An Annotated Bibliography, 1965–1985*, 1988; Jeanetta Boswell, *Emily Dickinson: A Bibliography of Secondary Sources, 1890–1987*, 1989; and Joseph Duchac, *The Poems of Emily Dickinson: An Annotated Guide to Commentary Published in English, 1978–1989*, 1993.

Annie Dillard

The Annie Dillard Library, collected in 1989, contains the following nonfiction works by Dillard: *Pilgrim at Tinker Creek* (1974), *Holy the Firm* (1978), *Living by Fiction* (1982), *Teaching a Stone to Talk: Expeditions and Encounters* (1982), and *An American Childhood* (1987); other nonfiction works include *Encounters with Chinese Writers* (1984) and *The Writing Life* (1989). *Tickets for a Prayer Wheel* (1974) is a book of poetry, and *The Living* (1992) is a novel. *The Annie Dillard Reader*, published in 1994, offers a selection of her works. Critical studies of Dillard are Linda Smith, *Annie Dillard*, 1991, and Sandra Humble Johnson, *The Space Between: Literary Epiphany in the Works of Annie Dillard*, 1992.

Isak Dinesen

Dinesen's books in English include *Seven Gothic Tales* (1934), *Out of Africa* (1937), *Winter's Tales* (1942), *Last Tales* (1957), *Anecdotes of Destiny* (1958), *Shadows on the Grass* (1961), and *Ehrengard* (1963).

Her *Letters from Africa, 1914–1931*, were edited by Frans Lasson and translated by Anne Born, 1981. Born also translated *On Modern Marriage and Other Observations*, 1986.

Biographies and memoirs include Clara Svendesen, *Isak Dinesen: A Memorial*, 1965; Migel Parmenia, *Titania: The Biography of Isak Dinesen*, 1967; Lasson, *The Life and Destiny of Isak Dinesen*, 1970; Thomas Dinesen, *My Sister, Isak Dinesen* (trans. Joan Tate), 1975; and Judith Thurman, *Isak Dinesen: The Life of a Storyteller*, 1982.

Among full-length critical studies are Robert W. Langbaum, *The Gayety of Vision: A Study of Isak Dinesen's Art*, 1965; Donald Hannah, "*Isak Dinesen*" *and Karen Blixer: The Mask and the Reality*, 1971; Thomas R. Whissen, *Isak Dinesen's Aesthetic*, 1973; Susan Aiken Hardy, *Isak Dinesen and the Engendering of Narrative*, 1990; and Olga Anastasia Pelensky, *Isak Dinesen: The Life and Imagination of a Seducer*, 1991. Pelensky also edited the recent *Isak Dinesen: Critical Views* 1993. Feminist perspectives are represented by Susan Gubar, "'The Blank Page' and the Issues of Female Creativity,' in *Writing and Sexual Difference*, 1982, ed. Elizabeth Abel; Susan Hardy Aiken, 'The Uses of Duplicity: Isak Dinesen and Questions of Feminist Criticism," *Scandinavian Studies* 57 (1985); Marilyn Johns Blackwell, "The Transforming Gaze: Identity and Sexuality in the Works of Isak Dinesen," *Scandinavian Studies* 63 (1991); and Sidonie Smith, "The Other Woman and the Racial Politics of Gender: Isak Dinesen and Beryl Markham in Kenya," in *De/Colonizing the Subject: The Politics of Gender in Women's Autobiography*, 1992, ed. Sidonie Smith and Julia Watson. See also Ca ol J. Clover, ed., "Isak Dinesen, 1885–1962," *Scandinavian Studies* 57 (1985), a special issue on Dinesen.

H. D. (Hilda Doolittle)

Louis Martz has edited *H D.: Collected Poems, 1912–1944*, 1983, which includes her major published (and some previously unpublished) work in verse except for the late volumes *Helen in Egypt* (1961) and *Hermetic Definition* (1972), both of which are available in paperback. He has also edited *Selected Poems*, 1988. Her prose fiction includes *Palimpsest* (1926), *Hedylus* (1928), and *Bid Me to Live* (1960). *By Avon River* (1949) celebrates Shakespeare in prose and verse. The autobiographical *HERmione*, with a forward by Perdita Schaffner, was published in 1981 and *The Gift* in 1982. *Tribute to Freud* (1944), her account of her psychoanalysis by Freud, and *End to Torment* (1979), a memoir of Ezra Pound, are available in paperback.

H. D. figures in *My Heart to Artemis: A Writer's Memoirs*, 1962, the autobiography of her closest friend and traveling companion, Bryher (Winifred Ellerman). Early critical studies include a chapter entitled "The Perfect Imagist" in Glenn Hughes, *Imagism and the Imagists*, 1931; Thomas Burnett Swann, *The Classical World of H. D.*, 1962; and Vincent Quinn, *Hilda Doolittle*, 1967. The Autumn 1969 issue of *Contemporary Literature* was devoted exclusively to H. D. and contains useful background information. The recent collection of correspondence *Richard Aldington and H. D.: The Early Years in Letters*, 1992, ed. Caroline Zilboorg, also provides useful biographical information.

Feminist interest in H. D.'s work has followed Susan Stanford Freidman's landmark essay, "Who Buried H. D.?" *College English* 36, (1975). The biography *H. D.: The Life and Work of an American Poet*, 1982, by Janice Robinson, is somewhat controversial, while *Herself Defined: The Poet H. D. and Her World*, 1984, by Barbara Guest, is useful. A valuable full-length critical study is Susan Stanford Friedman, *Psyche Reborn: The Emergence of H. D.*, 1981. More recently, Stanford has published *Penelope's Web: Gender, Modernity, H.D.'s Fiction*, 1990; "Portrait of the Artist as a Young Woman: H.D.'s Rescriptions of Joyce, Lawrence, and Pound," in *Writing the Woman Artist: Essays on Poetics, Politics, and Portraiture*, 1991, ed. Suzanne W. Jones; and has with Rachel Blau DuPlessis edited *Signets: Reading H. D.*, 1990. Other full-length studies are Gary Dean Burnett, *H. D. Between Image and Epic: The Mysteries of Her Poetics*, 1990; and Dianne Chisholm, *H. D.'s Freudian Poetics: Psychoanalysis in Translation*, 1992. Recent critical essays include Lawrence S. Rainey, "Canon, Gender, and Text: The Case of H. D." in *Representing Modernist Texts: Editing as Interpretation*, 1991, ed. George Bornstein; and Andrew Thacke, "Amy Lowell and H. D.: The Other Imagists," *Women: A Cultural Review* 4 (1993). A useful recent resource is Michael Boughn, *H. D.: A Bibliography, 1905–1990*, 1993.

Rita Dove

Dove's books of poetry include *The Yellow House on the Corner* (1980), *Museum* (1983), *Thomas and Beulah* (1986), *Grace Notes* (1989), *Selected Poems* (1993) and *Mother Love* (1995). She also has published a book of stories, *Fifth Sunday* (1985); a novel, *Through the Ivory Gate* (1992); and a verse play, *The Darker Side of the Earth* (1994). An interview is Steven Schneider, "Coming Home: An Interview with Rita Dove," *The Iowa Review* 19 (1989). Useful essays are Arnold Rampersad "The Poems of Rita Dove," *Callaloo* 9 (1986); Robert McDowell "The Assembling Vision of Rita Dove," in *Conversant Essays: Contemporary Poets on Poetry*, 1990, ed. James McCorkle; Ekaterini Georgoudaki, "Rita Dove: Crossing

Boundaries," *Callaloo* 14 (1991); Bonnie Costello, "Scars and Wings: Rita Dove's Grace Notes," *Callaloo* 14 (1991); Kirkland C. Jones, "Folk Idiom in the Literary Expression of Two African American Authors: Rita Dove and Yusef Komunyakaa," in *Language and Literature in the African American Imagination*, 1992, ed. Carol Aisha Blackshire Belay; and Patricia Wallace, "Divided Loyalties: Literal and Literary in the Poetry of Lorna Dee Cervantes, Cathy Song, and Rita Dove," *MELUS* 18 (1993).

Alice Dunbar-Nelson

Gloria T. Hull edited *The Works of Alice Dunbar-Nelson*, 1988, while Ruby Ora Williams edited *An Alice Dunbar-Nelson Reader*, 1978, with critical comments by Agnes Moreland. Also available are *The Goodness of St. Rocque, and Other Stories* (1899) and *Give Us Each Day: The Diary of Alice Dunbar-Nelson*, 1985, ed. Gloria T. Hull. Critical studies include an article by Roger Whitlow, "Alice Dunbar-Nelson: New Orleans Writer," *RFI* 4 (1978); an essay by Gloria T. Hull, "Alice Dunbar-Nelson: A Personal and Literary Perspective," in *Between Women: Biographers, Novelists, Critics, Teachers, and Artists Write about Their Work on Women*, 1984, ed. Carol Ascher; and a chapter in Gloria T. Hull, *Color, Sex, & Poetry: Three Women Writers of the Harlem Renaissance*, 1987. Ruby Ora Williams has also compiled a valuable bibliography in *College Language Association Journal* 19 (1976).

Maria Edgeworth

Ten volumes of Edgeworth's *Tales and Novels*, 1893—including *Castle Rackrent* (1800), *Belinda* (1801), *Leonora* (1806), *Tales of Fashionable Life* (1809), and *The Absentee* (1812)—were reprinted in 1967. *Belinda* and *Patronage* were reprinted in 1986, with introductions by Eva Figes. *Helen* was reprinted in 1987, with an introduction by Maggie Gee; *The Absentee* was reprinted in 1988, edited by W. J. McCormack and Kim Walker; *Castle Rackrent and Ennui* was reprinted in 1992, edited by Marilyn Butler; and *Dumb Andy* reappeared in 1992, edited by Jonathan Levy. Editions of her nonfiction and letters include *Letters from England, 1813–1844*, 1971, ed. Christina Colvin; *Letters for Literary Ladies*, 1974, with an introduction by Gina Luria; *The Education of the Heart: The Correspondence of Rachel Mordecai Lazarus and Maria Edgeworth*, 1977, ed. Edgar E. MacDonald; and *The Early Lessons. Part 10*, 1990, with an introduction by Mitzi Myers.

Among older biographical works are Isabel Constance Clarke, *Maria Edgeworth, Her Family and Friends*, 1950; and Marilyn Butler, *Maria Edgeworth*, 1971. A more recent biography is Oleta Elizabeth McWhorter Harden, *Maria Edgeworth*, 1984. In addition, James Newcomer has two full-length studies—*Maria Edgeworth, the Novelist, 1767–1849*, 1967, and *Maria Edgeworth*, 1973—while other studies include Mark D. Hawthorne, *Doubt and Dogma in Maria Edgeworth*, 1967; Michael Hurst, *Maria Edgeworth and the Public Scene*, 1969; and Harden, *Maria Edgeworth's Art of Prose Fiction*, 1971. Edgeworth is also discussed by Vineta Colby in *Yesterday's Women*, 1974, and by Patricia Voss-Clesly in *Tendencies of Character Depiction in the Domestic Novels of Burney, Edgeworth, and Austen*, 1979. Two useful critical essays are Mitzi Myers, "The Dilemmas of Gender as Double-Voiced Narrative; or, Maria Edgeworth Mothers the Bildungsroman," in *The Idea of the Novel in the Eighteenth Century*, 1988, ed. Robert W. Uphaus; and the recent W. J. McCormack, "Setting and Ideology: With Reference to the Fiction of Maria Edgeworth; A Collection of Interpretations," in *Ancestral Voices: The Big House in Anglo-Irish Literature*, 1992, ed. Otto Rauchbauer.

George Eliot

Eliot's publications include *Scenes of Clerical Life* (1858), *Adam Bede* (1859), *The Mill on the Floss* (1860), *Silas Marner* (1861), *Romola* (1863), *Felix Holt the Radical* (1866), *The Spanish Gypsy* (1868), *Armgart* (1871), *Middlemarch* (1872), *Daniel Deronda* (1876), and *Impressions of Theophrastus Such* (1876). Ten volumes of her works were published by Blackwood in the 1890s. Gordon S. Haight edited *The George Eliot Letters, 1954–1978*, and in 1985, edited *Selections from George Eliot's Letters*, a sampling from the larger volumes. Joseph Wiesenfarth edited *A Writer's Notebook*, and *Uncollected Writings*, 1981. Also useful is the three-volume *George Eliot's Life as Related in Her Letters and Journals*, 1885, arranged and edited by her husband, J. W. Cross. There are, of course, numerous editions of the novels, some of which, like the Penguins, contain valuable introductions and notes. There are two recent collections of Eliot's work: *Collected Poems*, 1989, with an introduction by Lucien Jenkins; and *Selected Essays, Poems, and Other Writings*, 1990, ed. A. S. Byatt and Nicholas Warren, with an introduction by Byatt. *Middlemarch* appears in a Norton Critical Edition, ed. Bert G. Hornback.

There have been many biographies; the best of them is Gordon S. Haight, *George Eliot*, 1968. Haight also wrote *George Eliot and John Chapman*, 1969, and edited *A Century of George Eliot Critics*, 1965. In addition, with Rosemary T. VanArsdel, he edited *George Eliot*,

A *Centenary Tribute*, 1982. Also useful is Ruby V. Redinger's biography, *George Eliot: The Emergent Self*, 1975, and a more recent biography is Ina Taylor, *A Woman of Correspondence: The Life of George Eliot*, 1989. *The Real Life of Mary Ann Evans: George Eliot, Her Letters, and Fiction*, ed. Rosemarie Bodenheimer, contains both biographical and critical information. Valuable full-length studies include Barbara Hardy, *The Novels of George Eliot: A Study in Form*, 1959; U. C. Knoepflmacher, *George Eliot's Early Novels: The Limits of Realism*, 1968; Felicia Bonaparte, *Will and Destiny: Morality and Tragedy in George Eliot's Novels*, 1975; Joseph Wiesenfarth, *George Eliot's Mythmaking*, 1977; Mary Ellen Doyle, *The Sympathetic Response: George Eliot's Fictional Rhetoric*, 1981; Karen S. Mann, *The Language That Makes George Eliot's Fiction*, 1983; Suzanne Graver, *George Eliot and Community: A Study in Social Theory and Fictional Form*, 1984; and Alan Feris, *A Return to the Primal Self: Identity in the Fiction of George Eliot*, 1989. Among feminist treatments are chapters in Patricia Meyer Spacks, *The Female Imagination*, 1975; Elaine Showalter, *A Literature of Their Own*, 1977; Sandra M. Gilbert and Susan Gubar, *The Madwoman in the Attic*, 1979; Diane F. Sadoff, *Monsters of Affection*, 1982; and Phyllis Rose, *Parallel Lives: Five Victorian Marriages*, 1983. Collections of critical essays include *Critical Essays on George Eliot*, 1970, ed. Barbara Hardy; *George Eliot: A Collection of Critical Essays*, 1970, ed. George R. Creeger; *George Eliot: The Critical Heritage*, 1971, ed. David Carroll; *The Critical Response to George Eliot*, 1994, ed. Karen L. Pangallo; *The Transformation of Rage: Mourning and Creativity in George Eliot's Fiction*, 1994, ed. Peggy Fitzhugh Johnstone; and *George Eliot and the Politics of National Inheritance*, 1994, ed. Bernard Semmel. There are also numerous collections on individual Eliot novels, such as the helpful *This Particular Web: Essays on Middlemarch*, 1975, ed. Ian Adam. A useful resource is *An Annotated Critical Biography of George Eliot*, 1988, ed. George Levine with Patricia O'Hara.

Queen Elizabeth I
The standard edition of Elizabeth's poems is Leicester Bradner, *The Poems of Queen Elizabeth I*, 1964. There are many collections of her letters; the most inclusive is *The Letters of Queen Elizabeth*, 1935, ed. G. B. Harrison, but forty previously unprinted letters were recently edited by E. I. Kour and titled *Elizabethan England and Europe*, 1982. George P. Rice Jr. published selected official addresses in *The Public Speaking of Queen Elizabeth*, 1951. Several literary figures have written about Elizabeth, including Thomas Heywood, *England's Elizabeth*, 1631; Lytton Strachey, *Elizabeth and Essex, a Tragic History*, 1928; and Edith Sitwell, *Fanfare for Elizabeth*, 1946. Elizabeth Jenkins, *Elizabeth the Great*, 1959, and *Elizabeth and Leicester*, 1962, are valuable studies, as are Paul Johnson, *Elizabeth I: A Study in Power and Intellect*, 1974; and Alison Plowden, *Elizabeth Regina: The Age of Triumph, 1588–1603*, 1980. See also Wallace T. MacCaffery's recent biography, *Elizabeth I*, 1993; and Susan Doran's study *Elizabeth I and Religion, 1558–1603*, 1994. Susan Frye's interesting book *Elizabeth I: The Competition for Representation*, 1993, discusses representations of the queen in literature. Steven W. May's article "Recent Studies in Elizabeth I," *English Literary Renaissance* 23 (1993), is a helpful resource.

Buchi Emecheta
Among Emecheta's literary achievement are *Second-Class Citizen* (1975), *The Bride Price* (1976), *The Slave Girl* (1977), *The Joys of Motherhood* (1979), *Nowhere to Play* (1980), *Our Own Freedom* (1981), *Destination Biafra* (1982), *Adah's Story* (1983), *The Wrestling Match* (1983), *The Rape of Shavi* (1983), *The Moonlight Bride* (1983), *Double Yoke* (1983), *A Kind of Marriage* (1986), *Gwendolyn* (1989), *The Family* (1990), *In the Ditch* (1994), and *Kehinde* (1994). She has also published an autobiography, *Head above Water* (1991). Emecheta is discussed in Susan Z. Andrade, "Rewriting History, Motherhood, and Rebellion: Naming an African Women's History Literary Tradition," *Research in African Literatures* 21 (1990); and Eva Lennox Birch, "Autobiography: The Art of Self-Definition," in *Black Women's Writing*, 1993, ed. Gina Wisker. Useful critical essays are Afam Ebeogu, "Enter the Iconoclast: Buchi Emecheta and the Igbo Culture," *Commonwealth Essays and Studies* 7 (1985); Abioseh Michael Porter, "Second Class Citizen: The Point of Departure for Understanding Buchi Emecheta's Major Fiction," *International Fiction Review* 15 (1983); M. J Daymond, "Buchi Emecheta, Laughter and Silence: Changes in the Concepts 'Woman' and 'Mother,'" *Journal of Literary Studies* 4 (1988); Christina Davis, "Mother and Writer: Means of Empowerment in the Works of Buchi Emecheta," *Commonwealth Essays and Studies* 13 (1990); and Cynthia Ward, "What They Told Buchi Emecheta: Oral Subjectivity and the Joys of 'Otherhood,'" *PMLA* 105 (1990).

Louise Erdrich
Erdrich's novels include *Love Medicine* (1984; expanded ed. 1993), *The Beet Queen* (1986),

Tracks (1988), and The Crown of Columbus (with Michael Dorris, 1991). The Blue Jay's Dance: A Birth Year (1995) is her first major nonfictional work. Her books of poetry are Jacklight (1984) and Baptism of Desire (1989). Useful critical sources are Mickey Pearlman, "A Bibliography of Writings about Louise Erdrich," in American Women Writing Fiction: Memory, Identity, Family, Space, 1989, ed. Pearlman; and Conversations with Louise Erdrich and Michael Dorris, 1994, ed. Allan Chavkin and Nancy Feyl Chavkin.

Ursula Fanthorpe
Fanthorpe's books of poetry include Side Effects (1978), Four Dogs (1980), Standing To (1982), Voices Off (1984), Selected Poems (1986), A Watching Brief (1987), and Neck-Verse (1992). Poems by Fanthorpe also appear in The Faber Book of Twentieth-Century Women's Poetry, 1987, ed. Fleur Adcock. An autobiographical essay, "Observations of a Clerk," Poetry Review 75 (1985), includes interesting background information. A helpful critical essay is Marilyn Hacker, "Unauthorized Voices: Ursula Fanthorpe and Elma Mitchell," Grand Street 8 (1989).

Fanny Fern
Among the editions of Fern's collected newspaper articles are Fern Leaves from Fanny's Portfolio (1853), Caper-Sauce: A Volume of Chit-Chat about Men, Women, and Things (1872), and Fanny Fern: A Memorial Volume (1872). Her novel, Ruth Hall, was first published in 1855, and reissued in 1986 in the collection Ruth Hall and Other Writings, ed. Joyce W. Warren. A second novel, Rose Clark, was published in 1856. For interesting biographical information, see Joyce Warren's important full-length study of Fern's life and work, Fanny Fern: An Independent Woman, 1992, as well as her profile of Fern in Legacy 2 (1985), and her critical introduction to Ruth Hall and Other Writings (1986). A useful critical article is Lauren Berlant, "The Female Woman: Fanny Fern and the Form of Sentiment," American Literary History 3 (1991).

Anne Finch
Myra Reynolds's The Poems of Anne, Countess of Winchilsea, 1903, is out of print, but Katharine M. Rogers edited Selected Poems of Anne Finch in 1979. Rogers also wrote an essay on Finch, "An Augustan Woman Poet," in Shakespeare's Sisters, 1979, ed. Sandra M. Gilbert and Susan Gubar, as well as "Finch's 'Candid Account' vs. Eighteenth-Century Theories of the Spleen," Mosaic 22 (1989). In addition, Finch's work appears in Rogers's own anthology, Before Their Time: Six Women Writers of the Eighteenth Century, 1979. Never

previously published, the Wellesley Manuscript Poems of Anne, Countess of Winchilsea, ed. J. M. Ellis d'Alessandro, became available to Finch scholars in 1988. A new selection with a useful introduction, Selected Poems of Anne Finch, ed. Denys Thompson, appeared in 1987. Elizabeth Hampsten has written the introduction "Poems by Anne Finch," Women's Studies 7 (1980); and Barbara McGovern's valuable biography, Anne Finch and Her Poetry, was published in 1992.

Critical studies include discussions of Smith in Hilda Smith, Reason's Disciples, 1982; Ann Messenger, His and Hers: Essays in Restoration and Eighteenth-Century Literature, 1986; and Ruth Salvaggio, Enlightened Absence: Neoclassical Configurations of the Feminine, 1988. Other useful articles include Lucy Brashear, "Finch's 'The Bird and the Arras,'" Explicator (1981); Ann Messenger, "Publishing without Perishing: Lady Winchilsea's Miscellany Poems of 1713," Restoration (1981); Dorothy Mermin, "Women Becoming Poets: Katherine Philips, Aphra Behn, Anne Finch," ELH 57 (1990); Jean Mallinson, "Anne Finch: A Woman Poet and the Tradition" in Gender at Work: Four Women Writers of the Eighteenth Century, 1990, ed. Messenger; Charles H. Hinnant, "Song and Speech in Anne Finch's 'To the Nightingale,'" Studies in English Literature, 1500–1900 31 (1991); and Hinnant, "Feminism and Femininity: A Reconsideration of Anne Finch's 'Ardelia's Answer to Ephelia,'" The Eighteenth Century 33 (1992).

M. F. K. Fisher
Fisher's twenty-one books include gastronomy, memoirs, travel writing, short stories, and essays. Her first five books were collected as The Art of Eating: The Collected Gastronomical Works of M. F. K. Fisher in 1954. Later collections of memoirs, stories, and journal entries include As They Were (1982), Sister Age (1983), Long Ago in France: The Years in Dijon (1991), and Legends of Love: Stories and Memoirs (1992). Fisher's last books—To Begin Again: Stories and Memoirs, 1908–1929 (1992) and Stay Me, Oh Comfort Me: Journals and Stories, 1933–1941 (1993)—assemble both short fiction and autobiographical pieces. David Lazar edited Conversations with M. F. K. Fisher in 1992. For interesting biographical information, see also Lazar's "The Usable Past of M. F. K. Fisher: An Essay on Projects," Southwest Review 77 (1992), and Norah Kennedy Barr's introduction to Stay Me, Oh Comfort Me.

Mary E. Wilkins Freeman
Of the six volumes of short stories Freeman published, the two best known are A Humble Romance (1887) and A New England Nun

(1891). Three collections of Freeman's work are *The Best Stories of Mary E. Wilkins*, 1927, ed. Henry W. Lanier; *Selected Stories of Mary E. Wilkins Freeman*, 1983, ed. Marjorie Pryse; and *The Uncollected Stories of Mary Wilkins Freeman*, 1992, ed. Mary Reichardt. Freeman also wrote a number of novels, including *Pembroke* (1894), *By the Light of the Soul* (1906), *The Portion of Labor* (1901), and *The Shoulders of Atlas* (1908). A volume of Freeman's correspondence, *The Infant Sphinx: The Collected Letters of Mary E. Wilkins Freeman*, ed. Brent L. Kendrick, appeared in 1985.

Full-length critical/biographical studies include Edward Foster *Mary E. Wilkins Freeman*, 1956; Abigail Ann Hamblen, *The New England Art of Mary E. Wilkins Freeman*. 1966; and Perry D. Westbrook, *Mary Wilkins Freeman*, 1967. See also Marjorie Pryse, "Mary E. Wilkins Freeman," in *Modern American Women Writers*, 1990, ed. Elaine Showalter. In recent years, Mary R. Reichardt has published widely on Freeman, see her useful full-length study *A Web of Relationship: Women in the Short Stories of Mary Wilkins Freeman*, 1992; and her essays "Mary Wilkins Freeman: One Hundred Years of Criticism," *Legacy: A Journal of Nineteenth-Century American Women Writers* 4 (1987); "A Checklist of Uncollected Short Fiction by Mary Wilkins Freeman," *American Literary Realism, 1870–1910* 23 (1990), co-authored with Philip Eppard; "'Friend of My Heart': Women as Friends and Rivals in the Short Stories of Mary Wilkins Freeman," *American Literary Realism, 1870–1910* 22 (1990); and "The Web of Self-Strangulation: Mothers, Daughters, and the Question of Marriage in the Short Stories of Mary Wilkins Freeman," in *Joinings and Disjoinings: The Significance of Marital Status in Literature*, 1991, ed. JoAnna Stephens Mink and Janet Doubler Ward. Among other articles, especially useful are Ann Douglas Wood, "The Literature of Impoverishment: The Women Local Colorists in America, 1865–1914," *Women's Studies* 1 (1972); Alice G. Brand, "Mary Wilkins Freeman: Misanthropy as Propaganda," *New England Quarterly* 50 (1977); Joseph E. McElrath Jr., "The Artistry of Mary E. Wilkins Freeman's 'The Revolt,'" *Studies in Short Fiction* 17 (1980); Sarah W. Sherman, "The Great Goddess in New England: Mary Wilkins Freeman's 'Christmas Jenny,'" *Studies in Short Fiction* 17 (1980); Kate Gardner, "The Subversion of Genre in the Short Stories of Mary Wilkins Freeman," *The New England Quarterly* 65 (1992) Martha J. Cutter, "Beyond Stereotypes: Mary Wilkins Freeman's Radical Critique of Nineteenth-Century Cults of Femininity," *Women's Studies* 21 (1992); and Monika M. Elbert, "Mary

Wilkins Freeman's Devious Women, *Harper's Bazaar*, and the Rhetoric of Advertising," *Essays in Literature* 20 (1993).

Margaret Fuller

Fuller's works include *Summer on the Lakes* (1844), *Woman in the Nineteenth Century* (1845), *Papers on Literature and Art* (1846). and numerous magazine essays and newspaper articles, some of which appear in the posthumous collections *At Home and Abroad* (1856) and *Life Without and Life Within* (1859), both edited by her brother, Arthur B. Fuller. *The Letters of Margaret Fuller*, 5 vols., 1983–88, was edited by Robert N. Hudspeth. The somewhat bowdlerized *Memoirs of Margaret Fuller Ossoli*, 1852, was prepared by W. H. Channing, James Freeman Clarke, and Ralph Waldo Emerson; however, accurate and substantial recent collections of Fuller's writings are Bell Gale Chevigny, *The Woman and the Myth: Margaret Fuller's Life and Writings*, 1994; *The Portable Margaret Fuller*, 1994; and *Women in the Nineteenth Century and Other Writings*, 1994.

Biographies include Joseph J. Deiss, *The Roman Years of Margaret Fuller*, 1969; Charles Capper, *Margaret Fuller: An American Romantic Life*, 1992; and Donna Dickenson, *Margaret Fuller: Writing a Woman's Life*, 1993.

Full-length critical studies include Paula Blanchard, *Margaret Fuller, from Transcendentalism to Revolution*, 1978; Margaret Allen, *The Achievement of Margaret Fuller*, 1979; and Marie Urbanski, *Margaret Fuller's "Woman in the 19th Century": A Literary Study of Form and Content, of Sources and Influence*, 1980. For a discussion of Fuller's relation to romanticism, see Julie K. Ellison, *Delicate Subjects: Romanticism, Gender, and the Ethics of Understanding*, 1990. Joel Myerson has published annotated bibliographies of secondary material, 1977, and of Fuller's own work, 1978.

Elizabeth Gaskell

The standard edition of Gaskell's novels—including *Mary Barton* (1848), *Cranford* (1853), *Ruth* (1853), *North and South* (1955), *Sylvia's Lovers* (1863), and *Wives and Daughters* (1866)—is *The Works of Mrs. Gaskell*, 1906–20, with an introduction by A. W. Ward. In addition, much of this fiction, along with Gaskell's *The Life of Charlotte Brontë* (1857), has been published in modern editions, most notably a Penguin series with good critical introductions. The author's letters appear in *The Letters of Mrs. Gaskell*, 1966, ed. J. A. V. Chapple and Arthur Pollard; *Letters of Mrs. Gaskell and Charles Eliot Norton, 1855–1865*, 1973, ed. with an introduction by Jane Whitehill; and *Elizabeth Gaskell: A Portrait in Letters*, 1980, ed. J. A. V. Chapple. There are many biogra-

phies, the best of which is Winifred Gérin, *Elizabeth Gaskell*, 1976. A helpful recent biography is Jennifer Uglow, *Elizabeth Gaskell: A Habit of Stories*, 1993. Full-length critical studies include Aina Rubenius, *The Woman Question in Mrs. Gaskell's Life and Works*, 1950; A. B. Hopkins, *Elizabeth Gaskell: Her Life and Work*, 1952; Edgar Wright, *Mrs. Gaskell: The Basis for Reassessment*, 1965; Margaret Ganz, *Elizabeth Gaskell: The Artist in Conflict*, 1969; J. G. Sharps, *Mrs. Gaskell's Observation and Invention*, 1970; Angus Easson, *Elizabeth Gaskell*, 1979; Enid Lowry Duthie, *The Themes of Elizabeth Gaskell*, 1980; Patsy Stoneman, *Elizabeth Gaskell*, 1987; and Hilary Margo Schor, *Scheherezade in the Marketplace: Elizabeth Gaskell and the Victorian Novel*, 1992. Angus Easson edited *Elizabeth Gaskell: The Critical Heritage* in 1991. Nina Auerbach takes a feminist approach to *Cranford* in *Communities of Women: An Idea in Fiction*, 1978; and valuable discussions of Gaskell appear in Pauline Nestor, *Female Friendships and Communities: Charlotte Brontë, George Eliot, Elizabeth Gaskell*, 1985; Margaret Homans, *Bearing the Word: Language and Female Experience in Nineteenth-Century Women's Writing*, 1986; Rosemarie Bodenheimer, *The Politics of Story in Victorian Social Fiction*, 1988; and Elsie B. Michie, *Outside the Pale: Cultural Exclusion, Gender Difference, and the Victorian Woman Writer*, 1993. Useful reference works are Robert L. Selig, *Elizabeth Gaskell: A Reference Guide*, 1977, and Jeffrey Welch, *Elizabeth Gaskell: An Annotated Bibliography, 1929–1975*, 1977.

Charlotte Perkins Gilman

A collection of Gilman's fiction is *The Charlotte Perkins Gilman Reader: The Yellow Wallpaper, and Other Fiction*, 1980, ed. and with an introduction by Ann J. Lane, who also wrote the introduction for the 1979 Pantheon edition of *Herland* (1915). Another volume of Gilman's collected fiction is *"The Yellow Wall-Paper" and Selected Stories of Charlotte Perkins Gilman*, 1994, ed. Denise D. Knight; and a recent collection of Gilman's nonfiction is *Charlotte Perkins Gilman: A Nonfiction Reader*, 1991, ed. Larry Ceplair. Other reprinted works include the Feminist Press edition of *The Yellow Wallpaper* (1892), with an afterword by Elaine R. Hedges; *Women and Economics: A Study of the Economic Relation between Men and Women as a Factor in Social Evolution* (1898); *The Home, Its Work and Influence* (1903); and *The Man-Made World; or, Our Androcentric Culture* (1911). Of great interest is the writer's autobiography, *The Living of Charlotte Perkins Gilman* (1935). A recent helpful biography is Ann J. Lane, *To "Herland"*

and Beyond: The Life and Work of Charlotte Perkins Gilman, 1990.

Three useful collections of critical essays are *Charlotte Perkins Gilman: The Woman and Her Work*, 1989, ed. Sheryl L. Meyering; *Critical Essays on Charlotte Perkins Gilman*, 1992, ed. Joanne B. Karpinski; and *The Captive Imagination: A Casebook on "The Yellow Wallpaper,"* 1992, ed. Catherine Golden. Helpful feminist studies are Carl N. Degler, "Charlotte Perkins Gilman on the Theory and Practice of Feminism," *American Quarterly* (1956); Mary A. Hill, "Charlotte Perkins Gilman: A Feminist Struggle with Womanhood," *Massachusetts Review* 23 (1980); Hill, *Charlotte Perkins Gilman: The Making of a Radical Feminist, 1860–1896*; Laura E. Donaldson, "The Eve of De-Struction: Charlotte Perkins Gilman and the Feminist Recreation of Paradise," *Women's Studies* 16 (1989); and Georgia Johnston, "Exploring Lack and Absence in the Body/Text: Charlotte Perkins Gilman Prewriting Irigary," *Women's Studies* 21 (1992). Gilman is also discussed in *Modern American Women Writers*, 1991, ed. Elaine Showalter. A useful resource is Gary Scharnhorst, *Charlotte Perkins Gilman: A Bibliography*, 1985.

Susan Glaspell

A collection of Glaspell's short dramas, *Plays*, was published in 1920. Her three-act plays include *The Verge* (1921), *The Comic Artist* (1927), and *Alison's House* (1930); among her novels are *The Visioning* (1911), *Fidelity* (1915), *Ambrose Holt and Family* (1931), and *The Morning Is Near Us* (1939). Glaspell's biography of George Cram Cook, *A Road to the Temple* (1927), includes useful background information on the Provincetown Players. Another collection, *Plays by Susan Glaspell*, appeared in 1987, with a useful critical introduction by C. W. E. Bigsby. The recent *Lifted Masks and Other Works*, ed. Eric S. Rabkin, was issued in 1993.

Susan Glaspell, 1966, by Arthur E. Waterman, is a helpful introduction to her life and work; also by Waterman is "Susan Glaspell's *The Verge*: An Experiment in Feminism," *Great Lakes Review* 6 (1979). A recent and helpful full-length study is Veronica Makowsky, *Susan Glaspell's Century of American Women: A Critical Interpretation of Her Work*, 1993. Of interest are Marcia Noe, "Susan Glaspell's Analysis of the Midwestern Character," *Books at Iowa* 27 (1977); Cynthia Sutherland, "American Women Playwrights as Mediators of the 'Woman Problem,'" *Modern Drama* 21 (1978); Christine Dymkowski, "On the Edge: The Plays of Susan Glaspell," *Modern Drama* 1 (1988); Linda Ben-Zvi,

'Susan Glaspell's Contributions to Contemporary Women Playwrights," in *Feminine Focus: The New Women Playwrights*, 1989, ed. Enoch Brater; and Barbara Ozieblo, "Rebellion and Rejection: The Plays of Susan Glaspell," in *Modern American Drama: The Female Canon*, 1990, ed. June Schlueter. *Books at Iowa* 27 also contains a Susan Glaspell checklist. Another bibliographical source is Gerhard Bach, "Susan Glaspell, (1876–1933): A Bibliography of Dramatic Criticism,' *Great Lakes Review* 8 (1977). Mary E. Papke's *Susan Glaspell: A Research and Production Sourcebook*, 1993, is a valuable historical resource.

Louise Glück

Glück's volumes of poetry are *Firstborn* (1969), *The House on Marshland* (1976), *The Garden* (1976), *Descending Figure* (1980), *The Triumph of Achilles* (1985), *Ararat* (1990), and *The Wild Iris* (1992). She has also published a collection of essays, *Proofs and Theories: Essays on Poetry* (1994). Critical essays include Calvin Bedient, "Birth, Not Death, Is the Hard Loss,' *Parnassus* 9 (1981); Robert Miklitsch, "Assembling a Landscape: The Poetry of Louise Glück,' *The Hollins Critic* 19 (1982); E. Laurie George, "The 'Harsher Figure' of *Descending Figure*: Louise Glück's 'Dive into the Wreck,'" *Women's Studies* 17 (1990); Diane S. Bonds, "Entering Language in Louise Glück's *The House on Marshland*: A Feminist Reading," *Contemporary Literature* 31 (1990); Lynn Keller, "'Free/Of Blossom and Suberfuge': Louise Glück and the Language of Renunciation," in *World, Self, Poem: Essays on Contemporary Poetry* 1990, ed. Leonard M. Trawick; Calvin Bedient, "'Man Is Altogether Desire?'" *Salmagundi* (1991); and Lynne McMahon, "The Sexual Swamp: Female Erotics and the Masculine Art," *The Southern Review* 28 (1992). See also the chapter on Glück in Alan Williamson, *Introspection and Contemporary Poetry*, 1984; and Elizabeth Dodd's recent study of Glück and other twentieth-century women poets. *The Veiled Mirror and the Woman Poet: H. D., Louise Bogan, Elizabeth Bishop, and Louise Glück* 1992. A helpful reference guide to Glück's publications is Paula Friedman, "Louise Glück: A Primary Source Bibliography," *Bulletin of Bibliography* 44 (1987).

Nadine Gordimer

Collections of Gordimer's short stories include *Selected Stories* (1976), *Something Out There* (1984), *Jump* (1991), *Why Haven't You Written?: Selected Stories, 1950–72* (1993). Among her best-known novels are *The Late Bourgeois World* (1965), *A Guest of Honor* (1970), *The Conservationist* (1974), *Burger's Daughter* (1979), *July's People* (1981), *A Sport of Nature* (1987), and *My Son's Story* (1990). *The Essential Gesture: Writing, Politics, and Places*, 1988, ed. Stephen Clingman, is a collection of her nonfiction from 1963 to 1985. Another nonfictional work is *Lifetimes under Apartheid*, 1986, written with David Goldblatt. She has also published a book of criticism, *The Black Interpreters* (1973).

Useful critical studies are John Cooke, *The Novels of Nadine Gordimer: Private Lives/Public Landscapes*, 1985; *Critical Essays on Nadine Gordimer*, 1990, ed. Rowland Smith; Stephen Clingman, *The Novels of Nadine Gordimer: History from the Inside*, 1993; and *The Later Fiction of Nadine Gordimer*, 1993, ed. Bruce Alvin King. Nancy Bazin edited *Conversations with Nadine Gordimer*, 1990, and Dorothy Driver has compiled *Nadine Gordimer: A Bibliography of Primary and Secondary Sources, 1937–1992*, 1993.

Jorie Graham

Graham's books of poetry include *Hybrids of Plants and of Ghosts* (1980), *Erosion* (1983), *The End of Beauty* (1987), *Region of Unlikeness* (1991), and *Materialism* (1993). Poems by Graham appear in *The Morrow Anthology of Younger American Poets*, 1985, ed. David Smith and David Bottoms; *The Faber Book of Contemporary American Poetry*, 1986, ed. Helen Vendler; *The Plough-Shares Poetry Reader*, 1987, ed. Joyce Peseroff; and *No More Masks! An Anthology of Twentieth-Century American Women Poets*, 1993, ed. Florence Howe. An interesting interview with Graham is Thomas Gardner, *Denver Quarterly* 26 (1992) See also Sven Birkets, "Jorie Graham I" and "Jorie Graham II," in his *The Electric Life: Essays on Modern Poetry*, 1989. Useful critical essays include Gardner, "Accurate Failures: The Work of Jorie Graham," *The Hollins Critic* 24 (1987); Lisa Issacson, "Mythic Composure and the Laughing Matter of Fact," *Denver Quarterly* 26 (1992); and Bonnie Costello, "Jorie Graham: Art and Erosion," *Contemporary Literature* 33 (1992). See also the discussion of Graham's poetry in Birkets, *The Electric Life: Essays on Modern Poetry*, 1989.

Lady Augusta Gregory

Gregory's plays—including *Spreading the News* (1909), *The Full Moon* (1913), *The Image* (1922), *The Dragon* (1923), *Aristotle's Bellows* (1923), and *Dave* (1928)—were edited in the four-volume *Collected Plays*, 1970, by Ann Saddlemyer. The Coole Edition, under the general editorship of T. R. Henn and Colin Smythe, also includes *Poets and Dreamers: Studies and Translations from the Irish* (1903), *Gods and Fighting Men: The Story of the Tuatha*

de Danaan and of the Fianna of Ireland (1904), Our Irish Theatre: A Chapter of Autobiography (1913), Lady Gregory's Journals (1946), and Seventy Years: Being the Autobiography of Lady Gregory, 1974, ed. Colin Smythe. Dan H. Laurence and Nicholas Grene edited a collection of letters, Shaw, Lady Gregory, and the Abbey: A Correspondence and a Record, in 1993.

Memoirs include Anne Gregory, Me and Nu: Childhood at Coole, 1970; and E. H. Mikhail, Lady Gregory: Interviews and Recollections, 1977. A helpful biography is Mary Lou Kohfeldt, Lady Gregory: The Woman behind the Irish Renaissance, 1985. Full-length critical studies are Elizabeth Coxhead, J. M. Synge and Lady Gregory, 1962, and her Lady Gregory: A Literary Portrait, 1966; Ann Saddlemyer, In Defense of Lady Gregory, Playwright, 1966; Hazard Adams, Lady Gregory, 1973; and Edward A. Kopper, Lady Isabella Persse Gregory, 1976. In addition, Ann Saddlemyer and Colin Smythe edited a useful collection of critical essays, Lady Gregory, Fifty Years After, 1987. Useful chapters on Lady Gregory appear in Herbert Howarth, The Irish Writers, 1880–1940, 1958; Elizabeth Coxhead, Daughters of Erin: Five Women of the Irish Renascence, 1965; Sean McCann, ed., The Story of the Abbey Theatre, 1967; Arra Garab, Beyond Byzantium: The Last Phase of Yeats's Career, 1969; Daniel Arthur Harris, Yeats: Coole Park and Ballylee, 1974; Elizabeth Hale Winkler, The Clown in Modern Anglo-Irish Drama, 1977; John Wilson Foster, Fictions of the Irish Literary Revival, 1987; and C. L. Innes, Woman and Nation in Irish Literature Society, 1993. Useful, too, are E. H. Mikhail, Lady Gregory: An Annotated Bibliography of Criticism, 1982; and Edward A. Kopper Jr., Lady Gregory: A Review of the Criticism, 1991.

Marilyn Hacker

Hacker's books of poetry include Presentation Piece (1974), Separations (1976), Taking Notice (1980), Assumptions (1985), Going Back to the River (1990), and Winter Numbers: Poems (1994). Love, Death, and the Changing of the Seasons (1986) is a verse novel. A recent collection, Selected Poems, 1965–1990 (1994), traces the poet's career and poetic development. For two interesting interviews with Hacker, see Karla Hammond, "An Interview with Marilyn Hacker," Frontiers 5 (1980); and Judith Johnson, "Poetics: A Conversation with Marilyn Hacker," 13th Moon 9 (1991). Reg Saner's essay "Studying Interior Architecture by Keyhole: Four Poets," Denver Quarterly 20 (1965), includes a discussion of Hacker's work.

Radclyffe Hall

Hall's novels and short story collections include The Unlit Lamp (1924), The Forge (1924), A Saturday Life (1925), Adam's Breed (1929), The Master of the House (1932), The Sixth Beatitude (1933), Miss Ogilvy Finds Herself (1934), as well as the famous The Well of Loneliness (1928), which has been reissued in a number of editions since its first printing; in addition, The Unlit Lamp has been reissued in a Virago Press edition, 1981. Hall also published several volumes of poetry, including The Forgotten Island (1915).

Vera M. Brittain discusses Hall's life as well as the Well of Loneliness trial in Radclyffe Hall: A Case of Obscenity, 1969. Fuller biographies include Lady Una Troubridge's memoir, The Life and Death of Radclyffe Hall, 1961, and Lovat Dickson, Radclyffe Hall at the Well of Loneliness: A Sapphic Chronicle, 1975. A helpful full-length study of Hall's work is Claudia S. Franks, Beyond the Well of Loneliness: The Fiction of Radclyffe Hall, 1982, but Hall is also discussed in Lillian Faderman, Surpassing the Love of Men: Romantic Friendship and Love between Women from the Renaissance to the Present, 1981, and in a useful essay, Catharine R. Stimpson, "Zero Degree Deviancy: The Lesbian Novel in English," Critical Inquiry 8 (1981). Esther Newton's "The Mythic Mannish Lesbian: Radclyffe Hall and the New Woman," in Hidden from History: Reclaiming the Lesbian Past, 1989, ed. Martin Bauml Duberman, is a particularly valuable essay, while other useful critical essays dealing specifically with Hall are Gillian Whitlock, "'Everything Is Out of Place': Radclyffe Hall and the Lesbian Literary Tradition," Feminist Studies 13 (1987); Joanne Glasgow, "What's a Nice Lesbian Like You Doing in the Church of Torquemada? Radclyffe Hall and Other Catholic Converts," in Lesbian Texts and Contexts, 1990, ed. Carla Jay and Joanne Glasgow; and Sherrie A. Inness, "Who's Afraid of Stephen Gordon? The Lesbian in the United States Popular Imagination," NWSA Journal 4 (1992).

Frances E. W. Harper

Harper's published works include Poems on Miscellaneous Subjects (1854), Poems (1871), Sketches of Southern Life (1872), Iola Leroy; or, Shadows Uplifted (1892), and The Martyr of Alabama and Other Poems (c. 1894). Her best-known work, Iola Leroy, was reissued in 1988 by the Schomburg Library of Nineteenth-Century Black Women Writers, with an introduction by Frances Smith Foster, and is also included in two collections: Three Classic African-American Novels, 1990, ed. and with an introduction by Henry Louis Gates Jr.; and The African-American Novel in the Age of Reaction: Three Classics, 1992, ed. and with an introduction by William L. Andrews. The Complete Poems of Frances E. W. Harper, ed. Maryemma

Graham, appeared in 1938; and A *Brighter Coming Day: A Frances Ellen Watkins Harper Reader*, ed. Frances Smith Foster, was issued in 1990. Harper is discussed in three broad studies: William H. Robinson Jr., *Early Black American Poets*, 1971; Joan Sherman, *Invisible Poets: Afro-American Women of the Nineteenth Century*, 1974; and Gloria Hull, "Afro-American Women Poets: A Bio-Critical Survey," in *Shakespeare's Sisters*, 1979, ed. Sandra M. Gilbert and Susan Gubar. She is also discussed within a more narrow context in the recent study, by Elizabeth Ammons, *Conflicting Stories: American Women Writers at the Turn into the Twentieth Century*, 1991. A valuable essay is Patricia L. Hill, "Let Me Make the Songs for the People: A Study of Frances W. Harper's Poetry," *Black American Literature Forum* 15 (1981). See also the interesting essays by Paul Lauter, "Is Frances Ellen Watkins Harper Good Enough to Teach?" *Legacy* 5 (1988); Farah Jasmine Griffin, "Frances Ellen Watkins Harper in the Reconstruction South," *SAGE: A Scholarly Journal on Black Women* (1988); Claudia Tate, "Allegories of Black Female Desire; or, Rereading Nineteenth-Century Sentimental Narratives of Black Female Authority," in *Changing Our Words: Essays on Criticism, Theory, and Writing by Black Women*, 1989, ed. Cheryl A. Wall; and Lauren Berlant, "The Queen of America Goes to Washington City: Harriet Jacobs, Frances Harper, Anita Hill," *American Literature* 65 (1993).

Gwen Harwood

Harwood's collections of poems are *Poems* (1963), *Poems: Volume Two* (1968), *Selected Poems* (1975, 1985, 1990), *The Lion's Bride* (1981), *Bone Scan* (1988), and *Collected Poems* (1991). She is also the author of *Blessed City: The Letters of Gwen Harwood to Thomas Riddel, January to September 1943* (1990) and of librettos for the opera *The Golem* (1990) and the comic opera *Fiery Tales* (1992), both composed by Larry Sitsky. Critical work includes R. F. Brissenden, *A Fire-Talented Tongue: Some Notes on the Poetry of Gwen Harwood*, 1978; Robert Selleck, ed., *Gwen Harwood*, 1987; Jennifer Strauss, "Elegies for Mothers: Reflections on Gwen Harwood's 'Mother Who Gave Me Life,'" and Les Murray, "'Three Poems in Memory of My Mother,'" both in *Westerly* 34 (1989). Also valuable are Elizabeth Lawson, *The Poetry of Gwen Harwood*, 1991; Alison Hoddinott, *Gwen Harwood: The Real and the Imagined World*, 1991; Jennifer Strauss, "She/I/You/It—Constructing Mothers and Motherhood in the Writing of Gwen Harwood," *Southerly Journal—A Review of Australian Literature* 52 (1991); Strauss, *Boundary Conditions: The Poetry of Gwen*

Harwood, 1992; and Stephanie Trigg, *Gwen Harwood*, 1994.

Eliza Haywood

Haywood's works include *The Fortunate Foundlings* (1744) and *The History of Miss Betsy Thoughtless*, with an introduction by Dale Spender, 1986. Mary Anne Schofield has introduced two collections of Haywood's novels: *The Masquerade Novels of Eliza Haywood*, 1986, which includes *The Masqueraders*, *Fantomina*, *The Fatal Secret*, and *Idalia*; and *Four Novels of Eliza Haywood: Photoreprints*, 1983. *The Plays of Eliza Haywood*, ed. Valerie C. Rudolph, appeared in 1983; and *Selections from "The Female Spectator,"* ed. Gabrielle M. Firmager, was printed in 1993. For valuable biographical information, see Mary Anne Schofield, *Eliza Haywood*, 1985. Critical articles include Schofield, "Exposé of the Popular Heroine: The Female Protagonists of Eliza Haywood," *Studies in Eighteenth-Century Culture* 12 (1983); Kathryn Shevelow, "Re-Writing the Moral Essay: Eliza Haywood's Female Spectator," *Reader* 13 (1985); April London, "Placing the Female: The Metonymic Garden in Amatory and Pious Narrative, 1700–1740," in *Fetter'd or Free? British Women Novelists, 1670–1815*, 1986, ed. Mary Anne Schofield; Christine Blouch, "Eliza Haywood and the Romance of Obscurity," *Studies in English Literature, 1500–1900* 31 (1991); and Polly Stevens Fields, "Manly Vigor and Women's Wit: Dialoguing Gender in the Plays of Eliza Haywood," in *Compendious Conversations: The Method of Dialogue in the Early Enlightenment*, 1992, ed. Kevin L. Cope. See also the full-length study Rosalind Ballaster, *Seductive Forms: Women's Amatory Fiction from 1684–1740: with Particular Reference to Aphra Behn, Delarivier Manley, and Eliza Haywood*, 1992.

Bessie Head

Head's works include *When Rain Clouds Gather* (1968), *Maru* (1971), *A Question of Power* (1974), *Life* (1975), *The Collector of Treasures, and Other Botswana Village Tales* (1977), *Serowe, Village of the Rainwind* (1981), *A Bewitched Crossroad: An African Saga* (1984), *Tales of Tenderness and Power* (1989), and *The Cardinals: with Meditations and Stories* (1993). Her autobiographical collection, *A Woman Alone: Autobiographical Writings*, appeared in 1990; and her collection of correspondence, *A Gesture of Belonging: Letters from Bessie Head, 1965–1979*, was published in 1991. Biographical information may be found in Craig MacKenzie, *Bessie Head: An Introduction*, 1989; and Virginia Uzoma Ola, *The Life and Works of Bessie Head*, 1994. Useful critical essays are Susan Gardiner, "Bessie

Head: Production under Drought Conditions," in *Women and Writing in South Africa: A Critical Anthology*, 1989, ed. Cherry Clayton; Teresa Dovey, "A Question of Power: Susan Gardiner's Biography versus Bessie Head's Autobiography," *English in Africa* 16 (1989); Linda Susan Beard, "Bessie Head's Syncretic Fictions: The Reconceptualization of Power and the Recovery of the Ordinary," *Modern Fiction Studies* 37 (1991); and Dorothy Driver, "Reconstructing the Past, Shaping the Future: Bessie Head and the Question of Feminism in a New South Africa," in *Black Women's Writing*, 1993, ed. Gina Wisker. A valuable critical resource is Craig MacKenzie, *Bessie Head: A Bibliography*, 1992.

Mary Sidney Herbert, Countess of Pembroke
Herbert's published works include *The Psalms of Sir Philip Sidney and the Countess of Pembroke*, 1963, ed. J. C. A. Rathmell; *Two Poems by the Countess of Pembroke*, 1962, ed. Bent Juel-Jensen; *The Triumph of Death, and Other Unpublished and Uncollected Poems*, 1977, ed. G. F. Waller; *The Countess of Pembroke's Antonie*, 1897, ed. Alice Luce; and *The Countess of Pembroke's Emanuell*, ed. A. B. Grosart, in *Miscellanies*, 1871. Herbert is included in George Ballard, *Memoirs of Several Ladies of Great Britain*, 1752, and Louisa Costello, *Memoirs of Eminent Englishwomen*, 1844. Biographical materials include M. M. Bulloch, *Mary Sidney, Countess of Pembroke, an Elizabethan Historiette*, 1895; and the useful Frances B. Young, *Mary Sidney, Countess of Pembroke*, 1912. G. F. Waller has written the more recent *Mary Sidney, Countess of Pembroke, a Critical Study of Her Writings and Literary Milieu*, 1979. In addition, her work is discussed in Coburn Freer, "The Countess of Pembroke in a World of Words," *Style* 5 (1980); Margaret Hannay Patterson, "'Doo What Men May Sing': Mary Sidney and the Tradition of Admonitory Dedication," in her *Silent but for the Word: Tudor Women as Patrons, Translators, and Writers of Religious Works*, 1985; and Beth Wynne Fisken, "'The Art of Sacred Parody' in Mary Sidney's Psalmes," *Tulsa Studies in Women's Literature* 8 (1989). A full-length study is Mary Ellen Lamb, *Gender and Authorship in the Sidney Circle*, 1990.

Linda Hogan
Hogan's volumes of poetry are *Calling Myself Home* (1978), *Daughters, I Love You* (1981), *Eclipse* (1983), *Seeing Through the Sun* (1985), *Savings* (1988), *Red Clay: Poems & Stories* (1991), and *The Book of Medicines* (1993). Hogan's works of prose include *Mean Spirit* (1990, 1992), *Dwellings: Reflections on the Natural World* (1995), *From Women's Experience to Feminist Theology* (1995), and *Solar Storms* (1995). Hogan also co-edited, with Carol Bruchac and Judith McDaniel, *The Stories We Hold Secret: Tales of Women's Spiritual Development* (1986). Critical essays include Mark Vogel, "Hands, Feet and Soul: Linda Hogan's 'The Truth Is,'" *English Journal* 83 (1994); and June Jordan, "The Book of Medicines," *Ms. Magazine* 4 (1994).

Zora Neale Hurston
Hurston's volumes include *Jonah's Gourd Vine* (1934), *Mules and Men* (1935), *Their Eyes Were Watching God* (1937), *Tell My Horse* (1938), *Moses, Man of the Mountain* (1939), *Dust Tracks on a Road* (1942), and *Seraph on the Suwanee* (1948). An excellent anthology of Hurston's work, ed. and with useful introductions by Alice Walker and Mary Helen Washington, is *I Love Myself When I Am Laughing . . . And Then Again When I Am Looking Mean and Impressive: A Zora Neale Hurston Reader*, 1979.

A good biography, Robert E. Hemenway, *Zora Neale Hurston*, appeared in 1977, and Lillie P. Howard wrote *Zora Neale Hurston*, 1980. Two more recent biographies are N. Y. Nathiri, *Zora! Zora Neale Hurston, a Woman and Her Community*, 1991; and Janelle Yates, *Zora Neale Hurston: A Storyteller's Life*, 1993. A useful full-length study is Karla F. C. Holloway, *The Character of the Word: The Texts of Zora Neale Hurston*, 1987. Three collections of critical essays are Michael Awkward, ed., *New Essays on Their Eyes Were Watching God*, 1990; Lillie P. Howard, ed., *Alice Walker and Zora Neale Hurston: The Common Bond*, 1993; and Henry Louis Gates Jr. and Anthony Appiah, ed., *Zora Neale Hurston: Critical Perspectives Past and Present*, 1993. Individual articles include Erlene Stetson, "Their Eyes Were Watching God: A Woman's Story," *Regionalism and the Female Imagination* 4 (1978); Florence E. Borders, "Zora Neale Hurston: Hidden Woman," *Callaloo* 2 (May 1979); Mary Jane Lupton, "Zora Neale Hurston and the Survival of the Female," *Southern Literary Journal* 15 (1982); Cheryl A. Wall, "Zora Neale Hurston: Changing Her Own Words," in *American Novelists Revisited: Essays in Feminist Criticism*, 1982, ed. Fritz Fleischmann; Pearlie Peters, "Women and Assertive Voice in Hurston's Fiction and Folklore," *The Literary Griot* 4 (1992); and Mae Gwendolyn Henderson, "Speaking in Tongues: Dialogics, Dialectics, and the Black Woman Writer's Literary Tradition," in *Aesthetics in Feminist Perspective*, 1993, ed. Hilde Hein and Carolyn Korsmeyer. A helpful but somewhat dated resource is Adele S. Newson, *Zora Neale Hurston: A Reference Guide*, 1987.

Rebecca Cox Jackson

Jackson's work has been collected in *Gifts of Power: The Writings of Rebecca Jackson, Black Visionary, Shaker Eldress*, 1981, ed. and with an introduction by Jean McMahon Humez. Richard E. Williams's biography, *Called and Chosen: The Story of Mother Rebecca Jackson and the Philadelphia Shakers*, has been edited by Cheryl Dorschner and republished in 1981. A valuable essay, occasioned by the publication of *Gifts of Power*, appears in Alice Walker's recent volume *In Search of Our Mothers' Gardens*, 1983; and Diane Sasson's essay "Life as Vision: The Autobiography of Mother Rebecca Jackson" appeared in *The Shaker Spiritual Narrative*, 1983, ed. Sarah D. Sasson. Jackson is also discussed in Joanne Braxton, *Black Women Writing Autobiography*, 1989; and Darlene Clark Hines, ed., *Black Women in America: An Historical Encyclopedia*, 1993.

Harriet Jacobs

A reprint of Jacobs's *Incidents in the Life of a Slave Girl* (1861) was edited by Walter Teller in 1973. In 1987 Jean Fagan Yellin edited an edition containing Yellin's valuable introduction and photographs of historical documents. Jacobs is discussed in William L. Andrews, *To Tell a Free Story: The First Century of Afro-American Autobiography, 1760–1865*, 1986; Valerie Smith, *Self-Discovery and Authority in Afro-American Narrative*, 1988; Sidonie Smith, "Resisting the Gaze of Embodiment: Women's Autobiography in the Nineteenth Century," in *American Women's Autobiography: Fea(s)ts of Memory*, 1992, ed. Margo Culley; Frances Smith Foster, *Written by Herself: Literary Production of African American Women, 1746–1892*, 1993; and Karen Sanchez-Eppler, *Touching Liberty: Abolition, Feminism, and the Politics of the Body*, 1993. Useful critical essays are Mary Ellen Washington, "Meditations on History: The Slave Narrative of Linda Brent," in her *Invented Lives: Narratives of Black Women, 1860–1960*, 1987; Beth Maclay Doriani, "Black Womanhood in Nineteenth-Century America: Subversion and Self-Construction in Two Women's Autobiographies," *American Quarterly* 43 (1991), which discusses Jacobs and Harriet Wilson; and Carla Kaplan, "Narrative Contracts and Emancipatory Readers: Incidents in the Life of a Slave Girl," *The Yale Journal of Criticism* 6 (1993).

Alice James

James's work can be found in *Alice James, Her Brothers—Her Journal*, 1934, ed. and with an introduction by Anna Robeson Burr; *The Diary of Alice James*, 1964, ed. and with an introduction by Leon Edel; and *The Death and Letters of Alice James*, 1981, ed. and with a biographical essay by Ruth Bernard Yeazell.

Secondary material includes Francis Otto Matthiessen, *The James Family*, 1947; Jean Strouse, *Alice James: A Biography*, 1980; and R. W. B. Lewis, *The Jameses: A Family Narrative*, 1991.

Sarah Orne Jewett

Jewett's work includes *Deephaven* (1877), *A Country Doctor* (1884), *A White Heron and Other Stories* (1886), and *The Country of the Pointed Firs* (1896). Her *Stories and Tales* were published in seven volumes in 1910, but a more readily available collection, *The Best Stories of Sarah Orne Jewett* (1925), was edited in two volumes with a preface by Willa Cather. In 1988, Charles Waugh et al. edited another *The Best Stories*, with an introduction by Josephine Donovan. *The Country of the Pointed Firs, and Other Stories* was edited by Mary Ellen Chase in 1968 and reissued, with an introduction by Marjorie Pryse, in 1981. Richard Cary edited *The Uncollected Short Stories of Sarah Orne Jewett* 1971, as well as the *Sarah Orne Jewett Letters*, revised and enlarged in 1967.

Critical biographies include F. O. Matthiessen, *Sarah Orne Jewett*, 1929; Richard Cary, *Sarah Orne Jewett*, 1962; Margaret Thorp, *Sarah Orne Jewett*, 1966; and Elizabeth Silverthorne, *Sarah Orne Jewett: A Writer's Life*, 1993. Cary also edited a collection of essays, *Appreciation of Sarah Orne Jewett*, 1973. Other critical studies are Josephine Donovan, *Sarah Orne Jewett*, 1980; Perry Westbrook, *Acres of Flint: Sarah Orne Jewett and Her Contemporaries*, 1981; and Sarah Way Sherman, *Sarah Orne Jewett: An American Persephone*, 1989. Gwen L. Nagel has edited *Critical Essays on Sarah Orne Jewett*, 1984, as well as a valuable reference guide, *Sarah Orne Jewett*, 1978.

Julian of Norwich

Marion Glasscoe has edited a reliable edition of the Middle English text of Julian's *A Revelation of Divine Love*, 1976, but a more readable modern version is *A Book of Showings*, 1978, ed. and trans. Edmund Colledge and James Walsh. P. Franklin in Chambers, *Juliana of Norwich*, 1955, and Paul Molinari, *Julian of Norwich*, 1958, are general introductions to her work; Robert Stone, *Middle English Prose Style*, 1970, treats both Julian and Margery Kempe. Critical essays are Brant Pelphrey, *Love Was His Meaning: The Theology and Mysticism of Julian of Norwich*, 1982; Jennifer P. Hummel, "God Is Our Mother": Julian of Norwich, and the Medieval Image of Feminine Divinity, 1982; Ritamary Bradley, "Mysticism in the Motherhood Similitude of Julian of Norwich," *Studia-*

Mystica 8 (1985); Marion Glasscoe, "Visions and Revisions: A Further Look at the Manuscripts of Julian of Norwich," *Studies in Bibliography* 42 (1989); Lynn Staley Johnson, "The Trope of the Scribe and the Question of Literary Authority in the Works of Julian of Norwich and Margery Kempe," *Speculum* 66 (1991); and Elizabeth Robertson, "Medieval Medical Views of Women and Female Spirituality in the *Ancrene Wisse* and Julian of Norwich's Showings," in *Feminist Approaches to the Body in Medieval Literature*, 1993, ed. Linda Lomperis and Sarah Stanbury. Mary Mason's useful article "The Other Voice: Autobiography of Women Writers," in *Autobiography*, ed. James Olney, 1980, puts Julian's work in the context of women's autobiography.

Margery Kempe
Colonel W. E. I. Butler-Bowdon edited and modernized *The Book of Margery Kempe*, 1936. In 1940, Sanford Brown Meech edited a transcription of the Butler-Bowdon manuscript, which includes a prefatory note by Hope Emily Allen, and in 1985, B. A. Windeatt edited an edition. Valuable introductions are Katharine Cholmeley, *Margery Kempe, Genius and Mystic*, 1947; Martin Thornton, *Margery Kempe, an Example in the English Pastoral Tradition*, 1960; Louise Collis, *Memoirs of a Medieval Woman: The Life and Times of Margery Kempe*, 1964; and Clarissa W. Atkinson, *Mystic and Pilgrim: The Book and the World of Margery Kempe*, 1983. Two recent valuable full-length studies are Karma Lochrie, *Margery Kempe and Translations of the Flesh*, 1991; and Lynn Staley Johnson *Margery Kempe's Dissenting Fictions*, 1994. Sandra J. McEntire edited the collection *Margery Kempe: A Book of Essays*, 1992. Robert Stone discusses her in his *Middle English Prose Style*, 1970; as do Mary Mason in "The Other Voice: Autobiography of Women's Writers," in *Autobiography*, 1980, ed. James Olney, and Hope Phyllis Weissman, in "Margery Kempe in Jerusalem: *Hysterica Compassio* in the Late Middle Ages," in *Acts of Interpretation*, ed. Mary J. Carruthers and Elizabeth D. Kirk. Useful recent essays are François Le Saux, " 'Hir not Lettyrd': Margery Kempe and Writing," in *Writing and Culture*, 1992, ed. Balz Engler; Robert C. Ross, "Oral Life, Written Text: The Genesis of the *Book of Margery Kempe*," *Yearbook of English Studies* 22 (1992); Lynn Staley Johnson, "Margery Kempe: Social Critic," *Journal of Medieval and Renaissance Studies* 22 (1992); and Wendy Harding, "Body into Text: *The Book of Margery Kempe*," in *Feminist Approaches to the Body in Medieval Literature*, 1993, ed. Sarah Stansbury.

Anne Killigrew
Killigrew's work is collected in *Poems* (1686). A facsimile reproduction, with an introduction by Richard Morton, was published in 1967. A valuable essay on Killigrew's poetry is Kristina Straub, "Indecent Liberties with a Poet: Audience and the Metaphor of Rape in Killigrew's 'Upon the Saying That My Verses . . .' and Pope's 'Arbuthnot,' " *Tulsa Studies in Women's Literature* 6 (1987). See also the discussions of Killigrew in Ann Messenger, *His and Hers: Essays in Restoration and Eighteenth-Century Literature*, 1986; and Elaine Hobby, *Virtue of Necessity: English Women's Writing, 1646–1688*, 1988.

Jamaica Kincaid
Kincaid's novels are *Annie John* (1985), *Lucy* (1990), and *The Autobiography of My Mother* (1996); her short story collection is *At the Bottom of the River* (1983); her book-length essay about her native island, Antigua, is *A Small Place* (1988); and her literature for children is *Annie, Gwen, Lilly, Pam, and Tulip*, 1986. Useful critical works are Diane Simmons, *Jamaica Kincaid*, 1994; and Moira Ferguson, *Jamaica Kincaid: Where the Land Meets the Body*, 1994. Allan Vorda's interview with Kincaid, "I Come From a Place That's Very Unreal: An Interview with Jamaica Kincaid," is published in *Face to Face: Interviews with Contemporary Novelists*, 1993, ed. Vorda.

Maxine Hong Kingston
Kingston's works are *The Woman Warrior* (1976), *China Men* (1980), and *Tripmaster Monkey: His Fake Book* (1989). She also has an important article, "Cultural Misreading by American Reviewers," *Asian and Western Writers in Dialogue: New Cultural Identities* (1982). Useful background information on Kingston can be found in Paula Rabinowitz, "Eccentric Memories: A Conversation with Maxine Hong Kingston," *Michigan Quarterly Review* 26 (1987); and in Shelley Fisher Fishkin, "An Interview with Maxine Hong Kingston," *American Literary History* 3 (1991). An interesting critical study is King-kok Cheung, *Articulate Silences: Hisaye Yamamoto, Maxine Hong Kingston, Joy Kogawa*, 1993. See also discussions of Kingston in John Paul Eakin, *Fictions in Autobiography: Studies in the Art of Self-Invention*, 1985; Roberta Rubenstein, *Boundaries of the Self: Gender, Culture, Fiction*, 1987; G. Thomas Couser, *Altered Egos: Authority in American Autobiography*, 1989; Amy Ling, *Between Worlds: Women Writers of Chinese Ancestry*, 1990; and Bonnie C. Winsbro, *Supernatural Forces: Belief, Difference, and Power in Contemporary Works by Ethnic Women*, 1993. Critical essays on

Kingston include Patricia Lin Blinde, "The Icicle in the Desert: Perspective and Form in the Works of Two Chinese-American Women Writers," MELUS 6 (1979); and two essays in *Modern Chinese Women Writers: Critical Appraisals*, 1989, ed. Michael S. Duke. Feminist perspectives on Kingston include Sidonie Smith, "Maxine Hong Kingston's *The Woman Warrior*: Filiality and Women's Autobiographical Story-telling," in her *A Poetics of Women's Autobiography: Marginality and the Fictions of Self-Representation*, 1987; and Bonnie Tu Smith, "Literary Tricksterism," in *Anxious Power: Reading, Writing, and Ambivalence in Narrative by Women*, 1993, ed. Carol J. Singley and Susan Elizabeth Sweeney.

Carolyn Kizer

Kizer's books of poetry include *The Ungrateful Garden* (1961), *Knock upon Silence: Poems* (1965), *Midnight Was My Cry: New and Selected Poems* (1971), *Yin* (1984), and *Mermaids in the Basement: Poems for Women* (1984). *The Nearness of You* (1986) contains new poems as well as selections from Kizer's first three books. A recent collection, *Proses: On Poems and Poets* (1993), includes an autobiographical narrative as well as essays on twentieth-century poetry. See also the interview with Earl Ingersoll and Stan Rubin, "'The Very Separateness of Things': A Conversation with Carolyn Kizer," *Webster Review* 11 (1986). An interesting essay on her work is Dominic Cheung, "Carolyn Kizer and Her Chinese Imitations," in *China and the West: Comparative Literature Studies*, 1980, ed. William Tay, Chou Ying-hsiung, and Yuan Heh-hsiang; David Rigsbee edited a useful collection of essays, *An Answering Music: On the Poetry of Carolyn Kizer*, 1990.

Maxine Kumin

Kumin's works include children's books, novels, and verse collections; some of the most notable are *Through Dooms of Love* (1965), *Up Country* (1972), *The Designated Heir* (1974), *House, Bridge, Fountain, Gate* (1975), *The Retrieval System* (1978), and *Our Ground Time Here Will Be Brief* (1982). Her recent books of poetry are *The Long Approach* (1985), *Nurture* (1989), and *Looking for Luck* (1992). She has three books of essays: *To Make a Prairie* (1979); *In Deep: Country Essays* (1987), which includes both new and previously published prose; and *Women, Animals, and Vegetables* (1994), which also contains short stories.

Two interesting interviews are Karla Hammond, "An Interview with Maxine Kumin," *Western Humanities Review* 33 (1979); and Shelley Armitage, "An Interview

with Maxine Kumin," *Paintbrush* 7–8 (1980–81). Critical pieces include Philip Booth, "Maxine Kumin's Survival," *American Poetry Review* (1978); Sybil P. Estess, "Past Halfway: The Retrieval System by Maxine Kumin," *Iowa Review* 10 (1979); Alicia Ostriker's discussion in her *Stealing the Language: The Emergence of Women's Poetry in America*, 1986; Peter Harris, "Poetry Chronicle: Hunger, Hope, and Nurture: Poetry from Michael Ryan, the Chinese Democracy Movement, and Maxine Kumin," *Virginia Quarterly Review* 67 (1991); and Diana Hume George, "Keeping Our Working Distance: Maxine Kumin's Poetry of Loss and Survival," in *Aging and Gender in Literature: Studies in Creativity*, 1993, ed. Anne M. Wyatt-Brown and Janice Rossen.

Dilys Laing

Laing's books include the poetry collections *Another England* (1941), *Birth Is Farewell* (1944), *Walk through Two Landscapes* (1949), and *Poems from a Cage* (1961), as well as a novel, *The Great Year* (1948). Her posthumous *Collected Poems* (1967) contains some previously unpublished poems and an introduction by M. L. Rosenthal. Poems by Laing appear in *The World Split Open: Four Centuries of Women Poets in England and America, 1552–1950*, 1974, ed. Louise Bernikow; *Parallels: Artists/Poets*, 1993, ed. Grace Glueck; and in *The Massachusetts Review* 34 (1993).

Aemilia Lanyer

Lanyer's long poem, *Salve Deus Rex Judaeorum* (1611), appears as *The Poems of Shakespeare's Dark Lady*, 1979, ed. and with an introduction by A. L. Rouse. Suzanne Woods edited *The Poems of Aemilia Lanyer* in 1993. Some of Lanyer's work is included in *The Female Spectator*, 1977, ed. Mary R. Mahl and Helene Koon. She is discussed in George Ballard, *Memoirs of Several Ladies of Great Britain*, 1752; H. T. C. de la Fontaine, *The King's Musick*, 1909; and Eric Blom, *Grove's Dictionary of Music and Musicians*, 1954 (supplement 1961). Helpful critical studies include Barbara K. Lewalski, "Of God and Good Women: The Poems of Aemilia Lanyer," in *Silent but for the Word: Tudor Women as Patrons, Translators, and Writers of Religious Works*, 1985, ed. Margaret Patterson Hannay; Ann Baynes Coiro, "Writing in Service: Sexual Politics and Class Position in the Poetry of Aemilia Lanyer and Ben Johnson," *Criticism* 35 (1993); Lewalski, "Re-Writing Patriarchy and Patronage: Margaret Clifford, Anne Clifford, and Aemilia Lanyer," in *Patronage, Politics, and Literary Tradition in England, 1558–1578*, 1993, ed. Cedric C. Brown; and Wendy Wall,

"Our Bodies/Our Texts? Renaissance Women and the Trials of Authorship," in *Anxious Power: Reading, Writing, and Ambivalence in Narrative by Women*, 1993, ed. Carol J. Singley and Susan Elizabeth Sweeney. See also Elaine V. Beilin's valuable discussion of Lanyer in *Redeeming Eve: Women Writers of the English Renaissance*, 1987.

Margaret Laurence

Laurence's novels include *This Side Jordan* (1960), *The Stone Angel* (1964), *A Jest of God* (1966), *The Fire-Dwellers* (1969), and *The Diviners* (1974). She has several books of short stories, such as *The Olden-Days Coat* (1979). Other works include literary studies, children's books, and a collection of essays, *Heart of a Stranger* (1976). Her autobiographical *Dance on the Earth: A Memoir* appeared in 1989, and a collection of letters: *Margaret Laurence–Al Purdy, A Friendship in Letters*, ed. and with an introduction by John Lennox, was published in 1993. George Woodcock's collection, *A Place to Stand On: Essays by and about Margaret Laurence*, appeared in 1983. Full-length critical studies are Patricia Morley, *Margaret Laurence*, 1981; Morley, *Margaret Laurence: The Long Journey*, 1991; Fiona Sparran, *Into Africa with Margaret Laurence*, 1992; and Nora Foster Stovel, *Rachel's Children: Margaret Laurence's "A Jest of God,"* 1992. Useful collections of critical essays are *Margaret Laurence: An Appreciation*, 1988, ed. Chrystl Verdun; and *Critical Approaches to the Fiction of Margaret Laurence*, 1990, ed. Colin Nicholson. Four helpful essays are Judy Kearns, "Rachel and Social Determinism: A Feminist Reading of *A Jest of God*," *Journal of Canadian Fiction* 27 (1980); Harriet Blodgett, "The Real Lives of Margaret Laurence's Women," *Critique* 23 (1981); and Jean Gandesbury, "Shaping Myths: The Manawaka Novels of Margaret Laurence," *Commonwealth Novel in English* 5 (1992). There is an annotated, though dated, bibliography of Laurence by Susan J. Warwick in *The Annotated Bibliography of Canada's Major Authors I*, 1979, ed. Robert Lecker and Jack David.

Mary Lavin

Lavin's collections of short stories include *Tales from Bective Bridge* (1942), *The Long Ago* (1944), *The Becker Wives* (1946; published in the United States as *At Sallylgap* in 1947), *The Patriot Son* (1956), *The Great Wave* (1961), *In the Middle of the Fields* (1967), *A Memory* (1973), *The Shrine* (1977), and *A Family Likeness* (1985). *Selected Stories* appeared in 1959 and 1984; *The Collected Stories* in 1971; and *The Stories of Mary Lavin*, 3 vols., in 1964, 1973, and 1985. Lavin has also published two novels, *The House in Clewe Street* (1945) and *Mary O'Grady* (1950). Full-length studies of Lavin's work include Zack Brown, *Mary Lavin*, 1975; Richard F. Peterson, *Mary Lavin*, 1978; and A. A. Kelly, *Mary Lavin, Quiet Rebel: A Study of Her Short Stories*, 1980. See also the "Mary Lavin Issue," *Irish University Review* 9 (1979). Other useful essays on Lavin's achievement include V. S. Prichett's introduction to the *Collected Stories*, 1971; Patricia Meszaros, "Woman as Artist: The Fiction of Mary Lavin," *Critique* 24 (1982); Maria Gottwald, "Narrative Strategies in the *Selected Stories* of Mary Lavin," in *Anglo-Irish and Irish Literature: Aspects of Language and Culture*, 1988, ed. Birgit Bramsback and Martin Croghan.

Jane Lead

Lead's published works include *A Fountain of Gardens Watered by the River of Divine Pleasure and Springing Up in All Variety of Spiritual Plants* (1677–1701) and *Wars of David* (1700). Most of the studies are by Catherine F. Smith and include "A Note on Jane Lead with Selections from Her Writings," *Studia Mystica* 3; "Mysticism and Feminism: Jacob Boehme and Jane Lead," in *Women and Men: The Consequences of Power*, 1977, ed. Dana V. Hiller and Robin Ann Sheets; "Jane Lead: The Feminist Mind and Art of a 17th-Century Protestant Mystic," in *Women of Spirit*, 1979, ed. Rosemary Ruether and Eleanor McLaughlin; "Jane Lead: Mysticism and the Woman Clothed with the Sun," in *Shakespeare's Sisters*, 1979, ed. Sandra M. Gilbert and Susan Gubar; "Jane Lead's Wisdom: Women and Prophecy in Seventeenth-Century England," in *Poetic Prophecy in Western Literature*, 1984, ed. Jan Wojick and Raymond Jean Fontain; and "Three Guineas: Virginia Woolf's Prophecy," in *Virginia Woolf and Bloomsbury: A Centenary Celebration*, 1987, ed. Jane Marcus, which compares Woolf's prophetic writings with those of Lead.

Ursula Le Guin

Le Guin's works include *Rocannon's World* (1966), *A Wizard of Earthsea* (1968), *The Left Hand of Darkness* (1969), *The Dispossessed* (1974), *The Wind's Twelve Quarters* (1975), *Orsinian Tales* (1976), *Malafrena* (1979), *The Beginning Place* (1980), *The Compass Rose* (1982), *Women of Vision* (1988), *Dancing at the Edge of the World: Thoughts on Words, Women, and Places* (1988), *Tehanu: The Last Book of Earthsea* (1990), and *Blue Moon over Thurman Street* (1993). She has written numerous essays and children's books as well as books of poetry, including *Hard Works, and Other Poems* (1981), *Wild Oats and Fireweed:*

New Poems (1988) and Going Out with Peacocks and Other Poems (1994). A multimedia work produced with Todd Barton, Margaret Chodos, and George Heish is Always Coming Home (1985). Le Guin has also edited two collections of science fiction: The Language of the Night: Essays on Fantasy and Science Fiction, 1992, and The Norton Book of Science Fiction: North American Science Fiction, 1960–1990, with Brian Attebery, 1993.

Full-length studies include George E. Slusser, The Farthest Shores of Ursula K. Le Guin, 1976; Barbara J. Bucknall, Ursula K. Le Guin, 1981; James W. Bittner, Approaches to the Fiction of Ursula K. Le Guin, 1984; Charlotte Spivack, Ursula K. Le Guin, 1984; Bernard Selinger, Le Guin and Identity in Contemporary Fiction, 1988; and Elizabeth Cummin Understanding Ursula K. Le Guin, 1990. Three collections of critical essays about her work are Ursula K. Le Guin 1979, ed. Joseph Olander and Martin Greenberg; Ursula K. Le Guin: Voyager to Inner Lands and to Outer Space, 1979, ed. Joe DeBolt; and Ursula K. Le Guin 1986, ed. Harold Bloom. Recent helpful essays are Elizabeth Cummin, "The Land-Lady's Homebirth: Revisiting Ursula K. Le Guin Worlds," Science Fiction Studies 17 (1990); Susan Bassnett, "Remaking the Old World: Ursula Le Guin and the American Tradition," in Where No Man Has Gone Before: Women and Science Fiction, 1991, ed. Lucie Armitt; and Kristine J. Anderson, "Places Where a Woman Could Talk: Ursula K. Le Guin and the Feminist Linguistic Utopia," Women and Language 15 (1992). Useful, but somewhat dated, is Elizabeth Cummins Cogell, Ursula K. Le Guin: A Primary and Secondary Bibliography, 1983.

Doris Lessing

Most of Lessing's collections of short stories and her novels—including the five-volume Children of Violence (1952–69), The Golden Notebook (1962), A Man and Two Women (1963), African Stories (1969), Briefing for a Descent into Hell (1971), and Summer before the Dark (1973)—are available in paperback. She has also written a series of science fiction novels, beginning with Shikasta (1979). Her most recent work includes nonfiction, novels, and short stories, such as Prisons We Choose to Live Inside (1987), The Wind Blows Away Our Words (1987), African Laughter: Four Visits to Zimbabwe (1992), Winter in July (1993), Under My Skin (1994), The Real Thing: Stories and Sketches (1992), and London Observed: Stories and Sketches (1992). A Small Personal Voice, 1974, ed. Paul Schlueter, is a selection of Lessing's essays on her life and writings, on other writers, and on Africa. Notebooks, Memoirs, Archives: Reading and Re-Reading Doris Lessing, ed. Jenny Taylor, came out in 1982; and The Doris Lessing Reader appeared in 1989.

Critical and biographical full-length studies include Dorothy Brewster, Doris Lessing, 1965; Paul Schlueter, The Novels of Doris Lessing, 1973; Mary Ann Singleton, The City and the Veld, 1977; Roberta Rubinstein, The Novelistic Vision of Doris Lessing, 1979; Lorna Sage, Doris Lessing, 1983; Betsy Draine, Substance under Pressure: Artistic Coherence and Evolving Form in the Novels of Doris Lessing, 1983; Mona Kapp, Doris Lessing, 1984; and Katherine Fishburn, The Unexpected Universe of Doris Lessing: A Study in Narrative Technique, 1985. Three useful essay collections are Doris Lessing: Critical Essays, 1974, ed. Annis Pratt and L. S. Dembo; Critical Essays on Doris Lessing, 1990, ed. Claire Sprague and Virginia Tiger; and In Pursuit of Doris Lessing: Nine Nations Reading, 1990, ed. Claire Sprague. Lessing is also discussed in Sally Robinson, Engendering the Subject: Gender and Self-Representation in Contemporary Women's Fiction, 1991. Dee Seligman compiled an annotated bibliography in 1981.

Meridel Le Sueur

Le Sueur's works include Annunciation (1935), Salute to Spring (1940), North Star Country (1945), Sparrow Hawk (1950), Crusaders (1955), Corn Village (1970), and Women on the Bread Lines (1978) Her novel The Girl, which was written in 1932 but not published until 1978, was reprinted in 1991. Song: Collected Essays and Stories (1977) was revised and enlarged in 1990. Harvest: Collected Stories appeared in 1977. Elaine Hedges includes important biographical background in her edition of and introduction to Ripening: Selected Work of Meridel Le Sueur, 1927–1980, 1982. Interesting critical essays are Blanche H. Gelfant's chapter on Le Sueur in Women Writing in America, 1985; Paula Rabinowitz, "Maternity as History: Gender and the Transformation of Gender in Meridel Le Sueur's The Girl," Contemporary Literature 29 (1988); Constance Coiner, "Literature of Resistance: The Intersection of Feminism and the Communist Left in Meridel Le Sueur and Tillie Olsen," in Left Politics and the Literary Profession, 1990, ed. Lennard J. Davis; and Phaedra Greenwood, "Post Cards from Meridel," in The Epistolary Form and the Letter as Artifact, 1991, ed. Jim Villani. Le Sueur is also discussed in Linda Wagner-Martin, The Modern American Novel, 1914–1945, 1990.

Denise Levertov

Levertov's books of poems include The Double

Image (1946), *Here and Now* (1957), *Overland to the Islands* (1958), *With Eyes at the Back of Our Heads* (1960), *The Jacob's Ladder* (1961), *O Taste and See* (1964), *The Sorrow Dance* (1967), *Relearning the Alphabet* (1970), *To Stay Alive* (1971), *Footprints* (1972), *The Freeing of the Dust* (1975), *Life in the Forest* (1978), *Candles in Babylon* (1982), *Breathing the Water* (1987), *A Door in the Hive* (1989), and *Evening Train* (1992). She also has three collections: *Collected Earlier Poems, 1940–1960* (1979), *Poems, 1960–1967* (1983), and *Poems, 1968–1972* (1987). *The Poet in the World* (1973), *Light Up the Cave* (1981), and *New and Selected Essays* (1992) are collections of her essays and reviews, as is *Denise Levertov: In Her Own Province*, 1979, ed. Linda Wagner-Martin. Levertov also published a translation of Jean Joubert's *Black Iris* in 1988.

Valuable analyses of Levertov's work include Rachel Blau DuPlessis, "The Critique of Consciousness and Myth in Levertov, Rich, and Rukeyser," in *Shakespeare's Sisters*, 1979, ed. Sandra M. Gilbert and Susan Gubar; Linda W. Wagner, "Levertov and Rich: The Later Poems," *South Carolina Review* 11 (1979); Diana Surman, "Inside and Outside in the Poetry of Denise Levertov," *Critical Quarterly* 22 (1980); Bonnie Costello, " 'Flooded with Otherness,' " *Parnassus* 8 (1980); John Felstiner, "Poetry and Political Experience: Denise Levertov," in *Coming to Light: American Women Poets in the Twentieth Century*, 1985, ed. Diane Wood Middlebrook and Marilyn Yalom; Paul A. Lacey, "Denise Levertov: A Poetry of Exploration," in *American Women Poets*, 1986, ed. Harold Bloom; and Sandra M. Gilbert, "Revolutionary Love: Denise Levertov and the Poetics of Politics," in *Conversant Essays: Contemporary Poets on Poetry*, 1990, ed. James McCorkle. A recent full-length study is Audrey T. Rodgers, *Denise Levertov*, 1993. In addition, see Linda A. Kinnahan, *Poetics of the Feminine: Authority and Literary Tradition in William Carlos Williams, Denise Levertov, and Kathleen Fraser*, 1994. Feminist perspectives on Levertov can be found in Alicia Ostriker, *Stealing the Language: The Emergence of Women's Poetry in America*, 1986. See also the useful collection *Critical Essays on Denise Levertov*, 1990, ed. Linda Wagner-Martin; and the special "Denise Levertov Issue" of *Twentieth-Century Literature* 38 (1992). A valuable resource is Liana Sakelliou-Schultz, *Denise Levertov: An Annotated Primary and Secondary Bibliography*, 1988.

Dorothy Livesay
Volumes of Livesay's poetry include *Selected Poems, 1926–1956* (1957), *The Documentaries: Selected Longer Poems* (1968), and *Collected Poems: The Two Seasons* (1972). Subsequent collections include *Nine Poems of Farewell, 1972–1973* (1973), *Ice Age* (1975), and *The Woman I Am* (1977), as well as a volume of short stories, *A Winnipeg Childhood* (1973). She has also recently published her autobiography, *Journey with My Selves; A Memoir, 1909–1963* (1991). For additional biographical information, see two interviews: Doug Beardsley and Rosemary Sullivan's piece in *Canadian Poetry* 3 (1978); and Jorn Carlsen's in *Kunapipi* 1 (1979); as well as the recently issued full-length biography *Dorothy Livesay: Patterns in a Poetic Life*, 1992, by Peter Stevens. Critical essays include Peter Stevens, "Out of Silence and Across the Distance: The Poetry of Dorothy Livesay," *Queen's Quarterly* 4 (1969) and his "Dorothy Livesay: The Love Poetry," *Canadian Literature* (1971); Debbie Foulks, "Livesay's Two Seasons of Love," *Canadian Literature* 74 (1977); Lee B. Thompson, "A Coat of Many Cultures: The Poetry of Dorothy Livesay," *Journal of Popular Culture* 15 (1981); and Fiona Sparrow, "The Self-Completing Tree: Livesay's African Poetry," *Canadian Poetry* 20 (1987). A volume containing useful critical essays on Livesay's career and history is *A Public and Private Voice: Essays on the Life and Work of Dorothy Livesay*, 1986, ed. Lindsay Dorney, Gerland Noonan, and Paul Tuessen.

Audre Lorde
The most nearly complete collection of Lorde's poetry is *Undersong: Chosen Poems, Old and New* (1992), which contains new poems and revisions from the earlier *Chosen Poems, Old and New* (1982). Other volumes include *First Cities* (1968), *Cables to Rage* (1970), *New York Headshop and Museum* (1974), *Coal* (1976), *The Black Unicorn* (1978), *The Cancer Journal* (1980), *Zami: A New Spelling of My Name* (1982), *Our Dead behind Us* (1986), and *The Marvelous Arithmetics of Distance: Poems, 1987–1992* (1993). She also produced two collections of essays and speeches: *Sister Outsider* (1986), which includes the pamphlet *Uses of the Erotic: The Erotic as Power*, and *A Burst of Light* (1988). See also "Audre Lorde: A Special Section" *Callaloo* 14 (1991).

Karla Hammond has a useful interview with Lorde in *Denver Quarterly* 16 (1981); and there is another interview in *Black Women Writers at Work*, 1984, ed. Claudia Tate. An interesting critical essay on Lorde and Maya Angelou is R. G. Stepto, "The Phenomenal Woman and the Severed Daughter," *Parnassus* 8 (1980). Helpful critical articles are Jerome Brooks, "In the Name of the Father: The Poetry of Audre Lorde," and Joan Martins, "The Unicorn is Black: Audre Lorde in Retrospect," both in *Black Women Writers (1950–1980)*, 1984, ed.

Mari Evans; Gloria T. Hull, "Living on the Line: Audre Lorde and *Our Dead behind Us's*," in *Changing Our Words: Essays on Criticism, Theory, and Writing by Black Women*, 1989, ed. Cheryl Wall; Estella Lauter, "Re-Visioning Creativity: Audre Lorde's Refiguration of Eros as the Black Mother Within," *Writing the Woman Artist: Essays on Poetics, Politics, and Portraiture*, 1991, ed. Suzanne W. Jones; Anna Wilson, "Audre Lorde and the African American Tradition: When the Family Is Not Enough," in *New Lesbian Criticism: Literary and Cultural Readings*, 1992, ed. Sally Munt; Ruth Ginzburg, "Audre Lorde's (Nonessentialist) Lesbian Eros," *Hypatia* 7 (1992); and Erin G. Carlston, "Zami and the Politics of Plural Identity," in *Sexual Practice, Textual Theory: Lesbian Cultural Criticism*, 1993, ed. Susan J. Wolfe and Julia Penelope.

Amy Lowell

Lowell's *The Complete Poetical Works* was published in 1955. Harley F. MacNair edited *Florence Asycough and Amy Lowell: Correspondence of a Friendship*, 1945; and E. Claire Healey and Keith Cushman edited *The Letters of D. H. Lawrence and Amy Lowell, 1914–1925* in 1985. Valuable background can be found in Clemens David Heymann, *American Aristocracy: The Lives and Times of James Russell, Amy, and Robert Lowell*, 1980. Full-length studies and biographies include Damon S. Foster, *Amy Lowell*, 1935; F. Cudworth Flint, *Amy Lowell*, 1969; Glenn R. Ruihley, *The Thorn of a Rose: Amy Lowell Reconsidered* 1975; Jean Gould, *Amy: The Word of Amy Lowell and the Imagist Movement*, 1975; and Richard Benvenuto, *Amy Lowell*, 1985. An analysis of Lowell's relationship to the lesbian tradition is offered in Lillian Faderman, "Warding Off the Watch and Ward Society: Amy Lowell's Treatment of the Lesbian Theme," *Gay Books Bulletin* (1979). Other critical essays on Lowell include Kathleen Flanagan, "Ezra Pound and Amy Lowell: English Poetics in Renditions of Chinese Poetry," *Paideuma* 15 (1986); Cheryl Walker, "Women and Feminine Literary Traditions: Amy Lowell and the Androgynous Persona," in her *Masks Outrageous and Austere: Culture, Psyche, and Persona in Modern Women Poets*, 1992; and Andrew Thacker, "Amy Lowell and H. D.: The Other Imagists," *Women: A Cultural Review* 4 (1993).

Mina Loy

Loy's volumes of poetry include *Lunar Baedeker* (1923), *Lunar Baedeker and Time-Tables* (1958), *At the Door of the House* (1980), *Love Songs* (1981), *Virgins Plus Curtains* (1981), and *The Last Lunar Baedeker* (1982), a nearly complete collection of her poems

printed to honor the centennial of her birth and edited by Roger L. Conover. New in 1996 is *The Lost Lunar Boedeker*, ed. Roger L. Conover. Loy also published *Insel* (1991), a *roman a clef*, edited by Elizabeth Arnold and with an introduction by Roger L. Conover, and has a great many unpublished works in the Collection of American Literature at the Beinecke Rare Book and Manuscript Library of Yale University. A full-length critical study is Virginia Kouidis, *Mina Loy: American Modernist Poet* (1980), which also includes an extensive bibliography of Loy's published poetry, drama, and prose. Loy is also discussed in Linda Kinnahan, *Poetics of the Feminine: Authority and Literary Tradition in William Carlos Williams, Mina Loy, Denise Levertov, and Kathleen Fraser*, 1994. Useful critical articles are Constance Hunting, "The Morality of Mina Loy," *Sagetrieb* 2 (1983); Carolyn Burke, "The New Poetry and the New Woman: Mina Loy," in *Coming to Light: American Women Poets in the Twentieth Century*, 1985, ec. Diane Wood Middlebrook and Marilyn Yalom; Melita Schaum, " 'Moon-flowers out of Muck': Mina Loy and the Female Autobiographical Epic," *Massachusetts Studies in English* 10 (1986); and Rachel Blau DuPlessis, " 'Seismic Orgasm': Sexual Intercourse, Gender Narratives, and Lyric Ideology in Mina Loy," in *Studies in Historical Change*, 1992, ed. Ralph Cohen.

Delarivier Manley

Manley's publications include the plays *The Lost Lover, or, the Jealous Husband* (1696), *The Royal Mischief* (1696), *Almyna; or, The Arabian Vow* (1707), *Lucius, the First Christian King of Britain* (1717); the political work *Memoirs of Europe* (1710), the satire *The Secret History of Queen Zarah and the Zarazians* (1705); and the two-volume work *Secret Memoirs and Manners of Several Persons of Quality of Both Sexes, from the New Atalantis, an Island in the Mediterranean* (1709), also known as *The New Atalantis*. A new edition was issued in 1991. Her fictional autobiography, *The Adventures of Rivella; or, The History of the Author of the "Atalantis"* (1714), was reissued as *Memoirs of the Life of Mrs. Manley* (1725). More recently, Fidelis Morgan edited *A Woman of No Character: An Autobiography of Mrs. Manley*, 1986. There is also a collection of correspondence, *Letters Written by Mrs. Manley* (1696), reissued as *A Stagecoach Journey to Exeter* (1725).

Two early essays on Manley are both by P. B. Anderson: "Mistress . . . Manley's Biography," *Modern Philology* 33 (1936), and "Delariviere Manley's Prose Fiction," *Philological Quarterly* 13 (1934). Manley is also discussed in Constance Clark, *Three Augustan Women*

Playwrights, 1986; and Ros Ballaster, *Seductive Forms: Women's Amatory Fiction, 1684–1740*, 1992. Also useful is *The Novels of Mary Delariviere Manley, 1705–1714*, 1971, ed. P. Köster.

Katherine Mansfield
Mansfield's stories appear in a complete one-volume edition, *The Short Stories of Katherine Mansfield*, 1937. Her *Journal*, 1954, was edited by J. Middleton Murry; and *Letters and Journals of Katherine Mansfield: A Selection*, 1977, was edited by C. K. Stead. *The Collected Letters of Katherine Mansfield* was edited in three volumes by Vincent O'Sullivan and Margaret Scott in 1984; vol. 1 covers 1903–17; vol. 2, 1918–19; and vol. 3, 1919–20.

Biographies, memoirs, and critical studies include S. Berkman, *Katherine Mansfield, a Critical Study*, 1951; Leslie Moore, *Katherine Mansfield*, 1971; John Carswell, *Lives and Letters*, 1978; Jeffrey Meyers, *Katherine Mansfield: A Biography*, 1978; Anthony Alpers, *The Life of Katherine Mansfield*, 1980; James Moore, *Gurdjieff and Mansfield*, 1980; Andrew Gurr, *Writers in Exile: The Identity of Home in Modern Literature*, 1981; Clare Hanson and Andrew Gurr, *Katherine Mansfield*, 1981; Nora Crone, *A Portrait of Katherine Mansfield*, 1985; Gillian Boddy, *Katherine Mansfield: The Woman and the Writer*, 1988; Jane Phillmore, *Katherine Mansfield*, 1989; Heather Murray, *Double Lives: Women in the Stories of Katherine Mansfield*, 1990; and Janet Sydney Kaplan, *Katherine Mansfield and the Origins of Modernist Fiction*, 1991. Mary Burgan, *Illness, Gender, and Writing: The Case of Katherine Mansfield*, 1994, is an important contribution. A recent collection of essays is *Critical Essays on Katherine Mansfield*, 1993, ed. Rhoda B. Nathan. For a useful resource, see Brownlee Jean Kirkpatrick, *A Bibliography of Katherine Mansfield*, 1989.

Paule Marshall
Marshall's novels are *Brown Girl, Brownstones* (1959), *The Chosen Place, the Timeless People* (1969), *Praisesong for the Widow* (1983), and *Daughters* (1991). Her novella *Merle*, as well as her short stories "The Valley Between," "Brooklyn," "Barbados," and "To Da-duh, in Memoriam," were originally collected in *Reena and Other Stories* (1983) and later reprinted as *Merle: A Novella and Other Stories* (1985). Another collection of short stories, *Soul Clap Hands and Sing* (1961), was reprinted in 1987. Marshall also authored a teleplay based on her novel *Brown Girl, Brownstones*.

A useful essay is Barbara Christian, "Sculpture and Space: The Interdependency of Character and Culture in the Novels of Paule Marshall," in *Black Women Novelists: The De-velopment of a Tradition, 1892–1976*, 1980. Other useful references are Harihar Kulkarni, "Paule Marshall: A Bibliography," *Callaloo* 16 (1993), and Darly Cumber Dance, "An Interview with Paule Marshall," *Southern Review* 28 (1992).

Bobbie Ann Mason
Mason's works of fiction are *Shiloh and Other Stories* (1982), *In Country* (1985), *Spence & Lila* (1988), *Love Life: Stories* (1989), and *Feather Crowns* (1993). She has also published a critical work, *Nabokov's Garden: A Guide to "Ada"* (1974), and a useful reference book, *The Girl Sleuth: A Feminist Guide* (1975). An interesting interview is Bonnie Lyons and Bill Oliver, "An Interview with Bobbie Ann Mason," *Contemporary Literature* 32 (1991). Helpful essays are Albert E. Wilhelm, "Making Over or Making Off: The Problem of Identity in Bobbie Ann Mason's Short Fiction," *Southern Literary Journal* 18 (1986); Robert H. Brinkmeyer Jr., "Finding One's History: Bobbie Ann Mason and Contemporary Southern Literature," *Southern Literary Journal* 19 (1987); Leslie White, "The Function of Popular Culture in Bobbie Ann Mason's *Shiloh and Other Stories* and *In Country*," *Southern Quarterly* 26 (1988); and Barbara Henning, "Minimalism and the American Dream: 'Shiloh' by Bobbie Ann Mason and 'Preservation' by Raymond Carver," *Modern Fiction Studies* 35 (1989).

Mary McCarthy
McCarthy published two collections of stories, *The Company She Keeps* (1942) and *Cast a Cold Eye* (1950). Her novels are *The Oasis* (1948), *The Groves of Academe* (1952), *A Charmed Life* (1955), *The Group* (1963), *Birds of America* (1971), and *Cannibals and Missionaries* (1979). Her autobiographical *Memories of a Catholic Girlhood* appeared in 1957. *On the Contrary* (1961) and *The Writings on the Wall* (1970) are collections of essays on literary and cultural topics. Travel books are *Venice Observed* (1956) and *The Stones of Florence* (1959). Her essays on Vietnam and the Watergate hearings are collected in *The Seventeenth Degree* (1974). *Sights and Spectacles* (1956) has been republished and enlarged as *Mary McCarthy's Theater Chronicles, 1937–1962* (1963). *Intellectual Memoirs: New York, 1936–1938*, with a foreword by Elizabeth Hardwick, was published in 1992.

Critical and biographical writings about her include Doris Grumbach, *The Company She Kept*, 1967; Irwin Stock, *Mary McCarthy*, 1967; Willena S. Hardy, *Mary McCarthy*, 1981; Carol Gelderman, *Mary McCarthy: A Life*, 1988; and Carol Brightman, *Writing Dangerously: A Critical Biography of Mary McCarthy*, 1992. Useful essays include Elizabeth Hardwick's

chapter in *A View of My Own*, 1963; and Rosalie Hewitt, "A 'Home Address for the Self': Mary McCarthy's Autobiographical Journey," *Journal of Narrative Technique* 12 (1982). Carol Gelderman edited *Conversations with Mary McCarthy*, 1991. Joy Bennett and Gabriella Hochmann have compiled *Mary McCarthy: An Annotated Bibliography*, 1992.

Carson McCullers

McCullers's works are *The Heart is a Lonely Hunter* (1940), *Reflections in a Golden Eye* (1941), *The Member of the Wedding* (1946), *The Ballad of the Sad Cafe* (1951), *The Square Root of Wonderful* (1958), *Clock without Hands* (1961), *Sweet as a Pickle and Clean as a Pig: Poems* (1964), and *The Mortgaged Heart*, 1971, ed. M. G. Smith. Her *Collected Works* appeared in 1987. There are two biographies: Virginia S. Carr, *The Lonely Hunter: A Biography of Carson McCullers*, 1975, and Richard Cook, *Carson McCullers*, 1975.

Critical studies include Oliver Evans, *The Ballad of Carson McCullers*, 1966; Margaret McDowell, *Carson McCullers*, 1980; and Virginia Spencer Carr, *Understanding Carson McCullers*, 1990. Harold Bloom edited an essay collection, *Carson McCullers*, in 1986. Among critical essays are Patricia S. Box, "Androgyny and the Musical Vision: A Study of Two Novels by Carson McCullers," *Southern Quarterly* 16 (1978); Louise Westling, "Carson McCullers's Amazon Nightmare," *Modern Fiction Studies* 28 (1982), and chapter 2 of *The War of the Words*, 1987, by Sandra M. Gilbert and Susan Gubar. A valuable annotated bibliography, *Carson McCullers*, comp. Adrian Shapiro, Jackson Bryer, and Kathleen Field, appeared in 1980.

Charlotte Mew

Two volumes of Mew's collected work have been produced since her death. *Collected Poems of Charlotte Mew*, 1953, with a memoir by Alida Monro; and *Collected Poems and Prose*, 1981, ed. and with a critical introduction and helpful critical bibliography by Val Warner. *Charlotte Mew and Her Friends* 1988, by Penelope Fitzgerald, contains a selection of poems and useful biographical information. Two of the few critical pieces on Mew are Val Warner, "Mary Magdalene and the Bride The Work of Charlotte Mew," *Poetry Nation* 4 (1975); and Linda Mizejewski, "Charlotte Mew and the Unrepentant Magdalene: A Myth in Transition," *Texas Studies in Literature and Language* 26 (1984).

Alice Meynell

Meynell's collected poems appear in *The Poems of Alice Meynell* (1923). *Alice Meynell, Prose and Poetry*, 1947, is a centenary volume edited by Frederick Page, with a biographical and critical introduction by Vita Sackville-West. A centenary collection of her essays, with an introduction by Sir Francis Meynell, was reprinted in 1970. Another selection of her essays, edited and introduced by P. M. Fraser, is *The Wares of Autolycus*, 1965.

For useful biographical information, see Viola Meynell, *Alice Meynell: A Memoir*, 1929; and June Badeni, *The Slender Tree: A Life of Alice Meynell*, 1981. A feminist approach is represented by Beverly Ann Schlack, "The 'Poetess of Poets': Alice Meynell Rediscovered," *Women's Studies* 7 (1980). Recent critical studies include John S. Anson, "'The Wind Is Blind': Power and Constraint in the Poetry of Alice Meynell," *Studia Mystica* 9 (1986); Shelly J. Crisp, "Meynell's 'The Return to Nature': Histories of Modern Poetry," *The Explicator* 50 (1991); and Sharon Smulders, "Feminism, Pacifism, and the Ethics of War: The Politics and Poetics of Alice Meynell's War Verse," *English Literature in Transition* 36 (1993). See also Angela Leighton's chapter on Meynell in her *Victorian Women Poets: Writing against the Heart*, 1992.

Edna St. Vincent Millay

Millay's *Collected Sonnets* (1941) and *Collected Lyrics* (1943) were followed by *Collected Poems: Edna St. Vincent Millay*, 1956, ed. Norma Millay. A revised and expanded version of the *Collected Sonnets* appeared in 1988, and Colin Falck edited *Selected Poems: The Centenary Edition* in 1991. Her prose sketches, *Distressing Dialogues*, published under the pseudonym Nancy Boyd, appeared in 1924. Her three verse plays—*Aria da Capo* (1920), *The Lamp and the Bell* (1921), *Two Slatterns and a King* (1921)—were collected in *Three Plays* (1926).

Allan Ross Macdougall edited *Letters of Edna St. Vincent Millay* in 1952. Biographical studies are Joan Dash, *A Life of One's Own: Three Gifted Women and the Men They Married*, 1973, and Anne Cheney, *Millay in Greenwich Village*, 1975. Fuller treatments are Miriam Gurko, *Restless Spirit*, 1957; and Jean Gould, *The Poet and Her Book*, 1969. Useful brief introductions are Norman A. Brittin, *Edna St. Vincent Millay*, 1967; James Gray, *Edna St. Vincent Millay*, 1967; and Norman A. Brittin, *Edna St. Vincent Millay*, 1982. Biographical information can also be found in William Drake, *The First Wave: Women Poets in America, 1915–1945*, 1987. A helpful collection of critical essays is *Critical Essays on Edna St. Vincent Millay*, 1993, ed. William B. Thesing. Other critical studies include Debra Fried, "Andromeda Unbound: Gender and Genre in Millay's Sonnets," *Twentieth-Century Literature* 32 (1986); Suzanne Clark, "The Unwarranted

Discourse: Sentimental Community, Modernist Women, and the Case of Millay," *Genre* 20 (1987); and Jean Gould, "Edna St. Vincent Millay: Saint of the Modern Sonnet," in *Faith of a (Woman) Writer*, 1988, ed. Alice Kressler Harris and William McBrien. In addition, see the discussions of Millay in Jan Montefiore, *Feminism and Poetry: Language, Experience, Identity in Women's Writing*, 1987; Clark, *Sentimental Modernism: Women Writers and the Revolution of the Word*, 1991; Susan M. Schweik, *A Gulf So Deeply Cut: American Women Poets and the Second World War*, 1991; Cheryl Walker, *Masks Outrageous and Austere: Culture, Psyche, and Persona in Modern Women Poets*, 1991; and Sandra M. Gilbert and Susan Gubar, *Letters from the Front*, 1994. A feminist approach is represented in Jane Stanbrough, "Edna St. Vincent Millay and the Language of Vulnerability," in *Shakespeare's Sisters*, 1979, ed. Sandra Gilbert and Susan Gubar. Karl Yost, *A Bibliography of the Works of Edna St. Vincent Millay*, appeared in 1973, and Judith Nierman, *Edna St. Vincent Millay: A Reference Guide*, in 1977.

Lady Mary Wortley Montagu

Lord J. S. W. Wharncliffe, Montagu's great grandson, edited *The Letters and Works of Lady Mary Wortley Montagu*, 1837. A modern edition of the *Complete Letters* is edited by Robert Halsband, 1965, who also edited Montagu's *The Nonsense of Common Sense*, 1947, and, with Isobel Grundy, *Essays and Poems of Lady Mary Wortley Montagu*, 1977. A new edition of *Letters* was published by Everyman's Library in 1992, and *Turkish Embassy Letters* appeared in 1993, edited by Malcolm Jack, and with an introduction by Anita Desai. Halsband also wrote a definitive biography, *The Life of Lady Mary Wortley Montagu*, 1956; and Cynthia Lowenthal has recently published a useful full-length study, *Lady Mary Wortley Montagu and the Eighteenth-Century Familiar Letter*, 1994. Critical articles include two by Grundy: "The Politics of Female Authorship: Lady Mary Wortley Montagu's Reaction to the Printing of Her Poems," *The Book Collector* (1982), and " 'Trash, Trumpery, and Idle Time': Lady Mary Wortley Montagu and Fiction," *Eighteenth-Century Fiction* 5 (1993); Jill Rubenstein, "Women's Biography as a Family Affair: Lady Louisa Stuart's 'Biographical Anecdotes' of Lady Wortley Montagu," *Prose Studies: History, Theory, Criticism* 9 (1986); Lowenthal, "The Veil of Romance: Lady Mary's Embassy Letters," *Eighteenth-Century Life* 14 (1990); and Cynthia Wall, "Editing Desire: Pope's Correspondence with (and without) Lady Mary," *Philological Quarterly* 71 (1992).

Marianne Moore

No collection of Moore's verse is definitive because each excluded some earlier poems while offering extensive revisions of others. Her separate volumes include *Poems* (1921), *Observations* (1924), *The Pangolin, and Other Verse* (1936), *What Are Years?* (1941), *Nevertheless* (1944), *Like a Bulwark* (1956), *O to Be a Dragon* (1959), and *Tell Me, Tell Me* (1966). Collections include *Selected Poems* (1935); *Collected Poems* (1951); and *The Complete Poems of Marianne Moore* (1967), which also offers selections from her translation of *The Fables of La Fontaine* (1954). In addition, she translated Adalbert Stifter's *Rock Crystal: A Christmas Tale* (1945); and a collection of her critical essays, *Predilections*, appeared in 1955. Patricia C. Willis edited *The Complete Prose of Marianne Moore* in 1986.

A recent biography is Charles Molesworth, *Marianne Moore: A Literary Life*, 1990. Four important and perceptive essays on Moore are by poet-critics: T. S. Eliot's introduction to Moore's *Selected Poems*; R. P. Blackmur, "The Method of Marianne Moore," in *The Double Agent*, 1935; Kenneth Burke, "Motives and Motifs in the Poetry of Marianne Moore," reprinted in *A Grammar of Motives*, 1945; and Randall Jarrell, "Thoughts about Marianne Moore," reprinted in *Poetry and the Age*, 1953. Hugh Kenner, "Disliking It," is in *A Homemade World: The American Modernist Writers*, 1975. Book-length studies include Bernard F. Engel, *Marianne Moore*, 1963; Jean Garrigue, *Marianne Moore*, 1965; George W. Nitchie, *Marianne Moore: An Introduction to the Poetry*, 1969; Donald Hall, *Marianne Moore: The Cage and the Animal*, 1970; Pamela W. Hadas, *Marianne Moore, Poet of Affection*, 1977; Laurence Stapleton, *Marianne Moore: The Poet's Advance*, 1978; Marie Borroff, *Language and the Poet: Verbal Artistry in Frost, Stevens, and Moore*, 1979; Bonnie Costello, *Marianne Moore: Imaginary Possessions*, 1981; Elizabeth Philips, *Marianne Moore*, 1982; Taffy Martin, *Marianne Moore: Subversive Modernist*, 1986; Grace Schulman, *Marianne Moore: The Poetry of Engagement*, 1986; John Slatin, *The Savage's Romance: The Poetry of Marianne Moore*, 1986; Margaret Holley, *The Poetry of Marianne Moore: A Study in Voice and Value*, 1987; Patricia C. Willis, *Marianne Moore: Vision into Verse*, 1987; and Celeste Goodridge, *Hints and Disguises: Marianne Moore and Her Contemporaries*, 1989. Two studies of Moore and Elizabeth Bishop are Jeredith Merrin, *An Enabling Humility: Marianne Moore, Elizabeth Bishop, and Two Uses of Tradition*, 1990; and Joanne Feit Diehl, *Elizabeth Bishop and Marianne Moore: The Psychodynamics of Creativity*, 1993. See also the discussions of

Moore in Alicia Ostriker, *Stealing the Language: The Emergence of Women's Poetry in America*, 1986; Lisa M. Steinman. *Made in America: Science, Technology, and American Modernist Poets*, 1987; Lynn Keller, *Re-Making It New: Contemporary American Poetry and the Modernist Tradition*. 1987; and Sandra M. Gilbert and Susan Gubar *Letters from the Front*, 1994. Essay collections are *Marianne Moore: The Art of a Modernist*, 1990, ed. Joseph Parisi; and *Marianne Moore: Woman and Poet*, 1990, ed. Patricia C Willis. Helpful, too, are Gary Lane, A *Concordance to the Poems of Marianne Moore*, 1972; Eugene P. Sheehy and Kenneth A. Lohf. *The Achievement of Marianne Moore: A Descriptive Bibliography*, 1977; and Craig S. Abbot. *Marianne Moore: A Reference Guide*, 1978.

Toni Morrison

Morrison's novels are *The Bluest Eyes* (1970), *Sula* (1973), *Song of Solomon* (1977), *Tar Baby* (1981), *Beloved* (1987), and *Jazz* (1992). Critical works by her include "Unspeakable Things Unspoken: The Afro-American Presence in American Literature," *Michigan Quarterly Review* 28 (1989), and *Playing in the Dark: Whiteness and Literary Imagination* (1992); she also edited and contributed the introductory essay to *Race-ing Justice, Engendering Power: Essays on Anita Hill, Clarence Thomas, and the Construction of Social Reality*, 1992, ed. Andrew Ross and Manning Marable. Morrison's *Lecture and Speech of Acceptance, Upon the Award of the Nobel Prize for Literature* was published in 1993. Three interesting interviews with Morrison are Robert B. Stepto, "'Intimate Things in Place': A Conversation with Toni Morrison," *Massachusetts Review* 18 (1977); Jane Bakerman, "The Seams Can't Show," *Black American Literature Forum* 12 (1978); and Bettye J. Parker, "Complexity Toni Morrison's Women: An Interview Essay," in *Sturdy Black Bridges: Visions of Black Women in Literature*, 1979, ed. Roseann Bell, Bettye Parker, and Beverly Guy-Sheftall.

Critical studies of Morrison include Karen F. C. Holloway and Stephanie A. Demetrakopoulos, *New Dimensions of Spirituality: The Novels of Toni Morrison*, 1987; *Critical Essays on Toni Morrison*, 1988, ed. Nellie McKay; Terry Otten, *The Crime of Innocence in the Fiction of Toni Morrison*, 1989; Wilfred D. Samuels and Clenora Hudson-Weems, *Toni Morrison*, 1990; *Toni Morrison: Modern Critical Views*, 1990, ed. Harold Bloom; Trudier Harris, *Fiction and Folklore: The Novels of Toni Morrison*, 1991; and Denise Heinze, *The Dilemma of "Double Consciousness": Toni Morrison's Novels*, 1993. *Callaloo* 13 (1990) is a special issue devoted to Toni Morrison. A useful bibliography is David L. Middleton, *Toni Morrison: An Annotated Bibliography*, 1987.

Bharati Mukherjee

Mukherjee's works include *The Tiger's Daughter* (1971), *Wife* (1975), *Darkness* (1985), *The Middleman and Other Stories* (1988), *Jasmine* (1989), and *The Holder of the World* (1993). *Days and Nights in Calcutta* (1977), with Clark Blaise, is an account of her time in India. A valuable collection of essays is Emmanuel S Nelson, *Bharati Mukherjee: Critical Perspectives*, 1993. Three useful critical articles are Sudha Pandya, "Bharati Mukherjee's Darkness: Exploring the Hyphenated Identity," *Quill* 2 (1990); Carmen Wickramagamage. "Relocation as Positive Act: The Immigrant Experience in Bharati Mukherjee's Novels," *Diaspora* 2 (1992); and Gail Ching Liang Low, "In a Free State: Post-Colonialism and Postmodernism in Bharati Mukherjee's Fiction," *Women: A Cultural Review* 4 (1993).

Alice Munro

Munro's fiction includes both short stories and novels: *Dance of the Happy Shades* (1968), *Lives of Girls and Women* (1971), *Something I've Been Meaning to Tell You* (1974), *The Beggar Maid* (1982), *The Moons of Jupiter* (1983), *The Progress of Love* (1986), *Friend of My Youth* (1990), and *Open Secrets* (1994). Geoffry Hancock has an interesting interview with the author in *Canadian Fiction Magazine* 63 (1982). A biography is Catherine Sheldrick Ross, *Alice Munro: A Double Life*, 1992.

Useful critical essays are Miriam Packer. "*Lives of Girls and Women*: A Creative Search for Completion," in *The Canadian Novel: Here and Now*, 1978, ed. John Moss; Bronwen Wallace, "Women's Lives: Alice Munro," in *The Human Elements: Critical Essays*, 1978, ed David Helwig; Nancy J. Bailey, "The Masculine Image in *Lives of Girls and Women*," *Canadian Literature* 80 (1979); Marlene Goldman. "Penning the Bodies: The Construction of Gendered Subjects in Alice Munro's 'Boys and Girls,'" *Studies in Canadian Literature* 15 (1990); and Karen Smythe, "Sad Stories: The Ethics of Epiphany in Munrovian Elegy," *University of Toronto Quarterly* 60 (1991). Valuable full-length studies are Louis MacKendrick, ed., *Probable Fictions: Alice Munro's Narrative Acts*, 1983; Walter R. Martin, *Alice Munro: Paradox and Parallel*, 1987; Beverly Jean Rasporich, *Dance of the Sexes: Art and Sexuality in the Fiction of Alice Munro*, 1990; and Magdalene Redekop, *Mothers and Other Clowns: The Stories of Alice Munro*, 1992. A useful collection is *The Art of Alice Munro: Seizing the Unseizable*, 1984, ed. Judith Miller, which consists of essays from the Waterloo

conference. Helpful is J. R. Struthers, "Some Highly Subversive Activities: A Brief Polemic and a Checklist of Works on Alice Munro," *Studies in Canadian Literature* 6 (1981).

Florence Nightingale
Nightingale's available works include *Florence Nightingale in Rome: Letters Written by Florence Nightingale in Rome in the Winter of 1847–1848,* 1981, ed. Mary Keele; and *Cassandra,* which originally appeared in the appendices of Ray Strachey's *The Cause: A Short History of the Women's Movement in Great Britain,* 1928, which has been published separately by the Feminist Press, 1978, ed. Myra Stark, and which has been included in *Cassandra and Other Selections for Thought,* 1992 ed. Mary Poovey. Also available are *"I Have Done My Duty": Florence Nightingale in the Crimean War, 1854–58,* 1987, ed. Sue M. Goldie; *Notes on Hospitals. Florence Nightingale on Hospital Reform,* 1989, ed. Charles E. Rosenberg; *Ever Yours, Florence Nightingale: Selected Letters,* 1990, ed. Martha Vicinus and Bea Merngarrd; *Notes on Nursing: What It Is and What It Is Not,* 1992, ed. Barbara Stevens Barnum; and *Selections for Thought,* 1994, ed. Michael D. Calabria and Janet A. Macrae. Biographies include Sir Edward Tyas Cook, *The Life of Florence Nightingale,* 1913; Cecil Woodham-Smith, *Florence Nightingale, 1820–1910,* 1951; Elspeth Huxley, *Florence Nightingale,* 1975; and Monica E. Baly, *Florence Nightingale and the Nursing Legacy,* 1986, which is also a study of nursing in Great Britain.

Lytton Strachey wrote a famous essay on Nightingale in *Eminent Victorians,* 1918, and more recently she is discussed in George Pickering, *Creative Malady,* 1974, and in Mary Poovey, *Uneven Developments: The Ideological Work of Gender in Mid-Victorian England,* 1988. Two full-length studies are Nancy Boyd, *Josephine Butler, Octavia Hill, Florence Nightingale: Three Victorian Women Who Changed Their World,* 1982; and F. B. Smith, *Florence Nightingale: Reputation and Power,* 1982. A useful collection of essays is *Florence Nightingale and Her Era: A Collection of New Scholarship,* 1990, ed. Vern Bullough, Bonnie Bullough, and Marietta P. Stanton. A valuable feminist essay is Elaine Showalter, "Florence Nightingale's Feminist Complaint: Women, Religion, and Suggestions for Thought," *Signs* 6 (1981), and three recent interesting essays are George P. Landow, "Aggressive (Re)Interpretations of the Female Sage: Florence Nightingale's Cassandra", in *Victorian Sages and Cultural Discourse: Renegotiating Gender and Power,* 1990, ed. Thais E. Morgan 1990; Showalter, "Miranda and Cassandra: The Discourse of the Feminist Intellectual" in *Tradition and the Talents of Women,* 1991, ed. Florence Howe; and Katherine V. Snyder, "From Novel to Essay: Gender and Revision in Florence Nightingale's 'Cassandra,'" in *The Politics of the Essay: Feminist Perspectives,* 1993, ed. Ruth Ellen Boetcher Joeres and Elizabeth Mittman.

Anaïs Nin
Nin's famous *Diary* has been published in several volumes from 1966 to 1980, ed. and with an introduction by Gunther Stuhlmann. *Linotte,* 1978–82, her early diary, is also available; as are *Journal of a Wife: The Early Diary of Anaïs Nin, 1923–27,* 1984; and *Incest—from a Journal of Love: The Unexpurgated Diary of Anaïs Nin, 1932–1934,* 1991. The *Anaïs Nin Reader,* ed. Philip K. Jason, was published in 1973; and a collection of Nin's correspondence with Henry Miller, *A Literate Passion: Letters of Anaïs Nin and Henry Miller, 1932–1951,* appeared in 1987. Wendy M. DuBow's essay, "The Elusive Text: Reading 'The Diary of Anaïs Nin, Volume I, 1931–1934,'" *Anaïs: An International Journal* 11 (1993), includes previously unpublished material. Nin's many other works, both fiction and nonfiction, include *The Winter of Artifice* (1939), *Ladders to Fire* (1946), *On Writing* (1947), *The Four-Chambered Heart* (1950), *A Spy in the House of Love* (1954), and *Collages* (1964), as well as *Paris Revisited* (1972).

Several full-length books have been written about Nin, including Oliver Evans, *Anaïs Nin,* 1968; Valerie Harms, ed., *Celebration with Anaïs Nin,* 1973; Evelyn J. Hinz, *The Mirror and the Garden,* 1973, and her *The World of Anaïs Nin,* 1978; Bettina L. Knapp, *Anaïs Nin,* 1978; Benjamin Franklin and Duane Schneider, *Anaïs Nin: An Introduction,* 1979; Sharon Spencer, *Collage of Dreams: The Writings of Anaïs Nin,* 1981; Nöel Riley Fitch, *Anaïs: The Erotic Life of Anaïs Nin,* 1993; and the interesting Philip K. Jason, *Anaïs Nin and Her Critics,* 1993. There is also a quarterly, which began in 1970, called *Under the Sign of Pisces: Anaïs Nin and Her Circle.* The useful *Anaïs Nin: A Reference Guide* by Rose Marie Cutting, 1978, has been updated yearly by Richard R. Centing in *Under the Sign of Pisces* and *Seahorse.* Two interesting recent essays are Kate Millett, "Anaïs—A Mother to Us All: The Birth of the Artist as a Woman," *Anaïs: An International Journal* 9 (1991); and Karen Brennan, "Anaïs Nin: Author(iz)ing the Erotic Body," *Genders* 14 (1992). For a useful but somewhat dated summary of criticism see Evelyn J. Hinz, "Recent Nin Criticism: Who's on First," *Canadian Review of American Studies* 13 (1982).

Joyce Carol Oates
Oates's more than sixty published works in-

clude the novels *them* (1969), *Do with Me What You Will* (1973), *Unholy Loves* (1979), *Bellefleur* (1980), *A Bloodsmoor Romance* (1982), *Solstice* (1985), *Marya: A Life* (1986), *You Must Remember This* (1987), *American Appetites* (1989), *Black Water* (1992), and *What I Lived For* (1994); as well as such short story collections as *Upon the Sweeping Flood. and Other Stories* (1966), *Marriages and Infidelities* (1972), *The Goddess and Other Women* 1974), *Raven's Wing* (1987), *The Assignation* (1989), *Where Is Here?* (1992), and *Haunted: Tales of the Grotesque* (1994). Her volumes of poetry are *Women in Love, and Other Poems* (1968), *Women Whose Lives are Money* (1978), and *The Time Traveller Poems 1983–1989* (1989). Her critical essays include *Contraries* (1981), *The Profane Art: Essays and Reviews* (1983), and (Woman) Writer Occasions and Opportunities (1988). Lee Milazzo edited *Conversations with Joyce Carol Oates* in 1989. Full-length studies include Mary K. Grant, *The Tragic Vision of Joyce Carol Oates,* 1978; Joanne V. Creighton, *Joyce Carol Oates,* 1979; Ellen G. Freidman, *Joyce Carol Oates,* 1980; Katherine Bastian, *Joyce Carol Oates's Short Stories: Between Tradition and Innovation,* 1983; Eileen T Bender, *Artist in Residence: The Phenomenon of Joyce Carol Oates,* 1987; Joanne V. Creighton, *Joyce Carol Oates: Novels of the Middle Years,* 1992; and Marilyn C. Wesley, *Refusal and Transgression in Joyce Carol Oates's Fiction,* 1993. Two useful collections of critical essays are *Critical Essays on Joyce Carol Oates,* 1979, ed. Linda W. Wagner; and *Joyce Carol Oates: Modern Critical Views,* 1986, ed. Harold Bloom. For feminist perspectives, see Elaine Showalter, "Joyce Carol Oates's 'The Dead' and Feminist Criticism," in *Faith of a (Woman) Writer,* 1988, ed. Alice Kessler-Harris and William McBrien; and Brenda O. Daly, "How Do We (Not) Become These People Who Victimize Us: Anxious Authorship in the Early Fiction of Joyce Carol Oates," in *Anxious Power: Reading, Writing, and Ambivalence in Narrative by Women,* 1993, ed. Carol J. Singley and Susan Elizabeth Sweeney. Three useful reference guides are Donald C. Dickson, "Joyce Carol Oates," *American Book Collector* 2 (1981); and two by Anne Hierstra, 'A Bibliography of Writings about Oates" and "A Bibliography of Writings by Oates," in *American Women Writing Fiction: Memory, Identity, Family, Space,* 1989, ed. Mickey Pearlman.

Edna O'Brien

O'Brien' works include the trilogy *The Country Girls* (1960), *The Lonely Girl* (1962), and *Girl in Their Married Bliss* (1964), as well as *A Pagan Place: A Play* (1973), *Mrs. Reinhart and Other Stories* (1980), and *James and Nora:*

A Portrait of Joyce's Marriage (1981). Her recent works of fiction include the novels *The High Road* (1988), *Time and Tide* (1992), and *House of Splendid Isolation* (1994); and the short story collections *A Fanatic Heart: Selected Stories* (1984) and *Lantern Slides* (1990). Her early trilogy was collected as *The Country Girls Trilogy and Epilogue* (1986). She has also written a play about Virginia Woolf, *Virginia* (1981). Critical articles about her work include Raymonde Popot, "Edna O'Brien's Paradise Lost," *Cahiers Irlandais* 4–5 (1976); Lotus Snow, "'That Trenchant Childhood Route?': Quest in Edna O'Brien's Novels," *Eire* 14 (1979); Darcy O'Brien, "Edna O'Brien: A Kind of Irish Childhood," in *Twentieth-Century Women Novelists,* 1982, ed. Thomas Staley; Lynette Carpenter, "Tragedies of Rembrance, Comedies of Endurance: The Novels of Edna O'Brien" in *Essays on the Contemporary British Novel,* 1986, ed Hedwig Bock and Albert Wertheim; Peggy O'Brien, "The Silly and the Serious: An Assessment of Edna O'Brien," *Massachusetts Review* 28 (1987); Tasmin Hargreaves, "Women's Consciousness and Identity in Four Irish Women Novelists," in *Cultural Contexts and Literary Idioms in Contemporary Irish Literature,* 1988, ed. Michael Kenneally; and Kiera O'Hara, "Love Objects: Love and Obsession in the Stories of Edna O'Brien," *Studies in Short Fiction* 30 (1993).

Flannery O'Connor

O'Connor's novels are *Wise Blood* (1952) and *The Violent Bear It Away* (1960). Two collections of stories—*A Good Man Is Hard to Find* (1955) and *Everything That Rises Must Converge* (1965)—are included with earlier, previously uncollected stories in *Complete Stories,* 1971. Her letters are collected in *The Habit of Being: The Letters of Flannery O'Connor,* 1979. A collection of O'Connor's nonfictional prose is *Mystery and Manners,* 1969, ed. Sally and Robert Fitzgerald, and a collection of her book reviews, *The Presence of Grace,* 1983, was compiled by Leo J. Zuber and ed. with an introduction by Carter W. Martin. Her *Collected Works* appeared in 1988, and Stephen G. Driggers edited *The Manuscripts of Flannery O'Connor at Georgia College* in 1989.

Robert Fitzgerald's memoir, prefaced to *Everything That Rises Must Converge,* offers a portrait of the artist. Other biographical material can be found in Robert Coles, *Flannery O'Connor's South,* 1980; Barbara McKenzie, *Flannery O'Connor's Georgia,* 1980; Lorine M. Getz, *Flannery O'Connor: Her Life, Library and Book Reviews,* 1950; and Marion Montgomery, *Why Flannery O'Connor Stayed Home,* 1981. *Conversations with Flannery O'Connor,* ed Rosemary Magee, appeared in 1987.

Full-length studies of O'Connor's fiction include Carol Schloss, *Flannery O'Connor's Dark Comedies: The Limits of Inference*, 1980; James M. Grimshaw Jr., *The Flannery O'Connor Companion*, 1981; Kathleen Feeley, *Flannery O'Connor: Voice of the Peacock*, 2nd ed. 1982; Frederick Asals, *Flannery O'Connor, the Imagination of Extremity*, 1982; Edward Kessler, *Flannery O'Connor and the Language of Apocalypse*, 1986; Suzanne Morrow Paulson, *Flannery O'Connor: A Study of the Short Fiction*, 1988; and Robert H. Brinkmeyer, *The Art and Vision of Flannery O'Connor*, 1989. Collections of essays are *The Added Dimension: The Art and Mind of Flannery O'Connor*, 1966, ed. M. J. Freedman and L. A. Lawson; and *Critical Essays on Flannery O'Connor*, 1985, ed. Melvin J. Friedman and Beverly Lyon Clark. *Flannery O'Connor: A Descriptive Bibliography*, 1980, by David R. Farmer, is very helpful.

Sharon Olds
As well as having published extensively in poetry magazines, Olds has composed several volumes of poetry, including *Satan Says* (1980), *The Dead and the Living* (1984), *The Gold Cell* (1987), *The Matter of This World: New and Selected Poems* (1987), *The Sign of Saturn: Poems, 1980–1987* (1991), and *The Father* (1992). For an essay from a feminist perspective, see Suzanne Matson, "Talking to Our Father: The Political and Mythical Appropriations of Adrienne Rich and Sharon Olds," *The American Poetry Review* 18 (1989). Two other useful essays are Brian Dillon, " 'Never Having Had You, I Cannot Let You Go': Sharon Olds' Poems of a Father-Daughter Relationship," *The Literary Review* 37 (1993); and Calvin Bedient, "Sentencing Eros," *Salmagundi* 97 (1993), both of which discuss Olds's portrayal of fathers.

Tillie Olsen
Olsen's works are *Tell Me a Riddle* (1961), *Yonnondio: From the Thirties* (1974), and *Silences* (1978). Virago has recently issued an edition of *Tell Me a Riddle and Yonnondio* (1990). Olsen has also edited *Mother to Daughter, Daughter to Mother: A Daybook and Reader* (1984) and *Mothers and Daughters: That Special Quality* (1987), a collection of photographs and remembrances, including Olsen's tribute to her mother, "Dream Vision." Critical essays include Deborah Rosenfelt, "From the Thirties: Tillie Olsen and the Radical Tradition," *Feminist Studies* 7 (1981); Joanne S. Frye, " 'I Stand Here Ironing': Motherhood as Experience and Metaphor," *Studies in Short Fiction* 18 (1981); and Erika Duncan, "Coming of Age in the Thirties: A Portrait of Tillie Olsen," *Book Forum* 6 (1982). Four recent useful full-length studies are

Elaine Neil Orr, *Tillie Olsen and a Feminist Spiritual Vision*, 1987; Mickey Pearlman and Abby H. P. Werlock, *Tillie Olsen*, 1991; Mara Faulkner, *Protest and Possibility in the Writing of Tillie Olsen*, 1993; and Kay Hoyle Nelson and Nancy Huse, *The Critical Response to Tillie Olsen*, 1994.

Cynthia Ozick
Ozick's works of fiction include *Trust* (1966), *The Pagan Rabbi and Other Stories* (1971), *Bloodshed and Three Novellas* (1976), *Levitation: Five Fictions* (1982), *The Cannibal Galaxy* (1983), *The Messiah of Stockholm* (1987), and *The Shawl* (1989). She is also the author of three collections of essays, *Art and Ardor* (1983), *Metaphor and Memory* (1989), and *What Henry James Knew and Other Essays on Writers* (1993). Critical work includes Harold Bloom, ed., *Cynthia Ozick*, 1986; Sanford Pinsker, *The Uncompromising Fictions of Cynthia Ozick*, 1987; Joseph Lowin, *Cynthia Ozick*, 1988; Lawrence S. Friedman, *Understanding Cynthia Ozick*, 1991; Norman Finkelstein, *The Ritual of New Creation: Jewish Tradition and Contemporary Literature*, 1992; Elaine M. Kaurar, *Cynthia Ozick's Fiction: Tradition and Invention*, 1993; Sarah Blacher Cohen, *Cynthia Ozick's Comic Art: From Levity to Liturgy*, 1994; and Victor H. Strandberg, *Greek Mind/Jewish Soul: The Conflicted Art of Cynthia Ozick*, 1994. Some valuable critical articles are B. Scrafford, "Nature's Silent Scream: A Commentary on Cynthia Ozick, 'The Shawl,' " *Critique—Studies in Contemporary Fiction* 31 (1989); Pinsker, "Jewish-American Literature's Lost and Found Department—How Philip Roth and Cynthia Ozick Reimagine Their Significant Dead," *Modern Fiction Studies* 35 (1989); M. Krupnick, "Cynthia Ozick as the Jewish T. S. Eliot," *Soundings* 74 (1991); A. F. Wilner, "The Jewish-American Woman as Artist: Cynthia Ozick and the Paleface Tradition," *College Literature* 20 (1993); A. Gordon, " 'The Shawl,' and Transitional Objects," *Literature and Psychology* 40 (1994); and A. Lakrits, "Cynthia Ozick at the End of the Modern," *Chicago Review* 40 (1994).

Grace Paley
The Collected Stories, published in 1994, includes Paley's two short story collections, *The Little Disturbances of Man* (1959) and *Enormous Changes at the Last Minute* (1974). *New and Collected Poems* was published in 1992. *Long Walks and Intimate Talks*, which includes poems and stories by Paley and paintings by Vera B. Williams, was published by the Feminist Press in 1991. Critical and biographical studies of Paley include Neil David Isaacs, *Grace Paley: A Study of the Short Fiction*, 1990;

Jacqueline Taylor, *Grace Paley: Illuminating the Dark Lives*, 1990; and Judith Arcana, *Grace Paley's Life Stories: A Literary Biography*, 1993. The May 1982 issue of *Delta*, ed. Kathleen Hulley, is devoted to Grace Paley and includes Hulley's interview with the writer. Other essays on this writer's work include Blanche Gelfant, "Grace Paley: Fragments for a Portrait in Collage," *New England Review* 3 (1980); John W. Crawford, "Archetypal Patterns in Grace Paley's 'Runner,'" *Notes on Contemporary Literature* 11 (1981); and Marianne DeKoven, "Mrs. Hegel-Shtein's Tears," *Partisan Review* 48 (1981).

Dorothy Parker

The Penguin Dorothy Parker, 1977, contains fiction, poetry, criticism, and journalism. Other collections include *Collected Stories of Dorothy Parker*, 1942; *Collected Poetry of Dorothy Parker*, 1944; *The Portable Dorothy Parker*, 1944; and most recently, *The Sayings of Dorothy Parker*, 1992, ed. S. T. Brownlow. Her *Constant Reader*, a collection of critical pieces, appeared in 1970.

Biographies include John Keats, *You Might as Well Live: The Life and Times of Dorothy Parker*, 1970; Arthur F. Kinney, *Dorothy Parker*, 1978; Leslie Fewin, *The Late Mrs. Dorothy Parker*, 1986; and Marion Meade, *Dorothy Parker: What Fresh Hell Is This?*, 1988. Randall Calhoun's *Dorothy Parker: A Bio-Bibliography*, 1993, is a valuable resource. Feminist approaches to Parker's work are taken in Suzanne L. Bunkers, " 'I Am Outraged Womanhood': Dorothy Parker as Feminist and Social Critic," *Regionalism and the Female Imagination* 4 (1978); and Paula Treichler, "Verbal Subversions in Dorothy Parker: 'Trapped Like a Trap in a Trap,'" *Language and Style* 13 (1980). A recent interesting article is Nina Miller. "Making Love Modern: Dorothy Parker and Her Public," *American Literature* 64 (1992).

Katherine Philips

Philips's poems appear in *Poems by the Most Deservedly Admired Mrs. Katherine Philips, the Matchless Orinda* (1669); *Selected Poems*, 1904–05, ed. L. I. Guiney; *Minor Poets of the Caroline Period*, vol. 1, 1905, ed. George Saintsbury. The definitive *Collected Works of Katherine Philips, the "Matchless Orinda"* appeared in 1990; Patrick Thomas edited vols. 1 and 2 (poems and letters), and G. Greer and R. Little edited vol. 3 (translations). A facsimile edition of *Poems* (1667) was published in 1992. A full-length study is Philip Webster Sower, *The Matchless Orinda*, 1931, but Philips is also included in Louisa Costello, *Memoirs of Eminent Englishwomen*, 1844. More recent discussions are Lucy Brashear, "The Forgotten Legacy of the 'Matchless Orinda,' " *Anglo-Welsh Review* 65; Catherine Cole Mambretti,

" 'Fugitive Papers': A New Orinda Poem and Problems in Her Canon," *Papers of the Bibliographical Society of America* 71; and Fidelis Morgan, *The Female Wits*, 1981. Three critical essays by Claudia A. Limbert include important biographical information: "Two Poems and a Prose Receipt: The Unpublished Juvenilia of Katherine Philips," *ELR* 16 (1986); "Katherine Philips: Controlling a Life and Reputation," *South Atlantic Review* 56 (1991); and " 'The Unison of Well-Tun'd Hearts': Katherine Philips' Friendships with Male Writers," *English Language Notes* 29 (1991). Also of interest are Elizabeth H. Hagerman, "Katherine Philips: The Matchless Orinda," in *Women Writers of the Renaissance and Reformation*, 1987, ed. Katharina M. Wilson; Harriette Andreadis, "The Sapphic Platonics of Katherine Philips, 1632–1664," *Signs* 15 (1989); Dorothy Mermin, "Women Becoming Poets: Katherine Philips, Aphra Behn, Anne Finch," *ELH* 57 (1990); Celia A. Easton, "Excusing the Breach of Nature's Laws: The Discourse of Denial and Disguise in Katherine Philips' Friendship Poetry," *Restoration* 14 (1990); and Arlene Stiebel, "Subversive Sexuality: Masking the Erotic in Poems by Katherine Philips and Aphra Behn," in *Renaissance Discourses of Desire*, 1993, ed. Claude J. Summers and Ted Larry Pebworth. See also the helpful discussion of Philips in Elaine Hobby, *Virtue of Necessity: English Women's Writing, 1646–1688*, 1988.

Ruth Pitter

Poems, 1926–1966 (1968) includes selections from *A Mad Lady's Garland* (1935), *A Trophy of Arms* (1936), *The Spirit Watchers* (1940), *The Rude Potato* (1941), *The Bridge* (1945), *Pitter on Cats* (1947), *Urania* (1951), *The Ermine* (1953), and *Still by Choice* (1966). *End of Drought* appeared in 1975. *A Heaven to Find* (1987) is a selection of previously unpublished poems and fragments gathered from the poet's notebooks, 1908–76. *Collected Poems*, with an introduction by the poet Elizabeth Jennings, appeared in 1990. Poems by Pitter appear in *The Faber Book of Twentieth-Century Women's Poetry*, 1987, ed. Fleur Adcock, and *The Things That Matter: An Anthology of Women's Spiritual Poetry*, 1990, ed. Julia Neuberger. An early critical work that contains material on Pitter is Rudolph Gilbert, *Four Living Poets*, 1944. *Ruth Pitter: Homage to a Poet*, 1969, ed. Arthur Russell, offers appreciative short essays and a biographical sketch.

Sylvia Plath

Plath's *The Collected Poems*—including *The Colossus and Other Poems* (1960) and *Ariel* (1965)—was edited by Ted Hughes in 1981. Plath's mother Aurelia Schober Plath, selected

and edited the useful *Letters Home: Correspondence, 1950–63*, 1975. Hughes, with Frances McCullough, edited *The Journals of Sylvia Plath*, 1982, and Hughes also edited *Johnny Panic and the Bible of Dreams, and Other Prose Writings*, 1978. Plath's novel, *The Bell Jar*, was published in 1963 and has appeared in several paperback editions.

Biographical studies include Linda Wagner-Martin, *Sylvia Plath: A Biography*, 1987; Anne Stevenson, *Bitter Fame: A Life of Sylvia Plath*, 1989; Paul Alexander, *Rough Magic: A Biography of Sylvia Plath*, 1991; Ronald Hayman, *The Death and Life of Sylvia Plath*, 1991; and Janet Malcolm, *The Silent Woman: Sylvia Plath and Ted Hughes*, 1993. Among full-length studies of Plath are two hostile but useful works: Edward Butscher, *Sylvia Plath: Method and Madness*, 1976, and David Holbrook, *Sylvia Plath: Poetry and Existence*, 1976. More positive are Eileen Aird, *Sylvia Plath: Her Life and Work*, 1975; Judith Kroll, *Chapters in a Mythology: The Poetry of Sylvia Plath*, 1976; Caroline King, *Sylvia Plath*, 1978; Jon Rosenblatt, *Sylvia Plath: The Poetry of Initiation*, 1979; Mary Lynn Broe, *Protean Poetic: The Poetry of Sylvia Plath*, 1980; Lynda K. Bundtzen, *Plath's Incarnations: Women and the Creative Process*, 1983; Other full-length critical works include Pamela J. Annas, *A Disturbance of Mirrors: The Poetry of Sylvia Plath*, 1988; Steven Gould Axelrod, *Sylvia Plath: The Wound and the Cure of Words*, 1990; Jacqueline Rose, *The Haunting of Sylvia Plath*, 1991; Toni Saldivar, *Sylvia Plath: Confessing the Fictive Self*, 1992; Susan R. Van Dyne, *Revising Life: Sylvia Plath's Ariel Poems*, 1993; and Nancy Duvall Hargrove, *The Journey toward Ariel: Sylvia Plath's Poems of 1956–1959*, 1994. See also the discussions of Plath in Alan Williamson, *Introspection and Contemporary Poetry*, 1984; Alan Sinfield, *Literature, Politics, and Culture in Postwar Britain*, 1989; Gayle Greene, *Changing the Story: Feminist Fiction and the Tradition*, 1991; and Sandra M. Gilbert and Susan Gubar, *Letters from the Front*, 1994. Two helpful collections of essays are *Ariel Ascending: Writings about Sylvia Plath*, 1985, ed. Paul Alexander; and *Sylvia Plath: Modern Critical Views*, 1989, ed. Harold Bloom;

Further biographical and critical material can be found in Margaret D. Uroff, *Sylvia Plath and Ted Hughes*, 1979. In addition, a number of informative essays appear in *The Art of Sylvia Plath*, 1970, ed. Charles Newman; *Sylvia Plath: New Views on the Poetry*, 1979, ed. Gary Lane; and *Critical Essays on Sylvia Plath*, 1984, ed. Linda W. Wagner. Linda Wagner edited *Sylvia Plath: The Critical Heritage* in 1988. Useful reference guides are Richard Matovitch, *A Concordance to the Collected Poems of Sylvia*

Plath, 1986; and two bibliographies: Stephen Tabor, *Sylvia Plath: An Analytical Bibliography*, 1987; and Sheryl L. Meyering, *Sylvia Plath: A Reference Guide, 1973–1988*, 1990.

Katherine Anne Porter

Porter's publications include volumes of short stories—*Flowering Judas* (1930), *Noon Wine* (1937), *Pale Horse, Pale Rider* (1939), and *The Leaning Tower, and Other Stories* (1944)—as well as the novel *Ship of Fools* (1962). Her *Collected Stories* appeared in 1965, and her *Collected Essays* in 1970. In 1993 Virginia Spencer Carr edited *Flowering Judas* for the series Women Writers: Texts and Contexts. The collection *Letters of Katherine Anne Porter*, ed. Isabel Bayley, appeared in 1990; and *This Strange Old World and Other Book Reviews by Katherine Anne Porter*, ed. Darlene Harbour Unrue, was published in 1991. A useful biography is Joan Givner, *Katherine Anne Porter: A Life*, 1982; but other biographical information can be found in Enrique Hank Lopez, *Conversations with Katherine Anne Porter, Refugee from Indian Creek*, 1981. An interview with Porter by George Plimpton appeared in the *Paris Review Interviews*, 1963.

For surveys of her career and writings, relevant texts include Harry J. Mooney, *The Fiction and Criticism of Katherine Anne Porter*, 1962; Ray West, *Katherine Anne Porter*, 1963; William L. Nance, *Katherine Anne Porter and the Art of Rejection*, 1964; George Hendrick, *Katherine Anne Porter*, 1965; W. S. Emmons, *Katherine Anne Porter: The Regional Stories*, 1967; Paul R. Baumgartner, *Katherine Anne Porter*, 1969; M. M. Liberman, *Katherine Anne Porter's Fiction*, 1971; Thomas Walsh, *Katherine Anne Porter and Mexico: The Illusion of Eden*, 1992; and Robert H. Brinkmeyer Jr., *Katherine Anne Porter's Artistic Development: Primitivism, Traditionalism, and Totalitarianism*, 1993. Darlene Harbour Unrue's scholarship has produced three useful sources on Porter: *Truth and Vision in Katherine Anne Porter's Fiction*, 1985; *Understanding Katherine Anne Porter*, 1988; and "Porter's Sources and Influences," in *Katherine Anne Porter and Texas: An Uneasy Relationship*, 1990, ed. Clinton Machann and William Bedford Clark. Important essays on Porter are in Robert Penn Warren, *Selected Essays*, 1958; Glenway Wescott, *Images of Truth*, 1962; *Katherine Anne Porter: A Critical Symposium*, 1969, ed. Lodwiej Hartley and George Gore; and Warren's more recent *Katherine Anne Porter: A Collection of Critical Essays*, 1979. For a feminist approach, see Jane K. Demouy, *Katherine Anne Porter's Women: The Eye of Her Fiction*, 1983. Bibliographies include *A Bibliography of the Works of Katherine Anne Porter*, 1969, ed.

Louise Waldrip and Shirley Ann Bauer; and the recent valuable resource, Kathryn Hilt, *Katherine Anne Porter: An Annotated Bibliography*, 1990.

Katharine Susannah Prichard

Prichard's fiction includes *The Pioneers* (1915), *Black Opal* (1921), *Working Bullocks* (1926), *Coonardoo: The Well in the Shadow* (1929), *Kiss on the Lips, and Other Stories* (1932), *Intimate Strangers* (1937), *Potch and Colour* (1944), and *Winged Seeds* (1950). She also published an autobiography, *Child of the Hurricane* (1963). *Coonardoo* was reissued in 1975. Ric Throssell edited *Tribute: Selected Short Stories of Katharine Susannah Prichard* in 1988. A selection of Prichard's correspondence appears in *As Good as a Yarn with You: Letters Between Miles Franklin, Katharine Susannah Prichard, Jean DeVanny, Marjorie Barnard, Flora Eldershaw, and Eleanor Dark*, 1992, ed. Carole Ferrier. John Hay and Brenda Walker edited *Katharine Susannah Prichard Centenary Essays* in 1984. For interesting biographical information, see Sandra Burchill, "The Early Years of Katharine Susannah Prichard The Growth of Her Political Consciousness," *Westerly* 33 (1988); and Hal Colebatch, "New Light on Katharine Susannah Prichard," *Antipodes* 4 (1990). Two valuable full-length studies are Henrietta Drake-Brockmar, *Katharine Susannah Prichard*, 1967; and Ric Throssell, *Wild Weeds and Wind Flowers: The Life and Letters of Katharine Susannah Prichard* 1975. Critical essays are Veronica Brady, "Katharine Susannah Prichard and the Tyranny of History: Intimate Strangers," *Westerly* 26 (1981); Pat Buckridge, "Katharine Susannah Prichard and the Literary Dynamics of Political Commitment," and Carole Ferrier, "Jean DeVanny, Katharine Susannah Prichard, and the 'Really Proletarian' Novel," both in *Gender Politics, and Fiction: Twentieth-Century Australian Women's Novels*, 1985, ed. Ferrier; Sue Thomas, "Interracial Encounters in Katharine Prichard's *Coonardoo*," *World Literature Written in English* 27 (1987); Ruth Morse, "Impossible Dreams: Miscegenation and Building Nations," *Southerly* 48 (Mar. 1988); and Ric Throssell, "Katharine Susannah Prichard A Reluctant Daughter of Mark Twain," *Antipodes* 3 (1989).

Jean Rhys

Rhys's published works include *The Left Bank: Sketches and Studies in Present-Day Bohemian Paris* (1927), *After Leaving Mr. MacKenzie* (1930), *Good Morning, Midnight* (1939), *Wide Sargasso Sea* (1966), *Tigers Are Better Looking* (1968), *Quartet* (first printed as *Postures*, 1928, rep. 1957, 1971), *My Day: Three Pieces* (1975),

Sleep It Off, Lady (1976), and *Smile Please: An Unfinished Autobiography* (1979). The *Collected Stories*, ed. Diana Athill, was published in 1987.

Francis Wyndham and Diana Melly edited *The Letters of Jean Rhys*, 1984, and David Plante, *Difficult Women: A Memoir of Three*, 1983, includes source material. Useful studies of Rhys's life and work are Peter Wolfe, *Jean Rhys*, 1980; Helen Nebeker, *Jean Rhys, Woman in Passage: A Critical Study of the Novels of Jean Rhys*, 1981; Teresa F. O'Connor, *Jean Rhys: The West Indian Novels*, 1986; Judith Kegan Gardiner, *Rhys, Stead, Lessing, and the Politics of Empathy*, 1989; Mary Lou Emery, *Jean Rhys at "World's End": Novels of Colonial and Sexual Exile*, 1990; Coral Ann Howells, *Jean Rhys*, 1991; and Carol Angier, *Jean Rhys: Life and Work*, 1991. Elgin Mellown compiled *A Descriptive and Annotated Bibliography of Works and Criticism* in 1984.

Adrienne Rich

Rich's *The Fact of a Doorframe: Poems Selected and New, 1950–84* (1984) draws upon poems from most of the poet's books during those years A *Change of World* (1951), *The Diamond Cutters* (1955), *Snapshots of a Daughter-in-Law* (1963, 1967), *Necessities of Life* (1966), *Leaflets* (1969), *The Will to Change* (1971), *Diving into the Wreck* (1973), *The Dream of a Common Language* (1978), and *A Wild Patience Has Taken Me This Far* (1981). She has also published *Poems Selected and New, 1950–1974* (1974), *Sources* (1983), *Your Native Land, Your Life* (1986), *Time's Power* (1989), and three recent collections: *An Atlas of the Difficult World: Poems, 1988–1991* (1991), *Collected Early Poems, 1950–1970* (1993); and *Dark Fields of the Republic* (1995). *Adrienne Rich's Poetry and Prose* (1993), with works selected and edited by Barbara Charlesworth Gelpi and Albert Gelpi, has also recently appeared. Rich is the author of the study *Of Woman Born: Motherhood as Experience and Institution* (1976), and she has collected her essays, lectures, and speeches in three volumes: *On Lies, Secrets, and Silence: Selected Prose, 1966–1978* (1979); *Blood, Bread, and Poetry: Selected Prose, 1979–1985* (1986), and *What Is Found There: Notebooks on Poetry and Politics* (1993).

Two useful full-length critical studies are Claire Keyes, *The Aesthetics of Power: The Poetry of Adrienne Rich*, 1986, and Craig Hansen Werner, *Adrienne Rich: The Poet and Her Critics*, 1988. There are valuable essays and an interview in the Norton Critical Edition of *Adrienne Rich's Poetry*, 1975, ed. Barbara Charlesworth Gelpi and Albert Gelpi. Other useful essays are Marilyn R. Farwell, "Adrienne

Rich and an Organic Feminist Criticism," *College English* 39 (1977); Dacia Maraini, "On *Of Woman Born*," *Signs* 4 (1979); Alicia Ostriker, "Her Cargo: Adrienne Rich and the Common Language," *American Poetry Review* 8 (1979); Diane Middlebrook, "Making Visible the Common World: Walt Whitman and Feminist Poetry," *Kenyon Review* 2 (1980); Joanne Feit Diehl, " 'Cartographies of Silence': Rich's Common Language and the Woman Poet," *Feminist Studies* 6 (1980); Adalaide Morris, "Imitations and Identities: Adrienne Rich's *A Change of World*," *Modern Poetry Studies* 10 (1981); Betty S. Flowers, "The 'I' in Adrienne Rich: Individuation and the Androgyne Archetype," in *Theory and Practice of Feminist Literary Criticism*, 1982, ed. Gabriela Mora and Karen S. van Hooft; Mary S. Strine, "The Politics of Asking Women's Questions: Voice and Value in the Poetry of Adrienne Rich," *Text and Performance Quarterly* 9 (1989); Helen M. Dennis, "Adrienne Rich: Consciousness Raising as Poetic Method," in *Contemporary Poetry Meets Modern Theory*, 1991, ed. Antony Easthope and John O. Thompson; and Alice Templeton, "Contradictions: Tracking Adrienne Rich's Poetry," *Tulsa Studies in Women's Literature* 12 (1993). In addition, useful critical analyses are included in Suzanne Juhasz, *Naked and Fiery Forms*, 1976; David Kalstone, *Five Temperaments*, 1977; Wendy Martin, *An American Triptych*, 1984; and *Reading Adrienne Rich: Reviews and Re-Visions, 1951–81*, 1984, ed. Jane Roberta Cooper.

Dorothy Richardson

The four volumes of Richardson's *Pilgrimage* (1915–38) have been published by Virago Press, 1979, with an introduction by Gillian E. Hanscombe. There is now also a prose collection, *Journey to Paradise: Short Stories and Autobiographical Sketches*, 1989, selected by Trudi Tate, and a series of letters, Gloria G. Fromm, ed., "Letters from Dorothy Richardson: Selected, with an Introduction," *The New Criterion* 10 (1992). A helpful introduction to Richardson's life and work is Thomas F. Staley, *Dorothy Richardson*, 1976. Two useful biographies are John D. Rosenberg, *Dorothy Richardson: The Genius They Forgot: A Critical Biography*, 1973, and Gloria G. Fromm, *Dorothy Richardson: A Biography*, 1977.

A feminist approach is offered in Gillian E. Hanscombe's recent full-length study *The Art of Life: Dorothy Richardson and the Development of Feminist Consciousness*, 1982. In addition, Richardson's achievement is analyzed in Sidney Janet Kaplan, *Feminine Consciousness in the Modern British Novel*,

1975; and in Jean Radford, *Dorothy Richardson*, 1991. Two useful essays are Hanscombe, "Dorothy Richardson versus the Novel," in *Breaking the Sequence: Women's Experimental Fiction*, 1989, ed. Ellen Friedman and Miriam Fuchs; and Sarah Schuyler, "Double-Dealing Fictions," *Genders* 9 (1990), which compares Richardson's *Pointed Roofs* with H. D.'s *HERmione*.

Henry Handel Richardson

Richardson's novels include *The Getting of Wisdom* (1910), *Maurice Guest* (1930), and *The Fortunes of Richard Mahony* (1931). The last two have been republished by Virago Press, with useful introductions. A valuable collection, *The End of a Childhood: The Complete Stories of Henry Handel Richardson*, appeared in 1992. Karl-Johan Rossing edited *Letters of Henry Handel Richardson to Nettie Palmer, 1953*.

Henry Handel Richardson, 1975, by William D. Elliott, offers a helpful overview of her work. Other biographical and critical studies include Nettie Palmer, *Henry Handel Richardson: A Study*, 1950; Vincent Buckley, *Henry Handel Richardson*, 1961; J. R. Nichols, *Art and Irony: The Tragic Vision of Henry Handel Richardson*, 1982; Eva Jarring Corones, *The Portrayal of Women in the Fiction of Henry Handel Richardson*, 1983; and Karen McLeod, *Henry Handel Richardson: A Critical Study*, 1985. Also of interest are three articles: Dorothy Green, "The Tradition of Social Responsibility in the Australian Novel: Richardson and Murphy," *Literary Criticism* 15 (1980); Margaret K. Butcher, "From *Maurice Guest* to *Martha Quest*: The Female *Bildungsroman* in Commonwealth Literature," *World Literature Written in English* 22 (1982); and Noel Macainsh, "Point of View and Consequent Naturalism in the Novels of Henry Handel Richardson," *Westerly* 29 (1984).

Mary Robinson

Robinson's novels include *Vancenza; or, The Dangers of Credulity* (1792), *Angelina* (1796), *Walsingham; or, The Pupil of Nature* (1797), *The Natural Daughter* (1799), and *The False Friend* (1799). Works of poetry include *Verses* (1775); three volumes of *Poems* (appearing in 1775, 1791, and 1794); a collection of sonnets, *Sappho and Phaon* (1796); and the posthumously published *The Poetical Works of the Late Mrs. Mary Robinson* (1806). Robinson also published a feminist essay, "Thoughts on the Condition of Women and on the Injustice of Mental Subordination" (1798). Her autobiography, *Memoirs of the Late Mrs. Mary Robinson, Written By Herself* (1801), appeared the year after her death. Although *Walsingham*

was reprinted in 1974 (with an introduction by
Gina Luria), Robinson's other works are not
available in modern editions.

Most of the scholarship on Robinson focuses
on her sensational life and on her circle of fa-
mous contemporaries. Biographical studies in-
clude Stanley Makower, *Perdita: A Romance in
Biography*, 1908; and Robert Bass, *The Green
Dragon: The Lives of Banastre Tarleton and
Mary Robinson*, 1957. More recent studies of
Robinson and her circle include Donald H.
Reiman, "The Beauty of Buttermere as Fact
and Romantic Symbol," *Criticism* 26 (1984);
Jan Fergus and Janice Farrar Thaddeus,
"Women, Publishers, and Money, 1790–1820,"
Studies in Eighteenth-Century Culture 17
(1987); Martin J. Levy, "Coleridge, Mary
Robinson, and 'Kubla Kahn,' " *The Charles
Lamb Bulletin* 77 (1992); Judith Pascoe, "The
Spectacular Flaneuse: Mary Robinson and the
City of London," *The Wordsworth Circle* 23
(1992); and Jacqueline Labbe, "Selling One's
Sorrows: Charlotte Smith, Mary Robinson, and
the Marketing of Poetry," *The Wordsworth
Circle* 25 (1994).

Christina Rossetti

Rossetti's volumes—including *Goblin Market,
and Other Poems* (1862), *The Prince's Progress*
(1866), *Sing-Song* (1872), and *New Poems*
(1896)—were collected in *The Poetical Works
of Christina Rossetti* 1904, ed. W. M. Rossetti;
and Rebecca Crump has edited three volumes
of *The Complete Poems of Christina Rossetti*:
vol. 1 appeared in 1979, vol. 2 in 1986, and vol.
3 in 1990. This variorum edition includes de-
tailed textual notes. Biographical studies in-
clude Mackenzie Bell, *Christina Rossetti: A
Biographical and Critical Study*, 1898; Marya
Zaturenska, *Christina Rossetti: A Portrait*,
1949; Lona M. Packer, *Christina Rossetti*, 1963;
Georgina Battiscombe, *Christina Rossetti*,
1965; Fredegond Shove, *Christina Rossetti: A
Study*, 1969; Margaret Sawtell, *Christina
Rossetti: Her Life and Religion*, 1974; Ralph A.
Bellas, *Christina Rossetti*, 1977; Georgina
Battiscombe, *Christina Rossetti: A Divided
Life*, 1981; and Kathleen Jones, *Learning Not to
Be First: The Life of Christina Rossetti*, 1990.

Critical essays on her life and work include
Virginia Woolf's appreciative " 'I Am Christina
Rossetti,' " in *The Second Common Reader*,
1932, as well as two recent pieces by Jerome J.
McGann: "Christina Rossetti's Poems: A New
Edition and Revaluation," *Victorian Studies* 23
(1980), and "The Religious Poetry of Christina
Rossetti," *Critical Inquiry* 10 (1983); and
David Kent edited a useful collection of essays,
The Achievement of Christina Rossetti,
in 1987. Full-length studies include Dolores
Rosenblum, *Christina Rossetti: The Poetry of

Endurance, 1986; Antony H. Harrison,
Christina Rossett in Context, 1988; and
Katherine J. Mayberry, *Christina Rossetti and
the Poetry of Discovery*, 1990. Other helpful
studies are Sharon Leder and Andrea Abbott,
*The Language of Exclusion: The Poetry of Emily
Dickinson and Christina Rossetti*, 1987; and
Mary E. Finn, *Writing the Incommensurable:
Kierkegaard, Rossetti, and Hopkins*, 1992.
Feminist approaches are represented by a chap-
ter in Ellen Moers, *Literary Women*, 1976; by a
chapter in Gilbert and Gubar, *The Madwoman
in the Attic*, 1979; by a section in Nina
Auerbach, *Woman and the Demon*,
1982; and by Sharon Smulders, "Women's
Enfranchisement in Christina Rossetti's
Poetry," *Texas Studies in Literature and
Language* 34 (1992). Three useful reference
works are Rebecca W. Crump, *Christina
Rossetti: A Reference Guide*, 1976; *The Bible
and the Poetry of Christina Rossetti: A
Concordance*, 1979, comp. Nilda Jimenez;
and Edna Kotin Charles, *Christina Rossetti:
Critical Perspectives, 1862–1982*, 1985.

Mary Rowlandson

Rowlandson's major work is *The Narrative of
the Captivity and Restoration of Mrs. Mary
Rowlandson* (1682). Richard Slotkin,
Regeneration through Violence, 1973, contains
a useful discussion of her captivity. See also
Captives among the Indians, 1915, ed. Horace
Kephart; and R. H. Pearce, "The Significances
of the Captivity Narrative," *American
Literature* 19 (1947). Among more recent criti-
cal studies of Rowlandson's life and work are
Tara Fitzpatrick, "The Figure of Captivity: The
Cultural Work of the Puritan Captivity
Narrative," *American Literary History* 3
(1991); Teresa Toulouse, "Mary Rowlandson
and the 'Rhetoric of Ambiguity,' " in *Sacvan
Bercovitch and the Puritan Imagination*, 1992,
ed. Michael Schuldiner; and Teresa Toulouse,
" 'My Own Credit': Strategies of (E)valuation
in Mary Rowlandson's Captivity Narrative,"
American Literature 64 (1992). See also "The
Captivity and Restoration of Mrs. Mary
Rowlandson" in Susan Howe, *The Birth-Mark:
Unsettling the Wilderness in American Literary
History*, 1993.

Muriel Rukeyser

The Collected Poems of Muriel Rukeyser ap-
peared in 1978; *Out of Silence: Selected Poems*,
ed. Kate Daniels—which includes selections of
poems from her first volume of poetry, *Theory
of Flight* (1935), through to her last volume,
The Gates (1978)—appeared in 1992. A *Muriel
Rukeyser Reader*, 1994, ed. Jan Heller Levi,
gathers both poetry and prose. Besides her own
poetry, Rukeyser published several translations,

including *Selected Poems of Octavio Paz* (1963). She also wrote biographies, including *Willard Gibbs* (1942), *One Life* (1957), and *The Traces of Thomas Hariot* (1971), as well as children's books. A full-length study is Louise Kertesz, *The Poetic Vision of Muriel Rukeyser*, 1980. Critical essays include Robert Coles, "Muriel Rukeyser's *The Gates*," *American Poetry Review* 7 (1978); and Rachel Blau DuPlessis, "The Critique of Consciousness and Myth in Levertov, Rich, and Rukeyser," in *Shakespeare's Sisters*, 1979, ed. Sandra M. Gilbert and Susan Gubar. *Poetry East*, 1985, issued a special edition on Rukeyser, ed. Kate Daniels and Richard Jones.

May Sarton

Among Sarton's many novels are *The Single Hound* (1938), *A Shower of Summer Days* (1952), *The Small Room* (1961), *Joanna and Ulysses* (1963), *Mrs. Stevens Hears the Mermaids Singing* (1965), and *Kinds of Love* (1970). Sarton's recent works include two novels—*The Magnificent Spinster* (1985) and *The Education of Harriet Hatfield* (1989)—and three books of poetry: *The Phoenix Again: New Poems* (1987), *The Silence Now: New and Uncollected Earlier Poems* (1988), and *Coming into Eighty: New Poems* (1992). Her *Collected Poems (1930–1973)* appeared in 1973 and an expanded volume, *Collected Poems: 1930–1993*, appeared in 1993. Her journal volumes include *Plant Dreaming Deep* (1968), *Journal of a Solitude* (1973), *The House by the Sea* (1977), *Recovering* (1980), *At Seventy* (1984), *After the Stroke: A Journal* (1988), *Endgame: A Journal of the Seventy-ninth Year* (1992), and *Encore: A Journal of the Eightieth Year* (1993). Marita Simpson and Martha Wheelock edited a selection of Sarton's autobiographical writings, *May Sarton: A Self-Portrait*, in 1986. In addition, *Sarton Selected: An Anthology of Novels, Journals, and Poetry*, ed. Bradford Dudley Daziel, appeared in 1991; and another collection, *May Sarton: Among the Usual Days*, ed. Susan Sherman, was published in 1993. Earl G. Ingersoll edited a selection of interviews, *Conversations with May Sarton*, in 1991. Constance Hunting edited *Writings on Writing*, 1980, and *May Sarton, Woman and Poet*, 1982. Other helpful biographical material appears in Sarton's own *I Knew a Phoenix: Sketches for an Autobiography* (1978), and in Dolores Shelley, "A Conversation with May Sarton," *Women and Literature* 7 (1979), as well as in Agnes Sibley, *May Sarton*, 1972.

A full-length study of Sarton's career is Elizabeth Evans, *May Sarton Revisited*, 1989. Essays on Sarton's work include Dawn Holt Anderson, "May Sarton's Women," in *Images of Women in Fiction*, 1972, ed. Susan Koppelman Cornillon; Doris L. Eder, "Woman Writer: May Sarton's *Mrs. Stevens Hears the Mermaids Singing*," *International Journal of Women's Studies* 1 (1978); Jane S. Bakerman, " 'Kinds of Love': Love and Friendship in the Novels of May Sarton," *Critique* 20 (1978); Marlene Springer, "As We Shall Be: May Sarton and Aging," *Frontiers* 5 (1980); Emily M. Nett, "The Naked Soul Comes Closer to the Surface: Old Age in the Gender Mirror of Contemporary Novels," *Women's Studies* 18 (1990); Henry Taylor, "May Sarton: Home to a Place Beyond Exile," in his *Compulsory Figures: Essays on Recent American Poets*, 1992; Janis P. Stout, "A Wordless Balm: Silent Communication in the Novels of May Sarton," *Essays in Literature* 20 (1993); and Anne Wyatt-Brown, "Another Model of the Aging Writer: Sarton's Politics of Old Age," in *Aging and Gender in Literature: Studies in Creativity*, 1993, ed. Anne Wyatt-Brown and Janice Rossen. See also Carolyn Heilbrun's discussion of Sarton in *Hamlet's Mother and Other Women*, 1990. Lenora Blouin compiled a bibliography, *May Sarton*, in 1978.

Olive Schreiner

Among the works published in Schreiner's lifetime, most important are *The Story of an African Farm* (1883), *Dreams* (1890), *Trooper Peter Halkett of Mashonoland* (1897), *Dream Life and Real Life* (1893, 1912), and *Woman and Labour* (1911); the last two have been reprinted by the Cassandra and Virago Presses, while *The Story of an African Farm* is available in a number of editions. *Stories, Dreams, and Allegories* (1924), *From Man to Man* (1926), and *Undine* (1919) were published posthumously and have also been reprinted. In addition, there are several collections of Schreiner's writing available: *Olive Schreiner, a Selection*, 1968, ed. Uys Krige; *A Track to the Water's Edge: The Olive Schreiner Reader*, 1973, ed. Howard Thurman; and *An Olive Schreiner Reader: Writings on Women and South Africa*, 1987, ed. and with an introduction by Carol Barash, and an afterword by Nadine Gordimer. Yaffa Claire Drazin has edited "My Other Self": The Letters of Olive Schreiner and Havelock Ellis, 1884–1920, 1992, and Richard Rive has edited *Olive Schreiner Letters*, 1988.

Biographical and critical studies include Vera Buchanan-Gould, *Not Without Honor: The Life and Writings of Olive Schreiner*, 1948; Daisy Lucie Hofman, *Olive Schreiner, Her Friends and Times*, 1955; Joyce Avrech Berkman, *Olive Schreiner: Feminism on the Frontier*, 1979; Ruth First and Ann Scott, *Olive Schreiner*, 1980; Ruth First, *Olive Schreiner: A Biography*, 1980; Douglas Ridley Beeton, *Facets of Olive Schreiner: A Manuscript Sourcebook*,

1987; Joyce Avrech Berkman, *The Healing Imagination of Olive Schreiner: Beyond South African Colonialism*, 1989; Carol Barash, "Virile Womanhood: Olive Schreiner's Narratives of a Master Race," in *Speaking of Gender* 1989, ed. Elaine Showalter; and Gerald Monsman, *Olive Schreiner's Fiction: Landscape and Power*, 1991.

Anne Sexton

Sexton's *The Complete Poems*, with a foreword by Maxine Kumin, was published in 1981. Two other useful collections are *Words for Dr. Y.: Uncollected Poems with Three Stories*, 1978, ed. Linda Sexton; and *Selected Poems of Anne Sexton*, 1988, ed. Diane Wood Middlebrook and Diana Hume George. *No Evil Star: Selected Essays, Interviews, and Prose*, ed. Steven E. Colburn, appeared in 1985. A *Self-Portrait in Letters*, 1977, and two recent books—Diane Wood Middlebrook, *Anne Sexton: A Biography*, 1991; and Linda Gray Sexton, *Searching for Mercy Street: My Journey back to My Mother*, 1994—provide useful biographical material. Important interviews and critical essays are to be found in J. D. McClatchy, *Anne Sexton: The Artist and Her Critics*, 1978; Diana Hume George, ed., *Sexton: Selected Criticism*, 1988; and Linda Wagner, *Critical Essays on Anne Sexton*, 1989. Critical essays include Suzanne Juhasz, "Seeking the Exit or the Home: Poetry and Salvation in the Career of Anne Sexton," in *Shakespeare's Sisters*, 1979, ed. Sandra M. Gilbert and Susan Gubar; Margaret Houton, "The Double Image and the Division of Parts: A Study of Mother/Daughter Relationships in the Poetry of Anne Sexton," *Journal of Women's Studies in Literature* (1979); Kathleen L. Nicholas, "The Hungry Beast Rowing toward God: Anne Sexton's Later Religious Poetry," *Notes on Modern American Literature* 21 (1979); Jeanne H. Kammer, "The Witches' Life: Confession and Control in the Early Poetry of Anne Sexton," *Language and Style* 13 (1980); Rosemary Johnson, "The Woman of Private (but Published) Hungers," *Parnassus* 8 (1980); and Alicia Ostriker, "That Story: Anne Sexton and Her Transformations," *American Poetry Review* 11 (1982). Valuable also is C. Northouse and R. P. Walsh, *Sylvia Plath and Anne Sexton: A Reference Guide*, 1974.

Mary Shelley

Although there is no collected edition of Mary Shelley's works, a number of titles have been republished. *Frankenstein* (1818) is available in many modern reprints; especially useful are the scholarly edition by James Rieger, 1974, and the Norton Critical Edition edited by J. Paul Hunter, 1996. *The Last Man* (1826) has been reprinted in an edition by Hugh J. Luke Jr.

1965; *Mathilda*, which the author left in manuscript, was printed for the first time by Elizabeth Nitchie, 1959; and Shelley's short fiction has been edited by Charles E. Robinson in *Mary Shelley: Collected Tales and Stories*, 1990. Robinson has also recently edited *Mythological Dramas: Proserpine and Midas*, 1992. *The Mary Shelley Reader*, ed. Betty T. Bennett and Robinson, contains *Frankenstein*, *Mathilda*, essays, reviews, and letters, and appeared in 1990. Her prefaces and notes to her husband's poems appear in *The Complete Poetical Works of Percy Bysshe Shelley*, 1970, ed. Thomas Hutchinson and rev. G. M. Matthews.

Frederick L. Jones has edited *The Letters of Mary W. Shelley*, 1946; and *Mary Shelley's Journal*, 1947. Paula R. Feldman and Diana Scott-Kilvert have edited *The Journals of Mary Shelley, 1814–1844*, 1987. Betty T. Bennett has edited two volumes of *The Letters of Mary Wollstonecraft Shelley*, 1980, 1983, and has recently published "Finding Mary Shelley in Her Letters" in *Romantic Revisions*, 1992, ed. Robert Brinkley and Keith Hanley. Biographies include R. Glynn Grylls, *Mary Shelley: A Biography*, 1938; Muriel Spark, *Child of Light: A Reassessment of Mary Shelley*, 1951; Elizabeth Nitchie, *Mary Shelley, Author of "Frankenstein,"* 1953; Jane Dunn, *Moon in Eclipse: A Life of Mary Shelley*, 1978; and Bonnie R. Neumann, *The Lonely Muse: A Critical Biography of Mary Shelley*, 1979. Much of the critical work on Shelley deals with *Frankenstein*. *The Endurance of Frankenstein*, 1979, ed. George Levine and U. C. Knoepflmacher, a collection of essays, is valuable, as is the St. Martin's Press 1992 edition of *Frankenstein*, which contains critical essays from five perspectives, including feminism, psychoanalysis, and cultural criticism. See also Mary A. Favret, "A Woman Writes the Fiction of the Body in *Frankenstein*," *Genders* 14 (1992); Margo V. Perkins, "The Nature of Otherness: Class and Difference in Mary Shelley's *Frankenstein*," *Studies in the Humanities* 19 (1992); James P. Davis, "*Frankenstein* and the Subversion of the Masculine Voice," *Women's Studies: An Interdisciplinary Journal* 21 (1992); Bette London, "Mary Shelley, *Frankenstein*, and the Spectacle of Masculinity," *PMLA* 108 (1993); and Colleen Hobbs, "Reading the Symptoms: An Exploration of Repression and Hysteria in Mary Shelley's *Frankenstein*," *Studies in the Novel* 25 (1993). Other feminist analyses are represented by chapters in Ellen Moers, *Literary Women*, 1976; Sandra M. Gilbert and Susan Gubar, *The Madwoman in the Attic*, 1979; and Mary Poovey, *The Proper Lady and the Woman Writer*, 1984. A recent collection of useful essays—*The Other Mary Shelley: Beyond*

Frankenstein, 1993, ed. Audrey A. Fisch, Anne K. Mellor, and Esther H. Schor—discusses Shelley's secondary writings. Earlier references may be found in W. H. Lyles's somewhat outdated *Mary Shelley: An Annotated Bibliography*, 1975.

Leslie Marmon Silko

Silko's works include *Laguna Woman* (1974), *Ceremony* (1977), *Storyteller* (1981), *Almanac of the Dead* (1991), and the autobiographical *Sacred Water: Narratives and Pictures* (1993). Anne Wright edited a collection of correspondence, *The Delicacy and Strength of Lace: Letters between Leslie Marmon Silko and James Wright*, in 1986. Useful background material is offered in Per Seyersted, "Two Interviews with Leslie Marmon Silko," *American Studies in Scandinavia* 13 (1981); Elaine Jahner, "The Novel and Oral Tradition: An Interview with Leslie Marmon Silko," *Book Forum* 5 (1981), and Linda Niemann, "Narratives of Survival," *Women's Review of Books* 9 (1992). In addition, Seyersted has written a full-length critical study, *Leslie Marmon Silko*, 1980, and there have been numerous critical essays, including Edith Blicksilver, "Traditionalism vs. Modernity: Leslie Silko on American Indian Women," *Southwest Review* 64 (1979); Ronald E. McFarland, "Leslie Silko's Story of Stories," *A Journal of Contemporary Literature* 4 (1979); A. LaVonne Ruoff, "Ritual and Renewal: Keres Traditions in the Short Fiction of Leslie Silko," *MELUS* 5 (1979); C. W. Truesdle, "Tradition and Ceremony: Leslie Marmon Silko as an American Novelist," *North Dakota Quarterly* 59 (1991); (1992); Edith Swan, "Feminine Perspectives at Laguna Pueblo: Silko's *Ceremony*," *Tulsa Studies in Women's Literature* 11 (1992); and Linda J. Krumholz, "To Understand This World Differently: Reading and Subversion in Leslie Marmon Silko's *Storyteller*," *Ariel* 25 (1994). Melody Graulich edited a volume of critical essays, *Yellow Woman*, in 1993. See also the helpful discussions of Silko in Roberta Rubenstein, *Boundaries of the Self: Gender, Culture, Fiction*, 1987; Arnold Krupat, *The Voice in the Margin: Native American Literature and the Canon*, 1989; Louis Owens, *Other Destinies: Understanding the American Indian Novel*, 1992; Hertha Dawn Wong, *Sending My Heart Back across the Years: Tradition and Innovation in Native American Autobiography*, 1992; and Bonnie C. Winsbro, *Supernatural Forces: Belief, Difference, and Power in Contemporary Works by Ethnic Women*, 1993.

May Sinclair

Sinclair's works include numerous volumes of poetry, criticism, philosophy, and short stories, as well as twenty-four novels, among them *The Divine Fire* (1904), *The Three Sisters* (1914), *The Tree of Heaven* (1917), *Mary Olivier: A Life* (1919), *Life and Death of Harriett Frean* (1922), and *Anne Severn and the Fieldings* (1924). *The Three Sisters, Mary Olivier,* and *Life and Death of Harriet Frean* have been republished by Virago Press, with helpful introductions.

Biographical studies include Theophilus Ernest Martin Boll, *Miss May Sinclair, Novelist: A Biographical and Critical Introduction*, 1973; and Hrisey D. Zegger, *May Sinclair*, 1976. In addition, Sinclair's work is extensively discussed in Sidney Janet Kaplan, *Feminine Consciousness in the Modern British Novel*, 1975. Useful articles include Diane F. Gillespie, "May Sinclair and the Stream of Consciousness: Metaphors and Metaphysics," *English Literature in Transition* 21 (1978), and Rebeccah Kinnamon Neff, " 'New Mysticism' in the Writings of May Sinclair and T. S. Eliot," *Twentieth-Century Literature* 26 (1979). Useful recent essays on May Sinclair include Laura Stempel Mumford, "May Sinclair's *The Tree of Heaven*: The Vortex of Feminism, the Community of War," in *Arms and the Woman: War, Gender, and Literary Representation*, 1989, ed. Helen M. Cooper, Adrienne Auslander Munich, and Susan Merrill Squier; Sandra Kemp, " 'But How Describe a World Seen Without a Self?': Feminism, Fiction, and Modernism," *Critical Quarterly* 32 (1990); Janice H. Harris, "Challenging the Script of the Heterosexual Couple: Three Marriage Novels by May Sinclair," *Papers on Language and Literature* 29 (1993); and Suzanne Stark, "Overcoming Butlerian Obstacles: May Sinclair and the Problem of Biological Determinism," *Women's Studies* 21 (1992).

Edith Sitwell

In addition to more than thirty volumes of poetry, culminating in *Collected Poems* (1957), *Selected Poems* (1965), with an introduction by John Lehmann, and most recently, *The Early Unpublished Poems of Edith Sitwell* (1994), ed. Gerald W. Morton and Karen P. Helgeson, Sitwell produced a variety of critical and other prose works. These include *Alexander Pope* (1930), *Aspects of Modern Poetry* (1934), *A Poet's Notebook* (1950), and *Taken Care Of: An Autobiography* (1965). John Lehmann and Derek Parker edited *Edith Sitwell: Selected Letters, 1919–1964*, and Lehmann has written an informative account of Sitwell's family and background in *A Nest of Tigers: Edith, Osbert, and Sacheverell Sitwell in Their Times*, 1968. Other biographical and critical works include J. D. Brophy, *Edith Sitwell: The Symbolist Order*, 1968; John Press, *A Map of Modern*

English Verse, 1969; Kenneth Rexroth, "Poets Old and New: Edith Sitwell," in Assays, 1961; E. Salter, The Last Years of a Rebel: A Memoir of Edith Sitwell, 1967; G. A. Cevasco, The Sitwells: Edith, Osbert, and Sacheverell, 1987; and Perdita Schaffner, "A Day at the St. Regis with Dame Edith," in American Scholar 60 (1991). Four full-length studies are John Pearson, Façades: Edith, Osbert, and Sacheverell Sitwell, 1978; Elizabeth Salter, Edith Sitwell, 1979; Geoffrey Elborn, Edith Sitwell: A Biography 1981; and Victoria Glendinning, Edith Sitwell: A Unicorn among Lions, 1981. Critical essays include Patricia Clements, "Edith Sitwell and Some Others: Departures from Decadence," in her Baudelaire and the English Tradition, 1985; and Cyrena N. Pondrom, "Influence? Or Intertextuality? The Complicated Connection of Edith Sitwell and Gertrude Stein," in Influence and Intertextuality in Literary History, 1991, ed. Jay Clayton and Eric Rothstein.

Charlotte Smith

Among Smith's numerous novels are Emmeline (1788), Ethelinde (1789), Celestina (1791), Desmond (1792), The Old Manor House (1793), and The Wanderings of Warwick (1794). Emmeline and The Old Manor House were reprinted in 1969 with an introduction by Anne Henry Ehrenpreis, and more recently, two new editions have appeared: Emmeline, 1988, with an introduction by Zoë Fairbairns; and The Old Manor House, 1989, with an introduction by Judith Stanton. Smith also published poetry in Elegiac Sonnets (1784) and Beachy Head: With Other Poems (1807). A collection, The Poems of Charlotte Smith, ed. Stuart Curran, was issued in 1993. The only biography is Florence May Anna Hilbish, Charlotte Smith, Poet and Novelist, 1941; however, Katharine M. Rogers includes a discussion of Smith in "Inhibitions in Eighteenth-Century Women Novelists," Eighteenth-Century Studies (1977) and in her anthology Before Their Time, 1979. In addition, Smith is discussed in Margaret Doody, "English Women Novelists and the French Revolution," in La Femme en Angleterre et dans les colonies Americaines aux XVIIe et XVIIIe siécles, 1975, and Matthew Bray's essay "Removing the Anglo-Saxon Yoke: The Francocentric Vision of Charlotte Smith's Later Works," The Wordsworth Circle 24 (1993), discusses the French influence on Smith's writing. Three useful essays are Judith Phillips Stanton, "Charlotte Smith's 'Literary Business': Income, Patronage, and Indigence," The Age of Johnson: A Scholarly Annual 1 (1987); Sarah Zimmerman, "Charlotte Smith's Letters and the Practice of Self-Presentation," Princeton University Library Chronicle 53 (1991); and

Jacqueline Labbe, "Selling One's Sorrows: Charlotte Smith, Mary Robinson, and the Marketing of Poetry," The Wordsworth Circle 25 (1994).

Stevie Smith

Smith's books of poetry include A Good Time Was Had by All (1937), Harold's Leap (1950), Not Waving but Drowning (1957), and Scorpion, and Other Poems, 1972, published posthumously with an introduction by Patrick Dickinson. Both the Selected Poems, 1962, and the Collected Poems, 1976, ed. James MacGibbon, reproduce many of the drawings she originally printed with her poems. Smith also wrote three novels: Novel on Yellow Paper; or, Work It Out for Yourself (1936), Over the Frontier (1938), and The Holiday (1949). All have been reissued in paperbound editions.

Frances Spalding's valuable biography, Stevie Smith, appeared in 1988. Another biography is Jack Barbera and William McBrien, Stevie: A Biography of Stevie Smith, 1985. See also the interviews in The Poet Speaks, 1966, ed. Peter Orr; and in Kay Dick, Ivy and Stevie, 1971. A full-length study of Smith's career is Arthur C. Rankin, The Poetry of Stevie Smith: "Little Girl Lost," 1985; and a helpful collection of critical essays is In Search of Stevie Smith, 1991, ed. Sanford Sternlicht. Useful essays are the chapter in Eight Contemporary Poets by Calvin Bedient, 1974; Philip Larkin, "Frivolous and Vulnerable," New Statesman (1962); an anonymous review, "The Voice of Genteel Decay," Times Literary Supplement (1972); Steven Helmling, "Delivered for a Time from Silence," Parnassus 6 (1977); Janice Thaddeus, "Stevie Smith and the Gleeful Macabre," Contemporary Poetry 3 (1978); Mark Storey, "Why Stevie Smith Matters," Critical Quarterly 21 (1979); Christopher B. Ricks, "Stevie Smith: The Art of Sinking in Poetry," in his The Force of Poetry, 1984; Lee Upton, "Stevie Smith and the Anxiety of Intimacy," CEA Critic 53 (1991); Richard Nemesvari, " 'Work It Out for Yourself': Language and Fictional Form in Stevie Smith's Novel on Yellow Paper," The Dalhousie Review 71 (1991); and Sheryl Stevenson, "Stevie Smith's Voices," Contemporary Literature 33 (1993). A feminist perspective on Smith's poetry is represented by Romana Huk, "Eccentric Concentrism: Traditional Poetic Forms and Refracted Discourse in Stevie Smith's Poetry," Contemporary Literature 43 (1993). Jack Barbera, William McBrien, and Helen Bajan compiled a reference guide, Stevie Smith: A Bibliography, in 1986.

Cathy Song

Song's books of poetry are Picture Bride (1983),

Frameless Windows, Squares of Light (1988), and *School Figures* (1994). Song has also edited (with Juliet S. Kono) an anthology of women's fiction and poetry, *Sister Stew* (1991). Two interesting articles on Song's poetry are Gayle K. Fujito-Sato, "'Third World' as Place and Paradigm in Cathy Song's *Picture Bride*," *MELUS* 15 (1988); and Patricia Wallace, "Divided Loyalties: Literal and Literary in the Poetry of Lorna Dee Cervantes, Cathy Song, and Rita Dove," *MELUS* 18 (1993). Kyhan Lee's "Korean-American Literature: The Next Generation," *Korea Journal* 34 (1994), examines Song's work in relation to her Korean-American heritage.

Muriel Spark
Spark's numerous works include *Memento Mori* (1959), *The Prime of Miss Jean Brodie* (1961), *Emily Brontë, Her Life and Work* (with Derek Stanford, 1966), *Collected Stories* (1967), *Collected Poems* (1967), *The Abbess of Crewe* (1974), *The Only Problem* (1984), *The Stories of Muriel Spark* (1985), *A Far Cry from Kensington* (1988), and *Symposium* (1990). The first installment of her autobiography is called *Curriculum Vitae: Autobiography* (1992). Studies of her life and work are Karl Malkoff, *Muriel Spark*, 1968; Patricia Stubb, *Muriel Spark*, 1973; Peter Kemp, *Muriel Spark*, 1974; Ruth Whittaker, *The Faith and Fiction of Muriel Spark*, 1982; Dorothea Walker, *Muriel Spark*, 1988; Norman Page, *Muriel Spark*, 1990; and Joseph Hynes, ed., *Critical Essays on Muriel Spark*, 1992.

Anne Spencer
Selections of Spencer's poems can be found in *Black Sister: Poetry by Black American Women, 1746–1980*, 1981, ed. Erlene Stetson; and *Shadowed Dreams: Women's Poetry of the Harlem Renaissance*, 1989, ed. Maureen Honey. The only full-length critical and biographical study of Spencer is J. Lee Greene, *Time's Unfading Garden: Anne Spencer's Life and Poetry*, 1977. Other useful information on Spencer can be found in Gloria T. Hull, "Afro-American Poets: A BioCritical Survey," in *Shakespeare's Sisters*, 1979, ed. Sandra Gilbert and Susan Gubar. A documentary film about Spencer, *Echoes from the Garden: The Anne Spencer Story*, was produced in 1980.

Elizabeth Cady Stanton
Stanton's *History of Woman Suffrage* (1881–86), ed. with Susan B. Anthony and Matilda Joslyn Gage, was reprinted in 1969; *The Woman's Bible* (1895, 1898) has been republished as *The Original Feminist Attack on the Bible*, with an introduction by Barbara Welter, 1974; *Elizabeth Cady Stanton* (1922), ed. Theodore Stanton and Harriot Stanton

Blatch, was reissued in 1969; *Eighty Years and More (1815–1897): Reminiscences of Elizabeth Cady Stanton* (1898) was reprinted in 1970. Also useful is *Elizabeth Cady Stanton, Susan B. Anthony: Correspondence, Writing, Speeches*, 1981, ed. and with critical commentary by Ellen Carol DuBois.

Biographies include Alma Lutz, *Created Equal: A Biography of Elizabeth Cady Stanton, 1815–1902*, 1940; Mary Ann B. Oakley, *Elizabeth Cady Stanton*, 1972; Lois W. Banner, *Elizabeth Cady Stanton: A Radical for Women's Rights*, 1980; and Elisabeth Griffith, *In Her Own Right: The Life of Elizabeth Cady Stanton*, 1984. A full-length study is Beth Marie Waggenspack, *The Search for Self-Sovereignty: The Oratory of Elizabeth Cady Stanton*, 1989. Useful critical essays are Ellen DuBois, "The Limitations of Sisterhood: Elizabeth Cady Stanton and Division in the American Suffrage Movement, 1875–1902," in *Women and the Structure of Society*, 1984, ed. Barbara Harris and JoAnn K. McNamara; Mary Loeffelholz, "Posing the Woman Citizen: The Contradictions of Stanton's Feminism," *Genders* 7 (1990); and Sidonie Smith, "Resisting the Gaze of Embodiment: Women's Autobiography in the Nineteenth Century," in *American Women's Autobiography: Fea(s)ts of Memory*, 1992, ed. Margo Culley, which compares Stanton's autobiography to Harriet Jacobs'. Stanton is also discussed in Lois J. Fowler and David H. Fowler, ed., *Revelations of Self: American Women in Autobiography*, 1990; and Mary D. Pellauer, *Toward a Tradition of Feminist Theology*, 1991, which discusses Stanton's religious-social thought.

Gertrude Stein
Although there is no complete edition of Stein's writings, *The Yale Edition of the Unpublished Writings of Gertrude Stein*, ed. Carl Van Vechten, 1951–58, contains eight volumes of poetry, prose fiction, portraits, and essays. Among the prose works published during Stein's lifetime are *Three Lives* (1909), *Tender Buttons* (1914), *The Making of Americans* (1925), the children's book *The World Is Round* (1926), *Lucy Church Amiably* (1930), *Ida: A Novel* (1941), and *Brewsie and Willie* (1946). *Geography and Plays* (1922), *Operas and Plays* (1932), and *Last Operas and Plays*, ed. Carl Van Vechten (1949), contain dramatic pieces. Autobiographical material may be found in *The Autobiography of Alice B. Toklas* (1933), *Portraits and Prayers* (1934), *Everybody's Autobiography* (1937), and *Wars I Have Seen* (1945). Other works, including meditations, essays, sketches, and sociolinguistic treatises, are *Useful Knowledge* (1928), *How to Write* (1931), *Lectures in America* (1935), *Narration: Four Lectures by Gertrude Stein* (1935), *What*

Are Masterpieces (1940), and *Four in America* (1947). Useful introductory collections of Stein's writings are *Selected Writings of Gertrude Stein*, 1962, ed. Carl Van Vechten, and *A Stein Reader*, 1993, ed. Ulla E. Dydo.

Donald C. Gallup has edited *Fernhurst, Q. E. D., and Other Early Writings by Gertrude Stein*, 1971, as well as a collection of letters to Gertrude Stein, *The Flowers of Friendship*, 1953. *Dear Sammy: Letters from Gertrude Stein and Alice B. Toklas*, ed. Samuel M. Steward, appeared in 1977, and *The Letters of Gertrude Stein and Carl Van Vechten, 1913–1946*, ed. Edward Burns, in 1986. Memoirs of Stein include W. G. Rogers, *When This You See Remember Me: Gertrude Stein in Person*, 1948, and Alice B. Toklas, *What Is Remembered*, 1953. Linda Simon, *The Biography of Alice B. Toklas*, 1977, provides useful background information.

Biographical studies of Stein are Elizabeth Sprigg, *Gertrude Stein: Her Life and Work*, 1957; John Malcolm Brinnin, *The Third Rose: Gertrude Stein and Her World*, 1959; James R. Mellow, *Charmed Circle: Gertrude Stein and Company*, 1974; and Janet Hobhouse, *Everybody Who Was Anybody*, 1975. Critical studies include Donald Sutherland, *Gertrude Stein: A Biography of Her Work*, 1951; Michael Hoffman, *The Development of Abstractionism in the Writings of Gertrude Stein*, 1965; Allegra Stewart, *Gertrude Stein and the Present*, 1967; Norman Weinstein, *Gertrude Stein and the Literature of Modern Consciousness*, 1970; Richard Bridgeman, *Gertrude Stein in Pieces*, 1970; Robert B. Haas, *A Primer for the Gradual Understanding of Gertrude Stein*, 1971; Carolyn F. Copeland, *Language and Time and Gertrude Stein*, 1975; Michael Hoffman, *Gertrude Stein*, 1976; Wendy Steiner, *Exact Resemblance to Exact Resemblance: The Literary Portraiture of Gertrude Stein's Experimental Writing*, 1983; Marianne DeKoven, *A Different Language: Gertrude Stein's Experimental Writing*, 1983; Harriet Scott Chessman, *The Public Is Invited to Dance: Representation, the Body, and Dialogue in Gertrude Stein*, 1989; Lisa Cole Ruddick, *Reading Gertrude Stein: Body, Text, Gnosis*, 1990; Ellen E. Berry, *Curved Thought and Textual Wandering: Gertrude Stein's Postmodernism*, 1992. Two valuable bibliographies are *Gertrude Stein*, 1979, by Maureen R. Liston, and *Gertrude Stein and Alice B. Toklas: A Reference Guide*, 1984, by Ray L. White. See also *A Gertrude Stein Companion: Content with Example*, 1988, ed. Bruce Kellner.

Ruth Stone

Stone's collections of poetry are *In an Iridescent Time* (1958), *Topography, and Other Poems* (1970), *Cheap: New Poems and Ballads* (1975), *Second Hand Coat: Poems New and Selected* (1987), *The Solution* (1989), *Who Is the Widow's Muse?* (1991), and *Simplicity* (1995). For a series of short, appreciative essays, see Sandra M. Gilbert et al., "On Ruth Stone," *Iowa Review* 12 (1981), as well as *The House Is Made of Poetry: The Art of Ruth Stone*, ed. Wendy Barker and Sandra M. Gilbert.

Harriet Beecher Stowe

Stowe's major works include *Uncle Tom's Cabin* (1851–52), *Sunny Memories of Foreign Lands* (1854), *Dred* (1856), *The Minister's Wooing* (1859), *The Pearl of Orr's Island* (1862), *Oldtown Folks* (1869), *Oldtown Fireside Stories* (1872), and *Poganuc People* (1878). The *Writings of Harriet Beecher Stowe*, 16 vols., 1896, is still the standard edition. More recently, John M. Moran edited *Collected Poems*, 1967, while Margaret G. Mair, Earl A. French, and Diana Royce produced *The Papers of Harriet Beecher Stowe*, 1977. An excellent edition of *Uncle Tom's Cabin*, with an introduction by Ann Douglas, appeared in 1981. Elizabeth Ammons edited a Norton Critical Edition of *Uncle Tom's Cabin*, which was published in 1994. Several memoirs were written during Stowe's lifetime or soon after she died. While Robert Forrest Wilson's *Crusader in Crinoline: The Life of Harriet Beecher Stowe*, 1941, has been considered the standard biography, Joan D. Hedrick's more recent *Harriet Beecher Stowe: A Life*, 1994, is also extremely useful. Johanna Johnston, *Runaway to Heaven: The Story of Harriet Beecher Stowe*, 1963, is a good popular biography. Others include Edward Wagenknecht, *Harriet Beecher Stowe: The Known and the Unknown*, 1965, and Noel B. Gerson, *Harriet Beecher Stowe: A Biography*, 1976.

Critical studies include Charles H. Foster, *The Rungless Ladder: Harriet Beecher Stowe and New England Puritanism*, 1954; John R. Adams, *Harriet Beecher Stowe*, 1963; Alice C. Crozier, *The Novels of Harriet Beecher Stowe*, 1980; Gayle Kimball, *The Religious Ideas of Harriet Beecher Stowe: Her Gospel of Womanhood*, 1982; and Jeanne Boydston, *The Limits of Sisterhood: The Beecher Sisters on Women's Rights and Women's Sphere*, 1988. Two valuable feminist articles are Jane P. Tompkins, "Sentimental Power: *Uncle Tom's Cabin* and the Politics of Literary History," *Glyph* (1981); and Laurie Crumpacker, "Four Novels of Harriet Beecher Stowe: A Study in 19th-Century Androgyny," in *American Novelists Revisited: Essays in Feminist Criticism*, 1982, ed. Fritz Fleischmann. Stowe's work is also treated in Ann Douglas, *The Feminization of American Culture*, 1977; Leslie Fiedler, *The Inadvertent Epic: From "Uncle Tom's Cabin" to "Roots,"* 1980; Thomas F.

Gossett, *Uncle Tom's Cabin and American Culture*, 1985. For other useful critical studies, see *New Essays on Uncle Tom's Cabin*, 1986, ed. Eric J. Sundquist; and Josephine Donovan, *Uncle Tom's Cabin: Evil, Affliction, and Redemptive Love*, 1991.

May Swenson

Swenson's volumes of poems include *Another Animal* (1954), *A Cage of Spines* (1958), *To Mix with Time: New and Selected Poems* (1963), *Poems to Solve* (1966), *Half Sun Half Sleep* (1967), *Iconographs* (1970), *More Poems to Solve* (1971), *The Guess and Spell Coloring Book* (1976), *New and Selected Things Taking Place* (1978), *In Other Words: New Poems* (1987), *The Love Poems of May Swenson* (1991), and *Nature: Poems Old and New* (1994). Swenson's comments are also included in *Poets on Poetry*, 1966, ed. Howard Nemerov, and Karla Hammond interviewed Swenson for *Parnassus 7* (1978). Useful critical essays are Ann Stanford, "The Art of Perceiving," *Southern Review* 6 (1969); Alicia Ostriker, "May Swenson and the Shapes of Speculation," in *Shakespeare's Sisters*, 1979, ed. Sandra M. Gilbert and Susan Gubar; and Ann S. Wicks, "Music, Meaning, and the Adaptation of Literature," *Literature in Performance* 2 (1981); and Dave Smith, "May Swenson: Perpetual Worlds Taking Place," in his *Local Assays: On Contemporary American Poetry*, 1985.

Luci Tapahonso

Tapahonso's collections of poems and stories include *Seasonal Woman*, with drawings by R. C. Gorman (1982); *A Breeze Swept Through* (1987); and *Saanii Dahataal, the Women Are Singing* (1993). Tapahonso also contributed an essay, "The Way It Is," to *Sign Language: Contemporary Southwest Native America* (1989).

Sojourner Truth

Truth's speeches can be found in Elizabeth Cady Stanton et al., *History of Woman Suffrage*, vols. I–III (1881–86). Truth's story is told in the *Narrative of Sojourner Truth, a Northern Slave, Emancipated from Bodily Servitude by the State of New York, in 1828*, an account written by Olive Gilbert in 1850 and reprinted several times—for instance, in 1991, with an introduction by Jeffrey C. Stewart, and in 1993, edited and with an introduction by Margaret Washington. Also reprinted is Arthur Huff Fauset, *Sojourner Truth: God's Faithful Pilgrim*, 1938, 1971. More recent biographies are Jacqueline Bernard, *Journey toward Freedom: The Story of Sojourner Truth*, 1967, and Carleton Mabee, *Sojourner Truth—Slave, Prophet, Legend*, 1993. An important interpre-

tation of Truth's life and work is Linda David and Erlene Stetson, *Glorying in Tribulation: The Lifework of Sojourner Truth* (1994). A useful article is Nell Irvin Painter, "Sojourner Truth in Life and Memory: Writing the Biography of an American Exotic," *Gender and History* 2 (1990).

Diane Wakoski

Wakoski's works include *Trilogy* (1974)—her first three books in one volume—as well as *The Motorcycle Betrayal Poems* (1971), *Waiting for the King of Spain* (1976), *Toward a New Poetry* (1980), *The Lady Who Drove Me to the Airport* (1982), *The Magician's Feastletters* (1982), and *The Complete Greed, Parts 1–13* (1984). Her recent books of poetry include *Why My Mother Likes Liberace* (1985), *The Rings of Saturn* (1986), *Emerald Ice: Selected Poems, 1962–1987* (1988), *Medea the Sorceress* (1990), and *Jason the Sailor* (1993). For interesting biographical information, see Taffy Martin, "An Interview with Diane Wakoski," *Dalhousie Review* 61 (1981); and the interview with Wakowski in Lee Bartlett, ed., *Talking Poetry: Conversations in the Workshop with Contemporary Poets*, 1987. Helpful critical articles include T. Olson, ed., "A Symposium on Diane Wakoski," *Margins* (1976); Evan Watkins, "Historical Criticism and Contemporary Poetry," *Contemporary Literature* 22 (1981); and Taffy W. Martin, "Diane Wakoski's Personal Mythology: Dionysian Music, Created Presence," *Boundary* 2 (1982). A helpful essay on Wakowski's development as a poet is Linda W. Wagner, "Wakowski's Early Poems: Moving Past Confession," in *Still the Frame Holds; Essays on Women Poets and Writers*, 1993, ed. Sheila Roberts and Yvonne Pacheo Tevis. See also the valuable discussions of Wakowski in Estella Lauter, *Women as Mythmakers: Poetry and Visual Art by Twentieth-Century Women*, 1984; and in two works by Alicia Ostriker: "'What are Patterns for?': Anger and Polarization in Women's Poetry," *Feminist Studies* 10 (1984), and *Stealing the Language: The Emergence of Women's Poetry in America*, 1986. A useful reference guide is Robert Newton, *Diane Wakowski: A Descriptive Bibliography*, 1987.

Alice Walker

Walker's works are *Once* (1968), *The Third Life of Grange Copeland* (1970), *Revolutionary Petunias* (1973), *Langston Hughes* (1974), *In Love and Trouble* (1973), *Meridian* (1976), *Good Night Willie Lee, I'll See You in the Morning* (1979), *You Can't Keep a Good Woman Down* (1981), *The Color Purple* (1982), *In Search of Our Mothers' Gardens: Womanist Prose* (1983), *Living by the Word: Selected*

Writings, 1973–1987 (1988), Her Blue Body Everything We Know: Earthling Poems, 1965–1990 (1991), and Warrior Marks: Female Genital Mutilation and the Sexual Binding of Women (1993), with Pratibha Parmar. A critical edition of Everyday Use appeared in 1994, edited and with an introduction by Barbara Christian. An interview appears in Black Women Writers at Work, 1984, ed. Claudia Tate.

Full-length studies include Elliott Butler-Evans, Race, Gender, and Desire. Narrative Strategies in the Fiction of Toni Cade Bambara, Toni Morrison, and Alice Walker. 1989; Donna Haisty Winchell, Alice Walker, 1992; and Alice Walker: Critical Perspectives Past and Present, 1993, ed. Henry Louis Gates Jr. and Kwame Anthony Appiah. Critical essays on Walker's work include Trudier Harris, "Folklore in the Fiction of Alice Walker," Black American Literature Forum 11 (1977). Chester J. Fantenot, "Alice Walker, 'The Diary of an African Nun' and Du Bois' Double Consciousness," and Mary Helen Washington, "An Essay on Alice Walker" both in Sturdy Black Bridges: Visions of Black Women in Literature, 1979, ed. Roseann Bell, Bettye Parker, and Beverly Guy-Sheftall; Deborah McDowell, "The Self in Bloom: Alice Walker's Meridian," College Language Association Journal 24 (1981); Trudier Harris, "Tiptoeing through Taboo: Incest in 'The Child Who Favored Daughter,'" Modern Fiction Studies 28 (1982); Barbara Christian, "Alice Walker," and Bettye J. Parker-Smith, "Alice Walker's Women," both in Black Women Writers (1950–1980), 1984, ed. Mari Evans; Lauren Berlant, "Race, Gender, and Nation in The Color Purple,'" Critical Inquiry 14 (1988), and bell hooks, "Writing the Subject: Reading The Color Purple," in Reading Black, Reading Feminist: A Critical Anthology, 1990, ed. Henry Louis Gates Jr. See also "Alice Walker: A Special Section," Callaloo 12 (1989). A useful, though somewhat dated, resource is Louise H. Pratt, Alice Walker: An Annotated Bibliography, 1968–1986, 1988.

Margaret Walker

Walker's works include For My People (1942), Jubilee (1966), Prophets for a New Day (1970), How I Wrote Jubilee (1972), October Journey (1973). A Poetic Equation: Conversations with Nikki Giovani (1974), The Daemonic Genius of Richard Wright (1934), This Is My Century: New and Collected Poems (1989), and How I Wrote "Jubilee" and Other Essays on Life and Literature (1990). For bibliographical information, see Jane Campbell, "Margaret Walker," in African American Writers, 1991, ed. Valerie Smith. Three helpful interviews are Charles H.

Robell, "Poetry, History, and Humanism: An Interview with Margaret Walker," Blackworld 25 (1975); Phanuel Egejuru and Robert E. Fox, "An Interview with Margaret Walker." Callaloo 2 (1979); and an interview in Black Women Writers at Work, 1984, ed. Claudia Tate. Critical essays on Walker include Phyllis R. Klotman, "'Oh Freedom': Women and History in Margaret Walker's Jubilee," Black American Literature Forum 11 (1977); James E. Spears, "Black Folk Elements in Margaret Walker's Jubilee," Mississippi Folklore Register 14 (1980); R. Baxter Miller, "The 'Etched Flame' of Margaret Walker: Biblical and Literary Recreation in Southern History," Tennessee Studies in Literature 26 (1981); two pieces in Black Women Writers (1950–1980), 1984, ed. Mari Evans—Eugenia Colliers, "Fields Watered with Blood: Myth and Ritual in the Poetry of Margaret Walker," and Eleanor Traylor, "Music as Theme: The Blues Mode in the Works of Margaret Walker"; Margaret B. McDowell, "The Black Woman as Artist and Critic: Four Versions," The Kentucky Review 7 (1987); and Charlotte Goodman, "From Uncle Tom's Cabin to Vyry's Kitchen: The Black Female Folk Tradition in Margaret Walker's Jubilee," in Tradition and the Talents of Women, 1991, ed. Florence Howe. Walker is also discussed in Southern Women Writers: The New Generation, 1990, ed. Tonette Bond Inge.

Eudora Welty

Welty's volumes of fiction include A Curtain of Green, and Other Stories (1941). The Wide Net, and Other Stories (1943), The Leaning Tower, and Other Stories (1944), Delta Wedding (1946), The Golden Apples (1949), The Bride of the Innisfallen, and Other Stories (1955), The Shoe Bird (1964), and The Optimist's Daughter (1972). The Collected Stories of Eudora Welty was published in 1989. The Selected Stories of Eudora Welty, 1954, has a valuable introduction by Katherine Anne Porter. Books of photographs by Welty include One Time and One Place (1971) and Eudora Welty: Photographs, 1989, with a foreword by Reynolds Price. One Writer's Beginnings (1983) is her literary autobiography. A Writer's Eye: Collected Book Reviews, 1994, edited and introduced by Pearl Amelia McHaney, is a collection of the sixty-seven book reviews written by Welty from 1942 to 1984.

Full-length studies of her writing include Ruth M. Vande Kieft, Eudora Welty, 1962, rev. 1987; Alfred Appel, A Season of Dreams: The Fiction of Eudora Welty, 1965; Elizabeth Evans, Eudora Welty, 1981; Albert J. Devlin, Eudora Welty's Chronicle: A Story of Mississippi Life, 1983; Peter Schmidt, The Heart of the Story: Eudora Welty's Short Fiction 1991; and Gail

Mortimer, *Daughter of the Swan: Love and Knowledge in Eudora Welty's Fiction*, 1994. Useful collections of critical essays are *A Still Moment: Essays on the Art of Eudora Welty*, 1978, ed. John F. Desmond; *Critical Essays on Eudora Welty*, 1989, ed. Craig Turner; and *The Critical Response to Eudora Welty's Fiction*, 1994, ed. Laurie Champion. *Welty: A Life in Literature*, ed. Albert J. Devlin, was published in 1987 to celebrate the fiftieth anniversary of Welty's first publication. Also available are Victor H. Thompson, *Eudora Welty: A Reference Guide*, 1976, and Noel Polk, *Eudora Welty, A Bibliography of Her Work*, 1994.

Rebecca West

West's numerous works include novels—notably *The Return of the Soldier* (1918), *The Judge* (1922), and *Harriet Hume* (1930)—a number of which have been reprinted, as well as several volumes of stories and many volumes of nonfictional prose, including books on Henry James and D. H. Lawrence. Works published posthumously include two novels, *Cousin Rosamond* (1985) and *Sunflower* (1986), and a collection of memoirs and auto-biographical narratives, *Family Memories*, 1987, ed. Faith Evans. In addition, Antonia Till has edited a collection that included short fiction and an unfinished novel: *The Only Poet and Short Stories*, (1992). A valuable anthology of her early journalism is *The Young Rebecca*, 1982, ed. Jane Marcus.

Full-length studies of her life and work include Peter Wolfe, *Rebecca West: Artist and Thinker*, 1971; Gordon N. Ray, *H. G. Wells and Rebecca West*, 1974; Motley F. Deakin, *Rebecca West*, 1980; and Harold Orel, *The Literary Achievement of Rebecca West*, 1986. Victoria Glendinning's biography, *Rebecca West: A Life*, appeared in 1987, and J. R. Hammond's *H. G. Wells and Rebecca West* was published in 1991. For feminist perspectives on West, see Jane Marcus, "A Wilderness of One's Own: Feminist Fantasy Novels of the Twenties: Rebecca West and Sylvia Townsend Warner," in *Women Writers and the City: Essays in Feminist Literary Criticism*, 1984, ed. Susan Merrill Squier; Bonnie Kime Scott, "Refiguring the Binary, Breaking the Cycle: Rebecca West as Feminist Modernist," *Twentieth-Century Literature* 37 (1991); and Sue Thomas, "Rebecca West's Second Thoughts on Feminism," *Genders* 13 (1992). Other helpful essays include Margaret Diane Stetz, "Rebecca West and the Visual Arts," *Tulsa Studies in Women's Literature* 8, (1989), and Jane Gledhill, "Impersonality and Amnesia: A Response to World War I in the Writings of H. D. and Rebecca West," in *Women and World War I: The Written Response*, 1993, ed. Dorothy Goldman. George E.

Hutchinson compiled *A Preliminary List of the Writings of Rebecca West*, 1957, which was followed by Motley F. Deakin, "Rebecca West: A Supplement to Hutchinson's Preliminary List," *Bulletin of Bibliography* (1982). A useful recent reference guide is Joan Garrett Packer, *Rebecca West: An Annotated Bibliography*, 1991.

Edith Wharton

Wharton's works include *The Decoration of Houses* (1897), *The House of Mirth* (1905), *Madame de Trêymes* (1907), *Tales of Men and Ghosts* (1910), *Ethan Frome* (1911), *The Custom of the Country* (1913), *Xingu* (1916), *Summer* (1917), *The Age of Innocence* (1920), and *Old New York* (1924), most of which have been reissued in the Scribner Library. In addition, Louis Auchincloss edited *The Edith Wharton Reader*, 1965, and R. W. B. Lewis edited in two volumes *The Collected Short Stories of Edith Wharton*, 1968. R. W. B. Lewis and Nancy Lewis edited *The Letters of Edith Wharton* in 1988. Another collection of correspondence is Lyall H. Powers, *Henry James and Edith Wharton: Letters, 1900–1915*, 1990.

Two major biographies are R. W. B. Lewis, *Edith Wharton: A Biography*, 1975; and Cynthia Griffin Wolff, *A Feast of Words: The Triumph of Edith Wharton*, 1977. Recent biographical studies of Wharton include Susan Goodman, *Edith Wharton's Women: Friends and Rivals*, 1990; Shari Benstock, *No Gifts from Chance: A Biography of Edith Wharton*, 1994; Eleanor Dwight, *Edith Wharton: An Extraordinary Life*, 1994; and Goodman, *Edith Wharton's Inner Circle*, 1994. Other useful biographical and critical studies include Blake Nevius, *Edith Wharton: A Study of Her Fiction*, 1953; Marilyn J. Lyde, *Edith Wharton: Convention and Morality in the Work of a Novelist*, 1959; Louis Auchincloss, *Edith Wharton*, 1961; Millicent Bell, *Edith Wharton and Henry James: The Story of Their Friendship*, 1965; Geoffrey Walton, *Edith Wharton: A Critical Interpretation*, 1971; Margaret B. McDowell, *Edith Wharton*, 1976; Richard H. Lawson, *Edith Wharton*, 1977; Elizabeth Ammons, *Edith Wharton's Argument with America*, 1980; Carol Wershaven, *The Female Intruder in the Novels of Edith Wharton*, 1982; Judith Fryer, *Felicitous Space: The Imaginative Structures of Edith Wharton and Willa Cather*, 1986; Josephine Donovan, *After the Fall: The Demeter-Persephone Myth in Wharton, Cather, and Glasgow*, 1988; Lev Raphael, *Edith Wharton's Prisoners of Shame: A New Perspective on Her Fiction*, 1990; Penelope Vita-Finzi, *Edith Wharton and the Unsatisfactory Man*, 1991; Candace Waid, *Edith Wharton's Letters from the Underworld: Fictions of Women*

and Writing, 1991; and Gloria C. Erlich, *The Sexual Education of Edith Wharton*, 1992. A valuable collection of critical essays is *Edith Wharton: New Critical Essays*, 1992, ed. Alfred Bendixen and Annette Zilversmith. For feminist perspectives on Wharton, see Sandra M. Gilbert and Susan Gubar, *Sexchanges*, 1989; and Elaine Showalter, *Sister's Choice: Tradition and Change in American Women's Writing*, 1991. Useful reference guides are Stephen Garrison, *Edith Wharton: A Descriptive Bibliography*, 1990; and Kristin O. Lauer, *Edith Wharton: An Annotated Secondary Bibliography*, 1990.

Phillis Wheatley

Wheatley's only book is *Poems on Various Subjects, Religious and Moral* (1773); a good current edition is the revised and enlarged *The Poems of Phillis Wheatley*, 1989, ed. Julian D. Mason Jr. See also *The Collected Works of Phillis Wheatley*, 1988, ed. John C. Shields. Shirley Graham, *The Story of Phillis Wheatley*, 1969; William G. Allen, *Wheatley, Banneker and Horton*, 1970; and Merle Richmond, *Phillis Wheatley*, 1988, are useful critical biographies. William Henry Robinson has four important contributions: *Phillis Wheatley in the Black American Beginnings*, 1975; *Phillis Wheatley: A Bio-Bibliography*, 1981; *Critical Essays on Phillis Wheatley*, 1982; and *Phillis Wheatley and Her Writings*, 1984. Another helpful secondary source is *Bid the Vassal Soar: Interpretive Essays on the Life and Poetry of Phillis Wheatley and George Moses*, 1974, ed. M. A. Richmond.

Anna Wickham

Wickham's *Selected Poems*—which appeared in many volumes during her lifetime—were edited with an introduction by David Garnett, 1971. R. D. Smith edited *The Writings of Anna Wickham: Free Woman and Poet* in 1984, a collection that includes the complete poems, an autobiographical fragment, and occasional pieces. Poems by Wickham appear in *The Faber Book of Twentieth-Century Women's Poetry*, 1987, ed. Fleur Adcock. Little critical work has been done, but see Margaret Newlin, "Anna Wickham: 'The Sexless Part Which is My Mind,'" *Southern Review* 14 (1978), and Myra Stark, "Feminist Themes in Anna Wickham's 'The Contemplative Quarry' and 'The Man with a Hammer,'" *Four Decades of Poetry* 2 (1978). A recent essay is Matt Holland, "Anna Wickham: Fettered Woman, Free Spirit," *Poetry Review* 78 (1988).

Harriet E. Adams Wilson

Wilson's book *Our Nig* (1859) was discovered by Henry Louis Gates Jr. and republished by Vintage Books in 1983, with a useful critical and biographical introduction by Gates. *Our Nig* is also included in *Three Classic African-American Novels*, 1990, ed. William L. Andrews. Important biographical material can be found in Barbara A. White, "Our Nig and the She-Devil: New Information about Harriet Wilson and the 'Bellmont' Family," *American Literature* 65 (1993). A valuable essay on Wilson's novel is Gates, "Parallel Discursive Universes: Fictions of the Self in Harriet Wilson's *Our Nig*," in his *Figures in Black: Words, Signs, and the "Racial" Self*, 1987. See also the discussions of Wilson in Bernard W. Bell, *The Afro-American Novel and Its Tradition*, 1987; Andrews, *To Tell a Free Story: The First Century of Afro-American Autobiography, 1760–1865*, 1988; and Claudia Tate, *Domestic Allegories of Political Desire: The Black Heroine's Text at the Turn of the Century*, 1992. Other useful studies include Frances S. Foster, "Adding Color and Contour to Early American Self-Portraitures: Autobiographical Writings of African-American Women," in *Conjuring: Black Women, Fiction, and Literary Tradition*, 1985, ed. Marjorie Pryse and Hortense Spillers; Beth Maclay Doriani, "Black Womanhood in Nineteenth-Century America: Subversion and Self-Construction in Two Women's Autobiographies," *American Quarterly* 43 (1991); Elizabeth Breau, "Identifying Satire: *Our Nig*," *Callaloo* 16 (1993); Cynthia J. Davis, "Speaking of the Body's Pain: Harriet Wilson's *Our Nig*," *African American Review* 27 (1993); Karla Holloway, "Economies of Space: Markets and Marketability in *Our Nig* and *Iola Leroy*," in *The (Other) American Traditions: Nineteenth-Century Women Writers*, 1993; and Margaret Lindgren, "Harriet Jacobs, Harriet Wilson, and the Redoubled Voice in Black Autobiography," *Obsidian II* 8 (1993).

Isabella Whitney

Whitney's two published works consist of a poem, *The Copy of a Letter* (1567), and a collection of verse, *A Sweet Nosegay or Pleasant Posye* (1573), which includes a poetic rewriting of Hugh Plat's maxims from *The Floures of Philosophie* (1572) a series of verse letters; and Whitney's "Will and Testament." Biographical and critical approaches to her career appear in three book-length studies: Elaine V. Beilin, *Redeeming Eve: Women Writers of the English Renaissance*, 1987; Ann Rosalind Jones, "Nets and Bridles: Early Modern Conduct Books and Sixteenth-Century Women's Lyrics," in *The Ideology of Conduct: Essays in Literature and the History of Sexuality*, 1987, ed. Nancy Armstrong and Leonard Tennenhouse; and Tina Krontiris, *Oppositional Voices: Women as*

Writers and Translators in the English Renaissance, 1992. See also "Isabella Whitney, Sir Hugh Plat, Geoffrey Whitney, and 'Sister Eldershae'," English Language Notes 21 (1983). Two useful critical essays are Betty Travitsky, "The Lady Doth Protest: Protest in the Popular Writings of Renaissance Englishwomen," English Literary Renaissance 14 (1984); and Wendy Wall, "Isabella Whitney and the Female Legacy," English Literary History 58 (1991).

Helen Maria Williams

Williams's work includes An Ode on the Peace (1783), Peru: A Poem (1784), Poems (1786), Julia: A Novel (1790), Letters on the French Revolution (1791–92), Letters From France (1794), Letters Containing a Sketch on the Politics of France (1796), A Tour of Switzerland (1798), Poems: Moral, Elegant and Pathetic (1801), Sketches of the State of Manners and Opinions in the French Republic Towards the Close of the Eighteenth Century (1801), The History of Perourou, The Bellows-Mender (1802), A Narrative of the Events Which Have Taken Place In France (1815), Poems on Various Subjects (1823), Memoirs of the Reign of Robespierre (1929), and Four New Letters of Mary Wollstonecraft and Helen M. Williams (1937), ed. Benjamin Kurtz and Carrie C. Autry. Williams also translated many books from the French, including Louis Sebastian Mercier, Seraphina: A Novel (1797); M. Ducray-Duminil, Ambrose and Eleanor: of the Adventures of Two Children Deserted on an Uninhabited Island (1799); Bernardin de Saint-Pierre, Paul and Virginia (1800); Francois Babie Barancy, The Political and Confidential Correspondence of Lewis XVI (1803); Alexander von Humboldt and Aime de Bonpland, Researches Concerning the Institutions and Monuments of the Ancient Inhabitants of America (1814); and Alexander von Humboldt and Aime de Bonpland, Personal Narrative of Travels to the Equinoctical Regions of the New Continent During the Years 1799–1804 (1815). Critical work includes Gary Kelly, Women, Writing and Revolution, 1790–1827 (1993), Deborah Kennedy, "Spectacle of the Guillotine: Helen Maria Williams and the Reign of Terror," Philological Quarterly 73 (1994), and Mary A. Farret, "Spectatrice as Spectacle: Helen Maria Williams at Home in the Revolution," Studies in Romanticism 32 (1993).

Mary Wollstonecraft

The seven-volume edition of The Works of Mary Wollstonecraft, ed. Janet M. Todd and Marilyn Butler, was published in 1989, as part of the Pickering Masters series; it includes all of Wollstonecraft's work published during her lifetime or immediately after her death. Of these works, the most important are the following three political writings: A Vindication of the Rights of Men (1790), A Vindication of the Rights of Woman (1792), and An Historical and Moral View of the French Revolution (1794), all of which are also collected even more recently in Political Writings, 1993, ed. Janet M. Todd; and her two novels, Mary, a Fiction (1788) and Maria; or, The Wrongs of Women (1797), the second of which she left unfinished at her death. The Collected Letters, ed. Ralph M. Wardle, was published in 1979.

Many biographers have drawn upon William Goodwin's "Memoirs of the Author of A Vindication of the Rights of Women," 1798. Modern critical biographies include Ralph Wardle, Mary Wollstonecraft, 1951; Eleanor Flexner, Mary Wollstonecraft: A Biography, 1972; Claire Tomlin, The Life and Death of Mary Wollstonecraft, 1975, rev. 1992; and Janet M. Todd and Moira Ferguson, Mary Wollstonecraft, 1984. Interesting appreciative essays include Virginia Woolf, "Mary Wollstonecraft," in The Second Common Reader, 1932, and Ruth Benedict, "Mary Wollstonecraft," in An Anthropologist at Work, 1959, ed. Margaret Mead. Among more recent critical studies of Wollstonecraft's life and work are Moira Ferguson, Mary Wollstonecraft, 1984, and Virginia Sapiro, A Vindication of Political Virtue: The Political Theory of Mary Wollstonecraft, 1992. Wollstonecraft is also treated in Mary Poovey, The Proper Lady and the Woman Writer, 1984; Laurie Langbauer, "An Early Romance: Motherhood and Women's Writing in Mary Wollstonecraft's Novels," in Romanticism and Feminism, 1988, ed. Anne Mellor; and Tom Furniss, "Mary Wollstonecraft (1759–97)," in A Handbook to English Romanticism, 1992, ed. Jean Raimond and J. R. Watson. Janet M. Todd compiled an annotated bibliography, Mary Wollstonecraft, 1976, and Leigh Williams and Rosemarie Johnstone produced Updating Mary Wollstonecraft: A Bibliography of Criticism, 1976–1989, Bulletin of Bibliography 48 (1991).

Virginia Woolf

Woolf's novels—which include The Voyage Out (1915), Night and Day (1919), Jacob's Room (1922), Mrs. Dalloway (1925), To the Lighthouse (1927), Orlando (1928), The Waves (1931), The Years (1937), and Between the Acts (1941)—have all been issued in paperback, as have her two major polemical volumes, A Room of One's Own (1929) and Three Guineas (1938). Susan Dick edited The Complete Shorter Fiction in 1985. Her Collected Essays, 4 vols., 1966–67, are supplemented by Books and Portraits, 1977, ed. Mary Lyon; Virginia Woolf on Women and Writing, 1979, ed. Michele

Barrett; and *Contemporary Writers* (with preface by Jean Guiget), 1966, a further collection of her book reviews. In addition, Andrew McNeillie edited *The Essays of Virginia Woolf* in three volumes, 1985–89. Woolf's *Moments of Being*, 1976, ed. Jeanne Schulkind, contains a group of memoirs, as well as a helpful introduction. *The Diary of Virginia Woolf*, ed. Anne Olivier Bell, began appearing in 1977, and two journal collections were published in 1990: *A Passionate Apprentice: The Early Journals, 1897–1909*, ed. Mitchell A. Leaska, and *A Moment's Liberty: The Shorter Diary*, ed. Anne Olivier Bell. *The Letters of Virginia Woolf*, 1975–80, ed. Nigel Nicholson and Joanne Trautmann, are available, as is a one-volume selection of Woolf's correspondence, *Congenial Spirits: The Selected Letters*, 1989, ed. Joanne Trautmann Banks.

Biographies include Quentin Bell, *Virginia Woolf*, 2 vols., 1972; Phyllis Rose, *Woman of Letters: A Life of Virginia Woolf*, 1978; Roger Poole, *The Unknown Virginia Woolf*, 1978; Louise De Salvo, *Virginia Woolf: The Impact of Childhood Sexual Abuse on Her Life and Work*, 1989; and James King *Virginia Woolf* (1995). Among the most useful of the many full-length critical studies of Woolf's work are Winifred Holtby, *Virginia Woolf*, 1978; David Daiches, *Virginia Woolf*, rev. 1963; Joan Bennett, *Virginia Woolf: Her Art as a Novelist*, 2nd ed. 1964; Jean Guiget, *Virginia Woolf and Her Works* (trans. Jean Stewart), 1965; Herbert Marder, *Feminism and Art: A Study of Virginia Woolf*, 1968; Harvena Richter, *Virginia Woolf: The Inward Voyage*, 1970; James Naremore, *The World without a Self*, 1973; Jean O. Love, *Virginia Woolf: Sources of Madness in Art*, 1977; Mark Spilka, *Virginia Woolf's Quarrel with Grieving*, 1980; Perry Meisel, *The Absent Father: Virginia Woolf and Walter Pater*, 1980; Maria DiBattista, *Virginia Woolf's Major Novels: The Fables of Anon.*, 1980; Susan Merrill Squier, *Woolf and London: The Sexual Politics of the City*, 1985; Mark Hussey, *The Singing of the Real World: The Philosophy of Woolf's Fiction*, 1985; Alex Zwerdling, *Virginia Woolf and the Real World*, 1986; Jane Marcus, *Virginia Woolf and the Languages of Patriarchy*, 1987; Makiko Minow-Pinkney, *Virginia Woolf and the Problem of the Subject*, 1987; Elizabeth Steele, *Virginia Woolf's Rediscovered Essays: Sources and Allusions*, 1987; Rachel Bowlby, *Virginia Woolf: Feminist Destinations*, 1988; Virginia R. Hyman, *To the Lighthouse and Beyond: Transformations in the Narratives of Virginia Woolf*, 1988; Elizabeth Abel, *Virginia Woolf and the Fictions of Psychoanalysis*, 1989; Alice Fox, *Virginia Woolf and the Literature of the English Renaissance*, 1990; and Alison Booth, *Greatness Engendered: George Eliot and Virginia Woolf*, 1992. See also Carolyn

Heilbrun, *Toward a Recognition of Androgyny*, 1973; Rachel Blau DuPlessis, *Writing beyond the Ending: Narrative Strategies of Twentieth-Century Women Writers*, 1985; Patricia Waugh, *Feminine Fictions: Revisiting the Postmodern*, 1988; and Sandra M. Gilbert and Susan Gubar, *Letters from the Front*, 1994.

Essay collections include *Virginia Woolf: A Collection of Critical Essays*, 1975, ed. Thomas Lewis; *Virginia Woolf: Reevaluation and Continuity*, 1980, ed. Ralph Freedman; *New Feminist Essays on Virginia Woolf*, 1981, and *Virginia Woolf: A Feminist Slant*, 1983, both ed. Jane Marcus; *Virginia Woolf: Modern Critical Views*, 1986, ed. Harold Bloom; *Virginia Woolf and Bloomsbury: A Centenary Celebration*, 1987, ed. Jane Marcus; *Virginia Woolf and War: Fiction, Reality, and Myth*, 1991, ed. Mark Hussey; *Virginia Woolf: A Collection of Critical Essays*, 1993, ed. Margaret Homans; and *New Essays on Virginia Woolf*, 1994, ed. Helen Wussow. For other books and articles, see Brownlee Jean Kirkpatrick, *A Bibliography of Virginia Woolf*, 1980. Useful reference works are Edward L. Bishop, *A Virginia Woolf Chronology*, 1989; and James M. Haule, *A Concordance to the Novels of Virginia Woolf*, 1991.

Constance Fenimore Woolson

An edition of Woolson's stories, *Women Artists, Women Exiles: "Miss Grief" and Other Stories*, ed. Joan Myers Weimar, became available in 1988. Some of Woolson's correspondence has been published in Alice Hall Petry, ed., "'Always, Your Attached Friend': The Unpublished Letters of Constance Fenimore Woolson to John and Clara Hay," *Books at Brown* 29–39 (1982–83). A valuable critical biography is Cheryl B. Torsney, *Constance Fenimore Woolson: The Grief of Artistry*, 1989. Torsney has also edited the useful collection *Critical Essays on Constance Fenimore Woolson*, 1992. Two critical articles are Sharon L. Dean, "Homeward Bound: The Novels of Constance Fenimore Woolson," *Legacy* 6 (1989); and Victoria Brehm, "Island Fortresses: The Landscape of the Imagination in the Great Lakes Fiction of Constance Fenimore Woolson," *American Literary Realism*, 1870–1910 22 (1990).

Dorothy Wordsworth

Mary Moorman edited *Journals: The Alfoxden Journal, 1798*, and *The Grasmere Journals, 1800–1803*, 1971, with an introduction by Helen Darbishire. Pamela Woof edited an edition of *Grasmere Journals*, 1991; and Paul Hamilton edited *Dorothy Wordsworth: Selections from the Journals*, 1992. Wordsworth's letters are collected with those of her brother in *The Letters of William Wordsworth and*

Dorothy Wordsworth, 6 vols., 1935–39 (rev. C. L. Shaver et al., 1967–82). The standard biography is Ernest de Selincourt, *Dorothy Wordsworth*, 1933. More recent are Elizabeth Gunn, *A Passion for the Particular: Dorothy Wordsworth, a Portrait*, 1981, and Pamela Woof, *Dorothy Wordsworth, Writer*, 1988. Also helpful is Sean Manley, *Dorothy and William Wordsworth: The Heart of a Circle of Friends*, 1974. A book-length study of Wordsworth's literary influence is Susan Levin, *Dorothy Wordsworth and Romanticism*, 1987. For useful feminist approaches to this writer's career and works, see the chapter in Margaret Homans, *Women Writers and Poetic Identity*, 1980; James Holt McGavran Jr., "Dorothy Wordsworth's Journals: Putting Herself Down," in *The Private Self: Theory and Practice of Women's Autobiographical Writings*, 1988, ed. Shari Benstock; and Pamela Woof, "Dorothy Wordsworth's Journals and the Engendering of Poetry," *Bucknell Review* 36 (1992).

Judith Wright

Wright's recent books of poetry are *Phantom Dwelling* (1985), *A Human Pattern: Selected Poems* (1990), and *Through Broken Glass* (1992). She has two major collections: *Collected Poems*, which appeared in 1971, and *Collected Poems: 1942–1985*, which appeared in 1994. Besides a number of books for children, Wright has written a critical biography, *Charles Harpur* (1963), as well as a critical volume, *Preoccupations in Australian Poetry* (1965). Articles on her work include Stephen Tatum, "Tradition of the Exile: Judith Wright's Australian 'West', " in *Women, Women Writers, and the West*, 1979; Leonie Kramer, "Judith Wright, Hope, McAuley," *The Literary Criterion* 15 (1980); Anne Godschalk, "The Australianness of Judith Wright: Landscape, Metaphor, and Analogy," *Dutch Quarterly Review of Anglo-American Letters* 12 (1982); Delip Kumar Sen, "The Poetry of Judith Wright: An Attempt at Interpretation," *Journal of the Department of English (Calcutta)* 18 (1982–83); Syed Anunuddan, "Judith Wright: A Major Australian Poet," *Creative Moment* 13/14; David Dawling, "Judith Wright's Delicate Balance," *Australian Literary Studies* 9; and Harry Heseltine, "Wrestling with the Angel: Judith Wright's Poetry in the 1950s," in his *The Uncertain Self: Essays in Australian Literature and Criticism*, 1986. For a feminist approach to Wright's poetry, see Jennifer Strauss, "Within the Bounds of Feminine Sensibility? The Poetry of Rosemary Dobson, Gwen Harwood, and Judith Wright," in *Still the Frame Holds: Essays on Women Poets and Writers*, 1993, ed. Sheila Roberts and Yvonne Pacheo Tevis.

Mary Wroth

The Poems of Lady Mary Wroth, 1983, ed. Josephine Roberts, includes most of Wroth's poems, an informative introduction, and detailed notes (as well as an appendix with selections from Wroth's correspondence). Wroth's romance *The Countesse of Montgomeries Urania* (1621) is not yet available in a complete modern edition, but the sonnet sequence *Pamphilia to Amphilanthus* (originally appended to *Urania*) was edited by Gary Waller in 1977. Wroth's pastoral drama *Love's Victory* (unpublished in her lifetime) was edited by Michael G. Brennan in 1988.

Critical studies that provide interesting biographical background are Waller's *The Sidney Family Romance: Mary Wroth, William Herbert, and the Early Modern Construction of Gender*, 1993; and Mary Ellen Lamb's *Gender and Authorship in the Sidney Circle*, 1990. A full-length study of Wroth's poetry is May N. Paulissen, *The Love Sonnets of Lady Mary Wroth: A Critical Introduction*, 1982. Feminist perspectives on Wroth can be found in a useful collection of critical essays, *The Renaissance Englishwoman in Print: Counterbalancing the Canon*, 1990. Another important collection, *Reading Mary Wroth: Representing Alternatives in Early Modern England*, ed. Naomi J. Miller and Gary Waller, appeared in 1991. See also the valuable discussions of Wroth in Paul Salzman, *English Prose Fiction, 1558–1700: A Critical History*, 1985; Elaine V. Beilin, *Redeeming Eve: Women Writers of the English Renaissance*, 1987; Ann Rosalind Jones, *The Currency of Eros: Women's Love Lyric in Europe, 1540–1620*, 1990; and Barbara Kiefer Lewalski, *Writing Women in Jacobean England*, 1993. Josephine Roberts has published three notable articles on Wroth: "Lady Mary Wroth's Sonnets: A Labyrinth of the Mind," *Journal of Women's Studies in Literature* 1 (1979); "The Biographical Problem of *Pamphilia to Amphilanthus*," *Tulsa Studies in Women's Literature* 1 (1982); and "Labyrinths of Desire: Lady Mary Wroth's Reconstruction of Romance," *Women's Studies* 19 (1991). Two essays by Maureen Quilligan are also helpful: "Lady Mary Wroth: Female Authority and the Family Romance," in *Unfolded Tales: Essays on Renaissance Romance*, 1989, ed. George Logan and Gordon Teskey; and "The Constant Subject: Instability and Female Authority in Wroth's *Urania* Poems," in *Soliciting Interpretation: Literary Theory and Seventeenth-Century Poetry*, 1990, ed. Elizabeth D. Harvey and Katharine Eisaman Maus.

Elinor Wylie

Wylie's books—published in a brief, eight-year period—include four collections of verse: *Nets*

to Catch the Wind (1921), Black Armour (1923), Trivial Breath (1928), and Angels and Earthly Creatures (1929). She also published four novels: Jennifer Lorn (1923), The Venetian Glass Nephew (1925), The Orphan Angel (1926), and Mr. Hodge and Mr. Hazard (1928). In 1912 her mother had privately printed in London Incidental Numbers, containing her youthful verse. The Collected Poems of Elinor Wylie, ed. William Rose Benét, appeared in 1932, and her Collected Prose came out the following year. Last Poems (1943) brought together previously uncollected poetry as well as some juvenilia from Incidental Numbers and transcriptions from manuscripts, with an appreciation by the English novelist Edith Olivier.

Memoirs and appreciations include Elizabeth S. Sergeant, Fire under the Andes: A Group of North American Portraits, 1927; William Rose Benét, The Prose and Poetry of Elinor Wylie, 1934; Nancy Hoyt's portrait of her sister, Elinor Wylie Portrait of an Unknown Lady, 1935; Carl Van Doren, Three Worlds, 1936; Mary Colum, Life and the Dream, 1947; and Edmund Wilson's essays in Shores of Light, 1952. A full-length biography is Elinor Wylie: A Life Apart by Stanley Olson, 1979. Recent critical studies are Thomas Gray, Elinor Wylie, 1969, and Judith Farr, The Life and Art of Elinor Wylie, 1983. Two interesting essays on Wylie's poetry are Anna Shannon Elfenbein and Terrence Allan Hoagwood, " 'Wild Peaches': Landscapes of Desire and Deprivation," Women's Studies 15 (1988); and Cheryl Walker, "Women and Aggression: Elinor Wylie and the Woman Warrior Persona," in her Masks Outrageous and Austere: Culture, Psyche, and Persona in Modern Women Poets, 1991. A useful reference guide appears in Bibliography of American Literature 9 (1991), ed. Jacob Blanck and Michael Winship.

Hisaye Yamamoto

Yamamoto's short stories are collected in Seventeen Syllables and Other Stories, 1988, with an introduction by King Kok Cheung. Yamamoto has also written the introduction to Toshio Mori, The Chauvinist and Other Stories, 1979. An interview by Charles L. Crow appeared in MELUS 14 (1987). A critical essay is Stan Yogi, "Rebels and Heroines: Subversive Narratives in the Stories of Wakako Yamauchi and Hisaye Yamamoto," in Reading the Literatures of Asian America, ed. and with an introduction by Shirley Geok-lin Lim and Amy Ling.

Anzia Yezierska

Alice Kessler-Harris edited and wrote an introduction for The Open Cage: An Anzia Yezierska Collection, 1979. She also edited and introduced the 1976 reprint of Bread Givers (1925). Other volumes by Yezierska include Hungry Hearts (1920), Salome of the Tenements (1922), Children of Loneliness (1923), Arrogant Beggar (1927), All I Could Never Be (1932), and Red Ribbon on a White Horse (1950). Vivian Gorwich wrote an introduction to How I Found America: Collected Short Stories of Anzia Yezierska, 1991. Good introductions to her life and work are Carol B. Shoe, Anzia Yezierska, 1982, and Louise Levitas Henriksen, Anzia Yezierska: A Writer's Life, 1988.

PERMISSIONS ACKNOWLEDGMENTS

Abigail Adams: Letters to John Adams reprinted by permission of the publishers from THE ADAMS FAMILY CORRESPONDENCE, Vol. I: Dec. 1761–May 1776, edited by L. H. Butterfield et al., Cambridge, Mass: The Belknap Press of Harvard University Press. Copyright © 1963 by the Massachusetts Historical Society.

Fleur Adcock: "Against Coupling," "The Voyage Out," "For a Five-Year-Old," "Miss Hamilton in London," "On the Border," "Street Song," from SELECTED POEMS (1983) by Fleur Adcock. Reprinted by permission of Oxford University Press.

Ama Ata Aidoo: "The Message" from NO SWEETNESS HERE. Copyright © 1970 by Ama Ata Aidoo.

Maya Angelou: "The Peckerwood Dentist and Momma's Incredible Powers" from I KNOW WHY THE CAGED BIRD SINGS by Maya Angelou. Copyright © 1969 by Maya Angelou. Reprinted by permission of Random House and Virago Press Limited.

Gloria Anzaldúa: Tlilli, Tlapalli: The Path of the Red and Black Ink from BORDER-LANDS/LA FRONTERA: THE NEW MESTIZA, © 1987 by Gloria Anzaldúa. Reprinted by permission of Aunt Lute Books.

Margaret Atwood: "This Is a Photograph of Me," © Margaret Atwood 1966 from CIRCLE GAME by Margaret Atwood. Reprinted by permission of Stoddart Publishing Co. Limited, Don Mills, Ontario. "The Little Red Hen Tells All" and "There Was Once" from GOOD BONES AND SIMPLE MURDERS by Margaret Atwood. Copyright © 1983, 1992, 1994 by O. W. Toad Ltd. A Nan A. Talese Book. Reprinted by permission of Doubleday, a division of Bantam Doubleday Publishing Group, Inc., Virago Press Limited. Reprinted by permission from GOOD BONES (Canada) by permission of Coach House Press. "Rape Fantasies" from DANCING GIRL & OTHER STORIES by Margaret Atwood. Reprinted by permission of Phoebe Larmore, the Canadian Publishers, McClelland & Stewart, Toronto, and Curtis Brown Brown Ltd., London. "Spelling" from TRUE STORIES by Margaret Atwood. Copyright © Margaret Atwood 1976. Reprinted by permission of Phoebe Larmore and Curtis Brown Ltd., London, on behalf of Margaret Atwood. "Waiting," "Asparagus," "Marsh Languages," "Morning in the Burned House" from MORNING IN THE BURNED HOUSE. Copyright © 1995 by Margaret Atwood. Reprinted by permission of Houghton Mifflin Company; the Canadian publishers, McClelland & Stewart, Toronto, and Curtis Brown Ltd., London on behalf of O. W. Toad Ltd.

Djuna Barnes: "Cassation" from SELECTED WORKS OF DJUNA BARNES. Copyright © 1962 by Djuna Barnes. Copyright renewed © 1986 by Saxon Barnes and Warner Lowey. Reprinted by permission of Farrar, Straus & Giroux, Inc.

Aphra Behn: "Oroonoko" published 1993 by W. W. Norton & Company, Inc. Reprinted by permission of Joanna Lipking.

Juliana Berners: selections from THE BOOK OF ST. ALBANS by Juliana Berners, translated into modern English by Dorothy Gilbert. Reprinted by permission of the translator.

Patricia Beer: "Witch," "Brunhild," "The Bull," "In Memory of Constance Markiewicz," "Mating Calls," "Transvestism in the Novels of Charlotte Brontë" from COLLECTED POEMS by Patricia Beer. Reprinted by permission of Carcanet Press Limited.

Elizabeth Bishop: "The Fish," In the Waiting Room," "One Art," "Pink Dog," and "Roosters" from THE COMPLETE POEMS 1927–1979 by Elizabeth Bishop. Copyright © 1979, 1983 by Alice Helen Methfessel. "Gwendolyn" from THE COLLECTED PROSE by Elizabeth Bishop, edited by Robert Giroux. Copyright © 1984 by Alice Helen Methfessel. Reprinted by permission of Farrar, Straus & Giroux, Inc.

Louise Bogan: "Medusa," "The Crows," "Women," "Cassandra," "The Crossed Apple," "Evening in the Sanitarium," "Several Voices Out of a Cloud," "The Dream" from THE BLUES ESTUARIES. Copyright © 1968 by Louise Bogan. Reprinted by permission of Farrar, Straus & Giroux, Inc.

Eavan Boland: "The Muse Mother," "Degas's Laundresses" reprinted from OUTSIDE HISTORY: SELECTED POEMS 1980–1990 by Eavan Boland, with the permission of W. W. Norton & Company, Inc. Copyright © 1990 by Eavan Boland. Reprinted by permission of Carcanet Press Limited from NIGHT FEED by Eavan Boland. "In His Own Image" and "Anorexic" from AN ORIGIN LIKE WATER: COLLECTED POEMS 1967–1987 by Eavan Boland. Copyright © 1996, 1980 by Eavan Boland. Reprinted by permission of W. W. Norton & Company, Inc. Reprinted by permission of Carcanet Press Limited from IN HER OWN IMAGE by Eavan Boland.

dream," "how he is coming then," "holy night," "a song of mary," "island mary" reprinted by permission of Curtis Brown Ltd. Copyright © 1980 by the University of Massachusetts. First appeared in *two-headed woman*, published by the University of Massachusetts Press. "if our grandchild be a girl" and "my dream about being white" copyright © 1987 by Lucille Clifton. Reprinted from NEXT: NEW POEMS, by Lucille Clifton, with the permission of BOA Editions Ltd., 92 Park Ave., Brockport, NY 14-20. "move" from THE BOOK OF LIGHT, © 1993 by Lucille Clifton. Reprinted by permission of Copper Canyon Press.

Kamala Das: "An Introduction" reprinted by permission of Kamala Das.

Emily Dickinson: Poems 24, 103, 209, 211, 249, 258, 271, 280, 288, 303, 312, 322, 327, 341, 365, 384, 401, 435, 441, 454, 465, 479, 505, 512, 520, 528, 569, 579, 593, 601, 613, 642, 657, 669, 670, 709, 712, 722, 732, 754, 858, 959, 986, 1129, 1138, 1282, 1317, 1445, 1562, 1651, 1657, 1670, 1705, 1732, 1737 reprinted by permission of the publishers and Trustees of Amherst College from THE POEMS OF EMILY DICKINSON, Thomas H. Johnson, ed., Cambridge, Mass.: The Belknap Press of Harvard University Press, copyright © 1951, 1955, 1979, 1983 by the President and Fellows of Harvard College. Poems 341, 392, 425, 462, 479, 569, 593, 601, 613, 642, 657, 709, 754 from THE COMPLETE POEMS OF EMILY DICKINSON, edited by Thomas H. Johnson. Copyright 1929, 1935 by Martha Dickinson Bianchi; copyright © renewed 1957, 1963 by Mary L. Hampson. Reprinted by permission of Little, Brown and Company. Poem 1072 from LIFE AND LETTERS OF EMILY DICKINSON, edited by Martha Dickinson Bianchi. Copyright 1924 by Martha Dickinson Bianchi, © renewed 1952 by Alfred Leete Hampson. Reprinted by permission of Houghton Mifflin Co. All rights reserved. Letters 233, 248, 26 , 265, 268 reprinted by permission of the publishers from THE LETTERS OF EMILY DICKINSON, edited by Thomas H. Johnson, Cambridge, Mass.: The Belknap Press of Harvard University Press, copyright © 1958, 1986 by the President and Fellows of Harvard College.

Annie Dillard: Excerpt from HOLY THE FIRM by Annie Dillard. Copyright © 1977 by Annie Dillard. Reprinted by permission of HarperCollins Publishers, Inc. and Blanche C. Gregory.

Isak Dinesen: "The Blank Page" from LAST TALES by Isak Dinesen. Copyright © 1957 by Random House, Inc. Reprinted by permission of Random House, Inc. and Florence Feiler.

H. D. (Hilda Doolittle): "Oread," "Sea Poppies," "Garden," "Orchard," "Eurydice," "Fragment Thirty-Six," "Helen," "The Master," selections from "Tribute to the Angels" from H. D.: COLLECTED POEMS, 1912–1944. Copyright © 1982 by The Estate of Hilda Doolittle. Reprinted by permission of New Directions Publishing Corp. and Carcanet Press Limited.

Rita Dove: "The House Slave," "Thomas and Beulah," "The Great Palaces of Versailles," "Wingfoot Lake" from SELECTED POEMS, Pantheon/Vintage, copyright © 1980, 1983, 1986, 1993 by Rita Dove. Reprinted by permission of the author. Also "Persephone Falling" first appeared in *Sequoia*. "Sonnet in Primary Colors" first appeared in *Sojourner*. Both from MOTHER LOVE. Copyright © 1995 by Rita Dove. Reprinted by permission of the author and W. W. Norton and Company.

Buchi Emecheta: "The Mother's Mother" from THE JOYS OF MOTHERHOOD by Buchi Emecheta. Reprinted by permission of George Braziller, Inc. and the author.

Louise Erdrich: "Saint Marie" from LOVE MEDICINE, new and expanded version, by Louise Erdrich. Copyright © 1984, 1993 by Louise Erdrich. Reprinted by permission of Henry Holt and Co., Inc.

Ursula Fanthorpe: "For Saint Peter," "After Visiting Hours," "Only Here for the Bier," "Mother-in-Law," "King's Daughter," "Women Laughing," "From the Third Storey" (Peterloo Poets).

M. F. K. Fisher: "The Flaw" from THE GASTRONOMICAL ME, reprinted by permission of Simon & Schuster, Inc. and Lescher & Lescher Ltd. (material also included in a collection of works by M. F. K. Fisher entitled THE ART OF EATING). Copyright 1943 by M. F. K. Fisher. Copyright renewed © 1971 by Mary Kenedy Friede.

Susan Glaspell: *Trifles* copyright © 1951 by Walter H. Baker Co. is the sole property of the author and is fully protected under the copyright laws of the United States, the British Empire including the Dominion of Canada, and all other countries of the Copyright Union, and is subject to royalty. The play may not be acted by professionals or amateurs without formal permission in writing and the payment of royalty. All rights, including professional, amateur, stock, radio, and television broadcasting, motion picture recitation,

Carolyn Kizer: "Pro Femina" (part three) from MERMAIDS IN THE BASEMENT by Carolyn Kizer. "Semele Recycled" from YIN: NEW POEMS by Carolyn Kizer. Reprinted by permission of Carolyn Kizer.

Maxine Kumin: "Making the Jam Without You," "The Envelope," and "How It Is" from OUR GROUND TIME HERE WILL BE BRIEF. Reprinted by permisson of Curtis Brown Ltd. Copyright © 1982. First published by The Viking Press.

Dilys Laing: "The Double Goer," "Let Them Ask Their Husbands," "Sonnet to a Sister in Error," "Prayer of an Ovulating Female" from THE COLLECTED POEMS OF DILYS LAING. Reprinted by permission of David B. Laing.

Aemilia Lanyer: "To the Virtuous Reader," "The Description of Cooke-ham," "Salve Deus Rex Judaeorum" from THE POEMS OF AEMILIA LANYER, ed. Susanne Woods. Oxford University Press.

Margaret Laurence: "The Loons" from A BIRD IN THE HOUSE, © 1963 by Margaret Laurence. Reprinted with the permission of New End Inc., the Canadian Publishers, McClelland & Stewart, Toronto, and A. P. Watt Ltd.

Mary Lavin: "In a Café" from THE STORIES OF MARY LAVIN, volume I (London: Constable, 1964). Reprinted by permission of the author and Sanford J. Greenburger Associates.

Ursula K. Le Guin: "Sur" from THE COMPASS ROSE: SHORT STORIES. Copyright © 1982 by Ursula K. Le Guin; first appeared in *The New Yorker*. "She Unnames Them" from WE ARE THE STORIES WE TELL. Copyright © 1985 by Ursula K. Le Guin; first appeared in *The New Yorker*. Both selections reprinted by permission of the author and the author's agent, Virginia Kidd.

Meridel Le Sueur: "Annunciation" from SALUTE TO SPRING. Reprinted by permission of International Publishers Co.

Doris Lessing: "One Off the Short List" from STORIES by Doris Lessing. Copyright © 1978 by Doris Lessing. Reprinted by permission of Alfred A. Knopf. Copyright © 1963 Doris Lessing. Reprinted by kind permission of Jonathan Clowes Ltd., London, on behalf of Doris Lessing.

Denise Levertov: "The Son," "The Ache of Marriage," "Song for Ishtar," "Hypocrite Women," "In Mind," "The Wings," "Abel's Bride," "Stepping Westward," "The Mutes," "Eros at Temple Stream" from POEMS 1960–1967. Copyright © 1966 by Denise Levertov. "The Goddess" from COLLECTED EARLIER POEMS 1940–1960. Copyright © 1957 by Denise Levertov. "Cancion," "Divorcing" from THE FREEING OF THE DUST. Copyright © 1975 by Denise Levertov. "The Dragon-Fly Mother" from CANDLES IN BABYLON. Copyright © 1982 by Denise Levertov. "Dyptich," "Ancient Airs and Dances," "Evening Train" from EVENING TRAIN. Copyright © 1992 by Denise Levertov. Reprinted by permission of New Directions Publishing Corp. and Laurence Pollinger Limited.

Dorothy Livesay: "Green Rain," "Eve," "The Three Emily's," "The Children's Letters" reprinted by permission of Dorothy Livesay.

Audre Lorde: "Kitchen Linoleum," "The Electric Slide Boogie" reprinted from THE MARVELOUS ARITHMETICS OF DISTANCE: POEMS 1987–1992 by Audre Lorde. Copyright © 1993 by Audre Lorde. "From the House of Yemanja," "The Women of Dan Dance with Swords in Their Hands to Mark the Time When They Were Warriors" reprinted from THE BLACK UNICORN by Audre Lorde. Copyright © 1978 by Audre Lorde. "Coal," "On a Night of the Full Moon," "Now That I Am Forever with Child" reprinted from COAL by Audre Lorde. Copyright © 1968, 1970, 1976 by Audre Lorde. Reprinted by permission of W. W. Norton and Company, Inc., and the Charlotte Sheedy Literary Agency. "Zami" from ZAMI. Copyright © 1982 by Audre Lorde. Reprinted by permission of the Crossing Press.

Amy Lowell: "The Sisters" from WHAT'S O'CLOCK: THE COMPLETE POETICAL WORKS OF AMY LOWELL. Copyright © 1955 by Houghton Mifflin Company, Brinton P. Roberts and G. D'Andelot Belin, Esquire. Reprinted by permission of Houghton Mifflin Co. All rights reserved.

Mina Loy: "Gertrude Stein," "Three Moments in Paris," "Photo after Pogrom," "Omen of Victory," "Songge Byrd," "Nancy Cunard," and "Feminist Manifesto" reprinted from THE LOST LUNAR BAEDEKER: POEMS OF MINA LOY, edited by Roger L. Conover (Farrar, Straus & Giroux, 1996). Reprinted by permission of Roger L. Conover.

Delarivier Manley: NEW ATALANTIS, edited by Rosalind Ballaster. New York University Press, 1992. Reprinted by permission.

Katherine Mansfield: "The Daughters of the Late Colonel" and "The Fly" from THE SHORT STORIES OF KATHERINE MANSFIELD by Katherine Mansfield. Copyright 1922 by Alfred A. Knopf, Inc. and renewed 1950 by John Middleton Murry. Reprinted by permission of the publisher.

Paule Marshall: "The Making of a Writer": from "Poets in the Kitchen" (pages 3–12 of REENA AND OTHER STORIES). Reprinted by permission of the author and Faith Childs Agency.

Bobbie Ann Mason: "Wish" from LOVE LIFE by Bobbie Ann Mason. Copyright © 1990 by Bobbie Ann Mason. Reprinted by permission of HarperCollins Publishers, Inc. and Random Century.

Mary McCarthy: "Names" from MEMORIES OF A CATHOLIC GIRLHOOD. Copyright © 1957 and renewed 1985 by Mary McCarthy. Reprinted by permission of Harcourt Brace & Company and A. M. Heath. Copyright © the estate of the late Mary McCarthy.

Carson McCullers: "Ballad of the Sad Café," copyright © 1987 by the Estate of Carson McCullers. Used by permission of the Estate.

Charlotte Mew: "The Farmer's Bride," "The Quiet House" from COLLECTED POEMS by Charlotte Mew. Reprinted by permission of Carcanet Press Limited.

Edna S. Vincent Millay: "First Fig" and "Second Fig," copyright 1922, 1950 by Edna St. Vincent Millay. "Oh, oh, you will be sorry for that word!," "I, being born a woman and distressed," and "Sonnets from an Ungrafted Tree," copyright 1923, 1951 by Edna St. Vincent Millay and Norma Millay Ellis. "The Buck in the Snow" and "To Inez Milholland," copyright © 1928, 1955 by Edna St. Vincent Millay and Norma Millay Ellis. "Women have loved before as I love now" and "Oh, sleep forever in the Latmian cave," copyright © 1931, 1958 by Edna St. Vincent Millay and Norma Millay Ellis. "Childhood Is the Kingdom Where Nobody Dies" and "Apostrophe to Man," copyright © 1934, 1962 by Edna St. Vincent Millay and Norma Millay Ellis. "Rendezvous," "I too beneath your moon, almighty Sex" and "The Fitting," copyright © 1939, 1967 by Edna St. Vincent Millay and Norma Millay Ellis. "The courage that my mother had" and "An Ancient Gesture," copyright © 1954, 1982 by Norma Millay Ellis. Aria Da Capo, copyright © 1920, 1948 by Edna St. Vincent Millay. Reprinted by permission of Elizabeth Barnett, literary executor.

Lady Mary Wortley Montagu: selections reprinted by permission of Dr. Isobel Grundy.

Marianne Moore: "O to be a Dragon," copyright © 1957 by Marianne Moore, renewed 1985 by Lawrence E. Brinn and Louise Crane, Executors of the Estate of Marianne Moore. From THE COMPLETE POEMS OF MARIANNE MOORE by Marianne Moore. Used by permission of Viking Penguin, a division of Penguin Books USA Inc. "To a Snail," "Poetry," "Sojourn in the Whale," "Sea Unicorns and Land Unicorns," "An Egyptian Pulled Glass Bottle in the Shape of a Fish," "Silence," "No Swan So Fine," "The Jerboa," "Those Various Scalpels" reprinted with permission of Simon & Schuster, Inc. from COLLECTED POEMS OF MARIANNE MOORE. Copyright © 1935 by Marianne Moore, renewed 1963 by Marianne Moore and T. S. Eliot. "The Paper Nautilus" reprinted with permission of Simon and Schuster, Inc. from COLLECTED POEMS OF MARIANNE MOORE. Copyright © 1941, and renewed 1969 by Marianne Moore. "His Shield" reprinted with permission of Simon & Schuster, Inc. from COLLECTED POEMS OF MARIANNE MOORE. Copyright © 1951 by Marianne Moore, renewed 1979 by Lawrence E. Brinn and Louise Crane. All poems also reprinted by permission of Faber and Faber Ltd.

Toni Morrison: "Sula" from SULA by Toni Morrison. Reprinted by permission of International Creative Management, Inc. Copyright © 1973 by Toni Morrison.

Bharati Mukherjee: "The Management of Grief" from THE MIDDLEMAN AND OTHER STORIES. Copyright © Bharati Mukherjee, 1988. Reprinted by permission of the author, Penguin Books Canada Limited and Virago Press Limited.

Alice Munro: "Wild Swans" from THE BEGGAR MAIDS by Alice Munro. Copyright © 1977, 1978 by Alice Munro. Reprinted by permission of Alfred A. Knopf, Inc. and Penguin Books Ltd.

Anaïs Nin: "Birth" from UNDER A GLASS BELL, reprinted by permission of Gunther Stuhlmann and Peter Owen, Ltd., Publishers.

Edna O'Brien: "A Rose in the Heart" from A FANATIC HEART by Edna O'Brien. Copyright © 1984 by Edna O'Brien. Reprinted by permission of Farrar, Straus & Giroux, Inc.

Flannery O'Connor: "Good Country People" from A GOOD MAN IS HARD TO FIND AND OTHER STORIES, copyright © 1955 by Flannery O'Connor and renewed 1983 by

Regina O'Connor. Reprinted by permission of Harcourt Brace & Company and Faber & Faber Ltd.

Joyce Carol Oates: "Where Are You Going, Where Have You Been?" from THE WHEEL OF LOVE AND OTHER STORIES by Joyce Carol Oates. Copyright ©1970 by Joyce Carol Oates. Reprinted by permission of John Hawkins & Associates, Inc.

Sharon Olds: "The Language of the Brag" from SATAN SAYS by Sharon Olds, copyright © 1980 by Sharon Olds. Reprinted by permission of The University of Pittsburgh Press. "The One Girl at the Boys Party" from THE DEAD AND THE LIVING by Sharon Olds. Copyright © 1983 by Sharon Olds. "This" and "Rite of Passage" from THE GOLD CELL by Sharon Olds. "The Mortal One" from THE FATHER by Sharon Olds. Copyright 1992 by Sharon Olds. Reprinted by permission of Alfred A. Knopf, Inc.

Tillie Olsen: "Tell Me a Riddle" from TELL ME A RIDDLE by Tillie Olsen. Introduction by John Leonard. Copyright © 1956, 1957, 1960, 1961 by Tillie Olsen. Introduction 1994, by Dell Publishing. Reprinted by permission of Delacorte Press/Seymour Lawrence a division of Bantam Doubleday Dell Publishing Group, Inc. and the Elaine Markson Agency.

Cynthia Ozick: "The Shawl" from THE SHAWL by Cynthia Ozick. Copyright ©1980, 1983 by Cynthia Ozick. Reprinted by permission of Alfred A. Knopf and Raines & Raines as agents for the author.

Grace Paley: "Enormous Changes at the Last Minute" from ENORMOUS CHANGES AT THE LAST MINUTE by Grace Paley. Copyright © 1972 by Grace Paley. Reprinted by permission of Farrar, Straus & Giroux, Inc. and Elaine Markson Agency.

Dorothy Parker: "Resumé" by Dorothy Parker, copyright © 1926, 1928, renewed 1954, copyright © 1956 by Dorothy Parker. "One Perfect Rose" by Dorothy Parker, copyright © 1929, renewed copyright © 1957 by Dorothy Parker. "News Item" by Dorothy Parker, copyright © 1926, renewed copyright ©1954 by Dorothy Parker. "Song of One of the Girls" by Dorothy Parker. "A Pigs-Eye View of Literature" by Dorothy Parker, copyright © 1928, renewed copyright ©1956 by Dorothy Parker. "Oscar Wilde" copyright ©1928, renewed copyright ©1956 by Dorothy Parker. "Harriet Beecher Stowe" copyright © 1928, renewed copyright ©1956 by Dorothy Parker. "D. G. Rosetti" copyright © 1928, renewed copyright © 1956 by Dorothy Parker. "Thomas Carlisle" copyright ©1928, renewed copyright © 1956 by Dorothy Parker. "Alfred Lord Tennyson" copyright © 1928, renewed copyright © 1956 by Dorothy Parker. "Walter Savage Landor" copyright © 1928, renewed copyright © 1956 by Dorothy Parker. "George Sand" copyright 1928, renewed © 1956 by Dorothy Parker. "The Waltz" by Dorothy Parker, copyright © 1933, renewed copyright © 1961 by Dorothy Parker from THE PORTABLE DOROTHY PARKER by Dorothy Parker, introduction by Brendan Gill. Reprinted by permission of Viking Penguin, a division of Penguin Books USA Inc. and Gerald Duckworth and Company, Ltd.

Ruth Pitter: "The Military Harpist," "The Irish Patriarch," "Old Nelly's Birthday," "Yorkshire Wife's Saga" from RUTH PITTER: THE COLLECTED POEMS. Reprinted by permission of Mark Pitter.

Sylvia Plath: "The Distinguishing Muses," copyright © 1962 by Sylvia Plath. "The Colossus," copyright © 1961 by Sylvia Plath. Both from THE COLOSSUS AND OTHER POEMS by Sylvia Plath. Reprinted by permission of Alfred A. Knopf, Inc. and Faber and Faber Ltd. "You're" copyright © 1961 by Ted Hughes; "Mirror," "The Bee Meeting," "The Arrival of the Bee Box," "Stings," "The Swarm," "Wintering," "Daddy," "Lady Lazarus," "Edge," copyright © 1963 by Ted Hughes; "Words" copyright © 1966 by Ted Hughes. All from ARIEL by Sylvia Plath. Reprinted by permission of HarperCollins Publishers, Inc. "Nick and the Candlestick" from the COLLECTED POEMS OF SYLVIA PLATH by Sylvia Plath. Copyright © 1966 by Ted Hughes. Copyright renewed. Reprinted by permission of HarperCollins Publishers, Inc. All of the above also reprinted by permission of Faber and Faber Ltd.

Katherine Anne Porter: "The Jilting of Granny Weatherall" from FLOWERING JUDAS AND OTHER STORIES, copyright © 1930 and renewed 1958 by Katherine Anne Porter. Reprinted by permission of Harcourt Brace & Company, the Estate of Katherine Anne Porter and Jonathan Cape.

Katharine Susannah Prichard: "The Cooboo" from TRIBUTE: SELECTED STORIES OF KATHARINE SUSANNAH PRICHARD. Reprinted by permission of the copyright owner, R. P. Throssell, c/o Curtis Brown (Aust.) Pty Ltd., Sydney.

Jean Rhys: "The Insect World" from SLEEP IT OFF LADY by Jean Rhys (Penguin Books, 1979, first published by André Deutsch). Copyright © Jean Rhys, 1976.

Adrienne Rich: From "Twenty-One Love Poems" XI, (The Floating Poem, Unnumbered),

Elinor Wylie: "The Eagle and The Mole," "Atavism," "Wild Peaches," copyright © 1921 by Alfred A. Knopf, Inc., renewed 1949 by William Rose Benet. "To a Lady's Countenance," copyright © 1929 by Alfred A. Knopf, Inc., renewed 1957 by Edwina C. Rubenstein. "Let No Charitable Hope," "Full Moon," "From One Person," "Pastiche," copyright © 1932 by Alfred A. Knopf, Inc., and renewed 1960 by Edwina C. Rubenstein. Reprinted by permission of Alfred A. Knopf, Inc.

Hisaye Yamamoto: "Seventeen Syllables" from SEVENTEEN SYLLABLES AND OTHER STORIES. Copyright © Partisan Review 1949, © renewed Hisaye Yamamoto DeSoto, 1976. Copyright © 1988 by Hisaye Yamamoto. Reprinted by permission of the author and of Kitchen Table: Women of Color Press, Box 40-4920, Brooklyn, NY 11240.

Anzia Yezierska: "Where Lovers Dream" from HUNGRY HEARTS & OTHER STORIES by Anzia Yezierska. Copyright © 1985 by Louise Levitas Henriksen. Reprinted by permission of Persea Books, Inc.

Index